THE
OXFORD COMPANION
TO THE
THEATRE

THE OXFORD
COMPANION
TO THE
THEATRE

Edited by
PHYLLIS HARTNOLL
L.-ès-L., M.A. (Oxon.)

SECOND EDITION

LONDON
OXFORD UNIVERSITY PRESS
NEW YORK TORONTO
1957

Oxford University Press, Amen House, London E.C.4

GLASGOW NEW YORK TORONTO MELBOURNE WELLINGTON
BOMBAY CALCUTTA MADRAS KARACHI
CAPE TOWN IBADAN NAIROBI ACCRA SINGAPORE

First edition 1951
Reprinted (with revisions) 1952
Second edition (with illustrated supplement) 1957

PREFACE

IN compiling a book which deals with the theatre in all ages and in all countries, the difficulty has been to decide what to omit. Since completeness was not to be thought of, a representative selection of what was most likely to interest the English-speaking reader was aimed at, and the emphasis throughout has been on the popular rather than on the literary theatre. More space has been devoted to melodrama and the music-hall than to comedy and tragedy, literary quarrels have been ignored, actors have been rated above dramatists. In short, this is a companion to the playhouse, and is meant for those who would rather see a play than read it, for those whose interest is as much in the production and setting of a drama as in its literary content. For such a study of the theatre as entertainment and not as literature we have the support of the great French critic, Ferdinand Brunetière, who said: 'Il n'est pas du tout nécessaire qu'une pièce de théâtre soit littéraire pour être "du théâtre". L'histoire est là pour nous prouver que le théâtre s'est passé plus d'une fois d'avoir aucune valeur proprement littéraire.' This, then, accounts for such entries as Boulevard du Temple, Burlesque, Gaff, Haupt- und Staatsaktionen, Music-Hall, Vaudeville, Zarzuela, and for the number of minor dramatists, low comedians, and obscure theatres that lie cheek by jowl with Shakespeare and Aristophanes, Kean and Irving, Drury Lane and the Comédie-Française.

While thus limiting our range to the theatrical theatre, it has nevertheless proved impossible to ignore completely the sister arts of music, dancing, and design. Opera and Ballet, which have vast literatures of their own, have each been dealt with in a single article, as has Incidental Music in the Theatre. No attempt has been made to include individual composers, though a few librettists have short notes, as have some ballet-dancers and choreographers. Costume and Scenery are fully dealt with in articles covering Europe and America, as are Architecture, Acoustics, Make-Up, and Lighting; but few individual names have been singled out in these fields. On the other hand, space has been largely allotted to the development of the specifically English playhouse under its component parts—Auditorium, Proscenium, Stage—and a number of technical terms, both modern and historic, have been explained at length.

The theatres of the Far East—China, India, Japan, Malay (with Java)—have each one article, as have such European countries as Belgium, Holland, and Hungary, all supplemented by cross-references. The classical theatres of Greece and Rome have, in addition to their main articles, supplementary articles on their dramatists under their own names, and on such points of interest as Didascalia, Mime, Pantomimus, Satyr-Drama; the larger countries of Europe—England, France, Germany (with Austria), Italy, Russia, Scandinavia (Denmark, Norway, and Sweden), and Spain—have each their long main article, but in addition are furnished with a large

[v]

number of supplementary articles on dramatists, actors, and theatre buildings under their own names. The history of the theatre in the United States has been minutely recorded, both in its territorial expansion and in its actors and dramatists; South America is dealt with in one article; while Canada, taken in conjunction with the Amateur Theatre in Great Britain and the Nationwide Theatre in the United States, deals with the bulk of the English-speaking amateur movement. Finally, standing somewhat apart from the above classifications, are the special articles, which range from Jesuit and Jewish Drama to Marionette, Mumming Play, and Toy Theatre.

Although cross-references are plentiful in the main alphabet, they have been used sparingly in the text, and serve to direct the reader's attention to another main article, and not to biographies or short articles. Every effort has been made to give each play mentioned its date of first production. Where this was not possible, the date of publication is indicated. In the biographical articles, the years of birth and death have been given where possible. It is hoped that those that are missing may eventually be found. Brackets indicate the subject's real name, as opposed to stage or pen-name, and Christian names not in general use, as CONWAY [RUGG] and WOFFINGTON, PEG [MARGARET]. It has not proved practicable to exclude all living actors and dramatists, but as few as possible have been included, and their biographies are in the main factual rather than critical.

The Cinema has been deliberately ignored, as being a totally different art which requires a book to itself. Lack of space has been responsible for the exclusion of the Circus, except for the short period in which it mingled with the play proper. For the same reason the lighter forms of entertainment—Cabaret, Café-Chantant, Revue—outside England and the United States have been drastically curtailed. Other omissions there are which were not intended. For these the chaotic state of Europe during the last ten years, and the difficulty of communications, must be held partly responsible. It is hoped that some gaps may be filled later, and that names, dates, facts of all kinds now sought in vain may come to light. I am well aware of these deficiencies, as of many others that mar the book, and shall welcome corrections and supplementary information on any subject. And I apologize in advance for any mistakes or misstatements that may have crept in, and hope for the opportunity to amend them.

The editor of such a book as this is laid under a heavy burden of gratitude to all those scholars and theatre historians of the past whose work has made possible such a compilation. In addition, I have a pleasant duty to fulfil in acknowledging the help I have received from the many contributors whose names will be found in the contributors' index. I thank them for undertaking the work in the first place, and even more for their patience and forbearance in dealing with the many queries that arose, for constantly revising the modern sections of their articles during the ten years that have elapsed since the book was started, and particularly for allowing me to cut and alter their material in order to make it fit the pattern of the work as a whole. Uniformity was obviously desirable in a book of reference—though even now it is not completely attained, and could not be attempted (where nearly sixty persons were working independently) without some sacrifice of individuality in the writing. To those who have so patiently borne with me I am indeed grateful. Among the contributors a special word of appreciation is due to Mr. George Freedley of New York and Mr. Macqueen-Pope of London, whose help has gone far beyond the boundaries of their allotted tasks, and whose knowledge of the theatre has been unstintedly at my disposal. I also acknowledge my debt to the works of Professor Allardyce Nicoll; and thank Mrs. Gabrielle Enthoven, O.B.E., and Miss M. St. Clare Byrne, Miss Sybil Rosenfeld, and Mr. Richard Southern, contributors and fellow-members of the Society for Theatre Research, who, with the other members of the Society, have given me inestimable help in my researches.

Among those who are not contributors to the book my first thanks must go to the great modern scholars of the English and American theatres, and particularly to Sir E. K. Chambers and Professor George C. D. Odell. I am also greatly indebted to Mr. John Parker. The many editions of his *Who's Who in the Theatre* have been a constant help and guide, as they are to all who deal with the modern theatre. Nor must I forget Mr. Hubert Foss, with whom this book was first discussed and planned in 1939–40.

For help with the articles on the French theatre I am indebted to the Société d'Histoire du Théâtre, and particularly to my good friend Monsieur J. G. Prod'homme, and to Madame Horn-Monval of the Bibliothèque de l'Arsenal. The articles on the Spanish theatre have had the expert assistance of Don Alberto Jiménez, Lecturer in Spanish in the University of Oxford, and of Miss Elizabeth Watson, while my ignorance of the Russian language has led me to rely gratefully on the help of Mr. Herbert Marshall, who translated for me long extracts from manuals of Russian theatre history and memoirs; of Mr. Hubert Griffith, who revised all the articles dealing with Russia; of Mr. Joseph Macleod and Mr. André van Gyseghem, who have made available to English readers so much material on the Russian theatre; of Miss Bertha Malnick, who gave me access to her Papers on the early Russian theatre, and allowed me to quote from one of them; and of Miss Eleanor Fox, Librarian of the Society for Cultural Relations with the U.S.S.R.

My work on the American theatre would not have been possible without the generous co-operation of Dr. Van Lennep, who opened to me the treasures of the Harvard Theatre Collection; of the Director and Staff of the Drama Department at Yale; of Miss May Davenport Seymour of the Museum of the City of New York; of Mrs. Sarah Chokla Gross of the Theatre Library Association; and of Miss Mary Virginia Heinlein of Vassar. I must also express my thanks to those good friends who smoothed my path in New York: Mr. Ben Lucien Burman, who helped me with the history of the Showboat; Miss Ruth May; and Miss Elsa Shelley. Above all I must acknowledge the help given me at every point, and particularly over the bibliographies, by Mrs. Elizabeth Barrett, Mr. Paul Myers, and their helpers in the Theatre Department of the New York Public Library, where I spent many happy and fruitful hours. I also acknowledge gratefully the help given me in England by the staffs of the British Museum, the Victoria and Albert Museum, the Bodleian Library, Oxford, and the Director and staff of the Shakespeare Memorial Theatre, Stratford-on-Avon. A special word of thanks is due to Mr. R. C. Maasz, Assistant Librarian of the Taylor Institution, Oxford, for his help in preparing the bibliographies of European countries. I am indebted also to members of the staff of the Oxford University Press both in London and in New York. To the Principal of St. Hugh's College, Oxford, and to the members of the Senior Common Room, particularly my Tutor and the Librarian, my thanks are due for help and encouragement—as much material as spiritual—over a long period. And finally a more personal word of gratitude is due to my mother, who first introduced me to the theatre, and implanted in me at an early age that love of plays and players which has sustained me throughout my task; and to Miss Winifred Kimberley, whose constant care over many years has enabled me to complete it. To all these, and to the many friends, inside the theatre and out, who have borne with my ruling passion and encouraged me to give free rein to it, I here make full and heartfelt acknowledgement of many acts of unrecorded kindness.

PHYLLIS HARTNOLL

OXFORD 1950

PREFACE TO THE SECOND EDITION

THE history of the theatre is now accepted in England as a reasonable subject for scholarly research. In the years since this book was first published the Society for Theatre Research, then in its infancy, has been firmly established, and one of the first-fruits of its endeavours has been the foundation of an International Federation for Theatre Research. My work in preparing this new edition has been greatly eased by the help and encouragement of members of both these bodies. I am also grateful to the many other theatre enthusiasts who have sent me material from all over the world. For particular help with the illustrations I must acknowledge my debt to Miss M. St. Clare Byrne, Mr. James Laver, and Professor Kenneth Macgowan.

PHYLLIS HARTNOLL

LONDON 1957

CONTRIBUTORS' INDEX BY NAME

CONTRIBUTORS' INDEX BY INITIAL

A. L.	The late Alfred Loewenberg	L. G. A.	L. G. Applebee, London
A. N.	Professor Allardyce Nicoll, Birmingham	L. S.	Lee Simonson, New York
A. V. C.	A. V. Cookman, London	M. A.	Miss Mildred Adams, New York
		M. E. B.	Miss M. Elizabeth Barber, London
B. H. C.	Barrett H. Clark, New York	M. R.	Miss Margaret Rubel, London
B. S.	Bernard Sobel, New York	M. St. C. B.	Miss M. St. Clare Byrne, O.B.E., London
C. W. B.	C. W. Bickmore, London	M. W. D.	Maurice Willson Disher, London
D. G.	Douglas Gilbert, New York		
D. H.	Dyneley Hussey, London	O. R.	The late Owen Rutter
E. B.	Eric Blom, C.B.E., London	P. L.	Petr Lotar, Czechoslovakia
E. C.	Edward Carrick (Craig), London		
E. F.	The late Elsie Fogerty	R. G.	Miss Rosamond Gilder, New York
E. H.	E. Harris, Israel		
E. P.	Professor Edna Purdie, London	R. S.	Dr. Richard Southern, London
F. S.	Francis Schiller, Oxford	S. A. B.	Professor Sterling A. Brown, Washington, D.C.
G. E.	The late Mrs. Gabrielle Enthoven	S. F.	Sawyer Falk, Syracuse, N.Y.
G. F.	George Freedley, New York	S. McC.	Stanley McCandless, New York
G. S.	George Speaight, London	S. R.	Miss Sybil Rosenfeld, London
G. W.	The late Geoffrey Whitworth	S. R. L.	Sam R. Littlewood, London
H. A.	Harold Acton, London	T. B.	Professor T. Burrow, Oxford
H. B.	Hope Bagenal, F.R.I.B.A., London	T. C. K.	The late T. C. Kemp
		T. Q. C.	Thomas Quinn Curtiss, New York
H. C.	Herbert Cahoon, New York		
H. D. F. K.	Professor H. D. F. Kitto, Bristol	U. E.-F.	Professor Una Ellis-Fermor, London
H. F. D.	Mrs. Hallie Flanagan Davis, Northampton, Mass.		
		V. G.	Val Gielgud, O.B.E., London
J. A.	John Andrews, London	V. M. S.	The late Violet M. Saunders
J. G.	John Gassner, New York		
J. L.	James Laver, C.B.E., London	W. A.	The late William Armstrong
J. R. S.	Professor J. R. Sutherland, London	W. B.	Professor William Beare, Bristol
		W. E. D.	Dr. Wilhelmina E. Delp, London
		W. G. B. C.	Professor William Glasgow Bruce Carson, St. Louis
K. M. L.	Miss K. M. Lea, Oxford		
L. E. T.	Laurence E. Tanner, C.V.O., London	W. J.	The late William Jeffrey
		W. M. P.	W. Macqueen-Pope, London

A

AASEN, IVAR (1813–96), Norwegian linguist and philologist, and the author of a musical play, *Ervingen*, which proved extremely popular when first produced in 1855. (See SCANDINAVIA, 2.)

ABBEY, HENRY EUGÈNE (1846–96), American theatre manager, and one of the most courageous and consistently successful in New York in his day. He first worked as ticket-seller in the opera-house at Akron, and within two years he was lessee of the theatre, and arranging tours of good companies. In 1876 he was in management in Buffalo, and in the following year went to New York. The elder Sothern played under him, and he brought together for the first time William H. Crane and Stuart Robson. In 1880 he visited Europe, and on his return sealed his growing reputation by presenting Sarah Bernhardt for the first time in New York. In subsequent years he was responsible for the visits of the London Gaiety company, of Coquelin, and of Irving, who with Ellen Terry played at Abbey's Theatre (see KNICKERBOCKER THEATRE) on its opening in 1893. Abbey was one of the first to present good theatre and opera outside New York, and to engage Continental stars for the United States.

ABBEY THEATRE, DUBLIN, see IRELAND.

ABBOTT, GEORGE (1887–   ), American playwright and director, who became interested in the theatre while at the University of Rochester, and went to Harvard in 1912 to work under Professor Baker. Some success there, and a prize for a one-act comedy, led in 1913 to a job at Keith's Theatre, and a subsequent appearance in New York at the Fulton Theatre. Five years in various parts followed, and some work for John Golden, and in 1925 *The Fall Guy*, written in collaboration with James Gleason, was put on successfully. Soon after this Abbott left the stage to devote all his energies to writing, producing, and directing, and became one of the outstanding men on Broadway. Between 1925 and 1939 he was responsible for over thirty productions, many of which were extremely successful. Among them were *Boy Meets Girl*, *Room Service*, and *The Boys from Syracuse* (based on *The Comedy of Errors*). Most of his own plays, which include *Broadway*, *Love 'em and Leave 'em*, *Three Men on a Horse* (also a success in London), and *Coquette*, which established Helen Hayes as a star, have been written in collaboration, and Abbott's reputation as a play-doctor stands high, owing to his ability to get the best out of his material, and his competent and experienced work in direction. One of his few failures was *Sweet River* (1936), based on *Uncle Tom's Cabin*. He worked for some time in films, but in 1932 returned to Broadway and launched out as an independent producer.

The hallmarks of an Abbott show are pace and humour, and a steady level of efficient action.

ABBOT, WILLIAM (1789–1843), an English actor of whom Hazlitt said 'he never acts ill'. He first appeared at Bath in 1806, and came to London a few years later. By 1813 he was known at Covent Garden as a successful exponent of comedy and melodrama. He played Pylades to Macready's Orestes in *The Distressed Mother* when Macready made his first appearance at Covent Garden in 1816, and created the part of Appius Claudius in *Virginius* in 1820. Two melodramas by Abbot were given at Covent Garden. It may have been he who organized the English company which visited Paris in 1827; he was certainly a member of it, and played Charles Surface. Back in London, he played Romeo to Fanny Kemble's Juliet in 1830, and then went to America, where he appeared as Hamlet in Philadelphia in 1836. He was not a success in America, and died there in poverty.

ABBOT OF MISRULE, OF UNREASON, see MISRULE.

ABELL, KJELD (1902–   ), contemporary Danish dramatist, author of a number of plays which combine the style of the later Strindberg with that of the German expressionists to produce a unique blend of fantasy. The best-known of his plays is *Melodien, den blev væk* (1935), which, as *The Melody that Got Lost*, was produced in London in 1936.

ABERCROMBIE, LASCELLES (1881–1938), English poet, author of *The End of the World* (1914) and other plays in verse.

ABINGTON, FRANCES (1737–1815), English actress, the daughter of a soldier named Barton. She was first a flower-girl (Nosegay Fan) and street singer, and, after a little polishing by a French milliner who employed her temporarily, she took to the stage. Her first appearance was as Miranda in *The Busybody* at the Haymarket in 1755. On the recommendation of Foote she was taken on at Drury Lane, where she found herself overshadowed by Kitty Clive and Mrs. Pritchard. It was at this time, apparently, that she made an ill-judged and unhappy marriage with her music-master, and from Fanny Barton became Mrs. Abington. Despairing of finding success in London, she went to Dublin, where she remained for five years, returning to Drury Lane only at the express invitation of Garrick, who disliked her but judged her to be a good actress. During the eighteen years that she remained there she played a number of important roles, and was the first Lady Teazle (1777). She is said to have been excellent as Beatrice. She also revived Anne Oldfield's part of Lady Betty Modish in *The Careless Husband*, and was much admired as Miss Prue in *Love for Love*, in which character she was painted by Reynolds. In 1782 she went to Covent Garden, where she remained until 1790. After her retirement she made a few appearances between 1797 and 1799, but left the stage for good in the latter year. She was an ambitious, clever, and witty woman, and in spite of her humble origins she achieved an enviable position in distinguished society, where the womenfolk paid her the supreme honour of copying her clothes.

ABOVE, see STAGE DIRECTIONS.

ACADEMY OF MUSIC, NEW YORK, see BROADWAY.

ACCESI, THE, a company of *commedia dell'arte* actors who are first found in 1590. Records of their early activity are scarce, but in 1600 they were led by Tristano Martinelli and Pier Maria Cecchini, who took them to France. Among the actors were Martinelli's brother Drusiano, Flaminio Scala, and possibly Diana, formerly of the Desiosi. They returned to Italy, and on their next visit to France some years later (1608) were without their Harlequin (Tristano Martinelli), who had for some time been at loggerheads with Cecchini. In spite of this they gave a good account of themselves, and were much admired by the Court and by Marie de' Medici. Shortly afterwards Cecchini joined forces with the younger Andreini (see FEDELI), but the constant quarrelling of Cecchini's and Andreini's wives caused the two parties to separate. Cecchini retained the old name of Accesi, but little is known of his subsequent activities. Silvio Fiorillo, the first Captain Mattamoras, was with the Accesi in 1621 and 1632.

ACCIUS, LUCIUS (c. 170–86 B.C.), Roman dramatist, and the last important writer of tragedy for the Roman stage. The titles of over forty of his plays have survived, and show that he dealt with every field of tragedy open to a Latin writer, from the translation of Greek works of the fifth century and later to the composition of two *praetextae*. The outstanding quality of his style was force; here he excelled all Roman dramatists, though inferior to Pacuvius in learning and care. Characteristic of him are plots of a violent, melodramatic nature, flamboyant personages, majestic utterance, and powerful repartee; when we can compare him with his Greek models we find that he works up the rhetorical possibilities of each situation to the highest degree. Thus while Eteocles's command to Polynices is simply expressed in the Greek: 'Then get thee from these walls, or thou shalt die', Accius gives us four imperatives in six words: 'egredere, exi, ecfer te, elimina urbe!' The most famous example of his style is the tyrant's retort: 'oderint dum metuant' (Let them hate me, provided they fear me). The continual search for rhetorical effect, the eagerness to exploit each situation to the full, is characteristic of Roman tragedy as a whole, and seems to reach its culminating point in

Accius. Inevitably it tends to eliminate the half-tones of nature and reduce all portraiture to glaring white and black. Still, we may admit that Accius's heroes are grand and striking, while sometimes they seem to surpass their Greek prototypes, not merely in Stoic fortitude but in a certain grave humanity and sympathy with misfortune. On the other hand, we have no evidence that he ventured to alter the structure given him by his originals, though he seems to have remodelled certain passages and occasionally to have inserted lines from other sources. In Accius we have Roman tragedy at its climax, before a change of fashion drove it from the theatre. Comparing his extant lines with the plays of Seneca we see at once that Accius is still under the salutary discipline of having to write for a real stage. Stage technique is taken into due account; rhetoric and melodrama are kept within bounds. Accius's plays may seem stiff and strained versions of their Greek originals, but they are real plays and as such far different from the purely literary drama of the Empire.   W. B.

ACEVEDO, PEDRO DE, see JESUIT DRAMA.

ACHURCH, JANET (1864–1916), English actress, who made her first appearance at the Olympic in 1883, and later appeared in pantomime. She toured with Benson for some time, playing leading parts in Shakespeare, and was also seen at the Adelphi in *Harbour Lights*. It is, however, as one of the first actresses in England to play Ibsen that she is remembered. She was Nora in *A Doll's House* at the Novelty Theatre in 1889, and in 1896 produced *Little Eyolf* at the Avenue Theatre with herself as Rita, Mrs. Patrick Campbell as the Ratwife, and Elizabeth Robins as Asta. She was also seen as Shaw's heroine in *Candida* and as Lady Cecily Waynflete in *Captain Brassbound's Conversion* (both Strand, 1900). With her husband, Charles Charrington, she toured extensively, and was the first English actress to appear in the Khedivial Theatre, Cairo. A beautiful woman, with a superb carriage and lovely voice, she was called by Shaw 'the only tragic actress of genius we now possess'. Some excellent descriptions of her acting can be found in his *Our Theatres in the Nineties*. She retired from the stage in 1913.

ACKERMANN, a family of actors of eighteenth-century Germany whose work was of the highest importance in the development of German theatrical art. The father, (1) KONRAD ERNST (1710–71), was nearing thirty when he joined Schönemann's company, and it is not known what made him take to the stage. He had already served with some distinction as a soldier, and was a man of parts—a good fencer and horseman, a painter, and a dancer. He was a fine-looking man, with a restless, vagabond temperament which often did him ill service, and the life of a strolling player suited him. In later years he became fat and indolent, but was on the whole popular with his actors and audience because of his good nature. He was good in comedy, and in such parts as Major von Tellheim in *Minna von Barnhelm*. After serving his apprenticeship with Schönemann he left to form his own company, taking with him Schönemann's leading lady, whom he later married. This was (2) SOPHIA CHARLOTTA SCHRÖDER (née Biereichel) (1714–92). She was married young to a drunken organist, but left him after a few years, and supported herself by doing gold embroidery. She became friendly with young Ekhof, and was persuaded to join him in Schönemann's company, making her début at Lüneburg as Monime in an adaptation of Racine's *Mithridate* on 15 Jan. 1740. She was immediately successful and was regarded as the leading lady of the company. A handsome woman, with a majestic presence, she had enthusiasm and an artistic sense which aided her materially in her career. She was also practical and businesslike, traits which came uppermost in later life, causing her to be accused of parsimony. Soon after she had joined Ackermann's company her husband sought her out, and a short reconciliation took place, which resulted in the birth of one of Germany's greatest actors (see SCHRÖDER). But the husband was unable to overcome his intemperance, and Sophia returned to the stage, marrying Ackermann soon after.

For many years the Ackermanns toured unceasingly, with no outstanding success, but equally with no overwhelming losses. They visited Russia, Prussia, and Switzerland, with a varied repertory which included a number of Holberg's plays as well as adaptations from the French and some indigenous drama. In 1764 they were joined by their old friend Ekhof, then at the height of his fame, and with a strong company, which included Sophia's son, now a fine actor of about 20, they played at the first German National Theatre, established at Hamburg and inseparably connected with Lessing's *Hamburgische Dramaturgie*, corner-stone of modern dramatic criticism. Unfortunately this enterprise was ruined by internal dissension, and by the antagonism between young Schröder, who, after an unhappy childhood, was proving a thorn in the flesh to his stepfather, and Ekhof, who did not care to find himself the rival and butt of a youngster, however gifted. He left, as did Schröder, but the latter returned after a time to take over the Hamburg company, supplanting his stepfather, who died shortly after. In the company, which was still financially in the grip of his mother, who had given up acting for management and for the training of young actors, many of whom owed her a great debt of gratitude, were Schröder's two half-sisters. The elder, (3) DOROTHEA (1752–1821), had been acting for many years with her parents, and at 13 had played young girls' parts, some of them too difficult for her, which had earned her much adverse criticism. She was twenty when her half-brother took over, and already tired of the stage. Appreciation of her great gifts, which had by this time matured, came too late, and though Schröder managed to keep her with him a few more years, she abandoned her career when she married in 1778. She was a great loss to the company, and was much mourned by her audiences, who had admired her as Minna von Barnhelm, as the Countess Orsina in *Emilia Galotti*, and as the young roguish girl-lovers of French comedy. Her younger sister, (4) CHARLOTTE (1757–74), a frail and beautiful child with a touch of genius, made her first appearance on the stage at the age of 4, as Louison in an adaptation of *Le Malade imaginaire*. She rapidly obtained complete mastery of her art, matured young, and at 14 gave a most moving performance as Emilia Galotti. By the time she was 17 she was one of the greatest and most admired actresses of Germany. But her half-brother drove her too hard, and the strain of new parts and constant appearances took their toll. She died before her eighteenth birthday, and Schröder was much blamed for her death, since there was more than a suspicion that she had committed suicide.

ACOUSTICS, THEATRE. 1. ACOUSTICS AND ORATORY. Early drama was an art not of fireside conversation but of speech projected across a distance. 'Sit in a full theatre,' says Overbury (*Character of an excellent Actor*, 1614), 'and you will think you see so many lines drawn from the circumference of so many ears while the actor is the centre.' And the building has an effect on the voice. It expands some vowels to tones and suppresses others, it can add overtones, it can alter, emphasize, repeat. That is to say it is an instrument; it can be a good or bad instrument; it can be learned and made use of, or ignored. Add also that the larger the building the more marked is the acoustic effect. To-day it can be said that on the wireless and in the Little Theatre the extreme intimacy of fireside conditions can be reproduced. And yet in few theatres can acoustics be truly ignored to-day, any more than in the past, and there are a large number of theatres of considerable size. The response of the voice to the building as an instrument has produced oratory and often fine oratory—something that is an art in itself. But the oratorical tradition is really inseparable from stage playing, in theatres of any size, however much it may be ignored by actors and dramatic writers, and by the general taste of the time.

The form of the theatre has developed from a complex of causes in all periods. We may note the dependence of oratory in the Graeco-Roman world on a building without echo or reverberation. In an inflected language, if word-endings are obscured the sense is lost, and the sense is equally lost if the verb at the end of the sentence is obscured. In the classical theatre both loudness and distinctness were necessary and were achieved. But excessive loudness can be a serious fault. It is curious that the evidence from Shakespeare is that he feared too loud a voice—a voice that can 'split the ears of the groundlings'. Also there are the words—'O there be players . . . that have so strutted and bellowed . . .'. The passage in

Hamlet is doubtless the dramatist's warning against over-emphasis, a plea for the use instead of the abuse of a convention, but it points also to the oratorical facility of Elizabethan drama and to the acoustics of the theatres. The Elizabethan theatre was of a shape and dimension that generally avoided echoes, and being largely unroofed there was no reverberation. Therefore sheer loudness would not have tended to the prolonging of syllables such as can occur in a modern theatre. There is another interesting passage in the *Character of an excellent Actor*: 'He doth not strive to make Nature monstrous; she is often seen in the same scene with him, but neither on stilts nor on crutches, and for his voice it is not lower than the prompter nor louder than the foil and target.' Here is set a common-sense standard of loudness very valuable both for players and for students of acoustics.

Another factor to be noted is the contribution made by verse. This can best be realized by reciting Shakespeare in the open air to a remote listener. The rhythm of the verse clearly contributes to the carrying power. The physical strain of conveying the sense is noticeable, and it is also noticeable that the reciter is relying on one or two vowel sounds in each line to convey the sense. A range-testing experiment of this kind brings home to speaker and listener alike some of the formative factors in the growth of drama. Certainly two great schools of dramatic verse, the Greek and the Elizabethan, developed in an unroofed auditorium and in response to exacting physical requirements.

But when we turn from England to France, and compare the development of French dramatic verse and the alexandrine line to the English, we must be astonished at the difference. By comparison alexandrines are inflexible and impose a much more rigid technique. The endings of the rhymed couplets must be heard, because the rhymed words are often significant for the sense; at the same time they impose a pause at the end of each line, so that lines cannot easily be run on as in Shakespeare. The French language does not carry in the open air; the modified vowels are too delicate, there are no open *i*s (English *high*), and the nasal vowels (as *enfin*) seem to need the resonance of an enclosed building. French dramatic verse, in fact, demands short reverberation conditions but within doors. One might note that early French drama developed in the halls of palaces and in converted tennis-courts: but add also that Racine was performed at Versailles or St. Cloud out of doors, although it is difficult to believe that the plays were well heard. The clue to the problem is doubtless the fact that alexandrine verse as developed in the sixteenth century was an oratorical instrument so perfectly adapted to French language and genius that it triumphed over all obstacles and has survived to this day.

2. GREEK THEATRE ACOUSTICS. When we turn to the origin of the drama we might begin by noting that some spots in the open air are much better for hearing than others, and natural amphitheatres were probably selected in ancient, as in modern, times for ritual ceremonies, out of which Greek dramatic representations developed. A smooth dancing-floor, the wall of the little temple or shrine, and finally some kind of raised platform in front of it, would then give the essentials of the Greek theatre. And each of these contributes to the acoustics. A man speaking in the open air in front of a wall can be heard further away, and if the floor in front of him be hard paved and he can raise himself a little above it his voice will be reflected upwards and the reflections will reinforce the direct sound. Also, the higher his speaking position, the greater will be the angle of impact of sound upon his audience. This is what is meant by the statement that the Greeks developed the principle of sound reflection. From the interaction of these physical facts the Greek theatre developed, with its long narrow *logeion* (platform) increasing in height in successive periods, with its temple wall background with doors, and hard paved orchestra floor. Also, since the theatre was not an enclosed space, the chances of long-path echoes were small, and reverberation or inter-reflection due to the action of opposite plane surfaces did not exist. There was therefore no loss of distinctness. The value of these simple reflectors close to the source can be tested to-day in Athens in the Odeion of Herodes Atticus, where the shell of the building remains. A person reading a book at ordinary conversation loudness can be heard perfectly in the remotest seats, some 150 ft. distant. The strain on the voice, however, must have been considerable in large theatres such as Epidauros, where the remotest seats were some 200 ft. from the stage, and it is not surprising to read of the tradition of the players' masks which are supposed to have contained some kind of megaphone mouthpiece. (See also GREECE, 3. EXTERNALS.)

3. VITRUVIUS AND THE GRAECO-ROMAN THEATRE. The Greek theatre may be said then to give open-air conditions modified and improved. Such conditions have the advantages we have noted, but they give no response to tones. Response is given in enclosed buildings by a slight reverberation causing a moderate prolonging of vowel sounds. But there is another kind of response caused by the resonance of wood panelling—a fact well known and employed in the design of concert halls and of musical instruments. And we find in fact evidence of an attempt on the part of Hellenistic theatre-builders to provide a resonant system in the shape of *echeia* or acoustic vases. The chief evidence for the *echeia* is found in Vitruvius (*c.* 70–15 B.C.), a Roman architect who wrote about a generation before the beginning of the Christian era, and who attempts to sum up the traditions of Hellenistic building. In his Book V, which treats of theatres, he recognizes that sound is propagated in waves, also that obstacles must be avoided, and he connects with this the admirable rule that the ascent of

seats must be stepped in a straight incline without noticeable breaks. In the chapter on harmony he distinguishes between reciting in a monotone and reciting with modulations, and although the subject is obscure, it is clear that the *echeia* were intended for the purpose of enhancing vowel tones. The vases are described as being of bronze or earthenware, placed in cavities under the seats of the amphitheatre, and in an inverted position with an air space around them. They were tuned in response to the notes of the tetrachord and were arranged in a certain sequence in three tiers. Vitruvius's words are: 'By the adoption of this plan the voice which issues from the *scena*, expanding as from a centre, and striking against the cavity of each vase, will sound with increased clearness and harmony from its unison with one or other of them.' They are used, therefore, to introduce into a masonry building some special resonance factor. The disadvantage of such resonators depending on enclosed air-spaces must be their sharpness of resonance, that is to say, they will respond at a very small range of pitch: whereas wood panelling will respond over a fairly wide range. In the same chapter Vitruvius states clearly that theatres built of wood do not need *echeia*. The comedies of Terence (*c.* 190–159 B.C.) included music for pipes; bass and treble pipes are mentioned. In the Roman theatre the orchestra floor was a semicircle, rather than the Greek circle, and was occupied by senators' seats, with a sloping roof, to protect against rain, over the stage. The Roman stage was greater in width, and there is mention in Vitruvius of *periaktoi*, a series of tall prisms set in the wings, triangular on plan, which could rotate about their axes and provide three sets of scenes. Vitruvius also notes the practice of singers to the harp turning towards the *valvas scenae* (some part of the stage scenery) in order to project their voices. If the *periaktoi* were set at an angle of about 45° they would in fact serve to reflect sound outwards to the auditorium. (See also GREECE, 3 *b*, and ROME.)

We have then in the acoustics of the classical theatre some criteria of reinforcement by reflection, of absence of echo and reverberation, and of the function of resonance. These can be applied in reviewing later types.

4. THE ELIZABETHAN PLAYHOUSE. To return to the Elizabethan playhouse, the plan and section of the Fortune Theatre, reconstructed by W. H. Godfrey from the specification, which survives, strongly suggest its origin, namely the platform set up by strolling players in the inn-yard. Here again is a natural auditorium. A large part of the audience is well above the players, and the floor of stage and paved yard acts as a reflector. Sound is said to rise only because the floor, if it be hard, is the first and nearest reflector, and this explains why hearing in London theatres to-day is often much better in the gallery than at the rear of the pit. The Elizabethan stage roof, known as the 'shadow' or 'testa', was probably intended

to keep off rain and sun. It would have reinforced sound by reflection in the lower part of the house but would have tended to screen it from top side seats. Also it would have reduced the loudness of players as heard from the stage balcony for listeners in the top gallery; that is to say, in these seats Juliet would not be as well heard as Romeo. For the players on the boards the testa would have served to return tone upon the stage, enabling them to hear themselves well, a useful thing for sustained recital. The musicians in the Elizabethan theatre appear to have occupied a position immediately on one side of the stage and at the level of the first tier. Here, and on the left as seen from the house, they are shown in Van Buchell's view of the Swan Theatre and are labelled 'orchestra'. (See also ELIZABETHAN PLAYHOUSE.)

The polygonal plan of the Elizabethan Globe and Swan theatres was carried on in a theatre plan attributed to Inigo Jones (1573–1652) in the Worcester College Collection, consisting of an octagon set in a square. But the tradition actually survives to-day in Wren's Sheldonian Theatre in Oxford. Here we find also the wooden galleries, but combined with the classic rostrum for oratorical exercises, and with a large ceremonial entrance door. The ceiling of the Sheldonian, as though to provide as much sound-absorption as possible and imitate open-air acoustics, was originally designed by Wren of canvas panels. As a result the reverberation was very short. The building is largely of wood and is noted for its good acoustics.

5. THE PALACE HALL AND MASQUE HOUSE. The palace hall and the moot hall were also used for stage plays. They were medieval or Tudor buildings resembling the college halls surviving at Oxford and Cambridge. We know that *Othello* was first performed in the Old Palace Hall at Whitehall in 1604. In the Lansdowne MSS. in the British Museum there survives the plan of this building set for a pastoral. The layout closely resembles that shown in a plan for a Masque House by Inigo Jones (also in the British Museum), and the two give evidence of the general arrangement for Court performances in which movable scenery was beginning to dominate the design. Inigo Jones, Surveyor to the King, was the chief contriver of masques in James I's reign, and the masque relied upon music, upon effects produced by machines, and upon classical scenic architecture in perspective (see ARCHITECTURE, LIGHTING, MACHINERY, MASQUE, and SCENERY). The general arrangement, as shown in the plan, was dominated by the royal dais with a central floor space in front of it for processions of homage, or for dancing, and having a flight of steps beyond, leading to the world of the stage at a higher level. On either hand were banks of seats and 'Musicians' are marked in a recessed position on the left of the stage. In the Whitehall plan various pens or 'boxes' are shown railed off for important persons, including 'Mr. Surveyor' (probably Inigo Jones himself). Tennis-courts were also used both in England and France for dramatic performances, their

pent-house side galleries at floor level providing some side seats.

It is interesting that this general arrangement of banked seats and pens survived to 1938 in the arrangement for the Westminster play in the School Dormitory building (see WESTMINSTER PLAY). The headmaster's seat, later in a forward position, probably corresponded originally with the royal dais, in the position shown in Inigo Jones's Masque House plan. At the Westminster play the doors on the fore-stage were part of the Plautian tradition: the scenes were at the crossing of a city street, and the two opposite houses, with their doors, were the dwellings of the characters. This tradition may be the origin of the doors on the fore-stage which are a noticeable feature of English Restoration and of the English eighteenth-century playhouses, and which survived at Drury Lane until 1822. If this be correct we have here an English tradition lingering from Roman adaptations of Greek comedy.

In Inigo Jones's design for a Masque House we have an embodiment of the true art theatre at its fullest as a plastic and acoustic instrument. The various factors are: the *scena stabile* which yet admitted of some scenic changes in the background; the stage; the processional steps; and also the floor for ritual or dancing, which was not covered with seats and therefore gave a useful sound-reflector as in the Greek theatre. This arrangement was possible because the musicians, though essential to the masque and to the opera, were not as yet interposed in front of the stage.

6. THE RESTORATION PLAYHOUSE. The Restoration playhouse in London witnessed the struggle for position of the musicians, and the first domination of the stage by movable scenery. The original London playhouses were the Duke's Theatre, home of Davenant and the Duke of York's players, and the Theatre Royal or King's Theatre, home of Killigrew and the King's players.

At this formative period there must have been discussions on rival claims to space of actors, musicians, and artists in perspective, and we find that Wren, when he built the new playhouse for Davenant and the Duke's players at Dorset Garden in 1671, made a large box or small gallery, presumably for the musicians, above the proscenium opening. But in this position there must have been little room, though having the theatre ceiling above them they would have been well heard. By 1674 the musicians at Dorset Garden appear to have been moved down to the modern position in front of the stage, where there was room for a much larger orchestra than before, '24 strings with harpsichord and theorbos'. An impression of the interiors of the two rival Restoration playhouses can be had from Pepys. The plans as shown on maps and engravings were long and narrow: there were pit benches, boxes of all prices, and probably a top gallery. The performance was in the afternoon, and the theatre was lighted by side windows and by candles on the stage. Killigrew, telling Pepys (in 1667) about the improvements he had effected at the Theatre Royal, said:

That the stage is now by his pains a thousand times better and more glorious than ever heretofore. Now wax candles and many of them; then not above 3 lbs. of tallow: now all things civil, no rudeness anywhere; then as in a bear garden: then two or three fiddlers, now nine or ten of the best: then nothing but rushes upon the floor and everything else mean; now all otherwise.

There survives at All Souls Library, Oxford, a design by Wren for a theatre called 'Drury House', thought to be for Killigrew's new Theatre Royal (1674) in Drury Lane. (It is illustrated in vol. xii, pl. 23 of the Wren Society publications.) It is interesting to compare this with the Dorset Garden Theatre. At Dorset Garden there is a full proscenium picture frame ornamented by Grinling Gibbons. In the All Souls design by Wren there is no evidence of side windows; the proscenium frame is not emphasized; there is no orchestra place shown, and there is a kind of classical *scena stabile* in the Italian mode in the form of side columns diminishing in height and a sloping cornice to emphasize the illusion of perspective. The English mode is acknowledged in the large fore-stage and doors opening upon it. An examination of Wren's very varied theatre designs would make an interesting study. (See also ENGLISH PLAYHOUSE.)

7. EIGHTEENTH-CENTURY THEATRES. Meanwhile in Italy the theatre had developed from the classical reconstructions of Palladio and Scamozzi, at Vicenza and Sabbionetta, into the large ramped spectacle house such as Aleotti's theatre at Parma, and later into the fully developed Italian theatre with its horseshoe plan, having boxes or *loges* in tiers one above another (see ARCHITECTURE). To this day, it might be remarked, the Italian opera house retains something of the spectacle house—the spectacle being the crowd, anxious to see itself, as well as to see and hear what goes on on the stage. It is likely that the floor was preserved for some time for ballet and processions. In a seventeenth-century engraving (in the Theatre Museum in Munich) a large Masque House in Florence is represented with the floor occupied by the ballet and connected with the stage by a flight of steps. Also, as late as 1745 at Versailles a temporary *Salle de Spectacles* was erected for a fête performance of Voltaire's *Princesse de Navarre*, and an engraving shows a cleared floor space in front of the royal personages. But this floor space is now, in the French example, cut off from the stage by a large orchestral enclosure. The Royal Opera House at Bayreuth, built by the Bibienas in 1748, had a flat floor kept clear for ballet, and ballet doors placed to left and right in the proscenium. Above these doors were boxes resembling stage boxes, known as *trompetenlogen*. When the royal personage entered, three trumpeters appeared in each box and blew a blast. For the ballet the doors below were opened and the dancers defiled upon the floor. The theatre is a beautiful example of the art of

the Bibiena family. (In a later historical period Wagner and his family would sometimes occupy the great centrally-placed royal box.) On the continent the development of the orchestra pit tended to cut back the fore-stage. But in England this was not the case, and Handel made use of the fore-stage at Covent Garden for his choir in performance of oratorio. In England also we find the sloping auditorium ceiling, as in Vanbrugh's design for a theatre (reproduced by Edward Craig and exhibited at Burlington House by the British Drama League, 1945), and in the surviving Theatre Royal at Bristol, built in 1766. A ceiling of this kind acts as an efficient reflector of sound, but it was probably designed in this form to give height over the upper gallery at the rear of the theatre. The splayed proscenium ceiling is found in Adam's design for the King's Theatre, Haymarket (Soane Collection). On the continent the flat ceiling was customary; true domes were not introduced until the nineteenth century (although we find a dome painted on the flat in Adam's Drury Lane).

As often happens in the history of buildings, fortuitous circumstances produced in the eighteenth-century theatre all over Europe a good acoustical instrument and a home for the development of an art. The reverberation was short owing to the tiers of *loges* with their drapery; echoes were avoided owing to the diffusing of sound by baroque and Louis Quinze ornament, and owing to the flat ceilings and absence of domes; but orchestral tone was good owing to the large amount of wood construction. In these theatres Garrick performed Shakespeare to large audiences, in them the astonishing art of *bel canto* was developed in opera, and the Italian *aria*, with its 'introduction' and accompaniment on strings, carried music forward from the church cantata to the operas of Mozart. This was made possible by the short reverberation and bright tone of the Italian theatre form. Modern acoustic studies have also shown the useful effect of the mixture of resonant, reflecting, and absorbing materials in a hall and of their equal distribution over the interior surface, all of which are characteristic of this type of theatre. The theatres were often very large. The Scala at Milan had six tiers above floor-level, Covent Garden in 1808 seated 2,800 persons. For instrumental music the theatre form was generally satisfactory, and evidence of this is shown in the influence exerted by it on the form of early concert rooms. Leopold Mozart, writing from Milan in 1770, says of the Mantua concert hall:

I wish you could see the hall where the concert took place, the so-called *Teatrino della Accademia Filarmonica*. In all my life I have never seen anything more beautiful of its kind. It is not a theatre but a hall built with boxes like an opera house. Where the stage ought to be there is a raised platform for the orchestra and behind the orchestra another gallery built with boxes for the audience.

The old Gewandhaus at Leipzig (1780) was also somewhat of this shape.

But for the purpose of developing the full tone of the chorus the Italian opera house was not good, owing to the considerable sound-absorption and consequent short reverberation. Covent Garden, under John Rich's management, was used for pantomimes, plays, operas, and oratorios. Handel opened at Covent Garden in 1734 and in his first season gave fourteen performances of oratorio. The Pugin and Rowlandson view of Covent Garden about 1808, on the occasion of an oratorio, shows Handel's organ on the stage with the orchestra surrounding it and the choir in front on the fore-stage. There is evidence that Handel was sensitive to acoustic effects. On one occasion, behind the scenes at Covent Garden, he was told the audience was small and replied, 'My music will sound the better.' The significance of this is that the audience is generally the chief sound-absorbing factor in a hall and therefore the smaller the audience the longer the reverberation. Handel implied that he preferred conditions which gave a fuller tone. It is probable that the characteristic theatre acoustics of Covent Garden, with its considerable sound-absorption, contributed to the broad, loud, choral tone called Handelian.

For opera, however, the short reverberation permitted the great rapidity and animation of Mozart's and Rossini's vocal music. A Mozart opera is at its best with a weight of orchestra of about 30 players, and before 1939 it could be heard performed thus at the Residenz Theater in Munich. The conductor sat at the piano and played the recitatives. The Residenz Theater was the first theatre in Europe to increase its lighting by putting little mirrors behind the candles. The acoustics remained practically as when it was built in 1751 and from the *loges* the true effect could be studied. The extreme rapidity of the vocal ensembles of 'Don Giovanni' and 'Figaro' assumes both the tripping Italian tongue and the extremely short theatre reverberation.

8. THE WAGNER THEATRE. When the orchestra in an Italian theatre increased in size, as occurred during the nineteenth century, the unresolved problem of the orchestra position became acute in opera. The weight of instrumental tone then began to screen the singers on the stage and especially so for listeners in stall seats. At the Scala in Milan in recent times during a Verdi opera the huge orchestra was found seated far out on the floor; and consequently hearing was far better in the upper galleries than in expensive stall seats. In Wagner the loudness of the brass under these conditions is often deafening. One result of this is that Wagner singers are forced to develop the reed tones of their voices and sing sharp in order to make themselves heard, and consequently accuracy of pitch is often sacrificed. Wagner recognized the failure of the Italian theatre as an instrument for his own music-dramas, and so evolved the Wagner theatre at Bayreuth. In it the ramped floor seats beginning at stage level, the double proscenium arch, the baffled side-walls, and

especially the placing of an orchestra of 110 instruments in a pit extending under the stage instead of into the stalls, combine to give a characteristic interior. The boxes are situated only on the rear wall. The roof is flat, and the building is constructed largely of wood. But what gives it acoustic character is the longer reverberation, much more that of a German concert hall, namely 2·2 seconds approximately (by the Sabine formula) as compared to the 1·4 seconds of a typical Italian theatre like Covent Garden. This longer reverberation is the result of the absence of side galleries, which gives a larger cubic air-space per seat and therefore a greater volume relative to audience-absorption. This gives a 'fullness' of tone, as distinguished from 'brightness', but requires a slower tempo. Also, the mixing and subduing of instrumental tone in the concealed orchestra pit gives a balance and unity of artistic effect, impossible for Wagner opera in an Italian theatre. It is not too much to say that it is impossible to realize the dramatic and musical quality of a Wagner opera unless the enormous tone energy produced is properly controlled, as at Bayreuth. Why then, it may be asked, is the Wagner Theatre at Munich (the Prinz Regent) so much criticized? The reason is clear. The reverberation is far too long to permit of the rapid tempo of Mozart or Puccini, or Gilbert and Sullivan. It is also quite unsuited to stage plays. That is to say, it is unsuited to repertory purposes unless precautions are taken to compensate for the lack of galleries by adding special sound-absorbents and reducing the reverberation by special means.

9. NINETEENTH-CENTURY THEATRES. In the nineteenth-century commercial theatre the horseshoe plan was preserved. The plan-form suggested the domed ceiling, and there was probably a movement after the introduction of gas-lighting for more air and better ventilation. But this led to some notable echoes focussed from a particular stage position, such as that of the old Alhambra in Leicester Square. The 'Irving Safety Theatre' designed as an ideal auditorium for Sir Henry Irving, but not built, had a large dome which would certainly have caused trouble. Even when echoes were not noticeable, curved ceilings gave an unequal distribution of reflected sound, so that some seats were noticeably better than others, and the myth of the 'blind spot' became fashionable. But the baroque tradition of heavy theatre ornament, of stage boxes and plenty of drapery, continued, and this tended to keep reverberation short. At the same time the smaller 'comedy' theatres came to be built, in which a sentimental society could more intimately enjoy domestic rather than heroic emotions. Thus while the larger theatres preserved an oratorical tradition in Shakespeare, in old-fashioned melodrama, and in the pantomime, there developed a greater tendency towards naturalism in gesture and voice and with it a demand for the acoustics of the fireside. Clearly modern comedy demands a smaller

theatre than Drury Lane or the Winter Garden, in which nuances of tone and of facial expression can hardly be detected in rear seats, and the standard of loudness, without an oratorical technique, tended to decline. Thus when a drawing-room comedy by Henry Arthur Jones went on tour from the Criterion and was performed in a large old-fashioned provincial theatre it was not well heard in the recesses of pit and gallery, but on the whole stalls and dress circle could hear well enough.

10. ACOUSTICS AND THE MODERN THEATRE. In the twentieth century, between 1919 and 1939, a remarkable change occurred in the design of theatres. This was due to two things: (i) a style change, and (ii) the application of building acoustics to theatre design. The modern style swept away baroque ornament; large continuous surfaces in hard plaster, ingeniously lit, took their place. At the same time the stage boxes were removed, likewise a large area of proscenium pelmets, curtains, and velvet tympana. Then the fan-shaped plan was found to seat more persons at a medium distance from the stage, and to give better sight lines both for legitimate theatre and cinema. The smooth tunnel interior with splayed walls and ceiling thus superseded the Victorian baroque building with its broken-up surfaces interspersed with curtains. At first the new acoustic studies approved the fan-shaped plan and splayed proscenium on account of the useful reflecting surfaces provided. Loudness was considerably increased by that means in rear seats. But it was also discovered that any return of sound from surfaces at the rear, including balcony fronts, ceiling coves, balustrades, &c., found its way to front seats, and the complaints registered were no longer from cheap rear seats but from expensive seats in the stalls, especially from front side seats. Now acoustic theory assumed powerful sound-absorbing material on the rear wall behind the audience to prevent any return of sound; but in practice it was found that commercial sound-absorbents, often covered with paint, were not nearly as efficient as the modern hard plasters of the reflecting walls and ceiling. Another factor is that the fan-shaped plan gives a relatively large area to the rear wall, and that this wall was often given the most dangerous curve possible, namely a curve struck from a centre on or near the stage. Thus, whatever remainder of sound was returned, as not absorbed, was focussed towards the front of the house, or, if touching the side walls on its return course, was not diffused by ornament, or absorbed by side galleries, boxes, and curtains. The result was not necessarily a complete echo (that is to say, a distinct repetition) but a prolonging of word-endings liable to obscure rapid speech. A parallel symptom was that coughs and noises in galleries tended to concentrate also on stall seats. The result was to show the value of the breaking-up of sound by heavy ornament, that is to say, the value of the principle of diffusion, and to impress again on modern designers the paramount importance of absorption in the theatre auditorium, where

speech is often very rapid and where the syllable intervals (about one-twentieth of a second in duration) must not be obscured by any prolonging of tone.

The modern theatre type therefore requires some modification. Large radius concave surfaces whether on plan or section must be avoided, and this especially applies to the rear wall. On the other hand, convex surfaces will diffuse sound, and should be deliberately designed to prevent sound concentrations, and thus take the place functionally of the heavy ornament of former times. Convex shapes are therefore specially desirable on proscenium areas, and we often find that cinema theatre designers treat these areas with ribs and grilles. Another danger is that the large volume in the front of the house without side galleries and boxes tends to give a longer reverberation than in galleries, and inter-reflection is increased by the fore-stage. Therefore large sound-absorbing panels on front side walls, as in the New Hippodrome at Coventry, are necessary. Also, if the ceiling be stepped, instead of sloped, it is not minimized as a useful reflector, but yet interposes some obstacles to the return of sound. Finally, a proscenium well draped or rendered absorbent is highly desirable, as is the stage box. Apart from acoustics, the stage box is useful for pantomime and vaudeville, and one might note that the ingenious modern dramatists Auden and Isherwood made good use of it in their play, *The Ascent of F.6*, as part of the theatral area. Indeed, it is fairly well recognized that the development of the theatre lies in the direction of extending the theatral area and escaping from the rigidity of the picture-frame proscenium. Earlier in this article the Masque House plan of Inigo Jones has been mentioned as representing the art theatre at its fullest; it gave the greatest scope for the plastic designer. An advantage of the *scena stabile* is that it gives a home for the mind—a something familiar and unifying, yet impersonal. An advantage of the fore-stage is that it increases depth and dimension and links up auditorium with *scena*: while by means of steps and floor space, processions, ritual, and dance are given room. It should be recalled that Shakespeare is the drama of the procession as well as of the group, and constantly tends to come out beyond the proscenium arch. All this is recognized by theatre designers. What is not so well recognized is that these spatial elements require some care in acoustics owing to the character of the modern hard lining materials which tend to cause inter-reflections: the principle of ample distributed sound-absorbents over the whole house and of diffusing surfaces should be the general guide. (See also AUDITORIUM, COSTUME, and PROSCENIUM.)

H. B.

ACT. (1) In early times the music between the parts of an English play was called the Act. It was beaten by a drummer, with the later addition of pipe or trumpet. In time it came to be called the Act- or Curtain-Tune or -Music, and then simply the Music.

(2) The divisions of a play are now known as Acts, each of which may contain one or more scenes. Greek plays were continuous, the only pauses being marked by the chorus. Horace was the first to insist on the importance of five acts, probably from experience. With the Renaissance, the division into five acts became classic, and was adopted by the great French dramatists, from whence it passed into England via Ben Jonson. It should be noted that there is no proof that Shakespeare divided his plays thus. The divisions in the printed copies were probably introduced by the editors in imitation of Jonson. In comedy more licence was allowed to the individual, two or three acts being quite usual, even in Molière. Modern drama usually keeps to three acts, as being convenient for actors and audience alike, but two acts are sometimes found, and many Shakespeare revivals have had only one interval in each play. A division into four acts is unusual.

ACT-DROP, the name given in the late eighteenth century to the painted cloth which closed the proscenium opening between the acts of a play (see CURTAIN).

ACTOR, ACTRESS, ACTING. The art of acting, and the profession of actor, is as old as man, showing itself first in ritual dance and song and somewhat later in dialogue. Of the very early actors nothing is known, but in Greece, where they took part in a religious ceremony, they were evidently men of some repute (see GREECE, 3). In Rome their status was low, and they were often recruited from the ranks of slaves, a circumstance which may be linked with the decadence of the theatre there and the decline from classical tragedy and comedy to pantomime (see ROME, *passim*). With the coming of Christianity they were finally proscribed and sank into obscurity, handing on some mutilated traditions through the little bands of itinerant acrobats and jugglers who catered for the crowds at fairs and in the larger cities. The medieval minstrels, however, occupied a special place in the social scale, and were welcome at Court and in noble houses, forming themselves into Guilds for mutual help and protection and being assured of at least a decent livelihood (see MINSTREL). They were not actors, but when the revival of the theatre came in Europe, first in the Church and later in the market-place (see ECCLESIASTICAL DRAMA), they may have given advice and practical help to the big amateur groups that performed the Mystery cycles.

With the emergence of a vernacular drama in each country, as distinct from the universal Latin drama, the time was ripe for the rise of the professional actor. He came slowly, and it is almost impossible to fix a date for his arrival in any particular country. In general one might safely say that he established himself in most countries during the sixteenth century, which saw the formation of the *commedia dell'arte* troupes in Italy (see ITALY, 2), the work of the first professional actor-manager in Spain, Lope de Rueda (1510–60), the building of the first permanent playhouse in London, Burbage's Theatre (1576), and, at the end of the century, the establishment of the first professional troupe at the Hôtel de Bourgogne in Paris (see FRANCE, 3). Germany, owing to internal dissension and division, had to wait longer for a settled theatre, and not until the eighteenth century were any of her actors famous enough to be known by name. Russia, whose early theatrical history is as yet imperfectly known, can hardly be said to have had a national and professional theatre much before the middle of the nineteenth century.

Women did not act in Greece at all, and in Rome only if very depraved. The medieval stage may have employed a few women, but they were still amateurs. The professional actress emerges first in Italy, the best-known being Isabella Andreini (1562–1604), and in France appears at the same time as the professional actor, Marie Vernier or Venier being a member of the company at the Hôtel de Bourgogne from the start. Elizabethan drama made no use of women at all, and all the heroines of Shakespeare and other playwrights were played by boys and young men. It was not until the Restoration in 1660 that women were first seen on the London stage. The name of the first English actress is not known; there are several claimants, but whoever she was, she played Desdemona on 8 Dec. 1660, and paved the way for the actresses of the Patent theatres. It is interesting to note, in passing, that the first great name in the annals of the German theatre is that of a woman, Caroline Neuber (1697–1760), who tried to put into effect the reforms of Gottsched. But she was probably not the first German actress, since Jolly had one in his company of English comedians in Germany in 1654.

The position of the actor was for a long time precarious. In Catholic countries he was refused the sacraments, and an anomalous situation arose by which a man like Molière could be wealthy, respected, received by the king and patronized by the nobility, and yet be buried in unconsecrated ground. Legally even Shakespeare and his great contemporaries were still liable to be classed as rogues and vagabonds, and it was not until the nineteenth century that the actor achieved a definite place in society, which culminated in the knighthood bestowed on Henry Irving in 1895. In becoming respectable the actor no doubt lost something of his mystery and picturesqueness, qualities which may have appealed more to the non-theatrical mind than to the harassed professional, who was for many centuries at the mercy of any jack-in-office who chose to interpret the strict letter of the law, and might find his means of livelihood taken from him overnight.

Fashions in acting change as in everything else, and the whole history of the theatre shows one method giving way to another, one convention succeeding another. Only in the Far East,

which lies outside the range of this article (see CHINA and JAPAN), have traditions in acting remained unbroken down the centuries, and even they are now in a state of flux. In Greece, the tragic actor was static—a voice and a presence; in Rome he was lively, and, in the last resort, an acrobat. The commedia dell'arte demanded above all a quick wit and a nimble body; French tragedy once again asked for a fine presence and a sonorous voice; Restoration comedy must have called for a polished brilliance and a gentlemanly insolence. The melodrama of the nineteenth century could only make its full effect when its actors 'tore a passion to tatters', and the modern comedy which replaced it gives little scope for gesture or raised voices. Yet the true actor still needs to be a little of everything—singer, dancer, mimic, acrobat, tragedian, comedian—and to have at his command a good physique, a retentive memory, an alert brain, a clear, resonant voice with good articulation and controlled breathing (see SPEECH). Some actors have achieved fame lacking one or more of these essentials, but only at the cost of much hard work, and by the impress of their personality, amounting, as in the case of Garrick and Kean, to genius. Often the price of their victory has been an early collapse. Much of an actor's art must be born in him; something may be taught. The ideal is a good balance of intuition and hard work, tempered by all-round experience.

ACTORS' THEATRE. (1) A membership group which developed from the first Equity Players' Group of New York, formed in 1922 for actor-controlled presentation of good classic and new plays. Dudley Digges was one of the first directors, and among the plays of the first seasons were *Candida* and *The Wild Duck*. In 1925 the organization fused with that of the Greenwich Village Group under Kenneth Macgowan.

(2) Another group under the same name was formed in 1939, and gave plays at the Provincetown Playhouse. It was intended as a Little Theatre organization for the tryout of new plays and young actors. Its activities were suspended on the outbreak of war in 1941.

ADAM DE LA HALLE (c. 1240–c. 1286), also known as Le Bossu d'Arras, one of the few medieval minstrels known to us by name. He was intended for the Church, but a rash marriage prevented him from taking orders, and he turned to literature. Among his works is *Le Jeu de la feuillée*, given at Puy in 1262–3, held by competent critics to mark the beginning of lay, as distinct from ecclesiastical, drama in France. A reference in it to Hellequin, king of the underworld, has also been cited as one of the sources of the later Harlequin. It was for the Court of Robert II, Count of Artois, that Adam de la Halle wrote the charming *Jeu de Robin et Marion*, a picture of thirteenth-century rustic happiness which by virtue of its music—for Adam was as good a musician as he was a poet—may be considered the first French light opera, as it certainly was the first French pastoral. Through the medium of wandering minstrels it may have given to England some details of the Robin Hood story.

ADAMS, EDWIN (1834–77), American actor, who made his first appearance at Boston in 1853 in *The Hunchback*. He was later seen in Philadelphia and Baltimore, and toured extensively, being well received as an excellent light comedian. At the opening performance of Booth's Theatre, New York, he played Mercutio to Booth's Romeo, and remained there for some time, playing also Iago, and appearing in modern plays. His most successful part was Enoch Arden in a dramatization of Tennyson's poem, which, said Jefferson, 'so far as the character is related to the stage, was a creation entirely his own, and one too that touched the sympathy of his audience'. He toured in the part all over the United States, but made his last appearance in San Francisco, shortly before his early death, as Iago to the Othello of John McCullough. His loss was deplored by actors and audience alike. 'Everybody loved him,' said William Winter. 'He was one of the blithest spirits of the stage.'

ADAMS, DR. JOSEPH QUINCY (1881–1946), American Shakespearian scholar, who at the time of his death was Director of the famous Folger Library devoted primarily to works by or about Shakespeare. Son of a Baptist minister, Adams studied in London and Berlin, and from 1919 until his appointment to the Folger Library in 1931 was Professor of English at Cornell University, of which he was a graduate. He devoted most of his leisure to the study of the Elizabethan drama, and was editor of the New Variorum Shakespeare, of a number of pre-Shakespearean dramas, and of the Folger Shakespeare Reprints. His own works included *Shakespearian Playhouses* (1917) and a life of Shakespeare published in 1923. In 1937 he edited a facsimile reproduction of Thomas Middleton's *The Ghost of Lucrece*, of which the only existing copy is in the Folger Library.

ADAMS, MAUDE (1872–   ), an American actress, daughter of the leading lady of the Salt Lake City stock company. She was on the stage as a child, and at the age of 5 scored a signal triumph as Little Schneider in *Fritz*, at the San Francisco Theatre. Young David Belasco was also a member of the cast. She played all the usual child-roles, including Eva in *Uncle Tom's Cabin*, and, after an interval for education, returned to the stage. At 16 she played with Sothern, and in 1892 was engaged by the Frohmans to appear opposite John Drew, who had just left Daly. She remained with them for many years. One of her most famous parts was that of Lady Babbie in *The Little Minister*, which Barrie enlarged specially for her, at the suggestion, it is said, of Elizabeth Marbury, his agent. He was fortunate in his interpreter, for her quaint, elfin personality suited his work to perfection, as was later seen

in *Peter Pan*, *What Every Woman Knows*, *Quality Street*, and *A Kiss for Cinderella*. She was also much admired as Juliet, Viola, Rosalind, Joan of Arc, and L'Aiglon. One of the most popular actresses of her day, she was modest and retiring, and much averse to publicity, and in 1918 left the stage, not returning until 1931, when she appeared on tour as Portia to Otis Skinner's Shylock. She also toured in 1937 as Maria in *Twelfth Night*. As a young girl she was not strictly beautiful, but had a frail and wistful appearance which later matured into true loveliness, the outward sign of her gracious and endearing personality.

A.D.C., see CAMBRIDGE.

ADDISON, JOSEPH (1672–1719), English politician and man of letters, friend and collaborator of Richard Steele in the *Spectator* and the *Tatler*. He was also the author of two plays, *Cato* (1713), a tragedy on the French classical model, and *The Drummer* (1715), a moral comedy which obtained little success. *Cato*, on the other hand, which was well supported by the Whigs for political reasons, and the Tories for effect, was extremely successful, and exerted a powerful restraint on the natural exuberance of English drama, so powerful, says one critic, 'that it emasculated the art of play-writing and well-nigh bereft the stage of originality of thought or freedom of expression'. Written in unrhymed heroic couplets, it contains some fine polished poetry, but cannot be esteemed good theatre. The part of Cato was originally offered to Colley Cibber, who declined it, and it was finally played by Barton Booth, with Anne Oldfield as Lucia. It ran for thirty-five nights, and was then given at Oxford, Addison's university, with equal success, the actors donating £50 out of the profits towards the repair of St. Mary's Church. Addison's dramatic theories and criticisms are found in several papers of the *Spectator*, while the *Tatler*, No. 42 (1709), contains an amusing mock inventory of the properties and furnishings of Drury Lane.

ADE, GEORGE (1866–1944), an American journalist, humorist and playwright, whose 'fables in slang' brought a new and refreshing idiom to American literature. Famous for his wisecracks, his plays of contemporary life were full of the homely humour and wit that had already become associated with him. Among them were *College Widow*, which added a new phrase to contemporary language, *Father and the Boys*, *Just Out of College*, and *Speaking to Father*. He was also responsible for the books of several musical comedies, among them *The Fair Co-Ed*, which made Elsie Janis a star.

ADELPHI THEATRE. (1) LONDON, was originally the Sans Pareil, and was built and opened on 27 Nov. 1806 by John Scott, a colour-maker who had invented a washing-blue. It cost £10,000, and was used to exploit the talent of his daughter, who gave a one-woman entertainment written and performed by herself, ending with a display of fireworks.

Mr. Scott and his daughter succeeded, and in 1819 sold the theatre to Jones and Rodwell for £25,000, having also made a good deal of money out of it in the meantime.

The new tenants renamed the theatre the Adelphi and opened on 18 Oct. 1819. The fare was melodrama and adaptations of Scott's novels. They prospered, and the theatre was redecorated in 1821. Keeley made his début there, as 'Little Keeley', and the first stage version of Pierce Egan's *Tom and Jerry; or, Life in London* was produced there with enormous success, with Keeley, Reeve, and Wrench. It was frequently revived. A sequel called *Green in France; or, Tom and Jerry's Tour*, produced at great expense, shared the fate of most sequels, but a third play, based on Egan's *Life of an Actor*, was more successful.

Rodwell died, from the strain, it is said, of a horrific drama, *Valmondi; or, the Unhallowed Sepulchre*, Jones retired, and Terry and Yates took over successfully, especially with *The Pilot*, adapted by Fitzball from Fenimore Cooper's novel. T. P. Cooke made a great hit in this play and remained at the Adelphi for some time. In 1827 the theatre was enlarged, and in the following year Terry retired, being replaced by Charles Mathews. Although good plays and companies were presented, both managers were poor business men and got into difficulties. Mathews died in 1835 and was replaced for a season by his son, who was succeeded by one Gladstone. In 1842 Yates died, but Gladstone managed to make the theatre pay. Madame Céleste appeared there, and when Reeve, who had been a pillar of the house, died, he was replaced by Edgar Wright, an accomplished comedian. A dramatic version of Ainsworth's *Jack Sheppard*, with Mrs. Keeley as the house- and prison-breaker, was a big success. In 1844 Madame Céleste and Webster took the Adelphi and started there what became known as 'Adelphi Drama'. The plays were mostly written by Buckstone, the best-remembered being *Green Bushes* and *The Flowers of the Forest*, in which Madame Céleste and O. Smith were outstanding. In 1853 Webster left the Haymarket (he had been running both theatres) to devote all his time to the Adelphi. He gave a fine performance in *The Dead Heart*. On the recommendation of Dickens, Toole succeeded Wright in 1858, making a name for himself in *Good for Nothing* and *Ici on parle français*. In the summer of that year the old theatre was pulled down and a new one built, which opened on Boxing Day. It made a promising beginning with *The Colleen Bawn* and *The Octoroon*. In 1863 Kate Bateman made a great success in *Leah*, which ran for 210 nights, and in 1865 Jefferson was a sensation in *Rip Van Winkle*. Fechter was at the Adelphi in 1868. Webster, having taken Chatterton into partnership, retired in 1872, after a reign of twenty-eight years. Nothing of importance occurred until the Gattis took over and, with William Terriss as their leading man, started a new type of 'Adelphi Drama'. Terriss was the idol of the town, and his assassination by a madman in 1897, while entering the theatre, caused widespread mourning.

In 1901 the house was rebuilt and opened by Tom B. Davis as the Century Theatre with an American variety show called *The Whirl of the Town*. It failed, and the theatre reverted to its old name. Sarah Bernhardt appeared there on two occasions, also Wilson Barrett in *The Christian King*. Two highly coloured melodramas, *The Worst Woman in London* and *Her Second Time on Earth*, were big successes.

In 1910 George Edwardes inaugurated a series of musical plays with Gertie Millar and Joseph Coyne in *The Quaker Girl*, a policy continued by Alfred Butt during the war of 1914–18, when W. H. Berry was the chief comedian. In 1930 the house was again reconstructed and redecorated. Ivor Novello's *The Dancing Years*, transferred there in 1942 from Drury Lane, ran for over two years. (See AUDITORIUM, 4.)   W. M. P.

(2) NEW YORK, on Fifty-Fourth Street between Sixth and Seventh Avenues. This was originally named the Craig Theatre, and opened on 24 Dec. 1928 with *Potiphar's Wife*, in which Frances Carson and Barry O'Neill played the leading parts. The play was unsuccessful, as were several that followed, and after standing empty for some time the theatre re-opened under its present name on 27 Nov. 1934, with *The Lord Blesses the Bishop*, which had only seven performances. After a short session of American Ballet, the theatre was taken over by the Federal Theatre Project, who, on 19 May 1936, produced there *The Dance of Death*, followed by several performances of the negro *Macbeth*, originally produced by Orson Welles at the Lafayette Theatre in Harlem, and by the anti-Fascist play, *It Can't Happen Here*. A children's play, *The Revolt of the Beavers*, condemned as Communist propaganda by those who opposed the Federal Theatre Project, was also seen in the summer of 1936, and in the early days of the following year came the overwhelming success of Arthur Arent's Living Newspaper on housing, *One-Third of a Nation*. Produced by Philip Barber, this ran for 237 performances. The last play staged at the Adelphi by the Federal Theatre Project was the ill-fated *Sing for Your Supper* (1939), whose sixty performances, only achieved after arduous and acrimonious rehearsals, were brought to an end by the dissolution of the sponsoring body. In 1947 the Adelphi came back into the news with the production of the Theatre Guild's musical version of *Street Scene*.   G. F.

ADMIRAL'S MEN, the theatrical company that shared the honours of the Elizabethan stage with the Chamberlain's Men, with whom Shakespeare was associated. Their star actor, rival of Richard Burbage, was Edward Alleyn, who joined them possibly in 1587, in which case he would have been the original Tamburlaine. Lord Howard, their patron, had had a company of players in 1576–9, known as Lord Howard's Men. He became Admiral in 1585, and at Christmas in the same year the 'Admiral's players' made their first appearance at Court. In November 1587 they were concerned in a sad accident, when a bullet fired in the course of a play killed a child and a pregnant woman and severely injured a man in the audience. They are not heard of again for a year or so, but in 1590-1 they were housed in James Burbage's Theatre with Strange's Men. Richard Burbage, then only a boy, may have appeared in small parts in some of their plays, but it is not certain. After a quarrel with James Burbage over finance, the two companies moved to the Rose, under Henslowe, whose stepdaughter married Alleyn. When the Chamberlain's Men were formed in 1594 some of the Admiral's Men joined them, while the rest formed themselves into an independent company under Alleyn, with Henslowe as their landlord and 'banker'. The fact that Henslowe kept a combined diary and account book enables us to follow the fortunes of the Admiral's Men very closely from 1594-1604. They were apparently very successful, and had a large repertory of new and old plays, most of which, except for Marlowe's, have been lost or forgotten. The company also performed some of Chapman's early works and plays by Dekker and Chettle. They were badly handicapped by the retirement in 1597 of Alleyn, whose roles were shared among two lesser men, neither of whom came up to his excellence. However, he returned three years later, apparently at the express wish of Queen Elizabeth, who commanded him to play at Court, and the company took a fresh lease of life, moving into Henslowe's new playhouse, the Fortune. Here they continued after the death of Elizabeth, when they were renamed Prince Henry's Men, and again lost Alleyn, this time for good, though from his retirement in Dulwich he continued to advise and assist the company. In 1612 their young patron died, and was replaced by the Elector Palatine, the company now being known as the Palsgrave's Men. In 1621 the Fortune was burnt down, and all the wardrobe and playbooks were lost, a calamity indeed. It nearly broke them, but with Alleyn's help they struggled along and a new Fortune was opened in 1623 with practically the same company as before. New plays were bought, one by Dekker, several by Rowley, and four by an actor in the company, Gunnell; but none of them proved successful, and after two difficult years the combination of plague and the death of James I proved too much. The company disbanded, after a long and honourable career, and its remnants were probably absorbed into other existing organizations.

ADVERTISEMENT CURTAIN, an outer curtain or act-drop used mostly in smaller theatres, covered with advertisements of local shops and manufacturers.

AE [George William Russell] (1867-1935), see IRELAND.

AESCHYLUS (525-456 B.C.), Greek dramatist, son of Euphorion, was born of noble parents in Eleusis, near Athens, and died at Gela in Sicily. He fought against the Persians in the battle of Marathon; possibly at Salamis and Plataea too. Like Pindar and other poets of his time, he visited the Court of Hiero, Tyrant of Syracuse; he composed a (lost) tragedy in honour of his founding of the new city of Etna. There seems to be no reason for believing ancient statements that Aeschylus withdrew from Athens for political reasons, or that he was killed by an eagle's dropping a tortoise upon his bald head. His epitaph at Gela is recorded; it is said to have been composed by Aeschylus himself. It may be translated: 'Here, in the fertile soil of Gela, lies Aeschylus, son of Euphorion. Of his notable courage the field of Marathon could speak, and the long-haired Mede; for he knows it well.' He was commemorated as a citizen, not as a poet.

Aeschylus is said to have written 90 plays, and he gained 13 victories. The titles of 79 plays are known: only seven are extant—the *Suppliants* (c. 490 B.C.), the *Persians* (472), the *Seven against Thebes* (469), the *Prometheus Bound* (? c. 460), and the trilogy known as the *Oresteia* (458), viz. the *Agamemnon*, the *Choephori* (Libation-bearers), and the *Eumenides*. About a quarter of these 90 plays must have been satyr-plays, in which riotous form of drama Aeschylus was an acknowledged master. Nothing of these survives except a few fragments.

Aeschylus may reasonably be regarded as the real founder of European drama, and no one but Shakespeare can seriously be considered his equal as a dramatic poet. At the time of Aeschylus's birth the tragic festival in Athens was only ten years old. A play was represented by a chorus of singers and dancers, and one actor only (who of course might 'double'); except that the leader of the chorus, speaking strictly in the name of the chorus, might engage in dialogue with the actor proper. Drama therefore must have been predominantly lyrical; development of plot and of character could have been only slight. Aeschylus, by introducing a second actor, made (gradually) the histrionic part as important as the lyric, and (as it has been said) turned oratorio into drama. The transition can be seen in the early plays: in the *Suppliants* the chorus is the chief actor; the *Persians* still opens with the entrance-song of the chorus, the actors still first address themselves to the chorus and not to the other actor, and it is still through the chorus that the play gets its formal unity; the *Seven against Thebes* opens with a speech from an actor, not with a choral ode, and the play is clearly dominated by the chief actor. In his later plays Aeschylus used (though in a highly individual way) Sophocles' invention of the third actor. Even so, the proportion of lyrics to the whole play remained large; in the *Agamemnon* they form as much as one-half of the play.

Aeschylus also reduced the size of the chorus from fifty. His third innovation, one which died with him, was his use of the statutory tetralogy. Competing poets had to present three serious plays and one satyr-play; Aeschylus normally made the three plays a connected 'trilogy' in the modern sense of the word: not always, for the *Persians* is an independent play, having no connexion with the two that were presented with it. In the Aeschylean trilogy each play is a complete unity, yet each is a coherent part of a larger unity. This device gave his drama an amplitude which has never been approached since—an amplitude which his vast conceptions needed, and which only his magnificent structural sense could control. The normal scheme might be very baldly summarized as the offence, the counter-offence, and the resolution; sin provokes sin, until justice asserts itself. Thus, the *Agamemnon* deals (though in no pedestrian chronological order) with the crime of Thyestes against his brother Atreus (Agamemnon's father), and the terrible revenge of Atreus; and with the crime of Paris and Helen against Menelaus. Agamemnon, by the will of Zeus, seeks a just vengeance, but his cause is stained by personal ambition: to this he sacrifices his own daughter, and he also behaves with impiety when he has captured Troy. Clytemnestra, seeking a just revenge, kills him: but her vengeance too is stained by murder and adultery, and only promises more blood. The play shows again and again how sin begets sin, and raises, with increasing insistence, the question how and where a final act of justice can be found. All this, thanks to Aeschylus's constructional skill, is brought to a brilliant focus in the crimes and death of Agamemnon. In the second play Orestes appears to avenge his father by killing his mother. After a long preparation the horrible deed is done in two or three swift scenes. Orestes, unlike the previous avengers, is disinterested; his motives are pure, and he is acting under the direct command of Delphian Apollo, who is the mouthpiece of Zeus. But for all that, he rushes out at the end of the play, pursued by his mother's Furies. There is no solution yet. The third play shows Orestes protected by Apollo but pursued by the Furies; Apollo is acting for Zeus, the Furies claim an even more august authority. Issue is joined before Athena (embodying Divine Wisdom) on the Acropolis. She declines to judge in so weighty a case; and it is decided by a jury of Athenian citizens under her presidency. Orestes is acquitted, by her casting-vote. Apollo and Orestes disappear. The Furies, indignant, threaten Athens with ruin, but are persuaded by Athena to relent and to accept an honoured place in her city. Disinterested justice is at last achieved, and the final plan of Zeus revealed, in the usages of civic life. Thus the *Oresteia* is, among other things, a drama of human civilization.

Of the other plays, the *Suppliants* and the *Prometheus* were the first plays of their trilogies, the *Seven against Thebes* the third of its; and, judging by what can be recovered, the scale of these trilogies was hardly less majestic than that of the *Oresteia*.

These conceptions were matched by a bold dramatic technique, an immense concentration, a wonderful sense of structure, and magnificent poetry. Aeschylus made the utmost use of spectacle and colour; and, in virtue of the beauty and strength of his choral odes, he might well be regarded as one of the greatest of lyric poets, as well as, possibly, the greatest of dramatists.

As a unique honour to him, it was enacted in Athens after his death not only that his plays might be revived at the festivals (to which normally only new plays were admitted) but also that anyone proposing to do this should be 'given a chorus' without question (see also GREECE, 1 *b*). H. D. F. K.

AESOPUS, CLAUDIUS, a celebrated Roman tragic actor of the first century B.C., much admired by Horace. He was a friend of Cicero, who speaks of him as having great powers of facial expression and fluent gesture. During Cicero's exile Aesopus would often allude to him on the stage, in the hope of swaying public opinion in his favour.

AFINOGENOV, ALEXANDER MIKOLAEVICH (1904–41), Soviet dramatist, who began writing in 1926. His first important play was *Fear* (translated into English by Charles Malamuth and published in *Six Soviet Plays*, 1936), which was first performed at the Leningrad Theatre of Drama in 1931. Later in the same year it was seen at the Moscow Art Theatre, produced by Sudakov with settings by Shifrin. It was one of the earliest Soviet plays to combine good technique and dramatic tension with party propaganda, and deals with the conversion to Socialism of an irritable psychologist who has propounded the theory that fear governs the U.S.S.R. This fusion of socialist propaganda with the long tradition of classical and pre-Revolutionary playwriting, whereby humanity, with its faults, foibles, courage, and idiosyncrasies, its basic lovableness and everlasting interest, is shown as being as important as the play's message, is even more clearly seen in a later play, *Distant Point*, given at the Vakhtangov Theatre in 1934. This is a fine character-study of a Far-Eastern general on his way to western Russia, who stops at a remote Siberian railway station to give its inhabitants a much-needed lesson in unselfishness, dying in the process. The play, which has been given four separate productions in London, was first seen at the Gate Theatre in 1937 in a translation by Hubert Griffith. It has been produced by many British provincial repertory theatres and several times broadcast by the B.B.C.

Shortly after the production of *Distant Point* Afinogenov was in trouble with the authorities, but returned to favour on the outbreak of war, and in 1940 had a light comedy, *Mashenka*, produced by Zavadsky at the Mossoviet Theatre. A year later he was killed in an air-raid, leaving his last play, *On the Eve*, to be produced posthumously. Set in a Moscow suburb, it shows how a typical family there played their part in the stemming of the German advance. By the early death of Afinogenov

Russia lost one of her few post-Revolutionary dramatists who might have had a world-wide appeal.

AFRANIUS, Lucius, writer of Roman comedies (see FABULA (9) *Togata*).

AFRICAN ROSCIUS, see ALDRIDGE, IRA.

AFTER-PIECE, see ENGLAND, 5.

AGATE. (1) JAMES EVERSHED (1877-1947), English dramatic critic and author, who began his career as dramatic critic on the staff of the *Manchester Guardian*, and went on to the *Saturday Review*. From 1923 to 1947 he was dramatic critic of the *Sunday Times*; he also contributed to other periodicals, besides broadcasting on drama for the B.B.C.

Few critics wrote more entertainingly for their contemporaries than James Agate, and no English critic served posterity so extensively by reprinting his newspaper criticisms in book form. He published more than a dozen volumes covering the years between the 1914 and the 1939 wars. He also published *Brief Chronicles* (1943), a survey of performances of Shakespeare and the Elizabethans; *Red-Letter Nights* (1944), a survey of post-Elizabethan drama, 1921-43; and *Immoment Toys* (1945), a survey of light entertainment on the London stage, 1920-43. In 1943 he published also *These were Actors*, extracts from a newspaper-cuttings book, 1811-33. In *The English Dramatic Critics* (1932) he compiled an anthology of criticism selected from critics writing between 1660 and 1932.

In all his writings James Agate fulfilled the first principle of criticism in that his views were as individual as his method of expression. He was fond of quoting his predecessors, but this was merely a work of supererogation, for he could score his own points smartly enough. He had also a tremendous respect for the great actors on whom he was brought up. He saw Irving and Bernhardt and walked in the light of their genius ever after. However frequently his findings were questioned, his integrity always went free. The manner of his criticisms was always as good as, and not infrequently better than, the matter on which they were based.

In the *Ego* series Agate published his diary, kept since 1932. One of his reasons for keeping a diary was that 'it is part of the insane desire to perpetuate oneself.' Time will show whether he will be remembered more for his diary than for his dramatic criticisms. But one thing is certain: he recorded the theatre of his time with more vigour and interest than any other critic, except Bernard Shaw, brought to any period. In 1935 he composed an epitaph for himself: 'Though, in his declining years, he used the words Great, First-Class, Pre-eminent, indiscriminately like everybody else, James Agate at his unclouded best, remembering what great acting was, allowed no second-rate player to get past him.' With few lapses he lived up to his epitaph. His sister (2) MAY (1892-   ) studied for the stage under Sarah Bernhardt, on whom she has published a volume of reminiscences, *Madame Sarah* (1945). She appeared with her in Paris and London in 1912, and in 1916 joined Miss Horniman's company at the Gaiety Theatre, Manchester. She has appeared constantly in London and the provinces, and worked also in films and for the B.B.C.   T. C. K.

AGATHON, of Athens, a tragic poet and a younger contemporary of Euripides, won the first of his two victories in 416 B.C. He was the first to invent his own plots, instead of taking them from legend. Also, according to Aristotle, he was the first to write choral odes, unconnected with the plot, as *entr'actes*. Few fragments of his work survive, but he seems to have written romantic drama. Aristophanes laughs at him for effeminacy, but on his death laments the loss of a 'good poet and a good friend'. There is a character-sketch of Agathon in Plato's *Symposium*.   H. D. F. K.

AGGAS, ROBERT (c. 1619-79), English scene-painter, much esteemed in the Restoration theatre. He worked for the second Theatre Royal under Killigrew, and with Samuel Towers painted the elaborate scenery used there for *The Destruction of Jerusalem* in 1677, later suing the theatre for payments overdue. His name is occasionally found with the spelling Angus.

AGNAN SARAT, see SARAT.

AGRELL, ALFHILD (1849-1923), Swedish dramatist (see SCANDINAVIA, 3).

AIKEN, GEORGE L. (1830-76), American actor and playwright, who made his first appearance on the stage in 1848. His first play, a dramatization of a popular novel, was done in New York in 1851, but he is chiefly remembered for his adaptation—the best of many—of *Uncle Tom's Cabin*. This was prepared at the request of George C. Howard, who wished to star in it his wife, Aiken's cousin, as Topsy, and his daughter as Eva. It was first given at Troy in 1852, and in New York a year later, and was constantly toured, its latest revival being in 1924. Apart from its entertainment value, it is important in the history of abolitionist propaganda. Aiken wrote or adapted a number of other plays, none of which has survived, and continued to act until 1867.

AINLEY, HENRY (1879-1945), English actor, possessed of a remarkably fine voice and great personal beauty and charm. He was introduced to the stage by George Alexander, under whom, after a short apprenticeship with Benson's company, he made his first success. This was as Paolo in Phillips's *Paolo and Francesca* (1902), a part to which he was eminently suited in every way. He soon made a name for himself as a romantic and Shakespearian actor, and was seen in such plays as *If I were King*, *Old Heidelberg*, and *The Prisoner of Zenda*, and as Bassanio, Orlando, Cassio, Orestes, and Hippolytus. In 1912 he made a great impression as Malvolio in Granville-Barker's production of *Twelfth Night*, and a year later showed his versatility by his playing of Ilam Carve in *The Great Adventure*. A wide range of parts followed, interrupted by war service from 1916 to 1919, after which he returned to the theatre. He was for a time associated in the management of the St. James's, the New, and His Majesty's Theatres, appearing at the last as Oliver Cromwell and Hassan, the latter one of his finest parts. Ainley would undoubtedly have ranked as one of the great actors of his generation had not serious illness twice kept him from the stage for several years. After his first absence he returned in 1929 to score an instantaneous success as James Fraser in *The First Mrs. Fraser*, which, with Marie Tempest in the name-part, ran for eighteen months. A year later he was seen as Hamlet at a Command Performance, and finally retired in 1932. His son Richard, who has inherited his striking presence and fine voice, is also an actor.

AKHUNDOV, ILYA ELVIN, see RUSSIA, 2 *e*.

AKIMOV, NIKOLAI PAVLOVICH (1901–), Soviet producer, who began his theatrical career as a scenic designer. His first work was done in 1922, and was followed by a bewildering variety of designs in various genres, mostly experimental and revolutionary, and not always successful. The first settings which drew general attention to his work were those for Popov's production of *Razlom* (1927) at the Vakhtangov Theatre. Three years later came his famous designs for Antokolosky's production of *Kabale und Liebe* at the same theatre. In 1932 he turned to production himself, with a *Hamlet* at the Vakhtangov which aroused a storm of controversy by its interpretation of the text—Hamlet fakes the ghost, and Ophelia, a bright young thing, is not mad but drunk, and is drowned after a drunken orgy. The play was taken off in deference to public opinion. Yet even in his mistakes Akimov was interesting, and his work was bound to be important to the Soviet theatre as he matured. In 1934 he returned to Leningrad, his birth-place, and opened his own experimental theatre, becoming director of the Leningrad Theatre of Comedy in 1936. Here he produced a number of excellent comedies, among them an outstanding *Twelfth Night* (1938), and designed settings for others (*Monday at Eight, Dangerous Corner*).

ALARCÓN, JUAN RUIZ DE (*c*. 1580–1639), Spanish dramatist of the Golden Age, contemporary and bitter enemy of Lope de Vega, alienated from many of his contemporaries by their ridicule of his physical deformities. His most original contribution to Spanish drama is the 'comedy of ethics', in which the comic element underlines a moral conclusion. With Alarcón, however, the moral is generally quite personal. He was less prolific than other dramatists of his time, since he wrote only twenty-four plays (some in collaboration with Tirso de Molina), but he excelled all his contemporaries in the perfect finish of his work and the deliberate portrayal of character. His best comedy, *La verdad sospechosa*, which deals with

a young man much given to lying, supplied Corneille with the plot of *Le Menteur*, without which, as Molière himself told Boileau, *Le Misanthrope* would never have been written. Alarcón's romantic drama, *El tejedor de Segovia*, has for hero a character of great individuality, faintly reminiscent of Robin Hood.

ALBEE, EDWARD FRANKLIN (1857–1930), an American theatre manager, who was for some years a tent boy with Barnum's 'Greatest Show on Earth'. In 1885 he joined with B. F. Keith in the presentation of variety shows in Boston and elsewhere, and did his best to improve not only the standard of the stage shows, but also the conditions of employment and housing backstage for vaudeville artists. He was concerned with the building of a number of variety theatres in the leading cities of the East and Middle West, including the Keith, erected in Boston in 1894, and also set up an agency for the engagement of variety turns. By 1920 he was accounted one of the leading purveyors of light amusement in the United States, with a vaudeville circuit of some seventy houses, and an interest in about 300 others.

ALBERT SALOON, LONDON, built in 1844, stood near the Grecian in Shepherdess Walk, City Road. It had two stages, one with an open-air auditorium.

ALBERY. (1) JAMES (1838–89), English dramatist, author of a number of plays, of which *Two Roses*, produced at the Vaudeville in 1870, provided Henry Irving, as Digby Grant, with one of his earliest successes. Albery also made a number of adaptations, including *Jingle* (a version of *Pickwick*), done at the Lyceum in 1878, and translations from the French, mainly for the Criterion Theatre, where his wife, Mary Moore (see WYNDHAM, 2), was playing leading parts. His son (2) Sir BRONSON (1881–), theatre manager, made his first ventures at the Criterion, and on the death of his mother, who had married as her second husband Sir Charles Wyndham, took control, together with his half-brother Howard (see WYNDHAM, 3) of the Criterion, Wyndham's, and New Theatres. This joint management proved a vital and important influence in the London theatre of the 1930s, and many interesting productions took place at all three theatres, including *Richard of Bordeaux, Hamlet, Romeo and Juliet, Noah*, and *The Seagull* (all with John Gielgud) at the New, *Musical Chairs* and *French Without Tears* at the Criterion, and *Service* and *The Maitlands* at Wyndham's. After the bombing of the Old Vic the company found a temporary home in Albery's New Theatre.

ALBION THEATRE, LONDON, in Windmill Street. This was opened in 1832. Three years later, after an obscure career, it became the New Queen's. Sally Booth, the tragedienne, appeared there, but the staple fare was melodrama. The theatre was demolished in 1836.

The Oriental Theatre in Poplar (1867) was also known as The Albion.

ALCAZAR, London, see CONNAUGHT THEATRE.

ALDRICH, LOUIS (1843–1901), American actor, whose real name was Lyon. He was an infant prodigy, and as the Ohio Roscius toured in such parts as Richard III, Macbeth, Shylock, Jack Sheppard, and Young Norval. He was later known as Master Moses, McCarthy, or Kean, and after a break for schooling returned to the stage as an adult under the name of Aldrich. After five years in St. Louis he appeared in New York, playing in Charles Kean's farewell performance, and then went to Boston as a member of the stock company there. From 1873 to 1874 he was leading man of Mrs. John Drew's Arch Street Theatre company in Philadelphia. He then toured for many years in his greatest part, Joe Saunders in *My Partner*, first produced in 1879, which brought him a fortune. He was also good as Shoulders, a drunken creature in *The Kaffir Diamond* (1888). In 1897 he became President of the Actors' Fund of America, and was the first to suggest the building of a home for destitute actors. He made his last appearance on the stage in New York in 1899, and was about to appear under Belasco's management when he died suddenly of apoplexy.

ALDRIDGE, IRA FREDERICK (1804–67), the first great American negro actor, who in 1863 became a naturalized Englishman. Little is known of his early years, but he is believed to have been Kean's servant on his first American tour, to have been taken by him to London and encouraged in his love for the stage. Billed as the African Roscius, he made his début as Othello at the Royalty Theatre, London, in 1826. He then went on tour, and in Belfast had as his Iago Charles Kean. He was also good as Lear, Macbeth, Zanga (in *The Revenge*), Rolla, and Mungo (in *The Padlock*). He was generally regarded as one of the finest actors of the day, and was the recipient of many honours. He amassed a large fortune and married a white woman. It was at one time thought that he had never acted in the United States, but he is believed to have made an unsuccessful attempt to do so at Baltimore in the 1830s. He was last seen in England in 1865, and then returned to the continent, where he had first toured in 1853. He was immensely popular in Germany, where he played in English with a supporting cast playing in German.

ALDWYCH THEATRE, LONDON, was opened on 23 Dec. 1905 by Charles Frohman, with Seymour Hicks and Ellaline Terriss in a revival of *Bluebell in Fairyland*, which had a considerable success. In 1909 a lurid melodrama called *The Bad Girl of the Family* had a big success there, followed by *The Girl who took the Wrong Turning*. *The Ever Open Door*, a play of a different kind, prospered in 1913, as did *Sacred and Profane Love* in 1919. With the transfer of *Tons of Money* from the Shaftes-

bury Theatre, the Aldwych began to make theatre history, as Tom Walls and Ralph Lynn, who brought the play there, produced a series of successful farces, mainly written by Ben Travers, in which they played together. The association, which was one of the outstanding theatrical attractions of London and made the Aldwych a most popular theatre, ended in 1933. Later successes there have been *The Watch on the Rhine* and the Lunts in *There Shall Be No Night*.   W. M. P.

ALEICHEM, SHOLOM [really RABINOVICH] (1859–1916), Jewish writer and dramatist. Born in Pereiaslav (Poltava), he was educated with a view to becoming a rabbi, but at 18 took to journalism, first in Hebrew, later in Yiddish. By 1888 he was owner and editor of a newspaper in Kiev. In 1905 he emigrated to America, and died while on a visit to Copenhagen. He wrote few plays, and his connexion with the stage has been through the dramatization of his numerous novels and short stories, which deal with life in the Jewish communities of the Ukrainian villages. His characters are generous, kindly, simple folk with considerable native shrewdness, the chief being Tuvia the Milkman, the dreamer, the poor, hard-working, unsuccessful little man with an infinite trust in God, and Menahem Mendel, whose dreams are of 'big business' schemes which never come off. Their wives are the practical partners. A Sholom Aleichem cult has grown up in the Yiddish Art Theatres, fostered by Maurice Schwartz in America, and by the State Jewish Theatre in Moscow, both of which see his people as national Jewish types. These offer great scope to actors of intelligence, and it is interesting to note that Mikhoels in the U.S.S.R. and Muni Wiesenfreund (known in the cinema as Paul Muni) in Germany first emerged from obscurity in Sholom Aleichem's plays. Some idea of his work may be obtained from Maurice Samuel's *The World of Sholom Aleichem* (1943).   E. H.

ALENCAR, JOSÉ MARINIANO DE (1829–77), see SOUTH AMERICA, 2.

ALEOTTI, GIAMBATTISTA (1546–1636), Italian theatre architect, designer of the Teatro Farnese (see ARCHITECTURE and SCENERY, 3).

ALEXANDER, SIR GEORGE [really GEORGE ALEXANDER GIBB SAMSON] (1858–1918), English actor, and manager of the St. James's Theatre from 1891 till his death. He made his first appearance at Nottingham, and in 1881 joined Irving's company at the Lyceum as Caleb Deecie in a revival of Albery's *Two Roses*. He remained with Irving, except for a short session under Kendal and Hare at the St. James's in 1883, until 1889, when he entered into management on his own, a venture which was to prove financially and artistically a success. Alexander had a definite policy. At a time when English dramatic literature was at a low ebb, and the stage was cluttered up with adaptations of French farces, he deliberately encouraged English writers. Of over eighty plays which he produced at the St. James's only eight were by foreign authors. A man of distinguished appearance and great charm, Alexander succeeded in investing any part he played with romance and dignity. His greatest success was in the dual role of Rudolf Rassendyll and the King in *The Prisoner of Zenda*, to which may be added the equally picturesque parts of Villon in *If I Were King* and Karl Heinrich in *Old Heidelberg*. In 1906 he produced Pinero's *His House in Order*, perhaps the most typical 'St. James's play'; but Alexander's net was widely cast, and his productions ranged from Shakespeare to Pinero, from Stephen Phillips's verse drama, *Paolo and Francesca*, to Oscar Wilde's *Lady Windermere's Fan* and *The Importance of Being Earnest*. In the latter he was admirable as John Worthing; 'he never', says A. E. W. Mason in his *Sir George Alexander and the St. James's Theatre* (1935), 'acted with a lighter or more confident touch'.

Alexander was not only a good actor, but also a good business man, as the account books of his theatre indicate. In 1907 he was elected to the L.C.C. as member for South St. Pancras, a position he held with distinction until 1912. He also contemplated standing for Parliament, and might have been equally successful there had not increasing ill-health caused him to reconsider his decision. In 1911, the year of the Coronation of George V, he was knighted, and during the war of 1914–18 he was indefatigable in his efforts on behalf of the Red Cross and other charities. His early death, from diabetes, was a great loss to the stage which he had graced with his presence and upon which he had maintained a consistently high standard.

ALEXANDRA THEATRE, LONDON. (1) Highbury Barn, a concert hall in the grounds of an open-air pleasure resort of a kind common round London. It was converted into a theatre in 1861 by Edward Giovanelli, who staged farces and burlesques there and ruined himself. E. T. Smith, the great showman, tried to run it, but it was finally closed, with the gardens, in 1871. J. G. Tayler, Danvers, and Rachel Sanger played there.

(2) Camden Town, probably opened in 1874 (some authorities give 1871) when Thorpe Pede, a musician, staged a double bill there on 31 May—an operetta 'Marguerite' composed by himself, and a play entitled *Friendship; or, Golding's Debt*. Apparently the theatre cost £20,000 to build, and it stood near two famous taverns, 'The Mother Redcap' and 'The Britannia'. In 1875 Walter Bentley and a Miss Clayton played there, and in 1877 an old play, *The Rake's Progress*, was revived. In the same year Madame St. Claire took over the theatre, chiefly to show herself off in the part of Romeo, but without success. In 1879 the theatre became known as The Park Theatre, from its proximity to Regent's Park. It mostly gave straight plays, and Stella Brereton and the celebrated Odell appeared there in a version of

Jane Eyre. The house was burned down after a performance of Bellini's 'La Sonnambula' by the National Grand Opera Co. in 1882 and never rebuilt.

(3) Stoke Newington. See SUBURBAN THEATRES.   W. M. P.

ALEXANDRINSKY THEATRE, LENINGRAD. This theatre, which has since been renamed the Pushkin Theatre, was founded in 1824, in the same year as the Maly Theatre in Moscow. It had a fine actor in Vasily Karatygin (1802–53), but it had no authors of the calibre of Gogol and Ostrovsky, then holding the stage at the Maly, and never developed a settled policy. Also its audiences were more influenced by the Court life of St. Petersburg, and had none of the liberalism and intellectual curiosity of the middle-class merchant audiences of Moscow. For this reason it staged a good deal of ballet and opera, until the former was transferred to the Bolshoy and was replaced by the popular vaudeville of the time, or by translations of French melodramas. Later the patriotic dramas written to order by Polevoy and Kukolik were seen at the Alexandrinsky, and after a long, blank period the first stirrings of realism came with such plays as *The Father*, in which the actor Mamont Dalsky (1865–1918) scored a personal triumph. But on the whole the theatre and its audience did not want new works, and continued to play for safety. Its first and last attempt at Chekhov, *The Seagull* in 1896, was a dismal failure, the theatre's oldfashioned technique being unable to convey the subtlety of the author's characterization. Just before the October Revolution Meyerhold was working at the Alexandrinsky, his last production there being a somewhat frigid and abstract *Masquerade*.

Amid the stress of the Revolution the Alexandrinsky clung desperately to a repertory of welltried classics, the only new play being *Faust and the City*, by the Commissar for Education, Lunacharsky, under whose care and vigilance the Alexandrinsky, like the Moscow Art and other pre-Soviet theatres, gradually found its feet in the new world. By 1924 it was ready to include new plays in its repertory, some Soviet, some from Europe. Among the producers who worked there were Radlov, Solovyov, and Rappoport, while in 1937 Meyerhold returned, to produce *Masquerade* again. Outstanding productions since then have been *Antony and Cleopatra*, a revival of *The Forest*, *Lenin in 1918*, a remarkable performance of *Macbeth*, and, during the Second World War, when the theatre was evacuated and went on tour up to the front line, *Othello*, *Oedipus Tyrannus*, and the new plays, *The Russian People* and *Kremlin Chimes*. Some interesting revivals of old plays were done under Leonid Vivien, with a somewhat more accurate historical bias than formerly, and the policy of the theatre tended to show a heightened consciousness of the social problems of present-day life—a far cry from the conventional and easy-going attitude of the Imperial Alexandrinsky, which received its new name in 1937. Among its outstanding actors are Yuryev, who gave fine performances as Oedipus and Othello, and Cherkasov and Babochkin, both well known outside Russia for their work in Russian films.

ALEXIS, a Greek comic poet of the period of Middle Comedy (*c.* 400 B.C.) (see GREECE, 2 *b*). He was uncle to Menander. Only a few fragments of his work survive.

ALFIERI, VITTORIO AMEDEO (1749–1803), one of the greatest Italian dramatists, mainly remembered as a writer of tragedies in verse. Born in Turin of a noble and wealthy family, he had an unhappy childhood, and at an early age left home to travel widely in Europe. For a long time French was his only language, but when in his twenties his thoughts turned to literature, he went to Tuscany and worked hard to perfect himself in Italian, which he henceforth championed against the influence of French. His first play, *Cleopatra*, was given at Turin in 1775 with great success, and was followed by a number of others, on classical, biblical, or, occasionally, romantic subjects. His two best tragedies are *Saul* (1782–4) and *Mirra* (1784–6). His verse, which owes much to Cesarotti, is austere, but fits well with his conception of tragedy as a dramatic presentation of a great theme from which all lesser matters must be banished. It has been said of his tragedies that their action flies like an arrow to its mark. He also wrote half a dozen comedies, mainly satiric, which are now forgotten, and a remarkable autobiography, in which he depicts himself more as he wished to be than as he was. For many years Alfieri was the devoted lover of the Countess of Albany, wife of the Young Pretender. He visited London on several occasions, chiefly to buy horses, for which he had a passion. He was in France at the time of the Revolution, which he first welcomed, and later abhorred. When he returned to Italy the French treated him as an *émigré*, and confiscated his goods and practically all his money. His books and manuscripts were given to the painter Fabre by the Countess of Albany, and Fabre bequeathed them to the University of Montpelier (see also ITALY, 3 *a*).

ALHAMBRA, LONDON. Opened in 1854 as the Panopticon, the Alhambra housed many kinds of shows, from scientific demonstrations and circuses to music-hall and variety. In 1871 it became a theatre, and for ten years staged opéra bouffe. In 1882 it was burned down, but was rebuilt and opened again on 3 Dec. 1883, still with opéra bouffe, but less successfully. It then became a music-hall once more, with ballet as the main attraction. In 1911 it went over to revue, and 1916 saw *The Bing Boys are Here*, one of the most popular revues of the war of 1914–18, in which Violet Loraine and George Robey starred. The Alhambra then reverted to variety, with intervals of revue and seasons of Russian Ballet. Towards the end it had no settled policy, but presented revue,

ballet, plays, and, in 1934, Shakespeare. It was finally demolished in Nov. 1936, and a cinema, the Odeon, was erected on the site of the old theatre, whose Moorish-style architecture had dominated the east side of Leicester Square for so long (see MUSIC-HALL).   W. M. P.

ALIZON (*fl.* 1610–48), an early French actor who specialized in the playing of comic women-servants, particularly in farces, or of the heroine's nurse in more serious plays. He was with Montdory when he first came to Paris, but was later transferred to the Hôtel de Bourgogne. As with his equally popular companion, Jodelet, his own name was frequently given to the parts destined for him.

ALLAN, LOUISE ROSALIE (*née* Despréaux) (1810–56), French actress, and the first to discover the excellence of Alfred de Musset as a dramatist. At the age of ten she appeared with Talma at Brussels, and was later, on his recommendation, engaged for minor parts at the Comédie-Française, where she played the page Iaguëz in the first production of *Hernani* (1830). Coming into conflict with Mlle Mars, at that time the reigning star of the company, she left the Comédie-Française in 1831 and went to the Gymnase, where she scored a notable triumph, at the same time marrying a fellow actor named Allan. She was then engaged to appear at the French theatre in St. Petersburg, and tradition has it that while there she saw, and may have acted in, a charming trifle which she planned to have translated into French, only to find that it was a Russian translation of Alfred de Musset's *Un Caprice*. This story is now considered apocryphal, but it is certain that *Un Caprice*, with Mme Allan and Mlle Judith, was warmly received at the Comédie-Française in 1847, seven years after its publication. Mme Allan then remained at the Comédie-Française until her early death. She was the contemporary there of Mlle Rachel, and maintained, even against such a rival, a claim to be considered an actress of the first rank.

ALLARD, MARIE (1742–1802), a dancer at the Paris Opéra, and the mother of the great dancer Auguste Vestris (see VESTRIS, 1 and 2).

ALLEN, VIOLA (1869–1948), American actress, who made her first appearance on the stage in 1882, succeeding Annie Russell in the part of Esmeralda at the Madison Square Theatre. A year or two later she was leading lady to John McCullough, and in 1886 played with Salvini. From 1891 to 1898 she was a member of Frohman's stock company at the Empire, where she appeared in many old and new parts and gained a great reputation as one of the leading actresses of the day. On leaving Frohman she toured for some time as a star, her first venture being Gloria Quayle in *The Christian*. She was also excellent as her namesake in *Twelfth Night*, and appeared in *The Winter's Tale*, *Cymbeline*, and *As You Like It*. In 1915 she toured with J. K. Hackett as Lady Macbeth, and made her last appearance in 1916 as

Mistress Ford in *The Merry Wives of Windsor*. In 1946 the Museum of the City of New York Drama Department organized an exhibition devoted to her, at which many of her stage costumes and other mementoes of her long and distinguished career were on view.

ALLEN, WILLIAM (?–1647), English actor, and an important member of Queen Henrietta's Men at the Cockpit, where he played leading parts in *The Renegado* and *Hannibal and Scipio*. After the dissolution of the company in 1636 he joined the powerful King's Men. He married the daughter of a fellow actor, and may have been apprenticed as a young man to Christopher Beeston. He has been confused with a William Allen who was a Major in the Civil War.

ALLEYN, EDWARD (1566–1626), founder of Dulwich College (originally the College and Hospital of God's Gift), and one of the first English actors of whom we have any substantial knowledge. In 1583 he was a member of the Earl of Worcester's players, and already accounted a good actor. In 1592 he married Joan Woodward, stepdaughter of the theatrical manager Henslowe, and so laid the foundations of his later fortune. He became part-owner in Henslowe's ventures, and later sole proprietor of several playhouses and places of entertainment, including the Paris Garden and the Rose and Fortune theatres. He had a high reputation, being much praised by Nashe and Jonson, and was considered the only rival of Burbage. He was the chief actor of the Admiral's Men, and may have joined them in 1587. He played at the Rose from 1594–7, and at the Fortune from 1599 till his retirement, probably at the accession of James I. Marlowe was his chief dramatist, and plays in which he is known to have appeared include *Tamburlaine*, *Faustus*, *The Jew of Malta*, as well as Greene's *Orlando Furioso*, and, no doubt, many others lost or unrecorded. Two legends —that he retired from the stage and founded Dulwich College in a fit of remorse after seeing the Devil while playing Faustus, and that he died a pauper in his own charitable institution —are now discredited. He was, in fact, a man of substance to the end, and only three years before his death he was able to settle on his second wife, the daughter of John Donne, the sum of £1,500. A Frenchman who saw him act described him as having 'a pleasing voice, a good figure and a fine presence' and credited him with having raised the art of acting to a level hitherto unknown.

ALLGOOD. (1) SARA (1883–1950), Irish actress, whose early career is bound up with the history of the Abbey Theatre. After studying for the stage with Frank J. Fay, she made her first appearance in Dublin and London with the Irish National Theatre Society, playing Cathleen in *Riders to the Sea* and Princess Buan in *The King's Threshold*. She also appeared in the same year in the opening productions of the Abbey Theatre, some of her best parts being Deirdre, Mrs. Delane in *Hyacinth Halvey*, Widow Quin in *The Playboy of the Western World*, and Cathleen in *Cathleen ni Houlihan*. In 1913 she joined the Liverpool Repertory Theatre, and was in Miss Horniman's company at Manchester, playing Isabella in the opening production of *Measure for Measure*, a part which she later repeated at Stratford. She had appeared many times in London with the Abbey Players, and in 1920, after a long tour in Australia, was seen there as Mrs. Geoghegan in *The White-Headed Boy*; the finest performance of her career was undoubtedly Juno Boyle in *Juno and the Paycock* (1925), in which she also appeared in America, together with Bessie Burgess in *The Plough and the Stars* (1926). Among her later successes were Julia Hardy in *Things That Are Caesar's*, Honoria Flanagan in *Storm in a Teacup*, and Jemima Cooney in *Shadow and Substance*. She made her last appearance on the stage in New York in 1940, and has since appeared only in films. Her younger sister (2) MAIRE O'NEILL also appeared first at the Abbey Theatre and was seen in London with the Abbey Players as Margaret Flaherty in *The Playboy of the Western World*. She remained at the Abbey until 1913, and Gwynn, in his *Irish Literature and Drama*, says she and her sister 'made the company stronger in its actresses than it ever had been or has been since they left'. She appeared subsequently with the Liverpool Repertory Theatre, and during a long and distinguished career was seen in London and New York, often in Irish plays in conjunction with her sister and her second husband, Arthur Sinclair.

ALMA TADEMA, see TADEMA.

ALMQUIST, CARL JONAS LOVE (1793–1866), Swedish dramatist (see SCANDINAVIA, 3).

ALPHONSINE [FLEURY] (1829–83), French actress, daughter of a flower-seller on the Boulevard du Temple. She appeared at the theatres there as a child, and at the Petit-Lazzari, where she was extremely popular; as a young girl she was the idol of the little theatres, and was nicknamed the Déjazet of the Boulevards. A fine comedienne, never falling into farce or caricature, but always subtle and witty, she was a pretty woman, with an elegant figure, good voice, and abundant high spirits. She was for many years at the Porte-Saint-Martin and the Variétés, and then went to the Palais-Royal, where she was one of the company sent on 13 Nov. 1869 to play before the Court at Compiègne—the last time French actors appeared before Napoleon III. She was playing at the Gymnase when she retired owing to ill health. In private life she was an excellent woman, and in spite of her vivacity and charm she gave no occasion for scandal.

A. L. S. TRAVELLING THEATRE, see ARTS LEAGUE OF SERVICE.

ALVIN THEATRE, NEW YORK, a handsome edifice with an Adam interior. It opened on 22 Nov. 1927, taking its name from a combina-

AMATEUR THEATRE

tion of the first syllables of Alex A. Aarons and Vinton Freedley, partners in musical comedy production, who retained control of the theatre until 1932. It was then taken over by the Pincus Brothers, who are still in occupation. The size of the theatre made it particularly suitable for musical shows, with such stars as the Astaires, Ginger Rogers, and Ethel Merman, but straight plays were also seen there, including *The Apple Cart*, *Mourning Becomes Electra*, a revival of *Uncle Tom's Cabin* with Otis Skinner, and Maxwell Anderson's *Mary of Scotland*. Gershwin's musical adaptation of *Porgy and Bess* delighted the critics in 1935, but did not prove as attractive to the public as had been hoped. It was left to *I'd Rather Be Right* (1938), with George M. Cohan in his spirited impersonation of Franklin D. Roosevelt, to inaugurate a series of successful productions which included *Anything Goes*, *The Boys from Syracuse*, and *There Shall Be No Night*, this last graced by the fine acting of the Lunts. In 1945 Margaret Webster produced *The Tempest* with Canada Lee as Caliban, and the following year Ingrid Bergman made a great success at the Alvin in *Joan of Lorraine*.

G. F.

AMATEUR THEATRE IN GREAT BRITAIN. 1. GENERAL SURVEY. The history of the British amateur stage goes back to the beginnings of British drama. Actors in the Mystery plays were ordinary working folk from the Guilds, and although they sometimes received small payments for their services, they were not regular professional players. More than a century later the masques were the recreation of the Court or the big country houses. In the nineteenth century, home amateur theatricals became the rage of the upper and middle classes, at the same time as many public amateur dramatic societies were being formed. To-day there are various estimates of the number of amateur societies in existence, and the figure cannot be less than thirty thousand groups, which put on at least one production (if only a sketch or one-act play) during the season.

Without detailed research, it is difficult to decide which society possesses the longest history of play production. The Old Stagers have given regular annual performances, closely associated with the Canterbury Cricket Festival, dating back to 1842. They only perform at one season of the year, in contrast to the Manchester Atheneum Dramatic Society, who in 1946 celebrated their centenary, although admitting that for the first eight years, owing to a dispute on the question of the appearance of ladies on the stage, their activities were limited to play-readings. Since 1854 this Society has presented plays regularly and in most recent seasons given four or more productions. In 1855 the Cambridge University A.D.C. was formed, followed in 1885 by the O.U.D.S. (See CAMBRIDGE and OXFORD.)

Those who wish to disparage amateur drama enthusiasts say their motive is exhibitionism or a desire for the social pleasure that can be derived from the presentation of a play with, and before, one's friends and acquaintances. There are undoubtedly many societies with such motives as their *raison d'être*, but they often give performances of fair quality of productions devised with some care. They are important in the social life of the middle class of their towns, and have raised vast sums for charity. The need to raise funds for worthy charities has, in fact, often been the reason for the formation of a Dramatic Club which has gone on to develop a worthwhile artistic existence.

The amateur dramatic movement in Great Britain can be divided into four categories:

(*a*) Occasional groups formed for the production of short or long plays for a single occasion at irregular intervals or every season, the cast being assembled from the members of a church or school, factory or other organization, for the purpose of producing the entertainment. Such groups have no continuous existence or overall policy.

(*b*) The small groups which may put on one, two, or more productions a year, or a series of one-act plays. They have an organized life, and are often drama sections of voluntary organizations which exist for another purpose, such as Women's Institutes, Youth Clubs, Welfare Clubs, Community Centres, and churches or schools. In number their activities probably constitute the major part of the whole amateur dramatic movement in the British Isles. They are frequent competitors at the one-act play festivals held all over the country. Their production policy is inclined to be opportunist, and few give any real consideration to the literary value or dramatic content of the play. Comedy and farce are very popular with these groups, who are the principal producers of one-act plays.

(*c*) The larger Dramatic Societies, including the Operatic Societies, of which there will normally be at least one in every town, and several in each of the larger towns and cities. Such societies constitute the second largest part of the amateur movement, and it is against them that most of the allegations of exhibitionism and preoccupation with social life are directed. Some have made important contributions to the culture of their towns by presenting plays of real value. Others have contented themselves with repeating West End successes. Most prepare their productions with great care and many reach a very high standard, perhaps even better than some provincial professional repertory companies. The Bournemouth Dramatic and Operatic Society, now the Bournemouth Little Theatre Society, raised a large sum of money to build a small theatre, which is used not only for their own productions but also for visits by smaller professional touring companies, and for the performances of other amateur societies. Similar small theatres are to be found in Southport, Nottingham, and other centres.

(*d*) The fourth group are the Little Theatres,

which although few in number are important for artistic and aesthetic reasons. The Little Theatre Society usually owns or leases its own building, and presents every season a number of productions which vary from three or four to a dozen or more. One would have thought that the creation of a Little Theatre would result from the development of a large society. Historically this has not been the case, for most were founded by people who originally gathered together for the express purpose of starting such a theatre.

Of the leading Little Theatres, the Maddermarket at Norwich has the only Elizabethan stage in the country. Under the direction of Nugent Monck, a dozen or so productions are presented annually, ranging from the classics to the ultra-modern. All the plays of Shakespeare have been presented, together with representative dramas from the theatre of many lands, including Japan and China. At the Maddermarket social ambition is curbed by anonymity and the theatre has become a most important centre of education and artistic inspiration for the whole country.

The Bradford Civic Playhouse, an offshoot of the now defunct Leeds Civic Theatre, presenting plays in a great industrial area, draws on a large acting membership which includes members of other societies. The production of plays of quality is alternated with the exhibition of cinematograph films to provide a continuous programme of entertainment throughout the whole year. The People's Theatre, Newcastle, founded in 1911, has presented an unusually varied repertoire, including continental and American plays, and many first performances. Its Arts Group provides concerts, film shows, and lectures, and publishes a magazine, *The Phoenix*. The members of the Highbury Little Theatre, at Sutton Coldfield, distinguished themselves during the 1939–45 war by building a theatre literally with their own hands.

The productions of these amateur Little Theatres and of some others are of professional standard. They show considerable enterprise in play selection and some employ professional producers and have other paid officials on their staff. Some have training schools which are not only a source of new material for their own acting companies, but also provide the first training for those who wish to go on the professional stage.

The most significant amateur activity in the theatre is outside London. This is to be expected in view of the paucity of theatrical entertainment of any quality in most provincial towns and cities. There is only one amateur Little Theatre in the whole of London—the Questors at Ealing. Before the war, the St. Pancras People's Theatre and the Tavistock Repertory Theatre were important, but the first is now defunct and the second operating on a much-reduced scale.

In London, however, Unity Theatre, an important group, originally amateur, later professional, and, owing to economic circumstances, amateur again, was formed in 1936 for the primary purpose of performing plays of political and social significance. With their own theatre in a converted chapel in Goldington Street, King's Cross, they occupy a unique place in the theatrical life of the metropolis. Up to the outbreak of war in 1939, at a time when the London theatre was moribund and unenterprising, these amateurs, under skilled direction, staged productions of the highest quality. Producers such as John Allen, André Van Gyseghem, and Herbert Marshall have made names in the professional theatre, as have many of the amateurs from the early casts who gave up all their free time to the work of the theatre.

In association with the theatre in London, federated through the Unity Theatre Society, there are Unity Theatre Groups in centres throughout the country but they have, on the whole, had a chequered existence. In Scotland, Glasgow Unity Theatre is almost fully professional, and therefore outside the scope of this article. Beginning as amateurs, they were by 1947 the second most significant play-producing unit in the whole of Scotland (see UNITY THEATRE).

This survey has indicated the vast extent of the amateur theatre in the British Isles, and the importance of the leading societies and Little Theatres to the development of the drama. Thirty thousand amateur play-producing groups have an important effect on the economics of playwrights, publishers, theatrical costumiers, wig-makers, and the like, besides contributing no small part of the revenue of the public halls and institutes which they use for their productions. The importance of the amateur stage can be appreciated particularly when it is realized that the activities of the local dramatic society provide the only 'live' theatre for many sizeable towns.

Membership of a drama group, however small, offers a useful cultural occupation for the leisure hours of folk in cities, small towns, or country districts, providing a means of artistic self-expression and a relief from the permanently 'workbound' state of the average mortal. Drama as an activity of schools and Youth Clubs is recognized as a legitimate part of education and as such can receive considerable assistance from national and local funds. Under the 1944 Education Act, Local Authorities are empowered to provide theatres, club rooms, rehearsal rooms, training classes, and other facilities.

2. ORGANIZATION. The British Drama League was founded by Geoffrey Whitworth in 1919, and although by no means limited to the amateur theatre, has five thousand affiliated members drawn from a representative cross-section of the amateur movement. The League holds an annual conference, publishes a magazine, *Drama*, provides its affiliated members with a library and information service, and organizes schools and training courses for producers and actors, some full time, some in the vacation or at week-ends. Through a system of regional federations, the League organizes

an annual Community Theatre Festival on a competitive basis for one-act plays, the finals of which are held in London. More recently a full-length play competition has been held, in which the preliminary adjudication is carried out on a regional basis and the annual finals are held in different provincial centres.

In Scotland the counterpart of the British Drama League is the Scottish Community Drama Association. Their annual festival of one-act plays dominates the whole of the amateur drama of Scotland to the extent that comparatively few societies produce anything but these short plays. The S.C.D.A., through its area organization, probably organizes a higher percentage of societies in Scotland than does the British Drama League in England and Wales, and, although independent, acts as the Scottish regional organization for the national competitions.

The national organization second in importance to the B.D.L. is the National Operatic and Dramatic Association, Ltd., which includes amongst its eight hundred members most of the big amateur societies which stage elaborate musical productions. A quarterly *N.O.D.A. Bulletin* is published, and facilities offered to members are similar to those of the B.D.L., but with an emphasis towards the musical stage.

Smaller are the local Theatre Guilds which federate societies in towns and districts to plan production programmes, to share equipment and facilities, and to promote joint performances.

The British Drama League, S.C.D.A., and N.O.D.A. provide for societies which are established and which have a more or less permanent existence. Many new and smaller groups, particularly those in rural areas, have received help through the more recently formed County Drama Committees. Inspired by the Carnegie United Kingdom Trust, who give important financial aid, they are on similar lines to the successful County Music Committees, and include representatives of education authorities and voluntary educational or social service organizations. Their purpose is to develop and advise amateur societies and the drama sections of adult education or youth clubs, or of voluntary organizations such as the Women's Institutes and the Townswomen's Guilds. They are financed partly by grants from Local Authorities, partly from funds raised through local affiliations. They employ advisers, whose salaries are subject to grants from the Carnegie United Kingdom Trustees, and from the Local Education Authority.

The work of the County Drama Committees is more positive than the work of the regional federations of the British Drama League, and the advisers actively promote the formation of new groups. They give advice, and arrange for training courses for producers, actors, and stage managers. The County Drama Committees are federated into a national organization, the Standing Conference of Drama Associations, which holds an annual meeting in London.

The Guild of Little Theatres was formed in 1946, and restricts membership to Little Theatres whose work reaches an approved artistic standard. Quarterly meetings are held in rotation at the premises of the member theatres, numbering thirteen in 1947.

3. PLAYS. The size and scope of the British Amateur Theatre makes it an important market for plays, and a strong influence on the work of the playwright. As has been indicated above, the amateurs provide 90 per cent. of the market for one-act plays, the balance being taken up by school productions and a few performances in the professional theatre. The short play is the starting-point for most new amateur groups, and the competitive festivals stimulate the demand for new plays. Authors, therefore, find a ready market for their work, and it is feared that many attempt to cash in on the demand, for a number of the plays published are of extremely poor quality; but the natural processes of intelligent selection operate, and there is a constant gradual improvement in the standard of plays written and selected for production. County Drama Advisers are working toward an improvement of standards.

The amateur theatre offers many opportunities to authors of full-length plays. Some authors have found the amateur market most receptive, and have written plays which suit amateur societies and are technically within the scope of their members and stage facilities. Dr. Falkland Carey has disclosed some astonishing figures as to the financial reward the author may get from this field. Playwrights writing for the professional stage have the comfortable knowledge that when their success has exhausted the commercial possibilities of the West End and the provinces it may then bring in a good steady revenue in royalties from the amateur societies. A play which has been a comparative failure in the West End may afterwards become extremely popular with the amateurs.

The societies are also important producers of revivals, and frequently turn to the works of Galsworthy, Drinkwater, Pinero, and others as a change from the more up-to-date West End successes. The Little Theatres and some of the leading societies and Unity groups present the experimental work of new playwrights, and also produce some of the great classics of the world theatre which rarely appear on the professional stage.   J. A.

For the Amateur Theatre in the U.S.A., see NATIONWIDE THEATRE.

AMBASSADOR THEATRE, NEW YORK, on 49th Street west of Broadway. This opened on 29 Sept. 1921 with *Blossom Time*, under the management of the Shubert brothers. It has had a fair measure of success, and has been used frequently for visiting foreign actors, including Moissi in Reinhardt's production of *Redemption*, Maurice Schwartz playing Sholem Aleichem in Yiddish, the Argentine Players in a number of Spanish plays, and the Abbey Players from Dublin in a repertory of modern Irish plays. For a time the theatre was given over to radio, but it later reverted to straight plays, and is still in use.

AMBASSADORS' THEATRE, LONDON, in West Street, near St. Martin's Lane, was opened under the management of Durrant Swan in June 1913, with *Panthea*. It is a small intimate playhouse, which has been the home of revue and of straight plays. In 1914 Cochran took the theatre for several years, and in 1931, after many notable productions had been staged there, Robert E. Sherwood's comedy, *The Queen's Husband*, had a long run. In 1934 there was a revival of *The Country Wife*, followed by a new play, *Family Affairs*. In 1936 *Children to Bless You* and *The Two Bouquets* were both successful, as was *Spring Meeting* in 1938 and *The Gate Revue* in 1939. Later revue became very popular at this theatre, with the *Sweet and Low* series. For some time the theatre was controlled by H. M. Harwood, the dramatist.   W. M. P.

AMBIGU-COMIQUE, THÉÂTRE DE L', PARIS. This was founded by Audinot, as a marionette and children's theatre, in 1769, on the Boulevard du Temple, where it remained until it was destroyed by fire in 1827. It gave all types of entertainments at first, and from 1797 onwards mainly melodrama, by Pixerécourt, Bouchardy, and others. A theatre of the same name, still in use, opened in 1828 to replace the old one, whose site was taken over by the Folies-Dramatiques, and this has since had a long and flourishing career.

AMEIPSIAS, a Greek comic poet of Old Comedy, contemporary and rival of Aristophanes (see GREECE, 2 *b*). His *Revellers* defeated Aristophanes' *Birds* in 414 B.C. One of his plays ridiculed Socrates. Only fragments of his work survive.

AMERICA, NORTH, see CANADA and UNITED STATES OF AMERICA.

AMERICA, SOUTH, see SOUTH AMERICA.

AMERICAN COMPANY, THE, a troupe of professional actors, made up of the remnants of the elder Hallam's company, and a company under David Douglass, with Hallam's widow as their leading lady and his son Lewis as their leading man. The name by which they are usually known was first used in a notice of their presence at Charleston in 1763–4, and they retained it during successive changes of management, John Henry and the younger Hallam succeeding Douglass, and being in turn succeeded by Hodgkinson and Dunlap. The American Company played an important part in the development of early American drama, being the first professional company to produce a play by an American—*The Prince of Parthia*, by Thomas Godfrey. It was also responsible for the production of several plays by Dunlap. The company underwent many vicissitudes before its reorganization in 1776 under Dunlap, when he engaged the first Joseph Jefferson and took possession of the

Park Theatre, New York. Its identity was finally lost when in 1805 Dunlap went bankrupt and retired, the Park Theatre being taken over by Thomas Abthorpe Cooper, who had been a member of the company for some years. The American Company had practically the monopoly of acting in the United States for many years, its only rival being Wignell's company in Philadelphia.

AMERICAN MUSEUM, a show-place opened by P. T. Barnum in 1842, which by 1849 had become a theatre with a good stock company and some stars, among them the Bateman children. On 17 June 1850, much enlarged and embellished, it opened with an excellent company in a highly moral play entitled *The Drunkard*, which had a record run for that time. Barnum soon found himself at the head of a reputable theatre, which gave two performances a day, and paid its actors well. He sold it in 1855, but plays were still given there, and in 1860 its former owner, being once more financially stable, was able to buy it back. He continued to present a certain number of plays, but they were gradually ousted by freaks, baby-shows, and boxing contests, until on 13 July 1865 the old Museum was burnt down. Barnum went temporarily to the Winter Garden, and on 6 Sept. opened a new Museum, also on Broadway, with a similar mixture of freaks and plays, and pantomime in the summer. In 1867 Barnum finally withdrew from management, and Van Amburgh took over with his menagerie, though evidently plays were still given occasionally, as it was during a run of *Uncle Tom's Cabin* that on 3 Mar. 1868 the second Museum was burnt to the ground. It was never rebuilt.

AMERICAN NATIONAL THEATRE AND ACADEMY (ANTA). This organization came into being on 5 July 1935 when President Roosevelt signed the Charter which Congress had just enacted. This important document permits the establishment of a nation-wide, tax-exempt institution which, in the words of its preamble, was to be:

A people's project, organized and conducted in their interest, free from commercialism, but with the firm intent of being as far as possible self-supporting. A national theatre should bring to the people throughout the country their heritage of the great drama of the past and the best of the present, which has been too frequently unavailable to them under existing conditions.

The Charter was secured by a group of public-spirited citizens who were actuated by enthusiasm for the theatre but were not themselves connected with it. Though authorized by Congress, it carried no government grant; money was to be raised by private subscription as soon as a working plan could be proposed. At about the time the Charter was signed the Federal Theatre, a project of the Works Progress Administration (WPA), was in operation, and it was impractical to raise private funds for a nation-wide theatre at that juncture. The Second World War delayed action still further.

After 1945, however, the Board of Directors was reorganized to include leading theatre people and the heads of such organizations as Actors' Equity, the Dramatists' Guild, the craft unions, and such non-professional groups as the National Theatre Conference, the American Educational Theatre Association, and the Theatre Library Association. A membership structure consisting of 500 corporate (or voting) members, as well as several types of individual and group memberships, was set up, and a long-range programme was decided on. It had as its major objective the furthering of the best in the theatre, both professional and non-professional; the fostering of a decentralized theatre, that is to say, the encouragement of professional resident theatres outside New York; the development of experimental theatres; the training of young theatre talents in the fields of acting, directing, and playwriting; and the founding of a post-graduate Academy or theatre school. ANTA will also represent the American theatre in its international relations. It was represented at the meetings of the UNESCO committee of experts held in Paris in 1947, when preliminary steps were taken toward the founding of an International Theatre Institute, and it will work with UNESCO and the Institute on all future theatre plans. In order to implement so extensive a programme ANTA will raise a National Theatre Fund, seeking through private donations and through the income derived from special performances and benefits to build up a Foundation which will operate for the benefit of the theatre in the same way that the Rockefeller and Carnegie Foundations have helped in the development of education, medicine, and science. The work of the British Arts Council has also been studied as a sound method of approach to the complex problems of the theatre. The foundation technique which assists and encourages individual initiative while maintaining standards and offering a great variety of opportunities for assistance can best serve the interest of the far-flung American theatre.   R. G.

AMERICAN OPERA HOUSE, NEW YORK, see CHATHAM THEATRE (1).

AMERICAN THEATRE, NEW YORK, on 42nd Street. This opened on 22 May 1893 with *The Prodigal Daughter*. It had a somewhat chequered career, and in 1908 became a music-hall. It was closed in 1929, but shortly afterwards reopened with burlesque, which remained its staple fare until on 18 Dec. 1930 it was badly damaged by fire. It was finally demolished in 1932.

Burton's first theatre (see CHAMBERS STREET) was called the American for a season under Davenport in 1857. For the American Theatre, Bowery, see BOWERY THEATRE (1).

AMERICAN THEATRICAL COMMONWEALTH COMPANY, see LUDLOW, NOAH, and SMITH, SOL.

AMES, WINTHROP (1871–1937), American theatre director, who used the money inherited from his father, a railroad capitalist, to back non-commercial ventures in the theatre. In 1904 he took over the Castle Square Theatre, Boston, and later made a gallant but unsuccessful attempt to establish a true repertory theatre in New York, at the New Theatre, and finally at the Little and Booth Theatres, both of which he built. Among his productions were a number of Shakespeare plays and other classics, some revivals of Gilbert and Sullivan, and such modern plays as *Prunella, The Betrothal, Old English,* and *Will Shakespeare.* In 1914 Ames offered a prize of 10,000 dollars for the best play by an American, which was won by *Children of Earth.* This was produced in the following year, but was not very successful, since the author, Alice Brown, was, according to Quinn, 'a novelist rather than a playwright'. Ames did good work for the American theatre over a long period of years, and retired in 1932.

AMPHITHEATRE. (1) LONDON, see CONNAUGHT THEATRE. (2) NEW YORK, see CHATHAM THEATRE (1).

ANCEY, GEORGES [really GEORGES DE CURNIEU] (1860–1926), French dramatist, and one of the best of the naturalistic writers who followed in the steps of Henri Becque. His plays, which were produced by Antoine at the Théâtre Libre, were even franker than Becque's, but they were popular in their time. The best of them were *Les Inséparables,* in which two friends share the same mistress, and *L'École des veufs* (both 1889), in which a father and son find themselves in the same position. Ancey's plays went out of fashion with the decline of naturalism and have not been revived.

ANDERSON, JUDITH (1898–), American actress, born and educated in Australia, where she made her first appearance at Sydney in 1915. Three years later she was in New York, playing small parts in stock there and in other American cities. Her first outstanding success was made as Elise in *Cobra,* with which she toured Australia, returning to New York to play in *As You Desire Me* and *Mourning Becomes Electra.* In 1936 she played the Queen to John Gielgud's Hamlet in New York, and a year later made her first appearance in London, where she gave an outstanding performance as Lady Macbeth with Laurence Olivier at the Old Vic. In 1947 she electrified New York with a superb rendering of the name-part in *Medea,* in a new adaptation prepared by Robinson Jeffers and produced by John Gielgud. Rosamond Gilder in *Theatre Arts* said of her:

Her Medea is pure evil, dark, dangerous, cruel, raging, ruthless. From beginning to end she maintains an almost incredible intensity, yet she varies her moods so constantly, she moves with such skill through unexplored regions of pain and despair that she can hold her audience in suspense throughout the evening.

ANDERSON, MARY (1859–1940), an American actress of great charm and beauty, who made her first appearance at the age of 16 at Louisville, playing Juliet. She toured the United States for some years in a wide variety of parts, being much admired as Julia in *The Hunchback,* as Pauline in *The Lady of Lyons,* and as Parthenia in *Ingomar.* It was in this last part that she made her first appearance in London, at the Lyceum in 1883. In 1885 she was seen at Stratford-on-Avon as Rosalind, one of her best parts, and in 1887 toured in a production of *The Winter's Tale,* in which she was the first actress to double the parts of Perdita and Hermione. She appeared in several plays by W. S. Gilbert, *Comedy and Tragedy* (1884) being specially written for her. She retired in 1889, and was not seen again on the professional stage, though during the First World War she appeared at some charity matinées, notably as Juliet in the Balcony Scene. In 1890 she married Antonio de Navarro, and settled at Broadway in Worcestershire, where she died. She was the author of *A Few Memories* (1896) and *A Few More Memories* (1936), and part-author of the play based on Hichens's *Garden of Allah.*

ANDERSON, MAXWELL (1888–   ), American dramatist, received his early schooling in various States, and after graduating from the University of North Dakota in 1911, taught college for a short time and worked on three newspapers. His first-produced play was *White Desert* (1923), a failure in the theatre. Written partly in verse, it is a tragic study of a lonely woman on a farm. *What Price Glory?* (1924), written with Laurence Stallings, was a great popular hit, which portrayed realistically and sympathetically the common American soldier in action during World War I. There followed two historical plays, also written with Stallings; then came *Saturday's Children* (1927), by Anderson alone—a mature 'serious comedy', dealing with the problem of marriage as it affects two young people. This was an outstanding popular success. Following this were a dramatization of a book about tramp life, and (with Harold Hickerson) the passionately written thesis play, *Gods of the Lightning* (1928), neither of which was a success in the theatre. Another realistic play of modern city life, *Gypsy* (1929), preceded a series of historical and pseudo-historical plays, idealistic in conception and on the whole effectively poetic in language. The best of these were *Elizabeth the Queen* (1930), *Night Over Taos* (1932), *Mary of Scotland* (1933), *Valley Forge* (1934), and *The Wingless Victory* (1936). But Anderson has never been content to follow any one dramatic or artistic formula, and he has varied his themes and styles to conform with his aims as thinker and practical playwright intent upon providing entertainment for the public. His realistic satires on political subjects and the problems of man trying to adjust himself to a modern world are among his most effective works. This is especially true of *Both Your Houses* (1933), a savage attack on political corruption. He has combined poetic drama with formal verse, philosophy and political commentary, in several other plays, notably in *High Tor* (1936), *The Masque of Kings* (1937) (two of his best plays), *Knickerbocker Holiday* (1938), and *Key Largo* (1939). In *Winterset* (1935), a mood piece and a study in conscience —among other things—the author has sought, as he says in his preface, 'to make tragic poetry out of the stuff' of his own times. He has always held that without great poetry there is no great drama. 'If we are going to have a great theater in this country somebody has to write verse, even if it is written badly.' His later plays, *The Eve of St. Mark* (1942), *Storm Operation* (1944), *Truckline Cafe,* and *Joan of Lorraine* (both 1946), however distinguished and poetic in mood and conception, are, except in the case of the first-named, devoid of formal verse. In the last-named, where verse might have been expected, there is none at all. It seems likely that the playwright, more and more concerned with the basic problems of faith and morals, has concluded that verse as a medium of speech does not necessarily create poetic drama. Though Anderson was loath to make public his ideas on art and life during the first part of his career, he has written and spoken at length about poetry in the theatre and the ends of tragedy in speeches and articles, several of which he collected into a volume in 1929, under the title *The Essence of Tragedy and Other Footnotes and Papers.* In spite of his growing concern over the problems of modern civilization and his lifelong preoccupation with poetic form, it should be noted that Maxwell Anderson has remained substantially a man of the theatre, a conscientious workman who knows that the theatre is basically a medium of inspiration and entertainment.

B. H. C.

ANDREINI. (1) FRANCESCO (1548–1624), one of the outstanding actors and authors of the *commedia dell'arte.* He was originally a soldier, and was captured by the Turks, spending several years in slavery. He was famous chiefly as Capitan Spavento, and evidence of the way in which he played this part may be seen in the *Bravure del Capitano Spavento* (1607). Before he made the mask of the Captain his own Andreini seems to have played a lover's part. He was one of the leaders of the Gelosi, with whom he went to Paris in 1600. He married in 1578 (2) ISABELLA CANALI (1562–1604), one of the most famous actresses of her time, unreservedly praised in many contemporary documents. She was the leading lady of the Gelosi, and went with her husband to France, dying in childbirth on the return journey. She had seven children, of whom the most famous was (3) GIAMBATTISTA (c. 1578–1654), known as Lelio. He was a great actor, very popular in France, and appeared mainly with the Fedeli company. He was also a prolific author. He was twice married, in 1601 to (4) VIRGINIA RAMPONI (1583–c. 1627/30), who acted with him in the Fedeli company as Florinda, and after her death to (5) VIRGINIA ROTARI, also an actress, known as Lidia.

ANDREYEV, LEONID NIKOLAIVICH (1871–1919), Russian dramatist, who graduated in the faculty of Law in the Moscow and St. Petersburg Universities, and became a journalist on a Moscow paper. A short story published in 1897 attracted the attention of Gorky, and started Andreyev on the road to success. In his early days he was attracted to the Revolutionary movement, but he drifted away, and after the October Revolution emigrated to Finland, where he died. His plays, which express the deterioration and bitterness of the period between 1905 and 1917, fall into two groups, realistic and symbolic, of which the latter are the most important. Among them are *The Sabine Women* (1911), a satire on political compromise, *The Life of Man* (1906), *The Seven Who Were Hanged* (1908), and the theatrically effective *He Who Gets Slapped* (1914), which has been produced in England and America. Himself a man who had lost his way, his work is permeated with a bitter pessimism, as of a lost soul wandering in a cruel and unpredictable world. This may be the reason for the total eclipse of all his plays, with the exception of *He Who Gets Slapped*, which was unsuccessfully revived in a new adaptation by Judith Guthrie in 1947.

ANDRONICUS, LUCIUS LIVIUS (*c.* 284–204 B.C.), founded Latin drama in 240 B.C. by producing at Rome the first Latin version of a Greek play. The only other known date in his career is 207 B.C., when he composed the state hymn celebrating the victory of the Metaurus. His name shows that he was a Greek, probably from southern Italy, who had become a dependent of the Livian *gens*. Up to his time the Roman stage seems to have known only a formless medley of dance, song, and buffoonery. The introduction of plays with a regular plot was successful, and Andronicus continued to translate and produce pieces taken from Greek tragedy and New Comedy until his death. His importance is as a pioneer; Cicero pronounced his plays unworthy of a second reading, and the fragments of his dramas and his translation of the *Odyssey* which have come down to us indicate that his style was uncouth. Nevertheless later Roman dramatists continued to work on his lines and to use the metres which, so far as we know, he was the first to employ.

W. B.

ANGEL, EDWARD (*fl.* 1660–73), Restoration actor, an excellent comedian, who is referred to in *The Dancing Master* (1671), where Hippolita says: 'Angel is a good fool.' He was first with Rhodes at the Cockpit, and later joined Davenant at Dorset Garden, where he paired excellently with that great comedian, Nokes. Angel specialized in parts of low comedy, particularly French valets. He is not heard of after 1673.

ANGIOLINI, GASPARE (1723–96), Italian *maître de ballet* and theorist, who attacked the theories of Noverre, carrying on a long and acrimonious pamphlet war with him. Angiolini, who was the choreographer of Gluck's 'Don Juan', went to Russia under Catherine the Great and contributed not a little to the development of the Russian Imperial Ballet.

ANGLIN, MARGARET (1876–   ), American actress, accounted one of the finest of her day. Born and educated in Canada, she was a pupil at the Empire Dramatic School, New York, when Charles Frohman engaged her for *Shenandoah*, in which she made her first professional appearance in 1894. After touring with James O'Neill, Sothern, and others, she made her first outstanding success as Roxane in Mansfield's production of *Cyrano de Bergerac* (1898). She was later leading lady of Frohman's stock company at the Empire, where she remained for several years, appearing in a wide variety of plays, including *Mrs. Dane's Defence*, *Diplomacy*, and *The Importance of Being Earnest*. Among her later successes were *The Devil's Disciple* and *Camille*, in which she appeared with Henry Miller; Moody's *The Great Divide*, both under that title and in its original form as *The Sabine Woman*; new translations of *Antigone* and *Hippolytus*, *Iphigenia in Tauris* and *Medea*, *Electra* and *Iphigenia in Aulis*; and such Shakespearian parts as Viola, Rosalind, Cleopatra, and Katharine, many of which she played on tour. In later years she was excellent as Mrs. Malaprop.

ANGUS, ROBERT, see AGGAS, ROBERT.

ANNAPOLIS, one of the earliest towns in America to welcome the players, and one regularly visited by the companies of Hallam and Douglass. They had at first to adapt an existing building for their shows, as Douglass did in 1759, when he produced *The Orphan* and *Venice Preserved*, but in 1771 he built a brick theatre holding 600 persons, in which a number of plays were given, including *Cymbeline* with Beatrice Hallam as Imogen. The first permanent modern theatre was built in 1831.

ANNUNZIO, GABRIELE D', see D'ANNUNZIO.

ANOUILH, JEAN (1910–   ), French dramatist, whose first plays were given by Pitoëff, among them *Le Voyageur sans bagage* (1937) and *Le Sauvage* (1938). His *Bal des voleurs* was one of the great successes of the 1939 season, and during the war his work, already noted for its freshness and vigour, took on a deeper maturity. In 1940 he produced a fine version of the old story of Orpheus and Eurydice, while his *Antigone* (1944), the study of a woman's stand against tyranny, served as the mouthpiece of young France under the rigours of the German occupation. It was given in New York in 1945 with Katharine Cornell in the name part, and in London by the Old Vic in 1949. Anouilh is not only a dramatist, but also a poet, in whose tense, concentrated style and insistence on the dignity and grandeur of man lies a great hope for the future of the French theatre.

ANSKY [SALOMON RAPPOPORT] (1863–1920), Jewish ethnologist and man of letters, whose researches into folk-lore in Russia, Paris, and Central Europe resulted in the writing of his one well-known play, *The Dybbuk, or Between Two Worlds*, a study of demoniac possession and the Hassidic doctrine of pre-ordained relationship. It is more folk-lore than drama, and owes much of its renown to the manner of its production, first in Yiddish by David Hermann for the Vilna Troupe in 1920, and two years later in Hebrew by Vakhtangov for the Moscow Habima company. It has also been played in Yiddish by Maurice Schwartz in New York, and in London in both Hebrew and Yiddish, by Habima and the New Yiddish Theatre respectively. Ansky was also the author of an unfinished play, again Hassidic in theme, and of a satirical poem on the popular conception of Heaven and Hell. He was keenly interested in politics, but after the purge consequent on the attempted assassination of Lenin in 1918 he retired to Vilna, where he died.   E. H.

ANTA, see AMERICAN NATIONAL THEATRE AND ACADEMY.

ANTHONY STREET THEATRE, NEW YORK. This famous theatre, in which Edmund Kean first appeared in New York in a succession of fine parts, was originally a circus, and in 1812 was opened as the Olympic Theatre by a company from Philadelphia, headed by Mrs. Melmoth and Twaits, after some delay caused by a carriage accident in which the leading lady broke her arm. Among the plays, interspersed with circus turns, which were given during this season was the famous equestrian melodrama *Timour the Tartar*, then seen for the first time in the United States. In 1813 Twaits again opened the theatre, redecorated and enlarged and renamed the Anthony Street Theatre, with a passable company which included the young Placides and a Mrs. Beaumont, who was excellent in tragedy. This group survived until 1814, when the theatre passed through various hands and was named successively the Commonwealth and the Pavilion, opening only for the summer. After the destruction by fire of the Park Theatre in May 1820 its company moved to the Anthony Street Theatre, which soon proved too small to hold the crowds that flocked to see Kean. He made his first appearance there as guest-artist on 29 Nov. 1820, as Richard III. When the Park Theatre was rebuilt the company moved back, and the Anthony Street Theatre closed.

ANTI-MASQUE, see JONSON and MASQUE.

ANTOINE, ANDRÉ (1858–1943), French actor, producer, and manager, and one of the outstanding figures in the theatrical reforms of the late nineteenth century. In 1887, while working for the Paris Gas Company and employing his leisure hours in amateur acting, he founded the Théâtre Libre for the production of the new naturalistic drama then coming to the fore in Europe. Here he produced in 1890 Ibsen's *Ghosts*, playing Oswald himself, and followed it with plays by Hauptmann, Strindberg, Björnsen, Verga, de Curel, Becque, Brieux, and Porto-Riche. Here, too, he revolutionized French acting and inaugurated a new era of scenic design. Inspired by him Otto Brahm founded the Freie Bühne in Berlin, and Grein the Independent Theatre in London. In 1894 Antoine's first venture failed financially, though it had had an immense cultural value, and in 1897, after working at the Odéon for a while, he took over the Théâtre des Menus-Plaisirs, and, renaming it the Théâtre Antoine, made it a rallying-point for the young and aspiring dramatists. From 1906–16 Antoine was director of the Odéon, retiring from active work in the theatre at the end of that period. His influence, not only in France, but all over Europe and in America, has been incalculable, and he helped more than anyone to deliver Europe from the domination of the 'well-made' play and to establish the reputation of Ibsen and his followers in France. Among the outstanding figures of the next generation who owed much to him was Jacques Copeau, founder of the Vieux-Colombier.

ANZENGRUBER, LUDWIG (1839–89), Austrian actor and dramatist. He was for some years a strolling player, and his first plays were written in dialect. They dealt with problems of the ordinary man, particularly of the peasants, though his *Der Pfarrer von Kirchfeld* (1867) is a plea for the exercise of a tolerant religious spirit. He also proved in his *Der Meineidbauer* (1871), where the figure of the old farmer who has cheated two orphans of their heritage assumes demoniac stature, that peasant life can furnish matter for true tragedy. A comic battle for matrimonial supremacy, with a vague background of clerical dissension, is exploited in *Die Kreuzelschreiber* (1872), where a number of peasants are induced to append their signatures—in the form of crosses—to a document much resented by the village priest. Egged on by the latter and by a vagrant wag—a figure dear to this dramatist—who engineers the whole affair for his own amusement, the wives shut out their husbands, and induce them to embark on a penitentiary pilgrimage to Rome. When they find out that, in addition to taking the family purse, the men are to be accompanied by a train of virgins, the wives change their minds and each firmly leads home her husband.

In contrast to the vein of humour, *Der Doppelselbstmord* is a rustic version of *Romeo and Juliet*, while in his best-known play, *Das vierte Gebot* (1877)—which incidentally was the first German play to be produced by Otto Brahm's Freie Bühne—Anzengruber deserts his rural solitudes for the teeming life of the city, proving himself, however, as rugged a realist in one place as in the other. Eventually his unselfconscious rural humanity went out of fashion, and his popularity waned; but he holds an important place in theatre history, and was one of the few good dramatists produced by the German-speaking stage of his day.

APOLLODORUS, of Carystos, a Greek comic poet of New Comedy (see GREECE, 2 *b*), of whose works only a few fragments remain. Terence modelled his *Phormio* and *Hecyra* on plays by this author.

APOLLO THEATRE. (1) LONDON, in Shaftesbury Avenue. This opened in 1901, under the management of Henry Lowenfeld. Its first production, *The Belle of Bohemia*, was a failure. Then Martin-Harvey took two of his assured successes, *The Cigarette Maker's Romance* and *The Only Way*, there, and in Sept. 1901 George Edwardes produced a musical version of *Kitty Grey* (previously played as a comedy at the Vaudeville) which, with Evie Greene, Edna May, Maurice Farkoa, and G. P. Huntley in the cast, was an immediate success and ran for 220 performances. *The Girl from Kays*, in the following year, under the same management, ran for 432 performances. The Apollo, although never the permanent home of a great management, has been a consistently successful theatre. It is well situated and the right size for either musical or straight plays. The Pélissier Follies were staged there, each season exceeding 500 performances. In 1939 Alec L. Rea, after leaving the St. Martin's Theatre, took over the Apollo, but the outbreak of war interrupted his management. Among later productions were *The Light of Heart*, *Old Acquaintance*, and *Flare Path*.   W. M. P.

(2) NEW YORK, on 42nd Street, between 7th and 8th Avenues. It opened as the Bryant in 1910, for films and vaudeville acts, and was renamed the Apollo on 17 Nov. 1920. One of its early productions was Hopkins's revival of *Macbeth* in 1921, with a notable cast headed by Lionel Barrymore, and triangular settings by Robert Edmond Jones. A series of musical comedies followed, and for many years the house was occupied by *George White's Scandals.* It became a cinema again in 1933.

(3) The Third Avenue Variety Theatre was known as the Apollo for a short time in 1885, when it opened on 5 Jan. with plays in German.

(4) A mixed film and stage playhouse, on Chuter Street, New York, which opened in Oct. 1926, was known as the Apollo, as was a burlesque house on 125th Street.

APPIA, ADOLPHE (1862–1928), Swiss scenic designer, whose theories on the use of light in stage production govern much of the best modern work in this medium (see LIGHTING, 1 *d* and SCENERY).

APRON STAGE, see FORESTAGE.

AQUARIUM THEATRE, LONDON. The Royal Aquarium and Winter Garden, Westminster, built as an exhibition-amusement palace in 1876, on the site of the old Westminster Theatre, once a plague pit, had an annexe which was called the Aquarium—also the Afternoon—Theatre. It soon became a regular theatre, and Labouchère seems to have had a hand in its management, as did Edgar Bruce. Jennie Lee appeared there as Jo in *Bleak House* with great success. Jennie Hill, later a variety star, appeared as a child in one of J. A. Cave's pantomimes there, in which she played the hind legs of an animal; the framework gave way, leaving her stranded on the stage. In 1878 Phelps made his last appearance on any stage at the Aquarium, breaking down in Wolsey's farewell speech, and being carried off, never to appear again. He died in the same year. The theatre was then under the management of Marie Litton. In April–May 1879 the Vokes family appeared in sketches and the theatre was renamed the Imperial. Miss Litton, afterwards Mrs. Wybrow Robertson, did some excellent productions there with fine casts. In 1880 a Dutch company from Rotterdam made a success in *Anne Mie*, and two years later Mrs. Langtry appeared in *An Unequal Match* and as Rosalind. In 1885 the theatre closed. Mrs. Langtry took it over, rebuilt it lavishly on the model of a Greek temple in marble and gilt, and opened it in April 1900 with *The Queen's Necklace*, but without success. Neither Herbert Waring, who followed her, nor Ellen Terry, who in 1903 produced Ibsen's *The Vikings* there, fared better, though Ellen Terry herself appeared in the latter play and her son Gordon Craig was responsible for the production, scenery, and lighting. In Nov. 1903 Lewis Waller became actor-manager of the theatre, and did better than the former tenants, opening with a revival of *Monsieur Beaucaire*, followed by an English version of Hugo's *Ruy Blas*, which was a failure in spite of Mrs. Patrick Campbell. *Brigadier Gerard* was his greatest success during his three years' tenancy. Mrs. Langtry eventually disposed of the theatre to the Wesleyan Methodists, and on its site the Central Hall, Westminster, now stands. The theatre was pulled down in 1908, and taken away to Canning Town to be re-erected as a cinema.   W. M. P.

AQUATIC DRAMA, see CIRCUS and SADLER'S WELLS.

ARCH BORDER, see BORDER and STAGE, 3.

ARCHER, WILLIAM (1856–1924), a Scottish journalist who became a London dramatic critic and who brought to his work what H. G. Wells called an 'unscrupulous integrity'. He worked first on the staff of the *Edinburgh Evening News*, and settled in London in 1878. He became dramatic critic successively to *Figaro*, the *World*, the *Tribune*, and the *Nation*. Archer took the theatre seriously as an art and helped to bring in the 'new drama' of the nineties by his translations of the plays of Ibsen, whose collected works he edited in 1906–8. He had an astringent sense of humour which was probably responsible for his long friendship with Bernard Shaw.

Archer claimed that the drama of his day was at least as fine a product of the human spirit as the Elizabethan drama—Shakespeare only apart—and that it was incomparably superior technically, intellectually, and morally to the drama of the Restoration. He was always protesting at the critical overvaluation of ancient drama and the undervaluation of the modern.

His publications included editions of the dramatic essays of Leigh Hunt and Hazlitt, *English Dramatists of Today* (1882), *Henry Irving* (1883), *Masks or Faces* (1888), *William Charles Macready* (1890), *Study and Stage* (1899), *America Today* (1900), *The Old Drama and the New* (1923), and, with Granville Barker, *A National Theatre : Scheme and Estimates* (1907). His dramatic criticisms in the *World*, from 1893 to 1897, were reissued in annual volumes as *The Theatrical World*. In 1923 his play, *The Green Goddess*, was produced at the St. James's Theatre. This improbable melodrama ran for 416 performances and has since been filmed.   T. C. K.

ARCHITECTURE, THEATRE. (For Greek and Roman Theatres see ACOUSTICS, 2 and 3, GREECE, 3 *b*, and ROME.)

The shape of English theatres in the sixteenth century was accidental, for when the drama ceased to be of a religious nature it left the precincts of the church and went to the open inn-yard. This, surrounded by two or three tiers of galleries, was a convenient shape and had a ready-made audience, so it became the pattern for all English playhouses until 1674. When a theatre was required a builder or a carpenter was called in, and he adapted the inn-yard, adding benches to the galleries and a platform with a trap-door to one end of the yard (see also ELIZABETHAN PLAYHOUSE).

The first Italian theatres, however, were planned—planned by architects—and during their development from the original half-circle of gradines to five tiers of boxes in the shape of a horseshoe these plans were gradually adopted throughout the whole of Europe for over four centuries.

Italian theatre building began about the year 1486 at the Court of Ferrara, the seat of the Este family and centre of the humanistic movement in Italy, where the Greek and Latin comedies had been 'rediscovered' by the Duke Ercole d'Este. The Duke's sudden interest in these plays caused him to have them acted in what he thought would have been the Greek or Roman style. He treated the matter seriously and called in his architect to build him a theatre based on the writings of Vitruvius, whose works had also come to light again through this new desire to study the ancients. The example set by Ercole d'Este was followed by the Dukes of Milan and Florence, and gradually spread through the whole of northern Italy, one princely Court vying with another in this revival of classic drama, each Court building a theatre to house it. The architect was generally given some vast hall, riding-school, or granary in which to build, and in these early days he also designed and built the scenes.

The development of the French theatre, until the arrival in Paris in 1645 of Giacomo Torelli (1608–78), the architect and machinist from Fano, consisted merely in the more or less luxurious conversion of one tennis-court after another, the French tennis-court being an oblong wooden building with a few high seats or boxes for spectators at either end of the courts and sometimes some benches running down one of the long sides as well. It had only one advantage over the English inn-yard in that it was covered. Torelli brought with him the most elaborate ideas about movable scenery and machines, for which a vast stage was necessary. This resulted in the remodelling of Richelieu's old theatre (later the Palais-Royal), and led to the conversion of a room in the Tuileries into the so-called Salle des Machines under another Italian stage-designer, Gaspare Vigarani (1586–1663). This was completed by 1662, and opened with the performance of an elaborate opera. In Holland, however, when the first theatre was built by Jacob Van Campen (*c.* 1590–1657) in Amsterdam in 1637, it was quite original in shape. The auditorium was like that of the Teatro Olimpico in Vicenza, built by Andrea Palladio (1518–80), but it had two tiers of boxes surmounted by a big public gallery; the stage had a built scene on medieval lines but in classic style. In 1674 when Sir Christopher Wren (1632–1723) rebuilt Drury Lane theatre it was obviously Van Campen's little theatre in Amsterdam and Vigarani's Salle des Machines in Paris that influenced him most, plans and sections of both having been published by that time.

Before 1637 the Italian public had to stand in the market-squares to see travelling actors perform a comedy on an improvised stage of planks, except on special occasions when they were admitted free to the theatres which were the private property of their princes. In England, from the start, the playhouses had always been public, and so a more democratic building was evolved. Boxes were introduced because that was the fashion abroad but, following the lead of Van Campen, Wren's great gallery in his first Drury Lane set the pattern for all future theatres in England. A few boxes were kept on either side of the proscenium and a second, as well as a first, gallery was developed. The development of these galleries was peculiar to England and forms a very interesting study (see also ENGLISH PLAYHOUSE).

Spain's drama, like England's, started democratically. Stages were put up in the courtyards formed by the backs of a number of vast palaces in which many different families lived. The windows looking on to the courts became boxes, the yard being filled with benches, and a semi-permanent theatre was established during certain festive periods in the year (see SPAIN); but the Italian influence was too great to be resisted for long and architects were soon imported to build what became some of the most ornate opera houses in Europe.

In the whole of Europe the only country that has been able to preserve any of its sixteenth- or seventeenth-century theatres has been Italy. Three of these are well worth studying—the Teatro Olimpico referred to above, which was built in 1579, the Court theatre at Sabbionetta built by Vincenzo Scamozzi (1552–1616) in 1588, and the Farnese theatre at Parma built by Giambattista Aleotti (1546–1636) in 1618, now partially destroyed by bombing. Palladio's building in Vicenza, which is the best known of the three, is not a very good example of a theatre. He had to work for a society of academicians who insisted on his adhering very strictly to Vitruvius, so he built them an 'antique' on a quite inadequate site. But the theatres at Parma and Sabbionetta, although very little is generally known about them, are probably the most important of two distinctive forms of the Italian seventeenth-century theatres, the one at Parma, holding some 3,500 spectators, being a house for spectacle and ballet, and the one at Sabbionetta, holding only 250 spectators, a house for intimate drama.

By 1600 the revival of classic drama had been taken up with such interest throughout Italy that Peri and his friends in Florence, in their attempts to re-create an original Greek pastoral accompanied by music, evolved a form of *dramma con musica* which was to spread like wildfire through the whole of Europe and develop into the grand opera of to-day. Up to the beginning of the seventeenth century all performances were given at the expense of the princes and rich courtiers for the purpose of entertaining their friends at marriage ceremonies, coronations, and other state occasions, and the audience was divided as follows: 'The best seats for the ladies, next best seats for the foreign gentlemen, and standing room or whatever could be found to sit on for the gentlemen of the Court.' When the prince was particularly generous and the show particularly good an extra performance was given, sometimes three or four performances, and then the townspeople were admitted for nothing. The public was so taken with the idea of opera that it decided to build permanent theatres of its own. From this point in the history of the modern revival of drama we see nothing but elaboration, until over-elaboration brings the theatre to a state of gaudy decay.

With the public's desire for opera the architect was confronted with the problem of how to house it, and this forced him to concoct a building that can only be described as a mess of conglomerated architectural forms. Among his many problems was that of building a theatre containing a number of private boxes. Boxes there had to be, in order to induce the autocratic merchants of those times to subscribe money towards building the theatres, their subscriptions entitling them to use a special section of the theatre for a definite period. As these sections of the theatre had to be marked off, the box was evolved, first with low barriers dividing up two or three tiers of seats, which gradually rose and became walls enclosing little rooms, the floor of the auditorium and the top gallery being left for the non-subscribing general public. Of course this brought up the question of acoustics, and over

this (as many hundreds of documents show) one architect vied with another in trying to invent a new shape of auditorium that would hold more people who could all, theoretically, see and hear everything that happened on the stage (see ACOUSTICS).

Before the introduction of the completely musical drama, or opera, light intermezzi, or interludes, had been introduced into plays, thus offering the audience a kind of musical plum to make the rest of the cake more attractive. These interludes were such things as four shepherds dancing a moresco, or Aurora and attendant nymphs singing a song in praise of the princes present. In the early days the intermezzi were performed on the fore-stage, or in the auditorium (which was reached by means of ramps from the stage), either while the scenery was being re-dressed behind, or to mark a lapse of time. When opera became the only fashionable form of entertainment the intermezzi were still retained but, whereas once Aurora and her nymphs had walked on to the stage, or moved on in some charming little chariot, they now had to descend from the clouds borne by swans and peacocks, and the music had to get louder and louder to drown the creaking of the ropes; and when one architect surpassed himself by bringing on fifteen people at one fell swoop, the neighbouring prince, notified of this by his ambassador or spies, told the architect or engineer in charge of his performance that when Juno next appeared in her chariot from the skies she must be accompanied by no less than sixteen attendants and at least four extra cupids. This went on and on until the machines became more important than the play or the music, while the stages became larger and larger to accommodate them. Intermezzi now took the form of great ballets; sometimes horses and other animals performed dances in the auditorium, which became a kind of circus.

Nearly all the early public theatres on the continent opened with opera, the first being the San Cassiano in the Republic of Venice in 1637. These theatres tried for some time to supply the public with their favourite new machines, but this became so costly that they had to be content with revamping the old ones, and eventually these fell out of use to a great extent. With the eighteenth century came the Bibienas, a family of scenographers led by Ferdinando Galli (1657–1743), who introduced a new form of painted scenery which was the answer to the popular demand for 'show'. This was the *scene al angolo*—instead of having the one and only vanishing point in the centre of the stage, they moved the point of sight to the sides so that the audience looked at it, as it were, from a different angle. Rococo decoration lending itself so magnificently to this art, scene-painting and perspectives became popular in place of machines. The Bibienas also designed a new bell-shaped auditorium and built many theatres to this pattern in southern Germany as well as in northern Italy.

The end of the eighteenth century saw

Italian opera houses built by Italians all over Europe from Spain to Russia.

By the end of the seventeenth century, the theatres having all supplied themselves with stock scenery and stock costumes which were used for every performance without regard to place or period, the public became apathetic and turned its attention to the star performer—the singer. These virtuosi, mostly pets of the cardinals and local aristocracy, had by now reached such a pitch of arrogance that it was common for them to loll against the proscenium and beat time with their canes or fans while waiting for their cues, sometimes chatting with the people in the stage boxes, or taking snuff with gentlemen acquaintances in the pit, and now and then shouting some rude joke at the prompter, and adding improvised flourishes to their parts wherever they thought fit. We have extraordinarily good records of theatre life in Rome at this time, and conditions do not seem to have differed much elsewhere in Europe. The theatre was now a place of reunion for genial conversation and social gossip. Boxes were like little drawing-rooms full of chattering people. In some of them, instead of chattering, they would play cards or dominoes. During the evening gentlemen paid visits to the ladies, going from one box to another. The persistent chatter, and the popping in and out of boxes, made the architect Francesco Milizia (1725-98) liken theatres to beehives, and it went on right through the performance, except for a break here and there, when all would stop while they craned their heads to listen to one of their favourite *castrati* singing some special aria. Priests and cardinals were great frequenters of the theatre and were no better behaved than any other members of society. The passages behind the boxes were very small and badly illuminated by oil lamps at distant intervals. They were described by a contemporary author as being more like sewers, for lackeys and linkboys who brought the picnics which the gentry ate in the boxes, when not able to crowd into the *colombaia*, or dove-cot, as the top of the gallery was called, congregated together in throngs under those little lights in the passages and played at dice to pass the time. Also, as there would probably be no more than three lavatories in a theatre holding between 2,000 and 3,000 spectators, the servants (and even their masters) found the passages the next most convenient place for their purpose. Those who thronged the pit only paid a small entrance fee and went in and out of the theatre during the performance, staying merely to listen to one or two arias that attracted them. The ladies and gentlemen in the boxes, who partook of meals during the performance, would throw chicken-bones and peelings into the pit, and it is recorded that there were those amongst the pittites who were so superstitious that they fought for positions beneath the box of some prince of the Holy Church, and kept as sacred possessions anything he might throw out; they even considered it a great honour to be spat upon, which was a

habit frequently resorted to by the gentry in the boxes.

The wax candles, which numbered many hundreds in front of the curtain, and as many as two or three thousand behind, illuminating the scene and audience alike, were made daily, by a man specially employed for this purpose, in a room with a boiler under the stage. The tallow used in these candles was usually made from mutton fat. When they had been burning for some time a haze hung between the audience and the stage, which, some say, lent an air of mystery to the performance. It may also have been the reason why actors and singers alike had to shout their lines to make themselves heard through the fog of candle smoke, which got into their lungs and caused them to spit continuously. At the Comédie-Française in Paris giant spittoons were built into the stage on either side of the proscenium. Candle smoke also acted as a gauze between the audience and the scenery, so that the tonal values in the scenery had to be emphasized to counteract it. The smells from the candles in front and the passages behind must have made the theatre a very unsavoury place in the eighteenth century, and for this reason the ladies scented themselves profusely, and ladies and gentlemen alike sniffed pomanders the entire time, the gentlemen alternating with snuff and sneezing violently into little silk handkerchiefs.

In the private theatres in the palaces everything was much more spacious and the audience more select, and this was one of the reasons why, towards the end of the eighteenth century, the public theatre grew into such disfavour with the gentry, and private theatricals were resorted to once more. During these private shows sherbets and lemonades and sweetmeats were handed round to the guests from time to time by little black boys, but in spite of the fizzing and tinkling of glasses the actors found them quiet after the noise of the public theatres. Nevertheless, by the beginning of the nineteenth century, except for the few private theatres dotted about Europe which had been built and were maintained by princely lovers of the theatre, all other buildings that were to house drama had been built as opera houses with vast tiers of boxes—social centres for the middle and upper classes.

In England things were somewhat different. Opera never became as popular as on the continent, and the tiers of little boxes were replaced by the two galleries required by the large merchant class. These really evolved from the narrow galleries round the old inn-yard, and when Sir Christopher Wren rebuilt Drury Lane in 1674 he introduced the deep gallery which has remained the most noticeable feature of the English theatre ever since. Plans of the first theatre in Covent Garden, built in 1732 by one of our best theatre architects, Edward Shepherd (c. 1670-1747), shows giant galleries, and when Sir John Vanbrugh (1664-1726) built his opera house in the Haymarket in 1705 he also put in the two galleries. The aristocracy was catered for by six to nine private boxes, together with a few open boxes, on either side of the proscenium. There is an interesting account of a visit to Vanbrugh's theatre made in 1782 by a German cleric named Charles Moritz; it is worth quoting, since it gives such a very clear picture of an English theatre in the eighteenth century.

. . . For a seat in the boxes you pay five shillings, in the pit three, in the first gallery two, and in the second or upper gallery, one shilling. And it is the tenants in this upper gallery who, for their shilling, make all that noise and uproar for which the English play-houses are so famous. I was in the pit, which gradually rises, amphitheatre-wise, from the orchestra, and is furnished with benches, one above another, from the top to the bottom. Often and often, whilst I sat here, did a rotten orange, or pieces of the peel of an orange, fly past me, or past some of my neighbours, and once one of them actually hit my hat, without my daring to look round, for fear another might then hit me on my face.

. . . Besides this perpetual pelting from the gallery, which renders an English play-house so uncomfortable, there is no end to their calling out and knocking with their sticks till the curtain is drawn up. I saw a miller's boy, or a baker's boy, thus, like a huge booby, leaning over the rails and knocking again and again on the outside, with all his might, so that he was seen by everybody, without being in the least ashamed or abashed. I sometimes heard, too, the people in the lower or middle gallery quarrelling with those of the upper one.

. . . In the boxes, quite in a corner, sat several servants, who were said to be placed there to keep the seats for the families they served till they should arrive; they seemed to sit remarkably close and still, the reason of which, I was told, was their apprehension of being pelted; for if one of them dares but to look out of the box, he is immediately saluted with a shower of orange peel from the gallery.

On the stages of these buildings actors tried to keep alive a lovely art that was once the drama. The architects who built these theatres were not much to blame; they had done their best with the aid of good builders and contemporary decorators. What was bad in theatre architecture was mostly due to the impresarios' or showmen's attempts to get as much money for as little as possible, by pandering to the tastes of those to whom display has always meant 'class'. It was not until two German architects approached the subject in the nineteenth century that a modern theatre to house drama was evolved. These two men were Max Littman (1862–   ), who seriously tackled acoustics and developed the idea of a steadily rising bank of seats and movable prosceniums, and Gottfried Semper (1803–79), who built the Opera House at Dresden and planned a theatre for Wagner at Munich. This was never built, but many of its features were incorporated into the plan for the Festspielhaus at Bayreuth, among them the so-called 'fan-shaped' auditorium which has been used as the basis of most theatre designs ever since. The strange thing about this fan-shaped plan is that it was first used by our own Edward Shepherd in 1732.

The study of theatre buildings in the past and the present proves that no good comes of trying to house opera, spectacle, and intimate drama all under the same roof—each requires separate study and a separate theatre. (See also ACOUSTICS, AUDITORIUM, ENGLISH PLAYHOUSE, MACHINERY, PROSCENIUM, STAGE.)   E. C.

ARCH STREET THEATRE, see DREW (1) and PHILADELPHIA.

ARETINO, PIETRO (1492–1556), Italian dramatist, who began life as a lackey, and nearly ended as a Cardinal. His one tragedy, *Orazio* (1546), is probably the best of those written at that time, but as a dramatist he is chiefly remembered for his comedies, which are exceptionally free from neo-classical conventions, and thoroughly Italian in their realistic and satiric thought and presentation. Although his plays were written in haste, and lack finish, they were original and amusing, and his public asked for nothing more; hence his popularity. He provides us with much light on the less creditable aspects of the social life of his day. It has been suggested that Ben Jonson's *Epicoene* may owe something to Aretino's second comedy, *Il Marescalco* (1533). (See also ITALY, 1.)

ARGENTINA, see SOUTH AMERICA, 1.

ARGYLL ROOMS, LONDON, in Regent Street. These were fitted up as a private theatre and run by subscription from 1819 to 1823, for French plays under aristocratic patronage. Performances were given every Friday from March to September. Plays began at 9 and ended at midnight when the company adjourned to the public ballroom and joined the dancing.

ARION, of Lesbos (c. 625–585 B.C.), an important, though vague, figure in the development of Greek music and dramatic poetry. He reorganized the dithyrambic dance (see DITHYRAMB), and was the first to give literary shape both to the dithyramb and to the satyr-revel. He was also the inventor of the 'tragic mode' (? musical mode), and, according to one tradition, the first tragic poet. He is credited with a miraculous escape from death by drowning at the hands of pirates, being conveyed to land on the back of a dolphin charmed by his singing.   H. D. F. K.

ARIOSTO, LODOVICO (1474–1533), famous Italian poet, author of the romantic epic, *Orlando Furioso*, written in honour of his patrons, the family of the d'Este, in whose service he spent most of his life at Ferrara. He was one of the first and the greatest of the writers of Italian comedy, and did much to establish it in its literary form of the *commedia erudita*. The structure of his plays is modelled upon Roman comedies; their content is of Renaissance city life. His first plays, *Cassaria* and *I Suppositi*, were given in Ferrara in 1508 and 1509, in a permanent building of classical style erected under the influence of Vitruvius's *De Architectura*, with scenery by Raphael (this building was destroyed in 1533). These were in prose, but were later re-written in verse, and

I Suppositi, in its revised form, was given in 1513 before Pope Leo X, in his new theatre in Rome. Ariosto's next play, *Il Negromante*, written in 1520, also in verse, was performed at Ferrara in 1530. A further play was left unfinished (see also ITALY, 1 *b* iii).

ARISTOPHANES (*c.* 448–*c.* 380 B.C.), Greek dramatist, son of Philippus, of Athens. The comic poet of Old Comedy (see GREECE, 2), he wrote some 40 comedies, of which 11 are extant (the only Greek comedies to be preserved entire): the *Acharnians* (425 B.C.), *Knights* (424), *Clouds* (423), *Wasps* (422), *Peace* (421), *Birds* (414), *Lysistrata* (411), *Thesmophoriazousae* (Women at the Festival) (410), *Frogs* (405), *Ecclesiazousae* (Women in Parliament) (392), and *Plutus* (Wealth) (388).

Aristophanes' name is joined with those of Eupolis and Cratinus in the well-known Horatian verse (*Satires*, Book 1, Satire 4, line 1), but we have no reason to suspect the good judgement of the ancient critics who regarded him as the greatest of the Attic comic poets. His direct influence on drama has been slight, simply because both the form and the spirit of his comedy were so intensely local that they offered no models and but little material to comic dramatists of other times and places (see MENANDER); on the other hand, his purely literary influence has been great, particularly on Rabelais and Fielding.

The form of Aristophanes' comedy is in some respects exceedingly strict, in others exceedingly loose. One element was a series of scenes (in which the chorus took part) where correspondence was strict: e.g. opposing speeches were of exactly the same length. This element was derived from a traditional animal-masquerade or revel. It will be noticed how many of the plays got their titles from the disguise assumed in them by the chorus, which became wasps, clouds, frogs, &c. A second element was the *parabasis*, the 'coming-forward' of the chorus. This was a long address of the chorus to the audience, again in a most elaborately strict form. Naturally the parabasis is quite undramatic; in it the poet harangues the audience quite openly in his own person. A third element is a series of loosely attached scenes in a different metre (a colloquial version of the tragic iambic verse); these have no set form.

In the earlier plays, which are more characteristic of Old Comedy, there is little development of plot; rather, some fantastic situation was quickly developed—it often involved a contest or struggle between hero and chorus, or between two halves of the chorus—and then the situation was exploited in a series of loosely connected scenes. The central situation was normally one that had direct reference to the political situation of the moment or to some urgent social question; in the *Acharnians*, for example, an Athenian citizen, weary of the war, makes a private treaty with the enemy and consequently enjoys the advantages of trading with them. The iambic scenes develop the ludicrous possibilities of this invention, and

enable Aristophanes to hit out right and left at people he dislikes—politicians, busybodies, philosophers, Euripides.

These earlier plays are an astonishing mixture of fantasy, unsparing (and often, to our minds, violently unfair) satire, brilliant verbal wit, literary and musical parody, exquisite lyrics, hard-hitting political propaganda, and uproarious farce. There is an uncertain tradition that an attempt was made to limit the licence of Old Comedy, but the matter and the manner of Aristophanes shows that the attempt, if made, failed.

The *Frogs* marks the transition to the much quieter Middle Comedy, in which personal and political invective plays a smaller part, the element of the fantastic is much reduced, and plot becomes more elaborate. The chorus, in consequence, is made much less prominent. The two last plays make fun of current ideas of feminism and communism; the *Frogs* is important in the history of criticism, for it stages a contest, in Hades, between Aeschylus and Euripides, as to which shall be brought back to earth to revive the dying art of tragedy. Dionysus is umpire, and Sophocles sits by to take on the winner.   H. D. F. K.

(For the English Aristophanes, see FOOTE, SAMUEL.)

ARISTOTLE (384–322 B.C.) of Stagira, Greek philosopher and scientist. His *Poetics* analyses the function and structural principles of tragedy and (to some extent) of epic; a second book, on comedy, has been lost. The *Poetics* is a reply to the criticisms of Plato and of Socrates, who says (in Plato's *Apology*) that the poets are unable to give a coherent account of what they do. To the latter criticism Aristotle replies by working out a logical theory of poetic composition; to Plato, who condemns poetry and drama for what it does not do (viz. inculcate virtue), he replies by inquiring quite objectively what it does do. It aims at pleasure, but at the rational pleasure which is a part of the good life; by its representation of serious action it does indeed excite emotions, but only to purge them and so to leave the spectator strengthened; since art represents universals and not particulars, it is nearer to the truth than actual events and objects are, not farther from it, as Plato maintained. 'Poetry is more philosophical than history.'

Aristotle's account of the historical development of tragedy and comedy is extremely brief. His analysis of the form of tragedy is clear and penetrating, but, because of his biological bias, it is something less than an account of the existing types of tragedy; for Aristotle regarded tragedy as an organism which, like other organisms, developed until it achieved its 'natural' form, and then decayed; its basic laws are therefore to be disclosed by an analysis of the mature, not of the immature or the enfeebled, stages of the art. The 'complete' form of tragedy, the one in which all its structural features are fully developed and most vigorously used, is the Sophoclean (see SOPHOCLES); it is, therefore, the Sophoclean tragedy, in all essentials, that Aristotle analyses, and his dicta are not necessarily true of Aeschylus or even Euripides. Within these limits his criticism is penetrating and in many ways final.

The neo-classical critics of the seventeenth and eighteenth centuries, especially those in France, were anxious to claim Aristotle's authority for their own doctrines, some of which Aristotle never thought of. Their interpretations of Aristotle were therefore often ludicrous. For example, of the famous Three Unities Aristotle mentions only one and a half; he insists on the Unity of Action, and he remarks parenthetically, comparing tragedy with epic, that tragedy (but not the early tragedy) 'tries as far as possible to confine itself to twenty-four hours or thereabouts'. About the Unity of Place he says nothing, and several extant Greek plays disregard it, if it was convenient and plausible to move the chorus from one (dramatic) place to another.

Aristotle also compiled a list of the prize-winning tragedies and comedies (see DIDASCALIA.)   H. D. F. K.

ARLECCHINO, one of the comic, quick-witted servants of the *commedia dell'arte*. The name may have been picked up by the Italians when they visited France in the late sixteenth century, where, in the form Herlequin, it denoted a personage akin to the comic devils of the medieval Mystery play. Probably the first Italian actor to adopt the name, in its Italian form, was Tristano Martinelli. As Arlequin, still a comic servant, the character crops up in later French comedy and in the dumb shows of the fairs, while, in the familiar form of Harlequin, it survives to-day in the harlequinade of the English pantomime, metamorphosed into the young lover of Columbine. (For a more detailed discussion of this point, see HARLEQUINADE and ITALY, 2.)

ARLISS, GEORGE (1868–1946), English actor, whose later career was almost entirely connected with films. He had, however, already made a name for himself on the stage before he went to Hollywood, some of his finest parts being Zakkuri in *The Darling of the Gods* (1902), the title-role in *Disraeli* (1911), and the Rajah in *The Green Goddess* (1921). It was in the last part that he reappeared in London after a long absence in America, where he first went in 1901 with Mrs. Patrick Campbell. He was an excellent delineator of suave villainy, but his versatility enabled him to play with equal success the elderly gentleman in *Old English* (1924). He was also seen in Pinero, Ibsen, and Shakespeare, and was the author of several plays and of an autobiography entitled *Up the Years from Bloomsbury* (1927).

ARMIN, ROBERT (c. 1568–c. 1611), an Elizabethan clown, pupil and successor of Tarlton, who was first with the Lord Chandos's Men, later with the Lord Chamberlain's. He appears in the list of actors in Shakespeare's plays, and was certainly at the Globe. He probably played Dogberry in succession to Kempe, and his name is found in the actor-list of *The Alchemist* (1610). It is as a writer, however, that Armin is best known. His *Foole upon Foole, or Six Sortes of Sottes* appeared in 1600, and on the title-page he describes himself as 'Clonnico de Curtanio Snuffe', changed in a later edition, by which time he had probably moved from the Curtain to the Globe, to 'Clonnico del Mondo Snuffe'. These publications were anonymous, but Armin's name is found on an enlarged edition published in 1608 as *A Nest of Ninnies*. He was probably the author of *Quips upon Questions* (also 1600), a collection of quatrains on stage 'themes', or improvisations on subjects suggested by the audience, and can certainly be credited with at least one play, *Two Maids of Moreclacke*, produced by the King's Revels in 1609.

ARMSTRONG, PAUL (1869–1915), American dramatist who was for a time purser in the Merchant Navy, and later a journalist. His early plays were not successful, but in 1905 he scored a triumph with *The Heir to the Hoorah*, and became one of the most popular and prolific playwrights of the day. Among his later successes, some of which were written in collaboration, were *Blue Grass* (1908), *Alias Jimmy Valentine* (1909), the first of a long line of crook plays, and *The Deep Purple* (1910). His dialogue was crisp, with strong situations and grim humour, but his work had little literary merit, and was in the melodramatic style now successfully exploited by the cinema.

ARMSTRONG, WILLIAM (1882–), English actor and producer, who was for many years connected with the Liverpool Playhouse, the oldest existing repertory company in Great Britain. He began his acting career under Benson, and made his first appearance at Stratford-on-Avon in 1908. He later toured extensively in England and America, and was successively with the Glasgow, the Liverpool, the Birmingham, and the Everyman Repertory companies. In 1922, after touring with Mrs. Patrick Campbell in *Hedda Gabler*, he went to Liverpool as director and producer at the Playhouse, and remained there until 1941, when the theatre closed owing to heavy air-raids. He did not return on its re-opening, but was responsible for a number of outstanding productions in London theatres, including *Old Acquaintance*, a revival of *The Circle, Uncle Harry*, and *Claudia*. In 1945 he was appointed producer and assistant director, under Sir Barry Jackson, of the Birmingham Repertory theatre. In a letter to Norman Marshall, quoted in the latter's *The Other Theatre*, he says: 'My heart has always been in repertory and the theatre with a definite policy.... There is a lovely spirit of adventure and excitement in repertory which one never gets elsewhere.' His work in Liverpool was of great value to the repertory movement, and to the English theatre as a whole, many of his company going on to become leading actors in London.

ARNOLD, MATTHEW (1822–88), English poet, educationist, and critic, whose interest in the drama led him, as far back as 1880, to put the case for its official support. His two poetic plays, *Empedocles on Etna* (1852) and *Merope* (1858), were both written on classical lines. Arnold said that in his endeavours to learn and practise what was sound and true in poetical art he found the only sure guidance and solid footing among the ancients. His plays are for the study rather than the stage, yet he did the drama some service by arguing its claims as an important cultural influence. In 1882 he published an essay on *The French Play in London*, and was for a short time dramatic critic of the *Pall Mall Gazette*.   T. C. K.

ART, THÉÂTRE D', see LUGNÉ-POË.

ARTEF THEATRE, NEW YORK, see COMEDY THEATRE.

ARTILLERY THEATRE, LONDON. This theatre, at Woolwich, was built by subscription with the help of the War Office, and was opened by Lord Roberts in 1904. It was controlled by various people until 1909, when a lease was granted to Mrs. Agnes Littler. She continued in management very successfully up to September 1940, when the theatre was taken over for use by various Service units in entertaining the troops. Many famous actors appeared there, including Lily Langtry, Belle Bilton, George Robey, Albert Chevalier, Oscar Asche, and Violet Vanbrugh. The first wounded men to arrive in this country from the war of 1914–18 were entertained there by Mrs. Littler, who, with her husband, was badly injured when in March 1918 a bomb was dropped just outside the theatre while they were in the foyer.
                                                          W. M. P.

ARTS COUNCIL OF GREAT BRITAIN. Originally known as the Council for the Encouragement of Music and the Arts (C.E.M.A.), this was set up at the beginning of 1940 with the aid of a grant from the Pilgrim Trust, and from the Treasury on the vote of the then Board of Education. Its avowed intention was to bring concerts and plays to the crowded evacuation areas where entertainment was limited or nonexistent. In 1942 the Pilgrim Trust withdrew, leaving the Treasury to provide the whole of C.E.M.A.'s income, and Lord Keynes was appointed Chairman. It was largely due to his enthusiasm and unceasing activity that the good work done by C.E.M.A. did not end with the war, but was put on a permanent basis, with a direct Treasury grant. The defined purposes of the Arts Council, as it was then called, are 'to develop a greater knowledge, understanding and practice of the Fine Arts, to increase their accessibility to the public and to improve their standard of execution'. It assists drama through associated companies which enjoy a large measure of autonomy within the Council's general artistic and financial policy, and also by means of directly managed companies in theatreless towns and areas. The Council is also responsible for the Theatre Royal, Bristol, and the Arts Theatre, Salisbury.

ARTS LEAGUE OF SERVICE TRAVELLING THEATRE, GREAT BRITAIN, was founded on 28 April 1919 as a drama section of the A.L.S. From the beginning it was linked to an art movement rather than a theatrical tradition, which allowed great freedom in choice of material and experimentation. The members of the company, among whom were the young Angela and Hermione Baddeley, toured the country, giving a varied programme of mimed folk-song, dances, short plays, sketches, &c. Props and scenery were reduced to a minimum, all being comfortably carried in a van which also served for transport. The company, although doing excellent work in bringing varied and wholesome entertainment to remote corners of rural England and Scotland, was always in financial difficulties, in spite of a grant from the Carnegie Trust, and was finally disbanded in 1937. It may be said that its very success was its undoing, for it stimulated local interest in drama, and soon found itself ousted by the amateur companies it had helped to bring into being. Among its constant supporters were Judith Wogan, Eleanor Elder, who later (1943) wrote a short history of the movement, and Hugh Mackay, well known for his singing of Hebridean folk-songs.

ARTS THEATRE, LONDON, a well-equipped private theatre for members of the Arts Theatre Club in Great Newport Street, Charing Cross Road, where many interesting revivals and new plays have been produced, a number subsequently finding their way to regular West End stages (see also CAMBRIDGE).

ASCH, SHOLOM (1880–   ), Jewish dramatist and novelist, born at Kutno in Poland. In 1900 he was working as a journalist in both Hebrew and Yiddish, and two years later published a volume of short stories in Hebrew. He is the author of several plays in Yiddish, of which the best-known is *God of Vengeance*. This could not be performed in Russia in the original, because of the ban on Yiddish plays at that time, and, as *Gott der Rache*, it was given its first production by Reinhardt in Berlin in 1907. It immediately attracted the attention of the literary and theatrical world to the possibilities of Yiddish drama, and has since been translated and produced in many countries. Some of Asch's Yiddish novels have also been dramatized or adapted for the stage. He was at one time President of the Yiddish Section of the P.E.N. Club, and travelled constantly between Europe and America. He has now settled in the United States. Interested in religious problems, he has written lives of Jesus and of St. Paul, and is the author of an Open Letter to Christians. More than anyone else Sholom Asch has raised the standard of Yiddish writing and helped to place it on a literary basis. To non-Jews he is undoubtedly the best-known Yiddish author, since his works have frequently appeared in translation.

E. H.

ASCHE. (1) OSCAR [JOHN STANGER HEISS] (1871–1936), English actor, of Scandinavian descent, born in Australia, who is mainly remembered in connexion with his own oriental fantasy with music, *Chu-Chin-Chow*. First given in 1916, this ran for five years without a break, setting up a record for its own day. Asche appeared in it himself as Abu Hasan, and followed it by another play of the same type, *Cairo* (1921), which was not, however, so successful. Asche made his first appearance on the stage in 1893, and was for some years with Benson's company, and with Tree at His Majesty's, being himself manager of that theatre in 1907, when he produced *As You Like It*, *Othello*, and *The Taming of the Shrew*. He made several tours of Australia, playing Petruchio, Shylock, and other parts, and in South Africa added Antony to his repertory. In 1911 he appeared as Falstaff, and in the same year made a great success in the part of Hajj in *Kismet*. He published his autobiography in 1929. His wife (2) LILY BRAYTON (1876–   ), who appeared with him in *Chu-Chin-Chow* and many other plays, and was associated with him in management in London and on tour, made her first appearance on the stage in 1896, with Benson, remaining with him for some time. In 1904 she was seen as Yo-San in *The Darling of the Gods*, and subsequently her career followed that of her husband. She made her last appearance on the stage in 1932, playing Portia in *Julius Caesar*.

ASHTON, FREDERICK (1906–   ), English ballet-dancer and choreographer. A pupil of Marie Rambert, he worked with her Ballet Club and the Camargo Society, and later joined the Sadler's Wells Company. Among his best works are 'Façade', 'Horoscope', 'Apparitions', 'Dante Sonata', and 'Symphonic Variations'.

ASHWELL [POCOCK], LENA (1872–   ), English actress, who was studying music when on the advice of Ellen Terry she abandoned it for the stage. She made her first appearance in 1891, and after playing a wide variety of parts, in London and on tour, made a great success in 1900 in *Mrs. Dane's Defence*, which she frequently revived. Among her later successes were Yo-San in *The Darling of the Gods*, Leah Kleschna in the play of that name, Jacqueline in *Madame X*, and Deborah in *The Shulamite*. She made her first appearance in America in this last part, together with *Mrs. Dane's Defence*, and on her return to England took over the Kingsway Theatre, inaugurating in 1907 a season of successful repertory with *Irene Wycherley*. She remained in management until 1915, when she relinquished all her other activities in order to organize companies for the entertainment of the troops in France and later in Germany, for which work she was awarded the O.B.E. Similar companies, under

the title of the Lena Ashwell Players, continued after the war to appear in halls throughout London, and Miss Ashwell was also active in the foundation of the British Drama League. In 1924 she took over the Bijou Theatre, Bayswater, renamed it the Century, and produced there several new plays, including her own adaptations of *Crime and Punishment* and *Dr. Jekyll and Mr. Hyde*. She is the author of several books, including an autobiography, *Myself a Player*, published in 1936.

ASPHALEIAN SYSTEM, see STAGE, 5.

ASSEMBLY THEATRE, NEW YORK, see PRINCESS THEATRE.

ASTLEY'S AMPHITHEATRE, LONDON. Best known as Astley's, and immortalized by Charles Dickens, this curious theatre had many names. In 1770 Philip Astley (1742–1814), who had been a sergeant-major and breaker-in in General Elliott's Light Horse in 1759, opened what he called a riding-school just by Westminster Bridge, and used it as a circus. It had a ring surrounded by seats. Proceedings were instituted against him by the authorities, but he had the good fortune to help George III in the matter of a restive horse and was granted a licence. In 1780 he erected a wooden building with a gallery, pit, and boxes—all constructed out of waste timber—decorated the interior so that it looked like a grove of trees, and called it 'The Royal Grove'. It remained a circus, but in 1787 Astley added burlettas and pantomime to its attractions. It was burned down in 1794, rebuilt in less than seven months, and again destroyed by fire in 1803. Astley moved to the Olympic (Astley's Middlesex Amphitheatre) in Wych Street while he rebuilt yet again, and the new house opened in 1803 with a great equestrian spectacle, for which type of performance it became famous.

Having built similar places of entertainment all over Britain, France, and Ireland (19 in all), Astley died in 1814, and was succeeded by his son, John, who retired three years later in favour of his partner Davis. The theatre was now known as Davis's Amphitheatre, and equestrian spectacle reached great heights with *The Blood-Red Knight, The Battle of Waterloo*, and *The Burning of Moscow*, in which the chief actor was Gomersal, enshrined by Thackeray in *The Newcomes*.

The famous Andrew Ducrow—perhaps the finest circus rider of all time—followed Davis. He was so illiterate that he seldom played a speaking part, but excelled in riding, stage management, and production. In 1841 fire again destroyed the amphitheatre, with great loss, and Ducrow died soon after. William Batty then rebuilt it, and gave it his name. He was followed by William Cooke, who made *Macbeth* and *Richard III* into equestrian dramas, giving White Surrey, Richard's horse, a leading part.

In 1863 Dion Boucicault turned the Amphitheatre into the Theatre Royal, Westminster, but the result was a dismal failure in spite of a spirited representation of *The Relief of Lucknow*, and an adaptation of *The Heart of Midlothian*, called *The Trial of Effie Deans*. Boucicault left, heavily in debt, and was succeeded by E. T. Smith, the remarkable showman who was also a Patentee of Drury Lane. He drew the whole of London across the river to see Adah Isaacs Menken in *Mazeppa*. Later the theatre passed under the management of 'Lord' George Sanger, was known as Sanger's Amphitheatre, and was finally closed in 1895. No trace of it remains.   W. M. P.

ASTON, ANTHONY (*fl.* first half of the eighteenth century), commonly called Tony, and known also as Matt Medley, an English actor to whom, in default of more precise information, goes the honour of having been the first professional actor to appear in the New World. A wild, irresponsible Irishman, of mercurial disposition, he tried his hands at many things, but soon wearied of them. At one time he appeared at Drury Lane, and in the preface to his *Fool's Opera*, printed in about 1730, he refers to his appearances in 'New York, East and West Jersey, Maryland, Virginia (on both sides Cheesapeek), North and South Carolina, South Florida, the Bahamas, Jamaica, and Hispaniola'. He is known to have appeared in Charleston in 1703, and later in the same year in New York, but we have no knowledge of what he played, or whether he was alone or with a company of other actors. He may have given a sort of Variety entertainment like the 'Medley' in which he appeared in the English provinces in 1717. His stay in the New World was short, and he returned to tour England and Scotland. He was still alive in 1735, when he protested against the proposed bill for regulating the stage, and in 1749 Chetwood spoke of him as 'travelling still and as well known as the post-horse that carries the mail'. There are references to him in O. G. Sonneck's *Early Opera in America* (1915), and his life was written by Watson Nicholson.

ASTOR PLACE OPERA HOUSE, NEW YORK, one block east of Broadway, a house built for Italian opera, which opened on 22 Nov. 1847. During the summer of 1848 Niblo, burnt out of his Garden, leased it and put on some good plays with an excellent stock company. After this it reverted to opera, except for Macready's season, which began on 4 Sept. and, owing to the jealousy of Edwin Forrest, terminated on 10 May 1849 with the anti-British Astor Place Riot, in which 22 people were killed and 36 wounded by shots fired by the militia. The theatre then closed for repairs, and reopened on 24 Sept. 1849, with Jean Davenport as Juliet. Other actors who came during the intervals of opera were Vandenhoff, Julia Dean, and Charlotte Cushman, the last as Romeo with Fanny Wallack as Juliet. The theatre was never successful, however, in spite of the efforts of Charles R. Thorne and Frank Chanfrau, and it finally closed on 4 Apr. 1854, the furniture, scenery, and props being sold at auction.

ASTOR THEATRE, NEW YORK, on Broadway at 45th Street. This opened on 21 Sept. 1906 with *A Midsummer Night's Dream*, followed by *Cymbeline*. Two musical plays proved successful in 1908, but the theatre's first long run was achieved by a melodrama, *Paid in Full*, which ran throughout 1908, followed by the equally successful *The Man From Home*. *Seven Keys to Baldpate* (1912) had 320 performances, and the theatre's record run of 680 performances was scored by *East is West* (1918). Seven years later the Astor saw its last legitimate production with a musical play, *June Days*, and then became a cinema.   G. F.

ASTRACANADAS, see GÉNERO CHICO.

AŚVAGHOṢA, see INDIA.

ATELLAN FARCE, see FABULA (1) *Atellana* and ROME.

ATKINS, ROBERT (1886–   ), English actor and producer, whose career has been mainly spent in the service of Shakespeare. He was a pupil at the R.A.D.A. when in 1906 he was engaged by Tree for His Majesty's, making his first appearance there in *Henry IV, Part I*. He later toured with Martin-Harvey in *The Only Way*, and was in the companies of Forbes-Robertson and Frank Benson. He joined the Old Vic company in 1915, and returned there in 1920, after war service, as producer. He remained until 1925, during which time he produced and appeared in a number of Shakespearian and other plays, including the rarely seen *Titus Andronicus* and *Troilus and Cressida*, and staged, for the first time in England, Ibsen's *Peer Gynt*. In later years he took his own Shakespeare company on tour, founded the Bankside Players for the production of Shakespeare under Elizabethan conditions at the Ring, Blackfriars, and was producer at the Stratford-on-Avon Memorial Theatre, and at the Open Air Theatre, Regent's Park. Among his best parts have been Sir Toby Belch, Touchstone, Caliban, and James Telfer in *Trelawny of the 'Wells'*.

ATKINSON, BROOKS (1894–   ), American dramatic critic, born in Melrose, Massachusetts, and educated at Harvard. He served under H. T. Parker as assistant dramatic critic for *The Boston Transcript* in 1918, and became literary editor of *The New York Times* in 1922. He has been dramatic critic of *The New York Times* since 1926 (with a brief leave of absence during World War II when he went to China and later on to Russia as a correspondent) and has maintained a fine record of honest and intelligent observation of the American theatre. He has written *Henry Thoreau, East of the Hudson*, *Skyline Promenades*, and *The Cingalese Prince*.   T. Q. C.

ATTA, see FABULA (9) *Togata*.

ATTERBOM, PER DANIEL AMADEUS (1790–1835), Swedish poet (see SCANDINAVIA, 3).

[38]

ATTWELL, HUGH (?–1621), English actor, originally with the Queen's Revels. He later joined Prince Charles's Men, and remained with them until his death. An elegy on him by William Rowley tells us that he was a little man, probably with a fine speaking-voice—"Mongst living Princes it hath sweetly sung (While they have sung his praise)', and later 'his toung a silver bell'; while it ends, 'He changed his *Hugh*, yet he remains At-Well'. He had a brother George, who was probably the author of and a performer in *Mr. Attowel's Jigge*.

AUBIGNAC, FRANÇOIS HÉDELIN, ABBÉ D' (1604–76), one of the first important French writers on the drama. His *Pratique du théâtre*, published in 1657, upheld the Unities, and criticized with much acerbity those who departed from them. It marks a decisive step in the formation of the French classical style, and was translated into English in 1684. D'Aubignac's own plays, of which the first was the tragedy *Zénobie* (1640), were intended as models for aspiring dramatists, but they were not particularly successful, partly owing to the mediocrity of their style, and partly to the many enemies which d'Aubignac's criticisms had made for him.

AUDE, JOSEPH (1755–1841), French dramatist, who came of a working-class family and was educated by the kindness of his bishop. He was for some time secretary to Buffon, whose memoirs he edited, and in 1793 returned to the theatre (for which as a young man he had written a number of ephemeral plays) with a series of farces based on Cadet Roussel. These, played by Brunet in the minor theatres, particularly the Montansier, had an enormous vogue, though they are now forgotten. Aude, who was a friend of Dorvigny and equally witty, quarrelsome, penniless, and drunken, wasted what might have been an outstanding talent in comedy. He had a nephew of the same name as himself, who also wrote farces and vaudevilles, frequently attributed to the uncle.

AUDEN, WYSTAN HUGH (1907–   ), English poet (now an American citizen) and author with Christopher Isherwood of several plays in verse and prose, *The Dog Beneath the Skin* (1935), *The Ascent of F.6* (1936), and *On the Frontier* (1938), given by the Group Theatre at the Westminster, London.

AUDIENCE ON THE STAGE. The practice, common in Elizabethan and continental theatres of the sixteenth and seventeenth centuries, of allowing members of the audience to buy seats on the stage was a fertile source of disorder and of acute irritation to both actor and dramatist. The places were usually occupied by young fops, who took occasion to show off their fine clothes and display their insensitiveness to any form of theatrical art by their constant chatter and restlessness. The practice was first noticed in England in 1596 and in France in 1649, but at both dates was well established. The theory has been advanced that in France it helped to do away with the old multiple setting, and to confine French tragedy in a small open space, making it a series of bravura recitations given before a backcloth. It had a less restrictive effect on the English theatre, where its influence on dramatic convention can be seen in the Induction to *The Taming of the Shrew*, and—a final vestige—in *The Beggar's Opera*. It was the development of the 'Machine Play' which finally made the audience on the stage intolerable, and Voltaire, who attributed the failure of his early plays to their presence, finally got them banished in 1759 at the Comédie-Française, other French theatres following suit at intervals. Garrick drove them from the English stage in 1762. It is said that Molière once sat on the stage of the Hôtel de Bourgogne to watch a play in which he and his company were satirized, and that the closeness of the original somewhat embarrassed the actor who was representing him, a fact which no doubt afforded Molière some quiet amusement.

AUDITORIUM, the hall in a theatre designed for the accommodation of the people witnessing the performance. The word in its present usage dates from about 1727, though Auditory and Spectatory are also to be found. In English procedure the design of the auditorium was marked by unique characteristics, and in this, as in the system of its stage machinery (see ENGLISH PLAYHOUSE, 1 c and MACHINERY), the English playhouse originally differed from the continental. Failure to note this is a hindrance to a proper understanding of English stage history (see also ARCHITECTURE.)

The root of the difference is national. It is an expression of the dramatic nature of the English theatrical genius as against the operatic tendency of the continent. The English theatre produced plays first and operas second. It used the theatre as a vivid platform for the performance of direct action, and the delivery of crisp, highly developed dialogue, with wide and human characterization, minutely noted. Music was always the servant and never the master of the show. Scenic spectacle was primarily ingenious and mobile rather than superb and elaborate; plain and bluff, rather than magnificent; a fancy, trimming deeds and actions, rather than a phantasy, enshrining music and song. It is not therefore to be wondered at that the English theatre bore the imprint of the national characteristics.

This point at length established, after so long a period of vain and puzzled endeavour to reconcile the English theatre with continental taste, it is not surprising to find that in form the playhouse built to serve the English theatre was also individual, with scenery and machinery on an unusual system of 'flats' and 'grooves', and that its main characteristics must be traced to other than continental sources. The English theatre indeed took note of these, but went its own way.

This essential fact, which has been lying at our doorstep for 300 years, has already been remarked on by Soviet Russian research. In *Teatr* (Nov. 1940) Bogoslovsky, in 'Notes of an Architect on the Spectacle and the Theatre Auditorium', observes: 'If in Italy, France and Germany, in the eighteenth century, buildings were constructed, with rare exceptions, primarily for opera, in England, on the other hand, of the three big London theatres, two—Drury Lane and Covent Garden—were dramatic, and only one—Vanbrugh's theatre in the Haymarket—was for opera. This fact illustrates the leading place held by drama on the English stage since the days of Shakespeare. . . . The auditoriums of the two above-named London theatres were differentiated by special details of structure from the continental theatres.' The writer then refers to Dumont's *Parallèle de plans des Salles de Spectacles* (1763) and Patté's *Essai sur l'architecture théâtrale* (1782), and quotes Patté's remarks on the 'unusual planning' of the English fan-shaped auditorium, on the three tiers of boxes along the side walls holding only four boxes in each tier, on the raked pit, on the three galleries or amphitheatres, and on the sloping ceiling—all indigenous features of the English auditorium. Patté concludes that it is well designed for seeing, but does not fit his idea of classic taste, and tends to isolate the various portions of the audience from one another.

The characteristic English playhouse found its greatest period in the Georgian era, and in the progress of its auditorium design there are five phases—Restoration, Georgian, Regency, Victorian, and Modern—though a narrow insistence on the exclusiveness of these would be misleading.

1. RESTORATION. The first phase—that of the Restoration—is one of experiment in form. Four theatres were built or adapted in quick succession—the Duke's House in Lincoln's Inn Fields (1661), the Theatre Royal in Bridges Street (1663), the Duke's House in Dorset Garden (1671), and the Theatre Royal in Drury Lane (1674). There is then a pause until 1695, when Betterton reconstructed Lincoln's Inn Fields; ten years later Vanbrugh led off in a new direction with his Opera House in the Haymarket, and two theatres followed which probably formed a link with the Georgian period proper, but still bore marked Restoration features—Shepherd's theatre for Rich in Lincoln's Inn Fields (1714) and his Covent Garden (1732). Of Potter's Little Theatre in the Haymarket (1720) we know little till later, but it would appear rather to herald the Georgian era than close that of the Restoration.

The characteristic details of the auditorium in these theatres may be summarized under the contemporary names of its parts. The three words most commonly used to-day in this connexion are the oldest. The terms Pit, Box, and Gallery all go back to the seventeenth century, and, with a couple of variants, sum up the primal English auditorium, which in its design, it appears, was often conceived in lines of artificial perspective. Thus, in Wren's section, supposed to be for Drury Lane, only one line is horizontal—that cutting the centre of the upper box fronts. All lines above slope down towards the proscenium and all lines below slope up, to converge in a point some 75 ft. beyond the back wall of the stage. Though no ground-plan exists for this building, the Adams' drawing for the redecoration of its ceiling in 1775 provides evidence that the pit sides also converged towards the stage. It may be that this perspective tendency led to the fan-shaped auditorium which Patté in the late eighteenth century noted as a peculiarity of the English playhouse, and it may have arisen from an attempt to confer on the limited size of the converted tennis-court the impression of a more imposing interior.

(*a*) *The Pit.* This was the floor of the house, which was usually sunk below ground-level and treated from the first as a basement of independent design in the decorative scheme of the theatre interior. It was described by Misson in 1698 as an 'amphitheatre', and it had a sloping floor rising from the foot of the stage to the base of what he called 'another amphitheatre' beyond (see below, *b*). It took various forms—'nearly of a circular form', a magnet-shape, a broad fan-shape, or a rectangle. It was 'fill'd with Benches without Backboards and cover'd with green Cloth'—which green became the traditional colour of many parts of the English auditorium for nearly two centuries. The pit was entered by doors in the side walls near the stage, where the head-room under the boxes was greatest because of the slope, and the doors communicated with passages running beside the pit to the front of the house. A seat in the pit—which was occasionally given the French name of *parterre*—cost 2*s.* 6*d.*, but the price might be doubled or trebled for a first performance.

(*b*) *The Boxes.* At the brink of the pit, and on the level of the stage, stood the chief, and possibly the most controversial, feature of the Restoration playhouse—the boxes. In some theatres, especially those adapted from tennis-courts, these boxes probably ran continuously round all three sides of the pit. The Theatre Royal, Bridges St., is said to have 'been surrounded in the inside by boxes separated from each other and divided into several rows of seats'. Further, Dorset Garden is said to have had seven of these boxes, each holding twenty people; this uneven number of boxes does not allow of equal division into two sides, and so suggests they ran all round the pit, perhaps two on either side and three at the end facing the stage. In all theatres the actual railing of this tier probably ran continuously round the pit, but in Drury Lane and Covent Garden the 'boxes' opposite the stage were of so different a nature from those at the sides as to suggest limiting the name 'box' to the sides only, as was hinted in Misson's phrase, where the end portion of the auditorium was likened to 'another amphitheatre'. Thus, in Wren's drawing for Drury Lane no subdivisions at all are seen in the central part of the lower tier, and the curved benches in it are exactly similar to those of the pit, while in Shepherd's plan for Covent Garden, though radial partitions are to be seen, yet the segments they enclose are far deeper than the Side Boxes (the term is found as early as 1685), and these segments each contain as many as six rows of benches. It appears, then, that in what we may call the immediately post-Restoration period the boxes facing the stage were larger and more open than those at the sides. It is probably this variability of arrangement that elucidates, at the end of the century, the uncertainty of phrase in George Saunders's *A Treatise on Theatres* (1799), where he talks of the habitual 'disposition of our theatres' as being 'three galleries, i.e. boxes and two galleries above', so classifying the boxes as a 'gallery'.

The normal price of a seat in a Restoration box (the seats were sold separately) was 4s., the most expensive seat in the house. A variant of the word already in use in the Restoration was King's Box, which was apparently always situated facing the stage. It was not, like the Georgian 'royal box', at the side. It had no regular exclusiveness and, in the absence of the king, was sold in the normal way, but, says W. J. Lawrence, at the slightly higher price of 5s. per seat. He also gives the usual charge for the whole box as £10. A further qualification of the name is found at least as far back as 1710 in Stage Box, or that box at either side of the lower tier which stood on the stage itself.

Above the lower row of boxes was a second tier, or, as Pepys calls it, a 'belcone'. This may have been an unbroken, open gallery in some theatres, but in others (see Wren's presumed Drury Lane section) the sides at least were divided into boxes, like those below. They were the Upper Boxes. The central part of this tier was probably in all theatres an open gallery.

Thus though early Restoration theatres present experimental variations, in general the side boxes on both floors were combined into one architectural façade on either side of the pit, related in design with the proscenium, and usually marked by heavy columnular treatment. A tier comprised about four boxes, which were separated by partitions. The Front Boxes, on the first tier, might approximate to the modern open circle. They contained more benches than the side boxes, and had only dwarf partitions just over elbow height.

There was a custom in the early eighteenth century, and afterwards, by which, upon special occasions, 'the boxes and pit were all thrown into one, so that all sat in common', or were 'laid together', box prices being charged for all seats. The nature of the expression, together with the sentence 'all sat in common' suggests that, in some theatres at least, the box fronts and partitions on the lower tier may have been removable.

(c) *The Galleries.* Above the first tier of boxes was a second tier of which, though the sides may sometimes have contained boxes, the centre portion fronting the stage was undoubtedly an open gallery. This gallery was known either as the Eighteenpenny Places, the Middle Gallery, or the First Gallery, all of which terms belong to the 1670s or earlier. The Middle Gallery was the popular part of the house. Above it there was generally the Twelvepenny Places or Upper Gallery, but this occupied only the end of the house, and was not continued along the sides over the tier below. 'The galleries', says Misson (1698), 'whereof there are only two Rows, are filled with none but ordinary People, particularly the Upper one.' (See also FOOTMEN'S GALLERY.)

The orchestra of the Restoration theatre was frequently situated in the Musique Room, as Pepys calls it, a sort of high bow-gallery projecting from above the top of the proscenium opening. At Dorset Garden it is represented as having casement windows. The placing of the orchestra under the fore part of the stage was tried by Killigrew at Bridges Street, but not at the time tolerated.

2. GEORGIAN. This period saw the building of several new theatres, and the altering of the old ones. The first theatre of typically Georgian character appears to have been Potter's Little Theatre in the Haymarket (1720—though pictorial evidence dates only from late in the century). There followed two theatres in Goodman's Fields, Whitechapel, about the thirties but information on them is scanty. It is not until the sixties, seventies, and eighties that Covent Garden was altered, Drury Lane was entirely rearranged by the Adam brothers, Novosielski altered Vanbrugh's Opera House; and Astley's, the Pantheon, the King's Concert Rooms, the Royal Circus, and the Royalty were built. Then the last decade of the century saw the culmination of the phase in Holland's redecoration of Covent Garden, and his rebuilding of Wren's Drury Lane, which was demolished to give place to this theatre of a hitherto unapproached vastness. Also, a burnt-out Opera House was rebuilt by Novosielski, a burnt Astley's raised again, and a new Pantheon reared on the ashes of the old, built, like the first, by James Wyatt. Characteristics of this period were the final perfecting of the Restoration form and then extension upon it, with a simplification of the architectural treatment of the side boxes and the whole style lighter and more related to structural requirements. A great profusion of spiked railings is introduced to keep the members of the audience from climbing to the stage or to superior parts of the house. The tiers are increased in number. At the culmination, in Holland's Drury Lane (1794), there were no less than five towering above the great pit. But, possibly most characteristic of all, there is a tendency to carry at any rate the lowest tier of boxes right round the pit in unbroken succession, and to increase the side boxes to three, or four, on each side, and run the tiers of boxes up

three or four storeys. In the majority of theatres the two galleries were strictly isolated from the side boxes.

The auditorium above the pit had always been designed and decorated in a totally different scheme from that of the pit itself, rising from a base-line level with the stage, and cutting along the bottom of the lower box fronts. This may recall the old tennis-court tradition, where the boxes rose from the original floor-level which corresponded with the stage while the pit was hollowed out below it. Be that as it may, there is evidence from the year 1785 that it was the custom to floor over the pit of a theatre for balls and dances, so as to present one unbroken expanse continuous with the stage. This must have exerted a strong influence on English playhouse design.

Several new parts, or usages of parts, are found in the Georgian playhouse. By the middle of the eighteenth century the term Front Boxes was used to distinguish those facing the stage from those at the side, and the Private Box makes its appearance. This, reserved for a private party of individuals, had its own excluding walls and its own door, possibly even a curtain to draw across its front, or at least a lattice to obscure the inward view. Such boxes were indeed sometimes called Lattices or Lettices. The Box Lobby at the rear of the boxes came into use towards the end of the century, to serve the increasing social life of the boxes, and to supply a corridor or promenade where the box-holders could stroll about and yet see the stage through peep-holes in the box doors. By 1751 the term Green Box is in use, and in 1788 two tiers of these were erected above the Lettices at the rebuilding of Crow St. Theatre, Dublin. The name would appear to designate those side boxes at, or near, the top of the house (perhaps called 'green' because they partook of the general greenish decoration of the Georgian auditorium and were not, like the more sumptuous lower boxes, provided with crimson curtains or linings). But the Green Boxes were not invariably the topmost ones, for a playbill of the Ipswich Theatre in 1786 states that the box seats were 3s. and the 'Green Boxes (Lower) 2s. 6d.' The plain terms seen on bills to distinguish the rows of boxes are most commonly 'upper' and 'lower'.

One other feature essentially related to the auditorium may be mentioned here—the Pay-Box. Of these small cubicles for the taking of money, a medium-sized theatre would possibly have three, one beyond each of the three entrance doors to boxes, pit, and gallery. A smaller theatre might have two, one situated at the junction of two ways of access from a common entrance, and it is possible that by ingenious alteration of the internal structure (as at Richmond, Yorks.) one money-taker might check the whole audience.

It does not appear that a great extension of these front-of-house rooms and offices was typical of the playhouse until the next century.

The term 'Gods' as referring to the upper gallery, or its occupants, dates from 1752, while the orchestra is found from the beginning of this period in the pit, or well, before the stage front, which it still occupies.

3. REGENCY. This period seems to fit with the beginning of the nineteenth century. In the first fifteen years a new Covent Garden was built by Smirke and a new Drury Lane by Benjamin Wyatt (both after disastrous fires), and an English Opera House was instituted at what was to be the Lyceum; the King's Concert Rooms, as the Regency Theatre (see SCALA), the Royalty, and the Olympic all offer us valuable pictorial information on the new fashion, and Nash's Theatre Royal in the Haymarket followed in 1821. Finally, a new little theatre, at first called the Sans Pareil (1806, see ADELPHI), presents an important fresh trend in design; this theatre and Wyatt's Drury Lane offer us the two extremes of Regency development.

Up to 1823 it had been the custom to keep the lights burning in the auditorium throughout the performance, but at this date it was found possible, by means of a gas chandelier suspended from the roof, to control the lighting. It was then dimmed at the rise of the curtain and the audience was left in comparative darkness during the run of the scene. At this time too there was an increase in the number of social rooms built in front of the house—saloons, coffee-rooms, lobbies, and rotundas—where fashion and parade, lost in the obscurity of the house, could once more have free play. It is interesting to note that in Wyatt's own *Observations on the Design for the Theatre Royal, Drury Lane* (1813), his considerations are grouped under four heads, of which the last is social—they are (1) Size and Capacity of Building, (2) Shape for Distinct Sound and Vision, (3) Convenience and Safety of Exits and Entrances, and (4) Decorum among the Classes. He spent much thought on an arrangement of social rooms such as would (without the intention being too obvious) segregate the classes, and permit those who desired to watch the play to do so in undisturbed seclusion (could they afford it) and avoid contact with those who desired to enjoy themselves, and each other, first and the play second. Hence the attractiveness of his coffee-rooms and the seclusion of what he calls the Dress Boxes. His auditorium contained first, a pit approximating to three-quarters of a circle, then around it a ring containing seven Private Boxes on either side, and a lobby round the front. Directly above was an unbroken circle of Dress Boxes, intended for occupation by a dignified and responsible company, who entered by an approach well away from the blaze and conviviality of the coffee-rooms— thence arises our Dress Circle. These boxes —26 in all—were open, with dwarf partitions, as suited an embankment of fashion. Above ran an exactly similar circle, called the First Tier of Boxes (as who should say, the first row of *ordinary* boxes, those below having a special character). At either stage extremity of this circle were two Private Boxes. The corridor behind this tier gave directly on to the Rotunda, and thence to the Great Saloon in front of the house. Above came a similar circle called the Second Tier of Boxes, and above this again a circle at whose sides were seven Slip Boxes, but from whose centre extended the rise of the Lower Gallery, with its ten curved rows of seats. Slip Box appears to be the name now given to the old Green Box. The Slips was a term already in use to designate the 'horns', or near-stage extremities, of an upper circle. This concluded the house on the sides, but above the cornice which crowned it arose at the back an Upper Gallery of six rows of benches. It is interesting to note that Wyatt says there had formerly been, at the back of the Dress Circle, what were vulgarly termed Baskets or Basket Boxes, with a poor reputation (the 'basket' may have been a screen after the nature of the 'lattice'). Finally there were the Proscenium Boxes, four in number, two built either side in the Proscenium.

Further varieties of the box found at this period, or within the first half of the nineteenth century, are the Royal Box, now generally on the stage right of the first circle of boxes, the large Omnibus Box near the stage where congregated a select group of influential patrons, as at the Opera House, then called Her Majesty's, in the Haymarket in 1842, and the Family Box, a variety of the Private Box. Lastly we may mention the Pigeon Holes, a term not necessarily restricted to any special part of the house, but applied to any box framed by a small arched opening. There was a series of these above the top of the side tiers in Smirke's Covent Garden in 1809, and a row of four is mentioned on either side of the pit, under the Dress Boxes, in Beazley's Lyceum.

The chief theatres of this time show a slight reduction upon the mammoth size of Holland's Drury Lane, where the comfortable range for the capacity of an actor's voice seemed to have been overreached.

In the little Sans Pareil Theatre in the Strand, built in 1806, the first step was taken towards the transformation of the old Georgian auditorium into that which we know to-day. The bond between boxes and pit is broken at last, and no ground-floor side boxes are to be seen. The first circle is clear above the heads of the pit, which spreads underneath it like seeping water. This spread of the pit outwards, however, was no gain for the pittites; their territory was not increased, for hard upon the extension outwards came a pressing back from the direction of the orchestra. Now that the lower boxes had gone, the first rows of the pit gained in importance for those who wanted to be near the stage, and Stalls came into being about the thirties and forties—especially comfortable seats as opposed to the old benches —followed by Orchestra Stalls and, later, Balcony Stalls, though their coming, and the displacement of the front rows of the old pit seats, was not effected without opposition from the displaced. About the middle of the century the French term Fauteuil was introduced to designate comfortable individual seats, similar to stalls, and it was later used sometimes to refer to a particular part of the house—generally the orchestra stalls.

The Coburg (later the Old Vic) was built in 1818 in this same pit-under-balcony form, as was Bushill's reconstruction of the Olympic (1850), and the Surrey which rose after the fire in 1861. Many other theatres followed the fashion till the custom became general, so that the box-tier directly flanking the pit is now a rare curiosity where it was once the Georgian commonplace. It is probably only to be seen to-day in the Theatre Royal, Bristol, the Richmond Theatre, Yorkshire, and to some extent in the Theatre Royal, Bath.

The dying Regency period saw a burst of theatre-building about the 1830s, when numerous theatres opened in quick succession, ending just over the decade with the great 'Brit', the Britannia, Hoxton.

4. VICTORIAN. The 1840s saw no such spate of theatre-building as had characterized the previous ten years, but from 1866 onwards the increase was so extraordinary that in the ensuing seventy years, that is, up to 1936, no fewer than eighty new theatres opened in London, without counting music-halls. The first half-dozen of these open a fresh chapter in design, with the removal of the columns supporting the tiers. These had been a characteristic feature of the earlier playhouse, but they must always have seriously obstructed the view of the stage for the spectator who sat behind them; yet to do away with them was to leave the circles unsupported. The first solution was to build one very shallow Dress Circle with only two or three rows of seats and a row of boxes directly behind, and then to set back the upper circles and galleries to the level of the box façades, thus leaving the Dress Circle projecting, free and unobstructed like a half-open drawer from a chest. Phipps's theatres—the Queen's (1866), the Gaiety (1868), and the Vaudeville (1870)—all give evidence of a move in this direction, and from that it was a short step to the abolition of columns in other parts of the auditorium. By the 1880s such theatres as the Savoy (1881), the Prince's (1884), Terry's (1887), and the Garrick (1889) had done away with most or all of them. In 1901 Wyatt's old Adelphi was transformed by Runtz into the Century, and all traces of supporting pillars were removed. The modern era in playhouse design had begun, to be confirmed in 1921 by the reconstruction of the interior of Wyatt's Drury Lane, when the columns were replaced by cantilever construction.

The Adelphi, long before this date, had achieved another landmark in playhouse history, which forms the second great feature of the Victorian period. When Wyatt in 1858 opened the new and splendid building whose history went back to the revolutionary little Sans Pareil of 1806, his auditorium was labelled with an adjective which has since become a commonplace in describing any theatre, but which could never have been applied to any Georgian playhouse—it was called *luxurious*. Henceforth the arms of the patron's fauteuil are padded, he leans back on springs, his feet are flattered by thick pile carpet, and he is far removed from backless benches covered in green baize. The era of voluptuous comfort for the playgoer had dawned. With it came also a series of new names applied to different parts of the house, each striving to outdo the other in splendour, but whose definition or distinction defies investigation. There are balconies, circles and dress circles, royal circles, upper circles, grand circles, family circles, amphitheatre stalls, grand tiers, grand tier stalls, balcony stalls, fauteuils, imperial fauteuils, imperial grand circles, and even more high-sounding combinations which signify little beyond the mounting ambition of the managers.

5. MODERN. Of the modern phase, with its resources of cantilever construction and its reaction towards simpler decoration, the historian can say little as yet. He must confine his work to the collection of contemporary evidence that may later form the foundation of an account. In anticipation, however, it seems likely that the box, which segregated small groups of spectators, will vanish, and the auditorium become a place of sweeping, unbroken curves of massed ranks of seats (sometimes so unified as to be all in one single spreading tier), and that the skeleton of these rising amphitheatres will be so carefully planned with regard to the comfortable sight-lines of the spectator as to provide a saucer-shaped section, so that not only will those at the back see clear above the heads in front, but those at the sides will see clear over the heads of those in the centre. The 'side-box position' has become no more than a slight eminence on the fringe of a concave pit.

It is likely that other motives will also be at work. The great playhouse must be accompanied by the small one. The English idiom of the intimate, cosy, small theatre is probably too deep-rooted to die. Benjamin Wyatt, planning the Drury Lane of 1812, was 'aware of the existence of a very popular notion, that our Theatres ought to be *very small*' (the italics are his own), and it seemed almost with regret that he planned a theatre big enough to hold an audience whose entrance-money would cover nightly a fixed figure of expenditure (he set this at £600, exclusive of Private Boxes). Thus, though the great theatres of our chief towns have a purpose of their own to fulfil, an equally worthy place in playhouse history may be held by the prospective small halls and civic theatres, which the trend of the times leads us to expect in the second half of the twentieth century. (See also ACOUSTICS, ARCHITECTURE, ENGLISH PLAYHOUSE, LIGHTING, MACHINERY, PROSCENIUM, PROVINCIAL THEATRES, and London theatres under their own names.) R. S.

AUDITORY, see AUDITORIUM.

AUGIER, GUILLAUME VICTOR ÉMILE (1820–89), French dramatist and, with Ponsard, the first to revolt against the excesses of the Romantics. He was intended for the law, but after the success of his first play, *La Cigüe* (1844), at the Odéon he devoted himself to writing, either alone or in collaboration. After a few plays in verse, he found his true vocation in the writing of a series of honest domestic dramas dealing with social questions of the moment, of which *Le Gendre de Monsieur Poirier* (1854) is the best known. Among others which were successful in their day were *Le Mariage d'Olympe* (1855), which paints the courtesan as she is, and not as the younger Dumas had idealized her in his *Dame aux camélias* a few years previously; *Les Lionnes pauvres* (1858), which shows the disruption of home life consequent on the adultery of the wife; and the political comedies, *Les Effrontés* (1861) and *Le Fils de Giboyer* (1862). Augier, who had a solid bourgeois background and a good education, came at a moment of transition in the French theatre, when Romanticism had failed with *Les Burgraves* (1843) and people, tiring of the 'well-made' plays of Scribe, were turning back to the seventeenth-century classics, ably interpreted by the great actress Mlle Rachel. From a neo-classicist he became a social dramatist, and ended his career, under the influence of the new currents of thought then running across Europe, with two problem plays, *Mme Caverlet* (1876) and *Les Fourchambault* (1879). In the latter an illegitimate son saves his father and his father's legitimate offspring from ruin. Although Augier was scorned by Zola, Jules Lemaître, a surer judge, thought well of him, and his plays, though not without their faults, were well written and well adapted to the theatrical conventions of his time. He was more of a realist than either the younger Dumas or Sardou.

AUGUSTUS DRURIOLANUS, see HARRIS (2) AUGUSTUS.

AUSTIN, CHARLES (1878–1944), a famous music-hall comedian who for many years featured a character of his own invention, Parker, P.C., in a series of sketches built round this amusing member of the police force. He was also a well-known figure in pantomime, and was very popular in his profession. On one occasion he ran a horse, named after his famous character, in the Derby, but it was unplaced.

AUSTRALIA. The early history of the Australian theatre seems to have paralleled, in broad outline and at a distance of nearly a hundred years, that of the American. Just as the Hallams in the mid-eighteenth century went from London to establish the professional theatre in the American Colonies, so in the mid-nineteenth century actors from England inaugurated theatrical activities in Australia. In both countries they were preceded by amateurs, since the first recorded play in Australia was *The Recruiting Officer*, given in

Sydney on 4 June 1789 by a cast of convicts. A few years later *Henry IV* was produced by a semi-professional company in Sydney's first theatre building, but the venture failed, and little but amateur and military performances are recorded for the next thirty years. In Oct. 1833 a Theatre Royal was opened in Sydney by Barnett Levey (1798–1837) with the famous melodrama *The Miller and his Men*, and it was at this theatre that *Richard III* (doubtless in Colley Cibber's version) was first seen in Australia. Hobart had a theatre in the same year, Adelaide in 1838, Melbourne in 1841. These, and several others, were at some time under the control of George Selth Coppin (1819–1906), who also inaugurated the second phase of the Australian theatre by introducing the pernicious 'starring tours' by visiting celebrities which had already threatened to wreck the American theatre. The first European star to be imported was G. V. Brooke, followed by such diverse players as Joseph Jefferson, the Charles Keans, Mme Céleste, Ristori, and the younger Mathews. Theatrical memoirs of the period contain many illuminating glimpses of the Australian theatre in the latter half of the nineteenth century, and reference should also be made to Paul McGuire's *The Australian Theatre* (published in 1949), from which many of the above details have been taken. Later the great names of the music-hall made their way to Australia, under the auspices of the English comedian Harry Rickards (really Henry Benjamin Leete)(1845–1911). But the war of 1914–18, and the subsequent competition of the cinema, caused the theatre to languish all over the country. Good work was, however, done by a number of amateur Little and Repertory Theatres, particularly in Adelaide, Melbourne, and Sydney, and great interest was aroused by the visit in 1948 of the Old Vic Company, followed in 1949 by the Stratford-on-Avon Festival Company. This led to proposals for an Australian National Theatre, and to the prospect of a new phase in the theatre there, corresponding to the preceding fifty years in America—the emergence, that is, of a truly local theatre—with its own performers and playwrights.

AUSTRALIAN MARIE LLOYD, see FORD, FLORRIE.

AUSTRIA, see CZECHOSLOVAKIA, GERMANY, HUNGARY, and VIENNA; also Austrian dramatists and actors under their own names.

AUTHOR'S NIGHT, see ROYALTY.

AUTO, the name given to the religious play of the medieval Spanish theatre (see SPAIN). At first it indicated any piece to be acted, but with the growth of secular drama it became confined to religious plays. In Spain, unlike other European countries, these continued to be acted side by side with the secular drama during the Golden Age, particularly the *auto*

sacramental, which dealt allegorically with the Mystery of the Mass, and was generally performed on the feast of Corpus Christi. The greatest composer of *autos sacramentales* was Calderón, who found in them a form peculiarly suited to his native genius. The *auto* is a direct development of the medieval Morality play, but as the feast of Corpus Christi was not associated with any particular passages of the Bible, as were the feasts of Christmas and Easter, the development was allegorical rather than liturgical, and represented dogma symbolically. These plays were sumptuously produced, and accompanied by fine music. They continued to be given until the eighteenth century, but finally pious opposition caused their suppression by the Archbishop of Toledo on 11 June 1765. The nineteenth century saw a revival, mostly of Calderón's *autos*.

AVANCINUS, NICOLAUS (1612–86), see JESUIT DRAMA.

AVENUE THEATRE, LONDON, see PLAYHOUSE (1).

AVON THEATRE, NEW YORK, see KLAW THEATRE.

AYALA, ADELARDO LÓPEZ DE (1828–79), was, with Tamayo, the chief representative in Spanish drama of the transition period from romanticism to realism. His historical drama, *Un hombre de estado* (1851), is purely romantic, while his modern comedies, particularly *El tanto por ciento* (1861) and *Consuelo* (1878), are social homilies in the style of Augier. They nevertheless give evidence of a certain delicate poetic power, and are extremely witty and colourful.

AYRENHOFF, CORNELIUS VON (1733–1819), Austrian dramatist, whose serious dramas, in contrast to the light fare of Vienna at the time, were intended to raise the standard of the theatre. They were given at the newly founded Hofburgtheater, under the able management of Joseph von Sonnenfels, but proved unequal to the task of weaning the public from the light diet provided by harlequinade, farce, and operetta.

AYRER, JAKOB (*c.* 1543–1605), an early German dramatist, successor of Hans Sachs, and like him a voluminous author of long Carnival plays and *Singspiele*, of which about seventy were published in 1618 as *Opus Theatricum*. Ayrer, who was much influenced by the English Comedians, spent most of his life in Nuremberg, and was probably a Mastersinger. His *Phänicia* and *Sidea* are related to *Much Ado about Nothing* and *The Tempest* respectively by a common source, but direct influence by one dramatist on the other is not now credited. Ayrer's plays, popular in his own day, are not distinguished by any particular literary merit.

AZERBAIJAN, see RUSSIA, 2 *e.*

B

BABANOVA, Maria Ivanovna (1900–), Soviet actress and Honoured Artist of the Republic (equivalent to the English D.B.E.). She began her career under the direction of Theodore Komisarjevsky and in 1920 was taken by Meyerhold into his Theatre Workshop, where she was soon playing leading roles. In 1922 she appeared as Pauline in Meyerhold's production of Ostrovsky's *Place of Profit* for the Theatre of the Revolution, but continued to work in the Meyerhold Theatre. In 1927 she again appeared at the Theatre of the Revolution in Faiko's *The Man with the Portfolio*, working for the first time under a producer from the Moscow Art Theatre, A. Dikie. This proved a turning-point in her career, since she was able to achieve a successful synthesis of the two methods, and she has since become the leading actress of the Theatre of the Revolution, making a notable appearance as Juliet in Popov's production of *Romeo and Juliet*. She was also considered outstanding as the heroine in *Tanya*, by Arbuzov, and was awarded a Stalin prize in 1941 for her performance in this part.

BACKCLOTH, a flat painted canvas which hangs at the back of the scene, suspended from the grid. It is used in combination with wings (see DROP and ENGLISH PLAYHOUSE, 3).

BACKING FLAT, a canvas-covered frame, or hinged screen, set outside a door or other opening on the stage to conceal the view beyond.

BACKSTAGE, a term applied to the parts of the theatre behind the stage, such as the actors' dressing-rooms; visitors going there are said 'to go backstage'. The word is applied also to a recess in the back wall of the stage used for the last pieces of scenery in a deep spectacular vista, and at other times used as an extra storage place for scenery.

BACON, Frank (1864–1922), American actor and playwright, who made his first appearance on the stage at the age of 25, in *Ten Nights in a Bar Room*. He was for some years at San Francisco, where he played a variety of parts, and was seen in vaudeville with his wife and family. After the earthquake he moved to New York, where in 1918 he scored a triumph with his play *Lightnin'*, written in collaboration with Winchell Smith, which ran for nearly three years. In this Bacon played Bill Jones, a lovable rascal with a taste for strong drink and a great gift for exaggeration, a part eminently suited to his homely simplicity and humour and quaint, engaging personality.

BADDELEY. (1) Robert (1732–94), English actor, who was first a pastrycook and then a gentleman's gentleman, in which capacity he toured the Continent for three years, acquiring a knowledge of foreign manners and accents which he later turned to good account. He was first seen on the stage in 1761 at Drury Lane, with his wife (2) Sophia (1745–86), the daughter of the trumpeter Valentine Snow. She was a beautiful woman, excellent in such parts as Ophelia, Desdemona, Imogen, and Mrs. Beverley. Zoffany painted her as Fanny in *The Clandestine Marriage*. Unfortunately she was very dissipated and extravagant and Baddeley soon left her, though he later fought a duel on her behalf with the brother of David Garrick. She was last seen in London in 1781, and then played in the provinces, mainly at York and Edinburgh. Her husband remained on the stage until his death, being taken ill while dressing for his most famous part, Moses in *The School for Scandal*, which he was the first to play. He was excellent in all broken English parts, among them Fluellen, and Canton in *The Clandestine Marriage*, and in such comic parts as Brainworm in *Every Man in His Humour*, and Grumio in *The Taming of the Shrew*. He was the last actor to wear the royal livery of scarlet and gold as one of the King's Servants. On his death he left a cottage at Moulsey to the Drury Lane Fund, for the benefit of four poor actors, and a sum of money for a cake and wine to be partaken of by the company in the green room annually, a custom still observed at Drury Lane on Twelfth Night.

BAHR, Hermann (1863–1934), Austrian dramatist and critic, who, after nearly twenty years of journalism and playwriting in Vienna, became manager of the Berlin Deutsches Theater in 1906. He was one of the first to rally to the naturalism of Ibsen, and has been described as a 'lesser Schnitzler, softening the sharp edges of realism by his scrupulous art' (Sobel). He is unmistakably Austrian in his mixture of flippant gaiety, warm-heartedness, and witty acumen, and his best play is a comedy entitled *Das Konzert* (1910), which deals with the matrimonial difficulties of a musician and his wife. Among his other plays, which amount to nearly eighty all told, *Das Tschaperl* (1898) is outstanding.

BAIRD, Dorothea (1875–1933), see IRVING (3).

BAKER, Benjamin A. (1818–90), American actor-manager and playwright. Apprenticed to a sadler, he escaped to join a travelling company, and was soon playing Brabantio to the elder Booth's Othello. In 1839 he appeared in New York, and was engaged for the company which opened the Olympic. He had already written a number of farces when on 15 Feb. 1848 he produced, for his own benefit night, *A Glance at New York in 1848*, in which the actor Frank Chanfrau made a great success as the hero Mose, a New York volunteer fireman. Mose soon had many imitators, in New York and elsewhere, and gave rise to an offshoot of melodrama, strong action played against a background of local conditions. Further plays by Baker in the same vein were *New York As It Is* (1848), again with Chanfrau, *Three Years After* (1849) and *Mose in China* (1850). Baker was manager successively of several theatres, including the Metropolitan in San Francisco, returning to New York in 1856 as manager of Edwin Booth's company. In 1885 he became assistant secretary of the Actors' Fund. He continued to work as manager and theatrical agent until his death. Known as Uncle Ben Baker, he was a well-loved figure in American theatrical circles.

BAKER, GEORGE PIERCE (1866–1935), one of the most vital influences in the formation of modern American dramatic literature and theatre. He was educated at Harvard, where he later became the first professor of Dramatic Literature. Intensely interested in everything theatrical and himself a good amateur actor, he inaugurated, first at Radcliffe, in 1905, and a year later at Harvard, a course in practical playwriting. This in turn led to the foundation of his famous '47 Workshop' for the staging of plays written under his tuition. One of the immediately successful results of Baker's enterprise was the professional production by Mrs. Fiske in 1906 of *Salvation Nell*, by Baker's pupil Edward Sheldon. Among other playwrights who attended Baker's special courses were Eugene O'Neill, Sidney Howard, and George Abbott. In 1919 Baker gave a series of lectures at the Lowell Institute, published in the same year as *Dramatic Technique*, a standard work for aspiring playwrights. He had previously written *The Development of Shakespeare as a Dramatist* and edited some unpublished letters of David Garrick. In 1925, by which time he had had the pleasure of seeing his pioneer work bear fruit in many other centres of learning, often under his own old pupils, Baker left Harvard, where his practical methods were considered perhaps a little unorthodox, and went to Yale, where Edward Harkness had provided and endowed a fine little experimental theatre. Here he remained as Director of the post-graduate Department of Drama until his retirement in 1933. Combining in a rare degree the attributes of the scholar and the practical man of the theatre, he had an immense influence not only in his own country, but throughout Europe, an influence which is yet felt, and to the end of his life was unremitting in his industry, accuracy, and perseverance on behalf of his students.

BAKER, HENRIETTA (1837–1907), see CHANFRAU (2).

BAKST, LÉON (1866–1924), Russian artist who did some of his best work for Diaghilev's Ballets Russes. His brilliant, exotic colouring, as in the décor for 'Cléopâtre' and 'Schéhérazade', had a great influence on contemporary art. He was also responsible for the décor of Diaghilev's London production of 'The Sleeping Beauty' (see BALLET, 7 and COSTUME, 9).

BALCONY, see PROSCENIUM.

BALCONY STALL, see AUDITORIUM, 3 and STALL.

BALE, JOHN (1495–1563), Bishop of Ossory in Ireland, and author of a number of anti-Catholic plays, of which the greater part formed a long Miracle play, now lost. His existing works, which include Morality plays and a translation of Kirchmayer's *Pammachius*, are filled with coarse and incessant abuse of popery and priests. The most important is *Kynge Johan* (1538), which may claim to rank as the first historical drama in English literature. In its mingling of such abstract figures as Sedition, Clergy, and England, and the historical King John and Cardinal Pandolphus, the play forms a link between the medieval and the Elizabethan drama. It may have been first acted at St. Stephen's, Canterbury, and was revived at Ipswich as late as 1561. The only extant manuscript is in the Huntington Library. A Malone Society reprint was issued in 1931 under the editorship of Dr. Greg.

BALIEFF, NIKITA (1877–1936), deviser and compère of a Russian cabaret entertainment, La Chauve-Souris, first seen in Paris soon after the First World War. It was taken to London in 1921 by Charles B. Cochran, and though it did not immediately achieve the success he had hoped for, repeated visits (sometimes in theatres unsuited to such intimate entertainment) brought it into notice, and it became part of the London theatrical scene. In New York its success was instant and unflagging. In both places Balieff, a monkey-faced little man who eked out his slender store of English with most expressive shrugs and gestures, gained immense personal popularity. His 'turns', costumed and set with a richness reminiscent of the Russian ballet, consisted of short burlesques, and small, often mimed, sketches based on old ballads, folk-songs, prints, engravings, the woodenness of a toy soldier or the delicacy of a china shepherdess, rendered amusing by very slight and subtle guying of the material. Agate, who called the show 'pure theatre', said of its actors: 'Barbarian ecstasy, gallantry under French Louis, naïve buffoonery, the porcelain sentimentality of Sèvres or Dresden—all come alike to these superb artists.'

BALLAD OPERA, see GAY and OPERA, 7.

BALLET, a dramatic spectacle in which the action is presented in dancing and in mime to the accompaniment of music.

1. ORIGINS. Within the terms of this definition the history of the ballet begins in seventeenth-century France. For, although from much earlier times records of elaborate spectacular performances—of which the masque fashionable in Elizabethan and Jacobean times is the most familiar type—prove that dances played an important part in the entertainments of royal and noble personages, the dances were adjuncts to the poetry and drama, even as they have remained in latter times adjuncts in opera. In these performances the

ladies and gentlemen of the Court took part and they were in no sense professional affairs, resembling rather the pageants which were in vogue in England during the early years of the twentieth century. It was, nevertheless, the personal enthusiasm for dancing of that versatile genius, King Louis XIV, that gave the impetus to the establishment of ballet as an independent dramatic form. Among the entertainments in which he took part was 'Le Ballet de la nuit' (1653), in which he appeared as Le Roi Soleil—an impersonation which he continued to sustain after his dancing days were over. Among those who contributed to these Court ballets were Molière and Lully, whose collaboration began with *Le Mariage forcé* in 1664 and continued until 1670, ending with *Le Bourgeois gentilhomme* (see also BALLET DE COUR).

By this date Louis had retired from the stage and his Court followed him; but the taste for ballet had become established and, besides being incorporated into opera by Lully and Rameau, it continued to have an independent existence with professional dancers in place of amateurs. The ballets remained stately, not to say pompous and somewhat turgid, spectacles, in which elaborate costumes, masks, high heels, and heavy skirts forbade any swift or agile movement and any play of facial expression. In the first half of the eighteenth century these stiff conventions were gradually broken down by dancers like Camargo (1710–70), who dared to shorten her skirt and introduced the *entrechat*, and Marie Sallé (1710–56), who in 1734 forestalled Isadora Duncan by appearing on the stage in simple muslin draperies designed to represent classical Greek costume. The dancers were able at last literally to get off the ground to which they had been tied down by their long and heavy costumes.

2. DEVELOPMENT. It was not, however, until the second half of the eighteenth century that the reform of the ballet was completed and an attempt made to establish its main principles as an art. What Gluck did for opera in his preface to 'Alceste', Jean Georges Noverre (1727–1810) did for ballet in his manifesto, *Lettres sur la danse et les ballets*, which was published in 1760. As was natural for a theorist working in Paris, Noverre wrote under the influence of Rousseau, and advocated the same ideals of a 'return to nature' and to the simpler virtues of classical antiquity. The inconsistency of the idea of the 'noble savage' with that of the highly organized cultures of Greece and Rome was overlooked by the theorists in their enthusiasm for any means of getting as far away as possible from the artificialities of contemporary fashion.

In practice, Noverre's reforms amounted to the simplification of both costume and movement, and resulted in greater importance being given to the expression of feeling, and to the plausible narration of a story in mime, than to technical virtuosity. The reaction went, as usually happens, too far, and Noverre laid himself open to the criticism of overloading his ballets with dramatic action involving long written explanations. He was indeed strongly criticized on this score by Gaspare Angiolini (1723–96), who was working in Vienna and produced Gluck's ballet 'Don Juan' there in 1761. Angiolini maintained that a work of art should be complete in itself and self-explanatory, and that the necessity for a programme was a confession of failure. The disputations of the two great ballet-masters, like the contemporary arguments of the operatic theorists, served both to stimulate public interest in the art and to clarify the ideas of the contestants.

Notwithstanding Noverre's insistence upon dramatic propriety in the choreography, it was under his aegis that many of the steps and movements that have become the conventions of classical ballet were invented by the dancers. Among them was the *pirouette*, first exploited by Anne Heinel (1753–1808), and only made possible by the abolition of the heavy skirts of the old style, and the *rond de jambes* developed and perfected by Pierre Gabriel Gardel (1758–1840)—whose father, incidentally, was the first dancer to dance without a mask (in 1772)—and by Gaetan Vestris (1729–1808), whose son Auguste (1760–1842) became the most famous male dancer of his time (see also VESTRIS).

3. FRANCE. The French Revolution naturally accelerated both the emancipation of the dancers from the old conventions and the tendency of the artists to derive their themes, their costumes, and their movements from what they knew of classical antiquity. Their knowledge being in fact very imperfect and mostly derived at third hand from inferior examples of ancient art, they did not reproduce the dramatic style of the age of Sophocles and Euripides with any more exactitude than artists like David and Ingres achieved in their 'classical' paintings the kind of draughtsmanship that was employed by the Athenian painters. But the classical vogue had one important effect upon the ballet. When ladies went about in thin gauze draperies and sandals *à la grecque*, it was natural for the dancers to adopt low-cut bodices and diaphanous material; and since it was necessary to wear under this something less revealing, the *maillot*, or tights, which cover the whole body in flesh-coloured silk,[1] was invented by the costumier of the Paris Opéra. In this way was established the conventional costume of the ballerina which has persisted ever since through all the changes of artistic styles and costumier's fashions. This costume, exposing as it did the movement of every part of the body, imposed new tests upon the dancer's technique. Where nothing is concealed, everything must be perfect. It is not a little due to the invention of the new costume that the art of dancing developed so rapidly and to so high a pitch of excellence in the first quarter of the nineteenth century.

It has been said that the classical vogue in

[1] In Rome dancers were at first prohibited from wearing the *maillot* unless it were blue, so that there should be no misunderstanding on the part of the spectator as to what was and what was not naked flesh.

art which came in with the French Revolution and persisted through Napoleon's Empire was not at all exact in its imitation of the antique. It was not even, in spirit, classical. For the antique was viewed as something strange and exotic; it was romantically admired. And the ballets, like the operas composed in the same mode (Bellini's 'Norma' (1831) is the most familiar example, though its subject is not classical), were romantic in spirit. When therefore in the following generation the full tide of Romanticism swept over Latin Europe from Germany and Great Britain, there was no need for the ballet to undergo any very drastic reform. All that happened was that the nymph dancing before a Doric temple donned a pair of quite insufficient wings and became a sylph pursued through a gloomy glade by one of Sir Walter Scott's kilted compatriots.

'La Sylphide' (1832), the most famous of the earlier romantic ballets (not to be confused with the later 'Les Sylphides', for which see below), was the production of Filippo Taglioni (1777–1871), an Italian ballet-master who had worked at the Theatre Royal, Stockholm, where he married the daughter of a Swedish singer. By her he had a daughter, Marie (1804/9–84), who became the most celebrated dancer of her time, the first real practitioner of the *danse d'élévation* (which we commonly call nowadays the 'classical' style of ballet-dancing) and its most accomplished exponent. She was also the first dancer of repute to use *les pointes*. Notwithstanding the rivalry of such excellent younger dancers as Carlotta Grisi (1819–99), Fanny Elssler (1810–84), and, loveliest in looks, Fanny Cerrito (1821–*c.* 1895), Marie Taglioni occupied the position, *hors concours*, that we have seen accorded to Anna Pavlova in our own time.

4. ITALY. It will be observed that of the dancers mentioned most have Italian names; none is French, though Paris was still the chief centre of their activities. The creative leadership in ballet, as in opera, has passed to Italy, and for the remainder of the century Italian fashions, musical and dramatic, dominate the ballet. The most remarkable work was done in Milan, where, with the enormous resources of La Scala at his disposal, Salvatore Vigano (1769–1821) produced a series of grand spectacular ballets that seem to have anticipated the splendours of the 'grand' operas of Rossini, Meyerbeer, and Verdi. In these productions, which were on the musical side *pastiches* (see OPERA, 4) he was assisted by a scenic artist of exceptional ability and imagination, Alessandro Sanquirico (1780–1849).

5. NINETEENTH CENTURY. This spectacular element persisted as a natural ingredient in the romantic ballets of the nineteenth century, but the musical and dramatic elements were strengthened by the provision of books and music specially composed. The most famous of these ballets and the earliest surviving in the modern repertory is the 'Giselle' of Jean Coralli (1779–1854), for which Théophile Gautier provided the dramatic idea and Adolphe Adam composed

the music. 'Giselle', which was produced in 1841 with Grisi in the title-part, is the exact counterpart in ballet of the contemporary Donizettian tragic opera, 'mad' scene and all. The dancers' solos are the equivalent of the arias, in which the singer sums up the emotions of the dramatic situation, and are connected by recitative-like passages of miming in which the story is developed. Once the convention is accepted, 'Giselle' remains a beautiful and affecting drama, to whose effect the innocent naïveté of Adam's music contributes its share. Ballet had at last found its equilibrium and become a fully grown and independent form of dramatic art.

As always happens when that position is reached in the development of an art, the conventions tended to harden into formulas and so to lose real significance. They became, in fact, conventional. One of the most unfortunate results of the apotheosis of the ballerina was the complete subordination of the male dancer, who was reduced to the role of attendant and supporter. Indeed, by the end of the century the male dancer had almost disappeared from Paris, his roles being performed by women *en travesti*.

So, of the great mass of nineteenth-century ballets, little has survived and nothing deserves our attention, except the productions of the French *maître de ballet*, Marius Petipa (1822–1910), with Tchaikovsky's music, the two masterpieces of the late romantic ballet—'Le Lac des Cygnes' (1877, rev. Petipa 1894), in which the sylphs and wilis[1] have become swan-princesses, and 'La Belle au Bois Dormant' (1890), which retells with every imaginable splendour of pantomime the immortal story of the Sleeping Beauty. To these must be added Tchaikovsky's third ballet 'La Casse-Noisette' (1892), a variant on the theme of dancing dolls which has been used with success in so many ballets, including 'Coppélia' (1870), 'Petrouchka' (1911), and 'La Boutique fantasque' (1919).

6. RUSSIA. Just as in the early part of the nineteenth century the centre of gravity had moved from France to Italy, so now it began to shift to Russia. Ever since Peter the Great had encouraged the cultivation of Western manners, dancing and the ballet had played an increasing part in the entertainments of the Imperial Court and of the wealthy Russian nobles on their own estates. Hence, although the artistic direction of the Imperial Ballet at St. Petersburg was more often than not in the hands of a foreign expert, the dancers themselves were recruited from native sources and brought with them the exciting vigour of the peasant dances, which came to form the basis of so much in the true *ballets russes*, (e.g. 'Petrouchka', the dances in 'Prince Igor', and 'Children's Tales'). For the nobles naturally recruited their private companies from among their serfs, who would know only the folk-dances of the region where

[1] In Germanic legend, wilis are young girls who have died before their wedding-day, and who come out of their graves to dance by night in their wedding-dresses.

they dwelt and the style of these dances inevitably affected the general development of ballet-dancing in the schools to which the dancers were sent to learn their technique. Moreover the Russians never acquiesed in the complete subordination of the male dancer which has been noticed in Western Europe. It was precisely because the Russian dancers had roots deep in their native soil that the ballet was able to develop there into so splendid and vigorous and original an art in the first decades of the twentieth century.

This magnificent flowering was no sudden miracle. Indeed, already in the latter years of the nineteenth century the Imperial Ballet under the direction of Petipa had given to the world such masterpieces as 'Le Lac des Cygnes' and 'La Belle au Bois Dormant'. When every allowance has been made for the admirable dramatic invention shown in the 'books' of these ballets and in their choreography, the element that has ensured their survival, as it has rescued from among many pieces not inferior in other respects the works of Delibes, is the music. Tchaikovsky was not, perhaps, a great composer in his own right, but he was certainly a great composer of ballet music. He could take instructions from the choreographers—so many bars in 6-8 time—and write something that was fresh, characteristic of the scene in question, and delightful for its own sake. His ballets maintain their popularity and indeed have joined 'Giselle' as classics, the touchstones on which are tested the merits of the companies of dancers.

The Tchaikovsky ballet was a three-act drama occupying the whole evening. Structurally it resembled the contemporary opera in which recitative and aria tended to lose some of their differentiation and to merge into a more continuous melodic *cantilena*, though of course the lyrical climaxes remained equally for singers and dancers. So although scenes of conventional miming were still necessary to explain and to carry on the story, and although the principals had their important solos and duets, the action tended to be more fluid and continuously interesting than in the older romantic ballets. One feature of these dramas, necessary both to fill out the evening and to introduce variety into what might have become too monotonous an entertainment, is the *divertissement*, which performs, on a rather more elaborate scale, the function of the ballet in contemporary opera. These *divertissements* consist of a series of 'characteristic' dances, usually national—a Hungarian czardas, a Polish mazurka, a Spanish tarantella, and so on—danced supposedly for the entertainment of the personages of the drama on the stage, and incidentally for that of the audience in the theatre. Later, as we shall see, the *divertissement* developed into an independent type of ballet.

Without the genius of Tchaikovsky, and with the inevitable hardening of the conventions into formulas that always follows upon any successful artistic development, the Russian Imperial Ballet in the years between 1895

and 1909 lost its vitality. It continued to produce ballets on the same scale—Glazounov's 'Raymonda' (1898) will serve as an example because it has been given in England within memory, and is a favourable specimen of an uninspired period—and its school turned out a succession of superb dancers who could sustain the public interest in the old ballets.

7. BALLETS RUSSES. A visit to Russia of the American dancer, Isadora Duncan (1878–1927), who performed barefoot in flowing Grecian draperies, was the occasion rather than the cause of the reaction against the current conventions that occurred about the year 1908. The mere appearance of a solo dancer, however talented and beautiful, who eschewed *pointes* and all the other artificialities of the classical style of ballet-dancing, would not have been sufficient to cause something in the nature of an artistic upheaval, unless there had been explosive matter ready to be touched off. Such material did exist in a group of young men, led by Serge Diaghilev (1872–1929)—an amateur of painting and music who had been for a while assistant to Prince Volkonsky, Director of the Imperial Theatres—Michel Fokine (1880–1944), a dancer of the Imperial Ballet, and Alexandre Benois (1870–   ), a painter who seems to have provided most of the creative ideas.

In 1909 Diaghilev obtained permission to take a company of dancers from the Imperial Ballet to Paris for a season. The company included Anna Pavlova (1882–1931), Tamara Karsavina (1885–   ), Vaslav Nijinsky (1890–1950), a young Polish dancer, with Fokine as choreographer and Enrico Cecchetti (1850–1928), Petipa's successor at the Marinsky Theatre, as *maître de ballet*. The repertory contained 'Les Sylphides', which as 'Chopiniana' had been produced at a charity performance in St. Petersburg a year before, the dances from 'Prince Igor', 'Le Pavillon d'Armide', one of Fokine's contributions to the Marinsky repertory, and 'Cléopâtre'. Here was, indeed, a revelation to the Parisian public, accustomed to the old-fashioned insipidities of the Opéra ballet, of the potentialities of the dance! In place of a three- or four-act drama, a number of short pieces, varied in style from the melodramatic to the purely lyrical, and each a considered attempt to obtain a synthesis of the three arts of dancing, painting, and music. Not all these ballets were equally successful, 'Cléopâtre', which was the first of a line of exotic creations decorated by Léon Bakst (1866–1924), was set to a tasteless pot-pourri of music by various composers. 'Les Sylphides', on the other hand, was a completely successful gloss upon the music of Chopin as well as being a beautiful summary of all that was best in the art of Taglioni and Grisi and Fanny Cerrito; it has become one of the classics of the repertory, surviving every injury to its butterfly wings and every travesty of Alexandre Benois's stage-design. The dances from Borodin's opera 'Prince Igor' were perhaps the most startling revelation of all, bringing into the theatre an intoxicating breath of savagery from the far Caucasian steppes.

In the following year (1910) Fokine added to the repertory three new masterpieces: 'Schéhérazade', in which the more than oriental splendours of Léon Bakst's art found their finest expression in the adornment of a tale of passionate sensuality; 'Carnaval', which applied to Schumann's music in a slightly more dramatic manner and with no less success the method of 'Les Sylphides'; and 'L'Oiseau de Feu', a fairy-tale with music by the young composer Igor Stravinsky, which carried a stage further the exploitation of native Russian dancing. The success of this last ballet resulted in the composer being commissioned to write the music for a new ballet in the following year. This work, 'Petrouchka' (1911), was the product of collaboration between Benois, the scenic designer who also provided the outline of the story, Fokine, and Stravinsky, under the co-ordinating chairmanship of Diaghilev. The result is the exception to the rule that works of art are not produced by committees. It was an unqualified success and remains the chief masterpiece of the Ballets Russes. The charming *pas de deux* for Karsavina and Nijinsky to Weber's 'Invitation to the Dance', entitled 'Le Spectre de la Rose', belongs to the same year.

In a couple of years the art of Fokine had reached its summit. From then on he could only strive to attain the same level of achievement, and too often, handicapped by a pretentious score, as in Richard Strauss's 'Eine Joseph-Legende' (1914), his aim fell short. But still in 'Thamar' and 'Papillons' (both 1912), and in the sumptuous and satirical opera-ballet 'Le Coq d'Or' (1914) by Rimsky-Korsakov, in which the singers were duplicated by dancers, he created new variations upon the themes of oriental passion and cruelty, of romantic poetry and of Russian fairyland. In 1912 he essayed a large classical theme in 'Daphnis and Chloe', for which the music was commissioned from Maurice Ravel. Unfortunately the large orchestra and the difficult nature of the music, together with the employment of the chorus (which was indeed omitted from the London production in 1914, to the annoyance of the composer), have militated against the retention in the repertory of this ballet, whose beauty remains treasured in the memories of those who saw it then.

The Graeco-Roman motif, interest in which was undoubtedly stimulated by Isadora Duncan's art, also appeared in the production of Debussy's 'L'Après-midi d'un Faune' (1912), the choreography of which was entrusted to Nijinsky. Paradoxically, the nimblest dancer of the age, whose greatest technical accomplishment consisted in his extraordinary power of elevation by which he appeared to hang suspended in the air, composed as his first essay a ballet in which the dancers' feet are flat on the ground throughout, and their movements are confined to angular gestures in profile, in order to create the illusion of a frieze in *bas-relief*.

The ballet created something of a sensation in Paris on account of the alleged lasciviousness of the action. The Parisian audience was even more deeply shocked in the following year by the production of Stravinksy's 'Le Sacre du Printemps', for which Nijinsky devised movements in the Cubist manner, then fashionable in advanced artistic circles, which seemed to the majority of spectators to be merely uncouth and ugly. No greater contrast to the romantic beauty and sensuous colour of Fokine's ballets could have been imagined than this harsh, sub-human ritual performed upon a grey and empty waste. But Nijinsky's career as choreographer was soon over. During a tour in South America he married one of the dancers in the company, and, having quarrelled with Diaghilev, was dismissed.

The Ballets Russes of Diaghilev had by now completely severed their connexion with the Imperial Ballet in St. Petersburg and from 1914, when the outbreak of war caught them at the end of their fourth season in London, they remained in exile, cut off from their homeland first by war and then by the Revolution of 1917. During the war years of 1914–18 the company toured in Europe and America, collecting, especially in Spain, materials in the form of local colour that were to prove valuable in the future. Paris became their spiritual home. Fokine had left the company, which found a new choreographer in Leonide Massine (1896–   ), who had first appeared with the Ballets Russes as little more than a boy in Strauss's 'Eine Joseph-Legende'. In this ballet the part of Potiphar's wife was created by Ida Rubinstein, who was the original Schéhérazade in the 1910 Paris production of Fokine's ballet.

Ida Rubenstein, a strikingly beautiful woman, was an actress and mime rather than a dancer. But she was later to play an important part in the history of ballet, when she formed her own company in Paris and commissioned a number of ballets, including Stravinsky's 'Le Baiser de la Fée' and Ravel's 'Bolero' (both 1928), for which Bronislawa Nijinska (1891–   ) arranged the choreography and Benois designed the décor. Her repertory also included Ravel's 'La Valse' (1920) in versions by Fokine and Nijinska.

After one or two essays in the Russian style, of which 'Contes Russes' (1917) is an excellent example, Massine broke new ground in 'Les Femmes de Bonne Humeur' (also 1917), and 'La Boutique Fantasque' and 'Le Tricorne' (both 1919). These are all *ballets d'action*, comic in theme, and satirical or grotesque in manner. In place of the flowing, graceful movements that characterize the older ballets, Massine tended to use quick, angular gestures which gave spontaneity to the action and served as an admirable vehicle for the robust humour of the characters. Moreover, Massine completed that fusion of mime and dancing proper which had been begun by Fokine in ballets like 'Carnaval'. The *corps de ballet*, too, was used by Massine not as a chorus performing uniform gestures simultaneously but as a group of individual characters each with its own life to live within the framework of the action. Fokine had, indeed, worked towards this emancipation of the *coryphées*, particularly in 'Petrouchka', but generally his advance in this line amounted to no more than devising contrapuntal movements for groups of dancers, as in the 'Prince Igor' dances and the *Ronde des Princesses* in 'L'Oiseau de Feu'.

During the years immediately following the Peace of Versailles Diaghilev tended for a while, out of a genuine desire to foster young talent and explore new paths, to follow one after another the most advanced artistic fashions of the French capital, and that during a period when, emotionally exhausted by the war and its consequences, the minds of young artists tended to concentrate upon trivialities. The productions of this period were conspicuous chiefly for their silliness, though one or two, like Massine's 'Les Matelots' (1925), had wit and vigour enough to preserve them from immediate oblivion.

Massine had severed his connexion with Diaghilev in 1921, but returned to his company as choreographer in 1924. During the interval Diaghilev apparently perceived that his search after novelty for its own sake was taking the art of the ballet into the desert, besides threatening him and his company with financial ruin. He endeavoured to avert the former disaster, while at the same time easing the latter, by staging at the Alhambra Theatre, which had become his company's London home, a revival of Tchaikovsky's 'La Belle au Bois Dormant' of unparalleled sumptuousness. The cast included a galaxy of distinguished dancers, the décor was in Bakst's most lavish manner, and his costume designs were executed in the most expensive materials. Unfortunately the London public, which would later throng any second-rate performance of ballet, displayed no appetite for this Lucullan feast.

When Diaghilev died in 1929 the Ballets Russes were both artistically and financially in low water, and admirers of their art might well despair of the possibility of a revival. For, whatever the incidental lapses of taste, their art was admirable and their achievement, under Diaghilev's direction, extraordinary. They had transformed the ballet from a trivial entertainment into a serious dramatic art, laying under contribution the most original musicians and painters of the period. Music was, perhaps, the most important constituent, and it is worth remarking that the ballets which have survived in the permanent repertory are those with music that has lasting merits of its own, whether composed expressly as for 'Petrouchka' or 'Le Tricorne', or adapted for the purpose like that of Chopin for 'Les Sylphides', Schumann for 'Carnaval', Scarlatti for 'Les Femmes de Bonne Humeur', and Rossini for 'La Boutique Fantasque'. The same consideration applies also to the older ballets of Tchaikovsky, Delibes, and Adam, whose score for 'Giselle' admirably portrays within the operatic conventions of a hundred years ago the pathos of the story.

8. ENGLAND. It is the lack of any pretension to musical or, for that matter, scenic distinction that makes it unnecessary to discuss at any length the English Ballet before 1930. Before the advent of the Ballets Russes, ballet in London was indeed a somewhat raffish entertainment, designed mainly for the display of the female dancers' persons. Occasionally the company was led by a dancer of real merit, like the adorable Adeline Genée, who was from 1897 to 1907 the ballerina at the Empire Theatre, or Catherine Geltzer, who appeared at the rival Alhambra. The ballets were elaborate and tasteless pantomimes in four or five acts, with music by a theatre musician and décor in the realistic manner. A typical example is 'The Press', produced at the Empire in 1898, which surveyed the history of printing, from Caxton to *Ally Sloper* and *The Pink 'Un*, in terms of tip-toe dancing to music by Leopold Wenzel.

The interest created by the Ballets Russes, and the apparent probability of the dispersion of the company at Diaghilev's death, stimulated a number of musicians, artists, and amateurs interested in the art to form the Camargo Society in order to give performances of ballet in London, and especially to afford opportunities to young English dancers and choreographers. Among the society's productions were Vaughan Williams's 'Job' (1931), with choreography by Ninette de Valois (1898–), an Irish dancer from Diaghilev's company who had lately been appointed to train the dancers at the Old Vic Theatre, and William Walton's 'Façade' (1931), for which Frederick Ashton (1906–), a pupil of Mme Rambert, was responsible. At one stroke an English Ballet, as distinct from the cosmopolitan confections of the Empire and the Alhambra, seemed to have been created—on the one hand a grave mimed drama on a religious theme designed to re-create in living form the illustrations of William Blake, and on the other a gay, satirical *divertissement* that owed more than a little of its wit to that essentially English institution, the music-hall.

The Camargo Society succeeded beyond all expectation, for London was soon embarrassed by the choice of ballets.[1] The Old Vic Ballet quickly developed, from very modest beginnings as a provider of dancers for the operatic performances, into a company capable of giving independent performances of its own. When the Sadler's Wells Theatre, reopened by Miss Lilian Baylis in 1931, had become well established, the ballet made that theatre its headquarters. During the first years of its existence the company was led by two British-born dancers who had served their apprenticeship with Diaghilev, Alicia Markova and Anton Dolin. Later its own dancers came to the fore, led by Margot Fonteyn and Robert Helpmann.

In the meantime two companies of Russian,

[1] When the Vic-Wells Ballet was firmly established, the Society was dissolved and its repertory and funds were made over to Sadler's Wells.

or mainly Russian, dancers, recruited on the continent and trained in Paris by exiled ballerinas of the Imperial Ballet, visited London. The first of these companies was managed by Col. de Basil and had Massine as its choreographer and *maître de ballet*. The company arrived in London in 1933 with a new repertory, including 'Jeux d'Enfants' (music by Bizet), 'Les Présages', an elaborate symbolic drama danced to the music of Tchaikovsky's Fifth Symphony, and 'Le Beau Danube', a delightful Viennese fantasia that owed something to the ballet in Smetana's 'The Bartered Bride'. The decadence and triviality into which the Russians had fallen in the last years of Diaghilev's reign had disappeared, and there was a fresh outcrop of productions that were either spontaneously delightful or of serious artistic intention. 'Les Présages', indeed, proved a portent, the forerunner of a series of symphonic ballets that laid Brahms, Berlioz, and Beethoven successively under contribution. Musicians were inclined to look askance at these invasions of almost sacrosanct territory. The real fault of these ballets, however, was not that they outraged great music, but that in fact they were unable to sustain the interest of the spectator through a long symphonic movement or to build up the choreographic action to a climax comparable with that in the music. By the end of the exposition of the first movement in Brahms's E minor Symphony the possibilities of choreography were seen to be exhausted; during the rest of the movement the dancers, repeating more or less what they had already done, remained earthbound while the music soared away. On the experience of these ballets and of some later productions, such as Massine's 'Nobilissima Visione' (1939), with music by Hindemith, and Ashton's 'Wanderer Fantasia' (1941), it may be questioned whether such symbolic and quasi-religious subjects are really within the scope of ballet's powers of presentation. 'Job' might seem to be an exception; but that remarkable and unique work owed its success (apart from the beauty of Vaughan Williams's music) to its careful adherence to the pictorial imagination of William Blake.

The second Russian company was under the direction of René Blum[1] and had Fokine as its choreographer. He revived a number of the ballets he had created for Diaghilev, revealing their full beauty to audiences that had become accustomed to imperfect reproductions and garbled versions. He also produced a few new ballets, of which 'L'Épreuve d'Amour' (1936), a delightful *chinoiserie* with music by Mozart and décor by André Derain, and Gluck's 'Don Juan' (1936), produced as nearly as possible in the manner of Gaspare Angiolini, its original choreographer, were the most memorable. Later, having joined Col. de Basil's company, Fokine revived 'Le Coq d'Or', but to an arrangement of the music that omitted the vocal parts and so deprived the production of some of its piquancy, though not of its garish splendour.

In 1939 both Massine and Fokine, together with the companies with which they were associated, went to America. Fokine, who died there in 1944, added nothing important to the repertory after 'Paganini', produced in London in 1939, while Massine appears to have oscillated between repetitions of Viennese and Spanish motifs and essays in surrealism.

When Markova and Dolin left the Sadler's Wells Ballet in 1935 the company was in a position to replace them with dancers trained in its own school. Its repertory, hitherto consisting of established classics in addition to the ballets taken over from the Camargo Society, and a few novelties, of which the most important were 'The Haunted Ballroom' (1934) and 'The Rake's Progress' (1935), was soon enlarged by a number of new ballets arranged by Ninette de Valois and Frederick Ashton.

In the course of the following decade the Sadler's Wells company explored the whole range of ballet, from the classics, including 'Giselle' and complete productions of Tchaikovsky's three masterpieces, onwards. The company's own creations covered every form and style, from the romantic, of which Ashton's 'Apparitions' (1936) and 'Horoscope' (1938) are good examples, to the light fantasy of his 'Patineurs' (1937), the robust satire of de Valois's 'The Prospect Before Us' (1940), the neo-classicism of Ashton's 'Baiser de la Fée' (1935), and the serious semi-political drama of de Valois's 'Checkmate' (with music composed by Arthur Bliss), the first performance of which was given in Paris in 1937. The company has also paid tribute to the fashion for symphonic ballet in an arrangement of Schubert's 'Wanderer Fantasia'. A more successful essay in the same vein was Ashton's 'Dante Sonata' (1940), with music by Liszt which lent itself better than Schubert's to the choreographer's imagination and to dramatic treatment. More recently Robert Helpmann (1911–), who succeeded Dolin as the company's chief male dancer, has produced a number of ballets, of which the most notable are a version of Milton's *Comus* with music by Purcell, and a 'Hamlet' to Tchaikovsky's overture (both 1942). The last was a most interesting gloss on Shakespeare's play, presenting the whole action of the tragedy in a vision supposed to take place in the dying Hamlet's brain. This ballet must be reckoned one of the most thoughtful contributions to the repertory.

To these productions a number of able designers contributed their share—Rex Whistler ('The Rake's Progress'), McKnight Kauffer ('Checkmate'), Oliver Messel ('Comus'), John Armstrong ('Façade'), William Chappell ('Les Patineurs'), John Piper ('The Quest'), and Leslie Hurry ('Hamlet' and 'Swan Lake'). A large number of the ballets have consciously followed the precedent of 'Job' and transferred

---

[1] René Blum died in an internment camp during the German occupation of France in 1940–44. As a Jew and a brother of the Socialist Prime Minister, he was subjected to ill-usage which he bore with great courage.

to the stage the style and characteristics of a given painter, as Rowlandson in 'The Prospect before Us', Flaxman in 'Dante Sonata', and Hogarth in 'The Rake's Progress'. Further examples of the practice may be found in the repertory of Mme Marie Rambert's Ballet Club, which in the small Mercury Theatre has trained a number of accomplished dancers and choreographers.

9. BALLET JOOSS. Among a number of companies, visiting or resident, the Ballet Jooss deserves particular mention. Kurt Jooss (1901–), formerly ballet-master at Münster and at Essen, left Germany when the Nazis came into power and established a school of ballet at Dartington Hall, Devon. A pupil of Rudolf von Laban who was much influenced by Isadora Duncan, Jooss makes little or no use of the classical technique of dancing. The barefoot style is obviously adapted to the expression of the vague transcendentalism dear to German hearts. But it has its dangers—not the least being that of appearing ridiculous. Jooss has avoided that danger in most of his ballets, because he possesses a sharp critical mind and has disciplined his company no less than an Italian *maître de ballet*. His best productions have a satirical tang, the most notable being 'The Green Table', a political caricature of international conferences, produced in Paris in 1926. That Jooss has never been able to match this early production is perhaps the best indication of the limitations of his style. None the less his ballets have had an influence upon the productions of other companies, e.g. 'Job', 'Checkmate', 'Nobilissima Visione', and Helpmann's 'Miracle in the Gorbals' (1944).

D. H.

BALLET CLUB, see RAMBERT, MARIE.

BALLET DE COUR (or Ballet à Entrées). Though belonging more properly to the domain of music, the French *ballet de cour* deserves mention here for its connexion with the great dramatist Molière. This form of entertainment, in which music, dancing, and drama all played an equal part, developed out of the French Court festivities of the fifteenth century, particularly the mascarades. It was reshaped under the influence of the classical revival of the late sixteenth century, Jodelle being the first dramatist of the new form, in collaboration with the foremost musicians of the day. These ballets-mascarades, as they were then called, consisted of songs and dances, loosely strung together with no central unifying idea. Early in the seventeenth century, under the influence of the new Italian form of opera, connecting links of sung recitative were added, but this proved unsatisfactory. With the collaboration of Lully and Molière—great musician and great poet—the 'entrées' took their place within the framework of a dramatic entity, and the new genre, which began with *Le Mariage forcé* (1664) in which Louis XIV danced, reached its peak of perfection in *Le Bourgeois gentilhomme* (1670). After the breach between Lully and Molière the genre declined, in spite

of later efforts to revive it, and the *ballet de cour* became merged in the *opéra-ballet*. (See also BALLET, 1 and OPERA, 3.)

BALLET JOOSS, see BALLET, 9.

BALLET RAMBERT, see RAMBERT, MARIE.

BALLETS RUSSES, see BALLET, 7.

BALTIMORE, one of the first towns in America to show hospitality to theatrical companies. The first theatre building was raised there after the War of Independence, by a former member of the American Company, one Wall, and opened on 1 Jan. 1782, but performances in adapted halls had frequently been given there before that date. The town continued to be visited regularly by the early companies, and to-day retains its position as an important date in the tours of the best American and foreign companies.

BALUSTRADE-PIECE, see FLAT.

BANCROFT. (1) SIR SQUIRE (1841–1926), English actor-manager, a tall, distinguished-looking man of great ability, who, with his wife (2) MARIE EFFIE (née Wilton) (1839–1921), introduced a number of reforms on the British stage, both as regards acting and the type of play produced. To them is attributable the vogue of the drawing-room comedy and drama as it is known to-day, together with its typical stage-setting and décor.

Marie Wilton was the daughter of provincial actors, and was on the stage from early childhood. She played with many famous actors of the time, including Macready on his farewell performance in the provinces, when she appeared as Fleance to his Macbeth. She was also much praised by Charles Kean for her Prince Arthur in *King John*. She first appeared in London in 1856, at the Lyceum, as Henri to Dillon's Belphegor in the play of that name, in which Toole, then still unknown, played Fanfaronade. As Perdita in Brough's extravaganza on *The Winter's Tale* she quickly made a success, and continued to play in burlesque, notably at the Strand in H. J. Byron's plays, until she decided to go into management on her own account.

Meanwhile Squire Bancroft, who had no family associations with the stage, had made his first appearance in the Birmingham stock company in pantomime in Jan. 1861, and for the next four years was gaining experience of all types of parts in stock and touring companies. Towards the end of this period he played with Marie Wilton, who went to Liverpool in burlesque, and on her return to London she invited him to join her company. On a borrowed capital of £1,000, of which little remained when the curtain went up, they opened the old Queen's Theatre (now the Scala), which, situated in an unfashionable part of London, had fallen into disrepute, and was nicknamed the 'Dust Hole'. Renamed the Prince of Wales's, charmingly decorated, and excellently run, it opened on 15 Apr. 1865, with Bancroft in Wooler's *A Winning Hazard*, while Marie Wilton appeared as Alessio in a burlesque by Byron entitled *La! Sonnambula!; or, the Supper, the Sleeper, and the Merry Swiss Boy.* The venture was a success, consolidated two years later by the marriage of the joint managers. The despised Dust Hole became one of the most popular theatres in London, and there the Bancrofts presented and played in the plays of Tom Robertson, domestic comedies more credible and true to life than the melodrama which had been so much in vogue previously. As Captain Hawtree in *Caste* (1867) Bancroft gave one of his best performances, only equalled by his Orloff in *Diplomacy* and his revival of Webster's old role of Triplet in *Masks and Faces.* His wife was brilliant in the leading female roles, and was accounted one of the best actresses of her day. The company was carefully chosen and the object of much solicitude, since the Bancrofts did much to raise the economic status of their actors. Leading players were paid £60–£100 a week, as against a previous scale of £5–£10 elsewhere, and the theatre also paid for the ladies' dresses, an unusual arrangement at that time. Among other innovations the Bancrofts adopted Mme Vestris's idea of practicable scenery—real doors and windows in solid three-wall rooms with a ceiling (see BOX SET). In 1880 they moved to the Haymarket and continued their successful career, in spite of a first-night riot caused by the abolishing of the pit. They retired in 1885, their last appearance being on Monday, 20 July, in a mixed bill consisting of the first act of *Money*, a scene from *London Assurance*, and the second and third acts of *Masks and Faces.* In after years they both appeared intermittently under other managements, but the main bulk of their work was done before 1885. There can be no doubt that they had a great and salutary influence upon the English stage. Happily married and of congenial temperaments, they commanded the highest respect from their staff and audiences, and the knighthood conferred upon Bancroft in 1897 was a recognition of the services of both to their profession. Their collaboration extended to three plays and a joint autobiography, while Lady Bancroft was also the author of a novel.   W. M. P.

BANDBOX THEATRE, NEW YORK, originally Adolf Phillipp's, at 205 East 57th Street, opened on 23 Nov. 1912. Two years later it was re-christened, and it finally closed on 28 Apr. 1917, a cinema being built on the site. It was at this theatre that the Washington Square Players, forerunners of the Theatre Guild, first appeared in New York in 1915, in a series of one-act plays, mainly by American authors, under the direction of Philip Moeller, Robert Edmond Jones, Edward Goodman, and Helen Westley.

BAND-ROOM, a small retiring-room under the front of the stage used by the members of the theatre orchestra.

BANGS, FRANK C. (1833–1908), American

actor, who was serving his apprenticeship in a newspaper office when he saw the elder Booth as Richard III and decided to go on the stage. He made his début in Washington in 1851, and worked as general utility in a number of good companies, including those of the Ravel pantomimists and of Mrs. John Drew. In 1858 he made his first appearance in New York at Laura Keene's Theatre, and then went to Wallack's, where he shared juvenile leads with Lester. During the war he was a Confederate soldier, but returned to the stage and in 1867 made a great success in *After Dark*, at Niblo's. He retired following a dispute with the management, and spent his time lecturing and teaching elocution. In 1870 he returned to the stage, and was seen in the company of many good actors, playing Mark Antony to the Brutus of Edwin Booth and the Cassius of Lawrence Barrett with great success. In later life he was less successful, and appeared in a number of ephemeral plays, his last outstanding production being a revival in 1892 of Boker's *Francesca da Rimini.*

BANKS, JOHN (c. 1650–1706), English dramatist, author of eight tragedies, of which the best is probably *Virtue Betrayed; or, Anna Bullen* (1682). Banks, of whose life very little is known, has been somewhat under-rated, according to Allardyce Nicoll, who considers him a writer of undoubted merit, worthy to rank next to Otway 'in the imaging of emotional and pathetic scenes'. His early works were heroic dramas in the style of Dryden, but he later shows traces of pathos and intimate tragedy which mark him as a precursor of Rowe.

BANNISTER. (1) CHARLES (c. 1738–1804), English actor, who after some years in the provinces appeared with Foote at the Haymarket, and established an enviable reputation as a comedian and a mimic of fashionable singers. He was engaged by Garrick to play Merlin in *Cymon* (1767), and his Caliban was considered outstanding. A pleasant, easygoing man, he was often in financial trouble, and towards the end of his life was forced to rely for supplies on an annual benefit at the Haymarket, of which Colman allowed him the use. At his 1800 benefit Lord Nelson, fresh from his victory at the Nile, was present with Sir William and Lady Hamilton. Charles's modest reputation was eclipsed by that of his son (2) JOHN (1760–1836), who was in his youth an art student at the Royal Academy with Rowlandson the caricaturist. In 1778, with the encouragement of Garrick, he went on the stage, and made his first appearance at the Haymarket in a part made famous by Woodward, who had just died. Bannister, however, did well in it, in spite of his youth and inexperience, and was engaged for Drury Lane, where he appeared mainly in tragedy. In this he was soon overshadowed by the rising fame of Henderson and Kemble, and it was in comedy that he found his true bent. He was the first Don Ferolo Whiskerandos in *The Critic* (1779), in which he later played Sir

Fretful Plagiary, and was also good in such parts as Sir Anthony Absolute, Tony Lumpkin, Scrub, and Doctor Pangloss. The eminence of King in first comic parts was something of a bar to his advancement, and he took to making visits to the provinces, but he later returned to London and became one of the managers of Drury Lane, where he spent most of his career. He married in 1783 Elizabeth Harper, principal singer at the Haymarket, who retired in 1793 to take care of her increasing family. Bannister remained on the stage until 1815, and retired to spend 21 years of calm and happy family life. He always kept his taste for painting, and was intimate with Rowlandson, Morland, and Gainsborough. On his death it was said of him: 'The stage can point to few men of more solid virtue and unblemished character.' His life was written by John Adolphus in 1838.

BANNISTER, NATHANIEL HARRINGTON (1813–47), American actor and dramatist, who had a short and somewhat tragic life. He first appeared on the stage in Baltimore at the age of 16, playing Young Norval. In 1831 he went to New York, but in spite of his popularity in the south and west of America he never seemed to get a footing there, and died in poverty at the age of 34. He wrote a number of plays, but there also bad luck seemed to dog him, and he sold the most successful, *Putnam*, for fifty dollars. Of the rest only four have survived. They are romantic melodramas in the prevailing historical style, of small literary or theatrical merit.

BANVARD'S MUSEUM, NEW YORK, see DALY'S THEATRE (1).

BANVILLE, THÉODORE FAULLAIN DE (1823–91), French poet and playwright, son of a naval captain. It is on his poetry and on his numerous prose works that his reputation mainly rests, but he was also the author of a number of plays in verse produced at the Comédie-Française. Although written with distinction and refinement they are deficient in dramatic power, and have fallen out of the repertory. Among them were *Le Feuilleton d'Aristophane* (1852), *Gringoire* (1866), and *Deidamia* (1876). Banville, who numbered among his friends the critic Jules Janin and the actor Frédérick-Lemaître, was also dramatic critic to several papers, and by his temperate judgement and great charm exercised a wise and sound influence on the writers of the time.

BAR BELL, a warning to patrons in the theatre bars and foyers that the curtain is about to rise.

BARBIERI, NICCOLÒ (?–c. 1640), an actor and author of the *commedia dell'arte*, who played under the name of Beltrame. He is also credited with the invention of the character of Scapino. He is first found with the Gelosi at Paris in 1600–4, and then joined the Fedeli, of whom he became joint director with the younger Andreini. One of his plays, *L'Incanto*,

ovvero L'Inavvertito (1629), though originally only the usual summary for improvisation, was later published with dialogue in full, and was made use of by Molière for *L'Étourdi*. Barbieri also wrote his memoirs, and an account of the stage in his time, *La Supplica*, published in 1634.

BARD, WILKIE (1870–1944), a music-hall star who started work in a cotton-spinner's warehouse. He first appeared in Manchester at the famous 'Slip Inn', and afterwards at the Grand in 1893, singing coster songs. He then went to London, appearing at Collins's in a score of impersonations all featuring the high, domed forehead (modelled on Shakespeare's—whence Bard, his real name being Billie Smith) fringed with sparse hair, and the two black spots over the eyebrows, which were thereafter inseparably associated with him. He appeared in pantomime, playing Pantaloon in the harlequinade, and, with Will Evans, reviving much of its old spirit, while as Idle Jack in *Dick Whittington* at Drury Lane in 1908 he started the vogue for tongue-twister songs with his 'She Sells Sea-Shells On the Sea-Shore'.

BARKER, a character of the fairground or itinerant theatre company, whose job it was to stand at the door of the booth and by his vociferous and spell-binding patter to induce the audience to enter. He is probably as old as the theatre itself, and was known to the ancient world. He achieved notoriety in sixteenth-century France and in the later fairs and showgrounds of Europe.

BARKER, HARLEY GRANVILLE- (1877–1946). In the first decade of the twentieth century Granville-Barker was in the forefront of the progressive movement in England. As playwright, actor, and producer he displayed that alert intelligence which, combined with artistic taste and sound scholarship, did so much to revitalize the English theatre at the turn of the century. He was associated with the work of the Stage Society for several years, and at its performance of *Candida* in 1900 Barker made his first appearance in a Shaw play, as Marchbanks.

The Barker–Vedrenne management at the Court Theatre (1904–7) was one of the distinctive achievements of the modern stage. Plays by Euripides, Maeterlinck, Schnitzler, Hauptmann, Yeats, Hankin, Galsworthy, Masefield, and Barker himself were produced, together with plays by Shaw, who took the keenest interest in the Court Theatre venture and personally produced several of his own plays there. In 1912 Barker and his wife were at the Savoy Theatre, where Barker's productions set new standards in the choice staging, intelligent acting, and fluent speaking of Shakespeare's plays.

Barker was the author of several plays, chief of which are *The Marrying of Anne Leete* (1902), *The Voysey Inheritance* (1905), *Waste* (1907 privately, 1936 publicly), and *The Madras House* (1910). With William Archer he was responsible for *A National Theatre: Scheme and Estimates* (1907). With his second wife—his first was Lillah McCarthy—he translated several of the plays of Martinez Sierra and the Quintero brothers into English. He also edited (with G. B. Harrison) *The Companion to Shakespeare Studies* (1934). His retirement from active work in the theatre was a severe loss, but his contribution of *Prefaces to Shakespeare* retained him as an important ally to actors and producers undertaking Shakespeare. These are perfect combinations of practical stage directions and scholarship. He insists that the greatest tragedies are tragedies of character, and he traces what he calls the 'interior action' with skill and insight.

BARKER, JAMES NELSON (1784–1858), American dramatist, author of the first American play on an Indian theme, which was also the first play from America to be done in England. This was *The Indian Princess*, given in Philadelphia in 1808, and as *Pocahontas; or, the Indian Princess*, at Drury Lane in 1820. Of Barker's other plays, only four have survived, among them *Tears and Smiles*, a comedy of manners played in Philadelphia in 1807, and a dramatization of *Marmion*, which was at first announced as being by an English author. It held the stage for many years, being a favourite with James Wallack, and was last revived in 1848. Barker's last play was *Superstition* (1824), again based on American history. It deals in blank verse with the story of a Puritan refugee from England who leads his village against the Indians, mingled with a tale of intolerance and persecution for witchcraft. Barker had many interests, and playwriting was only a hobby. Quinn, in his *History of American Drama*, says of him: 'He showed a sense of dramatic values and a gift of expression in verse which cause us to wonder what the result might have been if he had devoted himself, under more favorable circumstances, to the drama as a profession.'

BARNES, CHARLOTTE MARY SANFORD (1818–63), American actress and dramatist, the daughter of John Barnes (1761–1841), who went with his wife Mary from Drury Lane to the Park Theatre, New York. They were both popular players for many years, the husband as a low comedian, the wife, who was the sister of Mrs. Baldwin, also an actress at the Park, in such parts as Jane Shore, Mrs. Haller, and Southerne's Isabella. Charlotte first appeared on the stage at the age of four, as the child in *The Castle Spectre*. In 1834 she made her adult début at the Tremont, Boston, and in New York, in the same play. On one occasion she played Juliet to her mother's Romeo, but was never accounted such a good actress as the older woman. In 1842 Charlotte appeared in London, playing, among other parts, Hamlet, in which she was well received. Four years later she married an actor-manager named Edmond S. Connor, and became his leading lady, being also associated with him in the management of the Arch Street Theatre, Philadelphia. She wrote her first play, *Octavia*

Bragaldi, at the age of 18, basing it on a recent murder case, but transferring the scene to Renaissance Italy. It was produced at the National Theatre, New York, with the author as the heroine, and frequently revived, the last time at the Bowery in 1854 under her husband's management. She also made several adaptations of French melodramas, and dramatizations of novels, but the only one of her plays, apart from the above, which has survived is *The Forest Princess* (1844), one of the many dramatizations of the story of Pocahontas.

BARNES, SIR KENNETH RALPH (1878–), brother of the English actresses Irene and Violet Vanbrugh, and since 1909 director of the Royal Academy of Dramatic Art, London. This institution, which gives a two-year course of training in all branches of theatre art, was founded in 1904 by Tree at His Majesty's Theatre, and a year later moved to Gower Street, where it has since remained. Under the beneficent rule of Sir Kenneth—knighted in 1938 for his services to the English stage—it has grown steadily both materially and in reputation. In 1921 a theatre with a full-sized stage, on ground adjoining the Gower Street premises but fronting on Malet Street, was added to its amenities, while in 1931 a new and more commodious building replaced the original houses in Gower Street. This also contained a small theatre; it was seriously damaged by blast in April 1941, when the larger theatre on Malet Street was completely destroyed. The financial difficulties of the war years were partly relieved by the action of Sir Kenneth in becoming part-time General Secretary of E.N.S.A. and devoting the salary he received for his work to the general well-being of the R.A.D.A. He has for many years campaigned strenuously on behalf of the status of the theatrical profession, and the recognition of the value of organized training for young actors.

BARNES, THOMAS (1785–1841), English editor and critic, educated at Christ's Hospital. 'He might', said Leigh Hunt, who was his school-fellow, 'have made himself a name in wit and literature, had he cared much for anything beyond his glass of wine and his Fielding.' To this it should most certainly be added that he cared also for the theatre, and still more for *The Times* newspaper, which he edited soundly from 1817 until his death. His love of the theatre is manifested in his early work in the *Examiner* under the signature 'Criticus'. In the same journal, during Leigh Hunt's term of imprisonment, he described Kean's famous first performance of Shylock at Drury Lane, 26 Jan. 1814. His account of this, though much less well known, bears comparison with that of Hazlitt.

BARNSTORMERS, a name given in the late nineteenth century to the early itinerant companies whose stages were often set up in large barns, and whose work was characterized by ranting and shouting and general violence in speech and gesture.

BARNUM, PHINEAS TAYLOR (1810–91), a great American showman, whose name is mainly connected with the circus. For fifty years he provided the world with entertainment, constantly gulling the public yet always finding them ready to be gulled again. His first great enterprise was the American Museum, known also as Barnum's Museum, which opened in 1842 and was burnt down in 1865 and 1868. Tom Thumb, Jenny Lind, freaks, giants, and curiosities of natural history were exhibited there impartially, and during most of its history it housed plays as well. In 1871 Barnum started his immense circus—'The Greatest Show on Earth'—which for twenty years began its spring season in Madison Square Gardens. He was twice married, but had no children.

BARON. (1) ANDRÉ (c. 1602–55), a French actor who changed his name from Boyron when Louis XIII inadvertently addressed him as 'le sieur Baron'. He was taken into Mondory's company at the Marais in 1634, to replace the actors drafted to the Hôtel de Bourgogne, where he himself went after Mondory's retirement. He played tragedy kings and peasants in comedy, and is reported to have died of a wound in the foot which he inflicted on himself with a property sword while playing Don Diègue in Le Cid too energetically. In 1641 he had married (2) JEANNE AUSOULT (1625–62), child of strolling players, who became an excellent actress. She was much admired in breeches parts and wore her male attire with an air. Her early death, during the run of Manlius Torquatus, was much regretted by Corneille, who had in his new play a role intended for her 'plein de tendresse'.

Of her six children the youngest (3) MICHEL (1653–1729) became a famous actor. Orphaned before he was ten, he was a child-actor in the juvenile Troupe du Dauphin formed by the elder Raisin, after whose death his widow took the company into the provinces and failed completely. Molière, with that generosity towards his fellow actors so characteristic of him, offered them the use of the Palais-Royal for three days, in order that she might make some money. Chancing to visit the theatre during a performance by the children, he was so struck by the good qualities of young Baron that he took him into his own company and treated him as a son, educating and training him for the stage, and eventually giving him small parts to play, among them Myrtil in Mélicerte (1666). Unfortunately Molière's wife took a dislike to the boy, and on one occasion slapped his face, whereupon he ran away and joined his former companions. He remained with them until 1670, when Molière wrote and asked him to return in order to play the part of Domitian in Tite et Bérénice. In the following year he played Cupid to the Psyche of Molière's wife, a juxtaposition which led to some

ill-natured gossip at Molière's expense. This seems to have been unjustified, since on Molière's death Baron left the company to go to the Hôtel de Bourgogne, where he married Charlotte (1661–1730) daughter of the actor La Thorillière. There he played Racine's young tragic heroes, and later became the chief actor of the newly formed Comédie-Française. He was liberally endowed by nature with a fine presence, a deep voice, amplitude of gesture, and a quick intelligence. To these gifts, ably fostered by his great teacher, he joined application, attention to detail, and a firm belief in the importance of his profession, and of his own place in it. 'Every hundred years may bring forth a Caesar; but it takes ten thousand to produce a Baron.' Baron did a great deal to raise the status of actors in his day, and helped many a struggling dramatist by his rendering of a poor part. He was himself the author of several comedies, of which the best is L'Homme à bonne fortune (1686). Le Rendezvous des Tuilleries (1685) is an amusing trifle which introduces some of the actors of the Comédie-Française under their own names, as well as a number of well-known dandies of Paris. In 1691, at the height of his powers, Baron suddenly retired. No reason for this was given, though it was thought at the time that his pride was beginning to chafe under the stigma of being 'only an actor' and that he hoped to achieve a dignified position in social and private life. He continued, however, to write plays, and occasionally acted at Court and in private theatricals until 1720, when he returned to the Comédie-Française, remaining there until his death. Except for his voice, which was a little quavery, he was as good as ever, and it says much for the hold he had on his public that he was able to play his old parts again. He initiated a number of reforms, and guided the early progress of Adrienne Lecouvreur, as well as playing the lead in Marivaux's first play. He was taken ill on the stage during a revival of Rotrou's Venceslas, and died shortly afterwards. He was the last actor who had known Molière to appear at the Comédie-Française. His son (4) ÉTIENNE (1676–1911) played several roles as a child, made his proper début in 1694, and died in the prime of life as the result of dissipation. He was a cold, though correct, actor, with none of the genius of his father. His daughter and one of his nephews were in the service of the Comédie-Française for many years.

BARRAULT, JEAN-LOUIS (1910–   ), French actor and producer, who began his career as a pupil of Charles Dullin at the Atelier, and for some years divided his time between the stage and the films. In 1940 he joined the Comédie-Française, making his début as Rodrigue in Le Cid, and giving proof of great talent and a freshness and speed of delivery which set him somewhat apart from his fellow actors. He remained there, however, only six years, leaving to direct and act in his own productions, of which the finest to date has been his Hamlet in a new translation by André Gide.

BARREL SYSTEM, a method of moving scenery, also known as the Drum-and-Shaft (see ENGLISH PLAYHOUSE, 2).

BARRETT, GEORGE HORTON (1794–1860), American actor, son of an English actor who went to New York in 1797, and of his wife, who as Mrs. Rivers had been well known in London previously. They both joined the company at the Park Theatre under Dunlap, and there, in 1798, young Barrett made his first appearance as the child in *The Stranger*, his mother playing Mrs. Haller. At the age of 11 he was seen as Young Norval, again with his parents in the cast as Old Norval and Lady Randolph. After an absence of some years, spent at school and on tour, Barrett returned as an adult actor, and became one of the best light comedians of his day. Among his best parts were Sir Andrew Aguecheek, young Absolute, Charles Surface, and Puff. He made his last appearance on the stage in 1855. He was for a long time stage manager of the Bowery Theatre, under Gilfert, and later of the Tremont Theatre in Boston, and of the Broadway Theatre, New York, from its opening in 1847. Familiarly known, from his elegant appearance and gracious manners, as 'Gentleman George', he married in 1825 an American actress named Mrs. Henry, and had two daughters, Georgina and Mary.

BARRETT, LAWRENCE (1838–91), American actor and producer, who was on the stage as a boy of 14, and travelled the United States with many outstanding companies, including that of Julia Dean. In 1857 he was seen in New York in *The Hunchback* and other plays, and was leading man under Burton at the Metropolitan, later the Winter Garden. In 1858 he was a member of the Boston Museum company, and was in the army during the Civil War. Afterwards he travelled widely, and became extremely popular. He managed Booth's Theatre in 1871, as the friend and associate of Edwin Booth, to whose Brutus he frequently played Cassius, his best-remembered part. While Irving was in America in 1884 Barrett took over the Lyceum in London, and though his visit was not a success financially, he was made welcome and fêted on all sides. He was a scrupulous and competent man of the theatre, careful, painstaking, and dependable. Winter called him an interpreter, not an impersonator. All the standard classics were in his repertory, and many new plays, since he tried to encourage American playwrights, though he drew the line at realism, and remained faithful to romantic and poetic drama. Tall, with classic features, and dark, deeply sunk eyes, he was probably at his best in Shakespeare, to whose interpretation he brought dignity, a dominant personality, and intellectual powers somewhat exceptional in an actor at that date. He was the author of several books on the theatre. Two of his grandchildren also went on the stage.

BARRETT. (1) WILSON (1847–1904), an English actor-manager, who had few equals in melodrama. After a varied career he took over the management of the Princess's Theatre in 1881, and among the successes which he produced during his five years there the first was G. R. Sims's *The Lights o' London*, which ran for 228 performances and then toured the world with unflagging vigour. Even this, however, was surpassed by the popularity of the two plays generally connected with Wilson Barrett—*The Sign of the Cross*, which he wrote himself, and Jones and Herman's *The Silver King*, in which, as Wilfred Denver, he gave an outstanding performance as a melodramatic hero, a part for which he was eminently fitted by nature. His face was strikingly handsome, his voice resonant, and his chest and arms powerfully developed; he lacked only height to make a perfect figure of a man. As Marcus Superbus (in *The Sign of the Cross*), a Roman patrician converted to Christianity by a beautiful Christian girl, with whom he goes into the arena to meet death from the lions, he gave a truly remarkable performance. The play was first produced in America, at a time when Barrett was on tour there and badly in need of money. It made a fortune for him, and when brought to England, first at the Grand, Leeds (which incidentally Barrett himself built), in 1895 and then at the Lyric, London, in the next year, it created a sensation. Clergymen preached sermons about it, and people who had never before entered a theatre crowded to see it. It was perennially successful on tour. Barrett was less successful in Shakespearian roles, which he often essayed, though his Mercutio was well thought of by Clement Scott. His Hamlet seems to have suffered from too much melodrama.

His brother (2) GEORGE EDWARD (1849–94) was also an actor, who made his début in the provinces in 1866. He first appeared in London in 1872 and, after a visit to India in support of C. J. Mathews, he joined his brother's company at the Princess's, and went with him to the United States. His son also joined Wilson Barrett's company, and the family was represented further by a grandson of Wilson Barrett, who spent some years in repertory with the Brandon-Thomas companies and in 1939 was manager of a repertory season at the King's Theatre, Hammersmith.   W. M. P.

BARRIE, SIR JAMES MATTHEW (1860–1937), Scottish dramatist and novelist. Born at Kirriemuir, Forfarshire, a poor handloom-weaver's son, he was educated at the Academy, Dumfries, and proceeded to Edinburgh University. Leader-writer on the *Nottingham Daily Journal*, he contributed articles to Frederick Greenwood's *St. James's Gazette* and commenced author in 1888 with *Auld Licht Idylls* and *A Window in Thrums* (1889). *When a Man's Single* was his first notable novel. *The Little Minister* (1891) gave the first glimpse of the laughter and tears, the strangeness and the naughtiness of a writer who could be at once sentimental and impish. His earliest plays were all unsuccessful, but *Walker, London* (1892) had Toole in the cast and caught on. *The Professor's Love Story* (1894) established Barrie as a successful playwright. In 1897 the play of *The Little Minister* established him as a wealthy man. More novels, *Sentimental Tommy* and *Tommy and Grizel,* appeared round the turn of the century, and in 1904 *Peter Pan* stepped out of a story-book and took the stage. In the theatre Barrie made his way by a series of surprises. The years before the war of 1914 produced *Quality Street* and *The Admirable Crichton* (both 1902), *Little Mary* (1903), *Alice Sit-By-The-Fire* (1905), *Josephine* (1906), *What Every Woman Knows* (1908), and *Rosalind* (1912), besides a number of short plays like *Pantaloon* (1905), *Punch* (1906), *The Twelve Pound Look* and *A Slice of Life* (both 1910), and *The Will* (1913). During the war he wrote *Rosy Rapture* (1915), a revue, for Gaby Deslys, some small occasional pieces, such as *The Old Lady Shows Her Medals* (1917) and *A Well Remembered Voice* (1918), and also *A Kiss for Cinderella* (1916) and *Dear Brutus* (1917). *The Truth About the Russian Dancers* (1920) was his first piece after the war. It was followed by *Mary Rose* (1920), a play that was almost passionately liked and disliked, a strange, creepy, harrowing, exquisitely painful play of the supernatural and the natural. *Shall We Join the Ladies?*, a delicately worked one-act puzzle, appeared in 1922. His last play, *The Boy David*, was written for Elisabeth Bergner and played by her in 1936. In 1913 Barrie was created a baronet; in 1922 he received the Order of Merit and in the same year he was elected Rector of St. Andrews University.

Barrie in his great moments was a stage magician. He would move his audience against the grain of their own reasoning, and charm them with fanciful variations on a theme of deepest pessimism. He had a boyish delight in playing with the theatre, but only a consummate craftsman could have brought off certain masterpieces of theatrical effect—the cooking-pot at the end of Act II of *The Admirable Crichton* and the boom of the gun during the dance in Act III, the opening scenes of *What Every Woman Knows* and of *Dear Brutus*, hard to equal for rousing curiosity, the disappearance of Mary Rose on the island in the second act, and the first sentence—'Mother, I have killed a lion!'—of *The Boy David*. He played not only with the theatre but with ideas, and most of his work reveals a mind queerly compounded of fancifulness, sentimentality, and dry pessimism; but in *Mary Rose* he is no longer afraid to say that life can be dreadful. He is brave enough for the first time to make beauty out of reality, and in *The Boy David* he treats not childishness, which in *Peter Pan* was something distinct from manhood, but the childhood which is at the core of all humanity. Barrie never saw life as anybody else has seen it: he revealed unsuspected shapes of beauty. He was something of a seer; and what he saw and showed had so little to do with time and fashion and

manners that it is unlikely to fade out of memory.   A. V. C.

BARRIÈRE, THÉODORE (1823–77), French dramatist, who left his work as a map-engraver after the success of a vaudeville which he had written for the Théâtre Beaumarchais. During the next thirty years he wrote over a hundred plays, of which the best are *La Vie de Bohême* (1849), based on Murger's book with the assistance of the author, *Manon Lescaut* (1851), again based on a novel, and *Les Malheureux vaincus* (1865), which was for some time forbidden by the censor. Barrière was a social dramatist, in the style of Augier, though with less vigour and more concern for the lighter side of drama.

BARRY, ELIZABETH (1658–1713), the first really outstanding English actress. She played opposite Betterton for many years, and created a number of famous roles—one biographer estimates it at 119—including the heroines of Otway's tragedies and Congreve's *Mourning Bride*. Otway all his life cherished a hopeless passion for her. Her first appearances on the stage were lamentable failures, but coached and encouraged by Rochester she appeared successfully in a revival of Orrery's *Mustapha* in 1673, and continued to improve, though she did not attain the full height of her powers until she was past her first youth. She was good in comedy, but better in tragedy, in which she displayed great power and dignity. She retired in 1710. In private life, if we are to believe contemporary accounts, she was not so estimable, and many scandals are attached to her name, some perhaps undeservedly. She was never married.

BARRY, PHILIP (1896–1949), American dramatist, who contributed to the American stage some distinguished high comedies and unique excursions into fantasy and serious drama. Born in Rochester, New York, he was graduated from Yale University in 1919, studied playwriting at Harvard under G. P. Baker, and served in the diplomatic service. His first professional production, *You and I* (1923), was a study of a father's effort to realize his artistic ambitions in his son. His next, unsuccessful, play, *The Youngest* (1924), was followed by an ingenious domestic comedy, *In a Garden* (1925), and a satirical extravaganza about people's resistance to change, *White Wings* (1926). After writing a biblical drama, *John* (1927), Barry returned to his métier with *Paris Bound* (1927), in which a husband wins his wife's forgiveness for an illicit affair after he overlooks her own weakness. Following a collaboration with Elmer Rice, *Cock Robin* (1928), Barry turned out *Holiday* (1928), a bright comedy concerning the revolt of youth against parental snobbery. Diverging from brittle themes in *Hotel Universe* (1930), he wrote a probing psychological drama in which several troubled characters achieved purgation, but the play proved too elusive for its audience. Barry, however, quickly recovered his public with the domestic comedies *Tomorrow and Tomorrow* (1931), which retells the story of Elisha and the Shunammite with a psychoanalyst in the role of the prophet, and *The Animal Kingdom* (1932), which reverses the roles of a wife and a mistress by making the latter the loyal companion and therefore the true wife. After the mishaps of *The Joyous Season* (1934), *Bright Star* (1935), and *Spring Dance* (1936), Barry won prestige with the mystifying but provocative allegory of good and evil, *Here Come the Clowns* (1938), and popularity with the deft comedy of manners and character, *The Philadelphia Story* (1939). The war in Europe inspired an allegory, *Liberty Jones* (1941), concerning the dangers threatening American democracy; *Without Love* (1942), a romantic comedy that strained a parallel between politics and love; and *The Foolish Notion* (1945), an ingeniously constructed theatrical fancy concerning a husband's return from the war in Europe. J. G.

BARRY, SPRANGER (1719–77), Irish actor, who was first seen on the stage in Dublin in 1743, playing Othello at Smock Alley Theatre. He remained there until 1746, and then went to Drury Lane, where he appeared as Othello to the Iago of Macklin. He became one of the finest young lovers on the English stage, and remained in the Drury Lane company when Garrick took over, playing Othello, Pierre, Bajazet, Henry V, and Orestes, while Garrick took for himself such parts as Lear, Richard III, Sir John Brute, Macbeth, and Abel Drugger. They both played Hamlet at different times, and proved a great attraction when they appeared together, as Jaffier and Pierre in *Venice Preserved*, Chamont and Castalio in *The Orphan*, Hastings and Dumont in *Jane Shore*, and Lothario and Horatio in *The Fair Penitent*. In 1750 Barry went to Covent Garden, where he engaged in rivalry with Garrick, playing Romeo, Lear, and Richard III. Of the first, Macklin said that Barry swaggered so, and talked so loud in the garden scene, that the servants ought to have come out and tossed him in a blanket; but Garrick sneaked in like a thief in the night. It was generally conceded that Barry was best in the garden scene and in the tomb, while Garrick was preferred in the scenes with the friar and the apothecary. As Lear Barry was impressive, dignified, and pathetic, but far inferior to Garrick in the mad scene. He also failed as Richard III, but made an excellent Young Norval, superb in white satin, to the Lady Randolph of Peg Woffington. His first leading lady was Mrs. Theophilus Cibber, who after one season, when she played Juliet, returned to Garrick at Drury Lane. Barry then engaged Miss Nossiter, who made a charming Cordelia. He fell in love with her, but she died almost immediately. In 1758 Barry ruined himself with the speculative building of a theatre in Dublin, and on his return to London went to the Haymarket, until in 1766 Garrick engaged him to play again at Drury Lane, together with his first wife, who

died shortly after. He married as his second wife in 1768 Ann Dancer (*née* Street) (1734–1801), who was good in tragedy and unsurpassed in comedy, particularly as Millamant, Mrs. Sullen, and Angelica. After the death of Spranger Barry she married a young man named Crawford, and retired from the stage in 1798.

BARRYMORE, an important family of American actors, allied with the Drews. The father (1) MAURICE (1847–1905) was an Englishman named Herbert Blythe, who took his stage name from an old playbill hanging in the Haymarket Theatre, London. Born in India and educated at Cambridge, he studied law, and was already well known as an amateur boxer before he decided to adopt the stage as a profession. He first appeared with a provincial company in 1875, and in the same year went to New York, where he played in Daly's *Under the Gaslight*. A handsome, well-built man, he was engaged by many of the leading actresses of the period, including Modjeska, for whom he wrote *Nadjezda* (1886). He played in it himself both in the States and in London, where he was also seen at the Haymarket in 1886 in *Diplomacy* and *Masks and Faces*. He later accused Sardou of having plagiarized his play in *Tosca*, and obtained an injunction to prevent Fanny Davenport doing the latter play in an English translation in the United States. He gave excellent performances in *Captain Smith* and *The Heart of Maryland*, and also appeared under the management of William A. Brady in his own *Roaring Dick*. Towards the end of his life he became a star of the vaudeville stage, where he made his last appearance before succumbing to a mental malady, brought on in part by his high spirits and convivial temperament. In 1876 he had married (2) GEORGIANA (1856–93), daughter of Mrs. John Drew and an actress of great ability. She appeared at the Arch Street Theatre, Philadelphia, then managed by her mother, at the age of 16, and remained in the stock company there for some years. She then went to New York and appeared at the Fifth Avenue Theatre under Daly. After her marriage she appeared with her husband in *Diplomacy* and in the repertory of Mme Modjeska's company, and was considered particularly good in *The Wages of Sin* and *The Senator*, the latter with William Crane. She also appeared with Lawrence Barrett and Edwin Booth, and under the management of the Frohmans, but her career was hampered by illness and she died young. Her three children were all on the stage. The eldest (3) LIONEL (1878–   ) made his first appearance at 15, also at the Arch Street Theatre, Philadelphia, under his grandmother, and later played with his uncle, John Drew, in *The Mummy and the Humming Bird*, making a great success as an Italian organ-grinder. Other plays followed, including Barrie's *Pantaloon*, but with his career well assured he suddenly threw it up to study art in Paris. He was later persuaded to return to the stage, and appeared in *Peter Ibbetson* and *The Jest*, and made an outstanding success in *The Copperhead*. He was accounted one of the leading actors of New York, but deserted the stage for film work, where he was equally successful. He was twice married, both his wives being actresses. His sister (4) ETHEL (1879–), one of the leading women of the American stage, also made her first appearance under the aegis of Mrs. John Drew, later going to London, where she appeared with Henry Irving in *The Bells* and *Peter the Great*. A tall and lovely woman, with remarkable eyes, she was as much esteemed for her acting as for her beauty, and her long career has been a succession of triumphs, broken only by an illness lasting three years, from which she recovered to star in a Theatre Guild production. Her first outstanding success was scored as Madame Trentoni in *Captain Jinks of the Horse Marines* (1901), after which she played a number of fashionable young ladies, including *Cousin Kate*, but also showed her mettle in such plays as *A Doll's House* and *The Silver Box*. She has appeared in such classic roles as Ophelia, Juliet, Portia, and Camille, and was also outstanding in modern plays, among them *Déclassée*, *Whiteoaks*, and *The Corn is Green*, which ran for four years. She has played in vaudeville in *The Twelve Pound Look*, and has done much film and radio work. In 1928 she opened the Ethel Barrymore Theatre in New York with *The Kingdom of God*, in which she played Sister Gracia, and later appeared there as Lady Teazle in *The School for Scandal*. Her three children by her marriage to Mr. R. G. Colt are also on the stage.

The youngest of Maurice Barrymore's children, (5) JOHN (1882–1942), was, at the height of his powers, accounted one of the finest actors of the English-speaking stage. He first appeared in *Magda* in 1903, at the Cleveland Theatre, and later successes were *Pantaloon* (1905) and *The Fortune Hunter* (1909). Aided by outstandingly good looks, inherent talent, and a debonair manner, he became a popular matinée idol and a good light comedian, but in 1916 proved himself a serious actor also by his performance as Falder in Galsworthy's *Justice*. This was followed by an excellent rendering of the title-role in *Peter Ibbetson*, by Gianetto Malespini in *The Jest*, and by Fedor in *Redemption*. He then took voice-production lessons from an opera singer, and in 1922 electrified New York by his *Hamlet*, in which Blanche Yurka appeared as Gertrude, and the settings were designed by Robert Edmond Jones. He repeated this success in London in 1925, giving a fine, meticulous, and scholarly reading of the part, whose beauty was enhanced by the depth and flexibility of his voice and the radiance of his personal appearance. Hopes for his future ran high, but he failed to maintain this standard, and for some time confined himself to films, which he had graced intermittently since 1912. His last years were feverish and unhappy, and except for a pitiful caricature of himself in a

poor play, given in 1939, he appeared mainly in films and on the radio. He was four times married and divorced, and his daughter by his second marriage has appeared on the stage and in films.

The Barrymore eccentricities, and their famous temper, as well as the majestic personality of their maternal grandmother, Mrs. John Drew, were incorporated into a play by Edna Ferber and George S. Kaufman entitled *The Royal Family* (1927), done in England in 1934 as *Theatre Royal*. Although the three Barrymores never appeared together on the stage, they were all seen in a film, and John and Lionel were together in *Peter Ibbetson* and *The Jest*. Both brothers were good artists and musicians, and John as a young man did a poster of Sothern as François Villon in *If I Were King* which was much admired. He was also a newspaper artist for some time.

There were two (6) WILLIAM BARRYMORES, no relation to the above actors, who appeared on the London and New York stages, one dying in 1830, the other in 1845. Little is known of their careers, though the second was esteemed 'a sound, useful actor' and wrote a number of plays. His wife also was an actress, who played in the United States for many years, dying in England in 1862.

(7) RICHARD BARRY, EARL OF BARRYMORE (1769–93), a great amateur of the theatre, maintained a private theatre in his house at Wargrave, Berks., and another in Savile Row, where he engaged professional stars to play with himself and his friends.

BARTHOLOMEW FAIR, see FAIRS.

BASIL, COLONEL DE, see BALLET, 8.

BASKET-BOX, see AUDITORIUM, 3 and BOX.

BASOCHE, LA, see FRANCE, 1.

BASSERMANN. (1) AUGUST (1848–1931), German actor, who made his début at Dresden in 1873 and later played under Laube at the Vienna Stadttheater, where he appeared in such parts as Rolla, Karl Moor, and in contemporary French comedy. He then went on tour throughout Germany, and in 1895 became manager and leading player of the Mannheim Theatre, where he appeared in both classic and modern parts, his personal preference being for the former. From 1904 until his death he was director of the theatre at Carlsruhe. He went to New York several times, and played in the German Theatre there, being much admired in classic and heroic parts. His nephew (2) ALBERT (1867–) made his first appearance at Mannheim at the age of 19. He was a well-disciplined actor, who studied his roles with great care, and under Otto Brahm, whom he joined in 1899, he became the outstanding interpreter of Ibsen in Germany. He later worked under Reinhardt, and was considered one of the greatest actors of Germany until the rise to power of the Nazi party drove him to America. He went to Hollywood to play in films, and in 1944 appeared on Broadway in his first English-speaking part, as the Pope in *Embezzled Heaven*.

BATEMAN, a family of actors important in the history of the English stage, since it was under (1) HEZEKIAH LINTHICUM BATEMAN (1812–75) that Irving first appeared at the Lyceum, and after some initial disappointments persuaded his manager to put on *The Bells* (1871). Bateman, who was an American, married the half-sister of the famous comic vocalist Sam Cowell, (2) SIDNEY FRANCES (1823–81), actress and author, who after her husband's death continued to manage the Lyceum until Irving took over in 1878. She then assumed the management of Sadler's Wells, where she remained until her death. She had six children, her four daughters being all on the stage. The eldest (3) KATE (1843–1917) made her first appearance in Louisville, Kentucky, at the age of four and with (4) ELLEN DOUGLAS (1844–1936) toured in adult parts which included Richmond, Portia, and Lady Macbeth to her younger sister's Richard III, Shylock, and Macbeth. They were first seen in London in 1851. Ellen retired on her marriage to Claude Greppo in 1860 and returned to the United States, but Kate, as an adult actress, made a success in *Leah* (1863), and played opposite Irving at the Lyceum in Lady Macbeth and other parts. She retired in 1892, and under her married name, Mrs. George Crowe, conducted a school of acting in London. The third Bateman daughter (5) VIRGINIA FRANCES (1853–1940) was also on the stage as a child, and appeared at the Lyceum under her parents' management. She married the actor Edward Compton and became the mother of a distinguished progeny (see COMPTON). The youngest daughter (6) ISABEL EMILIE (1854–1934) was also at the Lyceum, and was associated with her mother in the management of Sadler's Wells. She then toured with her own company. In 1898 she left the stage and joined the Community of St. Mary the Virgin, Wantage, Berks., of which she later became Reverend Mother General.

BATES, BLANCHE (1872–1941), American actress, daughter of the manager of a theatre in Portland, Oregon, who was murdered while on tour in Australia. Her mother, a small, dark, frail woman, was an excellent actress, her Camille being highly thought of. Blanche made her first appearances on the stage in California, where she toured from 1894 to 1898, and then made a brief appearance in New York under the management of Augustin Daly. It was, however, as the leading lady of Belasco's company that she made her name, particularly by her moving performance of Madame Butterfly in 1900. She then played Cigarette in a dramatization of *Under Two Flags* (1901), Yo-san in *The Darling of the Gods* (1902), and the title-role in *The Girl of the Golden West* (1905), her last important part, though she continued to act under her own and other managements until

her retirement in 1927, from which she emerged briefly in 1933.

BATHYLLUS, a pantomime actor of Imperial Rome referred to by Juvenal (vi. 63) (see PANTOMIMUS).

BATTEN, a length of timber used to stiffen a surface of canvas or boards, as by 'sandwich-battening' a cloth (i.e. fixing the upper and lower edges between pairs of 3 inch or 4 inch by 1 inch battens screwed together), or by 'battening-out' a section of boards, or a run of flats, with crossbars. A row of lights fixed rigidly together is also known as a Light Batten (for the American use of batten see LIGHTING, 3).

BATTY'S AMPHITHEATRE, LONDON, see ASTLEY'S AMPHITHEATRE.

BATY, GASTON (1885–   ), French producer, whose work had much influence on the theatre between 1920 and 1940. After studying production in Germany he returned to Paris, and worked in a number of theatres, where he was responsible for the production of many experimental dramas by new authors. He also travelled extensively, but in 1930 settled in Paris at the Théâtre Montparnasse, to which he gave his own name. Here he put on an imposing series of old and new plays, many of them foreign classics, and several dramatizations of novels, which he prepared himself. The best was probably his version of *Crime and Punishment*. His own play, *Dulcinée* (1938), was based on an episode in *Don Quixote*. Baty has been accused of subordinating the text of his productions to the décor, which with him is all-important. This has led to a tendency to substitute pictorial groupings for action, but it has also given the theatre some fine work, as in *Maya*, *Cyclone*, *Simoun*, and *Martine*. In 1936 Baty was appointed one of the producers of the Comédie-Française, where he brought his undoubted erudition and fine theatrical sense to re-animate the classical repertory.

BAXTER, RICHARD (1593–?1666), English actor who appeared at the Red Bull for some fifteen years, probably beginning as a young apprentice of about 14 years of age. He remained there until 1623, when he joined the King's Men, playing minor roles. He was acting at the Red Bull when he accidentally hurt with his sword an apprentice, presumably a member of the audience seated on or near the stage. A riot threatened, but all was smoothed over. After the suppression of the theatres in 1642 Baxter was one of those who defied the ban, acting secretly with some of his companions in 1648. Downes gives a Mr. Baxter among the first actors at the Restoration who assembled under Killigrew. This may have been the same man.

BAYLIS, LILIAN (1874–1937), founder of the Old Vic and Sadler's Wells companies, and one of the outstanding women of the English theatre. She was appointed Companion of Honour in 1929 and was the second woman outside the University to be given an Hon. M.A. at Oxford (1924). Daughter of Newton Baylis and Liebe (Elizabeth) Cons, both singers, she was given a musical education which resulted in a life-long devotion to opera, and appeared in London, her birthplace, as a child prodigy. At the age of 16 she went with her family to South Africa, touring in a combined musical and dramatic entertainment, and later settled in Johannesburg, where she was one of the first teachers of music. Recalled to England to assist her aunt, Emma Cons, who since 1880 had been running the old Victoria Theatre as a temperance hall under the name of the Royal Victorian Coffee Music Hall, she took over the management in 1914, and from then on the history of her life must be looked for in her work. An intensely religious and single-minded woman, she brought all her forces to bear on the achievement of her object—a popular home for opera and, incidentally, drama. When drama threatened to oust opera, she looked about for another theatre, and took over, rebuilt, and opened in 1931 the Sadler's Wells Theatre, where the popularity of opera has again been equalled, if not surpassed, by that of ballet. Lilian Baylis may have had some faults, but they were offset by the fervour of her belief in the destiny of her theatres, by her tireless work for them, by her uncanny knack of inspiring enthusiasm, and by her perspicuity in choosing her collaborators, as witness her choice of Ninette de Valois as ballet-mistress, and the subsequent rise of a hitherto undreamed-of English Ballet, or her selection of Charles Corri as musical director, a position which he held for over thirty years.

Under Lilian Baylis's management the whole of Shakespeare's plays were given at the Old Vic, from *The Taming of the Shrew* in 1914 to *Troilus and Cressida* in 1923. *Hamlet* in its entirety was also given several times, and in later years plays by other dramatists were occasionally included in the programmes. But it was as the home of Shakespeare that the Old Vic made its name, and it is a tribute to the soundness of the foundations on which Lilian Baylis built up its reputation that her death, which might have meant the end of its greatness, so closely was it identified with her, has proved merely a milestone in its prosperous career.

BAYREUTH, a German town near Nuremberg, formerly the capital of Franconia, where the famous opera-composer Richard Wagner (1813–83) settled when he was about sixty, and made a festival-centre for the performance of his works. This continued after his death under his widow and children, and later under his grandchildren. The operas are given in a theatre specially built for the purpose—the Festspielhaus, which was paid for by private subscriptions and donations from various Wagner Societies. It was built by the Bayreuth architect Wölfel and the stage machinist Karl Brandt, for whose use Wagner borrowed from King Ludwig of Bavaria the plans made

by Gottfried Semper for the abandoned site at Munich. It had no galleries, and made use of the fan-shaped auditorium, first employed by the English architect Edward Shepherd in 1733, with rising rows of seats all facing the stage directly. The orchestra and the conductor were out of sight in a sunk pit, and the whole attention of the audience was thus concentrated on the stage. Most of these features were planned by Wagner himself. Alterations have been made in recent years, but the main design remains the same. The Festspielhaus was opened in August 1876 with a complete production, on four evenings, of 'Der Ring des Nibelungen'. Since then, at two-yearly intervals, a number of Wagner operas have been given, and the town has become a place of pilgrimage for lovers of Wagner's music. The festival probably reached its heyday under the control of Wagner's widow, from 1886 to 1906, when its stagecraft was unequalled, and its discipline and subordination of all details to the main purpose of music-making was an example to all opera-houses (see also ACOUSTICS, 8). (See Ernest Newman, *Life of Wagner*, vol. iii, ch. 17.)

The Royal Opera House at Bayreuth was built by the Bibienas in 1748 (see ACOUSTICS, 7).

BEARD, JOHN (*c.* 1716–91), English singer, for whom Handel composed some of his finest tenor roles. He was also a good actor, making his first appearance at Drury Lane in 1737 in ballad opera. One of his best parts was Macheath. A happy marriage interrupted his career for a time, but after the death of his wife he returned to the stage, in about 1743, and later married the daughter of John Rich, taking over the management of Covent Garden on the death of his father-in-law in 1761. Like Garrick, he was beaten by the rioters who opposed the removal of half-prices after the third act, though he managed to hold out against them rather longer. A man of excellent character, universally popular, he was president of the Beefsteak Club, where his recitations were much admired. He retired in 1767.

BEAUBOUR. (1) PIERRE TROCHON DE (1662– 1725), French actor, third husband of (2) LOUISE PITEL (*c.* 1665–1740) daughter of Mlle Beauval, last survivor of Molière's company. His wife played only secondary roles, but Beaubour, who had been brought from the provinces in 1691 to replace Baron, was accounted good in tragedy, though somewhat noisy and declamatory. He also lacked all sense of theatrical illusion, but his good looks and excellent presence helped to compensate for the absence of real talent. His influence on French acting was unfortunate, since he tended to force it back to its former stiffness, a style later abolished by the more natural approach of his successor, Dufresne. He retired in 1718, at the same time as his wife.

BEAUCHÂTEAU. (1) [FRANÇOIS MATHIEU

CHASTELET] (*fl.* 1625–65), French actor who joined the company at the Hôtel de Bourgogne at the same time as Bellerose, and remained there until 1634, when he went with his wife, (2) MADELEINE DE POUGET (1615–83), an actress whom he had married a year previously, to the Théâtre du Marais. Both husband and wife were parodied, as the young lovers, by Molière in his *Impromptu de Versailles* (1664), but they had their admirers, though, like Bellerose, they were somewhat insipid and sentimental.

BEAUMARCHAIS, PIERRE AUGUSTIN CARON DE (1732–99), French dramatist, among other things. The son of a watchmaker, who brought him up to his own trade, he was handsome and assured, and soon decided to turn his undoubted talents to something more lucrative. As a first step he married the young widow of a Court official, and took over her late husband's position. It was at this time that he added Beaumarchais to his original surname of Caron. A year later he was a widower, giving lessons on the harp to the daughters of Louis XV—Coche, Loque, Chiffe, and Graille, as their father called them—and directing the music of the Court concerts. He indulged in speculation under the able guidance of the financier Paris-Duverney, and after the latter's death engaged in unprofitable litigation. His interest in Spanish literature was first aroused when in 1764 he went to Madrid on behalf of his sister, entangled there in an unhappy love-affair. On his return he wrote his first play, *Eugénie*, which had a somewhat cool reception when produced at the Comédie-Française in 1767. He altered it considerably and it was then successful, as was *Les Deux Amis* (1770). Meanwhile Beaumarchais had been making himself heard outside the theatre, first by his quarrels with the Duc de Chaulnes over Mlle Ménard, an actress at the Comédie-Italienne, and particularly by his sallies against Goëzmann in his famous *Mémoires*, whose style and humour aroused the envy of Voltaire. Beaumarchais was fighting a popular battle, and though he lost it he became the idol of the people. All this was reflected in the turmoil which greeted his first great play, *Le Barbier de Séville* (1775). Originally intended as a play with music, and later used as the basis of an opera by Rossini, it was refused by the Comédie-Italienne, who thought its barber-hero a caricature of their leading actor, who had formerly been a barber himself. It was accepted by the Comédie-Française, but it took a long time to get permission for its production. Politically it was considered hazardous, and the censorship had no use for the outspokenness of the upstart valet. Beaumarchais fought hard for his play, and is reported to have said in conversation with Louis XVI that he would bring down the Bastille rather than see it kept off the stage. The Bastille was safe for a few more years, and the play was finally acted before an audience which still felt secure from the Revolution which it presaged. Nine years later, when *Le Mariage de Figaro* (1784)—used

by Mozart for his famous opera—was first given, again after a hard struggle, the situation was somewhat different. The public was beginning to realize the dangers that lay before it, and Figaro, older and wiser, criticizes not an individual man, as in the earlier play, but society as a whole. No wonder it needed, as was said at the time, more wit to get it put on the stage than to write it. These two plays sum up Beaumarchais's whole life and character. He is himself the precocious page, the handsome Almaviva—he was three times married—and above all he is Figaro, jack-of-all-trades, watchmaker, musician, financier, courtier, gun-runner, author, secret agent; in prison, ruined, embroiled with the law, libelled, harassed, hunted across Europe—all this according to his own account of his life—and yet always imperturbable, landing on his feet, clever, and unscrupulous.

His later dramatic works, *La Mère coupable*, a lachrymose play produced 1792, and an opera 'Tarare' (1787), which under cover of a story of Eastern despotism attacks the vices of the monarchy and the Church, are less interesting. More important was his part in breaking the stranglehold of the actors on their authors. Like many other dramatists of the day, he objected to the rules governing the financial relations of theatre and playwright, and was instrumental in getting them altered, though not as fundamentally as he wished. His later years were spent in the turmoil of the Revolution, of whose early utterances he had been the mouthpiece, and he was only saved from the guillotine by the fall of Robespierre. A few years later he died, 'suddenly and without illness, as he had aged without infirmity'.

BEAUMENARD, ROSE-PERRINE LE ROY (1730–99), French actress, wife of the actor Bellecourt. She made her début at the Opéra-Comique in 1743 with some success, and then toured the provinces, being a member of the company taken on his campaigns by Marshal Saxe. In 1749 she joined the Comédie-Française, where she excelled in the soubrettes of Regnard and Molière, being considered the perfect Nicole in *Le Bourgeois gentilhomme*. She was variously nicknamed La Rieuse and Gogo, and was a great favourite with the public. She retired from 1756 to 1761, but on her reappearance proved as good an actress as ever. After the Revolution she again retired, this time with no intention of returning, but by 1799 she was penniless, and forced to take up her former profession. She attempted to play Nicole, but was only a shadow of her former self, and died in the August of that year.

BEAUMONT, SIR FRANCIS (*c.* 1584–1616), English dramatist, whose name is so associated with that of John Fletcher (1579–1625) that they are usually spoken of in one breath, and scholars are still disentangling their separate contributions from the bulk of work that passes under their joint names. Beaumont had had some connexion with the stage, and written *The Woman Hater* and possibly *The Knight of* *the Burning Pestle,* before his name was first linked with Fletcher's in laudatory verses affixed to Jonson's *Volpone.* Their collaboration began in about 1608–9, and covered, according to some authorities, some six or seven plays, though in collections published in 1647 and 1679 fifty-three are assigned to them. Later investigations have attributed large parts of these to Massinger, Jonson, Tourneur, Middleton, Rowley, and Shirley, either in their original form or in later revisions. It is thought that Beaumont ceased to write for the stage on his marriage in 1613, although his work was once or twice seen at Court entertainments (for further details see FLETCHER).

BEAUPRÉ. (1) [NICOLAS LION] (*fl.* 1624–30), French actor, who with his wife (2) MADELEINE LEMOINE (*fl.* 1624–50) was in a somewhat obscure company which came to Paris in 1624. They both went to the Hôtel d'Argent and in 1630 Bellerose took the wife (the husband having just died) into his company at the Hôtel de Bourgogne, where she proved an excellent actress in both comedy and farce. At some point she returned to the company she had been with previously, which was now established at the Théâtre du Marais, for she played there in Corneille's *Cinna* (1640), and was still there when the troubles of the Fronde a couple of years later closed the theatres and sent the actors back into the provinces. She joined a provincial company, probably that of Filandre, which was going to the Low Countries, and was not heard of again in Paris. Her niece, (3) MAROTTE (*fl.* 1662–70), was in Molière's company.

BEAUVAL. (1) [JEAN PITEL] (*c.* 1635–1709), a French actor who was in the provincial troupe of Filandre in 1661. Here he met and married in about 1665 (2) JEANNE OLIVIER BOURGIGNON (*c.* 1648–1720), of whose early life little is known. She is said to have been an orphan who was adopted by a kind-hearted Dutch washerwoman and taken at the age of ten into Filandre's company as maid-of-all-work. Filandre taught her to read and write, and eventually entrusted her with small parts. After her marriage she and her husband joined another troupe and from it went to Molière's company in 1670. Beauval was a mediocre actor, though he was apparently good as Thomas Diafoirus in *Le Malade imaginaire,* more by nature than art. His wife, however, though rather coarse-featured and bad-tempered, was an excellent comic actress, and profited much by Molière's teaching. She was given to irresistible fits of laughter, which Molière incorporated into her part of Nicole in *Le Bourgeois gentilhomme.* She also played Zerbinette in *Les Fourberies de Scapin* and Toinette in *Le Malade imaginaire.* After Molière's death the Beauvals went to the Hôtel de Bourgogne, where the wife, who was competent in tragedy, played Oenone in *Phèdre,* and Cleopatra in *Rodogune.* She also took over the part of Hermione from Mlle Champmeslé. Both she and her husband became members

of the newly formed Comédie-Française, from which they retired in 1704, thus breaking the last direct link with Molière. Of Mlle Beauval's numerous children—she is thought to have had at least ten—one, (3) LOUISE (*c.* 1665–1740), played the part of Louison in *Le Malade imaginaire,* and later married, as her third husband, the actor Beaubour, both retiring in 1718.

BEAZLEY, SAMUEL (1786–1851), English architect, designer particularly of theatres, among them the Lyceum, the St. James's, the City of London, that part of the Adelphi fronting on the Strand, and the colonnade of Drury Lane. He left plans for theatres in several English provincial towns, and for places abroad. His buildings, though plain and somewhat uninteresting, were good and well adapted for their purpose. A prolific dramatist, mainly of ephemeral farces and short comedies, Beazley was also responsible for the translation of several operatic libretti.

BECCARI, AGOSTINO (?–1598), Italian dramatist, author of an early pastoral, *Il Sacrifizio,* which was performed at Ferrara in 1554–5, before the Duke and his Court. Although it contains some happy imitations of classical pastoral poetry, it is mainly important as having preceded and perhaps inspired the *Aminta* of Torquato Tasso. (See ITALY, 1 *b* ii.)

BECHER, LADY, see O'NEILL, ELIZA.

BECK, HEINRICH (1760–1803), a German actor, born in Gotha and intended for the Church, who began his career under Ekhof in his native town in 1777, at the same time as Beil and Iffland. He was tall and slim, and eminently suitable for juvenile leads. After Ekhof's death he went with the company to Mannheim under Dalberg, and became a friend of Schiller, playing the part of Ferdinand in the first production of *Kabale und Liebe,* in which his wife, an excellent little actress (Karoline Siegler), played Louise. He was also a life-long friend of Iffland, and was associated with him in his work at Mannheim, where he was on the administrative committee.

BECQUE, HENRI FRANÇOIS (1837–99), French dramatist, and one of the outstanding exponents of naturalistic drama. He had a hard life, which was reflected in his plays, and was of a somewhat quarrelsome and misanthropic turn of mind. His first work was a libretto, based on Byron's *Sardanapalus,* written in 1867 for Joncières. This was followed by a somewhat bitter comedy, *L'Enfant prodigue* (1868), and by *Michel Pauper* (1870), an important play which was overlooked on its first production, and only appreciated in a revival of 1886. Meanwhile Becque had written the two plays with which his name is usually associated, *Les Corbeaux* (1882) and *La Parisienne* (1885), both naturalistic dramas of great force and uncompromising honesty. They present rapacious or amoral characters who are unaware even of their own degradation, and unlike the 'well-made' play, against which they were a reaction, they leave it to the audience to draw their own conclusions, merely presenting the facts and not commenting on them. This was in the tradition of Zola's 'slice of life', of which Becque's *comédies rosses*, as they were called, were the natural outcome. Becque, who never again reached the heights of these two plays, though he continued to write until his death, was not fully appreciated until Antoine's Théâtre Libre had provided a stage for the new drama. He had a number of followers, of whom the most important was probably Georges Ancey.

BEDFORD, PAUL (*c.* 1792–1871), English actor who had already been many years on the stage as a singer in light and ballad opera when in 1838 he was engaged by Yates for the Adelphi to play second low-comedy parts. Here he made a great reputation in such parts as Blueskin in *Jack Sheppard* (1839), Jack Gong in *Green Bushes* (1845), and the Kinchin Cove in *Flowers of the Forest* (1847). Portly in later life, with a deep, rolling voice, he was a sound, reliable actor, who spent more than fifty years on the stage.

BEDLOW STREET THEATRE, NEW YORK, see GROVE THEATRE.

BEEKMAN STREET THEATRE, NEW YORK, see CHAPEL STREET THEATRE.

BEERBOHM, SIR MAX (1872–   ), English dramatic critic and half-brother of Sir Herbert Tree. He was dramatic critic of the *Saturday Review* from 1898 to 1910, succeeding Bernard Shaw, who, in his Valedictory, spoke of the younger generation knocking at the door, 'and as I open it, there steps spritely in the incomparable Max'.

Max lived up to this introduction. 'For my own part, I am a dilettante, a *petit maître*. I love best in literature delicate and elaborate ingenuities of form and style.' Yet he realized that, without personality, artistry goes for little, and his appreciation of the art of the theatre embraced almost every type of personality from the dignified actor of the legitimate stage to the homely humorist of the halls. The elegance of Max Beerbohm was that of the natural aristocrat which rises above snobbery. He held that vulgarity is an implicit element of the true music-hall. For all the enchanting lightness of his critical pen, it ran always to sincerity and often to wisdom. His twelve years of criticism brought distinction to the theatrical journalism of his time. Some of his best work reappeared in *Around Theatres* (1924). His one-act play, *The Happy Hypocrite*, based on one of his own short stories, was produced at the Royalty Theatre in 1900 by Mrs. Patrick Campbell, and a three-act version by Clemence Dane was seen at His Majesty's in 1936. His short play, *A Social Success*, was put on at the Palace Theatre in 1913 and in it George Alexander made his first music-hall appearance. In 1902 *The Fly on the Wheel*,

which Max wrote with Murray Carson, was produced at the Coronet Theatre. Beerbohm was knighted in 1939 for his services to literature.   T. C. K.

BEESTON. (1) CHRISTOPHER (?1570–1638), an important figure of the Jacobean and Caroline stage. He began his career as a member of Strange's Men, with whom Shakespeare was also connected. Though not named in the list of actors in Shakespeare's plays, Beeston was probably a minor member of the famous Chamberlain's Men, for Phillips, who left a legacy to Shakespeare and others of the company, left one also to Beeston. In 1602 Beeston was with Worcester's Men at the Rose and stayed with them when they became the Queen's Men on the accession of James I. He was appointed their business manager on the death in 1612 of Thomas Greene, the actor who had hitherto held this position. A few years later, in about 1616–17, he built or acquired the Cockpit in Drury Lane, also known as the Phoenix, which he leased to various companies, himself ceasing to act. He was apparently an excellent manager, but suspected of being more shrewd than honest in his dealings with the actors. In 1637 he collected and trained a young company called Beeston's Boys, some of whom later made their name in the Restoration Theatre. Beeston was a life-long friend and admirer of the dramatist-actor Thomas Heywood, many of whose plays were given at the Cockpit. When Beeston died his son (2) WILLIAM (?1606–82), who had acted with his father probably from boyhood, succeeded him as head of Beeston's Boys, but soon got into trouble with the authorities for performing an unlicensed play which gave offence to James I. William was imprisoned, and his place taken by Davenant, who was later to play so important a part in the history of the Restoration theatre; but in 1641, when Davenant had to leave England owing to his political activities, Beeston returned to the Cockpit. On the closing of the theatres in the following year his activities ceased, but he managed to acquire Salisbury Court, where he trained a company of boys. This theatre was one of the first to reopen in 1660, with a licence from Sir Henry Herbert, Master of the Revels, still under the control of Beeston, who also opened the Cockpit again, leasing it to John Rhodes's company, and probably to a company under the joint control of Davenant and Killigrew. With the granting of Royal Patents to the two last, however, Beeston was put out of business, and nothing further is known about him. He left a mark on the theatre, as being a link between the Elizabethan and Restoration stages, and his ability in training young actors, which is several times referred to in contemporary records, must have meant that some of the traditional business of the old actors reappeared in the work of many of the leading Restoration actors. He is suspected, perhaps unjustly, of being the 'ill Beest' who betrayed to Commonwealth soldiers the actors who were appearing secretly at Gibbon's Tennis-Court in 1652.

BEHN, Mrs. Aphra (1640–89), playwright and novelist and the first Englishwoman to earn a living by her pen. Brought up in the West Indies, the scene of her novel *Oroonoko* (dramatized in 1696 by Southerne), she returned to England in 1658 and married a merchant of Dutch extraction. Soon widowed, she went to Holland during the Dutch war as a spy, and did good work, for which she does not appear to have been paid. In any case, she was shortly afterwards imprisoned for debt, from which she may have been saved by the intervention of Killigrew. Her first play, *The Forced Marriage; or, the Jealous Bridegroom* (1670), was a tragi-comedy given at Dorset Garden with Betterton and his wife in the leading parts. Otway, the dramatist, also made his first and last appearance on the stage in this play, with such conspicuous lack of success that he gave up all thought of being an actor. It was, however, in comedies of intrigue that Mrs. Behn did her best work, and her first substantial success came with *The Rover; or, the Banished Cavalier* (1677), with Betterton in the name part and Lee and Underhill as the comedians. The play, in a modified version, was often revived, the part of Willmore the Rover being a favourite one with leading actors. It was followed by several other comedies, of which *The Feign'd Curtizans; or, a Night's Intrigue* (1678), was a complicated affair dedicated to Nell Gwynn, while *The Roundheads; or, the Good Old Cause* (1681), and *The City-Heiress; or, Sir Timothy Treat-All* (1682), owed most of their success to their topicality. Her later plays were less successful, though *The Emperor of the Moon* (1687), a pantomime-farce based on a *commedia dell' arte* scenario recently given in Paris, is historically interesting. Anthony Leigh played Scaramouche and Jevon Harlequin; the play was frequently revived and was the forerunner of the many harlequinades which later led to the English pantomime.

Aphra Behn, whose plays have been edited by Montague Summers, is said to have introduced milk punch into England. Witty and high-spirited, she was the friend of Dryden, Otway, Southerne, and other prominent literary men of the time. She worked hard, and was more prolific than any dramatist of her day except Dryden, and the coarseness of her work is often compensated by excellent lyrics. It has been the fashion to consider her a loose-living creature, a scandal in a scandalous age, but her unremitting industry argues at least some time taken from the pursuit of pleasure, and on examination her plays are found to be somewhat better than those of the average playwright of the day. Much of their indecency is due to the fashion of the time, and to the necessity for writing with masculine pungency if they were to be given a hearing. Allardyce Nicoll says:

Indecent, free, sometimes positively vulgar, she was in several of her plays; but, on the whole, when we compare her works with similar productions of D'Urfey, and Shadwell, even of Dryden, we must be prepared to admit the comparative purity of her dialogue. She has, moreover, on many occasions introduced thoughts and ideas which not only display her unconventional and modern attitude towards life's relations, but also formed the basis for not a few moralisations in the sentimental eighteenth century to come!

BEHRMAN, Samuel Nathaniel (1893–   ), American dramatist, who combines deft characterization and sparkling dialogue in the pursuit of high comedy. Born in Worcester, he attended Clark University, Baker's playwriting workshop at Harvard, and Columbia University; then wrote criticism, read plays professionally, acted as a theatrical press agent, and collaborated with Kenyon Nicholson on the trifles *Bedside Manner* (1923) and *Love Is Like That* (1927). His apprenticeship ended with *The Second Man* (1927), a bright comedy of manners concerning a young girl's infatuation with a cynical novelist. It was followed by *Serena Blandish* (1929), a comedy based on a novel (by Enid Bagnold) about a girl's adventures in Mayfair society, and *Meteor* (1929), a tantalizing study of an egotist in the world of business enterprise. *Brief Moment* (1931) dramatized the romance and misalliance of a socially prominent young man. *Biography* (1932) provided a provocative study of contrasts of temperament in the romance of a carefree woman portrait-painter and a crusading journalist who leaves her when she proves too indulgent toward reactionary politicians. *Rain From Heaven* (1934) used conflicting viewpoints at an English house-party to establish the untenability of civilized detachment in a strife-ridden world. *End of Summer* (1936) described the bankruptcy of the idle rich. As a pleasant interlude between this play and *Wine of Choice* (1938), a wavering political comedy, Behrman adapted Jean Giraudoux's *Amphitryon 38* for the Lunts. With *No Time for Comedy* (1939), however, the playwright returned to a social problem in the dilemma of a writer who wants to express the tragedy of his times but has a talent only for light comedy. The problem was, in a sense, a personal one, since *The Talley Method* (1940), the study of a domestic tyrant, and *Dunnigan's Daughter* (1945), an exposé of a ruthless capitalist, proved unrewarding, whereas his next trifle for the Lunts, *The Pirate* (1942), adapted from a play by Fulda, succeeded. Behrman was able to fuse comedy and the serious subject of the fall of France in an adaptation of Franz Werfel's *Jacobowsky and the Colonel* (1944), but *Jane* (1947), a dramatization of the Somerset Maugham story, was another light comedy.

J. G.

BEIL, Johann David (1754–94), German actor who, after several years in small touring companies, went to Gotha to act under the great Ekhof in 1777, the same year as Iffland. He was excellent in comic parts, a good mimic and lively observer. In person he was round-faced and jolly. He went with the company to Mannheim under Dalberg after Ekhof's death, and played in Schiller's early works, and in the plays of Iffland, to whom he proved a loyal friend and colleague during the great days of the Mannheim stage. Unfortunately he was much given to drink and fell a victim to it at the early age of forty, much to the despair of Iffland, who had just been appointed producer to the theatre, and in addition had to take on a number of Beil's leading roles.

BÉJART, a family of actors intimately associated with Molière. The eldest daughter, (1) MADELEINE (1618–72), was already an actress of some repute in the provinces when Molière met her, and it is usually assumed that it was for love of her that he became an actor. Together they formed a company which played in Paris without success under the name of the Illustre-Théâtre. They then went into the provinces, where they amalgamated with a troupe under Dufresne, of which Molière soon became the leader. Madeleine returned to Paris with Molière in 1658, shared in his success, and remained with him at the Palais-Royal until her death a year before his. In her early years she played the heroines of classical tragedy, and in later life created a number of Molière's witty maids who ridicule the follies of their mistresses. At one time she managed the finances of the company. It is impossible to assess how much Molière owed to her constant affection and support over a period of thirty years. Associated with her in the Illustre-Théâtre were her brother (2) JOSEPH (c. 1620–59) and her sister (3) GENEVIÈVE (c. 1622–75). In spite of a stammer Joseph was a useful actor, and a popular member of the company. His death soon after they were established in Paris was a great blow. He was taken ill during a performance of L'Étourdi. Little is known of Geneviève, who was called Mlle Hervé from her mother's maiden name, beyond the fact that she was twice married and was probably better in tragedy than in comedy. During its travels Molière's company was augmented by the arrival of another brother, (4) LOUIS (1625–78), who was known as L'Éguisé on account of his sharp tongue. He also accompanied Molière to Paris, and did yeoman service in the company until his retirement in 1670. He was lame in the right leg, a trait which Molière incorporated into the part of La Flèche in L'Avare, where Harpagon calls him 'lame dog', and the limp has remained traditional for this character. He was the first of Molière's actors to draw a pension. The last, and in some ways most important, member of the family was (5) ARMANDE GRÉSINDE CLAIRE ÉLISABETH (1642–1700), whom Molière married in 1662 in the church from which the signal for the massacre of St. Bartholomew was given. She had been brought up by Madeleine, who had herself lost a girl-child at the time of Armande's birth, and contemporary gossip believed her to be Madeleine's daughter. Molière was therefore accused of having married the child of his late mistress, and even, by the rival actor Montfleury, his own daughter

by Madeleine, a calumny which has never been expressly disproved, though it is no longer credited. The marriage was an unhappy one, and after Molière's death his young widow married an actor named Guérin d'Étriché, and was apparently happy with him. She was an excellent actress, who owed all her training to Molière. She first appeared on the stage as Élise in his Critique de l'École des femmes and as herself in L'Impromptu de Versailles (both 1663). In the following year she played a gipsy woman in Le Mariage forcé, when she had the honour of dancing with Louis XIV, and had her first important part as the heroine in La Princesse d'Élide. After 1664 she played most of Molière's heroines. Whatever her faults, she was an able and energetic woman, and contemporaries admired the firm way in which she kept her company together after her husband's death. She had three children of whom only one, a girl, survived.

BELASCO, DAVID (1859–1931), American actor-manager and playwright, and for many years one of the outstanding personalities of the American stage. Born in California, of a Portuguese-Hebrew family originally named Valasco, he inherited his good looks from his father, who had been a harlequin at various London theatres, and his strong-willed and imperious temperament from his mother. His love for the stage showed itself in early days, and as a child he appeared at the local theatre in Pizarro, East Lynne, and Richard III, playing the little Duke of York to Charles Kean's Richard on the latter's farewell tour. Belasco later joined the stock company of the San Francisco Theatre, where he played with John McCullough, Booth, and other famous actors. He married at 20, dabbled in journalism, and for several years led the usual life of the itinerant actor, travelling the Pacific Coast. He served his apprenticeship to playwriting by dramatizing novels, poems, and stories, and by adapting old plays, a task made less onerous by the lack of any copyright laws. As stage-manager at various theatres he devised some spectacular melodramas, with battles, fires, and other calamities, and produced an overwhelming Passion Play with real sheep. All this served as a useful introduction to his career in New York, where he later became the outstanding purveyor of 'sensation drama'. He first appeared there with Herne in 1879 in Hearts of Oak (also known as Chums), a joint adaptation of an old melodrama entitled The Mariner's Compass. It was not a success, and Belasco returned to California to continue his stage-management and play-doctoring, until shortly afterwards he was called to New York again by the Frohmans to succeed Steele Mackaye as director of the Madison Square Theatre. Here his first venture was Young Mrs. Winthrop (1882), and in 1884 he produced his own May Blossom, in which year he also made his first visit to England. In 1886 he was engaged by Daniel Frohman to manage the Lyceum, where he remained until 1890, continuing to turn out a number of plays, mainly in collaboration. Success finally came with *The Girl I Left Behind Me* (1893), written in collaboration with Franklyn Fyles, and *The Heart of Maryland* (1895), based on the American Civil War, in which Maurice Barrymore was excellent as the hero. *Zaza* (1898), an adaptation from the French, starred Mrs. Carter, whom Belasco had launched on a spectacular career some years before. It was a success both in New York and in London, and was followed by *Madame Butterfly* (1900), in which Blanche Bates, another of Belasco's stars, gave a fine performance as the Japanese girl, a part played in London by Evelyn Millard. This dramatization of a story by John Luther Long was seen by Puccini, and used as the basis of an opera, as was *The Girl of the Golden West* (1905). Meanwhile Belasco had begun his association with the actor David Warfield, whom he took from the Variety stage and starred in *The Auctioneer* (1901). He also achieved a lifelong ambition by leasing the Republic Theatre from Hammerstein. Completely rebuilt, and re-christened the Belasco, it opened with a revival of *Du Barry*, with Mrs. Carter, which had previously been seen at the Criterion Theatre. This was followed by *The Darling of the Gods* (1902), another Japanese story written in collaboration with John Luther Long, in which Blanche Bates played the heroine and George Arliss the villainous Minister for War, and by *Sweet Kitty Bellairs* (1903). Other successes at this first Belasco theatre were *Adrea* (1905), with Mrs. Carter, and *The Rose of the Rancho* (1906), while Warfield scored a triumph in *The Music Master* (1904), in which he toured for many years.

In 1906 Belasco built his own theatre, known first as the Stuyvesant, under which name it opened in 1907 with *A Grand Army Man*. It took the name of Belasco in 1910, when the former Belasco reverted to its original title of the Republic. Here Belasco remained until his death, and his private rooms in the theatre, where priceless *objets d'art* were jumbled up with theatrical properties in artistic disorder, presided over by the owner with his deceptively benign and clerical appearance, have passed into legend. Here he produced *The Return of Peter Grimm* (1911) with Warfield as the old man who returns after death to rectify the errors of his life; *The Case of Becky* (1912) with Frances Starr, dealing with a dual personality and hypnotism; *Kiki* (1921) with Leonora Ulric; *Laugh, Clown, Laugh* (1923), based on an Italian play; and, his last production as well as his last play, *Mini* (1928), adapted from *The Red Mill* by Ferenc Molnar.

It will be seen that Belasco ended his career as he began it, adapting the work of another. He contributed little that was original to the American stage, and can in no sense be said to have encouraged the national American drama which was growing up round him. He belongs to the great age of American stagecraft, when the subject-matter of drama was imported from Europe, and his great contribution to the American scene lay in his elaborate scenic displays, his passion for realism, which led him in *The Governor's Lady* (1912) to place an exact replica of a Child's restaurant on the stage, and in the strong vehicles which he provided for the stars of the day, many of them becoming stars only through his efforts. He was in the widest sense a man of the theatre, though he himself never acted after 1880, and even his weaknesses, his vanity, his craving for admiration and his constant posturing, were products of his intensely dramatic nature. As a stage-director he was meticulous, a hard master but a just one, and he should be judged on what he did for the American stage, and not on what he failed to do. His long career covers a transition period in the history of American drama, and it was inevitable that he should give the weight of his authority to the older, romantic, flamboyant period, rather than to the less spectacular though more truly realistic drama of the new age. Yet he did not disdain the mechanical inventions of the day, and made interesting and often far-reaching experiments in the use of light. Perhaps the greatest achievement of his career was his production in 1922 of *The Merchant of Venice*, with Warfield as Shylock. Nor should his long fight against the stranglehold of the Theatrical Syndicate, and his ultimate triumph, go unrecorded, since it involved the whole question of the freedom of the American theatre, and the independence of the artist in the theatre. His large collection of theatrical material is now housed in the New York Public Library. The second Belasco Theatre (for the first see also REPUBLIC) is still owned by his estate, though controlled for bookings by the Shuberts. It was at one time leased to Katharine Cornell, who produced there *Alien Corn* and a translation of Obey's *Le Viol de Lucrèce*. Two of Elmer Rice's plays were first given at the Belasco, while for six years the Group Theatre had their headquarters there, producing the plays of Odets. In 1945 *Trio*, a play on an equivocal theme which caused a good deal of trouble, was seen at the Belasco for a short run which was terminated by the censor.

BELCARI, FEO (1410–84), early Italian dramatist, author of a number of religious dramas written about 1450 (see ITALY, 1 *a* ii).

BEL GEDDES, NORMAN-, see COSTUME, 10 *b*, SCENERY, 6 and U.S.A., 2.

BELGIUM. The early history of Belgium provided little opportunity for a peaceful development of a native drama, and the bilingual nature of its people has led to progress in two directions—French and Flemish. The first followed fairly closely the general trend of the theatre in Paris, and tragedies written in the early seventeenth century are modelled on the earlier French examples. It was not until the late nineteenth-century spread of naturalism on the one hand and symbolism on the other that the Belgian-French theatre took on a separate existence, and, with the works of its greatest poet and dramatist, Maurice Maeterlinck (1862–1949), entered the main stream of European literature. Other dramatists of this period worthy of mention are Émile Verhaeren (1855–1916), whose most successful play was *Les Aubes* (1898), and Georges Rodenback (1855–98), author of the poetic drama *Le Mirage* (1901), taken from one of his novels; both these men are better known by their other works, however, and Maeterlinck remains the outstanding dramatist of Belgium.

In spite of poor audiences and the lack of first-rate authors and actors, many of whom have migrated to Paris, there has always been a great deal of theatrical activity in Belgium, particularly in Brussels, where the two most famous theatres are the Théâtre de la Monnaie and the Théâtre du Parc. The early years of the twentieth century saw a rapid increase in the number of playhouses, mainly of the Little or Art Theatre type, and in 1945 a Belgian National Theatre was founded under the direction of the Huisman brothers, who had formerly been directors of the Comédiens Routiers, founded in 1934. This group, influenced by the work of the Russian theatre and of Jacques Copeau, toured Belgium with a repertory of classics and fairy-tale plays. They continued their work during the war, when they achieved immense popularity with a production of *Les Quatre Fils Aymon*, banned by the Germans but successfully played more than a hundred times. It is to be hoped that their courage and enterprise will prove useful to the Belgian National Theatre, which has made a good start, not only in Brussels, but as a centre for the co-ordination of theatrical activities all over Belgium.

The Flemish stage, whose history is linked with that of the Dutch, has also its part in the new National Theatre, and a Flemish-speaking company plays in Antwerp, Brussels, and other large towns, as well as touring the country-side.

BELGRAVIA THEATRE, LONDON, see COURT THEATRE.

BELL, JOHN (1745–1831), English publisher and bookseller, who, though quite uneducated, was a pioneer of good printing with excellent engravings. One of his most important ventures was the publication of *Bell's British Theatre*, a comprehensive selection of plays, each prefaced by an interesting character portrait. His 1773 acting edition of Shakespeare, edited by Francis Gentleman—not to be confused with the 1788 edition of Johnson and Steevens—was based on the prompt-books of the Theatres Royal, and is interesting as showing what was actually performed on the stage at the time. He was also the publisher of *Bell's Weekly Messenger*, which appeared on Sundays from 1801 until well after the accession of Queen Victoria, and of several other papers and journals, including *La Belle Assemblée*, a monthly review of fashion. He was the first to discard the long s, and Leigh Hunt said of him: 'His taste in putting forth a publication, and

getting the best artists to adorn it, was new in those times and may be admired in any.'

BELL, JOHN JOY (1871–1938), Scottish dramatist, and one of the pioneer writers of plays in the Scots vernacular. His work was represented in the repertory of the Glasgow Repertory Theatre under Alfred Wareing's management. In *The Thread o' Scarlet* (1923) Bell made a definite contribution to the series of thrillers and Grand Guignol pieces that Edgar Wallace and others supplied to the theatre in the years immediately following the war of 1914–18. His other plays include *Wee Macgregor*, a classic of Glasgow working-class life, *The Pie in the Oven*, and *The Coortin' o' Kirsteen*.   W. J.

BELLAMY, GEORGE ANNE (*c.* 1727–88), English actress, rival of Mrs. Cibber in the heroines of tragedy, who received her first names from a mishearing of Georgiana at her christening. She was the child of Lord Tyrawley by a Quakeress, Miss Seal, who eloped with him from boarding school and later married a sea-captain named Bellamy. Tyrawley, however, acknowledged his daughter, had her educated, and would have done much for her had she not disobeyed him by going to live with her mother. Introduced to Rich, she appeared at Covent Garden, possibly in 1744 as Miss Prue in *Love for Love*, and certainly, as her early biographies say, two years later with Quin in *The Orphan*. Taken up by her father's relatives, she was much petted and spoiled, and at one time administered a severe snub to Garrick, who had thought her too young to play Constance with him in *King John*. Beautiful, arrogant, and extravagant, she was twice married, once bigamously, and much public scandal attached itself to her name. As an actress she was at her best in romantic and tragic parts, being an admirable Juliet to the Romeo of Garrick, who admired her acting sufficiently to make her one of his leading ladies at Drury Lane; but she had none of the professional probity of Peg Woffington or indeed of Mrs. Cibber, and much of her success was due to her youth and beauty. When these left her, the more quickly for her riotous pursuit of pleasure, managers were chary of engaging her, and an appearance in Dublin in 1780 was a complete failure. She continued to act intermittently until her retirement in 1785, when a benefit was organized for her at Covent Garden, but was constantly harassed by her creditors and held in very little esteem by the public or her fellow actors. In 1785 appeared her *Apology* for her life, in six volumes, edited by another hand, a sensational affair, readable rather than reliable.

BELLECOURT [JEAN CLAUDE GILLES COLSON] (1725–78), French actor, husband of Mlle Beaumenard. He was in his youth a painter, and studied under Carl Van Loo. At the same time he appeared in several amateur dramatic productions with a success which, joined to a secret predilection for the stage, decided him to become an actor. He went into the provinces, and by dint of hard work made so much progress that in 1750 he was accepted by the Comédie-Française instead of Lekain, who presented himself at the same time. This was chiefly owing to his fine stage presence, for Lekain was undoubtedly the better actor. When Lekain was finally admitted to the company Bellecourt, who had no aptitude for tragedy, was happy to hand over to him all the tragic roles, reserving for himself the fine gentlemen of comedy, in which he excelled.

BELLEROSE [PIERRE LE MESSIER] (c. 1600–70), French actor, first found in a provincial company in 1619 and in Paris three years later. After bitter controversy with the Confraternity of the Passion, holders of the old monopoly of acting in Paris, a company of which Bellerose was a member took permanent possession of the Hôtel de Bourgogne, where it remained until the foundation of the Comédie-Française in 1673, and some time between 1630–4 Bellerose became its acknowledged head. He was an excellent actor both in comedy and tragedy, though some critics found him insipid and sentimental. Unlike his rival Montdory, he was not a ranter. His style was quiet and rhetorical rather than declamatory, and the name part in Corneille's *Le Menteur* (1643), with which he is particularly associated, though he was not the first to play it, was probably well suited to his style. Bellerose's acting may have helped to raise the prestige of the serious actor and oust from public favour the older generation of farce-players. He figures as himself in *La Comédie des comédiens* (1633), and created a number of roles in pastoral and tragi-comedy during the years of transition from early farce to French classical tragedy. He controlled the Hôtel de Bourgogne for many years, and his traditions were carried on by his successors Montfleury and Floridor. His wife, Nicole Gassot (?–1680), widow of an actor named Meslier, had red hair and was an excellent actress. She retired in 1660 with a pension.

BELLEVILLE, the name under which the great French comedian Turlupin played serious parts at the Hôtel de Bourgogne from 1612 to 1627.

BELLEW, HAROLD KYRLE (1855–1911), English actor, who was for some time in the navy. He made his first appearance on the stage in Australia in 1874, and in the following year went to England, appearing at Brighton under the name of Harold Kyrle. He reverted to his own name in 1878, when he joined Irving at the Lyceum, having previously been with the Bancrofts and Adelaide Neilson. In 1885 he was first seen in New York, appearing at Wallack's in old comedy, in which he was at his best, his finest parts being Orlando and Charles Surface. He was for a long time associated with Mrs. Brown-Potter, in whose company he toured extensively, leaving it to settle in Australia, where he made money in mining. In 1902 he returned to the New York stage and

remained there until his death, two of his best-remembered parts being Raffles and Brigadier Gerard. He was a man of great charm, handsome, with clear-cut features and a gentlemanly ease of address, added to an extremely beautiful voice and fine elocution.

BELL INN, see INNS USED AS THEATRES.

BELLOY, PIERRE LAURENT BUIRETTE DE (1727–75), French dramatist, known by one play only, *Le Siège de Calais*, given at the Comédie-Française in 1765. It owed its great and unexpected success to the acting of Lekain, Molé, and Mlle Clairon, but above all to its topicality. France had just signed a humiliating peace, and the audience were consoled by seeing themselves, on the stage, forcing the admiration of their conquerors by their moral virtues. The play itself is of little value, and shows only too clearly the continued decline of classical French tragedy. It contains little or no psychology, the speeches are trivial and narrative rather than poetic; but it came at the right moment, and after a successful start in Paris it was often revived in the provinces, being played before soldier audiences to arouse their patriotism. De Belloy, who was early orphaned and brought up by an uncle for the law, ran away and became an actor under the name of Dormont de Belloy. He was for some years in a French company at the Court of St. Petersburg. He wrote a number of other plays which had little success at the time, and are now forgotten.

BELLWOOD, BESSIE (1847–96), a music-hall performer, best remembered for her singing of 'What Cheer, Riah!' As Bessie Mahoney she was for some time a rabbit-skinner in the New Cut, near the Old Vic. After a riotous first appearance at the Star, Bermondsey, she was given an audition at the Holborn, and turned down as being 'too quiet', a judgement which her later career did much to disprove. She had a happy knack of indulging in repartee with members of the audience, usually in the gallery, who invariably got as good as they gave. In private life a warm-hearted, generous woman and a fervent Catholic, she was one of the most high-spirited stars of the day, both on and off the stage, and many racy stories, some probably apocryphal, are associated with her name.

BELMONT THEATRE, NEW YORK, a small, intimate playhouse which opened on 18 Jan. 1918 as the Norworth, with Jack Norworth, one-time husband and partner of Nora Bayes, as owner and star. It received its present name a few months later, but its early years were not successful. Its first real hit was scored by the Pulitzer Prize-winner for 1920–1, *Miss Lulu Bett*. In the following season *The Hero* also had a respectable run, and was included by Burns Mantle among the ten best plays of the season. A more popular success was scored by *Tarnish* (1923), and in the same year the Belmont saw *You and I*, the first play by Philip Barry, fresh from study under Baker at the '47

Workshop', and later one of America's outstanding dramatists. Two more successes were *Young Woodley* in 1925 and a revue in 1926, after which the fortunes of the house appeared to decline, in spite of redecoration and many determined bids for popularity.   G. F.

BELOW, see STAGE DIRECTIONS.

BEL SAVAGE INN, see INNS USED AS THEATRES.

BELTRAME, see BARBIERI.

BENAVENTE, JACINTO (1866–), the outstanding contemporary Spanish dramatist, winner of the Nobel Prize for Literature, 1922. He brought to the stage an impeccable technique and a wide knowledge of the works of contemporary European dramatists, translating into Spanish some of the plays of Shakespeare and Molière. His own works, which are numerous, range from light comedies, as in the one-act collection *Teatro fantástico* (published in 1892), to the Freudian intensity of *La malquerida* (1913), and include satire, sentiment, philosophy, wit, and symbolism. His acknowledged masterpiece is *Los Intereses creados* (1907), done in English as *The Bonds of Interest*, in which he works out his conception of the world as a place in which aesthetic values only can help mankind on his pilgrimage, and love alone give him a glimpse of the divine. Of his other plays, the most important are *Gente conocida* (1896), *El marido de la Tellez* (1897), *Los malhechores del bien* (1905), and *Más fuerte que el amor* (1906)—penetrating studies of contemporary society, exposing its follies and vices with smiling irony.

BENCHLEY, ROBERT CHARLES (1889–1945), American man of letters, a fine humorist turned dramatic critic. Though he wrote in a light vein, his judgement of actors and plays was very sound, and he was a discerning reporter. Born in Worcester, Massachusetts, he graduated from Harvard in 1912. He was editor of *The New York Tribune Sunday Magazine* in 1916 and managing editor of *Vanity Fair* in 1919. In 1920 he became dramatic critic of *Life*, and his witty work at once attracted wide attention, boosting the magazine's circulation considerably. In 1929 he joined *The New Yorker* as dramatic critic, but retired in 1939 to devote his time to motion picture acting. Before this he had appeared on the stage as an actor in *The Music Box Revue of 1924*. Unfortunately, there is no collected volume of his criticisms, but many of them may be found scattered through his books: *After 1903—What?*, *My Ten Years in a Quandary*, *The Early Worm*, and *Inside Benchley*.   T. Q. C.

BENDINELLI, GIACINTO (?–1668), an actor of the *commedia dell'arte*, who played the part of a young lover under the name of Valerio. He is first noted in the Modena troupe in 1651, and went to Paris in 1660, where he married a French actress, Jeanne-Marie Poulain, retiring a few years later.

BENEFIT, a performance of a play, the entire financial proceeds of which were given to one— or at the most two—members of the company. In the days of the sharing system and the stock company an actor might rely almost entirely on his benefit night to provide him with ready money, his weekly 'share' hardly paying current expenses. Doran, in *Their Majesties' Servants*, says that the first actor's, as distinct from author's (see ROYALTY), benefit was given for Mrs. Barry on the order of King James, and that 'what was commenced as a compliment soon passed into a custom'. In France the first benefit is believed to have been given in 1735 for Mlle Gaussin after she had lost all she possessed in a fire. It was a vicious system, which exposed the actor to constant humiliation and kept him in a vacillating condition of affluence and penury. It lingered on in the provinces long after it had been abandoned in London, as can be seen from the accounts of the Crummles family in *Nicholas Nickleby*, and the abuse of the system in the early American theatre can be studied in Odell's *Annals of the New York Stage*. It was abolished at Wallack's in 1867–8, salaries being raised instead. A slightly more dignified method of making money was the Bespeak Performance, whereby a wealthy patron would take up most of the tickets and sell or give them to his friends, choosing his own play from the company's repertory. Exceptional benefit nights might be given for the family of an actor or actress who had recently died, or for one in retirement who had fallen on bad times; but in general the proceeds of a benefit night went to an acting member of the company, who might choose the play in which he wished to appear, and often took the opportunity of introducing one of his own (see also PROVINCIAL THEATRES, 1 *d*).

BENELLI, SEM (1875–1949), Italian dramatist, considered in some ways the only outstanding follower of the methods of d'Annunzio, with less poetry, perhaps, but more strength and subtlety. Among his plays, which were first brought into prominence by the Compagnia Stabile Argentina, founded in 1906, the most important is probably *La Cena delle beffe* (1909), a Renaissance melodrama of jealousy and fratricide which, as *The Jest*, was done in New York by John Barrymore and his brother Lionel in 1919. It was in blank verse, as was Benelli's *L'Amore dei Tre Re* (1910). His other works included the modern prose comedy, *La Tignola* (1908).

BENFIELD, ROBERT (?–1649), English actor, who joined the famous King's Men in about 1615. He replaced Ostler, in whose part of Antonio in *The Duchess of Malfi* he appeared in the 1619 revival. Before that he had been with two or three other companies, and was probably not a young man when he joined the King's, since he regularly took such elderly and dignified parts as Kings, Counsellors, and Noble Old Men. His name appears in the list of actors in Shakespeare's plays, and in those of Beaumont and Fletcher. He also played the part of Junius Rusticus in *The Roman Actor* (1626) and of Ladislaus King of Hungarie in *The Picture* (1629), both by Massinger. Benfield was not an original shareholder in the Globe or the Blackfriars, but he later acquired some interest in both.

BENGER, SIR THOMAS, see MASTER OF THE REVELS.

BENINI, FERRUCCIO (1854–1925), Italian dramatist and actor, author of a number of plays in Venetian dialect played by his own company. He himself was a comedian of repute, with an ugly, mobile face and expressive gesture, one of his best parts being the untruthful, but fascinating, hero of Goldoni's *Il Bugiardo*. His repertory extended over the comedies of Goldoni and Gallina and a few modern pieces, including his own, written specially for him.

BENNETT, (ENOCH) ARNOLD (1867–1931), English novelist and dramatist, whose reputation rests more upon his novels than upon his plays, although he enjoyed considerable success in the theatre. His plots were ingeniously constructed, and his character-drawing had vitality and was mellowed by a homely humour. *The Great Adventure* (1913) had much success and owed a great deal to the fine acting of Henry Ainley and Wish Wynne. *Milestones* (written in collaboration with Edward Knoblock) was produced at the Royalty Theatre in 1912 and ran for 607 performances. It was revived at the same theatre in 1920. Bennett's other plays include: *Cupid and Commonsense* (1908), *What the Public Wants* (1909), *The Honeymoon* (1911), *Rivals for Rosamund* (1914), *The Title* (1918), *Judith* and *Sacred and Profane Love* (both 1919), *The Love Match* and *Body and Soul* (both 1922), and *London Life* (1924), written with Edward Knoblock.   T. C. K.

BENOIS, ALEXANDRE (1870–   ), Russian artist, who, with Diaghilev, was responsible for taking the Russian Imperial Ballet to Western Europe. He himself did the décor for many of the early ballets, including 'Les Sylphides', and was responsible for the artistic policy of the Ballets Russes until 1914 (see BALLET, 7 and COSTUME, 9).

BENSERADE, ISAAC DE (1613–91), French poet and dramatist, related to Cardinal Richelieu, who gave him a pension. He came of a good Norman family, and was intended for the Church. But a passion for the wife of the actor Bellerose, contracted while he was studying theology in Paris, turned his thoughts to the theatre, and in 1635 he produced his first play, a comedy of little account, followed in the next year by a tragedy, *Cléopâtre*, the best of his not very considerable output. On the death of Richelieu he gave up writing plays, and devoted himself to the composition of libretti for ballets, then much in favour at Court. He excelled at this, and collaborated with Molière and Lully in *Les Fêtes de l'Amour et de Bacchus.*

BENSLEY, ROBERT (*c.* 1738–1817), English actor, who went on the stage after seeing service as a marine. After some years in the provinces he appeared at Drury Lane in 1765, and was seen there and at Covent Garden, retiring in 1796. He played few new parts, since little of any value was being written at the time, and his best work was done in such characters as Malvolio, Pierre in *Venice Preserved*, and Evander in *The Grecian Daughter*, which he played, just before his retirement, to the Euphrasia of Mrs. Siddons. A man of unblemished character and a sound actor, he was often severely criticized, and seems to have had to overcome several physical disabilities. Lamb, however, speaks feelingly of him.

BENSON, SIR FRANK ROBERT (1858–1939), English actor-manager best remembered for the Shakespearian company which he founded. With this he toured the provinces, keeping the plays of Shakespeare always before the public, and at the same time providing a fine training for countless young actors and actresses, all of whom in later years were proud of being Old Bensonians. A man of breeding and culture, Benson, who was the son of a wealthy barrister, was educated at Winchester and Oxford, where he was a prominent member of O.U.D.S. Among the parts he played there was Clytemnestra in his own production of the *Agamemnon* of Aeschylus in the original. He made his first appearance on the professional stage in 1882, at the Lyceum under Irving, as Paris, and in the following year took his own company on tour, producing in due course all Shakespeare's plays with the exception of *Titus Andronicus* and *Troilus and Cressida*. The first of his numerous London seasons took place in 1889–90, at the Globe, and in 1916, on the occasion of the Shakespeare Tercentenary Celebrations at the Theatre Royal, Drury Lane, he was knighted by King George V for his services to his profession. There was nearly a disaster on that occasion because, when the King sent for Benson to come to the Royal Box for his accolade (he was the only actor ever to be knighted in a theatre), there was no suitable sword available, and one had hastily to be borrowed from a military outfitters' near by. In 1933 Sir Frank was granted a Civil List pension in recognition of his work for the drama. In addition he was a Governor of the Shakespeare Memorial Theatre, a trustee of the Shakespeare Birthplace, and a freeman of Stratford-on-Avon. His success as a manager and trainer of young actors somewhat obscured his personal performances, yet in certain parts he was more than capable. He had a noble appearance, with handsome aquiline features, and had about him much of an 'antique Roman'. He married in 1886 a member of his company, Constance Featherstonhaugh (1860–1946), who continued to play leading parts with him for many years. In 1930 he published his reminiscences, and was also the author of a handbook on acting.   W. M. P.

BENZON, Otto (1856–1927), Danish dramatist, with Edvard Brandes one of the earliest exponents of modern social drama in that country (see SCANDINAVIA, 1).

BEOLCO, Angelo (*fl.* 1520–42), one of the earliest Italian actors and dramatists connected with the origins of the *commedia dell'arte*. He was born in about 1501–2, and, though in all probability never a professional actor, is found acting in 1520 at Venice. Most of his activities occurred there in carnival season, under the name of Ruzzante, 'the gossip', a shrewd peasant who indulges in long and amusing soliloquies. His plays were written in the dialect of Padua; they have been edited by Lovarini, and translated into French by Ruzzante's biographer, A. Mortier (pub. 1925–6). Riccoboni, who probably knew very little of Beolco's work, attributed to him the invention of the *commedia dell'arte*, but modern scholarship discounts this, though rating highly his own plays, which are fully written out and not scenarios for improvisation (see ITALY, 2).

BÉRAIN. (1) Jean (1637–1711), French theatrical designer, who replaced Vigarani at the Salle des Machines and as scenic designer to the Paris Opéra. In 1674 he succeeded Gissey as designer to the king, and the costumes and decorations which he prepared for Court spectacles had a great influence on the ornamentation of rooms and furniture (see COSTUME, 5). His son (2) Jean (1678–1726) succeeded him in his official functions, but though industrious and inventive, lacked his skill.

BERGELSON, David (1884–   ), Russian-Jewish writer of plays on contemporary themes, produced at the Moscow State Jewish Theatre (see JEWISH DRAMA, 6).

BERGERAC, Savinien de Cyrano de (1619–55), French author, who was in the Compagnie des Gardes under M. de Carbon de Casteljaloux. He was a great duellist, ready to run through at a moment's notice anyone who dared to remark on his abnormally large nose. After being twice badly wounded in the wars, he left the army and settled in Paris, intending to cultivate his undoubted gifts for literature and science. He followed the lectures of Gassendi and wrote on scientific subjects. But his friendship with Molière and Scarron turned his thoughts to the stage, and he produced a tragedy, *La Mort d'Agrippine* (1653), which was not a success. He was also the author of a comedy, *Le Pédant joué*, written between 1645 and 1649, which does not seem to have been performed. There is no contemporary reference to it, though it is often spoken of by later critics as a great success. It was, however, given in an expurgated version in America in 1899, and deserves to be remembered, since Molière took from it a scene for his *Fourberies de Scapin*, and it is thought that Cyrano's Gareau, the dialect-speaking peasant, was the model for several of Molière's Lubins and Pierrots. Scarron may also have been indebted

to Cyrano's play for some of his *Dom Japhet*. Cyrano, who thought Molière the greatest actor and dramatist of France, agreed with him in his dislike of the actor Montfleury, then the star of the rival theatre, the Hôtel de Bourgogne, and once forbade him to appear on the stage for a month. When Montfleury disobeyed, Cyrano went to the theatre and enforced obedience. He was killed by a wooden beam which fell on his head. Both these incidents are made use of by Edmond Rostand in his play, *Cyrano de Bergerac*, in which the elder Coquelin made a great success as Cyrano.

BERGMAN, Hjalmar (1883–1931), Swedish dramatist and novelist, was one of the most influential writers in the Swedish theatre from the death of Strindberg to his own death in 1931. His early work, like that of his younger contemporary Pär Lagerkvist, was strongly influenced by Strindberg, though in Bergman's case the influence of Maeterlinck and Ibsen must also be allowed for. The experiments in dramatic and theatrical technique, which characterize his work throughout, were also of great value as a stimulus to the renaissance of the Swedish theatre. Although he began his career as a playwright as early as 1905, he was first widely known by the 'Marionette Plays' of 1917, *Dödens Arlekin* (*Death's Harlequin*) and the exquisite psychological tragedy *Herr Sleeman kommer* (*Mr. Sleeman is Coming*), and their immediate successors, *Ett Experiment* (*An Experiment*) (1918) and the three published in 1923, *Vävaren i Bagdad* (*The Weaver of Bagdad*), *Spelhuset* (*The Gambling House*), and *Porten* (*The Doorway*). His most successful later plays were *Swedenhielms* (1925) and *Patrasket* (*The Rabble*) (1928) and in these and his final works for the stage, the dialogue, mood, and structure of comedy have replaced the tragic mood of his earlier work.

BERGOPZOOMER, Johann Baptist (1742–1804), an Austrian actor who made his début in his native town of Vienna in 1764, where he played in improvised comedy and in the old popular farces. He went to Germany with the company of Joseph von Kürz, and was with him on the arrival of the great actor Schröder, then a youngster, who played the valet to his Don Juan. The two men, who were much of an age and temperamentally suited, became fast friends, and when Schröder in after years went to Vienna he was delighted to find Bergopzoomer installed as one of the chief tragedians of the Burgtheater there. Bergopzoomer was an old-fashioned, ranting actor, but was highly thought of in his day.

BERGSTRÖM, Hjalmar (1868–1914), Danish dramatist, one of the best-known of his period outside his own country. In his plays he deals, under the influence of Ibsen, with such social problems as feminine emancipation, as in *Karen Bornemann* (1907), for example, and the struggle between the classes, as in *Lynggaard & Co.* (1905).

BERLIN. After several attempts elsewhere, a German National Theatre was established in 1796 in Berlin, which was later the home of the Freie Bühne and of the Deutsches Theater (see GERMANY and IFFLAND).

BERNARD. (1) TRISTAN (1866–1947), French dramatist, author of innumerable light farces, satires, comedies, and melodramas, of which the first was produced in 1897. Several of them have been translated into English, and *Triplepatte* (1905), adapted by Clyde Fitch as *Toddles*, was popular both in London and New York, where it was played by John Barrymore. These plays have little literary value, but are deftly constructed and amusing, and mainly serve to show man in his less heroic moments, entangled in petty intrigues from which the author extricates him with superb craftsmanship and no little ingenuity. If any moral can be drawn from this thistledown work, it is that success or failure in life depend more upon a man's character than upon his circumstances. Bernard's son, (2) JEAN-JACQUES (1888–   ), is also a dramatist, but in a very different style. His work, which deals with the tragedies of unrequited or unacknowledged love, derives from the *école intimiste* founded by Maeterlinck, and though contemporary in form and matter, is essentially lyric in tone. A number of his plays have been seen in translation in London and New York, among them *Le Feu qui reprend mal* (1921) as *The Sulky Fire*, *Martine* (1922), the story of the wooing and desertion of a country girl by an educated man, *L'Invitation au voyage* (1924), which deals with a woman's self-deception in love, and *L'Âme en peine* (1926), done in London as *The Unquiet Spirit*.

BERNHARDT [BERNARD], SARAH HENRIETTE ROSINE (1845–1923), French actress, and one of the best known, not only in Europe but in America, both North and South, in Australia, and in Egypt, where she frequently appeared on tour. Numerous legends about her eccentricities were in circulation, some provoked by her undoubted unconventionality, others apocryphal. She was probably one of the finest actresses the world has ever seen, and had a voice which, though likened to a 'golden bell', or the 'silver sound of running water', can never be adequately described to those who have not heard it. It constituted one of her main charms, added to a slim, romantic figure, dark eyes, and a consummate mastery of her art. She began her training for the stage at the age of 13, and in 1862 made her first appearance at the Comédie-Française, where she was destined to make many a brief and stormy appearance, her free spirit not accommodating itself easily to the traditions of that venerable establishment. She left it for good in 1880, and the rest of her career was passed in other theatres. After an unsuccessful attempt to sing in burlesque, she first attracted attention by her performance in Coppée's *Le Passant*, given at the Odéon in 1869. Her career was interrupted by the Franco-Prussian

war, but in 1872 she returned to the Comédie-Française and played Cordelia in a French version of *King Lear*, and the queen in *Ruy Blas*. This double triumph brought her to the head of her profession, and she consolidated her position by outstanding performances as Phèdre, and Doña Sol in *Hernani*, where for the sombre *femme fatale* of Hugo she substituted an adorable creature all tenderness and charm. She then set out on her travels, making her first appearance in London in 1879 in *Phèdre*, and in New York in 1880 in *Adrienne Lecouvreur*, scoring an immediate triumph in both capitals. She returned to them many times in later years, and always with success, her last appearance in London being in *Daniel* not long before her death. In Paris she managed several theatres, including the Ambigu and the Porte-Saint-Martin, before opening the old Théâtre des Nations as the Théâtre Sarah Bernhardt. There she revived a number of her former successes and also appeared in some outstanding new plays. Among the plays in which she scored her greatest successes, apart from *Phèdre*, were *La Dame aux camélias*, Sardou's *Fédora*, *Théodora*, and *La Tosca*, the plays of Edmond Rostand, particularly *L'Aiglon*, with which her name is always associated, and *Hamlet*. She was an accomplished painter and sculptress, and wrote poetry and plays, appearing in the latter herself. Among them were *L'Aveu* (1898), *Un Cœur d'homme* (1909), and the unpublished *Dans les nuages*, the manuscript of which is in Harvard College library. A volume of reminiscences was published in English in 1907.

BERNINI, GIOVANNI LORENZO (1598–1680), see MACHINERY and SCENERY, 3.

BERNSTEIN, ALINE (1882–   ), American scenic designer, and founder, with Irene Lewisohn, of the Museum of Costume Art in New York. Opened in 1937, this houses actual costumes, as well as a library of books and other documents devoted to the history of costume, which are available for study by research workers. Aline Bernstein's first work for the theatre was done in connexion with the Neighborhood Playhouse, and she has since been responsible for a number of important productions (see also U.S.A., 2).

BERSENEV, IVAN (1889–   ), Soviet actor and producer, sometime director of the Lenkom Theatre (formerly T.R.A.M.), whose principal actress is Serafina Birman. He studied at the Moscow Art Theatre, and in 1935 produced *The Spanish Priest* for the Moscow Theatre Festival. One of his best productions there was *Twelfth Night*, while his performance as Cyrano, under the direction of Birman at the Lenkom, has been warmly praised.

BERTANI, GIAMBATTISTA (*fl.* 16th cent.), see MACHINERY.

BERTINAZZI, CARLO (1710–83), the last of the great Arlequins of the Comédie-Italienne, where he was known as Carlin, and one of the last Italians to join the company (1741), which later became composed almost entirely of French actors. Bertinazzi was much admired by Garrick, who said that his back wore the expression his face would have shown had not the mask covered it.

BESKOW, BERNHARD VON (1796–1868), Swedish dramatist and dramatic critic (see SCANDINAVIA, 3).

BESPEAK PERFORMANCE, see BENEFIT.

BESSENYEI, GYÖRGY (1747–1811), Hungarian writer, author of *Agis Tragédiája* (*The Tragedy of Agis*) (pub. 1772), a play which marks the beginning of Hungarian literature.

BETTERTON. (1) THOMAS (?1635–1710), English actor, and the greatest figure of the Restoration stage. He was apprenticed young to a bookseller, John Rhodes, who had a great love for the theatre and reopened the Cockpit as soon as the Restoration was an accomplished fact. When Killigrew and Davenant obtained patents from the king, they took over all existing companies of actors. Rhodes's men, including the young Betterton, fell to the share of Davenant, and went with him to the theatre in Lincoln's Inn Fields. In 1671, after Davenant's death, the company, of which Betterton was now the head, moved to a new theatre in Dorset Garden, and remained there until the union of the two companies at the Theatre Royal in 1682. In 1695 Betterton broke with the management of the Theatre Royal, and reopened the theatre in Lincoln's Inn Fields most successfully with the first performance of Congreve's *Love for Love*, moving ten years later to Vanbrugh's new theatre in the Haymarket.

Cibber had a high opinion of Betterton, and considered him 'without competitors'. He was admirable in both comedy and tragedy, his Hamlet and Sir Toby Belch being equally admired. Though not perhaps so well suited to the requirements of Restoration comedy, he excelled in the high-flown rhetoric of the heroic drama of the day, and created many famous parts by well-known dramatists, who, for their part, were always ready to profit by his advice. The great Dryden himself cut twelve hundred lines of his *Don Sebastian* in rehearsal, 'judiciously lopt by Mr. Betterton'. He adapted a number of plays, including some of Shakespeare's, to suit the taste of the time, and turned Fletcher's *The Prophetess* into an opera with music by Purcell (1690). This was most successful, and ended with an elaborate masque whose stage directions show to what a pitch stage mechanism had been brought by this time, influenced no doubt by the machinery of opera, and Betterton's own study in Paris of French theatrical effects.

Betterton married one of the first English actresses, (2) MARY SANDERSON (?–1712), whom Pepys always refers to as Ianthe, from her excellent playing of that part in Davenant's *Siege*

of Rhodes. She seems to have been at her best in Shakespearian roles, and as Lady Macbeth Cibber thought her superior to her successor, Mrs. Barry. Both she and her husband were much esteemed by their contemporaries, both as actors and as private individuals, and were noted for their kindness to young and aspiring players, particularly Anne Bracegirdle.

BETTY, WILLIAM HENRY WEST (1791–1874), an English child prodigy, known as the Young Roscius, who for a season, from 1804 to 1805, took London by storm. He had already played with great success in Ireland and Scotland when he went to Covent Garden on 1 December. There, and at Drury Lane, he appeared in all the great tragic roles of Shakespeare and others, ousting even Mrs. Siddons and Kemble from public favour. The House of Commons adjourned on a motion of the younger Pitt to see him as Hamlet, and Northcote painted him as Norval in *Douglas*. After a brief and hectic success, however, opinion turned against him, and he was hissed off the stage when he attempted Richard III. He went to Cambridge in 1808, and three years later again attempted the stage, without success. He was ignored, his father squandered his money, and the rest of his long life—he was well over eighty when he died—was passed in complete obscurity.

BEVERLEY, WILLIAM ROXBY (c. 1814–89), English scene-painter, son and brother of actors, who painted his first scenery for the Theatre Royal, Manchester, then under the management of his father, William Roxby (1765–1842). He was for some time an actor on the Durham circuit, playing heavy comedy, but his chief interest lay in scenic design and in 1842 he was engaged by Knowles for the Theatre Royal, Manchester, painting for him a beautiful act drop which remained in use for twenty-five years. Some years later he did good work for the Vestris–Mathews management at the Lyceum, achieving his greatest success in *The Island of Jewels* (1849). He perfected the transformation scene in pantomime, and was engaged by the entertainer, Albert Smith, to paint the dioramic views for his 'Ascent of Mont Blanc'. Beverley's long and fruitful association with Drury Lane began in 1854 and lasted through successive managements until 1884. His best work was done in pantomime, but he worked intermittently for other theatres, and was responsible for several of the important Shakespearian revivals at the Princess's, including *King John*, *Henry IV*, *Part I*, and *Macbeth*, as well as for an elaborate production of *Comus*. He was a frequent exhibitor at the Royal Academy, mostly of seascapes. Next to Stanfield, Beverley may be accounted the most distinguished scene-painter of the nineteenth century in England, and much assisted the development of the art of scene-painting by his original methods and use of new inventions. A one-surface painter, he was all his life opposed to the innovation of built stuff. His last work was done in 1885 for the pantomime at Drury Lane.

BHARATA, see INDIA.

BHĀṢA, see INDIA.

BHAṬṬA NĀRĀYAṆA, see INDIA.

BHAVABHŪTI, see INDIA.

BIANCOLELLI, a family of actors of the *commedia dell'arte.* (1) ISABELLA FRANCHINI (*fl.* 1630–50), the daughter of an actor who played Pantalone, acted servant parts under the name of Columbina, and was a member of the troupe at Modena. She had previously married an actor named Biancolelli, who died in 1640 leaving her with a small boy. She married as her second husband Carlo Cantù, an actor who played as Buffetto. A certain (2) NICCOLO, who is said to have played a young lover about 1650, may have been her brother-in-law. Her son (3) GIUSEPPE DO-MENICO (*c.* 1637–88), who was also a playwright, became famous as Dominique, playing the role of Arlequin. From his youth he was accounted a good actor, and he became a particular favourite of Louis XIV when on Mazarin's invitation he joined the Italian troupe in Paris. It was under him that the Italians first began to play in French. His early death was a great loss to the stage, and he was deeply mourned. He became a naturalized Frenchman, and in 1663 married (4) ORSOLA CORTESI (*c.* 1636–1718), an actress who was also in the Paris troupe, where she became leading lady under the name of Eularia on the death of Brigida Bianchi (see ROMAGNESI, 2). Soon after the death of her husband she retired, and later entered a convent, where she died. She had eight children, one of whom, the god-son of Louis XIV, although not an actor, left a manuscript collection of *scenarii.* Two daughters and one other son are known. The eldest, (5) FRANCESCA MARIA APOLLINE (1664–1747), made her début in *Arlequino Proteo* in 1683. She acted in Paris until 1695, marrying a few years before her retirement an officer in the Guards, who died in 1706. Her younger sister (6) CATERINA (1665–1716) also made her début in *Arlequino Proteo,* as Colum-bina, the name under which her grandmother played. She married in 1685 an actor of the Comédie-Française, Pierre Lenoir de la Thorillière, and continued to act in Paris until her retirement in 1697. The youngest child of Dominique, (7) PIETRO FRANCESCO (1680–1734), played for a while in Paris, both as Arlequin and as Pierrot, but on the closing of the Théâtre-Italien in 1697 he went to the pro-vinces. As Dominique le Jeune he was a member of the company which Riccoboni (Lelio) took back to Paris in 1716, and he remained with it till his death.

BIBBIENA, BERNARDO DOVIZI DA (1470–1520), an Italian cardinal, author in his youth of a comedy, the *Calandria,* freely adapting the *Menaechmi* of Plautus. The twin brothers are replaced by twins of different sexes, and a sub-plot uses as a comic figure Boccaccio's Calandrino. In situation and language the play is more witty than decent. It was first per-formed at Urbino during the carnival of 1506. A year later it was given in Rome, and it made its appearance at most of the princely Courts of Italy, delighting its audiences, as is apparent from the contemporary descriptions of its productions which survive.

BIBIENA (BIBBIENA, DA BIBBIENA). A family of scenic artists and architects, originally of Florence, whose work, in pure baroque style, is found all over Europe, though Parma and Vienna probably saw their greatest achieve-ments. The family name was Galli, and Bibiena (or Bibbiena) was added later, from the birth-place of the father of (1) FERDINANDO (1657–1743) and (2) FRANCESCO (1659–1739), who together founded the family fortunes and renown. Orphaned at an early age, they were trained first in the studio of a Bolognese painter, and later under Rivani, a stage engineer respon-sible for some of the machinery in Louis XIV's Court theatre at Versailles. While still a young man, Ferdinando was employed by the Dukes of Parma, for whom he worked in the beautiful Teatro Farnese built by Aleotti. Early in the eighteenth century he left Parma, at the com-mand of the Emperor Charles VI, to go to Vienna, where, with the help of his brother and his sons, he was responsible for the decorations of the Court fêtes and theatrical performances. Of his sons (3) ALESSANDRO (1687–*c.* 1769) was an architect, but concerned himself less with theatrical work than his three brothers—(4) GIUSEPPE (1696–1757), designer of a fine opera-house in Bayreuth and the first to use transpar-ent scenery lighted from behind (in 1723), (5) ANTONIO (1700–74), designer of the Teatro Communale in Bologna, which opened in 1763, and (6) GIOVANNI MARIA (*c.* 1704–69), who is believed to have built a theatre near Lisbon. Giuseppe's son (7) CARLO (1728–87), also a famous designer of stage settings, one of which is preserved in the old Royal Theatre at Drott-ningholm, was associated with his father in the decoration of the Bayreuth opera-house. The whole family worked so much in the same tradition, and so often in collaboration, that it is sometimes impossible to apportion their work individually. They introduced many modifica-tions and reforms into scenic design and acous-tics, working not only for their royal patrons, but for the powerful Jesuit colleges which in-cluded dramatic work in their educational pro-grammes (see JESUIT DRAMA), for the Church, wherever the tradition of religious plays was continued, and for the rich municipalities of Italy. They made their home at Bologna, but were more often than not to be found in every corner of Europe, working on Court spectacles for royal weddings, accessions, and funerals, and in the public and private theatres of the time, where their new diagonal perspective, which had taken the place of the central per-spective beloved of the seventeenth century, opened up new vistas and made possible the elaborate architectural stage settings so charac-teristic of the family style (see also SCENERY).

BIBLE-HISTORIES, a name given by modern scholarship to the medieval plays based on Scripture and formerly known as Miracle or Mystery plays.

BIBLIOTECA DE AUTORES ESPAÑOLES, a series of Spanish plays, edited by various hands, which appeared from 1850 to 1860, and revived an interest in the drama of the Spanish Golden Age which had suffered an eclipse under the neo-classicism of the eighteenth century.

BICKERSTAFFE, ISAAC (1735–1812), English dramatist, considered in his day the equal of John Gay as a writer of lyric comedy. The first of these, *Thomas and Sally; or, the Sailor's Return*, described as a 'musical entertainment', was given at Covent Garden in 1760. It was followed by *Love in a Village* (1762), a ballad opera based on *The Village Opera* (1728) of Charles Johnson, which has been described as a musical amalgamation of *The Gentleman Dancing Master* and *Le Jeu de l'amour et du hasard*. It has been frequently revived down to the present day. Another piece of the same nature, *The Maid of the Mill* (1765), based on the novel *Pamela*, also held the stage for many years, and must have been popular in the early nineteenth century, to judge from its frequent inclusion in the repertory of the Juvenile Drama. Among Bickerstaffe's later productions, many of them written in collaboration with Foote and Dibdin, the best was *Lionel and Clarissa* (1768), which again has often been revived. Four years after its production the author, who enjoyed the friendship of Dr. Johnson, Goldsmith, and Garrick, was suspected of some heinous offence, and fled to the continent, where he led a long life of misery and exile, and died in poverty.

BIDERMANN, JAKOB (1578–1639), see JESUIT DRAMA.

BIEDERMANN, JOSEPH (1800–?), Austrian Jew, author of a number of plays in Yiddish, performed in Vienna by amateurs in about 1850 (see JEWISH DRAMA, 4).

BIJOU THEATRE. (1) LONDON. A small theatre of this name was attached to Her Majesty's Opera House (The Royal Italian Opera House) in the Haymarket. It was mostly used for concerts and sometimes for dramatic performances of a light nature. Charles Mathews the younger appeared there in 1862 with his wife. It was also used by amateurs, and on one occasion Palgrave Simpson, the dramatist, staged *Macbeth* there with Clement Scott, afterwards the well-known dramatic critic, as Fleance. The theatre was burned down with the Opera House in 1867.

(2) A small theatre in Bayswater, used occasionally for performances of a special nature and by amateurs, was also known as the Bijou. In 1905 Oscar Wilde's *Salome* had its first London production there. In 1924 Lena Ashwell took it over and renamed it the Century,

producing plays and appearing in them herself. Among these were *A Mirror of Souls*, *The Ship*, *Crime and Punishment*, and *Dr. Jekyll and Mr. Hyde*, all of which she adapted from novels. As the Century, this theatre still stands, and is occasionally used for plays. W. M. P.

(3) NEW YORK, a small playhouse devoted to operetta and light entertainment. Situated at 1239 Broadway, it opened with variety, as the Brighton, in 1878. It then became Wood's Broadway Theatre, and the Broadway Opera House. On 31 Mar. 1880 it was renamed the Bijou Opera House. Lilian Russell, coming from Tony Pastor's in 1882, appeared there in several musical plays, including *Patience*. The theatre was occasionally used for visiting companies and straight plays, until 7 July 1883, when it was pulled down and a larger one built, opening 1 Dec. 1883 with Offenbach. It was at this theatre that Julia Marlowe made her début as an adult actress. It continued in use, mainly as a home of musical and light entertainment, until 1911.

(4) On Forty-Fifth Street west of Broadway. This was opened by the Shuberts on 12 Apr. 1917. Its smallness and consequent heavy overhead expenses mitigated against its usefulness, and in 1938 it turned to films, being only occasionally used after that for plays. It is, however, interesting to note that *Life With Father* ended its phenomenal run at the Bijou in 1947. Among the plays produced at this theatre during its twenty years of legitimate activity were *Sleeping Partners* (1918), *The Skin Game* (1920), *The Dover Road* (1921), *Uptown West* (1921), a problem drama of a Japanese-American marriage, and *What Every Woman Knows* (1926), with Helen Hayes. Later came Blanche Yurka in *The Lady from the Sea*, and *Springtime for Henry*, which was the Bijou's last successful production. G. F.

BILL-BELOTSERKOVSKY, VLADIMIR NAUMOVICH (1884–), Soviet dramatist, whose early play, *Hurricane*, written, as a Russian critic said, 'with his heart's blood', was produced in 1926 at the Mossoviet Theatre, then known as M.O.S.P.S. (The Moscow Trades Unions' Theatre). This was a fine, stirring piece of propaganda about the struggles of a Revolutionary leader in a small village during the Civil War. His later plays have been somewhat quieter, but *Life is Calling* (1934), published in 1938 in an English translation by Anthony Wixley, marked a step forward in the development of the Mossoviet Theatre, which had lost its early fervour and tended to lapse into dullness and stagnation. The plot of *Life is Calling* (or, as it is also called, *Life Goes Forward*) is somewhat conventional, on the 'eternal triangle' theme, but the tension is heightened by the conflict, not only between the characters' emotions, but between social duty and personal happiness. It is enlivened by the acid comments of the old grandfather, who, before his death at the end of the play, shows the younger generation that their trivial quarrels are as nothing beside the great tide of new life surging outside, which they must accept if they wish to survive. A later play treats of the same theme from a different angle, showing the adjustment of an old Russian intellectual to the new social order. This was produced in 1936, since when Bill-Belotserkovsky seems to have written little.

BILTMORE THEATRE, NEW YORK, on 47th Street between Broadway and 8th Avenue. It was built by the Chanins as one of a chain of playhouses with which to challenge the Shubert brothers' supremacy in Broadway management, and opened on 7 Dec. 1925. It had an undistinguished career until 1929, when it found itself in trouble over Mae West's *Pleasure Man,* which was closed by the police after two performances. A further period of fluctuating fortunes was ended in 1936, when the Federal Theatre Project took over the theatre and presented there, with some success, their experimental Living Newspapers. A Yiddish version of *It Can't Happen Here* was the last production before the theatre was bought by Warner Brothers, to become the happy hunting ground of George Abbott. *Brother Rat* ran for 577 performances, and was followed by the equally successful *What a Life!* Among later successes at this theatre were *My Sister Eileen* and *Kiss and Tell.*   G. F.

BINYON, LAURENCE (1869–1946), English poet, whose verse-drama *Paris and Oenone* (1906) was produced by Gertrude Kingston. *Attila* (1907) was done at His Majesty's by Oscar Asche, while *Arthur,* written for Martin-Harvey, with music by Elgar, was given at the Old Vic in 1923. Of his other plays, *The Young King* and *Boadicea* were produced privately by John Masefield in his theatre on Boars Hill, Oxford, while the rest have been published but not produced.

BIO-MECHANICS, the name given to Meyerhold's system of production. Reducing the actor to the status of puppet, to be thrown into attitudes at the producer's whim, it calls for the complete elimination of personality, and the subjugation of mind and body to a series of acrobatic turns. It further demands the stripping of the stage to the bare bones, the elimination of 'detail' scenery, and the willing co-operation of the audience in building up the desired stage-picture by association. Meyerhold himself admitted that his system was in a large measure based on Pavlov's theory of association. It has also, in its insistence on conventional and stylized gesture, been compared to the *kabuki* theatre of Japan. A mental rather than an emotional theatre, it served its purpose in the early days of the October Revolution in clearing away the inessentials of production which cluttered up the old theatres; but it was fated to be outstripped by the forces it had liberated, and finally became outmoded, the new, untrained, but highly perceptive Soviet audiences demanding more warmth, colour, and above all, humanity.

BIRD, ROBERT MONTGOMERY (1806–54), American playwright, leader of the Philadelphia group of dramatists, and by profession a doctor. He had already written a number of unacted plays when in 1831 Edwin Forrest produced his romantic tragedy, *The Gladiator,* playing Spartacus, the hero. It was an immediate success, and Forrest selected it for his first appearance at Drury Lane in 1836, continuing to act in it until his retirement in 1872. It was also done by John McCullough, who made his last appearance in it in 1884, and it was seen on the stage as late as 1892. Bird wrote two more plays for Forrest, another romantic tragedy, *Oralloossa* (1832), and a domestic drama entitled *The Broker of Bogota* (1834), and revised for him Stone's *Metamora.* All these were popular and frequently revived, but owing to the chaotic state of the copyright laws at that time Bird made no money from their production, and Forrest would not allow them to be printed. Bird consequently withdrew from the theatre and sought a livelihood elsewhere, writing several successful novels, later dramatized by other hands, and engaging in journalism and politics. Quinn says of him: 'Had he lived in a time when the American playwright received fair treatment, it is not easy to put a limit to his possible achievements. For he had a rare sense of dramatic effect, a power to visualize historic scenes and characters, to seize the spirit of the past out of the mass of facts and, in a few brief lines, to fuse those facts into life.'

BIRD (BOURNE). (1) WILLIAM (?–1624), English actor and an important member of the Admiral's Men, since he frequently figures in Henslowe's *Diary* as their agent. Before joining them he may have been with the short-lived Pembroke's Men. He remained one of the leading figures of the Admiral's Men when they became the Palsgrave's Men, retiring a year or so before his death. His son (2) THEOPHILUS (1608–64) may have appeared as a child with his father, but is first found playing female parts for Queen Henrietta's Men. In 1635 he was Massinissa in *Hannibal and Scipio,* and shortly afterwards he married Anne, the eldest daughter of Christopher Beeston. In 1637, when the theatres opened after the plague, he joined the King's Men at Blackfriars, remaining with them until the closing of the theatres in 1642. He still retained his interest in the theatre, however, since it was he, as brother-in-law of William Beeston, who negotiated the transfer of Salisbury Court to Beeston in 1647. Bird is named first in Downes's list of actors who appeared immediately on the opening of the theatres in 1660, and Pepys notes a rumour that he had broken his leg while fencing in *Aglaura* in 1662.

BIRMAN, SERAFIMA GERMANOVNA (1890–), one of the outstanding actresses of the Soviet stage, who has also several fine productions to her credit. She studied at the Moscow Art Theatre, and was one of the group which set up independently under Vakhtangov and later under Bersenev. She then became leading lady of the Lenkom Theatre, where she produced *The Living Corpse,* and a new translation of *Cyrano de Bergerac* with Bersenev as Cyrano.

BIRMINGHAM REPERTORY THEATRE. In intention and achievement the Birmingham Repertory Theatre is one of the most significant enterprises launched in the English theatre during the present century. High ideals inspired its inception and have been maintained in face of many difficulties.

It began with private theatricals at The Grange, the Birmingham home of Barry Vincent Jackson. From these, in 1907, emerged the Pilgrim Players, who, at local halls, put on plays rarely or never seen in the commercial theatre. Beginning with *The Interlude of Youth,* an old Morality play, and ending with Shakespeare's *Twelfth Night,* the company put on twenty-eight productions between 1907 and 1913. This early organization was entirely amateur, and included among its fifty or so members John Drinkwater, Scott Sunderland, Cecily Byrne, Margaret Chatwin, and Isabel Thornton. The success of this early venture was due to a catholic choice of plays, the enthusiasm of Barry Jackson, and a single-minded attention to artistic essentials. It soon became apparent that the conversion of Birmingham to the cause of intelligent drama would be a full-time job, demanding a permanent theatre and a professional company. Fortunately, Barry Jackson was a wealthy man. He was able to build and equip a playhouse that fulfilled several conditions often overlooked by architects in the theatre. A clear view of the stage was to be had from every seat. Intimacy between actors and audience was established by the high rake of the auditorium and the inclusion of an apron stage. Sicilian marble and a scheme of decoration in old-gold and oak replaced the customary cherubs and nymphs. On 5 Feb. 1913 the curtain went up at the new theatre on a production of *Twelfth Night.*

The policy of the Birmingham Repertory Theatre was to serve an art instead of making that art serve a commercial purpose. This meant that playwright rather than player was master when play selection was afoot. For years the London theatre had been sole arbiter and source of supply in dramatic matters and the metropolitan monopoly extended to the provinces, where London successes toured in endless round. The old stock companies had almost disappeared. Actor-managers travelled the country, swelling out poor plays to richly remunerative proportions by flamboyant feats of acting. The Birmingham Repertory Theatre set out to explore little-trodden ways, and its founder was in a position to allay undue anxiety over means. To increase the aesthetic sense of the public in the theatre was its avowed object, and in that it has definitely succeeded.

During the first ten years, the classics, new plays, translations from continental drama, and even opera, were staged. Drinkwater's *Abraham Lincoln* made money, and the first English performance of Shaw's *Back to Methuselah* was a landmark in theatre history. The production of *Cymbeline* in modern dress, later to be followed by similar treatment of *Macbeth, Hamlet,* and *The Taming of the Shrew,* stressed the essential Shakespeare who was in definite danger of being swamped by excess of scenery and stagecraft. Seventeen Shakespearian plays, a dozen Shavian pieces, much of Hankin, Ibsen, Galsworthy, Masefield, Molière, Kaiser, and Andreyev offered Birmingham a decade of comprehensive playgoing to which it was only partly alive. Intensive support from the perceptive few was outbalanced by the indifference of the city as a whole. In 1924 Jackson threatened to close the theatre. The Birmingham Civic Society took action and guaranteed a sufficient body of season-ticket holders to keep the theatre open.

Work went on in an even more enterprising spirit. The success of such productions as *The Farmer's Wife, Back to Methuselah, The Marvellous History of St. Bernard,* and *The Barretts of Wimpole Street* induced Jackson (now Sir Barry) to transfer the best of the Birmingham productions to London. For ten years the 'artistic capital' made available in Birmingham was extended to London. In 1929 the Malvern Festival was founded, the Birmingham Company forming the nucleus of the Festival company until 1938.

The Birmingham Repertory Theatre has been a rallying-point for those willing to serve rather than to take from the theatre. Producers have included John Drinkwater, H. K. Ayliff, A. E. Filmer, W. G. Fay, and H. M. Prentice. A host of now well-known players served their apprenticeship on its stage, among them Felix Aylmer, Ivor Barnard, Eileen Beldon, Melville Cooper, Gwen Ffrangcon-Davies, Cedric Hardwicke, Laurence Olivier, Ralph Richardson, Ion Swinley, and Isabel Thornton. Settings and costumes designed by Paul Shelving have set new standards in English stage decoration.

In 1935 Sir Barry transferred the Birmingham Repertory Theatre to a Board of Trustees. He himself remained at the head as Director, and ensured the faithful observance of the all-important condition that the Birmingham Repertory Theatre should inspire and lead rather than travel in the wake of popular taste. In that spirit some five hundred plays have been presented. Few have been without artistic merit; many have proved notable additions to English drama.   T. C. K.

BIRÓ, LAJOS (1890–1948), see HUNGARY.

BJERREGAARD, HENRIK (1792–1842), Norwegian dramatist (see SCANDINAVIA 2).

BJØRNSON, BJØRNSTJERNE (1832–1910), Norwegian novelist, poet, and dramatist, was born in the bleak upland district of Kvikne and early went to live at Romsdal. The changes in the formative years of his life are thus the reverse of those in Ibsen's. His biographers have remarked upon the joy and delight with which Bjørnson, as a child, looked at the new and unexpected beauty of the world to which he found himself transferred, and something from the mood of that moment seems to have remained with him throughout his life.

For Bjørnson, although his work as journalist, novelist, poet, and dramatist reflected the same ideals of truth and freedom as did Ibsen's, differed widely from him as a man and as an artist, showing those very qualities of happiness and optimism, a certain sweetness and radiance of temperament, which Ibsen lacked, and lacking also Ibsen's profundity and power. His contribution to Norwegian drama is affected at every point by these factors. He was a fertile innovator, exploring territory such as the moral diseases of contemporary society before Ibsen himself actually did so. In all his work, however apparently unpropitious the theme, there is a frank and firm confidence in the love of God and the potential goodness of man, which is often explicit: 'Where good men walk, there are God's ways.' His criticism of the evil in society, though uncompromising, as befitted a Liberal leader, has that confidence in redemptive forces which in Ibsen's work is rare and seldom more than implicit. As a dramatic artist he shows the skill born of years of theatrical experience—he is a true man of the theatre—but his technique is swift and effective rather than architectural. Withal, to the stranger, his plays seem more foreign than do Ibsen's; they have in them, that is to say, more of the immediate and local and less of the ageless and universal.

His plays are too numerous to describe in detail, but they may be roughly grouped in three periods. In the earliest, to which belong also his novel *Synnøve Solbakken* and other tales of country life in Norway, besides his two years' experience (1857–9) as Director of the Bergen Theatre, comes the group which is mainly historical and patriotic: *Mellem Slagene* (*Between the Battles*) (1855); *Kong Sverre* (*King Sverre*) (1861); *Sigurd Slembe* (*Sigurd the Boisterous*) (1862); and *Maria Stuart i Skotland* (1864) and others. From 1865 to 1867 he was a director of the Christiania Theatre, edited a newspaper, and became a leader of the Liberal party. He was away from Norway for a few years and during and after this he wrote his second group of plays, the realistic social dramas which often treat material like that Ibsen was to use a few years later (in the group beginning with *Pillars of Society*) and are often compared with Ibsen's. Such a comparison, if pushed at all closely, must inevitably be detrimental to Bjørnson, who is by contrast an eager poet and an able theatre-artist, using the stage skilfully as a pulpit for his liberal, and often noble, thought. Between 1867 and 1883

he produced *De Nygifte* (*The Newly Married*) (1865); *Redaktøren* (*The Editor*) (1874); *En Fallit* (*A Bankruptcy*, generally translated as *The Bankrupt*) (1875); *Kongen* (*The King*) (1877); *Leonarda* and *Det ny System* (*The New System*) (both 1879); and, after an interval of lecturing in America (1880–1), *En Handske* (*A Gauntlet*) (1883), perhaps the height of his achievement in this kind and too bold for immediate production.

The second play of that year, *Over Ævne I* (1883) (given at the Royalty in London in 1901 as *Beyond Human Power*), one of Bjørnson's greatest plays, marks the increasing interest in spiritual rather than social problems which characterizes much of his last phase and is clearly seen also in the novel *Paa Guds Veje* (*In God's Ways*) published in 1889. The other plays of this period are *Over Ævne II* (1895); *Paul Lange og Tora Parsberg* (1898); *Laboremus* (1901); *Daglannet* (*Dayland Farm*) (1904); and *Naar den ny Vin blomstrer* (*When the Vineyards are in Blossom*) (1905). He received the Nobel prize in 1903 and died in Paris in 1910.

U. E.-F.

BLACK, GEORGE (1890–1945), a Northern music-hall manager, went to London in 1928 as director of the General Theatre Corporation Ltd. In 1933 he joined Moss Empires Ltd., of which he later became joint managing-director. Next to C. B. Cochran he was the outstanding figure in the music-hall world between the two wars, and his Crazy Gang shows at the Palladium, with Flanagan and Allen and Nervo and Knox as their moving spirits, caused a minor revolution in the profession, bringing back some of the atmosphere of the old 'halls'. Black was also responsible for a number of shows at the Hippodrome, notably *The Fleet's Lit Up*, *Black Velvet*, and *Black Vanities*, and after the outbreak of war in 1939 he took over the Prince of Wales's. He was excellent at spotting nascent talent, and was at all times receptive to new ideas, but later became somewhat intolerant of criticism, and after the poor notices given to *Jenny Jones* (1944) he refrained from inviting the critics to his next production.

BLACKFRIARS THEATRE, LONDON. There were two Blackfriars theatres, one succeeding the other, both built within the boundaries of the old Blackfriars monastery, the site of which is now covered by the offices of *The Times* and Playhouse Yard.

(1) On the dissolution of the monasteries part of the Blackfriars building was granted to Sir Thomas Cawarden, Master of the Revels for Henry VIII, and the first holder of that office, who already had the use of several rooms there for the storing of properties and costumes used at Court entertainments. He may also have used the rooms for rehearsals. In 1576 or 1577 Richard Farrant, Master of the Children of Windsor Chapel, adapted part of the building, probably the frater, as a theatre which was used by the Children of the Chapel Royal and of Windsor Chapel from 1577 until

Farrant's death in 1580. From 1583 to 1584 it was used by a mixed company of children from the Earl of Oxford's company, Paul's, and the Chapel. It then lapsed and was let out as lodgings.

(2) In 1597 James Burbage bought part of the old monastery, including that part used by Farrant, and adapted it as a roofed theatre, to be used by his company in the winter when inclement weather prevented them from playing in the roofless playhouses like the Theatre and the Curtain. His company included Richard Burbage, Lowin, Condell, Armin, Heminge, and Shakespeare. It was probably at Blackfriars that Shakespeare played the Ghost in *Hamlet*, Adam in *As You Like It*, and other small parts. Later the Blackfriars company, then the King's Men, sought to restrain the players at the Red Bull from performing Shakespeare's plays.

There is some difference of opinion as to the dimensions of the Blackfriars Theatre, but it was either 45 × 52 ft. or 46 × 66 ft. It had several galleries, and was lit by candlelight. Its prices were higher than at the open-air theatres. Jonson refers to the stools on its stage as being 'twelve penny' seats. Seating was also provided for pit patrons in the form of benches. The orchestra was a great feature, the performers actually paying to play there in the hope of attracting patronage from the nobility in the audience. That scenery of some sort was used is certain, for there are references to it in connexion with Suckling's *Aglaura* (1637). One of the scenes was jeered at in a contemporary play by another author. Habington's *Queen of Aragon* (1640) also had scenery, which had been in use for Court masques for some time.

The 'private' theatres, for so those with a roof were called, had the advantage, from the managerial and actors' point of view, of being outside the jurisdiction of the City Corporation. Nevertheless the Blackfriars Theatre had a stormy time, for the citizens who lived around it objected very much to its presence in their midst. In 1631 there was a definite move to suppress it. The actors demanded the sum of £21,000 as compensation, the referee assessed the value at £3,000, and the neighbours cheerfully agreed to contribute £100 towards that sum. But the movement failed, and the theatre remained open. It was one of the best patronized of all the pre-Restoration playhouses. Henry Evans, who had leased it from the Burbages, and had got permission to 'erect or sett up a company of boys ... to play playes and interludes in the said playhouse in such sort as before time had been there used', testified to the popularity of the Blackfriars when he stated that 'during such time as the said defendants Heminges and Burbage and their company contined playes and interludes in the said great hall of ffryers ... they gott, and as yet doth, more in one winter in the said Great Hall by a thousand powndes than they were used to get in the Banckside'. Evans was then trying to get out of his

lease of the theatre, of which in his pleadings he says he 'grewe wearye'. He had been hit by the plague of 1603-4, and was in trouble with the Court of the Star Chamber for 'his unorderlie carriage and behaviour in takinge up of gentlemens children against their wills and to employe them for playes'. It is not clear whether he offended against the wills of the children or their parents. These juvenile performers had a great following and were very talented. Their popularity gave rise to a great deal of jealousy and uneasiness on the part of the adult actors. They gave the first performances of many famous plays, including Jonson's *Cynthia's Revels* and *The Poetaster*, done by the Children of the Chapel Royal in 1600 and 1601.

Apart from the Boy Companies the chief tenants of the Blackfriars Theatre were the King's Men, who used it as a winter house from 1609 until the closing of the theatres in 1642. The building was finally dismantled in 1655.

In 1629 a French company played at the Blackfriars, when actresses appeared on the stage to the scandal of the populace and the pelting of the daring women, who speedily retired.

W. M. P.

BLAGROVE, Thomas, see MASTER OF THE REVELS.

BLANCHARD. (1) WILLIAM (1769–1835), English actor, who in 1785 joined a travelling company under the name of Bentley. He reverted to his own name in 1789 and was for many years an actor and manager in the provinces. He made his first appearance in London at Covent Garden, playing Bob Acres, on 1 Oct. 1800, and remained there until his death, except for a short visit to the United States in 1831, when he played at the Bowery under his son-in-law Hamblin. He was at his best in heavy comedy, and in character parts, particularly those of drunkards and old men. Oxberry gives special praise to his Polonius, Pistol, Fluellen, and Sir Andrew Aguecheek. He was also good as Peachum, and as Mungo in *The Padlock*. His wife and daughter were on the stage, and his son (2) EDWARD LEMAN (1820–89) became famous as a writer of pantomime and Christmas extravaganzas. From 1844 until his death he wrote at least one pantomime a year, most of which were given at Drury Lane, the others at such minor theatres as the Surrey, Astley's, and the Olympic. He was also responsible for a number of farces, some burlesques, including one of Dickens as *The Cricket on Our Own Hearth* (1846), and a comedy, *The Road of Life*, given at the Olympic in 1843. For many years he contributed articles on theatrical matters to the *Era*, the *Era Almanack*, and the *Daily Telegraph*, and edited an edition of Shakespeare. His diary, edited by Clement Scott, was published in 1891. Nothing of his work, which was mainly topical and spectacular, has survived on the stage.

Two actors, father and son, both named Thomas Blanchard, of whom the first died in

1797 and the second in 1859, do not appear to have been related to the above.

BLANCHARD'S AMPHITHEATRE, NEW YORK, see CHATHAM THEATRE (1).

BLANCHE, AUGUST THEODORE (1811–68), Swedish dramatist (see SCANDINAVIA, 3).

BLAND. (1) GEORGE (?–1807), English actor, the brother of Mrs. Jordan, and the illegitimate son of Francis Bland, whose name he adopted when he went on the stage. He was not a particularly good actor, and died in penurious circumstances in America, where he acted under the name of Wilson at the Park Theatre in 1801 and at the Grove in 1805. His wife (2) MARIA THERESA ROMANZINI (1769–1838) had been an actress in Dublin at the same time as Mrs. Jordan. She later became a well-known ballad-singer at Vauxhall and was attached for forty years to the Drury Lane company. She married Bland in 1790. Of her two sons the elder, Charles, was a singer, but the younger (3) JAMES (1798–1861), though he was first a singer, later appeared at the Olympic in burlesque, and played the fathers and similar parts in the extravaganzas of Planché. He died suddenly at the Strand Theatre.

BLOOD-TUB, see GAFF.

BLUES, a Victorian term for plain sky borders (see BORDER).

BLUM, RENÉ, see BALLET, 8.

BOADEN, JAMES (1762–1839), English playwright, critic, and journalist, who became editor of the *Oracle*, a paper started in opposition to the *World*. He was intensely interested in drama, and had several plays to his credit: *Fontainville Forest* (1794), *The Secret Tribunal* (1795), *The Italian Monk* (1797), founded on Mrs. Radcliffe's novel, *Cambro-Britons* and *Aurelio and Miranda* (both 1798).

Boaden was a keen Shakespearian and took part in the correspondence on the Ireland forgeries. In 1837 he published a pamphlet on the authorship of the sonnets in which he identified the 'Mr. W. H.' of the dedication as William Herbert, Earl of Pembroke. His knowledge of the theatre is apparent in his biographies of famous actors. His *Life of Kemble* appeared in 1825, *The Life of Mrs. Siddons* in 1827, and *The Life of Mrs. Jordan* in 1831.   T. C. K.

BOARDS. A term used of the theatrical profession by extension from the wooden boards forming the stage floor. Thus 'to tread the boards' is to act, while to be 'on the boards' is to be an actor by profession (see STAGE, 1).

BOARS HEAD INN, see INNS USED AS THEATRES.

BOAT TRUCKS, large low platforms on castors, on which large sections of scenery can be mounted and run or pivoted on or off the stage (see STAGE, 5).

BOBÈCHE [ANTOINE MANDELOT] (1791–c. 1840), a farce-player of the boulevards, who, with his companion Galimafré [Auguste Guérin] (1790–1870), amused the holiday crowds with his *parades*. They were both young workmen, Bobèche the son of an upholsterer and Galimafré of a carpenter, when they were taken up and trained by the acrobat Dromale. They became extremely popular, and were invited to private houses to entertain the guests, but Bobèche, whose red jacket and grey tricorne hat with butterfly antennae were familiar sights on the Boulevard du Temple, offended Napoleon by the topicality of his jokes and was banished from Paris. He returned under the Restoration, and was again successful, but he had a hankering for serious drama, and took over the management of a provincial theatre—Mlle Flore in her memoirs says it was at Rouen. He failed, and was not heard of again. Galimafré, who refused to act after 1814, joined the stage-staff of the Gaîté and later of the Opéra-Comique, and died in retirement. A play based on the lives of these two comedians, by the brothers Cogniard, was given at the Palais-Royal in 1837.

BOBO, the rustic clown of early Spanish plays, who amused the noble audiences with his naïve witticisms and malapropisms.

BOCAGE. (1) [PIERRE-FRANÇOIS TOUSEZ] (1797–1863), celebrated French actor, one of the finest of the Romantic period. He tried a wide variety of trades before joining a travelling troupe in the provinces, and had a hard apprenticeship to acting before in 1821 he went to Paris. His efforts to join the Comédie-Française proved unavailing, and he returned to the provinces for a short time and then went to the Odéon. He found his métier in the new drama and melodrama, which suited him better than the old comedy and tragedy. A forceful personality, with a fine physique and sonorous voice, he revelled in the plays of the elder Dumas, particularly *Antony* and *La Tour de Nesle*. He once again tried for the Comédie-Française, but its somewhat arid atmosphere proved too confining for him, and he returned to the boulevards, where his popularity was greater than ever. In 1845 he became director of the Odéon, and died in the midst of success, much of which he owed to the dramatists of the Romantic movement. He was not as good an actor as Frédérick-Lemaître but, handsome, passionate, and debonair, he had a huge following among the youth of the day. His nephew (2) PAUL (1824–87) was the author of several plays, mostly written in collaboration, and editor of the *Mousquetaire*, a paper founded by Dumas, in much of whose work the younger Bocage is believed to have had a hand.

BODEL, JEAN (*fl.* thirteenth century), a contemporary of the minstrel Adam de la Halle, and with him one of the founders of French secular drama. He wrote a *Jeu de Saint Nicholas* which was given on the vigil of the saint.

It contains a number of contemporary allusions, some of which seem to indicate that Bodel had been on a crusade, and though from a literary point of view it is not as good as the best of Adam de la Halle's work, it is more dramatic, and probably seemed better in performance. Bodel was preparing to go on a second crusade when he was stricken with leprosy, and retired from the world. The date of his death is uncertain.

BOECK, JOHANN MICHAEL (1743–93), German actor who played young lovers in Ackermann's National Theatre company at Hamburg. He later made theatre history by being the first to play Karl Moor in *Die Räuber* when it was put on under Dalberg at Mannheim, where Boeck had gone with his wife after the death of Ekhof. He was not a particularly intelligent or subtle actor, but he had a fine presence, a passionate style, and a strong repertory of theatrical tricks which made him acceptable to the more uncritical section of the audience. He was a staunch supporter of Iffland at Mannheim, and was sadly missed when he died of drink soon after the latter had been appointed producer to the theatre. His wife (Sophia Schulze) had received her early training under Schönemann, and always retained something of the early affected style, but she was very popular, particularly in her youth in breeches parts.

BOILEAU-DESPRÉAUX, NICOLAS (1636–1711), a French critic who exercised a great influence on French literature and drama. He was intended for the Church, but studied law and in 1660 took to literature. His criticism brought a new and invigorating atmosphere into the literary debates of Paris. He was not a poet, but a writer of verse, and a good one. He had no imagination, no warmth, but plenty of common sense and an uncanny flair for the best in art. He appreciated and was the friend of the great men of his time, of Racine—whom he taught to write verse—of La Fontaine, and particularly of Molière, whose satire matched his, and whom Boileau called *le contemplateur.* It was at the height of his friendship with Boileau that Molière wrote his greatest plays, *Tartuffe* and *Le Misanthrope*, as well as *Don Juan.* It was said of Boileau that his criticisms were mordant, but always justified, and that those whom he attacked never recovered.

BOINDIN, NICOLAS (1676–1751), French dramatist and man of letters, whose lonely and delicate childhood developed in him habits of study and reflection beyond his years and a decided bent towards atheism. After a year in the army, which he left owing to ill health, he frequented the literary cafés of Paris and became a friend of Saurin and La Motte. He wrote a number of plays, of which the most successful, *Le Bal d'Auteuil* (1702), caused a tightening-up of the censorship laws by its equivocal plot. His work in other directions, which included a number of volumes on French theatre history, would have earned him a seat in the French Academy, but he was denied it owing to his irreligion, which later led the clergy to refuse him Christian burial. After quarrelling with La Motte, Boindin founded a new literary clique which had its headquarters at the Café Procope. He was an excellent talker, at his best when he was in the wrong, and Voltaire, who disliked him intensely, drew a savage picture of him as Bardon in *Le Temple du goût.*

BOISROBERT, FRANÇOIS LE METEL DE, ABBÉ (1592–1662), a great talker, a pleasant companion, a priest who preferred the pleasures of the world to the duties of his office, a friend of Richelieu, and a foundation member of the French Academy. In addition to all this he found time to be a dramatist, producing his first play at the age of 40. Since it was successful he continued to write for the stage until he had nearly twenty plays to his credit. He was one of the dramatists chosen by Richelieu to write his plays for him, and in the eyes of his contemporaries he was no doubt the most important, although his collaborators included Corneille. Boisrobert's continued success in the theatre may have done something to disgust Corneille with play-writing, especially after the failure of *Pertharite* in 1662. Yet, since Molière found some of *L'Avare*, and a hint of *L'École des maris*, in Boisrobert's forgotten comedies he cannot be said to have lived in vain. He was the younger brother of the profligate playwright d'Ouville.

BOITO, ARRIGO (1842–1918), Italian poet and composer, and the first to realize that the libretto of an opera should have some literary value. His own opera 'Mefistofele' (1868), based on Goethe's *Faust*, was not at first a success, though in a revised form it later won acceptance; but it is as the librettist of Verdi's 'Otello' (1887) and 'Falstaff' (1893) that he is chiefly remembered. His handling of the themes is excellent, and his translations keep closely to the Shakespearian originals, without sacrificing the sense to the music.

BOKER, GEORGE HENRY (1823–90), American dramatist, who imported into the early drama of the United States themes of historical romance, interpreted in blank verse. Two of these were on incidents in Spanish history, *Calaynos* (1849) and *Leonor de Guzman* (1853), but his most famous play, and the only one to be extensively acted and revived, was Italian, *Francesca da Rimini.* This was first given at New York in 1855, and in 1882 was revived by Lawrence Barrett with himself as Lanciotto, Francesca's husband, who in Boker's version becomes the chief character in the play. It remained in his repertory for many years and was again revived in 1901 by Otis Skinner. The text was frequently revised, notably by William Winter in 1882, and has never been acted from the printed version, since Boker himself altered it extensively for production. He later wrote two other plays in the style of

Francesca da Rimini, but they were not produced. His comedies, of which he wrote three,
are less important, and it is as one of the few
successful exponents of blank verse tragedy
that he is chiefly remembered (see POETIC
DRAMA). Boker was a poet of some standing,
and from 1871 to 1875 and 1875 to 1878 served
as American envoy to Turkey and Russia.

BOLIVIA, see SOUTH AMERICA, 1.

BONARELLI DELLA ROVERE, GUIDO-
BALDO (1563–1608), Italian dramatist, author of
the best-known pastoral of the seventeenth
century, the *Filli di Sciro*, produced at Ferrara
in 1607. (See ITALY, 1 *b* ii and PASTORAL.)
This was given at Cambridge in a Latin translation by Samuel Brooke before Henry, Prince
of Wales, on 2 or 3 Mar. 1613, and in an English
translation about twenty years later before the
Court in London. A second English translation, by Gilbert Talbot, was played in London
in 1657. The first was printed in 1655, the
second remains in manuscript.

BOND, THOMAS (?–1635), English actor, whose
portrait is at Dulwich, somewhat surprisingly,
since he does not appear to figure with any
great prominence in the theatrical records of the
time. He was a provincial actor in 1624, when
he appeared at Norwich and Exeter, and played
small parts in two London companies, at the
Red Bull and Salisbury Court. Kemble was
certainly mistaken in saying that Bond (or Band,
as he is sometimes called) was the third actor to
play Bussy d'Ambois, since he was never with
the King's Men, who owned the play.

BONSTELLE, JESSIE (1872–1932), American
actress and theatre manager, nicknamed the
Maker of Stars. Her real name was Laura
Justine Bonesteele, and she began her career as
a child, reciting at concerts and playing in
amateur productions. In 1890 she started her
professional career in a touring company under
Augustin Daly. At the age of 19 she was already
managing the Shuberts' theatre in Syracuse,
and after several similar ventures in other
towns, including Toronto, she became lessee
of the Garrick Theatre in Detroit from 1910 to
1922, and then purchased the Playhouse in the
same city. She opened it in 1925, and three
years later, having aroused the interest of the
townsfolk, was able to make it one of America's
first Civic Playhouses, run on the lines of the
Theatre Guild. Under her many-sided control
it flourished until her death. She was responsible for the fostering of much native American
talent, and among her discoveries was Katharine
Cornell. In 1892 she married an actor, Alexander Hamilton Stuart, who died in 1911.

BOOKED FLAT, two flats hinged together.
They may also be used as a Booked Wing (not
to be confused with Book Wing below).

BOOKHOLDER, the Elizabethan name for
the prompter, not to be confused with the Book-
keeper, an important functionary for whom see
below. In addition to prompting the actors in
their parts the bookholder saw that they were
ready for their entrances, and was responsible
for their props.

BOOK-KEEPER, an important member of
an Elizabethan company, who was responsible
for the manuscript copies of plays and of actors'
parts. He might also, though not necessarily,
be an actor, and was in any case likely to be
concerned with the finance and management of
the company.

BOOK WING, used on the English Victorian
stage, usually four at each entrance, each
quartet hanging on its own central upright
spindle. This passed down through a hole in
the stage, and at its lower end was a grooved
wheel. By means of a connecting rope passing
over these wheels, all the spindles could be
rotated and all the wings of a scene changed
simultaneously by means of one master handle.

BOOMERANG, see LIGHTING, 2.

BOOTH, a family of actors, of English origin,
but important in the history of the American
theatre, and indeed in world history generally,
since one member of it was responsible
for the assassination of President Lincoln
on 14 Apr. 1865. The first of the family to
achieve eminence on the stage was (1) JUNIUS
BRUTUS (1796–1852), who owed his Christian
names to the republican sentiments of his
lawyer father. He was given a good education,
and destined for the law, but went on the stage
at 17. After touring for some years he appeared
at Covent Garden as Richard III, and almost
immediately entered into rivalry with Edmund
Kean, the reigning favourite of the London
stage. He was seen at Covent Garden as Sir
Giles Overreach, Leonatus Posthumus, and,
in 1818, as Shylock. Two years later he was
seen as Lear, and shortly afterwards went to
Drury Lane, where he played Iago to Kean's
Othello, Edgar to his Lear, and Pierre to his
Jaffier. In 1821 he deserted his legal wife, by
whom he had one son, and with Mary Ann
Holmes, a flower-seller in Bow Street, went
to America, making his first appearance as
Richard III at Richmond, Va. From then
until his death, except for two short visits to
Drury Lane, he was constantly seen in America,
where he may be said to have founded the
tradition of tragic acting. He made his first
appearance in New York late in 1821, again
as Richard III, and was seen in a number of
classic, as well as modern, parts. He was also
manager of several theatres. Among his other
achievements was the playing, in French, of
Orestes in Racine's *Andromaque*, and he is said
to have played Shylock in Hebrew. He was
on tour in the West when he died on board
a Mississippi steamboat, and was buried at
Baltimore. He made his last appearance at the
St. Charles Theatre, New Orleans. He was a
superb actor, rough and unpolished, but full
of grandeur and eloquence, with a resonant
voice and ample gesture. There was, however,
a streak of insanity in him, aggravated by his
intemperate habits, which he appears to have

passed on to his sons. He and Mary Ann had ten children before, in 1851, his first wife divorced him and they were able to marry. Several of them died young, a fact which contributed not a little to Booth's habitual melancholy. The eldest, however, (2) JUNIUS BRUTUS junior (1821–83), survived to make the stage his profession, and though never so good an actor as his father, he was accounted an excellent manager and producer. He acted with the elder Booth in 1835, and again in 1852, playing Iago to his father's Othello. He was for many years a useful member of the stock company at the Bowery Theatre, New York, and later of that at Booth's Theatre. One of his best parts was Dan Lowrie in Frances Hodgson Burnett's *That Lass o' Lowrie's* (1878), which he also played on tour. He was three times married, and had two sons on the stage. The elder shot himself and his wife in a London hotel, but the younger, (3) SYDNEY BARTON (1873–1937), who made his début at Wallack's in 1892, was a successful leading man with such actresses as Maude Adams, Lillian Russell, Jane Cowl, Ruth Chatterton, Grace George, and Alice Brady. In 1902 he went into vaudeville for two seasons.

The second surviving son of the elder Booth was (4) EDWIN THOMAS (1833–93), one of the first great American actors, and the first to win a European reputation. He was an unhappy man, prone to melancholia and much affected by the insanity of his father, brother, and second wife. But as a tragic actor he had few equals. He made his first appearance in his father's company at the age of 16, and remained with him until the latter's death, playing Richard III at 18. He soon established a fine reputation, one of his best parts being Sir Giles Overreach. He toured Australia in 1854 with Laura Keene, and in 1861 was seen at the Haymarket, London, as Shylock, Overreach, and Richelieu. It was during this visit that his daughter Edwina was born, his wife Mary Devlin (1840–63) dying two years later. He returned to the United States, and from 1863 to 1867 was manager of the Winter Garden Theatre, where in 1864 he set up a record with a hundred consecutive performances of *Hamlet*, which was not broken until John Barrymore's one hundred and one in 1923. After the destruction by fire of the Winter Garden Theatre, he built his own theatre, opening it with a fine production of *Romeo and Juliet* on 3 Feb. 1869. The actress who played Juliet, Miss McVicker, later became his second wife, dying in 1881. Both remained there with a fine company in a distinguished list of plays until 1873, when he went bankrupt. Nothing daunted, he embarked on a series of starring tours throughout the United States, and built up a new and enviable reputation. He was seen in England between 1880 and 1882, and also went to Germany, where his fine acting was much appreciated. In London he appeared at the Lyceum by invitation of Henry Irving, and the two actors alternated the roles of Othello and Iago. In 1888 he presented his

house in Gramercy Park to the newly founded Players' Club, and continued to occupy his rooms there until his death. A good deal of Edwin's moodiness and despair must be ascribed to the shock consequent on the assassination of Lincoln by his youngest brother (5) JOHN WILKES (1839–65), during a performance at Ford's Theatre, Washington, of *Our American Cousin*. There are two conflicting theories current about this mad act. The one presents John Wilkes as a wild, undisciplined, and embittered madman, jealous of his brother's success, and seeking notoriety through crime; the other considers him an excellent actor, though eccentric, and ascribes his action to motives of mistaken patriotism. For a systematic survey of the whole question, see *The Mad Booths of Maryland* (1940) by Stanley Kimmel.

The elder Booth's only daughter, Asia, married the actor-manager John Sleeper Clarke (1834–99).

BOOTH, BARTON (1681–1733), English actor, of good family and well educated, whose aptitude for the stage showed itself early in a fine performance in the *Andria* of Terence while he was at Westminster School. His theatrical ambitions not meeting with much encouragement from his family, he went to Dublin, and after two seasons at the theatre there, and possibly a short tour of the English provinces, was engaged by Betterton for Lincoln's Inn Fields Theatre in 1700. Here he proved himself a fine tragic actor, worthy to carry on the traditions of Betterton, but he was slow in establishing himself, even when the company moved to Vanbrugh's new theatre in the Haymarket. This was possibly due to the jealousy of Wilks, who was, however, unable to prevent Booth's success as Pyrrhus in *The Distressed Mother* (1712), and as Addison's Cato, his greatest part, in the following year. These successes, coupled with that of his Othello, brought him money as well as reputation, and he became one of the managers of Drury Lane with Cibber and Wilks, Doggett retiring in disgust on political grounds. Booth played a wide range of tragic roles, and though not tall, was dignified in appearance, with a rich, well-trained voice. He is believed to have regretted his decision to become an actor, but persevered in his profession for many years, though in later life he proved somewhat lazy. The most striking features of his acting were his 'attitudes', the pose, for instance, in which he listened, with appropriate gestures, to Emilia's address to her dying mistress. In these he was unexcelled, and even those who were jealous of his popularity conceded his effectiveness at such points. After the death of his first wife he married, in 1719, Hester Santlow, a dancer and actress of some repute, with whom he lived happily, though accused of marrying her for her money.

BOOTH THEATRE, NEW YORK, on 45th Street. This was built by Winthrop Ames, and opened 16 Oct. 1913 with *The Great*

Adventure, based by Arnold Bennett on his novel *Buried Alive*. Lyn Harding and Janet Beecher headed the cast, and a minor part was played by Guthrie McClintic, later to figure so prominently in the New York theatre. The Booth is still (1949) in use, and has had a fair number of successes, including *The Green Goddess* (1921) and *You Can't Take It With You* (1936), which ran for two years. Two distinguished failures were *White Wings* (1926) and *For Services Rendered* (1933). In 1925 a production of *Hamlet* in modern dress was seen at the Booth, with Basil Sidney in the title-role supported by a fine cast. Among its later successes have been *Claudia* and a fantastic production of *Le Bourgeois gentilhomme* with the comedian Bobby Clark as M. Jourdain.

BOOTH'S THEATRE, NEW YORK, on the south-west corner of 6th Avenue and 23rd Street. It was built for Edwin Booth, and opened on 3 Feb. 1869, with Booth and Mary McVicker, later his second wife, as Romeo and Juliet. The stage was the finest yet seen in New York, splendidly equipped, and wings and flats were discarded in favour of solid sets. After the opening production came *Othello*, and subsequent seasons saw Booth in many of his finest parts, as well as such outstanding actors as Kate Bateman—her last appearance in New York before her departure to London as Mrs. Crowe—Hackett, also in his last regular New York season, Jefferson in *Rip Van Winkle*, Lawrence Barrett, who played Cassius to Booth's Brutus, and Charlotte Cushman, who played opposite Booth in *Macbeth* and *Henry VIII*. Booth had hoped to establish a great national theatre for the production of poetic drama, but after a good start the venture failed, and in 1873 he withdrew from the management on which he had embarked with such high hopes. He frequently appeared at the theatre as a guest-star, in common with other outstanding actors of the day, and it was at Booth's that Adelaide Neilson made her first appearance in New York, and the younger Wallack his last. Fanny Janauschek appeared in a version of *Bleak House*, made by herself, and Minnie Maddern, later the famous Mrs. Fiske, played Arthur in *King John*. After Edwin's withdrawal, his brother, Junius Brutus, had endeavoured to manage the theatre, but on 30 May 1874 it passed out of the control of the Booth family, and was opened by Jarrett and Palmer with plays by Boucicault. Later in the same year Charlotte Cushman made her farewell appearances, ending with Lady Macbeth on 7 Nov. The great event of 1875 was the importation from the Theatre Royal, Manchester, of Calvert's production of *Henry V*, with George Rignold in the name part, and Mrs. Charles Calvert as Rumour. Calvert's production of Byron's *Sardanapalus* was also seen, with scenery by Telbin, but it was much hampered by adventitious ballet and spectacle, and was not a great success, though it ran for 113 performances. The theatre continued to house visiting stars, and saw the last appearance of E. L. Davenport, as Edgar in Lawrence Barrett's *King Lear*. In 1879 Dion Boucicault became its lessee. Under him Rose Coghlan, John Brougham, Robert B. Mantell, Helena Modjeska, with Maurice Barrymore and many other stars, gave successful seasons, and Charles R. Thorne junior made his last appearance on any stage in *The Corsican Brothers*. He played only two nights, and died shortly after. The theatre was then sold, and disappeared in a blaze of glory, with Salvini, Clara Morris, and Modjeska in quick succession. Its last production was *Romeo and Juliet*, with Modjeska and Maurice Barrymore. It closed on 30 Apr. 1883, and was pulled down, a large department store being built on the site.

BORDER, a narrow strip of painted cloth, battened at the top edge only, used to mask-in, or hide, the top of the stage as seen from the auditorium. The lower edge is often cut to a shape, and the whole is then known as an Arch, Beam, Cloud, Sky, or Tree Border. The use of clouds for masking the top of almost any scene was formerly common (see CLOUDINGS). In Victorian times plain sky borders were sometimes known as Blues. Tails, or Legs, on a border are long vertically hanging extensions at each end, forming with the border an arch over the scene.   R. S.

BÖRJESSEN, JOHAN (1790–1866), Swedish dramatist, one of the first to write under the influence of Shakespeare, whose works had recently appeared in translation (see SCANDINAVIA, 3).

BOSSU D'ARRAS, LE, see ADAM DE LA HALLE.

BOSTON, a town important in the history of the American theatre, though the early companies had much opposition to contend with. Even after the building of the New Exhibition Room (1792), later the Board Alley Theatre, plays had still to be given as 'Moral Lectures'. In 1794 the Federal Street Theatre was built, rebuilt after a fire four years later, and finally destroyed, after a long and chequered career, in 1852. Two years later the present Boston Theatre was built. The Haymarket, built in 1796, was unable to rival the popularity of the Federal Theatre, and was pulled down in 1803. The Tremont Theatre, which opened in 1827, was able for a short time to take over and close the Federal, its only rival, but was itself outshone by the Boston Museum, which opened in 1841; the Tremont closed in 1843 and was used as a church, and for concerts and lectures, until destroyed by fire in 1852. Other Boston theatres were the Howard Athenaeum, opened by Hackett in 1846, and the National, which opened in 1832 as the American Amphitheatre, later became the Warren, and was destroyed by fire in 1852. The Boston Museum, which had a long and glorious history, reached the height of its popularity in 1873–83, with a fine stock company and good visiting stars. It finally closed in 1893.

BOTTOMLEY, GORDON (1874–1948), English poet, and one of the few to bring verse-plays successfully into the professional theatre. His *King Lear's Wife* (1915), *Britain's Daughters* (1922), *Gruach* (1923), and *Laodice and Danae* (1930) were all seen in London, while *Gruach* was awarded the Femina–Vie Heureuse Prize. He was in no way a neo-Elizabethan, although the influence of Shakespeare can be seen in his work, as can that of the Japanese No play. But his themes are taken mainly from Celtic and Northern legend and early history, and he introduced to England, as Yeats did to Ireland, the Celtic and Northern twilight, the old world of fear and evil. He was an important figure in the evolution of the modern poetic drama, and wrote also a number of one-act plays, and the Exeter Cathedral Festival play for 1933, *The Acts of St. Peter*.

BOUCHER, FRANÇOIS (1703–70), famous French artist, who in 1744 succeeded Servandony as decorator at the Paris Opéra, remaining there until 1748 (see COSTUME, 7).

BOUCICAULT [BOURCICAULT and BOURSIQUOT]. (1) DIONYSIUS LARDNER (1822–90), actor and dramatist of Irish extraction, whose life and works were divided between England and the U.S.A. He was a prolific author, being credited with some 150 plays, many of them translations from the French or adaptations of novels. The former, which began with *The Corsican Brothers* in 1852, were given mainly at the Princess's under Charles Kean or at the Adelphi, where they set a standard for romantic melodrama; the latter included *The Colleen Bawn* (1860), one of Boucicault's most successful plays. More than any other dramatist of the time he had 'the trick of the theatre' and his material, wherever he found it, was shaped to fit the taste and fashion of the day. Professor Allardyce Nicoll, who has a great admiration for Boucicault's undoubted gifts, says of him (*Nineteenth Century Drama*, i. 84), '[His] importance as a dramatist rests on two things—his uncanny sense of theatrical values and his keenly observant eye. No man knew better than he just what would appeal on the stage. The construction of his plays, if we make allowance for their frankly melodramatic framework, is excellent; and of countless theatrical devices he was the eager inventor. . . . Crude as many of his effects may seem to us, he had an acute eye for oddity in real life, and many of his best scenes rely, not on scenic splendour, but on the depiction, through laughter or tears, of domestic interiors. It was this—the cultivation of naturalistically conceived scenes allied to melodramatic excitement—which gave him his contemporary importance.' He was also the first, and for a long time the only, dramatist to treat the American negro seriously on the stage, in *The Octoroon; or, Life in Louisiana* (1859). Many of his plays, in which he acted himself, were also graced by the presence of his wife (2) AGNES KELLY ROBERTSON (1833–1916), who appeared on the stage in Scotland as a child, and in 1850, under the tuition of the Charles Keans, was first seen in London. She accompanied her husband on his tours to America, where she was immensely popular, and though a Scotswoman by birth, played to the life the Irish heroines of *The Colleen Bawn*, *Arrah-na-Pogue*, and *The Shaughraun*, as well as Jessie Brown in a drama based on the Relief of Lucknow and Jeanie Deans in a dramatization of *The Heart of Midlothian*. A sweet, gentle woman, she was universally beloved and respected. Several of her children were on the stage, the eldest, (3) DIONYSIUS GEORGE (1859–1929), being also a dramatist. He made his first appearance in his father's company in New York in 1879, and in London played with Hawtrey. He was for many years in Australia, in partnership with Robert Brough, and from 1901 to 1915 he produced all the plays given at the Duke of York's Theatre, London, under the management of Charles Frohman. His best parts were Sir William Gower in *Trelawny of the 'Wells'* (1898) and Carraway Pim in *Mr. Pim Passes By* (1920). In 1901 he married Irene Vanbrugh, who appeared in many of his productions at the Duke of York's, and was Olivia to his Mr. Pim (see VANBRUGH, 2).

BOUFFE, OPÉRA, see OPERA, 5.

BOUFFES-PARISIENS, a theatre opened by Offenbach in 1855, first in the Champs-Élysées, in the old Salle Lacaze, and on its present site at the end of the same year. It is mainly used for light opera, of which the most successful was 'Orphée aux Enfers', and for musical plays.

BOULEVARD DU TEMPLE, a fair-ground in Paris which took the place of the earlier fairs of Saint-Germain and Saint-Laurent, and under the Revolution saw the building of a number of small permanent playhouses, of which the first was that of Nicolet, later the Gaîté. The whole area became a centre of entertainment, having also in its precincts the Ambigu-Comique, the Folies-Dramatiques, the Funambules, as well as circuses and booths for acrobats and puppet-shows. The whole picturesque scene was swept away in 1862, in the rebuilding scheme of Haussmann, and the Boulevard Voltaire now occupies most of the site. Many famous actors, including Deburau, Frédérick-Lemaître, Mme Dorval, and Bocage, were seen in its theatres, while Dumas and Gautier were among those who wrote for it in its later years. But its main purveyors were the prolific and second-rate authors of melodrama, Pixérécourt, Bouchardy, and others, from whose works it took its nickname of the Boulevard of Crime. In its earlier days the two farce-players Bobèche and Galimafré revived memories of the earlier *parades*, and children's companies played in the little theatres which were later to house some of the greatest actors of France. And always there were innumerable sideshows, wild beasts, fireworks, waxworks, and museums, as well as the cafés with their concerts and the perambulating musicians and ballad-singers.

BOURCHIER, ARTHUR (1863–1927), English actor, husband of Violet Vanbrugh, whom he married in 1894. Educated at Eton and Oxford, he was one of the founders of the Oxford University Dramatic Society (O.U.D.S.), playing Hotspur, Feste, Falstaff, and Brutus in its first productions. On leaving the university he joined the company of Mrs. Langtry, and made his first professional appearance as Jaques at Wolverhampton. After his marriage he toured with his wife, who played the leading parts in his farces and comedies, many of them adapted from the French. From 1900 to 1906 he was in management at the Garrick Theatre, London, playing Shylock, Macbeth, and new plays by Pinero, Gilbert, H. A. Jones, and others. In 1910 he joined Tree at His Majesty's Theatre, and was seen in a number of Shakespearian parts, being particularly admired as Henry VIII. He later appeared at the Oxford Music-Hall as Old Bill in a sketch based on Bairnsfather's *The Better 'Ole*. He was devoted to the theatre, and frequently lectured on it. He was at his best in truculent, fiery, or broad, hearty parts, but had little subtlety and hotly resented criticism, spoiling much of his best work by impatience and over-eagerness. He died in South Africa while on tour. His second wife, whom he married in 1918, was Violet Marion Kyrle Bellew.

BOURDET, ÉDOUARD (1877–1945), French dramatist, whose plays, written under the influence of Becque, are subtle and penetrating portrayals of social and moral disequilibrium. The first, *Le Rubicon* (1910), was a light comedy based on the complications of a wedding-night, but with his succeeding works Bourdet became more serious, until by way of *La Cage ouverte* (1920) and *L'Heure du berger* (1922) he reached his peak of analysis and penetration with a study of Lesbianism entitled *La Prisonnière* (1926). Some years later he followed this with a study of homosexuality in *La Fleur des pois* (1932), but developed his theme as comedy instead of tragedy, as previously. One of his most penetrating plays was *Vient de paraître* (1927), a satire on the modern commercialism of literature. Most of Bourdet's plays have been translated into English, and have been seen in London and New York. It has been said of him that his 'conflicts of the heart were situated often on the borderline of the forbidden, but he managed with consummate art not to overstep the line of dramatic propriety'. He brought wit and irony to his satires, which made no pretence at propaganda, and struck out at corruption wherever he found it without seeking to point the moral.

BOURSAULT, EDMÉ (1638–1701), French man of letters, who went to Paris at the age of 13, entirely uneducated, and by dint of study and application, joined to a natural aptitude for literature, soon made a name for himself. In 1661 his first play, a farce entitled *Le Médecin volant*, was given at the Hôtel de Bourgogne. It was followed by several others, and then, thinking himself attacked in the

character of Licidas in Molière's *La Critique de l'École des femmes*—which was mainly aimed at d'Aubigné—he replied with *Le Portrait du peintre* (1663), in which he accuses Molière of putting recognizable contemporary characters on the stage. The dispute threatened to become acrimonious, but Boursault, who really admired Molière and knew how much he owed him, capitulated, and they became friends. Boursault also attacked and then became friendly with Boileau, who at one time rated him soundly for his bad style, and congratulated him when he improved. Boursault, who was happily married and father of a large family, had none of the faults of the self-made man, but was modest, kindly, and good-mannered. For many years he was taken up with literary work for the Court, and wrote no plays, but in 1683 he reappeared with *La Comédie sans titre; ou, le Mercure Galant*, which shows an immense improvement on his earlier works, as did two later plays, based on the life and fables of Aesop. They are interesting as being the first instance of direct moral teaching in French drama, forerunners of the eighteenth-century *drames sérieux*. The more successful of the two, *Ésope à la cour* (1701), was produced after Boursault's death, and was adapted in English by Vanbrugh.

BOUSCHET, JAN, see ENGLISH COMEDIANS.

BOWER SALOON, LONDON, at Stangate St., Lambeth, was built and opened in 1838 by a scene-painter named Phillips. East End actors who were afterwards to please the West End made their débuts there, and West End actors out of work were glad to find employment there in its early days. George Hodson, father of Henrietta Hodson, was an early manager; so was Biddles, father of Mrs. Calvert, who made her first appearance at the Bower Saloon as Adelaide Biddles. James Fernandez for some time a member of the company. Eventually it sank very low, with rowdy audiences, and plays—from *Macbeth* to *Maria Marten*—done in the roughest and most barnstorming manner. It came to an end in 1879.

W. M. P.

BOWERY THEATRE, NEW YORK. (1) A theatre was first projected for the Bowery in 1823, when it was to have been called the Bull's Head Theatre from the name of a tavern on the intended site. It finally opened on 23 Oct. 1826 with *The Road to Ruin*, as the New York Theatre, Bowery, but it was always known simply as the Bowery. Gilfert and George H. Barrett were the first managers, and they had gathered round them a fine cast. The theatre was lit by gas, not with naked jets, as previously at the Chatham, but with the flames enclosed in glass shades. One of the earliest productions of the Bowery was a fine *School for Scandal*, with Mrs. Gilfert as Lady Teazle and Barrett as Charles. Edwin Forrest, whose name is for ever associated with the Bowery, where he had many of his early triumphs, made his first appearance there as Othello, and shortly afterwards Hamblin, its manager for many years, appeared as Virginius. At first the new theatre proved stronger in comedy than in tragedy, but it later became the home of melodrama. Among highlights in its early history were the French ballet dancers introduced by Gilfert to New York, which had seen nothing like them before, and the appearance of Louisa Lane, later Mrs. John Drew, at the age of 8. Cooper and Forrest then starred in a joint engagement, but on 26 May 1828 the theatre was burnt down, and the actors had to migrate to Niblo's Sans Souci. A second Bowery Theatre opened on 20 Aug. of the same year, again under Gilfert, with Forrest as its star, but soon declined into melodrama and spectacle, as with Dunlap's *Trip to Niagara*, which was merely the excuse for the employment of dioramic scenery. On 30 July 1829 Gilfert died, and after a period during which the Bowery was managed jointly with the Park, Hamblin entered on his 20 years of management. Under him melodrama flourished, and the Bowery was the first theatre in New York to start continuous runs, in opposition to the constant changes of bill as still practised at the old-fashioned Park Theatre. Hamblin tried to rechristen the theatre, naming it the American Theatre, Bowery, but it was always referred to by its old name. Rice appeared there in his famous Jim Crow song and dance, Louisa Lane, now aged 13, came back as 'general utility', and a great success was scored by *Mazeppa*, and by Céleste, appearing for the first time in her famous *French Spy*. The Bowery saw, in the season of 1835–6, the last appearance in New York of the great actor, Cooper, and the first of Charlotte Cushman, as Lady Macbeth. In Sept. 1836 the theatre was once again burnt down, but a third Bowery was ready by the following New Year's Day. It was destined to have a short and uninteresting history, as it was again destroyed by fire on 18 Feb. 1838, and not reopened until 6 May 1839, once more under the management of Hamblin, who had been absent in England during the lifetime of the third Bowery. Among the successful melodramas of the fourth Bowery was *Jack Sheppard*, with Mrs. Shaw, who later appeared on her benefit night as Hamlet. John Gilbert made his first appearance in New York as Sir Edward Mortimer in *The Iron Chest*, but the fortunes of the theatre appeared to decline. Circus, boxing, aquatic drama, unsuccessful plays, and constant cuts in the price of admission, had brought the theatre to a very low ebb when on 25 Apr. 1845, for the fourth time in less than 17 years, it was once more destroyed by fire, just prior to a benefit for the Davenports. The actors went to Tryon's Amphitheatre, and the Bowery was again rebuilt. It opened on 4 Aug. 1845, continuing its policy of melodrama, and Hamblin, still its manager, undertook also the management of the Park Theatre after the death of Simpson until it too was destroyed by fire.

In 1851 an actor who was long to be the

idol of the Bowery audiences made his first appearance in a series of strong parts. This was Edward Eddy, who after the death of Hamblin in 1853 and the consequent decline of the theatre under several unsuitable managers, took over himself in 1857. He too was unable to restore prosperity to the old theatre and left after one season. On 7 Aug. 1858 the theatre reopened under George L. Fox and James W. Lingard with a curious mixture of plays and pantomimes, and a series of melodramas by Boucicault. When they left to open the New Bowery in the following year the old Bowery, now the oldest playhouse in New York, was once again subjected to a series of incompetent managers. During the Civil War it was occupied by the military, and then became a circus. After thorough renovation, which it badly needed, Fox reopened it as Fox's Old Bowery, and put on a rapid succession of novelties including a pantomime of Old Dame Trot and her Wonderful Cat. Long after the old-fashioned farce had vanished from New York's newer playhouses it continued to flourish at the old Bowery, but melodrama was always its staple fare. On 2 Nov. 1868 Boucicault's *After Dark* was put on at the Bowery, but was stopped on the complaint of Niblo's managers, who held the American rights. The theatre then fell a victim to the prevalent craze for burlesque, and finally closed in 1878, having seen the New York début of Ada Rehan in melodrama and farce, a curious beginning for the future star of Daly's. In Sept. 1879 the old Bowery, which had spanned more than 50 years of the young American theatre, was reopened as the Thalia for plays in German, and was finally destroyed by its old enemy, fire, in 1929.

(2) The New Bowery opened on 5 Sept. 1859, under Fox and Lingard, with a good company, some filched from the Old Bowery, where the managers had been in office for the previous year. The theatre had a short and somewhat undistinguished career, enlivened only by visits from guest-stars and the inevitable *Uncle Tom's Cabin*. When Fox returned to the Old Bowery, Lingard carried on alone, with a stock company in an undistinguished repertory, and the season of 1866–7 was well under way, mainly with melodrama and pantomime, when on 18 Dec. 1866 the theatre was destroyed by fire and never rebuilt.

BOWYER, MICHAEL (?–1645), English actor, who, after several years on the stage, played leading romantic roles with the Queen's Men, a company organized at the Cockpit in 1625. He was apparently considered the leader of the company after Beeston, but some years later (about 1637) he left it for the King's Men, with whom he remained until the closing of the theatres in 1642. He was evidently a man of means, and he left a large legacy to his fellow player, Richard Perkins.

BOX, a term used in the modern theatre for small compartments on each side of the stage, in the auditorium, adjoining the circles and holding four to six people each. These are usually the most expensive but least adequate seats in the house, since one obtains from them a distorted sideways view of the stage. They were often filled by those who wished to be seen as much as to see. They were previously known as Side Boxes, since in earlier times boxes ran all round the pit—a custom which still obtains in opera-houses—and held up to twenty people each. The Royal, or King's Box, originally facing the stage, shifted in Georgian times to the side, where it remains, save in exceptional cases. The nineteenth-century Dress Box gave rise to the modern Dress Circle, while such variants as Family Box, Omnibus Box, Private Box, and Front Box (the two latter being of the eighteenth century) are self-explanatory. Slip Boxes were originally those at the end of the circles, nearest the stage, while Proscenium Boxes, first built into the proscenium itself, gave way to the modern Stage Boxes, those of the lowest tier on each side of the stage. Green Boxes were those near the top of the house, probably furnished in green, and not, like the more sumptuous lower boxes, in crimson, while Private Boxes might be provided with a lattice or screen, and were then known as Lattice (or Lettice) Boxes, and later as Baskets. The Pay-Boxes in early theatres were small cubicles for the taking of money. Their function has now been largely usurped by the Box-Office (see below), the name being reserved in the modern theatre for those places where money is taken at the door. (See also AUDITORIUM.)   R. S.

BOX-OFFICE, that part of a theatre devoted to the selling of seats. The name dates from the time when the majority of seats in the house, except in the gallery, were in boxes. The staff of the Box-Office may consist of from one to six persons, according to the size of the house, some of the larger theatres having separate divisions for differently priced seats, and for booking in advance. The term Pay-Box, used in the eighteenth century for the recesses at which entrance money was paid, is now generally reserved for those windows (i.e. gallery, amphitheatre, pit) which collect money at the door, and do no advance booking. But customs may vary from one theatre to another. The Box-Office is under the control of a Box-Office Manager, an important member of the theatre staff, who may remain attached to one theatre for many years and become, as it were, a repository of its history and traditions. He works long hours, and usually has three telephones to attend to at once, and half a dozen more in connexion with the 'libraries', or ticket-selling agencies. A quick mind, a cheerful disposition, and great patience and tact are requisites for this job, while the holder of it must be an accurate accountant and ready reckoner as well. The term 'box-office' is used metaphorically to indicate the appeal of a play to the public, and 'good box-office' may indicate a drawing power in money incommensurate with the excellence of the fare

offered. In happier circumstances the two may be combined, and good drama prove equally good box-office.

BOX SET, a scene representing the three walls and ceiling of a room, not by means of perspective painting on wings, backcloth, and borders, as in early scenery, but by an arrangement of flats which form continuous walls, with practicable doors and windows, completely covered in by a ceiling cloth. The flats are lined-and-cleated together, edge to edge, on any desired ground plan, with Reveals, or false thickness-pieces, to give solidity to the openings, and Returns, or setbacks, in the walls. The bottoms of openings in a door or arch flat are strengthened by flat metal strips called Sill Irons. The Box Set, first used in 1841 by the younger Mathews and Mme Vestris, is now in general use for most modern plays.   R. S.

BOY BISHOP, THE, a choirboy appointed to be the chief personage in the children's revels held either on St. Nicholas's Day (6 Dec.) or on Holy Innocents (28 Dec.) in cathedral and monastic schools, and song schools. Earlier in origin than the Feast of Fools, with which it was sometimes amalgamated, this festival probably began as a serious church service conducted by the choirboys, but soon developed a secular, merry-making character, with plays—usually in Latin—given by the children, and considered as part of their education. It can be traced all over Europe and was extremely popular in England, where the first note of it (at York) is earlier than 1221. The custom of appointing a Boy Bishop survived till the Reformation.

BOY COMPANIES. During the sixteenth century plays were frequently given at Court by boy actors, particularly those attached to the choir schools and known as the Children of the Chapel and the Children of Paul's. In 1576 the former made their first public appearance at the Blackfriars, which for some time after was used exclusively as a children's theatre. The popularity of the boy players is attested by Hamlet's reference to them as 'an aerie of children, little eyases'. They achieved a quasi-professional status, and gave performances of many important plays, including some by Jonson, Lyly, and Marston.

BOYLE, ROGER, see ORRERY.

BOYLE, WILLIAM (1853–1923), see IRELAND.

BRACE, see STAGE BRACE.

BRACEGIRDLE, ANNE (?1663–1748), one of the first and loveliest of English actresses, who was as much esteemed for the austerity of her private life as for the excellence of her acting. She first appeared on the stage as a child, and was a pupil of Betterton, to whom, and to his wife, she was much indebted for kindness and encouragement. She made her greatest successes as the heroines of Congreve's comedies, and was particularly applauded as Millamant. From 1680 until her retirement in 1707 she was universally admired and beloved, by her fellow actors as much as by the public, and deeply regretted when she left the stage at the height of her fame. But a new star had risen in the person of Anne Oldfield, and the older actress preferred to leave the field rather than be driven from it.

BRACKENRIDGE, HUGH HENRY (1748–1816), an early American dramatist, author of two plays on the American Revolution, *The Battle of Bunkers Hill*, published in 1776, and *The Death of General Montgomery*, published in 1777. Brackenridge is perhaps more important in the history of the American novel than of the drama, but his verse is flexible and dignified, and he is faithful to the old traditions of blank verse and the three Unities. His plays were probably given an amateur production at the Maryland Academy, where Brackenridge was a master. He was later a chaplain in the army.

BRADFORD CIVIC PLAYHOUSE, see AMATEUR THEATRE IN GREAT BRITAIN, 1 *d*.

BRADY. (1) WILLIAM A. (1863–1950), American actor and theatre manager, who made his first appearance on the stage in San Francisco in 1882. He later toured successfully with his own company, and was for a considerable time seen as Svengali in *Trilby*. Among the New York theatres with which he was associated were the Forty-Eighth Street, the Manhattan, which he managed from 1896 until its demolition, and the Playhouse, which he built in 1911. He was responsible for a number of outstanding productions, in many of which his second wife, (2) GRACE GEORGE (1879–   ), whom he married in 1899, appeared in leading parts. By his first wife Brady was the father of (3) ALICE (1892–1939), who studied singing at the Boston Conservatory of Music, and appeared in a number of operettas, including Gilbert and Sullivan. Her first appearance as an actress was made in 1909, after which she was frequently seen in straight parts, both tragic and comic. She, like her father, was connected with the early days of the film industry, in which much of her later career was passed.

BRAHM [ABRAHAMSOHN], OTTO (1856–1912), a German literary critic with a marked interest in the theatre, who founded the journal *Die Freie Bühne* (later *Neue deutsche Rundschau*), and in 1889 the dramatic enterprise of the same name. This was inspired by the work of Antoine's Théâtre Libre in Paris, and its main purpose, in marked contrast to that of the Devrients, was to further the work of the new naturalistic playwrights. For this a new type of actor had to be trained, and Brahm, already well known for his penetrating criticisms of contemporary acting, succeeded in getting together a noteworthy company, among whom the outstanding figure was Emanuel Reicher. In 1894 Brahm, realizing that the sporadic

efforts of his new venture were insufficient, affiliated it to the larger Deutsches Theater group, established in 1883, and continued to produce both old and new plays in the new naturalistic style, brought to perfection in Russia by Stanislavsky. This method was admirable for new plays written for this particular type of theatre, as was proved by such successes as *Die Familie Selicke* and *Vor Sonnenaufgang*. It failed when applied to older plays by classic or romantic writers, since it was inadequate to convey passion or exalted emotion or even polished comedy. Brahm, however, did good work in clearing the German stage of outmoded traditions, and affiliating it to the main current of European drama.

BRAITHWAITE, LILIAN (1873–1948), English actress, who in 1943 was created D.B.E. for her services to the stage. She had already had some experience in amateur productions when in 1897 she appeared in a series of Shakespeare productions in Natal, and during her long and distinguished career she was seen in many revivals of the classics, as well as in a number of new plays. In her early years she was with Julia Neilson, and Frank Benson, and with Alexander at the St. James's for several seasons; she played Mrs. Gregory in *Mr. Wu*, both on its first production and in subsequent revivals, and in 1924 was Florence Lancaster in *The Vortex*. In later years she gave some excellent performances, notably as Queen Elizabeth in *La Femme sans Homme*, and as the eccentric Abby Brewster in the English production of *Arsenic and Old Lace*, which ran for over three years.

BRANDANE, JOHN [DR. JOHN MACINTYRE] (1869–   ), Scottish dramatist, born of working-class parents in Bute. His father was of Highland descent, his mother of Lowland. As a boy he worked twelve hours a day in a cotton mill in Glasgow, and later, from his fifteenth to his twenty-seventh year, he was a clerk in a warehouse. During part of that time he studied medicine, qualifying as a doctor in 1901. He then became a general practitioner in various parts of England and Scotland. His interest in drama was stimulated by performances given by the Abbey Theatre Players during their visits to London, and after he settled in Glasgow he began writing plays for the Scottish National Players, a company formed to foster Scottish drama (see SCOTLAND). He fought uncompromisingly for his ideal school of Scottish dramatists and actors who would derive sustenance from their native soil. In *The Glen is Mine* he contributed to that movement its best Scots comedy. He has also written a number of other plays, some of which have been translated into Erse, Gaelic, German, and Norse. Brandane's plays are strongly constructed and alive with acute observation and humour, while the dialogue has a natural unaffected Highland lilt. It was largely due to Brandane's influence that James Bridie became a playwright.   W. J.

BRANDES. (1) GEORG MORRIS COHEN (1842–1927), Danish critic, was an aesthetician, philosopher, and writer of articles for the contemporary Danish press, whose influence as a dramatic critic was felt throughout Denmark and beyond. He succeeded Hauch in the Chair of Aesthetics at Copenhagen in 1872 and in the same year he founded the Litteraturselskabet (The Society of Literature), gathering round him a circle of critics and writers. Among them was his brother (2) EDVARD (1847–1931), who, with Otto Benzon, was one of the earliest exponents of modern social drama in Denmark (see SCANDINAVIA, 1). Georg Brandes gathered into his mind the best of contemporary European thought and culture and eventually became famous for his *Hovedstrømninger (Main Currents of Nineteenth Century Literature)* (6 vols., 1872–90), in which he traced the tendencies and development of European culture. He departed from the systematic criticism of the schools of Hegel and Heiberg and developed instead the psychological criticism of Taine, maintaining that literature must be related to the problems of its time and can best be interpreted in the light of that background. This aesthetic creed made him quickly appreciate Ibsen's work and ranged him on Ibsen's side when the criticism of his work became controversial. Throughout that period Brandes was one of the most constant, as he was the most penetrating, of Ibsen's defenders, and for many modern readers he is remembered primarily as the author of a series of essays on the drama of Ibsen and Bjørnson and for his volume *Henrik Ibsen* (1898).

BRANDES. (1) JOHANN CHRISTIAN (1735–99), a German actor and playwright, whose reminiscences, *Meine Lebensgeschichte*, published in 1800, give a fairly clear idea of the organization and vicissitudes of theatrical companies during the eighteenth century. After a miserable boyhood he became a manservant, which gave him the opportunity of improving his manners and his education, and in 1757 joined Schönemann's company, of which the celebrated Ekhof was then a member. He was not successful, and when the troupe broke up was obliged to return to domestic service. His first settled engagement came later, with the company of the old harlequin-player Schuch, who was an excellent friend to him. It was while he was with Schuch that Brandes in 1764 married the sister of a fellow actor, (2) ESTHER CHARLOTTE HENRIETTA (née Koch) (1746–84), who soon proved herself a good actress, particularly in grand tragic parts. This brought her into continual conflict with the redoubtable Sop ie Hensel, particularly at Mannheim and at Hamburg, where her husband was for a short time, during Schröder's stay in Vienna, appointed manager. His easy-going ways and weak affability helped to bring the theatre into disrepute, which was only checked by the return of Schröder. Brandes, as he confesses in his memoirs, was at best a poor actor, but he prided

himself on his plays, which are now forgotten. The most successful of them were probably *Miss Fanny*, which had a thrilling shipwreck with appropriate music, and the monodrama (a genre of his own invention) *Ariadne auf Naxos*. Of his three children the eldest (3) MINNA (1765–88), who was Lessing's godchild, made her first appearance on the stage in one of her father's plays. She later developed a fine voice, and was highly thought of in opera as well as in straight plays. She died when she was only 23, and was much missed by the Hamburg audiences. Brandes, having lost his wife and only son a year or so previously, retired to Berlin, where he lived on the proceeds of his literary labours and occasionally appeared at the National Theatre under Iffland.

BRANSBY WILLIAMS, see WILLIAMS, BRANSBY.

BRAYTON, LILY (1876–   ), see ASCHE (2).

BRAZIL, see SOUTH AMERICA, 2.

BRECHT, BERTOLT (1898–   ), German dramatist, who mingled expressionism with satire on the new political tendencies, as in his prize-winning *Trommeln in der Nacht* (1922), an indictment of war profiteers. Brecht, a rebellious spirit with a darting tongue, made a stir with his adaptation of *The Beggar's Opera* as *Die Dreigroschenoper* (1928) with music by Kurt Weill, for whom Brecht also wrote the libretto of 'Happy End' (1929), of 'Aufstieg und Fall der Stadt Mahagonny' (1930), and of 'Der Jasager' (1930). His later plays, which give evidence of his adherence to Communism, are in the nature of social documents, the most striking of which is *Die Massnahme* (1931), with its large chorus and cinema technique. In these thesis plays Brecht sought to educate and enlighten his audience rather than touch its emotions, but he was unable to suppress his lyrical and sensuous gifts, which break out in the poetry underlying the grim realities of his theme. One of his plays, *Die Spitzköpfe und die Rundköpfe*, acted in Copenhagen in 1936, is a biting satire on the racial theories of the Nazi party, reduced to absurdity.

BRÉCOURT [GUILLAUME MARCOUREAU] (1638–85), French actor and dramatist, child of strolling players, who had an adventurous and nomadic life. He was playing in the provinces in 1659 when he married an actress, Étiennette Des Urlis (c. 1630–1713), whose two sisters, Madeleine and Catherine, and brother Jean, were at the Théâtre du Marais, where the newly married couple joined them. Catherine Des Urlis had been with Molière in his first venture, the Illustre-Théâtre, and in 1660 Brécourt, probably introduced to Molière by his sister-in-law, joined the company at the Palais-Royal. He remained only two years, however, and left unregretted, owing to his quarrelsome temper, going to join Floridor at the Hôtel de Bourgogne. After Molière's death Brécourt wrote a one-act play about him, *L'Ombre de Molière* (1674), in which he spoke most feelingly of the great actor-dramatist's good qualities. Brécourt, who was the first to play Britannicus in Racine's play, had the misfortune in 1680 to kill a coachman in a fit of temper, and was forced to take refuge in Holland. Pardoned by Louis XIV, whose life he is said to have saved in a boar-hunt, he entered the Comédie-Française and remained there until his death. In 1682 he was arrested for debt, and had to attend rehearsals and performances in charge of a jailer, who took him to and from his prison cell. Among his plays, some of which are lost, the best was *La Feinte mort de Jodelet*, given at the Marais in 1659, just before the comedian named in the title left there to join Molière.

BREDERO, GERBRAND ADRIAENZ (1585–1618), see HOLLAND.

BREECHES PARTS, the name given to roles written for men—usually handsome heroes—and played by women. The classic example is Sir Harry Wildair in *The Constant Couple* as played by Peg Woffington, and later by Mrs. Jordan. Nell Gwynn also essayed the genre with no little success. These parts are not to be confused with the temporary assumption of male attire by such characters as Rosalind in *As You Like It* and Viola in *Twelfth Night*, who begin and end in petticoats. A humbler form of breeches part is that of the Principal Boy in the pantomime.

BRETÓN DE LOS HERREROS, MANUEL (1796–1873), Spanish playwright, author of nearly 200 comedies written in easy, flowing verse, of which the best known is *Marcela, o ¿cual de los tres?* (1831). He is interesting as being a follower of Moratín as well as of the Romantics, and, with Ventura de la Vega, he kept alive the old Spanish comedy of intrigue during the spate of dramas and melodramas produced by the emulators of Hugo and Dumas.

BRIDGE, a mechanical device by means of which large groups of posed figures or heavy scenery can be raised to stage level from below (see STAGE, 1).

BRIDGES, JOHN, see STEVENSON, WILLIAM.

BRIDIE, JAMES [DR. OSBORNE HENRY MAVOR] (1888–1951), Scottish dramatist, born in Glasgow, where his father conducted an engineering business. From a childhood and youth spent in middle-class and artistic circles typical of place and period, and slightly moulded by his education in Glasgow Academy, he passed to the medical faculty at Glasgow University. There he lingered longer than is usual, talking, larking, producing with the aid of Walter Elliot and a few other wits the University magazine (in which he spread himself in prose, verse, and black-and-white drawings) and laboriously collecting his class tickets, till in his twenty-fifth year he qualified as a medical practitioner. Meanwhile the Abbey Theatre Players, and other itinerant theatrical attractions, had aroused his latent interest in the theatre, and he began to cover paper with dialogue. He

was invited to write a play for the Glasgow Repertory Theatre, and did so, but it was never produced. He became in turn a successful general practitioner, a consulting physician at a large hospital and, from 1914 to 1918, a doctor in the army. This took him far afield in Mesopotamia, Persia, and Russia, on journeys which he has described in a whimsical book, *Some Talk of Alexander*, and from which he drew local colour for his comedy *Marriage is no Joke* (1934) and for his Biblical plays. After the war he resumed his medical career in Glasgow.

James Bridie's first success in the theatre was made through the Scottish National Players, who, largely under John Brandane's example and fatherly advice, were striving to nurse a Scottish drama into life (see SCOTLAND). Brandane drew Dr. Mavor into the circle as playwright and reader of plays, and so James Bridie was born. His first pen-name, however, was Mary Henderson, to whom was accredited *The Sunlight Sonata*, produced by the Scottish National Players in Glasgow in 1928 with Elliot Mason and Morland Graham in the cast and Tyrone Guthrie as producer. Once set in motion, Bridie's pen seemed tireless, and plays followed each other in quick succession, including *The Anatomist* and *Tobias and the Angel* (both 1930), *Jonah and the Whale* (1932), *A Sleeping Clergyman* (1933), *The Black Eye* (1935), *Storm in a Teacup* (an adaptation of Bruno Frank's *Sturm im Wasserglas* with a Scots setting) (1936), *Susannah and the Elders* (1937), *The King of Nowhere* (1938), and *What Say They?* (1939).

In addition to these plays James Bridie has written a witty autobiography, *One Way of Living*, two books of essays, and a book for children. On the outbreak of war in 1939 he rejoined the Army Medical Corps with the rank of Major, but continued to write plays, as witness *Mr. Bolfry* (1943), *It Depends What You Mean*, and *The Forrigan Reel* (both 1944), and *Dr. Angelus* (1946). He returned to civilian life before the end of the war, became the head of C.E.M.A.'s Scottish Committee, and played a leading part in the founding of the Glasgow Citizens' Theatre.

Just as Shaw's, Barrie's, and Maugham's plays have their own atmosphere, so Bridie's plays are *sui generis*, their distinguishing marks being a wit which sees the obvious in the extraordinary, and a devastating moral sense. The latter has grown in power and purpose. In character after character Bridie has laid bare the peacocking, boasting, and shouting of our species, sometimes with a rapier stroke, sometimes with a cudgel blow, but always with a laugh. His technique has not always been equal to his ambition. An over-facile pen has been his bugbear, and he is wilful and wasteful in his use of excellent material. Plays with good first acts (*The Last Trump* and *The King of Nowhere*) go into a decline in the second act and wilt away in the third. But on the whole his influence in the theatre has been salutary. When it seemed as if modern comedy was about to commit hara-kiri by reducing speech to a minimum, along came Bridie with a train of characters, every one of whom will talk twenty to the dozen and deave the welkin. All in all, Bridie has devised plays rich in entertainment and generous in their number of good parts for players.   w. j.

BRIEUX, Eugène (1858–1932), French dramatist whose plays are naturalistic dramas in the tradition of Zola and Henri Becque. In him, however, bitterness and misery were tempered by a deep pity for humanity, and he railed not so much at the sins of the flesh as at the social conditions which produced them. Each of his plays is, as it were, a plea for the amelioration of some particular evil, which sometimes degenerates into a sermon lacking in dramatic action. This tendency to mistake the theatre for a pulpit was Brieux's greatest weakness, as he himself realized. But in his best plays he combined his didactic outlook with a fierce pity for individual victims which produced some fine and lasting pieces of work. Chief among them are *Les Trois Filles de M. Dupont* (1898), which portrays the dangers of a marriage of convenience; *La Robe rouge* (1900), which exposes the abuses of the judiciary system; *Les Avariés* (1902), a study of venereal disease which, as *Damaged Goods*, created a sensation in England and America; and *Maternité* (1903), which deals with the question of legalized birth-control. Most of Brieux's plays will be forgotten as the conditions he writes of pass away, but these four will probably continue to be revived, since they represent the best works of an undoubted talent, and their general interest far exceeds that of the momentary problems they attack.

BRIGHELLA, one of the *zanni* or servant roles of the *commedia dell'arte*. Like Arlecchino, he has some connexion with Bergamo, but has in him much of the Neapolitan streetcorner boy. Originally a thief, a bully, and an intriguer, he gradually quietened down until he became a lackey, retaining his love of intrigue and lying. Through the influence of the Italian popular comedy in France, he may have had some part in the shaping of the French valets of Marivaux and others, and so entered into the composition of Figaro.

BRIGHOUSE, Harold, see HORNIMAN, A. E. F.

BRIGHTON THEATRE, New York, see BIJOU THEATRE (3).

BRISTOL, Theatre Royal, see PROVINCIAL THEATRES, 2 *d*.

BRITANNIA THEATRE, London, stood in High Street, Hoxton, on the site of an Elizabethan tavern called the Pimlico, to which Shakespeare is said to have resorted. Sam Lane (1804–71) built it as the Britannia Saloon in 1841, and ran it as a place of entertainment, charging only for refreshments, until in 1843 the abolition of the old Patents enabled him to stage complete plays, mainly farce and strong drama. The Britannia, or the Brit., as it was usually called, prospered, and in 1850 Lane enlarged and improved it, making it a true theatre. Among other attractions, James Anderson appeared in a number of Shakespeare plays at a weekly salary of £120. In 1858 the theatre was again enlarged to hold 3,000 people. After Lane's death his widow, Sara Lane (1823–99), an excellent actress related by marriage to the Lupino family, continued in management, and ran it successfully until her death, over a quarter of a century later. The Britannia was an institution, with its own traditions, and its history is unique in London's theatrical annals. No theatre has ever been for so long under one management. Authors wrote for it exclusively, actors joined it as boys and remained until old age. Its main support came from the people of the surrounding neighbourhood, who loved it and reverenced its manageress. In its pantomimes (which always ran till Easter) Sara Lane played the Principal Boy until she was in her seventies. In these magnificent spectacles the transformation scene was an outstanding feature. The Britannia was the last London theatre to give up its own local and democratic drama and take in touring companies. After the death of Mrs. Lane, mourned by the entire neighbourhood, the theatre passed into the hands of relatives and became a cinema. In 1927 three generations of the Lupino family, who had so often played there, went to the Britannia, gave a farewell show, and addressed the audience amid scenes of the wildest enthusiasm. But the old days were over, and the theatre remains a cinema.   w. m. p.

BRITISH COUNCIL. Founded in 1934 for the purpose of making the life and thought of Britain more widely known abroad, the British Council established its Drama Department in 1937. In this field the Council's main activities are the sponsoring of overseas tours by leading British companies, the distribution of copies of British plays with a view to their performance overseas by local professional and amateur companies, and the sponsoring of visits to Britain by eminent personalities of the theatre for professional studies and contacts with representatives of the British theatre. Among the United Kingdom scholarships awarded by the Council to graduates and others of like status from overseas there are a number for studies relating to drama and the theatre. Brochures specially produced by the Council for overseas readers include one on the British Theatre, and another on British Drama since 1939, designed to meet the demand for information in countries that were cut off during the war.

Before the war tours sponsored by the Council included those of the Old Vic and Dublin Gate Theatre Companies in European countries, Egypt, and Malta; a performance of *Hamlet* by John Gielgud and his company at Elsinore, and in 1940 a visit by the Sadler's Wells Ballet to Holland. Under the Council's auspices from 1945 to 1947 the Old Vic, the

English Arts Theatre, and the Sadler's Wells Ballet Companies visited a number of European countries, John Gielgud played in Canada and the United States, and the Ballet Rambert toured Australia. In 1948 the Old Vic Company visited Australia. Exchange visits included that of the Comédie-Française to Britain in 1945.

BRITISH DRAMA LEAGUE (B.D.L.), see AMATEUR THEATRE IN GREAT BRITAIN, 2.

BRITTON, HUTIN (1876–), see LANG (2).

BRIZARD [BRITARD], JEAN-BAPTISTE (1721–91), French actor, of good family and well educated. He had a decided talent for painting, which, like Bellecourt, he studied under Van Loo, but gave it up for the stage. He had been for ten years in the provinces when in 1756 he attracted the attention of Mlle Clairon and Mlle Dumesnil, who happened to be in Lyons during his appearance there. The following year he joined the company of the Comédie-Française and, owing to being prematurely white, could play old men's parts without a wig. Of a dignified presence, with a good voice and a natural style of acting, he was much admired, particularly as Henry of Navarre in *La Partie de chasse d'Henri IV* when in 1774 it was finally passed by the censor. Brizard was also the first French actor to play Lear, in the adaptation by Ducis, in 1782. He retired in 1786, much regretted by the public and by his companions, and employed his leisure by again taking up his painting, which he had abandoned for the theatre forty years previously.

BROADCASTING, see RADIO DRAMA.

BROADHURST, GEORGE H. (1866–), American dramatist, born in London, who at the age of 20 went to the United States and became manager of several provincial theatres. His work marks the transition in American drama at the turn of the twentieth century from the old melodrama to modern comedy, and though his early plays were farcical comedies like *What Happened to Jones* (1897) and *Why Smith Left Home* (1899), a more serious note is struck later, notably in *The Man of the Hour* (1906), probably his best play. He did not, however, entirely desert his earlier melodramatic style, as is shown by his production in 1911 of *Bought and Paid For*. On 26 Sept. 1918 Broadhurst opened his own theatre at West 44th Street with *Misalliance*. His first outstanding venture was *39 East*, which ran for 160 performances, and then moved elsewhere to make room for the first play by Broadhurst to be seen at his own theatre, *The Crimson Alibi* (1919). Later successes at this theatre include *Beggar on Horseback*, produced by Winthrop Ames, the record-making *Broadway*, first of a long series of gangster plays, a revival of *The Merchant of Venice*, and, in 1930, a fine production of *Hamlet* with Raymond Massey and Colin Keith-Johnston, in a vast setting designed by Norman-Bel Geddes. This, however, had less success than the series of

light musical comedies to which the theatre was later devoted, though in 1934 the Pulitzer Prize-winner, *Men in White*, was seen there, as was *Victoria Regina*, in which Helen Hayes gave an outstanding performance as the Queen.

BROADWAY, the symbol for the commercial theatre in the United States, as London's West End is in England. This is not surprising, since almost from the beginning of theatre history in New York the playhouses have been located on Broadway, or in the side-streets just off that famous thoroughfare. Where Tony Aston played in the season of 1703–4 will probably never be determined by scholars. Rip Van Dam's warehouse was the scene of *The Recruiting Officer*, the first definitely known public performance in New York, in 1732. By 1750 Thomas Kean and Walter Murray had established the first professional theatre in Nassau Street. These two young Englishmen introduced Shakespeare to New York with a performance of *Richard III*. David Douglass in 1761 opened the Theatre in Chapel Street where *Hamlet* was first performed in Manhattan. By 7 Dec. 1767 the pressing need for a larger playhouse was realized, and the John Street Theatre opened with *The Beaux' Stratagem*. This theatre, together with all places of amusement in America, was closed by act of the Continental Congress in 1775 'until the aims of the Revolution have been attained'. The British reopened it after the capture of New York, and performances were given there by military actors and such Tory ladies as were willing to perform. With the ending of the war Lewis Hallam, Thomas Wignell, John Hodgkinson, and William Dunlap were prominently associated with the John Street Theatre.

In 1798 the need for a larger and more imposing theatre was met by the opening of the Park Theatre, on Park Row, facing the City Hall, and a short block from Broadway. First called the New Theatre, it was opened on 29 Jan. with *As You Like It*, the cast including Hallam, Hodgkinson, and Mrs. Johnson. Destroyed by fire and twice rebuilt, the sole memory to-day of that famous playhouse remains in Theatre Alley, upon which the stage door opened.

In 1813 the Anthony Street Theatre, located on the present Worth Street near Broadway, opened with a company which included the Placides. It was at this theatre that in 1820 Edmund Kean made his first appearance in New York, after the burning of the Park. In 1824 the Chatham Theatre opened, and in 1839 the New Chatham, later famous as Purdy's National. In 1841 P. T. Barnum inaugurated his famous American Museum, in which he presented both plays and musical entertainment. This was situated on Ann Street, still in the City Hall section of Broadway. After its destruction by fire in 1865 Barnum's Museum moved to 537 Broadway. This building was also burnt down, during a run of *Uncle Tom's Cabin* in 1868.

Though not precisely on Broadway, the Bowery Theatre deserves mention. Famous under Hamblin as the home of melodrama, it opened in 1826, and was four times destroyed by fire and rebuilt. It ended its career as the Thalia, a theatre for plays in German, and was finally burnt down in 1929. The name of the great actor Edwin Forrest is irrevocably associated with the Bowery.

William Niblo erected in 1830 at the corner of Broadway and Prince Street the famous Niblo's Garden in which the Ravels appeared. In popular imagination this theatre will always be associated with the dance-melodrama of *The Black Crook*, which began a year's run on 12 Sept. 1866, and was several times revived.

In 1847 the old Broadway, located at 326–8 Broadway at Pearl Street, opened with *The School for Scandal*. It had seats for 4,000 and could accommodate 4,500 people. There was an immense pit to which only men and boys were admitted.

One block east of Broadway, on Astor Place just below Eighth Street, the Astor Place Opera House opened on 22 Nov. 1847. It was here that Macready was playing in 1849, on the occasion of the disgraceful Astor Place Riot. At least 22 people were killed when the militia fired on the anti-British mobs who out of mistaken loyalty to the American actor, Forrest, were trying to break up the performance.

Burton's famous theatre opened in 1848 and on 23 Dec. 1850 the Lyceum, first known as Brougham's but famous later as Wallack's, opened on the west side of Broadway two doors below Broome Street. It was here that the celebrated Wallack company performed until 1861. In 1865 it was re-christened the Broadway and functioned under that name until its demolition four years later. Just east of Broadway on 14th Street was the handsome Academy of Music, erected at a cost of $335,000 with a seating capacity of 4,600. It opened on 2 Oct. 1854 with 'Norma', the admission scale running from $3 to $40. The public bitterly resented this, and only 1,500 people attended the opening night. The next day the prices were halved. The Academy of Music continued to be the centre of opera in New York, even though rivalled by Pike's Opera House, later known as the Grand Opera House, far west at 23rd and Eighth Avenue, until the opening in 1883 of the Metropolitan Opera House, 25 blocks farther north on Broadway. In 1926 the beautiful old Academy, which had become a cinema, was torn down. Its establishment had made 14th Street and its neighbourhood New York's Rialto. In nearby Irving Place were located two theatres, the Amberg, built as Irving Hall in 1860, and the Irving Place Theatre, opened in 1893. These were the seats of the German language theatre in New York, where many fine actors played, including Possart, Rudolph Christians, Heinrich Conried, and Albert Brunning.

A block south of the Academy of Music James W. Wallack, after relinquishing the Lyceum, established a theatre named for himself on the north-east corner of Broadway and 13th Street, and opened it in 1861. Such actors as E. L. Davenport, Dion Boucicault, Rose Eytinge, and Maurice Barrymore were long identified with this theatre. By 1880 fashion was moving northward, and Wallack's failed. James's son, Lester Wallack, resumed possession of it two years later, however, and renamed it the Star. Up to 1901 many famous actors appeared there, though towards the end it was used for short engagements of plays which had already been performed farther north on Broadway.

Augustin Daly with his Fifth Avenue Theatres, curiously enough located on 24th Street near Broadway (opened 1869) and on Broadway itself at 28th Street (opened 1873), and Steele Mackaye with his famous Madison Square Theatre (opened 1879) just two blocks away, were two new theatre managers who recognized the fact that the centre of gravity on Broadway was shifting from Union Square (14th Street), where in 1872 A. M. Palmer opened his celebrated theatre, to Herald Square (34th Street). Incidentally, Daly's own theatre, formerly Wood's Museum on Broadway, opened in 1879, the same year as Madison Square. The great actor-manager, Edwin Booth, anticipated the northward trend when he established his famous theatre, named for himself, at 23rd and Sixth Avenue, just one block west of Broadway. He opened it on 3 Feb. 1869 with *Romeo and Juliet*.

One of New York's most important playhouses was on the west side of Broadway, between 32nd and 33rd Streets. This was the Eagle, which opened in 1875 and became famous three years later as the Standard. In 1897 it was renamed the Manhattan, opening with *What Happened to Jones*.

Continuing the concentration of theatres in the Herald Square area, 1239 Broadway, near 31st Street, became the Brighton, later the Bijou Opera House, and, much more importantly, the Bijou Theatre, which continued until 1911. Its name was perpetuated by an intimate playhouse on 45th Street west of Broadway, which opened in 1917.

In 1882 Lester Wallack opened a new theatre at 30th Street and Broadway, under his own name, with a brilliant revival of *The School for Scandal*, and remained there until 1887. The theatre's last season in 1914–15 was graced by the Granville-Barker productions of Shaw and Shakespeare which proved an innovation in staging in New York.

At the peak of Herald Square was erected in 1873 the Colosseum, later the Park, and finally, until its demise, the Herald Square Theatre with which Richard Mansfield was prominently identified. On the corner of 41st and Broadway was erected yet another Broadway Theatre, which opened on 3 Mar. 1888 with Fanny Davenport in Sardou's *La Tosca*.

Back in 1884 on Fourth Avenue, two blocks east of Broadway, Steele Mackaye had opened the celebrated Lyceum which was later taken over by Daniel Frohman and managed by him until 1902, when he opened a second Lyceum on 45th Street east of Broadway. The move from Herald Square to Times Square (42nd to 47th Streets) was emphasized by the erection of the Casino, famous as a musical house from 1882 to 1930. Directly opposite the Metropolitan Opera House, which is located on Broadway between 39th and 40th Streets, is situated the Empire Theatre, which is now (1949) the oldest playhouse devoted to the drama in New York City. *The Girl I Left Behind Me*, by David Belasco and Franklin Fyles, was the initial attraction when the Empire opened on 25 Jan. 1893. Abbey's Theatre, better known as the Knickerbocker, at the corner of 38th Street, was opened by Irving and Ellen Terry in the same year with Tennyson's *Becket*; it was demolished in 1930. Times Square came into its own with Hammerstein's Olympic, a music-hall which later became the Criterion. Beside it was the Lyric, which opened in 1895, with a roof garden over the two theatres for promenading. These were situated on the east side of Broadway between 44th and 45th Streets.

On 42nd Street west of Broadway, which once gave room to eight of New York's handsomest theatres (now 'grind', i.e. non-stop, movie houses), was established the famous New Amsterdam Theatre long associated with the Ziegfeld Follies. In 1903, however, it was opened with Nat Goodwin and Chrystal Herne in *A Midsummer Night's Dream*, thus continuing the tradition of Shakespearian initiation. Three years later, in 1906, the Astor, at the corner of 45th Street and Broadway, opened with the same play, this time starring Annie Russell.

Not content with populating the side-streets off Broadway with the Plymouth (1917), the Music Box (1921), the Martin Beck (1924), the Mansfield (1926), and the Ethel Barrymore (1928), some brave souls were moving up the Great White Way, as it came to be called, and in 1903 the Majestic on Columbus Circle at 59th Street opened with *The Wizard of Oz*. In 1946–7, as the International, this house played host to the American Repertory Theatre.

The Winter Garden on Broadway between 50th and 51st Streets, which began its career in 1911, was long one of New York's most celebrated houses for musical comedies and revues. It is still in use.

The long march up Broadway seems ended, though Walter Hampden once operated the Colonial at 62nd Street, and the Shuberts utilized the Riviera at 97th Street as a second-run house. Washington Heights boasts another playhouse of this type in the Audubon at 161st Street. Playgoers, however, are reluctant to traverse Broadway above Columbus Circle, and the future trend seems aimed at the section lying east of Broadway, and in the general direction of the site of the capital of the United Nations.   G. F.

(For more detailed information on the above and other New York theatres, see under their own names.)

BROADWAY MUSIC-HALL, NEW YORK, see BROADWAY THEATRE (2).

BROADWAY OPERA HOUSE, NEW YORK, see BIJOU THEATRE (3).

BROADWAY THEATRE, NEW YORK. (1) The first Broadway was a bright, cheerful theatre, with gold and white decorations, built by Trimble, architect of the Olympic. It opened on 27 Sept. 1847 with Henry Wallack and Rose Telbin as the Teazles in *The School for Scandal*, while Lester (Wallack) played in the afterpiece, his first appearance in New York. The Broadway had been intended as a stock house, but after the final destruction by fire of the old Park Theatre took its place as a home of visiting stars. Forrest was there when the Astor Place Riot took place, caused, it was believed, by his jealousy of Macready. Charlotte Cushman, after four years in England, reappeared at the Broadway as America's greatest tragic actress, and in the same year, 1849, the Bateman children, Kate aged 6 and Ellen aged 4, appeared as Portia and Shylock, Richmond and Richard III, Macbeth and Lady Macbeth. Later stars seen at the Broadway included Lola Montez, Julia Dean, and Mr. and Mrs. Barney Williams, and it was there that Boker's fine poetic play, *Francesca da Rimini*, was first seen, in 1855. Shortly afterwards, when workmen were excavating for a new building next door, the walls of the theatre fell down and had to be rebuilt, but it seemed as if the prestige of the house, which had never really taken the place of the old Park, was fatally injured, for after a poor season in 1857–8, redeemed only by a visit from the younger Mathews, it sank to circus and variety, and the theatre closed with a spectacular show on 2 Apr. 1859.

(2) On 2 Sept. 1861 Wallack's old theatre opened as the Broadway Music-Hall. It had a chequered career, under a variety of names, and saw one of the few appearances in New York of the assassin of Lincoln, John Wilkes Booth, in Richard III and other parts. It was for some time known as the Olympic, but finally, renovated and redecorated, it opened as the Broadway Theatre under George Wood. It had a short life, and the main incidents were the emergence of John E. Owens as a fine comedian in *The People's Lawyer*, in which he played Solon Shingle, the truly rural old Yankee farmer, and as Caleb Plummer in *Dot*, Boucicault's version of *The Cricket on the Hearth*; the farewell appearance in New York of the Charles Keans, and of Julia Dean; and the production by Florence of *Caste*. This was first seen on 5 Aug. 1867, and caused trouble, as Lester Wallack thought he held the American rights in the play. It subsequently transpired that Florence had seen and memorized the play in London, and in the absence of international copyright laws, he won the case which Lester Wallack brought against him. In later years he is known to have regretted his action. A year later the site of the theatre was required

for shops, and it closed on 28 Apr. 1869, being subsequently demolished.

(3) A concert hall on 41st Street, originally known as the Metropolitan Casino, which opened on 27 May 1880 and saw, among other things, the famous Hanlon-Lees troupe in their *Voyage en Suisse*, was rebuilt and opened as the Broadway on 3 Mar. 1888, with Fanny and Harry Davenport in Sardou's *La Tosca*. In 1890 Mrs. Leslie Carter made her first professional appearance at this theatre in *The Ugly Duckling*, and in 1899 came the successful run of *Ben Hur*. An English pantomime had a long run in 1901, but all previous records were eclipsed by the popularity of *Little Lord Fauntleroy* in 1907. Among the European actors who visited this theatre were Modjeska, Salvini, and Mlle Rhéa, while Helen Hayes appeared there as a child. Weber and Fields occupied the house with variety for a while, and after the failure of a Sousa operetta in the early part of 1913, it became a cinema. Closed in 1928, it was pulled down a year later.

Daly's Theatre, originally Banvard's Museum, was also known as the Broadway for the season of 1877–8, as was the Euterpean Hall for a few unsuccessful weeks.

BROCHET, HENRI (1898–), see GHÉON.

BROCKMANN, JOHANN FRANZ HIERONYMUS (1745–1812), German actor. He was a barber's apprentice who took to the stage and became the friend and pupil of Schröder, to whose company he belonged in Hamburg. He played Hamlet in the first production there of a German version of the play in 1776, with Schröder as the Ghost. He later went to the Burgtheater in Vienna, where he was highly thought of. He had great natural gifts, but lacked control, and in the absence of a firm hand, such as Schröder's had been, he proved less successful. In spite of this, and of increasing girth, however, he remained an honoured member of the Burgtheater until his death.

BRODY SINGERS, see JEWISH DRAMA, 5.

BROME, RICHARD (c. 1590–1653), English dramatist, who was at one time in the service of Ben Jonson, where he no doubt learned much that later stood him in good stead. His comedies, on which his reputation mainly rests, show plainly Jonson's influence, though Brome has a greater insistence on plot than his mentor, and seems in his later work—which was interrupted by the closing of the theatres in 1642— to be working towards a more individual style. His best plays are generally thought to be *The City Wit; or, the Woman Wears the Breeches* (1628), *The Northern Lass* (1629), *The Sparagus Garden* (1635), *The Antipodes* (1638), and *A Joviall Crew* (1641). The last was often revived, and was later turned into an operetta. Brome also collaborated with Heywood, or perhaps revised some of his plays for revivals, and wrote some romantic dramas in imitation of Fletcher and Middleton.

BROOKE, GUSTAVUS VAUGHAN (1818–66),

English actor, who made his first appearance on the stage in Dublin as a boy of 14, and subsequently toured England and Scotland as the Dublin (or Hibernian) Roscius. A tall, handsome man with an excellent voice and everything in his favour, he yet failed to fulfil the promise of his youth, and spent many years starring in the provinces, where he played with Macready (with whom he had quarrelled over an engagement for Drury Lane) as well as Forrest, Helen Faucit, Lester Wallack, and Charlotte Cushman. In 1848, at the height of his powers, he appeared at the Olympic in London as Othello, and had a most enthusiastic reception, being hailed as the successor of Kean. He also played Sir Giles Overreach, Richard III (in Cibber's version), Hamlet, Shylock (his only appearance in the part), and Virginius, which he had played as a boy of 14. Success seemed within his grasp, but with a careless, happy-go-lucky spirit, he dissipated himself in conviviality, fell into low water financially, and finally was ill-advised enough to refuse an offer from Webster to star at the Haymarket, returning eventually to the provinces. Here, his voice much altered and his physique impaired, he soon found himself in financial difficulties which an unfortunate experience at the New Olympic in London did nothing to alleviate, and he was twice arrested for debt. He decided to seek his fortune in New York, appearing on 15 Dec. 1851 at the Broadway Theatre in *Othello*. After a successful tour of the principal cities of the United States, he embarked on the management of the Astor Place Opera House with disastrous results. He returned to England, where he finally appeared at Drury Lane with unexpected success in 1853, in a round of his well-known parts, and was then persuaded to go to Australia. This he did, appearing in the principal cities with some success, marred occasionally by his return to old habits of insobriety. On his return to England these rapidly became worse and led him into even greater difficulties, until he finally found himself in Warwick jail. Determined to rehabilitate himself, he once more set sail for Australia and was drowned in the sinking of the S.S. *London* in the Bay of Biscay. He was twice married, his second wife being the American actress Avonia Jones (1839–67), whose death was hastened by grief at his loss. Brooke's *Life* was written by W. J. Lawrence (1892).

BROOKLYN THEATRE, NEW YORK, the second playhouse in this district, which was opened on 2 Oct. 1871 by Mrs. Conway, who had previously managed the Park, Brooklyn. She continued her policy of engaging stars to play with her stock company, and gave mainly standard comedies, revivals, and some contemporary melodrama. In 1873 Daly's company, while waiting for the completion of their new theatre, came for a season. Mrs. Conway remained at the Brooklyn until her death in 1875, her husband having died the previous year. Her daughter Minnie attempted to take over the management of the theatre, but was unsuccessful, and left after a few months. On 20 Sept. 1875 it reopened under Palmer for a brief but exciting season, and on 5 Dec. 1876 it was burnt down during a performance of *The Two Orphans*. Two actors lost their lives, and about 300 of the audience. This was one of the worst theatre fires in the United States, equalled only by that at the Richmond Theatre in 1811 and the Iroquois, Chicago, in 1903.

BROUGH, a family of English actors, descended from a dramatist named Barnabas Brough. Two of his sons, (1) WILLIAM (1826–70) and (2) ROBERT BARNABAS (1828–60), were also dramatists, writing alone or in collaboration a number of burlesques, extravaganzas, and pantomimes, in one of which, by William, Robert's daughter (3) FANNY WHITESIDE (1854–1914) made her first appearance on the stage in 1869 in Manchester. She appeared in the same town as Ophelia to the Hamlet of Barry Sullivan, and a year later was seen in London at the St. James's Theatre under Mrs. John Wood. During her subsequent career she was associated with all the outstanding managements of the day, and was unrivalled in certain lines of comedy. Her brother Robert was also an actor and theatre manager. Barnabas's youngest son (4) LIONEL (1836–1900) was a distinguished actor, who also made his first appearance in one of William's plays. He was for a time in journalism, being assistant publisher to the *Daily Telegraph* and the first man to organize newsboys selling papers in the street. He returned to the stage seriously in 1864, and in 1873 was the principal low comedian of the Gaiety under Hollingshead. He was not a character actor, but a clown in the best sense, his gift of improvisation and rich sense of humour making him excellent in burlesque. Two of his finest parts were Tony Lumpkin and Bob Acres, but he was also good in Shakespeare, and played with Tree at His Majesty's. He toured extensively, and was popular in the United States and South Africa. His four children were all on the stage, two of them dying young. But (5) MARY (1863–1934) was an excellent comedy actress, particularly in later years, when she was associated with the Aldwych farces. She also had a distinguished film career. Her brother (6) SYDNEY (1868–1911) made his first appearance in 1885, and remained on the stage until his death, being seen mainly in comedy parts in London and New York.

BROUGHAM, JOHN (1810–80), American actor and dramatist, who was born in Ireland. He was intended for the medical profession, but forsook it for the stage, making his first appearance in London in July 1830 in Egan's *Tom and Jerry*. After a long engagement with Mme Vestris he became manager of the Lyceum, and in 1842 went to America. Here he made his début at the famous Park Theatre, and later was at Burton's and Niblo's. On 23 Dec. 1850 he opened his own theatre on Broadway, Brougham's Lyceum, in the hope of rivalling the success of Mitchell's Olympic. Brougham was a fine actor, an experienced manager, and a jovial, popular personality, and his venture ought to have succeeded. Unfortunately Mitchell's formula for success—a varied bill of short burlesques and farces, which had served him so well in the heyday of the Olympic—was now outmoded, and in spite of the success of Florence in his first New York hit, and of a hurried importation of such stars as Charlotte Cushman, circumstances proved too strong for Brougham. In less than two years the theatre had passed into the control of the elder Wallack, who started it on a glorious career.

Brougham continued to act, reviving *King John* at the Bowery, appearing at most of the big Broadway theatres, and spending several years in England, before he opened his second playhouse, on the site of the present Madison Square Theatre, on 25 Jan. 1869. This again was not a success. Brougham retired from management in a few months, and up to his death appeared with various stock companies in New York, his last appearance being on 25 Oct. 1879 at Booth's. He was essentially a comedian, and his best parts were the stage Irishmen of tradition, Sir Lucius O'Trigger, Dennis Brulgruddery, O'Grady, O'Callaghan, and such parts as Captain Cuttle, Micawber, and Dazzle in *London Assurance*, of which he was long believed to be part author. He wrote copiously, mainly ephemeral farces, burlesques, and adaptations of novels and stories, and none of his works has survived. He was twice married, and both his wives, who were also on the stage, predeceased him.

BROWN, IVOR (1891–   ), English dramatic critic and author who, in 1913, relinquished a post in the Civil Service in order to devote himself to writing theatre criticisms for the *Manchester Guardian*. In 1928 he became dramatic critic to the *Observer*. He has also written for the *Saturday Review*, *Illustrated London News*, and the *Sketch*. In 1942 he was appointed editor of the *Observer*, but continued as its dramatic critic.

Ivor Brown himself wrote in the *Observer*: 'The first business of criticism, in any art, is to assist and extend the enjoyment of that art by writing about it intelligently, agreeably, and with sensitive response to its beauties, and with a good-tempered and, if possible, witty dismissal of its follies.' He has certainly lived up to his definition. He regards the theatre as a contribution to the full life and, in looking at a play, sees it steadily and sees it whole. He brings sound judgement to the theatre and expresses his findings in lively and witty style.

In 1925 he wrote *Smithfield Preserved* (a play). His other writings on the theatre include *Masques and Phases* (1926), *First Player* (1927), *Parties of the Play* (1928), and (with George Fearon) *Amazing Monument, A Short History of the Shakespeare Industry* (1939).

                                                      T. C. K.

BROWN, JOHN MASON (1900–   ), American dramatic critic, born in Louisville, Kentucky. He was graduated from Harvard, and in 1924 he became an associate editor and dramatic critic of *Theatre Arts Monthly*. In 1929 he took to newspaper work, becoming the dramatic critic of *The New York Evening Post*, and in 1939 he went to *The World-Telegram*, a post he held until he entered the U.S. Navy during World War II. Since the war he has deserted daily reviewing to become dramatic critic of the weekly *Saturday Review of Literature*. His refreshing and vivid writings have won him a large public, and in recent years he has had conspicuous success on the lecture platform, delivering talks on the theatre. The best of his newspaper reviews may be found in *Two on the Aisle*, while *Upstage : The American Theatre in Performance* is a rewarding and accurate picture of the American stage and its personalities. Among his other books are *The Modern Theatre in Revolt*, *Letters from Greenroom Ghosts*, *The Art of Playgoing*, *Many a Watchful Night* (a book of war experiences), and *Accustomed as I Am* (a book of lecturing experiences).

T. Q. C.

BROWNE, E(LLIOTT) MARTIN (1900–   ), English actor and producer, who has been closely connected with the revival of poetic, and particularly religious, drama in England. He directs the Pilgrim Players, who in association with the Arts Council have toured England in a repertory of religious plays, and in 1945 took over the Mercury Theatre for a series of plays by poets, among which have been *The Old Man of the Mountains*, *This Way to the Tomb*, *The Shadow Factory*, *A Phoenix Too Frequent*, and *Happy as Larry*. He had previously been associated with Ashley Dukes in the production of poetic plays at the Mercury, including *Panic* and *In Theatre Street*, and was responsible for the first production, in 1935, of *Murder in the Cathedral*, in which he played the Fourth Tempter and Knight. The play was originally given in the Chapter House of Canterbury Cathedral, and, after a run at the Mercury, was seen at the Duchess, at the Old Vic, and on tour in England. It was also given in New York in 1938. It had an unexpected and unprecedented success, and inaugurated a new era of poetry in the theatre. E. Martin Browne, who made his first appearance on the stage in 1927 and then spent some years in America, has also been responsible for the production of T. S. Eliot's other verse-plays, *The Rock* and *The Family Reunion*. In 1948 he succeeded Geoffrey Whitworth as Director of the British Drama League.

BROWNE, ROBERT (*fl.* 1583–1620), an English actor who was, more than anyone, responsible for the vogue for the English Comedians in Germany during the late sixteenth and early seventeenth centuries. He was active there from 1590 to 1620, taking with him relays of English actors who often split up into independent companies. Before that he had been one

of Worcester's Men with Alleyn, with whom he remained connected until his first visit abroad, and to whom he wrote on his return to England in 1612. Browne's repertory included a number of jigs, plays by Marlowe and others, and several biblical plays, and he was succeeded as chief English Comedian abroad by his pupil and companion, John Green. His last appearance on the continent was in 1618–20 (see ENGLISH COMEDIANS).

BROWNING, ROBERT (1812–89), English poet, two of whose verse-plays were seen on the stage: *Strafford* (1837), written for Macready, and *A Blot on the 'Scutcheon* (1843). Neither of these was particularly successful, and they serve only to mark the great cleavage between poetry and the stage in the nineteenth century. His other plays were written to be read, and are part of English literature rather than drama.

BROWN-POTTER, MRS., see POTTER.

BRÜCKNER, JOHANNES (1730–86), German actor, a member of the company of Koch, who married his sister. He was trained for the stage by Lessing and Ekhof, and was one of the best tragedians of his time. His Mellefont in *Miss Sara Sampson* was considered superior even to Ekhof's, particularly when the latter grew too old for the part and yet insisted on playing it. One of Brückner's greatest triumphs was his portrayal of Götz von Berlichingen in Goethe's play of that name.

BRUEYS, DAVID AUGUSTIN DE (1640–1723), French dramatist, a lawyer of good family, who later became a priest. In 1686 he met and later collaborated with Palaprat, a writer of comedies to which Brueys gave an added substance and firmness. They wrote several plays for the Comédie-Française, of which the best were *Le Grondeur* and *Le Muet* (both 1691), and their collaboration persisted until Palaprat left Paris in the service of the Duc de Vendôme. Brueys also wrote a number of plays on his own, including three tragedies of which only one reached the stage, and a new and most successful version of the farce of Maistre Pierre Pathelin. As *L'Avocat Pathelin* (1706), this remained in the repertory of the Comédie-Française for many years.

BRUN, NORDAHL (1745–1816), Norwegian dramatist (see SCANDINAVIA, 2).

BRUNELLESCHI, FILIPPO (1377–1446), Italian machinist, designer of a piece of stage mechanism known as a 'Paradiso' (see MACHINERY).

BRUNO, GIORDANO (1548–1600), Italian philosopher, author of a fine play, *Il Candelaio* (*c.* 1582), which probably never saw the stage. It is a brilliant, mordant piece of work, a comedy which discloses the corrupt customs of the time with unbated candour. During his travels through Europe Bruno went to England, and visited Oxford at the invitation of Sir Philip Sidney, to whom some of his works are dedicated. Among the contemporary

English authors who were cognizant of him may perhaps be reckoned Thomas Carew, whose masque *Coelum Britannicum*, performed at Whitehall in 1634, shows traces of Bruno's influence. At one time scholars were anxious, perhaps too anxious, to find a like influence in Shakespeare, particularly in *Hamlet*. The resemblance is probably fortuitous. More informed criticism sees something in Bruno's comic genius akin to Ben Jonson's. Bruno was burnt at the stake by order of the Inquisition in 1600.

BRUNSWICK THEATRE, LONDON, see ROYALTY THEATRE (1).

BRUNTON, a family of English actors, of whom the first was (1) JOHN (1741–1822), a grocer in Drury Lane, who appeared at Covent Garden in 1774 as Hamlet. He was afterwards in the Norwich and Bath stock companies and manager of the Norwich circuit. He had three children on the stage, of whom the eldest, (2) ANN (1768–1808), first appeared in Bath at the age of 15, and was so well received that in 1785 she was engaged to play at Covent Garden. There the future American dramatist and theatre manager, Dunlap, saw and described her début. In 1792 she retired from the stage to marry Robert Merry, but he lost his money, and a few years later she accepted Wignell's offer to go to the Chestnut Street Theatre in Philadelphia. Here she appeared on 5 Dec. 1796 as Juliet, and as Mrs. Merry was soon the leading actress of the time, equally successful in New York, where she first appeared in the season of 1797, and in Philadelphia. Many contemporary accounts testify to her beauty and success, particularly in Mrs. Siddons's great part of Belvidera in *Venice Preserved*. She was widowed in 1798 and in 1802 married Wignell, who died a couple of months after the marriage. She later married William Warren, who had succeeded, jointly with Wood, to the management of the Chestnut Street Theatre, made several successful appearances in New York at the Park Theatre under Dunlap, and died in childbirth at the age of 40. Her loss was a great blow to the American stage.

Her brother (3) JOHN (1775–1849) first appeared on the stage at Lincoln, at the age of 18. He made his début at Covent Garden in 1800, and remained in London for some years, being at one time manager of the West London Theatre. He was also manager of several provincial theatres. He married an actress, Anna Ross (1773– ?), and was the father of Elizabeth, later Mrs. Frederick Yates. The youngest Brunton, (4) LOUISA (1779–1860), made her début at Covent Garden in 1803. She excelled in light comedy, and was considered a worthy successor to Elizabeth Farren. Among her best parts were Beatrice, Lady Anne in *Richard III*, and Dorinda in *The Beaux' Stratagem*. She was also the original Emily in *The Wheel of Fortune* and Julia in *The School of Reform*. She retired from the stage in 1807, on her marriage with the Earl of Craven.

BRUSCAMBILLE [JEAN DESLAURIERS] (*fl.* 1610–34), a mountebank at the Paris fairs in the early seventeenth century who went with Jean Farine to the Hôtel de Bourgogne to play in farce. He won fame as a speaker of witty prologues and harangues to the rowdy audiences, which he composed himself. These are extant, and give an interesting picture of the tribulations of the actor before his profession became respectable, summed up in Bruscambille's oft-quoted epigram, *une vie sans soucis et quelque fois sans six sous*.

BÜCHNER, GEORG (1813–37), a German dramatist who, in a general dearth of talent, stands out as one of the best playwrights of his day. His strongest and best play, *Dantons Tod*, first given in 1835, retains its vitality to-day, as was proved by two later revivals, in Berlin in 1927 by Max Reinhardt, and in New York in 1938 by Orson Welles. It depicts Danton as a disillusioned man, sickened by the bloodshed which he has helped to start, and is amazingly objective for a young revolutionary. Büchner had little in common with the romantic writers of his day, and, had he not died before his powers came to maturity, he might have been one of the earliest of the naturalistic writers. Little else remains of his work, except the dramatic fragments on which Alban Berg later based his opera 'Wozzeck' (1925).

BUCK, SIR GEORGE, see MASTER OF THE REVELS.

BUCKINGHAM, GEORGE VILLIERS, second Duke of (1628–87), English nobleman and a prominent literary figure of the Restoration. He was the original of Zimri in Dryden's *Absalom and Achitophel*. Keenly interested in contemporary drama, he satirized Dryden and the heroic verse-play in *The Rehearsal* (1671). This provided a model for many later burlesques, of which the best was *The Critic; or, a Tragedy Rehearsed* (1779). Buckingham was also the author of a comedy entitled *The Chances* (1666) and of a quantity of satiric and other verses.

BUCKSTONE, JOHN BALDWIN (1802–79), English actor and dramatist, who was articled to a solicitor, but left the law for the stage. He made his first appearance in the famous melodrama, *The Dog of Montargis*, in a barn at Peckham, and spent several years in the provinces, where he acquired an excellent reputation as a low comedian. Kean, who saw him act, encouraged him in his profession, and Buckstone eventually appeared in London, first at the Coburg, and, in 1827, at the Adelphi. Here he was seen in his own play *Luke the Labourer*, which had previously been given anonymously because the manager, Daniel Terry, had lost the author's name and address. He was also seen at the Surrey, as Gnatbrain in *Black-Eyed Susan* (1829), and during the summer seasons of 1833–9 at the Haymarket, of which he later became manager. It was here that many of his plays were first produced, with himself and an excellent company, and his ghost is said still to haunt the theatre. As an actor he had great breadth and humour, and the mere sound of his voice, a mixture of chuckle and drawl, heard off-stage was enough to set the audience laughing. For fifty years he was one of London's most popular comedians and most prolific playwrights, writing some 200 plays of all kinds, chiefly melodramas and farces. The best were *Married Life* (1834), *Single Life* (1839), *The Green Bushes; or, a Hundred Years Ago* (1845), and *The Flowers of the Forest* (1847). He also dramatized a number of contemporary novels, and in later life wrote pantomimes.

BUDAPEST, see HUNGARY.

BUEN RETIRO, the theatre of the Spanish Court, where many of Calderón's plays were first produced. It was later given over entirely to opera.

BUFFA, OPERA, see OPERA, 5.

BUFFALO BILL, see CODY, W. F.

BUILT STUFF, a scenic term comprising all specially carpentered, three-dimensional objects, from banks and rostrums to columns and complete scenes on trucks. The most common is perhaps the Rostrum, which may vary in size from a small throne-dais to an 8 ft. high platform, approached by steps or a ramp. Beyond this, by way of porches and mantelpieces, one reaches all the ingenious applications of light carpentry, of chicken-wire reinforcement, of glued and shaped canvas, and of papier mâché, which enable a room complete in all details, or a wood scene with every tree in the round and every leaf separate, to take shape upon the stage. R. S.

BULGAKOV, MICHAEL AFANASYEV (1891–), Soviet dramatist, who graduated from Kiev University in 1916 with the intention of becoming a doctor. In 1920, however, he turned to literature, and became a journalist in Moscow. He wrote a novel, *The White Guard*, dealing with the Civil War in the Ukraine, which he later turned into a play. This, as *The Days of the Turbins* (or *The Last of the Turbins*), was produced by the Moscow Art Theatre under Stanislavsky in 1926. In its delicacy and restraint, and its handling of personal rather than national problems, it was an advance on earlier Soviet plays, and was successful. But its sympathetic treatment of the bewildered White Russian aristocrats, at a time when feeling still ran high, made it suspect for a time. As *The White Guard* it was produced in London in 1938 in an adaptation by Rodney Ackland. In 1928 Bulgakov, who had joined the staff of the Moscow Art Theatre, prepared for it an excellent dramatization of Gogol's *Dead Souls*—one of the few examples of a novel turned successfully into a play, and a most moving experience—and in 1936 wrote a play based on the life of Molière.

BULL INN, see INNS USED AS THEATRES.

BULL, OLE BORNEMAN (1810–80), famous Norwegian violinist, and the founder of the first National Theatre in Norway. After five years of negotiation, this opened in 1850 at Bergen, Bull's birthplace, and was the first theatre in Norway to be staffed by Norwegians, since earlier ventures had been in the hands of Danes.

BULWER-LYTTON, see LYTTON.

BUNN. (1) ALFRED (1798–1860), English theatrical manager, best remembered for his numerous quarrels, particularly for his brawl with Macready, whom he tried to force into a triple bill in a mutilated version of *Richard III*, and for his attacks on Douglas Jerrold, Gilbert à Beckett, and Mark Lemon—as Wronghead, Sleekhead, and Thickhead—in a pamphlet, *A Word With Punch*, got up to look like *Punch*, in which he had been criticized. He was considered an adventurer and an impostor, and coming at a time when the London theatre was at a low ebb, he debased it still further by his methods and manners. Appointed stage-manager to Drury Lane by Elliston in 1823, he later went to Birmingham. In 1833 he tried to control both Drury Lane and Covent Garden, a policy which ended in failure, and caused him to write his apologia in *The Stage; Before and Behind the Curtain*, published in 1840, in which year he went bankrupt. He made great efforts to establish English opera, with the help of the composers Balfe and Wallace, but defeated his own ends by the poorness of his libretti, of which 'The Bohemian Girl' is a fair sample; he also made some weak translations of foreign libretti, and of a number of Scribe's plays, now forgotten. His facile though flat versification, and his pretensions to poetry, caused him to be nicknamed derisively 'Poet Bunn'. In 1819 he married (2) MARGARET AGNES SOMERVILLE (1799–1883), an actress who had been engaged for Drury Lane three years previously by Byron and Kinnaird. She was at her best in heavy tragedy, but Macready and Kean disliked her, the latter finding her too tall and overpowering to play with. She soon left the stage, though her marriage does not appear to have been very happy.

BUONTALENTI, BERNARDO (1536–1608), Italian theatre architect and scenic designer, who spent all his life in the service of the Medici family. He was the architect of a theatre in Florence, which opened in 1585 (see also MACHINERY and SCENERY, 2).

BURBAGE (BURBADGE, BURBEGE). (1) James (c. 1530–97), a joiner by trade, became an actor in the Earl of Leicester's company in 1572 or thereabouts. Opposition from the Lord Mayor of London to actors playing in open inn-yards within the City boundary led Burbage in 1576 to build the Theatre—the first English building entirely devoted to the presentation of plays—an enclosed structure of wood situated outside the City boundary in Finsbury Fields. In 1596 James also took over and rebuilt the Blackfriars Theatre, but died before he had obtained permission to use it. All his life he was harassed and beset by financial and other difficulties, but he never wavered in his allegiance to the theatre. In *A Note on Burbage*, Mrs. Stopes says: '[James] did more than build the first theatre; he raised and purified the stage, and honoured his profession; he selected and trained his fellow-actors, among them Shakespeare and his own son Richard.' James appears to have been a man of violent temper, stubborn and unscrupulous, but devoted to the theatre, though probably a poor actor. His eldest son, (2) CUTHBERT (*c.* 1566–1636), inherited the Theatre, and after a dispute with his rivals, Alleyn and Henslowe, dismantled it, and used the timber to build (in 1599) the Globe, on the Bankside, Southwark. This was the scene of the greatest triumphs of Cuthbert's brother, (3) RICHARD (*c.* 1567–1619), who was the first great English actor, and the original player of Shakespeare's Hamlet, Lear, Othello, Richard III, and other characters. He also appeared in plays by Jonson, Kyd, Webster, and others. His acting career began early, probably in 1584 with the Admiral's Men at the Theatre. He had a high reputation both during his lifetime and afterwards. There are numerous references to him in contemporary verse and prose (see Jonson's *Bartholomew Fair*: 'Which is your Burbage now?... your best actor?'), and his name long remained synonymous with all that was best in acting.

BURGTHEATER, see VIENNA.

BURKE, CHARLES (1832–54), see JEFFERSON (4) and (5).

BURLA (pl. *burle*), the longer comic interlude of the *commedia dell'arte*, usually involving a practical joke, perhaps the tripping up of one character by another, or a certain amount of horseplay. The slighter decoration of a comic touch was known as a *lazzo* (pl. *lazzi*).

BURLESQUE. 1. A satiric play, usually based on some well-known contemporary drama, or dramatic fashion, which offered elements fit for parody. The prototype of the burlesque was Buckingham's *The Rehearsal* (1671), which made fun of Dryden and the heroic drama, and set the pattern for future writers. The genre was finally crystallized in *The Critic* (1779), where Sheridan amused himself at the expense of the sentimental drama and the literary foibles of the day. In the meantime the traditions of burlesque had been worthily upheld by Gay's *Beggar's Opera* (1728), by Henry Carey, who burlesqued both opera and drama, and by Fielding's *Tragedy of Tragedies; or, the Life and Death of Tom Thumb the Great* (1730).

In the nineteenth century a new type of burlesque flourished. It retained enough consciousness of its origin to hang, where possible, its nonsense and high spirits on the convenient peg provided by some popular play, such as *The Maid and the Magpie* or *Black-Eyed Susan*;

but the original impulse of criticism was lacking. This may have been due to the increase in the size of the audience and the lowering of its general educational level, since the success of the earlier type of burlesque had depended on the familiarity of the greater part of the audience with the play or prevailing mode which was under dissection. One of the best writers of the new burlesques was H. J. Byron, with such things as *Aladdin; or, the Wonderful Scamp* (1861), *The Corsican 'Bothers'; or, the Troublesome Twins* (1869), *Robert MacMaire; or, the Roadside Inn turned inside out* (1870). It was possibly Byron's execrable puns, as well as the reform of the stage initiated by Robertson, that finally killed the burlesque, though not before it had provided Londoners with a good deal of amusement at the old Gaiety, with the famous quartet headed by Nellie Farren. It survives only as a short scene in such revues as *The Gate, The Little,* and the *Sweet and Low* series, parodying a current Shakespearian production or some long-running London success. (For the American use of the word in the sense of a variety entertainment see below, 4.)

2. EXTRAVAGANZA. It is almost impossible to disentangle the Extravaganza from the Burlesque, since many of the latter, so called in memoirs of the day and reminiscences of old playgoers, are listed by Allardyce Nicoll in his *Nineteenth-Century Drama* as extravaganzas. The original distinction seems to be that the extravaganza had no particular satiric object but was a fantastic affair intended solely for amusement, and that its subject was taken from mythology or fairy tale. The great purveyor of extravaganzas was Planché, who wrote a long series of them for Madame Vestris and others, while Byron also produced a number currently with his burlesques. The extravaganza has now entirely disappeared from the London theatre.

3. BURLETTA. Closely allied to both Burlesque and Extravaganza is the Burletta, which began in the middle of the eighteenth century as 'a poor relation to an Opera' and 'a drama in rhyme, which is entirely musical'. It was the efforts of the smaller theatres to evade the licensing laws which led to a broadening of the term in the nineteenth century. This led Planché to sub-title one of his plays 'A Most Extravagant Extravaganza, or Rum-Antic Burletta'. Legally, any piece in three acts with at least five songs was a burletta, and could be performed at the minor theatres. This allowed the adaptation and presentation of plays by Shakespeare and other 'legitimate' dramatists, and accounts for the odd interpolations found in some nineteenth-century productions.   ED.

4. IN THE U.S.A. American burlesque, a native sex and comedy entertainment for men only, was devised by Michael Bennett Leavitt (1843–1935) in about 1865 and known popularly as 'burleycue' and 'leg show'. The comedy was reminiscent of the bawdy days of Aristophanes, and the sex feature, the display

of girls in tights, was borrowed from Lydia Thompson's troupe of visiting British Blondes and the notorious 'Black Crook' extravaganza. The show opened with a 'spiel'—or patter-talk—by the 'candy butcher', who walked down to the front of the theatre just before the curtain rose, sold picture-books revealing 'woman's hidden charms', and promised fabulous prizes to purchasers of ten-cent boxes of candy. The performance which followed was divided into three parts on the pattern of the American minstrel show. Part I was a combination of chorus numbers, comedy sketches, called the 'bits', and monologues. Part II, the 'olio', was made up of variety acts: acrobats, instrumentalists, magicians, freak entertainers, and sentimental song singers. Part III consisted also of chorus numbers, 'bits', and an occasional travesty on politics and current plays, the only claim which the show had to the title Burlesque (see above).

The final number was called the Extra Added Attraction, and was usually the 'hootchy-kootchy' or *danse du ventre*. Certain managers, however, occasionally substituted a boxing bout or some other exhibition of manly skill and prowess.

Burleycue comedy material consisted largely of monologues and the 'bits', which were identified either by the trick apparatus employed, like bladders, or by opening lines like 'I'll meet you 'round the corner'. The intervening dialogue the comedian supplied, giving it his own personal type of humour, with the aid of comic make-up—putty nose, scare wig, false feet, drooping trousers, and grotesque headgear. He was assisted also, from time to time, by two or three other comedians, known as the dude, the Chinaman, the tramp, and the straight man or 'feeder', who was dressed in perfect evening attire.

One of the most famous 'bits' was the courtroom scene. It showed a judge, lawyers, witnesses, and jury all busy considering the case of a lady guilty of a misdemeanour. As the trial progressed the judge shot peas at the jury, hit himself on the head with the gavel while calling for order, and finally collapsed in the pandemonium which he had himself created. Though the 'bits' were old and familiar, the audience loved the double-entendres, the suggestive stage business, the slapstick and bladders. Between scenes and drinks the patrons laughed, applauded, and participated actively in the performance, sang the sentimental songs, ogled the girls, dated them up, and handed them presents when they strutted down the runway. Burlesque became the natural, extemporaneous school for most of the great American stage, screen, and radio comedians. Among these were Al Jolson, W. C. Fields, Fannie Brice, Sophie Tucker, Jack Pearl, Jimmy Barton, Leon Errol, Bobby Clark, Willie Howard, Bert Lahr, and Weber and Fields. The training was difficult, an ordeal by fire, for the rowdy audience heckled the comedian, hurled vegetables across the footlights, and often shouted 'Get the hook!'

Sometimes a fist-fight in the front aisle interrupted the comic in the midst of a monologue, but he had to carry on or get off. Sometimes the police rushed in, raided the show, and carried him off along with the other performers, on charges of indecency.

About 1920 the strip-tease, an innovation of uncertain origin, startled audiences who eventually turned the theatre into a disrobing arena by inducing the dancer to remove more and more of her scant attire by applauding and shouting, 'Take 'em off!' The dance, ostensibly simple, had an involved routine, requiring skill and personality. First came the 'parade', in which the so-called dancer promenaded back and forth across the stage. Then came the 'grinds', vigorous twistings of the torso, and the 'bumps', a forward thrusting of the abdomen, and finally 'the flash', with the girl exposing herself for one moment, completely nude except for the G-string. Gypsy Rose Lee broke down puritanic convention by establishing the scandalous burlesque number as a conventional Broadway revue speciality. Her subsequent career as novelist, actress, découpé artist, and social favourite made her, for a time, the most-talked-of woman in the United States.

Burlesque reached its peak of popularity just before the outbreak of war in 1914. At that time resident companies like Minsky's Winter Garden, New York City, played to packed houses; and two rival syndicates, or 'wheels', the Mutual and the Columbia, had companies touring the entire United States successfully. Among the best-known companies were Rentz-Santley's, Sam T. Jack's, Billy Watson's 'Beef Trust', 'Wine, Woman and Song', and Rose Sydell's 'London Belles', which ran twenty years. Among the stars, who had large followings, season after season, were Al Reeves, 'Bozo' Snyder, 'Sliding' Billy Watson, and 'Snuffy' the cabman.

With the enforcement of prohibition, burlesque lost its hold for a time, being finally barred from New York City in April 1942. The causes for the breakdown were numerous. Broadway revues appropriated the bawdy 'bits' under the title of 'black-outs', and also the exploitation of female nudity. The invention of motion pictures provided a new, cheaper, and more accessible amusement. Finally, the shows lost their male appeal when Columbia cleaned them up, and made them suitable for ladies and children.   B. S.

BURNACINI. (1) GIOVANNI (? –1655), architect of a theatre in Vienna, for which he also designed the scenery. His son (2) LODOVICO OTTAVIO (1636–1707) was also a scenic designer, and a representative of stage baroque at its richest and most typical. Some of his best work was done in Vienna, where he worked for Leopold I (see also COSTUME, 7, OPERA, 2 and SCENERY 3).

BURNAND, SIR FRANCIS COWLEY (1836–1917), editor of *Punch* from 1880 to 1906. He was closely connected with the theatre, and in 1855 was instrumental in founding the Cambridge Amateur Dramatic Club (A.D.C.). He wrote over a hundred plays, mainly burlesques of popular drama, or adaptations of French farces. He had little profundity or originality, but much wit and agility, and was a great punster and player on words. The success of his works was mainly due to their topicality, and none has survived.

BURNS MANTLE, see MANTLE, ROBERT BURNS.

BURNT CORK MINSTRELS, see NIGGER MINSTRELS.

BURTON, WILLIAM EVANS (1804–60), an actor-manager and dramatist, born and educated in England, whose professional life was passed in the United States, where he went in 1834. Son of a printer, he inherited his father's business and became editor of a monthly magazine, but gave it up to go on the stage. He first appeared in London in 1831, and in the following year was at the Haymarket, where he played with Edmund Kean. His American début was made at the Arch Street Theatre, Philadelphia, and he first appeared in New York in 1837. After converting a circus in Philadelphia into a theatre, and running it successfully as the National, he returned to New York and took over Palmo's Opera House in Chambers Street, which had degenerated into a home of variety. Renovated and redecorated, it opened on 10 July 1848 as Burton's, and was one of the most important theatres of the day. Odell, in his *Annals of the New York Stage*, dates the beginning of modern times from the opening of Burton's, four years before Wallack's. It had a talented company, which flourished under a genial management, and Burton, himself a supreme comedian, appeared there in a number of richly characteristic parts, of which the most popular were Timothy in *Toodles*, Aminadab Sleek in *The Serious Family*, and Captain Cuttle in Brougham's adaptation of *Dombey and Son*, which was the theatre's first outstanding success. Dickens was always popular at Burton's, and Oliver B. Raymond's Toots and Johnston's Uriah Heep were both memorable, as was a series of old English comedies with Henry Placide. The arrival in 1851 of Mrs. Warner from Sadler's Wells led to a revival of several Shakespearian plays, beginning with *The Winter's Tale*. In the following year Burton began to suffer from the success of Wallack's, which took some of his best actors from him. But before Burton finally deserted his theatre in 1856 it had seen the début of Agnes Robinson in a long run of *To Parents and Guardians*, and fine productions of *A Midsummer Night's Dream* and *The Tempest*, with Burton as Bottom and Caliban. On 8 Sept. 1856 Burton took over the Metropolitan, and opened with *The Rivals*. But he was never so successful there as in his old theatre. The competition of

Wallack's was too keen, and the theatre was too big to stand up to the financial crisis of 1857. In spite of some successful new plays and the appearance of such guest-actors as Booth, the Florences, Charlotte Cushman, Brougham, Mathews, and the Davenports, the theatre was put up for sale in 1858 and finally closed on 9 Sept. It reverted to its original name, and was only used intermittently (for its later history, see WINTER GARDEN, 1).

Meanwhile Burton made his last appearance on the New York stage at Niblo's in 1859, and then went to Canada, returning to New York to die in 1860. His life was written in 1885 by W. L. Keese. He was the author of several plays, none of which has survived. On his death he left behind a substantial fortune, a splendid library, as befitted one educated at St. Paul's School, London, and a reputation as actor and manager which time has in no way diminished.

BUSKIN, the European term for the thick-soled boot worn by the Greek actor in tragedy only (see COTHURNUS), hence used to imply writing, or acting in, tragedy. The itinerant actors of the English country-side were called Buskers, a name derived from Buskin.

BUZARIO, ANTONIO (*fl.* fifteenth century), early Italian dramatist, author of the *Cauteriaria* (1469), a comedy in Latin which borders on tragedy. It turns on the misdemeanours of an erring wife, whose husband punishes her infidelity with torture, and is in turn to be tortured by her priest-lover. But on the wife's pleading he relents, and the play ends grossly (see ITALY, 1 *b* iii).

BYRON, GEORGE GORDON, LORD (1788–1824), English poet, and author of several plays in verse which were staged in the hope of reviving poetry in the English theatre, but with little success. Only one was produced during his lifetime, *Marino Faliero* (1821), done at Drury Lane, where after his death *Werner* was given in 1830, and *Sardanapalus* by Charles Kean in 1834. *Manfred*, a dramatic poem, and *The Two Foscari* were given at Covent Garden in 1834 and 1837 respectively. Byron joined the Committee of Drury Lane in 1814, and his letters are full of references to theatrical matters of the day; but his plays read better than they act, in spite of his undoubted dramatic talents, and stand somewhat apart from the main stream of nineteenth-century theatre development.

BYRON, HENRY JAMES (1834–84), English actor and dramatist, best known for his series of burlesques, of which the first was seen in 1857, the last in about 1881. They were usually given at the smaller London theatres, the Olympic, Adelphi, Strand, and others. Intended for medicine, which he hated, and then for the law, which bored him, he joined a provincial company, and in 1869 made his first appearance in London in one of his own comedies. He continued to appear almost entirely in his own plays, one of the exceptions being at his last appearance on the stage in 1881, in Gilbert's *Engaged*. In 1865 he joined Marie Wilton (Lady Bancroft) in the management of the renovated Dust Hole, to whose opening programme as the Prince of Wales's he contributed a burlesque of 'La Sonnambula'. He was under contract to write exclusively for this theatre, and two of his three-act comedies, *War to the Knife* (1865) and *A Hundred Thousand Pounds* (1866), were given there, as were several burlesques and extravaganzas. In 1867 he took over the management of the Alexandra Theatre, Liverpool, where some of his best work was done, but with little financial success. He returned to management in London in 1874 at the Criterion and in the following year, on 16 Jan. 1875, produced his famous *Our Boys*, which ran till 18 Apr. 1879, and set up a record which lasted for many years—1,362 performances.

Byron's work—he was responsible for nearly 150 plays, ranging from sentimental comedy to pantomime—owed little to the prevalent pilfering from French and German drama, but can hardly be called original, for all that. His themes were taken from mythology, nursery tale, opera, legend, and topical events; his style was ingenious, but heavily overloaded with wearisome puns, and with smart repartee which somehow lacked wit. In his serious plays he tended to create stock types, which recur constantly throughout his work, and he had no originality. At his best he reflected the prevailing taste of the day, against which T. W. Robertson rebelled, and that, and his own charming personality, accounted for much of his ephemeral success. Hibbert, in *A Playgoer's Memoirs*, says of him: 'His habit of word contortion, or punning, in burlesque is tiresome to us now, and seems laborious, but it was natural to him. His humour is homely, and even vulgar. His characters are mostly conventional creatures of the stage. But he never set up a suggestive situation, or wrote an indecorous line.' He also adds that he was 'a tall, handsome, heavily moustached man, who was hardly ever known to lose his temper, who was universally beloved for his charm and for his ready wit' and as an actor 'he rejected makeup and would step from a cab on to the stage'.

C

CAECILIUS STATIUS (*c.* 219–*c.* 166 B.C.), Roman dramatist, said to have been a Gaul from north Italy. During the years between the death of Plautus and the advent of Terence, he translated Greek comedies for the Roman stage. Some 40 titles and about 300 lines have survived. Cicero thought Caecilius's latinity bad. In one of the most interesting passages in Latin literary criticism Aulus Gellius sets extracts from Caecilius's *Plocium* side by side with their original by Menander to show how inferior the Latin writer is in style, wit, simplicity, and truth to nature. It is certainly illuminating to see how widely a Latin 'translation' can differ from the original. We may grant that Caecilius has coarsened his material (the theme of the peccant husband and the jealous wife), yet claim that he has lent it a lively pungency which was probably more in keeping with Roman taste than all the subtle grace of Menander. Here as elsewhere in Latin drama we see how the translator has used every trick of rhetoric to make a situation instantaneously effective. In Menander the wife's triumph is stated in matter-of-fact language: 'Out of the house she has cast the troublesome girl'; in Caecilius we can hear her nagging accents: 'ita plor*ando* or*ando* inst*ando* atque obiurg*ando* me optudit.' We notice also that the Latin writer has introduced a broad jest (a reference to the lady's unpleasant breath) for which there is no justification in the Greek. It would seem, then, that Caecilius allowed himself considerable freedom in expression and style, just as his predecessors, Naevius and Plautus, had done; nevertheless his plays were at first unpopular and only succeeded because of the steady support given them by the famous actor-producer Ambivius Turpio. Caecilius seems to have set the new fashion of leaving titles for the most part in the Greek; he favoured Menander, the most refined of the Greek authors of New Comedy; his plots, we are told, were good, which presumably means that he chose originals with good plots and did not tamper with them; he was something of a moralist. It would appear, then, that he had at least set foot on the road which led from the careless gaiety of Naevius and Plautus to the more Hellenic and sentimental comedy of Terence and his successors.   W. B.

CAFÉ-CONCERT, the name given to the French restaurant where singers and orchestra amuse the diners, sometimes with a simple programme of ballads and light music, sometimes with an elaborate operetta. A number of good singers and actors have come to the legitimate stage from the cafés-concerts, which were originally known by their Dutch name as Musicos. They were a product of the Revolution, and flourished until their licences were restricted under the Empire, reappearing under Louis-Philippe. The destruction under the Second Empire of so many small popular theatres along the Boulevard du Temple gave new life to many cafés-concerts elsewhere.

The café-spectacle was run on the same lines, but offered its clients more solid fare, with acrobats, conjuring, short sketches, and dancing.

CAFÉ FLAMENCO, a type of entertainment popular in Spain, native to Andalusia, and corresponding to the French *café-concert*. The patrons of the café are regaled with songs and dances, in folk-lore and gipsy tradition, which have a vaguely oriental flavour, due no doubt to the persistent influence of the Moors, comparable to that of café-singers in Algiers and Tunis. (See Sargent's painting *El Jaleo*, which was in the Salon of 1882.)

CAIN, ANDREW (*fl.* 1620–1644), English actor, a goldsmith by profession, who became a player in 1622, first as one of Lady Elizabeth's Men and then as a Palsgrave's Man. He was evidently a comedian, for he is frequently referred to as 'Cane the Clown', and in 1631 (by which date he had evidently joined the Prince's Men at Salisbury Court) he played the part of Trimalchio, a humorous gallant, in *Holland's Leaguer*. He was one of the actors who continued playing surreptitiously at the Red Bull after the closing of the theatres in 1642. In 1641 *The Stage-Players' Complaint* was published, with the sub-title *In a Pleasant Dialogue between Cane of the Fortune and Reed of the Friers* (Timothy Read was another popular comedian of the day), and woodcut portraits of both men. During the Civil War Cain (whose name is found in numerous spellings, including Keyne and Kein) returned to his trade, and engraved dies at Oxford for the debased coinage of the Royalists. Thirty years later he was still remembered for his jigs at the Fortune, and at the Red Bull, where the Prince's Men spent their last active years.

CALDERÓN DE LA BARCA, PEDRO (1600–81), Spanish dramatist, successor of Lope de Vega and with him one of the finest exponents of Spanish dramatic art. He wrote his first play at the age of 14, and was appointed official playwright and Master of the Revels to Philip IV, by whom he was knighted. About 100 of his plays survive, out of a possible 200 odd, many of them *autos sacramentales* written for the festival of Corpus Christi. These contain some of his most exquisite poetry, combined with excellent stage-craft, which unite to clothe the abstract ideas of Catholic theology in great dramatic beauty. A. A. Parker, in his study of Calderón's religious plays, says: 'Calderón is not a dramatist who was forced by his environment to retail theological clichés and to distort the nature of his medium. He is a theological poet and dramatist in a deep and legitimate sense, and as such his achievement is not only valuable, but also unique in literature.' Of these plays, the best known are *El gran teatro del mundo* (*c.* 1645) and *La cena de Baltasar* (*c.* 1634).

Of Calderón's other plays, the most important are the historical *El alcalde de Zalamea* and *La vida es sueño* (1673), the latter a philosophical fantasy containing some fine poetry. *El mágico prodigioso* is a version of the Faust-legend. These three plays, together with five of the *comedias*, were freely translated into English by Edward Fitzgerald, and *La vida es sueño*, as *Such Stuff as Dreams are Made of*, was privately performed by the Elizabethan Stage Society in May 1899. Shelley was also an enthusiastic admirer and translator of Calderón, as were Tieck and Schlegel in Germany. Another of Calderón's plays, *El médico de su honra*, deals with the *pundonor*, or 'point of honour' so dear to Spanish dramatists. More robust than Lope de Vega, though lacking his spontaneity, Calderón is the more finished playwright, and exercised a great influence over European drama. A number of his plays were translated into French and so found their way into Restoration England, not without acknowledgement from the adapters.

CALIFORNIA, see PIONEER THEATRE IN THE U.S.A.

CALL DOOR, see PROSCENIUM.

CALLIPIDES, a Greek actor of the fifth century B.C. (see GREECE, 3 *e*).

CALMO, ANDREA (1509/10–c. 1561), a Venetian gondolier, and an early Italian dramatist and amateur actor, contemporary and rival of Ruzzante (see BEOLCO). He seems to have exercised considerable influence on the literary development of the *commedia dell'arte*. As an actor he specialized in old men, and may have played a part comparable to Pantalone, though the name is not yet in use. His plays were edited by Rossi in 1888 (see ITALY, 2).

CALVERT. (1) CHARLES (1828–79), English actor and manager, who made his first appearances in the provinces, before going to London in 1855. In 1859 he became manager of the Theatre Royal, Manchester, and was the first manager of the Prince's Theatre there when it opened in 1864. He remained until 1875, when he went to New York to produce *Henry V.* On a previous visit to the U.S.A. in 1871 he had been responsible for the production of *Richard III* at Niblo's Garden. On his return to England he continued to appear in the provinces until his death. It was, however, at Manchester that his main work was done, with the production of a number of Shakespeare and other plays which were much admired by discerning critics of the day. In 1856 he married (2) ADELAIDE HELEN (née Biddles or Bedells) (1837–1921), daughter of a provincial actor, who had been on the stage since, as a child of six, she appeared with the Charles Keans, going with them to America. After her marriage she appeared in leading parts under her husband's management with great success, and also accompanied him to America. She returned there after his death and toured with Edwin Booth, Mrs. Langtry, and Mary Anderson. She was the author of two plays, *Trotty Veck* (1872), based on Dickens's *The Chimes*, and *Can*

He Forgive Her? (1891). All her eight children went on the stage, but only one achieved any great eminence. This was (3) LOUIS (1859–1923), who made his first appearance in Durban, Natal, in 1879, and from there went to Australia. On his return to England in 1880 he joined Sarah Thorne's famous stock company at Margate. He appeared at Drury Lane in 1886, and at the Lyceum with Irving in the following year, and was subsequently associated with most of the leading managements of London, including that of Fred Terry and Julia Neilson, with whom he gave a splendid performance as an old actor in *Sweet Nell of Old Drury*. He was a leading member of the company at the Court Theatre during the Vedrenne–Barker management, playing Broadbent in *John Bull's Other Island*, and William the Waiter in *You Never Can Tell*, with marked success. He several times formed and managed his own company, in London and on tour in England and America. He was at one time producer at the New Theatre, New York, and appeared there also in several revivals of the classics and Shakespeare. Besides being a splendid actor, robust, with a fine voice and a complete knowledge of his art, he was an excellent producer, and a successful and highly respected manager. Whether in Shakespeare, Shaw, costume plays or modern comedy, he was equally at home and always in the front rank. His Mercutio and Casca were memorable, as was his Creon in the Reinhardt production of *Oedipus Rex* at Covent Garden in 1912. At his best in parts requiring dramatic strength which gave his fine voice full play, he could also play comedy roles with ease and polish. He was the author of a handbook to acting, *Problems of the Actor*, published in 1918.

W. M. P.

CALZABIGI, RANIERO DA (1714–95), Italian poet, and the librettist of Gluck, whom he encouraged in his attempts to reform opera. The first result of their collaboration was 'Orfeo' (1762), followed by 'Alceste' (1767) and 'Paride ed Elena' (1770).

CAMARGO, MARIE ANNE DE CUPIS DE (1710–70), one of the first and most famous dancers of the eighteenth century. She is chiefly remembered now for her daring in shortening the cumbersome skirts then worn, and so allowing the dancer greater freedom, and for the introduction of the *entrechat*. The Camargo Society, named after her, was founded in 1930, when Diaghilev's death seemed as if it might deprive London of all classical ballet. Its aim was to encourage young English dancers and choreographers, in which it succeeded admirably. Its productions included 'Job' and 'Façade', and these, together with the rest of the Society's properties and funds, were presented to the Sadler's Wells Ballet when the success of the latter showed that the Camargo Society had done its work well, and was no longer needed.

CAMBRIDGE. Although medieval religious plays were in all probability given at Cambridge as elsewhere, the first recorded performance there appears to be that of the early English comedy, *Gammer Gurton's Needle*, which at some time between 1552 and 1563 was given at Christ's College. At about the same time Latin plays were common, and were doubtless regarded as part of the educational curriculum. Elizabeth, on her only visit to Cambridge, in 1564, was entertained with a comedy by Plautus and an original tragedy in Latin on the subject of Dido. An English play by Udall was also given, but this was apparently not to the taste of the authorities, since a letter of 1592 from the Vice-Chancellor asks the Queen to allow a Latin play to be prepared in honour of her approaching visit—which did not materialize—instead of the English play which she had commanded, the latter not being customary and 'nothing beseminge our students'. Later records show a preponderance of Latin plays, several of them translated from contemporary Italian works, either directly or through the French. St. John's seems to have been particularly addicted to play-acting, and it was there that the *Pilgrimage to Parnassus* and the two parts of the *Return to Parnassus* were first performed, in the years between 1598 and 1603. King's, however, can claim to have been the first to present a translation—albeit in Latin—of Guarini's famous *Pastor Fido*, round about the turn of the century. It was with a Latin translation from the Italian that Trinity men entertained the young Prince Charles when with his sister Elizabeth and her husband, the Elector Palatine, he visited Cambridge in 1613, while the visit of James I in 1615 was made memorable by the performance, among other plays, of Ruggle's *Ignoramus*, which so delighted the King that, being unable to get the actors up to Whitehall, he returned to Cambridge some weeks later to see it again.

There were, of course, occasional visits to Cambridge by the professional companies, particularly in the summer and when plague closed the London theatres. On the whole, however, they were not encouraged, though the Lord Chamberlain's Men are believed to have played *Hamlet* at Cambridge in 1603. Traces of Latin plays grow fewer as the Commonwealth approaches, and the Restoration did little to bring back the academic play. For a serious revival of acting in the University we have to wait for the foundation of the A.D.C. by F. C. Burnand, the first performance taking place in the May term of 1855. Unlike the later O.U.D.S., the A.D.C. did not confine itself to Shakespeare, but during its first fifty years played mainly comedy and burlesque. One of its early ventures was *The Overland Route*, an ambitious production which led to further essays in the same style, including a version of *The Lyons Mail* with no female characters. One of the early A.D.C. actors to win fame on the professional stage was Charles Brookfield, who was first seen in *Money* in 1877.

The A.D.C. now has a permanent and well-equipped theatre, built in 1935, and since 1947

has admitted women as full members. The introduction of more solid fare into its programmes dates from the early 1920s, and owes much to the influence of Frank Birch. The Marlowe Society, founded in 1908, has also done good work, particularly under George Rylands, who combines in himself the attributes of scholar and practical producer. Mention should also be made of the Arts Theatre, which under the guidance of the late John Maynard Keynes (Lord Keynes) and his wife, Lydia Lopokova, did much to stimulate interest in good plays, well acted and carefully produced, while retaining its function as a repertory theatre for the ordinary playgoer. The Arts Theatre is also one of the participating bodies in the Company of Four at the Lyric Theatre, Hammersmith.

It was the influence of the Greek play at Oxford, first given in 1880, which stimulated interest in a similar venture at Cambridge, and Sophocles' *Ajax* was given at the end of 1882. A year later *The Birds*, with music by Parry, was performed, and in 1884 a society was definitely established for the continued production of plays in Greek, not necessarily every year. Among later productions were the *Eumenides*, *Oedipus Tyrannus*, and *The Wasps*.

A theatrical venture not connected with the University, but of some interest in the history of the English stage, was the establishment by Terence Gray in 1926 of the Festival Theatre, founded 'to attack the realistic tradition of acting and production'. It had no proscenium, a stage on several levels with numerous outlets, and a curved auditorium which met the fore-stage at each side. Here some interesting and unusual productions were staged, the plays ranging from Greek drama to modern comedy, and embracing examples of most ages and European countries. Props and scenery were abolished, the lighting was deliberately unrealistic, and all the attention was concentrated on the actors and the broad general sweep of the plot. This method succeeded admirably with Greek and Elizabethan plays, less well with Ibsen and the moderns, but the Festival Theatre provided a stimulating training-ground for young actors, among whom were Maurice Evans and Flora Robson. Unfortunately it had little effect on the English theatre as a whole, and in 1933 became an ordinary repertory theatre, later becoming derelict.

CAMBRIDGE THEATRE, LONDON, in Seven Dials, built by Bertie A. Meyer and opened by him on 4 Sept. 1930 with Charlot's revue, *Masquerade*. Though a charming playhouse, the Cambridge has as yet contributed little to theatre history. The Chauve-Souris company played a season there soon after its opening, and other productions were *Elizabeth of England* and a revival of *Night Must Fall*. Seasons of ballet and classical music have also been given there, and successful plays transferred there from other theatres. It was later used for opera. W. M. P.

CAMERON, BEATRICE (1868–1940), see MANSFIELD (2).

CAMINELLI, ANTONIO (1436–1502), author of the first Italian play to bear the formal name of 'tragedy'. This was *Filostrato e Panfile* (1499), and in it Caminelli, who was known as 'Il Pistoia', tried to force a story from the Decameron into the mould of Senecan tragedy, while retaining much of the tradition of the old medieval religious play.

CAMPBELL, BARTLEY (1843–88), one of the first American dramatists to make playwriting his only profession. He even retired from journalism when his first play was given in 1871, on the ground that a playwright could not also be a critic. He wrote a number of melodramas, of which the first was *Through Fire* (1871), and directed a theatre in Chicago where many of his later works were produced, including *Fate* (1872), and a domestic drama, *Risks* (1873). It was the visit of the Chicago company to San Francisco which inspired Campbell's best play, *My Partner* (1879), a drama of the American frontier, which owes much to the stories of Bret Harte. It was first played with Louis Aldrich in the chief part, and was translated into German. Among Campbell's later plays were *The Galley Slave* (1879) and *The White Slave* (1882), both emotional melodramas, which he directed and financed himself, thus losing the fortune which *My Partner* had brought him. He died insane, of overwork and worry, and none of his plays has been published. They have little literary quality, but are interesting in the history of the late nineteenth-century American stage.

CAMPBELL, HERBERT (1844–1904), a music-hall performer, who began his career as a member of a burnt-cork trio during the Nigger Minstrel boom, and then went on the halls as a solo turn. He appeared regularly in Drury Lane pantomimes from Boxing Night, 1882, until the year of his death, and with his large fat figure and jolly red face proved a wonderful foil to diminutive Dan Leno during the many years they played together.

CAMPBELL, MRS. PATRICK [*née* BEATRICE STELLA TANNER] (1865–1940), English actress, who made her first appearance on the stage in 1888 at Liverpool. After touring with Ben Greet, she appeared in London in 1890, playing in *The Hunchback, The School for Scandal*, and *As You Like It*. A season at the Adelphi was followed by her outstanding performance as Paula in *The Second Mrs Tanqueray* at the St. James's, and she was soon considered one of the leading actresses of the day. Among her later successes were Agnes in *The Notorious Mrs. Ebbsmith*, Juliet and Ophelia to the Romeo and Hamlet of Forbes-Robertson, Mélisande in English and in French—the latter to the Pelléas of Sarah Bernhardt—and a number of leading roles in Ibsen. She also appeared in London and in New York in the title-role of *Magda*, in which Matheson Lang thought her superior to Duse. Shaw, however, in *Our Theatres in the Nineties*, pours scorn on it, as he does on her Rita in *Little Eyolf*, though he wrote for her the part of Eliza Doolittle in *Pygmalion*, which she played at the first production in 1914 and at subsequent revivals. Among her other parts were Fedora, Bella Donna, Lady Macbeth, and—one of her finest creations—Anastasia Rakonitz in *The Matriarch*, a play based on the novel by G. B. Stern. A beautiful woman—Shaw calls her 'perilously bewitching'—she had a devastating wit, and became a legend long before her death. In spite of long absences from the stage, she was one of the great theatrical figures of her generation. Her daughter Stella was also on the stage.

CAMPDEN HOUSE, Kensington. This had a well-appointed private theatre where frequent amateur performances were given in the 1850s and 1860s.

CAMPEN, JACOB VAN, see VAN CAMPEN, JACOB.

CAMPION, THOMAS (1567–1620), English poet and musician, who at one time practised as a doctor. He was connected with Philip Rosseter, also a musician, who was lessee of Whitefriars theatre, and manager of the Queen's Revels, and may have made contact with the public stage through him, though there is no evidence that he ever wrote for it. His masques for performance at Court, however, place him next to Jonson in the history of the genre during Jacobean days. The words of these are printed in the 1909 edition of Campion's works, edited by Percival Vivian.

CAMPISTRON, JEAN GALBERT DE (1656–1723), French dramatist who, after a stormy and precocious youth, went to Paris and was befriended by the actor J. B. Raisin. His first two plays having been produced at the Comédie-Française, Campistron was engaged on the recommendation of Racine to write the libretto for Lully's last opera 'Acis et Galatée'. Its success brought him recognition and a lucrative position with a noble house. Campistron's most important play, *Andronic*, given in 1685, is, like so many plays of the time, contemporary history under a Roman guise, and it marks the extent of the influence exercised on drama by the historical novel, to the detriment of the former. The continued decadence of classical tragedy is also apparent in its exaggerated and improbable intrigue. Of his other plays *Alcibiade* (1685) was momentarily successful, owing to the excellent acting of Baron, but his later plays were failures, being weak in execution and overweighted with intrigue. In 1686 a play entitled *Phraate* was given four performances, but was then stopped by the authorities, possibly on account of some fancied slight to the king. No copy of it exists, and it is said that Campistron was made to burn the only manuscript copy. Though the plan and conception of Campistron's plays were good, his style was poor, owing to laziness. He wrote also two comedies, which are of no importance. The poverty of French drama at this time is revealed by the fact that from 1683 to 1693 Campistron was considered its leading tragic writer. Like Racine, he gave up the theatre to enter the king's service.

CANADA. This vast Dominion, with its scattered population and its division into French- and English-speaking groups, offers the paradox of a country which combines the complete lack of a professional theatre with an immense theatrical activity. Forced by the conditions of their life to depend very much upon themselves for amusement, Canadians in town and country have been enthusiastic advocates of the Little, Amateur, or Community Theatre movement. The infrequent visits of English and American touring companies have been welcomed in the larger towns, often with keen appreciation and informed criticism, and have no doubt done much to encourage the local amateur groups. But it is on these latter that the main burden of theatrical entertainment falls, particularly in the more isolated regions, and it is from the stronger and more energetic of them that, it is hoped, a professional and national theatre will one day arise. What is needed before such a theatre can be established is self-confidence, training, experience, and, above all, the unshackling of professional theatrical enterprise from the present heavy economic burdens of wages and rents. Enthusiasm, ability, and a keen recognition of the place of the drama in social life are not lacking. It only remains for the financial problems to be solved, and for the rising generation of Canadian writers and actors to resist the lure of Hollywood, New York, or London, and to establish, on their own soil and in their own fashion, a professional theatre which shall be as truly native as that of any other land.

The ground has been well prepared. One of the first towns to become theatre-conscious was Toronto, where in the early years of the twentieth century Earl Grey encouraged the organization of music and drama festivals. Just previous to the First World War the Arts and Letters Club of Toronto University had its own group of players which, under its American-trained producer Roy Mitchell, gave a number of interesting performances. But an organized amateur movement may be said to have begun in 1919, with the opening of Hart House Theatre, an integral part of the central students' building donated by the Massey Foundation. This theatre, which was one of the finest Little Theatres on the North American continent, with an excellently equipped stage and an auditorium seating some 300, was organized on a semi-independent basis, with a subscription membership drawn both from the University and the surrounding neighbourhood. It had a professional producer,

electrician, and stage-manager, and an amateur cast of both undergraduates and townspeople, all jointly responsible for the making of scenery, costumes, and properties. Until well into the 1930s the theatre maintained a consistently high standard, producing a variety of established classics, as well as some experimental plays and new plays by Canadian authors, a form of dramatic activity which it directly encouraged with fruitful results. The first productions were given by the Players' Club under Roy Mitchell, but almost from its foundation the theatre was under the control of a Board of Syndics, with Vincent Massey, after whose father Hart House had been named, as its first chairman, a position he retained until 1935. In addition he directed and appeared in several plays, as did his younger brother Raymond, later a well-known professional actor of stage and screen.

The status of Hart House Theatre at that time may be considered that of a good amateur repertory theatre, with a settled policy and the beginnings of a stabilizing tradition. Under a succession of directors, Roy Mitchell, Bertram Forsyth, Walter Sinclair, Carroll Aikens, Edgar Stone, and Nancy Pyper, much interesting work was done, and the theatre won golden opinions at home and abroad.

Towards 1939 Hart House Theatre fell somewhat from its high estate. The competition of radio and cinema, and economic and other difficulties, mitigated against the usefulness of what had been the most outstanding venture in the Canadian amateur theatre, and for some time the stage was used fitfully by various outside amateur groups and for lectures and concerts, which had indeed always formed part of its programme. On the outbreak of the Second World War it was closed, and on its reopening in 1946 gave up its quasi-independent status and became wholly affiliated to the University, as an undergraduate theatre connected, though not too crampingly, with the main English curriculum. It is to be hoped that the new departure, sustained by the enthusiasm of staff and students alike and stimulated by frequent visits of outstanding English and American companies to the Alexandra Theatre, will inaugurate a new and brilliant period in the theatre's history.

Other Toronto activities of which mention may be made are the local amateur repertory theatre, which unassumingly does good steady work, and the Toronto Children Players, founded in 1930. Playing on Saturdays, morning and afternoon, this organization, with a mixed company of children and adults, aims at providing good entertainment for children during a season running from October to May. Nor should the Margaret Eaton Theatre School be forgotten, since it was there that Bertram Forsyth worked after leaving Hart House Theatre, while a prize-winning play by a Canadian dramatist, Isabel Ecclestone Mackay, *Two Too Many*, had its first performance there in 1928. Toronto also had its Masquers' Club, which, like those of Montreal and Winnipeg, travelled the country during the war, playing to service audiences.

Winnipeg has for many years been a centre of theatrical activity, and her Masquers' Club was awarded first prize in the first Dominion Drama Festival, an enterprise which has undoubtedly been the greatest incentive to the development and co-ordination of the theatre in Canada. Founded in 1932 at the instance of the then Governor-General, Lord Bessborough, the Dominion Drama Festival was first held in 1933, and thereafter yearly until the outbreak of war in 1939. As stated in its Charter, the objects of the Festival are 'to encourage dramatic art in Canada by the holding of a Dominion Drama Festival and such regional or other subsidiary festivals as may be deemed advisable, and by the granting of prizes and awards for distinctive effort in any of the arts relating to the drama, including among others the writing of plays, their presentation, mounting, costuming and lighting'. In order to cover the vast area quickly and concisely, the country is divided into eleven regions, and the winners of these regional festivals attend the final festival, held in early summer, usually at Ottawa, though the 1947 festival, the first since the war, was held in London, Ontario, one of the most active theatrical regions in the country. Its Little Theatre, formed in 1934 by the amalgamation of four small amateur groups, now numbers 7,000 members, and owns and operates its own playhouse, having in 1945 purchased the old Grand Theatre, which had housed its earlier productions. It also runs a theatre school and, in association with the University of Western Ontario, a Summer School, while an Extension Department of the University gives help to small church, school, and rural groups. The Grand Theatre is also used by other local amateur and university groups, and prepares them for participation in the Dominion Drama Festival.

Although London, Ontario, is outstandingly successful in its dramatic work, it is only symptomatic of what is going on all over the country. Vancouver, whose stock company, flourishing during the 1920s, was disbanded after its best actors had gone to Hollywood, has nevertheless a good Little Theatre group, founded in 1922, which makes intermittent use of a small theatre, the York, with a seating capacity of about 400. This, though often used as a cinema, also provides a centre for the activities of the many drama clubs scattered throughout British Columbia, and has housed the Labour Arts Guild and the productions of the School and Community Drama Department run by the British Columbia Provincial Government. A Summer School University Extension Course is also in operation, while the University Players' Club has done good productions of Shakespeare and modern plays. In the summer open-air shows are given in Stanley Park. The province of Saskatchewan has also had a sustained theatrical history. In 1912 the Regina Amateur Dramatic Society

was started by a group of talented new-comers from England, and lasted until the outbreak of war in 1914. Re-formed in 1923, it was re-organized three years later, when W. I. Read and Captain Chetwynd started the Regina Little Theatre Society, which still flourishes. Amateur clubs were then organized in other towns of the province, and in 1932, on Read's suggestion, the methods of the British Drama League were used to form the Saskatchewan Drama League, under the patronage of Lord Bessborough. This organization now has well over a hundred affiliated clubs, and during the war was able to run its own local festival.

Nothing has so far been said about the French theatre, which flourishes mainly in Montreal and Quebec. The Dominion Drama Festival, which caters for plays in both French and English, and awards a separate prize in each section, as well as the Bessborough trophy, which may be won by either language-group, has given a great stimulus to the production of French plays, and interest in the French theatre has been quickened by the visits of such eminent theatre historians as Gustave Cohen, and the wartime tour of Ludmilla Pitoëff and her company. To the existing theatrical activity of Quebec and Montreal has now been added a cultural activity which has resulted in the publication of a number of excellent books on the theatre, and in the formation of such groups as the Compagnons de Saint-Laurent under Father Émile Legault, on the lines of similar groups in France, for the production of early French religious and secular plays. One of the most original manifestations of the French spirit in Canada, however, has undoubtedly been the revue, staged and devised in Montreal by the excellent comedian known as Fridolin. The wit and gaiety of his work give evidence of its Gallic origin, and Fridolin himself, inimitable comedian and master of mime, may well rank among the best professional actors of the day. It seems as if the future is bright for an active and scholarly French theatre in Canada, which will add its vivacity and colour to the future shaping of theatrical life there.

That professional actors can come from the ranks of Canadian amateurs is amply proved by such actors as Raymond Massey, Walter Huston, Margaret Anglin, Beatrice Lillie, and Mary Pickford, to mention only a few, all Canadian-born, and all forced to seek a wider sphere for the development of their talents. One essential for the retention of young actors in the Dominion is a sufficiency of good plays drawn from the life and history of the country and best interpreted by its own people. Apart from the serious encouragement given to Canadian authors by the Dominion Drama Festival, which resulted in twelve new plays in 1935 and sixteen in 1936, of which four reached the finals, a further effort to unearth native talent working on native themes has been made at the Banff School of Fine Arts. In 1933 an extension course in playwriting and production was started by the

University of Alberta, on the lines of the Carolina Playmakers, whose director, Frederick Koch, came himself to the Banff Summer School for several consecutive years. He was assisted by the most considerable playwright the course has yet produced, Gwen Pharis, author of some half-dozen plays on Canadian themes and editor of a volume of Folk Plays chosen from among those played at Banff. The subjects of these indigenous dramas range from the Peace River country to the fisherfolk of Vancouver, and cover mining, logging, farming, and the Okanagan Indians.

In conclusion it may be said that Canada, a young country, has a young theatre, which cannot as yet claim professional status. Yet it is probably no more amateur than were the first plays of medieval Europe, and from its present manifestations and constant activity it may, in due course, give rise to a firmly based national theatre which will give employment and entertainment to many thousands of people.

CANE, ANDREW, see CAIN, ANDREW.

CANEVAS, the French name for the outline plot or *scenario* of the *commedia dell'arte*.

CAÑOS DEL PERAL, see MADRID THEATRES, I.

CANTERBURY MUSIC-HALL. (1) LONDON (see MUSIC-HALL). (2) NEW YORK. This was originally the Canterbury Concert Hall at 663 Broadway, which opened in 1860 and was shortly afterwards destroyed by fire. On 15 Apr. 1861 it opened at 585 Broadway in what had been the French theatre, and was closed on 7 Apr. 1862 by legislation.

CAPA Y ESPADA, COMEDIAS DE, see CLOAK-AND-SWORD PLAYS.

ČAPEK, KAREL (1890–1938), Czech dramatist, and one of the few to be widely played in translation outside his own country. Among his plays, some of which were written in collaboration with his artist-brother, Josef, the best known are *R.U.R.* (Rossum's Universal Robots) and *The Insect Play* (both 1921). The latter has also been staged as *The World We Live In* and *And So Ad Infinitum*. Both are satires on the contemporary world, depicting the horrors of regimentation and the terrible end that awaits the regimented, and both have been extremely successful all over Europe and in America. Čapek also wrote *The Makropoulos Affair* (1923), which deals with the desirability or otherwise of long life, and *Adam the Creator* (1927), which serves as a sequel to *R.U.R.* in that it shows man endeavouring to rebuild the world which the robots have destroyed. His last plays, written just before the entry of Hitler into Czechoslovakia, deal with the rise of dictatorship and the terrible consequences of war. Čapek's plays were always a reflection of the world he lived in, and served as a comment on its grosser follies. He also wrote an amusing short monograph, *How a Play is Produced*.

CAPITANO, IL, the braggart soldier of the *commedia dell'arte*, vainglorious and cowardly. Andreini was one of the first to play him, as Capitan Spavento, while Silvio Fiorillo made him a Spaniard, Mattamoros (death to the Moors, anglicized as Captain Matamore). The mask of Scarramuccia, though more properly a *zanni* role, had something of the captain in it (see ITALY, 2).

CAPON, WILLIAM (1757–1827), English architect and painter, who in 1791 was appointed scenic director of the new Drury Lane by John Philip Kemble. He started with a clear field, the new theatre being too large for the scenery left over from Garrick's day, and his historical scenes introduced a radical change in the scenic system, doing away with the old flats and wings. Of a plodding, pedestrian temperament, he was a painstaking antiquarian, which accorded well with Kemble's plans for scenic reform, and he designed a number of approximately correct scenes and costumes for many of the latter's productions, including streets of ancient houses copied with careful accuracy from actual remains of the period. The banquet scene in *Macbeth*, with which the new theatre opened in April 1794, was spoken of as 'a thing to go and see of itself', while a later setting, in 1799, showed a fourteenth-century cathedral with nave, choir, and side aisles superbly decorated, the whole being about 56 ft. wide, 52 ft. deep, and 37 ft. high. One serious drawback to Capon's work was, incidentally, the difficulty of shifting such heavy and cumbersome pieces. He was nevertheless held in high regard, and continued to work at Drury Lane after Kemble's departure in 1802, until in 1809 the theatre was burnt down, involving Capon in a severe monetary loss, since much of the scenery destroyed in the fire had not been paid for. He then worked for Kemble again at the new Covent Garden Theatre, which became noted for the splendour of its Shakespearian revivals. Many of his sets remained in use in the theatre for years, and, with a little touching-up, served for stock pieces until the arrival of Macready. The precursor of Charles Kean in the application of archaeological studies to the stage, Capon had also something of Kean's pedantic inaccuracy, and delighted the public with his Anglo-Norman hall for *Hamlet*, which was made up of fragments from the periods of Edward the Confessor, Rufus, and Henry I.

CARLIN, see BERTINAZZI.

CARLTON THEATRE, LONDON. (1) Greenwich, built by Sefton Parry in 1864 to replace the derelict Theatre Royal, Deptford. It was well built and compact, but attained no special eminence. It fell into disuse when the Broadway Theatre, Deptford, was built in 1897.

(2) Haymarket, opened on 27 Apr. 1927, with *Lady Luck*, under the management of Laddie Cliff and Edgar O'Brien. It had a short theatrical history, presenting *Good News* and *The Yellow Mask* in 1928, and a revival of *The*

Merry Widow and a revue with George Robey in the following year. It then became a cinema.

W. M. P.

CARNEY, KATE (1868–1950), a much-loved star of the music-halls, who made her début on 10 Feb. 1890 at the Albert as a singer of Irish melodies. These, however, quickly gave way to the Cockney songs for which she is best remembered. She sang them dressed in a coster suit of 'pearlies' and a vast hat with towering feathers—a feminine pendant to Albert Chevalier's costermonger. Her most popular songs, still remembered, were 'Liza Johnson' and 'Three Pots a Shilling'. In 1885 she married George Barclay, a Cockney step-dancer who became one of the leading music-hall agents and a successful racehorse owner, and retired after the 1914–18 war, returning later to the halls with a mouth-organ band. In 1935, just after the celebration of her golden wedding, she appeared at the Royal Variety Performance and sang two of her old coster ditties, the audience joining heartily in the choruses.

CAROLINA PLAYMAKERS, see KOCH, F. H.

CARPENTER'S SCENE, a short front scene, usually devoted to the sub-plot, and containing matter irrelevant to the development of the main plot, used in Victorian times to enable elaborate scenery to be prepared behind its backcloth, out of sight of the audience. With the practice of dropping the front curtain between changes it became obsolete, and was at no time anything more than a makeshift device. It is, however, still properly and effectively used in pantomime and in big spectacular musical shows.

CARPET CUT, a device by which a stage carpet can be neatly and safely secured (see STAGE, 1).

CARRETTO, GALEOTTO DEL (*fl.* 1497–1530), early Italian dramatist, whose tragedies *Timon* (1497) and *Sofonisba* (1502), though influenced by Senecan models, retained much of the freedom of composition of the early religious dramas (see ITALY, 1 *b* i).

CARRIAGE-AND-FRAME, a device for changing the scenery wings, used on the continent and occasionally in England (see ENGLISH PLAYHOUSE, 2 *c*). It was also known as the Chariot-and-Pole system.

CARROLL, PAUL VINCENT (1900–   ), modern Irish dramatist. His plays take their own line, as distinctive as that of any of his predecessors in the Irish Dramatic Movement (see IRELAND). The setting of the earlier ones, the little-exploited area around Dundalk, is somewhat akin to the Midlands of William Boyle, Padraic Colum, and Brinsley Macnamara. The series of studies of priests, the profound interest in the relations of religion and daily life, the sympathy with the rebel against convention imposed from within or from without, touch upon the territory now of T. C. Murray,

now of Sean O'Casey, now of Teresa Deevy. But these things apart, Carroll stands alone among modern dramatists both in his attitude to his material and in the balance of his qualities. The sympathy, humour, and above all the discernment of subtle but significant distinctions which makes memorable his studies of priests extends also to the other characters, so that, especially in the later plays, Carroll begins to reach the balance of genuine drama, attained only when the dramatist identifies himself not with one or two of his characters but with all. In this, as in other ways, Carroll's art would appear to be steadily developing, and that without loss of the passion and clarity that he has had from the beginning.

His plays have had considerable success in Dublin, New York, London, and Glasgow. *Things that are Caesar's* was produced at the Abbey Theatre, Dublin, in 1932; *The Wise Have not Spoken* followed. *Shadow and Substance*, produced at the Abbey in 1937, had immense popularity in New York later as the best foreign play of the year. *The White Steed* was first produced in New York in 1939 and *The Strings My Lord are False* at the Olympia in Dublin in 1942.

U. E.-F.

CARTE, RICHARD D'OYLY, see D'OYLY CARTE.

CARTER, MRS. LESLIE [*née* CAROLINE LOUISE DUDLEY] (1862–1937), an American actress, who is chiefly remembered for her appearances in Belasco's productions. Married in 1880 and divorced nine years later, she decided to adopt the stage as a profession, and asked Belasco to train and launch her. There was a certain amount of opposition to her on account of her divorce, but she was an able woman, and eventually achieved her object. After an arduous course of training she made her first appearance in *The Ugly Duckling* (1890), a poor play in which she achieved a moderate success. Her first outstanding part was as the heroine in Belasco's *The Heart of Maryland* (1895), in which she appeared in New York and London, as she did in *Zaza* (1899). She then played the heroine in *Du Barry* (1901), and in *Adrea* (1904) (which were not seen in London), her last appearances under Belasco's management, as two years later she remarried, touring under her own and other managements with some success.

CARTON [CRITCHETT]. (1) RICHARD CLAUDE (1856–1928), English dramatist, who had a short career as an actor from 1875 to 1885 and then turned to playwriting. His first plays were much influenced by Dickens, the best being *Liberty Hall* (1892), but in 1898 he scored a success with *Lord and Lady Algy*, and continued to write comedies, bordering on farce, which poked discreet fun at the aristocracy, and were much enjoyed by the occupants of the London stalls. Elegantly staged, they served as starring vehicles for his wife (2) KATHERINE MACKENZIE COMPTON (1853–1928), who played almost exclusively in his plays from 1885 onwards, and was a great factor in their success. She was adept at portraying the society woman of shrewd wit and few scruples. The daughter of Henry Compton, she made her first appearance in London in 1877 as Julia in *The Rivals*, and was for some years at the St. James's Theatre.

CARTWRIGHT, WILLIAM. There were apparently two, if not three, actors of this name, of whom the first appears with great frequency in Henslowe's Diary, and was presumably an important member of the Admiral's Men. He is thought to have died in 1650, and there is a portrait of him at Dulwich College. His son was born c. 1606, and may have acted as a boy at the Fortune with his father; but his first recorded appearance is in 1634, when he is noted with a band of King's Revels Men at Norwich. He was at Salisbury Court when the theatres were closed in 1642, and was one of the actors who later played surreptitiously at the Cockpit. Aubrey says of him that he was also a bookseller and that he gave a collection of plays to Dulwich College, where there are two portraits of him. He was still alive in his eightieth year.

CASINO THEATRE, NEW YORK, on the south-east corner of Broadway and 39th Street. This was for almost fifty years the leading musical comedy house of New York, maintaining a consistently high standard in spite of financial stringency. Built in a massively Moorish style, it held 1,300 people, and was equipped with a fine staircase leading to the auditorium. Rudolph Aronson opened it on 21 Oct. 1883, in an unfinished state, which necessitated an almost immediate closing for final touches, when a fine roof garden was added for summer evening concerts. Marie Tempest was seen at the Casino in 1892, and among the musical plays produced were *Floradora* (1900), *A Chinese Honeymoon* (1902), *Wildflower* (1922), and *The Vagabond King* (1925), which, with Dennis King as Villon, ran for 511 performances. The house's last hit was *The Desert Song* (1926), and after a performance by the American Opera Company of 'Faust' on 18 Jan. 1930 it was pulled down.   G. F.

For Metropolitan Casino, New York, see BROADWAY THEATRE (3); for the London Casino, see PRINCE EDWARD THEATRE.

CASSON, SIR LEWIS (1875–   ), English actor, husband of Dame Sybil Thorndike, who made his first appearance on the stage in 1903, after some amateur successes in Charles Fry's productions of Shakespeare. He was at the Court Theatre under the Barker–Vedrenne management, where he appeared in a number of Shaw's plays, and later at the Duke of York's in Charles Frohman's repertory season. His career was interrupted by the war of 1914–18, but he returned to the stage, and in conjunction with his wife produced a season of Greek tragedy at the Holborn Empire and of Grand Guignol at the Little Theatre. For some years he concentrated mainly on production, though continuing to act, and toured widely in South

Africa and Australia with his wife, being co-director with Esmé Church of the Old Vic Mediterranean tour in 1939. He accompanied Dame Sybil on her tour of the mining towns during the Second World War, and was for some years connected with C.E.M.A. and E.N.S.A. He was knighted in the Birthday Honours of 1945 for his services to the theatre.

CASTRO Y BELLVÍS, GUILLÉN DE (1569–1631), a Spanish dramatist of Valencia, friend and follower of Lope de Vega. His main claim to fame rests on his dramatization of the ballads celebrating Spain's national hero, *Las mocedades del Cid*, from which Corneille took the main outline of his *Le Cid* (1636). This was a turning-point in the history of European drama, and the first play of the French classic theatre, which was later to prove so detrimental to that of eighteenth-century Spain. Its sequel, *Las hazañas del Cid*, was also successful, as were a number of other plays, including *Los Malcasados de Valencia*, *El Narciso en su opinión*, and *El Conde de Alarcos*, in all of which Castro followed in the steps of Lope de Vega, though with less charm and vitality. Castro's drama is almost purely national, and his style is admirably suited to his subjects.

CATHERINE STREET THEATRE, LONDON, see ROYAL PANTHEON.

CATWALK, a narrow bridge slung on iron stirrups from the grid, running from one fly-floor to another to enable the fly-men to reach and adjust any portion of the hung scenery.

CAULDRON TRAP, see STAGE, 1 and TRAP.

CAUSSIN, NICOLAS (1580–1651), see JESUIT DRAMA.

CAVE, JOE A. (1823–1912), an early music-hall performer who started as a juvenile, and then became a black-faced singer and violin player. He later became a prominent music-hall proprietor and manager, running, among other places, the West London and the Old Vic.

CAWARDEN, SIR THOMAS, see MASTER OF THE REVELS.

CECCHETTI, ENRICO (1850–1928), Italian *maître de ballet*, the successor of Petipa at the Imperial Russian Ballet School, who went to Western Europe with Diaghilev's Ballets Russes. He was an exceptionally gifted teacher, through whom the tradition of the classical Russian training was transmitted to the English ballet.

CECCHI, GIOVANNI MARIA (1518–87), an early and prolific Italian dramatist, whose work ranged from religious plays (*drammi spirituali*) to comedies of which the best is possibly the *Assiuolo* (prod. 1550). The secularization of Italian drama was carried a step farther by his interpolation into Bible stories of extraneous characters, usually farcical, borrowed from classical comedy, and incidents taken from contemporary life (see ITALY, 1 *a*).

CECCHINI. (1) PIER MARIA (1575–1645), an actor and author of the *commedia dell'arte*, who was apparently an amateur before he joined a professional company about 1591. After appearing in various Italian cities he went to Paris, returning there again later with his own company. His stage name was Fritellino. His wife (2) ORSOLA (*fl.* 1590–?), whom he married in 1594, may have been the daughter of Flaminio Scala. Her stage name was Flaminia, and with her husband she was associated with the Accesi troupe. She was much praised for her beauty and her acting, and seems to have been the bitter rival of Virginia Andreini (Florinda).

CEILING, a canvas stretch, battened-out and suspended flat over the top of a Box Set. Ceilings were often 'booked' transversely to enable them to be the more easily flown.

CÉLESTE, CÉLINE (1814–82), a famous French dancer and pantomimist, who appeared with much success on the Parisian stage as a child, and in 1827 went with a troupe of dancers to New York. Here she was seen at the Bowery, then known as the American, Theatre, and was much admired for her exquisite dancing and expressive gesture. Shortly afterwards she made an unhappy marriage with a Mr. Elliott, but soon separated from him, and in 1830 she was seen in London and the provinces. In spite of her years in England and the United States, she was a long time learning the language, and did not attempt a speaking part until 1838, relying until then on dumb-show. She created a number of parts in new plays, few of them of any lasting value, and was manager of the Adelphi and Lyceum Theatres in London for a short time, the former in association with Ben Webster. She was frequently seen in the United States, where her farewell performances are said to have outnumbered even those of Charlotte Cushman. She made her last appearance there in 1865, and in London in 1874, reappearing for one performance as Miami in *Green Bushes*, one of her best parts, at a benefit night at Drury Lane in 1878. She was also the original Madame Defarge in *A Tale of Two Cities* (1860), and scored triumphs in *The Woman in Red* and *The French Spy*. From her photographs she appears to have been an extremely plain woman, but intelligent, and contemporary accounts leave no doubt of the beauty and expressiveness of her dancing and acting.

CELLAR, the space below the acting area, which houses some of the machinery necessary for stage effects and scene shifting (see STAGE, 2).

CELLE, a small German town, between Hanover and Hamburg, whose castle contains a private theatre, built in 1670, and thus the oldest still in existence in the country. The Kings of Hanover, after the extinction of the dukedom of Celle, used the theatre as a ballroom, concert-hall, and playhouse during their summer residence at the castle. It was built in the style of a Renaissance opera-house, and was elaborately decorated, with side boxes for the musicians, a pit for standing auditors, two tiers of boxes, and a gallery, holding 300 in all. In 1935 it was modernized, its stage much enlarged, and a fly-floor added, making the theatre capable of handling scenery for lavish productions. It escaped damage during the 1939–45 war, and is still in good order, though it is now mainly used for concerts.

C.E.M.A., see ARTS COUNCIL.

CENSORSHIP, see DRAMATIC CENSORSHIP.

CENTLIVRE, MRS. SUSANNAH (1667–1723), English actress and dramatist, a masculine-looking woman who delighted to play men's parts. After two unhappy marriages she went to Windsor to play Alexander the Great and there met and married (in 1706) Joseph Centlivre, cook to Queen Anne. She was more successful as a writer than as an actress, and among her many comedies of intrigue, in which she rivalled the verve and ingenuity of Aphra Behn, the best are *The Busie Body* (1709), *The Wonder, a Woman keeps a Secret* (1714), and *A Bold Stroke for a Wife* (1718). All three were frequently revived, and the second later provided a fine part for Garrick in the part of Don Felix, while its initial success was largely due to the fine acting of Anne Oldfield as Violante. The last is perhaps better classified as a comedy of manners, in which Mrs. Centlivre shows the influence of Congreve. Some of the scenes may have been written by John Mottley. Mrs. Centlivre was also the author of the sentimental drama, *The Gamester* (1705), based to some extent on Regnard's *Le Joueur* (1696), but with the moral tone of Cibber and Steele. It was closely followed by a similar play entitled *The Bassett-Table*. Mrs. Centlivre's early plays were published under her second married name, Mrs. Carroll.

CENTRAL AMERICA, see SOUTH AMERICA.

CENTRAL PARK THEATRE, NEW YORK, see CENTURY THEATRE (2).

CENTRAL SCHOOL OF SPEECH-TRAINING AND DRAMATIC ART, see FOGERTY, ELSIE.

CENTRAL THEATRE, NEW YORK, on the west side of Broadway near 47th Street. This was opened on 9 Sept. 1918 by William A. Brady, with Owen Davis's *Forever After*, starring Alice Brady and Conrad Nagel. Under the management of Weber and Fields the theatre had several successes, but from about 1920 onwards it was used for continuing runs of successful plays produced elsewhere rather than for new productions, and in 1928 it became a cinema.

CENTRAL THEATRE OF THE RED ARMY, MOSCOW, see RED ARMY THEATRE.

CENTRE THEATRE, in the Rockefeller Centre, New York. This holds 3,700 people, and was opened on 29 Dec. 1932 as a cinema, the R. K. O. Roxy. This name was already in use, and was changed a year later to R. K. O. Centre. In 1934 the stage was rebuilt and used for spectacular musical shows, and for ballet, opera and pageant. In 1940 came the first ice-show, which was successful enough to warrant an annual edition.

CENTURY THEATRE, NEW YORK. (1) Originally the New Theatre, on Central Park West at 62nd Street, this was intended as a home of modern repertory. It opened on 6 Nov. 1909 with Julia Marlowe and E. H. Sothern in *Antony and Cleopatra*, and gave two seasons of Shakespeare and foreign plays. In spite of a large and expensive company and the reputation and experience of those connected with the enterprise—Ames and Lee Shubert— the venture was not a success. The general public felt that it was a theatre for the few, and stayed away. It closed, and reopened as an ordinary playhouse under the name of the Century on 15 Sept. 1911. Its main successes were musical shows, for which it was eminently suitable, having been planned as an opera house; but in 1916 the Shakespeare Tercentenary was celebrated in a fine production of *The Tempest*, while in 1921 Martin-Harvey's *Hamlet*, and in 1924 *The Miracle*, with Norman-Bel Geddes's fine scenery, were both successful. In 1927 Reinhardt, who had produced *The Miracle*, brought his own company to the Century in *A Midsummer Night's Dream*, *Everyman*, and *Dantons Tod*. It closed in 1929 and was pulled down a year later. There was a small theatre on the roof of the Century, known as the Cocoanut Grove, and as the Century Grove, where intimate revue was given.

(2) On Seventh Avenue just below Central Park South, a big theatre which was opened by the Shuberts as the Jolson on 6 Oct. 1921. An early production was that of *The Insect Play*, given as *The World We Live In*, while in 1923 came the epoch-making visit of the Moscow Art Theatre under Stanislavsky. These fine actors, of whom three—Varvara Bulgakova, Maria Ouspenskaya, and Akim Tamiroff—remained in the U.S.A. and contributed largely to its theatrical life, were seen in Tolstoy, Gorky, Chekhov, and Turgeniev, and the influence of their productions can still be traced on the American stage. They remained for 12 weeks, and were followed later in the year by Julia Marlowe and Sothern in several Shakespearian plays. The following year saw the arrival of another great foreign actor, Firmin Gémier of the Odéon in Paris. His repertory included some Shakespeare translations, Molière's *Le Bourgeois gentilhomme*, and several modern French plays. Later came the long run of *The Student Prince*, whose 608 performances constituted a record for this house. In 1932–3 the Shakespeare Theatre occupied the Century, giving fifteen of Shakespeare's plays at low prices to an audience mainly composed of students. The theatre, which has also been known as the Venice and the Central Park, has housed a negro operetta, an Italian company,

the Federal Theatre Project, and Maurice Schwartz with his Yiddish Players, while in 1946 the Old Vic company from London, headed by Laurence Olivier and Ralph Richardson, appeared in *Henry IV, Parts I* and *II, Oedipus,* and *The Critic.*

For the Century Theatre, London, see ADELPHI THEATRE and BIJOU THEATRE (2).

CERRITO, FANNY (1821–c.1895), famous ballerina, and the loveliest dancer of her day. She was much admired in London, and was one of the famous quartette that danced at His Majesty's in 1845—with Taglioni, Grisi, and Grahn.

CERVANTES SAAVEDRA, MIGUEL DE (1547–1616), the author of *Don Quixote,* was also a dramatist of some repute. From his youth he had a passion for the theatre, and saw and much admired the famous actor-manager Lope de Rueda, who died when Cervantes was only eighteen. There are numerous references to contemporary actors and acting in *Don Quixote,* and in Cervantes' other writings, particularly in the preface to his published plays. These appeared in 1615, and consist of 8 comedies and 8 *entremeses* or comic interludes. Cervantes himself says that he wrote nearly 30 plays, but if so, some must be lost, since, in addition to the above 16, only one tragedy and one other comedy have survived. The tragedy, *El cerco de Numancia,* is founded on the history of the Spanish town of that name which so heroically resisted the power of Rome, a struggle which still has power to move a Spanish audience, as was proved at a revival of Cervantes' play, in Madrid in 1937. Of the other plays, *El trato de Argel* deals with the sufferings of men captured by pirates, and is based on the author's own five-year captivity at Algiers, while *El rufián dichoso* gives an excellent picture of contemporary Spanish life. The *entremeses,* of which *El viejo celoso* and *El retablo de las maravillas* are perhaps the best, are models of realistic and dramatic truth and profound satire.

CHAIRMAN, an important feature of the early music-hall, and a link with the 'free-and-easy' of the public-house. He sat at the head of a table in front of the footlights, with his back to the stage, in full evening dress with top hat. Equipped with a mirror (to see the stage), a clock (to time the performers), and a gavel, he announced the 'turns' and kept the somewhat unruly audience in order. It was considered an honour to be allowed to sit at his table and buy him a drink, and one of his assets was an ability to imbibe freely and remain sober. The last London music-hall to have a Chairman was the Old Mo.

CHAMBERLAIN'S MEN, the theatrical company with which Shakespeare was mainly connected, and for which he wrote the bulk of his plays. It first emerges when the actors were regrouped after the disastrous plague of 1594. The repertory already included *Titus Andronicus, The Taming of the Shrew,* and a *Hamlet* (either an early draft or by someone other than Shakespeare, whose *Hamlet* as we know it was not given until 1601). After a joint session at the Rose with the Admiral's Men, the players moved to James Burbage's Theatre, with his son Richard as their chief actor, and for some years appeared there, later at the Curtain, and regularly at Court, giving plays by Shakespeare (for the chronology of these see SHAKESPEARE) and others, including Jonson, whose *Every Man in His Humour* was done by them in 1598. There is, however, no evidence that Jonson, who was reputed a poor actor, ever played with the Chamberlain's Men, since he was at this time concerned in the scandal over *The Isle of Dogs*, in which he appeared at the Swan. Shakespeare, who probably made his early appearances with Strange's or Pembroke's Men, played also with the Chamberlain's, in his own plays and in Jonson's *Every Man in His Humour* and *Sejanus*, his last traceable appearance being in the cast of the latter in 1603. In 1599 the company left the Theatre, and migrated to the Globe, which was built by the younger Burbages from the timbers of the old playhouse. The Globe was owned by a group of actors in the company, of whom Shakespeare was one. *Henry V* may have been produced there (or at the Theatre before the removal); *Julius Caesar* certainly was, as was Jonson's *Every Man out of His Humour*. In 1601 the actors got into trouble for performing *Richard II*, which, taken in conjunction with the Earl of Essex's unsuccessful rebellion, smacked of treason; but they got off lightly, though they may have had to take to the provinces for a while. It is conjectured that they played *Hamlet* at this period in Oxford and Cambridge. They played at Court not long before Elizabeth's death in 1603, and shortly afterwards became the King's Men, under the direct patronage of James I. A new actor who joined them at this time was Lawrence Fletcher, who had taken some English actors on tour in Scotland, and become a favourite of James I; but it was probably more in the capacity of a royal servant than as an actor, for he does not appear in any of the cast-lists, nor in the list of actors appended to the Shakespeare Folio. As the King's Men these players, who already had an excellent reputation, outshone all the other Jacobean and Caroline companies, not excepting Alleyn's, which now became the Palsgrave's Men (see ADMIRAL'S MEN). They continued to act Shakespeare's plays as they were written, but from 1608 onwards he gradually withdrew more and more from London and the theatre, his place being inadequately filled by Beaumont and Fletcher, whose earliest play for the King's Men, *Philaster*, dates from about this time. At the same period they took over Blackfriars, which had been leased to the Children of the Chapel, and shares were allotted among the actors, Shakespeare being one of the 'sharers', together with Burbage, Heminge, Condell, and Sly, who died while the business was in hand. The company continued, however, to use the Globe, which caught fire during a performance of *Henry VIII*, Shakespeare's

last play, in 1613 and was burnt to the ground. It was rebuilt in the following year, and saw the first production of Webster's *Duchess of Malfi*, in which Burbage played Ferdinand. The death of Shakespeare in 1616, and of Burbage three years later, broke up the company, and some of its members are traceable in other theatrical organizations. Taylor took Burbage's place, and Heminge and Condell, who had been the company's business managers for so long, were replaced by Lowin and Taylor. A great event in the company's history was the publication in 1623 of Shakespeare's 'First Folio' of plays, the largest collection of contemporary plays yet to appear in print. The following year saw the production of Middleton's *A Game of Chess*, aimed at the Spaniards, whose Ambassador took umbrage. The players were restrained from acting, admonished, and fined, and the play shelved; but its immense popular success long remained a topic in theatrical circles. The company, in spite of being in disgrace, continued to prosper, and at the death of James I, when it came under the patronage of his son, it numbered at least thirty-five men, with an unknown number of boys. During the new reign they continued to do well, though they had trouble over the lease of the Globe, which was finally extended to 1644, and with the Puritan inhabitants of Blackfriars, who tried to get the theatre closed. That this was not done was probably due to the interest which the King, and particularly the Queen, took in the players. They were constantly commanded to Court, and the Queen, at any rate, paid several visits to Blackfriars, which became the haunt of wit and nobility. Meanwhile the Cockpit at Whitehall had been refashioned as an indoor theatre, and the King's Men appeared there frequently. Massinger was their main dramatist, and was succeeded on his death by James Shirley. Evil times, however, were coming, and in 1642 the theatres were shut, the players disbanded, and, in spite of clandestine acting, organized theatrical activity ceased, to be resumed in 1660 under totally different circumstances.

CHAMBERS STREET THEATRE, NEW YORK. This was Burton's first theatre, originally Palmo's Opera House. When Burton left to go to the Metropolitan, his old theatre was taken by Eddy, renamed the Chambers Street, and opened with *Othello*. It soon degenerated into melodrama and farce, and on 13 Feb. 1857 it was taken over by E. L. Davenport. He rechristened it the American Theatre, and did a season there, during which Fanny Davenport made her first appearance in New York. The theatre finally closed on 30 March.

CHAMPAGNE CHARLIE, see LEYBOURNE, GEORGE.

CHAMPION, HARRY (1866–1942), a musichall performer who appeared originally as a black-faced comedian under the name of Will Conray, his first discoverable appearances being at the Queen's, Poplar, and the Parthenon, Greenwich, in Feb. 1888, though he may have been working before that. As Harry Champion he reappeared with a white face, and became famous as the singer of 'Ginger, Ye're Barmy', 'Enerey the Eighth I am, I am', 'When the Old Dun Cow caught fire', 'Any Old Iron', and other well-remembered ballads. He sang his songs at terrific speed and with tremendous zest and vitality right up to the day of his death, and for some years specialized in ditties about food, such as 'Boiled Beef and Carrots', 'Baked Sheep's Heart, Stuffed with Sage and Onions', 'Hot Tripe and Onions', and 'Hot Meat Pies, Saveloys, and Trotters'. At the Palladium after the 1914–18 war he appeared as himself in a scene where young actors had given imitations of old stars, and was received with riotous applause. As a side-line to his music-hall performances he ran a very successful jobmaster's business in North London.

CHAMPMESLÉ. (1) CHARLES CHEVILLET (1642–1701), French actor and dramatist, who began his career in a provincial company at Rouen. He then went to the Marais, and later to the Hôtel de Bourgogne, where he played mostly in tragedy. A handsome man, with excellent taste, he soon became popular, and many authors profited by his recommendations. He was a friend of La Fontaine, to whom several of Champmeslé's plays have been attributed. Among his many comedies the best is probably *Crispin chevalier*, a one-act version of an earlier play given in 1682, though *Le Florentin* (1685) was the most popular. It was given in Paris as late as the 1920s, as was *La Coupe enchantée* (1688). Champmeslé was one of the members of the Comédie-Française on its foundation, as was his celebrated wife (2) MARIE DESMARES (1642–98), the chief tragic actress of the troupe. She was already in a provincial troupe, which she had probably joined on the death of her first husband, when she met and married Champmeslé in 1665. They went to the Marais in 1669, where the husband was at first accounted the better actor. His wife, however, profited so much by the lessons of Laroque that in six months she was playing leading roles. A year later she went to the Hôtel de Bourgogne, where she replaced Mlle Desœillets, and became so popular that the rival troupes competed for her services. In 1679 she joined the amalgamated Molière–Marais company, thus depriving the Hôtel de Bourgogne of its pre-eminence in tragedy, and from there became the leading lady of the Comédie-Française, playing opposite Baron, a position which she retained until her death. She created many famous tragic roles, including Racine's Phèdre and Bérénice, and the Ariane of Thomas Corneille, and was much esteemed for her wit and charm by many famous men of her time. She had a fine figure, an expressive face, and a voice which served her equally well in tenderness, passion, or rage. La Fontaine dedicated his *Belphégor* to her, and she was the mistress, in his youth, of Racine, who owed so much to her acting. She favoured a chanting, sing-song declamation which she

taught to her niece (see DESMARES) and to Mlle Duclos, the leading actresses of the next generation. The tradition lingered on at the Comédie-Française until the time of Sarah Bernhardt. Her husband, from whom she was for some time separated on a mutual charge of adultery, died suddenly in a café while endeavouring to reconcile Baron and Sallé, who had quarrelled over the distribution of roles.

CHANCEREL, LÉON (1886–   ), French dramatist and producer, pupil of Jacques Copeau, whose most important work has been done with his Comédiens Routiers, a company founded in 1929 to bring good religious and other plays to Boy Scout camps. In 1935 Chancerel opened a theatre for children, Le Théâtre de l'Oncle Sébastien (previously the Vieux-Colombier), for which he himself wrote or adapted the plays.

CHANFRAU. (1) FRANK S. (1824–84), American actor, closely identified with the success of Benjamin Baker's *A Glance at New York* (1848) and similar productions, in which he played Mose, the New York fireman. The plays had little literary value, and depended on swift action and caricature, and on the personality of the chief actor. Chanfrau played Mose to the life, and many of the Bowery Boys he impersonated were delighted spectators of his mimicry. He then wrote *New York As It Is* (1848), also for Mose, and on the profits took over the Chatham Theatre, rechristened it the National, and continued Mose's adventures in *The Mysteries and Miseries of New York* (1848) and other plays, all of which were successful. Chanfrau was henceforth identified with Mose, but he was also good as the pioneer Kit Redding in *Kit the Arkansas Traveller* (1870), which he played until 1882, and his son Henry, also an actor, until 1890. In 1858 Chanfrau married the actress (2) HENRIETTA BAKER (1837–1909), whose real name was Jeannette Davis. She usually appeared apart from her husband, starring with most of the famous actors of the day, but they were together in *London Assurance*. She played Portia in the 1864 production of *Julius Caesar* which brought together for the only time the three Booth brothers. After her husband's death she retired from the stage, but in 1886 embarked on a tour of Europe.

CHANINS THEATRE, NEW YORK, see FORTY-SIXTH STREET THEATRE.

CHAPEL STREET THEATRE, NEW YORK. This was opened by David Douglass in 1761, in what was later Beekman Street, by which name the theatre is often called. It was at this playhouse that the first known performance of *Hamlet* in New York was given, on 26 Nov., with the younger Hallam as Hamlet. The repertory was extensive, but contained few plays that had not been seen before. The actors, we learn from contemporary documents, were often incommoded, as in Europe earlier, by members of the audience who insisted on sitting on the stage, which must have been a small one, as the entire theatre measured only ninety feet in length by forty feet wide. After the departure of Douglass's company in May 1762, the theatre was used occasionally by amateur companies, and possibly also by the officers of the British garrison in New York. In May 1766 a company, whether Douglass's or not is uncertain, but certainly a professional company, were playing *The King and the Miller of Mansfield* when the Sons of Liberty, an unruly band of anti-Britishers to whom all players were suspect, broke up the performance, routed the players, and greatly damaged the building, which fell into desuetude.

CHAPMAN, George (c. 1560–1634), English poet and dramatist, author of the translation of Homer which inspired Keats's sonnet. He is believed by some critics to be the 'rival poet' referred to in Shakespeare's sonnets, and the original of Holofernes and Thersites, but this lacks proof. Little is known of Chapman's early life. In 1596 he was accredited dramatist to the Admiral's Men, in the pay of Henslowe. Most of his early plays are lost, but enough of his later work remains to substantiate the claims which have been made for him as a fine playwright. Among his tragedies the most important is *Bussy d'Ambois*, based on the story which Dumas *père* later used in *La Dame de Montsoreau*. It was given in about 1604 by the Children of Paul's, who also acted *Eastward Ho!* (1605), written by Chapman in collaboration with Jonson and Marston. This gave offence to James I and caused the imprisonment of the authors. In comedy Chapman's best work was done in *All Fools* (c. 1604) and *May Day* (1609), both given at Blackfriars. The former, called by Swinburne one of the best comedies in the English language, is based on Terence. Among Chapman's other plays are *Charles, Duke of Byron* (1608), which gave offence to the French Ambassador, *The Revenge of Bussy d'Ambois* (c. 1610), *Chabot, Admiral of France* (c. 1613), and *Caesar and Pompey* (c. 1613), all tragedies. He was also the author of a masque played by the Middle Temple and Lincoln's Inn in 1613, for which he complained he was insufficiently paid, being ranked merely 'with taylors and shoomakers and such snipperados'. Chapman was Sewer in Ordinary to Henry Prince of Wales, on whose early death he wrote a pathetic ode.

CHAPMAN, William (1764–1839), one of the earliest and possibly the first of the American showboat managers. Born in England, he was as a young man a member of a travelling company under one Richardson, visiting the fairs. In 1803 he made his début on the London stage, and in 1827 appeared at the Bowery Theatre, New York. With his wife and large family he started on tour for the south-west, and in Pittsburg had built for him by a Captain Brown a 'floating theatre', on which he played up and down the Ohio and the Mississippi (see SHOWBOAT). He died on board, and his widow continued to run the business for some years, finally selling it in about 1847 to Sol Smith.

CHAPPUZEAU, Samuel (1625–1701), a French man of letters, well educated and widely travelled, who wrote some mediocre and forgotten plays, and is best remembered for his *Théâtre françois* (1674), which consisted of three parts, (1) *De l'usage de la comédie*—a defence of the theatre, (2) *Des auteurs qui soutiennent le théâtre*, a dictionary of dramatists, and (3) *De la conduite des comédiens*, an apology for players, with lives of many of the best-known up to the date of publication. This third part contains a long chapter on Molière, who had just died. Though somewhat inaccurate in regard to detail, particularly for the earlier history, the work as a whole remains important as a source book, indispensable to students of the seventeenth-century French theatre. There is a possibility that an early farce by Chappuzeau, published in Lyons in 1656, may have been done by Molière's company while they were touring the provinces, or alternatively that Molière may have seen or read it, since it appears to have influenced *Les Précieuses ridicules*.

CHARING CROSS THEATRE, London, see TOOLE'S THEATRE.

CHARIOT-AND-POLE SYSTEM, see ENGLISH PLAYHOUSE, 2 c.

CHARLES HOPKINS THEATRE, New York, see PUNCH AND JUDY THEATRE.

CHARLESTON, a town important in the early history of American drama. It saw a production of *The Orphan* in 1736, and of *The Recruiting Officer* a year later, when the actors performed in the first theatre in Dock Street. This remained intermittently in use until 1763, when Douglass built a new theatre to house the American Company, to which they returned in 1766. After the War of Independence Charleston was one of the first towns to be visited by a theatrical company, that of Wall, which under Ryan continued to play there in opposition to the company of young Hallam and Henry. The theatre in Charleston continued to flourish, and in the early years of the nineteenth century had its own group of dramatists, writing plays which were put on under the management of Placide.

CHÂSSIS À DÉVELOPPEMENT, see TRICKWORK ON THE ENGLISH STAGE.

CHÂTELET, THÉÂTRE DU, Paris. Built in 1862, this theatre held 3,000 people and was intended for spectacular and musical shows. Among its early productions were *Les Mystères du vieux Paris*, *Le Tour du monde en 80 jours*, and such fairy plays as *La Poudre de Perlinpinpin*. In 1874 Colonne started his famous symphony concerts at this theatre.

CHATHAM THEATRE, New York. (1) A summer resort in Chatham Gardens, opened by a pastrycook named Barrière in 1819, with ice-cream, punch, and open-air music. Plays were first given there in 1822, and in 1823 a theatre, known as the Pavilion, was opened for a summer season with a company strong in farce and operetta. In 1824 this gave place to the Chatham Theatre, opened all the year round, which soon proved a serious rival to the old-established Park Theatre. The Chatham, which seated 1,300, was the first theatre in New York to be lit by gas-jets. Its architect and scenic designer was Hugh Reinagle, its machinist George Conklin. The company included George Barrett and his future wife, Henry Wallack and his wife, formerly a dancer, and young Jefferson and his father, who made his last appearance in New York at this theatre on 4 Oct. 1825. It flourished until the death of Barrière on 18 Feb. 1826, when Henry Wallack took over. He proved unsuccessful, as did a number of other managers, among them Cooper, Hackett, who renamed the theatre the American Opera House, and Blanchard, who ran it as the Amphitheatre in 1830 with a mixture of equestrian and straight drama. It finally closed in 1832, under Hamblin, and became a Presbyterian Chapel and a centre for Sacred Concerts.

(2) On the south-east side of Chatham Street. Known as the New Chatham Theatre, it was built for Thomas Flynn and H. E. Willard from designs by Samuel Purdy, and held 2,200 people. It was first managed by James Anderson from the Bowery Theatre, and opened on 11 Sept. 1839. After a successful start, the theatre found itself in financial difficulties, until Charles R. Thorne became sole manager, and brought it a modicum of prosperity. Its bills were somewhat mixed, Booth and Shakespeare one week being followed by Rice and negro farce the next. In 1843 Thorne retired, and a number of ephemeral managements followed. The main event of these years was the emergence as a great American comedian of Frank Chanfrau, who in 1848 took over the theatre, and renamed it Chanfrau's New National Theatre. It was henceforth known as the National, and Purdy, its next manager, kept the name. It was at this theatre that Edwin Booth made his first appearance in New York (27 Sept. 1850), and the elder Booth his last. Fanny Wallack also made her farewell appearance here. One of the greatest successes of the National was *Uncle Tom's Cabin*, which ran intermittently from 1852 to 1854. The fortunes of the theatre then began to wane, and Purdy had recourse to circus, dog dramas, and pantomime. His last success in legitimate drama was *Ten Nights in a Bar Room*, which opened on 23 Aug. 1858, and his last production a revival of *Black-Eyed Susan* on 21 Mar. 1859. During Purdy's last season Adah Isaacs Menken made her first appearance in New York, under his management, as a young and untried actress. After Purdy's departure the National had a number of short-lived managements. A fire, on 9 July 1860, damaged much of the building, but it continued in use, as the Union Theatre, the National Concert Hall, and once again the Chatham. It finally became the National Music Hall, and in Oct. 1862 it was pulled down.

CHAUVE-SOURIS, LA, see BALIEFF, NIKITA.

CHEKHOV. (1) ANTON PAVLOVICH (1860–1904), Russian dramatist, possibly the one best known outside Russia, whose plays are in the repertory of every country. He came of humble parentage (his grandfather had been a serf), but graduated as a doctor from Moscow University in 1884. As he himself has pointed out, his study of medical science affected his approach to literature, and he always thought of himself more as a doctor than a writer. His short stories, published during his student days, caused something of a stir, and through them he became acquainted with the literary figures of his time, notably Tolstoy and Gorky, resigning his membership of the Russian Academy when the latter was dismissed from it by order of the Tsar.

Chekhov was early attracted by the theatre, particularly by the then popular vaudeville and French farce, and his first dramatic essays were one-act comedies such as *The Bear* (1888) and *The Proposal* (1889), for which he always retained an amused affection. A deeper note was struck in *On the Road*, a study in nomadic derelicts, which was banned by the censor. His first full-length play, *Ivanov* (1887), was written for the Korsh Theatre, but was not a success. A second, *The Wood Goblin* (1889), also done by a private theatre, was unremarked. And finally *The Seagull* (1896), when done by the old-fashioned Imperial Theatre, the Alexandrinsky, was a complete failure. Chekhov now made up his mind to leave play-writing and concentrate on other things, and he would have done so, thus robbing the world of his fine later plays, had not Nemirovich-Danchenko persuaded him to let the newly founded Moscow Art Theatre revive the ill-fated *Seagull*. Nemirovich-Danchenko had realized that this new dramatist needed a new style of presentation, which the old stereotyped actors could not give him, but which the Moscow Art Theatre, with its delicate and subtle technique, could. The revival was successful, and was followed by *Uncle Vanya* (1899), *Three Sisters* (1901), and *The Cherry Orchard* (1904), of which the last is often considered to be Chekhov's masterpiece. He died shortly afterwards, at the height of his powers.

The reasons for Chekhov's apparent failure at first are not far to seek. His sense of tragedy was no longer that of the old melodrama and grand heroic drama, but a feeling for the constant attrition of daily life and the futile waste, particularly in Old Russia, of youth and talent hampered and stifled by a maleficent social order. This demands a delicacy of apprehension from the audience and a subtlety of ensemble playing by the actors which was not available in Russia until the Moscow Art Theatre developed it. Even then they needed to perfect their technique, and the audience had to rise to the demands made upon it, before Chekhov could be fully understood. He may still, particularly in translation abroad, be falsified—early English productions made his characters irresponsible weaklings groping in a gloomy fog—but gradually the truth of his work, both for his own time and for ever, is imposing itself on his interpreters. As an American critic (John Gassner) has said: 'We have heard a good deal about the plotlessness and irresolution of Chekhov's work. But we have not heard enough about the secret strength and drive, the portentous hunger for life and positiveness, in his plays. We hear a great deal about Chekhov's simplicity, but overlook the terrible power that often resides in such simplicity.' And when we consider that the forces at work, however obscurely, in Chekhov's dramas, are those which produced the Russia of to-day, it must be admitted that there is a great deal of truth in that summing-up. It is not without interest that the great speech by the student Trofimov at the end of Act II of *The Cherry Orchard*—the celebrated 'All Russia is our garden'—is not only a concise and accurate review of then recent Russian history, but an astonishingly and fiercely accurate prediction of the Revolution itself.

Among the first actors of the Moscow Art Theatre was a young student who had come from Nemirovich-Danchenko's class at the Moscow Philharmonic Society, (2) OLGA KNIPPER (1870–). She appeared in Chekhov's plays, and was married to him in 1901. After his death she remained with the Moscow Art Theatre as one of its leading actresses, and in 1943, at the 300th performance of *The Cherry Orchard*, was still playing the part of Madame Ranevsky which she created in 1904. Madame Knipper-Chekhova is one of the outstanding figures of the Soviet stage, and an important link with pre-Revolutionary days.

(3) MICHAEL ALEXANDROVICH (1891–), nephew of Anton Chekhov, is also an actor and producer. He first appeared on the stage in St. Petersburg, and in 1910 joined the Moscow Art Theatre, where he became a member of the group Studio One. Here he played his best parts, Tackleton in *The Cricket on the Hearth*, Hamlet, and Erik XIV. After the departure of Vakhtangov he remained for a while as the leader of the group, but he was unable to adjust himself to the new régime, and in 1927 emigrated to America, where he opened a studio for dramatic training.

CHELSEA THEATRE, LONDON, see COURT THEATRE.

CHÉNIER, MARIE JOSEPH (1764–1811), French dramatist (younger brother of the poet André Chénier, who was guillotined in 1794) and one of the few important literary figures of the French Revolution. He had already produced some unimportant and unsuccessful plays when, after a battle with the censor lasting two years, his *Charles IX* was given in 1789. It had a strong republican bias, disguised as history, and was enthusiastically received. Its triumph was in some measure due to the magnificent acting of Talma, who later opened the Théâtre de la République with Chénier's *Henri VIII* (1791), following it in the same year with *Jean Calas*, and in 1792 with *Caius Gracchus*, another revolutionary

play well suited to the temper of the time. Chénier was now at the height of his popularity, and was as active in politics as in drama. A member of the Convention, he voted for the death of Louis XVI, but his political career came to an end in 1802, when he opposed the rising star of Napoleon. He continued to write, but without success, and his *Timoléon*, first given in 1794, was proscribed and burnt by order of the censor. Only one copy, saved by Mme Vestris, escaped destruction. Chénier's work marks an important step in the evolution of historical drama in France, and has the merit, rare at this period, of moderation and some literary grace. Chénier has been much blamed for not using his influence to save his elder brother's life, but he had the wit to see that obscurity best served André's turn, and it was the father's ill-judged interference that brought André to the scaffold.

CHÉRI, ROSE [ROSE-MARIE CIZOS] (1824–61), French actress, daughter of actors, who played as a child in a provincial travelling company. On 6 July 1842 she made her début at the Gymnase and remained there for twenty years, marrying the director in 1847 and continuing as his leading lady, playing opposite Bressant. With a lovely face and figure she combined much intelligence, and a willingness to profit by experience and teaching which soon brought her to the front, and she became one of the best-loved actresses of Paris. She was also much admired in London, where she appeared several times. She was at her best in the ingénue parts of vaudeville, had a fresh, clear singing voice, and was a good dancer. Her elder sister Anna was also in the company at the Gymnase, and proved a reliable actress, particularly when she took over elderly parts. She married an actor and retired in 1875, having made her début at the Gymnase in 1842.

CHESTER CYCLE, see ENGLAND, 1 and MYSTERY PLAY.

CHESTNUT STREET THEATRE, PHILADELPHIA, built in 1791 for the company brought from England by Thomas Wignell, formerly leading comedian of the American Company. Owing to an epidemic of yellow fever, it was not opened until 17 Feb. 1794. A copy of the Theatre Royal at Bath, it was an elegant and impressive building, holding about 2,000 people. Here Wignell remained until his death, being succeeded by Warren and Wood as joint managers, and the Chestnut Street Theatre had practically a monopoly of acting in Philadelphia until the opening of the Walnut Street Theatre in 1811. Under Warren and Wood it prospered, and its fine company, with such actors as Henry Wallack and his wife, and Joseph, John, and Thomas Jefferson, was unequalled in light comedy. From its prominent position in the American theatre world it was sometimes known as 'Old Drury'. It was one of the first theatres in the United States to be lit by gas, and in every way it was superior to the theatres of New York. It was not until

1828 that Wood's retirement from management, and the rivalry of the Walnut Street and Arch Street Theatres, brought about the dissolution of the company, which went bankrupt in 1829. From this time onwards the theatre had a stock company which served to support visiting stars, and the supremacy of Philadelphia passed to New York. Under Maywood in the early 1830s it started on a disastrous policy of employing foreign stars, at fabulous sums which, however profitable the evening, left the management out of pocket.

CHETTLE, HENRY (c. 1560–1607), a prolific playwright, who is credited by Henslowe in his diary with a long list of plays, mostly written in collaboration, and now lost. Of his surviving works, the only one which he appears to have produced unaided is *Hoffman*, known also as *Revenge for a Father* (c. 1602), which follows the pattern of the 'revenge tragedy' set by Kyd. With Anthony Munday he wrote two plays on Robert Earl of Huntingdon, or Robin Hood, and with Day a comedy entitled *The Blind Beggar of Bethnal Green*, to which Day subsequently wrote two sequels. Chettle, who was also a printer, was concerned with the publication of Nashe's pamphlets as well as Greene's *Groatsworth of Wit*, which he edited in 1592. From the numerous small sums lent him by Henslowe as advances on his plays he appears to have been both needy and improvident.

CHEVALIER, ALBERT (1861–1923), a music-hall performer best remembered for his coster songs. He was first an actor under the Bancrofts and Kendals, and even appeared in grand opera. He was persuaded by Charlie Coborn, with great difficulty, to sing some of his own songs on the halls, and his début at the London Pavilion in 1891 singing 'The Coster's Serenade' was a great success. He became the great exponent of Cockney humour and pathos in such perennial favourites as 'Knocked 'em in the Old Kent Road', 'The Nasty Way 'e Sez It', 'It Gits me Talked Abaht', ''Appy 'Ampstead', and, best-loved of all, 'My Old Dutch'. He wrote and appeared in a number of serious and sentimental sketches and ballads, which the audience tolerated for the sake of the coster songs, and was the author of an ill-fated musical play, *The Land of Nod*, which after a successful run of nine months in the provinces was withdrawn in London after a week. He also published a volume of memoirs entitled *Before I Forget*. He was one of the few music-hall stars who did not appear in pantomime.

CHICAGO, see PIONEER THEATRE IN THE U.S.A.

CHILDREN OF THE CHAPEL, OF PAUL'S, see BOY COMPANIES.

CHILE, see SOUTH AMERICA.

CHIMNEY, an opening practised in the thickness of the side wall of the stage to house the counterweights which control the working of the scenery (see ENGLISH PLAYHOUSE, 2).

CHINA. Popular Chinese drama, perfected in Peking during the nineteenth century, is a flexible and harmonious combination of spoken dialogue, operatic singing, dancing, and acrobatics; and the play or libretto, roughly classified as civil (*wên*) and military (*wu*), is little more than a framework for skilled actors to complete. The language is a hybrid of colloquial and literary Chinese, a purely theatrical dialect which is easily acquired and understood: vocal passages are in verse; spoken dialogue breaks the tension, elucidates the plot, and gives the singer a rest. When the protagonist appears, he chants a prologue and prefatory poem and proceeds to render a full account of himself, his names, family, circumstances, motives, and intentions. A character speaks until his gathering emotions plunge him into melody, and the last word spoken is prolonged *crescendo* as a signal to the orchestra.

The same plays are performed again and again to tireless audiences far more critical than our own. They are divided not into acts but into numerous scenes of varying length. While unities of time and place are disregarded and stage properties are simplified, an elaborate set of conventions has been evolved which, like the written symbols for speech, are as logical as they are imaginative. This unlocalized drama allows the Chinese playwright, as it allowed the Elizabethan, to indulge in loose flowing construction, episodic plots, and complex action. Although incongruous changes are creeping in, the stage still mirrors the life and thought of China through the centuries: the subject-matter is mainly traditional, derived from legends, historical anecdotes, and famous novels, and always makes some pretence of pointing a moral. Goodness is rewarded, wrongs are redressed, and evil punished—eventually. There is no clear distinction between comedy and tragedy, and the majority of Chinese plays may be described as melodramas with happy endings.

As in Greece, dramatic performances were of ancient ritual origin. According to the experts, it was not until the Northern Ch'i dynasty (A.D. 557–81) that singing and dancing were combined with the dramatizing of a story. The practice of wearing masks originated in the same period, and engraved reliefs from contemporary tombs bear witness to the stylized grace of the dancers. The famous T'ang Emperor Ming Huang is credited with the foundation of the first dramatic school, known as the 'Pear Garden', in A.D. 720.

Chinese actors have developed a technique that renders scenery superfluous. To indicate change of place they have only to tread in a circle. The projecting stage is almost square with an embroidered curtain or flat painted background, flanked by two curtained doors, the left for entrances and the right for exits. Stage properties are symbolic and, like almost everything connected with the Chinese theatre, strictly conventional. An ordinary table may represent an altar, a judge's bench, a bridge, a banquet-board, &c., and can serve for climbing mountains or scaling battlements: by jumping over it the actor may be jumping over a wall. The position of chairs is also significant: circumstance and social status are conveyed by the manner of sitting, the left being invariably the place of honour. Two or three chairs covered with a curtain may represent a bed. An arched gate with bricks painted in white on a square blue cloth is held up by stage hands when characters are to enter or leave a city: this and the screen-like panels on which formal rocks are depicted for a mountain range are the nearest equivalents to scenery. Among important properties are the tasselled horse-whip which enables an actor to ride an invisible horse; the horse-hair duster which symbolizes spirituality and is held by deities and religious characters; and the oar which represents a boat. Painted flags serve many purposes: four black flags are flourished when a violent wind is required; four flags depicted with waves represent water; two yellow flags with wheels a chariot. Large banners in groups of four represent armies; inscribed with characters, they denote military rank. A hat wrapped in red cloth does duty for a decapitated head, a bench with hat and robe flung over it for a corpse. A woman's diminutive red shoe represents needlework, a cube wrapped in yellow silk an official seal. A fan is usually a sign of frivolity. Other properties, such as military weapons, state umbrellas, imperial mandates, arrows of command, shop-signs, lanterns and candles (not necessarily lighted), are mostly realistic.

Scenic problems are solved by vivid pantomime: the actor is the cynosure of the performance. Standing on a bare projecting stage, he is seen in space. Hence all his movements are sculptured to combine grace with maximum significance. He is his own producer: he must be a skilful singer, dancer, mime, and acrobat. His strenuous training begins at the age of twelve or earlier; from his physique and the talents he displays it is soon decided in which type he shall specialize, and for seven years or more he is coached in every detail of his craft.

Characters are classified under four types: *shêng*, males in general; *tan*, females in general; *ching* or *hua-lien*, robust males with faces painted like masks; and *ch'ou*, broad comedians. But these have a number of precise subdivisions. The righteous elderly bearded male role (*lao-shêng*) was the most important from about 1850 till the first decade of this century, and there were no less than four distinct schools of interpreting it. But with the meteoric rise of Mei Lan-fang, the role of female impersonator assumed a greater importance. As in Elizabethan England, boys had impersonated girls since the origin of drama. Neo-Confucian prejudice against the mingling of sexes on the stage encouraged this practice, facilitated by a slender build and an exiguous growth of whiskers. Until recently the actors were all of one sex,

usually male, and though there is a modern tendency for women to appear in feminine roles, the finest critics prefer female impersonators, since theirs is the subtler triumph of art over nature.

Except broad comedians and those vigorous males with mask-like make-up who sing in a forced bass, most characters speak and sing in falsetto. The music must have been influenced by the open-air conditions of primitive theatres, which resembled the temporary mat-shed structures in villages and at temple fairs. The orchestra is accommodated on the stage. A hard wooden instrument like castanets beats the time; a fiddle called *hu-ch'in*, with a hollow cylindrical body of varying size, the smallest with two strings bowed horizontally, is the leading instrument of vocal accompaniment; and the volume of sound which a small Chinese orchestra can produce when the *so-na*, or clarinet, and the brass instruments of percussion are in full force, is more astonishing than agreeable to the average Western ear.

The costumes are generally adapted from the styles of the T'ang, Sung, Yüan, and Ming dynasties: they are sumptuous but seldom historically accurate. The main colours indicate social rank, character, and occasion: Emperors wear yellow, high officials red, civilian worthies blue, elderly people brown, and rough characters black. For ceremonial occasions high officials don satin robes with capacious 'rippling water' sleeves, embroidered with dragons and bordered with wave-patterns, and a big jade belt dangling a little below the waist. There is a saying, 'the longer the sleeves, the better the dance', and their adroit manipulation is a salient part of the actor's technique. White silk cuffs about two feet long, left open at the seam, are sewn to sleeves which would otherwise be too heavy for rapid motion. Their flowing lines accentuate physical grace and the delicacy of hands, and enhance dramatic expression. For 'asides' the right hand is raised level with the cheek and the sleeve hangs down like a curtain between the character and his immediate neighbour. When a character weeps, a corner of the left sleeve is held up to the eyes. The stage warrior's costume could scarcely be more magnificent. Embroidered tiger heads are attached to the heavily padded shoulders and waist, long scalloped panniers sweep down between the legs, and a 'heart-protecting' mirror glitters on the chest. Four triangular pennons, fixed between the shoulders, are worn on the backs of generals, and their head-dress of brilliant pompons, spangles, and imitation jewels, is often surmounted by two pheasant-plumes, which may be six or seven feet long. The swirling and twirling of these noble plumes intensify the exuberant pride of a victorious commander.

Painted-face roles (*hua-lien*) wear the most complicated make-up and shave their foreheads to lengthen or broaden their features. Temperament is expressed by certain lines about the eyes, nose, and mouth, and by symbolical combinations of colours. Since the Ming dynasty these have increased in elaboration and decreased in significance, but the main background and predominant colours remain the same: all white indicating treachery; black, straightforwardness and tough integrity; red, loyalty and courage; blue, stubbornness and ferocity; green, outlaws, brigands, and demons; yellow, strength and hidden cunning; gold, gods and immortals; dull pink and grey, advanced age. This unique art upon which Chinese actors have lavished so much taste and ingenuity requires careful study. The great historical roles have been chiselled and polished for generations, from facial make-up to the most trivial mannerisms. Ts'ao Ts'ao, for instance, has become a classical monument of villainy. Tou Erh-tun, perhaps the most gorgeous of theatrical brigand chiefs, is made up like a ferocious monster beetle. Indigo blue is the main colour, with scarlet eyebrows and curving lines of black and white of various thicknesses about the eyes to represent the tiger-head hooks which were his most formidable weapon, and another pair of eyes are painted beneath his own to denote his remarkable powers of vision, while the forehead appears as if encrusted with gems. An enormous scarlet beard completes this masterpiece. 'Iron Face' Pao Chêng, the Sung dynasty judge who never smiled, has a jet-black make-up except for the striking silhouette of his arched eyebrows and the crescent moon on his forehead to symbolize his supernatural acumen. His diction is hard and rasping, and all his movements are calculated to inspire awe. But the awe is blended with a certain affection, and the audience revels in his fulminations against wickedness in high places. The make-up of Sun the Monkey God, 'Discoverer of Secrets', is wonderfully expressive, though hardly more than an inverted triangle of bright crimson with touches of gold about the nostrils and golden circles round the blinking, mischievous eyes. His every twitch is realistic and formal at the same time, and the result is far subtler than an imitation of monkey cunning; it is a synthesis and sublimation of the whole simian tribe. The veteran actor Hao Chên-chi gave uncanny demonstrations of metempsychosis in this fascinating role.

Numerous types of beard also help to indicate age and character, and owing to their prestige in ancient China, the longest and fullest, covering the mouth, denote heroism and prosperity; tripartite beards, culture and refinement; red and blue beards, supernatural beings (announced by flashes of fire), while moustaches are generally a sign of coarseness or cunning. In anger the foot is stamped and the beard swept upward.

The broad comic roles with white patches on the nose are the most realistic, and the domestic farce, equivalent to our curtain-raiser, bears a closer relation to the Western theatre than any other type of Chinese play.

The actors walk on and off stage to a tempo set by the orchestra; every movement should follow a strict convention. A small hand-gong heralds a civil play, a large gong and the clash of cymbals a military play. Naturally the difference between the sexes is emphasized by all sorts of appropriate devices. Every finger of the female impersonator must contribute to the effect of fragile femininity. A genius for doing the right thing in the right way, supreme theatrical instinct, is the final test. 'She whose movements are disciplined, she who is a living harmony, a lyric in flesh and blood', wrote Sarcey of Sarah Bernhardt. Alter the pronoun, and these words apply to Mei Lan-fang. Fortunately the essentials of the Chinese theatre still remain intact, even in Shanghai, where actor-managers have made numerous concessions to the vulgar. H. A.

CHINA HALL THEATRE, LONDON. This stood in the pleasure-grounds of a public-house in Rotherhithe in the eighteenth century. George Frederick Cooke played there in 1778. The prices were Boxes, 3s.; Pit, 2s.; Gallery, 1s. There had evidently been a place of entertainment there long before, as Pepys mentions it in his Diary.

CHIONIDES, a very early Athenian comic poet of *c.* 500 B.C. (see GREECE, 2 *b*).

CHIRGWIN, GEORGE H. (1854–1922), a Nigger Minstrel, originally known as the White-Eyed Musical Moke, who from 1877 was billed as 'the White-Eyed Kaffir' because of the white lozenge-shaped patch round his right eye. He made his first appearance at the age of six at the Swallow Rooms, Piccadilly, with a Minstrel Troupe, and later made a name for himself as a solo turn on the 'halls', celebrating his jubilee at the Oxford in 1911. He sang sentimental coon songs—the two favourites being 'The Blind Boy' and 'My Fiddle is My Sweetheart'—in a high-pitched, piping voice, accompanying himself on the banjo, and later on the one-stringed fiddle.

CHOCOLATE-COLOURED COON, see ELLIOTT, G. H.

CHOERILUS, an Attic tragic poet of the generation before Aeschylus. Beyond the fact that his first production took place about 520 B.C., practically nothing is known of him.

CHOREGUS. Under the Athenian democracy, certain specific financial burdens (liturgies) were imposed in rotation on citizens whose wealth exceeded a certain sum. These included the equipping of a man-o'-war, defraying the cost of certain religious ceremonies, and, the one that comes into question here, the equipping and paying of a chorus for a tragic, comic, or dithyrambic contest. Hence the name *choregus*, or chorus-leader. The dramatic contests were therefore contests between choregi as well as between poets, and, later, actors. It was important to the poet that his choregus should not be stingy, since the proper presentation of the play depended on him; choregi therefore were assigned to the poets by lot (see GREECE, 3).   H. D. F. K.

CHOREOGRAPHY, the term applied to the creating of a ballet, that is, to the choice and grouping of the various movements, with their intermediate positions, which will best interpret both the music and the drama of the subject. The creator of a ballet is known as a choreographer, and his work calls for a rare combination of talents, since he must be an expert in music, dancing, anatomy, aesthetics, and in artistic appreciation. Only thus can he adequately interpret his thought in movement. He must also be a student of human nature as well as of the theatre, and an inspired teacher. Choreography is not an art that can be taught; it is the irresistible expression of the personality of the dancer, working through the medium which he knows, understands, and can manipulate at will. The early choreographers, of whose work nothing remains but 'Giselle', were also *maîtres de ballet*, often in their youth dancers, though they may later have given up active participation in their ballets; modern choreographers, of whom the greatest are perhaps Fokine, Massine, Ninette de Valois, Ashton, and Helpmann, have been active dancers who appeared in the leading roles, which they thus 'created' in a double sense. Choreography is a complex subject, and a part of ballet-dancing which still remains mysterious to the inquiring layman.

CHORUS, in Greek drama a group of actors who stood aside from the main action of the play and commented on it (see GREECE, 1 c). In Elizabethan phraseology the Chorus was the speaker of the introductory prologue, as in Shakespeare's *Henry V*, a legacy from Euripides via Seneca. In the modern theatre the word is usually taken to mean the chorus of a musical comedy, which reached its apogee in the late nineteenth century, particularly at the Gaiety Theatre. It consisted of a number of beautiful young women who could sing and dance a little, stand and move gracefully, and wear lovely clothes. As their attire became scantier their activities increased, until in the 1920s they wore practically nothing at all and reached an exceedingly high standard, particularly in the clockwork precision of their dancing. The male members of the musical comedy chorus have, on the other hand, remained almost static throughout, merely acting as foils for the women, and being entirely dispensed with in some plays and in revue. Under the influence of the modern American musical play the chorus tends to have a greater share in the actual development of the plot, and to attain, in both sexes, a good standard in singing, dancing, and acting. The use of the Chorus in the Greek sense has been revived in some recent poetic plays, notably T. S. Eliot's *Murder in the Cathedral* (1935).

CHRISTY MINSTRELS, see NEGRO IN THE AMERICAN THEATRE.

CHRONEGK, LUDWIG, see MEININGEN PLAYERS.

CIBBER. (1) COLLEY (1671–1757), English actor, theatre manager, and playwright, now chiefly remembered for his *Apology for the Life of Mr. Colley Cibber, Comedian*, published in 1740, and for its admirable descriptions of Restoration actors. The son of a Danish sculptor who had settled in England, Cibber was well educated and went on the stage in 1690 against the wishes of his family. He had few advantages of voice or person, but quickly improved and became an excellent comedian, particularly in the fops of Restoration comedy and of his own plays. The needs of a young family turned his thoughts to playwriting, and in 1696 his first play, *Love's Last Shift; or, the Fool in Fashion* was given at Drury Lane with some success. Striking a happy balance between the Restoration comedy of manners and the new vogue for sentiment and morality, this is now considered the first sentimental comedy, and undoubtedly influenced Steele and Farquhar, as well as setting the pattern for Cibber's later plays. It is also worthy of note in that it inspired the young Vanbrugh to write *The Relapse*, where the elegant fop Sir Novelty Fashion becomes in Vanbrugh's hands the cynical rake Lord Foppington, a part which Cibber played brilliantly, thus establishing his reputation as an actor. Among his later plays the best was *The Careless Husband* (1704), of which it has been said 'it played an important part in the development of sentimental comedy . . . and helped to fix standards of gentility and politeness which were profoundly to influence comic writing throughout most of the 18th century'. With this, and the earlier *She Would and She Would Not; or, the Kind Impostor* (1702) —revived as late as 1886 by Daly in New York, with Ada Rehan and John Drew—Cibber achieved a reputation for the writing of scenes of high life, which are, however, found to be somewhat spurious when compared with those of Congreve. A snob and a social climber, Cibber was only on the fringe of the society he strove to depict, yet for a hundred years his comedies were taken as representative of English high society. His tragedies were mostly failures, but he achieved success with his famous adaptation of *Richard III* (1700), which remained the standard acting text, in Europe and later in America, until well into the nineteenth century, and with his adaptation of Molière's *Tartuffe* as *The Non-Juror* (1717). Cibber chose to think that it was his championship of the Hanoverian cause in this latter play that brought him the coveted position of Poet Laureate in 1730; but the general opinion seems to have been that it was due to his friendship with great men, and to a certain flat facility in the composition of state verse which was happily lacking in greater poets. The appointment caused no little dismay, in spite of the fact that Cibber's predecessors had included

Shadwell, Tate, and Rowe, none of whom were poets.

The greater part of Colley Cibber's life was spent at Drury Lane. He early insinuated himself into the good graces of the miserly and eccentric Christopher Rich, and later became one of the Triumvirate which ruled the fortunes of the theatre—with Doggett and Wilks. This establishment of the actor-manager was not very successful, and Cibber spent most of his time trying to keep the peace between his co-partners, until the arrival of Barton Booth drove Doggett out (see DRURY LANE). Cibber himself, though the theatre prospered under him, and he was instrumental in accepting a number of good new plays—choosing them always for their theatrical effectiveness rather than their literary merit—was unpopular, and for so eminent and in many ways able a man had remarkably few friends. He was tactless, rude to minor actors and playwrights, supremely self-confident, and given to posing as an expert on subjects of which he knew little. He was savagely ridiculed by critics of the time, by Pope in *The Dunciad*, by Dr. Johnson, and by Fielding in several of his plays, and again in the opening chapter of *Joseph Andrews*. He was a competent rather than an inspired playwright, good at doctoring other men's plays, and his methods can best be studied in his completion of Vanbrugh's unfinished *Journey to London*, which was produced at Drury Lane in 1728 as *The Provoked Husband*, with Anne Oldfield, the greatest actress of Cibber's period, as Lady Townley.

Cibber married young and had several children, of whom two went on the stage. His son (2) THEOPHILUS (1703–58) was born in one storm and died in another, being drowned in the Irish Sea on his way to act at the Smock Alley Theatre, Dublin. He was a wild and eccentric character, who went on the stage at 16, and seemed as if he might have the making of a good actor, especially in such parts as Ancient Pistol. But his imprudences and extravagant manner of living were his undoing. He was for some time co-manager of Drury Lane in succession to his father, but soon forfeited all claim to respect by his insolence and complacency, while the scandal of his second marriage drove him eventually from London. Having first married an actress who died young, he took as his second wife in 1734 the sister of Dr. Arne, (3) SUSANNA MARIA (1714–66), who was then known as a singer at the Haymarket. The elder Cibber, however, saw in her the makings of a good tragic actress, and coached her to such effect that she appeared in 1736 in *Zara* with much success. Unfortunately her husband embroiled her with the other ladies of the company by trying to take for her the part of Polly in *The Beggar's Opera*, hitherto the perquisite of Kitty Clive. He then, to escape his creditors, allowed her to be drawn into an intimacy with one John Sloper, in return for substantial payments, all three living together in London until Theophilus was able to withdraw to France. The outcome of this affair was an unsavoury lawsuit which drove Mrs. Cibber from the stage for some years, and caused Sloper to retire to the country under an assumed name. Theophilus continued to appear in minor parts for a while, but gradually sank to the status of a hack-writer, without losing any of his effrontery and self-confidence. His wife later returned to the stage with some success, and was for a long time at Drury Lane with Garrick, who said, when he heard of her death, 'Then tragedy has expired on one side.' Though at her best in tragedy, she was sometimes seen in comedy, and her last part was that of Lady Brute in *The Provoked Wife*. She was buried in the Cloisters in Westminster Abbey.

One of Colley Cibber's daughters, (4) CHARLOTTE (?–c. 1760), had her full share of her family's eccentricity, and made herself extremely conspicuous in London. She was intensely masculine, and scorned all pursuits except hunting and shooting, spending most of her time in the company of the stable-boys. Married young to Richard Charke, a violinist at Drury Lane, in the hope of taming her, she went on the stage, quarrelled with the managers, and ran away, communicating with her family from time to time in order to borrow money from them. She disguised herself as a man, acted men's and women's parts indifferently in strolling companies, was a conjuror's assistant in Petticoat Lane, a puppet-master, a performer at fairs, and kept a tavern in Drury Lane. She published a remarkable *Narrative of the Life of Mrs. Charlotte Charke*. Odell believes that the Mrs. Harman who acted in New York towards the end of her life and was buried in Trinity Churchyard there, in 1773, was a daughter of Charlotte Charke. One of Theophilus's daughters by his first marriage was also on the stage for a short time, but with no great success.

CICOGNINI, GIACINTO ANDREA (1606–60), Italian dramatist, a prolific and popular provider of theatrical fare in the seventeenth century. He was much influenced by the Spanish theatre, which had come into Italy by way of Naples, where, under a Spanish viceroy, the plays of Lope de Vega and Calderón were frequently performed by visiting Spanish companies. Cicognini, who is credited with over forty compositions, of which perhaps only half were really his own, is also believed to have been the first Italian dramatist to handle the legend of Don Juan (for further details on Cicognini, see ITALY, 1 *b*).

CINCINNATI, see PIONEER THEATRE IN THE U.S.A.

CINQUEVALLI, PAUL (1859–1918), probably the greatest juggler the music-halls ever knew. He juggled with anything, from cannon balls to billiard balls, with equal skill, and was top of the bill for over twenty years. A Pole by birth, he was unjustly accused of German sympathies during the 1914–18 war, and this, preying on his mind, is believed to have caused his death.

CINTHIO, IL, see GIRALDI.

CIRCUIT, see PROVINCIAL THEATRES, 1 *b*.

CIRCUS, in Roman times a place of exhibition for chariot-racing and athletic contests. In its modern sense a circus is an entertainment of a particular kind, which lies outside the scope of this book. It is cosmopolitan and itinerant (though Europe has some permanent circuses), and is performed in the central area of a tent (known as the Big Top) or in the arena of a building specially adapted to its needs. Its programme is built up of separate turns, mainly featuring performing animals or acrobatics, loosely correlated by the antics of the Clown or Auguste. Owing to the specialized nature of their work, circus performers tend to remain a class apart, with much intermarrying. The great names of the American circus are Barnum and Sand, of the English Sanger and Bertram Mills; but the circus is universal and, since it places little dependence on the spoken word, can be at home anywhere. Its history is fully documented, and a list of books in which further information can be found is given in the Bibliography.

There was, however, a time in the late eighteenth and early nineteenth centuries when stage and circus mingled. Philip Astley, who is credited with introducing the circus to England, opened in 1770 an Amphitheatre, in which both theatrical performances and displays of horsemanship were given. They were apparently kept separate, however, and it was not until the early years of the nineteenth century that Equestrian Drama, as it was called, became popular. As the spectacular side of the theatre increased in these years, so the employment of horses, and even lions, became more general. *Richard III* offered an admirable claimant for fame in the person of Richard's horse, White Surrey, but horses could be, and were, introduced everywhere, even into *Macbeth*. Two famous equestrian dramas were *Mazeppa* and *Dick Turpin's Ride to York*, but horses were used most effectively in such melodramas as *Timour the Tartar* and *The Blood-Red Knight*. The invasion was not confined to the minor theatres, but attacked Drury Lane and Covent Garden, who also succumbed to a further innovation which came from the circuses of Paris, the Aquatic Drama. For this the stage was flooded, and fine mimic sea-fights took place, particularly in plays based on the victories of Lord Nelson. The use of an entire menagerie in *Hyder Ali; or, the Lions of Mysore*, also connected the theatre with the circus in its widest sense, as did the sudden craze for Dog Drama which swept England and America in the nineteenth century. This probably had its origin—though there had of course been performing dogs before—in a little afterpiece at Drury Lane where a real dog, Carlos, effected a rescue from a tank of water. The most famous Dog Drama, however, was written by Pixérécourt in 1814, and given in several English versions as *The Dog of*

Montargis, or *The Forest of Bondy*. It is said that the Duke of Weimar's insistence on seeing a German version of this play, with a performing poodle, caused Goethe's retirement from the Court theatre in disgust. There can be no doubt that the admixture of circus with theatrical elements had a bad influence on the drama, and that both are far better when confined to their separate spheres.

CITÉ, THÉÂTRE DE LA, PARIS, a large playhouse for spectacle and music built during the French Revolution. It opened as the Palais-Variétés on 20 Oct. 1792, but failed to achieve its purpose and devoted itself mainly to broad farce and pantomime, one of its most popular actors being Brunet. It took the name Cité in 1793, became a circus, reopened as a theatre in 1800 under Saint-Aubin, and passed from hand to hand with constant changes of name until in 1807 it closed and later became a famous dance hall known as Prado.

CITIZEN HOUSE, BATH, founded as a resident Community Art Centre by Councillor Helen Hope, J.P., of Bath, was also a pioneer force in the development of community and institutional drama. Its Little Theatre, founded in 1913 by Miss Consuelo de Reyes, who controlled it till her death in 1948, began in a lecture room, but is now housed in its own building, complete with simplified theatre equipment which makes ample provision for the courses in acting and production which are a feature of its activities. There is also an Open-air Theatre. A fine theatrical library and museum, a collection of costumes which may be borrowed for group productions (some unfortunately lost in 1944 by fire), and an advisory bureau dealing with all aspects of community drama, make up a comprehensive service at the disposal of those concerned with drama whether in schools, colleges, institutions, clubs, or local societies. In 1930, hoping to establish a permanent centre in London, Citizen House purchased the Everyman Theatre, Hampstead. This was used for vacation courses in dramatic art, and for productions by amateurs attending the courses, but was later sold. After Miss de Reyes' death the work of Citizen House continued under her husband, Peter King, and Marion Radford.

CITIZENS' THEATRE, THE, Glasgow, was founded in 1943 by an influential body of citizens and with the support of C.E.M.A. Its directors included James Bridie, Paul Vincent Carroll, and Dr. J. J. Honeyman. It was accommodated in the Athenaeum Theatre, and from the first proved successful. It has a permanent professional company, and is conducted on repertory lines. Among its productions have been Massinger's *A New Way to Pay Old Debts*, Goldsmith's *The Good-Natured Man*, P. V. Carroll's *Shadow and Substance*, and James Bridie's *Mr. Bolfry*.

w. J.

CITY OF LONDON THEATRE. This stood in Norton Folgate, adjoining Bishopsgate. It was built by Beazley, architect of the Lyceum, and opened on 27 Mar. 1837 under the management of Cockerton with a version of *Pickwick* by Edward Stirling. In 1837 Mrs. Honey, a popular actress, appeared there in *Don Juan*, with Miss Pincott (Mrs. Alfred Wigan) also in the cast. In the same year Mrs. Honey became manageress. In 1838 Osbaldiston succeeded her and ran the theatre for three years. Then Cockerton returned, with Shepherd (afterwards at the Surrey) as his partner and Nelson Lee as his dramatist. In 1846 Mr. and Mrs. Honnor appeared there in Shakespeare and other plays, of which *The Battle of Life*, based on Dickens, was a success. The palmiest days of this theatre came in 1848 under Nelson Lee and Johnson, who controlled it for many years with great sucess and made it well known. These two men had succeeded Richardson in his famous booth, or portable theatre, and knew their business. They worked on cheap prices—the gallery was threepence and the pit sixpence—and they gave good value for money. Nelson Lee's pantomimes were a great attraction. When the Patent Theatres' rights were broken many leading actors and actresses visited the City of London. Constance Loseby made a very early appearance there. When Nelson Lee retired the place began to decline, though Sarah Thorne was there in 1867, and Burton's Christy Minstrels later in the same year. By 1868 the house had fallen to a lowly position, and the land on which the stage stood being required for an extension of the railway, the theatre closed. The auditorium became a soup kitchen and later a Temperance Hall.   W. M. P.

CITY PANTHEON, LONDON, see CITY THEATRE (2).

CITY THEATRE. (1) NEW YORK, a small playhouse at 15 Warren Street, which was opened on 2 July 1822 by Mrs. Baldwin. This lady, with her husband, her sister Mrs. Barnes, and her brother-in-law, left England in 1816 and became a member of the company at the Park Theatre, where she was first seen as Juliet's nurse, and later as Mrs. Malaprop. Unfortunately her first season at the City Theatre was stopped by an outbreak of yellow fever, and though for her second season she engaged Hilson and other good actors, she never recovered from her initial setback, and the theatre closed in 1823.   G. F.

(2) LONDON, a disused chapel in Grub Street, E.C. (later Milton Street), which in 1829–30 was converted into a theatre. Its name was afterwards changed to the City Pantheon. John Bedford, a popular comedian, was its first manager, and was succeeded by Chapman. It was there that Fanny Clifton (the stage name of Mary Anne Kehl), afterwards Mrs. Stirling, made her first appearance. In 1831 Edmund Kean played there, and in the same year Ellen Tree and James Vining appeared in *Eily O'Connor*, a play based on

Griffin's novel *The Collegians*, which supplied Boucicault with the foundation of his successful *Colleen Bawn*. *Love in a Village* and *Black-Eyed Susan* were also given there with excellent casts. In 1831 Chapman retired in favour of Davidge, and a working arrangement was come to with the Coburg (later the Old Vic) by which the same companies appeared at both theatres, being taken to and fro in hackney coaches. Harriet Smithson, who married Berlioz, appeared at the theatre in 1832, *The Rake* was produced there, and, with Webster as manager, Mrs. Waylett starred there. Moncrieff the dramatist also ran it for a while, selling tickets off the premises to evade the Patent Act. It was last used as a theatre in 1836, and then became a warehouse.   W. M. P.

(3) NEW YORK, in the upper part of the City Saloon on Broadway. It opened on 13 July 1837 under the management of J. J. Adams, with Joseph Cowell as Crack, his famous part in *The Turnpike Gate*. Cowell had not been seen in New York for nine years, but in spite of a good supporting company and a repertory of popular plays, the venture soon failed.

CIVIC REPERTORY THEATRE, NEW YORK, see LE GALLIENNE, EVA.

CIVIC THEATRE, U.S.A., see NATION-WIDE THEATRE.

CLAIRON, CLAIRE JOSÈPHE HIPPOLYTE LÉRIS (Leyris) DE LA TUDE (1723–1803), outstanding French actress. She was the daughter of a sempstress, and, according to her own memoirs, which are not very reliable, had a hard childhood. At 12 she showed signs of precocious ability, and joined the troupe of the Comédie-Italienne, where she played minor roles for a year or so before going to La Noue at Rouen. Later she developed a fine singing voice, and in 1743 went to the Opéra. But her real talent was for acting, and she was transferred to the Comédie-Française to understudy Mlle Dangeville. When asked, as was customary, to chose the role for her début, she horrified the entire company by demanding to play the title-role in Racine's *Phèdre*, in which at that time Mlle Dumesnil excelled. Thinking she would fail, and that the lesson would be salutary, they allowed her to tackle it. Her performance on 19 Sept. 1743 was a triumph, and led to her being entrusted with important tragic roles. Contemporary accounts show that her first appearances were hailed everywhere with acclamation, particularly by Voltaire, in many of whose plays she was destined to appear. This early success did not, however, prevent her from studying her parts with fervour and determination. With the great actor Lekain, also a protégé of Voltaire, she was responsible for introducing some much-needed modifications into the contemporary costumes worn on the stage for any and every play, mainly by adding some historical note in keeping with the character she portrayed. The time was not yet ripe for complete historical accuracy, but she made a tentative step towards it, and also, on the good advice of Marmontel, abandoned in about 1753 her somewhat stiff and declamatory style of acting for a freer and more natural method. The naturally tragic depth of her voice prevented her from lapsing into triviality, and the new departure was a success. In 1765 Clairon, with Lekain and other members of the Comédie-Française, was imprisoned for quite rightly refusing to play with an actor who had brought disgrace on the company, and after this did not return to the theatre. Instead she took refuge with Voltaire at Ferney, and acted in his private theatre there. On her return to Paris she retired from public life and appeared only in private theatricals and at Court. She was fifty when she went by invitation to the Court of the Margrave of Anspach, and it was there that she wrote her *Mémoires et réflexions sur l'art dramatique*. On the outbreak of the Revolution her pension ceased and, the Margrave also dying about this time, Clairon found herself almost penniless. She returned to Paris, where she remained until her death, living on the proceeds of her book, published in 1799. Among her pupils were Larive and Mlle Raucourt. Garrick, on a visit to Paris in 1764, saw and admired Clairon, though there is apparently no reason to believe that they were intimately acquainted.

CLARENCE THEATRE, LONDON, see PANHARMONIUM.

CLARK, HUGH (?–1653), English actor who was probably apprenticed to the stage as a child, since he played the leading feminine roles in *The Wedding* (1626) and *The Fair Maid of the West* (1630), in between which he appears to have got married. A few years later he was playing men's parts, and transferred from the Queen's Men to the King's, with whom he signed the dedication of the Beaumont and Fletcher folio in 1647.

CLARKE, JOHN SLEEPER (1833–99), American actor, who made his début in 1851 at Boston, became the principal comedian at Baltimore, and was joint lessee of the Arch Street Theatre, Philadelphia. With Edwin Booth, whose sister he married, he managed several theatres. He was first seen in London in Oct. 1867, and in 1872 opened the Charing Cross Theatre. He later took over the Haymarket and the Strand, appearing in all three theatres under his own management. Two of his sons were on the stage.

CLAUDEL, PAUL (1868–   ), French poet-dramatist, whose work has, owing to the devotion of his few but enthusiastic admirers, been performed in many countries. He was born in Picardy, but later went to Paris, where he was a disciple of Mallarmé. He joined the French consular and diplomatic service, and at 24 went to America, where he seems to have come under the influence of Walt Whitman. The scene of *L'Échange*, one of his earliest plays, is 'America: The East Coast'. While in China he wrote his *Grandes Odes*. In 1908 he

was appointed French consul at Prague, and held similar posts in German cities until the summer of 1914. He was appointed French Ambassador at Tokyo in 1921, at Washington in 1927, and at Brussels in 1933. His earlier publications were anonymous; their ardent Catholicism might have proved damaging at that time to his career. Little, in fact, was known of his plays until the Théâtre de l'Œuvre staged *L'Annonce faite à Marie* in Paris in 1912. This was followed by *L'Échange* —written in 1893—at the Vieux-Colombier. When these plays were given in Germany they excited enthusiasm among the reformers of theatrical presentation. The Little Theatres of the United States also gave a number of Claudel performances. The first in London were directed by Edith Craig, whose Pioneer Players gave *Exchange* at the Little Theatre on 2 May 1915; she was also responsible for a performance of *The Tidings brought to Mary* at the Strand the following year, and for *The Hostage*, a translation of *L'Otage*—the most theatrically effective of Claudel's dramas—at the Scala in 1919, when the heroine, Synge du Coûfontaine, became one of the outstanding achievements of Sybil Thorndike's career. Among Claudel's other works are *Le Pain dur*, *Le Père humilié*, and the best-known, *Le Soulier de satin*. This was written between 1919–24, but was not performed until 1943, when it was done at the Comédie-Française. It was translated by John O'Connor as *The Satin Slipper*. After the outbreak of war in 1939 Ludmilla Pitoëff, who had played in many of Claudel's plays in Paris, took them to Canada and America, where they were well received. Claudel needs audiences that are familiar with his work before they come to the theatre—a demand more easily satisfied in French- than in English-speaking countries, where published translations are scarce as yet. *The Tidings brought to Mary*, the first and for a long time the only one available, has now been joined by *The Hostage*, *Crusts*, and *The Humiliation of the Father* (1946), in translations by John Heard.

CLAXTON, KATE (1848–1924), American actress, who made her début at Chicago in 1869, after which she joined Lotta on tour. From 1870 to 1873 she was a member of Daly's company at his Fifth Avenue Theatre. In 1874 she scored an outstanding success as Louise, the blind girl in *The Two Orphans*, a melodrama adapted from the French, and for the rest of her life she was identified with this part, which she acted all over the United States. She was appearing in it at the Brooklyn Theatre in 1876 when the latter was destroyed by fire, with the loss of 200 lives.

CLEANDER, a Greek actor associated with Aeschylus.

CLIFTON, HARRY (1832–72), a music-hall singer of 'motto' songs of unimpeachable respectability and moral fervour, which were as popular in Victorian drawing-rooms as on the halls, especially 'Pulling Hard against the Stream', 'Work, Boys, Work', and 'Paddle Your Own Canoe'. He also sang comic songs, of which 'The Weepin' Willer', written by himself, is the best known.

CLIVE, KITTY [CATHERINE RAFTOR] (1711–85), English actress, who though not strictly beautiful was so charming and animated that she achieved a great reputation in the playing of high-spirited comedy and farce. She was early attracted to the stage and at 17 appeared under Colley Cibber at Drury Lane in minor parts. She first charmed the audience by her singing, and by 1731 was established as a fine comic actress, her first outstanding success being as Nell in the farce of *The Devil to Pay*, a part later played with equal brilliance by Mrs. Jordan. She married a barrister named George Clive, but the marriage soon broke up, though merely through incompatibility, and no scandal ever attached itself to her name. Most of her career was spent at Drury Lane, where she and Garrick, with much admiration for each other's powers, were nevertheless constantly at loggerheads, and she is said to have been the only actress of whose temper Garrick stood in awe. She was passionate and vulgar, but always generous and quite without pride or ostentation. Her one fault was a constant desire to appear in tragedy, or even in genteel comedy, for which she was quite unfitted. Her excellence in low comedy, and in burlesques of Italian opera, endeared her so much to the public that they were willing to tolerate her as Portia, though she burlesqued the Trial Scene by mimicking famous lawyers of the day. But as Zara and Ophelia she was less successful, and much of her animosity against Garrick came from his preventing her appearing in such unsuitable parts. One of her great admirers was Horace Walpole, who on her retirement in 1769 presented her with a small house —Clive's-Den—on Strawberry Hill, where her company and conversation were much relished by his friends, particularly Dr. Johnson. Kitty Clive was frequently painted, notably by Hogarth, and was the author of several short farces.

CLOAK-AND-SWORD PLAYS (*Comedias de capa y espada*), the name given to a type of Spanish drama which has often been taken as characteristic of the whole. Originally the phrase indicated only the external nature of the play—the characters were drawn from the nobility, and their dress was typified by the cloak and the sword. The action dealt with their private lives and intrigues, usually amorous, and did not require the elaborate staging of the *comedia de teatro*, where the characters were kings and princes. However, in later criticism the flamboyance of the title became associated with the subject-matter of the play, helped no doubt by the recurrence in Spanish plots of the *pundonor*, the elaborate and exacting 'point of honour'. Nineteenth-century dramatists found a great attraction in this type of play,

which is often taken to mean any sort of romantic costume play with a strong love interest and a certain amount of sword-play.

CLOSET DRAMA, see PLAY and ROME, 2.

CLOTH, a term used for any large unframed expanse of canvas or material used for scenery. A modern cloth is generally made of widths of canvas, seamed horizontally together, and attached at top and bottom to a sandwich batten, or one formed of two lengths of 4×1 in. timber, screwed together with the cloth between. A Cut-cloth is one with cut openings. The shape of the opening, if it is elaborately fretted, may need the reinforcement of a piece of netting, glued on behind. A Gauze-cloth is used for special effects, and consists of an unbroken stretch of fine net, which appears opaque when lit from the front, but is transparent, almost to vanishing point, when lit from behind. Such a cloth can be painted in dye to appear as a normal cloth.

A distant cousin of the hanging cloth is the Stage-cloth, which is an expanse of painted canvas, not attached to battens, laid on the stage as a floor covering. It is painted a plain colour, or patterned to suit a scene, and further and self-describing varieties of it are known, such as Sand-cloth, for desert and other scenes.

A variant of the framed cloth is the Ceiling, a canvas stretch battened out and suspended flat over the top of the Box Set.   R. S.

CLOUDINGS, a term formerly applied to cloud borders, which were used to mask the top of almost any scene. They could be drawn off sideways by hooked poles, and are mentioned as late as 1743. The detail of their arrangement is not clear, but they recall the form of border used by Inigo Jones in his last masque, *Salmacida Spolia* (1640). This had not only 'the Clouds of ye heaven which went crosse ye sceane', and were like the modern cloud border, but also, at either end of each of these, to left and right, further independent 'peeces of Clouds which came downe from ye roofe before ye upper part of ye syde shutters whereby ye grooues aboue were hidden and also ye howse behind them'. The sectional drawing of the stage for this masque, preserved in the Landsdowne manuscripts in the British Museum, shows these to have been deeper than the borders proper, turning them into a species of arch. These 'side-clouds' were not left unchanged throughout the show as were the borders themselves, for 'these Clouds also' (like the shutters) 'went in grooues . . . and changed with ye sceanes below'. They could presumably be slid off sideways to reveal a second set behind, thus transforming a stormy sky into a calm sky, or vice versa.   R. S.

CLOWN is not as simple as he looks. No other stage figure has such complexity. 'Clod, clot, lump' explains his origin in the unconscious humour of the village idiot and in representations of this upon the stage. Just as the natural fool of real life could become the hired jester of entertainments, so the clown has always tended to be both the part and the player, which is merely one of his peculiarities among *dramatis personae*. This overlapping of life and art creates such legendary figures as Harlequin, Pierrot, Joey, and Auguste, whose gradual metamorphosis from humble butts into idols of the motley, and thence into glamorous immortals, affords a curious insight into the workings of mass imagination. Their evolution reveals in its stages the chief types of clowns, (*a*) the simpleton, such as the one upon whom Shakespeare bestows his own Christian name in *As You Like It*, (*b*) the knave, who is usually more temperate in his habits than Punch in the puppet-show, though this is his apotheosis, (*c*) the jester or professional fool, like Touchstone, invested in his motley and given leave to speak his mind, (*d*) the transcendental spirit of mirth, such ghosts of departed clowns as Harlequin. Encounters between knave and butt occur throughout the history of clowning, notably in the tricks played by the Vice upon the Devil in the religious drama of the Middle Ages. The triple partnership whereby the butt vainly tries to delude the jester with the tricks of the knave is a modern convention.

'Merry Andrew', one of the earliest nicknames for clowns in England, was derived from Andrew Borde, an ex-Carthusian monk whose amusing *Breviare of Health* was published in 1547. Thomas Heywood, court jester of Henry VIII, wrote comic interludes now studied as foundations of the drama. Richard Tarleton, first clown of the professional theatre in England, kept the Tabard in Southwark, where the young Shakespeare may have seen this fellow of infinite jest set the table on a roar. William Kempe was clown and shareholder of the Globe. Because he left the company for a time the unflattering portrait of a clown in the First Quarto, omitted in all other versions of *Hamlet*, is supposed to be his. The scene between clown and musicians in *Romeo and Juliet*, staged before he left, resembles the scene between clown and musicians in *Othello*, staged at the time of his return. In *The Travels of Three English Brothers* (1607) he appears under his own name to flout a dolt from Italy—Harlequin on his arrival in English drama. Here begins the long struggle between the British idea of individual humour and the foreign delight in perpetuated type. Harlequin was known merely as clown to travelling mountebanks who sold quack nostrums, and was so represented in the masque of *Britannia Triumphans* at Whitehall in 1637. The Italians triumphed when Tiberio Fiorello played Scaramouche in London in 1673, and this braggart in black was the first figure of the *commedia dell'arte* to acclimatize the pattern of mirth in this country. In *Scaramouche a Philosopher, Harlequin a Schoolboy, Bravo, Merchant and Magician*, staged at Drury Lane four years later, Harlequin was a simpleton, mocked and beaten even by infants, and yet before the end he caused his

opponents to hit each other when aiming blows at him—which indicates how the butt inevitably turns into the knave. As the change progressed another butt had to be provided—another clown hatched from a clod. Either Pierrot or 'a farmer's man' served the purpose, while Harlequin, imitating Dominique's Arlequin in Paris, took on the graces of a dancer. Comparison between his English and French evolutions is instructive. The sentimental Arlequin of Marivaux at last became the insipidly moral, impeccably respectable Arlequin of Florian's comedies for the propagation of domestic virtue under Louis XVI. John Rich (who billed himself at Lincoln's Inn Fields and Covent Garden as 'Lun') kept Harlequin's rascality alive while representing him in dance and dumbshow as a lover and a magician, until the vogue of virtue affected him also; in the Christmas pantomimes of England henceforward there was nothing to laugh at in Harlequin. Pierrot became the chief character of these harlequinades when he was played by Delpini, an Italian who gave him the stamp of the over-grown schoolboy which English audiences have always loved. Dubois, his humble rival, added colour to the costume, and shortened legs and sleeves in a compromise with the motley of the Merry Andrew. Hitherto Pantaloon's blundering servant had been either Pierrot or a ragged yokel (a clown in the older sense), but this mongrel had an overwhelming popularity when played by Joseph Grimaldi. The new character took Clown as his proper name, and was affectionately called Joey. In his acrobatic heyday his costume was spare; his wig was a single crest like that on the helmets, fashioned after an antique style, of the Household Cavalry. Changes in his appearance reflected changes in his character. In rebellion against the vogue of virtue he was villainous; he persecuted true love and had all the mentionable vices—particularly gluttony, covetousness, drunkenness, avarice, vanity, craft, and cruelty. His trunks were widened by pockets for stolen food, and his wig became triple-tufted, each with a frozen-pigtail like the one worn by his master. Pantaloon was now the butt and Clown the knave—more cunning even than Punch, whom he outwitted when they met in the puppet-show at street-corners. Joey now had an existence outside the harlequinade where he was born. He was still in his prime when Grimaldi retired and bequeathed the part to his son, and when both were dead, the harlequinade existed solely as the vehicle for his pranks. In modified forms—wearing a conical cap for juggling—but still called Clown and Joey, he was the pet of circuses in all lands, until metamorphosis overtook him. The affection lavished upon him transformed him first into the 'Shakespearian Jester' and then into a glamorous being in silk and spangles too elegant for horseplay. Blows and drenching needed a new type, and fell upon some clumsy attendant in the ring. One of these won fame under the name of Auguste; instead of his semi-military uniform he took to wearing cast-off clothes the better to receive rough treatment—thus naturally obeying the so-called tradition that the butt wears rags. Grock took the Auguste from the circus to the music-hall. Beneath a vast greatcoat he wore dress clothes many sizes too small; inside a 'cello case was a tiny dancing-master's fiddle; his bald dome had a short fringe of hair. His inarticulate speech consisted of gurgles and growls. He exhausted himself pushing the piano towards the stool. He fell through a chair when he stood upon it to reach the spot-light for his accordion, and then played master-fully while displaying an oafish grin of beati-tude. The Fratellini (three brothers, members of a veritable dynasty of clowns) established themselves as the chief clowns of the circus, mainly at the Cirque d'Hiver in Paris. These three conformed to the pattern which was customary on the Continent between 1918 and 1939; one was elegant in satin, spangles, and face-powder, another was a bulbous-nosed, doltish Auguste, and the other a shabby-genteel Auguste who blundered more through ill luck than downright stupidity. The white faces of elegant clowns in the French circus maintain an ancient Paris tradition. In Molière's childhood three clowns (Gros-Guillaume, Turlupin, and Gaultier-Garguille) made such play with their death-like pallor that they were said to have been bakers who discovered their comic powers while throwing flour at each other. Similarly Pierrot (after disappearing from the English harlequinades) fascinated Paris as a being 'pale as the moon'. Jean-Gaspard Deburau had created, before he died in 1846, a legend of sentimental romance which was carried on by his son Charles, by Paul Legrand, and by Severin, who died in 1930.

Perpetuated type still continues in clown-ship. Individual humour has been equally productive, especially on the music-halls, where clowns are miscalled comedians to dis-tinguish them from the players of Clown. The 'red-nosed' comic, being both the player and his part, is essentially a clown, which the man who doffs his mirth with his motley is not. This ingrained quality of clownship, richly possessed by Whimsical Walker and Joe Cras-ton, has been strongly marked in those who were stars of music-hall and pantomime. They have been in real life what they are on the boards, freely giving their spirit to add to the zest in life of their duller fellows. The music-halls have not produced one definite type to be perpetuated, but the comic characters which their comedians have added to children's stories, such as Widow Twankey in *Aladdin*, Idle Jack in *Dick Whittington*, and Buttons in *Cinderella*, are worthy to be set by the side of the immortal Joey. Like him they are no author's work. Year by year they are nourished by the spirit of the clowns who pretend to be them; and they are likely—particularly the now utterly devoted Buttons—to inspire feelings too deep for laughter. What we mean by

'clown' cannot be clipped. It has grown into a magical word.   M. W. D.

COAL HOLE, LONDON, see TERRY'S THEATRE.

COATES, ROBERT (1772–1848), a wealthy and eccentric gentleman from the West Indies, who believed himself to be a superb actor. In 1810 he rented the Theatre Royal, Bath, and dis-played himself as Romeo, whence his nick-name of 'Romeo' Coates. Taking the hilarity of the audience as a tribute to his genius, he toured the provinces and finally appeared at the Haymarket in London, again as Romeo, wear-ing a sky-blue spangled cloak, tight red panta-loons, a muslin vest, a full-bottomed wig and a tall hat. He was also seen as Lothario in *The Fair Penitent*. He had a brief blaze of notoriety, but the public soon tired of his absurdities, and he relapsed into poverty and obscurity.

COBORN, CHARLIE (1852–1945), music-hall star whose real name was Colin Whitton McCallum. He was first on the halls as an Irish comedian, calling himself Charles Lawrie. A friend advising him to change his name, he adopted that of Coborn Street, Poplar, where they were standing. His most famous songs were 'Two Lovely Black Eyes' (1886) and 'The Man Who Broke the Bank at Monte Carlo' (1890). Coborn was one of the founders of the Music-Hall Benevolent Fund in 1888, and during the Second World War was in-defatigable in entertaining the troops, singing almost to the day of his death with unimpaired vigour.

COBURG THEATRE, LONDON, see OLD VIC.

COBURN. (1) CHARLES DOUVILLE (1877–), American actor and manager, who at 17 was in charge of the Savannah Theatre, where he had begun his career as a programme boy. He was for some years with a stock company in Chicago, and in 1901 made his first appearance in New York, subsequently touring the United States in *The Christian*. He married (2) IVAH WILLS (1882–1937), an actress, with whom he organized in 1905 the Coburn Shakespearian Players, both playing leading parts in it for many years. He was outstanding as Falstaff, but he also scored a success as Old Bill in *The Better 'Ole* (1918), which ran for nearly two years, and in 1925 he played James Telfer in an all-star revival in New York of *Trelawny of the 'Wells'*. One of his greatest successes otherwise was *The Yellow Jacket*, a play in the Chinese manner which he frequently revived, himself playing the hero Wu Hoo Git. In 1934 the Coburns inaugurated the Mohawk Dramatic Summer Festival at Union College, Schenectady, which became an annual event, and in the same year Coburn appeared in *The First Legion*. He retired from the stage on his wife's death, but in 1946 returned to play Falstaff for the Theatre Guild.

COBURN'S THEATRE, NEW YORK, see DALY'S THEATRE (3).

COCHRAN, Sir Charles Blake (1873–1951), master-showman of his time, began as an actor, playing in America with Comstock, Joseph Jefferson, and others, and was for three years personal representative for Richard Mansfield. He was also attached to theatres, circuses, and exhibitions in the United States, and so laid that foundation of showmanship to which was added his own personal genius. As an agent in England he represented Hackenschmidt, and created a vast boom in wrestling, and also popularized Houdini, the Handcuff King, and other stars. He was one of the promoters of the roller-skating boom in the 1900s, and there are indeed few branches of the entertainment industry in which he has not made his mark. In 1911 he promoted and managed the production of *The Miracle* by Reinhardt at Olympia, and in the following year presented Carl Hagenbeck's Wonder Zoo there. His first theatrical production was Ibsen's *John Gabriel Borkman* in 1897 in New York, and his first London production *Sporting Simpson* at the Royalty in 1902. In 1914 he became prominent in promoting revue, of which he is the supreme producer and presenter, starting at the Ambassadors' with *Odds and Ends*, followed by *More*, and *Pell Mell*; but his best revues were those which he presented at the London Pavilion between 1918 and 1931, perfect specimens of wit, taste, and the right kind of music—*As You Were*; *London, Paris, and New York*; *This Year of Grace*; *Wake Up and Dream*. He was equally successful with musical comedy and with straight plays, of which *Damaged Goods* is perhaps the most memorable, and his long association with Noel Coward was responsible, among other things, for *Bitter Sweet* at His Majesty's and *Cavalcade* at Drury Lane. Among his many other activities Cochran has been General Manager of the Albert Hall, converted the old Oxford Music-Hall into a theatre, imported a real Rodeo into the British Empire Exhibition at Wembley in 1924, and has been connected with practically every theatre in London. During 1919–20 he was instrumental in causing a boom in boxing, and in 1934 he was elected Governor of the Council of the Shakespeare Memorial Theatre at Stratford-on-Avon. During the most troubled part of the 1939–45 war he was responsible for a series of broadcast programmes which were immensely successful in spite of bombs, black-out, and other attendant horrors of the times, which hampered him at every turn. In 1948 he was knighted for his services to the theatre. It may truly be said that no one has left a deeper imprint on the entertainment world of his time than this many-sided, much-travelled man, who has written his reminiscences in *Secrets of a Showman* (1925), *I Had Almost Forgotten* (1932), and *Cock-a-Doodle-Do* (1941).   W. M. P.

COCKPIT, London (later the Phoenix), situated in Drury Lane, where for many years its name was perpetuated in Pitt-Place. It should not be confused with the Cockpit at Whitehall, which was only occasionally used for the presentation of plays before the Court. The Drury Lane Cockpit was built, for cock-fights, by John Best in 1609, but was converted into a roofed or 'private' theatre in 1616 by Christopher Beeston. It was about the same size as and very similar to the Blackfriars theatre. It soon met with disaster, for on Shrove Tuesday 1617 the London apprentices, in the course of their usual rowdy merrymaking on that day, sacked and set fire to it. It was quickly rebuilt and named, appropriately enough, the Phoenix, though the old name continued in use. It was very nearly the first Theatre Royal, for in 1636/7 Beeston was sworn in as Governor of the King and Queen's Young Company, popularly known as Beeston's Boys. In 1639 he died and his son William succeeded to the title. A year later William was foolish enough to produce an unlicensed play which offended Their Majesties. He was arrested and lodged in the Marshalsea, and his post was given to Sir William Davenant, who was later to make his mark in the Restoration theatre. The Cockpit was closed with all the other theatres in 1642, but illicit performances were occasionally given there, as is shown by a raid made by Parliamentary soldiers in 1649, when the audience was fined on the spot. The amount collected was £3. 11s. 4d. Two of Davenant's 'Plays with Music' (or early operas) were performed at the Cockpit, *The Cruelty of the Spaniards* and *Sir Francis Drake*, the former probably with the connivance of Cromwell, as political propaganda. When the theatres reopened Rhodes, at one time prompter at the Blackfriars theatre, played at the Cockpit with a troupe of youngsters, many of whom became famous, and a joint company under Killigrew and Davenant may have played there before the granting of the two Patents. In 1661 a company of French actors gave at the Cockpit Chapoton's *Mariage d'Orphée et d'Eurydice*, with a profusion of 'Great Machines', and it was occupied from 1661 to 1665 by a troupe under George Jolly, who had previously made a name for himself in Germany; but when the Theatre Royal, Drury Lane, opened in 1663 the fortunes of the Cockpit declined.   W. M. P.

COCOANUT GROVE, New York, see CENTURY THEATRE (1).

COCTEAU, Jean (1892–   ), French dramatist, who first attracted attention with his *Orphée*, produced by Pitoëff in 1924 at the Théâtre des Arts. A new version of Sophocles' *Antigone*, given by Dullin at the Atelier in 1922, was also well received. A further excursion into Greek mythology, with *La Machine infernale*, on the story of Oedipus, was given by Louis Jouvet at his own theatre in 1934, with the author playing the part of A Voice. A parable on modern lines, *Les Mariés de la Tour Eiffel*, was given in 1924. Cocteau was one of the most significant figures of the French theatre between the two wars, and his work, a singular blend of poetry, irony, and fantasy, did much to redeem it from triviality and staleness.

CODY, WILLIAM FREDERICK (1846–1917), American showman, better known as Buffalo Bill. Born on a farm in Iowa, he was at the Colorado gold-mines as a boy, and then became a pony express rider and a Civil War scout. He afterwards went on the stage, playing in Western plays specially written for him. In 1883 he first embarked on the Wild West show which made him famous all over the world. This, however, partook more of the nature of the circus than the theatre, and is outside the scope of the present volume.

COGHLAN. (1) CHARLES F. (1842–99), English actor, much of whose professional life was spent in the United States. Hibbert, in *A Playgoer's Memories*, calls him 'handsome, fascinating, selfish, spendthrift Charles Coghlan, whose death was a mystery, and whose body was washed up on the Pacific shore'. He had a daughter, also on the stage in New York. He made his first appearance at the Haymarket under Buckstone, in 1860, and subsequently played a number of parts, including Charles Surface, Shylock, and the name part in Burnand's *The Colonel*, before going to New York, where he was seen at Wallack's with his sister (2) ROSE (1851–1932). A distinguished actress, she had made her first appearance on the stage as a child, playing one of the witches in *Macbeth*, and in 1869 made her adult début under Hollingshead at the old Gaiety Theatre, London. Two years later she was seen in New York with Lydia Thompson, where she made an immediate success, and, after a few years in London and the provinces, returned in 1877 to settle down, becoming an American citizen in 1902. She was for many years leading lady at Wallack's Theatre, one of her most successful roles being Lady Teazle. She also appeared in such modern productions as *The Silver King*, *Masks and Faces*, and *Diplomacy*, and was good as Rosalind, and, in 1893, in *A Woman of No Importance*. Towards the end of the nineteenth century her fortunes declined somewhat, and her style was considered outmoded. But her fine voice, distinguished presence, and technical ability kept her in demand, and in 1916 she celebrated her stage jubilee. She was frequently seen in vaudeville, and in 1921 made her last appearance in Belasco's production of *Deburau*.

COHAN, GEORGE MICHAEL (1878–1942), American actor, dramatist, and manager. Son of vaudeville actors, he appeared as a child with his parents and sister in an act billed as The Four Cohans, and by the time he was 15 he was writing skits and songs for vaudeville performance. In 1901 his first full-length play was seen in New York, and he soon built up a big reputation, both as actor and author, with such shows as *Little Johnny Jones* (1904) and *Forty-Five Minutes from Broadway* (1906). In 1911 he opened his own theatre with

The Little Millionaire, and two years later scored a success with *Seven Keys to Baldpate*, based on a story by Earl Biggers. Apart from his own plays, which included *The Song and Dance Man* (1923), in which he played the part of a second-rate Variety performer who thinks himself perfect, he also appeared with success in such plays as *Ah, Wilderness!* and *I'd Rather Be Right*, and as a manager was responsible for a wide variety of productions. Cohan was essentially a man of the theatre, as he reveals in his autobiography, published in 1925, and his work had great entertainment value, though it is of little interest otherwise. It is to his credit, however, that he made full use of his gifts, and was not content to remain in vaudeville.

COHEN, GUSTAVE (1879–   ), French scholar, whose researches on the medieval theatre of France have materially added to our knowledge of liturgical drama as a whole. His *Histoire de la mise en scène dans le théâtre religieux français au moyen âge*, first published in 1906, was re-edited and brought up to date in 1926, after the discovery of the documents relating to the Mystery of the Passion given at Mons in 1501. These were also published separately in 1925. Appointed to the staff of the Sorbonne, Cohen formed a group of students, known as the Theophilians, who produced in one of the lecture halls of the university a number of medieval plays, adapted and slightly modernized by Cohen himself. The first of these, from which the little company took its name, was *Le Mystère de Théophile*, by Rutebeuf, given in 1933. It was followed by *Le Jeu de Robin et Marion*, by Adam de la Halle, and by a reconstruction of the earliest known French play, the *Mystère d'Adam*. On the outbreak of war in 1939 Cohen retired from his post, and went to live in America, from whence he made several visits to Canada, returning to France after 1945. He continued his work of bringing back to life the old medieval plays which had for too long been considered only as texts for examination purposes, and is also the author of numerous books on other aspects and authors of the Middle Ages and Renaissance, and on the theatre of the seventeenth century.

COLERIDGE, SAMUEL TAYLOR (1772–1834), English poet, critic, and philosopher. He was the author of several plays in verse, of which one, *Remorse*, written in 1797 as *Osorio*, was produced at Drury Lane in 1813 with moderate success. The rest, among which are several translations from the German, remain unacted, except for a Christmas entertainment which, with alterations by Dibdin, was given at the Surrey in 1818. Coleridge's chief importance in theatre history lies in his critical and editorial work on Shakespeare, though even there he was handicapped by his ignorance of Elizabethan theatre conditions, which Malone was only gradually bringing to light.

COLISEUM, THE, LONDON, Sir Oswald Stoll's famous music-hall in St. Martin's Lane, became a theatre in 1931, with the production of the successful *White Horse Inn*, which ran for 651 performances. Other spectacular productions which followed were not so successful, but the Coliseum remained a theatre, with musical shows, both new and revivals—including *The Vagabond King* in 1937—straight plays and ice shows. There were also seasons of ballet and of Variety, and a circus. From 1936 onwards pantomimes were staged at the Coliseum, which remains a theatre under the control of Prince Littler (see also under MUSIC-HALL).												W. M. P.

COLISSEUM, LONDON, in Albany Street, Regent's Park. This was open as a theatre for a few months only, when James Howard Tully (1814–68), composer and conductor, appeared there as a comedian. It should not be confused with the Colisseum, Regent's Park, which was not used as a theatre.

COLLÉ, CHARLES (1709–83), French writer of whose private life little is known. He was one of the members of the famous 'société du caveau', a dining-club renowned, among other things, for its wit and good company. He wrote admirable, though not always very circumspect, verses, and for twenty years produced for the Regent, the Duke of Orleans, who was an excellent comic actor, the plays collected in his *Théâtre de société* (printed in Amsterdam and not intended for publication), and in the *Théâtre des boulevards*. These were imitations of the medieval *parade*, which survived during the eighteenth century at the Paris fairs, and though somewhat modified in tone, were still extremely licentious. Apart from these, of which the best is perhaps *La Vérité dans le vin*, Collé wrote two serious plays. The first, a sentimental comedy entitled *Dupuis et Desronais*, was given at the Comédie-Française in 1763 with some success, but the second, *La Partie de chasse d'Henri IV*, based on Dodsley's *The King and the Miller*, was forbidden by the censor on the orders of Louis XV, and was not played in public until 1774, though it had been printed and played in the provinces much earlier. It was this charming little essay in democracy, in which a king incognito is taught his duty by a humble subject, which was given by some actors from the Comédie-Française, including Préville, at the house of the retired actress, Mlle Dangerville, as a surprise for her birthday.

COLLECTIONS, THEATRE. The ephemeral literature of the theatre—playbills, programmes, pamphlets, scenic designs, even the plays themselves—was treated with scant respect in the old days, and even where it survived was often left to moulder in garrets and cellars, or on inaccessible library shelves. At the beginning of the twentieth century the fresh impetus given to the study of theatre history led to a revival of interest in these fugitive memorabilia. Libraries, museums, and theatres turned over their treasures and began systematically to docket them, to allow scholars access to them, to reprint or reproduce them, and in some cases to gather them together in a definite theatre collection.

Practically all public and university libraries contain a varying amount of theatre material. This may be scattered, as in the British Museum, London, and the Bibliothèque Nationale, Paris, or collected, as in the Public Library, New York, the Nationalbibliothek, Vienna, and the Victoria and Albert Museum, London. Old-established theatres, like the Comédie-Française, Paris, the Scala, Milan, the Art Theatre, Moscow, have their archives, which are rich store-houses of material relating to their own history and to the theatre in general. Collections made by private persons have been donated to or purchased by libraries, as the Gabrielle Enthoven Collection in the Victoria and Albert Museum, the Douce Collection in the Bodleian, Oxford, the Rondel and Soleinne Collections in the Bibliothèque de l'Arsenal, Paris, the Hamilton Collection of English Plays in Stockholm, and the numerous collections housed in the great libraries of America. Sometimes collections may relate to one person, as the Victor Hugo Museum in Paris, the Lessing and Clara Ziegler Museums in Germany, the Folger Shakespeare Library in Washington, and the big Shakespearian collection of the Birmingham Public Library. Lastly there are collections which still remain in private hands, among them the Duke of Devonshire's, at Chatsworth.

Most art galleries contain theatre paintings and portraits, while the Garrick Club, London, and the Players' Club, New York, own fine collections of theatre portraits. There are also a number in the drama collection of Harvard University which have been catalogued in 4 vols. by Lillian A. Hall (1930–32).

COLLIER, CONSTANCE (1878–   ), English actress, whose long and distinguished career began at the age of 3, when she appeared as the Fairy Peas-Blossom in *A Midsummer Night's Dream*. She later played the child in *The Silver King* with Wilson Barrett, and in 1893 first appeared in London. She was for some years one of the famous Gaiety Girls, but left to play serious parts. From 1901 to 1908 she was with Tree at His Majesty's, where she appeared in all his major productions, and accompanied him to Germany, playing before the German Emperor. In 1908 she made her first appearance in New York, and has since divided her time between London and the United States, being equally popular in both. She played the Queen to Barrymore's Hamlet in London, and among her other parts have been Nancy in *Oliver Twist*, the Duchess of Towers in *Peter Ibbetson*, Mrs. Cheveley in *An Ideal Husband*, the Duchess de Surennes in *Our Betters*, and Anastasia in *The Matriarch*. She is part-author of *The Rat*, has been responsible for the production of several plays, and in 1929 published her reminiscences as *Harlequinade*.

COLLIER, JEREMY (1656–1726), a Non-juror and pamphleteer, best known for his attack on the theatre in his *Short View of the Immorality and Profaneness of the English Stage*, published in 1697–8. It strikes out most forcibly at the contemporary drama, not without reason, and Collier had many sensible and courageous things to say. His work is, however, marred by excessive pedantry and an ignorance of theatrical matters, both historical and technical. He also made the mistake of accusing the Restoration stage of corrupting English morals, instead of realizing that it was itself a reflection of a corrupt society, and lent himself to ridicule by his lack of proportion and literary ability. Nevertheless, his work had a salutary effect, and reflected, and perhaps helped in, the reform which was in any case overdue.

COLLIER, JOHN PAYNE (1789–1883), English dramatic and literary critic, the value of whose work was ruined by his forgery of entries in Elizabethan documents, many of which still persist, in spite of the rectifications of later scholars. Originally a journalist and law-student, Collier was much attracted by the Elizabethan dramatists, some of whom he edited for a new edition of Dodsley's *Old Plays*, published in 1825–7. He also wrote a volume on the puppet-play of Punch and Judy, in which he gave a reconstructed text, combining several in use by puppet showmen. His three-volume history of the stage, published in 1831, seemed full of new and interesting material, for much of which he was himself responsible, and his falsifications extended to his several volumes on Shakespeare, thus rendering them useless. He also edited for the Shakespeare Society, of which he was an enthusiastic supporter, the papers of Henslowe and Alleyn, again with his additions, thus ruining what might have been an excellent and useful piece of research. It is impossible to say how far Collier's forgeries extended—he is known to have made some manuscript additions to a second folio of Shakespeare, which first aroused the suspicions of such scholars as Dyce, Knight, and Halliwell—and they are still being refuted. They extended even to the State Papers, and are all the worse in that he had access to many private collections and so abused the confidence of his employers. In everything else his behaviour was irreproachable. He seems to have had no literary conscience whatsoever, and to have been actuated merely by vanity. In consequence of his aberration, all his statements and every document he handled are open to suspicion. Proof of his guilt, which he never admitted, was found in his papers after his death.

COLLIER'S COMEDY, NEW YORK, see COMEDY THEATRE (2).

COLLIN D'HARLEVILLE, see HARLEVILLE.

COLLINS. (1) LOTTIE (1866–1910), a well-known music-hall performer who gained fame through one song—'Ta-Ra-Ra-Boom-De-Ay'. This was written by Harry Sayers, manager of an American Nigger Minstrel troupe, who died in 1934 at the age of 77, and was first sung by Thatcher's Minstrels in a show called *Tuxedo* (from the Tuxedo Club, New York); but it had no great success until Lottie Collins introduced it, in an English version written by B. M. Batchelor, into the pantomime of *Dick Whittington* at the Grand, Islington, in 1891. It was then an enormous hit, so much so that while the pantomime was still running George Edwardes engaged the singer to perform it at the Gaiety Theatre as well, in the burlesque *Cinder-Ellen-Up-Too-Late*. Lottie Collins would rush from Islington to the Strand to sing this famous song, and do her terrific dance, starting gently on a low note, and suddenly placing her hands on her hips and whirling into the high-kicking, swift dance. She did it for years, and was paid £200 a week for it all over America, where the song had originally failed. Her daughter (2) JOSÉ (1887–) was a fine singer, who appeared with great success in many musical comedies, the best-known being *The Maid of the Mountains*, under which title she wrote her reminiscences in 1932. The play ran for three years, and was later revived with José Collins in her original part of Teresa. She toured the halls also, both in England and America, and occasionally appeared in straight plays.   W. M. P.

COLLINS, SAM (1826–65), a chimney-sweep whose real name was Samuel Vagg. He was the original music-hall Irish Comedian, first appearing at Evans's Song-and-Supper Rooms to sing 'Paddy's Wedding' and 'The Limerick Races', and then starring at all the London halls, including the first of them, the Canterbury. He was later proprietor of the Marylebone Music-Hall, and then opened at Islington Green the music-hall which still bears his name, though it is sometimes used as a repertory theatre. On his tomb in Kensal Green Cemetery are carved pictures of the hat, the shillelagh, and the shamrock with which he always appeared.

COLMAN. (1) GEORGE the elder (1732–94), English dramatist, who, after a good education at Westminster and Oxford, and some legal studies, became a well-known man of letters, and by his friendship with Garrick was attracted to the stage. His first play, given at Drury Lane in 1760, was a farce, attributed to Garrick. It was not acknowledged by its author until after the success of his *Jealous Wife* (1761), one of the most popular comedies of its time, which was played by a remarkably strong cast—Garrick, Yates, Palmer, King, Moody, Mrs. Pritchard, and Kitty Clive. This, with *The Clandestine Marriage* (1766), probably represents Colman's best work, and both plays were frequently revived, and translated into French and German, the second being used also as the basis of an Italian comic opera. Colman received some help in its composition from Garrick, but its production led to a breach between the two friends, as Garrick refused the part of Ogleby, played by King. Colman, to mark his displeasure, took a lease of Covent Garden with three associates, with whom he almost immediately found himself involved in litigation, Colman and Powell against Harris and Rutherford. After many troubles, including the death of his wife and of Powell, Colman retired from Covent Garden in 1774. During his reign Spranger Barry had made his appearance, and several good plays had been put on, including those of Goldsmith. Colman also revived *Cymbeline*, and produced a *King Lear* with his own alterations instead of those of Nahum Tate; several of his own plays were produced during this time, including *The Oxonian in Town* (1767). In 1776 Colman took over the Haymarket from Foote, engaged a good company, headed by John Henderson, and did well for several seasons. He was an energetic manager of strict probity, and a good dramatist. His adaptation of *Philaster* was the first play in which Powell appeared in London, while Tattle, in his farce *The Deuce is in Him* (1763), played by King, may be considered the first of those 'patter-parts' in which Mathews was later to excel. His translations of Terence, published in 1765, also met with approval. Among the plays which he produced at the Haymarket during his managership there was the first work of his son (2) GEORGE the younger (1762–1836), a negligible farce which had only one performance. Some later works, however, also given at the Haymarket, were more successful, and included the musical play *Inkle and Yarico* (1787). In 1789 the younger Colman succeeded his father as manager of the theatre, and remained there for some years, though with less success. He was reckless and extravagant, and was constantly involved in lawsuits, which had a bad effect on the conduct of the theatre. He was also hampered by a secret marriage which he had contracted in 1784 with a young actress, Clara Morris. He had powerful friends, however, and from 1824 until his death was Examiner of Plays, in which capacity he showed a prudery and strictness which were unexpected from the general tenor of his own works, particularly his comic poems. He had none of the rectitude and stability of his father, but was profligate and disorderly, though some scurrilous publications have been attributed to him without cause. He was a good dramatist, excelling in comic characters, many of which have remained favourite parts with comedians—among them Dr. Pangloss and Dennis Brulgruddery. His best plays are probably *The Iron Chest* (1796), which, after an initial failure ascribed by Colman to Kemble, was later revived and supplied Kean and other tragedians with a fine part; *The Heir at Law* (1797); *Bluebeard; or, Female Curiosity* (1798); and *John Bull; or, the Englishman's Fireside* (1803), considered his masterpiece by his contemporaries, and a great favourite in America. Colman also wrote for Mathews *The Actor of All Work; or, First and Second Floor* (1817), in which two rooms were shown on the stage simultaneously, something of an innovation in those days.

Colman is believed to have married as his second wife his leading lady, (3) MARY LOGAN

(1770–1844). Of unknown parentage, she was the godchild of John Palmer, with whom she appeared at the Haymarket at the age of 13. She was first billed as Mrs. Gibbs at Goodman's Fields in 1787, and retained that name for over fifty years. Fair, plump, with blue eyes and a sweet singing voice, she had good looks, good taste, and a good temper. She played heroines at the Haymarket for many years, eventually succeeding Mrs. Mattocks in duenna parts in old comedy. She retired to Brighton on the death of the younger Colman, and died there. Peake called her 'a kind, unaffected woman, who, with very considerable acquirements and much accurate study of her art, is yet more admired for the cheerfulness of her mind and the goodness of her heart'.

COLOMBIA, see SOUTH AMERICA, 1.

COLOMBIER, MARIE (*c.* 1842–1910), French actress, who studied at the Conservatoire and made her début in 1863 at the Châtelet, going later to the Gaîté and Porte-Saint-Martin. She went with Sarah Bernhardt to tour in the United States, and on her return published a violent attack on her manageress which led to an acrimonious lawsuit. Marie Colombier then left the theatre and attracted attention as the author of a number of novels, continuing at the same time her attacks on Bernhardt (whom she called Sarah Barnum). One of the latter's supporters retaliated with a somewhat scandalous *Vie de Marie Pigeonnier* (1884). These skirmishes between the two actresses seem somewhat to have obscured Marie Colombier's gifts for the theatre, and the abrupt ending of her career gave her little time to develop them fully.

COLON, JENNY [MARGUERITE] (1808–42), a lovely little French actress, whose short career was spent in an atmosphere of gaiety and affection. She made her first appearance at the Opéra-Comique in 1822, and two years later toured England, marrying at Gretna Green a French actor named Lafont, whom she left the following year. She was seen at several Parisian theatres, and Janin, reviewing her work in a new part at the Variétés, called her 'queen and fairy, compound at once of songs and smiles'. She was capricious and self-willed, but kept her hold on the public until her early death. Her elder sister was also on the stage, and was for many years a useful member of the company at the Opéra-Comique.

COLOSSEUM THEATRE, NEW YORK, opened on 10 Jan. 1874. Renamed the Criterion in 1882, Harrigan's Park in 1885, and the Park in 1889, it had an undistinguished career until, rebuilt as Herald Square Theatre, it opened on 17 Sept. 1894 with Richard Mansfield in *Arms and the Man*. It was for some years an important link in the opposition to the powerful Theatrical Syndicate, but was burnt down in 1908, and finally demolished in 1915.

COLOUR CIRCUITS, see LIGHTING, 2 *f.*

COLUM, PADRAIC (1881–   ), though generally known now as a writer in other fields, contributed, in the early years of the Irish Dramatic Movement, three plays that, together with those of Boyle and Robinson, had a strong influence upon the realistic development that followed. The first play that left its mark was *Broken Soil*, produced at the Abbey in 1903 and later revised as *The Fiddler's House* (see below). *The Land* (also 1903) is a firmly drawn study of farming life in the grip of the agrarian problems. There is a double conflict, on the one hand between the older and the younger generations and, on the other, between the love of the Irish soil and the longing for the adventure of emigration in the minds of the young. The characters are memorable and though the speech is plain and literal, the poetry that is never wholly absent in the Irish dramatists is revealed in the passion of the conflict. *The Fiddler's House* (1907) is a moving and imaginative study of the instinct of a vagrant artist in conflict with the practical demands of the life of a small farmer. The sympathy felt for all the characters simultaneously gives tragic balance to the play and makes it probably the finest Colum wrote. In *Thomas Muskerry* (1910) the setting is small-town life and the play, though it has less power than the two earlier, shows that the author could reveal the drab life of such towns as clearly as he could the more powerful passions of those who live on the land. His work gave a strong impetus to the second phase of the movement and when he abandoned the theatre for other forms of literature, one of the leaders of the realistic drama was lost to the Irish theatre. U. E.-F.

COLUMBINE, the young girl of the English harlequinade, usually the daughter, ward or wife of the old man Pantaloon, in love with Harlequin, with whom she eventually elopes. She was a late mask in the *commedia dell'arte*, and the name, Columbina, was used by several actresses of the Italian company in Paris in the latter half of the seventeenth century. Originally she was not one of the pairs of stage lovers, but was classed among the maid-servants, with Rosetta, Fiammetta, Pimpinella, or Puparella, as the counterparts of the *zanni*, one of whom, Harlequin, has turned into her youthful lover. Columbine is usually dressed in a conventional ballet dress, the *tutu*, with a wreath of small roses on her hair, and came into England in the eighteenth century with the growing popularity of pantomime.

COLUMBUS CIRCLE THEATRE, NEW YORK, see MAJESTIC THEATRE (1).

COMBEROUSSE, ALEXIS DE (1793–1862), a French dramatist, typical in his facility, his contemporary successes, and his later oblivion, of the many indefatigable vaudevillists of his day—Mélesville, Dupeuty, Bayard, Ancelot, Théaulon, Miéville, and, greatest of them all, Scribe—whose names crop up in different combinations throughout the lighter side of French theatrical life in the first half of the nineteenth century. Comberousse's love for the theatre was said to have been kindled when, at the age of 14, he played truant from school to see Talma in *Britannicus*. While studying law in Paris he had several plays put on with some success, and, encouraged by Picard, gave up the law for literature. He wrote more than seventy-five plays, in which many of the outstanding actors of the day—outside the Comédie-Française—appeared with success, including Frédérick-Lemaître, Léontine Faÿ, Mlle Déjazet, and Mlle Dorval. But, like all his contemporaries except Scribe, he was first submerged in the torrent of Romanticism, and then outdistanced by the social drama of Augier and the younger Dumas, and it is doubtful if any of his plays would bear revival. The best of them were collected in three volumes and published in 1864 with a preface by Jules Janin.

COMÉDIE-FRANÇAISE, LA. This national institution, which is at once the glory and despair of the French theatre, was officially founded in 1680 by the fusion of the company of the Hôtel de Bourgogne with the already amalgamated troupes of Molière, who had died in 1673, and the Théâtre du Marais. In honour of France's great actor-dramatist the theatre is also known as La Maison de Molière. Its other name is the Théâtre-Français. It was apparently first called the Comédie-Française to distinguish it from the Italian actors at the Hôtel de Bourgogne, usually referred to as the Comédie-Italienne. At first the new company continued to play in the theatre of the rue Guénégaud, with Mlle Champmeslé, Mlle Guérin (formerly Molière's wife) and her husband, Baron, Hauteroche, and the elder Poisson as its chief members. In 1689 they moved to a new theatre, specially built for them by François d'Orbay in the tennis-court of the Étoile, rue Neuve des Fossés, St-Germain-des-Prés, where they remained until 1770, the chief actors of that period being Beaubour, Mlle Duclos, Mlle Desmares, Mlle Dangeville, Adrienne Lecouvreur, and Legrand, followed by Mlle Clairon and Lekain, whose partnership made theatre history, with Préville, Grandval, Bellecour, the Dugazons, and Molé. After some years in the Salle des Machines at the Tuileries the company, which now included Mlle Raucourt and Louise Contat, again moved to a new theatre on the present site of the Odéon. The Revolution caused a split, the more revolutionary actors, headed by the great Talma, going to the Palais-Royal as the Théâtre de la République, while the others under Molé remained *in situ* as the Théâtre de la Nation. The second group soon lost the favour of the public, who considered them 'aristos', and first Laya's *Ami des lois* and then Neufchâteau's *Paméla*, based on Richardson's novel, caused riots, which culminated in the arrest and imprisonment of the actors concerned for nearly a year. For the next few years the history of the theatre in Paris is confused and the actors were dispersed over many stages. But in 1803 the company of the Comédie-Française was reconstituted in the theatre occupied by Talma and has since remained stable, though in the upheaval it lost the monopoly which it had enjoyed for so long.

The organization of the Comédie-Française is interesting, as being the last remaining example of the system on which all French theatrical companies were organized from the far-distant days of the medieval Confrérie de la Passion. On its formation it was minutely regulated by Royal command, and through all its vicissitudes the essentials have remained unchanged. The company, whose constitution was redrafted by Napoleon on his way to Moscow, is a co-operative society in which each actor holds a share, or, in the case of younger or less important actors, a half or quarter share. Admission depends on merit, and the aspiring actor is allowed to choose his own part in tragedy and comedy for his first essay. If successful he is then considered to be 'on probation' and is called a *pensionnaire*, drawing a fixed salary. After a time, which may vary from weeks to years, he may be admitted to the company as a full member, or *sociétaire*, taking the place of a former member who has resigned or died. On retirement, which is not usually permitted under twenty years' service, the *sociétaire* is entitled to a pension for the rest of his life. The oldest actor, in years of service, not in age, is the head of the company, and known as the Doyen. The green-room is a meeting-place for actors and distinguished visitors, where each member of the company in turn performs the duties of host. Its library and archives house a rich collection of theatre material.

The value of the Comédie-Française lies in the stabilizing influence of tradition, the keeping alive of a varied repertory, representing all that is best in the history of French dramatic literature, and the excellent team-work which results from the working together of a number of actors who know each others' ways, and who are securely placed at the head of their profession. Its disadvantages lie in the numbing weight of that same tradition, which tends to lie heavily on young and aspiring talents, and discourages initiative and the trying-out of new methods, whether of acting or production, the retention of a number of outworn plays, and the carelessness that security sometimes brings in its train. Yet, weighing the good against the bad, it must be agreed that on the whole the influence of the Comédie-Française has been beneficial to the development of the French theatre. At times its inertia and pontifical attitude has caused a sudden uprush of young life in some other part of Paris, but the great talents thrown to the surface in such an upheaval, as with Antoine's Théâtre Libre and Copeau's Théâtre du Vieux-Colombier, have usually ended by placing themselves at the service of the National Theatre, to the ultimate benefit of both.

COMÉDIE-ITALIENNE, LA. The Italian *commedia dell'arte* companies (for a history of the *commedia dell'arte* see Italy, 2) were often in France, and naturally included Paris in their itinerary. The first mention of them there is in 1570–1, when Ganassa and his company paid a short visit, succeeded in 1571 by the Gelosi. In 1577 the Gelosi, who had been summoned to Blois by Henri III during the assembly of Parliament there, again came to Paris, and probably had with them the famous Isabella and Francisco Andreini. Other companies followed, for long or short stays, playing either at the Hôtel de Bourgogne, or at the Petit-Bourbon, on payment of a levy to the Confraternity of the Passion, holders of the monopoly of acting in Paris. They were popular at Court, where Italian was in the ascendant, and also with the populace, whom they amused by their antics in spite of playing in a foreign tongue. It was on returning from a visit to Paris in 1604 that Isabella Andreini died at Lyons in childbirth. Many years later her son, Giovanni Battista, known as Lelio, was leader of the Fedeli when at the invitation of Louis XIII they also went to Paris and made a long stay. In the company at that time were Tristano Martinelli, known as Arlequin, and Niccolò Barbieri, known as Beltrame, both popular with Parisian audiences.

The Italian actors first became prominent in French dramatic history when in 1658 Molière obtained permission to settle in Paris, and was allowed to share the Petit-Bourbon with an Italian company already settled there, paying them a yearly rental for the theatre, which he used on Mondays, Wednesdays, Thursdays, and Saturdays, while the Italians kept their usual days, Tuesdays and Sundays. Little is known of Molière's relations with the Italians, whose famous leader was the famous Tiberio Fiorillo (or Fiorilli), better known as Scaramouche, but they were evidently cordial. It is unlikely, however, that Molière profited, as has been said, from watching the Italians, since he was already an experienced actor when he came to Paris; any profit he may have gained from contact with Italian acting, and such influence as his plays show of *commedia dell'arte* scenarii and methods, must date from the earlier years of touring, when he would no doubt have had many opportunities of seeing the various *commedia dell'arte* companies that regularly visited the larger provincial cities.

In 1660, after the destruction of the Petit-Bourbon, the Italians, who had been away from Paris, returned and found themselves obliged to pay rent to Molière for a part-share in his theatre, the Palais-Royal. Here they remained until the foundation of the Comédie-Française in 1680, when they were allowed sole possession of the now-vacated Hôtel de Bourgogne, playing there every day except Friday. In the company, besides Scaramouche, now an old man but still incredibly active, were Domenico Biancolelli, known as Dominique, and, like Scaramouche, a naturalized Frenchman, and his two daughters, together with Romagnesi, and Angelo Constantini, known as Mezzetin.

The Comédie-Italienne, as it was now known,

to distinguish it from the Comédie-Française, had for some years before 1680 begun to interlard its Italian with French songs and phrases, and even whole scenes. This innovation was opposed by the French actors, but Dominique, who was popular with Louis XIV, persuaded him to allow the Italians a modicum of French in their performances. This soon led to the acting of some plays entirely in French, and contemporary dramatists, led by Fatouville, Dufresny, Regnard, and Palaprat, were not slow to take advantage of this new market for their wares. The acting, however, continued to be purely that of the *commedia dell'arte*, and even in French plays the actors figured under their own names and were allowed ample scope for improvisation. They fell victims ultimately to their high spirits, and after having been warned several times for transgressing, they were expelled from France in 1697 because, it is said, they offended Mme de Maintenon by playing *La Fausse prude*, which the audience took the greatest delight in applying to her.

While Louis XIV lived the Italians stayed away from Paris, but in 1716 they returned under the leadership of the elder Riccoboni. The Hôtel de Bourgogne was put in order, and the company set to work to regain their former status. They found, however, that the time for harlequinades was past, while Italian was definitely out of favour. Even the French plays of their earlier repertory seemed old-fashioned, and the company, afraid of being forced to leave Paris again, looked round for fresh material. They lighted on the first play of an elderly painter, Jacques Autreau. This was a comedy entitled *Le Port-à-l'Anglais*, with musical interludes by Joseph Mouret. It was an immediate success, and once more the Italians had a permanent place in French theatrical life. The younger dramatists were ready to write for them, and they gave, among other things, many of Marivaux's finest plays. It was, however, no longer, even remotely, *commedia dell'arte* that they played, but a mixture of foreign art and native material which produced a specialized type of play and player. Seeking to extend their popularity they leased in the summer of July 1721 a newly built theatre at the Foire St-Laurent, where they found the holiday crowd in the humour for them. Two years later, on the death of the Regent, they were given the title of *comédiens ordinaires du roi*, with a yearly grant from public funds, paid to-day to their successors, the Opéra-Comique. From this time they were Italian only in name, and shared the theatre-going public with the Comédie-Française. They produced an astonishing variety of shows, from true comedy to ballet-pantomime, last relic of the harlequinade, and the newly fashionable vaudevilles. Gradually French actors joined the company and ousted the Italians, of whom the last—and incidentally the last Arlequin—was Carlin Bertinazzi, whom Garrick considered one of the best actors in Paris. The arrival in 1752 of an Italian opera buffa company (see OPERA, 5), and its success, together with that of its

imitators, the Opéra-Comique de la Foire under Monnet, led the Comédie-Italienne to venture into this new territory. This they did with such success that they were able to absorb their rivals, but at the expense of their former repertory and individuality. The rest of their history belongs to the domain of music. In April 1783 they left the Hôtel de Bourgogne and opened a fine new theatre on the Boulevard des Italiens, to which they gave its name. In 1789, soon after their change of policy, a danger threatened them in the success of the Théâtre de Monsieur (later, under the Revolution, the Théâtre Feydeau, while the Italians were known as the Théâtre Favart), which was being run by Viotti and Léonard, hairdresser to Marie-Antoinette. The intense rivalry between these two theatres produced many excellent works at both, but nearly ruined them. In 1801 they amalgamated as the Opéra-Comique, a name that was given to the new theatre, built in 1835 after the destruction of the older one by fire, and the Comédie-Italienne, which had held an important place in French theatre history, then ceased to exist in name as well as in fact.

COMÉDIENS ROUTIERS, see CHANCEREL.

COMEDY, a term which, in its modern use, covers a wide variety of plays. These differ from tragedy in that they have a happy ending, and from farce in that they contain some subtlety and character-drawing. The word, of Greek origin (see GREECE, 2), was applied to the satiric plays of Aristophanes and to the works of Terence and Plautus (see FABULA and ROME, *passim*), but by medieval times had lost its connexion with drama, and merely indicated any tale with a happy ending, particularly one written in a colloquial style and dealing with the love-affairs of lesser folk. The Renaissance brought back the term to the theatre, but without its former satiric connotation; it also lost in course of time its connexion with 'comic' and 'comedian', terms now reserved for low humour, though on the continent the latter term in the generic sense of actor was used later than in England, where from the eighteenth century onwards it was applied to players of farcical parts, as in the stock companies.

It has been said that comedy is, by its very nature, incapable of translation. Its appeal depends, far more than with tragedy, on local and topical interest, and on its preoccupation with the immediate concerns of its audience. Thus the greater its appeal to its contemporaries the less its impact on future ages, and the history of the theatre shows innumerable instances of comedies enormously successful in their own day and soon forgotten. This handicap is, of course, subject to the overriding force of genius, and the comedies of Aristophanes, Shakespeare, and Molière can still be enjoyed, though they demand from the audience a certain amount of co-operation in recapturing the spirit of their time, and in translation suffer a loss which it is impossible to assess.

Students of dramatic literature group comedies under various headings, as Comedy of Character, of Humours, of Intrigue, of Manners, and of Morals. The Comedy of Humours is possibly the one most congenial to the English temperament, and might, in the hands of Ben Jonson and of Fletcher, have developed a truly native English comedy, had it not been deflected by the Commonwealth and Restoration. The Comedy of Intrigue, which subordinates character to plot, originated in Spain, and was practised in England by Mrs. Aphra Behn. With it may be classed Romantic Comedy, which also came from Spain and reached its highest point in France during the Romantic Revival. It is marked by exaggeration and violence, and by an overpowering use of local colour, costume, and scenery. In the hands of a great poet it may give an illusion of greatness, but easily degenerates into melodrama. The Comedy of Manners originated in France with Molière's *Les Précieuses ridicules* (1658), and Molière himself defined it when he said 'correction of social absurdities must at all times be the matter of true comedy'. Pushing it to its logical extreme, he adventured into the Comedy of Morals—the correction of abuse by the lash of ridicule—of which the greatest exemplar is *Tartuffe*, a play which could not be written or understood outside its own country. The Comedy of Manners, however, proved fertile in Restoration England, and gave us the plays of Congreve. This artificial comedy, or Old Comedy, as it was later called, was at its best delicate and disarming, at its worst equivocal and indecent, but always witty and intellectually remote from reality. It has been called 'the sublimation of the trivial', and after seeming to vanish from the English stage with the death of Farquhar in 1707, it revived under Sheridan with much wit and less indelicacy. But even Sheridan tended to be influenced by the prevalence of Sentimental Comedy, a type of pathetic play which reflected the false sensibility of the rising eighteenth-century middle class. In France this led to the *comédie larmoyante*, which reached its height in the plays of Nivelle de la Chaussée, and, after blurring the distinction between tragedy and comedy and ousting them from the stage, was in its turn eclipsed by the *drame bourgeois*.

Modern comedy turns mainly upon the trivial complications of sex, and has lost both its robust humour and its wit. The last true English comedy was *The Importance of Being Earnest*. Some of the best elements of comedy have, however, been imported into the modern serious play, which deals lightly and yet persuasively with social problems of the day. The playing of old comedy makes heavy demands on the actor, who must be able, without affectation or pedantry, to suggest elegance, leisure, and a nimble wit. Its broader forms may demand great mobility of countenance and a command of dialect. In the nineteenth century the acting of comedy was regarded as a separate branch of the art, and comedian and tragedian rarely trespassed on each other's territory, but the distinction is now seldom maintained.

COMEDY, OLD, MIDDLE, AND NEW, see GREECE, 2 and OLD COMEDY.

COMEDY THEATRE. (1) LONDON. In Panton Street, Haymarket. It opened on 15 Oct. 1881, under the management of Alexander Henderson, with Audran's light opera 'La Mascotte', the cast including Lionel Brough and Violet Cameron. It was a great success, as were the productions which followed it. In 1884 Violet Melnotte, soon to build her own theatre, took over the management and produced, among other things, *The Silver Shield*, with Arthur Roberts and Kate Rorke, and a comic opera 'Erminie' with Marie Tempest in the title role. In 1887 Tree ventured into management for the first time at the Comedy, producing one of his greatest successes, *The Red Lamp*. He then went to the Haymarket, and from 1887 to 1892 Charles Hawtrey was at the Comedy. He was succeeded by Comyns Carr, under whose management Winifred Emery made a great success in *Sowing the Wind* (1893) with Cyril Maude and Brandon Thomas, as she did also in *The New Woman* (1894) and *The Benefit of the Doubt* (1895).

Ada Rehan made one of her last London appearances at the Comedy in 1896. Charles Hawtrey controlled it for some time, producing several of H. V. Esmond's plays, but it fell upon bad days, until on 28 Oct. 1902 Lewis Waller went there with a play which, intended as a mere stopgap, proved a big success— *Monsieur Beaucaire*. Arthur Chudleigh, who had been manager at the Court Theatre, ran the Comedy for many years. Gerald du Maurier made a hit there in 1906 with *Raffles*, in which he played the title role, and on 10 Oct. 1914 Alfred Butt presented Laurette Taylor in *Peg o' My Heart*. This had a long run and was then transferred to the Globe. From 1914 to 1918 Charlot produced revue at the Comedy, and afterwards Norman McKinnel had a short managerial season there. Among the successful plays of recent years was *Busman's Honeymoon*, produced in 1936. The theatre was one of the last in London to keep its old-time green baize act-drop. W. M. P.

(2) NEW YORK, on West 41st Street, between Sixth Avenue and Broadway. Built by the Shuberts as a small, intimate playhouse, it opened on 9 Sept. 1909. It was leased to the comedian William Collier for three years, and later saw the first production in New York of *Fanny's First Play*, produced by Granville-Barker, fresh from his guest directorship at Yale's Department of Drama. It was at this theatre that the Washington Square Players, forerunners of the present Theatre Guild, made in 1917 some of their early appearances, and in the same year Ruth Draper first appeared there in her one-woman show. She returned in 1928 and 1929, creating a record of five months' solo playing. An exciting moment in the history of the Comedy was the brief but stimulating management of Orson Welles in 1937, when as the Mercury the theatre saw

the modern-dress production of *Julius Caesar*, a revival of *The Shoemaker's Holiday*, and an interesting production of *Heartbreak House*. In Sept. 1939 the theatre was taken over by the Artef Players for the production of Yiddish dramas, but reverted to its original name on their departure. It was demolished in 1942.

G. F.

COMELLA, LUCIANO FRANCISCO (1716–79), Spanish dramatist, extremely prolific and very successful in his own day, whose works are now forgotten. Most of his plays, which numbered over a hundred, were based on contemporary history, falsified to satisfy popular taste, often to the extent of being unrecognizable, and were heavily over-weighted with romanticism. His plots were skilfully woven, and his dialogue good, but his characters lacked reality and his style was deplorable. His popularity was killed by the younger Moratín, who satirized him in his first play, and rendered his extravagances ridiculous.

COMIC OPERA, see OPERA, 5.

COMMEDIA DELL'ARTE, thenameusually given to the Italian popular improvised comedy which flourished from the sixteenth to the early eighteenth centuries. Its history is somewhat obscure, and must be pieced together from fragments, but its influence was felt all over Europe, and penetrated even to England, where its ebbing tide left behind the harlequinade of the Christmas pantomime, and the perambulating Punch and Judy show. Other names for this particular style of acting are *a soggetto*, since it was acted in accordance with a *scenario* or pre-arranged synopsis; *all'improvviso*, since the actors made up some at least of their speeches as they went along; *dei zanni*, from the comic servants who later gave us Harlequin and Punch; *dei maschere*, since most of the actors wore masks; and *all'italiana*, since its home was Italy. *Dell'arte*, the only phrase to survive in general use, is hard to translate exactly, but means substantially 'of the profession', since its actors were trained professionals (see ITALY, 2 for a detailed account of the *commedia dell'arte*).

The *commedia dell'arte* had a great influence in France, and the company which settled in Paris produced what was virtually a separate genre, the *comédie-italienne*. Through successive French playwrights, particularly Molière and Marivaux, many of the features of the *commedia dell'arte* became naturalized and passed into French literary drama (see COMÉDIE-ITALIENNE, FRANCE, MARIVAUX, and MOLIÈRE).

To distinguish it from the improvised comedy, the written drama of this period in Italy was known as the *commedia erudita*.

COMMONWEALTH, see THEATRICAL COMMONWEALTH.

COMMONWEALTH THEATRE, NEW YORK, see ANTHONY STREET THEATRE.

COMMUNITY THEATRE, U.S.A., see NATIONWIDE THEATRE.

COMPAGNIE DES QUINZE, see COPEAU, OBEY, and SAINT-DENIS.

COMPAGNONS DE JEUX, DE NOTRE-DAME, see GHÉON.

COMPTON, a family of English actors, allied with the Batemans, which has given many notable players to the English and American stages. The family name was originally Mackenzie, but when Charles, son of a Scottish minister, decided to go on the stage, he took his grandmother's maiden name, and it was as (1) HENRY COMPTON (1805–77) that he embarked on his new profession. He married an actress and had seven children, all connected with the theatre, his daughter Katharine being the wife of the dramatist R. C. Carton. His memoirs were published in 1879 by two of his sons, of whom (2) EDWARD (1854–1918) was an elegant and subtle actor whose talents received insufficient recognition. He was the moving spirit of the Compton Comedy Company, which from 1881 until his death toured the provinces, and sometimes appeared in London, in a repertory of Foote, Sheridan, Goldsmith, and other standard comedies. He married in 1882 (3) VIRGINIA FRANCES BATEMAN (1853–1940), who made her first appearance on the stage at the age of 12, and later, as Virginia Francis, was seen at the Lyceum under her parents' management, with her sisters Kate and Isabel, and young Henry Irving. She was her husband's leading lady in the Compton Comedy Company, and continued to manage it after his death. She was the mother of the novelist Compton Mackenzie, and had four other children on the stage, of whom (4) FAY (1895–) had a distinguished career, making her début in 'The Follies' of her first husband, H. G. Pélissier. Among her later successes have been the name-part in Barrie's *Mary Rose* (1920), Phoebe Throssel in *Quality Street* (1921), The Lady in *The Man with a Load of Mischief* (1925), Fanny Grey in *Autumn Crocus* (1931), Dorothy Hilton in *Call It a Day* (1935), and Martha Dacre in *No Medals* (1944). She was Ophelia to the Hamlet of John Barrymore and of John Gielgud, has played a number of Shakespearian parts at the Open-Air Theatre, and has appeared in pantomime and variety. In 1926 she published a volume of reminiscences, *Rosemary*. She was at one time the wife of Leon Quartermaine.

CONCERT THEATRE, NEW YORK, at 202 West 58th Street. This was originally the John Golden—the first to bear that name. Seating 900 people, it opened on 1 Nov. 1926, and shortly afterwards was taken over by the Theatre Guild, who staged there two plays by Sidney Howard, *Ned McCobb's Daughter* and *The Silver Cord*. In 1927 they were also responsible for the production of O'Neill's *Strange Interlude*, directed by Philip Moeller. Lynn Fontanne played Nina Leeds and the décor was designed by Jo Mielziner. The play reached 426 performances, and was the Theatre Guild's greatest success up to that time. After a short period as the 58th Street Theatre in 1935–6, the Concert Theatre, as the Film-arte, became the home of foreign films, making a brief return to live entertainment in 1942 with intimate revue, for which it is eminently suitable.   G. F.

CONDELL, HENRY (?–1627), Elizabethan actor, first mentioned in 1598 as playing in *Every Man in His Humour*. His only other known role was the Cardinal in *The Duchess of Malfi*, but he is believed to have played in Shakespeare's plays, in such parts as Horatio in *Hamlet*. He was one of the original sharers in the Blackfriars theatre in 1608, and by 1612 had acquired, with his fellow actor Heminge, a large part of the Globe shares. These two men are noted in the list of players who were granted a licence by Charles I in 1625, and to them we owe the printing of Shakespeare's complete works, since the author made no provision for it himself, and the quarto copies of single plays were more often than not incomplete and badly mutilated. The complete collection of 36 plays was published in 1623, price twenty shillings. Although there is no record of how many copies were first printed, a second edition was not called for until 1636, by which time both editors were dead. Though Condell was not an outstanding actor—he left the stage to devote himself to business matters in about 1616—it has been surmised that he was a well-known and respected figure of Jacobean theatre society. (See also HEMINGE.)

CONFIDENTI, THE. There were two *commedia dell'arte* troupes of this name. The first seems to have been associated in some way with the Uniti, and the same actors are frequently found in both. The first definite mention of the Confidenti, who may have been in existence then for some years, is found in 1574. Some years later Vittoria Piissimi and Pellesini (Pedrolino) (who may have been husband and wife) became the leaders of the Confidenti, whose wanderings took them all over Italy, and into France, and Spain. Towards the end of the century little is heard of them, though some of the Gelosi actors may have joined them on the death of Isabella Andreini. The second Confidenti troupe, which emerges about 1610, had Flaminio Scala (Flavio) at its head, more as business manager and author than as actor. In the company were Domenico Bruni (Fulvio), Marc'Antonio Romagnesi (Pantalone), Niccolò Barbieri (Beltrame), and two actresses whose rivalry caused a lot of trouble, Lavinia and Valeria. It seems likely that the Confidenti travelled chiefly in Italy, and after the break-up of the company about 1621 a number of the actors are found with the younger Andreini in Paris.

CONFRATERNITY OF THE PASSION (Confrérie de la Passion), an association of the burghers of Paris, formed in 1402 for the performance of religious plays. Their first permanent theatre was in the disused hall of the Guest-House of the Trinity outside the walls of Paris, in the direction of the Porte Saint-Denis. In 1518 they were confirmed in their privileges, and given a monopoly of acting in Paris which later proved a serious hindrance to the establishment of a permanent professional theatre there. When the Confraternity, who had abused their position by an increasing licence in the matter of farce and innuendo, were driven from their first home, they built themselves a theatre in the ruins of the Palace of the Dukes of Burgundy, ornamenting its doors with the emblems of the Passion (see HÔTEL DE BOURGOGNE). No sooner was it ready for their occupation in 1548 than they were forbidden to act religious plays, though still retaining their monopoly. Thus deprived of the major part of their repertory, they gave up acting, and from about 1570 onwards leased their theatre to travelling and foreign companies, always retaining, however, a couple of boxes and the right of free entry. The Confraternity kept a jealous eye on any company that tried to establish itself in Paris, and usually succeeded in having it sent away. When the pressure of circumstances grew too strong for them, and the actors of the Hôtel de Bourgogne became their permanent tenants, they still insisted on the payment of a levy for every performance, and were constantly engaged in recriminations and lawsuits with outside companies, as well as with their own tenants. The first breach in their privileges was made when in 1595 the fairs of St. Germain and St. Laurent were thrown open to provincial actors, but the monopoly lingered on until 1675, after the death of Molière and only a few years before the foundation of the present Comédie-Française.

CONGREVE, WILLIAM (1670–1729), the greatest English writer of the Restoration comedy of manners. He was educated in Ireland, first at Kilkenny, where Swift was his schoolfellow, later at Trinity College, Dublin, where he frequented the theatre in Smock Alley more than the lecture-halls. In 1689 he went to England, and spent a couple of years in the country, writing his first play, *The Old Bachelor*. This, revised by Southerne and Dryden, was produced at Drury Lane in March 1693, with a fine cast headed by Betterton and Mrs. Bracegirdle. The play, which gave a sharper edge of wit to the theatrical conventions of the time, was well received, and was followed by *The Double-Dealer*, given in 1694 by the same company. This was less successful, perhaps because of the intricacies of the plot, but the commendation of Queen Mary improved its reception. The following year saw Betterton's secession from Drury Lane and his reopening of the old theatre in Lincoln's Inn Fields with *Love for Love*, with himself as Valentine and Mrs. Bracegirdle as Angelica. This was Congreve's most successful play. It contains some of his best writing, and calls for a high degree of skill in the acting. It continued to hold the stage, and still does. On the tide of good fortune Congreve made his one essay in tragedy, *The Mourning Bride* (1697). It was a success with the public and the actors,—the part of Almeria, first played by Bracegirdle, was long a favourite with tragedy queens—but not with the critics. Congreve now became entangled, not very successfully, in controversy with Jeremy Collier. This, or some caprice on the part of the public, caused his best and last, play, *The Way of the World* (Lincoln's Inn, 1700), to be coldly received. Pique, laziness, or ill health, or a combination of all three, drove Congreve from the theatre, and, except for some words for a masque and a translation of Molière in collaboration with Vanbrugh, he wrote no more. In 1707 he was for a short period manager of the Haymarket Theatre, again with Vanbrugh, opening with an opera in deference to the public demand for this 'prevailing Novelty'. The last years of his life were clouded by ill health and failing sight. He died of injuries received when his coach overturned on the way to Bath, and was buried in Westminster Abbey.

CONNAUGHT THEATRE, LONDON, opened as the Amphitheatre, Holborn, in 1868. It became a playhouse in 1874, under John Hollingshead, at cheap prices. He mixed his attractions in a curious manner, staging pantomime with *The Maid's Tragedy*, and companies of straight actors with some of his burlesque artists from the Gaiety. George Rignold produced a version of *Adam Bede*, and the career of the theatre, which had meanwhile been known as the Alcazar, and the Theatre Royal, Holborn (alternatively the New Royal Theatre, Holborn), ended in 1888.

CONNELLY, MARC(US) COOK, see KAUFMAN and U.S.A., 1. 8.

CONQUEST, a family of English actors and pantomimists, the first of whom, (1) BENJAMIN OLIVER (1805–72), adopted the name Conquest when he first went on the stage. He was for some time manager of the Garrick Theatre in Leman Street, which he rebuilt after a fire in 1846. He married a member of the Lupino family who was a dancer, by whom he had six daughters. They were all on the stage and one, Clara (1825–88), married the actor Charles Dillon. Ben's only son, (2) GEORGE AUGUSTUS (1837–1901), was also on the stage as a child, but was later sent to France to be educated and was at the same school as the famous French actor Coquelin. George, who translated and adapted a number of French plays given under his father's management, was intended for the musical profession, but preferred to be an acrobat and pantomimist. He produced nearly 50 pantomimes and was a master of trickery, in one play alone using 30 traps. He is also credited with the invention of flying on invisible wires. Off-stage he had a slight impediment in his speech which disappeared when he was acting. He was good in melodramatic parts, and was an excellent animal impersonator. With his father he managed the

Grecian, and later took over the Surrey. He also made several visits to America, where on one occasion he was seriously injured by the intentional carelessness of the stage-hands during one of his tricks. His three sons followed in his steps, one of them taking over the Surrey, while another became manager of the Britannia, and the third went to Drury Lane in pantomime. His six daughters were also on the stage, appearing mainly at the Surrey under the management of their father and brother.

CONTAMINATION is a term used nowadays to denote the combining of two original works so as to make one borrowed work, and it is generally supposed that both this sense of the word and the practice it denotes are Roman. *Contaminare* properly means 'to stain', 'to spoil'. Terence was accused of 'spoiling' his Greek originals by departing from them in translation. His reply was that his predecessors in Latin drama had themselves departed from their originals (owing to carelessness), and that all that he had done was to insert a few passages from a second Greek work. In this reply Terence is trying to disguise the difference between the liberties taken by earlier Roman dramatists and his own deliberate attempts to improve on his Greek originals. Misled by Terence, Donatus, in his commentary, actually gives 'to combine' as one sense of *contaminare*.

W. B.

CONTAT, LOUISE (1760–1813), French actress, who first appeared at the Comédie-Française in 1776. She was not at first considered remarkable, and in tragedy was, like her friend and tutor Préville, distinguished but cold. Her real bent was for comedy, at that time in the capable hands of Mlle Dangeville. Beaumarchais, however, gave her the role of Suzanne in *Le Mariage de Figaro*, which set the seal on her growing reputation, and she continued to play coquettes with intelligence and grace, particularly in the plays of Marivaux when they eventually reached the stage of the Comédie-Française. She retired at the age of 50, much regretted by her companions and by the public, having for some years previously given up youthful parts in favour of elderly matrons owing to her increasing size. During the Revolution she narrowly escaped being guillotined, the pretext for her arrest being a phrase in a letter she had written to Marie-Antoinette in 1789. Having, to please the Queen, learnt a long part in twenty-four hours, she says, in mentioning this fact: 'J'ignorais où était le siège de la mémoire; je sais à présent qu'il est dans le cœur.' She was the daughter of a linen-draper who served the actresses of the Comédie-Française, and had many opportunities in her youth of watching them from the wings. Her younger sister was also an actress, making her first appearance as Franchette in *Le Mariage de Figaro* at the age of 13.

CONTI, ITALIA (1874–1946), English actress, founder and head of the school for training stage children which bore her name. She made her first appearance on the stage in 1891 at the Lyceum, and was later with Benson, playing small parts in Shakespearian repertory, and gaining useful experience. After a long tour of Australia with the Robert Brough Company, she returned to London and was seen in a variety of parts, which included Mirra in *Paolo and Francesca*, Rosalind in *As You Like It*, Marie Gaubert in *Maternité*, and Tulpe in *Hannele*. It was, however, her engagement by Charles Hawtrey in 1911 for the training of the children in *Where the Rainbow Ends* that decided her future vocation, and although she was later seen intermittently on the stage, she devoted most of her energies to the work of her theatre school, from which came a succession of notable theatre personalities, including Noel Coward, Gertrude Lawrence, June, and Anton Dolin, as well as several film stars.

CONTROL, see LIGHTING, 2 *j*.

CONWAY [RUGG]. (1) WILLIAM AUGUSTUS 1789–1828), English actor, known as 'Handsome' Conway, from his exceptional good looks and fine carriage. He was first seen on the stage in Dublin in 1812, and later went to England. He was¡ a good actor, but morbidly sensitive, and is said to have thrown up his part in London because of adverse criticism. In 1824 he went to New York and appeared at the Park Theatre as Hamlet, Coriolanus, Romeo, and Othello with great success. He also played Edgar to the Lear of Cooper, then at the height of his fame, Faulconbridge to his King John, and Joseph Surface to his Charles. An actor of the Kemble school, Conway seemed on the threshold of a brilliant career; but his morbidity increasing, he threw himself overboard on the way to Charleston and was drowned. His son (2) FREDERICK BARTLETT (1819–74) was also an actor, who with his wife (3) SARAH CROCKER (1834–75), the sister of Mrs. Bowers, was important in the development of the theatre in Brooklyn, since in 1864 they took over the Park, the first theatre erected there, and in 1871 opened the larger Brooklyn Theatre. Here, with a good stock company and frequent visits from stars, they provided excellent entertainment until they died within a year of each other. Their daughter (4) MINNIE (MARIANNE) (1854–96) made her first appearance on the stage under their management in 1869 (see TEARLE).

COOK, EDWARD DUTTON (1829–83), English dramatic critic, who was on the *Pall Mall Gazette* from 1867 to 1875 and the *World* from 1875 to 1883. His writings on the theatre include *A Book of the Play* (1876), *Hours with the Players* (2 vols., 1881), *Nights at the Play* and *On the Stage* (both 2 vols. 1883). He also contributed articles on actors and dramatists to the Dictionary of National Biography, and with Leopold Lewis was the author of a play entitled *The Dove and the Serpent*, which was produced at the City of London Theatre in 1859.

Nights at the Play contains many of Cook's notices of the early London appearances of Irving and Ellen Terry. Of Irving's first Hamlet he wrote: 'Mr. Irving's Hamlet is the conscientious effort of an intelligent and experienced player, and presents just claims to respectful consideration and a fair measure of approval . . . his voice seems somewhat artificially treble in quality and to be jerked out with effort: his movements are angular, and his bearing is deficient in dignity and courtliness, though not without a certain refinement of its own.'   T. C. K.

COOKE, GEORGE FREDERICK (1756–1812), an eccentric and unstable English actor, who made his first appearance at Brentford in 1776, and then, except for a fleeting engagement at the Haymarket two years later, spent twenty years as a strolling player in the provinces. In 1786 he found himself playing opposite Mrs. Siddons, and later he was with John Philip Kemble in Dublin. He had already contracted the habit of intemperance which was to be his ruin when, on 31 Oct. 1800, he appeared at Covent Garden as Richard III. He was immediately successful, and it is said that after this Kemble never appeared in the part again, for fear of invidious comparisons. Cooke remained at Covent Garden for ten years, playing a wide range of parts, and constantly in trouble with the management, who never knew whether he would arrive in time, or be sober enough to go on the stage. When he played, he played well, but he was undisciplined and dissipated, usually in debt and often in prison. He seemed to play better when drunk, and was probably somewhat insane with constant inebriation. In 1810 he went to New York, appearing at the Park Theatre before a crowded and enthusiastic audience who, however, fell away during his second season when he proved himself as undependable as in England. Under the management of Dunlap he toured America, but he was already a dying man, and but for his good constitution would not have lasted so long. He was buried in New York, where Edmund Kean, who though his rival had a high opinion of his capabilities, erected a monument to his memory. Cooke was a powerful but coarse actor, at his best in villainous parts—Richard III, Iago, Stukely, the hypocritical Sir Archy MacSarcasm, or the impudent Sir Pertinax MacSycophant, in which he was considered the equal of the original interpreter, Macklin. He had a strongly marked face, with long and somewhat hooked nose, an uncommon breadth between the eyes, which were fiery, dark, and tremendously expressive, a lofty forehead, and a powerful voice of great depth and compass. He had no grace or nobility, but was unequalled at expressing the worst passions of mankind. Careless in studying his parts, he picked them up quickly, and played them intuitively. He had great gifts, and an earlier success in London might have given him the opportunity of conquering his bad habits and developing his genius to the full.

COOKE, JOHN ESTEN (1830–86), American writer, whose novel, *The Virginian Comedians* (1854), is based on the adventures of the first professional actors to appear in the New World (see HALLAM), with Beatrice Hallam as its heroine.

COOKE, THOMAS POTTER (1786–1864), an English actor who in his youth was in the Navy. He played in the provinces, and was engaged by Elliston for the Surrey, where in 1829 he appeared as William in the 400 consecutive performances of *Black-Eyed Susan*, the part with which his name is always associated. As William, and as Harry Halyard in *Poll and My Partner Joe* (1857), he frequently figures in the theatrical portraits and tinsel pictures of the time. He acted in many of the minor theatres of London and in both Patent Theatres. A man of strong physique and great energy, he was at his best in such parts as Ruthven in *The Vampire* (1820), his first outstanding success, and the Monster in *Frankenstein* (1823). It was in this latter play that little Louisa Lane, later the famous American actress, Mrs. John Drew, appeared with Cooke on tour, playing Frankenstein's young brother. Cooke, whose nickname was 'Tippy', made his last appearance at Covent Garden in 1860.

COOKMAN, ALBERT VICTOR (1894–), English dramatic critic, on the staff of *The Times*. He began his career as journalist with the *Salisbury and Winchester Journal*. In 1919 he joined the staff of the *Manchester Guardian* as a reporter. In 1925 he became a member of the staff of *The Times*, and in 1928 was appointed assistant dramatic critic to Charles Morgan, whom he succeeded as dramatic critic in 1939. He also writes theatre criticisms for the *Tatler* as 'Anthony Cookman'. His criticisms in *The Times* have the literary quality that we have come to expect of the distinguished succession of critics that has served this great newspaper.   T. C. K.

COON, see NIGGER MINSTRELS.

COOPER, THOMAS ABTHORPE (1776–1849), an English actor, son of a surgeon, who made his début at Edinburgh in 1792, appearing in London three years later at Covent Garden, where he played Hamlet, Macbeth, and Lothario in *The Fair Penitent*. In 1796 he went with Wignell to Philadelphia, and spent the rest of his life in the United States, except for visits to Drury Lane in 1803 and 1827. He soon became a firm favourite with the American public, and, having quarrelled with Wignell, joined Dunlap's American Company, where he played a number of tragic parts. In 1806 Cooper, who had taken a lease of the Park Theatre, New York, on the bankruptcy of Dunlap, employed the latter as his assistant stage manager, and with Stephen Price as his partner toured the eastern circuit—New York, Philadelphia, and Charleston, S.C. He appeared in most of the big tragic roles of Shakespeare, his best part being Macbeth. He was also outstanding as Jaffier in *Venice*

Preserved, in which he made his New York début in 1797. A handsome man, with a fine voice and much eloquence and dignity, he unfortunately continued to act too long, and towards the end of his life his popularity declined. He holds an important place in the early history of the American theatre, and was one of the first outstanding English actors to become an American citizen.

COPEAU, JACQUES (1878–1949), French actor and producer, whose work had much influence in the European and American theatres. Although interested in the work of Antoine at the Théâtre Libre, Copeau was as antagonistic to the realist theatre as to the 'well-made' plays of Scribe's emulators, and in 1913, after being associated with André Gide in the foundation of *La Nouvelle Revue Française*, he opened his own theatre, the Vieux-Colombier, in an effort to bring back truth, beauty, and poetry to the French stage. Among his actors were Louis Jouvet and Charles Dullin, and later Valentine Tessier, while the main strength of his repertory lay in his productions of Molière and Shakespeare. The latter's *Twelfth Night* proved to be one of his greatest successes, but he was also instrumental in bringing before the public the work of a number of young dramatists. He instituted major reforms in scenic design, which he simplified to the point of symbolism, and in acting, training his company himself. Indeed, after his return from New York, where his troupe had been installed in the Garrick Theatre from 1917 to 1919 as part of France's propaganda programme, he tended to concentrate more and more on the training of his students, finally giving up the direction of the Vieux-Colombier and retiring to the country with a band of youngsters, later famous as the Compagnie des Quinze. In 1936 Copeau, whose work was at last beginning to bear fruit, was appointed one of the producers at the Comédie-Française, retiring in 1941. Copeau wrote a number of articles and books on the theatre, translated some of Shakespeare's plays, and published an annotated edition of the plays of Molière. His Vieux-Colombier is now a theatre for young children.

COPYRIGHT IN A DRAMATIC WORK.
1. GREAT BRITAIN. Medieval law recognized virtually no distinction between a literary work and the material upon which it was written. The underlying Common Law principle that a man should be allowed undisturbed enjoyment of his property applied equally to both. When the invention of printing, however, made it possible for a literary work to be appropriated without theft of the manuscript, a revolution in the practical and legal aspect of the position began which, accelerated as each new method of reproduction came into being, led finally to the abstract legal conception, now known as 'copyright'. To-day the manuscript of an author's work is but the outward symbol of a network of rights and interests—rights of publication in any form in any language; stage, film, broadcasting, and television rights

—which time and the law have brought into being.

The law always lags a little behind events, and the branch of the law governing the protection of literary property is no exception. The first Act to concern itself with copyright in the modern sense was passed in the reign of Queen Anne. For two centuries previously there had been legislation governing the publication of literary works, but its primary purpose was to enforce State control over freedom of expression. From 1556, with short intermissions, until 1694, no book might be published without a licence from the Stationers' Company. As entry on the register of the Company of the work to be published was necessary as an indication of ownership, the public was, it is true, gradually familiarized with the idea of ownership of a literary work as distinct from ownership of the manuscript, but as such entries could be made only in the name of a member of the Company, which consisted exclusively of printers and publishers, the author himself was not directly protected.

However, it was in the general interest of authors to see that there was some more effective safeguard against piracy than their cumbersome and ill-defined Common Law property right, so that, when the Licensing Act of 1662, which had been revived in 1685 and continued in 1693, expired in 1694, authors joined with booksellers and publishers in an agitation for statutory protection against printers who were 'stealing' their 'copies'. The result of their efforts was a bill 'for the Encouragement of Learning, by vesting the Copies of printed Books in the Authors or Purchasers of such Copies during the Time therein mentioned', drafted, it is said, in its original form by Dean Swift, which took its place on the Statute Book in 1709 as 8 Anne, c. 19.

Under this Act the authors of books already printed who had not transferred their rights, and booksellers or other persons who had acquired copies of books with a view to reprinting them, were given the sole right of printing those books for a period of twenty-one years from 10 April 1710; in the case of books not already printed the right endured for only fourteen years, but was extended for a further fourteen years if the author were living at the end of the first period. The title of every book printed had still to be registered at Stationers' Hall, but registration could now be taken out in the author's name. Copies had also to be deposited at certain libraries, and a fine and forfeiture of the infringing copies were the penalties provided for a breach of the Act.

As soon as the twenty-one year period granted under the Act expired disputes arose as to whether an author's proprietary right at Common Law was extinguished with the statutory right acquired under the Act, and for the next forty years there followed a series of lawsuits on this point, culminating with the case of *Donaldson* v. *Becket* (1774), 4 Burr 2408, in which the House of Lords decided

by a bare majority that so far as published works were concerned the Common Law right had been destroyed by the Act of Anne, the Common Law right in the case of unpublished works being unaffected.

In 1810 the civil remedy of damages was made available in cases of infringement and in 1814, by 54 Geo. 3, c. 156, the period of protection was extended to twenty-eight years from publication or the life of the author, whichever was the longer.

Thus by the beginning of the nineteenth century Parliament had recognized the right of the proprietor of a literary work, dramatic or non-dramatic, to prevent for a limited period any unauthorized person from making copies of it. As the performance of a dramatic work did not necessitate the making of a copy of it, there was no statutory protection as yet against an unauthorized stage production, and although the author of an unpublished play could theoretically at Common Law prevent its production without his consent, there does not seem to have been any case where this argument was used successfully.

In 1833, however, the position was regularized by the *Dramatic Copyright Act* of that year (3 & 4 Will. 4, c. 15), commonly known as *Bulwer Lytton's Act*, which gave to the author of 'any tragedy, comedy, play, opera, farce or other dramatic piece or entertainment' the sole liberty of representing it 'or causing it to be represented at any place or places of dramatic entertainment whatsoever' in Great Britain and the Dominions for twenty-eight years from publication, with a reversionary period to the author for the rest of his life.

In 1842 *The Literary Copyright Act* (5 & 6 Vict., c. 45) consolidated the law relating to the protection of literary, dramatic, and musical property and brought within the terms of a single statute the two rights so far recognized, 'copyright' or the right of 'multiplying' copies and 'performing right' or the right of representation.

It provided that copyright should endure for forty-two years from publication or for the life of the author and seven years, whichever was the longer, and laid down that 'the sole liberty of representing dramatic pieces' should last for a similar period. A 'dramatic piece' was now defined as 'every tragedy, comedy, play, opera, farce, or other scenic, musical or dramatic entertainment'.

Under Bulwer Lytton's Act an unauthorized presentation in order to constitute an infringement of copyright had to be given in a 'place of dramatic entertainment'; the Literary Copyright Act made no such condition, but in *Russell* v. *Smith* (1848), 12 Q.B. 217, it was held that a building 'when used for the public representation and performance of "a dramatic piece" for profit, became a place of dramatic entertainment'. The term of protection in the case of an unpublished play was still left open.

A play had to be registered before an action for infringement of copyright could be brought. No registration, however, was necessary as a condition precedent to an action for infringement of the performing right.

Although the Act was in general a great advance on earlier legislation, a number of flaws in its drafting soon came to light.

In the first place, 'the sole liberty of representing' a work attached only to 'dramatic pieces'. Unauthorized performances of dramatizations of non-dramatic works could therefore be given with impunity and were judicially sanctioned in such cases as *Reade* v. *Conquest* (1861), 9 C.B. (N.S.) 755, although the multiplication of copies of such dramatizations where passages were copied verbatim was held to amount to an infringement of copyright (*Warne & Co.* v. *Seebohm* (1886), 39 Ch.D. 73).

In *Reade* v. *Lacy* (1861), 1 J & H 524, it was decided that an author could protect himself against these unauthorized dramatic representations of his non-dramatic works by himself making dramatizations of them before they were published, and so acquiring the sole liberty of representation in them as 'dramatic pieces'. This practice was, therefore, followed by many authors as the only practical safeguard against such exploitation of their work.

Another cumbersome institution brought into being by ambiguous phrasing in the Act was the 'copyright performance'. It was generally believed, though the belief seems to have had no clear legal support, that if a play were published before it was performed, the performing right in it was irretrievably lost. Actors were therefore hired to give what amounted to public readings of manuscript plays. Normally no costumes were worn and no scenery used.

These and other inconsistencies and ambiguities in Statute and Common Law forced a Commission, appointed to investigate the position, to report in 1878 that 'the law is wholly destitute of any sort of arrangement, incomplete, often obscure and, even where it is intelligible upon long study, it is in many parts so ill-expressed that none who does not devote study to it can expect to understand it'.

It was not, however, until some thirty years later that any steps were taken to remedy the position.

In 1909 a Committee was appointed to recommend changes in the law to enable Great Britain to keep abreast of the trend of international opinion and legislation, and in particular to give effect to the Revised International Convention signed at Berlin in the previous year. Three years later a new Copyright Act was passed—the *Copyright Act 1911*—which incorporated in modified form the more important of the Committee's recommendations.

This Act, which repealed with one or two minor exceptions all previous legislation relating to copyright property, is the Statute upon which practically the whole of the copyright law of this country to-day depends. Perhaps the simplest way, therefore, of outlining the present position will be to refer the reader to those sections of the Act which lay down the fundamental principles of protection for a dramatic work.

For the first time the two separate rights, the right of multiplying copies and the right of representation, are merged in the general term 'copyright', which now includes in its meaning the right of reproduction by any means whatsoever. For the first time no formalities of any kind are necessary either to obtain copyright or as a condition precedent to the institution of proceedings.

Under Section 1 (1) of the Act 'copyright shall subsist throughout the parts of His Majesty's Dominions to which this Act extends . . . in every original . . . dramatic work' if (a) 'in the case of a published work, the work was first published within such parts of His Majesty's Dominions as aforesaid' and (b) 'in the case of an unpublished work, the author was at the date of the making of the work a British subject or resident within such parts of His Majesty's Dominions as aforesaid'. Section 1 (2) goes on to define copyright as 'the sole right to produce or re-produce the work or any substantial part thereof in any material form whatsoever, to perform . . . the work or any substantial part thereof in public; if the work is unpublished to publish the work or any substantial part thereof'. Subsection (2) (b) and (c) lay down specifically that copyright includes the right 'in the case of a dramatic work, to convert it into a novel or other non-dramatic work' and 'in the case of a novel or other non-dramatic work to convert it into a dramatic work by way of performance in public or otherwise'.

As the gramophone and film were in their infancy at the time of the passing of the Act, a provision was inserted expressly stating that it is an infringement of copyright, in the case of *inter alia* a dramatic work, to make any record, perforated roll, cinematograph film, or other contrivance by means of which the work may be mechanically performed or delivered (Section 1, subsection 1 (d)).

Unfortunately Section 35 of the Act (the interpretation section) does not define the term 'original dramatic work'. Judges, however, have emphasized in a number of cases that this term must be given a much wider meaning than it has in everyday use. A work need show no originality of thought in the ordinary sense in order to be entitled to copyright protection. It is 'the product of the labour, skill and capital of one man which must not be appropriated by another'. Thus, for example, protection is given to a new edition or adaptation of a play which is itself out of copyright.

The first owner of the copyright in a dramatic work is normally the dramatist. Where, however, a work is composed in the course of the dramatist's employment by some other person that other person is, in the absence of any agreement to the contrary, the first owner of the copyright (Copyright Act 1911, Section 5 (1) (b)). The interpretation of this subsection was one of the points at issue in the case of *Massine* v. *de Basil*, Macg. C.C. (1938), 223, where Massine sued Col. de Basil for a declaration that he was the owner of the copyright by him to the choreographic work contributed by him to certain ballets.

The period for which copyright endures is governed by Section 3 of the Act. The general rule is that protection lasts for the life of the author and for fifty years from his death. Where there are joint authors the fifty-year period runs from the death of the author who dies first, but if at the end of that time the joint author is living the period is extended to last for his lifetime and ends simultaneously with his death (Copyright Act 1911, Section 16 (1)).

Where a work is not published or publicly performed during the author's life, the period of protection lasts until the date of first publication or public performance, whichever is the earlier, and fifty years thereafter (Copyright Act 1911, Section 17).

Under Section 3 of the Act, after the expiration of twenty-five years, or, in the case of a work in copyright at the date of passing of the Act, thirty years from the death of the author, any person may reproduce the work on giving notice to the copyright owner in the form prescribed by the Board of Trade and paying to him royalties on all copies sold at the rate of 10 per cent. of the published price of such copies. This 'statutory licence period' relates only to reproduction by publishing and has no application to reproduction by performance. It should be noted that under Section 4, if after the death of the author of a dramatic work, which has been published or performed in public, the owner of the copyright refuses to allow the republication or public performance of the work, with the result that it is withheld from the public, the Judicial Committee of the Privy Council has power to order the copyright owner to allow the work to be published or performed on such terms and conditions as the Judicial Committee may think fit. This power has, however, never been exercised.

Section 2 (1) of the Act deals with the ways in which copyright may be infringed. 'Copyright in a work,' it says, 'is deemed to be infringed by any person, who without the consent of the owner of the copyright does anything the sole right to do which is by this Act conferred on the owner of the copyright.'

It will be remembered that Section 1 (2) of the Act defines 'copyright' as including 'the sole right to perform the work or any substantial part thereof in public'. Regrettably neither the words 'substantial part' nor the words 'in public' are defined in the Act. On many occasions, therefore, the courts have been called in to interpret both of these terms. In cases of verbatim copying stress has been laid on the fact that quantity is not the sole criterion by which to judge whether a substantial part of a work has been copied. The quality and importance of the passage taken

must also be given consideration. For this reason, four lines from Kipling's thirty-two line poem *If* were held to amount to a substantial part of the poem in *Kipling* v. *Genatosan Ltd.*, Macg. C.C. (1920), 203, and in *Hawkes & Son Ltd.* v. *Paramount Film Services Ltd.*, Macg. C.C. (1933), 473, twenty-eight bars, the playing time of which was twenty seconds, were held to amount to a substantial part of a musical work the playing time of which in its entirety was four minutes.

Where there is no verbatim copying 'both the plot (including in that word the idea and the arrangement of the incidents) and the dialogue and working out of the play must be regarded in order to see whether one play is a reproduction of the other or a substantial part of it, and regard must also be had to the extent to which both plays include stock incidents' (*Rees* v. *Melville*, Macg. C.C. (1911–1916), 168). In this case it was decided that the basic idea of a young man marrying a beggar girl to comply with the terms of a will and acquire a fortune did not constitute a substantial part of a play.

It has been emphasized in many cases that, particularly in the field of melodrama, there are certain stock characters and stock situations the inclusion of which in two plays does not of itself give the author of the earlier play a good cause of action against the author of the later play, 'though the combination of these ordinary materials may nevertheless be original, and when such combination has arrived at a certain degree of complexity it becomes practically impossible that they should have been arrived at independently by a second individual' with the result that there is a presumption that there has been infringement.

As copyright is not a monopoly, proof that a later author had no knowledge of an earlier author's work and arrived at his results independently of it will be a good defence, however similar the two works may be.

The most recent cases in which the meaning of 'performance in public' came before the courts occurred in 1943, when it was held in *The Performing Right Society* v. *Gillette Industries Ltd.* and *Ernest Turner Electrical Instruments Ltd.* v. *The Performing Right Society Ltd.* (1943), Ch. 167, that the relaying of wireless programmes to workers in factories were performances in public. In these cases, and in previous cases where the same point was at issue, the courts made it clear that the question to be decided narrows down to an analysis of the nature of the audience before whom the performance is given. Whether performers are paid, whether admission is charged, and whether the hall in which the performance is given is part of a private house or is a public building are now held to be irrelevant except in so far as these facts are a guide to the nature of the audience. Lord Justice Romer in *Jennings* v. *Stevens* (1936), 1 Ch. 469, where a performance to a Women's Institute of Gertrude Jennings's play *The Rest Cure* was held to be a performance in public, said that the difference between a performance in public and a performance in private is that 'in the latter case the entertainment forms part of the domestic or home life of the person who provides it and none the less because of the presence of his guests. They are for the time being members of his home circle. In the former case, however, the entertainment is in no sense part of the domestic or home life of the members of the audience. It forms part of what may be called, in contradistinction, their non-domestic or outside life. . . . The home circle may, of course, in some cases be a large one. The section of the public may in some cases be a small one. But this can make no difference, though it may sometimes be difficult to decide whether a particular collection of persons can properly be regarded as constituting a domestic circle.'

In addition to the general liability for infringement by public performance, a special liability falls upon the person who lets for hire a place of entertainment. Section 2, subsection 3, of the Copyright Act 1911 provides that 'copyright in a work shall also be deemed to be infringed by any person who for his private profit permits a theatre or other place of entertainment to be used for the performance in public of the work without the consent of the owner of the copyright, unless he was not aware, and had no reasonable ground for suspecting that the performance would be an infringement of copyright.' There need be no express permission or authorization but a general authority to use a theatre for public performance is not sufficient. (*Performing Right Society* v. *Ciryl Syndicate* (1924), 1 K.B. 1.)

It should be briefly noted that 'the reading or recitation in public by one person of a reasonable extract from any published work' does not constitute an infringement of copyright (Copyright Act 1911, Section 2, subsection (1) (vi)).

Infringement of copyright is now primarily a civil offence for which the remedies are an injunction and damages. Proceedings must be instituted within three years of the date of the infringement (Copyright Act 1911, Section 10). In the case of infringement by performing each production constitutes a separate act of infringement so that the three-year period runs from the date of the latest performance. Criminal proceedings lie only if the infringer can be proved to have 'knowingly' made, distributed, or imported infringing copies or caused a work in which copyright exists to be publicly performed (Copyright Act 1911, Section 11).

2. THE UNITED STATES OF AMERICA. The Copyright Law of the United States of America is a direct legacy from Great Britain. The differences which to-day exist between the Copyright Laws of the two countries are largely due to the fact that American theory and practice in the copyright field have changed and developed in their essentials very much less than have our own during the two centuries

that have elapsed since America won her independence. The Copyright Act in force in 1783 was the Statute of 1710 and it is the characteristics of that Act—the formalities of registration and deposit of copies—which still underlie American Copyright Law today.

Shortly after the end of the American War of Independence twelve of the American states passed laws giving protection to their authors based on that afforded by the statute of Anne. These state laws gave no protection outside the boundaries of each state. In 1790, however, a clause in the United States Constitution empowering Congress 'to promote the progress of science and useful arts, by securing for limited times to authors and inventors the exclusive right to their respective writings and discoveries' was put into effect.

On 31 May 1790 the first United States Copyright Act was passed 'to encourage learning'. Its substance, no less than its preamble, followed very closely the Statute of Anne. Protection was given to the author of any 'book, map or chart' for fourteen years from registration in the Register Book of the local District Court renewable for a further fourteen-year period if the author were living at the end of the first period.

During the next sixty years the scope of the Copyright Act was enlarged to cover wider categories of literary and artistic material, but the general basis and period of protection remained the same, until in 1831 the first term was extended to twenty-eight years, renewable for a further fourteen years at the request of the author, his widow, or his children.

In *Wheaton* v. *Peters*, 8 U.S. 591 (1834), the American courts reached the same decision as that to which the British courts came in *Donaldson* v. *Becket*, namely that an author lost on publication whatever Common Law rights he had in his unpublished manuscript.

It was not until 1856 that dramatic compositions with the right of performance in public were brought under statutory protection (11 St. L. 138), and in 1870 registration formalities were transferred from the local district courts to the Library of Congress at Washington.

By the early years of the twentieth century the mass of piecemeal copyright legislation and case law had reached very much the same confused state as that obtaining in Great Britain in the latter part of the nineteenth century, and a report on the position was made by the first Register of Copyrights in 1903. This paved the way for the passage of the Copyright Act of 4 Mar. 1909—the statute which, with certain amendments, is the law in force to-day.

The principal improvements made by this Act were the extension of the term of copyright protection, a slight relaxation in the copyright formalities, and the expansion of copyright protection to 'all the writings of an author' (Copyright Act 1909, Section 4).

Under Section 1 of the Act of 1909, any

F

person entitled to copyright in a dramatic work has the exclusive right:

(a) To print, reprint, publish, copy, and vend the copyrighted work;

(b) ... to dramatize it if it be a nondramatic work; to convert it into a novel or other nondramatic work if it be a drama. . . .

(d) To perform or represent the copyrighted work publicly if it be a drama, or, if it be a dramatic work and not reproduced in copies for sale, to vend any manuscript or any record whatsoever thereof; to make or to procure the making of any transcription or record thereof by or from which, in whole or in part, it may in any manner or by any method be exhibited, performed, represented, produced, or reproduced; and to exhibit, perform, represent, produce, or reproduce it in any manner or by any method whatsoever.

The term of copyright protection under this Act endures for twenty-eight years from publication, plus a renewal period of twenty-eight years, bringing the total maximum of protection up to fifty-six years from publication (Copyright Act 1909, Sections 23 and 24).

Under the Act of 1909, as under all previous United States copyright legislation, it is necessary that all books and periodicals written in the English language and seeking protection in the U.S.A. should be completely manufactured in the United States. This provision of the Act does not, however, apply to dramatic or dramatico-musical compositions. These works, to obtain protection in the U.S.A., have, however, to comply with the other copyright formalities necessary. In the case of a published play the word 'Copyright' or the abbreviation 'Copr.' accompanied by the name of the copyright proprietor and the year of publication must appear on the title-page or the page immediately following (Copyright Act 1909, Section 18). Plays published in England may be registered by sending to the Register of Copyrights at Washington an application and at the election of the applicant either one copy of the play and four dollars or two copies and a catalogue card. This latter alternative is available only for six months after publication.

If the play is unpublished, a complete copy of the typescript has to be sent to Washington with a fee of four dollars and the appropriate registration form.

The time limit within which the formalities necessary to secure protection in the United States for works first published or produced in Great Britain must be complied with was extended by a Presidential proclamation of 10 March 1944 'until the day on which the President of the U.S.A. . . . shall . . . terminate . . . the present . . . proclamation.' The proclamation is still (1949) in force.

3. THE CONTINENT OF EUROPE. The development of legal protection for intellectual property on the Continent of Europe follows very closely in its general outline that of the development of British Copyright Law.

A number of countries were readier than was Great Britain to cast aside registration formalities and to provide for automatic copyright protection. No other European country has the anomalous 'statutory licence' period provided by Section 3 of the British Copyright Act of 1911, and every European country, with the exception of Bulgaria, Liechtenstein, Rumania, Sweden, Switzerland, Spain, and Portugal, grants protection for the author's life and fifty years after his death. The first four of these countries give protection for the author's life and only thirty years after his death. Spain protects the copyright works of its nationals for the author's life and eighty years after his death, and Portugal alone of all the countries in the world gives protection in perpetuity.

The International Convention of 1886, the Additional Act of 1896, the International Convention of 1908, the Protocol of 1914, and the International Conventions of 1928 and 1948 are largely responsible for assimilating the basic principles of copyright protection in all the European countries. The first of these conventions brought into being The International Copyright Union with nine original members. To-day the Union has over forty members and includes in its membership all the European countries, their colonies and mandated territories, and Great Britain and the British Empire. Although individual countries in joining the Union have made certain special reservations and stipulations, all adhere to the principle that a national of any member-country of the Union enjoys in every other country of the Union the rights and privileges of a national of that country.

The most prominent absentees from the Union are the United States of America and the U.S.S.R. Efforts have been made in the past to bring these two countries into the Union membership, and at the time of writing similar movements are again on foot. Whether they will meet with greater success than their predecessors remains to be seen.

M. E. B.

COQUELIN. (1) CONSTANT-BENOÎT (1841–1909), French actor, known as Coquelin aîné to distinguish him from his brother (see below, 3). A pupil of Régnier at the Conservatoire, he first appeared at the Comédie-Française in 1860, and remained there until 1886, when he left for a prolonged tour of Europe and America. After a further session at the Comédie-Française, he left it finally in 1892, went to the Renaissance, and later became director of the Théâtre de la Porte-Saint-Martin, where he first played the part always associated with his name, that of Cyrano de Bergerac in Rostand's play. His son (2) JEAN (1865–1944), also an actor, appeared in this play as Ragueneau, the pastrycook, having previously been with his father at the Comédie-Française, where he first appeared in 1890. In 1900 Coquelin aîné toured with Sarah Bernhardt, with whom he appeared at her own theatre in *L'Aiglon*,

Towards the end of his life he was much in London, where he was extremely popular; he founded a home for aged actors near Paris where he himself retired to die. A big man, with a mobile visage, piercing eyes, and an excellent voice, Coquelin aîné was outstanding in the great comic roles of Molière and other classics, and in modern parts of a romantic, flamboyant type. He was also the author of a number of books on the theatre, including *L'Art et le comédien* (1880) and *Les Comédiens par un comédien* (1882). His younger brother (3) ERNEST ALEXANDRE HONORÉ (1848–1909), known as Coquelin cadet, first appeared at the Comédie-Française in 1868, after a year at the Odéon, and remained there until his death. He was at his best in secondary comic parts, and in 1881 appeared with Gôt in a modernized version of the old farce of Pierre Pathelin with much success. He was the author of several amusing books, some of which he published under the pseudonym of Pirouette, and his monologues were also very popular. He died about a fortnight after his elder brother.

CORALLI, JEAN (1779–1854), the choreographer of 'Giselle' (1841) (see BALLET, 5).

CORCORAN, KATHARINE (1857–1943), see HERNE, JAMES A.

CORNEILLE. (1) PIERRE (1606–84), France's first great tragic dramatist. He wrote his first play, *Mélite*, a comedy, for a strolling company under Lenoir, with Montdory as its star, which was appearing in Rouen, Corneille's birthplace, in some of Alexandre Hardy's plays. In 1630 the company was in Paris, and *Mélite* was given in a converted tennis-court near the Porte-Saint-Martin. After a slow start it was a success, in spite of the fact that it contained none of the stock personages of farce, and that it violated the Unities, then coming into fashion under the influence of Jean Mairet.

Piqued by some of the criticisms levelled at *Mélite*, Corneille next wrote a tragi-comedy, *Clitandre* (1631), and it was said 'the critics were then ready to implore him to return to his earlier style'. This he did, and his next four plays were comedies—*La Veuve* (1631–2), *La Galerie du Palais* (1632), *La Suivante* (1633), and *La Place Royale* (1633). In 1635 came his first tragedy, *Médée*, written probably as a result of the success of Mairet's *Sophonisbe* at the Marais the previous year, followed by *L'Illusion comique* (1636), again a comedy. Meanwhile Corneille, who had settled in Paris, had been chosen by Richelieu as one of the five authors commissioned to write his plays for him, probably on account of his success as an author of comedies. But he was not temperamentally fitted for such servitude, and after incurring the wrath of Richelieu by altering some part of the plot allotted to him, Corneille retired again to Rouen. He had as yet done nothing to justify any extravagant hopes being placed on him, and ranked merely as one among

a number of good contemporary dramatists who were experimenting with new forms in French dramatic literature. Back in Rouen, however, Corneille dipped again into Spanish literature, with which he had already shown himself familiar in *L'Illusion comique*, and on *Las mocedades del Cid* by Guillen de Castro y Bellvis he based *Le Cid*, which has been described by George Saintsbury as 'perhaps the most epoch-making play in all literature'. Certainly it has become the custom to date the great age of French dramatic literature from its production in 1636 (though modern research indicates the first days of 1637 as a more likely date). Like its predecessors, this play was first given at the now flourishing Théâtre du Marais, with Montdory in the name part. It was an immediate success, and was translated into English by Joseph Rutter, tutor to the Duke of Dorset. The English version was played by Beeston's Boys in 1637. Madrid also saw and admired a translation, though Spaniards were amused at the scene being laid in Seville, which at the time of the play's action was in the hands of the Moors. According to Corneille's nephew, Fontenelle, Turkey was soon the only country to lack a translation of *Le Cid*, a want now supplied.

The success of *Le Cid* raised up a number of enemies for Corneille, chief among them Mairet and Scudéry, and a fierce pamphlet war raged round it, in which Richelieu played a part which later laid him open to a charge of jealousy. This was possibly a calumny, since two performances of the play were given in Richelieu's private theatre, later to be the stage of Molière. In any case the public, and Rotrou, to his credit, remained faithful to Corneille, and were ready to applaud his *Horace* (1640), *Cinna* (1641), and *Polyeucte* (1642). These were all given at the Marais, but with Floridor in the name-parts, since Montdory had retired from the stage in 1637, owing to ill health.

In 1643, which saw the production of another tragedy, *La Mort de Pompée*, Corneille produced his finest comedy, *Le Menteur*, based on Alarcón's *La verdad sospechosa*. Floridor played Dorante, with Jodelet as Cliton. It had a great success, which unfortunately was not repeated with its sequel in the following year, *La Suite du menteur*.

The place of production of Corneille's next group of plays—*Rodogune*, *Théodore* (both 1645), and *Héraclitus* (1646)—is uncertain, and depends on the date of Floridor's removal to the Hôtel de Bourgogne, which took place somewhere between 1643 and 1653. Corneille was now established as France's major dramatist, and in 1647 was elected a member of the French Academy. *Nicomède* (1651), one of his best and most popular plays, which Molière chose for his reappearance in Paris in 1658, was preceded by the rather weak *Don Sanche d'Aragon* (1649), and by *Andromède*, a spectacle-opera written at the request of Mazarin to show off the machinery of Torelli. This was produced by the actors of the Hôtel de Bourgogne at the Petit-Bourbon in 1650.

By now Corneille was showing signs of that fatigue which led to the poor productions of his later years, and this, added to the troubles of the Fronde, probably accounted for the disastrous failure of *Pertharite* (1652), after which Corneille abandoned the theatre for some years.

It was not until 1659 that Paris again saw a play by its veteran dramatist. This was *Oedipe*, done at the Hôtel de Bourgogne, where Floridor was now firmly established in succession to Bellerose. Tradition has it that the subject was suggested to Corneille by Fouquet. It was a moderate success, and Louis XIV enjoyed it, while it was sufficiently well known for Molière to quote from it in his *Impromptu de Versailles*. It was followed by another spectacle-play, *La Toison d'or*, written for the marriage of Louis XIV, and played by the actors of the Marais at the castle of the Marquis de Sourdéac in Nov. 1660. Later, having been given the scenery and machines by their generous patron, the actors were able to put the play on in their own theatre. *Sertorius* (1661) was also given there, though *Sophonisbe* (1663) and *Othon* (1664) were done at the Hôtel de Bourgogne, without much success.

In 1663 Corneille finally deserted Rouen for Paris, but his plays became less and less successful, particularly in view of the rising popularity of Racine. *Agésilas* (1666) was hampered by the author's employment of a new verse-form, while *Attila* (1667) was overshadowed by the success of Racine's *Andromaque* in the same year. It was done by Molière, who had a great admiration for Corneille and is reported to have said that without *Le Menteur* he might have written *L'Étourdi*, but never *Le Misanthrope*. He followed it by a production of *Tite et Bérénice* (1670), given at the same time as Racine's play on the same subject at the rival Hôtel de Bourgogne. This circumstance gave rise to much gossip, particularly as it was said that Henrietta, sister of Charles II and sister-in-law of Louis XIV, had deliberately suggested the same subject to both authors in order to enjoy their rivalry. There is no evidence for this, but the two men certainly were rivals, and may have been seeking to outshine each other. It was in Corneille's play that the young Baron, later to be so famous an actor, had his first adult part, as Domitien. La Thorillière played Tite, and Molière's wife Bérénice. The play was moderately successful, and was followed by some of Corneille's most charming work, done for *Psyché* (1671) in collaboration with Molière and Quinault. *Pulchérie* (1672), done at the Marais, and *Suréna* (1674), done at the Hôtel de Bourgogne, are Corneille's last plays, and both, though successful for a short time, soon fell out of the repertory.

Corneille was not an easy person. He was brusque and shy with strangers, had none of Racine's easy graces—but was probably a far finer character—and was sometimes too pleased with himself and his work. His domestic life was happy, and he had not to wait for posterity to give him his due, since in his lifetime he was successful (though never wealthy), honoured, fêted, and called *le grand Corneille*. Even Racine at his best could not easily prevail against the popularity of Corneille in his decline, which did not prevent his making a memorable eulogy of the older dramatist at the Academy on the reception of Thomas Corneille in his brother's stead. Corneille's fame was a little eclipsed in the eighteenth century, but the nineteenth restored him to his true place. His work is unequal, and it may be that he would have been happier working for a freer theatre. He had not, as Racine had, the art of making an asset out of the limitations imposed on him. It is ironical that the form of French tragedy which he adopted and did so much to further was not really suited to his genius. But he rightly ranks first among French dramatists, and the best of his plays still hold the stage.

His brother (2) THOMAS (1625–1709), referred to above, was also a playwright. He had undoubted talent as a poet, great facility, and untiring industry. He was also more attractive in manner and conversation than his elder brother, and a favourite in Parisian drawing-rooms. He married a younger sister of his brother's wife, and nothing is more charming than the account of their lives, the two families living in the same or adjoining houses, completely in harmony. All the evidence goes to show that Pierre rejoiced in his younger brother's popularity, and never showed to him the anxious jealousy with which he sometimes regarded another's success. Thomas wrote over forty plays, all successful and all forgotten. He had not his brother's genius. The first of his productions was a comedy, *Les Engagements du hasard* (1647), based on a Spanish play and given, in the year of Pierre's election to the French Academy, at the Hôtel de Bourgogne. His first tragedy, *Timocrate* (1656), was done at the Marais, and helped to restore the genre to popularity after the troubles of the Fronde. Altogether the younger Corneille is an interesting person, and deserves a little pity for having had such a famous brother, beside whom his fires naturally pale. His best plays are usually considered to be *Ariane* (1672), in which Mlle Champmeslé and later Rachel were outstanding, and *Le Comte d'Essex* (1678), given at the Hôtel de Bourgogne, again with Champmeslé.

To distinguish him from Pierre, Thomas was known as Monsieur Corneille de L'Isle.

CORNELL, KATHARINE (1898–), see McCLINTIC (2).

CORNER TRAP, see STAGE, 1 and TRAP.

CORONET THEATRE, NEW YORK. This opened as the Forrest on 24 Nov. 1925 with a musical play which had a moderate run of some eighty performances. It was followed by a series of unremarkable plays, and in May 1927 the theatre housed a brief season of the Spanish Art Theatre, under Crosby Gaige. The first production to achieve a hundred performances was *Women Go On Forever*, a melodrama of dubious morality which had a number of out-standing actors in its cast. A spate of thrillers was followed by revivals of recent successes, until on 17 Sept. 1934 *Tobacco Road* moved to the Forrest—having opened on 4 Dec. 1933 at the Masque Theatre—and remained until 31 May 1941, setting up a record which was later broken by *Life With Father*. The theatre received its present name in 1945, when it was taken over by the City Playhouses Inc., and remodelled.   G. F.

CORPS DE BALLET, the group of dancers who form, as it were, the chorus of the ballet, commenting in concerted action on the main theme as enunciated by the solo dancers. It was Vigano who first made them disciplined individuals, instead of mechanical robots, and although they reverted to unintelligent uniformity during the decadence of the late nineteenth and early twentieth centuries in France and England, when dancing was one of the least of their preoccupations, the modern *corps de ballet* is composed of highly trained, technically accomplished dancers working in harmonious co-operation. They are known individually as 'les coryphées' and, familiarly, at the Paris Opéra, as 'les rats'.

CORRAL, de la Cruz, de la Pacheca, del Príncipe, see SPAIN.

CORREA, JULIO, see SOUTH AMERICA, 1.

CORRIE, JOE (1894–   ), Scottish dramatist, who has supplied the modern Scottish dramatic movement, and especially that branch of it associated with the Community Drama Festivals (see SCOTLAND), with some of its most representative one-act plays. He began writing verse while working in the coal-mines in Fife, and had his first plays, *The Shillin'-a-Week Man* and *The Poacher*, performed by the Bowhill Village Players during the General Strike in 1926. This group of actor-miners, of which Corrie himself was one, toured the music-halls of Scotland and the north of England with Corrie's plays during 1929–30, and for the first time in the history of the music-hall succeeded in putting on a three-act play there (*In Time o' Strife*). During the next ten years Corrie's plays were welcome additions to the repertory of the amateur stage. They include kitchen comedy, tragedy, and history. Many have been festival prize-winners, and some have been translated into French and Russian. Corrie has also written a three-act play on Robert Burns, a novel, and a volume of poems.
                                                   W. J.

CORSICAN TRAP, a piece of stage mechanism first used for the apparition in *The Corsican Brothers*, by means of which it rose slowly, at the same time appearing to drift across the stage. It was also known as the Ghost Glide (see ENGLISH PLAYHOUSE, 2).

CORT THEATRE, NEW YORK, opened 2 Dec. 1912 with Laurette Taylor in the immensely successful *Peg o' My Heart*. After

several successes, the theatre was taken by Charles Coburn and his wife, who appeared in revivals of *The Yellow Jacket* and *The Better 'Ole*. A notable event in the history of this theatre was a successful production there in 1919 of Drinkwater's *Abraham Lincoln*. A series of unremarkable plays followed, though *Behold the Bridegroom*, with Judith Anderson, was listed by Burns Mantle among the ten best plays of 1927. In the following year Katharine Hepburn made her first appearance on Broadway at the Cort, and in 1930 came a magnificent revival of *Uncle Vanya*, superbly acted by a fine cast. Other successes were *Five Star Final* (1930) and *The Green Bay Tree* (1932), the latter with Laurence Olivier and Jill Esmond, and an elegant setting by Robert Edmond Jones; *Boy Meets Girl* (1935) and *Room Service* (1937), both of which had long runs; the fine war-play *A Bell for Adano* (1944), and a translation of Anouilh's resistance play, *Antigone*, with Katharine Cornell in the name-part.
                                                   G. F.

CORT'S 63rd STREET THEATRE, NEW YORK, see DALY'S THEATRE (3).

COSMOPOLITAN   THEATRE, NEW YORK, see MAJESTIC THEATRE (1).

COSSA, PIETRO (1830–81), Italian dramatist, whose tragedy, *Nerone*, was coldly received on its first production in Rome in 1870, but revived with success in Milan, and later acclaimed throughout Italy. It has remained his most popular contribution to the theatre, though responsible critics have shown a preference for *Messalina* (1876), which he wrote after the success of his earlier play had encouraged him to persevere in his dramatic career.

COSTANTINI. A family of actors of the *commedia dell'arte*, of whom (1) COSTANTINO (*fl.* 1668–96) played under the name of Gradelino, and was for some time in Paris. He married (2) DOMENICA (*fl.* 1675–?), also an actress, and was the father of the famous Mezzetino, (3) ANGELO (*c.* 1655–1729), author of a life of Tiberio Fiorelli (Scaramuccia). Angelo was in Paris from 1683–97, and after the death of Dominique took over the role of Arlequin, retaining however his own soubriquet. While appearing in Brunswick he had the misfortune to be the successful rival in love of the Elector of Saxony, which cost him twenty years in prison. His brother (4) GIOVAN BATTISTA (?–1720) was also an actor, and played second young lover parts under the name of Cintio. He was in Paris in 1688, and succeeded Marc'Antonio Romagnesi when the latter abandoned the 'young lover' for the 'Pedant-Doctor'.

COSTELLO, TOM (1863–1945), a music-hall performer who went to London from Birmingham in 1886 and played in melodrama at the old Surrey. He later made his name on the halls with a song 'Comrades', but is probably better remembered as the hen-pecked husband singing 'At Trinity Church I met me Doom'. He was also a fine singer of stirring patriotic ballads, often in naval officer's uniform. He retired from the halls at the time of the 1914–18 war, but returned with the Veterans of Variety in the 1920s.

COSTUME, THEATRICAL. Theatrical costume is of much more ancient date than theatrical scenery. It is possible for the theatre to do without a stage, but 'acting' *must* mean 'assuming a character', and assuming a character means dressing up. Every ritual dance (and what people are so primitive as to have no ritual dances?) involves its appropriate costume, its animal disguise, its dignifying feathered headdress, or its appropriate mask. The actor assumes the god, impersonates the hero, or affects the garb of men like himself. This descent to realism, which is that of the drama itself, is necessarily reflected in the history of stage costume.

1. GREEK. We must, however, attempt to distinguish in a field where distinction becomes progressively more difficult the earlier we take up the story. We must attempt to strip theatrical costume of its religious and magical elements at a time when the theatre itself was still full of both. The point of departure must be an arbitrary one, and perhaps none better can be found than the Greek theatre of Aeschylus on the one hand and Aristophanes on the other. For tragedy and comedy, having different origins, had different systems of dress, both quite different again from the ordinary dress of the day. The tragedies of Aeschylus were played in the long, rich, Asiatic robes of the priests of Dionysus, the tragedies of Sophocles and Euripides in the decorated Ionian costumes which the Greeks had abandoned in favour of the plainer Doric modes at the time of the Persian wars. In the fifth century B.C. tragedy costumes became stereotyped, a traditional dress being provided for each of the different roles. The cothurnus, afterwards regarded as the mark of the tragic actor, was at first an Asiatic leg-boot. It was only later that its sole was so much increased in thickness that it became a kind of stilt. The chorus wore no high boots, as they had to dance, and their clothes, for the same reason, were shorter and less voluminous. But they were often equally rich. Both actors and chorus wore the mask.

In Old Comedy the actors all wore clothes grotesquely padded, and each was provided with an enormous phallus of red leather. The female characters too were padded, and over the padding wore the long *chiton* if they belonged to the upper classes, and the short one if they belonged to the lower, in the contemporary manner of ordinary life. Several of Aristophanes' plays demanded a chorus of beasts, birds, or allegorical figures, and these were represented, not by complete disguises, but by suitable accessories such as feathered wings or horses' heads and tails.

The Attic New Comedy, represented by

Menander, abandoned the phallus and the mythological elements. Its intention was to reflect the life of the day, and the clothes worn were those of the ordinary citizens of Athens, except that a regular tradition seems to have grown up of colouring the clothes differently for the different characters. The masks also were stereotyped in a regular series of character parts, and used over and over again for different plays. (See also GREECE, 3 d.)

2. ROMAN. Greek tragedy and comedy were imported into Rome in the middle of the third century B.C., and with them the whole system of Greek stage costume, including the cothurnus in its most exaggerated form. When the Romans developed a drama of their own they naturally added such typically Roman garments as the *toga* and the *stola*. By the time of the Caesars stage costumes, especially in tragedy, had become very gorgeous. The same colour symbolism was adopted as the Greeks had used to express the characters or the moods of the players.

Pantomime and mime were very popular in Rome. In the former very scanty clothing was worn, and when women began to take part in it the effect must have been something similar to a modern revue or cabaret. In mimes, or farces played without masks, women appeared from the beginning, and these entertainments soon became more popular than the regular drama. The most interesting dress in the mimes was the patchwork garment worn by the Fool, an interesting parallel with the Harlequin costume to be worn in the Italian Comedy more than a thousand years later.

Similar parallels with the characters, if not with the costumes, of the *commedia dell'arte* are to be found in the Atellanae, the improvised farces of the Roman Campagna, in which we find five permanent types or characters closely corresponding with the Capitano, the Dottore, the Pantalone, &c. of the sixteenth century. The strolling Atellan players were masked like their later counterparts.

The mimes became ever more popular as the Empire moved towards its dissolution, and the costumes of the players steadily more gorgeous. We hear in the sixth century of actresses' dresses adorned with pearls and enriched with cloth of gold. These extravagances excited the hatred of the Church, and after the collapse of the Empire public performances in regular theatres ceased altogether, although some of the traditions must have been carried on by strolling players throughout the Dark Ages. (See also ROME.)

3. MEDIEVAL. Drama was reborn in the Mystery and Miracle plays of the Church. The earliest of these performances were given inside the sacred edifice itself, and were performed by the priests wearing their usual sacerdotal robes. These, since the ninth century, had become very elaborate. Female characters were indicated by the simple expedient of placing a kerchief on the head and draping a cloak over the shoulder. Secular costumes,

however, and even false beards soon began to creep in, and with the progressive secularization of the plays, this tendency was accentuated. Finally the priests were forbidden to take part and the drama moved out of the church, first to a place in front of the great doorway, and then into the markets or other open spaces of the towns. (See also ECCLESIASTICAL DRAMA.)

Once the plays had been abandoned to the laity, some of the minor roles, played in the ordinary costume of the day, took on a new importance, and very soon developed into comic characters. The devils too were comic. This obviously gave some scope for fantasy in costume, and there is plenty of evidence to show that the opportunity was eagerly seized. Some of the performances of the later Middle Ages were most gorgeously mounted and extremely expensive, but, except for a slight orientalism in some of the costumes, there was, of course, no attempt at any kind of historical or geographical accuracy, the necessary knowledge being completely lacking. Realism, however, in so far as it could be obtained by such devices as painted wounds or tights of white leather, was much in vogue. Towards the end of the Medieval period martyrs or damned souls were sometimes presented quite naked.

In the Morality plays, which dealt with allegorical figures of Virtues and Vices, the costumes were sometimes extremely rich. The characters were clothed in fantasticated contemporary dress, with the exception of the Devil, taken over with all his accessories from the Miracle plays, and the 'Vice', a new character usually clothed as a fool or jester. The French *soties* were regular fool-plays, the costumes being contemporary dress with certain fantastic or archaic elements such as long donkey's ears on the hood, cockscombs, and bells. Some of these details, together with the deformity which former ages considered comic, have survived into our own day in the costume of Punch.

4. RENAISSANCE. By the middle of the sixteenth century the medieval theatre was in full decay. Its place was taken by attempts in academic circles to revive the classical drama, and also by that astonishing flowering of the Elizabethan stage which culminated in the achievement of Shakespeare. The same period was the Golden Age of the Spanish drama, but very few records have survived of either its costume or scenery. It is probable that both followed the same course as in the presentation of Shakespeare. The Elizabethan theatre took over some of the elements of the Miracle and Morality plays. Its stage was as bare as theirs, its costumes no less gorgeous. Little attempt was made at historical accuracy, the players wearing contemporary costume with such minor modifications as might be suggested by the knowledge that orientals were in the habit of wearing long robes and turbans. The players' wardrobes were enriched by gifts from aristocratic patrons, so that the stage kings and queens were almost if not quite as finely clad as their counterparts in real life.

It was impossible, however, for the public theatres to compete in magnificence with the masques presented at Court. Elizabeth was fond of such shows, but very few records of them have survived. James I had a passion for them, and for the entertainments at Whitehall under him and under Charles I we have a mass of material preserved in the library of the Duke of Devonshire at Chatsworth. Inigo Jones (1573–1652) was the architect-designer in charge, and it was through him that all the recent Italian developments were reproduced in England. As in Italy, mythological subjects were highly in favour and gave considerable scope to the artist's fantasy. The male costumes were, in general, of the 'Roman' pattern, the Roman breastplate moulded to the form of the body and some variation of the Roman kilt being an essential part of it, modified by elements of contemporary fashion. The female costumes followed the dress of the period more closely, but strove for a looseness and even a transparency supposed to be typical of 'classical' dress. Every advantage was taken of décolletage, and some of the dresses, with their low-cut bodices or bosoms veiled with gauze, would not be out of place in a modern revue. The grotesque characters show elements of costume continued from the Morality plays or borrowed from the ever more popular *commedia dell'arte*. The cost of the dresses being borne by the wearers (the lords and ladies of the Court) there was almost no limit to their magnificence and luxury. (See also MASQUE.)

5. SEVENTEENTH CENTURY. This splendour, however, was as nothing compared with that of similar shows on the continent. At the Courts of Italy, of Germany (up to the outbreak of the Thirty Years War), and of France the most extravagant entertainments were used with the deliberate policy of enhancing the prestige of the Prince, and they reached a new height of elaboration in France in the early years of the reign of Louis XIV. Italian scenography had by this time spread almost all over Europe, and Mazarin had called in numerous Italian artists, of which the most celebrated was Giacomo Torelli (1608–78). It is possible that he was responsible for the splendid costumes in the *Noces de Thétis et de Pélée*, given by the Cardinal at the Petit-Bourbon in 1654, but the French, with their innate talent for anything relating to costume, soon had this field in their own hands. The *Grand Carrousel* of 1662, a kind of mock-tournament in fantasticated *habits à la Romaine*, was designed by Henri Gissey (1621–1673), and the appearance of the costumes has been preserved in an admirable series of engravings by Chauveau. So great was the enthusiasm and emulation provoked by this entertainment that every monarch in Europe wished to stage something of the kind, the most notable being the fête given in Vienna a few years later. After his death Gissey was succeeded as *Dessinateur du Cabinet du Roi* by the great Jean Bérain

the Elder (1637–1711). The influence of this artist was not confined to the restricted area of theatrical costume but extended over the whole field of the decorative arts. In fact it would not be much of an exaggeration to say that the *style Louis XIV* is the *style Bérain*. Numerous examples of his designs have been preserved in the Louvre, in the Musée de l'Opéra in Paris, in the Library of Versailles, in the Victoria and Albert Museum, and elsewhere. It is possible that many of these are copies or tracings by the pious hand of Jean Bérain the Younger (1678–1726), but they enable us to gain a very complete idea of the evolution of theatrical costume during the greater part of the reign of the *Roi Soleil*. The most striking characteristic of Bérain's work is the complete blend of fantasy and contemporary taste. Even when the costumes are those of Romans, Turks, or mythological personages, the exotic elements are, as it were, absorbed and digested into one supreme manifestation of style. There was no attempt at realism or archaeological reconstruction. Bérain's style is at once intensely personal and completely contemporary, and perhaps this makes him the greatest designer of stage costume that has ever lived. His influence both on his contemporaries in other European countries and his successors in France was immense. (See also ACOUSTICS and ARCHITECTURE.)

6. COMMEDIA DELL'ARTE. Before dealing further with this, however, it is necessary to say something of the costumes of the *commedia dell' arte*, that astonishing manifestation of theatrical activity which swept over Europe and spread its influence everywhere during the whole of the seventeenth century. As a dramatic form the improvised Italian Comedy is dealt with elsewhere (see ITALY, 2). We are concerned merely with its traditional costumes. Some of the elements of these go back, it is thought, to the Atellanae of Roman times, but when the Comedy re-emerges, towards the end of the sixteenth century, we find certain definite traditional types. While the plays changed (indeed, as they were improvised no two performances could be exactly alike) the characters remained constant. The most famous of these were il Capitano, il Dottore, Brighella, Pantalone, Pulcinella, and, of course, Arlecchino. It is one of the curiosities of the *commedia dell'arte* that all the characters (with the exception of the 'straight' parts, the lovers and the female servants, who played in contemporary dress) wore the costumes of different Italian towns or provinces. Pulcinella was a Neapolitan, Brighella and Arlecchino were from Bergamo, Pantalone was a Venetian, il Capitano a swaggering Spaniard—for the Spaniards still held considerable territory in Italy. Arlecchino's costume was 'a thing of shreds and patches', but these patches gradually became stylized and decorative, until we reach the familiar lozenge-shaped pattern of parti-coloured cloth which has survived to our own day. Pierrot represented a French development of a minor character,

and his traditional costume was stereotyped by Watteau. But Watteau or anyone familiar with the Italian Comedy would have been astonished at the notion of a 'troupe' of Pierrots, for Pierrot was essentially one character among others of strongly contrasting types. The characters of the *commedia dell'arte* have a long history, and have found their way into many unexpected places, but they were too traditional and unchanging to have much influence on the evolution of theatrical costume in general.

7. ROCOCO and EIGHTEENTH CENTURY. So long as the desire for historical accuracy played an altogether minor part in the minds of theatrical designers, that evolution followed the main lines of the taste of the time. The Austrian equivalent of Bérain was the great Italian designer Lodovico Ottavio Burnacini (1636–1707), who flourished at Vienna under the cultivated Emperor Leopold I. In France the work of Bérain was carried on by his son and other disciples, but the *style Louis XIV* gradually merged into the *style Régence* and was dissipated in the fantasies of rococo. Claude Gillot (1673–1722), the master of Watteau, was responsible for some of the costumes of the Court ballets in the early years of the eighteenth century, but the great name of the middle of the century is that of François Boucher (1703–70). As early as 1734 we find him designing a whole series of theatrical costumes to illustrate a new edition of the works of Molière. It may have been these which brought him to the notice of the authorities. He was certainly working for the Opéra in 1737, and in 1744 he succeeded Jean Nicholas Servandony (1695–1766) as official decorator. His style is sufficiently familiar to need no description, and his painting and non-theatrical work in general seems to have absorbed more and more of his time, for in 1748 he abandoned his post at the Opéra to Jean Baptiste Martin (*fl.* 1748–57), chiefly remembered for his rococo shepherds and shepherdesses. The rococo style was to find its completest development, however, in the designs of Louis René Boquet (*fl.* 1760–82), who worked both for the Opéra and the Menus-Plaisirs, that is, the Court entertainments at Versailles and Fontainebleau. A good many of his designs have been preserved, and they show that he was, like Bérain, content to suggest character or period by some small decorative accessory and, for the rest, brought everything under the domination of the contemporary style. His designs have great charm and his costumes, both male and female, are characterized by his use of wide paniers, forming a kind of ballet-skirt covered with rococo detail.

These wide paniers haunted the stage not only in France, and not only in ballet or opera. The English actor Quin played Coriolanus in just such a ballet-skirt as we find depicted in the drawings of Boquet, and one of Garrick's most 'realistic' reforms was the abolition of such garments. England could offer, in the eighteenth century, no such opportunities for the theatrical designer as were enjoyed on the continent, and of what records may have existed very few have come down to us. The main story of development still lies in France.

Boquet worked for the Opéra from about 1760 until 1780, and towards the end of his reign a notable change in taste began to make itself felt. In classical plays at any rate a real effort was made to approximate more closely to what was known of the costumes of antiquity. The first real costumes à l'antique are said to have been due to the collaboration of the famous singer Mlle Saint-Huberty and the artist Moreau le Jeune (1741–1814). This was in 1782. By 1785 it was possible to find quite a number of correct classical costumes on the French stage, and the French Revolution, with its passion for the Ancients, powerfully reinforced a tendency that had already set in.

The reform of stage costume had been strongly advocated for some years by authors of the calibre of Voltaire and Diderot, and the actress Mlle Favart and the actor Lekain had made efforts in the same direction. In Voltaire's L'Orphelin de la Chine the famous Mlle Clairon appeared with bare arms and without paniers, although how this made the costume more 'Chinese' than it would otherwise have been it is difficult to say. However, she played the part of Roxane in a fairly close approximation to Turkish costume.

In England Garrick's reforms consisted in abandoning the traditional stylization of costume, and playing Shakespeare, for example, in contemporary dress (i.e. the dress of Garrick's day, not Shakespeare's). It is odd to reflect that he acted Macbeth in the scarlet of the King's livery. Komisarjevsky, in his Costume of the Theatre, has recorded that when Garrick, in 1758, was playing the part of the ancient Greek, Aegis, 'he wore the costume of a Venetian gondolier, on the ground that the majority of Venetian gondoliers at that time were of Greek origin'. It is perhaps sufficient commentary on the accuracy of eighteenth-century stage costume to say that Garrick passed as a realist. English tragic actresses of the same period wore contemporary dress with a few accessories, such as a turban, a crown, or a veil. Engravings have survived of an Electra, in the high headdress of the seventeen-seventies, and in her hand an elegant urn in the taste of the period, purporting to contain the ashes of her brother. In Germany we find the same system adopted in the productions of Iffland.

8. NINETEENTH CENTURY. As we have seen, France was in the van of the reforming movement, and the first real step forward was taken by the famous Talma, supported by the painter David. When, however, in the very year of the Revolution, he appeared as Brutus with bare arms and legs, the reaction of the public was anything but favourable. But by the end of the century classical costumes, at least for women, were the fashion in ordinary life, and so appeared less incongruous on the stage.

It is the same story in the first quarter of the nineteenth century. There was considerably more interest in 'historical' costume, and following the success of the novels of Scott, 'Elizabethan' details began to take their place in ordinary fashions. The Restoration period in France is marked by an outbreak of ruffles à la Marie Stuart, somewhat incongruously attached to dresses which still followed in their main outlines the 'classical' Empire modes. The same was true of stage costumes, which indeed were hardly distinguishable from those of the street and the ballroom. The new rage for historical plays merely meant the addition of a jumble of sixteenth- and seventeenth-century details to early nineteenth-century dress. The resulting mixture is not without its charm (the charm we are beginning to discover in late eighteenth- and early nineteenth-century Gothic), but it bore, it is perhaps needless to say, very little relation to any kind of historical accuracy.

It is of course arguable that the quest for historical accuracy is a mistake. As Carlos Fischer remarks, regretfully, in his Costumes de l'Opéra, 'le costume d'opéra, étant désormais consacré à l'Histoire, n'a plus d'histoire'. But this is not quite true. It was not until the very end of the nineteenth century that historical costume on the stage made any very close approximation to reality. During the whole of the crinoline period, at least, the forms of stage dress followed the contemporary mode. As Hermione in Charles Kean's production of The Winter's Tale in the fifties, Mrs. Kean wore a perfectly correct Greek costume, but she wore it over a crinoline! None the less the archaeological research undertaken by Charles Kean had its effect, and his work in England was paralleled by that of Paul Lormier in France. Lormier's long reign as designer for the Paris Opéra lasted forty-five years, and he strove unceasingly to make the costumes of the principal singers and figurantes as accurate as possible.

However successful he was with these, he was completely defeated as regards the ballet by the curious convention of clothing the danseuses in the tutu, the short powder-puff skirt of many layers of gauze or tarlatan, which lasted as the inevitable ballet costume until the reforms of Diaghilev. This dress was very convenient for dancing in, but it owed its origin to the enormous success of Taglioni in 'La Sylphide'. Her costume in this was perhaps designed by Eugène Lorris Lami (1800–90), but in essentials it was merely the dress of the day, white and somewhat shortened. Its persistence in every ballet whatever the theme or period made any attempt at historical verisimilitude quite impossible.

It is necessary when considering female stage costume of past periods to remember how difficult it is to escape, even with the best intentions, from the prevailing mode. The Bancrofts prided themselves upon their realism, and Mrs. Bancroft twice played Peg Woffington in what she fondly imagined was eighteenth-century costume. To the modern eye the photographs which have come down to us bear no suggestion of eighteenth-century costume at all. They show merely the dress of the different dates of production. It is particularly difficult for any actress to abandon an attractive (i.e. a contemporary) style of hair-dressing, and this alone is sufficient to throw the most painstakingly 'accurate' costume out of focus.

Towards the end of the nineteenth century, realism took on a new meaning. On the one hand it was an attempt, as with the company of players organized by the Duke of Saxe-Meiningen, at an almost pedantic degree of accuracy in historical plays; on the other an abandonment of historical themes altogether and a concentration upon the problems of everyday modern life. In the plays inspired by this ideal there was obviously no place for the costume designer at all. The actresses had dresses made for them by fashionable dressmakers and the men wore their own clothes.

The designer, excluded almost entirely from the 'legitimate' stage, let his fancy run riot in the lighter musical productions. In England such men as Attilio Comelli (1858–1925) and Wilhelm—whose real name was William John Charles Pitcher (1859–1925)—designed innumerable dresses for *figurantes* in the early years of the twentieth century, and large collections of these have survived. They are valuable social documents, indicating as they do the whole erotic-aesthetic of the day; the elaborate plumed hats, the ample bosoms dripping with lace and jewels, the tight-clad thighs, the open-work stockings. Much earlier in France, *La Vie Parisienne* artists, men like Alfred Grévin (1827–92), had been called in for a similar purpose. From the point of view of the history of manners, 'show-girl' costumes have perhaps hardly received the attention they deserve. The 'Empire' ballets of the Edwardian epoch provide an almost complete summary of the taste of the time.

9. BALLET. For the history of stage costume much more important was the movement inaugurated by Diaghilev. He had at his command all the resources of the 'classical' ballet, but he broke completely with the traditional manner of presentation, in particular with the slavery to the *tutu*, the flounced white ballet skirt which had lasted so long. In Alexandre Benois (1870–   ) and Léon Bakst (1866–1924) he had two giants of theatrical art, and if the talents of the former were shown most effectively in décor, those of Bakst were pre-eminently those of the costume designer. Bakst brought to western Europe a riot of oriental colour which first dazzled and then delighted audiences in London and Paris. His costumes were not historically 'accurate'; they represented rather a synthesis of the place and period suggested by the theme of the ballet. (See also BALLET, 7.)

In addition to Russian artists like Larinov, Roerich, and Gontcharova, Diaghilev brought in French painters of the stature of Braque, Derain, and Picasso. The drawings of Picasso for 'The Three-Cornered Hat' are among the masterpieces of costume design. His cubism found its way on to the stage in the much-criticized 'Parade'. Juan Gris, Marie Laurencin, Rouault, and G. de Chirico also designed costumes for the Russian Ballet; the last named worked also for the Swedish Ballet, as did Fernand Léger and Irène Lagut.

10. MODERN PERIOD. (*a*) *European*. The French state theatres commissioned costumes from Valdo Barbey and Maxime Dethomas; the Théâtre des Arts employed Desvallières; the Vieux-Colombier, Luc-Albert Moreau and others; the Atelier, Barsacq and Jean Victor-Hugo. The last named, however, had his greatest success with his costumes for *Romeo and Juliet* for the Soirées de Paris. The number of French experimental theatres in the period between the two wars gave ample scope for the talents of designers of theatrical costume.

In Germany Ernst Stern continued, at the beginning of the same period, the traditions of stylized realism instituted by Reinhardt. The movement known as Expressionism had perhaps more effect on stage settings than on stage costume. Artists like Oscar Schlemmer inaugurated some interesting experiments of an abstract-mechanical kind, but the human figure places very definite limits to the process of abstraction; the actors themselves always tend to rebel against too rigid a style, and so-called cubist costumes tend when worn to become merely the fantastic–historical. A production such as that of *Saint Joan* at the Kamerny Theatre, Moscow, shows this clearly enough. At the same theatre the Sternberg costumes for *All God's Chillun Got Wings*, and those of I. Nivinsky for Puccini's opera 'Turan', dot show the breadth and variety of the Russian approach to the problem of stage-costuming. Very interesting work has been done in Moscow by Varpekh for the Theatre of the Young Spectator. (See RUSSIA, 2 *d*.)

(*b*) *American*. In America as elsewhere the 'Modern Movement' found expression more easily in décor than in costume. The costumes of Norman-Bel Geddes for *Lysistrata* were considerably less abstract than his settings. His method, as also in *Boudoir* and *The Miracle*, is a witty commentary on the styles of the past. Many plays in which the setting was highly formalized clothed the actors in the dress of every day, and indeed it is difficult to see how they could have done anything else. Historical plays, especially where the scene represents a period the dresses of which are more or less known to the public, allow a certain fantastication or formalization of Elizabethan or 'classical' dress, and this fact has been taken advantage of by such artists as Woodman Thompson (*Iphigenia in Aulis*), Robert Edmond Jones (*Othello*), and Walter René Fuerst (*The Oresteia*). Robert Edmond Jones has made some interesting experiments in showing one age through the eyes of another, as when he set and costumed *Lucrèce* in terms of Renaissance Rome. As in other countries, the American lighter stage gave the designers of costume opportunities for which they would have waited long elsewhere. Some of the great spectacular 'musicals' have provided almost a cross-section of all the aesthetic impulses of the contemporary theatre. (See also UNITED STATES OF AMERICA, 2.)

(c) *English.* In England one of the most talented of the designers of stage costume during the early years of the twentieth century was Charles Ricketts (1866–1931). Even before the appearance of Diaghilev, Ricketts was already a pioneer in the protest against an unimaginative realism. Some of his costumes were devised for the sheer love of imagining a stage picture, and many of them were never used, but already in 1906 we find him decorating *Salome* and *A Florentine Tragedy. Don Juan in Hell* and *The Man of Destiny* were among the first of his professional tasks, but it was not until some sixteen years later that he really caught the attention of the public with his costumes for *Saint Joan.* Then followed *Henry VIII* and *Macbeth.* His attempt to re-dress *The Mikado* had a less favourable reception. His last work was for *Elizabeth of England* in 1929.

A much shorter, but almost equally brilliant career was that of Claud Lovat Fraser (1890–1921). His fame rests chiefly on his designs for the costumes (as well as the scenery) of the Hammersmith revival of *The Beggar's Opera.* So successful was his stylizing of the period that a Lovat Fraser influence can be traced in almost all eighteenth-century plays produced in England since. His early death deprived the English theatre of one of its major artists.

Norman Wilkinson of Four Oaks (1882–1934) first attracted attention with his designs for Granville-Barker's productions of Shakespeare at the Savoy Theatre in 1913. In the following year he was concerned in the production of *The Dynasts* at the Kingsway; and under Playfair's management of the Lyric Theatre, Hammersmith, he decorated *Lionel and Clarissa, The Rivals,* and *The Would-be Gentleman.* The same management employed no less an artist than Sir William Nicholson for *Polly,* the sequel to *The Beggar's Opera.* Other artists who were tempted into occasional work for the theatres were James Pryde, Albert Rutherston, F. Cayley Robinson, Paul Nash, and E. McKnight Kauffer.

George Sheringham (1884–1937) employed his delicate talent for Playfair and other managements; Paul Shelving worked mostly for Sir Barry Jackson at Birmingham and elsewhere; the more naturalistic style of George W. Harris (1880–1929) found scope in a wide variety of plays. Among the most successful scenic designers of the nineteen-twenties was Aubrey Hammond, who decorated, among other plays, *The Man with a Load of Mischief* and *The Circle of Chalk.*

The period between the two Great Wars was marked by the emergence of a number of talented women designers: Gladys Calthrop (who did much work for Noel Coward's productions); the Motleys, three young women who did some of their best work for John Gielgud; Nadia Benois (the niece of the great Alexandre), Molly McArthur, and Doris Zinkeisen. The last-named designed the costumes for *The Insect Play,* but most of her work has been done for the lighter stage. Cochran revues often provided opportunities for the artist denied him by the legitimate stage. Such an artist is Oliver Messel, who seems to display his gifts most successfully when the play offers the artist scope for fantasy, as in *Helen.* His costumes for the revival of *The Miracle* were also justly admired. Rex Whistler (1905–44) was an admirable stage-designer whose death in action was a great loss to the English theatre; and among others who should be mentioned in a survey, however cursory, of modern stage-costume design in England are John Gower Parkes, Roger Furse, Michael Weight, Reginald Leefe, John Garside, and John Armstrong. Many of these artists are still young and it is to be hoped that the theatre of the period following the Second World War will be sufficiently imaginative to make use of their talents.   J. L.

COTHURNUS, the thick-soled boot worn by the Greek tragic actor (see GREECE, 3 *d*). The word is occasionally used as a synonym for an elevated, high-flown style, and for tragedy (see also BUSKIN).

COULDOCK, CHARLES WALTER (1815–98), American actor. Born in London, he decided to adopt the stage as a profession after seeing Macready. In 1836 he made his début in a provincial company, later playing in Birmingham and Liverpool with most of the leading actors of the day. Among them was Charlotte Cushman, who engaged him for her New York company, where he made an immediate success in *The Stranger.* After several seasons at the Walnut Street Theatre, Philadelphia, he went on tour, making a great reputation in *The Willow Copse* (1853) and *The Chimney Corner* (1861). He played Abel Murcott in *Our American Cousin* (1858), and was outstanding as Dunstan Kirke in *Hazel Kirke* (1880). He was for more than sixty years on the stage, and was the friend of Booth, Macready, and Jefferson, a man of great vitality and energy, and a witty, genial companion.

COUNCIL FOR THE ENCOURAGEMENT OF MUSIC AND THE ARTS, see ARTS COUNCIL.

COUNTERWEIGHT HOUSE, the name given to a theatre where the scenery is worked by a modern system of endless lines and counterweights, as opposed to the traditional system of lines from a fly-floor used in Rope, or Hand-worked, Houses (see ENGLISH PLAYHOUSE, 2 *a* and STAGE).

COURTELINE [MOINEAUX], GEORGES (1861–1929), French dramatist, author of a number of amusing farces, some of which were produced by Antoine before finding their way eventually into the repertory of the Comédie-Française. They deal with the humours of military life, as in *Lidoire* (1891) and *Les Gaietés de l'escadron* (1895), and of the law, as in *L'Article 330* (1901); or, as in what is perhaps his best play, *Boubouroche* (1893), with episodes in the life of ordinary people, salted with much wit and a certain gross brutality which recalls the farces of the early French theatre.

COURT THEATRE, LONDON, opened as the New Chelsea in 1870, under the management of Morgan and Oliver, with cheap prices and a mixture of stage-show and music-hall. It was a badly transformed Nonconformist Chapel, and had no success at all, in spite of changing its name to the Belgravia, until Marie Litton took it over, reconstructed it, and reopened it as the Royal Court Theatre in Jan. 1871 with *Randal's Thumb*, by W. S. Gilbert, who provided further successes with *The Wedding March* and *The Happy Land*. In the last of these he burlesqued contemporary politicians so mercilessly that the Lord Chamberlain intervened, and the actors' make-up had to be altered.

In 1875 Hare became manager of the Court, bringing with him the Kendals, John Clayton, Henry Kemble, and a good company, and produced a number of successful plays. Wilson Barrett appeared in 1879, and in 1880 Modjeska played Juliet. A year later Clayton became manager, in association with Arthur Cecil. The company included Marion Terry, Mrs. John Wood, and Brandon Thomas, and achieved its first success in March 1885, with Pinero's *The Magistrate*, a farce English in spirit and not adapted from the French or German. It was followed by *The Schoolmistress* and *Dandy Dick*, in the same tradition. The old theatre was pulled down in 1887, and reopened a year later under the management of Mrs. John Wood and Arthur Chudleigh. It was less successful for a while, in spite of the popularity of *The Cabinet Minister*, but in 1897 Hare returned for a short season, the Prince and Princess of Wales being present at his opening night. A year later, on 20 Jan., came the successful production of Pinero's *Trelawny of the 'Wells'*. The fortunes of the theatre, which had been laid by the Pinero farces, now took another turn. A brilliant partnership, and one outstanding in British theatrical history, began in 1904 when J. E. Vedrenne and H. Granville-Barker took the theatre, and produced a remarkable series of new plays and revivals, all superbly acted, ranging from the Greek dramatists to Shaw, Galsworthy, and the plays of Barker himself. This memorable period of theatrical enterprise ran until 1907, and its influence on the English drama was incalculable.

A later notable production at the Court was *The Farmer's Wife*, presented by Barry Jackson, which, after a bad start, ran for 1,329 performances. The theatre was partially destroyed by bombing in 1941, but it is hoped that it will be rebuilt.   W. M. P.

COVENT GARDEN THEATRE, LONDON. At the end of 1731 John Rich, finding that his theatre had fallen into disrepair (see LINCOLN'S INN FIELDS THEATRE), opened a subscription for building a new playhouse in Bow Street, Covent Garden. Six thousand pounds was quickly raised, and building began at once. The project caused great excitement, and fashionable people gathered daily to watch the workmen. Rich paid the Duke of Bedford £100 as ground-rent, which by 1792 had risen to £940.

The theatre was a small one, 51 ft. long, holding about £200 when full. Space for seating was restricted to 21 in. per person. The admission prices were: boxes, 5s.; pit, 3s. 6d.; galleries, 2s. and 1s.; seats on the stage, 10s. 6d. There were two entrances, one under the famous Piazza, the other in Bow Street. The new house was decorated in magnificent style by an Italian artist named Amiconi, and the scenery also was very fine. The theatre opened on 7 Dec. 1732, with *The Way of the World*, and so great was the demand for admission that 5s. was charged for the pit. A revival of *The Beggar's Opera* followed.

Little of interest happened in the early years. Old plays and tragedies were revived, while the company remained the same as that which had played at Lincoln's Inn Fields, with Quin as its star. The first piece of excitement was the engagement, by the eccentric Rich, of Peg Woffington. She appeared on 8 Nov. 1740 as Sylvia in *The Recruiting Officer*, and on 20 Nov. electrified the town in a breeches part—Sir Harry Wildair in *The Constant Couple*. Later she went to Drury Lane, but she returned to Covent Garden, and collapsed on its stage in 1757, while playing Rosalind. She died three years later.

In 1744 George Anne Bellamy appeared at Covent Garden as Monimia in *The Orphan*. She was such a child that Quin at first objected to playing with her, but afterwards encouraged her greatly. She played Juliet to Spranger Barry's Romeo at Covent Garden during his rivalry with Garrick, who staged the same play at Drury Lane.

Rich, a great Harlequin under the name of Lun, played pantomime at Covent Garden, doing it most extravagantly with wild beasts, tumblers, and contortionists. He fancied himself as a tragedian, but the public disagreed. Quin, the leading man, ruled with a rod of iron, and all trembled before him. In 1746 Garrick accepted an engagement to play against him at Covent Garden and beat him, as he did Barry later. Barry joined the Covent Garden company in 1750 and proved a serious menace to Garrick at the Lane, as he was handsome and 'silver-voiced'. He was the better Othello, but Garrick the better Romeo and Lear.

Rich died in 1761 and his son-in-law John Beard, the famous vocalist, succeeded him. Under Beard the theatre was mostly given over to opera—Dibdin made his start there. Rich, in his will, had provided that the theatre and Patent should be sold when it would fetch £60,000. This sum was realized in 1767 when George Colman the elder, Harris, Rutherford, and Powell bought it.

When they took over the company included Powell, a fine actor, 'Gentleman' Smith, Bensley, Shuter, Macklin, Woodward, Yates, Hull, Mrs. Yates, Mrs. Bellamy, Mrs. Mattocks, Mrs. Ward, Miss Macklin, and Mrs. Buckley. The partners soon fell out, and Colman locked Harris out of the theatre. Harris, with Rutherford and some hired toughs, broke in through a window and removed most of the wardrobe, books, and other properties. A lawsuit took place, and in the end Colman was made sole manager.

On 15 Mar. 1773 *She Stoops to Conquer* was produced, after Colman had been persuaded by Dr. Johnson that it was a good play. Some of the company objected that it was 'not genteel', but it was a great success. In the same year Macklin appeared as Macbeth for the first time, at the age of 84. He introduced the wearing of kilts and tartans.

Colman sold out in 1774. Powell was dead and Rutherford of no importance, so Harris took possession. Spranger Barry appeared for the last time in 1776, and in 1780 Macklin, as a very old man, played Sir Pertinax Macsycophant in his own play, *The Man of the World*, on its first production in London. In 1779 John Henderson, the great actor who died too soon, was the star. In 1787 Covent Garden was rebuilt and five years later greatly enlarged. On 7 May 1789 Macklin bade farewell to the stage, breaking down half-way through Shylock.

Charles Incledon, a famous tenor, was at Covent Garden in 1790, and Mrs. Glover made her London début there in 1797. In 1800 George Frederick Cooke, a genius who was to waste himself, made his London début there as Richard III. In 1803 John Philip Kemble, after breaking with Sheridan at Drury Lane, bought a sixth share of the Covent Garden Patent and appeared there, soon followed by his sister, Mrs. Siddons.

At the end of 1804 Master Betty, the Young Roscius, flamed from the stage, drawing a tremendous crowd. Parliament adjourned so that the Members might see him act. On 30 Sept. 1808 the theatre was burnt down, twenty-three firemen losing their lives. The loss was estimated at £150,000, of which only £50,000 was covered by insurance. Eight months later a new and more splendid theatre arose. It cost £150,000, two-thirds of which was raised by £500 shares. Robert Smirke, the architect, modelled it on the Temple of Minerva on the Acropolis, and it had statuary by Flaxman.

On account of the great expense incurred Kemble raised the prices. This, and his engagement of Madame Catalani, led to the celebrated O.P. (Old Prices) riots which broke out on the opening night, 18 Sept. 1809, as soon as Kemble stepped forward to speak. The plays were *Macbeth* and *The Quaker*. Pandemonium broke out, and the air was filled with cries of 'Old Prices!' Police and soldiers were called in, the Riot Act was read, but riot-

ing went on for sixty-one nights. The whole town took sides, men wearing the letters O.P. on their hats and waistcoats and women sporting medals similarly adorned. Kemble eventually gave way.

The ordinary expenses of the theatre at this time were £300 a night, and there was a quadruple company for tragedy, comedy, opera, and ballet. Between 1809 and 1821 most of the famous tragedians and comedians of the day appeared at Covent Garden, as well as noted opera-singers and famous pantomimists like Byrne, Farley, Bologna, Ellar, and Grimaldi. The receipts averaged £80,000 a season. On 29 June 1812 Mrs. Siddons made her farewell appearance, though she reappeared in 1817 and 1819, and in 1817 John Philip Kemble gave a farewell performance as Coriolanus—his favourite part—and he never played it better. His last appearance was almost as impressive as Garrick's. The previous year Macready had made his London début, being well received, though he did not create a sensation. In 1824 Charles Kemble, who had taken charge of Covent Garden on his elder brother's retirement, produced *King John* with 'historically accurate' scenery and costumes. This was the first attempt at such realism, John Philip having refused to do it, saying he did not want to be taken for an antiquary.

Disagreements now led to lawsuits, and the theatre suffered, Drury Lane reaping the benefit. By 1829 the bailiffs were in possession. Charles Kemble's daughter Fanny stepped into the breach. So great was her success that she enabled her father to pay off his debts to the extent of £13,000 in one season. But she soon left the stage, having no liking for it. In May 1832 Laporte took command, and Young, the tragedian, made his farewell. In the following year, on 25 Mar., Edmund Kean, who had been at Covent Garden since 1827, made his dramatic last appearance as Othello with his son Charles as Iago. In 1833 also the theatre was taken over by Bunn, of Drury Lane, and two years later by Osbaldiston, who engaged Macready and Charles Kean, reduced the prices, and introduced Helen Faucit to London. But the public stayed away.

In Sept. 1837 Macready, as manager and actor, tried to re-establish the theatre, engaging fine actors and putting on good plays. But his obstinacy in refusing to keep successes running, and his determination to have his own way in everything, ruined him, and he left Covent Garden in 1839.

Then came Madame Vestris, who opened with *Love's Labour's Lost* on 30 Sept. 1839. She began badly by closing the 1s. gallery, whose patrons filled the pit and lower gallery and booed heartily, but she scored a great success with *Love*, in which Anderson and Ellen Tree appeared. She also staged *Romeo and Juliet* with Shakespeare's text for the first time since Caroline days, and produced a beautiful version of *A Midsummer Night's Dream*. The greatest success during her tenancy was Boucicault's *London Assurance*. She did magnificent work altogether, particularly in the staging and dressing of her shows.

In 1842 Charles Kemble took over again, and his daughter Adelaide proved a fine singer. Bunn came back also for a short time, and with that the story of Covent Garden as a theatre really closes. It became an Opera House, and although on one or two occasions it staged panto-mimes, and made a notable contribution to theatre history when Martin-Harvey played *Oedipus Rex* in Reinhardt's production there in 1912, it has since been, save for occasional ventures into cinema and revue, and one prize-fight, entirely devoted to opera and ballet.

The old theatre was burnt down in 1856, and the present one dates from 1858.

W. M. P.

COVENTRY CYCLE, see ENGLAND, 1 and MYSTERY PLAY.

COVENTRY HOCKTIDE PLAY, see HOCKTIDE PLAY.

COWARD, NOEL (1899–   ), English actor, producer and composer, and a prolific drama-tist, who has been on the stage since childhood, making his first appearance on 27 Jan. 1911 in a fairy play, and later playing with Charles Hawtrey at the Prince of Wales's. His early plays, which include *The Young Idea* (1921), *The Vortex* (1924), and *Fallen Angels* (1925), aroused a great deal of controversy and were considered typical of the post-war generation, as was the successful *Hay Fever* (also 1925). They were, however, well suited to the taste of the time and in 1925 Coward had five plays running in London, including the revue *On With the Dance*, for which he wrote most of the music as well as the words, as he did later for *This Year of Grace* (1928). The inevitable reaction to his sudden success came with a riot on the first night of *Sirocco* (1927), but in 1929 Coward was winning golden opinions with the romantic sentiment of *Bitter Sweet*, and two years later he consolidated his position with the patriotic *Cavalcade*. Among later suc-cesses have been *Design for Living* (1932), the nine one-act plays of *To-night at 8.30* (1935), *Blithe Spirit* (1941), which has set up a record run for a non-musical play in England with 1,997 performances, *Present Laughter* (1942), and *Peace in Our Time* (1947). He has appeared in many of his own plays, and has published a diary of his war-time experiences and an auto-biography, *Present Indicative* (1937). It is as yet too early to assess his ultimate place in English drama, on which he has exercised a certain influence, but he is essentially a man of the theatre in all its aspects.

COWELL, a family of actors in England and America, of whom the first was (1) JOSEPH LEATHLEY (1792–1863), born in England and intended for the navy. At 19, however, he took to the stage, and after appearing in Plymouth and other provincial towns he joined the Drury Lane company. In 1821 he made his first appearance in America, making a great success as Crack in *The Turnpike Gate*, a part ever

after associated with his name. He was later in Philadelphia with William Warren, and from 1826 until his return to England in 1844, in which year he also published his auto-biography, he was one of the most popular comedians in America, though a short venture into management in 1837 proved unsuccessful. In 1850 he reappeared in New York, making his final appearance in the part of Crack, and then returned to England to die. Through his wife he was connected with the Kembles, as her sister married Henry, son of Sarah Siddons. His son (2) SAMUEL HOUGHTON (1820–64) was one of the earliest stars of the English music-halls. Born in London, he grew up in America, and was billed originally as the Young American Roscius. He played in Edinburgh in 1840 and later in London. But it was as the singer of 'Villikins and his Dinah' and 'The Ratcatcher's Daughter' that he became popular, making a big hit at the Grecian in 1851 and later at the Canterbury. In 1860 he embarked on a star-ring tour of America which brought about his death from consumption. His wife, an actress whom he married while in Edinburgh, kept a diary of the tour, published in 1934 by M. Willson Disher as *The Cowells in America*. Her two daughters, (3) SYDNEY (1846–1925) and (4) FLORENCE (1852–1925), were both on the stage, the former making her first appearances in London and the provinces. While still a young woman she went to the United States with Charles Wyndham, and remained there, subsequently marrying an American. She was at her best in such parts as Maggie Mac-Farlane in *Engaged* and Dolly Dutton in *Hazel Kirke*, which ran for a year at the Madison Square Theatre, and was afterwards seen all over the United States. In 1900 she retired, but returned to the stage five years later, play-ing small parts. Florence, who is best known as Mrs. A. B. Tapping, was for many years with the Kendals. Her daughter (5) SYDNEY (1872–1941), by a previous marriage with the actor John Parselle (1820–85), appeared on the stage under her great-grandmother's name, as Sydney Fairbrother, and was successful in a wide variety of plays, from *Two Little Vaga-bonds* to *Chu-Chin-Chow*, besides Shakespeare and Shaw. She was a fine character actress in her later years, one of her best parts being Mrs. Badger in *The Young Person in Pink* (1920). She also toured the music-halls with the elder Fred Emney in the sketch *A Sister to Assist 'Er.*

Sam Cowell's half-sister, (6) SIDNEY FRANCES (1823–81), married the actor-manager H. L. Bateman, under whom Irving first appeared at the Lyceum (see BATEMAN).

COWLEY, ABRAHAM (1618–67), English poet and Royalist spy, who was also the author of a play which, as *The Guardian*, was given at Cambridge before Prince Charles just before the outbreak of the Civil War. As *Cutter of Coleman Street*, this was one of the first plays performed publicly at the Restoration. It was given at the Duke's House by Davenant's company at the end of 1661. A comedy of contemporary manners, it satirized both the Puritans and the Cavaliers, and was much enjoyed by Pepys, who was present at its first London performance. Its satire was not, however, everywhere acceptable. In spite of this it was given at Court, and was revived in 1668, 1702, and 1723. Cowley, whose first volume of verse was published when he was only 15, was also the author of a pastoral comedy composed while he was at school, and probably not acted, and of a Latin play given at Cambridge in 1639.

COWLEY, HANNAH (neé PARKHOUSE) (1743–1809), one of the first women playwrights of England, whose work marks the transition from Restoration to eighteenth-century comedy, though without too strong an infusion of sentimentality. She was at her best in the comedy of manners, and her first play, *The Runaway*, given at Covent Garden in 1776, is said to have been improved by Garrick. Of her later plays, which include *Which is the Man?* (1782), *A Bold Stroke for a Husband* (1783), and *The Town Before You* (1794), all given at Covent Garden, the best is *The Belle's Stratagem* (1780), based on *La Fausse Agnès*, by Destouches. This was revived several times, notably by the Kembles and by Irving, Ellen Terry playing Letitia, one of Mrs. Jordan's finest parts. It was last seen in London at the Court Theatre in 1913, and was one of the earliest comedies to be given in the New World, being in the repertory of the Hallams and Hodgkinson in New York in 1794. There also it was frequently revived, Ada Rehan playing Letitia to Arthur Bourchier's Doricourt in 1893. In 1813 a number of Mrs. Cowley's plays were published with a biographical notice.

COWLEY, RICHARD (?–1619), an Elizabethan actor who was the first man to play Verges, probably to the Dogberry of Kempe. He was one of Lord Strange's Men in 1593, and joined the Lord Chamberlain's Men on their formation in the following year. He is in the actor-list of Shakespeare's plays, but does not appear to have been a sharer in either the Globe or Blackfriars.

COX, ROBERT (?–1655), an English actor of the time of Charles I, who, on the closing of the playhouses in 1642, managed to evade the ban by playing drolls, or short farcical pieces, with himself in the chief parts, interspersed with rope-dancing and conjuring. He appeared at country fairs, and at the Red Bull playhouse in London where, with several companions, he was apprehended in 1653 by Commonwealth soldiers, and imprisoned. Apart from one or two drolls which he is presumed to have written himself, his repertory consisted mainly of extracts from popular plays (i.e. 'Bottom the Weaver' from *A Midsummer Night's Dream*). These were published by Francis Kirkman as *The Wits; or, Sport upon Sport* (1662, new ed. 1672) with a laudatory preface. Cox was a great favourite with his audiences, and

apparently a good actor, upon whom the closing of the theatres fell heavily.

CRABTREE, CHARLOTTE (1847–1924), an American actress, known on the stage simply as Lotta. Born in New York, she was taken to California at the age of 6, where she was taught to dance by the famous Lola Montez. An attractive child, tiny, with black eyes and a mop of red hair, she toured the mining-camps from the age of 8, singing, dancing, and reciting, and becoming, in ten years of this nomadic and often dangerous life, a well-known and much-loved figure. In 1865 she went to New York, and there made her first success in Brougham's dramatization of *The Old Curiosity Shop* (1867), in which she played Little Nell and the Marchioness. Throughout her career she preserved a look of youth and innocence, even in her most daring dances and by-play. She was outstanding in burlesque and extravaganza, and in slight plays specially written to give scope for her comic powers, among which were *Zip* and *Musette*, in which she toured indefatigably. She retired in 1891, having amassed a large fortune, which she left to charity. She was never married.

CRAIG. (1) EDITH (1869–1947), daughter of Ellen Terry and E. W. Godwin. She appeared on the stage as a child, and as a young woman played with her mother and Irving at the Lyceum. She also appeared with the former in *The Good Hope* and *Alice Sit-by-the-Fire*. During Ellen Terry's tour in America in 1907 she acted as her stage-manager, and later studied music at the R.A.M. and in Berlin. She then turned her attention to production, and from 1911 directed the Pioneer Players, for whom she also designed costumes and scenery. In 1929 she inaugurated an annual Shakespeare matinée on the anniversary of Ellen Terry's death, when performances were given in the converted barn adjacent to the house at Small Hythe where Ellen Terry spent her last years. This has now been made into an Ellen Terry Museum. Her brother (2) EDWARD GORDON (1872–   ) also appeared on the stage as a child, and in 1889 joined Irving's company at the Lyceum, where he remained for 9 years. During this time he played also many leading parts on tour, and in 1897 gave 6 performances of Hamlet at the Olympic. In 1903 he designed 3 scenes for Fred Terry's production of *For Sword or Song*, with some interesting and unusual lighting effects, and with, in one scene, a curious and most effective appearance of mist rising from the ground. He also did the designs for his mother's productions of *The Vikings* and *Much Ado About Nothing*, and from that time deserted the stage for design and production. Among his productions were *Venice Preserved* (1905) in Berlin, *Rosmersholm* (1906) for Eleonora Duse in Florence, and *Hamlet* (1912) at the Moscow Art Theatre. In 1908 he settled in Florence, where he founded and edited *The Mask*, a journal devoted to the art of the theatre, and also ran a school of acting in the Arena Goldoni. He has had an immense influence on production methods in Europe and America, more by his originality and prodigality of ideas than by his actual achievements. His theories, which cannot be briefly summarized, are best studied in his publications, *The Art of the Theatre* (1905); *On the Art of the Theatre* (1911), incorporating the previous book and frequently translated; *Towards a New Theatre* (1913), which contains 40 plates of scenic designs; *The Marionette* (1918); *The Theatre Advancing* (1921); *Books and Theatres* (1925). He has also written a volume on Irving and one on Ellen Terry, and published an edition of *Hamlet* with woodcuts. His theory of acting has been much criticized as reducing the actor to the status of a puppet working under the instruction of a mastermind 'capable of inventing and rehearsing a play; capable of designing and superintending the construction of both scenery and costume; of writing any necessary music; of inventing such machinery as is needed and the lighting that is to be used'. In 1926 he produced *The Pretenders* at Copenhagen, his designs for the production being subsequently published in portfolio. His influence has been most apparent in Germany and America, but has been somewhat overlooked in England, from whose theatre he seems to have been divorced by more than distance. His son (3) EDWARD ANTHONY (1905–) is a scenic designer and student of theatre architecture, under the name of Edward Carrick.

CRAIG THEATRE, NEW YORK, see ADELPHI THEATRE (2).

CRANE, RALPH (*c.* 1550/60–after 1621), in early life a household servant to the Osbornes, and later an underwriter in the Privy Seal Office. He added to his income by copying plays, either for their authors or for the actors. His copy of *Sir John van Olden Barnavelt*, made for the King's Men in 1619, was used as a prompt copy, and his two copies of *A Game of Chess* are in the Bodleian and the British Museum respectively. He also made the copy of *The Witch* which is in the Bodleian. There must have been an immense amount of this work done for the playhouses, and it is curious that more names and facts are not known in connexion with it. It was probably poorly paid, and done by hacks and hangers-on of the literary profession.

CRANE, WILLIAM HENRY (1845–1928), American actor, who had had some amateur experience before joining a light opera company. He had a fine bass voice, and intended to become an opera singer, but he proved so good in comedy that he finally devoted himself to it. In 1877 he joined forces with Stuart Robson, and they appeared as the two Dromios in *The Comedy of Errors*. Among their other successful plays were *Our Boarding House*, *Our Bachelors*, and *The Henrietta*, the last being specially written for them. Crane also played Falstaff and Sir Toby Belch, and after parting amicably from his companion in 1888 he con-

tinued to appear in bluff, kindly American parts. Among his later successes were *David Harum* and *Business is Business*. He retired in 1916.

CRATES, of Athens, one of the masters of Old Comedy, who won his first prize in 450 B.C. He was a contemporary of Aristophanes, who praised him in the *Knights* for his wit and graceful style. Fragments of his work survive (see GREECE, 2 *b*).   H. D. F. K.

CRATINUS (*c.* 520–*c.* 423 B.C.), of Athens, Greek dramatist, one of the masters of Old Comedy, and an elder contemporary of Aristophanes. Only fragments of his works survive. In the *Knights* Aristophanes makes fun of Cratinus as a worn-out drunkard; in the following year (424 B.C.) Cratinus had his revenge by defeating Aristophanes' *Clouds* with his own *Wine-Flask*, probably his last play. Aristophanes also speaks of Cratinus's torrential style, and of the popularity of his lyrics.
                                                       H. D. F. K.

CRAVEN, FRANK (1880–1945), American actor, dramatist, and producer, who made his first appearances on the stage as a child in Boston, where his parents were members of the stock company. He returned to the stage after some years' schooling, and toured extensively. His first New York success was James Gilley in *Bought and Paid For* (1911), in which he was also seen in London for the first time. During the long run of this play he wrote his first comedy, *Too Many Cooks*, in which he appeared himself in 1914. The most important of his later works was *The First Year* (1920), a comedy of domestic life which has been called 'a milestone in the American theatre', in that the 'matter and the manner, characters, dialogue and situation were all treated with a like gaiety and understanding'. He appeared in it himself, and was also seen as the Stage Manager in *Our Town*. Much of his later work was done in films.

CRAVEN, HAWES [HENRY HAWES CRAVEN GREEN] (1837–1910), English scene-painter, son of a pantomime actor and an actress. As a young boy he played in the provinces, but showed a preference for art and was apprenticed to the scene-painter of the Britannia, Hoxton. His first outstanding work was done for *The Lighthouse*, given at the Olympic in 1857. Befriended by Stanfield and Beverley, he worked at Covent Garden and Drury Lane, and from 1862 to 1864 was at the Theatre Royal, Dublin. He is, however, chiefly remembered for his connexion with Irving at the Lyceum, and his finest work was done for *Faust*, *Romeo and Juliet*, *Becket*, and *Coriolanus*, the last from designs by Alma Tadema. He was much admired, being considered the equal of Stanfield and Beverley in craftsmanship, and their superior in his grasp of theatrical essentials. As an innovator he ranks with de Loutherbourg, and was held by a contemporary critic to have 'carried scenic realism and stage illusion to their utmost limits, much helped by the recent introduction of electric lighting'. Ellen Terry, who knew his work well from her connexion with the Lyceum, called him 'dear Mr. Craven, who so loved his garden and could paint the flicker of golden sunshine for the stage better than anyone'.

CRÉBILLON, PROSPER JOLYOT DE (1674–1762), French dramatist, who in his own day enjoyed enormous prestige, no one being considered worthy to figure between him and Racine, thus conveniently forgetting Pradon, Longepierre, Genest, Campistron, and La Fosse, who were, perhaps, not worth remembering. Crébillon was 32 when his first play was given at the Comédie-Française. It was followed by three more, the last of which, *Rhadamiste et Zénobie* (1711), is usually considered his best. By this time he was lauded as the French Aeschylus, and it was commonly said that he had revived the great days of Corneille and Racine. But he had his detractors. Boileau called him 'Racine drunk' and 'a Visigoth in an age of good taste'. His poetry was certainly crude, but the audience bore with it for the sake of the romantic element, and the atmosphere of terror which he succeeded so well in imparting. His plays are, strictly speaking, not tragedies but melodramas, and they remained popular up to the time of the Romantics, when they were ousted by the works of the elder Dumas, on the principle that one corpse is good, but two are better. Crébillon's early plays, in spite of their success, brought him little money, and his later ones were failures. Continually hampered by poverty and by the consequences of an imprudent marriage, Crébillon became embittered and a recluse. He used his position as dramatic censor to oppose Voltaire, while the latter, to prove his superiority in verse-writing, took for the subjects of five of his tragedies plots already treated by Crébillon. The only good thing Crébillon got from his rivalry with Voltaire was a pension, granted him at the age of 72 at the instance of Voltaire's enemies, who chose to exalt the work of the older man at the expense of the younger.

CREPIDATA, see FABULA (2).

CRISPIN, a character of French comedy who derives from the *commedia dell'arte* mask, Scaramuccia (Scaramouche). As originally played by Raymond Poisson, he had in him something of the braggart captain, as witness his enormous rapier, and a good deal of the *zanni* or servant. Succeeding generations of Poissons played the part until 1753, making him more and more a quick-witted unscrupulous valet. Molière used the character but not the name, which was introduced by Scarron. It later figured largely in French comedy, as in *Crispin rival de son maître*, *Crispin musicien*, *Crispin gentilhomme*, and as a character in *Le Légataire universel* and *Le Chevalier à la mode*.

CRITERION THEATRE. (1) LONDON, in Piccadilly Circus. This theatre stands on historic ground, for its site was once St. James's

Market, where stood the Mitre Tavern, in which Farquhar discovered Nance Oldfield, and where George III first met Hannah Lightfoot. The theatre was originally an adjunct to Spiers and Pond's restaurant, and opened in 1874 with *An American Lady*, with Mrs. John Wood in the title role. It was—as it still is—an underground theatre, and air had to be pumped into it. Success did not come until 1877, with the production of *The Pink Dominos*, a farce adapted from the French. In the cast was Charles Wyndham, who in 1879 took over the theatre, inaugurating his management with *Truth*. He reconstructed and greatly improved the theatre, which was one of the first to be lit by electricity. Among his successful productions were *Betsy* (1879) and *Little Miss Muffet* (1882), also adaptations of French farce. In the latter Beerbohm Tree attracted attention. In 1886 Wyndham himself made a great personal success in *David Garrick*, outshining Sothern, the original player of the part. In 1899 Wyndham left the theatre to go to his own new playhouse, named after him (see WYNDHAM'S THEATRE), but remained lessee of the Criterion till his death. He reappeared there from time to time, notably in 1907 in *The Mollusc*, a triumph for himself and for his wife, Mary Moore. Among the successful plays staged at this theatre mention must be made of *Ambrose Applejohn's Adventure*, *Lord Richard in the Pantry*, and, during the war of 1914–18, *A Little Bit of Fluff*, which ran for 1,241 performances. Among more recent successes was *French Without Tears*, produced in 1936, which ran for 1,039 performances. The Criterion was in use as a theatre up to the outbreak of war in 1939, and for a short time after that, until the B.B.C. took it over as a studio. It is still under the control of Wyndham's family, and is a theatre again.   W. M. P.

(2) NEW YORK, opened as the Lyric on 25 Nov. 1895, as part of Hammerstein's Olympia. It seated 2,800 and had a roof garden for promenading. In 1899, having been sold at auction, it reopened as the Criterion under Charles Frohman. Among its early productions were Julia Marlowe in *Barbara Frietchie* (1899), John Hare and Irene Vanbrugh in *The Gay Lord Quex* (1900), and Mrs. Leslie Carter in *Zaza* (1901). In 1903 Charles Hawtrey opened the season with *The Man from Blankley's*, while the following year *The Dictator*, with Willam Collier and John Barrymore, ran for three months. In 1908 Isadora Duncan was seen at the Criterion; Laurette Taylor was successful in *Happiness* (1917) and *One Night in Rome* (1919), and the last production, before the house became a cinema, was a version of Brieux's *La Robe Rouge*, as *The Letter of the Law*, with Lionel Barrymore.

(3) The Herald Square Theatre, New York, originally the Colosseum, was named the Criterion from 1882 to 1885.   G. F.

CRITICISM, see DRAMATIC CRITICISM.

CROSS KEYS INN, see INNS USED AS THEATRES.

CROTHERS, RACHEL (1878–   ), American dramatist, whose first short plays were produced while she was a student at a dramatic school. She subsequently appeared on the stage, and has been responsible for the production of all her own plays. These include *The Three of Us* (1906); *A Man's World* (1909), an attack on the 'double standard of morality' which has been regarded as one of the most significant plays of its time; *He and She* (also known as *The Herfords*) (1911), in which Rachel Crothers herself played the lead in a revival in 1920; *A Little Journey* (1918); *Nice People* (1920), a study of post-war youth; *Expressing Willie* (1924); *As Husbands Go* (1931), which contrasts the English and the American conception of marriage; *When Ladies Meet* (1932), a deft study of feminine psychology; and *Susan and God* (1937). Miss Crothers, who has had a long and distinguished career in the American theatre, has always been in the vanguard of public opinion, yet has never allowed her feminist viewpoint to weaken the theatrical effectiveness of her writing. Quinn, who calls her a 'craftsman' of the theatre, says of her:

Without inventive power of the highest order, she is a keen observer of life, especially in the concrete, and her plays are filled with minor characters who indeed at times attract attention more easily than the major ones. Her view of life is sane and progressive . . . This ability to progress, to keep abreast of the fashions of the theatre and the conditions of life, reveals the flexibility and adaptability which are her most characteristic traits.

CROW STREET THEATRE, see DUBLIN.

CROWNE, JOHN (?1640–1703 or 1714), a Restoration dramatist and a favourite of Charles II, whose birth, death, and parentage are all equally obscure. His best work was done in comedy, with the creation of Sir Courtly Nice in the play of that name (1685) based on Moreto—a favourite part with many actors; but he also contributed a two-part *Destruction of Jerusalem* (1677) to the contemporary spate of heroic drama. This was given at the Theatre Royal, with most elaborate scenery and dresses, at vast expense. The scenery was probably painted by Aggas and Towers, who later sued the theatre for payment. Indeed, it is possible that many of Crowne's successful but forgotten plays owed much to the resources of scenic art. Crowne was also the author of a masque, a tragedy in rhyme, and a verse comedy which, in the opinion of competent critics, shows a return to a late Elizabethan style. He may therefore be regarded as a synthesis of the dramatic styles and types prevalent in his day. He was part author, with Dryden and Shadwell, of the satirical *Notes and Observations* on Settle's *Empress of Morocco*.

CRUGER'S WHARF THEATRE, NEW YORK, built in 1758 by David Douglass, who appeared there with a company formed of the remnants of that of the elder Hallam, whose widow he had married, and some English actors brought to Jamaica by Moody. The younger Hallam was leading man, and his brother and sister were also in the company. They opened in *Jane Shore*, probably with Mrs. Douglass as the heroine, and after a season of two months ended up with *Richard III*, after which 'the Theatre on Mr. Cruger's Wharff' was used no more. It was sometimes referred to as the Wharf Theatre.

CRUMMLES, VINCENT, see LANDER, JEAN.

CRUZ, SOR JUANA INÉS DE LA (1651–95), see SOUTH AMERICA, 1.

CRUZ Y OLMEDILLA, RAMÓN DE LA (1731–94), a Spanish dramatist who deserves mention for his excellence in a time of general apathy with regard to the theatre. He refused to succumb to the prevailing influence of French neo-classicism, and produced a number of short one-act farces, or *sainetes*, a genre developed from the *paso* of Lope de Rueda, which are purely Spanish in subject and treatment. They portray in vivid but economical lines the daily life of the lower classes of Madrid, and for nearly fifty years were the only plays acceptable alike to the unlettered public and the erudite neo-classicists.

CSIKY, GERGELY (1841–91), Hungarian dramatist, and the first to put on the stage social problems of the Hungarian middle class.

CUEVA, JUAN DE LA (1550–1610), Spanish dramatist and the chief writer of the Sevillan school of drama. Some of his plays are on themes of classical antiquity, but he was one of the first to draw on Spanish history for his subjects (as in the *Siete Infantes de Lara*), and so paved the way for the great Spanish dramas of Lope de Vega and others. He mingled Italian metres with Spanish, varying them to suit the exigencies of plot and character, and drew freely on popular poetry to enliven his historical plays. He was also an innovator in the comedy of manners with his *El viejo enamorado* and *El infamador*.

CUMBERLAND, RICHARD (1732–1811), English dramatist, well educated, and a grandson of the great Richard Bentley, Master of Trinity College, Cambridge. He had spent some years in politics before in 1761 he embarked on a career as a prolific playwright, mainly because he was in need of money. He wrote a number of poor tragedies, including reworkings of *Timon of Athens* with a new fifth act, and of two plays by Massinger, but it is in sentimental domestic comedy that his most characteristic work is found. He first achieved recognition with *The Brothers* (1769), but his best-known play is *The West Indian* (1771), produced with great success by Garrick, and typical of the whole school of sentimental comedy. Among his later plays were *The Fashionable Lover* (1772) and *The Jew* (1794), the latter one of the earliest plays to plead the cause of Jewry. It was frequently revived, and translated into several languages, providing a fine part for outstanding actors of the day.

Cumberland, whose success made him an important figure in the literary world of London, was extremely sensitive to criticism, and figures in *The Critic* as Sir Fretful Plagiary, a portrait which his own memoirs, published in 1807, show to be substantially true. A study of his life and works by S. T. Williams was published in 1917 by the Yale University Press. With Hugh Kelly he is perhaps the most typical exponent of the eighteenth-century style which received its death-blow at the hands of Goldsmith and Sheridan.

CUREL, FRANÇOIS DE (1854–1929), French dramatist, whose plays belong to the naturalistic movement, and were first produced at Antoine's Théâtre Libre. A wealthy man of good family, he was trained as a scientist, and brought his analytical faculties to bear on the problems of social life. His first three plays dealt with feminine psychology, and were somewhat limited in scope, though giving promise of the excellence shown in his later works, of which the best was *Le Repas du lion* (1897). This was a study of the struggle between tradition and socialism, which he later returned to and revised. De Curel, who was a somewhat remote and unconventional playwright, never became popular, but his work ranks high for its integrity and its subtle delineation of souls in torment.

CURTAIN. Within the proscenium opening (see PROSCENIUM) hangs the curtain, unknown in the Elizabethan theatre. In the Restoration theatre it rose at the conclusion of the Prologue (spoken on the forestage) and remained out of sight till the play was ended and the Epilogue spoken, when it fell to mark the finish of the performance. During the play the end of an act was marked by an empty stage, and the end of a scene merely by the changing of the scenery, often with the actors still on the stage ready to walk straight into the next action, and so sustain the flow of the play. This curtain was at first, and remained for many decades, green. Its commonest form was probably that of the 'french valance', in which a series of lines descend at the back through rows of rings. When the lines are pulled the curtain rises vertically in a series of bunching, shallow festoons. It might occasionally, and for special effects, be dropped during a performance, but it was not until about the mid-eighteenth century that it began to be used regularly to mark the end of the act, and to hide the stage during an interval. Shortly after, this function was transferred to the Act-Drop, a painted cloth descending in the proscenium opening, and bearing some decorative picture which became associated with the theatre and was not directly related to the play being performed. By 1895 the Act-Drop had become such a recognized feature of the theatre that popular articles were written on its proper design.

This drop, however, only marked the acts; the scene-transitions were still at this time unconcealed. It was not till Irving's revival of *The Corsican Brothers* in 1880 that a crimson velvet curtain was set in the proscenium to hide scene-changes, and even then the master-manager saw to it that the heaviest change was so well organized as to be performed in only 38 seconds.

The Front Curtain, often called the House Curtain, has to-day a variety of possible forms of working, including straightforward 'flying', or vertical ascent; side-parting on the traverse principle; and bunching up sideways to the outer top corners—a form often called Tabs (short for Tableau Curtain). This name is now applied to any front curtain, and is sometimes misapplied to the curtain setting on the stage itself.

Another curtain in the proscenium opening is the Safety or Fireproof Curtain, sometimes nicknamed the Iron, of which an example was present at Drury Lane as early as 1800. The Advertisement Curtain made its appearance as an act-drop in the smaller theatres, and bore, in various panels, painted notices of local manufacturers and their wares. (See also ENGLISH PLAYHOUSE, 3.) R. S.

CURTAIN-RAISER, a one-act play, usually farcical, which in the nineteenth century served to whet the appetite of the audience before the main five-act drama of the evening. It continued into the early years of the twentieth century, and was the last relic of the days when a full evening's entertainment included several plays to which late-comers were admitted on payment of a reduced fee. Together with the After-piece (see ENGLAND, 5), a one-act farce intended to mitigate the horrors of the preceding tragedy, it is now seldom seen, owing to the modern professional theatre's determined adherence to the single bill, and the one-act play survives only in the productions of the amateur theatre in England and America.

CURTAIN SET, see ENGLISH PLAYHOUSE, 3.

CURTAIN THEATRE. (1) LONDON. The first Curtain was London's second playhouse, opened in 1577, the year after the Theatre. There is no definite information as to who built it, how much it cost, or the actual date of its opening. It may be that Burbage was responsible for it as well as for the Theatre, for the two stood very close together. The Curtain seems to have been a more peaceful house than its neighbour. It took its name, not from a theatre curtain or act-drop, but from the fact that it stood on a piece of land called the Curtain, or Curtain Close, and later Curtain Court. The name survives to-day in Curtain Road, Shoreditch. The choice of Finsbury Fields was a wise one. It was the playground of London. The citizens practised archery there, train-band musters were held there, and the Artillery Company (now the H.A.C.) were near by. This place of public resort was the very spot for theatres.

In shape, form, and design the Curtain was the same as the Theatre, but its dimensions are not known. That it was crowded more often than not is proved by numerous entries in the legal records concerning pickpockets caught there red-handed, lifting the purses of members of the public gaping at the show; and at first it was probably a venue, as was the Theatre, for exhibitions of swordplay, fencing, quarterstaff, and the like. Theatrically it has a much more distinguished record than its older rival. Some of the most notable companies of the time appeared there under Elizabeth, including the Lord Chamberlain's, which on the accession of James I became the King's. Pope, who had a share in the theatre, was a member of this company, as were Tarleton and Armin, under the control of Burbage. They were specially licensed to appear at the Curtain in 1603. There were many attempts to suppress the Curtain, and it was seriously threatened with extinction when the Fortune was opened in 1600. The opponents of theatres, having succeeded in abolishing the Theatre itself, suddenly realized that the Fortune, another playhouse, was to be erected. They petitioned the Privy Council, who replied that it was not proposed to increase the number of theatres, and that should the Fortune arise, it would be in lieu of the Curtain. But nothing came of that, and the Curtain continued its existence. Its greatest glory is that it was associated with Shakespeare. It is claimed, with some justification, that *Henry V* was first played at the Curtain, and that it was 'the wooden O' referred to by the chorus. *Romeo and Juliet* may also have had its first production there, and Jonson's *Every Man in His Humour*, as it was by that time (1600) a home of legitimate drama.

In 1615, in spite of the opposition of the City Fathers, certain young men of the City, presumably talented amateurs, gave a performance of *Hector of Germany* at the Curtain. At that time it could be hired for such performances, or by any company who so desired. In 1617 the Prince's Company occupied it. In *Vox Graculi, or The Jackdaw's Prognostications for 1623*, it is said: 'about this time new plays will be more in request than old, and if company come current to the Bull and Curtain, there will be more money gathered in one afternoon than will be given to Kingsland and Spittle in a whole month.'

The last traceable reference to the Curtain is none too happy—a prosecution in 1627 of one Richard Burford 'for defiling a sewer near the Curtain Playhouse'. After that reference it vanishes from knowledge, but it is quite likely that it stood until the general suppression of theatres in 1642, in which case it lasted the longest of all the old playhouses.   w. m. p.

(2) LONDON. At one period the Holborn Theatre (1866-80) was called the Curtain.

(3) GLASGOW, founded by amateurs to facilitate the production of new plays by Scottish authors. It opened in January 1933 with a four nights' run in its own miniature theatre. After nearly three years' work in private, public presentations began in the autumn of 1935, and the last play to be presented was given in the spring of 1940. A number of interesting new plays were produced, among them Robert

McLellan's, with their vital grip of the vernacular, and two of Robins Millar's. The producer of most of the Curtain Theatre productions was Grace Ballantine, and careful attention was given to décor.   w. j.

(4) The name 'Curtain Theatre' was later taken by a small professional touring company under Ann Casson, younger daughter of Dame Sybil and Sir Lewis Casson, which toured the camps and civilian halls of the Orkneys, Scotland, and the north of England in the winter of 1943-4. Among the actors was Frank Baker, whose book, *Playing with Punch*, describes the tour and gives the text of his new version of the Punch and Judy play which was used by the company.

CURTAIN-TUNE, see ACT (1).

CUSHMAN. (1) CHARLOTTE SAUNDERS (1816-76), American actress, outstanding in tragic or character parts. She made her first appearance in opera, but had the misfortune to lose her voice and turned to straight acting. She made her first appearance on the legitimate stage in 1836, as Lady Macbeth, in which she was considered to be unequalled. At the Park Theatre, New York, she played a number of parts, including Romeo, but was at her best as Meg Merrilies in a dramatization of *Guy Mannering*, and as Nancy Sikes in *Oliver Twist*. She later played Oberon, and Lady Gay Spanker in the first American production of *London Assurance* (1841). A turning-point in her career came with a season in New York when she played opposite Macready, who noted in his diary: 'The Miss Cushman who acted Lady Macbeth interested me much. She has to learn her art, but she showed mind and sympathy with me; a novelty so refreshing to me on the stage.' According to a contemporary critic, her acting improved enormously after this experience, and on Macready's advice she went to London, where she was well received. She made her first appearance at the Princess's on 13 Feb. 1845, being seen as Lady Macbeth, Rosalind, Mrs. Haller, Beatrice, Meg Merrilies, and Portia. At the Haymarket later in the same year she was seen as Romeo to the Juliet of her sister (2) SUSAN (1822-59), who after an unhappy marriage with a Mr. Merriman had joined her sister on the stage. They played together in the provinces and in Dublin, and in 1848 Susan was married again, to an Englishman named Muspratt. Before returning to America in the following year Charlotte was seen as Queen Katharine to Macready's Wolsey at Drury Lane, for his benefit night. She repeated this part in New York, and also played Claude Melnotte. In 1852 she gave the first of many farewell performances, but remained before the public until a year before her death, being seen in 1857 as Cardinal Wolsey. Among the other great parts attempted by this intrepid woman were Hamlet, Phèdre, and Bianca. But her greatest part was undoubtedly Meg Merrilies, which she practically created, being criticized by some purists for her departures from the original novel. Dutton Cook wrote of her: 'Her performances lacked femineity, to use Coleridge's word; but in power to stir an audience, to touch their sympathies, to kindle their enthusiasm, and compel their applause, she takes rank among the finest players.' Joseph Jefferson, who admired her very much, praised her warm and charitable disposition, and described her as 'tall and commanding in person, with an expressive face, whose features might have been called plain but for their strength and character'. During the last years of her life, though she continued to act intermittently, she was mainly occupied with Shakespeare readings, which proved very successful.

CUT, a division practised in the floor-boards of a stage to allow the passage of flat scenery (see STAGE, 1).

CUT-CLOTH, see CLOTH.

CYCLORAMA. This scenic device has had a short and not entirely happy history. In principle it is the solution to half a scene-designer's difficulties, but in practice its design and accommodation on any given stage are matters demanding the greatest forethought. The cyclorama is, in essence, a curved wall, or section of a dome, built at the back of the stage, and demanding one quality—an absolutely unbroken surface. Upon it light can be thrown, and the effects thus achieved are amazing; but to present that perfect surface a cyclorama has to be rigidly and heavily built, and it should generally be of hard cement. Thus it becomes a completely immobile part of the stage, and so a potential obstacle when not needed. Movable cycloramas have been invented, but never widely adopted. A full cyclorama interferes with access to the stage from the sides, and with the suspension of scenery from above. It thus tends to limit the scenery used on the stage to one given style only, and to restrict or forbid the use of other, traditional, types of scene arrangement. A partial, or shallow, cyclorama—even a plain, uncurved, distempered back wall—is often used instead of a full cyclorama, and has proved effective and less restrictive. A well-planned cyclorama may considerably reduce the amount of scenery needed to mask a stage, but only if the types of scenes are such as can widely include the cyclorama effect. In most other cases it is useless, and the scenery must stand in front of it and hide it. (See also LIGHTING and SCENERY.)   R. S.

CYRANO DE BERGERAC, see BERGERAC.

CZECHOSLOVAKIA. 1. DRAMA. Owing to the multilingual character of Czecho-slovakia the history of her theatre divides into three main currents of language and culture, (a) German, (b) Slovak, and (c) Czech.

(a) The achievements of the German minority are bound up with the history of the German theatre as a whole, and must be sought within that framework (see GERMANY).

(b) The Slovaks were able to build up a theatrical culture of their own only after the foundation of the Czechoslovakian Republic in 1918, since their Hungarian overlords had previously suppressed with a ruthless hand any sign of cultural life on their part. Aided by the State, Drašar, a Czech, founded and directed the Slovak National Theatre in Bratislava, using for the purpose the municipal theatre which had formerly housed exclusively Hungarian or German theatrical companies. As only a few Slovak-speaking actors were at first available, a bilingual Czech and Slovak repertory was organized. Opera was under the control of Oskar Nedbal, the composer of 'Polish Blood', and after his death under that of his son Karel. Victor Šulc (who died in a German concentration camp) led the Czech, Janko Borodáč the Slovak, company. In the twenty years till 1938 a number of excellent Slovak actors came to the fore, especially in the realm of traditional popular art, capable of taking into their own hands the development of the Slovak theatre. The tragic actress Olga Orszaghová-Borodáčová deserves mention in this connexion, and such actors as Andrej Bagar and Ján Sýkora.

(c) The main interest, however, focuses on the Czech theatre. International art has already given a place of honour to the musicians of this small nation, such as Smetana, Dvořák, and Janáček, and it may be that only language difficulties have hindered a like appreciation of the astonishing development of Czech dramatic art. This has followed a somewhat different course from that of other European nations, owing to the unfavourable position of the Czechs in history. The tradition of the native Passion play was submerged in the Hussite wars of religion in the early part of the fifteenth century. The promising beginnings of humanist drama were smothered, together with many other expressions of Czech national life, by the tyranny of the Habsburgs from the onset of the Thirty Years War. After the battle of Bílá Hora (1620) the Czech nobility and intelligentsia were either executed or forced to emigrate. For more than 150 years Czech culture was apparently dead.

After an unsuccessful attempt by von Brunian in 1771, František Bulla, in 1785, was the first to give performances of plays in Czech. Manager of the Prague Theatre, hitherto devoted to Italian opera and German plays, Bulla's intention was to contribute to the revival of Czech national culture by means of the spoken word sounding from the stage. From this 'period of awakening', which lasted for more than half a century, dates the prevalent idea of the theatre as an important instrument in the furthering of Czech national culture. This awareness of responsibility is one of the main reasons for the high standing of contemporary dramatic art in Czechoslovakia.

Until the end of the eighteenth century Czech language and culture had been preserved almost entirely by the obstinate efforts of the peasantry and lower middle classes. Consequently their way of life forms the subject of the first popular dramatic pieces by such authors as J. K. Tyl, V. K. Klicpera, J. N. Štěpánek, S. K. Macháček, and others. There can be no doubt that Czech drama owes its naïve charm, its vivacity, and much of its force to this source. It is interesting to note that a lyric from the unassuming musical play *Fidlovačka* (The Fair), written in 1834 by Tyl with music by František Škroup, has become the Czech national anthem, 'Kde domov můj' (Where is my home?).

It took a long time, however, before the Czech theatre found its own home. Mostly it languished in primitive suburban halls, or in the inn-yards of small towns much frequented by local amateur companies, which, by the way, have remained a continual source of inspiration both to the amateur and professional stage to this day. Performances in Czech were only sporadically tolerated in the splendid Theatre of the Corporation of Bohemia, built in 1783 by Count Nostitz-Rieneck. It was not until 1862 that a Provisional Theatre was erected from private funds, by the Czech for the Czech. On the same site, twenty-one years later, arose a representative National Theatre, seating 1,800, built by contributions from the entire nation. On the frieze above the stage runs the proud inscription 'Národ Sobě' (The nation to itself), and to this day the Czechs consider this so-called 'little golden chapel' one of the highest symbols of their national independence and culture.

This is the starting-point of the evolution of the Czech national theatre, from its awakening to full artistic achievement under the management of F. A. Šubrt, which lasted from 1883 to 1900. The first generation of eminent actors and actresses, Kollár, Šamberk, Šmaha, and Sklenářová-Malá and Laudová, still modelled their style on the powerful rhetoric of the Viennese Burgtheater; but they were soon joined, and in some cases superseded, by the advocates of dramatic realism, among whom were Mošna, Sedláček, Slukov, Vávra, Želenský, and Benionová, Danzerová, and Grégrová. At the same time a generation of realistic dramatists arose, who combined the new technique with subjects of the national renaissance—as Šubrt's *Jan Výrava* (1886) and L. Stroupežnický's *Wenceslas Hrobčický of Hrobčic* (1888)—or transformed rural subjects into broad pictures of life with social undertones—as A. Jirásek's *The Father* (1894), the brothers Mrštík's *Maryša* (1894), and G. Preissová's *Její pastorkyna* (1890)—which last provided the libretto for Janáček's opera 'Jenufa'.

Against this realist movement the romantic and poetic dramatists, such as Julius Zeyer and Jaroslav Vrchlický, found it difficult to prevail; but the latter has enriched the nation's heritage by his admirable translations of great world literature. He, with J. V. Sládek, gave the Czech language its own version of Shakespeare, and his translations of the classics have not been superseded even by the more modern

interpretations in prose of E. A. Saudek and B. Štepánek.

The presentation of Shakespeare on the Czech stage began with the actor and producer J. J. Kollár, and found its most passionate and outstanding interpreter in Jaroslav Kvapil, who succeeded Šubrt as manager of the National Theatre from 1900 till 1927. The climax of Kvapíl's life and work was his production of twenty-eight of Shakespeare's plays, of which fifteen were performed in 1916 to mark the Tercentenary, as an expression of Czech admiration for this great dramatist and as a hint of solidarity with his country.

Before Kvapil, German and Austrian influence had been paramount in the Czech theatre, but he brought it under the influence of Western and Russian classical and modern drama, and of impressionism. Under his guidance a new generation of actors grew up, culminating in the overwhelming personality of Edward Vojan, accounted the greatest Czech tragedian of all time, and in the delicacy of Hana Kvapilová, Kvapil's wife and his most subtle interpreter. Other eminent actors of this time were Dejl, Hašler, Hurt, Schlaghammer, Steimar, and Viesner, while Kvapil discovered and developed such diametrically opposed talents as that of Marie Huebnerová (who died in 1931), unsurpassed exponent of women of the people in popular drama, and Anna Sedláčková, probably one of the most elegant and entrancing leading ladies of the Central European stage.

Kvapil was succeeded by K. H. Hilar, who had the outstanding personality necessary for success. Whereas Kvapil's concern had been all for harmony and delicacy, Hilar was ready for the forcible expression and revolutionary experiment which characterized the post-war period. He had been, since 1914, director of the Municipal Theatre of Královské Vinohrady (situated in one of the boroughs which make up the city of Prague), founded in 1907 under Šubrt and V. Štech. Under Hilar it had become one of the most important theatres in the country.

Up to his death in 1935, Hilar passed through several successive stages without damage, however, to his creative power. He began with expressionism, went over to collectivistic interpretation of great drama, including, among other things, Marlowe's *Edward II* and Shakespeare's *Romeo and Juliet*, *Hamlet*, and *Coriolanus*, and ended up with civilism, and the new 'matter-of-fact' style. It is to Hilar, even more than to Kvapil, that the majority of Czech dramatists of the last two generations owe much of their vigour and variety, and the furthering of their work in performance. Perhaps the most important of them was Karel Čapek (1890–1938), author of *The Insect Play* and *R.U.R.*, both given in London.

A new generation of psychological actors, formed under Hilar, reached their maturity in the nineteen-thirties. Even the younger ones of the following decades have not entirely escaped his influence; and to him also is due the rise of scenic design in the Czech theatre. Even before 1914 conventionalism, and the slavish copying of reality in décor, was considered a thing of the past. The new stage, seen three-dimensionally, with aesthetic laws of its own, has produced one of the foremost scenic artists of the day, Hilar's most fervent collaborator, Vlastislav Hofman. With him are a score of others, who have enriched the European theatre with their impressionist, constructivist, or surrealist scenes.

After Kvapil and Hilar came E. F. Burian, a strong personality in Czech stagecraft. Equally outstanding as actor, stage director, composer, and choreographer, he aimed at a fusion of language, movement, music, lighting, painting, and sculpture, giving to each of them an equally important function in his productions, in which he has been ably seconded by the stage designs of Kouřil. Thanks to exceptional talent, untiring energy, and uncompromising directness, he came near to realizing his ideals. From its opening in 1934 his small experimental theatre, where he formed his own company of actors trained in his own methods, gradually overshadowed the official institutes.

Besides Burian the leading theatre directors of Czechoslovakia were J. Honzl, an ardent surrealist, A. Kurš, a pupil of the Moscow Art Theatre, J. Frejka and A. Podhorský, exponents of ultra-modern ideas at the National Theatre. Their more conservative colleagues at the theatres run by the State were K. Dostál, V. Novák, and Jan Bor, Director of the Municipal Theatres from 1927 to 1936, and successor of O. Fischer as Director of the National Theatre. Bor's predilections were for the Russian authors. His successor as Director of the Municipal Theatres in 1936 was Bohuš Stejskal, a cultivated, delicate, and precise man.

Prague's theatre history would not be complete without the mention of two outstanding private permanent theatres. The first was the 'Osvobozené Divadlo' (The Unfettered Theatre) run by two most original comedians, Voskovec and Werich, who, under the mask of ingenious clowning, had since 1926 been ardent advocates of cultural and political progress. After Munich they were forced to transfer their highly successful activities to New York's Broadway. The second theatre was dominated by Vlasta Burian, popular comedian of the middle classes. Incidentally, both these theatres, and a few cinemas, were built underground.

Before 1939 Prague had fifteen to twenty professional theatres, performing on weekdays, Sundays, and most holidays. The non-private ones were repertory theatres. Tickets were relatively inexpensive. Outside Prague the most important theatres were those at Brno, the capital of Moravia, the National Theatre of Moravia and Silesia at Moravská Ostrava, and the municipal theatres of Pilsen and Olomouc.

2. OPERA. Czech opera, too, had great difficulties to overcome at first. Up to 1724 only occasional performances of opera were given in Prague, by Italian companies. In that year the Italian opera-house of Count Šporck was opened, and later Italian opera found a permanent home in Count Nostitz's theatre, acquired in 1798 by the Corporation of Bohemia. The climax of this period came when Mozart conducted a festival performance of his 'Marriage of Figaro' on 14 Oct. 1787, followed by the first performance, on 29 Oct., of 'Don Giovanni', an event which has for ever established a bond between the memory of Mozart and the musical world of Prague.

The Italians were superseded by German romantic opera, particularly during Karl Maria von Weber's appointment as conductor to the Theatre of the Corporation, from 1813 to 1816. Meanwhile Czech composers had to seek their fortune abroad, especially in Italy and Germany. These included, among others, Josef Mysliveček, who had some influence on Mozart, Jiří Benda, and Václav Pichl. The first opera given at Prague in Czech was Weigl's 'The Swiss Family' (1823), and the first genuinely Czech opera was František Škroup's 'Dráteník' (The Tinker), first performed on 2 Feb. 1826, and it was not until the opening of the Provisional Theatre in 1862 that Czech opera found a permanent abiding-place. There, despite the modest scenic resources available, it soared to the heights in which Czech music culminated—the works of Bedřich Smetana (1824–84). His admiration for Wagner is most pronounced in his earliest opera, 'Braniboři v Čechách' (The Brandenburgers in Bohemia) (1863), also in his heroic opera 'Dalibor' (1868) and the pageant of 'Libuše' (1872); but his own and his country's musical reputation throughout the world was established by his 'Prodaná Nevěsta' (The Bartered Bride) (1866), which, together with the slighter but equally melodious 'Hubička' (The Kiss) (1876), and 'Tajemství' (The Secret) (1878), is drawn from the inexhaustible fountain of Czech folk-song and folk-lore. The tale of Smetana's operas is completed with 'Dvě vdovy' (The Two Widows) (1874) and the tragic 'Čertova Stěna' (The Devil's Wall) (1882).

The Provisional Theatre is associated also with Smetana as a conductor, with the composers V. Blodek and K. Bendl, and with the first operas of Zdeněk Fibich (1850–1900) and Antonín Dvořák (1841–1904). The world knows Dvořák almost exclusively by his instrumental music, but in his own country his 'Rusalka' (libretto by Kvapil) (1901) is, after 'The Bartered Bride', the opera most frequently performed. This and his other operas, particularly the delightfully gay 'Tvrdé palice' (The Pigheaded Peasants) (1881) and 'Šelma sedlák' (The Peasant a Rogue) (1878), the tragic operas 'Vanda' (1876), 'Dimitrij' (1882), and 'Armida' (1904), and the legendary 'Čert a Káča' (The Devil and Kate) (1899), show the vigour of his musical genius. Fibich, much influenced by Wagner, was nevertheless an exponent of national music. His best operas were 'Bouře (The Tempest, based on Shakespeare) (1894), 'Hedy' (Haidée, from Byron's *Don Juan*) (1895), and Šárka (on a national legend) (1897).

The opening of the National Theatre in 1883, and the great success obtained by its company with 'Dalibor' and 'The Bartered Bride', given in Czech at the Vienna Exhibition in 1892, inaugurated a period of brilliant performances of Czech and other operas under the outstanding conductor, Karel Kavařovic, supported by such excellent stage directors as Polák, and splendid singers, among them Emmy Destinn (Ema Destinová). Further eminent Czech composers came to the fore. Besides Kovařovic himself, these included such names as J. B. Foerster, Novák, Suk, and above all

Leoš Janáček (1854–1928), whose 'Jenufa', after an unnoticed first performance in Brno in 1904, was brilliantly successful under Kovařovic in 1916. Janáček's other operas, too, are masterpieces of dramatic eloquence, their music springing naturally from the melody of the spoken word.

A young composer, Otokar Ostrčil (1879–1935), formerly conductor at the Municipal Theatre, succeeded Kovařovic. His outstanding characteristics were an almost fanatical adherence to the score, great artistic integrity, and a liking for modern scenic and musical experiments. With his stage director Pujman he directly influenced the younger generation of composers—among them Jaromír Weinberger (1896–   ), whose 'Švanda dudák' (Schwanda the Bagpiper) (1927) had a sensational success all over Europe. P. L. (*tr.* F. S.)

D

DAHLGREN, FREDRIK AUGUST (1816–95), Swedish dramatist (see SCANDINAVIA, 3).

DAKOTA PLAYMAKERS, see KOCH, F. H.

DALBERG, BARON WOLFGANG HERIBERT VON (1750–1806), a wealthy and aristocratic amateur of the theatre who was also a playwright. His interest in theatrical matters led to his appointment in 1779 as honorary director of the newly opened Mannheim National Theatre. Here his inexperience led to his making a bad start by engaging Seyler and his redoubtable wife Sophie Hensel at the same time as her bitter rival, the wife of Brandes. Their quarrels led to the speedy departure of both couples, and a new democratic rule was instituted. After the death of Ekhof in Gotha in 1778 Dalberg arranged for his actors to be transferred to Mannheim, and with a fine company headed by Iffland the theatre flourished. Iffland's first plays were given there, as was *Julius Caesar* for the first time in Germany in an adaptation by Dalberg. But the chief glory of this period was the production of the young and then unknown Schiller's first play, *Die Räuber*, and his appointment as theatre poet from 1783–4, during which time *Fiesco* and *Kabale und Liebe* also appeared. The enterprise continued to prosper until the rigours of war reached Mannheim in 1796, when it was disbanded and Iffland left to go to Berlin.

DALIN, OLOF (1708–63), Swedish dramatist, the first to introduce contemporary French classic tragedy to the Swedish stage. He was also the author of a number of comedies, which show the influence of Molière and Holberg.

DALY, (JOHN) AUGUSTIN (1839–99), American dramatist and manager. At 21 he became a dramatic critic, and by the time he was 30 had served in that capacity on several leading papers. He also wrote and adapted a number of plays, among them the London melodrama, *Under the Gaslight*, and *Leah the Forsaken* (from Mosenthal's *Deborah*). In 1869 he went into management, opening the Fifth Avenue Theatre, New York, where he produced a season of Shakespearian and other plays. In 1873 the theatre was burned down, but he rebuilt it, retiring from its management in 1878. He then spent a short time in England, but returned to New York to open his own theatre (see below) with a fine company headed by John Drew and Ada Rehan, which in 1884, under the management of William Terriss, played at Toole's Theatre in London. Although previously unknown, Ada Rehan scored such a success there that the company became welcome visitors, returning to the old Strand Theatre in 1886, to the Gaiety in 1888, and the Lyceum in 1890. Daly then decided to have his own theatre in London (see below). After his return to New York in 1894, Daly made one more visit to London before his death. Both in New York and in London his first nights were important events, and he was one of the outstanding managers of his day on both sides of the Atlantic. He accomplished much, and had a high standard, in spite of his tendency to tamper with the text of established classics.

W. M. P.

DALY, (PETER CHRISTOPHER) ARNOLD (1875–1927), American actor, who had already had some success on the stage, where he made his first appearance in 1892, when in 1903 he came into prominence with his production of *Candida*, in which he played Marchbanks. This was the first production of one of Shaw's plays in the United States since Mansfield's tour of *The Devil's Disciple* in 1897, and Daly, who was intensely interested in Shaw's work, and ready to further it by every means in his power, followed the success of *Candida* with a production of *Mrs. Warren's Profession* which led to an uproar and prosecution by the police. In spite of this Daly produced *You Never Can Tell*, *Arms and the Man*, and a double bill consisting of *The Man of Destiny* and a trifle written specially for him by Shaw, *How He Lied to Her Husband*. He also played this last sketch in vaudeville. Opposition eventually proved too much for him and he became soured by ill usage and the attacks of prudish journalists and city fathers. An effort to run a 'theatre of ideas' failed financially, and Daly, who was a good actor, though inclined to be somewhat temperamental, went back to the usual run-of-the-mill life of the theatre, dying in a fire in his early fifties.

DALY'S THEATRE. (1) NEW YORK (for Daly's first theatres in New York, see FIFTH AVENUE THEATRE). Daly's last theatre was originally Banvard's, and later Wood's, Museum. Plays were first given there in 1867, and under Wood in 1868 Lydia Thompson and her Blondes started the vogue for British burlesque. It was at this theatre that Laura Keene made her last appearance, on 27 Apr. 1872, dying the following year, but in spite of a sprinkling of stars in straight plays, it relied mainly on extravaganza, burlesque, variety, and melodrama. Odell, in his *Annals of the New York Stage*, calls it 'a Broadway Bowery' and says that its early history is but the 'cluttered story of a humble house'. A series of revivals in the season of 1874–5 was notable for the first appearance of Ada Rehan at the theatre she was afterwards to adorn for so long. This was on 26 Apr. 1875, in *Thoroughbred*. After the removal of the museum exhibits, the theatre, as the New Broadway, was rented to travelling companies, and from 1877 to 1878, under James Duff, it had a good season as the Broadway. Finally, on 17 Sept. 1879, entirely remodelled and redecorated, it opened as

Daly's, of glorious memory, and in spite of a slow start became one of the leading theatres of New York, particularly after the burning of the Park and the break-up of Wallack's and Union Square. By 1882–3 Daly was firmly established as the most enterprising and successful manager on Broadway. The same season saw Ada Rehan, who with John Drew was the star of Daly's fine company, as Donna Hypolita in a revival of Cibber's *She Would and She Would Not*. She was also extremely good in an expurgated edition of *The Country Girl*, but scored her greatest triumph in the revival of *The Taming of the Shrew*, given on 17 Jan. 1887. This was only one of Daly's great revivals of Shakespeare. Other notable productions were *The Merry Wives of Windsor*, on 14 Jan. 1885, and a lovely *Midsummer Night's Dream*, with scenery by Henry Hoyt. Daly remained at this theatre until his death, and it still retained his name until it was demolished in 1920, having for the last five years of its life been a cinema.   G. F.

(2) LONDON, in Cranbourn Street, Leicester Square. This was built by George Edwardes for Augustin Daly, the American manager, at a cost of £40,000, with a rental of £5,000 a year. The foundation stone was laid by Ada Rehan on 30 Oct. 1891, before a large and distinguished gathering, and Lady Bancroft christened the theatre by breaking a bottle of champagne over the stone and speaking some lines specially written for the occasion by Clement Scott. Strikes in the building trade nearly prevented its opening on the agreed date, but the tact of Edwardes and the drive of Daly prevailed, and on 12 Mar. 1893 *The Taming of the Shrew* was given, with Ada Rehan as Katharina, supported by Daly's own company, —sixty-one strong with nineteen walk-ons— with a special ode of welcome written by Irving. Daly, who believed in frequent changes of bill, then presented *The Hunchback* with Bourchier and Violet Vanbrugh, *Love in Tandem*, and *Dollars and Sense*, followed by a play by Tennyson called *The Foresters*, which failed, though it deserves a note as being the first play to be lit entirely by electric light. Before his departure in 1894 Daly put on a number of other plays, including Shakespeare, with which, it may be said in passing, he took as many liberties as Colley Cibber had done. He promised to return, and his company did in fact make one more short visit to the theatre. But George Edwardes took it over and presented Duse in the younger Dumas's *La Dame aux camélias*. The critics, however, preferred Bernhardt in the part. On 26 Dec. 1894 Edwardes staged his first musical production at Daly's, presenting the Carl Rosa Opera Company in Humperdinck's 'Hansel and Gretel' for the first time in London. After a visit from Bernhardt, with Lucien Guitry, Daly's became the home of musical comedy, starting with *An Artist's Model*, on 2 Feb. 1895, which ran for 405 performances. In the cast were Marie Tempest, Letty Lind, Lottie Venne, and Hayden Coffin. It was followed by *The Geisha* on

25 Apr. 1896, which ran for 760 performances. In the cast was Huntley Wright, who spent nearly a lifetime at this theatre. During the next fifteen years Daly's became one of the most fashionable and successful theatres in London, being rivalled only by the Gaiety, George Edwardes's other home of musical comedy. Among the eleven productions which occupied the theatre during this time were *San Toy*, *A Country Girl*, *The Merry Widow*, with Lily Elsie and Joseph Coyne, and *The Dollar Princess*. George Edwardes's last production at Daly's was *The Marriage Market*. War broke out in 1914, and he died on 4 Oct. of that year. His daughter, Mrs. Sherbrooke, and Robert Evett carried on, and among their productions was *The Maid of the Mountains* in 1917. It ran for 1,352 performances, and in the cast were José Collins, Lauri de Frece, Mark Lester, Thorpe Bates, Arthur Wontner, and Mabel Sealby. This, and *A Southern Maid*, which ran for 306 performance, were produced by Oscar Asche. Then came *Sybil*, produced by Seymour Hicks, *The Lady of the Rose*, with Harry Welchman and Phyllis Dare, and *Madame Pompadour*, with Evelyn Laye, Bertram Wallis, and Derek Oldham. The last two productions were given under James White, ex-bricklayer and millionaire, who flashed across the financial world during and after the war of 1914–18, and bought Daly's for £200,000. Robert Evett remained with him for a while, but eventually left, for White, like so many new-comers to the theatre, did not consider that experience was essential to success. He lost a good deal of money, though his suicide on 29 June 1927 was attributable not to his theatrical activities but to the collapse of the vast structure of his gamble with fortune. The tide of success was now flowing away from Daly's. *Sirocco* led to a riot, revivals and new plays alike failed, and in May 1929 the theatre was offered for sale by the Westminster Bank, who had taken it over for White's creditors. It was bought by Isadore W. Schlesinger of South Africa. From 1931 to 1932 J. Bannister Howard produced revivals of old musical plays, and in July 1932 non-stop variety was the attraction. At Christmas a pantomime, *Mother Goose*, was put on by Francis Laidler, but Daly's was nearing its end. Straight plays of no great importance had runs there, the last production being *The First Legion*, and on 25 Sept. 1937 the curtain fell for the last time, with no ceremony, not even a speech, to mark the passing of this famous theatre. It was pulled down and a cinema erected on the site.   W. M. P.

(3) NEW YORK, on 63rd Street. This was built as the Davenport in 1909, but became a music-hall in 1913, and was a home of musical comedy, as Cort's, when in 1922 it was rechristened Daly's. Its first important production was a revival of *Love for Love* in 1925. It was known successively as Coburn's, when it saw Mr. and Mrs. Coburn in a revival of *The Yellow Jacket*, as the Recital, when *Lady Windermere's Fan* was seen there, as the Park

Lane, and in 1935 as Gilmore's, with Paul Gilmore and his daughter Virginia in popular and cut-rate revivals. It became the Experimental on 4 Mar. 1936, when the Federal Theatre Project leased it, and produced there a number of new plays and revivals, including Shaw's *On the Rocks* for the first time in New York. The Yiddish Theatre Project also occupied the house for a time, but with the passing of the Federal Theatre Project in 1939 the theatre closed, to open again in 1941 under its old name of Daly's.   G. F.

DANCE, SIR GEORGE (1858–1932), English theatrical manager, author, and song-writer, whose early song, 'Girls are the Ruin of Men', was one of Vesta Tilley's successes. From composition he turned to the writing of libretti for musical plays, and his 'books', which include *The Nautch Girl* (1891) and *A Chinese Honeymoon* (1901), are models of their kind. The former immediately succeeded the series of Gilbert and Sullivan works at the Savoy, while the latter, first seen at Hanley in 1899, had a long run at the old Strand Theatre. Dance became one of the most successful and most powerful theatre managers in the United Kingdom, and often had as many as twenty-four companies on tour at once. He was behind the scenes financially at many of the big West End theatres in the days preceding the First World War, and had a keen eye for a rising man or woman of talent, either artistically or managerially. He was a tireless worker, a forceful personality, and a man of vision. His knighthood was given him in recognition of his services to the theatre, which included a gift of £30,000 for the reconstruction of the Old Vic in 1924. His son, Eric, who died in a prison camp during the Second World War, was responsible for the building of the new repertory theatre in Oxford, which opened in 1938.   W. M. P.

DANCHENKO, VLADIMIR NEMIROVICH-, see NEMIROVICH-DANCHENKO.

DANCOURT. (1) FLORENT CARTON (1661–1725), French dramatist and actor. He was studying law in Paris when he fell in love with the actress (2) MARIE THÉRÈSE LENOIR (1663–1725), daughter of La Thorillière, and goddaughter of Molière. He married her in 1680, and adopted her profession. He had a good face and figure, and a natural liveliness of disposition which was an asset in comedy, though in the playing of tragedy he was judged cold and monotonous. After some years in the provinces Dancourt, with his wife, joined the Comédie-Française, and remained there until 1718. During this time he wrote more than fifty comedies, many of them ephemeral, based on small scandals or topicalities of the day. But his better plays, though never approaching the true comedy of Molière, show wit and observation, and much skill in etching the contemporary scene. He was particularly good in his delineation of the

rising middle class, with its love of money, its desire for political power, its shrewdness in taking advantage of a corrupt government, and its avidity for easy pleasure. There is no bitterness in Dancourt's writing, but under the superficial wit and good humour much brutality and selfishness are apparent. His best play is *Le Chevalier à la mode* (1687), written in collaboration with Saint-Yon, an excellent portrait of contemporary life with much satire at the expense of parvenu financiers. Others worthy of note are *La Maison de campagne* (1688), and the one-act *Vendanges de Suresnes* (1695), the most frequently revived of all his works. In *La Foire de Bezons*, also given in 1695, Dancourt's two daughters, (3) MARIE-ANNE-ARMANDE (1684–1745), known as Manon, and (4) MARIE-ANNE-MICHELLE (1685–1780), known as Mimi, made their first appearance on the stage. They were both precocious, talented children, and their father continued to write plays for them, in which they were much admired. In 1701 they became members of the Comédie-Française. Manon retired a year later on her marriage, but Mimi remained, and was still drawing her pension at the age of 95. Dancourt was not as versatile as Dufresny, nor as poetic as Regnard, but more than any one after Molière he was a dramatist who was also a man of the theatre. His dialogue was easy and humorous, and he was a keen observer of contemporary manners, either in town or in the country.

DANGEVILLE, MARIE ANNE BOTOT (1714–96), French actress, and the most important member of a family of actors who served the Comédie-Française for three generations. She was on the stage at an early age, playing child-roles with much success, and in 1730 joined the company for comedy roles, in which she excelled. She occasionally attempted tragedy, but without much success. Some of her greatest triumphs were gained in Marivaux's plays, in which she was ably supported by Préville, and Garrick considered her the leading French actress of the day, ranking her even above Mlle Clairon. She was a woman of great integrity. No breath of scandal ever touched her private or public life, and she was as kind-hearted as she was virtuous. In old age she adopted a granddaughter of the great actor Baron, whom she found living in poverty. Her retirement in 1763 was much regretted by the public and by her fellow actors, who lost no opportunity of testifying their fondness for her by arranging parties and surprise visits for her birthdays and other festive occasions. It was at her house in Vaugirard that some of the actors of the Comédie-Française first performed Collé's *Partie de chasse d'Henri IV*, which Louis XV had banned from the public stage.

DANIEL, SAMUEL (c. 1563–1619), English poet and dramatist, author of an unacted tragedy in the classical manner on the subject of Cleopatra, and of *Philotas* (1604), which got him into trouble on account of some fancied resemblance to the unhappy fate of the Earl of Essex. Daniel was at this time in charge of the Children of the Queen's Revels, and was implicated in the trouble over their production of *Eastward Ho!* (1605), where a reference to Scotland annoyed James I. He was also the author of two pastorals, and of a number of Court masques which contain some excellent poetry, little relished by Jonson, Daniel's rival in this field, but highly praised by many of his contemporaries and later by S. T. Coleridge.

DANIELS, Frank Albert (1856–1935), an American musical comedy star, who, after a successful début in light opera in 1879, became second comedian of the Gaiety, Boston. He first sprang into prominence with a farce entitled *The Electric Doll* (or *Spark*), with which he visited London, returning to New York to star as Old Sport in Hoyt's first success, *The Rag Baby* (Tony Pastor's Theatre, 14 Apr. 1884). He later went into management. In 1887 he had another long run in *Little Puck* (based on *Vice Versa*), and in 1895 appeared in *The Wizard of the Nile*, by Harry B. Smith, with music by Victor Herbert, dancing, singing and clowning. The same authors supplied him with *The Idol's Eye*. Daniels continued to appear in a series of similar productions, including *Miss Hook of Holland*, the last being *The Pink Lady*. In 1913 he retired. He had a round, irresistibly comic face, a short, stout body, and most expressive eyebrows. He was a good dancer and singer, and a fine exponent of patter songs.

DAN LENO, see LENO.

D'ANNUNZIO, Gabriele (1863–1938), Italian poet, novelist, and dramatist, whose real name was Rapagnetta. He was one of the most discussed and controversial figures of his day. His first volume of poems was published when he was 15, and in 1919 he figured largely in politics when he raided and captured the port of Fiume for Italy, relinquishing his authority a year later. His plays, which are simple in structure but rich in poetry and sensuality, have been both praised and condemned. The stage directions, written with a wealth of detail, reveal the extent and accuracy of d'Annunzio's archaeological knowledge. But his people are puppets, driven by elemental passions, and his works live by their poetry rather than their humanity. Among the best known are *La Città morta* and *La Gioconda* (both 1898), *Francesca da Rimini* (1902), *La Figlia di Jorio* (1904), and his last play, *La Piave* (1918). Many of his heroines were first played by Eleonora Duse, who scored an outstanding success in *La Città morta* and *La Gioconda*, and contributed not a little to d'Annunzio's success as a dramatist (see also ITALY, 3 *b*).

DANVERS, Johnnie (1860–1939), a music-hall performer, uncle of the famous Dan Leno, who was a month younger than himself.

Danvers made his first appearance at the Alexandra, Sheffield, then toured with the Leno family, and later went into pantomime with Dan Leno at the Surrey. After this he joined the Mohawk Minstrels, and remained with them for twenty years, during which time he also appeared in many Drury Lane pantomimes, in musical comedy, and in light opera. He was a masterly performer on the tambourine, and despite his size—for he was a heavily built man—remarkably light on his feet.

DARLINGTON, William Aubrey (1890–), English dramatic critic, on the *Daily Telegraph* since 1920. He was appointed examiner for the Diploma of Dramatic Art, University of London, in 1929, and member of the Advisory Committee for the Diploma in 1931. In 1919 he wrote *Alf's Button*, an extravaganza which was first produced in 1924 at the Prince's Theatre, and has been twice filmed; it was filmed again in 1937 in a modernized version, as *Alf's Button Afloat*.

W. A. Darlington is also the author of the following plays: *Carpet Slippers* (1930), *A Knight Passed By* (1931), a burlesque version of Boucicault's *The Streets of London* (1932), and *Marcia Gets Her Own Back* (1938). In 1932 appeared his *Sheridan* (Great Lives Series), and in 1938 *J. M. Barrie* ('Order of Merit' Series). His critical works on the theatre include *Through the Fourth Wall* (1922) and *Literature in the Theatre* (1925). In 1947 he published a volume of reminiscences entitled *I Do What I Like*.

W. A. Darlington looks at the drama with a clear objective eye, and writes on what he sees with wit and understanding.   T. C. K.

DAUVILLIERS. (1) Nicolas Dorné (? – 1690), French actor who went from the provinces to the Marais in 1670. Two years later he married (2) Victoire Françoise (c. 1657–1733), daughter of the famous comedian Raymond Poisson. They both joined the depleted company at the rue Guénégaud after Molière's death, but the wife retired from the stage on the foundation of the Comédie-Française on account of ill health. Dauvilliers continued to play until his death. It was said of him that he was not a good actor in comedy, and had no advantage of person, but in tragedy he sometimes showed a genius akin to madness. He was evidently a somewhat wild and undisciplined actor, and tradition has it that he went mad on the stage, and tried to kill himself with a property sword while playing Eros in *Cléopâtre*, subsequently dying in an asylum. His daughter Anne was also an actress, and married an actor.

DAVENANT, Sir William (1606–68), English dramatist and theatre manager. Born and educated at Oxford, he was reputed to be the natural son of Shakespeare by the hostess of the Crown Inn, Cornmarket. There is no proof of this, though Shakespeare was certainly his godfather and well acquainted with his family. There can be no doubt that Davenant had a great love for the theatre, and before the closing of the playhouses by the Puritans in 1642 had made a name for himself as a writer and producer of Court masques in the tradition of Ben Jonson. In 1638 he was made Poet Laureate. He was the first to evade the ban on play-acting by presenting it as 'music and instruction', and by this means managed to get permission to put on *The Siege of Rhodes* in 1656, considered by competent authorities the first English opera. This was followed by *The Spaniards in Peru* (1658) and *Sir Francis Drake* (1659).

As soon as the Restoration was an accomplished fact, Davenant and Killigrew obtained from Charles II patents giving them a monopoly of acting in London. While Killigrew took most of the veteran actors into his company at the Theatre Royal, or King's House, Davenant recruited his actors mainly among the younger generation, and took them to Lincoln's Inn Fields, to the Duke's House. Among his youngsters was Thomas Betterton, destined to become the foremost actor of his day, Mrs. Sanderson, later Betterton's wife, the comedians Jevon and Nokes. A fine new theatre in Dorset Garden was built for the Duke's Men, but Davenant died before it could be opened.

With Dryden, Davenant was responsible for adaptations of Shakespeare to suit the new tastes of the day, thus, according to one irate critic, turning Shakespeare into pantomime. Hand in hand with the new proscenium stage, with its greater reliance on scenery and its lack of intimate action, went the new taste for elaborate machinery, ballet, and music, which Davenant had been one of the first to foster. There can be no doubt that the English theatre received a great impetus from the work of Davenant and Killigrew, even if it was not always in a direction favoured by later critics. In founding a training school for young actors at Hatton Garden, Davenant continued the work begun by Burbage in apprenticing young actors to the stage. He was originally the person aimed at in the character of Bayes in Buckingham's *The Rehearsal*, transferred after his death to Dryden.

DAVENPORT, a family of American actors, of whom the father (1) EDWARD LOOMIS (1815–77) was the son of an innkeeper. He made his first appearance on the stage in 1837, playing at Providence, R.I., with Junius Brutus Booth in *A New Way to Pay Old Debts*, billed as Mr. E. Dee. After some years on tour he appeared in New York in 1843, supporting Mrs. John Drew in a series of Shakespearian and other revivals. He visited England in 1848 with Mrs. Anna Cora Mowatt, remaining for some years, and being accounted a fine actor in such parts as Othello, Richard III, Sir Giles Overreach, Claude Melnotte, and the Corsican Brothers. Returning to New York, he appeared as Hamlet, engaged in theatre management, and starred at a number of theatres with his

own company. A distinguished actor and an indefatigable worker, he seemed destined for great things. William Winter said of him: 'Davenport was an actor of extraordinary versatility. I have seen him act, in one evening, Shakespeare's Brutus and Roaring Ralph Stockpole. . . . He was massive and weird in Macbeth. His Duke Aranza in *The Honeymoon* was peerless. . . . His Sir Giles Overreach was a sinister and grisly embodiment of worldly craft and insensate villainy. His Othello was, in construction, as nearly perfect as a work of art may be. Mind, grace, force, variety, and occasional flashes of fire were characteristic of Davenport's acting.' Yet with all these gifts he failed to attain the eminence which seemed his due, and some lack of sympathy between himself and his audiences led him to pass the greater part of his career outside New York. He made his last appearance as Dan'l Druce at the National Theatre, Washington, D.C., in April 1877. While in England he married, in Jan. 1849, (2) FANNY ELIZABETH VINING (1829–91), member of a famous theatrical family. She was on the stage as a child, and was already an accomplished actress when she accompanied her husband to New York. She appeared with him in leading parts until his death. Of her nine children, five went on the stage. The most distinguished of them was (3) FANNY LILY GYPSY (1850–98). Born in England, she played child parts with her father at the Howard Athenaeum in Boston, and at fifteen made her adult début as Mrs. Mildmay in *Still Waters Run Deep*, also in Boston. In 1869 she joined Augustin Daly's company in New York, and was his leading lady until 1877, when she formed her own company, starring with it in the principal theatres of the United States. Her range of parts was wide, including Shakespeare's heroines and such modern women as Polly Eccles and Lady Gay Spanker, while between 1883 and 1895 she produced and played in four of Sardou's plays, *Fédora*, *La Tosca*, *Cléopâtre*, and *Gismonda*. Of her sisters Blanche was an opera singer, while (4) MAY (1856–1927) made her first appearance on the stage at the age of six, playing the Duke of York in *Richard III*. She then went to school until 1872, and made her adult début at sixteen at the Chestnut Street Theatre, Philadelphia, under her father's management. At the same theatre she created the part of Libbie Ray in *The Mighty Dollar* (1876), and later joined Daly's company. She retired on her marriage to William Seymour, returning to the Boston Museum in 1885, and making her last professional appearance at a benefit for the Actors' Fund in 1894. Her daughter May was also on the stage (see SEYMOUR). Fanny's younger brother (5) EDGAR LONGFELLOW (1862–1918) made his first appearance as a child at the Chestnut Street Theatre. He was at the Walnut Street Theatre from 1878 to 1879, supporting his sister Fanny in a season there, and for several years toured as leading man with a number of companies, including those of Kate Claxton and McKee Rankin.

From 1887 to 1892 he was leading juvenile at the Boston Museum, appearing with Julia Marlowe, Viola Allen, and other great actresses of the day. His brother (6) HARRY GEORGE BRYANT (1866–1949) made his first appearance at the age of five, under his father's management, playing Damon's son in *Damon and Pythias*. He continued to play children's parts in the companies of Jefferson, McCullough, and Frank Mayo, and in 1879 made his first appearance in New York as Sir Joseph Porter in a children's production of *H.M.S. Pinafore*. As an adult actor he played leading parts in New York and on tour, and in 1898 made his first appearance in London in *The Belle of New York*. He married Phyllis Rankin, who was with him in this play, and for many years appeared with her in vaudeville. He was one of the first actors to appear in films, being engaged by the Vitagraph Picture Company in 1912, and his later career was mainly in Hollywood.

DAVENPORT, JEAN and **T. D.,** see LANDER.

DAVENPORT THEATRE, NEW YORK, see DALY'S THEATRE (3).

DAVIS, OWEN (1874–   ), American dramatist, who as a young graduate from Harvard, finding no market for his tragedies in verse, turned to more remunerative branches of the theatre and wrote over a hundred ephemeral melodramas for the popular-priced circuit. Prompted, however, by Ibsen, and the new spirit abroad in the theatre, he wrote in 1921 a sincere and moving play, *The Detour*, which was recognized as one of the best of the year, in spite of its lack of financial success when compared with his earlier works. This was followed by *Ice Bound*, a study of New England farming folk which was awarded the Pulitzer Prize for 1923. Davis's later work has hardly maintained the promise of these two plays, though in 1936 he made, with his son, a good dramatization of Edith Wharton's novel, *Ethan Frome*. In 1931 he published his autobiography, *I'd Like To Do It Again*.

DAVIS'S AMPHITHEATRE, see ASTLEY'S.

DAY, JOHN (*c.* 1574–*c.* 1640), English dramatist, noted in Henslowe's diary as writing plays for the Admiral's Men and later for Worcester's, mainly in collaboration with Chettle, with whom he wrote the first part of *The Blind Beggar of Bethnal Green*. To this he later added two further parts, possibly with a different collaborator. This play is also known as *Thomas Strowd*, and is all that survives of Day's early dramatic work. His later plays, which Chambers says 'are of finer literary quality than his early record would suggest', include *The Travels of Three English Brothers* (1607), *The Parliament of Bees* (1608), and the ill-fated *Isle of Gulls*, given in 1606 by the Children at Blackfriars. This, because of its satire on English and Scottish relations, caused the imprisonment of those connected with its production.

DEAN, JULIA (1830–68), American actress, granddaughter of the English actor Samuel Drake (1769–1854), who went to the United States in 1810 and became a pioneer theatre manager in Kentucky. With her father and step-mother (her mother, Julia Drake, also an actress, having died when she was two) Julia Dean appeared as a child under the management of Ludlow and Smith, and in 1846 made her adult début in New York as Julia in *The Hunchback*. A beautiful woman, with a gentle personality and great charm of manner, she had a few years of immense popularity, though she was not perhaps a great actress. She could on occasion rise to great heights of passion, but was at her best in roles of tenderness and pathos, such as Adrienne Lecouvreur and Mrs. Haller. She made an unhappy marriage in 1855, and her acting declined. A tour of California in 1856 was a success, but she never regained her position in New York, where she returned after her divorce. In 1867 she married again, dying the following year in childbirth. It was with Julia Dean that Belasco, as a small boy, made his first appearance on the stage in 1856, when he was carried on as the child in *Pizarro*. Later he played Little Willie in her production of *East Lynne*.

DE ANGELIS, THOMAS JEFFERSON (1859–1933), an American actor, son of one of the original members of the San Francisco Minstrel Company. With a younger sister he appeared on the stage as a child, and travelled extensively, giving performances at small cities and mining camps from St. Louis to the coast. He has vividly portrayed this life in his autobiography, *A Vagabond Trouper* (1931). He was never a star actor, but always a reliable and likeable one, who appeared in light opera, musical shows, straight plays, and vaudeville with equal facility. He was the first American to sing the part of Sir Despard Murgatroyd in *Ruddigore* and his greatest personal success was the song 'Tammany', which he sang in his own production of *Fantana*. In 1927 he was in *The Royal Family* (*Theatre Royal*) and his last part was in *Apron Strings* in the same year.

DE BRIE. (1) EDMÉ VILLEQUIN (1607–1676), a mediocre actor who was in Molière's company in the provinces and later in Paris. He played various small parts, such as the fencing-master in *Le Bourgeois gentilhomme* and the river-god in *Psyché*. His main claim to fame is that he married, in about 1651, the charming actress (2) CATHERINE LECLERC DU ROZET (*c.* 1630–1706), who as Mlle de Rose had joined Molière a year previously. A gentle, affectionate woman, and a fine actress in comedy, she was destined to create many of Molière's best women's parts, and remained his friend and companion all his life, though there is no proof that she was ever his mistress. Her first important part was Cathos in *Les Précieuses ridicules*, and among her many fine performances Agnès in *L'École des femmes* was considered the best. She continued to play it for nearly fifty years, and when in later life she was replaced by a younger actress the audience clamoured for her return. Tradition has it that she was sent for after the curtain had risen, in such haste that she had to play the part in her ordinary clothes. She retired on pension in 1685, having been one of the original members of the Comédie-Française.

DEBURAU. (1) JEAN GASPARD (1796–1846), famous French pantomimist, creator of the long, pale, lovesick Pierrot who has since remained a popular figure in the public imagination. He was born in Bohemia, member of an acrobatic family with whom he toured the continent. In 1811 they played at the Parisian fairs, and Deburau was engaged for the Funambules on the Boulevard du Temple, a home of tumblers and tight-rope walkers. His subsequent history is bound up with that of this theatre, where he remained until his death. He was at first an inconspicuous member of the company, but as he developed, with great subtlety and many delicate touches, his conception of Pierrot as the ever hopeful and disappointed lover, as the child, the prince, the poet, and the eternal seeker, all Paris flocked to see him, and his praises were sung by all the critics, particularly by Jules Janin, who devoted a whole volume to his work. He died a few days after his last appearance on the stage, some said from the effects of a fall, others of consumption. His son (2) CHARLES (1829–73) carried on the tradition of the white-faced white-robed Pierrot after his creator's death, without his father's genius, but with a vast store of goodwill and popularity to draw on. He remained at the Funambules until it was destroyed, and then opened a theatre under his own name. It was not very successful, and he took to the provinces until his death.

DECORATION, THEATRE, see ACOUSTICS, ARCHITECTURE, and SCENERY.

DÉJAZET, PAULINE VIRGINIE (1798–1875), French actress, who made her first appearance on the stage at the age of 5. Gardel, the ballet master, would have made a ballerina of her, but her real aptitude was for acting, and, after appearing with several children's companies, she went for her training to the Théâtre des Jeunes Élèves. In 1807 she was at the Vaudeville, and later at the Variétés under Brunet, where her success in the part of a young boy so displeased the reigning star that her engagement was terminated. She then went into the provinces, and dropping the name of Virginie, by which she had hitherto been known, she used that of Déjazet for the first time. In 1821 she returned to Paris and appeared with some success in a vaudeville by Scribe at the Gymnase, where she remained for some time, playing male roles. The arrival of Jenny Vertpré from the Vaudeville robbed her of the parts she had considered hers by right, and she left. Her reputation really dates from the opening of the Palais-Royal in 1831. She stayed there thirteen years, and became one of the most popular actresses in Paris. After an argument over her salary she continued her triumphant career at the Variétés and the Gaîté, still playing masculine roles—soldiers, collegians, students—as well as great ladies and pretty peasant girls. Some idea of her versatility is given by the fact that her parts included Voltaire, Rousseau, Napoleon, Henri IV, Ninon de l'Enclos, Sophie Arnould, Mlle Champmeslé, and Mme Favart. In 1859 she took over the Folies-Nouvelles, which she renamed Théâtre Déjazet, and appeared there in a number of new plays under the management of her son Eugène. At the age of 62 she made a great hit in a male part in Sardou's *Monsieur Garat*. She made her last appearance in Paris in 1870, and in the same year was seen in London at the Opéra-Comique in a season of French plays. Her last years were unhappy, and, harassed by financial difficulties, she played continuously in the provinces to support her children and grandchildren. Two of her sisters were also on the stage, one as a singer, one as a dancer.

DEKKER, THOMAS (c. 1572–c. 1632), English dramatist, about whose life very little is known. He was working for Henslowe towards the end of the sixteenth century, and had a hand in more than forty plays, of which about fifteen survive. The most important, which has an honoured place in the evolution of English comedy, is *The Shoemaker's Holiday*, which tells how one Simon Eyre, a master shoemaker, became Lord Mayor of London. It was first given at the Rose towards the end of 1599, and at Court on the following New Year's Day. Robust and full-blooded, this play of London characters reveals a promise which Dekker's later work unfortunately did little to fulfil. His other plays include *Satiromastix* (1601), written in collaboration with Marston, in which Jonson, who had satirized the authors in his *Poetaster*, is ridiculed as Horace; *The Honest Whore* (1604), and *The Roaring Girl* (1610), both with Middleton; and two plays which he apparently wrote by himself—*If It be not Good, the Devil is in It* (1610) and *Match Me in London* (c. 1611). With Massinger he also wrote a tragedy, *The Virgin Martyr*, given at the Red Bull playhouse in 1620, but probably dating in a different version from some ten years earlier. Dekker is also believed to have had a hand in *The Witch of Edmonton* (1621). In his later years he wrote a number of pamphlets in imitation of Nashe, and in 1609 published *The Gull's Handbook*, a satiric account of the fops and gallants of the day, which gives some interesting information about the contemporary theatre. It has been said of Dekker that he was of a sunny and sympathetic nature, with much simplicity, and an unusual feeling for the poor and oppressed.

DELAUNAY, LOUIS ARSÈNE (1826–1903), French actor, son of a wine merchant, who entered the Conservatoire as a student in 1844 and a year later, impatient of further study, made an unauthorized début (as M. Ernest) in a vaudeville at the Gymnase. This experience taught him that he was not yet ready for the stage, and he returned to the Conservatoire, making his proper début at the Odéon, where his youth and precocity in classical comedy caught the attention of the Comédie-Française. He appeared there on 25 Apr. 1848 and had a long and brilliant career, playing young lovers till he was nearly sixty, seldom knowing failure and becoming the idol of the public. His first outstanding success was made in a little one-act play, *Le Moineau de Lesbie*, in which he appeared with Rachel, and he was the original Fortunio in Alfred de Musset's *Le Chandelier*. He was also good in *Les Caprices de Marianne*, which went out of the repertory for many years after his retirement in 1886. He played in Marivaux, Regnard, in Hugo's *Hernani* when it was first given at the Comédie-Française, and in new plays by Augier, Ponsard, Legouvé, and Pailleron. His son was also a member of the Comédie-Française.

DELLA PORTA, GIAMBATTISTA (1538–1613), a Neapolitan scientist and philosopher, who amused himself in his leisure by writing plays, fourteen of which survive out of a possible thirty-three. These are all written in prose, and take their subjects from authors both of classical Rome and the Italian Renaissance, particularly Plautus and Boccaccio. His *Il due fratelli rivali* is taken from a tale of Bandello's which supplied Shakespeare with *Much Ado About Nothing*. In all his plays, the dates of which are unknown, the dialogue is vivacious and the satire keen. This *commedia erudita* was much imitated by later seventeenth-century dramatists, none of whom, however, brought to their material the freshness and deft handling of their original. Della Porta is accessible in excellent critical editions. His *La Cintia*, *La Fantesca*, and *Astrologo* were given in Latin translations at Trinity College, Cambridge, between 1598 and 1615.

DE LOUTHERBOURG, PHILIPPE JACQUES, see LOUTHERBOURG.

DELPINI, see CLOWN.

DELYSIA [LAPIZE], ALICE (1889–   ), French actress and singer, who made her first appearance in 1903 at the Moulin Rouge under Flers, being engaged by him for the chorus of *The Belle of New York*. She was later seen at the Variétés, and at the Folies-Bergère with Yvonne Printemps, and in 1905 made her first appearance in the United States at Daly's. She married as her first husband the Anglo-French music-hall artist Harry Fragson, and retired from the stage for a while, returning after his death in 1913. She was then seen in London in revue, where her success was instantaneous, and she has since continued her career with equal brilliance in all three capitals, appearing mainly in revue or spectacle, under the management of C. B. Cochran, who first engaged her for London. During the 1939–45 war she toured the Middle East entertaining the troops under the auspices of E.N.S.A. A beautiful and witty woman, she has been the mainspring of many of Cochran's most success-ful revues, and in his volumes of memoirs he constantly pays tribute to her loyalty and good nature.

DEMILLE, HENRY C. (1850–93), see BELASCO.

DENMARK, see SCANDINAVIA, 1.

DERY, JOHANNÉ JASZBERÉNY (1793–1872), Hungarian actress, leading lady of the company of the first Hungarian National Theatre opened in Budapest in 1837.

DESCLÉE, AIMÉE OLYMPE (1836–74), French actress, who studied at the Conservatoire, but, finding the discipline irksome, left it to make her début at the Gymnase in 1855. After appearing at several other Parisian theatres, and meeting with little success, she retired and went to Italy and elsewhere, appearing in a repertory of French plays. Dumas *fils*, seeing her in his *Diane de Lys* at Brussels in 1867, brought her back to Paris and persuaded the Gymnase to re-engage her. The hard years of touring bore fruit, and she was an immediate success in *Frou-Frou*, becoming overnight the idol of the Parisian public. Her gratitude to Dumas knew no bounds, but, he being at this time a fervent moral reformer, she could only show it by her excellent performances in his plays, being particularly good as the heroines of *Visite de noces* (1871) and *La Femme de Claude* (1873). She died suddenly at the height of her success.

DESEINE, MLLE (?–1759), see DUFRESNE (2).

DESIOSI, THE, a company of *commedia dell'arte* actors led by Diana (da Ponti) which first emerges in 1580. In 1595 Tristano Martinelli is found with them, after breaking away from Pellesini's troupe. The company appears to have broken up some years later, when the two chief actors are found with the Accesi.

DESJARDINS, MARIE CATHERINE HORTENSE (1632–83), one of the first women playwrights of France. She left home after a love-affair with a cousin, and may have become an actress, possibly in Molière's provincial company. She was later taken under the protection of the Duchesse de Rohan, and wrote poetry, novels, and plays, of which *Manlius Torquatus*, a tragedy, was given at the Hôtel de Bourgogne in 1662. It was while appearing in this play that Mlle Baron, mother of the famous actor, died. Mlle Desjardins was also the author of a comedy, *Le Favory* (1665), given by Molière at the Palais-Royal. As Mme de Villedieu, bigamous wife of an absconding officer, Mlle Desjardins became a figure in Parisian society, and later married the aged Marquis de Chasté, giving him a son whose godparents were the Dauphin and Mlle de Montpensier. After the death of the Marquis she reverted to her first married name, retired to the country, and died, it is said, of over-indulgence in drink. *Manlius Torquatus*, which had been successful on its first appearance, remained in the repertory of the Comédie-Française until the time of the French Revolution.

DESLYS, GABY [GABRIELLE] (1884–1920), a celebrated French singer and music-hall artist, around whom some fantastic stories have accumulated, particularly the tale of her famous pearls, said to have caused a revolution in Portugal, from whence she escaped in a hay-cart. She appeared in Paris and New York, and was first seen in London at the Gaiety in 1906 under George Edwardes. She had no great stage talent, but any amount of glamour, being a blonde with a small but perfect figure and large appealing blue eyes. She had a short and successful career, making her last appearance in London in 1917. On her death she left a considerable sum of money to the poor of Marseilles, where she was born.			W. M. P.

DESMARES. (1) NICOLAS (*c.* 1645–1714), French actor and dramatist, brother of the celebrated actress Mlle Champmeslé. He spent some years in a French company at the Court in Copenhagen, and was also a member in 1680 of a provincial company under the patronage of the great Condé. Five years later he became a member of the Comédie-Française, where he remained until his retirement in 1712. His range was somewhat limited, but he was unsurpassed in the playing of peasant characters. His plays are forgotten. He married a granddaughter of the actor Montfleury, and his daughter (2) CHRISTINE ANTOINETTE CHARLOTTE (1682–1753), profiting by the tuition of her aunt, Mlle Champmeslé, to many of whose parts she succeeded, became an excellent actress, sharing feminine roles with Mlle Duclos. She retired in 1721, having seen herself surpassed by the young and lovely Adrienne Lecouvreur. Charlotte Desmares was at her best in pathetic and tender roles, and was particularly admired in Voltaire's *Oedipe*, in which she played opposite Quinault-Dufresne.

DESMARETZ DE SAINT-SORLIN, JEAN (1595–1676), French novelist, poet, and dramatist, one of the original members of the French Academy, and a frequenter of the Hôtel de Rambouillet. Urged by his patron, Richelieu, to attempt the theatre, he wrote *Aspasie* (1636), a somewhat mediocre play given in the same year as *Le Cid*. Desmaretz, who helped Richelieu in his extensive systems of reform, is best remembered, however, for his comedy, *Les Visionnaires* (1637), probably the most important before Corneille's *Le Menteur*. A witty comment on the foibles of fashionable society, it was produced at the Marais with Montdory as the hallucinated old-fashioned poet who believes himself to be a great modernist. It had some influence on Molière, who revived it twice at the Palais-Royal. Desmaretz wrote several other plays, including the greater part of *Mirame* (1641), the first production to be staged in Richelieu's new private theatre.

DESŒILLETS [ALIX FAVIOT], Mlle (1621–70), French actress, who served a long apprenticeship in the provinces, where she married an actor, before she was seen in Paris in her late thirties. She was for a short time at the Marais,

where Corneille admired her acting as Viriate in his *Sertorius* (1662), and later in the same year she joined the company at the Hôtel de Bourgogne, taking the place of Mlle Baron, mother of the famous actor, Michel Baron. Neither young nor pretty, and of short stature, Mlle Desœillets was nevertheless an excellent actress, most moving in tragedy, and in high favour with the audience. She created a number of tragic roles, among them Corneille's Sophonisbe and Racine's Hermione. During an illness she was replaced in the latter part by the young Mlle Champmeslé, who was so good that the elder actress retired from the theatre in tears, and never acted again.

DESTOUCHES, PHILIPPE NÉRICAULT (1680–1754), French dramatist, and an important link in the development of eighteenth-century *drame* from seventeenth-century comedy. He was an imitator of Molière, but spoilt his plays by emphasizing the moral, which Molière had allowed to emerge naturally in the course of the action. Even his titles—*L'Ingrat*, *L'Irrésolu*, *Le Médisant*—read, as it has been said, 'like sub-titles to Molière'. There is a tradition that Destouches was, in his youth, an actor, but proof of this is wanting. He must, however, have left the stage fairly soon for diplomacy, for in 1716 he was at the French Embassy in London, where he was well received. He also contracted at this time a secret marriage with an Englishwoman, which later supplied material for one of his best plays, *Le Philosophe marié* (1727). Before his visit to London he had written several moderately successful comedies, and on his return he retired to the country and gave himself up wholly to writing. His stay in England had helped to heighten his taste for gothic romance, and accounts for the mingling of sentiment and tragedy with comedy in his later plays, though many of them, particularly towards the end of his career, were spoilt by sententiousness. His most important play is undoubtedly *Le Glorieux* (1732), which was translated into English in 1791. It pictures the struggle between the old nobility and the newly rich who are rising to power, and some traits of the central character are said to have been taken from the actor Dufresne, who played the part. Destouches became a member of the French Academy in 1723, in succession to Campistron. He was a man of a serious, even a religious, turn of mind, and at 60 he turned his attention entirely to theology, though he left several plays in manuscript, of which one, *La Fausse Agnès*, was given after his death with some success.

DES URLIS, see BRÉCOURT.

DETAIL SCENERY, the name given to small, changeable pieces of scenery used for a particular scene in or before a formalized setting (see ENGLISH PLAYHOUSE, 3). This system was successfully used in Lovat Fraser's designs for *The Beggar's Opera* at the Lyric Theatre, Hammersmith, in 1920.

DEUS EX MACHINA, see GREECE, 3 *c.*

DEUTERAGONIST, see PROTAGONIST.

DEUTSCHES THEATER, a private play-producing society founded in Berlin in 1883 for the purpose of staging a repertory of good plays, old and new, as a protest against the deadening effect of long runs and outmoded theatrical tradition. Under its chief promoters, Adolf L'Arronge and Ludwig Barnay, ably assisted by the actors Josef Kainz and Agnes Sorma, it presented classical historical plays in the style inaugurated by the Meiningen company. In 1895, by which time the enterprise was well established and flourishing, it was given a new direction by its affiliation with the Freie Bühne, under the latter's founder and director Otto Brahm. He brought to it the naturalistic methods which had proved so excellent with Ibsen and Hauptmann, less successful with the classics and romantics. The Deutsches Theater knew another period of fame under the direction of Max Reinhardt, who went there in 1905 from the Neues Theater, with a band of keen young actors trained in his methods. Here he was able to realize some of his ambitious schemes of production, in which music, scenery, ballet, and mime all played their parts. In the crisis following on the First World War the theatre collapsed, but was later revived under Heinz Hilpert.

DE VALOIS, NINETTE, see VALOIS, NINETTE DE.

DE VILLIERS, see VILLIERS.

DEVRIENT, a family of German actors of whom the first (1) LUDWIG (1784–1832), of Dutch origin, was a brilliant actor, but of a fiery temperament, unamenable to discipline. An inimitable comedian, he was considered at his finest in Falstaff, but he himself preferred tragedy, and Franz Moor, Shylock, and Richard III were his favourite parts. He appeared in the chief theatres of Germany until 1815, when he took Iffland's place in Berlin, remaining there until he died. He had three nephews on the stage. The eldest (2) KARL (1797–1872) excelled in heroic and character parts—Wallenstein, Faust, Lear, Shylock. He was for many years attached to the Court theatre in Dresden and later joined the companies of Carlsruhe and Hanover. In 1823 he married the opera singer Wilhelmine Schröder-Devrient (1804–60), from whom he was divorced five years later. The second nephew (3) EDUARD (1801–77) began his career as a singer, and with Mendelssohn-Bartholdy revived Bach's 'St. Matthew Passion', himself taking the part of Christ. In 1852 he was appointed director of the Hoftheater at Carlsruhe, and was the first professional man of the theatre to be appointed to such a post. Of conservative tastes, but thoroughly competent and reliable, he made good team-work his first aim, and brought his company to a high pitch of excellence. He also induced his public to accept a number of German classics and Shakespearian plays in the repertory, and his German versions of Shakespeare—*Deutscher Bühnen- und Familien-Shakespeare*—published from 1869 to 1871, though somewhat bowdlerized, proved more suitable for the stage than Schlegel's and other literary translations. He was also the first to write a detailed account of the development of the German stage in his *Geschichte der deutschen Schauspielkunst* (1848). His youngest brother (4) EMIL (1803–72) was a handsome and polished actor, at his best in youthful heroic parts. He was for nearly forty years attached to the Dresden Court theatre, but was frequently given leave of absence to star elsewhere, including London, where his Hamlet was well received. His excellent acting was somewhat marred by virtuoso mannerisms, but his Tasso, Egmont, and Essex were considered outstanding. His son (5) OTTO (1838–94) played under him in Carlsruhe in the 1850s and 1860s, and in 1873 went as character actor to the Weimar Court theatre. Here, in 1876, his staging of both parts of Goethe's *Faust* as a Mystery play, on a stage on three levels, aroused much interest. Seven years later he was at Jena, where, for a festival in honour of Luther, he wrote and staged a pageant play. From 1884 until his death he was in Oldenburg, except for a season in Berlin. He was the author of several tragedies. His son (6) ERNEST (1873–   ) was also on the stage.

One of the outstanding members of the family was (7) MAX (1857–1929), the son of Karl and his second wife Ida Block, who made his début in Dresden in 1878 as Bertrand in *Die Jungfrau von Orleans*. He played extensively all over Germany, and was for many years at the Vienna Burgtheater, joining the company in 1882, and making his first appearance there in *Die Räuber*. A handsome man, of commanding presence, he excelled in big tragic roles, particularly in Goethe, Schiller, and Shakespeare. He was also considered good in comedy, and was much admired as Petruchio in *The Taming of the Shrew*. Another member of the family (8) HANS (1878–   ), though not on the stage, became editor of the *Archiv der Gesellschaft für Theatergeschichte.*

DIAGHILEV, SERGE (1872–1929), a Russian impresario, and a great lover of the ballet, who was responsible for introducing to Western Europe the splendours of the Imperial Russian Ballet. His company, known as the Ballets Russes, danced in Paris and London before the 1914–18 war, and opened up new worlds to artists, dancers, and critics alike. Having with great difficulty kept the company together during the war, Diaghilev continued to manage it until his death, and, through those whom he had trained and encouraged during his life-time, continued to exert untold influence on the history of the ballet, particularly in England (see BALLET, 7, COSTUME, 9, and SCENERY).

DIANA, see PONTI, DIANA DA.

DIBDIN. (1) CHARLES (1745–1814), English

dramatist, actor, and song-writer, whose ballads of ships and sailors, among them 'Tom Bowling' and 'The Lass that Loves a Sailor', were said to have 'brought more men into the Navy in war than all the press-gangs could'. They were probably inspired by Charles's brother Thomas, a naval captain for whom he had a great affection. Charles was a good actor, though he preferred light opera to straight comedy, and made a hit as Mungo in *The Padlock*. He wrote a number of ballad operas, of which *The Waterman* (1774) long remained a favourite and passed into the repertory of the Juvenile Drama. He quarrelled constantly with the managers, and his relations with Garrick are dwelt on at length in his autobiography, *The Professional Life of Mr. Dibdin*. From 1788 to 1793 he gave one-man entertainments, playing, singing, and reciting monologues. Handsome, but quarrelsome and bad-tempered, he left his wife after he had spent all her money, and by his association with the actress Harriet Pitt had three children, of whom the eldest (2) CHARLES ISAAC MUNGO PITT (1768–1833) was a popular and successful writer of plays and pantomimes, and was for some time proprietor and manager of Sadler's Wells Theatre. He also wrote a history of the London theatres, published in 1826, and had two children who were both musicians. His younger brother (3) THOMAS JOHN PITT (1771–1841) first appeared on the stage at the age of 4, as Cupid to the Venus of young Sarah Siddons. He was a choirboy at St. Paul's, and later ran away from his apprenticeship to an upholsterer to become an actor, occasionally a scene-painter, and always 'a dramatist of a fatal facility'. When he was first on the stage he called himself S. Merchant, but in about 1800 took the name of Dibdin, much to his father's annoyance. Thomas, who in his early years was genial and good-tempered, was devoted to his mother, and though proud of his father's work was resentful of his neglect. In later life he became sour and embittered. He was the composer of some 2,000 songs in the style of the elder Dibdin, to whom they are often attributed, and his most successful dramatic work was the pantomime of *Mother Goose*, done at Covent Garden in 1806–7 with Grimaldi as Clown. His theatrical glorifications of the Navy, as in *The Mouth of the Nile* (1798) and *Nelson's Glory* (1805), were also extremely popular. He married an actress named Nancy Hilliar and had four children, who under their grandmother's name of Pitt were all connected with the stage. Some of their children went to the United States, where there are still several Pitts in theatre management.

DICKENS, CHARLES (1812–70), the great English novelist, was all his life intimately connected with the stage, and had an immense influence on it through the numerous dramatizations of his books. As a young man he had serious thoughts of becoming an actor, and there is a stubborn tradition that he was at one time in the company of T. D. Davenport at the Portsmouth Theatre, where he obtained the material which later went to the fashioning of the Crummles family, little Jean Davenport being the original of the Infant Phenomenon. Those who saw Dickens in his many amateur appearances, notably as Captain Bobadil and Shallow, considered that he would have made a fine eccentric comedian, and his famous readings from his own works were in a way solo dramatic performances. In his London home, Tavistock House, he had a small theatre, perfectly fitted up, where with his friends and family he gave private performances before a distinguished audience. Two of Wilkie Collins's plays were given there before their professional productions at the Olympic. Dickens also collaborated with Collins in *No Thoroughfare*, which was given in 1867 with Fechter and Ben Webster in the cast, and wrote, early in his career, several operatic burlettas which he did not later wish to see revived. One of them, *The Strange Gentleman* (1836), was the opening production of Braham's St. James's Theatre.

It would be impossible to catalogue here the plays based on Dickens's novels, many of which were done before the books had finished appearing in fortnightly parts. The most persistent adapters were W. T. Moncrieff and Edward Stirling, but Dickens entrusted Albert Smith with the Christmas Books, and himself dramatized *Great Expectations*, hoping Toole would play Joe Gargery. His version was not acted, however, and the first to appear on the stage was that prepared by W. S. Gilbert, and given at the Court Theatre in May 1871. Owing to the absence of copyright laws, Dickens's novels were pirated for the American stage, and he received nothing from the numerous adaptations in common use.

Dickens's characters are so vivid, his plots so dramatic, that it is not surprising that they found favour with actors and audience alike. At Christmas 1845 versions of *The Cricket on the Hearth* were being given at twelve London theatres, all of which were later surpassed by Boucicault's excellent adaptation entitled *Dot* (1862). Among the outstanding actors who appeared in Dickens's characters were Toole as The Artful Dodger and Bob Cratchit, Mrs. Keeley as Oliver Twist, Smike, Little Nell, and Dot, Joseph Jefferson as Newman Noggs and Caleb Plummer, George Fawcett Rowe and John Brougham as Micawber, the latter in his own version of *David Copperfield*, Lotta as Little Nell and the Marchioness, Mme Céleste as Mme Defarge, Irving as Jingle, Tree as Fagin, Seymour Hicks as Scrooge in a music-hall sketch, and, most famous of all, Sir John Martin-Harvey as Sidney Carton in *The Only Way*, a dramatization of *A Tale of Two Cities*. Bransby Williams had a whole gallery of Dickens characters, while Betsey Prig and Sairey Gamp were for a long time acted by men, the most popular exponent of the latter being John Clarke.

DIDASCALIA, from the Greek *didaskalos*,

meaning teacher, and, by extension, dramatic poet, since in the earliest times of Greek drama the poet 'taught' his chorus its part and produced his own play. Hence *didascalia* meaning production, while *didascaliae* was the title given to catalogues, made by Aristotle and others, of dramatists, plays, and victories. Fragments of these survive in the ancient Arguments prefixed, in the manuscripts, to most Greek plays.

H. D. F. K.

DIDEROT, Denis (1713–84), French man of letters. Compared with his labours over his Encyclopaedia, and his numerous writings on any and every subject, Diderot's plays are but a minor feature of his busy literary life. Yet they are important, as is his *Paradoxe sur le comédien*, for they helped to diffuse the new ideas of the time, and had a great influence on Lessing, and through him on the European drama of the nineteenth century. Diderot was an exponent of bourgeois drama, that offshoot of *comédie larmoyante* whose mixed sentiment, virtue, and sheer priggishness appealed so strongly to the middle-class audiences of the eighteenth century. The titles of his plays—*Le Fils naturel, Le Père de famille*—are sufficiently revealing, and, in spite of some feeling for dialogue, they degenerate all too quickly into didactic expositions of philosophical theories. They were in some cases published years before they were acted, while some, like *Est-il bon, est-il méchant?*, were seen only on private stages. Yet the extent of his influence may be gauged by the fact that during his lifetime they were translated into German, English, Dutch, and Italian. But the best of Diderot's work for the theatre must be looked for elsewhere; in his *Observations sur Garrick*, his *Essai sur la poésie dramatique*, and his *Entretien avec Dorval*, which tell us, far better than his somewhat weak and confused plays, what he is aiming at. Among other things he endeavoured to place the actor as a member of a united company, and pleaded for greater unity between actor and dramatist.

DIDRING, Ernst (1868–1931), modern Swedish dramatist, whose *Elna Hall* (1917) was given with much success throughout Europe (see SCANDINAVIA, 3).

DIGGES, Dudley (1879–1947), Irish actor, who made his first appearances with the Irish National Players in 1901–3. He was trained for the stage by Frank J. Fay, and was in the original production of *Deirdre* and other plays, being particularly good as The Wise Man in *The Hourglass*. After the second visit of the Irish company to London Digges, with two other members, accepted an invitation to America, where he spent the rest of his life, becoming one of the outstanding actors of New York, and a potent force in the theatre there. His departure was a great loss to the Irish players, since he had a good presence, and was equally at home in comedy and romance. He began his New York career in 1904 in *John Bull's Other Island*, and was later with Ben

Greet, Mrs. Fiske, and George Arliss, acting as stage manager for the last for seven years. He was in the first productions of the Theatre Guild in 1919, and remained with it until 1930, playing a wide variety of parts, and producing some of the plays, notably *Pygmalion* and The *Doctor's Dilemma*. He later produced the all-star revival of *Becky Sharp*, and in 1937 was seen as Franz Joseph in *The Masque of Kings*. His last, and one of his finest, parts was Harry Hope in *The Iceman Cometh*.

DIGGES, (John) Dudley West (1720–86), English actor, who served his apprenticeship in Dublin and Edinburgh, where he remained from 1749 to 1764, and was the first to play Young Norval in *Douglas* (1756). By a curious twist of fortune he played Old Norval at the Haymarket in 1780. Meanwhile he had been seen at the same theatre between 1777–81 as Macbeth, Lear, Shylock, Wolsey, Cato, Sir John Brute, and Lord Townley, showing a remarkable versatility. He then went to Dublin and acted there till incapacitated by paralysis in 1784. In his prime he had a noble presence, and a fine manly figure.

DIKIE, Alexei Denisovich (1889–   ), Soviet actor and producer. The son of a peasant, he trained at the Moscow Art Theatre, where his first appearance was in *The Lower Depths*. After the October Revolution he concentrated on production, and worked in various theatres until in 1932 he was appointed director of the V.Ts.P.S. theatre, where his finest productions were Wolf's *Sailors of Cattaro* and Finn's *Nonsense*. When this theatre finally closed, Dikie went on the staff of the Maly, and later became one of three producers at the Vakhtangov. At one time he worked in the Theatre of the Revolution, and he also opened a studio where he was responsible for some interesting productions, notably of Shakespeare, and of Shostakovich's opera 'Lady Macbeth of Mtsensk'.

DILLINGHAM, Charles Bancroft (1868–1934), American theatre manager, who, after some years as a journalist, made his first contact with the stage when he was appointed dramatic critic of *The New York Sun*. A somewhat poor play led to a friendship with Charles Frohman and to the managership of Julia Marlowe. Later he managed many eminent actors, some of them on their first visits to the U.S. He was responsible, with Howard Gould, for the building of the Globe Theatre, 1910, in New York, and for twenty years was responsible for productions there, mainly musical shows and revues, in most of which Fred Stone appeared. For Herbert's *The Red Mill* Dillingham put up the first moving electric sign seen on Broadway. He was head of the Dillingham Theatre Corporation and associated also with Erlanger and Ziegfeld. Among straight plays, he was responsible for Shaw's *Man and Superman* in 1905, and for introducing Lonsdale's comedies to New York. At the height of his prosperity he had as many as six plays running at once. In 1914 he took over the Hippodrome for lavish vaudeville shows, which included trained elephants, Anna Pavlova on her first visit to New York, Gaby Deslys, and performing seals. He produced over 200 plays, but later failed and in 1933 became bankrupt, dying a year later.

DIMMER, see LIGHTING.

DINGELSTEDT, FRANZ (1814–81), German theatre director, who was appointed to the control of the Munich theatre at the time of the big industrial exhibition held there in 1854. Here he made theatre history by his elaborate productions, for which he imported actors from all over the country. The experiment, however, ended disastrously, owing to a combination of cholera and slighted native talent, and Dingelstedt withdrew to Weimar. Later he was appointed director of the Vienna Burgtheater, and in both places staged remarkable productions of Shakespeare's chronicle plays.

DIONYSUS, a Greek nature-god (Bacchus being a roughly equivalent name), who was associated particularly, but by no means exclusively, with wine. His worship took many forms. The most remarkable was the orgiastic revels in which his votaries, women in particular, withdrew for a time into the wild and experienced a mystical communion with Nature (see Euripides' *Bacchae*). As Dionysus was a vegetation-spirit, who died and was reborn each year, he was associated not only with all kinds of rites designed to promote fertility but also with mystery-religions, of which an important part was teaching about death, purgation, and rebirth. The death and 'sufferings' of Dionysus were commonly presented in quasi-dramatic ritual; his rebirth, presumably, in ritual of a more cheerful kind; while as god of plenty, and of wine, intoxication, and ecstasy, he was honoured with rites that may be mildly described as jolly.

In so dynamic a worship there are obviously all sorts of contacts with every form of drama, and in fact drama in Athens, whether tragic, satyric, or comic, was always strictly associated with the festivals of Dionysus (see GREECE, 3 *a*). In Old Comedy the phallus (as symbol of fertility) and the Dionysiac 'comus' or revel (whence 'comedy') are constant features; and another element, the 'contest' (*agôn*), is by some scholars derived from the 'agony' of Dionysus. In the satyric-drama too, direct Dionysiac influence is obvious; the satyrs, or 'horse-men', imaginary creatures of the wild, had come to be regarded as attendants on Dionysus, though apparently they were not that originally.

With tragedy the connexion is less clear, and may be more indirect. Attempts have been made to trace, in the basic form of tragedy, a Dionysiac ritual-sequence, but they are not very convincing. It is possible, though it cannot be proved, that the earliest tragedy in Athens dealt exclusively or mainly with Dionysiac subjects; but when we begin to have knowledge of it, some thirty years after its inception, it certainly does not. Dionysiac subjects are common (though only one Dionysiac play, the *Bacchae*, happens to have survived), but not more common than the dramatic nature of the Dionysus-legends would lead us to expect. When Aristotle says that tragedy originated in the dithyramb (a type of hymn to Dionysus), he is obviously thinking of the form of tragedy, that it grew out of a choral performance with dialogue interspersed; he cannot be held to mean that the new art was Dionysiac in spirit or content, though it may have been. He states also that tragedy developed 'out of the satyr-drama' (which was undoubtedly very closely connected with the more boisterous side of Dionysus-worship) by discarding its rollicking metres, its ridiculous diction, and its insignificant plots; it might therefore be argued that tragedy became itself actually by getting rid of Dionysiac elements. The whole question remains obscure because, though there is an abundance of analogies and possibilities, there is little direct and trustworthy evidence; but at the very least it is certain that the worship of Dionysus stimulated, in a most catholic way, the lively dramatic sense of the Greeks, and gave to the Athenians, in its festivals, a congenial home in which diverse forms of the drama could grow to maturity.   H. D. F. K.

DIPHILUS (*d.* 290 B.C.) of Sinope, Greek poet of the New Comedy, contemporary with Menander (see GREECE, 2 *b*). He was frequently imitated by Plautus and Terence. Only fragments of his work survive.

DIPS, see LIGHTING, 2 *f*.

DIRECTOR, see PRODUCER, 2.

DISGUISING, a term used in the fifteenth and sixteenth centuries in England to cover any sort of entertainment which included mummery or dice-play and the wearing of masks. The word was later (1512) replaced by mask, or masque, and was obsolete by 1544. 'Disguise', says Ben Jonson, 'was the old English word for a mask.'

DITHYRAMB, a type of hymn in honour, originally, of the Greek god Dionysus, then of other deities. It was performed by a chorus of fifty, and would normally relate some incident in the life of the deity to whom it was addressed. The leader of the chorus later became semi-detached, as a soloist; and in the question-and-answer that might pass between him and the rest of the chorus lies, almost certainly, the origin, or one of the origins, of drama. (See further GREECE, 1.)   H. D. F. K.

DIVERTISSEMENT, see BALLET, 6.

DMITREVSKY, IVAN AFANASYEVICH (1733–1821), one of the first important actors in the Russian theatre. He appeared with the amateur company founded by Fedor Volkov, and went with him to play before the Court in January 1752. He was then sent to the Cadet College to be trained for the Court theatre, and was a member of the company organized by Sumarokov. After the untimely death of Volkov in 1763 Dmitrevsky was appointed Inspector of Theatres, and took a leading part in the running of the State playhouses. Between 1765 and 1768 he twice went abroad to complete his theatrical education, and spent most of the time in Paris with the leading French actors of the day. On his return he occupied the highest position in the St. Petersburg theatre, both as actor and administrator, being known as 'the ornament of the Russian stage'. He was extremely gifted, and appeared with equal success in tragic and comic parts. His best performances were considered to be the title-roles of *Le Misanthrope* and Sumarokov's *Dmitri the Self-named*, and Starodum in *The Minor* by Fonvizin. He wrote and translated plays, prepared a history of the Russian theatre, and was elected a member of the Russian Academy. These activities set him apart from the general run of Russian actors, who at that time were usually lacking in education. Dmitrevsky played a big part in the development of the theatre in Russia. As head of the State theatres he determined its artistic development, chose its repertory, formed its companies, and rehearsed the actors in their parts. Among his pupils was Alexei Yakovlev.

DÖBBELIN, KARL THEOPHILUS (1727–93), German actor-manager, who started his career in the company of Caroline Neuber and later of Ackermann; he found his true vocation, however, in the several troupes of wandering harlequin-players which he afterwards joined. He was a boastful and unscrupulous man, who started his own company on money won at cards, and kept it by going by blatant publicity and somewhat underhand means. He settled in Leipzig, and for some time proved a serious rival to Koch, who was established there. Döbbelin was a great noisy cheerful creature who played all his parts, whether tragic or comic, in the same style, thundering out his lines in a roar, and rushing about the stage to the great danger of the scenery and his fellow actors. This pleased the groundlings mightily, and for the rest he was indifferent. It should, however, be said in his favour that he had a good repertory of plays and kept his company well under control. None of his actors was outstanding, with the exception of his wife, a gentle, charming woman, whose quiet, subtle style was a great contrast to her husband's. Nevertheless Döbbelin, by sheer personality, carried his company to the point where it was taken seriously by contemporary critics. In 1765 he took over the management of Schuch's company, which had gone to pieces under the management of the old harlequin-player's three sons, took it to Berlin, re-formed it, and again forced it and himself on the attention of the critics. On the opening of the National Theatre in Berlin he was replaced by Fleck, though he retained a nominal position as stage-manager till his death.

DOCK STREET THEATRE, see CHARLESTON.

DÓCZY, LAJOS (1845–1918), Hungarian dramatist, and with Rákosi founder of the neo-romantic drama, which abandoned the realistic social problems of the day for fantasy and legend. His best play was probably *A Csók* (*The Kiss*), which had a great success on its production in 1874.

DODD, JAMES WILLIAM (1734–96), English comedian, the last of the fops who started with Cibber, all lace, frills, and snuff-boxes. After a hard apprenticeship in the provinces he appeared at Drury Lane in 1765, where he was the original Sir Benjamin Backbite in *The School for Scandal*. One of his finest parts was Sir Andrew Aguecheek, of which Lamb has left an excellent description: 'Dodd was *it*, as it came out of nature's hands.... In expressing slowness of apprehension this actor surpassed all others. You could see the first dawn of an idea stealing slowly over his countenance, climbing up little and little, with a painful process. . . . The balloon takes less time in filling, than it took to cover the expansion of his broad moony face over all its quarters with expression.' Boaden described him as 'the soul of empty eminence'. He was good as Lord Foppington, as Tattle, as Bob Acres, and in such parts as Fribble. Off-stage he was serious and a great student, leaving at his death a fine library which was bought chiefly by the King, the Duke of Roxburghe, and John Kemble.

DODD, LEE WILSON (1879–1933), American man of letters, who, in addition to poetry and novels, wrote several plays. Among them the most important were *Speed* (1911), a satire on the early motor-car craze, *The Changelings* (1923), and a satiric comedy, *A Stranger in the House* (1931), which met with disaster when its leading man, Henry Miller, died on the first night in New York. After some financial losses in the slump of 1920, Dodd turned successfully to the teaching of English, and at the time of his death had just been invited to succeed Professor Baker, whose assistant he had been for some time, in his playwriting course at Yale.

DODSLEY, ROBERT (1703–64), an interesting figure in the English literary world of the early eighteenth century. The son of a Mansfield schoolmaster, he was apprenticed to a weaver, but ran away and went into domestic service. While working as a footman in London he attracted notice by some occasional verses, was taken up and patronized by the nobility, and became the friend and protégé of Defoe and Pope. He appears to have been a charming and attractive young man, whose head was in no way turned by his success, though he knew how to profit by it. On the proceeds of his first play, *The Toy Shop* (1735), and other literary works, he established himself as a bookseller and publisher at the sign of Tully's Head in Pall Mall, where he issued works by Pope, Dr.

Johnson, and his own important *Select Collection of Old Plays*, later revised and edited by Hazlitt. His best-known play was *The King and the Miller of Mansfield* (1737), which, with its sequel, *Sir John Cockle at Court* (1738), was given at Drury Lane, and frequently revived. It provided the basis for Collé's *Partie de chasse d'Henri IV*, and is still obtainable in the repertory of the nineteenth-century Juvenile Drama. Dodsley's last play, *Cleone* (1758), was a tragedy which owed much of its success to the acting of George Anne Bellamy, and was revived by Mrs. Siddons in 1786. He also wrote the libretto of a ballad opera, *The Blind Beggar of Bethnal Green* (1741).

DOG DRAMA, see CIRCUS.

DOGGETT, THOMAS (*c.* 1670–1721), English actor, who first appeared in London after some years in the provinces, and soon made a reputation in the playing of low comedy. Congreve admired him exceedingly, and wrote for him the parts of Fondlewife in *The Old Bachelor* and Ben in *Love for Love*. Doggett, of whom Cibber has left an excellent pen-portrait in his *Apology*, had the good sense never to step outside his own line of characters. He was joint manager of Drury Lane with Cibber and Wilks, retiring in disgust when Barton Booth, whose politics he disliked, was allowed a share in the Patent. In 1696 he wrote a farce which was played at Lincoln's Inn Fields Theatre, and later revived in an adaptation by Colley Cibber. He also instituted the Doggett Coat and Badge for Thames watermen, a race which is still rowed, in honour of the accession of George I. It takes place on 1 August, and figures in *The Waterman* (1774) by Dibdin. Doggett was the friend of Addison, Steele, and Pope, whom he met daily at Button's Coffee-house, where he had also to encounter Cibber, whom after his retirement from Drury Lane he ignored for a year. They eventually became friends again, and made common cause against the insufferable and extravagant Wilks.

DOLCE, LODOVICO (1508–68), Italian dramatist of whom Walker, in his *Historical Memoir on Italian Tragedy* (1799), says scathingly 'little is known that can be related with pleasure'. He was one of those who 'supped full of horrors', and his tragedies, drawn from classical drama, are only a degree less distasteful than the famous *Canace* of Speroni. One of the most successful, which was given to great applause in 1565, was *Marianna*, a rehandling of the story of Herod and Mariamne which is, for its period, unusually subtle. By some critics it is considered the most representative tragedy of the sixteenth century. His *Giocasta*, based on Euripides' *Phoenician Women*, was given in translation at Gray's Inn in 1566.

DOLIN, ANTON [really PATRICK HEALEY-KAY] (1904–), see BALLET, 8.

DOMINION DRAMA FESTIVAL, a yearly competitive festival held in Canada, in which amateur groups from all over the country

participate. Founded in 1932 by the then Governor-General, Lord Bessborough, who was well aware of the widespread interest in community drama and its value as a civilizing and educative influence, it has as its aim the encouragement of acting and play-production all over the Dominion, and the writing of new plays by Canadians. In order to cover the vast area of Canada thoroughly and yet quickly, the country is divided into eleven regions, and these again where necessary into sub-regions, and the winners from each area are invited to participate in the final festival, held in April or May, usually at Ottawa, though the 1947 festival, the first since the outbreak of war in 1939, was held at London, Ontario. At first only one-act plays were admissible, but this has now been changed, and three-act plays are accepted for competition. At the final festival about five full-length and nine or ten short plays are seen, representing the best available talent from all over the country. The awards include the Bessborough Trophy for the most outstanding production, which may be in French or English; separate French and English Trophies; and the Sir Barry Jackson Trophy for the best play by a Canadian to reach the finals. Canadian authorship is also encouraged by a cash prize to the author of the best play produced in any of the regional festivals or in the final festival. This, coupled with the opportunity of production which the festival affords, has proved very stimulating to Canadian dramatists, resulting in twelve new plays in 1935, and sixteen in 1936, of which four reached the finals. Individual awards are also given for outstanding performances by actors and actresses (see also CANADA).

DOMINION THEATRE, LONDON, a large playhouse on the site of a famous brewery at the junction of Tottenham Court Road and Oxford Street. It opened on 3 Oct. 1929 with *Follow Through*. Other productions there were Julian Wylie's pantomime *Aladdin*, and a musical play called *Silver Wings* (both 1930). The theatre then became a cinema.

DOMINIQUE, see BIANCOLELLI (3).

DON JUAN, a character derived from an old Spanish legend, who first found vital expression in Tirso's *El Burlador de Sevilla y Convidado de Piedra* (1630), and has since become a constantly recurring figure in European literature. There is no evidence for the existence of Don Juan as an historical figure, though tradition usually connects him with Seville. Tirso's play is in two parts, the first concerned with the character and activities of the hero, the second with his mocking invitation to dinner given to the marble statue, who accepts it and brings retribution by supernatural means upon Don Juan in punishment of his many crimes. Each part derives from a separate source, but is so linked with the other as to present a convincing whole. Don Juan is not portrayed as a merely sensual man; he is the embodiment of self-will, unable to curb his desires although he knows they are evil. There is no lack of Catholic belief in him, as there is in Molière's version of the story. He does not doubt that retribution will come, but he continually puts off repentance, hoping through God's mercy and long-suffering to remain immune as long as possible. Among the many works on the same theme are Mozart's opera 'Don Giovanni', Byron's poem *Don Juan*, Molière's *Festin de Pierre*, Goldoni's *El dissoluto*, a Russian version by Pushkin, and frequent versions in Spanish, the best being Zorrilla's *Don Juan Tenorio*. Don Juan also appears in the third act of Shaw's *Man and Superman*.

DOOR OF ENTRANCE, or Proscenium Door, see PROSCENIUM.

D'ORGEMONT [ADRIEN DES BARRES] (?–*c.* 1665), French actor, who was at the Théâtre du Marais with Montdory and succeeded him as Orator of the troupe. Little is known of his acting, though he was favourably compared with Bellerose and was a good comedian. In 1638 he married the widow of the farce-player Turlupin and went to the Hôtel de Bourgogne, where he remained until his death. He is believed to have played Don Diègue in the first production of *Le Cid*.

DORIMOND [NICHOLAS DROUIN] (*c.* 1628–*c.* 1664), a French provincial actor-manager, whose early career bears some resemblance to that of Molière, though, unlike his famous contemporary, he never succeeded in establishing himself in Paris. With his wife, who after his death appeared at the Marais, he directed the Troupe of Mademoiselle, in which the son of Floridor also played for a short time. Dorimond was the author of nine plays, including one on the subject of Don Juan, which were given by the above company, probably between 1657 and 1660, and his farces may have been seen by, and had some influence on, Molière, who no doubt encountered Dorimond's company on his wanderings.

DORSET GARDEN THEATRE, LONDON (the second Duke's House), was planned by Davenant, who died before it was completed. Designed by Wren, it cost £9,000, the money being subscribed by people known not as 'backers', the term in use to-day, but much more picturesquely as 'adventurers'. It stood by the river, just to the south of Salisbury Court, and was larger than either Davenant's old house in Lincoln's Inn Fields or the Theatre Royal, Bridges Street (Drury Lane). It had a river frontage and steps for those landing by boat, called Dorset Stairs. Over the front were the arms of the Duke of York, for he was its patron, and its players were known as the Duke's Men. The building, which was of a magnificence never before seen in a London theatre, was decorated with statues of Melpomene and Thalia, and had a striking proscenium arch. Over the theatre were apartments, where lived Betterton, the chief actor—known as the Keeper. He and Harris were the artistic

directors of a fine company, while the business arrangements were in the capable hands of Davenant's widow, Dame Marie de Tremblay Davenant, and later of her sons.

The theatre opened on 9 Nov. 1671 with *Sir Martin Mar-All*, a tried favourite. The first new play was *King Charles VIII of France*, which, says Downes the prompter in his *Roscius Anglicanus*, though 'all new cloathed, yet lasted but 6 days together'. *Mamamouchi; or, the Citizen turned Gentleman*, the next new play, had Harris, Haines, Nokes, Sandford, Underhill, Mrs. Betterton, and Mrs. Leigh in the cast. The critics described it as foolish, but it ran nine days to full houses. Opera, for which the theatre later became famous, began with Davenant's adaptation of *Macbeth*. Shadwell's operatic version of *The Tempest* was given a spectacular revival, with great success, and Locke's opera 'Psyche', which cost £800 to produce, ran for eight days and proved very remunerative. Two dramatists made unsuccessful appearances as actors during this time, Lee in *Macbeth*, Otway in *The Jealous Bridegroom*. Betterton's reputation was much enhanced by his performance in Shadwell's version of *Timon of Athens*, and his *Libertine* and *Virtuoso*, while Otway's *The Orphan* and *Venice Preserved*, with Southerne's *The Fatal Marriage*, made the name of the famous Mrs. Barry, for whom Otway's plays were written.

Under Betterton's skilful direction the theatre proved a thorn in the side of Drury Lane, and from 1672, when the latter was burnt down, until 1674, when it was reopened, Dorset Garden was the only first-class theatre in London. Although most of Dryden's plays were done at Drury Lane, his *Spanish Friar* and *Mr. Limberham; or, the Kind Keeper* were first done at Dorset Garden. Other dramatists who wrote for this theatre were D'Urfey, Settle, Aphra Behn, Etherege, and Ravenscroft.

Things got bad for both houses eventually, and in 1682 the two companies combined, making Drury Lane their head-quarters, with Betterton as leading man displacing Hart and Mohun. After the union Dorset Garden declined. It gave operas occasionally, and in 1689 was called the Queen's Theatre, out of compliment to Queen Mary (William and Mary). But it descended the scale gradually, and was finally used for acrobatic and wild beast shows. The last mention of it is in 1706. W. M. P.

DORVAL [MARIE THOMASE AMÉLIE DELAUNAY] (1798–1849), French actress, child of strolling players, orphaned at 15, married in the following year, and soon widowed. She played in the provinces for some years, and was first seen in Paris at the Porte-Saint-Martin in a poor melodrama to which her excellent acting gave a momentary success. It was, however, as Amélie in *Trente Ans, ou la Vie d'un Joueur* that she made her first hit, playing opposite Frédérick-Lemaître as Georges. At the same theatre she was superb in the elder Dumas's *Antony*, with Bocage, appearing with the same actor in *Marion Delorme*. This brought her to the notice of the Comédie-Française, where she made her début on 21 Apr. 1834, as Kitty Bell in *Chatterton*. She played with Mlle Mars in *Angelo*, and might have remained at the Comédie-Française until her retirement, but finding the restrictions irksome she left in 1838 and went back to the Gymnase and Renaissance. She was seen at the Odéon in 1842 and later at the Ambigu, but she was already ill, and soon retired.

DORVIGNY [LOUIS FRANÇOIS ARCHAMBAULT] (1742–1812), French actor and dramatist, a reputed son of Louis XV, whom he certainly resembled in looks. He played for some time on the boulevards under Nicolet, but being idle and dissipated he soon turned to playwriting as a less arduous occupation, and turned out some 300 light comedies and farces, many of which were never printed. Most of them were done at the Foire Saint-Laurent in the 1770s, and his Janot, played by Volange, and Jocrisse, played by Brunet, delighted uncritical audiences for years. The Comédie-Française, hoping to profit by his success elsewhere, finally did two of his plays, but the academic atmosphere of this great theatre was not suited to his genius, and they were comparative failures. Usually penniless, often drunk, a bohemian and a wit, Dorvigny was a friend of the dramatist Aude, who became his boon companion in dissipation. His life was written by Charles Monselet.

DOSTOIEVSKY, FEODOR MIKHAILOVICH (1821–81), distinguished Russian novelist, several of whose novels have been dramatized, notably *The Idiot* and *The Brothers Karamazov*. Both these were done before 1917, and have been revived since. *The Insulted and Injured* (also known in English as *The Despised and Rejected*) was adapted for the Moscow Art Theatre by V. A. Solovyov, and in 1946 an adaptation of *Crime and Punishment* was given with some success in London.

DOTTORE, IL, the pedant and second agèd parent of the *commedia dell'arte*. He was usually depicted as a Bolognese lawyer, and frequently confused with the Pedant. His name was often Graziano (see ITALY, 2). Unlike his companion, Pantalone (Pantaloon), he has left no trace in the English harlequinade, though he passed into French dramatic literature via Molière.

DOUBLE MASQUE, see MASQUE.

DOUGLASS, DAVID (?–1786), the first American actor-manager, who in 1758 met and married the widow of the elder Hallam in Jamaica, where he was touring with a company. He took her and her family, with his own actors, back to New York, later calling them the American Company. He was an excellent manager, and seems to have found his work most profitable, in spite of some opposition from the more Puritan elements of the population in New York and Philadelphia. He built a temporary theatre on Cruger's Wharf, another in Beekman Street and a third in John Street, all in New York, and was also responsible for the erection of the first permanent theatre in the United States, the Southwark, in Philadelphia, which opened in 1766. It was under Douglass's management that the American Company did *The Prince of Parthia*, the first American play to have a professional production, and that John Henry, later to succeed Douglass as manager, first joined the company in New York.

DOWNES, JOHN (*fl.* 1662–1710), author of *Roscius Anglicanus*, a volume of scattered theatrical notes which is one of the rare sources of information on the early Restoration theatre. Downes, who was connected with the theatre all his life, wanted to be an actor, but his first appearance on the stage, in Davenant's *Siege of Rhodes* in 1661, was such a fiasco that he gave up, and worked backstage. He was connected with Davenant's company, and later with Betterton's at Lincoln's Inn Fields, as prompter and book-keeper, in which capacity he had charge of the play scripts, copied the actors' parts, and attended all rehearsals and performances. His *Roscius Anglicanus* was first published in 1708. It was edited in 1886 by Joseph Knight, and in 1930 by Montague Summers.

DOWNSTAGE (the acting area nearest the audience), see STAGE DIRECTIONS.

DOWTON, WILLIAM (1764–1851), English actor, who was intended for architecture but was led by some successful appearances in amateur theatricals to take to the stage. After working in the provinces he made his first appearance in London in 1795, and soon became an excellent player of such elderly characters as Sir Anthony Absolute and Dr. Cantwell, Hardcastle and Old Dornton. He was also extremely good as Falstaff, in which part he made his New York début at the Park Theatre in 1836. A thorough artist, of the Garrick school, he was considered by Leigh Hunt one of the finest comic geniuses of the day, while Hazlitt described him as 'a genuine and excellent comedian'. He had two sons, both of whom were on the stage.

D'OYLY CARTE, RICHARD (1844–1901), theatrical impresario, who encouraged the early collaboration of Gilbert and Sullivan and with the profits which accrued to him therefrom built the Savoy Theatre, London, the first to be lighted by electricity. It opened with *Patience*, and became a home of light opera. D'Oyly Carte also built the Royal English Opera House, Cambridge Circus (now the Palace Theatre), in an endeavour to encourage the writing and production of English opera. He did much to raise the musical taste of his generation, gave employment to young singers, and founded the company for the production of Gilbert and Sullivan which still bears his name.

DRACHMANN, HOLGER HENRIK HER-
HOLDT (1846–1908), Danish poet and dramatist,
was born in Copenhagen, went to the university
and the Academy of Fine Arts, and for many
years was simultaneously a writer and a painter.
He came for a time under the influence of
Georg Brandes, travelled widely in England
and on the continent, and wrote a good deal
of prose and verse before he attempted
dramatic work. When he did so his wide
experience of men and nations gave him
wealth of material, though his form remained
to the end lyrical rather than dramatic. His
poetry was already famous (from the time
of *Daempede Melodier* (*Muffled Melodies*) in
1875) when he began writing plays in 1882.
Three plays were written between 1882 and
1884 and then the well-known *Der var en Gang*
(*Once upon a Time*) in 1885. Two dramatic
poems and two more plays followed and then,
in 1894, *Vølund Smed* (*Wayland the Smith*),
the first of his melodramas, a collected volume
of which appeared in 1895. His popularity as
a playwright was now very high and it was
increased by his *Brav Karl* in 1898. Two more
plays followed in 1898 and then the last plays,
Gurre, a romantic play, in 1899, *Hallfred
Vandraadeskjald*, a lyrical drama, in 1900, and
Det grönne Haab (*The Evergreen Hope*) in
1903. He died in Copenhagen early in 1908.
                                                               U. E.-F.

DRAKE, SAMUEL (1769–1854), see DEAN.

DRAMA. (1) A term applied loosely to the
whole body of work written for the theatre, as
English drama, French drama, or to a group
of plays related by their style or content, as
Restoration Drama, Realistic Drama.

(2) A term applicable to any situation in
which there is conflict and, for theatrical purposes, resolution of that conflict with the
assumption of character. This implies the co-
operation of at least two actors, and rules out
narrative and monologue. The dramatic instinct is inherent in man, and the most rudimentary dialogue with song and dance may be
classed as drama. In a narrower sense the
word is applied to plays of high emotional
content, which at their best may give us
literary masterpieces, and at their worst degenerate into melodrama. The term dramatist
is not necessarily restricted to a writer of such
dramas, but serves, like playwright, to designate
anyone writing for the theatre.

DRAMATIC CENSORSHIP. 1. GREAT
BRITAIN. The wide powers of supervision and
control over the stage in this country which are
to-day vested in the Lord Chamberlain are an
elaboration of the functions of the Master of
the King's Revels of Tudor times. He was
appointed in the reign of Henry VII to supervise the entertainments of the Court, his duty
being, in part, to ensure that such entertainments were carried on in an orderly manner
and contained no matter offensive to the King.
With the growth of the Tudor and Stuart policy
of suppressing in the drama, as elsewhere,

opinions which were unorthodox or tended to
heresy or sedition, the work which devolved
upon him outgrew his administrative capabilities and was gradually taken over by his superior
officer in the Royal Household, the Lord Chamberlain, whose primary duty it became to give
effect to the royal will in these matters as it
varied from reign to reign. His appointment
depended upon no statutory enactment and
there were no statutes defining the extent of his
authority in the theatre. The first statute
directly concerned with control over the stage
was passed in the reign of James I (3 Jac. I, c. 21)
—'an Act to restrain the abuses of players . . .
for preventing and avoiding of the great abuse
of the Holy name of God in Stage Plays, Enter-
ludes, May-Games, Shews, and such like'.

For over two centuries there was little change
in the general situation. The Lord Chamberlain concerned himself almost exclusively with
political and religious issues, paying attention
to the moral aspect of the theatre only to the
extent of prohibiting riotous or immoral conduct at dramatic performances.

With the emergence of the theatre from its
extinction under the Commonwealth, the reaction towards a general unruliness in the
theatre became pronounced and resulted in the
passing of an Act in 1713 (12 Anne, stat. 2,
c. 23) 'for reducing the laws relating to rogues,
vagabonds, sturdy beggars and vagrants, into
one act of Parliament; and for the more effectual
punishing such rogues, vagabonds, sturdy
beggars and vagrants, and sending them
whither they ought to be sent'. 'Common
players of Interludes' were deemed 'under the
Act to be 'rogues and vagabonds'.

In 1737, however, a development occurred.
For the first time the Lord Chamberlain's
prerogative powers received statutory recognition and his dual function in the theatre was
clearly defined. Under Section 1 of 10 Geo. II,
c. 28, any person acting 'for hire, gain or
reward' in any place where they have not a
settlement, or 'without licence from the Lord
Chamberlain of His Majesty's Household for
the time being, shall be deemed a rogue and
vagabond'; while under Section 2 no new
plays or additions to old plays might be acted
unless and until a copy of such plays or additions had obtained the approval of the Lord
Chamberlain.

In 1843, matters were taken a stage farther,
when the Theatres Act of that year (6 & 7 Vict.,
c. 68) repealed all previous acts relevant to the
control of the stage, and consolidated the law
on the whole subject. Under this Act, which
is still in force, detailed regulations are laid
down as to the structural and other requirements necessary before premises can be licensed
by the Lord Chamberlain as suitable for the
production of stage plays. The Lord Chamberlain is the licensing authority for this purpose
for all theatres in London other than Drury
Lane and Covent Garden, and for all theatres
in Windsor and other places of Royal residence.
Elsewhere the licensing of theatres comes under
the jurisdiction of the local authorities.

As this article is concerned with the Lord Chamberlain's second function—as Censor of plays—it is to Section 12 of the Act and the sections which amplify it that the reader should refer. Section 12 provides that:

One copy of every new stage play, and of every new act, scene, or other part added to an old stage play, and of every new prologue or epilogue, and of every new part added to an old prologue or epilogue, intended to be produced and acted for hire at any theatre in Great Britain, shall be sent to the Lord Chamberlain of Her Majesty's household for the time being, seven days at least before the first acting or presenting thereof, with an account of the theatre where and the time when the same is intended to be first acted or presented, signed by the master or manager, or one of the masters or managers of such theatre; and during the said seven days no person shall for hire act or present the same, or cause the same to be acted or presented; and in case the Lord Chamberlain, either before or after the expiration of the said period of seven days, shall disallow any play, or any act, scene, or part thereof, or any prologue or epilogue, or any part thereof, it shall not be lawful for any person to act or present the same, or cause the same to be acted or presented, contrary to such disallowance.

The term 'stage play' is defined by Section 23 of the Act as including 'every tragedy, comedy, farce, opera, burletta, interlude, melodrama, pantomime or other entertainment of the stage, or any part thereof'.

The application of any definition gives rise to disputes in borderline cases and the interpretation of Section 23 has led to a certain amount of litigation during the century since the passing of the Act. In *Wigan* v. *Strange* (1865 L.R. I.C.P. 175) where a 'ballet divertissement' in contradistinction to a 'ballet d'action' was held not to constitute a stage play, Erle, C.J., in dealing with the particular issues involved, gave a general indication of the position. He said 'the ballet divertissement involves no consecutive train of ideas, but consists merely of poses and evolutions by a number of persons, elegant in shape and graceful in action. On the other hand, the ballet d'action has a regular dramatic story which may give rise to all manner of emotions incident to tragedy, comedy, or farce, accompanied by elegance of form and grace of motion.' Willis, J., in the same case, in associating himself with the Lord Chief Justice's decision, said of the ballet divertissement: 'In strictness, it is not an entertainment of, but on the stage.'

Provided that a performance is a performance 'of the stage' and has 'a regular dramatic story' it is not necessary for all the performers to be 'on the stage'. In *Day* v. *Simpson* (1865 18 C.B.N.S. 680) only two of the characters were 'on the stage'; the rest were below the stage, their reflections only appearing in front of the footlights.

As Section 12 relates to every 'new stage play', plays written before the passing of the Theatres Act need not be submitted to the Lord Chamberlain. Such plays, however, can be suppressed by the Lord Chamberlain under powers vested in him by Section 14 of the Act. This section reads:

It shall be lawful for the Lord Chamberlain for the time being, whenever he shall be of opinion that it is fitting for the preservation of good manners, decorum, or of the public peace so to do, to forbid the acting or presenting any stage play, or any act, scene, or part thereof, or any prologue or epilogue, or any part thereof, anywhere in Great Britain, or in such theatres as he shall specify, and either absolutely or for such time as he shall think fit.

Under the terms of the same section the Lord Chamberlain can also withdraw a licence already granted. This power is, however, exercised only in exceptional cases.

Paragraphs 88, 89, and 90 of the *Rules and Regulations with regard to Theatres in the Jurisdiction of the Lord Chamberlain* lay down that no profanity or impropriety of language; no indecency of dress, dance, or gesture; and no offensive personalities or representations of living persons are permitted on the stage, or anything calculated to produce riot or breach of the peace.

At the time of writing the Lord Chamberlain has two readers, who read and report upon the works submitted. Although the Lord Chamberlain's power to withhold or withdraw a licence is absolute and he is under no legal obligation to disclose the reasons which led his readers to come to their decision, as a matter of practice the Lord Chamberlain's office when refusing a licence is normally ready to indicate changes in the text that would enable a licence to be issued. There is no appeal against the Lord Chamberlain's decision in such matters.

The penalty for performing an unlicensed play is a fine not exceeding £50 for every offence, and, in addition, Section 15 of the Act, now amended by Section 43 of the Criminal Justice Act 1925, gives discretionary power to the court dealing with the case to suspend the licence of a theatre where an unlicensed play is produced. Prosecutions for such offences must begin within six months after the offence is committed and may be brought against any persons who 'for hire shall act or present or cause, permit or suffer to be acted or presented' the unlicensed play. This definition covers the licensee of the theatre, the manager, producer, and actors.

The Lord Chamberlain's power over the licensing of plays is not territorially limited as is his authority to license theatres. He is the sole authority in Great Britain with power to give or withhold his licence for a play intended for 'presentation for hire'. 'Presentation for hire' is defined under Section 16 of the Act in the following way:

In every case in which any money or other reward shall be taken or charged, directly or indirectly, or in which the purchase of any article is made a condition for the admission of any person into any theatre to see any stage play, and also in every case in which any stage play shall be acted or presented in any house, room, or place in which distilled or fermented excisable liquor shall be sold, every actor therein shall be deemed to be acting for hire.

Although within the strict terms of the Act the Lord Chamberlain has control over plays produced by play-producing societies who draw their income indirectly in the form of annual subscriptions, rather than directly from the sale of tickets for each performance, the Lord Chamberlain does not always exercise his full powers in such cases and has always shown himself inclined to lenience in this respect in the case of societies 'bona fide established for the private performance of stage plays' where tickets are issued to members of such societies and 'no payment, directly or indirectly, beyond an honorarium' is paid to the actors.

The formalities necessary to apply for the Lord Chamberlain's licence are as follows:

One copy of the work to be performed must be sent to the Lord Chamberlain's office at least seven days before the first performance, accompanied by the appropriate fee—£1. 1s. 0d. in the case of 1-act plays, or single additional scenes, £2. 2s. 0d. in the case of other plays—and a statement giving the name of the theatre where, and the time when, the work is first to be presented. Manager, producer, author, or anyone interested in a particular production may submit a play to the Lord Chamberlain for a licence. The licence is, however, always sent by the Lord Chamberlain to the licensee of the theatre.

The controversial question of the desirability or the reverse of any form of dramatic censorship lies outside the scope of this article. It should, however, be noted that in 1853, 1866, and 1892 Select Committees of the House of Commons investigated the position and reported that the system was working satisfactorily. There was no protest from any individual or organization at either of the first two investigations, but in 1892 one dramatic critic put forward the case against censorship in the form prescribed under the Act of 1843. In 1909 a Joint Committee of the House of Lords and House of Commons again looked into the question, and on that occasion most of the leading dramatists individually and through their representative organization asked for drastic modifications in the existing machinery. Some of the witnesses who appeared before the Committee asked for the total abolition of any form of pre-production censorship, while others asked either for the censorship of plays to be optional only or alternatively for there to be an appeal from the Lord Chamberlain's decision.

Although the Lord Chamberlain has absolute power to decide whether any play shall **or** shall not be 'presented for hire', he has no powers of censorship whatsoever over the *publication* of dramatic works, which are in this respect treated in exactly the same way as any other literary work: that is to say, they are subject to no pre-publication censorship whatsoever, but are liable to suppression if they contain anything which is in the eyes of the Law blasphemous, seditious, or obscene. Prosecutions for sedition and blasphemy are so rare nowadays that they can be ignored for the purpose of this article, but a word must be said about the crime of publishing an obscene libel.

Until the end of the eighteenth century the Law took notice of only those forms of im-

morality which tended to a breach of the peace, and criminal proceedings brought in a number of cases against the publishers of obscene literature were unsuccessful.

By the beginning of the nineteenth century, however (the Society for the Suppression of Vice was founded in 1802), public opinion was changing and, with it, the law. In 1857 the Obscene Publications Act (commonly called Lord Campbell's Act) was passed. Its intention was largely to create machinery for the more effective enforcement of the Common Law as it then stood, and it was passed by Parliament only on Lord Campbell's assurance that 'the measure was intended to apply exclusively to works written for the single purpose of corrupting the morals of youth and of a nature calculated to shock common feelings of decency in any well-regulated mind'. The test of obscenity was to be 'what was indictable under the present law'. Under Lord Campbell's successor in office, Lord Chief Justice Cockburn, however, the Act was given a very much more 'puritanical' interpretation. In *R*. v. *Hicklin* (1868 L.R. 3. Q.B. 360) he said: 'The test of obscenity is this, whether the tendency of the matter charged as obscene is to deprave and corrupt those whose minds are open to such immoral influences and into whose hands a publication of this sort may fall.' This dictum, widely phrased and difficult to apply as it is, has remained the test of obscenity in all subsequent cases.

2. THE UNITED STATES OF AMERICA. There is no office in the United States corresponding to that of the Lord Chamberlain in this country and no pre-production censorship of any kind. The law relating to dramatic works is, therefore, to be found in the Federal and State laws dealing with literary works as a whole. The Federal Acts are principally concerned with the prevention of the importation of obscene literature into the United States, and the sending of obscene literature by post, while the State Acts, although varying in detail, contain provisions similar in substance to the dictum of Lord Cockburn in *R*. v. *Hicklin*. A typical State law makes it a crime

to sell, lend, give away, or show, or have in possession with intent to sell, lend, or give away, or to show, or advertise in any manner, or to otherwise offer for loan, gift, sale, or distribution any obscene, lewd, lascivious, filthy, indecent, or disgusting book, magazine, pamphlet, newspaper, story paper, writing, paper or any written or printed matter of an indecent character.   M. E. B.

DRAMATIC COPYRIGHT, see COPYRIGHT IN A DRAMATIC WORK.

DRAMATIC CRITICISM. If one considers dramatic criticism in a broad sense, as anything said or written about the theatre, the earliest surviving example dates back to a time before 3000 B.C. It is the testament inscribed at Abydos by the Egyptian actor, I-kher-nefert, giving a personal impression of the Passion Play of Osiris, which he himself produced. Herodotus's account (Book II, ch. 63) of the ritual drama at Papremis, as it was in the fifth century B.C., may also claim to be dramatic criticism; and so might the Biblical record of the exhibition of Samson in the temple at Gaza (Judges xvi. 27).

The *Poetics* of Aristotle (384–322 B.C.), vulnerable as it is, remains the first known attempt at analytical and comparative criticism. It is one of the ironies of history that this 'salvaged' assortment of lecture-notes, evolving supposed laws for the theatre by impersonal deduction from incomplete data, should have been for so many centuries regarded as infallible. Of the three Unities ultimately put forward on Aristotle's authority as essentials to drama, those of time and place had in view the Attic theatre, where the scene could never be entirely changed and the same chorus was to be seen all the while. A 'unity', or coherence, of action remains obviously desirable, as each drama is still framed by its beginning and its end—now, as then, the source of countless conventions. Opinion continues divided over the exact meaning of Aristotle's definition of tragedy as effecting, 'through pity and fear', a 'purge of like passions'. The points in question are as to whether actual fright is meant, what are the 'like passions', and how and why they should be purged.

The *Ars Poetica* of Horace (65–8 B.C.) extended Aristotle with arbitrary maxims in undying verse. Juvenal, Martial, Lucian, and Petronius have useful references to the theatre of their time. Plutarch and Quintilian give critical surveys. But the father of dramatic criticism as an art was Longinus (*c*. A.D. 220–73), doubtfully identified with Queen Zenobia's adviser. His demand for sincere expression on the part of dramatist and critic alike has only recently found full appreciation, though Boileau translated him in 1674 and Burke owed him some points in his *Essay on the Sublime and Beautiful* (1756). Amid the chaos of the enslaved world of the third century A.D., Longinus tempers the onslaughts made upon the theatre by Tertullian—and afterwards by St. Augustine—as the temple of false gods, which it most certainly was, both officially and otherwise. For the rest, the Dark Ages were as barren of enlightened criticism as they were of good drama, save for Hroswitha, the nun of Gandersheim, who has left a revealing note upon her plays.

With the awakening of drama at the Renaissance came the awakening also of criticism—primarily in Italy, with Scaliger (1484–1558), Minturno (?–1574), and not least Castelvetro (1505–71), who first formulated the Unities out of Aristotle. Erasmus and Sir Thomas More both wrote with insight upon the theatre. Sir Philip Sidney's *Apologie for Poetrie* (pub. 1595) has its disappointments. He did not foresee the romantic outburst which was at hand. Stephen Gosson's *School of Abuse* (1579), which provoked him, was a vigorous and, at heart, sympathetic satire—a far better work than William Prynne's dreary *Histriomastix* (1632). Thomas Coryate, in 1611, gave a vivid description of the Venetian theatre, with a sidelight upon the

Italian 'impromptu comedy' (see ITALY, 2). John Dryden's *Essay of Dramatic Poesy* (1668), with his *Defence* of that essay, and the *Discours* and *Examens* of Pierre Corneille (1606–84), flog the dead horse of the *Poetics*. Jeremy Collier's *Short View of the Immorality and Profaneness of the English Stage* (1698) stands out in its period as a well-reasoned call for good taste, to be echoed ten years later by Steele in *The Spectator*.

From Jonson's ode and Heminge and Condell's First Folio preface down to the last of several thousand volumes, criticism has been on the whole helpful to the true life of Shakespeare's plays—this, even at the cost of such controversies as the Baconian and Oxfordian. Hazlitt, Coleridge, Leigh Hunt, and De Quincey did much to rescue Shakespeare from eighteenth-century travesty, to which Johnson and Mrs. Inchbald in her *British Theatre* had been complacent. Goethe, Lessing, Schlegel, and a host of laborious successors spread the light of a closer understanding in Germany. The later work of Dowden, Furnivall, Ward, Chambers, Lee, Gollancz, Dover Wilson, Boas, and others in England, and Bradley and Brander Matthews in America, has kept Shakespeare as man and dramatist faithfully and intimately before the minds of readers and playgoers. Hence it is probable that modern English and American productions are—with some freakish exceptions—nearer Shakespeare's intentions than those of any intervening period (see SHAKE-SPEARE, 2).

With the eighteenth century, criticism of the individual actor began to be conscious of its value in the survival of the written word. The genius of Charles Lamb (1775–1834), who had already revived interest in the lesser-known Elizabethan dramatists, graced the very falsity of the later eighteenth-century theatre with the charm of his own style. Thanks to this, the art of Munden and other old actors has won immortality, deserved or not. Colley Cibber's *Apology* (1740) gives us the best idea of Betterton, Lichtenberg of Garrick, Hazlitt (in conjunction with Crabb Robinson) of Kean. Churchill's *Rosciad* (1761) makes Quin live in satiric verse. The account in the *English Review* of Mrs. Siddons's performances at Drury Lane in 1782 by Thomas Holcroft, author of *The Road to Ruin*, was one of the earliest critical heraldings of its kind. Victorian criticism also, for the most part, centred upon the actor. George Henry Lewes's *On Actors and the Art of Acting* set a fruitful example. The inspiring effect which the rise of Henry Irving had upon criticism in the seventies was followed by the visit of the Comédie-Française company to London in 1879. In the same year was published George Meredith's *Essay on Comedy*, with its illuminating tributes to Congreve and Molière.

On both sides of the Atlantic criticism benefited in some respects from the fact that it became a recognized branch of journalism for practical news-purposes. At the same time it developed as an art far beyond the demands of its immediate professional task. The critics who brought a vast new public into the English theatre in the eighties and nineties of the last century did so by their own self-expression rather than as reliable judges. Clement Scott's utterly unfair abuse of Ibsen did not prevent him from being of immense use to the romantic stage of his time. William Archer's invaluable work as Ibsen's champion and translator was coupled with a certain lack of sympathy for popular farces and conventional dramas, which were human and not necessarily without merit in their own kind. Walkley and Shaw both attracted by their own idiosyncrasies of wit and of purpose, sometimes quite regardless of the play under consideration. None the less, they interested people in the theatre. J. T. Grein is to be remembered for his passionate enthusiasm, faith, and breadth of sympathy and of modern knowledge as a critic-manager. Nor should Sir Max Beerbohm be forgotten, nor C. E. Montague and the Mancunian tradition.

The saying of Anatole France, that criticism tells of 'the adventures of a soul among masterpieces', entails a reservation that adventures cannot always be among masterpieces for the professional critic. No critics survived this more adroitly than his fellow-countrymen. Sainte-Beuve, when he turned his attention to the drama, Janin, Sarcey, Lemaître, Faguet, Filon, and other Parisian critics of the nineteenth century, though often limited in their outlook, were past masters in the art of enticing the reader to join in their own spiritual experiences, whatever the theme. They were the first 'columnists'.

It may have been largely due to the existence of the Comédie-Française that French criticism had kept a tradition of its own through all political changes. The dicta of Horace and Aristotle, as approved by Boileau and Voltaire, did stifle the drama, but they afforded a perpetual topic for critical discussion. The influence of Rousseau made itself felt through Sébastien Mercier, author of *Le Tableau de Paris* (1781–9), who made a candid comparison between the hidebound state of the French theatre and the freedom of the English. Diderot's *De la poésie dramatique* (1758), and his critical upholding of domestic drama and comedy—*larmoyante* and otherwise—and Beaumarchais's *Essai sur le genre dramatique sérieux* (1767) signalled a more popular appeal, quite apart from their work as dramatists. In 1827 came the Romantic outburst, with Victor Hugo's famous preface to *Cromwell*. In 1873 Zola claimed that 'naturalism' was 'stammering its first accents'. In 1894 Ferdinand Brunetière, in *La Loi du théâtre*, was discovering yet another formula, based on the 'quality of will'; but he was careful to call it a 'law' and not a 'rule'.

Without the stabilizing focus of a central theatre like the Comédie-Française, criticism in Italy has been more volatile and sporadic, but extremely alive. The duel of words between Carlo Goldini (1707–93) and Carlo Gozzi (1720–1806) over the *commedia dell' arte*—to

which both, as well as the world's theatre, were so profoundly indebted—still affords bright reading. Also, political events have had a far closer relation in Italy than in France both with the theatre itself—from Alfieri to D'Annunzio —and with dramatic criticism. The national struggles were the direct and confessed inspiration of Francesco de Sanctis (1817–83) and his fellow-romanticists of the latter half of the nineteenth century. For the same reason, to some extent, criticism in Italy has tended to be philosophic rather than technical. It has been said of Benedetto Croce (1866–   )— whose importance to Italian drama, as to every side of Italian culture, cannot be doubted—that for him neither theatre nor actor nor audience exist. His belief in the intuitive nature of dramatic genius remains none the less sound. It has a bearing upon Wagner's suggestion that all true dramatic art, whether expressed in verse or prose or no words at all, and with music or without, is at its birth an improvisation—unconcerned with any conscious technique. Neither the 'futurism' of Marinetti nor the 'expressionism' which still has to seek its critical classic in Nietzsche has founded any enduring school of criticism. External events have been, possibly, too absorbing. The psychological masks of Pirandello are tantalizing; but the despair for humanity that lies behind them hardly invites their removal by others than himself.

During the twentieth century the possibility of professional criticism in England having something more than a news-value has lessened considerably so far as daily journalism is concerned. There are fewer newspapers, but these have a much larger circulation, and news is drawn from a much larger area. The result is that time and space on daily papers have been minimized to a point at which a full and considered over-night criticism of a first performance is seldom feasible. In these circumstances the average daily-paper dramatic critic has become little more than a paragraphist. None the less, in weekly and monthly journals dramatic criticism still keeps to a high level of sincerity and scholarship. More English books about the theatre were published during the decade before the 1939–45 war than in any corresponding period.

One of the characteristics of present-day criticism is the extent to which it is combined with dramatic authorship, though, as we have seen, the combination is in itself no new thing. Generally speaking, it is good for the critic to have had some experience as a dramatist. At the same time it has proved bad for the dramatist, as such, to relapse in any large degree upon the easier method of expression. Shaw's critical habit, continued in his prefaces, has sometimes made him less careful over the creative content of the plays themselves. The prefaces of Hugo and the younger Dumas can no longer transfuse life into many of their plays. Henry Arthur Jones's value as a dramatist noticeably declined when he took to prose of a different kind—fine prose though it was.

Somerset Maugham announced the end of his career as a dramatist in bringing out his critical book, *The Summing Up*. St. John Ervine, as manager, critic, and novelist, and Ashley Dukes, who forsook regular criticism before entering management, have divided their energies, not always to the benefit of their work as dramatists. Among other English critic-dramatists must be numbered the late James Agate and Horace Horsnell, Charles Morgan, W. A. Darlington, Ivor Brown, Willson Disher —all of them also novelists—and the late Herbert Farjeon, manager, dramatist, and lyrist, who left novel-writing to other members of his family.

Some intensely valuable dramatic criticism has come from theatrical producers. The books upon the stage written by Gordon Craig, William Poel, Granville-Barker, Stanislavsky, Komisarjevsky, and Jacques Copeau are rich in suggestion as well as record.

In America daily criticism has not suffered anything like so disastrous a reduction as in England—indeed, it has improved greatly during the present generation, alike in style, purpose, and opportunity. The official interest in drama shown by the American universities has been important—particularly the stimulus given by Professor Baker, and his English successor at Yale, Professor Allardyce Nicoll. Such critics as Brooks Atkinson and John Mason Brown in New York dailies, and George Jean Nathan in weekly reviews—not to mention the late Robert Benchley and particularly the late Alexander Woollcott, probably the best known of them all in England have a scope and power appropriate to the advancing value of American drama. Some excellent critical and historical work has been done by American women, e.g. Winifred Smith's study of the *commedia dell'arte*, Hallie Flanagan's *Shifting Scenes of the Modern European Theatre*, and criticism in *Theatre Arts Monthly* by Rosamond Gilder.   S. R. L.

DRAME BOURGEOIS, a type of play which arose in eighteenth-century France from the blending of the hitherto incompatible forms of tragedy and comedy, and may be defined as 'tragedy in low places'. It differs, however, from the earlier *tragédie bourgeoise* in that its prevailing tone is serious rather than tragic, and it may end happily, after extolling the virtues of home life and leading the erring to repentance. It eschews comedy, however, and appeals purely to the emotions. Its popularity had much influence on the art of acting, causing the break-up of the declamatory line, and the toning-down of gesture. It also led to the adoption of dress and scenery conforming to time and character.

DRESS BOX, see AUDITORIUM, 3 and BOX.

DRESS CIRCLE, in the modern theatre the first tier of seats, the lineal descendant of the Regency Dress Boxes (see AUDITORIUM, 3).

DRESSLER, MARIE (1871–1934), an American actress probably best remembered for her work in the cinema. But she served a long apprenticeship to the stage, and at 14 joined a succession of light opera companies, taking the name of an aunt because of family opposition to her stage career. Her real name was Leila Koerber. She toured for many years, and in 1892 appeared in New York, in Maurice Barrymore's *The Robber of the Rhine* (Fifth Avenue Theatre, 28 May), and when it failed remained to sing in vaudeville. In the following year she joined Lillian Russell's company and later made a great success as Flo Honeydew in *The Lady Slavey* (1896). In 1905 she was again in vaudeville and in 1907 had a great success in London, appearing at the Palace, though later her American humour failed to get across. After further tours she found fame with the part of Tillie Blobbs, a boarding-house drudge in *Tillie's Nightmare* (1909), in which she sang 'Heaven will Protect the Working Girl', a song ever after associated with her. The play had a phenomenal run and incidentally led to her first appearance in films in 1914 under Mack Sennett, in which from 1927 till her death she had an outstanding career.

DREW, a family of actors, important in the history of the development of the American theatre, and allied by marriage with the Barrymores. The first outstanding member of the family was (1) LOUISA LANE [really CRANE] (1820–97), daughter of English actors who could trace their theatrical ancestry back to Elizabethan days. Born in Lambeth, she went on the stage as a small child and played with such actors as Macready, Cooke, and Maria Foote. In 1827, her father having died, she was taken by her mother to New York, where she appeared as many characters in one play, in the style of Clara Fisher, with much success. She was also seen with the elder Booth, with the first Joseph Jefferson, then a very old man, and with Edwin Forrest, who much admired her precocious talent. She spent practically the whole of her long life on the stage, playing Lady Macbeth and the Widow Melnotte at 16, and appearing all over the United States in a variety of parts. From 1860 to 1892 she was manageress of the Arch Street Theatre, Philadelphia, which flourished under her firm rule, and from 1880 to 1892 was constantly seen on tour as Mrs. Malaprop, one of her best parts, with Joseph Jefferson as Bob Acres. A woman of strong, almost masculine, personality, she ruled her theatre and family with an unwavering rectitude and energy, and contributed not a little to the establishment of the American theatre during the nineteenth century. She had already had three or four husbands, being first married at 16, before in 1850 she married (2) JOHN DREW (1827–62), and it was as Mrs. John Drew that she was generally known. John Drew was an Irish actor who in his brief career was considered an excellent portrayer of Irish and eccentric characters, among them Sir Lucius O'Trigger and Handy Andy.

Mrs. John Drew had three children, of

whom the youngest became an actress and the wife of Maurice Barrymore (see BARRYMORE, 2). A son (3) JOHN (1853–1927) was one of the outstanding actors of his day. He had already appeared in his mother's stock company in Philadelphia when in 1875 he was engaged by Augustin Daly to play opposite Fanny Davenport in *The Big Bonanza*, in which he appeared as Bob Ruggles, the young lover. Under the same management he later scored a success as Alexander Spinkle in *An Arabian Night; or, Haroun al Raschid and his Mother-in-Law*. He remained with Daly for many years, playing opposite Ada Rehan, and visited London several times in the 1880s, being seen in such classics as *As You Like It*, *The School for Scandal*, and *The Taming of the Shrew*. His Petruchio was considered remarkable. In 1892 he agreed to appear under the management of the Frohmans, for which Daly found it hard to forgive him, and appeared in many modern comedies, often with Maude Adams, making frequent visits to the larger cities of the United States. In 1893 his *Twelfth Night* had a long run in London. One of his finest performances in later life was as Major Pendennis in a dramatization of Thackeray's novel, and he was last seen in a tour of *Trelawny of the 'Wells'*. A handsome man, of distinguished presence, he was for many years President of the Players' Club, and in 1903 presented the library of Robert W. Lowe, which he had acquired, to Harvard University, thus inaugurating the fine Theatre Collection there. He was the author of *My Years on the Stage* (1922). His daughter Louise was also an actress.

An adopted son of Mrs. John Drew, (4) SIDNEY WHITE (1868–1919), was also on the stage, and appeared in vaudeville with his first wife in sketches written by her. She was also the author of several melodramas and farces. With his second wife he appeared on the stage, but his later career was mainly in films.

DRINKWATER, JOHN (1882–1937), English poet and dramatist, whose work did much to strengthen and popularize the modern poetic play. He was one of the foundation members of Sir Barry Jackson's Pilgrim Players, which later gave rise to the Birmingham Repertory Theatre, where he was for some years producer, actor, and general manager. His early plays in verse were taut and economical in dialogue, without false romanticism; the most successful was $X = O$, an episode of the Trojan War. But it was in his prose play, *Abraham Lincoln*, that Drinkwater did his finest work. Transferred to the Lyric, Hammersmith, in 1919 under the management of Nigel Playfair, it ran for a year, and has been frequently revived. It was also well received in New York, where Drinkwater, who had appeared in the original production, played the Chronicler. Later, but less successful, chronicle plays were *Mary Stuart* (1922), *Oliver Cromwell*, and *Robert E. Lee* (both 1923). In 1927 Drinkwater's first comedy, *Bird in Hand*, opened the season at the Birmingham Repertory Theatre. It was revived there in 1931 and again for the theatre's silver jubilee. It also had a long run in London.

DROLL, the name given to a short, comic sketch, usually a scene taken from a longer play. Its origin must be looked for during the lean years of the Puritan interregnum (1642–60), when the actors, deprived of the right to act, of scenery, of costumes, and often of their playhouses, nevertheless managed to give a certain amount of entertainment. For their illicit purposes long plays were useless, so they invented or hashed up these 'drolls'—the term is short for Droll Humours or Drolleries—rounding them off with dancing in the manner of the Jig. Some of the most famous are 'Bottom the Weaver' from *A Midsummer Night's Dream* and 'The Grave-diggers' from *Hamlet*. Others were from Biblical sources. The actor Robert Cox was a noted player of drolls, and his repertory was printed in 1662 by Kirkman as *The Wits; or, Sport upon Sport*. Droll was also the name applied to early puppet shows, and was given to collections of humorous or satiric verse, not dramatic, as in 'Westminster Drolleries' (1672). It was sometimes used to designate actors, particularly players of humorous parts, and men of quick wit and good company. Pepys uses it in this sense of Killigrew.

DROP, an unframed piece of scenery, first used about 1690, usually a canvas backcloth. It had the advantage of offering an unbroken plain surface for painting, free from any central join such as marked the alternative 'pair of flats'. Initially it had the disadvantage that no doors or practicable windows could be used with it. To-day a cloth or drop can be made into a framed cloth by the addition of battens at the back, with the doors hinged to the framing so afforded, thus making the piece, in a sense, a large single flat which can be flown like an ordinary cloth. The early theatre, however, possessed no height for such flying of an entire cloth, which had to be rolled. The framed cloth was, therefore, impossible.

The early method of handling a loose drop was to roll it on a bottom roller, which ascended by means of lines, furling up the cloth as it went. This system had a disadvantage in that, as records show, the ends of swords and cloaks, or even the hem of a petticoat, might be snatched by the ascending roller and swallowed in the turns, to the detriment of dramatic dignity.

Another method of getting rid of a cloth was by 'tumbling'—when a batten was fixed across the back a third of the way up, and the cloth taken away in bights, with a loose roller, or tumbler, inside the bight to weight the cloth, and keep the bend straight.

The term Top Drop was occasionally used for borders.   R. S.

DRUM-AND-SHAFT, an early system, based on the principle of the lever, used for the moving of theatre scenery. It is also known as the Barrel System (see ENGLISH PLAYHOUSE, 2).

DRURIOLANUS, Augustus, see HARRIS (2) AUGUSTUS.

DRURY LANE. The Theatre Royal, Drury Lane, known also in its early days as the King's House and Theatre Royal, Bridges Street, is the most famous of English theatres, and the oldest still in use. It was built by Thomas Killigrew under a direct Charter or Patent from Charles II 'to erect a Company of Players which shall be Our own Company'. Killigrew, who at the Restoration had taken over Gibbon's Tennis-Court as a theatre (see VERE STREET THEATRE), had previously made up his mind to build his own. He leased a piece of ground 'scituate in Pach. Sct. Martins-in-the-Fields and St. Paul's Covent Garden, known by the name of The Riding Yarde'. From east to west it measured 112 ft.; it was 58 ft. wide at its eastern end and 59 ft. wide at the western end. The lease was dated 20 Dec. 1661, the ground-rent was £50, and a condition of the lease was that a playhouse should be erected thereon by Christmas 1662 and that £1,500 should be expended on the building. On 25 Apr. 1662 Killigrew got from Charles II a further charter, making his new theatre the Theatre Royal and its company the King's Servants. Certain of them were sworn in as Members of the Royal Household and termed Gentlemen of the Great Chamber. They had an allowance of scarlet cloth and gold lace for their liveries. The Royal Livery is still worn by the footmen at Drury Lane. The charter, which has varied much in value, is still in existence, held at the bank and annually inspected. It is an integral part of the lease of the theatre.

Killigrew built his theatre and opened it on 7 May 1663 with a performance of *The Humorous Lieutenant*. It cost about £2,400 to build, and when finished its total dimensions were almost the same as those of the stage of the present theatre. It was divided into Boxes, which cost 4s., Pit, 2s. 6d., Middle Gallery, 1s. 6d., and Upper Gallery, 1s. (but see FOOTMEN'S GALLERY). The pit benches were covered with green cloth and the floor was steeply raked, so that people at the back of the pit could converse with the occupants of the boxes behind. There were six proscenium doors and an apron stage. The lighting was by chandeliers. There was a glazed cupola over the pit, and windows—the cupola let in the draught, and leaked too, for Pepys, who has left us a description of the theatre in his Diary, caught a cold there in June 1663. A French visitor who went to the theatre soon after its opening says it was the best he had ever seen, with a finely equipped and most ingenious stage; he was especially charmed by the decoration and arrangement of the boxes and tiers, and the gilded leather of the upholstery. The refreshments were looked after by a woman known as Orange Moll (see MEGGS), who paid £100 down for a thirty-nine years' agreement and 6s. 8d. a day when the theatre was open. She was not allowed to sell in the upper gallery, probably

because fruit was a handy missile. The regulation price of an orange was 6d.

Killigrew's 'bookkeeper' (prompter and stage manager) was Charles Booth; Hart (who trained Nell Gwynn) and Mohun (the latter a great favourite with Charles II) were his chief actors. Good fortune at first attended the theatre, though it had to be closed on account of the plague from 5 June 1665 to 29 Nov. 1666, during which time Killigrew made many useful alterations. But on the evening of 25 Jan. 1672, between seven and eight o'clock, fire broke out and spread rapidly. It destroyed half the theatre, all the scenery and wardrobe, wiped out the houses from the Rose Tavern in Russell Street to Vinegar Yard, and caused destruction to the yard itself. Gunpowder was used to blow up houses standing in the path of the fire, and in one of these explosions Richard Bell, an actor at the theatre, was killed. The damage was estimated at £20,000.

Killigrew opened temporarily at the now deserted theatre in Lisle's Tennis-Court (see LINCOLN'S INN FIELDS THEATRE), and set about rebuilding Drury Lane, with Christopher Wren as his architect. On the site occupied by this new theatre, which cost £4,200 and was much larger than the former one, Drury Lane Theatre stands to-day.

The new playhouse opened on 26 Mar. 1674 with *The Beggar's Bush* and the King and Queen in the Royal Box. No attempt had been made to rival the exterior and interior magnificence of Davenant's new theatre (see DORSET GARDEN) which had opened in 1671, and in his prologue for the opening night of Drury Lane Dryden contrasted the 'plain built house' with the rival theatre 'shining all with gold', where, he said, 'scenes, machines and empty Operas reign'. He implied that the quality of acting and plays at Drury Lane was so good that it needed no ornate gilding!

In many ways the second Theatre Royal was a great improvement on the first. The stage now projected in a semi-oval right up to the front row of the pit, there were side wings instead of stage boxes, and the whole action of the play took place beyond the proscenium pillars. The orchestra played above instead of below the stage. For a time things went well. The theatre had the best actors and Dryden was its playwright. But soon dissension crept in and actors and actresses were lured away to the rival house. Killigrew had left the management in the hands of Hart and Mohun, who were getting old, and the younger men wanted a chance. In 1676 the situation was so bad that the theatre had to be closed. The Lord Chamberlain, intervening, fell back on that fine British institution, a Committee, consisting of Hart, Mohun, Kynaston, and Cartwright; but it got nowhere. Eventually Charles Killigrew, worthless son of Thomas and a great source of trouble, took his brother Henry into partnership. Both were useless fellows, but the young actors, led by Cardell (commonly called Scum) Goodman and Thomas Clarke, sided with them. Still things went from bad to worse, and playwrights began to take their plays to Dorset Garden. In 1681 the theatre was again shut for a time, and in April of the following year, in spite of an occasional good house when Mohun and Hart appeared together, and a successful production of *The Loyal Brother; or, the Persian Prince*, Drury Lane had to close.

It was not altogether the fault of the management. The times were out of joint, and Dorset Garden was in low water too. After protracted negotiations a union between the two companies was agreed upon, with Drury Lane as its theatre, and the joint company opened there on 16 Nov. 1682 with Betterton in charge. Matters did not, however, greatly improve. The first fine careless rapture of the Restoration had evaporated. Times were troublous, and, as usual, the theatre suffered. And Charles II, that great pillar of the playhouse, was dead.

In 1690 a crisis took place and Davenant's son, Charles, who held the patent, sold out to Christopher Rich, a lawyer, father of John Rich, who later built Covent Garden and popularized pantomime, playing Harlequin under the name of Lun. Rich got a fine bargain, as he procured the Patent and the entire interest for £80. But he had only one idea—to make money for himself at the expense of everyone else. He broke all agreements when it suited him to do so, and scandalously underpaid his actors—when he paid them at all. Two of his leading men, Verbruggen and Powell, both fine actors, received only £2 a week, and even that not regularly, while Goodman and Griffin had to share a bed and a shirt. Rich had an iniquitous system of getting young men to play for nothing under pretence of learning the business. One of these was Colley Cibber, later a power in the theatre, who received his first salary of 10s. a week through the kindness of Betterton, and then had to pay back 5s. as a fine.

Eventually, in 1695, Betterton, who seems to have been the only actor to stand up for his rights, led a revolt and laid the actors' grievances before William III, who gave them a licence to break away from Drury Lane and play at Lincoln's Inn Fields Theatre. Betterton took the best of the company with him, including Mrs. Barry and Mrs. Bracegirdle. Congreve gave them his plays, which had been contracted for by Drury Lane, and it was soon war to the knife between the two houses. Powell now reigned at Drury Lane, but his company was second-rate compared with Betterton's, which, besides the actresses mentioned, contained Doggett, Underhill, Sandford, and Mrs. Bowman. Both theatres got into trouble for licentiousness, but for ten years Betterton gave Rich a good drubbing, until in 1705 he went to Sir John Vanbrugh's theatre in the Haymarket. The Restoration actors were now long past their prime. New people like Wilks, Cibber, Barton Booth, Mrs. Porter, and Mrs. Oldfield were arising to take their place. In 1709 Rich, who had been constantly in trouble, lost his Patent and Drury Lane was

closed. William Collier, a Member of Parliament who had obtained a licence from Queen Anne to reopen it, had the greatest difficulty in ejecting Rich, and then found, after a forcible entry, that he had sold all the portable property in the place (for a mock inventory of the sale, see *The Tatler*, No. 42). Collier had no success and transferred his interest to Cibber, Doggett, and Wilks—the Triumvirate. They formed an excellent combination, each supplying what the others lacked. All were first-class actors. Cibber was a fop and fine gentleman, happy in the company of a lord, and the only actor for many years to be a member of White's Club. Wilks, in spite of drawbacks, was the best light comedian of his day. Doggett was a master of make-up and character parts, and careful in money matters. With Anne Oldfield as their leading lady, the Triumvirate prospered, and inaugurated one of the brightest periods in the annals of the English stage.

The first split came when Barton Booth joined the Triumvirate and Doggett, on political grounds, left it. Booth took Betterton's place, and Anne Oldfield succeeded to the throne of Mrs. Bracegirdle. There was trouble with Sir Richard Steele, in which Cibber was involved, that caused a temporary suspension of the licence, but things were restored to normal in 1721. Steele, who had got the Patent made out in his name, received a salary of £700 a year for his lifetime, and during the Triumvirate's twenty years of brilliance each manager made at least £1,500 a year—a very good sum in those days.

Wilks died, then Booth, and Cibber, now Poet Laureate, retired. A man called Highmore purchased Cibber's share in 1732 for £3,000, and shortly after acquired Wilks's share from his widow. But Highmore was doomed to failure, caused very largely by Theophilus, Colley Cibber's worthless son, and he sold out at great loss to Charles Fleetwood, a young man of good breeding, who with Giffard, of Goodman's Fields Theatre, bought Booth's share from his widow, and so stood possessed of all the Patent rights. But Fleetwood was a gambler with no money sense, always in debt. He threw away a golden opportunity, and Drury Lane sank to a very low level indeed. The one bright spot was Macklin, who pressed for a revival of *The Merchant of Venice*, which had not been seen for many years, with himself as Shylock. At length Fleetwood consented, and on 11 Jan. 1741, with considerable trepidation on the part of everyone save himself, Macklin took the stage as the Jew. It was a revelation, for Macklin threw over the accredited idea that Shylock was a comic part and played it as we know it now. His performance was of such intensity that he thrilled his audience where they were accustomed to laugh, and so impressed George II that he could not sleep after seeing it. Pope immortalized it in the couplet, 'This is the Jew, That Shakespeare drew'. It put Macklin, a very great actor, in the front rank. Had he been of a less quarrelsome nature he might have been the leader of the stage. As it was, he was the forerunner of a new school of acting which Garrick was to glorify.

Garrick, whose success at Goodman's Fields Theatre had been phenomenal, was engaged by Fleetwood at 600 guineas for the season. He made his first appearance at Drury Lane on 11 May 1742 as Chaumont in *The Orphan*. After that he played for six nights at Goodman's Fields Theatre, probably the last nights of its existence, and then returned to the Lane to play Lear and Richard III.

Macklin, who was managing Drury Lane, was able to keep it going in spite of Fleetwood's extravagance, but in 1743 things came to a head. The bailiffs were in, debts were mounting, and the actors' salaries were unpaid. They petitioned the Lord Chamberlain to be allowed to go to the Haymarket and play there, but they were refused. They went on strike, but there was no other work; the power of the Patent was too great. Fleetwood, having thus beaten them, agreed to take them all back except Macklin, whom he regarded as the ringleader. Garrick, who felt that Macklin had been badly treated, offered to pay his salary out of his own pocket. The fiery Irish Macklin refused, and on the first night of the season, 5 Dec. 1743, he and his friends hissed Garrick and caused a riot. This went on, accompanied by free fights in the theatre, until Macklin was re-engaged. But Fleetwood had shot his bolt; he was ruined and advertised the Patent for sale. It was bought by two City men, on condition that James Lacy, who had been manager at Covent Garden, should take charge. He eventually agreed and asked Garrick to go into partnership with him. Garrick accepted, and the Patent was endorsed to both of them on equal terms, Garrick to have a salary also as actor.

Now followed great days for Drury Lane, where incidentally, on an evening in 1746, George II in the Royal Box first heard of the defeat of Prince Charles Edward at Culloden Moor. He attempted to address the audience, but his English was not equal to the task, and he could only shout and wave the dispatches. An equerry made the announcement, and so England learnt the news from Drury Lane Theatre.

Garrick and Lacy opened on 15 Sept. 1746, Garrick supervising the stage and productions. He introduced many reforms, insisted on order and decency as well as proper rehearsals, excluded the public from the stage—though that took time—introduced new lighting, founded a Pension Fund which still functions, and surrounded himself with a wonderful company, including Spranger Barry, Mrs. Pritchard, Mrs. Theophilus Cibber, Peg Woffington, and Kitty Clive. He also undertook to restore the mutilated texts of Shakespeare, which had suffered much from rewriting. His *Othello* failed, but his *Macbeth* in 1748 was a huge success, although he wore a scarlet coat, silk stockings, and powdered wig, while Mrs. Pritchard, one of the greatest of Lady Macbeths, dressed her as a lady of the period in black satin.

In 1750 Spranger Barry was at Covent Garden with Mrs. Cibber, and he and Garrick embarked on rival productions of *Romeo and Juliet*, each appearing as Romeo. Garrick was considered superior in the part, as he was in *King Lear*, another rival production. But Barry was the better Othello.

Garrick did not disdain pantomimes, of which Drury Lane had become the traditional home; he even wrote some himself. His capacity for work was remarkable, but he had his setbacks. In 1755 he was preparing a great musical spectacle, *The Chinese Festival*, when war broke out between England and France. He had some Swiss dancers, whom he had billed as French, and he retained them. A terrific riot ensued, and although the King was present, the enraged audience broke up the theatre. In the end troops were sent for to keep order, and from then until 1896 a guard was mounted at Drury Lane every night.

In 1776 Garrick announced his retirement. The scenes during his last season were remarkable, and his farewell performance moved the audience to tears. He had shed dignity and lustre not only on Drury Lane but upon his entire profession, which had never stood higher in public esteem. On 21 Sept. 1776 Sheridan took over the reins of government in partnership with his father-in-law, Thomas Linley, and Dr. Ford. His first season in 1777, which included the first production of *The School for Scandal*, was memorable.

On 10 Oct. 1782 Mrs. Siddons, who had made a short and unsuccessful appearance at Drury Lane under Garrick, reappeared in *Isabella; or, the Fatal Marriage*. Her success was instantaneous, and as Lady Macbeth she outshone even the memory of Mrs. Pritchard, hitherto considered incomparable in the part. John Philip Kemble, her brother, appeared for the first time at Drury Lane in 1783, and in 1785 Mrs. Jordan joined the company.

In 1791 the theatre, which had stood since 1674, was in such bad repair that it was decided to rebuild it. The new theatre, which incorporated much of the old, opened on 12 Mar. 1794, part of the performance being a selection from Handel's oratorios performed in a stage setting of a Gothic cathedral. The new house held 3,611 people as against 2,000 in the old—about six or seven hundred more than the present theatre.

On 21 Apr. 1794 Kemble and Mrs. Siddons played *Macbeth*, with Charles Kemble, their younger brother, as Malcolm. An epilogue, written by George Colman, was spoken by Miss Farren, informing the audience that they were now safe from fire, and a safety curtain was lowered upon which a man beat with a hammer. It is interesting to note that the theatre was burned down fifteen years later.

On Thursday, 15 May 1800, there was an attempted assassination of George III while he was watching from the Royal Box a performance of *She Would and She Wouldn't*. A man called James Hadfield fired two shots from the front row of the pit. He was discovered to be an old soldier, mentally deranged, and ended his days in Bedlam.

Sheridan was still in charge of the theatre and, in spite of the attempts of King, and later John Philip Kemble, to manage it for him, always in a state of bankruptcy, no matter how large the audiences. Kemble finally left him to go to Covent Garden in 1802 and took Mrs. Siddons with him. Sheridan carried on with plays from the German, which had a vogue, and gruesome melodrama and spectacle. Real elephants and performing dogs now trod Garrick's hallowed stage, until on 24 Feb. 1809 the theatre was destroyed by fire. And that might have been the end of it, for no funds were available; but a public-spirited man, Samuel Whitbread, one of Sheridan's shareholders, made tremendous exertions and raised the sum of £400,000 for rebuilding.

The new theatre, built by Holland, took three years to erect and opened on 10 Oct. 1812 under the control of a committee which included Whitbread, the Earls of Dudley and Essex, Doughty, Kinnaird, and Lord Byron. The manager was Samuel James Arnold. Sheridan had been superseded. But although the company included Elliston, Dowton, Robert Palmer, Pope, Bannister, Wrench, and Mrs. Glover, the first season incurred a very heavy loss; nor was the second much better.

Then an obscure country tragedian, engaged at a small salary and treated very shabbily by the directorate, made his début at Drury Lane to a half-full house on 26 Jan. 1814, a bitter winter's night. Like Charles Macklin, he played Shylock, and he went even farther than Macklin had, for he discarded the traditional red beard and wig. Yet such was the enthusiasm he aroused that his success was even greater than that of Mrs. Siddons. The next morning all London rang with the news of the new actor. His name was Edmund Kean.

The theatre filled, and Kean's salary was raised. In his first season £68,329 was taken, yet so bad was the management that the loss was £20,000. Whitbread committed suicide. The next season Kean filled the place again, and for six years he bore the whole weight of the theatre on his shoulders, packing it whenever he appeared. Yet still the directorate continued to lose money. They retired, and Robert William Elliston, called the Great Lessee, took over. His success was considerable, but his ideas were so extravagant—he spent £20,000 in remodelling the interior of the theatre—that by 1826 he was bankrupt.

He was succeeded by Stephen Price, from America, who ran the theatre for four seasons and then retired. Under his management Edmund's son Charles Kean made an unsuccessful appearance, and the great Grimaldi gave his farewell performance in 1828.

The next tenant was Alexander Lee, a music composer and publisher, who engaged the rising star Macready. Lee had no money, and Captain Polhill, who backed him, eventually ousted him, handing over the reins to the amazing Alfred Bunn. By 1834 Bunn had got complete control and reduced the place to the level of a fairground booth. He had been stage manager for Elliston and had quarrelled with Macready, then a young actor who was challenging Kean and getting slightly the worst of it. Kean was now gone, but Macready remained, and the result was a bout of fisticuffs in Bunn's office. Bunn, who had also got control of Covent Garden, made the same actors play at both houses, and gave more attention to musical plays and performing animals than to drama. He staged Shakespeare for Macready and Phelps, promenade concerts, *tableaux vivants*, brought over the great Malibran, and gave Balfe, composer of 'The Bohemian Girl', his first opportunity in the theatre. At the end of five years, practically ruined, he retired in favour of Hammond, who, although he engaged Macready, Elton, Phelps, and Mrs. Warner, was soon forced to give up.

At Christmas 1841 Macready himself took over the theatre. He swept away many abuses and introduced reforms. His first company included, in addition to himself, James Anderson, Phelps, Keeley and Mrs. Keeley, Harley, Elton, Mrs. Nesbitt, Mrs. Stirling, and Miss Horton, as good a galaxy of stars as London could show. He alternated tragedy with Handel's 'Acis and Galatea'. His second season included *As You Like It*, with a wonderful cast, *King John*, *The Patrician's Daughter*, and *The Blot on the 'Scutcheon*. At Christmas 1842 a revival of Purcell's 'King Arthur' resulted in the discovery of Sims Reeves. Macready staged Milton's masque, *Comus*, in Feb. 1843 and, finding that opera paid better than tragedy, engaged Clara Novello in Apr. 1843. But his enormous overhead expenses, to say nothing of the shareholders' free admission, forced him to give up.

The resilient Alfred Bunn returned and engaged Charles Kean, who did well this time. Bunn preferred opera and ballet to drama, and during his reign Drury Lane was more opera house than theatre. He wrote many of the libretti himself, and in 1845 had a great popular success with 'The Bohemian Girl'. He then tried a new departure—serial plays—and made *The Count of Monte Cristo*, played by a French company, extend over two nights. This caused a riot, so he fell back on circuses and opera. But it was too late, and he retired to Boulogne, a ruined man. On 26 Dec. 1850 James Anderson took over Drury Lane. He produced *Ingomar* and *Azael* with wonderful settings, but the Great Exhibition in the summer of the following year brought about his ruin, and an American circus took over the theatre, making a big profit. In 1851 Macready bade farewell to the stage from Drury Lane, after playing Macbeth. It was an impressive but not an emotional evening. Then Gye, of Covent Garden, ventured opera at Drury Lane, calling it the National Opera House, but met with no response. Things became so bad that between July and Oct. 1852 Drury Lane saw three managers come and go—Sheridan Smith, de Vere, and George Bolton, none of whom lasted more than a week. At the end of that year an extraordinary showman named E. T. Smith, publican and ex-policeman, entered into possession. The rental had been considerably reduced—Drury Lane was going at bargain rates. Smith lowered the price of seats and ran the Lane for seven years, beginning with *Uncle Tom's Cabin*. He then followed in Bunn's footsteps and made the great theatre into a fairground. Italian opera at cheap prices, Gustavus Brooke, and Charles Mathews were sandwiched between Chinese conjurors and a man called the Human Fly, who walked across the ceiling. Rachel, the great tragedienne, followed a circus. Eventually Smith's multitudinous activities landed him in the Bankruptcy Court.

In 1862 Dion Boucicault opened at Drury Lane with *The Colleen Bawn*, with himself, his wife, and Madame Céleste. He followed this with *The Relief of Lucknow*. Then came Edmund Falconer, who had made a fortune at the Lyceum and promptly lost it at the Lane. He joined forces with his manager, F. B. Chatterton, and they produced *King John*, *Henry IV*, *Manfred*, *Faust*, and *Comus*, with a company which included Phelps, Walter Montgomery, Mrs. Hermann Vezin, and other good players. When Falconer's money was gone Chatterton worked alone. He made a noble effort, with Shakespeare, Byron, and the old comedies, and produced *The Great City*, first of all the great Drury Lane 'realistic' melodramas—also dramatized versions of Scott's novels, with Adelaide Neilson and Phelps. These, and pantomimes with the Vokes family and Beverley's wonderful scenery, kept things going for a while. But the rent was going up, and when in Feb. 1879 even the pantomime failed, Chatterton was beaten. He laid it down that 'Shakespeare spelt ruin and Byron bankruptcy'.

The theatre was now closed, and a young and ambitious man, with less than five pounds in his pocket, proposed himself as a tenant. He was told he would be accepted if he deposited £1,000. He got the money within twenty-four hours, and starting with a revival of *Henry V*, followed by a pantomime, he began a new page in the history of Drury Lane. His name was Augustus Harris.

Harris pinned his faith to big shows and pantomime. He brought over distinguished foreign companies, like the Saxe-Meiningen, the Comédie-Française, and Ristori herself. In 1886 he gave opera with the De Reszkes, Melba, Lassalle, Nordicaa, and others; and always he did his vast realistic melodramas with big spectacular scenes, and always his gigantic pantomimes. He had many other interests, but it is as the great impresario of Drury Lane that he will be remembered. It was under his management that Dan Leno—who first appeared at the Lane in 1869—and Herbert Campbell played together in pantomime. Harris was knighted in the same year, not for his services to the theatre, but because he was Under-Sheriff of London when the Ger-

man Emperor visited the City. He died in 1896, at the age of 45. His widow carried on for a season, but Harris's right-hand man, Arthur Collins, took the theatre over with a syndicate, under circumstances almost as romantic as Harris's had been. Pantomimes and dramas became more and more elaborate, sensation was piled on sensation. Prosperity reigned, and the theatre once more held a high position. Irving's seasons in 1903 and 1905, Ellen Terry's Jubilee, Forbes-Robertson's farewell, when he mingled with the audience, Beecham's great opera seasons in 1913 and 1914, and many similar events took place there. Films too were shown for the first time, including *The Birth of a Nation* and *Intolerance*, (both during the 1914–18 war) and the Shakespeare Tercentenary in 1916 was celebrated by a performance of *Julius Caesar*. In 1919 peace was celebrated by the *Pageant of Drury Lane*. Pavlova danced there for a season. In 1921 the auditorium was rebuilt and Collins retired two years later, his last production being appriately named *Good Luck*. He had reigned for twenty-seven years.

Sir Alfred Butt then took charge, and for a short time Basil Dean was associated with him, but it was not until the policy of great musical shows, starting with *Rose Marie*, was inaugurated that fortune smiled once more. Pantomime, banished since 1919, came back to its traditional home in 1929, when Julian Wylie presented *The Sleeping Beauty*. In 1931 Butt retired and *The Land of Smiles* introduced Richard Tauber to this country. It was followed by Noel Coward's *Cavalcade*, produced by himself and C. B. Cochran. After that luck seemed to desert Drury Lane again until pantomime in 1934 revived it. Then came Ivor Novello, who, understanding the needs of the great house, wrote, composed, and acted in a series of successful plays with music—*Glamorous Night*, *Careless Rapture*, *Crest of the Wave*, and *The Dancing Years*. This last, presented by Tom Arnold, who had also been responsible for *Henry V* with Ivor Novello in the title role, still held the stage when the theatres were closed for a brief period on the outbreak of war in 1939. On their reopening it ran elsewhere for six years, the longest run of any Drury Lane-produced show.

On 8 Sept. 1939 Drury Lane was taken over by Ensa as their head-quarters, and in spite of being bombed in 1940 continued to be used by them. After the war it returned to its proper use as a theatre and had a great success with the American musical comedy, *Oklahoma!*

W. M. P.

Little Drury Lane was the name given by Elliston to the Olympic Theatre in 1813.

DRUTEN, JOHN VAN, see VAN DRUTEN.

DRYDEN, JOHN (1631–1700), English writer, critic, poet, and satirist, and the outstanding dramatist of the Restoration stage, though his best work was done in other fields. He was very prolific, being responsible, alone and in collaboration, for nearly thirty plays of all kinds. Of his comedies the most successful were *Sir Martin Mar-All* (1667), *Marriage à la Mode* (1672), in which the part of Melantha was finely played by Mrs. Mountfort, and yet another version of *Amphitryon* (1690). His wit was mordant, but lacked humanity. *Marriage à la Mode* was revived by the Phoenix Society in 1920, and by the Birmingham Repertory Theatre in 1928. Two other comedies, *The Spanish Friar*, in which Antony Leigh later made a great hit, and *Mr. Limberham; or, the Kind Keeper*, are perhaps better left in oblivion.

Dryden's tragi-comedies include *The Rival Ladies* (1664), from the Spanish, and *Secret Love* (1667), based partly on Madame de Scudéry's famous novel *Le Grand Cyrus*. The parts of Florimel and Celadon, played by Nell Gwynn and Charles Hart, have sometimes been considered the prototypes of Congreve's Mirabell and Millamant. Dryden's most characteristic work, however, was done in the heroic drama, a new development in the history of the English theatre, which rose, flourished, and fell with him. Written in rhymed couplets, and dealing with the conflict in noble bosoms between love and honour, on the lines of Corneille's *Le Cid*, this genre had perhaps been foreshadowed by Davenant, and to a certain extent by Fletcher and Quarles. But Dryden was its greatest exponent, though his contemporaries shared in its vogue.

His first serious essay in rhymed verse, *The Indian Queen* (1664), was written in collaboration with Sir Robert Howard, whose sister, Elizabeth, Dryden had married in the previous year. This was followed by *The Indian Emperor* (1665), by Dryden alone, by *Tyrannic Love* (1669), and by the greatest of his heroic dramas, *Almanzor and Almahide*, usually called, from its sub-title, *The Conquest of Granada*. This vast and complicated play, in two parts (1669, 1670), contains all the elements, good and bad, of the heroic drama—rant, bombast, poetry, vigour, battle, murder, and sudden death. It was guyed unmercifully in Buckingham's *The Rehearsal* (1671), and the species soon died a natural death. Dryden's last effort was *Aureng-Zebe* (1675), and from the restraints of rhyme he then turned to blank verse for the play which, in the opinion of posterity no less than in that of his contemporaries, was his masterpiece—*All for Love* (1678), a retelling of the story of Antony and Cleopatra, which takes only its plot from Shakespeare. All the rest is Dryden's own. It is well constructed, contains some fine poetry, and observes more strictly than any other English tragedy the Unities of time, place, and action. It has been called 'the happiest result of French influence on English tragedy'. Above all, it provides excellent theatrical material, and was frequently revived in the eighteenth century, with such actors as Mrs. Oldfield and Booth (1718), Mrs. Yates and Holland (1766), Mrs. Hartley and Smith (1773). In 1922 the Phoenix Society gave two performances of it, with Edith Evans and Ion Swinley.

Dryden's last play was a comedy, *Love Triumphant* (1694). He also, in the course of a busy lifetime, wrote numerous Prologues and Epilogues, then very much in fashion, both for his own and other people's plays. These are not only a mine of theatrical information, but a notable contribution to English poetry. Less admirable are the Shakespeare adaptations in which Dryden had a hand. He helped Davenant to make a perversion of *The Tempest* (1670), and in later years rewrote *Troilus and Cressida* (1679) but without the success which attended *All For Love*. In his prefaces and critical writings Dryden contributed largely to literary and theatrical controversies which need not detain us here; nor need his pamphlet war with another popular dramatist, Elkanah Settle.

DUBLIN. The first theatre in Dublin was built in 1635 and closed under the Commonwealth, as did the London theatres. After the Restoration the famous Smock Alley, known also as the Orange Street Theatre, was opened, but it was not until the eighteenth century that Dublin society became enamoured of play-going. Even then all the plays and most of the chief actors were imported from London, and it was the Irish Literary Movement that first gave the country an indigenous drama (see IRELAND).

The first outstanding actor to appear at Smock Alley was Wilks, in 1692, but it reached its heyday, after extensive rebuilding, in the 1730s and 1740s, when Quin and Woodward, Garrick and Peg Woffington, gave extensive seasons, followed by the ten-year management of Thomas Sheridan, father of the dramatist, and himself an excellent actor. Towards the end of the eighteenth century Smock Alley fell into disrepair and was finally converted into a corn store. Almost its only rival was the Crow Street Theatre, opened in 1758 by Spranger Barry, who had at one time as partner in his enterprise the Irish actor Macklin. Another Irish actor, Henry Mossop, was in control of both theatres for some time, and after the disappearance of Smock Alley the Crow Street Theatre remained in sole charge of all professional enterprises in Dublin until in about 1819 Harris, an actor from Covent Garden, opened the Theatre Royal. The Crow Street Theatre then closed and was pulled down in the early 1830s, while the Theatre Royal perished by fire in 1880.

DUBOIS, see CLOWN and GRIMALDI.

DUCHESS THEATRE, LONDON, in Catherine Street, a medium-sized playhouse which was opened on 25 Nov. 1929 by J. and D. de Leon with *Tunnel Trench*. In Mar. 1930 it staged one of the shortest runs ever known, when the *Intimate Revue* lasted for one night. But it recovered from this, and has had a high percentage of good runs. In 1934-5 J. B. Priestley, several of whose plays were first produced at the Duchess, was associated with its management, and in 1939 Emlyn Williams's

The Corn is Green started a successful run, brought to an end by the outbreak of war. Since then *Life Line* has been staged there (1941), and the theatre was then occupied for some years by Noel Coward's *Blithe Spirit*, followed by Margaret Rawlings and Robert Helpmann in *The White Devil*. The theatre later became the headquarters of the Mask Theatre, whose first production was *The Linden Tree*. W. M. P.

DUCIS, JEAN FRANÇOIS (1733–1816), French dramatist, best known as the first adapter of Shakespeare for the French stage. He was the son of a linen-draper, and remained all his life a sturdy, independent bourgeois of simple tastes, having nothing to do with the Revolution, refusing the overtures of Napoleon, and welcoming with pleasure the re-establishment of the monarchy. As a young man he served in the Seven Years War, and returned home to live quietly and amuse himself with plays and poetry. His *Amélise* (1764) was not successful, but he consoled himself with the plays of Shakespeare, which he probably read in the deplorable translations of Le Tourneur and Laplace, since there is no proof that he himself knew English. Profiting by the vogue for all things English he adapted Shakespeare for the Comédie-Française, often so drastically that nothing remained of the original but the title. He well understood, however, the temper of his audience, and knew that they would only accept Shakespeare with modifications. Beginning with *Hamlet* in 1769, in which Molé appeared in the title-role, he dealt faithfully, after his own methods, with *Romeo and Juliet*, *King Lear*, *Macbeth*, *King John*, and *Othello*. This last, given in 1792, owed much of its success to the fine acting of Talma. When we remember that none of Ducis's own plays have survived, it is interesting to note that in connexion with his adaptation of *King John* a contemporary critic deplored his wasting his undoubted talents on such rubbish. Ducis became a member of the French Academy in succession to Voltaire, and after the failure of his last play in 1801 retired quietly to Versailles.

DUCLOS [MARIE ANNE DE CHÂTEAUNEUF] (1668–1748), French actress, who, after an unsuccessful attempt to join the company at the Opéra, was accepted by the Comédie-Française in 1693 for tragic roles, in which she later replaced Mlle Champmeslé, sharing feminine leads with Mlle Desmares. Her strength lay in declamation, and her acting was stiff and artificial, in opposition to the traditions of Molière and Baron. Mlle Duclos was not at all popular in the theatre on account of her violent temper and strong passions, which she vented freely on the young and lovely Adrienne Lecouvreur when the latter was allotted some of her roles. She was also most undisciplined in her private life, and at the age of 55 married a young boy, who soon left her. This involved her in a lawsuit, whose speeches make curious reading. She retired at the age of 72, by which time the artificiality of her acting

seemed sadly old-fashioned beside the freer methods of the younger generation.

DU CROISY, PHILIBERT GASSOT (1626–95), French actor, who may have been related to the tragedian Bellerose. After touring the provinces he joined Molière at the Petit-Bourbon in 1659, with his wife, a mediocre actress who retired a few years later. It seems from some remarks in *L'Impromptu de Versailles* that Molière disliked her. Du Croisy, however, remained with the company until 1689, and was the first to play Tartuffe, both in 1667, when the character was called Panulphe, and, under its original name, in 1669. A handsome man, though somewhat fat, he was a good comedian, and played poets and pedants in Molière's comedies. He was also good in tragedy. After Molière's death he remained with the company, retiring in 1689. He had two daughters, both actresses, of whom one married Paul Poisson, and in her old age wrote articles on Molière and his company for the *Mercure de France*, 1738.

DUFF, MARY ANN (*née* DYKE) (1794–1857), American actress, born in London. With her sister Elizabeth, later the wife of Tom Moore, she appeared in Dublin as a dancer, and then married William Murray of the Theatre Royal, Edinburgh, brother of Mrs. Henry Siddons. He died almost immediately, however, and his widow re-married, her second husband being an Irish actor, John Duff (1787–1831), with whom she went to America. They appeared in Boston in 1810 as Romeo and Juliet, and were both considered excellent actors. It was in Boston, and later in Philadelphia, that Mrs. Duff made her reputation, for in spite of the approbation of the critics she was never wholly accepted by audiences in New York, where she made her first appearance in 1823, as Hermione in *The Distressed Mother* to the Orestes of the elder Booth. A tall, dark, graceful woman, she was at her best in tragedy—Ophelia, Constance, Lady Macbeth, Jane Shore—and in the pathetic heroines of such plays as *The Maid and the Magpie* and *The Innkeeper's Daughter*. The early death of her second husband left her with seven small children, of whom one, also Mary, became a good actress, and the wife of J. J. Addams. In spite of constant tours throughout America Mrs. Duff's financial distress became acute, and in a moment of mental aberration she married the actor Charles Young. The marriage was never consummated and was soon after annulled. Mrs. Duff retired into obscurity for some time, but eventually returned to the stage, and in 1835 married a lawyer of New Orleans named Seaver, making her last appearances there in the following year as Jane Shore and Portia.

DUFRESNE. (1) [ABRAHAM ALEXIS QUINAULT] (1693–1767), French actor, whose father, brother, and three sisters were members with him of the Comédie-Française (see QUINAULT). He is sometimes referred to as Quinault-Dufresne. He made his début as

Oreste in Crébillon's *Électre* in 1712, and was engaged to play young heroes and lovers. He was extremely handsome, and, as a contemporary said of him, had the good fortune to please the ladies in an age when they took little trouble to fight against their inclinations. At first the simplicity of his acting was against him, and it was not until the retirement of Beaubour, a somewhat pompous actor, that Dufresne came into his own. He had a fine voice, and a good presence, reminding many of the great Michel Baron, whose traditions he had inherited through the teaching of Ponteuil. Dufresne was the first to play the name-part in Voltaire's *Œdipe* (1718), and Destouches wrote for him his best comedy, *Le Glorieux* (1732), in which Dufresne hardly had to act, so completely was he the person Destouches was satirizing. His companions, who had suffered much from his arrogance, must have got a good deal of quiet amusement out of seeing him as the hero of this play. His wife (2) CATHERINE MARIE JEANNE DUPRÉ (?-1759), known as Mlle Deseine, was a good actress, overshadowed by several outstanding actresses of the period. She first appeared at Fontainebleau in 1724, and from there went to the Comédie-Française. She had much charm and a delightfully natural style of acting, but a weak voice. She was delicate in health, and after several prolonged absences from the stage finally retired in 1736, four years before her husband.

DUFRESNE, CHARLES (c. 1611–c. 1684), a French actor-manager, first found in the provinces in about 1643, as leader of a company under the patronage of the Duc d'Éperon. A year or two later he was joined by the remnants of the ill-starred Illustre-Théâtre, and soon ceded his leadership to Molière, with whom he returned to Paris in 1658, retiring a year later. Son of a Court painter, Dufresne played second lead in tragedy, but does not appear to have shone in comedy. Even before the arrival of Molière and the Béjarts his company was considered one of the best in France.

DUFRESNY, CHARLES RIVIÈRE (1654–1724), French dramatist, reputed to be a great-grandson of Henri IV, a relationship which procured him many privileges at Court. His inveterate habit of gambling, however, and his lighthearted lack of thought for the morrow, not to mention two imprudent marriages, kept him poor all his life. But he was always happy, had no great ambitions, and no enemies. He began his dramatic career by writing for the Italian actors established at the Hôtel de Bourgogne, and after their departure from Paris in 1697 turned his undoubted talents to the service of the Comédie-Française. Of his numerous plays the best was the one-act *Esprit de contradiction* (1700). Others, successful when first produced, were *Le Double veuvage* (1702), *La Coquette du village* (1715), and *Le Mariage fait et rompu* (1721), all of which kept their place in the repertory for some time. Dufresny was very conscious of the weight of tradition in comedy, and made some effort to shake it off,

as may be seen from his prologue to *Le Négligent* (1692), in which he complains that a good comic writer is blamed for copying Molière, and a bad for not. Dufresny shrank from hard work, however, and with all his qualities his plays were never more than witty and superficial. Many of them, in accordance with the fashion of the time, had a number of interpolated songs, which he composed himself.

DUGAZON. (1) MARIE MARGUERITE GOURGAUD (1742–99), French actress, daughter of a provincial manager who had aspired unsuccessfully to the Comédie-Française in 1739. She made her first appearance there in 1767, playing secondary soubrette roles. With her was her younger sister, who had married the brother of the celebrated dancer Vestris (for her career, see VESTRIS, 5), and a younger brother (2) JEAN BAPTISTE HENRI GOURGAUD (1746–1809), who joined the company in 1771. He was a most amusing comedian, at his best in somewhat farcical roles, particularly in the comedies of Scarron and Legrand. He was one of the first professors of acting at the newly formed Conservatoire, in 1793, with Préville, Molé, and Fleury. He later supported Talma in the upheavals consequent on the Revolution, and followed him to the Comédie-Française when it was reconstituted under Napoleon.

DUKE OF YORK'S THEATRE, LONDON, in St. Martin's Lane, near Trafalgar Square. This was built by Violet Melnotte as the Trafalgar Square Theatre. St. Martin's Lane was then little more than a slum, and for her enterprise she was known as 'Mad Melnotte'; but a few years later there were two other theatres in St. Martin's Lane—the New and the Coliseum. The theatre opened on 10 Sept. 1892 with a comic opera called 'The Wedding Eve', which failed, and *Dorothy* was revived almost immediately. It was then closed, owing to a lawsuit—Miss Melnotte being rather a difficult person—and reopened in Feb. 1893 with a farcical comedy, *The County Councillor*, in which Yorke Stephens, Cyril Maude, and Fanny Brough appeared. Two months later May Yohe appeared in *Mlle Nitouche*. In Sept. 1895 the theatre took its present name, the Duke of York's. Its first success was *The Gay Parisienne* in which that quaint droll, Louie Freer, made a sensational success; produced on 4 Apr. 1896, it ran for 369 performances. Nothing further happened of note until Charles Frohman took over the theatre in 1897 and, with the younger Dion Boucicault as his dramatist-producer and Irene Vanbrugh as his leading lady, began a brilliant tenancy of nineteen years which included (in 1910) a remarkable repertory season under Granville-Barker—*Misalliance, What Every Woman Knows,* and *The Madras House.* When Frohman left things were not so successful. Miss Melnotte had a way of quarrelling with her associates which did not make for long partnerships. On one occasion she evicted a tenant after an exciting week-end siege. She sold the theatre in 1928 to William Hutter, but regained possession a few years later and controlled it until her death in 1935. Her own most notable production was *Thunder in the Air* in 1928. Among other successful productions there were Archie de Bear's revue *Punchbowl*, which ran for 585 performances, and Charlot's production of Noel Coward's revue, *London Calling. Such Men are Dangerous, The Chinese Bungalow,* and *Jew Süss,* all with Matheson Lang, followed, and a season of non-stop Grand Guignol was given in 1933. Several translations of continental plays were given at this theatre in 1937–8 by the London International Theatre Club, who were also responsible for the first production in London of Bridie's *Susannah and the Elders* and other new plays. In 1943 *Pink String and Sealing Wax* began its long run at the Duke of York's, followed in 1944 by the successful farce *Is Your Honeymoon really Necessary?*, which ran for nearly 1,000 performances. W. M. P.

DUKE'S HOUSE, LONDON, see DORSET GARDEN and LINCOLN'S INN FIELDS THEATRE.

DUKE'S THEATRE, LONDON, see HOLBORN THEATRE.

DUKES, ASHLEY (1885–　　), English dramatist, theatre manager, and dramatic critic, in which last capacity he worked for the *Star* and the *Illustrated London News.* He was also English editor of *Theatre Arts* for many years. In 1933 he opened the Mercury Theatre, a small playhouse in which he has done excellent work with the production of new and foreign plays, particularly poetic drama. The theatre is also used for ballet, directed by his wife (see RAMBERT, MARIE). Dukes's wide knowledge and appreciation of continental drama has been turned to good account in the adaptation of French and German plays for the London theatre. The best-known of these are *The Man Who Married a Dumb Wife* and *Mozart,* from the French, and *From Morn till Midnight, The Machine Wreckers, Such Men are Dangerous,* and *Jew Süss,* from the German. He has also adapted from the Italian Machiavelli's *Mandragola,* and from the Spanish part of *La Celestina* as *The Matchmaker's Arms.* Of his own plays the most successful was the charming and romantic *Man with a Load of Mischief.* He is the author of several books on the theatre, including *Drama* in the Home University Library, and of an autobiography, *The Scene is Changed,* published in 1943. He is an honorary member of the Critics' Circle, from which he was British Delegate at several International Congresses of Critics, and in 1945 was appointed head of the Entertainments Branch of the Control Commission for Germany.

DULLIN, CHARLES (1885–1949), French actor and producer, who, after some appearances in melodrama, became one of the original actors of Copeau's company at the Vieux-Colombier, remaining with him until the return of the troupe from America after the 1914–18 war. He then collected his own company, and after some preliminary training, took it on a long tour in the provinces. Back in Paris, confronted by many difficulties, and always short of money, Dullin nevertheless succeeded finally in establishing himself and his actors in the Théâtre de l'Atelier, which soon gained a reputation as one of the outstanding experimental theatres of Paris, worthy to rank with the Vieux-Colombier which had given Dullin his first training. The list of plays produced at the Atelier covers the classics of France, the comedies of Aristophanes, translations of famous foreign plays, including Shakespeare and Ben Jonson, Pirandello for the first time in France, and the works of some new authors. Dullin sought first in his productions to engender that current of sympathy between actors and audience, without which no play can come to life, and then to bring to the stage, with the help of dancing, décor, and, above all, poetry, the sense of wonder and imagination which the 'well-made' play had banished for so long. Himself an excellent actor, he ran a school of acting connected with his theatre, and in 1936 was invited to become one of the producers of the Comédie-Française. During the occupation of France he toured the unoccupied zone with Molière's *L'Avare.*

DUMAS. (1) ALEXANDRE *père* (1803–70), a prolific writer, of Creole parentage, who is now mainly remembered for his novels, but whose plays were an important part of the Romantic movement in the French theatre. He began by writing vaudevilles, but in accordance with the contemporary orientation, and influenced in part by the visit to Paris of an English company in Shakespeare, turned to historical romance, and his *Henri III et sa cour* (1829) was the first triumph of the Romantic theatre. In the prevailing decadence of the stage the colour and movement of Dumas's plays delighted the audience, and brought the author the friendship and admiration of Alfred de Vigny and Victor Hugo. A play on Napoleon was followed by *Antony* (1831), given at the Théâtre de la Porte-Saint-Martin, where many of Dumas's more melodramatic pieces were first produced. It was extremely successful, owing in part to the excellent acting of Bocage and Mlle Dorval. The Porte-Saint-Martin saw also the first production of Dumas's most famous play, *La Tour de Nesle* (1832), which for terror and rapidity of action—not to mention the number of corpses—surpassed anything seen on the French stage since the days of Alexandre Hardy. When Dumas had run the gamut of history, alone or in collaboration, from Roman times to the contemporary scene, he turned to his own novels and made them into plays, of which in all he wrote nearly a hundred. Some of them were given at the Théâtre Historique, which he built and financed himself, and which nearly ruined him when it failed in 1850, for in spite of his enormous earnings Dumas was continually harassed by his creditors, and a prey to harpies and hangers-on. He was finally rescued by his daughter, who came to live with him in 1868. Meanwhile his natural son (2) ALEXANDRE, known as

Dumas *fils* (1824–95), had also turned to the theatre. He was a complete contrast to his father, who seems to have had practically no influence on his literary career, though they lived in harmony together, the younger man often supporting and shielding the elder from the consequences of his own folly. The younger Dumas approached the theatre by way of a dramatization of his own novel, *La Dame aux camélias*, which, first acted in 1852, became one of the outstanding theatrical successes of the second half of the nineteenth century, and is occasionally revived to-day. But this romantic presentation of the repentant courtesan was destined to remain unique among his dramatic works, for he later turned to social questions, and became the leading exponent of what has been called 'the useful theatre', which regards the stage as a pulpit for the expounding of moral principles. Himself an agnostic, he sought to enforce Christian virtues and conventional morality by dramatic examples. He had little liking for the bohemian society in which his childhood had been passed, and to which he gave a permanent label in the title of his play *Le Demi-Monde* (1855). The bitterness of his illegitimacy found expression in *Le Fils naturel* (1858) and *Un Père prodigue* (1859), while social problems of the day were ventilated in such plays as *La Question d'argent* (1857), *L'Étrangère* (1876), and his last play, *Francillon* (1887). The sanctity of home life was his constant theme and, by a curious reversal of ideas, the prostitute became his whipping-boy. Unlike his father, he had no thought of rebelling against society, but sought to ameliorate conditions by the inculcation of moral standards. Much of his theatre has disappeared with the conditions which gave rise to it, and later enactments on paternity and illegitimacy have outdistanced many of his arguments. In his own day a popular and powerful social dramatist, he is now only remembered by his least typical work, mainly because the consumptive and pathetic figure of Marguerite Gautier offers a fine part for an ambitious and passionate actress.

DU MAURIER. (1) GEORGE LOUIS PALMELLA BUSSON (1834–96), English artist, best remembered for his work on *Punch*, and for his novels *Peter Ibbetson* and *Trilby*. The latter was dramatized by Salter and produced in 1895 with much success. Of George's two sons, the eldest (2) GUY (1865–1916), a soldier by profession, was killed in action in France. He was the author of *An Englishman's Home*, produced anonymously in 1909, a patriotic play which provided a great stimulus to the recruiting of the Territorial Army; the younger son (3) SIR GERALD HUBERT EDWARD (1873–1934), who was responsible for the production of his brother's play, was a famous actor-manager. He made his first appearance at the Garrick in 1894, went on tour with Forbes-Robertson, and in 1895 appeared under Tree at the Haymarket in a small part in *Trilby*. He remained with Tree for some years, both at His

Majesty's and in America, but his real talent became apparent when he went to the Duke of York's Theatre under Charles Frohman. There, in *The Admirable Crichton* and as the original Mr. Darling and Captain Hook in *Peter Pan*, he did excellent work. His great success, however, came in 1906 with *Raffles*, where he destroyed all the old traditions of drama by making the villain of the piece the hero. As the gentleman crook his performance was memorable, and the part is always associated with his name. Following it with *Arsène Lupin* and *Alias Jimmy Valentine*, he seemed doomed to crook plays for the rest of his career; but in 1910 he broke away, and took over the management of Wyndham's Theatre in association with Frank Curzon, making it a home of light comedy for many years. At this time Du Maurier, who was a great exponent of natural acting, and of the art that conceals art, was virtually the leader of the English stage. Striking rather than good-looking, with a strongly marked face, gaunt and thin, he had compelling power and great charm. His voice was not strong, but he knew how to use it. His style tended to be somewhat monotonous, and his range of parts limited; but within those limits he was seldom excelled, and he could on occasion step beyond them, as was proved by his portrayal of Harry Dearth in *Dear Brutus* in 1917. A more typical part, and one which brought him solid success, was *Bull-Dog Drummond* in 1921. A year later Du Maurier was knighted for his services to his profession, and shortly afterwards left Wyndham's for the St. James's Theatre, where his last two outstanding appearances were in *The Last of Mrs. Cheyney* and *Interference*. A memoir, *Gerald, a Portrait*, was published in 1934 by his daughter (4) DAPHNE (1907–   ), novelist, and author of the stage version of her novel *Rebecca*, and of two plays, *The Years Between* (1945) and *September Tide* (1949).   W. M. P.

DUMB BALLET, see TRICKWORK ON THE ENGLISH STAGE.

DUMESNIL, MARIE FRANÇOISE (1713–1803), French actress, rival and contemporary of Mlle Clairon. She first appeared in the provinces, and joined the company of the Comédie-Française in 1737. She was a fine actress, excellent in passionate roles, and was by some critics acclaimed above Mlle Clairon, who with more art had less range. Voltaire attributed much of the success of his *Mérope* (1743) to the acting of Mlle Dumesnil, who, unlike Mlle Clairon, had no interest in the reform of theatrical costume, and aimed at magnificence rather than correctness, being always robed in rich stuffs, made in contemporary styles, and loaded with jewels. She retired in 1775, and passed the rest of her long life at Boulogne. She remained in full possession of her faculties until the end, and was able to remember and pass on to younger actors many traditions temporarily lost during the upheavals of the Revolution. Towards the end of her life she published a book of memoirs, mainly in reply to the many injurious references made to her in Mlle Clairon's *Mémoires*. It is not particularly interesting, though some passages have a technical value. There are also some useful notes on the theatrical slang of the time, which constituted a language of its own, and in which, says Dumesnil, Préville excelled.

DUNCAN, ISADORA(1878–1927), an American dancer who discarded the stiffened sandal and conventional dress of ballet for the Greek chiton and bare feet. She had much influence on the trend of dancing in her day, and it was her visit to Russia in the early part of the twentieth century which provided the spark needed to stimulate the innovating forces that led to the formation of Diaghilev's Ballets Russes (see BALLET, 7).

DUNDREARY, see SOTHERN (1).

DUNLAP, WILLIAM (1766–1839), one of the first outstanding figures of the American stage, and its dominating force from 1790 to 1810. He at first intended to become a painter, and went to England in 1784 to study under Benjamin West. Once in London, however, he neglected his work for the theatre, with which he had first made contact through the productions of British officers in New York. He soon saw most of Shakespeare's plays, a good many contemporary comedies, and the work of such actors as Charles Kemble and Mrs. Siddons. It was at this period that Dunlap imbibed that sense of dramatic and theatrical values which was later to stand him in good stead. Late in 1787 he returned to the United States, and, inspired by the success of Tyler's *The Contrast*, wrote a comedy for the American Company. This was accepted but never played, owing mainly to the lack of suitable parts for the manager, John Henry, and his wife. A second comedy, *The Father; or, American Shandyism*, remedied this defect, and was produced at the John Street Theatre, New York, on 7 Sept. 1789.

Dunlap continued to write for the American Company, and in 1796 became one of its managers, in partnership with Hallam and Hodgkinson, whose joint management had led to constant bickering between themselves and their wives. Dunlap strengthened the company by the inclusion of the first Joseph Jefferson, and did all he could to keep the peace among his co-partners. In 1797 Hallam withdrew from active management, and Hodgkinson and Dunlap opened the Park Theatre, New York, on 29 Jan. 1798, with *As You Like It*. One of the first plays to be done there was *André*, a tragedy which Dunlap based on an incident in the War of Independence, thus making it the first native tragedy on American material. Hodgkinson played André, and the part of Bland, his friend, was taken by a newly imported young English actor, Thomas Abthorpe Cooper, who was later to succeed Dunlap as lessee and manager of the theatre.

In 1798 Hodgkinson left the management of the Park Theatre, and Dunlap continued alone, producing a number of his own plays, many of them translations and adaptations of the highly popular Kotzebue. Among these the most successful were *The Stranger*, which has not survived, *Lovers' Vows*, *The Wild Goose Chase*, *The Virgin of the Sun*, and its sequel *Pizarro*. Dunlap also translated a number of French plays, and wrote some original works, of which the early ones mentioned above were the best, though *Leicester* and *The Italian Father* have much to recommend them. Many of them were performed also in Boston, where Dunlap had leased the Haymarket Theatre, and in Philadelphia under Warren and Wood at the Chestnut Street Theatre. Meanwhile Dunlap struggled on at the Park Theatre, hampered by the temperaments of his actors and recurrent epidemics of yellow fever, until in Feb. 1805, he went bankrupt and was forced to close down. He returned to painting, but a year later agreed to become assistant stage manager of the Park under Cooper, in which capacity he engaged in 1809 Mr. and Mrs. Poe, the parents of Edgar Allan Poe, for parts in Monk Lewis's *Castle Spectre*. In 1812 he accompanied George Frederick Cooke on his American tour, and then retired finally from the stage to devote himself entirely to literature and painting. He contemplated the publication of his plays in a uniform edition, but produced only the first volume, and in 1832 published his invaluable *History of the American Theatre*. Quinn, who devotes a chapter of his *History of the American Drama from the Beginning to the Civil War* to the career of William Dunlap, sums him up as follows: '(He) had the soul of an artist and the intrepidity of the pioneer, and his place in our dramatic literature will remain secure.'

DUNLOP STREET THEATRE, see GLASGOW.

DUNSANY, LORD (1878–   ), see IRELAND.

DUNVILLE, T. E. (*c.* 1870–1924), an eccentric music-hall comedian whose real name was Wallon. He specialized in songs made up of short terse sentences, which left much to the imagination and were delivered in an explosive manner. A typical one was 'Little boy, Pair of skates, Broken ice, Heaven's gates'. He became stage-struck as a youngster after seeing a performance of Pepper's Ghost at Coventry Fair. After practising high kicks in the counting-house of a silk merchant where he was employed he joined a Nigger Minstrel troupe, and then went into pantomime at obscure theatres. He and a partner gained their first success through their carefully rehearsed act going wrong and causing the audience to laugh so much that they continued the mistakes as the real act. It was when appearing as an extra turn at Bolton in 1899 that Dunville first caught the eye of an enterprising manager, and his luck turned. For years he was top of the bill, wearing the extraordinary make-up—

long black coat, small hat, baggy trousers, big boots, and ugly face with red nose—which he often tried vainly to alter. His bills always announced him as 'Sticking Here for a Week', and showed him suspended from the wall. When the music-halls began to slump after the 1914–18 war it preyed on his mind. One night in 1924, in a saloon bar, he overheard someone referring to him as a 'fallen star'. Some days later his body was recovered from the Thames near Reading.   W. M. P.

DU PARC. (1) RENÉ BERTHELOT (c. 1630–64), French comic actor, known as Gros-René, who was with Molière in the provinces and went to Paris with him. He was a good actor, but was overshadowed by his wife (2) MARQUISE-THÉRÈSE DE GORLA (1633–68), who had already had some experience in a travelling company before she married Gros-René and joined Molière. A woman of great beauty and majestic presence, she was excellent in tragedy, less good in comedy, and probably for this reason left Molière in 1666 to join the company at the Hôtel de Bourgogne, where she played the title-role in Racine's *Andromaque* (1667). She died suddenly, and Racine, whose mistress she had been, was later accused of having poisoned her to make way for Mlle Champmeslé. According to contemporary gossip, Mlle du Parc was loved by Corneille and by his younger brother Thomas, by Molière, whom she disdained, by Racine, and by La Fontaine.

D'URFEY, THOMAS (1653–1723), Restoration dramatist and song-writer, a favourite with Charles II and James II, whom he ardently supported in his writings. He wrote a number of plays, mainly based on earlier English or foreign dramatists, none of which has survived on the stage. The earlier ones are purely farcical, but later ones are tinged with the sentimentality which was soon to bulk so large in English drama. D'Urfey was one of the writers most savagely attacked for indecency by Collier in his *Short View*, and in 1698 he was prosecuted for profanity. In 1719 he published a collection of songs and ballads called 'Wit and Mirth, or Pills to Purge Melancholy'.

DUSE, ELEONORA (1859–1924), famous Italian actress, and one of the great tragediennes of the international theatre. She had a hard and unhappy childhood, much saddened by the death of her mother. Daughter and granddaughter of strolling players, she was on the stage from her earliest years, playing Cosette at the age of 4, and Juliet at 14. In 1878, after a popular success as the heroine in *Les Fourchambault*, she was engaged by Ernesto Rossi as his leading lady, and went on tour with him, soon taking her place as one of the greatest actresses of the day. In 1885 she toured South America, though she was not seen in the United States until just before her death, when she played at the Metropolitan Opera House, and on tour. In London in 1895 she and Sarah Bernhardt both appeared as Magda, an event which

caused much excitement among public and critics alike. Shaw, at that time dramatic critic of the *Saturday Review*, unhesitatingly proclaimed the supremacy of Duse, while Clement Scott preferred Bernhardt. Duse had a certain statuesque way of playing, a slowness and subtlety which was not always to the taste of her audience. A slender woman, with a dark, mobile face, melancholy in repose, and long slender hands and arms, she was noted for the beauty and expressiveness of her gestures, but her excessive nervousness and overwrought temperament led at times to too much restlessness on the stage, and it was in her rare moments of immobility that one best realized her greatness. She was probably at her best in big emotional parts—Tosca, Fédora, Théodora, Camille—though she was much admired, even by Clement Scott, as the Hostess in *La Locandiera*, one of the most popular pieces in her repertory, in spite of her inability to present a buxom, vigorous woman, as the part demands. In her late thirties, when she stood in the forefront of her profession, she ardently championed the cause of D'Annunzio's poetic drama, and made him famous as a dramatist by her playing in *La Gioconda, Francesca da Rimini*, and *La Città morta*. Even after the failure of his *Gloria* at Naples in 1899, she continued to appear in his plays, often with much loss of money and reputation. She retired shortly before 1914, but returned to play in London and New York in 1923, dying in Pittsburgh the following year.

Shaw, who always had the greatest admiration for her, much to the fury of those who preferred Sarah Bernhardt, said, with reference to her Magda:

When it is remembered that the majority of tragic actors excel only in explosions of those passions which are common to man and brute, there will be no difficulty in understanding the indescribable distinction which Duse's acting acquires from the fact that behind every stroke of it is a distinctively human idea. In nothing is this more apparent than in the vigilance in her of that high human instinct which seeks to awaken the deepest responsive feeling without giving pain. (See *Our Theatres in the Nineties*.)

Unlike Bernhardt, Duse professed a great hatred of publicity, but in seeking to avoid it made herself even more conspicuous. She was an enigmatic personality, who captured the imagination of the theatre-going public and even in her own lifetime became a legend. Yet, with all her faults, she was a superb actress, and it was finally the sterling truth of her representation which fired public imagination. She disdained the use of make-up on the stage, and was noted for her ability to blush or turn pale at will.

DUST HOLE, see SCALA THEATRE.

DUTCH DRAMA, see HOLLAND.

DUTTON COOK, see COOK, EDWARD DUTTON.

DYMOV, OSSIP (1878–), see JEWISH DRAMA, 6.

E

EAGLE THEATRE, NEW YORK, see STAN-
DARD THEATRE (2).

EARL OF DERBY'S MEN, see STRANGE'S
MEN.

EARL OF LEICESTER'S MEN, see
LEICESTER'S MEN.

EARL OF LINCOLN'S MEN, see LIN-
COLN'S MEN.

EARL OF OXFORD'S MEN, see OXFORD'S
MEN.

EARL OF PEMBROKE'S MEN, see PEM-
BROKE'S MEN.

EARL OF SUSSEX'S MEN, see SUSSEX'S
MEN.

EAST LONDON THEATRE, see EFFING-
HAM SALOON and ROYALTY THEATRE (1).

ECCLESIASTICAL DRAMA. It is an
interesting and ironic fact that modern drama
in Europe evolved from the services of that
Church which had done so much to suppress
the last vestiges of classical drama, and which
has throughout the centuries battled with varying success against the manifestations of its
secularized offspring. The dramatic instinct
in man, driven underground by the ordinances
of the Early Fathers, was bound to break out
somewhere, and when one considers the drama
inherent in Christianity it is not surprising that
mimetic tendencies should early have shown
themselves in the services of its cult. The
celebration of the Mass was a highly dramatic
spectacle, enhanced by ceremonial and symbolic ritual, and the use of antiphonal singing;
so were the services of Easter and Christmas,
and such specialized festivities as the dedication
of a church or the enthronement of a bishop.
Antiphonal singing, which may owe something
to the influence of the Greek tragic chorus,
lends itself readily to dialogue, and so has in
it the germ of drama. As church services became more elaborate the earlier antiphons were
supplemented by additional melodies, first sung
to vowel sounds only (neumes), later to specially
written texts, or tropes, many of which took on
a dialogue form.

One of these tropes, from the Benedictine
Abbey of St. Gall, is for Easter, and follows
closely the Gospel account of the interview
between the Angel at the Tomb and the three
Maries on Easter morning. It is known shortly
as the *Quem quaeritis* (Whom seek ye?), and
from it liturgical drama was born. At some
point this trope got detached from its proper
place at the beginning of the Easter Mass,
either as an Introit trope or as a processional
chant, and reappeared as a separate little scene
at Matins on Easter morning, with four persons
to act the parts of the women and the angel,

and with a building, temporary or permanent,
to represent the empty tomb (for the complete
scenario see Chambers, *Mediaeval Stage*, ii,
pp. 14–15). This symbolic representation of
the sepulchre had already been used, says St.
Ethelwold, 'for the strengthening of faith in
the unlearned vulgar and in neophytes'. In it
the Cross was laid on Good Friday, and removed before Easter morning. This ceremony
ended in England with Elizabeth (1559), and
on the continent was later fused with the
Adoration of the Reserved Host on Maundy
Thursday. It cannot be said at what date this
little drama of the *Quem quaeritis* started, but
it is certain that, aided perhaps by the interchange of ideas of the wandering scholars, it
gave ever fuller expression to the dramatic
instinct which had first prompted it. Anthems
were added to the original trope, then proses,
and finally metrical hymns took their place in
the dialogue, the most important being the
Victimae paschali written by Wipo of St. Gall in
1125–50, which found its way into the scenario
of the *Quem quaeritis* during the thirteenth
century. There were now two scenes—the
angel showing the empty sepulchre to the
Maries, and they in turn announcing the Resurrection to the rest of the congregation. The
Victimae paschali formed part of the second
little scene, and new voices were introduced
to represent the disciples. A third scene was
added when the apostles John and Peter were
shown going themselves to the sepulchre. This
occurred probably at the end of the eleventh
or beginning of the twelfth century, and in
most churches brought the drama to a close;
in a few a fourth scene or dramatic moment
was added with the person of the Risen Christ
and His dialogue with Mary Magdalene. An
important step in dramatic evolution was the
singing by the Maries of lyric laments as they
approached the sepulchre. An interpolation
(probably of the 13th or 14th century) with no
scriptural basis was a short scene between the
Maries and the Seller of Spices. But it is
possible that this character, who is important
in the vernacular religious drama of Germany,
and who brings in the first hint of secularized
humour, is a counter-influence on the late
liturgical play of the vernacular drama which
had by now developed from it.

Materials for a study of the evolution of
the liturgical play are fragmentary, but it is
found all over Europe. It seems to have been
most common in Germany and France, Spain
and Italy developing somewhat differently.
Even in the early days some attempt at costume
was made, with robes for women, angels, and
apostles, and properties were used, such as a
palm and wings for the angel, and a box for the
spices. But the *Quem quaeritis* always remained
part of the Liturgy, and the actors were priests,
nuns, and choirboys. The dialogue was chanted,

[213]

not spoken, and the hymns and proses were sung by the choir without the intervention of the congregation. The scene was immediately followed by the *Te Deum*, and so merged into Matins.

A further Easter play, called the *Peregrinus* and modelled perhaps on the above, was that which showed the Risen Christ with the disciples at Emmaus, with in some cases the addition of the three Maries and Doubting Thomas. This had its place at Vespers, and was performed in the church, as was a longer version, preserved at Tours, which blended the scene at the sepulchre, the *Quem quaeritis*, and the *Peregrinus* in one. Gradually the details coalesced and further ones were brought in, notably the Lamentations of those stationed by the Cross on Good Friday. This led to a drama on the Passion of Christ, distinct from that of the Resurrection, which extended from the preparations for the Last Supper to the burial of Christ. It was given only in a rudimentary form inside the church, mostly in dumb show with dialogue restricted to passages from the Vulgate, but it developed in importance when it moved to the market-place (see PASSION PLAY).

The services of Christmas gave scope for a drama of the Nativity, centring on the crib with Mary, Joseph, the ox and ass, shepherds, and angels. The practice of dressing a crib, which was the focal point of the Nativity play, has never ceased on the continent, and has recently returned in force to England. But the Nativity play does not seem to have attained in ecclesiastical drama the importance of the Easter play, and, with a further short scene dealing with Rachel and the massacre of the Innocents, was soon absorbed into an Epiphany play where the interest centred on the Wise Men and their gifts. The evolution of this play was probably complete by the end of the eleventh century. It began with the journey of the Magi, their visit to Jerusalem and interview with Herod, their meeting with the shepherds, the presentation of their gifts at the manger, their return home by a different route after a warning by an angel, Herod's rage at being outwitted, the massacre of the Innocents, and ended with the Flight into Egypt. Occasionally a further scene was added, showing the death of Herod and the return of the Holy Family from exile. Herod, so important in later secular plays on religious subjects, was from the first a noisy, blustering fellow, whence Hamlet's phrase 'to out-Herod Herod'. He was probably played by the 'king' chosen from among the minor clergy for the Feast of Fools, and may be an importation from extra-ecclesiastical gaieties at Christmastide. The textual evolution of the Epiphany play can be studied from collated fragments, and begins with antiphons and prose sentences based on Scripture only. The influence of the wandering scholars led later to the writing of new metrical texts with occasional tags from Sallust or Virgil, débris thrown up by the submerged classical learning and used by the Church for her own purposes.

Another Christmas play, and the most important for the future development of the drama, was based on a narrative sermon attributed to St. Augustine, and known as the Prophet play. This made use of the Old Testament prophets, as well as of Virgil and the Erythraean Sibyl, listing their prophecies concerning the coming of the Messiah. In the eleventh century it was converted into a metrical dramatic dialogue, in some cases enriched by the appearance of Balaam and his Ass, and the Three Children in the Fiery Furnace. The ass was probably another importation from the Feast of Fools, and its use may mark a determined effort by the Church to canalize the irrepressible licence of Christmas merry-making by incorporating into its own more orderly proceedings an undoubted element of buffoonery.

Apart from these Christmas and Easter plays, which grew up organically within the Church, and developed in accordance with certain rules and limitations, others exist on the same lines, deliberately written for performance in a church. The manuscript works of a wandering scholar, Hilarius, pupil of Abelard, contain three plays of this kind, a Miracle of St. Nicholas, the Raising of Lazarus, and a two-part play on Daniel, probably detached from the Prophet play. There are in addition a number of anonymous plays on these subjects, those dealing with St. Nicholas being particularly connected with the children's scholastic feast and the Boy Bishop. There are traces of other subjects—John the Baptist, Isaac and Rebecca, the Conversion of St. Paul—and a French play on the Wise and Foolish Virgins has, as many of these later plays had, speeches in the vernacular. An Advent play from Germany, *Antichristus*, demanded a number of actors, and much space, probably the nave of some great church. It is well written, dramatically conceived, and probably had some significance in church politics of the time. It introduces allegorical as well as biblical figures, and its date is about 1160. We are here far from the simplicity of the angel and the three Maries, and it is hard to avoid the suspicion that the amateur actors of early days have now been reinforced by those to whom acting was no novelty, no part of a ritual church service, but a means of livelihood—the lineal descendants of those *mimi* whom the Church had tried to suppress. Certainly the wandering scholars, as witness Hilarius, had some practice in the mimetic art and, having once written their plays, may have called upon their acquaintances among the travelling tumblers to eke out the shortcomings of the local clergy. The participants in local folk-plays, too, may have been pressed into service, to dance, to sing, to bear a part with experienced assurance. But all this is conjecture. What can be said with certainty is merely that liturgical drama, as it evolved from the simple antiphon of Easter or Christmas, was complete by the end of the thirteenth century, and that in its later development it necessarily ceased to be liturgical. Plays were given in churches, mostly in the vernacular, right up to the fifteenth century, and in isolated cases even later, but they were intermixed with, and influenced by, the secular plays of the market-place to such an extent that they can no longer be considered purely, or even, as time went on, partly, ecclesiastical. Having given back the drama to Europe the Church again withdrew, and prepared to do battle with the theatre it had engendered. (For the later developments of the drama see the separate countries of Europe.)

ECCLESTON (Eglestone), William (?–?1625 or 1652), an actor in the lists of those who played in Shakespeare's plays, and a member in 1610 of the King's Men, with whom he remained, with one break, until about 1623. Baldwin, in his *Organization and Personnel of the Shakespearian Company* (1927), assigns to him the roles of sprightly youth with a penchant for sword-play. He also assumes that he played, as an apprentice, a number of Shakespeare's female roles, but there is no proof of this. Eccleston may have died in 1625, when his name disappears from the actor lists, or may conceivably have lived to be the W. E. who contributed some verses to the 1652 edition of *The Wild Goose Chase*, in which Lowin acted in 1632.

ECHEGARAY, José (1832–1916), the most important Spanish dramatist of the later nineteenth century, who was awarded the Nobel Prize for Literature in 1904. His plays, which retain the verse-form and much of the fire and imagery of the Romantics, deal nevertheless with questions of social import, which often arise indirectly in the unfolding of the plot. They aroused fierce controversy, but were enthusiastically received, and had a great influence, not only in Spain, but on the European theatre generally. Echegaray's best-known plays are *O locura o santidad* (1877), *El loco Dios* (1900), *El hijo de Don Juan* (1892), a study of inherited disease which owes something to Ibsen's *Ghosts*, and, most important of all, *El gran Galeoto* (1881), given in England as *Calumny*. Its theme is that slanderous tongues may cause the downfall of the most virtuous, since a woman wrongfully accused of being a poet's mistress becomes so in good earnest, driven to it by the oppression of unfounded scandal.

ECHEIA, see ACOUSTICS, 3.

ECKENBERG, Johann Carl (1685–1748), a German strolling actor, an acrobat and juggler of great dexterity, who with his wife, a rope-dancer, led a company of acrobats and actors up and down Europe. He was once the successful rival of the great actress Caroline Neuber, at Hamburg, his varied entertainment proving more acceptable to the public than her classic plays.

EDDY, Edward (1822–75), American actor, long popular at the Bowery Theatre, where he first appeared on 13 Mar. 1851 as Richelieu. He followed this with such parts as Othello, Claude Melnotte, and Belphegor, and with his

greatest success of this first season, Edmond Dantès in *The Count of Monte Cristo*. Tall, handsome, and extremely vigorous in his acting, he was at his best in youthful, melodramatic parts, and though he never attained great eminence in New York he was a good actor with a wide range. He appeared occasionally in Shakespeare, but was also seen in less reputable works, even taking part in the Dog dramas which were such a feature of the popular stage at this time, and earning for himself the sobriquet of 'robustious Eddy'. He was at Burton's in 1855 with Chanfrau and Holland, and also at the New Metropolitan, but his style was not suited to the fashionable theatres, and he went back to the Bowery as Richard III. Further ventures into management ended in the same way, with a return to the Bowery and pure melodrama. Towards the end his popularity waned and he was seen fleetingly at a number of theatres.

EDESON, Robert (1868–1931), American actor, whose later career was in films, but who spent many years on the stage. Son of an actor-manager and his wife, Marion Taliaferro, he started work at 16 in the office of the Park Theatre, appearing there a year later as an understudy. By 1892 he was leading man at the Boston Museum, where he was seen and engaged by Charles Frohman during a performance of *Our Boys*. Frohman took him to the Empire in New York, where he played for many years, making a great hit as the Rev. Gavin Dishart in *The Little Minister* (1897) with Maude Adams. Two years later he made his first appearance in London, as David Brandon in *The Children of the Ghetto*, and appeared there again in 1907 in his most successful part, Soangataha in *Strongheart* by William C. de Mille. After a further series of successes, including two plays by himself, he made his last appearance as The Vagrant in *The Insect Play* (done as *The World We Live In*) in 1922. Edeson was one of the earliest stage stars to go into motion pictures, in which he was most successful. He had four wives, the third, 1917–24, being the actress Mary Newcomb. In person he was quiet and friendly, and a man of fine presence.

EDINBURGH. There appear to be indications that Edinburgh might have developed as the centre of an indigenous Scottish drama during the sixteenth century, but the troubled state of the country and the heavy hand of England prevented it, and in spite of some sporadic outbursts like that of the poet Allan Ramsay in 1736–7, who ran a theatre in Carruthers' Close for six months, it was not until 1767 that the first patent was granted for a playhouse in Edinburgh. The law was, however, evaded by the erection of a so-called 'concert hall', which issued tickets for a musical entertainment, and afterwards gave a 'free' performance of a play. It was at such a 'concert-hall' in the Canongate, under the control of the actor West Digges, that Home's *Douglas* was produced in

1756. The patent Theatre Royal opened in 1769 with the patentee, David Ross, as leading man, and here were given mainly plays from London with English actors in the chief roles. Among the distinguished visitors were the Yateses, the Barrys, Shuter, Samuel Foote, and, in 1781, John Kemble, whose brother Stephen controlled the theatre from 1791 to 1800. The family connexion with Edinburgh was continued by Henry, son of Mrs. Siddons, who was there from 1809 till his death in 1815, with his wife as his leading lady, and such visitors as Munden and the elder Mathews. From 1815 to 1850 the theatre was most successful, with an excellent stock company and visits from practically all the stars of the day. It was pulled down in 1859, Toole and Irving being members of its last stock company, and the General Post Office was built on the site. Meanwhile a second theatre, known as the Adelphi, had emerged from an earlier Circus, but this was burnt down in 1853. On its rebuilding the patent of the Theatre Royal was transferred to it, and it was known as the Royal through all its vicissitudes, being burnt down in 1865, 1875, and 1884, and always rebuilt on the same site. Other theatres in Edinburgh included the Princess's, which was first a music-hall, and flourished from 1860 to 1888, and the Edinburgh, which had a short life, 1875 to 1877, but saw Salvini's first appearances in the United Kingdom. The Lyceum opened in 1883. For a long time the theatrical life of Scotland seems to have centred in Edinburgh and Glasgow, and depended heavily on the English stage and actors, but present indications seem to point to a widespread revival of a Scottish National Drama (for further details see SCOTLAND). The Edinburgh Festival, founded in 1947, concedes a large part to drama, and in 1948 a revival of Lyndsay's old morality play, *The Three Estates* (1549), was an outstanding success.

EDOUIN, WILLIE [WILLIAM FREDERICK BRYER] (1846–1908), English comedian, son of a dancing-master. With his five brothers and sisters he gave children's shows in Brighton and London, and appeared in pantomime. As an actor he played in Australia and in New York, and was associated with Lydia Thompson and her burlesque troupe, one of whom he married. At Wallack's in 1871 he appeared in a burlesque of Bluebeard in his famous character of Wishee-Washee. He then returned to London and made his first adult appearance there in 1874 at the Charing Cross Theatre. After a further visit to America, he opened Toole's Theatre, London, in 1884, with Brough as his co-manager. He was also at one time manager of the Strand, but was not successful financially, being a poor business man. He was excellent in certain grotesque and whimsical parts, but his main successes were made in burlesque and extravaganza.

EDWARDES, GEORGE (1852–1915), English theatre manager, to whom we owe the form of entertainment known as Musical Comedy. Even if he did not invent it, it was through him that it came into being, and his influence that gave it its final form, while his name is indissolubly linked with its history. Edwardes was intended for the army, but drifted into theatre management in Ireland, his native country, at the Gaiety Theatre, Dublin, in 1875. He became business manager of the Savoy Theatre, London, when D'Oyly Carte opened it in 1881, but left there in 1885 to go into partnership with John Hollingshead at the old Gaiety. In the following year Hollingshead retired, and Edwardes ran the theatre on his own account. His flair for what the public wanted, his genius in finding talent and bringing out the best in it, his imagination in supplanting burlesque by musical comedy, made the Gaiety even more famous than it had previously been, while a 'Gaiety Girl' from his carefully chosen and well-trained chorus was a recognized type of beauty and ability. In 1893 Edwardes built Daly's for Augustin Daly, afterwards taking control of it himself, and making it as great a theatrical landmark in London as the Gaiety. He made stars by the score, his chorus-girls married into the peerage, and he made few mistakes in the choice of plays and casts. His list of successes at Daly's, the Gaiety, the Prince of Wales's, the Apollo, and elsewhere, is remarkable, and includes most of the musical comedies whose titles and tunes are still known to-day—*The Geisha, San Toy, The Merry Widow, The Country Girl, The Shop Girl, The Runaway Girl, The Quaker Girl* (he always maintained that there was magic in the word 'girl'). To his staff and companies, who adored him, he was always known as 'The Guv'nor'. Tall, good-looking and burly, he had a curiously sleepy, almost complaining, voice, that was very characteristic, as was his disregard of expense. He wanted the best for his theatres, and cared little what it cost. He was rewarded by packed houses and almost constant prosperity, and his popularity with the public was as great as with his own profession.   W. M. P.

EDWARDS, HILTON (1903–), see IRELAND.

EDWIN. (1) JOHN the elder (1749–90), English actor who was appearing in amateur theatricals when he made the acquaintance of the comedian Ned Shuter. This led to an engagement in Manchester to play Shuter's parts, and to further work in the provinces and in Dublin. Edwin was naturally unable to establish himself in London while Shuter was there, but he became a favourite actor in Bath. Later he was extremely successful at the Haymarket during the summer seasons, appearing in a number of plays by O'Keefe, who also wrote the comic songs for which Edwin became famous. A good, reliable actor, with a face which contrived to be both humorous and handsome, he was accounted the best burletta singer of the day, his voice being naturally good. He was not a buffoon, and seems to have played with

great subtlety, in spite of a sad propensity to
over-indulgence in drink. Among his best
parts in comedy were Dogberry, First Grave-
digger, Launcelot Gobbo, Sir Hugh Evans, and
Sir Anthony Absolute. His son, (2) JOHN the
younger (1768–1803), was the child of a Bath
milliner, and was first on the stage as a youngster, playing with his father at Bath and at the
Haymarket. As an adult, he made his début at
Covent Garden in 1788, and was taken up by
Lord Barrymore, for whom he devised private
theatricals at Wargrave. He died young as a
result of dissipation, which prevented him from
realizing his full powers as an actor. He married
(3) ELIZABETH REBECCA RICHARDS (c. 1771–
1854), an actress who had played with her
parents in Dublin while still quite young. She
returned to the stage after some schooling, and
was in Tate Wilkinson's provincial company,
being excellent in comedy and farce. After her
husband's death she was at Drury Lane and
other London theatres, and retired early. The
loss of her money caused her to return, when,
being too old for her previous parts, she appeared in such characters as Sheridan's
Duenna. She was small, fair, with an expressive
face, and had some of the charm and vivacity
of Mrs. Jordan, though without her excellence.

EFFINGHAM SALOON, LONDON. This
opened as a music-hall in the 1840s. In 1867
it was rebuilt and became the East London
Theatre, with one of the roughest audiences on
record and plays to suit their taste. It was burnt
down in 1879, and later a building called
Wonderland rose on the site, which housed
plays in Yiddish and then became a boxing
saloon.

EGAN, PIERCE (1772–1849), English journalist
and reporter of sporting events, author of *Life
in London*, first published in shilling parts in
1821 with illustrations by the Cruikshank
brothers. It was an immediate success, and
was at once dramatized by many hands as *Tom
and Jerry; or, Life in London*. Versions by
Barrymore at the Royal Amphitheatre, and
by the younger Dibdin at the Olympic, were
superseded by that of Moncrieff, first given
at the Adelphi and later frequently revived.
This version was also popular in America.
Egan himself prepared a version for Sadler's
Wells, and wrote a sequel, *Finish to the Adventures of Tom, Jerry and Logic*, both books
doubtless suggesting to Dickens the rough
idea of *The Pickwick Papers*. Egan was also
the author of *The Life of an Actor*, an amusing
survey of the progress of young Peregrine
Proteus from poverty and the provinces to the
honour of a performance before royalty. Dedicated to Kean, it was published in 1824, with
illustrations by Theodore Lane, and proved
almost as popular as *Tom and Jerry*.

EGRESSY, GÁBOR (1808–66), Hungarian
actor, the leading man, with Szerdahelyi, of
the company of the first Hungarian National
Theatre opened in Budapest in 1837.

EICHELBAUM, SAMUEL (1894–), see
SOUTH AMERICA, 1.

EIGHTEENPENNY PLACES, see AUDI-
TORIUM 1 c.

EKHOF, KONRAD (1720–1778), great German
actor who did more than anyone, after Caroline
Neuber, to raise the status of the professional
actor in Germany, and to prepare the way for
the reforms and triumphs of the great F. L.
Schröder. He was originally a clerk, but
an overwhelming love of the theatre led him
to go on the stage. He joined Schönemann's
newly formed company in 1740, taking with
him Sophie Schröder, at that time separated
from her drunken husband. Being short and
ungraceful, with a plain face, he was not at first
thought much of, and made himself generally
useful. But he had a fine speaking voice, which
later developed into a mighty organ of which
Iffland said 'the like was never heard on the
German stage'. He made his début in a small
role in *Mithridate* on 15 Jan. 1740, and remained with Schönemann for seventeen years,
deepening and perfecting his art by study and
observation, till from the wooden declamation
and stiff posturings of Caroline Neuber's school
he had evolved a supple and natural style of
acting, which, though already known elsewhere
in Europe, was something new in Germany.
During this time he married a young actress in
the company, the daughter of Frau Spiegelberg-
Denner, and trained her in his own methods.
He was the first professional theorist on German dramatic art—since Gottsched was no
actor—and the first to think of giving young
actors formal training, for which purpose he
founded, in 1753, a short-lived Academy of
Actors for classes in reading and discussion of
plays. As Schönemann became more and more
immersed in horse-dealing, which was his
passion, he left the running of the company to
Ekhof, who was unable to stave off disaster.
He left, but after a short tour with a harlequin
company, which was not at all suitable for him,
returned to take over the remnants of the old
company. He had no taste or talent for business management, and soon called in the actor-
manager Koch to take control. They spent six
years together, but there was continual friction,
and in 1764 Ekhof left to join the Ackermann
company. He was now at the height of his
powers, with a flexible voice, expressive gesture,
and a fully controlled technique. He was a
great asset to Ackermann, who had just taken
over the newly opened National Theatre—
Germany's first—at Hamburg, and he remained
with them five years, leaving only because he
could not stomach the rudeness and bad manners
of the youthful and arrogant Schröder. He
spent several miserable years touring in the
company of Abel Seyler, husband of the redoubtable Sophie Hensel, who tormented him
with her professional jealousy, until he found
a permanent home at the Court theatre of
Weimar. Here he pursued a cautious but
acceptable policy, gaining the affection and

esteem of his audience, until a disastrous fire at Weimar caused a removal to Gotha. There, as chief actor and stage director, he spent his last happy and honoured years, dying in 1778, the year after he had taken Iffland into the company. Just before his death he went to Weimar to appear in private Court theatricals with Goethe, when he probably imparted to him some of the reminiscences which were incorporated in *Wilhelm Meister*, and he made his last appearance on the stage at Gotha as the Ghost in *Hamlet*, in an adaptation made by his old enemy, Schröder, now the uncontested head of his profession. To Schröder Ekhof also entrusted the organization of an Actors' Benevolent Fund which he had been instrumental in starting.

Ekhof excelled in the mingled tragi-comic and pathetic roles, the rough but good-natured, crusty but noble, characters which the new drama had brought in its train. His best parts were Old Barnwell in Lillo's *London Merchant*, the father in Diderot's *Père de famille*, and Odoardo in *Emilia Galotti*. In spite of his physical shortcomings he was also outstanding in tragedy, as Schröder found when, expecting some travesty of the part, he first saw Ekhof play Oedipus. In comedy Ekhof was subtle and discreet, and his portrayal of north-German peasants was good enough to wring a tribute from one of them. In his early days he was adequate in juvenile leads, but unfortunately continued to play them until late in life, which called forth some caustic remarks from contemporary critics. This, however, was a minor blemish in a man who commanded the respect and affection of audiences all over Germany, and lived to see his fellow actors, in great part through his own exertions, raised from the misery of strolling players to the dignity of an assured profession under noble patronage.

ELECTOR PALATINE'S MEN, see ADMIRAL'S MEN.

ELECTRIC LIGHTING, see LIGHTING, 1 *d*, 2, and 3.

ELEN, GUS [really ERNEST AUGUSTUS] (1862–1940), a music-hall performer who first appeared in the old taverns of the 1880s. He became famous as the singer of London cockney ditties, especially 'Never Introduce yer Donah to a Pal' and 'You Could Almost Shut yer Eyes and 'ear 'em Grow'. His presentations of Cockney character were true to life, whereas those of Chevalier had been idealized. Elen's songs were the true songs of London, and his characters had a Dickensian touch. ''E Dunno Where 'E Are', 'Down the Road', 'If It Wasn't For the 'Ouses in Between', and 'Wait Till the Work Comes Round' are music-hall classics. Elen retired a successful man, but came back to the Palladium to a Command Performance in 1935 to show a delighted audience that he was as good as ever.

W. M. P.

ELEPHANT AND CASTLE THEATRE, LONDON, at the northern end of the New Kent Road. This was built in 1872, and staged 'transpontine melodrama', with pantomime at Christmas. It is said to stand on the site of the old theatre at Newington Butts, of which little is known. The Elephant and Castle closed in 1900, but was reconstructed and opened again in Aug. 1902. It became a cinema in 1928.

ELIOT, THOMAS STEARNS (1888–), English poet (of American birth), author of plays in verse of which *Murder in the Cathedral*, dealing with the murder of Thomas à Becket, was written for production in the Chapter House of Canterbury Cathedral in 1935. It achieved an immense success in the commercial theatre, being several times revived with Robert Speaight in his original role of Becket. Eliot's second play, *The Family Reunion* (1939), though it contained some fine poetry, was less successful, possibly because of the modern setting. He was, nevertheless, responsible for a widespread interest in the possibilities of modern poetic drama, and in 1948 was awarded the O.M. for his services to literature. In 1949 a new verse-play with a modern setting, *The Cocktail Party*, was given at the Edinburgh Festival and subsequently transferred to New York and London.

ELIZABETHAN PLAYHOUSE. Before English actors had any settled homes they played chiefly in inn-yards (see INNS USED AS THEATRES), and their first permanent buildings bore the unmistakable impress of inn-yard architecture. They were wooden structures, roughly circular, with a raised platform stage backing on to the wall and jutting out into the open space, still called a 'yard'. Round the walls rose two, or usually three, galleries, reminiscent of the balconies and chamber-windows of the inn. The first of these probably continued behind the stage, and so formed an inner room below, which could be used for intimate interior scenes, as in *The Tempest*, and an upper room which might house the musicians, or serve as a stretch of battlements or an upper-storey window. Behind this was the tiring-house, or actors' dressing-room. Beneath the back of the stage, hidden from view by boarding, was a cellar-space, used for storage, or for lurking apparitions who were due to arrive on the stage via the traps which were in constant use in the Elizabethan theatre, and were probably used in the temporary erections put up before the building of playhouses—of which the first, the Theatre, dates from 1576. The platform stage itself was partly railed off, and privileged spectators could buy seats on it, an inconvenience which lasted in the English theatre until the days of Garrick. On three sides of the platform stood the 'groundlings', in close proximity to the actors, while the galleries were filled with those who, on payment of a fee over and above their original entrance fee, which admitted to the 'yard' only, lounged or sat about on rough benches and stools. In all parts of the house people amused themselves by cracking and eating nuts, and munching apples and pears, often throwing the cores at any actor who displeased them.

Performances were given during the afternoon, beginning at 2 p.m., and though at first they were countenanced on Sundays, much to the disgust of the already vociferous Puritan element, this was later discontinued, and they were limited to week-days. The audience was summoned by a trumpet blown from the highest point of the building, above the stage, and during the performance a flag was flown there. Scenery on the stage was kept to the barest minimum—a throne, a bench, a tree, a tent—except in the inner stage, where a previously arranged scene might be disclosed by the drawing of a curtain; but costumes, many of which came to the players from their courtly patrons, might be gorgeous, though often inappropriate, since contemporary dress was used for any place or period. There were, however, some conventional touches which served to distinguish foreigners, as a breastplate for a Roman or a turban for a Turk, and the even tenor of the plot was often interrupted by music, processions, and bouts of most realistic fencing or fisticuffs.

The foregoing applies in general to the public theatres (for which see the CURTAIN, FORTUNE, GLOBE, HOPE, NEWINGTON BUTTS, RED BULL, ROSE, SWAN, and THEATRE) where such actors as Burbage and Alleyn, Kempe and Tarleton, interpreted the works of Shakespeare and his contemporaries; but mention must also be made of the 'private' theatres—Blackfriars, the Cockpit, Whitefriars—which differed from the public ones in being roofed buildings, probably rectangular in shape, with all the spectators seated, and in charging higher prices. Indeed, it is probable that admission to the 'private' theatres could only be obtained by paying for one's seat beforehand, and not at the door, as elsewhere. These indoor theatres were first used by the Boy Companies who caused the adult players so much uneasiness, but were later used by the men, particularly during bad weather when the unroofed 'public' theatres became uninhabitable. Scenery was more extensively used in the private theatres, under the influence of the Court masque, than in the public playhouses, and it was from them that the Restoration theatre developed after the closing of the playhouses from 1642–60 (for their later history see ENGLISH PLAYHOUSE).

The financial affairs of the Elizabethan stage were so involved that it is impossible to give details here; but each company, which took its name from the great lord under whose protection it existed (as the Earl of Pembroke's, the Earl of Leicester's, Lord Strange's, the Lord Admiral's, the Lord Chamberlain's), was an association of partners, or 'sharers', who acted together, and had a joint stock of plays and clothes. One man might be appointed to act as manager for the rest, but all received a share in the profits, though some might be full sharers, others only half- or quarter-sharers.

The owner of the playhouse was allotted part of the entrance-money, usually the takings in some particular part of the house, and for this purpose he appointed 'gatherers', or money-takers, to collect up his due portion. Certain actors might also have a share in this entrance-money, and they were then known as 'house-keepers'. This at any rate was the method used by the Burbages and their chief rivals. A different system was in force at the Rose, where Henslowe was virtually an 'outside capitalist', since he paid all the bills on behalf of the actors and frequently made loans to them and to their playwrights, reimbursing himself from the takings in all parts of the house.

Not all actors were necessarily 'sharers', since the boys, who in the absence of actresses played the women's parts, were usually apprenticed to the older men, while extra actors could be hired by the sharers; and it was possible for a man to be a 'housekeeper' in a playhouse at which he did not necessarily act. Also the shares could be bought and sold, or left as legacies, which enabled Heminge and Condell, for instance, to buy up those Globe shares which were not held by the Burbage family. The housekeepers were responsible for the upkeep of the building, while the sharers met all other incidental expenses, the minor ones of lights and music, and the major charges of playwrights and wardrobe.

ELLIOTT, GEORGE H. (1884–   ), a music-hall comedian, known as the Chocolate-Coloured Coon. A fine singer and dancer, and an excellent pantomime performer, he was the successor of Eugene Stratton. One of his best-known songs was 'I Used to Sigh for the Silvery Moon'.

ELLIOTT. (1) MAXINE (1871–1940), an American actress, and a woman of great personal charm and beauty. Born in Rockland, Maine, the daughter of a sea-captain, her real name was Jessie Dermot. She made her début on the stage in *The Middleman*, with E. S. Willard, adopting her stage name at the suggestion of Dion Boucicault. From Willard's company she went to that of Rose Coghlan, playing among other parts Dora in *Diplomacy*. In 1895 she became a member of Augustin Daly's company, appearing in his Shakespearian and other productions, both in London and New York. Some years later she married the comedian, Nat Goodwin, with whom she toured Australia, and appeared with him in a number of plays by Clyde Fitch. It was in the latter's *Her Own Way* that she made her first independent starring venture in 1903, following it by *Her Great Match* (1905). In 1908 she built and managed her own theatre in New York (see MAXINE ELLIOTT THEATRE). A personal friend of Edward VII, she was extremely popular in England, and retired there shortly before the 1914–18 war. During the war years she was active in war-work both in England and Belgium, for which she received official recognition. In 1920, impoverished by her relief work for Belgium, she returned to the films and stage, and was once again one of the best-loved stars of the American theatre. One of her first appearances was with William Faversham in a revival of *Lord and Lady Algy*. She was later able to retire definitely, and spent the rest of her life in England and France. Her sister (2) GERTRUDE (1874–1950) made her first appearance in 1894 in Rose Coghlan's company at Saratoga in *A Woman of No Importance*. She appeared in New York at the Star Theatre in the same year, and was engaged by Nat Goodwin for his company; she appeared at the Duke of York's Theatre in London in 1899, as Midge in *The Cowboy and the Lady*, supporting her sister. In 1900 she was engaged by Forbes-Robertson, with whom she went on tour, marrying him at the end of the year. She appeared subsequently as her husband's leading lady, toured with him in America, Canada, and the English provinces, and was with him during his farewell season at Drury Lane in 1913. After her husband's death she appeared in London under her own management, and undertook extensive tours of South Africa, Australia, and New Zealand. She was not seen in New York after the 1914–18 war until 1936, when she played the Queen in Leslie Howard's production of *Hamlet* at the Imperial Theatre. (For her husband and daughter, see FORBES-ROBERTSON.)

ELLISTON, ROBERT WILLIAM (1774–1831), English actor, who was intended for the Church, but, after a taste of amateur theatricals, left home in 1791 and went to Bath, playing there and on the York circuit. At some point he was reconciled with his family, met Kemble, who encouraged him in his ambitions, and eloped with a teacher of dancing, making his London début in 1796 at the Haymarket under Colman, while still retaining his position as leading man at Bath under Dimond. Dibdin wrote a number of entertainments for him, and he was frequently seen at Drury Lane, being one of the most popular actors of the day. Leigh Hunt placed him second only to Garrick in tragedy, and accounted him one of the best lovers on the stage. He was also good as Doricourt, Charles Surface, Ranger, Hamlet, Romeo, and Hotspur, and one of his greatest parts in later life was Falstaff. He was an eccentric and extravagant man, much given to drink, of whose odd behaviour many entertaining stories are told, and he had a passion for management. After trying unsuccessfully to open a theatre in Oxford, he took over innumerable provincial theatres, and in 1809 became lessee of the Surrey, London. Ten years later he achieved his ambition of managing Drury Lane. He opened with Kean in *King Lear*, put on Byron's *Marino Faliero* (1821) in the face of much opposition, and engaged Clarkson Stanfield and David Roberts, whose work gave the theatre a great reputation for scenery. He also surrounded himself with a fine company, and engaged Kean both before

and after his visit to America. His resources could not, however, stand up to his extravagances and his outside speculations, and in 1826 he went bankrupt. A year later he reinstated himself with the production at the Surrey of *Black-Eyed Susan*, starring T. P. Cooke, an immediate success which netted him a large sum. His last appearance on the stage was made about a fortnight before his death. All contemporary critics were loud in his praise. He had a fine voice, noble face, and gallant bearing, and was unrivalled as gentlemanly rakes and agreeable rattles. A brilliant, fascinating personality, of whom Lamb said: 'Wherever Elliston walked, sat, or stood still, there was the theatre.'

ELSSLER, FANNY (1810–84), famous ballerina of the Romantic period, a more energetic and flamboyant dancer than her contemporary Taglioni. She excelled in character—particularly Spanish—dances.

ELTINGE THEATRE, NEW YORK, on the south side of 42nd Street between Seventh and Eighth Avenues. This was named by Al Woods after his popular female impersonator, Julian Eltinge, and opened on 11 Sept. 1912 with a melodrama, *Within the Law*, sponsored by the American Play Company. It ran for 541 performances, and established Jane Cowl as a star. The theatre housed a number of interesting straight plays, as well as farces, before, in 1930, it became a home of burlesque, notorious for the daring and vulgarity of its strip-tease acts and its dubious jokes. It was closed in 1942 and later became a cinema.   G. F.

ELTON, EDWARD WILLIAM (1794–1843), English actor, whose real name was Elt. His father, a schoolmaster, was interested in acting and staged several productions by his pupils, in some of which young Elt appeared. This gave him a taste for the stage, and in a short time he had changed his name to Elton and joined a company of strolling players. In 1823 he was seen at the Olympic, but it was not until he had been brought back to London from the provinces by Charles Mayne Young that he really established himself. At the Garrick Theatre in Whitechapel under Conquest he played Richard III, and was seen at several minor theatres before in 1837 he made an outstanding success in the name part of *Walter Tyrrell* at Covent Garden. He was the original Beauséant in *The Lady of Lyons* (1838), and from 1841 to 1842 was at Drury Lane under Macready, playing Romeo, Rolla, and Rizzio. He then went to Ireland, and on his way back was drowned in the wreck of the *Pegasus*, leaving seven small children for whom a benefit was later given at the Haymarket. Elton, who was excellent as Edgar in *King Lear*, and in the plays of Sheridan Knowles, also wrote a little and lectured on the theatre.

ELVIN, JOE (1862–1935), the son of an old actor named Matthew Keegan. He specialized in music-hall sketches, some of which, like *'Appy 'Ampstead*, were most spectacular. He was a quaint, eccentric comedian, with a white face and red wig, whose uncouth antics, in his constant stage battles with misfortune, made him extremely popular. He did much for his profession, and was a man of great integrity and goodness of heart. First President of the Variety Artistes' Benevolent Fund, he gave £300 towards the purchase of a home for old music-hall performers at Brinsmead, and was one of the founders of the music-hall institution, the Grand Order of Water Rats. In later years he was himself in need of assistance, and on the fiftieth anniversary of his début a matinée was organized for his benefit which resulted in an annuity of £5 a week.

EMBASSY THEATRE, LONDON, at Hampstead. This opened as a try-out theatre for new plays on 11 Sept. 1928, with *The Yellow Streak*, under the management of Herbert Jay and Sybil Arundale. From 1930–2 Alec. L. Rea ran it as a repertory theatre. It has sent many successful plays to the West End, including *The Dominant Sex* and *Ten Minute Alibi*. It was damaged by enemy action, but has been repaired and reopened, and continued to do good work under Anthony Hawtrey.

W. M. P.

EMERY. (1) JOHN (1777–1822), English actor, son of Mackle Emery (1740–1825), himself a competent player, whose wife took small parts at Covent Garden. Even as a youngster John had a remarkable faculty for portraying old men, and at 15 was considered by Tate Wilkinson to be already an outstanding actor. In 1798 he was engaged for Covent Garden to take the place of the comedian Quick, and played every sort of stage countryman, making good use of his knowledge of the Yorkshire dialect, and of 'the loutish cunning of the three Ridings'. After a short engagement at the Haymarket, he returned to Covent Garden and remained there until his sudden death. Hazlitt said of him: 'In his line of rustic characters he is a perfect actor. His Hodge is an absolute reality . . . his Robert Tyke the sublime of tragedy in low life.' His Caliban was highly praised, and he was good as Sir Toby, the First Gravedigger, and Dogberry. He was also an artist, and between 1801–17 exhibited frequently at the Royal Academy. His son (2) SAMUEL ANDERSON (1817–81) inherited much of his father's talent. After some years in the provinces, he was at the Lyceum with the Keeleys, where he was the first to play Jonas in *Martin Chuzzlewit*, Will Fern in *The Chimes*, and John Peerybingle in *The Cricket on the Hearth*. In 1853 he went to the Olympic, and in the following year became lessee of the Marylebone Theatre, making his last appearance in London in 1878. He was good as Sir Peter Teazle, Robert Macaire, and in many new plays of the period.

His daughter (3) WINIFRED (1862–1924) began her long and distinguished career in 1870

in Liverpool, when she appeared as the child Geraldine in *Green Bushes*. Four years later she was in London in pantomime, at the Princess's, and made her début as an adult actress at the Imperial in 1879. She appeared with Wilson Barrett, Hare, and Irving—with whom she went to America—and in 1888 married Cyril Maude, becoming his leading lady when he went into management at the Haymarket in 1896. A beautiful woman of great charm, Winifred Emery adorned every part she played, and was one of the most versatile and popular actresses of her generation. Among her best parts were Lady Windermere in Wilde's comedy, and Lady Babbie in *The Little Minister* (see also MAUDE, CYRIL).

W. M. P.

EMNEY. (1) FRED (1865–1917), English actor, who, after many years in light opera and musical comedy, toured the music-halls with the famous sketches *A Sister to Assist 'Er* (with Sydney Fairbrother), *Getting Over a Stile*, and the riotous *Plumbers*. He also appeared in many Drury Lane Pantomimes, and was the supreme exponent of the 'Dame'. He died of injuries received on the stage in *Cinderella* when he slipped on the soap-suds in a knock-about comedy scene. His son (2) FRED (1900–   ), starting on the halls with a partner and a piano (he is a fine pianist), made for himself a definite place as a leading comedian on the musical comedy stage and in revue. His heavyweight personality, his imperturbable face and manner, his eyeglass and his eternal cigar, make up an unforgettable character—and his comic powers equal those of his father.   W. M. P.

EMPIRE, LONDON, in Leicester Square, a famous music-hall, originally a theatre. It opened in 1884 with a spectacular production of a comic opera, 'Chilperic'. In 1884 John Hollingshead brought the Gaiety company there in a burlesque entitled *The Forty Thieves*, and in the following year Hayden Coffin and J. L. Shine appeared in a comic opera, 'The Lady of the Locket'. In 1886 a very elaborate version of Jules Verne's *Round the World in Eighty Days* was staged under the direction of Marius, with Charles Cartwright, Colette, and Kate Vaughan; also a spectacle called *The Palace of Pearl*. After that the Empire became a Theatre of Varieties.

It began to stage revue a year or two before the outbreak of war in 1914, and in 1918, under Alfred Butt, it became a theatre again with the production of *The Lilac Domino*. This was a success, as was *Irene*, which followed in 1920. Other successful productions there were *Henry VIII* with Sybil Thorndike as Queen Katharine in 1925, and *Lady Be Good* in 1926. At the end of 1927 the Empire was entirely reconstructed and became a cinema. (See also under MUSIC-HALL.)   W. M. P.

EMPIRE THEATRE, the oldest surviving playhouse in New York. Built for Charles Frohman, it opened on 25 Jan. 1893 with *The*

Girl I Left Behind Me, which ran for 288 performances. This was followed by *Liberty
Hall*, in which Viola Allen, Henry Miller, and
May Robson, names always associated with
this theatre, all appeared. During the next few
years the theatre built up a reputation for
sophisticated comedy, with occasional incursions into sentiment and whimsey. Three
permanent companies shared it, the Empire
stock, the John Drew, and the Maude Adams,
while in the summer the theatre was let to
travelling companies. Few outstanding plays
were presented at the Empire during its first
thirty years, but whatever came was sure of
an adequate run. They were mainly by Henry
Arthur Jones, Haddon Chambers, or Paul M.
Potter. In 1899 Maude Adams appeared as
Juliet to Faversham's Romeo, and in the same
year John Drew scored a great personal
success in *Richard Carvel*. One of the most
popular plays ever seen at the Empire was
When Knighthood was in Flower, with Julia
Marlowe, while 1905 brought Maude Adams
in *Peter Pan*. *Captain Brassbound's Conversion*
was seen in 1907 with Ellen Terry, for whom it
was written, followed by *The Good Hope*, in
which Edith Craig and Beatrice Forbes-Robertson also appeared. Ethel Barrymore was seen
at this theatre in *Mid-Channel* (1910) and
Déclassée (1919). Further interesting productions were *Mary Rose* with Ruth Chatterton,
Blood and Sand with Otis Skinner and his
daughter, and Doris Keane in *The Czarina*.
It was in 1923 that a name frequently associated
with the Empire first appeared on its bills—
Katharine Cornell, who was seen there later in
*The Age of Innocence, The Barretts of Wimpole
Street*, and *Candida*. Judith Anderson in *The
Dove* (1924) and Jane Cowl in *Easy Virtue*
(1925) also made their names at this theatre,
which in 1926 found itself in trouble over *The
Captive*, a translation of Édouard Bourdet's
La Prisonnière. Athough seriously designed
and intended, and graced by a superb performance by Helen Menken, this was considered disturbing in its implications, and was
closed by the authorities. Two important productions of later years were the socially significant *We The People* (1933), with settings by
Aline Bernstein, and a startling revival of
Ghosts, with sets by Stewart Chaney and fine
performances by Nazimova and Harry Ellerbe.
One of the outstanding events in the life of this
theatre was its first *Hamlet*, in 1936, with John
Gielgud, Lillian Gish, Judith Anderson, and
Malcolm Keen. The play was directed by
Guthrie McClintic, and its 132 performances
broke the records set up by Booth and Barrymore. On 8 Nov. 1939 came the first night of
the record-breaking *Life With Father*, which
occupied the theatre for six years. On its
removal to the Bijou, the Empire saw the Lunts
in Rattigan's *O Mistress Mine* (done in London
as *Love in Idleness*).   G. F.

ENCINA, Juan del (1468–c. 1537), known as
the *Patriarca del Teatro español*. With his later
contemporaries Naharro and Vicente, he was

the founder of Spanish drama, which he helped
to secularize. Little is known of his life, though
he was in Italy in the early part of the sixteenth
century, and was at one time a chorister in the
chapel of Pope Leo X. His *églogas*, or pastoral
dialogues between shepherds and shepherdesses, are based on Christmas, Easter, and biblical themes, and, though they contain vivid
scenes of daily life, with characters speaking a
rustic dialect, they were intended for performance at Court and in the private houses of the
nobility, not for the people, who still found their
amusement in the spectacles provided by the
clergy, either in the church or the market-place.
Encina's plays may originally have been given
by talented amateurs of high rank or by their
servants, but they were also the first serious
plays to be acted by the professional actors
of the strolling companies which were by now
beginning to travel the countryside. Apart
from religious dramas, reminiscent of the
medieval Mystery and Morality plays, Encina
also wrote on mythological subjects. One of
these plays, probably the *Égloga de Plácida y
Victoriano*, was given in Italy in 1513 before
a brilliant audience which included the Spanish
ambassador. In all his plays Encina introduced
villancicos or rustic songs, and his work in
general owed much to his musical talent.

ENFANTS SANS SOUCI, see FRANCE, 1.

ENGLAND. 1. Medieval. If English drama,
like that of other European countries, may be
said to have originated in the dramatic presentation of certain elements in the Church service
(see ECCLESIASTICAL DRAMA), it had little freedom for growth in such a soil, and was cultivated only for its usefulness in strengthening
the faith of humble worshippers. The priest,
after all, was bound to handle his material in
much the same spirit as a scholar deals with
his sources; he was not really free to invent, to
draw upon his imagination, or to depart very
far from the words of scripture. The opportunities for acting were limited, and while the
liturgical play remained within the church and
the words spoken were not English but Latin
there was no chance of humanizing the biblical story by means of humour or of idiomatic
and colloquial expression. The real opportunity came when the plays passed out of the
hands of the priests into those of the people.
The change was gradual: from the church to
the churchyard, and later, when the crowds
became too large, to the market-place. Once
in the market-place the plays were no longer
under the direct control of the Church, and the
process of secularization could begin. (The
clergy were forbidden by a papal edict of 1210
to appear on a public stage.) Without losing
their religious significance the plays, in which
the priestly Latin had been replaced by the
vernacular, now began to reflect the purely
secular interests of medieval folk, and were
often vitalized by a broad humour in which it
would have been indecorous for priests to
participate.

In the well-ordered life of the Middle Ages it would have been surprising if the religious plays, after leaving the Church, had not come under the control of some other authority. In fact they were taken over by the Trade Guilds of the various towns all over England, and as far north as Aberdeen in Scotland. They became linked, too, to one particular day in the Church calendar: in 1311 the Council of Vienne had ordained that Corpus Christi Day, on the Thursday after Trinity Sunday, should be strictly observed as a feast day, and it was accordingly with Corpus Christi Day (one of the longest days in the year, when the weather was most likely to be fine) that the religious plays became associated. Starting about sunrise, performances continued till sunset. These plays have been variously referred to in the past as Miracle and Mystery plays; they are best described (a modern scholar has suggested) as 'Bible-histories', since they invariably deal with some part of the Bible story. Plays based on the lives of saints were also written and performed, but they can be left out of account here since no English example has survived. Of Bible-history plays, on the other hand, we possess four collections (or 'cycles'): the York (with 48 pieces), the Chester (25), the Towneley (32), and the Coventry (42). The Towneley plays are so named because the manuscript in which they are preserved was for long in the possession of the Towneley family; the plays themselves probably belong to the Wakefield (Yorks.) cycle. The Coventry plays may be wrongly designated: they appear on linguistic grounds to belong to some town in the north-east Midlands, though a Latin inscription on the fly-leaf assigns them to Coventry.

These guild plays were at their height from about 1300 to 1450. In an important town such as York each of the larger guilds made itself responsible for the performance of one play; the smaller guilds would combine their resources in groups of anything up to half a dozen. The plays were performed on pageants, that is, large timber structures on four wheels that could be drawn through the streets from one place to another, so that spectators gathered at different points in the town had a chance of seeing many different plays during the course of the day. The often-quoted account of Archdeacon Rogers, describing a performance in Chester as late as 1594, will clear up some obscurities:

Every company had his pagiant or parte, which pagiants weare a high scafolde with two rowmes, a higher and a lower, upon four wheeles. In the lower they apparelled themselves, and in the higher rowme they played, being all open on the tope, that all behoulders mighte heare and see them. The places where they played them was in every streete. They begane first at the abay gates, and when the firste pagiante was played it was wheeled to the highe crosse before the mayor, and so to every streete: and so every streete had a pagiant playing before them at one time, till all the pagiantes for the day appointed weare played.

It will be realized that considerable organization was required to get through the day's programme on time. Discipline was maintained by the guilds, and we hear of players being fined for not having memorized their parts satisfactorily. Details from the accounts of expenses incurred show that costume ('God's Coat of white leather'; 'jackets of black buckram with nails and dice upon them for the Tormentors') and stage properties ('The Cross with a Rope to draw it up, and a Curtain hanging before it') formed an important part of the dramatic appeal. Actors were paid, and so too was the author of the 'book'.

The Chester plays dealing with Noah's Flood and the Sacrifice of Isaac are good early examples of the humour and pathos which the medieval playwright had always at his command. The Towneley *Secunda Pastorum*, dealing with the three shepherds at the Nativity, develops into the delightful comedy of Mak the sheep-stealer and his wife. The process of secularization is here almost complete.

2. TUDOR. Side by side with the Bible-history plays there developed another form of religious drama, the Morality play, which appears to date from the late fourteenth century. In this the characters are for the most part personified virtues and vices, such as Ignorance, Humility, Covetousness, Good Deeds, Riot, and so on, and these (sometimes with the aid of Good Angel and Bad Angel) are shown characteristically as contending for the soul of Man (variously referred to as Mankind, Humanum Genus, Everyman). Here, in however wooden a fashion, we have a dramatic action: a struggle between irreconcilable adversaries, a human soul wavering in the balance, a choice to be made between two lines of conduct, a climax to be reached when the decision is at last taken. To the medieval spectator, delighting in allegory and familiar with personification, the Morality play offered an intellectual entertainment to which the twentieth-century reader is probably slow to respond. Some of them, such as the anonymous *Castell of Perseverance* and Skelton's *Magnyfycence* (both of considerable length), are indeed heavy going; but the well-known *Everyman* (an English version of a Dutch original) is far more interesting and moving than any summary of its simple action would be likely to suggest. The fact is that in spite of the personified abstractions the Morality play at its best contains many touches of human nature; the abstractions (as in Bunyan's *The Pilgrim's Progress*) come to life, and we find that we are listening not to Poverty or Sensual Appetite, but to Englishmen of the fifteenth and sixteenth centuries. The deep seriousness of the issue involved, too, can hardly fail to impress anyone whose religious instincts are not atrophied. As we might expect, the vices rather than the virtues provide the most lively examples of character-drawing. In *Hickscorner* (*temp.* Henry VIII) Freewill and Imagination are two rollicking and shameless characters, coarse and vigorous, speaking in the idiom of the early sixteenth century. By 1550 the Morality play had developed so far that we get a play such as *Nice Wanton*

(on the theme of 'Spare the rod and spoil the child'), in which some of the characters are still abstractions and others have become fully individualized.

A very faint line divides the Morality play from the Moral Interlude; and if any distinction may properly be made it is that the Moral Interlude introduces more mirth than the Morality play proper. The *Interlude of Youth* and *Lusty Juventus* may be cited as examples. The latter (*c.* 1550) has a further interest: it was an anti-Catholic play. There are several other extant Morality plays which were written to propagate either Protestant or (as in *Respublica*, 1553) Catholic views.

If the distinction between Morality plays and Moral Interludes is almost imperceptible, that between Morality plays and Interludes is easier to define. The precise significance of the term 'interlude' has long been in dispute; it may indicate, as the word suggests, a play given in the pauses between other entertainments during a banquet. At all events a distinct genre of dramatic entertainment was produced in the late fifteenth and early sixteenth centuries to which the term is usually applied: this was a development of the Morality play in which the matter treated is of intellectual rather than moral interest, and so reflects the new stirring of thought among the English humanists of the Renaissance. Several writers of these Interludes are known to us. John Rastell, who had a little theatre built in the grounds of his house and possessed a stock of players' costumes, wrote an Interlude called *The Four Elements*, in which he sought to impart both learning and entertainment in dramatic form. John Redford's *Wit and Science* follows the same lines. The liveliest writer of Interludes was undoubtedly John Heywood (?–1580). His best-known work, *The Four PP.*, a dialogue between a Palmer, Pardoner, Poticary, and Pedlar, turning on the question of which can tell the greatest lie, and his *Play of the Wether* (in which various people with contending interests pray to Jove for the weather they would like) are designed more for pure entertainment than instruction. Heywood's Interludes have few purely dramatic qualities, but they do at least progress to a climax or conclusion, and the dialogue is animated and natural. Rather earlier than any of these last-mentioned writers is Henry Medwall, whose *Fulgens and Lucrece* (*c.* 1500) came to light in 1919 in a London sale-room. This odd and for its time remarkable play has been dated by its editors 1497; it is an example of the purely secular drama at a date considerably earlier than anything hitherto known. For this Interlude, performed in two parts as an entertainment at a banquet, Medwall dramatized the story of Lucretia, a Roman lady, who was wooed by two very different suitors, an idle patrician and a virtuous young man of humble birth. To this story he added a comic sub-plot, involving two servants and Lucretia's maid. Medwall's play, in fact, foreshadows that mixture of a serious with a comic

plot which was to be a feature of Elizabethan romantic comedy.

From what has been said it will be seen that the Interludes were written for a more educated audience than the plays performed by the Trade Guilds. Heywood's little plays were all written for performance at Court. The Morality plays, too, were probably acted for the most part in the halls or gardens of noblemen's houses, though there is evidence that they were also performed by professional actors in country towns. By the early years of the sixteenth century there were a considerable number of companies of players in the service of the Court or of the great noblemen: in the account books of Thomas Cromwell (*c.* 1530) we read of the King's players, the Queen's, the Lord Chamberlain's, the Marquis of Exeter's, the Lord Cobham's, and several others. A generation earlier Cardinal Morton had his company of players, and we learn that young Thomas More would sometimes 'slip in among the players' and 'make a part of his own' *ex tempore*. Under the Tudors, bands of actors who were not the servants of some nobleman were looked upon as 'rogues and vagabonds', and subject to severe penalties when found performing plays. These restrictions were still in force in Shakespeare's time; the company of which he was a member came under the protection of the Lord Chamberlain in 1594, and in 1603 was reconstituted as the King's Men.

3. ELIZABETHAN. The development of the drama in the early years of Queen Elizabeth's reign has to be pieced together from such imperfect evidence as still remains. Not many plays found their way into print, and of those that did by no means all have survived. The influence of classical comedy had begun to appear in Nicholas Udall's *Ralph Roister Doister*. Written about 1550, this was in all probability intended for performance by schoolboys. So, too, was *Jacke Jugeler*, described on the title-page as 'A new Enterlude for Chyldren to playe', and derived from the first scene of Plautus's *Amphitruo*. The classical influence appears at second hand in Gascoigne's *Supposes*, acted at Gray's Inn in 1566; this play was based on Ariosto's *I Suppositi*, which in turn was derived from the *Captivi* of Plautus. *Gammer Gurton's Needle* (*c.* 1560) is an entirely English farce, though the author (his identity is uncertain) has learnt something of plot construction from classical comedy. Writers of academic tragedy were also turning to classical models, though not to the tragedy of ancient Greece, at this time almost unknown in England, but to the Latin tragedies (written to be read or recited rather than acted) of Seneca. In *Gorboduc*, first acted in 1562 in the presence of Queen Elizabeth by members of the Inner Temple, Thomas Norton and Thomas Sackville produced what is by common consent the first English tragedy; a five-act drama in blank verse, it has many features of the Senecan play. These 'classical' plays, it will be noticed, were for the most part performed in the Inns

of Court before an audience of lawyers and
their friends, or in schools and universities;
in no sense were they popular. For popular
drama we must go rather to such tragi-
comedies as the *Cambyses* (c. 1570) of Thomas
Preston. This 'lamentable tragedie, mixed
full of plesant mirth' is the sort of play that the
classically-minded Sidney objected to in his
Defence of Poesie; it was 'neither right tragedy,
nor right comedy, mingling kings and clowns'.
Equally objectionable in Sidney's eyes was
another popular type of play, the chronicle
history. As early as 1538 John Bale had written
Kynge Johan, a kind of cross between the
Morality and the history play; and in the second
half of the sixteenth century many more plays
loosely dramatizing the reigns of English kings
were written and produced. Shakespeare's
Histories, while still dramatizing a series of
historical events which may stretch over a
number of years, are much more artistically
constructed; the events are knit together into a
genuine plot, and though the hero is still apt
to tower in importance above the other characters he is not (as in the old chronicle histories)
the sole means of giving the play unity.

The sudden leap forward which English
drama made in the last two decades of the
sixteenth century is phenomenal; perhaps the
nearest parallel to it is the advance made by
the cinema between 1910 and 1930. Right up
to the time of Marlowe and Kyd the English
drama, for all its earnestness and animal
vigour, had shown little sign of growing up;
there is much that is not fully adult about such
a play as *Cambyses*, much that is naïve, and
home-made, and hopelessly awkward. The
crudeness is partly due to the metrical form
('the jigging vein of rhyming mother-wits'),
which in itself makes any real dignity of expression almost impossible, but partly also to
the jerkiness of the dramatic movement,
the spineless plot, and the rapid and haphazard
alternation between tragedy (or, more precisely,
bloodshed) and farcical comedy. Of *Gorboduc*,
it is true, such complaints cannot be made. But
though *Gorboduc* is indeed adult, we may perhaps be excused for feeling that it was born old.
There is dignity in its stiff, unyielding blank
verse, in its grave, sententious speeches, in its
coherent plot; but it is the dignity of a marble
monument. The characters are wholly without
interest, and the dialogue has not the accent of
living speech.

It was, however, from those two oddly
assorted parents—the crude popular tragedy
like *Cambyses*, and the academic tragedy like
Gorboduc—that the tragedy of Christopher
Marlowe (1564–93) sprang. It might be
enough to account for the great gap that lies
between *Tamburlaine* and those earlier plays
by saying that Marlowe was a great poet
and dramatist, while his predecessors were
only well-meaning purveyors of entertainment.
But though this is true enough, it is not quite
the whole truth. The great advance made
by Marlowe had been rendered easier by
what is certainly not a comparable, yet none

the less a real, advance in the physical conditions under which plays were performed. The
first regular London playhouse, the Theatre,
had been built by James Burbage in 1576. It
was erected in Shoreditch, outside the jurisdiction of the City magistrates; and it was
in this neighbourhood or on the Bankside,
south of the Thames, that the sixteenth-
century London theatres were built. For
various reasons, but chiefly because they
regarded them as detrimental to public morality, the civic authorities, among whom the
Puritan element was strongly represented,
were hostile to the theatres. By 1587—the
year in which *Tamburlaine* was first performed
—two other houses, the Curtain and the Rose,
had been built, and by 1600 their number had
been increased by the Swan, the Globe, and
the Fortune. All of these theatres were open
to the air, and therefore unlighted and un-
heated. Up to this time the players had been
forced to play wherever they could find a
pitch, most commonly in the yards of inns.
Among London inns the Red Lion in Stepney,
the Bell and the Cross Keys, both in Gracechurch Street, the Bull in Bishopsgate Street,
and the Bel Savage on Ludgate Hill were all
being used for the performance of plays before
Burbage built his theatre. An inn-yard, after
all, is a kind of natural theatre, enclosed on all
sides and therefore reasonably quiet, with
room for a platform or 'scaffold' round which
the spectators could group themselves, and
with more comfortable accommodation for the
better-class auditors at windows and balconies
overlooking the courtyard. If any plays came
to Stratford when Shakespeare was a boy it
was probably in such surroundings that he
saw them acted. Those surroundings were
good enough in their way, but they were undeniably crude. No doubt great drama does
not depend on the existence of luxuriously
equipped theatres, but to put the issue so is
beside the point. There was no question of
luxury here; the English drama was contending
with primitive staging and makeshift accommodation which almost necessarily retarded
its growth and kept it on an amateur footing.
Now at last buildings specially adapted for the
performance of plays were being erected,
though with their platform stage and seating
arrangements they reproduced the main
features of the inn-yard. A regular play-going
public was already in being and steadily
increasing in numbers, a public that no longer
looked on a play as a rare event but that could,
and did, attend the theatre frequently. With
the growth of this public (at once metropolitan
and sophisticated) the dramatist had not
merely a less casual audience; he had one that
was more experienced and more critical, for
whose entertainment it was worth exerting
himself seriously, and who could respond by
appreciating his fine things. Marlowe and
Kyd certainly gave much to the English theatre,
but the influence was reciprocal: a new
audience (which could hardly be said to exist
in the 1560s) called forth their powers and

encouraged them to do still better. Almost certainly, too, this audience exercised a similar influence on the acting and producing of plays; it expected more, and got it.

Tamburlaine is a real landmark. With the sound of Marlowe's blank verse in their ears— that 'great and thundering speech'—the Elizabethans could never again be content with the homelier rhythms of the earlier drama. There was, too, a grandeur in Marlowe's Scythian warrior, a feeling of inevitability in his triumphant progress, a sense of vastness in the events and their setting, that gave the English drama a new importance. No less significant than the confidence of Tamburlaine is the confidence of Marlowe himself: the fumbling and uncertain workmanship that gave the older drama the atmosphere of amateur theatricals has almost entirely disappeared; the professional writer has arrived, perfectly sure of himself, and making the effects that he intended to make. In *Dr. Faustus* (1588) Marlowe found an even finer tragic theme; and in *Edward II* (1592) he revealed a hitherto unsuspected interest in character, and also showed his ability to handle a more intricate plot.

Thomas Kyd (1558–94) was not, like Marlowe, a thinker, but he was a born playwright. In *The Spanish Tragedy* (*c.* 1589) he adopted and popularized some of the main features of the Senecan play, and with this full-blooded drama, with its revenge motive, its ghost, its murders, and its madness, he not only delighted the Elizabethans but gave to later dramatists a successful prototype for the Revenge play.

What Marlowe did for tragedy, John Lyly (*c.* 1554–1606) did in some degree for comedy. For doggerel verse he substituted a delicate and sensitive prose, and for rollicking humour a refined wit and fantasy. His plays, which were performed by the Children of the Chapel Royal and the Children of Paul's between 1584 and 1595, are a unique blending of the classical and the Elizabethan, the fantastic and the real; we get the impression that we are listening to an echo coming back from life rather than looking on at life itself. Lyly's world is oddly Arcadian; his characters have almost the remoteness of fairies, whose movements may delight us but whose concerns do not touch us. He left no direct descendants; but he taught his successors the value for comedy of wit and repartee, and of disguise and mistaken identity for complicating a plot. Above all, he refined comedy, and showed the possibility of combining humour with sentiment, the witty with the romantic. In *The Old Wives' Tale* (*c.* 1590) of George Peele (*c.* 1558–*c.* 1597) we meet again with fantasy and humour, and something of the same effect reappears later in the *Old Fortunatus* of Thomas Dekker (*c.* 1572–*c.* 1632). In *Friar Bacon and Friar Bungay* (*c.* 1589) by Robert Greene (*c.* 1560–92) we have a prototype of that romantic comedy which Shakespeare was to make peculiarly his own. In Greene's play an upper-class world of refinement and a lower-class world of comedy

alternate and occasionally mingle, the scene shifting between Court and countryside. Into this fabric Greene also weaves magic, poetry, and a romantic love story.

When, therefore, William Shakespeare (1564–1616) began writing for the stage about 1590, he found several types of drama already firmly established. In *Titus Andronicus* (*c.* 1594) he offered his own version (still crude) of the Revenge play, and recurred in his maturity to this genre in *Hamlet* (1601). The influence of Marlowe can be seen in *Richard III* (*c.* 1593), whose hero is a superman of the Machiavellian kind, and in *Richard II* (*c.* 1595), which has some resemblance to *Edward II*. Lyly's influence can be traced in Shakespeare's nimble-witted young women, often wandering about disguised as boys, and in his fondness for word-play. Shakespeare's history plays, as we have seen, are a development of the old rambling chronicle history. Indeed, his vast contribution to English drama was made rather by example than by technical innovation. Time after time he showed what might be done with a form of drama which had hitherto yielded only moderate results. Towards the end of his career, in the group of plays which closed with *The Tempest* (1611), he was experimenting with a new kind of tragicomedy in which the clouds of grief and misfortune which have gathered about the heads of an erring generation are dispersed by the mutual love and reconciliation of the next. This, then, may be Shakespeare's own special contribution to the dramatic 'kinds'; though even here we cannot be certain that he was not at his old practice of doing better what had already been attempted by others.

The theatre for which Shakespeare wrote was in the fullest sense a place of popular resort. The audience at the Globe about 1600 was a representative cross-section of the London population, with no important absentees except the growing body of Puritans, whose hostility to the theatres was made abundantly clear in sermons and pamphlets. No doubt, therefore, Shakespeare's audiences were a very mixed lot; but it is a common mistake to rate their intelligence too low, and to think too exclusively of the 'groundlings', whistling, cracking nuts, shouting, and caring only for blustering rhetoric and bawdy jokes. Recent research has tended to suggest that the Elizabethan playgoer was a trained listener, that a considerable part of the audience consisted of people of some education, and that if it was predominantly male there was nevertheless a considerable sprinkling of respectable women present, citizens' wives and the like. There is surprisingly little on record to suggest riots or disturbances of any kind at the Elizabethan theatre; indeed there is good evidence that the audience were normally attentive and well behaved, and in many ways more civilized than English audiences in the eighteenth and nineteenth centuries. The fact that plays were generally performed in the afternoon (and therefore in broad daylight) may have had something to do with this good behaviour; the play had not yet become the prelude to a night's debauchery. Prices, too, though relatively 'popular', were not particularly low when related to the average wages of the period, and no reasonable man will refuse to listen to a play that he has paid good money to hear, or permit his neighbours to ruin it by their interruptions.

For this mixed audience the Elizabethan dramatist had to cater as best he could, and the varied appeal of Elizabethan tragedy and comedy reflects the composition of the audience at the Globe and the Swan. Romance, realism, intellectual comedy, rough humour, bawdry, satire, horror, pathos, ghosts and fairies, kings and clowns, poetry, patriotic sentiment, social and political problems, fantasy, history, murder, love, brawling, melancholy gentlemen and plain country wenches—all this and much more we meet in the drama of the period; in the same play curiously mixed (and, to all but the Elizabethan, incompatible) effects are constantly to be found. Clearly the Elizabethans retained some of that medieval facility for passing easily from one emotional state to another; they loved variety, they were not interested in decorum, or unity of action, or any of those classical restraints and decencies that a Sidney or a Jonson thought so important. They wanted plenty of action, too, but they also enjoyed rhetoric, and they could stand a good deal of poetry. Sometimes they got a play like *Othello*, in which the action moved steadily and consistently to a tragic climax; but next week they might get a play like *Antony and Cleopatra*, in which the interest was split up between world history and the passion of a man and a woman, in which Lepidus got drunk, and Cleopatra's ladies talked bawdry with a eunuch, Antony died upon his sword, and Cleopatra put the asp to her bosom. If one thinks only of the infinite variety of Cleopatra —passionate, witty, dreaming romantically of the absent Antony, striking the messenger, rising at last to tragic grandeur, 'everything by starts and nothing long'—one has the very soul of the Elizabethan drama. It was a drama vibrating with action and passion, racing along in witty badinage or dawdling delightfully in scenes of slow and almost bovine humour: a brief abstract of life, heightened for the purposes of an afternoon's entertainment, and so (like life) very rarely all tragedy or all comedy, but a blending of both.

If Shakespeare may be said to have gone with the tide, Ben Jonson (1572–1637) spent much of his energy in swimming against it. In an age which cared little for dramatic rules and found it so easy to reconcile opposites, Jonson is rather a lonely figure. It was his aim in comedy to 'sport with human follies, not with crimes', but to sport with them in such a way as to render them contemptible. He set himself, therefore, to write a realistic comedy (with 'deeds and language such as men do use') in which he could expose and correct the follies of the day. In *The Alchemist* (1610), for instance, he lays bare greed and credulity in different walks of life: these are the particular 'humours' in this comedy on which he has chosen to concentrate his satire, and he shows their results in a series of highly effective scenes which culminate in the wholesale exposure of the last act. For all his realism Jonson has also a strain of fantasy and extravagance which occasionally lands him in absurdity; but his ingenious plotting, his clear characterization, and his conscientious craftsmanship are in striking contrast with the 'sluttish incoherence' of some of his less painstaking contemporaries.

By the end of the first decade of the new century certain changes began to make themselves felt. While Shakespeare's company still played at the Globe, they had also come into possession of another theatre at Blackfriars, considerably nearer to the Court. At the Blackfriars, which was roofed in, prices were higher; the atmosphere, too, was more intimate, and a quieter type of acting was possible. In time the roofed-in theatres (known to the Elizabethans as 'private' theatres) ousted the open-air or 'public' theatres altogether, and the decline of the latter coincides with a gradual change in the composition of the audience. In the Jacobean and Caroline period it becomes less representative of the middle classes, and the drama begins to reflect increasingly the tastes of the more sophisticated upper class. It was for this audience that Francis Beaumont (1584–1616) and John Fletcher (1579–1625) wrote *The Knight of the Burning Pestle* (1607), in which the citizen and his wife come in for good-humoured ridicule. For this audience, too, were written their tragicomedies, and John Ford's (1586–1639) *'Tis Pity She's a Whore* (c. 1627), which turns on the incestuous love of a brother and sister, and James Shirley's (1596–1666) fashionable comedies of wit and intrigue. An air of gallantry begins to creep into the drama which was wholly absent from the plays of Shakespeare and Jonson; the honest bawdiness of the Elizabethans is transformed into a more furtive indecency; the high argument and the ruthless facing of facts of Elizabethan tragedy—still to be met with in the work of Marston, Webster, Tourneur, and the early Middleton—give place to a shirking of tragic issues, or an excess of pathos, or the exploitation of unnatural vice. The dish has now to be more highly seasoned. In the work of Beaumont and Fletcher or of Philip Massinger (1583–1640) there is much ingenuity of construction and plenty of entertainment, but there is a new willingness to subordinate everything to excitement. Effects become theatrical rather than dramatic; character is sacrificed to plot, and plot is anything the dramatists care to make it. One ceases to anticipate the behaviour of characters when the only certainty is that they will do something unexpected. A typical example of the new drama is Beaumont and Fletcher's *Philaster* (c. 1610), in which the hero rushes impetuously from one unpremeditated action to another, until in the end we care very little what happens to him. In Massinger's *Duke of Milan* (*c.* 1620) there is more consistency of character and a more natural development of the action; yet here too the chief character seems to be an entirely different person in the second part of the play from what he was in the first.

The contemporaries of Shakespeare and Jonson—Chapman, Marston, Dekker, Massinger, Middleton, Webster, Tourneur, Heywood, Ford, Shirley, and the rest—are dealt with separately. Here it is sufficient to indicate some of the main types of drama which the age evolved. The Revenge play enjoyed a new lease of popularity in the early seventeenth century; the action was often set in Italy, which to the Elizabethans was the proper milieu for poisonings and stabbings and deeds of horror of all kinds. Among the finest plays of the period which turn on revenge or bloody deeds leading to retribution, are Chapman's *Revenge of Bussy D'Ambois* (*c.* 1610), Webster's *The White Devil* (*c.* 1612) and *The Duchess of Malfi* (1614), and Middleton's *The Changeling* (1622). Elizabethan and Jacobean tragedy concerned itself usually with the misfortunes of the great, but a minor genre in this period was Domestic Tragedy, as seen in *Arden of Feversham* (*c.* 1591) and Heywood's *A Woman Killed with Kindness* (1603). Tragi-comedy has already been noted as a form increasingly popular in the Jacobean period. The History play lost some of its popularity as the years passed; Ford's *Perkin Warbeck* (*c.* 1630) is an interesting late example. Romantic comedy continues with some modifications (e.g. with a strong infusion of middle-class manners in *The Shoemaker's Holiday* of Dekker) throughout the period, but some of the best comedy written by Jacobean dramatists comes nearer to the Jonsonian satirical kind, as Chapman's *All Fools* (*c.* 1604), Massinger's *A New Way to Pay Old Debts* (1625), and Middleton's *A Trick to Catch the Old One* (*c.* 1605). Some of the plays of Beaumont and Fletcher also belong to this kind, while others again are closer to the upper-class comedy of intrigue which Shirley was writing in the 1630s. Among minor genres the Pastoral play is represented by Fletcher's *The Faithful Shepherdess* (1608) and Jonson's *The Sad Shepherd* (*c.* 1637). Many plays, of course, fall outside any category, for the dramatists were fertile in invention and not browbeaten by critical canons. A word may be said, in conclusion, of the masques. These elaborate entertainments, performed at the Court of James I and Charles I by ladies and gentlemen for their own diversion, left their mark on the drama. There is, for instance, a masque in *The Tempest*. Apart from Milton's *Comus* (1634), written for performance at Ludlow Castle to celebrate the inauguration of the Earl of Bridgewater as Lord President of Wales, the highest achievement of the English masque was reached in the collaboration of Ben Jonson and Inigo Jones. The scenes and machines designed by Jones for performances at Court were often elaborate,

and he introduced many innovations which ultimately affected the setting and production of stage plays (see ENGLISH PLAYHOUSE and SCENERY). Here the name of Sir William Davenant should be remembered, for Davenant, who had been associated with the production of masques for the Court of Charles I, was also the first to introduce scenery on the English stage. When the Civil War broke out in 1642 the drama was one of the first casualties. The London theatres, so long frowned upon by the Puritans, were closed by Act of Parliament, and dramatic performances practically ceased in England. Towards the end of the Commonwealth period, however, there was a partial relaxation of the ban, and Davenant, for instance, was permitted in 1656 to stage a musical play, *The Siege of Rhodes*, at Rutland House. (See PURITAN INTERREGNUM.)

4. RESTORATION. With the return of Charles II in 1660 the drama was quickly revived, but with a difference. It was no longer in any important sense a national drama. For the rest of the century the theatrical needs of Londoners were met by two playhouses and two companies of players, and even so the theatres often had difficulty in showing a profit. Less than three months after his return the King had issued patents to Thomas Killigrew (1612–83) and Sir William Davenant (1606–68) enabling them to form two companies of players, and forbidding any other company to act in London. Killigrew was the first in the field: on 8 Nov. his company, the King's Players, opened at Gibbon's Tennis-Court in Clare Market, and in May 1663 he moved to the newly built Theatre Royal in Bridges Street—the site of the present Drury Lane Theatre. Davenant, who had taken the old Salisbury Court Theatre as a temporary house, moved with his actors (the Duke's Players) into his new theatre in Lincoln's Inn Fields in the summer of 1661. The most striking innovation since the closing of the theatres was the introduction of female actors in place of the old boy players; and several of them, such as Nell Gwynn, and, rather later, Mrs. Barry and Mrs. Bracegirdle, became celebrated either for their acting, or for less professional reasons, or for both. How well they must sometimes have acted may be seen from Colley Cibber's description in his *Apology* (1740) of Mrs. Mountfort playing the part of Melantha in Dryden's *Marriage à la Mode*: the whole scene lives before us, as it had lived in Cibber's memory for fifty years. Of the men the finest actor (and one of the great English actors) was Thomas Betterton (? 1635–1710), who also exercised a steadying influence on the theatre. Considerable advances were made at this time in scenic effects and stage machines, and the old Elizabethan platform stage was being gradually modified to a less prominent apron stage, which still jutted out, however, for a good distance beyond the proscenium (see AUDITORIUM, PROSCENIUM, and STAGE).

Among large sections of the community the habit of theatre-going had been lost, and was not in fact to be recovered during the next two centuries. In the Restoration period the theatres became almost exclusively a rendezvous of the fashionable class and their hangers-on, the rakes and bullies, the ladies of pleasure, the young inns-of-court men, and a smattering of the *nouveau riche* class. For this specialized audience a specialized drama was required, and in a year or two the dramatists were meeting the demand. For the first few years the managers had to draw upon the pre-Commonwealth drama for most of their plays, and it is significant that the dramatists who proved most acceptable to this new audience were not Shakespeare and Jonson, but Beaumont and Fletcher and others of their type. 'They understood and imitated the conversation of gentlemen much better', is one of Dryden's explanations (*Essay of Dramatic Poesy*); and no doubt Shakespeare's dialogue had a rather old-fashioned ring in the ears of up-to-date young men in the 1660s, whereas Fletcher and Shirley were nearer to their own time. But there were other, and perhaps deeper, reasons. This new age (much influenced by French standards) found the Elizabethans altogether too poetical; Shakespeare's metaphor was too rich for the modern taste, and the liberties he took with language offended against the new standards of correctness. In Fletcher and Shirley the stream of metaphor is much thinner, and the metaphor itself is often of a conventional kind and therefore much easier to assimilate; intellectually, too, they made smaller demands on an audience anxious only to be easily amused and not made to think.

The most important contribution made by the Restoration theatre to English drama was the comedy of manners; here it found its liveliest and most natural expression. It should not be forgotten, however, that only a small part of this comedy falls within the Restoration period proper; it reached its highest expression in the plays of William Congreve (1670–1729) (written and produced in the reign of William and Mary), and came to an end in the first decade of Queen Anne's reign with the death of George Farquhar (1678–1707). Congreve wrote nothing for the stage after 1700, and John Vanbrugh (1664–1726) nothing after 1706 (though he left an unfinished play which Colley Cibber completed in 1728 as *The Provoked Husband* and produced at Drury Lane with great success, Wilks and Anne Oldfield playing Lord and Lady Townly). This early drying up of their dramatic productivity cannot be dissociated from a change in the tastes of the public, which by 1700 was beginning to be shocked by, or otherwise dissatisfied with, the dry intellectual comedy of Congreve and his predecessors. At its best that comedy had wit and poise, delicacy of phrase, and an engaging impudence; it held the mirror up to one small and incorrigible segment of the London scene. In *Love in a Tub* (1664) and still more in *She Would if She Could* (1668) by George Etherege (1634–91) we meet with early examples of those

gay young men and witty, assured young women who are going to reappear with little variation or distinction of personality in the comedies of the next forty years. Etherege has an air of innocence that disarms criticism; it is all so obviously fun for him that we scarcely consider the moral implications of what is going on. But with *The Country Wife* (1675) and *The Plain Dealer* (1676) of William Wycherley (1640–1716) we do. In his plays cuckolding has become almost the serious business of life; we are in a world of inverted moral values, with the dramatist not quite certain whether to accept or satirize it. Congreve, the most accomplished artist of the group, works the same vein, but with greater detachment. Here again we have the battle of the sexes, the successful management of an intrigue, the ridicule of marriage, the nice discrimination between fools and men of sense—all this reaching its culmination in his last and subtlest play, *The Way of the World* (1700). His aristocratic detachment, his flawless style, and a certain remoteness from reality enable Congreve to skate over the thinnest of ice; this is the intellectual comedy at its best. He is not a satirist, but he is always, however unemphatically, a critic of life. Vanbrugh, a jollier man, is more of a realist; his situations (as in *The Relapse*, 1696; *The Provoked Wife*, 1697) are no more and no less indecent than those of Congreve, but we feel the indecency more because his characters are made of flesh and blood and are not the exquisitely artificial phantoms that Charles Lamb would persuade us *all* the characters in this artificial comedy are. He has, however, genuine humour, and his dialogue is delightfully easy and natural. Farquhar has little of Congreve's deliberate perfection; he is boisterous and high spirited rather than witty or critical. In *The Recruiting Officer* (1706) and *The Beaux' Stratagem* (1707) the intellectual comedy is beginning to dissolve; his young men are still rakes and scamps, but they are not heartless. The change is no doubt mainly due to Farquhar's warm-hearted Irish temperament; but it is probable, too, that the celebrated attack by Jeremy Collier, *A Short View of the Immorality and Profaneness of the English Stage* (1698), was having its effect. At all events, with the turn of the century comedy becomes progressively more decent, if also a good deal less witty.

Of the other types of comedy written in the period just surveyed the most interesting is Shadwell's revival of the comedy of humours. Thomas Shadwell (c. 1642–92), who never tired of announcing himself as a follower of Jonson, has been unduly disparaged ever since Dryden ridiculed him in *Macflecknoe*; but he was a shrewd observer of contemporary life, and his comedies, such as *The Squire of Alsatia* (1688) and *Bury Fair* (1689), have point and sense. The comedy of intrigue (often borrowed from Spanish sources) was the specialty of Mrs. Aphra Behn (1640–89). This comedy of cuckolding and closets, of midnight assignations and panting lovers, becomes excessively tedious; it is rarely leavened with much wit (though it has plenty of impudence), and relies for most of its interest on the comic vicissitudes of the plot. The lower levels of the drama at this period are best forgotten, and indeed are singularly easy to forget. An occasional comedy such as Sir Samuel Tuke's *Adventures of Five Hours* (1663), or Otway's *The Soldier's Fortune* (1680), or Crowne's *Sir Courtly Nice* (1685), stands out from the rest, but only the specialist is likely to interest himself today in the D'Urfeys and Tates who wrote so industriously in the manner of the period.

The late seventeenth century was not a heroic age, and it is not surprising to find that its tragic drama is on the whole inferior to its comedy. The period produced a form peculiar to itself, the rhymed Heroic play, so wittily satirized in Buckingham's *Rehearsal* (1671). The author who had most success with this form of drama was John Dryden (1631–1700), whose *Conquest of Granada* (in two parts, 1671) gave the English stage the celebrated boasting hero, Almanzor. The Heroic play reverberates with rant and hyperbole; it is characterized, too, by the constant juxtaposition of Love and Honour, between which the hero must decide, and by violent action and startling reversals of fortune. Read in a cool hour in the scholar's study, these plays are no doubt sufficiently absurd; but in justice to them we ought to see and, still more, hear them, for their appeal is mainly rhetorical. Besides writing several plays of this type, Dryden turned out several comedies, the worst of which rank about as low as anything written in the period, but one of which, *Marriage à la Mode* (1671), is among the more memorable Restoration plays. In tragedy he had at least two successes, *All for Love* (1677), based on *Antony and Cleopatra*, and *Don Sebastian* (1689). Both these are in blank verse, the fashion for rhymed plays having passed after only a few years. He also wrote a number of operas, the best known of which, 'King Arthur', owes its fame to the composer, Henry Purcell: the libretto is not much above the usual level of such things.

In the general dearth of good tragedy two plays, *The Orphan* (1680) and *Venice Preserved* (1682), by Thomas Otway (1652–85), stand out prominently; they continued to move English audiences well into the nineteenth century. The new note in Otway, pathos, must have been welcome after much heroic bluster. Rant and hyperbole blow as furiously as ever in the plays of Nathaniel Lee (*c.* 1653–92) (*The Rival Queens*, 1677), but Lee keeps a precarious hold on immortality by reason of a daring imagination which flames out fiercely from time to time in an age which was growing more and more rationalistic. Mention may also be made of John Banks (*c.* 1650–1706), whose plays were rather looked down upon by the critics, but who succeeded in *The Earl of Essex* (1681) in writing a tragedy which long held the stage on account of its dramatic rather than literary qualities.

5. EIGHTEENTH CENTURY. Entering the eighteenth century we find that London playgoers are still restricted to their two houses (both rebuilt), the Theatre Royal and the New Theatre in Lincoln's Inn Fields. In 1705 another theatre, built by Vanbrugh, opened in the Haymarket; it was found acoustically unsuitable for plays, however, and became the home of opera. The Covent Garden theatre dates from 1732. It opened under the management of John Rich, famous as the producer of *The Beggar's Opera* (1728), and much satirized in his own day for his highly successful development of pantomime, in which many people saw a serious threat to the regular drama. Rich himself was a popular Harlequin. Equally gloomy misgivings were aroused in many quarters by the growing taste for Italian opera, which became popular in the reign of Queen Anne and was supported by large numbers of the nobility and the people of fashion. According to Addison, 'Arsinoe' (by Motteux, 1705) 'was the first opera that gave us a taste of Italian music.' Handel, who came to London in 1710, was promptly commissioned to write an opera for the Haymarket. The opera which he wrote, 'Rinaldo', had a phenomenal success, and ran from 24 Feb. 1711 to the end of the season in June. Joseph Addison's English opera, 'Rosamund' (1707), was written with the intention of making English lovers of opera take some interest in the words, since to the great majority of the audience Italian was unintelligible. But the public cared only for the music and continued to patronize Italian opera, or sometimes (strangely enough) opera in which the chief parts were sung in Italian and the less important parts were performed by Englishmen in English. Italian singers—Nicolini, Margharita de L'Épine, and (in the next generation) Cuzzoni, Faustina, and Farinelli—made vast sums of money and quarrelled like cats. Not all the singers were foreign: Mrs. Katherine Tofts shared the honours in the first decade of the century with L'Épine. Opera under the management of the Swiss, John James Heidegger, was carried on successfully at the Haymarket in the reigns of the first two Georges; but the prices charged (seats cost as much as a guinea) kept the audience select, and prevented opera from becoming widely popular (see OPERA).

The early part of the century saw another interesting development: the introduction of after-pieces. These were generally short comedies or farces. From the beginning of the century and even earlier the play notices contain references to 'entertainments of singing and dancing' which were often thrown in as an additional attraction to the playgoer. Such supplementary entertainments point to competition for a public which was willing to be easily amused, or which relished some light diversion after sitting through a five-act tragedy. The after-piece may be looked upon as a development from this light diversion. But it must also be related to the contemporary social background: the customary hour for a performance to begin in the theatre was six o'clock—in the first years of the century even five o'clock—and this was altogether too early for the middle classes and for anyone else who had business to do. It had long been the practice to charge a second price at the close of the third act of a five-act play, and at that later hour a number of additional spectators would drop in. The after-piece is therefore to be regarded as a bid to attract the middle-class public to the theatre by providing them with a solid entertainment, and not with a few musical scraps or odds and ends of farce, at an hour at which they could attend. The after-piece was often a five-act comedy cut to the required length, but many short plays were specially written by Garrick, Murphy, Foote, and others.

The eighteenth century's contribution to English drama is various, but if we compare it with that of the previous century it shows a sharp decline. Tragedy in the first decade was represented most favourably by the plays of Nicholas Rowe (1674–1718), who followed as a respectful distance behind Otway. In *The Fair Penitent* (1703) and *Jane Shore* (1714) Rowe concentrated on heroines and was more successful at moving pity than fear. Joseph Addison's (1672–1719) celebrated *Cato* (1713) is a good example of that French neo-classical tragedy which found favour all through the century; the action was slight, the speeches were long, and 'Declamation roar'd while Passion slept'. Edward Young, James Thomson, David Mallet, Aaron Hill, and many other contemporary poets, often with little knowledge of the theatre, contributed their quota to the tragic pool; but most of their plays are now forgotten. Dr. Johnson is not remembered for his *Irene* (1749), but *Irene* for Dr. Johnson, and Home's *Douglas* (1756) is preserved rather by the enthusiasm of the anonymous Scotsman who shouted 'Whaur's your Wully Shakespeare noo?', and by the popularity as a recitation of the passage beginning 'My name is Norval', than by its own vitality. A more interesting development was that of bourgeois tragedy in the plays of George Lillo (1693–1739) (*The London Merchant*, 1731) and in *The Gamester* (1753), by Edward Moore (1712–57). In these there is a good deal of the sentiment noted below in the comedies of Steele, and a strong insistence on the middle-class virtues; but no great dramatist arrived to lift this genre above interesting mediocrity.

In comedy the record is not quite so depressing. At the beginning of the century Mrs. Centlivre (c. 1667–1723) was writing slightly chastened comedies of intrigue such as *The Busybody* (1709) and *A Bold Stroke for a Wife* (1718), and Colley Cibber (1671–1757) was allowing the rake in *Love's Last Shift* (1696) to run the old course for four acts, but pulling him up in the fifth act and dismissing him as a converted character. Societies for the Reformation of Manners, started in the reign of William and Mary, give evidence of a new, if modified, Puritanism, and in the reign of Queen Anne the

moral tone of the drama is distinctly less libertine. Sir Richard Steele (1672–1729), whose *Tatler* and *Spectator* did so much to amend contemporary morals and manners, did not shrink from using comedy for the same ends. His four sentimental comedies, culminating in *The Conscious Lovers* (1722), were all written to render vice contemptible and virtue attractive. They suffer, however, from the faults of the genre: virtue becomes too much a matter of pious sentiments, laughter is drowned in tears of forgiveness or repentance, and while the characters are all breathing good resolutions reality unobtrusively escapes. Yet Steele's comedies are robust when compared with the mawkish plays of Hugh Kelly (1739–77) and Richard Cumberland (1732–1811) in the 1770s. Here eighteenth-century sentimentalism sobs itself out; and the success of *She Stoops to Conquer* (1773) by Oliver Goldsmith (1730–74) is some indication that public taste was willing to react from such sentimental refinements. In his first comedy, *The Good-Natured Man* (1768), Goldsmith had shown rather tentatively the dangers of excessive delicacy, but in his later comedy he ridicules it unsparingly in the person of Tony Lumpkin. In the plays of Richard Brinsley Sheridan (1751–1816) we return to the comedy of manners, with all the traditional wit and perfection of phrase, but with none of the indecency. In characterization and in management of plot and situation Sheridan loses nothing in comparison with Wycherley and Congreve: what he does in *The Rivals* (1775) and *The School for Scandal* (1777) could hardly be done better. *The Suspicious Husband* (1747) of Benjamin Hoadly (1706–57), and *The Jealous Wife* (1761) of George Colman the Elder (1732–94), are favourable examples of the more ordinary run of eighteenth-century comedy.

Among the minor things which this century did well are the burlesque play—Carey's *Chrononhotonthologos* (1734), Fielding's *Tom Thumb* (1730), above all, Sheridan's *Critic* (1779)—and the ballad opera (see OPERA, 7). A word should be said, too, of the continuing popularity of the Prologue and Epilogue throughout the century; they point to an age in which the theatre was still very much a social rendezvous and the audience could still be addressed directly and made pleasantly conscious of itself.

The eighteenth century brought some interesting changes in theatrical representation and acting, some of which must be credited to David Garrick (1717–79). After a long struggle playgoers were finally banished from the stage, where they had sat intermittently from Elizabethan times. Under Garrick's management a new system of lighting the stage from the wings was introduced (see LIGHTING). Actors and actresses were regularly dressed in contemporary costume whatever part they might be playing, but towards the end of the century period costumes had begun to supplant the hooped petticoat for Juliet and the wig and velvet breeches for Romeo. In the early part of the century tragic acting was still declamatory and formal, but under the influence of Garrick (and perhaps of the improved lighting) it became much more naturalistic.

6. NINETEENTH CENTURY. At the beginning of the nineteenth century there were still only the same two theatres (both rebuilt) licensed for the performance of legitimate drama. These were, for economic reasons, so large that a critic of 1840 complained that it was difficult 'to see the countenances of the performers without the aid of a pocket telescope', and hard to hear anything 'except the ranted speeches'. In such conditions intimate or naturalistic acting was almost impossible, and plays with frequent and violent action and comparatively little dialogue—in short, melodrama—flourished in the early decades of the century. The theatres tended, too, to concentrate on spectacular effects; and such attractions as Mount Vesuvius in eruption or the Grand Falls of Tivoli were offered to the gaping spectators. Tragedy and comedy could hardly thrive in this environment; and the dramatist gave place to such journeyman entertainers as Charles Dibdin (1743–1814), J. R. Planché (1764–1841), and Frederick Reynolds (1796–1880), who kept turning out farces, burlesques, operettas, pantomimes, and extravaganzas. Besides the two licensed theatres there were various unlicensed houses in London and the suburbs, and these were permitted to stage musical plays, for musical plays did not infringe the monopoly held since 1660 by Drury Lane and Covent Garden (see ASTLEY'S, OLYMPIC, SADLER'S WELLS, SURREY). More and more, however, those secondary theatres were contriving to circumvent the law by putting on 'straight' plays with a few pieces of incidental music and not less than six songs added, and calling them 'burlettas'. In 1812, for instance, the Surrey Theatre included among its burlettas *Antony and Cleopatra*, *The Beaux' Stratagem*, *A Bold Stroke for a Wife*, *The Merry Wives of Windsor*, *King Lear*, and *Richard III*. Finally, in 1843, as a result of prolonged agitation, came an Act for Regulating the Theatres, and the old cramping monopoly came to an end. If there was little immediate effect on the quality of the plays produced, the lifting of the monopoly undoubtedly contributed to the dramatic revival in the later decades of the nineteenth century (see COPYRIGHT and DRAMATIC CENSORSHIP).

Among the more serious dramatists of the first half of the century were Lord Byron, James Sheridan Knowles, Thomas Noon Talfourd, and Sir Henry Taylor, but they were working in an outworn convention. Yet Sheridan Knowles (1784–1862) and, still more, Bulwer Lytton (1803–73) in *Money* (1840) were feeling their way towards a more naturalistic drama in which real human issues were at least raised. Apart from such plays as were written for performance, there were many others intended to be read rather than acted. Wordsworth, Coleridge, Scott, Shelley, Keats, Landor, and Beddoes all tried their hand at poetic drama, and later in the century Browning, Tennyson, Arnold, Swinburne, and many others, dwindling at last to the once celebrated Stephen Phillips (1864–1913), continued the practice of writing for the Victorians as if they were Elizabethans or ancient Greeks. When such plays had any success on the stage it was due rather to actor and producer than to the dramatist, as when Irving put on Tennyson's *Becket* (1893) and Alexander staged Phillips's *Paolo and Francesca* (1902). Contrary to popular belief, too, people are willing to be bored—for some time, at least—by what they have been led to believe is great drama, and as few people expect to enjoy poetic drama few people can tell if it is good or merely bogus.

In the work of Dion Boucicault (1822–90) there was at least some character study and some technical skill. But more important are Tom Taylor (1817–80) (*The Ticket-of-Leave Man*, 1863) and Thomas William Robertson (1829–71) (*Caste*, 1867), who both deal with life as it was being lived in their own day, and put contemporary characters on the stage involved in contemporary dilemmas. About this time the influence of the French dramatist Sardou was making itself felt in the London theatre; the 'well-made' plays of Sardou and other French playwrights were acted in English versions, and for some time dominated the work of English dramatists. Two of those, Henry Arthur Jones (1851–1929) and Arthur Wing Pinero (1855–1934), were now bringing a good deal of fresh air into the theatre; at least they had opened a window or two, and one could hear the authentic sounds of life coming in from outside. Jones in particular (his work is most unequal) was a serious dramatist, a conscious pioneer, who not only wrote plays that were intended to startle his contemporaries, but followed them up with a considerable amount of dramatic criticism. Jones startled the Victorians in 1884 with *Saints and Sinners*, a play which (in spite of some melodramatic features) introduced them to a naturalism that they had not known in the theatre, though they were perfectly familiar with it in prose fiction. Pinero's *The Second Mrs. Tanqueray* came in 1893 as another delightful shock to them, and it was followed two years later by *The Notorious Mrs. Ebbsmith*. In the work of both Jones and Pinero, however, there is a tendency (as Bernard Shaw pointed out) to run away at the last moment from the issues which they have raised, and the behaviour of their characters is still usually governed by the conventions of the theatre rather than by life itself. They had, in fact, the sort of success that comes to men of talent who walk ahead, but not too far ahead, of their contemporaries. The success of Bernard Shaw (1856–1950), who made a more absolute break with the past, was harder to achieve, but more decisive and valuable when it was finally won.

While Jones and Pinero were sailing rather tentatively down the main stream of the intellectual drama in the 1890s, Oscar Wilde (1854–1900) was writing in quick succession a number of brilliant artificial comedies, of which

The Importance of Being Earnest (1895) is the most likely to survive. Wilde had impudence and gaiety and epigram at his command, and (what seems to come naturally to Irishmen) an ear for the rhythms of speech which enabled him to write the most sparkling dialogue in English drama since Sheridan. Victorian wit found a more typical expression in the comic operas which William Schwenck Gilbert (1836–1911) wrote with Arthur Seymour Sullivan (1842–1900), beginning with *Trial by Jury* in 1875. Beside irradiating the English theatre with his fantastic humour and good-natured satire, Gilbert set new standards of precision for acting and producing.

Something more drastic than this was needed, however, if English drama was to do more than stir in its sleep. The real awakening came when the English public began to grow aware of Ibsen in the 1890s. In 1889 William Archer's translation of *A Doll's House* was produced in London, and *Ghosts* followed in 1891. The critics were aghast and indignant; but their moral indignation was anticipated and turned against them by the brilliant polemics of Bernard Shaw, a man who took the theatre seriously and who was determined to make it once again a place of adult entertainment. In *The Quintessence of Ibsenism* (1891) he stated his case against the frivolous English drama of the day, and commended Ibsen's work to the attention of the English playgoer. From 1895–8, as dramatic critic of the *Saturday Review*, he ridiculed unsparingly the 'well-made' play, the old tradition of melodramatic acting, the taste for spectacular performances of Shakespeare, and much else. In 1892 his first play, *Widowers' Houses*, was produced by J. T. Grein at the Independent Theatre. By collecting and editing his own plays (*Plays: Pleasant and Unpleasant*, 2 vols., 1898; *Three Plays for Puritans*, 1901) Shaw succeeded in reaching a wider public than the few thousand people who had seen them acted; but it was not until the Vedrenne–Barker partnership at the Court Theatre from 1904–7 that—first with *John Bull's Other Island*—he became really popular as a playwright. A series of fine plays from *Man and Superman* (1903) to *St. Joan* (1924) gave him a world reputation.

7. TWENTIETH CENTURY. If Shaw's early plays sometimes owed a good deal to Ibsen, he was never in any strict sense a disciple, and in his later work the influence of Ibsen ceased to count for much. Closer to Ibsen is a group of playwrights who were writing, in the early years of the new century, some fine plays which were neither tragedy nor comedy, and can be best described as *drame*. Harley Granville-Barker (1877–1946) in *Waste* (1906), John Galsworthy (1867–1933) in *The Silver Box* (1909) and *Justice* (1910), Stanley Houghton (1881–1913) in *Hindle Wakes* (1912), St. John Hankin (1869–1909) in *The Return of the Prodigal* (1904), and St. John Ervine (1883–) in *Mixed Marriage* (1911) were dramatizing the conflict of the individual with society, and consciously directing attention to injustices

and maladjustments and preventible evils of many kinds. 'What would *you* do about it?' they seem to ask their audiences; or even, 'What are you going to do about it?'

This new post-Ibsen drama required a new kind of audience. One of the most notable features of the twentieth-century theatre in England has been the deliberate and successful cultivation of a new type of playgoer, chiefly by the creation of repertory and 'intimate' theatres, by the organization of theatre societies and dramatic festivals, and by the training of players in a new technique. In 1891 J. T. Grein founded his Independent Theatre in London; the Abbey Theatre, Dublin, was opened in 1904 for the Irish Players; the Vedrenne–Barker seasons at the Court Theatre awakened many thousands of Londoners to the fact that drama could be at once serious and entertaining; Miss A. E. F. Horniman, whose humane and enlightening influence was felt all over England, opened her repertory theatre in Manchester in 1907; and rather later came the great days of the Old Vic under Miss Lilian Baylis. The repertory movement spread to Norwich, Birmingham, Glasgow, Liverpool, and other large towns, and in the 1930s the annual Malvern Festival was attracting a growing number of visitors. It is difficult to overestimate the importance of those new theatres if we are thinking of the drama they produced, for most of the plays of the early twentieth century that are likely to survive were written for those non-commercial theatres. On the other hand, it is easy to over-estimate the extent to which they have succeeded in leavening the doughy lump of the West End theatre, which in many ways has remained resolutely Edwardian. Even Shaw has not gained more than a precarious foothold in the West End; his plays are more likely to be met with in the outskirts than in the heart of London. (See also REPERTORY THEATRE MOVEMENT.)

Nevertheless, the standard of expectation has risen all round, and intelligence in the English theatre is no longer so suspect as it used to be. An important contribution to the raising of dramatic standards has been made by the growth all over the country of amateur dramatic societies, whose work has been greatly encouraged by the British Drama League (see AMATEUR THEATRE IN GREAT BRITAIN). A further sign that the theatrical needs of English audiences are not completely met by *A Little Bit of Fluff* and *Chu-Chin-Chow* is the very real interest shown in the drama of other countries. French, Spanish, Italian, German, Czech, Russian, Scandinavian, Irish, American, and even Chinese plays have been successfully produced in the English theatre, though often, admittedly, to select audiences, and the technique of foreign dramatists has had some influence on modern English drama. Visiting companies of foreign players, too, have met with considerable support. Finally, the fact that the printed play of the twentieth century usually contains a good deal more commentary and explanatory matter than the bare stage directions which were formerly supplied has made the reading of plays more interesting, and for that and other reasons a larger public is reading plays to-day than read them a hundred, or even fifty, years ago.

For one sort of play, the poetic drama, readers were always to be found. But the twentieth century has seen the return to a poetic drama that has managed to establish itself with some success in the theatre, and which was never intended to interest the reader alone. The reaction against the realistic drama was first seen in the plays of Yeats, Synge, and other Irish dramatists (see IRELAND); and their example was followed (though with widely different results) in such plays as Masefield's *Tragedy of Nan* (1909), Lascelles Abercrombie's *The End of the World* (1914), Gordon Bottomley's *Lear's Wife* (1915), and Drinkwater's *Abraham Lincoln* (1918). Hardy, whose *Dynasts* appeared in print from 1904–8, stands rather apart. This modern poetic drama is sometimes poetical in content but not in form: blank verse, which tended to drive the dramatist back to outworn conventions of thought and expression, is no longer an essential, or even usual, feature of the modern poetic play. In more recent times a number of interesting religious plays have been written by T. S. Eliot, Charles Williams, Dorothy Sayers, Christopher Hassall, and Christopher Fry, some for performance in Canterbury Cathedral. Poetic drama has also taken a very different turn in the political and surrealistic plays of Auden and Isherwood, such as *The Dog beneath the Skin* (1935) and *The Ascent of F.6* (1936). In pure tragedy the modern English theatre has little to boast about.

In comedy the first decade of the new century saw Jones and Pinero continuing to write what was virtually a comedy of manners, and this genre was carried on in the work of such men as Somerset Maugham (1874–   ) and Noel Coward (1899–   ). The whimsical comedies of Sir James Barrie (1860–1937) are difficult to place in any category, and are therefore perhaps in some danger of being underestimated by the historian of the drama.

The English theatre now faces a rapidly changing world in which old ways of thinking are being discarded more rapidly than is usual. It finds itself, too, in growing competition with the cinema, and to some extent with the wireless transmission of plays, whose popularity will no doubt be increased by television (see RADIO DRAMA). Its future must depend upon many factors, social, economic, and spiritual, as well as upon the biological accident that produces great dramatists and actors. If there is no Bernard Shaw writing for the English theatre to-day (except, indeed, Shaw himself) there are several thoughtful dramatists, such as James Bridie, John Van Druten, J. B. Priestley, Emlyn Williams, Terence Rattigan, and Peter Ustinov, who have something to say, and can say it effectively in dramatic form. But just as important as intelligent dramatists are intelligent and thoughtful audiences, and

it argues well for the future of English drama that at the present time there is a playgoing public which is a good deal more serious than any that the twentieth century has hitherto known (see also MELODRAMA, MUSICAL COMEDY, MUSIC-HALL, PANTOMIME, POETIC DRAMA, and REVUE; also English actors and dramatists under their own names). J. R. S.

ENGLISH ARISTOPHANES, THE, see FOOTE, SAMUEL.

ENGLISH COMEDIANS, THE. During the late sixteenth and early seventeenth centuries a number of English actors went abroad, and soon made a name for themselves, especially in Germany, where the so-called *Englische Komödianten* had a great influence on the development of the German theatre, the prose form of their dialogue indicating the break with tradition. The first records of English players abroad is of a company of instrumentalists at the Danish Court in 1579–80, while five years later English actors appeared at Elsinore under Kempe. In the following year they were invited to Dresden, and thereafter they crop up in the archives of many German towns. They probably performed short comic musical sketches or jigs, whose humour was broad enough to be obvious even to a foreign audience, and acrobatic and other feats. Though they played in English, their clown pattered in Low German. The outstanding name in connexion with later English companies is Robert Browne, who made a short visit to Leyden in 1590, and in 1592 took a company on an extended tour, in the course of which he played some of Marlowe's plays, *Gammer Gurton's Needle*, and several biblical plays at Frankfort fair. A company, probably under Sackville, one of Browne's companions, was at Wolfenbüttel, capital of Heinrich Julius of Brunswick, himself author of several plays in which an English influence is apparent, particularly in the character of the Fool, played by Sackville under the name of Jan Bouschet (Posset). Sackville later went into business in Frankfort and prospered exceedingly. Meanwhile Browne continued his tours, and stayed for some time at the Court of Count Moritz of Hesse, another princely enthusiast of the drama, who in 1606 built a private theatre for the amusement of his guests. Browne was succeeded on tour by a company under John Green, and at Cassel by a company under Ralph Reeve. The next notable name to crop up in these records is that of Robert Reynolds, who made a great reputation as a clown under the name of Pickelherring, while John Spencer, known as Stockfisch, with headquarters in Berlin, went as far afield as The Hague and Dresden.

The repertory of all these companies was in the main similar. The titles of many of their plays are known, but as the names of the authors conveyed nothing to the audience they were usually omitted. Two collections of texts were printed, one in 1620, one in 1630, the first being plays of English origin, while the second is wholly German. Some idea of the English Comedians in action can be gained if the following points are borne in mind: subtlety and poetic language could not be appreciated by a foreign audience, and are therefore dropped; pirated editions and older versions of plays are often used; since visual action alone could convey the plot there was a strong incentive to exaggeration, horseplay, and lurid horrors; the audience was kept amused by music and ballet interpolated into the action for the benefit of the more sophisticated spectators, and by the introduction of fooling for the groundlings; the actors who sought employment abroad, though obviously adventurous spirits, were perhaps not in the front rank of their profession. Their acting would therefore tend to be violent and declamatory, with much boisterous action and broad effects in comedy. From the literary point of view therefore the influence of the English actors was on the whole deplorable; but it must be admitted that they first acquainted the German public with passion on the stage, and so paved the way for an appreciation of tragedy, and further they counteracted the German tendency to excessive discussion; for them the play was the thing, to the exclusion of all else. In these respects they revolutionized German drama in a manner long overdue.

The Thirty Years War baulked their activity somewhat, but a number of English companies continued to play on the continent, particularly during the Puritan Interregnum of 1642–60. The last authenticated record of an English troupe is in 1659, but such was their prestige that the name *Englische Komödianten* was used for publicity purposes as late as the eighteenth century. The constant passage of actors to and from the continent, and the consequent interchange of ideas and subjects for drama, produced some interesting problems of comparative literature, of which the theme of Faustus is a case in point.

ENGLISH FAIRGROUND AND PORT-ABLE THEATRES.

The provision of an adequate stage has always been one of the chief difficulties of theatrical touring companies. It is said that Thespis acted on a cart; and, in essence, this solution has often been adopted since. The medieval pageants, upon which incidents from the Mystery plays were performed, were, in fact, built-up carts, usually of two storeys, that were drawn round the streets of a town from one assembled audience to another. The tableaux displayed in carnivals and the Lord Mayor's Show are, to a certain extent, relics of the same tradition.

By the end of the sixteenth century there were several companies of players touring the country towns and villages of England, and in the seventeenth century their number was greatly increased; but as theatrical productions grew more ambitious, and the London theatres more elaborately fitted up, the actors and the audiences must have grown dissatisfied with the meagre stage accommodation provided at country inns and rustic barns; there were, of course, at this period no such things as provincial theatres. The creation of portable theatres, as completely self-contained units, was a natural growth to satisfy an obvious need.

The earliest travelling theatres in England seem to have grown up in the fairs during the seventeenth century; at first they were probably little more than tents, housing a small stage, and presenting crude popular drolls, intermixed with turns of juggling and rope dancing. Later some of these became more elaborate, and by the eighteenth century quite ambitious stage productions were being presented at Lee and Harper's and Fielding's Theatrical Booths, and many good actors served their time upon their boards; besides these there were many smaller companies—Hippisley, Yeates, Mme Violante, and so on. At least one 'Great Theatrical Boothe' always attended at Bartholomew Fair, and the London theatres used to close down during its celebration, lending their audiences and sometimes their actors to the fairground (see also FAIRS).

Between the great London fairs of Bartholomew, Smithfield, Southwark, Mayfair, and Greenwich, the theatrical booths would spend the summer making the round of the country wakes. This tradition was sustained for over 200 years; during the nineteenth century Richardson's Theatre was by far the largest concern on the road, but there were dozens of other 'portable theatres' that continued to cover the country after that great enterprise was broken up in the middle of the century—'Johnson's Thespian Temple', 'Baker's Pavilion', 'Douglass's Travelling Shakespearean Saloon', Holloway's, Wadbrook and Scard's, Maggie Morton's, and many another. With the spread of the cinema the old 'portable fit-ups' lost their importance, but even to-day an obscure theatrical road show may still occasionally be found trouping the English countryside.

The fairground theatres of the eighteenth and nineteenth centuries seem to have conformed to a general pattern; the stage itself was solidly constructed, sometimes upon the carts that carried the show round, and was furnished with a few simple backcloths and properties; the auditorium consisted of a canvas tent that could be easily rolled up and transported on the wagons; the seats were almost always plain wooden planks. If the show was at all pretentious there might be a built-up front of gaudily painted canvas flats, and a platform outside upon which some of the performers would parade as an advertisement for the marvels within. These parades were often very elaborate, and sometimes even superior to the actual performance.

The performances themselves were often conducted with the main idea of getting through the piece as quickly as possible and clearing the seats for another audience; on a busy day a play might be run through as often as a dozen times. The plays were, for the most part, strong dramatic stuff, based on popular legends and stories from the classics, the Bible, or English history; sometimes they dramatized sensational topical murders (Maria Marten is, of course, the most famous example), presented pantomimes, or adapted current theatrical successes. There was hardly ever any written script; the actors were given the stock situations and were expected to improvise the stock speeches, and the result usually bore very slight verbal resemblance to any dramatic original. Like the puppet-show, whose repertory was very similar, the fairground theatre preserved some interesting elements of the Elizabethan stage tradition.

Despite their crudities the theatrical booths and the portable theatres played a great part in carrying the English drama throughout the English countryside to the English people, and they deserve a fuller recognition than they have received from theatre historians. The ordinary stage histories ignore them almost entirely, but some information may be gleaned from Morley's *Bartholomew Fair*, Frost's *Old English Showmen*, Peter Paterson's *Glimpses of Real Life*, and similar theatrical reminiscences.

There are indications that the travelling theatre has not exhausted its usefulness to-day; for several years the Arts League of Service toured the country with an easily portable entertainment of traditional English song and drama, and under the stress of war, and the consequent dispersal from the towns, there was a growing movement to carry the theatre into the country. Well-appointed provincial theatres and village halls will reduce, but never perhaps entirely destroy, the scope of the genuine portable theatre.　　　　　G. S.

ENGLISH OPERA HOUSE, see LYCEUM THEATRE (1), PALACE THEATRE, and ROYALTY THEATRE (2).

ENGLISH PLAYHOUSE. 1. STRUCTURE. The modern English theatre (the general word having unfortunately ousted the more specific 'playhouse') is a roofed building designed exclusively for the presentation and witnessing of theatrical shows. It contains an auditorium with provision for seating spectators, a stage fitted with all the gear necessary for the presentation of a play, and offices for the running of all these, and in its present form it goes back directly to the Restoration playhouse (for pre-Restoration theatre buildings, which show significant differences in form and use, see ELIZABETHAN PLAYHOUSE).

When the theatres reopened after the Puritan interregnum (1642–60) the break with tradition was complete, and Restoration London had two playhouses only, as against the fifteen of Elizabethan times, both built on an entirely new plan. These were Killigrew's Theatre Royal (ater to be Drury Lane) and Davenant's Lincoln's Inn Fields Theatre, also known as the Duke's House. The most important feature of the new age was the introduction of scenery. Before this there had been no public playhouse equipped for the regular presentation of shows

with scenery; but in June 1661 Sir William Davenant's *Siege of Rhodes*, was given at the Duke's House with elaborate scenery specially designed for it by Webb, pupil of Inigo Jones. This was not the first presentation of *The Siege of Rhodes*—regarded by some authorities as the first English opera—for it had been given at Rutland House in 1656, nor was it the first presentation in England of an elaborate scenic show, for there had been many such in the privacy of the Court (see MASQUE); but it does appear to have been the first production with elaborate scenery given before an audience in a public theatre shaped and equipped for regular scenic productions.

The success of Davenant's playhouse, and of Killigrew's rival theatre, when re-designed to use scenery, laid the foundations of the new style, and the Elizabethan platform stage was henceforth out of fashion. In 1671 Wren built a new theatre for Davenant, who there proposed—though he died before its completion—to mount even more elaborate spectacles, and a year later Killigrew also commissioned Wren to build a new theatre to replace his old one, destroyed by fire. Four main factors contributed to the final form of the Restoration playhouse, and thus of the modern English theatre. These were (*a*) the scenery of the Court masques, (*b*) the long-oblong shape of the converted tennis-courts, (*c*) the doors, balconies, and stage of the Elizabethan open theatre, and (*d*) the architectural schemes devised by Inigo Jones and John Webb for the performance at Court of dramatic shows as distinct from masques.

From the form, details, and working of the Court-masque scenery the design of the whole stage was derived (see STAGE); and to the shape of the Jacobean tennis-court building is probably due much of the form of the early auditorium (see AUDITORIUM), since both Killigrew and Davenant, before their theatres were built, made use of temporarily converted tennis-courts, Gibbon's Tennis-Court in Vere Street and Lisle's in Lincoln's Inn Fields. Hence their conversion into theatres permitted no more alteration than could have been removed to return them to their use as tennis-courts.

It would be of considerable interest to find a contemporary account of expenses indicating the nature of work involved in converting a tennis-court into a theatre, but lacking such information we must be content to make the following suggestions: First, the tennis-court, as opposed to the more or less circular Elizabethan playhouse, was a long, narrow building and seems to have lent its character to the first regular Restoration auditoriums. Secondly, since the 'pent-house' of the tennis-court—a sort of covered way along one side and one end of the room—offered such convenient seating for the audience, a similar feature was possibly built symmetrically on the other side of the hall, and the sloping roof of each balustraded to accommodate a further, upper, gallery of spectators.

To associate a raised stage, however, with

such side seats at ground-level in the pent-house would result in uncomfortable sight-lines, and the three or four feet permissible to stage-height would not allow sufficient working room under the stage for traps. If now the stage were, instead, planned on floor-level, and a cellar dug beneath for traps, the central floor could be removed, and an excavation made for seats in sloping ranks. The central auditorium could be floored in again and the building returned to tennis-court uses without any need to remove the sunk seats. It is significant that the accepted name for the part of the auditorium so produced was, and has remained to this day, the pit, and that the ground-level of most English theatres is nearer the first circle than it is to the pit floor.

Such a treatment of the tennis-court is conjectural, but the result compares well, in every significant feature, with the disposition of the Georgian playhouse which survives at Richmond, Yorks. Moreover, one part of the pent-house face was pierced by doors which, if the theatre were divided about half-way (as was normal) into stage and auditorium, would come remarkably near the situation of the proscenium doors (see PROSCENIUM). If this theory is at all correct, the Georgian playhouse form owes much to the Jacobean tennis-court building.

The remaining features that chiefly charac-terize the new Restoration playhouse are closely enough related to be taken under one head. They are the perpetuation in the new type of building of certain features to which the pro-fessional actors had all been accustomed on their Elizabethan playhouse stages and perhaps to some extent in the private theatres. The four most important of these traditional features were the players' doors of entrance, the balconies which they might need for the action of certain scenes, the 'inner stage'—a recess in the tiring-house wall behind the stage—and, lastly, the 'peninsular' nature of the stage itself, which jutted into the curve of the audience, so that the players might be watched from three sides, and whereby the audience would perceive them in relief against the background.

The intimate effect which these traditional features had on the form of the drama and the style of the acting is worth remark. No doubt the designers of the new playhouses were wise to incorporate and continue some adaptation of each one of these since they were so much a creed of the players. The forms which the adaptations took are interesting, and have left their mark on the playhouse even to the present day.

The transition by which the final form was reached is suggested in those curious indeter-minate theatres, of which drawings exist by Inigo Jones and John Webb, designed for the presentation at Court of dramatic perform-ances as against masque performances. When, as often happened, a troupe of professional players came to Court to present a typical 'inn-yard' play, written in quick short scenes,

and never intended for full scenery, but abounding in occasions where the players were on different levels (as scenes between street and window, or field and castle-wall), they clearly would find so much modification of their production necessary as to throw the whole show out of gear, had they performed on a masque stage. So a form of theatre was pro-jected which related the Court taste for elaborate painted or modelled classical-archi-tectural background with the players' need for doors and balconies, and provided them at the same time with their indispensable Eliza-bethan 'inner stage'.

Jones's project (see 'A Theatre Project by Inigo Jones', by W. G. Keith, *Burlington Magazine*, Aug. and Sept. 1917) and Webb's design for the Cockpit in Whitehall Court (see 'John Webb and the Court Theatre of Charles II', by W. G. Keith, *Architectural Review*, Feb. 1925), though different in many details, have this in common—in an architectural façade at the back of the stage is a principal central opening, capable of use as an inner stage; on either side of this opening are one or more doors, in the façade, or in the advancing wings of that façade, and above some at least of these openings a balcony is present. Before all this lies the main acting area. Here seems to have been an attempt to adapt the 'inn-yard' stage to what was to become the Restora-tion playhouse.

The next step might have been as follows. Firstly, full scenery had to be accommodated; some small scenic detail may have hitherto been used behind the central opening and its presumed doors or curtain, but now it would appear that the acting area was flanked by side scenes, the doors of the central opening were replaced by the masque shutters, and the space behind the opening developed to take the 'scene of relief'. In such an arrangement the doors and balconies would of course be hidden by the side scenes. Accordingly the doors and bal-conies were brought forward and set in front of the side scenes and the scenic area. Now some sort of framing element was required to mask the off-stage spaces to left and right and above the scenes, and to cover their working. Into this frame the doors were incorporated structurally, and the balconies above them were related (as they had been in the Elizabethan playhouse) to the upper rows of seats in the auditorium.

From such a transition, probably, was born the modern playhouse with its auditorium, its stage, and the relating (yet separating) feature of the proscenium between them. The further history of these three elements is outlined under their separate headings (see AUDITORIUM, PROSCENIUM, STAGE).

2. MACHINERY. Machines on the typical English stage have been so reduced that there remains to-day only one mechanical system in wide general use—the flying system, by which scenery is hung, and by which it is raised out of sight, or lowered into the acting position, during scene changes. The manifold and com-plex devices that once made the stage one of

the largest and most elaborate tools employed in the expression of any art are now matters of history, or expensive luxuries attainable by only the largest theatres. Elaboration in the mechanical department of a typical theatre is now rather to be found in the lighting plant than in the machinery (see LIGHTING). Time was when the working of machines in the theatre was a feature of the performance seen and marvelled at by the audience. Now the last widely used machine that remains is probably scarcely dreamed of by the general spectator, for its action is purely utilitarian, and its movement of the scenery is always hidden by the curtain, not made a feature of the show.

Thus, the subject of English theatrical machines may be divided under three heads: (a) the flying system, essential in some form to almost every modern stage and still a part of normal, general procedure; (b) the elaborate developments of mechanics and engineering, comparable with any achievements of the past, now found only in a few highly specialized, or very large, theatres; (c) stage machinery as it used to be, in all its visible and impressive development from the adaptations by Davenant of Inigo Jones's experiments, through the staggering intricacies of Dryden's 'operas', and the widely established, standard equipment of the Georgian and Regency stages, to its last lingering home and expression in the single appearance of the Demon King through a star trap, or an even rarer transformation-scene of the older type, in a pantomime of to-day.

(a) In the Flying System, the piece of scenery—let us suppose a backcloth, for instance—is hung by means of a Set of Lines, generally three in number, and known as the Long, Short, and Centre Lines respectively, which ascend to pass over three pulley blocks in the grid. The lines are then taken to a triple headblock at the side of the stage, and their ends descend together to be made fast to a cleat on the Fly Rail, or Pin Rail, which is the railing along the fly-gallery edge (see STAGE). Borders and ceilings are also flown like cloths, and, at need, almost any other element of a stage set. Even a complete box set may be battened together, with property furniture attached to its walls, and the whole flown entire on a number of sets of lines.

The above is the older form of flying system, used in the so-called Hand-worked or Rope Houses, where the power to raise the scenery is manual alone. In Counterweight Houses the sets of lines, generally of wire rope, are attached to a steel barrel, and the scenery is strapped to this barrel. The lines, after leaving the headblock, are clewed together and attached to a Counterweight Cradle, which may be loaded to balance the weight of the scene piece, and which is raised and lowered by means of an endless line, passing over pulleys and working (generally) from the floor of the stage, where a system of brakes is installed for each line. The fly gallery in such an arrangement may be done away with (see also STAGE, under Fly-floor).

(b) For the modern experiments and elaborations of mechanical stage construction, and the incorporation of numberless devices in a few highly specialized stages, certain standard works should be consulted, since little of the procedure is yet general, while to study in adequate detail the comparative qualities of all would make a highly specialized work, for which the materials to-day are still not properly assembled. The initial experiments may be studied in the monumental *Modern Opera Houses and Theatres* of Edwin O. Sachs and E. A. Woodward (3 vols., 1896–8), with its supplement *Stage Construction* (1898), and later developments in Friedrich Kranich's *Bühnentechnik der Gegenwart* (2 vols., 1929).

(c) For the tradition and detail of English stage machinery in the past no standard work is available, and some attempt will therefore be made to give a brief review of the subject.

The normal machines of the traditional English stage were: the Grooves, the Drum-and-Shaft systems, Traps in their varieties, the Sloats, and finally the machines for 'flyings'. These were all more or less standard equipment and were to be found, in part at least, in even the small theatres of the provinces. Besides these there were a number of special machines, not designed for general use but reserved for occasional effects, which were more in the nature of tricks.

The main function of machinery in the theatre is to change the scenery. It may be widely employed in special effects, but though the most elaborate engines have been invented for such effects, yet the normal function of scene-changing is, in the long run, the most important office of stage machinery.

The usual changing of scenes in the English theatre was, until about the 1880s, a visible affair, taking place in sight of the audience, and arranged as part of the action of the show. No proper estimate of the drama of those times can be made unless this characteristic of visible scene-change, with all that it means for continuous and vividly pursued action, is appreciated. English scene-change took place by the aid of a 'machine' differing very greatly from any method widely accepted on the continent (save perhaps occasionally in Holland, whose theatre often had a close link with ours). This, the English groove system, had its rise with Inigo Jones, and maintained a steady development till near the end of the nineteenth century. It then suffered a sudden eclipse, and fifty years later its history and its very existence were nearly forgotten.

In the groove system the scenery was changed by sliding the pieces in and out. The wings of the old scene went off to right and left and new wings came on to replace them, the borders rose upwards and others were substituted, and the back scene parted centrally, the two parts sliding outwards, to be replaced by another pair of halves closing in. To support and guide the parts of the scenery in these movements, grooved timbers were used, built into the skeleton of the stage structure. The design, number, and placing of these grooved timbers varied greatly at various periods, and they were capable of a high degree of complexity and ingenuity.

The system is seen in its infancy in Inigo Jones's designs for masques at Court. In these shows, there was fixed to the stage floor, at the position of the back scenes (called Backshutters), a number of strips of wood, an inch or so apart, making a row of grooves across the stage, one groove for each pair of shutters. Similarly, at the level of the shutter-tops, there was suspended a flat timber, bearing corresponding grooves on its under face. The shutters stood in the bottom grooves, and were supported at the top by the upper grooves, and they were opened or closed at need by being pulled off, or pushed on, in their grooves, which were soaped to lessen friction. Such a system was used for the pastoral *Florimène* in 1635. By the time of the last and greatest of the masques, *Salmacida Spolia*, in 1640, not only was such a set of long grooves across the stage used to take the back scenes, but further sets of short grooves were to be found, one set at each wing-position, and hence the wings might also be slid on or off, to change with the changing back scene. In *Salmacida Spolia* there were four parallel grooves above and below each wing-position, and also at the position of the back scenes, so supplying means to accommodate the scenery for four complete changes of back scene and four corresponding changes of back scene.

Moreover, the Side Borders and Upper Backshutters were all hung from special top grooves, and could be drawn off, or on, in a similar way.

Our knowledge of grooves at the culmination of this opening period of their history, that is in the year 1640, may be summarized as follows: Jones employed four varieties of groove: (*a*) the Backshutter Grooves, a group of long grooves running right across the stage at the position of the backshutters; an upper and a lower groove was provided for each separate shutter scene to be used in the play; (*b*) the Side Shutter or Wing Grooves, a series of groups of much shorter grooves, one group above and one below, at each wing-position, each group containing sufficient grooves to accommodate all the changes of wings required in the show; (*c*) the Upper Backshutter Grooves, a group of long grooves, situated face down across the stage above the shutter scenes; these were slightly different in detail in that they were unaccompanied by lower grooves: the upper backshutters hung in them and received no support from below; and (*d*) the Side-Cloud Grooves, a series of groups of short grooves, designed like (*c*) to take hanging scenery, and of which one group was situated, face down, above every wing-position (see CLOUDINGS).

All grooves were parallel to the front of the stage, consequently all pieces of scenery had to face the audience directly, and this later became one of the limitations of the groove system, since an oblique setting of scene pieces was made impossible owing to the difficulty of adjustment arising in any attempt to use oblique grooves on a raked stage. Oblique wings are, however, much more advantageously placed than those squarely facing the audience, so far as masking is concerned. But it appears to be certain that formerly the parallel position imposed by the groove system led to a very low regard for the proper masking of the sides of the scene, and spectators in side boxes must have regularly seen far more of the waiting actors than is possible to-day.

In the early arrangements the opposite pairs of wing-groove groups were fixed to converge as one went up-stage, so that the avenue of wings might form a perspective vista. Similarly the upper wing-grooves were successively placed lower as one approached the back, a shorter wing being used at each position, again in accordance with perspective effect. Thus, no wing could be used at any position of grooves other than the one it was built to fit, and interchangeability was impossible.

Each set of Jones's grooves consisted of a number of slats fixed parallel on a single bed, whose thickness, in the case of the bottom grooves, raised the foot of each scene-piece an inch or so above the stage.

Though the scenes were most probably moved in the grooves by direct manual pushing or pulling, yet there are ambiguous references to ropes which may indicate a use of some system of linking the pieces for simultaneous movement by means of a winch.

A further disadvantage in the early groove arrangement, which was later conquered by an ingenious and characteristic modification, concerned the grooves used to hold the top of the back scenes. It will be realized, upon consideration, that in such a scheme as that used in the masques, when the upper and the lower backshutters were opened at the same time, the tall vista beyond, thereby disclosed, would be marred by the top member of the lower backshutter grooves, cutting across the middle of the scene like the cross-bar of an H. This delicate problem was at first solved, and the intruder hidden, by a wraith of scenic cloud, tacked across to hide the timber. But a far more practical solution was later to be found.

During the Commonwealth, a considerably simplified system of grooves was used by John Webb, to work the backshutters only, for his scenery in *The Siege of Rhodes* in 1656. Here, the tiny back scenes measured only 9 ft. by 7 ft., and the grooves consisted of a set of three lower ones, 9 ft. long, lying face up on the floor of the stage, with a corresponding set hung face down 7 ft. above them from the ceiling. The two sets were probably connected at the ends by uprights into one frame. Between the sides of the frame and the two great upright timbers which supported it at the back came a pair of additional upright grooves through which were slid the narrow framing elements which commonly introduced the vista of the relieve scenes behind.

Following the Commonwealth, evidence for the use of grooves in the Restoration public theatre is obtainable at first only from play-directions. But these supply many examples of the use of scenery of a type similar to the masque shutters, and there can be little doubt that grooves were used. The first direct mention of grooves is in 1743, at Covent Garden. Both top and bottom grooves are referred to, the top grooves fixed to the under side of the fly-floor. There were probably six sets a side at Covent Garden. The bottom grooves, at least, were of different sizes; possibly some short to accommodate wings, and some long for back scenes.

There is definite evidence in 1748 (and presumptive evidence from as far back at least as 1678) that grooves for back scenes were now used at positions near the front of the stage, as well as farther back, where Jones had confined them in his masques. Thus the use of front scenes in grooves was possible. The groove-sets were numbered from the front of the stage—1st grooves, 2nd grooves, and so forth—and the position of a piece of scenery might be described by specifying the number of the groove it occupied, as 'Palace, 3rd groove'.

In 1776 we hear of the upper grooves being connected with a system of 'barrels' or shafts (for which see below).

About the end of the eighteenth century several criticisms were made of the groove system, and of the rigid form of setting which it enforced, but it persisted because, better than any other, it permitted the swift, mobile succession of scenes which so suited the flexible, lively, and human, contemporary British drama. Several innovations were made to surmount some at least of the limitations of the grooves. When the scenes were drawn open, the bottom grooves offered an awkward step, or barrier, across the floor of the stage, over which the actor had to stride, and whose apertures might trap his heel. So by 1790 at least lower grooves were divided into 'loose' and 'fixed' types. Loose grooves could be lifted up from the stage (where they were held by pegs, projecting into holes in the floor-boards) when they were not needed for the flat scenes. The fixed grooves were probably the wing-grooves, and perhaps the offstage extremities of the longer flat-grooves, which, owing to their size, were divided into two sections, the inner section being 'loose'. Being on the sides of the stage these fixed grooves could remain in position without hindering the players.

Similarly the upper flat-grooves offered serious ground for objection, of which an anticipation was already to be found in the intrusive bar crossing the vista of some of the masque scenes when upper and lower back-shutters were open together. For just as the Restoration theatre employed deep set scenes as well as shallow flat scenes, so it had variation in respect of height, and low, straight-bordered scenes were interspersed with high, arch-bordered scenes. The low scene with a straight border was generally a flat scene, consequently the low-hung border was available to mask the upper groove, holding the top of the flat scene. But when the flat scene was withdrawn to discover a deep set scene behind, and the low borders rose to reveal a dignified succession of tall arches, the grand effect (comparable with the 'magnascope' of the modern cinema) would be sadly marred by the row of empty grooves left high and dry over the stage, and cutting the vista like a succession of rafters.

Consequently the upper flat-grooves were early arranged in a new way. Instead of running clear across the stage, they were made in two halves, with a central interval between of several feet, and each half consisted of a 'fixed' and a 'loose' part. The outer part in each case was fixed, being firmly attached under the fly-floor, as were the wing grooves, but to its inner extremity the loose, and major, portion was connected by hinges. This hinged arm projected over the stage in its normal position, but could be raised like a drawbridge by means of a line when it was not needed. Thus the upper space of the stage could be cleared, and left free for an uninterrupted vista of arches. Upon reversion to a flat scene, the straight borders descended again, and the groove-arms were once more lowered on the tops of the closing flats.

Sometimes the two lines working the pair of groove-arms in each set were brought together to a cleat on the fly-rail, in which case any pair of groove-arms could be dropped at need; and sometimes all the lines from all the groove-arms on the stage were taken to one long shaft, and upon the rotation of this each groove-arm rose or fell simultaneously with the others in one operation (see below, DRUM-AND-SHAFT SYSTEM).

The plans for the Theatre Royal, Plymouth, in 1811, well exemplify these arrangements. Here the wing-sets contained three grooves each, and the flat-sets varied from three to five, the larger number belonging to the sets at the front of the stage, where, it appears, the greatest number of scenes was used. The earlier perspective convergence of opposite pairs of wing-grooves was abandoned; the tips are parallel. A set of flat-grooves appears behind each set of wing-grooves, and there are four sets either side.

The number of individual grooves in each group varied in different theatres. It might seem that two grooves alone were all that could be needed in any wing position, one for the wing in use at the moment and one for the withdrawn wing, which could be taken away after use, and the next wing put in its place ready for the next change. But such an apparently simple arrangement does not seem to have been widely used. On the other hand, since the number of sets of wings needed in a show may vary considerably, it was clearly impossible in the regular, professional theatre to design a groove-group containing sufficient grooves to house all the wings ever likely to be needed for any one show. For heavy shows, some substitution of 'live' wings for 'dead' wings in the grooves would have to be effected. How then was the number of grooves arrived at? It seems likely that one governing factor was the number of typical Stock Sets of wings likely to be most frequently employed. It appears that, in the past, scenery was regarded commonly as a stock thing, and that to have a scene, or a set of scenes, specially prepared for a show was unusual. For a fresh season a complete new set of scenes might possibly be advertised, but for each given show the material in stock was drawn upon, and specially designed scenery was comparatively rare. Thus at Ipswich, in the first half of the nineteenth century, there were four types of wing kept in readiness at each position—Palace interior, Wood or Tree wing, Cottage interior, and Cave or Rock wing. Plymouth, at the beginning of the same century, appears to have stocked three wing sets—Palace, Tree, and Chamber wings. Hence it is likely that the number of wing-grooves was dependent upon the number of varieties of stock scene most commonly in use at that theatre.

Objections continued to be raised against grooves in 1818, and representations were made that the continental system of machinery (see below) should be used. It appears that the scenes sometimes stuck in the grooves, and the actors had to play with a gap in the back scene. A further objection, commented on as far back as Fielding, turned on the great difficulty of moving all pieces in a scene-change at the same time, which led to ragged variations in the movement.

About this time bottom grooves began to decline. First they became isolated single strips separating the feet of the scenes which now stood directly on the stage itself, and then they disappeared altogether, leaving the guidance of the sliding solely to the upper grooves.

These upper grooves were often built in open-work construction to save weight. It was of the utmost importance that an exactly correct level should be maintained for the hinged arms of the upper grooves, and we find this achieved by a chain, suspended from above and acting as a check to their fall—a chain being less subject to alteration with atmospheric changes than a rope. These chains, and the heavy falling arms, made a characteristic noise in the scene changes of their time.

In some later theatres these upper grooves reached vast dimensions, and must indeed have been heavy. In one case the fixed portion was itself 9 ft. long, and to it was attached, not one hinged arm, but two, successively, the first 6 ft. 6 in. long, and the last reaching the amazing figure of 12 ft., so that the whole groove was 27 ft. 6 in. long. The distance between the opposite tips of each pair was 15 ft. 6 in., and the stage accommodating such members was 85 ft. wide.

By 1857 the continental method (see below) had replaced grooves at Covent Garden. In 1863 Charles Fechter did away with the groove system at the Lyceum, and installed the continental method, but the innovation was not maintained, and grooves returned. In 1880 Irving again removed the grooves from the Lyceum, to use instead what became the modern method of scene-support by braces, and, incidentally, at the same time initiated the custom of dropping the curtain for scene-changes.

Grooves remained, however, for some years in smaller theatres, and a pivoted variant is found in the 1880s which surmounted the objection to their rigidly enforcing a position parallel to the footlights on all wings, for wing and groove could now be twisted to any angle. Eventually even this modification was superseded by the Forks, in which the tops of the wings were held as by an inverted garden-fork. This idea is still occasionally to be found, for instance in a form where the prongs are replaced by short, vertical, rubber-covered rollers projecting down from a headboard. But the device is rarely used to-day, though ingenious examples of it are to be found in the late nineteenth century.

The groove system was also employed in the American theatre, where it was quoted as old-fashioned by 1897. Otherwise it is unknown in any other country in the world (with the possible exception of Holland) after the Renaissance period.

In the above account of the English groove mention was made of the continental method of wing movement. It is necessary to give a very brief account of this system in any study of English machines, for it was more than once introduced into this country, and later research may prove that it was imported earlier than might be supposed. In this system each wing-piece is hung on a frame (or sometimes a simple mast) so as to be suspended just clear of the stage floor. Each frame (or mast) projects downwards through a long slit in the stage, and is borne on a wheeled carriage, running on rails in the mezzanine floor. At every wing-position this arrangement exists in duplicate, and the two carriages at each position are connected by ropes, working in opposite directions, to a common shaft serving the whole series, in such a way that one carriage of each pair moves off as its neighbour moves on, thus exchanging one set of wings for another. The withdrawn wing may then be replaced by the wing for the next scene and the process repeated when required.

A passage in Chetwood's *General History of the Stage* (Dublin, 1749) mentions his importation in 1741 to Smock Alley Theatre, Dublin, from Drury Lane, of a 'Machine to move the Scenes regularly altogether', which involved altering the stage 'after the manner of the Theatres in *France* and *England*'. It may well be then that, before the middle of the eighteenth century, an alternative method to grooves was known. But references to it are all inconclusive, and it seems never to have taken root in English tradition. It can only be said that the Carriage-and-Frame, or Chariot-and-Pole system, described above, was known in England. Some writers have gone so far as to ask whether Betterton himself might not have brought back something of the principle in 1673, when he returned to the Duke's Theatre after a study of machinery in France. This, however, has still to be substantiated, and however frequent and early the intermissions, the groove system was the standard English system till the end of the nineteenth century.

Another application of the groove system in theatrical machinery is found in the Sloat, or Slote. Here, within the throat of a vertical groove, a tongue slides up and down, to the face of which the scene-piece or object to be moved may be fixed. In early times—for instance at an English Court performance in 1574—such a groove might be used horizontally, to guide the movement of a drifting cloud. In established procedure it was used vertically to lift pieces into view, generally from under the stage. A row of two or more sloats was attached to the timbers in the cellar under any of the stage cuts (see STAGE, 1), and a piece of scenery, such as a long groundrow, attached across to the tongue of each. A line passed up from the base of each tongue, lying adjacent to it until near the top, where it passed out over a pulley and was led to a winch, in some convenient position, in company with the lines of any other sloats in the same set. On the turning of the winch the tongues simultaneously rose and lifted the scene through the cut up to the stage-level.

The next important system of early stage machinery is the Drum-and-Shaft, or Barrel, System, which is an application of the principle of the lever. Its purpose is to draw in, or let out, a rope actuating some piece of scenery. The rope is fixed to the cylindrical shaft. In order to turn this shaft a lever might have been inserted through the shaft and the whole twisted thereby like a corkscrew. A more apt arrangement, however, was to build a circular drum round part of the shaft, but of a diameter considerably greater than that of the shaft. Then the shaft might be rotated by pulling on a line wound round the drum, and in this way the lever principle would be the more easily and steadily applied.

Where a number of pieces have to be moved simultaneously the drum-and-shaft system has many advantages. Take, for instance, a set of five borders. The lines of each go up to pulleys vertically over them in the grid, where they pass to a long shaft running the length of the stage. Upon the drum of this shaft a line is wound in the opposite direction to the border lines, and its free end attached to a winch. On the turning of the winch the drum may be revolved, and hence the shaft, upon which there are now rolled up all the border-lines at once, and the borders of the set themselves, rise steadily and simultaneously. Not only this, but by winding an independent

rope round the drum in a contrary direction, leading it by pulleys to a convenient place for descent, and by attaching a counterweight to the end of this line, the original weight of the borders to be lifted can be easily worked by a hand-line.

Sometimes it is convenient for counterweights to be arranged slightly to exceed the pull of the scenery; then the working line becomes a check line, and is paid out slowly to steady the rate of rise. The lowering of the scenery is then achieved by pulling up the counterweight by steady pressure on the working line. Conversely, the scenery may slightly exceed the counterweight, and the working line is used, in this case, to overcome its excess weight and raise the whole. It is lowered again merely by a release of the working line. When at rest, the working line is made off round a cleat. The counterweights are generally housed in chimneys built in the thickness of the side walls of the stage, so as to prevent accidents in the case of a rope breaking.

Applications of this system are found in many parts of the stage—below, for working traps, bridges, and sloats; above, for working borders and cloud machines; and, later, cloths. It may be varied by drums of different diameters used on the same shaft, and separate pieces of scenery attached to the different drums, when, upon the rotation of the shaft, the individual pieces move at various speeds. This is exemplified in gradually unfolding cloud effects, where a number of clustered cloud-pieces expand to a great aureole.

To-day, when visible scene-changes are no longer made, simultaneity of movement is not necessary and the drum-and-shaft system has been abandoned, all pieces of flown scenery now being worked independently.

Bridges and Traps, which are also part of stage machinery, are dealt with at length under STAGE, 1. The mechanism of the traps, which worked in conjunction with particular openings, is varied in detail, but they mostly consist of a rigidly built platform on strong legs which slides up and down between four uprights, or corner posts. In a few smaller traps the platform slides between two posts only, which are grooved down the inner face to take two projections from the sides of the platform.

From the framework of the platform itself, ropes are led up to pulleys at the head of the uprights, and over these to some sort of counterweight. In the large and slower-moving traps the counterweight approximately balances the trap and its load, and the rising movement is achieved by means of a hand winch on the mezzanine floor, actuating a rope passing to a drum-and-shaft system below the trap, which is connected with the trap itself by further ropes wound in the opposite direction. In a small, fast-moving trap, such as a star trap, the arrangement is a little different; the weight of the trap, with the figure it is to carry, is heavily over-counterweighted, and the trap itself retained in position by a lever. Upon the turn of the lever, the counter-weights rapidly fall and the trap leaps up. It is clear that some considerable shock is likely to be sustained when the swiftly rising platform reaches the limit of its travel, and has to be checked sharply at the level of the stage. Several methods of lessening the shock are used. One of the simplest and most ingenious is that in which the counterweight consists of a series, or chain, of iron balls, each about nine inches in diameter, hung one below another. At the beginning of the run this chain of balls falls swiftly through the air, exerting all its dead weight on the movement of the trap. But the length of the 'chain' is so adjusted that towards the latter part of the run the first of the balls has reached the limit of its descent and come to rest on a ledge, or floor. Its weight is thus deducted from the motive power exerted upon the trap; in a fraction of a second the next ball in the chain has come to rest, and then the next, and so forth, until, when the summit of the ascent is nearly reached, all the counterweight balls are 'dead' upon the floor, and the trap is travelling for the last few inches practically on its momentum alone. Though described in some detail here, the whole action is in practice so quick as to be over in a moment. The player is shot through the opening, but the platform comes to rest in its position with far less of a shock than if the full counterweight force had been equally exerted through the whole length of its run.

Most traps can be dismantled and moved to another position or substituted for one of a different type as need arises. A grave trap may, for instance, be removed and its place taken by a pair of traps of the type usually seen in a corner trap; or a special aperture may be cut in the stage beside an existing corner trap to allow of the placing of a duplicate mechanism close beside it. The use of such a double trap was for the substitution of characters to suggest the magic transformation of a person. The two adjacent platforms were so geared that one rose as the other fell. Upon his cue, the player on the stage moved to his position upon the platform of the first trap, now raised and appearing as part of the stage floor, while his partner in the change stood ready waiting upon the other trap, lowered to its starting position. At the crucial moment a diversion was caused, or a cloak waved in front of the figure on the stage; the traps were released, one fell and, simultaneously, the other rose. In a second, a different figure stepped from a part of the stage floor so near the original spot as to be indistinguishable from it. To complete the effect, the trap door of the second opening was arranged to flap over, or slide, into a new position covering the aperture left by the descent of the first trap, all as part of the one concerted movement.

One of the most ingenious trap mechanisms was that devised for the apparition in *The Corsican Brothers*, which had to appear out of the earth so slowly that it was not possible to rely on the quickness of action which deceives

the eye to conceal the working of the trick. It was therefore necessary that no square opening, or aperture of any sort, should appear round the ghost as he was rising; and, most difficult of all, the figure did not rise steadily at one fixed spot, but appeared to drift slowly across the full width of the stage.

The brilliant solution of this problem, in which skilled and judicious use was made of the existing possibilities of stage mechanism, became known as the Corsican Trap, or Ghost Glide. Its mechanism was as follows: First, the slider fillings were removed from a complete cut, leaving a long, narrow aperture across the full width of the stage. Into this a new filling was fitted, capable of sliding, not in two pieces to either side, but in one piece to one side only. (One method of accommodating such a long piece under the floor of a very much narrower wing-space would be to build it on the system of a roll-top desk, and coil it up under the stage as it drew off to the side.) To the far extremity of this sliding floor the trap-door itself was fitted, to be drawn along with it, and beyond that a further, and similar, length of filling was attached. This was drawn from under the opposite side of the stage and pulled across to cover the aperture that would otherwise have been left behind the travelling trap as it followed the first slider off-stage.

Below this cut an inclined railway was built to accommodate a small truck, upon which stood the ghost. The truck rose from a point some six feet below stage at the beginning of its travel to the level of the stage itself at the end of it. It was drawn by a line working simultaneously with that drawing the trap door and its attached sliders across the stage, so that the truck was continuously under the trap but rose nearer and nearer to it as the travel proceeded.

The final ingenuity was the construction of a trap door which would allow the figure to pass slowly through the stage floor, without, at any time, being visible in the shape of an aperture. For this the Bristle Trap (see STAGE, 1) was used. The aperture of the trap-opening was lined with a fringe of inward projecting bristles which were coloured to resemble the stage cloth. The player's body pushed these aside as he rose, and they immediately returned to their position when the pressure was released. No aperture was ever perceptible and the ghost did indeed appear to rise through the stage.

So popular did the effect become that a Corsican Trap was installed in 1858 even at the little Theatre Royal, Ipswich.

Since the first days of the theatre, the ingenuity of mechanists has been directed to flying effects. Of these, the simplest is a direct descent, where four lines over pulleys in the grid suspend a platform decorated with clouds and bearing a figure. The lines are taken to a windlass on the fly-floor. But such a merely vertical rise or fall was not enough, and the flying figure was moved across the stage as well as up or down. Many ingenious systems may be found, whose basis was usually as follows: a small 'carriage' was arranged— either on a taut rope, or on a specially built railway—capable of moving across above the stage from side to side at the level of the fly-floors. The motive power was manual, or supplied by counterweight and check-line. The 'carriage' was situated above one side of the stage, and carried pulleys, down past which ran the lines bearing the flying car or figure. These lines ascended straight from the object to be flown, through the carriage above, directly up to points in the grid. To begin the flight, these suspending lines were not touched, but the carriage through which they ran was drawn across the stage, so that the pulleys in the carriage bore against the vertically hanging lines as it moved and pushed them sideways, thus progressively raising the object from the stage as the carriage was drawn across, and thereby achieving a diagonal cross-ascent. A reverse movement of the carriage achieved a descent. A rearrangement of the parts, and an alteration of the points of suspension, would produce a sweeping curve, where the figure descended to the centre and rose again to the other side. A different arrangement produced a similar flight, but in two straight lines, down and up, so that the path of the flight was in the shape of a V. A further arrangement would produce an undulating flight.

Such ingenuities were well known in the theatre by the Restoration period, where frequent references to 'flyings' are found. Actual diagrams exist of English procedure at the end of the eighteenth century. By the mid-nineteenth century many elaborations are found, including a most complicated machine for controlling the circulatory gyrations of a pair of flying figures. Individual flying artists, too, can be traced about this time and immediately following. One of the most famous was Mlle Aenea, with her husband, W. P. Dando, who used a simple windlass with stout, stretched, rubber cords, which allowed Mlle Aenea to achieve the famous act of *La Mouche d'Or* on the continent in the 1890s, and at the Palace Theatre, London, in 1894. The fascinations of flying continue into the present century where, for instance, in the pantomime *Red Riding Hood*, at Covent Garden in 1938, Kirby's Flying Ballet gave a brilliant and graceful performance in which two figures, suspended by lines worked from a winch above the centre of the auditorium, rose from the stage—their lines shortening on the winch as they swung forward, so that their level was controlled—flew hand in hand directly over the heads of the audience in the stalls, turned at the limit of their travel by a neat movement of exchange of hands, and, as gracefully, swung back to the stage and lightly stood upon it again.

In these effects, where no chariot or cloud is used to bear the figure, the line is attached to a hook at the player's back which forms part of a harness worn under the costume. It is easily fixed or discarded, but a safety device prevents the line leaving the hook in flight.

Many forms of motive power are used, from the manual or the counterweight in earlier times, to the stretched rubber of Dando, and the electric motor of to-day. An article published at the beginning of the nineteenth century says of flying effects: 'The cords are very slender and painted black, to elude the eye of the spectator. The lights also are strong in front, and dim behind, to assist the optical deception. To give the cords sufficient strength without increasing their diameter, they are spun of the best hemp, mixed with brass wire well annealed. Those used at Covent Garden for the flying horse, in the Pantomimic Spectacle of *Valentine and Orson* . . . although less in diameter than a common quill, were said to possess sufficient strength to suspend a ton weight' (see also TRICKWORK ON THE ENGLISH STAGE).

3. SCENERY. A theatrical scene is a composition of pieces in three dimensions. Two considerations govern the composition to-day: first, the provision of a back, sides, and top, to the acting area; second, the creation of an appearance which shall be a fitting theatrical accompaniment to the scene performed. Liberties may be taken with either of these considerations in the modern theatre, but, generally, the setting has to supply (i) the surround and (ii) the picture.

The two functions may be separated and performed by different pieces, or they may be combined in one unified design. The distinction is valuable to understanding and is worth defining at the outset. Thus, the term Stage Setting may be reserved for the treatment of a stage so as to provide a general background suitable for any play. It is merely the decking of a stage and the establishment of essential entrances and aids to the actor's performance. No special representation of a given place is involved. It is the preparation of a stage in the sense that a table is laid or set for a meal, or a jeweller's setting is prepared for a stone. It is the oldest theatrical system and it is to be seen in the formalized tiring-house façade of the Elizabethans (see ELIZABETHAN PLAYHOUSE). The same function exactly is performed by the plain curtain surround on the simple stages of to-day. Its key quality is that it has a sense of permanence and bears no reference to any particular play or scene. Scenery, on the other hand, is a term to cover all elements which refer to one scene and one scene only, and which must be changed to render the stage suitable for another scene. Scenery may either be a small element, a changeable detail in, or before, a formalized setting (which system it is convenient to call Detail Scenery), or the functions of setting and scenery may be combined, and the surround wholly painted, or otherwise treated, to become scenic in all its area, and hence require to be totally changed between the performance of one scene and the next; such a system may be termed Full Scenery. Its essence is that it supplies the whole stage picture, refers to one scene only, and is totally changeable.

However the functions may be finally expressed, and whatever principles obtained in the past, there are five main systems of arranging a scene to-day.

The first gives nothing but a pure surround —it may be simple curtains, it may be an elaborate architectural composition. Its only essential is that it shall provide a theatrical background suitable for any scene likely to be played. Without addition, this system has no scenic function at all. The Pure Curtain Set— the commonest form of this system to-day —is reducible to three components: Side Curtains, a Back Curtain, and Borders, which latter are narrow, hanging strips to mask-in the top. It may also include a Traverse Curtain, one centrally divided and running off to the sides of the stage on a wire or railway. The Curtain Set is a favourite stand-by of amateurs and Little Theatres, and can be used with remarkable ingenuity, but it frequently fails to rival, in theatrical effect, the wide possibilities of painted canvas (for the varieties of Front Curtain, see CURTAIN).

The scenic function arises when, in the second system, this surround is specially modified, or added to, in such a way as to adapt it for the playing of a given scene. It then becomes characterized by that additional, modifying, detail, and so remains until the detail is changed. An example is a simple detail setting whose scenic character is pro- vided by a small set-piece placed before curtains.

The third system came into general use at the Restoration, and, with modifications, still survives. It is the Wing and Backcloth Scene. Here the back consists of a painted cloth, the top is masked by a set of borders, and the sides are formed by wings, an arrangement of two rows of side scenes, each separate from its neighbours, and framing the back scene in a vista. This system may include other varieties of pieces, and can reach a high degree of elaboration and of pictorial representation. It is essentially a system of full scenery.

The fourth system of scene arrangement is much more recent, and is called the Box Set. In it the separate pieces are joined, edge to edge, to form the three walls of a room, and the top is masked not by borders but by a flat canvas ceiling, framed out and laid upon the top of the walls. In this system it is possible to achieve that exact imitation of a room which is demanded by so many nineteenth- and early twentieth-century dramas.

The fifth, and most recent, system arose from a development of stage lighting. It consists of a large, plain, curved back-wall, or half-dome, designed purely to receive effects of light, and termed a Cyclorama. Here the upper part of the stage is masked by the great height and curve-forward of the top of the cyclorama; thus no borders or ceiling are required. The sides are similarly masked either by the deep curving-forward of the ends of an embracing cyclorama, or by combining a shallower cyclorama with an Inner, or False, Proscenium Arch, built inside the normal proscenium (see PROSCENIUM).

The basic elements from which all these varieties of scene are built can therefore be reduced to five groups: (a) the Flat, and its variants, fundamentally a simple, canvassed frame; (b) the Drop and its cousin, the Border —a suspended, vertical stretch of loose canvas; (c) the Curtain in its many forms; (d) the Cyclorama; and finally (e) a varied group of Built Pieces for special needs, to supplement the above.

These five fundamentals of modern scenery are discussed separately under their own head- ings (see BUILT STUFF, CURTAIN, CYCLORAMA, DROP, and FLAT).   R. S.

ENNIUS, QUINTUS (239–169 B.C.), one of the greatest of Latin poets, and an important figure in the history of Latin drama. Born at Rudiae in the south of Italy, he went to Rome in 204 B.C. A man of versatile genius and broad human sympathies, he brought into Latin literature a fresh impulse of Hellenism. In the absence of a reading public at Rome it was inevitable that Ennius should turn to drama; here the death of Andronicus and the disgrace of Naevius left the way clear for him in tragedy, and fragments from no fewer than twenty of his tragedies have come down to us. He seems to have taken many of his plays from Euripides, a writer in whom he found a questioning spirit and humanitarian outlook like his own. Like other Roman dramatists Ennius kept, or tried to keep, close to the sense of the Greek he was translating, though allowing himself consider- able freedom in expression and in metre; of original construction we have no evidence, ex- cept that in his *Iphigenia* he introduced a chorus of soldiers. The fragments illustrate his poetic power; compared with the Greek they may strike us as rhetorical, but they are free from the excesses of later Roman tragedy in this respect, and they contain much that is beautiful and moving. The influence of his tragedies on the Romans of his generation must have been great. His contemporary Plautus burlesques his style—a proof that his plays were well known—and in the next generation Terence refers to him as one of the 'careless' but never- theless admirable dramatists of the past. His plays continued to be read down to the end of the Republic, though Roman opinion seems to have ranked Pacuvius and Accius higher as writers of tragedy. He also attempted comedy, though, it would appear, without much suc- cess, and two *praetextae* are doubtfully assigned to him—the *Sabinae*, dealing presumably with the Rape of the Sabines, and the *Ambracia*, which perhaps told of the conquest of that region by Ennius's patron, M. Fulvius Nobilior. There are few losses in Latin literature which we have to regret more than the disappearance of the tragedies of this gifted and warm-hearted man.   W. B.

ENSA. THE ENTERTAINMENTS NATIONAL

SERVICE ASSOCIATION, commonly known as Ensa, grew according to its Director, Basil Dean, 'from a simple idea, discussed round the table one Sunday morning in the far-off days of Munich, into an organization so large that it numbered its members by the thousand, its performances by the tens of thousands, and its audiences by many millions'.

The outbreak of hostilities in Sept. 1939 found Ensa ready to start its work of entertaining the armed forces. Under the financial supervision of the Navy, Army, and Air Force Institute (Naafi), it gave its first performance on 9 Sept. 1939. Two days later it took over Drury Lane Theatre as its headquarters, and by the end of September twelve fully equipped concert parties were sent out to entertain the troops, with portable stages and lighting, so that the companies could perform anywhere and at any time. Mobile cinemas were promptly organized, giving performances in tents, barns, and village halls. From all over the country Ensa was inundated with requests for entertainments. Soon it was realized that much more would be required than these concert parties and cinemas. Speedily, and with expert help, camp halls built by the War Department or taken over by Naafi were fully equipped both for cinema and living performances. During 1943 it was possible for Ensa companies to present various types of entertainment, including serious plays, musical plays, variety, revues, and concert parties. A company could perform for nearly a year, visiting these semi-permanent theatres, without repeating a single visit.

In 1943 also Ensa supplied entertainment to all war-fronts—Gibraltar, Malta, Italy, Middle East, Palestine, Africa, India, Iceland, and the Faroes. Ensa and Naafi worked in partnership. The former recruited the artists and created the shows, while the latter provided administration, buildings, transport, hostels (in Great Britain there were nearly sixty special hostels, many of them being Jacobean and Georgian mansions), cinemas, fit-up stages, seating, and equipment. Naafi financed Ensa, and in 1943 the annual bill for Naafi-Ensa entertainment for the Forces was over two million pounds.

Classical concerts under distinguished conductors—broadcasts to overseas—entertainments by International Concert Parties for the Allied Forces in Great Britain (Belgian, Dutch, Polish, Norwegian, French, Greek, Czech) —daily performances in war factories and hostels—plays with star artists such as Edith Evans, Robert Donat, John Gielgud, John Clements, and Constance Cummings—concerts in coal mines—the supply of costumes, scenery, gramophone records for productions by the Forces themselves—all these by no means exhaust the record of inestimable services to the war effort rendered by the joint efforts of Naafi and Ensa.

ENTHOVEN, MRS. GABRIELLE, O.B.E. (1868–1950), English theatre historian, who in 1924 presented to the Victoria and Albert Museum in London the vast collection of theatre material which bears her name. This included innumerable playbills, engravings, prints, books, models, and newspaper cuttings covering the history of theatrical production in London from the eighteenth century onwards. Mrs. Enthoven continued to administer and work on it for the benefit of research students, constantly revising and adding to its resources. She was herself an amateur actress and a dramatist, appearing for many years with such companies as the Old Stagers and the Windsor Strollers, and writing several plays, including an English adaptation of one of d'Annunzio's poetic dramas.

ENTREMÉS, in the early Spanish theatre a short comic interlude, often ending in music and dancing, played between the *jornadas* or acts of a long play. It developed into a separate one-act play, still amusing and indeed often farcical in treatment, in the tradition of Lope de Rueda's *pasos*. Among the more famous *entremeses* are those of Cervantes, and the works of Luis Quiñones de Benevente.

EPICHARMUS (*c.* 550–460 B.C.) of Syracuse, Greek comic poet and the most important figure in Sicilian-Greek comedy, which influenced the Old Comedy of Athens (see GREECE, 2 and MIME, 1 *b*). His work survives only in a few fragments and in some doubtful traditions; the traditions make him something of a philosopher, and the fragments suggest that mythological burlesque was an important element in his comedy. According to Horace (*Epistles*, ii. 1. 58) Plautus was said to have imitated the fast-moving style of Epicharmus ('dicitur . . . Plautus ad exemplar Siculi properare Epicharmi'). H. D. F. K.

EPILOGUE, see PROLOGUE.

EPISODE, see GREECE, 1 *c*.

EQUESTRIAN DRAMA, see CIRCUS.

ERCKMANN-CHATRIAN, the pseudonym of two French authors, Émile Erckmann (1822–99) and Louis Gratien Charles Alexandre Chatrian (1826–90), who wrote a series of novels dealing with the French Revolution and the Napoleonic period seen from the point of view of the private soldier. Some of these were dramatized, but the collaborators are best remembered for their play, *Le Juif polonais*, which, in an English adaptation by Leopold Lewis as *The Bells*, provided Irving with a fine part in which he made his first great success.

ERLANGER THEATRE, NEW YORK, see ST. JAMES THEATRE.

ERNST, PAUL (1866–1933), German dramatist, a writer of great austerity who forsook naturalism because it did not satisfy his innate sense of form. In his tragedies, which he wrote for the Düsseldorf theatre, where he was employed for a time, he isolates the inner action and reaction in a timeless sphere, and is inclined to reduce drama to dialogue. There is more movement in his comedies, *Eine Nacht in Florenz* (1904), *Der heilige Crispin* (1910), *Pantalon und seine Söhne* (1916), where the characters, though traditional, are seen from a new angle, while the comic situation, often arising out of a confusion of identity, provokes reflection rather than laughter.

ERVINE, St. John Greer (1883–   ), Irish dramatist and critic, whose early work was produced at the Abbey Theatre, Dublin, where he was for a short time manager. He later settled in England. He served as dramatic critic on a number of papers, notably the *Morning Post* and the *Observer*, while from 1928 to 1929 he was guest critic of the *New York World*. A controversial and outspoken writer, he has not hesitated to use the theatre for the furtherance of his ideas on social problems, as in *Robert's Wife* (1937), in which Edith Evans gave a fine performance, and *Private Enterprise* (1947). He has also written a number of light comedies, including *Antony and Anna* (1926), and *The First Mrs. Fraser* (1929), which ran for two years with Marie Tempest in the title-role. More serious themes are dealt with in *Mixed Marriage* (1911) and *John Ferguson* (1915), which were both given originally in Dublin, and *Jane Clegg*, given at Manchester in 1913 with Sybil Thorndike in the title-role. Ervine has written several books on the theatre, including *The Theatre in My Time* and *How to Write a Play*; he has received honorary degrees from St. Andrews and Belfast, and in 1937 became President of the League of British Dramatists.

ESLAVA, Fernán González de, see SOUTH AMERICA, 1.

ESLAVA THEATRE, see MADRID THEATRES (3).

ESMOND, Henry V. (1869–1922), English actor-manager and dramatist whose real name was H. V. Jack. The son of a doctor, he was born at Hampton Court and educated privately. He went on the stage in 1885, and after gaining experience on tour was seen in London in 1889, appearing at the Opera Comique, the Globe, the Princess's, and several other theatres which have now vanished. He was for a time associated with E. S. Willard and Edward Terry, and then joined George Alexander at the St. James's, where he scored a big success as Cayley Drummle in *The Second Mrs. Tanqueray* (1893). He was also Little Billee in the first production of *Trilby* (1895). While at the St. James's he began writing plays, sentimental comedies of the period which had a great vogue, and in which he toured with much success, his wife, Eva Moore (1870–   ), whom he married in 1891, playing opposite him. The best known of these are *One*

Summer's Day (1897), *The Wilderness* and *When we were Twenty-One* (both 1901), *My Lady Virtue* (1902), *Billy's Little Love Affair* (1903), and *Eliza Comes to Stay* (1913). His last play, which had a considerable success, was *The Law Divine*, produced at Wyndham's in 1918.   W. M. P.

ESPAÑOL THEATRE, see MADRID THEATRES (2).

ESPY, L' [François Bedeau] (*fl.* 1610–64), French actor, the elder brother of the clown Jodelet, with whom he is usually found, first in Lenoir's company at the Hôtel d'Argent, then at the Hôtel de Bourgogne, and finally at the Théâtre du Marais. He joined Molière's company in 1659, but was already somewhat old and soon gave up acting in favour of management. It was he who was responsible for the alterations made in Richelieu's old theatre, the Palais-Royal, before Molière took possession of it in 1661. He retired in 1664, being then well over 60.

ESSLAIR, Ferdinand (1772–1840), German actor, of good family, whose passion for the theatre declared itself at an early age. He made his début at Innsbruck and for many years travelled from one town to another, poor, overworked, early married, and soon widowed. As his second wife he married a young actress, with whom he continued to tour until, after a short period as manager of the theatre in Stuttgart, he was in 1820 appointed leading actor and manager of the Court theatre in Munich. Here he remained for a long time. He relied more on inspiration than on study, but his passionate acting allied to exceptional graces of person and voice made him one of the most popular actors in Germany. At the height of his fame he again undertook a tour of the chief towns in the country, being everywhere fêted and applauded. He was at his best in Schiller, particularly as Wilhelm Tell and Wallenstein.

ESTCOURT, Dick (1668–1712), a Restoration actor immortalized by Steele in *The Spectator*. He does not appear to have been a particularly good actor, but he was an amazing mimic, and his natural good humour and vivacity made him a favourite with any company. Shortly before his death he became landlord of the Bumper Tavern in St. James's Street. For an excellent account of Estcourt, see *The Spectator*, no. 468, which also records his death.

ETHEL BARRYMORE THEATRE, New York. This was built by Lee Shubert, and opened on 20 Dec. 1928 with *The Kingdom of God*. It seats 1,100 people, and its history, though not sensational, has almost invariably been one of success. The actress after whom the theatre was named first appeared at it as Lady Teazle in a brief revival of *The School for Scandal*. Among outstanding productions there were Noel Coward and the Lunts in

Design for Living, the latter pair in *Point Valaine*, and Margaret Rawlings in *Parnell*. Emlyn Williams, with Dame May Whitty and Angela Baddeley, in his own *Night Must Fall*, was followed by Clare Boothe's scathing comedy, *The Women*, which set up a record for the theatre of 657 performances.   G. F.

ETHEREGE, SIR GEORGE (1634–91), English dramatist, the first to attempt the social comedy of manners developed by Congreve and later perfected by Sheridan. Etherege spent part of his early years in France, and was doubtless influenced by memories of Molière when he came to write his first play, *The Comical Revenge; or, Love in a Tub* (1664), a serious verse drama with a comic prose sub-plot. It was this latter style that Etherege explored further in his two later comedies, *She Would if She Could* (1668) and *The Man of Mode* (1676). The latter, which may be taken as typical of Restoration Comedy, is Etherege's best play, a picture of a society living exclusively for amusement, with a tenuous plot of entangled love-affairs offering an opportunity for brilliant dialogue and character-drawing. It contains the 'prince of fops', Sir Fopling Flutter, and the heartless, witty Dorimant, often considered a portrait of Lord Rochester, just as the poet Bellair is supposed to be Etherege himself.

ETHIOPIAN OPERA, a turn in the Nigger Minstrel show, consisting of burlesques on Shakespeare and opera, with negro melodies inserted. It was modelled on the early burlesques of T. D. Rice (Jim Crow), of which the best were *Bone Squash Diavolo* (on 'Fra Diavolo'), *Jumbo Jim*, *Jim Crow in London*, and a burlesque of *Othello*.

EUPHORION. (1) The father of Aeschylus. (2) The son of Aeschylus, and himself a tragic poet, apparently of some merit.

EUPOLIS (*c.* 446–*c.* 411 B.C.), of Athens, one of the leading poets of Old Comedy, and a contemporary of Aristophanes (cf. Horace: 'Eupolis atque Cratinus, Aristophanesque poetas'). Eupolis is said to have won seven victories. Many fragments of his work survive, but no complete play.

EURIPIDES (484–406/7 B.C.), Athenian tragic poet, son of Muesarchus (or Muesarchides), born, probably, in the Athenian island of Salamis. His parents were well-to-do, his mother apparently of good family. Aristophanes' standing joke that she was a greengrocer was funny perhaps because it was so remote from the truth. Of Euripides' life little is known, and still less can be believed. Thus statements that he had matrimonial troubles may be based only on the supposed misogyny of his plays; and the story that he had a study fitted up in a cave on the coast of Salamis sounds like a plausible invention. He is said to have been morose; he was certainly deeply interested in the philosophic and scientific movements of his day. He seems to have played little part in public life, being in this respect an interesting contrast with Aeschylus and Sophocles, for in many ways Euripides was a forerunner of the greater individualism of the next and following centuries. He is said to have written 92 plays, of which there survive 17 tragedies, one quite entertaining satyr-play, the *Cyclops*, and a very large number of fragments (an indication of his later popularity), which include substantial parts of the *Hypsipyle* (on papyrus). The extant plays are: *Cyclops*, *Alcestis* (438 B.C.), *Medea* (431), *Hippolytus* (428), *Children of Heracles* (? *c.* 428), *Andromache*, *Hecuba*, *Heracles Furens*, *Suppliants*, *Ion*, *Electra*, *Trojan Women* (415), *Iphigenia in Tauris* (? 414), *Helen* (412), *Phoenician Women* (411), *Orestes* (408), and the *Bacchae* and *Iphigenia in Aulis*, both produced posthumously. Included with these plays in the manuscripts is a weak play, *Rhesus*, sometimes thought to be an early play by Euripides, more probably a fourth-century work.

Euripides gained five victories (compared with Sophocles' eighteen). In 408 he visited (like Agathon) the Court of Archelaus, King of Macedonia, much as Aeschylus visited Hiero of Syracuse; and he died there soon afterwards. Sophocles, who outlived him by a few months, is said to have dressed his next chorus in mourning as a mark of respect. Aristophanes, in the *Frogs* (405 B.C.), compares Euripides very unfavourably with Aeschylus, but he obviously felt that the death of Euripides and Sophocles had left Athens with no worthy successors to them.

Though contemporary, Sophocles and Euripides seem to belong to different ages. Sophocles is the last of the 'classics', carrying into a democratic age the traditions and outlook of an aristocratic society; Euripides is critical, sceptical, individualistic, in a sense cosmopolitan. His drama deals less with the community than with the individual, less with broad questions of religion and morality than with the emotions and passions—love, hate, revenge—and with specific social questions, like war. In this respect he looks forward to the thought and art of the cosmopolitan Hellenistic age and of Rome; Seneca could imitate the emotionalism, sententiousness, pathos, and rhetoric of Euripides, but very little in Aeschylus or Sophocles. In his lifetime Euripides aroused great interest and great opposition; his realism, his interest in abnormal psychology, his portraits of women in love, his new and emotional music, his unorthodoxy, his argumentativeness, all gave offence; on the other hand, Aristophanes, by continually parodying not only his manner but also particular scenes and verses, is good evidence for the great interest that he aroused. His immense fame did not begin until after his death; he soon eclipsed both Aeschylus and Sophocles, for he was the only one of the great three who could speak directly to the new world established by Alexander's conquests. In modern times his reputation has fluctuated.

He has been unduly disparaged by critics of a neo-classic turn of mind, perhaps overpraised by 'advanced' thinkers. His work is uneven, his manner can become tiresome; few would put him on a level with Aeschylus or Sophocles, but many would echo Aristotle's description of him as 'the most tragic of the poets'.

His plays fall into two clearly marked kinds, tragedies (in the modern sense) and plays which may variously be called tragi-comedies, romantic drama, melodrama, or high comedy The tragedies are of unequal merit; in most of them Euripides' episodic plot-construction is —at any rate at first sight—a stumbling-block. The best are the *Medea*, *Hippolytus*, *Bacchae*, *Trojan Women*, and *Hecuba*. The *Children of Heracles* and the *Suppliants* are weak, and the *Heracles Furens* is hardly a success. It is in the tragedies that most of the puzzl'ng features of Euripides' work are to be found—episodic plots, irrelevant philosophizing, over-simplified characterization, a poetic style that sometimes becomes tediously rhetorical. Of the other plays, the *Electra* and the *Orestes* (completely misunderstood by many critics of the nineteenth century) are powerful studies in morbidity and insanity; the *Alcestis*, *Ion*, and *Iphigenia in Tauris* are excellent tragi-comedy or romantic drama—the *Alcestis* was the fourth play of its tetralogy, taking the place of the usual satyr-play; the *Helen* is most delightful high comedy, and the *Phoenician Women* is a kind of pageant-play. All these plays (except the last) show a skill in construction, and a delicacy and wit both in the dialogue and in the characterization, which are of the very highest order. Euripides was the earliest master in this non-tragic genre, and remains unsurpassed. It is through these plays that he, and not the contemporary writers of Old Comedy, point forward to the New Comedy of the fourth century (see GREECE, 2 *b* and MENANDER).

Euripides continued to use the three actors and chorus as finally established by Sophocles, but one innovation of his, the 'prologue', has been important in the history of the drama. Early Greek tragedies began with the entrance-song of the chorus; Aeschylus's later plays, and all the extant plays of Sophocles, begin with a histrionic scene, whether in dramatic soliloquy or dialogue, the chorus entering later. Any such scene was, in Greek, a 'prologos'; what Euripides did was to invent a quite formal 'prologue' spoken sometimes by a character in the play, sometimes by an external god, which did little more than summarize the story up to the point where the action begins. This, via Seneca, is the origin of the 'prologue' in Elizabethan drama.

Another development in Euripides' drama was that the chorus came to be less closely connected with the action. This was inevitable when plays began to deal with private rather than public issues (e.g. the conjugal difficulties of Medea and Jason), and when the plot was very largely intrigue (as in the *Iphigenia in Tauris* and *Helen*) the presence of a chorus might be a positive embarrassment. It there-

fore tended to become (and in the younger dramatist Agathon did become) a quite conventional lyrical decoration, having no close connexion with the plot. A similar thing happened to the comic chorus (see GREECE, 2 *b*). Hence the Elizabethan idea of an extraneous person called the 'Chorus' speaking a 'prologue'.   H. D. F. K.

EVANS, EDITH (1888–   ), English actress, created D.B.E. in 1946 for her services to the English theatre. She made her first appearance on the stage in 1912 as an amateur, playing Cressida in William Poel's production of *Troilus and Cressida* for the Elizabethan Stage Society. She then became a professional actress and toured with Ellen Terry. After varied experience—mainly in modern plays, though in 1922 she played Cleopatra in *All for Love*, and other seventeenth-century parts, for the Phoenix Society—she first came prominently before the public with her fine performance of Millamant in *The Way of the World* at the Lyric, Hammersmith, in 1924. She was with the Old Vic for the 1925–6 season, playing among other characters Portia, Cleopatra, Beatrice, Rosalind, and the Nurse in *Romeo and Juliet*, and in 1927 went back to Hammersmith to play Mrs. Sullen in *The Beaux' Stratagem*. Other outstanding parts of her distinguished career have been the Serpent and the She-Ancient in *Back to Methuselah*, Florence Nightingale in *The Lady with a Lamp*, Orinthia in *The Apple Cart*, which she first played at the Malvern Festival, Irela in *Evensong*, the name-part in *Viceroy Sarah*, Agatha Payne in *The Old Ladies*, and Sanchia Carson in *Robert's Wife*. She was also excellent as Lady Bracknell in the 1939 revival of *The Importance of Being Earnest* and as Mrs. Malaprop in *The Rivals*. In 1936 she was again with the Old Vic company, playing Lady Fidget in *The Country Wife*, Rosalind, and the Witch in *The Witch of Edmonton*. During the war of 1939–45 she toured extensively overseas under the auspices of E.N.S.A.

EVANS, MAURICE (1901–   ), English actor, whose first appearances on the stage were in amateur dramatizations of Hardy's novels. His début on the professional stage was made at Cambridge, but he first came prominently before the public with his performance as Raleigh in *Journey's End* in 1928. He joined the Old Vic company in 1934 and was seen in a variety of parts, including *Hamlet* in its entirety, which he later played in New York with great success. He first went to America in 1935, and has since remained there, becoming an American citizen in 1941. Among his outstanding parts have been Romeo, with Katharine Cornell, Richard II, Falstaff, Malvolio, and Macbeth in productions by Margaret Webster. During the Second World War he entertained the troops with the so-called G.I. version of *Hamlet*, which he subsequently published.

EVANS, WILL (1875–1931), one of the

funniest comedians of the London stage, both
on the halls and in pantomime, was the son
of Will Evans, a clown in the Grimaldi tradition. The younger Will, who made his first
appearance at Drury Lane in 1881, was
particularly good in kitchen scenes in pantomime, where he performed small tasks with
an immense amount of superfluous energy,
bungling them thoroughly, and accompanying
them with a lot of spilling and slopping about
of soft dough or flour paste. Among his most
amusing music-hall sketches were *Building a
Chicken House, Whitewashing the Ceiling*, and
Papering a House. He was part-author of the
successful farce, *Tons of Money*, which was
produced in 1922, ran for nearly 800 performances, and has since been revived.

EVERYMAN THEATRE, LONDON, at
Hampstead. This was opened by Norman
Macdermott in 1920, with *Bonds of Interest*.
It staged revivals, and try-outs of new plays,
many of which later went to the West End,
and in return received from the West End
such productions as *The Vortex, At Mrs.
Beam's, Outward Bound*. It was not used by
touring companies, but had its own company,
in which many young actors began successful
careers. It is now a cinema.   W. M. P.

EVREINOV, NIKOLAI NIKOLAIVICH (1879–
), Russian dramatist, a symbolist who was
an able exponent of non-realistic stagecraft.
He held that each play should be a projection
of the inner self, a theory which he exemplified
in *The Theatre of the Soul*, a 'monodrama' in
which various aspects of the same person appear
as separate entities. The idea was further expanded in his controversial book, *The Theatre
for Oneself*. A later play, *The Chief Thing*
(1921), which has some affinity with Pirandello,
affirms the healing power of illusion. It was
the best of Evreinov's work, as his later output
was negligible, and was in any case quickly
submerged in the new 'socialist realism' of the
Soviet era, in which Evreinov's theories had no
place. Two short plays, translated by C. E.
Bechhofer, *A Merry Death* and *The Beautiful
Despot*, were published in *Five Russian Plays*
(1916).

EWALD, JOHANNES (1743–81), Danish lyric
poet and dramatist (see SCANDINAVIA, 1).

EXIT, 'he goes out', see STAGE DIRECTIONS.

EXPERIMENTAL THEATRE, NEW YORK,
see DALY'S THEATRE (3).

EXPRESSIONISM, the name given to a
phase of playwriting and production which
sought to present the inner life of humanity
rather than its outward appearance, in contrast
to Naturalism, which tended to concentrate
exclusively upon the external details of reality
and environment. It may be said to have
originated with Strindberg in his later symbolic
works, but found its spiritual home in Germany,
particularly after the war of 1914–18, with
such authors as Wedekind, Kaiser, Fritz von
Unruh, and Toller, who marks the transition
period. This movement had its repercussions
in other countries, with the plays of Čapek, of
Lenormand and Gantillon, of O'Casey and
O'Neill. Since expressionism, with its insistence on the unseen and the subconscious, on
the evocative and symbolic, offered golden
opportunities to scenic designers and producers, it is not surprising to find that they
bulk large in the movement, and indeed have
imparted to many of the plays produced under
their aegis a personal flavour which it is often
difficult to reproduce in revivals. Indeed, it
may be said that expressionism owes as much
to them as to its playwrights and actors, since
their insistence on new methods of production
gave the dramatists freedom to conceive, and
the actors to execute, an interpretation of
humanity in one of its many aspects which
might not otherwise have found its way to the
stage.

EYSOLDT, GERTRUD (1870–   ), German
actress, who made her first appearance on the
stage at Meiningen in 1890 in *King Henry IV*.
After touring in Germany and Russia she
appeared in Berlin in 1899, and later played
under Reinhardt. An extremely clever and
subtle player, she was at her best in modern
realistic parts, particularly in the works of
Wedekind, in which she played opposite the
author. She was also good in Ibsen, in such
parts as Salome and Cleopatra, and in the plays
of Maeterlinck.

F

FABBRICHESI, SALVATORE (1760–1827), see MODENA.

FABRE D'ÉGLANTINE, PHILIPPE FRANÇOIS NAZAIRE (1755–94), French dramatist and revolutionary who took the name 'Églantine' after winning a prize at the Floral Games of Toulouse for his verses. His origin is unknown, but he was for some time an actor. Although he had a good voice and presence, he was unsuccessful, and soon forsook the stage in order to devote himself to the Revolution. In this he took an active part, being a member of the Convention with Danton, Marat, and Robespierre. His excesses led to his downfall, and he was guillotined in April 1794. He wrote several poor plays and a number of libretti for the little theatres. In 1790 he produced *Le Philinte de Molière*, which showed what he could do, and gave promise of great things in the future. But he had time for nothing more. He was very much a child of the Revolution which destroyed him, and his faults were more those of his age than of his character.

FABULA. 1. ATELLANA. Like their Neapolitan descendants at the present day, the inhabitants of the pleasant land of Campania had in antiquity a reputation for love of jest and merriment. At an early period there grew up here a rustic farce which displayed certain traditional characters in ridiculous situations. This farce seems to have been designed to suit the taste of the crowds which gathered on market days in country towns, and its Latin name is apparently connected with the small town of Atella, nine miles from Capua on the road to Naples. Greek influence was widespread along the Campanian coast, but the Campanian farce was always sharply distinguished by the Romans from Greek performances of a farcical nature such as the mime. The essential feature of the *atellana* was the appearance of certain traditional characters, Maccus and Bucco, both clowns, Pappus the Old Fool, Manducus the Ogre, Dossennus. All these have a family resemblance as coarse, greedy clowns, whose animal characteristics were such as might amuse a primitive and rustic audience, ever ready to laugh at guzzling and drunkenness, horseplay and obscene jest. Manducus was certainly an ogre with champing jaws; *manducare*, to champ the jaws, is the slang word for 'to eat' from which is derived the French *manger*. It has been thought that Bucco means 'Fat-cheeks' (*buccae*) and Dossennus 'Hunchback' (*dorsum*), but this is uncertain. These stock roles would require stock costumes and masks. Indeed, a recurring motif of the *atellana* was disguise and masquerade. Hence arose those complications, *tricae Atellanae* (the origin of our word 'intrigue'), indi-

cated by such titles as *Maccus the Maiden.* Atellan pieces were apparently of no great length; the number of characters is said to have been small. The use of *atellanae* as *exodia* or interludes would suggest that in length they corresponded to our curtain-raisers, and they were in all probability impromptu performances until they received literary form in the time of Sulla. Originally given in the Oscan tongue, they assumed Latin dress when they came to Rome. The performers must have been professionals; Plautus makes a character, whose teeth are chattering with cold, propose to 'hire himself out as a Manducus at the games'. Plautus also uses the word *bucco* in the sense of fool, and the prologues to the *Mercator* and *Asinaria* give the author's name as Maccus. Livy's account of theatrical origins in Rome seems to be largely theorizing, but he does assert that in his own day the Atellani (professional performers of Atellan plays) were of citizen status. Most of our information about the *atellanae* is derived from the literary *Atellanae* of Pomponius and Novius, who belong to the opening decades of the first century B.C. But the very assumption of literary form must necessarily have altered the character of this type of farce; though Pomponius and Novius strove to retain the traditional characters and the rustic style of jest, the surviving titles and fragments remind us at times of other forms of drama, the *palliata*, the mime, the Greek satyric play, and the mythological burlesque of Tarentum, the so-called *rhinthonica* or *hilarotragoedia*. At the beginning of the first century B.C. farce seems to gain at the expense of higher forms of drama; from now on we hear of no writer who made a living by writing tragedy or comedy for the stage. From Pomponius we have the titles of 70 *atellanae*, with fragments amounting to 200 lines or parts of lines; from Novius we have 44 titles with over 100 lines of fragments. To distinguish between the styles of these two writers seems impossible, so meagre is our information. The stock characters frequently appear. Maccus appears to be the most popular; we hear of *Maccus the Soldier, Maccus the Inn-keeper, Maccus the Maiden, Maccus in Exile,* and even *The Twin Macci.* We have also such titles as *Bucco the Gladiator, Bucco Adopted, Pappus the Farmer, The Bride of Pappus, Pappus Defeated at the Poll,* and *The Two Dossenni.* Other titles point to the maintenance of the primitive rustic atmosphere: *The Pig, The Sow, Hog(g) Sick, Hog(g) Well* (companion pieces these, one would imagine), *The Farmer, The Woodpile, A-Hoeing, The Vine-Gatherers, The She-Ass, The She-Goat.* Others suggest the life of the town: *The Candidate, The Fullers, The Inspector of Morals, The Pimp.* Such characters might easily be imagined in any fair-sized town of Campania, and indeed some of the fragments remind us of the scribblings on the walls of Pompeii. Here, then, the *atellana* approached the boundaries of the *togata* (see below, 9); other titles remind us of the *palliata* (see below, 3)—*Synephebi, Adelphi, Hetaera*; yet others of the *hilarotragoedia* (see below, 5)—*The Counterfeit Agamemnon, Marsyas, Phoenissae*. That Maccus might be dressed up as a maiden is shown by the title *Maccus Virgo*; and the feelings of someone who is deceived by such a trick are expressed in a fragment of the *Macci Gemini* of Pomponius. Elsewhere we find someone being coached to adapt his voice to a woman's role; this kind of impersonation must have been popular with the Romans, witness the concluding and very Roman scenes in the *Casina* of Plautus. Bucco's clownish wit appears in his over-literal interpretation of a request to 'Handle the job cleanly', to which he replies 'I have already washed my hands'. In Pappus the disadvantages of old age were satirized without mercy; whether as a candidate for election, a lover, or a husband, he is sure to be unlucky. We cannot tell how many of these stock characters appeared in any one piece. The language is homely; a peasant defines wealth as 'a short-lived blessing, like Sardinian cheese'. As contrasted with the *palliata*, the *atellana* was vulgar and rustic; this rustic quality, as well as the use of masks, differentiated it from the equally vulgar mime. There were plenty of jokes; Cicero, when discussing the subject of jest, turns for examples to the *Atellanae* of Novius. The scantiness of literary fragments from *atellanae* after the days of Pomponius and Novius suggests that the *atellana* returned to its improvised character. We have a few lines of Atellan songs from the Early Empire, e.g. Datus, an Atellan actor in the time of Nero, sang in Greek a song containing the words 'Health to you, father; health to you, mother', at the same time indicating by gestures the acts of drinking and swimming—the point being that Claudius, Nero's stepfather, had been poisoned, and Nero had tried to bring about Agrippina's death by drowning. Songs of this kind would no doubt have to be written down, and so might outlive the dialogue, which may have consisted largely of 'patter'. The line quoted also illustrates the perennial, often fatal, interest of the Atellan performers in politics. In spite of all extraneous influence which acted on it, this masked farce seems to have retained something of its primitive, rustic, Italian character, and on the stages of the Early Empire its performers, though social outcasts, enjoyed considerable popularity. Eventually, it would seem, they had to yield place to the mime.

2. CREPIDATA. The meaning of this rare term is not clear, but as the *crepida* was a Greek shoe, regularly worn with the *pallium*, the word was probably a synonym for *palliata* (see below, 3). The *cothurnus*, or boot worn by tragic actors, was quite different from the *crepida*.

3. PALLIATA, a play translated from Greek New Comedy (see GREECE, 2 *b* and MENANDER),

from *pallium*, the Greek cloak of everyday wear. For authors of *palliatae* see Andronicus, Caecilius, Naevius, Plautus, and Terence. The last writer of *palliatae* for the stage was Turpilius, who died in 103 B.C.

4. PRAETEXTA or PRAETEXTATA, an original Latin play of serious character on a theme taken from Roman legend or contemporary history; from *toga praetextata*, the purple-bordered toga worn by Roman magistrates. This form of drama was created by Naevius, but we know of only about half-a-dozen fairly certain examples from the time of the Republic. It may be that those *praetextae* which dealt with recent events were intended for production at the funeral games of the heroes whose victories they celebrated, thus avoiding a violation of the general principle that the names of living men must not be mentioned on the stage. To deal with affairs and personalities fresh in the minds of all present must have been a delicate matter, as we see from the fate of Naevius himself. Accius, Ennius, and Pacuvius are thought to have written *praetextae*. In 43 B.C. L. Cornelius Balbus illustrated his lack of good taste by producing at Gades a *praetexta* on his own achievements in the Civil War. Other *praetextae* intended for reading only were written under the Empire; we possess only the *Octavia*.

5. RHINTHONICA, a burlesque of tragedy, named after the Greek writer Rhinthon of Tarentum (*fl. c.* 300 B.C.). Another name for it was *hilarotragoedia*, or Merry Tragedy. The popularity of such plays among the Greeks of southern Italy is illustrated by the so-called phlyax vases, which show, for example, Zeus on a love-adventure about to climb a ladder to the window from which a lady is looking out, while Hermes holds a lantern to assist him. Our nearest example in Latin is the *Amphitruo* of Plautus.

6. RICINIATA, a synonym of mime (see MIME, 2), from *ricinium*, the hood worn in the characteristic mime-costume.

7. SALTICA, a 'play for dancing', that is, the libretto to be sung by the chorus in a pantomime (see PANTOMIME, 1 and PANTOMIMUS).

8. TABERNARIA, apparently a synonym for *togata* (see below), from *taberna*, a poor man's house.

9. TOGATA, or Roman Comedy, arose out of the irrepressible Italian instinct for social satire and topical allusion—an instinct which failed to find satisfaction in the imported *palliata*, especially in its later and more strictly Hellenic form. But as the ruling classes at Rome would have reacted vigorously to any political or personal attacks on them, the *togata* seems to have found its themes in the life of ordinary folk in Italian towns or among the lower classes in Rome. We have the names of three writers of *togatae*—Titinius (15 titles of his and 180 lines are preserved), Atta (11 titles, 20 lines), and Afranius (44 titles, 400 lines); they all seem to have lived in the second century B.C. Afranius seems to have been the ablest; we hear further that he introduced into

his plays the theme of homosexuality; but the material does not enable us to distinguish very clearly between the three writers. The extant titles bring us into a brisk world of business, amusement, matchmaking, and family relationship: *The Weavers, The Games the Aedile Gave, The Matchmaker, The Aunt, The Mother-in-Law, The Clown's Adoption, The Divorce, The Hairdresser, The Butler, Tit for Tat, Neck or Nothing, Fire!* It would seem that the plot might be fairly complex. The *Vopiscus* of Afranius introduces the parents of the 'twin that lived', a newly married pair (scarcely to be identified with these parents), a husband whose wife has left him, a woman who feigns submission while really playing on the violence of a man's temper, a trusted parasite, a pampered slave, a door-keeper, a lady's maid. The *Fullonia* of Titinius shows us a wrangle between fullers and weavers, a wife who complains that her husband is squandering her dowry, and a philanderer who, in fear of capture by an angry husband, is about to commit himself (like brave Horatius) to the Tiber. On the other hand, we have a statement by a scholiast that the cast of a *togata*, like that of an *atellana*, was smaller than that of a *palliata*; and on general grounds we should suspect that an average *togata* would be both shorter and simpler than a comedy taken from the Greek. We are told by Donatus that in the *togata* slaves were not allowed to be cleverer than their masters; it would seem, then, that in the *togata* we must have none of those swindling slaves who extract money from their old masters and assume control of their young masters' affairs. The wheels of the *palliata* were set in motion by love; yet, as Athenian convention prevented young women of good class from appearing in public, the dramatists have to employ various devices—midnight festivals, kidnapping, exposure of children, recognition scenes—if a love-plot, leading to marriage, is to be at all possible. In Roman life women of the citizen class had much more freedom; and indeed in the fragments of the *togata* we find that they can appear in public, can meet eligible suitors, and can accompany their fiancés on social calls. It would seem, then, that the typical plots of the *palliata* would be out of place in the *togata*, in which we find an atmosphere of family life not altogether unlike our own, where marriage is to some extent based on mutual attraction, and where relatives, male and female, express their opinions about a projected match. There is no sign of a romantic interest in Afranius's *Setina*, where the reluctant suitor doubts the wisdom of aspiring to a maiden of superior fortune, or in the family councils of the *Fratriae*, where it is calculated that a pretty girl will need less dowry, and a hope is expressed for possible advantages in kind if she marries the confectioner. In general we should suspect that the *togata* was not sentimental but lively, amusing, and satirical. The opening scene of Afranius's *Epistula* shows some eager gallant or belated reveller, bareheaded and be-slippered, out of

doors in the cold air of a winter's dawn; the other fragments of this play give us glimpses of a drinking-party, of someone escaping from a street-bully, of someone dressed up as a girl, of a girl who can hardly restrain her laughter while her mother storms in fury, and of a general state of domestic turmoil. In *The Divorce* a father forces his daughters to leave their husbands, in *The Pretender* another father is advised to follow a similar course. Elsewhere we hear of husbands trying to play the gallant —a stock theme in the *palliata*, it is true, but in the *togata* there is this curious difference: the erring husband chooses not the town but the country for his amours. Afranius's use of sodomy as a theme shows that the *togata* was unfettered by the sexual conventions which the *palliata* had taken over from New Comedy. In the *palliata* a man may love anyone except 'maiden, wife or widow, youths or boys' (*Curculio*, ll. 37–8)—in other words, love-affairs can only occur between the hero and a girl who for some reason is not regarded as his social equal. In the *togata* we hear of adultery involving women of respectable position. What the fragments do not tell us is how a coherent plot was built up around such themes; indeed, in the whole range of Latin stage-drama, we have no knowledge of the course of so much as one plot invented by a Latin writer. The *togata* must have enjoyed some popularity, at least during the lifetime of its authors, for we have the titles of seventy pieces. Revivals at a later period are not often recorded. The purely literary *togata* continued to be written down to Juvenal's day.

10. TRABEATA, a form of *togata* dealing with Roman knights, from *trabea*, the official robe of the equestrian order. Invented by Melissus, the freedman of Maecenas, it was probably short-lived; at all events we know nothing else about it.

W. B.

FAGAN, JAMES BERNARD (1873–1933), English playwright and producer, who in 1923 founded a repertory theatre in the old Big-Game Museum on the Woodstock Road, Oxford, and for two seasons produced there a series of excellent plays with a young company which included at various times Flora Robson, Dorothy Green, Molly McArthur, John Gielgud, Tyrone Guthrie, and Raymond Massey. Fagan himself had begun his career in Benson's company, making his first appearance in 1895; he then played two seasons under Tree at His Majesty's and after some years in retirement took over the management of the Court Theatre, where he gave some notable productions of Shakespeare, including *The Merchant of Venice* with Moskovitch as Shylock. In 1929 he became director of the Festival Theatre, Cambridge, and he was also responsible for many productions by the Irish Players. Among his own plays the most successful were *The Wheel* (1922), *And So To Bed* (1926), and *The Improper Duchess* (1931). A kindly, lovable man, widely read and extremely cultured, he worked tirelessly for the betterment of the

English theatre, on which his unobtrusive work had a profound influence.

FAIKO, ALEXEI MIKHAILOVICH (1893–   ), Soviet dramatist, whose most important play to date, *The Man with the Portfolio*, was produced in 1928. It deals for the first time in Soviet drama with the problem, not of the worker nor of the aristocrat, but of the intellectual man confronted with the new régime to which he is largely hostile. The hero, a professor in a Moscow college, tries to make the best of both worlds by conforming in public, and abusing the Government in private, but everything works against him, and finally, a spiritual bankrupt, he commits suicide. The play has its melodramatic moments, and the ending is somewhat contrived, but its production marked an immense step forward in Soviet dramatic history. Unfortunately Faiko does not seem to have touched such heights again, and his later work has been somewhat trivial.

FAIR, WILLIAM B. (1851–1909), music-hall performer. He is best remembered as the singer of 'Tommy, Make Room for your Uncle', with which he made a fortune, singing it at as many as six halls a night. With the money thus earned he bought the Surrey Music-Hall (renamed the Winchester), lost every penny, returned to the halls as Chairman, and ended as link-man outside the Coliseum.

FAIRBROTHER, SYDNEY (1872–1941), see COWELL (5).

FAIRS. In England and Europe the big fairs, held usually in the spring and autumn, were from the beginning associated with theatrical enterprise, just as the small country fairs were never without their little groups of acrobats, dancers, and singers. The assembling of a number of people in one place for a definite time provided a ready-made audience for the travelling companies of the fifteenth and sixteenth centuries, and finally provided them with a site on which to build a permanent theatre. This was most noticeable in the case of the Parisian fairs, particularly that of Saint-Germain in early spring, and that of Saint-Laurent in August and September. Some of the best-known farce-players of seventeenth-century Paris are believed to have graduated from the fairs, or to have been the children of fair-ground actors, but the main development of the Forains, as they were called, came at the end of the seventeenth and in the eighteenth centuries, when they gradually extended their season beyond that of the fairs proper, and replaced their wooden booths with permanent playhouses. Their popularity, and the fact that during the fairs provincial companies were allowed to play in Paris without further permission, gave constant annoyance to the Comédie-Française and the Comédie-Italienne. The latter finally made common cause with the enemy and combined with the Forains to form the Opéra-Comique, occupying during the summer months the Théâtre de la Foire Saint-Laurent, built in 1721 and finally destroyed in the rebuilding of the Opéra-Comique in 1761.

The old French farce survived at the fairs in the form of the *parade*, a rough sketch played on a long narrow balcony, traditionally the one overlooking the courtyard of the Foire Saint-Germain. This was destroyed in 1756, but the plots of the *parades* were printed in a volume entitled *Théâtre des Boulevards*, in which the genre is explained. They were meant to arouse the interest of the spectator in the play to be given inside the booth or, later, playhouse, and by the names of the characters show their affinity with the *commedia dell'arte*. After the French Revolution the freedom accorded to the theatres led the Forains to settle permanently on the Boulevard du Temple, where Bobèche and Galimafré revived the *parade*, and where a number of small but important playhouses were built, including Deburau's Funambules, the Gaîté, the Ambigu-Comique, and the Cirque Franconi, as well as innumerable small booths of acrobats and marionettes. The whole thing was swept away at the height of its success by Haussmann in his rebuilding scheme in 1862, thus breaking the last link between the modern theatre and the old fairground actor.

In England the fairs of Saint Bartholomew, Smithfield, and Southwark, as well as the smaller Greenwich and May fairs, were always connected with theatrical entertainments, particularly puppet shows, and there were also booths for the accommodation of living actors. The dramatist Elkanah Settle is believed to have ended his days as a green dragon in Mrs. Myn's booth at Southwark, and he also wrote drolls and short sketches for Bartholomew Fair. The theatrical development of the English fairs was, however, less noticeable than in France, perhaps owing to the greater inclemency of the weather, which must often have precluded open-air entertainment, and there is no record of any permanent playhouses being built on fair-sites. The English fair is portrayed in Jonson's *Bartholomew Fair* (1614) and in some of the plays of Shadwell (see also ENGLISH FAIRGROUND AND PORTABLE THEATRES).

Of the German fairs, held in different towns, those of Leipzig and Frankfurt are best known in connexion with theatrical matters. It was at Frankfurt that the English Comedians appeared most frequently and had, if anywhere, a permanent home, while Leipzig saw the reforms of Gottsched first put into action by the great actress Caroline Neuber. Fairs also played a big part in the history of the early Russian theatre, which, however, developed somewhat differently from the rest of Europe. Little information seems to be available on the fairs of Italy and Spain, but no doubt the *commedia dell'arte* in the first, and the travelling companies of such actor-managers as Lope de Rueda in the second, were to be found wherever they saw the chance of a ready-made audience.

FALLING FLAPS, see TRICKWORK ON THE ENGLISH STAGE.

FALSE PROSCENIUM, see PROSCENIUM.

FAMILY BOX, see AUDITORIUM, 3 and BOX.

FAN EFFECT, a method of scene-changing used in the Transformation Scene (see TRICKWORK ON THE ENGLISH STAGE).

FARCE, an extreme form of comedy in which laughter is raised at the expense of probability, particularly by horse-play and bodily assault. It must, however, retain its hold on humanity, even if only in depicting the grosser faults of mankind; otherwise it degenerates into travesty and burlesque. Its subject is the inherent stupidity of man at odds with his environment, and it belongs in its origins to the great submerged stream of folk-drama of which little written record remains. It stands at the beginning of classical drama (see GREECE, 2 and FABULA, 1) as of modern European, and was most popular in France, where in the seventeenth century the great farce-players, Turlupin, Gros-Guillaume, and Gaultier-Garguille, kept alive the old traditions. These gradually died out, and the farce was last seen at the Théâtre du Marais, in the lifetime of Jodelet. It had a great influence on Molière, who must often have seen and played in old farces, particularly in the districts round Lyons, and whose own early plays followed the old pattern. Among the many that were long current, of which the greater part no doubt were never written down, the best known is *Maître Pierre Pathelin*, which has survived revision, adaptation, and even translation, without losing its savour and robust humour. There were elements of farce in early English biblical plays, and later farcical interludes were written by scholars for production in schools and other places, but, as in Italy and Germany, it was the influence of the French farce that was paramount in its development, culminating in the works of John Heywood.

In the eighteenth and nineteenth centuries short one-act farces were popular on the English and American stages, usually as part of a bill which included also a five-act tragedy. They were ephemeral productions, though some of them achieved a great success, mainly through the acting of some particular comedian. A few might bear revival. In modern usage the word farce is applied to a full-length play dealing with some absurd situation hingeing generally on extra-marital relations—hence the term bedroom farce. Farce has small literary merit, but great entertainment value, and owing to its lack of subtlety can be translated from one language to another more easily than comedy.

FARINE, JEAN (*fl.* 1600–35), a mountebank in the style of Tabarin, who is believed to have been originally a travelling quack doctor. After having served his apprenticeship at the Paris fairs he went to the Hôtel de Bourgogne with Bruscambille, and together they played improvised farces in the manner of Turlupin and his associates, with whom they are often mentioned approvingly in contemporary doggerel.

FARJEON, HERBERT (1887–1945), see JEFFERSON (7).

FARNESE THEATRE, PARMA, see SPECTACLE THEATRES.

FARQUHAR, GEORGE (1678–1707), English dramatist, usually classed among the writers of Restoration Comedy, though chronologically and spiritually he stands a little apart from them, showing more variety of plot and depth of feeling, and, in his later and best plays, a more conscious effort to adapt the licentiousness of the early comedy of manners to the changing taste of the time. Born in Ireland and educated at Trinity College, Dublin, Farquhar was for a short time an actor, but left the stage after accidentally wounding a fellow actor in the last act of Dryden's *The Indian Emperor* by attacking him with a real instead of a property sword. He may also have had some doubts as to his abilities, and believed himself more fitted for writing than acting. With the assistance of Wilks, who remained his firm friend in later life, he went to London, where his first play was successfully produced at Drury Lane in 1698. With the second, *The Constant Couple; or, a Trip to the Jubilee* (1699), Farquhar established his reputation as one of the outstanding dramatists of the day, and the play held the stage throughout the eighteenth century, the hero, Sir Harry Wildair, first played by Wilks, being a favourite breeches part with Peg Woffington and Dorothy Jordan. A sequel to it proved less successful, as did a revision of one of Fletcher's comedies, and a melodrama entitled *The Twin Rivals* (1702), and Farquhar left London for some time, after a sudden marriage with a penniless lady whom he believed to be an heiress. He bore this misfortune with what his contemporaries regarded as noble resignation, and appears to have been happy in his family life, though always harassed by financial entanglements and two daughters. He returned to the theatre in 1706 with a fine comedy entitled *The Recruiting Officer*, based on his own experiences in that capacity in Shropshire, where he was sent to get together a company for the War of the Spanish Succession. This was an immediate success, and was followed by what many critics regard as Farquhar's finest play, *The Beaux' Stratagem*, given at Drury Lane in 1707 with Wilks as Archer, and Anne Oldfield —with whom the dramatist was at one time in love—as Mrs. Sullen. It has since been frequently revived, notably at the Lyric, Hammersmith (1927), and at the Royalty (1930), with Edith Evans as Mrs. Sullen. The play has a wholesome, open-air humour in which, says Professor Strauss in his study of it, Farquhar 'blended the essentials of character, plot, and situation in juster proportions than any previous writer of realistic comedy. . . . The result was a form of comedy unsurpassed for naturalness and fidelity to life: the form adopted and perfected by Sheridan and Goldsmith.'

This was Farquhar's last work, written in six weeks while he was lying ill and harassed in mean lodgings, with no encouragement but that of the faithful Wilks. His early death was a great loss to the stage, since *The Beaux' Stratagem* shows clearly the way in which he might have developed, with subsequent benefit to the history of English comedy.

FARREN, ELIZABETH (1759–1829), English actress, child of strolling players, with whom she appeared from her earliest years. She made her first appearance in London on 9 June 1777 at the Haymarket, as Miss Hardcastle, and then went to Drury Lane. She was not immediately successful, owing to the popularity of Mrs. Abington, but she soon became recognized as the outstanding player of fine ladies, to which her natural elegance, tall, slim figure, and beautiful voice rendered her particularly suitable. Horace Walpole considered her the best actress he had ever seen, and was enchanted by her keen wit. She was received everywhere on an equal footing with women of birth and fashion, and at one time organized private theatricals for the Duke of Richmond. The Earl of Derby was in love with her for many years, and married her on the death of his wife in 1797, in which year she made her last appearance on the stage as Lady Teazle. She was much regretted, and Boaden considered that her loss 'produced the degeneracy of comedy into farce'. Her elder sister was also an actress, known as Mrs. Knight.

FARREN. (1) WILLIAM (1725–95), English actor, head of a distinguished theatrical family, who was at Drury Lane from 1776 to 1784, and then at Covent Garden until his death. He was the first to play Careless in *The School for Scandal* and Leicester in *The Critic*, and also had some success in Shakespeare in such parts as Hotspur, the Ghost in *Hamlet*, and Buckingham in *Henry VIII*. His two sons (2) PERCIVAL (1784–1843) and (3) WILLIAM (1786–1861) were also on the stage, though the elder afterwards deserted the boards for stage-management. He was the friend and tutor of Helen Faucit, whom he prepared for her first appearance in 1833, by which time a severe asthmatical condition had caused his retirement from the theatre. William made his début at Plymouth, under his brother's management, and first appeared in London at Covent Garden in 1818 as Sir Peter Teazle, always one of his finest parts. Vandenhoff, writing of him in this role, said: 'I have never seen any representation of Sir Peter that could compare with him in animation, ease, naturalness of manner and piquancy of effect.' He was equally good in such parts as Lord Ogleby, and during his long career he appeared also in a number of Shakespearian

roles, Aguecheek, Shallow, Malvolio, Polonius, and Dogberry being perhaps his best. He retired in 1853, his last years on the stage having been overshadowed by the effects of a stroke. Contemporary critics were loud in his praise, Lewes going so far as to compare him for quickness of apprehension and natural elegance to the best French actors of the day. William's two sons, (4) WILLIAM (1825–1908) and (5) HENRY (1826–60), were both actors, the former being connected with the Haymarket from 1853 to 1867. He played a number of original roles in Tom Taylor's plays, and was the first Sir Geoffrey Champneys in *Our Boys*. His son (6) WILLIAM (Percival) (1853–1937) was also an actor and dramatist. Henry made his London début under his father before going to America, where he remained until his early death while managing the theatre at St. Louis. Of his three daughters, all actresses, one married the brother of Mary Moore, while the most famous was (7) ELLEN (1848–1904), known as Nellie, a favourite at the old Gaiety Theatre, London, from 1868 until her retirement in 1891. She was a member of the famous burlesque quartette with Edward Terry, Kate Vaughan, and Edward Royce. She specialized in the playing of boys' parts—Smike, Sam Willoughby in *The Ticket-of-Leave Man*, and the Cockney and cheeky boys in Byron's burlesques and extravaganzas. A contemporary critic said of her: 'Miss Farren may be a wife and a mother, but she is certainly one of the best boys in existence.' Her husband, Robert Soutar, and her two sons were all on the stage. Towards the end of her career she contemplated a return to serious comedy, but ill health forced her to retire before she had achieved this ambition.

FASTNACHTSSPIEL, the German Carnival or Shrovetide play of the fifteenth century, performed mainly by students and artisans. It shows, in its somewhat crude couplets, a mingling of religious and popular elements interesting in the light of later developments in German drama, and is somewhat akin to the French *sotie* (see also GERMANY, 1).

FATE DRAMA, the name given to a type of early nineteenth-century German play, inaugurated by Werner's *Der vierundzwanzigste Februar* (1809), in which a malignant fate is shown to be dogging the footsteps of some unfortunate and fear-ridden mortal, driving him, by a chain of fortuitous circumstances, to commit a horrible crime. In Werner's play, for instance, a father unsuspectingly kills his own son, the fatal instrument, a dagger, falling from the wall at the fatal moment. The genre was further exploited by Adolf Müllner in *Der neunundzwanzigste Februar* (1812), and by the young Grillparzer in *Die Ahnfrau* (1817), his first play, which has been described as having 'all the *frissons* of Gothic romance'.

FATHER OF THE HALLS, see MORTON, CHARLES.

FAUCIT, HELEN [HELENA SAVILLE] (1817–98), English actress of great beauty and charm, whose best work was done in revivals of Shakespeare and in new verse dramas, many of them written specially for her. She first appeared in London in 1836, in *The Hunchback*, and was much admired, though some critics found her acting somewhat exaggerated. In the dearth of fine actresses at that period she shone even more brightly, and appeared with Macready and Phelps, one of her finest parts being Pauline in *The Lady of Lyons*. She appeared in several other plays by Bulwer Lytton, and in Browning's *Strafford* (1837), *A Blot on the 'Scutcheon* (1843), and *Colombe's Birthday* (1853). It is said that her refusal to appear in Matthew Arnold's *Merope* caused him to abandon its production. She appeared in Paris with great success, and embodied her experiences as an interpreter of Shakespeare in a volume entitled *On Some of Shakespeare's Female Characters* (1885). She married in 1851, becoming Lady Martin when her husband was knighted in 1880. In later life she acted almost entirely on behalf of various charities and was a friend and guest of Queen Victoria.

FAUST. A medieval legend of a man who sells his soul to the devil became linked up in the sixteenth century with the name and adventures of a wandering conjuror, Johann Faust (*c.* 1488–1541). His story was published in a chapbook produced in Frankfort in 1587, and found its way to England in translation, to provide the material for Marlowe's *Tragical History of Doctor Faustus* (*c.* 1588, publ. 1601 or 1604). It returned to its country of origin via the English Comedians, and lived on until the eighteenth century in a popular puppet show which greatly disgusted the literary precisian, Gottsched. It was first taken up seriously in Germany in 1759 by Lessing, who saw in it a reflection of his own problem, that of a scholar's inquiring mind in conflict with the limits imposed by the Almighty. Only two scenes of Lessing's version appeared during his lifetime, but it is clear from fragments and from accounts of it published posthumously that Faust's soul was to be saved. One account speaks of an angelic voice declaring that man's noblest impulse was not given him in order to lead him to eternal pain.

During the *Sturm und Drang* period the legend made an instant appeal, and was taken up by Goethe, Müller, and Klinger, each treating it in the light of his own temperament. The scenes Müller wrote have an unromantic realism, Faust being driven to make his pact with the devil largely through pecuniary difficulties. In Klinger's novel Faust attempts to use his powers to right the wrongs of this world, only to find that he has caused more evil than he has countered. He ends in the deepest confines of hell, cursing the Almighty.

In Goethe's version, of which Part I was begun about 1774 and published in 1808, while Part II did not appear until 1832, the year of his death, Faust is possessed by a thirst not only for knowledge but for experience. Mephistopheles fosters his illicit relations with Gretchen (Margaret), an innocent, loving girl, who perishes on the scaffold for child-murder (end of Part I). Mephistopheles had reckoned that Faust's impulse to action would be choked by despair and remorse; but Goethe's Faust, who, far from striking a bargain with hell, had defied the devil to bring him satisfaction, never flags. His energies are directed to wider spheres, and he finally embarks on the reclamation of land from the sea, an enterprise which will benefit mankind. The initiative has passed from Mephistopheles to Faust, and though in the closing scene of his life the latter declares himself satisfied, this satisfaction is not the result of the devil's efforts. Consequently hell has no power over his soul, and by the grace of God it is borne away to heaven.

Since Goethe's *Faust* the subject has been treated again by Lenau, Heine, Grabbe, and others. It has also formed the subject of operas by Gounod and Boito (based on Goethe) and by Spohr and Busoni (in new versions).

FAVART. (1) CHARLES SIMON (1710–92), French dramatist, the son of a pastrycook, and the first man to make a solid reputation out of the writing of libretti for light opera, in which genre he was the mentor and forerunner of Marmontel and Sedaine. He had much in common with La Fontaine as regards style and easy versification and had also something of his wit and good humour. Favart's best works are written to be sung, and read poorly. His one straight play was an amusing trifle entitled *L'Anglais à Bordeaux*, given at the Comédie-Française in 1763. He married a charming actress, (2) MARIE JUSTINE BENOISTE DURONCERAY (1727–72), known before her marriage as Mlle Chantilly. She played for many years at the Comédie-Italienne, and is credited with the first introduction there of historical and local details into her costume, a practice soon to be inaugurated at the Comédie-Française by Lekain and Mlle Clairon. She and her husband were at one time members of the private company maintained by the Maréchal de Saxe.

FAVART, THÉÂTRE, see COMÉDIE-ITALIENNE.

FAVERSHAM, WILLIAM (1868–1940), American actor-manager, who was born in London and studied for the stage under Carlotta Leclercq. After a brief appearance in London he went to New York, and made his début there in 1887. He played small parts at the Lyceum with Daniel Frohman's company, and was for two years with Mrs. Fiske. In 1893 he was engaged by Charles Frohman for the Empire Theatre company, and remained there for eight years, playing a wide variety of parts, including Gil de Berault in *Under the Red Robe*, Lord Algernon in *Lord and Lady Algy*, Henry Beauclerc in *Diplomacy*, and Romeo to the Juliet of Maude Adams. He then starred in a number of modern plays, and in 1909 made his first independent venture with the production of *Herod*, in which he played the name part. It was, however, his production of *Julius Caesar* in 1912, in which he played Mark Antony, that set the seal on his growing reputation both as actor and director. With a fine cast, the play ran for some time in New York, and then went on tour, being followed by productions of *Othello* and *Romeo and Juliet*. After a further series of new plays, Faversham toured Australia, and on his return was seen in several more Shakespeare plays, and as Jeeter Lester in *Tobacco Road*.

FAY. (1) FRANK J. (1870–1931) and (2) WILLIAM GEORGE (1872–1947), Irish actors, who as amateurs produced and played in *Deirdre* and *Cathleen ni Houlihan* in Dublin in April 1902, and so, with Padraic Colum, Maude Gonne, Dudley Digges, and others, inaugurated the Irish National Theatre movement. They were also connected with the later productions of that group, the younger brother being particularly good in *The Pot of Broth*, and with the early years of the Abbey Theatre, Frank being primarily responsible for voice production and W. G. for stage direction. Stephen Gwynn, in *Irish Literature and Drama*, says of these first productions: 'The style of acting identified with the Abbey Theatre is due to the genius of the Fays—and of W. G. Fay especially.' It was a style which Fay himself defined when he wrote that he had endeavoured 'to enforce the most rigid economy of gesture and movement, to make the speaking quite abstract, and at the same time to keep a music in it by having all the voices harmonized'. Both brothers appeared in the most significant production of this period, *The Playboy of the Western World*, W. G. playing Christy Mahon and Frank his rival Shawn Keogh, as well as in most of the other plays seen at the Abbey. They left in 1908 and went to America, where they were responsible for the production of a repertory of Irish plays for Charles Frohman, in which they also appeared. Back in London in 1914, W. G. was seen in several new parts, and was successively producer at the Nottingham and the Birmingham Repertory theatres. Among his later parts were the Tramp in *The Shadow of the Glen*; Mr. Cassidy in *Storm in a Teacup*, which he also produced; Johnny Mahoney in *Spring Meeting*; and the name part in *Father Malachy's Miracle*. He produced a number of plays at the Arts Theatre, and in 1940 was seen as Stephano in the Old Vic production of *The Tempest*. He was the author of *The Fays of the Abbey Theatre* (1935), and of a volume of reminiscences, *Merely Players*, and in 1932 published *A Short Glossary of Theatrical Terms*.

FEAST OF FOOLS, see FOOLS, FEAST OF.

FECHTER, CHARLES ALBERT (1824–79), an actor who played in French and English, in Europe and America, with equal success. He first appeared in Paris at the Salle Molière in

1840, and made his début at the Comédie-Française in the same year. He soon left there, however, and his reputation was made at the smaller theatres, including the Porte-Saint-Martin. He was the first to play Armand Duval in *La Dame aux camélias* (1852). At this time he was the leading *jeune premier* of Paris, and co-director of the Odéon, but, chafing at the restrictions imposed on him by the Government in favour of the Comédie-Française, he came to England, where he had already appeared some years earlier, and played Ruy Blas in an English translation. Although his accent was never very good, he had confidence and fluency, and was much admired in London. It was his revolutionary Hamlet in 1861, however, which first brought him into prominence. Joseph Knight said of his performance that 'the text gained greatly in beauty and intelligibility by the abandonment of old traditions'. Fechter's reading brought out the subtlety and depth of the part, and even those who clung to the older view of Hamlet were impressed by his interpretation, while his admirers were fervent in his praise. His next venture was not so successful, and Lewes remarked that while his Hamlet was one of the best, his Othello was one of the worst he had ever seen. In a subsequent revival Fechter played Iago. In 1863 he took over the management of the London Lyceum, and appeared in a series of melodramas in which he proved himself a powerful actor, and one of the best exponents of youthful heroes on the English stage. He went to America in 1869, and after a successful tour opened the old Globe Theatre in New York as Fechter's. He was responsible for a number of improvements and innovations there, and appeared in a number of his old successes as well as in new plays; but his imperious and quarrelsome nature made him many enemies. He left for a short visit to England, and on his return to New York appeared only in revivals. In 1876 he retired to die on a farm near Philadelphia. He was the author of several dramatizations of novels, which he produced himself.

FEDELI, THE, a company of *commedia dell'arte* actors, formed probably by the younger Andreini in the last years of the sixteenth century, and always connected with him. Early records are scanty, and the company first comes into prominence in 1603. It was later strengthened by the inclusion of some of the actors from the disbanded Gelosi company, and between 1606 and 1608 several attempts were made to fuse the Fedeli with Cecchini's company, the Accesi, but without success, mainly owing to quarrels between the two men's wives and their mutual jealousies. These animosities continued to embitter relations between the two companies, and finally the Fedeli, without Cecchini, but with Tristano Martinelli as their Harlequin, returned to Paris for a long stay. Andreini (Lelio), Barbieri (Beltrame), and Gabrielli (Scapino) were particular favourites of the

Parisians and their king, Louis XIII. The company continued for some years, under the direction of Andreini, to tour Italy, but he and his companions were ageing, and the Fedeli seem to have been disbanded before Andreini, in his old age, made a final visit to Paris to play with Mazarin's company in 1644. The Fedeli had made for itself a fine reputation during the first quarter of the seventeenth century, and was accounted one of the best troupes of its time.

FEDERAL STREET THEATRE, see BOSTON.

FEDERAL THEATRE (1 Oct. 1935–1 July 1939). This was the first nation-wide federally sponsored theatre in the United States. It was a project of the Works Progress Administration to give employment to needy professional theatre people in socially useful jobs.

Directed nationally from Washington, it operated through regional assistants throughout the country. Payment at the security wage was less than prevailing pay for corresponding work in industry, but was adjusted through hours to meet that wage in order not to lower standards in the theatrical unions to which most of its personnel belonged. Nine out of ten of its members came from relief rolls, and nine dollars out of ten were spent for wages. In the beginning the Government paid, in addition to labour costs, all non-labour costs; by the end of the project, admissions (never higher than a dollar) totalled approximately $2,000,000 and were paying the equivalent of all non-labour costs—scenery, costumes, royalties, rentals, advertising—although 65 per cent. of the productions were free. At its peak employment Federal Theatre employed 10,000 people, 2,600 of whom were returned to private industry; operated theatres in 40 states; published a nationally distributed theatre magazine; conducted a play and research bureau serving not only its own theatres but 20,000 schools, churches, and community theatres throughout America; and played to audiences totalling many millions.

From the first Federal Theatre offered an ambitious programme of classical and modern plays, dance drama, musical comedy, children's plays, religious plays, marionette shows, and cycles of plays by distinguished dramatists and by young playwrights. Dramatic critics gave increasing approval and between 1936 and 1939 the Federal Theatre had successful plays running simultaneously on Broadway and throughout the country.

Drawing on various techniques, Federal Theatre invented the Living Newspaper, a terse, cinematic type of production dealing with such social and economic subjects as agriculture, flood control, and housing. *Triple A Plowed Under, Power*, and *One-Third of a Nation* pioneered in an art form still widely used in theatrical, cinematic, and radio production.

Other artistic achievements of the Project

included the development of a Negro theatre responsible for such productions as *Macbeth, Haiti, The Swing Mikado*; classical revivals such as *The Tragical History of Doctor Faustus*, Miracle and Morality plays, and a long line of Shakespeare revivals; an international cycle of plays from Euripides through Ibsen; simultaneous production in twenty-one cities of Sinclair Lewis's *It Can't Happen Here*; over national networks such well-known series as the *Epic of America, Men Against Death, Women of America*; nation-wide productions of plays by Elmer Rice, Eugene O'Neill, and Bernard Shaw, including the American première of *On the Rocks*; regional productions, such as *The Sun Rises in the West* in Los Angeles, and Paul Green's *The Lost Colony* on Manteo Island in North Carolina, which still plays to thousands of people each summer. On *Treasure Island* at the San Francisco Exposition, Federal Theatre built and equipped out of its own box-office receipts a modern theatre.

Sponsorship of Federal Theatre was wide and varied: theatre and other unions; schools and universities; churches—Catholic, Jewish, and Protestant; civic and community groups; industrial and philanthropic organizations; a great following of youth never before (or since) able to afford theatre-going. In *Federal Theatre Magazine* this audience speaks:

We're a hundred thousand kids who never saw a play before. We're students in colleges, house-wives in the Bronx, lumberjacks in Oregon, share-croppers in Georgia. We're rich and poor, old and young, sick and well. We're America and this is our theatre.

And in the same article:

We're the Caravan theatre in the parks, Shake-speare on a hillside, Gilbert and Sullivan on a lagoon, the circus under canvas, Toller on a hill. We're the theatre for the children of the steel mills in Gary; we're the theatre for the blind in Oklahoma. We're dramatic companies and vaudeville com-panies and marionette companies touring the C.C.C. camps, touring the flood areas, playing in schools, playgrounds, prisons, reformatories, hospitals. We're the Living Newspaper; we're the Negro theatre, the Yiddish theatre and theatres throughout America playing not only in English but in French, German, Italian, and Spanish; we're the file, we're the record, we're theatre history.

Emphatically a people's theatre, the candour of its comment on economic issues, especially in the Living Newspapers, led to criticism by witnesses before the House Committee to investigate un-American activities and before the sub-committee of the House Committee on Appropriations. All major units of screen, stage, and radio, many schools, churches, and sponsoring bodies spoke in favour of Federal Theatre. There was a struggle in Congress. The House voted to liquidate the project; the Senate voted to restore it. On 30 June 1939 the Federal Theatre was ended by Congres-sional action.   H. F. D.

FELLOWES, AMY, see TERRISS (1).

FENN, EZEKIEL (1620–?), a boy actor who at

the age of 15 played Sophonisba, the chief female part in *Hannibal and Scipio*. He must already have had a good deal of experience, since at about the same time he played Winifred, an even more exacting role, in a revival of *The Witch of Edmonton*. He was with the Queen's Men at the Cockpit, and stayed on with Beeston after their removal, possibly as one of the older members of Beeston's Boys. He must have had a good reputation and been very popular with his audience, since Henry Glapthorne wrote him a prologue in 1639 'at his first Acting a Man's Part'. It is not known what happened to Fenn on the closing of the theatres in 1642.

FENNELL, JAMES (1766–1816), an English actor, intended for the law, who went on the stage in 1787 at Edinburgh, as Mr. Cambray, his first part being Othello. Later in the same year he was at Covent Garden, but he was not outstandingly successful in London, and preferred to tour the provinces. In 1792 he went to America, where he was very popular. He was a member of the American Company, and also of Wignell's company in Philadelphia. His best part was always considered to be Othello, though he appeared in most of the tragic roles of the current repertory, including Jaffier. This he played at the Park Theatre, New York, in 1799, in company with Cooper and Mrs. Melmoth. He speculated heavily in salt, and fell into debt, retiring, after several farewell performances, in 1810. A fine man, six feet tall, with an expressive face, he was an excellent actor, and was also the author of a comedy and editor of a theatre magazine. In 1814 he published his autobiography, entitled *An Apology for the Life of James Fennell*.

FENTON, LAVINIA (1708–60), English actress, and the first to play Polly Peachum in *The Beggar's Opera*. She was the daughter of a naval lieutenant named Beswick, but took her name from her widowed mother's second husband, a coffee-house-keeper in Charing Cross. She made her first appearance on the stage at the Haymarket in 1726, as Monimia in *The Orphan*, followed by Cherry in *The Beaux' Stratagem*, and was an immediate success, being pretty, witty, and only 18. Her appearance as Polly at Lincoln's Inn Fields on 29 Jan. 1728 sealed her reputation, and she became one of the most-talked-of women of the London stage. She made her last appearance on 28 June 1728, and retired to live with the Duke of Bolton, whom she married in 1751.

FERBER, EDNA, see KAUFMAN and SHOWBOAT.

FERRARI, PAOLO (1822–89), one of the most popular Italian dramatists of his time. He studied law, and was engaged in its practice when his first plays were produced. He won fame when in 1853 his play about Goldoni, *Goldoni e le sue sedici commedie*, won a prize

offered by a Florentine dramatic academy. It was followed by several other plays, of which *Il Suicidio* (1875) held the stage for many years; but his best-known work is undoubtedly *La Satira e Parini* (1856), of which one character, Marchese Colombi, is as familiar to Italian audiences as Mrs. Malaprop to English.

FERRAVILLA, EDOARDO (1846–1915), Italian actor, trained by Modena, in whose company he played young lovers. He later developed as a great comedian and character-actor, and although he could when he wished play in pure Italian, it was in the comic exploitation of the Milanese dialect that he made his reputation, frequently writing his own plays. In 1870 he was joint founder with Arrighi of the Milanese Theatre.

FERREIRA, PROCÓPIO, see SOUTH AMERICA, 2.

FESTIVAL THEATRE, see CAMBRIDGE.

FESTSPIELHAUS, see ACOUSTICS, 8, BAYREUTH and OPERA, 11.

FEYDEAU, THÉÂTRE, see COMÉDIE-ITALIENNE.

FIABE, LE, the name given by Gozzi to his 'fairy-tale' plays (see ITALY, 2 vi).

FIELD, NATHAN (1587–1620), English actor and playwright, the son of a preacher who fulminated against the players. He was a scholar at St. Paul's in 1600, when the Master of the Children of the Chapel Royal, abusing the powers conferred upon him to impress singing-boys, snatched him away to become a boy actor. He went to Blackfriars, where he appeared in *Cynthia's Revels*, and later in the *Poetaster* and *Epicoene*. He also continued his education under Ben Jonson, reading Horace and Martial with him. Nat, or Nid Field, as he was commonly called (the modern form of Nathaniel is incorrect), was a wild and dissolute young man, constantly in debt, from which he was more than once rescued by Henslowe, but apparently an excellent actor, playing the parts of young lovers, and noted as excelling in the title-role of *Bussy d'Ambois*. He was absorbed into the company of the Lady Elizabeth's Men in 1613, and two years later joined the King's Men, possibly in succession to Shakespeare. He was the author of two plays, *A Woman is a Weathercock* (1609) and *Amends for Ladies* (1611), and collaborated in several works with Massinger and Fletcher. A portrait of him in Dulwich College shows him as a dark and handsome young man.

FIELDING, HENRY (1707–54), famous English novelist who in his early years played an important part in the development of the theatre, when he supported himself in London by writing comedies and farces in various styles. The best remembered of these is his burlesque on the serious drama of the day, *Tom Thumb, a Tragedy*, or, as it was called in a later revision, *The Tragedy of Tragedies; or, the Life and Death of Tom Thumb the Great.* This was first given in 1730 at the Haymarket, of which theatre Fielding was lessee from 1736 to 1737. He also produced there his political satires, *Pasquin* and *The Historical Register for 1736.* In these he attacked Walpole, as well as the Cibbers, to such an extent that the former was moved to restrict the liberty of the London theatres, reducing them by the Licensing Act to two only, Covent Garden and Drury Lane, and bringing all stage performances under the authority and censorship of the Lord Chamberlain. This brought to an end the dramatic career of Fielding, who henceforth turned to the less restricted form of the novel.

FIFTH AVENUE THEATRE, NEW YORK. (1) This was originally the Fifth Avenue Opera House, on 24th Street near Broadway, home of negro minstrelsy. On 2 Sept. 1867 it opened as a theatre with light entertainment and burlesques, of which the best was Talfourd's *Shylock; or, the Merchant of Venice Preserved*, with Leffingwell as Shylock. The theatre closed abruptly after a dispute in the auditorium which ended in the death of a member of the audience, and did not open again until 25 Jan. 1869, when John Brougham appeared there in one of his own plays. After another interval of idleness it finally opened on 16 Aug. 1869 as Daly's Fifth Avenue Theatre, with a good company which included Mrs. Gilbert and Fanny Davenport. A number of plays by Robertson, some old comedies, and Boucicault's *London Assurance*, with Fanny Davenport as Lady Gay Spanker, were seen in the first season, as was Mrs. Scott-Siddons as Viola and Rosalind. Daly's first outstanding success at this theatre was *Frou-Frou*, but he was anxious to encourage American dramatists, and on 21 Dec. 1870 produced Bronson Howard's first play, *Saratoga*, which had a long run. The theatre was by now firmly established, and in 1872 was redecorated and much improved. Some fine productions followed, but on New Year's Day 1873 it was burnt down. The company went to 728 Broadway temporarily, where *Alixe*, with Clara Morris, was produced.

(2) On 3 Dec. 1873 Daly opened his second Fifth Avenue Theatre at Broadway and 28th, but with little success. Among other failures was that of a costly and elaborate production on 21 Feb. 1874 of *Love's Labour's Lost*, which had not previously been seen in New York. The financial panic of 1873–4 had a bad effect on the theatre, but success came with the production on 17 Feb. 1875 of *The Big Bonanza*, in which John Drew made his New York début as Bob Ruggles. The following season saw the popular London success, *Our Boys*, with Maurice Barrymore, Fanny Davenport, Mrs. Gilbert, and Sydney Cowell, while Daly's *Pique*, in which Fanny Davenport had her first big starring role, was also a success. It was during the run of this play that Georgiana Drew, later the wife of Maurice Barrymore, made her first appearance in New York.

The season of 1876–7 was memorable for the first appearance of Charles Coghlan in New York as a leading man of distinction and charm. He played Orlando to Fanny Davenport's Rosalind, and appeared in a revival of *The School for Scandal* on 5 Dec. 1876, whose opening night success was marred by the disastrous Brooklyn Theatre fire in which over 300 people lost their lives. In 1877 Adelaide Neilson was seen at the Fifth Avenue as Viola, as Imogen, new to New York audiences, and as Juliet. Daly was now finding the financial loss on his theatre too great, and in 1878, after several failures, he found himself unable to pay the rent, and so left. The Fifth Avenue was taken over by Stephen Fiske, and Mary Anderson, at the age of 18, made her début there, followed by Helena Modjeska. The theatre was then leased to various travelling companies, and frequently housed light opera, including several of the Gilbert and Sullivan under D'Oyly Carte. After many changes of name this famous theatre was pulled down in 1908.

FIFTY-EIGHTH STREET THEATRE, NEW YORK, see CONCERT THEATRE.

FIFTY-FIRST STREET THEATRE, NEW YORK, see HOLLYWOOD THEATRE.

FILANDRE [JEAN BAPTISTE DE MOUCHAINGRE] (1616–91), a French actor-manager whose long and active life was spent entirely in the provinces, where he led a company which toured northern France, Holland, and Belgium. He is believed to have served as a model for Léandre in Scarron's novel, *Le Roman comique.* Floridor, the actor, who took a company to London in 1635, and was subsequently one of the stars of the Hôtel de Bourgogne, was for a short time associated with Filandre, as was Mlle Beauval, creator of some of Molière's most charming feminine roles.

FINN, HENRY JAMES (c. 1790–1840), American actor and playwright, who studied law at Princeton University, but deserted his profession to go on the stage. He was at the Charleston Theatre for some time, and in management in Boston with Thomas Kilner. After the burning of the Park Theatre, New York, in 1820, where he was a member of the resident company, he appeared at the Anthony Street Theatre as Hamlet, a part which he also played at Chatham Garden Theatre in the great season of 1824. He was also seen as Andrew Aguecheek, and finally deserted tragedy for comedy, in which he was inimitable. In 1825 he played Sergeant Welcome Sobersides in his own play *Montgomery; or, the Falls of Montmorency*, an amusing Yankee character who was later incorporated into *The Indian Wife* (1830), and played by James H. Hackett. Finn, who was also the author of an amusing farce, died in the destruction by fire of the S.S. *Lexington* in Long Island Sound.

FINN [KHALFIN], KONSTANTIN YAKOVLEVICH, (1904–), Soviet dramatist, whose comedies have a light ironic and lyrical touch, while dealing with the conflict of individual and environment, social outlook, and personal feelings. His greatest success to date has been *Nonsense*, produced in 1933 by V.Ts.P.S., which ridicules those who make love the only thing in life, while pointing the moral that hard work will go far to assuage a man's emotional pangs. Finn's later plays, particularly those produced during the Second World War, such as *Peter Krymov*, seem to point to his emergence as a playwright of considerable importance.

FIORILLO. A family of actors of the *commedia dell'arte*, of whom (1) SILVIO (?–*c*. 1632), the original Capitano Mattamoros, was probably the first Pulcinella. He had a company of his own in Naples, his birthplace, in the last years of the sixteenth century, and later appeared with other companies. He was the author of several plays, and of *scenarii* in the *commedia dell'arte* tradition. He had a son (2) GIOVAN BATTISTA (*fl.* 1614–51), who played the parts of Trappolino and Scaramuccia, and was married to (3) BEATRICE VITELLI (*fl.* 1638–54), also an actress.

It is now thought unlikely that (4) TIBERIO (1608–94) was also Silvio's son. His surname is also found as Fiurelli and Fiorilli. One of the most famous actors of his day, he was first in a poor company, but left it to make a name for himself elsewhere. He paid many visits to Paris, and was one of the Italian company at the Petit-Bourbon in 1658, when Molière's company was playing there on alternate days. He was the greatest, if not the first, actor of Scaramuccia (Scaramouche), which he played unmasked. His life was written by Angelo Costantini (Mezzetin), in 1695, and edited from the original impression, with introduction and notes, by Louis Moland in 1876. He visited London several times, notably in 1673, when he became the rage, displacing French puppets and English actors in the affections of fashionable society. He was a fine dancer and acrobat, and at the age of 80 was still so supple that he could tap a man's cheek with his foot.

FIRST GALLERY, see AUDITORIUM, 1 *c*.

FIRST PIPE, see LIGHTING, 3.

FISHER, CLARA (1811–98), a child prodigy who made her first appearance on the stage at the age of 6, being much admired as Richard III, Shylock, and Young Norval, as well as in such parts as Young Pickle and the Actress of All Work, in which she impersonated a series of characters. Having appeared at Drury Lane, Covent Garden, and in the provinces, she went in 1827 to New York, making her début at the Park Theatre as the four Mowbrays in *Old and Young*. For the next few years she toured in light opera and vaudeville, and in 1834 married a musician, James G. Maeder. She continued to act, however,

though with less than her former success, and was seen in a number of classic parts, such as Ophelia, Viola, Lady Teazle, and in modern comedies and musical comedy. She retired from the stage in 1844, but later returned to star in opera bouffe, finally retiring in 1880. Her brother John, and two sisters, Jane (Mrs. George Vernon) and Amelia, were also on the stage, appearing at the Park Theatre, New York, in the late 1830s. Jane, who died in 1869, was also at Wallack's, where she played old ladies and elderly secondary roles.

FISKE, MINNIE MADDERN (1865–1932), one of the outstanding women of the American stage, daughter of a theatrical agent in New Orleans. At the age of 3 she appeared on the stage, billed as Little Minnie Maddern, a name which she afterwards retained, her real name being Marie Augusta Davey. At 5 she was in New York, where her early appearances included Little Eva in *Uncle Tom's Cabin*, the Duke of York in Cibber's version of *Richard III*, Little Alice in *Kit the Arkansas Traveller*, and Arthur in *King John*. At 13, after some schooling and several tours in the South and Mid-West, she played the Widow Melnotte in *The Lady of Lyons*, and reappeared in New York on 15 May 1882, in a poor play in which she was much admired for the vivacity and naturalness of her acting. Several later productions served only to enhance her success, but in 1890 she retired from the stage on her marriage to Harrison Grey Fiske (1861–1942), editor of *The New York Dramatic Mirror*. The theatre at this time was in a state of transition, and in 1893 Mrs. Fiske, as she was now known, returned to the stage to star in her husband's *Hester Crewe*, an attempt to establish the new tradition in play-writing. She also appeared in *A Doll's House*, but it was her Tess in a dramatization of Hardy's novel by Lorrimer Stoddard, on 2 Mar. 1897 at the Fifth Avenue Theatre, that again won over the public. Charles Coghlan played Alec. Mrs. Fiske's versatility embraced Dora, Magda, and both light and musical comedy, one of her great successes at this time being in Langdon Mitchell's *Becky Sharp*, with Maurice Barrymore as Rawdon and Tyrone Power as Steyne. Since her husband's opposition to the powerful Theatrical Syndicate prevented her from appearing in their theatres, the Fiskes rented the Manhattan in 1901. For six years she played there with a splendid company, putting on a series of fine plays which were not equalled until the early years of the Theatre Guild. Among them were *Hedda Gabler* and *Rosmersholm*. Mrs. Fiske was also responsible for the first professional production of a play from Professor Baker's '47 Workshop', *Salvation Nell* (1908) by Sheldon. She also starred in his *High Road* (1912). A short but unsuccessful attempt at films resulted in her return to New York, where for some years she appeared in light comedies, followed by a long tour as Mrs. Malaprop, the finest since Mrs. John Drew. In 1927 she toured as Mrs. Alving in *Ghosts*, and one of her last productions was *Much Ado About Nothing*, in which she played Beatrice. In her last years she seldom appeared in New York, but revived her early successes on tour. Her acting was instinctively natural, and from 1893 on she was one of the most potent forces in the battle for realism on the New York stage. Even those who detested Ibsen had to admire her greatness in playing him, while she was, significantly, much admired by members of her own profession. During her six years in her own theatre she gave proof of great ability as a director, and she was always encouraging to young playwrights. In tragedy she was good, though not universally admired, but in comedy she had no peer among her contemporaries.

FITCH, WILLIAM CLYDE (1865–1909), one of America's best-loved and most prolific dramatists, who before his death at the age of 44 had written fifty plays. He began his career with *Beau Brummell*, commissioned from him by Richard Mansfield, who produced it in 1890 with himself in the title-role and retained it in his repertory until his retirement. Once launched Fitch continued to pour out plays, the best of his early ones being *Nathan Hale* (1898) and *Barbara Frietchie* (1899), based on American history, and showing in their mingling of personal and political problems a strength which might have taken Fitch far had he not been content to dabble in light comedy. He was at the height of his popularity in 1901, when *The Climbers* and *Lovers' Lane*, social comedies of life in New York, and *Captain Jinks of the Horse Marines*, in which Ethel Barrymore first appeared as a star under Charles Frohman, were running simultaneously in New York, while in London Tree was producing *The Last of the Dandies*. Among Fitch's other plays, many of which were written to order for certain stars, were *The Moth and the Flame* (1898), and *The Cowboy and the Lady* (1899), both melodramas, *The Stubbornness of Geraldine*, dealing with the American abroad, *The Girl with the Green Eyes*, a broad comedy (both 1902), *The Truth* (1906), which is sometimes considered to be his best play, and *The Woman in the Case* (1909). Fitch, who was one of the first American playwrights to publish his plays, was excellent at seizing certain phases of contemporary and domestic life, but his work as a social historian was spoilt by the introduction of melodrama in deference to the prevailing fashion.

FITZBALL, EDWARD (1792–1873), English dramatist, author of a vast number of melodramas given at the minor theatres of London, and now forgotten. He dramatized most of the novels of Sir Walter Scott, and is credited with the invention of Nautical drama, which had as its hero a typical Jolly Jack Tar. His *Jonathan Bradford* (1833), based on a sensational murder case, made a fortune for the managers of the Surrey, where it was first produced. Fitzball was appointed dramatist to Covent Garden under Osbaldiston, and

later went to Drury Lane, where he provided libretti for the light operas staged by Alfred Bunn. In 1859 he summed up his years of hack-work in *Thirty-Five Years of a Dramatic Author's Life*. A master of theatrical trick and artifice, and the creator of many terrifying devils, villains, murders, conflagrations, and suicides, he was in private life a mild little man, whose facility prevented his bothering much about good terms for his plays, since he could always earn more money with little effort. Several of his melodramas, notably *The Red Rover* (1829) and *Paul Clifford* (1835), passed into the repertory of the Juvenile Drama. In 1827 he wrote a version of *The Flying Dutchman* which was given at the Adelphi, full, says its author, 'of horrors and blue fire'. He had little originality, and wrote too quickly, but his work suited the taste of the time, and for over fifty years he was a prodigal purveyor of what the public wanted.

FITZROY THEATRE, LONDON, see SCALA THEATRE.

FLANAGAN, HALLIE [MRS. PHILIP H. DAVIS, née FERGUSON] (1890–   ), theatre historian and organizer, author of *Shifting Scenes of the Modern European Theatre* (1928). After working as production assistant in Professor Baker's '47 Workshop' she was appointed Professor of Drama and Director of the experimental theatre at Vassar in 1925, leaving there in 1941 to occupy the same position in Smith College, Northampton, Mass. In 1935 she became Director of the Federal Theatre Project of the Works Progress Administration, in which capacity she was responsible for the working of the project in some forty towns, and for the overseeing of more than a thousand productions up to 1939, when the organization was disbanded (see FEDERAL THEATRE PROJECT). She has also been a prolific contributor on theatrical topics to many leading American magazines.

FLAT, a frame, made of 3 × 1 in. timber, generally covered with canvas (though modern stage designers have introduced a variety of surfaces). It is possibly the most important single element of the designer's equipment, and is the solution to the problem that scenes must be made up of separate parts, which should be as light as possible. The standard full-sized flat is 18 ft. high; in small theatres it may be lower, and in large ones may reach 24 ft. Its width may vary from 1 to 6 ft., or more rarely 8 ft. For widths above this, two or more flats, hinged together, are used; these are known as Booked Flats. Flats may be plain, or may contain openings; they may be straight edged, or may bear profiling boards of wood ¼ in. thick, fixed to the side of the frame and sawn to a required shape. They may be used as one of a set of wings (or a Booked Flat may be used as a Booked Wing), and may then carry on their on-stage edge an extension of profiling known as a Flipper. This is hinged so that it may face the audience even if the flat is set at an angle, and so that it may be folded in for packing. Flats may be used to form the three walls of a Box Set. Those at the back may be battened together, and the whole wall is then flown like a cloth (see DROP) in a scene change. Such a group is termed a French Flat.

Variants of the flat are the Groundrow, which may be likened to a flat on its side, lying across the stage, and the Set Piece. This latter is a low flat, profiled all round and probably cut to the silhouette of some representational or decorative shape. The term is, however, applied also to similar 'built' pieces (see SET PIECE, 2). A flat, when standing separately, is supported by a Stage Brace—a rod, generally extensible, hooked to the back of the flat at one end, and screwed into the floor at the other by means of a Stage Screw (a sort of corkscrew), or weighted with a Braceweight (a weight shaped to fit over the foot of the brace). Sometimes, however, the support of the flat takes the form of a framework of wood shaped like a right-angled triangle and hinged to the back of the piece, to be opened out and weighted as it is needed; this is termed a French Brace. A flat forming a wall with others is connected with its neighbours by a Throwline, a 16-ft. length of sashcord, fixed at the back of the left-hand stile near the top, and tossed over a cleat in a similar position behind the right-hand stile of the next flat. The line is then brought across the join and made off below by taking a turn round a pair of cleats, one on either flat, and finished in a 'slippery hitch'. The join between the two flats may then be 'broken', when it is required to 'strike' them, by a single tug at the end of the line and an upward toss to clear the cleat at the top, the operation being practically instantaneous.

A Backing Flat is a small flat, or booked flat, set outside a door or other opening to stop the view beyond.

There remain a number of small pieces that belong to the 'flat' family in that they are canvas-covered frames—such as rostrum-fronts, balustrade-pieces, staircase-sides, and raking pieces (that is, pieces with a sloping top edge, used either independently as small groundrows, or as fillings before ramps).

Since no full account of the construction of the traditional English flat is readily available, the following description may be of interest, and may serve as a record of a nice piece of traditional design which the commercial speed of modern production-methods may soon render obsolete. (For American flat see Burris-Meyer and Cole's *Scenery for the Theatre*, 1939.)

The frame of an English flat consists of four 3 × 1 in. timbers, of which the two vertical side-pieces are the Stiles, and the others, the top and bottom Rails. The corners are morticed-and-tenoned. It is essential that the stiles always bear the tenons, and the rails the mortises, since the Running, or sliding of the flat on its lower edge during shifting, would split up the foot of the stile if it were carried through to form the mortise with the bottom

rail tenoned into it. The mortises on the rails are of the 'closed' variety; the tenons on the stiles are 'shouldered' and the mortises made to fit. No glue or screws are used in the assembly; the parts are put together and 'dry-pinned' with wooden pins. Thus, any flat can be altered, transformed into a door flat, or shortened, without the waste of cutting away glued joints. The canvas is laid back, the pins struck out, and the parts then easily separated for alteration. It is vital to keep the stiles dead straight, or adjacent flats will not join properly, and in that case the edges will need to be shot with a plane. Since the contracting draw of size paint on the canvas of the flat when drying is so powerful as to pull the sides concave, two or three horizontal Toggle Rails are 'jumped in' between the stiles as stays. These are of timber slightly thinner than the outer frame, so as not to touch the back of the canvas and cause a ridge under the pressure of the painter's brush. Each rail is tenoned and pinned, at either end, into the mortise of a triangular Toggle, or cross-piece, about 18 in. long. These toggles fit just between the inner edges of the stiles, and are screwed into their thickness. This method of inserting the rails tends both to resist the twisting strain exerted when the flat is handled, and to avoid any cutting into the material of the stile, which is a prime fault, since every such cut becomes a point of weakness that may eventually break in handling. To preserve squareness at the corners, a diagonal, cross-corner brace, about 3 ft. long, is shouldered across at one, or two, of the corners, but here again the outer frame is not cut, and the brace is halve-jointed at the ends, planted on, and screwed from the back face, from which it now stands proud by about ½ in. If the flat is to be profiled, the necessary profile board (or, nowadays, fireproof plywood) is attached to the stile at this stage. The flat is then canvased by tacking the canvas to the face, keeping the tacks near the inner edge of the frame. The waste canvas is roughly trimmed off, and the edges beyond the tacks are laid back while the frame is glued. The edges of the canvas are then pressed back in position on the glue. Finally a sharp knife is run round ⅛ in. from the edge of the flat, cutting the canvas clean, and at the same time making a slight incision into which the cut edge of the glued canvas tends to be pressed, and so sealed. If the flat is to be used in a box set it is provided with a Throwline, fixed near the top of the left-hand stile, and a cleat of special pattern in a corresponding position on the right-hand stile. The flat is now ready for priming and painting. So closely is this piece of carpentry adapted for the work it has to do, for the considerable strains of twisting that it must suffer in changes, and for the highly essential requirement of lightness and good balance consistent with strength, to ease the labour of those changes, that tall flats in big productions are sometimes made with the stiles slightly tapering in thickness throughout their whole length, so that they balance more easily in 'running'. Many quicker or cheaper alternatives are known for various parts of the construction, but none gives a lighter, stronger, finished article than the above traditional method.

Historically, the word Flat is possibly one of the most interesting in stage parlance. Its present meaning is explained above; in the mid-nineteenth century, however, it had a different application. It was then used in the phrase 'a pair of flats', and was confined to the two separate halves of a back scene, which then, unlike ours to-day, parted centrally in the middle of the picture, and drew off to either side. Farther back, the word is used only adjectivally, and the full term is Flat Scene. Formerly, scenes were divided into two sorts, of which the flat scene, consisting of a painted cloth, or of a pair of painted 'flats', was distinguished from the Scene of Relief (a word found in many spellings). To discover the origin of this distinction, it is necessary to go back to the Court masques of Inigo Jones. The scenic system of the masques—the origin of our modern scenery—was in its final form briefly this: behind a decorative frontispiece, or Proscenium Arch, was placed a set of wings, called Side Scenes or Side Shutters, to frame the back scene on either side. These were masked-in with borders, or Clouds. The wings were either permanent throughout the performance, or were in groups working in grooves, and changeable with the changing back scenes, which consisted of centrally divided pairs of shutters, from two to four in number, sliding in grooves about the middle of the stage. A point to note here is that, very early in the later Restoration theatre, the position of the back shutters was extended beyond their old central position, for there are indications that they could be closed at other positions farther down-stage—there was possibly provision made for them behind every pair of wings—thus permitting shallow Front Scenes as well as the deeper scene. Behind such front scenes it was possible to set furniture, or groups of players, for discovery at the opening of the flats.

In some masques the shutters were further divided horizontally into two storeys. The Upper Back Shutters might then open independently to show a view beyond into heaven, or on to a mountain-top, while the Lower Back Shutters parted to disclose a distant landscape beneath, or the interior of a cave in the mountain. This system may have persisted well into the next century, for in 1736 Fielding has an interesting allusion to an imaginary scene-painter named Mynheer Van Bottom-Flat.

Most scene changes in the masques were achieved by the opening and closing of the shutters described above; but, at specially dramatic moments, the shutters might all be opened to disclose the deeper half of the stage, and so reveal what came to be known as the Scene of Relief—that is, a scene which was not flat. It was composed of cut-out pieces in

various planes, set, like modern groundrows, before a backcloth, and often framed by a narrow pair of wings, set in a special groove immediately behind the shutters. That these 'groundrows' were made in wood is suggested by a note on the back of one of Inigo Jones's drawings (No. 286 in the Duke of Devonshire's collection) where there is an account for 'putting bourdes togeather for sceanes of releaue'. This joining of boards edge to edge to make a continuous sheet is so like the method of making old-fashioned profiling (as described for instance in F. Lloyds's *Practical Guide to Scene Painting, c.* 1875) that it seems likely that the scenes of relief were constructed in a manner similar to the Set Scenes, with their successive, profiled groundrows, of a modern pantomime.

Such a scene could not be neatly changed before the eyes of the audience, as the shutter scene could be. Its component pieces were set in place beforehand, and revealed, as a discovery, by opening a pair of shutters upon them; it was, in short, a previously set scene, or, to give it the name which eventually became one of the principal terms in the stage vocabulary, it was a Set Scene. To-day a 'set' is any complete scene, and the true meaning of the word is thus obscured, since it was originally a verbal adjective applying only to a scene previously prepared, as against a flat scene whose two simple parts slid on and off in view of the audience, according to the method of visible scene-change normal in the English theatre up to the time of Irving.

The flat scene, as far back as the Restoration, might be either plain, or a Cut Flat or Open Flat Scene—that is, its two halves might each be a plain painted surface, or might contain openings for doors, windows, arches, or the interstices between the trees of a Cut Wood Scene. With such open flats another piece of scenery was needed behind, to mask the opening. Any small scene behind a central opening was later termed an Inset, or an Inset Scene.

In Chamber Scenes, or room interiors, which might have to travel on circuit, the pairs of central flats might be comparatively narrow. A pair still in existence in Oxfordshire is only 8 ft. wide in all. If need arose, additional pieces could be pushed in from either side as Close-Ins. Such an arrangement is apparently visible in Hogarth's painting of the juvenile performance, at Mr. Conduit's, of *The Indian Emperour*. This system of a back-wall in several pieces approaches the Box Set of to-day, and in both a perfect join between the pieces is very important. Frequent references are found in literature to lights showing through the cracks of bad joins.   R. S.

FLAT SCENE, see FLAT and SET.

FLAVIO, see SCALA, FLAMINIO.

FLECK, JOHANN FRIEDRICH FERDINAND (1757–1801), an excellent German actor who forsook theology for the stage and was stage-director at the Berlin National Theatre shortly before Iffland went there in 1796. He was a gifted but eccentric personality and first made his mark as Gloucester to Schröder's Lear. His fine presence, resonant voice, and fiery artistic temperament made him eminently suitable to interpret the stormy heroes of the *Sturm und Drang* period. In such parts as Karl Moor and Don Carlos he excelled Schröder, and was the idol of the young Romantics. But his capricious and unstable character, which caused him to act well one night and badly another, was often a sore trial to his fellow actors, and an irritation to his audience, who never knew if they would, as they said, see the 'little' or the 'big' Fleck. Such was his magnetism, however, that he could in a moment win over an audience which he had previously alienated by his behaviour. He died at the comparatively early age of 45, and was a sad loss to the Berlin theatre, where he might have helped to counterbalance Iffland's cautious and old-fashioned repertory, and satisfy the young Romantic generation who railed against it. The last part he played was his greatest—Wallenstein in Schiller's trilogy.

FLECKER, (HERMAN) JAMES ELROY (1884–1915), English poet, and author of the fine poetic plays *Hassan* and *Don Juan*. The first was brilliantly produced at His Majesty's in 1922, with music by Delius, and proved a success, owing as much to the splendour of its Oriental costumes and scenery, and the excellence of a fine cast, as to its inherent poetic beauty. Had Flecker lived longer he might have proved an important influence in the renaissance of poetic drama, but *Don Juan*, (written 1910–11), more modern and realistic than *Hassan*, had only a private production by the Three Hundred Club, and *Hassan* remained for many years the only poetic play to have a full-scale West End production without a preliminary production in the provinces or at one of the smaller London theatres.

FLEETWOOD, CHARLES (?–c. 1745), a wealthy gentleman who took an interest in the theatre and became manager of Drury Lane, first with Cibber and later with Macklin, who was also his leading man. They were both gamblers by temperament, and eventually ruined each other and everyone who came into contact with them. It was, however, under the management of Fleetwood that Macklin played his epoch-making Shylock in 1741, and that Garrick came from Goodman's Fields, where his success had been endangering the receipts of Drury Lane. Fleetwood also abolished in 1737 the free entry of lackeys into the Footmen's Gallery, thus doing away with a constant source of annoyance and disorder. He was constantly in the hands of money-lenders, but by his charm and his repentant manner he continually staved off disaster and wheedled his actors into playing with their salaries still unpaid. He finally gave up, and sold his Patent in about 1744 to two city men, Green and Amber. It was said of Fleetwood that he

was 'a gentleman by birth, a coarser Sheridan, pleasant and fascinating, but addicted to low company, a gambler and a spendthrift'. He certainly played havoc with the finances of Drury Lane, in spite of Garrick's popularity.

FLESCHELLES, the name under which the great French comedian Gaultier-Garguille played serious parts at the Hôtel de Bourgogne from 1621 until his death in 1633. He was good in light comedy, and made an excellent tragedy king.

FLETCHER, JOHN (1579–1625), English poet and dramatist, who spent most of his life actively writing for the stage, either alone or in collaboration. His name is so indissolubly linked with that of Sir Francis Beaumont (*c.* 1584–1616) that more than fifty plays have been ascribed to their joint authorship, of which Chambers believes only some six or seven are authentical. The rest were either by other hands, by Fletcher alone, or by Fletcher in collaboration with other contemporary dramatists, particularly Massinger. Fletcher had already written for the Queen's Revels *The Woman's Prize* and *The Faithful Shepherdess*, both given in the early years of the seventeenth century, before his name was first linked with Beaumont's in some commendatory verses prefixed to Jonson's *Volpone*. The chief plays of Beaumont and Fletcher were *Philaster* (1610), *A Maid's Tragedy* (1611), *A King and No King* (1611), and *The Scornful Lady* (1613). It has been said of the collaborators that Beaumont, influenced by Jonson's comedy of humours, shows a more conservative and moral outlook in style and versification, together with greater power in tragedy, while Fletcher, starting from Middleton's comedy of manners, was the finer poet and more inventive mind. Together they stand as the chief exponents in English literature of the romantic tragi-comedy. Beaumont seems to have ceased writing on his marriage in 1613, but Fletcher continued with such comedies as *Monsieur Thomas*, *Wit without Money*, and the tragedy, *Bonduca*, in which Burbage played the lead. Fletcher has been credited with collaboration with Shakespeare in *The Two Noble Kinsmen* and *Henry VIII*. The former is doubtful, and Beaumont or Massinger has been substituted for Shakespeare, but there seems reason to believe that Fletcher had a hand in parts of *Henry VIII*.

FLEURY [ABRAHAM-JOSEPH BÉNARD] (1750–1822), French actor, son of the manager of a theatre at Nancy, where he made his first appearances. He was at first considered to be fit only for minor parts, but with his sister, who with her husband was on the stage under the name of Sainville, he went to Geneva and was invited to play at Ferney. Encouraged by Voltaire, who discerned great promise in him, he made his first attempt at the Comédie-Française in 1774, helped by Lekain, who had known his father. He was thought promising, but was advised to return to the provinces for further practice, which he did, playing chiefly at Lyons. In 1778 he made a second successful attempt, and remained at the Comédie-Française until his retirement in 1818, being its seventeenth Doyen. During the Revolution he was imprisoned, together with a number of his companions, but after his release returned to the stage, and was one of the members of the company reconstituted in 1799. An excellent actor, he owed his position to hard work and a certain innate feeling for the theatre, being almost totally uneducated.

FLIES, the name given to the space above the stage, hidden from the audience, where scenery can be lifted clear from the stage or 'flown' by the manipulation of ropes. The men in charge of these are known as Fly-men, and they work on a Fly-floor or Gallery (see STAGE, 3), while the railing to which the ropes are attached is known as the Fly- or Pin-rail (see ENGLISH PLAYHOUSE, 2).

FLIPPER, a hinged extension at the on-stage edge of a wing, usually with a cut profile (see FLAT).

FLOATS, see LIGHTING.

FLOOD BATTENS, see LIGHTING, 2 e.

FLORENCE, WILLIAM JERMYN (or JAMES) (1831–91), American actor, whose real name was Bernard Conlin. He began his career as call-boy at the Old Bowery, but his excellent powers of mimicry and exceptional memory soon took him on to the stage, and he made his New York début in 1849 at Niblo's Garden in dialect impersonations. Two years later, while appearing at the Broadway Theatre, he married the actress Malvina Pray, sister of Mrs. Barney Williams, and with her toured the United States in a repertory of Irish plays. Husband and wife were first seen in London in 1856, when they appeared at Drury Lane in *The Yankee Housekeeper* with great success. Among Florence's best parts were Captain Cuttle in *Dombey and Son*, in which he followed and reproduced with some fidelity the acting of W. E. Burton, Bob Brierly in *The Ticket-of-Leave Man*, which he was the first to play in America, and Bardwell Slote in *The Mighty Dollar*, a play which remained in his repertory for many years. He was good in burlesque, and as a comedian ranked with Jefferson, appearing with the latter as Sir Lucius O'Trigger in *The Rivals* and Zekiel Homespun in *The Heir-at-Law*. He also gave the first production in New York of *Caste*, which he had memorized while in London, staging it at the Broadway Theatre on 5 Aug. 1867, with all the realistic scenery and atmosphere of the Bancroft production. He himself played D'Alroy, one of his best parts, with his wife as Polly, Mrs. Chanfrau as Esther, Davidge as Eccles, and Mrs. Gilbert as the Marquise de St. Maur, her first important part in New York. The production caused a good deal of controversy,

as Lester Wallack had bought the American rights of the play, but in the absence of copyright laws had no redress against piracy, and did not put it on himself until 1875, probably fearing to challenge comparison with Florence's excellent production. Florence, who was at first inclined to justify his behaviour on the score of expediency, later regretted it, but maintained that he did not know Wallack had already bought the play for New York. His feat of memory, which extended to the words and business, recalls that of Holcroft in memorizing for translation Beaumarchais's *Mariage de Figaro* nearly a hundred years before.

FLORIDOR [JOSIAS DE SOULAS, SIEUR DE PRIMEFOSSE] (1608–72), French actor, of good family, who left the army to join a company of strolling players. He soon became their leader, and in 1635 took them to London, where they appeared before the Court and at a theatre in Drury Lane. Three years later Floridor toured the provinces with Filandre, and shortly before or after that joined the company of the Théâtre du Marais, becoming Orator of the troupe after the departure of d'Orgemont. He had all the attributes of a good actor, aided by an excellent education, and was equally good in tragedy and comedy. Some of his best performances were given in the plays of Corneille, who was godfather to one of his children, and it may have been Floridor's move to the Hôtel de Bourgogne, which took place some time between 1643 and 1653, which induced Corneille to give his later plays to that theatre rather than the Marais. At the Hôtel de Bourgogne Floridor took the place of Bellerose and soon became leader of the company. His quiet, authoritative acting was in marked contrast to the bombastic style of his colleague, Montfleury, and he was the only actor spared by Molière in his mockery of the rival troupe in *L'Impromptu de Versailles* (1663). In 1671 he fell ill, and on the advice of his confessor renounced the stage, dying shortly afterwards.

FLYING BALLET, see ENGLISH PLAYHOUSE, 2.

FOGERTY, ELSIE (1866–1945), English actress, who trained for the stage in London and Paris, and made her first appearance in 1879. She was, however, keenly interested in the problems of diction, which led her to lecture on elocution and speech-training, and finally to found the Central School of Speech Training and Dramatic Art which she directed until her death. In pursuance of her efforts to further the study and adoption of choral speaking she adapted and produced a number of Greek plays, and was the author of several manuals of speech-craft and of *The Speaking of English Verse*. She was closely concerned with the development of the British Drama League, and was a member of the Advisory Committee for the Diploma in Dramatic Art established by the University of London in 1923.

FOIRE SAINT-GERMAIN, SAINT-LAURENT, PARIS, see FAIRS.

FOKINE, MICHEL (1880–1944), Russian dancer and choreographer, who went to Western Europe with Diaghilev's Ballets Russes, and was responsible for many of their outstanding productions, including 'Les Sylphides', 'Schéhérazade', and 'Petrouchka'. He was later with de Basil and René Blum (see BALLET, 7 and 8).

FOLGER, HENRY CLAY (1857–1930), American business man, founder of the great Shakespeare library in Washington which bears his name. As an undergraduate at Amherst he heard Emerson lecture on English literature, and was led through him to take an interest in the works of Shakespeare. From a modest set of the plays in thirteen volumes he went on to make the finest collection of Shakespeariana in the world, which after his death was donated to the nation. Under Dr. Joseph Quincy Adams, the great Shakespearian scholar who became its first director, the collection, administered by Amherst College, increased rapidly in size and scope. It now contains a series of English manuscripts from 1475 to 1640 which is exceeded in value and rarity only by those in the British Museum and the Bodleian. Fellowships were established in connexion with work on Shakespeare and his contemporaries, exhibitions arranged, lectures given, and a series of Folger Shakespeare Reprints inaugurated under the general editorship of Dr. Adams.

FOLIES-BERGÈRE, a famous music-hall in Paris, built in 1869 on the site of a livery-stable, and intended as a vast café-spectacle. It opened on 1 May with a mixed bill of light opera and pantomime in which Paul Legrand appeared as Pierrot, and soon became the rendezvous of the young men of the town, who either watched the successive turns on the stage, or loitered in the immense promenade which was one of the attractions of the house. It caters to a large extent for visitors, whether French or foreign, and one of the main features of its programme is a bevy of young and beautiful women, either stark naked or clad only in inessentials. For the rest its turns consist of acrobats, singers, and sketches, the last extremely vulgar or surpassingly beautiful, the scenic resources of the theatre being immense though its stage is small. Many of the greatest names of the entertainment world have appeared on its bills.

For the Folies-Bergère, New York, see FULTON THEATRE.

FOLIES-DRAMATIQUES, THÉÂTRE DES, PARIS, on the Boulevard du Temple. This was built on the site of the first Ambigu-Comique (destroyed by fire in 1827) and opened with melodrama on 22 Jan. 1831. Under its first proprietor Mourier it had twenty-five years of unbroken success, catering mainly for a local audience, and playing each new piece about thirty times. Many young actors found the theatre a convenient stepping-stone to higher things, since Mourier would only pay them a certain sum and when they asked, or deserved, more was ready to let them go elsewhere, taking in their place a new batch of youngsters. The repertory consisted mainly of patriotic and melodramatic plays, written by the Cogniard brothers, Comberousse, de Kock, Théaulon, and others. In 1834 the great Frédérick-Lemaître had one of his first successes at this theatre in *Robert Macaire*. It continued to be one of the best-conducted and most popular theatres in Paris until Mourier's death in 1857. Harel then took over, and when the Boulevard du Temple was demolished in 1862 built a new Folies-Dramatiques in the rue de Bondy. It ruined him, however, and under new management became a home of light musical shows, rival of the Bouffes-Parisiens and Variétés.

For the Folies-Dramatiques in London, see KINGSWAY THEATRE.

FOLIES-MARIGNY, THÉÂTRE DES, PARIS, a small playhouse, originally the Salle Lacaze, used by the Bouffes-Parisiens. In 1858 the son of the great pantomimist Deburau opened it under his own name, but it was not a success, and became the Théâtre des Champs-Élysées and finally the Folies-Marigny under the director of the Délassements-Comiques, who had lost his own theatre in the demolition of the Boulevard du Temple. It became a home of vaudeville, and was fairly successful until 1869. It then passed from hand to hand, and was finally destroyed in 1881.

FOLIES-NOUVELLES, THÉÂTRE DES, PARIS, a small theatre which had a short but brilliant career. It opened in 1852 and under several successive names was a home of pantomime, with Paul Legrand as Pierrot and Vauthier as Punch. It also put on light opera with good singers and dancers and a small but adequate orchestra. Two years later it became the Folies-Nouvelles, and was given a licence which allowed it to use four people in operetta instead of the original two. Its programmes were like those of the old fair-ground theatres, simple, crude, and naïvely charming. It had a great vogue until 1859 and then became an ordinary theatre under the son of the great actress Virginie Déjazet, opening with plays by Sardou and others as the Théâtre Déjazet.

FOLK FESTIVALS, connected with the activities of the agricultural year, must have existed from the time of the first organized communities. In Europe they survived the rise and fall of Greece and Rome, and the coming of Christianity, but lost much of their significance, and were often kept up merely 'for fun' or 'for luck'. The Church, considering them an undesirable pagan survival, tried either to suppress them or to graft them on to its own festivals. But they were irrepressible, and constantly broke out again, often under the aegis of the parish priest. Wandering minstrels may have had some slight share in them, but they depended mainly on local talent, and the details varied from one district to another. The main folk festivals of England, and elsewhere, were Plough Monday, May-day, Midsummer Day, and Harvest Home, of which May-day longest retained its importance, with its May Queen, Maypole, garlanded processions, its Morris dancers, Jack-in-the-Green or Jack-a'-lantern, and its Hobby Horse, often with the addition of Robin Hood and his Merry Men. Most of the festivities were athletic rather than dramatic, but traces of a rudimentary play can be found (see PLOUGH MONDAY and MUMMING PLAY). The folk element in modern literary drama is very slight.

FOLK PLAY. Under this heading may be grouped the rough-and-ready dramatic entertainments given at village festivals by the villagers themselves. These were derived, with the minimum of literary intervention, from the dramatic tendencies inherent in primitive folk festivals, and should not be confused with the productions of professional minstrels. They were given either at the May-games, at Harvest Home, or at Christmas, and to the central theme of a symbolic death and resurrection were added the names and feats of local worthies. Later, though not before 1596, these were replaced by the Seven Champions of Christendom, or other heroes, probably under the influence of the village schoolmaster (cf. Holofernes). St. George may have figured in them from the earliest times, as patron saint of England. With some dramatic action went a good deal of song and dance, of which the Sword Dance and the Morris Dance are the main survivals, except for the Mumming Play, usually given between Christmas and Twelfth Night, at Easter, or on Plough Monday (for further details see MUMMING PLAY). Practically no written records of the folk play survive, as is to be expected of an unliterary and impromptu form of drama, and it contributed only a small stream to the main current of modern drama; but its influence should not on that account be entirely disregarded.

FOLLIES, see PÉLISSIER and ZIEGFELD.

FOLLOWING SPOTS, see LIGHTING, 2 *d*.

FOLLY THEATRE, LONDON, see CHARING CROSS THEATRE.

FOLZ, HANS (*fl.* fifteenth century), a writer of German popular farces (see GERMANY, 1) who lived in Nuremberg, and was a Mastersinger of that town.

FONTANNE, LYNN (1887–), see LUNT (2).

FONTENELLE, BERNARD LE BOVIER DE (1657–1757), French man of letters, and

nephew of Corneille, to whom we are indebted for many, mostly inaccurate, anecdotes of his famous uncle. He wrote with ease in many styles but, having failed in tragedy and comedy, he wisely retired from playwriting. His libretto for the opera 'Thétis et Pélée', written in 1689, was much admired by Voltaire, but has not otherwise survived.

FONVIZIN, DENIS IVANOVICH (1744–92), early Russian dramatist who forms the link between the neo-classical literary plays of Sumarokov and the social comedies of Ostrovsky. Son of a nobleman, he was educated at Moscow University, and his first work, a translation, appeared in print when he was 18. In the same year (1762) he went to St. Petersburg, where he became an official translator, and was later attached to the staff of the Supervisor of Theatres. His first attempt at play-writing was a comedy, *The Minor*, contrasting the crude provincial nobility, with their lack of education, with the cultured nobility of the city. He put it aside unfinished in favour of a second play, *The Brigadier-general*, which he himself, being a fine elocutionist, read before the Court in 1766 with great success. It satirized the illiterate newly rich men who were filtering into Russian society, and at the same time attacked the existing fashion for praising everything from western Europe at the expense of everything Russian.

It was not until 1781 that Fonvizin took up *The Minor* again and rewrote it, sharpening the satire on the landowners and their politics. As this party was then predominant in the government, Fonvizin's daring was his downfall. After the death of his patron Panin in 1783 he was forced to retire from public life, and his works were refused publication. Nevertheless, *The Minor* remains a small classic in its own way, and is still in the repertory of the Soviet theatre. Although Fonvizin wrote in the comic tradition of Molière and the French eighteenth century, he infused into his work a native Russian element of folk comedy which was to come to fruition in his successors.

FOOL. (1) The licensed buffoon of the medieval Feast of Fools, and later a member of the French *sociétés joyeuses*; not to be confused with (2) the Court Fool or King's Jester, a permanent member of the Royal Household, whose origin has been variously traced to the Court of Haroun-al-Raschid, to the classical dwarf-buffoon, or to the inspired madman of Celtic and Teutonic legend. The traditional costume of the fool, adopted by the Court Fool at some unknown date in imitation of his humbler rival, is a cap with horns or ass's ears, and sometimes bells, covering the head and shoulders; a parti-coloured jacket and trousers, usually tight-fitting, and occasionally a tail. He carries a marotte or bauble, either a replica of a fool's head on a stick, or a bladder filled with dried peas; exceptionally a wooden sword or 'dagger of lath', a relic of his predecessor the Vice (or buffoon) in medieval drama (see *Twelfth Night*,

'Like to the old Vice, . . . Who with dagger of lath, In his rage and his wrath, Cries, Ah, ah! to the devil'). It is surmised that this costume is a survival of the head and skin of the sacrificial animal worn by the worshipper at the primitive folk festival, while the ass's ears were imported from the ass used in the procession of the Feast of Fools. The grotesque fool of the Morris dancers and of village festivities invariably had a tail. Shakespeare's Fools have nothing to do with the Feast of Fools or with the Folk revellers, but derive from the Court Fool, already by his time a tradition in Europe and England. In dramatic use fools are vehicles of social satire. (See also CLOWN.)

FOOLS, FEAST OF, the generic name given to the New Year revels of the minor clergy in cathedrals and collegiate churches, which Chambers summarizes as 'the ebullition of the natural lout beneath the cassock'. The feast seems to have originated in France in about the twelfth century, and may have had in it some dim remembrance of the festivities of the Roman Kalends. During the feast the minor clergy usurped the functions of their superiors and gave free rein to their turbulence and high spirits. The entertainments from the beginning seem to have included some form of crude drama, with much tippling, noise, and burlesque ceremonies. A 'king' was appointed from among the participants (in schools his function was usurped by the Boy Bishop), and the ceremonies included a procession headed by the 'king' riding on a donkey, an innovation taken over by ecclesiastical drama with the introduction of Balaam's ass and the Flight into Egypt into the liturgical plays. The Feast of Fools, which is known to have been held in England at Lincoln, Beverley, Salisbury, and St. Paul's, died out in the fourteenth century, though it continued intermittently in France until the sixteenth century, by which time it had passed from the church to the street, and was finally absorbed into the *compagnies des fous* or *sociétés joyeuses* (see FRANCE).

FOOTE, LYDIA (1844–92), see KEELEY (3).

FOOTE, MARIA (*c.* 1797–1867), English actress, daughter of a Samuel Foote who claimed some relationship with the dramatist (see below). He was manager of the theatre at Plymouth, where his daughter made her first appearances as a child, playing Juliet while still quite young. In 1814 she was at Covent Garden, playing Amanthis in *The Child of Nature* with such success that she was engaged permanently, playing Miranda and, in 1815, Statira to the Alexander the Great of Master Betty. She was not a great actress, but beautiful and talented enough to secure steady engagements, travelling constantly to Ireland, Scotland, and in the provinces. Her love affairs, particularly her breach of promise case against Haynes, caused much scandal, but she had powerful friends who secured her prefer-

ment at both Patent Houses until in 1831 she retired to marry the Earl of Harrington.

FOOTE, SAMUEL (1720–77), English actor and dramatist, well born and well educated but so extravagant that lack of money drove him to adopt the stage as a profession in 1744. He had had some experience as an amateur, but his first appearances at the Haymarket were not particularly successful, and he went to Ireland, where he was well received. On his return he went to Drury Lane, but seemed fit neither for tragedy nor for comedy. Yet it was in the latter that his strength lay, as he discovered when he took over the Haymarket in 1747. Here, with great ingenuity, he evaded the Licensing Act by inviting his friends to a dish of tea or chocolate, their invitation-card giving admittance to an entertainment in which Foote mimicked his fellow actors and other public characters. In 1749, having inherited a second fortune, he went to Paris, spent it, and returned to take up in earnest a life of hard work as actor-manager and playwright. He had already written a few farces, but his first success was *The Englishman in Paris* (1753), with its sequel, *The Englishman Returned from Paris* (1756). After acting at both Patent Houses, in Dublin, where he was always welcome, and Scotland, Foote again took over the Haymarket. He staged there, in the summer of 1760, his best play, *The Minor*, which had had its first performance earlier in the year at the Crow Street Theatre, Dublin. In this satire on Whitefield and the Methodists he himself played Shift, a character intended to ridicule Tate Wilkinson. Foote remained at the Haymarket, appearing in his own comedies in afternoon performances, for many years, but still without a licence, until he lost a leg through some ducal horseplay (see HAYMARKET), and the Duke of York, who was present, procured him a Royal Patent in compensation. He was then able to buy the old Haymarket, pull it down, and reopen it in 1767 with Spranger Barry and his wife in leading parts.

Foote had a bitter wit, and his plays were mainly devised with the idea of caricaturing one person, which he did most successfully, judging to a nicety how far he could go without chastisement or open rebuke. He disliked Garrick, and missed no opportunity of lampooning him, though Garrick disdained to reply to his shafts. He had such wonderful powers of mimicry and repartee that even his victims found themselves bound to laugh at him. He was often in trouble, but evaded it for many years, until Nemesis finally overtook him, and he disposed of his Patent to Colman, dying shortly after on his way to France. His plays were successful through their topicality, and have not survived. He had a keen eye for character, and wrote brilliant sketches of contemporary manners, which caused him to be nicknamed 'the English Aristophanes'. Short, fat, flabby, with an ugly but intelligent face and a bright eye, he was at once feared and admired by his contemporaries, Dr. Johnson being one of the few who despised him without any wish to placate, though he said of him: 'Sir, he was irresistible.' Foote's portrait was painted by Zoffany and Reynolds.

FOOTLIGHTS, see LIGHTING.

FOOTLIGHTS TRAP, see STAGE, 1 and TRAP.

FOOTMEN'S GALLERY. At the Restoration the usual charge for the Upper Gallery was a shilling, but footmen waiting for their masters were admitted free at the end of the fourth act, at any rate at Dorset Garden, and probably at the Theatre Royal also. The latter theatre, however, under Christopher Rich, hoping to curry favour with the rougher element, allowed the footmen from 1697 onwards to occupy the gallery gratis from the opening of the play, which led to much noise and disorder. This abuse was finally abolished, not without much rioting and opposition, by Fleetwood in 1737.

FORBES-ROBERTSON. (1) SIR JOHNSTON (1853–1937), English actor-manager, son of an art critic and journalist. Educated at Charterhouse, he first studied art, but abandoned it for the stage, learning his perfect elocution from Samuel Phelps. He made his first appearance in 1874, and from then until his retirement in 1913 he had a long and varied career. His first big success was at the Haymarket in *Dan'l Druce, Blacksmith*, in 1876. Two years later he joined the Bancrofts at the Prince of Wales's, scoring a great success in *Diplomacy, Duty*, and *Ours*. Wilson Barrett then engaged him to play opposite Madame Modjeska at the Court and Princess's Theatres, where he appeared as Romeo, as Armand Duval in *Heartsease* (a version of *La Dame aux camélias*), and as Maurice de Saxe in *Adrienne Lecouvreur*. In 1882 he went to the Lyceum under Irving. Then followed a tour in England and America as leading man to Mary Anderson, with whom he made his first appearance in New York—as Orlando—at the Star Theatre in 1885. He went into management in 1895 at the London Lyceum, playing Romeo to the Juliet of Mrs. Pat Campbell. At the same theatre he produced and appeared in *Hamlet*, and made a deep impression, proving to be one of the greatest Hamlets of his time. It is indeed doubtful if modern times have seen a better. Forbes-Robertson had one of the finest voices ever heard on the stage, and was an actor of great sensibility and delicacy of imagination. His ascetic fine-featured face made him a notable figure, while his repose, his power, and his understanding of his art placed him in the forefront of English actors. His performance as The Stranger in *The Passing of the Third-Floor Back*, with which he opened his season at the St. James's in 1908, was considered by many to be memorable—reverent, yet exciting. That, with his Hamlet, Buckingham (*Henry VIII*), Mark Embury (*Mice and Men*), and Dick Helder (*The Light that Failed*), made up

a gallery of exquisite stage portraits. Forbes-Robertson was knighted in 1913, during the last week of his farewell performances at Drury Lane Theatre. Those privileged to be present at his final appearance long remembered the emotion of the evening, and his coming down among the audience to say his last farewell.

Sir Johnston's younger brothers (2) IAN (1858–1936), (3) NORMAN (1859–1932), and (4) ERIC (1865–1935) were also actors. Norman was seen on the stage for the first time at the Gaiety in 1875, under the name of Norman Forbes. He appeared under most of the outstanding managements of the day, and was at one time manager of the Globe. He was the author of several plays, and of dramatic versions of *The Scarlet Letter* and *The Man in the Iron Mask*, himself playing Louis XIV and Marchiali in the latter. His son Frank was also on the stage. Eric, who was also a painter, took the name of John Kelt.

In 1900 Sir Johnston married Gertrude Elliott, an American actress (see ELLIOTT, 2), a beautiful and accomplished woman who was on many occasions his leading lady. Their daughter (5) JEAN (1905–) is also an excellent actress, who has been on the stage since 1921. Among her outstanding performances have been Peter Pan, which she played for many years in succession, a series of Shakespearian parts with the Old Vic and elsewhere, and, in modern plays, Helen Pettigrew in *Berkeley Square*, Jenny Lyndon in *Strange Orchestra*, and Kay in *Time and the Conways*.   W. M. P.

FORD, JOHN (1586–1639), English dramatist, four of whose plays are lost, destroyed by Warburton's cook. Little is known of his life, except that he was born and died in Devonshire, and was admitted to the Inner Temple in 1602. It has been said that the prevailing note of his work is 'the powerful depiction of sorrow and despair', which caused him to be surnamed 'melancholy John Ford'. He is believed to have been part-author with Dekker and Rowley of *The Witch of Edmonton* and *The Sun's Darling*, but his own work, which is more important, includes the four romantic and somewhat effeminate dramas which contributed not a little to the continued emasculation of the English stage before the closing of the theatres in 1642—*The Lovers' Melancholy* (c. 1625–6), *Love's Sacrifice* (c. 1627), *The Broken Heart* (1629), and, his best-known work, *'Tis Pity She's a Whore* (c. 1625–33). In all these plays Ford shows a totally different attitude towards morality from that of Shakespeare or Jonson, and his more modern point of view makes it difficult to assess his originality. He has been called a romantic rebel, a believer in the divine impulse of human passion which leads in the end to self-destruction.

FORD, JOHN THOMSON (1829–94), American theatre manager, who was in charge of the theatre in Washington where Abraham Lincoln was assassinated on 14 Apr. 1865 by the actor

Wilkes Booth. With his brother he was imprisoned for thirty-nine days, but was later acquitted of complicity in the crime, and continued his career, managing a number of other theatres, and being for some forty years an active and honourable member of the American theatrical profession.

FORDE, FLORRIE (1876–1940), music-hall singer, came from Melbourne, where she appeared in pantomime and was known as the Australian Marie Lloyd, her real name being Florence Flanagan. She appeared in London on August Bank Holiday 1897, and was particularly good at putting over a chorus. On one occasion the audience made her repeat an old favourite thirty-three times. A massive woman, she was in her time a famous Principal Boy and a great star. 'Down at the Old Bull and Bush', 'Has Anybody Here Seen Kelly?' 'Hold Your Hand Out, Naughty Boy', and 'Oh, Oh, Antonio' are her best-remembered songs. Her voice and delivery matched her ample figure.   W. M. P.

FORESTAGE, a term applied in the modern theatre to the small area of the stage in front of the proscenium arch and the front curtain. This is the final vestige of what was once the main acting area, the apron stage of the English Restoration theatre, itself a modified form of the Elizabethan platform stage. It served the purpose of an unlocalized 'platea', the actors approaching it from the inner stage or through the proscenium doors. Its loss has proved a great handicap in staging revivals of Elizabethan and Restoration drama in modern theatres, and consideration is now being given to the provision of a large forestage, either permanent or temporary, in new theatre buildings, particularly those intended for experimental or academic work.

FORK, a device used in the English nineteenth-century theatre to replace the upper groove by which a wing of scenery was supported (see ENGLISH PLAYHOUSE, 2 c).

FORMALISM, the name given to a theatrical method popular in Russia soon after the October Revolution, and put into practice by Taïrov (in a lesser degree), Meyerhold, and Akimov in his earlier period. It implies a negation of humanity, the schooling of the actor so that he becomes the producer's puppet, and the insistence on exterior symbolism at the expense of inner truth. Though in its origin it served its purpose in helping to clear the stage of the old falsities and conventions of pre-Revolutionary days, when pushed too far it resulted in á complete lack of harmony between stage and audience. Joseph Macleod says of Formalist producers: 'Their brains are in front of their eyes', and in the long run intellectual isolation so cut them off from the new audiences that they had either to return to the warmth and intimacy of normal human relationships or leave the theatre. This Meyerhold did for a short time after his theatre was closed in 1937, but he returned, and, like Taïrov and Akimov, found his place within the scheme of Socialist Realism.

FORREST, EDWIN (1806–72), one of the finest American tragic actors of the nineteenth century. He appeared in an amateur performance at the age of 10, and four years later played Young Norval at the Walnut Street Theatre in Philadelphia, his birthplace. His early years were hard, and overshadowed by poverty and thwarted ambition, but in the end he triumphed and became the acknowledged head of his profession for nearly thirty years, and the idol of the public. Yet even then the defects of his character made him as many enemies as friends, and no one received more abuse mingled with the praise which was his due. William Winter, who characterized him as 'utterly selfish' and said that the motives of his conduct 'were vanity, pride, self-assertion, and avarice of power, praise and wealth', also called him a 'vast animal, bewildered by a grain of genius', and his portraits show him as a heavy, brooding man with a sombre expression. Yet Mrs. John Drew, who appeared with him in *William Tell* at the age of 8, spoke feelingly of his good qualities, and praised his unselfishness in allowing other actors to gain the attention of the audience during their important moments. He certainly had great advantages of person, expressive features, and a powerful voice, which he used unsparingly, but his acting, though bold and forceful, lacked delicacy, and in his early years he was much criticized for 'ranting'. This he later cured to some extent, and was then outstanding as Lear, Hamlet, Macbeth, and Richelieu. Among his other parts were Spartacus and Metamora, written specially for him and well suited to his art and personality, Jaffier, Othello, Rolla, Mark Antony, and Virginius. He appeared in London in 1836 with some success, but on a later visit in 1845 was received with marked hostility, which he attributed to the machinations of Macready. Their quarrel led eventually to the fatal Astor Place riot in New York in 1848, when Macready barely escaped with his life. This caused Forrest to be ostracized by the more sober members of the community, but he was the idol of the masses, who looked on him as their champion against the tyranny of English superiority.

In 1837 Forrest married Catharine Norton Sinclair (1817–91), who was on the stage and later became manager of a theatre in California. The marriage proved an unhappy one, and he was divorced in 1850. In his last years Forrest knew again the bitterness of failure, and died a lonely, unhappy man. He last appeared on the stage at the Globe Theatre, Boston, on 2 Apr. 1872, as Richelieu.

FORREST THEATRE, NEW YORK, see CORONET THEATRE.

FORSTER, JOHN (1812–76), English historian, biographer, and editor, who from an early age took a keen delight in the theatre. While still a youth, he wrote a play, *Charles at*

FORTUNE THEATRE

Tunbridge; or, the Cavalier of Wildinghurst, which was performed at his native Newcastle. He became dramatic critic of the *True Sun* in 1832. In the same year he began editing a weekly collection of essays called *The Reflector,* to which Lamb and Leigh Hunt were contributors. In 1833 Forster became chief literary and dramatic critic to the *Examiner,* and in 1846 he succeeded Dickens as editor of the *Daily News.* In the general run of literature, Forster is remembered principally for his biographical writings; but he brought to dramatic criticism a well-stored mind and a warm enthusiasm for the theatre.   T. C. K.

FORTUNE THEATRE, LONDON. (1) Built by Henslowe as a countermove to the building of the Globe on Bankside by his rival Burbage. Before the Globe was opened Henslowe and his star actor Alleyn had reigned supreme on the south bank of the river while the Burbages ruled in the north. After the opening of the Globe Henslowe decided, apparently, to invade the enemy territory. The Fortune stood in Cripplegate on a site afterwards called Playhouse Yard, between Whitecross Street and Golden Lane. It was modelled on the Globe, and its dimensions were almost identical. Unlike the Globe, however, it was constructed of plain unpainted timber. It cost £550, and took its name from a statue of the Goddess of Fortune over its entrance. It opened in the autumn of 1600 with a performance by the Admiral's Men, who occupied it continuously for many years, first as the Admiral's Men, then as Prince Henry's Men until his death in 1612, then as the Palsgrave's Men. In 1621 the theatre was burnt down and rebuilt in brick the following year. After the closing of the theatres in 1642 the Fortune was used for surreptitious performances, until in 1649 Commonwealth soldiers entered and destroyed its fittings. They were said to have pulled it down, but it stood after that, being finally destroyed about 1656. Some idea of the area it occupied may be gained from the fact that a street was cut through it and twenty-three houses with gardens erected on the site. An old wall, said to be part of the theatre, existed, and may still exist, in a factory adjoining the site.

(2) A small, intimate theatre in Russell Street, Drury Lane, built by Lawrence Cowan. Externally it was intended to resemble the old Fortune, but the likeness was based upon a print of doubtful authenticity. It opened on 8 Nov. 1924, with Ida Molesworth and Templar Powell in *Sinners,* and so far its name has not been of happy augury, for it has had few successes. It was for some time used for amateur productions. In 1927 Tom Walls took it over and presented *On Approval,* which ran for 469 performances—the only long run the theatre has known. Other plays given under Walls's management were *Cape Forlorn, The Last Enemy,* and Chekhov revivals. After the outbreak of war in 1939 the theatre was taken over by Ensa, but has now reverted to its former status.   W. M. P.

FORTY-NINTH STREET THEATRE

FORTUNY, MARIANO (1871–   ), Italian scenic designer and lighting expert, and inventor of the diffused-lighting system which bears his name (see LIGHTING, 1 d and SCENERY, 6).

FORTY-EIGHTH STREET THEATRE, NEW YORK. This opened on 12 Aug. 1912, and housed opera and musical comedy, including Gilbert and Sullivan, as well as a number of successful straight plays. In 1922 came Kelly's delightful satire on Little Theatres, *The Torch Bearers,* which ran for 17 weeks, and was transferred elsewhere to make room for the Equity Players in *Malvaloca.* Later successes were *The Squall* (1926) with Blanche Yurka, which had 444 performances, a revival of *The Streets of New York* in 1931, and the Pulitzer Prize-winner, *Harvey* (1944). This theatre was for a short time known as the Windsor.   G. F.

FORTY-FOURTH STREET THEATRE, NEW YORK. This was built by the Shuberts, and opened on 21 Nov. 1912 as the Weber and Fields New Music-Hall. Seating 1,463 people, the building housed in its basement for some time the famous Little Club, while on its roof was a smaller theatre, later known as the Nora Bayes. This little playhouse had few successes, which led to its being considered unlucky, but Little Theatre Tournaments were held there, and in Dec. 1922 some of Gershwin's first tunes were heard in a 'musical melodrama'. In 1935 it was occupied for a short time by the Yale Puppeteers, and two years later it was taken over by the Federal Theatre Project. It was scheduled for demolition in 1945, together with its parent house, which was re-opened in 1914 with a successful revival of *The Geisha.* In 1915 Robert B. Mantell appeared in his classical repertory, which showed, among other things, what the nineteenth century demanded of an actor's memory. Mantell's parts in this season included Lear, Richelieu, Louis XI, King John, Macbeth, Hamlet, Shylock, Richard III, and Romeo. After this excursion into the classics, the theatre returned to light opera and musical plays, varied by the Marx Brothers in a long run of *Animal Crackers.* An outstanding production seen in 1930 was that of Gilbert Seldes's adaptation of *Lysistrata,* played by an excellent cast. Other plays seen at this theatre included *The Good Companions* (1931), a fleeting glimpse of Pierre Fresnay and Yvonne Printemps in *Conversation Piece* in 1934, Walter Hampden in a four-weeks' classical repertory, the short-lived but memorable *Johnny Johnson* (1936), and, in 1943, *Winged Victory.*   G. F.

FORTY-NINTH STREET THEATRE, New York, on the north side between Broadway and Eighth Avenue. This was opened by Lee Shubert on 26 Dec. 1921. Early in the following year Morris Gest presented the Chauve-Souris for a season which continued during the summer on the roof of the old Century Theatre. A series of successful new plays followed, though Wedekind's *Lulu* was a failure, as was Coward's *Fallen Angels*. In 1928 came a fine revival of *The Wild Duck* with Blanche Yurka, followed by *Hedda Gabler*, and a year later the public were delighted by the great Chinese actor, Mei Lan-Fang. Among later productions were *Marigold, Bird in Hand*, a revival of *The Father* with Robert Loraine, a season of Yiddish plays with Maurice Schwartz, and three productions by the Federal Theatre Project. The last play seen there was a modern-dress revival of *The Wild Duck* in Apr. 1938, after which the theatre became a cinema.

G. F.

47 WORKSHOP, see BAKER, G. P. and NATIONWIDE THEATRE, 2.

FORTY-SIXTH STREET THEATRE, NEW YORK, west of Broadway. This was built by the Chanins, whose name it bore until 1932. It was intended for musical shows, and opened on 24 Dec. 1925, since when it has been consistently successful. Among the straight plays produced at this theatre have been *The First Legion* (1934), a sensitive portrayal of the Jesuit life, and a Group Theatre production of *Weep for the Virgin* (1935) which, though not particularly successful, first brought into prominence a young actor named Jules (later John) Garfield. The theatre is, however, mainly associated with such musical hits as *Hellzapoppin* (1938), *Du Barry Was a Lady* (1939), *Panama Hattie* (1940), and *Finian's Rainbow* (1947).

G. F.

FOURTEENTH STREET THEATRE, NEW YORK, see LYCEUM THEATRE (2).

FOWLER, RICHARD (?–1643), English actor, and one of the chief players at the Fortune Theatre from 1618 until the closing of the theatres in 1642. He figures in two anecdotes of a later date, which represent him as playing heroic parts—conquering captains and mighty fighters—which helped to give the theatre a bad reputation for noisy plays, and apparently noisy audiences, since on one Shrove Tuesday they rioted, and threw nuts, apples, and oranges at the actors.

FOX. (1) GEORGE WASHINGTON LAFAYETTE (1825–77), American actor and pantomimist, who at various times used several variants of his name, but is generally known as G. L. Fox. He was on the stage as a child, and from 1850 to 1858 was a stalwart member of the National Theatre company. While there he persuaded the management to put on Aiken's adaptation of *Uncle Tom's Cabin*, which ran for a year, and was the best of many versions. In 1858 he went into partnership with Lingard, and took over the management of the Bowery, the New Bowery, and in 1862 the Lyceum, which he rechristened Fox's Olympic. From 1862 to 1867 he staged a long series of successful pantomimes at the Old Bowery, and in 1867 gave a fine performance as Bottom in Mrs. John Wood's production of *A Midsummer Night's Dream* at Laura Keene's old theatre.

A year later he produced at the same theatre his pantomime *Humpty-Dumpty*, and a travesty of *Hamlet* which Edwin Booth is said to have seen and enjoyed. He continued to appear in successive editions of *Humpty-Dumpty* until his death, and was accounted a competent actor, and 'the peer of pantomimists'. Much of the pantomime 'business' in his shows was devised by his brother (2) CHARLES KEMBLE (1833–75), who with his parents and brothers and sister played as a child in the Howard-Fox company. He was also in Aiken's version of *Uncle Tom's Cabin*, as was his mother, and played Pantaloon in his elder brother's pantomimes.

FOX'S BOWERY, NEW YORK, see BOWERY THEATRE (1).

FOX'S BROADWAY, NEW YORK, see NEW YORK THEATRE (1).

FOX WEDGES are those used under the side flats of a Box Set on a raked stage (see STAGE, 1).

FOY, EDDIE (1856–1928), American actor and vaudeville player, whose real name was Edwin Fitzgerald. He was a singer and entertainer from childhood, and in 1878 sang and danced in the Western boom towns with a minstrel troupe. Later he was seen in comedy and melodrama, and from 1888 to 1894 he played leading parts in a long series of extravaganzas in Chicago. He was acting in the Iroquois Theatre there in 1903 when fire broke out, and did his best to calm the audience, but without success, the panic resulting in the loss of 600 lives. Foy, who was an eccentric comedian with many mannerisms and a distinctive clown make-up, played in musical comedy until 1913 and then went into vaudeville, accompanied by his seven children, with whom he made his last appearance in 1927. He subsequently wrote his autobiography as *Clowning Through Life* (1928).

FRAGSON, HARRY (1869–1913), a music-hall performer, whose real name was Potts. He was as popular in Paris with his Cockney accent as in London with his French accent. His songs were witty and well-observed, the best-remembered being 'Billie, Billie Brown of London' and 'The Other Department'. He appeared before Royalty on several occasions, and played in pantomime at Drury Lane. When he played Dandini in *Cinderella*, the character, out of compliment to his Anglo-French reputation, was rechristened Dandigny. Fragson was shot by his father in a fit of insanity.

W. M. P.

FRANÇA JUNIOR, JOAQUIM JOSÉ DA, see SOUTH AMERICA, 2.

FRANCE. 1. MEDIEVAL. In France, as elsewhere in Europe, national drama evolved from the liturgical drama of the Church (see

ECCLESIASTICAL DRAMA), with some slight but definite accretions from the folk-play and the ministrel tradition. The evolution of the play based on the liturgy, and performed wholly or mainly by the clergy inside the church, was complete by the middle of the thirteenth century, and any further development was bound to intensify the secular elements which had already crept in. This process began when exigencies of space, and a growing sense of the limitations imposed by the church walls, forced the play from the nave and choir to the churchyard and, eventually, to the market-place. In France this move was made early, for a twelfth-century Anglo-Norman play on the subject of Adam was clearly intended for outdoor performance, and while plays continued no doubt to be given in churches long after this date, they were gradually over-shadowed and replaced by their secularized open-air offspring.

Once the drama escaped from the church it grew and altered rapidly. The details of the transition period are confused and obscure, and must be studied in the works of scholars who have collected and collated the scattered fragments which are all that remain to us. It is, however, clear that from the early days of secularization the plays were taken over by the guilds, that important feature of medieval civic life, who first supplied the extra actors needed, and later were entirely responsible for the financing and production of the plays. These fell into two main groups—those based on the Old and New Testament stories, a series of episodes strung together to cover the whole span of creation from the Fall to the Last Judgement; and those based on the lives of the Saints and, in France particularly, on that of the Virgin Mary (see MIRACLE PLAY). These still remained linked with the Church Festivals, and could be played either on a stationary platform raised against the church wall or in the market-place, or in procession, when each scene was enacted on a wheeled stage, or pageant, which visited different parts of the city in turn. On the evidence available it would seem that the stationary stage was more common in France, while England favoured the succession of pageants. In both countries the practice of acting in the open air, at the mercy of the elements, caused the plays to be given mainly in the summer, since, as Chambers says in his *Mediaeval Stage*: 'Even in sunny France, Christmas is not exactly the season to hang about the market-place, looking at an interminable drama.' So Whitsun, and particularly the Feast of Corpus Christi (the Thursday after Trinity Sunday), were the favourite times for theatrical activity.

The staging of medieval plays developed from that of liturgical drama, where various sites in the church had symbolized the different scenes of the action. As many localities as were needed—and these might range from four to forty—were denoted by booths, or 'mansions' grouped behind or around a central, un-localized acting space, which for the stationary stage was merely the unencumbered front of the platform, but for the perambulating pageants included also a roped-off portion of the street. The most ornate and elevated mansion represented Heaven, while Hell, as far removed from Heaven as possible, was usually shown in the shape of a dragon's mouth. In between these two extremes were the earthly 'mansions'—houses, shops, rooms, gardens—appropriately draped and furnished. Pulleys, trap-doors, and other mechanical devices were freely used, costumes were elaborate and brightly coloured, singing and dancing had their place in the general scheme. A few plays might be given on one day, or the whole cycle might be spread over a week, the latter perhaps at intervals of several years, a reasonable supposition when one considers the time and energy that must have been expended in rehearsals, carpentry, and dressmaking, as well as the heavy expense involved.

The outstanding results of the passing of drama from the hands of the clergy into those of the laity, and the most important for the future of the theatre, were the extended use of the vernacular, already present in the twelfth-century play on Adam referred to above, which inevitably produced a national, as opposed to a cosmopolitan, drama, and an intensification of the comic and rowdy elements which had already begun to make their appearance inside the church, and were later strengthened there also by a reciprocal influence from the secular plays. There were plenty of opportunities for comedy in these early productions, mainly in connexion with the extraneous personages grafted on to the Bible story—wives, merchants, servants—and with the imps and devils attendant upon Satan. By the thirteenth century, as can be seen from the *Jeu de Saint Nicolas* by Jean Bodel (*fl.* thirteenth century), scenes of everyday life were already being incorporated into the religious plays, thus further weakening their original liturgical character. A further influence at work in the direction of humour was that of the purely secular farce, a twofold inheritance from the almost submerged traditions of the classical *mimi* preserved in the repertory of the minstrels, and from the licensed buffoonery of the Feast of Fools. Just as the serious religious play became the concern of the town guilds and literary societies, so the farcical horseplay of the minor clergy became the perquisite of the *sociétés joyeuses*, those bands of light-hearted, irreverent youths who, when the ecclesiastical merry-making fell into disrepute and desuetude, took it upon themselves to provide amusement for their fellow townsmen. They, and such similar societies as the *clercs de la basoche*, formed by the law-students in the universities under Philippe le Bel, and the student society of the Parisian *enfants sans souci*, formed under Charles VI, were primarily associations of amateurs, and must not be confused with the professional corporations of minstrels. These latter, however, were not excluded from participation in the revels and, though there is no proof of their association with them, professional entertainers may have been employed by the guilds to assist in the religious plays, particularly in the domain of music. They certainly played a part in the production of the non-religious plays, where their experience and ready pens would be most welcome. To a minstrel, Adam de la Halle (c. 1240–c. 1286), goes the honour of having written in the late thirteenth century the earliest-known French secular plays—a link between folk-song and drama—the *Jeu de Robin et Marion* and the *Jeu de la feuillée*. Another thirteenth-century minstrel whose work is extant is Rutebeuf (c. 1230–c. 1285). He, Adam, and Bodel, are lone figures surging above the sea of anonymity which covers most of medieval drama.

2. THE PERIOD OF TRANSITION. These various influences, working together, shaped the early destiny of French drama, which by the fifteenth century emerges as a national entity, capable of classification and of more detailed study than was possible in the earlier confused period. Drama has now utterly forsaken the Church, and been forsaken by it. The Confraternity of the Passion, a guild of amateur actors formed in 1402 for the performance of Mystery plays in and around Paris, probably indoors and for a small entrance fee, was the model for many similar associations up and down the country. The literary societies (the *puys*) and the student companies had their allegorical drama (see MORALITY PLAY) and their topical satiric drama (see SOTIE), the first a fourteenth-century offshoot of the religious play, whose characters were abstractions of vice and virtue dealing not specifically with religion, but with morality in general, the latter a short topical skit, spiced with pungent wit, often political and wholly irreligious. The best-known writer of these *soties*, as they were called, was Pierre Gringore (*fl.* sixteenth century), the *mère-sotte*, or chief fool, of the Parisian *enfants sans souci*, in whose *Jeu du Prince des sots* (1511) may be seen a fusion of the morality and the *sotie* pure. The *sotie* was not a farce, though it had elements in common with it, for its plot was weak, and its content mainly topical, which may account for the frequency with which its actors found themselves in trouble with the authorities. The farce, that perennial and unliterary form of popular drama, flourished also, the most famous example being the anonymous fifteenth-century *Maître Pierre Pathelin*, done by the *enfants sans souci* in 1470, whose robust humour survives modernization and even translation. During the whole of the fifteenth and sixteenth centuries in France Mystery, Miracle, and Morality plays, *soties* and farces, continued to be performed, often by the same actors and on the same programme. On the whole the actors were probably still amateurs, though modern critics incline to the view that *soties* may have been done by semi-permanent bands of actors, who thus take on a somewhat professional air.

This mingling of the genres had its dangers, the most obvious being the final swamping of

the religious element by the secular. That the actors of the Confraternity of the Passion did not escape this snare is proved by a decree of 17 Nov. 1548, which, while confirming the brotherhood in its monopoly of acting in Paris, at the same time forbade the performance of anything but secular pieces, on the ground that the admixture of sacred and profane elements, and the consequent disorder and licence, brought religion into disrepute. The Confraternity was thus deprived of the greater part of its repertory, and with the ban the history of early religious drama in France comes to an end. The secular theatre is now free to develop in its own way along literary and popular lines.

3. THE ESTABLISHMENT OF A NATIONAL AND PROFESSIONAL THEATRE. Owing to the ravages of civil war, however, the secular theatre took a long time to establish itself and the sixteenth century, which saw the emergence of a fine national drama in Spain and England with Lope de Vega and Shakespeare, was still in France a period of confusion and experiment. It is interesting, though useless, to speculate on what direction the popular element in drama might have taken had it not been caught up and overwhelmed by the tide of new learning sweeping in from Italy. The influence of the Renaissance triumphed in the end over the old farces and *soties* as much as over the complicated and out-moded Bible-histories. Drawing not only their inspiration but also their form and content from classical antiquity, the writers of the French Renaissance were students first and playwrights almost by accident. Étienne Jodelle (1532–73), whose tragedy, *Cléopâtre captive*, given in 1552 together with a comedy on classic lines, is generally held to be the first neo-classic drama of France, opened the way for the great drama of the seventeenth century. Among his contemporaries, who all looked to Greece and Rome for their models, the best was probably Robert Garnier (c. 1535–c. 1600), a fine poet and scholar, who made good use of the chorus, but hampered himself by slavish adherence to the drama of antiquity, which he envisaged through Roman eyes. A later dramatist, Antoine de Montchrétien (c. 1575–1621), continued the vogue for tragedy. He was also a fine poet and one of the first playwrights to deal with modern history, making Mary Queen of Scots the heroine of his *L'Écossaise* (1603).

True to what they believed to be the principle of their Greek models—a view since somewhat modified—these early French dramatists allowed themselves no mingling of the serious and the gay. The old medieval mixture of high tragedy and low farce was no longer permissible, and the genres were sharply defined. The same author might adventure in both, as Jodelle himself did, and as did Jacques Grévin (c. 1538–c. 1570), whose tragedy on Julius Caesar is overshadowed by the popularity of his comedy *Les Esbahis* (1560); but this owes nothing to the popular farce of old France, nor do the comedies of Pierre Larivey (c. 1540–c. 1612), an Italian turned Frenchman, who saw the Italian *commedia dell' arte* company, the Gelosi, play at Blois in 1577, and was inspired to write a number of comedies in French based on Italian models. This early association of French with Italian comedy is interesting, since it foreshadows the connexion between the *commedia dell'arte* scenarii and the early plays of that great writer of French comedies, Molière. Also from Italy came the Pastoral, the delight of a courtly society, which shared the popularity of tragedy.

The years which saw the gradual shaping and perfecting of French drama in a form which was to reach its height in the plays of Corneille and Racine saw also the emergence of a body of professional actors to interpret them. The early writers, Jodelle, Garnier, Grévin, relied on amateurs, on themselves and their friends, or on the schools, particularly in those run by Jesuits, where Latin plays and occasionally comedies in the vernacular formed part of the educational curriculum (see JESUIT DRAMA). Jodelle himself played the heroine in his *Cléopâtre captive*, while Grévin's plays were given at the Collège de Beauvais. While the new drama was thus establishing itself as literature, the old discredited drama was still played in the provinces, by bands of strolling actors who were, by the 1570s, beginning to form permanent professional companies. They had as yet no foothold in Paris. Apart from the monopoly still held, and jealously exercised, by the Confraternity of the Passion, the country was in too troublous a state to allow of the establishment of permanent theatre-buildings. Peace came with the accession of Henri IV in 1594, but it was not until Richelieu came into power some thirty years later that the theatre could flourish in the capital, and Paris achieve that pre-eminence which she has since retained. Until then she had to be content with visits from foreign companies, mainly Italian, brought in expressly for the amusement of the Court, and from French provincial companies which included the town in their itineraries, and took the old theatre of the Confraternity of the Passion, the Hôtel de Bourgogne, on a short lease. One such company is noted in 1578 under Agnan Sarat (?–1613), an actor-manager who became the comedian of the first professional company which can really be said to have established itself in Paris. Led by Valleran-Lecomte (*fl.* 1590–*c.* 1613), this company has two other claims to distinction. Its leading lady was Marie Venier (*fl.* 1590–1619), the first French actress to be known by name, and it had as its dramatist Alexandre Hardy (*c.* 1575–*c.* 1631), a prolific dramatist who, with a spark of genius, might have changed the course of French dramatic literature. His numerous plays, which subordinated character to action, were mainly tragi-comedies. They were extremely popular, and many future dramatists of the great age of French drama, including Corneille, owed their first glimpse of the theatre to Hardy.

The Hôtel de Bourgogne was at this time in much the same state as when the Confra-

ternity of the Passion had used it for their medieval Bible-histories. A long, narrow room, it had rising tiers of benches at one end, opposite the stage, and boxes on each side. A pit, for standing spectators only, ran half the length of the room, and the stage and auditorium alike were lit by candles, which had frequently to be snuffed during the performance. The old system of simultaneous, or multiple, settings was still in use, at least during the early seventeenth century, and each actor played his part as a solo, advancing to the edge of the stage to declaim, and retiring to make way for his successor.

Since the Confraternity of the Passion still clung to their monopoly of acting, it followed that only companies to whom they leased their theatre at the Hôtel de Bourgogne could legally act in Paris. A breach was, however, made in their privileges by an edict of 1595, which permitted other companies to play at the fairs, at that of St. Germain in the spring and of St. Laurent in the autumn. The father of Valleran-Lecomte's leading lady, himself a provincial actor-manager of long standing, was quick to profit by this, and took his company from the spring fair to the Hôtel d'Argent, where he was allowed to remain on payment of a levy to the Confraternity. On a later visit there he was joined for a time by his daughter and her husband, also an actor, and author of some lost plays, under the name of Laporte.

The opening years of the seventeenth century thus found Paris with two semi-permanent and wholly professional companies. The fortunes of both fluctuated, as did their composition, for actors constantly migrated from one group to another, while a political upheaval, such as the assassination of Henri IV in 1610, was sufficient to uproot them all and send them back into the provinces again. But by 1629 the *Comédiens du roi*, as the company once headed by Valleran-Lecomte was now called, had established itself firmly at the Hôtel de Bourgogne, while a rival company under Charles Lenoir (*fl.* 1610–37) was competing for public favour elsewhere.

The establishment of the French professional actor in the capital led to an increase in the number of plays written, but little of permanent value was produced. Some of the plays that survive, many of them anonymous, have scenes of merit but little form. They are intended to entertain or amuse, and are not yet subject to criticism or bound by laws of dramatic composition. In spite of a slight ascendancy, Paris has not yet attained complete control of theatrical activity, and good companies are still found in the provinces, particularly in Normandy, while an increasing number of plays are published in Rouen. A study of the repertory, where indications of it can be found, discloses a curious mingling of the old medieval play with those written under classical or Italian influence. The actors who leased the Hôtel de Bourgogne in the early years of the century showed a marked preference for plots derived from medieval romance epics. Scenes of violence, later to be banned by the purists, are often found, and were apparently much enjoyed by the audience. The pastoral continued in high favour, with tragi-comedy not far behind. Comedy is practically non-existent. Hardy's neglect of it may have caused others to disdain it also. Farces were no doubt abundant, but as they were seldom printed, perhaps hardly even written down, few have survived. We can, however, judge of their popularity by the fact that the outstanding actors of the period are farce-players. Some of them are reputed to have come to the professional theatre from the booths of the fairs, among them Bruscambille (*fl.* 1610–34), famous for his amusing prologues and epilogues; his partner Jean Farine (*fl.* 1600–35), and the famous trio Turlupin (*c.* 1587–1637), Gaultier-Garguille (*c.* 1573–1633), and Gros-Guillaume (*fl.* 1600–34), delight of the audiences at the Hôtel de Bourgogne for many years, and actors, under the names of Belleville, Fleschelles, and Lafleur, of serious parts also. An actor who never achieved the dignity of the Hôtel de Bourgogne, but whose clowning on the Pont-Neuf was long a feature of Paris life, was Tabarin (?–1626), whose name passed into the colloquial language of France, while one of his jokes was later used by no less a person than Molière.

The leader of the company at the Hôtel de Bourgogne, whose acting in pastoral and tragi-comedy did much to raise the status of the profession and oust the farce-players from public favour, was Bellerose (*c.* 1600–70). Under him such clowns as Guillot-Gorju (1600–48), though still popular, were content with a secondary place, while an interesting feature of this period is the sudden flowering of feminine talent with such actresses as Mlle Beauchâteau (1615–83) and Mlle Beaupré (*fl.* 1624–50), both wives of actors. At the newly established Théâtre du Marais, too, where the great actor Montdory (1594–1651) was building up a fine reputation in tragedy, there was an excellent actress, Mlle de Villiers (?–1670). She and Montdory, with an able and experienced company, were called upon to interpret the early plays of the French classical period, which Corneille is generally held to have inaugurated with his tragi-comedy, *Le Cid* (1636), in which they played Chimène and Rodrigue respectively.

4. THE GREAT AGE OF FRENCH DRAMA. (*a*) *Corneille.* Many influences had been at work, however, before Corneille produced his masterpiece, the most important being the establishment of the Unities—of time, place, and action. These Unities, codified by French logic from the precepts of Aristotle, were destined to have a great influence on French drama and to lead to much argument, both at the time and in succeeding generations. Their history belongs mainly to the domain of literature, where they are represented either as a code imposed on dramatists against their will, which thwarted their natural develop-

ment, or as a formulating of theatrical devices which had already proved successful in action, and were therefore adopted by contemporary dramatists. It has been remarked, in support of the latter theory, that plays of the early classical period written in accordance with the Unities were more successful in performance than those that were not, a fact which would provide sufficient incentive for their adoption by other writers.

The Unities were first adhered to in the Pastoral, a genre which had proved popular ever since the publication in 1584 of a translation of Tasso's *Aminta*, and which was to achieve a sudden blaze of glory before it disappeared for ever. Courtly poets, like the Marquis de Racan (1589–1670) and Théophile de Viau (1590–1626), had already brought to the art of playwriting some distinction in style and versification, and a greater insistence on emotion than on action, while raising at the same time the prestige of the dramatist, when a young writer, Jean Mairet (1604–86), influenced and encouraged by them, brought out his *Sylvanire* (1630). The success of this play induced other writers to adopt the rules which Mairet had set out in his preface, and the triumph of the Unities was assured by the reception given to his *Sophonisbe* (1634). This play, which provided Montdory with a fine part as Massinisse, brought about a return to popular favour of the tragedy after its partial eclipse by tragi-comedy, and had a marked influence on other writers of the period. One of the best plays written under its influence was the *Mariamne* (1636) of Tristan l'Hermite (1601–55), who followed it with a number of other plays without again equalling its excellence. It, too, gave scope for Montdory's powers in the part of Herod, which he was playing when paralysis of the tongue caused his premature retirement from the stage.

Before this melancholy event, however, Montdory had been instrumental in introducing to the public the plays of Pierre Corneille (1606–84). He had already given eight of them at the Marais, mainly comedies of intrigue, of a type new to the Parisian stage, when he put on *Le Cid* (1636). This tragi-comedy, based on the story of Spain's national hero, proved popular, as did many others of the same type written at this time; but, unlike its emulators, *Le Cid* had a permanent value, and is to-day recognized as one of the outstanding works of French literature.

Its present position, however, and the popular acclaim with which it was first received, should not blind us to the fact that contemporary criticism of it was not wholly favourable. Corneille was accused of violating the Unities, and a fierce quarrel broke out among the literary figures of Paris. Mairet, possibly through jealousy, stood firm for his beloved rules, as did such lesser writers as Georges de Scudéry (1601–67), who nevertheless violated them in his own plays, and Jean Gombauld (1570–1666), while those who had already some perception of Corneille's stature argued that genius makes its own rules and may discard those of lesser men where it pleases. The question was finally brought for arbitration to Cardinal Richelieu (1585–1642), who added an interest in the theatre, an urge to organize it, and a desire to shine as a playwright, to his many other preoccupations. The point never was, indeed never could be, settled, but posterity has given the verdict to Corneille against his opponents.

Undeterred by the storm of criticism he had aroused Corneille continued to write, but it is interesting to note that his next plays, among them *Horace* (1640) and *Cinna* (1641), were mainly tragedies, as though he wished to prove that he could beat his opponents at their own game. Tragedy was now established as the recognized vehicle for classical French drama, and many fine ones were written at this period, among them those of Pierre du Ryer (*c.* 1600–58) and Jean Rotrou (1609–50). The former had been an early adherent to the theory of the Unities, and had followed some early tragicomedies in the style of Hardy with tragedies written strictly in accordance with the rules of Mairet. The best of these was *Scévole* (1644), which remained in the repertory of the Comédie-Française until the middle of the eighteenth century, as did Rotrou's *Venceslas* (1647). Rotrou was an excellent dramatist, whose first play was produced when he was only 19. His popularity, and also his industry, can be judged from the fact that he had four plays produced in the year of *Le Cid*, and throughout his career he never failed to provide good parts for Bellerose and the company of the Hôtel de Bourgogne, to which he was attached as official dramatist in succession to Hardy.

An interesting dramatist, contemporary with Corneille's early years, was Gautier de Costes de La Calprenède (*c.* 1610–63), who, unlike his companions, looked to English rather than Roman history for the subjects of his tragedies. The best of these, and certainly the most interesting, was *Le Comte d'Essex* (1637), in which he introduces for the first time the episode of the ring given by Elizabeth to Essex. An earlier play by La Calprenède had dealt with Lady Jane Grey. La Calprenède later deserted the theatre for the novel, and his success in that genre has somewhat overshadowed his reputation as a dramatist.

Tragedy was still in the ascendant when the troubles of the Fronde overwhelmed France, and caused a slowing-down of theatrical activity, and a slight but noticeable change in the development of drama. Among Corneille's plays at this time are *Rodogune* (1645), with which is associated the name of a much lesser dramatist, Gabriel Gilbert (*c.* 1620–*c.* 1680), who was later accused, with some justification, of having plagiarized Corneille's play in his own *Rhodogune*, done early in the following year; *Andromède* (1650), the first 'machine-play', embellished by the mechanical inventions of Torelli; and the unfortunate *Pertharite* (1652), whose failure, added to the troublous

times, led Corneille temporarily to abandon the theatre. His retirement coincided with that of du Ryer and the death of Rotrou. The public taste was for lighter fare, and new dramatists came forward to satisfy it, among them Corneille's younger brother, Thomas Corneille (1625–1709), whose first play was produced in 1647, Philippe Quinault (1635–88), friend and protégé of Tristan l'Hermite, and the prolific and elderly Abbé Boisrobert (1592–1662), who had already contributed a number of plays to the repertory, the first at the age of 40, but whose main activity was confined to the 1650s.

Although all the later dramatists mentioned above wrote tragedies, their work in the period under review was mainly done in comedy, a genre which for the first time comes into prominence, and seeks to rival and even outdo tragedy and tragi-comedy. Its development through the first half of the seventeenth century was to culminate in the work of the actor-dramatist, Molière, one of France's greatest dramatists and perhaps one of the greatest writers of comedy in the history of the European theatre.

(b) *Molière.* In the early years of the seventeenth century playgoers relied for humour mainly on the rough horseplay of the farce, or on the incidental comic scenes and characters in the pastorals and tragi-comedies. The 1630s saw a few isolated examples of comedy by such established authors as Rotrou, du Ryer, and Scudéry, but it was Corneille, with the series of plays which preceded *Le Cid*, who liberated true comedy from the entanglements of farce and melodrama, and made it a genre worthy of serious attention. Later, having proved himself a great writer of tragedies, he returned to this earlier form, and produced in *Le Menteur* (1643), based on a play by Alarcón, the best French comedy of the period. Its success, however, was not repeated by its sequel in the following year, and the failure of *La Suite du Menteur* may have decided Corneille to return to tragedy. Whatever the reason, he wrote no more comedies; but he had blazed a trail which others were not slow to follow.

Among the few notable comedies before *Le Menteur* was *Les Visionnaires* (1637) by Jean Desmaretz de Saint-Sorlin (1595–1676), one of Richelieu's protégés, in which plot is subordinated to the study of a series of comic characters, monomaniacs who think of themselves as brave, rich, poetic, or adored, when in reality they are cowardly, poor, prosaic, or ridiculous. French comedy might, after this, have concentrated on character rather than intrigue, had it not been for the influence of Antoine d'Ouville (*c.* 1590–1656/77), brother of the Abbé Boisrobert, and like him a dramatist. He had lived much in Spain, and most of his comedies were based on Spanish models, as were those of his brother, and of Paul Scarron (1610–60), friend of Corneille and first husband of the future Mme de Maintenon. Better known for his novels, which included one on the life of a travelling company, *Le Roman comique*, Scarron nevertheless ranks high in the history of French comedy, since to him is due the introduction, in his *L'Écolier de Salamanque* (1654), of the valet Crispin. Another writer who owed much to Spain was the younger Corneille; like his brother, he began by writing a series of comedies, but since they are drawn from Spanish sources they are all comedies of intrigue. For a revival of true French comedy, as indicated by Corneille, but with its roots in the indigenous farce, we must turn to Molière.

Jean-Baptiste Poquelin, known as Molière (1622–73), came of a good family of the upper middle class and, as far as is known, had no affiliations with the stage. Yet before he was 21 he had renounced his succession to his father's position as Court upholsterer, and gone off with a family of young actors, drawn perhaps by love for the eldest girl, but more probably by the irresistible attraction of the theatre, which he never again deserted. After an unsuccessful start in Paris, where they were billed as the Illustre-Théâtre, the young company left for the provinces, and remained there until 1658, playing stock Italian farces, knockabout comedies written by Molière himself, who had soon become the leader of the troupe, and tragedies by contemporary dramatists, particularly Corneille, whom Molière much admired. Little is known of these years in the provinces, but the experience gained in them proved useful when Molière brought his company back to Paris in 1658. In addition to himself and the Béjarts, Madeleine (1618–72), Joseph (*c.* 1620–59), Geneviève (*c.* 1622–75), and Louis (1625–78), remnants of the original company, he had two good actresses in Mlle du Parc (*c.* 1633–68) and Mlle de Brie (?–1707), a staunch veteran in Charles Dufresne (*fl.* 1643–60), once leader of the troupe and soon to leave it, and a good comedian in Gros-René (*c.* 1600–64), husband of Mlle du Parc.

The company first appeared at Court, before the king, in *Nicomède*, but without much success. They redeemed themselves, however, by a splendid performance of one of Molière's early farces, *Le Docteur amoureux*, now lost. In consideration of their success they were allowed to remain in Paris and share the stage of the Petit-Bourbon with an Italian *commedia dell' arte* company established there under Scaramouche (Tiberio Fiorelli), where they remained until their removal to the Palais-Royal in 1660.

Paris now had three permanent troupes of actors—the Hôtel de Bourgogne, which, under the successors of Bellerose, Floridor (1608–72) and Montfleury (*c.* 1600–67), had achieved supremacy in tragedy; the Marais, fallen from its high estate but still able, under Laroque (*c.* 1595–1676), to tempt away two of Molière's best actors, the du Parcs, and already beginning to specialize in 'machine-plays'; and Molière's company, which, after another abortive attempt at tragedy, found its true vocation in the acting of Molière's comedies. These,

which range from the one-act *Précieuses ridicules* of 1658 to the three-act *Malade imaginaire* of 1673, mark the development and flowering of French comedy of character, and added a number of masterpieces to the repertory of French dramatic literature. It is almost impossible to over-estimate the influence of Molière, not only in his own country, but on European literature in general. Before him comedy had been a neglected art, too often relegated to the status of a farce in a fair-booth; he made it a genre worthy to rank with tragedy. His genius was peculiarly his own, and though like Shakespeare he borrowed freely, yet he adorned everything he touched. In spite of the speed with which he wrote, and his many other preoccupations as actor and leader of a company, his comedy is in no way superficial. His most ridiculous characters have about them some touch of pathos, some sense of lost and bewildered humanity which gives them a universal appeal. He was never deliberately malicious, though his satire cut deep; it was directed against those who sought to dupe or entangle the ordinary man, in whose innate goodness and kindliness he firmly believed. He attacked hypocrisy and pretension wherever he found it and did not scruple to bring down on himself the wrath of those in high places, as when he attacked the false piety of the religious hypocrite in *Tartuffe*, whose stormy history shows the forces he had to contend with.

Apart from his straightforward plays, which were usually given for the first time on the public stage, and included such light-hearted comedies as *L'École des maris* (1661), *L'École des femmes* (1662), *Le Médecin malgré lui* (1666), *Le Malade imaginaire* (1673), and those two great comedies of character, *Le Misanthrope* (1666) and *L'Avare* (1668) Molière was also responsible for a large number of entertainments written for the amusement of the Court. These, known as *comédies-ballets*, show a judicious mingling of speech, song, and dance, and many of Molière's plays, including *Le Bourgeois gentilhomme* (1671), were originally written for these elaborate spectacles in which the King and his courtiers took part as dancers and actors. Though Molière cannot claim to have invented the *comédie-ballet*, which was much in vogue at Court before his day, he extended and developed it, and gave it a literary, as well as a musical, importance. His collaborators were Lully, who eventually obtained a monopoly of music in Paris which effectually put an end to the development of plays with music, and hastened the overwhelming popularity of opera and operetta, and Isaac de Benserade (1613–91), protégé and kinsman of Richelieu, whose inconsiderable early plays were overshadowed by the later popularity of his libretti; and, on one occasion, in *Psyché* (1671), the great Corneille himself, who had returned to the stage in 1659 with *Œdipe*.

Molière's work for the Court and for his own theatre completely filled his life, and from his arrival in Paris in 1658 until his untimely death in 1673 he had no interests and no affiliations outside. He even took a wife from among his actors, marrying in 1662 Armande Béjart (1642–1700), youngest sister of Madeleine, and an excellent actress who was the first to play many of Molière's delightful heroines. It was an unhappy marriage, and many critics have sought in Molière's plays a reflection of his domestic troubles. The parallel does not seem to have struck contemporary audiences overmuch. As with many authors, Molière's plays through the centuries have gathered an accretion of interpretation and application perhaps foreign to his original intention. He was too good a judge of what was theatrically effective to risk boring his audience with a purely personal problem, and it may be coincidence that his situations and speeches, with their universal appeal, apply also to his own life.

(c) *Racine*. Although he was sufficient in himself to sustain the burden of writing for his own theatre for many years, Molière did not neglect the work of contemporary dramatists, and among the plays which he imported into the Palais-Royal was the first tragedy of a young man whose fame was soon to overshadow that of Corneille himself. This was *La Thébaïde* (1664), by Jean Racine (1639–99). Early orphaned, educated at the Collège de Beauvais and at Port-Royal, Racine was already known as a poet, and had made the acquaintance of the actors of the Marais and the Hôtel de Bourgogne, was a friend of La Fontaine, and at some point met Molière.

His first venture was a success, and it is interesting to see that, in spite of its somewhat brutal subject and the inexperience of its author, the play contains already the germ of Racine's future theatre. Though it lacks the poetic charm and psychological insight of some of his later work, its Greek theme, its technical excellence, and its insistence on the love-interest, show the way he is going.

At the time of Racine's début French tragedy was becalmed. Comedy flourished under Molière, whose success had raised up a host of imitators, some of them actors also. But to the new names in comedy, tragedy could oppose only such established authors as the ageing Corneille; his brother Thomas, whose *Timocrate* (1656) heralded the return of tragedy after the upheaval of the Fronde, and was followed by a number of other tragedies, mostly on classical themes; the mediocre works of Jean Magnon (1620–62) and Claude Boyer (1618–98); the one tragedy, *Manlius Torquatus* (1662), of Mlle Desjardins (1632–83), one of the few women dramatists of the period; and Quinault, who after four successful comedies and a number of tragedies, of which *Astrate* (1665) is usually considered the best, gave himself up entirely to the writing of libretti for opera, mainly set to music by Lully. The time was therefore ripe for a new talent, and Racine came at his hour. *La Thébaïde* was followed by *Alexandre et*

Porus (1665), which Racine, with a callous disregard of Molière's kindness that cost him the older man's friendship, gave to the actors at the Hôtel de Bourgogne a fortnight after it had opened at the Palais-Royal. Molière's insufficiency in tragedy has been advanced as the cause of this double-dealing; whatever the explanation, Racine's plays were henceforth given at the rival theatre, which also took from Laroque Molière's former star, Mlle du Parc, now the mistress of Racine. She was at the Hôtel de Bourgogne in time to play the title-role in *Andromaque* (1667), a fine play which established Racine as the leading dramatist of the day, superior even to the great Corneille, whose *Agésilaus* (1666) and *Attila* (1667) had been coolly received. The rivalry between them came to a head when in 1670 both authors produced plays on the same subject, Racine's *Bérénice* being given at the Hôtel de Bourgogne a week before Corneille's *Tite et Bérénice* at the Palais-Royal. Racine's play, with its simplicity and fine poetry, and the added attraction of the great tragic actress Mlle Champmeslé (1642–98) in the title-role, was judged the better of the two, in spite of the excellence of Molière's wife as Corneille's heroine, and the fine Domitien of young Michel Baron (1653–1729), later to be the foremost actor of France, and now appearing in his first adult part after a childhood spent on the stage.

While Corneille was bringing his honourable career to a close with two rather frigid tragedies, which showed to great disadvantage against the warmer, more passionate, works of his young rival, Racine turned to oriental subjects in his *Bajazet* (1672) and *Mithridate* (1673), treating them in a contemporary style that was purely French, and then went back, as his only rivals Thomas Corneille and Quinault were doing, to Greek mythology. *Iphigénie* (1674) was followed by Racine's masterpiece, *Phèdre* (1677), which has been acclaimed as one of the greatest plays ever written. The success Racine might well have looked for at this culminating point in his career was, however, vitiated by the efforts of a powerful cabal. Jealous of his growing prestige, this group extolled a mediocre play on the same subject by a second-rate dramatist, Nicolas Pradon (1632–98), author of a number of tragedies which suffer by comparison with Racine's. Pradon's temporary success, however, added to Racine's official appointment at Court, and perhaps some private scruples, combined to make the latter forsake the theatre. He retained an interest in it for many years, but his only connexion with it after *Phèdre* was through the two biblical plays, *Esther* (1689) and *Athalie* (1690), written at the request of Mme de Maintenon for private performance by the young ladies of Saint-Cyr, and never publicly produced in Racine's lifetime.

Unlike Corneille, Racine wrote only one comedy, *Les Plaideurs* (1668), a satire on the law, based to some extent on Aristophanes' *Wasps* and intended for the Italian *commedia dell' arte* troupe. Owing to Scaramouche's absence from Paris, it was given at the Hôtel de Bourgogne with some success, and it has often been regretted that Racine did not further develop his undoubted comic vein. Perhaps he hesitated to enter into competition with Molière, whose chief rivals in comedy were his brother-actors. Claude de Villiers (1600–81), husband of the first Chimène, wrote farces and a version of Don Juan. A better actor and dramatist was Raymond Poisson (*c.* 1630–90), whose numerous plays were successfully performed at the Hôtel de Bourgogne, where the author appeared as a farce-player under the name of Philipin, and was the first to immortalize the valet, Crispin. Of his plays, several of which deal with theatrical people or situations, the most interesting is *Le Baron de la Crasse* (1663). It portrays a provincial nobleman being entertained by a travelling company, whose leader may be intended as a caricature of Molière. Poisson, even more than Molière, was influenced by the form and content of the old French farce, with its short lines, violent action, and elementary humour. He understood his audience, and his plays proved most successful in performance, having a more individual stamp than those of most of Molière's imitators. Like Molière, he was a good comic actor, a tradition carried on through several generations by his numerous children and grandchildren.

A restless actor, Guillaume Brécourt (1638–86), who is found in all three Parisian troupes and in the provinces, wrote several comedies, of which *L'Ombre de Molière* (1674) was a tribute to the great dramatist, and owed perhaps more to him than to its author. *La Feinte Mort de Jodelet* (1659) was one of a series intended to give scope for the comic powers of the actor Jodelet (*c.* 1604–60), who had appeared in *Le Menteur* and its sequel, and was for a year before his death in Molière's company at the Palais-Royal. The plays of Charles Champmeslé (1642–1701) were for a long time attributed to La Fontaine or the Abbé Abeille, but have recently been restored to him. Those attributed to La Fontaine, *Le Florentin* (1685) and *La Coupe enchantée* (1688), were still being given in Paris in the early twentieth century. Champmeslé's main claim to fame, however, is his marriage to the outstanding tragic actress of her day, who was the first to play Racine's later heroines, and replaced Mlle du Parc in the dramatist's affections.

Of the many writers of comedy at this time the only one to approach Molière, either in quantity or quality, was an actor at the Hôtel de Bourgogne, Noël de Hauteroche (*c.* 1616–1707). He was at his best in simple, often one-act, sketches based on a single humorous situation, and among his most successful plays were those that gave the chief part to the valet Crispin, played by his colleague Raymond Poisson. Another author closely connected with the stage, though not himself an actor, was Antoine de Montfleury (1639–85), son of

the great tragedian, a lawyer and dramatist, who found himself in continual competition with Molière, mainly owing to the pressing need for the actors at the Hôtel de Bourgogne to put on a comedy each time Molière produced one. Even the titles are similar, as in *L'École des jaloux* (1661) and *L'Impromptu de l'Hôtel de Condé* (1663), the latter intended as a counterblast to the satire of *L'Impromptu de Versailles*, in which Molière had hard things to say of the elder Montfleury and his associates.

Apart from Boisrobert and the younger Corneille, the only other writer of comedies at this period who deserves a passing mention is Edmé Boursault (1638–1701), who at various times found himself quarrelling with Molière and with Boileau, two redoubtable enemies. His attack on Boileau was not acted, but that on Molière—*Le Portrait du peintre*—was given at the Hôtel de Bourgogne in 1663. Boursault, however, was destined to do his best work after Molière's death, with *La Comédie sans titre, ou Le Mercure galant* (1683) and two comedies based on the life and fables of Aesop.

The great age of French drama, which opened with *Le Cid* in 1636, closed with *Phèdre* in 1677. Corneille had gathered up the strands woven by those who preceded him, and of them fashioned the French classical drama, seen at its best in the conflict of love and honour in *Le Cid*, and in the lofty and noble diction of such tragedies as *Horace*, *Cinna*, and *Nicomède*. Racine, taking up the challenge of the older man, narrowed the range of tragedy but deepened it immeasurably with the introduction of passion and poetry. He also made extensive use of the theatrically effective device of raising the curtain on a situation which is about to be resolved, and then handling with consummate art the various pretexts which delay the catastrophe until the end of the fifth act. It is idle to compare Corneille and Racine. They are two different facets of the same jewel. Between them stands Molière, who chose for his début in Paris one of Corneille's tragedies, and was the first man of the theatre to recognize and encourage the genius of Racine. He was never their rival, since he never adventured into tragedy himself; but his comedies form the perfect pendant to their tragedies, and all three together represent the summit of French dramatic art.

During his lifetime Molière saw great changes come over the French theatre, some of which he helped to bring about. Apart from assisting in the literary development of farce into comedy, and the evolution of French tragedy, Molière lived through three eras of stage-craft. In his early days he saw, and may have used, the medieval system of simultaneous or multiple settings, which long continued to be popular at the Hôtel de Bourgogne, and may have been employed, in a modified form, for *Le Cid*. This gradually gave way to an unlocalized set scene suitable for the formal acting of French tragedy, usually summed up as *palais à volonté*. During this period, as in

England, the actors were hampered by the presence on the stage of a number of spectators, who were not finally dislodged until the eighteenth century. The setting of comedy was influenced by the scenery of the *commedia dell'arte* troupe with whom Molière had to share his stage. This showed a street or square in perspective, with houses grouped round from which the actors issued to transact their most intimate affairs in the open air—domestic quarrels, signing of wills, consultations with doctors, and so on. This fairly simple setting, which employed stylized scenery of painted and folding screens, was at first taken by Molière to Court, but he was soon influenced by the spectacular effects necessitated by Court spectacles and by the fashionable opera, and one of the last things he did was to rebuild the stage of the Palais-Royal to accommodate elaborate scene-shifting and machines. *Psyché* (1671) was the first play to be given there with all the effects which had been possible at Court. Earlier elaborate plays of this type had been Corneille's *Andromède* and *Toison d'or*, and the Marais had specialized in such spectacles. After Molière's death his new stage proved very useful to the wily Lully, who managed to get it assigned to him, under his monopoly of music, for the production of opera.

It is more difficult to assess the changes which had come over acting during this period, but there can be no doubt that great advances had been made, and that the early unpolished hit-or-miss methods of the itinerant companies had given way to a more studied technique. Bellerose and Montdory, the one gentle and somewhat insipid, the other forceful and declamatory, had raised the art of acting to a high level, and their work was continued by Floridor and Montfleury, both excellent actors in their different styles. Molière, though never a good actor in tragedy, excelled in comedy, and it was doubtless a far cry from the horseplay and acrobatic buffoonery of the early farces to his subtle and more natural style of acting, while his discarding of the mask, which he originally wore in imitation of the *commedia dell' arte*, as did all the farce-players, allowed full play to facial expression. Some of his company have already been mentioned. Others worthy of note were La Grange (1639–92), Molière's close friend, editor of his works, and keeper of a daily register of the theatre which has proved invaluable to later students of the period; Philibert Gassot du Croisy (*c.* 1630–95), who with his wife joined Molière soon after his arrival in Paris, and was the first to play the part of Tartuffe; and François Lenoir de La Thorillière (1626–80), who played a number of important roles in Molière's comedies, went to the Hôtel de Bourgogne after his death, and by the marriages of his sons and daughters, all on the stage, became the founder of a big theatrical family. Lesser parts in Molière's plays were taken by André Hubert (*c.* 1634–1700), a good impersonator of old women, and

the first to play Mme Jourdain in *Le Bourgeois gentilhomme*; by L'Espy (*fl.* 1610–64), the brother of Jodelet, and by Beauval (*c.* 1640–1709), a mediocre actor whose one great success, more by nature than by art, was the part of Thomas Diafoirus in *Le Malade imaginaire*. His wife, Mlle Beauval (*c.* 1649–1720), was, however, an excellent actress, both in comedy and tragedy, worthy to rank with Mlle de Brie and Mlle du Parc, mentioned above. The former played the part of Agnès in *L'École des femmes* for nearly fifty years, from its first production, while the latter, who died at the height of her powers, had the distinction of being admired by Corneille, trained by Molière, and loved by Racine.

At the Hôtel de Bourgogne two actors not yet mentioned were Jean de la Tuillerie (1650–88), a fine actor in tragedy, who married a daughter of Raymond Poisson, and wrote comedies about the valet Crispin for his father-in-law; and Mlle Desœillets (1621–70), who took the place of Michel Baron's mother at the Hôtel de Bourgogne, and created a number of tragic roles, including Corneille's Sophonisbe and Racine's Hermione. She was replaced in the latter part by Mlle Champmeslé.

Although Paris had, by the end of the century, attained complete supremacy in theatrical matters as in all else, provincial companies continued to circulate, and some of their actor-managers achieved a certain reputation. Among these was Filandre (1616–91), who is credited with the early training of Mlle Beauval and possibly of Floridor; Dorimond (?–*c.* 1664), whose career resembles that of Molière in his early years (though he never attained Paris), in that he headed his own company on their wanderings, and supplied them with farces and comedies written by himself; and Rosimond (*c.* 1640–86), who eventually came to the Marais, and afterwards joined the remnants of Molière's company, playing a number of Molière's roles. He, too, wrote several plays, among them one on Don Juan.

5. AFTERMATH AND EIGHTEENTH CENTURY. After Molière's death his company, under the leadership of his widow and La Grange, amalgamated with the actors at the Théâtre du Marais, and in 1680, as a result of Louis XIV's passion for centralization and monopolies, was again amalgamated with the actors of the Hôtel de Bourgogne to form what was eventually called the Comédie-Française (also known as the Théâtre-Français and the Maison de Molière). The name seems to have arisen in an effort to distinguish the French actors from the Italian (see COMÉDIE-ITALIENNE) who, after intermittent but increasingly lengthened visits to Paris during the past hundred years, took complete possession of the now disused Hôtel de Bourgogne, and began to mingle French with their Italian.

The Comédie-Française, which is still the National Theatre of France, had the sole right of acting and producing plays in Paris, and first call upon the services of provincial actors.

Its constitution was in the main that of the old Confraternity of the Passion, on which Molière's first abortive venture, the Illustre-Théâtre, had also based its articles of association. Roughly speaking, it is a co-operative enterprise, in which each member is entitled to a certain share in the proceeds and to a pension after some fixed period of service, has definite rights and obligations, and is subject to a discipline administered by general agreement in the common interest.

The most important members of the Comédie-Française on its foundation were Baron, Raymond Poisson, Hauteroche, Mlle Beauval, and Mlle Champmeslé, with the latter's husband, the widow of Molière and her second husband, Guérin d'Étriché (c. 1636-1728), whom she had married in 1677. A new-comer who was to prove so good in comic parts that he was nicknamed 'le petit Molière' was Jean-Baptiste Raisin (1655-93), whose brother, sister, and wife were also members of the company. A few years later a second generation of actors was represented by Paul Poisson (1658-1735), son of Raymond, by his wife, daughter of Molière's du Croisy, and by Pierre Lenoir de La Thorillière (1659-1731), whose father's death in 1680 is generally held to have accelerated the formation of a single troupe, to which he had been strongly opposed. This younger La Thorillière married the daughter of Dominique, leader with Scaramouche of the Italian actors at the Hôtel de Bourgogne, while his sisters were the wives respectively of Baron and of the actor-dramatist Dancourt (see below).

At the one theatre with which they now had to be content, Parisian audiences could see revivals of Molière, Corneille, and Racine, together with some older plays, and a host of inferior imitations. Some of the blame for the aridity of this period must lie with the authors, who were afraid to venture into new paths; some with the actors, who used their monopoly as an excuse to avoid anything but variations on an old theme. Tragedies on classical and exotic subjects continued to be written, often by those whose aptitudes were for some other form of art, but began to lose their hold on the public, who looked for something new. In the same way, comedy, while appearing to flourish in new hands, is no longer the fine comedy of character perfected by Molière, but a superficial imitation, a comedy of manners which no longer holds an audience whose milieu has altered.

Among the few writers of tragedy who make some small showing in the period are Jean de La Chapelle (1655-1723), whose Cléopâtre (1681) provided Baron with an effective part, and Hilaire Bernard de Roqueleyne Longepierre (1659-1731), whose only successful play was a re-writing of Corneille's Médée, done in 1694. La Chapelle might have kept classical tragedy alive after Racine's retirement, but he soon became immersed in politics and wrote no more, while Longepierre's main interest lay in criticism. A more prolific dramatist was Jean Galbert de Campistron (1656-1723), several of whose plays dealt with contemporary history under a Roman guise. The most successful were Virginie (1683), Arminius (1684), and Andronic (1685), all early works in which Baron and Mlle Champmeslé were excellent. Campistron's later tragedies were weaker in structure, and the subjects were unfortunately chosen.

A writer whose best tragedy marks the end of the seventeenth century was Antoine de La Fosse (1654-1708). His first play was not produced until he was over 40, and it was often said that had he turned to playwriting earlier he might have rivalled Racine. As it was, only one of his plays, Manlius Capitolinus (1698), based to some extent on Otway's Venice Preserved, remained in the repertory, after a resounding initial success. La Fosse's later plays were less interesting and were overshadowed by the works of the infant prodigy Joseph de La Grange-Chancel (1677-1758), whose first play was written at the age of 13, and who, by 1700, had had four tragedies performed at the Comédie-Française. This young author was helped and encouraged by Racine, but does not seem to have profited by his advice as he might have done, and his plays, of which Amasis (1701) and Ino et Mélicerte (1713) were the most successful, could only have appealed to an audience that had lost the taste for grand tragedy. Yet La Grange-Chancel had good qualities, and might have kept tragedy from some of its later excesses had he continued writing. Unfortunately he came into conflict with the authorities and was exiled from France for many years. Meanwhile, in the hands of Prosper Jolyot de Crébillon (1674-1762), tragedy was turning to melodrama, its force and dignity to the horrors of incest and child-murder, its psychological realism to the puerilities of intrigue and romance. All these traits are observable in Crébillon's early works, of which the best, and perhaps the best of his long career, was Rhadamiste et Zénobie (1711).

Unlike Crébillon, who devoted himself entirely to tragedy, La Grange-Chancel and Campistron both produced comedies. But these were isolated examples and it is to two actors that we must look for the largest output in comedy. Baron, famous for his acting in tragedy, wrote only comedies, of which the best was L'Homme à bonne fortune (1686). This study of contemporary life, in which Baron himself played the leading part, Moncade, shows an adventurer living by his wits in a society where love is no longer a passion but a pastime. In this, and in La Coquette (1686), there is a part for a precocious boy, written for and acted by Baron's son Étienne (1676-1711), who later joined the Comédie-Française and proved a difficult and undisciplined actor, dying in the prime of life as the result of dissipation. Baron's plays owe much to Molière, with whom he was so closely associated in his youth, but he tended to concentrate too much on his main role at the expense of the rest. His lesser personages have nothing of the life and individuality of Molière's.

Baron's attempt to keep alive in some measure the comedy of character was frustrated by the concentration of his fellow-actor and brother-in-law, Florent Carton Dancourt (1661–1725), on the comedy of manners. Dancourt's plays cover a wide field, and though they are, on the whole, superficial and lack permanence, they give an interesting picture of Parisian life at the time. The best is *Le Chevalier à la mode* (1687), which shows the penniless aristocrat at grips with the newly-rich, This was one of the few occasions when Dancourt ventured on a full-length play. The success of his *Maison de campagne* (1688) and *Opéra du village* (1692)—the latter the first of a long series of *comédies-vaudevilles*—induced him to confine himself mostly to one act. Of these shorter plays, many dealt with seasonal amusements and in one, *La Foire de Bezons* (1695), Dancourt's two young daughters first appeared on the stage. The younger, known as Mimi (1685–1779), later joined the Comédie-Française and remained a member of it all her long life.

While Dancourt was dramatizing with much skill and gaiety something of the social struggle implicit in the changing conditions of his day, and his fellow actor Marc Antoine Legrand (1673–1728) was basing his ephemeral comedies on contemporary events, other writers were catering for the Italian actors, who were becoming increasingly important in the theatrical life of Paris as their use of French was extended. Permission to use French at all had only been achieved with a struggle, and was strenuously opposed by the Comédie-Française. With the help of Dominique, who himself wrote several plays for his companions, the Italians won their case before no less a person than Louis XIV, and looked increasingly to French dramatists to supply them with material. In course of time they evolved what was virtually a new method, foreign art working on native material, a combination which was destined to have important results in the later history of French comedy. Among their collaborators the most important were Charles Rivière Dufresny (1654–1724) and Jean François Regnard (1655–1709), who both contributed largely to the repertory of the Comédie-Française also. Their first plays, however, were written for the Italians, and they might have continued to work there had not Louis XIV dismissed the company in 1697, annoyed at some fancied slight to Mme de Maintenon, and also, perhaps, not unwilling to lighten his budget by withdrawing the large subsidy which the Italians had enjoyed for so many years, often at the expense of their French rivals.

Deprived of their Italian interpreters, Regnard and Dufresny were forced to depend entirely on the Comédie-Française, where they had already made a start. The best of Regnard's comedies were *Le Joueur* (1696) and *Le Légataire universel* (1708), but Dufresny, who was the reputed great-grandson of Henri IV, wrote little of permanent merit. He had good qualities, but grudged the time given to playwriting, preferring to gamble. His light comedies, however, many of them interspersed with songs which he wrote himself, were successful, and appealed to the light-minded audience of the time.

Two authors who collaborated in comedy for the French actors, though one at least wrote for the Italians also, were Jean de Bigot Palaprat (1650–1721) and David Augustin de Brueys (1640–1723). The finest result of their joint labours was *Le Grondeur* (1691), a comedy of character worthy to rank with some of Molière's. Brueys, who also wrote several tragedies on his own account, was the author of a refurbishing of the old farce of Pathelin, which, as *L'Avocat Pathelin* (1706), became one of the most popular plays in the repertory of the French theatre.

With such comedies as these, dramatists succeeded for a time in persuading their contemporaries that the great art of Molière was still flourishing. But the finest comedy of the time was to come from a novelist, Alain-René Le Sage (1668–1747), whose early plays had been drawn from Spanish cape-and-sword dramas, and proved little to the taste of the audience. He then turned to more native themes, and made a success with *Crispin rival de son maître* (1707). But his most important contribution to drama was undoubtedly *Turcaret* (1709), a scathing attack on the financiers and *nouveaux riches* who embittered the last years of the reign of Louis XIV. Its production was delayed by the machinations of those it satirized, and either this or quarrels with the actors of the Comédie-Française over a later play led Le Sage to waste his great talents in writing for the ephemeral productions of the fair-booths.

Two writers of slight comedies were Nicolas Boindin (1676–1751), whose *Bal d'Auteuil* (1702) caused a tightening-up of the censorship laws through its somewhat equivocal plot, and Antoine Houdard de La Motte (1672–1731), who also made one notable contribution to post-classical tragedy with his *Inès de Castro* (1723). The last outstanding writer of tragedy, however, was Voltaire (1694–1778), whose universal genius applied itself to the theatre as to every other aspect of eighteenth-century thought. His first play, *Œdipe* (1718), and such later tragedies as *Brutus* (1730) and *Zaïre* (1732), which both owe something to Shakespeare, are classical in form, and continue the illusion of greatness. But Voltaire had a far more disintegrating influence on tragedy than his lifelong enemy Crébillon, now censor of plays and still a prolific dramatist. Crébillon kept, in however pedestrian a style, to the old ways in form and content, while Voltaire, whose sense of tradition led him to follow Racine for the form of his plays, found no difficulty in reconciling that form with the liberal ideas of his time, which looked on the theatre as a school of morals. At the same time his use of spectacular effects and the intrusion of sentiment and emotion contributed to the development of the *drame* (or *tragédie bourgeoise*) which, with the *comédie larmoyante*, constitutes the main offering of the eighteenth century to the evolution of the French theatre. Both are the logical outcome of the influx into the theatre of the middle class, with its toleration for moral teaching and its desire for strong emotional situations, placed in a recognizable décor of modern society. The doctrine of the equality of man brought the heroes of tragedy from the palace to the parlour, while the sensibility of the age needed something to weep at even in comedy. This in itself was not fatal to the theatre, but it was France's misfortune at this time to have no dramatist of genius capable of making great drama out of the material to hand.

The germ of *comédie larmoyante*, and so of *drame*, can be found in the plays of Philippe Néricault Destouches (1680–1754), who detracted from the vigour of his comedies by too much insistence on the moral virtues. In spite of the humour of his valet Pasquin, and a gift for comic situations, he was too anxious to move his audience to be able to impart a cutting edge to his satire. His best play is *Le Glorieux* (1732), which dramatizes once more the struggle between the old nobility and the wealthy parvenu. It provided an excellent part for Abraham Alexis Quinault, known on the stage as Dufresne (1690–1767). This illustrious member of a family which gave many actors to the Comédie-Française was one of the few outstanding players of his time. Beaubour (1662–1725), though good in some parts, could not adequately take the place of Baron, while Mlle Champmeslé had been replaced, but not equalled, by her niece Charlotte Desmares (1682–1753) and her pupil Marie Anne Châteauneuf, known as Mlle Duclos (1664–1748). The Comédie-Française had also to suffer the competition of the unlicensed actors in the well-built, permanent theatres of the fairs, open nearly all the year round, where the plays of Le Sage, and other less eminent dramatists, were put on by enterprising managers, among them the widow of Étienne Baron, herself the daughter of a German fair-ground actor. In spite of constant complaint and litigation, the Forains, as they were called, flourished, and evaded each new law as it was passed with an ingenuity which merely served to enhance their popularity. The early history of the fair-theatres is obscure, and little is known of their actors and managers beyond a few names and anecdotes, but they could not be suppressed, and by the 1770s had fused with the Comédie-Italienne to form the Opéra-Comique, whose history belongs to the domain of music. The Italian actors were recalled by the Regent in 1716, and returned under Lélio and the younger Dominique to reap new triumphs, and to become completely assimilated into the theatrical life of France; how completely can be realized

when we remember that the finest plays of Pierre Carlet de Chamblain de Marivaux (1688–1763) were written for and performed at the Comédie-Italienne. He did, at times, write for the Comédie-Française; but he found the actors there overbearing and narrow-minded, and much preferred the gaiety and freedom of the Italians, whose acting, in any case, was more suited to the quick wit and subtlety of his dialogue. His plays are fine, penetrating analyses of young love, a restricted subject from which he drew a remarkable amount of material. His characters have the same names, taken from the actors who played them, as was the tradition of the Italian company. The heroines of *La Double inconstance* (1723) and of *Le Jeu de l'amour et du hasard* (1730) are both Silvias, while the hero of the second is Mario, from the stage-names of the actors who took the parts, the enchanting Rosa Zanetta Benozzi and her husband. But in spite of a similarity of name, they are all clearly defined, presenting to the audience innumerable facets of the stock pair of lovers, whose difficulties, though usually of their own making, are poignant enough for the moment, and universally applicable. No one ever laid bare with greater insight and delicacy than Marivaux the fluctuations of the proud, foolish, wilful human heart.

Yet, in spite of wit, gaiety, and good humour, aided by fine acting, Marivaux was not much appreciated by his contemporaries. He belonged to no stream of tradition, he had no imitators. His style, which was so much his own that the word *marivaudage* was coined to describe it, though it looked easy, was a pitfall to the unwary, and few ventured on it. Marivaux remains an isolated phenomenon in French dramatic literature, the one great exponent of that fusion of French and Italian art which arose from the acclimatization of the *commedia dell'arte*.

Much more to the taste of eighteenth-century audiences were the tearful comedies of Pierre Claude Nivelle de La Chaussée (1692–1754). Pathos was *à la mode*, and reached its apotheosis in the plays of a wealthy, middle-aged man whose own tastes were decidedly more libertine and scabrous than those of his virtuous stage parents and children. Equally averse to classical tragedy and to the wit and characterization of comedy, he sought to amalgamate the two in a form which brought tears to the eyes of the audience, particularly of the women, who now frequented the theatre in far greater numbers than in the previous century. They brought their husbands to be edified by the spectacle of a patient wife in *Le Préjugé à la mode* (1735), and laughed and wept alternately at *L'École des mères* (1744). Later they were to forgo even a modicum of amusement in favour of an excess of sensibility, for La Chaussée's later plays, though still called comedies, are more allied to those moral effusions which went under the name of *drame*.

Although La Chaussée's name is always

associated with the *comédie larmoyante*, others essayed the genre, notably Alexis Piron (1689–1773), best known for his comedy *La Métromanie* (1738), Jean Baptiste Louis Gresset (1709–77), and even Voltaire with *L'Enfant prodigue* (1736) and *Nanine* (1749). Voltaire, however, continued to write tragedies in his own manner, and was fortunate in being able to call on a new generation of actors to appear in them. First among them was the lovely and ill-fated Adrienne Lecouvreur (1692–1730), who died in his arms, and who was, like Molière, refused Christian burial, a fact not calculated to soften Voltaire in his attitude to the Church. Her early death was a great loss, but she was replaced by Mlle Dumesnil (1711–1803), for whom Voltaire wrote *Mérope* (1743), and by Mlle Dangeville (1714–96), who, with Préville, excelled in the plays of Marivaux when they eventually attained the boards of the Comèdie-Francaise.

The greatest players of the period were, however, Hippolyte Clairon (1723–1803), an actress from childhood, and Henri Louis Lekain (1728–78), friend and protégé of Voltaire. They played opposite each other in many of Voltaire's plays, and were instrumental in effecting some slight reforms in the theatre, notably in the adoption of a modified form of historical costume. After Mlle Clairon had played Roxane in oriental draperies instead of in paniers and seventeenth-century head-dress, Lekain appeared as Orestes with some attempt at Greek costume, and in *L'Orphelin de la Chine* (1755) both made a determined effort to simplify clothes, acting, and scenery. Under the influence of Jean François Marmontel (1723–99), in whose *Denys le tyran* she played in 1748, Mlle Clairon dropped her declamatory style for a more natural tone, and induced her companions to do likewise. Lekain and Voltaire were also responsible jointly for the long over-due clearance of the stage, which had been cluttered up with audience for nearly a hundred years. This encroachment on the acting space, which had been tolerated by French classical tragedy, had already proved impossible in the 'machine' plays, and matters finally came to a head with the introduction, under the influence of Shakespeare, of crowd scenes and spectacular effects in some of Voltaire's later tragedies, when, in opposition to his old enemy Crébillon, he took up the subjects of six of the latter's plays and rewrote them, the best being *Sémiramis* (1748).

Another actor associated with Voltaire was Jean de La Noue (1701–61), director of a provincial company in which Mlle Clairon played for a short time. He had had a play on Mahomet accepted by the Comédie-Française, and Voltaire acknowledged what his own *Mahomet, ou le fanatisme* (1741) owed to it by allowing La Noue to put it on at Lille before it was done, without much success, in Paris. La Noue later joined the Comédie-Française for secondary roles. Among his companions were Grandval (1711–84), preferred by some to

Lekain, and Bellecour (1725–78), excellent in comedy.

Voltaire, though living in exile, was still writing for the French stage, and had just sent *Tancrède* (1760) to the Comédie-Française when Denis Diderot (1713–84) saw his first play in production. This was *Le Père de famille*, written and published two years earlier. *Le Fils naturel*, Diderot's other important play, though published in 1757, was not acted until 1772, a curious reversal of the earlier practice by which plays were not seen in print until some time after their first production. Both these plays, typical of the *drame bourgeois*, as was the *Brouette du vinaigrier* (1784) of Sébastien Mercier (1740–1814), are written in an exalted, declamatory prose, weighed down with moral sentiments, which now appears somewhat ludicrous in connexion with its homely application. Yet both Diderot and Mercier brought something to French drama which even La Chaussée had not adumbrated—man in relation to his social life. Grimm thought it likely that Diderot would bring back morality to France by force of dramatic examples, but he had to wait for his successors until the rhetoric of the Romantics had had its day. Mercier's plays were technically better than Diderot's, and his translation of Lillo's *London Merchant* as *Jenneval* (1768) reduced it to some order and unity of purpose. But his quarrels with the actors, and his unpopular political ideas, mitigated against his success, though his plays, when read, seem not to deserve the oblivion which has overtaken them.

The plays of Michel Jean Sedaine (1719–97), though equally moral, are written with greater simplicity. Most of his work was done for the Opéra-Comique, and consisted of libretti for rustic comedies, sprung from the fashionable cult of the simple life. His best work, however, was *Le Philosophe sans le savoir* (1765). It has several dramatic moments, and even some touches of humour, a quality noticeably lacking in the *Béverlei* (1768) of Bernard Joseph Saurin (1706–81), a *drame bourgeois* based on Moore's *The Gamester*. A tragedy by this author, *Blanche et Guisard* (1763) was expected to do well, but Mlle Clairon, who acted in it, says it was coldly received. The actors were, however, consoled for their disappointment by the sudden success, on patriotic grounds, of a poor play entitled *Le Siège de Calais* (1766), by Pierre Laurent Buirette de Belloy (1727–75). Another dramatist who had some success at this time was Jean François de La Harpe (1739–1802) who is, however, mainly remembered as a critic.

The Comédie-Française now decided to move, and leaving in 1770 the theatre which they had occupied since 1689, they went first to the Tuileries and, in 1782, to a new theatre on the present site of the Odéon. Mlle Clairon retired shortly before the first removal, and was replaced by two sisters, one known as Mlle Dugazon (1742–99), the other as Mlle Vestris (1743–1804), sister-in-law of the famous dancer. Her husband was an actor at the Comédie-Italienne. The outstanding actor of comedy at this time, Molé (1734–1802), was, by a curious irony, destined to be the first French Hamlet. Struck by the overwhelming popularity of everything English, an unsuccessful dramatist, Jean François Ducis (1733–1816), conceived the idea of refashioning the plays of Shakespeare, probably from an existing translation, to the taste of the time. This he did so successfully that *Hamlet* was produced in 1769, and was followed at short intervals by *Roméo et Juliette*, *Le Roi Lear*, *Macbeth*, *Jean sans terre*, and *Othello*.

In the welter of tears, piety, blood, sentimentality, and sheer dullness that characterizes most of the theatre of the second half of the eighteenth century, one writer of comedy stands out, Pierre-Augustin Caron de Beaumarchais (1732–99). This extraordinary man, whose life would provide material for half a dozen picaresque novels, was destined to be the one memorable name in the theatre of his time. This, however, was not immediately apparent. His first play, *Eugénie* (1767), written under the double influence of Diderot and Spain, was only moderately successful, as was *Les Deux amis* (1770), a somewhat arid financial drama. Then Beaumarchais, fresh from his encounters with Goezman and the French judicial system, wrote a light opera which he offered to the Comédie-Italienne. It was refused; the leading actor of the company had been a barber, and thought Beaumarchais's hero, also a barber, was intended as a caricature of himself. Rewritten as a five-act comedy in prose, *Le Barbier de Séville* was accepted by the Comédie-Française in 1772, but had to wait three years before it could be produced. It roused a storm of criticism such as the French theatre had not known since the days of *Tartuffe*. Complaints of its length, among other things, caused Beaumarchais to shorten it by one act, and in its final form it continued to be played successfully. It led Beaumarchais into arguments with the actors, however, since he had the temerity to question their traditional system of payments to authors, and the tenacity to get it altered. In spite of this first attack on their privileges, forerunner of many shocks which the established monopolists of the theatre were to suffer before the end of the century, the actors accepted *La Folle journée*, better known as *Le Mariage de Figaro*, which again had to wait three years, from 1781 to 1784, before it could be produced. It was read in the salons and at Court, and even asked for in Russia, before permission could be obtained for a public production. Its first night, with Dazincourt (1747–1809) as Figaro, and the charming Louise Contat (1760–1813) as Suzanne, assisted by Molé and Préville (the original Figaro), was a triumph. Dazzled by its wit, attracted by curiosity, and perhaps a little defiant, blind to its political significance, the audience that applauded it represented the very people who were later to suffer under the Revolution it presages.

Against the blaze of notoriety achieved by Beaumarchais, other writers of comedy stood little chance; but one charming little play deserves mention, *Les Châteaux en Espagne* (1789) by Collin d'Harleville (1755–1806), who might have written more and even better comedies had he not been overwhelmed by the Revolution, and persecuted by his rival, the revolutionary Fabre d'Églantine (1755–94), who paid for his excesses under the guillotine.

6. REVOLUTION, ROMANTICISM, AND REALISM. The Revolution, which produced only one playwright, Marie-Joseph Chénier (1764–1811), whose historical dramas were contemporary events in disguise, first closed the theatres and then opened them to all comers. It did not cause as great a shock to theatrical life as did the Puritan interregnum in England. The French theatre was too firmly established for that, and had a longer tradition behind it. It did, however, put an end to the monopoly of the Comédie-Française, which had already suffered much, in the latter part of the century, from the activities of the unlicensed theatres, particularly those on the Boulevard du Temple, where even Nicolet with his performing monkey drew greater audiences than the king's players. The activities of Mlle Montansier (1730–1820), friend of Marie Antoinette and manageress of numerous provincial and suburban theatres, also caused the Comédie-Française some concern, particularly when she opened her own theatre in the grounds of the Palais-Royal. With the removal of all restrictions, theatres sprang up in every corner of Paris, and soon numbered nearly forty. The most important of the newcomers was the Odéon, which now ranks second only to the Comédie-Française. Founded and managed by Louis Baptiste Picard (1769–1828), a capable man of the theatre who wrote most of its repertory himself, the Odéon provided light amusing plays which suited the taste of its audience and avoided giving offence to the censorship, re-established in 1804. Napoleon, though interested in the theatre, was too ready to suppress any manifestations of originality, and did not allow his authors that liberty accorded to Molière by Louis XIV. Consequently his Empire proved singularly barren in playwrights, and the one man who might have adorned it, Népomucène Lemercier (1771–1840), who tried unsuccessfully to establish historical romance, broke with his patron when he saw where ambition was taking him. Satire and comedy could not flourish, tragedy was out of date. The chief and most popular genre of the time, apart from operetta, was the vaudeville, child of the old theatres of the fair. Given at the secondary theatres, the Gaîté, Ambigu-Comique, Variétés, and Vaudeville, it provided light entertainment for the vast new theatre-going public, and at the same time served as the echo and mirror of the times. Under the Republic, the Empire, and the Restoration it continued undisturbed, its authors adapting their subjects to the prevailing

ideology, with many a backward glance to the seemingly heroic ages of the past. But the great delight of the new, often illiterate, audiences who crowded the popular theatres were the melodramas of the prolific Guilbert de Pixérécourt (1773–1844), which delighted the uncritical with their swift, violent action, their mingling of bloodshed and sentimentality, their elaborate settings and stage effects, and their expert manipulations of well-worn themes, in which, after the pleasurable excitements of villainy, virtue rose triumphant. Many of Pixérécourt's works, which were influenced by the contemporary German theatre, found their way to London in adaptations, often without acknowledgement, and became the staple fare of the smaller theatres, and so of the Penny Plain, Tuppence Coloured Toy Theatre.

Pixérécourt wrote, as he himself said, for those who could not read. Meanwhile the elderly and learned formed a fast-diminishing audience for the frigid tragedies and dull comedies which were all that the Comédie-Française could offer. The time was ripe for a revival of French literary drama, and it came with the onslaught of Romanticism. The leader of the new movement was Victor Hugo (1802–85), its manifesto was contained in the Preface to his *Cromwell*, published in 1827, and its battle-cry was his *Hernani* (1830), whose first night was one of the most tempestuous the Comédie-Française had seen for a long time. *Ruy Blas* (1838), first seen at the Théâtre de la Renaissance, set the seal on the triumph of the new drama. But Hugo was more a poet than a dramatist. His plays pleased by their fine verses, by the audacity of their challenge to the Unities and the outmoded restrictions of the classical theatre, and by their appeal to the youthful adherents of Romanticism. A far better dramatist, and the first to see his work on the stage, was Alexandre Dumas (1803–70), whose *Henri III et sa cour* was given in 1829. It was followed by a number of others, on subjects taken from all sides, from history, from legend, from the English stage (Kean), and finally from his own novels. Among them the best and most characteristic of Dumas's varied styles are the melodrama, *La Tour de Nesle* (1832), and *Antony* (1831), a study of the Romantic hero, *l'homme maudit*, driven to murder by the conventions of an unsympathetic environment.

Among the other dramatists of the Romantic period must be reckoned Alfred de Vigny (1797–1863), whose translation of *Othello* (1829) marked a step further in the acclimatization of Shakespeare in France, and yet another triumph for the Romantics. His best-known play, *Chatterton* (1835), based on the short life and tragic death of the English poet Thomas Chatterton, is a play of the emotions. It has little action, but appeals by its imaginative and psychological insight, showing, as it does, the anguish of the poet at grips with society.

The plays of Alfred de Musset (1810–57), charming trifles often based on popular sayings —*Il ne faut jurer de rien, Il faut qu'une porte soit ouverte ou fermée*, and *On ne badine pas avec l'amour*—together with such lyric fantasies as *Lorenzaccio* or *Fantasio*, were written at this time, but after the failure of his first play, *La Nuit vénitienne* (1830), were not acted. They had to be translated into Russian and discovered by the actress Mlle Allan-Despréaux (1810–56), who brought them back to Paris, before the French theatre would accept their delicate wit and melancholy, their mingling of imagination and caprice. Once acted, they proved popular, but they were written with no thought of the stage, and de Musset, child of Romanticism in his prose and poetry, had no influence on the drama of his time.

In any case the life of the Romantic theatre was short. It left behind it some fine works, but on the whole it was antipathetic to the true genius of France. The public, once so enthusiastic, wearied of its excesses, and in 1843 Hugo's *Les Burgraves* failed completely, while the calm neo-classicism of *Lucrèce*, by François Ponsard (1814–67), was acclaimed. It seemed as if there might be a classical revival, but the real taste of the time was shown in the popularity of the *comédie-vaudeville*, the light opera, and the 'well-made' plays of that prolific dramatist, Eugène Scribe, (1791–1861), who, during the whole of the Romantic period, continued to turn out an inexhaustible supply of bourgeois comedies, beautifully constructed, optimistic, platitudinous, and no longer acted. Unlike the Romantics, who made high tragedy of everyday events, Scribe excelled in bringing great historical events down to the level of a second-rate boarding-house. Witness his *Verre d'eau* (1820), where the struggle of Whig and Tory under Queen Anne is reduced to an amorous intrigue more suited to a back drawing-room than an English Court. Yet Scribe should not be despised. His technique was superb. He had none of the lavish disregard for probability and the general untidiness of the Romantics. His plots are so closely knit and so well dovetailed that no single incident can be omitted, and when the curtain comes down all the loose ends are gathered together and tied off. This was a great satisfaction to an audience which had been somewhat hurriedly introduced to the splendid irrelevancies of Shakespeare and his imitators, and brought Scribe and his numerous collaborators, of whom the best was Ernest Legouvé (1807–1903), a vast fortune and an undisputed eminence in the theatre of their time.

During the nineteenth century the French theatre slips away in all directions. The old signposts have gone. No longer can one follow the steady evolution of tragedy and comedy. Their component parts are broken up and scattered among a hundred different genres, ranging from the flamboyant historical romances of the early Romantics, through the staid bourgeois comedies of Scribe, to the farcical productions of the théâtres des boulevards. No longer is the Comédie-Française the only theatre whose actors are worthy of notice. Great reputations can be made elsewhere, as witness the careers of Frédérick-Lemaître (1800–76), the first portrayer of Ruy Blas, of Jean Gaspard Deburau (1796–1846), beloved Pierrot of the Funambules, of Mlle Dorval (1798–1849), star of the Porte-Saint-Martin, and of many other favourites of the Parisian public too numerous to mention. Even the members of the Comédie-Française itself were not averse to seeking more remunerative employment elsewhere. Samson (1793–1871) signed a contract with another theatre which he was not, however, allowed to implement, and the greatest actress of the day, Rachel (1821–58), who had succeeded Mlle Mars (1779–1847), the Desdemona and Doña Sol of the Romantic theatre, as leading lady of the Comédie-Française, was more often in the provinces or abroad than in Paris. Yet her influence was considerable, and she revived the fine tradition of French classic acting which had almost been lost sight of in the upheavals of the Revolution and the vagaries of Romanticism. She was not immediately successful, but helped by the notices of the great critic and theatre historian Jules Janin (1804–74) in *Le Journal des débats*, she finally triumphed and brought a modicum of prosperity to the tottering fortunes of the French National Theatre. Reviving *Phèdre*, she revived at the same time the glories of French classical literature for an audience that had never known them. She could not, however, sustain alone the burden of a classic repertory, and received little support from her comrades, many of whom were jealous of her prestige, and not a little sarcastic over her frequent absences, and the Comédie-Française was glad to take over plays which had proved popular elsewhere. This was done in the case of *Le Gendre de M. Poirier* (1854), the best-known play of Émile Augier (1820–89), which had made a successful début at the Gymnase.

The Revolution of 1848 brought new preoccupations to the theatre, and the comedies of Scribe were replaced by a more serious type of social drama, though it was long before French dramatists broke away from the tradition of the well-made play in matters of form. The first exponent of the new drama was Augier, who had been associated with Ponsard in the short-lived classical reaction against Romanticism. After writing a few plays in verse, he turned to prose and, basing his work on the doctrine of common sense, produced a number of *pièces à thèse* which glorified the virtues of the bourgeoisie and attacked the social problems of the day. It was in his political plays, many of them based on contemporary problems, that he scored his greatest triumphs. There was much in the régime of the Second Empire that merited his attention, and he was not slow to profit by his observations. *Les Effrontés* (1861) is an attack on contemporary journalism, *Le Fils de Giboyer* (1862) on contemporary politics. The latter, which is usually ranked as Augier's best

play, had important repercussions, and was considered to be the manifesto of the liberal party. Of his other works, the best was probably *Les Lionnes pauvres* (1858), which dealt with the current social phenomenon of the wealthy courtesan, a subject taken up in a different spirit by the younger Dumas (1824–95) in his *Dame aux camélias* (1852). He, too, with perhaps even more success in his own day than Augier, treated social problems, and in *Le Demi-Monde* (1855), *Une Question d'argent* (1857), *Le Fils naturel* (1858), and right on to his last play, *Francillon* (1887), accustomed his audience to discussions of social and ethical problems, a habit which proved useful to later exponents of social drama.

It might be said of Augier and the younger Dumas that they set out to reform society by showing morality in action. They were seconded, rather faintly, by Octave Feuillet (1821–90) and Théodore Barrière (1823–77), while farcical comedy was kept alive by Eugène Labiche (1815–88), who set out frankly to amuse, and succeeded admirably, so well, in fact, that he was compared by his grateful contemporaries to Molière. The best of his plays, *Le Chapeau de paille d'Italie* (1851) and *Le Voyage de M. Perrichon* (1860), are still amusing, and bear revival. Their continued success may have been a tacit protest against the serious preoccupations of his rivals. But without doubt the spirit of the Second Empire finds its truest expression in light opera and in the musical burlesques of Henri Meilhac (1831–97) and Ludovic Halévy (1834–1908), whose collaboration produced *La Vie parisienne* (1866) and *Frou-Frou* (1869), as well as operettas like 'La Belle Hélène', with music by Offenbach. Better than anything they sum up the light-hearted, corrupt, and amusing world which came to an end in 1870.

Meanwhile the work of Scribe was continued by Victorien Sardou (1831–1908), who was at home in all types of play. Comedy of contemporary manners, historical romance, political satire, social drama—he brought to all of them the same technical ability and the same poverty of thought. In his hands any subject lost whatever depth it might have, and became simply a vehicle for a series of complicated intrigues. Yet Sardou must be credited with having provided some excellent parts for that incomparable actress Sarah Bernhardt (1845–1923), who, like Rachel, was a member of the Comédie-Française, but had her greatest triumphs elsewhere. Indeed, much of the history of the French theatre from this time onwards must be sought outside the Comédie-Française, which tended to lag further and further behind the times, in spite of the excellence of such actors as Edmond Got (1822–1901) and the elder Coquelin (1841–1909) who appeared together in an amusing comedy by Édouard Pailleron (1834–99), *Le Monde où l'on s'ennuie* (1881), and who were responsible for the first visit of the Comédie-Française to London; the younger Coquelin (1848–1909); Jean Mounet-Sully (1841–1916),

the outstanding tragic actor of his day; and
Gustave Hippolyte Worms (1836–1910), together with many excellent actresses. From
time to time the venerable National Theatre
suffered the shocks of modernization, and its opponents became its directors, but in the main it
served as a repository of tradition. Like others
before her, the fine tragedienne Gabrielle
Réjane (1857–1920) carried the glories of
French art and acting all over Europe and
America without ever setting foot in the
National Theatre. The full tide of theatrical
life must be looked for elsewhere, particularly
in the experimental theatres of the end of the
nineteenth century which herald a new era.

7. THE CONTEMPORARY THEATRE. It is
noticeable that during the nineteenth century
the outstanding dramatists are not wholly
addicted to the theatre, but are also poets, like
Hugo, and, above all, novelists, like Dumas.
Drama is no longer the pre-eminent literary
genre as it was in the seventeenth and to a
certain extent in the eighteenth century. It is
therefore not surprising that the impulse
towards a new realism in the theatre should
have come from the novelists. Balzac, Flau-
bert, and the Goncourts had made tentative
efforts in this direction, but it was Émile Zola
(1840–1902) who first put their ideas into
practice. He rejected with equal fierceness the
problem plays of Augier and the younger
Dumas, and the well-conducted intrigues of
Scribe and Sardou, substituting for their
artifices the naturalistic slogan of 'a slice of
life'. His dramatization of his own novel,
Thérèse Raquin (1873), was the first consciously
naturalistic play, and paid for its temerity by
being hissed off the stage. Yet the seed had
been sown, and the harvest was reaped by
Henri Becque (1832–99), whose plays were
uncompromisingly naturalistic, the best
known being Les Corbeaux (1882) and La
Parisienne (1885).

Becque's work might, however, have rested
without result had it not been for the efforts
of André Antoine (1858–1943), who in 1887
founded the Théâtre Libre, and later the
Théâtre Antoine (previously the Théâtre des
Menus-Plaisirs), for the production of the
new drama. Here, with actors trained in a new
style of acting and with a new type of stage
setting, he produced the plays of such great
contemporary foreign dramatists as Ibsen,
Strindberg, Hauptmann, and Tolstoy, as well
as of his own countrymen, notably Georges
Ancey (1860–1926), Octave Mirbeau (1850–
1917), author of Les Affaires sont les affaires
(1903), a sordid study of the lust for money,
and Eugène Brieux (1858–1932). Antoine had
a great influence on the European theatre, and
his Théâtre Libre was a model for the Freie
Bühne founded in Berlin in 1889, and the
Independent Theatre which was established
in London in 1891.

Of Antoine's authors the most important
was Brieux, who was primarily a moralist and
a reformer. His plays deal with specific
problems and offer concrete remedies. This
concentration on actualities dates many of
them, but since most of the problems he
treated are always with us, the best of his
plays will bear revival. Among them are Les
Trois Filles de M. Dupont (1897), which deals
with the dangers of a marriage of convenience,
and Les Avariés (1901), a study of the ravages
of venereal disease. The latter, given in
England and America as Damaged Goods,
aroused much controversy on its first production.

Among the other exponents of naturalism in
France, albeit in a somewhat diluted form,
were François de Curel (1854–1929), who
brought an austere intellect to bear on social
problems; Paul Hervieu (1857–1915), a writer
in the tradition of the younger Dumas; and
Henri Lavedan (1859–1940), whose work
shows a curious mingling of realism and
fantasy.

As was inevitable, a wave of reaction against
naturalism soon set in, in which the Belgian
poet Maurice Maeterlinck (1862–1949) was the
leading figure. His symbolic dramas, which
include Pelléas et Mélisande (1892), L'Oiseau
bleu (1908) (well known in English as The
Blue Bird, with its sequel, The Betrothal),
brought back poetry and a sense of wonder to
a theatre which was in danger of losing both.
The reaction was intensified by the distinguished talent of Edmond Rostand (1868–
1918), whose fine verse plays, intensely theatrical and full of vitality, ensured him an
enormous popularity which seems in no danger
of diminishing. The best known are Cyrano
de Bergerac (1897), a swashbuckling romance
written for the elder Coquelin after he had left
the Comédie-Française, and L'Aiglon (1900),
a poignant evocation of Napoleon's young son,
in which Sarah Bernhardt gave a most moving
performance.

An author of the early twentieth century
whose work defies classification and is only
now becoming known and admired is Paul
Claudel (1868–   ). Among his plays, which
bear traces of symbolist influence, but are
deeply impregnated with his fervent Catholicism, are L'Otage (1911) and L'Annonce faite à
Marie (1912), while his Soulier de satin, written
between 1919 and 1924, was given at the
Comédie-Française in 1943.

The production of Amoureuse (1894), by
Georges de Porto-Riche (1849–1923), in which
Gabrielle Réjane gave an outstanding performance, set the fashion for plays dedicated to the
penetrating analysis of love and marriage,
among them those of Maurice Donnay
(1860–1945), Henri Bataille (1872–1922), and
Henri Bernstein (1877–   ), while a more
light-hearted approach to the subject is to be
found in the comedies of Alfred Capus (1858–
1922) and of Tristan Bernard (1866–1947),
author of L'Anglais tel qu'on le parle (1899).
A master of French farce was undoubtedly
Georges Courteline (1861–1929), whose first
plays were put on by Antoine, while Lucien
Guitry (1860–1925) and his son Sacha (1885–
) continue the tradition of many French

actors by appearing in their own light comedies. Sacha in particular was the author of a number of amusing trifles, in which Yvonne Printemps (1895–   ), at one time his wife, appeared with him.

Shortly before the outbreak of war in 1914 Jacques Copeau (1878–1949) started an experimental theatre known as the Vieux-Colombier, where fine work was done in the production of new authors, among them Charles Vildrac (1882–   ), whose *Paquebot Tenacity* was given in 1922, and in new productions of Shakespeare and other classics. An offshoot of this venture was the foundation of the Compagnie des Quinze under Michel Saint-Denis (1897–   ) for which André Obey (1892–   ) wrote *Noé* and *Le Viol de Lucrèce* (both 1931), the latter serving as the basis for Benjamin Britten's opera. At the same time the work of Antoine was being carried on by Aurélien-Marie Lugné-Poë (1869–1940) at the Théâtre de l'Œuvre, and by Georges Pitoëff (1886–1939), a Russian refugee who, with his wife Ludmilla, enriched the French stage with a number of productions of foreign authors, and some fine performances in his own subtle and delicately nuanced style.

The partnership of the actor Louis Jouvet (1887–1951) with the playwright Jean Giraudoux (1882–1944) produced some fine work, including *Amphitryon 38* (1936), in which the American actor Alfred Lunt and his wife Lynn Fontanne were later extremely successful in an English translation. It was at Jouvet's theatre too (formerly the Comédie des Champs-Élysées) that *La Machine infernale* (1934) by Jean Cocteau (1892–   ) was first produced. Cocteau, a versatile author, wrote also *Les Parents terribles* (1938), and symbolist dramas which turn to surrealism, while the work of Maeterlinck was developed and intensified in the expressionist plays of Henri René Lenormand (1882–1938) and the subtle psychological dramas of Jean-Jacques Bernard (1888–   ). Three important events of the late 1930s were the appointment of Jouvet to a professorship at the Conservatoire, the invitation to Jouvet and Édouard Bourdet (1887–1945) to produce at the Comédie-Française, and the formation, with financial assistance from the State, of a combination of theatre directors known as the Cartel, and including, with Jouvet and Pitoëff, the actor Charles Dullin (1885–1949) and the producer Gaston Baty (1885–   ). It seemed as if the Comédie-Française might once more take a leading part in the theatrical life of Paris, and although the German occupation of France from 1940 to 1945 shattered a great many hopes, this one was in part realized. It is as yet too soon to estimate the gains and losses of the war years. One outstanding talent which emerged was that of Jean Paul Sartre, several of whose plays have been seen in translation in London and New York, notably *Huis-Clos*, *La Putain respectueuse* and *Les Mains sales*. Jean Anouilh, noted before the war as a promising young playwright, put on under the German occupation an *Antigone* (1944) which provided a rallying-point for the aspirations of insurgent youth. No doubt other new talents will come to light, both among the playwrights and the actors, all the richer for the temporary setbacks of the years of repression and disillusion. An interesting point is the reappearance of religious drama, whose leader in the period between the two wars was Henri Ghéon (1875–1943), ably assisted by Léon Chancerel (1886–   ). This is a development which has immense possibilities and may lead to much enrichment of the theatre.

In a brief survey of the French theatre during the last fifty or more years, no space has been given to those lesser but typically Parisian amusements, the revue, the *café-chantant*, the cabaret. They deserve a whole volume to themselves, and have produced a number of stars, like Mistinguett (1875–   ), Yvette Guilbert (1865–1944), Maurice Chevalier (1889–   ), and many others, known and loved far beyond the confines of Paris. They are an integral part of the theatre, though they stand a little outside the main stream which we have been considering here, and their work is often so much a matter of improvisation and atmosphere, their material, in its topicality, so ephemeral, that it would seem an impossible task to pin down their excellence on paper. They should be remembered, however, since they represent the quintessence of that Gallic wit and gaiety which is one of the outstanding characteristics of the French theatre.

FRANK, BRUNO (1887–1946), modern German playwright who, in reaction from the extreme drama of the realists and expressionists, wrote a number of light, sophisticated comedies. Of these *Sturm im Wasserglas* (1930) was successfully given in England in an adaptation by James Bridie as *Storm in a Teacup* and in America as *Storm over Patsy*. Frank has also written some historical dramas, of which the best and most characteristic is *Zwölftausend* (1927). In an English translation this was successful in New York, and was seen in London in 1931.

FRANKLIN THEATRE, NEW YORK, a small building at 175 Chatham Street, holding about 600 people. It opened 7 Sept. 1835 with a good company in *The School of Reform*, followed by some classic comedies. It soon degenerated into melodrama and farce, however, in spite of a long visit by Booth in 1836–7; but this theatre is memorable as being the first at which the famous Joseph Jefferson, then aged 8, appeared on a New York play-bill. It closed for a time in late 1837 and reopened under a succession of managers, who were never able to achieve its initial popularity. It was finally vanquished by the success of the New Chatham Theatre, and in 1840 was taken over by a semi-professional group of German actors. It later housed variety, and was run for a short time by the great Yankee actor Hill. Early in 1841 the actors from the Park, which was at that time given over to balls and concerts, gave a successful season at the Franklin Theatre, which also saw the first productions in New York of *Fifteen Years of a New York Fireman's Life* and *Money*. It then struggled along under various names, but forsook legitimate drama and ended up as a home of pantomime and minstrel shows.

FRANZ, ELLEN, see MEININGEN PLAYERS.

FRASER, CLAUDE LOVAT (1890–1921), English artist and stage-designer, many of whose early and most imaginative designs were published in *Flying Fame* (1913). The first of his settings to impress the theatre-going public were those for *As You Like It* and *The Beggar's Opera*, at the Lyric Theatre, Hammersmith, in 1920. The latter, in particular, may be said to have inaugurated a new era in stage design. He also worked extensively for ballet and opera. Albert Rutherston, who in 1923 collaborated with John Drinkwater in a memoir of Fraser, said of him that his inspiration came 'especially from the 18th and early 19th century. His work stands for a gay, brightly-coloured romanticism.' His early death was a great loss to English art and to the theatre, and his influence, when one considers how brief was his career, has been phenomenal.

FRÉDÉRICK-LEMAÎTRE, see LEMAÎTRE, FRÉDÉRICK.

FREIE BÜHNE, DIE, was founded by Otto Brahm in 1889 on the lines of Antoine's Théâtre Libre in Paris, for the production of the plays of the new naturalistic school of writers inspired by Ibsen. The society had no fixed theatre, and gave only matinées. Its first production was Ibsen's *Ghosts*, followed by translations of plays by Tolstoy, Strindberg, and Zola. The first German play to be given was Anzengruber's *Das vierte Gebot*, but the real manifesto of the new movement was *Die Familie Selicke*, a sordid picture of lower middle-class life, played in a realistic manner against an equally realistic background. The actors of Brahm's company had to be trained anew to interpret characters so far removed from the conventional heroes and heroines of the contemporary theatre, and this led to the formation of a permanent company, whose chief actor was Emanuel Reicher. This in turn led to a growing desire for something more stable than the sporadic employment afforded by the Freie Bühne, and the consequent amalgamation in 1895 with the older and well-established Deutsches Theater. The movement, however, had achieved its object and its impulse continued to be felt. One of its most notable achievements had been the production of the earlier plays of Gerhart Hauptmann, particularly of his study of drink, immorality, and greed, *Vor Sonnenaufgang*.

In 1890 the Freie Volksbühne was founded for the purpose of bringing good plays at low prices within the reach of the working-class population. Admittance was limited to subscribers, who drew lots for their seats.

FRENCH BRACE, see STAGE BRACE.

FRENCH FLAT, the name given to a series of flats battened together and 'flown' as one piece (see FLAT).

FRENCH PLAYERS' THEATRE, a temporary playhouse fitted up in a riding school in Drury Lane, kept by a Frenchman, N. Le Febure. It was used between 1635 and 1636 by a company of French actors under Floridor (Josias de Soulas).

FRESNEL SPOTLIGHT, see LIGHTING, 3.

FREYTAG, GUSTAV (1816–95), German writer. Best known as the author of sociological and historical novels, he began his literary career as a dramatist. He was the German exponent of the 'well-made' play of France, and two somewhat artificial serious plays, exalting the sterling qualities of the bourgeoisie in contrast to the flightiness of the gentry, were followed by an excellent comedy, *Die Journalisten* (1852), a good-humoured portrayal of party politics in a small town during an election. This can still be read with pleasure, but his attempt at an historical tragedy in verse is less attractive. In 1863 Freytag published his *Technik des Dramas*, with its famous pyramid, or diagrammatic plot of a well-made play.

FRIDOLIN, see CANADA.

FROHMAN. (1) DANIEL (1851–1941), American theatre manager. In his early days he was a journalist, but in 1880 became business manager of the Madison Square Theatre, where he remained for some years. He first went into management on his own account in 1885, when he took the old Lyceum Theatre, New York. Here he brought together an excellent stock company, and was responsible for a number of outstanding productions, including plays by Pinero and H. A. Jones. It was under Daniel Frohman's management that E. H. Sothern scored his earliest successes. When the old Lyceum closed in 1902, Frohman became owner of the new theatre bearing the same name. He was also manager of Daly's New York Theatre from 1899 to 1903. In 1911 he published a volume of reminiscences, *Memories of a Manager*, and followed it in 1935 by *Daniel Frohman Presents*. On the death of his youngest brother (see below (3) CHARLES) he took over the administration of his affairs in America. He was also active in the film world. His brother (2) GUSTAVE (1855–1930) was also a theatre manager. The best known of the family, however, is the youngest brother (3) CHARLES (1860–1915), who was as well-known and as well-liked in England as in America. Like his brothers, he inherited a love of the theatre, and made it his life. From selling souvenirs and programmes he graduated to walking-on, and then to various grades of executive rank, learning all there was to know about theatrical business, and storing it away in his extremely alert and lively mind. He first visited England in 1880 as business manager of Haverley's Minstrels, for whom he achieved great things, including Royal patronage. He liked England, and decided to return. Back in America he became a manager, a dramatic agent, and an organizer of touring companies. His first great success came in 1888–9, with the production of *Shenandoah*. This had a long run and laid the foundations of his fortune, since he had had the acumen to purchase the American rights. In 1893 he opened the Empire Theatre with a fine stock company, which he maintained for many years, and he soon had a controlling interest in many other theatres, in New York and elsewhere. His first venture in London was not a success, but his second, when he produced *A Night Out* at the Vaudeville in 1896, made up for it. He then joined forces with the Gattis, with George Edwardes and with Barrie, taking Edwardes's musical comedies and Barrie's plays to America. Feeling the need for a permanent theatre in London, he leased the Duke of York's from Violet Melnotte, and made many notable productions there, including Barrie's *Peter Pan* (1905). At one time he had five London theatres under his control, but his efforts to establish a repertory theatre at the Duke of York's in 1910 were unavailing. He was drowned when the *Lusitania* was torpedoed in 1915. A memorial to him was later erected in Marlow churchyard. A small, odd-looking man, very like a little Buddha, he was charming, kindly, helpful to everyone, and never had a contract with anyone; his word was good enough. He was sincerely mourned in England, a country to which he was deeply attached, and left behind him a name for honour and fair dealing, and a record of remarkable achievements in both London and New York.   W. M. P.

FRONT BOX, see AUDITORIUM, 2 and BOX.

FRONT CURTAIN, see CURTAIN.

FRONT OF HOUSE, a term applied to those parts of a theatre which appertain to the audience as apart from the performers. These include the auditorium, the passages, lobbies and foyers, the bars, cloakrooms and refreshment-rooms, and the box-office or pay-box for the booking of seats, the whole being under the supervision of a front-of-house manager.

FRY, CHRISTOPHER (1907–   ), English dramatist, of whom it has been said that 'his invaluable achievement consists in the long-needed reinstatement of the Comic Spirit in English poetic drama'. He first came into prominence in 1949, when his medieval verse-fantasy, *The Lady's Not for Burning*, had a long run in London with John Gielgud and Pamela Brown in the chief parts. This was followed by *Venus Observed* (1950), written for Sir Laurence Olivier, and by a translation of a play by Anouilh, *L'Invitation au Château*, as *Ring*

Round the Moon (also 1950). In addition to these, Fry—who has been a schoolmaster, an actor, and director of a repertory theatre—is the author of religious verse-dramas, *The Boy with a Cart* (1937), *The Firstborn* (1947), and *Thor, With Angels* (1948), and of a one-act *jeu d'esprit*, *A Phoenix Too Frequent*, produced at the Mercury Theatre, London, in 1946.

FULLER, ISAAC (1606–72), English scene-painter, who studied in Paris under François Perrier, probably at the new Academy there. He worked for the Restoration theatre, and in 1669 painted a scene of Paradise for the Theatre Royal's production of *Tyrannic Love*, later suing the company for payment. He was awarded £335. 10s. 0d.—a large sum in those days, but his scene may have been utilized for other plays.

FULL SCENERY, that system of setting where all the parts of the stage picture belong to the current scene only and must be changed for another scene, as against Detail Scenery or Permanent Setting, where the scenic element amounts only to a part of the whole picture, the rest being a neutral or generalized background remaining in place for the whole of the performance (see ENGLISH PLAYHOUSE, 3).

FULTON THEATRE, NEW YORK, originally the Folies-Bergère, the first theatre-restaurant on Broadway. It opened on 26 Apr. 1911, but its prices were considered too high, and it soon closed. Remodelled as a regular playhouse, and renamed the Fulton, it opened again on 20 Oct. 1911 with a series of short-lived comedies. Its first hit was *The Yellow Jacket*, which ran for ten weeks. Equally good, though in a more serious vein, was Brieux's *Damaged Goods*. A record for the theatre of 411 performances was set up by the farce *Twin Beds*. A revival of *A Woman of No Importance* in 1916 was moderately successful, while in 1921 *Abie's Irish Rose* started its record run here, before moving to the Republic. Among later interesting productions were *The High Road* (1928) with Edna Best and Herbert Marshall, *Oscar Wilde* (1930) with Robert Morley, and *Arsenic and Old Lace* (1941), which set up a new record with 1,437 performances. A moving play on the negro problem, *Deep are the Roots*, was seen at this theatre in 1945.
                                              G. F.

FUNAMBULES, THÉÂTRE DES, PARIS, situated on the Boulevard du Temple. The name of this theatre was derived from the Latin name for rope-dancers, and it began as a booth for acrobats and pantomime. In 1816 the booth was replaced by a permanent playhouse which, under the existing laws, had to have a barker outside, while the actors, even in slightly serious roles, had to indulge in somersaults and handsprings. In 1820 Deburau was in the company, but had not yet made his name as Pierrot, and most of the pantomimes still had Arlequin as hero. It was here too that the great actor Frédérick-Lemaître made his first appearances, playing in pantomime. In 1830 the new liberty of the theatres allowed the Funambules to play vaudeville and to do away with the tight-rope and acrobatics. Then came the great vogue of Deburau as Pierrot, celebrated by Jules Janin and visited by all Paris, and by other great actors, who were not ashamed to admire this unique pantomimist. The Funambules offered to its patrons no other star but Deburau until his death, though he was always surrounded by a good company. Fairy-plays were given with wonderful scenery, transformations, and tricks. The stage was excellently equipped, and even had apparatus for the production of a real waterfall. When Bertrand, the original owner, retired, his son took over until 1843, when the theatre was rebuilt, with 500 more places, and the prices raised. It continued to flourish, still with Deburau, for whom good writers turned out pantomimes, mimes, and fairy-plays. Everything was going well when Deburau died on 17 June 1846. Luckily the theatre was able to continue, with Charles Deburau and Paul Legrand successively as Pierrot, until it was destroyed by Haussmann in 1862.

FURNITURE STORE, a room opening from the stage, where stage furniture, as distinct from scenery or properties, is stored.

FURTENBACH, JOSEF (1591–1667), see JESUIT DRAMA, LIGHTING, 1 *a*, and SCENERY, 2.

FUZELIER, LOUIS (1672–1752), French author, whose plays were written mainly for the small theatres of the Paris fairs, with Piron, Dorneval, and Le Sage. The Comédie-Française having tried to stop their performances, regarding them as an infringement of their monopoly, Fuzelier and his companions solved their difficulties by writing the verses on long placards, held up by two children dressed as cupids, so that the audience could sing them to a popular air while the actors mimed the action. Many of Fuzelier's plays, written for this convention, are very charming and have been reprinted in numerous collections. He also wrote several serious plays, done at the Comédie-Française, of which none has survived. He was editor of the *Mercure* from 1744 to 1752, and wrote widely for it on the theatre and other subjects.

FYFFE, WILL (1885–1947), music-hall comedian, who was born in Dundee and as a boy toured Scotland in a stock company run by his father. Here he played all sorts of parts, including Shakespeare, but made his first appearance as Little Willie in *East Lynne*. He played Polonius at the age of fifteen. He then went into revue, and when some ideas for Scottish character sketches had been refused by Harry Lauder and Neil Kenyon, he decided to go on the halls and use them himself. He was a great success, and by 1921 was at the top of the bill, where he remained till his death. His art lay in his grasp of character and his really fine acting. His people lived, whether they were an engineer on a liner, a guard on a Highland railway, or a centenarian desiring to ride a motor-bicycle. He was also one of the best pantomime comedians of his day. During the war of 1939–45 he was given the C.B.E. for his tireless war work. W. M. P.

G

GABRIELLI. A family of actors of the *commedia dell'arte*, of whom the father (1) GIOVANNI (*c.* 1588–*c.* 1635) played under the name of Sivello. He was a whole company in himself, taking each personage of a comedy in turn, either with or without a mask. His son (2) FRANCESCO (?–1654), the creator of Scapino, played with most of the important companies, and is first found in the Accesi in 1612. For many years he was one of the outstanding members of the Confidenti, but went with the younger Andreini and the Fedeli to Paris in 1624, later rejoining the Accesi. He appears to have been a skilful musician, and also a maker of musical instruments. A number of his letters, which have been preserved, give interesting information on the internal affairs of the companies, and on the theatrical life of the time. He had a daughter (3) GIULIA (*fl.* 1639–45), who appeared as Diana with the company in Paris, and possibly a son (4) GIROLAMO (*fl.* 1687), who played Pantalone. It is not certain that two other actresses, Luisa, who married Domenico Locatelli, and Ippolita, were related to the above. They may have been daughters of Francesco.

GAELIC DRAMA, see IRELAND, 4.

GAFF, a nineteenth-century term for an improvised theatre, in the poorer quarters of London and other large towns, on whose stage an inadequate company dealt robustly with a repertory of melodrama. The entrance fee was a penny or twopence. The lowest type of gaff was known as a blood-tub.

GAIETY THEATRE. (1) LONDON, stood in the Strand (its site is now in Aldwych) and had an entrance there, a pit and a gallery entrance in Catherine Street, a stage-door entrance in Wellington Street, and a Royal Entrance in Exeter Street. It was built on the site of the Strand Music-Hall by Lionel Lawson, of the *Daily Telegraph*; but the man who opened it and made it famous was John Hollingshead. He wanted a restaurant under the same roof, so that diners could go straight to the play, but the authorities refused to allow a connecting door between theatre and restaurant.

Many troubles were encountered during the erection of the theatre, but Hollingshead overcame them all. He lost all his scenery by fire shortly before the opening date, Monday, 21 Dec. 1868, and only got possession of the stage three hours before the curtain went up on the first night. Much of the paint was still wet, and some eighty workmen who had not quite finished their jobs took possession of the front rows of the upper circle and refused to move, demanding to see the theatre they had helped to build launched on its career.

The theatre opened with a successful triple bill, a comedy, *On the Cards*, an operetta, *The Two Harlequins*, and an extravaganza, *Robert the Devil*. Hollingshead had a fine company, with Nellie Farren and Madge Robertson (Mrs. Kendal) as leading ladies and Charles Wigan as leading man, and he began his reforms by paying salaries large enough to make the old-fashioned system of benefit nights unnecessary. He had a flair for success and, though he made mistakes, his reign was on the whole a prosperous and exciting one. Dickens saw his last play at this theatre—*Uncle Dick's Darling*—and prophesied the future greatness of a young actor in it, Henry Irving. Mr. Gladstone visited it and made an exhaustive tour behind the scenes. Phelps played Shakespeare, and a company came from France under the Commune to play to the many French refugees in London. But the great feature of the Gaiety was its burlesques, many of them written by Burnand and Byron, in which appeared the famous quartette, Edward Terry, Kate Vaughan, E. W. Royce, and Nellie Farren, who first played together in 1876 in *Little Don Caesar de Bazan*. They became steadily more and more popular, as did the Gaiety girls, famous for their looks.

In 1885 Fred Leslie joined the company. He was the perfect foil to Nellie Farren, with whom he first appeared in *Little Jack Shephard*, the only joint production of Hollingshead and George Edwardes, who was to be his successor. In 1886 Hollingshead retired and Edwardes, who had come from the Savoy, took over. His first production was *Dorothy*, which became a success when Hayden Coffin sang an interpolated song, 'Queen of My Heart'. Burlesque continued, one, *Ruy Blas; or, the Blasé Roué*, containing the famous *pas de quatre*, with Fred Leslie, C. Danby, Ben Nathan, and Fred Storey dressed as ballet girls and made up to look like Irving, Toole, Edward Terry, and Wilson Barrett. Irving protested and the make-up was altered. In 1891 Nellie Farren left the Gaiety through illness, and her place in *Cinder-Ellen* was taken by Kate James, while Lottie Collins joined the cast to sing and dance 'Ta-Ra-Ra-Boom-De-Ay'. In 1892 Fred Leslie (whose real name was Frederick Hobson) died suddenly of typhoid fever, aged 37, and was replaced by Arthur Roberts. Nellie Farren, who had been at the Gaiety for twenty-three years, lived on and had a benefit at Drury Lane in 1898.

Edwardes transferred from the Prince of Wales's a new type of show called *In Town*, now considered the first musical comedy. It was followed by many similar, and successful, shows, most of which had the word 'girl' in their titles. The end of the old Gaiety was now approaching; the site was required for the Aldwych reconstruction. The last play to be produced was *The Toreador*, which introduced a star destined to shine at the new Gaiety—Gertie Millar. The end of the old theatre was celebrated by a special show written by George Grossmith, jr., entitled *The Linkman*, in which many of the great stars who in their early days had played at the Gaiety returned to say farewell. It was a wonderful cavalcade, and Irving, forgetting his previous displeasure, gave the farewell address in July 1902.

(2) LONDON. The New Gaiety Theatre was built by Edwardes on the Aldwych-Strand corner, and opened on 26 Oct. 1903, with *The Orchid*. The early first-nighters lined up at 5 a.m. and King Edward VII and Queen Alexandra occupied the Royal Box. The cast included Gertie Millar, George Grossmith, jr., Edmund Payne, Connie Ediss, Arthur Hatherton, Robert Nainby, and Gabrielle Ray, who formed what was practically a stock company. Gaiety composers were Lionel Monckton, Ivan Caryll, Leslie Stuart, and Paul Rubens, whose musical shows ran successfully, especially *Our Miss Gibbs*. When George Edwardes died the fortunes of the Gaiety declined somewhat and the company split up. Things revived in 1915 when *To-Night's the Night* was put on, and a new comedian, Leslie Henson, burst upon London. When he, with Grossmith and Laurillard, went to the Winter Garden, much of the old Gaiety spirit went with them, though Butt had some success there with Evelyn Laye as his leading lady. The Gaiety became more its old self when Henson returned under the management of Firth Shephard, and a new team consisting of himself, Richard Hearne, and the younger Fred Emney. They were still in possession of the theatre when it closed in 1939, the last play there being *Running Riot*.

W. M. P.

(3) NEW YORK, a most attractive playhouse on Broadway's west side at Forty-sixth Street. It opened on 4 Sept. 1909 with John Barrymore in *The Fortune Hunter*. This and the productions which followed, including one with the then novel setting of a Pullman car, had good runs, as did the popular *Daddy-Long-Legs* in 1914, *Turn to the Right* in 1916, and *The Country Cousin* in 1917. A year later came the house's record run with the 1,291 performances of *Lightin'*, which brought stardom to old Frank Bacon, and proved to be his last part, as he died during the Chicago run which followed. Among later successes at this theatre were *Loyalties, Aren't We All*, a revival of *Rain* with Jeanne Eagels, and *The Youngest*, which passed the century mark. In 1932 the Gaiety was given over to burlesque and films.

G. F.

GAÎTÉ, THÉÂTRE DE LA, PARIS, the first of the French theatres which was not state-aided. It stood on the Boulevard du Temple, and was originally Nicolet's marionette theatre, and then a theatre for living actors, which, after the upheaval of the Revolution, became the Gaîté. From 1808 until its destruction in 1862 it flourished, sharing the vast output of melodrama with the Ambigu-Comique, and putting on elaborate fairy-plays, pantomimes, and vaudevilles. Pixérécourt was its manager from 1825 to 1834, and in 1835 it was rebuilt after a disastrous fire. When the Boulevard du Temple was pulled down in 1862 the Gaîté took its old name to a new building, which under Offenbach became the home of light operetta and big spectacular musical shows.

GALANTY SHOW, see SHADOW SHOW.

GALDÓS, BENITO PÉREZ (1843–1920), the 'father' of the modern Spanish novel. He was also a dramatist of some repute, bringing to the theatre his own dramatizations of some of his novels. His approach, however, is always that of the novelist, and his power lies in the slow unravelling of character rather than in the selection and synthesis of the stage. His themes are mainly taken from the social problems of modern life, and he shows the influence of both Ibsen and Björnson. His most interesting plays are *Realidad* (1889) and *La loca de la casa* (1893), the latter presenting a dramatic conflict between a selfish, self-made man and an imaginative and religious girl. Among his other plays *Electra* (1901) obtained an enormous vogue because of its anti-clericalism, while *El abuelo* (1897), probably his best work for the stage, deals with the problems of heredity.

GALIMAFRÉ, see BOBÈCHE.

GALLERY, in the modern theatre, the highest and cheapest seats in the house, usually unbookable. The seating generally consists of wooden benches, in some cases without backs. The occupants of the gallery, from their elevated position, have been nicknamed 'the Gods', and form often the most perceptive and certainly the most vociferous part of the audience (see also AUDITORIUM and FOOTMEN'S GALLERY).

GALLIARI FAMILY, see SCENERY, 3.

GALLI-BIBIENA, GALLI-BIBBIENA, GALLI DA BIBBIENA, see BIBIENA.

GALLIENNE, EVA LE, see LE GALLIENNE.

GALSWORTHY, JOHN, O.M. (1867–1933), English dramatist and novelist. Born into an old and well-to-do Devon family, he was educated at Harrow and at New College, Oxford. He was called to the Bar in 1890, but did not engage in serious practice; instead he travelled widely. *The Island Pharisees* (1904) was the first work published under his own name fully to reveal gifts as a novelist which, exercised effectively in *Fraternity, The Patrician, The Country House*, and other studies of the social conscience, came to maturity and power in *The Forsyte Saga*, his great claim to abiding importance. Here he traced the decline of the upper middle classes to which he himself belonged, and worked out in detail his sense of the universal struggle between the desire for possession and the instinct of beauty which mocks at bolts and bars. Galsworthy entered the theatre in 1906. Shaw's plays and the brilliant Vedrenne–Barker season at the Court had just brought the drama of social discussion into fashion. *The Silver Box* (1909), which draws a disquieting contrast between the treatment given by the law to a poor man and a rich man guilty of theft, impressed itself as a masterpiece of realistic observation. *Joy*, his second play, was only a qualified success, but *Strife* (both 1909), giving tense and moving dramatic form to the meaning of a great strike, at once established Galsworthy among the first dramatists of the day. The sombre tragedy of *Justice* (1910), with the famous scene depicting the torture of solitary confinement when endured by a nervous prisoner, led to a reform of prison practice, and its success in this respect may have encouraged the reformer in Galsworthy at the expense of the dramatist. At all events, his next group of plays, *The Pigeon* and *The Eldest Son* (both 1912), *The Fugitive* (1913), and *The Mob* (1914), hardly marked an advance of his talent, and it was not until after the 1914–18 war that, with *The Skin Game* (1920) and *Loyalties* (1922), he recovered an impulse as purely dramatic as his nature would allow. Though he continued to write plays as well as novels, *Windows* (1922), *The Forest* (1924), *Escape* (1926), and others all fell some way below his own high standard. He began, like his Forsytes, to 'date'.

There were qualities of greatness in Galsworthy the dramatist. They may be seen in the first and last acts of *Justice*, in the masterly control of the whole action of *Strife*, and in many other well-remembered scenes. His dialogue, significant, clean, actual without ever being trivial, dramatically characteristic and emotionally rich, is the dialogue of enduring drama. Yet there is somehow a lack of vitality in the *corpus* of his work for the theatre. He renders the errors, the cruelty, and the ugliness of life as it is, but seems to withhold his own vision of what life might be, as though he lacked confidence in that side of his sensibility. The hiatus is filled with indignation and pity which, though sometimes noble, is often rooted in squeamishness. The beauty which is a pervading presence in the finer novels is absent from the plays and, perhaps for that reason, his dramatic vision of life seems incomplete.

A. V. C.

GALWAY THEATRE, see IRELAND, 4.

GAMMER GURTON'S NEEDLE, see STEVENSON, WILLIAM.

GANASSA, ZAN [real name probably Alberto Naseli] (*fl.* 1568–83), one of the earliest actors of the *commedia dell'arte* to take a company abroad. He was in Paris in 1571–2, but his most successful tours were in Spain, where he is found frequently during the 1570s. A curious painting in the Bayeux Museum, reproduced in Duchartre, *The Italian Comedy* (p. 84), is believed by him to represent a performance by Ganassa's troupe, assisted by some French courtiers.

GARCÍA DE LA HUERTA, VICENTE

(1734–87), a Spanish dramatist who revolted against the eighteenth-century neglect of the Spanish classics in favour of French translations, though in his own edition of forgotten plays (1785) he did not always choose the best, and entirely omitted Lope de Vega, Tirso de Molina, and Alarcón. He was in spite of himself much influenced by the Unities imposed on Spain by the *Poética* of Luzán (1737), and among his own plays the one which enjoyed the greatest success, *La Raquel* (1778), was modelled on French lines; but its inspiration was entirely Spanish, and it stands out, in the general poverty of eighteenth-century Spanish drama, as a worthy successor to the plays of the Golden Age.

GARCÍA GUTIÉRREZ, ANTONIO (1812–84), Spanish dramatist of the Romantic period, whose somewhat inferior play *El Trovador* (1836) achieved world-wide popularity when it was used by Verdi as the basis of his opera 'Il Trovatore'. García Gutiérrez was also the author of a number of other plays, including *Juan Lorenzo* and *Venganza Catalana*, both superior in conception and execution to his better-known *El Trovador*. His work shows the influence of Dumas *père*, two of whose melodramas he translated into Spanish. He also translated several plays by Scribe.

GARDEL. There were two dancers of this name at the Paris Opéra in the eighteenth century, contemporary with the older and younger Vestris. The father, whose name may have been (1) PIERRE (?–1776), and the son (2) PIERRE GABRIEL (1758–1840), seem to have been confused, since the younger Gardel is credited with having abolished the mask worn by dancers, when in 1772 he replaced Vestris at short notice and refused to put it on. This led to dancers appearing bare-faced, and to a much greater range of pantomime. Since, however, the son would at this time have been only 14, and not of an age or experience to replace Vestris, either the date of the incident must be wrong or the abolition of the mask must be attributed to the father.

GARDEN THEATRE, NEW YORK, at 61 Madison Avenue. This opened on 27 Sept. 1890 and in the following year saw the reappearance in New York of Sarah Bernhardt in *La Tosca*, in its original French form as a play. Other interesting productions were *The Mountebanks* (1893), *Under Two Flags* (1901), and Hauptmann's *The Weavers* (1915) in a translation by Mary Morrison, while in Jan. 1910 the Ben Greet Players from England were seen in a number of Shakespeare's plays. In 1919 the theatre became the Jewish (later Yiddish) Art Theatre (see JEWISH DRAMA, 6) and was demolished in 1925.   G. F.

GARNIER, ROBERT (*c.* 1535–*c.* 1600), a lawyer who by his adaptations of Greek plays prepared the way for French classical tragedy. He began writing for the theatre in 1568, and produced eight tragedies, all on Greek models, which give proof of wide reading, keen perception, and great lyric power. The best was *Sédécie*, usually known by its sub-title as *Les Juives*, which was also his last. He had a vigorous and supple style, which occasionally reads like Corneille. To scholarship he united imagination and a deep sense of moral dignity. His choruses are particularly fine, and he made many important innovations adopted by later dramatists. But he suffered, as did his contemporaries of the French Renaissance, from a belief that to follow the best models was necessarily to excel, and he saw Greece through Roman eyes.

GARRICK, DAVID (1717–79), one of the greatest of English actors, of whom Burke said that 'he raised the character of his profession to the rank of a liberal art'. He was responsible for a radical change in the style of English acting in his day, and instituted many reforms before and behind the curtain, the most important being the introduction of stage-lighting concealed from the audience (see LIGHTING, I) and the abolition of the audience from the stage, a measure long overdue and achieved at about the same time by Voltaire in Paris. Garrick has also been credited with the revival of Shakespeare's texts, freed from the gross corruptions of the seventeenth century, but this assertion must be taken with caution. He was himself responsible for a production of *Hamlet* with the Grave-diggers omitted, a bad precedent followed in our own day by Maurice Evans in his *G.I. Hamlet*; a *Lear* without the Fool; and a new version of *Romeo and Juliet* which allowed the lovers a scene together in the tomb before dying. He also concocted a *Catherine and Petruchio* and a *Florizel and Perdita* (both 1756) from *The Taming of the Shrew* and *The Winter's Tale*, and did not scruple to add to, or alter, scenes and speeches in any play by Shakespeare which he put on. He had, however, to contend with the taste of the time, and the ignorance and lack of appreciation of Shakespeare's genius which was then prevalent, and even in his worst excesses he seems to have had a deep and sincere appreciation of the dramatist he was tampering with.

Garrick, who was of Huguenot descent, early showed an inclination for the stage, and at 11 appeared with some success as Sergeant Kite in a schoolboy production of *The Recruiting Officer*. Later, being sent to study under Dr. Johnson at Lichfield, he accompanied the latter to London, and there indulged in amateur theatricals at the expense of his business career in the wine trade, which he soon abandoned. Some obscurity surrounds his early appearances on the professional stage, but in 1741 he was playing small parts at Goodman's Fields Theatre, and went with the manager, Giffard, to Ipswich. There, under the name of Lyddal, he was received in a variety of parts with sufficient acclaim to justify his continuing on the stage, and he looked forward confidently to an engagement in London. Being rejected by the managers of both Drury Lane and Covent Garden, he again fell back on Goodman's Fields, and there, on 19 Oct. 1741, made his formal début as Richard III, with such success that playgoers crowded to see him, leaving the Patent Theatres to repent of their obtuseness. Garrick's first biographer, Davies, says of this performance that the actor at first took the audience by surprise, his 'easy and familiar, yet forcible style in speaking and acting', and the 'concurring expression of the features from the genuine workings of nature' being novelties for which the declamatory and laboured manner of Quin, then the greatest exponent of tragedy, had not prepared them. They were soon won over, however, and Garrick embarked on a triumphant career which suffered no serious check until his retirement in 1776. In person he might have seemed unsuited to tragedy—he is described as being 'a small man of middle height, with good mobile features and flashing expressive eyes' and a clear but not particularly resonant voice. But his genius rose superior to all disadvantages, and he was unsurpassed, not only in the tragic heroes of the contemporary theatre, but in such parts as Hamlet, Macbeth, and particularly Lear—which he apparently played in a scarlet coat. Murphy, who published a life of Garrick in 1801, said of him: 'It was in Lear's madness that Garrick's genius was remarkably distinguished. His movements were slow and feeble; misery was depicted in his countenance. . . . During the whole time he presented a sight of woe and misery, and a total alienation of mind from every idea, but that of his unkind daughters.' Garrick himself has related how he modelled the madness of Lear on that of an unfortunate man who had accidentally killed his two-year-old child by dropping it from a window. It was to this 'copying of nature' that much of Garrick's success was due, and with it he brought a fresh lease of life to the English stage, which at the time of his first appearance was at a very low ebb. He was equally admired in comedy, one of his earliest parts being Abel Drugger in *The Alchemist*; he was good as Benedict, and as Ranger in *The Suspicious Husband*, in which part he was much admired by Fanny Burney, while as Bayes in *The Rehearsal* he scored a signal triumph with his mimicry of well-known actors of the time. He exempted from his mockery his rival Quin, however, and was always careful to give the older actor his due, admitting his greatness in Falstaff, and in such heroic parts as Cato, while he filched from him the great parts in which he had hitherto reigned supreme. Garrick was also generous in his admiration of Spranger Barry, often his rival for public favour, and in later years resigned to him the parts of Romeo, in which he excelled, and Othello, a part in which Garrick was not successful, chiefly, says Murphy, because the blacking of his face deprived him of that marvellously expressive play of features which constituted one of his greatest assets and made him intelligible even to a spectator who was deaf. With Macklin, another great actor of the day, Garrick's relations were less happy, an unfortunate quarrel at the outset of his career preventing any close friendship.

Garrick's fiery temper, vanity, and snobbishness, as well as his sudden rise to fame, naturally brought him many enemies. The worst of these was the malicious Samuel Foote, to whom many bitter criticisms of Garrick are due; it may possibly be from that source that Garrick got his somewhat undeserved reputation for meanness; he had also to contend with the petulance of unacted authors and disappointed small-part actors. He was not always responsible for the quarrels in which he found himself involved, notably those with Dr. Johnson over the failure of *Irene* (1749) and with Colman the elder, whom he offended by refusing to play the part of Lord Ogleby in *The Clandestine Marriage* (1766), a comedy in which they collaborated. As a result Colman took his later plays to Covent Garden, of which he assumed the management in rivalry with Garrick at Drury Lane.

Apart from his collaboration with Colman, and his adaptations of Shakespeare, Garrick was also the author of several plays, of which the farces *Miss in her Teens* (1747), in which he played Fribble, and *Bon Ton; or, High Life Above Stairs* (1775), were the most successful. He was a vivacious and competent dramatist, at his best about equal to Colley Cibber, but much of his work was mere hack-writing and adapting of old plays. His rewriting of Wycherley's *The Country Wife* as *The Country Girl* (1766) was most successful, and held the stage for many years. Garrick was also a prolific writer of epilogues and prologues, published with his other works in a three-volume edition in 1785. One of his most publicized achievements, and the one which has occasioned much malice at his expense, was his Shakespeare Jubilee at Stratford in 1769, to which, it was said, 'the wits and the weather were equally unkind'; it was remarkable for a number of odes, songs, speeches, and other effusions by David Garrick, of which the manuscript has been lost, and for the complete absence of anything by Shakespeare.

It was in 1747 that Garrick first took part in the management of Drury Lane, where the major part of his career was spent. On the death of Lacy he became sole manager, resigning his share of the Patent on his retirement to Sheridan, Linley, and Ford. During his time many reforms were introduced, and he gathered round him a good company, his leading ladies being Peg Woffington (also his mistress for some years), Mrs. Cibber, who was said to resemble him like a sister, Mrs. Bellamy, whom he trained up to play Juliet to his Romeo, and Mrs. Abington. Among the men, apart from intermittent appearances by Quin and Barry, his chief supports were the unfortunate Mossop, Woodward, who wrote the Drury Lane pantomimes and appeared in them as Harlequin, Yates, a fine comedian and character actor, and Tom King, who took over

Lord Ogleby when Garrick refused it, and was the original Sir Peter Teazle of *The School for Scandal*. Garrick's management was marred by two serious riots, one caused by the abolition of half-price at the end of the third act, a time-hallowed concession which the manager was forced to restore, and the other by his importation of French dancers into *The Chinese Festival* shortly before the outbreak of war with France. The former caused Garrick, described as 'a peaceful, long-suffering man, petted and rather spoilt by the distinguished men to whose society he was admitted, who shrank from dependence upon the mob', to retire for a time, and from 1763 to 1765 he travelled on the continent with his wife, Eva Marie Violetti (1724–1822), a dancer at the Haymarket whom he had married in 1749. He was well received everywhere, particularly in France, and his reputation shed much lustre upon the contemporary English stage. He returned, greatly refreshed, and a public surfeited with musical spectacles was glad to see him in a succession of his greatest parts. He made his farewell appearance on 10 June 1776 as Don Felix in *The Wonder, a Woman never Vexed*, and retired to Hampton to enjoy the society of his friends until his death, which was felt as a personal loss by many, and called from Dr. Johnson the memorable epitaph: 'I am disappointed by that stroke of death which has eclipsed the gaiety of nations and impoverished the public stock of harmless pleasure.' He was buried in Westminster Abbey (where Henderson and Irving later joined him), and the carriages of the mourners reached as far as the Strand. His brother George, who had been his right-hand man at Drury Lane for many years, died a few days later, because, said the wits of the time with rueful humour, 'Davy wanted him'.

Garrick was several times painted by Sir Joshua Reynolds, one of whose portraits of him hangs in the Garrick Club, named in honour of the great actor, as was the Garrick Theatre, London. A fine portrait by Gainsborough, done in 1766, and said by Mrs. Garrick to be the best ever painted, was lost when the Stratford-on-Avon Town Hall was destroyed by fire in 1946.

GARRICK CLUB, LONDON, which has numbered among its members many great names of the English stage, owes its inception to the Duke of Sussex, who, according to T. H. Escott, 'recognized the need for furthering the literary industry in England by the formation of a Club on less formal lines than the Athenæum, recruited from the most active caterers for the public taste with pen and pencil, in the studio and on the stage'. The first committee consisted of Colonel Sir Andrew F. Barnard, equerry to George IV, Lord Kinnaird, Samuel James Arnold, manager of Drury Lane Theatre, Francis Mills, Henry Broadwood, and Samuel Beazley. Most of the work necessitated by the formation of the club was done by Mills and Broadwood.

The first committee meeting was held on 17 Aug. 1831, and the club, with the Duke of Sussex as its patron, opened in November of the same year, though its premises (Probatt's Family Hotel, King Street) were not ready for the use of members until Feb. 1832. The present club-house, opened on 4 July 1864, stands on part of old Rose Street, and in that warren of crowded alleys which lay between King Street and St. Martin's Lane, home of Curll, the bookseller at the 'Pope's Head'—associated too with Samuel Butler and Samuel Johnson. The club, which is restricted to 700 members, has a fine collection of theatrical portraits, of which an annotated catalogue was prepared in 1908 by Robert Walters. In 1896 the Rev. R. H. Barham, author of *The Ingoldsby Legends*, published a collection of short biographies of 135 of its former members. (See also Percy Fitzgerald's *History of the Garrick Club*.)

GARRICK THEATRE. (1) LONDON, at Leman Street, E., opened in 1830, and took its name from its proximity to the o d theatre in Goodman's Fields where Garrick made his début. Wyman and Conquest (father of George Conquest) were its first managers. In 1845 it was burned down and rebuilt. It held a very low position, even among East End theatres, and was practically a 'gaff'. In 1873–4 J. B. Howe, a great local favourite, took it, and with redecoration and better companies made a gallant bid for popularity. But he went bankrupt in 1875, and there are no further records of the theatre.

(2) LONDON, in the Charing Cross Road, opposite the statue of Irving and the National Portrait Gallery. This was opened in Apr. 1889 by Hare, with himself, Forbes-Robertson, Lewis Waller, and Kate Rorke in *The Profligate*. *La Tosca* followed, with Mrs. Bernard Beere, and then in 1890 *A Pair of Spectacles*, which ran for 335 performances. Later *The Notorious Mrs. Ebbsmith*, with Hare and Mrs. Patrick Campbell, caused a sensation, and a woman of that name was found drowned in the Thames with a ticket for the theatre in her pocket; she had written to a friend that the play had preyed on her mind. When Hare left the theatre its standing declined until in 1902 Arthur Bourchier and his wife, Violet Vanbrugh, leased it and inaugurated a long and brilliant period, with productions ranging from Shakespeare to farce. Oscar Asche and Lily Brayton occupied the Garrick for some time, notable productions being *Kismet* (1911), which ran for 328 performances, and a revival of *The Merry Wives of Windsor*. For some years the theatre had no regular policy or management, and at one time, shortly before the outbreak of war in 1939, it ran a season of Old Time Varieties. It has also been used for revue.　　　　　　　　　　　　　　　W. M. P.

(3) NEW YORK, in 35th Street between Fifth and Sixth Avenues. It opened as Harrigan's Theatre on 29 Dec. 1890 with a play by Harrigan in which he himself appeared. In 1895 Richard Mansfield took it over, renamed it the Garrick, and appeared there with his wife in repertory. He was not particularly successful, and the theatre housed other attractions, the longest run under Mansfield's management being that of William Gillette in his own play, *Secret Service*, which lasted for five months. The same actor appeared later at the Garrick as Sherlock Holmes, a part always associated with the last years of his life. Among later productions at the Garrick were *Captain Jinks of the Horse Marines*, which made Ethel Barrymore a star, *The Stubbornness of Geraldine*, and *Her Own Way*, all by Clyde Fitch, while 1905 saw a successful run of *You Never Can Tell*. A distinguished failure was Percy Mackaye's fine drama, *The Scarecrow*, which had only 23 performances in 1911, and was followed by Paul Orleneff and his company in a repertory of Russian plays. In 1919 a great American subscription theatre was established at the Garrick when the Theatre Guild opened there on 19 Apr. with Benavente's *Bonds of Interest*, in a new translation by J. G. Underhill. This was followed by *John Ferguson* and later *Jane Clegg*, both by St. John Ervine. Among later productions were *Heartbreak House*, *Mr. Pim Passes By*, *Liliom*, *He Who Gets Slapped*, *R.U.R.*, *Peer Gynt*, and *The Adding Machine*. In 1924 came the Lunts in *The Guardsman*, and *They Knew What They Wanted* with Pauline Lord. The Theatre Guild moved into its own playhouse in 1925, and the Garrick had only two more important productions, *The Mystery Ship* and the modern-dress *Taming of the Shrew* (both 1927), before it was pulled down in 1929. It was at this theatre that the Provincetown Players made their last appearance, shortly before its destruction.　　　　　G. F.

GASCOIGNE, GEORGE (*c.* 1535–77), a scholar of Cambridge, and a versifier of some reputation, who helped in the preparation of the entertainments given before Elizabeth at Kenilworth and Woodstock in 1575. He was also the author of a translation of Lodovico Dolce's *Giocasta* (based on Euripides' *Phoenician Women*), and of Ariosto's *I Suppositi* (based on Plautus's *Captivi*), both done at Gray's Inn in 1566. The latter was also given at Trinity College, Oxford, in 1582.

GAS LIGHTING, see LIGHTING, 1 *b*.

GATE THEATRE, LONDON. This stood in Villiers Street, Strand, in one of the bars of the former music-hall, Gatti's-Under-The-Arches, below Charing Cross Station. It was a small private venture, founded in 1925 by Peter Godfrey. Under his direction, and later under that of Norman Marshall (from 1934 onwards), it did important work in the production of unlicensed or uncommercial plays, often in translation. Many of these, as well as the witty Gate Revues, found their way subsequently to regular West End theatres. The Gate was badly damaged by enemy action, and needs extensive repair.

For the Dublin Gate Theatre, see IRELAND.

GATHERER, a functionary of the Elizabethan playhouse whose task it was to collect the money from that part of the house, usually the upper gallery and the boxes, allotted to the owner of the building.

GAULTIER-GARGUILLE, [HUGUES GUÉRU] (*c.* 1573–1633), French actor and chief farce-player, with Gros-Guillaume and Turlupin, of the company at the Hôtel de Bourgogne, to which he may have graduated from the Paris fairs. He was a tall, thin man with a dry humour, much appreciated by Parisians. As Fleschelles he also played serious parts, but it is as a low comedian that he is best remembered. He figures as himself, with other members of the company, in Gougenot's *La Comédie des comédiens*, given at the Hôtel de Bourgogne in 1633, the year of his death. He married Aliénor Salomon, who was at one time thought to be the daughter of the mountebank Tabarin. This, however, is not certain.

GAUSSIN, JEANNE CATHERINE (1711–67), French actress, daughter of Antoine Gaussem, valet to the great actor Baron. As a child she had the opportunity of watching Adrienne Lecouvreur and other actresses from the wings of the Comédie-Française, and profited so well from what she saw that while quite young she was taken on tour by a travelling company. She made her first appearance at the Comédie-Française in 1730, later succeeding Mlle Duclos in tragedy. She was particularly good in roles demanding tenderness and grief rather than the portrayal of the sterner passions, which had to await the arrival of Mlle Dumesnil and Mlle Clairon. Dark, with languorous eyes and a rich voice, which, as La Harpe said, 'had tears in it', she never lost her youthful look, and at the age of 50 could still play young girls. She appeared in several of Voltaire's plays, notably *Zaïre* (1732), and was considered outstanding in the sentimental comedies of La Chaussée. In 1759 she made an unhappy marriage with a dancer at the Opéra, and retired from the stage four years later, at the same time as Mlle Dangeville. Off-stage Mlle Gaussin was modest, amusing, kind, and most generous. While playing Berenice in 1752 she was so heart-rending that a soldier on guard in the wings dropped his musket and burst into tears, a tribute to the pathos of her acting which was commemorated in numerous poor verses of the time.

GAUZE-CLOTH, see CLOTH.

GAY, JOHN (1685–1732), English poet and satirist, friend of Pope, to whom he dedicated his first book, and author of the famous ballad opera, *The Beggar's Opera*, first given at Lincoln's Inn Fields in 1728 under John Rich, thus, as it was said, 'making Gay rich and Rich gay'. A light-hearted mixture of political satire and burlesque of Italian opera, then a fashionable craze, it has frequently been revived, notably at the Lyric, Hammersmith, in 1920 and 1925. In 1929 it was done into German by Bert Brecht as *Die Dreigroschenoper* with music by Kurt Weill. Its sequel, *Polly*, was not produced for many years owing to political censorship, but was finally given at the Haymarket in 1777 with alterations by Colman. Gay was also the author of several comedies and of the libretto of Handel's 'Acis and Galatea', but his fame rests almost entirely on *The Beggar's Opera*.

GEDDES, NORMAN-BEL (1893–   ), American scenic designer, and one of the outstanding figures of the American stage (see COSTUME, 10 *b*, SCENERY, 6 and U.S.A., 2).

GELOSI, THE, one of the earliest and best-known *commedia dell'arte* companies. After an initial visit to France in 1571, it was summoned to play before the French King, Henri III, at Blois in 1577, and from there went to Paris, thus inaugurating the visits of the Italian players which later had such a marked influence on the French theatre. In the company at this time were Franceso Andreini and his beautiful and talented wife, Isabella, accounted one of the best actresses of her day. Vittoria Piissimi, later of the Uniti and Confidenti troupes, was also with it in its early days, and reappeared with it intermittently in after years, indulging in much rivalry with Isabella. After constant travelling and much shifting of personnel, the Gelosi, with the Andreini in charge, returned to Paris in 1602, and it was on their return journey to Italy that Isabella died and her husband disbanded the troupe. The players scattered to other companies and the history of the Gelosi, which had been the best company of the day, came to an end.

GELTZER, CATHERINE, *première danseuse* in the Alhambra ballets, 1871–1914 (see BALLET, 8).

GENÉE, ADELINE (1878–   ), a Danish dancer, from 1897 to 1915 *première danseuse* of the Empire ballets. She also appeared with much success at the Coliseum in half-hour programmes, and was later a teacher of dancing in London (see BALLET, 8).

GENERAL UTILITY, see STOCK COMPANY.

GÉNERO CHICO, or *Teatro por horas*, a generic term applied in Spain to the lesser and lighter types of dramatic entertainment. In its present form it dates from about 1868, when the performance of one-act pieces became popular. It has its own authors, too numerous to mention, and was at its best in the late nineteenth century, being now practically defunct. The first productions of this genre were short comic scenes of daily life, usually in Madrid, heightened to the point of caricature, but the fashion developed for musical accompaniments, until *género chico* became synonymous with one-act *zarzuela*. It was treated with scorn by academic critics and the more conventional dramatists, but was nevertheless a living and popular entertainment, with a distinguished ancestry, since it derives from the old *sainete* or *entremés*, and is thus connected with the earliest traditions of drama in Spain. It has been superseded by the *astracanadas*, or sketches with wildly improbable plots and a dialogue thick with untranslatable puns and plays on words (see also ZARZUELA).

GENGENBACH, PAMPHILUS (*fl.* sixteenth century), a Swiss printer of Basle whose *Totenfresser* (1521) is a savage attack on the Roman Catholic Church (see GERMANY, 2).

GENTLEMAN, FRANCIS (1728–84), who was born and died in Dublin, is best remembered by his dramatic criticism, which appeared in 1770 in two anonymous volumes called *The Dramatic Censor*. The first volume is dedicated to Garrick, the second to Foote. As a critic Gentleman dealt judiciously but verbosely with various plays of Shakespeare and of his own day. His remarks on actors, at the end of each article, are more valuable and informative. He was for some years a soldier, and then became a player, succeeding in spite of what he himself called 'an unconsequential figure and uncommon timidity'. On his way to London from his native city he acted with Macklin at Chester, and had two tragedies of his own composition presented at Bath. It is known also that he acted Othello in Edinburgh, met James Boswell at Glasgow, and appeared in the first production of the best of his own plays, *The Modish Wife* (1761), at Chester. Among many other adaptations *The Tobacconist* (*c.* 1760), watered down from Ben Jonson's *The Alchemist*, was the most successful and was reprinted in the collections of Dibdin and Oxberry. Gentleman appears to have been prone to self-pity and ingratitude to his helpers. Garrick called him a 'dirty dedicating knave' on the latter account. In his forties Gentleman retired to Yorkshire for five years, and married there. His wife died in 1773, leaving him with two infants. He repaired finally to Dublin, and the last seven years of his life brought him nothing but sickness and abject poverty. Professor C. H. Gray justly says of Gentleman's *Dramatic Censor*: 'He wrote much as other men of his day wrote and with many echoes of Dr. Johnson's criticisms, except that here and there he expressed opinions that have an air of fresh discovery about them. . . . His criticisms of the actors are full of vivid descriptions of the way certain parts were played by different men.'

GEORGE, GRACE (1879–   ), see BRADY (2).

GEORGE M. COHAN THEATRE, NEW YORK, on Broadway at 43rd Street. This opened on 25 Sept. 1911 with Cohan's play *The Little Millionaire*, the author and his parents being in the cast. It was followed by a revival of

45 Minutes from Broadway, while the following year saw *Broadway Jones*, again with the three Cohans. Among later successes were *Potash and Perlmutter*, which had 441 performances, *It Pays to Advertise*, *Come Out of the Kitchen*, and a number of musical shows, including *Two Little Girls in Blue* in 1921. Clemence Dane's *Bill of Divorcement*, in the same year, established Katharine Cornell as a star, and was moved to Times Square to make way for Ed Wynn in *The Perfect Fool*, by which sobriquet he has continued to be known. The last years of the theatre were uneventful, and its swansong was *The Dubarry*, with Grace Moore. A year later it became a cinema, and has since been pulled down.   G. F.

GEORGE, Mlle [MARGUERITE JOSÉPHINE WEIMER] (1787–1867), French tragic actress, and one of the best of her day, in spite of the handicap of a wilful and imperious temper which made her many enemies and spoilt her acting. Child of actors, she was befriended by Mlle Raucourt of the Comédie-Française, and made her début there in 1802. Her majestic bearing and fine voice assured her instant success in tragic parts, but in 1808 she eloped suddenly with a dancer named Duport and went to Russia, where she acted with a French company for five years. Back at the Comédie-Française, she was again successful until her fellow actors, tiring of her temper and her caprice, asked her to resign in 1818. She then went to London and on tour, and in 1822 returned to Paris to star at the Odéon. She was reputed to have been the mistress of Napoleon, and for many years lived with the manager Harel, following him into the provinces and to the Porte-Saint-Martin, where she acted with great success in romantic drama. Increasing stoutness led her to retire, and she became a teacher of elocution, but her extravagance forced her back to the stage, where she found herself outmoded and forgotten. She struggled on for some time, and finally retired to die in obscurity.

GEORGE II OF SAXE-MEININGEN, see MEININGEN PLAYERS.

GEORGIA, see RUSSIA, 2 *e*.

GERMANY. 1. PRE-REFORMATION DRAMA. The precise origin of secular drama in Germany, as elsewhere, is still under discussion. Direct descent from the ancient classical theatre through the *mimi* is no longer claimed, and recent criticism in Germany tends to regard the indigenous pagan rites as being of far greater importance in the growth of religious as well as of secular drama than was formerly conceded, a theory which affords a convenient explanation for the presence of grotesque and comic elements in religious plays. Thus the *Fastnachtsspiel* (originally a Carnival play, later acted at any season) which emerges in the fifteenth century, far from being a mere offshoot of the Church play (see ECCLESIASTICAL DRAMA), frequently shows cognate native elements in an unchristianized form. No doubt the wandering minstrel was also instrumental in the propagation of medieval farce, at any rate before it became the preserve of the burghers, while the Church, by admitting the practice of the Feast of Fools, in which young clerics were allowed to vent their high spirits, and their grievances, also furthered its development.

The Carnival plays, which form the pre-Reformation secular drama of Germany, were governed by the taste of the audiences before which they were performed. They attack what the burgher dislikes or despises, but they lack the satirical pungency and the political element of the French *sotie*, as well as the charm of the English Interlude, for they had little contact before the sixteenth century with either School Drama or with Courts, petty or imperial. This is perhaps an early instance of the way in which German drama has always been affected by the absence of a central focus of culture such as Paris or London.

Religious subjects still appear in these secular farces, as for example in the Debate between Church and Synagogue, but the punishments meted out to the losing party are so revolting as to preclude ecclesiastical patronage. The learned Aristotle on all fours with a lady on his back preserves a trickle of classical tradition. Contemporary events are reflected in a play about the Turkish wars. There are also links with ancient pagan festivals, as in the Austrian *Neidhartspiel*, in which the minnesinger Neidhart von Reuental, having seen the first violet of the year, herald of spring, marks the spot with his hat and hastens to call his lady so that she may admire it, and the courtiers dance round it. He has been spied on by some peasants, who hate him for mocking their ways and decoying their women. They pick the flower and, after putting something offensive in its place, tie it to a pole and caper round it. Neidhart, utterly discomforted in the presence of his mistress, suspects the trick and, with a few followers, pounces on his foes. A scrimmage ensues in which the peasants are routed, whereupon Neidhart leads his lady to the dance.

In all these plays the weaknesses of lawyers and their clients, doctors and their patients, are drastically portrayed, and the illicit relations of the clergy with women are shown up with gusto. But by far the most popular themes were those within the experience of the spectators themselves. All the human failings that undermine domestic peace—unfaithfulness, quarrelling, gluttony, avarice, bullying, lack of physical self-control—are described with disconcerting frankness. In the fifteenth-century farces these family crises are not usually shown in action. The problem is ventilated before a magistrate or some other person of authority; or else the help of a doctor or a friend is sought, in which case the advice given often redounds upon the adviser.

A delightful example of the former type is found in *Rumpolt und Marecht*. It is a breach-of-promise case, in which Rumpolt desires to rid himself of Marecht, who declares that she has just cause to demand marriage. Rumpolt is staunchly supported by his father, even to the extent of financial aid; Marecht by her nimble-tongued mother and a hussy, her friend. Each party pays cash down—heavily—for legal assistance. Rumpolt stoutly denies Marecht's insinuations, but unfortunately gives himself away. His attempts to turn upon his lawyer are unavailing, and he is about to submit with a bad grace when, on the banns being called, an earlier claimant to Marecht's favours appears. Rumpolt's possessive instincts are aroused; he champions his lady, and the warring parties join in a dance. This witty little sketch is a masterpiece of characterization, and shows dramatic qualities to which few of these plays attain.

A variable feature of many fifteenth- and sixteenth-century German farces is the *Narr* or fool. The word originally meant those who live foolishly, that is, not as befits their hope of salvation or their true interest, a conception immortalized by Brant in his *Narrenschiff* (*Ship of Fools*). This personage is not necessarily funny, but in the Carnival plays is usually made to appear so. He may also stand for the quality of folly regarded as a disease which may be cured by exorcism, by purging, or by the use of the knife. This *Narr* is always the central figure of the action. A secondary form of the type is the dullard who cannot see the sun at noonday. Further, assumed stupidity may cover slyness, and the *Narr* may either hoist his master with his own petard, or in some way succeed in feathering his own nest. Lastly the existence of the Court fool leads to the introduction of the *Narr* in plays where the scene is laid in high places. Here he may simply be vulgar, but he may have a certain gravity, and in one fifteenth-century farce at least he shows far more sense than his betters.

These early farces were probably acted by youths, usually artisans, from the neighbourhood, and their jokes were doubtless largely personal. Gradually the plays assumed a more general significance, and groups of such actors, having gained a certain competence, occasionally visited other places; but no organized companies on the scale of the Parisian *enfants sans souci* are recorded in Germany. At first the presentation of the plays must have been extremely simple, performers and audience being almost one, both joining in the final round dance. A 'precursor' or crier begs for hospitality and a hearing, and gives instructions for a space to be cleared. He, or another, afterwards conveys the thanks of the company, and craves pardon for any licence of speech. In the most primitive form of farce, which resembles the modern revue, the actors step forward one by one from a row or semicircle, usually addressing an authoritative central figure who comments on each person in turn, and winds up the discussion (see MUMMING PLAY for parallel English production). There is no setting, but there must have been some rudimentary indication of character by costume, gesture, speech, or perhaps by masks. When action was introduced, properties such as chairs, tables, and so on would be required, and soon, as there was something to see as well as to hear, it became more convenient to raise the actors above the level of the floor on tables and trestles, thus setting the play at a greater distance from the audience; but the practice of having all the actors on the stage from start to finish continued, and as the action grew more elaborate accommodation had to be found for more than one group of actors at a time. The stage was therefore erected in the open, or, if permission could be obtained, in the halls of public buildings. With few exceptions the medieval farces are in one act only, though they vary greatly in length, and the scene is not localized. The *Neidhartspiel* has two actions going on simultaneously, one with courtiers, one with peasants, the speeches coming sometimes from one group, sometimes from the other. As the process of elaboration continued there was no doubt some idea of emulating the magnificence of the religious plays or the richer setting of the School Drama, but it must have been held in check by lack of funds, for the performance of popular farces was not for some time an institution which had any claim on public money, and only small contributions could be collected from the audience. Not until the middle of the fifteenth century, when the guilds undertook the performances, was more money forthcoming under the stimulus of local pride. The most active of these guilds were the Mastersingers, who flourished in the large towns of south Germany. Two of the few authors of fifteenth-century farces known by name, Hans Rosenblüt and Hans Folz, lived in Nuremberg about the middle of the century, and Folz was certainly a Mastersinger. Serious secular drama was hardly known in Germany at this period. The *Tellspiel* from Uri, celebrating the winning of Swiss independence, probably belongs to the sixteenth century.

2. THE REFORMATION AND LATER SIXTEENTH-CENTURY SECULAR DRAMA. Since the days of Hroswitha of Gandersheim (*c.* 970), who wrote plays on the model of Terence, but of Christian content, Latin drama had lain fallow in Germany; but in 1450 the University of Heidelberg acquired some manuscripts of Terence and Seneca, and intensive study of these authors ensued. For a time admiration for the early Renaissance drama in Latin as it developed in Italy, and the use of the Dialogue for argument, retarded the adoption of classical dramatic form. In 1497, however, Reuchlin, in his *Henno*, dressed up a popular farce (on the theme of *Maistre Pierre Pathelin*) in five acts, complete with prologue and choruses. The neo-Latin drama is of its nature international, and there was considerable give and take in it all over western Europe. The most notable contributions by German humanists were probably those pertaining to the religious struggle (see below). Latin comedy and its derivatives were first in the field. Tragedy, it may be said, did not on the whole flourish in sixteenth-

century Germany. Seneca was republished, commented on, and translated, but purely for educational purposes. Of the Greek tragedians Euripides was the first to evoke interest, Erasmus and Melanchthon making translations of which performances are recorded. The contemplative mind of Sophocles could find no echo during the turmoil of the Reformation. The humanist drama is thus important rather as a model of form, and for the importation of classical themes, than for positive achievement, though Nicodemus Frischlin, an alert mind, gained fame and imprisonment for his spirited but indiscreet comedies.

By the end of the fifteenth century religious drama, though widespread, had largely deteriorated into pageantry, and was beginning to yield to the onslaught of the Reformation, while the old farces were also losing their vitality. Though still popular, they relied on a rehandling of old material, and gave increasing offence by their coarseness. The Reformation brought new life and fresh material. Certain practices of the Church were attacked, particularly in the free cities of Switzerland, with a violence as yet unknown in German drama. In Basle the printer Pamphilus Gengenbach in his *Totenfresser* (1521) shows the Church battening on the dead, growing rich on the money paid by credulous relatives in order to save the souls of the departed from purgatory. The Pope, a bishop, a lay brother, a monk, and a nun sit round a table carving up a corpse, while the devil plays the fiddle. In the foreground the laity, led by a parson, cry for deliverance. The play, if it can be so called, is primitive in form, but anger imparts fire to the uncouth speeches.

In the same year the painter-poet Niklas Manuel of Berne used an even simpler but no less effective device. Two men, a naïve peasant and his more knowledgeable town cousin, are watching two processions entering the market-place. On the one hand are seen richly caparisoned horses, their riders crowned and mitred, wearing costly cloaks and gazing disdainfully upon the crowd. On the other there is one riding upon an ass, meanly clad and attended by rough fishermen, while the poor and humble throng round him. The country lad is dazzled at first by the display of wealth and power, but his companion soon draws the moral. Here pageantry and dialogue are happily combined, and the words are plain-spoken but restrained. In a later play, *Der Ablasskrämer* (1525), Manuel gives us almost a foretaste of the French Revolution. A certain Ricardus Hinterlist (Dick Trickster), a seller of indulgences, unwarily returns to a former field of action. His female customers have, however, seen through him, and supported by their husbands they arrive armed with shovels, distaffs, and rusty weapons, setting upon him with torrents of abuse. His entreaties and his threats are alike unavailing. Having thrashed him they tie his hands together and hoist him up repeatedly until he has confessed all his tricks one by one, and disgorged his ill-gotten gains. For concentrated fury this little sketch, which was acted in the market-place of Berne, would be hard to beat.

Elsewhere in Germany too the old dramatic forms were used in support of the Reformation. In Riga the former monk Burkhart Waldis points the parable of the prodigal son against the Catholics. The prodigal is robbed of his fortune in a papist house of ill repute, at the instigation of the devil. His brother, trusting in the virtue of his own good works, represents a doctrine Luther seeks to frustrate. The wicked are converted and in a final chorus join in Luther's hymn. This play in two acts, written in a Low German dialect, is not without its lively moments, but action is subordinated to argument. It was performed on a stage similar to that required for the *Neidhartspiel*, with the two actions located on opposite sides of the available space; but they do not in this case proceed simultaneously.

It was only to be expected that Protestant dramatists would make use of the *mise en scène* of the Passion Plays. A striking example of this occurs in the *Pammachius* (1538) of the humanist Naogeorg (1511–63) (really Thomas Kirchmayer). Originally written in Latin, this play was soon translated into racy German and performed at Zwickau. The first act opens in heaven, the second in hell. Pope Pammachius is shown to be utterly perverted by the acquisition of secular power. St. Peter, who had believed in him, and the emperor Julian, who had sponsored him, are much distressed. His deeds cry to heaven. Christ, having sent Truth and her outspoken maid, Bold, to investigate matters, comforts them on their return by pointing to the little town of Wittenberg in Germany where one, 'God's Word', will shortly arise and set matters right. For the concluding fifth act Naogeorg bids his audience look around them. This play, inordinately long, was doubtless cut for performance. It was played in Latin at Christ's College, Cambridge, in 1545, and was translated into English by John Bale.

The greatest zest in the struggle was clearly displayed by the attackers. Nothing of comparable vigour was produced by the Catholics until the second half of the sixteenth century, when the Jesuit schools instituted play-acting as an effective method of training and propaganda (see JESUIT DRAMA). In plays such as *Pammachius* the stage is clearly used as a pulpit, while many others, without so definite an argument, show unmistakable Protestant, or more rarely Catholic, bias. The increasing number of printed copies shows too that their authors could now count on a reading public.

The early dramatists of the Reformation had been content to use popular or traditional forms, but sporadic division into acts and scenes reveals the influence of classical studies. The humanist movement had been gaining ground in Germany towards the end of the fifteenth century, and though the religious upheaval hindered anything like a renaissance of poetry for the time being, the mere fact that Latin plays were acted in the schools and universities with much

pomp and ceremony led to a wider acquaintance with the form of classical drama, and incidentally to somewhat novel staging. In the *Fastnachtsspiel* any stage there was was neutral; it could represent any place, and did not alter, though the introduction of a throne, for example, might underline the locality. The religious drama had required a far more elaborate structure, and the action moved from one part of the stage to another. For the performances of Terence, however, a special type of stage had been evolved in Renaissance Italy, ostensibly on a classical pattern: the back of the stage showed a number of curtained openings, or cells, flanked by pillars, leading to the various localities required for the action, and from these the characters entered and departed. This arrangement, known as the Terence-stage, marks a deliberate attempt to counteract both elaboration and naturalism. Later in the sixteenth century the desire for realism again prevailed, and a series of scenic houses on both sides of a sharply converging central prospect was used, terminating in a painted backcloth. This technique also was of Italian origin, and it was rendered more flexible by the use of *telari* or triangular prisms revolving on pivots (see SCENERY). Such a stage may have been used by Paul Rebhun (c. 1500–46) when in 1535 he presented his *Susanna*, written with direct encouragement from Luther, though the intimacy of many scenes suggests rather an approximation to the medieval stage with its multiple setting as the characters come and go from their several houses. The action falls naturally into five acts, each followed by a lyrical chorus in varying measures; in the body of the play Rebhun uses lines of different length and rhythm, according to the effect he wishes to create. The play has a delightful simplicity and homeliness combined with dignity.

Although Rebhun had imitators, no other sixteenth-century dramatist rose to such a height; in most of the longer plays (the Carnival play meanwhile retaining tenaciously its one-act anecdotal character) the division into acts is purely mechanical and rarely corresponds to any break in the organic structure. This applies also to Hans Sachs (1494–1576), the master-cobbler, mastersinger, and master of ceremonies of the Carnival play in Nuremberg. He was probably stimulated to his more ambitious dramatic efforts by witnessing academic entertainments in his native town. He recognized no virtue in the five-act play as distinct from the two-, seven- or eleven-act play, and frequently begins his new act precisely where the previous one left off. His four-beat doggerel verse contrasts oddly with the attempted dignity of many of his productions. But to Hans Sachs belongs the honour of having instituted the first German theatre building. In 1550 he took over the Marthakirche, disused since Nuremberg had adopted Protestantism. There has been much speculation as to the detailed arrangement of his stage. It was certainly a simple one. Curtains with slits screened the sides and back; visible steps led from the floor-level to the sides, hidden steps to the back; there was a floor trap, and a pulpit and existing steps may have been incorporated. Isolated features such as doors were probably of painted wood. Incidental properties were brought on to the stage and removed by the characters in the course of the play. It should be noted that here, as in the case of School Drama, the audience sat facing the stage, and not on three sides of it. As Hans Sachs staged his own plays, his methods, ascertainable to some extent from his stage directions, are of interest. In the Carnival play, which he purged of indecency without abating a jot of its fun, the acting must have been fairly realistic. Not so in the serious plays. Here he could hardly follow the example of the School Drama, which laid its principal emphasis on delivery and facial expression, and so probably fell back on the stylized gestures of the old religious plays. As his stage was small, mass scenes must have been resolved into single incidents. In the case of persons of exalted rank the costume seems to have been traditional, while the lesser characters wore their ordinary garments. Hans Sachs clearly gave some training to his actors but they can in no sense be regarded as professionals.

Thus by the 1580s German drama was gropingly making headway, hampered by tradition. There is evidence that by slightly raising a portion of the stage and using a partition with an exit to a lower level, interior scenes were made practicable alongside the usual scenes in public places; there were other experiments too. In the *Comedi vom Crocodilstechen* (*c.* 1596) a stone crocodile in effigy on a wall scares the beholders, and sets the whole of Nuremberg, including authentic notabilities, by the ears. If this racy little satire was actually performed, it must have necessitated quite elaborate scenery. Apart from its personal element, it is well in the Hans Sachs tradition. It is a Carnival play in two parts, though the use of the term *comedi* implies that the earlier name was being dropped.

The real quickening of dramatic life in Germany came, however, from the English Comedians whose first performances of plays in Germany under Robert Browne are recorded in 1592. Many German princes, among them Heinrich Julius, Duke of Brunswick, engaged these strolling players for periods varying in length, and undertook their remuneration and lodging. Otherwise, for performances in towns, permission had to be obtained from the authorities, usually after much bargaining as to the price to be charged for entrance and seats. Town halls, school halls, fencing grounds, and, as a last resort, inn yards were hired. The players carried all their apparatus with them, so the scenery must have been modest; but their costumes were colourful and picturesque, and their devices manifold. The characteristic features of their Shakespearian stage, which had to be constructed locally, were the projecting apron stage, the space to the rear which could be used for interior scenes, and, when practicable, the gallery above either for the

musicians or for balcony and window scenes. This clearly gave a stage which had more possibilities than that used by Hans Sachs. Their repertory, in which most of the Elizabethan dramatists were represented, is characterized by the complete absence of the moralizing tendency so prevalent in contemporary German drama, and by the element of excitement it provided, translated into more energized dramatic form. The actors had quickly learned Low German, which they used for comic interludes, and were soon acting in German entirely, helped by local men who gradually took over the whole concern. The original companies were small, which meant that doubling was frequent and crowd scenes had to be cut, but the vivid acting of these professionals, masters of gesture and facial expression, supported by superb fooling, expert dancing, fencing, and acrobatics, carried the day. Sackville evolved Jan Bouschet (John Posset), who has all the characteristics of the later sixteenth-century *Narr*. He was by no means squeamish, got plenty of humour out of linguistic misunderstandings, and was a master of repartee; he is always commenting on or parodying the main action, or taking part in it with exaggerated zeal. Though a secondary character he doubtless held the stage and was given free rein to improvise. Similar types were created by other leading actors—Hans Stockfisch by John Spencer, Pickelherring by Robert Reynolds—and eventually the specifically German Hanswurst or Kasperle came into being, with his likeable clumsy ingenuousness. The vivaciousness and self-assurance of these English players, enhanced by the practice of improvisation which had reached England with the *commedia dell'arte*, raised the standard of acting in Germany for all time.

Clearly German authors could no longer afford to ignore this new importation. In the south Sachs still had a great following, and Jakob Ayrer (*c.* 1543–1605), his successor, retained much of his manner, including the doggerel verse and the old verbosity; but several of his subjects are of English origin, and a certain increase in pace shows that he had profited by the visits of the English Comedians to his native town from 1593 onwards. The English fool, recognizable under his many disguises by his first name of Jan, appears in a number of the longer plays, and is even the hero of a few Carnival sketches. Although Ayrer's actors were amateurs, he aimed at big spectacular effects. He learned many tricks of the trade from the English Comedians, and his stage must have been of a fair size to accommodate his large casts.

Heinrich Julius of Brunswick (1564–1613), reigning Duke from 1589 till his death, was less influenced by tradition than Ayrer. He wrote to supply his English company with plays, and adopted their prose form and manner of staging. Like them, he shrank from no horror.

Given the popularity of the English Comedians, and the slow progress of the Renaissance in Germany owing to the Reformation and the strife of religious wars, it is not surprising that the general trend of drama about 1600 was towards noisy hilarity or gory sensationalism. It was not until the turn of the century that comparison with the achievements of other countries opened the eyes of patriots to the backwardness of the German stage.

3. THE SEVENTEENTH CENTURY. The opening years of the century, however, even before the outbreak of war in 1618, were a period of growing disintegration in which nothing of value could flourish. The well-meant efforts of numerous literary societies modelled on the *Accademia della Crusca* were unavailing until a short handbook of poetics by Martin Opitz (1597–1639) bade the budding poet look to the classics, France, and Italy for guidance. His almost unchallenged authority resulted in a complete break with national tradition, and an academic literature, smooth, not ungraceful at times, but devoid of all life and action. His translations from Seneca into monotonous, if stately, alexandrines awakened no echo. Once again the element of passion was lacking, and the genre primarily affected was the lyric. Towards the middle of the seventeenth century, however, under the stress of suffering and religious perplexity, the more highly coloured exuberance of the Italian *Seicento* gained ground in Germany, mainly through the influence of the Jesuit Counter-Reformation. It produced a rhetorical style, expressive of pent-up emotion controlled by rationalistic stoicism, and this baroque mentality, as it may be termed, whatever its merits or demerits, produced in its turn German tragedy.

A taste for the serious plays of Andreas Gryphius (1616–64), the chief dramatist of this time, needs to be acquired, yet they are epoch-making and reveal an inner life of great depth. In five usually well-balanced acts, separated by allegorical lyrical choruses, they relate the clash of imperious desires and stoic endurance. They deserve respect as the first literary German dramas, however much they may try the patience of the modern reader by their sustained loftiness of language, by pages of stichomythia, and by the all too rhythmic ebb and flow of the rhymed alexandrines. Although a staunch Protestant, Gryphius owes much to the Jesuit productions, as well as to performances of plays by Corneille and others which he witnessed during his travels from 1644–6, while a double comedy of intrigue, in which four scenes of a musical play of Italian flavour alternate with four richly comic prose scenes in Low German, prove that he had had contact with the strolling players; this is even more noticeable in two other comedies closely allied to the popular repertory in form and subject-matter, though distinguished by their well-pointed dialogue.

Gryphius is the first German dramatist to handle his material with conscious artistry. He wrote at a time when high and low, after the strain of war, craved entertainment as never before. Yet—and this is the tragic element in his career—there was no permanent theatre in which his plays could be given to the public,

and only sporadic performances, mostly by schoolboys, are recorded.

There were at this time three main types of theatrical performances in Germany, though no very sharp line of demarcation can be drawn between them, since their conditions were governed by circumstances. At the lower end of the scale the strolling players struggled on, being rapidly eclipsed by their more moneyed rivals, the Court opera and operetta, and the Jesuit school productions. Their decline is indicated by the significant fact that the middle of the seventeenth century saw the managers resorting to marionettes. The most splendid productions of the day were those at the Courts. Here the Italian machines, and scenic devices painted by famous artists, were much in favour. Of almost equal importance were the Jesuit school plays, mostly given in Latin, and forming part of the regular educational curriculum. Apart from religious propaganda they were considered useful for training in deportment and articulation for public occasions. No efforts were spared to create powerful effects. The austere Terence-stage no longer sufficed and was replaced by a deep stage divided into three sections by curtains, sometimes painted, or by shutter-like flats carrying painted scenery, and moved on ropes. The full depth of the stage was used for important scenes which demanded elaborate settings; the two front sections allowed the use of a restricted number of properties, while the foremost section was used for un-defined localities and the less important scenes. A front curtain was not in regular use. The Protestant School Drama, also active, could not allow itself to be entirely outshone by its Catholic rivals, but it evinced greater sobriety, both by necessity and on purpose. It was for the latter stage that Gryphius's plays were written.

With the increased interest in the past and in other countries characteristic of this age, costumes were more carefully differentiated, and lighting effects were freely used. The prevalent martyr-plays demanded flaming stakes, descending clouds, and so on. Opera was even more exacting. Music, especially vocal music, was then of a high standard, and was freely used, even outside opera, for choruses and arias supported by instrumentalists. Gryphius, avoiding in his tragedies the ultra-rhetorical gestures of the Jesuits, appears to have aimed at as much expressiveness as was consistent with dignity. Comedy allowed of more realistic acting. Women now appeared in opera, and in a few strolling companies. Generally speaking the aim of the theatre in the seventeenth century was to create an illusion as far removed as possible from drab reality.

The baroque drama proper reached its peak in the work of Daniel Caspar von Lohenstein (1635–83) and his imitators. His *Cleopatra* (1661) and *Sophonisbe* (pub. 1680) have theatrical qualities, but their bombastic language, overburdened with far-fetched similes and interlarded with erudite references, covers no depth. It is not surprising to find towards the close of the century a sharp reversal of taste in the direction of realism on the one hand and simplicity on the other.

The former tendency is manifest in the productions of Christian Weise (1642–1708), headmaster of a large school at Zittau. He is the author of a prodigious number of lengthy plays with enormous casts, written for his pupils, in which all the characters, whether historical, biblical, fanciful, or farcical, are made to speak in the same vein of home-spun prose. His *Böse Catherina* (undated) is a crude version of the main plot in Shakespeare's *Taming of the Shrew*. Weise used a simple stage, and readily admitted the fool into his plays. In place of declamation he demanded clear delivery and individualized characterization.

The second tendency is marked by an increasing number of translations and adaptations from French classical drama, and culminates in the plays of Gottsched in the following century. It is first revealed in the work of Johannes Velten (1640–92), who strove to improve the status of actors by raising their standard of living, both social and moral, and to educate them and the public by the performance of plays derived from French classical drama. He wanted to do away with improvisation and to make the play an artistic entity, and he insisted that female parts should be played by women. Like many such attempts made without sufficient financial backing, Velten's failed, and he had to turn again to the popular plays (see HAUPT- UND STAATSAKTIONEN) to replenish his coffers. Nevertheless in the last decade of the century French classical tragedies were performed at the Court of Brunswick in imitation of the Parisian style.

4. THE EIGHTEENTH CENTURY. The seventeenth century had seen the emergence of the professional actor whose improvisations invaded the domain of the dramatist; in contrast the eighteenth century sees the dramatist reinstated, and an advance made towards the establishment of the German theatre on a permanent basis. The theatre formed only part of the vast programme in which Johann Christoph Gottsched (1700–66) joined forces with the philosopher Wolff and other advocates of enlightenment in their endeavours to educate the German public. In the 1720s he had launched some periodicals on English models, and when in 1730 he issued his *Critische Dichtkunst* he had every reason to think himself the dictator of German letters. A thoroughgoing rationalist, he saw salvation only in the application of reason—in his case a synonym for common sense. His bugbears were the disorderly popular plays with their improvisations, their Hanswurst, and their rowdy fooling. Boileau was his lodestar and the French theatre with its decorum and its easily formulated rules his ideal. French actors were at that time much in favour with all the emulators of Versailles at petty German Courts, and in Berlin, where Voltaire had brought in a French company for Frederick the Great. Owing to their detachment from Paris these actors were largely

uninfluenced by the more natural style of acting instituted by Molière, and adhered to the declamation suitable to the works of Corneille.

The German theatre as Gottsched found it was undoubtedly in a poor way. The public was dazzled by the splendour of opera, and its taste vitiated by crude dramatic fare. In the absence of satisfactory German plays, Gottsched, assisted by his wife, tried to fill the gap with works in the French classical style, both translations and original plays, all written in sober prosaic alexandrines. Good fortune brought him into contact with the best theatrical company of his day—that of Caroline Neuber (1697–1760)—'die Neuberin', as she was called. Their alliance dates from 1727, when her company was playing during the Leipzig fair, and was strengthened by a later visit to Strasbourg, where the actress had the opportunity of studying the work of a French company. She was greatly impressed by their style, and resolved to emulate it—a decision which fitted in well with Gottsched's reforms. It was, however, not an easy task to convert the largely mercantile public of Leipzig to highbrow drama; her temporary success was due partly to Gottsched's authority, partly to the regard in which all things French were held at that time, but largely to her own vivacious charm. The collaboration could not, however, last, for Gottsched was a stickler for detail, Caroline Neuber a temperamental woman with a good sense of theatre and a desperate need of funds. Her famous enactment of Harlequin's banishment from the stage was not so much a tribute to Gottsched as a thrust at an inconvenient rival—the harlequin-player Müller; she had the audacity to reject Frau Gottsched's translation of Voltaire's *Alzire* for one less polished but more lively; they bickered over the costumes in *Der sterbende Cato* (1732)—in brief, the rift between them was inevitable. She came to Leipzig again in 1746 and was heartened by the enthusiasm of the young Lessing, but he had as yet neither fame nor influence, and with the passing of time her star waned. It must, however, be credited to her that in combining French stateliness with German emotion she had inaugurated a new era in German acting.

Gottsched found compensation for her loss in the companies of Heinrich Koch (1703–75) and Johann Schönemann (1704–82), both of whom had worked under Caroline Neuber, but his day too was over. By 1740 his overbearing arrogance had alienated even his own Leipzig followers, and his Zurich opponents were acclaiming the superiority of English imaginative poetry. The most gifted of his disciples, Johann Elias Schlegel (1719–49), cautiously compared *Julius Caesar*, recently translated into German and condemned by Gottsched as a wretched thing, with the work of Andreas Gryphius, and while conceding all the 'faults' of Shakespeare's play, firmly declared the latter to be superior in character-drawing. A new star had arisen on the horizon, destined to eclipse Gottsched's life-work. Lessing's oft-quoted remark that it would have been better if Gottsched had never meddled with the German theatre need not be accepted nowadays. The discipline he imposed was necessary and salutary, and first induced in the German public some recognition of artistic form, and if Schlegel later urged that the theatre should be regarded as a civic institution, his high conception of its value may ultimately be traced back to the influence of Gottsched. How firmly the latter had impressed himself on the German theatre may be gauged by the fact that Schlegel himself in his plays adhered strictly to Gottsched's ideal of French classical drama, and also by the violence with which Lessing, Herder, and others attacked it.

Schlegel's comedies are pleasant; his tragedies are remarkable chiefly for the fact that several, such as *Hermann* (1743), deal with episodes from German history. This vein was also exploited by the poet Klopstock, who celebrated Hermann and his victory over Quintilius Varus in A.D. 9, and his struggle against disunion among his own people, in a trilogy (1769–87) in the bardic, that is Ossianic, style. Written in rhythmic prose of studied simplicity, interspersed with lyrical choruses, these richly emotional scenes lack dramatic life, but the theme is symptomatic of a rising national consciousness.

Though Gottsched had all unsuspectingly signed his own death-warrant in damning *Julius Caesar*, Shakespeare was neither the first nor the only factor which militated against the stilted heroes and heroines of French origin; the play-going public was being further deflected from them by the converging streams of the *comédie larmoyante*, the *drame sérieux*, and the domestic tragedy, in all of which a strong middle-class element was asserting itself. In the domestic tragedy the moralizing sentimentality of Richardson's novels, then very popular in Germany, fused with the sterner accents of Lillo's *London Merchant* to produce, in the hands of Lessing, Schiller, and others, a type of drama truly German in character, and of vivid actuality. In all these plays verse gives way to prose.

The first milestone on this journey was the *Miss Sara Sampson* (1755) of Gotthold Ephraim Lessing (1729–81), which drew many tears, much to the satisfaction of the author, and had many equally tearful successors. Lessing himself made no further concession to Richardsonian soulfulness, and when he later returned to this genre with *Emilia Galotti* (1772) he imbued it with a far greater robustness. Sentimentality has vanished, and the main emphasis falls on the difference of outlook between the licentious despot and the commoner. If Emilia chooses to die for fear of her own weakness, and if the libertine is punished only by remorse, we may still see in Lessing, not indeed a revolutionary, but none the less an audacious critic of contemporary social conditions. Certain characters in this play, the stern, upright father, the more worldly-minded mother, the virtuous daughter, the high-born seducer, and the dis-

carded mistress, set the pattern for this type of tragedy until our own day.

Between *Miss Sara Sampson* and *Emilia Galotti* appeared *Minna von Barnhelm* (1767), a comedy in which laughter results from humour rather than from ridicule, and in which middle classes are made to inspire affection and respect. For the first time in German drama the characters are truly three-dimensional, and German to the core. The play is new also in that it deals with a topical subject, the aftermath of the Seven Years War.

Lessing's last play, *Nathan der Weise* (1779), is the first to voice the great humanitarian message of this epoch, and fitly ushers in the blank-verse form.

As a dramatic critic Lessing demolished Gottsched and all he stood for in his *Briefe die neueste Litteratur betreffend* (1759), when he declared Shakespeare to be essentially nearer to the ancients than Corneille, in spite of the latter's classical form, and more likely to kindle indigenous talent. Nevertheless, in his *Hamburgische Dramaturgie* (1767–8) he seeks only to rid German drama of outworn conventions, and not to substitute for it the Shakespearian form, the inner scaffolding of which he does not seem to have understood. He insists on close logical linking of every scene, so much so that his *Emilia Galotti* drew from a Romantic critic the witty criticism: 'An excellent example of dramatic algebra.'

Comments on acting appear only in the earlier sections, but they are enough to show that he was a connoisseur, and could have given helpful advice. He sought grace and dignity rather than statuesque stylization, expressiveness rather than naturalism. Here as elsewhere the law of beauty must not be transgressed. Lessing believed with Riccoboni that the actor must never be carried away by his part, and also that the simulation of emotion may engender enough feeling to give warmth to the performance.

From the time of Caroline Neuber until the late 1760s the German theatre presents in its development a confused picture of companies formed, broken up, and reshuffled, all homeless, all dependent on the whim of the public or a patron, all wandering incessantly from Court to town, and town to Court, mostly in Germany but with excursions abroad to Zurich, Vienna, Russia. Entertaining glimpses of this way of life may be gained from the autobiographies of the actors Brandes and Iffland, or from Goethe's *Wilhelm Meister*. There were bitter feuds among the actors, but also much healthy emulation, and the standard of acting was continually being raised. After Schönemann and Koch, who mainly carried on the work of Caroline Neuber, came a number of eminent actors who in the course of the century brought the German theatre to the front rank of European art.

Konrad Ekhof (1720–78) was successful in overcoming the tendency to declamation imported from France, and by 1767 he had acquired a natural style which delighted Lessing. To Ekhof falls the honour of having founded the first academy of acting in Germany, in 1757, thus raising his calling to the status of a profession. The programme included lectures, discussions and analyses of plays to be performed. Guiding principles were laid down to ensure high standards, collaboration between actors, and social recognition. Ekhof laboured unceasingly for this, and shortly before his death was busy with a scheme of pensions and insurances for actors. What he accomplished may be measured by the fact that while in 1692 a priest refused the sacrament to Velten because he was a comedian, Ekhof was accorded something resembling a public funeral.

Konrad Ackermann (1710–71) deserves a place in the history of the German stage because he first sought to establish in Germany a 'national' theatre, one, that is, that eschewed private, profit-making ownership, and set itself a high standard of plays and productions. In 1765 Ackermann settled in Hamburg which, on account of its active literary life and its contact with English letters, was rapidly outstripping Leipzig, formerly the intellectual centre of Germany. Here, prompted by his own needs and by the recent posthumous publication of Schlegel's thoughts on the theatre, he sought to establish a permanent playhouse, backed by a number of prominent business men and notabilities of the town. Only plays of repute were to be performed, preferably by German writers. Ballet, hitherto a sure source of revenue, was to be curtailed. Lessing, foremost critic and playwright of the day, was to be the mouthpiece of the new order, and in support of it a certain F. L. Löwen wrote the first history of the German theatre.

Much of this ambitious programme went unrealized. Ackermann was not a good business man and, disheartened by numerous cabals and lack of public appreciation, soon lost interest; his second-in-command, the aforesaid Löwen, had no control over the actors. The repertory proved inadequate, ballet inevitably reappeared, and Lessing, having failed to enlist general interest in the art of drama, gave up the attempt, and in his last Hamburg article of 4 April 1768 scoffed at the naïve idea of giving the Germans a national theatre when they were not yet a nation. Nevertheless the idea lived on and bore fruit in Gotha, Mannheim, and Vienna, though not under municipal patronage.

It was at Gotha that the great actor August Wilhelm Iffland (1759–1814) got his first serious training for the stage. A group of writers, musicians, and connoisseurs had gathered there at the Court of Duke Ludwig Ernst, a man of taste and a patron of the arts. In 1774 a fire gutted the Weimar theatre where a company which included Ekhof and other actors of repute was then installed under Abel Seyler (1730–1801), and they were invited to Gotha, where they gave great satisfaction. The actor-dramatist Johann Christian Brandes (1735–99), developing the lyrical element introduced into German drama by Klopstock and intensified by the influence of Rousseau's *Pygmalion*,

devised the monodrama, incidentally creating effective parts for his wife. For some five years these short *tours de force*, useful because with ballet they eked out the then customary triple bill, had an immense vogue. Libretti were provided for them by many leading writers, including F. W. Gotter, one of the outstanding literary men of Gotha. The fame of the theatre spread abroad, and there was general consternation when Seyler announced that he was going permanently to Dresden. At this point the composer Johann Friedrich Reichardt (1752–1814), an able schemer, suggested to the Duke that a 'national' theatre should be formed under his royal patronage, independent of private enterprise. Reichardt succeeded in detaching some of Seyler's company, and with Ekhof as his partner became managing director of the concern. This second 'national' theatre aroused much interest at first, Reichardt's *Theaterkalender* was widely read, and the introduction of a pension scheme was felt to meet a great need among actors. After two years, however, enthusiasm died down. The somewhat conservative repertory—only two of the least stormy of the *Sturm und Drang* plays were given—quarrels between the management and the actors, the death of Ekhof in 1778, and the danger inherent in a repertory company playing continuously to the same limited public, all combined to wreck the scheme, and in 1779 the theatre closed.

Iffland, who had done excellent work at Gotha, and two of his companions there, Heinrich Beck (1760–1803) and Johann David Beil (1754–94), were engaged by Count Dalberg to go to Mannheim, then embarking on the third German 'national' theatre. The Duke of the Palatinate, having succeeded in 1778 to the kingdom of Bavaria, was obliged to remove his court to Munich, and, by way of compensation to his Mannheim subjects, had decided to equip a theatre for them under the direction of Dalberg. It was a happy choice, for the Count was a man of culture, energy, and resource. For two years the actual work of production was in the hands of Seyler, but in 1781 Dalberg himself took over, and the theatre forged ahead. Some memorable performances by Schröder in 1780 established Shakespeare in the repertory, and the theatre opened its doors to the younger generation. In 1781 *Die Räuber* by Friedrich Schiller (1759–1805), its turbulence somewhat toned down but its vitality unimpaired, was staged there. There was no lack of variety. Iffland, by his writing and acting in the genre, established the domestic drama, while Dalberg leaned to the polished French style, which accounts somewhat for the uncongenial atmosphere the young Schiller found there.

A close rival to these 'national' theatres was to be found in Vienna, where serious drama had hitherto waged a losing battle against French and Italian players, ballet and, last but not least, against the local type of farce, raised to a great height of popularity by Joseph Anton Stranitzky (1676–1726). In the hope of improving popular taste Maria Theresa instituted the first public censor of the theatre, and in 1776 the Emperor Joseph II dismissed the foreign actors and dancers and established the Hofburgtheater to encourage 'regular drama of improving tenor', such as the work of Cornelius von Ayrenhoff (1733–1819). He committed the theatre to the expert guidance of Joseph von Sonnenfels (1733–1817), and made its welfare his personal concern. But the great days of the Hofburgtheater were not yet. The democratic method of control broke down; the change to highbrow fare had been too sudden, and Italian opera and ballet soon crept back. In 1781 the Leopoldstädter Theater began its joyous career, uniting actors and audiences in hilarious burlesque and delicate fantasy. Gems like Mozart's 'Die Zauberflöte' were among its productions.

Friedrich Ludwig Schröder (1744–1816), mentioned above in connexion with the Mannheim theatre, is important in the history of German drama as the manager who first established Shakespeare in Germany. He alone was an actor of sufficient calibre to undertake such parts as Lear, Othello, and Richard III. Herder, an earlier admirer of Shakespeare, had not wished to see him acted, and indeed the German stage at that time was not ready for him. Some attempts had been made to force *Hamlet* or *Romeo and Juliet* into the prevailing mould, but it was not until the *Götz von Berlichingen* (1773) of Johann Wolfgang Goethe (1749–1832) had broken the barriers of the 'regular' play that Shakespeare could be acted and appreciated. Schröder, who had seen *Hamlet* in Austria, though accommodated *à la viennoise*, took the bold step of putting it on for an astonished Hamburg audience in 1776. It was much adapted, Hamlet being allowed to survive, as was Cordelia in a later version of *King Lear*, but an initial success had been gained, and other German theatres followed it up.

By now the *Sturm und Drang* movement, unleashed as far as drama was concerned by *Götz von Berlichingen*, was in full swing. The boldness with which the characters are sketched, their wide range, the utter disregard of the Unities, the historical perspective, all proclaim the influence of Shakespeare. In this picture of the sixteenth century, 'natural man', hearty, healthy, staunch, stands out against the encroachment of civilization and its shams, while in Schiller's *Die Räuber* (1781) and *Kabale und Liebe* (1784), which close the movement, the author challenges the perverted social order of his day. The Faust legend is dramatized no less than three times, proof that the divine order is no longer accepted submissively. The younger generation, resentful of the tyranny of reason over aspiration and fervent ardour, rebels against regimentation and restraint. The tragic implications of rebellion—inescapable guilt and its retribution—are squarely faced, and it may be said that a new sense of tragedy is dawning, that of the tragedy inherent in the march of progress.

In many of these productions the poetic licence of Shakespeare is outdistanced, and even where the form is not irregular, the quickened pace sweeps the audience into a different world. In short, vivid scenes the action is spotlighted, or a mood reflected. Reinhold Lenz (1751–92) uses this technique with good effect in order to stress successive aspects of whatever evil he happens to be attacking in such plays as *Der Hofmeister* (1774) and *Die Soldaten* (1776). The break with classicism is complete, and it is obvious that the informality, even slovenliness, of the language called for increased realism in acting. An incidental change brought about in theatres by *Götz von Berlichingen* and the historical dramas (see RITTERDRAMA) which followed it was the acquisition by a number of companies of wardrobes of medieval costumes, which led to a greater use of the picturesque element in production.

By the time of the French Revolution the literary upheaval in Germany had spent itself. In *Egmont* (1789) Goethe abandoned the practice of scrappy scenes and rough-hewn language, and having achieved serenity in Italy, and a love of artistic shapeliness, returned in *Iphigenie* (1787) and *Tasso* (1790) to a regular form and blank verse of exquisite mellowness. Schiller, still avid for freedom, sought it now in the realm of thought and conscience, and gave it expression in verse even more vibrant than Goethe's. *Don Carlos* (1787), structurally the weakest of Schiller's plays owing to the shifting of emphasis from personal suffering to political and humanitarian issues, nevertheless heralds a change of outlook. During the subsequent ten years, a period of ill health but concentrated study, Schiller gained objectivity and aesthetic insight. His friendship with Goethe, which began in 1794, inaugurated a decade of intensive production. The year 1799 saw the completion of *Wallenstein*, a trilogy in which the turmoil of the Thirty Years War is woven into a lucid pattern. *Maria Stuart* (1800) followed, equally well knit, and with an impressive array of finely contrasted personalities. Here, for the first time, is explored the theme of the soul freed by the acceptance of suffering. It appears again in the romanticized setting of *Die Jungfrau von Orleans* (1802), the most operatic of Schiller's plays, and in *Die Braut von Messina* (1803), the closest approximation of the age to the form of ancient drama. Fate, or Nemesis, assails a princely house; two hostile brothers are drawn to the same woman, who, too late to avert catastrophe, is discovered to be their sister; death is the penalty of fratricide. In this distillation of human passions, written in chiselled verse with superb lyrical choruses, Schiller's characteristic conception of tragedy is clearly portrayed; adverse fate is seen as a steppingstone to sublimation, leaving a final sense of victory in defeat. His last completed play, *Wilhelm Tell* (1804), is not a tragedy, but for sheer stagecraft it surpasses its predecessors. This tale of the liberation of the Swiss cantons from the Austrian yoke by unity and singleness of purpose is told with dignified simplicity, in language which has cast off the last trammels of rhetoric.

The 'classical' dramas of Goethe, unlike Schiller's clarion calls, make an intimate and personal appeal. *Iphigenie* is bathed in a cool and tranquillizing light; in *Tasso* the characters quiver at a touch. Here staging can add little, and rarely satisfies, while Schiller's personages gain when the actor fills them out. It was Iffland, ably assisted by Johann Ferdinand Fleck (1757–1801), who first presented Schiller's later work to the public beyond Weimar. In the 1790s the campaign against the French revolutionaries had caused much disorganization in the Mannheim theatre. Iffland, then in charge of production, went on tour. In 1796 he appeared with great success in Berlin, until then much in the rear of theatrical development, and was promptly appointed director, by royal decree, of a National Theatre, the culminating honour of his career. The public flocked to his productions, and a better building had to be provided, more worthy of Schiller's masterpieces. During the French occupation Iffland, bereft of his state subsidy, had to adapt his repertory to the demands of the authorities, but loyalty led him to refuse a flattering summons to Vienna. The return of the royal family assured him once again of financial support, and music and ballet, as well as drama, were entrusted to his care. Overwork and the hostility of the rising Romantic generation undermined his health, and he died in harness in 1814.

In the meantime an experiment of great importance and interest was being carried out in Weimar. Goethe's dramatic work of the 1790s and after, though dealing with problems made actual by the French Revolution, is highly stylized; the characters have paled to symbols. This development finds its parallel in his work as director of the Weimar theatre. When in 1792 Goethe was entrusted by the Grand Duke with the entire responsibility for the Weimar Court theatre, he went to work with his usual thoroughness and circumspection. By this time the naturalism fostered by the domestic conversation-piece and the *Sturm und Drang* plays had become rampant among actors, to the exclusion of all else. Goethe regarded this as a degradation of the theatre, and resolved to combat it with the same determination with which he and Schiller opposed all pandering to the public taste in the literary sphere. The worst offender in both respects was August von Kotzebue (1761–1819), a prolific writer and master of stage effect, whose clever but shallow and often risqué plays outshone their own in public favour. He was a great thorn in Goethe's flesh, as his works had perforce to be included in the Weimar repertory to swell the box-office takings.

As the years went by Goethe's horror of realism increased. The Greece of Sophocles became his mental refuge. His essay *Shakespeare und kein Ende* (1813) relegated Shakespeare from the visual scene to the realm of the inner eye. He sought to inculcate in his actors a technique of dignified gesture, differing from the French style prevalent at the beginning of the century by the absence of rhetorical declamation. Already in 1785 J. J. Engel, in his treatise *Ideen zu einer Mimik*, had defined gesture as 'music for the eye', and had worked out elaborate patterns of movements conveying every shade and grade of emotion without transgressing the laws of beauty. Engel, however, had no belief in verse drama, and Goethe could only use him as a starting-point. The actors, speaking in cadenced phrasing, were not allowed to turn away from the spectator, nor to diverge from carefully prescribed groupings, nor to attract undue attention to themselves. Thus an artistic ensemble for the first time made the prime purpose of dramatic presentation, and it is much to be regretted that the tendency to artificiality increased after Schiller's death, so that the rugged humour of such a play as Kleist's *Der zerbrochene Krug* was smoothed out. Goethe's aim, however, if not the manner of its execution, commands respect, and the Weimar tradition was taken to Berlin by Pius Alexander Wolff (1782–1828), the most accomplished actor of this school.

5. THE NINETEENTH CENTURY. The achievement of the eighteenth century in the German theatre had been the employment, in the absence of centralization in the country, of drama as one of the main vehicles of culture, and as a potentially great factor in social and literary life. On the other hand, the profession of acting was still hampered by insecurity and lack of funds, with all their attendant evils, and there was a disquieting cleavage between the intellectual leaders and the general public. Nor could the Romantic School, which arose in about 1798, be looked to to bridge the gap. The highly intellectual and individualistic outlook of its writers was not favourable to drama. The Schlegels, Arnim, Brentano, Fouqué, Eichendorff, produced no dramatic work of lasting value; the recurring features of their work are the frequent use of the supernatural, the mythical, and the mysterious, the accentuation of abnormality and indefiniteness of form. The ironical twist which Ludwig Tieck (1773–1853) gave to his dramatized folk-tales robbed them of their vigour, while the not unattractive church-window transparency of his more ambitious medieval plays denied to his characters the attributes of flesh and blood. His intensive study of Elizabethan drama bore no dramatic fruit, though his public readings from Shakespeare's plays probably did more than all the Romantic theorizing to make the latter's genius appreciated in Germany. As critical adviser to the Dresden theatre Tieck stimulated artistic endeavour as far as the prevailing conditions would allow, though a performance of *A Midsummer Night's Dream* on a specially constructed Shakespearian stage, as Tieck imagined it to have been, remained an isolated experiment.

Meanwhile the authors of the so-called Fate Dramas—Zacharias Werner (1768–1823) with his one-act tragedy *Der vierundzwanzigste Februar* (1809), Adolf Müllner (1774–1829) with *Der neunundzwanzigste Februar* (1812) and the successful *Die Schuld* (1816), and the young Grillparzer with *Die Ahnfrau* (1817)—wallowed in morbid perversions, and turned into sheer malignance the power Schiller had revered in Sophocles. Yet one dramatist of genius did appear—Heinrich von Kleist (1777–1811), who pursued his lonely way determined to unite in his work the grandeur of the fate element in antiquity with Shakespearian character-drama. In *Penthesilea* (1808) the warring impulses in the heroine of the amazon and the woman brought Kleist very near his goal, though the savagery of her passion has no parallel in classical tragedy. In this play, and in his comedy of village life, *Der zerbrochene Krug* (1808), Kleist sought to increase the pace by substituting the ebb and flow of action for the conventional division into acts, an experiment which he later abandoned. His highly nervous temperament led him to create heroes of a like mould, self-willed, excitable, equally capable of collapse or heroism. The supporting characters were of tougher fibre; only in some of his women did he prove that he could use a softer touch. He showed himself a true Romantic in his use of sleep-walking scenes, dreams, and second sight. His masterpiece, *Der Prinz von Homburg* (published in 1821), with its gallery of brilliantly characterized military types, reveals most clearly his gift of individualization with the utmost economy of effort. Kleist's language is terse and pregnant, bursting into vivid imagery at moments of heightened emotion. During his lifetime he failed almost entirely to establish contact with the stage; neither Goethe, averse by nature to tragedy, nor his Romantic contemporaries suspected his quality.

The German theatre in the opening decades of the nineteenth century seemed to be in a state of stagnation. The Napoleonic wars hampered enterprise, and the nation that was soon to rise in arms against the invader could slake its thirst for freedom on nothing more 'actual' than Schiller's plays. After the battle of Waterloo the reactionary Metternich régime, which excluded social, political, and religious subjects from public discussion, reduced the theatre to a mere place of entertainment; importations from France—'well-made' plays by Scribe, Delavigne, and the vaudevillists—and from Denmark—the dramas of Oehlenschlaeger—occupied a considerable place in the repertory. The chief German purveyors of light refreshment were Eduard von Bauernfeld (1802–90) with his conversation pieces, Roderich Benedix (1811–73) with his bourgeois domestic interiors, Ernest Raupach (1784–1852) with plays in the Kotzebue tradition, and Friedrich Halm (1806–71), would-be successor to Schiller. To these must be added such writers of dialect farce as Johann Nepomuk Nestroy (1801–62), master of parody, in Vienna, and Elias Niebergall (1815–43) in Frankfort; and lastly Charlotte Birch-Pfeiffer (1800–68), wholesale purveyor of other people's goods (her *Die Waise von Lowood* of 1856 is based on *Jane Eyre*), who outshone even Bauernfeld in popularity. The only people to rebel against this emasculation of the stage were the politically minded members

of the 'Young Germany' movement, with the result that vigilance in high quarters increased until the troubles of 1848 produced some relaxation. The movement produced at least two dramatists who, without writing masterpieces, showed at any rate vigour and vitality—Christian Dietrich Grabbe (1801–36) and Georg Büchner (1813–37). Both rebels, one by temperament, the other by disillusioned conviction, they have some affinity in form and style to the *Sturm und Drang* writers. Karl Gutzkow (1811–78) and Heinrich Laube (1806–84), also connected with the movement, ventilated their political views in lengthy novels; Gutzkow's plays, except for *Uriel Acosta* (1847), are of little account, but Laube, who later became manager of the Vienna Hofburgtheater, wrote some effective, if not profound, dramas. Their contemporary Gustav Freytag (1816–95) marks the transition from unrest to constructive endeavour on a bourgeois basis, characteristic of the so-called 'Biedermeierzeit'.

If drama in Germany during the inter-revolutionary years was on the whole mediocre, some enterprise is visible in the theatrical field. There was able and even brilliant acting by Ferdinand Esslair (1772–1840) and Ludwig Devrient (1784–1832), but the individual actor still tended to display his powers to the detriment of artistic unity. Moreover, the dispersion of German theatrical companies among many small states meant that only in a few large towns possessing several theatres could they cultivate a style of their own. Tieck's work in Dresden has already been mentioned. In Düsseldorf Karl Immermann (1796–1840) founded a little colony of artistically minded men, convinced of the potential influence of a good theatre. From 1834 to 1837 he was director of the Stadttheater, and provided a number of 'subscription performances' of standard plays, intended to serve as models and show what could be achieved. He laid the main stress on delivery, emulating in this respect Goethe, whose results at Weimar had impressed him, but avoided the latter's exaggerations. The press and the bulk of the public were, however, indifferent to his efforts, and to his intense disappointment his experiment ended in bankruptcy. Certain technical improvements were also made at this time. Scenery was lighter and more easily moved, gas-lighting was introduced after 1830—though Cologne still considered it too dazzling in 1837—and in Berlin, most highly subsidized of the Court theatres, Iffland's successor, Count von Brühl, insisted on greater accuracy than hitherto in historical costume.

By the 1820s Austria, and more particularly Vienna, had definitely come to the fore in matters theatrical. One of Nestroy's main butts was his rival Ferdinand Raimund (1790–1836), who first won popularity through his portrayal of the comic types which evolved from Stranitzky's Hanswurst. He then became manager and finally director of the Leopoldstädter Theater, achieving considerable success with his own plays, which, unlike the customary Viennese farce, were inspired exclusively by folk-lore, traditional allegory, and mother wit. Even when more sophisticated and literary elements crept in, Raimund retained a simplicity and soundness of mind, and a high standard of human conduct, which gave his plays lasting value.

The Vienna Hofburgtheater was also entering upon its most flourishing period at this time, under the able and energetic guidance of Josef Schreyvogel (1768–1832), who had been connected with this and other theatres since 1802, and from 1814 was responsible for the choice of play, casting, and production. He separated the spoken drama from opera, both for finance and personnel, manœuvred standard works past the censor and assured them a permanent place in the repertory, fired his actors with the enthusiasm necessary to ensure artistic execution, and at the same time, by his critical articles, fostered understanding in his audience. He laboured indefatigably to secure the best actors, and struggled on, often in financial difficulties, until in 1832 his outspokenness earned him summary dismissal.

One of Schreyvogel's greatest achievements was the encouragement he gave to the young Franz Grillparzer (1791–1872), who, after an initial excursion into Romantic fate-drama, showed his true powers in classical dramas of great and seemingly effortless beauty—*Sappho* (1819), *Das goldene Vliess* (1822), and *Des Meeres und der Liebe Wellen* (1831). In 1825 he embarked with equal skill and success on historical tragedy in *König Ottokars Glück und Ende*, where a large but finely individualized cast and a complex action are dexterously handled with the minimum of deviation from historical fact. Although the play celebrates the founding of the Hapsburg dynasty and recalls the fall of Napoleon, it lingered in the censor's office for many years. Meanwhile Grillparzer had embarked on *Der Traum ein Leben*, inspired by Calderón's *La vida es sueño*, which bordered on the traditional Austrian fairy-tale drama, and was written in lively trochaics which assisted the nightmare atmosphere. This was produced in 1834, under Schreyvogel's successor. Grillparzer was demanding more and more delicate perception from his public and was on the whole well supported, but when in his deliciously whimsical comedy, *Weh dem, der lügt* (1838), he seemed to be holding the Austrian nobility up to ridicule, the audience loudly manifested its displeasure; whereupon Grillparzer turned his back on the stage and continued to write plays for his own satisfaction only.

The direction of the Vienna Hofburgtheater had now passed to Heinrich Laube, who had an intimate knowledge of the Parisian stage, spared no pains to engage actors of promise, insisted on careful rehearsals, and made the Hofburg productions justly famous for their finish. He still, however, sacrificed the pictorial aspect to the close study of word and character; but adroitness and persistence enabled him to serve at the same time the public desire for entertainment and the cause of higher drama.

More artistic, but less single-minded, was Franz Dingelstedt (1814–81), who in 1851 was appointed director of the Munich theatre. King Max of Bavaria aspired to make Munich the intellectual hub of Germany, and in view of this, and of the industrial exhibition to be held there in 1854, ambitious plans were made. Dingelstedt, having collected actors from all over Germany, certainly made theatre history with his brilliant settings, and the poetic atmosphere of his productions, but aroused much resentment among native talent. An epidemic of cholera brought the enterprise to a sudden close with a heavy deficit, and Dingelstedt left for Weimar. Both there, and later at the Burgtheater, Dingelstedt staged Shakespeare's chronicle plays in the new style with great success.

Richard Wagner (1813–83) belongs mainly to the domain of music, but the texts of his operas, all written by himself, have considerable merit. His works may be regarded as the fulfilment of the Romantic ideal—the perfect fusion of poetry, music, and the pictorial arts. The buried treasures of medieval myth and epic, unearthed during the Romantic period, were fused into a clear-cut action, working up to a sublime close, and imbued with some moral or philosophical idea which ensured their appeal to a modern audience. In his revival of Old High German alliterative verse Wagner skilfully made use of sound and rhythm to convey both thought and mood.

His greatest contemporary in the field of pure drama was Friedrich Hebbel (1813–63), whose first play, *Judith*, was produced in 1840, and his last, *Die Nibelungen*, in 1861. Hebbel's style lacks the mellow clarity of Grillparzer's. It is allusive, syncopated, image-laden, and leaves the reader still searching for motive and implication beneath the words. In this, as in his questioning mind, his sense of the complexity of life, his understanding of women, Hebbel is essentially modern, and Ibsen and many others are greatly in his debt.

Less successful was Hebbel's contemporary, Otto Ludwig (1813–65). His characters, magnificently alive and self-willed, were often unamenable to the demands of dramatic structure; hence his plots tended to become involved and even obscure, and a number of promising first drafts came to nothing. His best play, *Der Erbförster* (1850), is linked by some of its characters to traditional domestic tragedy while anticipating the future in its vigorous realism, as seen in the tricks of speech by which the characters betray themselves.

By the time Hebbel and Ludwig died a great change was coming over Germany. Successful wars had brought her political supremacy, unification had stimulated industrial enterprise and the all too sudden rise in prosperity created extravagant hopes, naïve national self-conceit and rampant materialism. This was poor soil for serious drama. The nation's mentality was expressed in the plays of Ernst von Wildenbruch (1845–1909). An ardent admirer of the Hohenzollerns, and proud of his nation's past, he wrote historical dramas which proved extremely popular, mainly on account of his great gift for effective crowd scenes, racy dialogue, and picturesque lower-class characters. Wildenbruch's work is undoubtedly sincere, and it is to be deplored that he descended at times to sheer claptrap, as in his trilogy on the story of Canossa, *Heinrich und Heinrichs Geschlecht* (1896).

Austria was little touched by these developments, and was mainly preoccupied by the clash between conservative and progressive opinion within the Church. This struggle exercised many minds and inspired the dramatist Ludwig Anzengruber (1839–89). Since 1840 German fiction had drawn new sustenance from peasant life. It was fitting that Vienna, the home of popular drama, should see the first village plays, written by one sprung from village folk. *Der Pfarrer von Kirchfeld* (1870) attacks the burning question of the day with great sincerity. It has the fault of thesis drama, but its author went on to depict peasant life in its comic as well as its tragic aspects. His characters, with their pithy speech, are rooted in their natural surroundings. The healthy outlook and fine moral fibre of these plays make them the most refreshing literary phenomenon of the time. The peasant play became popular. In 1891 a theatre was founded at Schliersee in Bavaria; during the summer months a peasant company played in the village, and in winter went on tour. Karl Schönherr (1869–1943) achieved much success with his Austrian village plays, which have, however, an element of pity derived from Hauptmann's *Die Weber*, and a tendency to sensationalism foreign to Anzengruber.

No dramatist of outstanding merit marked the opening years of the new empire in Germany, but a number of theatrical enterprises deserve mention at a time when the commercial spirit invaded the artistic as well as every other sphere. Duke George II of Saxe-Meiningen (1826–1914), an artist of considerable talent, and a devotee of the theatre, took to designing for his Court company scenery and costumes depicted with the utmost accuracy after exhaustive study. Inspired by the actress Ellen Franz, later his wife, he concentrated not on the acquisition of great actors, but on continuous rehearsal in costume, particularly of crowd and battle scenes, and on silent by-play, in which the leading characters, if not otherwise occupied, were obliged to share. The scene-painter and the stage mechanic, supplied with first-class material, came into their own. The result of all this was that many historical and romantic plays came to life for the first time. The earlier endeavours of von Brühl in Berlin and Dingelstedt in Weimar were combined with a new desire for verisimilitude, and by 1874 the fame of the new company had spread. In that year it took *Julius Caesar* and *As You Like It* to Berlin, and met with unqualified success. Plays by Kleist and Schiller followed, not only in Berlin but in an increasing number of towns in Germany and abroad. In 1878 the company earned many laurels in London. In 1890 the

indefatigable director, Ludwig Chronegk, broke down, and the tours, having accomplished their mission, were discontinued. The greatest actor developed by Meiningen was Albert Bassermann (1867–   ), who later supported Otto Brahm. In course of time the Meiningen players were accused of excessive attention to detail, but there is no doubt that they set an entirely new standard of ensemble playing and pictorial effect, which had great and far-reaching results. The chief difficulty of their method is the necessity for avoiding frequent changes of scenery, and this was not finally overcome until Karl Lautenschläger invented the revolving stage in 1896.

Although in 1876 the opening of the new opera-house at Bayreuth had been hailed as an important event which raised high hopes of artistic progress, by 1883, in Berlin at any rate, there was a feeling of stagnation, intensified by the increasing practice of long runs. The new movement in drama, known as Naturalism, being a movement of revolt, was naturally in bad odour politically and socially. Yet the more thoughtful of the younger generation were shocked by the national complacency and by the misery of the working class under the new industrialism. Ibsen's plays gave further impetus to their discontent. The Deutsches Theater, founded by Adolf L'Arronge and Ludwig Barnay, with the actors Josef Kainz and Agnes Sorma, would have opened its doors to the new dramatists, but there was trouble with the censor, and in 1889 a private company, the Freie Bühne, modelled on Antoine's Théâtre Libre in Paris, came into being under the aegis of the critic Otto Brahm. It had no fixed habitat, and played at matinées only. The campaign opened with Ibsen's *Ghosts*, followed by plays of Tolstoy, Strindberg, and Zola. Anzengruber's *Das vierte Gebot* was the first German play to be performed, but the real manifesto of the new school was *Die Familie Selicke* (1890), by Arno Holz (1863–1929), a sordid picture of mental, moral, and physical decay, in which man appears as the helpless plaything of circumstance. The fame of the movement rests, however, on the work of the young Gerhart Hauptmann (1862–1946). He did not disdain squalor but neither did he seek it. His early plays vibrate with actuality, but the comparative failure of his historical drama, *Florian Geyer* (1895), whose violent and stirring action was not well served by the naturalistic approach, caused him to forsake Naturalism for Symbolism, as in his next play, *Die versunkene Glocke* (1896). His subsequent work, tending sometimes to one style, sometimes to the other, conformed more and more to normal dramatic procedure. It opened up no new avenues, but served to confirm the excellence of his gift for creating characters in the round, and dialogue that rings true.

Hauptmann's chief rival in popularity was Hermann Sudermann (1857–1928), a clever playwright with an unfailing sense of the theatre. His plays reflect the problems of contemporary society from a progressive angle.

His manner is realistic, but submits to no scientific discipline; compared with Hauptmann his situations often appear forced in order to ensure an effect.

The founding of the Freie Bühne was followed, when the need for providing good plays at low prices for the working class was realized, by the Neue Freie Volksbühne in 1890, limited to subscribers who drew lots for their seats, and by the Schillertheater in 1894. In the new drama that was sweeping across Europe Berlin was well to the fore. The Meiningen methods of staging could be adapted to the requirements of Naturalism, provided such conventions as facing the audience, speaking standard German, and so on, were scrapped. The stress laid on the darker side of life and on the endless frailties of human nature demanded from the actor, as from the dramatist, the most minute observation; all self-expression was an offence against the first principles of Naturalism, which demanded the subordination of the actor to his role, and made of the whole play 'a slice of life'.

No artist, however, will long remain satisfied with photography, and by 1900 reaction had set in. The revolt against sordidness came, as might be expected, from Vienna. The pessimism of the naturalistic writers reached Austria, as witness the work of Anton Wildgans (1881–1932), but was repudiated by a group of young, hyper-sensitive impressionists, foremost among them Hugo von Hofmannsthal (1874–1929). His short lyrical plays have a luminous, pensive remoteness which gains little by staging. With 'Elektra' (1909) begins his partnership with the composer Richard Strauss, of which 'Der Rosenkavalier' (1911), that quintessence of old Vienna, is the choicest fruit. For Max Reinhardt he revived the old morality play *Jedermann* (1912), with a few discreet evocations of modern problems. But for Hofmannsthal life spelt weariness. His contemporary Arthur Schnitzler (1862–1931) was never tired of viewing it, particularly in its Viennese aspect, with a discerning but not malevolent eye. His witty one-act sketches, often in series, and his more serious longer plays, have this much in common: they reveal the discrepancy between our motives as we imagine them to be and as they really are. The result can be ludicrous or pathetic, though too slight for tragedy. His brilliant dialogue and light touch give Schnitzler's plays a quality all too rarely found in German comedy.

A further reaction against Naturalism originated in Munich, and is a sign of the gradual ascendance of the southern capital. Frank Wedekind (1864–1918), in flouting the philistine, gave his characters the significance of types rather than individuals, and thus pointed the way to Expressionism. This Bohemian, with his predilection for animal passions, however amoral, and his eye for the grotesque, acted his own heroes, ably supported by Gertrud Eysoldt (1870–   ), with flamboyant irony, in garish settings which suggested the cabaret, that product of modernity which was about to become a serious rival to the theatre. Akin to Wedekind was Karl Sternheim (1878–1943), whose virulent anti-bourgeois satires laid bare the follies and flayed the conditions which led to the war of 1914.

6. THE TWENTIETH CENTURY. The nineteenth century closed in a welter of warring, shallow-rooted tendencies. Expressionism, the revolt from Naturalism, reached its peak during the First World War, and in its German manifestations was at least as extreme as Naturalism had been. Once again Scandinavia, in the person of Strindberg, was the directive force, while from Belgium came the influence of Maeterlinck. Two distinct tendencies may be noted, one leading to intellectual abstraction, the other to emotional concentration. They have in common the desire to render only the vital essence of life, stripped of all accidental accretions, or to show man in relation to cosmic force. In order to do this a new language had to be created, an ejaculatory rhythmic language of bald but explosive statement, dispensing with all but the basic elements of the sentence (*geballter Stil*), and accompanied on the stage by staccato gestures of cubist simplicity. The yearning for a new world order and a new religious orientation is manifest; biblical and classical Greek subjects appear beside the timeless or the ultra-modern.

A pioneer of the movement was Reinhard Sorge (1892–1916), whose *Der Bettler* (written in 1912, but not performed until 1917) reveals the growth and mission of the poet (i.e. the beggar of the title) as seen from within and without. We witness the moulding of the hero by his experiences, his struggles against the powers of darkness, his unflinching resistance to compromise, his emergence into ecstatic certainty. Played on a stage of varied levels, with shifting spotlights, and curtains allowing glimpses into visionary distances, the scenes betray their symbolic meaning.

The leader of the expressionists was Georg Kaiser (1878–1945), whose impressive analysis of self-sacrificing patriotism, *Die Bürger von Calais* (1914), marks the return to energy and will-power in place of the defeatist attitude common to Naturalists and Impressionists alike. His most memorable work is probably *Gas* (in two parts, 1918, 1920), a vision of man mastered by the machine to the point of self-annihilation. In Kaiser the intellect reigns supreme; Ernst Toller (1893–1939) is more lyrical. His *Masse-Mensch* (1920), which shows the pacifist at grips with the multitude, alternates between realistic scenes and cinematographic dream pictures, and was one of the best plays to come out of post-war Germany. A number of other writers deserve mention—Ernst Barlach (1870–1938), the sculptor-poet, in whose *Der tote Tag* (1912) Mother and Son contend in semi-darkness, impelled by a mysterious voice or assuaged by a stranger from the unknown; Max Mell (1882–   ), whose religious plays recapture something of the simplicity and sincerity of the medieval mystery play; Fritz von Unruh (1885–   ), in whose *Ein Geschlecht* (1916) the younger generation accuses its elders with cries of horror and despair; Reinhard Goering (1887–1936), author of plays in free verse; and finally Franz Werfel (1890–1945), Austrian novelist and poet, who grappled with many of the same problems as the expressionists in his powerful symbolic trilogy, *Der Spiegelmensch* (1921), but avoids their extreme mannerisms, and reverts to more normal methods of presentation in his historical *Juarez und Maximilian* (1924).

A further stand against Naturalism was made by writers of classicist or romanticist tendencies, such as Paul Ernst (1866–1933), who returned to the blank-verse tragedy of Schiller and Hebbel; Wilhelm von Scholz (1874–   ), who in polished prose explored the mysteries of psychic interaction; Ernst Hardt (1876–1947), who returned to the Middle Ages for his subjects, infusing into them much modern feeling; and Herbert Eulenberg (1876–   ), who sought to galvanize his audience by a forced cultivation of passion, as in *Anna Walewska* (1899).

This complete revolution in the purpose of dramatic art, this dismissal of any attempt to create an illusion of reality, demanded drastic changes in staging, just as, in their turn, new scenic possibilities affected the dramatist. It is therefore not surprising to find that the salient fact of this period is the emergence of the producer as the most important figure in the theatre, made necessary by changes in theatre management, by mechanical devices, by improved lighting, and by ever-increasing emphasis on the visual aspect. Max Reinhardt (1873–1943) was the first to co-ordinate the producer's functions. He staged plays in circuses, in front of Salzburg Cathedral, and in London's Olympia. At the same time he fostered the intimacy of the small playhouse, where he addressed himself to the connoisseur, and gave to many masterpieces a subtly individualized atmosphere. Among the notable actors who worked for him were Max Pallenberg, Alexander Moissi, and Emil Jannings, while his assistants and disciples were legion.

Reinhardt's success gave an immense impetus to theatrical enterprise in Germany and elsewhere. The most arresting of his emulators were Leopold Jessner (1878–   ), who pursued a more exclusively intellectual line, replacing warmth by reasoned detachment, and made great use of the stairway (*Spieltreppe*) on which the players traced as it were a graph symbolic of the play's action; and Erwin Piscator (1893–   ), who reduced his actors to marionettes, freely mingled stage and screen, and at times approached an almost surrealistic dadaism, effective in ultra-modernistic subjects, but less successful elsewhere.

The time was ripe for a further reaction. Less violently, but quite definitely, the pendulum swung back towards a modified realism with the plays of Carl Zuckmayer (1896–   ), who took his audience into the woods and vineyards and showed them the ordinary folk who live and laugh heartily; with the more sophisticated plays of Bruno Frank (1887–1946), the humour of whose *Sturm im Wasserglas* survived

translation into English and on the screen as *Storm in a Teacup*; and with the mocking wit of Bertolt Brecht (1898–   ), adapter of *The Beggar's Opera* as *Die Dreigroschenoper* (1928), who stands a little apart, with his sharply pointed dialogue interspersed with songs.

With the slump in the early 1930s there swept over Germany a renewed fear of economic disintegration and a general restlessness which brought the Nazi party into power. As early as 1925, by which time the main impulses of Expressionism, Symbolism, Abstractionism, and Impressionism had spent themselves, Herbert Ihering, the dramatic critic, had called for greater actuality in the theatre, and for the re-evocation of the past with an eye to present-day social and political problems. This was but the first step, as the Nazi party were not slow to realize, towards the use of the theatre as a means of political propaganda. Domestic virtues and the self-sacrifice of the individual for the good of the State were themes to be preached. Plays by internationally minded or 'non-Aryan' writers disappeared from the repertory, historical scenes were reconstructed with deliberately calculated political implications. The most obvious manifestation of the new régime was the rapid development of open-air theatres, traceable in many ways to the influence of Reinhardt. Spacious natural sites, often termed *Thingstätten* (places for national festivals), with a background of hilly slopes, woodland trees, or ancient ruins, were utilized for choric dramas of expressionist technique, with specially trained mass choruses exercising an almost hypnotic power over the audience. Against this blatant propaganda, however, must be set the remarkable performances of *Die Nibelungen* and *Götz von Berlichingen* in the castle courtyard at Heidelberg, and of *Faust* in the Römerplatz at Frankfort-on-Main, experiments of unquestionable artistic quality.

Among the more talented of the many who responded to the official demand for suitable dramatic material was Hanns Johst (1890–   ), whose early play *Der Einsame* (1925), based on the life of the poet Grabbe, indicated a return to natural, almost naturalistic, modes of expression, while retaining the expressionist practice of using successive 'pictures' without interlinking. His *Schlageter* (1934), dedicated to Adolf Hitler, celebrated the heroes of German resistance during the French occupation of the Ruhr. It had considerable repercussions, and earned him the Presidency of two important literary societies.

It is to be hoped that when the now shattered theatrical buildings of Germany rise again from the dust a new freedom will be wedded to the high endeavour of the past.   W. E. D.

GHÉON, HENRI (1875–1943), French dramatist, and leader of the modern revival of religious drama in France. His plays, though written after those of Claudel, were performed before them, and were the first to combine the reforms envisaged by Copeau with the expression of a newly awakened Catholicism. The early ones, of which the most important was *Le Pauvre sous l'escalier* (1913), were given at the Théâtre du Vieux-Colombier, but it was not until after the 1914–18 war, during which Ghéon returned to the Church, that he embarked on the work with which he was afterwards associated, the writing and production of plays on religious and biblical themes in provincial parishes, colleges, and schools. Among the many works which he produced for this purpose, running into nearly a hundred, the best-known outside France is *Le Noël sur la place* (1935), which, as *Christmas in the Market Place*, in a translation by Eric Crozier, has several times been given in England. It was originally played by Les Compagnons de Jeux, a semi-amateur company organized in 1932 by Henri Brochet (1898–   ), himself an excellent actor and religious dramatist, to take the place of Ghéon's earlier troupe, Les Compagnons de Notre-Dame. In recent years a number of Ghéon's plays, which combine fine poetry and an excellent theatrical sense with great simplicity and religious feeling, have been given in the smaller theatres of Paris, and, on one occasion, at the Odéon.

GHERARDI. (1) GIOVANNI (*fl.* 1675–?), actor of the *commedia dell'arte*, whose great accomplishment was his imitation of a flute, from which he took the name of Flautino. He joined the company in Paris in 1675, but his misdemeanours caused him to be imprisoned and later expelled. He was the father of (2) EVARISTO (1663–1700), a famous Harlequin, whose professional career was spent entirely in Paris, where he made his début in 1689 in Regnard's *Le Divorce forcé*. He is chiefly remembered now for his collection of plays given by the Italian comedians in Paris.

GHOST GLIDE, another name for the trap first used in *The Corsican Brothers*, by means of which the apparition appeared to drift across the stage while rising slowly from beneath it (see ENGLISH PLAYHOUSE, 2).

GIACOMETTI, PAOLO (1816–82), Italian dramatist, whose plays are of a homely popular type, known as *Teatro da Arena*—a phrase which may be said to cover drama appealing to 'simple minds and honest hearts'. His reputation is widespread in his own country. His best play is probably *La Morte civile* (1861), a dramatization of a social theme, which has as its hero an escaped convict who, unable to return to his wife and daughter, commits suicide.

GIACOSA, GIUSEPPE (1847–1906), Italian dramatist. He was a lawyer, but the success of a one-act comedy in verse, *La Partita a scacchi*, produced in 1871, caused him to abandon a legal career for the theatre. He took up his residence in Milan, and there wrote a number of plays, none of which was very successful until the production in 1890 of *Tristi amori*, a problem play of homely provincial life. *Come le foglie*, first produced in 1900, has been suc-

cessfully given in translation in America and England. Giacosa also wrote a play in French for Sarah Bernhardt, *L'Âme de Challant*, which, in an Italian translation, was given by Eleonora Duse's company in 1898. In collaboration with Luigi Illica, Giacosa wrote the libretti of three of Puccini's operas, 'Madame Butterfly', 'Tosca', and 'La Bohème'.

GIBBON'S TENNIS-COURT, see VERE STREET THEATRE.

GIBBS, MRS. (1770–1844), see COLMAN (3).

GIBBS, WOLCOTT (1902–   ), American dramatic critic, born in New York City. He worked as an architect's apprentice, as a railroad conductor, and as a rural newspaper reporter before becoming a copy-reader on *The New Yorker* in 1927. In 1939 he replaced Robert Benchley as drama critic of that magazine and is recognized as a most valuable addition to the ranks of American critics. A shrewd and alert playgoer, he often writes more brilliantly of bad plays than of good ones; but his irony is a tonic Broadway badly needs. Sometimes he will err in judging a play by its production. Once, for example, when there appeared an incompetent version of *Uncle Vanya*, and a poor and confused one of *He Who Gets Slapped*, he seemed to find Chekhov and Andreyev at fault. On the other hand, he is never to be won over—as are so many of his colleagues—by the 'sincerity' of inept and bogus dramas dealing with vital problems of the day, and though he writes with humorous and sardonic detachment he never descends to 'wise-crack' reviewing. He is an excellent parodist—admiring Max Beerbohm above all other models—and his book, *Season in the Sun*, contains a dozen biting burlesques of modern novelists and playwrights.

T. Q. C.

GIELGUD, (ARTHUR) JOHN (1904–   ), English actor and producer, grand-nephew of Ellen Terry. After studying under Lady Benson he made his first appearance on the stage at the Old Vic in 1921 as the Herald in *Henry V*, returning there some years later to star in a fine series of Shakespeare productions. He was by then accounted one of the most promising young actors of the English stage, but his first popular success came with *Richard of Bordeaux* (1932), which he also produced. An actor of commanding presence, with a fine speaking voice, he is at his best in Shakespeare, and his Hamlet, which has achieved record runs in London and New York, is accounted by some critics the finest of this generation. He has, however, also given a good account of himself in such plays as *Love for Love* and *The Importance of Being Earnest*, and has appeared in some modern plays, among them *Noah* (1935) and *The Lady's Not for Burning* (1949). He has produced many plays besides those in which he himself appeared, and was responsible for two important repertory seasons, at the Queen's Theatre in 1937–8, and the Haymarket in

1944–5. At the opening of Sadler's Wells Theatre in 1931 he appeared as Malvolio, and played Hamlet at the Lyceum in 1939, subsequently taking his company to Elsinore. He is the author of an autobiography, *Early Stages* (1939). In 1949–50 he produced at Stratford-on-Avon and acted there in the latter year.

GIFFARD, HENRY (1694–1772), English actor and manager, in whose company Garrick made his first appearances on the stage. He was lessee of an unlicensed playhouse in Goodman's Fields, Whitechapel, where for some years he had a good company, headed by Yates. He also held, for a short time, part of the patent of Drury Lane, but gave it up because he could not stomach the extravagances of Fleetwood, his co-manager. When Garrick's success brought all London to Whitechapel, to the detriment of Drury Lane, Fleetwood stifled the opposition by engaging Garrick for his own theatre, and with him Mr. and Mrs. Giffard. The latter, a fine actress, played Lady Macbeth and other parts opposite Garrick, but after his removal to Drury Lane little is heard of Giffard.

GILBERT, GABRIEL (c. 1620–c. 1680), French dramatist, author of numerous plays, but best known through Fontenelle's accusation that his *Rhodogune* was stolen from the *Rodogune* of Corneille. It is certain that he must either have seen Corneille's play, or heard it read, since the resemblances between the two are too obvious to be the result of chance. *Rhodogune* was probably given in 1646, a year later than Corneille's play, and is a very inferior piece of work, particularly in the fifth act. Gilbert's other plays are equally negligible, though *Téléphonte* (1641) may have been given in Richelieu's private theatre. Gilbert's origins are obscure. Well educated and patronized by several women of high rank, including Queen Christina of Sweden, whose secretary he was for a short time, he nevertheless died in poverty in the house of a kindly benefactor, M. d'Hervart, where La Fontaine also subsequently found shelter.

GILBERT, MRS. GEORGE H. (*née* ANN HARTLEY) (1821–1904), a much-loved American actress, who in her later years was extremely popular as a player of eccentric spinsters and aristocratic dowagers. She was in her youth a ballet dancer in London, where in 1846 she married George Gilbert, an actor, with whom she toured England and Ireland. Having saved enough to emigrate, they went to Wisconsin, but failed to make a success of farming and in 1850 returned to the stage, touring the larger cities. Gilbert, who was pre-eminently a dancer, injured himself falling through a trap, and though he continued to work in the theatre, he was unable to appear on the stage, and died in 1866. His wife had already given up dancing in favour of straight acting, and almost immediately found her niche in the playing of comic elderly women, in which capacity she was with Mrs. John Wood's company at the Olympic, New York, in 1864. Her first important part was the Marquise de St. Maur in Florence's pirated production of *Caste* in 1867. The period of her greatest fame, however, was from 1869 to 1899, when she was in Daly's company, and with Ada Rehan, John Drew, and John Lewis formed a unique combination of artistic and technical skill. When Daly died she was engaged by Frohman, with whom she remained until her death. During her long career she played with most of the famous actors and managements of her time. Her angular body and homely features prevented her from attempting tragedy, but proved assets in comedy. She played well and carefully every part she was given, and to the end of her days was conscientious in studying and rehearsing, being a reliable as well as a rare and distinguished actress.

GILBERT, JOHN [really GIBBS] (1810–89), American actor, who made his début in Boston in 1828. He then toured the Mississippi river towns until 1834, and returned to the Tremont Theatre, Boston, until it closed, playing the parts of elderly men, in which he later became a great favourite in New York as a member of Wallack's company. He was particularly good as Sir Anthony Absolute and Sir Peter Teazle. In 1847 he had a successful season in London, and studied for a while in Paris, returning to play at the Park Theatre, New York, until it was destroyed by fire. He first joined Wallack's in 1861, and remained until the company was disbanded in 1888, dying the following year during a tour of *The Rivals* with Jefferson. Although an excellent comic actor, and exceedingly popular both with the audience and his fellow players, off-stage he was somewhat formal and unhumorous. He was a man of some erudition, and after his death his widow presented his fine collection of books to the Boston Public Library.

GILBERT, SIR WILLIAM SCHWENCK (1836–1911), English dramatist whose name is always associated in the public mind with that of Sir Arthur Sullivan, for whose music he wrote the libretti of their famous light operas. As a young man he was called to the Bar and was also a journalist, contributing regularly to many of the humorous papers of the day. He was encouraged to write for the stage by T. W. Robertson, and his first play was a burlesque commissioned for a Christmas entertainment. He also wrote dramatic sketches for the entertainers, Mr. and Mrs. German Reed. In 1870 Buckstone produced his *Palace of Truth* at the Haymarket, with himself, Madge Robertson, and W. H. Kendal in the cast. It was followed by *Pygmalion and Galatea* (1871), a somewhat artificial classical romance which was nevertheless a great success. The part of Galatea was played by many lovely young actresses of the day, including Mary Anderson and Julia Neilson. Gilbert then embarked on a series of comedies for Marie Litton, which were given at the Court Theatre. Among his more serious plays may be cited *Sweethearts* (1874), *Broken Hearts* (1875), *Dan'l Druce, Blacksmith* (1876), long a favourite part with character actors, and *Engaged* (1877). His collaboration with Sullivan began with *Trial by Jury* (1875) and ended with *The Grand Duke* (1896), though *The Gondoliers* (1889) was the last of those which still hold the stage. The others are *The Sorcerer* (1877), *H.M.S. Pinafore* (1878), *The Pirates of Penzance* (1880), *Patience* (1881), *Iolanthe* (1882), *Princess Ida* (1884), *The Mikado* (1885), *Ruddigore* (1887), and *The Yeomen of the Guard* (1888). *Utopia Limited* (1893) has not been revived.

Gilbert wrote libretti for other composers, but with little success, just as Sullivan wrote music for other dramatists but failed to recapture the brilliance of the Savoy operas—so called because the later ones were given at the Savoy Theatre. Their partnership was not happy, Gilbert being a man of irascible temperament and a martinet in the theatre. He believed in long and arduous rehearsals and in the dominance of the playwright, which led him into many disagreements with his actors, particularly Miss Hodson. He used the profits from his plays to build the Garrick Theatre, which was opened by Sir John Hare in 1889, and he was knighted in 1907. He was an outstanding figure among the playwrights of the Victorian era, having much literary grace and finish and a wit second to none. Yet of all his theatrical work, admired as it was in his own day, only the libretti for Sullivan have survived.

GILCHRIST, CONNIE (1865–1946), English actress, a very lovely woman, who made her first appearance on the stage as a child in pantomime and in later years was at the Gaiety as a skipping-rope dancer. In 1880 she made a hit as Libby Ray in *The Mighty Dollar*, but she preferred burlesque to straight comedy and had a brief but glorious career before she left the stage in the late eighties to become the Countess of Orkney. Her name is best remembered in connexion with the supreme example of 'judicial ignorance', when Mr. Justice Coleridge in *Scott* v. *Sampson* asked 'Who is Miss Connie Gilchrist?'

GILDER, ROSAMOND (1900–), American dramatic critic. She was born in New York City, and is the daughter of Richard Watson Gilder, the celebrated editor of the eighteen-nineties, whose letters she has edited. From 1924 to 1948 she was on the staff of *Theatre Arts*, the outstanding American theatre magazine, being appointed its dramatic critic in 1938, and editor in 1945. Her monthly report on Broadway was a valuable record and often contained excellent criticism of plays and players. She has written *Enter the Actress, A Theatre Library* (notes on 100 books), and *Gielgud's Hamlet* (the record of a performance she greatly admired). She was director of the Playwrights Bureau of the Federal Theatre in 1935–6, and is Secretary of the New York Drama Critics' Circle and of Anta. T. Q. C.

GILLETTE, WILLIAM (1855–1937), American actor and dramatist, author of a number of adaptations from foreign sources, and dramatizations of novels, in most of which he appeared himself. The most important of these were *Esmeralda* (1881), which ran for a year, and *Sherlock Holmes* (1899), with which Gillette's name is usually associated. He played it with outstanding success both in England and America, and frequently revived it up to his retirement in 1932. Of his original plays best were the spy-stories of the Civil War, *Held by the Enemy* (1886) and *Secret Service* (1895), strong melodramatic plays of action in which his own forceful personality found a suitable medium. He also wrote a comedy, *Too Much Jonson* (1894). He appeared in *The Admirable Crichton* and *Dear Brutus*; but his best work was done in his own plays, which remained on the stage while he played them, but would probably not bear revival.

GILMORE'S THEATRE, NEW YORK, see DALY'S THEATRE (3).

GILPIN, CHARLES SIDNEY (1878–1930), American Negro actor, who spent many years as a minstrel in vaudeville. From 1903 to 1913 he toured with various companies, and in 1916 became manager of the first all-Negro stock company in New York, at the Lafayette Theatre, Harlem. Among his later Broadway parts were the Negro clergyman in *Abraham Lincoln* (1919) and Brutus Jones in *The Emperor Jones* (1921), which ran for three years and was frequently revived. It provided Gilpin with a great emotional part, in which he was at once powerful, terrifying, and extremely moving. He retired in 1926, but occasionally reappeared in revivals of *The Emperor Jones* until his death.

GIL Y ZARATE, ANTONIO (1796–1861), a minor Spanish dramatist of the Romantic period, and a staunch adversary of the French classical influence which did so much harm to the Spanish theatre. His most important work is a melodrama, *Carlos II et Hechizado* (1837), which, following on the success of Saavedra's play *Don Álvaro*, definitely assured the momentary triumph of Romanticism. It was enthusiastically received, and ran for some months. Gil y Zárate was also the author of a *Manual de literatura*, which contains a good deal of information about Spanish drama. His plays, which included a number of historical romantic dramas and some charming comedies, seem to have fallen into oblivion.

GIRALDI, GIAMBATTISTA (1504–73), an Italian writer of the Renaissance better known as 'Il Cinthio'. His collection of short stories, or 'novelle', entitled the *Hecatonmiti*, is chiefly remembered, but he was also a dramatist, whose 'horror' tragedies are modelled on Seneca. The first, and most violent, was acted before the Duke of Ferrara and his court in 1541, at the author's house. Music was specially composed for the occasion and the scenery was designed by Carpi. His later plays, commissioned also by the Duke, were not quite so blood-thirsty, and some were conceded a happy ending (see also ITALY, 1 *b*).

GIRAUDOUX, JEAN (1882–1944), French novelist and dramatist, whose best work was done in collaboration with the actor Louis Jouvet, who produced Giraudoux's first play, *Siegfried* (1928). A year later actor and author scored a resounding success with a witty and extremely elegant retelling of an old legend in *Amphitryon 38*, done in England and America by the Lunts, with equal success, in an adaptation by S. N. Behrman. These plays were followed by others, equally polished, and written in a fine nervous style which brought back to the theatre both dignity and poetry. The most successful were *La Guerre de Troie n'aura pas lieu* (1935) and *Ondine* (1939).

GIRL. George Edwardes was of the opinion that there was magic in the word 'girl', and this seems to have been borne out by the titles of many successful productions of the late nineteenth and early twentieth centuries—the melodrama *The Girl Who Took the Wrong Turning*, the musical play *The Girl in the Taxi*, the musical comedy *The Girls of Gottenberg*, the music-hall song 'The Girl in the Clogs and Shawl'. In the 1920s the word was usually applied to the chorus, especially to well-trained precision dancers like the Tiller Girls. An exception to this rule was C. B. Cochran, who billed his beautiful and talented chorus at the Pavilion politely as 'Mr. Cochran's Young Ladies'. Many of them later became famous in the theatre, among them Florence Desmond and Anna Neagle.

GISSEY, HENRI (1621–73), see COSTUME, 5.

GLASGOW. Like her sister-city Edinburgh, Glasgow had a long struggle before she achieved a permanent playhouse, the first three, erected in the mid-eighteenth century, being burnt down by fanatics. The first to survive, and the most famous, was the Dunlop Street, which opened in 1782 and for a long time depended on Edinburgh for its company and repertoire, the same man being manager of both. It underwent an eclipse when the Queen Street Theatre was built in 1805, and was sold to a merchant as a warehouse. Part of the building was, however, used for miscellaneous entertainments, and in 1829 it was rebuilt, considerably enlarged, and again used as a theatre. All the great stars of the day appeared there, and it had a fine stock company. It flourished under successive managements until 1863, when it was burnt down and not rebuilt. Meanwhile the Queen Street Theatre had had a successful career, and in 1818 was lighted by gas. It too was burnt down in 1829. Other theatres in Glasgow were the Adelphi, which opened in 1842, and was destroyed by fire in 1848, the City, which opened and was burnt

down in 1845, the Queen's, and the Prince's. In 1867 a music-hall was built which in 1869 became the Theatre Royal, Glasgow, and was rebuilt on the same site after its destruction by fire in 1879. In the same way the Prince of Wales's became the Grand, and the end of the nineteenth century saw Glasgow in possession of several other theatres, including a Lyceum and a King's. They still provided mainly English fare, however, and the widespread desire for a purely national theatre had to wait for expression until the founding in 1909 of the Glasgow Repertory Theatre, under the direction of Alfred Wareing and a committee that included Professors John Phillimore and Macneile Dixon. It opened with a production of Galsworthy's *Strife*, and from 1909 to 1914 produced plays by many English and continental dramatists. In its prospectus it announced a desire to foster 'a purely Scottish drama by the production of plays national in character, written by Scottish men and women of letters'. This was the first intimation of a desire in Scotland for the creation of a national drama. The theatre did in fact produce a few Scottish plays, the most notable being John Ferguson's *Campbell of Kilmohr*. The venture was well on its way to success—the annual losses for the first four years were successively £3,000, £1,500, £300, and £125, while the fifth year showed a profit of £780—when the outbreak of war in 1914 forced it to close down. The remaining funds were transferred to the St. Andrew's Society, and later used to launch the movement that produced the Scottish National Players (see also SCOTLAND).   W. J.

GLASPELL, SUSAN (1882–1948), American novelist and dramatist, one of whose early plays was given by the Neighborhood Playhouse. She was also active in the formation of the Provincetown Players, who produced several of her one-act plays, and in 1915 her first three-act play, *Bernice*, in which she herself played the devoted servant, Abbie. Her finest work for the theatre was *Alison's House* (1930), prompted partly by the life of Emily Dickinson. This deals with the efforts of the family to keep back from publication the poems of one of its members who has recently died, and with the impact of a love-affair with a married man on an older and a younger woman. This play, produced by Eva Le Gallienne at the Civic Repertory Theatre, was awarded the Pulitzer Prize.

GLEEMAN, the singer of songs and teller of tales in Anglo-Saxon England. He went underground at the Norman Conquest, but reappeared in the fourteenth century, when he descended somewhat in the social scale, becoming more of a buffoon or itinerant minstrel. In early days the gleeman was a privileged person, and partook of some of the respect accorded to the Teutonic *scôp* or bard.

GLOBE THEATRE. (1) LONDON. Of all the old theatres of London the Globe has the strongest hold on the popular imagination. It was certainly in its time a very important playhouse, and its Shakespearian associations have made it famous. Yet Shakespeare was as intimately connected with the Blackfriars, whose name is less well known.

The Globe was built in 1599 on the Bankside, Southwark, by Cuthbert Burbage with timber from London's first playhouse, the Theatre, built by his father, James. Chambers says 'it was almost certainly round', while Mrs. Thrale, who later lived near the site, says that 'though hexagonal in form without, it was round within'. The cost of erection was £600. The stage was 43 ft. wide, and, including the 'tiring house' or dressing-room at the back, the depth was 39½ ft. Although the structure was only 32 ft. high from floor to ceiling it had three tiers of galleries. The Globe was painted —in contrast to most other playhouses, which were of plain timber. It was an open theatre, and such roof as there was, over the stage and galleries, was thatched. Being only partly roofed, it was a 'summer' house. The company played at the Blackfriars in winter.

On the roof over the stage was a tower or penthouse, with a flagstaff from which a flag was flown when the theatre was open, and from which trumpets were blown to announce the beginning of the play or the opening of the doors. At the Globe, as elsewhere, a spectator who paid a penny and stood in the pit was referred to as a groundling; a further penny would admit him to a gallery; and for yet another penny he could have a seat. The stools on the stage were for privileged people, who were allowed to enter through the stage door. (Jonson refers to the stage stools at the Blackfriars as 'twelvepenny' seats.) In common with most other theatres, the Globe had two doors only, a front entrance which served the whole of the auditorium, and a stage door.

The glamour which surrounds the Globe comes from the fact that its actors and its playwrights were the finest of their time. Led by Richard Burbage, a strong company presented most of the plays of Shakespeare for the first time, as well as those of other contemporary dramatists. Their chief rivals were Henslowe's company under Alleyn.

In 1613 the original Globe was burnt down, owing to the thatched roof taking fire from the wadding in a gun discharged during a performance of what is thought to have been Shakespeare's *Henry VIII*. It was rebuilt with the help of public subscriptions and a royal grant, and reopened in 1614, this time with a tiled roof. For many years it continued as a flourishing theatre, but in 1644 it was pulled down by the ground landlord, Sir Matthew Brand. Globe Alley perpetuated its memory, and its site is now occupied by a brewery.

(2) LONDON. Sefton Parry, who had a hand in many London theatres, built a Globe Theatre in Newcastle Street, Strand, which was swept away by the Aldwych alterations. It stood on the site of Lyon's Inn, an old Inn of Court dating from Henry VIII which had be-come the centre of a very disreputable neighbourhood. The new building was close to the Opera Comique, the two theatres being known as the Rickety Twins. It opened in Dec. 1868 with H. J. Byron's *Cyril's Success*, which lived up to its name. But it was a solitary success.

In 1871 Harry Montague, having left the Vaudeville, took over the Globe. He was the idol of women playgoers, and a man of fascinating personality. But none of his productions at the Globe succeeded, and he left England for America. He was succeeded by Edgar Bruce, who transferred *Bleak House*, in which Jennie Lee made a great success as Jo, from the Aquarium. Edward Righton followed, presenting revivals with excellent companies. In 1882 *Far From the Madding Crowd*, with Mrs. Bernard Beere, failed to emulate the success of the novel on which it was based. Mrs. Beere later became manageress of the theatre, presenting *The Promise of May*, which failed. There was a sensation on the second night of its run when the Marquis of Queensberry rose in the stalls and, proclaiming himself an agnostic, denounced the characterization of one of the people in the play who was similarly described. Nor was Mrs. Beere any more successful with a version of *Jane Eyre* by Wills. In 1884 Charles Hawtrey transferred *The Private Secretary* to the Globe from the Prince's, where it had not done well. With Penley in the lead it was a success, and became one of the classic stage farces.

The Globe changed hands frequently. Richard Mansfield was there in 1889, F. R. Benson played his first London season there in 1890. *Charley's Aunt*, transferred from the Royalty in 1893, ran for four years, though an American counterpart, *Miss Frances of Yale*, failed in 1897. Lewis Waller, John Hare, and Wilson Barrett all appeared there with varying success, and in 1902 the old theatre finally closed its doors. Its last production was a revival of *Sweet Nell of Old Drury*, originally produced at the Haymarket, with Fred Terry and Julia Neilson. The Globe was a badly built house, and had fire broken out it would have been a death-trap. It held about 1,000 people.

(3) LONDON. The present Globe Theatre was originally the Hicks (after Seymour Hicks). It opened in 1906 under the management of Charles Frohman with *The Beauty of Bath*, transferred from the Aldwych, with Ellaline Terriss in the cast. *Brewster's Millions* was produced there in the following year and *The Waltz Dream* in 1908. The theatre was then renamed the Globe, and was Charles Frohman's headquarters during the last years of his London management. In 1916 Alfred Butt acquired it and transferred *Peg o' My Heart* there. In the following year Gaby Deslys made her last London appearance there in a musical play called *Suzette*, which had a disturbed first night but was eventually a success. A series of successful productions was given under the management of H. M. Tennent, Ltd., including *Call it a Day*, *Robert's Wife*, and a revival

of *Candida*. There was also an interesting revival of *The Importance of Being Earnest*, with
John Gielgud, Edith Evans, and an all-star
cast.   W. M. P.

(4) NEW YORK, an attractive playhouse on
Broadway just north of 46th Street, which was
opened on 10 Jan. 1910 by Charles Dillingham,
whose name was always associated with it. In
the main it has housed musical shows, many of
them extremely successful, though early in its
career it saw five weeks of Sarah Bernhardt,
with Lou Tellegen. Among other things seen
at this theatre were Ziegfeld's Follies and
several editions of George White's Scandals.
The final legitimate production at the Globe
was *The Cat and the Fiddle*, on 15 Oct. 1931,
which set up a record for the house of 395 performances. It then became a cinema, though
there are hopes that it may revert to the big
musical shows for which it is eminently suited
(see also NEW YORK THEATRE, 1).   G. F.

See also ROTUNDA.

GLOVE-PUPPET, see PUNCH AND JUDY and
PUPPET.

GLOVER. (1) JULIA (née Betterton) (1781–
1850), an English actress who was said to be descended from the great Betterton, her father
being a respectable provincial player who made
several appearances at Sadler's Wells. She was
on the stage as a child and remained there until
her death, making her last appearance as Mrs.
Malaprop. After some years on the York circuit she made her first appearance in London
at Covent Garden in 1797. Her marriage to
Samuel Glover took place three years later.
She was at Covent Garden with Kemble, and
in June 1832 appeared as Hamlet for her own
benefit, and was congratulated on her performance by Edmund Kean. She appears to
have been an excellent actress, much admired
for her fine voice and her serious approach to
her profession, being completely dependable,
'a rare thinking actress', said Macready. Her
son (2) EDMUND (1813–60) was for many years
manager of the Theatre Royal, Glasgow, and
his wife and three children were also connected
with the stage, one being a scenic artist and
another a musician.

GODFREY, CHARLES (1851–1900), a music-
hall singer whose real name was Paul Lacey.
He started his career in melodrama at the
Pavilion, Whitechapel, but later went on the
halls and became famous as a singer of stirring
patriotic ballads—'The Royal Fusiliers', 'On
Guard', 'Nelson', and 'The Last Shot'. He
also sang 'After the Ball', and one of his most
popular songs in a more frivolous vein was
'Hi-Tiddley-Hi-Ti!'

GODFREY, THOMAS (1736–63), the first
playwright of the United States. Apprenticed
in his youth to a watchmaker, he was befriended
and educated by Provost William Smith of the
College of Philadelphia, who also encouraged
his love of poetry and the drama by various

college and academic productions. In 1759
Godfrey wrote a tragedy entitled *The Prince
of Parthia*, which he sent to Douglass, manager
of the American Company. It was received
too late for production during the season in
Philadelphia, and Godfrey died before it was
either acted or printed. Douglass gave it for
one night at the Southwark Theatre in 1767,
and it was then not acted again until its revival
at the University of Pennsylvania in 1915. It
was issued in 1765 with other poems by Godfrey, and shows plainly the influence of Shakespeare, and of the plays which were in the
repertory of the elder Hallam in about 1754.

GODS, The, a term, dating from 1752, used
of the upper gallery of a theatre and, by extension, of its occupants (see also GALLERY).

GODWIN, EDWARD WILLIAM (1833–86),
archaeologist, architect, and theatrical designer,
father of Edith and Gordon Craig. By the age
of 25 he was already well known and had
designed several important buildings. While
living in Bristol he met the 15-year-old Ellen
Terry, and it was at his house, she says in
her memoirs, that 'for the first time I began
to appreciate beauty, to observe, to feel the
splendour of things, to aspire'. After the breakdown of her early marriage with G. F. Watts
she lived in retirement with Godwin from 1868
to 1875, during which time her two children
were born (see CRAIG). Later, in London,
Godwin supervised the Bancrofts' production
of *The Merchant of Venice* in which Ellen Terry
played Portia, and from then on was much
absorbed by work for the theatre. He wrote
a good deal on archaeology in relation to the
theatre, and for a production of a Greek play
designed a classical theatre which was built
inside the existing structure of Hengler's
Circus. In 1908 Gordon Craig reprinted in
The Mask his father's articles on 'The Architecture and Costumes of Shakespeare's Plays',
first published in *The Architect* in 1875.

GOETHE, JOHANN WOLFGANG (1749–1832),
Germany's greatest man of letters, was the son
of a well-to-do and respected Frankfort family.
He was educated chiefly by his father, who gave
him an excellent grounding in languages, while
the presence in the house of a French officer
during the occupation of 1759–62 gave him the
opportunity of acquiring complete fluency in
that language. At the same time a French company whose performances he regularly visited
instilled into him that admiration of French
dramatic literature which survived his later
enthusiasm for Shakespeare. Leipzig, that
'miniature Paris', where he went to continue
his studies, confirmed this taste. Here Goethe,
like his prototype, the young student in *Faust*,
wanted to learn 'all about everything', but this
mental orgy, added to the strain of a hectic love
affair, brought on a severe illness. A long rest
at home followed, during which time his inquiring nature sought orientation in mystic speculation and the study of alchemy, seed of his

later scientific research. When he was finally restored to health he was sent to Strasbourg to study law, in which he eventually took his degree, though medicine, and above all literature, absorbed his interest. It was at Strasbourg that Goethe had his momentous meeting with Herder. The latter, then burning with enthusiasm for Shakespeare and folk-song, was confined to a darkened room with eye trouble, and the young poet, visiting him, drank inspiration from his lips. The trappings of the rococo period fell from him; nature, truth, spontaneity, became his watchwords. Already *Faust* and *Götz von Berlichingen* were germinating, and in the meantime he poured his love for the village parson's daughter, Friederike, into lyrics which have all the simplicity and lilt of folk-song. The tie between the lovers was broken when Goethe found himself on the threshold of a wider life into which she could not have fitted, but the remorse which he felt at this desertion colours his portrait of the unfaithful lover in his first play, *Götz von Berlichingen* (1773). This play, the first to be written in Germany in a Shakespearian manner, and the first of the *Sturm und Drang* pieces, is a somewhat idealized portrait of a robber baron, who is shown as an honourable and upright man in revolt against tyranny. The play suffers from diffuseness and the action is badly broken in the middle, but it became the spearhead of revolt for the *Sturm und Drang* movement, and a pattern for young dramatists, including Klinger, Lenz, and Schiller.

Goethe's next plays—which were preceded by the epoch-making *Die Leiden des jungen Werther*—were *Clavigo, Stella* (first version), and *Egmont*, the latter dealing with the revolt of the Netherlands against Spain. Lessing had declared the poet to be under no obligation to historical fact, and *Egmont* in Goethe's hands becomes not a circumspect Fleming of heroic mould—portrayed in the play by William of Orange—but a warm-hearted believer in fundamental goodness of man and of life. With sublime indifference he walks into the snare set for him and goes to the scaffold dreaming of his country's liberation. A captivating personality, he reflects Goethe's belief in his own 'daimon' at this turning-point in his career, when he was about to accept an invitation to Weimar, given by the young Duke, against the advice of his friends and family. Goethe has been blamed for the riotous gaiety at the Court of Weimar which shocked more sedate minds in Germany, but in fact he was the first to tire of it, and to endeavour to restrain the young Duke. The projected visit developed into a permanent sojourn, and finding Goethe unwilling to act as Court entertainer his master, recognizing his outstanding energy and ability, entrusted him with one office after another. Gradually he found himself responsible for agriculture, mining, forestry, with a seat in the Cabinet and the Chairmanship of the Treasury, all in the teeth of the old ministerial guard, whom he succeeded in propitiating by tact and efficiency. The poet in him chafed,

however, in spite of the outlet afforded by the writing of the earlier drafts of later poetic plays and the companionship of Charlotte von Stein, a woman of sensitive discernment. At last he could bear it no longer, and in 1786 went to Italy, where he remained nearly two years. The fruits of this sojourn in the land of art and sunshine were *Iphigenie auf Tauris* and *Torquato Tasso*. The former, inspired by the *Iphigenia* of Euripides, and covering the same episode, has a definitely eighteenth-century flavour. Iphigenia owes her position as priestess and adviser to King Thoas to her personality and not to her rank. Believing in the goodness of the gods she avoids human sacrifice until the time comes when her brother Orestes is to be killed. Then, staking all on her trust in the fundamental humanity of Thoas, and in divine clemency, she reveals their situation, and wins from the king an unequivocal pardon. The play, which is one of the masterpieces of European literature, is an expression of Goethe's belief that the salvation of mankind can come only through renunciation and humanity. It remains, however, a poem to be read rather than a play to be acted.

In *Torquato Tasso* Goethe portrays the difficulties of the poetic temperament in conflict with the world of action. Introspective self-pity and other shortcomings are not glossed over, nor the limitations of the man of action. In the princess whom Tasso loves can be discerned traces of Charlotte von Stein. She is depicted as an intellectual woman, of delicate health and reserved disposition. The poet brings her happiness, but she would never contemplate marriage with a commoner, and imposes on him an intolerable strain. He breaks into her reserve, and loses her. Apart from this the action is inconclusive, a cross-section of life rather than an elucidation, but it serves to show Goethe's idea of the place of the poet in the scheme of things. Again this is a play for the study rather than the stage.

During Goethe's visit to Italy his nature had expanded and consolidated. The feverish element, which had troubled him, but had made him feel akin to all things human, was eliminated, and the first signs of Olympian aloofness, very marked in his old age, began to appear. A sense of isolation came upon him, and he turned to scientific research, seeking always the inner unity of nature in the various fields in which he has left his mark. The first draft of *Wilhelm Meister*, written at Weimar, is taken up again, and becomes an illustrated treatise rather than an echo of life. In the new version, *Wilhelm Meister's Lehrjahre* (1796), the quest for the perfect stage has given place to the quest for true citizenship; the events of 1789 had put theatrical problems in the shade.

It was Schiller who won Goethe back to poetic creation, if not to drama. *Faust* (Part I) was published in 1808; the completed version appeared only after his death. As a drama it defies classification. It is the precipitate of a long life and a great man. Its language and style vary from harsh prose and lively four-beat doggerel to radiant iambics, flamboyant alexandrines, and stately trimeters. It has scenes of undying comedy and heartrending tragedy in Part I, of detached satire and philosophical symbolism in Part II. It has been successfully staged in its entirety, but it cannot adequately be contained in the theatre, in spite of the greatness (from a dramatic point of view) of several episodes, such as the prison scene in Part I and the blinding of Faust in Part II; Gretchen, and Faust himself, are fine dramatic figures, but the vastness of the conception, and strength of the execution, of this panorama of man's spirit make it impossible to judge it from the point of view of an ordinary play.

The last twenty years of Goethe's life were taken up with his autobiographical retrospect and with the writing of a fine novel, *Die Wahlverwandtschaften*, while a continuation of *Wilhelm Meister* served as the mouthpiece of an old man's garnered wisdom. In his last years he was, as it were, the mirror of intellectual life far beyond the borders of Germany. He dreamed of a world-literature in which the contributions of all nations could take their place. He had long ago outgrown the *Sturm und Drang* phase to which his own early play gave the impetus, and whose reverberations can be studied in the life and work of his contemporaries, not only in Germany, but all over the continent and in England.   W. E. D.

GOGOL, NIKOLAI VASILIEVICH (1809–52), Russian writer and dramatist, and the first great realist of the Russian theatre. In his youth he attempted to go on the stage, but without success, and he turned to literature. His early work was highly praised by Pushkin, and in 1832 he made the acquaintance of the actor Shchepkin, a friendship which was of value to them both. It was at this time that Gogol began work on his first play, a satire on bureaucracy which he abandoned because he knew it would not pass the censor. Some scenes, slightly altered, were later published. The complete manuscript was destroyed by Gogol during the mental illness which overshadowed the end of his life. Two other plays, both satires, were started and left, to be finished in 1842, but Gogol's dramatic masterpiece, *The Inspector-General* (or *The Government Inspector*, also known as *Revizor*), had a curious history, since it was actually produced at the Court theatre, in the presence of the Tsar, in 1836. The authorities were disposed to be lenient to it, since it amused the Tsar. It dealt with official corruption in a small town, where an impecunious impostor is mistaken for a government official and treated accordingly, and so came opportunely at a moment when the authorities were engaged in reorganizing municipal affairs. But it proved too biting in production and was viciously attacked, as a result of which Gogol left Russia, not to return till 1848, already broken in health. He himself said of *The Inspector-General*: 'I decided to gather into a heap all that was wrong inside Russia, as far as I knew of it, all injustice committed in those places and in those cases where more than anywhere justice is demanded of man, and to deride them all at once.' This play, in its unsparing realism, had a great influence in Russia, and has been translated and produced in Europe and America.

In 1932 Gogol's novel, *Dead Souls*, was dramatized and presented by Stanislavsky at the Moscow Art Theatre.

GOLDEN THEATRE, NEW YORK, see CONCERT THEATRE, JOHN GOLDEN THEATRE, and ROYALE THEATRE.

GOLDFADEN, ABRAHAM (1840–1908), the first important Yiddish dramatist, and founder of the Yiddish theatre. Born in Russia, at Old Constantine (Volhynia), the son of a watchmaker with literary ambitions who gave him a good education, he was first apprenticed to his father's trade, but later entered the Rabbinical college in Zhitomir. Here he took part in the memorable first public performance of Ettinger's *Serkele*, in 1862, playing the title-role—a foreshadowing of his later life-work. Before he left college in 1866 he had published volumes of poetry in Hebrew and Yiddish, and was already known as a writer of popular folksongs. A volume of dramatic sketches which appeared in 1869 went into a second edition, and one of its pieces was successfully performed by the Brody Singers, the itinerant Jewish musicians of Poland (see JEWISH DRAMA, 5) who were destined to play so large a part in Goldfaden's later work. He essayed several professions, including teaching, but after a short stay in Munich in 1875 with the intention of studying medicine, he turned to journalism. Several failures brought him at last to Jassy, where he found his songs well established in the repertory of the Brody Singers, and it was there, in Simon Marks' Wine Cellar, some time between 5 and 8 Oct. 1876, that he produced the two-act musical entertainment on which his claim to be the founder of the Yiddish theatre chiefly rests. The Brody Singers had formerly confined themselves to one-act sketches. The success of this attempt encouraged Goldfaden to collect a company, to train actors, and to produce a succession of his own works, ranging from the early farces to full-length plays, liberally interspersed with songs. A man of imperious temper, he frequently quarrelled with his actors, who left him to form their own troupes, and so spread the idea of a Yiddish theatre. He toured Rumania, Russia, and Poland, and in 1887 went to America, where he found a Yiddish theatre already established in New York, from which he encountered strong opposition. In 1889 he was in London, where he reorganized the Yiddish theatre established a year previously, but found that the actors refused to put on his plays, preferring those of other Yiddish dramatists, of whom there were now a number in Europe and America. After further travels on the continent he settled in New York in 1903 and opened a dramatic school. One of his students was the great Jewish actor, Maurice Moskowitz (1871–1940). In later life he adopted Hebrew as his medium, and wrote in that language *David at War*, which was given an amateur production in 1904 by members of a Zionist Club, and was the first Hebrew play to be seen in the United States. Goldfaden, who died in New York and was buried in Washington Cemetery there, was the author of about four hundred plays. Among the best-known are *The Recruits* (1877), *The Witch* (1879), *The Two Kune Lemels* and *Shulamit* (both 1880) (the latter is usually considered his masterpiece, and has been translated into many languages, including Hebrew and English), *Dr. Almosado* (1882), and *Bar Kochba* (1883). His last play, *Son of My People* (1908), was running in New York at the Yiddish People's Theatre under Thomashefsky at the time of Goldfaden's death.   E. H.

GOLDONI, CARLO (1707–93), one of the greatest dramatists of Italy, who strove to reform the Italian theatre of the eighteenth century by substituting written comedies for the debased remnants of the old improvised comedy, or *commedia dell' arte*. He was bitterly opposed by Gozzi, who in his turn was trying to reform the contemporary stage by making use of what was left of the *commedia dell' arte*, and adapting it to his own purposes. Gozzi was the more successful for a time, but Goldoni's comedies live, and are still to be seen on the stage, while those of Gozzi are forgotten.

Goldoni, who was a typical Venetian, and wrote of what he saw and heard around him, is credited with more than 300 plays. Some of these, however, are duplicates, since the same play was given under different titles in Italian and French. He himself wrote a number in French, during his long stay in Paris, of which *Le Bourru bienfaisant* (1771) is accounted the best. Of those in Italian *Il Bugiardo* and *La Bottega del Caffè* (both 1750), *Il Moliere* (1751), *La Locandiera* (1753), *Un curioso accidente* (1757), and *Il Ventaglio* are the most important. *I Rusteghi* (1760), *Todero Brontolon* (1761), and *Le Baruffe Chiozzotte* (1762) rank first among the plays in Venetian dialect. Translations of Goldoni's plays are numerous, and there are about seven versions in English of *La Locandiera*, for example. The part was a favourite one with Eleonora Duse, who played it in London at the Savoy Theatre and elsewhere. A translation of *I Rusteghi* as *The Four Bears*, by Ferruccio Bonavia, was given in London by an amateur company in 1939. Many of Goldoni's texts have served as libretti for composers of opera, among them *Le Donne curiose* and *I Rusteghi*, set by the Venetian composer, Ermanno Wolf-Ferrari, in 1903 and 1906 respectively. The latter was given at Sadler's Wells in 1939, in an English translation by Professor E. J. Dent.

One of Goldoni's most significant points is his attitude to women. His men are more conventional, types which had served the *commedia dell'arte* before him. But his young women, whether married and in revolt against the tyranny of their husbands, or single and insisting on their right to marry where they will, are something new and charming. In most of his plays the aristocracy come off badly. He castigates their gambling, duelling, and licentiousness, while reserving his approval for the thrifty, close-knit, sensible bourgeois family, the most important unit of society. He wrote good parts for actors, having himself at one time in his youth tried to become one. Most of his plays were given at the Sant' Angelo and San Luca (now Goldoni) Theatres in Venice, and at the Comédie-Italienne in Paris, where he settled in 1761, remaining until his death (see also ITALY, 3 *a*).

GOLDSMITH, OLIVER (1730–74), English poet, novelist, and dramatist, whose two plays, *The Good-Natured Man* (1768) and *She Stoops to Conquer* (1773) stand, like the works of Sheridan his contemporary, far in advance of the drama of his time. The first, produced by Colman at Covent Garden, had a cool reception, and was over-shadowed by the success of a forgotten comedy, *False Delicacy*, at the rival theatre; but the second, also given at Covent Garden, made amends by its instantaneous appeal, Dr. Johnson, who had been instrumental in getting the play put on, leading the applause. This masterpiece has little in common with the genteel comedy of the day, or even with that of the Restoration dramatists, to which it has often been compared, but, says Nicoll (*Eighteenth Century Drama*), 'is close to the mood which is prevalent in the works of Greene and Lyly, and the young Shakespeare'. It has been constantly revived, and has a sure place in the affections of the English playgoer. Goldsmith wrote no more for the theatre, but in 1878 his novel, *The Vicar of Wakefield*, was made into a charming play, with Ellen Terry as Olivia.

GOLIARD, a name given to the wandering scholars and clerks of the early Middle Ages, who, unamenable to discipline, joined themselves to the nomadic entertainers of the time, and were often confused with them, as in an order of 1281 that 'no clerks shall be jongleurs, goliards or buffoons'. They imparted a flavour of classical learning to the often crude performances of their less erudite fellows, and even when, as happened in the fourteenth century, the word was used for 'minstrel' without any clerical association, the goliard is still shown rhyming in Latin (cf. *Piers Plowman*).

GOMBAULD, JEAN (1570–1666), one of the original members of the French Academy, and a frequenter of the Hôtel de Rambouillet. He was also well received at Court, being in favour with the Queen-Mother. Among his literary works was a pastoral, given in 1630; it was of little account, but helped by its example to enforce a regard for the Unities which Mairet had recently been advocating. Its success at the time of its production was probably due more to its author's reputation on other counts than to its own merits.

GONCOURT. (1) EDMOND LOUIS ANTOINE HUOT DE (1822–96) and (2) JULES ALFRED HUOT DE (1830–70), French novelists and men of letters, whose careers cannot be separated, since they lived and wrote in collaboration. The theatre held an important place in their work, although their own plays are negligible. *Henriette Maréchal* (1865) failed in an atmosphere of political recrimination, and *La Patrie en danger*, written in 1873, had to wait until 1889 before it was put on at Antoine's Théâtre Libre. Several plays taken from their own novels fared no better, and it would seem on the face of it as if their influence on the French theatre was very slight. Indeed, they themselves considered the theatre inferior to the novel, but they were nevertheless fascinated by it, and it is in the field of ideas that their influence must be sought. They were the apostles of realism, and Zola, among others, owed much to them. They were also interested in the history of the French theatre and wrote a number of books on the actresses of the eighteenth century.

GONGORISM, associated with 'cultism' and 'conceptism', has been described as the Spanish form of 'an epidemic which broke out in England with euphuism, in Italy with Marinism', and to a lesser degree in France with preciosity, though France was saved from the worst excesses by the stern remedies of Malherbe and Boileau. Gongorism takes its name from the poet Luis de Góngora (1561–1627), and corresponds to the baroque style in the plastic arts and in architecture. In poetry, this style is essentially metaphorical, both in imagery and in the organization of thought. Upon a basis of common and accepted metaphor is built an edifice of supermetaphor. An object under examination is frequently represented by its attribute, the connexion between this attribute and a second object then occurs to the poet, and the new material is presented without explanation, so that generally a change of metaphor within the phrase, or the word itself, may be understood only through following the association of ideas. Gongorism is never content with a commonplace effect; it must emphasize, press the effect further. Exaggeration, hyperbole, are incidental to it; and by using compression and concision it attains an emotional effect of extreme and stylized beauty. Góngora enriched the Spanish language with neologisms and syntactical constructions taken directly from the Latin. There is no attempt to disguise their artificiality or their intricacy, for these do not detract from, but emphasize, the emotional effect. Gongorism affected the literary style of most dramatists of the Golden Age, and explains the rhetorical structure of many passages in Calderón's plays.

GOODMAN, CARDELL (or CARDONNEL) (c. 1649–99), an actor in Killigrew's company at Drury Lane, whose less endearing attributes were probably responsible for his nickname of 'Scum'. His manners and habits seem to have been reprehensible, and he was the acknowledged pet of the notorious Duchess of Cleveland, repaying her by trying to murder two of her children. The son of a clergyman, 'Scum' turned to the stage after he had been expelled from Cambridge, and was first seen in 1677, his best parts being apparently Julius Caesar and Alexander. He later turned highwayman, was captured, and pardoned by James II; in return for this magnanimity he became implicated in a plot to kill William III, and fled to Paris, where he died in obscurity.

GOODMAN'S FIELDS THEATRE, LONDON. There were two, or possibly three, theatres of this name. In 1729 Thomas Odell, having been made Deputy Licenser of Plays, converted a shop in Leman Street, Whitechapel, into a theatre. Here Fielding's second play, *The Temple Beau*, was first produced. Odell made Henry Giffard, an actor from Dublin, his stage manager, and, not having much knowledge of theatrical affairs, soon retired. He transferred his rights to Giffard, who, according to Chetwood, 'in the year 1733 caused to be built an entirely new, beautiful, convenient theatre, by the same architect with that at Covent Garden; where dramatic pieces were performed with the utmost elegance and propriety'. This theatre apparently stood in Ayliffe Street.

A play called *The Golden Rump* being sent to Giffard frightened him so much by its abuse of the King and his Ministers that he sent it on to Sir Robert Walpole. This resulted in the passing of the Licensing Act of 1737. Giffard was given £1,000, but lost the licence of his theatre under the new Act.

He had had a good company, which included Walker, the original Macheath, Yates, later of Drury Lane, Bullock, a low comedian, and Woodward, then a boy but afterwards famous. Giffard tried a season at Lincoln's Inn Fields, but returned to Goodman's Fields, and to evade the law issued tickets of admission at 1s., 2s., and 3s. for a concert 'at the late theatre in Ayliffe Street'. He then performed a play, for which there was no extra charge, between the two halves of the concert. In this way he revived *The Winter's Tale*, which had not been seen for 100 years.

It was at this theatre that young David Garrick deputized for Yates, and then made his professional début on 9 Oct. 1741 as Richard III, being billed as 'a young gentleman who never appeared on any stage', though, under the name of Lyddal, he had previously played for Giffard at Ipswich. At the end of his season, in 1742, the theatre closed, never to reopen. Meanwhile at Odell's theatre in Leman Street exhibitions of rope-walking and acrobatics had been given. It now tried its fortune as a theatre again, but very obscurely, and it closed in 1751. It became a warehouse, and was burned down in 1802.

There would seem to have been yet another and older theatre hereabouts, for a periodical called *The Observator* stated in 1703 that 'the great playhouse has calved a young one in Goodman's Fields, in the passage by the Ship Tavern, between Prescot Street and Chambers Street'. But of this there is no other record.

W. M. P.

GORDIN, JACOB (1853–1909), Jewish dramatist, born in the Ukraine, the son of a well-to-do merchant, who gave him a good education on liberal principles. At seventeen he became a journalist and a member of a Jewish community run on Tolstoyan lines, which advocated manual labour and a return to the land. This proved unsuccessful, and in 1891 Gordin emigrated to America in the hope of continuing its work there. He was, however, soon drawn into the orbit of the newly founded Yiddish theatre in New York, and within a year had produced his first play, *Siberia*. Its success encouraged him to continue, and in all he wrote some eighty plays, of which *The Jewish King Lear* (1892), *Mirele Efros* (1898), a feminine pendant of Lear, and *God, Man and Devil* (1900), based to some extent on Goethe's *Faust*, are the best-known. Although, like his contemporaries, Gordin took much of his material from non-Jewish plays, adapting and re-writing them with Jewish characters against a Jewish background, his work marks a great advance on that of such men as Hurwitch and Lateiner, in its simplicity, seriousness, and characterization. A man of strong character, with a clear conception of the problems of the Yiddish theatre, and also of what he wanted that theatre to become, Gordin opposed improvisation, and insisted on strict adherence by the actors to the printed text. He was one of the directors of Goldfaden's dramatic school in New York, and towards the end of his life fought the 'star' system which he foresaw would be a danger to the theatre.

E. H.

GORKY, MAXIM [ALEXEI MAXIMOVICH PYESHKOV] (1868–1936), one of the greatest Russian dramatists, and the only one to belong equally to the Tsarist and Soviet epochs, between which he serves as a bridge. Of his plays the two most important were staged under the different régimes, *The Lower Depths* in 1902 and *Yegor Bulichev* in 1932. By temperament and conviction, however, Gorky belongs wholeheartedly to Soviet Russia, and by his work helped to bring about the establishment of the new régime. In acknowledgement of the debt owed to him his grateful country has renamed his birth-place, Nizhni-Novogorod, after him, and also the Moscow Art Theatre.

Gorky had a hard, unhappy childhood, and a youth overshadowed by brutality. His pseudonym of Gorky—the Bitter—well typifies his attitude at this time. Painfully (encouraged first by a ship's cook, and later by the writer V. G. Korolenko) he educated himself and began to write. His first short story was published in 1892, and was followed by a succession of works in which he became the outspoken champion of the under-dog, and the bitter opponent of 'man's inhumanity to man'. This led to his imprisonment and banishment. He spent many years in Italy, and organized a Bolshevik Party School on the Isle of Capri to which Lenin and Lunacharsky came to lecture. To such a man the October Revolution could mean nothing but good, and though he deplored some of its early excesses, he was always a whole-hearted advocate of its constructive work. A realist in his view of the worst in human nature, he was a romantic in his faith in the brotherhood of man and the hopefulness of the new generation. In 1929 he returned to Soviet Russia for good, and took a keen interest in the work of the younger writers, whom he befriended on all occasions.

It was Chekhov who was instrumental in bringing together Gorky and the Moscow Art Theatre, which in 1902 produced his first play. Since Gorky was already in the bad books of the authorities, this was given in a cut version, but even so it was sufficiently outspoken to get him into trouble, particularly when it was followed by that masterpiece of Russian realism, *The Lower Depths*, depicting the life of the Moscow underworld, huddled in a cellar. It is not surprising that Gorky's election to the Imperial Academy of Russian Artists was annulled. The performance of *The Lower Depths*, in Dec. 1902 (it has also been produced in England and America), was one of the glories of the Moscow Art Theatre's history, and to Stanislavsky, who produced it, it came to mean 'Freedom at any price!' It was followed by a number of lesser plays, all dealing with the class struggle (of which *The Enemies* was produced at the Moscow Art Theatre in 1935), but not until Gorky began his trilogy on the decay of the Russian bourgeoisie did he again attain the dramatic stature reached by *The Lower Depths*. Of this projected trilogy only two parts were completed, *Yegor Bulichev*, produced at the Moscow Art Theatre in 1934 by Nemirovich-Danchenko, and *Dostigayev*, produced by the Vakhtangov Theatre.

Gorky's work is not as well known outside Russia as it should be, but it is to be hoped that adequate translations, and careful production, will make him accessible to those who cannot read Russian.

GOSET, see JEWISH DRAMA, 6 and MOSCOW STATE JEWISH THEATRE.

GÔT, EDMOND FRANÇOIS JULES (1822–1901), French actor, who passed the whole of his long and honourable career at the Comédie-Française, of which he was the twenty-ninth Doyen. He made his début on 17 July 1844 in comedy roles, playing Mascarille in *Les Précieuses ridicules*, and became a member of the company in 1850. He was one of the finest and most dependable actors of his day, and played in innumerable new parts, as well as in the whole classic repertory.

GOTHA, the home of Germany's second attempt at a National Theatre (see EKHOF and GERMANY, 4).

GOTTSCHED, JOHANN CHRISTOPH (1700–66), German literary critic, who endeavoured to reform the German stage and remodel it on the lines of the French classical theatre. In this he was much helped by the actress Caroline Neuber, who put his theories into action, and replaced, as far as she was able, the old plays and farces, and particularly the clowning of Hanswurst, by translations of French classics. Gottsched, who had become professor of poetry at Leipzig in 1730, although he had no great talent for literature or criticism, prepared a model repertory for her, which was later published as the *Deutsche Schaubühne nach den Regeln der alten Griechen und Römer eingerichtet.* This consisted of adaptations from the French, by himself, his wife, and some picked collaborators, and a few original plays, of which by far the best were the comedies and tragedies of J. E. Schlegel. Of Gottsched's own plays, *Der sterbende Cato* (1732) was successful with Kohlhardt in the title-role, but was later discredited by Gottsched's Swiss opponents, who claimed that it was an amalgamation of Addison's *Cato* with one by Deschamps on the same subject. His *Agis*, which makes dreary reading, is important as the first treatment of a social problem on the German stage.

One of Gottsched's first periodicals, *Die vernünftigen Tadlerinnen,* contained an article on the theatre—probably the first of its kind in Germany—with a favourable allusion to Neuber's company. Unfortunately trouble arose between him and the actress who had done so much to further his ideas, and they parted company. By 1740 Gottsched had ceased to exercise any determining influence on the German theatre, or indeed on her literature in general, but he laboured on undaunted to the end. His *Nöthiger Vorrath zur Geschichte der deutschen dramatischen Dichtkunst,* which appeared from 1757–65, is a well-documented bibliography of German drama from the sixteenth century onwards.   W. E. D.

GOUGH. (1) ROBERT (?–1625), English actor and the brother-in-law of Augustine Phillips. He first appears in about 1592, playing a woman's part. It has been conjectured, on slender evidence, that he played a number of Shakespeare's female parts, including Juliet and Portia, and with greater probability that he succeeded to Phillips's share in the company. He was one of the earliest King's Men, and his name appears in the actor-list in the Shakespeare Folio. His younger son (2) ALEXANDER (1614–?) was evidently apprenticed to the stage at an early age, since he appeared in an important female role in *The Roman Actor* at the age of 12. He continued to play important women's parts up to 1632, but on graduating to men's roles he appears to have lost his excellence, since he is scarcely mentioned in the company's casts, and a reference to him after the Restoration, saying that he was responsible for giving

the word to 'Persons of Quality' when the actors were going to perform surreptitiously under the Commonwealth, refers to him as the 'Woman Actor'. He appears to have been a publisher of plays during the 1650s.

GOZZI, CARLO (1720–1806), Italian dramatist, who endeavoured in the eighteenth century to adapt the masks of the *commedia dell'arte,* then in its decline, to the purposes of a written and literary theatre. In this he was partly inspired by his hatred and jealousy of Goldoni, who was trying to reform the stage by substituting written comedy of character and intrigue for the old improvised plays.

His first play, performed in 1761, when Goldoni was just taking leave of Venice before settling in Paris, was *Gli Amore delle tre melarance,* which was partly written, partly improvised. This, and his later plays, were given by the troupe of Sacchi, one of the best-known actors of the day, whose leading lady was Teodora Ricci.

Gozzi's *fiabe,* or fairy-tale plays, gained more applause in Germany and France, where he was regarded as a harbinger of Romanticism, than in Italy, where, though he succeeded in capturing the attention of his audience for a short time, he was considered extravagant and fantastic. In his desire to parody Goldoni, he was led into absurdities which hardly bear revival. The best of his plays is perhaps *L'Augellino belverde* (1764), though *Turandot* (1762), which was used as the basis of an opera by Puccini, proved extremely successful when given a fine production at the Vakhtangov Theatre in Moscow in 1922. It was also produced in America a few years later (see also ITALY, 2 vi).

GRABBE, CHRISTIAN DIETRICH (1801–36), German poet and dramatist, who with Büchner was the dramatic mouthpiece of the 'Young Germany' movement. His ambitious *Don Juan und Faust* (1829), which strives to emulate both Mozart and Goethe, has some striking scenes. A later play, *Napoleon, oder die hundert Tage* (1831), consists of little more than a long series of sketches, loosely strung together. Grabbe led an unhappy, harassed life and died young. He was later made the hero of a play, *Der Einsame* (1925), by Hanns Johst.

GRACIOSO, the comic servant in Spanish drama of the Golden Age, corresponding to the valet in France, or the Elizabethan fool in England. According to Menéndez y Pelayo, he first appears sketched in in the character of Lenicio in Torres Naharro's *Comedia Serafina,* and by the time of Lope and Calderón is an indispensable figure. His language is generally lively and popular, and his behaviour is governed by a common sense often so at variance with the main plot that it seems almost a parody. He represents the realistic note recurrent in Spanish literature, and nearly always confined in drama to the minor characters or minor genres, which offers a contrast to the artificial code of the *dama* and the *galán.*

GRAFTON THEATRE, LONDON, a play-house in Tottenham Court Road, was opened in 1931 with a revival of *The Lilies of the Field* by Helena Pickard (Lady Hardwicke) and Beatrix Thomson. A few plays were revived and then the venture was given up. Productions were occasionally seen there in the next few years, and from 1939–45 the theatre was occupied by the B.B.C. It is no longer in use.

GRAND GORKY THEATRE, LENINGRAD. This theatre was founded in 1919, under the direction of the poet, Alexander Blok, by amalgamating the two independent but short-lived ventures, the Theatre of Artistic Drama and the Theatre of Tragedy. Gorky took a great interest in it, advised it on policy, and guided it through its early troubles. Its first production was *Don Carlos*, followed by a number of classic and a few modern plays. Then came a period of expressionism, when Toller, Kaiser, Shaw, and O'Neill were produced in the constructivist style. From 1925 onwards Soviet plays were introduced into the repertory, and in 1933 Gorky's *Enemies* was given its first production. All Gorky's plays were first done in Leningrad by this theatre. It continued to waver between different styles, and to flirt with every novelty, until the appointment in 1938 of B. A. Babochkin as its director. Among its early scenic designers were Alexander Benois, who left Russia to join Diaghilev's Russian Ballet company, and Akimov, who remained and made a name for himself later as a producer. During the war the theatre was evacuated, and returned to find its buildings damaged. These, however, were soon repaired, and the theatre embarked on an ambitious programme, including a revival of a fine production of *King Lear*, cut short by the outbreak of war.

GRAND GUIGNOL, see GUIGNOL.

GRAND OPERA HOUSE, NEW YORK, opened on 9 Jan. 1868 by Samuel J. Pike of Cincinnati. Its early years were somewhat unsuccessful, and it was often closed between short visits from travelling stars. Daly took it over for two seasons, 1872–4, and under him Mrs. John Wood made her last appearance in New York as Peachblossom in *Under the Gaslight*, Fechter was seen as the Count of Monte Cristo, and Fay Templeton, later a star of variety under Weber and Fields, played Puck. In 1875 E. L. Davenport was seen in the parts then being played by Barry Sullivan at Booth's, and the theatre closed, to reopen under Poole and Donnelly after redecoration, with seats at greatly reduced prices, as a local 'family' house for the visits of Broadway successes with a generous sprinkling of stars—a policy which proved successful for many years.

GRAND THEATRE, LONDON, in Upper Street, Islington. This started its career as a music-hall called the Philharmonic. At the end of 1870 it became a theatre under the management of Head, a bookmaker, and Charles Morton, the 'father' of the halls. It became the

home of opéra bouffe, with Emily Soldene as the star, and West End audiences, even royalty, flocked to North London to see her. The theatre burned down in Sept. 1882. One notable event in its life had been the temporary loss of its licence through the introduction of the can-can. Rebuilt, redecorated, improved, and enlarged, the theatre reopened in the autumn of 1883 as the Grand, but was burned down again in Dec. 1887. Rebuilt more elaborately still, it rose again in the same year to perish by fire once more in 1900. Again reopened, it became a theatre which relied on touring companies, though many West End stars included it in their circuits. Its Christmas pantomimes were famous, and Harry Randall played in them for many seasons. It finally reverted to variety, and is now a cinema.

W. M. P.

GRANDVAL, CHARLES FRANÇOIS RACOT DE (1711–84), French actor, who made his début at the Comédie-Française at the age of 19 as Andronic in Campistron's tragedy of that name. He had one great fault—he rolled his r's badly; but the public soon got used to that, and he became a great favourite with them. He played some of Baron's roles, and succeeded Dufresne in tragedy with a force and intelligence considered by some to be the equal of the great Lekain himself. Grandval retired at 52, but lack of money brought him back to the stage, where he was again successful. This, however, was his undoing, and some of his fellow actors, jealous of his return, were suspected of hiring a gang of toughs to howl him down in *Alzire*. In disgust Grandval again retired, and went to live near Mlle Dumesnil, enjoying her company, and that of his many friends, until his death. He wrote a certain amount of witty verse, and some scurrilous but amusing comedies are attributed to him.

GRANOVSKY, ALEXANDER [really ABRAHAM OZARK] (1890–1937), Jewish actor and producer, who received his theatrical training in Germany. In 1919 he founded in Leningrad the Jewish Theatre Studio, which later moved to Moscow and became the State Jewish Theatre (known also as Melucha and Goset). Granovsky's first production was Maeterlinck's *Les Aveugles*, with the text freely adapted to his own theories of dramatic effect. His opening evening in Moscow in 1921 was, however, devoted to short sketches by Sholom Aleichem, and the theatre then concentrated on the production of plays by Yiddish dramatists. Granovsky's methods were perhaps most clearly shown in his own dramatization of Peretz's poem, *Night in the Old Market* (1925). With no more than a thousand words of text to work on, he made music the basic element, while a subtle use of lighting evoked the presence of the dead, who, with the market people and the *badchan*, or professional jester, made up the characters of the play. In 1928, while on a European tour, Granovsky resigned his directorship of the theatre, being succeeded by his chief actor, Mikhoels, and in 1930 produced *Uriel Acosta* for Habima in Berlin.

E. H.

GRAN TEATRO, see MADRID THEATRES (1).

GRANVILLE-BARKER, HARLEY, see BARKER.

GRASSO, GIOVANNI (1875–1930), a Sicilian actor, son and grandson of puppet-masters, who was encouraged to go on to the stage by the great Italian actor, Rossi, under whom he trained. He was seen all over Europe, and was considered a fine actor of the realistic school, being at his best in the plays of Pirandello. He was several times seen in London, where his Othello was considered excellent.

GRAVE TRAP, see STAGE, 1 and TRAP.

GRAY, TERENCE, see CAMBRIDGE.

GRAZIANO, the most usual name of the Pedant-Doctor of the *commedia dell'arte* (see ITALY, 2).

GREAT QUEEN STREET THEATRE, LONDON, see KINGSWAY THEATRE.

GRECIAN THEATRE, LONDON, built in the grounds of the Eagle Saloon, in Shepherdess Walk, City Road (a summer resort for al fresco entertainment). It opened as a theatre in 1832 under Thomas, nicknamed 'Brayvo', Rouse. He had good actors, singers, orchestra, and chorus, and presented light opera, himself sitting in a box every night to maintain order. He lost much money in his endeavours to improve musical taste, recouping himself, however, by the profits on the tavern. Robson had his first London engagement at the Grecian in 1844, remaining there for five years before being discovered by managers and playgoers farther west. Sims Reeves sang in the Grecian chorus. In 1851 Benjamin Conquest succeeded Rouse. The huge theatre with its enormous pit was then used for Shakespeare, comedy and tragedy, but money was lost. The Grecian was rebuilt, with two tiers instead of one, and a gallery, and held 3,400 people. Ballet was given under the direction of Mrs. Conquest, herself a fine dancer, and there was still al fresco entertainment in the grounds. All through the Conquest management drama and pantomime played a big part. Conquest was a superb pantomimist and the Grecian pantomimes became one of the Christmas attractions of London. In 1876 the theatre was rebuilt at a cost of £8,000–£9,000, and three years later Conquest sold it for £21,000 to Clarke, a marine-store dealer and one-time lessee of the Adelphi. Clarke managed to lose a fortune and finally sold out to the Salvation Army. Among the actors who appeared at the Grecian were Kate Vaughan, Harry Nicholls, Herbert Campbell, and Arthur Roberts.   W. M. P.

GREECE. Greek drama is in fact Athenian drama; for although every Greek city and many a large village came to have its theatre, and although some dramatic forms (see MIME) originated and flourished elsewhere, Athens established and maintained a complete pre-eminence among the Greek states both in tragedy and in comedy, and all the Greek drama that we possess was written by Athenians for Athens. The question of the origin of tragedy, and of comedy too, is obscure and difficult, but of little practical importance when compared with the major fact that both forms of drama were, from their inception, a part of a religious festival; that is (since the word 'religious' in this context can be misleading to modern ears), a serious and splendid civic and national celebration. Both arts were, from the beginning, addressed to a whole community which came to the theatre as the community, not as individuals; and to a community which was its own political master and its own government.

Tragedy was formed while the Athenian democracy was being formed; it ennobled itself while the Athenian people were ennobling themselves by the part they played in repelling the Persians (490–479); it lost its vigour at the end of the fifth century, under the double strain of the long Peloponnesian War and an age of criticism and self-consciousness. During this century it moved, on the whole, from communal to individual or private themes. The typical Aeschylean theme, shown in his earliest surviving play, the *Suppliants* (*c.* 490; part of a lost trilogy) and his latest, the Orestes-trilogy (458), is the moral government of the universe; sin produces suffering and counter-sin, that produces more sin and suffering, until a resolution is reached in Justice. Sophocles (first victory, 468) brought to perfection the tragedy of the individual hero—this being the form of tragedy that Aristotle analyses in the *Poetics*; in Euripides, and in some of Sophocles' later work, we find the study of the abnormal, and the exploitation of dramatic situation for its own sake (romantic drama, melodrama, even high comedy, as in Euripides' *Helen*, 412).

Comedy followed a roughly parallel course, but some fifty years later. Old Comedy (*c.* 435–405) was a riotous burlesque and criticism of current personalities and movements in political life (this is represented for us by the first nine plays of Aristophanes). Middle Comedy was still strongly satirical, but quieter, more coherent, and with a social rather than a political background. New Comedy (*c.* 350–292, death of Menander) was a delicate, sometimes sentimental, comedy of manners.

The stylistic reflection of this is that in both forms of drama the chorus, that is, the communal element, is originally very prominent, and the movement of plot restricted; and in both forms, the histrionic element and plot grow in importance, while the chorus becomes more and more out of place and finally disappears.

1. TRAGEDY. (*a*) *Origins.* It is beyond

question that tragedy developed out of the choral lyric, an art which, during the sixth century, reached a high degree of perfection, particularly among the Dorian peoples of the Peloponnese; this was a poem, religious or otherwise, which was sung and danced by a chorus. Beyond this, nothing can be said without qualification. Aristotle's authority must stand high; unfortunately, his account of the origin of tragedy, and of comedy too, is bald and perfunctory. He derives tragedy from the 'leaders of the dithyramb'; it was, he says, at first an improvisation; then, passing out of the satyric stage (see SATYR-DRAMA), and abandoning short plots and ludicrous diction, gradually attained dignity. These statements accord with the facts that in Athens, the home of tragedy, it was performed only at festivals of Dionysus, to whom the dithyramb belonged, and that the statutory tragic trilogy ended regularly with a satyr-play. It has indeed been suggested that what Aristotle says is only an inference drawn from these facts. In modern times many detailed theories have been advanced; the whole world has been scoured for 'ritual-sequences' similar to those of Dionysus; the plays themselves have been diligently read and misread to yield evidence; but little that is secure has emerged. The Dionysiac origin is generally accepted. Dionysus was a nature-god, connected particularly, though not exclusively, with wine. As a nature-god, he died and was reborn each year, and these events were celebrated in a variety of ritual; but attempts to trace the outlines of any such ritual in existing tragedy must be pronounced a failure. We cannot profitably look farther back than the dithyramb, originally a hymn to Dionysus, performed by a chorus of fifty. It would be a natural development, and in accord with Aristotle's statement, if the leader of this chorus engaged in a simple form of dialogue with his fellows (compare the soloist and chorus in oratorio); here would be the germ of the histrionic element in drama. But if ever tragedy had a special association with Dionysiac subjects (as distinct from the Dionysus-festival), this association was lost before tragedy reached maturity.

Since the worship of Dionysus celebrated the rebirth of the god in the spring as well as his death in the autumn; since the wine-god had his jovial aspect; and since Greek ritual was tolerant of features which seem to us undignified, even indecent, it would not be surprising if the developing art of drama was now serious, now comic; and in fact the burlesque and often indecent satyr-drama was associated with tragedy from at least 500 B.C. onwards. (The origin of comedy was quite distinct; see below.) In spite of this, Aristotle's statement that tragedy itself went through a satyric stage is difficult and has been called in question.

The word tragedy means 'goat-song'. The role of the goat is also obscure; probably it was a prize—'a song for a goat'.

(b) *Development.* The sixth century B.C. was the formative period, but we know very little

about it, as the evidence is scanty, and most of it very late. For example, ancient authorities state variously that the first tragic poet was Epigênes of Sicyon (*c.* 590 B.C.) or Thespis of Athens, or that Thespis was the second or the sixteenth. Such mathematical statements are obviously derived from earlier histories of literature, and they reflect also the difficulty of defining the term 'tragic poet' in the period before 534, when Pisistratus first instituted the regular contests (see below, 3 *a*, FESTIVALS).

At the first of these contests Thespis won the prize, appropriately, since it was he who had taken the decisive step of introducing an actor, as distinct from the chorus-leader. Aeschylus introduced a second actor; he is already in use in our earliest extant play, Aeschylus's *Suppliants*, so that we have no specimen of the earlier one-actor tragedy. It happens, however, that during a considerable part of the *Suppliants* one of the actors, playing Danaus, is quite idle on the stage; for all practical purposes therefore we do possess here drama composed for a single actor (the King) and the chorus (the Suppliants), and—if we can overlook the uselessness of Danaus—the scene is extremely dramatic. It is long, and formal, and contains practically no development of plot, but it does contain a most effective intensification, on quasi-musical lines, of the already existing situation. The early drama is often compared to oratorio, and indeed it must have consisted very largely of singing and dancing, with only the very simplest and shortest of plots, but obviously it could be intensely dramatic.

It was Aeschylus, still the world's grandest dramatist, who brought tragedy to its maturity. His introduction of the second actor had the effect of making the histrionic part of the play as prominent and significant as the choral, and the chorus gradually loses its primacy. It enabled him also to develop plot, though length and complexity of plot was never one of his objects. Aeschylus knew better than to try simply to dramatize a myth: he dramatized certain implications of the myth. He did not use his highly individual trilogy-form (see AESCHYLUS) to tell a story; each of the three plays was, in all essentials, the dramatization of a crisis, with but little movement of plot. His dramatic resources (especially the chorus), and the material that the myth could be made to provide, were so deployed as to intensify steadily the significance of that crisis. The *Agamemnon* is a very long play, but its actual plot is extremely short; in spite of the new histrionic possibilities, half the bulk of the play is lyrics. Characterization is not subtle, but catastrophic: there is little interplay between the characters, only head-on collisions; though minor characters, like the Watchman and the Nurse in the *Oresteia*, are drawn with a vividness quite Shakespearian.

The dramatists of this period, and Aeschylus in particular, made considerable use of spectacle, for which the vast theatre and the big orchestra offered such facilities. For instance,

Agamemnon enters in a chariot; and the ancient story that the chorus of Furies so terrified the audience that women miscarried is probably true to everything but fact.

At some time, perhaps after he wrote the *Suppliants*, Aeschylus reduced the number of the chorus from fifty to twelve, perhaps by simply dividing the original fifty among the four plays of the tetralogy. As we know so little about this aspect of Greek drama, we do not know why he did this, nor what the effect was. Though Aeschylus's music and dances are lost, the metrical rhythms of the odes remain, and often suggest something of the original effect: for instance, the odes in the *Agamemnon* are pervaded by variations on a slow iambic rhythm which by its sheer persistence becomes very dramatic and moving.

It should be observed that each of the actors could play more than one role. In the *Agamemnon*, using three actors, Aeschylus has six characters—an unusually large number for him. Further, apart from the statutory two, later three, actors who were paid by the city, the dramatist could employ any number of 'supers' (dumb persons) who were paid by the *choregus*. Thus, if the chorus in the *Suppliants* was still the old dithyrambic chorus of fifty, as seems probable, then there were in one scene the fifty daughters of Danaus (the chorus), fifty suitors, the two actors, and probably the King's bodyguard.

In Sophocles, above all others the 'classical' dramatist, a new balance is struck between chorus and actors, and a very different type of drama and production appears. Sophocles was interested in the tragic interplay between different characters, or between a character and circumstance, or between the different aspects of a single character—a quieter, less catastrophic, but even more tense type of drama. He needed therefore much more complex characterization, a much more subtle plot, and a much more detailed and naturalistic treatment; and these were made possible by his introduction of a third actor (borrowed by Aeschylus in his later plays). His plots are masterpieces of construction: complex, beautifully controlled, with every detail made to contribute to the central idea of the play. The same is true of his characterization, which is subtle, strong, and never merely decorative. Working in this more detailed way, Sophocles naturally abandoned the vast canvas of the Aeschylean trilogy, and always presented three separate plays.

He both reduced and altered the scope of the chorus. It plays a very small part in the action, though it is always relevant to it, and may intervene effectively. Its chief function is now purely lyrical; it is used between histrionic scenes, which now begin to resemble 'acts', to carry on the dramatic rhythm—to emphasize a climax, or to prepare the way for a sudden change of mood. See, for example, the ecstatic ode in the *Antigone* which stands immediately before the messenger's tale of death.

Sophocles increased the number of the chorus from twelve to fifteen, at which number

it remained. This seems to have been a purely technical development. Finally, according to Aristotle, it was Sophocles who introduced 'scene-painting'; again a natural result of his dramatic methods and aims. This means, probably, that landscape-paintings were arranged on revolving screens (*periaktoi*) set up at the sides of the proscenium; they could be changed between, or even during, plays—as in the *Ajax*—to indicate a change of scene.

After Sophocles there were no important changes in the externals of tragedy, though it seems that in the (late) *Oedipus Coloneus* Sophocles employed a fourth actor. Euripides' innovations were concerned with style and treatment—much more realism, more pathos, a new and more emotional style of music. In his non-tragic plays plot becomes more elaborate and important; in some plays indeed the interest lies almost entirely in the succession of the events, not in their moral or intellectual significance. The actors therefore gain still more ground at the expense of the chorus. The number of roles tends to increase. In the *Phoenician Women* there are eleven. The choral odes are sometimes only decorative, and there are fewer of them—notably in the *Helen* and in the (late) *Philoctetes* of Sophocles. The chorus was now becoming an encumbrance. The last we hear of it is Aristotle's statement that it was Agathon—a younger contemporary of Euripides—who first introduced odes that had no connexion with the plot, and were mere lyrical interludes.

(*c*) *Form.* A Greek tragedy had traditional features rather than a set form, and these are most easily understood when its choral origin is borne in mind. Originally a play was a series of choral odes on a dramatic theme, punctuated by histrionic interludes (called 'episodes', literally 'additional entrances', because the actor, as it were, came in on top of the chorus). In the classical period a balance was attained between the lyrical and the histrionic parts; the dramatic ideas presented through the action were caught up and amplified in the successive odes. The odes therefore knit the play together; there was no question of the division of the play into 'acts'. This came with the decadence, when the chorus provided only interludes, which separated rather than linked scenes. Hence the 'five acts' recognized by Horace.

Our earliest plays begin with the entrance-song of the chorus, the 'parodos'. This was written in anapaests, the marching-rhythm. (Not always, however. The chorus in the *Seven against Thebes* of Aeschylus comes pouring in to the most uneven dochmiac rhythm. The idea that Greek tragedy was always statuesque is a delusion.) Soon, as the histrionic element increased in significance, there was prefixed to the parodos a scene for the actor or actors; this was the 'prologos'. (The 'prologue' in the modern sense of an introductory monologue was a convention first adopted by Euripides.) As tragedy became more realistic, the formal parodos was replaced by lyrical conversation between members of the incoming chorus, or between the chorus and the actor on the stage. Formal odes after the parodos were (later) given the name 'stasimon', the exact interpretation of which is uncertain. The number of stasima, and therefore of the episodes which came between them, varied considerably; Sophocles wrote five (besides the parodos) in the *Antigone*, only three in the *Electra*. Everything that followed the last stasimon was called the 'exodos' (exit).

A stasimon consisted of one or more strophes with the corresponding antistrophes, and might end with an independent 'epode'. Antistrophe corresponded to strophe exactly in metre, therefore in the music and dance too, but no strophe ever corresponded with another. (The choral strophe was, in fact, not a literary but a musical form.) As the rhythms were music- and not speech-rhythms, it is rarely possible to represent them at all in translation.

But the lyrics were by no means confined to the stasima, or to the chorus. Lyrical dialogue between actor and chorus was common; this was a 'commos' (lament); or, at a crisis, a striking effect might be got by making the actor sing and the chorus reply in spoken verse. (When the chorus engaged in spoken dialogue, the chorus-leader only spoke, that is, the chorus-leader spoke for it; the Greek chorus never attempted the preposterous feat of speaking in unison.) Again, an actor might be given a solo to sing (a 'monody') before the chorus had appeared. In the decadence, such solos became much commoner and purely decorative.

Another constant feature, lyrical in origin, was strict line-by-line dialogue, 'stichomythia'. The iambic verse of ordinary dialogue was never divided between two speakers, except occasionally, and for special dramatic reasons, by Sophocles.

Of the three Unities, the only one that has any essential connexion with Greek tragedy is the Unity of Action—and Euripides disregarded even that. The Unity of Time was entirely overlooked, and although Unity of Place was normally imposed by the continuous presence of a chorus, if circumstances made it necessary and possible to move the chorus, it was moved, and the Unity of Place disappeared. The scene of the *Eumenides* shifts from Delphi to Athens, and the change of place implies also an interval of about a year.

2. COMEDY. (*a*) *Origins*. Attic comedy had a much stricter and more complex form than Attic tragedy, but its origins are not less obscure. Like tragedy, it was a blend of two elements, the choral and the histrionic; but while in tragedy it is easy to see how the histrionic part may have grown naturally out of the leader of the chorus, in comedy we seem to have rather a fusion of two separate elements. For Old Comedy (represented now by Aristophanes only) exhibits, though naturally with variations, a curiously complex and elaborate form. There is, on the one hand, a succession of scenes in which form is strict; the chorus enters; there is a dispute between the

chorus and an actor, or between two actors each supported by a semi-chorus; there is a formal 'contest' (*agôn*) or debate; and finally an address made by the chorus direct to the audience (the parabasis—'coming-forward'). All this, but especially the parabasis, tends to be elaborately symmetrical in structure, and the contest is usually composed in metres other than the iambic trimeter of ordinary dramatic dialogue.

Besides this element, essentially choral in form, there is another; scenes for actors alone precede the entry of the chorus and follow the parabasis, these using the iambic trimeter and showing no trace of symmetrical structure.

It seems clear then that comedy had a dual origin. Without going into detail, we may say that the histrionic scenes have an obvious affinity with such things as the Sicilian mime and the burlesque performers whose masks or representations of them have been dug up in great numbers at Sparta; while the formal part must have been developed out of some ritual performance by a chorus. The name comedy means 'revel-song' (*cômos* and *ôdê*). One form of revel was associated with fertility-rites; it was a mixture of singing, dancing, scurrilous jesting against bystanders, and ribaldry. Aristotle derives comedy from this, and certainly comedy contained all these elements, including the use of the phallus, the symbol of fertility. Another form of *cômos*, well represented on vase-paintings, was the masquerade, in which revellers disguised themselves as animals or birds. Since the comic chorus was often of this type (cf. Aristophanes' *Wasps*, *Birds*, *Frogs*), the influence of this kind of revel on comedy seems clear enough. Our evidence does not enable us to say which, if either, of these forms was the lineal ancestor of comedy.

(*b*) *Development*. Aristotle says that it was not until late that comedy was taken seriously enough to be admitted to the civic festivals. The first contest seems to have taken place in 486, some fifty years later than the first tragic contest. Among the early masters were Chionides, Magnes, and Crates. Crates is said by Aristotle to have been the first to abandon the 'lampoon-form' and to write 'generalized plots'. This, emphatically, does not mean that Crates gave up direct personalities and built his plays on neatly contrived plots. Comedy did not reach this degree of sophistication until well on in the fourth century, and Aristophanes was always lampooning individuals (Cleon in the *Knights*, Socrates in the *Clouds*). It means, probably, that until the time of Crates comedy had kept up the atmosphere and style of the original revel, with its sudden and disconnected attacks on members of the audience, and that Crates reduced this to order by introducing elements of plot and a unifying theme.

Comedy came to maturity during the second half of the fifth century and continued vigorous until Menander's death in 292. Ancient critics divided it into Old, Middle, and New. Old Comedy was the comedy of Athens in her prime, and is represented now by the first nine plays of Aristophanes. (Other masters of whom only fragments survive were Eupolis and Cratinus.) These plays often baffle the modern reader, who is disconcerted by their lack of plot and by their extreme topicality. Old Comedy is the most local form of drama that has ever reached literary rank; it was, to speak very roughly, a national 'rag', in which anything prominent in the life of the city, whether persons or ideas, was unsparingly ridiculed; it was a unique mixture of fantasy, criticism, wit, burlesque, obscenity, parody, invective, and the most exquisite lyricism. To-day much of it would be obnoxious to the laws of libel, blasphemy, or indecency, and of the rest, a great deal would be rejected as too 'high-brow'. The atmosphere of the whole is well suggested by the story that during the performance of the *Clouds* Socrates rose from his seat to give the audience an opportunity of comparing the mask of the stage-Socrates with the appearance of the real Socrates.

Instead of plot Aristophanes uses a single fantastic situation, which is quickly developed and then exploited in a series of loosely connected scenes. The most remarkable feature is the parabasis, for in it the dramatist drops all dramatic illusion, suspends the plot, and speaks directly to the audience on matters— sometimes purely personal—which are quite unconnected with the play. Thus, in the parabasis of the *Knights* Aristophanes gives a brilliant account of his predecessors and of his rival Cratinus.

Aristophanes' last two plays, the *Ecclesiazusae* (Women in Parliament; 392 B.C.) and the *Plutus* (Wealth; 388 B.C.), mark the transition to Middle Comedy. In this, little is left of the strict form of Old Comedy, and not much of its spirit of revelry. Plot grows, and the chorus shrinks; in particular, the parabasis disappears, and dramatic illusion is taken more seriously. These plays are still strongly political—they ridicule feminism and communism—but they are less personal and fantastic. Judging from the remaining fragments, Middle Comedy in general was social rather than political, with a background of private life. By the middle of the fourth century it had passed into New Comedy.

New Comedy is of the highest importance in the history of the drama, as it became the model and the quarry for Roman comedy. Its greatest exponent was Menander, who had an enormous fame in antiquity, but was little more than a name to us until considerable portions of several of his plays (but no complete play) were discovered among the papyri from Egypt. New Comedy was pure comedy of manners. It used stock characters—the testy old man, the interfering slave, and so on—and conventional turns of plot—the foundling was a constant figure—but these, at least in Menander's hands, are treated with a delicacy of feeling and observation which make a drama of great charm. The chorus survives, but has nothing to do with the plot; Menander sometimes treats it as a band of tipsy revellers who come in singing songs.

As always in Greek drama, the scene represented a public place, usually a street, with houses as the background. This led to many conventions which were used with great discretion—e.g. that two persons can be on the stage and yet not be able to overhear each other. These were taken over by Roman comedy, including one which in Athens was topographically true, that the right-hand exit led to the town, the left-hand to the harbour or country. In general, New Comedy was much less boisterous than its Roman counterpart and paid much more attention to elegance of plot.

3. EXTERNALS. (*a*) *The Festivals*. As was said above, it was of decisive importance in the development of Greek drama that, except in its extreme infancy, it was never a private venture, given to attract a crowd or to please a coterie. It was always part of a festival. Originally, tragedy was played at the City Dionysia, comedy at another Dionysiac festival, the Lenaea. The former was a spring festival, held in the month March–April, when the sailing-season had begun and Athens was normally full of visitors; the latter was a winter festival, January–February, and therefore a more domestic affair. Early in the fifth century contests in comedy were added to the City Dionysia, and later contests in tragedy to the Lenaea. As the arrangements for all the contests were similar, it is unnecessary to do more than outline those for tragedy at the City Dionysia.

Early in the official year, which in Athens began soon after midsummer, the magistrate in charge of the festivals had to choose from among the applicants three poets who should compete at the ensuing festival. As it was already an honour to be chosen, there was a prize, first, second, or third, for each poet. It is conjectured that the lesser-known poets had to submit their script, and established poets only a scenario; certainly Aristophanes makes one or two topical references which could only have been inserted at the last minute. Young poets would have had opportunities of learning their complex trade and making their reputations at local festivals in Attica.

To each selected poet a 'choregus' was assigned by lot. He would be one of a rota of wealthy citizens on whom the State laid from time to time special, and very honourable, burdens, such as equipping a warship, or the annual state-representation at Delphi, or a play. The chorus and the three statutory actors for each play (five for a comedy) were paid by the State; the other expenses, including the payment of supers, fell upon the choregus. It was an advantage to the poet to have a generous choregus; hence the use of the lot.

The poet wrote his own music and invented his own dances. He also produced the play and originally trained the chorus and acted as well, but the last two functions were early handed over to specialists. In the early days of the fifth century individual actors seem to have been associated with particular poets, but when the importance of the actor increased, it was considered fairer to distribute the actors too, or at least the three chief ones (the 'protagonists'), by lot.

The festival lasted for five or six days, it is uncertain which. The first day was taken up by a solemn and splendid procession, parts of which are represented on the Parthenon frieze. On the next three days (apparently) a tragic trilogy with its satyr-play was given in the morning, and a comedy later in the day; on the last day, or two days, the dithyrambic contests were held. The contest was a double one, between the choregi and the poets. After the middle of the century contests between the chief actors were added. The prizes were awarded on the vote of a small jury.

The seat of honour, in the centre of the bottom row, was assigned to the priest of Dionysus. (In the *Frogs* Dionysus, from the edge of the orchestra, makes frantic appeals to him for help!) A few other seats were reserved for state officers and such foreigners as Athens wished to compliment; between the other seats no distinction was made. Originally all seats were free; then, to prevent abuses, a charge of 2 obols (say ninepence) was made; and later still a state theatre fund was instituted to provide the admission fee to any who cared to ask for it.

During the fifth century original plays only were performed in Athens, except that in compliment to Aeschylus it was decreed, after his death, that anyone might compete by offering to revive one of his plays. Plays which had been a success at the festival were commonly reproduced in the local theatres of Attica.

(b) *The Theatre.* The Greek theatre was always an open-air structure, built against a hill-side, the auditorium forming a semicircle, or a little more. (The 'Amphitheatre', a complete circle or ellipse, built on the flat, was a Roman invention; see ROME, 3.) The theatres of Athens, Epidaurus, and Megalopolis all held about 16,000 spectators, but in spite of their size their acoustics are admirable (see ACOUSTICS, 3).

As drama began with the chorus, so did the theatre with the dancing-floor, the 'orchestra'. This was always a full circle, the diameter of which was, in Athens, 64 feet. The architectural history of the Greek theatre is very troublesome. Our chief interest is naturally in the theatre of the fifth century, but though many theatres have been excavated, none of them offers any feature which goes back farther than 400 B.C., so that we have to rely on late literary notices, often doubtful, and on the evidence of the plays themselves. It has even been disputed whether in the fifth century there was a stage.

The first addition to the simple dancing-floor must have been a hut or booth for the actor to change in—the *skênê*, whence our word scene. This gradually developed into a permanent two-storey building immediately behind the orchestra, which gave a back-scene and an elevated stage from which such as gods could speak. At each end of the *skênê* short wings projected towards the auditorium, *paraskênia*.

Between these *paraskênia*, and against the *skênê*, ran the stage, if there was one. The evidence excludes a high stage; actors and chorus mingle much too freely for that to have been possible. The better view seems to be that there was a low stage, probably descending into the orchestra by steps; it may well have been for some time a temporary structure, easily removable. (In Hellenistic times, when the chorus had disappeared, a stage some 12 feet high became usual.) The *skênê* provided at least three entrances to the stage and orchestra; two others were given by passages between the *paraskênia* and the auditorium—passages which were used also by the audience. Chorus and actors used all or any of these entrances as circumstances suggested; as the chorus, naturally, did not often appear out of the building, it almost always used these passages, as also did actors supposed to arrive from a distance.

The usual back-scene was the *skênê* itself, for an architectural background is implied in most extant plays—a temple or palace in tragedy, a house or row of houses in comedy. The 'scene-painting' which Aristotle says Sophocles introduced was probably applied to movable screens used to hide this architectural back-scene when the action was laid in the open country. Certainly there can have been no thought of realistic scenery until the decadence.

(c) *Stage machinery.* This was of the simplest. Fifth-century tragedy relied for its effects on poetry, dancing, and colour; mechanical realism would have been incongruous. In open-air theatres lighting effects were impossible; in compensation, free use was made of effects impossible indoors, such as the arrival of a character in his chariot. We hear of a simple thunder-machine—this must have been used in the *Oedipus Coloneus*—and of a lightning-machine of unknown date and contrivance.

Apart from these incidental effects, two machines were used. The first, the *eccyclema* (wheel-out), was a device for showing, by convention, an interior scene. It was a low platform which was either wheeled out or swung out on a pivot, on which a tableau could be arranged. The other device was a crane used to simulate flight through the air (from whence the expression *deus ex machinâ*). Both machines were used freely by Euripides and parodied most amusingly by Aristophanes.

(d) *Costumes.* The costume of the tragic actor was very elaborate—a long tunic reaching to the ground, a mantle or short cloak worn over this, the tragic buskin (*kothornos*, a boot with a sole several inches thick), and a mask. Normally the costume was brilliantly coloured. The mask (Dionysiac in origin) was boldly modelled, and represented the facial type of the character represented—the old man, the tyrant, &c. A character might change his mask during the play, to represent for instance a change from happiness to unhappiness. It is possible also that the mouthpiece of the mask served as an amplifier. The boot gave the actor abnormal stature, to accord with which his body was padded. It is usually assumed that the actor's stature was exaggerated in this way because at first his normal role was that of a god or hero. It is, however, obvious that a practical advantage was gained; in the earliest times at least there was no stage, actors and chorus both using the orchestra; this costume would enable the audience to see the actor more easily among the chorus.

Not much is known about the actor's costume in Old Comedy, except that he too wore a mask and (usually) the phallus, and was grotesquely padded. The comic mask, naturally, might be extremely grotesque. The use of the mask was never dropped, though it is a little more difficult to appreciate in the intimate New Comedy than in either tragedy or Old Comedy. The size of the theatre, however, would reduce the value of facial expression, and must have restrained the tendency towards naturalism.

The tragic chorus normally represented ordinary citizens, and so wore ordinary dress, with a mask. If it represented anyone else, foreigners for instance, its costume was modified accordingly.

(e) *The Actors*. Very little is known about individual Greek actors. In early tragedy, in which only one actor was employed, the poet was his own actor; acting as a profession began when Aeschylus introduced parts for a second actor. For some time individual actors were associated with individual poets—Cleander and Mynniscus with Aeschylus, Cleidimides and Tlepolemus with Sophocles. Later, actors were assigned to the poets by lot.

With the decline of tragedy in the fourth century, actors became more prominent. The most famous was Polus, who is said to have taught Demosthenes elocution. In the scene in Sophocles' *Electra* in which Electra receives an urn supposed to contain her brother's ashes, Polus is said to have used, on one occasion, an urn containing the ashes of his recently deceased son, with excellent effect. Other names of actors to which anecdotes are attached are Theodorus, Aristodemus, Neoptolemus, Thessalus, and Athenodorus. Little is known, however, of individual styles and methods. Aristotle (*Poetics*, c. 26), speaking of overacting, whether by actors, members of the chorus, or the flute-players, records that Mynniscus used to call a younger actor, Callippides, an 'ape' because of his extravagant style. A degree of specialization is suggested by the fact that a certain Nicostratos became proverbial for his excellence in delivering messenger-speeches.

The profession of acting was confined to men, and was of good repute. Since the drama had religious associations, actors enjoyed immunity of person, and because of this were often used as diplomatic envoys in disputes between Greek states. During the fourth century, to protect their privileges and interests, they organized themselves into a guild, the 'Craftsmen of Dionysus'.

About actors in Greek comedy nothing is known beyond a few names and the fact that they were quite distinct from tragic actors. Women never appeared on the Greek stage.

4. CENSORSHIP. A censorship on Greek plays did not in fact exist, though a dramatist who seriously offended might be punished by special decree. Thus Phrynichus the tragedian was fined for his *Capture of Miletus*, a play based on a recent event very painful to Athens, and it was decreed that the play should never be revived. Similarly, the demagogue Cleon prosecuted Aristophanes for denouncing the policy of Athens towards the subject-allies, and apparently had some success. A scholiast records a decree that comic poets should not satirize individuals by name; if such a decree was ever made, it had singularly little effect, for, until the spirit went out of it, Old Comedy was often extremely libellous. It should not be overlooked that since a magistrate chose the tragedies and the comedies that were to proceed to the competition, he could in fact exercise a censorship; but we never hear that he did, and it seems that the choice was made purely on literary grounds.

5. HELLENISTIC AGE. In the Greek or Hellenizing cities which sprang up everywhere in the Near and Middle East in the wake of Alexander's conquests, a theatre was an indispensable public building, and it was often of great beauty. It is from this period that most of the extant remains date. Little original drama of any merit was produced, except, early in the period, the continuation of New Comedy in Athens. In Alexandria there was an artificial revival of tragedy among a group of seven writers known as the Pleiad (from the seven bright stars in the Pleiades), of whom Lycophron is the best-known figure. The greatest contribution of this age to drama, and indeed to literature as a whole, was the work of Alexandrian scholars in collecting, purifying, annotating, and preserving texts of the great dramatists of the fifth century. The tragic drama of the fifth century (not the comedy, which was too purely Athenian) became classical and was regularly performed. More attention was given to acting, and purely spectacular productions became common. The characteristic and only vital form of dramatic art was the mime.   H. D. F. K.

6. MODERN GREECE. A renascence of the theatre began with the struggle for independence in the early nineteenth century, typified in the plays of Jacob Rizos Nerulos (1778–1850). But it took a long time to overcome the handicaps of poverty and a dual language, and it was not until well into the nineteenth century that the vernacular triumphed over the earlier literary language. The influence of Ibsen was important, particularly in the plays of Joannes Kambisis (1872–1902). In 1937 the Greek National Theatre was formed. It was seen in London in 1938 in Shakespeare and Sophocles and was much admired. Closed in 1939, this and other theatres in Athens which have survived the war are gathering themselves together, and there is hope that Greece may yet have a modern theatre worthy of her great past.

GREEN BOX, see AUDITORIUM, 2 and BOX.

GREEN-COAT MEN, footmen in green liveries who, in the early Restoration theatre, placed or removed essential pieces of furniture in full view of the audience.

GREEN, JOHN (?), an English actor, well known on the continent from 1606 to 1627. He first went there with Robert Browne, and later succeeded to Browne's position as chief of the English actors abroad. He and his company played jigs, farces, short episodes from longer plays, and a number of plays by Shakespeare, Marlowe, and others (see ENGLISH COMEDIANS).

GREEN, PAUL ELIOT (1894–   ), American dramatist, who studied under Professor Koch at the University of North Carolina, where he is now a member of the faculty, and had his first plays produced by the Carolina Playmakers. These were mainly in one act, and dealt with the problems of the negroes and poor whites in the South, as did his later full-length plays, of which the most outstanding is *In Abraham's Bosom.* This was awarded the Pulitzer Prize when it was given professional production at the Provincetown Theatre in 1926, and was based on two earlier one-act plays done by the Carolina Playmakers. It deals with the attempts of an ambitious but illiterate negro, son of a white man, to found a school for negro children, and portrays poignantly the heartbreaks and disappointments which harass him until his violent death at the hands of an infuriated mob. Other full-length plays are *The Field God* (1927), a study of religious repression among the farmer folk of eastern North Carolina, *Tread the Green Grass* (1929), *Roll, Sweet Chariot* (1934), another negro play based on the earlier *Potter's Field,* and *The House of Connelly* (1932), which presents a vivid contrast between the decadent southern planter family and the vigour of the new generation of tenant farmers. *Johnny Johnson,* with music by Kurt Weill, was given in 1937, and was a forerunner of Green's symphonic plays with music, which have not yet been seen in the professional theatre. In spite of a certain tendency to propaganda, and to epic rather than dramatic situations, Green remains the most significant figure in the drama of the American provinces. His best one-act plays of negro life were published in 1926 in *Lonesome Road,* with a preface which shows a deep and unfailing sympathy for the negro in his struggle with life. A further collection of plays was published in *Out of the South* (1939). In 1941 Green dramatized *Native Son,* by the negro novelist Richard Wright, which was produced by Orson Welles.

GREENE, ROBERT (c. 1560–92), English dramatist, who studied at Oxford and Cambridge, travelled widely on the continent, and returned to London to lead a wild and dissipated life. He was the author of numerous pamphlets and prose romances, and of some autobiographical sketches which describe with pungent detail the London rogues and swindlers of his time. Shortly before his early death from over-indulgence he wrote his famous recantation, *A Groatsworth of Wit bought with a Million of Repentance,* chiefly remembered now for its attack on Shakespeare—the earliest allusion to his standing as a dramatist. Greene's malicious remark may have been prompted by the consciousness of his own failings as a playwright, and of his own wasted gifts, or he may sincerely have believed that Shakespeare had profited by the work of other men, including Greene himself. He is thought to have had a hand in the *Henry VI* which Shakespeare later re-wrote, as well as in Kyd's *Spanish Tragedy,* and many other plays of the time. Among those plays which can be definitely ascribed to him—and these include a chronicle play on James IV of Scotland, and an *Orlando Furioso,* a romantic drama influenced by Marlowe's *Tamburlaine,* and probably given the year after it—the most important is the charming *Honorable History of Friar Bacon and Friar Bungay,* a study of white magic probably intended as a counterblast to the black magic of *Dr. Faustus.* This comedy, important in the development of the genre in English dramatic literature, was first published in 1594, and was probably acted a few years previously. It was constantly revived up to 1630, at least, and is still occasionally given by amateur and university societies, when it proves as popular with its audiences as its early stage history shows it to have been before the closing of the theatres in 1642. Although much of Greene's work suffers from carelessness and poor construction, it has many merits, chief among them an excellent portrayal of the English scene, passages of great poetic beauty, and characters of interest and vitality. With a little more application and a little less wastefulness he might have ranked high among the dramatists of the day, and proved a formidable rival to Shakespeare. As it is, he can be regarded only as a precursor of the great age of Elizabethan drama.

GREEN ROOM. The name given to the room behind the stage in which the actors and actresses gathered before and after the performance to chat or entertain their friends. It is regrettable that the green room has almost disappeared from the modern English theatre, actors preferring to receive their friends in their dressing-rooms. It still exists, in a modified form, at Drury Lane. The first reference to a theatre Green Room occurs in Shadwell's informatory *A True Widow,* given at Dorset Garden in Dec. 1678. In Cibber's *Love Makes a Man* (Drury Lane, 1700), Clodio says: 'I do know London pretty well . . . ay, and the Green Room, and all the Girls and Women-actresses there.' It seems probable that the Green Room was so called simply because it was hung or painted in green (see also STAGE, 5).

GREENWICH VILLAGE THEATRE, NEW YORK, see PROVINCETOWN PLAYERS.

GREET, SIR (PHILIP) BEN (1857–1936), English actor-manager, knighted in 1929 for his services to the theatre, one of the greatest being his work on behalf of Shakespeare. He first appeared on the stage in 1879, and after some years with Sarah Thorne at Margate came to London, where he appeared with a number of outstanding actors, including Lawrence Barrett and Mary Anderson. It was in 1886 that he gave the first of his many open-air productions of Shakespearean plays, and formed the company with which he toured the United Kingdom and America, many stars making their early appearances with him. As a training-ground for young actors his company rivalled that of Benson, while many school-children owe their introduction to the theatre to his visits in the 1920s and 1930s to L.C.C. and other centres, with a repertory in which Shakespeare predominated. He was for many years in New York, but returned in 1914, and was one of those responsible for the founding of the Old Vic, where between 1915 and 1918 he produced twenty-four of Shakespeare's plays, including *Hamlet* in its entirety, and a number of other classics. In his later years he concentrated mainly on production of plays for schools and open-air performances, but was seen as the First Grave-digger at the Lyceum in 1926 in aid of the Sadler's Wells Fund, and as Egeus in a charity matinée of *A Midsummer Night's Dream* (1927). In 1929 he celebrated his jubilee, but continued active until his death. A capable, hard-working, and essentially practical man, he achieved a great deal in an unobtrusive way, and left the theatres of England and America very much in his debt.

GREGORY, AUGUSTA, LADY (1852–1932), entered the theatre in middle age with an unsuspected gift for comedy-writing, which, but for her contact with Yeats and the Irish Dramatic Movement (see IRELAND), would presumably never have been realized. She had a wide experience of life and literature and, as a great landowner, of the west of Ireland peasants out of whose lives her best comedies were made and whose way of speech she acclimatized in the Irish Theatre. She proved an indefatigable and spirited worker in the movement whose early years she described in *Our Irish Theatre* (1914). In 1909 she won a notable victory for the Abbey and its Patent by frustrating the attempt to suppress the production of *Blanco Posnet*, and in 1911 she took the company on its famous, stormy, and triumphant visit to America. She withdrew from active theatre work in 1928 and died in 1932 on her estate at Coole in Galway, a close friend to the end of Yeats and of Irish drama.

Her plays are numerous, but the greater number are short. The most widely known are her comedies of peasant life based on what she herself calls 'our incorrigible genius for myth-making': *The Pot of Broth* (with Yeats, 1902), *Spreading the News* (1904), *Hyacinth Halvey* (1906), and *The Workhouse Ward* (1908). But she is also known for two fine, short, patriotic

plays, *Cathleen ni Houlihan* (with Yeats, 1902) and *The Rising of the Moon* (1907), and for one brief peasant tragedy, *The Gaol Gate* (1906). Later, she wrote fantasies of mingled humour, pathos, and poetic imagination, *The Travelling Man* (1910), *The Dragon* (1919), *Aristotle's Bellows* (1921), and others. She also wrote plays on Irish history or legend which are still esteemed by many readers. These are all full- or nearly full-length plays: the three 'tragic-comedies', *The Canavans* (1906), *The White Cockade* (1905), and *The Deliverer* (1911), and the tragedies, *Grania* (not produced), *Kincora* (1905), *Dervorgilla* (1907). She also contributed to the Abbey repertory many translations, of which *The Kiltartan Molière*, a version of several of Molière's plays in west of Ireland speech, is the best known.

Her fame as a dramatist rests chiefly upon her portrayal of Irish peasants and the habits of their speech. The comedies for which she is most esteemed derive directly from character and her highest skill is shown in the designing of a brief ecstasy of comic complication. In this kind of one-act comedy of errors she is a mistress of form, character, dialogue, and technique.   U. E.-F.

GREIN, JACK THOMAS (1862–1935), a Dutchman who became a naturalized Englishman in 1895, and who, as playwright, critic, and manager, did much to bring about the revival in the English theatre at the turn of the century. He began his career as critic by writing articles on the modern English stage for the *Dutch Art Chronicle*; and from sheer enthusiasm acted as an international intermediary for the exchange of plays between England and the continent.

Inspired by the example of Antoine and his Théâtre Libre, Grein founded the Independent Theatre of London in 1891. The declared object of the Independent Theatre was 'to give special performances of plays which have a literary and artistic rather than a commercial value'. It was launched at the Royalty Theatre with an 'invitation' performance of Ibsen's *Ghosts*. The critics, with few exceptions, turned every gun they had upon the play and its sponsor, and Grein became the 'best abused man in London'. The Independent Theatre continued to produce 'literary and artistic plays', and in 1892 put on *Widowers' Houses*, the first of Bernard Shaw's plays to be seen in London. Grein's interest extended also to the Stage Society, and out of the Stage Society sprang the Vedrenne–Barker management at the Court Theatre.

Grein was dramatic critic of *Life* from 1889 to 1893. He followed this by writing in French, German, and Dutch for continental journals. He was also critic to the *Sunday Special*, which afterwards merged with the *Sunday Times*, for which Grein wrote until 1918. He also wrote for the *Illustrated London News*. Five published volumes of *Dramatic Criticism* cover the years from 1898 to 1903. Two other books of criticisms appeared in 1921 and 1924. His wife ('Michael Orme') wrote his biography, *J. T. Grein; the Story of a Pioneer*, published in 1936.

T. C. K.

GRESSET, JEAN BAPTISTE LOUIS (1709–77), French dramatist, and author in his youth of a charming poem, *Vert-Vert*, published in 1734, dealing with the adventures of a parrot in a convent, which he spent the rest of his life in regretting. It was considered impious, particularly as the author was an abbé, and he was expelled from the Jesuit order on account of it. Thrown on his own resources in Paris, Gresset wrote several plays, not of any great importance, and intended mainly for the amusement of a small literary circle. The best of them is *Le Méchant* (1754), which some critics consider superior even to Piron's *La Métromanie*. An earlier play, *Édouard III* (1740), though subtitled 'a tragedy', is really a sentimental bourgeois drama, and, like all Gresset's other works, shows the influence of the artificial cult of the day for the simple life. This is particularly noticeable in *Sidneï* (1745), which takes place in an English village. The hero, in love with the unresponsive Rosalie, drinks poison, as he thinks. But his valet—sole survivor of the old French comedy in this morass of sentiment—has substituted some harmless beverage, and all ends well. The play is worth reading for amusement, though it would probably not bear revival. It was well received at the time of its first production, and is yet another manifestation of the anglomania of eighteenth-century France.

GRÉVIN, JACQUES (*c.* 1538–*c.* 1570), one of the precursors of French classical tragedy. His serious plays, however, have been overshadowed by his one comedy, *Les Esbahis*, given before the Court at the Collège de Beauvais in 1560 in honour of the marriage of the young Duchess of Lorraine, who was present at the performance with her father, Henri II. Grévin was also the author of a number of poems. He was a doctor by profession, and at the time of his death was attached to the household of the Duchess of Savoy.

GRIBOYEDOV, ALEXANDER SERGEIVICH (1795–1829), Russian dramatist, who was educated at home and later went to Moscow University. He served in the army against Napoleon and in 1815 went to St. Petersburg, where he associated with writers and became interested in the theatre. He joined the diplomatic service and went abroad, but in 1826 was arrested for his friendship with the Decembrists. Released for lack of evidence, he resumed his career, and participated in the drawing up of the Russo-Turkish treaty of 1829. He was then appointed ambassador to Persia, where he was assassinated during an attack on the Russian embassy.

Griboyedov's literary works were the fruit of his leisure time, and with one exception were comedies translated from the French or written in collaboration with his friends. The exception is the classic play *Woe From Wit* (also known as *Wit Works Woe, Too Clever by Half, The Misfortunes of Reason*, and *The Disadvantages of Being Clever*, though *Woe to the Wise* would perhaps be nearer the mark, since the original word represented by 'wit' contains the sense also of sincerity, intelligence, farsighted liberalism). The play's title gives a clue to its contents, for it deals with the struggle of a young man, arriving in Moscow full of liberal and progressive ideas, against the stupidity and trickery of a corrupt society. Hounded and derided by the self-seekers, reactionaries, and petty-minded officials, he is labelled mad, and even his fiancée, as superficial as her associates, turns against him, driving him away from a society which has nothing to offer him. This play, which has remained in the repertory of the Soviet theatre, and is frequently revived, was the first dramatic protest against the rotten structure of Tsarist society, against corruption, bribery, ignorance, and cupidity in high places. Human and dramatic, classic in form yet realistic and satiric in content, written with sparkling wit and yet truthful insight, it is one of the great plays of the Russian dramaturgy. Griboyedov worked on it all his life, perfecting and augmenting it until it became as it were a poetic diary which he was always bringing up to date. It was banned during his lifetime, but circulated in manuscript, and was printed four years after his death. It was first performed by the Bolshoy Theatre in St. Petersburg in 1831, and no doubt the audience regarded the hero, Chatsky, as a peculiar young man with dangerous ideas, who deserved all he got. It was produced by the Moscow Art Theatre in 1906, and when it was revived in 1938 Kachalov and Moskvin again played their former parts in it. At the same time it was revived at the Maly. The part of Chatsky is to young Russian actors what Hamlet is to English, and Famusov, the conservative father, has been a favourite role with all the older actors of Russia.

GRID, an open framework above the stage from which suspended scenery is hung (see STAGE).

GRIEG, NORDAHL (1902–43), Norwegian dramatist, whose early death in action was a great loss to the European theatre. His outstanding works are *Vår Aere og Vår Makt* (1935), an anti-war play, and *Nederlaget* (1936), dealing with the Paris Commune (see SCANDINAVIA, 2).

GRIEVE, a family of English scene-painters, of whom the father (1) JOHN HENDERSON (1770–1845) was long associated with Covent Garden, and was responsible for the scenery of spectacle plays and pantomime under the Kemble régime. Of his two sons (2) THOMAS (1799–1882) was principal scenic artist at Covent Garden under the Vestris–Mathews management in 1839, and later went to Drury Lane, while (3) WILLIAM (1800–44) was in his youth employed at Covent Garden, but did his best work for Drury Lane. After the retirement of Stanfield he was considered the finest scenic artist of the day, and his early death was a great loss to the theatre. His moonlit scenes were particularly remarked, and he was the first theatre artist to be called before the curtain by the applause of the audience. Thomas was for a long time assisted by his son (4) THOMAS WALFORD (1841– ?), whose work was remarkable for the brilliance of its style and the artistic beauty of its composition.

GRIFFITH, HUBERT (1896–), English dramatic critic and dramatist, who began his journalistic career on the *Daily Chronicle* in 1922, and has since been connected with the *Observer* and the *Evening Standard*. In 1945 he was appointed dramatic critic of the *Sunday Graphic*, and of the *New English Review*. His first play, *Tunnel Trench*, which dealt with events in the war of 1914–18, was produced in 1925, and was followed by several others, including *Red Sunday* (1929), and *Youth at the Helm* (1934), an adaptation from the German of Paul Vulpius. Among a number of later adaptations were *Return to Yesterday*, *Young Madame Conti* (both 1936) with Benn W. Levy, and *Distant Point* (1937) from the Russian of Afinogenov. An interest in Soviet Russia has led to the publication of several books, including *Seeing Soviet Russia* (1932). He is also the author of *Iconoclastes, or the Future of Shakespeare* (1928) and of a translation of the memoirs of Mistinguett, published in 1938.

GRILLPARZER, FRANZ (1791–1872), Austrian dramatist, who inherited from his father his shrewd intelligence, and from his mother his love of music and a tendency to melancholy. His first play, written at the height of German romanticism, was *Die Ahnfrau* (1817), a sombre tragedy which brought him to the notice of the public. It was followed by *Sappho* (1819), a retelling of Sappho's love-story which combines dignity with warmth, and shows in its heroine the poetic temperament at odds with the everyday world, the mature woman fighting a losing battle against rosebud maidenhood. In *Das goldene Vliess* (1822), a trilogy dealing with the story of Jason and Medea, only the last section corresponds to Euripides' *Medea*, the earlier parts showing Medea before the arrival of Jason. In spite of a slightly sentimentalized portrait of the heroine, Medea towers over her ineffectual husband, and their relationship is shown in acuter form than that of Sappho to her lover Phaon. Grillparzer next attempted historical tragedy in the style of Schiller with the story of a Bohemian king's arrogant aspiration to the Empire in *König Ottokars Glück und Ende* (1825); though less vicious, Ottokar is reminiscent of Shakespeare's Richard III, while his successful opponent Rudolf von Hapsburg has something of the blunt simplicity of Bolingbroke in *Richard II*. As with Medea, the impact of the character is deliberately lessened towards the end. A positive counterpart to Ottokar is given in the unassuming and ultra-scrupulous regent in *Ein treuer Diener seines Herrn* (1826), where Grillparzer skirts the ridiculous in order to exemplify his ideal of humble heroism. With increasing frequency Grillparzer chooses to cheat expectation by unconventional methods. Thus Hero, in his retelling of the story of Hero and Leander, *Des Meeres und der Liebe Wellen* (1831), has a distinct element of tartness in her composition, which eliminates sentimentality. In the same tragedy Grillparzer introduces slight comic elements, not in contrasting scenes, as in Shakespeare, but embedded in the main action, and fading away before the approaching catastrophe. For his next play Grillparzer turns to Spain, whose dramatists had much influence on him, and in his *Der Traum ein Leben* (1834), based on Calderón's *La vida es sueño*, a young man is cured of ambition by seeing the results of it in a dream. His most whimsical comedy, *Weh' dem, der lügt* (1838), shows an early Christian bishop, an idealist of the front rank, entrusting a ticklish mission to his scullion, a near relative of Figaro, with strict injunctions to tell no lies. This play was suppressed, after a preliminary production at the Vienna Burgtheater, and Grillparzer renounced the theatre, writing for his own pleasure and interest a further play on the Hapsburgs, *Ein Bruderzwist in Habsburg*, in which the Emperor Rudolf II is depicted as an aged philosopher, of deep humanity, wearily conscious of his own impotence to prevent the outbreak of the Thirty Years War which he clearly foresees. To this period belongs also *Libussa*, dealing with the mythical origins of Bohemia. It was never acted, but is considered by some critics to be Grillparzer's best work.   W. E. D.

GRIMALDI, JOSEPH (1778–1837) is traditionally the funniest of clowns. His surname, that of an illustrious family of Genoa, where it is common, was borne on the English stage in the time of *The Spectator* by Nicolini Grimaldi, but this operatic falsetto was nobody's ancestor. Neither should an eminent dentist of this name be dragged into the story. It begins with Giuseppe Grimaldi, a pantomimist noted for his sardonic humour on and off the stage, who was ballet-master at Drury Lane from 1758 until his death thirty years later. He lived with Mrs. Brooker, a dancer, and they had two sons and a daughter. Joseph, born on 18 December 1778 (though the date given by himself was a year later), danced at Sadler's Wells when he was two years and four months of age. In his boyhood he played dwarfs and old hags in pantomimes which had Dubois for the chief comic character. It was Dubois who changed the clown in harlequinades from a country bumpkin into a coloured Pierrot. At the Lane in winter and at the Wells in summer Joe was becoming noted for his silent acting in dramatic spectacles, particularly when broadsword combats evidenced his powers in grim fights to the death. What changed his fortunes was a quarrel with the Lane and an engagement at Covent Garden in the autumn of 1806, when he took over from Dubois the part of the bear-suckled Orson. At Christmas *Harlequin and Mother Goose; or, the Golden Egg* gave Joe full scope to display his comic powers as Clown—the type who has been called Joey ever since. This must not be judged by dwindled survivals of his tradition that have been cherished for old time's sake. Grimaldi was the most popular comic singer of his day, a finished dancer qualified to burlesque ballerinas, an acrobat of astonishing agility, an actor and a serious pantomimist admired by actors, and a past master in the 'wit of goods and chattels', as well as the inexplicable personality that because of him is called Clown. Knave and butt, stupidity and cunning, were fused by him; he feared and was feared, he was criminal and innocent dupe in one. Later Joeys were plain rascals, but Grimaldi was more of a mischievous schoolboy mounted, to borrow Lamb's phrase, into the firmament. The clue to his humour is in the new joke he invented. Old harlequinades made much of transformations. The Bank of Paris would be changed into a balloon, and the clown who stole into a hothouse would become a water-melon. In place of such magic Joe would painfully and laboriously, in a mood of profound thought, construct a post-chaise out of basket and cheeses, or a hussar's uniform out of coal-scuttles, a pelisse, and muff. Despite these leisurely jokes the essence of his humour was dynamic energy. When his strength began to fail men waited in the wings to massage his legs directly he came off; he shook with sobs from exhaustion. At Christmas 1823 he retired, and Clown in Covent Garden's next pantomime was his son, Joseph S. (1802–32), whose easily won success was soon destroyed by debauchery. The father took his farewell of the public at Sadler's Wells on 17 March 1828. Covent Garden denied him a benefit, but Drury Lane came to his rescue, and there, on the following 27 June, a crowded audience heard him sing while he was seated at the footlights. His son drank himself to death. Then Grimaldi lost his wife and was alone in the world. He moved to Southampton Street, Pentonville Hill, and spent his evenings by a tavern fireside surrounded by old cronies. The landlord carried him home pick-a-back. On the evening of 31 May 1837 he called, 'God bless you, my boy, I shall be ready for you to-morrow night', then went to bed and 'died by the visitation of God' in his sleep. He was buried by St. James's Chapel on Pentonville Hill, where his tombstone has been cared for though the ground has become a public garden. 'Hot Codlins', his song about an old woman who sold roasted apples and drank too much gin, was regularly sung in pantomimes for thirty years after Grimaldi's death, by command of 'the Gods'.   M. W. D.

GRIMM, FRIEDRICH MELCHIOR, BARON VON (1723–1807), a German turned Frenchman,

who, through his friendship with Rousseau and the Encyclopædists, and his voluminous correspondence on every possible literary and philosophical subject with at least three crowned heads of Europe and innumerable friends, is an important factor in the development of European drama in the eighteenth century. He did much to diffuse the ideas of his time, both by his admiration of bourgeois tragedy and by his championship of Italian as opposed to French opera. A man of great integrity, he brought to his observation of life and literature an excellent critical faculty and an unbiased judgement.

GRINGORE, PIERRE (*fl.* sixteenth century), one of the best-known writers of *soties*, or medieval French topical farces. He was master of ceremonies for most of the plays given in Paris from 1502 to 1515, in collaboration with the master-carpenter Jean Marchand, who built the stage while Gringore was writing or adapting the play destined to be performed on it. Practically nothing is known of Gringore's origins or early life (the spelling Gringoire, often found, proceeds from an error in Victor Hugo's *Notre-Dame de Paris*), and he had already a number of works to his credit before he became associated with the student society of the *enfants sans souci*. His best-known play, *Le Jeu du Prince des sots* (a political satire on Pope Julius II), was given in the Halles on Shrove Tuesday 1511, with Gringore himself playing second lead, *la mère-sotte*. Successful under Louis XII, Gringore was regarded with suspicion by François I as a political agitator. He therefore left Paris and attached himself to the household of Lorraine, producing only one more play, a *Mystère de Saint Louis*, the first to be written on a national theme. The place and date of his death are uncertain.

GRISI, CARLOTTA (1819–99), a famous ballerina of the Romantic period, and the first to dance the role of Giselle, in the ballet of that name written for her by Théophile Gautier, with choreography by Jean Coralli and music by Adolph Adam (1841). She appeared in England with great success, and with Taglioni, Cerrito, and Grahn danced a *pas de quatre* at His Majesty's Theatre in 1845.

GROCK (1880–   ), whose real name was Adrien Wettach, was the supreme clown of his generation. He was born in Switzerland, the son of a watchmaker, and was trained in a circus. Later he toured with his sister and his parents, who were fine Tyrolean singers, and after innumerable jobs and much hardship, became the partner of a clown named Brick, and changed his name to Grock. That was in 1903. For some years they toured Europe, and when Brick married, Grock joined Antonnet. It was in Berlin that they first appeared on a music-hall stage instead of in a circus, and at first were a complete failure. But they soon got the measure of their new medium, and were seen there by Cochran, who engaged them for the Palace Theatre in 1911, after which Grock appeared almost continuously in London for many years, though with many different partners. His clowning was magnificent, wordless but so expressive that no one had any doubt what he meant. Although he was an expert performer on eight instruments, his 'act' consisted in failing in everything he did. He would sit on a chair to play a concertina, and the chair would collapse and entangle him. A massive portmanteau would hold the tiniest violin. If he attempted to play the piano —and he was a fine pianist—the stool was too far away. It never occurred to him to move the stool. The piano must be shifted and he exhausted himself pushing it towards the stool. He slid over the piano in an attempt to stop his hat falling off and so revealing his baldness; his woe when this became apparent was one of the most impressive pieces of tragi-comedy the stage has seen. Grock kept his head shaved specially for this 'gag', and wore a wig in private life.   W. M. P.

GROOVE, a characteristic of English, as opposed to continental, stage machinery, which enabled wings and flats to be slid on or off the stage sideways in view of the audience, as required by the system of visible scene-changing obtaining up to the end of the nineteenth century (see ENGLISH PLAYHOUSE, 2 c and STAGE, 2).

GROS-GUILLAUME [ROBERT GUÉRIN] (*fl.* 1600–34), one of the great farce-players, with Turlupin and Gaultier-Garguille, of the permanent company at the Hôtel de Bourgogne. He was already an actor in 1600, though he is said to have been originally a baker, and he may have appeared in the Paris fairs before going to the Hôtel de Bourgogne. He was a fat man, with black eyes and a very mobile face. After being associated with Laporte and Valleran-Lecomte in the early years of the seventeenth century he became one of the leading members of the company and was its acknowledged head from 1622 until his death. Tradition says that, having mocked a magistrate in one of his parts, he was thrown into prison, where he died. He was known as *le fariné* from his habit of covering his face with flour, and was much admired by Henri IV. He figures as himself in Gougenot's *La Comédie des comédiens* (1633). As La Fleur he also played serious parts, but it is as a low comedian that he is best remembered.

GROSSMITH. (1) GEORGE (1847–1912), English actor, primarily an entertainer, who is best remembered for his sketches at the piano, and for his connexion with Gilbert and Sullivan. He was at the Savoy from its opening in 1881 until 1889. He was the author of an autobiography, *A Society Clown*, and with his brother (2) WALTER WEEDON (1852–1919) of the inimitable *Diary of a Nobody*. The younger Grossmith was also an actor, making his first

appearance on the stage at Liverpool in 1885. He then went to America, but returned to London in 1887 and was at the Lyceum with Irving, and at the Royalty with Alexander. In 1901 he made a great hit in his own play, *The Night of the Party*, in which he toured England and the United States. He was also the author of *The Duffer* (1905), and was an excellent artist, exhibiting at the Royal Academy and contributing frequently to the *Art Journal*. George's two sons, (3) GEORGE (1874–1935) and (4) LAWRENCE (1877–1944), were both on the stage, the latter, originally an engineer, making his first appearance in 1896 at the Court Theatre, London. He had a long and distinguished career in London and New York, and was the brother-in-law of Vernon and Irene Castle. George junior made his first appearance in 1892 at the Criterion, and became famous as the impersonator of the 'dude' or man-about-town in musical comedy. He was often seen in revue, and was part-author of *The Bing Boys* and *The Cabaret Girl*, being associated with Laurillard in the management of several London theatres. His son and daughter were both connected with the stage.

GROTO, LUIGI (1541–85), Italian dramatist and poet, known as the blind man of Adria (Cieco d'Adria). He was possibly the first to put on the stage the story of Romeo and Juliet, from a *novello* of Bandello, as *Adriana* (1578). He also wrote tragedies such as *Dalida* (1572), in which horrors abounded, much to the taste of his time, and is credited with a number of pastorals and comedies. *Dalida* was given at Cambridge in 1592 in a Latin translation by William Alabaster.

GROUNDROW, originally a strip of gas lights, laid flat along the stage to illuminate the foot of a back scene, and then, by transference, the low, cut-out strip of scenery placed in front to mask them. It is now applied to all long, low pieces of scenery, made of canvas stretched on wood, cut along the upper edge to represent, for example, a hedge with a stile in it, or a bank topped by low bushes (see FLAT).
R. S.

GROUP THEATRE, NEW YORK, an organization which evolved from the Theatre Guild, under whose auspices it produced *Red Rust* at the Martin Beck Theatre in 1929. Two years later, after a production of *The House of Connelly*, it became an independent entity, and during the 1930s was responsible for some of the most interesting plays seen in New York, including *Night Over Taos* (1932), *Men in White* (1933), *Thunder Rock*, and *My Heart's in the Highlands* (both 1939). The Group also sponsored the work of the young dramatist Clifford Odets. A permanent repertory company has been built up, of which several members have been constant from the beginning, dedicated to the principles of group acting as formulated by Stanislavsky and practised at the Moscow Art Theatre.

GROVE THEATRE, NEW YORK, a small playhouse in Bedlow Street, which opened in 1804 with a company of little-known actors, including Bland, the brother of Mrs. Jordan, and Mr. and Mrs. Frederick Wheatley, who later joined the stock company at the Park, together with several of their associates. The Grove Theatre, which gave chiefly farce and light comedy, was open only on the nights when the all-powerful Park Theatre was closed, and it lasted only a couple of seasons. Among its attractions was a pantomime staged by Signor Bologna, from London's Covent Garden, in which he himself played Clown.

GRUNDY, SYDNEY (1848–1914), English dramatist, who was for some years a barrister in his native town of Manchester. His first play was a short comedy entitled *A Little Change* (1872), which was done at the Haymarket under Buckstone with the Kendals in the leading parts. Encouraged by its success Grundy continued to write comedies and farces, but in later years he became infected with the prevailing taste for melodrama and sentiment, and his more serious plays, of which the best are *The Silver Shield* (1885) and *Sowing the Wind* (1893), show a curious mingling of old and new fashions. He lacked the skill to handle realistic situations with any depth of insight, cramping them into the conventions of an outworn method, and the only play of his which has survived is his adaptation of a French farce as *A Pair of Spectacles* (1890). This was immensely successful, and provided Hare, as Benjamin Goldfinch, with a part which he played to perfection and revived many times, both in London and on tour.

GRYPHIUS, ANDREAS (1616–64), a seventeenth-century German dramatist (born in Silesia, where he returned in 1647) who grew up in the shadow of war. He is notable as a lyric playwright, and his religious poetry, much of which dates from his early years, reveals a soul obsessed to the point of morbidity by a sense of sin, and reaching out incessantly to the Eternal. The conviction that earthly existence is vanity pervades his work. Catherine, Queen of Georgia, a martyr for her faith, Charles I of England, Papinianus, the righteous counsellor of Caracalla, are his heroes, in their passive, but unshakable, fortitude. Yet greater interest is aroused by their opponents, who grow in complexity until in the Emperor Bassanius (Caracalla) Gryphius depicts the mixed character so essential to true tragedy. Having stabbed his half-brother in a fit of anger, he is caught in the meshes of his crime until he is forced to commit his incorruptible mentor to the executioner, knowing all the time that his conscience will never let him rest. *Papinianus* (1659) is a well-knit play with firmly contrasted personalities, in which we may discern tenderness, passion, and forthright integrity. *Carolus Stuardus, oder die Ermordete Majestät* (pub. 1657), though interesting as a treatment of a contemporary event viewed with strong royalist sympathies, is the weakest of Gryphius's plays. Much in advance of his time, Gryphius also wrote a middle-class play, *Cardenio und Celinde* (1647), in which, despite visions and churchyard horrors, the characters are human, and resolve their conflicting desires by abnegation. Gryphius's comedies are all in prose, except for the doggerel of the Pyramus and Thisbe scenes in *Peter Squentz* (pub. 1663). The best of them, *Horribilicribrifax* (pub. 1663), gives a lively picture of contemporary follies—bombastic conceit, pedantry, self-seeking—as seen by a naturally austere mind with a sense of humour.   W. E. D.

GUARINI, BATTISTA (1538–1612), Italian dramatist, author of *Il Pastor Fido*, a pastoral tragi-comedy which stands with Tasso's *Aminta* as the outstanding achievement of the Italian pastoral drama. It was begun in 1569, and finally published in 1590, and after some delay was produced at Mantua in 1598, with much splendour and success. Frequently reprinted and translated, it had a great influence on the pastoral and romantic literature of England and France in the seventeenth century, and was given in English in 1601, and in a Latin translation at Cambridge, by King's College men, in 1605 (see ITALY, 1 *b* ii and PASTORAL).

GUÉRIN D'ÉTRICHÉ, ISAAC FRANÇOIS (*c.* 1636–1728), French actor, who in 1677 married Molière's widow. Son of an actor, he was a member of the troupe at the Théâtre du Marais when it fused with that of Molière, and was already known as a good actor in light comedy. He became a member of the Comédie-Française on its foundation, and was its third Doyen, continuing to act until he was well over eighty. He was much admired in elderly parts, as in *L'Avare* and *Le Grondeur*. He also created a number of roles in early eighteenth-century plays. He was stricken with paralysis in 1717 while waiting in the wings to go on.

GUIGNOL, the name of a French marionette, originating in Lyons, with the local characteristics of the peasant and provincial man of the Dauphiné. He probably dates from the last years of the eighteenth century, and may have been invented by a puppet-master named Laurent Mourquet (1744–1844), grafting native humour on to Polichinelle (Punch). By some twist of nomenclature, perhaps because of the horrors and general heartlessness of the puppet show, as exemplified in our Punch and Judy, the name attached itself in Paris to cabarets which catered for an over-sophisticated and decadent taste, later centralized in the Théâtre du Grand Guignol. This specialized in short plays of violence, murder, rape, ghostly apparitions, and suicide, all intended to chill and delight the spectator. In a modified form it made its appearance in England in 1908, and has appeared sporadically ever since, apart from Grand Guignol elements in such plays as *Gaslight* and *Duet for Two Hands*. Subtlety, psychology, love interest, all must be sacrificed to the overriding considerations of pain and terror. English Grand Guignol has never reached the intensity of the French, however, and its true home is in the small theatres of Montmartre. In the French theatre a 'guignol' is also a small room just beside the stage, with mirror and washbasin, used for quick changes or hasty repairs.

GUILBERT, YVETTE (1869–1944), French 'diseuse', whose wit, vivacity, and charm made a profound impression in London, Paris, and New York. She made her début at the Théâtre des Variétés in 1889, and was heard at various cafés-concerts in songs specially written for her. Tall, thin to the point of emaciation, with a voice to match, she became the rage of Paris, and her long black gloves, originally a result of her poverty, became a mark of distinction which she retained till the end. She was a favourite at the old Empire, London, and at the Coliseum, and reappeared in London in the 1920s, after a long stay in America, in a series of recitals. She was the author of a volume of reminiscences entitled *The Song of My Life*.

GUILD THEATRE, NEW YORK. This was built to house the activities of the Theatre Guild, and opened on 13 Apr. 1925, with Helen Hayes in *Caesar and Cleopatra*. It ran for 129 performances, but was not an outstanding success, many of the audience coming as much to see the new playhouse as the play. Later productions included the Lunts in *Arms and the Man*, and the controversial *Goat Song*, considered by some critics the outstanding venture of the Theatre Guild. Another play by Werfel, *Juarez and Maximilian*, was an artistic though not a commercial success, and was followed by a revival of *Pygmalion* with Lynn Fontanne as Eliza Doolittle. This was the first play to be produced by the Theatre Guild outside New York, with a success that justified a continuance of the policy. Other outstanding productions at this theatre were *The Brothers Karamazov* (1927), adapted and directed by Jacques Copeau, *Porgy, Marco Millions* (the first O'Neill play to be done by the Theatre Guild), and revivals of *The Doctor's Dilemma* and *Volpone*. *Faust, Part I*, with a German director, proved unsuccessful, as did *Major Barbara*. In 1929 Alice Brady appeared for the first time under the auspices of the Guild, who later presented Nazimova in *A Month in the Country*. The following year saw the first musical play at the Guild Theatre, and the poetic *Elizabeth the Queen*, again with the Lunts, who, after *Green Grow the Lilacs* and *Mourning Becomes Electra*, the latter with Alice Brady and Nazimova, were seen again in *The Taming of the Shrew*. Later productions were *Too True to be Good*, with Beatrice Lillie, Behrman's *Biography* and *End of Summer*, and O'Neill's *Ah, Wilderness!*   G. F.

GUILLOT-GORJU [BERTRAND HARDOUIN DE ST. JACQUES] (1600–48), French actor,

originally a medical student who had abandoned his studies and earned a precarious living as a 'barker' for quack-doctors at the Paris fairs. He had great wit and powers of repartee, and Bellerose, seeing in him the makings of an actor, took him into the company at the Hôtel de Bourgogne, where he played in farce in succession to Turlupin and his companions. He was excellent as the pedantic doctor, which he played masked. He married the sister of Bellerose in 1636, and in 1641 retired from the stage to take up his old profession of medicine.

GUIMARD, MADELEINE (1743–1816), a celebrated *danseuse* at the Paris Opéra, where she was contemporary with the great Vestris. Her life was written by Edmond de Goncourt.

GUIMERÁ, ÁNGEL (1847–1924), a Spanish dramatist, who with Galdós represents the impact of realism on the Spanish stage. His plays were first produced in Barcelona, where he spent most of his life. They fall into two groups, the first, influenced by Shakespeare and the French Romantics, being historical dramas, a genre to which Guimerá returned in later years, while the plays of his intervening period are realistic representations of contemporary life, often with a working-class setting, and showing clearly the influence of the Scandinavians, particularly Ibsen. The best known of these is *Terra baixa* (1897).

GUISARD, GUISER, another name for the Christmas mummer (see MUMMING PLAY), probably from 'disguise'. The modern slang term 'geezer' may be derived from it.

GUITRY. (1) LUCIEN (1860–1925), French actor and dramatist, trained at the Conservatoire, who made his first appearance on the stage as Armand in a revival of *La Dame aux camélias* in 1878, at the Gymnase. He was later in Russia, and toured the continent for many years, returning to the Odéon in 1891, and appearing with Sarah Bernhardt at the Porte-Saint-Martin in 1893. He was for several years manager of the Renaissance, where he also appeared in many of his own productions and plays. His son (2) SACHA (1885–   ) was also an actor and a most prolific author, having written nearly a hundred plays, mainly light comedies, many of which have been translated into English. He first appeared under his father's management in St. Petersburg, where he was born, and was seen in Paris at the Renaissance, again with his father, in 1902. He came to London in 1920 and proved extremely popular, appearing in a number of his own plays and sketches with (3) YVONNE PRINTEMPS (1895–   ), a charming French actress, the second of his five wives, who delighted English audiences with her performance in *Nono*, a play written by her husband when he was sixteen. She has since had a distinguished career in Paris, where she directs her own theatre.

GUNNELL, RICHARD (?–1634), one of the outstanding personalities of the English theatre from about 1623 to his death. He was with the Palsgrave's Men on their taking that name in 1612, and was a friend of Alleyn, in whose diary he often figures. He held shares in the new Fortune, rebuilt in 1618 after the disastrous fire, and he appears later as a dramatist for the company there, since two plays by him, both lost, were licensed in 1623 and 1624. At this time he seems to have given up acting and taken over the management of the Fortune, but does not appear to have prospered, since he was several times in debt. In 1629 he was associated with Blagrove in the building of Salisbury Court, where he remained in management until his death.

GUSTAV III (1746–1792), King of Sweden, took a great interest in the theatre, and had much influence on its development in Sweden in the latter part of the eighteenth century. Himself the author, or part-author, of a number of plays given at Court, he also supported the National Theatre opened in Stockholm in 1773, and encouraged the work of young dramatists (see SCANDINAVIA, 3).

GUSYEV, VICTOR MIKHAILOVICH (1908–44), Soviet dramatist, whose early plays were written for the Red Army Theatre, and were about soldiers. *Friendship*, which was in rhyme, and dealt with the unselfish affection of five friends on the Soviet frontier, was produced in 1938. During the war Gusyev came to the fore with several plays, of which *A Moscow Girl*, also in rhyme, was considered outstanding. The author's sudden death at the early age of 35 has been a great loss to the Soviet stage.

GUTHRIE, TYRONE (1900–   ), English actor and producer, who made his first appearance on the stage in 1924 with the Oxford Repertory Company under Fagan. Relinquishing acting for production, he directed the plays given by Anmer Hall at the Festival Theatre, Cambridge, from 1929 to 1930, and for the same management produced his first play in London, James Bridie's *The Anatomist*, with which the Westminster Theatre opened in 1931. Much of Guthrie's finest work has been done in Shakespeare; he was twice appointed producer at the Old Vic, in 1933 and in 1936, and from 1939 to 1945 was Administrator of the Old Vic and Sadler's Wells Theatres. A creative and experimental artist, he is not afraid to approach his material from a new angle, often with unexpected success, as in his delightful *Midsummer Night's Dream* and a 'modern dress' *Hamlet* starring Alec Guinness. Among other notable productions have been a more orthodox *Hamlet*, with Laurence Olivier, which was later seen at Elsinore; *Measure for Measure*, with Charles Laughton (1933) and Emlyn Williams (1937) as Angelo; *Peer Gynt* in 1944, all for the Old Vic; and, for the Edinburgh Festivals of 1948 and 1949, the old Scottish plays, *The Three Estates* by Lyndsay and *The Gentle Shepherd* by Ramsay. After leaving the Old Vic, Guthrie, one of the most interesting of the younger English producers, became a director of the Company of Four at the Lyric Theatre, Hammersmith, and a guest producer of opera at Sadler's Wells. He was one of the first to write plays specifically for broadcasting, and is the author of *Theatre Prospect* (1932).

GUTZKOW, KARL FERDINAND (1811–78), German writer, and a prominent member of the 'Young Germany' literary movement. He is, however, mainly remembered as the author of the great Jewish play, *Uriel Acosta*, written in 1847, which has become a recognized classic of world drama, and is in the repertory of the main Soviet and Jewish theatres. Dealing with the tragedy of a Jewish heretic, it is a moving and terrible picture of the struggle for intellectual freedom. It was first seen in England in 1905, and has been played, both in the original and in translation, in most European countries and in America.

GWYNN, NELL (ELEANOR) (1650–87), English actress and, during her short stage career, one of the best-loved of her day. After a stormy childhood, she became an orange-wench at Drury Lane, perhaps under the redoubtable Mrs. Meggs, and with the help of Charles Hart made her first appearance on the boards at the age of fifteen in *The Indian Emperor*. She was not a good actress; in tragedy she was a failure, and in comedy she owed her success more to her charm and vivacity than to her histrionic powers. Her best part seems to have been Florimel in Dryden's *Secret Love*, where she was much admired in male attire. She was much in demand as a speaker of Prologues and Epilogues and took Charles II by storm when she spoke the witty Epilogue to *Tyrannic Love* (1669). She then became his mistress, and made her last appearance on the stage in *The Conquest of Granada* (1669), as Almahide to Hart's Almanzor. Tradition has it that the founding of Chelsea Hospital was due to her influence. She is the subject of a number of plays, including Paul Kester's *Sweet Nell of Old Drury*, a part indissolubly linked with the name of Julia Neilson.

GYLLENBORG, CARL (1679–1746), Swedish dramatist, author of *Den Svenska sprätthöken*, the first play to be given at the newly opened Royal Swedish Theatre in Stockholm in 1737.

GYMNASE-DRAMATIQUE, THÉÂTRE DU, PARIS. This opened on 23 Dec. 1820 under Delestre-Poirson, a mediocre actor but a good manager, who conducted it successfully until 1844. Scribe was its dramatist and its company included Virginie Déjazet and the 11-year-old Léontine Fay. It was at first intended as a nursery for young talent coming from the Conservatoire, and was licensed to play classical plays if condensed into one act. That soon proved impracticable, and the theatre turned to vaudevilles. The Gymnase, as it was usually called, was one of the first theatres in Paris to be lit by gas. For a short time it was known as the Théâtre de Madame, under the patronage of the Duchesse de Berry, but in 1830, the Revolution having taken away its title, it was closed for repairs and reopened under its old name. During the next few years it saw the débuts of Madame Allan-Despréaux, Rachel, and Rose Chéri, the last marrying its second director Monsigny and remaining as its leading lady for twenty years. Under Monsigny the theatre, which had suffered from Poirson's dispute with the Society of Authors, once more established itself, and gradually came to accept more serious plays. In 1850 *La Dame aux camélias* was given there, followed by other plays by Dumas *fils*, and by Sand, Augier, and Feuillet. The Gymnase now became a serious rival of the Comédie-Française, and under successive directors has retained its position among the important theatres of Paris.

There was a small children's theatre known as the Gymnase-Enfantin, founded by Joly in 1829, which was burnt down in 1843.

H

HABIMA, a company formed in Moscow in 1917 for the production of plays in Hebrew (*habima* meaning stage). Its first members came from the short-lived Warsaw and Bialystok Hebrew theatres, and soon attracted the attention of Stanislavsky, who entrusted their training to his assistant, Vakhtangov. The company's first public performance, in 1918, consisted of four one-act plays by various Jewish writers, and proved so successful that Habima became one of the four studios affiliated to the Moscow Art Theatre. Vakhtangov's best work for Habima was done with the production of the Hebrew version of *The Dybbuk* in 1922; already a sick man, he died a few months later. In 1925 Habima played *The Eternal Jew* and *The Dybbuk* in Leningrad for three weeks; Riga was visited in 1926, and the company then went on tour in America. It had always been the intention of Habima to settle in Palestine, and a first visit there was made in 1928. In the following year an extended European tour was made, during which the company was seen in the last two plays to be produced abroad, *Twelfth Night* and *Uriel Acosta*, the latter directed by Granovsky. Since 1931, except for another European tour in 1937–8, during which it visited London, Habima has been permanently resident in Palestine. Its theatre building, which also comprises a dramatic school and library, was opened in 1945 in Tel Aviv.

E. H.

HACKETT. (1) JAMES HENRY (1800–71), American character actor, who made his first appearance in 1826, and became famous for his portrayal of Yankee characters, many of which he interpolated into new or existing plays. In this way he re-wrote Finn's *Montgomery* as *The Indian Wife*, and turned the French cockney in *Paul Pry* into a Yankee, rechristening the piece *Jonathan in England*. One of his finest parts was Nimrod Wildfire in *The Lion of the West*, a play which owed much of its success to his acting. Like many other plays in which Hackett appeared, this is now lost, as he objected to the printing of play manuscripts in case other actors should appropriate his parts. Long before Jefferson made *Rip Van Winkle* his own, Hackett had appeared in a version of it which he continued to play for some years after Jefferson's début. He was the first American actor to appear in London as a star, which he did in 1833, playing Falstaff, one of his best parts, and several of his Yankee characterizations, which were well received. By his encouragement of American dramatists, and his offer of prizes for new American plays, he had a definite influence on the development of a native drama in the United States. He was also a keen student of Shakespeare, and published his correspondence with Quincy Adams on the subject of Shakespeare's plays. Hackett was manager of the Astor Place Opera House on the occasion of the Macready riot. He was always a scholarly, genial, and hard-working actor, handsome in his youth, who served the theatre conscientiously, if not with overmuch genius. His first wife was the actress (2) CATHARINE LEE SUGG (1797–1848), who came from the Theatre Royal, Birmingham, to the Park Theatre, New York, in 1818, and proved herself a good versatile actress, with an excellent contralto voice. She appeared with her husband for a short while after her marriage in 1819, and then retired. By his second wife Hackett had a son (3) JAMES KETELTAS (1869–1926), who became a fine romantic actor, playing leading Shakespearian and Sheridan roles under Daly in 1892. In 1895 he joined Daniel Frohman's company at the Lyceum, where he appeared in *The Prisoner of Zenda* and similar plays. In his youth he was a tall, slim figure, with dark hair and fine features, exactly suited to the heroes of dashing melodrama and romance; a certain picturesque artificiality and lack of training, however, prevented him from doing serious work later in his career, though with the profits of his production of *The Walls of Jericho* he opened his own theatre in New York, and later, with the proceeds of a legacy, put on an *Othello* with sets by Urban which marked an important step forward in the history of American stage-craft and scenic design.

HAINES, JOSEPH (?–1701), English actor, was an excellent comedian, an inveterate practical joker, and a writer of scurrilous verse and lampoons which on several occasions got him into trouble. He was a dancing-master in France, but went to England and set up a booth at Bartholomew Fair. He eventually joined Killigrew's company at the Theatre Royal, and played clowns and buffoons. He was one of the first English Harlequins, in Ravenscroft's adaptation of *Les Fourberies de Scapin*, which, being forestalled by Otway's at Dorset Garden, was renamed and remodelled on the lines of Fiorelli's *commedia dell'arte* productions in Paris. Haines made a special journey to Paris to study the methods and machinery of the French stage.

HALE, LOUISE (*née* CLOSSER) (1872–1933), American actress and author, whose later career was entirely in films. She was, however, on the legitimate stage for many years, first appearing at Detroit in the mid-'90s in *In Old Kentucky*. Her first great success came as Prossy in *Candida* with Arnold Daly in 1903. In 1907 she appeared in London as Miss Hazy in *Mrs. Wiggs of the Cabbage Patch*, and before she left the stage to go to Hollywood she appeared in many other excellent productions, including *The Blue Bird*, *Ruggles of Red Gap*, *Beyond the Horizon*, and *Peer Gynt*. She wrote a number of novels, many of them dealing with theatrical life, and some travel books, the latter illustrated by her husband, Walter Hale (1869–1917).

HALLAM, a family of English actors, closely connected with the earliest beginnings of a professional theatre in the United States. The first was (1) LEWIS (1714–56), son of Adam Hallam, who was at Covent Garden from 1734 to 1741, and later at Drury Lane, and brother of the manager of a theatre in Leman Street (either Goodman's Fields or the Wells). In 1752 he took his wife and children, with a company of ten actors, to Williamsburg, Virginia, and on 15 Sept. gave *The Merchant of Venice* and *The Alchemist.* A year later he was in New York, where he built the first theatre there, on Nassau Street. In it his company, in the face of some opposition, appeared in a fine repertory which included Shakespeare, Rowe, Lillo, Moore, Farquhar, Addison, Cibber, Vanbrugh, Steele, and Gay, together with a number of farces and after-pieces. Later in Philadelphia Hallam's company played in a building previously occupied by Kean and Murray, which was not demolished until 1849, and then, after a visit to Charleston, went to Jamaica. There the elder Hallam died, and his widow married David Douglass, also manager of a company touring there. The remnants of Hallam's company joined that of Douglass, and with the younger (2) LEWIS (c. 1740–1808) as leading man, went back to New York. They were billed as the American Company, and played in a temporary theatre on Cruger's Wharf where, in 1759, the younger Hallam played Romeo to his mother's Juliet, his younger brother and sister Beatrice being also in the cast. Lewis was an excellent actor, and appeared in *The Prince of Parthia,* the first American play to be given a professional production. After the death of Douglass he took over the management of the American Company, in partnership with John Henry. Bringing it back from the West Indies, where it had taken refuge during the War of Independence, he reopened the Southwark Theatre in Philadelphia and the John Street in New York, playing also in Baltimore and Annapolis. Hallam remained a manager of the American Company, first with Henry and later with Hodgkinson and Dunlap, until 1797, when he became merely a salaried actor, continuing on the stage until his death. He married, as his second wife, an actress named Miss Tuke, who became an important member of the company, but caused much trouble by her intemperate habits and quarrelsomeness. By a former marriage he had a son Mirvan, who was on the stage till his death in 1811, but was accounted a mediocre actor.

The stepmother of the elder Hallam was a well-known actress in London, first as Mrs. Parker, then as Mrs. Berriman, and finally as Mrs. Adam Hallam, while one of his children (3) ISABELLA (1746–1826), left behind in London when the family embarked for Williamsburg, became well known as Mrs. Mattocks. Two younger members of the Hallam family were Nancy, who played children's parts in Philadelphia in 1759–61, and Sarah, who became leading lady of the company in 1770, and in 1775 opened a dancing-school in Williamsburg. She was much appreciated during her short reign, and many poems were addressed to her. She is believed to have been a niece of the elder Hallam, and therefore cousin to young Lewis.

HALLS, a generic term for the music-halls, including those in London and in the provinces.

HALLSTRÖM, PER (1866–   ), Swedish dramatist, produced in the course of his career lyric and romantic poetry, novels and studies, drama, essays, and some significant aesthetic criticism. His plays belong almost entirely to the twentieth century: *Grefven af Antwerpen* (*The Count of Antwerp*) (1898); a tragedy, *Bianco Capello* (1900); *En veneziansk komedi* (A Venetian Comedy) (1901); a comedy, *Erotikon* (1908); two legend-plays, *Alkestis* and *Ahasverus* (also 1908); two saga-plays, *Önskningarna* (*Wishes*) and *Tusen och en natt* (*The Thousand and One Nights*) (1910): *Karl den elfte* (*Carl XI*) and *Gustaf den tredje* (*Gustave III*) (both 1918); *Nessusdräkten* (*The Shirt of Nessus*) (1919). Hallström's chief contribution to drama after 1919 was the translation of the plays of Shakespeare made between 1922 and 1931.   U. E.-F.

HAMBLIN, THOMAS SOWERBY (1800–53), actor and theatre manager, who is chiefly remembered as manager and leading man of the Bowery Theatre, New York, in its most successful years. He was born in London and, after some years in the provinces, appeared at Drury Lane in leading parts. He went to America in 1825, and made his first appearance at the Park Theatre as Hamlet, later touring the United States as a tragedian. He was a fine, though somewhat melodramatic, actor, but in later years his acting was hindered by frequent bouts of asthma. He became lessee of the Bowery in 1830, rebuilt it after the disastrous fire of 1836, and only relinquished it after two further fires, in 1838 and 1845. Ill luck seemed to dog him, for in 1848 he rented and redecorated the old Park Theatre and opened it on 4 Sept., only to see it destroyed by fire three months later. He then retired, and lived quietly until his death. He was twice married, his first wife being a daughter of the English actor William Blanchard. She was herself a good actress, and was for many years her husband's leading lady.

HAMBURG, a town important in the development of the German theatre, since it saw in 1765 the first attempt to establish a German National Theatre, with Lessing as its accredited critic. The enterprise failed after three years (see ACKERMANN, GERMANY, 4, LESSING, and SCHRÖDER).

HAMMERSTEIN'S OLYMPIA, NEW YORK, see NEW YORK THEATRE (2).

HAMMERSTEIN'S THEATRE, New York, see MANHATTAN THEATRE.

HAMMERTON, Stephen (*fl.* 1630–47), English actor of whom it was said that he 'was at first a most noted and beautiful Woman Actor, but afterwards he acted with equal Grace and Applause a Young Lover's part' (Wright). He is known to have been an excellent boy-actor, and must have appeared at Salisbury Court, for in 1632 Beeston, the manager, and Blagrove, one of the landlords, petitioned for his return from the King's Men, who had inveigled him away. There is no record of whether they got him back or not, and he next appears in adult male parts, as King Ferdinand in *The Doubtful Heir*, and Orsabin in *The Goblin* (both Shirley, 1640). He signed the dedication of the Beaumont and Fletcher folio in 1647, but nothing more is known of him.

HAMPDEN, Walter (1879–), American actor, whose full name was Walter Hampden Dougherty. He made his first appearances on the stage in England, where he was for some years a member of Benson's company, and played leading parts at the Adelphi, London. In 1907 he returned to the United States, and made his New York début when he appeared with Nazimova in a season of Ibsen and other plays. Among his later successes were Manson in *The Servant in the House*, Hippolytus, and a number of Shakespearian parts which included Caliban, Oberon, Macbeth, Romeo, Hamlet, Othello, and Shylock, while in 1923 he first played in *Cyrano de Bergerac*, which he several times revived. In 1925 he took over the Colonial Theatre, which he renamed Hampden's, and appeared there in an interesting repertory of Shakespeare, Ibsen, and other plays, including *Henry V*, *The Bonds of Interest*, and *Richelieu*. He remained in his own theatre until 1930, and then toured, mainly in revivals of his previous successes. In 1939 he played the Stage Manager in *Our Town*, and in 1947 was associated with the American Repertory Theatre, playing Cardinal Wolsey in *Henry VIII*.

HAND-PROPS, see PROPS.

HAND-PUPPET, see PUNCH AND JUDY and PUPPET.

HAND-WORKED HOUSE, see ENGLISH PLAYHOUSE, 2 *a* and STAGE.

HANKIN, Edward Charles St. John (1869–1909), English dramatist, of whom it was said that 'his plays, shot through with a cynical pessimism, made even Ibsen seem good-humoured'. He had great talent, but in revolt against the sentimentalism of the nineteenth-century theatre he renounced all faith in human nature, attacking abuses but in no way suggesting remedies for them. Among his plays were *The Two Mr. Wetherbys* (1903); *The Return of the Prodigal* (1905), in which the central figure, a young wastrel, is supported by his father and brother in case he should damage their reputations; *The Charity that Began at Home* (1906), a bitter attack on indiscriminate benevolence; *The Cassilis Engagement* (1907), where a misalliance is avoided when the bookmaker's daughter is invited to visit her fiancé's country-house family, and breaks off her engagement because of the dullness of their lives; and *The Last of the De Mullins* (1908), which deals with the opposition of her family to the New Woman of the period, who chooses to earn her own living.

HANLON-LEES, a troupe of acrobatic actors, composed originally of the six sons of an actor named Thomas Hanlon, manager of the Theatre Royal, Manchester. They worked in combination with the famous acrobat, 'Professor' John Lees, and in 1889, after some thirty years of work, the three surviving brothers, George (1839– ?), William (1844–1923), and Edward (1854–1931), were in New York with a show called *Fantasma*. This was first produced at the Fifth Avenue Theatre in 1883, at which time William Hanlon's home at Cohasset was said to resemble a museum, so crowded was it 'with curios and the models of their many productions'. Their most famous show was possibly the *Voyage en Suisse*, presented at the Théâtre des Variétés in Paris in 1879, and at the Gaiety, London, in 1880. 'It included a bus smash, a chaotic scene on board a ship in a storm, an exploding Pullman car, a banquet transformed into a wholesale juggling party after one of the Hanlons had crashed through the ceiling on to the table, and one of the cleverest drunk scenes ever presented on the stage.' *The Times* critic was moved to describe the drunken scene as 'so dreadfully true to nature and withal so genuinely diverting, that one gazes on it with an enthralled interest more fittingly applied to some burst of passion at the Lyceum'. An account, from which the above is quoted, is given by Dr. Thomas Walton in an article entitled 'Entortillationists' in *Life and Letters To-day* for April 1941, and an analysis of the technical trickwork of the drunken scene in the September 1941 number of the same journal, by Richard Southern.   R. S.

HANSEN, Christiern (?–post 1545), early Danish dramatist (see SCANDINAVIA, 1).

HANS STOCKFISCH, see ENGLISH COMEDIANS and SPENCER, JOHN.

HANSWURST, the seventeenth- and eighteenth-century German stage jester, the lineal descendant of the *Narr* of medieval times. He came to typify the jolly, beer-drinking, broadly farcical humour of German as distinct from the imported vivacity and drollery of Italian, French, or English wit. He was most popular in Vienna, where he was evolved and portrayed by the comedian Stranitzky as a Salzburg peasant, but he soon found his way all over Austria and Germany, and became a familiar figure, butting his way through all the plays of the time, and always hailed with uproarious delight. Eventually his clowning became a tyranny, and he was banished by Gottsched from the serious stage, only to reappear as Kasperl in the puppet-shows of Vienna, where he still survives.

HARCOURT WILLIAMS, see WILLIAMS, (ERNEST GEORGE) HARCOURT.

HARDWICKE, SIR CEDRIC (1893–   ), English actor, knighted in 1934 for his services to the stage. He studied at the R.A.D.A., as did his wife, Helena Pickard, who was one of the earliest members of the Birmingham Repertory company, and for a short time concerned in the management of the Grafton Theatre, London. Hardwicke made his first appearance on the stage in 1912, joining Benson's company on tour a year later. In 1914 he was at the Old Vic, but his career was interrupted by war service, and he was not seen again on the stage until 1922, when he was with the Birmingham Repertory. Here he laid the foundations of a notable career with a variety of performances, of which the most important were Churdles Ash in *The Farmer's Wife* and Caesar in *Caesar and Cleopatra*, in both of which he was subsequently seen in London. Some of his best work was done at the Malvern Festival, where he played Magnus in *The Apple Cart* and, among other parts, Edward Moulton-Barrett in *The Barretts of Wimpole Street*, which he continued to play during a long run in London and on tour. Later parts were the Burglar in *Too True to be Good*, Dr. Haggett in *The Late Christopher Bean*, and Mikail in *Tovarich*. He then went to New York and was seen in the title-role of *The Amazing Dr. Clitterhouse*, and as Canon Skerritt in *Shadow and Substance*. After several years in Hollywood he returned to England to tour for E.N.S.A. in a revival of *Yellow Sands*. In 1932 he published a volume of reminiscences, *Let's Pretend*.

HARDY, ALEXANDRE (*c.* 1575–*c.* 1631), an early French dramatist, and perhaps the most important before Corneille. Very little is known of his life, and his date of birth is variously given as 1560, 1569, and 1575, the latest research inclining towards 1575. He was of good family, born in Paris, and well educated. Although there is no evidence that he was ever an actor, he was certainly attached as paid dramatist to a provincial company, that of Valleran-Lecomte, which was in Paris in the early years of the seventeenth century. He had begun to write in about 1595, and was a most prolific author, turning out between 600 and 700 plays, of which some 34 survive. They were of every conceivable type, and would serve to illustrate the catalogue of Polonius, but because of their mixture of genres they are generally classed as tragi-comedies, though many of them verged on melodrama. Action rather than narrative was Hardy's aim, which he achieved with a complete disregard for the

unities of time and place. With a spark of the genius of Shakespeare or Lope de Vega he might have changed the course of French dramatic literature, but his facility and easy successes told against him, and he lived just long enough to see the Unities triumph. Ironically enough, Corneille's first contact with the theatre was through Hardy, whose plays he saw in Rouen. In view of Hardy's definite connexion with a professional company of actors, and of the fact that unlike most contemporary dramatists he did nothing but write plays, he may perhaps be called the first professional playwright of France. His plays were given with the old-fashioned simultaneous setting of the medieval religious drama, and called for the presentation of many different localities.

HARE [FAIRS], SIR JOHN (1844–1921), English actor-manager, knighted in 1907 for his services to the stage. He made his first appearance in Liverpool in 1864 and was first seen in London on 25 Sept. 1865 at the Prince of Wales's in *Naval Engagements*, under the management of H. J. Byron and the Bancrofts. He made a success in Robertson's *Society* (1865), and stayed at the Prince of Wales's for many years, being mainly identified with the plays of Robertson. He left to assume the management of the Court Theatre, where he produced, but did not play in, *Olivia*, and appeared in a series of successful new plays from 1875 to 1879. He then went into partnership with Kendal at the St. James's for eight years, producing and playing in Pinero's *The Money Spinners* (1881). Hare then went to the Garrick, which W. S. Gilbert built for him, and opened on 24 April 1889 with *The Profligate*. It was at this theatre, where he remained until 1895, that he made such a success as Benjamin Goldfinch in *A Pair of Spectacles*, a part with which his name is always associated. He made his first appearance in New York on 23 Dec. 1895 in *The Notorious Mrs. Ebbsmith*, and then revived several of his successes. He toured as Old Eccles in *Caste*, in which he had originally played Sam Gerridge, and made his farewell performances in 1907–8, retiring finally in 1911.

HARLEQUIN, the young lover of Columbine in the English harlequinade. His name, though not his status, derives from the Arlecchino of the *commedia dell'arte*, where he was one of the *zanni* or quick-witted, unscrupulous serving-men; and so he remained in Italy. But Marivaux turned him into a pretty simpleton, while in the harlequinade he was first a romantic magician and later a languishing, lackadaisical lover, foppishly dressed in a close-fitting suit of bright silk diamonds (derived from the patches on his original rags), sometimes with lace frill and ruffles. He retains from his origins the small black cat-faced mask, and a lath or bat of thin wood, which in English pantomimes served, when slapped lightly on the floor or wall, as a signal for the transformation scene (see ARLECCHINO and HARLEQUINADE).

HARLEQUINADE, as distinct from *Arlequinade*, which means a sample of Arlequin's wit, is used as the label for scenes acted by Harlequin, although *the* harlequinade refers to a special kind (see CLOWN and PANTOMIME). In Ravenscroft's *Scaramouche, a Philosopher* (1677) and Mountford's *Dr. Faustus* (1685/6), Harlequin and Scaramouche already show how the *commedia dell'arte* is translated into horseplay by the English theatre. Another change originated in restrictions upon dramatic performances at Paris fairs (see COMÉDIE-ITALIENNE). Arlequins, forbidden dialogue when acting in booths, invented a new style of comic dancing which the patent theatres of London billed as 'Italian Night Scenes'. Thus Harlequin became permanently a dancer, who was voiceless except in freakish pieces. His bat or slapstick was replaced by a magic wand of similar pattern; in Paris Arlequin had been armed, in parodies of fairy tales, with the conjurer's baguette, and the uses of this were exploited in London when Harlequin was demonstrating the latest devices of transformation scenes. The two 'hand-props' were fused into one because the pliant bat gave an effective slap upon sidewing or stage as a signal to scene-shifters. There was a still more curious translation. At the Hotel de Bourgogne Arlequin had the licence *x* enjoys in mathematics of presenting himself as any number of other personages, usually leading characters in contemporary plays which the Italians were burlesquing. In London this convention was not understood. Thurmond's *Harlequin Dr. Faustus* (1723) and *Harlequin Sheppard* (1724), which duplicated characters without burlesque, established a tradition that Harlequin must be someone other than himself. In the harlequinade-pantomimes which developed from the Italian Night Scenes, it was customary for Harlequin and Columbine, as eloping lovers, to be pursued by her father (Pantaloon) and his blundering servant (at first Pierrot and then Clown). There had to be an 'opening' scene for Harlequin to receive his magic wand from some immortal, and this part of the plot had to be novel. The taxing of authors' brains was evident in titles alone until the duplicate-character idea was accepted. Towards the end of the eighteenth century the design was established that the 'opening' should tell a well-known story of persecuted lovers rescued by a good fairy and changed by her into Harlequin and Columbine. In the early years of the nineteenth century Grimaldi made Clown the chief character of the harlequinade, and so began the tendency which later diminished the love scenes into an occasional *pas de deux* by Harlequin and Columbine between bouts of horseplay—shop-lifting with Pantaloon as a weak-witted accomplice whom the policeman caught red-handed, the buttered slide for angry shopkeepers to fall upon, the pail of paste emptied over a dandy's head, the red-hot poker frequently laid upon

unsuspecting trousers, and the 'spill and pelt' when vegetables were flung in battle. Throughout Victoria's reign the 'opening' increased in length, and when fairy-tales were regularly dramatized for this purpose the older delights dwindled into a plotless epilogue known as the harlequinade because it was no longer the pantomime. Harlequin was not allowed to be the hero in the fairy-tale (who had become even before this the Principal Boy for an actress to play), although for some years there was a pretence of changing one character into the other by means of traps to lower the hero out of sight and set Harlequin on the stage at the same instant. Children of the *fin de siècle* had no interest in this hocus-pocus; the harlequinade, all links severed, was usually an advertising medium after the grand finale (though introduced mid-way in one or two pantomimes). There were still vestiges of the harlequinade in London up to and during the Second World War.   M. W. D.

HARLEVILLE, (JEAN FRANÇOIS) COLLIN D' (1755–1806), French dramatist, who was intended for the law, but haunted the Paris theatres and got into debt. His family called him home, and he was over thirty before he again succeeded in escaping. Back in Paris, he was brought to the notice of Marie Antoinette by Mme Campan, who persuaded the queen to allow his first play, *L'Inconstant*, to be performed at Versailles. It was then given at the Comédie-Française (1786), and was followed by *L'Optimiste* (1788), in which d'Harleville criticizes Rousseau's *homme sensible*, showing that such a man can only be happy by closing his eyes to facts. D'Harleville's best-known play is *Les Châteaux en Espagne* (1789), an amusing study of a man who, like Candide, thinks everything is for the best in the best of all possible worlds. Its success nearly cost d'Harleville his head, for it aroused the jealousy of Fabre d'Églantine, who had just failed with a play based on a similar idea, and d'Harleville was arrested as an enemy of the Republic. But he escaped the guillotine, and lived to write several more plays, none of them as good as his earlier ones. The best is *Le Vieux célibataire* (1792), which again deals with the pitfalls that beset *l'homme sensible*. D'Harleville was a popular, though not a particularly good, dramatist, and his light-hearted comedies were much appreciated by an audience caught up in the toils of the Revolution.

HARRIGAN. (1) EDWARD (1845–1911), American actor, manager, and dramatist, who was born in New York, but ran away from home to go on the stage, and first appeared in San Francisco. It was his partnership with Tony Hart (1857–91), a female impersonator whose real name was Anthony Cannon, which first brought him into prominence, and as the comedy team of Harrigan and Hart they established themselves in New York in 1872. Here, under their own management at various theatres, they produced many successful shows, particularly the Mulligan Guards series in which Ned Harrigan played Dan Mulligan and Hart his wife Cordelia. They parted company after a fire in 1884 had destroyed their theatre, but Harrigan continued to act, appearing in a number of his own plays, such as *Old Lavender* and *The Major* (1881), and made his last appearance on the stage in 1908. He is credited with the composition of over eighty vaudeville sketches in ten years, on which some of his later full-length plays were based. His characters are recognizable types of old New York life, chiefly Irish- and German-Americans and negroes, and he wrote for his own productions a number of delightful songs, set to music by David Braham, his father-in-law. His son (2) WILLIAM (1893–) also became an actor, making his first appearance as a child of 5 with his father in the latter's *Reilly and the 400*. He was first seen in London in 1934, and twice toured Australia.

HARRIGAN'S THEATRE, NEW YORK, see GARRICK THEATRE (3).

HARRINGTON, COUNTESS OF, see FOOTE, MARIA.

HARRIS. (1) AUGUSTUS GLOSSOP (1825–73), English theatre manager, son of an opera singer known as Madame Féron, and of the Joseph Glossop who built the Coburg Theatre (later the Old Vic). Augustus first appeared on the stage in America at the age of 8, in *Cinderella*. He went to London and played at the Princess's under Maddox, and became manager of the theatre when Charles Kean retired, opening in Sept. 1859 with *Ivy Hall*. His management lasted until Oct. 1862, and during it he introduced Fechter to London; but it is as a manager of opera and ballet that Harris is chiefly remembered. He was for twenty-seven years connected with Covent Garden, and directed opera in Madrid, Paris, Berlin, and St. Petersburg. He had a good eye for colour, and was an excellent stage-manager. His son (2) AUGUSTUS (1851–96), nicknamed Druriolanus from his connexion with that famous theatre, was knighted in 1891, not for his services to the theatre, but because he was a Sheriff of the City of London when the German Emperor paid a visit there. He took over Drury Lane in the 1880s, and made a success of spectacular melodrama and elaborate pantomimes. Although his efforts in the latter direction were by some held responsible for the vulgarizing of pantomime, he had a feeling for the old harlequinade, and always made it a feature of his shows, with such clowns as Whimsical Walker and others. He also equipped his pantomimes with lavish scenery and machines, and was the first to import into them tried favourites from the music-halls as Principal Boys, Dames, and knockabout comedians.

HARRIS, HENRY (?–*c.* 1682), an English actor of the Restoration, who played with Betterton, and was ranked by some above him. Chappuzeau, the historian of the French theatre, saw him act, and was much struck by his energetic playing of the name part in Orrery's *Mustapha* (1668). Pepys, though he thought him proud and overweeningly conceited, admired him immensely, and took great delight in his company, calling him 'a man of fine conversation'. One of his finest parts was Cardinal Wolsey, in which character his portrait was painted and engraved by Greenhill.

HARRISON, RICHARD BERRY (1864–1935), an American negro actor, son of slaves who escaped to Canada. Returning to Detroit, Harrison, who had always shown a great love for the theatre, was befriended by L. E. Behymer, and after some training in elocution, toured the Behymer and Chautauqua circuits with a repertory of Shakespearian and other recitations. He was working as a teacher of dramatics and elocution when he was persuaded to play De Lawd in *Green Pastures* (1930), in which he immediately made a great success. He appeared in the part nearly 2,000 times before his death, and in 1931 was awarded the Spingarn medal for his performance. A man of medium build, with a soft, resonant voice, he was for the greater part of his life a lecturer, teacher, and arranger of festivals for coloured schools and churches. An intensely humble man, his one great regret was that he had never appeared in any of the plays of Shakespeare, whose works he knew so well.

HARṢA, see INDIA.

HART, CHARLES (?–1683), English actor who was in Killigrew's company at the Theatre Royal with Mohun. He was on the stage as a boy, playing the important role of the Duchess in *The Cardinal* in 1641, apparently with much success. He later became a soldier, returning to the stage at the Restoration. He was the original Celadon in Dryden's *Secret Love,* in which he played opposite Nell Gwynn as Florimel. He excelled in heroic parts, particularly as Alexander in *The Rival Queens,* and when on the stage became so absorbed in his parts that it was almost impossible to distract his attention. He retired on pension when the two companies amalgamated in 1682, being perhaps unwilling to enter into competition with Betterton, and died shortly afterwards.

HART, MOSS (1908–), see KAUFMAN and U.S.A., 8.

HART, TONY (1857–91), see HARRIGAN, EDWARD.

HART HOUSE THEATRE, a small but excellently equipped playhouse which forms part of the central students' building, Hart House, built by the Massey Foundation for the University of Toronto, Canada. The theatre owed its inception to the enthusiasm of Vincent Massey, who was Chairman of its Board of Syndics from 1919 until his appointment as Canadian High Commissioner in London in 1935. Both he and his brother Raymond, later a professional actor, acted and produced at

Hart House Theatre, which was founded 'to provide an experimental art theatre for the use of the University of Toronto and the wider community'—a function which it continued to perform until well into the 1930s, under a succession of able directors. Its first programme, put on by the Players' Club, shows an interesting variety of plays, including *The Trojan Women, The Farce of Master Pierre Patelin, The Alchemist,* and *Love's Labour's Lost,* each preceded by a professorial lecture and by talks on various aspects of drama by the first director, Roy Mitchell, founder of the Players' Club. In later seasons plays were given by Shakespeare, Shaw, O'Neill, Yeats, Synge, and Sutton Vane, whose *Outward Bound* was directed by Vincent Massey. In 1923 a new play by a contemporary Japanese playwright was given, and a year later, under Bertram Forsyth, who did much to raise the standard of acting, fine performances were seen of *The Bonds of Interest* and Claudel's *The Hostage.* Forsyth was followed as director by Walter Sinclair, who had previously managed the Hongkong Amateur Dramatic Society with much success. The encouragement of Canadian playwrights had always been one of the functions of the Hart House Theatre, and it was during Sinclair's term of office that in May 1927 the first all-Canadian bill was presented, consisting of one-act plays by Isabel Ecclestone Mackay, author also of full-length Canadian plays, Duncan Campbell Scott, winner of the Lorne Pierce Gold Medal for distinguished service to Canadian literature in 1927, and Mazo de la Roche, well known as a novelist, whose Canadian *Whiteoaks* series formed the basis of a successful play given in London in 1936. Sinclair was also responsible for excellent productions of *Turandot* and *Twelfth Night,* and invited as guest-producer for *Antony and Cleopatra* the Canadian dramatist, Carroll Aikins. Aikins, whose *God of Gods* was done by the Birmingham Repertory Theatre in 1920, succeeded Sinclair as Director of Hart House Theatre, his chief productions being *Romeo and Juliet* and *The Doctor's Dilemma.* Later directors were Edgar Stone, who had worked for many years at Hart House, and Mary Piper, the only woman yet appointed, whose work as producer was commended, though her choice of play was somewhat adversely criticized.

On the outbreak of war in 1939 the theatre, which had somewhat fallen from its high estate and been used mainly for concerts, lectures, and the activities of outside bodies, was closed until 1946. It then reopened on a new basis, having relinquished its former semi-independent status and become an integral part of the university. It is hoped that in its capacity as an undergraduate theatre it will continue to prove a stimulating and educative force in the rapidly developing theatrical life of the whole country. (See also CANADA.)

HARTLEY, ELIZABETH (1751–1824), English actress of such remarkable beauty that she was the favourite model of Sir Joshua Reynolds. He used her frequently for his paintings, and three professed portraits of her are in the Mathews Collection in the Garrick Club. After her death an unknown admirer wrote of her: 'Her complexion was beautifully fair, her hair was auburn, and her eyes more like those of doves than any I remember to have seen.' As an actress, she was best in pathetic and tender parts, and her Elfrida, Jane Shore, and Rosamund were more highly praised than her Lady Macbeth, Desdemona, or Cleopatra (in *All for Love*). She was very reticent about her personal affairs, and little is known of her life beyond the fact that she was born in the north of England, married young to an unknown Mr. Hartley (her maiden name being White), and that after a successful career untouched by scandal she retired to Woolwich to live comfortably on her savings. She made a first fleeting appearance in London, at the Haymarket under Foote, in 1769, but went into the provinces for several years, and in 1772 made her first appearance at Covent Garden as Jane Shore, remaining there for the rest of her career. She appears to have been good in comedy, and was the original Lady Touchwood in *The Belle's Stratagem* (1780).

HARTZENBUSCH, JUAN EUGENIO (1806–80), the son of a German carpenter, born and brought up in Spain, who translated many foreign plays into Spanish and adapted for the contemporary theatre a number of old Castilian dramas. He worked for a long time without success, until the production in 1837 of his masterpiece, *Los Amantes de Teruel,* a romantic drama on a traditional Spanish theme which remained in the repertory of the Madrid theatre for many years. Hartzenbusch followed up this success with many others, though none of his later plays deserves to rank with *Los Amantes.* He was also the author of several comedies, and of fairy plays, of which the most successful was *Los polvos de la madre Celestina* (1841). Hartzenbusch was the editor of a number of plays by the older dramatists (Lope de Vega, Calderón, Tirso de Molina, and Alarcón) in the series *Biblioteca de autores epañoles,* which appeared from 1850 to 1860, and helped to reveal the richness of the Golden Age of Spanish drama to those who had for so long neglected it.

HARVARD. Plays were given at Harvard in its very early days, since a graduate of the college records in his diary several amateur and no doubt surreptitious performances by students between 1758 and 1761 of such plays as *Cato, The Roman Father,* and *The Orphan.* Later a certain amount of amateur acting was encouraged by the authorities, and the Hasty Pudding Club was formed, its productions now being mainly musicals. The Harvard Dramatic Club was started in 1908, and for many years produced only plays written by its members. It later concentrated on outstanding foreign plays. It was at Harvard that Professor Baker first organized, in 1906, his famous course of play-writing and play-production known as '47 Workshop', moving to Yale in 1925. Harvard possesses one of the finest theatre collections in the world. It was started in 1903 by John Drew, who presented to the university the library of Robert W. Lowe, theatre bibliographer of London. In 1915 it was increased by the collection of Robert Gould Shaw, who became the first (honorary) Curator of the collection, for which he later left a liberal endowment. It is now housed in the Houghton Library under the administration of Dr. Van Lennep, and is constantly being added to by purchase and bequest. A descriptive catalogue of the engraved portraits in the collection was issued in four volumes (1930–4) under the editorship of Mrs. Lillian A. Hall, and a comprehensive system of filing, which is continually being improved, makes the material, on which much work remains to be done, easily accessible to research workers.

HARVEY, SIR JOHN MARTIN- (1863–1944), English actor-manager, who in 1921 was knighted for his services to the theatre. He made his first appearance on the stage in 1881, and in the following year joined Irving's company at the Lyceum, where he remained for some fourteen years. During that time he made rapid strides in his profession, and was already marked out for eminence when in 1899 he inaugurated his own management of the Lyceum with an adaptation of *A Tale of Two Cities* as *The Only Way*, in which he played Sydney Carton, a part with which he was associated for the rest of his life. He had previously toured in several plays of Irving's repertory, including *The Corsican Brothers* and *The Lady of Lyons*, and had made a success as Pelléas to the Mélisande of Mrs. Patrick Campbell; but it was the production of *The Only Way* which started him on his career as a romantic actor and outstanding manager. Among his later productions were *A Cigarette Maker's Romance* (1901), *The Breed of the Treshams* (1903), *The Burgomaster of Stilemonde* (1918), and *Everyman* (1923); *Hamlet*, which he played for the first time in 1904 and frequently revived; *Richard III*, *The Taming of the Shrew*, and *Henry V*. In 1912 he gave a magnificent performance as Oedipus Rex in Reinhardt's production of this play, and toured all over the world in a repertory of his favourite parts. Harvey, who was a handsome man with clear-cut sensitive features and a distinguished presence, was regarded by many as the lineal descendant of Irving, and his death broke the last link with the Victorian stage. His acting in *Oedipus Rex*, which Macqueen-Pope called 'savage in its stark horror of relentlessness, heart-moving in its sorrow and grief', showed to what heights he might have risen had he not been so closely identified with the somewhat melodramatic role of Sydney Carton, which he was constantly forced to revive in order to satisfy an adoring public. He was, however, a man of scholarly and scrupulous taste, and on the occasion of his seventy-fifth birthday

received the degree of Hon. LL.D. from Glasgow University. He published his autobiography in 1933. He married in 1889 Angelita Helena de Silva (1869–1949), who was his leading lady for many years.

HARWOOD, JOHN E. (1771–1809), American actor, celebrated for his portrayal of Falstaff, which he first played at the Park Theatre, New York, in 1806, with Cooper, manager and leading man of the company, as Hotspur. Harwood was for some years at the Chestnut Street Theatre, Philadelphia, under Wignell, and was with the company when it appeared in New York in 1797, being much admired in low-comedy parts. He was engaged by Dunlap for the Park Theatre in 1803, and made his first great success there as Dennis Brulgruddery in the younger Colman's *John Bull; or, an Englishman's Fireside*. Dunlap, in his *History of the American Stage*, characterized this as 'one of the richest pieces of comic acting we have ever witnessed'. He later changed his style of acting, appearing as polished gentlemen, for which his fine presence and handsome countenance made him eminently suitable. He remained at the Park Theatre until his death, except for a short session in Philadelphia after Dunlap's bankruptcy, and the company, as well as the public, felt his loss keenly. He married the granddaughter of Benjamin Franklin.

HAUCH, JOHANNES CARSTEN (1790–1872), Danish dramatist, succeeded Oehlenschlaeger as Professor of Aesthetics in Copenhagen University, and in his youth attacked the romantic poetry and philosophy of the school of the dramatist Ingemann. While thus exerting influence at most periods of his life through his criticism, he was at the same time an active and, at the height of his power, a highly esteemed dramatist. His admiration for Oehlenschlaeger was strong from his early years. His first plays were remarkable rather for their psychological insight than for their dramatic structure; *Bajazet* (1828), *Tiberius* (1828), and *Gregorius den Syvende* (*Gregory the Seventh*) (1829) perhaps represent the best of his first phase. He reached the height of his popularity in *Søstrene paa Kinnekullen* (*The Sisters at Kinnekullen*) (1849), *Marsk Stig* (*Marshall Stig*) (1850), and *Tycho Brahe's Ungdom* (*The Youth of Tycho Brahe*) (1852).

U. E.-F.

HAUPTMANN, GERHART (1862–1946), German dramatist, a Silesian by birth, who often used his native dialect in his plays. He first intended to become a sculptor, and attended art schools in Germany and Italy, but he was attracted by the activities of the Freie Bühne in Berlin, and his first play, *Vor Sonnenaufgang*, a grim naturalistic drama much influenced by Holz's *Familie Selicke*, was given there in 1889. This was followed by other plays in the same genre, including *Einsame Menschen* (1891), a study of marital incompatibility which had its echoes in his own life, since he had recently separated from his wife, whom he had married in 1885. But Hauptmann was at heart a romantic, and this first period, which ended in 1892 with the historical drama *Die Weber*—on the revolt of the Silesian weavers in 1844—was followed by a series of comedies, of which the best was *Der Biberpelz* (1893), and by the fantasy of *Hanneles Himmelfahrt* (1893). This led to essays in the then-fashionable symbolic style with *Die versunkene Glocke* (1896) and other less successful plays. Hauptmann's later output varied between his earlier realism and his later fantasies, with occasional excursions into history; but he never again reached the heights of *Die Weber*, for which he was awarded the Nobel Prize in 1912. Yet many of his plays will live by the freshness of his verse and prose. A keen eye, a feeling heart, and a creative imagination endow his characters with life. In his naturalistic, and best, period, he deliberately subordinated action to circumstances, and his characters are more often sinned against than sinning. In his comedies he displays human foibles with engaging benevolence, while his tragedies inspire sympathy rather than admiration.   W. E. D.

HAUPT- UND STAATSAKTIONEN, the name given to popular seventeenth-century plays in Germany dealing with events in high places. No complete texts of these have survived, since, as in the *commedia dell'arte*, only the main outline of the plot was laid down, the dialogue being left to the ingenuity of the actors who, assisted by the fool, Hanswurst, interpreted their parts in flowery prose, in accordance with established conventions. This practice arose in Germany in imitation of the English Comedians, and was also directly influenced by Italy. The subjects of the plays were drawn from opera, from English, and from German drama, even such a serious play as Gryphius's *Papinianus* being laid under contribution. They were particularly popular in Vienna, and continued to hold the stage until the literary reforms of Gottsched.

HAUTEROCHE, Noël Jacques le Breton de (c. 1616–1707), a French actor and dramatist, believed to have been of good family and certainly well educated. He was at the Marais for some time, probably joining the company there in about 1654 and leaving in 1663, when he went to the Hôtel de Bourgogne. A man of upright character, he was tall and elegant and a good actor, though Molière satirized him in *L'Impromptu de Versailles*. He succeeded Floridor as Orator of the troupe, and was one of the original members of the Comédie-Française, retiring in 1684 and being later stricken with blindness. He was the author of a number of successful comedies, reminiscent of Molière, some of which remained in the repertory until late in the nineteenth century. Among them were *Crispin médecin* (1670) and *Crispin musicien* (1674), written perhaps for Raymond Poisson, and *La Dame invisible* (1684), a rewriting of d'Ouville's adaptation of *La Dama Duende* by Calderón, given over forty years previously as *L'Esprit folet*. Many

years later this play provided the actor Préville with one of his greatest successes.

HAWTREY, Sir Charles H. (1858–1923), English actor-manager, a fine light comedian. The son of a clergyman who was a master at Eton, where he himself was educated, Hawtrey was typical of the English gentleman and man-about-town of his time. He always wore a moustache (on the only occasion when he shaved it off the play failed), he had perfect poise and sang-froid, and was, on the stage, naturalness itself. He excelled in parts where he had to tell lies, which he did with such ease and brilliance that he afforded the audience, in the secret, the most unbounded delight. He was a much better actor than his public would allow him to be, since he was so popular in what were known as 'Hawtrey' parts that he seldom had the opportunity to play anything else. But in his particular line he had no equal. He made his first appearance on the stage, under the assumed name of Bankes, at the old Prince of Wales's Theatre in 1881, and soon went into management on his own account. Among the many successful plays which he produced and appeared in were *Lord and Lady Algy*, *The Man from Blankley's*, *A Message from Mars*, and, in later life, *General John Regan* and *Ambrose Applejohn's Adventure*. In 1883 he adapted a play by Von Moser as *The Private Secretary*, and tried it out in Cambridge, playing the part of David Cattermole himself. When first brought to London (at the old Prince's Theatre, 1884) it was not a success, but Hawtrey believed in it, and transferred it to the Globe, returning to the cast himself, and replacing Tree, as the Private Secretary, by W. S. Penley. It ran until 1886, and was frequently revived, rivalling even *Charley's Aunt* in popularity.

In spite of his many successes Hawtrey was often in distress financially, for money meant little to him. Always well dressed and immaculate, he was a man of great charm and culture, and a keen student of the Bible, with a text for every occasion. He was knighted in 1922 for services to his profession.   W. M. P.

HAYES, Helen (1900–   ), American actress who was on the stage as a child, making her first appearance in Washington at the age of 5. Three years later she was seen in New York under the management of Lew Fields. Among her successful child roles of this period were Pollyanna, in which she toured extensively, and Margaret in *Dear Brutus*. She continued her career without a break, stepping easily into adult roles from about 1920 onwards. She made a great success in the long-running *To the Ladies* (1922), and appeared at various times for the Theatre Guild as Cleopatra, Viola, and Mary Queen of Scots. Her greatest triumph, however, was the name-part in the American production of *Victoria Regina* (1936), in which she was seen in New York and throughout the United States, being awarded the medal of the Drama League of New York for the most distinguished performance of the year. Among her later appearances were Harriet Beecher Stowe in *Harriet*, and the leading role in a hilarious farce by Anita Loos entitled *Happy Birthday*. In 1948 she made her first appearance in London as the Mother in *The Glass Menagerie*, produced by John Gielgud at the Haymarket.

HAYMARKET THEATRE, LONDON. This is the second oldest London playhouse still in use. It was built in 1720 by a carpenter named John Potter, who erected a small theatre on the site of an inn called 'The King's Head'. The whole building, including decorations, fittings, scenery, and wardrobe, cost £1,500. It had no licence or Patent, it stood in what was still almost a rural district, and its first few years were uneventful. The first recorded performance there was on 29 Dec. 1720, by a French company under the patronage of the Duke of Montague. In 1726 it was occupied by acrobats, including Madame Violante, the rope-walker who discovered Peg Woffington. In 1729 a dancing-master, Samuel Johnson of Cheshire, put on a wild, extraordinary burlesque called *Hurlothrumbo*, which proved most popular and ran for thirty nights.

In 1730 Fielding took over the theatre, which was known as 'the Little Theatre in the Hay', and there produced his famous satire, *The Tragedy of Tragedies; or, the Life and Death of Tom Thumb the Great*. Altogether about eight of Fielding's plays were produced at the Haymarket. He gave up on account of licensing troubles, and Theophilus Cibber, worthless son of Colley Cibber, who had led a revolt at Drury Lane, brought his rebellious company there.

Fielding re-entered into possession in 1734, with a company which included Macklin. He defied the licensing law as enforced by Drury Lane's Patent, and sold tickets for the play outside the theatre at the coffee-houses. But in 1737 the new Licensing Act of Sir Robert Walpole, whom he had satirized bitterly, caused him to close again. This Act was very unpopular with the public, and when a French company took possession of the Haymarket they rioted, and the French players were howled down, in spite of appeals by J.P.s, threats of the Riot Act, and a display of military power.

For several years after this the theatre was practically derelict, save for short seasons by Macklin and Cibber, rebels both, until Samuel Foote, a clever actor and playwright and a master mimic, took over in 1747 and started a new phase. He invited people to attend 'The Diversions of the Morning'—tickets for which could be obtained at the coffee-houses. As his diversions included an act of *The Old Bachelor*, Drury Lane intervened, and he was forced to close after the second performance. But nobody could defeat Foote. He had set his heart on making the Haymarket a great theatre, and on rivalling Garrick as a Patent-holder. So he invited his friends to come and take a cup of chocolate with him (tickets at George's Coffee House, Temple Bar), and this

time he pretended to be training young people for the stage. He made his own imitations the great feature of the entertainment, which soon became the rage. Foote carried on with variations of this scheme for some years, making the theatre famous, but never getting any nearer his heart's desire, a Royal Patent, until in 1766, when he was the guest of Lord Mexborough, his host and friends, amongst whom was the Duke of York, mounted him for a joke on an unmanageable horse. It threw him and broke his leg. The limb had to be amputated, and to make amends his tormentors begged the King to grant him a Patent for the Haymarket. This the King did, but only for the summer months, and only for Foote's lifetime. So the little theatre finally became a Theatre Royal.

Foote sold the theatre to the elder George Colman in 1777, and died soon after. Colman re-roofed it and carried out many improvements, and the Haymarket entered upon a second period of prosperity. All the great actors of the day played there during the summer months, when the two big Patent theatres were closed. In 1789 Colman handed over the management to his son, George Colman the Younger. In 1794 there was a great calamity, for when on 3 Feb. Their Majesties commanded a performance there—the first in the history of the Haymarket—such an enormous crowd collected that fifteen people were trampled to death and many injured.

Elliston made his début at the Haymarket in 1796, Charles Mathews the elder in 1803, Liston in 1805. That year was marked by another curious riot. A play was staged to which the tailors of London took exception. Dowton was the star, and they attended in vast numbers, howling him down, throwing shears on the stage, and rioting outside until dispersed by the Life Guards.

In 1807 Charles Mayne Young the tragedian made a big success at this theatre, and in 1810 'Romeo' Coates, an eccentric amateur, caused the loudest laughter the theatre had ever heard by his attempted portrayal of Romeo.

Although the theatre was so prosperous Colman was always in difficulties, and finally his imprisonment for debt caused the theatre to be closed for a whole season. In 1820 Morris demolished the old building, and built the stately Haymarket theatre we know to-day. It opened on 4 July 1821 with *The Rivals*. In 1825 the farce *Paul Pry* was produced with Farren, Mrs. Waylett, Mrs. Glover, Mme Vestris, and Liston. It ran for fourteen nights; but Morris relied mainly on revivals of old favourites with excellent casts, Farren in the lead, and Liston, always a success, in comedy.

In 1837 Benjamin Webster, who had been a member of the company since 1829, became manager. Under him the theatre was again successful. Phelps made his London début there in 1837, Barry Sullivan in 1853, and between those two dates all the great players of the day appeared there. Among many fine plays was *Masks and Faces*, in which Webster and Mrs. Stirling made such a success. Webster brought the theatre to a very high level and left in 1853 to take over the Adelphi. He was succeeded by Buckstone, a magnificent comedian, whose ghost is still said to haunt the theatre he loved. Drury Lane at this time was little better than a show-booth and Covent Garden was given over to opera, so the Haymarket became the foremost comedy house of London. Buckstone gathered a fine company round him, and in five years the theatre was not closed on any night when the law allowed it to remain open. It frequently kept open until 1 a.m., people flocking in after other shows to see Wright in a farce.

In 1861 Edwin Booth made his first London appearance at the Haymarket. Then things took a bad turn, and Buckstone's fortunes were at a low ebb when he produced *Our American Cousin*. In this comedy Edward Sothern made such a success as Lord Dundreary—a part which he had played in the original production in New York, and largely built up himself—that it ran for 400 nights, and Buckstone made a profit of £30,000. Sothern remained with him, making a further success in *David Garrick* by the then unknown T. W. Robertson, and by 1865 Buckstone had virtually handed over control to him.

In 1870 *The Palace of Truth* was produced, followed by *Pygmalion and Galatea*, in which Madge Robertson (Mrs. Kendal) had her first big success. She had made her first appearance at the Haymarket five years earlier, playing Ophelia to the Hamlet of Walter Montgomery. Buckstone, who was not a good business man, was again in difficulties and Clarke, a comedian of the grotesque school, took over. The only notable event during his tenancy was the appearance at the theatre of Adelaide Neilson. In 1880 Mr. and Mrs. Bancroft took possession and remodelled the interior of the theatre, doing away with the pit, which led to a first-night riot. They ran the theatre splendidly for five years, adding to its prestige, until they retired from the stage in July 1885. In September of that year Bashford, who had been their manager, took over in partnership with Russell, but with little success, and in the autumn of 1887 the theatre passed into the hands of Herbert Beerbohm Tree. His most striking success there was *Trilby*, with himself as Svengali and Dorothea Baird in the title role.

In 1896 Tree moved to his own theatre—His Majesty's—across the way, and Frederick Harrison and Cyril Maude became managers of the Haymarket, the former attending to the business, and the latter to the artistic, side. Opening on 17 Oct. 1896 with *Under the Red Robe*, they continued in association for nine years, with magnificent plays, casts, and settings. In 1905 Cyril Maude left, and Harrison carried on until his death in 1926 with the same regard for tradition, being succeeded by Horace Watson, and he in turn by his son Stuart Watson. The theatre escaped damage from enemy action during the war of 1939-45; in 1944-5 it housed a brilliant company in repertory under John Gielgud, and in 1948 his production of the

American success *The Glass Menagerie*, in which that fine actress Helen Hayes made her London début.   W. M. P.

HAZLITT, WILLIAM (1778–1830), English essayist and critic, and the first of the great dramatic critics, who wrote in an age when literary criticism was flourishing at the hands of a group of masters which included Leigh Hunt, Coleridge, and Lamb. Hazlitt's period of dramatic criticism coincided with the dearth of new dramatic writing that fell on the English theatre during the first quarter of the nineteenth century. From 1813 to 1818 Hazlitt wrote for the *Examiner*, the *Morning Chronicle*, the *Champion*, and *The Times*, and it was his good fortune to survey a distinguished period of acting exercised chiefly in revivals of Shakespeare, on which the theatre relied during the lean years. A selection of these criticisms was collected in *A View of the English Stage* (1818).

In *The Characters of Shakespeare's Plays* (1817) and *The Literature of the Age of Elizabeth* (1820) he took the conceit out of his own age by pointing to the glories of the past: 'Pavilioned in the glittering pride of our superficial accomplishments and upstart pretentions, we fancy that everything beyond that magic circle is prejudice and error, and all before the present enlightened period but a dull and useless blank in the great map of Time.' In his zeal for bygone dramatists Hazlitt was once led to say he loved the written drama more than acted drama: but no one who has read his essay *On Actors and Acting* will be misled by that temporary reaction which at times comes to most dramatic critics, tethered to their stalls year in and year out. Whatever may have been Hazlitt's pleasure at performances taking place in the theatre of his own mind, there is no doubt that he also took a vivid delight in acting, and in writing about it. 'There is no class of society whom so many persons regard with affection as actors. We greet them on the stage: we like to meet them on the streets; they always recall to us pleasant associations; and we feel our gratitude excited without the uneasiness of a sense of obligation.'

But Hazlitt's affection for actors never prejudiced his opinions as a critic. His knowledge of plays enabled him to assess a player with unerring accuracy, as he assessed Macready in *Macbeth*: 'There is not a weight of superstitious terror loading the atmosphere and overhanging the stage when Mr. Macready plays the part. He has cast the cumbrous slough of Gothic tragedy, and comes out a mere modern, agitated by common means and intelligible motives.' There was no one like Hazlitt for finding the right word for the wrong action. No wonder he has been called 'the critics' critic'.   T. C. K.

HEAVY FATHER — LEAD — WOMAN, see STOCK COMPANY.

HEBBEL, FRIEDRICH (1813–63), German dramatist, was the son of a poor North German mason, and the bitter struggles of his youth left their mark on his work. Obsessed by the tragedy of life, Hebbel probed ceaselessly for its cause; he found it less in the realm of guilt and human frailty than in the very process of life and progress. What the *Sturm und Drang* writers had rebelliously suspected became in his case philosophical conviction. The consciousness of his own imperious nature led him to analyse the reactions of the woman wronged. Hence a gallery of subtle portraits in *Judith* (1840), his first play, in *Maria Magdalena* (1844), a powerful middle-class tragedy which anticipates the later naturalism of Ibsen, in *Herodes und Mariamne* (1850), a fierce tragedy of jealousy, in *Gyges und sein Ring* (1856), and in the trilogy of *Die Nibelungen* (1861), his last work. Hebbel was fortunate in finding an excellent interpreter of his heroines in his wife, Christine Enghausen.   W. E. D.

HEBREW DRAMA, see JEWISH DRAMA.

HEDBERG, TOR (1862–1931), Swedish dramatist, was the son of Franz Hedberg, a popular dramatist of the mid-nineteenth century in Sweden, whose interest in the lives of the work-people of Stockholm he shared and continued to use in his work. Hedberg's earliest works were novels and stories. The plays began in 1886, the earliest of note being perhaps *En Tvekamp* (*Single Combat*) in 1892. The comedy *Nattrocken* (*The Dressing-Gown*) followed in 1893; *Judas*, a drama, in 1895; *Gerhard Grim*, a dramatic poem, in 1897; *Giorgione* and *Antonios frestelse* (*Antonio's Temptation*) in 1901; *Guld och gröna skogar* (*Gold and Green Forests*), a comedy, in 1903; *Amor och Hymen*, a comedy, in 1904; *Ett hems drama* (*The Drama of a Home*) in 1906; *Johan Ulfstjerna*, a five-act tragedy, in 1907; *Michael*, a drama in four acts, in 1908; *Karlavagnen* (*Charles's Wain*), a comedy, in 1910; *Borga gård*, a tragedy in four acts, in 1915; *Perseus och vidundret* (*Perseus and the Miracle*) in 1917. In 1910 he became a director of the Royal Dramatic Theatre in Stockholm. Later plays are *Teseus konungen* (*King Theseus*), *Nationalmonumentet*, *Vad kvinan vill* (*What Woman Wants*), *Rembrandt's son*, *Talias barn* (*Talias's Child*), *På andras vägnar* (*On Behalf of Others*), *Er vårmorgon* (*A Spring Morning*). Hedberg also contributed a certain amount of dramatic criticism which was collected, together with other essays and articles, in *Ett decennium* (*A Decade*) in 1912–13.   U. E.-F.

HEIBERG, GUNNAR (1857–1929), Norwegian dramatist, whose work shows the influence of Ibsen's later style. He was for a time director of the Norwegian theatre at Bergen, and wrote some volumes of dramatic criticism. He was the author of a number of light, satiric comedies, but his best-known works are *Balkonen* (1894) and *Kjaerlighedens Tragedie* (1904), both serious studies of contemporary social problems (see also SCANDINAVIA, 2).

HEIBERG, JOHAN LUDVIG (1791–1860),

Danish poet, dramatist, aesthetic critic, journalist, and theatre director, had an influence on the Danish drama that to some extent counteracted Oehlenschlaeger's, much as Oehlenschlaeger's had that of Holberg before him. Though he was capable of writing romantic drama, especially romantic comedy, he was strongly influenced by the French and Spanish theatres and transmitted much of their thought and ideas through his comedy, his vaudevilles, and his dramatic criticism. Heiberg was simultaneously a practising dramatist and an active critic. He on the one hand defined the nature of the vaudeville, which he had himself fostered in Denmark, in his *Om Vaudevillen som Dramatisk Digtart* in 1826, and, in 1827, on the other, founded the *Kjøbenhavns flyvende Post* in which appeared those criticisms of the dramatic art of Oehlenschlaeger and his school which had a stronger influence than any similar body of work before Brandes'. Heiberg's importance as a critic in dramatic aesthetics is considerable.

The titles of a few only of his plays can be listed. His vaudevilles began in 1825 with *Kong Salomon og Jørgen Hattemager*, and were followed, between 1826 and 1836, by eight more. The last of these, *Nej* (*No*), is a masterpiece of miniature technique and fine witty vaudeville-monologue. His longer and more nearly traditional drama extends over the whole of his life, beginning with *Dristig vovet halvt er vundet* (*Well Ventured is Half Won*), a romantic drama written under the influence of Calderón, and *Psyche*, a mythological play, in 1816. After the period of the principal vaudevilles come *Elverhøj* (*The Elf-Hill*) (1828), a highly popular romantic play; *Fata Morgana* (1838); *Syvsoverdag* (*The Day of the Seven Sleepers*) and *En Sjael efter Døden* (*A Soul after Death*) (both 1841); *Nøddeknakkerne* (*The Nutcrackers*) (1845), a satire on newspapers and critics and the new tendencies in politics and literature; and *Valgerda* (1849), a comedy.   U. E.-F.

HEIBERG, PETER ANDREAS (1758–1841), Danish dramatist (see SCANDINAVIA, 1).

HEIJERMANS, HERMAN (1864–1924), see HOLLAND.

HEINEL, ANNE FRÉDÉRIQUE (1752–1808), a famous ballerina, who was a pupil of Noverre, and the first to exploit the possibilities of the pirouette which the abandonment of heavy draperies had made possible. Born at Bayreuth, she went as a young dancer to Stuttgart, to join the troupe of the Duke of Württemberg. She first appeared at the Paris Opéra in 1768, and was immediately successful, remaining there for the rest of her life. She made occasional appearances in London, and during one of them married, but soon left her husband, returning to Paris. She was a contemporary there of the great dancer Vestris, with whom she had an impassioned love affair and many violent quarrels. Later in life, however, they set up house together, retiring on their pensions, and marrying in 1792 in order to legitimatize their son (see VESTRIS, 1).

HEINRICH JULIUS, DUKE OF BRUNSWICK (1564–1613), a royal playwright whose favourite theme was matrimonial discord, usually with the onus on the female side, unless the husband, through sheer stupidity, deserved his punishment. The Duke, who succeeded to his title in 1589, was much attracted to the English Comedians, who may have visited his capital of Wolfenbüttel some time early in the 1590s, and a company of English actors, under Sackville, was definitely attached to the royal household from 1596 intermittently until the Duke's death. His plays show considerable English influence. The first of them, *Susanna* (1590–3), with its large cast, its wailings, and the manifold activities of the fool Jan Clant or Bouschet (from the English Clown and Posset respectively), marks the complete change which has taken place in the approach to religious subjects since Rebhun. In all the Duke's plays the fool is endowed with sound common sense, and talks humorously in Low German. One of his most successful comedies was *Vincentius Ladislaus* (1594), in which the braggart soldier of the *commedia dell'arte* is tripped up by the fool.

HELLMAN, LILLIAN (1905–   ), American dramatist, born in New Orleans, but educated at Columbia and New York Universities. She entered the theatre as a press agent, and as a play-reader for the Broadway producer Herman Shumlin. Her first play, *The Children's Hour* (1934), aroused extraordinary interest with its story of a neurotic schoolgirl's defamation of her teachers, whom she accuses of lesbianism, and compelled attention on both psychological and social levels. Miss Hellman failed with her next play, *Days to Come* (1936), a penetrative if also unwieldy study of a labour strike, but fulfilled the promise of her début with *The Little Foxes* (1939) and *Watch on the Rhine* (1941). The former exposed a predatory family of industrial entrepreneurs, comparable to the little foxes that destroy the vineyards. *Watch on the Rhine* dramatized the mortal struggle of an anti-Nazi leader against his betrayer, a Rumanian aristocrat living with the hero's American mother-in-law near Washington, and implied that America could not long remain neutral in the struggle against Fascism. *The Searching Wind* (1944), an incompletely integrated chronicle, reviewed the errors of an American career diplomat whose moral fibre was no stronger in his private life than in his public policy of appeasement. In *Another Part of the Forest* (1946) Miss Hellman returned to the antecedent history of her 'little foxes' with a Jonsonian picaresque comedy of villains outsmarting one another. Miss Hellman's preoccupation with the problem of evil drew accusations of misanthropy, and her tightly knit plots caused her to be charged with the outmoded technique of the 'well-made' play of Sardou. Her work is, nevertheless, invigorated by sharp characterization and by respect for active idealism.   J. G.

HELPMANN, ROBERT (1911–   ), English actor, ballet dancer, and choreographer, a member of the Sadler's Wells Ballet since its inception, and previously a pupil of the school there. A superb dancer, he is also well known as a choreographer, having been responsible for such thoughtful and important ballets as 'Comus', 'Hamlet', 'Miracle in the Gorbals', and 'Adam Zero', in all of which he danced himself. He was also seen as an eerie and impressive Oberon in *A Midsummer Night's Dream* and has given interesting performances of Hamlet, Shylock, and King John.

HELTAI, JENŐ (1871–   ), Hungarian dramatist, well known for his light comedies, which show the gayer side of life in Budapest. One of them, *Jó Üzlet*, has been translated into English as *A Good Bargain*, while a verse-play, *A Néma Levente*, given in Budapest in 1936, was translated into verse by Humbert Wolfe, and given in London at the St. James's Theatre in 1937 as *The Silent Knight*.

HEMINGE (HEMINGES, HEMMINGS), JOHN (1556–1630), English actor, was in Burbage's company, and probably the first player of Falstaff. When this company became the King's Men, he probably acted as their business manager. He held considerable shares in the Globe and Blackfriars playhouses. He lived in the parish of St. Mary, Aldermanbury, near the theatre in Shoreditch. In his will he describes himself as 'citizen and grocer', but his wife probably ran the business while he was off play-acting. To him, with Condell, we owe the printing of the Shakespeare Folio. Fault has been found with these first editors for their arbitrary division of the plays into five acts, regardless of sense, on the classic model of Ben Jonson, and for many sins of omission and commission which have given headaches to literary historians and caused much ink to flow. But since Shakespeare himself made no efforts to get his plays printed, they would probably have been lost entirely or survived only in mutilated fragments—for no complete Shakespeare manuscript has ever come to light—had it not been for the labour of love undertaken by his friends and fellow-actors. (See also CONDELL.)

HENDERSON, JOHN (1747–85), English actor whose early passion for the stage was fostered by Garrick, who had recently retired, and to whose literary gatherings in Beckett's bookshop the young Henderson, at that time apprenticed to a jeweller and silversmith, was a frequent visitor. He got an introduction to Garrick's brother George at Drury Lane when he was 21, but was refused on account of his weak voice and unprepossessing appearance, due in great part to his extreme poverty. However, he was determined to act, and after several amateur appearances, in which he imitated Garrick to the life, the latter gave him a letter of recommendation to Palmer at Bath, where he was engaged at a guinea a week. He made his first appearance on 6 Oct. 1772 as

Hamlet, and was successful. Several years of hard work followed, during which he was painted by Gainsborough as Macbeth, a portrait which shows him to be a stoutly-built, fair-haired man with a strong, determined face —not handsome, but commanding. In 1777 his years of labour were justified, as he was engaged by Colman to appear at the Haymarket in London, which he did on 11 June as Shylock. His success was instantaneous, and even Macklin, that great player of Shylock, congratulated him. He returned to Bath, but in the following year Sheridan wanted him for Drury Lane, which had three times shut its doors to him, and to induce Palmer to release him gave the latter the sole right of playing *The School for Scandal* in Bath. Henderson stayed at Drury Lane for two years, going from there to Covent Garden, and never again left London except on tour. He appeared in Edinburgh with Mrs. Siddons with great success. One of his greatest parts was Falstaff. He died young, before his fortieth birthday, of overwork and early privation, and was buried in Westminster Abbey, near Garrick. It was his rendering of *John Gilpin* at a series of readings in the Freemasons' Hall in 1785 that first launched Cowper's poem on its successful career.   W. M. P.

HENRY, JOHN (1738–94), an actor who was for many years one of the leading men of the American Company, which he joined in 1767 at the John Street Theatre, New York, under Douglass. He was an Irishman, and had already appeared in Dublin and London before he sailed for the New World. On the return of the American Company from the West Indies, where they took refuge during the War of Independence, Henry assumed the management, jointly with the younger Hallam. He accepted and played in Dunlap's first play, and was responsible in 1792 for the importation from England of that excellent actor John Hodgkinson, by whom he was soon forced into the background, retiring from management and acting shortly before his death. He was twice married. His first wife, an actress named Storer, was lost at sea before the company came back from the West Indies, and was never seen in New York. After living for some time with her sister, Ann or Nancy (?–1816) (later Mrs. Hogg), by whom he had a child, Henry married a younger member of the Storer family, Maria (c. 1760–95). She was first on the stage as a child, and later became a member of the American Company, where her imperious temper caused much trouble. She retired from the theatre at the same time as her husband, and went mad after his sudden death on board ship, surviving him by only a year. Yet another Storer, Fanny, was also an actress, though not a very remarkable one. Later, as Mrs. Mechtler, she gave concerts in New York.

HENRY MILLER'S THEATRE, NEW YORK, on 43rd Street east of Broadway. This opened on 1 Apr. 1918. Its first successes were Mrs. Fiske in *Mis' Nelly of N'Orleans* (1919) and Blanche Bates and Henry Miller in *The*

Famous Mrs. Fair (1920). A succession of moderate successes, with strong casts, followed, and in 1922 Mme Simone gave a short season of French plays. Soon after this the theatre embarked on the production of the sophisticated drama with which its name is now connected, including *The Vortex* (1925). In 1929 came the overwhelming success of *Journey's End*, and in 1932 Pauline Lord in *The Late Christopher Bean*. The Theatre Guild produced *Days Without End* (1934), destined to be O'Neill's last play for many years, and in 1936 came a revival of *The Country Wife*, with Ruth Gordon, and settings and costumes by Oliver Messel. *French Without Tears* followed, but failed to repeat its London success, and in 1938 *Our Town* opened on 4 Feb., subsequently moving to the Morosco for a long run. In 1944 the theatre broke its own records with the 680 performances of *Dear Ruth*.   G. F.

HENSEL, SOPHIE FRIEDERIKE (née Sparmann) (1738–89), a German actress, and one of Ackermann's company at the Hamburg National Theatre. She had an adventurous girlhood, and at seventeen married a comedian, from whom she later separated to live a dissipated life. Built on generous lines, with a face and figure of majestic beauty, she was much admired, and filled admirably the roles of noble heroines in German classical drama. Even Lessing, who detested her, had to admit that she was, in her own line, a fine actress, and Schröder too thought well of her. In private life she was a malicious and intriguing character, who caused trouble wherever she went, and was undoubtedly one of the factors which brought about the downfall of the Hamburg enterprise. She then married Abel Seyler, who had for a short time been one of the managers of the theatre, and set out on tour, taking Ekhof with her. Her jealousy of his acting was so profound, however, that when he took over the leadership of the company she left and went to Vienna. Returning to Germany, she found herself at Mannheim, and later at Hamburg, confronted with her bitterest enemy, the wife of the actor-playwright Brandes, against whom she continued to intrigue until her death. She was known and feared all over Germany, but the infatuated Seyler remained faithful to her, though she was a constant source of anxiety and financial ruin to him, and it was only after her death that he retired to the peace of Schröder's country estate.

HENSLOWE, PHILIP (?–1616), important in the history of the Elizabethan stage as being the owner of the Rose, Fortune, and Hope playhouses. He may also have been the lessee of Whitefriars. He married the wealthy widow of a dyer to whom he had been apprenticed, and his stepdaughter Joan married Alleyn, the great actor and rival of Burbage. Henslowe was a shrewd business man, and gradually amassed a good deal of property in London, in addition to the playhouses. On his death his papers (with other property) passed to Alleyn, and are now housed in Dulwich College. Among them is his Diary, a capital document for the study of Elizabethan theatre organization. In it he entered accounts for his various theatres, loans made to actors, payments made to dramatists, and various private memoranda. Unlike other outstanding theatre men of this period, Henslowe was not an actor. Greg, to whom we owe most of our knowledge of him, calls him the 'banker' of the company. He did not take a fixed rent for his playhouses, but a sum allotted from the daily takings, originally half the proceeds of the galleries and later the whole. He appears to have paid all bills, including the purchase of plays, and of clothes and properties, for the companies acting in the theatre for the time being. These varied from time to time, but the Admiral's Men were at the Rose from 1594 to 1600, and when they moved to the Fortune were succeeded by Lord Worcester's Men. The upkeep of the structure, and the licensing fees paid to the Master of the Revels, appear to have been Henslowe's only liabilities as landlord, and it follows that the players were constantly in his debt. Since some of the individual actors were contracted to Henslowe personally, and not, as was usually the case in Elizabethan companies, to their fellow actors, and as he paid the dramatists for their work, it follows that he had a large say in the policy of the company. That his relations with his actors were not always cordial is proved by a document headed *Articles of Grieuance, and Articles of Oppression, against Mr. Hinchlowe*, drawn up in 1615, in which he is accused of embezzling their money, and unlawfully retaining their property. He is even accused of having bribed Nathan Field, who was acting as the company's representative, to testify in his favour. There is no note of how the controversy ended, and apart from this document there is no evidence of Henslowe's having done more than keep the actors in his debt in order to retain his hold over them. There can be no doubt that such an arrangement was not so good, nor did it make for such stability, as that in force in the Burbages' company, where the actors were joint owners of their own theatre, and responsible to each other and not to any 'outside capitalist', as Chambers calls Henslowe.

HERALD SQUARE THEATRE, NEW YORK, see COLOSSEUM THEATRE.

HERBERT, SIR HENRY (1596–1673), Master of the Revels from 1623, in which capacity he controlled the actors and licensed the theatres. He was also responsible for the censorship of plays, which he read personally, and for collecting the fees due for each performance of licensed drama at the official playhouses. The extant passages taken from the lost manuscript of his office book, which he kept from 1622 to 1642, have been collected in Professor J. Q. Adams's *Dramatic Records of Sir Henry Herbert* (1917), and form a precious deposit of material on the stage history of the period. At the Restoration Sir Henry made strenuous efforts to recover the powers of his office, and issued

licences to William Beeston for the Cockpit and also to Mohun for a company at the Red Bull; but he was routed by the Royal monopoly granted to Killigrew and Davenant, and although he kept up a continual skirmishing with them until his death, his importance in stage matters was constantly whittled away, until he was left with nothing but a token payment from the players, and no real authority over them. Killigrew, who was more amenable to Sir Henry's attempts at discipline than Davenant, inherited his title of Master of the Revels on his death, and later passed it on to his son, but the office was of no importance, and its main function, the censorship of plays, passed to the Lord Chamberlain (see DRAMATIC CENSORSHIP).

HERCZEG, FERENC (1863–), one of Hungary's leading dramatists, author of many excellent comedies and satires on contemporary life, and also of historical dramas on subjects taken from Hungarian history.

HERMANN, DAVID (1876–1930), see JEWISH DRAMA, 6 and VILNA TROUPE.

HERNÁNDEZ, ANTONIO ACEVEDO Y, see SOUTH AMERICA, I.

HERNE, JAMES A. (originally AHEARN) (1839–1901), American actor and dramatist, who made his first appearance on the stage in 1859, and was later leading man for Lucille Western, his sister-in-law. He was for some time stage manager of Maguire's New Theatre in San Francisco, where he appeared in a number of adaptations of Dickens's novels, which later had a great influence on his own writing. He was leading man of the Baldwin Theatre in the same town, where he worked with Belasco, collaborating with him in a number of plays, including *Hearts of Oak* (see BELASCO). This was purely melodrama, but Herne's later works show a deflexion towards realism and sobriety, mainly under the influence of his wife, Katharine Corcoran (1857–1943), a fine actress who played most of his heroines. His first important play was the sombre drama of marital infidelity, *Margaret Fleming* (1890), which was at first too far ahead of its time to appeal to the public, in spite of the fine acting of Mrs. Herne in the title-role. It was revived in 1894, in 1907, with Herne's daughter Chrystal as Margaret Fleming, and in 1915. It was followed by *Shore Acres* (1892), which had a hard struggle to establish itself, but ended by being one of the most popular plays of the day, mainly through the character of Uncle Nathaniel Berry. *The Reverend Griffith Davenport* (1899), a tale of the Civil War of which no complete copy remains, and *Sag Harbour* (1899), a re-writing of the old *Hearts of Oak*, in which Herne was acting when he died, complete the number of his works. They have little literary value, but, particularly in *Margaret Fleming*, they mark a great advance on contemporary drama, which led to the best of them being unsuccessful in their own day. This was mainly due to the realistic treatment of even the most conventional types, like Uncle Nat, and to the simplicity and sincerity with which Herne approached his subjects.

HERODAS (or HERONDAS) (c. 300–250 B.C.), Greek dramatist, a writer of semi-dramatic mimes, nine of which were discovered, whole or in part, on an Egyptian papyrus in 1891. They represent very vividly, and with some coarseness, scenes from ordinary life. (See also MIME, 1 b.)

HEROIC DRAMA, a type of play in rhymed couplets, in vogue in England from 1664 to 1678. Influenced by the French classical forms, and dealing with the theme of 'love and honour' from Spain's Golden Age, it found its greatest exponent in Dryden, though it could be stretched to include Davenant and some earlier writers. The heroic play was satirized by Buckingham in *The Rehearsal* (1672), and later by Sheridan in *The Critic* (1779).

HERON, MATILDA AGNES (1830–77), American actress, who made her début in Philadelphia in 1851, and after a brief visit to New York went to California, where she made an immediate success in such parts as Juliet, Mrs. Haller, Juliana in *The Honeymoon*, and Bianca in *Fazio*. It was, however, as Marguerite Gautier that she achieved widest recognition, though she was not the first to play the part in America, Jean Davenport having forestalled her with an innocuous adaptation entitled *Camille; or, the Fate of a Coquette*. In 1855 Matilda Heron, while on a visit to Paris, saw *La Dame aux camélias* in its original form, made a fairly accurate version of it herself, and played it all over the United States. It was particularly successful in New York, and the author-actress made a fortune out of it, most of which she spent or gave away. She later played Medea, and Nancy in a dramatization of *Oliver Twist*, and was seen in several of her own plays. It was said of her that in a few good parts she displayed a 'strange wild beauty and elemental passion, and much influenced the actresses of her time'. Among those whom she trained for the stage was her daughter by her second marriage, Hélène Stoepel, known as Bijou Heron, who married Henry Miller.

HERRERA, ERNESTO (1887–1917), see SOUTH AMERICA, 1.

HERTZ, HENRIK (1798–1870), a Danish dramatist of Jewish parentage, is chiefly remembered for his highly popular *Kong René's Datter* (*King René's Daughter*), for his comedies, his national, romantic, and historical dramas, and for his dramatic criticism in defence of and collaboration with J. L. Heiberg. In his early work he reverts to Holberg against the tendencies of the 1820s and throughout his life some of his most popular work was character comedy after the tradition of French drama. In all, he wrote some twenty-five plays, of which the best-known are: *Herr Burchardt og hans Familie* (*Mr. Burchardt and his Family*) (1827); *Amor's Genistreger* (*Amor's Strokes of*

Genius) (1830); a number of vaudevilles produced between 1827 and 1835; *Sparekassen* (*The Savings Bank*) (1836), a popular and highly skilful comedy; *Svend Dyrings Hus* (1837), a romantic tragedy; the lyrical drama *Kong René's Datter* (1845), seen in London in 1908; *Nixon* (1848), *Den Ingste* (*The Youngest*) (1854); *En Kurmethode* (*The Cure*) (1861), and *Tre Dage i Padua* (*Three Days in Padua*) (1869), his last play.

Of his remaining twenty-two plays a few only can be mentioned: *Flyttedagen* (*Quarter-days*) (1827); *Tonietta* (1849); *Et Offer* (*The Sacrifice*) (1854); and *Juvelskrinet* (*The Jewel Box*) (1866).   U. E.-F.

HERVIEU, PAUL (1857–1915), French dramatist, whose plays resemble those of Brieux in their preoccupation with social problems, but are free from the somewhat didactic tendencies of the latter dramatist. Realizing that the sorrows of human life, though no longer expressed in the grandeur of classic verse, are as poignant and immutable as ever, he sought to introduce into a modern setting the ancient elements of tragedy. He was concerned not so much with the fugitive inequalities of social custom, as with the unchangeable vices of individuals—egotism, vanity, indifference, deceit. He was constantly preoccupied with the problems of divorce and the child, as in *Les Tenailles* (1895) and *La Loi de l'homme* (1897), usually considered his best plays, and in *Le Dédale* (1903) and *Connais-toi* (1909). One of his most interesting plays is *Les Paroles restent* (1892), which traces the destructive course of a slanderous rumour which ruins several lives, while his *La Course du flambeau* (1901) is devoted to the perennial problem of maternal love and filial ingratitude.

HEVESI, DR. SANDOR (1873–   ), Hungarian producer and theatre manager, who in 1904 founded his own company, Thalia, and produced a number of modern Hungarian plays, and translations of foreign dramatists. He was much influenced by the theories of Gordon Craig, which he endeavoured to put into effect when he was appointed Director of the State Theatre in Budapest.

HEYWOOD, JOHN (c. 1497–1580), early English dramatist, author of a number of interludes which mark the transition from the medieval Morality and Mystery plays to the comedy of the Elizabethans. Heywood, who was an accomplished singer and player of the virginals, much in favour at Court, married Elizabeth Rastell, niece of Sir Thomas More, and there is little reason to doubt that he owed much to the influence of More, whose love and encouragement of acting are well known. His most famous play is *The Playe called the foure P.P.; a newe and a very mery enterlude of a palmer, a pardoner, a potycary, a pedler*, each of whom tries to outdo the others in lying. The palmer wins when he says that in all his travels he never yet knew one woman out of patience. This was given in about 1520, probably at Court, and was published some twenty years later by his brother-in-law, William Rastell, as were *The Play of the Wether* and *The Play of Love* (both 1533). *The Dialogue of Wit and Folly*, which probably dates from the same year, remained in manuscript until 1846, when it was issued by the Percy Reprint Society. Two further interludes are sometimes attributed to Heywood, *The Pardoner and the Frere* and *Johan Johan*, which were both published anonymously by Rastell in 1533, while A. W. Pollard considers him a likely author of *Thersites*, also attributed to Udall. Heywood left England on the accession of Elizabeth and died at Malines.

HEYWOOD, THOMAS (c. 1570–1641), English actor and dramatist, who may be connected with the older dramatist, John Heywood (see above), though there is no certain proof of this. Thomas Heywood worked for Henslowe, and was a member both of the Admiral's Men and of Worcester's until their dissolution in 1619 on the death of Queen Anne, to whose patronage Worcester's Men had been transferred. After a period of retirement, during which he wrote a good deal of non-dramatic prose and poetry, including the *Apology for Actors* (pub. 1612) and a lost and unfinished collection of *Lives of All the Poets*, Heywood returned to the theatre, and produced a number of new plays and revivals of his older ones, as well as pageants for the Lord Mayor's Show for many years. He says himself that he had a hand in 220 plays, most of which are lost. He wrote entirely for the moment, and did not trouble to print his plays until driven to it by piracy and, possibly, the growth of a demand for plays in print for reading. Of those that survive the best is undoubtedly *A Woman Killed with Kindness* (1603), a domestic tragedy whose excellence may almost entitle it to rank with some of Shakespeare's work. Other plays by Heywood are *The Fair Maid of the West*, *The English Traveller*, *The Wise Woman of Hogsdon*, and *The Rape of Lucrece*, all of which appear in a volume in the Mermaid Series edited by Verity in 1888. Heywood's *Four Prentices of London* (c. 1600), a somewhat absurd romantic drama, was satirized by Beaumont in his *Knight of the Burning Pestle*. In spite of his many excellences Heywood undoubtedly contributed to the decadence of the later Elizabethan drama, particularly by the almost complete separation between his main and sub-plots and by the weakness of his poetic diction. His industry was applied to many types of drama, including the chronicle play with *Edward IV* and with the rambling *If You Know Not Me, You Know Nobody* (1605), a two-part survey of the 'Troubles of Queen Elizabeth'; but it was in the drama of everyday life that he was most successful.

HIÄRNE, URBAN (1641–1724), early Swedish dramatist, author of a School Drama, *Rosimunda* (1665).

HICKS, SIR (EDWARD) SEYMOUR (1871–1949), English actor-manager and dramatist, who has been described as the 'Admirable Crichton' of the British stage. He was the author of a number of plays which included *Bluebell in Fairyland*, *The Gay Gordons*, and *Sleeping Partners*, and part-author of others, including adaptations from French drama such as *The Man in Dress Clothes*. With Charles Brookfield he produced the first revue seen in London, *Under the Clock*. He published several volumes of reminiscences, and was the first actor to take a party of entertainers to France in the 1914–18 war, and again in 1939. In 1931 he received the Legion of Honour from the French Government in recognition of his services to French drama in London, and he was knighted in 1935. He began his career in 1887 by walking-on at the Grand, Islington, and was for a long time with the Kendals, both in England and America. In the course of his long and varied life he topped the bill in the music-halls, and appeared with equal success in musical comedy and straight plays. Among the latter will be remembered his performances in *Sleeping Partners*—a tour de force of silent acting—and in *Quality Street*. He married Ellaline Terriss, who appeared with him in many of his plays (see TERRISS, 2), and formed with him an ideal couple, both on and off stage.   W. M. P.

For Hicks Theatre see GLOBE (3).

HIGHBURY LITTLE THEATRE, see AMATEUR THEATRE IN GREAT BRITAIN, 1 *d.*

HILAROTRAGOEDIA, see FABULA (5).

HILL, JENNY (1851–96), early music-hall performer, the daughter of a Marylebone cabdriver. She first worked in a North Country public-house, where, in the intervals of serving the beer, she amused the customers by her songs and dances. She married an acrobat, who nearly killed her by teaching her his trade, and left her with a child to support. She went to London and, after heartbreaking delays and poverty, got an audition at the Pavilion, where she was an immediate success. Billed as the Vital Spark, she sang and danced and did male impersonations, eventually earning enough to buy a large estate in Streatham, where she gave extravagant parties, and where she eventually retired, broken in health, to lead the life of an invalid until her death at the early age of 44.

HINDU DRAMA, see INDIA.

HIPPODROME, LONDON. This opened on 15 Jan. 1900 as a circus, and later became a music-hall. In about 1912 it staged revue under Albert de Courville, and pantomime and revue later for many years under Julian Wylie. In 1925, under R. H. Gillespie, Chairman of Moss Empires, Ltd., who own the theatre, it went over to musical comedy, varied with revue and pantomime, and became a consistently successful theatre, staging many notable productions. After 1939 the theatre was under the direction of George Black until his death in 1945. (See also under MUSIC-HALL.)

W. M. P.

HIRSCHBEIN, PERETZ (1881–1949), Jewish actor and dramatist, and founder of the first Yiddish Art Theatre in Odessa (see JEWISH DRAMA, 6). Born near Grodno, in Poland, he spent his early years in the country, and in 1905 published his first play, *Miriam*. This was written in Hebrew, as were his early poems. His company was formed in 1908 for the production of plays in Yiddish, however, as the Russian ban against them had just been rescinded, and Hirschbein wrote thereafter in Yiddish, translating his plays into Hebrew himself. Among the most important of them are *The Smith's Daughters* (1915) and *Green Fields* (1916), both idylls of Jewish country life. The latter is considered one of the finest plays in Yiddish literature, and Samuel J. Citron, in an article on Yiddish and Hebrew drama in *A History of Modern Drama* (1948) said of Hirschbein that 'his simple and honest treatment of his subjects have endeared to theatre audiences the country Jew, the simple man of the soil, a type which has been all too rare in Jewish life until the recent return to the land in Palestine'.

HIS MAJESTY'S THEATRE, LONDON, stands on part of the site of Vanbrugh's old theatre (see QUEEN'S THEATRE, 1), at the corner of King Charles II Street and the Haymarket. It was built by Beerbohm Tree, who always referred to it, with some justification, as 'my beautiful theatre'. During his management of the Haymarket, Tree had planned to have his own playhouse, and this was made possible by the success of *Trilby*. When he entered on the management of His Majesty's he began an era of English theatre history comparable to that of Garrick at Drury Lane, or Irving at the Lyceum. He opened the theatre, then called Her Majesty's, on 19 Apr. 1897 with an adaptation of *The Seats of the Mighty* by Gilbert Parker. This ran until the following June, when Tree revived several of his old successes, including *Trilby*. These were followed by a succession of brilliant productions, of Shakespeare and of new plays, which formed a distinguished repertory. Tree disliked long runs, and referred to his production of *Henry VIII*, which ran for nearly nine months, as 'an obstinate success'. His rooms in the dome of the theatre were a centre for artistic London. The name of the theatre was altered to His Majesty's on the succession of Edward VII, and it was while managing it in 1909 that Tree received his knighthood. He left the theatre in 1915 and did not play there again, dying as the result of an accident in 1917, aged 63. With his departure His Majesty's lost that pre-eminence which Tree had given it, but still achieved distinction. Bourchier and Martin-Harvey did seasons there in 1916, and in the same year Oscar Asche produced the record-making *Chu-Chin-Chow*, which ran for 2,238 performances.

For some time the theatre staged mostly musical productions. The most notable were *Cairo*, *Hassan* with Delius's music, two seasons of *The Co-Optimists*, *Bitter Sweet*, which ran for 697 performances, the Knoblock adaptation of Priestley's *Good Companions*, and *The Happy Hypocrite*, adapted from Max Beerbohm's story by Clemence Dane, with Ivor Novello in the leading part. Later Jack Hylton took over the theatre and was responsible for many interesting productions, including the negro play *Anna Lucasta*.

W. M. P.

HMELEV, HMELYOV, see KHMELEV.

HOADLY, BENJAMIN (1706–57), a well-known English physician, son of a bishop, who had a certain partiality for the stage and in 1747 offered Garrick a comedy entitled *The Suspicious Husband*. With Garrick in the part of Ranger— in which he was much admired by, among others, Fanny Burney's Evelina—the play made an unexpected success, and was often revived, though it reads poorly. Nicoll, in his *Eighteenth Century Drama*, says of it: 'It shows the weakening of the genteel comedy inaugurated by Cibber when that genteel comedy had become transfused with sentimental emotions.' This is Hoadly's only important contribution to the theatre, though he is believed to have written another comedy, now lost, and to have collaborated in a third.

HOBBY-HORSE, a character common in folk festivals throughout Europe, and probably a survival of the primitive worshipper clad in the skin of a sacrificial animal. He rode a wooden or wicker framework shaped like a horse, usually with a green saddle-cloth. In England the hobby-horse became a necessary accompaniment of the Morris dancers, and sometimes of the Mummers. By Elizabethan times he was already beginning to be 'forgot', as Shakespeare and Ben Jonson bear witness. For his survival in the company of the Christmas mummers, see MUMMING PLAY. Hobby-horses were also used to represent horsemen, as in the Coventry Hocktide play.

HOCKTIDE PLAY, COVENTRY, given on Hock Tuesday (the third Tuesday after Easter Sunday), and revived as a pleasant antiquity in the Kenilworth Revels prepared for the visit of Queen Elizabeth in July 1575. It began with a Captain Cox leading in a band of English knights (on hobby-horses) to fight against the Danes, and ended with the leading away of the Danish prisoners by the English women. It was intended to represent the massacre of the Danes by Ethelred in 1002, but this is probably a late literary assimilation of an earlier folk-festival custom, traceable in other places (Worcester, Shrewsbury, Hungerford), by which the women 'hocked' or caught the men and exacted a forfeit from them on one day, the men's turn coming the following day. The practice was forbidden at Worcester in 1450. This ceremony may in its turn be merely a survival of the symbolic capture of a victim for human sacrifice.

HODGE, William Thomas (1874–1932), American actor and playwright, who after some years on tour appeared in New York in 1898, and had his first success in *Sag Harbour* (1900). Several years later he made a great personal success as the Indiana lawyer, Pike, in *The Man from Home* (1907), and based all his future parts on this character, writing his plays himself. These were pleasant homely tales of American life, in which Hodge figured as the slow but shrewd countryman, and though they proved too unsophisticated for Broadway, they had a faithful audience elsewhere. Hodge, who married a musical comedy actress, retired in 1931.

HODGKINSON, John (*c.* 1765–1805), an English actor, son of a publican in Manchester named Meadowcroft. At an early age he ran away from home and joined the Bristol stock company, later touring the Midland circuit. He appeared several times in support of Mrs. Siddons, but in 1792 accepted an offer from John Henry to join the American Company, and spent the rest of his life in America. With him in the company were his wife and her sister, Arabella Brett. Hodgkinson soon became extremely popular, ousting the younger Hallam and Henry himself from management as well as from public favour, and he was joint manager with Dunlap of the Park Theatre, New York, when it first opened. A handsome man, with a good memory and a fine stage presence, Hodgkinson excelled both in tragedy and comedy. Among his outstanding parts were André in Dunlap's tragedy of that name, and Rolla in an adaptation of *Pizarro*, also made by Dunlap. His early death from yellow fever was a great loss to the American stage. Under him the John Street Theatre, New York's first permanent playhouse, had its most brilliant period, and it had been hoped that he would long prove an ornament to the Park Theatre. His wife, who was accounted a charming actress, died in 1803 of consumption, as did her sister. His two daughters, Rosina and Fanny, were both on the stage. Hodgkinson had also a brother, Thomas, who was licensee of the Shakespeare Tavern, New York.

HODSON, Henrietta (1841–1910), English actress, who made her first appearances on the stage in Glasgow and Greenock, where she was in the same company as the young Irving. They went together to Manchester to join the stock company of the Theatre Royal under Knowles, and she then went to Bath and Bristol, where she appeared with Madge Robertson, later Mrs. Kendal, and Kate and Ellen Terry. She retired from the stage on marriage, but, being soon widowed, returned, and in 1866 was seen in London in extravaganza. She then went to the Queen's Theatre, and in 1868 married Henry Labouchère, one of the proprietors. She continued to act, however, under her maiden name, and in 1871 appeared as Imogen in *Cymbeline*. She later took over the management of the Royalty, and engaged

in some skirmishes with W. S. Gilbert, whose dictatorial manner, when she produced some of his plays, she much resented. A good singer and dancer, and an actress of highly individual style and technical accomplishment, she was at her best in demure humour or the farcical characters of burlesque, pathos and deep sentiment lying outside her range. She retired in 1878, and three years later was instrumental in introducing Mrs. Langtry to the stage.

HOFFMAN, François Benoît (1760–1828), French dramatist and man of letters, chiefly remembered as an incorruptible critic. His plays were not important, being mainly libretti for light opera, but he was the author of an excellent one-act comedy, *Le Roman d'une heure, ou la folle gageure*, given in Paris in 1809.

HOFMANNSTHAL, Hugo von (1874–1929), Austrian poet and playwright, chiefly known as the librettist of Richard Strauss's operas, 'Der Rosenkavalier', 'Ariadne auf Naxos', 'Die Frau ohne Schatten', 'Die aegyptische Helena' adapted from an earlier play by Hofmannsthal, and finally 'Arabella'. Apart from this collaboration Hofmannsthal, who was in the forefront of the reaction against naturalism, wrote a number of poetic plays—*Gestern* and *Der Tod des Tizian* (both 1891), *Der Tor und der Tod* (1893), and *Das kleine Welttheater* (1903) —which reveal in exquisite poetry his craving for beauty and his awareness of its dangers, his thirst for life and his shrinking from it, his sense of the merging of time and eternity. His other plays, which are somewhat more concrete, but still imbued with poetic sensitiveness, include *Jedermann*, a rehandling of the old Morality play which became a feature of the Salzburg Festival, where it was produced annually by Reinhardt in front of the cathedral.

HOLBERG, Ludvig (1684–1754), was born at Bergen, in Norway, studied at the University of Copenhagen and then at Oxford, travelled through Europe on foot, came into close and sympathetic contact with the culture of England, France, and Italy, and returned to Denmark to become professor of metaphysics in Copenhagen University and to reach fame as an historian, philosopher, and man of letters throughout Scandinavia and beyond.

His connexion with the theatre was relatively brief, but of immense effect in Dano-Norwegian literature, for he created a native comedy in the native language, bringing to it a mind disciplined by his love of Plautus, Molière, the *commedia dell' arte*, and contemporary English prose-writers. His art is in the tradition of the first three of these; his material he sought at home in native Danish and sometimes Norwegian types, which had not appeared upon the stage before. It can indeed be said of him, more truly than of many writers to whom the words are applied, that his plays call no man father but himself.

When, in 1721, he became Director of the

Danish Theatre in Copenhagen, French and German drama was habitually played there. There was no Danish drama, the vernacular School Drama having died out, at least in the cultural centres (see SCANDINAVIA, 1). But he resolved that Denmark like other countries should have a drama in its own language and with new material peculiar to Denmark and Norway and never used before. He was by now a man of considerable experience and clearly defined tastes; his letters show him, in an age which worshipped Terence, placing Plautus far above him and believing he had no equal again until Molière. He was, admittedly, a moralist in dramatic form, but, in an age which enjoyed this tendency and in general practised its moralizing with grace, this in no way hindered his immense popularity; Holberg's comedies were known not only in Denmark, but in Sweden, Germany, Holland, and even France. The greater number of them were written during the six years of his directorship (1721–8). These, with five that had not been acted, were published in 1731, four years after the closing of the Danish Theatre. When the theatre was re-opened in 1747, he returned for a time to his earlier interests and wrote six more. The first play in Danish, a translation of L'Avare, was performed on 23 Sept. 1722, and a week later came Holberg's first original play, Den Politiske Kandestøber (The Political Tinker). His rapidity of production in his newly-found and congenial art was remarkable: five comedies in 1722, ten in 1723, and ten more by 1725. The most notable of them are probably the first five, Jeppe paa Bjerget (Jeppe of the Hill), Barselstuen (The Birth Room), Erasmus Montanus, Ulysses von Ithacia, and Det lykkelige Skibbrud (The Lucky Shipwreck). A few only of the remaining twenty-one can be mentioned: these are, in the probable order of writing, Den Vaegelsindede (Scatterbrains), Jean de France, Gert Westphaler, Julestuen (The Christmas Room), Maskaraden, Jacob von Thyboe, Melampe, Uden Hoved og Hale (Without Head or Tail), Henrik og Pernille, Diderich Menschenskraek, Pernille's korte Frøkenstand (Pernille's Short Spinsterhood), Den Danske Komedies Ligbegaengelse (The Funeral of Danish Comedy), De Usynlige (The Invisible People), Plutus, Sganarel's Rejse til det filosofiske Land (Sganarel's Journey to the Land of Philosophers), Don Ranudo, Republiken, Philosophus udi egen Indbildning (The Self-styled Philosopher), and the posthumous Den forvandlede Brudgom (The Bridegroom Bewitched).

U. E.-F.

HOLBORN EMPIRE, LONDON, in High Holborn. This famous music-hall, which had existed under many names since the middle of the nineteenth century, was sometimes used as a theatre for matinées. From Feb. to Apr. 1920 Sybil Thorndike appeared there in The Trojan Women, Medea, Candida, Tom Trouble, and The Showroom. For several years Italia Conti staged Christmas matinées of Where the Rainbow Ends and also a season of Shakespeare.

The Holborn Empire was destroyed by enemy action in 1941. (See also MUSIC-HALL.)

W. M. P.

HOLBORN THEATRE, LONDON, erected in 1866 by Sefton Parry, on the site of what had been stables and was later to become the First Avenue Hotel. It opened in October with The Flying Scud, in which George Belmore scored a success; but subsequent productions failed, and in 1868 Fanny Josephs took over the theatre from Parry, with equal lack of good fortune. Barry Sullivan followed and, with Mrs. Herman Vezin, played a round of old plays which ended in 1871. In 1875 Horace Wigan assumed control, and renamed the theatre the Mirror. His management saw the production of the first of the plays based on A Tale of Two Cities, which was called All For Her, and in which John Clayton made a hit; but though an artistic success it made no money. The house was again renamed, this time the Duke's Theatre, but remained unsuccessful, though in 1879, under Holt and Wilmot, The New Babylon was well received. On 4 June 1880 the building was burned down. At one time in its short career it was called the Curtain.

W. M. P.

HOLCROFT, THOMAS (1744–1809), English dramatist who is usually credited with the introduction of melodrama on the London stage with his Tale of Mystery (1802), an adaptation of Pixérécourt, though the main ingredients of the mixture had been used before (see MELODRAMA). The son of a shoemaker, he became an actor and had a hard struggle until in 1778 he reached Drury Lane. After the success of his first play, Duplicity (1781), a sentimental comedy on the evils of gambling, he gave up acting and devoted himself to literature. His most famous play is The Road to Ruin (1792), with its excellent roles of Goldfinch, first played by Lewis, and Old Dornton, a favourite part with many elderly character actors, both in London and in America, where the play was frequently revived. It was last seen in London in 1937. Holcroft, who was entirely self-educated, was a very good French scholar, and had a phenomenal memory, a combination which enabled him while in Paris to learn by heart Le Mariage de Figaro, and to put it on the London stage in 1784 as The Follies of a Day. He also translated Destouches's Le Glorieux as The School for Arrogance (1791). Among his other comedies the most successful was Love's Frailties (1794), based on a German original. Holcroft, who was a friend of Lamb, was editor of the Theatrical Recorder, which appeared monthly from 1805 and contained play-texts translated from French and Spanish. A somewhat irritable man, but extremely hardworking and one of the few good dramatists of his day, he was four times married, his last wife surviving him and marrying the actor Kenney. Holcroft's Memoirs were edited by Hazlitt and published posthumously in 1816.

HOLLAND. In common with other European nations, Holland's early plays sprang from the services of the Church, and resulted in a drama in the vernacular on religious themes, of which the earliest extant texts date from the late fourteenth and early fifteenth centuries. There are also in existence some serious secular plays of this period on themes of chivalry drawn from the medieval romances, which, when performed, were given some light relief by the introduction of farcical interludes or comedies of daily life. Of the Morality plays the most famous was *Elckerlijk* (printed 1495), which as *Everyman* is known and frequently revived in English, and as *Jedermann* was given annually at the Salzburg Festival, in an open-air production by Reinhardt in front of the Cathedral. It is probable that both the latter versions are based on the Dutch original, which has thus provided one of the most universal and vigorous dramas in European theatre history. Apart from the Morality play, the farce continued to flourish during the sixteenth and early seventeenth century, providing a relatively rough folk-drama presented by corporations, both indoors and in the open air on trestle stages at the big annual fairs. There was also a certain development at this time of Latin School Drama, which had relatively little influence on the secular Dutch theatre.

Holland was fated to undergo so many political upheavals that steady development of a national theatre was for a long time hardly possible, and playwrights were bound to feel the pressure of outside influences. The dramatist Gerbrand Adriaenz Bredero (1585–1618) was much under the influence of Spain's Golden Age, and produced a number of romantic comedies in the style of Lope de Vega, as well as comic interludes and farces of a more pronounced Dutch origin. It was at this time that Amsterdam became a centre for the establishment of a Hebrew drama (see JEWISH DRAMA, 3) which borrowed its religious themes from the works of Joost van Vondel (1587–1679), leader of the Dutch humanists, who also translated and imitated the comedies of Terence and Plautus. Of his thirty-two plays, the finest is *Lucifer* (1654), which had some influence on *Paradise Lost*.

The end of the seventeenth century saw the complete domination of Dutch drama by French classical tragedy, for whose exponents Andries Pel wrote a modern Dutch version of Horace's *Ars poetica*. The influence of the stately alexandrine doubtless did something to curb the exuberances and soften the crudities of native Dutch drama, but took from it all originality, and only in imitations of Molière, of which the best were by Pieter Langendijk, did something of the natural savour of the folk-drama come through.

French influence was again paramount in the eighteenth century, this time with the pathos and sentiment of the *tragédie bourgeoise*. The romanticism of the nineteenth century was exemplified by the triumphs of Hendrik Jan Schimmel (1823–1906), but it was not until the European theatre had been dominated by the doctrine of realism that Holland finally produced a dramatist worthy to rank with the great names of the theatre. This was Herman Heijermans (1864–1924), whose plays explore the miseries and inequalities of the modern social system. The best known of them is *The Good Hope* (1900), which has been translated into several languages and frequently revived. Since then little has been heard of Holland outside her own boundaries, but the art of the theatre flourishes, and has not been unmindful of later theory and practice, in particular of the scenic reforms of Gordon Craig.

HOLLAND. (1) GEORGE (1791–1870), an English actor, son of a dancing-master, who after seven years on the London stage went to New York and founded a family of American actors. He made his first appearance in New York at the Bowery in 1827, and became a popular comedian. He travelled extensively, and was well known in the South, was for some years in management with Ludlow and Sol Smith, and was for six years at Mitchell's famous Olympic in burlesque. From 1855 to 1867 he played character parts in Wallack's company, being outstanding as Tony Lumpkin, which he was still playing at the age of 75. In 1869 he was with Daly. Jefferson, who knew him well, writes feelingly of his 'bright and cheerful spirit' and says that he was 'an actor of the old school, introducing even into modern characters its traditions and conventionalities; his effects were broadly given, and his personality was essentially comic'. It was in connexion with his funeral that the famous New York 'Little Church Around the Corner' first received its name, since Jefferson was directed to it under that title by a clergyman who refused to bury an actor in his own churchyard. By his second wife Holland had three sons, and a daughter who died just as she was beginning her career under Daly. Of his sons (2) EDMUND MILTON (1848–1913) made his first appearance on the stage as a child, and was call-boy at Mrs. John Wood's Olympic. He was with Jefferson in the first New York production of *Rip Van Winkle*, and as E. Milton became a member of Wallack's, where he stayed for thirteen years, later reverting to his family name. He was excellent in comedy, and in the parts of elderly men. In 1879 he was seen in London with McKee Rankin, playing the Judge in *The Danites*. He was later at Madison Square under Palmer, with Frohman at the New York Lyceum, and for three years with Kyrle Bellew in *Raffles*. He had just joined Belasco's company when he died. A clean-shaven man, with thin mobile features and a high forehead, he was a comedian of a dry and subtle humour, who relied on gait, gesture, and expression for his effects. He had two children on the stage. His brother (3) JOSEPH JEFFERSON (1860–1926), named after his famous godfather, was also on the stage as a child, and in spite of partial deafness made his adult début in 1878, playing in Daly's company from 1886 to 1889, and touring with many famous actors and with his elder brother. In 1904 he became paralysed, but for the rest of his life remained in close touch with the stage, being responsible for the direction of several amateur societies. In his heyday a versatile light comedian, dignified and attentive to detail, he made light of his subsequent disabilities, and was respected and loved by his many friends both within and without the theatrical profession.

HOLLINGSHEAD, JOHN (1827–1904), English theatre manager, who in his young days was a journalist, an early contributor to the *Cornhill*, and on the staff of Dickens's *Household Words*. He also succeeded Edmund Yates as dramatic critic of the *Daily News* and wrote for *Punch*. He was a staunch upholder of the reform of copyright laws, particularly those intended to prevent the dramatization of novels without the author's consent, from which Dickens suffered so severely, and was against the closing of the theatres on Ash Wednesday. He became stage manager of the Alhambra in 1865, but it was with the Gaiety that his name was chiefly associated. He opened this newly-built theatre on 21 Dec. 1868. He was there for eighteen years, and was succeeded by George Edwardes, who was to make the theatre a home of musical comedy. Under Hollingshead it had been used mainly for burlesque. Hollingshead is credited with the introduction of matinées, and with being the first manager to use electric light both outside and inside his theatre, which was well conducted and had always a good company. In 1880 at the Gaiety Hollingshead staged a translation by Archer of Ibsen's *Pillars of Society* as *Quicksands; or, the Pillars of Society*, the first Ibsen play to be seen in London.

HOLLYWOOD THEATRE, NEW YORK, on 51st Street. Originally a cinema, this was opened by Warner Brothers on 22 Apr. 1930. It ventured into legitimate drama, as the 51st Street Theatre, and in 1936 saw the production of *Sweet River*, George Abbott's new version of *Uncle Tom's Cabin*, with fine settings by Donald Oenslager. This can best be described as a distinguished failure, since it was taken off after five performances, and the theatre reverted to its old name and policy, except for a short run of *Romeo and Juliet*, with Laurence Olivier and Vivien Leigh, in 1940.   G. F.

HOLZ, ARNO (1863–1929), German novelist and dramatist, whose *Die Familie Selicke* (1890), written in collaboration with his friend Johannes Schlaf, was the manifesto of the new school of naturalistic drama. Given by the recently founded Freie Bühne, this dreary catalogue of misery, rape, disease, and death, set against a sordidly realistic background, and devoid of all theatrical tricks, proved a rallying point for the younger dramatists. Among them was Gerhard Hauptmann, whose first play, *Vor Sonnenaufgang*, given in the same season, shows very clearly the influence of Holz's realism. Holz wrote a number of other plays, but, lacking the collaboration of Schlaf, without success.

HOME, THE REV. JOHN (1722–1808), a Scottish minister, author of the famous tragedy, *Douglas* (1756), given in Edinburgh with Digges as Young Norval and Sarah Ward, who had encouraged the author in its production, as Lady Randolph. The play caused much controversy, the clergy and elders of the Church of Scotland being against the theatre, prosecuting any ministers seen there, and horrified that one of their number should write for it. But it was a triumph with the audience, and on the first night a voice from the pit cried: 'Where's yer Wully Shakespeare noo?' Offered to Garrick at Drury Lane, the play was refused, possibly because Garrick feared that Mrs. Cibber would be too good as Lady Randolph; but Rich accepted it for Covent Garden, and there Barry, 'six feet high and in a suit of white puckered satin', says Doran, played Young Norval to the Lady Randolph of Peg Woffington. The play was constantly revived, Lady Randolph being a favourite part with Sarah Siddons, while many young actors in England and America, including Masters Betty and Howard Payne, delighted in Young Norval. The speech beginning 'My name is Norval' was always to be found in recitation books and in the repertory of youthful elocutionists, while the play found its way into the stock of the Juvenile Drama, and can still be given on a Toy Theatre. Its author wrote further tragedies, but they were not successful, and *Douglas* remains his one claim to fame.

HONYMAN. (1) JOHN (1613–36), one of the most important boy-actors of the King's Men, with whom he is found playing female parts as early as 1626, when he appeared in *The Roman Actor*. For the next few years he continued to appear in actor-lists, graduating from women to adult parts in about 1630. He died before he had the opportunity of showing whether he would do as well as was expected, but his contemporaries appear to have considered him an actor of great promise. Some later references to him indicate that he may have written a play, but so far it has not been found. Honyman had a younger brother (2) RICHARD (1618–?), who also acted with the King's Men, though probably in a minor capacity only, since he was not a member, but a hired man. He died some time in his thirties, since his widow remarried in 1657.

HOPE THEATRE, LONDON, started life as the Bear Garden, an amphitheatre in which bulls and bears were baited. In or about 1613 Henslowe and Jacob Meade, a waterman and his partner in the project, entered into an agreement with Gilbert Katherens, a carpenter and builder who seems to have been kept busy on theatre construction at that time, to convert the Bear Garden into the Hope—or, as the agreement states, 'into a game place or plaiehouse'. It was to have a dual use, both for plays and for bull- and bear-baiting. The form and size were to be the same as the Swan, but with a movable stage which could be dismantled for the baitings; and there was to be a bull house and stable capable of holding six bulls and three horses.

Henslowe and Alleyn, who were already Masters of His Majesty's Games of Bulls, Bears, and Dogs, were probably desirous of getting all the custom which could not go to the burnt-out Globe, and thereby stealing a march on their theatrical rival, Burbage. They engaged the company known as the Lady Elizabeth's Men, headed by Nathan Field, who played at the Hope in 1614-15, presenting, among other plays, *Bartholomew Fair*. John Taylor, the water-poet, challenged William Fennor, who called himself 'The Kings Majesties Riming Poet', to a trial of wit at the Hope in October 1614. Fennor paid Taylor 10s. in earnest of the contest, and Taylor had 1,000 bills printed announcing it. He got a full house for this very popular form of entertainment, but Fennor failed to appear, and Taylor had to face a disappointed audience—and audiences in those days had a way of speaking their minds. He himself said: 'Then this companion for an Asse ran away and left me for a Foole, amongst thousands of critical censurers, where I was ill thought of by my friends, scorned by my foes . . . besides the summe of Twenty Pounds in money I lost my reputation amongst many and gained disgrace in stead of my better expectations.'

Henslowe died in Jan. 1616, and a new agreement was executed between Edward Alleyn, Jacob Meade, and others, probably actors in the company, now known as the Prince's Men. Matters did not prosper, for Meade quarrelled with the actors and also with Alleyn, and legal business and disputes occupied them until 1619, to the detriment of the Hope. The Globe had meanwhile been rebuilt, and the Hope now reverted to bear- and bull-baiting. It was dismantled in 1656, but the building may still have been standing in 1682-3.   W. M. P.

HOPKINS THEATRE, NEW YORK, see PUNCH AND JUDY THEATRE.

HOPPER, DE WOLF (WILLIAM D'WOLF) (1858-1935), an American actor, who at 21 deserted the study of the law to tour in his own company. He then played in light opera for some years, establishing a reputation as an eccentric comedian with a fine bass voice. In 1891 he produced and appeared in musical comedy, being responsible five years later for Sousa's *El Capitan*, in which he also appeared in London in 1899. After a couple of years at Weber and Fields' Music-Hall he returned to light opera, and was excellent in Gilbert and Sullivan, where his fine voice and clear diction made him outstanding in the patter songs, notably the Nightmare song in *Iolanthe*. His favourite part, however, was the jester in *The Yeomen of the Guard*. From 1918 onwards, the vogue for light opera having waned, he mainly toured in revivals. He was famous for his recital of *Casey at the Bat*, which he first gave at Wallack's on 13 May 1888, and thereafter repeated some 10,000 times. He was married six times. In 1927 he published his memoirs, *Once a Clown, Always a Clown*.

HORNIMAN, ANNIE ELIZABETH FREDERICKA (1860-1937), theatre manager and patron, one of the first to organize and encourage the modern repertory theatre movement, and a vivifying influence in the English and Irish theatres at the beginning of the twentieth century. She was for some years an art student at the Slade School, and later became secretary to W. B. Yeats. In 1894 she sponsored the production at the Avenue Theatre, London, of *Arms and the Man*, and in 1903, impressed by the work of the young Irish Theatre Movement, she built and equipped, at an estimated cost of £13,000, the Abbey Theatre, Dublin, with which she was associated until 1910. Meanwhile she had bought and refurbished the Gaiety Theatre, Manchester—now a cinema—where from 1907 to 1921 she maintained an excellent repertory company, and put on some 200 plays, of which more than half were new ones. Among her productions were many by the so-called Manchester School, which included Stanley Houghton, author of *Hindle Wakes* (1912), and Harold Brighouse, author of *Hobson's Choice* (1916) and other realistic plays of provincial life. She was also responsible for the production of St. John Ervine's *Jane Clegg* (1913), and materially assisted by her example the growth of similar repertory ventures in other provincial towns of England. In 1921 she sold the theatre, which had served its purpose and was becoming something of a financial burden, and presented her library of plays to the British Drama League (see also REPERTORY THEATRE MOVEMENT).

HOSTRUP, JENS CHRISTIAN (1818-92), Danish dramatist (see SCANDINAVIA, 1).

HÔTEL D'ARGENT, THÉÂTRE DE L'. In the early days of the professional theatre in Paris the only building legally licensed for the performance of stage-plays was the Hôtel de Bourgogne, whose owners, the Confraternity of the Passion, put down all opposition with a heavy hand. But towards the end of the sixteenth century a breach had been made in their privilege by allowing provincial companies to play at the Paris fairs, and in 1598 an actor-manager from the provinces, Pierre Venier, father of the first French actress to be known by name, appeared at the Foire St. Germain and then took his company to an improvised theatre in the Hôtel d'Argent in the rue de la Verrerie. He was allowed to remain there for a short time, on condition that he paid a tax to the Confraternity for every performance. This theatre must have remained in use intermittently for many years, for in 1607 Venier is found there again, this time with his daughter and her husband, who had temporarily left the company at the Hôtel de Bourgogne where they had been acting under Valleran-Lecomte. The assassination of Henri IV in 1610 caused both troupes to leave Paris, and on their return they all went together to the Hôtel de Bourgogne, while a new company, later to be famous, leased the Hôtel d'Argent. This was the troupe of Montdory, then led by the Lenoirs. Later they are found in different quarters of Paris, and in 1634 Montdory opened the famous Théâtre du Marais. The history of the Hôtel d'Argent has been dwelt on at some length, as it was thought, before the recent researches of the theatre historian Rigal, that it was synonymous with the Théâtre du Marais, whose foundation was wrongly assigned to 1600.

HÔTEL DE BOURGOGNE, THÉÂTRE DE L', the first and most important theatre of Paris, and one of the components of the later Comédie-Française. When in the mid-sixteenth century the Confraternity of the Passion, who held the monopoly of acting in Paris, were turned out of their old quarters in the guest-house of the Trinity, they built themselves a new theatre in the ruins of the palace of the Dukes of Burgundy, which had been uninhabited since the death of Charles the Bold. Situated in the rue Mauconseil, it was ready for occupation in 1548, but the Confraternity got little good from it, for in the same year they were forbidden to act religious plays and so saw themselves deprived of the greater part of their repertory. They struggled along as best they could with productions of farces and with secular plays drawn from the *chansons de geste* and the romances of the Middle Ages, but they gradually lost their audiences, and towards the end of the sixteenth century were glad to hire out their hall to travelling companies from the provinces which included Paris in their itinerary. As early as 1578 Agnan Sarat was there, while twenty years later an English company under Jean Sehais (possibly Shaa) is traditionally believed to have played there. The first more or less permanent company to occupy the theatre was that of the provincial actor-manager Valleran-Lecomte, usually known as the King's Players. Among its members were Marie Venier, the first French actress to be known by name, and her husband Laporte. For many years the relationships between the actors and the proprietors of the theatre were troubled, and the hall was often let to rival French or visiting Italian companies. But the King's Players gradually asserted their pre-eminence, and for a time reigned supreme in Paris, with Belle-ville as their star, until in 1634 a second theatre, that of the Marais, was established under Montdory. The two theatres were bitter rivals, but Montdory's early retirement again left the Hôtel de Bourgogne, under Belleville's successors, Floridor and Mont-fleury, in an unchallenged position until the arrival of Molière in Paris in 1658. Many of the outstanding plays of the seventeenth century, with the exception of *Le Cid*, were first seen at the Hôtel de Bourgogne, until the company was finally merged with the other actors of Paris to form the Comédie-Française

in 1673. The new company moved to the theatre in the rue Guénégaud, and the stage of the Hôtel de Bourgogne was occupied inter-mittently by the Italian actors until 1783 (see COMÉDIE-ITALIENNE).

HOUGHTON, (WILLIAM) STANLEY (1881–1913), English playwright, and the best of the so-called Manchester School of realistic drama-tists, much influenced by Ibsen. He was in cotton, and practised literature in his spare time, writing for the *Manchester Guardian* on theatrical matters. His plays, which deal with the revolt against parental authority and the struggle between the generations, were mainly given in Manchester, except for his best piece of work, *Hindle Wakes*, which was also seen at the Aldwych, London, in 1912. In it Fanny, a working girl, refuses to marry the cowardly, vacillating rich man's son who has seduced her, a reversal of things which took contem-porary playgoers by surprise. This, with Houghton's other plays, particularly *The Dear Departed* (1908) and *The Younger Generation* (1910), has proved popular with amateur and repertory societies.

HOUSE CURTAIN, see CURTAIN.

HOUSEKEEPER, the term used to denote an Elizabethan actor, or other person, who had a share in the playhouse building, as distinct from the sharer, whose part was in the clothes and playbooks of the company.

HOWARD, BRONSON (1842–1908), American playwright, and one of the first to make use of native material with any skill and assiduity. He had no social purpose in writing, and never forgot the necessity of amusing his audience, but his work is significant in the development of the modern American theatre. He was also the first American dramatist to make his living solely by play-writing, since his predecessors, like Bird and Boker, had other sources of income. He was originally a journalist in Detroit, where his first play was produced in 1864. He continued in journalism in New York while waiting for success in the theatre, which came finally in 1870 with the production of *Saratoga*, a farcical comedy produced by Daly which ran for over a hun-dred nights. As *Brighton* (1874) it was adapted for the English stage with Wyndham in the chief part of Bob Sackett. Howard then wrote several other comedies, including *A Banker's Daughter* (1878), which, as *Lilian's Last Love*, was first performed in 1873 and as *The Old Love and the New*, with revisions by Albery, was successfully given in London in 1879. But his most important play was probably *Young Mrs. Winthrop* (1882), in which, says Quinn in his *History of the American Drama*, he 'placed on the stage for the first time in America a group of characters whose actions are deter-mined by the power of social laws and the interruption of social distractions without making the prevailing note one of satire'. It marks a great advance in Howard's own development as well as in that of the American stage, and was the first of its author's plays to be done in England without alteration or adaptation. The most successful of Howard's later plays were *The Henrietta* (1887), a satire on financial life, and *Shenandoah* (1888), a drama of the War between the States. The latter was at first a failure, but in a revival by Charles Frohman it established itself as an outstanding success, both in New York and on tour. Howard worked hard for the betterment of the lot of American playwrights, and in 1891 founded the American Dramatists Club, which later became the Society of American Dramatists and Composers, and was instrumental in amending the copyright laws of the period. He encouraged younger writers, and on his death bequeathed his library to the society he had helped to found.

HOWARD, SIDNEY COE (1891–1939), American dramatist, born at Oakland, California, of pioneer parents. After his graduation from the University of California in 1915 he studied playwriting under Professor G. P. Baker at Harvard. Early during World War I he went overseas and served in many capacities, ending up as captain of an American air squadron. He returned to his native country and by 1919 was busily engaged in newspaper and editorial work. He had done a good deal of writing in his student days, including drama and poetry, but his first play to be produced professionally was *Swords* (1922), a romantic drama in verse on an Italian Renaissance theme. It failed. His first popular success was *They Knew What They Wanted* (1924), a comedy that combined the writer's immense zest for life and his tolerant philosophy toward human beings seeking happiness within themselves. The background he chose was the grapegrowers' country in his native state. Both before and after the production of this comedy, Howard was constantly at work, alone or in collaboration, adapting, translating, or dramatizing plays from novels and stories. Among the best of these products were *Sancho Panza* (1923), *S.S. Tenacity* (1922) (from the French of Vildrac), and *Salvation* (1928), the last-named in collaboration with Charles MacArthur. *Lucky Sam McCarver* (1925), a more serious work than *They Knew What They Wanted*, was memorable chiefly as a study in character, being the portrait of a night-club proprietor in New York. Two other successes followed: *Ned McCobb's Daughter* and *The Silver Cord* (both 1926). The first is a sympathetic study of a New England woman at odds with rum-runners, while the second, though largely concerned with character, is something of a thesis play, being based on a 'mother complex'. *Half-Gods* (1929), a failure in the theatre, is the author's most deliberate attempt to preach a sermon. It is a passionate, and in places vastly amusing, protest against the idea that woman's fundamental place is anywhere but in the home. *Alien Corn* (1933) is another dramatic plea, or rather the exposition of a problem, in which the position

of an artist in an unsympathetic community is made the basis of a somewhat melodramatic and unconvincing drama. But the play was an outstanding success, perhaps by reason of the incidental details and the acting of Katharine Cornell, who starred in it. Two adaptations belong to the period now under discussion: *The Late Christopher Bean* (1932), an amusing character-comedy derived from the French of Fauchois (*Prenez garde à la peinture*); and *Dodsworth* (1934), a clever dramatic condensation of the Sinclair Lewis novel. *Yellow Jack* (1934), based on scientific data furnished by De Kruif and dealing with the heroic story of the 'discovery of the means by which yellow fever is carried and controlled', was not a success when first produced, but it is one of the most distinguished dramatic works of our time. Several adaptations followed, none of them very successful, though *Paths of Glory* (1935), based on a novel, revealed Howard's attitude toward war and war-mongering. *The Ghost of Yankee Doodle* (1937), though only moderately successful on the stage, is one of the most satisfactory of Howard's plays. Here, though he is ostensibly concerned over the chaotic state of the world on the eve of global conflict, he seems to have returned to what was always his chief concern as a playwright, what he once said was of paramount importance to him, 'the value and significance of flesh'. He had determined, he claimed, to ask of the life he was reporting no more concessions than 'my limited skill as a reporter forced me to ask'. Howard had just finished work on his play, *Madam Will You Walk?*, when he was killed in an accident. The piece was tried out briefly on the road, and then withdrawn. The manuscript would, of course, have been drastically revised if Howard had lived a few weeks longer. It is an entertaining fantasy on good and evil, and shows the playwright to have been in complete control of his vigorous talents.

B. H. C.

HOWE, HENRY (1812–96), English actor, whose real name was Hutchinson. He had appeared several times as an amateur before he made his professional début in Oct. 1834, playing a round of small parts. In 1837 he was with Macready at Covent Garden, and played an Officer in the first production of *The Lady of Lyons*. He then went to the Haymarket under Webster, and remained there without a break for 40 years. He soon rose high in his profession, and was excellent in such parts as Malvolio, Jaques, Macduff, Old Absolute, Sir Peter Teazle, Dornton, and others. In 1881 he was at the Lyceum, playing elderly parts, and went with Irving on tour in the United States, where he died. Known as 'Daddy' Howe, he was universally beloved, a conscientious actor and a most worthy man, who took great pride in his lovely garden at Isleworth.

HOYT, CHARLES HALE (1860–1900), American dramatist, whose numerous and forgotten plays were mainly farcical comedies depicting characters of the cities and small towns of the day.

They all have large casts, improbable but infectious humour, and a rapid succession of incidents, often only faintly connected, with a generous smattering of songs, sometimes written by other hands. They have little literary quality, and their wit evaporates in print, but in their day they gave pleasure to thousands, and were an important part of New York's entertainment in the last twenty years of the nineteenth century. Among the most popular were *The Texas Steer; or, Money Makes the Mare Go* (1890), first given in 1882 as *A Case of Wine; A Trip to Chinatown* (1891), whose 650 consecutive performances set up a record for the day; and *A Day and a Night in New York* (1898).

HROSWITHA (Hrotsvitha, Roswitha), a Benedictine abbess of Gandersheim in Saxony, who in the tenth century, finding herself drawn by the excellence of his style to read the pagan plays of Terence, much esteemed at that time as a scholastic author, and fearing their influence on a Christian world, set out to provide a suitable alternative. This she did in six original prose plays modelled on Terence, but dealing with subjects drawn from Christian history and morality—*Paphnutius, Dulcitius, Gallicanus, Callimachus, Abraham,* and *Sapientia.* These were intended for reading rather than production, but their use of miracles and abstract characters links this isolated survival of classical drama with the later Mystery and Morality plays. The Latin is poor, but the dialogue is vivacious and elements of farce are not lacking. The plays were published in 1923 in an English translation by H. J. W. Tillyard, and *Paphnutius,* which deals with the conversion of Thaïs, was produced in London in 1914 by Edith Craig in a translation by Christopher St. John.

HUBERT, ANDRÉ (*c.* 1634–1700), French actor who after serving his apprenticeship in the provinces was at the Théâtre du Marais, and joined Molière's company in 1664, taking the place of Brécourt. After playing a number of secondary young lovers and other parts, he created Mme Jourdain in *Le Bourgeois gentilhomme,* playing also the Music-Master. In Molière's last play, *Le Malade imaginaire,* Hubert played M. Diafoirus. He was evidently a dependable, though not outstanding, actor, but he was not a very brave man, for on one occasion when the musketeers rioted at the Palais-Royal he vanished, and was later found stuck fast in a hole in the back wall. After Molière's death he became responsible, with La Grange, for the finance and administration of the company, and retired in 1685. His wife also served the theatre in a minor capacity, probably in the box-office.

HUDSON THEATRE, NEW YORK, on West 44th Street. Built by Henry B. Harris, this opened on 19 Oct. 1903 with Ethel Barrymore in *Cousin Kate.* It was handsomely furnished in sober taste, and was considered a fine example of the new theatre architecture of its day.

Among its early productions were *The Marriage of Kitty* with Marie Tempest, Pinero's *Letty,* a short version of *Man and Superman* with Robert Loraine, and the world première of Henry Arthur Jones's *The Hypocrite* (1906), with Jessie Milward and the young Doris Keane. In 1908 came the success of *Lady Frederick,* with Ethel Barrymore and Bruce McRae, and in 1910 Belasco filled the theatre with *Nobody's Widow.* Among further productions were the sharply contrasted *Pollyanna* and *Our Betters,* and a record for the theatre of 440 performances was set up by a popular sentimental comedy, *Friendly Enemies,* which made a fortune for Al Woods. *Clarence,* a delightful comedy by Booth Tarkington, almost equalled its success, but had only 300 performances. Its cast included Helen Hayes and Alfred Lunt. *The Plough and the Stars,* with Arthur Sinclair, Maire O'Neill, and Sara Allgood, ran only a month, but success attended a negro musical, Cedric Hardwicke in *The Amazing Dr. Clitterhouse,* and Ethel Barrymore in *Whiteoaks.* In 1940 the Players staged an interesting revival of *Love for Love.* The Pulitzer Prize-winner, *State of the Union,* opened at the Hudson in 1946.   G. F.

HUGO, VICTOR MARIE (1802–85), one of France's greatest lyric poets, and leader of the French Romantic movement. He was also a dramatist, of whose plays it has been said that they are masterpieces in all but their fitness for the stage. Indeed, the first, *Cromwell,* was not intended for production, and would take six hours to act. It was a battle-cry, and its Preface was the manifesto of the young school. A second play, *Marion Delorme,* intended for the stage, was forbidden by the censor on political grounds, and not acted until 1831, a year later than *Hernani,* whose first night at the Comédie-Française led to a riot in the theatre. This play, with *Ruy Blas* (1838), is the best known of Hugo's dramatic output, which includes also the prose melodramas *Lucrèce Borgia, Marie Tudor* (both 1833) and *Angelo, tyran de Padoue* (1835). All alike suffer from overloading, from a plethora of words and details, from too much erudition and not enough emotion. The characters fail to come to life, and even when one is under the spell of the rhetoric of *Hernani* and *Ruy Blas* one still sees them as puppets, jerking uneasily against their rich historical background. Yet by their vigour, and by the new life which they brought into the theatre, they operated a revolution in French theatre history. They are plays of youth—a young man and a young movement—and must be judged as such. Of them all *Ruy Blas* is the most theatrical, with two excellent acts, the second and the fourth, and a superb ending. But it fails to convince, since Ruy Blas kills himself because he is a lackey, yet has nothing of the lackey in his composition, which is purely that of a well-born romantic hero.

Hugo's plays mark the entry of melodrama into the serious theatre. His plots come from the boulevards, but his language is that of the author of *Les Quatre vents de l'esprit*, breaking like a trumpet-call into the fusty atmosphere of outworn classicism. Yet it is difficult, even in Hugo's finest dramatic moments, to disentangle the dramatist from the poet, and both from the novelist and politician. The Romantic theatre carried in itself the germ of its decay, and its vogue was bound to be short. The failure of *Les Burgraves*, in 1843, showed that the tide had turned in favour of prose and common sense, and Hugo withdrew from the stage. His later plays were written to be read, and form part of his poetic works. Of them all *Ruy Blas* and *Hernani*, and the ill-fated *Le Roi s'amuse*, forbidden after one performance in 1832, can still bear revival. The first particularly, given sincerity and force in the actors, allied with impeccable technique, retains the power to move and enthral by the passion of its lyric poetry.

HUNEKER, JAMES GIBBONS (1860–1921), American dramatic critic, and a pioneer of immense importance. Beside him such popular educators of the 1890s as Brander Matthews and William Dean Howells fade away completely. He was not particularly concerned—as George Jean Nathan later was—with upsetting the theatre's apple-cart of prosperous mediocrity; he was a reformer only indirectly. He wrote chiefly of what interested him and what he found of value in the theatres of America and Europe, and maintained a determined silence about the second- and third-rate. He was perhaps more of an interpreter than a critic, an impressionistic ambassador of belles-lettres. In drama his tastes were very catholic, and it is difficult to discover his sympathies. Maeterlinck, Sudermann, Hervieu, and Wedekind—he praised and explained them all and taught Americans more about foreign literature than any other man of his time.

Huneker was born in Philadelphia, of Irish-Hungarian extraction. He studied law for a short period, but gave it up to become a concert pianist. This he never achieved, but he later became a music critic of international renown, writing definitive biographies of Chopin and Franz Liszt. As a young man he lived in Paris and it was there he learned his trade. Both in style—he was an admirable stylist—and in his approach there are obvious traces of French influence. His critical essays, composed in the Parisian manner, are packed with gossip about the private lives of artists, for he believed that a man's private life is often the key to his work. In 1890 he became the music and drama critic of *The Morning Advertiser* and *The New York Recorder*. In 1902 he joined the staff of *The Sun* and in 1912 left it for *The New York Times*. As a journalist he touched on everything from architecture to zoology, and his learning—though he carried it lightly—was extraordinary. He battled in print with William Winter over Ibsen and Shaw, and his gusto and worldly knowledge shocked the Puritans of the day. He edited a two-volume edition of Shaw's criticisms from the *Saturday Review* and acted as advance man for Richard Strauss, then unheard-of in America. His own books are still remarkably alive, and his studies of Becque, Hauptmann, D'Annunzio, and other dramatists are keen, thorough, and very entertaining. Though an excessively modest man, he could never resign himself to being 'a mere critic'. On various occasions he tried becoming a musician, a novelist, and a short-story teller, but in the end he always returned to criticism. 'I am Jack of the Seven Arts, master of none', he wrote in his amusing autobiography, *Steeplejack*.

Among his critical books are *Iconoclasts*, *A Book of Dramatists*, *Egoists*, *Mezzotints in Modern Music*, *Promenades of an Impressionist*, *Bedouins*, and *Ivory Apes and Peacocks*. He also wrote a novel, *Painted Veils*, the biography of an imaginary prima donna, and a volume of short stories, *Melomaniacs*.   T. Q. C.

HUNGARY. In Great Britain and the United States the theatre has always been regarded primarily as a medium of entertainment. In Hungary both government and people regard it as a matter of public concern, and recognize it as a valuable instrument for the reconstruction of Hungarian history, for the preservation and dissemination of the language, and for the presentation of national ideas and ideals both at home and abroad.

Modern Hungarian drama has its origin in the nineteenth century. In earlier days Morality and Mystery plays were performed, but whereas the Mystery plays survived in their original form in the unwritten traditions of the peasants, the Morality plays did not develop as in western Europe, since there was no Hungarian middle class and the intellectual life of the towns was not Hungarian. Such theatres as existed were German. The Hungarians' natural feeling for drama was fostered, however, by plays performed in the schools. Hungarian students, returning from abroad, made these plays known in their own country, and their popularity was mainly due to the fact that they encouraged the practice of Latin (see JESUIT DRAMA). Later, during the Reformation and afterwards, these plays ceased to have a purely educative aim. The dramatic element developed and national peasant types were introduced. Besides the translations, original plays, written by priests and university professors, were performed by students.

Towards the end of the eighteenth century Hungarian nationalism began to stir. The leaders of the movement were the young lawyers and the law students, who realized that if they were to succeed in establishing a truly Hungarian culture they could not afford to disregard the stage. Many difficulties confronted them, not least the jealousy and competition of the existing German theatres. Failing in their attempts to induce the Hungarian government to found a national theatre, they obtained private support and in 1791 produced, at the German playhouse in Buda, the first public dramatic performance to be given in Hungarian. The company continued to play in Buda for two years, and toured the provinces, but was dissolved in 1796. A similar experiment was more successful in Transylvania, where there was no German theatre, and in 1792 a company began playing in Kolozsvár, the capital. A performance of *Hamlet*, translated into Hungarian by Francis Kazinczy from Schröder's German version, was given as early as 1794.

In 1803, with the generous support of the Transylvanian aristocracy, a Transylvanian National Theatre was founded; but although the pioneers of Kolozsvár continued their activities in Pest it was not until 1837 that the Hungarian National Theatre was opened, the most prominent players of the day being Gábor Egressy (1808–66), Kálmán Szerdahelyi (1829–72), and Johanné Jászberény Déry (1793–1872). From that period until the present day the State Theatre has played an important part in the intellectual life of the country. The Hungarian government owns and maintains both the National Theatre and the Royal Hungarian Opera House in Budapest. In addition to this, various towns and villages make contributions towards the upkeep of a local theatre. Besides the university town of Debrecen, which provides and maintains its own playhouse, no less than forty other theatres receive aid from the local municipal authorities.

It follows that the training of both the directorate and the players receives serious attention unknown in English-speaking countries. The post of theatre director is regarded as an honour and a responsibility, as well as a career, a goal towards which a man may work for the greater part of a lifetime. The Ministry of Education issues licences for the directors of all theatres save the dozen private playhouses in Budapest; these may be revoked for due cause, and not even a private theatrical enterprise may be started until its aims and resources have been approved by the mayor, on the recommendation of the police. Similar supervision is exercised over the selection of candidates for the stage, who must undergo three years' training at the Royal Academy of Dramatic Art in Budapest before they are allowed to appear professionally.

Although the theatre in Hungary is largely state-controlled or state-aided, nevertheless the private theatres in Budapest are both active and flourishing, always eager to present new experiments in playwriting or production. The Vigazinház Theatre has been successful in performing light French comedies in the realistic manner. Sandor Hevesi (1873–   ), who founded the Thalia company in 1904, also produced a number of modern plays and introduced many foreign playwrights to Hungarian audiences. Later in his career he became Director of the National Theatre.

Having no subsidies to sustain them, the managements of the private Hungarian theatres must, like their British and American equivalents, learn perforce to judge the taste and temper of their audiences, or pay the penalty of extinction. Their method of gauging the public taste is ingenious and unusual. The first two productions of the season are put into rehearsal at the same time. If the first play presented does not prove a success it is not withdrawn immediately, but the second production is introduced into the bill for several performances a week while the company sets to work on a third play, which is then inserted when it appears desirable. As one play develops its appeal the number of its performances is increased, while those of its companion plays are reduced. In this way players are given continuous work, and audiences find available the plays in which they are most interested.

In spite of the Hungarians' intense interest in the theatre, however, there has in recent years been a dearth of contemporary playwrights of the first rank. Ferenc Molnár (1878–   ), one of the best known of Hungarian dramatists, is still an outstanding name, but he is no longer active, and during his later productive years his plays were written for the international theatre rather than for the Hungarian stage. In twentieth-century Hungary there is a sufficiency of competent playwrights, but few significant voices with something important to say. This may be one reason for the prevalence of Shakespeare's plays on the boards of Hungary's theatres.

Apart from Molnár and Jenö Heltai (1871–   ), whose verse play *A Néma Levente* was seen in London as *The Silent Knight* in 1937, the most important Hungarian dramatists are György Bessenyei (1747–1811), whose book-drama, *Agis Tragédiája* (*The Tragedy of Agis*) (pub. 1772), is significant as marking the beginning of modern Hungarian literature; Károly Kisfaludy (1788–1830), author of several historical tragedies and a number of successful comedies, who was the first to introduce the peasant types which later became so popular on the Hungarian stage; Jozsef Katona (1791–1830), whose tragedy, *Bánk Bán* (*The Viceroy*) (pub. 1820; prod. 1826), deals with Hungary's eternal problem, the national attitude to the foreign ruler, and is of great importance; Imre Madách (1823–64), who achieved international renown with his *Az Ember Tragédiája* (pub. 1862, prod. 1883), which has been twice translated into English as *The Tragedy of Man*; Ede Szigligeti (1814–78), founder of the Hungarian popular play, peasant musical comedies in which the peasants are portrayed in an idealized form; Gergely Csiky (1841–91), the first playwright to study the problems of the Hungarian middle class; Jenö Rákosi (1842–1928) and Lajos Dóczy (1845–1918), who together founded the neo-romantic school in Hungary, attempting to escape from materialism into a world of legendary heroes and fantasy; Ferenc Herczeg (1863–   ), who has written excellent comedies and historical tragedies, among them *A Hid* (*The Bridge*, 1925), a study in national problems, and *Gyurkovits Lányok* (*The Gyurkovits Girls*, 1899), a good picture of the life of the Hungarian gentry; Dezsö Szömöry (1869–1945), a playwright with an individual style, who writes on both general human problems and on Hungarian historical themes; Zsigmond Móricz (1879–1942), whose peasants are not the idealized creatures of the earlier popular plays, but sharply drawn men and women; Lajos Zilahy (1891–   ), whose plays deal with the problems of Hungarian life in the 1920s and 30s, in a more realistic manner than Herczeg; and finally, among the other modern playwrights who deal with social questions, must be mentioned Lajos Biró (1890–1948) and János Kodolányi (1899–   ). The former's *Our Katie* was given in London in 1946.

O. R.

HUNT, (JAMES HENRY) LEIGH (1784–1859), English poet, essayist, and critic, and one of the pioneers of modern dramatic criticism. He probably had a keener appreciation of acting than any of his contemporaries, and to-day his criticisms re-create the art of the great players who brought acting distinction to the theatre of his day. He took his profession as seriously as he expected the players to take theirs, and insisted that the player could not express passion perfectly unless that passion had first been felt. 'It is from feebleness of emotion that so many dull actors endeavour to supply passion with vehemence of voice and action, as jugglers are talkative and bustling to beguile scrutiny.'

But with all his knowledge of actors' work, Hunt maintained an unusual honesty and independence: 'To know an actor personally appeared to me a vice not to be thought of; and I would as lief have taken poison as accepted a ticket from the theatres.'

Leigh Hunt was the first regular critic of quality who made it his business to report upon all the principal theatrical events of the day. He was critic of the *News* from 1805 to 1807. He and his brother John ran their own paper, the *Examiner*, and Leigh wrote criticisms for it from 1808 to 1813. His play, *A Legend of Florence*, was produced at Covent Garden Theatre in 1840. In the same year he published the dramatic works of Sheridan, and those of Wycherley, Congreve, Vanbrugh, and Farquhar, with biographical notes. These drew from Macaulay, in the *Edinburgh Review*, the famous essay 'The Comic Dramatists of the Restoration'. Macaulay wrote of Hunt: 'We have a kindness for Mr. Leigh Hunt. Unless we are mistaken, he is a very clever, a very honest, and a very good-natured man.' The cream of Leigh Hunt's theatre criticism is contained in a volume prepared by William Archer—*Dramatic Essays* (1894)—with a long and valuable introduction by the editor.

T. C. K.

HURLEY, ALEC (?–1913), a music-hall singer, with a remarkably fine tenor voice, who specialized in bright and breezy coster songs of a more robust style than those of Albert Chevalier. One of the most famous was 'The Lambeth Walk', not to be confused with the later song of that name featured in *Me and My Girl*. He was the second husband of Marie Lloyd.

W. M. P.

I

IBSEN, Henrik Johan (1828–1906), Norwegian dramatist, was born at Skien of wealthy parents who soon lost their wealth, so that his early years were spent in poverty and his youth in a slow fight for recognition.

The reputation of Henrik Ibsen is recovering from the reaction liable to occur in the half-century after a great poet's death, and the more sober judgement of a later generation now finds less perishable matter in his work than was once supposed. What will endure (all the work, that is, of his maturity and much of that of his youth) will probably be found to place him among the greatest dramatists of the world. His interpretation of life, even when it speaks in terms of the parochial and immediate, is, in fact, concerned with the universal and the unchanging; his art, which has the economy and stability of architecture, having outlived its host of imitators, can now be seen for what it is, the inevitable expression in form of profound and passionate poetic thought. Never, even in the most seemingly prosaic pictures of small-town life (with which his name is all too closely associated in England), does Ibsen speak otherwise than as a profound, passionate, and meditative poet. He himself asked that his readers should look at his works as a whole, should read them chronologically, and should leave none out. And indeed it is only by so doing that we can hope to see the continuity and breadth of his estimate of human experience, his profound apprehension of its significance. A few only of his plays are tragic in form; most of them are tragic in mood, if we include in the tragic mood the solemn, the stern, and the prophetic. It is sometimes said that his lack of humour brings him short of ultimate greatness. He had, it is true, less than Shakespeare. But he had more than Milton or Dante or Aeschylus; and it is as they see it that he sees man's nature.

His first play, *Catilina* (1850), is a melodrama full of crude strength, and of promise easier for us to recognize than for his contemporaries. In 1851 he went to the Bergen theatre as Ole Bull's assistant and travelled to Denmark and Germany. In 1854 he wrote *Fru Inger til Østraat* (*Lady Inger of Østraat*), a play set in medieval Norway with a theme that, nevertheless, bears closely on the history of his own time. Already Ibsen sees the life and national policy of his country against a background of European culture and thought. In 1855 he wrote *Gildet paa Solhaug* (*The Feast at Solhaug*), a medieval play, romantic and poetic this time, and full of the past glories of Norway. It was the first to have any measure of success. *Haermaendene paa Helgeland* (*The Warriors* (or *Vikings*) *at Helgeland*) is set in the world of the sagas, the greatest age of Norway. It is a severe, simple, and moving tragedy, and structure, character, and dialogue reveal the remarkable artistic progress made in these seven years. After this he only twice used the past as a setting for his plays and then primarily for the light thrown by it upon his own times.

In 1862 the theatre at Bergen became bankrupt and Ibsen went, as sub-manager, to the Christiania Theatre. *Kjaerlighedens Komedie* (*Love's Comedy*) was produced there in the same year, a satirical verse play on contemporary life, revealing a totally different side of Ibsen's power. Though received with some hostility it made a sharp impression. *Kongsemnerne* (*The Pretenders*) was produced in 1863, an impressive historical play whose interest is psychological and poetic. In 1863 also he received a travelling fellowship which allowed him to visit Italy and Germany and removed the worst of his financial difficulties. Two years later, after the appearance of *Brand* (1865), he received a state pension and his future as a poet was assured. Although he spent much of the rest of his life abroad, his interest in Norwegian politics remained keen, fierce, and often critical. He never, in any essential respect, ceased to be a Norwegian.

After the political events of 1864 he went south and settled in Rome, where *Brand* was written. This great poetic drama, the first of his major works, established his fame throughout Europe. For the first time we meet in their full power his characteristic sternness, strength, and searching questioning of motive and deed. The method, which he never wholly forsook after, of implying the nature of truth by a series of unanswered questions and seeming negations, is here felt in all its bleakness. It is a play of unsurpassed grandeur and of profound understanding. *Peer Gynt* (1867) is in some ways a complementary study of Norwegian character (and through that of universal humanity); much of it is happy, gay, and even humorous poetry; the mountain landscape, grim in *Brand*, is often radiant with sunshine. Few plays have bewildered more critics or led to more discussion; the truths it tells are not always comfortable to live with.

After *Peer Gynt*, Ibsen wrote no more plays in verse. *De Unges Forbund* (*The League of Youth*), finished in 1869, is an unexpectedly light-hearted satire on a theme on which Ibsen usually showed himself implacable—dishonesty and insincerity. The colossal *Kejser og Galilaeer* (*Emperor and Galilean*), begun in 1869, was finished in 1873. It is a highly interesting and complex study of the struggle between paganism and early Christianity under the Emperor Julian. It reveals a powerful historical imagination, but is the last play of Ibsen's to be set in the past.

The four plays that follow are realistic pictures of the small-town life of Ibsen's own day, revealing mercilessly the lies upon which certain societies, self-righteous and self-contained, are and always have been founded. They are the images of ageless and universal parochialism. *Samfundets Støtter* (*The Pillars of Society*) (1875–7) is a study of public life rooted in a lie and, by implication, of the truth that finally frees it; *Et Dukkehjem* (*A Doll's House*) (1878–9), of the insidious destruction worked by a lie in domestic life; *Gengangere* (*Ghosts*) (1881), of the lingering poison of another marriage rooted in a lie; *En Folkefiende* (*An Enemy of the People*) (1882), of the man of truth in conflict with a corrupt society. All have the structural economy and simplicity that is reached only by a skilled and experienced artist concentrating all his powers. Their influence, both in thought and technique, was probably greater than that of any other group of Ibsen's plays.

On the threshold of the last group stands *Vildanden* (*The Wild Duck*) (1883–4), a group in which symbolism plays an increasingly large part and the interest shifts gradually from the individual in society to the individual exploring strange areas of experience, isolated and alone. *Rosmersholm* (1885–6) traces the growth of a mind in contact with a tradition of nobility; *Fruen fra Havet* (*The Lady from the Sea*) (1888), the overcoming of obsession by freedom and responsibility. *Hedda Gabler* (1890) is a subtle and skilful study of the effects of artificial society and, by contrast, of the virtue of nature and normality. The symbolism of *Bygmester Solness* (*The Master Builder*) (1891–2) is stronger than that of any earlier play, and much of it is concerned with the relation of the artist and the man within an individual. *Lille Eyolf* (*Little Eyolf*) (1894) is a study of married relations, of the nature of love and the distinctions between its kinds; *John Gabriel Borkman* (1895–6), of unfulfilled genius and of the relation of the genius to society. *Naar vi Døde Vaagner* (*When We Dead Awaken*) (1897–9) is Ibsen's last pronouncement on the artist's relation to life and to truth. He died in April 1906.   U. E.-F.

IFFLAND, August Wilhelm (1759–1814), German actor and playwright, was a member of a cultured middle-class family, and was intended for the Church. An irresistible attraction, however, drew him to the stage, and caused him to leave home, wandering from place to place in search of an opening, pursued everywhere by his father's anger. In 1777 he was taken on by Ekhof in Gotha, and a year later went with the company, on Ekhof's death, to Mannheim, where Dalberg had recently taken charge of the newly opened National Theatre. Iffland was given a large part in the management of theatrical affairs, and his first plays were produced with much success. He played the part of Franz Moor in the first production of *Die Räuber*, which remained one of his best parts, and one in which he was warmly praised by the author. At the same time, his own plays, now forgotten, were more popular than Schiller's. Their simple, unsophisticated characters, well-made plots, and superficial nobility and ecstasy caught the taste of public and critics alike. He toured in them

with much success, and even acted at Hamburg with the great Schröder, who, however, thought little of him. Iffland, conscious of this, was not at his best, and preferred the atmosphere of Weimar, where, inspired by the kindness of Goethe, he played sixteen of his best parts to great applause. As an actor he developed a fine technique, but no depth. It was said of him that he was a virtuoso, capable of great moments but not of sustained effort, and he had an unfortunate predilection for tragic parts—Lear and Wallenstein—for which he was not suited. He was at his best in dignified comedy, in the parts of retired officers, elderly councillors, indulgent parents, reverend and witty old men. His character, unlike his acting, never changed, and the faults and virtues of his youth were those of his old age. He was a curious mixture —a *bon viveur* yet fond of solitude, eager for money yet always in debt, indolent yet a prolific playwright, companionable yet sensitive. He left his mark on the German theatre by his work at Mannheim, which he practically controlled throughout its heyday. He then went to Berlin, where he remained until his death. His policy was cautious, and his repertory restricted. This led to trouble with the extremists among the rising generation, and Iffland was often embittered by their attacks. But he trained a number of young actors, not in his own virtuosity, but in the serious, sober style of Schröder, and shortly before his death took on Ludwig Devrient, destined to be the greatest German actor of the Romantic period.

ILLICA, Luigi (1857–1919), Italian writer, author with Giacosa of the libretti for the operas of Puccini (see OPERA, 15).

ILLINGTON, Margaret (1879–1934), an American actress who made her first appearances in Chicago. Engaged by Daniel Frohman, who coined her stage name—her real name being Maude Ellen Light—she first appeared at the Criterion Theatre, New York, in Sept. 1900. Three years later she married Frohman, from whom she was divorced in 1909. She remained on the stage, and later toured under the management of her second husband, Major Bowes, making her last appearance in 1919. A woman of strong personality, she was at her best in forceful, passionate parts, and one of her biggest successes was Marie Louise Voysin in *The Thief*.

ILLUSTRE-THÉÂTRE, the name taken by the company with which Molière, drawn into it by his friendship with Madeleine Béjart, made his first appearance on the professional stage. The contract drawn up between the first members, among whom were three of the Béjart family, is dated 30 June 1643, and was modelled upon that of the Confrérie de la Passion. In essentials, it has remained the basic constitution of the Comédie-Française. The company leased a tennis-court in Paris, and while alterations were in progress there, played for a time in the provinces, possibly at Rouen, where they may have given a play by Corneille, a native of that town. On 1 January 1644 they opened in Paris, but without great success. It was early in the course of that year that Poquelin first signed himself 'Molière', a choice of name for which no explanation has been given. The company, all young and inexperienced, led a harried and precarious life, and in January 1645 changed their quarters in the hope of improvement. Financial affairs, however, went from bad to worse, and in the end Molière found himself imprisoned for debt, a predicament from which he was rescued by his father. By August 1645 the Illustre-Théâtre had come to an ignominious end, and vanished without leaving a trace in contemporary records. Its repertory included plays by Corneille, du Ryer, and Tristan l'Hermite, and some specially written by a member of the company, Nicholas Desfontaines, all of which had the word *illustre* in the title. There was a marked lack of comedy, in which the company, after a provincial tour which lasted until 1658, was later to excel in Paris, under the leadership of Molière, and with several of its original members.

ILYINSKY, IGOR VLADIMIROVICH (1901–), outstanding comedian of the Soviet stage, who began his career under Theodore Komisarjevsky in 1917. In 1920 he joined the Meyerhold Theatre, where, according to André van Gyseghem in *Theatre in Soviet Russia*, he was the one good actor, 'as near to genius as anyone content to work under the heavy firing of Meyerhold's terrific personality and barrage of ideas could ever be'. When the theatre was closed in 1938 Ilyinsky went to the Maly Theatre. Among his best roles were Arkashka Neschastlivstev in *The Forest*, Prisipkin in *The Bug*, and Raspluev in *The Wedding of Krechinsky*.

IMMERMANN, KARL (1796–1840), director of the Düsseldorf theatre from 1834–7. Under the influence of Goethe's work at Weimar he tried to raise the standard of theatrical performance, insisted on clear diction, and made many technical improvements in scenery, costume, and lighting. The public, however, was apathetic, and his experiment ended in failure.

IMPERIAL THEATRE, NEW YORK, on 45th Street between Broadway and Eighth Avenue. One of the most consistently successful theatres in New York, this was opened by the Shuberts on 24 Dec. 1923. It has mainly been used for musical shows, but in 1936 it had its first Shakespeare production with Leslie Howard in *Hamlet*, settings by Stewart Chaney. This, however, was no match for the Gielgud *Hamlet*, which was running at the same time, and soon took to the road. It was followed by further musicals, and in 1946 came the successful *Annie Get Your Gun*.   G. F.

For the Imperial Theatre, London, see AQUARIUM THEATRE.

IMPRESSIONISM, a theory of modern art which has some bearing on the theatre, since it maintains that to reproduce a thing faithfully or realistically focuses the eye on misleading externals, whereas to reproduce the impression made by the thing approximates the reproduction to reality. In play-writing and production this leads to the use of symbolic scenery, undramatic dialogue, and to the extension of impressionism to the inner realm of thought, leading to expressionism.

INCHBALD, ELIZABETH (*née* SIMPSON) (1753–1821), English actress and one of the earliest English women dramatists. She had a brother George on the stage, and decided to join him, in spite of an impediment in her speech which she never wholly overcame. A very beautiful and spirited young woman, though without any money, she ran away from home and had many adventures before she married Joseph Inchbald (? –1779), an inoffensive little man who painted and acted indifferently, and only survived his marriage by seven years. He was at his best in old men. His wife was first seen on the stage in the provinces, where she acted Cordelia to his Lear; she became the friend of Mrs. Siddons and Tate Wilkinson, and was acting with the latter when her husband died. She later appeared at Covent Garden, but in 1789 retired from a profession in which she had made little mark, and devoted herself to the more lucrative employment of playwriting. A tall, fair woman, beautifully dressed, with a somewhat angular figure, she was extremely popular in private life, and had many opportunities of remarriage. She refused them all, but in spite of high spirits and a witty tongue no scandal attaches itself to her name. She was a capable writer of sentimental comedy, and though none of her plays has survived, they were successful in their own day, being mainly adaptations of contemporary French or German models. The best were probably *I'll Tell You What* (1785), *Wives as They Were, and Maids as They Are* (1797), and her last comedy, *To Marry or Not to Marry* (1805). She had a good sense of humour and some wit, but her plays, which are very characteristic of their time, are spoilt by an obvious moral purpose and too much sentiment. She was also the author of a number of novels, and edited several important collections of English tragedies and comedies. Among her many activities she was a notable contributor to the *Edinburgh Journal*. An account of her life and times was written by S. R. Littlewood in 1921.

INCIDENTAL MUSIC. Strictly speaking, any music written for and used in the production of a spoken play is in the nature of incidental music, even if not technically so described. Such music may amount to too little for such description, or to too much. Thus, for example, Linley's song 'Here's to the Maiden' in *The School for Scandal* or Beethoven's 'Coriolan' Overture, the only piece of music written by him for von Collin's play, come technically under the head of incidental music, but would hardly be so called; nor would, on the other hand, such works as those in which Lully collaborated with Molière, which amount to intermezzi, indeed almost to *opéras-ballets* (see BALLET DE COUR), where the music is as important as the play; and the same is true of eighteenth-century English musical stage pieces, of French vaudevilles and of German *Singspiele*. These, although not operas—which even the English ballad operas are not—(see OPERA, 7 and 8) are sufficiently important types of musical composition, as distinct from dramatic pieces with added music, to have acquired names of their own.

Incidental music, then, may be defined as any kind of stage music expressly written for use in a dramatic performance that would still be in all its essentials complete without it (even the songs could be spoken as poetry without damage to the dramatic context), music that would not have come into existence independently of the play to which it is attached, though portions of it may afterwards be extracted for use at concert performances, especially in the form of suites. Mendelssohn's *Midsummer Night's Dream* Overture, written at the age of 17, was not in itself incidental music, but rather a symphonic poem for concert performance based on the subject of Shakespeare's play; but the pieces Mendelssohn wrote for the play later are incidental music properly speaking, and the overture became part of it.

From what has been said it will have become obvious that the historical origins of incidental music are complicated and indefinite. Courtly Italian spectacles, before the rise of opera in Italy at the opening of the seventeenth century, were full of music for singing and dancing; but they were distinctive types of stage entertainment with music as an integral part. The same is true of the seventeenth-century English masque. Milton's *Comus*, for instance, although it may be regarded as containing music merely as an adjunct, cannot be imagined to have been written in the first place as a self-sufficient play to which music could subsequently have been added by way of an expedient or for greater effectiveness—if not by Henry Lawes, then by any other competent composer. Up to a point it was distinctly a musical entertainment, and indeed would have become an opera if opera had by its time taken a firm foothold in England.

Plays with incidental music are in no sense primarily musical works except, precisely, 'incidentally'. Thus we must not look for the rise of incidental music in the stage entertainments of Renaissance Italy, nor in those which plainly derived from them in England (see MASQUE). We see traces of it, however, in the independent English drama of the Elizabethans, and also in the classical Spanish drama. It is clear that Shakespeare's plays asked for a good deal of music, not only interpolated songs, which the poet fortunately made an integral part of his work by himself providing the words for them,

nor merely the sennets (a word probably derived from *sonata*) and tuckets (from *toccata*) he prescribed, but also interludes and dances. It is evident that there must have been music, perhaps for a consort of viols, if not a 'broken consort' of wind and strings for greater effectiveness in the theatre, at the opening of *Twelfth Night*; and since a Bergomask is called for in the last act of *A Midsummer Night's Dream* and Benedick asks the pipers to strike up for a dance at the end of *Much Ado About Nothing*, there must have been players provided. In Spain the plays of Cervantes, Lope de Vega, Calderón, Moreto, and many other classics continually called for music of various sorts; yet they have too much action and dialogue and self-sufficient verse to become anything like operas. Their music is not casual, but it is plainly incidental.

In English Restoration plays it has been said to be casual. Indeed, Grove's *Dictionary of Music and Musicians* will not admit that their 'act-tunes'—it makes no mention of the songs —come properly under the head of incidental music at all. Nevertheless, it is difficult to maintain that the contributions to the play-house made by so important a composer as Purcell are to be ignored as contributions to the development of that species of theatre music also, and no doubt J. A. Westrup, in his book on Purcell, is justified in cataloguing the comedies and tragedies coming into this category under the head of 'Plays with Incidental Music and Songs'. These plays include works by Beaumont and Fletcher, Dryden, Congreve and others, as well as a number of melodramatic adaptations from Shakespeare. Thus forty-four of Purcell's fifty stage works, the other six of which either are or may, at any rate, be fairly accurately called operas, decidedly remain literary dramatic pieces: their music, which as such has a classical importance, must therefore be called incidental music and marks, indeed, an important historical advance in that domain.

The fact that this advance was made in England and not in any other European country of comparable musical culture is unquestionably due to two interdependent causes: the flourishing condition of the spoken drama and the failure of opera to thrive, as it was by that time doing in Italy and France, and was soon to do in Austria and Germany as well. Purcell's early death further postponed the development of English opera at the very moment when it promised a brilliant and nationally independent future. But nowhere else had incidental music resulted in anything as fine as it had done in Purcell's hands. It might have done so in Spain if the only condition in its favour had been the drying-up of early sources of opera; but it failed there because the Spanish drama too had declined by that time.

There was not much call for incidental music anywhere during the eighteenth century. The five chief musical countries, Italy, France, Germany, Austria, and England, now developed light operatic types of stage entertainment of various sorts, in which the music, though often very flimsy, was still essential, not incidental. Handel, however, provided music for a London revival of *The Alchemist* and later for *Alceste*; Haydn for *King Lear*, which seems to have been staged at the Esterház palace in 1776; and Mozart for an obscure play called *Thamos, King of Egypt*, which is now of some interest only because his score for it, in some ways, foreshadows his later great 'Egyptian' opera, 'The Magic Flute'. But the eighteenth century did something to nourish a rich soil for developments in the next. It enlarged and improved the orchestral resources, and, through the intermediary of opera on a more or less grand scale, established the orchestra in the theatre. The opera orchestras in London and Paris were the best obtainable in their time and place, while in Italy, except perhaps at one or two Courts, they were the only existing ones.

The German Courts all had their operatic establishments, and therefore their orchestras. But here conditions were rather different and, as it happened, most favourable to the development of incidental music. Although the Courts vied with each other in keeping opera going lavishly, the majority of them were situated in quite small provincial towns, such as Mannheim, Weimar, Bonn, Brunswick, Cassel, or Carlsruhe. However great their cultural ambitions, they were, on the whole, confined to the Courts and sometimes the universities. Even the few princely residences which happened to be large centres, like Berlin, Dresden, and Munich, were still restricted in size as seats of culture, for the Court theatres were wholly inaccessible to the masses and almost as much so to the middle classes. This meant that the princes who wished to cultivate both opera and the drama were obliged to do so in a single Court theatre, with very few exceptions, one of which was Vienna, where the Court theatres kept open house more democratically.

Now an operatic establishment meant a large and good orchestra, whereas a dramatic one did not necessarily call for anything of the kind. But the latter sometimes required music of sorts, if only accompaniments for songs or some dance measures; and as on play-nights the opera orchestra was necessarily kept idle where there was only one theatre, intendants and managers naturally began to think of using it when music was called for in a play. Such a generous supply could not fail before long to lead to increasingly greedy demands. If a large orchestra was used for songs and dances in plays, it might as well be employed to the full to perform an overture and interludes between the acts. This in turn led to commissions given to composers to write such overtures and interludes and, again, it was not long before it occurred to playwrights to make the most of these orchestral opportunities by inserting into their new plays scenes actually requiring musical accompaniments, such as processions and what they called 'melodramas'—particularly exciting or moving scenes in which the spoken words were accompanied by an orchestral undercurrent. The later English 'melodrama', where attempts at robbery or murder were accompanied by appropriate music provided by a theatre composer like Jimmy Glover, was nothing else than a debased offspring of such scenes (see MELODRAMA).

The German theatre now developed along two lines in this field. There was incidental music written for plays, as for instance when the Burgtheater in Vienna, intending to produce Goethe's *Egmont*, asked Beethoven to write an overture and other pieces, and to set Clärchen's songs for it; and there were plays written with the intention of using incidental music, as when Helmina von Chézy turned out her preposterous *Rosamunde* (also for Vienna) and the Theater an der Wien called on Schubert to provide music for it, with the result that we are left with some delicious music by that master for a play which has vanished off the face of the earth.

Not all the German princes were necessarily enlightened, but they all felt it incumbent on them to live up to the obligations of Courts. There was much vainglorious rivalry, but it did result in a serious cultivation of opera and classical drama, the latter including translations of Greek tragedy, Shakespeare, and other non-German classics. The competition spread to the municipal theatres of some of the cities which had no Court, such as Hamburg and Leipzig, where there was probably less ostentation and more genuine endeavour.

By chance or design the greater Germanic masters of the first half of the nineteenth century wrote incidental music more conspicuously for translations than for the indigenous classics, Lessing, Goethe, Schiller, Grillparzer, and the rest. Goethe's *Faust*, for instance, was for a long time furnished with nothing better than music by an aristocratic amateur, Prince Radziwill. On the other hand, Weber contributed music to Schiller's version of Gozzi's *Turandot*, including an earlier overture on Chinese themes. Nearer the middle of the century, Schumann's score for *Manfred* appeared, and Mendelssohn was commissioned by the Prussian Court to write music for translations of Sophocles' *Antigone* and *Oedipus Coloneus*, Racine's *Athalie*, and Victor Hugo's *Ruy Blas*, as well as his extensive additions to the *Midsummer 'Night's Dream* Overture.

By the second half of the nineteenth century incidental music was established as a musical category of some importance, and that importance has grown ever since. It was not to be cultivated as systematically by other countries as by Germany and Austria until the present century, but important works of the kind appeared sporadically here and there. In France, Bizet's music for Alphonse Daudet's rather over-wrought but extremely well-constructed tragedy of *L'Arlésienne* comes next in importance to 'Carmen' among his works, and it is a remarkable example of what may be called 'regional music'. That is true also of Grieg's congenial, if not quite commensurate, contribution to the success of Ibsen's *Peer Gynt*, the original production of which was so exceptional an event in the Norwegian theatre as to justify the unusual extravagance of a full orchestra. Another commission for music to one of Ibsen's poetic dramas, *The Feast at Solhaug*, was issued later in Vienna to Hugo Wolf. Ibsen's sociological plays, of course, attracted no composers, and indeed they are unimaginable with music; and it is noticeable that everywhere poetic drama—which does not necessarily mean verse drama—was the type of play that called for music and most often had its call answered by famous composers. It is not to be wondered at that, for example, Bernard Shaw's plays were left without incidental music, though it seems almost unbelievable now that, by way of exception, *Saint Joan* was not provided with a score from the hand of a distinguished British composer at its original production.

Other poetic plays that may be singled out in this connexion from the stage history of about the turn of the nineteenth century are Rostand's *Cyrano de Bergerac*, with music by Jean Nouguès, and Maeterlinck's *Pelléas et Mélisande*, for which both Fauré in France (though the commission came from the Prince of Wales's Theatre in London) and Sibelius in Finland wrote music that has remained valuable in the concert-room in the form of suites, even if they are less familiar than those from the music to *Peer Gynt* and *L'Arlésienne*. In the theatre *Pelléas et Mélisande* as a play has been eclipsed by Debussy's setting of it as a music-drama. There is also one case at least of a composer's superseding his own incidental music to a play by a later opera on the same subject: Humperdinck's 'Königskinder'. Italy's foremost dramatic poet of recent years, Gabriele d'Annunzio, has been given his share of incidental music, among which Pizzetti's score for *La Pisanella* takes a high place. But the outstanding one written for him was for his drama in French, *Le Martyre de Saint Sébastien*, composed by Debussy, which turned out to be one of that master's most arresting later works.

In France, as to a smaller extent in England, intrigue, vested interests, and log-rolling have produced much waste in second-rate production and much neglect of first-rate talent in the world of both the stage and music; and these evils could not fail to do harm where these two worlds intersect as inevitably as they do in the domain of incidental music. All the same, it is in these two countries, with Russia and the U.S.A. as perhaps equal partners, that this kind of theatre music shows signs of being most likely to thrive in the near future. The French stage has been fruitfully active in this direction, and once again it is the poetic drama which has benefited most, particularly the translations and adaptations of Greek and Shakespearian plays by André Gide and others, for which many remarkable scores have been drawn from Florent Schmitt, Darius Milhaud, Arthur Honegger, and many more composers of distinction. A remarkable case of collaboration is the music by Honegger, Albert Roussel, and

Jacques Ibert, for Romain Rolland's dramatic trilogy, *Le Théâtre de la Révolution*.

Imperial Russia produced some interesting work, beginning rather humbly and obscurely with Glinka's music for Count Kukolnik's drama of *Prince Kholmsky*. Mussorgsky set to work on music for an Oedipus drama by Ozerov, but left it unfinished and used up what he had written in later works; and so little was known of it even to specialists that they continued for a long time in the belief that it had been intended for Sophocles. Balakirev's music for *King Lear* and Tchaikovsky's for *Hamlet* were later examples of good work produced under the old régime, which could afford large orchestras as well as great actors and lavish productions. But the U.S.S.R. too, if not extravagant, are generous in this matter, and it is evident from the catalogues of living Russian composers alone that orchestral music is expected as a matter of course in the theatre of Soviet Russia. Not many of these numerous composers—who cannot all be good, but who are at any rate all kept busy—have failed to produce at least one score of incidental music, and among these, again, every other seems to have composed one or more for the production of Shakespeare plays. In America the most interesting examples of modern incidental music are those written for the new indigenous drama of Eugene O'Neill and others.

In England incidental music was rarely taken seriously until the present century. In the eighteenth century such slender things as Arne's delightful Shakespeare songs were exceptional, though these were actually written for stage productions. Nothing of much importance emerged during the nineteenth; but something in the nature of a false start was made towards its close. It began with music commissioned from Sullivan for productions of *The Tempest*, *The Merchant of Venice*, *The Merry Wives of Windsor*, *Henry VIII*, and *Macbeth*, as well as for *The Foresters* and *King Arthur*. All this has now gone to waste, though a London production of *The Tempest* in the early 1920s, which used some of Sullivan's pieces and Arne's songs incongruously with new and very striking music by Arthur Bliss, showed how good Sullivan could be in his own much milder way at theatre music of this kind. He was certainly superior to Edward German, whom later actor-managers discovered as a purveyor of all they conceived incidental music to need—a talent for easy entertainment and agreeably picturesque, if distant, period imitation. Of German's scores for plays nothing has survived but his dances for Shakespeare's *Henry VIII* and those for Anthony Hope's romanticized *Nell Gwynn*. Little else produced before 1900 can be taken much more seriously than Glover's music, which provided stealthy undercurrents for the villain's exploits in the Drury Lane melodramas, though exceptions could be mentioned, such as Stanford's music for *The Eumenides* and *Oedipus Tyrannus* and for *Queen Mary* and *Becket*.

After that date things began to improve.

Norman O'Neill's contributions to many plays produced at the Haymarket Theatre, where he was musical director, were still slight, but they showed a special aptitude for the requirements of the stage combined with graceful, sometimes fanciful, invention. But on the whole the dramatic societies at the universities were quicker in the uptake than the professional theatres. The undergraduates at Oxford and Cambridge were encouraged to have highbrow fun (in Greek) with Aristophanes, and some of the foremost composers took pleasure in writing music for these ephemeral productions, Parry being among the earliest, Vaughan Williams coming later, and one of the most recent being Walter Leigh. However, for a London production, though hardly a commercial one, Elgar was invited to write music for *Grania and Diarmid*, and thereafter interesting things happened periodically. Elgar again appeared with lovely music for *The Starlight Express*, a play based by Algernon Blackwood on his own novel, *A Prisoner in Fairyland*, and later with a rather insignificant *Beau Brummell*. Bliss's music for *The Tempest* has been mentioned; Bantock's for *Macbeth*, Goossens's for Maugham's *East of Suez*, Armstrong Gibbs's for Maeterlinck's *The Betrothal*, and Frederic Austin's for Čapek's *The Insect Play*, should be referred to. Delius had a more than ordinary success with what was once again music for the poetic drama, *Hassan*, of which some has been saved for the concert-room.

There have been some deplorable lapses, such as that of the music for the spectacular oriental fantasy, *Chu-Chin-Chow*, now heard mainly from band-stands and pier pavilions; but modern producers, if they consider incidental music at all, are increasingly inclined to take it seriously. John Gielgud's productions of *Macbeth* (1942) and *Hamlet* (1944) with music, respectively, by William Walton and Leslie Bridgewater, showed enterprise promising extremely well for the future of the British theatre in this direction. True, Walton's music, scored for a large symphony orchestra, was relayed by amplifiers from gramophone records, a procedure that was satisfactory neither to the audiences artistically nor to the orchestras economically. But this method, although probably a war-time economy, points to possible developments of the greatest interest to future producers, among whom there will always be many who cannot in any circumstances call upon the services of an orchestra, but whose artistic sense revolts against the compromise only too light-heartedly resorted to by theatrical managements in the past, and sometimes still in the present. It must be recorded with regret, for example, that the Shakespeare Memorial Theatre at Stratford-on-Avon, which ought as a matter of course to maintain international festival standards in every particular, including its music, has never, up to the time of writing, kept anything a professional musician would call an orchestra at all, nor always insisted on adequate standards of performance.

Another interesting recent development is that of a return to—or rather, in England, a new departure in the direction of—a combination of the artistic interests of drama and opera (in this case including ballet as well), achieved in London by the Old Vic and Sadler's Wells theatres. It is this which made the wonderful production of Ibsen's *Peer Gynt*, with a full orchestra to play Grieg's music, possible in 1944–5, in spite of harassing war conditions. And beyond that date the English theatre may look to a future in which the drama may, and probably will, call confidently for the assistance of music and musicians.   E. B.

INCORPORATED STAGE SOCIETY, see STAGE SOCIETY.

INDEPENDENT THEATRE, LONDON, see GREIN, J. T.

INDIA. The origin and early history of the classical Hindu (Sanskrit) drama remain matters on which little reliable information can be found. When, about A.D. 100, the first surviving dramas were composed, the form of the drama had already developed to that which was stereotyped for later times, and the period of growth and development lies before this date. Mention of actors (*naṭa*) and other kinds of performers appears sporadically in earlier texts, but few details are available as to the nature of their performances. It would seem, from what slight evidence is available, that the drama proper developed fairly rapidly in the centuries immediately preceding the Christian era, growing out of earlier dramatic dances and mimetic representations, the tradition of which may go back indefinitely. Controversy as to whether its origin was religious or secular has little meaning in a country like India, though it is certain that it had nothing to do with the official Vedic religion of the ruling orders. The suggestion that its origin is due to Greek influence has no evidence to support it; nevertheless it is convenient in point of time, and it is possible that knowledge that plays were performed at the Courts of Greek invaders may have stimulated Indians to develop their own drama, though direct influence of classical models is certainly out of the question.

The earliest dramatist of whom anything has survived is Aśvaghoṣa (*c.* A.D. 100). Fragments of three of his plays have been found in the sands of Central Asia. They are interesting because in them we find the drama being used for purposes of propaganda for the Buddhist religion. Since this was far from being the original purpose of the drama, it is an indication that the drama had been established for some considerable time. Later come Bhāsa and Śūdraka (fourth century) and Kālidāsa (fifth century). In the three plays of Kālidāsa, particularly in the *Śakuntalā*, the Sanskrit drama reaches its highest state of perfection. It was the translation of this play by Sir William Jones (Calcutta, 1789) that first awoke an interest in Sanskrit literature in Europe, and in particular stirred the admiration of the poet Goethe. Later works of merit are the *Mudrā-rākṣasa* of Viśākhadatta, based on a story of complicated political intrigue, and the *Veṇi-saṃhāra* of Bhaṭṭa Nārāyaṇa who draws his inspiration from the Mahābhārata, the national epic of India. King Harṣa of Kanauj wrote two comedies of Court intrigue and one play with a Buddhist theme. Second in order of merit to Kālidāsa comes Bhavabhūti, whose works are more exalted but less spontaneous than those of his predecessor. Later dramas are more artificial and often have the appearance of literary exercises meant to be read rather than performed. By A.D. 1000 the drama is in a full state of decline, and little of value is produced after that date.

The earliest treatise on the theory and practice of the drama is the *Nāṭya-śāstra* of Bharata, which is probably to be dated in the third century A.D., that is to say, earlier than the bulk of the existing dramas. It is an extensive work dealing exhaustively with every branch of the subject, the erection of theatres, the production of plays, the composition of plays, music, dancing, costume, and so forth. The rules of this work were quickly accepted as canonical, and the practice of all later dramatists and performers is dominated by it. Later treatises on the drama contain essentially the same material and add little that is new. Some are valuable as preserving fragments of lost dramas which otherwise would be unknown. Some of the commentaries on the dramas contain useful details about the production of the plays.

Regular theatres do not appear to have existed. Bharata's account implies that the hall and stage were erected specially for the performance. This would take place in connexion with some festival or public celebration, or the king, or some rich patron, would summon the actors to perform for his benefit. Temples and palaces were frequently adapted for the occasion, and we even hear in an inscription of a cave being used for this purpose. The playhouse was constructed in accordance with certain specified measurements, divided into the two sections: stage and auditorium. The latter was divided by pillars into sections to be occupied by the four castes. The rows of seats were made of either brick or wood. In front was the seat of honour occupied by the patron and his entourage. The stage (*ranga*) was decorated by pictures and reliefs. At the back of the stage was the curtain which separated it from the dressing-rooms of the artists. Behind the curtain were performed various noises off, sounds of tumult, &c., and voices of gods which could not suitably be represented on the stage.

It was not the general custom to represent on the stage the scenery of the action. The curtain remained the background and the rest was for the most part left to the imagination of the spectators. To indicate that certain actions were being performed, the actors would go through various conventional gestures. Thus, when a character representing a king had to mount a chariot, instead of a chariot being brought on to the stage, he would indicate by a particular set of gestures, with which the audience was familiar, that a chariot was being mounted; similarly when an actress went through the operation of watering flowers, and so on. At the same time use was made of certain minor stage properties, some accounts of which are available. Thus we hear that the toy cart which gave its name to the *Mṛcchaka-ṭikā* actually appeared on the stage. In another performance an artificial elephant was constructed in connexion with a certain scene in the story of Udayana, which was a popular subject of drama.

Great care was taken with costume to indicate the class, profession, and nationality of the characters. Princes wore elaborate and many-coloured garments; ascetics garments of bark or rags. Maidens of the cow-herd class wore garments of dark blue, and so on. Dirty and ragged clothes indicated madness, distraction, or misery; sober and uncoloured garments were worn by people engaged in religious service; while gods, demigods, &c., appeared brightly arrayed like kings. For the same purposes paint was regularly employed. Peoples of the north-west were painted reddish-yellow, as also were brahmins and kings. Those of the Ganges valley as well as the two lower castes, Vaiśyas and Śūdras, were painted dark brown. Men from the south and representatives of primitive tribes appeared as black. In the same way different kinds of decorations, jewellery, garlands, &c., were adapted to the varying types of character.

The actors (*naṭa*) formed a distinct caste of their own and, to judge from numerous references, their social status was not very high, nor their morals much esteemed. At the same time instances are on record of actors enjoying the friendship of distinguished personages. Their life was to a large extent itinerant and they would wander about in troupes with their repertory of plays seeking patronage from city to city. These troupes worked under a leader called the Sūtradhāra, whose business it was to supervise the construction of the theatre and the production of the play, as well as acting one of the principal parts. He always appeared first on the stage to introduce the play with a few remarks on its author, the occasion of its production, &c., to which a few complimentary remarks about the audience, as being men of good taste, were usually added. He was usually married to one of the actresses (*naṭī*) with whom he appears in conversation in the introduction of the play, with reference as a rule to the domestic arrangements of his household. The Sūtradhāra was assisted by his deputy or right-hand man (*pāripārśvika*), and we also hear of a figure called the *sthāpaka* whose duties seem to have been connected with the construction and management of the stage. The other actors and actresses worked under these. Normally male parts were taken by men, and female parts by women.

The production of the play was preceded by a series of introductory performances (*purvaranga*). This consisted of a programme of instrumental music, song, and dance, by which the spectators were entertained before the play began. To judge by the description this programme was long and complicated, and must have formed a considerable part of the day's proceedings. In addition certain ritual acts of worship and prayers to the gods had to be performed. These were brought to an end by the *nāndī* or benedictory stanza, which heralded the approach of the play proper, and was followed by the appearance on the stage of the Sūtradhāra in the introductory scene.

Characters were early stereotyped into certain well-recognized types. First comes the *nāyaka* or hero, usually a king or some other exalted personage. He was of various types but must be noble, handsome, brave, &c. The enemy of the hero (*pratināyaka*) is represented as courageous and resourceful, but violent, stubborn, and wicked. The heroine (*nāyikā*) could be of various kinds—goddess, queen, lady of noble birth, and, in certain types of drama, courtesan—with various characteristics according to her position, but always beautiful and accomplished. Other types frequently mentioned are the *piṭhamarda*, companion or hanger-on of the hero, the *viṭa* or rake, who assists the hero in any less reputable ventures, the *ceṭa*, manservant, and so on. Curious is the *viduṣaka*, who appears as a disreputable and illiterate brahmin, with an insatiable appetite for food, providing the comic relief of the piece.

The drama was divided into acts which varied in number but were not usually more than ten. The plays were written partly in prose, partly in verse. The background of the dialogue is prose, but verse is introduced when anything is to be said that appears deserving of poetic expression. The language of the characters differs according to their rank and station. Kings and brahmins speak Sanskrit; people of lower stations and women speak Prakrit, that is to say, the ordinary vernacular current in the early centuries A.D. This accurately represents the prevailing social conventions of the time. The subject-matter of the play was most frequently based on heroic and religious legend, though in certain types the story could be invented by the author. A happy ending was the rule and tragedy was never developed in India.

A large number of types of drama are classified, not all of which are represented among the surviving texts. In the most important, the *nāṭaka*, the story was based on mythology or heroic legend, its hero a king or divine person. It should have not less than five acts and not more than ten; not more than five main characters should appear in the play. The *prakaraṇa* or bourgeois comedy dealt with the activities of less exalted people, ministers, brahmins, merchants, &c., and the subject of the plot

could be invented by the author. The *samavakāra* was a play dealing exclusively with the activities of gods and divine persons. The *nāṭikā* is like the *nāṭaka*, but slighter in subject and extent. It is usually a comedy dealing with the amours of the hero. The *prahasana* is usually a short piece, and specializes in the tricks and intrigues of low characters of various kinds. The *bhāṇa* is a monologue, in which one character, the *viṭa* or rake, walks through the less respectable part of the town, and holds imaginary conversations with the people he meets.

After the onset of the Mohammedan invasions the drama in India underwent a rapid decline. We still hear of its being popular in eleventh-century Kashmir, but after that date the tradition of dramatic performances gradually began to die out. The new rulers were naturally averse to such things, and to an art which depended so largely on patronage this was a fatal blow. In the end the tradition almost totally vanished, so that we are dependent for our knowledge of it on books, and to some extent on artistic representations. Only in remote Malabar has some trace of the old tradition been preserved, among the Cākkiyar, a caste of actors and performers, but that is not a great deal.

In the nineteenth century a movement began to resuscitate the classical drama. The *Śakuntalā* (in Bengali translation) was produced in 1857 after an interval of many centuries, and other similar examples followed. Since then the modern dramatic writers of India, particularly Sir Rabindranath Tagore, have drawn on the classical tradition for their inspiration, as well as welcoming the very different influences that they have received from the West.

T. B.

INGEGNERI, ANGELO (*c.* 1550–*c.* 1613), see LIGHTING, I *a*.

INGEMANN, BERNHARD SEVERIN (1789–1862), Danish dramatist, whose sentimental dramas were extremely popular in his day. The best of his many works—he was a prolific writer—is *Sulamith og Salomon* (1839).

INNER PROSCENIUM, see PROSCENIUM.

INNER STAGE, see ELIZABETHAN PLAY-HOUSE and STAGE, I.

INNS USED AS THEATRES, LONDON. These may have been converted, or merely equipped with a trestle stage at one end of the yard. The best known were:

(1) The Bell Inn, in Gracious (Gracechurch) Street in the City of London. It was used for plays in 1576, and by the Queen's Men in 1583.

(2) The Bel Savage Inn, on Ludgate Hill in the City of London. Plays were performed there from 1579 to 1588 and later. The Queen's Men also played there.

(3) The Boars Head Inn, in Aldgate, where a play called *A Sack Full of News* was suppressed in 1557. The players were under arrest for twenty-four hours, and thereafter all plays

to be performed had to be submitted first to the Ordinary. This was the first act of real censorship the English theatre had known. Another Boars Head Inn or playhouse somewhere in Middlesex was in use between 1602 and 1608.

(4) The Bull Inn, in Bishopsgate Street, in the City of London. It was used for plays before 1575 and until after 1594. The Queen's Men played there in 1583 and probably later.

(5) The Cross Keys Inn, also in Gracious Street. Plays were performed there before 1579 and up to about 1596. Lord Strange's Men played there in 1589 and 1594.

(6) The Red Lion, in Stepney. A play called *Samson* was performed there in 1567.

INSET, a small scene set behind a central opening (see FLAT).

INTERLUDE, the early English name for a short dramatic sketch, from the late Latin *interludium*. It is often taken as the starting-point of English drama, and seems to have some affinity with the Italian *tramesso*, signifying something extra inserted into a banquet, and so an entertainment given during a banquet. By extension it passed to short pieces played between the acts of a long play, for which Renaissance Italy adopted the term *intermedio* or *intermezzo*, the latter exclusively for musical entertainments (see below), while the former gave rise to the French *entremets* or *intermède*, meaning a short comedy or farce. In Spain the *entremes*, while having a somewhat similar origin, became a distinct dramatic genre. The first to make the English Interlude a complete and independent dramatic form was John Heywood (*c.* 1497–1580) (see also ENGLAND, 2). The Players of the King's Interludes (Lusores Regis) had half a century of history behind them when Elizabeth came to the throne. They are first recorded under Henry VII in 1493, and then consisted of four to five men, who were paid an annual fee by the Exchequer, with additional sums for performances. They later increased in numbers. They went up to Scotland with Princess Margaret to play at her wedding festivities when she married James IV. They also played in private houses, and may be the company referred to in *Sir Thomas More*. They dwindled away during the later years of Mary, and disappeared entirely under Elizabeth, the last survivor dying in 1580. During their last years they were sometimes referred to as the Queen's Players, but should not be confused with Queen Elizabeth's Men, the best-known London company of the 1580s, founded in 1583.

INTERMEZZI (INTERMEDII), interpolations of a light, often comic, character performed between the acts of serious drama or opera in Italy in the late fifteenth and early sixteenth centuries. They usually dealt with mythological subjects, and could be given as independent entertainments for guests at royal or noble festivals, on the lines of the English 'disguising' and dumb-show, or the French

momeries and *entremets* and the Spanish *entremeses* (see also ARCHITECTURE, INTERLUDE, OPERA, 5 and SCENERY, 2).

INTERNATIONAL THEATRE, NEW YORK, see MAJESTIC THEATRE (1).

INTIMATE THEATRE, LONDON, at Palmers Green, see SUBURBAN THEATRES.

ION, of Chios, a tragic poet of some note, who lived in the fifth century B.C. Longinus compares him with Sophocles, saying that he was elegant and faultless, but not powerful. He wrote, besides tragedies, other forms of poetry, and a volume of memoirs often cited by later writers.

IRELAND. 1. GENERAL SURVEY AND ABBEY THEATRE. The history of Irish drama may be said to begin with the Irish Literary Movement, itself a part of the National movement, at the end of the nineteenth century. There are, it is true, certain medieval manuscripts (of liturgical plays) which are of Irish origin, and this suggests that Ireland had a share also in the composition of those religious dramas of the Church which spread over the greater part of Europe (see ECCLESIASTICAL DRAMA). But there is no continuity of tradition, and at the end of the nineteenth century the Dublin theatre depended upon English touring companies who brought over the current London successes (see DUBLIN).

But the Irish Dramatic Movement, begun by William Butler Yeats (1865–1939) and Lady Gregory (1852–1932) in 1899, offered from the beginning plays by native dramatists upon native subjects; after their union with the Fays' company in 1901 the players were Irish too. After 1904 Miss Horniman's help resulted in the procuring of the now famous Abbey Theatre and the setting up of the Abbey Theatre company. The theatre became financially independent in 1910, and now receives a small annual subsidy from the government. It won and maintained a world-wide reputation as a repertory theatre of a specialized kind, comparable with others in England, on the continent, and later in America, but differing from them in being wholly or mainly national in its repertory. Its international fame began in 1903 with two performances given in London and was rapidly extended by other English tours and by the American tours of 1911 and later. After 1904 the Ulster Theatre (see below) formed an important part of the movement; its aims and methods, though independent, were fundamentally akin.

The ideals of the movement, which have been described by Yeats ('The Irish Dramatic Movement', in *Plays and Controversies*) and by Lady Gregory (*Our Irish Theatre*) were revolutionary; though fervently and fundamentally national, it was independent of all political parties; though a literary theatre it was independent of European fashions; though only scantily subsidized (if at all) it was independent of the box-office and popular control. 'We went on giving what we thought good until it became popular', said Lady Gregory, and Yeats declared, 'Literature must take the responsibilities of its power and keep all its freedom.' While honouring Ibsen himself, the leaders of the movement had no illusions as to the value of 'Ibsenism' and determined that their material, whether tragedy or comedy, prose or verse, contemporary or historical, should be native and poetic. Besides Yeats and Lady Gregory, John Millington Synge (1871–1909), AE (George William Russell, 1867–1935), Edward Martyn (1859–1924), and many writers of the Ulster Theatre, drew upon the legendary and historical material which the great Gaelic scholars of their own and the preceding generation had made accessible by translation from Old and Middle Irish, while Lady Gregory's comedies, most of the work of Martyn, and later of Synge, drew also from contemporary Irish life. Lady Gregory, followed in this by Synge, used from the first in her dialogues the 'language of the folk', the English idiom of the Irish-speaking peasants of the West. Here, Yeats too believed, could be found the 'living language', a way of speech which did not stifle the 'living imagination' as did contemporary English speech. This principle of realism in dialogue (which was yet essentially poetic, since the speech from which it was drawn was rich in poetry) has been adopted by a long succession of Irish dramatists down to the present day, and the dialects of nearly all parts of Ireland have by now been acclimatized upon the Irish stage.

Producing, setting, and acting were also revolutionary and have, in their turn, established a fine tradition. The actors were at first amateurs (the Abbey company has continued to the present day to carry a proportion of these); their acting was that of a naturally dramatic people unspoiled by the conventions of the European stage. It has had a wide influence, reaching far beyond Ireland. Setting and dressing were necessarily strictly economical, but this economy was exercised both in Dublin and Ulster by highly intelligent artists and craftsmen and resulted in beauty and simplicity little known at that time, though, again, widely appreciated since.

Some of the original leaders—AE, Martyn George Moore, and Padraic Colum—were either men of letters who contributed an occasional play, or writers who began as playwrights and afterwards developed along other lines. As the movement gathered power, new writers were drawn to it and some, such as Synge and Lennox Robinson, remained. When Yeats drew up his well-known 'Advice to Playwrights' he was able to define clearly the aesthetic principles reached in the workshop of the theatre during those early years: criticism of life or a vision of life as the substance, the logic of carefully wrought form as the means, and, in general, freedom from all conventional aesthetic prepossessions. The movement eventually developed into something quite other than its original founders foresaw, but it has never abandoned these principles, and if its standards wavered for a time during the difficult years 1916–22, they recovered as soon as conditions made it possible.

It was a sign of the vitality of the movement that the mood of its drama began to change within the first ten years of its life. With the entry of new writers—William Boyle (1853–1923), T. C. Murray (1873–   ), Lennox Robinson (1886–   ), Padraic Colum (1881–   ) in Dublin, St. John Ervine (1883–   ) and Rutherford Mayne (1878–   ) in Belfast—naturalism and objectivity, sometimes gay, sometimes bitter, sometimes satirical, began to find their place in the new drama. Between 1903 and 1912 some twenty plays by these six writers were produced; original, independent, clear-sighted plays, ranging wide in mood and subject, finding their material no longer in the heroes of a splendid mythology and the primitive tragedy or fantastic comedy of the life of the Western peasant only, but in the hard fight of the peasant everywhere in Ireland, in the world of the small farmer and the small-town man, in the people of the Dublin or Belfast suburbs. With Colum's *The Land* (1905), Boyle's *The Building Fund* (1905), Robinson's *The Clancy Name* (1908), Murray's *Birthright* (1910), St. John Ervine's *Mixed Marriage* (1911), and Rutherford Mayne's *Red Turf* (1911) added to the work, to that date, of Yeats, Lady Gregory, and Synge, little more pioneering in extending the setting remained to be done except for the inclusion of the Dublin slums, later to be made his own by Sean O'Casey.

To the names of these dramatists should be added those of certain others who wrote before 1916. (And 1916 is the natural pausing-place for any survey of recent Irish affairs.) These, though taking each his own line in theme and setting, tend in general to belong to the later tradition rather than the earlier one of the original founders, though both Lady Gregory and Yeats, it should be remembered, continued to take an active part in the direction of the theatre and from time to time to contribute plays until their deaths in 1932 and 1939. Between 1907 and 1916 we may notice, as also representative of their authors, George Fitzmaurice's *The Country Dressmaker* (1907), Conal O'Riordan's *The Piper* (1908), W. F. Casey's *The Suburban Groove* (1908), R. J. Ray's *The White Feather* (1909), Seumas O'Kelly's *The Shuiler's Child* (1910), John Guinan's *The Cuckoo's Nest* (1913), J. B. MacCarthy's *Kinship* (1914), and Bernard Duffy's *The Coiner* (1916), and this list could be extended to include several more playwrights who contributed one play apiece. During these years, also, Lord Dunsany (1878–   ) began his connexion with the Irish theatre with *The Glittering Gate* (1909) and Bernard Shaw (1856–1950) his—when *Blanco Posnet* was produced in Dublin in 1909 while still forbidden by the censor in England.

The Abbey Theatre was seriously damaged by fire in 1951.

The history of the Irish drama since 1916 is one of inevitable retardation during the years 1916–22, of slow recovery after, and of what now appears to be a healthy and progressive phase of development.

In 1928 the Gate Theatre (see below) opened in Dublin, bringing in a fresh range of drama and a different type of technique. Certain new playwrights appeared at one or other of the two theatres after 1916 with plays which, in every case, marked the beginning of an original and sometimes of a long-continued series of contributions. Brinsley Macnamara (1890–) wrote *The Rebellion in Ballycullen* (1919); George Shiels (1886–1949), *Bedmates* (1921); Sean O'Casey (1884–), *The Shadow of a Gunman* (1923); Denis Johnston (1901–), *The Moon in the Yellow River* (1931); Paul Vincent Carroll (1900–), *Things that are Caesar's* (1932). The work of Lennox Robinson, with its variety of mood, theme, and subject, continued to bridge the gap between the periods, no less than did his lifelong association with the Abbey Theatre either as playwright, actor, manager, producer, or director. The Abbey Theatre Festival of 1938 showed no signs of senility in drama or tradition and there has since been much activity in North and South, professional and amateur companies alike producing native drama (English and Gaelic) and large numbers of translations from foreign drama.

The years immediately before and during the war saw Teresa Deevy's *Katie Roche* (1936)—perhaps the most popular of a number of plays which include *Reapers* (1930), *A Disciple* (1931), *Temporal Powers* (1932), *The King of Spain's Daughter* (1935), and *The Wild Goose* (1936)—and the work of Margaret O'Leary (*The Coloured Balloon*), Joseph Tomelty (*The End House*), Ralph Kenny (*The Railway House*), Louis D'Alton (*The Money Doesn't Matter*), Roger McHugh (*Rossa*), M. J. Molloy, and B. G. MacCarthy.

2. DUBLIN GATE THEATRE. Because of its slightly different aims and technique separate mention must be made of the work of the Dublin Gate Theatre. This was founded in 1928 by Hilton Edwards (1903–) and Micheál MacLiammóir (1899–), playing first at the Peacock Theatre and opening at the Rotunda in 1929. Its work is distinct from that of the Abbey; indeed, the two theatres are complementary, the Abbey continuing to present the picture of Irish life in all its phases while the Gate programmes include drama of every period and every country from Aeschylus to the present day—Shakespeare, Goethe, Ibsen, Strindberg, Chekhov, Shaw, O'Neill, the Čapeks, Elmer Rice, and many others. The aim of the founders was twofold, to create a standard of presentation comparable with that of the best in Europe and to lay the foundations of a new Irish school of writers different in subject, style, and setting from those of the Abbey; such, for instance, as was Denis Johnston's in *The Old Lady Says No!* (1929), *A Bride for the Unicorn* (1933), *Storm*

Song (1934), and *The Dreaming Dust* (1940). This twofold aim has been widely recognized by critics and audiences. When the time came for the company to travel abroad, the brilliance of their presentation and technical skill was immediately acknowledged in successive visits to England, Egypt, and the Balkans. And the growing list of Irish dramatists first produced by them indicates the need and welcome for such a theatre: Denis Johnston, Lord and Lady Longford, An Philibin, Hazel Ellis, Robert Collis, Mary Manning (with *Youth's the Season*, 1931; *Storm over Wicklow*, 1933; *Happy Family*, 1934, and *Lark in the Clear Air*), David Sears (with *Juggernaut*, 1929; *The Dead Ride Fast*, 1931; *Grania of the Ships*, 1933), and Ulick Burke (*Bride*, 1931).

Since 1936 a second company, 'Longford Productions', having similar aims and scope, has alternated at the Rotunda at six-monthly intervals with the earlier company.

In the beginning, Lady Gregory had said 'What we wanted was to create for Ireland a theatre with a base of realism and an apex of beauty', and even in the subsequent drama, which she and Yeats had not foreseen, this was, paradoxically, achieved. For the realism of the Irish dramatists has never, by reason of the poetic imagination of the plays it draws, lost the beauty inherent in its content. Out of Easter week of 1916, as Yeats himself said, 'A terrible beauty is born.' And though this was not immediately apparent in the theatre, it became clear in the mature work of Sean O'Casey and others. In the most recent Irish drama, whether in the Abbey repertory or at the Gate, beauty is taking new forms. Despite Denis Johnston's implication (*The Old Lady Says No!*), something like a full revolution of the circle seems to be taking place, not only in his own plays and in those of Lennox Robinson, but in the work of such new writers as Paul Vincent Carroll and Teresa Deevy. The 'apex of beauty' again dominates, without destroying, the 'base of realism'. The achievement of half a century in Irish drama may still be summed up in Lady Gregory's judgement part-way through its career: 'They have won much praise for themselves and raised the dignity of Ireland.' Not once, but several times, Irishmen of genius have given to this movement their work, their names (and in some cases the chance of prosperity elsewhere), because it was Irish.

3. ULSTER THEATRE. Though essentially a part of Irish drama, the Ulster Theatre (since 1939, the Ulster Group Theatre) has so nearly independent a history that it claims a separate notice. The work of several dramatists well known in Ireland and outside, such as St. John Ervine, Rutherford Mayne, Patrick Hamilton, and George Shiels, is closely associated either with its earlier or with its later years. In the fundamental ideals from which it grew it was so closely allied to the Dublin movement that what has been said earlier of that is in general true of the parallel development of Belfast. Like the Dublin movement, it has produced

its own group of actors and drawn into its service some notable dramatists. Its history has been nearly as long. Its contribution to the picture of Irish life forms a necessary complement to that of the Dublin group. There has been, too, a frequent interchange of plays and playwrights, so that the two movements may be considered aesthetically as two aspects of one.

The beginnings of the Ulster Theatre are contemporary with those of the Dublin movement; Yeats, Lady Gregory, and Edward Martyn lent their support to an Ulster Branch of the Irish National Theatre and members of the Dublin Company took part in a performance of *Cathleen ni Houlihan* in 1902.

The history of the actual Ulster Theatre, however, starts in 1904 with the production of Lewis Purcell's *The Reformers* and Bulmer Hobson's *Brian of Banba*, and for some twenty-five years the Theatre continued to produce plays written by its own group of authors for its own company, treating Irish subjects and in general representing the life of the North as the Abbey plays in the beginning represented that of the South. A group of playwrights was soon associated with the movement and its plays were written by Mrs. Donn Byrne, Sean Bulloch, Joseph Campbell, Robert Christie, Helen Dobbs, William Dobbyn, Lynn Doyle, Bernard Duffy, Charles Eyre, James Winder Good, H. Richard Hayward, Bulmer Hobson, Rutherford Mayne, Harry C. Morrow, Lewis Purcell, George Shiels, and Helen Waddell. In all, the Theatre gave first productions of nearly 100 plays and had support and encouragement from artists and men of letters in both parts of Ireland and in England.

After a few years the Ulster Theatre was firmly enough established to visit Dublin (1907 and 1908, at the Abbey), Liverpool, Manchester (1911), London (1913), the U.S.A. (1913), and again London in 1923. The impression left in every case was of a movement original and individual in its material and in its approach.

In 1939 it became merged with other dramatic groups, to become known since as the Ulster Group Theatre in Belfast.

Some of the most notable of its plays are those of Rutherford Mayne and George Shiels, together with Lewis Purcell's contributions at the beginning and, later, those of Lynn Doyle (*Turncoats, Love and Land, The Lilac Ribbon*) and of Bernard Duffy (*Paid in His Own Coin, The Old Lady*).

4. GAELIC DRAMA. A special branch of modern Irish drama is the drama in Gaelic. Some of its plays were originally produced at the Abbey Theatre, but the greater part of its history belongs to the work of the Gaelic Drama League in Dublin, Galway, and the provinces and country districts. The pioneer of this drama was Douglas Hyde, one of the original founders of the Gaelic League in 1893, whose *Casadh an tSúgáin* (*The Twisting of the Rope*), produced at the Abbey in 1901, was the first play in Irish to appear on any stage. His dramatic work and that of his followers became well known throughout Ireland. Once established, the drama in Irish never flagged and some half-dozen later names may be mentioned: Piaras Béaslaoi (*An Danar* and *An Bhean Chródha*), Séamus ó n-Aodha (*An Luch Tuaithe*), Mícheál Brethnach (*Cor in Aghaidh an Chaim*), Mícheál ó Siochfhrada (*Cuchulainn agus Aoife*), Micheál MacLiammóir, one of the founders of the Gate Theatre, Dublin (*Diarmuid agus Gráinne*), and Séamus Wilmot (*Barabbas*).

An interesting feature of this drama in recent years was the Taibhdhearc na Gaillimhe (Galway Theatre) built up by Micheál MacLiammóir from 1928 to 1931, opening with his *Diarmuid agus Gráinne* and producing about twenty-five plays, either original Irish work or translations into Irish of such authors as Shaw. Several European dramatists have also been translated into Irish for An Comhar Drámuíochta. The only Irish plays to have been translated and played in English are those of Douglas Hyde at the beginning of the century and later MacLiammóir's *Diarmuid agus Gráinne*.

U. E.-F.

IRELAND, WILLIAM HENRY (1775–1835), a brilliant but eccentric Englishman who, at the age of nineteen, forged with the greatest ease and accuracy a number of legal and personal documents relating to Shakespeare. These, he explained, he had found in the house of a friend who wished to remain anonymous. Ireland successfully deceived his father, a dealer in prints and rare books, and also a number of scholars and experts. The crowning achievement of his career was the forging of an entire Shakespeare play, *Vortigern and Rowena*, which after many difficulties and delays was put on at Drury Lane on 2 Apr. 1796 by Sheridan, with Kemble and Mrs. Jordan in the cast. The play was already suspect, and was damned by a riotous audience. This failure prevented Ireland from going on with a series of similar forgeries, of which *Henry II* was already written and *William the Conqueror* nearly completed. Ireland's forgeries were published by his father, who never ceased to believe in them, maintaining that his son was too stupid to have composed them. They were easily demolished by the great Shakespearian scholar Malone, and Ireland found himself forced to confess his ingenious deception. After this short blaze of glory he lived for another forty years in ignominious retirement, doing nothing but hackwork. The whole story has been well told in John Mair's *The Fourth Forger* (1938).

IRON, THE, see SAFETY CURTAIN.

IRVING. (1) SIR HENRY [JOHN HENRY BRODRIBB] (1838–1905), English actor-manager who dominated the London stage for the last thirty years of Queen Victoria's reign. Of Cornish extraction, he was born at Keinton, Somerset, educated at the City Commercial School, off Lombard Street, and at the age of 18, after four years in a Newgate Street counting-house, made his first appearance at the Lyceum Theatre, Sunderland. For the next nine years he worked in various stock companies in the provinces. In 1866 Dion Boucicault offered him the part of Rawdon Scudamore in his *Hunted Down* at the St. James's Theatre. His success there both as actor and as stage manager was sufficient to keep him in London. From the St. James's he passed to the Queen's Theatre in Long Acre, where in a shortened version of *The Taming of the Shrew* he first acted with Ellen Terry. He went to the Lyceum in 1871, joining the Bateman management. This theatre had long been unlucky, and Irving's Jingle, in Albery's adaptation of *The Pickwick Papers*, did nothing to restore its fortunes. The management, almost in despair, allowed him to force upon them *The Bells*, an adaptation by Leopold Lewis of Erckmann-Chatrian's *Le Juif polonais*. The audience on the first night was scanty, but by the next morning Henry Irving was famous.

The Polish Jew, a study in terror, was succeeded by Charles I, a figure of pathos enabling Irving to make noble and restrained use of all the romantic, pitiful, and tender associations of the Stuart legend. *Eugene Aram* repeated the triumph of *The Bells*. The brilliant new actor had found himself, and as Richelieu he deliberately pitted his own conception of acting against that of Macready and his school. Although everything about his performance was by some accounted wrong, there were influential critics who perceived in him a genius struggling powerfully for self-vindication. Comedy was being regenerated by the Bancrofts at the Haymarket; here at the Lyceum, it seemed to Clement Scott and John Oxenford, was the champion for which tragedy had been waiting. In 1874 Irving played Hamlet. He presented him as a gentle prince who failed to do the great things demanded of him not so much from weakness of will as from excess of tenderness. The reading, so different from the popular method of illumining tragic character by flashes from a dark lantern, puzzled the audience and was hotly contested by the coteries.

It was Irving's fate to gain immense prestige and never to be free from critical attack. He was not easily and in his nature popular. Few of his performances in classic parts were universally accepted. At the height of his renown there were people who found his mannerisms unsympathetic and even slightly ludicrous. Yet they also were drawn to see him, and they discussed him eagerly, because the acting he chose to give them was overwhelming in its intensity. Superseding the heavily pointed style of his predecessors, his own style was equally far removed from the subjective quietness of a Duse. To Irving acting was movement. He drew a character in sharp, sudden, delicate, superb movements, each guided by a craftsmanship on which he had worked with what seemed to his associates almost inhuman concentration. There is the ring of truth in Ellen Terry's account of his

qualities. 'He was', she wrote, 'quiet, patient, tolerant, impersonal, gentle, close, crafty, incapable of caring for anything outside his work.' The picture he drew of a Louis XI, a Dubosc, a Shylock, or a Vanderdecken challenged rather than reproduced nature. It had the splendid liberating madness of a dream in the remembered light of which the world's sanity looked drab and unreal. The tall figure, the beautiful, intense, ascetic face angled by nature for tragedy—now embodying a noble pride, now malignant horror, now sardonic impudence, now the grotesque at that point where it turns grim—threw a spell over his audience. It was a spell not so much of emotional sympathy as of intellectual curiosity; and under this spell it seemed that his peculiar pronunciation, his crabbed elocution, his halting gait, the queer intonations of his never very powerful or melodious voice, were the right and true expression of a strange, exciting, and dominating personality. Occasionally the homely and tender charm of a Dr. Primrose would solicit his imagination, and he kept an equable level of good acting, but nearly always his native grandeur would out. Even his Macaires became quasi-regal in their villainy, and when he played a Charles I, a Richelieu, a Wolsey, or a Becket, the irresistible impression was that greatness was impersonating greatness. Dominating spirit called to dominating spirit across the centuries, hidalgo to hidalgo.

Irving's management of the Lyceum began in 1878. It did little for the original work of contemporary English playwrights, but Irving was a great manager as well as a great actor. He was not content until he had enlisted in the service of his theatre some of the first archaeologists and painters and musicians of the day. All he did was done with a certain magnificence. Ellen Terry was only one of the glories of a theatrical reign that melted away the remains of Puritan prejudice against the playhouse and made each new production a universal topic of late Victorian conversation. The chief of these productions were *The Merchant of Venice* and *The Lady of Lyons* (both 1879), *The Corsican Brothers* (1880), *The Cup* and *Two Roses* (both 1881), *Romeo and Juliet* and *Much Ado about Nothing* (both 1882), *Twelfth Night* (1884), *King Henry VIII* and *King Lear* (both 1892), *Becket* (1893), *King Arthur, A Story of Waterloo*, and *Don Quixote* (all 1895), *Madame Sans-Gêne* and *Cymbeline* (both 1896), and *Peter the Great* (1898). In 1899 Irving nominally gave up management, and in 1901, after a production of *Coriolanus* and two revivals, his tenancy expired. The only other production in London was Sardou's *Dante* (1903). Irving received in 1895 the first knighthood that was ever won by an actor.

Irving had two sons, both on the stage. The elder (2) HENRY BRODRIBB (1870–1919) studied law, but after appearing with the O.U.D.S. made his first appearance on the professional stage in 1891 under Hare. In the course of his career he revived many of his father's famous parts, both in England and America. His wife, (3) DOROTHEA BAIRD (1875–1933), also made her first appearance on the stage with O.U.D.S., and was later with Ben Greet. She made her first outstanding success in the name part of *Trilby* (1895), and later accompanied her husband to America and Australia. Irving's younger son, (4) LAURENCE SIDNEY (1871–1914), was in the diplomatic service before taking to the stage, where he made his first appearance in 1891 in Benson's company. Later performances, among them Skule in Ibsen's *The Pretenders* in 1913, indicated that he would have developed into a great actor but for his untimely death by drowning (with his wife, Mabel Hackney) when the *Empress of Ireland* sank after a collision in the St. Lawrence. He was the author of a number of plays, of which the most successful was *The Unwritten Law* (1910), and translated for his father Sardou's *Robespierre* and *Dante*.   A. V. C.

ISAACS, EDITH JULIET (*née* RICH) (1878–), for a quarter of a century one of the leading forces in the American theatre. Born in Milwaukee, Wisconsin, she went to live in New York in 1904, the year of her marriage to Lewis M. Isaacs, and in 1913 was drama critic for *Ainslee's Magazine*. As editor of *Theatre Arts* from 1919 to 1945 (and for many years its chief stock-holder), she exercised a unique and beneficial influence on the theatre as a whole. She saw the American theatre as something more than a passing show. She saw it with its roots in the educational and community theatres throughout the country and in the perspective of its own historical past. She saw it constantly and steadily as an art form enriched by all the other arts and related to the world-theatre of which it is an integral part. Through the pages of *Theatre Arts* she exercised not only her remarkable editorial faculties, her taste in literature, her gift of discovering and developing young talent, her openness of mind and readiness of access, but also her own very keen faculties as a critic. She wrote with discernment on the theatre, dance, and music, and was an excellent judge of the graphic arts. She was also a clear-headed business woman who understood the economic as well as the aesthetic problems of the theatre, and was in the forefront of the theatre's practical as well as spiritual battles. Among the manifold activities in which she took a leading part were the founding of the National Theatre Conference, of which she was executive head from 1932 to 1936; the campaign for better theatre buildings in New York which led to improvements in the building code; assistance in the difficult first days of the Federal Theatre, when the offices of *Theatre Arts* were guest headquarters for the newly appointed director, Hallie Flanagan; assistance in organizing the first Board of Directors and professional advisory committee of the American National Theatre and Academy, of which she was first Vice-President.

Among the many theatre artists whose early work appeared in *Theatre Arts*, and to whom its editor gave encouragement and often practical guidance at a crucial stage, only a few can be listed here. The pages of the magazine are the best record of a rich and fruitful life which was prolonged after her retirement as editor by her activities as critic and author. But no record would be complete without the names of Eugene O'Neill, Thornton Wilder, and Paul Green, some of whose earliest work she published; without those of Ashley Dukes, Stark Young, Kenneth Macgowan, John Mason Brown, John Hutchens, Carl Carmer, Rosamond Gilder, who were at one time or another dramatic critics and associate editors of the magazine; without those of Joseph Urban, Robert Edmond Jones, Norman-Bel Geddes, Lee Simonson, Jo Mielziner, Donald Oenslager, Stewart Chaney, whose theatre designs she published; or Martha Graham, Argentina, Isadora Duncan, whose art she recognized and valued. A host of *Theatre Arts* contributors, from Bernard Shaw and D. H. Lawrence to Robert Sherwood and William Saroyan, includes writers from many of the sixty-seven lands to which the magazine found its way. Among the books she edited or wrote are: *Theatre* (1927), *Architecture for the New Theatre* (1935), and *The Negro in the American Theatre* (1947).

R. G.

ISRAEL, see JEWISH DRAMA, 7.

ITALY. Italian drama is here dealt with in three sections:

1. The literary drama from the beginning to the eighteenth century.

2. The improvised drama or *commedia dell' arte*.

3. The literary drama from the eighteenth century to the present day.

The first section may be regarded as subdivided into the drama of (*a*) the Middle Ages, and (*b*) the Renaissance, a term which is here very broadly taken as stretching from the early sixteenth to the late seventeenth century and even, for a special reason, in Section 2 extending to cover Gozzi's quixotic use of the *commedia dell' arte*, which is strictly eighteenth-century work.

1. FROM THE BEGINNING TO THE EIGHTEENTH CENTURY. The main medieval drama was liturgical; such lay forms as have survived were sporadic and rudimentary and consisted chiefly of the semi-dramatic entertainment provided by minstrels and tumblers, by verse dialogues, by festival celebrations and dances. The Renaissance represents an enormous process of expansion and secularization by which the ecclesiastical gives way to academic, courtly, and popular patronage. The changes occur roughly in this order, but no exact date can or should be given to the overlapping phases. It is significant and perhaps slightly sinister that by the seventeenth century Italian drama has three masters; scholars and, in league with them, the critics, with their passionately pedantic concern for classical precedent; the Courts, with their avidity for spectacle and subsequently for music; and thirdly, the common

people feeding fat on the scraps from both these tables, served up by the genius of two or three generations of actors professing a distinctive method of improvisation.

The sixteenth and seventeenth centuries will be taken together because of the more real distinction to be made between the two styles, known as the *commedia erudita* and the *commedia dell'arte*; for this contrast Shakespeare through Polonius provided the most neatly descriptive terms when he referred to the visiting players as 'for the law of writ and the liberty'.

Medieval religious drama is anonymous; in the Renaissance period there is many a fine, rather than one superlative, figure, form, place, or phase upon which to focus. Critics have worked along various lines, concentrating now upon an individual, now on a city, a period, or a form, in each case with profit and limitation; their peaks of interest will not coincide. Warned of this we may make use of their researches, and choose the division by 'kinds'.

The history of Italian drama does not begin or end in Italy; it is important to conceive of it in relation to European drama to appreciate its full significance. It transmits the ancient to the modern stage, so that it is impossible to account for the development of the greater drama of France, and partly for that of England, without allowing for the influences, theoretical or practical, good or bad, of Italy. Spain too takes, and later repays, in fair measure. This can only be indicated in passing, but it is fundamentally important. During the Renaissance especially Italy is the exchange and mart of dramatic forms. She has not many golden pieces. Her wealth is mainly in silver and in bonds.

(*a*) *Middle Ages.* (i) *Laudi.* There is evidence that something was known indirectly, and a little perhaps directly, at least of Latin comedy during the Middle Ages, but the references do not indicate any activities or compositions that can properly be called dramatic. Writing that has more real affinity with drama is found in such collections of stories as the *Decamerone*, and in the graver counterpart that Boccaccio provided in *De Casibus Virorum Illustrium*, but here impersonation, the determining factor of drama, is only invited.

In the opinion of D'Ancona what instances survive of the liturgical drama in manuscripts of Italian provenance do not suggest anything distinctively national. This was still the drama of the Church, and it can be viewed best in Professor Karl Young's comprehensive work on the drama of the medieval Church (see ECCLESIASTICAL DRAMA). The first impulse that is unmistakably Italian in origin and issue comes in the middle of the thirteenth century, and is due to the amazing penitential movement of the Flagellanti. The *laudi* or praises which they and their followers sang were primarily devotional and in form lyric at first and then narrative, using almost literally the stories and phrases of the Gospels; but it is easy to understand how recitation led to dialogue, and then to dramatic impersonation. A list of the properties possessed by the Company of the Disciplinati in Perugia shows how far the process had gone by 1339.

The choice of episodes, their elaboration and grouping were designed to follow the seasons of the Church's year. Manuscripts, mainly of the sixteenth century, preserve the cycles of *laudi* for districts of Umbria and the Abruzzi. The authors remain anonymous and their purpose was still religious rather than artistic. A recent critic, M. Apollonio, illustrates his study with reproductions of contemporary paintings, assuming some connexion between the arts in their graphic, naïve representation of incidents, but he insists that the trend of the *laudi* was choral and by this distinguishes it from the second medieval form, the *sacre rappresentazioni*, which developed later with special spectacular splendour.

(ii) *Sacre Rappresentazioni.* These constitute the religious and subsequently the artistic expression of the fifteenth century, and were particularly the pride of Florence. In 1454 M. Palmieri described the festival for St. John's Day, with its procession of clergy and religious companies involving twenty-two 'edifizi' for the enacting of episodes from the Old and New Testaments. In Siena there was a sequence in honour of Santa Caterina. While the *sacre rappresentazioni* are comparable to the French and English Mystery plays, Sanesi claims for them a Florentine sense of form and moderation. They were played by religious and educational 'companies' of young citizens in churches, refectories, or in the open, on a multiple stage. D'Ancona shows how comic and realistic characters gradually intruded to relieve the sameness of the traditional or stiffly typed figures; such chances were taken in exploiting brawls, grotesque names, the caricaturing of foreigners and certain professions, and even with satire of convent life. Occasionally there emerge individual authors such as Feo Belcari (1410–84) or Lorenzo de' Medici (c. 1449–92) with his *San Giovanni e Paolo* (1489). In plays based on the lives of saints some romance material is incorporated.

The simple episodic method could not hold its own against the pressure of the conscious revival of classical forms, but critics are reminded of the tradition of the *sacre rappresentazioni* as they find the early humanists plotting according to narrative sequence in defiance of the classical Unities, or again when Poliziano (Angelo Ambrozini, 1454–91) substitutes a mythological for a scriptural theme, and yet again, but this time in intention rather than in form, with the *drammi spirituali* of Giovanni Maria Cecchi (1518–87) and with Counter-Reformation plays; in convents and in some seasonal country festivities other traces remain.

The *sacre rappresentazioni* gave scope to the related tastes and capacities for music, spectacle, and for two kinds of acting, grave and ribald, and so seem to have absorbed the talents which can otherwise only be descried in undeveloped arts and diversions of the Middle Ages.

(b) *Renaissance and Seventeenth Century.*
(i) *Tragedy.* In recognition of its debt to the
dramatic artists of the Italian Renaissance
Europe might say 'they gave us patterns' and
'they set us bounds', and then proceed to
reckon more precisely the cost of the tragic,
comic, and pastoral patterns, and the bounds
of the neo-Aristotelian criticism. It is easy to
imagine how desirable the acquisition of some
standard, form, rule, or model, must have
seemed to the generation of Petrarch, and how
hard to foresee the imminent tyranny of this
benevolent classical rule.

The first signs of the tragic form as well as
the term in Italy are found at the end of the
thirteenth century when Albertino Mussato
(1261–1329), Giovanni Manzini (*fl.* 1387), and
Laudivio de' Nobili, (*fl.* 1464) [these latter are
the dates of their tragedies], sharing Boccaccio's
conception of tragedy as concerned with the
fall of princes, attempt to give to the full stories
of Ezzelino, Antonio della Scala, and Piccinino
respectively at least the external features of
Senecan tragedy, but they come short of the
rigorous selection needed for classical unity.
Other plays, also in Latin, still only half out of
the *sacre rappresentazioni* tradition, use medieval
history and ancient mythology more for moral
and literary than for dramatic purposes.

In 1472 Poliziano took a turn away from
scriptural drama by using its method to
present the story of Orpheus, and twenty-
three years later an unknown author (? Antonio
Tebaldeo) gave his work another classical
twist by refashioning it into *Orphei tragedia.*
The two significant facts are that anyone
should have wished to make the formal
changes and yet not have attempted any
fundamental reconception.

Apart from these experiments the first work
in the vernacular said to bear the title of
tragedy is *Filostrato e Panfile* (1499) by Antonio
Caminelli, called 'il Pistoia' (1436–1502). It is
shaped from Boccaccio's story of Tancred and
Gismond, but neither Caminelli nor his
successor Galeotto del Carretto (*fl.* 1497–1530)
really forsook the older method.

During the second decade of the sixteenth
century the rare, scholarly pleasure of direct
contact with Greek drama made its mark on
the vernacular in the *Sofonisba* (prod. 1524)
of Gian Giorgio Trissino (1478–1550). It is a
frigid and famous play, achieving unity of time
by formal redisposition of the material drawn
from Livy by means of narration, chorus, and
act-division. It has the form, but not the
pressure, of its models. As a play there seems
to be no life in *Sofonisba*, but as a sign-post it
has a commanding position.

Trissino stimulated Giovanni Rucellai (1475–
1525) to press Gothic material and turn out
Rosmunda (1516) and then to squeeze from
Greek mythology an *Oreste.* Meanwhile the
work of translating Aristotle's criticism and
the tragedies themselves went on parallel to the
free imitations, but for a very limited public. It
is hardly surprising that it needed the ulterior
attraction of spectacle and inter-act dancing to

draw an audience to plays in which horror was
held to be indispensable, and rhetoric came
before action. If an English reader could
realize what Sidney saw and admired in
Gorboduc, he would presumably be drawn into
sympathy with what Italian humanists sought
to provide.

In the middle of the century Giambattista
Giraldi, called 'il Cinthio' (1504–73), faced and
dealt with this depressing situation theoretically in treatise and preface, and practically in
nine plays. When his public had been sated
with distended Senecan atrocities in *Orbecche*
(1541), Giraldi began to find his own style.
There is said to be less of Seneca in *Dido* and
Cleopatra, but there is never any retraction
from the Senecan conception of a moral function and sententious speech. In *L'Altile* (1543)
Giraldi presented a dramatic version of one of
the medieval stories from his own *Eccatonmiti*,
where the persons were noble but not royal,
with the further concession of a happy ending
to encourage his audience. Here too he asserts
a modern independence of Aristotle, but he
did not care to take much advantage of the
freedom he claimed. In this respect his
practice is typical of the period. Stories drawn
from widely varied sources, mostly but not
exclusively old, were pulped down and poured
into the mould which had been made carefully
and patiently to Aristotelian specifications,
and in the process much, if not all, of what
was the spirit of drama evaporated. To see how
the rich dramatic potentialities of Giraldi's
store of *novelle* could be exploited by another
method it is instructive to turn to Greene and
Shakespeare, and to compare *James IV* with
Giraldi's *Arrenopia*, *Measure for Measure* with
Epizia, and *Othello* with its narrative source.
For English dramatists Giraldi opened up
chivalric sources and romantic situations by
broaching sentiment for tragedy and tragi-
comedy, but for Italy, in Bertana's estimate,
he consolidated the neo-classical model. He
was content to further the moral and sensational
purposes of tragedy, holding his public by
minor concessions of novelty and sentiment,
relaxing the imitation of the classical chorus a
little, treating his women with unusual sympathy and observing strict poetic justice. His
tragedy asks no ultimate questions, and it seems,
at least to an English reader, that he is too
ready to supply his own answers. It is exas-
peratingly competent.

Giraldi's work was so central, comprehensive, and influential that one has the illusion of
being able to predict what was to follow.
Since it was his ambition to give tragedy
greater currency on the Renaissance stage he
must be called successful. It would be a
penance to read all that was written; even so
thorough a critic as Bertana finds it hard to
make a satisfactory classification of the productions of the second half of the sixteenth and
the seventeenth centuries, and attempts a grouping only according to historical, romantic,
classical, and a characterization of the themes
as horrific.

What happened may be illustrated by another method by leaping forward to Giacinto Andrea Cicognini (1606–60), who was probably the most popular provider and generally representative playwright of the next generation. It is symptomatic that he is credited with over forty compositions, but the list varies and much published in his name is palpably made over from Spanish drama. Giraldi's achieved purpose had been to adapt the classical form just so much and no more as would commend it to his own age; Cicognini's was to cater for his public by excitement in more exotic styles. Giraldi provides the concentration of neoclassical serious drama, Cicognini touches the bounds of its diffusion and dissipation. Giraldi's style is plain, Cicognini's cheaply coloured.

But Cicognini does not travel thus far on his own; along the lines of protraction from Giraldi lie scores of other tragedies, and some more correctly termed *tragicommedie* and *opere sceniche*. The range of material is considerable; *argomenti* are drawn from myths, or from ancient and modern history, frequent use is made of Ariosto, Tasso, and the *novelle*. The apparent variety is enormous, but once the stories have been 'processed' they taste much the same. It is interesting, at least to the critic, to see how the pressure of the content combining with the general temptations of popularity and in certain cases a special pressure of religious propaganda gradually affect the neo-Aristotelian rigidity. First one and then another of the classical conventions are ruptured, but the freedom gained is rarely used creatively; it is won as expedience and has the effect of licence. Authors go on writing, but have little to say, and they produce, as other generations before and since, only nominal tragedies. In some, however, the dynamic force of the dramatist's conception gives him a truer claim to independence.

To return to Bertana's thematic classification: among those plays drawn from Roman history the *Orazio* (1546) of Pietro Aretino (1492–1556) stands out. To a modern Italian this Renaissance presentation of ancient Rome rings true, at least in the main and in the treatment of the crowd. The style is more direct and figurative than is usual.

Occasionally the drama latent in a modern story has its way, as, for instance, when Giovanni Francesco Savarro (*fl.* early seventeenth century) takes his chance with Anne Boleyn or Mary Stuart, and Girolamo Graziani (1604–75) is nerved to refuse to be bound by Aristotle's rule in *Cromuele* (*c.* 1671).

Among the horror tragedies the notorious *Canace* (1543) of Sperone Speroni (1500–88) shocked his age and it shocks ours, but not for the same reasons. It was attacked and defended in the name of Aristotle until Speroni's death, and meanwhile others, Luigi Groto (1541–85) especially, and rather less grossly Lodovico Dolce (1508–68), waded on in blood.

Those who risked romance material found the attractions and the dangers of love as a tragic motive. Erotic tragedies were popular at the turn of the century. One of the most elaborate is that of Torquato Tasso (1544–95), but it is with deference to his poetic rather than to his tragic gift that *Torrismondo* (1586) is famous. In the *seicento* many minister to this taste. Some concede to love-plots a happy ending; some venture to let the lovers speak for themselves.

As a general rule, however, care was devoted to plotting, to the impoverishment of characterization and the delineation of the more inward conflicts of motive and passion. To judge from the topics of critical controversy this was not felt as a loss. Few can pretend now that the result was very acceptable. Tragedy was expensive, and the displays in the great theatre at Vicenza were exceptional. The comparative unpopularity of the style was openly acknowledged by Ingegneri in 1598.

In the seventeenth century, at the price of concessions to popular taste and by subserving propaganda purposes, the Jesuits found uses for the form and gave it some temporary support. Since the connexion with *Paradise Lost* has been mooted, *L'Adamo* (1613) of Giambattista Andreini (*c.* 1578–1654) is probably the religious drama of the seventeenth century that an Englishman would wish to have seen, but *L'Adamo* is entitled *sacra rappresentazione* and is not typical. In itself it is more suggestive of the coming *melodramma*. Spain led the way for most playwrights, and martyrdom was more to their purpose. Massinger's *Virgin Martyr* would bring an English reader nearest to the general effect. The combination of sensation, emotion, and piety makes a nauseating mixture with a distinct flavour, but no form, of its own. One of the most prolific exploiters was Ortensio Scammacca (1562–1648), who has nearly fifty plays to his credit. Others did not trouble to develop plots beyond the 'scenario'.

Italian Renaissance tragedy had great possessions; good stories, good models, some patronage, much critical attention, much practice, but it lacked one thing, the power to make contact with the imagination. Its weaknesses are as various and sporadic as its merits. It is tempting but useless to speculate on its prospective promise or its retrospective dreariness. One plea remains. We are ill-placed to judge. We read too much and see too little. But the fact that there is no acting tradition is not encouraging.

(ii) *Pastoral*. If we are tempted to plead specially for Italian Renaissance tragedy, some consideration, though in another kind and degree, may be claimed for its rival the pastoral. According to contemporary critics the pastoral drew attention from the severer mode; that is easily understood, but if we then find it hard to appreciate the new form we may apply a rough analogy, and think of it as the cinema of the age. It was largely because it *was* new that it was rated so highly. The parallel is, of course, very rough. The novelty was apparently the result of crossing Renaissance eclogue and drama, not, as in the modern case, of the application of a new technique. It was, primarily at least, a courtly, sophisticated entertainment with a limited scope, not for the populace; but it was the age's own invention and gave them a sense of superiority over the ancients, their betters.

The exact stages of the development of pastoral as a third dramatic form have been disputed. Dr. Greg's admirable summary will be found in Appendix I of his *Pastoral Poetry and Pastoral Drama* (1906).

It is generally agreed that the chief pattern was Tasso's and its enlargement Guarini's, but there were earlier experiments in lyrical, spectacular, and rhetorical entertainments which should be mentioned. If we return to Poliziano's *Orfeo* (1471) and follow its lead we come to the *Cefalo* (1487) of Niccolo da Correggio (1450–1508). The mythological drama is in a sense a sidetrack. Looking back, some would prefer to regard it as a shoot from the old wood of the *sacre rappresentazioni*, and not as radically related to the new growth. Looking forward and reading the *libretti* it is tempting to descry *melodramma* before its time. Whatever the relations in conscious artistic experiments may have been, the affinities are obvious, and these three forms, and with them perhaps the Carnival masques, Triumphs, and such semi-dramatic shows, may be reckoned together as several ways of ministering to the delight in any sensuous blending of music, movement, impersonation, and lyrical speech.

A Jacobean who could remember seeing plays by Peele, Lyly, and Daniel, and some masques, would have understood the Renaissance variety in Italy, and perhaps suspected that England owed Italy many small debts. The relative popularity of the various forms is different, and the opera is a separate story. Only the Italian pastoral realized to the full its dramatic possibilities, and it is tempting to describe it as drama pastoralized rather than pastoral dramatized.

Guarini reckons that the *pastorale favola*, *Il Sacrifizio* (1554–5), by Agostino Beccari (?–1598) was the first of the new kind. It was followed by *Lo Sfortunato* of Agostino Argenti (?–1576) in 1568. This Tasso saw, and his own *L'Aminta* was acted in Ferrara in 1573. From Tasso's delicate single flower Battista Guarini (1538–1612) cultivated a rich double variety. *Il Pastor Fido* (prod. 1598) is more than three times as long as *L'Aminta*, and Guarini is as proud of its complicated plotting as Tasso might be of his own simplicity. No attempt is made here to do justice either to *L'Aminta*, which is of a poet's substance, or to the artfulness of Guarini's contrivances. There are plenty of good versions and critiques of both, and summaries of the pamphlet war between the author and the critics which opened in 1587, three years before Guarini published, and went on until 1602. Superficially these plays are easy to imitate, fatally easy. The marvel is that the small Arcadian world of nymphs, shepherds,

satyrs, rustics, and enchanters, with the artificiality of its sentimental concerns, its dependence upon oracles, metamorphoses, and other 'ancientry', should have stood up to so many repeats and re-combinings. The best of these, and the representative pastoral of the next generation, is the *Filli di Sciro* (1607) of Guidobaldo Bonarelli (1563–1608). Its admirers liked to regard the pastoral as the third dramatic form, but it is hardly on a level with tragedy and comedy, and has not the monopoly of the tragi-comic modification. It is rather the most prolific of period forms, and in addition to the intrinsic value of a few of the plays it can claim some part in the *melodramma* which was the great contribution of the *seicento*. The pastoral slips quietly into the stronger current and is hardly missed.

(iii) *Comedy*. What the humanists attempted for the promotion of classical form in tragedy they achieved rather more congenially with comedy. Petrarch's contribution is not extant, so that pride of place is given to the *Paulus* (*c.* 1389) of Pier Paolo Vergerio (1370–1444), where the presentation of medieval university society is intended for the correction of youth; it is only superficially classical. The content of these Latin plays is chiefly students' follies, light or gross, sharpened by national or personal satire, or, in the *Cauteriaria* (? 1469) of Antonio Buzario (*fl.* fifteenth century) by brutal realism. Others use the comedy of matrimonial misfits, as in *Comedia Bile* (first half of fifteenth century). One Dominican friar, in *Comoedia sine nomine* (? 1450–60), attempts to use a more romantic theme, but hardly with success. For some, comedy was a graver affair, and intended for moral improvement; a few, but only a few, were adroit enough to maintain the burlesque style while discharging this purpose. It is not until the turn of the century that the formative influence of classical models is apparent, but Sanesi claims that in the *Chrysis* (1444) of Enea Silvio Piccolomini (1405–64) the Latin types are recognizable. Slowly but surely the Romans came back, conquered, and were seen.

Alongside this more creative work there was a steady increase in the acquisition, mastery, and translation of classical comedy. Glosses and commentaries were recovered, and in 1429 twelve of Plautus's plays were added to the eight already known. There was also some attention paid to Aristophanes.

For educational purposes acting was encouraged. Isabella d'Este admits in a letter of 1502 that the *intermezzi* had compensated for the play which had bored her. It is clear that what was decorative and complimentary was used to make the more intellectual provision acceptable. The character and splendour of such display depended upon the resources in money and talent at the various Courts.

When Lodovico Ariosto (1474–1533) comes into view what had shone before now seems tentative and dim. He occupied himself with comedy for the Court of Ferrara twice, in the first decade with *Cassaria* (1508) and *I Suppositi*

(1509), and in the third when he re-wrote these in verse, worked out an earlier idea in *Il Negromante* (written 1520, prod. 1530), added *La Lena* (written 1529), and left *Gli Studenti* to be finished by his brother as *La Scolastica*, and by his son as *L'Imperfetta*. Comedy was evidently a congenial, though not his favourite, form for the expression of that 'sunlight of the mind', that 'mental richness' which Meredith might have claimed for him in virtue of *Orlando Furioso*.

Ariosto used the classics with masterly freedom, and there are credible legends of how he took copy from his own father while the latter reprimanded him; ancient and modern materials are creatively welded. Even in the bareness of reading, deprived of Raphael's scenery and all the social circumstances, when we can no longer test the excitement of finding what was recognizably old made realistically new, the quality of his comedy is evident.

The proper preparation for the *commedia erudita* as it was instituted by Ariosto and his generation is to acquire a taste for Plautus and Terence, a good working knowledge of the *Decamerone* and other *novelle*, a relish for realism in the close representation of men and manners, and a callous, quick enjoyment of human folly. It is a critical comedy worked by intrigue, and showing types, if not caricatures, of city life.

In the interval between the two periods of Ariosto's activity others were discovering what could be done with the good method and rich resources now released and encouraged by patronage. *La Calandria* was published in 1521, a year after the death of its author Cardinal Bernardo Dovizi da Bibbiena (1470–1520), but it was seen at Urbino in 1506. This gross, boisterous, witty comedy is famous to us because of contemporary descriptions of its reception which make it live in the terms of the society which it delighted. To read it is another admirable way of initiation into the fashion for playing variations upon the stage twins (real or faked) and the traditional booby (Boccaccio's Calandrio). It is coarser fare than Ariosto's and more clumsily served, but it had immense popularity then, and it has some substance and flavour still.

Niccolo Machiavelli (1469–1527) is said to have worked on an Aristophanic model at first in his lost *Le Maschere*; he too reverted to Terence in *L'Andria* (date unknown) and to Plautus's *Casina* in *La Clizia* (after 1513), but in *La Mandragola* (? 1513) all is his own. It made no mould for his own use or anyone else's. No formula can be drawn from it, its form is vital, and consists in that apparently effortless fitting of means to an end which Henry James called the artist's 'deep-breathing economy'. Machiavelli's touch is so wickedly nice that each remark betrays its speaker to us. They give themselves away, so that in doing all the author seems to be doing nothing. We think we are seeing life for ourselves, but we are seeing it with his eyes, appraising it with his intellect, shirking nothing and yet not

unduly shocked. Only the deft ironic verses between the acts remind us of his invisible presence. His detachment disinfects the noisome theme so that in reflection we proceed beyond it, until, imperceptibly, his Frate Timoteo, Messer Nicia, Callimaco, and Lucrezia come to count for more than types, stage or social, and are found to possess baffling but unmistakable individuality. They are not conceived as Shakespeare or Molière or Congreve would have conceived them, but they are of the same order of imaginative being. Machiavelli can only be judged by his peers, though among such he is himself and no other. Such individuality comes again in *Il Candelaio* (c. 1582), by Giordano Bruno (1548–1600), where the form is used effectively once and once only. Meanwhile to provide patterns Ariosto was more useful, with his imitable blending of common materials and forms.

Machiavelli's style is curt Tuscan, 'expurgate and sober, with scarcely an "issimo".' *La Mandragola* stands up like a rock-needle, emphasizing the contrast with the gross fertility of Pietro Aretino (1492–1556). We may marvel with how few words Machiavelli can say so much, and how much Aretino can find to say about so little. He had a knack for finding real life racier than fiction, and used its flavour and substance five times: in *La Cortigiana* (1525, prod. 1534), *Il Marescalco* (1526–7, prod. 1533), *La Talanta* and *L'Ipocrito* (1541–2), and *Il Filosofo* (1544, prod. 1546). Fantastic situations are accepted as his means, but the end is the presentation of men and women, mostly foolish with love or greed, but vividly alive. Practical jokes old and new, romantic complications, sustained burlesques, actual scandals—nothing was safe with Aretino about, and nothing was dull when he had worked it up. Only Jonson working at a great figure such as Subtle or a huge scene such as Bartholomew Fair can compete with Aretino as a comic artist, but as artist and man Jonson had a conscience and Aretino had not.

The originality of these plays moves Sanesi to contend that Renaissance comedy was not so formalized as to make it inflexible for the expression of vehement individual power, but no one could deny that by the mid-*cinquecento* there were already enough standard patterns to support the many who had some talent and a few who had none. The first quarter-century provided models, and later critics reduced to rules what the artistic sense of this generation had found to be expedient. This was only too helpful for mediocrity. It is hard to test the real merit of this supply; the conformity of so much that is second-rate is apt to dull the wits of the reader, still more of the modern reader, and, most of all, the foreign reader, but the plays to be mentioned below are good in their kind and very fairly representative of the favourite situations of amorous intrigue, of the chief comic types, and of the dexterous, firm way in which they had trained themselves to plot. Alongside the Italian efficiency the homeliness and romance of the

English method seems naïve in all but the best of Elizabethan comedies, and yet, for this very quality, they are refreshing. Gosson has a damaging summary of the content of Italianate comedies which, allowing for his Puritan malice, is not inaptly phrased: 'Love, cosenedge, flatterie, bawderie, slye conveighance of whordome; the persons, cookes, queanes, knaves, baudes, parasites, courtezannes, lecherous old men, amorous young men with such lyke of infinite varietie.'

Trading with plots, sub-plots, situations, devices, and types was brisk. Anyone might draw upon Plautus and Terence, and much of the modern work was pooled in a common stock to which most of the chief cities had something to contribute. Venice has less to offer at this stage than, as we shall see, she had earlier and in other kinds, but Dolce, Bentivoglio, and later Loredano were productive. Brescia had Niccolo Secchi; Adria its blind playwright, Luigi Groto; Ricchi, who wrote *I Tre Tiranni* at the age of 18, came from Lucca. Florentines were the most prolific, with Giannotti, Firenzuola, Lorenzo de' Medici, Landi, Gelli, d'Ambra, Razzi, Varchi, Salviati, Cini, Borghini, while Cecchi and Grazzini even strike out, or protest that they will strike out, on lines of their own. Siena's output was more select: three comedies for the Accademici Intronati, *Gl'Ingannati* (anon., 1531), and *L'Amor Costante* (1536) and *L'Alessandro* (1543–4), both by Alessandro Piccolomini (1508–78), are excellent and particularly interesting to an English reader because of the likeness that the first bears to *Twelfth Night*, and the relation between the third and Chapman's *May Day*. Belo, a Roman, may have preceded Aretino in satirizing pedants, in *Il Pedante* (1529). Sanesi is full of admiration of the vivid realistic detail and the adroit handling of a most complicated intrigue drawn from Tatius by A. Caro in *Gl'Straccioni* (1544). In Perugia Sforza degl'Oddi also uses Tatius, and pursues more sentimental issues in *L'Erofilomachia* (1572) and *Prigioni d'amore* (1590); tears, he argues, are not incompatible with laughter when comedy chooses noble themes. Naples, with Giambattista Della Porta (1538–1613), seems to sum up the first phases and lead the way into the seventeenth century.

Giambattista Della Porta, in spite of all his other preoccupations (he was also a scientist), is said to have composed three tragedies, one tragi-comedy, and twenty-nine comedies; fourteen plays survive. Wherever he finds anything good he takes it. If you want the best plots, Della Porta has them, and deserves them. He contrives capital situations, and handles disguises, substitutions, misconceptions, talk at cross-purposes, with an exhilarating deftness. His plays were packed tight with good things, and if he used stock figures he did it so well that he gave them a new lease of life. He creamed the sixteenth century, and many a seventeenth-century dramatist lived on him. The best way of testing how far and in what directions comedy had expanded since Ariosto's time is

to read Della Porta. He has been admirably edited by Spampanato; *Albumazar*, Tomkis's Latin version of *L'Astrologo* (1606), done for the amusement of Cambridge in 1615, has now had the attentions of H. G. Dick. Where many are so good it is hard to choose as between *L'Olimpia*, *La Fantesca*, *La Cintia*, *La Turca*, *La Trappolaria*, *La Carbonaria*, *Il Moro*, *La Furiosa*, *I Due Fratelli Simili*, but perhaps the most rewarding and illuminating essay in comparison would put *I Due Fratelli Rivali* alongside *Much Ado About Nothing* and summon Bandello, whose tale it is, to judge between them.

Yet we would give all that Della Porta has in silver for the one gold piece of Bruno's *Il Candelaio*, which probably never saw the stage. Here is comedy which is truly critical of life. It is almost incredible that the familiar situations and types should be made to tell so differently. Bruno's comedy is still read by critics looking for Shakespeare's footprints, but it would be more to the purpose to match him boldly with Ben Jonson. The difference of tone between Shakespeare's treatment of the pedant and Bruno's is more striking than the butt they have in common: the likeness between Jonson and Bruno is inward. It is not suggested that anything passed between them, but there is the same fluency, trenchant accuracy of terms, and authentic ring. Manfurio's quotations have roots, his absurd etymologies are freshly drawn, the alchemical jargon is genuine; mockery goes home. Bruno can make more comedy out of two rogues recounting a gross story than many more practised playwrights with a handful of disguises. We have an uneasy feeling that the animus is personal, and for this reason obscurities must be given the benefit of the doubt; but the satire goes beyond personalities, and seems to express the author's restless brilliant intelligence. He is more interested in character than plot; an *argomento* takes the form of an analysis of the three chief persons—Manfurio, Bonifacio, and Bartolommeo. At a glance one might be in danger of dismissing *Il Candelaio* as another tangle of worn threads. Here are pedant, alchemist, and amorous old man; here are rogues dressed as officers, a serving-maid touting for the penurious courtesan, a wife dressed as her husband's mistress to catch him at his tricks; here are beatings and brawls, and yet, what is faded elsewhere, and much that is crude anywhere, has been transformed by vigorous realism and by the direction of a critical purpose. This is not a comedy of relaxation. It is for exercising the mind. If we think, Bruno tells us, we may either weep with Heracleitus or laugh with Democritus. *Il Candelaio* is primarily for those who are interested in genius and Bruno; meanwhile *commedie erudite* continued to come from the talent and industry of more ordinary men.

2. COMMEDIA DELL'ARTE. In so far as it was improvised it is impossible to recover an accurate impression of the *commedia dell'arte*. We lack a vital part of experience; we have not

seen it. A plea which has already been hinted must now be urged with emphasis: 'Piece out' its 'imperfections with your thoughts'. Yet there is danger that our thoughts may be too kind. The only safeguard is an informed imagining, and there is much left for our instruction, given patience to recover and connect the fragments.

The separate treatment accorded here to the improvised comedy underlines the most important point about it: it was a distinct style; as soon as this is said it is essential to remark certain exceptions which bring the generalization nearer to the truth. The players who came to Elsinore had two styles—'for the law of writ and the liberty'—but were one company. So with Italy's drama; she has one drama, not two, but that one, in comedy at least, is twofold. Unless the difference and the relationship are recognized it is impossible to account for the nature, development, and effect of the *commedia dell'arte*. Several other terms are used to describe it: *a soggetto* or *all'improviso, dei zanni, dei maschere, all'italiana*. They remind us of its distinguishing marks, but each is subject to an occasional exception. Thus, it was 'of the profession' (*dell'arte*) but it was also cultivated by academic amateurs; it was improvised, but it had its documents and discipline; it used masks, mainly but not invariably; it was Italian, but it also flourished abroad, and at the end of the seventeenth century was at least half French; between it and the *commedia erudita* there were many transactions. Puzzling as this may be to its critics and historians, it is in reality easily explained on practical considerations.

(i) *Origins*. There are three possible ways of investigating the origins of the *commedia dell'arte*: by seeking for it a tradition, or an inventor, or by studying the dramatic conditions at the time of its appearance. Neither the first nor the second inquiry has yielded a fully satisfactory answer, but they have not been unprofitable. It seems impossible to establish continuity between later Roman, and especially Atellan, mimes and the Renaissance buffoons; and it is hardly consistent with the character of what is being studied that it should have a single founder if it is, as its names indicate, the way that was devised by professional actors for making a living out of the art of the theatre. But there is something to be gained from both these researches into its heredity which may supplement the attempt to account for it by re-imagining the Renaissance conditions which encouraged the experiment.

Advocates of the more far-fetched connexions in time and space (Riccoboni, Quadrio, de Amicis, and Reich) make it clear that something like the *commedia dell'arte* has amused mankind before and elsewhere, but they do not prove that these manifestations were identical or connected with it. The slightness of the evidence from the Middle Ages weakens their case. Those who have sought to find it a 'father' have at least promoted the study of a body of drama which has not so far been mentioned,

the record in literary form of the vigorous rustic or semi-rustic farce of districts round Naples, Asti, Siena, and Padua. It is time that we recognized the talent of Carracciolo, Braca, Alione, Calmo, Beolco, and the importance of small associations of enthusiasts such as the *Rozzi* of Siena and friendly groups playing in Venice.

From among these actor-dramatists two stand out—Calmo, because his work and reputation suggest some close connexion with what was soon to become the dominant form of popular comedy, and Beolco (Ruzzante) for the same reason, and still more for the quality of what survives of his work. 'Ruzzante' was the stage-name of Angelo Beolco (*fl.* 1520–42), who invented for himself the character-mask of a loquacious Paduan countryman and used it with immediate and lasting success to rejuvenate old Plautine material in *La Piovana* and *La Vaccaria*, and a neo-classical plot in *L'Anconitana*, and to support the slighter but more original compositions such as *La Commedia Senza Titulo* and two 'dialoghi'. In the Carnival season Ruzzante would take a holiday from managing the family estates and entertain his patron, Alvise Cornaro, and other friends. He collected a few companions, and devised parts for them. Thanks to the work of Lovarini, his Italian editor, and Mortier, his French translator, the Paduan dialect, in which much of the attraction lay, is less of an obstacle than it used to be. His plays have the appearance of farce, but they leave the impression of comedy, and for this reason their intrinsic excellence transcends the interest of their reputed connexion with the *commedia dell'arte*. From a distance, in synopsis or by a summary account, it is true that they seem to have everything in common with the professional comedy, and it is no wonder that Maurice Sand (following Riccoboni) was tempted to proclaim him as its 'father'. But the more Ruzzante's work is known in detail the more individual and inimitable it appears. It is arguable that by improvisation such born comedians as Martinelli, Cecchini, or Biancolleli gave performances of comparable excellence, and that this is why they were so much in general and royal demand. This can neither be denied nor proved; it is indeed very probable, but one difference remains. These men were content with their functions as actors. Their secret died with them, or was committed only partially and privately to the inheritors of their masks. Ruzzante's was also a literary gift, and we can judge for ourselves. Some of his plays were printed in his lifetime, Cornaro had access to manuscripts for a posthumous publication in 1551, Lovarini added one in 1894. No true critical purpose is served by drawing the work of Ruzzante and the professional companies too close together. His example as an improviser was undoubtedly a contributory but not a determining factor.

When Beolco died his mantle fell upon Andrea Calmo (1509/10–*c.* 1561), but only with half a portion of Ruzzante's art. They had, it seems, been friendly rivals and Calmo had other literary ambitions. Some of their work was confused by contemporaries, but when it is sorted out it is plain that Calmo's is of a coarser grain. The likeness between Calmo's old Venetians and the mask of Pantalone has tempted many to identify them, but the proper name does not appear. Again Calmo's is mainly premeditated work, and there is no direct succession of *persona*, but nobody could deny that in its use of farcical situation, dialect, buffoonery, the caricatures of local types, and possibly, in the original instance, even of some improvisation, it is certainly as close as anything we could expect to find to the *commedia dell'arte*. He had collected stuffs and designs, and perhaps experimented with the method which others were to popularize and, in a sense, perfect, but we do not know that he intended or envisaged what was to follow so soon. When it is closely examined there is not one of these farce-writers whose work exhibits simultaneously or in true proportion the distinguishing characteristics of the *commedia dell'arte*.

(ii) *Acting Companies*. The determining factor is the rise of companies of professionals who sought and found enough encouragement to make modern comedy their livelihood. Their method was devised as they went along; they felt out their way, using whatever talent and luck they had. Their talents were the very talents their predecessors the Atellan mimes and medieval jesters had had, they were recruited from their counterparts, the strolling tumblers and the charlatan's boys, as well as from adventurous enthusiasts of better education. Their chances were the demand for entertainment by all classes, in Italy and abroad; the comic vulnerability of certain common types or of droll individuals as they were detected by the first Arlecchino or Pulcinella; and finally the prevailing taste for a comedy with plots that could be easily and cheaply imitated. They might also reckon that their necessity was part of their luck; they had to be quick-witted, tough, and adaptable, or they perished. For a generation or two enough of them found the risk stimulating and throve on it. If we refuse to believe that there was a single founder we may acknowledge many benefactors. Each of those mentioned has some responsibility for it, no one, it seems, has it all. The *commedia dell'arte* was the major theatrical experiment of the age, combining the minor experiments in a collective effort. In its simplest form it is represented by the single actor playing many parts, as old Giovanni Gabrielli (*c.* 1588–*c.* 1635) continued to do, but in its most developed form by such a company as the one to which his son Francesco (?–1654) belonged, in which each player knew the others' ways so well that all could collaborate harmoniously.

No attempt will be made here to follow the intricacies of the make-up and itineraries of the companies. Two principles seem to have determined their constitution: the need for

unity within, among themselves, to make smooth and intelligible improvisation possible, and the temptation from without when patrons bribed the best from several groups to make an 'all-star' cast to grace a special season. The intrigues and complications that resulted when actresses were making their reputations and were jealous of them may be imagined or amply illustrated from documents—letters, licences, ecclesiastical and civil protests— collected by Luigi Rasi in his biographical dictionary, *I Comici Italiani*. The earliest notice of a travelling professional company is for 1545. The chief companies of the sixteenth century were the *Gelosi*, with the Andreini (Francesco, 1548–1624; Isabella, 1562–1604) as their mainstay; the *Desiosi*, led by 'Diana' (*fl.* 1582–1605) and sometimes including Tristano Martinelli (*c.* 1557–1630); the *Confidenti*, with Vittoria Piissimi (*fl.* 1575–94) and 'Pedrolino' (Pellesini) (*c.* 1526–1612); the *Uniti*, under Drusiano Martinelli (?–1606/8) and his wife Angelica (*fl.* 1580–94). These gradually give place to the next generation, who carried on the tradition in the competing groups of the second *Confidenti*, directed by Flaminio Scala (*fl.* 1600–21); the troupe of Pier Maria Cecchini (1575–1645), the *Accesi*; and the *Fedeli*, giving scope to the many talents of the younger Andreini, 'Lelio' (*c.* 1578–1654) (all of which see also under their own names).

The patronage of Mantua continued, and later in the seventeenth century companies associated with Modena and Parma came to the fore and were in demand even beyond Italy. The earliest records of professional companies show that they were often in Paris. Their frequent journeys thither gave place to the permanent establishment of an Italian company in 1661, which flourished until in 1697 the actors trespassed upon a royal scandal and were evicted for their impertinence. In 1716 Italian comedians came back and stayed until the end of the century. The mingling of languages, styles, and resources, and especially the connexions with the art of Molière, make this phase of the *commedia dell'arte* as much a part of the history of French as of Italian drama, and much critical research has been lavished upon it (see COMÉDIE-ITALIENNE, FRANCE, and MOLIÈRE).

(iii) *Economy of the Companies*. Takings and expenses seem to have been shared between the leading members, while a few younger actors were hired. In some cities *stanze* or public rooms could be rented for a few weeks at a time. Some patrons provided better stage accommodation now and then, including the reversion of the equipment of the *commedia erudita*. On such occasions the leaders looked for individual rewards in money, goods, and personal favours. The better companies are often found at the French Court. There are traces of their visits to Bavaria, Spain, and England, but Paris was their second home, especially towards the end of the seventeenth century.

The average company needed as a minimum

two who could take old men's parts, two lovers and their ladies, two *zanni* for servants, a braggart captain, a serving-maid, and one or two extras for minor parts. Doubling was also possible, but the main masks were fixed.

(iv) *Masks.* The peculiarity of a 'mask' character is that it is transferable from one company and one generation to another while at the same time it is also subject to modification. Since it is still a matter of dispute who were the inventors of many of the chief masks, and the succession of their changes is partly conjectural, it is only possible here to remark the best-known impersonators without trying to record the individual and period modifications of dress or behaviour. They may be grouped according to their functions in the plots as parents, lovers, servants, and miscellaneous caricatures or 'oddities'.

The toughest of the parents was Pantalone de' Bisognosi, in dress and dialect a Venetian Magnifico given to reprimands, tirades, and long-winded advice; according to Cecchini it should be taken as a grave part, relaxing into absurdity only when treating of love and feasting with the servants. This was a counsel of perfection, and the comical possibilities of an amorous and avaricious old man were freely exploited. Variants were introduced as time went on, and the roles of fathers and counsellors were sometimes taken by Coviello, Pincastro, Pandolpho, Ubaldino, Prospero, Lattanzio, and others, but they had little staying power. Pasquati and Braga in the sixteenth century, Ricci, Romagnesi, and Riccoboni in the seventeenth, are known to have made the mask their own.

The favourite mask for the second parent was of a Bolognese lawyer, usually Dr. Graziano. Here, as elsewhere, an origin in a personal skit is suspected, but it was soon submerged in the professional type. He too was amorous and gullible, but grosser than Pantalone. There were two levels of caricature; when the better Graziani expounded, what they said made sense; but the cheaper imitations lapsed into *Spropositi* and tongue-twisters that were sheer nonsense. The local dialect gave way to the habit of 'saying everything the wrong way round'. Strictly, the doctor was distinct from the stage pedant, who belonged to the *commedia erudita*, but they had many characteristics in common and were confounded by foreigners. 'Luz' Burchiella, Lodovico de' Bianchi, and a certain 'Andreazzo' (?Zenari) used the mask with credit in the sixteenth century. Bongiovanni, Bruni, and Lolli were among their distinguished successors.

The lovers, usually the lost or erring children of Pantalone and Graziano, did not use masks, and their parts were hardly characters, still less caricatures. Some stylization was convenient, but their behaviour was determined by the situations of the love intrigues, and their attraction was left to their personal eloquence and grace. They were recommended to read good authors to form a

style for the laments, addresses, dialogues, conceits, soliloquies for several occasions, and for the *pazzie* (ravings). It was said of Antonazzoni by a fellow actor that he was too lazy to study for the lover's part and so changed to the captain's. Many had literary ambitions, but for those who could not compose there was provision made in the *zibaldoni* or commonplace books.

It was among the professionals that actresses came into their own. The *commedia erudita* concealed, the *commedia dell'arte* displayed, their talents, and tragi-comedies and pastorals gave them many chances. When the first and second ladies conducted their own affairs in public the part of the 'confidante' dwindled, but a waiting-woman, often Franceschina or Olivetta, still found enough to do pairing off with the *zanni* servant. This was sometimes a man's mask.

The captain was often used as a rival, but he had also an independent role. As a braggart and coward he went as near as he dared in satirizing the alien soldier, chiefly the Spaniard, but in Venice the Greek *stradiotto*. Francesco Andreini made this mask his own, and during the first three years of his widowhood (Isabella died in 1604 and he retired from the stage) he collected and published his famous *Bravure del Capitano Spavento del Vall' Inferno*. From this it is plain that Andreini preferred to play to the height of a literary fancy and not realistically. The *Bravure* were republished, translated, and worked into plays by later admirers such as Belando. Fornaris as a *capitano* was Andreini's contemporary, a certain 'Cardone' seems to have been his successor, and in the seventeenth century Silvio Fiorillo (?–*c.* 1632) played as Mattamoros, and Tiberio Fiorillo (1608–94) as Scaramuccia, a part which to some is more comparable to that of the *zanni*. Its fame was individual.

The servants who gave the comedy one of its names, *dei zanni*, took over the functions of the slaves of classical comedy, and discharged them with the physical skill of acrobats and the impudence of their immediate prototypes, the Bergomask *facchini*, odd-jobbers in the piazza, witty rogues and literally jacks-of-all-trades. Zanni is the Bergomask pronunciation of Gianni, diminutive of Giovanni. It became a common prefix, and individuals made themselves reputations within the group, as Panzanino, Zan Ganassa, Buratino, Francatrippe, Arlecchino, Pedrolino, Scapino, Fritellino, Beltrame, Brighella, Mezzettino, and Trappolino. They found it convenient to pair off wit against stupidity, with infinite possibility for surprise and reversal in the *burle* or practical jokes, and the smaller pieces of comic business known as *lazzi*, which were their stock-in-trade.

Greed and shrewdness were their staple characteristics; beyond this it is impossible to generalize. For a few we can recover from contemporary references or illustrations some idea of their individuality, but many are merely names now. Not all handed on their masks, but of those which persisted the luckiest were Arlecchino (Harlequin), and Pulcinella (Punch), who represents the droll wit of the countryside near Naples as it was exploited for the stage early in the seventeenth century by some genius, probably Silvio Fiorillo. Much has been written of and for these two masks, conjecturing their origins, recovering their characteristics, marvelling at their adaptability. They have lost all but a savour of local caricature, and survive as symbols of the humour of their acquired nationalities. They are perhaps the most tangible and also the subtlest part of our inheritance from the *commedia dell'arte*.

The most exhaustive study of Arlecchino's origins is Driesen's, of Pulcinella Dieterich's and Croce's. Tristano Martinelli, if he was not actually the first, was certainly the dominant Arlecchino of the sixteenth and early seventeenth centuries; to judge by his letters he could turn their Majesties of France round his little finger. Giuseppe Domenico Biancolleli (Dominique) (*c.* 1637–88) and Evariste Gherardi (1663–1700) were among the last Italian Arlecchini flourishing in Paris.

Pulcinella developed into as distinct a person among the *zanni* as the captain among the lovers. He stole many of the jokes and devices that the doctors had used, but gave them a new twist, and specialized in animal noises. Uncertainty was his chief characteristic; no one ever knew where to have him, in what disguise he would turn up, or how he would wriggle out of outrageous situations. His sweetheart or wife was a Rosetta, a Pimpinella, a Colombina, his *zanni* pair usually Coviello.

Some plays needed a few tradesmen or peasants or foreigners, but these parts, though repeatable, can hardly be counted as masks. Often variety enough was provided by doubling and disguise. There were a number of Neapolitan skits and considerable play with dialects other than those monopolized by the main masks.

(v) *Repertories of scenarii and miscellanies.* Since the licences and letters use masks as often as proper names it is comparatively easy to work out the membership of a company, but it is harder to determine their repertories exactly, because the surviving collections of *scenarii* more often represent the taste of private and non-professional admirers of the art of improvisation. We can only imagine in general terms what plays were given.

Flaminio Scala's *Teatro* (1611) is exceptional in many ways; it is printed, and it represents his taste, if not always his invention, and is closely associated with the *Gelosi*. It contains thirty-nine comedies, one tragedy, a tragicomedy, a mixed entertainment, a pastoral, and a few fairy-tale plays.

Other *scenarii* are in manuscripts in libraries in Rome, Florence, Naples, Venice, Perugia, Modena, Paris, and some even in Leningrad. In the larger collections comedy, or more properly farce, has the largest provision; much is drawn at second- or third-hand from classical and neo-classical plays, and, in the

seventeenth century, the taste for Spanish drama enlarges the proportion of melodramatic and sentimental plots. Pastorals with a strong infusion of buffoonery did well.

The resources might be more neatly reckoned by breaking up the plays into stock situations, allowing for variety and for the ingenious shuffling and renovation by minor changes. This was notoriously part of the economy of improvisation. The *scenarii* are often referred to as 'skeleton-plays'; they would be better described as dried plays. How they were put to soak and swell is explained by Perucci in his *L'Arte Rappresentativa* (1699), an invaluable handbook much of which has been reprinted by Petraccone in his *La Commedia dell'arte, storia, tecnica, scenari* (1927). Perucci's manual is the best of its kind, but not unique. Several *zibaldoni* have turned up which assemble the necessary equipment of spare prologues, speeches, jokes, and *lazzi* provided by the ingenuity and industry of the more literary members of the companies, often for their general use. One of the amplest and most informative was the property of an amateur enthusiast, D. Placido Adriano. It is now in Perugia.

Other hints come in semi-critical treatises of such players as Cecchini, Barbieri, and Riccoboni. If we hesitate or flag in piecing the parts together, it is possible to find models in a number of plays, some by actors such as Fornaris, Cecchini, Fiorillo, Andreini, Barbieri; some by interested amateurs, among them Bricci, Verucci, and Locatelli. These may be used to control our conjectural reconstructions.

(vi) *Decadence; a revival. General estimate.* In the eighteenth century Goldoni's way of meeting the reproach of the decadence of Italian drama was to struggle to substitute premeditation for improvisation. He was for reforming the actors by the dramatist's control (see below, 3). Carlo Gozzi (1722–1806), in an animated opposition to Goldoni, took another way, and blew upon the ashes of the *commedia dell'arte* by using its masks and methods for his own purposes. The rough opportunist bargain was fair enough. Gozzi gave Sacchi's company their chance in 1761, when he provided them with the first of a series of plays—*fiabe*—in which in a bold, ingenious way he mingled fairy tales with farce. He used the professionals' talents, and even allowed them some scope for improvisation, while he parodied his rivals, shot his satire, and, most important, rediscovered the attraction of this blend of fooling and fantasy. He followed up *L'Amore delle tre melarance* (1761) with *Il Corvo* in the same year; in 1762 came *Il Re Cervo, Turandot,* and *Donna Serpente*; *Zobeide* came in 1763, *Pitocchi fortunati, Nostro Turchino,* and *L'Augellino belverde* in 1764, and finally *Zeim, re de' Genj* in 1765.

A precedent for this mixed kind might be found in a few of the *scenarii* of Scala's *Teatro*, but it is not necessary to suppose that Gozzi looked back. He was bent on meeting an occasion, he wanted to worst Goldoni, and for a time he did so. Parody and satire served his present purpose, but they are perishable. The fairy tales and his way of touching on reality by forsaking realism still stir the imagination if they do not satisfy it. Many have felt that in the *fiabe* is achieved a kind of imaginative release not only for the irascible author but for audiences otherwise sad and sober. Inadvertently perhaps Gozzi gave the *commedia dell'arte* its final flourish; with him it 'made a good end'. It was invented for gaiety—as Il Lasca had it 'per passatempo, burla, giuoco e festa, e fare il mondo star lieto e beato'—and its last triumph was in the true style. It is impossible at this distance to generalize fairly about the extent and quality of the improvisation, but we may mark the extremes. At its best it was, as Barbieri insisted, a serious art, a corporate discipline chosen by men and women of remarkable talents, but, as Riccoboni, another player, regretfully observes, by the eighteenth century it was a lost art, and consisted too often of a mere piecing together of stock material. The danger of the declension of a comedy into a series of practical jokes is obvious. The *commedia dell'arte* could originate farcical episodes, but in everything else it was dependent upon the support of literary forms. Unashamedly it borrowed, cut, twisted, stretched, and finally wore out all that the drama of the Renaissance had to offer; in return it gave a longer life and greater popularity to much that would otherwise have been merely literary drama. Its importance lay in the economy of its method, which made the best use of histrionic talent of several varieties. At its highest it was the actors' art *par excellence*; at its lowest, mere clowning. It survives now in an attenuated form in puppet-shows, in mask names, in harlequinades, and above all in reputation. There have been some attempts to revive it, but they rest upon a mistaken notion. The masks might be revived and *scenarii* prepared; two or three actors with an *ex tempore* faculty might collaborate. It happened so with Maurice Sand and his family. There have been experiments in Prague and at Queen Mary's College, London. But these are not the *commedia dell'arte*; the tradition has gone.

Basilio Locatelli, in a preface to his collection of *scenarii*, remarks that 'the player's function is one thing, and the poet's another'. This states half the truth; but if drama is to be great and lasting it is necessary that the player and poet should meet on honourable terms. The plays of Ruzzante, and for some those of Gozzi, are evidence of one kind; the mirth of which we have only echoes is evidence of another kind, testifying to this hard truth.

K. M. L.

3. LITERARY DRAMA FROM THE EIGHTEENTH CENTURY TO THE PRESENT DAY. (*a*) In the early years of the eighteenth century a threefold attempt was made to produce a tragic theatre which, if it could not rival the glory of Corneille and Racine, should at least give Italy a tragedy worthy of the name. The first was by Pier Jacopo Martelli (1665–1727), who drew on classical subjects for inspiration, but followed the French writers in the structure of his tragedies. He attempted to reproduce the dignified alexandrine by means of a rhyming couplet composed of a pair of 'settenari doppi'. These have been given his name, and are known as 'versi martelliani'. He was followed by Gian Vincenzo Gravina (1664–1718), who looked solely to the Greeks for his themes, and in vain attempted to bring to life an Italian tragedy based on the ancients. His *Tragedie Cinque* (1712) reveal that Gravina the poet was greatly inferior to Gravina the critic.

The third attempt, that of Scipione Maffei (1675–1755), produced a slight measure of success. His reform of tragedy lay in his endeavour to draw at the same time from the French and from the Greeks. Maffei's *Merope* (1713) in blank verse won considerable praise in its day. Voltaire wrote to Maffei, after meeting him in 1733, that he planned to translate the work, but the plan ended there, for instead Voltaire wrote, in 1736, a *Mérope* of his own. Maffei's *Merope* is the sole tragedy of significance in the years preceding Alfieri.

The Jesuits were responsible for the representation of many plays, but few of their tragedies have survived on account of intrinsic worth. Among the best of them are those of Saverio Bettinelli (1718–1808). The four Roman tragedies of Antonio Conti (1677–1749) are mediocre, though their author claimed to have been inspired by Shakespeare.

Pastoral drama had already produced a new dramatic development, the *melodramma*, in which equal weight was given to the lines of poetry and to the music which accompanied them. Apostolo Zeno (1668–1750), an erudite Venetian, attempted to give *melodramma* all the dignity of the regular classical tragedy. It was left to a poet of astonishing facility and productivity, the Arcadian Pietro Trapassi, or Metastasio, as he preferred to style himself, to carry the genre to the height of its possibilities. Metastasio (1698–1782) began his successful career in Naples, and in 1730 became 'poeta cesareo' at the Court of Vienna. Between 1731 and 1750 he wrote eleven of his masterpieces, among them *La Clemenza di Tito* (produced in 1734 with music by Caldara), *Achille in Sciro* and *Temistocle* (both 1736, with music again by Caldara), and *Attilio Regolo* (1750, music by Hasse). These, and many of his other works, have been used as opera libretti, some of them fifty or sixty times (see OPERA).

In comedy three minor writers attempted to break away from the conventions of the *commedia dell'arte*. Giambattista Fagiuoli (1660–1742) set on the stage realistic scenes of village life; Girolamo Gigli (1660–1722) in his *Don Pilone* (1711) revealed his debt to Molière; while Iacopo Angelo Nelli (1673–1767) mildly satirized middle-class life. But it was Goldoni who later carried out the reform of comedy.

The two outstanding figures of the eighteenth century have already been mentioned. They are, in tragedy, Vittorio Amedeo Alfieri

(1749–1803), and in comedy Carlo Goldoni (1707–93). Alfieri, who was born at Asti, in Piedmont, travelled continuously in Europe from 1766 to 1772, visiting France, England, the Low Countries, Germany, Russia, Spain, and Portugal. In 1772 he returned to Turin, and, following the fashion of his day, attempted to compose a tragedy in blank verse, *Cleopatra*. This was performed on 16 June 1775; its success fired him with ambition, and marks the beginning of a successful career. From 1775 to 1790 Alfieri immersed himself in the study of the greatest Italian writers to acquaint himself with Tuscan ways of speech, and of the classics, to make up for the deficiences of his education, and above all to perfect his style.

When he came to compose his tragedies he chose chiefly subjects which introduced heroic figures of Greek or Roman history, Antigone, Agamemnon, Orestes, Merope, Sofonisba, Brutus, Mirra. Royal or princely personages were the heroes of his tragedies drawn from European history and the Bible—Mary Stuart, Don Garcia, Saul. In many of his plays Alfieri set out to awaken in his countrymen a political consciousness; he taught the need to abhor and overthrow tyranny, and to inculcate the craving for liberty. 'In su la scena mosse guerra ai tiranni.'

It is ironical that this apostle of political freedom should have bowed willingly to the literary yoke of the classics, and unquestioningly have adhered strictly to their conventions. In structure his tragedies were more rigidly classical than his classical models. He limited the number of characters to those who were absolutely essential. He observed the Unities; he ruled out episodes and scenes which did not contribute to the development of the main theme. His blank verse, often unadorned to the point of harshness, and often broken into short, jerky phrases, nevertheless in its concision and rapidity contributes greatly to the dramatic tension. His tragedies have moving eloquence. For intensity of feeling, vigour, and power Alfieri is unsurpassed. *Saul* (1782–4) and *Mirra* (1784–6) are generally recognized as his masterpieces. He wrote also sonnets and *canzoni*, satires in verse, epigrams, and a poem in *ottava rima*, *L'Etruria Vendicata*. Between 1800 and 1803 he wrote six comedies and a 'tramelogedia' on political subjects. He also wrote his autobiography.

Goldoni, who was born in Venice, and destined by his parents to become a lawyer, showed from his childhood that he had a vocation for the theatre, and spent much of his leisure in reading classical plays. He took his lawyer's degree in 1731 and began to practise, but turned to a theatrical career soon afterwards. His first play, a tragi-comedy, *Belisario*, was played by Imer's Company in the Arena at Verona on 24 Nov. 1734, to an audience which listened in perfect silence, and, says Goldoni, 'its reception could not have been a more brilliant novelty, nor more satisfactory to me'. Goldoni early cherished hopes of reforming the Italian theatre. He wished to

substitute for the improvised and fantastic adventure plays of the *commedia dell'arte* a regular comedy, written instead of improvised, without masks, without obscenities, without *lazzi* or horseplay and mere buffoonery. Above all he aimed at a comedy of character based on close observation of real life.

He began his reform in 1738 with *Momolo Cortesan*, which had one part written. In 1746 he signed a five-year agreement with Medebac, whose company was playing in Venice at the Teatro Sant' Angelo. To those years belong his early successes, *La Vedova Scaltra* (1748), *La Buona Moglie* (1749), and *Il Cavaliere e la Dama* (1749).

In 1750 Goldoni announced that he would undertake to compose sixteen new comedies to be played the following season. This pledge he kept, and opened the autumn season with the *Teatro Comico*, a polemical play which explains his reform; like Pirandello's later *Sei Personaggi*, it sent up its curtain on a bare stage set for a rehearsal, and had for its cast a troupe of actors about to begin rehearsing. Some of Goldoni's best works belong to this season, including *La Bottega del Caffè*, *Il Vero Amico*, *La Finta Malata*, and *I Pettegolezzi*. The years 1748–53 saw Goldoni at the height of his glory, beloved by all Venice, aristocrats, bourgeoisie, common people alike—from doge to gondolier. In 1752 he composed *La Locandiera*, a picture of feminine coquetry which has pleased audiences all over Europe and America, particularly when Mirandolina was played in recent times by Eleonora Duse. In 1753 came *Le Donne Curiose*, whose plot foreshadows *Are You a Mason?*

In 1753 Goldoni left Medebac to join Vendramin's company at the Teatro San Luca, and remained with him till 1761. Difficulties presented themselves almost at once. The San Luca Theatre was larger and more suited to spectacular plays. The rivalry and open hostility of the Abate Piero Chiari (1711–85) divided Venice into two camps, Chiaristi and Goldonisti. Chiari followed Goldoni at the Teatro Sant' Angelo, and saw to it that every new work by Goldoni at the San Luca was immediately followed by a parody at the Sant'Angelo. In 1756 Carlo Gozzi (1720–1805) joined in the quarrel, vowing that any fairy tale would attract an audience to a theatre (see above, 2 vi).

Though embittered by strain and strife, these years saw some of Goldoni's best works, *I Rusteghi* (1760) in the Venetian dialect, *Gli Innamorati* (1759), *La Casa Nova* (1758), *Le Baruffe Chiozzotte* (1762), *Tòdero Brontolon* (1762), and *Il Campiello* (1756).

In April 1761 Goldoni agreed to go to Paris to the Italian company (see COMÉDIE-ITALIENNE) for two years only, but remained there till his death. In Paris fresh problems confronted him, not least the old struggle against actors who clung to improvisation, and resented change. The first plays he presented were badly received. He composed many works in these years, among them two masterpieces,

L'Éventail (1763), a comedy of manners, and *Le Bourru bienfaisant* (1771). Hard times then overtook him. For some years he acted as tutor to the royal family, and was granted a pension. The French Revolution took this from him, and he died in dire poverty in 1793. He left behind him his autobiography, some 150 comedies in verse and prose, 10 tragedies, and 83 *operette* or *melodrammi*. He has been called the Italian Molière, but the title does not suit him, for his genius was of a different kind. He excels in the comedy of manners, or 'ambiente'. He was struck by the ridiculous in human beings, and drew his comedy from that without attempting deeper commentary in the form of satire. He has been admirably summed up by Browning in his sonnet on the erection of Goldoni's monument in Venice in 1833:

Goldoni good, gay, sunniest of souls,
Glassing half Venice in that verse of thine,
What though it just reflects the shade and shine
Of common life, nor renders, as it rolls,
Grandeur and gloom? Sufficient for thy shoals
Was Carnival . . .

though Browning hardly does justice to the technical perfection of Goldoni's work, which, together with the sparkling and incisive wit of his dialogue, has kept his comedies still alive and keenly appreciated even in our own day.

(*b*) *Nineteenth Century to Modern Times*. With few exceptions plays of the early nineteenth century belong to the history of literature rather than to the history of the theatre. In some cases the drama represents the mediocre achievement of poets or prose-writers who made themselves famous for excellence in other genres. That Italy wished to improve the quality of her dramatic output is indicated by the number of prizes offered for the best plays. From 1770 onwards, the Duke of Parma offered annually a prize for the best tragedy. In 1786 this was won by Vincenzo Monti (1754–1828), the most representative poet of Italy's Napoleonic era. His tragedy, entitled *Aristodemo*, followed the model established by Alfieri. In 1778 Monti produced also *Caio Gracco*, in which the handling of certain scenes, and the portraying of character, reveal that the author had studied Shakespeare. Ugo Foscolo (1778–1827), one of Italy's finest lyric poets, composed tragedies on the Alfierian model, but they are the least attractive of all his works, and have more lyric than dramatic value.

A tragedy which won great fame for its author when played in 1815 was the *Francesca da Rimini* of Silvio Pellico (1789–1854), better known for his prose work, the account of his sufferings at the hand of his Austrian jailers, entitled *Le Mie Prigioni* (1832). *Francesca da Rimini*, modelled in part on Alfieri's tragedies, now seems insipid and insignificant, yet in its day it owed its success to the author's pronounced appeal to the national spirit, and to a pathos which now seems sentimental.

The most brilliant writer of the nineteenth century, Alessandro Manzoni (1785–1873), author of the historical novel *I Promessi Sposi*, broke away from the classical conventions which had enslaved tragedy. In the *Conte di Carmagnola* (begun in 1816 and published in 1820) and in *Adelchi* (begun in 1820 and published in 1822) he set Italian tragedy on a new path. A fervent admirer of Shakespeare, and of Goethe and Schiller, Manzoni created the Italian romantic drama. He was no longer content, as Alfieri had been, to distort history in order to illustrate his own ideas and ideals; rather, he aimed at drawing the poetry out of history. His tragedies appeared in print in company with essays entitled *Notizie Storiche*, researches into aspects of the historical background. His conclusions on the Unities are to be found in his *Lettre sur l'unité de temps et de lieu dans la tragédie* (1823), addressed to his friend Chauvet. In spite of great qualities as works of art, the two romantic tragedies of Manzoni nevertheless lack dramatic power; the lyric note predominates, and the works can be best enjoyed for their poetry.

A strong political current runs through the bulk of Italian literature of the Risorgimento before 1848. Italian Romanticism was essentially political. The drama was no exception, and the most famous romantic tragedies were written by a university professor who regarded poetry as a vehicle of expression for his political opinions and patriotic sentiments. This was Giambattista Niccolini (1782–1861), who at first wrote classical tragedies but later came under romantic influences. In 1815 he wrote *Matilde*, which owed something to John Home's *Douglas* (1756). His *Beatrice Cenci* (1838–44) derived inspiration from Shelley's tragedy. *Nabuco*, composed in 1816, and published in London in 1819 by Foscolo and Gino Capponi, is an allegory on the fall of Napoleon. *Antonio Foscarini* (1827), like *Filippo Strozzi* (1847), contains an attack on despotism. *Giovanni da Procida* (1830) and *Lodovico Sforza* (1833) aimed at furthering the achievement of the independence and unification of Italy. *Arnaldo da Brescia* (1843) added to this same aim an attack on the temporal power of the Pope and on the corruption of his clergy. It is generally recognized as Niccolini's masterpiece, though it is essentially a dramatic poem of great beauty divided into five acts rather than a tragedy for the stage.

While the vogue for tragedy prevailed in Italy, comedy suffered neglect. A few insipid imitators of Goldoni produced comedies, but little worthy of survival. *Il Cavaliere d'Industria* by Vincenzo Martini (1803–62) won a prize in Turin in 1854, and one of the best comedies of the time proved to be his *Donna di Quarant'anni* (1853). Pietro Cossa (1830–81) infused a certain vigour into his romantic dramas based on historical subjects, *Nerone* (1871) and *Messalina* (1876). Paolo Giacometti (1817–82) attempted historical plays, such as *Elisabetta, Regina d'Inghilterra* (1853), and comedies of manners such as *Maria Antonietta, Regina di Francia* (1867). Most successful were the comedies of Paolo Ferrari (1822–89). Inspired by the sane vigour and sober realism of Goldoni, he wrote a comedy with an historical setting entitled *Goldoni e le sue sedici commedie nuove*, a play which set on the stage the society and atmosphere of Goldoni's day. This won the prize offered by the Ginnasio Drammatico of Florence in 1852. An equally brilliant masterpiece of historical comedy was *La Satira e Parini* (1854–6), a picture of *settecento* life and manners. Ferrari then turned to the drama of social criticism, and wrote between 1856 and 1888 a number of *commedie a tesi*, or thesis dramas.

Though Italy achieved political unity in 1870 the regional spirit did not cease, and has not yet ceased, to dominate her literature. In the theatre the most original works of the 'Veristi' or naturalistic writers depict the life and atmosphere of different provinces: some were written in dialect.

Giacinto Gallina (1852–97) gave Venice comedies in dialect which pleased his age no less than those of Goldoni had pleased his fellow citizens. Gallina's plays fall into two groups: those of the early period, romantic and sentimental, for example *Teleri Vecchi* (1877), *Mia Fia* (1879), and *I Oci del Cor* (1880); and those of the second phase, in which he gives a more naturalistic colouring to his view of Venetian life. Amongst these is his masterpiece, *Serenissima* (1891).

Sicilian life was magnificently portrayed by Giovanni Verga (1840–1922). *Cavalleria Rusticana* and *La Lupa*, based on two of Verga's short stories, depict in all its violence the bitter reality which governed the daily life and passions of the Sicilian peasant. Luigi Capuana (1839–1915) achieved an equal measure of success with *Malia* and *Giacinta* (dramatized 1888) and other plays set in Sicily.

Carlo Bertolazzi (1870–1916) wrote in the Milanese dialect some of his best plays, such as *El Nost Milan* (1894) and *La Gibigianna* (1898). Augusto Novelli (1868–1927) showed great insight and skill in setting on the stage the life of the popular quarters of Florence, as in *L'Acqua Cheta* (1908). He scored his greatest success with *Il Cupolone* (1913), set in the Florence of the *quattrocento*, presenting the heroic struggle of Brunelleschi to complete the construction of the famous cupola for the cathedral of Florence.

Girolamo Rovetta (1851–1910) composed one of the most successful of Italy's historical plays in *Romanticismo* (1901), in which he depicts the sufferings and heroism of the followers of Mazzini during the struggle for Italy's freedom. Rovetta wrote also *La Trilogia di Dorina* (1889), *Il Poeta*, *Re Burlone* (1905), *Molière e sua Moglie*, and *Papà Eccellenza* (1906).

Giuseppe Giacosa (1847–1906), a Piedmontese, won success with a group of historical comedies in which a fantastic story unfolded in a romantic medieval setting, as in *Una Partita a scacchi* (1871) and the *Trionfo d'amore* (1875), written in 'martelliani'. He later turned to a realistic picture of history in *Conte Rosso* (1880) and *La Signora di Challant* (1891). The

psychological drama, the commentary on social problems and customs, then claimed his attention. *Tristi amori* (1888), *Diritti del'anima* (1894), *Come le foglie* (1900), and *Il più Forte* (1905) won a place for Giacosa among the most successful writers of realistic plays of middle-class life.

In spite of repeated attempts to cut adrift from foreign influences, an almost slavish adherence to the French theatre characterizes modern Italian drama. The influence of Henri Becque and the Théâtre Libre is apparent in Carlo Bertolazzi's *L'Egoista* (1901), in *Lulù* (1903), and in *Il Focolare Domestico* (1910), while the influence of Bernstein is faithfully reflected in the work of Dario Niccodemi, whose first plays were produced in Paris. These include *Le Refuge* (1909), *L'Aigrette* (1912), and *Les Requins* (1913). His best work is perhaps *Scampolo* (1916).

When Ibsen shook Europe by introducing to the stage an entirely new attitude to social problems and to the commonplace in man, Italy did not escape his influence. An Italian version of *Ghosts* was played in Florence by Zacconi in 1892. Enrico Annibale Butti (1868–1912) reproduced certain features of Ibsen's work in *Il Vortice* (1892), *L'Utopia* (1894), and *Fiamme nell' ombra* (1904). Ibsen was better understood by Roberto Bracco (1862–1943), amongst whose finest works were *Fantasmi* (1906), *La Piccola Fonte* (1905), *Il Piccolo Santo* (1909), and *I Pazzi* (1921). Bracco was a feminist and many of his works depict the evils of the enslavement of woman by man. He excels in plays which depict in strong colouring and melodramatic situations the life of the dregs of the populace in Naples, as, for example, *Maschere* (1893) and *Don Pietro Caruso* (1895). His masterpiece is generally considered to be *Sperduti nel Buio* (1901).

Italy has had few dramatists able to achieve fame outside their own country. Gabriele D'Annunzio (1863–1938) won a world-wide reputation, though his best work is not to be found amongst his tragedies, *La Città morta* (1898), *La Gioconda* (1899), *Più che l'amore* (1907), and *Fedra* (1909). In these, descriptive and lyrical passages abound: passages which please the ear but delay the development of the plot. His characters are animated by his own attitude to life, rather than by any vitality of their own: as, for example, Settala in *La Gioconda*, who reflects D'Annunzio's belief in the artist as a superman, a creature above conventions and social laws.

His *Francesca da Rimini* (1902) and *La Figlia di Iorio* (1904) are tragedies in verse, magnificent reconstructions of medieval life in the duecento and peasant life in the Abruzzi. D'Annunzio's theatre has been aptly designated *Teatro di Poesia*, but the poetical qualities of his plays cannot render acceptable the morbid sensuality and brutality of his themes, nor bring to life his characters.

Like D'Annunzio, Sem Benelli (1875–1949) succeeded in depicting the violence and brutality of a bygone age: his *Maschera di Bruto*

(1908) was inspired by the figure of Lorenzino, who in 1537 murdered his cousin Alessandro de' Medici. Benelli's *Cena delle beffe* (1909), a play in verse founded on a short story of Anton Francesco Grazzini, was entitled a dramatic poem but is nevertheless powerful in its intensity, and one of the most successful of modern Italian plays.

Equally fortunate in capturing the public imagination was another poet, Ercole Luigi Morselli (1882–1921). His *Glauco* (played in 1911) pleased his age for the ingenuous freshness of its idyllic quality. Though it could be called a tragedy of the superman, *Glauco* has a robust sanity which sets it in a different world from the world of morbid supermen created by D'Annunzio. The ancient myth of Glauco is created anew to symbolize the double tragedy, of the hero whose ambition compels him to set out on a life of adventure, and of the devoted woman to whom he returns too late with all ambition fulfilled.

In the years before the First World War the Futurist movement came into being. Its aims were largely destructive, a campaign against classicism and romanticism alike, and against all academic values, all traditions and conventions. Sentimentality and syntax were treated with equal contempt.

The leader of the Futurists was Filippo Tommaso Marinetti (1876–1944). His earliest work, *Mafarka le Futuriste* (1910), was suppressed and he was prosecuted in Milan for offending the morals of the community. He was acquitted but left Milan for Paris, and soon afterwards the manifesto of the Futurists was published in *Figaro*. In the theatre there were to be sweeping innovations. For the orderly, well-constructed play, they united to substitute a series of unrelated scenes and visions, accompanied by much noise and brilliant lighting.

Il Re Baldoria almost created a riot when played at Lugné-Poë's Théâtre de l'Œuvre in 1909. Most of Marinetti's work was written in French. The Futurists looked for a return of vaudeville or variety theatres, just as D'Annunzio believed that the cinema would bring salvation to the stage.

The 'Intimistes' or 'Crepuscolari' also found exponents in the theatre. The poet Fausto Maria Martini (1886–1931), at one time dramatic critic attached to the *Tribuna*, and from 1925 to 1929 to the *Giornale d'Italia*, wrote *Il Giglio Nero* in 1920, *Il Fiore sotto gli occhi* in 1922, and *I drammi dell' insignificante* in 1928. His plays were competent reconstructions of drab provincial life, with the humdrum adventures of every day set in an atmosphere of resigned melancholy.

During the First World War the 'Teatro del grottesco' emerged. This type of play took its name from Luigi Chiarelli's (1884–   ) tragical farce *La maschera e il volto* (given on 31 May 1916 at the Teatro dell' Argentina in Rome) which he entitled *Grottesco in tre atti*. The theme has much affinity with the plot of Pirandello's novel *Il Fu Mattia Pascal* (1904),

which ran on the same lines as *Buried Alive*, by Arnold Bennett, in taking as its hero a man who quits society, allowing himself to be presumed dead, and meets consequent complications when he wishes again to become a member of society.

The 'Grottesco' throws into relief the automaton in mankind, the being who acts as society expects him to act. In contrast Chiarelli shows the man behind the social being: the human being as he really is, the face behind the mask. There came into being the two planes of drama, appearance and reality, which Synge had developed in his *Playboy of the Western World* (1907). Chiarelli wrote many other plays, none of which was successful.

Other writers of 'Grotteschi' were Luigi Antonelli (1882–   ) and Enrico Cavacchioli (1884–   ). Antonelli's best work was *L'Uomo che incontrò se stesso* (1918), which develops a plot similar to that of Barrie's *Dear Brutus* (1917); but the Italian play is heavy, grim, and sinister, its characters gross, and its spirit bitter. Cavacchioli emphasizes the contrast between reality and illusion in his play *L'Uccello del Paradiso* (1919), which has one character, Lui, who recalls the Man in Grey of Andreyev's *Life of Man*. *La Danza del Ventre* (1920) creates the impression that life is a puppet show.

Massimo Bontempelli (1878–   ) similarly presented in a satire on woman, *Nostra Dea* (1925), a heroine who was admittedly a puppet, donning different clothes, and acquiring her personality from her garments.

His heroine appears as a mere mannequin in her underclothes, but dons temperaments and personality with the different garments she puts on, acquiring her spiritual life and adventures through her dressmaker. This play has been designated an early 'experiment in relativity'.

Last of the 'Grotteschi' and by far the most interesting was Pier Maria Rosso di San Secondo (1887–   ), a Sicilian and a romantic. His first successful play was *Marionette! che Passione!* (1918). The first act is set in a telegraph office of the General Post Office in Milan on a rainy Sunday evening. The chief characters are The Lady in the Blue Fox Fur, The Man in Grey, and The Man in Mourning, and later 'He who should not have come'. All the characters are puppets, victims of passion, and each symbolizes a different stage on the road to despair.

La Scala (1926) was more successful. The setting of the first act is the staircase of a block of flats: the theme, the contrast between the life of the tenants as seen from the staircase, and in the intimacy of family life between four walls. *La Bella Addormentata* (1919), 'a play in colours', and *La Roccia e i Monumenti* (1923), have charm in spite of their uneven qualities.

Alessandro de Stefani's (1891–   ) *I Pazzi della Montagna*, set in a madhouse, was mediocre, but he won fame with *Il Calzolaio di Messina*, given 11 Apr. 1925, in Rome at the

Teatro Odescalchi by the Compagnia del Teatro d'Arte di Roma, and produced by Luigi Pirandello. A tragedy with entirely modern sentiments in an eighteenth-century setting, it treats the problem of injustice; it illustrates the impossibility of achieving an ideal of absolute justice, and is one aspect of the denial of the absolute in any form. The Cobbler of Messina suffered to see 'captive good attending captain ill' (son. LXVI. Shakespeare). He took on himself to dispense justice: whenever a criminal went undetected the Cobbler sought him out and shot him by night. One victim is proved to have been no criminal, and the Cobbler's system stands condemned. The play ends with the Cobbler sitting in the midst of a semi-circle of the ghosts of those he has killed, with his madness and his suicide.

Amongst minor writers who seemed at one time to be striking an original note is Orio Vergani (1899–   ). He began his career as a journalist attached to the *Corriere della Sera*. His *Cammino sulle Acque* (1927) shows the influence of the Expressionists, and experiments with the divided stage, one part for reality and one part for what is going on in the mind of the characters. The play is a presentation of the thoughts of a man whose wife has lost her reason; by living the past again he tries to find out why she went mad, reconstructing in particular the tragic events in her life, the death of her baby, and the suicide of her father because his second wife proved unfaithful to him. Vergani's play is probably more suitable for the cinema than the theatre.

The best-known of Italy's modern playwrights, however, is Luigi Pirandello (1867–1936). He studied in Bonn and Rome, and taught in a women's training college for teachers in Rome. Luigi Capuana encouraged him to devote himself to the writing of short stories and novels, and his first novel, *L'Esclusa*, published in 1901, deals, like some of his early plays, with Sicilian life, and reveals in style and matter the influence of Capuana.

Misfortune overshadowed the early years of Pirandello's career. Disaster overtook his father's sulphur mines in 1896, but loss of money was nothing compared with the domestic misery which resulted from his marriage in 1894. His wife, for some years afflicted by hysteria, developed a mental illness bordering on insanity, and until her death in 1918 Pirandello cherished her, and gave up his life to her care. Doubtless the tragedy in his own home accounts for Pirandello's preoccupation with the mentally unbalanced.

Some of Pirandello's finest works are his short stories, and it is on them that his fame in his own country rests. Outside Italy he is best known as a playwright. In many cases his greatest plays are founded on an earlier short story, as in the case of *Così è, se vi pare* (1918), founded on a story from the collection entitled *È Domani, Lunedì*.

Novels and short stories occupied Pirandello until 1916, when he turned his attention to the theatre. His plays have been published under the general title of *Maschere nude*, and this gives the key to his subject-matter, for Pirandello's obsession was the problem of reality and illusion, of mask and face.

According to varying aspects of this problem, Pirandello's plays fall into different groups. Some lead to the conclusion that reality in the absolute does not exist; truth is as you like it, as you make it. Others illustrate the coexistence of two planes of reality: life as it is lived, and life hidden by an appearance or a mask assumed by man, the crystallization into a form. In some of these, as *Tutto per bene* (1920), *Il piacere dell' onestà* (1917), *Ma non è una cosa seria* (1918), the mask is torn aside, and life is triumphant. In others, *Il berretto a sonagli* (1916), *La Patente* (1917), *Il Gioco delle Parti* (1918), the mask becomes more firmly fixed, and avenges itself on the life it has suffocated. In *Enrico IV* (1922) the triumph of the mask turns to starkest tragedy.

In yet another group, exemplified by *Come tu mi vuoi* (1925) (known in the English-speaking world as *As You Desire Me*), the problem of reality takes on a more puzzling aspect and develops into a riddle of personality, or even of identity. A later group deals with the artistic creation of personalities, and the relative values of the real and the fictitious character. This includes *Ciascuno a suo modo* (1924) and *Trovarsi* (1932); *Quando si è qualcuno* (1934) won for Pirandello the Nobel Prize in 1935, and has an ending which recalls Galsworthy's *The Mob*. *Lazzaro* was given at Huddersfield for the first time on any stage in 1929.

In 1925 Pirandello founded the Art Theatre in Rome, at the Teatro Odescalchi, which had once been used by Guido Podrecca for his marionettes. The first play given there was his own *Sagra della Signora della Nave*.

Pirandello has set out no new philosophy in his plays; his view of life is acridly pessimistic and his humour bitter. The novelty of his theatre lies rather in his extension of the realm of drama to express the psychological discoveries of his age. Whether he is giving expression to spiritual problems arising from double or multiple personality, whether he is probing the relations between reality and illusion, or assessing the shifting values of mask and face, and the non-permanence of identity, Pirandello is always dramatic, always technically sound. The sparkling wit and brilliant dialogue of the short stories become most effective in the plays. It is an amazing technique which can dramatize so intangible a thing as an exploration into the subconscious, or an analysis of thought-processes. Pirandello is at once an expert technician and a great artist, and his plays may be the most significant thing that modern Italy has given to the European theatre.

v. m. s.

IVANOV, VSEVOLOD VYACHESLAVICH (1895–   ), Soviet dramatist, who, after running away from home at the age of 15, had a hard and adventurous youth. He began writing in

1915, served first in the White Army and then in the Red, and in 1920, with the help of Maxim Gorky, settled in Leningrad. His first play, *Armoured Train 14–69*, is an important landmark, since it was the first definitely Soviet play to be successfully produced by the Moscow Art Theatre. This was in 1927, by which time this pre-Revolutionary theatre had made the necessary adjustments to the new régime, and was able to go ahead with confidence. The play, which deals with the capture of a train-load of ammunition during the Civil War, is a melodramatic but effective piece of propaganda, which perhaps suffered a little from the determined naturalism of the Moscow Art Theatre production. It has been revived since, but the author does not yet seem to have produced anything comparable to it. His latest play, about events in the Far East, is *The Doves See the Cruisers Departing*.

J

JACK-IN-THE-GREEN, see FOLK FESTI-VALS, MORRIS DANCE, and ROBIN HOOD.

JACKSON, SIR BARRY VINCENT (1879–), founder of the Birmingham Repertory Theatre and of the Malvern Festival. Though originally trained as an architect, Sir Barry's dramatic mission soon showed itself, and his father's house became the rallying-place for the Pilgrim Players, a company of ardent amateurs who assumed professional status when Sir Barry built the Repertory Theatre in 1913. For twenty-two years he maintained this creative playhouse in the face of local indifference to the fact that a miracle of high patronage was being performed by one who was willing to back his faith in the intelligent theatre with his own money. The varied fare he provided bears witness to his liberal view of the function of the theatre. Classics and new plays, tragedy and farce, pantomime and ballet, opera, and even marionettes were presented on the Repertory Theatre stage. Sir Barry has always been on the alert for worthy material and has himself adapted several foreign pieces, including *The Marriage of Figaro* and *He Who Gets Slapped*. In addition to these, he translated Ghéon's *The Marvellous History of St. Bernard* for presentation in Birmingham and London, where it was hailed as 'one of the loveliest productions in the modern theatre'. He wrote *The Christmas Party*, a real children's pantomime, adapted Wyss's *The Swiss Family Robinson*, and contributed revue sketches to Birmingham's Christmas entertainment. Sir Barry has always regarded the theatre as a workshop for artistic experiment rather than as a museum for the preservation of tradition. His productions of Shakespeare in modern dress were a sincere, and on the whole successful, attempt to break free from cumbersome convention. For Shaw (on Shaw's own admission) Sir Barry did what no commercial manager could have done by the production of *Back to Methuselah* in Birmingham and in London. By founding the Malvern Festival in 1929 he initiated the English theatre into the festival habit, and provided an entertaining month of drama in enchanting surroundings. From 1945–8 Sir Barry was Director of the Memorial Theatre at Stratford-on-Avon, and of the Shakespeare Festival plays given there.

In 1935 Sir Barry made over the Birmingham Repertory Theatre to the Sir Barry Jackson Trust, of which he remains the Governing Director. Eight trustees now share the responsibility. In 1922 Sir Barry received the Gold Medal of the Birmingham Civic Society. In 1923 he was made Master of Arts by Birmingham University; in 1925 national recognition came in the form of knighthood.

T. C. K.

JADOT, JACQUEMIN (*fl.* 1610–60). French actor, who played serious parts under the name of La France, and farce as Michau. He was originally with the company headed by Lenoir which went to Paris in 1610, and was transferred with Lenoir, Jodelet, and others to the Hôtel de Bourgogne in 1643, where he replaced Gaultier-Garguille as a clown. Little is known about him, but he was still acting in 1658.

JAMES, „DAVID (1839–93), English actor, brother of the harlequin Humphrey Belasco, and so uncle of the famous American manager, who was called after him. James made his first appearance as a super at the Princess's Theatre, London, in 1857, under Charles Kean, and then went into burlesque at the Strand and elsewhere, being much admired as Mercury in *Ixion* (1863) at the Royalty. In 1870 he built and opened the Vaudeville Theatre, in partnership with Montague and Thomas Thorne. Their intention was to make it a home of burlesque, but their first productions having proved unsuccessful they put on *Two Roses*, in which young Henry Irving, as Digby Grant, attracted the attention of Colonel Bateman, and was engaged for the Lyceum, thus inaugurating his brilliant career as London's outstanding actor-manager. James was also responsible for the production of the phenomenally successful *Our Boys* (1875), which made a fortune for him and his associates. After leaving the Vaudeville, which in 1891 was taken over by the Gattis, James was seen at a number of theatres, and eventually returned to burlesque—in *Little Jack Sheppard* at the Gaiety. One of his best parts in later years was Old Eccles, in *Caste*, and he was also good as Stout in *Money*. His son David was also on the stage.

JAMES, HENRY (1843–1916), who was born in New York, spent most of his life in England, and in 1915 became a British subject. Though he is chiefly remembered as a novelist, he had an ardent love for the theatre, as can be seen from his correspondence, and from the essays contributed to various journals, reprinted in 1949 in one volume as *The Scenic Art*. He wrote a number of plays, but few of them were produced during his lifetime, and those unsuccessfully. After the hostile reception given to *Guy Domville* (1895), which George Alexander put on in London at the St. James's, he wrote no more for the stage. The success he had longed for came later to dramatizations of his works made by other hands—notably *Berkeley Square* (1928), suggested by his unfinished novel *The Sense of the Past*; *The Heiress* (1947), based on *Washington Square*; and *The Innocents* (1950), based on *The Turn of the Screw*. James's own plays were published in a one-volume edition in 1948 with an excellent introduction and notes by Leon Edel.

JAMES, LOUIS (1842–1910), American actor, who made his début in 1863, and was for some years with Mrs. John Drew at the Arch Street Theatre, Philadelphia. In 1871 he joined Daly at the Fifth Avenue Theatre, and during the next four or five years appeared there in a wide variety of parts, being good in light comedy. From 1880 to 1885 he was leading man with Lawrence Barrett, with whom he first appeared in London as Master Heywood in *Yorick's Love*. With Marie Wainwright (1853–1923) as his leading lady he toured extensively in a repertory of Shakespearian and other classics, and remained on the stage until his death, which occurred while he was dressing to play Wolsey in *Henry VIII*.

JAMES STREET THEATRE. This small eighteenth-century theatre or amusement hall stood between the Haymarket and Whitcomb Street. It was used mostly for variety, but pantomimes were given there, and occasionally plays. Its prices seem to have been 3*d*., 4*d*., 6*d*., and 1*s*.

JANAUSCHEK, FRANCESCA ROMANA MAGDALENA (1830–1904), Czech actress, who made her début in Prague in 1846, and two years later became leading lady of the Frankfort Stadt-Theater. She remained there for some years, and then went to Dresden, building up a great reputation as an interpreter of tragic drama in such parts as Medea, Iphigenia, Marie Stuart, and Lady Macbeth. She toured extensively in Europe, and in the United States, where she was highly thought of. In 1873 she undertook to play in English, appearing in a number of Shakespearian and other roles. Her later years were spent mainly in America, where she died four years after suffering a stroke which paralysed her. She was one of the last of the great international actresses in the grand tragic style.

JANIN, JULES GABRIEL (1804–74), French journalist and dramatic critic, most of whose best work was done for the *Journal des Débats*, where he succeeded Geoffroy. For forty years he wrote a Monday article which dealt as much with personal and national affairs as with the theatre, and his outspokenness frequently landed him in lawsuits and quarrels. But his enthusiasm for good acting, wherever he found it, made him a powerful advocate, and it was his articles that first drew the attention of the Parisian public to Rachel and to Deburau. A prolific writer, he published lives of both these actors, and also a history of French dramatic literature, as well as innumerable works of criticism and several novels. Celebrated and feared during his lifetime, he was soon forgotten, but his books are useful sources for contemporary theatrical and social history.

JAPAN. The present-day Japanese theatre takes three distinct although related forms, the *Nō* or lyrical drama, *Ningyō-shibai* or marionettes, and *Kabuki*, the popular theatre.

The first printed texts of the *Nō* date from about 1600, but their composition is attributed to Kwanami and his son Seami, who lived at the end of the fourteenth and beginning of the fifteenth centuries. The language, however, in which they are written is the Court colloquial of the fourteenth century and they represent an art already mature; the *Nō* must therefore have been an established art form soon after the Ashikaga line of *Shōguns* began to rule at Kyōto (in 1334) and may even date from the later years of the first shogunate, set up at Kamakura thirty miles south of the modern Tōkyō at the end of the twelfth century. The language of the *kyōgen* or comic interludes which accompany their performance is the vernacular of the second half of the sixteenth century. The marionette theatre and the popular drama were established art forms by the time the centre of power had shifted once more to the east with the setting up of the Tōkugawa shogunate, which lasted until the Restoration in 1868, at Edo, the modern Tōkyō, at the beginning of the seventeenth century. They reached their highest point of development in the second half of the century, and have remained more or less static since that time. The *Nō* has been static since the beginning of the same century.

The *Nō* drew its forms and materials from the ritual dances of the temples and the folk dances of the countryside; from the Buddhist scriptures, and from the abundant sources of Chinese and Japanese poetry, myth, and legend. But it was from the first an aristocratic art, and with the passage of time this tendency grew until it became a close preserve of the ruling caste. On the overthrow of the shogunate in 1868 and the consequent disappearance of the feudal system, the *Nō* survived precariously at first, but has since taken a new lease of life; its enjoyment, however, is still confined to the upper classes of society. The marionettes, although their sources were ultimately the same, were influenced more directly by the *hanashi-ka* or story-tellers; their appeal was to the populace, but with the development of the popular stage, which appropriated their best dramas, interest in them has dwindled until there is only one stage for their exhibition, the Bunraku-za at Ōsaka, the commercial metropolis of Japan, not far from Kyōto. The popular stage drew not merely on the *Nō*, but more extensively on the range of marionette drama, especially in the *jōruri* form in which the chanting of the story by a chorus accompanies the action. It has from early days been the apanage of the Edo (Tōkyō) townsfolk; indeed, access to it was forbidden to the *samurai*, the warrior caste of old Japan.

The marionettes are displayed on a wide, shallow stage of no great height; although it does not reach the same pitch of realism as on the *kabuki* stage, the scenery is elaborate, and cunningly contrived to allow for the movements of the puppets and their handlers on different planes of depth and height. The puppets are two-thirds life size and the principal characters need for their display a chief handler, who wears a ceremonial costume and is not masked, and two assistants in hoods; the minor characters are handled by a single hooded assistant. All these handlers are visible to the audience; the technique of manipulation from above by strings, although it has its exponents in Japan, has not succeeded in establishing its right to a stage of its own. The action is accompanied by the chanting of the story by a chorus of five singers to the music of five *samisen*, or Japanese guitars; the chorus sings in unison, and the music has no independent existence apart from the chanting to which it forms a rhythmical background.

The *kabuki* stage is also wide, shallow, and not very high; its depth is limited by the adoption of the device of the revolving stage which dates from 1760, and is an integral part of the scenic presentment. Another special device characteristic of the *kabuki* stage, although adapted from the *Nō*, is the *hana-michi*, the 'flower way', running on the left-hand side from the back of the hall to the stage at the level of the spectators' heads. Along this the characters make their entrances and exits, and to it they sometimes withdraw for an aside; it is sometimes duplicated by a similar though narrower passage on the right-hand side. The curtain does not rise but rolls back to one side. The scenery is elaborate and complete to the last detail; but since the scene is Japan, where simplicity to the point of asceticism is the rule, this over-elaboration does not serve to distract the attention. The costumes are similarly fitted to the part; rich brocaded silks in historical subjects, plain where the scenes are drawn from common life. The performers are not masked, unless for performance of an actual *Nō*, when a replica of the *Nō* stage is sometimes constructed on the stage; but in the classical plays they are heavily made up in conventional style appropriate to the character represented. Female parts are taken exclusively by male actors who specialize in these roles. Music and sound-effects are provided by a small party of instrumentalists inconspicuously placed behind a lattice on the left of the stage; where the play is adapted from the marionette theatre a *jōruri* reciter and a *samisen* player sit in open view on the right; if from the *Nō*, in addition to the chorus and a number of *samisen* players seated on the stage, there will be the special *Nō* musicians seated in front of them. Finally, mention may be made of the stage assistants, the *kurogo* and *kōken*, the one hooded and the other not. Like the handlers of the marionettes they are conventionally invisible; they survive from a time when the actor had a 'shadow' who crouched behind him with a light on the end of a bamboo to illuminate the play of his features.

As in the Chinese theatre, it is the rule for individual scenes from several plays to be acted in the course of one performance; these scenes have their own names and enjoy a semi-independent existence apart from the play of which they form a part. The Japanese theatre recognizes three main classes, the *jidaimono* or histories, with a subdivision composed of scenes of exaggerated action, the *aragoto* (it is of these last that the '18 masterpieces' of the Ichikawa school of actors consist); the *sewa-mono* or melodramas; and the *shosagoto* or dances. A typical programme would thus consist of a selection of scenes from one of the histories followed by a dance; and a second half consisting of a melodrama followed by another dance.

The *Nō* stage has a floor of highly polished cypress 18 feet square, raised 3 feet from the ground; it projects into the auditorium so that it is surrounded by the audience on two sides, separated from them only by a narrow path of loose pebbles. Four stout pillars support a temple roof, the eaves of which are some 12 feet from the ground and the ridge 20 feet. The front pillar on the right is the pillar of the Second Actor (*waki*) and diagonally across from it at the left rear is the pillar of the First Actor (*shite*, *shtay*). On the right a balcony some 3 feet wide accommodates the chorus of ten singers; at the back a transverse back-stage half the width of the main stage accommodates the four musicians and the two stage assistants; from its left-hand edge runs at a backward slant a passage of the same width, some 40 feet long, the *hashi-gakari*, by which the performers enter and leave the stage, closed at the far end by a narrow curtain.

There is no scenery; on the back wall of the rear stage is painted a stylized pine-tree, and along the bridge railing are three small pine-trees or branches. The properties are equally exiguous, a frame 2 feet square from which spring four light posts to support a roof representing a house, a temple, or a palace, as the play may require. The costumes are of a great richness, and the First Actor, especially in the second part where he performs the dance which is the kernel of the play, wears a mask. None of the other players is masked; essentially there are only the two actors, of whom the second occupies a minor role, but they have companions, *tsure*, so that there may occasionally be as many as ten performers on the stage at once. The music, consisting of a transverse flute, two hand-drums—of which the smaller, held on the right shoulder, is played with a thimble, the other on the knee with the flat of the hand—and a larger flat drum resting on the floor and played with two sticks, provides a rhythmical background only.

The play normally opens with a short introductory chant delivered by the Second Actor from the bridge, indicative of the 'order' to which the play belongs. Advancing to the traditional position he recites his name or description and purpose; then follows the journey-song, at the close of which he retires to his pillar. This is the cue for the entrance of the First Actor in his first impersonation, with a chant similar to the Second Actor's, but more developed. As he enters the stage after this chant the Second Actor addresses him, and the theme of the play and the emotions it evokes are developed in exchanges between the two; the first part of the play is rounded off by a chant, more or less prolonged, by the chorus, at the close of which the First Actor (his real character now made known) retires.

Then follows an interlude during which an actor in ordinary costume, and bearing the same name as the performers in the three comic interludes which separate the individual plays, once more relates the story of the play in a prose recitative. The second part of the play opens with the Second Actor's waiting-song; the First Actor then reappears in his real person as god or hero, and performs the great dance or dances for which the rest of the play provides a setting.

Although there are special movements within it which are more animated and even exaggerated, in general the dance is a stately gliding to and fro, without raising the heel, in a series of three, five, or seven steps in a line, accompanied by gestures, of which the most striking is the throwing up of the great brocade sleeve. The dancer is in stockinged feet, the floor is highly polished and specially constructed for resonance; the tapping, beating, and stamping of the feet, accompanied by the syncopated rhythm of the drums, the piercing notes of the flute, and the sharp ejaculations of the musicians, all go to make up the total effect. The dance normally is composed of five movements, each accompanied by the use of a special accessory such as a fan, a sword, or a sacred wand.

Between the individual plays which go to compose a *Nō* sequence there are interposed, in order to relieve the emotional tension, short comic interludes or farces, *kyōgen*, performed in ordinary dress and without masks. That is not to say that there are not parts which call for costume or a wig, that the use of a mask is not sometimes the point of a scene, that parodies of the *Nō* and its masks are not common. Nothing is sacred to the *kyōgen*, the *daimyō* or feudal lord, the monk, the friar, not even the dread ruler of the lower regions; and every object of popular fun finds a place, the drunken or impudent or dishonest or stupid servant, the boaster, the glutton, the shrew, the gallant; almost it might be said that every precept of the classical canon of education is turned to ridicule. If the purpose of the *Nō* is magical, here is counter-magic.

The modern classification of the *Nō*, on which is based the selection of pieces to form a programme, divides them into:
(1) The god piece;
(2) The battle piece;
(3) The wig piece;
(4) The mad piece;
(5) The melodrama;
(6) The finale.

The ordinary day's programme of five pieces contains in addition three *kyōgen*, and lasts for six or seven hours, beginning at nine or ten in the morning or at one in the afternoon. Although not selected to form a programme, the following summaries will give some indication of the content of the individual classes:

Oimatsu, or The Ancient Pine. The ninth-century poet-minister Sugawara no Michizane, unjustly exiled through a palace intrigue, was miraculously followed into exile by his favourite trees. He was subsequently deified as the god of calligraphy. In the first part the spirits of the trees are represented by their attendant gardeners; in the second the spirit of the aged pine tree performs the solemn, stately *Ṣhin no jo* dance.

Atsumori. In the great war of the twelfth century which has furnished the Japanese stage with so many of its themes the young hero turned back to face the gnarled veteran and was slain; but the slayer shaved his head and became a monk. In the first part the monk appears in person and the hero as a young reaper. The first dance of the second part is symbolic of the dance and song with which the elegants of the defeated clan whiled away the night before the battle; the second mimes the hand-to-hand fight, ending with the absolution of the monk.

Ha-goromo, or The Feather Robe. A fisherman finds an angel's feather robe, without which she cannot return to heaven, and is persuaded reluctantly to return it to her. In gratitude she performs the 'dances that are danced in heaven'.

Aoi no Ue, or Lady Aoi. Drawn from the eleventh-century romance of Genji, the Japanese Don Juan, another fertile source of inspiration for the stage, Aoi is possessed by the jealous spirit of a rival. In the first part the incantations of a sorceress evoke the jealous spirit in her natural form; in the second she is incarnate as the devil of jealousy.

Ataka, or The Barrier of Ataka. The youthful hero on the opposing side in the battle in which Atsumori lost his life quarrelled with his brother, the founder of the Kamakura shogunate, and was forced to flee in disguise. Led by his faithful supporter, the gigantic monk Benkei, the party come to a barrier, which they are allowed to pass on the production by Benkei of a subscription list, *kanjinchō*, in proof of their bona fides as mendicant friars. When they are called back for a second scrutiny, Benkei dances the *Ennen no mai*, the dance of longevity, one of the temple dances from which the *Nō* form descends.

Ko-kaji. The swordsmith Munechika is commanded to forge a blade for the emperor and invokes the aid of Inari, the god of rice-cultivation, whose symbol is the fox. In the second part the god mimes the forging of the sword in the *hataraki*, a dance of agitated movement.   **C. W. B.**

JAVA. The theatre of the Javanese embraces the dance drama, which lies outside the scope of this volume, the shadow show, and the puppet play. The shadow show is of great antiquity, the first reference to it dating from the seventh century, when it was already an established art-form. It has had a wide-spread influence throughout the East (see also MALAY and SHADOW SHOW).

JEFFERSON, a family of actors, of English origin, but important in the history of the American stage. The first to be known by name is (1) THOMAS (1732–1797), who was at Drury Lane under Garrick, and was accounted a good actor. He was for some time manager of the Plymouth theatre, and was twice married, having a large family, most of whom were on the stage. By his first wife, a charming and beautiful woman who died young, he had a son (2) JOSEPH (1774–1832), the first of that name. This son was trained for the stage by his father, and in 1795 went to America. After a short stay in Boston he was at the John Street and later Park Theatres, New York, from 1796 until 1803, where he was popular with the company and the public alike, particularly in comedy, and in the parts of humorous elderly gentlemen. He was, however, somewhat held back by the pre-eminence of Hodgkinson, and in 1803 went to the Chestnut Street Theatre, Philadelphia, where he remained until a few years before his death. He then fell on hard times, and from about 1830 was seen mostly on tour in the big cities. Yet his career as a whole had been successful, and his influence on the stage was salutary. Walter Prichard Eaton in the *Dictionary of American Biography* says of him: 'He brought to the theatre the best traditions, and to private life dignity and kindliness and virtue.' He and William Warren married two sisters, thus connecting two families of importance in American stage history. Jefferson had a large family, all of whom were on the stage, including a second Thomas and four daughters. The best-remembered of them is, however, (3) JOSEPH (1804–42), the second of the name, who inherited his father's happy nature and strong sense of integrity, but not his genius. He was on the stage, but had a decided bent for art, and did a good deal of scene-painting. He married (4) CORNELIA FRANCES THOMÁS (1796–1849), an actress and singer of great ability who by her first marriage was the mother of the actor Charles Burke (1822–54), and had by her two children, of whom (5) JOSEPH (1829–1905), third of the name, was destined to become one of the outstanding figures of the American stage. He made his début at the age of 4, in Washington, being tumbled out of a sack by the famous Jim Crow, whose song and dance he then mimicked. With his family he toured extensively, living the hard life of pioneer players. He had little schooling outside the theatre, and at 13 lost his father. Long years of labour with little reward at last bore fruit, and in 1849 he achieved some eminence. By 1856 he was able

to afford a trip to Europe and on his return joined Laura Keene's company, where he made a great success as Dr. Pangloss in *The Heir-at-Law*, and as Asa Trenchard in *Our American Cousin*. This proved a turning-point in his career, as in that of E. A. Sothern, who played Lord Dundreary, and after a short starring tour he went to the Winter Garden under Boucicault, where he played among other parts Caleb Plummer in *Dot* and Salem Scudder in *The Octoroon*. On the death of his first wife in 1861 he went on a four-year tour of Australia, and it was on his return that he first played the part with which he is always identified—*Rip Van Winkle*. There had already been several dramatizations of Irving's story, notably by Kerr, and by Jefferson's half-brother Charles Burke in 1850, in which Jefferson himself played the innkeeper. He based his own version partly on the above and partly on the original tale, and produced it in 1859, but found it unsatisfactory. The final version was done by Boucicault in 1865, while Jefferson was in England, but during the many years in which the latter appeared in it he made so many alterations that in the end the character became his own creation, and the play lived only as long as he did. He first played it in Boucicault's version at the Adelphi in London in 1865, and in New York a year later. It was during this visit to London that Jefferson was entertained by the son of his great-uncle Frank, and went with twenty-four relations to see the pantomime at Astley's. The size of the party gives some idea of the ramifications of the family, whose members in America were even more numerous. Until 1880 Jefferson played little but *Rip Van Winkle*, which was acknowledged everywhere to be a masterpiece; he then revived *The Rivals*, making Bob Acres a little more witty and a little less boorish than his predecessors in the part had done. With Mrs. John Drew as Mrs. Malaprop, and a good supporting company, this toured successfully for many years. Jefferson, whose charming, humorous personality made him typical of all that was best in the America of his time, made his last appearance on 7 May 1904, as Caleb Plummer, and then retired after seventy-one years on the stage. In 1893 he had succeeded Booth as President of the Players' Club, and so became the recognized head of his profession. He did a good deal of lecturing, and in 1890 published a delightful autobiography, from which many of the above details are taken. He strengthened the family tie with the Warrens by marrying as his second wife the granddaughter of the first William. The eldest of his children (6) CHARLES BURKE (1851–1908) was for many years his manager, and was also an actor, as were three other sons, among them a third Thomas. His only daughter, by her marriage with the novelist B. L. Farjeon, was the mother of the composer Harry, the novelists and playwrights Joseph Jefferson and Eleanor, and of (7) HERBERT FARJEON (1887–1945), actor, author, and dramatic critic, pre-eminently a writer and producer of intimate witty revues, staged mainly at the Little Theatre, London. He was a scholarly man, editor of the Nonesuch and other editions of Shakespeare, and of the *Shakespeare Journal* from 1922 to 1925, and had much of the charm and geniality of his famous grandfather.

JEROME, JEROME KLAPKA (1859–1927), English humorist, novelist, and playwright, who was also for a short time an actor. It was no doubt his experiences then that led to the compilation of his *Stageland: Curious Habits and Customs of its Inhabitants*, which was published in 1890 with amusing illustrations by Bernard Partridge. He also wrote *On the Stage and Off* (1888), and several plays which have not survived, the first being *Barbara* (1886), produced by Charles Hawtrey at the Globe. Jerome's theatrical fame, however, rests mainly on *The Passing of the Third Floor Back* (1908), in which Forbes-Robertson scored a signal triumph as the mysterious and Christ-like stranger whose sojourn in a Bloomsbury lodging-house changes the lives of all its inhabitants. The play has been several times revived.

JERROLD. (1) DOUGLAS WILLIAM (1803–57), English man of letters, whose early experiences in the Navy, where he was a shipmate of the scene-painter Stanfield, were turned to good account in his best-known play, *Black-Eyed Susan; or, All in the Downs* (1829), in which the actor T. P. Cooke made a great hit. Jerrold was then engaged by Elliston as dramatic author to the Surrey Theatre, a position he had formerly held at the Coburg Theatre under Davidge, where his farce, *Paul Pry* (1827), and his melodrama, *Fifteen Years of a Drunkard's Life* (1828), were produced. Some of his later plays, notably *The Rent Day* (1832), were given at Drury Lane, while in 1836 he took over the management of the Strand Theatre and produced his own plays there. He also acted occasionally, but had little taste or talent for it. He was associated from its foundation in 1841 with *Punch*, and in later years was more engaged in journalism than play-writing; none of his plays has survived on the stage, though in the lighter forms of burlesque and comedy, and occasionally in melodrama, he had a good deal of contemporary success. Jerrold's son (2) WILLIAM BLANCHARD (1826–84) was also a prolific writer, and his farce, *Cool as a Cucumber* (1851), gave the younger Mathews one of his best parts. His other plays are negligible.

JESSNER, LEOPOLD (1878–   ), German producer, a disciple of Reinhardt, who abandoned the use of scenery in his productions in favour of different levels connected by stairways (*Spieltreppe*). A man of stern purpose and high intelligence, Jessner was a staunch republican. In art he was an expressionist, and during his years as director of the Berlin State Theatre (1919–25) he was considered one of the most advanced exponents of that creed. Among his most notable productions were *Wilhelm Tell*, *Richard III*, and *Der Marquis von Keith*.

JESSOP'S HALL, LONDON, see ROYAL PANTHEON THEATRE.

JESTER, see CLOWN and FOOL.

JESUIT DRAMA. In origin, the drama of the Jesuit schools and colleges is similar to other forms of scholastic drama; it was the product of a didactic purpose. The aim of the Jesuit plays was both educational and theological; they were directed to the improvement of the pupils who acted them and of the audience that watched them. At the same time, the degree of emphasis laid on those visual means of conveying purpose which are characteristic of the theatre, differentiates Jesuit dramas to a very considerable extent from such scholastic dramas as relied mainly on the power and argument of the spoken word.

In the curriculum of study for the numerous educational institutions of the Society of Jesus, the staging of a drama, or at the least a dialogue, in Latin was laid down as an appropriate public exercise at the beginning or end of the school year; by this means the study of grammar and rhetoric was to be enlivened, the pupils were to be given an opportunity of showing their progress and abilities, and the doctrines of true religion and morals were to be effectively shown forth. In the first full *Ratio atque Institutio Studiorum* of 1586, the acting of comedies and tragedies was included among the aids to the study of the humanities, but it was to be in moderation, and without undue elaboration; an earlier rule (1577) had already laid down that plays might be acted, infrequently, and only in Latin, that they must be decorous, and in no case performed in church. In the revised *Ratio Studiorum* of 1599, Rectors were charged to see that the subject-matter of tragedies and comedies—which must only be acted rarely, and in Latin—was of a sacred and pious nature, that nothing intervened between the acts which was not in the Latin tongue, and decorous, and that no female character or feminine costume was introduced on to the stage (*nec persona ulla muliebris vel habitus introducatur*). Between the lines of these regulations and prohibitions, something of the relationship between the drama of the Jesuit schools and contemporary developments may be read; and also something of the conflict between scholastic principle and the need for adaptability. The history of drama in Jesuit institutions is in some measure a history of the transformation of a school exercise into an almost professional spectacle, showing a high degree of technical skill.

The earliest mention of the acting of a Jesuit play appears to date from 1551, only three years after the establishment of the first Jesuit college in Europe solely designed for the instruction of outside pupils—the Collegio Mamertino at Messina. A tragedy was performed there in 1551; but we know nothing of its character, and it is possible that it may in fact have been little more than a dialogue. But in 1558 a comedy by a Spanish Jesuit, P. Francesco Stefano, was acted at Messina: *Philoplutus, seu de misero avaritiae exitu*, and this was followed in 1561 and subsequent years by other plays (*Hercules, Nabuchodonosor, Goliath, Juditha*, &c.). Meanwhile, the first performance of a play by the pupils of the Jesuit College in Vienna took place in 1555 (*Euripus sive de inanitate rerum omnium*, by a Franciscan, Levinus Brechtanus of Antwerp), and this inaugurated a long series of performances of Jesuit dramas in Vienna; at Cordoba in 1556 a play by P. Pedro de Acevedo, *Metanea*, was acted. Performances of plays were given early at Ingolstadt in 1558, and at Munich in 1560.

At this period Jesuit colleges had been and were being established in great numbers throughout Europe—in Spain, Portugal, Italy, Sicily, France, Germany, Austria, Poland, Switzerland, and the Netherlands. At the death of Ignatius of Loyola in 1556, there were already 33 colleges open for the instruction of pupils; the number catering for outside pupils had increased to 148 by 1587, and this number was nearly doubled before the seventeenth century was far advanced. In these numerous colleges of Europe, for over two centuries, at least one play—and for the most part more than one—was performed by the pupils each year. Only the best of them were allowed to be published; for by far the greater number of performances only programmes, or *periochae*, were printed, of which numerous examples survived in various European libraries. Within the last sixty years, however, the researches of scholars in many countries have brought to light manuscript versions of Jesuit plays; some of these have been published, of others detailed descriptions have been given, and a considerable number still await adequate investigation.

Records of early dramatic performances are to be found in the histories of all the better-known Jesuit colleges. In 1568 a play on the martyrdom of St. Catherine was given at the Collegio Romano in Rome; two years earlier the second great college in Rome, established for students from the German-speaking lands, had staged a drama, *Saul*. In 1561 at Ocaña there was a play on the subject of Judith, at Seville in 1562 a representation of great magnificence was given at Corpus Christi (*Comedia habita Hispali*) and at Medina in the same year a drama, *Absalon*. At Trier a play was acted in 1562, and one at Innsbruck in 1563. The famous Collège de Clermont in Paris, founded in 1564, was the scene of a representation of a *Herod* tragedy at the opening of the session in 1579. In 1578 *Achab* was acted in the college at Pultusk; in 1580 a Faust drama was given at Liége, in 1596 *Philopater seu Pietas* at Vilna, in 1599 a play on St. Elizabeth of Hungary at Antwerp, in 1601

Philomusus Aquisgranensis at Aachen. These are only a few examples of the practice which by the end of the sixteenth century had become well established, indeed practically universal, in the Jesuit schools and colleges.

The last quarter of the sixteenth and the whole of the seventeenth century were a period of development in Jesuit drama which was very important both from a dramatic and a theatrical standpoint. There was a continuous process of elaboration of the technical aspects of production; moreover, in the different countries and regions where it flourished, interesting divergences within the general type can be observed. On the one hand, a degree of approximation to the characteristics of indigenous drama was combined with the maintenance of a general international pattern; on the other, changes of emphasis in the different regions led to new variations of the pattern. Such an approximation can be observed, for example, in Spain, where the characteristic verse forms of the national drama soon found an entry into the Jesuit plays; while the development of the ballet-interlude and of the mechanism of décor reinforced the evolution of ballet in France and of opera in South Germany and Austria. In England religious policy precluded the development of Jesuit scholastic drama; but it flourished on the continent through the seventeenth century into the eighteenth; and indeed its development was only cut short at the suppression of the Order in 1773.

The early pattern of Jesuit drama was simple in outline and purpose. There were two main types of play; *tragoediae* in five acts, on the classical model, which were generally performed either at the opening of courses after the reassembly of pupils for the session, or at a final prize-distribution at the end of the scholastic year; and shorter plays, which were acted at Carnival time or on other suitable occasions. There were also in many places special performances of plays in connexion with royal or princely festivities. The tragedies (*ludi solemnes*) were performed by the senior classes, the less exacting plays (*ludi priores*) by the younger boys. Normally the play was written by the professor of rhetoric; and it was deliberately constructed in order to afford the pupils exercise in the Latin tongue, in declamation, and in gesture and deportment. (Sometimes, however, the pupils themselves composed, or partially composed, the play, as for example at Medina in 1562, when *Absalon* was performed.) The number of actors was large, and choruses and arias gave opportunity to many who were not chosen for individual parts. *Juditha*, by the Sicilian P. Stefano Tuccio (1564), has 32 characters (apart from an angel, a demon, and the chorus); in the *San Hermenegildo* play performed at Seville in 1580 there were likewise 32 personages (including abstract characters), together with soldiers, pages, &c.; in the *Theseus* (acted at Paris in 1663) there were 25, and in the *Mauritius* tragedy at Aachen (1716) 67 in all. In the later period of Jesuit drama, the addition of ballets and interludes of various kinds also swelled the list of performers: in the *Tartaria Christiana* performed in Paris in 1657 there were 28 characters and 13 in the accompanying ballet (entitled *drama mutum* in the programme). In the *Pietas Victrix* of Avancinus (Vienna, 1659) there was a grand array of 36 personages and 10 abstract characters, together with the Senatus, members of the army and the fleet, operatives, choruses of soldiers, youths, Roman citizens, Naiads and Tritons, and angels, *gloriae* and masks.

The early prohibition of female personages and costumes was modified in a revision of the rules in 1591; female roles were to be limited to what was absolutely necessary. In the final *Ratio* of 1599 the general prohibition remained, but in reply to comments submitted by the Provinces of the Rhine, Upper Germany, and Austria, pointing out the difficulty of such a rule both for secular and religious plays, a dispensation was granted in 1602, as long as the women characters were modest and serious and were only very rarely introduced. An exception to the general rule must indeed always have been made for the numerous dramas on Judith (of which there are early examples in the sixteenth century) or on Esther, and for some of the martyr tragedies (e.g. St. Catherine). Other roles gradually came to be accepted. In Tuccio's *Juditha* (1564) there had been five female parts besides that of the heroine. In *San Hermenegildo* (1580) there were five feminine roles; in a play on William the Pious of Aquitaine performed at Graz in 1612 in the presence of the Duke of Bavaria, there were as many as ten. Eight nymphs appeared in *Dapiferi* (Constance, 1629); of the 45 characters in *Tabropana Christiana* (Paris, 1650) two were women; and in *Athalia* (Paris, 1658) there were three. The increasingly frequent introduction of abstract characters (Felicitas, Castitia, Pietas, Fides, Industria, Pax, Fama, Ecclesia, &c.) no doubt contributed also to a modification of the regulation against feminine costume; thus gradually in practice the rule came to imply simply the absence of love interest in the plays.

The names of the actors were usually appended (with the list of *dramatis personae*) to the programmes which were prepared for distribution to the audience. These programmes contained a general summary of the plot, together with brief summaries for each of the acts, indications of the scene, and frequently the text of arias or choruses. From a scrutiny of the very numerous extant examples an idea of the prevailing pattern of Jesuit drama can be gained; but the more interesting details of its adaptation to various regions and traditions must be sought mainly in the manuscripts and reprints of complete plays.

That the themes chosen must be sacred and of a pious nature was a rule which in general governed the choice of subjects, but it was interpreted more or less widely at different stages. The Old Testament and biblical history, and the lives of saints and martyrs, provided a large number of themes which were constantly treated. Such figures as those of Joseph, Saul, Herod, Nebuchadnezzar, Judith, Esther, familiar to early scholastic drama, appear again and again, as do those of numerous saints and martyrs. The great drama of the New Testament and the Apocalypse inspired an early trilogy—Stefano Tuccio's *Christus Natus, Christus Patiens, Christus Judex*. It was recorded that at the performance of the third of these plays at Messina in 1569 the spectators were in tears; and that contrition and miraculous conversions were experienced there, and in other places where the drama was acted. The history of antiquity and the Middle Ages also provided many subjects, especially later—as for example Pompey, Brutus, Croesus, Cyrus, Alexander, Damocles, Constantine the Great, Theodoric, Hermenegildus. Subjects were drawn from national or regional history and given appropriate moral colour—*Messana liberata* for example (acted in 1594) celebrated the victory over the Saracens at Messina in 1060; at Regensburg in 1598 a drama, *Tragoedia de infelicis Herodis obitu*, acted in the presence of the Archduke of Austria, showed Herod as a symbol of Turkish tyranny and gave encouragement in the Epilogue to resist the Turks; and the liberation of Vienna in 1683 was the subject of dramas acted at Cologne in 1684 and Münster in 1689. They were drawn also from mythological sources, which were then reinterpreted allegorically (e.g. *Partus Iovis, sive ortus Palladis* at Messina in 1585). The heroic aspect of the religious ideal was increasingly emphasized. Personages such as *Theophilus* (Munich, 1582), *Faust* (Liége, 1581–2), or *Cenodoxus* (Augsburg, 1602), showed the tension between good and evil, between this world and the next; dramas celebrating the founder of the Society of Jesus gave opportunity to display the victory of religious fervour and spiritual purpose over the forces of this world. The Christian virtues were exalted in such plays as *Clementia christiana*, or P. Acevedo's *Bellum virtutum et vitiorum*; pictures of impenitent sinners or a late repentance were drawn, as in *Udo*, or Bidermann's *Jacobus Usurarius*.

There were, however, in addition to the *tragoediae* and *comoediae* of serious intention, a smaller number of comic plays, usually performed by the *secundani*, or members of the lower school classes. There was a certain hesitancy over the adoption of the comic form; P. Jouvancy, for instance, in the treatise *De ratione discendi et docendi* (1703), expressed the view that it should only be used with great discretion in Christian schools, since the buffoonery proper to this genre was incompatible with the pious and liberal education of youth. Moreover—and the argument is worth noting—the gestures, customs, and jests of servants (*valets de comédie*) were unsuitable for the pupils whose education was confided to the care of the Society. But there were, nevertheless, some discreetly composed comedies—as for example *Adolescens poenitens* (MS. preserved at Messina), *Conaxa* (acted at Rennes, probably in 1710), or *Les Incommodités de la grandeur*, a five-act comedy in French verse by P. du Cerceau (performed at Paris in 1721). In France in the eighteenth century there was a considerable increase in the number of such comedies.

A Spanish farce, *Triumphus Circuncisionis* (acted at Medina del Campo) throws light on the social customs of students in Spain in the sixteenth century; and in Germany as well as Spain a mixed genre is to be found: *Ambitio infelix sive Adonias . . . oppressus* (Hildesheim, 1669) is described in the synopsis as 'Comico-Tragoedia, Vermischtes Frewden- und Trawr-Spiel'. Interludes related to the main action in substance but contrasting in mood are described on the programme of a drama on Boleslaus II, King of Poland (Jülich, 1699). A comic scene would likewise be interpolated on occasion in a serious play (as in *Rogerius, sive Panhormus liberata*, acted at Palermo in 1599, or in *Faustinianus*, Milan, 1610). Frequently there were comic interludes or entr'actes contrasting in mood with the main play; a burlesque of the classic canon is inserted in an anonymous drama at Salamanca, *Comoedia quae inscribitur Margarita*, and in P. Acevedo's *Athanasia* (Seville, 1566) there is a dialogue in Spanish popular verse form between a rustic character and the *Parcae*. In the German Provinces, interludes in German of a character contrasting with the tragedy are found frequently in the later period (as, for example, *Von einem hintergangenen Schornsteinfeger* in a drama, *Felicitas*, at Aachen, 1771).

The rule concerning Latin prevailed in general during the sixteenth century, but with some notable modifications and exceptions. The humanistic trend of the Jesuit system of education, and in particular the regulation that Latin should be the medium of communication between masters and pupils, ensured its general observance; moreover, the models from which most of the plays were derived were Latin. But certain concessions, to the audience if not to the actors, crept in early. The Latin drama by Tuccio, *Christus Judex* (1569), was translated into Italian verse at Bari in 1584; a second translation of 1596 was reprinted at Venice in 1606, and a further much revised version appeared at Rome in 1698. This last translation was adapted into a sacred drama set to music, in three acts with intermezzi, *L'ultima scena del mondo*, in 1721; while a more faithful rendering in Italian prose was made by a Jesuit Father in 1727. A German version of *Christus Judex* was acted at Olmütz in 1603; a Polish one at Warsaw in 1752.

The *tragoediae* produced in the French colleges were generally in Latin, as were most of the comedies—and, as in Italy, not only the language of the dialogue but also the different lyric metres of the choruses followed classical patterns. But as early as 1580, at Pont-à-Mousson, a *Pucelle d'Orléans* is recorded, by P. Fronton du Duc, and there also, a French *Conversion de Saint Ignace* in 1623. P. Le Jay's *Joseph venditus a fratribus* (1698) was translated into French and performed at Paris in 1704. During the seventeenth century, interludes in French became the rule; and in Italy there were plays in Italian. In the eighteenth century, both in France and in Italy, dramas were more frequently written in the native tongue. In the Netherlands likewise exceptions to the rule are recorded; dramas in Flemish were represented at Ghent and Hal in 1640. In that same year, with obvious intention, a tragedy in Spanish, *Joab*, was played by the pupils of the college at Tournai.

In Spain the mixture of Latin and Spanish appears early. Not many of the Jesuit dramas in Spain seem to have been wholly in Latin; some indeed were wholly in Spanish. The mixture conformed to medieval precedents; and it is interesting evidence for the incorporation of indigenous dramatic tradition. A Prologue in Spanish, or in Spanish and Latin (with two 'interpreters'), is sometimes found; in the *Actio quae inscribitur Examen Sacrum* acted in Salamanca in the sixteenth century there is even a discussion, mainly in Spanish, as to the language in which the play should be performed. On occasion, the compromise of a hybrid language was adopted. In the dramatic dialogue, both languages were sometimes used, with the object of distinguishing serious and noble personages from secondary and plebeian characters—again a notable instance of adaptation to a dramatic tradition. Spanish, Italian, and Latin are all used in the drama *San Hermenegildo* represented at Seville in 1591. The earliest well-known Spanish Jesuit dramatist, P. Acevedo, observed in the main the Latin rule; but as early as 1556 the mixture of Latin prose and Spanish verse which was to become the prevalent mode is to be found in his *Metanea*; while in his *Comoedia habita Hispali in feste Corporis Christi* of 1562 the prologue and arguments are translated into Spanish hendecasyllables. Four years later his *Athanasia*, written in Latin prose, had three entr'actes in Spanish verse. The evolution of the Jesuit drama in Spain shows in fact both an early admixture of the vernacular tongue and a progressive diminution of the Latin and learned elements under the influence of the native tradition of drama; in Acevedo's *Bellum virtutum et vitiorum* quintillas and redondillas are to be found; and in the *Tragedia de San Hermenegildo* a great variety of Spanish verse-forms appears.

In the German-speaking lands the process of gradual modification of the Latin rule can also be observed. As early as 1582 a request was made on behalf of Lucerne for a play in German, if necessary a translation of a Latin drama; and the reply gave reluctant consent. In 1588 the Austrian Province was allowed to produce interludes in the vernacular, on condition that no unsuitable buffoonery was admitted. The Rhine Province petitioned in 1600 for a relaxation, which was granted on condition that liberty was sparingly used. At first the relaxation may well have been made in respect of the open-air performances which catered specifically for a mass audience; and only later in respect of the plays acted in the college buildings. Prologues in German, however, were prefixed to each of the five acts of a *Tragœdia de regibus Achab et Jezabel* given at Paderborn in 1604. Gradually the practice grew up of inserting German arias into the Latin text, and plays wholly in German are extant from the end of the seventeenth century (in 1697 a 'musical tragedy' in German, *Julius Maximinus*, was acted at Cologne).

In addition to the lyric airs which were an integral part of the plays in all regions from the beginning, there was a development of the interlude, intermezzo, or other forms of entr'acte which varied in kind and in frequency in different areas. Music and dance formed part of the earliest dramatic performances in the colleges of Spain; *entretenimientos de música y danza* are recorded of the production of the *tragicomoedia* of *Joseph* at Ocaña in 1558. Elsewhere, the intermezzo came to flourish rather later. An intermezzo was given in Scammacca's *Amira* acted at Palermo in 1610 for the festival of St. Ignatius. In France, both intermezzo and ballet became very important elements in the Jesuit drama. The great vogue of dancing at the Court and among the nobility no doubt contributed to the cultivation of the ballet in the dramatic performances of the French Jesuit schools, where young noblemen were being educated. P. Menestrier in 1682 and P. Le Jay in 1725 both wrote important treatises on the ballet; the latter observes that it need not conform to the strict rules of drama, the only requirement being that all its parts should conform to the general idea which is the design of the whole. Thus the ballet rested on allegory; and where there was a link between it and the tragedy the link was one of allegorical interpretation (e.g. a tragedy on the fall of the Assyrian Empire was accompanied by a ballet 'Les Songes', because that fall was predicted in dreams; *Cyrus* was embellished by a ballet on the Empire of the Sun). Sometimes, however, the ballet would be topical; the marriage of Louis XIV in 1660 was the occasion for one entitled 'Mariage du Lys et de l'Impériale'; the Peace of Nijmegen in 1679 was alluded to in a 'Ballet de la Paix'; and Louis le Grand was glorified in many ballets on the stage of the college which came to bear his name. Décor and costumes were of immense importance in these elaborate ballets, and P. Menestrier (*Des ballets anciens et modernes*, Paris, 1682) gives details of the costumes proper to Roman, Greek, Persian, Moorish, Turkish, Saracen, 'American', and Japanese personages, as well as to many allegorical figures. The historical accuracy thus demanded for the ballet at the height of its popularity on the college stages in France was of a piece with the elaborate conditions of décor and production in contemporary opera. The scenery and effects of the theatre at the college of Louis-le-Grand in the seventeenth century are stated to have been considerably more varied and numerous than those of the Théâtre-Français,

even if they fell short of those of the Opéra.

The ballet was of course by no means confined to the French productions. It appears early in the records of performances at Munich (an elaborate one was inserted in the drama *Samson* acted there in 1568), and its popularity is attested in many of the *periochae* of plays in the German Provinces. But it is the parallel with opera, which had begun to penetrate from Italy in the early period of the seventeenth century, that is perhaps most characteristic of the Jesuit drama in South Germany and Austria. In these regions Jesuit plays, operas in the Italian style, and the popular melodramas of the *Englische Komödianten* were all being offered to the public—sometimes side by side. In the year 1608 the Archduke Ferdinand in Graz attended performances both by the pupils of the Jesuit college and by Greene's troupe of English players. In Munich, where Jesuit plays had been acted since 1560, the coincidence of their performance of the music-drama of *Philothea* in 1643 with the building of an opera house in 1657 may be noted. In 1666, at a time when performances of great splendour were being given both at the Court theatre and at the Jesuit college in Vienna, the Imperial opera house was erected.

With equal and characteristic skill, the Jesuit theatre accommodated itself to the mentality of the masses or to the customs of a Court, while consistently pursuing its own purposes. Influences of many kinds thus bore upon its development, and its practitioners sprang from many lands. The works of the Spaniard Pedro de Acevedo (*fl.* 1560), the Italian Stefano Tuccio (1540–97), the German Jakob Bidermann (1578–1639), the Frenchman Nicolas Caussin (1580–1651), the Englishman Joseph Simon (Simeon) writing in Rome (1594–1671), the Austrian Nicolaus Avancinus (1612–86)—to name only a few representative authors of plays—all bear witness to an early expansion and elaboration of the theatrical aspects of drama; the rapid development of the means for change of scene and transformation was matched by the increased variety of visual and musical adornments. As early as 1573, a play on the Last Judgement acted at Rome made so deep an impression with its strange apparitions and fearful vistas of destruction and damnation that it was repeated the next year. A sumptuous décor is recorded of the play of *San Hermenegildo* given at Seville in 1580 to celebrate the solemn opening of the extended college; a great frontispiece represented the city of Seville, with two high towers on each side, one of which served as the Saint's place of imprisonment, the other as a '*castillo de los entretenimientos*'—which appear to have consisted of fireworks and varied mechanical devices. The high degree of technical development reached in the Jesuit theatre in Vienna in the seventeenth century is shown by the nine illustrations to an edition of *Pietas Victrix* by Avancinus (Vienna, 1658). It is clear from these that the play was acted on an elaborate transformation-scene stage. A comparison with the staging of earlier Jesuit plays at the end of the sixteenth century in the German Provinces reveals striking developments in the variety of scene and decoration, and in the possibilities of change of scene within the acts. In 1653, indeed, the stage of the college in Vienna was equipped with seven transformation scenes. The new technical means influenced the structure and composition of the plays themselves; they may well account in part for the prevalence of dream scenes, which could be effectively combined with music, dance, and mechanical effects of all kinds. In its luxuriance of decoration the seventeenth-century Jesuit theatre affords clear evidence of its approximation to contemporary taste; and the influence exerted by its widespread dramatic activities in the development of that taste has come to be recognized. The links with plastic and pictorial art are obvious. It is interesting in this connexion to note the prevalence in the *tragicomoediae* of landscape as well as architectural settings; and the spectacle of the sea in movement, decorated with ships, marine creatures, Naiads, or Tritons, rivalled the effects of fire and lightning, flying machines, and suspense mechanisms which were almost universal in seventeenth-century Jesuit plays. *Dum mare turbatum fremit, et coelum fulminat, apparet Xaverius naufragus* is a stage direction in Avancinus's *Zelus, sive Franciscus Xaverius* (IV, 3); and in the huge drama acted at Lisbon for Philip II of Portugal in 1619, the sea was a constant motif both in the text and in the elaborate décor. In a play produced for the festival of the canonization of St. Ignatius at Pont-à-Mousson in 1623, the figure of the Saint appeared on the stage, and by a sudden transformation changed into a tower, from which fireworks issued. At the end of the play, the Saint appeared above a neighbouring roof and descending, by a mechanism, as if from the sky, set fire to a castle filled with fireworks.

In the course of the seventeenth century, lighting effects were increasingly used. While it seems clear that the plays were most frequently performed in daylight—one or two o'clock in the afternoon was a favourite time for the performances to begin, just after the midday *prandium*—their length frequently made it necessary to conclude them by the light of torches. (The duration seems to have varied from two to seven hours—a regulation for the Rhine Province set a limit of four, but there was no consistent practice in the matter.) Large windows often let in light upon the stage, so that artificial light should not be needed. [Cp. the plan and description of this kind of stage in J. Furtenbach: *Mannhaffter Kunst-Spiegel*, Augsburg 1663, p. 113.] But necessary or not, it was used, and was regarded as an additional attraction to the spectacle. Lighting effects were frequently indicated in the plays; concealed lamps would irradiate the clouds, a 'gloria' would appear in the empyrean, the light of sun, moon, stars, comets would be thrown by mechanical means upon the

stage. Similarly, auditory effects were achieved: thunder and other terrifying noises were used to sharpen the susceptibilities of the audience. Gruesome deeds were not always carried out behind the scenes; in the German-speaking Provinces during the seventeenth century, they more and more frequently became part of the action, thus showing once again the close association of the Jesuit theatre with contemporary customs and taste. In *Judith* dramas, for example, the head of Holofernes was a standing stage effect (in the drama of Avancinus (V, 9) it is a target for the insults of the chorus of Bethulians), and in seventeenth-century Jesuit plays in the German-speaking lands, executions and murders took place upon the stage as they did in the popular dramas of the wandering players. A puppet figure of Jezebel, decked out in realistic detail, was torn to pieces by dogs upon the stage in Graz in 1640. Costumes and stage adornments corresponded in magnificence to the customs of the particular environment—in those cities which were also Court residences, the theatre at the Jesuit college was often the recipient of munificent gifts such as were commonly made at this period to the Court operas and theatres. There were conventional costumes for the different categories of personages, but within this convention the producers aimed at accuracy. The numerous allegorical characters afforded scope for decorative invention; much of the detail was naturally borrowed from contemporary paintings.

The musical element was present in the Jesuit dramas from the beginning, but, like the other embellishments, it grew in importance as the productions became more elaborate. The presence of a chorus, on the classical model, gave rise from the outset to lyric passages which took the form of arias; while the *tableau* or *scena muta*, always a frequent accompaniment to the action, was often suitable for choreographic treatment. The influence of Italian opera can be argued from the inclusion (particularly in South Germany and Austria) of solo singing in the action of the plays. (An Italian *Singspiel*, *Tobias*, is recorded as having been given at the Innsbruck college as early as 1582.) But the powerful tradition of church music in the Order itself must not be forgotten. The songs of the different choruses in the more ambitious plays frequently approximated to the form of cantata or oratorio. They required, in their developed form, the accompaniment of instrumental music, and many of the schools had a school orchestra trained to a high degree of proficiency. At the performance of *Theophilus* in Munich in 1643 there were 32 instrumentalists as well as 40 singers. It is probable that on some occasions professional musicians also assisted in the performances.

The elaborate nature of these arrangements made it necessary to have adequate accommodation for actors and audience alike. In the early period of any given institution, plays were frequently performed in the open—partly, no doubt, in order to attract the mass of spectators so frequently recorded. The splendid *Esther* drama given at Munich in 1577 was acted in the market-place with great magnificence of décor, the play lasted three days and 300 persons took part in it. In Vienna, the court-yard of the college served as stage until 1650, when a large interior theatre and a small rehearsal stage were opened. When an established school gave performances within its own precincts, the accommodation would vary from a simple hall—such as that in the college at Pau, where a curtain was let down to separate the audience from the stage—to such ample provision as the stage in the college at Vienna built on Italian models, or the three separate theatres at the college of Louis-le-Grand. Here there was a large theatre, a smaller theatre for the less important spectacles given in the course of the school year, and finally an interior theatre, used for the plays given in winter and for rehearsals for the grand August performances. At these last there was always a large public audience, with a high proportion of exalted personages. Jean Loret writes in 1651 (*La Muse historique*, II, letter 32):

La Reine et messieurs ses deux fils,
Lundy dernier, à jour préfix,
Allèrent, avec grandes suites,
Au collège des Jézuites,
Pour, sur un téâtre fort beau
Voir un poëme tout nouveau
Que pluzieurs jeunes philozofes,
Vêtus de brillantes étofes,
Reprézentèrent en latin,
Moitié figue, moitié raizin.
On y vit aussi pluzieurs dances,
Balets, postures et cadances,
Où maint fils de prince et seigneur
Y parurent avec honneur. . . .

The same chronicler records two years later that not only Louis XIV and his mother and brother, but also the exiled heir to the English throne, the later Charles II, and the young Duke of Gloucester, were present at the Jesuit play. In addition, he adds, there were many blonde and brunette Court beauties. Eminent personages such as cardinals, legates, and members of other religious orders, were also frequently among the spectators.

In Vienna also the Jesuit plays in the seventeenth century attracted an audience of high rank. Leopold I would be present not only at the grand performances but even at the minor plays, thus attending six or seven performances in the school year. Indeed, the Jesuit theatre during the reigns of Leopold I and Joseph I, and in the early years of Charles VI, fulfilled many of the functions of a Court theatre.

The composition of the audience varied in different regions and periods. Especially in the matter of admitting women to the performances, the practice appears to have been adapted to current social usage. Where there was a Court in residence (or even when members of a Court were passing travellers) its customs were decisive. The visits of the Queen to the performances at Louis-le-Grand clearly were enough to determine the usage in Paris. Elsewhere, the question was variously solved. As early as the late sixteenth century there was a relaxation in the German Provinces—at the discretion of the Superior and if custom demanded it—of the rule prohibiting the attendance of women; and although difficulties frequently arose, this relaxation clearly continued. (In 1680, at Hildesheim, for example, the presence of *viri et foeminae honoratiores* was recorded.) Sometimes the dress rehearsal was turned into a special performance for an audience of women (as at Freiburg in Switzerland in 1644). In the French Provinces at the end of the seventeenth century there seem frequently to have been two performances of the main play of the year, the first for a feminine, the second for a masculine, audience (the programmes of a performance at La Flèche in 1680 refer to this as the established practice).

That the Jesuit form of drama with its peculiar combination of entertainment and moral purpose, of classic pattern and flamboyant execution, was an integral part of the life of a Jesuit school is abundantly clear. But if further evidence were needed, it could be gathered from an examination of the comments that were made upon it within the Order itself, and of the attacks launched against it from without. Protests against luxuriance of décor were made in Spain in the sixteenth century. In the German-speaking Provinces, throughout the seventeenth century, decrees issued at intervals sought to curtail the number and diminish the extravagant splendour of performances; the frequency of these decrees attests the strength of the impulses which they endeavoured to control. The work of the school was said to suffer through the excessive labour and concentration on preparations for acting the plays; the expenditure on production was censured as excessive and unsuitable. (*Pietas Victrix*, for example, in Vienna in 1659, cost between three and four thousand florins—defrayed on this occasion by the Emperor. At the jubilee celebrations in 1640, a great allegorical drama on St. Francis Xavier with many accompaniments of music and pageantry had cost about 13,000 gulden.) In 1714 interludes were forbidden because of their satiric and sometimes unsuitable allusions; in 1770 in Hildesheim a decree prohibited music and dancing. The number of performances had steadily increased, until it was not unusual to have as many as five repetitions of a successful play, or even, on occasion, to arrange for performances to be repeated in other places—as when the Rector and the Professor of Rhetoric at Emmerich took all the actors to Cleves in 1647 to act a play before the Elector of Brandenburg. In France also, the college pupils might be called on to give a performance at Court, or in the house of some great personage, and in the age of Louis XIV the elaborate setting and accompaniments of the plays were in close conformity with prevailing taste. It was perhaps for this reason as well as for others that the opponents of the Jesuits in France seized upon their cult of the theatre and attacked it fiercely. The highly developed ballet in particular was sharply criticized, and plays and ballets alike were severely censured by the University of Paris, and in numerous polemical writings. The attempt to defend and illustrate the theatre in a didactic ballet *L'Homme instruit par les spectacles ou Le Théâtre changé en école de vertu* by P. Charles Porée (Paris, 1726) failed to convince such confirmed opponents; and in 1762, when taking possession of the college after the Jesuits had had to give it up, the Rector of the University openly rejoiced at the cessation of such entertainments.

While controversy was thus acute in France, Jesuit dramatists in Italy during the eighteenth century had fewer rivals. The name *teatro gesuitico* appears indeed to be rather generic than specific; the Jesuit dramas of the period were written in a recognized form—a variant, subject to the general principles and particular dramatic aims of the Jesuit system, of the accepted classical pattern, under the dominant influence of France. The Jesuit authors Giovanni Granelli and Saverio Bettinelli (writing in Italian) have a recognized place among the not over-numerous pseudo-classic dramatists of this period in Italy; the *Sedecia, Manasse, Dione* of the former, the *Demetrio* and *Serse* of the latter certainly enjoyed in their own day great popularity—not only on the scholastic stage—and they find a place in histories of Italian literature.

It is not easy to make any precise estimate of the direct contribution made by the Jesuit cult of the dramatic art to the general development of drama and the theatre in Europe—not easy to determine exactly how far it helped to form taste at any given period, or simply conformed to it and developed it further. In content and form the dramas appear on the whole conservative; though in the matter of the preservation of the unities of time and place, or where they adopt and adapt characteristic features of indigenous drama, they do not in the main follow rigid pseudo-classic conventions. But their prevailingly allegorical form and their consistently didactic purpose perpetuated through two centuries modes of approach to life which secular drama had in many regions abandoned before the first of those centuries had come to an end; and the discouragement of women's parts—even though it was by no means consistent—tended to limit both range of subject and mode of treatment. Yet it was perhaps just the allegorical element in the plays which stimulated advance in another direction. The desire to present abstract conceptions in visually attractive and therefore easily acceptable form was a powerful factor in the development of technical methods of production. And in this aspect of the art of the theatre the Jesuit drama was pre-eminent, its only contemporary rival being the opera. To what degree each of these two forms influenced the other is a question to which different

answers might be given in respect of different countries; but at least their inter-action is clear. Technical devices and elaborate transformations, the development of music and dancing as integral parts of a dramatic whole, were common to both; setting and costume were also of paramount importance in the artistic ensemble. If in Paris the college of Louis-le-Grand provided spectacles which rivalled those of the *Académie de danse* founded by its royal patron, in Vienna during the seventeenth and earlier eighteenth centuries the stage of the Jesuit college was the scene of *ludi caesarii* whose only counterparts in splendour of production were the operas given at the Court theatre. And in the smaller Court cities of the German-speaking lands a similar parallel could be drawn. The music-dramas, cantatas, and oratorios of the Jesuits dating from the first half of the seventeenth century were the forerunners of the cult of opera which developed at the German Courts; opera in its turn suggested some of the more potent scenic and auditory effects of the later Jesuit dramas. At the least, the plays at the Jesuit colleges may be said to have constituted in the seventeenth and early eighteenth centuries a link between opera and drama, and to have furthered technical advances in the production of both. It is of some interest also to note the number of well-known dramatists who were educated in Jesuit schools. Some doubt has been cast, it is true, on statements that Lope de Vega was for a time at the college at Madrid, and that Cervantes studied at Seville when P. Acevedo's plays were being performed there. But Maffei and Goldoni (as well as Tasso) were pupils of the Jesuits, and so were the two brothers Corneille, Molière, the elder Crébillon, Dancourt, Le Sage, and Voltaire. Thomas Corneille acted in a play on Jezebel at the college at Rouen about 1642; Pierre Corneille and Voltaire both received prizes for Latin verse during their school-days, and it is tempting to think that they were rewarded by parts in the Latin play at the prize distribution. Voltaire indeed, in a letter to Dr. Bianchi of 1761, recalled the dramatic performances given by the pupils at the college in Paris as the best thing in the education he received there from the Jesuits.   E. P.

JEVON, THOMAS (?–1688), one of the first English Harlequins, playing the part at Dorset Garden in *The Emperor of the Moon* (1687). He was an excellent dancer, and was credited in a contemporary satire with 'heels of cork and brains of lead'. He wrote a farce, *The Devil of a Wife; or, a Comical Transformation*, which was given at Dorset Garden in 1686 with some success. In 1731 it was made into a three-act play with music as *The Devil to Pay*, and later, curtailed to one act by Theophilus Cibber, it became one of the most popular of English ballad operas.

JEWISH DRAMA. Jewish drama has no territorial limits. Its sole boundaries are linguistic—Hebrew, the historical and religious language which has never ceased to be written and has now been reborn as a living tongue; Yiddish, the vernacular of the vast Jewish communities lying between the Baltic and Black Seas, one which emigrants have spread over the world; and Ladino (Judaeo-Spanish), the speech of the Jews who live round the Aegean Sea. Even the linguistic frontiers are not clearly defined. Israel Zangwill (1864–1926) wrote Jewish plays in English; Alexander Granach (1890–1945) began as a Yiddish actor, won fame in the German theatre, and, after 1933, returned to the Yiddish stage in Poland. Thus any study of Jewish drama must be viewed in the light of the Jewish approach to the theatre in general.

1. THE BACKGROUND. Drama was not indigenous to the Jew. The commandment in Deuteronomy, xxii. 5, 'A man shall not put on a woman's garment', and the connexion between early drama and the rites of idol-worship, were strong arguments against the establishment of a theatre, and were invoked by many leading Jews as late as the nineteenth century. Yet the classical theatre, low as it had fallen by the time the Jew came into contact with Hellenism, exercised an immediate attraction. Jewish actors were found in Rome under the Empire, and Ezekiel of Alexandria, who flourished in the second century A.D., taking Euripides as his model, wrote a Greek tragedy in hexameters on the Exodus, though there is no reason to suppose that this was ever acted or indeed intended for the stage.

2. THE ORIGINS. It was from the Jewish jugglers, dancers, and mimics of the Middle Ages, and from the emphatic intonation of the Cantor and the questions and responses in the Synagogue services, that the Jewish theatre slowly evolved. Itinerant musicians and professional jesters (the badchans of modern Yiddish literature) also played their part in its development. A more serious contribution can be found in the Hebrew philosophical dialogues, dating back to Ibn Ezra (fl. 12th century) and popular down to the end of the eighteenth century—Beer's Conversation of the Spirit of Poverty with that of Good Reputation (1674), Fiammetta's Duet between Grace and Truth (1697), with musical accompaniment, and Norzi's Conversation with Death (1800).

The travelling minstrels were much in demand at Jewish festivals, and by the fifteenth century their vernacular songs were already being dramatized under the influence of German Court drama and the plays of the Nuremberg Mastersingers. Typical examples are The Play of the Devil, the Doctor and the Apothecary, the farce A Play of Food- and Drink-loving Youth, and a fragment of a burlesque, The Beggar's Wedding. Philosophical dialogues, after the style of those mentioned above, were performed in the vernacular, and religious plays appeared, on such subjects as Adam and Eve, the sacrifice of Isaac, or the death of Moses, modelled on the lines of the South German Carnival play. The earliest extant manuscript of such a play

is one on the Prophet Jonah, based on a similar work by the Mastersingers Simon Rothen and Balthasar Klein, and dating from 1582.

Play-acting at festivals gradually centred on Purim, the holiday observed on 14 Adar (very roughly about early March) to celebrate the events recorded in the Book of Esther—the downfall of the anti-Semite Haman through the intercession of Queen Esther. The plays given then (for further details see PURIM PLAYS), with their set plots, costumes, and characters, continue to the present day. Their extensive use of interpolated songs, and their mixture of tradition and improvisation, provide elements which can be traced in contemporary Jewish drama.

3. EARLY HEBREW DRAMA. Yiddish drama was born in Germany, Hebrew in Italy and among the Spanish Jews in Holland. The first Hebrew play was The Comedy of a Marriage, ascribed to Leone de Somi (1527–92), which shows very clearly the influence of the commedia dell' arte; the dramatis personae consist of the pining lover, his beloved, her crafty maid, the broad-humoured servant, and the unscrupulous lawyer. The introduction to the earliest extant manuscript (1618) states that the play was intended for presentation at Purim.

It was, however, in Amsterdam, in the early seventeenth century, that Hebrew drama first became established. Marrano refugees filled the city, and their leaders saw in the drama one way of restoring their self-respect. They knew no Dutch, and Spanish was suspect in recently liberated Holland. The medium of the new drama had therefore to be Hebrew. Its content was borrowed from the religious plays of the Dutch dramatist Joost van Vondel, its form from the comedia and auto of Lope de Vega and Calderón. It was the use of the auto which permitted the dramatization of the allegory inherent in the philosophical dialogues referred to above.

Throughout the whole of the seventeenth and eighteenth centuries the Dutch and Italian communities were closely connected. Yesod Olam, an auto by Moses Zacuto (1625–97), an Amsterdam Kabbalist, may have been performed in Italy, where Jewish actors could be found. It describes Abraham's rescue by an angel from the furnace into which he had been thrown after destroying his father's idols, and shows strongly the influence of van Vondel. Zacuto's Tuftei Olam, a mystery-play dealing with a journey to the next world, was certainly acted by synagogue worshippers in Ferrara about 1700. It was imitated by Jacob Olmo (1690–1755) in his Eden Aruch about 1720. The first Hebrew play to be printed was a Morality play by Joseph Penço de la Vega (1650–1703), Asiré Hatiqva, published in 1673 at Amsterdam, and reprinted at Leghorn in 1770. In it a serious-minded king is led astray by Satan, by his wife, and by his passions; his reason and an angel guide him back to virtue. Songs are included in this play, which is believed to have been intended for a festivity at a religious school.

Moses Hazim Luzzatto (1707–47), the out-standing figure of the period, was an Italian Jew resident in Amsterdam. His *Migdal Oz* (1727), a pastoral play in four acts modelled on Guarini's *Pastor Fido*, compares the Law of Moses to a king's daughter who, hidden in a strong tower (the Migdal Oz of the title), shows herself only to her lover. The language and style of this drama, written for his uncle's wedding, have placed Luzzatto among the great Hebrew poets. His other important play, *Tehilla Leyisharim* (pub. 1743), written for the marriage of one of his pupils, tells how Pride tries, with the help of Falsehood, to win Praise (Tehilla), who, however, weds Righteousness. Luzzatto was also the author of a third play, dating from 1724, which deals with Samson among the Philistines, and of a book of gram-mar in which he devotes a section to the defini-tion of drama—an early attempt at dramatic criticism.

Eighteenth-century Italy saw a great increase in the number of Hebrew playwrights. Samuel Romanelli of Mantua (1757–1814) translated the works of several Italian authors, including Metastasio, and took the plots of his own plays from Ovid. There was a general tendency to utilize classical mythology under Hebrew names. But in spite of the increased output plays were still performed only on religious holidays and on special occasions. The wide-spread imitation of outside sources did not result in the establishment of a permanent theatre, and drama in general remained a literary exercise remote from stage presenta-tion.

4. THE HASKALA (ENLIGHTENMENT) MOVE-MENT. As a result of the period of religious tolerance which followed the Thirty Years War, the German Jews were able to enjoy a fairly normal life. This fostered the rise of the Haskala Movement in the second half of the eighteenth century, under the influence of the German-Jewish philosopher Moses Mendels-sohn. It aimed at introducing the Jew to the language, literature, and science of other nations, while stimulating a revival of his own culture. The principles of the Haskala Move-ment spread eastward slowly, reaching the more remote regions only in the second half of the nineteenth century, and for over a hundred years provided the dominating feature in the history of Central and Eastern European Jewry.

One of the results of the movement was a renewed interest in the writing of Hebrew plays. Imitations of Luzzatto are to be found in such works as *Yaldut Ubahrut*, by Menahem Mendel Bresselau (1760–1827), written in 1786 for performance at a Barmitzva (or confirma-tion), and in *Amal and Tirza* (1812), written by Shalom Cohen (1772–1845) for a wedding. Knowledge of the drama was also increased by translations. Racine's *Esther* and *Athalie* were frequently translated, both on account of their subjects and because the choral structure of the plays appealed to the Jewish love for com-bined dialogue and song. Goethe's *Faust*, and the plays of Schiller and Lessing, were also drawn on, as were those of Metastasio, Molière, and others. Even Shakespeare was imitated by Joseph Ephrati of Toplowitz (1770–1840) in his *Reign of Saul*, which, first published in 1794, was often reprinted.

These plays were, however, mainly intended for reading or occasional private performance. The day of the Hebrew theatre had not yet dawned, and the Yiddish theatre was destined to be established first, mainly in an attempt to check the growing vulgarity of the Purim play. Two of these early Yiddish plays were written by followers of Moses Mendelssohn in Ger-many: *Reb Henoch* (c. 1793), by Isaac Eichel (1756–1804), and *Leichtsin und Fremmelai* (1796), by Ahron Halle [Wolfsohn] (1754–1835); others by Joseph Biedermann (1800–?) in Vienna, where they were performed by amateurs about 1850. But they flourished best in Russia, with such writers as Israel Axenfeld (c. 1795–1868), Solomon Ettinger (c. 1803–56), whose *Serkele*, written in about 1825, long remained popular, Abraham Ber Gottlober (1811–99), and Ludwig Levinsohn (1842–1904).

5. THE PERMANENT YIDDISH THEATRE. While the above playwrights were laying the foundations of a Yiddish repertory, an audience for the future theatre was being created by the Brody Singers, wandering musicians who took their name from the Polish town of Brody. These lineal descendants of the medieval pro-fessional jesters became extremely popular in Galicia and the Carpathians about 1850, and during the next twenty years evolved a new type of entertainment, with popular comic and sentimental Yiddish songs linked by dialogue and dance, evolving finally into one-act sketches. They provided almost all the theatri-cal entertainment available until in 1876 Abraham Goldfaden (1840–1908) founded the first permanent Yiddish theatre. The date is usually given as between 5 and 8 October, when, with the help of two Brody Singers, he presented a two-act musical sketch in a tavern in Jassy. Its title, if it ever had one, has not been preserved. Its songs were written by Goldfaden, who also provided the scenario on which the actors improvised their dialogue. From these humble beginnings the new theatre progressed rapidly. Goldfaden, who was actor, dramatist, song-writer, producer, and manager, enlarged his company, trained his actors, em-ployed women on the stage for the first time in Jewish history, and from the slight skits of his early days passed to the writing of full-length plays, some of which—*The Witch* (1879), *The Two Kune Lemels*, and the histori-cal drama *Shulamit* (both 1880)—still remain in the repertory of the Yiddish theatre. He gave his audiences what they wanted, and what they could at that time assimilate—a mixture of song and Purim play, with plots and music borrowed from all over Europe, racy dialogue and broad characterization, much action and little analysis. He lacked what the established theatres of Europe could have given him—

training, tradition, and experience—and much of his undoubted genius was wasted in the struggle to establish and maintain a theatre under primitive conditions. This he did, in the teeth of all opposition, and even raised up rivals in his own field. While he was in Bucharest, the Russian headquarters during the Russo-Turkish War, one of his original actors, Israel Gradner, broke away and established his own company. Its playwright was Joseph Lateiner (1853–1935), who was later to be one of the founders of a Yiddish theatre in New York. Another troupe formed at this time found a playwright in Moses Hurwitch (1844–1910), who also emigrated to New York. In Odessa, where Goldfaden went at the end of the war in 1879, his plays were considered too rough by the more sophisticated members of the Jewish community, to whom the theatre was no novelty, and they found a more congenial playwright in Joseph Yehuda Lerner (c. 1849–1907). He sought his material in non-Jewish works dealing with Jewish heroes, and is chiefly remembered for his translation into Yiddish of *Uriel Acosta*, by Karl Ferdinand Gutzkow (1811–78).

All this activity was brought to a sudden close by the anti-Semitic measures taken in Russia after the assassination of the Tsar Alexander II. In September 1883 all plays in Yiddish were expressly forbidden, and the Yiddish theatre existed precariously until the Revolution of 1917. Many actors and dramatists left the country for England and America, and New York became the centre of Yiddish drama. The first attempt at its establishment there was made by Boris Thomashefsky (1886–1939), and it found its feet with the arrival of Lateiner and Hurwitch, both prolific but unoriginal dramatists, under whom the Yiddish theatre lost much of the ground it had gained in Russia. Playing mainly to a bewildered and illiterate immigrant audience, it tended to rely on the stock themes of the old Jewish life in Europe, which became increasingly out-moded as americanization proceeded, as did the alternation of broad farce and sentimental melodrama which had proved acceptable in the early days of immigration. Even Goldfaden, who had emigrated to New York in 1887, found himself out of touch with the new régime, and it was left to a new dramatist, Jacob Gordin (1853–1909), to revitalize the American Yiddish theatre. Realizing that its weak point was the use of unsuitable material, he endeavoured to broaden its outlook by free adaptations, into Jewish terms, of the plays of the great European dramatists from Shakespeare to Ibsen. He also tried to raise the standards of the Yiddish stage by discouraging improvisation and insisting on respect for the dramatist's text as given to the actors. Among his many plays the best known are his *Jewish King Lear* (1892), *Mirele Efros* (1898), a feminine pendant to Lear, and *God, Man and Devil* (1900), based on Goethe's *Faust*. Gordin has been criticized for failing to make his plays Jewish in spirit as well as in setting, but his

work is important in the development of the Yiddish theatre in America. Among those who followed him in the path of social drama, concerned mainly with the breakdown of the traditional Jewish family, may be mentioned Leo Kobrin (1872–   ), whose *Riverside Drive* was produced by Maurice Schwartz in 1927, and Solomon Libin (1872–   ), author of some fifty plays dealing with the life of the immigrant Jewish worker in New York, of which *Broken Hearts* (1903) was the most successful.

6. THE ART THEATRE PERIOD. Meanwhile in Europe the Yiddish theatre had been making headway. In 1907 Max Reinhardt's production of *Gott der Rache*—a German translation of *God of Vengeance* by Sholom Asch (1880–   ) —and of one of the plays of David Pinsky (1872–   )—later done as *The Treasure* by the New York Theatre Guild—had called the attention of the general theatre public to the possibilities of Yiddish drama. The Russian ban on plays in Yiddish had been relaxed in 1908, thus enabling the dramatist Peretz Hirschbein (1881–1949) to found in Odessa the first Yiddish Art Theatre for the production of his own and other plays, notably those of Gordin, Asch, and Isaac Loeb Peretz (1852–1915), poet and symbolist, and author of a number of one-act sketches which have proved very successful on the stage.

Hirschbein's venture failed after two years, but it was not forgotten, and early in 1916 the Vilna Troupe, founded by David Hermann (1876–1930), endeavoured to carry on his ideas. Like Hirschbein, Hermann was preoccupied with folk-drama—Jewish themes treated in a Jewish spirit, as with Sholom Asch—and respected the printed word, without improvisation. The acting of his young company was influenced by the methods of Stanislavsky; but much of its initial success was doubtless due to the fact that it was working in harmony with a Yiddish background, and not against an alien one, as in America. When the Vilna Troupe finally split, one section remained in Europe with Hermann, while the other went to New York. There it associated itself with Maurice Schwartz (1888–   ), who in 1905 had emerged from an amateur dramatic society to reform and refashion the New York Yiddish theatre, then at a low ebb. Entirely ignorant of theatre management and production, he started once again from the popular theatre. The turning-point in his career came when he first encountered the idyllic folk-romances of Hirschbein, but his greatest discovery was the work of Sholom Aleichem (1859–1916), the quintessence of Jewish folk-humour and characterization. Schwartz also introduced to the stage the works of Ossip Dymov (1878–   ), author of *Bronx Express* (1919), of Moses Nadir (1885–1943), author of *The Last Jew* (1919), and of Halper Levick (1888–   ), considered by some critics the outstanding Yiddish literary figure of modern America. Some of his most important plays are *The Golem*, which has been played in Hebrew, Yiddish,

Polish, and English (as *Poet Lore*), and made the basis of an oratorio; and his social dramas, *Rags* (1921), *Shop* (1926), and *Chains* (1930). In 1945 he produced his *Miracle of the Warsaw Ghetto*, which dealt with the struggle of the Polish Jews against the Nazis.

Schwartz's example brought into being other smaller Art Theatres, including that of Rudolf Schildkraut (1862–1930), founded in 1925; Our Theatre, founded in the same year; the New York Dramatic Troupe of 1934; and the workmen's studio, Artef, which adopted the methods of the Jewish State Theatre in Moscow (see below), and staged works by Soviet-Jewish writers. Wherever young actors have been able to provide topical ideas there has been a temporary revival of the American Yiddish theatre, but the widespread adoption of English in Yiddish homes and the slackening in immigration are potent factors in its continued decline. Schwartz's efforts to enlarge his repertory by playing European classics in Yiddish, which took him from Second Avenue to Broadway, was not successful; nor was his playing of Yiddish plays in English.

The third important Yiddish Art Theatre (the other two being the Vilna Troupe's and Schwartz's) is the Moscow State Jewish Theatre, known in Yiddish as the Melucha Teater, and in Russian as Goset. Its first director was Alexander Granovsky (1890–1937), and, like the Vilna Troupe and Maurice Schwartz, it found its most suitable material in the plays of Sholom Aleichem. Granovsky reintroduced the *commedia dell' arte* methods of improvisation, adapting tales of Jewish life in the Ukrainian villages to the current Soviet doctrines without losing touch with the work of such modern producers as Meyerhold. In 1927, when new trends of political thought in Russia affected literature and drama equally, Granovsky's leading actor, Salomon Mikhoels (1890–1948), became director of the theatre. He continued much of Granovsky's work, but also produced a number of new plays including those of David Bergelson (1884–   ) and Peretz Markish (1895–   ).

7. THE NEW HEBREW THEATRE. The popularity of the Yiddish theatre among the Jewish masses made it clear that the revival of spoken Hebrew aimed at by Zionism could be encouraged by the provision of a permanent company for the production of plays in Hebrew. In 1907 Isaac Katzenelson (1886–c. 1941) founded a Hebrew theatre in Warsaw, followed by that of Nahum Zemach (1887–1939), which functioned in Bialystok from 1911 to 1914. Already suggestions were being made for the provision of drama for the infant communities in Palestine, and in 1917 the Habima (*habima* meaning stage) was founded in Moscow with the intention of transferring eventually to Palestine. Its first three productions were *The Eternal Jew*, *The Golem*, and *The Dybbuk*. This last, by Solomon Ansky (1863–1920), had already been given in Yiddish by the Vilna Troupe, and served more than anything else to set the Habima style. It

was produced by Vakhtangov, Stanislavsky's assistant, who was in charge of the training of Habima, with décor by Nathan Altman, Granovsky's scenic designer.

It was 1928 before Habima first appeared in Palestine, and efforts had already been made to found a theatre there. Plays had been produced by Menahem Gnessin (1882–   ), one of the original members of the Warsaw and Bialystok Hebrew companies, and later a member of Habima. Isaac Daniel (1895–   ) had also, with very limited resources, been active on lines suggested by Reinhardt and the French stage. And in 1926 the Ohel (or Tent) Theatre, established in 1925, had begun giving public performances.

Since 1928 the development of the Hebrew theatre has been confined to Palestine, where, in the absence of a repertory—the old Hebrew plays being useless for a modern audience—it made its mark originally as a theatre of production. By moving to Palestine (now Israel) it acquired a territorial background and a positive line of development based on composite Jewish elements from the whole world. There were thus three principal companies, Ohel, Habima, and the Chamber Theatre. All encouraged original work, which, though popular, often suffered from technical inexperience and from the lack of an objective viewpoint.

8. OTHER JEWISH THEATRES. The Ladino-speaking Jews emigrated from Spain after the first expulsion of 1491, before the Golden Age of Lope de Vega and Calderón. Consequently they had no dramatic tradition, nor did they achieve one. Purim and other festival plays appear to have been performed for popular amusement, but no records were kept. In modern times there has been a certain amount of printed drama—the poetical plays of Yakim Behar, the one-act comedies of Alexander Ben Giyat, and a fantasy and two biblical plays, on Deborah and Jephthah respectively, by Joseph Jaen. Where plays have actually been performed, it has always been by amateurs, mostly at Salonica. There are translations in Ladino of some European classics, including *Le Malade imaginaire* and *Esther*, and two versions of Sholom Aleichem's *Mazal Tov*.

The Argentine, home of a large Jewish community, has two permanent Yiddish theatres in Buenos Aires. London, which had its first Yiddish theatre in 1888, now has two, both in Whitechapel. The New Jewish, founded in 1943 on a non-profit-making basis, has been recognized by the Arts Council. Its repertory consists of the Yiddish classics. Paris, where Goldfaden founded a company in 1890, with Anna Held (1865–1918) as its leading lady, now has a company which plays the more popular operettas from the New York Yiddish stage, giving one performance a week of a different work each time. Poland, scene of the activities of the Vilna Troupe, has always maintained a Yiddish theatre. Its present one, the Jewish Miniature Theatre, usually known as Mikkt, was evacuated to Russia in 1941, and became part of the Moscow State Jewish Theatre (as did the Yiddish theatres of the Baltic States after the war). In 1945 it returned to Poland, and a year later toured Germany. Vienna, home of the Biedermann theatre, has had several notable companies, including the Free Jewish Folk Theatre, which flourished from 1918–19. It worked on the lines of the Vilna Troupe, under two directors, I. Deutsch and E. Brecher. The latter later organized the Jewish Ensemble Art Theatre in New York.

E. H.

JIG, an Elizabethan after-piece, given in the public theatres only, consisting of a rhymed farce, sung and danced by three or four characters, of whom the clown was usually one. The best-known exponents of the jig are Tarleton and Kempe. The songs were sung to existing popular tunes, and the subject-matter was often libellous or lewd. The jig disappeared from the legitimate theatre with the Restoration, but remained in the repertory of strolling players and actors in fair-booths, while it became increasingly popular in Germany from the late sixteenth century onwards, being taken there by the various companies of English comedians who toured the continent. Some critics have inclined to see in it a formative element in the development of the German *Singspiel*, as well as in the English ballad opera.

JIM CROW, see RICE, T. D.

JODELET [JULIEN BEDEAU] (c. 1600–60), a French comedian who was in the company of Montdory shortly before the opening of the Théâtre du Marais. With several of his companions he was transferred by Louis XIII to the Hôtel de Bourgogne, but at some point he returned to the Marais, since he played Cliton in *Le Menteur* (1643) and its sequel. He then appeared in a series of farces written for him, mostly with his name in the title—as *Jodelet, ou le maître-valet, Jodelet duelliste, Jodelet astrologue*. He was extremely popular, and had only to show his flour-whitened face to raise a laugh, while he frequently added gags of his own to the author's lines. When Molière first established himself in Paris he induced Jodelet to join him at the Palais-Royal, thus assuring the co-operation of the one comedian whose rivalry he had reason to fear, and gave him the part of the valet in *Les Précieuses ridicules*. He may have intended the role of Sganarelle in his next play for Jodelet, but unfortunately the comedian died before its production, and Molière took the part himself. Jodelet's brother was also an actor, and was usually to be found in the same company (see ESPY).

JODELLE, ÉTIENNE (1532–73), French Renaissance writer, and a member of the famous Pléiade to which Ronsard belonged. He was intended for the army, but escaped, and divided his time equally between pleasure and literature. His *Cléopâtre captive* was the first French tragedy to be constructed on classical lines. Together with a comedy, also on a classical model, it was given before Henri II and his Court in 1552, with Jodelle, not yet 21, as Cleopatra. Remi Belleau, Jean de la Péruse, and other distinguished amateurs were also in the cast. It was a great success, and was subsequently given by a professional company at the Hôtel de Bourgogne, as were some later plays of which only *Didon* (1558) survives. The Pléiade, overjoyed at the dramatic success of one of its members, organized a festival in Jodelle's honour, at which he was presented with a goat garlanded with ivy. The Church, suspecting nameless orgies, took umbrage at this revival of paganism, and Jodelle bore the brunt of its displeasure. He died in poverty, having successfully blazed the trail for Corneille and Racine.

JODRELL THEATRE, LONDON, see KINGS-WAY THEATRE.

JOG, the American term for the narrow flat used in a Box Set to produce a 'return' or break.

JOHN GOLDEN THEATRE, NEW YORK, Built by the Chanins as the Masque Theatre, this opened on 24 Feb. 1927 with a translation of an Italian play which had only 12 performances. It was at this theatre that on 4 Dec. 1933 *Tobacco Road* had its first night in New York. It was transferred to another theatre for its record run, and in 1937 John Golden took over the theatre, named it after himself, and opened with *And Now Good-bye*. Success eluded him until 1938, when Carroll's *Shadow and Substance* won the Critics' Prize for the most distinguished foreign play of the season. This intensely moving drama of the Catholic faith had Cedric Hardwicke, Sara Allgood, and many other fine actors in its cast, and set up a record for the house of 274 performances.

G. F.

For an earlier John Golden Theatre, see CONCERT THEATRE.

JOHNSON, ELIZABETH (*fl.* 1790–1810), American actress, who made her first appearance in Boston in 1795 with the American Company, and went with them to the John Street Theatre, New York, the following year. A tall, elegant woman, she played Rosalind on the opening night of the Park Theatre, and was later seen as Juliet and Imogen to the Romeo and Iachimo of Cooper. In 1798 she appeared in London, but returned to the Park Theatre in 1802, and made a great success in fashionable ladies of high comedy, quite ousting Mrs. Whitlock, who had joined the company in her absence. Among her best parts were Lady Teazle, Beatrice, Rosalind, and Imogen. She was one of the first actresses in New York to play male parts seriously, appearing in 1804 as Young Norval. Her husband, John, was a good utility actor, specializing in old men, and he was for a short time joint manager of the Park, where his daughter Ellen, later the charming Mrs. Hilson, made her first appearance as a child of 5.

JOHNSON, Dr. Samuel (1709–84), the great English lexicographer, was the author of a five-act tragedy *Irene*, which his friend and fellow townsman David Garrick produced at Drury Lane in 1749, with little success. After its failure Johnson never again essayed the stage, though he made more money from the proceeds of the third, sixth, and ninth nights of his play than by anything he had previously done. His edition of Shakespeare is valuable for the light it throws on the editor rather than on the author, since Johnson had little knowledge of Elizabethan drama or stage conditions, and was not temperamentally a research worker. He should not be confused with Samuel Johnson of Cheshire, author of *Hurlothrumbo* (1729) and other burlesques.

JOHNSTON, Henry Erskine (1777–1845), English actor, who at 17 played Hamlet, with no training and no previous experience, at the Theatre Royal, Edinburgh. He then created a profound sensation as Young Norval, and was called the Scottish Roscius; unqualified adulation, which he had done little to deserve, much of his success being due to his youth and beauty, turned his head, and he suffered in after life from an excess of complacency. This prevented him from taking his work seriously, and he relied almost entirely on his external abilities to carry him through his parts. Leigh Hunt, who regretted seeing his good qualities going to waste, said of him that he was 'always on stilts'. He went to Covent Garden in 1797 and was the original Henry in *Speed the Plough* and Ronaldi in *A Tale of Mystery*. He was at his best in melodrama, where his graceful and effective acting made up for his lack of intelligence and humility.

JOHNSTON, (William) Denis (1901–   ), Irish dramatist of originality and versatility whose work has been received with interest in Ireland, England, and America. He is equally at home in direct delineation of character, essentially and distinctively Irish, the analysis of the conflicting moods of a difficult transition period (the years succeeding the war of 1922–3), and in the revelation of the more obscure territories of the mind bordering upon the unconscious, after the manner of Toller, Kaiser, and their forerunners. He has produced a good many plays, continental and American, in Dublin and was at one time a director of the Dublin Gate Theatre (see IRELAND, 2). He has also written much broadcast drama and was well known as a war correspondent.

The first of his plays to be produced, *The Old Lady Says No!* (1929), is a satiric review of certain dominant elements in Irish life, thought, political history, and literature, and an acute exposure of the sentimentality inherent in some of them. The author has said that, for a non-Irish audience, the play 'requires in a sense to be translated', but this in fact cannot be done, for it is not knowledge of fact but association that is required to appreciate the significance of the social criticism in its rapid allusions. His second play, *The Moon in the Yellow River* (1931), earned wide popularity for the richness of its characters and the preciseness with which the author has diagnosed the mood of the middle nineteen-twenties in Ireland. Though much of the material is so recent as to be used here for the first time, there is mastery and harmony in form and grouping. In *A Bride for the Unicorn* (1933) he produced one of the most original pieces of dramatic technique in modern English. The play, as he expressly states, is 'not an expressionist or constructivist drama'. If it suggests a preceding dramatist at all, it is Strindberg at the period of *The Dream Play*, but in general it appears rather to carry dramatic technique towards that of music. *Storm Song* (1934) is, like *The Moon in the Yellow River*, a straightforward play on an original theme. His later plays are *The Golden Cuckoo* (1939) and *The Dreaming Dust* (1940), to which must be added *Blind Man's Buff* (1936), from Toller's *Die Blinde Göttin*.   U. E.-F.

JOHN STREET THEATRE, the first permanent playhouse of New York. It was opened by David Douglass in Dec. 1767, and is described in some detail by Dunlap in his *History of the American Stage*, where he says that its stage was equal in size to that of the Haymarket, London, under Colman. There is extant a print of the theatre dated 1791, now known to be a forgery. There is also a reference to it in *The Contrast*, performed at the John Street Theatre in 1787, where Jonathan, the country bumpkin, describes his first visit to the playhouse.

The first play to be given at the John Street Theatre was *The Beaux' Stratagem*, with the younger Hallam as Archer and John Henry, making his first appearance in New York, as Aimwell. Up to the outbreak of the War of Independence the theatre was used intermittently for winter seasons by the old American Company under Douglass, and saw the first productions in New York of such plays as *The Merchant of Venice*, *Macbeth*, *King John*, *Every Man in His Humour*, and *All for Love*, as well as a large repertory of contemporary plays and after-pieces. During the war the playhouse was rechristened Theatre Royal, and was used for productions by the officers of the English garrison, among them Major John André—later the subject of a play by Dunlap—whose scene-painting was much admired. Just before the British evacuated New York a professional company under Dennis Ryan came from Baltimore and stayed for a time at the John Street Theatre, but without much success.

Two years after the British evacuation, in 1785, the American Company, now under the control of the younger Hallam and John Henry, returned to New York and took possession of the theatre again. The company was shortly afterwards reinforced by Thomas Wignell and the second wife of Owen Morris, who proved herself a fine actress. During the next few years the company gave regular seasons, and produced for the first time in New York *The School for Scandal*, *The Critic*, *Much Ado About Nothing*, and *As You Like It*. This theatre also saw the first productions of two works important in the history of the American drama—Royall Tyler's *The Contrast* (1787) and Dunlap's *The Father; or, American Shandyism* (1789). The American Company also gave a performance of Garrick's version of *Hamlet*, omitting the Grave-diggers and Osric, which had been done in London in 1772, but dropped after Garrick's death. Washington, who was fond of the theatre, visited John Street three times in the year of his inauguration (1789). On 6 May he saw *The School for Scandal* and a popular farce entitled *The Poor Soldier*, in which Wignell was much applauded as Darby; on 5 June he saw *The Clandestine Marriage*; and on 24 Nov. he attended Wignell's benefit night, and heard himself alluded to on the stage in *Darby's Return* by Dunlap.

After this Wignell and Mrs. Morris left the company to found one of their own (see CHESTNUT STREET THEATRE), and when the American Company returned to the John Street Theatre in 1791 a new period in its history was inaugurated with the arrival of John Hodgkinson. This actor, fresh from England, soon became so popular, and so grasping, that he ousted both Hallam and Henry from management and from the affections of the public. Henry and his wife withdrew from the company in 1794, Hallam in 1797, leaving Hodgkinson in command with Dunlap, who had been added to the management in 1796. The previous year had seen the first appearance with the company of the first Joseph Jefferson, who remained until 1803, when he went to Philadelphia.

In the autumn of 1797 Sollee, a theatre manager of Boston and Philadelphia, rented the John Street Theatre, and there entered on an intense rivalry with Wignell's company from Philadelphia, established for a season in Ricketts's Circus. In the company were Miss Arnold, later the mother of Edgar Allan Poe, and Mrs. Whitlock, sister of Sarah Siddons. In spite of this, the season was not a success, and the old company returned while waiting to move into their new Park Theatre, built by Dunlap. The theatre was used for the last time on 13 Jan. 1798, and was later sold by Hallam for £115.

JOLLY, GEORGE (*fl.* 1640–73), English actor, the last of the English strolling players who exerted so great an influence on the German theatre (see ENGLISH COMEDIANS). An entry in the St. Giles's register of the birth and death of his son John in 1640 suggests that he may have been employed at the Fortune Theatre near by, where Prince Charles's Men were playing at that time, and it is possible that he was apprenticed to Matthew Smith, one of their outstanding members. He was certainly in Germany in 1648, and may have gone there earlier to escape the rigours of the Commonwealth. He was particularly active in

Frankfurt, where Prince Charles (later Charles II) probably saw him act. He appears to have anticipated Davenant's use of music and scenery on the public stage, and already had women in his company in 1654. He returned to England at the Restoration, and in spite of the monopoly granted to Killigrew and Davenant, got permission to open a theatre. He went to the Cockpit, where the French theatre historian Chappuzeau saw him in 1665, but by some chicanery on the part of Davenant and Killigrew he was deprived of his patent, and had to content himself with the overseeing of their training school for young actors, the Nursery.

JOLSON THEATRE, NEW YORK, see CENTURY THEATRE (2).

JONES, HENRY ARTHUR (1851–1929), English dramatist, born at Grandborough, Buckingham, the eldest son of a farmer of Welsh descent. At the age of 12 he was sent to work in a draper's shop kept by his uncle at Ramsgate. Six years later, after a spell with another draper at Gravesend, he found employment in a London warehouse, and subsequently became for ten years a commercial traveller in the London, Exeter, and Bradford districts, his leisure being devoted to private study and widely varied reading. After the rejection of several one-act plays as well as a novel, Jones's *It's Only Round the Corner* was performed at the Theatre Royal, Exeter, in Dec. 1878. Thus encouraged, he abandoned business for playwriting, and on 16 Oct. in the next year *A Clerical Error* was put on at the Court Theatre in London by Wilson Barrett, who afterwards found one of his most successful parts in Wilfred Denver in *The Silver King* by Jones and Henry Herman, produced at the Princess's on 16 Nov. 1882. The run of 289 performances of that melodrama established Jones's reputation. He then turned to plays with a more serious intention, but there continued to be a strong melodramatic current in his work, even though his contemporaries accepted him as one of the new school of dramatists who in the closing decades of the century were propagating the drama of ideas and using the stage as a platform for social criticism. Among Jones's very numerous pieces, public attention was attracted chiefly by *Saints and Sinners* (1884), *The Dancing Girl* (1891), *The Case of Rebellious Susan* (1894), *The Triumph of the Philistines* (1895), *Michael and His Lost Angel* (1896), *The Liars* (1897), and *Mrs. Dane's Defence* (1900). Beerbohm Tree, Charles Wyndham, Forbes-Robertson, George Alexander, Fred Terry, Marion Terry, Violet Vanbrugh, Julia Neilson, and Sybil Thorndike appeared with success in first productions and revivals of Jones's works. The withdrawal of Mrs. Patrick Campbell from the role of Audrie Lesden before the opening performance at the Lyceum on 15 Jan. 1896 of *Michael and His Lost Angel* was symptomatic of the wide antagonism provoked by that play, which was withdrawn after ten performances, mainly on account of the church scene in which the priest, standing before the altar, makes public confession of adultery, after having some years before exacted a similar penance from a girl member of his congregation.

With Pinero and Bernard Shaw, Henry Arthur Jones was one of the three most considerable playwrights in the period when Ibsen's influence was penetrating the English theatre, but there is no reason to doubt Jones's insistence that he was not a conscious disciple of Ibsen. Ibsenism was in the air and established a climate of opinion to which all serious and would-be serious playwrights were susceptible through either attraction or repulsion. Though Shaw praised Jones at the expense of Pinero in the 1890s, on the ground that he drew faithful portraits of men and women in society whereas Pinero merely flattered them with reflections of their own imaginings, the verdict of time on Jones's plays has been harder. His exceptional skill in naturalistic dialogue and in the creation of dramatic tension remains impressive (in these respects Act III of *Mrs. Dane's Defence* is a classic fragment), but his social and moral criticism lacked a firm philosophical basis. Towards the end of his life he ventured rashly upon sustained controversy with Bernard Shaw and H. G. Wells. He was also the author of *The Renaissance of the English Drama* (1895), *Foundations of a National Drama* (1913), and *The Theatre of Ideas* (1915).

JONES, INIGO (1573–1652), English architect and artist, and the first to be associated with scenic decoration in England. Before his day the designing and decorating of Court masques had pertained to the Office of the Revels, who employed for the purpose any artist who happened to be about the Court. Jones, having studied in Italy and worked in Denmark, was in 1604–5 attached to the household of Prince Henry, and, in addition to his work as an architect, took entire control of the masques. Of the thirteen given at Court from 1605 to 1613, nine were certainly of his devising, the others probably, the first being Jonson's *Mask of Blackness*. He was also in charge of the plays given at Oxford in Christ Church Hall in Aug. 1605, where he first used revolving screens in the Italian manner. He later used as many as five changes of scenery, with backcloths, shutters, or flats painted and arranged in perspective. These ran in grooves and were supplemented by a turn-table (*machina versatilis*) which presented to the audience different facets of a solid structure. Jones also introduced to England the picture-stage framed in the proscenium arch. His increasing power and responsibility brought him into conflict with the Court poets, particularly Jonson, who satirized him in many of his plays. The smouldering hostility between them broke out under Charles I. During the Civil War Jones was heavily fined, fell out of favour, and died in poverty. Many of his designs have been preserved in the library of the Duke of Devonshire at Chatsworth. (See also ACOUSTICS, 4 and 5, COSTUME, 4, ENGLISH PLAYHOUSE, 1, MACHINERY, MASQUE, SCENERY, 2.)

JONES, JOSEPH STEVENS (1809–77), American actor and author, creator of a number of Yankee characters, of whom Solon Shingle in *The People's Lawyer* (1839) was the most popular. It was played by Hill, Charles Burke, and John E. Owens, the last making his final appearance in it in New York in 1864. The Honorable Jefferson S. Batkins, another Yankee character in *The Silver Spoon* (1852), was first played by William Warren at the Boston Museum, and survived until well into the twentieth century. Jones wrote a number of other plays, some of them wildly improbable melodramas, and was for a time manager of the Tremont Theatre, Boston, where he had made some of his earliest appearances on the stage.

JONES, RICHARD (*fl.* 1590–1615), English actor, who was with the Admiral's Men from 1594 to 1602, and had probably been an actor before he joined them. In about 1610 he went to Germany with Robert Browne, leader of the first company of English Comedians to become popular on the continent, and remained there until a few years before his death (see ENGLISH COMEDIANS).

JONES, ROBERT EDMOND (1887–   ), outstanding American scenic designer, of whom it was said that his first designs, in 1915, 'sounded the note that began the American revolution in stage scenery' (see COSTUME, 10 *b*, SCENERY, and U.S.A., 2). Jones was also associated with Kenneth Macgowan in the direction of the Greenwich Village Playhouse from 1925 onwards, and collaborated with him in a volume entitled *Continental Stagecraft*.

JONSON, BEN(JAMIN) (1572–1637), English dramatist, and one of the outstanding men of his day, possibly the only one who may claim to rank with Shakespeare. His life was eventful and he was several times in prison or in danger of imprisonment for his outspokenness. Much of his energy was consumed in literary wrangles—usually summarized as the 'war of the theatres'—with contemporary dramatists, most of whom, always excepting Shakespeare, he appears to have despised as uneducated hack-writers. He himself was at Westminster, but was deprived of the university education his attainments warranted by the action of his stepfather, who apprenticed him to his own trade of bricklaying. Finding this intolerable, Jonson went soldiering in the Netherlands, and returned in about 1597 to connect himself with the London stage. As actor and part-author he was probably involved in the production at the Swan of the lost *Isle of Dogs*, a play which so incensed the authorities that they closed the theatres and put Jonson in prison. He is not henceforward found as an actor, but his first comedy, *Every Man in His Humour* (1598), had Shakespeare in its cast playing Knowell. It was followed by some fine satiric plays which left an enduring mark upon the development of English comedy. These include *Every Man Out of His Humour* and *The Case is Altered* (both 1599), and *Cynthia's Revels* (1600), done at Blackfriars by the Children of the Chapel. They also did *The Poetaster* (1601), in which Jonson vents his spleen on some of his contemporaries, ridiculing Marston as Crispinus and Dekker as Demetrius Fannius, while Horace represents Jonson himself. The play also contains a generalized criticism of actors, and a side hit at lawyers and soldiers respectively. It provoked a reply in *Satiromastix*, by Dekker, possibly with some help from Marston, with whom Jonson, however, collaborated in *Eastward Ho!* (1605). This again landed him in prison, owing to some reflections in it on James I's Scottish policy. He had already been in trouble over his first tragedy, *Sejanus* (1603), which the authorities judged seditious and full of popery.

Jonson's best work was done in the ten years from the production of *Volpone, or The Fox* in 1606 to that of *The Devil is an Ass* in 1616, the failure of the latter causing his retirement from the public stage for some years. The intervening period saw the production of *Epicoene, or the Silent Woman* (1609), *The Alchemist* (1610), a second tragedy, *Cataline* (1611), and the farcical *Batholomew Fair* (1614), whose slight plot strings together a number of scenes laid in a typical London holiday crowd. The first three of these plays are those which have been most frequently revived in recent years, *Volpone* having almost a permanent place in the repertory of Donald Wolfit, and being one of his best parts.

It was not until 1625, when he had lost Court patronage, that Jonson again wrote for public presentation, with the four comedies, *The Staple of News* (1625), *The New Inn* (1629), *The Magnetic Lady* (1632), and *A Tale of A Tub* (1633). These were not on a level with his previous works and are little known. There is, however, a further aspect of Jonson's dramatic work which cannot be ignored—the fine series of Court masques, an entertainment which in his hands reached the summit of its excellence, foreshadowing Milton's *Comus*, and to which he added the anti-masque, often a scene of Aristophanic comedy. Jonson had already introduced a masque into *Cynthia's Revels* with some success, and on the strength of it hoped to become Court poet, a position temporarily filched from him by Daniel. His genius was not to be withstood, however, and between 1605 and 1612 he was responsible, with the collaboration of Inigo Jones for scenic design and costume, for some eight Court masques. The young Prince Henry appeared in the title-role of one of these—*Oberon, the Faery Prince*—shortly before his death in 1611.

It has been said of Jonson by his great critic and editor, C. H. Herford, that he is 'probably the most signal example in literature of power without charm. He impresses, without greatly attracting, posterity; and his dominating position in the contemporary theatrical world was won in the teeth of hostile currents of opinion which almost always had a germ of reason on their side. . . . Jonson's services to English comedy were beyond question great, though his very reforms contained an element of decadence and tended to hasten its decay.' In person he was arrogant and quarrelsome, a good fighter but a staunch friend, warm-hearted, fearless, and intellectually honest. His merits are best summed up in the epitaph by one of his contemporaries, 'O rare Ben Jonson'.

JOOSS, KURT (1901–   ), see BALLET, 9.

JORDAN, DOROTHY (1761–1816), English actress, supreme in the realm of comedy, and, as Byron said, superlative in hoyden, or high-spirited tomboy, parts. She was the illegitimate daughter of an actress, Grace Phillips, and a gentleman, Francis Bland, and was originally billed as Miss Francis, since the Bland family had made her mother an allowance for some time on condition that the children did not use their father's name. When the allowance ceased, Dorothy's brother George took his father's name (see BLAND).

Mrs. Jordan's first recorded appearance was at the Crow Street Theatre, Dublin, on 3 Nov. 1779, in *The Virgin Unmasked*, and she was first billed on 20 May of the following year, when *The Governess* was given for O'Keefe's benefit. She was a great success, especially in breeches parts, and sang interpolated songs in most of the plays to great applause. In 1780 she was engaged by Daly for Smock Alley Theatre, but in 1782, after being seduced by him, she left secretly and fled to England with her mother and sister. Here she was befriended by Tate Wilkinson, who had acted with her mother in Dublin, and he agreed to give her a trial. She changed her name to Jordan, some say at the suggestion of Wilkinson himself, and on 11 July 1782 appeared at Leeds as Calista in *The Fair Penitent*, continuing to appear at the theatres in Wilkinson's circuit up to, and after, the birth of her first child, Daly's, at the end of the year. While playing at York during race week she had the good fortune to be seen and admired by 'Gentleman' Smith of Drury Lane, who was later responsible for her move to London. There she was engaged by Sheridan to play second to Mrs. Siddons, who had thought poorly of her on a visit to Hull. In spite of the preference of audiences at that time for tragedy, Mrs. Jordan chose to make her first appearance at Drury Lane as Peggy in *The Country Girl*, which she did with great success on 15 Oct. 1785. This became one of her most celebrated parts, and Leigh Hunt has left an excellent description of her in it in his preface to Wycherley's works. Realizing that her true métier lay in comedy, she wisely abandoned tragedy, and continued to delight her audiences in such parts as Priscilla Tomboy in *The Romp*, in which Romney later painted her, Miss Hoyden in *A Trip to Scarborough*, Sir Harry Wildair in *The Constant Couple*, and Miss Prue in *Love for Love*.

During her early years at Drury Lane Mrs. Jordan became entangled with a young man named Richard Ford, who promised marriage at some future date, but baulked after several years of intimacy, during which she bore him four children. In 1791 she at last left him to become the mistress of the Duke of Clarence, later William IV, by whom she had ten children, continuing to act, however, intermittently either in London or on tour. She was one of the company which performed Ireland's Shakespeare forgery, *Vortigern and Rowena*, in 1795, and in 1800 she appeared as Lady Teazle. She was painted by Hoppner as the Comic Muse, and by Chalmers as Sir Harry Wildair. In 1811 she was separated from the Duke, to whom she had proved a faithful and affectionate companion, and the last years of her life were overshadowed by anxiety about her children, and financial difficulties. Her last appearance in London was at Covent Garden on 20 April 1814, when she played in *Debtor and Creditor*, a new play, and in a revival of *As You Like It*, and in August of the following year she made her final appearance, at Margate. She was then involved in the financial ruin of her son-in-law, Edward Marsh, who had married one of her Ford daughters, and fled to France, where she died. Her grave in Paris vanished during rebuilding in the early 1930s.

JORNADA, the name given in Spain to each division of a play, corresponding to our Act. It probably comes from the Italian *giornata*, found occasionally in the *sacre rappresentazioni*. The word in its present form was first used by Torres Naharro: 'The division (of comedy) into 5 acts is in my opinion not only good, but absolutely necessary, although I call them *jornadas* and not acts, because they seem resting-places more than anything else.'

JOUVET, Louis (1887–1951), French actor and producer, and one of the most important figures of the French theatre in the years before the war of 1939–45. He had already had some experience of acting and management when, in 1913, he joined Copeau's Théâtre du Vieux-Colombier as actor and stage manager. In both capacities he proved invaluable, his finest work being done as Philinte in *Le Misanthrope*. Jouvet went with Copeau to America in 1917–19, and in 1922 left him to establish his own theatre. After several tentatives he settled at the Comédie des Champs-Élysées, going in 1934 to L'Athénée, to which he added his own name. He joined the staff of the Conservatoire in 1935, and a year later was appointed one of the producers of the Comédie-Française. To Jouvet goes the honour of having first encouraged and shown to the public the plays of Jean Giraudoux, in which he gave some of his finest performances, as well as being responsible for some excellent décor, where his own methods of lighting proved a revelation. In 1939 he published a volume entitled *Refléxions du comédien*.

JUDAEO-SPANISH DRAMA, see JEWISH DRAMA, 8.

JUDEU [ANTÓNIO JOSÉ DA SILVA] (1705–39), see SOUTH AMERICA, 2.

JUGGLER is the lexicographer's nightmare. Many English dictionaries stress its strictly secondary meaning of deceiver, which may be implied in such phrases as *juggling with finance*, or *juggling with words*. What it means in everyday life is explained by Hazlitt in his essay 'The Indian Jugglers', but who could reduce his opening paragraph into a phrase? During the war of 1914–18 objection was raised to it in Germany as a foreign word; showmen who tried to replace it on their programmes could invent nothing better than the equivalent of 'knowing-how-to-play-at-throwing'. The juggler is not concerned with the conjurer's principle, 'the quickness of the hand deceives the eye'. When his quickness is not noticed by the eye, his effects are spoilt. To keep balls or clubs or plates or batons passing through the air from one hand to the other is the most familiar of his feats, and the expert wishes his audience to observe how many more of these objects he keeps moving than his less dexterous rivals. What were once known as the feats of the 'Balance Master', later called 'polandric tricks' owing to the success of the Little Polander over a hundred years ago, have become part of the repertoire of the juggler. Likewise 'Antipodean' displays on the soles of the feet while he lies on his back with legs in the air are often included in his performance, but only when inanimate objects are so balanced, rotated, or bounced. Paul Cinquevalli, a favourite in British music-halls from the eighteen-eighties onwards, was a strong man and a humorist as well as a juggler. In popularity he was never surpassed, but Rastelli had greater skill in pure juggling. His experience was that British audiences were unable to observe the exceptional skill of his performances. Comedians who use simple feats to offset their humour have been credited with expert dexterity. Rich Hayes, who wore a Robinson Crusoe costume in a scene set to represent a tropical island, had both humour and uncommon skill. W. C. Fields used juggling as the medium for his humour on the halls before he became a film star. The accidental discovery on the Californian coast of the sea-lion's natural aptitude for catching things on his snout, and tossing and catching them in play, brought 'performing seals' into music-halls and circuses as rivals to the human juggler towards the end of the nineteenth century.　　　　　　　　　　　　　　M. W. D.

JUVENILE DRAMA, see TOY THEATRE.

JUVENILE LEAD, see STOCK COMPANY.

K

KABUKI, see JAPAN.

KACHALOV, VASILI IVANOVICH [SHVERUBO-VICH] (1875–1948), Russian actor, and one of the original members of the Moscow Art Theatre. He studied at the St. Petersburg University, and began his stage career as a super at the Suvorin Theatre. From 1897 onwards he worked in the provinces, where he played every kind of role from tragedy heroes to vaudeville ancients, until in 1900 he made his début at the Moscow Art Theatre, playing in *Tsar Feodor Ivanovich*. His talent was quickly recognized and he became a permanent member of the company, playing the leading roles in many of their outstanding productions, including Julius Caesar, Brand, Hamlet, Ivan Karamazov, Vershinin in *Armoured Train 14–69* and the Reader in the dramatization of Tolstoy's *Resurrection*, one of his best parts. Possessed of a fine voice and an excellent presence, Kachalov was one of the actors whose career marked the transition from Imperialist to Soviet Russia. At the revival of *Woe from Wit* by the Moscow Art Theatre in 1938 he again played Chatsky, the part he had taken in the same theatre's production of 1906.

KAINZ, JOSEF (1858–1910), German actor, famed for the richness and beauty of his voice, and the purity of his diction. He was trained with the Meiningen company and made his first appearance on the stage in 1874, in Vienna, where in 1899 he returned to end his days as a leading member of the Imperial Theatre. He was for some time in Munich, where he was the friend and favourite actor of King Ludwig II of Bavaria, and in 1883 played opposite Agnes Sorma in the newly founded Deutsches Theater in Berlin. He toured extensively in America, where he appeared in many of his best parts, which included Romeo, Hamlet, and the heroes of Grillparzer. He was also good as Tartuffe, Oswald in *Ghosts*, and Cyrano de Bergerac.

KAISER, GEORG (1878–1945), one of the most important German dramatists of modern times, and the leader of the so-called expressionist school of drama. His early plays, of which *Die jüdische Witwe* (1911) is typical, were satirical comedies directed against romanticism. The 1914–18 war led him, however, to question the ethical foundations of a society blindly rushing to perdition, and his *Von Morgens bis Mitternachts* (1916) satirizes both the futility of modern civilization and the robot-like men who are caught in its meshes. This sombre history of a bank clerk whose bid for freedom led to suicide was followed by the powerful plays *Gas I* and *II* (1918–20), a symbolic picture of industrialism crashing to destruction, and taking with it the civilization which it has ruined. Kaiser, whose other plays include the melodramatic *Der Brand im Opernhaus* (1919) and the historical drama *Die Bürger von Calais*

(1914), had a great influence on the European and American theatres between the two wars.

KĀLIDĀSA, see INDIA.

KAMERNY THEATRE, Moscow. This theatre, whose name means Chamber, or Intimate, Theatre, was founded in 1914 by Alexander Taïrov, and rebuilt in 1930 with a seating capacity of 1,210. It was intended as an experimental theatre for those to whom the naturalistic methods of the Moscow Art Theatre and the conventional classics of the Maly no longer appealed. In it, particularly after the October Revolution, Taïrov sought to work out his theory of 'synthetic theatre', in which all theatrical arts and forms were to be fused into an organic whole. This, in contradiction to Meyerhold's 'conditioned theatre', where the actor was a puppet, made him the centre of everything, and demanded in his person an acrobat, singer, dancer, pantomimist, comedian, and tragedian. Although Taïrov's work caught and held the attention of the theatrical world outside Russia, he was not completely successful in Moscow until the production in 1934 of *An Optimistic Tragedy*, in which his wife, Alice Koonen, played the part of the heroine. This production showed Taïrov's acceptance of the principles of Socialist Realism, upon which he has continued to work ever since. A further claim to fame of the Kamerny, and of its director, is that since its foundation it has been Moscow's chief link with Western drama, whose masterpieces have been continually in its repertory. Taïrov even made the interesting if not entirely successful experiment of linking a version of Shaw's *Caesar and Cleopatra* with Shakespeare's *Antony and Cleopatra* in a single evening, with a fragment of Pushkin thrown in for good measure. Like other Moscow theatres, the Kamerny was evacuated during the Second World War, but returned with two new plays, *Moscow Skies* and *At the Walls of Leningrad*, and an imposing list of revivals.

KARATYGIN, VASILY ANDREYEVICH (1802–53), famous Russian tragedian, son of an actor and producer at the St. Petersburg Dramatic Theatre. His father opposed his wish for a theatrical career, but he played with an amateur company at home and later at the Cadet College. His performance in a production of *Oedipus Rex* was so remarkable that he was invited to join the Imperial company. He refused, and continued his studies, finally making his début as a professional actor in May 1820, as Fingal. All his life he was noted for the care with which he studied his roles, returning where possible to the original sources, and labouring for historical accuracy in costume and décor, though he was opposed to the realistic style of acting and the innovations of Shchepkin. In contrast to Mochalov he developed a subtle and calculated technique which enabled him to play the most varied roles, though his preference was always for classical tragedy. He was also much admired in the patriotic drama of the day, and the tradition of his personal style persisted on the Russian stage until modern times.

KARNO, FRED (1866–1941), a notable figure in the music-halls, whose 'Jail Birds' and 'Mumming Birds' will be remembered as the training-ground of many well-known stars, including Fred Kitchen, Harry Weldon, and Charlie Chaplin. Born at Exeter, he worked as a child in a Nottingham factory, and then became a plumber's boy. His real name was Wescott. With two friends he went on the halls as an acrobatic turn billed as the Karno Trio. But his most original contribution to music-hall history was the elaboration of the 'sketches' or wordless plays mentioned above. Karno ruined himself in an attempt to popularize a Thames-side resort under the name of Karsino, and started life again in trade, but not before he had left his mark on the history of the music-hall, and, through Charlie Chaplin, on the cinema.   W. M. P.

KARSAVINA, TAMARA (1885–   ), a famous ballerina, trained in the Russian Imperial School, who joined Diaghilev's Ballets Russes after Pavlova left, and became the standard of excellence for all European ballerinas. A versatile dancer, equally outstanding in classical and character roles, she will be particularly remembered for her young girl in 'Spectre de la Rose', a ballet which she and Nijinsky made their own. Karsavina has written her autobiography in *Theatre Street* (1929).

KASPERLE, the name given to the typical Viennese peasant-clown after Gottsched's reforms had banished Hanswurst (or Harlequin) from the eighteenth-century stage. The Kasperltheater in Vienna was named after him, and formed the scene of his many farcical exploits. He still survives in puppet-booths in an attenuated repertory.

KATAYEV, VALENTIN PETROVICH (1897–   ), Soviet dramatist, who was born in Odessa, the son of a school-teacher. He took part in the Civil War, and since 1922 has lived in Moscow. His most successful play, which has been produced in many countries, was *Squaring the Circle*, an amusing comedy about two ill-assorted married couples who, owing to the housing shortage, are compelled to live in one room, and finally change partners. It was produced at the Moscow Art Theatre in 1928 under Nemirovich-Danchenko, and was done in English in 1938 at the Mercury in a translation by N. Goould-Verschoyle. Katayev is the author of a number of other plays, mostly light-hearted comedies like *The Blue Scarf*, an amusing trifle about a soldier at the front who receives a blue scarf from a bundle of comforts, and is all prepared to fall in love with the youthful donor, only to discover when on leave that it is a schoolboy. This was produced in 1943, in the rear of the front line.

KATONA, JOZSEF (1791–1830), Hungarian dramatist, author of a number of historical dramas dealing with Hungarian history, and of an important play, *Bánk Bán* (*The Viceroy*), which is concerned with Hungary's eternal problem, the national attitude to the foreign ruler.

KAUFMAN, GEORGE S. (1889–   ), American journalist and dramatist, whose first plays were written in collaboration with Marc(us) Cook Connelly (1890–   ), the most successful being *Beggar on Horseback* (1924), in which a satire upon existing conditions is worked out in a dream-sequence. Their collaboration then ended, and Kaufman alone wrote *The Butter and Egg Man* (1925), a clever farce, but otherwise insignificant, while Connelly wrote the fine negro play, *The Green Pastures* (1930). Kaufman then wrote a number of light-hearted plays which include several collaborations with Moss Hart (1904–   ), among them *Once in a Lifetime* (1930), *Merrily We Roll Along* (1934), *You Can't Take It with You* (1936), *I'd Rather Be Right* (1937), and *The Man Who Came to Dinner* (1939), a portrait of Woollcott in which Woollcott himself appeared on tour. Kaufman, who is known as 'the Great Collaborator', is also the author, with Edna Ferber, of *The Royal Family* (1927), a play of the theatre based apparently on the lives of the Drews and the Barrymores, and done in England as *Theatre Royal*. An expert technician and an excellent director, Kaufman has a keen sense of satire and a thorough knowledge of the theatre.

KEAN. (1) EDMUND (1787–1833), English tragedian, who appeals more strongly to the imagination than almost any other actor. The sympathy excited by his sufferings and the glamour of his meteoric success are dangerous to critical judgement. He should not be set above Garrick, whose wide range he lacked; nor should Kemble, exponent of virtue, suffer by false comparison with the exponent of villainy. Kean's was the fierce flame of crime exultant, and the true contrast is with Irving's baleful glow of crime repentant. To separate fact from fiction in Kean's life seems wasted labour. What is known to be true is so bizarre that legends cause no astonishment. The fantastic novels of his time had no stranger hero. The mysterious circumstances of his birth have been described in a biography by Giles Playfair. Was he descended, as Macaulay declared, from George Savile, Marquis of Halifax? The story, more easily believed than disbelieved, is that Halifax's natural son, Henry Carey, passed on the spark of genius to George Savile Carey, whose daughter Anne inherited little more than the wildness in their blood. At fifteen she turned strolling player. As a hawker in London she caught the eye of Aaron Kean—architect, tailor, or stage carpenter—who took just enough interest in her to tell her friends when she was with child so that they should find clothes and take her to George Savile Carey in Gray's Inn. They had—supposing we may believe their story that she was the mother—only her word for it that Kean was the father. No record of the birth (Hawkins's date is 4 November 1787) has been found and nothing is known of 'Master Carey's' infancy until he was found in a doorway by a kindly pair who brought him up in Frith Street, Soho. Soon Anne Carey dragged him off to be a wage-earner, and he posed as Cupid in a Covent Garden ballet. Fantastic stories of his infancy on the stage cannot be ignored; they chime with known facts. At length he found a guardian in Moses Kean, once a tailor, now a mimic and ventriloquist, the brother of Aaron. Anne Carey's friend, Miss Tidswell, also helped in gaining for the boy the freedom of the stage, which meant that he was given expert training in dancing, fencing, singing, and acting by its generous spirits. Well-meaning people adopted him and dropped him. Instinctive vagabondage drew him to the fairs. As 'The Pupil of Nature' he was a successful infant prodigy before he had to face the bitter trials of a strolling player, tramping the country with his wife, two small sons (until the elder died), and 'props' for their performance. On 26 January 1814 he played Shylock at Drury Lane. The audience acclaimed the genius of his performance, and Hazlitt recorded it for posterity. The technical novelty of his acting is revealed in the statement that by-play was one of his greatest excellences; he relied less on his voice, so harsh that at times it 'creaked', than on facial expression. In spirit the change was still greater. While Kemble was 'the statue on the pedestal that cannot come down without danger of shaming its worshippers', Kean was deficient in dignity, grace, and tenderness; his acting was not of the patrician order. He was 'one of the people, and what might be termed a *radical* performer'. These were contemporary comments. At this distance of time a more vital difference becomes plain. That Kemble excelled in nobility and virtue was evident in all his favourite parts, from Hamlet and Coriolanus to Earl Percy and Rolla. That Kean failed when he tried to assume such qualities, or when he essayed suffering innocence, was admitted. There had to be a touch of the malign, of murderous frenzy, to inspire him. His Lear caused very considerable disappointment. As Romeo he stood beneath Juliet's balcony like a lump of lead. His Hamlet, no 'sweet prince', showed a severity amounting to virulence. Abel Drugger, Garrick's favourite comic part, he played but three times. As for polished comedy, he would have none of it. When offered the part of Joseph Surface he returned it 'with the just indignation of insulted talent'. Mild villainy made no appeal to him. At his first London appearance as a star he caused the vast, half-empty auditorium of Drury Lane to vibrate with the shouts of those who now saw Shylock as a swarthy fiend with a huge butcher's knife in his grasp and blood-lust in his eyes. Richard Crookback and Iago

were the finest performances of this 'little ill-looking vagabond' magnetized by an anarchy of passions. Even his magnificent Othello was 'too often in the highest key of passion, too uniformly on the verge of extravagance, too constantly on the rack'. As Macbeth he was heart-rending. On coming to himself after the murder, his voice clung to his throat at the sight of his bloody hands. Two of his greatest masterpieces were Sir Giles Overreach, with his ruthless frenzy of miserliness in Massinger's *A New Way to Pay Old Debts*, and that barbarous fiend, Barabas, in Marlowe's *Jew of Malta*.

Biographers who whitewash Kean must surely miss the clue to his art and his character. His spirit was untamably wild. Unpublished diaries kept by Winston, Elliston's housemanager at Drury Lane, give a day-to-day account of uncouth exploits. The scandal caused by Kean's amour with the wife of Alderman Cox turned playgoers against their idol, but not before his frequent non-appearances had forfeited their respect. He played Othello at Covent Garden on 25 March 1833 to the Iago of his son. 'I am dying—speak to them for me' he moaned as he fell into Charles Kean's arms. His wife came to his house at Richmond, and they were reconciled before he died on 15 May 1833. He was buried in Richmond Old Church in a vault difficult to discover. On the church wall is a memorial with a medallion portrait set up by his son. This son, (2) CHARLES (1811–68), had been sent to Eton with the idea of detaching him from the stage, but Drury Lane engaged him at the time of his father's break both with that theatre and his home. Father and son acted together finally on that memorable occasion referred to above. With his wife, (3) ELLEN TREE (1806–80), Charles rose to the head of his profession at the Princess's Theatre, 1851–9, where he set his stamp upon a style of management which lasted for the rest of the century. Lavish spectacle which laid claim to historical accuracy embellished all types of drama from *Pizarro* to *Sardanapalus*, and brought the new Gallic drama into line with Shakespeare. Praises of Charles's style in 'gentlemanly melodrama' have tended to damn him as an actor, but his place in theatre history cannot be ignored. M. W. D.

KEAN, THOMAS (*fl.* mid-eighteenth century), manager of a troupe which in 1749 acted *Cato* and other plays in a converted warehouse in Philadelphia, later the home of Hallam's company. Kean, who was partnered by Walter Murray, also took his troupe to New York, and in 1751, in a theatre in Nassau Street, gave a number of plays which included *Richard III*, *Love for Love*, *The Orphan*, and *George Barnwell*. From there he went to Virginia with a company of comedians which played in Williamsburg and Annapolis, and at some places found itself rivalling the American Company. There is no information available at present of the composition of Kean and

Murray's company, nor of the exact status of its members, who may have been amateurs acting for pleasure, or the first professional players of the New World. Nor is anything known of their history after 1752–3 or of the circumstances in which they were disbanded.

KEELEY. (1) ROBERT (1793–1869), English actor, who ran away from his apprenticeship to join a strolling company in Richmond. His early days are obscure, but in 1818 he was at the Olympic, and later at the Adelphi, where he made a hit as Jemmy Green in *Tom and Jerry*, and played Jerry in the sequel, *Life in London*, at Sadler's Wells in 1822. In later years he was a fine low comedian, his stolid look and slow, jerky speech adding much to the humour of his acting. Dickens said of his Dogberry:

The blunders of the old constable fell from his lips with the most immovable and pompous stolidity. . . . As we write, we see again the wonderful expression of his face at the supreme moment when he was called an ass. No other catastrophe on earth . . . could have aroused in living man such an amazing exposition of stupendous astonishment, indignation, and incredulity, as that insult wrung from Dogberry as Keeley drew him. But his Verges was even finer.

He was also a master of pathos and, Dickens continues, 'our most delightful memories of him are connected with characters into which, by a few words or a little touch, he threw a certain homely tenderness quite his own'. Among his most famous parts were Jacob Earwig in *Boots at the Swan* and Sairey Gamp. He was, however, somewhat overshadowed by the excellence of his wife, (2) MARY ANN GOWARD (1806–99), who was trained as a singer, and appeared in 1825 at the Royal Opera House, London (later the Lyceum). She soon took to the stage, however, and had already made a name for herself when in 1829 she married Keeley, and thereafter appeared with him. She was a small, neatly made person, at her best in pathetic, appealing parts, Nydia in *The Last Days of Pompeii* and Smike in Stirling's adaptation of *Nicholas Nickleby*. But her greatest part was the title-role in *Jack Sheppard*, in which the highwayman was portrayed as a wild youngster, defrauded of his heritage and driven to bad ways by the animosity of Jonathan Wild the thief-taker. From 1844 to 1847 the Keeleys managed the Lyceum; they were with Charles Kean and Webster at the Haymarket, and for five years played at the Adelphi. Mrs. Keeley retired on the death of her husband, whom she survived by thirty years. She had two daughters of whom one, Mary, married the humorist and entertainer, Albert Smith. A niece of the Keeleys, (3) LYDIA ALICE LEGGE (1844–92), was also on the stage, as Lydia Foote, and proved herself a good actress, particularly in pathetic parts.

KEENE, LAURA [MARY MOSS] (*c.* 1820–73), American actress and theatre manager, who was born in England and made her first appearances in London, playing there until 1851. In the following year she was first seen in New York on her way to tour Australia, and she returned in 1855, spending the rest of her life in the United States. On 18 Nov. 1856 she opened her own theatre, a beautiful playhouse with a white and gold interior, upholstered in gold damask. The first production was *As You Like It*, in which she herself played Rosalind, supported by a good company. She remained at this theatre until 1863, and but for the outbreak of the Civil War might have continued to flourish. She presented good foreign and American plays with a well-balanced stock company, eschewing the destructive practice of importing visiting stars, and among her actors were Joseph Jefferson and Sothern. The latter finally brought the theatre an outstanding success in 1858 with *Our American Cousin*, whose long run, in the opinion of Odell, finally established New York as the metropolitan theatre centre of the United States. By July 1861 Laura Keene's was the only theatre open in New York, owing to the war, but she was forced to lower her standards and give poor, showy spectacles. She never recovered her prestige or buoyancy and, leaving genuine comedy to the newly established Wallack's Theatre, she relied more and more on melodrama and spectacle. Her last season opened in 1862 and in the autumn of the following year the theatre reopened under Mrs. John Wood (for its subsequent history see OLYMPIC, 3). Laura Keene, who was a good melodramatic actress and an excellent manager, continued to tour, and was seen at most of the important theatres of New York, but never again attained the heights of her previous management. Her company was playing *Our American Cousin* at Ford's Theatre, Washington, on the night Abraham Lincoln was assassinated there, 15 Apr. 1865.

The Fourteenth Street Theatre, formerly the Théâtre Français, was known as the Laura Keene from 1871 to 1873, but its history is negligible.

KEENE, THOMAS WALLACE (1840–98), American actor, whose real name was Eagleson. He started his career at the Old Bowery Theatre, and made his first successes while with Hackett. He toured England and the United States in support of most of the outstanding stars of the time, and from 1875 to 1880 was in the stock company at the California Theatre, where he proved his value during the engagement of Edwin Booth. He then went on tour as Coupeau in *Drink* with much success, and was seen up to the time of his death in a varied repertory, Richard III being one of his best parts. A big, florid man, of a kindly and quiet nature, he had little liking for modern plays or methods, and was somewhat old-fashioned in his acting, being most popular in the smaller and less sophisticated cities.

KEITH, BENJAMIN FRANKLIN (1846–1914), American theatre manager, who as a young man was connected with Barnum's and other circuses. He then took small shows on the road himself, and in 1883 began a long career as a vaudeville promoter. He was first active in Boston, where he inaugurated the original 'continuous performances', and eventually had a chain of popular-priced vaudeville theatres throughout the country. He paid good salaries, engaged good actors, and endeavoured to raise the standard of vaudeville and its working conditions.

KELLY, FRANCES MARIA (1790–1882), English actress and singer, who made her first appearance on the stage at the age of 7, with her uncle Michael Kelly, composer and singer, at Drury Lane. In 1800 she played Arthur in *King John* and the Duke of York in *Richard III* with great success. As an adult actress she revived some of the parts associated with Mrs. Jordan, and was for thirty-six years a favourite at Drury Lane, making occasional appearances elsewhere. In 1812 she acted with Kean at the newly built Drury Lane, being seen as Ophelia to his Hamlet. She also played leading roles in contemporary melodrama. On her retirement she endeavoured to found a school for the training of actresses, and built a theatre in Soho, later the Royalty, for this purpose. It was not, however, a financial success, and after several years of struggle and hardship she fell heavily into debt and lost her theatre. She then confined her activities to Shakespeare readings and the tuition of private pupils. She is the subject of the essay 'Barbara S——', by Charles Lamb, who was in love with her, proposing marriage in a letter of 20 July 1819.

KELLY, GEORGE (1887–   ), American dramatist, who gave the American stage a number of penetrative and austerely moralistic plays. Kelly entered the theatre when he became a vaudeville actor at the age of 21. His first full-length play, *The Torchbearers* (1922), was a satire on the pretentiousness of amateur theatricals. Two years later, he expanded his vaudeville skit *Poor Aubrey* into the comedy *The Show-Off* (1924), a hilarious satire on braggart philistinism as exemplified by the pompous success-worshipper Aubrey Piper. Next Kelly turned to the subject of home and marriage in the Pulitzer Prize-winner, *Craig's Wife* (1925), a relentless exposé of feminine possessiveness and lovelessness. The less successful *Daisy Mayme* (1926) was another study of selfishness, and applied the scalpel to an indulgent man's relatives. After writing an unimportant series of musical skits, the playwright composed the curiously moralistic drama *Behold the Bridegroom* (1927), in which a flighty 'modern' woman is punished with the contempt of her bridegroom, the first man she ever really loved. In *Maggie the Magnificent* (1929) Kelly treated the theme of integrity of character with unattractive coldness, and *Philip Goes Forth* (1931) exposed the limitations of a would-be playwright who fails to escape from the vulgar business world and becomes a phenomenally successful salesman. When this play failed, its author withdrew from the theatre, to which he returned unsuccessfully with *Reflected Glory*

(1936), the comedy of an actress who makes a lame attempt to leave the stage. The playwright himself did again retire from the theatre and was not heard from until he produced *The Deep Mrs. Sykes* (1945), a penetrative, if rather crabbed, satire on the follies of feminine 'intuition'. It was followed by *The Fatal Weakness* (1946), a knowing if not altogether unsympathetic treatment of feminine romanticism, in which a wife loses her husband when she becomes sentimentally absorbed in his romance with another woman.   J. G.

KELLY, HUGH (1739–77), English writer, whose sentimental comedy, *False Delicacy* (1768), was done by Garrick to offset Goldsmith's *Good-Natured Man* at the rival theatre, which it eclipsed for a short time, though it is now forgotten. It was played in the provinces, several times revived, and translated into French and German. Kelly wrote several other plays, of which *The School for Wives* (1773) was the least sentimental and almost approached the true spirit of the comedy of manners.

KEMBLE, a famous family of English actors, of whom the first, (1) ROGER (1721–1802), was a strolling actor-manager, formerly a hairdresser. He married the daughter of a provincial manager named Ward, who had at one time played with Betterton, and with her toured the country, his company being soon augmented by his numerous children, of whom the eldest became the great Sarah Siddons and is dealt with under her own name. Roger's eldest son (2) JOHN PHILIP (1757–1823), after a childhood spent on the stage, was sent to Douai to train for the priesthood, his father being a Roman Catholic. He abandoned his studies to return to the theatre, but not before he had acquired a certain habit of severity and asceticism which never left him. He became a stately, formal actor, at his best in heavily dramatic parts, and after several years in the provinces he made his London début at Drury Lane in 1783 as Hamlet, in which character he was painted by Lawrence. He gave an unusual reading of the part which at first puzzled the audience, but later captivated them by its gentleness and philosophy. Hazlitt, who had not at first appreciated him, spoke later of 'the sweet, the graceful, the gentlemanly Hamlet. . . . Later actors have played the part with more energy . . . but Kemble's sensible, lonely Hamlet has not been surpassed.' During his long career Kemble steadily improved, and the great tragic parts became linked with his name —Wolsey, the Stranger, Rolla, Brutus, Cato, and above all Coriolanus, in which he took leave of the stage on 23 June 1817. He was successively manager of Drury Lane and of Covent Garden, causing the O.P. Riots at the latter theatre when he raised the prices of admission after the disastrous fire of 1808, in which he and his sister Sarah suffered heavy personal losses. In 1787 he married Priscilla Hopkins (1755–1845), herself an actress and widow of an Irish actor. Her father was prompter at Drury Lane, and her mother a useful member of the company. She lived to a great age, and was proud of having been a member of Garrick's company in her early years. Kemble had a short and not very happy retirement. His years in management had not been a success financially, and he was forced to part with his fine library, the Duke of Devonshire buying his collection of old plays. Much troubled by gout, he went abroad and finally died in Lausanne. He had been a great actor in the grand manner, with no unexpected bursts of pathos or passion, but a steady and studied intensity of feeling. Walter Scott said of him that he was 'great in those parts where character is tinged by some acquired and systematic habit, like stoicism or misanthropy; but sudden turns and natural bursts of passion are not his forte'. He was ideally handsome, but had a harsh voice and laboured breathing, and his movements and gestures were stiff and unyielding. His somewhat pedantic approach to his work made him unfit for comedy, which he rarely attempted, and Lamb seems to have been the only critic who liked his playing of old comedy. It was said of him that 'even in his most convivial hours he was solemn and funereal'—a legacy of his priestly studies, no doubt. When he first took over Drury Lane from Sheridan he introduced a number of important reforms, both in the management of the theatre and in costumes and scenery. He was also responsible for the introduction of spectacular shows, with real animals and aquatic effects. He did much to improve the status of his profession, however, gracing it with nobility and decorum, and on the whole his influence was salutary.

His younger brother (3) STEPHEN (1758–1822) was born practically on the stage, his mother having just finished the part of Anne Boleyn. He played as a child in his father's company, became a chemist, returned to the stage when his sister Sarah became famous, and was always overshadowed by his elder brother. With reference to his great girth, which in later life enabled him to play Falstaff without padding, it was said that Covent Garden had the big, and Drury Lane the great, Kemble. Stephen had a somewhat roving life, being manager of a provincial company, of a theatre in Edinburgh, and of a company in Ireland. In 1818 he returned to manage Drury Lane, with little success, and retired after introducing his son Henry as Romeo. The latter soon sank to the Coburg and was heard of no more.

The youngest of the Kemble children was (4) CHARLES (1775–1854), who after the usual itinerant childhood became a civil servant, but left his job to return to the stage. At 17 he played Orlando at Sheffield, and first appeared in London as Malcolm in John Philip's revival of *Macbeth* for the opening of the new Drury Lane Theatre. He was not at first successful on the stage, being somewhat awkward, and having a weak voice. But in time he became an accomplished player of such parts as Mercutio, Mirabell, Orlando, Young Absolute, Charles

Surface, Benedick, and Romeo, which was considered his best role. Poetic rather than emotional, he was quite unfitted for tragedy, which he wisely left to his elders. He adorned the English stage for some 25 years, and then retired, troubled by increasing deafness, to give Shakespeare readings and become Examiner of Plays, a post he held until his death. In private life he was affable and much liked, and in America, which he visited in 1832, he was considered a typical 'English gentleman'. He married, in 1806, (5) THERESA (or Marie Thérèse de Camp) (1773–1838), an actress who had been a leading dancer at the Royal Surrey. She first appeared at Drury Lane in 1787, and in her twenty years on the stage created two parts always associated with her, Edmund in *The Blind Boy* and Lady Elizabeth Freelove in *The Day after the Wedding*, which she wrote herself. She was also good as Madge Wildfire in *The Heart of Midlothian*, and in all parts in which pantomime was needed. Her daughter (6) FRANCES ANNE (1809–93), usually known as Fanny, had no particular desire for a theatrical career, but in 1829 she appeared at Covent Garden, in order to save her father, who was then managing the theatre with little success, from bankruptcy. She was an immediate success, and for three years filled Covent Garden, bringing prosperity to everyone connected with it. She was first seen as Juliet, following it with Lady Teazle, Portia, Beatrice, and Bianca, as well as with Mrs. Siddons's great parts, Isabella, Euphrasia, Calista, and Belvidera. Unlike the other members of the Kemble family, Fanny appears to have been equally at home in tragedy and comedy. She was also the original Julia in *The Hunchback*. In Sept. 1832 she went with her father to America, and was received everywhere with acclamation. She left the stage in 1834 to marry Pierce Butler of Philadelphia, but the marriage proved unhappy, and she divorced him in 1845. For some time she travelled with her sister, the singer Adelaide Sartoris, and in 1857 began a series of popular readings in England and the U.S.A. She gave the last in New York in Oct. 1868 and then settled with her daughter in London and died there. In her youth she was a most beautiful girl, with dark eyes and hair, a wistful expression, and a slender, graceful figure. In later life her face retained its beauty, but with the added charm of a mature and thoughtful cast of countenance.

Fanny's nephew (7) HENRY (1848–1907), for whose education she made herself responsible, was also on the stage, making his first appearance at Dublin in 1867. He was for some years in the provinces, playing old men and character parts, and in 1874 he first appeared at Drury Lane. He was later with John Hare at the Court Theatre, and had a long association with the Bancrofts. He made his last appearance shortly before his death, in April 1907. A short, stout man, he was an excellent comedian, particularly in strong character parts, and an amusing and much-loved companion.

Three of Roger Kemble's daughters were also on the stage, Elizabeth (1761–1836) becoming well known, as Mrs. Whitlock, in America, where she first appeared in 1794. Her sister Anne, later Mrs. Hatton, settled in New York and became poetess to the Tammany Society. She was the author of an operatic spectacle entitled 'Tammany', done at the John Street Theatre on 3 March 1794. Dunlap has left a description of it, and the songs and scenario have been preserved. Henry Mason and his sons John Kemble and Charles Kemble, who all played at the Park Theatre, New York, in 1835, were related to the Kembles. The daughter, Miss Mason, married a scene-painter named Henry Hillyard.

KEMPE, WILLIAM (?–1603), a famous Elizabethan clown, the original Dogberry in *Much Ado About Nothing*, and a great player of jigs. He was a member of the company which went with the Earl of Leicester to Holland in 1585–6, and was at the Danish Court in Elsinore in the latter year. His reputation in London was already made by 1590, and he became one of the Chamberlain's Men on the formation of the company in 1594, remaining with them until 1600, in which year he danced his famous morris from London to Norwich. He then went to the continent, but returned, and in 1602 is noted in Henslowe's Diary as having borrowed some money. He may then have been with Worcester's Men at the Rose.

KENDAL. (1) WILLIAM HUNTER [really GRIMSTON] (1843–1917), English actor-manager, who made his first appearance on the stage on 6 Apr. 1861. He played in the provinces for some years, appearing with the Keans, G. V. Brooke, and Helen Faucit, and was a member of the Glasgow stock company. In 1866 he was engaged by Buckstone for the Haymarket, where he remained for eight years, playing leading parts in Shakespeare, Sheridan, and Gilbert. It was here that he met and married (2) MADGE [MARGARET] ROBERTSON (1848–1935); and from then on his career is inseparable from that of his wife. The twenty-second child of an actor-manager, and sister of the dramatist T. W. Robertson, she was on the stage from her early years, and had already made a name for herself before her marriage. She then went with her husband on tour and to the Court Theatre under John Hare, where by the excellence of her acting she gave a new lease of life to the old play *A Scrap of Paper*. With the Bancrofts at the Prince of Wales's she played Dora in *Diplomacy*, and appeared with Kendal in a revival of *London Assurance*. The Kendals then went into partnership with Hare at the St. James's and played leading parts in many notable productions, Kendal being somewhat overshadowed by the brilliance of his wife, but proving himself a fine actor and a good business man. His last years were uneventful and he retired in 1908, as did his wife. He was better in comedy than tragedy, and one of his finest

parts was Frank Maitland in *The Queen's Shilling*. His wife was also a fine comedienne, but she could on occasion play in a more gentle mood, as witness her success in *The Elder Miss Blossom*, a play which she frequently revived and took on tour. Clement Scott said of her in this part: 'We . . . can recall no creation at once so delicate, sympathetic and faultless as Dorothy Blossom. The artist speaks in every line, gesture, and movement. She has humour, change, variety; and when she wants to touch the human heart she crushes it with an infinite tenderness and truth.' In 1926 Mrs. Kendal was made Dame Commander of the British Empire and in 1927 received the Order of the Grand Cross (G.B.E.). She and her husband were long held up as a pattern of partnership, both on the stage and in their private lives, and with Sir Squire and Lady Bancroft did much to raise the status of the acting profession. The companies with which they were connected were admirably managed, and proved an invaluable training-ground for many young actors and actresses.

KESTER, PAUL (1870–1933), American playwright, whose first play, *The Countess Roudine*, was produced by Minnie Maddern Fiske in 1892. Kester's wide knowledge of European languages proved of great value to him when he came to adapt plays by foreign authors, which, in accordance with the practice of his time, he did prolifically. Among his original plays his first great success was *Sweet Nell of Old Drury* (1900), done first in London by Fred Terry and Julia Neilson, and later in the United States by Ada Rehan. It was taken on tour to Australia and the Far East, and revived in 1923. Many of Kester's plays were written for particular players of the period, including Salvini, Janauschek, Julia Marlowe, Mrs. Langtry, Marie Tempest, E. H. Sothern, Margaret Anglin, and others, and some of the most successful—*Guy Mannering*, *When Knighthood was in Flower*, *Dorothy Vernon of Haddon Hall*, *Lady Dedlock*, *Don Quixote*—were based on novels. Kester was fond of romantic and picturesque plots, and his hobby was the study of gipsy lore. He was never married.

KHMELEV, NIKOLAI PAVLOVICH (1901–1945), Soviet actor and producer, who joined the Moscow Art Theatre in 1919, where his first role was Fire in *The Blue Bird*. Here he subsequently played many important parts, including Firs in *The Cherry Orchard*, and Tusenbach in *Three Sisters*. He also worked at the Second Studio and was a producer at the Yermolova Theatre, of which he became director in 1937. In 1943, on the death of Nemirovich-Danchenko, Khmelev replaced him at the Moscow Art Theatre. Among his productions there were *The Russian People* and a revival of Ostrovsky's *The Last Sacrifice*, while at the Yermolova Theatre he directed a production of Fletcher's comedy, *The Woman's Prize; or, the Tamer Tamed*.

[439]

KILLIGREW. (1) Thomas (1612–83), English dramatist, theatre manager, and, from the death of Sir Henry Herbert in 1673, Master of the King's Revels. He had already written several plays before the closing of the theatres in 1642, among them *Claricilla*, *The Princess*, and *The Prisoners*, all tragi-comedies. Another, *The Parson's Wedding*, based on Calderón and first given in 1640, was revived in 1664 with a cast of women only and made even Pepys blush. It is not, however, as a dramatist that Killigrew ranks high in the history of the English theatre, but as a manager and administrator. He founded the present Drury Lane Theatre, as the Theatre Royal or the King's House, under a Charter from Charles II. With Davenant, holder of a Charter for the Duke's House, later transferred to Covent Garden, Killigrew held the monopoly of acting in Restoration London, and after a brief sojourn in a converted tennis-court in Vere Street, he opened the first Theatre Royal with a fine company, which included Mohun, Hart, and, for a short while, Nell Gwynn. The theatre was burnt down in 1672, but two years later a new theatre, designed by Wren, was ready for occupation. In it the company formed by the amalgamation of the two existing companies played from 1682. Killigrew also established a training school for young actors at the Barbican. He was, according to Pepys, 'a merry droll', and a great favourite of Charles II. He was not so good a business manager as Davenant, and was often in financial difficulties. His brother (2) Sir William (1606–95), and his son (3) Thomas (1657–1719), both wrote plays, while another son (4) Charles (1665–1725) took over the management of the Theatre Royal in 1671, assisted by his half-brother Henry, and became Master of the Revels on his father's death.

KINCK, Hans (1865–1926), Norwegian dramatist, author of a number of scholarly plays on Italian subjects, and of a two-part drama which is sometimes compared to *Peer Gynt* (see SCANDINAVIA, 2).

KING, Tom (1730–1804), English actor, one of the most famous members of Garrick's Drury Lane company, and the original Sir Peter Teazle, Puff, and Sir Anthony Absolute. At 17 he was a strolling player with Ned Shuter, and first appeared at Drury Lane under Garrick in Oct. 1748. He was ready to turn his hand to anything, but he was not suited to tragedy, and deciding to confine himself entirely to high comedy, he went to Dublin, worked under the elder Sheridan, and returned a finished comedian. His Malvolio and Touchstone were both admirable, but it was as Lord Ogleby, in *The Clandestine Marriage*, a part written for Garrick and refused, that he made his mark. He made his last appearance on the stage which he had so excellently served in 1802, again as Sir Peter. Hazlitt wrote a fine appreciation of him. 'His acting left a taste on the palate sharp and sweet like a quince. With

an old, hard, rough, withered face like a sour apple, puckered up into a thousand wrinkles . . . he was the real amorous, wheedling or hasty, choleric, peremptory old gentleman . . . and the true, that is pretended, clown in Touchstone.' He amassed a great deal of money, but a passion for gambling, and an unfortunate venture into management of the Bristol and Sadler's Wells Theatres, caused him to die poor.

KING OF MISRULE, see MISRULE.

KING'S BOX, see AUDITORIUM and BOX.

KING'S CONCERT ROOMS, London, see SCALA THEATRE.

KING'S HOUSE, see DRURY LANE.

KING'S MEN, see CHAMBERLAIN'S MEN.

KING'S THEATRE, London, see QUEEN'S THEATRE (1).

KINGSLEY, Sidney (1906–   ), American dramatist, who made his mark as a meticulous artist, social critic, and democratic idealist. After graduation from Cornell University in 1928 and a brief acting career, he wrote his first play, *Men in White*, in 1930. Produced in 1933, it won the Pulitzer Prize. It deals with an interne's wavering between private distractions and the exalted vocation of medical science, and provided a vivid picture of hospital life. The economic depression of the 1930s moved Kingsley to write *Dead End* (1935), a bleak but provocative study of crime-breeding slum conditions. His *Ten Million Ghosts* (1936) excoriated the international munitions cartels that had profited from the First World War. *The World We Make* (1939), a dramatization of a novel by Millen Brand, gave a moving account of a neurotic rich girl's discovery of comradeship and hope among the poor. Kingsley won the New York Drama Critics' award with *The Patriots* (1943), a chronicle of the formative years of American democracy in which Thomas Jefferson and Alexander Hamilton compound their differences in order to defend the nascent republic.   J. G.

KINGSTON [Konstam], Gertrude (1866–1937), English actress and theatre manager, for whom Bernard Shaw wrote *Great Catherine* (1913). She made her first appearance, after some amateur experience, in 1887, with Sarah Thorne's company in Margate, and a year later was seen in London at the Haymarket under Tree. After a long and varied career she built the Little Theatre in John Street, London, and opened it with *Lysistrata* in 1910, intending to make it a home of repertory. The venture was not an outstanding success, but her efforts, like those of Lena Ashwell at the Kingsway, later bore fruit in the establishment of the repertory system, mainly outside London. She then appeared in a number of plays by Shaw, including *Captain Brassbound's Conversion*, *The Dark Lady of the Sonnets*, and *You Never Can Tell*, and was several times seen in New York.

She was the author of several plays, some of which she herself produced, and wrote a number of books, including a volume of reminiscences.

KINGSWAY THEATRE, LONDON. This opened in Dec. 1882 as the Novelty Theatre, with a comic opera 'Melita; or, the Parson's Daughter', and closed the same month. Renamed the Folies-Dramatiques, it opened again in 1883 with Nellie Harris's name on the bills. Ada Cavendish appeared there in a revival of *The New Magdalen*, while Willie Edouin, Lionel Brough, and others tried plays there, but all without success. In 1888 it was again renamed, this time the Jodrell, after a lady so called who sought theatrical fame. The Russian National Opera Company appeared there, and then the theatre remained closed for some time, until in 1900 Penley took it, reconstructed and redecorated it, and opened it as the Great Queen Street Theatre with *A Little Ray of Sunshine*, transferred from the Royalty, followed by a revival of *The Private Secretary*. But still no good fortune attended the theatre. In 1907 Lena Ashwell took it over, and after more reconstruction and redecoration it opened as the Kingsway on 9 Oct. with *Irene Wycherley*. This was successful, as were *Diana of Dobson's* and other plays that followed. Notable Kingsway productions were *The Great Adventure*, with Henry Ainley and Wish Wynne, in 1913, which ran for 673 performances, Granville-Barker's version of Hardy's *The Dynasts* in 1914, and a revival of *Fanny's First Play* in 1915. In 1932, when the theatre was under the management of Jay and Littler, a group of theatrical enthusiasts took it over, surrendered the Lord Chamberlain's licence, and made it into the Independent Theatre Club for the production of unlicensed plays. In spite of a distinguished beginning the venture was not a success, and the Kingsway resumed its career as an ordinary theatre. It suffered damage by enemy action in 1940–1, but remained usable.

W. M. P.

KIRBY'S FLYING BALLET, see ENGLISH PLAYHOUSE, 2 c.

KIRCHMAYER, THOMAS (1511–63), German humanist and Protestant author, under the pseudonym of Naogeorg, of several anti-Catholic plays of which the most important is *Pammachius* (1538). It was written in Latin, in which language it was acted at Cambridge in 1545, and was translated into racy German for performance at Zwickau. It was later translated into English by John Bale of Ossory.

KIRKE, JOHN (?–1643), English actor who was at the Red Bull Theatre with Parry and Weekes, and later became one of Prince Charles's Men. He has been identified by W. J. Lawrence with the John Kirke who was a dramatist, since both men were attached to the Red Bull. His *Seven Champions of Christendome*, published in 1638, was given at the Red Bull and the Cockpit, and Herbert notes in his diary in 1642 that Kirke

brought him two other plays; but this may have been in his capacity as bookholder, or as manager of the company. Kirke evidently ceased to act on the closing of the theatres, and may have gone into business.

KIRSHON, VLADIMIR MIKHAILOVICH (1902–), Soviet dramatist, and author, with Ouspensky, of a play dealing with the problems of Russian youth at odds with the new régime. This was produced by M.O.S.P.S. in 1926, and was later given in America as *Red Rust* in a translation by V. and F. Vernon, which was published in 1930. Though discursive, and somewhat melodramatic, it is an interesting study of a transitional epoch. It was, however, too superficial to be of lasting value, a criticism which seems to apply to all Kirshon's later plays.

KISFALUDY, KÁROLY (1788–1830), Hungarian writer and dramatist, author of several historical tragedies, also of a number of successful comedies in which he first introduced to the Hungarian stage the peasant types which afterwards became so popular. The Kisfaludy Society, named after him, is Hungary's most important literary society, and was responsible for the translation and editing of a complete edition of Shakespeare's plays published in 1864. The translations were done by Hungary's outstanding poets and writers, and are still in general use on the Hungarian stage.

KJAER, NILS (1870–1924), Norwegian dramatist, author of satirical comedies and plays on contemporary themes (see SCANDINAVIA, 2).

KLAW THEATRE, NEW YORK, on 45th Street between Broadway and Eighth Avenue, one of the best houses for comedy in the city, which has unfortunately been unavailable since 1934, when it became a broadcasting studio. It opened on 2 Mar. 1921 with Tallulah Bankhead, Katharine Cornell, and a fine supporting cast in *Nice People*. This was followed by William Hurlburt's *Lilies of the Field* and *Meet the Wife*, by Lynn Starling, while Hatcher's *Hell-Bent for Heaven*, a mountaineering drama which won the Pulitzer Prize, was first seen at the Klaw for four matinées. In 1925–6 the Theatre Guild occupied this house with its Shavian double bill, *Androcles and the Lion* and *The Man of Destiny*. The theatre was later renamed the Avon, and on 15 Nov. 1931 Cornelia Otis Skinner appeared there in her monodrama, *The Wives of Henry VIII*, followed by Constance Collier and a fine cast in a revival of *Hay Fever*. The last legitimate production at this theatre was *Tight Breeches*, by John Tainter Foote and Hubert Hayes, which opened on 11 Sept. 1934.

G. F.

KLEIN, CHARLES (1867–1915), American dramatist. Born in London, he went to the United States at the age of 15, and was for some time an actor, his short stature enabling him to play juvenile parts. His first writing was done when he was asked to revise a play he was appearing in, but it was with *Heartsease* (1897) (not to be confused with Mortimer's version of *La Dame aux camélias*, done for Modjeska in 1880 under the same title) that he first came into prominence. Two later plays which had an enormous success were *The Auctioneer* (1901) and *The Music Master* (1904), both written for and produced by Belasco. They were quite trivial and unoriginal, and owed their success to the acting of David Warfield, for whom they were designed. Klein's later plays were mainly melodramas, which had a contemporary but ephemeral success. He was play-reader for Charles Frohman and was drowned with him in the sinking of the *Lusitania*.

KLEIST, HEINRICH VON (1777–1811), German dramatist, born of an East Prussian military family, who soon forsook the army for philosophy and literature. His first play, *Die Familie Schroffenstein* (1793), a gloomy fate-tragedy involving the destruction of two families, showed promise, but a more ambitious effort, *Robert Guiscard*, defied his powers, and he burnt the manuscript, of which only one beautifully written fragment survives. His best-known play, *Der zerbrochene Krug* (1808), is considered one of the finest comedies in the German language. In it a village magistrate with Falstaffian virtuosity in lying is made to try, in the presence of a visiting magistrate, a case in which he himself is the culprit. In its technique of progressive revelation in unbroken action it is a comic counterpart to *Oedipus Rex*. A similar form is used in *Penthesilea* (1808), a tragedy centring round the Amazon who, believing herself scorned by her lover Achilles, tears him limb from limb, and finds release only in death from the fatal dualism of her nature. In lighter vein is *Käthchen von Heilbronn* (1810), a study of a Griselda-like devotion in which supernatural and folk-tale elements are grafted upon the realistic medievalism of *Götz von Berlichingen*, but all imbued with Kleist's usual intensity. Here the continuous action of the earlier plays has given place to a Shakespearian interchange of verse and prose. By 1810 lack of recognition, and his own deep-seated pessimism and morbid introspection had brought Kleist to the verge of suicide; only his ardent patriotism, at this dark period of Germany's history, stayed his hand while he completed *Die Hermannschlacht*, dealing with the defeat of the Romans by the Germans under Arminius, but aimed at Napoleon, and *Der Prinz von Homburg*, in which the hero, carried away by impulse, disobeys a military command in an hour of national peril, but by wise handling is brought to accept before execution the necessity of discipline. Neither of these plays found a publisher, let alone a producer, and Kleist committed suicide in 1811.   W. E. D.

KNEPP, MARY (?–1677), one of the first English actresses. She was trained by Killigrew and appeared under him at the first Theatre Royal. She was a friend of Pepys, in whose diary she often figures, usually as the source of back-stage gossip. According to him, she was a merry, lively creature, at her best in comedy. She was also much in demand for the speaking of the witty prologues and epilogues in which the fashion of the time delighted, and was a good dancer. She was a friend and fellow-player of Nell Gwynn.

KNICKERBOCKER THEATRE, NEW YORK, a large playhouse on the north-east corner of 38th Street and Broadway. It was long a favourite home of big musical shows, but it was opened on 8 Nov. 1893 as Abbey's Theatre by no less a person than Henry Irving, on his fourth visit to New York. With Ellen Terry, Kate Phillips, and William Terriss, he appeared there in Tennyson's *Becket*. Later stars who were seen at Abbey's were Coquelin, Lillian Russell, the Kendals, and Sarah Bernhardt, while Mounet-Sully as Hernani, Réjane as Madame Sans-Gêne, and John Hare in *The Notorious Mrs. Ebbsmith* with Julia Neilson and C. Aubrey Smith, all made their New York débuts at this theatre. On 14 Sept. 1896 the theatre was taken over by Al Hayman and rechristened, but it continued to offer hospitality to visiting stars, notably Wilson Barrett in his famous melodrama *The Sign of the Cross*, and Beerbohm Tree in *The Seats of the Mighty*. Among later interesting productions were Maude Adams in *L'Aiglon* and *Quality Street*, Ada Rehan in *Sweet Nell of Old Drury*, Otis Skinner in *Land of Heart's Desire*, and Rostand's *Chantecler* in a translation by Louis N. Parker. *Kismet*, which opened on Christmas Night, 1911, was an instantaneous hit and the forerunner of many successful musical shows, while in 1929 the Players selected the Knickerbocker for their revival of *Becky Sharp*, with a superlative cast. In the same year this famous theatre closed, and in 1930 was pulled down.   G. F.

The Bowery Amphitheatre was called the Knickerbocker when for a short time in 1844 it was run as a theatre.

KNIGHT, JOSEPH (1829–1907), English dramatic critic and historian who wrote for the *Athenaeum* from 1867. We are indebted to him for detailed notices of the early work of Irving and Ellen Terry. Of Ellen Terry's performance as Pauline in *The Lady of Lyons*, at the Princess's Theatre in 1875, Knight wrote: 'One of the pleasantest, inasmuch as it is one of the rarest, tasks the critic is called upon to discharge is that of heralding to the world the advent of genius.' He had also a keen eye for the work of the Comédie-Française, and for the genius of Sarah Bernhardt.

Knight contributed many biographies of actors and actresses to the *Dictionary of National Biography*. A selection of his criticisms was published as *Theatrical Notes* in 1893.   T. C. K.

KNIPP, MARY, see KNEPP.

KNIPPER-CHEKHOVA, OLGA (1870–   ), see CHEKHOV (2).

KNOBLOCK [Knoblauch], Edward (1874–1945), a dramatist who, though born and educated in the United States, spent much of his life in England and on the continent. He was for a short time an actor, and had a thorough knowledge of the stage which he applied to the dramatization of novels with a skill which made him an admirable and reliable 'play carpenter' rather than an original dramatist. Of his own plays the most successful were *Kismet* (1911), an Arabian Nights fantasy done by Oscar Asche in England and Otis Skinner in New York and frequently revived, and *Marie-Odile* (1915), a tale of the Franco-Prussian war beautifully produced by David Belasco. Much of Knoblock's best work was, however, done in collaboration. With Arnold Bennett he wrote *Milestones* (1912), with Seymour Hicks *England Expects* (1914), with J. B. Priestley *The Good Companions* (1931), and with Beverley Nichols *Evensong* (1932), the last two from their novels. He also dramatized *Princess Priscilla's Fortnight* (1909), *Simon Called Peter* (1924), *Grand Hotel* (1931), and *Hatter's Castle* (1932). He translated a number of French plays, and in 1938 supervised the Irving Centenary Matinée at the Lyceum.

KNOWLES, James Sheridan (1784–1862), member of a literary family and friend of Hazlitt, Coleridge, and Lamb, was successively attracted by the army, medicine, and the teaching profession before, in emulation of his cousin Sheridan, he turned his attention to the stage. At 24 he was in the company at the Crow Street Theatre, Dublin, where he proved himself a passable comedian and singer. His first play, a melodrama now lost, was written for Kean, who was in the same company. Knowles later wrote a tragedy, *Virginius*, for the same actor, who refused it, allowing Macready to triumph in the part in 1820. Knowles was a prolific dramatist, who interpreted his classic tragedies in the light of nineteenth-century domesticity, and was more concerned with his characters' feelings than with their actions. In his own day he was much admired, but nothing of his work has survived in performance. His most successful play was *The Hunchback* (1832), whose heroine, Julia, was a favourite part with many young and lovely actresses. He reappeared in this play after many years off the stage, playing Master Walter, a part in which he made his first appearance in New York in 1834. He was not, however, a good actor, and it is as a dramatist that he is remembered. Allardyce Nicoll, in *Nineteenth Century Drama*, says of him: 'If only Knowles could have escaped from melodrama on the one hand and from Elizabethanism on the other, he might have done something notable for the stage. As it is, many of his plays are but glorified tales of black evil and white innocence. . . . Success, in Knowles's work, is near, yet is not attained.'

KNOWLES, Richard George (1858–1919), an outstanding figure of the old music-halls, who billed himself as the 'very peculiar American comedian' (he was born in Canada). He started his career in Chicago, and then went to New York, where he appeared in vaudeville, in plays, and in a minstrel troupe. In 1891 he went to London, and remained a firm favourite there until his death. He had a curiously quiet style, always wore a black frock coat, opera hat, and white duck trousers, and walked up and down across the stage. His best-remembered songs are 'Girlie, Girlie' and 'Brighton'.

KOCH, Frederick Henry (1877–1944), a university professor who is important in the history and development of the American theatre through his work with the Dakota and Carolina Playmakers. Like Professor George Pierce Baker, he introduced the serious study of playwriting and play production into the curriculum of the university student, but his main concern was with the 'folk-play' based on the regional life of the south. The Dakota Playmakers were founded in 1910, and did good work in the writing and production of plays on native themes, but it was with the Carolina Playmakers that Koch was able most fully to carry his ideas to fruition. The actors, drawn from the undergraduate body of the University of North Carolina, toured from Georgia to Washington, carrying their scenery and props with them, and produced plays, mainly in one act, written by themselves and their fellow students of the drama, on themes of Southern folk-lore, superstition, and local history. Although the acting of the students was less important than the plays they produced, which have been collected and published in several volumes, Koch's influence on the commercial theatre was probably greater than would at first appear, in spite of the fact that, unlike Baker, he did not aim to prepare playwrights for Broadway. But the first good plays about the Southern States, which began to appear about 1923, are probably due to him, and he can be credited with the training of at least one outstanding playwright, Paul Green, while the novelist Thomas Wolfe is also represented in the series of Carolina Folk-Plays. Nor should the influence of the Carolina Playmakers on the amateur and Little Theatres be forgotten, nor the impetus which Koch's work gave to the teaching of dramatics in American schools and colleges. Koch was also instrumental in founding and directing a Canadian school of playwriting at Banff, which is doing interesting work.

KOCH, Heinrich Gottfried (1703–75), German actor, who in 1728 joined Caroline Neuber's company, and soon proved his value, being most versatile and adaptable. He was a good scene-painter, a good translator and adapter of plays, and a competent actor. He adopted the new style of acting which Gottsched and Caroline Neuber were sponsoring, and was particularly popular in classical comedy, which he had an opportunity of studying at its best when he frequented the performances of a French company in Strasbourg. He was also acceptable in tragedy as long as the declamatory style favoured by Caroline Neuber remained in fashion. One of his best parts was the title role in *L'Avare*. After the break-up of the Neuber company he started on his own, and acquired her patent, quarrelling violently in the process with his old companion Schönemann, who had also broken away to start on his own. Some years later he took over the management of Schönemann's disbanded company, which included Ekhof as leading man, but after continual dissensions Ekhof left to join the Ackermanns. This gave Koch a free hand, and he continued steadily, in a quiet, old-fashioned way, gaining the respect of his audiences wherever he played, experiencing no great reverses of fortune and no spectacular successes. His actors, who included his wife, Christiane Henriette, née Merlick, the sister of his best tragic actor, were good. He treated them well, and was one of the few managers of his time, apart from Ackermann, to be esteemed generally. He travelled continuously, but made Leipzig his headquarters, where towards the end of his life he had the mortification of finding himself eclipsed by Döbbelin.

KOCH, SIEGFRIED GOTTHELF [really ECKARDT] (1754–1831), German actor who, having served his apprenticeship in a number of small travelling companies, was engaged by Iffland at Mannheim in 1790 to replace Boeck in tragic parts. He did well, and became one of the outstanding members of the company, being particularly active on the administrative side. His daughter Betty, who later married an actor named Rose, or Roose, was also a good actress, and appeared at Mannheim as Iphigenia with much success.

KODOLÁNYI, JÁNOS (1899–   ), see HUNGARY.

KOMISARJEVSKAYA, VERA FEDOROVNA (1864–1910), Russian actress and producer, daughter of a well-known opera singer, and sister of the producer Theodore Komisarjevsky (see below). She made her début in 1891 as Betsy in Tolstoy's *The Fruits of Enlightenment* in a production by Stanislavsky. She then toured the provinces, and in 1896 was accepted by the Alexandrinsky Theatre, where she soon occupied a leading position. The atmosphere of a Court theatre, however, was not to her taste, and she left to found her own theatre. There, in the midst of the social upheaval of 1905, she gave expression to the most advanced phases of Russian artistic life. Her early productions included plays by Gorky, Chekhov, and Ibsen. In the years of reaction, between 1906 and 1918, Komisarjevskaya came under the influence of the Symbolists, and invited Meyerhold to produce in her theatre. Disagreeing with his attitude to the actor, whom he regarded as a mere puppet, she soon broke with him, and in her later years decided, like Duse, to leave the stage and become a teacher of dramatic art. In order to settle her theatrical

debts she embarked on a last tour, during which she caught smallpox and died.

Komisarjevskaya's repertory consisted mainly of plays dealing with feminine problems, and her best parts were Gretchen (Margaret) in Goethe's *Faust*, Rosy in Sudermann's *The Battle of the Butterflies*, and Ibsen's Nora and Hedda Gabler. She was a woman of great charm, with a magnetic personality.

KOMISARJEVSKY, THEODORE (FEDOR) 1882–   ), brother of the famous Russian actress Vera Komisarjevskaya (see above), and an outstanding personality in the European theatre. He gained his initial experience in pre-Revolutionary Russia, where from 1907 he was a prolific producer of plays and operas, first at his sister's theatre, then at his own; and up to 1919 he was a director of the Imperial and State Theatres in Moscow, thus bridging the first phases of the Revolutionary change-over. In 1919 he went to England, and has since done a number of stage and operatic productions, chiefly in London, but also in New York, Paris, and other European capitals. As guest-producer at Stratford-on-Avon his experimental Shakespearian productions were usually startling, and frequently successful. His influence on the younger generation of European producers has been considerable, if for nothing else than his demonstration that Chekhov and other classics of the Russian stage are not necessarily dominated by gloom. He has written interestingly on the theatre, on theatrical costume, and on Stanislavsky.

KOONEN, ALICE, see TAÏROV.

KORNEICHUK, ALEXANDER EVDOKIMOVICH (1905–   ), Ukrainian dramatist, who started writing at an early age. The first play to bring him into prominence was *The Wreck of the Squadron* (1934), which dealt with the sinking of their fleet by the Red sailors to prevent its capture by the White Russians. It was first produced at the Red Army Theatre, and was awarded a prize in a nation-wide competition. This was followed by *Platon Krechet* (1935), the story of a young Soviet surgeon, and by *Truth* (1937), which shows a Ukrainian peasant led by his search for truth to Petrograd and Lenin at the moment of the October Revolution. Even more successful than these, however, was a historical play, *Bogdan Hmelnitsky* (1939), dealing with a Ukrainian hero who in 1648 led an insurrection against the Poles. Another play about his own country was *In the Steppes of the Ukraine* (1940), to which he later wrote a war-time sequel, *Partisans in the Steppes of the Ukraine* (1942). A war-play which has proved very popular is *The Front* (1943), while a satirical comedy, *Mr. Perkins' Mission to the Land of the Bolsheviks*, in which an American millionaire visits Russia to discover for himself the truth about the Soviet régime, was produced in 1944 by the Moscow Theatre of Satire. Korneichuk is outstanding among the younger Soviet dramatists, and more excellent work may be hoped for from him.

KOSTER AND BIAL'S, NEW YORK, on 23rd Street. Originally the St. James's and Dan Bryant's Opera House for Minstrel and Variety shows, this opened on 5 May 1879 as a concert hall. In 1881, after a distinguished musical history, it began to import outstanding vaudeville stars from abroad, and became a famous house of light entertainment. The original theatre closed on 26 Aug. 1893 and Koster and Bial moved to a site on 34th Street previously occupied by the Manhattan Theatre. There they successfully continued the policy of the earlier house until on 21 July 1901 the theatre finally closed, all the interior fittings being auctioned and the site sold to Macy's for their department store.   G. F.

KOTHORNOS, see GREECE, 3 d.

KOTZEBUE, AUGUST FRIEDRICH FERDINAND VON (1761–1819), German dramatist, who in his day was more popular than Schiller. From 1781–95 he was a civil servant at St. Petersburg. Then followed several years devoted largely to drama and the theatre in Vienna. On his return to Russia he was arrested and sent for a time to Siberia, but was later released and became director of the Court theatre in St. Petersburg. On the death of his patron Paul I he went to Weimar, and after the downfall of Napoleon, whom he had denounced violently, he became Russian Consul-General in Königsberg. His antipathy to the Youth Movement at German universities earned him the hatred of the students, one of whom, Karl Ludwig Sand, a fanatic, stabbed him to death in 1819, an ending as melodramatic as in any of his plays.

Kotzebue, who was vain and injudicious, but by no means without literary gifts, had an unerring flair for what the public wanted, and gave it to them. He wrote over 200 plays, and his vogue, not only in Germany but all over Europe, was immense. The most successful of his plays was possibly *Menschenhass und Reue* (1789), in which an erring wife gains forgiveness from her husband, turned misanthropist, by a life of atonement. It now dates badly, but as *The Stranger* it was successfully translated and adapted for Drury Lane in 1798 by Benjamin Thompson, who did the same for a number of other plays by Kotzebue. Sheridan himself adapted *Die Spanier in Peru* in the following year, with much success, under the title of *Pizarro*. Kotzebue provided excellent parts for the great actors of his day, including Mrs. Siddons and Kemble in England, and his plays arrived in America by way of adaptations made by America's first professional dramatist, William Dunlap. A delightful skit on provincialism, *Die deutschen Kleinstädter* (1803), is the best of Kotzebue's comedies, and still provides entertainment, but on the whole he appealed to the grosser instincts of his audience, and cheapened the major virtues in his endeavour to provide thrills and excitement. His influence on the development of melodrama was unfortunate, tending to lead it further down the paths of sensationalism, and as a result his plays,

lacking any depth of feeling or literary grace, have disappeared with the fashion that gave them contemporary popularity.

KRASNYA PRESNYA THEATRE, MOSCOW, see REALISTIC THEATRE.

KROG, HELGE (1889–   ), contemporary Norwegian dramatist, author of a number of fine plays (see SCANDINAVIA, 2).

KRUTCH, JOSEPH WOOD (1893–   ), American dramatic critic. He was born in Knoxville, Tennessee, and attended Columbia University, where he later became an instructor of English and journalism. He has been the dramatic critic of *The Nation* since 1924, and is one of the most scholarly and penetrating of the American writers. His standards are of a high order and he has not changed the fundamental principles of his criticism with the passing of the years. He is a critic of the drama—and the drama as literature—rather than a reporter of the playhouses, and his introduction to *Nine Plays* contains perhaps the fairest evaluation of O'Neill's work. He has also written *Samuel Johnson*, *The Modern Temper*, *Edgar Allan Poe* and *American Drama Since 1918*, a useful guide to the modern American stage.
                                                       T. Q. C.

KUMMERFELD, KAROLINE (née Schultze) (1745–1815), a German actress who in 1758 joined the Ackermann company, and made her début as Iphigenia—as she relates in her memoirs—without rehearsals and without having read more than her own part. She remained with the Ackermanns until they went to Hamburg, where her talents and popularity excited the animosity of Sophie Hensel, who soon engineered her dismissal. She and her brother, a ballet-master, then joined Koch in Leipzig, where she was much admired by the young Goethe. Later she went to Gotha under Ekhof, and was esteemed by him as a good actress and a loyal colleague. She accompanied the actors after his death to Mannheim at the invitation of Dalberg. Her memoirs, referred to above, give an interesting picture of the theatrical life of the period, and contain many sidelights on the great Ekhof, whom she blames in part for the controversy with Schröder at Hamburg.

KUPPELHORIZONT, see LIGHTING, 1 d.

KURZ, JOSEPH FELIX VON (1715–84), Austrian actor, who developed the typical Viennese peasant-clown Hanswurst into a personal type to which he gave the name Bernardon. He was the staunch champion of the old improvised comedy in its battle against the newly imported regular classic drama, and when the latter proved victorious he and his wife, an Italian, with a mixed company of Italians, Austrians, and South Germans, mostly young, took themselves off to the Rhineland. There they were joined by the young Schröder, who had just left Ackermann's company in Hamburg in disgust. He proved a great asset, but left after a year, harassed by the conflicting jealousies of the women of the company. Later von Kurz was divorced by his wife, and she continued to lead the old company while he returned to the Burgtheater in Vienna. The time for his Bernardoniades had, however, gone by, and the new drama had obtained so strong a hold that he was forced to retire before it.

KYD, THOMAS (1558–94), English dramatist, author of *The Spanish Tragedy* (*c.* 1585), one of the most popular plays of its day, and prototype of many succeeding 'tragedies of revenge'. It was constantly revived and revised, in one instance by Ben Jonson, and survived into Restoration days, being seen by Pepys in 1668. Some scholars have noted in it a strong relation to the later tragedy of *Hamlet*; it has also been suggested that Kyd was the author of an earlier *Hamlet*, now lost, which Shakespeare used as the basis of his play, written for the Lord Chamberlain's Men at the time when Jonson was revising *The Spanish Tragedy* for the Admiral's Men. Kyd is also one of the many contemporary authors credited with *The Taming of a Shrew*, again a lost play believed to have been used by Shakespeare. Apart from his translation of Garnier's

Cornélie (1574), no other plays can be definitely assigned to him, since *A First Part of Ieronimo* (printed in 1605), whose action precedes that of *The Spanish Tragedy*, is probably by someone else, and *Soliman and Perseda* (*c.* 1590) has by some been given to Peele. Traces of Kyd's work have been looked for in *Titus Andronicus* and *Arden of Feversham*. He was an intimate friend of Marlowe, with whom he was implicated in accusations of atheism, extricating himself in a not altogether creditable manner.

KYNASTON, EDWARD (NED) (*c.* 1640–1706), English actor and one of the last boy-players of feminine roles. Pepys said of him 'He made the loveliest lady that ever I saw', and it was the delight of fashionable ladies to take him, in his petticoats, driving in the Park after the play. Cibber recounts that Charles II had once to wait for the curtain to rise at the theatre because Kynaston, who played the tragedy queen, was being shaved. In later life he fulfilled the promise of his youth, and made many fine dignified appearances in heroic roles. He was particularly admired in *Henry IV*.

KYÖGEN, see JAPAN.

L

LABERIUS, Decimus, see MIME, 2 *b*.

LABICHE, Eugène (1815–88), French dramatist, who between 1838 and 1877 wrote, alone or in collaboration, more than a hundred and fifty light comedies. Of these the most successful were *Le Chapeau de paille d'Italie* (1851), *Le Voyage de M. Perrichon* (1860), *La Poudre aux yeux* (1861), and *La Cagnotte* (1864). The first two are still revived from time to time, and have been translated into English. The first was done in New York in 1936 as *Horse Eats Hat*. Some of Labiche's contemporary success, which was so great as to cause him to be compared, somewhat extravagantly, with Molière, may be looked for in a secret revolt of the lighter-minded audiences of Paris against the serious problem-plays of the younger Dumas and others. Labiche's humour is broad, his jokes time-worn, but acceptably presented and embellished. He raised French farce to a height which it has seldom attained since, and gave new life and gaiety to the vaudeville inherited from Scribe.

LABOUCHÈRE, Mrs. Henry, see HODSON, HENRIETTA.

LABOUR STAGE, New York, see PRINCESS THEATRE.

LA CALPRENÈDE, Gautier de Costes de (*c*. 1610–63), a French nobleman, well received at Court, author of several successful novels, and also a dramatist. He wrote several excellent tragedies, the first while still in the army. It was produced at the Hôtel de Bourgogne in 1635, and met with the approval of Richelieu. La Calprenède was rather ashamed of his plays, thinking playwriting beneath the dignity of a soldier and a courtier, but he was consoled by their success, and by the plaudits of the polite world. Three of his subjects were taken from English history, the most interesting being *Le Comte d'Essex* (1637), in which he introduces the episode of the ring given by Elizabeth to Essex, based on current tradition. La Calprenède was one of the little group of dramatists contemporary with the early plays of Corneille, and his work contributed to the moulding of the classical tradition in France.

LA CHAPELLE, Jean de (1655–1723), French nobleman who in his youth wrote plays, the first being a farce, followed by four tragedies. The latter were much influenced by Racine, and were given by the newly formed company of the Comédie-Française with Baron and Mlle Champmeslé. The most successful of them was probably *Cléopâtre* (1681), in which Baron gave an outstanding performance as Antony. It was sufficiently well known to be parodied a year or two later,

and remained in the repertory of the theatre until 1727. In 1684 La Chapelle abandoned dramatic composition for politics and history, but later wrote the libretto for an opera, which was considered a more elegant pastime for a gentleman than the writing of plays. La Chapelle, who helped to keep alive classical tragedy after Racine's retirement, might have done much for the French theatre had he continued to write, and taken his work seriously.

LA CHAUSSÉE, (Pierre Claude) Nivelle de (1692–1754), French dramatist, and the chief exponent of eighteenth-century *comédie larmoyante*. He was forty before he produced his first play, *La Fausse antipathie* (1733), though he was already a well-known figure in literary society. This and his *Préjugé à la mode* (1735) were both well received, and may be said, with their mingling of tragedy and comedy, to mark the end of old French comedy and the beginning of the *drame bourgeois*. La Chaussée was himself a wealthy man, with somewhat frank and licentious tastes, and it is obvious from his prologue to *La Fausse antipathie* that he wrote as he did deliberately, because he saw that that was what his audience wanted. His pictures of moral virtue and of the trials of domestic life exactly suited the new middle-class audience, with its preponderance of women and its disposition to indulge freely in sentimental tears. Having proved the success of his new method, La Chaussée produced some forty plays in the same vein, of which the most successful were *Mélanide* (1741), perhaps the most typical *comédie larmoyante*, *L'École des mères* (1744), and *La Gouvernante* (1747), a foretaste of *East Lynne*. If La Chaussée's plays are forgotten to-day it is not so much because their subject-matter dates, as because their simple central situations are involved in a conventional network of intrigue, and their action is impeded by much narrative. Also they are written in verse, which, though the finest medium for high tragedy, seems somehow wasted on domestic interiors. Yet in his own day La Chaussée was immensely successful and, in the wave of sentimentality which was sweeping across Europe at the time, his plays were translated into Dutch, Italian, and English.

LACKAYE, Wilton (1862–1932), American actor who was intended for the Church, but adopted the stage after a chance visit to Madison Square Theatre on his way to Rome. He was in an amateur company when Lawrence Barrett gave him a part in *Francesca da Rimini* at the Star Theatre, New York, on 27 Aug. 1883. He later appeared many times with Fanny Davenport, and in 1887 made a success in *She*. He was constantly in demand, being equally good in tragedy, comedy, romance, and melodrama. He appeared in a number of Shakespeare plays, and in many new productions. He was also Jean Valjean in his own dramatization of *Les Misérables*. But his greatest part was undoubtedly Svengali, which he played for two years and in many revivals. He retired from the stage in 1927, returning only once in support of Mrs. Fiske, two years later. A handsome man of fine presence, he founded the Catholic Actors' Guild, and helped to organize the Actors' Equity Association of New York. Though intolerant of indecency on the stage, he was opposed to censorship, and his caustic wit made him an opponent to be feared.

LACY, JOHN (?–1681), English actor, originally a dancing-master, went on the stage at the Restoration, and soon became a great favourite with Charles II. His portrait by Michael Wright, showing him in three different parts—as Teague in *The Committee*, Mr. Scruple in *The Cheats*, and Mr. Galliard in *The Variety*—still hangs in Hampton Court. He was the original Bayes in Buckingham's *The Rehearsal*, and was judged to have hit Dryden off to the life. Pepys admired his Teague exceedingly, and he was considered an excellent Falstaff. He was the author of four plays, of which one was based on *Le Médecin malgré lui* and another on *The Taming of the Shrew*.

LADINO DRAMA, see JEWISH DRAMA, 8.

LADY ELIZABETH'S MEN, a company of players formed in 1611, under John Townsend and Joseph Moore, which, after a provincial tour, appeared at Court in 1612. In the following year they were joined with the Revels Company, under Rossiter, and the joint company, of which Henslowe was manager, played together for some years. It was for them that Daborne wrote, and they appear to have acted at the Swan, the Rose, and Whitefriars. In 1614 the actor Nathan Field was their chief player, and in the same year they were established at the Hope, where they found they had much to complain of in Henslowe's treatment of them (see HENSLOWE). On his death in 1616 four of the chief members of the company joined Prince Charles's Men, a company newly formed by Alleyn; Field had already left them, as had other outstanding men, and the depleted group was reduced to the status of a provincial company. For four or five years they appear only in civic records, but some time in 1621–2 a new London company, known as the Lady Elizabeth's Men, but containing none of the provincial actors, appeared at the Phoenix. Beeston was one of the organizers of the new company, which prospered exceedingly for a short time, with a distinguished list of dramatists—Middleton, Rowley, Massinger, Ford, Dekker, Heywood, and Shirley—and some outstanding actors. In 1625, however, the company was finally broken by a disastrous epidemic

of plague, and disappears, its place being taken by the new Queen Henrietta's company. A later company, formed in 1628 as the Queen of Bohemia's players, seems to have had something fraudulent about it, but continued to exist intermittently until 1641.

LAFAYETTE THEATRE, NEW YORK. This was a circus, then an amphitheatre with spectacular drama, mainly equestrian, and in 1826 it opened as a regular playhouse, with newly installed gas-lighting. It had a good company, and in the summer some of the Chatham Theatre company joined it, Mrs. Duff appearing as Juliet and Mrs. Haller. The reopening of the Chatham, and the appearance of Macready and Kean at the Park, took away the Lafayette's audiences, and the theatre closed. In Sept. 1827 it reopened, enlarged and redecorated, with a company headed by Henry Wallack. It failed to maintain a high standard, however, and had sunk again to circus and melodrama when on 11 Apr. 1829 it was totally destroyed by fire and never rebuilt.

LA FLEUR. (1) The name under which the great French farce-player Gros-Guillaume played serious parts at the Hôtel de Bourgogne from 1621–4. His wife and daughter were both actresses, and the latter married an actor (2) FRANÇOIS JUVENON (*fl.* 1623–59), who also took the name of La Fleur. He played kings in tragedy, in succession to Montfleury, Gascons and ranting *capitanos* in comedy. He appeared in some of Racine's plays (for his son, see LA TUILLERIE).

LA FOSSE, ANTOINE D'AUBIGNY DE (1653–1708), French dramatist, nephew of a painter, by whom he was brought up. In his youth he went to Italy as secretary to Foucher, and later, in the service of Créqui, in company with another contemporary dramatist, Campistron, was present at the battle of Luzzara, where his master was killed. La Fosse was over 40 when he produced his first play, *Polixène* (1696). The style was accounted better than the subject, but a second play, *Manlius Capitolinus* (1698), was most successful, and remained in the repertory of the Comédie-Française until 1849. Talma, in particular, was later very good in the name part. The play was a frank imitation of Corneille and Racine, and under the guise of Roman names treated of contemporary history, being an account of the conspiracy of the Spaniards against Venice, a subject used some years earlier by Otway in *Venice Preserved* (1682). La Fosse's later plays were not successful, but many of his contemporaries thought he might have rivalled Racine had he begun his dramatic career earlier.

LA FRANCE, see JADOT.

LAGERKVIST, PÄR (1891–   ), Swedish dramatist and poet, is probably the most remarkable playwright of the modern Swedish theatre. Devoted as he is to Strindberg and sharing the profound despair implicit in Strindberg's early reading of life, he is nevertheless an independent and highly imaginative artist, original both in thought and technique. Characteristic of this side of his work are the early plays, *Sista människan* (*The Last Man*) (1917), *Himlens hemlighet* (*The Secret of Heaven*) (1919), and *Den osynlige* (*The Invisible*) (1923). Like Strindberg's before him, his mood and technique change in his second phase, though not necessarily in the same direction, for, while the gloom of his mood relents, his manner moves towards, not farther from, realism. Characteristic of these later plays are *Han som fick leva om sitt liv* (*The Man Who Lived His Life Again*) (1928); *Konungen* (*The King*) (1932); *Mannen utan själ* (*The Man Without a Soul*) (1936); and *Seger i mörker* (*Victory in the Dark* (1939).   U. E.-F.

LA GRANGE. (1) CHARLES VARLET (1639–92), a French actor, who joined the company of Molière from the provinces in 1659. He was young and handsome, of good presence and address, and played all Molière's young lovers, as well as the hero of Racine's *Alexandre*. A methodical man, he kept a register of the plays presented at the Palais-Royal and the receipts from each, interspersed with notes on the domestic affairs of the company which have proved invaluable to later students of the period. In 1664 he took over Molière's functions as Orator to the troupe, and was active in forwarding its affairs after Molière's death. As an act of piety to the memory of his friend he edited and wrote a preface to the first collected edition of Molière's works, published in 1682. He married (2) MARIE (1639–1737), daughter of the famous pastry-cook, amateur of the theatre, Cyprien Ragueneau, immortalized by Rostand in *Cyrano de Bergerac*. She was already a member of the company, and probably played the part of Marotte in *Les Précieuses ridicules*, by which name she was known on the stage. She also created the part of the Comtesse d'Escarbagnas, and retired from the amalgamated troupe of the Comédie-Française on the death of her husband. La Grange's eldest brother (3) ACHILLE (1636–1709) was also an actor, under the name of Verneuil, first at the Marais and later with the newly formed Comédie-Française. He, too, married an actress nicknamed Marotte.

LA GRANGE-CHANCEL, JOSEPH DE (1677–1758), French dramatist, writer of tragedies which rank with those of Campistron and Crébillon. He was a precocious child, whose first play was written when he was about 13. With the help of Racine, who was a friend and counsellor of the young writer, it was put on in 1694, but was not a great success. It was followed by several more tragedies, in which La Grange-Chancel again had the help and advice of Racine, but his work shows the continual decline of the classical ideal, and the tendency, which later becomes more marked,

to make sensationalism and not emotion the mainspring of the plot. The most successful of his plays were *Amasis* (1701) and *Ino et Mélicerte* (1713). A few years later he wrote some satirical verses about the Regent, and was imprisoned. He escaped and went into exile, not returning until after the Regent's death, when he settled in his native town of Antoniat and spent his time in alienating his friends and family by malicious epigrams. He also indulged in controversy with Voltaire. He seems to have been an embittered man, who suffered from his own precocity, and failed to redeem the promise of his youth.

LA HARPE, JEAN FRANÇOIS DE (1739–1802), French dramatist, whose plays, modelled on those of Voltaire, show the continued decline of classical tragedy during the eighteenth century. The first, *Le Comte de Warwick* (1763), is usually accounted the best, though *Philoctète* (1781) and *Coriolan* (1784) were well received. It is, however, as a critic that La Harpe is best remembered. His *Cours de littérature ancienne et moderne*, based on lectures given in 1786, is a standard work, full of interesting ideas and information, which has, however, to be corrected in the light of later literary judgements. He is at his best when dealing with the French seventeenth century, and wrote excellent commentaries on the plays of Racine. La Harpe also made a translation of Lillo's *London Merchant*, with alterations which entirely falsified the purpose and meaning of the plot. It was never acted.

LAMB, CHARLES (1775–1834), English critic and essayist who wrote about drama and dramatists with a warm affection which threw as much light on Lamb himself as upon his subject. He admits in *Imperfect Sympathies* that his mind was desultory, sadly lacking in system, 'suggestive merely, and content with fragments and scattered pieces of truth'. Yet on those 'fragments' for which he had a fondness Lamb held decided views.

Although he wrote four plays, none of them had any great success. His *John Woodvil* (1802) shows the influence of the Elizabethans, especially of Beaumont and Fletcher. His *Mr. H.*, a farce, was produced at Drury Lane in 1806 with Elliston in the title part. The play was soundly hissed, and was not revived until 1822, when it was performed at the Opera House in the Strand. It was revived also by the Society of Dramatic Students at the Globe Theatre in 1885. Lamb also wrote *The Wife's Trial; or, the Intruding Widow*, a play in poetic form which appeared in *Blackwood's Magazine* (1828), as did also his last play, *The Pawnbroker's Daughter* (1830). Neither was acted.

Lamb's dramatic essays were of more enduring stuff. His *Specimens of English Dramatic Poets who lived about the time of Shakespeare* appeared in 1808, and was designed to 'illustrate what might be called the moral sense of our ancestors'. In the essay *On the Tragedies of Shakespeare* he made out his famous case for reading Shakespeare's plays in preference to witnessing their performance on the stage. Yet the *Essays of Elia* recall more than one pleasure of playgoing. His references to old actors are tinged with the affection of one who has enjoyed the busy traffic of the stage as well as the calm seclusion of the study. His regard for Shakespeare led him to write the *Tales from Shakespeare* (1807) on which he worked with his sister Mary. In spite of his inability to see more in Lear on the stage than 'an old man tottering about the stage, turned out of doors by his daughters on a rainy night', Lamb was a man of the theatre. Put an old Drury Lane playbill before him, and 'how fresh to memory arise the magic and the manner of the gentle actor'.   T. C. K.

LAMI, EUGÈNE LOUIS (1800–90), French theatrical designer, who may have been responsible for Taglioni's costume in the ballet 'La Sylphide' (1832), from which the conventional ballet-dress, or *tutu*, was evolved (see COSTUME, 8).

LA MOTTE, ANTOINE HOUDARD DE (1672–1731), French dramatist, who was to have been a lawyer, but preferred literature. The failure of his first play in 1693 so disgusted him that he almost decided to become a monk, but the call of the theatre was too strong, and a few years later he was writing opera-libretti and lyrics for ballets, some of them the best since Quinault. His verses were graceful and charming, though lacking in vigour. His one important work is a tragedy, *Inès de Castro*, which was given with great success at the Comédie-Française in 1723, but he was also the author of several comedies, among them *La Matrone d'Éphèse* and *Italie galante*, and his works were well enough known to be parodied at the unlicensed theatres of the Parisian fairs. He was an excellent conversationalist, witty and warm-hearted, and was much sought after in society. But, having been preferred to J.-B. Rousseau in the contest for Thomas Corneille's seat in the French Academy in 1710, he made many enemies, and died friendless and in poverty.

LANDER, JEAN MARGARET DAVENPORT (1829–1903), the daughter of an English actor named Thomas Donald Davenport (1792–1851), who is believed to have been the model for Vincent Crummles, in which case his talented little daughter, who at 8 was playing Richard III, would be the original Infant Phenomenon. She went with her family to the United States in 1838 as a child prodigy, playing a number of unsuitable parts like Shylock, Sir Peter Teazle, and Sir Giles Overreach, was then privately educated, and made her adult début in 1844 as Juliet. She toured the continent, and in 1849 returned to the United States with such success that she settled there. She was the first actress in America to play Adrienne Lecouvreur and Marguerite Gautier, the latter with young

Edwin Booth as Armand. Her repertory also included *The Wife*, *The Hunchback*, *Love*, *Ingomar*, *The Lady of Lyons*, and the roles of Charlotte Corday and Peg Woffington, in all of which she appeared during her successful tours. These were interrupted in 1860 by her marriage to General Lander, but after his death in the Civil War two years later she returned to the stage, being billed for the first time as Mrs. Lander at Niblo's Garden in 1865 in her own adaptation of *Mésalliance*. On 1 Jan. 1877 she made her last appearance on the stage at Boston, again in her own dramatization, this time of *The Scarlet Letter*. A small, well-formed woman, with a sweet face, clear voice, and graceful figure, she was an actress of great talent and intellectual judgement, but lacked genius.

LANDRIANI, PAOLO (1770–1838), see SCENERY, 4.

LANE, LUPINO, see LUPINO (3).

LANE, SARAH (1823–99), see BRITANNIA THEATRE.

LANG. (1) MATHESON (1879–1948), English actor-manager and dramatist, son of a clerical family, cousin to Cosmo Lang, late Archbishop of Canterbury, and himself destined for the Church. As a boy, however, he was much attracted by the theatre, and his determination to go on the stage was strengthened by visits to Benson's and Irving's companies when they were on tour in Scotland. He first appeared with Calvert in Wolverhampton in 1897, and later joined Benson, being with him when the Theatre Royal, Newcastle, burnt down and all the company's wardrobe and properties were lost. After a visit to the United States with Mrs. Langtry, an English tour with Ellen Terry, and a Benson tour to the West Indies, he returned to London, where he had first appeared with Benson in 1900, and played under the Vedrenne–Barker management at the Court in Ibsen and Shaw. His first outstanding success, however, was scored in *The Christian* (1907) at the Lyceum, where he also gave fine performances as Romeo and Hamlet. He then took his own company on tour to South Africa, Australia, and India, playing Shakespeare and modern romantic drama with much success. It was on his return in 1913 that he appeared in a play with which his name was for a long time associated, *Mr. Wu*. First produced in Manchester, it ran for over a year in London, was subsequently seen all over the world with Lang as Wu Li Chang, and gave its title to his autobiography, *Mr. Wu Looks Back*, published in 1940. With his wife (2) HUTIN [NELLIE] BRITTON (1876–   ), who had been with him in Benson's and Ellen Terry's companies, and had subsequently toured as his leading lady, he inaugurated the Shakespeare productions at the Old Vic in 1914 with *The Taming of the Shrew*, *Hamlet*, and *The Merchant of Venice*. Among his later productions the most famous were *The Wandering Jew*, first produced in 1920, which ran for a year and was subsequently revived many times, *The Chinese Bungalow* (1925) in his own dramatization from a novel, *Such Men are Dangerous* (1928), and *Jew Süss* (1929), both dramatized by Ashley Dukes. Lang himself was the adapter of *The Purple Mask*, with which he opened his management at the Lyric Theatre, London, in 1918, and part-author of *Carnival*, seen at the New Theatre two years later. A tall, heavily built man, he was exceedingly handsome and had a fine, resonant voice. He attained eminence in the theatrical world through industry and application, making his way steadily, though without hardship, from the daily routine of the touring company to the cares of management, supported and assisted always by his wife, and by the constant affection and interest of the many audiences he catered for throughout the Empire.

LANGENDIJK, Pieter, see HOLLAND.

LANGTRY, Lillie (1852–1929), English actress, daughter of the Dean of Jersey, the Rev. W. C. le Breton, who from her surpassing beauty was known as the Jersey Lily. She married at the age of 22 Edward Langtry, a member of the Diplomatic Service, and became prominent in London society, being an intimate friend of Edward VII, then Prince of Wales. She was one of the first English society women to go on the stage, making her début under the Bancrofts at the Haymarket, as Kate Hardcastle, on 15 Dec. 1881. She caused a great sensation, but more on account of her looks and social position than by her acting, which for many years was not taken seriously by the critics. She organized her own company, being accounted a good manageress, and with it played at the Imperial and other London theatres and also toured the provinces and the United States. Although never a great actress, she was a pleasing one, being particularly acceptable in such parts as Rosalind. She maintained a large racing stable, and married as her second husband Sir Hugo de Bathe.

LA NOUE, Jean Sauve de (1701–61), French actor who for many years toured the provinces successfully with his own company. In 1739 he wrote a play, *Mahomet II*, which was given at the Comédie-Française, and Voltaire, who thought well of it, was indebted to it for some of his own *Mahomet, ou le fanatisme*. He acknowledged this debt by allowing La Noue to perform the play at Lille before it was given at the Comédie-Française, and then only allowed the latter to have it if La Noue were imported into the company to play the title-role, subject to his making a satisfactory début. This he did in 1742, remaining with the Comédie-Française until 1757. In the year before his retirement he wrote a comedy, *La Coquette corrigée*, given first at the Comédie-Italienne, which showed plainly the influence of Marivaux. Some critics indeed rank it above Marivaux's work, mainly on account of its greater realism. It was his last play, and La

Noue then left the stage to become Director of Court Theatricals, a post he held until his death.

LANTERN, see LIGHTING, 2.

LAPORTE [Mathieu le Febvre] (c. 1584–c. 1621), early French actor-manager, husband of Marie Venier, the first French actress to be known by name. With her he was a member of Valleran-Lecomte's provincial company which established itself at the Hôtel de Bourgogne in 1607–8, and was also for a time a member of his father-in-law's company. In 1610 he and his wife got into trouble for acting at the Hôtel d'Argent, and thus infringing the monopoly of the Hôtel de Bourgogne, and soon after Laporte retired. Little is known of his acting ability, but he was a good organizer and the author of a number of plays written for the travelling company to which he originally belonged.

LARIVEY, Pierre de (c. 1540–c. 1612), an early French dramatist, who may possibly have been born of Italian parents and formed his name from a translation of theirs, Giunti. In 1577 he saw the Italian *commedia dell' arte* company, the Gelosi, play at Blois, and inspired by them he wrote nine comedies, six of which were printed in 1579, the other three not until 1611. There may have been others, but if so they are lost. All those that survive are based on Italian models, but they are in no sense of the word translations, being adaptations which often contain much new material. They were played extensively in the provinces and also in Paris. Molière drew largely on Larivey, which is indeed the chief reason for the latter's importance in the history of French drama.

LAROQUE [Pierre Regnault Petit-Jean] (c. 1595–1676), French actor, a member of the company at the Marais under Montdory, and later its leader. When Floridor left to go to the Hôtel de Bourgogne Laroque took over his position as Orator to the troupe, and it was he who adroitly deprived Molière of the Du Parcs when they first came to Paris, though he was unable to keep them more than a year. Little is known of Laroque's abilities as an actor, but he was much esteemed as a fearless and efficient man of the theatre, and he piloted the Marais through many difficult years. He could not, however, stand up against the combined rivalry of Molière and the Hôtel de Bourgogne, and in the end his theatre was mostly given over to the newfangled 'machine' plays. On Molière's death he and his companions amalgamated with the company at the Palais-Royal, and so formed part of the original Comédie-Française. Laroque was the first to recognize and foster the talent of Mlle Champmeslé, whom he put through a systematic course of instruction when she first joined his company in 1669.

LARRA, Mariano José de (1809–37), a

famous Spanish journalist and satirist, a champion of the Romantic movement, and also a dramatist. His most important play, which preceded by a few months only the *Don Álvaro* of Saavedra and the definite triumph of Romanticism, was *Macías* (1834), a passionate and poetic drama which had a great influence on the theatre of its time. Larra wrote also several comedies and translated contemporary French plays by Scribe, Ducange, Delavigne, and others. He committed suicide at the age of 28 as the result of an unhappy love affair.

LATEINER, JOSEPH (1853–1935), writer of plays in Yiddish, and founder of the first regular Yiddish theatre in New York in 1883 (see JEWISH DRAMA, 5).

LATE JOYS, see PLAYERS' THEATRE.

LA THORILLIÈRE. (1) FRANÇOIS LENOIR DE (1626–80), French actor, who had already played in the provinces when he appeared at the Marais in about 1658–9, where he married the niece (or daughter) of the head of the company, Laroque. He later joined Molière at the Palais-Royal, played important parts in most of the latter's comedies, and himself composed a tragedy on the subject of Cleopatra which was given by Molière's troupe. On the death of Molière he went to the Hôtel de Bourgogne, and it was his death that precipitated the amalgamation of the companies to form the Comédie-Française, a course to which he had been opposed. His son (2) PIERRE (1659–1731) was also an actor, and joined the Comédie-Française in 1684. As a child he had appeared in Molière's *Psyché*, and he later replaced J. B. Raisin in some of Molière's parts, gaining a good reputation as a comic actor, and occasionally replaced Champmeslé in tragedy. He married Columbine, daughter of Dominique of the Comédie-Italienne. Their son (3) ANNE-MAURICE (*c.* 1697–1759) was also an actor, and Doyen of the Comédie-Française at the time of his death, having made his début there in 1722. He first played in tragedy, but later made an excellent reputation in romantic roles and in serious comedy. One of François's daughters, Charlotte, married the great actor Baron in 1675, while another, Thérèse, became the wife of Dancourt.

LATIN-AMERICAN THEATRE, see SOUTH AMERICA.

LATIN DRAMA, see FABULA, MIME, 2 and ROME; ECCLESIASTICAL DRAMA, JESUIT DRAMA and SCHOOL DRAMA.

LATTICE, see AUDITORIUM, 2.

LA TUILLERIE. (1), JEAN FRANÇOIS JUVENON (1650–88), French actor and dramatist, son of actors at the Hôtel de Bourgogne and grandson of the farce-player Gros-Guillaume (see LA-FLEUR). He himself was an actor at the Hôtel de Bourgogne by 1672, in which year he married (2) LOUISE CATHERINE (*c.* 1657–1706),

daughter of the celebrated comedian, Raymond Poisson. He was a tall, stately man, at his best in tragedy, where he often replaced Champmeslé, while in comedy he played minor roles, usually those requiring a fine physique. He was, for example, the statue in *Le Festin de Pierre*. His plays included tragedies which were mainly rewritings of older dramas, and farces, of which two, *Crispin précepteur* (1680) and *Crispin bel esprit* (1681), were produced at the Hôtel de Bourgogne with La Tuillerie's father-in-law in the title-roles. On the foundation of the Comédie-Française La Tuillerie's wife retired, but he remained with the company until his death a few years later. His plays were often attributed to the Abbé Abeille, author of some undistinguished works.

LAUBE, HEINRICH (1806–84), German theatre manager, who succeeded Schreyvogel as director of the Vienna Hofburgtheater. He had been a member of the 'Young Germany' movement, and a prolific novelist, while his plays, though uninspired, were effective in production. He brought to his task a profound knowledge of the European stage, particularly that of Paris, and, with an adroitness of which his predecessor had been incapable, managed to combine the staging of good plays with a lavishness and pictorial splendour which satisfied the public demand at that time for light entertainment. Laube was a friend of Wagner, who in 1843 wrote for a journal which Laube was then editing, the *Zeitung für die elegante Welt*, the autobiographical sketch which is reprinted in vol. i of his collected works.

LAUDER, SIR HARRY (1870–1950), one of the most famous stars of the music-hall stage, whose essentially Scots humour never failed to awaken a response in the most English bosom from his first appearance in London in 1900. He first gained fame at the Argyle, Birkenhead, as an Irish comedian. When, in response to the demand for encores, his Irish songs ran out, he sang Scots ones and from then on remained faithful to them. He was knighted in 1919 for his services during the First World War, and for the work he did in entertaining the troops on the French front. He made numerous tours of the United States, South Africa, and Australia, and wrote several volumes of reminiscences. Among his most famous songs may be mentioned 'I love a lassie', 'Roamin' in the Gloamin' ', 'A wee Deoch-and-Doris', 'It's nice to get up in the morning', and 'Stop yer tickling, Jock'. He invariably wore a kilt and glengarry, and carried a crooked stick. He appeared in revue, and in at least one straight play, *The Scrape of the Pen*.   W. M. P.

LAUDI, see ITALY, 1 *a* i.

LAUDIVIO, see NOBILI, LAUDIVIO DE'.

LAURA KEENE'S THEATRE, NEW YORK, see KEENE, LAURA, and OLYMPIC, 3.

LAVEDAN, HENRI (1859–1940), French dramatist, whose plays deal with social problems and contemporary manners, somewhat in the style of Becque and the naturalistic writers, but in a less downright and drastic manner. His best play is *Le Prince d'Aurec* (1894), in which a decadent young nobleman is saved from the consequences of his folly by the sacrifices of his bourgeois mother. It was followed by a sequel, *Les Deux Noblesses* (1897), in which the hero restores the family fortunes by going into trade. Among his other plays the comedies of manners, *Le Nouveau jeu* (1905) and *Le Goût du vice* (1911), were less serious, but had a breezy vitality which made them popular.

LAVER, JAMES (1899–   ), English theatre historian, lecturer, dramatist, and novelist. Since 1922 he has been in charge of the theatre collections of the Victoria and Albert Museum, and has produced a number of books on costume, one of his main interests, and on theatre design. He is also a lecturer and examiner in the history of theatre art. In 1933 his successful novel, *Nymph Errant*, was dramatized by another hand, while his own plays include *The House that went to Sea* (1936) and a study of Shelley entitled *The Heart was not Burned* (1938). In 1928 he adapted Klabund's *Der Kreidekreis* (1923), a modern romantic drama with a Chinese setting, as *The Circle of Chalk*. It is, however, as a writer, lecturer, and research worker that he has up to the present been most active in the theatre.

LAVINIA, see PONTI, DIANA DA.

LAWRENCE, SLINGSBY, see LEWES, G. H.

LAZZO (*pl. lazzi*), a word used for the byplay of the comic masks of the *commedia dell'arte*. It consisted in small items of comic decoration on the main plot, and there is no satisfactory etymology or translation of the word, which, says one authority, 'needs to be variously rendered as antics, gambols, tricks, actions, comic turns, according to the context'. The longer comic episode, usually involving a practical joke and some horseplay, was known as the *burla* (*pl. burle*), from which are derived the terms burletta and burlesque.

LEAP, the supreme test of an acrobatic player, by which he appears on or vanishes from the stage with magical effect (see TRICKWORK ON THE ENGLISH STAGE).

LECOUVREUR, ADRIENNE (1692–1730), French actress, the daughter of a poor hatter who settled near the Comédie-Française. She was thus brought into close contact with the actresses of the day, among them Mlle Duclos and Mlle Desmares, and, inspired by their example, she appeared in some amateur productions with no little success. She was then taken in hand by the actor-dramatist Legrand, and after a season at Strasbourg made her début at the Comédie-Française in 1717. The public took her to its heart at once, and never wavered in its allegiance, though she had much to suffer from the jealousy of her fellow-actresses, particularly Mlle Duclos. She is said to have been better in tragedy than in comedy, but it is difficult to assess her art, for her charm and beauty were such that even her faults were forgiven her, and the public looked with an indulgent eye on her love-affairs. She was for some time the mistress of Marshal Saxe, whose desertion of her in favour of the Princesse de Bouillon is said to have hastened her death. Her short but glorious reign lasted only thirteen years. She died suddenly, and was refused Christian burial, being interred secretly at night in a marshy corner of the Rue de Bourgogne. Voltaire, in some of whose plays she appeared, was with her when she died, and wrote a bitter poem on the attitude of the Church, which seemed to him even more monstrous when compared with the funeral of Anne Oldfield in Westminster Abbey in the same year. In 1849 Scribe and Legouvé wrote a play on Adrienne Lecouvreur, which, though hardly accurate, supplied Rachel, and later Sarah Bernhardt, with an excellent part.

LEE, NATHANIEL (*c.* 1653–92), English dramatist, author of a number of tragedies on subjects taken from ancient history—Nero, Mithridates, Sophonisba, Theodosius, Constantine—treated with much extravagance and bombast, though with occasional gleams of true poetic fire. The son of a clergyman, and well educated, he went to London with the intention of becoming an actor, but in spite of a fine voice and good elocution he was not successful. He turned to playwriting, confining himself entirely to tragedy, and that of the deepest dye, leaving his stage strewn with corpses, and many of his characters lunatic. He had a streak of morbidity, which later turned to insanity, and was towards the end of his life confined in Bedlam. His best and most successful play was *The Rival Queens; or, the Death of Alexander the Great*, dealing with the jealousy between Alexander's wives, Roxana and Statira. First produced in 1677, with Betterton and Mrs. Barry, it held the stage for over a hundred years, and was in the repertory of Kemble, Kean, and Mrs. Siddons. Cibber, in his *Apology*, attributes much of its original success to the splendid ranting of Betterton. Lee, who twice collaborated with Dryden, was one of the most popular writers of his day, and both his rhymed heroic dramas and his blank-verse tragedies, which sought to combine the passion of Shakespeare with the classical tradition of France, were frequently played and printed.

LEE SUGG, CATHARINE (1797–1848), see HACKETT (2).

LEFFLER, ANNE CHARLOTTE (1849–92), Swedish dramatist (see SCANDINAVIA, 3).

LE GALLIENNE, Eva (1899–), American actress and producer, daughter of the poet Richard Le Gallienne. Born in London, she studied at the Royal Academy of Dramatic Art, and after playing several small parts went to New York in 1915, where she has since remained. She made a great success as Julie in *Liliom* (1921), and among her later parts were Hannele in Hauptmann's play, Hilda Wangel in *The Master Builder*, and Ella Rentheim in *John Gabriel Borkman*. In 1926 she opened the Civic Repertory Theatre and during the next six years presented there a fine programme of foreign and American plays, appearing in most of them herself. She was also associated with the founding of the American Repertory Company, playing the Queen in the initial production of *Henry VIII*. She has been one of the outstanding interpreters of Ibsen in America, and by her acting and direction has done much to further the cause of international playwrights, and widen the horizon of the theatregoing public. In 1934 she published her autobiography, and is also part-author of a popular version of *Alice in Wonderland* for the stage, in which she gave an excellent performance as the White Queen.

LEGITIMATE DRAMA, sometimes abbreviated to 'the legit.', a term which arose in the eighteenth century during the struggle of the Patent Theatres—Covent Garden and Drury Lane—against the upstart and illegitimate playhouses springing up all over London. It covered in general those five-act plays (including Shakespeare) which had little or no singing, dancing, and spectacle, and depended entirely on acting. In the nineteenth century the term was widespread, and was used by actors of the old school as a defence against the encroachments of farce, musical comedy, and revue.

LEGOUVÉ, Ernest Gabriel Jean Baptiste (1807–1903), son and grandson of French writers, himself poet, novelist, and lecturer. He is best remembered for his collaboration with Scribe and Labiche, among others. With the first he produced in 1849 *Adrienne Lecouvreur*, a fictionized account of the life of the celebrated French actress, mistress of Marshal Saxe. By himself Legouvé wrote a tragedy on Medea, which he intended for Rachel. Refused by her, it was translated into Italian, and in 1856 provided a great part for Ristori. Legouvé also wrote a number of charming one-act comedies which held the stage for many years.

LEGRAND, Marc Antoine (1673–1728), French actor, the son of an army surgeon, who is traditionally said to have been born the day Molière died. He gained his experience in a French company under Sallé which played in Warsaw, and in 1702, having previously been refused, joined the Comédie-Française to play rustic and comic parts. Short and ugly in appearance, his wit made him popular. He sometimes insisted on playing tragedy, for

which he was quite unsuited. He was author as well as actor, and his numerous plays, given at the Comédie-Italienne and the Comédie-Française, were mainly based on contemporary events. The most notorious was *Cartouche*, which dealt with the career of a footpad arrested in Oct. 1721. Legrand's play was ready a week later. The actor who played the name part visited the condemned criminal in his cell and took lessons from him in the technicalities of his profession. The play was performed thirteen times, its last production being on the day before Cartouche was executed. The contemporary aspect of Legrand's plays, in which he sometimes had the collaboration of Dominique, means that they have fallen out of the repertory, but they were highly successful in their day, and helped to bring back to the Comédie-Française the audiences which were drifting away to the unlicensed theatres of the fairs. Legrand's stagecraft was good, though his dialogue was occasionally highly-flavoured. An obscene play, *Le Luxurieux*, published in London in 1738, is attributed to him (*Pièces libres de M. Ferrand*). If it is his, it corresponds to what is known of his morals. He was the teacher of Adrienne Lecouvreur, and his son and daughter were both members of the Comédie-Française.

LEG-SHOW, a slang term for a spectacular musical play, largely designed to display the charms of the chorus-girls in a series of scanty costumes and energetic dances.

LEGS, see BORDER.

LEGUIZAMÓN, Martínian (1858–1935), see SOUTH AMERICA, 1.

LEICESTER'S MEN, the earliest organized company of Elizabethan players, first mentioned in 1559. The actors were apparently on tour, having previously played in London, though not before the Queen, which they did at Christmas in the following year. They counted as Leicester's household servants, and among them was James Burbage, who in 1576 built the first theatre in London. From 1570 onwards they were in great favour at Court, and continued so until the formation in 1583 of the Queen's Men, in which many of the best actors from Leicester's company were incorporated. In 1585 the company was probably re-formed, as it accompanied Leicester to the Low Countries. Among the players was William Kempe, who with some others went to play in Elsinore before Frederick II of Denmark. The company continued to play in Leicester's name until his death, when many of its members joined the company of the Earl of Derby (see STRANGE'S MEN).

LEIGH, Anthony (? –1692), an actor in Davenant's company at Dorset Garden, much admired by Charles II, who called him 'his' actor. He created the part of Father Dominic in Dryden's *Spanish Friar*, and took over the part of Teague in Howard's *The Committee*, originally created by Lacy. He was an excellent foil to the comedian Nokes, with whom he often played. Cibber writes of him as 'of a mercurial kind . . . in humour, he loved to take a full career . . . he had great variety in his manner and was famous in very different characters . . . Characters that would have made the reader yawn in the closet, have by the strength of his action been lifted into the loudest laughter on the stage.'

LEIGH HUNT, see HUNT, (JAMES HENRY) LEIGH.

LEKAIN [CAÏN], HENRI LOUIS (1729–78), famous French actor, the son of a goldsmith, who brought him up to his own trade. But the boy's passion for the stage declared itself early, and he frequented the Comédie-Française, afterwards declaiming the plays for the benefit of his fellow-apprentices. In 1748 he organized some amateur productions, playing the leading parts himself, with much success. While appearing in a poor play, at the author's request, he was seen by Voltaire, who was much struck by his acting. In spite of this he attempted to dissuade the young man from making the stage his profession. When that proved impossible, however, he did all he could to help him; invited him to his house, built a theatre for him, and played there himself with his two nieces. The little company soon achieved an enviable reputation, and society clamoured for admission. Lekain stayed six years with Voltaire, and always said he owed him everything. Before Voltaire left Paris for Berlin in 1750 he was able to see Lekain's début at the Comédie-Française as Titus in *Rome sauvée*. Lekain was much applauded, but through intrigue and jealousy was not received as a member for a further eighteen months, the more spectacular but less gifted Bellecour and the elegant Grandval being preferred to him. The public wanted Lekain, however, though he was small, ugly, and had a harsh voice, for he knew how to overcome his faults, and on the stage they were forgotten. Like Kean and Rachel, he had that essential spark of genius which triumphs over disabilities. Lekain worked feverishly at his parts (for an account of his acting see Clairon's *Réflexions sur l'art théâtral*) and wore himself out playing them. He was one of the most popular actors of the day, and when he fell ill the bulletins of his progress were as eagerly awaited as those of a film star to-day. When he reappeared in 1770 it was remarked by many critics that he acted better than ever, as though the enforced leisure had led to a deepening of his talents. He went to Berlin on the invitation of Frederick II, and Voltaire, whose memories of French acting went back to Baron, called him the only truly tragic actor. He was highly praised also by Grimm and La Harpe, and frequently compared to Garrick. He was responsible for many reforms in the theatre, notably for the

introduction of some trace of historical costume, in which he was nobly supported by Mlle Clairon. He was three times in prison on account of his profession, once because, with a number of his colleagues, he refused to act with a man who had brought disgrace on the company. He suffered much from the ignominious status accorded to actors in his day, thought often of retiring, but loved his work too much. His death was tragic. After giving a magnificent performance as Vendôme in Voltaire's *Adélaïde du Guesclin*, he went out into the chill night air, took cold, and died just as his great benefactor and admirer was returning to Paris after thirty years of exile. The news of his funeral was the first thing Voltaire heard on his arrival.

LELIO, see ANDREINI (3) and RICCOBONI (2).

LEMAÎTRE, [ANTOINE LOUIS PROSPER] FRÉDÉRICK (1800–76), celebrated French actor, equally good in tragedy, melodrama, and farce. Usually known as Frédérick, he was a unique personality, his art proceeding from a judicious blending of application and intuition. He had a great influence on the French theatre, but never appeared at the Comédie-Française, where his forceful acting might have proved too overwhelming. He was encouraged by his parents in his early love for the theatre, and became a student at the Conservatoire, from which he escaped to play in vaudevilles and at the Funambules with Deburau. In 1820 he went to the Odéon, playing tragic roles, and in 1823 replaced Fresnoy at the Ambigu-Comique. It was there that he made his first successes, particularly as Robert Macaire in *L'Auberge des Adrets* (1823), a part always associated with him. It was intended as a serious melodrama, but Frédérick made it a success by burlesquing it. He was always at his best in strong parts, whether melodramatic or comic, and another of his outstanding roles was Cartouche, in a revival of Legrand's play of that name. He was for some time at the Porte-Saint-Martin, and there appeared with Mme Dorval in *Trente ans, ou la Vie d'un joueur* (1827), a powerful and sombre play on gambling in which he literally terrified his audience. He was considered the finest actor on the boulevards when Harel took him back to the Odéon, and there, in spite of a more critical and cultured audience, he was again a success, rising nobly to the demands made upon him and seeming to shed some of his earlier crudities. All his life he combined in an unusual degree the power to move the masses while retaining the respect of the critics. Among his most successful parts were Othello and several heroes of the elder Dumas, notably the title-role in *Kean, ou Désordre et Génie*, which he played at the Folies-Dramatiques. This theatre proved too small for him, however, and on the opening of the Renaissance he found greater scope for his gifts in the plays of the young Romantics. He was the first to play Hugo's Ruy Blas, which was one of his greatest achievements. He continued to act until his retirement in 1873, but never again reached such heights.

LEMAÎTRE, JULES FRANÇOIS ÉLIE (1854–1914), French author and dramatic critic, who was for many years attached to the *Journal des Débats* and *Le Temps*. One of his early works was a book on Molière. As a critic he was capable of extreme kindness, as in his appreciation of Victor Hugo, or of great cruelty, as in his treatment of Georges Ohnet; his opinions were usually sound, however, and taken as a whole his work was beneficial to the theatre. His articles were published in volume form as *Impressions de théâtre*. He was also the author of several plays, none of which proved successful, and his reputation rests mainly on his critical works.

LEMERCIER, (LOUIS JEAN) NÉPOMUCÈNE (1771–1840), French dramatist, who at one time seemed destined to be the great literary name of the Napoleonic era. Godson of the Princesse de Lamballe, he was befriended in his youth by Marie-Antoinette, and was later a protégé of Napoleon, the friend of Josephine, intimate with Cambacérès and Talleyrand. He had great gifts, and his first play was produced when he was only 16; but he was handicapped by bad health, and by his position, caught between the eighteenth century, which was no longer fashionable, and the nineteenth, which he lacked the power to comprehend. His plays belong to both epochs. His *Agamemnon* (1795) might be called the last French tragedy on a classical theme, while *Pinto* (1800), with its lackey who liberates Portugal, seems to anticipate Hugo's *Ruy Blas*. *Christophe Colomb* (1809), inspired by readings of Shakespeare, also seems, by its flagrant disregard of the Unities, to belong to the Romantic school. But Lemercier lacked the force and vitality which might have given life to his work, and is now totally forgotten. He apparently took no steps to safeguard his plays by printing them, and they have gradually been recovered in manuscript from various libraries and private collections, though one, which seems to have been an attack on the new Romantic school for which Lemercier had unwittingly opened the way, has not yet been found.

LEMON, MARK (1809–70), English man of letters, best remembered as the first editor of *Punch*, which he established financially in its difficult early years on the money he received for his numerous and now forgotten plays, mainly farces and melodramas. Lemon was a good amateur actor, and made his first appearance at Miss Kelly's theatre in Soho, later playing in Dickens's private theatricals at Tavistock House, and giving public dramatic readings.

LENKOM THEATRE, Moscow. This theatre, whose full name is the Moscow Theatre of the Leninist Komsomol, or Young Communist League, was founded in 1922 as the Theatre of Working Youth, known by its initials as T.R.A.M. Its original company was formed by a band of enthusiastic amateurs who trained themselves to become professional actors, writing their own topical plays dealing with such contemporary themes as life in a factory. The theatre passed through a difficult phase when success first came its way, and it seemed to be heading for a blind alley. Its reconstruction in 1933 under the leadership of the Moscow Committee of the Young Communist League, and the importation from the Moscow Art Theatre of experienced producers, including Simonov, gave it a new impetus, and with time it mellowed and matured. Under Ivan Bersenev and Serafima Birman it has given many notable productions, particularly of *My Son* (1939), a study in Fascist oppression in which Serafima Birman gave a moving performance as the mother of the condemned man. During the war the theatre was evacuated, but returned with a programme which included *The Winter's Tale* and a new play on the history of the Komsomol.

LENO, DAN (1860–1904), one of the best-loved and most famous stars of the English music-hall, whose real name was George Galvin. He was the epitome of Cockney comedy, of domestic humour, and resignation. His parents sang at early music-hall concerts as Mr. and Mrs. John Wilde, and when his father died his mother married a William Grant whose stage name was Leno. Dan Leno appeared at the age of 4 with his brother Jack and with his uncle Johnny Danvers, the same age as himself, dancing in public-houses all over England. At 18 Dan blossomed out as a champion clog-dancer, and was engaged by Conquest with Danvers for pantomime at the Surrey. In 1889 he went to Drury Lane under Augustus Harris, and appeared in pantomime there, returning for many years as Sister Anne, the Widow Twankey, Cinderella's stepmother, the Baroness, and other parts. He continued to appear on the halls, mostly at the London Pavilion, where he told, in quick, staccato style, long rambling anecdotes of incidents involving himself or some other member of his family, with frequent mutterings and asides, but always with an eager, startled look and wide smile. For his success when commanded by King Edward VII to Sandringham in 1901 he was called 'the King's Jester', and a comic paper was named after him. Towards the end of his life he broke down from overwork, and became insane.

LENOBLE, EUSTACHE (1643–1711), a French lawyer who was imprisoned for forgery, and later became a hack-writer. Among his miscellaneous works were some unsuccessful plays, including three done at the Hôtel de Bourgogne by the Italian actors there. One of them, *La Fausse prude*, was taken as a reflection on Mme de Maintenon, and was used as an excuse for the banishment of the Italian troupe from Paris in 1697.

LENOIR, CHARLES (*fl.* 1610–37), early French actor-manager, who in 1610 was a member of a company fined for playing in Paris without the permission of the Confraternity of the Passion. He became the leader of a provincial company under the patronage of the Prince of Orange which appeared intermittently in Paris from 1622–6, and had as one of its members the young actor Montdory, later to play the heroes of Corneille and rival the glory of Bellerose. The two men parted company in about 1624, but were together when in 1630 they brought a troupe, not that of the Prince of Orange, and settled permanently in Paris, where they were the first actors to appear in a play by Corneille. Just before this company settled, with Montdory at its head, at the Théâtre du Marais in 1634, Lenoir, his wife (an actress who had appeared in Mairet's plays), and several other actors were transferred to Bellerose's company at the Hôtel de Bourgogne. This was due to a sudden whim of Louis XIII, who thus revenged himself on Richelieu for a number of petty indignities which culminated in the Cardinal's marked preference for Montdory's troupe over the official King's Players. Little more is known of Lenoir, and his name is not mentioned after 1637, when his wife, who outlived him, retired from the stage.

LENSKY, ALEXANDER PAVLOVICH (1847–1908), Russian actor, and one of the leading members of the Imperial Maly Theatre company, which he joined from the provinces in 1876. He spent the rest of his life there, and eventually became its director. Lensky was a many-sided man, being at once actor, producer, teacher, artist, and sculptor. He trained many actors for the Maly, and introduced Ibsen to Russian audiences. Although he supported Yermolova and her companions in their efforts to revive the fortunes of the theatre in its difficult days at the beginning of the twentieth century by renewing the old classic repertory, he was enlightened enough to further many of Nemirovich-Danchenko's reforms, notably the introduction of more rehearsals and of a dress-rehearsal, and the abolition of the old-fashioned style of stilted acting in favour of a more natural and supple approach.

LEN-SOVIET THEATRE, Moscow. This theatre, which takes its name from a part of the city named after Lenin and governed by its local council, the Leninsky Soviet, was organized in 1926 by a group of graduates of the State Institute of Theatrical Art. Its first productions were classics studied by the young actors previously during their training, but later it included new Soviet plays in its repertory. It was successful enough to draw not only local audiences but people from the centre who found it worth while to pay a visit to this suburban theatre. Actors from the central theatres joined its company, and L. A. Zubov became its artistic director. Under him the theatre made great strides, combining realism with experimental production, not only of classical plays, but of contemporary events and problems of Soviet life.

LEONIDOV, LEONID MIRONOVICH (1873–1941), Russian actor and producer, and one of the leading members of the Moscow Art Theatre. He entered the school of the Maly Theatre in 1894, but did not finish there, preferring to leave it two years later to work in the provincial theatres of Kiev and Odessa. In 1901 he joined the Korsh Theatre in Moscow, and finally, in 1903, the Moscow Art Theatre. His most brilliant performance as a tragic actor was given in the part of Dmitri Karamazov in the dramatization of Dostoievsky's great novel. Among other parts he played Peer Gynt, Lopakhin in *The Cherry Orchard*, Solyony in *Three Sisters*, Professor Borodin in the early Soviet play, *Fear*, and Plushkin in the dramatic version of *Dead Souls*. At the time of his death he was engaged on the production, with Nemirovich-Danchenko, of a new play about Lenin, *Kremlin Chimes*, given by the Moscow Art Theatre in Jan. 1942.

LEONOV, LEONID MAXIMOVICH (1899–   ), Soviet dramatist, born in Moscow, the son of a self-taught peasant poet. He began writing very early, mostly poems, and is one of the outstanding Russian dramatists of the day, gaining in strength and popularity by his work during the Second World War. His *Untilovsk* (1926) was the first Soviet play to be produced by the Moscow Art Theatre, but it was not entirely successful. *Skutarevski*, which followed, was more promising, and dealt with the problems of an old scientist torn between his work and his family, and between the old and new régimes, as typified by his wife and his ward, complicated by the counter-Revolutionary activities of his son. This play was produced by the Maly Theatre in 1934. Interesting plays on contemporary themes are *The Orchards of the Polovtsi* (1938), done in 1948 by the Old Vic Bristol company as *The Apple Orchards*, and *The Wolf* (1939), which deals with the impact of the Soviet régime on personal problems; but the play which set the seal on Leonov's growing reputation was *Invasion* (1942). It was first produced, owing to the difficulties caused by the evacuation of the theatres, in a provincial theatre near Moscow, and was awarded a Stalin prize. Later it was produced by Sudakov at the Maly Theatre. It tells, with great force and pathos, the story of a Soviet village under Nazi rule, the reactions of the villagers, and their contribution to freedom and final victory. The play, which has been published in an English adaptation, was one of the most successful of the Soviet war-plays, and much may yet be expected from its author.

LERMONTOV, MIKHAIL YUREVICH (1814–41), famous Russian lyric poet, who also wrote three plays in verse, and had most of his work banned by the Tsarist censorship. He had a short and stormy life, being sent down from Moscow University in 1832, and exiled for his denunciation of contemporary society in his poem on the death of Pushkin in 1837. A year later he was pardoned and returned to St. Petersburg, but was again exiled in 1840 after a duel. While on active service in the Caucasus he quarrelled with a former student-friend and was killed at Pyatagorsk in the resultant duel.

He became interested in the theatre at a very early age. Writing to his aunt from Moscow when he was about 15 he said: 'You said that our Moscow actors were worse than the St. Petersburg ones. What a pity you didn't see *Die Räuber* done here. You would change your mind. Many St. Petersburg gentlemen agree that plays are better here than there, and that Mochalov in many ways is better than Karatygin.' He had no sympathy with the rules of French classical tragedy. His models were Schiller, and Shakespeare, whom he called 'that immeasurable genius'. His first play, a verse-tragedy, written in 1830, though it deals ostensibly with the Inquisition in Castille, is in reality aimed at the despotism of the Tsar, and was suppressed. It was first performed in Russia after the 1917 Revolution. His next play, in prose, was originally given a German title, to stress its kinship with the plays of the *Sturm und Drang* writers, particularly Schiller. Based on a family conflict which recalls Lermontov's own unhappy home life—his mother died when he was young, and he was brought up by his grandmother, who was constantly at odds with his father—it is again an indictment of contemporary society. He returned to this play later and re-wrote it, making it a 'romantic drama' in which, he said, 'all the characters are taken from life, and I want them to be recognized so that some repentance may come to their souls'. In the second version he emphasized the conflict of good and evil and the struggle of the rebellious hero confronting a hostile world.

Lermontov's greatest play, and the only one by which he is now remembered, is *Masquerade*. It was written in 1835, and again deals with the problem of good and evil, which Lermontov had begun to realize is no longer the problem of an individual only, but of the forces ranged for or against that individual. The climax of the play in which a man poisons his wife, whom he loves, is not the result of intrigue, but of the psychological state of the husband, driven to crime by the corrupt society in which he lives. In deference to the censor, Lermontov substituted a happy ending, but the play was not produced until 1852 at the Alexandrinsky Theatre and even then only in a mutilated text. The full version was given in 1864, but its history in the theatre may be said to have begun only in 1917 with Meyerhold's production at the Alexandrinsky, where it was the last play to be produced before the October Revolution. He later produced it at his own theatre, and again at the Alexandrinsky in 1938, and this 'masterpiece of sophisticated sarcasm', as it has been called, has found its way into the repertory of most Soviet theatres. It has not yet been seen in England or the U.S.

LERNER, JOSEPH YEHUDA (1849–1907), Jewish playwright, translator of *Uriel Acosta* into Yiddish (see JEWISH DRAMA, 5).

LE SAGE. (1) ALAIN RENÉ (1668–1747), French novelist and dramatist. He was orphaned at an early age and confided to an uncle who soon dissipated his ward's fortune. Left penniless, Le Sage managed to make a living somehow, though his early years are obscure. By 1694, however, he was established in Paris, and married. His fellow-student Danchet had already encouraged him to try his hand at literature, and Le Sage's brilliant career begins with a mediocre and not very successful translation. He also studied Spanish literature, and, inspired by it, wrote the novels, *Le Diable boiteux* and *Gil Blas*, which constitute his main claim to fame. But though pre-eminently a novelist, Le Sage is by no means negligible as a dramatist. His early plays were adaptations from the Spanish of Lope de Vega and Rojas, but his first success, in 1707, the year of the publication of *Le Diable boiteux*, was undoubtedly *Crispin rival de son maître*. Two years later a slight play, called *Les Étrennes*, which the actors refused, was remodelled as *Turcaret* (1709), Le Sage's masterpiece and one of the best comedies in the history of French drama. The play satirizes the gross, purse-proud parvenu, the financier battening on the miseries of the poor, who was in the ascendant at this time, and reflects that bitterness against taxation which came to a head under Louis XVI. Like many another good play, it met with great opposition, and those whom it attacked tried to bribe Le Sage and the actors to suppress it. But, with the support of Monseigneur, it was put on, and was successful. Some obscure quarrel between Le Sage and the actors of the Comédie-Française, due perhaps to arguments over another play, *Tontine*, then led Le Sage to break off his association with the official theatre, and for many years he wrote for the theatres of the Paris fairs, alone, or in collaboration with Piron, Autreau, Fuzelier, Dorneval, and others. He wrote 100 or more sketches, which had a purely ephemeral interest, since it was left to Piron to establish the 'play with one actor' called for by the various decrees promulgated against the fair-ground playhouses.

Le Sage's life, though laborious and unremunerative, since he was too proud to accept patronage, was mainly a happy one, as he had a devoted wife and four children, and enjoyed the esteem of his fellow-writers. His greatest sorrow was the decision of two of his sons to become actors, a profession he disdained. The eldest (2) René-André (1695–1743) took the name Montménil, and after some years in the provinces played at the Comédie-Française with great success. He was deservedly popular with the public, and was eventually reconciled with his father, after, it is said, the latter had seen him play Turcaret, one of his best parts. Father and son then became the best of friends, and Le Sage was heartbroken when Montménil died suddenly at the age of 48. Le Sage's third and youngest son (the second became a canon of Boulogne Cathedral) (3) François-Antoine (1700– ?) took the name of Pitténec, but was not as good an actor as his brother. Two plays by him were given at the Foire St. Germain, but they were only re-hashes of his father's works, and were not successful. On Le Sage's death Pitténec left the stage and retired to Boulogne, to be near his brother the canon, and the rest of his history is lost in obscurity.

LESSING, Gotthold Ephraim (1729–81), German playwright and dramatic critic, one of the most acute intelligences of the eighteenth century. Descended from a long line of Protestant pastors and theologians, he deserted theology for literature while a student at the university of Leipzig. This later critic and reformer of the German stage intended at first to become an actor-playwright like Molière, one of his heroes. He spent much time behind the scenes at Caroline Neuber's theatre, acquiring valuable knowledge when his first light comedies were produced there. Written in the traditional French style, these nevertheless reveal an alert, inquiring mind and a readiness to flout current opinions. He also embarked on various journalistic enterprises connected with the theatre, and translated several French and English treatises on acting and the drama, including Dryden's *Essay of Dramatic Poesy*. His own combative middle-class consciousness led him to prefer works in which such a milieu was studied, and he was well versed in English novels of this kind, as is apparent in his first important dramatic work, *Miss Sara Sampson* (1755), in which the influence of Richardson is particularly noticeable. This tragedy of a middle-class heroine, which with all its faults is superior to the 'bourgeois drama' of Diderot and Lillo, was the first modern German play to be taken from life and written in natural, unstilted dialogue. It was produced by Ackermann in Berlin. It tells the story of Sara, a virtuous girl, who has eloped with an unscrupulous lover and waits in vain for marriage. Her father traces her to an inn just as her lover's former mistress, a virago, is trying to regain his affections. The latter rebuffs her, but foolishly allows her to visit Sara, whom she poisons. Whereupon the conscience-stricken lover kills himself on Sara's corpse in the presence of the lamenting father. In 1759 Lessing with two collaborators launched the *Briefe die neueste Litteratur betreffend*, which set a new standard for literary criticism. Lessing's criterion was excellence, and with pungent wit he dissected those whose aim was low, insincere, or misguided. After serving for some years as secretary to the governor of Breslau, General Taudenzien, and so viewing the Seven Years War at close quarters, he returned to literature with his treatise on aesthetics, *Laokoon, oder die Grenzen der Malerei und der Dichtkunst* (1766), in which, countering inferences drawn from Horace's *ut pictura poesis*, he differentiates sharply between the sphere of art (space) and that of poetry (duration); in poetry he allows discreet use of ugliness, in art almost none. Only Part I of this work was completed, which is all the more regrettable since he might later have dealt fruitfully with acting as a combination of both spheres.

In 1767 appeared Lessing's first great play, a comedy which still retains much of its verve, *Minna von Barnhelm*. The heroine, hearing that her fiancé Tellheim intends to renounce her, he being penniless and under a cloud, pursues him, and finds him obdurate. She resorts to various subterfuges, but in the nick of time a letter from Frederick the Great clears Tellheim's name and all ends happily. The action, as in *Miss Sara Sampson*, takes place on one day, in various rooms of an inn. In view of this regularity it is not surprising that when in 1767 Lessing became official critic to the Hamburg Theatre, and made many onslaughts on the conventions of French classical tragedy in general and Corneille in particular, he nowhere advises wholesale imitation of Shakespeare, though he repeatedly acknowledges his supreme craftsmanship, his truth to nature in character-drawing, and his unerring sense of the theatre. The upshot of the *Hamburgische Dramaturgie* is that Aristotle's view of drama, provided it be intelligently interpreted, still holds good. In a discussion on catharsis and the aim of tragedy Lessing insists that both the fear and the pity, intimately linked, are felt by the onlooker as though he himself were in the place of the hero. He is clearly approaching tragedy from the angle of a predominantly middle-class audience, and rules out the admiration which heroic tragedy should evoke.

Unfortunate complications ruined the Hamburg Theatre, and in 1769 Lessing became keeper of the Duke of Brunswick's library at Wolffenbüttel. He set to work on a tragedy which should elucidate his arguments. The result was *Emilia Galotti* (1772), in which a young girl is abducted by a licentious prince on her way to her wedding. When her father finds that she is not insensible to the charms of her betrayer, he stabs her, at her own request, to preserve her honour. The story, in fact, is that of the middle-class Virginia brought up to date.

Lessing's last years were taken up with a prolonged struggle against narrow-minded orthodoxy, and with philosophy, which finds expression in his final work, *Nathan der Weise*, a noble plea for religious tolerance. It was not produced during Lessing's lifetime. Two years after his death it met with little success. It was not until Goethe produced it at Weimar in 1801 that it received the acclamation which was its due. It was translated into many languages, and, except during periods of dictatorship, has continued to form part of the German theatre's repertory.   W. E. D.

LETTICE, see AUDITORIUM, 2.

LEVICK, HALPER (1888–   ), writer of plays in Yiddish on modern themes, produced in New York by Maurice Schwartz (see JEWISH DRAMA, 6).

LEWES. (1) CHARLES LEE (1740–1803), English actor, whose first important part was Young Marlow in *She Stoops to Conquer* (1773), when he spoke an Epilogue specially written for him by Goldsmith. He was at Covent Garden until 1783, creating the part of Fag in *The Rivals*, and then went to Drury Lane, where he played a number of Shakespearian parts, including Touchstone and Falstaff. He was for some time assistant to Stephen Kemble at the Dundee Theatre, and from there went to Dublin, where he was not a success. Falling into financial difficulties, he was imprisoned for debt, and spent his enforced leisure in writing his memoirs.   ED.

His grandson (2) George Henry (1817–78) was a philosopher, dramatist, and dramatic critic. His plays were written under the pseudonym 'Slingsby Lawrence' and include one tragedy, *The Noble Heart* (1849), among the dramas, comedies, and farces which appeared up to 1856. Chief among these were *The Game of Speculation* (1851), *A Chain of Events* (with C. J. Matthews) and *Taking By Storm* (both 1852), *A Strange History in Nine Chapters* (with C. J. Matthews) and *The Lawyers* (both 1853), *Wanted, a She-Wolf*, *A Cozy Couple*, *Give a Dog a Bad Name*, *Sunshine through the Clouds* (all 1854), *Buckstone's Adventure with a Polish Princess* (1855), and *Stay at Home* (1856). He also published, in 1846, *The Spanish Drama, Lope de Vega and Calderón.*

His dramatic criticisms were written chiefly for the *Pall Mall Gazette*. Lewes had a keen eye for acting and in 1875 republished several articles under the title *On Actors and the Art of Acting*. In his analysis of Edmund Kean, Rachel, Macready, the Keeleys, and Salvini, he exhibited a sharp discernment between what the actor had to say and his method of saying it: 'It is the incalculable advantage of the actor that he stands in the suffused light of emotion kindled by the author, and is rewarded, as the bearer of glad tidings is rewarded, though he has had nothing to do with the facts which he narrates.'   T. C. K.

LEWIS, MATTHEW GREGORY (1775–1818), English novelist and dramatist, usually known as 'Monk' Lewis from the title of his most famous novel, written in ten weeks while Lewis was residing abroad, *Ambrosio, or The Monk* (1795). This provided material for a

number of sensational plays, which, together with *The Castle Spectre* (1797), a musical play of little literary merit which was immensely popular, and the famous equestrian melodrama *Timour the Tartar* (1811), found their way into the repertory of the nineteenth-century Juvenile Drama. Lewis's work, which was deliberately concocted to appeal to the prevailing taste for melodrama and spectacle, was somewhat crude, but offered great scope for effective acting and lavish scenery, enhanced by incidental music. His characters were all of a piece—villain, hero, romantic lover, or distressed maid—and his speeches, however much they may have moved or horrified audiences at the time of their production, read thinly on the printed page. He was of the school of Kotzebue, two of whose plays he translated, and most of his work has vanished with the fashion which gave rise to it.

LEWIS, WILLIAM THOMAS (1749–1811), English actor, whose elegance and affability earned him the soubriquet of 'Gentleman Lewis'. He made his first appearance on the stage at Dublin in 1770, and three years later went to Covent Garden, where he remained for the rest of his career. For twenty-one years he was acting-manager, and on his retirement in 1809 John Philip Kemble purchased from him his one-sixth share in the patent. He was the airiest and most mercurial of comedians, succeeding the famous Harlequin Harry Woodward in comedy parts. Boaden, in his memoirs of Kemble, calls him 'Lewis the sprightly, the gay, the exhilarating, the genteel . . . The charm of this really fine actor was in his animal spirits.' He was the first to play nearly all the rattling, hare-brained, and impossibly lively heroes of Reynolds and O'Keefe, and the creator of Jeremy Diddler in Kenney's *Raising the Wind*. He occasionally played tragedy in his early years, but his staccato utterance, restless gesticulation and light voice were totally unsuited for it, and he soon confined himself to comedy. He was a conscientious and hard-working manager, and was much liked by the company.

LEWISOHN, ALICE and IRENE, see NEIGHBORHOOD PLAYHOUSE.

LEYBOURNE, GEORGE (1842–84), a music-hall performer and the original 'lion comique'. His real name was Joe Saunders, and he was a mechanic from the midlands. He first sang in East End tavern 'free-and-easys' and was then engaged by Morton for the Canterbury at £25 a week, rising eventually to £120. He appeared always immaculately dressed as a man-about-town with monocle, whiskers, and fur collar, singing the delights of dissipation, an art which unfortunately he did not fail to practise in his spare time. His last years were a constant struggle with disillusionment and ill health, and he died at the age of 42, after a last appearance at the Queen's, Poplar. He was popularly known as 'Champagne Charlie' from his singing of the song of that name.

LIBERTY THEATRE, NEW YORK, on the south side of 42nd Street, between Seventh and Eighth Avenues. This theatre was for a long time famous for its farces. It opened on 14 Oct. 1904, and among its early productions were *Polly of the Circus*, which ran for nearly six months, and the great horse-racing drama *Wildfire*, with Lillian Russell. The season of 1909-10 included two important productions, Tarkington's *Springtime*, and *The Arcadians*, while a few years later *Milestones*, with 215 performances, and *The Purple Road*, with 136 performances, filled a successful season. Several musical successes were seen at this theatre, where the great negro musical, *Blackbirds of 1928*, had part of its long run, and the last legitimate production was given on 18 Mar. 1933, after which the building became a cinema.   G. F.

LIBRETTO (*pl.* libretti or librettos), 'little book', from the Italian, and used mainly to denote the words, as distinct from the music, of an opera or musical play. Though often the work of second-rate writers, with little to recommend them but their adaptability to the needs of the composer, some operatic libretti have been written by fine poets and dramatists, who successfully overcame the difficulties of combining the requirements of composer and singer with true poetic fervour and lyric beauty. Such were the early Italian librettists Rinuccini and Apostolo Zeno, and the great Metastasio, whose thirty-odd texts were set more than a thousand times, by many different composers. In France the dramatists Quinault, Sedaine, and Favart were excellent librettists, while the popular and prolific Scribe, like many of his contemporaries, added the writing of operatic texts to his other activities. Since opera never became acclimatized in England, no great names are connected with it, except that of Gay in ballad opera, for Nahum Tate, Alfred Bunn, and Edward Fitzball were never more than competent; but England can boast of the perfect collaboration of Gilbert and Sullivan in light opera. Dramatists in their own right whose plays have served as opera texts are Hugo von Hofmannsthal, Maurice Maeterlinck, and Oscar Wilde. Wagner avoided the dangers of collaboration by writing his own texts.

Even greater than the difficulty of writing a good libretto is the difficulty of translating it. In England, where poor translations for long did great disservice to the cause of opera, immense strides have recently been made, and it is noteworthy that the best work in this respect has been done by two distinguished music critics—Ernest Newman and Professor E. J. Dent.

LICENSING ACT, 1737, see DRAMATIC CENSORSHIP and PROVINCIAL THEATRES, I c.

LICENSING LAWS, see COPYRIGHT and DRAMATIC CENSORSHIP.

LIGHTING, STAGE. I. HISTORY. (*a*) *From the beginning to the introduction of gas.* In dealing with the history of stage lighting it is necessary to distinguish between the artificial illumination of theatre interiors and the use of lights on the stage. In all periods candles, torches, lamps, and lanterns have been used as stage properties to indicate night and darkness in performances given by daylight. For the unroofed theatres of Greece and Rome, for the open-air pageant stages of the religious drama in medieval Europe, and for the ordinary unroofed theatre of Elizabethan and Jacobean England, the practical problem of illumination to secure visibility was virtually non-existent. Until the advent of the so-called 'private' or indoor theatre, the Elizabethan stage demanded nothing beyond some kind of artificial light for the last part of the performance on a short winter afternoon, more especially when the time of opening was put on from 2 to 3 o'clock. For this purpose, apparently, cressets were used. Cotgrave's definition of the French *falot* in his 1611 *Dictionarie* is 'cresset light (such as they use in playhouses) made of ropes, wreathed, pitched and put into small and open cages of iron'.

When discussing the lighting resources of the sixteenth- and seventeenth-century theatres it may prove somewhat misleading to use the phrase 'stage lighting' if we think only in terms of the modern stage installation, which differs completely in principle and equipment from that required for front-of-house illumination. Until the increased size of both stage and auditorium in the latter part of the eighteenth century created a new set of conditions, the specific problem was not primarily how to light the stage, but how to light the interior of the theatre regarded as a whole. In normal theatre practice there was no question of extinguishing the 'house lights' during the performance; lighting was a matter of so many candelabra and candle-sconces for the auditorium and so many for the acting area; remembering that until the stage lost its apron and retreated behind the proscenium arch neither theory nor practice kept the action within the picture frame. For the most important parts of the action the actor deliberately came outside the effective range of the special stage lighting—footlights excepted.

The distinctive feature of the Elizabethan or Jacobean private playhouse was the roofed auditorium; but these buildings were well lighted by good-sized windows; such evidence as there is indicates that daylight was used whenever possible, and that the use of artificial light was matter for comment. As W. J. Lawrence originally pointed out, there is only one way to make sense of the *locus classicus* in Dekker's *Seven Deadly Sins of London* (1606), which describes the shuttered city, at the entry of Candlelight, looking 'like a private playhouse, when the windows are clapt down, as if some *Nocturnal*, or dismal *Tragedy* were presently to be acted'. The inference is, not that the private playhouses preferred or were compelled to use artificial light, but that it could be employed, on these special occasions, to create a more realistic impression of night or gloom, in contrast to the purely symbolic representation which was all the ordinary theatres could manage. A genuine drawback to artificial light, when not necessary, was the expense—a drawback of which the theatre itself remained very conscious until the introduction of gas.

That torches were sometimes used in the private theatres is evident from the reference in Lenton's *Young Gallant's Whirligig* (1629) to 'the torchy Friars', that is, the Blackfriars Theatre. Normally, however, chandeliers (branches) and candle-sconces provided the general illumination. The more usual form appears to have been that shown in the frontispiece to Francis Kirkman's 1672 edition of *The Wits; or, Sport upon Sport*, consisting of eight twisted branches each carrying one candle. In the eighteenth century this gave way to the simpler hoop or ring.

Apart from the very vague possibility that such a stage direction as 'Ici faict tenebres' (*Mystère de la Passion*, 1474) may indicate that some kind of smoke-screen effect was used in the medieval religious drama for the Crucifixion scenes, stage lighting proper, designed exclusively to enhance the stage spectacle, began in the theatre of renaissance Italy, where it was considered an integral part of the sumptuous entertainments with which the rulers and princelings of that country amused themselves. For the sixteenth and the first half of the seventeenth centuries, scenic precept and practice are embodied in the writings of Sebastiano Serlio (1475–1554), Leone di Somi (1527–92), Nicola Sabbattini (c. 1574–1654), and the German architect Josef Furtenbach (1591–1667). Taken together, they give a reasonably comprehensive idea of the lighting methods and resources of courtly entertainment.

Serlio, in his *Second Booke of Architecture* (1537; translated into French, 1545; into English, 1611), says the stage is 'adorned with innumerable lights, great, middle sort and small', cunningly set out to counterfeit precious stones. 'You place great part of the lights in the middle, hanging over the scene', and to add to the brilliance of the spectacle the windows of the lath and canvas houses of the tragic and the comic scenes should contain glass or paper, and have lights set behind them. Coloured lights are contrived by filling glasses or bottles with coloured liquids and placing 'great lamps' behind them, or—for extra brilliant illumination—torches with barbers' basins behind them for reflectors. Natural phenomena, such as the rising moon, can be admirably counterfeited.

Di Somi's *Dialogues on Stage Affairs*, translated by Allardyce Nicoll in the 1937 edition of his *Development of the Theatre* (Appendix B), gives the fullest early account of lighting as practised by an expert in the 1560s. He insists upon the careful placing of candles and lamps, upon the necessity for shading or concealing most of the lights, and upon reducing the amount of light in the auditorium. In common with others he uses small mirror reflectors fixed to the backs of his wings, and also set at the judiciously selected spots where concealed lights shone forth from behind columns and in the openings between the wings. He renders the stage as bright as possible, places only a few lamps in the auditorium, and deliberately sets these towards the back of the hall, because a man standing in the shade sees a distant and illuminated object much more clearly. Bright lighting helps to engender a mood of gaiety, and he has made experiments with the contrast between light and darkness to create atmosphere. Once, when he produced a tragedy, he says, he illuminated the stage brightly so long as the episodes were happy in key. Then, with the first tragic incident—the death of a queen—he contrived, '(by prearrangement, of course), that at that very instant most of the stage lights not used for the perspective were darkened or extinguished'. This made a profound impression of horror and won universal praise from the spectators.

Angelo Ingegneri (c. 1550–c. 1613), whose *Della Poesia Rappresentativa e del Modo di Rappresentare le favole sceniche* was printed in 1598, regards lighting as of 'supreme theatrical importance'. He goes even farther than di Somi, and would darken the auditorium completely. He believes in concealing the stage lights, and, to light the faces of the actors and cast a glow over the scene, recommends the equivalent of a concert batten screened from the audience by a valance, and 'fitted with many lighted lamps, having tinsel reflectors to direct the beams upon the actors'. Care must be taken that none of this light is spilled over the auditorium (see Allardyce Nicoll: *Stuart Masques*, 1937).

Sabbattini in his *Pratica di fabricar scene e machine ne' teatri* (1638) points out from experience that lighting from either side of the stage gives more brightness and greater contrast than lighting from in front or behind. For obscuring the scene instantaneously he has tin cylinders suspended on wires over every lamp. These must be dropped simultaneously, and there must be very little light in front of the scenery or the effect will be lost. He also makes it clear that the equivalent of concealed footlights with reflectors were habitually used, but allows that smoke and smell are drawbacks to these lamps at stage level. They were screened from the audience by a parapet or wall—corresponding to the front of the modern orchestra, but a foot or so higher than the stage and built at a distance from it of anything from 1 to 10 feet. Furtenbach, in his *Architectura Civilis* (1628), gives a similar description of footlights, and further vouches for the use of a sunk strip, 6 feet wide, at the very back of the acting area,

in which also many oil lamps hang unseen, throwing their radiance up into the scene and thus causing many beautiful effects, particularly if the lamps are set on poles and are turned by appropriate means—a device by which very wondrous flashes of lightning and flames can be produced.

This could be used, in fact, both for effects of light and for lighting shutters or backcloths at the back of the scene behind the perspectives, and was also adapted 'to the passage not only of supposed coaches, horses, processions, marching of military formations, but also of ships, galleys, and suchlike'.

The Italian theatre used both candles and lamps. Sabbattini describes metal lamps with drip-pans and hooks to be attached to the lustres; and there were two kinds used for the scenes—the one a simple cruse lamp with a floating wick, the other specially made for theatrical use, specimens of which can still be seen in the Teatro Olimpico at Vicenza. This latter, the *bozze*, was a glass globe, blown so that it had a short handle opposite the hole left for the wick which was carried in a metal holder. The handles could be thrust into ring holders or holes drilled in a board, and two *bozzi* could be used as described above to give coloured light. Burnished reflectors and mirrors were used, both singly and in lengths.

From these writers we can establish the existence in the sixteenth- and seventeenth-century Italian theatre of the following stage lighting units: (1) chandeliers hung over the stage and in the auditorium, and standing candelabras; (2) concealed overhead and side lighting, including a No. 1 batten; (3) concealed or exposed footlights; (4) concealed sunk lighting comparable to the cyclorama trough; (5) exposed, shaded, and coloured lights on the stage. The lighting of the English masque of the seventeenth century was definitely based on Italian practice, and it is noticeable that foreign observers, when commenting on courtly entertainments, make it clear that for display and beauty England could hold her own with the European stage. Inigo Jones (1573–1652) used an abundance of coloured light, and the term he employs—'jewel glasses'—as well as the descriptions, shows that he aimed at the effect advocated by Serlio. He liked to conceal the source of his lighting, and was fully aware of the beauty and effectiveness of all kinds of reflected light. He also used transparencies, and such effects as moons, sunrises, sunsets, &c. The question is—at what period and how completely did the English playhouse stage adopt or adapt equipment similar to that used in the masque? Given the modified Elizabethan structure which was the early Restoration theatre, what evidence have we that the new conditions of 1660 definitely fostered the adoption and development of real stage lighting?

We can clear the ground at once by two statements. We know that until 1765 unconcealed chandeliers, hung over the stage, were the main source of lighting, and that *The Wits* frontispiece, which is the earliest English illustration to suggest the use of footlights, belongs to the year 1672. The placing of the chandeliers and the numbers used varied, naturally, from time to time in different theatres. For the pre-Restoration playhouses we have no pictorial evidence, unless we accept the above frontispiece as relating to that time. The second Drury Lane, designed by Wren and opened in 1674, had in Garrick's day a great central chandelier over the middle of the auditorium, and 'six chandeliers hanging over the stage, every one containing twelve candles in brass sockets' (Tate Wilkinson's *Memoirs*). Rich's Lincoln's Inn Fields theatre (1714–31) had six chandeliers, apparently iron rings hung on chains. Most theatrical prints of the eighteenth century show either a small chandelier or a two-branched candelabra over the proscenium doors, and double branches at regular intervals round the fronts of the circles. The better known of the two 'Fitzgiggo' illustrations of the Covent Garden stage in 1763 shows double branches between each of the stage boxes, a lofty central chandelier over the middle of the stage carrying six candles, and four rings of some sixteen candles each hung level with the tops of the proscenium doors well to the sides of the stage, the two in front being hung, apparently, in the actual arch of the proscenium. The other two illuminate the scenic area and hang upstage of the central lustre.

Similar conditions prevailed in the French theatre at the end of the seventeenth century. Dubech (*Histoire générale illustrée du théâtre*, 5 vols. 1931–4) has several good illustrations which show the arrangement of the chandeliers. One, depicting the stage of the Hôtel de Bourgogne in 1688, shows six large chandeliers hung in front of the proscenium arch over the apron, and six more to light the scenic area behind the arch, hung three on each side in line with the perspectives, so that each wing was illuminated (op. cit. ii. 288). Two others (1664 and 1674) show the stage and auditorium at Versailles, with five chandeliers hung in a line in the deep arch, illuminating the front of the stage very brightly and leaving the rear only dimly lit (iii. 240–1). Even more interesting is the reproduction of an anonymous painting of about 1670 in the Museum of the Comédie-Française, showing a stage illuminated by six chandeliers and a row of thirty-four footlights (iii. 126).

Flecknoe, in his *Short Discourse of the English Stage* (1664), asserts that the stages of France and Italy have the advantage of us in the matter of spectacle, 'we especially not knowing yet *how to place our lights* for the more advantage and illuminating the scene'. The drawbacks to unconcealed chandeliers hung over the stage—more particularly in a line in the proscenium arch—were that they impeded the view from the second circle of any upstage action, and that the glare from the naked candle-flames was very trying to the eyes. After a visit to the Duke of York's playhouse, where he sat in a side gallery 'over against the musick', Pepys records that 'the trouble of my eyes with the light of the candles did almost kill me' (12 May 1669). An improvement of the existing arrangements was the real substance of Garrick's famous lighting reforms of 1765 at Drury

Lane. It used to be said that his 'innovation' was the introduction of footlights to the English theatre. Tate Wilkinson in his *Memoirs*, however, makes it quite clear that footlights—he calls them 'the lamps'—which could be raised or lowered were in use at Drury Lane in 1758. Odell confirms Tate Wilkinson with a number of examples of the use of footlights in the English theatre between 1735 and 1765 (*Shakespeare from Betterton to Irving*, 1921, i. 281–2, 404–8); and W. J. Lawrence (*Stage Year Book*, 1927) cites *The Gentleman's and London Magazine* for Oct. 1765, which states explicitly that Garrick removed 'the six rings that used to be suspended over the stage in order to illuminate the house', indicating that though he took the hint from the French theatre he avoided its mistake of 'extremely faint and disagreeable lighting' and illuminated Drury Lane with 'a clear strong light'. Covent Garden, it adds, has been similarly improved, 'but not with the same success: instead of wax, they have given oil', which smells; and the stage is inadequately lit, having 'more of the gloom of the Comédie-Française than of the cheerfulness of Drury Lane'.

Perhaps the most helpful description of the new Drury Lane lighting, however, is that given by the *Annual Register* (Sept. 1765) which explains that it is done 'by the disposition of lights behind the scenes, which cast a reflection forwards exactly resembling sunshine'. This passage, cited by Odell, does not seem to have been noted by Lawrence, nor yet to have had its real significance sufficiently stressed. It does not tell us *how* the new lighting was done, but it certainly tells us *what* was done, and the well-known engraving of the 'screen scene' from *The School for Scandal* as performed at Drury Lane on 8 May 1777 (Enthoven Collection) undoubtedly records the artist's impression of the kind of effect which could be achieved with the 'new' lighting. It shows, firstly, brilliant lighting of the apron stage by footlights well masked from the pit; secondly, directed lighting on the prompt side, falling upon a considerable area of the main stage; thirdly, the absence of directed light on the O.P. side; and fourthly, the general all-over quality and amount of light still provided both for stage and auditorium by the house-lighting.

We are not told, either by this engraving or by contemporary accounts, whether Garrick retained any of the chandeliers for hidden overhead lighting of the scenic area: what we know is that from 1765 onwards all the stage lighting proper, except for the floats, came from behind the proscenium arch, and that it is the side-lighting which is stressed. Side-lighting, however, was no new thing in the English theatre. Garrick did not invent wing-ladders (perpendicular battens), nor did he take the idea from the French stage. An inventory of Covent Garden properties taken in Jan. 1744 lists '12 pairs of scene ladders fixt with ropes', with 24 scene blinds and 192 tin candlesticks for the same—items which make it clear that wing-ladders

equipped with eight candles each were in use in England at least twenty years earlier. It is possible that besides the hint about removing the chandeliers, Garrick may have obtained from France some brighter and more effective lamps, both for his floats and for his wing-ladders. His correspondence with Monnet in June and July 1765 makes it clear that the latter sent over from Paris specimens of a 'réverbères' (a lantern with reflectors), and two different kinds of lamp for the floats (see Boaden: *Private Correspondence of David Garrick*, 1831). There is no evidence that Garrick adopted any of these, but he was obviously looking for some means of increasing the strength of his concealed lighting to compensate for the removal of the chandeliers, and contemporary comment makes it clear that he succeeded.

Although Garrick did not introduce floats to the English theatre, it seems likely that he began the process of intensification which eventually gave us 'the glare of the footlights', and before leaving eighteenth-century stage lighting it is necessary to catch up on their earlier history. The float-wick lamp, best known to-day as the sanctuary lamp, is at least as old as the Mycenaean period. The wick can float in the oil or be threaded through a floating disk. For stage purposes it appears to have developed in two ways: as a spout-lamp with two or more wicks, and as a long narrow tin trough filled with fish-oil on which wicks threaded through broad pieces of cork were floated. Boaden called this 'the trap or floating light' and from at least the first half of the eighteenth century the floats were suspended on counterweights and could be lowered or raised through traps in the floor of the stage.

In the earliest known illustration of footlights candles take the place of lamps. This is a water-colour drawing in Harleian MS. 4325 showing the arrangement of a temporary stage in the Salle de la Diana at Montbrison in 1588, which was lighted from above by four three-branch chandeliers and a row of twelve smaller candles on flat bases attached to the tops of a row of framed portraits which embellished the back scene. In front it was lighted on stage level by six large candles like altar candles (see Sylvia England: 'An unrecognised document in the history of French Renaissance staging', *The Library*, Sept. 1935). How far this particular instance justifies us in assuming others in sixteenth-century France it is impossible to say; but Dubech (*op. cit.* iii. 139) reproduces an illustration of an early seventeenth-century French stage-setting showing a row of ten unscreened candles, and Molière at the Palais-Royal (1640–50) used a *rampe* of 48 small candles weighing eight to the livre. By the middle of the century the Hôtel de Bourgogne had a *rampe* of 'petits lampions espacés' and the painting of *c.* 1670, already mentioned in connexion with the chandeliers, depicts a row of thirty-four footlights divided into three groups, the one in the middle being made up of eighteen lamps. From the Dubech reproduction it looks as if the traps have been indicated by the painter. For a performance of *Psyché* at the Comédie-Française in 1703 there was a *rampe* 'formée par 80 lampions de 6 onces de cire à trois lumières chacun'; while at Versailles in 1704 there was one of forty *bougies*.

The evidence, in fact, points to the same continuity for footlights in the French seventeenth-century public theatre as is assumed for chandeliers, both being a direct inheritance from the Italian tradition by way of the French sixteenth-century courtly entertainment. It is generally thought, however, that in England the footlights were not used for the Jacobean and Caroline masques, which tended to retain traces of their original form and bring the masquers down to the floor of the hall for the concluding dance. This entailed the use of steps or ramps, and obviously precluded the use of the parapet advocated by Sabbattini and Furtenbach, to which, in foreign practice, the footlights were attached. For Court entertainments from 1670 onwards, however, there is evidence for their use in England. The accounts for a masque of 1670–1 have an entry 'for making a trough at the foot of the stage for lights to stand in'. Further entries show that candles were generally used, though one for 1679 is worded 'putting up a long trough to set the lamps in at the end of the stage against the Pit there' (see Boswell: *The Restoration Court Stage*, 1932).

The earliest English pictorial representation of footlights is *The Wits* frontispiece (1672) mentioned above. This, however, gives us neither a firm date nor an actual stage. It has been suggested that it probably represents the kind of makeshift stage which might have been used for surreptitious performances, possibly by strolling players, during the Commonwealth period. To whatever date previous to 1672 it should be assigned, the only clear implication of the drawing is that by then chandeliers and footlights were what was expected in a picture of a stage, however crude. There is no evidence whatever to suggest that it shows the stage of the old Red Bull Theatre. For the footlights, six lamps, each with two wicks, are shown: they are of the enclosed bowl type, with wick apertures but not spouts.

There is no definite evidence for the general assumption that footlights came to England from France, but it would be reasonable to believe—in the absence of any certainty about the use of them earlier—that they were introduced to the Restoration playhouse by men who knew the French stage and its mid-seventeenth century resources, and were bent on employing the scenery, decoration, and machinery already well established there. W. J. Lawrence (*op. cit.*) makes out a good case for 1671–4 as a probable date for their introduction. In 1671 the new Duke's Theatre in Dorset Garden was equipped with up-to-date French machinery, Betterton having previously visited Paris to pick up useful hints. In 1674 Wren's new Drury Lane was opened; and from then on both these theatres were able,

on the evidence of actual plays, to manage scenes of 'sudden darkness' not merely at the beginning of an act but during the course of the action. Given the chandeliers as the only source of controlled light this was obviously impossible, and Lawrence therefore infers some auxiliary source of controlled lighting which could be used to achieve this effect, provided the chandeliers had been put out or left unlighted. The natural inference is that the footlights with traps, vouched for in the early eighteenth-century English theatre, had already been adopted. There is no need to dispute this reasoning, but it does not, of itself, prove that footlights were the only source of concealed lighting in the late seventeenth century. The Court entertainments used lights attached to the backs of the wings (Boswell, *op. cit.*); and if the traps of the 1744 inventory are to be antedated for footlights, why not the scene-blinds of the scene-ladders for these earlier wing lights? (see above).

To sum up: the late seventeenth- and early eighteenth-century English stage was illuminated by the general theatre lighting, by the stage chandeliers, and by controlled stage lighting provided apparently by floats and wing-ladders. After 1765 the house lights and concealed footlights on traps cover the area in front of the proscenium; and controlled and directed side-lighting, with possibly some concealed overhead lighting, deals with the scenic area behind the arch. The lighting achievements of Garrick's scenic designer, Philippe Jacques de Loutherbourg (1740–1812), belong more properly to the history of stage effects, and include such things as fogs and the ever-popular conflagrations. The next milestone is the introduction of gas.

In passing, it is interesting to note that the floats, the lights beyond all others purely of the theatre, have always been the target of professional as well as critical abuse, and even in 1790 they were called 'that tormenting line of lamps at the front of the stage which wrongs everything it illuminates'. This early reformer, George Saunders (*A Treatise on Theatres*), recommended instead the use of M. Patte's reverberators (reflector lamps) fixed to each tier of the boxes at the front extremity of the stage to light the apron area, and asserts that they have been successfully used in small theatres, notably at Blenheim. Incidentally, he also recommends another set, again fixed to the boxes, immediately in front of the proscenium pillars, and others on the stage side of the arch, at the first and second shutters, to light the rest of the stage.

The argument that lighting from below is unnatural, that it calls attention to the soles of the actors' boots and the undersides of tables, and creates glare, does not condemn footlights but merely the unskilful use of them. They were born of experience—theatrical experience: of the desire to get more and better balanced lighting: and it is interesting to find no less an authority than Stanley McCandless asserting that in 'legitimate productions footlights should be used to illuminate the shadows on the actors' faces and to tone the setting at low intensity. . . . The practice of omitting them from a layout only limits the flexibility of lighting the stage for all occasions' (*A Method of Lighting the Stage*, 1932).

(*b*) *Gas to electricity*. It would appear that by a narrow margin of two days Drury Lane was the first English theatre to be entirely lighted by gas, when on 6 Sept. 1817 it re-opened for the autumn season. The Lyceum, however, was the first to light the *stage* by gas; its bill for 6 Aug. 1817 is headed 'The Gas Lights will this Evening be introduced over the whole Stage'. On 8 Sept. the bill announced that

the complete Success which, after a Trial of several Weeks, has attended the Experiment of Lighting the stage by Gas, has induced the Proprietors of this Theatre still further to consult the Improvement of the Public Accommodation; and this evening a new and brilliant Mode of illuminating the Audience Part of the Theatre by means of Gas Lights will be submitted to the Observation, and, it is respectfully hoped, to the Approbation of the Visitors of the English Opera House.

The statement made by Fuchs in *Stage Lighting* (1929) that gas was installed at the Lyceum by F. A. Winsor in 1803 rests upon a misunderstanding of the facts clearly given in Wm. Matthews's *An Historical Sketch of the Origin, Progress, and Present State of Gas Lighting* (1827):

In 1803 and 1804 Mr. Winsor publicly exhibited his plan of illumination by coal-gas at the Lyceum Theatre in London. Here he delivered lectures on the subject, which he illustrated by a number of entertaining and appropriate experiments. Among others he shewed the manner of conveying the gas from one part of a house to another. . . . Afterwards Mr. Winsor removed his exhibition to Pall Mall, where, early in 1807, he lighted up a part of one side of the street, which was the first instance of this kind of light being applied to such a purpose in London.

Covent Garden began to use gas in 1815, but not for the stage or auditorium. The playbill for the opening of the season on 11 Sept. 1815 announces that 'The Exterior, with the Grand Hall and Staircase, will be illuminated with Gas'. It is possible that the Olympic was actually the first theatre to use gas in the auditorium, as the playbill for 30 Oct. 1815 announces that 'The Exterior, the Saloon, and part of the Interior, will be lighted with Gas'. On 6 Sept. 1817 *The Times* gave the following account of the Drury Lane installation:

A very considerable improvement, we think, will be found in the introduction of *gas*-lights on the sides of the stage, on which there are 12 perpendicular lines of lamps, each containing 18, and before the proscenium a row of 80. The advantage anticipated from these lights consists mainly in the facility with which they can be instantly arranged so as to produce more or less of illumination, according to the particular description of the scene.

The Examiner, on the following day, praises the effect as being 'as mild as it is splendid—white, regular, and pervading', and describes the lights as being 'enclosed in glasses and blinded from the audience by side scenes and reflectors'.

Covent Garden Theatre was not far behind Drury Lane, and gave a preliminary demonstration on 6 Sept. *The Times* on the 7th reports that 'all the former chandeliers are removed, and a great central light descends from the centre of the ceiling, but not so far as to intercept the view of the stage, even from the one shilling gallery'; five magnificent five-armed branches, one on each side of the stage and three round the circle, supplement the central lustre; and 'the gas lamps have also been fixed upon the edges of the first wings on each side of the stage'. It comments that although gauze screens can be used, or the light diminished at will, 'it is not improbable that the whole illumination may prove too brilliant'. From this description it would appear that the stage was only partially lit by gas. This is confirmed by *Bell's Weekly Messenger* (7 Sept.), which repeats *The Times* description of Drury Lane's lighting almost verbatim, but adds that at Covent Garden the gas is only to be used in the front part of the house 'as yet'.

The Times review of the opening night (in the issue for 9 Sept.) was somewhat captious about the retention of the floats, and considered that the only advantage of the famous chandelier

that of throwing the light on the countenances of the actors from above instead of from below (which last method inverts the natural shadows of the face and distorts the expression) is defeated by the gas lights which are still retained between the stage and the orchestra. Nor do we know how these can well be dispensed with, as it is by raising or withdrawing them that the stage is enlightened or darkened as the occasion requires it.

The decade from 1817 to 1827 saw gas established, either partially or throughout, in all the more important theatres in London and the provinces. There were exceptions, of course. The Olympic, after being one of the first in the field, went back to wax-lights, and announced in 1822 that, among other improvements, the gas had been entirely removed from the interior (playbill, 28 Oct.). The rebuilt Haymarket of 1820 was lighted with oil lamps and spermaceti candles—the former in patent lamps round the upper circle, the latter in cut-glass chandeliers over the dress circle. Benjamin Webster introduced gas into the auditorium there in 1843. The playbill for 17 April announces that 'among the most important improvements is the introduction (for the first time) of GAS as the medium of light'. When the new Royal Coburg was opened in 1818 it was lighted by oil lamps. By 1832, however, and probably earlier, its stage was lighted by gas; but the playbill for 1 July 1833 announces that new lustres, to be lighted with wax, have been added to the dress-circle; and it is not until 15 Aug. 1836 that we are informed that 'a set of new and splendid chandeliers has been added to the dress-circle, lighted with gas'. In 1832 the Garrick, in

Leman Street, Whitechapel, possessed five handsome cut-glass chandeliers for gas.

In the provinces, Liverpool, Edinburgh, and Manchester appear to have led the way in the adoption of gas-lighting, the first in May 1818, the second in December of the same year, the third in December 1819. Gas was in use by 1820 for the auditorium of the Exeter Theatre, as *The Times* for 10 Mar. 1820, describing the fire which entirely destroyed the building on the 7th, says it is thought to have been caused 'by the concentration of gas lights in the centre, which were necessarily near the ceiling or the view of the stage from the gallery would have been impeded'. In its bill for 1 Jan. 1829 the Theatre Royal, Greenock, advertises 'the whole [house] Brilliantly Lighted with Gas'; while the theatre at Gloucester, opening after re-decoration in 1830, announces in its playbill of 14 Dec. that 'the Gas Fittings have also under-gone considerable Improvement—the whole of the Burners having been regulated—escapes stopped—and the *Footlights supplied with Glasses and Shades* to prevent the evil effects of so dazzling a body of light upon the eyes of the Auditors'.

The article on *The Theatre* in the 1867 edition of *Chambers's Encyclopaedia* gives a very succinct account of the gas-lighting system of the London theatres of the middle of the nineteenth century:

The prompter has command of all the lights of the house . . . he has a large brass plate in which a number of handles are fixed, with an index to each marking the high, low, etc. of the lights; and as each system of lights has a separate mainpipe from the prompt corner each can be managed independently. . . . The proscenium is lighted by a large lustre on each side and by the footlights which run along the whole of the front of the stage. These are sometimes provided with glasses of different colours, called mediums, which are used for throwing a red, green, or white light on the stage. The stage is lighted by rows of gas burners up each side and across the top at every entrance. The side-lights are called *gas-wings* or *ladders*; and the top ones *gas battens*. Each of them has a main from the prompt corner. They can be pushed in and out or up and down like the scenery. There is also provision at each entrance for fixing flexible hose and temporary lights, so as to produce a bright effect wherever required. The mediums for producing coloured light in this case are blinds of coloured cloth.

The gas battens, the writer explains, are hidden by borders, and are hoisted into position by ropes which pass over drums in the barrel loft and are worked from the flies.

As a rule the mains for lighting the stage and the front of house were entirely independent of each other. At the control, or 'gas-table', the main divided into smaller branch mains, each controlled by its own valve or stop-cock. Each of these branches was then carried to a 'water-joint' or stage-pocket, and thence by flexible rubber tubing to each separate piece of apparatus. 'In the French Opera-House', Percy Fitzgerald tells us, in his *World Behind the Scenes* (1881), 'there are no less than twenty-eight miles of gas-piping, while the controlling

"jeu d'orgue", as it is called, comprises no less than 88 "stops" or cocks . . . controlling 960 gas jets, etc.' That control of gas lighting was well established and genuinely adequate to theatrical needs by the 1860s is confirmed by an article in *The Builder* (13 Oct. 1866) in which the lighting equipment of the new Prince of Wales's Theatre in Liverpool is described. It obviously included a universal black-out 'switch': 'a single person, placed in front of a system of taps, effectually controls all the gas-lights of the stage and of the house, and he can, by a touch of an electric button, relight instantly, if needful, every burner in the house.' But if control was adequate, safety measures were not. Fitzgerald (*op. cit.*) gives some appalling statistics, which show theatre fires exactly doubling their numbers in the first decade following the introduction of gas—a total of 385 between 1801 and 1877, America, Great Britain, and France heading the list, in that order. As *The Builder* (5 Apr. 1856) gloomily remarks: 'The fate of a theatre is—to be burned. It seems simply a question of time.' Early gas floats were enclosed in glass chimneys and later ones were sometimes protected by ground glass or coloured glass mediums; but the open jets (generally fish-tail burners) used for wing lights were not always fenced even by wire guards.

From the first it was universally recognized that the great advantage of gas in the theatre was its susceptibility to control, but it is difficult to say how far, in its early years, it improved upon the artistic effects which had been achieved with candles and lamps. From criticisms of early gas lighting one might be inclined to think that it had brought the stage little except even more glare and brilliance. *The Theatrical Observer* (No. 1493) in 1826 complained of the lack of contrast in the stage-picture: 'The disposition of the lamps at present is such that no shadow whatever can be presented to the audience, everything upon the stage and in the audience part is a glare of undistinguished lights, painful to the eye. . . . A more concentrated light would be truly refreshing . . . and would give the objects on the stage the utmost beauty of which they are capable, by allowing them some degree of shadow.' In 1892 Percy Fitzgerald is still complaining that 'modern stage lighting is opposed to the exhibition of facial expression. There is such a flood of light, and the face is so bathed in effulgence, from above and below, that there is little relief. There are no shadows. The eye is distracted by the general garish-ness. . . . You cannot see the face for the light.' The glare is fatal to all illusion: 'with battens and footlights, each with two or three hundred jets all in one blaze, the figures seem part of a glittering tissue, and do not stand out' (*Art of Acting*).

These are not isolated complaints; they are, representative. Are we then to believe that those who worked with gas in the theatre completely lost or destroyed an earlier subtlety of light and shade? Was Dutton Cook (*A Book of the Play*, 1881) right to say that since Garrick's time little had been done 'beyond increasing the quantity of light', so that, as Bram Stoker claims, until Irving's reforms and experiments at the Lyceum in the 1880s, stage lighting by gas was 'crude and only partially effective'? Yes, in so far as the average fully illuminated scene in any large theatre was concerned; the theatres were larger than ever: gas was the first really powerful light the stage had acquired, and the obvious thing to do was to exploit its strength and brilliance. No, however, when certain specific lighting effects were the aim; as, for example, the moonlight, sunrise, and the coming of the morning light so 'exquisitely presented' in Phelps's 1853 *Midsummer Night's Dream* (see Odell, *op. cit.* ii for many quotations from contemporary journals). In the 1860s, moreover, efforts were made to combat glare by sinking the floats below stage level—an innovation generally credited to Fechter (see *Illustrated London News*, 7 Nov. 1863). On occasion, too, the auditorium was darkened for the sake of stage effect, as in Charles Kemble's 1832 Covent Garden production of *The Fiend Father*.

Gas, in fact, provided the theatre with means for achieving beautiful lighting effects, but until Irving nobody gave real thought or artistry to its general use, only to its use for the special effect. Bram Stoker claimed that because, under Irving's management, all gas could be regulated from the prompt corner, this in itself made a new era in theatrical lighting. Control, as we have seen, had been there since 1817; and by 1849, probably earlier, the gas-table had put the gas 'wholly under the control of the prompter' (*Theatrical Journal*, 13 Dec. 1849). It was not mechanical control which brought about the Lyceum lighting reforms; Irving was a creative lighting artist who made valuable experiments and gave personal superintendence to the whole business of lighting his productions. The foundation of his method was the consistent darkening of the auditorium throughout the performance—advocated by Ingegneri in 1598. Thanks to Irving, playhouse practice, after three centuries, caught up with Renaissance theory; though needless to say it took some time for the reform to become general.

The difficulty of knowing precisely which of the advances in lighting technique made by Irving relate to gas and which to electricity is increased by the directly conflicting evidence offered by Ellen Terry in her *Memoirs* (1933) and by Bram Stoker in his article on 'Irving and Stage Lighting' in *The Nineteenth Century* for May 1911. Stoker states that in 1891 Irving began to install electricity, beginning with the floats. Ellen Terry says, however:

We never had electricity installed at the Lyceum until Daly took the theatre. When I saw the effect on the faces of the electric footlights, I entreated Henry to have the gas restored, and he did. We used gas footlights and gas limes there until we left the theatre for good in 1902 . . . The thick softness of gaslight, with the lovely specks and motes in it,

so like *natural* light, gave illusion to many a scene which is now revealed in all its naked trashiness by electricity.

It is generally said that after gas-floats and battens were abandoned in most theatres, Irving took his own gas jets and apparatus with him on tour. His use of colour, both with gas and electricity, marked a genuine advance. In the 1870s the thin silk or 'scrim' mediums, used over wire guards, could be had in a few simple colours to give a dominant tone to the lighting, but little more. Irving broke up his floats into separate sections to get greater control of colour, intensity, and distribution; he also experimented with the mixing of colour on the stage, and consequently achieved a subtlety and delicacy 'hitherto unknown'. In his early experiments he used blue paper bags to dim his floats, and for fear of not being able to procure the exact shade even took a supply of these bags with him on his American tour. He is generally considered to have been the first to use transparent lacquers for the glasses of his limes and his electric-light bulbs.

His lighting was at times severely criticized by his contemporaries. The *Quarterly Review* (Apr. 1883) censured his sacrifice of truth and fitness to scenic effect, and quoted as 'a flagrant instance' the 'blaze of light in which Juliet's bedchamber was filled, when even the moon's light was waning, in order that the fierce ghastly livor of the limelight might fall upon the parting caresses of Romeo and Juliet'. The *Pall Mall Gazette* considered that the 'besetting sin' of his famous 1888–9 *Macbeth* was 'the arbitrary and unnatural disposition of the lights', and objected to the courtyard being lighted by 'a strong shaft of limelight obviously proceding from nowhere at all'. Against such English comments, however, must be set the tribute of Antoine of the Théâtre Libre, who saw the production on 9 Feb. 1889, and noted in his journal that the lighting was beyond anything known or thought of in France at that time. Impartial and professional contemporary criticism of this kind lends valuable support to Bram Stoker's contention that Irving's lighting effects were far ahead of anything generally known in the American theatre, where in 1883 only the Boston Theatre had equally good appliances. Whether Irving's partiality prolonged the life of gas in the theatre, and retarded the general adoption of electricity, it is impossible to say, but there can be little doubt that in him this medium found its most remarkable pioneer artist.

(c) *Limelight.* Associated with the era of gas lighting is the limelight which outlived it. The lime or calcium light, as developed by Drummond in 1816, gave a brilliant white light of a quality so excellent for stage purposes that nowadays we tend to associate it with the theatre and nothing else. 'It was the application of the limelight', says Fitzgerald, 'that really threw open the realms of glittering fairyland to the scenic artist.' It was at once radiant yet mellow, 'and by crossing the rays of different lamps and of different tints, strange twilight and soft moonlight effects' could be produced. In its early days it was much used for 'realistic' beams of sun, moon, or lamplight, directed through windows, doors, &c. A special limelight, invented by Frederic Gye, was used by Macready to give extra effect to the diorama by Clarkson Stanfield (1793–1867) of continental views used in his 1837–8 pantomime. It gave very good results, especially for moonlight, but was discontinued after a week's trial, as Macready considered that Gye's charge of 30s. a night was excessive. Ordinary limelight established itself in general use after the middle of the century, and is known to have been employed in the 1851 production of *Azael* at Drury Lane, which received high praise for its beautiful spectacular effects. Although the electric arc apparently gave the earliest lens-equipped spotlight apparatus, the lime was used for spot-lighting and following actors about the stage, and also for experiments with front-of-house lighting in the 1870s.

(d) *Electricity*. Gas had a run of over sixty years in the theatre before it was even challenged by electricity, although the latter had been used for arc-lighting, to counterfeit the disk of the rising sun, at the Paris Opéra as early as 1846, while the arc was used for spots and floods in its 1860 production of Rossini's 'Mosè in Egitto'. The arc, equipped with an enclosed hood, lens, and standard, was the prototype of the modern electric spotlight; and used with a parabolic mirror it could flood certain portions of the stage more intensely than others. It gave a brilliant incandescent light, but it never superseded the lime, because it needed just as much attention, and, moreover, was noisy in operation and apt to flicker. For spot-lighting, both limes and arcs continued in use long after the introduction of the electric bulb.

Like gas, electricity was tried out for entrances, staircases, and foyers before it was introduced to the stage and auditorium. It was the invention of the incandescent bulb which ensured its adoption for theatrical purposes, and the first public building in London to be illuminated throughout in this manner was the Savoy Theatre, built by D'Oyly Carte for the Gilbert and Sullivan operas. *The Times* (3 Oct. 1881) gave the new venture some excellent publicity:

It is worthy of notice that an attempt will be made here for the first time in London to light a theatre entirely by electricity. The system used is that of the "incandescent lamp" invented by Mr. J. W. Swan, and worked by an engine of Messrs. Siemens Bros. & Co. About 1200 lights are used, and the power to generate a sufficient current for these is obtained from large steam engines, giving about 120 horse power, placed on some open land near the theatre. The new light is not only used in the audience part of the theatre, but on the stage for footlights, side and top lights etc. . . . This is the first time that it has been attempted to light any public building entirely by electricity. What is being done is an experiment, and may succeed or fail.

The theatre should have opened on 6 Oct.

with a transfer of *Patience*, but owing to the difficulties involved by 'the application of electric light to theatrical purposes' this was postponed to 11 Oct., when for the 170th performance the electric lights of the auditorium were turned on and 'cheered to the very echo'. Clement Scott described the light as 'soft and pleasant', but found the glare too powerful and the audience illuminated at the expense of the stage. 'The Lyceum plan', he added, 'of a darkened auditorium and a brilliant stage is, I feel sure, the correct one.' At last, on 28 Dec. *The Times* carried a special notice: 'Electric Light on the Stage. Special Matinée this day at two o'clock. On this occasion the stage will be entirely lighted by incandescent lamps. This will be the first time that any theatre or any public building will have been illuminated in every part by electricity alone. . . .' On the following day *The Times* reported the complete success of the new lighting, and described how a resistance of 'open spiral coils of iron wire' was used in order to get gradations between full light and total darkness not possible with 'ordinary' electrical apparatus, but now made practicable by the Swan lamps. Dimmers, therefore, were used from the first with electrical stage-lighting in England, as also in France, according to Lefèvre's *L'Électricité au théâtre* (1895), a volume containing valuable illustrations of early electrical apparatus and installations, which should be consulted for further information.

It is necessary to distinguish between the lighting of theatres by electric arcs and lighting by incandescent bulbs. It is sometimes stated that the Paris Hippodrome was the first theatre to be lighted by electricity, and the date given is 1878. Actually, it was lighted by the Jablochkoff candle—an arc light with two side-by-side carbons insulated by kaolin. According to a contemporary account twenty of these 'candles', in globes, were used along the line dividing the audience from the arena, reinforced by another sixteen (with reflectors) and three twenty-burner gaslights; 'but with all these powerful lights the result was poor compared with the rich radiance we are accustomed to in the theatre' (J. T. Sprague: *Electric Lighting*, 1878). The Opéra was not completely lighted by incandescent bulbs until 1886. The Brünn Theatre in Austria had electricity by 1882; so had several theatres in America. According to Belasco (see his *Life* by W. Winter, 1918), who was playing there at the time, the first American theatre to use electricity was the California in San Francisco, from 21 to 28 Feb. 1879. Generally speaking, it may be said that between 1880 and 1887 electricity was installed in most of the important theatres of Europe, England, and America, and that after 1887—largely because the two disastrous theatre fires of that year, at the Opéra-Comique and the theatre at Exeter, had once again demonstrated the terrible risks of gas—it quickly gained favour everywhere.

Before leaving the nineteenth century we may notice in passing some of its anticipations of modern lighting practice. The abolition of the floats and front-of-house lighting go back to the first half of the century in England, and to 1872 in America; and in March 1879, in San Francisco at the Grand Opera, David Belasco began the experiments which were to lead to the lighting of *The Darling of the Gods* and *Peter Grimm*, when he got rid of the floats and for his production of *The Passion Play* by S. Morse lighted his stage from the front with old locomotive bull's-eye lanterns, thus anticipating the methods of Reinhardt and Granville-Barker by a quarter of a century. Even more unexpected, perhaps, are the mid-nineteenth-century experiments—again generally involving the abolition of the footlights—in which illusions of space and depth now associated with the cyclorama were to some extent realized. It looks as if they were developments of the panoramic and dioramic background effects popular on the London stage in the early years of the century. The most interesting of these occurred in the French ballet, 'Le Corsair', staged at Her Majesty's in July 1856, in which for the storm scene when the Corsair's vessel was wrecked something in the nature of a (canvas?) cyclorama was evidently used, if we may rely on the following description by *The Illustrated London News* (19 July):

> The complete withdrawal of what are technically called the wings, and the substitution of a broad expanse of panoramic atmosphere extending over the whole area of the stage, is a new, bold and successful idea.

Nothing, unfortunately, is said about the lighting except that the 'struggling moonbeams gleam' and that 'slowly the tempest comes on and the lurid and darkened clouds thicken'.

Gas-lighting was a practical business, begotten of experience; modern lighting is the result firstly of much theoretical examination of the principles which should govern the art of stage decoration, and secondly of the technical work which has produced the apparatus designed to carry out these new ideas. In his attempt to work out the problems of stage setting for Wagnerian opera Adolphe Appia (1862–1928) not only propounded what have since been universally accepted as fundamental principles of stage design, but, as an integral part of his aesthetic theory, set forth with specific and practical illustrations the basic ideas concerning the nature and function of stage lighting which virtually govern all the best modern work.

Envisaging a comprehensive artistic unity as the fundamental demand of a production, he rejected the painted scene in favour of the three-dimensional setting which is the only environment to which the three-dimensional actor can properly belong. To give both actor and setting their full plasticity, however, something other than the flat stage lighting of the end of the nineteenth century was required: if mass, form, and movement were to be self-expressive, to contribute their essential quality and meaning as a vital part of the drama, then shade as well as light was necessary: the light must behave as real light does. It is the unifying principle which links actor and setting in an artistic whole: consequently our emotional responses will be quickened—in both senses—by the light in which we are made to 'see': its colour, its stress, its comment will be in the full sense revelatory. Light, for Appia, is the visible counterpart of the music, interpreting to sensuous perception the dominant mood and following the pattern of the shift and play of feeling.

Appia did not invent apparatus, but the eighteen designs in *Die Musik und die Inscenierung* (1899) embodied his ideas so clearly and satisfactorily that they have enabled the theatre to put them into practice. Moreover, he pointed out that the movable arc lights of the then contemporary theatre provided a means for spotting or picking out the actor, emphasizing his importance, and giving him a shadow. Mobile lighting of this kind, breaking up the light and diversifying direction, intensity, and colour, has become the basis of modern interpretive dramatic lighting: atmosphere, suggestion, mood, and the stressing of the actor are so much the commonplaces of artistic direction to-day that the genius of Appia is honoured in theatre practice even by many who have no idea from whence the original stimulus derives.

The most important practical contribution to modern stage lighting was made at the beginning of the twentieth century, when Mariano Fortuny (1871–   ) put into operation in about 1902 the system which bears his name. Because there are two kinds of light in nature—the direct rays of the sun, or of any other light-source, and the diffused general light which is reflected from the atmosphere and from light-coloured surfaces—he believed that the basic illumination of the stage, which made actors, objects, and settings visible, should be provided by reflected light. To give reflected light he 'invented' the sky-dome to act as reflector; the light itself was thrown by high-powered arcs on to bands of coloured silk which reflected it back on to the dome and on to the stage. For all the direct lighting needed spots were used. The softness of the reflected diffused light is very beautiful, but the amount of current consumed is prohibitive. Fortuny's real gifts to the theatre, in fact, are ideas: the idea of the scope and beauty of indirect lighting, and the idea of the usefulness of the various kinds of reflecting surfaces that counterfeit what the nineteenth century called 'panoramic atmosphere' (see above), and which we call—loosely—the cyclorama. As used in Fortuny's own system it is the Kuppelhorizont, or true half-dome, made of silk or plaster: in its more usual form it is the semi-circular plaster or canvas wall surrounding the greater portion of the stage—the Rundhorizont, or cyclorama properly so-called; and finally there is the flat plaster wall or plain canvas cloth which can be lighted in the same way to give distance and good sky effects, but cannot give space and vastness because it still needs masking (see also SCENERY, 6).

On the continent the years 1900 to 1914 saw rapid technical and artistic advances in stage lighting, especially in Germany; England and America both lagged behind, though much of the progress made on the continent was due to the influence of an Englishman, Edward Gordon Craig (1872–   ), while in America David Belasco (1859–1931) made valuable experiments in the commercial theatre which solved specific lighting problems as they arose. His practical inventions and innovations gave to modern realistic spectacle some of its most beautiful early effects, and many years before the introduction of the Linnebach lantern for projecting from behind on to transparencies, Belasco, helped by a lucky accident (see Winter, *op. cit.*), achieved by somewhat similar methods the spectacular scene in *The Darling of the Gods*, mentioned above, where the bodies of the dead were seen floating and drifting on the River of Souls.

In 1910 *The Stage Year Book* summed up the situation in the London theatre by the sweeping statement that 'on the legitimate stage, with such exceptions as His Majesty's and one or two others, all lighting details are left to the Stage Manager and the Electrician', while in 1913 an American critic, H. K. Moderwell, in *The Theatre of Today*, was equally severe on his own countrymen, and, praising the charm and beauty of the lighting of any well-executed German stage-setting, asserted that it was difficult to realize the secret of it because 'it seems to an American imagination so impossible that a stage should be other than glaring white, that one does not dream of looking for the explanation in the lighting'.

From crude and glaring lighting both countries were to emancipate themselves in the nineteen-twenties, but it was only in such things as the Reinhardt productions, or Granville-Barker's Shakespearian work, or the experiments of small non-commercial theatre units, that they had previously encountered anything which could be compared with good contemporary work in Germany. For the English theatre of his day Barker's lighting of his 1912 and 1914 Shakespearian productions was unusual, but his abolition of the floats and his use of front-of-house lighting was not simply an endorsement of fashionable continental theory, but a practical solution of the problem of lighting the new acting areas created by the use of an apron over the orchestra pit and of a false proscenium which gave another plane between the stage proper and the apron. The description in *The Times* of 29 Sept. 1912 of his apparatus as 'search-lamps converging on the stage from the dress-circle' gives the measure of its novelty.

The fundamental principles governing the art of modern stage lighting were expounded by Appia, Craig, and others, and tried out on the continent between 1900 and 1910. With the advent of such things as the Schwabe-Haseit system, the Linnebach projector, the Gekape projecting process, Wilfred's colour-organ, the pure-colour media of Munroe R.

Pevear, and the immensely powerful lamps now used in the theatre, we are in the realm of scientific discovery and mechanical invention. Between them the theorists and the inventors have made modern stage lighting the most essential and the most sensitive of the mechanical means at the disposal of the theatre as a unifying and interpretive agent.

M. ST. C. B.

2. MODERN STAGE LIGHTING IN ENGLAND. (*a*) *General.* From the introduction of electricity into the first London theatre, the Savoy, in 1881, and the use of the electric arc spotlight in place of the limelight, there was little progress, beyond the increased efficiency of the electric lamp itself, until 1919. The general lighting of the scenery and the acting area was provided by rows of lights, known as battens (border lights in the U.S.A.), up among the sky borders, by footlights, and by strips of lights up each side of the proscenium arch and the wings, consisting of coloured or varnished lamps; hand-fed arc spotlights and floodlights provided all the highlights and directional light that were deemed necessary.

The first revolutionary step came with the invention of the gas-filled electric lamp, which had, however, a serious drawback in that the temperature of the glass bulb was so high that the coloured lacquer or varnish would not remain on it beyond a few minutes. Other methods of obtaining coloured light had to be found, and so was evolved the magazine compartment battens and footlights, in which each lamp has its own compartment with colour-runners for frames containing glass or gelatine colour media.

It was in 1922 that illuminating engineers began to look on stage lighting as a branch of their industry that called for scientific treatment and development, and methods were introduced for collecting as much as possible of the light given out by the lamp filament, and projecting it in the required direction. This was done by the use of scientifically designed reflectors. Many types of material were tried over a number of years, and mirrored glass with a broken surface was found to be the most successful, the reflection factor being 95 per cent. as against 65 per cent. for chromium-plated and 70 per cent. for white-enamelled iron. The reason for the broken surface is that owing to the irregularities the beam is dissected into dispersed rays of light, and this tends to soften and diffuse the beam and thus remove all striation or filament image. The advent of larger lamps of 500 and 1,000 watts led to the introduction of the high-powered flood lantern not only in the wings but hung among the sky borders for flooding backcloths and draperies.

About 1914 the introduction of a gas-filled lamp of high lumen (light) output, known as a projector lamp, was probably the most revolutionary step forward, and largely altered the whole technique of stage lighting. Previously all spotlighting had been by means of the hand-fed arc-lanterns mentioned above, each of which required an operator to 'feed' the carbons together. This naturally limited the positions in which the lanterns could be used. The projector lamp, however, has no need of an operator; it can be placed in any position and, being connected to a variable resistance known as a dimmer, its intensity can be varied at the wish of the producer. This incandescent spotlight, as it is also called, quickly became the most important lighting unit on the British and American stages. It has been aptly defined by Fuchs (*Stage Lighting*, 1929), as 'a piece of lighting mechanism used for lighting a small portion of the stage to a higher intensity than the remainder, and thus *unconsciously* focussing the attention of the audience to that part of the stage so lighted'. Its normal position on the stage is just upstage of the proscenium border and on the side walls of the proscenium, and its intelligent use provides the producer with a medium which will render his whole production stereoscopic, causing flat scenery to appear three-dimensional and the characters prominent (but not too much so) in their surroundings.

Since 1922 there have been many developments of this lighting unit. Originally it consisted of the lamp itself, the lens, and provision for moving the lamp towards or away from the lens to vary the beam; then came the introduction of reflectors of various types—optically worked mirrored glass, chromium plate, rhodium plate, &c.—together with stepped lenses and so on to increase the efficiency of the light output. Gradually it crept out into the auditorium so as to cover that area of the stage between the footlights, the spot-batten, and No. 1 batten, always a dark spot, where actors are drawn unconsciously towards the footlights so that, with illumination only from below, their facial expressions become grotesque. To overcome this spots were installed in the balcony fronts of theatres. At first, in order to reduce the distance from the stage, they were placed on the lowest circle, but as this is practically always level with the actors' faces, the result was not only to take all expression away from their features, but also to provide high and grotesque shadows on the backcloths. Removal of the spots to the second tier overcame these difficulties. The next problem was that of changing the colours in the lanterns so placed, which led to the development of remote control of the colour-frames by switch operation on the stage switchboard; actually electric magnets are attached to the lanterns.

These circle lanterns have become a big asset to the lighting of spectacular shows—revues, musical comedy, pantomime—and as these are mainly given in the bigger theatres, where the circle is some distance from the stage, increased efficiency was required. This led to the adoption of the lantern known as a mirror spot. This has a scientifically-designed eight-inch diameter optically-worked silvered glass reflector which projects an intense beam of light on a variable gate; this beam is focused by a six-inch diameter lens, in some cases a plain plano-convex and in others a stepped type. By means of the variable gate, rectangular spots of various sizes and shapes can be projected with an intensity of over double that obtained by the standard spotlight of the same size and wattage. This lantern is particularly successful for long throws, which are often as much as seventy feet where a 30-volt 30-ampere lamp is used, and where the variable shutter makes it possible to mask the light and therefore prevent it spilling into the orchestra.

Attempts have been made to use spot lanterns taking a larger lamp, e.g. the two-kilowatt; this has only proved successful for use in the wings of big spectacular shows. For the average stage play the lumen output is far too great and often has to be checked down by means of dimmers, while the excessive size of the lantern makes it a nuisance when hung up among the sky borders.

In addition to the now traditional spot-batten, groups of these lanterns are used on 'boomerangs', a steel barrel fixed to the stage floor and mounted upwards towards the fly floor. In straight plays these are usually mounted near the Prompt and O.P. corners, and may accommodate as many as twelve to fifteen spots in each.

In very large theatres the No. 1 spot-batten is apt to become difficult; in opera, for instance, it is sometimes necessary to move and reset the lanterns for each scene, and therefore a bridge is often provided, particularly in the big continental opera houses. The spots should be housed either underneath the bridge with access by means of a trap-door in the floor, or on the underside of the upstage rail of the bridge, which should be so designed that the rails slope towards the floor of the bridge from the upstage edge, and thus provide protection from scenery. The bridge should be, and often is, counter-weighted so that its height can be varied. It should be rigid, and there should be no vibration due to the operator passing over it when the curtain is up. The mobility of the bridge is allied in control with the 'perches' or ladder-type boomerangs, which can be moved on and off stage according to the width of the scene.

In the modern theatre there is a tendency to design a forward bridge out in the auditorium. An example of this can be seen at the London Coliseum. It is a very efficient method, and commends itself to the little playhouses such as those envisaged for civic centres, for example, where the circle or balcony, even if it exists, is usually too low.

(b) *Footlights*. The early history of the footlight has been traced in the first part of this article. Many important continental producers have maintained that their light is unnatural, and Appia once described them as 'the monstrosity of the theatre'. If, however, we light our actors entirely from above and ignore the 'under' lighting, we get an unnatural effect; there are pronounced shadows under the chin, nostril, and eyebrow of the actor, heavier than those produced by the light of day. The judicious use of some light from below corrects this. The footlight is of course always connected to a dimmer, which allows the intensity to be varied so that the correct balance may be obtained.

It is essential that the footlights should be placed in the correct position. They cause much consternation to theatre architects on account of the sight lines of the people who occupy the near stalls, and one finds frequently that architects, in designing their seating, ignore the fact that the footlights *must* project above the stage level. The light source of the lamp, namely, the filament, must be above the edge of the stage, otherwise there will be a rising shadow towards the back of the stage with resultant heavy shadows across the lower half of the backcloth. Also a ballet dancer's legs, for instance, would be in shadow when she was upstage. The footlights must therefore be set in such a position that the edge of the actor's boots is illuminated whenever he is standing in the acting area. Modern footlights, which usually project $3\frac{3}{4}$ inches above the stage level, are designed with reflectors that not only do this, but also light vertically up the curtain and nowhere else, for the light from the footlights must on no account illuminate any part of the auditorium.

(*c*) *Reflectors*. The design of the reflectors used in battens is also important, owing to the great number of drop scenes, draperies, borders, and so on, and to the fact that they are often very near the object they have to illuminate. The reflectors are therefore designed to give a very wide angle so that the resultant light is layer upon layer; they must also throw down a large amount of their intensity on to the acting area, though the increasing employment of a large number of directional lighting units is making the battens of secondary importance for this latter purpose.

(*d*) *Following Spots*, also known as 'the limes'. These, owing to the enormous intensity required, are practically the sole remaining electric arc-lanterns used in the theatre, mostly in spectacular shows and in opera. In the modern theatre they are usually placed at the back of the gallery or top circle in a special chamber, and therefore the throw of light is frequently as far as 100 feet. The increase in the general lighting intensity of the acting area since the early 1920s has necessitated the introduction of the high-intensity mirror arc, which uses a carbon combination similar to the cinematograph projector; this, with the specially designed reflector of mirrored glass and special lenses, has produced a most efficient lantern consuming about 100 amperes. It is fitted with various accessories to alter the shape and size of the beam, such as the 'barn door' shutters which vary the light horizontally and vertically, and iris diaphragms which give a circular variation of the light so that it can be reduced to a pinpoint. The arc-lantern usually employs a direct-current supply which is obtained either by a motor generator (though this is going out of date) or by a mercury arc-rectifier to convert the current from alternating to direct. The growth of alternating supply has led English designers to produce an arc-lantern that will operate satisfactorily on A.C. without the usual flicker, and this is rapidly replacing the old D.C. type. The use of the following spot is often described as unnatural, but to present the comedian in variety or the Fairy Queen in pantomime without the aid of this unit would be regarded by experts and public alike as bad showmanship.

(*e*) *Flood Battens*. Mention has already been made of flood lanterns using 500- and 1,000-watt lamps. These units are frequently used in place of the traditional batten on backcloths, as many as sixteen to twenty being used in an average-sized production. Like the batten, their reflectors are designed to give a wide angle of light and produce layer upon layer.

(*f*) *Colour Circuits*. In the early days of electric light a stage might be equipped with a 'three- or four-colour scheme' which provided the basis of the colour effects obtained. To-day the colour of the circuit merely differentiates one circuit from the other, since flexibility demands the grouping of the circuits into three or four sets independent of one another. The colour that is used is not fixed, but can be any one of the seventy hues obtainable, as desired by the producer. Nowadays the directional lighting units such as spots, which are not allied to any of the colour groups, are far in excess of the 'colour circuits' which are confined to foots, battens, and stage-floor connexions or dips (known as pockets in the U.S.A.).

(*g*) *Floor Apparatus*. There are numerous portable pieces of apparatus used in various parts of the stage, and mainly plugged into the dips, including strips for ground-row lighting which are, in England, similar to the footlights. There is also in the English theatre a lantern called a pageant which is somewhat similar to a small searchlight, giving an almost parallel beam; one might define it as a spot without the use of lenses. It is a very intense beam, and is used for sunbeams through a window, also in colour spectacles from a number of boomerangs; it has also been used for front lighting from the auditorium, for which spot lanterns are also frequently used.

(*h*) *The Cyclorama*. Though usually classed as scenery the cyclorama is so closely allied with stage lighting that it must be considered here. It is best described as a perfectly plain screen with a uniform surface on to which coloured light is projected to produce skies of various hues, often with clouds, moving or stationary, thrown on to the cyclorama from optical projectors. It can also be used for the projecting of symbolic designs and shadows. If efficiently illuminated the cyclorama gives the playgoer the illusion of a natural sky, and a feeling of infinite space. The method of lighting is by means of banks of flood lanterns, each of which produces a wide angle of light (i.e. a beam angle of not less than 100°) and thus projects layer upon layer of light on top of one another over the full width of the cyclorama. In English theatres the various colours are obtained by means of the additive method advocated by Professor Young in 1803, where, by taking three dominant colours of the spectrum and varying the intensity of the light behind each, any shade can be produced, even that of a November London fog. The colours used are No. 20 Blue, No. 16 Green-Blue, and No. 5a Orange. The incandescent electric lamp has a very low output of the blue end of the spectrum, only 3 per cent. of the lumen output of the lamp passing through the colour media. This means that there must be far more lighting in the blue circuit than in the other two.

Ideally the cyclorama should be illuminated at both the top and the bottom. The top lighting, which should cover the top two-thirds of the height, should be placed well away from the surface of the cyclorama, certainly, on a full stage, not less than twelve feet away, so that the angles of reflection and incidence are as large as possible. The lighting of the bottom should not rise more than a third of the total height, thus giving an illusion of distance. It can be much closer than the top lighting to the surface of the cyclorama and can come either from portable trucks or from a pit let into the stage.

The use of the cyclorama on the continent is practically universal. It stretches from the grid to the stage, and as it may be ninety feet in height, and any scenery that has to be flied for storing must be above it, it therefore follows that the grid is frequently as high as 120 feet. Starting from the Prompt corner, the cyclorama passes round the stage near to the back wall, ending at the Opposite Prompt corner, thus forming half a cylinder. Most continental cycloramas are made of canvas hanging from a track, and when not in use they can be rolled up in the Prompt and O.P. corners. They are not altogether satisfactory as they are susceptible to climatic conditions; only on a really hot day are they free from creases, while if a door is opened and a draught created, the illusion of looking into space is immediately shattered. For the average stage the cylindrical shape has many disadvantages, though it may be useful in a large opera house. Nor is the illusion of space due to the cyclorama's being curved, since the curving is only necessary to mask the sides of the stage.

Since the law in England does not allow of buildings being more than a certain height the abbreviated cyclorama has been evolved, though at Covent Garden and the London Coliseum the continental model is followed. The British method is in plan either perfectly flat, or has curved ends to a radius of approximately four to six feet. In a playhouse with a definite policy, e.g. a good repertory theatre, it should be a permanent structure of hard cement (*not* plaster) which is treated with a white water distemper, preferably applied

with a spray, the final result having the appearance of white blotting-paper. If temporary cycloramas of canvas have to be employed they should be attached to metal barrels at top and bottom and lashed to the stage with lacing to take up the slackness due to variations of temperature. With this type, borders will have to be used, but if their design is carefully considered they need not look unnatural. A cyclorama on these lines is more practicable than the continental type described above, particularly if it is also the back wall of the stage, as it leaves the full acting area available for use.

The spot lanterns at the front-of-house, and the spot batten and perches will, when a cyclorama is used, illuminate adequately the acting area to within a certain distance of the cyclorama. It is essential that no portion of this light should strike the cyclorama, which should be confined to its own lighting. It is therefore necessary to provide some overhead directional lighting for the area directly in front of the cyclorama. The type of lantern used for this, both in England and on the continent, is known as an acting area lantern. The English model is so designed that the beam angle and the lamp cut-off are identical, generally 24°. A number of these lanterns are used, generally to cover most of the acting area. In the big spectacular shows such as those given at the London Palladium and Coliseum, as well as in pantomimes and musical comedies, they have become one of the main lighting units (see also SCENERY).

(*i*) *Projected Scenery.* Projected effects have been used in connexion with the cyclorama on the continent by Strobach at Cologne, and by Messrs. Gayling, Kann, and Planer in Vienna. The latter is known as the G.K.P. system. In both methods the whole of the design is projected on to the big curved cycloramas from projectors fitted on a bridge over the proscenium arch. Optical effects such as clouds, snow, flames, and so on have long been in use on both cycloramas and ordinary scenery. They function in much the same way as a magic-lantern slide, and the mechanism for providing movement is either an electric motor or clockwork.

(*j*) *Control.* This, also known as the stage switchboard, is the brain of all stage lighting systems, and the electrical and mechanical contrivances which form the control unit must be carefully planned. They must also conform to the licensing requirements, which in England are largely based on the rules and regulations of the Institution of Electrical Engineers, and the fire regulations. They may be divided technically into two parts, the switching and fusing section, and the dimmer regulator. The latter is probably the most important point of the control, since it regulates the balance of stage lighting, and gives light and shade, life and realism, to the scenery and characters. The dimmer used in England is of the wire resistance type. It is relatively the least expensive, and satisfactory in every way where a fixed load has to be considered. On the continent the reactance dimmer, of the tapped trans-former type, has made much progress, while in the U.S.A. the direct current saturated choke finds favour. These last two are of course only operable when alternating current is available. They both have two advantages over the wire dimmer in that (1) flickerless dimming is obtained whatever the load, from fifteen watt up to as far as ten kilowatt, and (2) there is less wastage of current. Initial costs have some-what hindered the development of either of these types in England, but the tapped trans-former type of English design is in use in some of the larger theatres, and manufacturers are developing apparatus along these lines. It is on the mechanical operation of the dimmers that the biggest step forward has been made. The more dimmers employed the more flexible is the control, and so the lighting. In the average Lon-don theatre the number varies from eighty to two hundred. The mechanical operation of such a bank necessitates the design of each in-dividual dimmer handle being capable of being locked to shafting for gang control in such a way that it automatically releases itself both at the top and bottom of its travel. The collective operation of a number of shafts produced the 'Grand Master' control, where, by using bevels and 'spline' gears, the whole of the various dimmer shafts can be mechanically connected to the grand master wheel, each shaft being provided with gears (or electric clutches) for this purpose, so that it is possible for any shaft to be rotated in any direction irrespective of the direction in which its neighbours may be travelling. Remote control of main switch-gear, such as colour master black-outs, by magneti-cally operated contactors controlled by small switches on the stage board, has eliminated the noise that used to be heard on these occasions. Flexibility of switch control developed with the introduction of two-way and off switches, which allow any circuit to be pre-set so that it is in-dependent of the black-out.

The dimmer by its operation varies the volt-age (which to the uninitiated is the pressure), which varies the amount of light. This varia-tion of the light does not decrease in the same ratio as the pressure, and thus calls for careful design in the winding of the dimmer. In Eng-land dimmers are mostly wound to the Harold Ridge and F. S. Aldred formula, which, with a hundred-step dimmer, gives 50 per cent. lumen output at the thirtieth stud.

(k) *Remote Control.* An important develop-ment in control apparatus during the 1930s was the growth of complete remote control of the switches and the dimmers. The increase in the number of circuits to be controlled made the manually controlled switchboards in the larger theatres difficult to handle, and the various forms of remote control, whether operating mechanically by tracker wire, as in the German systems, or electrically, as in Britain and the U.S.A., have sought by reduc-tion in size of the levers and switches to reduce in turn the size of the control panel, the object of such reduction being to bring all controls under the hands of one operator, and to enable the panel to be sited so as to give the operator a better view of the stage.

It was soon found that miniature reproduc-tion of a normal switchboard did not of itself bring much advantage. A couple of hundred small levers, dials, and switches are no easier to work rapidly than their full-sized counter-parts—harder, in fact, since a small panel precludes the use of assistant operators work-ing simultaneously on different parts of the board. An attempt has therefore been made to enable one man to carry out large changes rapidly by giving him pre-set facilities, origin-ally for his switches, and latterly for his dimmer positions as well. The operator can make use of intervals to set several changes in advance, the controls for each circuit being repeated twice, or in some installations eight times; a master switch brings in the new settings of each series and takes out the old. Of this type of control the electronic board based on the thyratron valve, which originated in the U.S.A., is undoubtedly the most complete.

An entirely different approach to the problem has been made by Frederick Bentham with his Strand light console, which adopts the organ-type keyboards and stop keys. The operator uses his ten fingers instead of his two hands, and, as he is seated, in full view of the stage, pedal controls can be used as well. The second problem, that of reduction in size of the con-trol panel, is solved by providing each lighting circuit with one switch only, in the form of a stop key. By depressing a single stop key or combination of stop keys, lighting circuits are connected to a 'master' for operation. The 'masters' consist of keyboards, sub-divided into colours, where all the controls for dimming, switching, and black-outs are to be found. Thus whether one lighting circuit or a hundred are involved in a lighting change, the master con-trol is always used. The constant locking and unlocking of the lighting circuits is made effortless by the easy touch and semicircular arrangement of the stop keys. As a further aid there are the usual organ cancel and combina-tion pistons adjustable to move on and off large numbers of stop keys at a time. These and other devices are largely provided to help the operator through rehearsals and first nights, when the strain on one man in complete con-trol may be considerable. All remote controls are of necessity more expensive than a direct operated switchboard. The miniature switch-panel in the small theatre, and the console type in the larger houses, together with the 'Action' apparatus itself (usually low-voltage D.C.) which enables it to operate through motors and electro-magnets from a distance, constitute a heavy extra charge. But for a large stage in-stallation remote control is the only solution, and by 1948 the Strand light console had been installed in the London Palladium, the Theatre Royal, Bristol, the National Opera House, Lisbon, and the Opera House, Ankara.

L. G. A.

3. STAGE LIGHTING IN THE UNITED STATES. Since the beginning of the use of electricity in the theatre the development of equipment has been influenced largely by the availability of new light sources. These in turn are influenced by the fact that the electrical systems in the U.S.A. operate for the most part at 110 volts; in England commonly at 220. Sources for each range are therefore not interchangeable. The higher voltage system also requires a third wire (ground; in England, earth) on each piece of portable apparatus for safety, and requires larger filaments and bulbs (or the introduction of transformers and A.C. for low-voltage lamps). Low-voltage lamps are not used in the U.S.A. as extensively as they are in England. The compact ellipsoidal reflector spotlight (similar to, but smaller physically than, the English mirror spot, see above) has been made possible by the development of a T-12 (1½ in. diameter, tubular) lamp in a 500-watt biplane filament form, and recently even a 750-watt unit has been tested satisfactorily. This type of unit in its various forms (wide, 45°; medium, 30°; and narrow beams, 15°) is three to five times more powerful than the conventional plano-convex spotlight of equal wattage.

The Fresnel lens spotlight or step-lens spotlight seems to have had more development and use in the U.S.A. than in England. It is two to three times as powerful as the old plano-convex spotlight, and gives automatically a soft-edge beam. The soft-edge 'spill' or 'ghost' makes this instrument ('lantern' in England) useless for 'pin spot' or strictly localized 'spot lighting'.

The basic difference in type of equipment arises out of the 'portability' requirement for almost all instruments and even switchboards used in the 'legitimate' theatre in the U.S.A. A production carries with it not only actors, scenery, and properties, but all its lighting equipment. In England most theatres are fairly thoroughly equipped with permanent installations. Community, school, and motion-picture theatres and the opera houses are the only theatres in the U.S.A. so equipped.

Remote colour control permitting the moving of one or more of four or five colour filters in front of or out of an instrument electrically from the switchboard is found only in the non-travelling equipment.

Perhaps because of hazards in handling, very little glass is used in American equipment. Alzak (electrolytically treated aluminium) is almost universally used for reflectors. It has a high reflection coefficient and can be spun readily into accurate reflector forms, so that it seems more practical to use than silvered glass. It is almost as efficient. Colour filters in the U.S.A. (for which cinemoid is extensively used in England) generally consist of cheap films of dyed gelatine. They can be had in many hues and tints. Although they become brittle and fragile with use and fade rather rapidly, they seem to have more general use than more expensive, more permanent colour filters, except in certain strip lights (battens in England)

where the three primary colours in glass—red, green, and blue—are being used extensively.

There are several differences in method between English and U.S.A. practice. In the U.S.A., with a few exceptions, the designer assumes complete responsibility for the ultimate visual effect on the stage. In England, this is the duty of the 'stage director' (or producer). In the U.S.A. the designer works closely with the electrician or in a few cases with the so-called lighting specialist. Another difference in which the English practice is similar to the continental rather than the American lies in the use of so-called 'acting area' units. These provide a narrow beam of high-intensity illumination directly down on the acting area. In some respects they take the place of border lights as they are used in the U.S.A. In others they provide much the same effect as the 'projectors'—narrow beam units—used for backlighting in musical shows. 'Acting area lights' in the American theatre refer to the spotlights mounted out 'front', or on the bridge or first pipe, to light the actors from the front diagonal—not from directly overhead or from behind.

'Front lighting' in the U.S.A. is generally provided by 'ellipsoidal reflector spotlights' mounted in the open on the front of the first balcony. The English method of using the second balcony gives a much better angle, but many theatres in the U.S.A. do not have second balconies.

While on the subject of 'frontlights' the arc 'follow spot' (English 'following spot') and 'flood' are invariably direct-current instruments. The alternating-current arc such as is used in England has not had a satisfactory development in the U.S.A.

'Border lights' or 'X-rays' (battens in England) are used for much the same purpose in both countries, except that in England apparently 'acting area' lanterns are more often used to light the playing space, while battens and floods are used to light 'backcloths' ('backdrops' in the U.S.A.). Border lights, in fact all three-colour 'striplights' in use in the U.S.A., are generally equipped with compact etched Alzak reflectors, giving a narrow or medium beam spread. The introduction of the highly efficient 'reflector spot or flood lamp', with plain, coloured, or spread roundels (cover glasses), is meeting the need for more colour from a compact instrument. These lamps come in 150- and 300-watt sizes with spot or flood distribution. The shape of the bulb is roughly parabolic and about 5 inches in diameter so that it can be mounted in strips on 6-inch centres. These lamps are not yet available in voltages over 120.

The European tradition of large stages and considerable space given over to bridges and other lighting apparatus has made it possible to light cycloramas in England with efficient wide-angle floods mounted well downstage with no scenery cluttering the space between them and the cyclorama. This is seldom possible in the American theatre, where stages are not very deep. Cycloramas and backdrops are generally lighted by high-powered three-colour narrow beam striplights mounted close to the surface (not too smooth as a rule) at top and bottom. Where the English method has been used in the U.S.A. the results have generally been good.

The use of the high-powered 'fresnel' spotlight for sunlight, moonlight, and even backlighting restricts the use of the narrow beam 'projector' ('pageant lantern' in England) to back lighting or outdoor long-throw work.

The term 'batten' in the U.S.A. refers to the iron pipe on which lighting instruments ('lanterns' in England) and scenery are mounted. Ordinarily the horizontal pipe batten hung from the grid just back of the proscenium, on which lighting equipment is mounted, is called simply 'first pipe'. Wooden rails at the top and bottom of backdrops are also called 'battens'.

Control (switchboard) terminology and equipment vary considerably between the two countries. This is partly due to the two basic differences in operating voltage and portability. The variable rheostat ('wire resistance' in England) is still the dimmer most used in the U.S.A. It is almost never used with remote motor operation because if that amount of money is to be spent either an auto-transformer ('tapped transformer' in England) with a motor or a tube ('valve' in England) reactor combination is used. These are all for permanent installations, which are the exception rather than the rule. In New York the Metropolitan Opera and the Radio City Music Hall have elaborate tube-reactor pre-set boards. Recently (1947) a simplified pre-set dimmer board was demonstrated at the Yale University Theatre. In this board there are no reactors. The tube itself is the dimmer, and there are ten pre-sets with an automatic 'fader' which can be set for any speed between two seconds and four and a half minutes. (See also UNITED STATES OF AMERICA, II.)   S. MCC.

LIGHT OPERA, see OPERA, 14.

LILLO, GEORGE (1693–1739), English dramatist, best remembered for his play *The Merchant,* usually known as *The London Merchant; or, the History of George Barnwell,* which was done at Drury Lane in 1731. Based on an old ballad, it shows how a good young man's passion for a bad woman leads him to murder his old uncle for money, the murderer and his accomplice being subsequently hanged. The play was immensely successful, being warmly praised by no less a person than Alexander Pope, and it became the fashion to act it for the apprentices at holiday times, particularly on Shrove Tuesday. It was frequently revived at the Patent Theatres, notably by Mrs. Siddons, and was known well enough to be the butt of several burlesques. It was also the play given by the Crummles family in *When Crummles Played* (1927), based by Nigel Playfair on *Nicholas Nickleby.* It had a great vogue on the continent, and influenced the development of the sentimental comedy there, particularly in France. The printed copy has a scene at the place of execution, with a noble speech by the hapless Barnwell, which is usually omitted in production, but was done at Bath in 1817. Lillo wrote several other plays and ballad operas, of which the most important was *The Fatal Curiosity* (1736), again based on an old ballad about a murder done in Cornwall. It was first produced at the Haymarket by Fielding, and was the play chosen by Mrs. Siddons for her benefit in 1797, with John Philip and Charles Kemble. It also had a great influence abroad, particularly on the so-called German 'fate-drama', and was the inspiration for Werner's *24. Februar* (1809).

LIMELIGHT, see LIGHTING, 1 *c.*

LIMES, see LIGHTING, 2 *d.*

LINCOLN'S INN FIELDS THEATRE, LONDON, also known as Lisle's Tennis-Court or the Duke's House. This playhouse bulks large in theatre history. It was originally a tennis-court, built in 1656 by Anne Tyler and James Hooker, and it was converted into a theatre by Sir William Davenant in 1661. It stood in Portugal Street, and was about 75 ft. in length and 30 ft. wide. It was the first theatre to have a proscenium arch and to employ scenery which was 'set' and 'struck'. The stage projected in apron form beyond the proscenium into the auditorium. There was a large scene room, and next door were Davenant's own lodgings, where his principal actresses, including Mrs. Davenport and Mrs. Saunderson (later Mrs. Betterton), also boarded. Davenant had taken his company over from Rhodes, and in addition to the young Betterton he had six actors who as juveniles had played women's parts, the best known being Ned Kynaston. But both Davenant and Killigrew were empowered by their charters to engage women to act in their theatres.

The theatre opened, probably on 28 June 1661, with the first part of *The Siege of Rhodes.* The second part was given on the following day, and the two parts were acted alternately for a fortnight, always in the afternoon. They were followed by *The Wits,* and on 28 Aug. the play was *Hamlet,* which Pepys saw, 'done with scenes very well, but above all Betterton did the prince's part beyond imagination'. This was the first scenic production of *Hamlet.* Among other plays *The Adventures of Five Hours* was a great success, and there was a revival of *Romeo and Juliet* played alternately 'tragical one day' in Shakespeare's version, and 'tragicomical another' in a new version by James Howard which preserved the lovers alive. Dryden, although he belonged to Drury Lane, wrote *Sir Martin Mar-All* for Lincoln's Inn Fields. The comedian Nokes made a great success in it.

Davenant was an excellent manager. He never delegated authority as did the more mercurial and easy-going Killigrew, but kept the reins in his own hands, and his theatre prospered. His death on 7 Apr. 1668 was a great blow to it, though he had already found it too small for him, and was erecting a new one (see DORSET GARDEN). His widow, with Harris and Betterton, carried on at Lincoln's Inn Fields Theatre until the new theatre was ready in 1671, and the old theatre reverted to its former status as a tennis-court, except for an interval in 1672–4 when Killigrew's company played there after the destruction by fire of the Theatre Royal in Bridges Street. In 1695 Betterton, now leading man at Drury Lane, after a dispute with Christopher Rich, returned to Lincoln's Inn Fields with Mrs. Barry and Mrs. Brace-girdle, and began a ten-years tenancy with *Love for Love*. In 1705 Betterton and his company went to Vanbrugh's new theatre in the Hay (not the one we now know as the Haymarket Theatre), while Christopher Rich of Drury Lane, having lost his Patent, planned to use the Lincoln's Inn Fields Theatre. He died before his work was completed, but the theatre was reopened on 18 Dec. 1714 by his son John with *The Recruiting Officer*. It was described as a very handsome house, the interior having mirrors along each side; the stage was excellent and the scenery new. John Rich, an illiterate man and a curious character, tried acting in tragedy but failed. He was, however, an excellent Harlequin, and made a big successs at this theatre in 1717 with a pantomime called *Harlequin Executed*. The greatest event of Rich's career at Lincoln's Inn Fields was the production of *The Beggar's Opera* (1727–8), which took the town by storm.

In 1731, the theatre having fallen into decay, Rich started a subscription to build a new one in Bow Street, which eventually became Covent Garden Theatre. He left Lincoln's Inn Fields in 1732, and that was virtually the end of its career as a regular playhouse. In 1733–4 an Italian Opera Company under Porpora opened there in opposition to Handel at the King's (Haymarket). After that it was let for balls and concerts, and occasionally an actor, excluded from the two Patent Theatres, would try his luck there, as did Giffard for a short time when his theatre in Goodman's Fields was closed. It became in turn a barracks, an auction room, a china warehouse, and was pulled down in 1848.   W. M. P.

LINCOLN'S MEN, a small company of actors, led by Laurence Dutton, who were in the service of the first Earl of Lincoln, and of his son, Lord Clinton, whose name they some-times took. They appeared at Court before Queen Elizabeth several times between 1572 and 1575, and were active in the provinces up to 1577, as was a later company of the same name from 1599–1610.

LINDSAY, HOWARD (1899–), American actor, dramatist and producer, who collabo-rated with Russell Crouse (1893–) in a dramatization of Clarence Day's *Life with Father*. First produced in 1939, with Lindsay as Father, this set up a record with a seven-years run in New York. It was also seen on tour, and in London, where it was less success-ful. Most of Lindsay's work has been done in collaboration, and with Russell Crouse he was responsible for the Pulitzer Prize-winner, *State of the Union* (1945), and for the production of *Arsenic and Old Lace* (1941), which had a long run both in London and in New York.

LINE, the rope on which a piece of scenery is hung, and raised from or lowered to the stage (see ENGLISH PLAYHOUSE, 2 *a*).

LION COMIQUE, see LEYBOURNE, MUSIC-HALL and VANCE.

LISLE'S TENNIS-COURT, see LINCOLN'S INN FIELDS THEATRE.

LISTON, JOHN (1776–1846), English come-dian, whose early life is somewhat obscure, though he is believed to have been an usher in a provincial school. He first went on the stage at York, in Stephen Kemble's company, in succession to the elder Mathews, who said he was never known to smile. In private life he was nervous and melancholic, and much interested in the study of theology, but he had only to appear on the stage to set the audience laughing. He first appeared at the Haymarket under Colman in 1805, as Sheepface in *The Village Lawyer*, and for the next thirty years he was one of the leading players of London. He excelled in farce, and his Paul Pry, dress and all, was imitated by Wright and later by Toole. He made the fortune of several managers and authors—Pocock, Dibdin, Hook —and was the first comic actor to command a salary greater than that of a tragedian. He occa-sionally aspired to play tragedy himself, but without success. Boaden said of him, 'He must be seen to be comprehended. Other actors labour to be comic, I see nothing like labour in Liston.' He retired in 1837.

LISTON, VICTOR (1838–1913), a favourite comedian of the early days of music-hall, who began his career at the Old Bower Saloon, in Stangate Street. For some time he worked the small halls and supper-rooms, such as the Cyder Cellars and the Coal Hole, until one night, acting as a deputy turn at the Phil-harmonic, Islington, his song 'Shabby Gen-teel' made such a sensation that he stayed for seven months, going afterwards to the Metro-politan, Collins's, and Evans's Supper Rooms, where the Prince of Wales (later Edward VII) brought the Duke and Duchess of Sutherland specially to hear him. Later in life he became a music-hall proprietor.   W. M. P.

LITTLE CATHERINE STREET THEATRE, LONDON, see ROYAL PANTHEON.

LITTLE CLUB, NEW YORK, see FORTY-FOURTH STREET THEATRE.

LITTLE DRURY LANE, LONDON, see OLYMPIC THEATRE (1).

LITTLE THEATRE. (1) LONDON, in John Street, Adelphi. This was, as its name implies, one of London's smallest playhouses, holding only 350 people. There was no orchestra pit, and no pit or gallery, though a circle was added later, and an enclosure at the back, something like a jury box, was used for the cheaper seats. The theatre stood on the site of the old Coutts Bank, and the strong rooms formed the dressing rooms. It was opened in Oct. 1910 by Gertrude Kingston with *Lysistrata*, in which she herself appeared. She proposed to do a new play every month, withholding the author's name until after production, but though *Fanny's First Play* was put on anonymously, its run of 624 performances caused this scheme to be put aside. In 1922 the *Nine O'Clock Revue* was a successful innovation, and a season of Grand Guignol, with Sybil Thorndike, had a vogue, while later Herbert Farjeon staged some successful Little Revues. In 1927 the horrific *Dracula* was produced, followed by another 'horror' play, *Frankenstein*. In 1936 *Lady Precious Stream*, a traditional Chinese play translated and adapted by S. I. Hsiung, produced as part of Nancy Price's People's National Theatre Scheme, ran for 247 performances, and on revival for another 436. The Little Theatre was destroyed by enemy action on 16 Apr. 1941.   W. M. P.

(2) NEW YORK, standing between Broadway and Eighth Avenue, was built by Winthrop Ames as a try-out theatre. It held only 300 people, though its capacity was later enlarged to 600, and it proved somewhat unprofitable. Its present owners, the *New York Times*, use it as a lecture-hall and meeting-place only. Ames opened it on 12 Mar. 1912 with *The Pigeon*, followed later in the year by *Anatol* with John Barrymore and Doris Kean, and *Rutherford and Son*, *Prunella*, *The Philanderer*, and a revival of *Truth* followed, Guthrie McClintic appearing in the last in a small part. The Shuberts later took control of the theatre, which was enlarged and redecorated under their management, and produced among other things *The First Year* and *The Left Bank*, both successful. In 1935 the theatre was used as a broadcasting studio.   G. F.

LITTLE THEATRE IN THE HAY, LONDON, see HAYMARKET THEATRE.

LITTLE THEATRE MOVEMENT, ENGLAND, see AMATEUR THEATRE IN GREAT BRITAIN; U.S.A., see NATIONWIDE THEATRE.

LITTLE TICH (1868–1928), music-hall comedian, who was so named as a baby from his supposed likeness to the claimant in the famous Tichborne Case. His real name was Harry Relph. He first appeared as a child singer and performer on the tin whistle at Rosherville, near Gravesend, one of the last of London's pleasure grounds, and later appeared at London music-halls as a black-faced comedian. After a visit to America, where he found that Nigger Minstrels were no longer fashionable, he discarded this disguise, and returned to England to play in pantomimes at Drury Lane, and in music-halls, where he proved an immense success. His impersonations, which ranged from grocers, blacksmiths, and sailors on leave to fairy queens and Spanish dancers, usually ended, at least until his last years, with a dance in which he balanced on the tips of his preposterous boots, which were as long as he was high.

LITTLER. (1) BLANCHE (1899–   ), theatre manageress, and the wife of George Robey. With her brother (2) PRINCE (1901–   ) she began her career in the Royal Artillery Theatre, Woolwich, of which her parents were the lessees, and with him founded and directed a nation-wide network of touring companies. In 1927 Prince Littler joined the board of the New Theatre, Cambridge, and since then has become one of the most powerful men in the entertainment industry, being Managing Director of the Theatre Royal, Drury Lane, of the vast Stoll combination, including the London Coliseum, and of many other West End theatres. His younger brother (3) EMILE (1903–   ) is also a theatre manager, and began his career at the Ambassadors Theatre, Southend. Later he was stage-manager of the Birmingham Repertory Theatre, and went to America in 1927 as stage-manager for Shubert Bros. On his return he became manager of the Birmingham Repertory Theatre for Sir Barry Jackson, and was the first to install a broadcasting studio in a theatre. He started in management on his own account in 1934, and produced a number of successful musical comedies and pantomimes. He was licensee of the Prince of Wales's Theatre, Birmingham, when it was destroyed by bombing in 1942. He married Cora Goffin, a musical comedy star.

LITTLEWOOD, SAMUEL ROBINSON (1875–   ), English dramatic critic, who began his career on the *Morning Leader* in 1897, and since then has been actively engaged in journalism, becoming editor of *The Stage* in 1943. He served as dramatic and film critic on a number of London papers, including the *Pall Mall Gazette* and the *Morning Post*, and in 1935 was dramatic critic to the B.B.C. Among his books are several on the history of pantomime, one on Mrs. Inchbald, and one on Dramatic Criticism, while he has frequently lectured and written on Shakespeare, on whose plays he is an acknowledged authority.

LITURGICAL DRAMA, see ECCLESIASTICAL DRAMA.

LITURGY, in Athens, a public service required of wealthy citizens. One such duty was the staging of a play (see CHOREGUS and GREECE). In Europe the liturgy, or form of worship, of the early Christian Church gave rise to the performance of plays in Latin, for which see ECCLESIASTICAL DRAMA.

LIVERIGHT, HORACE BRISBIN (1886–1933), American publisher who was also active in the theatre, being the first to take an interest in the plays of O'Neill. At 17 he had written a light opera which failed to reach the stage, and it was not until 1924 that he again made contact with the theatre, one of his outstanding ventures being the controversial modern-dress *Hamlet.* He was opposed to censorship and constantly in trouble with the authorities. Among his productions were *An American Tragedy* (1926), *Dracula* (1927), and *The Dagger and the Rose* (1927). In 1930 he went to Hollywood as adviser to Paramount Studios.

LIVERPOOL REPERTORY THEATRE, now known as the Playhouse, is the oldest existing Repertory Theatre in Great Britain, and was the third to be opened. The history of this theatre is one of unusual interest, for during its existence it has had many changes of fortune. Shortly before war broke out in 1939 it had begun to triumph over its difficulties, and was not only paying its way, but even making a profit, no small achievement for a theatre whose weekly expenses amount to five hundred pounds and whose season is of forty-two weeks' duration.

The theatre traces its beginnings to the success of an experimental repertory season given at Kelly's Theatre, Paradise Street, in February 1911, under the direction of Miss Darragh and Basil Dean. The success of this venture showed that Liverpool wanted a Repertory Theatre, and a scheme was set on foot to give it a permanent one, which should make the city independent of London for its plays. The Star Theatre in Williamson Square, home of lurid melodrama, was acquired and completely reconstructed. It opened as Liverpool's Repertory Theatre on 11 Nov. 1911, since when it has closed only for short summer vacations.

Since the Playhouse has been almost entirely dependent on its box-office receipts, its directors have been unable to risk putting on many plays with a frankly limited appeal. They have nevertheless produced several hundred plays, many of them for the first time on any stage, and more often than not for the first time in Liverpool. In addition to plays by all the best-known modern British dramatists, many of Shakespeare's plays have been given, some of them in highly original settings, also the comedies of Sheridan and Goldsmith, and the works of many continental and American authors. The Playhouse is the only Repertory Theatre which has made a policy of doing one-act plays, and every Christmas there has been a new play specially written for children.

The Playhouse has been a notable school of acting. St. John Ervine said of it that 'it has enriched English acting to a quite extraordinary extent, and I believe it is true to say that more of the best actors and actresses learned their job in Williamson Square than in any other part of the country'. Basil Dean

was the theatre's first producer, Ronald Jeans's first plays and revues were done at the Playhouse, and another important author discovered there was Philip Johnson.

'The Playhouse Circle', which met on alternate Sunday evenings, was a valuable adjunct to the theatre's work for many years. It had a membership of over nine hundred, and many notabilities spoke at its meetings. Another collateral activity, which owes its existence indirectly to the theatre, is the Shute Lectureship in the Art of the Theatre at the University of Liverpool, founded in 1923 by Colonel Sir John Shute, Chairman of the Playhouse Directors.

Undeniably the theatre's success during later years was largely due to the work and enthusiasm of William Armstrong, its Director and Producer from 1922 to 1944, and Maud Carpenter, its Business Manager, who has been connected with the theatre since 1911.

The policy of the Playhouse is to produce plays which are outstanding and which, but for the Repertory Theatre, would not be seen in Liverpool. It caters for no definite class of audience, and is not run for any one type of playgoer. Its plays range from the lightest of comedies to works of such seriousness as Raynal's *The Unknown Warrior* and Susan Glaspell's *Inheritors*, which had its first performance in England at Liverpool. The encouragement which it has given to young and new authors has been one of the theatre's special activities. The Playhouse holds a unique place in the artistic life of Merseyside, enabling several thousand people a week to be 'decently entertained and often lifted above the grey atmosphere of this Northern city'.

LIVING NEWSPAPER, a stage production conceived in terms of the cinema, showing in short, swift-moving scenes problems of modern social life, and the methods of dealing with them. First evolved by the Federal Theatre in the United States, this technique was successfully used in England for adult education and propaganda in the armed forces during the Second World War.

LLOYD, ARTHUR (1840–1904), a music-hall performer of the early days, who was also a pioneer of the concert party, for he ran one as early as 1866. He came of theatrical stock, and in his early days was an actor. The possessor of a fine voice, he was skilled in selecting his songs, which included 'Not for Joe' and 'The Dark Girl Dressed in Blue'. On one occasion he and Jolly John Nash had the honour of appearing at a party given by a peer and singing before the Prince of Wales (later Edward VII). Between them they kept things going for hours with great success.

W. M. P.

LLOYD, MARIE (1870–1922), idol of the music-halls for many years. She was the daughter of a waiter at the old Grecian Saloon, and the eldest of nine children, her real name being Matilda

Alice Victoria Wood. She made her first appearance at the Royal Eagle Music Hall (as the Grecian was then called) in 1885, in an extra turn, billed as Bella Delmere, though it was not long before she discarded this for the name under which she became famous. She first made a hit at the Old Mo with Nellie Power's song 'The Boy I love sits up in the Gallery' and was then engaged for a year at the Oxford. Augustus Harris engaged her as 'principal girl' for his Drury Lane pantomime, where she appeared for several years. She was three times married: to Percy Courtney in 1887, from whom she was divorced in 1904, to Alec Hurley, the 'coster king', who died in 1913, and to Bernard Dillon the jockey. In spite of her success and popularity she had a hard life, which she faced with unassuming courage and unimpaired cheerfulness. In her work she was wittily improper, but never coarse or vulgar, and her humour lay less in her material than in her use of it. Though critics often railed, the public remained obstinately faithful. She appeared in all the leading music-halls of England, and in provincial and London pantomimes, and toured successfully in America, South Africa, and Australia. In 1920 her fiftieth birthday was celebrated by a special performance at the Bedford Music-Hall, and two years later she died, having continued on the stage until the last few days of her life. In her final years she was an almost legendary figure, and afterwards became the posthumous darling of Fleet Street.

LOA, the name given to the prologue, or compliment to the audience, which preceded the early Spanish theatrical performance. It ranged from a short introductory monologue to a miniature drama having some bearing on the play which was to follow; in certain cases it was even inseparable from it. It need not be by the author of the main play, and Agustín de Rojas in his *El Viaje Entretenido* (1630) indicates that a strolling company would generally have a variety of *loas* which could be fitted to any play. The *loa* fell out of use in the seventeenth century, except to serve as an introduction to an *auto*.

LOCATELLI. (1) DOMENICO (1613–71), a player of the *commedia dell'arte*, who, as Trivellino, had a *zanni* part somewhat akin to Harlequin's. Indeed, he is sometimes believed to have played Harlequin. He spent many years in Paris, going there first about 1644, and again from 1653 till his death. His first wife (2) LUISA GABRIELLI (*fl.* 1644–53) was also an actress, and went with her husband to Paris. They were playing in Modena together shortly before her death. Another Locatelli, (3) BASILEO (? –1650) was an amateur of the *commedia dell'arte* who collected and copied out over 100 *scenarii*, which are preserved in two manuscript volumes, dated 1618 and 1622, in the *Biblioteca Casanatense* in Rome.

LOFTUS, CISSIE [MARIE CECILIA] (1876–1943), English actress, the daughter of Marie Loftus, variety artist. She made her first ap-

pearance on the stage at the Oxford Music-Hall in 1893 and was immediately successful. In the same year she appeared at the Gaiety, and for some time oscillated between legitimate drama and the music-halls, where she gave a series of remarkable impersonations. She appeared in vaudeville in America in 1894, at the Lyceum, New York, in the following years, and later in light opera, with great success. She abandoned the music-hall for a time in 1900, and appeared in a number of straight plays with Mme Modjeska, Frohman, Sothern, and others. Irving brought her back from America to play Margaret (in *Faust*), Nerissa, and Jessica at the Lyceum. Later she appeared as Peter Pan, and as Nora in *A Doll's House*. She returned to the music-hall, both in England and America, and for many years alternated between both types and both countries, with equal success. An attractive, dark woman of great vivacity, she was a versatile and accomplished performer in both mediums.

W. M. P.

LOHENSTEIN, DANIEL CASPAR VON (1635–83), a dramatist in whom German baroque drama reached its height. Himself a scholar and a man of quiet abstemious life, his plays, which show much erudition, are nevertheless bloodthirsty melodramas couched in extravagant language, theatrical in the worst sense. It is not certain whether they were ever publicly performed, but as literary or 'closet' dramas they were read and acclaimed, since they fitted in with the prevailing taste for Gothic horrors. A new orientation in the direction of simplicity and realism caused them to be forgotten.

LONDON CASINO, see PRINCE EDWARD THEATRE.

LONDON COLISEUM, see COLISEUM.

LONDON HIPPODROME, see HIPPODROME.

LONDON OPERA HOUSE, see STOLL.

LONDON PAVILION, a famous music-hall, which started staging revue in 1916, but became a theatre under the direction of C. B. Cochran, whose musical productions and revues there were a feature of the London scene, the whole series from 1918 to 1931 being one of the most brilliant pages of the amusement world in the inter-war period. The Pavilion then became a home of non-stop variety and closed in 1933 to become a cinema. (See also under MUSIC-HALL.)

W. M. P.

LONDON THEATRE STUDIO, see SAINT-DENIS, MICHEL.

LONGACRE THEATRE, NEW YORK, on 48th Street between Broadway and Eighth Avenue. This opened on 1 May 1913, mainly for farces and musical comedy, among which were interpolated some matinées of *Ghosts* and of that fine play, *The Hero*. Ethel Barrymore was first seen at the Longacre in 1922, in several good parts, while the end of 1925 saw the successful run of *The Butter and Egg Man*. In spite of fine acting by Constance Collier, Derrick de Marney, and Jessica Tandy, making her first appearance in New York, *The Matriarch* was a comparative failure, and *Overture*, though included by Burns Mantle in his ten best plays of the 1931–2 season, also had a short run. This was true too of *Wednesday's Child*, and of the *Noah* of Obey, with Pierre Fresnay as Noah. Several of Odets's plays were given at this theatre under the auspices of the Group Theatre.   G. F.

LONGEPIERRE, HILAIRE BERNARD DE ROQUELEYNE (1659–1731), French dramatist, and the immediate successor of Racine in the history of French classical tragedy. From the great days of the genre he retains the form and to some extent the psychological conflict, as in his *Médée* (1694), and he gave an illusion of greatness before the final decadence of tragedy which was sufficiently strong for his contemporaries to rate him highly as a dramatist. In some places Longepierre is not unworthy of Racine, whose works inspired him to write for the stage. He was well educated and a student of antiquity, in the sense in which such study was understood at the time. In fact, he had everything of Racine but his genius, and his plays are forgotten.

LONGFORD, EDWARD ARTHUR HENRY PAKENHAM, 6TH EARL OF (1902–   ), author of several plays, was at one time a director of the Gate Theatre, Dublin and has been, since 1936, director of 'Longford Productions', playing alternately with 'Gate Theatre Productions' (see IRELAND, 2). The plays produced by 'Longford Productions' include several by Shakespeare, four or five by Chekhov, half a dozen or more by Shaw, and others by Molière, Sophocles, Euripides, Ibsen, Congreve, Sheridan, and translations from modern continental dramatists. Lord Longford's plays, produced in Dublin and London, include *The Melians* (1931), *Yahoo* (1933), *Ascendancy* (1935), *The Armlet of Jade* (1936), *Carmilla* (1937), *The Vineyard* (1938), and translations in verse of the *Oresteia* of Aeschylus, the *Oedipus* of Sophocles, and the *Bacchae* of Euripides, and in prose of *Tartuffe, Le Bourgeois gentilhomme*, and *Le Barbier de Séville*. Lord Longford's wife, Christine Patti (née Trew), is the author of several plays which have been produced by 'Gate Theatre Productions' or 'Longford Productions' in Dublin and London: *Mr. Jiggins of Jigginstown* (1933), *Anything but the Truth* (1937), *Sea Change* (1940), and adaptations of Jane Austen's *Pride and Prejudice*, Maria Edgeworth's *The Absentee*, and Sheridan Le Fanu's *The Watcher* and *The Avenger*.
                                              U. E.-F.

LONSDALE [LEONARD], FREDERICK (1881–   ), English dramatist, whose best plays, written in the 1920s, are comedies of contemporary manners in the style of Maugham, but with less subtlety. Their amusing situations, adroitly handled in easy and effective dialogue, made them immediately popular, and *The Last of Mrs. Cheyney* (1925), an unusually effective crook-play, proved successful in revival in 1944. Of the others the most important are *Spring Cleaning* (1923), *On Approval* and *The High Road* (both 1927), and *Canaries Sometimes Sing* (1929), all of which gave scope for good, brittle, sophisticated acting. Lonsdale was also the librettist of *The Maid of the Mountains, Madame Pompadour*, and other musical comedies, and of a version of *Monsieur Beaucaire*, with music by Messager, done in 1919.

LOPE DE VEGA, see VEGA CARPIO, LOPE FÉLIX DE.

LORAINE, ROBERT (1876–1935), English actor-manager, who made his first appearance on the stage in 1889, played with Tree and Alexander, and subsequently made a hit as d'Artagnan in *The Three Musketeers* (1899). After serving with distinction in the Boer War he went to America and made his first appearance there in *To Have and to Hold* (1901), returning to England to play Henry V. He was later associated with early productions of Shaw, playing John Tanner, Don Juan, and Bluntschli, the last with Lillah McCarthy, and opening his management of the Criterion in 1911 with a revival of *Man and Superman*, which he also took to America. During the 1914–18 war he made a great name for himself as an aviator, and was awarded the M.C. and D.S.O. for gallantry in action. His return to the stage in 1919 was made in the name part of *Cyrano de Bergerac*, which had a long run. Among his later parts were Deburau, the dual role of Rassendyl and Rudolf in a revival of *The Prisoner of Zenda*, the Nobleman in *The Man with a Load of Mischief* in its New York production, Adolph in *The Father*, and a number of Shakespeare parts, including Petruchio and Mercutio. He was essentially a romantic actor, but could subdue his flamboyance to such parts as John Tanner and Adolph. His life was written by his wife in 1938.

LORCA, FEDERICO GARCÍA (1898–1936), a young Spanish poet and dramatist of great promise, killed during the Spanish civil war. His plays include *Mariana de Pineda, Amor de Don Perlimplín con Belisa en su jardín* (1931), *Yerma*, a tragedy played in 1934 by the great Spanish actress Margarita Xirgu, *La zapatera prodigiosa*, an Andalusian farce, and the tense and passionate drama *Bodas de sangre*, given in London in 1939 as *The Marriage of Blood*. It has also been translated as *Blood Wedding*, and has been given in America and in the U.S.S.R. A few days before his death Lorca completed *La Casa de Bernarda Alba*, which was first given in London in a French translation by Jean-Marie Créach, and later in English in New York. As producer of his own plays, and for the student dramatic society La Barraca, Lorca had a great influence on the theatre of Republican Spain, and his early death was a great blow to it. A number of his poems have been translated into English.

LORD ADMIRAL'S MEN, see ADMIRAL'S MEN.

LORD CHAMBERLAIN, see DRAMATIC CENSORSHIP.

LORD CHAMBERLAIN'S MEN, see CHAMBERLAIN'S MEN.

LORD HOWARD'S MEN, see ADMIRAL'S MEN.

LORD HUNSDON'S MEN, see CHAMBERLAIN'S MEN.

LORD OF MISRULE, see MISRULE.

LORD STRANGE'S MEN, see STRANGE'S MEN.

LORENZI, GIAMBATTISTA (? –1805), an Italian actor famed for his gift as an improviser. It is said that when Joseph II visited Naples he gave Lorenzi the outline of a plot on which he improvised a complete play, delighting the Emperor and his audience. Lorenzi also wrote fifteen comedies in Neapolitan dialect. Settembrini calls him the Neapolitan Aristophanes, and declares that he is worthy of a place by the side of Metastasio.

LOTAR, PETR (1910–   ), outstanding Czech actor, who trained under Max Reinhardt in Berlin and later appeared with Barnowsky and Piscator. In 1931, after appearing in Breslau, he returned to Czechoslovakia and worked for two years in the provincial theatres there. He was then appointed to the Municipal Theatre, Prague, where he produced a Czech version of *The Shoemaker's Holiday*, and appeared in such parts as Lysander, Orsino, Tybalt, Antony, and Jaques. He was on the committee of the Czech Actors' Association, and was one of the founders of a club directed towards the association and co-operation of Czech and German democratic artists. In May 1939 he emigrated to Switzerland, where his work as actor and producer introduced Swiss audiences to the standard works of modern Czech drama. Of his own plays, one, a picture of the Czech national struggle shown in individual destinies in the days of Munich, was an outstanding success in the Swiss theatrical season of 1945.

LOTTA, see CRABTREE, CHARLOTTE.

LOUTHERBOURG, PHILIPPE JACQUES DE (1740–1812), a painter from Alsace, who worked for some time in Paris and Italy, making a special study of stage illusion and mechanics. Arriving in London in 1771, he met Garrick, who appointed him scenic director at Drury Lane, a position he also held under Sheridan after Garrick's retirement. He introduced a number of new devices, including the reproduction of fleeting effects on a landscape by the use of silk screens working on pivots before concentrated lights in the wings, and his cloud-effects were particularly admired. He introduced a series of head-lights or border battens behind the Drury Lane proscenium, which at once discouraged the actors from stepping too much outside the picture, and increased the importance of the scenery by the flood of illumination. His work was vivid and arresting, though his bizarre use of colour sometimes rendered it too glaring. But he was particularly successful in producing the illusion of fire, volcanoes, sun, moonlight, and cloud-effects, and invented strikingly effective devices for thunder, guns, wind, the lapping of waves, and the patter of hail and rain. He was the first to bring a breath of naturalism into the artificial scenic convention of the time, and paved the way for the realistic detail and local colour of Kemble. He is referred to by Mr. Puff in *The Critic*, for which he had executed a striking design of Tilbury Fort, and he was responsible for some excellent new transparent effects in a revival of *The Winter's Tale* in 1779. In the same year a visit to the Peaks resulted in some fine Derbyshire scenery for a pantomime, including an act-drop of a romantic landscape which remained in use until the theatre was destroyed by fire. W. J. Lawrence cites this as the earliest example of the use of an act-drop or scenic curtain in western Europe. Shortly after preparing the scenery for *Robinson Crusoe* on its first appearance on the stage—the first act alone had eight changes—de Loutherbourg, who had been elected to the Royal Academy in 1781, withdrew from the theatre, mainly on account of a dispute over his salary, and devoted most of his time to a remarkable scenic exhibition, 'Eidophusikon'. Although he seldom worked for the stage after this, his influence can be traced as late as 1820, when Elliston, in a revival of *King Lear* at Drury Lane, tried to reproduce some of the powerful effects of the storm scene in 'Eidophusikon'. De Loutherbourg has been credited with the breaking up of the scene by the use of perspective, and with being the first stage designer in England to make use of set scenes with raking pieces. But the time was not yet ripe for much practicable scenery, and he was for the most part sparing in his resort to built-up work. It is mainly as Garrick's scene designer that he is remembered, and his fine work gave momentary popularity to many an otherwise unremarkable piece.

LOW COMEDIAN, a term applied to a music-hall or pantomime player who specializes in a broad, somewhat vulgar, type of humour; sometimes known as a 'Red-nosed Comedian' from the traditional use of a fiery nose to indicate habitual insobriety. (See also STOCK COMPANY.)

LOWER GALLERY, see AUDITORIUM, 1 c.

LOWIN, JOHN (1576–1653), one of the best known of the actors in Shakespeare's plays, and an important link between the Elizabethan and

Restoration stages. He first appears as an actor in 1602, and a year later was one of the King's Men (the former Chamberlain's Men), with whom he remained until the closing of the theatres in 1642. He was often referred to as a big man, and played the parts of bluff soldiers and gruff villains. His Falstaff was much admired, as was his Volpone, and his Melancius in *The Maid's Tragedy*. He was probably Bosola in the first production of *The Duchess of Malfi* (1614), and played in several of Massinger's plays. He was one of the actors caught playing in the Cockpit during the Puritan interregnum, and Betterton is supposed to have been coached in his part of Henry VIII by Davenant on instructions from Lowin, 'who', says Downes in *Roscius Anglicanus*, 'had his Instructions from Mr. Shakespeare himself'. In his old age Lowin, who fell into dire poverty, kept an inn at Brentford.

LUCILLE LA VERNE THEATRE, NEW YORK, see PRINCESS THEATRE.

LUCY RUSHTON'S THEATRE, NEW YORK, see NEW YORK THEATRE (1).

LUDLOW, NOAH MILLER (1795–1886), one of the pioneer actor-managers of the American theatre. In 1815 he was engaged by Samuel Drake to go to Kentucky and later founded his own company, with which in 1817 he gave the first English plays in New Orleans. He travelled extensively, with his own or other companies, often being the first actor to penetrate to some of the more remote regions in the South and West. Going to New York in 1828 to recruit actors for his company, he was induced to take over the old Chatham Theatre with Cooper, but failed to make it pay, and returned to St. Louis. From 1835 to 1853 he was in partnership with Sol Smith as the American Theatrical Commonwealth Company, and ran several theatres simultaneously in St. Louis, New Orleans, Mobile, and other cities, often engaging outstanding stars. He was himself an excellent actor, particularly in comedy, and the author of an entertaining volume of reminiscences, *Dramatic Life as I Found It*.

LUDWIG, OTTO (1813–65), German novelist and dramatist, contemporary of Hebbel, whom he resembles in his passage from realistic prose to verse. In his best play, *Der Erbförster* (1850), a study of bourgeois life, a painful realism gains the upper hand, while an apocryphal drama, *Die Makkabäer* (1852), is written in a more romantic style. Ludwig, who studied music under Mendelssohn, was an ardent admirer of Shakespeare.

LUGNÉ-POË, AURÉLIEN-MARIE (1869–1940), French actor and manager, who studied at the Conservatoire, where he was a pupil of Worms, and obtained the second prize for comedy. He appeared at the Théâtre Libre under Antoine, and at the Théâtre d'Art with Paul Fort. He later took over this theatre and developed it into the celebrated Théâtre de l'Œuvre. Here, from 1892 to 1929, he worked as director and chief actor, and was responsible for introducing the work of many modern playwrights, of whom the first was Maeterlinck with *Pelléas et Mélisande, L'Intruse, Intérieur,* and *Monna Vanna*. He also staged Ibsen's plays, Björnson, Strindberg, Hauptmann, Wilde's *Salomé*, and plays by d'Annunzio and Echegaray. In later years Lugné-Poë was the first to bring into prominence the plays of Claudel, producing *L'Annonce faite à Marie* for the first time in 1912. He did much to encourage young playwrights, and at the same time helped forward the development of the modern French theatre by putting before it the best contemporary work of other countries. Himself an excellent actor, he was seen in London in 1908 in *Poil de Carotte*, and was for several seasons manager for Eleonora Duse.

LUNACHARSKY, ANATOLI VASILEVICH (1875–1933), first Commissar for Education in Soviet Russia, an able, cultured man, friend of Lenin, to whom the U.S.S.R. owes the preservation and renewed vigour of those Imperial theatrical institutions, notably the Moscow Art Theatre, which survived the October Revolution. When uninformed fervour would have swept them away, he protected them, and gave them the time and the money to find their feet in the new world. He was also responsible for the organization of the new Soviet theatres, which have sprung up in such vast numbers and made a name for themselves. He realized that the new audiences, many of whom had never been in a theatre before, would eventually demand new methods and new plays approximating to their own life. That he provided for. But he realized at the same time that the old plays, both Russian and European, were part of the heritage of the new world, and that to falsify or misinterpret them was to betray the people. This led to his exposition of the principles of Socialist Realism, which caused a reorientation of the Soviet theatre, a new respect for the classics, and a series of fresh, vivid, and important revivals (as well as productions of new plays) of which Popov's *Taming of the Shrew* in 1937 is the best example. Lunacharsky wrote a number of articles on the theatre, which were published in two volumes (in 1924 and 1926) in which his theories, and the attempts made to put them into practice, can be further studied. A third volume was published in 1936. He was also the author of several plays.

LUNT. (1) ALFRED (1893–   ), American actor, who made his début in 1913, toured with Margaret Anglin and Mrs. Langtry, and in 1919 made a great success as Clarence in Booth Tarkington's play of that name. With his wife, the English actress (2) LYNN FONTANNE (1887–   ), he has built up a big reputation in London and New York in the playing of intimate modern comedy. Miss Fontanne made her first appearance in London in 1905, and was with

Ellen Terry, Tree, Waller, and other actor-managers before she first went to New York in 1910. She had already had a distinguished career before, with her husband, she joined the company of the Theatre Guild from 1924 to 1929, and appeared with him in a succession of plays, including *The Guardsman, Arms and the Man, The Goat Song*, and *Pygmalion*. They were first seen together in London in *Caprice* in 1929, and among their later successes have been *Reunion in Vienna, Design for Living, Amphitryon 38*, and *Love in Idleness* (known in America as *O Mistress Mine*). The combination of these two excellent players produces acting of great subtlety and sophistication which is in itself sufficient to make a success even of flimsy material, and rises to great heights when they approach material worthy of their exceptional talents.

LUPINO, a vast family of English dancers, acrobats, pantomimists, and actors, who trace their descent from a line of Italian puppet-masters, one of whom came to England in the time of James I. His seventh descendant in direct succession had sixteen children, mostly on the stage, of whom two married into the family of Sara Lane, lessee of the old Britannia Theatre, one having children and grand-children on the stage. The eldest son was the father of (1) BARRY (1884–   ), who made his first appearance on the stage as a baby, was for some years stock comedian at the Britannia, toured extensively, and was seen in pantomime and musical comedy. His two children were also on the stage. His brother (2) STANLEY (1893–1942), also on the stage as a child, was in variety with an acrobat troupe and in pantomime for many years at Drury Lane. He was also seen in revue and musical comedy, was the author of several plays and novels, and of a volume of reminiscences, *From the Stocks to the Stars* (1934), from which many of the above details are taken. His nephew (3) HENRY GEORGE (1892–   ) took his great-aunt Sara's name of Lane, and is known as Lupino Lane. As Nipper Lane he made his first appearance on the stage at the age of 4, and as an adult toured extensively in variety. He was also seen in musical comedy, and in pantomime, and made a great hit as Bill Snibson in *Me and My Girl* (1937), in which he created the well-known dance 'The Lambeth Walk'. He also has a son on the stage, though some younger members of this illustrious family are now making their names in films.

LUZÁN, IGNACIO DE (1702–54), Spanish man of letters, was the theorist of the Spanish neo-classic theatre, and his *Poética*, published in 1737, was influenced by, if not directly imitated from, Boileau. It showed also the influence of the classic doctrines of the Italian renaissance, under whose yoke of Aristotelian unities Luzán endeavoured to subjugate Spanish poetry and drama. In spite of his dislike of the 'barbarous' work of Spain's Golden Age, and his criticism of Lope and Calderón, he did,

however, preserve some respect for the old masters, whom his followers condemned outright. Luzán's theories, which were perhaps useful at the time in cutting across the decadence of Spanish literature, had on the whole a harmful influence, for not only was he seeking to impose an alien aesthetic, but he was the cause of the traditional Spanish dramas being 'remodelled'. Only with the Romantic Revival were they again accessible in their original form.

LYCEUM THEATRE. (1) LONDON, originally a hall built by James Payne in 1765 for the use of the Society of Artists. Three years later the Society moved to Somerset House and the Lyceum was bought by Lingham, a breeches-maker in the Strand, who let it out for various purposes. In 1794 Dr. Arnold, the composer, rebuilt the interior for use as a theatre, but was prevented from obtaining a licence by the opposition of the Patent Theatres, and the premises reverted to Lingham. Arnold had added a large saloon, and there was room in the building for several exhibitions or entertainments to go on simultaneously. Astley occupied part of it during one of his rebuildings. Other attractions were the Musical Glasses, phantasmagoria, panoramas, a school of elocution, a concert hall, a Roman Catholic chapel, a porcupine man, and a white negress, while out-of-work actors gave performances for their own benefit. Charles Dibdin had a short and disastrous season there. In 1802, Madame Tussaud gave the first exhibition in this country of her waxworks, and in 1809 the Drury Lane company, their own home having been burned down, obtained a licence for the theatre, though they had previously opposed the application for it, and played there until the opening of the new Drury Lane in 1812. Samuel Arnold, son of Dr. Arnold, now succeeded in getting a licence for the production of English opera during the summer months, pleading that the theatre would serve as a nursery for the Patent Theatres. In 1810 the name of the building was changed to the English Opera House, and ballad operas, musical farces, and melodramas were given there with Braham, Liston, Fawcett, Oxberry, Mrs. Mountain, Mrs. Bland, and Fanny Kelly.

In 1815 Arnold, retiring from the management of Drury Lane, took a ninety years' lease of the Strand property, purchased more land adjoining it, and rebuilt at a cost of £80,000, the main entrance being from the Strand. At prices ranging from 1s. to 5s. the house held £350. The theatre was lavishly decorated and a large saloon was made scenic, sometimes representing a Winter Garden with flowers, sometimes an Italian terrace, a Chinese pavilion, or a representation of ancient Egypt. The Lyceum was the first London theatre to use gas-lighting for its stage, in Aug. 1817, though the Olympic had used it in the auditorium as early as 1815. Arnold opened on 15 June 1816 with two plays, *Up All Night* and *The Boarding House*, and an address by Fanny Kelly, who was the star of the house. Others in the company were Miss Love, Harley, and T. P. Cooke. The venture was a financial failure, and in 1817 the management tried the experiment of two houses a night. This, however, was speedily abandoned. In 1818 the elder Mathews gave his celebrated performance 'Mathews at Home'. Arnold engaged him for seven years at £1,000 a year, but so great was his success that more equitable terms had to be arranged. Masquerades and costume recitals filled the winter months, when the Patent Theatres prevented other forms of entertainment, though star performers were sometimes given special privileges. In 1820 Planché's melodrama *The Vampyre; or, the Bride of the Isles* was a success; Mrs. Glover played Hamlet in 1821, T. P. Cooke appeared as the Monster in *Frankenstein* in 1823, Kean came in 1828, and in 1830 the house was burned down.

It was rebuilt and reopened in 1834 as the New Theatre Royal Lyceum and English Opera House. When the building was finished it was discovered that Beazley, the architect, had forgotten to supply any stairs to the gallery, and a temporary wooden staircase had to be hastily installed. The main entrance was now in Wellington Street.

The new theatre started well, but ill fortune followed and much money was lost. A slight advantage, however, was gained over the Patent Theatres, for in 1835 the Lyceum was allowed to remain open from 17 Jan. to 6 April for a season of French plays with Frédérick-Lemaître. In Sept. 1842, after many vicissitudes, the theatre was renamed the American Amphitheatre and housed a wild beast show.

On 29 Jan. 1844, the Patent Rights of the two great theatres having been finally broken by the Licensing Act of 1843, the Lyceum went over to legitimate drama. It failed, but at Easter the Keeleys took over with a good company and made a success with dramatizations of Dickens, some extravaganzas, and the famous Caudle Curtain lectures. They left on 11 June 1847, and Mme Vestris, who had previously had a short season there, came back with a fine company. In one of Planché's extravaganzas given at this time, *The Island of Jewels* (1849), Beverley, the scenic artist, introduced the transformation scene to the modern West End theatre. Unfortunately for the Lyceum Mme Vestris was now past her prime, and her husband Charles J. Mathews, though a good actor, was no business man, nor could he cope with his wife's extravagance. He was made bankrupt and put in prison. A few days after his release his wife died.

Professor Anderson, and Ristori in opera (Covent Garden having been burned down), filled in the time until Charles Dillon took over and opened in 1856 with *Belphegor*. He could have risen to great heights, but he spent his time in taverns, was extravagant, and finally, in spite of good business, had to leave. In his time the orchestra stalls became a permanency at 5s. each.

After Falconer and Mme Céleste, Fechter took the Lyceum in 1863. He revolutionized stage settings and methods, started a fresh style of acting, and remained until 1867. Nothing of importance occurred until in 1871 Bateman took the Lyceum for his daughter Kate, and a young actor called Irving made a success as Jingle in *Pickwick*. Bateman fell upon bad times and as a stopgap *The Bells* was produced. Irving became famous and went from one success to another, Bateman, who was a good showman, publicizing him greatly. Finally, in 1875, when Irving was appearing in *Hamlet*, Bateman died. Irving continued his triumphant career under Mrs. Bateman's management until she gave up the Lyceum in Dec. 1878, and on 30 Dec. Irving took entire control. With Ellen Terry as his leading lady he inaugurated a series of fine productions, and made the Lyceum one of the most notable of London theatres. During his tours and frequent visits to America his tenants at the Lyceum included most of the famous actors of the day. In 1899 Martin-Harvey, who had been in Irving's company, produced *The Only Way* there. Irving left the Lyceum in 1902 and the theatre lost the glamour with which he had surrounded it. It was for a time a music-hall. In 1907 Smith and Carpenter produced Shakespeare (with Matheson Lang as their leading man), drama and pantomime, until in 1909 the Melvilles bought the theatre. They founded a new tradition, and under them it was most successful. They controlled it for thirty years, and died within a short time of each other. The Lyceum then closed, having been scheduled for demolition under a street improvement scheme. The last performances were given under the management of H. M. Tennent, Ltd., when from 28 June to 1 July 1939 John Gielgud appeared as Hamlet with a fine cast in a production later seen at Elsinore in Denmark. The theatre is still standing, as the outbreak of war prevented its demolition, and is now used as a dance hall.   w. m. p.

(2) NEW YORK, the old Fourteenth Street Theatre, which had for some time been the Théâtre Français. Fechter took it over and named it after the London Lyceum, hoping to establish it as the American national theatre; this proved impracticable, and under its new name the theatre finally opened on 11 Sept. 1873, with an English company in a version of *Notre-Dame de Paris*. This had little success and the theatre was mainly devoted to light opera, though Adelaide Neilson appeared there in 1874 and Booth, at the height of his glory, in the season of 1876–7.

(3) NEW YORK. The New Lyceum, on Fourth Avenue, was a small jewel-box of a theatre built by Steele Mackaye, which opened on Easter Monday, 6 Apr. 1885, with Robert B. Mantell and Viola Allen in a new play by Mackaye, *Dakola*. This was not a success, and Mackaye withdrew from management. The theatre was later taken over by Daniel Frohman, who had many brilliant successes there, and in 1902 it was pulled down.

(4) NEW YORK, on 45th Street east of Broadway, one of New York's most glamorous playhouses. It was built by Daniel Frohman, who named it after his old theatre (see above), and opened on 2 Nov. 1903 with E. H. Sothern in *The Proud Prince*, previously seen at the Herald Square Theatre. It is one of the few New York theatres to have a green room, and in the fine apartments on the top floor Frohman lived and entertained for many years. The first new play produced there was *The Admirable Crichton*, with William Gillette, and later Charles Wyndham and his wife brought their London company for a season of eight weeks. Among later successes were *The Lion and the Mouse*, *Arsène Lupin*, and several plays by Somerset Maugham. Lenore Ulric made her reputation at this theatre in *The Heart of Wetona* (1916) and *Tiger Rose* (1917), as did Jeanne Eagels in *Daddies*, transferred from the Belasco. Further productions by Belasco, who had been Frohman's first stage manager at the new Lyceum, heralded Warfield's Shylock in 1923, and the season ended with Ethel Barrymore in the Players' revival of *The School for Scandal*. *Antony and Cleopatra*, in 1924, was not a success, in spite of the fine acting of Jane Cowl, and the theatre had to wait for an outstanding success until *Berkeley Square* came in 1929. Later successes at the Lyceum were *George Washington Slept Here*, *Junior Miss*, *The Late George Apley*, and *Born Yesterday*, while Saroyan's *The Beautiful People* had an artistic, though not a commercial, success at this theatre.   G. F.

See also BROUGHAM and WALLACK.

LYCOPHRON (b. *c.* 324 B.C.), a learned Alexandrian poet, composer of tragedies, none of which survives. He was one of the original Pleiad (see GREECE, 5).

LYCOPODIUM FLASK, the name given to a blow-pipe of vegetable brimstone which added a white flame to the terrors of red fire in the conflagrations of melodrama.

LYLY, JOHN (*c.* 1554–1606), English dramatist, important as the first writer of sophisticated comedy, and for his first use of prose in drama. He is perhaps best known for his novels, *Euphues : The Anatomy of Wit* (1579) and *Euphues and his England* (1580), whose peculiarly involved and allusive style gave rise to the expression 'euphuism'; but by his contemporaries he was regarded as an outstanding dramatist, and his elegant writing had a salutary effect on some of the more full-blooded dramatists of the day. Lyly, who was an accomplished courtier and several times a Member of Parliament, wrote almost exclusively for a courtly audience, who delighted in the grace and artificiality of his style, and in the many sly allusions to contemporary scandal with which his plays are seasoned. His first two plays, *Alexander and Campaspe* and *Sappho and Phaon*, were given by the Children of Paul's and of the Chapel in 1583, at Blackfriars.

His most important play, *Endimion, the Man in the Moon*, has been ascribed by Chambers to 1588, when it may have been acted by the children before the Court 'on Candlemas Day at night', possibly with a multiple setting. It was first published in 1591. Of his other plays, several were pastoral comedies on mythological subjects, of ephemeral interest. Two comedies, *Midas* and *Mother Bombie*—the latter in the style of Terence—were given by the Children of Paul's, of whom Lyly was vice-master in about 1590, and a further comedy, *The Woman in the Moon*, may not have been acted. Lyly is also suspected of having had a hand in numerous other plays of the time, but nothing can be ascribed to him with any certainty. He outlived the popularity of his work, but may have had the satisfaction of knowing that he had materially helped to lay the foundations of the great age of Elizabethan drama.

LYRIC THEATRE. (1) LONDON, in Shaftesbury Avenue. This opened on 17 Dec. 1888 with *Dorothy*, transferred from the Prince of Wales's, where it had gone from the Gaiety. It was followed by light opera and burlesque. Duse made her first London appearance at the Lyric, in May 1893. A great success was inaugurated there on 4 Jan. 1896, when Wilson Barrett produced *The Sign of the Cross* with himself as Marcus Superbus. It ran for 435 performances, its religious theme bringing many people to the theatre who had never before entered one. Barrett afterwards produced *The Manxman*, *The Daughters of Babylon*, *Virginius*, and *Othello* at the Lyric. In 1898 Sarah Bernhardt was seen in a season of French plays, and Loie Fuller in *Little Miss Nobody*; then came *Floradora*, Leslie Stuart's outstanding musical comedy, which, produced on 11 Nov. 1899, ran for 455 performances. In 1902 Forbes-Robertson took the theatre, presenting *Mice and Men* with great success, and a dramatization of *The Light that Failed*. Musical comedy came back the following year with *The Duchess of Dantzig*. Lewis Waller was there in 1908, and in 1910 *The Chocolate Soldier* scored a big success. Another long run was that of *The Girl in the Taxi* in 1912. During the 1914–18 war *Romance* with Owen Nares and Doris Keane, transferred from the Duke of York's, ran for a long time. Since then a series of successful plays have been seen at this theatre, including *Lilac Time, Autumn Crocus, Dangerous Corner, Reunion in Vienna, Victoria Regina, The Flashing Stream, The Winslow Boy,* and *Edward, My Son.*

(2) LONDON, in Hammersmith (a western suburb of London). This opened on 17 Nov. 1890 under the management of Cordingley, with a triple bill—*The Waterman, His Last Legs,* and *Puck.* The theatre had a chequered career, became a home of melodrama, and was then closed for some time. In 1918 Nigel Playfair, helped by Arnold Bennett and Anmer Hall (A. B. Horne), took it over, and made this

remote and almost unknown theatre prosperous and fashionable, drawing large audiences from the West End and raising it far above local importance. For this management A. A. Milne wrote his first play, a Christmas entertainment called *Make Believe*. Lovat Fraser was responsible for the décor, and Hermione and Angela Baddeley, Herbert Marshall, and Leslie Banks, all young actors then, were in the cast. It was a success and the theatre was launched, though few realized how successful it was to become. The next attraction was a mixture—*The Younger Generation* by Stanley Houghton, and Pergolesi's 'La Serva Padrona', in which Mrs. Lovat Fraser sang and danced. Although a railway strike was in progress, Playfair decided to take what all thought a great risk and staged Drinkwater's *Abraham Lincoln*, which had been produced in Birmingham by Barry Jackson. It opened on 19 Feb. 1919 for a fortnight, but ran for 466 performances. A lovely revival of *The Beggar's Opera*, with décor by Lovat Fraser, ran for 1,463 performances. Notable productions were revivals of *The Way of the World* and *The Beaux' Stratagem*, in which Edith Evans made a great success, of *The Cherry Orchard* and *The Importance of Being Earnest*, of *Love in a Village*, *Lionel and Clarissa*, and *The Duenna*, and new light operas and revues, mostly by A. P. Herbert with music by Dunhill. The theatre was later taken over by the Company of Four, and is still in use.

W. M. P.

(3) NEW YORK, on 42nd Street. This opened on 12 Oct. 1903 with Richard Mansfield in *Old Heidelberg*. One of its earliest successes was *The Taming of the Shrew* with Ada Rehan and Otis Skinner, while in its second season Réjane and Novelli appeared with Italian companies. Plays by Sudermann, Hauptmann, and Ibsen were all seen at this theatre and, in 1907, Percy Mackaye's *Jeanne d'Arc*. *The Chocolate Soldier* was successful in 1909, scoring 296 performances, and two years later came the success of *The Deep Purple*. In Nov. 1911 Ibsen's *Lady from the Sea* had its first performance in America, while 1912 saw a revival of *Julius Caesar*. Among later productions the most important were probably the musical comedies produced by Ziegfeld, though in 1932 Vittorio Podrecca brought his musical marionettes, known as the Teatro dei Piccoli, to the Lyric for 129 performances. The theatre's last production, before it became a cinema, was a memorable negro drama with music, *Run, Little Chillun*.   G. F.

See also CRITERION THEATRE (2).

LYTTON, EDWARD GEORGE EARLE LYTTON BULWER-LYTTON, LORD (1803–73), primarily an English novelist, but important in the history of the theatre as the author of several plays. Of these the most successful was *The Lady of Lyons; or, Love and Pride* (1838), which was first done by Macready at Covent Garden, with Helen Faucit as Pauline. It was immensely popular and was many times revived, notably by the Charles Keans, by Phelps, by Wallack and by Laura Keene in New York, by Barry Sullivan, by Fechter, by the Kendals, and, in 1879, by Henry Irving with Ellen Terry. Its continued popularity led to a number of burlesques on the same theme. Though romantic and sentimental, it has a touching sincerity and wears well. Lytton essayed a more modern note in *Money* (1840), a serious comedy which seems to foreshadow the reforms of Robertson. It held the stage for many years, being given in 1911 at Drury Lane with an all-star cast for a Command Performance. Lytton's only other important play was *Richelieu* (1839), first done by Macready and again frequently revived, notably by Irving at the Lyceum no less than four times. Although Lytton's plays do not rank high in dramatic literature, he was almost the only dramatist of his day to write plays that have survived on the stage.

M

MACCARTHY, Desmond (1877–), English literary and dramatic critic who began to write on the theatre in 1904, when he joined the staff of *The Speaker*. In 1913 he moved to the *New Statesman*. He was also editor for some years of *Life and Letters*, and has published four volumes of collected essays, of which the last, *Drama*, appeared in 1940, and amounted, in its representative selection, to a review of the London theatre for the past quarter of a century. He also wrote *The Court Theatre, 1904–7*, published by A. H. Bullen in 1907.

McCLINTIC. (1) Guthrie (1893–), American director, responsible for many fine productions, among them Gielgud's *Hamlet* in 1936. He was for some years an actor, playing with Jessie Bonstelle and Grace George, and later became assistant to Winthrop Ames. He established himself as one of America's foremost men of the theatre with his production of *The Green Hat* in 1925 for his wife (2) Katharine Cornell (1898–), one of the leading actresses of the United States, whom he married in 1921. Both subsequently did fine work on their own, while their collaboration as director and leading lady was responsible for such excellent productions as *The Barretts of Wimpole Street*, which has frequently been revived on tour, *Candida*, *The Doctor's Dilemma*, and *Three Sisters*. Their gifts are complementary, and together they bring rare skill and a fine sense of theatrical values to the service of the American theatre.

McCULLOUGH, John (1832–85), American actor, born in Ireland, but an emigrant to the United States at the age of 15. He was self-taught, and had to make his way by hard work and study, gaining his experience first with amateur clubs and later in stock and touring companies. In 1861 he was taken by Forrest to play second lead, and later went with him to San Francisco, where he ran the California Theatre in partnership with Lawrence Barrett, and by himself, until financial difficulties caused him to give up management in 1875. He then toured until forced by illness to retire, making his last appearance as Spartacus in *The Gladiator* in 1884. McCullough, who was physically a big man, and a forceful personality, was often seen in New York, and in 1881 made a brief appearance in London. He had a high reputation in his own line of old-fashioned tragedy, in melodrama, and in some of Shakespeare's heroes, though his Hamlet was not good. He was noble and heroic rather than subtle, but maintained a good standard, and was much respected by his fellow actors and by the public which he served faithfully to the best of his ability.

MACDERMOTT, THE GREAT (1845–1901), a music-hall singer of patriotic songs—'We don't want to fight' and 'True Blues, stand to your Guns'. He was originally a bricklayer and a sailor, named G. H. Farrell, and went on the stage as Gilbert Hastings, from his Christian names. He was actor, author, and stage-manager at the Grecian and Britannia before blossoming out on the halls as the Great Macdermott. He later became a music-hall agent and manager.

MACGOWAN, Kenneth (1888–), American producer and theatre manager, who was for some years a dramatic critic, being associate-editor of *Theatre Arts* from 1919 to 1925. From 1923 to 1927 he was associated with the Provincetown Playhouse, the Greenwich Village Theatre, and the Actors' Theatre for the production of new and unusual plays, among them a number by Eugene O'Neill. He is the author of several books on the modern theatre, including *The Theatre of To-Morrow*, and, in collaboration with Robert Edmond Jones, *Continental Stagecraft*.

MACHIAVELLI, Niccolo di Bernardo dei (1469–1527), Florentine statesman and political philosopher, whose most famous work is *Il Principe*. Exiled from the service of the Medicis on suspicion of conspiracy, he gave some of his time and genius to the theatre. The best of his comedies is undoubtedly *La Mandragola*, written between 1513 and 1520, in sharp, precise prose. It is a pungent criticism of Florentine society, and portrays the gradual betrayal of its lovely heroine by her credulous husband, her ardent but unscrupulous lover, and her scheming mother, aided by the evil machinations of the corrupt priest, Fra Timoteo. Its audiences delighted in it, savouring its wit and accepting its portrayal of a rotten society as true. In a translation by Ashley Dukes it was successfully given at the Mercury Theatre in London during 1940. It was also published in New York in 1927 in a translation by Stark Young.

MACHINE PLAY, a name given to those seventeenth-century French plays which made excessive use of mechanical contrivances, especially for flights, and of elaborate changes of scenery. The development of these spectacular entertainments coincided with the popularity of opera, and is linked with the work of Torelli. The subjects were usually taken from classical mythology, which allowed the use of a *deus ex machinâ*, and, unlike the classical tragedies of the day, they were not usually written in regular alexandrines. The first French play of this type was Corneille's *Andromède* (1650), and it reached its peak with Molière's *Amphitryon* (1668) and *Psyché* (1671). By far the greater number of machine plays, though not the outstanding ones, were given at the Théâtre du Marais, which had a large and excellently equipped stage suitable for their presentation.

MACHINERY, THEATRE. Looking up from beneath the stage into the grid of a modern theatre one might be led to suppose that the mechanism there was very complicated—hundreds of ropes, winding-drums, pulleys, levers, counterweights, lifts, blocks, and tackles. Their purposes, however, are very limited, and the mechanism simple, but a lost tradition has turned many theatres into junk-shops of mechanical bric-à-brac.

Most theatre machines come into the following four categories:

(a) *Machines for Quick Changes.* These include *periaktoi* or prisms, pivots, trucks, trolleys, moving platforms, and turntable stages, on all of which scenery is mounted so that it can be moved into and out of sight quickly and easily. Derricks, levers, drums, rollers, and pulleys are for lifting out of sight, by means of ropes and wires, backcloths, frontcloths, set pieces, and the top parts of certain scenery so that it may be got rid of speedily.

(b) *Machines for Supernatural Appearances.* These include tracks above the stage, suspended ropes, wires, spring coils, and iron rods to which are attached persons, chariots, aeroplanes, &c., so that they can be held or transported in the air in view of the audience. Also included are traps, moving-stairs, and platforms on which persons or things may be placed so that they can travel across or descend below stage, either slowly or in an instant.

(c) *Machines for Controlling Light.* These include contrivances that attempt to imitate the colouring, brightening, and fading of light in nature or the imitations of lightning, fire, &c., also those for illuminating the actors for the simple purpose of making them visible to the audience in closed theatres.

(d) *Machines for Imitating the Sounds and Effects of Nature*, such as waterfalls, snowstorms, thunder, storms at sea, &c.

The study of theatre history shows that, as in the history of all arts and crafts, the earlier artists and craftsmen were content to say simple things and so required few implements with which to express themselves; but as time passed the desire to surpass one another in elaboration led to the use of more complex machinery, until in the end the mechanics overwhelmed the mechanic. But the story of how simple mechanics were applied to dramatic art is none the less interesting.

Machines were used in the earliest form of theatre, the pagan temples, when the great figures of gods were made to move their hands and eyes. They were brought to great perfection by the requirements of the Greek tragedies. With the Romans they became more and more spectacular; the sudden appearance of a full-sized galley or a mountain with sheep grazing upon it was familiar to the Roman audiences of A.D. 150. But when Rome faded out the theatre and all its trappings faded with it. After a long interval the old spirit of the 'theatrical' theatre slowly reappeared, this time in Christian temples—the great churches of northern Italy.

It was the Princes of the Church who brought about the revival. They wanted to help the people to believe by showing them the incredible in a material form, so great spectacles were given in the churches and the best architects of the time were called in to design the costumes and invent the machines or *ingegni*, as they were called.

Filippo Brunelleschi (1377–1446) led the way; it was he who, about 1400, made a machine commonly called a 'Paradiso'. Vasari has given a very long description of it in his life of Brunelleschi. The Paradiso was invented for the representation of the Annunciation which used to take place every year in the church of S. Felice in Florence during the month of March. It consisted of a 'nosegay' of singing cherubim suspended in a copper dome or 'heaven' in the roof of the church, from the centre of which an angel descended in a copper globe which opened—the whole accompanied by music, voices, incense, and mystery.

After Brunelleschi's death, a young carpenter called Il Cecca (really Francesco d'Angelo) (*fl.* 15th cent.) took his place. He was a genius at inventing machines either for war or peace. He added clouds or *nuvole* to theatre machinery. He was not content to see a 'Paradiso' suspended in the air with a single angel descending to make an announcement. He wanted things on a grander scale, with many more angels, cherubim, and seraphim all moving together, and as this required a tremendous number of ropes and pulleys he had to invent something that would hide them. Why not clouds? Clouds of cotton wool? He tried them at the Feast of the Ascension at the Chiesa degli Camini at Florence, and when the moment arrived on the evening of the performance, hundreds of little white clouds were seen clustered above the mountain on which stood Christ and the apostles; then, to the sound of beautiful voices, accompanied by lutes and viols, the clouds began to move apart and discovered a heaven full of angels in beautiful array, surrounded by cherubim and seraphim; these were seen gradually to descend until they reached the mountain, when the angels advanced and announced to Christ His ascension; then the clouds seemed to surround that piece of the mountain on which He stood and the whole ascended into a Paradise above. After this, clouds were used on every occasion when machinery had to be hidden, and when saints, represented by human figures, were carried in procession through the streets they were always surrounded by 'clouds' hiding their supports, thus making them seem more supernatural. After a while painted canvas, shaped and mounted on battens, took the place of cotton wool, and, as a form of screen for the mechanical working of any supernatural being, lasted until the end of the eighteenth century.

By the end of the fifteenth century the comedies of Greece and Rome, together with the books of Vitruvius, had been rediscovered, and classical drama began to creep back into the Courts of northern Italy. With the beginning of the sixteenth century sacred spectacles seemed to have gone out of favour, therefore architects studying the works of Vitruvius turned their attention to re-creating the Graeco-Roman stages with permanent scenes, *periaktoi*, and devices for transporting the deities through the air or making them appear from the earth.

Periaktoi were originally prism-shaped contrivances of varying sizes, made of wood, that turned on a central pivot behind certain openings in a fixed architectural scene built of stone. The three sides of the prism were painted with different visions or scenes, and by being turned to face the audience at different periods during the action of the drama a degree of change was introduced into the otherwise permanent scene. San Gallo (see below), when reviving this idea in later days, increased the size of the *periaktoi*, placing them behind each other like wings on either side of the proscenium, and in order to get more than three changes he reclothed these prisms in between acts or intervals with canvas coverings on which were painted still another three scenes.

The new theatres were usually erected in some big room in a palace—a semicircle of gradines at one end and a platform 3 ft. high at the other. The platform generally had a proscenium of some kind, without an arch. These prosceniums were of a very light construction with painted decorations, but as the machines they screened became more bulky, an arch was added. Through a succession of mis-statements it is now considered an historical fact that the first proscenium arch was that of the Teatro Farnese, built in Parma in 1617–18. Actually Francesco Salviati (1510–63), who designed some very beautiful scenes, designed them with quite the most beautiful proscenium arches that can be imagined, long before the Teatro Farnese was built. Until the arrival of opera most theatres had steps or some sort of ramp connecting the stage with the auditorium so that, like the Chorus of their Grecian ancestors, the performers could descend and perform their little ballets and other forms of intermezzi in between the acts.

It was opera that brought the orchestra from behind the scenes and placed it as a barrier between the actors and their audiences.

The theatre being established once again, the princes who had helped to bring this about first used it as a form of private entertainment, and later, on special occasions, admitted the public. They also collected around them the finest painters and architects in the land. This led to jealousy and competition, until the theatre became a factor of extreme political importance. Performances were given only in the event of visits from princes of neighbouring states, or from abroad, for the celebration of a marriage or when entertaining dignitaries of the Church. On these occasions the play was selected with great care, or composed specially to suit a certain political situation that was to be discussed. The same care was taken with the theatre itself, its symbolical decorations, and the placing of the guests. Ambassadors and spies were always present at these perform-

ances and usually sent to the princes or prelates whom they served detailed reports of the proceedings, many of which can still be studied to-day.

This situation, and the fact that Italy was so divided, prevented any steady growth in theatrical representation during the whole period from the beginning of the sixteenth century to the middle of the seventeenth century; instead it advanced by fits and starts. Special mechanical contrivances were made if a new effect was required for a particular occasion, but otherwise the machines left over from previous shows had to be adapted. Few, if any, of the architects and painters who prepared these spectacles studied the drama for its own sake. It was just part of the day's work, together with the building of churches and palaces, the draining of marshes, the designing of implements of war and state carriages; but although the theatre was only a side-line for these great artists, among whom may be numbered Mantegna, Leonardo da Vinci, Baldassare Peruzzi, Andrea del Sarto, Giulio Romano, and Cristoforo Gherardi, they did not treat it in an off-hand way. They joined in the excitement and allowed their fancy to run wild, not merely on paper but in practice. Thus in order to study the development of theatre machinery between the sixteenth and seventeenth centuries one has to follow the intricate political changes in Italy at the time, and follow also the different artists as they travelled from Court to Court.

It would seem that only one of the sixteenth-century artists ever gave his whole time and energy to the theatre, and that was Bastiano da San Gallo (1481–1551). He and his contemporary Baldassare Peruzzi (1481–1537) achieved great things for the theatre, Peruzzi by proving that painted perspective scenes could be as convincing as the built ones, San Gallo by his unceasing experiments with mechanics, for which he was given ample opportunity. San Gallo, who worked chiefly in Florence, developed, as mentioned above, the use of the old Roman idea of prisms, or *periaktoi*. These prisms used as wings, together with Peruzzi's perspective backcloths, were employed a great deal in Italy during the early part of the sixteenth century and appeared again at different times in the seventeenth century in the smaller towns of Italy, Germany, and France. They were first used in England at Christ Church, Oxford, by Inigo Jones (1573–1652) in 1605. An old French Jesuit, who published a book on perspective in 1649, totally ignored the inventions of Giacomo Torelli (1608–78), which at that time were astonishing the whole of Europe, and reproduced diagrams showing the working of this prism scenery, then just on 150 years old. Josef Furtenbach (1581–1667), the German architect, published a book seventeen years later in which this same arrangement of scene is still shown in plan and elevation as quite up to date. Eighteenth-century plans of the great College of Nobles established in Parma in 1600 show the existence of two private theatres for the use of the students, one for the performance of the classical or 'antient' drama with gradines for the audience and diminishing rows of *periaktoi* on the stage, and another 'modern' theatre with tiers of boxes for the audience and twelve rows of wings worked by Torelli's method on carriages under the stage.

San Gallo was also celebrated for his street scene built in perspective (Serlio's second book of architecture shows exactly what these scenes were like and describes them accurately, together with methods of lighting in use at the time). They required great skill to be successful as all the mouldings, cornices, and statues on the façades of the buildings had to be modelled in perspective. These street-scenes, when the hour permitted, were lighted from one side by daylight admitted through great windows, but more often than not by thousands of candles in crude holders stuck all over the backs of the scenes. The skies above were often represented by domed ceilings painted blue with little clouds floating about, but by the beginning of the seventeenth century 'sky borders'—strips of blue material one behind the other some 6 ft. apart and gradually getting lower towards the back of the stage—were generally in use; these were the forerunners of the more flexible Fortuny Panorama of to-day (see LIGHTING and SCENERY).

In 1514, to honour the arrival in Rome of Isabella Gonzaga, the *Calandria* of Cardinal Bibbiena was performed. Vasari says Baldassare Peruzzi's marvellous scenes painted in perspective on this occasion 'opened the way to all who came after him'. It then became cheaper and more fashionable to paint scenery, since the flexibility of the materials allowed for still more changes, and the variations in background helped to counteract the monotony of the academic plays. All the early scene-painters used paints ground in linseed oil. It was only at the beginning of the seventeenth century that size and whitening took the place of oil as a medium, but even to the end of the eighteenth century it was customary to paint scenery in a monotone and only glaze on colours in varnish or size.

After 1600 theatre machinery developed with great rapidity. Opera had been born in Florence in an attempt to revive the ancient form of pastoral play with a musical accompaniment, and everyone was enthusiastic about this new form of entertainment. It appealed to the more florid writers of the time who devised complicated plots requiring ever more complicated changes of scenery, apparatus, &c.

Up to the middle of the sixteenth century theatres were not permanent buildings. Few princes put on more than three or four performances a year and frequent wars caused gaps in between. The theatres therefore were always of a light construction fitted into a large hall, decorated with damask, paintings, or sometimes foliage and statues, and generally illuminated by giant candelabras, all put up to help the scenic illusion and taken down afterwards. But later, as plays became more frequent, one

after another the princes invested in permanent theatres; at the same time the impresario appeared, and, backed by public subscriptions, the first public theatres were built. By 1551 Mantua could boast one of the finest Court theatres in northern Italy, built by Giambattista Bertani (*fl.* 16th cent.). After Mantua came Siena with a theatre built by Bartolomeo Neroni (*c.* 1500–71/3) for the Academy of the Intronati. The theatre shown in Callot's superb pen and ink drawing, made in 1616 and preserved now in the Kupferstich Museum, Berlin, was built by Bernardo Buontalenti (1536–1608) in Florence in 1585. The scenery and machines used here were of a mixed kind, centre pieces built in relief, against painted backcloths and with wings at the sides run in grooves on the stage like those shown in Inigo Jones's section of the stage for *Salmacida Spolia* (1640). Italy got its first public theatre with the building of the San Cassiano in Venice in 1637.

Inigo Jones went to Florence between 1613 and 1614, and it was here that he must have met Buontalenti's pupil, Giulio Parigi (?–1635), who had been working on nearly every spectacle in the city for many years. Parigi had many pupils, and it was his methods that Jones brought back to the English Court where, until then, the old Chinese make-believe had been practised. Josef Furtenbach was in Florence at the same time as Jones and returning to Augsburg published there in 1663 *Des ältern Mannhaftern der Kunst-Spiegel*, which spread Parigi's methods through Germany.

After his achievements at the Teatro del Sole in Pesaro, Nicola Sabbattini (*c.* 1574–1654) published the first 89-page treatise on theatre machinery; in the Italian language it bore the title *Pratica de fabricar scene e machine ne' teatri*. Furtenbach often referred to this book, which, though published in 1638, was far behind the times. On page 72 (2nd edition) Sabbattini says, with regard to changing scenes, that you can make trumpets blare, or have an arrangement with someone in front to pretend that some of the seats are breaking down at the back of the theatre; this will attract the attention of the spectators away from the scene which can then be changed unperceived. He advises the use of the trumpets, however, as the other method may lead to a panic. This would seem to suggest that the Pesaro theatre had no curtain at that time.

Richard Lascelles, a contemporary of Furtenbach and Inigo Jones, who wrote *Italian Voyage* (1670), gives the following account of a performance he saw in Rome about 1630. This seems to show that Giovanni Lorenzo Bernini (1598–1680), who was master theatre mechanic in that town, was a little ahead of Sabbattini. It describes

the curious Opera, or musical Drammata, recited with such admirable art and set forth with such wonderful changes of scenes, that nothing can be more surprising. Here I have seen upon the stage, Rivers swelling, and Boats rowing upon them; waters overflowing their banks and stage; men flying in the air, Serpents crawling upon the stage,

Houses falling on the suddain, Temples and *Boscos* appearing, whole towns, known towns, starting up on a sudden with men walking in the streets, the Sun appearing and chasing away darkness, sugar plums fall upon the spectators' heads like Hail, Rubans flash in the ladies' faces like lightning, with a thousand like representations.

The performance of 1628 given in the vast Farnese Theatre in Parma (built by Giambattista Aleotti (1546–1636) in 1618) (see ARCHITECTURE) was the most spectacular in the history of the theatre; it inspired every contemporary designer and mechanic; it was a drama, opera, tournament, and regatta thrown into one. Archellini wrote the words, Monteverdi the music, Francesco Giutti, Luca Redi, and Carlo Renaldi designed the scenes, machines, and monsters. The performance, which was to celebrate the marriage between Ranuccio II and Margherita of Tuscany, took place on 21 Dec. The town was crowded, the whole Florentine Court having arrived, as well as all the most powerful princes and their followers from the neighbouring states. At 2 o'clock at night the doors of the theatre were thrown open and everyone took his seat on the gradines, leaving the vast parterre empty for the ballets that were to come; the chief princes rode upstairs into the theatre which was on the second floor, built over arches. When the newly married couple had taken their seats upon a special throne opposite the proscenium arch a symphony was started first by one orchestra and then by four others in different parts of the theatre, all eventually being joined by two powerful organs behind the stage. As their sound died away the curtains were drawn and Aurora appeared from the sea on a marvellous chariot drawn by fiery steeds; she sang of the happiness caused by the wedding. Every now and then an excuse was found for a 'Torneo' or 'Combattimiento', when warriors came dancing into the centre of the auditorium, and to the measured steps of a quadrille went through the antics of a combat. Twenty-one machines were made and used for this performance, and records exist of them all. The nineteenth intermezzo, or the entry of Neptune, was the climax of the evening, for suddenly, to the piercing notes of the organs, Neptune issued from the 'waves' on the stage, surrounded by singing tritons, and the sea, gradually swelling, overflowed through gullies into the auditorium, ever increasing in volume, until the whole floor was covered. Then through side doors entered great marine monsters and little islands, upon each of which sat warriors who fought until, at a given signal, they disappeared and all was dry. The gods ascended into heaven wishing everlasting happiness to the prince and his bride, while Discord was hurled down into an abyss. The water had been pumped up the day before into great iron tanks which had been prepared under the stage, and at a given signal it was released into the auditorium which had been made waterproof with lead sheeting to the height of about 3 ft. The sea on the stage was composed of a num-

ber of 'waves' that stretched right across between the proscenium arch, running far back and diminishing in perspective. These waves were made of wood and were exactly the same as the spiral columns so much used in the later Renaissance churches. Being laid on their sides and slowly turned, they gave a most beautiful effect. When the monsters and islands made their appearance through the side doors, they floated on the water but were guided by men who worked them from inside. Beneath the theatre a great walled and buttressed reservoir had been built, and at another signal Venetian sailors, who were in charge, knocked away a few poles which stopped up some sluice-holes, and the water ran away.

In 1608 was born in Fano Giacomo Torelli, the most important name in the history of theatre machinery. He studied architecture and mechanics and took to the theatre. Being rich, and longing to parade his talents, he built himself a public theatre in Venice in the year 1640. It was called the Teatro Novissimo, and in it he displayed the most extraordinary machines of his age. From this theatre came all the inventions that were used in the European theatre for the next two centuries; some are used even now. The most famous of his inventions was a device for achieving a quick change by making the wings on either side of the stage appear and disappear quickly. He mounted them on ladders which protruded through slits running across the stage, the ladders being mounted in turn on little carriages below the stage, which could all be pulled forward by one turn on a central drum and run back again by the action of counterweights. John Evelyn was in Venice in 1645 and saw some of these wonders. He wrote:

We went to the opera where comedies and other plays are represented in recitative music, by most excellent musicians, vocal and instrumental, with variety of scenes painted and contrived with no less art of perspective and machines for flying in the air, and other wonderful notions; taken together it is one of the most magnificent and expensive diversions the wit of man can invent.... The scenes changed thirteen times.... This held us by the eyes and ears until two in the morning.

His achievements soon acquired for Torelli the nickname of 'il gran stregone', the great wizard; at the same time his extreme conceit, and the fact that he was drawing away audiences from other theatres, were the cause of his being waylaid one night and his hands badly cut in a fight. In 1645 he went to France and introduced machines and footlights into the French theatre for the first time. The French went machine-mad and Torelli grew rich. Through intrigue, however, he was sent from the country in 1660, his place being taken by Gaspare Vigarani (1586–1663) who, out of jealousy, burned all Torelli had left behind. Torelli returned to Fano and there built himself another superb theatre. His innovations were not lost, for in 1772, when Diderot published his great *Encyclopédie* (M), under 'Machines du Théâtre' was a complete record of the theatre machinery of the time, all based on Torelli's ideas, some of which have not changed to-day, though we have lost the art of using others.

In France the Torelli tradition was carried on with a few additions by Vigarani (who destroyed Torelli's machines but kept his designs) and later by Jean Nicolas Servandony (1695–1766) and numerous French engineers who wrote theoretically on the subject. In Italy the Galli da Bibiena family carried on the Torelli tradition, but became known as the users of a greater number of cut cloths. They also painted their scenes at a different perspective angle, often putting the vanishing-point at the sides instead of in the middle as had always been done previously.

With the nineteenth century matters got worse as unskilled craftsmen were trying to manage machines a century old. Gustave Chougnet, writing about Rossini's 'Mosè in Egitto', produced in Naples in 1818, says:

The scene of the darkness was another step onwards, and the whole work was much applauded, with the exception of the passage of the Red Sea, the representation of which was always laughed at, owing to the imperfection of the theatrical appliances already spoken of. At the resumption of the piece therefore, in the following Lent, Rossini added a chorus to divert attention from the wretched attempt to represent the dividing waves, and it is to the sins of the Neapolitan stage machinists that we owe the universally popular prayer 'Dal tuo stellato soglio'.

With the arrival of the Social or Bourgeois Drama at the beginning of the nineteenth century dramatic action was confined to a few rooms and garden scenes, and the Japanese type of book wings came into use. Instead of the spectators being able to look off the scene by peering between the wings from the sides of the theatre, the scene became boxed in. By the end of the nineteenth century complicated machinery littered the theatres of the world and no use was made of it except in the annual pantomime or occasional spectacle show. And now, here we are in the Mechanical Age and, with the exception of our lighting equipment, our theatre machinery is years behind the times.

In the early years of the twentieth century a great deal of importance was attached to the use of turntable stages and hydraulic lifts, but Torelli used lifts loaded with actors and scenery, and the Japanese used vast turntable stages in the eighteenth century. Gordon Craig patented in 1913 the use of plain screens which could be painted with light, in an attempt to supply drama with an idealized background, but as his method of using them has never been tried out, except privately in his own theatre, this method of supplying scenic effects has not been seen by the public. When his experiments are eventually made use of the mechanics of changing the scene, and the art of painting the scene, may be completely revolutionized (see also ACOUSTICS, ENGLISH PLAYHOUSE, STAGE, and TRICKWORK ON THE ENGLISH STAGE).   E. C.

MACKAYE. (1) JAMES MORRISON STEELE (1842–94), American theatre designer, pioneer and inventor, whom Winter called 'a wayward genius of poetic temperament, enthusiastic, impetuous, fond of experiment'. While in the army in 1862 he made an amateur appearance as Hamlet, but it was not until ten years later, after studying in London and Paris, that he appeared in New York with a group of students whom he had trained in the methods of Delsarte. In order to carry out his ideas he remodelled the old Fifth Avenue Theatre, installing elaborate scenic apparatus, overhead and indirect stage lighting, and a double movable stage, and opened it in 1879 as the Madison Square Theatre. Here his best play, *Hazel Kirke*, was first put on, and ran for nearly two years, though owing to Mackaye's unbusinesslike methods he received very little money from it. It was frequently revived and was seen in London, where Mackaye's first plays, mainly adaptations and collaborations, had been done. Unable to continue working at the Madison Square Theatre, he went to the Lyceum on Fourth Avenue, installed electric lighting, and established there the first school of acting in New York, later known as the American Academy of Dramatic Art, which did much good work in training future generations of actors. Mackaye, who was thin, dark, nervous, and dynamic, was everything by turns—actor, dramatist, teacher, lecturer—and his erratic personality had a great influence on the trend of the American theatre. Shortly before his death from overwork and worry he had planned a vast playhouse for the Chicago World Fair, which was to have had a wonderful cyclorama and all the most modern continental stage equipment. It was never built, but later theatre architects were indebted to its plans for the introduction of many new ideas and methods. Mackaye influenced the theatre of his time and after, more by what he thought, dreamed of, and fought for, than by what he actually achieved, and none of his plays has survived. His life-story is told in *Epoch*, by his son (2) PERCY WALLACE (1875–   ), also a playwright, much of whose best work has been done in poetic drama, in modern masques and spectacles, and in the writing of operatic libretti. His independence of spirit, as well as his ideals of a free theatre, have led him away from the commercial theatre of his day, and he has developed his ideas in several volumes of criticism, *The Playhouse and the Play* (1909), *The Civic Theatre* (1912), and *Community Drama* (1917).

MACKINLAY, JEAN STERLING (1882–   ), see WILLIAMS, (ERNEST GEORGE) HARCOURT (2).

MACKLIN [M'LAUGHLAN], CHARLES (c. 1700–97), Irish actor, best remembered for having rescued Shylock from the crudities of the low comedian, to whom the part had been assigned since Restoration days. Macklin raised him to the status of a dignified and tragic figure, thus drawing from Pope the memorable couplet: 'This is the Jew, That Shakespeare drew.' The date of his birth is uncertain, and he was for a long time believed to have been at least a centenarian when he died, but recent evidence points to his having been born about 1700. He had a wild and restless boyhood, and at 20 joined a company of strolling players. In 1725 he was engaged by Rich for Lincoln's Inn Fields, but his natural delivery, in which he preceded Garrick's reforms, told against him in the high-toned tragedy of the day. He went back to the provinces and fairs, playing Harlequin at Sadler's Wells, and Clown when the part called for an actor and not, as later on, for a dancer. At this period of his life he was known as the Wild Irishman, a jovial boon companion, a famous fives-player, a great lover, boxer, and pedestrian. In the 1730s he went back to Lincoln's Inn Fields, and was the last great actor to appear there, since Rich soon deserted it for his new Covent Garden. Macklin went to Drury Lane under Fleetwood and with his wife played secondary parts, until in 1741 he persuaded the management to revive *The Merchant of Venice*, and became famous overnight for his Shylock. There is an excellent description of him in the part by the German critic Lichtenberg.

After this Macklin might have risen to even greater heights, but with advancing years he became extremely quarrelsome and jealous, and constantly moved from one theatre to another. At the Haymarket he played Iago to Foote's Othello, and the Ghost and Grave-digger to his Hamlet. At Covent Garden, where he appeared intermittently from 1770 to 1775, he played Mercutio to Barry's Romeo, and at Drury Lane in 1773 he played Macbeth, discarding Garrick's scarlet coat and appearing for the first time in the dress of a Highland chieftain. A good deal of his energy was expended off the stage. He was constantly engaged in litigation, often with his managers, he went bankrupt after opening a tavern, and he also founded a school, his serious but not very sensible lectures providing Foote with excellent material for burlesque at the Haymarket. Macklin also embarked on a speculation to build a theatre in Dublin, but soon quarrelled with his partners and withdrew. He was the author of a number of plays, of which two were excellent and survived well into the nineteenth century—*Love à la Mode* (1759), in which he himself played Sir Archy McSarcasm, and the famous comedy, *The Man of the World* (1781), which he based on one of his former farces, the two-act *The True-Born Scotsman*, given at Smock Alley, Dublin, in 1764. In this Macklin again played the chief character, Sir Pertinax McSycophant, though he was by then over 80. In 1788 his memory began to fail, but he still acted, and his last appearance on the stage was on 7 May 1789, when he attempted Shylock, but was unable to finish it. Neither a good tragedian, nor yet a good light comedian, he was at his best in his own plays, and in parts like Scrub and Peachum, which required a rough vigour. He was a complex personality, of whom it was said that he had a 'rough mind and rougher manner',

impatient of contradiction, dogmatic, a tyrant in the theatre, but of great critical acuity. He is variously represented as a disgustingly rude and obnoxious person, and as a man of great charm, quarrelling with other actors—notably Garrick and Quin—and managers and winning them back by a disarming apology. He was also an excellent teacher of acting, and a man of strict integrity, benevolence, and generosity. His energy was unbounded, but his restless disposition prevented him from making much mark on the theatre, and he lived always in the shadow of Garrick's greatness. He was twice married, his second wife surviving him, but his children all died before him. One of them, a daughter (1749–87), was a pretty, respectable girl, and though not a good actress was much admired in breeches parts.

MACKNEY, E. W. (1835–1909), an old-time music-hall performer who began his career in the supper-rooms, and was one of the first stars of the old Canterbury under Morton, also the first black-faced singer, accompanying himself on the banjo. He was also no mean dancer. His most famous songs were 'The Whole Hog or None' and 'I Wish I were with Nancy', sung to the tune of 'Dixie'. Unlike so many of the old music-hall favourites, he was a careful man, and retired when well advanced in years to live on a small farm at Enfield.   **W. M. P.**

MACLIAMMÓIR, MICHEÁL (1899–   ), Irish actor, scenic artist, and playwright in both Gaelic and English. He was on the London stage as a child, and then studied art. He exhibited in various parts of Europe, travelled widely, was familiar with the theatrical art and literature of several countries, and finally brought to the Dublin stage his combination of gifts as director and scenic artist. In 1928, in combination with Hilton Edwards, he founded the Gate Theatre, Dublin; he also created and directed from 1928 to 1931 the Galway Theatre (Taibhdhearc na Gaillimhe). He produced, for An Comhar Drámuíochta, a long list of foreign classics in Irish (himself being responsible for the translations of Chekhov, Guitry, and Shaw), and a number of original Irish plays. Among his own plays the best known are *Diarmuid and Grainne*, given both in English and Irish, *Ill Met by Moonlight*, seen in London in 1947, and *Where Stars Walk*. He is also the author of a theatrical autobiography, *All For Hecuba*.

MACREADY, WILLIAM CHARLES (1793–1873), English actor, and one of the finest tragedians of his own or any time. He was the son of a provincial actor-manager, and his father's financial difficulties caused him to leave Rugby, where he had already shown talent as an amateur actor and reciter, to go on the stage. He made his first appearance at Birmingham as Romeo in 1810, and then toured the provinces, playing Hamlet for the first time the following year at Newcastle. In 1816 he was engaged to appear at Covent

Garden as Orestes in *The Distressed Mother*, and there and in the provinces he subsequently played in a number of poor plays which gave him a lasting dislike for his profession. By 1819, however, he was firmly established as Kean's rival, and continued to appear at both Covent Garden and Drury Lane in a variety of parts. He was good in *Rob Roy*, *Gambia*, and *Virginius*, but it was his Lear, Hamlet, and Macbeth which were universally acclaimed, causing Hazlitt to say of him that he was the best tragic actor of his remembrance, except Kean. His rivalry with the latter was later transferred to Edwin Forrest, culminating in the Astor Place riot in New York (1848), in which several people were killed. Macready was a man of ungovernable temper, and on one occasion he and Alfred Bunn, then manager of Drury Lane, came to blows. Macready was himself manager at various times of both the Patent Theatres, where he sought always to improve current methods of production by subordinating scenery and costume to the play as a whole. His managements were artistically, though not always financially, a success. In 1837 he appeared with Helen Faucit in several outstanding new plays, including Browning's *Strafford*, and a year later produced *The Lady of Lyons*, playing Claude Melnotte to Helen Faucit's Pauline. Their fine acting did much to ensure the success of the play, and its subsequent reputation. Another of Bulwer Lytton's plays which gave Macready a fine part was *Richelieu* (1839), while among the new poetic plays which owed their appearance to his encouragement and initiative was Byron's *Two Foscari* (1838). Macready made his first appearance in America in 1826, and his last on the occasion of the riot mentioned above, and in 1828 was in Paris. He played an important part in the struggle to free the London stage from the monopoly of the Patent Theatres, and also worked to rescue the Shakespearian text from much of the Restoration emendations. A scrupulous and cultured man, enjoying the society of some of the greatest writers of the day, he nevertheless made many enemies, particularly by his constant disparagement of the profession which he adorned. Apart from the excellence of his acting, in which he was surpassed only by Garrick, and equalled only by Kean, he is important in theatre history for his efforts to encourage all that was best in the theatre of his day, and for his many reforms both of acting and of texts. His diary gives a lively picture of the society in which he moved, and reveals the man himself with all his virtues and shortcomings. It was published in two volumes in 1875, edited by Sir Frederick Pollock, and later supplemented by a little volume by Lady Pollock, entitled *Macready as I knew him*, much of which deals with his life after his retirement at Sherborne and Cheltenham. Macready's last performance was given at Drury Lane, where he appeared as Macbeth, on 26 Feb. 1851.

MACSWINEY, OWEN, see SWINEY.

MADACH, IMRE (1823–64), Hungarian dramatist, whose best play, twice translated into English as *The Tragedy of Man*, was *Az Ember Tragédidja* (1862). Conceived on a vast scale, somewhat on the lines of *Faust*, this deals with the struggle between the Devil and Adam for the possession of man's soul, and has won international recognition.

MADDERMARKET THEATRE, see AMATEUR THEATRE IN GREAT BRITAIN, 1 *d*, MONCK, and PROVINCIAL THEATRES, 2 *f*.

MADISON SQUARE THEATRE, NEW YORK. This was originally the Fifth Avenue Hall, on the site of Daly's first Fifth Avenue Theatre, and was adapted and renovated by the great inventive genius of the New York stage, Steele Mackaye, who intended to run it on the lines of the Comédie-Française, as a stock-company theatre with a picked repertory. The venture was a failure, but the theatre, which had opened on 23 Apr. 1879, was firmly established. With the Mallory brothers in command and Daniel Frohman as business manager, it opened again on 4 Feb. 1880 with *Hazel Kirke*, which scored 486 performances, the longest run on the New York stage up to that time. Viola Allen made her first appearance in New York at this theatre, in July 1882, and in the same year *Young Mrs. Winthrop*, one of the first good American plays, was staged there. Mansfield was seen at this theatre in several of his best parts, and in the season of 1889–90 produced *A Doll's House*, with Beatrice Cameron as Nora. On 15 Sept. 1891 it was taken over by Hoyt and Thomas and some years later was renamed Hoyt's Theatre, until on 1 Feb. 1905 its original name was restored. A year later *A Case of Arson*, by Heijermans, was produced there, and in March 1908 the theatre finally closed (see also U.S.A., 1. 6).   G. F.

MADRID THEATRES. 1. TEATRO REAL. This is Madrid's largest theatre. It stands on the site of the old *Caños del Peral*, which was founded in 1708 by Francisco Bartoli, the director of an Italian company then playing at the Court theatre of *El Buen Retiro*. In 1719 Bartoli's theatre was rebuilt by another Italian, the Marquis of Scotti, and, first as the *Gran Teatro*, later as *Caños del Peral* (after its site), it was chiefly important for Italian opera. However, at various periods it was occupied by the famous companies of Manuel Guerrero and of Isidore Máiquez, and in 1814 it was used by the Cortes (Spain's Parliament) for their assembly. In 1818 it was completely rebuilt, this time on a grander scale in an attempt to rival the Scala at Milan, in size as in achievement. The architect López Aquado designed the new building, and it took almost thirty years, and tremendous expense, to build. It is now in the forefront of European theatres for dimensions, dramatic convenience, and modern machinery.

2. TEATRO ESPAÑOL. This theatre, if not as large as the *Teatro Real*, is of equal importance

in Madrid. It stands on the site of the historic *Corral del Príncipe*, which was destroyed by fire in 1804. The new building was the work of the architect Villanueva, and reopened in 1806, retaining its old title until 1849. At this date there was strong feeling in dramatic circles against the prevalence of translations and foreign opera over original compositions, and there was a move to establish a national theatre. The early and definitely Spanish history of the *Corral del Príncipe*, in contrast to that of the *Teatro Real*, favoured its choice for the experiment, and in 1849 it was overhauled and renovated and renamed the *Teatro Español*. It is the property of the Ayuntamiento (the Council). However, in spite of many brilliant productions, notably of the plays of Echegaray, by Rafael Calvo and Antonio Vico, the *Teatro Español* has not achieved the national status enjoyed by the Comédie-Française, for example.

3. TEATRO ESLAVA. This is of more recent foundation than the other Madrid theatres, and on a far smaller scale. It was for many years in the hands of the dramatist Gregorio Martínez Sierra, under whose directorship it maintained a consistently high level of attainment.

MAEDER, MRS. JAMES, see FISHER, CLARA.

MAETERLINCK, MAURICE (1862–1949), Belgian poet and dramatist, whose symbolic plays were a challenge to both the ephemeral and the realistic drama of his time. In them he showed his characters as the instruments of some hidden force, emanating from the unseen reality which lies all around us. This is particularly true of the two plays best known in English, *L'Oiseau bleu* (1909) and *Les Fiançailles* (1919), which as *The Blue Bird* and *The Betrothal* were given in London and New York. Some critics, however, consider *The Burgomaster of Stilemonde*, given in London in 1918, to be his best work. Among his other plays, many of which were first given in Paris by Lugné-Poë, *Pelléas et Mélisande* was played by Mrs. Patrick Campbell in both English and French, the latter with Sarah Bernhardt. For the English version in 1898 the incidental music was composed by Fauré, while Debussy later used the play as the basis of an opera. Maeterlinck, who was much praised in his early years for having brought poetry and enchantment back to the stage, collaborated in 1907 with Paul Dukas in a 'conte-lyrique', *Ariane et Barbe-Bleue*, which had a considerable success.

MAFFEI. (1) SCIPIONE (1675–1755), Italian dramatist who in the early years of the eighteenth century tried to give Italy a tragic drama worthy of the name. In 1714 he published his tragedy *Merope*, which had been given the previous year both in Italy and at the Comédie-Italienne in Paris. It was much admired by Voltaire, who later essayed the same subject and dedicated his *Mérope* to Maffei. Maffei also wrote a *Trattato de' teatri antichi e moderni*, and some comedies of little importance. He visited England, where his reputation as a man of letters assured him a warm welcome

and an honorary Doctorate at Oxford. *Merope* was translated into English by Ayres in 1740. Scipione Maffei should not be confused with the later (2) ANDREA (1798–1885), who translated into Italian the plays of Schiller, Goethe's *Faust*, and Shakespeare's *Othello* and *The Tempest*.

MAGALHAES, DOMINGO JOSÉ GONÇALVES DE (1811–82), see SOUTH AMERICA, 2.

MAGNES, an early Athenian comic poet, mentioned by Aristophanes in the *Knights*. He won a victory in 472 B.C.

MAGNON, JEAN (1620–62), a mediocre French dramatist, of whom it was said, since he wrote with great facility, that his works were more easily written than read. But he deserves to be remembered, since his first play *Artaxerce* (1644) was given by a small company which included Jean-Baptiste Poquelin, later the immortal Molière, whose friend Magnon remained all his life. He wrote seven more plays, and a vast encyclopaedia called *La Science universelle*. He was assassinated on the Pont-Neuf by the hired bravos of his wife's marquis-lover. He had a son who opened a theatre in Copenhagen where Molière's plays were given and had much influence on the development of the Scandinavian dramatist, Holberg.

MAINTENON, MADAME DE (*née* Françoise d'Aubigné) (1635–1719), second wife of Louis XIV, deserves mention here on two counts. As a young and penniless girl she became the wife of the novelist and dramatist Scarron, and had a salutary effect on some of his later plays, and on the conduct of his house and conversation; and in 1689, as virtual mistress of France, she induced Racine, after twelve years' silence, to write for the young ladies of her school at Saint-Cyr his beautiful poetic dramas *Esther* and *Athalie*. She herself also composed, for the same young ladies, a number of one-act sketches illustrating well-known proverbs, a genre much in vogue in society at this time, and later made famous by Alfred de Musset. These, preserved in manuscript, were not published until 1829.

MAIRET, JEAN (1604–86), one of the most important of early French dramatists. He was well educated, and arrived in Paris with his first play, a tragi-comedy entitled *Chryséide et Arimand*, in 1625. This he sold to a troupe of actors, and it later figured in the repertory of the Hôtel de Bourgogne and of Montdory's troupe. Mairet then entered the service of the Duke of Montmorency, where he came into contact with Théophile and Racan, whose plays were already well known to him. They had a great influence on his development, and inspired his second play, a pastoral, given in 1626. Mairet was soon recognized as the leading dramatist of the day, and when his *Sophonisbe* (1634), the first French tragedy to be written in accordance with the Unities, was a success, contemporary dramatists were ready to imitate him. In form and content *Sophonisbe* was a complete contrast to the tragi-comedies and pastorals which had preceded it, and a forerunner of French classical tragedy. Unfortunately Mairet attacked Corneille bitterly in the quarrel over *Le Cid*, and the opprobrium this has brought him from later generations has tended to obscure his importance as a dramatist. In his own day he was as successful as, and even more highly thought of than, Corneille. He was attached as dramatist to Montdory's troupe for some years, but in 1640 he gave up writing for the stage and entered the diplomatic service.

MAISON DE MOLIÈRE, see COMÉDIE-FRANÇAISE.

MAJESTIC THEATRE, NEW YORK. (1) This theatre, on Columbus Circle, opened on 20 Jan. 1903 with a musical version of the famous children's book, *The Wizard of Oz*. This had a long run, and was followed by the equally successful *Babes in Toyland*. In 1911 the theatre was renamed the Park, reopening on 23 Oct. with Ina Claire in *The Quaker Girl*. Three years later Mrs. Patrick Campbell and Philip Merivale appeared there in *Pygmalion*, and a notable revival of *The Merry Wives of Windsor* was given in 1917 with Constance Collier. In the following year the Society of American Singers leased the theatre for a season of light opera, which included a long run of the seldom-seen *Ruddigore*. After some further plays and musicals the theatre was devoted to films and burlesque, until, in 1925, Florenz Ziegfeld took it over and renamed it the Cosmopolitan. It later housed Max Reinhardt's company. As the International it saw *Sing Out, Sweet Land* (1945) and the 1946–7 season of the American Repertory Company, while it was renamed the Columbus Circle for the production in early 1946 of Maurice Evans's *G.I. Hamlet*.

(2) A second Majestic, on 44th Street, between Broadway and Eighth Avenue, opened on 28 Mar. 1927 with an ephemeral production which soon gave way to musical comedy, for which this theatre is eminently suitable. In 1928, in spite of fine acting by Leslie Faber and Madge Titheradge, *The Patriot* had only a short run. John Gielgud made his first appearance in New York in a minor part in this play. After several more failures, the theatre reverted to musical comedy and light opera, and in 1935 was taken over by Michael Chekhov and his Moscow Art Players for a series of Russian plays. Several thrillers were revived here, beginning with *The Bat*, but success was mainly achieved by musical plays, and in 1945 the Theatre Guild presented a musical version of *Liliom* as *Carousel*, which had a long run.

G. F.

MAKE-UP. Until the introduction of gas and electricity and the invention of greasepaint, make-up in the theatre is the history first and foremost of the use of disguise, and only to a very minor extent the history of the use of cosmetics. Even as drama antedates the theatre, so disguise antedates the drama, following so hard upon the first expressions of the mimetic instinct as to be indistinguishable from them in point of time. The face-painting of the primitive ritual dance, equally with its animal- and spirit-masks, is disguise; and in the classical theatre it was for purposes of disguise that Thespis painted his face with white lead coloured with cinnabar, before he invented the unpainted linen mask.

In the religious drama of medieval Europe similar conditions prevailed. Grotesque masks and animal heads were used for devils; and visors—that is, vizards or face-masks—are frequently mentioned in accounts and lists of properties. It is generally stated that white lead and gold paint were used for painting the face and hands for God or Christ, in spite of their injurious effects on the skin. In Jean Michel's *Le Passion* (1490), when Jesus appears transfigured on Mount Tabor, he is clad all in white and has 'une face et des mains toute d'or bruny. Et ung gran soleil à rays par derrière.' It is unlikely that *face* and *mains* mean mask and gloves; 'face' is, indeed, sometimes used in English for a theatrical mask, and 'white gloves' for Christ are mentioned in some English accounts; but it is to be noted that in another French play, when gloves are wanted for God and the Holy Ghost, the word *gants* is used (see *Le Livre de Conduite du Régisseur . . . pour le Mystère de la Passion . . . à Mons en 1501*, ed. Gustave Cohen, 1925). How far this practice was usual the evidence does not show. Generalizations about the use of gilt paint would appear to derive from a few particular items, and especially, perhaps, from the famous example in Vasari's *Lives of the Painters*, where in the life of Jacopo di Pontormo he recounts how, in the carnival celebrations for the creation of Pope Leo X in 1513, 'a naked gilded child' represented the Golden Age, and adds that 'the gilt boy, the child of a baker who had been paid 10 crowns, died soon after of the effects'. Burckhardt (*Civilization of the Renaissance in Italy*) also cites another instance of a child being gilded from head to foot for celebrations in Rome in 1473. This use of gilt paint, however, for special effects in the elaborate Italian secular festivals does not necessarily derive from or even relate to the practices of the religious drama throughout Europe. Cennino Cennini instructs artists to temper their colours with egg, oil, or liquid varnish, if they should be required to paint performers' faces for plays or masquerades; but like all other writers who mention the subject he strongly condemns the use of paint for cosmetic purposes, and refuses to give any information on the subject (*Il Libro dell' Arte, c. 1437*, trans. by D. V. Thompson as *The Craftsman's Handbook*, 1923).

In some of the French plays the angels had their faces painted red, as if they were cherubim. One rubric has the stage-direction

'N.B. Warn a painter to go to Heaven to paint the face of Raphael red; and Raphael must have his face as entirely reddened as the painter can manage' (Cohen, *Le Théâtre en France au Moyen Âge*, i, 1928). This particular theological confusion—or theatrical licence —would appear to derive its sanction from literature rather than from medieval art. It is to be noted, for example, that in the Fouquet miniatures of the famous *Book of Hours* of Étienne Chevalier (1452–60; reproduced in *Verve*, Nos. 5–6, 1939) the seraphim are blue and the cherubim red, in Heaven; whereas the ordinary angels, adoring the Virgin and Child on earth, have flesh-coloured faces. In Dante, however, the angel of the sixth terrace of the *Purgatorio* is wholly red, face and all, 'e giammai non si videro in fornace vetri o metalli si lucenti e rossi' (and never in a furnace were glass or metals seen so glowing and red). In the *Paradiso* the visible angels of the Empyrean are all described, without distinction of hierarchy, as having 'le facce tutte . . . di fiamma viva' (their faces all of living flame); and it is possible that when the play representing Raphael as the angel at the tomb requires him to have a reddened face this is due not so much to a theatrical carelessness of theological detail as to an attempt to reproduce the 'face of living flame' of literary tradition.

Paint for beautifying the human face takes us to the history of cosmetics. Whether it is as old as the war-paint of the savage may be arguable; but it is certainly as old as Assyrian civilization (2250 B.C.). The Assyrian noblemen, who oiled and curled and dyed their beards and hair, also whitened their faces with white lead, and dyed their eyebrows and lashes black and darkened the edges of the lids with *stibium* (finely powdered antimony). Egypt anticipated the twentieth century in its use of green eye-shadow and hennaed finger-nails. Cleopatra darkened her lashes and eyebrows with *kohl*; Jezebel painted her face; and at the court of Nero men and women alike whitened the skin with white lead or chalk and rouged the cheeks. The Crusaders are generally saddled with the responsibility of introducing to their European women-folk the cosmetics of the harem, since when the West has used them continuously, although their respectability quotient has varied greatly from century to century and even decade to decade, both in different countries and in different classes of society. Literature abounds with references, mostly satiric in tone; and it is perhaps not altogether unfair to judge of the general effect by such names as 'Lady Stucco', and by Sir Benjamin Backbite's description of Mrs. Evergreen, in *The School for Scandal*: ' 'tis not that she paints so ill—but, when she has finished her face, she joins it on so badly to her neck that she looks like a mended statue, in which the connoisseur may see at once that the head's modern, though the trunk's antique.'

The colouring ingredients of all paints are the dry powders known as pigments, obtained from minerals, vegetables, animals, insects: as, for example, the ochres, oxides, and carbonate compounds of metals; the sepia of the cuttle-fish, the dried body of the cochineal insect; the madder and indigo blue of these plants. When used in this powder form paint has generally been considered harmful to the skin, particularly white and the chromes, owing to the amount of lead these contain. The powder can be applied dry, and can be rubbed into or dusted over the skin; or it can be painted on to the skin after being mixed with water or some other liquid. Apart from injurious effects the chief drawback to a completely dry powder make-up is that it tends to run if its wearer gets hot or perspires. In the past, western European cosmetics have required little save the pigments which would provide the smooth white lily complexions, the rosy cheeks, and the cherry—or ruby—lips of popular fancy and song: together with blue for tracing veins, and kohl or antimony for eye make-up.

Theoretically the Elizabethan theatre had at its disposal the same cosmetic resources as the lady of fashion, who used to paint freely, if not always with discretion, to judge by Hamlet's reference to painting 'an inch thick'. The actor could also have obtained any of the pigments then used by artists. It is worth noting, however, that none of the contemporary diatribes against the theatre mentions face-painting; and that Stephen Gosson (*Plays Confuted in Five Actions*, 1582), while explicitly condemning the wearing of women's apparel by boys, and their counterfeiting of women's gestures and passions, makes no allusion to face-painting, though the practice itself, as indulged in by women, is abundantly censured in contemporary literature and especially in the drama. Philip Stubbes (*Anatomy of Abuses*, 1583), who condemns boy-actors and face-painting, never couples them: it is 'the women of England, many of them, who use to colour their faces with certain oils, liquors, unguents and waters made to that end'; the boy-actors are 'trained up in filthy speeches, unnatural and unseemly gestures'. There is no positive evidence to show that the Elizabethan boy-actor, aged from ten to thirteen, who played young women's parts in a theatre lit by daylight, either needed to make up or was actually made up. That it would be quite unnecessary for an ordinary healthy child is, indeed, borne out by a passage in Ellen Terry's *Memoirs* where, speaking of her son Gordon Craig, she describes 'Teddy', then aged 10 or 11, playing in *Eugene Aram*, as 'associated in my mind with one of the most beautiful sights upon the stage that I ever saw in my life . . . as he tied up the stage roses, his cheeks, untouched by rouge, put the reddest of them to shame'. And this, it must be remembered, was in the gas-lit, lime-lit Victorian stage, not in Shakespeare's theatre. Lacking similar evidence for the Elizabethan stage, we can only say that if the boy who played Olivia in *Twelfth Night* was indeed made up it must have been excellently done: crudely done, it would have wrecked the passage in I. v, where she unveils herself to Viola:

Olivia. ... we will draw the curtain and show you the picture ... is 't not well done?
Viola. Excellently done, if God did all.
Olivia. 'Tis in grain, sir; 'twill endure wind and weather.
Viola. 'Tis beauty truly blent, whose red and white
Nature's own sweet and cunning hand laid on ...

On the evidence, in fact, it would appear that the Elizabethan actor, whether man or boy, did not use make-up except for purposes of disguise, even when—to us—the advantage of paint seems obvious and simple, as in the well-known reference in Dekker's *Guls Horne-booke* (1609): 'Present not yourself on the stage ... until the quaking Prologue hath (by rubbing) got colour into his cheeks.' Friction, rather than paint, is indicated; though the latter is obviously the simpler method, if paint was easily available in the tiring-house for making up the boy players. Ghosts and murderers whitened their faces with chalk (see below); and we know that negroes and Moors were represented with coal-black faces, hands, &c., for which the texts give ample evidence, as well as the *Titus Andronicus* sketch of 1595 (reproduced in *The Library*, v, 1925, and Nicoll's *Development of the Theatre*). That umber may have been used for certain characters in plays involving disguises is perhaps suggested by the reference in *The Wild Goose Chase* (III. i) when Mirabel, realizing that he has been taken in by De Gard disguised as a lord of Savoy, exclaims, 'Now I remember him; All the whole cast on 's face, though it were umber'd, And mask'd with patches.' Whether Celia in *As You Like It* actually followed up her own suggestion (I. iv) and with 'a kind of umber smirched her face' to counterfeit a peasant's sunburnt complexion, the text does not indicate. Red was obviously required for Bardolph's nose, unless we make what is on the whole the more likely assumption that a false nose was worn. Having regard to the force of tradition in the theatre it is quite likely that the practice of smearing Cassio's face with snuff to indicate his drunken condition in *Othello*, II, iii is Elizabethan in origin, but there is no evidence of this. It was apparently still usual in the middle of the eighteenth century, and is commented on by Lloyd in his poem *The Actor* (1762):

But Michael Cassio might be drunk enough, Though all his features were not grimed with snuff.

Evidence of the use of make-up in the sixteenth-century Italian theatre is to be found in the *Dialoghi in materialia rappresentazione scenica* of Leone di Somi (c. 1565). There is a complete translation in the 1937 edition of Nicoll's *Development of the Theatre* (App. B). When considering the actor's physical suitability for a part, di Somi does not trouble about the features, 'since so much

can be done by the aid of make-up ... simulating a scar, turning the cheeks pale or yellow, or rendering an appearance of vigor, ruddiness, weakness or darkness'. To enable a beardless actor to play an old man he would simply 'paint his chin to make him appear shaven, with a fringe of hair showing under his cap. I should give him a few touches with the make-up brush on his cheeks and forehead, and by so doing I should make him seem aged, decayed and wrinkled.' Apart from the references to long white beards and appropriate wigs, we have no evidence of a similar kind to satisfy our curiosity about the English boy-actors who impersonated old men or women. All that we know about Salathiel (or Salmon) Pavy, whose memory is preserved by Ben Jonson's epitaph, is that he was a very good-looking boy, 'the stage's jewel', who between the ages of ten and thirteen was able to act 'old men so duly, As sooth the Parcae thought him one, He play'd so truly'. It may not be significant, but it is certainly noticeable that what Jonson singles out for praise is the boy's power of acting, not his appearance.

The stage for which di Somi made up his actors was artificially illuminated. In general, the Elizabethan and Jacobean playhouses, including the so-called 'private' theatres, gave daylight performances. It was not, however, the advent of stage lighting which introduced make-up to the English theatre. Such evidence as there is, even if it does not prove, does strongly suggest that make-up for enhancing the natural appearance came in with the actress, and that in the English theatres of the seventeenth and early eighteenth centuries face-painting was confined to women, except in the case of young men called upon to play old men's parts. T. G.'s satiric poem, *The Playhouse* (1703), when describing the attire of the tragedy king makes no mention of make-up; but the tragedy queen is make-up and very little else:

His royal consort next consults her glass,
And out of twenty boxes culls a face.
The whitening first her ghastly look besmears,
All pale and wan the unfinished form appears,
Till on her cheeks the blushing purple glows,
And a false virgin modesty bestows:
Her ruddy lips, the deep vermilion dyes,
Length to her brows the pencil's touch supplies,
And with black bending arches shades her eyes.

'Every look the pencil's art betrays', is T. G.'s criticism; and when her admirer goes behind the scenes 'He sees the blended colours melt with heat, And all the trickling beauty run with sweat'.

One of the most helpful and interesting pieces of evidence is provided by the Italian actor Riccoboni who saw the English comedian James Spiller play the part of an old man in *Crispin médecin*, somewhere about 1727 (see his *Historical Account of the Theatres in Europe*, 1738, trans. 1741). At first he refused to believe he was watching a young man of about twenty-six: the impression given was that of an actor with at least forty years' experience:

Had he only used a trembling and broken voice, and had only an extreme weakness possessed his body...I conceived it possible for a young actor, by the help of art, to imitate that debility of nature to such a pitch of exactness; but the wrinkles of his face, his sunk eyes, and his loose and yellow cheeks, the most certain marks of a great old age, were incontestable proofs.

Nevertheless, Riccoboni had to accept the truth,

that the actor to fit himself for the part of the old man spent an hour in dressing himself, and that with the assistance of several pencils he disguised his face so nicely, and painted artificially a part of his eyebrows and eyelids, that at the distance of six paces it was impossible not to be deceived.

Apart from its intrinsic interest this comment has the further interest that it is the only one of its kind in Riccoboni's book. Coming from an Italian actor who knew the theatres of Europe it should allow us to presume a considerable degree of skill in the use of this kind of disguise make-up among English actors of the early eighteenth century. Further, it would seem to suggest either that the skill described by di Somi was unusual in the sixteenth century or else that the practice of the Italian theatre had degenerated or altered since his time. It would be rash, however, to claim too much credit for the English actor in general throughout the whole of the eighteenth century on the strength of this single tribute. It should be offset, for example, by the remarks of F. G. Waldron, the 1789 editor of Downes's *Roscius Anglicanus*, who adds the following note to the comment made by Downes in 1708 on the actor Benjamin Johnson's skill in 'the art of painting':

I apprehend this means the painting of the face and marking it with dark lines to imitate the wrinkles of old age; a custom formerly carried to excess on the stage, though now a good deal disused: I have seen actors who were really older than the characters they were to represent mark their faces with black lines of Indian ink to such a degree that they appeared as if looking through a mask of wire. Mr. Garrick's skill in the necessary preparation of his face for the aged and venerable Lear and Lusignan was as remarkable as his performance of those characters was admirable.

It seems to be generally agreed that Garrick used make-up for the purposes of disguise with extreme skill. According to the French actor Noverre, even his friends sometimes failed to recognize him. Alongside of this we have persisting throughout the century the traditional and obviously crude disguises. Steele in 1709 (*Tatler*, 42), in his humorous inventory of theatrical properties, lists 'The complexion of a murderer in a bandbox, consisting of a large piece of burnt cork and a coal-black peruke'; and in 1784 we have T. Davies (*Dramatic Miscellanies*) describing Hippesley's make-up for the first murderer in *Macbeth*: 'his face was made pale with chalk, distinguished with large whiskers and a long black wig.' In *Humphry Clinker* (1771) Mrs. Tabitha Bramble reminds the actor

Quin how she had once been 'vastly entertained with your playing the ghost of Gimlet at Drury Lane, when you rose up through the stage with a white face and red eyes and spoke of *quails upon the frightful porcupine*'.

Besides the murderer's complexion Steele lists 'a bale of red Spanish Wool'. Spanish Wool and the 'Spanish Paper' demanded by Lady Wishfort in *The Way of the World* (III. i) were two of the popular forms of rouge; and though Steele's intention is satiric there is obviously critical significance in his use of the word 'bale'. Nor was he alone in his opinion of the crudity of the make-up of the average actress who painted to enhance her beauty. Anthony Aston, writing in 1741 in praise of Mrs. Barry (*Supplement to Life of Colley Cibber*), refers scathingly to 'the actresses of late times' who are afraid to move a muscle or show any change of facial expression 'lest they should crack the cerum, white-wash or other cosmetic trowelled on'. That an embellishing make-up was essential, however, appears to have been accepted throughout the century. The anonymous admirer who in 1753 wrote *A Letter to Miss Nossiter* comments that nature has been kind to this lady above all other actresses on the stage, in that 'she hath so fine a natural bloom that she is under no necessity of wearing paint'—a fact which he discovered because at her first entry, as Juliet, 'she grew pale as cambric, but, as she recovered, her colour returned beyond what art could counterfeit'. Incidentally, his concluding remark confirms Aston's suggestion that the normal make-up was a complete coating of paint which inhibited facial expression, so that mobility of countenance was something which called for special comment: 'This [i.e. the lack of make-up] is no small assistance to her *surprising expression*; for I observed several times afterwards her colour came and went as the passion required it.' Steele in *The Spectator* (No. 41, 1711) also describes the 'dead, uninformed countenances' of ladies who paint: 'the muscles of a real face sometimes swell with soft passion, sudden surprise, and are flushed with agreeable confusions.' Not so with the Picts, as he terms them, who have a 'fixed insensibility'. The same impression is echoed by Fanny Burney's Lord Orville (*Evelina*, 1778), who observes that the difference between natural and artificial colour is very easily discerned: 'that of nature is mottled, and varying; that of art *set*, and *too* smooth; it wants that animation, that glow, that *indescribable something*' which he sees in Evelina's complexion. The italics are his lordship's.

Apart from the would-be embellishing make-up, the balance of the evidence suggests that the eighteenth-century actress did not, like the actor, use paint for the purpose of disguise. When Peg Woffington 'actually painted her handsome face with wrinkles and crowsfeet to give effect to a play of Shakespeare's' this was sufficiently unusual to excite comment; and that Mrs. Pritchard, when playing Jane Shore, did not make up in character is obvious from a criticism in John Hill's book, *The Actor* (1750): 'Nothing could be so unnatural as to see that plump and rosy figure endeavour to present us with a view of the utmost want and starving.' Two of Colley Cibber's anecdotes are equally helpful to indicate the normal procedure of the actor. When he first began to act, he tells us in his *Apology*, his ambition to play the hero and the lover was soon snubbed on account of the insufficiency of his voice, his 'meagre person', and his 'dismal *pale* countenance'. That the obvious remedy of a straight male make-up was never at this time envisaged as a possibility is emphasized by his further description of his own appearance in *The Orphan*, on the day when his death had been reported in *Mist's Journal*. He had 'that very day just crawl'd out, after having been some weeks laid up by a fever', and 'the surprise of the audience at my unexpected appearance on the very day I had been dead in the news, *and the paleness of my looks*, seem'd to make it a doubt whether I was not the ghost of my real self departed'. On the other hand, when at the beginning of his career he set out to imitate Doggett's performance of Fondlewife in *The Old Bachelor*, he tells us he 'laid the tint of forty years more than my real age upon my features', and impressed the audience by the likeness.

One of the best-known anecdotes of the eighteenth-century stage, told by every historian of the theatre, about Barton Booth's first appearance in Dublin in the name part of *Oroonoko*, throws interesting light not only upon the subject of negro make-up but also upon the use of grease in connexion with theatrical make-up. According to W. R. Chetwood, for twenty years prompter at Drury Lane (*A General History of the Stage*, 1749), 'It being very warm weather, in his last scene of the play, as he waited to go on, he inadvertently wiped his face, that when he entered he had the appearance of a chimney-sweeper (his own words).' For the next performance, therefore, an actress

fitted a crape to his face, with an opening proper for the mouth, and shaped in form for the nose; but in the first scene one part of the crape slipped off: 'And 'zounds', said he (he was a little apt to swear) 'I looked like a magpie! When I came off they lamp-blacked me for the rest of the night, that I was flayed before it could be got off again!'

Chetwood's own helpful footnote explains that the proper composition for blackening the face is 'ivory-black and pomatum, which is with some pains cleaned with fresh butter'.

It is clear from the many references, both precise and casual, in literature and in the literature of the subject, that the use of oils and fats and pomatums as preservatives and beautifiers of the skin is as old as the use of cosmetic pigments. It is also clear, from Chetwood's note, that the use of greasy substances in connexion with theatrical make-up is at least as old as the first half of the eighteenth

century, if not considerably older. Nevertheless, the introduction of grease paints as we know them, and as a commercial product, belongs to the latter half of the nineteenth century. Until then, all make-up, whether used with grease or some liquid medium, was basically a powder make-up.

Apart from references in literature, the earliest comprehensive account of the powder make-up as used in eighteenth-century society is that given in 1740 by Charles Lillie, perfumer, of Beaufort Buildings, in the Strand, in a manuscript embodying the results of his thirty years' business experience. His book, which was not actually published until 1822, is called *The British Perfumer, Snuff Manufacturer and Colourman's Guide*. It deals with every kind of cosmetic then in use and has a chapter (No. 51) on 'Paints, or Colours for the Face'. Carmine, which is the finest red colour, derives from cochineal, is safe to use, and comes from Germany; but there is also a cheap variety adulterated with vermilion and red lead, and definitely poisonous. The vermilion is made in England, and is chiefly used for wash balls. Dutch Pink is a yellow colour made from whitening or chalk, sold at 1s. a pound, and to be obtained—like yellow ochre and umber, powdered and sifted—at any colourman's shop. Ivory black is a black powder made from calcined ivory turnings. It is cheap, and so are white lead (ceruse), and flake white, which can also be had ready ground and powdered from the colourman.

Carmine he considers too high and glaring a colour for the complexion, 'notwithstanding the knowledge of which some ladies still continue to use it'. French Red is prepared from carmine in three shades: the palest is nearest to a flesh red. All these red powders are best put on with a fine camel-hair pencil. Spanish Wool is of several sorts, but that made in London by the Jews is by far the best, and is 'a bright pale red'. That which comes from Spain is a very dark red. It is made up in what he calls cakes (i.e. pads), 'which ought to be of the size and thickness of a crown piece'; and the best of them 'shine and glisten, between a green and a gold colour'. Spanish Papers, in which the colour is laid on the paper instead of tinging the wool, are made up for carrying in the pocket-book. Chinese Wool, which comes from China, is made up in large round loose cakes about 3 in. in diameter, as loose as carded wool. The finest kind gives 'a most lovely and agreeable blush to the cheek'. Portuguese Dishes, containing red paint for the face, are of two sorts: the one made in Portugal is scarce, the paint 'being of a fine pale pink hue and very beautiful in its application to the face'. The other, made in London, is of a 'dirty muddy red colour: it passes very well, however, with those who never saw the Portuguese Dishes, or who wish to be cheaply beautified'. The genuine dishes are rough on the outside: the London imitation is smoothly glazed. Chinese Boxes of Colour are not easily obtained. They are beautifully painted and japanned, and each contains two dozen papers, and inside each of these there are three smaller papers. One contains black for the eyebrows: the second is a paper of fine green colour, which when fresh makes a very fine red for the face; and the third contains about half an ounce of white powder, prepared from real pearls, for giving an alabaster colour to the neck and parts of the face. The colours in the dishes and wools and green papers 'are commonly laid on by the tip of the little finger, previously wetted'. All have some gum in them, so are apt to leave a shine on the cheek, 'which too plainly shews that artificial beauty has been resorted to'. For whitening the skin he recommends Pearl Powder. The best is made from genuine powdered pearls, the next best from bismuth and starch! Camphorated and chemical wash balls, which make no lather and are manufactured specially for ladies, 'are wholly designed to leave whiteness on the hands and face'.

The earliest comprehensive account of the use of make-up in the English theatre is that given by Leman Thomas Rede in his manual for theatrical aspirants, *The Road to the Stage* (1827). It remained a popular handbook for at least fifty years, and Rede's make-up instructions were freely borrowed, with or without acknowledgements, by most manuals of acting.

Rede begins by stating that make-up is an essential part of a performer's duty, and points out that 'the late introduction of gas into our theatres has rendered a more powerful colouring than that formerly used decidedly necessary'. He recommends 'too little rather than too much colour', but reminds actors that 'when heated, colour will sink, and it may be well in the course of a long part to retouch the countenance'. All paint being injurious to the skin one should 'neutralize its pernicious qualities as much as possible'. Rouge he condemns as an 'ineffective colour' which 'seldom lies well on the face'. 'Chinese vermilion boiled in milk, and then suffered to dry, and afterwards mixed with about half the quantity of carmine, is decidedly the best colour an actor can use.' He does not agree with the popular idea that this colour is 'too powerful for a female face'.

His instructions make it evident that it was already an established theatrical method to apply the pigment over some kind of greasy base:

previous to painting it is best to pass a napkin, with a little pomatum upon it, over the part to receive the colour, then touch the cheek with a little hair powder, which will set the colour, and then lay on the vermilion and carmine. A rabbit's foot is better than anything else for distributing the paint equally.

That individual actors, however, were experimenting along lines which were to lead them to grease paints proper, is obvious from his account of how

the late Mr. Knight [1774-1826] used to cover his cheek with a thin coat of pomatum, and paint

upon it, without rubbing the face dry; but this, which he effected cleverly, may be found difficult to perform: where it is necessary to have a powerful colour, as in Country Boys, Clowns, etc., it is decidedly the proper method.

Similarly, that grease or oil was also used to remove paint after the performance may be inferred from his notes on how to remove colour on the stage 'in any scene of fright or surprise'. If the face is turned away from the audience 'a greased napkin' can be employed: if in full view 'the thing can generally be sufficiently effected by oiling the inside of your gloves, and burying your face in your hands at the moment of accusation; colour adheres to oil immediately'.

Although he considers that 'to ladies it is of the utmost importance', Rede gives no instructions for female make-up; his reason being that 'ladies have generally sufficient knowledge of the arts of decking the human face divine'. Lining the face with the wrinkles of age, he asserts, is an art little understood on the English stage, although 'our Parisian neighbours are adepts'. For this purpose he recommends 'a round wire, like a black hairpin', held in the smoke of a candle, as giving 'a finer and more distinct line than can be made by dipping it in Indian ink'. He condemns 'the common though slovenly habit' of making moustaches and whiskers with a burnt cork, which involves 'the danger of transferring your lip ornaments to the mouth of a lady if it be necessary in the scene to salute her'. A 'camel's hair pencil and Indian ink' will give 'a more correct imitation of nature', and if the brush is wetted in gum water the ink will not rub.

He has no instructions to give for eye make-up, though he says that for situations such as Macbeth's return with the daggers after the murder of Duncan 'it is usual to whiten the face and blacken beneath the eyes, which gives them a hollow and sunken appearance'. He also describes the interesting trick-make-up work of 'a celebrated tragedian of the present day' when playing Richard III:

[he] always removes his colour in the dreaming scene, and applies pomatum to his countenance, and then drops water upon his forehead; and this he effects whilst tossing and tumbling in the assumed throes of mental agony, [so that] on rushing to the front at 'Give me another horse—bind up my wounds' his countenance is an exemplification of the text—'Cold drops of sweat hang on my trembling limbs.'

He is instructive, too, on the subject of Othello's make-up:

Othello used not in former days to sport a coloured countenance, but wore the same sables as Mungo in *The Padlock*; but this, as being destructive of the effect of the face, and preventing the possibility of the expression being noted, has become an obsolete custom. A tawny tinge is now the colour used for the gallant Moor, for Bajazet [in *Tamerlane*] and Zanga [in *The Revenge*]; Spanish brown [a red brown] is the best preparation.

Spanish brown should also be used for the Moor, Sadi, in *Barbarossa*, for Bulcazin in

The Mountaineers, and Rolla in *Pizarro*; though it is very common, in these parts, 'especially for comic performers, to use only an extraordinary quantity of vermilion or carmine spread over the whole of the face'. Previous to using the Spanish brown the whole of the face should be rubbed with pomatum, or the colour will not adhere. Some persons mix the colouring with carmine, and, wetting it, apply it to the face, but I never saw this plan answer.

For genuine negro parts the face, neck and hands should be covered with a thin coat of pomatum, or, what is better, though more disagreeable, of lard; then burn a cork to powder, wet it with beer (which will fix the colouring matter), and apply it with a hare's foot or a cloth. . . . A strong colouring of carmine should be laid upon the face after the black, as otherwise the expression of countenance and eye will be destroyed.

Black gloves he rejects as 'unnatural', because the colour is too intense to represent the skin; and considers that the 'arms of black silk, often worn in Hassan [in *The Castle Spectre*] have a very bad effect; armings dyed with a strong infusion of Spanish annatto [an orange-red dye] look much more natural'.

T. H. Lacy's *Art of Acting* (1863) quotes Rede freely, with and without acknowledgement, both on make-up and other subjects; but it is to be noticed that he insists on the importance of a dry, non-greasy surface: 'Every one, on entering the theatre at night, should wash his face, and after drying it thoroughly pass lightly a powder-puff over it. This is highly necessary to those whose skin is naturally greasy.' W. J. Sorrell in *The Amateur's Handbook* (1866) supplements Rede and Lacy with a few specific hints, such as, that rouge should be placed well under the eyes to make them sparkle, that cold cream and a dry towel should be used to remove make-up, and that sepia should be used for lining for old age and for sinking the eyes by painting underneath the lower lids.

The first comprehensive manual, illustrated, and devoted only to make-up, is *How to 'Make-Up'. A Practical Guide to the Art of 'Making-Up', for Amateurs, etc. . . . By 'Haresfoot and Rouge'. Copyrighted 1877. London: Samuel French.* The anonymous author explains that it has been written 'not so much with the idea of offering advice to Professionals' as with that of instructing amateurs and beginners, and to supply a long-felt want. It lists all the articles required, both in the text and in an advertisement which prices them. They represent the full resources of the powder make-up box of the nineteenth century, and are as follows: Pearl and Violet Powder, Prepared Whiting and Fuller's Earth, Rouge and Dark or Ruddy Rouge, Carmine, Mongolian, Crayon d'Italie for the Veins, Eyebrow Pencil, Powdered Antimony, Prepared Burnt Cork, Email Noir, Paste Powder, and Spirit Gum— all priced at 1*s.*: Chrome, Dutch Pink, Blue, Cosmetique, Joining Paste, Haresfoot, Powder Puff—all at 6*d.*: Burnt Umber, Indian Ink

and Lining Brush, at 2*d.* Good soap, a sponge, and towels are the only things recommended for removing the make-up; and the author follows Lacy in refusing to allow a greasy base: 'it is absolutely necessary that the face should be *clean shaved and thoroughly washed*, as it is impossible to "Make-Up" well if the skin is at all greasy.'

The instructions are given under the following headings: Youth, Manhood, Maturity, Old Age, Death; Low Comedy and Character Parts; Sailors, Soldiers and Countrymen; Clowns; Irish, Scotch, Frenchmen; Germans; Americans; Jews; Complexions—Pale and Wan, Pale and Sallow, Dark and Olive; Creoles, Indians, Mulattoes, Negroes; Chinese; Eyebrows and Whiskers, Nose and Chin, Mouth and Teeth, Hands and Arms. The last two sections deal with 'The Ladies' and 'Statuary'.

For Youth, Manhood, and Ladies, the rouge is applied on a base of Pearl or Violet Powder, and with a fine camel's hair brush a thin Burnt Umber line is painted under the lower eyelashes. A touch of rouge on the chin 'brightens and throws up the complexion'. The base for Maturity, Old Age, Low Comedy, Sailors, Soldiers, Countrymen, Irish, Scots, French, Germans, Americans, Jews, and Creoles is prepared Fuller's Earth. For Death and 'Pale and Wan' (e.g. Louis XI or Eugene Aram) the base is Prepared Whiting, as also for Clowns. That the powder, fuller's earth, and whiting bases were to some extent regarded as the equivalent of a modern grease base is evident from the directions for the Creole make-up, which conclude: 'Although it is not absolutely necessary to prepare the face first with Fuller's Earth, it is advisable to do so as the Mongolian is then more easily removed.' The only time grease is suggested is for Red Indians. Mongolian is advised as the chief ingredient, to give the characteristic rich tawny colour. One method is 'to mix it with beer or water and to apply it with a small piece of sponge, and when dry to add a strong colouring of Carmine to the cheeks. . . . The other, and by far the better plan, as it looks more natural and is much easier to wash off, is *first* to paint the line under the lower eyelashes, and any that may be required to indicate age, very strongly with Indian Ink; then to mix some of the Mongolian with a little Cold Cream and apply it well to the face, neck and throat, and finally to put a strong colouring of Carmine to the cheeks and to darken the eyebrows with Cosmetique.' For Othello 'a little of the Prepared Burnt Cork should be mixed with the Mongolian. The hands should be coloured to match the face, or a pair of Brown silk gloves may be worn.'

Under several of the headings special instructions are given for what are described as 'strongly-marked character parts'. If a strongly-marked Irishman, for example, is required, 'with a moderate-sized camel's hair brush paint the underpart of the eyebrows and well into the hollows of the eyes with Burnt

Umber to give them a deep-set appearance. Then fix on a pair of heavy black eyebrows, low down over the eyes, to give them a "beetle-browed" appearance. . . . Lastly, put just a tinge of Rouge on the eyelids and under the eyes, and rub the upper lip, chin and throat well with Powdered Blue, so as to give them a dirty and unshaved appearance.' The writer does not approve of the exaggerated dress and make-up usually employed for Americans, but Slave Owners are classified as strongly-marked and given a dark complexion with a slight tinge of Mongolian, also lines at the corners of the mouth with 'a downward tendency'. The make-up for ordinary Frenchmen 'differs very little from that of English characters of the same class, the foreign accent being the principal requirement'.

Detailed instructions are given for altering the shape of the nose for Low Comedy characters such as Bardolph and Blueskin, 'to give it that bloated, blotchy appearance so noticeable in drunkards'. A truly horrific illustration shows the exaggerated effect achieved. One method is 'to gum on to the end of the nose a piece of wool, press it down to the shape and size required, then powder it well with Rouge . . . the cheeks may also be enlarged in the same way. . . . Blotches, warts and pimples may be made by sticking on small pieces of wool and colouring them either red or brown.' The better way, however, is to use paste powder, mix it with water to the consistency of dough, and 'fix it to the nose with Spirit Gum', moulding it to the shape and size required, and powdering it with rouge. 'To impart to the nose the hooked appearance characteristic of the Jew, shade that portion of it just over the bridge, in between the eye-brows, slightly with Burnt Umber; also define very carefully the nostrils.' Mouth and teeth can also be altered. 'To give the mouth a one-sided appearance, for Coster-mongers, etc., paint a line upwards from one corner of the mouth, and another from the other corner downwards.' To 'stop-out' two or three front teeth for Old Men, Old Hags, Gipsies, or Witches, Email Noir could be used then as now, and is described as 'undoubtedly an improvement upon the old-fashioned method of sticking on Cobbler's Wax'.

The 'Death' make-up is intended for such characters as Lear, Werner, Louis XI, and Mathias, and is carefully described. The pre-pared whiting base is powdered with a good colouring of Dutch pink: the hollows of the eyes, underneath the eyes and under the brows, are darkened with powdered antimony, 'taking care, however, not to let any get on the eyelids'; and 'the hollows of the cheeks and temples, the throat, the chin, the upper lip (if no moustache be worn)' are similarly powdered, and a very slight touch of it given to the sides of the nose and in between the eyebrows. 'Put a little Chrome on the eyelids, nostrils, and down the front of the nose. Darken with Burnt Umber the hollow in the centre over the upper lip, also the hollows at the corners of the mouth. Put a little of the Powdered Blue on the lips in order to give them that ashy hue that is so noticeable in death, and paint the lines about the eyes, fore-head and mouth, etc., according to the age of the character to be represented. Then powder the whole slightly with Pearl Powder. This "Make-Up", with the addition of a pair of Gray eyebrows and a Grizzly beard will also apply to the Ghost in *Hamlet*.'

Like *The Road to the Stage*, the various editions of 'Haresfoot and Rouge' have been more or less thumbed out of existence. But there is one copy known to the present writer which has been largely reset, and which con-tains an extra section entitled 'Grease Paints'. It has the original imprint, 'Copyrighted 1877', and may be a later issue printed in that year. In the absence of contradictory evidence the obvious inference is that during 1877 grease paints first made their appearance in this country as a successful commercial product. At the most we need allow only a four years' margin-for-error in date, as L. Leichner's London, Ltd. (founded 1928) possess sticks known to have been imported in 1881.

That these paints described by 'Haresfoot and Rouge', and specified as German in all the early advertisements, were indeed Leich-ner's products admits of no real doubt. Until the turn of the century the firm had no com-petitors, either here or in Europe. Between the 1820s and the 1870s individual actors had experimented with the grease-paint idea; and S. J. A. Fitzgerald (*How to Make-Up*, 1902) singles out Hermann Vezin in particular, quoting his own statement, 'I know I mixed a lot of colour with melted tallow in Phila-delphia in 1857'. Grease paint as we know it, however, sold in round sticks, was the inven-tion of Ludwig Leichner (1836– ?), the Wag-nerian opera singer. About 1865 Leichner was in touch with the University of Würzburg, and either undertook some study of chemistry, or was given by the faculty such information and help as he needed to enable him to work out the formula which resulted in the original Leichner grease paints. He and his wife manufactured them at home, and they were used by Leichner and his fellow singers until a growing professional demand led to the founda-tion in 1873 of the business enterprise which has since become world-famous, and which still uses the original formula (information supplied by Messrs. Leichner).

The account given by 'Haresfoot and Rouge' in what may be called his Second Edition, Re-vised, (?) 1877, is the earliest description of grease paints as first used in the English theatre. Their introduction, he asserts, has very much simplified the art of making-up, and has ren-dered it more effective, compared with the old method. 'These paints impart a clearer and more lifelike appearance to the skin, the lights and shades . . . for old men and character parts being more easily graduated. . . . Being of a greasy nature they are to a great extent impervious to perspiration. This is in itself sufficient to recommend their use, especially for any very arduous character, as it enables the actor to go through his part without fear of his make-up being affected by his exertions. These paints are made by special machinery with chemically pure fat and purified colours free from lead. They will be found very soft to use, no hard rubbing or heating required in applying them.' A slight coating of cocoa butter, he says, should be used to prepare the skin: then, 'after removing a small portion of the foil, rub the paint on the cheeks and forehead, and then with the tips of the fingers smear the composition all over the face'. A 'liberal application' of the cocoa butter should be used to clean the face afterwards.

Only a general instruction is given: namely, to use the flesh tints in conjunction with the auxiliary colours, chrome, blue-black, red, and white. Each stick is numbered and described. No. 1 is 'the lightest flesh colour made', for ladies with delicate complexions; 1½ 'is also used by ladies, especially for chambermaid parts'. No. 2 can be used by ladies and gentlemen; 2½ is 'the most popular colour in use', invaluable for all youthful parts; 3 is 'a florid shade, very useful for character parts', and 3½ 'is somewhat darker, suitable for men of 30 to 35, being a little more sunburnt in appearance than No. 3'. No. 4 is the deepest flesh colour made, 'a dark, ruddy colour, suitable for soldiers, sailors, countrymen, etc.' No. 5 is a light yellow, used for old men; and No. 6, somewhat darker, can be used in conjunction with it. No. 7 is a brown, 'suitable for Mulattoes', and No. 8 a reddish brown for Indians. Chrome can be used with No. 7 for Chinamen. All these sticks are priced at 6d. Thin sticks, used for lining only, cost 4d. These numbers, still in use, are those originally given to the various colours by Leichner himself.

The instructions for using the liners are slightly more detailed. The black liner is intended for darkening the eyebrows and lids, also for 'very strong wrinkles'. Brown is 'more suitable for wrinkling the face where the characters are near the audience'. Lake is 'a new tint which has been lately introduced', has 'a very soft appearance when used for wrinkles, and is most effective and useful for blotches, etc., in drunken parts'. White is used 'for shading the wrinkles on the face, and for the high lights'. This is the only indication given anywhere in the book that the painting-in of high lights was an accepted part of make-up technique. Blue liners are to be used for the veins, and also for the eyes: 'a line made with this colour round the eyelashes, and a second line with the black will be found most effective.' 'An elegant tin case containing 14 of the most useful sticks' costs 7s.

From this time onwards the old-fashioned powder make-up was gradually superseded in the theatre by grease paint. That the powder had indeed been harmful and dangerous to use is asserted by all the authorities on cosmetics. Eugene Rimmel in his *Book of Perfumes* (1864) writes: 'Paints for the face I cannot conscientiously recommend. Rouge is innocuous in itself, being made of cochineal and safflower; but whites are often made of deadly poisons, such as cost poor Zelger his life a few months since.' This unfortunate Belgian opera singer died, according to *The Musical World* (23 July 1864), after a long and painful illness caused by blood-poisoning which he had contracted three years before from using a new composition containing white lead to whiten his beard and moustaches when playing Walter in 'Guillaume Tell' at Covent Garden. A. J. Cooley (*The Toilet and Cosmetic Arts*, 1866) is equally emphatic, though he adorns his tale with a less fatal moral. Deprecating the use by fashionable women of the metallic compounds which give greater brilliance to the complexion, he lists pearl powder (subchloride of bismuth), pearl white, and hydrated oxide of bismuth as containing poisonous elements, and points out that these preparations are darkened by sulphuretted hydrogen fumes and the smoke given off by coal fires, so that 'there are many instances recorded, and I have known more than one myself, of a whole company being suddenly alarmed by the fair complexion of one of its belles being thus in part transformed into a sickly gray or black'.

It is perhaps curious, therefore, that the use of powder make-up, both for the stage and in social life, should have taken such an unconscionable time a-dying. As late as 1882 Gustave Garcia in *The Actor's Art* refers only to powder make-up, although he recommends 'cold cream instead of water for the mixing of colours: not only does it spread evenly on the face without patches, but the perspiration does not affect it, nor does the skin get so easily injured'. In 1883 Dutton Cook in *On the Stage* gives powder make-up advice only, and does not even mention the existence of grease paints. Powder make-up boxes were advertised by make-up manuals as late as 1902; and a powder make-up is still used by a few actors to-day. By 1890, however, grease paint had obviously established itself. C. H. Fox in *The Art of Make-Up* (1890) speaks of its 'almost universal adoption' during the last ten years, points out the many advantages it has 'over the powders formerly employed', and recommends it as not merely innocuous but even positively beneficial to the skin. His book is the first to give detailed instructions for grease paint make-up, and he explains many points which were left obscure by 'Haresfoot and Rouge'. He deals clearly, for example, with high lights and shadows, pointing out that the former emphasize a feature while the latter make it less prominent: 'shadows and high lights should nearly always be used in conjunction', so that each heightens the other's effect. For high lights he recommends a flesh tint lighter than the ground colour: everything must be toned in, and 'no line, as such, should ever be left on the face'. For lining almost any colour except black can be used: crimson lake is the most popular. Cocoa butter or vaseline is recommended as the base, to be wiped off with a towel before the ground work is applied thinly and evenly, not forgetting the neck. 'The rouge: i.e. bright scarlet grease paint' is applied next after the ground colour. It must be smeared on the cheek bones and rubbed in, taking care not to leave a line. A touch of it on the chin and under the eyebrows is recommended. He favours white rather than a coloured powder, and recommends fuller's earth for old make-ups. He considers it is 'an open question how far expressions should be painted on the face; but as it is almost impossible that one expression can be required during a whole play it is advisable that, if painted at all, it should be done only so lightly as to help the face when it assumes that character. To do this it is necessary that the expression be assumed, and the lines so produced be painted in and toned down and the high lights added.'

By 1895 a wider range of colours could be obtained. To the sticks listed by 'Haresfoot and Rouge', *Lynn's Practical Hints on Making-Up* adds the following: No. 5½, for Chinese, Yankees, etc.; 6½ for Japanese; No. 8, now described as Armenian Bole, used for sinking the eyes, and with No. 5 for American Indians; No. 9, Dark Sunburnt, for old sailors and fishermen; No. 10, Brown, for Arabs, Negroes, Hindus; No. 11, Burnt Umber; No. 12, Black, for Minstrels, and with No. 10 for Negroes; No. 13, Red Brown; No. 14, Chocolate, for Mulattoes; No. 16, Dark Brown, for Indians; No. 20, White, for Clowns and Statuary. This particular manual recommends Mascaro for greying the moustache and eyebrows: defines *wig-paste* as 'another name for grease paint'; advises stumps instead of liners for broad work such as sinking the eyes, and vermilion for shading and enlarging the mouth; and lists both spirit-gum and wet-white, as well as nose-paste for building up the nose, cheeks, jaws, etc. It points out that make-up for electric light should not be as heavy as for gas, that more care is needed, and that all lines used for shading must be toned down by powdering. *Turner's Complete Guide to Theatrical Make-Up* (1898) gives both grease and powder instructions, and considers that for close effects the powder make-up is the better. He states that the powder is frequently used in conjunction with grease paints by professionals.

The instructions and hints given by the half-dozen or more books on make-up published between 1900 and 1920 vary little; but S. J. Adair Fitzgerald's *How to Make-Up* (1902) deserves special mention because it attempts the first concise sketch of the history of the subject. By 1926 Leichner's had added to the foregoing list of colours a No. 4½ Reddish Brown, an 8a Delicate Yellow, an 8b Deep Greenish Yellow, a 15 Fiery Light Brown (for Greeks and Romans), an entire new range of fourteen 'Lit.' shades—among them, Lit. K, the modern 'fleshing' shade,

a combination of Nos. 5 and 9, a range of three new shades for women, Star Girl, Star Lady, and Star Madam, described respectively as 'very delicate natural light-yellowish', 'yellowish pink for modern stage lighting', and 'warm yellowish shade for modern stage lighting'; also six 'special glaring shades' for revue, music-hall, and circus. By 1938 the *Leichner Handbook on Make-Up for Stage and Screen* listed a colour range of 54 sticks, 30 liners, 24 shades of eye-shadow, 15 shades of powder, 7 of water-black for darkening eyelashes, eyebrow pencils in 7 shades, and a range of 30 rouges—all these for theatrical use and distinguished from the special ranges which now cover film, colour-film, and television work. Grease paint is now packed in tubes and tins, but these have not superseded the ordinary sticks. Liquid make-up, applied with a sponge, is available in the same shades as the paints; and a recent innovation is the 'water-moist' make-up, greaseless, and packed in tubes. The descriptions of some of the colours now differ considerably from those attached to the same numbers at the beginning of the century. No. 5, for example, has become Ivory (used for groundwork), and 5½ is Dark Ivory (used for Hamlet); 6½ is Sallow Grey Brown, 10 is Dull Yellowish Brown (Spanish), and 11 Deep Dark Brown (African Native). Leichner's 13, Red Brown, for Mexicans in 1926, is now allotted to Old Fishermen, and a 13a has been added for Egyptians.

Modern grease paint, save in its cheaper forms, rules out for its fat base the lard or suet or tallow recommended for bases by Rede and other early writers and experimenters. Liquid or hard paraffin, beeswax, and almond- or peach-kernel oil are among the most favoured ingredients. Lanolin or white wax helps to give the necessary tackiness for powder. The dry base, with which the fat base and the pigment must be combined in suitable proportions, is generally made from precipitated chalk, kaolin, or zinc oxide. The pigment must be perfectly mixed with the dry base: this mixture is then added to the fat base and milled in a paint-mill. The liquid is then run into moulds, and the resultant sticks are wrapped in tinfoil or cellophane. In the Leichner process the grinding, milling, and mixing take as much as six weeks. Standard recipes for compounding typical paints are given by W. A. Poucher, in *Perfumes, Cosmetics and Soaps* (4th ed., 1932). The flesh tints from 1 to 3 are compounded from reds and yellows: the other flesh numbers are obtained by adding one or other of the lakes (as, crimson or geranium) and adjusting the other tones. No. 3½, for example, known as 'slightly sunburnt', uses crimson lake, golden ochre, and burnt sienna. For blues, cobalt, chinese, and ultramarine are used: in the carmines, the deeper tints are obtained by the addition of scarlet and vermilion: rose tints combine red lake and madder lake.

In the modern commercial theatre the

make-up that embellishes and the make-up that disguises are of equal importance. The first is the 'straight' make-up; the other is the 'character' make-up. The first aims at restoring natural colour by using paints that will stand up to the effects of artificial lighting as nature cannot, and at restoring natural line and features by emphasizing or bringing up the high lights, restoring 'natural' or accustomed shadows, and eliminating the 'unnatural'. The intensity and the quality and the colours of the artificial light, together with the methods used to concentrate it upon the acting area, are responsible for the effects which it is the business of make-up to conceal. Intensity destroys natural colour, and also natural light and shade, flattening the features and creating false lights and shadows. Normal daylight is reflected on to us: in the theatre light is generally directed on to the performer from floods, battens, spots, and floats (see LIGHTING). Under these conditions make-up is essential for the illusion of reality and 'naturalness'.

The actor's attitude to make-up has always varied. What is known in the profession as a 'Sadler's Wells make-up' could be encountered in the early years of the present century, and expresses perhaps not merely the economical mind but the grudging concession. All that is required for the Sadler's Wells make-up is a couple of tobacco tins, into which is scraped from the dressing-room walls white distemper and red or brown distemper: for shadow work one merely runs the finger along in the dust under the dressing-table shelf.

Now and again the individual refuses the aid of make-up entirely: the outstanding example is Eleonora Duse. Paul Schlenther, commenting on her first appearance in Berlin, describes how every emotion that stirs within her is reflected in her face, and considers that her whole bearing and figure is equally expressive. 'No living person has ever looked so like a corpse as Mme Duse in the character of Fedora feeling the effects of the poison in her body and in her soul. For these transformations she needs no external artifice, not even the artifice of paint, which she seems to despise. She achieves them solely through the force of her imagination.' Genius makes its own laws, in the theatre as elsewhere; but perhaps the wisest comment comes from Ellen Terry's *Memoirs*, in the passages where she discusses Henry Irving's use of make-up:

Make-up was, indeed, always his servant, not his master. He knew its uselessness when not informed by the spirit.... Irving's Lesurques was different from his Dubosc because of the way he held his shoulders, because of his expression.... He used to come on the stage looking precisely like the Vandyke portraits [of Charles I], but not because he had been building up his face with wig-paste and similar atrocities. His make-up in this, as in other parts, was the process of *assisting subtly and surely the expression from within*.

Nevertheless, make-up is an art. Interest, practice, and experience should enable anyone to become genuinely competent; but as in most things to do with the theatre, there is flair or inspiration, and some people have it and some have not. Talk to actors on the subject, and watch them at work, and the difference between the artist and the practitioner will be obvious. Always, the individual who excels has his own little tricks and devices and secrets—sometimes jealously guarded. He still makes his own experiments in mixing colours, trying new methods; aiming, nowadays, at the complete illusion of reality—the perfectly executed disguise of a character make-up, or the straight make-up which makes him look equally natural whether viewed from stalls or gallery. He may draw his inspiration from anything; from his own visualization of the person he presents; from a single item of make-up, such as a wig, which starts him off so that he gradually builds up a suitable and expressive countenance and bodily appearance; from a portrait once seen and perhaps half forgotten; from an impression seized upon in a glimpse of a casual passer-by; from a mere inquisitive delight in seeing what happens to his own face when he alters the shape of his jaw or the line or position of his eyebrows.

In itself both disguise and illusion, it is an essential element of 'theatre', ministering both to the realistic and to the 'larger-than-life' demands of theatrical art. The 'smell of the grease-paint' is almost a synonym for the glamour and attraction of the theatre; and it can even fascinate by 'twopence-coloured' methods, as anyone can testify who remembers the blatancy and crudity of much of the Victorian and Edwardian make-up as revealed by the view from a stage-box. Strong actinic lighting will always make it a necessity: strong lighting is an essential concession to size in the theatre, if the subtleties of facial expression are not to be lost. But there will always remain one thing which transcends the particular contribution of make-up and beats it at its own game, and that is the gift occasionally made by nature of a certain kind of face, figure, and personality which enables some players—not necessarily the greatest of their day—to assume as if by magic the very being and appearance of the character they present. There is the actor—great or mediocre—who is always himself: there is also the man or woman of whom we can say as Lamb does of Munden, 'There is one face of Farley, one of Knight ... but Munden has none that you can properly pin down and call *his*. ... He, and he alone, literally *makes faces*: applied to any other person, the phrase is a mere figure, denoting certain modifications of the human countenance. Out of some invisible wardrobe he dips for faces, as his friend Suett used for wigs, and fetches them out as easily.' It is not a gift that depends either upon a certain cast of feature or upon the shaping spirit of imagination at its most intense, though both have something to do with it. One cannot, by taking thought, add a cubit to one's stature, but the fortunate possessor of this true 'actor's face', though he will need the assistance of some straight make-up for modern conditions, has gone beyond the original disguise necessity which introduced make-up into the theatre.   M. ST. C. B.

MALAYA. Although the Malays delight in theatrical performances of any kind, the Malay drama has never reached a high standard, nor has it sprung from the natural genius of the people themselves, since it shows, almost invariably, traces of foreign origin. It developed from the dance, and for the most part is strictly bound by tradition and convention, being usually confined to representations of the classical Indian epics, particularly the Ramayana (see INDIA), which have been modified and adapted until they have become naturalized.

In the Peninsula the oldest form of theatrical entertainments are the *ma'yong* and other dance dramas of the ancient kingdom of Ligor. To students of the drama the *ma'yong* is chiefly significant as an example of primitive dramatic art which has been preserved almost intact through the ages.

The *ma'yong* is acted by a company of professional players, who tour the countryside, giving performances in the houses of the local rajahs or chiefs, or in the towns and villages for the general public. The stage is set in a palm-thatched shed, enclosed on three sides, the audience sitting or standing in the open air. There is no scenery, and the masks and costumes of the players are the only accessories. The company consists of four leading players, a few supernumeraries, and an orchestra of drums, gongs, a native flute, castanets, and a staccato instrument with a wooden keyboard.

Every company includes a *pawang*, the magician-priest who acts as the intermediary between gods and men. An invariable prelude to every performance are the prayers and invocations in which the *pawang* calls upon the god Siva to spare the actors and musicians, and implores the spirits of the countryside not to be incensed by the intrusion upon their domain.

The plots of the plays belong to a cycle of twelve stories akin to the Malay romances, with interludes of dancing and singing. A typical example is one in which the chief characters are a Malay noble and his henchman, a princess and her nurse. The hero (*pa'yong*) appears in princely dress: long wide trousers, silken waist-cloth, short, tight jacket, headdress with aigrette, coloured scarf flung over the left shoulder. He carries a *kris*, the wavy-bladed sword of Malaya, and a curious wand. On his fingers are tapering gold nail-protectors, and he has golden bracelets on his wrists and arms. Comic relief is supplied by his companion, a rough jester (*peran*) with whom he indulges in sallies of broad humour. To enhance his ridiculous aspect the clown wears a mask. He is naked to the waist and carries a wooden sword.

To this pair appears the princess (*ma'yong* or *putri*), dressed in a *sarong* of many colours, a close-fitting silken bodice, a tight girdle with jewelled buckle, and a long scarf trailing over one shoulder. She is decked with gold chains, earrings, bracelets and rings, and wears jewelled nail-protectors. She is attended by her aged nurse (played by a man), who is the feminine counterpart of the clown. Nurse and clown discuss betrothal negotiations, in a scene of low comedy dear to the Malay audience, this being followed by love passages, dancing, and singing by the two juvenile leads. The clown then provides the prince with a love potion to win the heart of the princess, but it results in her falling in love with the clown, while the nurse develops an embarrassing attachment to the prince. The prince, furious, belabours the clown, to the delight of the audience, but in the end all comes right, and the play closes with the princess's father bestowing his blessing upon the young couple.

Another theatrical performance which is of great antiquity is the shadow play, or *wayong kulit*, which had its origin in Java and is now common throughout the Peninsula and Siam (see SHADOW SHOW).

Like the *ma'yong*, it is played in a shed, the fourth side consisting of a white cloth, behind which the player manipulates the traditional figures, cut from deer-skin (*kulit*) or cardboard, before a hanging lamp which throws the silhouettes upon the screen. When not in use the puppets are stuck into lengths of banana pith, to be ready for the showman's hand. Behind the screen with the showman is the *compère*, who relates the story, with which every member of the audience is familiar. Usually the Ramayana cycle, which lasts seven nights, is played, in a form which has been handed down by word of mouth from one generation to another, with a mixture of local folklore in which traces of the old Indonesian beliefs are to be found. But the old Hindu tradition is paramount, and although the Malays are now followers of Islam, Mohammedanism has never influenced these shadow plays, except in the preliminary invocations (which are as invariable as those which precede the *ma'yong*), when the four archangels of the Koran may replace the ancient divinities.

The characters are easy for the audience to identify upon the screen. A profile with nose and receding forehead in an unbroken line is immediately recognized as one of the gods or heroes of old Java; a figure with a snub-nose and irregular features is a demon or evil spirit. As each appears the orchestra, consisting of drums and gongs and a clarinet (*serunai*), plays its appropriate tune. The Malays' love of comedy is catered for by the two comic characters (*Semar* and *Turas* or *Chemuras*), who keep up a running and irreverent commentary on the ways of gods and demons.

A purely modern form of entertainment, which has become increasingly popular in recent years, is the *bangsawan*, the equivalent of the modern musical comedy. It came to

Malaya from India. It is almost entirely devoid of any literary value, but it gives the Malay actor scope for his undoubted powers of mimicry and sense of comedy. It is at its best when it introduces a realistic element by portraying coolies, peasants, ricksha-pullers, and other country types, which the players burlesque to perfection. But while it is not faithful to classical tradition it has not yet cut adrift from romantic legend or produced original plays with local settings. The Malay impresario cares nothing for convention or criticism, but is concerned only with studying the predilections of his laughter-loving audience, so that in his hands *Hamlet* becomes a comedy in which the part of the ghost is played by a clown.   O. R.

MALONE, EDMOND (1741–1812), English man of letters, and one of the first scholars to study and annotate the works of Shakespeare. Born in Ireland, he came as a young man to London, intending even then to devote himself to literary criticism. He became the friend of Dr. Johnson, and was the first to perceive and denounce the Shakespeare forgeries of young Ireland. In spite of the many new facts which have been brought to light by later research, and an entirely new orientation in the study of Shakespeare as a dramatist, Malone's works, which include a biography, a chronology of the plays, and a history of the Elizabethan stage, are still valuable. The Malone Society, formed in 1907 to further the study of early English drama by reprinting texts and documents, was named after him in recognition of his eminence in the world of theatrical scholarship.

MALVERN FESTIVAL. A desire to bring together for a few days instead of the custom-ary few hours some of those having a sincere interest in the theatre was the basic inspiration that led Sir Barry Jackson to found the Malvern Festival. The choice of Malvern for such an enterprise was a happy one. The town possessed a theatre which, if not ideal, was at least adequate. It adjoined the Pump Room and Winter Gardens where players, audience, authors, and distinguished patrons could for-gather for lectures and informal talks; there the social side of the Festival found pleasant and ample scope. The townsfolk were accus-tomed to entertaining visitors in their lovely town; the broad sweep of the hills, pleasant gardens, and the wide panorama of the South-Midland counties conspired fittingly to set the scene for a pageant of English drama.

Festivals ran for a month, the complete cycle of plays being presented four times. Sir Barry's idea was to put on the best repre-sentative English plays, ancient and modern. In association with Mr. Roy Limbert, Director of the Malvern Theatre, he assembled a special Festival company of which the Birmingham Repertory Theatre Company formed the nucleus for several years. Distinguished players were engaged for special parts: in the course of eleven seasons these included Yvonne Arnaud, Elisabeth Bergner, Robert Donat, Edith Evans, Gwen Ffrangcon-Davies, Errol Flynn, Wendy Hiller, Curigwen Lewis, Herbert Lomas, Phyllis Neilson-Terry, Alas-tair Sim, Ernest Thesiger, Ralph Richardson, Cecil Trouncer, Irene Vanbrugh, Henry Wilcoxon, and Donald Wolfit.

Sir Barry's association with Bernard Shaw at Birmingham led to the dedication of the first year's programme to his works entirely. *The Apple Cart*, specially written for the Festival, *Back to Methuselah*, *Caesar and Cleopatra*, and *Heartbreak House* made up the bill for 1929. This exclusively Shavian in-auguration led to the adoption of Shaw as patron-in-chief, and subsequent festivals were announced as 'dedicated to Bernard Shaw'. Between 1929 and 1939, twenty Shaw plays were produced at Malvern Festival, seven of them for the first time in England. Five earlier Shaw plays and a revival of *The Apple Cart* were the substance of the second season. Play selection was not, however, exclusively confined to the works of the patron, and it was at Malvern that Besier's *Barretts of Wimpole Street* was launched on its distinguished career. In 1931 a series of chronological programmes was begun, and for three seasons the Festival was devoted to plays taken from five different centuries. Beginning with *Hickscorner*, a reli-gious play written in about 1513 by an unknown author, the 1931 season included *Ralph Roister Doister*, *A Woman Killed with Kindness*, *She Would if She Could*, *A Trip to Scarborough*, *Money*, and a new play, *The Switchback*, by James Bridie. The following season made a start with Heywood's *Play of the Wether*, fol-lowed chronologically with Udall, Ben Jonson, Southerne, Fielding, and Boucicault, and finished with Shaw's newly completed *Too True to be Good*. In 1933 the programme went back again to the primitives, beginning with the anonymous *Conversion of St. Paul*, and going on to *Gammer Gurton's Needle*, *The Fair Maid of the West*, *All For Love*, *The Love Chase*, *The Dancing Girl*, and finishing with the first performance of Bridie's *Sleeping Clergy-man*. These comprehensive sequences of English drama depended for full effect on audiences in regular and alert attendance. This was the distinguishing characteristic of the Malvern Festival. Pleasant as was its social side, climax came in the theatre itself, where an informed but open-minded audience surveyed the dramatic pageant with an atten-tion hardly possible in any other circumstances.

With the historical cycles came lectures. Every morning a talk on the play to be per-formed in the evening was given by a recog-nized authority. Professor F. S. Boas, Professor Ifor Evans, Principal A. E. Morgan, and Sir Barry Jackson were among the experts who clarified obscurities in the earlier drama-tists or enlarged upon method among the moderns. Tea-time talks were given on general aspects of drama and kindred arts.

In 1934 the austerities of the earlier drama-tists were tempered by more modern writings.

Drinkwater's *A Man's House*, Denis Johnston's *The Moon in the Yellow River*, and David Stewart's *Mutiny* took their place with *The Interlude of Youth, Doctor Faustus*, and Sir Barry's translation of Ghéon's *The Marvellous History of St. Bernard*. *You Never Can Tell* represented Shaw, who followed up his earlier masterpiece the next season with *The Simpleton of the Unexpected Isles*. The Shavian quota for 1935 was made up by *Fanny's First Play* and *Misalliance*, while *Volpone, Trelawny of the 'Wells'*, and Arkell's adaptation of *1066 and All That* maintained the Festival's reputation for catholicity of choice.

The next year found Shaw strongly represented by *Saint Joan, On the Rocks*, and *Pygmalion*. The author expressed himself as 'apologetically conscious that the year's programme has too much Shaw in it: but Malvern would be nothing if it had not a tradition of great acting as well as interesting dramatic literature. . . . My old plays and Garrick's old comedy will do as well as the next best to show what Malvern acting can do.' *The Clandestine Marriage, The Brontës of Haworth Parsonage, Jane Eyre*, and *Lady Precious Stream* completed the 1936 programme. In 1937 *Susanna, Gammer Gurton's Needle, Tom Thumb the Great, The School for Scandal*, and *Return to Sanity* were presented, together with two Shaw plays, *The Apple Cart* and *The Millionairess*.

At the end of 1937 Sir Barry Jackson withdrew from the Directorship of the Festival. For nine years he had made the Malvern meeting the most significant and attractive event in the English theatrical calendar. Roy Limbert, in association with Sir Cedric Hardwicke, then took over the direction and put on modern plays, all of which were new with the exception of *Saint Joan*. Shaw's long-awaited *Geneva* opened the 1938 Festival and was followed by new works by J. B. Priestley, C. K. Munro, Lord Dunsany, and James Bridie.

The Festival of 1939 was the last to be held before the outbreak of war caused a suspension. New plays by S. I. Hsiung, Sir Robert Vansittart, James Bridie, Alexander Knox, Evadne Price, and Ruby Miller were performed, but none of them aroused so much interest as the latest play by Shaw, *In Good King Charles's Golden Days*, easily the success of the season.   T. C. K.

In 1949 the Festival was revived by Roy Limbert, who had retained a skeleton organization at Malvern throughout the war. The six plays given included revivals of *The Apple Cart* (written for the 1929 Festival) and of *In Good King Charles's Golden Days* (written for the 1939 Festival) as well as *Buoyant Billions*, making its first appearance in England.

MALY THEATRE, Moscow. This theatre, whose name means 'small' (as opposed to *Bolshoy*—big) was opened on 14 Oct. 1824, on the site of a merchant's house, with a company which had been in existence as a corporate body since 1806, and is thus the oldest theatre in Moscow. The original building is still standing, and the theatre is the only one in Moscow to keep the old-fashioned drop curtain.

With its unbroken history the Maly is, not surprisingly, a theatre of tradition, and has been an important element in the history of Russian theatrical culture. It was well said that 'in Moscow one went to college but studied at the Maly'. Though an official Imperial Theatre, it represented the more liberal sections of society, and gave expression to progressive ideas. This was particularly noticeable in the 1840s, when *The Inspector-General* and *Woe from Wit* (or *Wit Works Woe*) were first produced, with that fine actor Mikhail Shchepkin (1788–1863) as the Governor, and as Famusov. Shchepkin, who worked in close collaboration with his authors, was the first exponent of realistic acting on the Russian stage, and trained his company in his own methods.

An actor of a different type, but quite as effective in his way, was Pavel Mochalov (1800–48), who excelled in the great classical and Shakespearian parts. His Hamlet was much admired, and he was the first to insist on translations of Shakespeare being made direct from English instead of from French. A true romantic, Mochalov relied on inspiration and intuition, rather than on study and observation, and his performances were consequently erratic.

Thirty years after its foundation the Maly Theatre produced the first play of Ostrovsky, and so began a brilliant partnership of author and company which lasted till 1885. The theatre is still known as the House of Ostrovsky, and nowhere, even in Russia, can finer interpretations of his plays be seen. The actor who first played many of the main roles, and who fought for the recognition of Ostrovsky's genius, was Prov Sadovsky (1818–72), who joined the company in 1839, and whose son and grandson were also members of it. The latter, also named Prov, became its Art Director and one of its outstanding actors—a close connexion of over one hundred years.

Other great names of the Maly are Alexander Lensky (1847–1908), who first introduced Ibsen to Russia, and Maria Yermolova (1853–1928), a fine tragedienne, who, in a difficult period of the theatre's existence, advocated a return to the classic plays of which she was so brilliant an interpreter. With the theatre she weathered the storm of the October Revolution and, after a few years of cautious experiment, the Maly took its rightful place in the theatrical life of Soviet Russia with the production of Trenev's *Lyubov Yarovaya* (first version, 1926). Since then it has given some fine performances of new plays on Soviet problems, among which are *Fighters, Skutarevski, In the Steppes of the Ukraine, Front*, and *Invasion*. It has also continued to produce the classics of Russia and Europe. Like all other Moscow theatres, the Maly was evacuated during the

Second World War, but afterwards returned to its old home. One of the outstanding productions of recent years has been *Othello* with the veteran actor Alexander Ostuzhev (1874–   ) in the title-role, as one of the finest Russian Othellos within living memory.

MANAGER, see PRODUCER.

MANCHESTER SCHOOL, see HORNIMAN, A. E. F.

MANET 'he remains', see STAGE DIRECTIONS.

MANHATTAN THEATRE, NEW YORK, on the west side of Broadway between 53rd and 54th Streets, a cathedral-like playhouse which, as Hammerstein's, opened on 30 Nov. 1927, and was used almost entirely for musical shows. In 1931 it was rechristened, but adhered to its musical policy, until in 1934, after a long period of idleness, it became a music-hall. It was not successful, and the theatre then remained empty until in 1936 the Federal Theatre Project took it over and, reverting to the name of Manhattan, opened with *American Holiday*, by E. L. and A. Barker. Shortly afterwards came T. S. Eliot's moving poetic drama, *Murder in the Cathedral*, for a limited run, and the theatre was then taken over for broadcasting.   G. F.

See also STANDARD THEATRE (2).

MANNERS. (1) JOHN HARTLEY (1870–1928), American dramatist, who was born in Ireland, made his first appearances on the stage in Australia, and up to 1902 was in London. There he appeared with Alexander, was Laertes to the Hamlet of Forbes-Robertson, and wrote his first play for Mrs. Langtry, playing in it himself. He went with her company to the United States, settled there, gave up acting, and between 1908 and 1928 was closely associated with the New York theatre, writing more than 30 plays. The best known is *Peg o' My Heart* (1912), which was translated into several European languages, produced with great success in London, and was at one time being played by five touring companies at once through several seasons. Its success overshadowed all his other work, and he never achieved his ambition to become a serious modern playwright. The heroine of *Peg o' My Heart* was his wife (2) LAURETTE TAYLOR (*née* COONEY) (1884–1946), an actress who had made her first appearance on the stage as a child, and had had a long and distinguished career before she was seen in New York and London as Peg, a part always associated with her. She was absent from the stage for some years, but in 1945 returned to give an outstanding performance as the Mother in *The Glass Menagerie*, which ran in New York for over a year.

MANNHEIM, home of Germany's third National Theatre, which was established in 1778, but failed to maintain itself beyond 1800 (see DALBERG and GERMANY, 4).

MANSFIELD. (1) RICHARD (1857–1907), American actor, son of a prima donna and a London wine merchant. He was born in Berlin, educated in England and on the continent, and after several attempts to earn a living in the London theatre, went on tour in the English provinces in Gilbert and Sullivan, and appeared in London in some minor parts. In 1882 he went to New York and made his first appearance there at the Standard Theatre on 27 Sept., again in light opera. It was, however, as Baron Chevrial in *A Parisian Romance* (1883) at the Union Square Theatre under Palmer that he first made his name, though struggles and disappointments still lay before him. Among his outstanding parts were Prince Karl, the dual role of Dr. Jekyll and Mr. Hyde, Beau Brummell in a play specially written for him by Clyde Fitch, Cyrano de Bergerac, and Monsieur Beaucaire. He also played the leading parts in his own play of *Monsieur* (1887), the romantic tale of a French refugee who earns his living by teaching music, in his own dramatization of *The First Violin* (1898), and in his own version of *Don Juan* in 1891, which was not, however, a success. He gave a fine performance as Nero in another unsuccessful play, and as Napoleon in a series of episodes based on the latter's career. During a visit to London in 1889 he first played Richard III, and among his other Shakespearian parts were Shylock, Brutus in *Julius Caesar*, and Henry V, which he produced with much pageantry in New York in 1900, making a spectacular appearance in the interpolated procession after Agincourt, riding a white horse. Mansfield was essentially a romantic actor at a time when the modern problem play was coming to the fore. But though he had little sympathy with the new drama as a whole, he much admired Ibsen's poetic drama, and in his last season of 1906–7 gave the first production in English of *Peer Gynt*, with himself in the title-role. He also introduced Shaw to America, appearing as Bluntschli in *Arms and the Man* in 1894, and Dick Dudgeon in *The Devil's Disciple* in 1897. He married in 1892 (2) BEATRICE CAMERON (1868–1940), who had played several small parts before in 1886 she appeared with him in *Prince Karl*. She continued in his company, playing Nora in *A Doll's House* in 1889–90, the first time the play had been done in the United States. After her marriage she played Raina and Judith Anderson in his productions of Shaw, and retired in 1898. Mansfield's career was something of a paradox. Though frequently successful, and a hard worker, he failed to achieve greatness. He was unpopular in London and spent much of his time outside New York, where in spite of several attempts at management he never had a permanent theatre. He had a hasty temper and a bitter tongue, which, allied with an air of conscious superiority, may have militated against his popularity.

MANSFIELD THEATRE, NEW YORK, on 47th Street between Broadway and Eighth Avenue. This has a wide, shallow auditorium which allows a very considerable seating capacity and yet preserves the intimacy usually found only in the smaller playhouses. It opened on 15 Feb. 1926 with an ephemeral play, and the only event of artistic importance during its early years was a visit from the Habima Players in *The Dybbuk* and other works in their repertory. Some successful musical comedies under Lew Fields brought temporary prosperity to the house, which in 1930 saw *Green Pastures*, directed by the author, with sets and costumes by Robert Edmond Jones. This had 640 performances, and was followed by another period of ill fortune. *Black Limelight* (1936) with Margaret Rawlings, which was an outstanding success in London, ran for two months. *Thunder Rock*, again a greater success in London than in New York, was also seen at the Mansfield, as was Ruth Gordon's nostalgic evocation of her early days, *Years Ago*.   G. F.

MANTEAU D'ARLEQUIN (Cloak or Mantle of Harlequin), the French name for the draped curtain frame inside the proscenium arch (see PROSCENIUM).

MANTELL, ROBERT BRUCE (1854–1928), American actor, born in Scotland, who made his first appearance on the stage in Belfast. Owing to family opposition to his chosen career, he called himself Robert Hudson, resuming his own name when in 1878 he went with Modjeska to the United States, playing Tybalt. He remained with her some time, then returned to England and after several years of hard work and little recognition went back to America, this time for good. In 1884 he played opposite Fanny Davenport with some success, and two years later took his own company on tour. As a young man he was essentially a romantic actor, handsome and passionate, at his best in such plays as *The Corsican Brothers*, *The Marble Heart*, and *The Lady of Lyons*. When with the years romance left him, he became somewhat heavy and uninspired, but he remained popular outside New York, where his careful studies of the chief Shakespearian characters won him respectful admiration. He was four times married, usually to actresses who were his leading ladies.

MANTLE, ROBERT BURNS (1873–1948), American dramatic critic, known as 'The Dean of the Dramatic Critics' until his retirement in 1943. He was born in Watertown, New York, and in 1898 became dramatic editor of *The Denver Times*. Later he worked as Sunday editor of *The Chicago Tribune* and from 1922 until his retirement he was dramatic critic of *The New York Daily News*. He edited till his death an annual volume of *The Best Plays*, a series he inaugurated in 1919. Each volume contains a lengthy condensation of ten of the season's plays together with an index of every play produced in New York during the year, with the date of its opening, its cast, its director, the number of performances it

achieved and a brief account of its plot. This useful history of the latter-day American theatre has been supplemented by two more volumes—somewhat less complete—covering the years from the beginning of the century to 1919. Burns Mantle was also the author of *American Playwrights of To-day* and edited *A Treasury of the Theatre* with John Gassner.

T. Q. C.

MANUEL, NIKLAS (1484–1530), a painter and poet of Berne, and a writer of anti-Catholic plays during the Reformation (see GERMANY, 2).

MANZINI, GIOVANNI (*fl.* fourteenth century), early Italian tragic dramatist (see ITALY, 1 *b* i).

MANZONI, ALESSANDRO (1785–1873), famous Italian poet and novelist, author also of two tragedies, *Il Conte di carmagnola* (pub. 1820) and *Adelchi* (pub. 1822). Both are historically more accurate than tragedies are wont to be, and both entirely disregard the Unities. They were written with the purpose of proving that dialogue need not be unnatural because it happens to be in verse, and to give the poet, particularly in the beautiful lyric choruses of *Adelchi*, 'a little corner where he can speak in his own person'.

MARAIS, THÉÂTRE DU. Recent research places the opening of this theatre, one of the forerunners of the Comédie-Française, at 31 December 1634, in a converted tennis-court in the rue Vieille-du-Temple, with a company under the great actor Montdory. This company had previously played at various sites in the town, and had given Corneille's first play, *Mélite*, its Paris première. Once established in the Marais, they continued to act Corneille's early comedies, and were responsible for the first production of *Le Cid* in 1636, Montdory playing the name-part. Having lost some of his best actors by a whim of Louis XIII, who sent them to join Bellerose at the rival theatre of the Hôtel de Bourgogne, Montdory took on the Barons, parents of the great actor Michel Baron. Among his other notable productions was Tristan's *Mariamne* in the same year as *Le Cid*, in which Montdory played Herod with great sound and fury, an effort which undoubtedly hastened his breakdown in health the following year.

After Montdory left the Marais it went through bad times. The best actors joined the rival company, to which Corneille also gave his new plays, and the remnants of a good company were forced to revert to the playing of old-fashioned crude popular farces. The one good thing that came to them at this time was the return of that excellent comedian, Jodelet, for whom Scarron, d'Ouville, and the younger Corneille wrote excellent farces. At a later date the Marais, which was a big theatre, specialized in spectacular performances with a good deal of the newly imported Italian machinery. But it never regained the place in public esteem which it had held under

Montdory, in spite of the efforts of Floridor (who in any case soon left to go to the Hôtel de Bourgogne), of Laroque, and of the Du Parcs, who left Molière's company a year after its arrival in Paris to join the Marais, but returned to him in despair. The theatre struggled on with little pleasure and few profits—though it continued to receive a small subsidy from the State—until 1673, when the company was amalgamated with that of Molière, who had just died. The combined company, which by its later fusion with that of the Hôtel de Bourgogne became part of the Comédie-Française, acted at the theatre in the rue Guénégaud which had been built for Lully's opera company, and the old Marais stage was abandoned.

MARBLE, DANFORTH (1810–49), American actor, famous for his Yankee characters. He was originally a silversmith, but was always interested in the theatre, and for some time played small parts in amateur societies. In 1831 he made his first appearance on the professional stage, and proved an excellent mimic of the Yankee dialect. He perfected this in four years' touring, until in 1836 he appeared, in a play specially written for him, as Sam Patch, always one of his most popular parts, particularly along the Mississippi and at the Bowery, New York. In 1844 he was received with enthusiasm in London and the provinces, and also visited Glasgow and Dublin, playing in such typical plays as *Jonathan in England* and *The People's Lawyer*, where full scope was given to his inimitable assumption of Yankee characteristics. He married the daughter of William Warren of Philadelphia, and died young at the height of his popularity.

MARBURY, ELIZABETH (1856–1933), an American theatrical agent who started her successful career by managing a theatrical performance for charity with such acumen that Daniel Frohman advised her to go into the business. This she did, her first client being Frances Hodgson Burnett, while she handled in America the plays of Victorien Sardou and, through him, of innumerable other French dramatists. She was twice decorated by the French Government for her services to French literature. She was also Shaw's agent, and was instrumental in introducing Mansfield to his plays. Among her other clients were Oscar Wilde, Hall Caine, Somerset Maugham, Stanley Weyman, and Sir James Barrie. It is said that it was she who persuaded Barrie to enlarge the part of Babbie in *The Little Minister* so as to make it acceptable to Maude Adams, who scored such a success in the part. Miss Marbury also handled the plays of Rachel Crothers and Clyde Fitch, brought the Castles to New York, and in partnership with Lee Shubert produced intimate revues with music by Jerome Kern and costumes designed by herself. In 1903 she bought a house in Paris which became a noted rendezvous for all connected with art and letters, and in 1914 incorporated her business as the American

Play Company. In 1923 she published an autobiography, *My Crystal Ball*.

MARIE RAMBERT BALLET CLUB, see RAMBERT, MARIE.

MARIONETTE. A marionette is a rounded full-length puppet controlled from above the stage. Originally the control was by a simple rod or strong wire to the centre of the head; sometimes another rod would go to one hand, used for fighting with; sometimes a string would be attached to each hand or to each leg. Marionettes controlled in this way are inevitably very crude, but they can be quite effective in their own tradition; folk-puppet theatres presenting this type of marionette are still open throughout Sicily, performing a series of plays based on the legends of Charlemagne, Roland, and their battles with the infidels, the cycle sometimes taking months to complete. A similar medieval tradition is found in Belgium, where, at Liége, a local peasant type—Tchantchès—has been introduced as hero or chorus. In France there are several local heroes of the puppet stage—Jacques at Lille, Lafleur at Amiens—who figure throughout the repertory of popular legends in the marionette theatres.

A great technical advance was achieved when marionettes were manipulated entirely by strings; this allows far greater flexibility for body and head movements and is less distracting to the audience. This was perhaps first done by the intricate Italian Fantoccini of the 1770s, but possibly not until a hundred years later by Thomas Holden. To-day marionettes are almost invariably strung in this manner, and literary allusions to 'puppet wires' have no relation to actuality. An ordinary standard marionette has a string to each leg and arm, two to the head, one to each shoulder (which take the weight of the body) and one to the back: i.e. nine strings (actually fine thread) in all. An elaborate figure will have twice or three times this number. These are gathered together on a wooden 'crutch' or control, held in one hand by the manipulator, while with the other he plucks at whatever strings are required. Marionettes are usually made of wood, but lighter materials such as papier mâché are sometimes now used; their size varies from 12 in. to 18 in. for home use up to 2 ft. to 3 ft. for public performance. With the exercise of great skill and ingenuity marionettes can be made that will reproduce almost every human movement—though simple and technically crude puppets will often convey an equally dramatic effect (see also JAPAN and PUPPETS).   G. S.

MARIVAUX, PIERRE CARLET DE CHAMBLAIN DE (1688–1763), French dramatist, who began his literary career by writing a number of plays and novels, much influenced by Spain, and completely forgotten. He was a friend of Fontenelle and La Motte, who helped to develop in him that peculiarly paradoxical and precious style later known as *marivaudage*, first reproachfully, later in admiration of its superb subtlety. Marivaux first made himself felt in the theatre in 1720, when his *Arlequin poli par l'amour* was given successfully at the Comédie-Italienne, and his *Annibal* less successfully at the Comédie-Française, in spite of the acting of Baron and Dufresne. Having lost all his money in an American investment, Marivaux for the next twenty years looked to the theatre for his main source of livelihood. He wrote chiefly for the Comédie-Italienne, and among the best of his plays given there were *La Surprise de l'amour* (1722), *La Double inconstance* (1723), *Le Jeu de l'amour et du hasard* (1730), *Les Fausses confidences* (1737), and *L'Épreuve* (1740). At the Comédie-Française several of his plays were given without much success, but the second *Surprise de l'amour* (1727), a totally different play from the first, and a much better one, was successful after a disastrous first night which nearly wrecked its career. Marivaux's best work for the Comédie-Française was *Le Legs* (1736), which was particularly successful when revived later by Molé and Mlle Contat. His last important play was *Le Préjugé vaincu* (1746), in which the actresses Jeanne Gaussin and Mlle Dangeville were so outstanding that the king increased their pensions forthwith. In his own day Marivaux had none of the pre-eminence accorded him at present. His work, which renounced the help of intrigue and conflict, substituting for them psychological and emotional action and reaction, stands a little apart from his time, which preferred the tearful comedies of La Chaussée. Unlike Molière, Marivaux confides his chief roles to women, and his plays are adapted to the needs of a sheltered, cultivated, subtle society, such as developed just prior to the Revolution, and crept back again in the following century, when Marivaux's plays were successfully revived, and had much influence on Alfred de Musset, again a dramatist who was in advance of his time.

MARKISH, Peretz (1895–   ), Russian-Jewish writer of plays on contemporary themes, produced at the Moscow State Jewish Theatre (see JEWISH DRAMA, 6).

MARKOVA, Alicia [really Lilian Alicia Marks] (1910–   ), see BALLET, 8.

MARLOWE, Christopher (1564–93), playwright of the English Renaissance, and an important figure in the development of the Elizabethan stage. Son of a Canterbury shoemaker and educated at Cambridge, he had a tragically short life, being stabbed in a tavern brawl before his thirtieth birthday, possibly during a dispute over the bill, but equally probably by a planned assassination due to his secret-service activities. His murderer was Ingram Frizer, with Skeres and the spy Robert Poley as accessories. Marlowe's first play was *Tamburlaine the Great, Part I*, given probably in 1587 by the Admiral's Men, with Edward Alleyn in the name-part. Written in flamboyant blank verse of great poetic beauty, it is a bold, passionate, and highly imaginative drama, which suffers from poor construction and the concentration of attention on the chief figure. A second part was given in the following year. Both were highly successful and had a great influence on Shakespeare, who no doubt saw them on his arrival in London a few years later, since they continued to be revived up to the closing of the theatres in 1642. They were followed by *The Tragical History of Dr. Faustus*, a treatment of the German medieval legend, which has survived in a fragmentary and much-mutilated condition. Though written and probably produced about 1589, it was not printed until 1604, by which time the development of the Devil as a comic character had led to interpolation and excision and the use of prose summaries for parts of the original verse. Though retaining all the fine poetry of *Tamburlaine*, *Dr. Faustus* is more consistently dramatic than the earlier play and shows Marlowe's great advance in stage-craft. It is the generally accepted opinion that the comic scenes are not from his pen, but were added later by Bird and Rowley at the instigation of Henslowe. As originally planned, the play was a vast dramatic poem which had much in common with the Morality play, infused with the genius of the new age. It continued to be acted in its mangled version until well into the eighteenth century, and was the inspiration of Goethe's *Faust*. Marlowe's last plays were *The Jew of Malta* and *Edward II*, the first a study of a crafty scoundrel who eventually over-reaches himself, the second a chronicle play which marks the highest point of Marlowe's development as a dramatist, though lacking in the fine lyricism of some of his earlier work. *The Jew of Malta*, which may have contributed something to Shakespeare's Shylock, was first produced in about 1590, but not printed until 1633, and here again the text has suffered considerable revision, probably at the hands of Thomas Heywood. It appears to have been the most popular of Marlowe's plays, and Edward Alleyn was much admired in its title-role. *Edward II*, acted in about 1591–2, was printed during its author's lifetime, and is consequently less corrupt than the other plays. It seems to have maintained its popularity for a few years and then fallen out of the repertory. It was revived in 1923 by the Phoenix Society.

Marlowe, who was acquainted with many of the leading men of his day, including Sir Walter Raleigh, was highly thought of as a scholar and poet, though often in danger of arrest through his atheistical and outspoken opinions. His death brought forth many expressions of regard and admiration from his fellow writers, and there is no doubt that his *Tamburlaine* gloriously inaugurated the first great age of English drama. He was a greater poet than dramatist, and by his use of blank verse for the expression of his heroes' mighty destinies he prepared the way for the fine tragedies of Shakespeare. Unable in the short time at his disposal to rise to great heights as a dramatist, he nevertheless stands at the threshold of Elizabethan drama, and did much to liberate it from the remnants of the medieval play and the Tudor interlude.

MARLOWE, JULIA (1866–1950), American actress, whose real name was Sarah Frances Frost. Born in England, she was taken to the United States at the age of 4, and, as Fanny Brough, made her first appearance on the stage in a juvenile *H.M.S. Pinafore* company in 1878. After some years on tour and a prolonged period of study she appeared in 1887 as Parthenia in *Ingomar*, in which she made her first appearance in New York. She was immediately successful, and began a long career as a leading actress, being at her best in such parts as Juliet, Viola, Rosalind, Beatrice, and Portia. She was also good in standard comedy, playing Lydia Languish in *The Rivals* with Jefferson and Mrs. John Drew, Lady Teazle, Julia in *The Hunchback*, and Pauline in *The Lady of Lyons*. She married as her second husband E. H. Sothern, playing Juliet to his Romeo in 1904. Three years later she made her first appearance in London, being well received in a series of Shakespearian and other parts, though a production of *When Knighthood was in Flower* was not a success. She toured for some years with her husband in a Shakespearian repertory, playing Lady Macbeth for the first time in 1910. She retired for a time in 1915, but returned to play mainly in Shakespeare until her final retirement in 1924. She received honorary degrees from the Columbia and George Washington Universities, and in 1926 gave to the Memorial Theatre, Stratford-on-Avon, the entire proceeds of the production of ten Shakespeare plays, done jointly with Sothern.

MARMONTEL, JEAN FRANÇOIS (1723–99), French man of letters, who was befriended in his youth by Voltaire, and was an *habitué* of the Comédie-Française. He had achieved some reputation as a poet when his first play, *Denys le Tyran*, was produced in 1748. In the existing dearth of good plays this pale reflection of classical French tragedy was well received. Some of its success was no doubt due to the acting of Mlle Clairon, who later became the mistress of its author, and was persuaded by him in about 1753 to discard her declamatory style for more natural acting, to the ultimate benefit of the French stage. Marmontel continued to write, with some success, until the failure of his *Égyptus* (1753) turned him from the theatre. None of his plays remained in the repertory, and it is mainly as a critic that he is now remembered. In 1758 he became editor of the *Mercure de France*, in which his *Contes moraux* had been appearing, and widely extended its scope and influence. Marmontel may be regarded as the founder of French dramatic criticism in journalism, and, in memory of Voltaire's kindness to him, he was always indulgent to young authors. He also wrote a number of libretti for light operas, mainly in order to help the composer Grétry,

and his only rival in this genre was Favart. In the quarrel between the adherents of Gluck and Piccini he was strongly on the side of the latter, with whom he also collaborated several times. He lived in Paris until the downfall of the Monarchy, and then retired to live in the country, returning only once to sit as deputy in the *conseil des anciens*, a post he lost in the upheaval of 18 fructidor.

MARS, Mlle [ANNE FRANÇOISE HIPPOLYTE] (1779–1847), French actress, younger daughter of the actor-dramatist Monvel (really Boutet) (1745–1812) by a provincial actress. She appeared on the stage as a child, with her elder sister, playing at Versailles and in Paris under Mlle Montansier, and in 1795 made her first appearance at the Comédie-Française, being befriended and tutored by Mlle Contat. Three years later she joined the reconstituted troupe, and began a long and glorious career, though she had first to compete with several talented and beautiful actresses whose names are now forgotten. She was equally good in tragedy and comedy, in the heroines of Molière and Beaumarchais, in the strong drama of Dumas and Hugo, and in the modern comedy of Scribe and Legouvé. She retired in 1841, her last appearance being on 31 Mar. as Elmire in *Tartuffe* and Silvia in *Le Jeu de l'amour et du hasard*. A year later she was seen at her benefit night as Célimène in *Le Misanthrope* and Armande in *Les Femmes savantes*. A beautiful woman, of great elegance and good taste, with exquisite manners and a lovely voice, she continued to play young parts until she was over 60. Her father was a good actor, to whom Talma admitted he owed much. Of his rather ephemeral plays, a comedy entitled *L'Amour bourru* and a drama, *Les Victimes cloîtrées*, were the most successful. His elder daughter was also a good actress, overshadowed by the fame of her younger sister.

MARSTON, JOHN (*c.* 1575–1634), English satirist and dramatist, son of an Italian mother, which may account for the influence of Italian literature discernible in his plays. He was at Oxford from 1602–1604 but refused to follow his father in the legal profession, and turned to literature. His theatrical career was compressed into some eight years, after which he renounced the stage and took holy orders. The immediate cause of his retirement seems to have been a play, now lost, in which he satirized James I, and for which he was sent to prison. He had narrowly escaped imprisonment for his share in *Eastward Ho!* (1605), where he appears to have been the chief offender, and only avoided the fate of his collaborators, Chapman and Jonson, by ignominious flight. In fact, the whole of Marston's theatrical career was stormy, owing in part to his satiric bent and self-consciousness, in part to his constant enmity with Jonson, whom he satirized in an early work, while Jonson retaliated by portraying Marston as Crispinus in *The Poetaster*. Marston wrote mainly for the Children's companies, his

Revenge tragedy, *Antonio and Mellida*, and its sequel, *Antonio's Revenge*, being done in 1599 by the Children of Paul's, who may also have produced a comedy, *What You Will* (1601), and a tragedy on the subject of Sophonisba. Among the plays done by the Children at Blackfriars was Marston's most important work, *The Malcontent* (1604), a somewhat sombre tragicomedy in which a deposed prince comes in disguise to the court of his usurper and so tests the character and loyalty of his subjects. *Eastward Ho!* was revived at Drury Lane in 1751 as *The Prentices*, and in 1775 as *Old City Manners*. It is said to have inspired Hogarth's 'Industrious and Idle Prentices'. Marston is thought to have had a hand in the writing of *Troilus and Cressida* (see *Englische Studien*, vol. xxx, 1901, article by R. Boyle).

MARSTON, JOHN WESTLAND (1819–90), English critic and playwright, who went from Lincolnshire to London, where he was a friend of Macready and Kean. He wrote, in succession to Bulwer Lytton and Sheridan Knowles, a number of plays in the then outmoded tradition of poetic drama, but they had little vigour and were soon forgotten. Marston's main claim to remembrance rests on his dramatic criticism for the *Athenaeum*, and a book entitled *Our Recent Actors* (1888).

MARTIN BECK THEATRE, NEW YORK, on 45th Street west of Eighth Avenue, the farthest west of all New York's legitimate playhouses. Built by the late Martin Beck of vaudeville fame, it opened on 11 Nov. 1924 with *Madame Pompadour*, and has since staged on an average a hit a year, many of them musical comedies. Among straight plays produced there have been *Spread Eagle* and *The Shannons of Broadway*, while the Theatre Guild used this house for their productions of *Wings over Europe*, finely directed by Mamoulian, *Red Rust*, done by the Theatre Guild Studio, later the Group Theatre, *The Apple Cart*, and *Hotel Universal* with Ruth Gordon. Two massive productions at this theatre were *Roar China* and *Miracle at Verdun*. In 1931 the Group Theatre produced *The House of Connelly*, and the Lunts followed in their highly successful *Reunion in Vienna*. Later productions included the Abbey Players, the D'Oyly Carte on their first visit to New York for 40 years, *Yellow Jack* in 1934, and Katharine Cornell in a repertory which included *Romeo and Juliet*, *The Barretts of Wimpole Street*, and *The Flowers of the Forest*. This theatre saw the first Critics' Prize play, *Winterset*, with Burgess Meredith, who again appeared there with Peggy Ashcroft in *High Tor*. Plays of interest in recent years have been *Watch on the Rhine*, again a Critics' Prize play, which set up a record run for the theatre, and *The Iceman Cometh*, with which O'Neill broke a long silence.   G. F.

MARTIN BROWNE, E., see BROWNE, E. MARTIN.

MARTINELLI. (1) DRUSIANO (?–1606/8), actor of the *commedia dell'arte*, who was probably in England in 1577–8 with the first regular Italian company to cross the Channel. He appears in the actor-lists of several companies after this, but his reputation was overshadowed by that of his wife, (2) ANGELICA ALBERIGI (or Alberghini) (*fl.* 1580–94), a fine actress who at one time had her own company, and by that of his brother, (3) TRISTANO (*c.* 1557–1630), who was probably the first to play Arlecchino. He was originally with Pedrolino's company, the Confidenti, but appears to have been of a roving and somewhat quarrelsome disposition, and is found in many places with different companies. He was popular in Paris, where he went several times, and was much admired for his wit, specimens of which are preserved in his *Compositions de rhétorique de M. Don Arlequin* (1600).

MARTÍNEZ DE LA ROSA, FRANCISCO (1787–1862), an important figure in the Spanish theatre, since he combined the classicism of the eighteenth century with the new spirit of Romanticism, and may be considered the first Romantic dramatist of the new era. His early plays were written in a conventional style, but with his *Aben-Humeya* (first written in French and given in 1830 in Paris, where he was Spanish ambassador) and *La Conjuración de Venecia* (1834) he openly declared himself on the side of the Romantics. These are typical Romantic prose dramas, with heavy local colour, and a mingling of tragedy and comedy. In his true comedies, of which the best is *La niña en casa y la madre en la máscara* (1821), he followed the traditions of Moratín the younger, still considered a master of comedy. One of his last plays, *El Español en Venecia* (1843), is in the style of the old Spanish *comedia*.

MARTÍNEZ SIERRA, GREGORIO (1881–1947), a modern Spanish dramatist, novelist, and poet, among whose plays are *Teatro de Ensueño* (1905); *Vida y dulzura* (1908); *La sombra del padre* (1909); *El ama de la casa* (1910); *Canción de cuna*—well known to English-speaking audiences as *The Cradle Song*—and *Primavera en otoño* (both 1911); *Mamá* and *Madama Pepita* (both 1912); *Las golondrinas* (1913); and *Don Juan de España* (1921). His work, in which he had the collaboration of his wife, is notable more for delicacy and quiet humour than for action or excitement, but it has been favourably received both in Spain and abroad, and has had some influence on the European and American theatre. From 1916 until his death Martínez Sierra was director of the Eslava Theatre in Madrid, and formed his own stock company. He translated the plays of Shaw into Spanish.

MARTIN-HARVEY, SIR JOHN, see HARVEY, JOHN MARTIN-.

MARTYN, EDWARD (1859–1924), see IRELAND.

MARYLEBONE THEATRE, LONDON, see WEST LONDON THEATRE.

MASEFIELD, JOHN (1878–   ), English poet and novelist, Poet Laureate since 1930. He is the author of several poetic dramas, which show the combined influence of the Greek tragic writers and the Japanese Nō play. Among them are several on biblical themes, including *A King's Daughter* (1928) on the subject of Jezebel, *Good Friday* (1917), and *The Trial of Jesus* (1926). The best-known of the others are *The Tragedy of Nan* (1908), *The Witch* (1910), adapted from a Norwegian tragedy and several times revived with success, and *Mellaney Holtspur* (1923). Some of Masefield's finest poetry is to be found in his plays, which, unlike those of many contemporary poets, are eminently suited to stage production. He is also the author of *A Macbeth Production* (1945), in which he gives some stimulating advice to a group of ex-service men about to produce the play, and incidentally ranges over a wide field of historical and literary criticism.

MASQUE, or more correctly Mask. The former spelling, which comes from sixteenth-century France, was first used extensively by Ben Jonson, and modern scholarship is reverting to the original term. This, however, tends to lead to confusion with mask, meaning a cover or disguise for the face, originally known in English as a visor. Both meanings are closely connected, since the players in a masque, known as the maskers, either blackened their faces or wore visors.

The origin of the masque is lost in obscurity, but is undoubtedly connected with primitive religious rites and folk-ceremonies. In essence it is the silent irruption into a festival of disguised guests, bearing presents, who then join with their hosts in a ceremonial dance. The latter point is important, since even in its most elaborate literary form the masque was designed to lead up to a dance or masked ball where the spectators mingled with the actors, who in Court masques were usually amateurs of high rank.

The early English mask, known as a Disguising or Mummery, gave rise to a traditional folk-play (see MUMMING PLAY), and also to an elaborate Court spectacle as practised in Renaissance Italy, where, mainly under the influence of Lorenzo de' Medici, it had become a vehicle for song, dance, scenery, and machinery, one of its non-dramatic offshoots being the elaborate Trionfo, or Triumph. From Italy it passed to France and at the Court of the French king gave rise to the simple *ballet de cour*, or the more spectacular *mascarade* (from which is derived masquerade); in the sixteenth century it came, under its new name, to Tudor England, where, forgetful of its humble origin, and the original 'guisers', it brought the maskers to play before the King in lovely dresses, with all the appurtenances of scenery, machinery, and rich allegorical speech.

In Elizabethan times the masque provided an excellent means of complimenting the Queen in her own palace, or entertaining her on her summer progresses through England.

The speeches were written by poets and scholars, often anonymously, and the main interest centred on the costumes, scenery, songs, and dances. The masque reached its height under the Stuarts, and became a literary rather than a social force in the hands of Ben Jonson, who in 1603 succeeded Samuel Daniel as Court poet. With him was associated the scene-designer and architect Inigo Jones, and their collaboration, which began with the Twelfth Night masque of 1605, produced some excellent work. Unfortunately their aims were incompatible, since Jonson saw the masque as an opportunity for the speaking of fine poetry, while Jones regarded it as a chance for trying out the stage innovations of Italy. Eventually Jones won, and Jonson retired, his last masque being produced in 1634. One of his innovations was the anti-masque, which he first employed in 1609. It introduced a grotesque element in contrast to the masque proper, as Hell before Heaven, Shipwreck before Peace, and was also known as the false masque. The form ante-masque is also found, presumably in reference to the fact that it preceded the main masque. It was not entirely new, since the earlier masques made use of grotesque elements in dancing, known as the antic, whence the suggestion that Jonson's innovation should properly be known as the antic masque. Whatever its origin, Jonson seems to have been the first to name it and make conscious use of it.

The double masque was one in which two sets of performers appeared, in different disguises, as Fishermen and Marketwomen, or Sailors and Countrymaids, as against the one disguise—Blackamoors, Wild Men, Shepherds, &c.—of the single and more usual masque. The later operatic development of the masque made an unfortunate division between the masque and the anti-masque, which tended to reduce it to farce and pantomime. It may be noted in passing that Milton's *Comus*, though called a masque, is considered by some scholars to be a pastoral—of which there are other less notable examples—done privately and probably so labelled to distinguish it from the plays of the public stage.

Lacking a poet of the calibre of Jonson, and having to provide for the entry of Henrietta Maria and Charles I as performers instead of spectators, the later masques became merely spectacular shows of small literary value, much under the influence of French courtly entertainment, particularly the *ballet à entrée* and *ballet de cour*. This led to a greater stress on dancing, and through Inigo Jones on spectacle. Shirley, as Court poet, merely had to provide a scenario and some rather dull speeches. The Civil War put an end to the masque, and later revivals were only belated imitations. The masque has an important place in theatre history, partly because of its influence on ballet, opera, and pantomime, but mainly because, when the London theatres reopened in 1660, they took their inspiration, their scenery, and some of their actors and dramatists from the Court masque. It cannot itself rank as drama, however, since it has practically no story, no action, no crisis, and no inevitable ending, but is merely an excuse for a compliment, a gift, and an entertainment. An earlier influence of the masque on the public theatre was brought about by the children who played in both, and the adult actors who were sometimes brought into the Court entertainments to play parts that had proved beyond the powers of an amateur. Shakespeare shows the influence of the masque in such plays as *As You Like It*, *A Midsummer Night's Dream* and particularly *The Tempest*, where all the accessories of the masque are described in pure poetry.

MASQUE THEATRE, New York, see JOHN GOLDEN THEATRE.

MASSEY, CHARLES (?–1625), an English actor, friend of Alleyn and of the actor-dramatist Samuel Rowley. He first appears with the Admiral's Men in 1597, and remained with them during their successive renamings until his death. He was one of the actors who leased the Fortune Theatre from Alleyn in 1618, and he was a shareholder in the new Fortune (1622), where he was one of the chief members of the company. He was also a dramatist, since two plays by him, now lost, were given by the Admiral's Men in 1602–3.

MASSINE, LEONIDE (1896–   ), one of the outstanding figures of modern ballet. He made his first appearance with Diaghilev's Ballets Russes in the place of Nijinsky as the young Joseph in 'Josephs Legende' (1914), and almost immediately began devising ballets for the company. It is as a choreographer that he is now best known, though his work in that direction should not be allowed to overshadow his fine dancing. Among his ballets for Diaghilev, under whom he succeeded Fokine as choreographer, are 'The Good-Humour'd Ladies' and 'The Three-Cornered Hat'. After Diaghilev's death Massine joined Colonel de Basil, for whom he created the first of the big 'symphonic' ballets, 'Les Présages', to the music of Tchaikovsky's Fifth Symphony (see also BALLET, 7 and 8).

MASSINGER, PHILIP (1583–1640), English dramatist, author of some forty plays, of which half are lost; the manuscripts of at least eight were destroyed by Warburton's cook, who used them to line pie-dishes. Of those that survive the most important is *A New Way to Pay Old Debts*, a satiric comedy which was first produced in about 1625. Allowed to lapse during the Restoration, it returned to the stage in the eighteenth century and has been constantly revived up to the present day. Sir Giles Overreach was a favourite part with many great actors, particularly Kean, who had an immense admiration for Massinger, and revived also his tragedy of *The Roman Actor* (1626). Among Massinger's other plays are the romantic dramas, *The Duke of Milan* (1620) and *The Great Duke of Florence* (1627), with its

charming idyll between Giovanni and Lidia; the comedies, *The City Madam* (1632) and *The Guardian* (1633); and the tragi-comedies, *The Bondman* (1623) and *The Renegado* (1624). *The Fatal Dowry* (1619) and *The Virgin Martyr* (1620) were written in collaboration, the first with Field, the second with Dekker, while Massinger had a hand in several of the plays ascribed to Beaumont and Fletcher, and may have worked with the latter on *Henry VIII* and possibly *Two Noble Kinsmen*. Massinger has received less attention than other dramatists of his day. Archer, in *The Old Drama and the New*, called him 'one of the best writers of the period', and ascribed his neglect to the absence of passages of lyric beauty in his plays, though his art as a dramatist is indisputable.

MASTER OF THE REVELS, an officer appointed under the Lord Chamberlain to supervise and pay for some particular entertainment at Court. He first appears in 1494, and was an intermittent official until 1545, when Sir Thomas Cawarden was appointed Master for life. He supervised the entertainments given for the coronation of Elizabeth, and was succeeded on his death in 1559 by Sir Thomas Benger. The powers of the Master were somewhat restricted, as a good deal of the financing of plays, and work in connexion with them, appertained to other departments of the Royal Household. After the death of Benger in 1572 there was a period of confusion and no new appointment was made, the work however continuing smoothly under the permanent under-officials, particularly Thomas Blagrove, the clerk, who served the Revels Office for 57 years. He had hoped to be given the Mastership, but in 1579 this went, probably through influence at Court, to Sir Edmund Tilney, who appears to have done very little work, though he retained his title until his death in 1610. He was not responsible for the masques given at the Court of James I, and seems to have been occupied only with the fittings and lighting. By decrees of 1581 and 1603, however, the Master of the Revels was made censor of plays, and drew acting fees for plays licensed for public performance. Tilney was succeeded by his nephew, Sir George Buck, who had been his deputy for some years, and on the death of Buck in 1622 the office passed to its most famous holder, Sir Henry Herbert. He held it until the closing of the theatres in 1642, and on the Restoration tried to uphold its importance, but was defeated by the patents granted to Killigrew and Davenant. Most of his powers were taken from him, but he retained his title, which passed on his death to Thomas Killigrew and then to the latter's son Charles. The censorship of plays had by 1737 become a direct responsibility of the Lord Chamberlain, as it is to-day, and the old office, dating from Tudor times, was virtually extinct (see DRAMATIC CENSORSHIP and HERBERT). For a detailed account of the Revels office in its palmy days, see Chambers, *Elizabethan Stage*, vol. i, ch. 3.

MASTERSINGERS, German musical and literary guilds which flourished in the larger towns, particularly in Nuremberg, in the fifteenth and sixteenth centuries. The activities of such a guild are portrayed in Wagner's opera 'Die Meistersinger von Nürnberg' (1868) (see GERMANY, 1).

MATHEWS. (1) CHARLES (1776–1835), English actor, who would perhaps be more accurately classified as an entertainer, since the best part of his work lay in his imitations and assumptions of different characters, particularly in his *At Homes*—a form peculiar to himself which has been described as 'a whole play in the person of one man'. The son of a bookseller, Mathews had from early childhood a most retentive memory and amazing powers of mimicry, coupled with an intense desire to go on the stage. This he eventually achieved, making his first appearances in Dublin in 1794. After some years in the provinces, spent mainly at York under Tate Wilkinson, during which time he married, lost his wife, and married as his second wife a young actress, he appeared in London at the Haymarket, and soon made a reputation as an eccentric comedian. Among his successes were Sir Fretful Plagiary, always one of his best parts, and Risk in *Love Laughs at Locksmiths*. In her biography of her husband Mrs. Mathews says, 'Risk may be recorded as his first great part, *written* for him; all characters besides, at least for many years, were in fact mere outlines left for him to fill up by dint of his genius. . . .' He later appeared at both Drury Lane and Covent Garden, and in addition to the many new parts which he created, estimated at about 400, he was seen as Falstaff, Sir Archy MacSarcasm, and Sir Peter Teazle. It was in 1808 that he first conceived the idea of the one-man entertainment with which his name is principally connected. It was originally a programme of comic songs linked together by descriptions of eccentric characters whom he had evolved, partly from observation, partly from intuition. During the years he performed his entertainments they gradually grew to be short plays, on the lines of *The Actor of All Work* (1817), which Colman wrote for him. This represents a country manager interviewing applicants for a place in his company, and gave Mathews an opportunity of portraying a bewildering series of totally dissimilar characters, and of showing his power of mimicry in an imitation of the French actor Talma. Among the most successful of the sketches which Mathews concocted himself were *The Trip to Paris, Mr. Mathews and his Youthful Days*, in which he gave an imitation of Macklin, and *The Trip to America*. He first visited the United States in 1822, making his first appearance in Baltimore, and playing in New York in his own sketches and in *The Heir-at-Law* and *The Road to Ruin*. He returned there in 1834, but was already in a precarious state of health and died at Liverpool on the return journey. He was for some years manager of the Adelphi with Yates,

which involved him in some financial difficulties, and he suffered all his life from a nervous irritability and tendency to melancholy which happily had no effect upon his work. He was also somewhat lame as the result of a carriage accident, and had a horror of publicity. Sir Walter Scott, who was his warm admirer, said that his imitations were of the mind, and that, far more than a mimic, he was an accurate and philosophic observer of human nature, blessed with the rare talent of identifying himself intuitively with the minds of others. This helps to explain the extraordinary success of his entertainments, which he played in London and all over the provinces for more than twenty years. By his second wife he had one son (2) CHARLES JAMES (1803–78), who was trained as an architect, and as a young man idled his time away pleasantly, travelling and occasionally appearing in amateur theatricals. He did not take to the stage professionally until 1835, when he replaced his father in the management of the Adelphi. This arrangement lasted only a short time, and he then went to the Olympic, making his appearance on 6 Nov. 1835 in his own play *The Humpbacked Lover*, and in a farce by Leman Rede, *The Old and Young Stager*, in which he played with Liston. Three years later he married Mme Vestris and with her went to New York, but they were not very well received at first. On their return to London they took over the management of Covent Garden, where they staged some brilliant productions, including *London Assurance* with Mathews as Dazzle, always one of his best parts. The venture was not, however, a success financially and hoping to recover their losses they moved to the Lyceum. This proved an even worse speculation and in the midst of their bankruptcy Mme Vestris died. Mathews continued to act, and made another visit to America, from which he returned with his second wife, an actress named Lizzie Davenport. With her help he extricated himself from his difficulties and embarked on a more successful, though less eventful, career which lasted until his death. He made several extended tours which took him to Australia and India, and remained to the end an elegant, lighthearted, and improvident creature. Tragedy and pathos were outside his range, but he was inimitable in such parts as Dazzle, Affable Hawk in *A Game of Speculation*, Plumper in *Cool as a Cucumber*, Puff, Flutter, and Young Wilding. 'With what ease,' says Coleman, 'what grace and distinction he carried his chapeau bras, took snuff, or fluttered his cambric.' Like his father he was a good mimic, and one of his most popular pieces was *Patter v. Clatter*, which he wrote himself and in which he played five parts. He also appeared with his second wife in an entertainment reminiscent of that of his father called *Mr. and Mrs. Mathews at Home*. He had not the solid gifts of the elder Mathews, but much charm and delicacy tempered his high spirits and made him within certain limits one of the best light comedians of the English stage. His reminiscences were edited with biographical notes by the younger Charles Dickens.

The younger Mathews's first wife (3) LUCIA ELIZABETH (or LUCY ELIZA) BARTOLOZZI (1797–1856) had already had a distinguished career before she married him. Daughter of a famous engraver, she was married at sixteen to Armand Vestris, one of the family of great French dancers, who left her in 1820. She was an excellent singer and might have made a career in grand opera, but preferred to limit herself to lighter entertainment. A fascinating woman, with large lustrous eyes and dark hair, she was at her best in burlesque, or in the fashionable ladies of high comedy. She made her first success in the title-role of Moncrieff's *Giovanni in London*, a burlesque of Mozart's 'Don Giovanni'. She played in Paris for several years, with such success that she was able to return to London on her own terms, playing alternately at Covent Garden and Drury Lane. In 1830 she took over the Olympic, with a strong cast which included Liston, Maria Foote (soon to become the Countess of Harrington), the Glovers, the Blands, and two members of the Vining family. The theatre opened with *Olympic Revels*, by Planché, who furnished Mme Vestris with a succession of farces and burlesques both at this theatre and later at the Lyceum. During her tenancy of the Olympic she engaged Charles Mathews the younger and the rest of her career ran parallel to his. She was an excellent manageress, known as 'Madame' to her company, whom she ruled with a rod of iron. She made many improvements in theatrical scenery and effects and had good taste in costume. She was responsible for the introduction of real, as opposed to fake, properties and by 1841 at the latest evolved the box set, complete with ceiling.

MATTHEWS, JAMES BRANDER (1852–1929), American theatre historian, playwright, and first Professor of Dramatic Literature in the United States, at the University of Columbia. With Laurence Hutton he edited *Actors and Actresses of Great Britain and the United States* in five volumes (1886), wrote widely on the history of the theatre, and had had several one-act plays produced, as well as collaborating in two full-length plays, when in 1892 he was appointed Professor of Literature at Columbia. From 1900 to 1924 he was Professor of Dramatic Literature, and by his writings and lectures had a great influence on the professional theatre, on the practice of dramatic criticism, and on the attitude of the general public. He had a wide knowledge of European drama, and a keen feeling for all that was best in the dramatic literature of his own and other countries. Among his own writings, which included several volumes of essays on New York, and an autobiography, *These Many Years* (1917), the most important were *The Development of the Drama* (1903), *Molière* (1910), *Shakespeare as a Playwright* (1913), and *Principles of Playmaking* (1919). Matthews was one of the founders of both the Authors' and the Players' Clubs. He

was also an original member of the National Institute of Arts and Letters and its President for a year.

MATTOCKS, MRS. ISABELLA (1746–1826), English actress, the youngest daughter of Lewis Hallam, senior. Left behind when the rest of the family went to the New World, she was brought up by an aunt who was an actress, and is believed to have been on the stage from the age of 5, playing small parts at Covent Garden. She made her adult début as Juliet in 1761, and a few years later married an actor named Mattocks, who became manager of the theatre in Liverpool, where Mrs. Mattocks played in the summer, spending the winter seasons, until her retirement in 1808, at Covent Garden. She also appeared at the Haymarket, and in Portsmouth. She had no aptitude for tragedy, and no singing voice, but was excellent in comedy, particularly in pert chambermaids. Her last appearance was as Flora in *The Wonder*.

MAUDE, CYRIL (1861–1951), English actor-manager of great charm and energy, who had a long and varied career in an epoch of great actor-managers. In his youth ill health sent him to Canada, after completing his education at Charterhouse. He was intended for the Church or the army, since he came of a military family, but he decided on the stage, and made his first appearance in 1884 in the United States, at Denver, Colorado, as the servant in *East Lynne*. In the following year he returned to England and appeared at the Criterion in 1886, and then went on tour. His first big success came in 1887, when he appeared as the Duke of Courtland in *Racing* at the Grand Theatre, Islington. A long round of successes finally brought him into management, and in 1896 he took over the Haymarket, where, first with Frederick Harrison, and later alone, he made theatre history with a series of fine productions, beautifully acted by a distinguished company with his wife, Winifred Emery, as leading lady. Maude excelled in old-men parts, and his performances in *The Clandestine Marriage* and *Beauty and the Barge* were unrivalled, while his Sir Peter Teazle was one of the finest in living memory. One of his later productions, *Grumpy*, brought him success on two continents. He could, however, play other parts, and was successful in the title-roles of such different plays as *The Little Minister* and *Toddles*. On leaving the Haymarket Maude became manager of the Playhouse, which was destroyed before he could open it by part of Charing Cross Station falling on it. He weathered the storm, however, and produced many successes there, including *The Flag Lieutenant*, which provided him with one of his best parts, and a fine performance of *Rip Van Winkle* (see also EMERY (3)).   W. M. P.

MAUGHAM, WILLIAM SOMERSET (1874–), English dramatist and novelist. Born in Paris, he was educated at King's School,

Canterbury, and at Heidelberg University and trained as a doctor at St. Thomas's Hospital, qualifying M.R.C.S. and L.R.C.P. He was a novelist before he was a playwright and has continued to write novels, short stories, travel books, and memoirs after appearing to have abandoned the theatre. The height of Maugham's popularity as a dramatist was reached in 1908 when he created a theatrical record by having four original plays performed in London concurrently, and from 1907, three years after the production at the Avenue Theatre of his first play, *A Man of Honour*, till the early thirties, he was prolific, fashionable, and popular. With *The Circle*, which has been described as an almost perfect 'serious' comedy, he made in 1921 what may be a permanent contribution to the theatre. Among the best-remembered of the pieces that entertained a large public over many years are *Lady Frederick* (1907), *The Land of Promise* (1914), *Caroline* 1916), *Our Betters* (1917), *Home and Beauty* (1919), *East of Suez* (1922), *The Letter* (1927), *The Constant Wife* (1927), *The Sacred Flame* (1928), *The Breadwinner* (1930), and *Sheppey* (1933).

There is a finish, a neatness, an air of accomplishment about every work of Maugham's, whatever its subject-matter, which ensures for playgoers and readers alike a certain quality of pleasure. He could always revive the oldest of themes, relacquer it, and make it look as good as new. He achieved popularity without being good-natured, expansive, optimistic, romantic, or soothing. His humour was sardonic, tending to hard epigram: his attitude towards the virtues mistrustful; but he took care to give the public what he himself liked, a good story. Situation in his plays was more important than character-drawing or philosophizing, but he was always capable of surprising those who looked to him for no more than cleverness and efficiency by sudden imaginative touches, as when the son in *For Services Rendered* (1932), hearing his mother's death sentence, crosses over to the sofa and without a word lightly kisses her; whereupon she says only, 'As you are up, Sydney, you might ring the bell.'   A. V. C.

MAURIER, see DU MAURIER.

MAURO FAMILY, see SCENERY, 3.

MAX, (ALEXANDRE) ÉDOUARD DE (1869–1925), French actor, a pupil of Worms at the Conservatoire, where he took first prizes for comedy and tragedy in 1891. He made his début at the Odéon, and was seen at a number of theatres in Paris, being already considered one of the foremost actors of the day when in 1915 he first appeared at the Comédie-Française, playing Nero in *Britannicus*. He had a short but glorious career there, dying of heart failure at the age of 56 after playing Orestes.

MAXINE ELLIOTT THEATRE, NEW YORK, on 39th Street between Broadway and Sixth Avenue. This was built by the actress after whom it is named, and opened on 30 Dec. 1908. The first outstanding success there was

The Passing of the Third Floor Back, which achieved 216 performances. A riot heralded the arrival of the Abbey Players from Dublin on 20 Nov. 1912, in a fine repertory of Irish plays. Doris Keane was seen in *Romance*, which later had a phenomenal run in London, while 1922 saw the 648 performances of *Rain*. Another Maugham success at this theatre was *The Constant Wife*, with Ethel Barrymore and C. Aubrey Smith, which had 295 performances. *Coquette* (1927), with Helen Hayes, ran for nearly a year. Later Jane Cowl appeared at this theatre in *Twelfth Night*, and in the same season Judith Anderson scored a success in *As You Desire Me*. In 1934 Shumlin was responsible for the production of *The Children's Hour*, with Florence McGee as the child who causes all the trouble. This set a record for the theatre with 691 performances, and the building was then taken over by the Federal Theatre Project with *Horse Eats Hat* and Orson Welles in *Dr. Faustus*. *Separate Rooms* began its long run at the Maxine Elliott, which only had time for a short season of Ballet Jooss before it was taken over for broadcasting and ceased to be a playhouse.   G. F.

MAYAKOVSKY, VLADIMIR VLADIMIROVICH (1894–1930), Soviet poet and dramatist, born in Georgia, the son of a forester. In 1908 he joined the Communist Party, and was twice arrested for underground activities, being also expelled from the School of Painting where he was a student. He was helped and encouraged in his writing by David Burlak and Maxim Gorky, and in 1913 produced and acted in his first play, which was followed, after the Revolution which he had helped to bring about, by the first Soviet play, *Mystery-Bouffe*. This, which shows the Revolution spreading over the whole world, was produced in Moscow in 1918, and in a revised version in 1921. It was also given in German at the Third Congress of the Comintern. In 1929 Mayakovsky wrote *The Bug*, a satire portraying a Soviet world of the future in which a pre-Revolutionary bourgeois and a bed-bug alone survive of the old world, and depicting the struggles and conflicts that result from their efforts to acclimatize themselves. A year later came *The Baths*, a satire on the last remnants of bourgeois elements in Soviet life. Both these plays were produced by Meyerhold, and with their symbolic settings, robots, mechanics, and angularities, typify the drama of the period. *The Bug* was later revived by Taïrov at the Kamerny Theatre. A good deal of Mayakovsky's poetry, some of which has been translated into English, is semi-dramatic in form, and intended for public declamation.

MAY-DAY PLAY, MAYINGS, see FOLK FESTIVALS and ROBIN HOOD.

MAYNE, CLARICE (1886–   ), a music-hall singer of great charm and wit, and a famous Principal Boy. With her first husband, James W. Tate (1876–1922), the song-writer and composer, at the piano and billed with her as 'Clarice Mayne and That', she sang songs which became the rage of the day. Tate, whose first wife was Lottie Collins, died as the result of a chill caught at rehearsal, and some years later Clarice Mayne married Teddie Knox, of Nervo and Knox, the knockabout comedians.

W. M. P.

MAYNE, RUTHERFORD (1878–   ), Irish dramatist, is associated chiefly with the Ulster Theatre (see IRELAND, 3). He began to write plays for it soon after its foundation in 1904 and remained throughout its career a strong supporter and its leading playwright. A few of his plays were first produced by the Abbey Theatre, Dublin, and many of them have had subsequent productions there or in London. He is concerned, like most Ulster dramatists, with what is individual and characteristic in the life of Northern Ireland, but plays such as *Red Turf* (1911) have a significance which is more than local, and the life of the peasant revealed there and the forces which bring about the tragedy are akin to similar ways of life and similar forces in other countries and other ages.

The plays of Rutherford Mayne are *The Turn of the Road* (1906), produced at the Ulster Theatre, Belfast; *The Drone* (1908), produced at the Ulster and Abbey Theatres, and in the U.S.A. in 1913; *The Troth* (London, 1908); *The Goneril* (Independent Theatre, Dublin, 1909); *Captain of the Hosts* (Ulster, 1909); *Red Turf* (Abbey, 1911); *Evening* and *Neil Gallina* (both Ulster, 1912); *If* (Ulster, 1913); *Industry* (Ulster, 1915); *Phantoms* (Ulster, and Gaiety, Dublin, 1928); *Peter* (Abbey, 1930); and *Bridgehead* (Abbey, 1934). Certain of these have been translated into Dutch, Swedish, and Norwegian and produced in those countries.   U. E.-F.

MAZARINE FLOOR, see MEZZANINE.

MEDICI. All the members of this famous Italian family were patrons of the arts, and extended their interest and protection to the theatre. Two of them were dramatists, (1) LORENZO (*c.* 1449–92), known as the Magnificent, author of a *sacra rappresentazione* on the lives of the saints John and Paul, produced in 1489, and patron of the humanist-dramatist Poliziano, and (2) LORENZINO DI PIER FRANCESCO (*fl.* early sixteenth century), one of the first Florentine writers of comedy, whose *Aridosia*, based on Plautus and Terence, was performed in 1536 with fine settings by San Gallo. Larivey later based his *Les Esprits* on this play.

MEDWALL, HENRY (*fl.* 1500), see ENGLAND, 2.

MEGGS, MRS. MARY (?–1691), known as Orange Moll, a well-known figure in the early days of the Restoration theatre. She was a widow, living in the parish of St. Paul, Covent Garden. On 10 Feb. 1662/3 the managers of the Theatre Royal, Bridges Street, granted her a licence for thirty-nine years to hawk oranges and other eatables in their theatre. For this privilege she paid £100 down and 6*s.* 8*d.* for every day the theatre was open, which seems to show that the business was a lucrative one. A contemporary description of the fatal fire which destroyed the theatre in 1672 says it started under the stairs 'where Orange Moll keeps her fruit'. Perhaps one of the lively orange-girls, of whom Nell Gwynn had been one, went searching for fresh supplies with a naked flame. Pepys refers to Orange Moll several times, and gleaned many items of theatrical scandal from her. She was involved in a dispute with the actress Rebecca Marshall, and towards the end of her life was frequently in trouble with the management of the theatre. In 1682 the companies of Drury Lane and Dorset Garden were amalgamated, and the joint management put in a new orange-woman. This led to endless disputes, and the matter was still unsettled when Orange Moll died.

MEILHAC, HENRI (1831–97), a prolific French dramatist, whose first play was done in 1855 at the Palais-Royal, for which theatre, and for the Gymnase, he wrote many comedies and vaudevilles. He collaborated with Halévy in writing libretti for Offenbach's light operas, and was for many years one of the outstanding figures of the French theatre. He had all the ephemeral gifts, and none of the durable ones, but he made a lot of people laugh and his work epitomizes the witty and slightly cynical spirit of the Second Empire, summed up in his nickname of 'the Marivaux of the Boulevards'.

MEININGEN PLAYERS, a private theatrical company formed and directed by George, Duke of Saxe-Meiningen, and his morganatic wife the actress Ellen Franz, which from 1874 to 1890 made theatre history by its reforms. These, as Lee Simonson says in *The Stage is Set*, were 'insistence on the continuous and direct relation between the design of a setting and the actor's movements within it' . . . 'consistent effort to add to the plastic possibilities of stage setting by breaking the monotonous surface of the stage floor into different levels' . . . and 'the handling of stage crowds'. This last was 'made an important part of productions at Meiningen by the characteristic thoroughness with which the duke integrated every detail of a performance into an ensemble'. The crowd became a personage in the drama, every member an actor in his own right yet the whole responding to the needs of the moment in a unifying thought. Great care was also lavished on costumes, which were made historically correct, on details of equipment, position, and intonation, in all of which the Meiningen company was an innovator and directly responsible for much of the fine costume and scenic design of later times. Through its protracted tours under Ludwig Chronegk it had an immense influence on the theatre all over Europe, making its first appearance outside its own town in May–June 1881, when it appeared at Drury Lane, and going as far afield as

Russia. Both the Moscow Art Theatre and Antoine's Théâtre Libre owed much to the precept and practice of the Meiningen players, and their influence can be traced all over Europe and America to-day (see also GERMANY, 5).

MELLON, MRS. ALFRED (née SARAH JANE WOOLGAR) (1824–1909), English actress, daughter of an actor who trained her himself and subsequently guided her whole career. She first appeared as a child prodigy in the provinces, and made her adult début in London on 9 Oct. 1843, appearing at the Adelphi under Webster, with whom she remained for many years. She was at that time known as 'Bella' Woolgar, from her playing of Bella Morton in *A Christmas Carol*. Subsequently, having married a musician, she was known as Mrs. Alfred Mellon. She was for some time at the Lyceum under Dillon, and in 1867 became manager of the Adelphi. She remained on the stage until 1883, retiring as the result of an illness which continued to harass her until her death. Towards the end of her career she was somewhat outmoded in style and lost the favour of the audience, but at her best she was a most accomplished all-round actress. In old comedy she lacked dignity, but she had plenty of high spirits and piquancy and some elegance. She was much admired as Mrs. Vane in *Masks and Faces*, and in *The Flowers of the Forest*. She appeared in a number of dramatizations of Dickens's novels, playing at various times Dot, Tilly, and Bertha in *The Cricket on the Hearth*, Mercy in *Martin Chuzzlewit*, and Mrs. Cratchit, one of her best parts, in *A Christmas Carol*. She was Black-Eyed Susan to T. P. Cooke on his last appearance, and played Anne Chute in the first production of *The Colleen Bawn*. In 1859 she was seen as Catherine Duval in *The Dead Heart*. Her daughter Mary was for some time on the stage.

MELLON, HARRIOT (1777–1837), English actress, who was with a strolling company at Stafford when Sheridan saw her and engaged her for Drury Lane. She appeared there as Lydia Languish in 1797, and remained until her retirement in 1815 on her marriage to the banker Mr. Coutts, playing mainly the light impertinent chambermaids of comedy, in which parts Leigh Hunt much admired her. After her first husband's death she married the Duke of St. Albans, leaving the vast Coutts fortune to the daughter of Sir Francis Burdett, later the Baroness Burdett-Coutts, friend and patron of Sir Henry Irving.

MELMOTH, CHARLOTTE (1749–1823), a fine tragic actress, important in the annals of the early American stage. As a young girl she ran away from school with an actor named Courtney Melmoth, really Samuel Jackson Pratt (1749–1814), author of a monody, *Shadows of Shakespeare, or Shakespeare's Characters paying Homage to Garrick*. They soon separated, but she continued to use his name, and became well known on the Dublin, Edinburgh, and provincial stages. She was at Covent Garden in 1784, and at Drury Lane the following year. In 1793 she appeared in New York, and after giving recitations at concerts, appeared at the John Street Theatre with the American Company, as Euphrasia in *The Grecian Daughter*, a favourite part of Sarah Siddons. At one point she got into trouble with her New York audience for refusing to recite a patriotic epilogue, but her excellent acting, particularly as Lady Macbeth, which caused many more tragedies to be added to the repertory, made her a universal favourite. She was one of the leading actresses at the Park Theatre, New York, when it first opened, leaving it in 1802 after a quarrel with Dunlap. She returned, however, the following season, and stayed until after Dunlap's bankruptcy, when she went to the Chestnut Street Theatre in Philadelphia. She made her last appearance in New York in 1812, and later opened a school of English diction and elocution.

MELNOTTE, VIOLET (1856–1935), English actress and theatre manager. Born in Birmingham, she took her stage name from *The Lady of Lyons*. She made her first appearance in pantomime under Sefton Parry, and also played opposite the younger Mathews. In 1880 she appeared in London under Sir Charles Wyndham and was subsequently seen at the Globe and the Folly Theatres. After touring with the Kendals she returned to London and was seen in light opera. She started in management in 1885 at the Avenue (now the Playhouse) and Comedy Theatres, and among her productions at the latter were Clement Scott's *Sister Mary*, and *The Red Lamp* with Beerbohm Tree. Wishing to have her own theatre, she built one in St. Martin's Lane, then an unfashionable thoroughfare, little more than a slum. This earned her the nickname of 'Mad Melnotte', in which she delighted, but she was eventually justified, as other theatres were built there and the despised Lane became an important feature in London theatrical life. Opened as the Trafalgar Square Theatre, the enterprise was at first unsuccessful, but later, as the Duke of York's, flourished, and was let for a long term to Charles Frohman. Eventually Miss Melnotte resumed control, and ran it herself with no supporting syndicate, quarrelling with every tenant or associate. She had a great love of litigation, and was constantly involved in, or threatened with, lawsuits. She was nearly always unfortunate in her choice of plays, which she produced herself, working on the formula that they must have not more than one scene or eight characters. If a play fulfilled those conditions she would produce it, regardless of its quality. She married Frank Wyatt (1852–1926) (the original Duke of Plaza Toro), outliving him and their son, Frank Gunning Wyatt (1890–1933), actor and dramatic critic. Known to everyone as 'Madam', she was a striking figure, dressed always in rather flamboyant mid-Victorian fashion, with, in later years, silver hair, a pale face, and ropes of pearls.

She had no settled home, living sometimes at the Hotel Metropole, Brighton, and at other times at the Piccadilly Hotel, London.   w. m. p.

MELODRAMA had a twin birth as contradictory musical terms round about 1780. In Germany it meant a passage in opera that was spoken to an orchestral accompaniment. In France *mélodrame* was applied to the device, invented some years earlier by Jean-Jacques Rousseau in his monologue 'Pygmalion', whereby music expressed a character's emotions when he was silent. There is no hint in 'Pygmalion' of the melodramatic spirit that Jean-Jacques made fashionable, but this influenced Schiller when he wrote *Die Räuber* (*The Robbers*), which set a character-pattern with falsely accused hero of noble birth, long-suffering heroine in captivity, tortured old age, and cold-blooded villain in usurped castle. This in turn influenced Mrs. Radcliffe, whose novels created a mountainous world infested by bandits, and under her influence 'Monk' Lewis wrote, besides the novel that gained him his nickname, a drama called *The Castle Spectre* which is *The Robbers* minus all meaning. Captives in castles had an intemperate vogue in the theatres of London and Paris. The usual climax was for prison walls to fall in flames by means of a stage-carpenter's device of wooden blocks easily pulled away. What effect this had on the revolutionary mob may be vaguely surmised. The Bastille fell, and then continued to fall nightly at theatres in both capitals. *The Robbers*, banned in England, was performed in Paris to shouts of 'Guerre aux châteaux!' But Mrs. Radcliffe prevailed over further endeavours to represent the triumph of liberty on the stage. When Napoleon ruled, the popular imagination was fed on tales of mystery and terror in her style. Newspaper feuilletons provided plots for lurid dramas; music between the dialogue gave them the new name of *mélodrame*. Guilbert de Pixerécourt wrote many; they had such power over audiences in the popular theatres that he was known as the Napoleon of the Boulevard. In the time of the empire he shaped and coloured a peculiarly picturesque country as the home of virtue triumphant. Mountains with mills, rivers with little bridges, pine forests with wayside inns or humble cottages, and Gothic castles with dungeons, were its regular features.

In Germany, where Schiller was regretting his undergraduate outburst, Kotzebue—destined to be shot by an undergraduate of *The Robbers* stamp—was writing popular plays that had a widespread vogue. *Menschenhass und Reue*, translated as *The Stranger*, a lasting success on the English stage, upset moral conventions by providing forgiveness for an erring wife—which was interpreted as the beating down of the barrier between comedy and tragedy. Similarly the heroine of *Die Sonnen-Jungfrau* (done as *Cora; or, the Virgin of the Sun*) married happily after breaking her vows. Kotzebue's sequel to this gave joy alike to Paris

under the Terror and to England under the threat of invasion, for in Sheridan's adaptation of *Die Spanier in Peru, oder Rollas Tod* as *Pizarro*, Peruvians expressed British sentiments of patriotic loyalty. What the Boulevard du Temple was to Paris, Lambeth was to London, and there Kotzebue's Peruvian romances and Mrs. Radcliffe's tales of mystery were dramatized as musical spectacles with songs, recitative, and the display of important statements (such as 'I swear to be thine') on notice-boards, to explain what was meant by the dumbshow. Cross, manager of the Royal Circus which later became famous as the Surrey, made such a stir with these that the Theatres Royal imitated his style in pieces labelled 'serious pantomime' or 'Ballet d'action' (see PANTO-MIME, 5). His outstanding success was *Black-beard the Pirate* (1798), a nautical drama with a Jolly Jack Tar for hero. This character can be traced to the singers, in costume, of sea songs at musick-houses in the early eighteenth century. The stage adopted the convention that he should land from a little boat, find somebody in need of protection, and rescue her, some years before Charles Dibdin's songs were composed. To Cross's dramas-without-dialogue the sailor-with-song was a ready-made hero, not only for dramas of the sea but for others in the Radcliffe manner. Thus true-blue adventure had already staked its claim on the popular stage before the first *mélodrame* was billed at Covent Garden on 13 November 1802 as *A Tale of Mystery*, by Thomas Holcroft. It was translated from Pixerécourt, whose name was not printed either on the playbills or in any published copy; all the many English melodramas adapted from his originals followed this example, so that he was unknown in England even when *The Dog of Montargis* (1814), vehicle for a dog star, was as celebrated as *Hamlet*. Theodore Hook likewise took the credit for *Tekeli* (1806). When Caigniez's *La Pie voleuse* came to London as *The Maid and the Magpie*, the original author's name was attached to one or two of the many translations. Some of the English plays of the 'twopence coloured' type may have plots of their own, notably Isaac Pocock's *The Miller and His Men* (1813), which is still acted to-day on Toy Theatres. Though Planché's *The Brigand* (1829) was the last of these banditti dramas to be written, they were constantly revived for many years.

Meanwhile Scott's poems and novels had inspired many melodramas that discarded Rousseau's musical device. The musick-houses and circuses which had used dumb-show as a means of avoiding the law had become burletta houses. According to the Lord Chamberlain's new ruling, a play which contained at least six songs could be classed as a burletta and be performed at these specially privileged places. Thomas Dibdin staged several of the Waverley Novels at the Surrey a week or two after publication. There was no 'insensibility to the absurd' in his work; his later plays, *Suil Dhuv the Coiner* (1828) and

The Banks of the Hudson (1829), provide masterly evidence of the new spirit in the drama of democracy. Previously its stage villains had been cast in the maudlin Gothic mould; human devilry became spirited after supernatural melodramas had proved how acceptable unrepentant evil in the forms of Frankenstein's charnel-house monster, Flying Dutchmen, and Vampires, could be. But this was but one of many new tendencies. Another important one was manifest in *The Lear of Private Life*, adapted by Moncrieff at the Coburg in 1820 from a story by Mrs. Opie, which set a fashion for domestic dramas.

With *Fifteen Years of a Drunkard's Life* at the Coburg in 1828, Douglas Jerrold made his earnestness apparent even in the midst of absurdity. His early life in the Navy inspired the light-hearted *Black-Eyed Susan* (Surrey, 1829); the next year he wrote *The Mutiny at the Nore; or, British Sailors in 1797* (Pavilion, Coburg, and Queen's) as a protest against flogging. In *Martha Willis, the Servant Maid* (Pavilion, 1831) and *The Rent Day* (Drury Lane, 1832) Jerrold championed democracy before succumbing to the pseudo-Shakespearian mode, but the drama of revolt was continued by others until 1840. Adaptations of *Oliver Twist* and *Les Mystères de Paris* are also to be included in these stage-echoes of the clamour for reform.

That ardour subsided. Social injustice was to playgoers merely a passing phase in the subject of crime, which was of permanent interest. *Maria Marten; or, the Murder in the Red Barn* is proof of this. It became a classic of melodrama round about 1830. None of its immediate rivals won such enduring popularity, though Edward FitzBall, that industrious hack who quickly sensed every new fashion, won success at the Surrey in 1833 with *Jonathan Bradford; or, the Murder at the Roadside Inn*. The romance of crime had a temporary vogue; it began with Rob Roy, whose appearance on the stage caused Gilderoy to be transformed into a transpontine hero by William Barrymore, who also made a circus spectacle of Dick Turpin's ride to York. Harrison Ainsworth and Bulwer Lytton raised a crop of thieving gallants who swaggered before the footlights. All such cut-throats, plain or coloured, were outdone when Dibdin Pitt (trained to the stage by his father's half-brother, Thomas Dibdin) borrowed the plot of a penny dreadful for his play at the Britannia in 1847 about Sweeney Todd.

In the patriotic style there was no rivalling the grand military and equestrian dramas of Astley's (circus and theatre combined) near the south side of Westminster Bridge. Though critics protested against an excessive admiration for Napoleon, the battles fought on its stage and in its ring celebrated many British victories from Waterloo to the Far East. *The Dumb Man of Manchester*, played here in 1837, was a factory drama which exhibited the skill in dumbshow of Andrew Ducrow, the famous wire-walker and trick-rider who ruled

over Astley's until it was burned down in 1841. In the new building the battles of the Crimea were represented while the war was in progress. But *Mazeppa; or, the Wild Horse of Tartary*, first equestrianized in 1831, was the regular stand-by of Astley's; Adah Isaacs Menken caused a stir there in the eighteensixties as one of the earliest and certainly the most notorious of many female Mazeppas.

The growth of the middle classes produced a new type of melodrama, notably at the Adelphi, where Buckstone became its chief exponent after making his name there in the democratic style with *Luke the Labourer* in 1826. For Madame Céleste he wrote *The Green Bushes* in 1845, and *The Flowers of the Forest* in 1847. They were sentimental and picturesque in contrast with the horrors of real life borrowed by the Surrey side from *Les Bohémiens de Paris*, which stirred the Boulevard in 1843. It changed from *The Scamps of London* to *London By Night*, then into *Under the Gaslight* in New York (1867) and next into *After Dark, A Tale of London Life* and *London by Gaslight* (both 1868), while its influence less directly shaped dozens of other dramas where heroes were bound to the railroad before the oncoming express. When working class and middle class were thus divided, a distinct type of melodrama was needed for the upper classes. This also came from Paris. It began when Frédérick-Lemaître, disgusted with his part of Robert Macaire in *L'Auberge des Adrets*, changed old-fashioned villainy into wild burlesque. Playwrights who had no wish to be guyed had to become more sophisticated, and the Gallic drama was the result. *Pauline*, from a story by the elder Dumas, was played at the Théâtre Historique in 1850, and the next year at the Princess's, where Queen Victoria was seen to clutch curtains of her box in terror as the heroine fell unsuspectingly into the clutches of a murderer with charming manners and merciless instincts. The Princess's, which was visited by Frédérick-Lemaître, came under the management of Charles Kean, whom the Queen specially favoured. From the Historique he brought another drama based on Dumas, and staged it as *The Corsican Brothers*. He also played Charles Reade's version of *The Lyons Mail* and Boucicault's of *Louis XI*. These three subjects stayed in the loftiest repertoires of the nineteenth century, side by side with Shakespeare's masterpieces, which were acted in the same manner. A melodramatic Hamlet (Fechter's) was acclaimed.

There was no challenging the 'Gallic' hold over the upper classes. Like opera and ballet it had the hot-house atmosphere which the world of fashion liked. Rachel radiated it—and later Bernhardt, with the *femme fatale* of Dumas *fils*. When the Victorian novelists wrote for the stage (Dickens, Wilkie Collins, and Charles Reade) they had to be content with the middle-class audiences of Drury Lane, Olympic, and Adelphi, where they were outshone by Boucicault. After an attempt at Miltonic blank verse, he won youthful fame with that comedy of conventions, *London Assurance* (Covent Garden, 1841), though John Brougham claimed to be the author. Boucicault left for America, where he wrote and played several adaptations. Among these was *The Poor of New York*—seen on the Boulevard as *Les Pauvres de Paris*, at the Strand as *Pride and Poverty*, and at Sadler's Wells as *Islington; or, Life in the Streets*—which he presented in Liverpool as *The Poor of Liverpool*, and at the Princess's as *The Streets of London*. Out of Gerald Griffin's novel *The Collegians* (already dramatized) Boucicault made *The Colleen Bawn*, which was rapturously received at the Adelphi in 1860 as the first 'sensation' drama because of the realistic drownings and rescuings in the cave scene. Among the other plays he brought back from America was *The Octoroon; or, Life in Louisiana*, which had the burning and blowing-up of a steamship as its sensation. Since the author and his wife played the leading parts at the Adelphi, he had the power to insist on a percentage of the takings instead of a fixed fee and so instituted the royalty system. *Arrah-na-Pogue* (Dublin, 1864) and *The Shaughraun* (Drury Lane, 1875) were the best of the many plays he wrote before he was outmoded by two important changes in the development of melodrama.

The first of these was the triumph of the woman novelist. Mrs. Beecher Stowe was the forerunner, as FitzBall realized when he dramatized *Uncle Tom's Cabin* for Drury Lane in 1853. A version of *East Lynne*, acted at the Effingham, Whitechapel, in 1864, was followed by others until a theatrical boom occurred in Mrs. Henry Wood's novel in 1879. In the eighteen-sixties she had had a formidable rival in Miss Braddon, whose *Lady Audley's Secret* and *Aurora Floyd* were denounced for interesting audiences in the 'unhealthy' subject of bigamy. Boucicault shared this profitable obloquy by making a bad woman his principal character in *Formosa; or, the Railroad to Ruin* at Drury Lane in 1869. But the second change was more difficult to withstand: it doomed all melodramatists who lived on other people's plots. (But not before such piracy produced, in Tom Taylor's *The Ticket-of-Leave Man*, at the Olympic in 1863, the best melodrama of all.) New laws of copyright, which protected novelists and foreign playwrights, made 'adaptation' a difficult career.

After collaborating with Dickens in *No Thoroughfare* at the Adelphi in 1867, Wilkie Collins dramatized his own novels, which increased the vogue of detective dramas and murder mysteries. Paul Merritt's *The Golden Plough* at the Surrey in 1877 proved that the trick of puzzling an audience concerning the identity of a criminal was soon mastered. Fergus Hume's *The Mystery of a Hansom Cab* was dramatized at the Princess's in 1888. But these did not destroy the vogue of virtue triumphant which was upheld by Wilson Barrett at the Princess's in plays by George R. Sims (*The Lights o' London and Romany Rye*)

and Hall Caine (*Ben-My-Chree*) and still more notably in *The Silver King*, by H. A. Jones and H. Herman in 1882, a drama on the old theme of falsely accused innocence (incidentally its novel idea of a hero who wrongly believed himself guilty had been used by 'Monk' Lewis in *Adelmorn the Outlaw*). Though acknowledged to be one of the best melodramas ever written, *The Silver King* came second as a source of financial profit to *The Sign of the Cross* by Wilson Barrett, who acted it in America before its first performance in England at the Grand, Leeds, in 1895.

From the first night of *The Bells* at the Lyceum in 1871, Henry Irving maintained melodrama in the highest dramatic sphere by the side of Shakespeare. Some plays in his repertoire had descended from the Boulevard du Temple by way of Charles Kean and Fechter—*Robert Macaire*, *The Lyons Mail*, *Louis XI*, and *The Corsican Brothers*—and these were among his greatest achievements. Members of his company established melodrama in companies of their own. William Terriss upheld the prestige of the Adelphi drama with *The Bells of Haslemere* in 1887. Martin-Harvey found in *The Only Way*, one of many versions of *A Tale of Two Cities*, the foundation of his managerial career. Arthur Wing Pinero, using the language, ethics, and characterization of melodrama, wrote plays that were accepted as an up-to-date criticism of life. London's leading actor-managers at the opening of the twentieth century relied mainly on melodrama—Tree with *Captain Swift*, *Oliver Twist*, and *Trilby*; Alexander with *Old Heidelberg*, *If I were King*, and *The Prisoner of Zenda*.

Because the word had become a term of abuse as soon as it had been associated with 'popular' audiences, melodrama usually appeared under heavy disguises. Less trouble was taken at Drury Lane, where 'autumn dramas' for fifty years kept to plots of the falsely-accused-innocence type as an excuse for spirited scene-shifting to represent shipwrecks, railroad crashes, earthquakes, and horse-racing. Walter and Frederick Melville, who took to writing melodramas for the masses after years of managerial experience, were franker still; their titles, such as *The Bad Girl of the Family*, *The Worst Woman in London*, and *The Ugliest Woman on Earth*, advertised their shock tactics. But twentieth-century melodrama, particularly at Drury Lane, strayed farther and farther from the fundamental idea of identifying virtue with poverty and simplicity; or perhaps the change was that 'poverty' now meant that heroes and heroines were reduced to the state of relying on a Derby winner to restore their fortunes. *Love on the Dole*, at the Garrick in 1935, was the true drama of democracy, and it discarded all the conventions of melodrama. These were employed *in toto* by Walter Reynolds (who played Virgil to Irving's Dante) in *Young England*, which was riotously received by busy mockers at theatre after theatre from 1934 onwards until withdrawn as a disturber of the peace. Virtue triumphant and crime exultant were jokes until the autumn of 1939. *Young England* was then revived; somehow it seemed rather less funny.

As a pair of contradictory technical terms 'melodrama' (what is spoken to music—the monologues of a *diseuse* for example) and 'mélodrame' (music accompanying dumb-show, as in Planquette's 'Rip Van Winkle')—are still in use, especially in France and Germany.   M. W. D.

MELODRAMMA, a play with music, each being given equal importance, which evolved in eighteenth-century Italy from the earlier pastoral. The chief writers connected with it are Apostolo Zeno and Metastasio, whose libretti have since been used by innumerable operatic composers.

MELPOMENE, the Muse of Tragedy.

MELUCHA TEATER, see JEWISH DRAMA, 6, and MOSCOW STATE JEWISH THEATRE.

MELVILLE. (1) WALTER (1875–1937) and (2) FREDERICK (1876–1938), sons of Andrew Melville, actor and theatre proprietor, under whom they both started their careers in Birmingham. For twenty-five years they were joint proprietors of the Lyceum Theatre, London, where they made their own tradition of Lyceum pantomimes. Mostly written by Fred, they were elaborate, expensive productions in which comedy predominated. No matter how absurd the situations, or how anachronistic the clothes, they were consistently successful, and taxed the capacity of the Lyceum every Christmas. The two brothers, who were also partners in other enterprises—they built the Prince's Theatre—amassed great wealth, which they made no effort to spend. They both had simple tastes, wore shabby clothes—Walter, who usually wore a white tie, was slightly better dressed than Fred, whose suits were seldom of one piece—lived plainly, and followed no fashionable pursuits. They were simply and solely men of the theatre. Their enterprises flourished, except when they were not on speaking terms, when everything stopped until the dispute was over. They then communicated through their excellent and trusted manager, Bert Hammond, while continuing to occupy the same office at the Lyceum, one of the oldest rooms in the building, furnished in an early Victorian manner. In spite of occasional disagreements there was a great bond between them, and if mutually attacked they stood firm together. They were good people to work for, in spite of the tales told of their economies—Fred's particularly—and their staff remained with them for years. Both brothers were successful writers of highly-coloured melodrama, simple, direct stories with virtue triumphant, much to the taste of the time. Walter was responsible for *The Worst Woman in London*, *The Girl Who Took the Wrong Turning*, and *The Girl Who*

Wrecked his Home, among others, and was a silent man, more reserved than his brother, but with a curious sense of humour which manifested itself in odd practical jokes which he much enjoyed. Fred, who early in his career was an actor, wrote *Her Forbidden Marriage*, *The Ugliest Woman on Earth*, and *The Bad Girl of the Family*, all lurid, and all successful in their day. His daughter (3) JUNE (1915–   ) is also an actress, and proprietor and manager of the Brixton Theatre.   W. M. P.

MENANDER (*c.* 342–292 B.C.), Greek dramatist, son of Diopeithes, and an Athenian poet of New Comedy (see GREECE, 2 *b*). For a time he studied philosophy with Theophrastus, pupil and successor of Aristotle. He was invited to the Court of Ptolemy I of Egypt, but preferred to remain in Athens. His comedies had an enormous reputation in antiquity; plays of his were closely imitated by Plautus and Terence; Caesar called Terence 'a half-Menander'; citations from his works are very numerous in later writers, and include a verse quoted by St. Paul, 'Evil communications corrupt good manners'. Until this century Menander was known only indirectly and in these fragments, but in 1905 a papyrus (now in Cairo) was discovered which contains considerable parts of four plays, with smaller fragments of a fifth; the four are *Hero*, *Samia*, the *Epitrepontes* (Arbitrators), and the *Periciromene*. The last was translated in 1941, with conjectural restorations, by Professor Gilbert Murray under the title *The Rape of the Locks*.

Because, very largely, of the change in the political status and atmosphere of Athens, the comedy of Menander is utterly unlike that of Aristophanes a hundred years earlier. It is a delicate comedy of manners and of neat intrigue drawn against a background of *bourgeois* city-life; the exuberant fancy, burlesque, and lampooning of Old Comedy are entirely absent. In fact, Menander is much closer, in form, matter, and style, to the later, non-tragic drama of Euripides than he is to Aristophanes.

As the earlier 'tragedy' was not always 'tragic' (in our sense of the word), so New Comedy was not regularly 'comic'; it is drama with a romantic flavour that turns usually on such things as the ill-used maiden and the slave-foundling who proves to be well born. The 'romance' is chastened by close observation of contemporary life, and by a tone of urbane philosophizing—another link with Euripides. The whole is distinguished by extreme elegance of composition and style, and by delicate and sympathetic characterization. Old Comedy was essentially local and topical; this was the opposite. Menander therefore gave to the Roman dramatists what Aristophanes could never have given—excellent models and useful material. It is in Menander that we meet the originals of some of the stock figures of later comedy—the irascible old man, the young rake with a good heart, the officious slave—portrayed with great delicacy and liveliness.

A drama which dealt exclusively with the

fortunes of private individuals obviously left no room for a chorus, which must in some sense represent the community. Accordingly, Menander's 'chorus' is nothing but a group of singers and dancers, who provide breaks between the acts; sometimes they are dramatically explained away as a band of tipsy revellers. Their songs are quite irrelevant to the play; in the papyrus there is only a heading 'Something for Chorus'.   H. D. F. K.

MENKEN, ADAH ISAACS (1835–68), American actress, whose real name was Dolores Adios Fuertes. Orphaned at 13, she became a dancer in her home town, New Orleans, with great success, and later decided to become an actress. The only part associated with her name is that of Mazeppa, though she was not, as is often asserted, the first woman to play the part. This equestrian drama had been first given in London in 1831, and continued to be popular during the next fifty years, though it was not until 1859 that a woman essayed the part of the hero. Menken played it in 1863 in California, then in New York, and in 1864 at Astley's in London. She had married in 1856 John Isaacs Menken, and retained her married name through subsequent matrimonial and other adventures. She appears to have exercised a fatal fascination over 'literary gentlemen', including Swinburne, Dickens, and the elder Dumas. She died in Paris, where she had first appeared in 1866. There are no records of her acting ability, and her theatrical reputation seems to rest entirely on the 'magnificent audacity' with which she displayed her person 'in a state of virtual nudity when she was bound to the back of the wild horse'.

MERCIER, LOUIS SÉBASTIEN (1740–1814), French dramatist, and an exponent of the *drame bourgeois* initiated by Diderot. A well-educated and much-travelled man, he was well versed in the dramatic literature of Europe, especially Shakespeare and Lope de Vega, and his book, *Du Théâtre*, makes interesting reading. His own plays, in which he gives elaborate directions for scenery, were not very successful in France, but in translation they were welcomed in England, Italy, Holland, and particularly in Germany, where they were very popular on account of their unimpeachable morality and their declamatory style. The most characteristic is *La Brouette du vinaigrier* (1784), the story of a marriage arranged between a wealthy girl and the son of a working-class man which brought tears to the eyes of its audiences, as did the earlier *Jenneval* (1768)—an adaptation of *The London Merchant* in which the hero escapes punishment by a last-minute conversion. Mercier was an optimist who believed that right would prevail and he had scant sympathy with tragedies in which the hero is at the mercy of forces outside his own control. In pursuance of this theory he gave his translation of *Romeo and Juliet* a happy ending, and reduced *King Lear* to a tale of a bourgeois household quarrelling over the misdeeds of the servants. His plays

possess unity, but not that conflict which is the essence of drama, and to quote one critic 'are no more interesting than the projects of a town councillor for municipal reform would be if dramatised'. It is interesting to note that this moral dramatist was a friend of the outcast Restif de la Bretonne, while of his fellow-authors, Beaumarchais was an adventurer, La Chaussée wrote *contes grivoises*, and Diderot equivocal novels. Yet they all posed as moralists. Mercier's political views were not looked on with favour before the Revolution, and he went to Switzerland to await the outburst which he boasted of having helped to prepare. He then returned and worked as a journalist. As a deputy he voted against the execution of Louis XVI in favour of a life sentence. He was later imprisoned, but, luckier than André Chénier, who was with him in prison, he was saved from the guillotine by the fall of Robespierre.

MERCURY THEATRE, LONDON, at Notting Hill Gate. This was opened by Ashley Dukes in 1933. It is a small but well-equipped theatre which has produced some excellent plays, often considered 'non-commercial'. It was at the Mercury that *Murder in the Cathedral* was first seen in London. The Mercury is also the home of the Ballet Rambert, run under the direction of Mrs. Ashley Dukes (Marie Rambert). For the Mercury Theatre, New York, see COMEDY THEATRE (2).

MERRY, MRS., see BRUNTON (2).

MERRYANDREW, see CLOWN.

MERSON, BILLY (1881–1947), a music-hall performer whose best-known songs were 'The Spaniard that Blighted my Life' and 'The Good Ship Yakihickidula'. Born in Nottingham, he was apprenticed to engineering, but ran away to join a circus, where he clowned as Ping-Pong. With a partner he went on the halls as Trewella and Snakella. Deciding to change the name of their act, they picked on two names that would look good on the bills, and tossed up for them. The partner became Keith, while William Henry Thompson became Billy Merson. He soon became famous, his shortness, his physical strength, and his ability to do acrobatics, added to a pleasing voice and an attractive personality, bringing him to the fore. He later went into pantomime and revue, and then starred at Drury Lane as Hard-Boiled Herman in *Rose Marie* (1925), in which he later toured. He went into management at the Shaftesbury, presenting and playing in a musical comedy called *My Son John*, and also played in some of Edgar Wallace's plays. During the war of 1939–45 he did fine service entertaining the troops.   W. M. P.

MESSENIUS, JOHANNES (1579–1636), early Swedish dramatist, one of the first to take his subjects from Swedish history and saga. He planned a series of fifty plays on the former, of which only six survive (see SCANDINAVIA, 3).

METASTASIO [PIETRO ARMANDO DOMINICO

TRAPASSI] (1698–1782), Italian poet and author of a number of libretti for plays with music which have been constantly used by operatic composers (see OPERA). He was a child of exceptional abilities, and was adopted by the Abbé Gravina. For some years he delighted Roman audiences by his rapid improvisations, and he wrote his first tragedy, *Il Giustino*, when he was 14. In 1729 he was appointed Court Poet at Vienna, in succession to Apostolo Zeno, a position which he retained under Charles VI and Maria Theresa. He wrote much, his lyrical vein appearing to be inexhaustible. Of his numerous libretti the best are *L'Adriano* (1731), *La Clemenza di Tito* (which has probably been set by more composers than any other text), and *Attilio Regolo*. These last were both written in 1732. The first was given in 1734 in Vienna, but the *Attilio Regolo*, considered Metastasio's masterpiece, was not performed until 1782 in Poland. Voltaire set Metastasio above all his contemporaries except Racine and Addison, whom he considered alone worthy of being compared to the classics. Rousseau was also a great admirer of Metastasio, but Alfieri, not without reason, attacked his style, which he found lacking in force and virility.

METROPOLITAN CASINO, NEW YORK, see BROADWAY THEATRE (3).

METROPOLITAN THEATRE, NEW YORK, originally Tripler Hall, and then used for opera. The original building was burnt down on 7 Jan. 1854, and a theatre was erected on the site for Henry Willard. This opened on 18 Sept. 1854 with a somewhat hackneyed bill, and by January of the next year had become a circus. It was still occasionally used for plays, and in Sept. 1855 Rachel appeared there with a French company in *Phèdre* and *Adrienne Lecouvreur*. On 27 Dec. the theatre reopened under Laura Keene, and, in spite of prejudice against a woman manager, it was progressing satisfactorily when, on a technical point of law, she lost her lease. She closed on 21 June 1856, and the theatre was bought by Burton, who remained there only two years. After his departure there was a short season of old comedies under Conway. For the later history of this theatre see WINTER GARDEN (2).

MEXICO, see SOUTH AMERICA, 1.

MEYERHOLD, VSEVOLOD EMILIEVICH (1874–), Soviet Russian actor and producer who began his theatrical career as a student in the Musical-Dramatic School of the Moscow Philharmonic Society under Nemirovich-Danchenko, and in 1898 was invited to join the newly founded Moscow Art Theatre. Here he worked until 1902, when he left and went to the provinces, acting and producing in the Society of New Drama founded by himself. His theatrical activity was intense and many-sided; he was actor, producer, artistic director, theoretician, and pedagogue. In 1905 Stanislavsky invited him to take charge of productions at the newly organized Studio which was

to be an experimental laboratory for the Moscow Art Theatre along the lines of the Symbolists. *La Mort de Tintagiles* was put into rehearsal, but was never shown to the public, and soon afterwards the Studio closed. From 1906 to 1907 Meyerhold was invited to produce at the Theatre of Vera Komisarjevskaya, where he was able to put into practice the symbolic or stylized method he had envisaged at the Moscow Art Theatre Studio. In effect this amounted to 'abstract' theatre, placing the human element, the actor, on a level with the other elements of production, thus reducing to nothing the actor's individual contribution to the ensemble, and making him merely a super-marionette in the hands of the producer—in fact, a realization of Gordon Craig's one-time ideal, and the source of Meyerhold's eventual theatrical bankruptcy. This treatment of the actor led inevitably to a break with Komisarjevskaya, and Meyerhold left. He staged some brilliant productions at the Imperial Theatres in Petrograd—the Marinsky and the Alexandrinsky—and at the same time continued experimental work in his own Studio, where from 1913 to 1917 he continued, under the influence of the improvisation and stylized traditions of the *commedia dell' arte*, to work out his own methods. On the outbreak of the Revolution Meyerhold was the first artist of the theatre to offer his services to the new Government, and in 1918 he became a member of the Bolshevik Party. Two years later he was appointed head of the Theatre Section of the People's Commissariat for Education, where he began a campaign to reorganize the theatre on Revolutionary lines. His views did not entirely coincide with those of the Soviet Government, since he was all for the immediate revolutionizing of the still existing pre-Revolutionary theatres, whereas the Government, and Lunacharsky in particular, saw that the revolutionizing of a delicate organism, such as the Moscow Art Theatre, could not be done by decree, or by sudden external change, but by its absorption into the general stream of Soviet activity, strengthening what was healthy and rejecting what was decadent. This was the plan actually followed, which twenty years later left Meyerhold high and dry. Yet nothing can take away from the flaming enthusiasm, daring sincerity, and originality of his early work, for he was the first producer to put on a Soviet play—*Mystery-Bouffe*—in 1920 in his newly formed First Theatre of R.S.F.S.R., which later became the Theatre of Meyerhold. In his own Theatre Workshop Meyerhold continued his teaching, and developed his famous 'bio-mechanics' system of acting. He trained a number of people who have since played an important part in the development of Soviet art, and was director till 1924 of the first Moscow theatre to specialize in Soviet plays—the Theatre of the Revolution. He also influenced the school of Stanislavsky, particularly in the Vakhtangov Theatre. In later years his productions became more experimental, his repertory less Soviet, and he became essentially a producer's producer. His actors left him, his audiences diminished. He was warned, from time to time over many years, what the end might be. No State, however sympathetic, can indefinitely subsidize unprofitable enterprise, and in 1938 the Theatre of Meyerhold was closed, and he was invited to work elsewhere.

MEZZANINE FLOOR. Albert Smith, in *The Natural History of the Ballet Girl*, says this, which he spells 'Mezzonine', is 'underneath the stage, halfway between the stage and nowhere, inhabited by those active spirits who send fairies and demons up and down the traps'. He says that it is also known in the theatre as the Mazarine floor (see STAGE, 2 *b*).

MEZZETINO, a *zanni* or servant of the *commedia dell'arte*, with many of the characteristics of Brighella or Scapino, though more polished. Towards the end of the seventeenth century (1682) the role was altered and elaborated by Angelo Costantini, who adopted red and white as the distinguishing mark of his costume, as opposed to the green and white stripes of Scapino. When, on the death of Dominique, he inherited that actor's role of Harlequin, he retained his name and costume. A later French Mezzetin was the actor Préville, of the Comédie-Française, who was painted by Van Loo in the part.

MICHAU, see JADOT.

MIDDLE COMEDY, see GREECE, 2.

MIDDLE GALLERY, see AUDITORIUM, 1 *c*.

MIDDLESEX AMPHITHEATRE, see OLYMPIC THEATRE (1).

MIDDLESEX MUSIC-HALL, LONDON, see MUSIC-HALL and WINTER GARDEN THEATRE (1).

MIDDLETON, THOMAS (*c.* 1570–1627), English dramatist, who began his career as one of Henslowe's hack-writers. Nothing survives of his work at this period, except some trace of collaboration with those other industrious workers, Dekker, Drayton, Munday, and Greene. He collaborated with Dekker in *The Honest Whore* (1604) and *The Roaring Girl* (1610), and by himself wrote a number of plays of which the best was *A Trick to Catch the Old One* (1604–5), to which Massinger may be indebted for the idea of his *New Way to Pay Old Debts*. Others were *A Mad World, my Masters* (1606), and *Your Five Gallants* (1607), both comedies of London manners, acted by the Children's companies; *A Chaste Maid in Cheapside* (1611); *No Wit, no Help like a Woman's* (? 1613); and the notorious political satire, *A Game at Chess* (1624). This dealt with the fruitless attempts which were being made to unite the royal houses of England and Spain, and, in spite of its popularity, Middleton was severely admonished for having written it and perhaps imprisoned. Middleton's best work was done in collaboration with Rowley, particularly in *The Changeling* (1622), and he was also responsible for a number of masques and pageants.

MIELZINER, JO (1901–   ), American scenic designer, who was for a short time an actor. Since 1924 he has devoted himself entirely to scenic design, and has been responsible for many fine productions, among them John Gielgud's New York *Hamlet* (see U.S.A., 11).

MIKHOELS, SALOMON [SALOMON MIKHAILOVICH VOVSKY] (1890–1948), Jewish actor and producer, and from 1928 until his death head of the Moscow State Jewish Theatre. Born at Dvinsk, he was educated at the Kiev Commercial Institute, and then studied at Petrograd University from 1915 to 1918 with the intention of becoming a teacher of mathematics. He was one of the original members of the Jewish Theatre Studio formed in Leningrad by Granovsky in 1919, and first came into prominence two years later with a performance in Sholom Aleichem's *Agents*. He became the company's leading actor, and in 1928 took over the directorship from Granovsky. One of his finest performances was given as King Lear in Radlov's production in 1935.

MIKKT, see JEWISH DRAMA, 8.

MILLAR, ROBINS (1889–   ), Scottish dramatist and journalist, born in British Columbia. His *Thunder in the Air*, a play dealing with the problem of communication between the living and the dead, combines the elements of the thriller with psychic drama, and met with considerable success when produced in 1928. His other plays include a fantasy, a satire, historical dramas, and comedies of Glasgow middle-class life, most of which have been performed by the Curtain Theatre, Glasgow, or the Scottish National Players.

w. J.

MILLER. (1) HENRY (1860–1926), American actor-manager, born in England, who was taken to Canada at an early age and at 15, after witnessing a performance of *Romeo and Juliet*, decided to go on the stage. He made his first appearance in Toronto and then went to New York, where, after touring with many leading actresses of the time, and with Boucicault, he became leading man of the Empire Theatre stock company. In 1899 he appeared as Sydney Carton in *The Only Way*, which had a long run, and in 1906 went into management, producing *The Great Divide* at the Princess Theatre. He was later seen in the same play in London. Among his other productions were *The Servant in the House* (1908) and *The Faith Healer* (1910), in both of which he himself played. In 1916 he opened his own theatre in New York (see HENRY MILLER'S THEATRE). He married Bijou, the daughter of the actress Matilda Heron, and their son (2) GILBERT HERON (1884–   ) became an actor and later a well-known theatre manager in London and New York, producing alone and in collaboration many outstanding plays, and fostering the exchange of new works across the Atlantic.

[531]

MIME(literally 'imitation' or 'representation').

1. GREEK. (*a*) *Popular*. The mime was originally a sketch of a dramatic, and often crudely realistic, kind (see below, the Latin mime).

(*b*) *Literary*. The popular mime had literary offshoots, some intended for dramatic performance, some not. Of these, the earliest seems to have been the Syracusan comedy of the early fifth century B.C., in which Epicharmus and Sophron were the most important figures. This comedy survives only in a few fragments and some doubtful traditions. It seems to have been a vigorous drama, and mythological burlesque seems to have been one of its sources of fun. It strongly influenced the slightly later Old Comedy of Athens, from which it differed in having no chorus and no political background. Sophron was associated especially with mime, and one purely literary development of this was the semi-dramatic dialogues of Plato. A still later development was the Alexandrian mime. Theocritus's *Women at the Festival of Adonis* (well translated by Matthew Arnold) is a good example of this, and is said to have been inspired by a mime of Sophron's on a similar subject. Herodas's mime is a rougher and more realistic form of the same genre.   H. D. F. K.

2. LATIN. (*a*) *Popular*. Of all the forms of dramatic entertainment known in classical times the mime was at once the most primitive and the most permanent. In its origins it cannot be classed as drama at all. All over the ancient world there were jugglers, acrobats, and public entertainers of all kinds, male and female, who displayed their skill in the market-places, at festivals in private houses, or wherever and whenever they could secure patrons. Among these nameless mountebanks there were some with a special gift for mimicry. They could imitate with their voices the neighing of horses, the sound of thunder, and so forth; even more important was their command of gesture, an art carried to a high pitch in the ancient world, involving the active use of every limb (the *mimi* were often themselves acrobats) and great control of facial expression. Such improvised performances were especially popular among the Doric peoples of Greece. The social status of the performers was low, and the performance was of the simplest kind. A rough platform served to raise the actors above the heads of the crowd; on it (at least in later times) was set up a movable curtain, behind which the actors stood until their turn came. Then, parting the folds in the middle, they stepped into the public gaze. While they performed, a colleague might collect coppers from the spectators, as we see in an Egyptian illustration. Xenophon gives us an admirable description of a performance by a boy and girl, the property of a Syracusan dancing-master, who by means of dance, gesture, and words represented the love of Dionysus and Ariadne. This performance was given at a banquet in a private house, and one of the guests was Socrates. The girl was an acrobat as well as an actress, and had already impressed the company by her

skill in the sword-dance. Her social class is indicated by the dancing-master's admission that she was his concubine. Wide indeed was the gulf between such performers and the actors who, in mask and costume, appeared in the theatre of Dionysus to present the tragedies of Euripides or the comedies of Menander. An element of indecency clung to the mime from the beginning; its aim was to amuse, no matter how. The mimes of Herodas (third century B.C.), which we still possess, are subtle, realistic, and sometimes sordid studies of certain social types, and were probably intended to be read, not acted.

Among the Dorians of Sicily and south Italy the mime was popular from an early period. Linguistic barriers were no hindrance to the art of gesture and facial expression; the simple requirements of the troupes of strolling *mimi* (a platform and a curtain) could be found anywhere. The contacts of Rome with Hellenism which arose out of the Pyrrhic War and the struggle for Sicily must have familiarized many Romans with the mime at a time when the literary drama of Rome had scarcely begun. Two years after the introduction of Greek drama to the Roman stage was founded the festival of Flora, which became a favourite occasion for the performance of mimes; the merry festival was riotously celebrated by the common folk, and licence went so far as to sanction the appearance of mime-actresses naked on the stage. The influence of mime on the development of Latin comedy must have been considerable; at any rate much of the jesting and buffoonery which Plautus introduced in his adaptations of Greek comedies would have been quite appropriate in the mime.

About this time the strolling companies of mimes ('birds of passage', as a Greek author calls them) were active all over the Graeco-Roman world. At its highest level the more elaborate form of mime, known as the 'hypothesis' and performed by a company, may have approached the level of drama, from which it differed chiefly in its preoccupation with character-drawing rather than plot, a necessary consequence of its more or less improvised nature. But we also hear of solo performers who prided themselves on being able to give the impression that they were several individuals in one. An epitaph found at Rome and dating from about the age of Sulla commemorates Eucharia, slave and later freedwoman of Licinia. Eucharia was a mime actress who had just achieved renown when she was cut down by death at the age of 14. The epitaph tells us that it is the record of a 'parent's love'.

We picture these small companies of strolling players, men, women, and children, setting up their simple curtain in some public place and giving their show. The manager (or manageress) took the leading role, to which the others were little more than foils; he was almost continuously present during the performance, and he kept the dialogue in his control, so that 'the second actor in the mime' was a phrase which denoted complete subservience. The distinctive costume was a hood (*ricinium*—whence the name *fabula riciniata* for mime) which could be drawn over the head or thrown back, a patchwork jacket, tights, and the phallus; the head was shaven, the feet were bare (hence the name *planipes* for the 'barefoot actor'). Perhaps only the *stupidus* or clown was so attired; the elegant philanderer of whom Ovid speaks must have been dressed as a man of fashion; a beautiful actress would appear in the most attractive and expensive clothes. The size of companies was perhaps not large; three actors are shown on a terra-cotta lamp from Athens as performers of *The Mother-in-law*, and Ovid speaks of a cast of three to take the roles of the foolish old husband, the erring wife, and the dandified lover.

The plots were simple, the endings often abrupt. A stock type was to show a character in a novel situation—a poor man suddenly become rich, for example. The riches might not last, and the ex-millionaire might have to disguise himself in his cloak and hurry off the stage. Abrupt endings of this kind were natural in what must have been fairly short pieces; Cicero tells us how, when the plot had reached a deadlock, someone would escape, the claqueurs would give the signal that the piece was over, and the drop-curtain would conceal the stage from view. So important was a curtain of some kind to the mime that we find Juvenal using the term 'curtain' as synonymous with 'mime'. The movable curtain (*siparium*) would serve as a back-cloth, and an actor appearing through its folds would be thought of as coming out of a doorway.

(*b*) *Literary.* In the age of Caesar the mime assumed literary importance. Decimus Laberius (106–43 B.C.) was the first Latin author to give the mime written form. As a respectable Roman knight he did not act in his own mimes; bitter then was the blow to his pride when, in his sixtieth year, he was compelled by Caesar to appear on the stage as the competitor of a young writer and actor of mimes, the ex-slave Publilius Syrus. We still possess the dignified and manly prologue which Laberius uttered on this occasion, with its significant warning to the dictator: 'Many he needs must fear whom many fear.' In all we possess 43 titles and about 140 lines or parts of lines from the works of Laberius. The fragments indicate that the mimes dealt with adultery and unnatural vice. The traditional fondness of the mime for biting topical allusions is illustrated by a reference to some governor who, like Verres, plundered his province; by an allusion to Caesar's supposed plan to legalize bigamy, and by a remark in the above-mentioned prologue: 'Roman citizens! We are losing our liberties!'

Publilius Syrus was, as his name implies, a native of Syria. He became famous as a writer and actor of mimes in the provincial towns of Italy; then, coming to Rome for the *ludi Caesaris* of 46 or 45 B.C., he challenged his rivals to extempore performances and vanquished them all, including Laberius. As we should expect in the case of pieces which seem to have been partly extempore, practically nothing is left of Publilius's mimes except the famous collection of maxims, made in the first century A.D., the high ethical standard of which surprised Seneca, who observes that they are worthy of tragedy rather than of mime.

(*c*) *Mime under the Roman Empire.* The composition of mimes for reading aloud was one of the amusements of literary dilettanti in the time of the Roman Empire, and Pliny's versatile friend, Vergilius Romanus, wrote character studies for recital, modelled on the *mimiambi* of Herodas. But the mime which all but drove other forms of spoken drama from the theatre was sub-literary, unmetrical, and largely impromptu. No Latin mimes of this type have survived; but in the Oxyrhynchus Mime we possess a Greek mime of the second century A.D., containing six or seven short scenes, supposed to take place in front of a house, the door of which could conveniently be represented by the opening in the portable curtain. The leading actress plays the part of a faithless wife. Where the text begins (the opening lines are lost) we find her attempting to seduce Aesopus, one of her slaves. But he is in love with a fellow slave, Apollonia, and rejects his mistress's advances. She then orders the lovers to be taken away and left to die. A later scene shows the body of Aesopus being brought in; the other slaves pretend that he has thrown himself from a height (in reality they have drugged him for his own safety); his mistress mourns his death, but soon consoles herself with the company of another slave, Malacus, with whom she conspires to poison her husband, whose 'corpse' is presently brought in. Now comes the turning-point. The old man gets up and denounces his guilty wife and Malacus; they are led off to punishment, while Aesopus and Apollonia are found to be alive and well, and all ends happily. The dialogue is in prose; probably the actors—or at least the *archimima*, who has by far the most important role—felt free to expand it at will. The sordid theme and the startling indecency of the language seem to be characteristic of the mime in general.

In indecency the mime of Imperial times reached incredible depths. Not only was adultery a stock theme, but the Emperor Heliogabalus appears to have ordered its realistic performance on the stage. If the plot included an execution, it was possible, by substituting a condemned criminal for the actor, to give the spectators the thrill of seeing the execution performed in fact. However popular the actors, they were socially and morally the lowest of the low. It was natural that the Christian Church should set itself against the mime, and equally natural that the actors should retaliate by mocking Christian sacraments, much to the delight of the crowd. Gradually the Church got the upper hand. In the fifth century it succeeded in excommunicating all performers of mime, and in the sixth century Justinian closed the theatres. Yet the mime lived on. Its simple requirements could be supplied in any public place or private house, and in such settings it continued to entertain audiences who were now nominally Christian. Though forced to drop its habit of burlesquing the sacraments, it still scandalized the Fathers by its indecency and the immorality of its performers. Yet, as one of the last strongholds of paganism, the mime did not lack defenders. About A.D. 500 Choricius of Gaza wrote his 'apology for actors' (i.e. performers of mime), while the lovely actress Theodora, whose daring performances had delighted the public of Byzantium, gave up the theatrical profession when she captured the affections of Justinian himself and sat beside him on the Imperial throne.

How far the mime survived the fall of ancient civilization is doubtful. So simple a type of performance might arise independently at different ages and in different countries. Yet precisely because of its primitive character it is hard to be sure that the classical mime ever became wholly extinct in Europe. Certainly the Middle Ages had their *mimi*. In its latest phase the classical mime was the last representative of classical drama; its strolling performers had taken over all that was left of a great tradition. Somehow or other they may have handed on their craft to their successors of the Dark and Middle Ages, and so to modern times. When the darkness clears we see a new drama arising. Perhaps its performers were in some sense the descendants of the strolling companies of mime-actors who had entertained the Roman world.   W. B.

3. MODERN. To-day the art of mime is arousing an ever-increasing interest both in the theatre and as an educational force. From the Roman period until the present day it has passed through varying degrees of popularity, reaching its height at the time of the *commedia dell'arte* of Italy in the sixteenth century, when a form of extempore comedy was in use in which the actors wore masks and employed the spoken word together with mime and gesture. The familiar figures of the harlequinade, which survives in a modified form to the present day, are based on the characters of the *commedia dell'arte*, and much of the traditional word-gesture of modern mime may be traced to the same source.

In 1576 a company of *commedia dell'arte* players, *I Gelosi*, under the direction of Flamino Scala, went from Italy to France, and the art of the impromptu player became immensely popular there. France soon produced companies of her own, and mime took its place as an important feature of the French stage. It lingered on until the nineteenth century, when the famous three-act mime play, *L'Enfant prodigue*, was produced, in which we find the forerunner of the modern mime play.

Mime has now become a purely silent art, in which the actor conveys his meaning by gesture, movement, and expression, and must be able, within the limits of that art, so to convey every thought and emotion that his audience is never at any time conscious of the lack of the spoken word. As in the French

mimes of the nineteenth century, so modern mime generally has a musical accompaniment (though this is not essential) which is co-ordinated with every movement and expression of the actor. Properties may be used as in a spoken play, but it is possible to leave them to the art of the actor and the imagination of the audience. Although the number of exponents of pure mime in England is at present small, the necessity for every actor to have a knowledge and understanding of the art is fully realized; mime has become an essential part of the training of every stage student, and is now to be found in the curriculum of all dramatic and ballet schools. The growing popularity of mime in the theatre is shown by its inclusion in many revues and variety entertainments, and by the tendency of present-day ballet to contain a far higher percentage of pure mime than was the case in the nineteenth century. The fact that mime is not without its following on the amateur stage, and that it has become an important feature in many a village entertainment, gives ample proof that it is gradually becoming understood and appreciated by a far wider public than if its performances were confined only to the professional stage.   M. R.

MINSTREL, the generic name for the professional entertainer of the Middle Ages (see also FOLK-PLAY, GLEEMAN, WAIT), whose origin must be sought in the fusion of the Teutonic *scôp*, or bard, with the floating debris of the Roman theatre, particularly the *mimi*. This process went on obscurely from the sixth to the eleventh century, helped by the wandering scholars, who brought to the mixture a certain leaven of classical erudition (see GOLIARD). The minstrel emerges in the eleventh century, and flourished till the fourteenth. Dressed in bright clothes, with flat-heeled shoes, clean-shaven face, and short hair—legacies of Rome —and with his instrument on his back, he tramped, alone or in company, all over Europe, sure everywhere of a welcome and an audience, though often harassed by the hostility of the Church and the restrictions of petty officialdom. In spite of this, he enlivened the festivities of religious fraternities, and may have had some small share in the development of ecclesiastical drama; he relieved the tedium of pilgrimages—it was only lack of a minstrel that set Chaucer's pilgrims story-telling—and frequented the market-place or the nobleman's hall with equal facility and success. There were different grades of minstrels, even before the formation of guilds, in France in 1321, in England in 1469. At the top of his profession was the accomplished poet and musician, permanently attached to a royal or noble household. Such were Blondel, the faithful servant of Richard Cœur de Lion, and Rahere, of Henry I. He and his like disappeared when the introduction of printing drew their audiences away to read romances. Next came the itinerant, but still respectable, bands of players whose repertory included some true drama, dialogued songs and debates, or rough farces in which it is tempting to see an echo of the farces of Imperial Rome. These made their contribution to literary drama in the *dits* and *fabliaux* of France and the English interludes, and continued into Elizabethan days and beyond. Lastly came the vast anonymous horde of little people—rope-walkers, acrobats, jugglers, conjurors, puppet-masters with crude wooden figures and some dramatic skill in their presentation, animal imitators and trainers—whose appeal was to the unlearned and therefore survived the Renaissance, and so continued down to the circus and music-hall performers of the present day. (For the modern Minstrel Show see NEGRO IN THE AMERICAN THEATRE.)

MIRACLE-PLAY, see AUTO; ENGLAND, 1; FRANCE, 1; ITALY, 1 *a* ii; MYSTERY PLAY; SACRA RAPPRESENTAZIONE and SPAIN, 1.

MIRANDA, FRANCISCO SÁ DE (1485–1558), see SOUTH AMERICA, 2.

MIRBEAU, OCTAVE (1848–1917), French dramatist, whose plays deal with contemporary problems, in the style of Henri Becque. Among them are *Les Mauvais bergers* (1897), a study of the struggle between labour and capital, and his best play, *Les Affaires sont les affaires* (1903), a mordant satire on the big-business man who is a slave to his wealth.

MIRROR SPOT, see LIGHTING, 2.

MIRROR THEATRE, LONDON, see HOLBORN THEATRE.

MISRULE, ABBOT, KING, OR LORD OF, a special officer (*dominus festi*) appointed to oversee the Christmas entertainments at Court and elsewhere in England in the late fifteenth and early sixteenth centuries. In Scotland he was also known as the Abbot of Unreason. His appointment was temporary and must not be confused with the permanent office of Master of the Revels, a Court official who first appears under Henry VIII in charge of masques and other set entertainments. Lords of Misrule were common in the colleges of the universities, particularly at Merton and St. John's, Oxford, where appointments were made as late as 1577. They are also found in the Inns of Court, intermittently until the time of Charles II. It was at the Gray's Inn Christmas Revels of 1594 that Shakespeare's *Comedy of Errors* was first given. The Lord of Misrule is a direct descendant of the 'king' in the Feast of Fools, and the equivalent in adult circles of the Boy Bishop of the schools.

MISS KELLY'S THEATRE, LONDON, see ROYALTY THEATRE (2).

MISTINGUETT [JEANNE BOURGEOIS] (1875–), French actress and dancer, the possessor of the reputedly most beautiful, and certainly most highly insured, legs in the entertainment world. She made her first appearances in music-hall, and in 1907 was seen in straight comedy, deserting it, however, to go to the Moulin-Rouge, of which she was for some years part-proprietor. With Maurice Chevalier as her partner, she appeared in some sensational dances at the Folies-Bergère. She was also seen at the Casino de Paris, where she first sang some of her most famous songs. She has written a volume of reminiscences, which was published in English in 1938. In her early days she was an eccentric comedienne of great originality, specializing in the portrayal of low-class Parisian women, but later she became the acknowledged queen of revue, and her fabulous hats and dresses attracted as much attention as her songs and sketches.

MITCHELL, LANGDON ELWYN (1862–1933), American poet and playwright, who in 1899 dramatized *Vanity Fair* for Mrs. Fiske, as *Becky Sharp*. It was a great success and was frequently revived. His finest play, however, was *The New York Idea*, a satire on divorce which has been cited as the best social comedy of the American stage in the early twentieth century. It was first produced by Mrs. Fiske at the Lyric Theatre, New York, on 19 Nov. 1906, with a remarkable cast, and was translated into German (production by Reinhardt), Dutch, Swedish, and Hungarian. In the same year Mitchell translated *The Kreutzer Sonata* from the Yiddish of Jacob Gordin, and later dramatized *Pendennis* for John Drew. As a successful playwright, he was invited to lecture at the University of Pennsylvania, and in 1928 became the first professor of playwriting at that university. He always retained his interest in the professional stage, but his high standards led him to be very critical of his own efforts, and he left a number of unfinished plays in manuscript.

MITCHELL, MAGGIE [MARGARET JULIA] (1837–1918), American actress, who made her first appearance on the stage in 1851, joining two sisters already established in the profession. She danced and played boy parts at the Bowery, being particularly admired as Oliver Twist. She then went on tour, becoming extremely popular in the south, and in 1857 became leading lady of Burton's company. It was in 1860 that she first played her famous role of Fanchon in an adaptation of George Sand's novel, *La Petite Fadette*. She continued to play it for the next twenty years, remaining always the same small, winsome, sprite-like child, piquant and overflowing with vitality. Although she was good in other parts, notably Jane Eyre, Pauline, Mignon, and Parthenia, it was Fanchon that the public wanted and invariably got.

MITCHELL, WILLIAM (1798–1856), American manager, born in England, where he had acted and worked as stage-manager for some fifteen years before in 1836 he went to New York. His real career began when in 1839 he took over the Olympic Theatre, previously considered unlucky, opened it with *High Life Below Stairs*, and embarked on a long series of triumphs, both as actor and manager, which made the Olympic one of the outstanding theatres of New York. He was excellent as Vincent Crummles, as Hamlet in a burlesque of that play, and in a burlesque of Fanny Elssler. But it was as a purveyor of light amusement that he won the heart of the New York public, and a contemporary reviewer said of him that his pieces, 'however trifling in incident, have always been produced admirably. ... He has contributed much to the enjoyment of the people of this city, and has always secured a company, which taken together, has been better than at any of the theatres.' He retired in 1850 and was sincerely mourned (see also OLYMPIC, 2).

MOCHALOV, PAVEL STEPANOVICH (1800–48), a famous Russian tragedian, and leading exponent of the 'intuitive' school of acting. He was born in Moscow, and was the son of a leading actor there. He attended the private academy of the Teslikov Brothers in Kostromov Province, where his family took refuge from the Napoleonic invasion, and made his début on the stage in 1817 with great success. His great roles were Hamlet and Lear, and the heroes of Schiller's *Die Räuber* and *Kabale und Liebe*. The critic Belinsky thought highly of him, and wrote a detailed description of his Hamlet. With great gifts of temperament and passion, Mochalov was antipathetic to any rational methods and relied entirely on the inspiration of the moment. He was consequently extremely uneven in his acting and in his effect on his audience. He later began to drink heavily, his talent weakened and his inspiration grew less, while he had no technique to fall back upon. His romantic quality was out of tune with the realistic tendency of the Russian theatre of the nineteenth century, and he deprecated the reforms of Shchepkin, but his influence nevertheless persisted for some time.

MODENA. (1) GIACOMO (1766–1841), Italian actor, who was for a long time in a travelling company, where he proved excellent in the comedies of Goldoni. He later turned to tragedy, and was the first to play the name part in Alfieri's *Saul*, in which he also made his last appearance, David being played on that occasion by his son (2) GUSTAVO (1803–61). Like his father, the younger Modena was accounted one of the best Italian actors of his day. In 1824 he was with Salvatore Fabbrichesi (1760–1827), an actor-manager who founded the first resident company in Milan, and with whom the elder Modena had often acted. He made his first success as David, and later proved excellent in both comedy and romance. He had his own company for some years. During the revolution he escaped to England, where he gave Dante recitals, but he returned to Milan in 1839 and again had his own company until 1846. Although not well known outside Italy, he was the tutor of Rossi and Novelli, both of whom toured Europe extensively. Though not handsome, the younger Modena had a fine figure and a nobly rugged and expressive face.

MODJESKA [MODRZEJEWSKA], HELENA (1844–1909), Polish actress, daughter of a musician named Opido. Though fond of the theatre from childhood, she did not act until after her marriage in 1861, when she joined a travelling company with her husband. On his death some years later she married again, and was then invited to the Warsaw theatre, where she remained for nearly ten years, proving herself a fine actress in tragedy and comedy, her repertory ranging from Shakespeare to the latest productions of Feuillet and Sardou. In 1876 she emigrated with her husband to California, where they met with little success, and lack of means soon caused her to desert the ranch for the stage. She played at the California Theatre, San Francisco, in 1877, and in spite of her poor command of the English language scored an immense success. She then toured extensively in the United States, England, and on the continent, and was considered one of the leading actresses of her generation, a woman of great charm and power, at her best in tragedy or strong emotional parts. She retired from the stage in 1905 after a farewell performance at the Metropolitan Opera House, New York.

MOHUN, MICHAEL (c. 1620–84), English actor, and, with Charles Hart, the leading man of Killigrew's company when it took possession of the Theatre Royal in 1662. He had been a boy-actor under Beeston, and was already playing adult parts before the closing of the theatres. He joined the Royalist army, became a major, and then returned to the stage. His Iago was much admired, and he created many Restoration roles in tragedy and comedy, including Abdelmelech in *The Conquest of Granada*, and Mithridates in Lee's play of that name.

MOISSI, ALEXANDER (1880–1935), German actor, of Italian origin, who was engaged as a super at the Vienna Burgtheater, and played his first speaking part in German at Prague in 1902. He remained there, playing leading parts, until 1905, when he went to Berlin. There his fine presence, and above all his rich, musical, speaking voice, soon brought him into prominence. At the Deutsches Theater under Reinhardt he played Romeo, Hamlet, the Fool in *Lear*, Oberon, and Touchstone; Faust, Mephistopheles, Posa in *Don Carlos*, Oswald in *Ghosts*, Louis Dubedat in *The Doctor's Dilemma*, and Marchbanks in *Candida*, as well as a number of less well-known parts. His Oedipus and Orestes in the Reinhardt productions in the Cirkus were exceptionally fine. In 1930 he came to London, playing Hamlet in W. V. Schlegel's translation at the Globe, John Gielgud's Hamlet in its entirety, from the Old Vic, playing next door at the Queen's.

MOLÉ [MOLET], FRANÇOIS RENÉ (1734–1802), French actor. Originally a notary's clerk, he engaged in amateur dramatics with such success that in 1754 he was allowed to appear at the Comédie-Française. He was considered promising, but was sent into the provinces to gain experience, returning at the beginning of 1760. Fleury says of him that he was the personification of youth, grace, and vivacity, so it is not surprising that he was received into the company to play young heroes and lovers. After a few successes, often in parts specially written for him, he became the idol of the public, and on the retirement of Grandval shared leading roles with Bellecour. He excelled in comedy, but was content to leave the great tragic roles to Larive. Yet, ironically enough, he was destined to be the first French Hamlet in 1769, in the adaptation made by Ducis, which was, however, nothing like the original. The French public liked it, and Molé was considered good in the part. In later life he got fat, but lost nothing of his agility of mind or body. A contemporary said of him that his wit was so quick, and his fooling so excellent, that he was capable of playing a part he did not know, relying entirely on the prompter, without the audience realizing it. Some of his mannerisms had an unfortunate influence on his younger companions, especially in tragedy, to which he unconsciously brought the technique of comedy. He was an adherent of the Revolution, and was not imprisoned with the rest of the company in 1793, going instead to play revolutionary drama at the theatre of Mlle Montansier. When the Comédie-Française re-opened he went back and remained there until his death. His wife was also an actress, doubling roles with the wife of Préville.

MOLIÈRE [JEAN-BAPTISTE POQUELIN] (1622–73), the greatest actor and dramatist of France, author of some of the finest comedies in the history of the theatre. He was the eldest son of a prosperous upholsterer of Paris attached to the service of the king. Little is known of his early years, though he is reported to have been an excellent mimic, and a great frequenter of theatres. He probably saw Belleville at the Hôtel de Bourgogne, while Montdory at the Marais introduced him to the tragedies of Corneille. He may also have watched the farce-players and barkers at the fairs or in the market-places amusing the crowds from their trestle-platforms. But nothing in his early life gave proof of that over-mastering passion for the stage which later possessed him. In about 1631 he became a pupil at the Jesuit College of Clermont (later Louis-le-Grand), and left in 1639 a good scholar, particularly in Latin, and an omnivorous reader of poetry and plays. While at school he probably took part in the plays—mainly adaptations of Latin authors—and ballets which formed part of the Jesuit educational curriculum (see JESUIT DRAMA). Among Molière's fellow students was the young Prince de Conti, who much later became his patron, and it may have been at Clermont that he met Cyrano de Bergerac, a lifelong friend and champion, who is known to have followed the lectures of Gassendi.

On leaving the College young Poquelin, who was destined to succeed his father, made a half-hearted attempt to study law, and in 1642 went to Narbonne in the suite of Louis XIII. This may have been a move designed to break up a somewhat undesirable friendship which he had formed with a family of actors, the Béjarts. If so, it was unsuccessful, for a year later the young man renounced his succession, and with the Béjarts and some of their actor-friends formed a small theatrical company, known as the Illustre-Théâtre, which took over and adapted a disused tennis-court. The driving force behind the enterprise was undoubtedly Madeleine Béjart, the eldest of the family, a woman of great attraction and talent, and already an experienced actress. Molière, as he had now become—no reason for the adoption of this particular name has yet been found—was merely an enthusiastic but untried aspirant, whose ambitions tended towards the playing of tragedy, for which he was physically and temperamentally unsuited. It has been surmised that he was at this time the lover of Madeleine, a relationship which was to have tragic repercussions in his later life.

The new company failed completely, and Molière was imprisoned for debt. The Illustre-Théâtre vanished overnight, without leaving a trace in contemporary gossip. Its scanty history has had to be pieced together from extant documents and later, often apocryphal, memoirs. But the young actors were not discouraged, and after some change of membership they set off for the provinces, remaining there from 1645 to 1658. These are the formative years of Molière's career, and must not be forgotten in the later blaze of glory in Paris. He achieved some distinction as an actor, and served his apprenticeship to play-writing by supplying the company, of which he soon became the virtual leader, with partly-improvised farces in the style of the *commedia dell'arte*. They appear to have been successful, though little of them survives beyond some stray titles, and fragments used again in later plays. Little more is known of the company's wanderings than a list of the towns they can be proved to have visited, under the patronage successively of the Duc d'Éperon and the Prince de Conti. There was no doubt a great deal of hard work and some hardship, but a corresponding degree of happiness and freedom. The company was reputable, usually well lodged and well received, and, with the later accession to its strength of the veteran actor Dufresne, of Gros-René, and of the two fine actresses Mlle du Parc and Mlle de Brie, capable of giving a good account of itself. These years in the provinces provided Molière with experience of men and of affairs, with a storehouse into which he dipped unendingly for his later plays, and with a nucleus of devoted friends and experienced actors who were to provide the backbone of his company in Paris. Above all they taught him to know, to love, and to laugh at human nature in all its frailty and stupidity.

So much spade-work was not to be wasted, as might so easily have happened. Helped by friends in high places the company once more approached Paris, and on 24 October 1658—a date memorable in French dramatic history—appeared in the Guard Room of the Old Louvre before the 20-year-old Louis XIV. In the audience of notables and courtiers were also the actors of the Hôtel de Bourgogne, which at this time had almost a monopoly of acting in Paris. The new company chose for their first play Corneille's *Nicomède*, in which everyone present had probably seen and admired the bombastic and ranting Montfleury. Molière's quieter and more natural style of acting failed to impress them. For a moment the future of the little company, and of French drama itself, hung in the balance. Then Molière came forward, and in a charmingly modest little speech introduced a farce of his own, *Le Docteur amoureux*. It was an immediate success. Molière, only a passable tragedian, was revealed as a comic actor of great gifts, ably supported by a company which had played together for many years. The actors of the Hôtel de Bourgogne, secure in their pre-eminence in tragedy, put no obstacles in the way, and the King granted Molière permission to remain in Paris, sharing the Petit-Bourbon, and later the Palais-Royal, with the *commedia dell'arte* troupe under Scaramouche (Tiberio Fiorelli) already installed there. The relationship between the two groups was most cordial, and Molière was always ready to acknowledge how much he had learnt from the Italians, though at first he suffered from their popularity. They retained the right to play on the most lucrative days, Tuesdays and Sundays, leaving the rest of the week for the new-comers. Molière had to pay them a heavy rent, and also adapt his plays to their fixed scenery—houses round a square. Much of the action had therefore to take place in the open air, even the signing of wills and consultations with doctors. Later, however, he was able to rebuild the Palais-Royal, with ample space for scenery and orchestra, and by then the Italians were paying him rent.

In spite of the failure of *Nicomède*, the company continued to appear in tragedies by Corneille, without success. In the last few weeks of the year Molière, in desperation, put on two plays of his own, *L'Étourdi, ou les contretemps* and *Le Dépit amoureux*. Both were successful, and drew the attention of the town to the merits of the struggling company. Meanwhile Molière, viewing the life of Paris with an acuteness sharpened by years of absence and experience, turned from the stock plots and time-worn artifices of the old comedy, and took a subject nearer at hand. The result was the one-act satire *Les Précieuses ridicules* (1658), which at one blow demolished the pretensions of the younger generation of the Hôtel de Rambouillet, and drew all Paris to laugh at their absurdities.

From now on Molière's life is that of his theatre. It led him into bitter controversies, and a struggle for freedom to attack social iniquities which ended only with his untimely death from overwork. On the other hand it gave him the devoted friendship of France's greatest men of letters, and the patronage of Louis XIV, without which he might have succumbed to the attacks of his enemies. This he paid for, however, in periods of feverish activity in connexion with Court festivities, for which he was in constant demand. His main function was the provision and production of a series of plays interspersed with music and dancing, for which Lully provided the music. The plays were given by Molière's company, while the notables of the Court, including the king himself, danced in the ballets.

The first of these Court entertainments was *Les Fâcheux*, in 1661. Two years later, at the king's command, came *L'Impromptu de Versailles*, a biting satire on the actors of the Hôtel de Bourgogne, who had sought to undermine Molière's influence at Court by attacking him not only in his profession but in his private life. It was a vulnerable spot, for in January 1662 Molière, so wise and balanced in his writing and in his conduct of business matters, had made a most injudicious marriage with the youngest sister of Madeleine, Armande Béjart, a spoilt child of 18, capricious, flirtatious, and entirely lacking in affection. The affair was complicated by the belief of most people, even Molière's friends, that Armande was the daughter, and not the sister, of Molière's former mistress, and Montfleury, in rage and jealousy, even went so far as to accuse Molière before the king of having married his own daughter. The royal reply to this accusation was the commissioning of *L'Impromptu de Versailles*, while Louis also stood godfather to Molière's first child, born in 1664, who died the same year. A second child, Esprit Magdeleine (1665-1723), was born before matters became so bad between the parents that Molière took himself off to Auteuil while Armande stayed in Paris, while a third child, a son, who lived only a few weeks, was born in 1672, after a reconciliation had been effected.

The old theatre of the Petit-Bourbon had seen only one more play by Molière, *Sganarelle, ou le cocu imaginaire* (1660), before it was demolished, and the company moved to Richelieu's theatre in the Palais-Royal, henceforth to be their permanent home. Here they opened in 1661 with Molière's one failure, a heroic drama entitled *Don Garcie de Navarre, ou le prince jaloux*. He redeemed himself in the eyes of his public by *L'École des maris* (1661), *L'École des femmes* (1662), and *La Critique de l'École des femmes*, in which he justifies his use of comedy, and replies to his critics. It was in this play that Armande, who was to prove an excellent actress, made her first appearance, as Élise.

In 1664 Molière, who had already earlier in the year provided the Court with *Le Mariage forcé*, in which the king danced the part of a gipsy, was responsible for the six-days' entertainment at Versailles given under the collective title of *Les Plaisirs de l'île enchantée*, for which he hurriedly wrote *La Princesse d'Élide*. It was during these celebrations that Molière produced privately the first version of

a play which was to cause him much distress—
Tartuffe. This attack on hypocrisy roused
against him the false *dévots* of Paris, who
succeeded in getting the play suppressed for
many years. Though frequently given in
private houses, it was not seen on the public
stage until 1667, and then in an altered version
as *L'Imposteur*. Another play which roused
almost as much opposition was *Don Juan, ou
le festin de pierre*, given at the Palais-Royal in
the same year as *L'Amour médecin* (1665). It
was followed by *Le Misanthrope* and *Le
Médecin malgré lui* in 1666 and by *Amphitryon*
and *L'Avare*, both written at Auteuil, in 1668,
while for the Court Molière provided *Le
Sicilien, ou l'amour peintre* (1667) and *Georges
Dandin, ou le mari confondu* (1668). These
were first given at Versailles, while *Monsieur
de Pourceaugnac* (1669) appeared at Chambord
and *Les Amants magnifiques* (1670) at Saint-
Germain, where Louis XIV, as Neptune and
Apollo, made his last appearances as an actor.

The best known of the Court plays is *Le
Bourgeois gentilhomme* (1671), written to provide the king with an entertainment *à la
turque*, a genre much in vogue at the time.
Psyché, a 'tragédie-ballet' in which Corneille
collaborated—written, tradition says, to make
use of some scenery representing Hell which
Louis hated to see lying idle—was also produced in 1671, as was the last play written for
the Court, *La Comtesse d'Escarbagnas*.

The Court plays, shorn of some of their
splendour, had also been given publicly at the
Palais-Royal, which in 1671 was rebuilt and
enlarged to take the scenery and machines of
Psyché. In the same year Molière reverted to
his earlier farcical manner in the light-hearted
Fourberies de Scapin. In 1672 came another of
the great satires, *Les Femmes savantes*, followed
by *Le Malade imaginaire*, Molière's last play,
in which he acted on the night of his death,
17 February 1673.

Molière's great achievement was that by his
own efforts he raised French comedy to the
heights of French tragedy. When he finally
settled in Paris tragedy was the only thing
worth watching or acting in; all the rest was
trifling, at its best good for an hour's amusement, at its worst left solely to the raucous
tumblers and travelling mountebanks. Molière
made comedy a polite entertainment, acceptable to the Court and to men of sense. He
raised it from the domain of farce, and made it
a vehicle of social satire, a supple, living organism capable of the nicest gradations of light and
shade, able at once to divert and admonish.
His plays are universal in their application, yet
untranslatable. In transit, the wit evaporates
and only a skeleton plot is left. This, however,
will not deter people from trying to translate
them—a fascinating occupation.

Molière was noted in his lifetime as an
excellent actor in comedy—though not in
tragedy—in spite of a slight impediment in his
speech to which one soon became accustomed.
He was a fine producer, both of his own and of
other people's plays, and as a working dramatist

knew how to suit his characters to his actors.
Like Shakespeare, he took his plots where he
pleased, and all through his works there are
echoes of Greek, Latin, Italian, and Spanish
comedies. Yet the result is unmistakably his own.

Molière should also be honoured for having
encouraged the genius of Racine, whose first
play, *La Thébaïde, ou les frères ennemis*, he
produced at the Palais-Royal in 1664. When
that ungrateful man, on a flimsy pretext, took
his *Alexandre et Porus* (1666) from the Palais-
Royal to the Hôtel de Bourgogne, and suborned
Molière's star actress, Mlle du Parc, to act in
it, Molière was so hurt by his behaviour that he
never spoke to him again.

MOLINA, TIRSO DE (1584–1648), a Spanish
ecclesiastic of high rank, whose real name was
Gabriel Téllez. He adopted for his secular
works the pseudonym by which he is best
known, and was the author of a number of
plays, of which 80 are extant, though he claimed
to have written 400. By their technique they
recall those of his contemporary Lope de Vega,
whom he much admired. Like Lope also,
Tirso excelled in the drawing of women, at
their wittiest and most intelligent in such
comedies as *Don Gil de las calzas verdes* and *El
vergonzoso en palacio*. His historical play, *La
prudencia en la mujer*, portrays excellently the
heroic queen Doña María. Tirso wrote also
a number of religious plays, and is doubtfully
credited with a theological drama, *El con-
denado por desconfiado*, which dramatizes the
theological 'sin of despair' and the power of
grace through faith. His fame chiefly rests on
El Burlador de Sevilla y convidado de piedra
(first ed. 1630), which is the first of the many
important dramatic works based on the legend
of Don Juan. Tirso has been considered the
Spanish dramatist with most affinity to Shakespeare, and after a period of temporary eclipse
he now takes his place in the front rank with
Lope de Vega and Calderón.

MOLNÁR, FERENC (1878–   ), Hungarian
dramatist, and one of the best known outside
his own country. He studied law, became a
journalist, and first attracted notice with some
light-hearted farces, in which he exploited for
the first time the humours of Hungarian town-
life. *The Devil*, a modern variation on the
Faust theme, was the first of his plays to be
done in England, France, and Germany, and it
was followed by his most famous work, *Liliom*
(1909), a mixture of realism and fantasy which
was a failure on its first production in Budapest,
and a resounding success ten years later. As
Carousel (1945) it was given in New York as a
play with music and had a long run. A long
series of comedies followed, none as successful,
but all acceptable, the most charming being
perhaps a version of the Cinderella story in
which the prince is a middle-aged cabinet-
maker. Molnár's sure technique and brilliant
dialogue have won him international admiration, and all his most important plays have
been translated into English.

[539]

MOMUS, the Greek god of ridicule, and by extension of clowns. The name was frequently used to denote a clown, as in Grimaldi's reference to himself as 'the once Merry Momus', and became attached to one of the figures in the harlequinade.

MONAKHOV, NIKOLAI FEDOROVICH (1875–1936), Russian actor whose career was mainly in the theatres of Leningrad (formerly St. Petersburg). He began in a café-chantant, singing satirical songs, and then played many roles in operetta. After seventeen years on the stage he joined the Free Theatre founded by Konstantin Mardjanov, where he had the opportunity of revealing his many-sided talent, in straight drama, in opera, and as a compère. When the Free Theatre went bankrupt, Monakhov could have gone to the Moscow Art Theatre, but he preferred to return to operetta for another five years. The October Revolution gave him a great chance. He joined the newly founded Leningrad Theatre, and appeared as Philip II in *Don Carlos* with great success, continuing to play leading parts until his death.

MONCK, NUGENT (1877–   ), English actor and producer, a disciple of William Poel, and founder of the famous Maddermarket Theatre, Norwich. His career as an actor, which had taken him from London to Ireland and New York, was cut short by the 1914–18 war, and it was in 1919 that he became producer to the long-established amateur group known as the Norwich Players. For them he bought and reconstructed a dilapidated building, giving it an Elizabethan stage complete with apron, and seats for about 250 people. Here the company, still amateur, play one week in every month, and have given all thirty-seven plays associated with Shakespeare, numerous early and Elizabethan comedies, foreign and adapted plays, Greek tragedy, and the works of Shaw and other modern writers. The Maddermarket celebrated its silver jubilee in 1946, and can look back with pride on the achievements of its first twenty-five years, during which time it has been entirely controlled by the guiding hand of Nugent Monck, who has himself appeared in many of the productions. He has also done a certain amount of theatrical work elsewhere, and has been responsible for a number of pageants in and around Norwich.

MONCRIEFF, WILLIAM (GEORGE) THOMAS (1794–1857), English dramatist and theatre manager, and a prolific writer of melodrama and burlesque for the minor theatres. There is little to distinguish him from a host of other scribblers of the time, except that he had a propensity for dramatizing novels before their authors had finished them, which drew down upon his head the wrath of Dickens, who had been one of the worst sufferers. He revenged himself, however, by depicting Moncrieff in *Nicholas Nickleby* as 'the literary gentleman . . . who had dramatized 247 novels as fast as they had come out—some of them faster than they had come out—and who *was* a literary

gentleman in consequence'. Moncrieff certainly had nearly 200 plays to his credit, of which *Tom and Jerry* (1821) was the most successful of the innumerable dramatizations of Egan's book, while *The Cataract of the Ganges* (1823) was given at Drury Lane with the added attraction of a real waterfall. The first of his Dickens adaptations was *Sam Weller; or, the Pickwickians* (1837). Moncrieff was manager of the Regency Theatre when it opened in 1810, and in 1819 was at the Coburg, where he staged innumerable melodramas of the most startling nature. In 1826 he produced the first plays given in Vauxhall Gardens, and had a short period in management at Astley's with equestrian drama.

MONODRAMA (sometimes called Melodrama, on account of its musical accompaniment). This short solo piece for one actor or actress supported by silent figures or by choruses was popularized in Germany between 1775 and 1780 by the actor Brandes. The Duodrama, a similar compilation, had two speaking characters. Both types of entertainment, which were useful in filling out the triple bill then in vogue, frequently consisted of scenes extracted and adapted from longer dramas.

MONTAGUE, CHARLES EDWARD (1867–1928), English provincial journalist whose dramatic criticisms in the *Manchester Guardian* were as distinguished as anything that appeared in any paper in the country. He was dramatic critic to that famous journal from 1890 to 1925. His artistic integrity was of the highest, and he always insisted that, to be of any worth at all, art must be individual. 'That is the truth of art, to be less true to facts without you than to yourself as stirred by facts. To find a glove-fit of words for your sense of "the glory and the freshness of a dream", to model the very form and pressure of an inward vision to the millionth of a hair's breadth.' Montague invariably followed his own precept. He turned an unclouded vision on to play or player and reported what he saw and felt with an honesty that permeated every line of his scrupulous writing.

Montague also wrote leading articles, novels, and a discerning work on the drama called *Dramatic Values* (1910). But it was his day-by-day dramatic criticisms in the *Manchester Guardian* that not only complimented drama in the north by the attentions of a fine mind, but also set an example to his critical colleagues throughout the country.   T. C. K.

MONTAGUE, HENRY JAMES (1844–78), American actor, whose real name was Mann. He appeared in London in the 1860s, and in 1870 opened the Vaudeville with James and Thorne. In 1874 he was seen at Wallack's, New York, where his good looks and well-bred air made him immensely popular with the audience. He was at his best in contemporary comedy—*Diplomacy, Caste, The Overland Route*—and for the whole of his short career was associated with Lester Wallack. It was probably his youthful assurance and personal magnetism that made him successful, and it was said of him that people liked him for himself, and not for his acting. His early death cut short a career which might not have lived up to the brilliance of its beginnings.

MONTALAND, Céline (1843–91), French actress, child of provincial actors, who was on the stage from her early years. At the age of seven she appeared at the Comédie-Française in children's parts, and was much admired. Going from there to the Palais-Royal she continued to attract the public in childish parts specially written for her, and after a few years in the provinces and in Italy reappeared in Paris and made her adult début in 1860 in the famous fairy-tale play, *Pied de mouton*, at the Porte-Saint-Martin. She was also seen at the Gymnase, where one of her finest parts was the mother in a dramatization of Daudet's *Jack*. She toured Europe and Russia several times, and in 1888 became a member of the Comédie-Française, remaining there until her death.

MONTANSIER, Marguerite (*née* Brunet) (1730–1820), French actress-manageress. She was orphaned at an early age, and was brought up in Paris by her mother's sister, from whom she took her stage-name. Beautiful and witty, she became the toast of the town, and having broken many hearts, suddenly lost her own to a young actor, Honoré Bourdon de Neuville (1736–1812). She decided to go on the stage, and helped by powerful friends took over the management of the theatre at Rouen. She was soon directing several others, with equal success, while Neuville, who was devoted to her, acted as her business manager. While in charge of the Versailles theatre, Mlle Montansier was presented to Marie Antoinette, who had a box there which she frequented incognito with the Princesse de Lamballe. The queen was charmed by the young actress's wit and gaiety, and made a favourite of her, even inviting her to play at Court. This she did successfully, though a strong provincial accent, which she never lost, kept her off the public stage in Paris. In 1777 she built a new theatre at Versailles, demolished in 1886, where many famous actors made their first appearances, since it was used to try out aspirants to the Comédie-Française. On the outbreak of the Revolution Mlle Montansier went to Paris, where her salon became the rendezvous of all the world. It was there that Napoleon, then an officer in the artillery, first met Talma, and laid the foundations of a friendship which lasted for many years. Accused by Fabre d'Églantine of royalist sympathies, owing to her friendship with Marie Antoinette, Mlle Montansier was arrested, but was saved from the guillotine by the fall of Robespierre. She immediately married her faithful Neuville and took up the management of the theatre she had just opened at the Palais-Royal, opposite the Bibliothèque Nationale, giving it her own name. It was closed in 1806 and became a café,

where its previous owner, now retired, was a constant visitor.

MONTCHRÉTIEN, Antoine de (*c.* 1575–1621), early French renaissance dramatist, who serves as a link between Garnier and Corneille. Son of an apothecary, he was early orphaned, and after being educated by wealthy friends was intended for the army. Instead he became a playwright. By 1600 he had written several plays on classical themes which had been given by the company at the Hôtel de Bourgogne. At the height of his success he laid siege to and successfully captured a rich widow, and took the name of Vasteville. In 1605 he had the misfortune to kill a man in a duel, and fled to Holland, and then to England. James I, to whom he had dedicated his play on Mary Queen of Scots, *L'Écossaise*, given at the Hôtel de Bourgogne in 1603, and incidentally one of the first French plays to deal with modern history, secured his pardon, and he returned to France in 1611. He then set up a factory for the manufacture of steel cutlery, and turned his attention to political economy. In 1621 he joined the Huguenots, and was killed by royalist soldiers while taking refuge in an inn. His plays are technically weak, but contain passages of great lyric beauty, and his choruses, like those of Garnier, are particularly fine, while the note of heroism so often sounded by his heroes is similar to that of Corneille.

MONTDORY [Guillaume Desgilberts] (1594–1651), with Bellerose the first outstanding French actor, friend and interpreter of Corneille. He is first heard of with the company of the Prince of Orange in 1610, under Lenoir, and probably remained with it until about 1622. After forming a company of his own, he again joined Lenoir and went with him to Paris in 1630, where he appeared in Corneille's first play, *Mélite*. This was probably given in a converted tennis-court near the Porte-Saint-Denis. It began quietly, but was soon an outstanding success, and the company, deciding to settle permanently in Paris, took over a tennis-court in the rue Vieille-du-Temple, known as the Marais. Just before they opened, Lenoir, his wife, and several other members of the company were drafted to the Hôtel de Bourgogne by Louis XIII, probably to annoy Richelieu, who had shown his preference for Montdory as opposed to Bellerose and the King's Players at the Hôtel de Bourgogne. This left Montdory in charge of the new theatre, which soon became a formidable rival to the established players, and had all the dramatists of the day, with the exception of Rotrou, working for it. Montdory was a man of great business ability, and a fine actor in the old, declamatory style, and to him goes the honour of having produced *Le Cid* (1636), in which he played the hero, Rodrigue. Another of his great roles was Herod in *Mariamne* (1637), in which he was acting before Richelieu, always a hard taskmaster, when he was stricken with paralysis of the tongue. His enforced retirement from the stage was a great blow, particularly for those authors who had in hand plays intended for his company. He had twice built up and controlled a good company in the face of much hostility, and he evidently trained and directed his actors well. Among them were the parents of Michel Baron, the first leading man of the Comédie-Française. It was said of Montdory that he was the first French actor who had never played in farce. He was also something of a poet.

MONTFLEURY. (1) [ZACHARIE JACOB] (c. 1600–67), French actor, who was in the company at the Hôtel de Bourgogne in 1639, where he was second only in importance to Bellerose, and later the companion of Floridor. He has been variously described as a nobleman, page to the Duc de Guise, and as the child of the strolling players Fleury Jacob and Colombe Venier, and thus the nephew of Marie Venier, the first French actress to be known by name. He was an enormously fat man, with a loud voice and a pompous delivery which Molière satirized in *L'Impromptu de Versailles* (1663). Montfleury had previously accused Molière before the King of having married his own daughter by Madeleine Béjart, but the accusation was not taken seriously, and Louis XIV showed how little credence he attached to it by standing godfather to Molière's next child. By his contemporaries Montfleury was considered a fine tragic actor, and was much sought after by authors. He was, however, disliked by Cyrano de Bergerac, friend of Molière, who is said to have ordered him off the stage, an incident made use of by Rostand in his play on Cyrano. In 1647 the Hôtel de Bourgogne put on a tragedy by Montfleury, *La Mort d'Asdrubal*, in which he played the lead. He married an actress, and his son (2) ANTOINE (1639–85) became a lawyer, but was also a well-known and successful dramatist. His first play was a one-act farce, but he came into prominence with a reply to Molière's *Impromptu de Versailles*, in which he satirized the company at the Palais-Royal. This was followed by a number of farces and comedies, often written in imitation of those of Molière, whom Montfleury hoped to surpass. But his plays, though written with much vivacity, and showing shrewd traits of wit and observation, lack permanence, and soon dropped from the repertory. He was probably induced to write most of them in order to supply the actors at the Hôtel de Bourgogne with something on the lines of Molière's successes, and a number of them have titles somewhat similar to Molière's. Montfleury's one serious play, *Trasibule* (1663), has some resemblance to *Hamlet*, but he is unlikely to have been acquainted with Shakespeare at so early a date, and probably adapted the story from a French work based on Saxo Grammaticus, one of Shakespeare's sources for *Hamlet*. Montfleury married the daughter of the actor Floridor, and two of his sisters were also on the stage. The elder (3) FRANÇOISE

(c. 1640–1708) married an inveterate gambler, and became an actress to support herself. As Mlle d'Ennebault she proved an asset to the company at the Hôtel de Bourgogne, playing several of Racine's young heroines. Her daughter Anne married the actor Desmares, brother of Mlle Champmeslé. Montfleury's younger sister (4) LOUISE (1649–1709) married a provincial actor who had been in the provinces with Dorimond, and went with him in 1670 to the Théâtre du Marais. With Mlle d'Ennebault they were both members of the newly formed Comédie-Française, the husband, a poor actor, retiring almost immediately, while the wife remained until the reorganization of 1685.

MONTMÉNIL, see LE SAGE (2).

MOOCK, ARMANDO, see SOUTH AMERICA, 1.

MOODY, WILLIAM VAUGHN (1869–1910), American dramatist, whose work marks a great step forward in the development of the native American playwright. Poet, scholar, and educationist, Moody had been for many years actively engaged in teaching when he decided that his real vocation lay in the theatre. His first plays, in verse, were not produced, but in 1906 *The Great Divide*, originally known as *The Sabine Woman*, was given by Margaret Anglin and Henry Miller with great success. It was seen in London in 1909. It was followed by *The Faith Healer* (1909), a somewhat better play which lacked the popular appeal of *The Great Divide*, but had a modified success, and was later used as the basis for a film. Both these plays are written in a dignified and poetic style, and mark the entrance into the American scene of the serious social dramatist, still somewhat crude and melodramatic, but moving in the right direction, away from the importations of French farce and the revamping of sentimental novelettes. Moody's early death was a great loss to the American stage, and it was unfortunate that none of his long poetic plays was produced during his lifetime.

MOORE, EDWARD (1712–57), English dramatist, author of two plays in the prevailing sentimental mode, of which the first, *The Foundling* (1747), bridges the gap, says Nicoll in his *Eighteenth Century Drama*, between the works of Cibber and Steele and those of Cumberland and Mrs. Inchbald. Moore's second important play—his *Gil Blas*, given at Drury Lane in 1751, was merely a dramatization of incidents from Le Sage's book—was *The Gamester* (1753), partly written by Garrick, who put it on at Drury Lane. It is a further essay in the vein of domestic tragedy exploited earlier by Lillo in *The London Merchant*, and though not at first successful, it proved so in revival and was translated into French, having a marked influence on the *tragédie bourgeoise*.

MOORE, JOSEPH (*fl*. first half of seventeenth century), an English actor who is first mentioned in 1611 as one of the chief men in the newly-formed Lady Elizabeth's Company.

After appearing at Court, and in several London playhouses, Moore lost several of his best men and took to the provinces, where he remained from 1615 to 1622. In 1617 he played before James I on his journey to Scotland, probably at some town in his usual circuit, and in 1622 he returned to the Cockpit in charge of a second Lady Elizabeth's Company—distinct from the previous company which had toured under that name, and certainly more prosperous—until their break-up during the plague in 1625. Moore then returned to the provinces, and was still acting in 1640.

MOORE, MARY (1862–1931), see WYNDHAM (2).

MORAL INTERLUDE, a short pedagogic drama of the sixteenth century, which has much of the character of a Morality play, but with more humour. Outstanding English examples are *Hickscorner*, produced anonymously in about 1513, and R. Wever's *Lusty Juventus* (*c.* 1550) (see also ENGLAND, 2).

MORALITY PLAY, a late medieval form of drama which aimed at instruction and moral teaching. Its characters are abstractions of vice and virtue, and the only trace of humour is provided by the Devil and the Old Vice, or buffoon. Played on a fixed stage, it was somewhat static and by modern standards dull. It has been said of Morality plays that 'their very name is like a yawn'. The only one to survive in performance is *Everyman*, originally written in Dutch in about 1495. This has been successfully given in English on the modern stage, and in German as part of the Salzburg Festival, in an open-air production by Reinhardt. Historically the Morality play is important and marks a big step forward in the secularization of the vernacular drama all over Europe. One of the best English examples is Skelton's *Magnyfycence*, the only play by this great satirist which has survived. (See also ENGLAND, 2.)

MORATÍN. (1) NICOLÁS FERNÁNDEZ DE (the elder) (1737–80), a Spanish dramatist of the eighteenth century whose translations of French plays helped to reinforce the theories of neo-classicism expounded by Luzán, and so further intensified the poverty of contemporary Spanish drama. His son, (2) LEANDRO FERNÁNDEZ (the younger) (1760–1828), was also a dramatist, and the outstanding exponent in original work of Luzán's theories. He combined the contemporary neo-classicism of France and the Venetian comedy of Goldoni with traditional Spanish elements, both in the presentation of character and of social background. His first success was a brilliant satire on the type of extravagant drama then delighting the public. The victim of this play (*El Café* or *La Comedia Nueva*) was recognizable as one Comella, whose plays, though of no great value, were at that time popular. Moratín's most famous play, however, was *El Sí de las Niñas* (1806), a piece of lively dialogue and excellent characterization in which the author defends the principle of a woman's freedom to marry the man she loves, a situation reminiscent of Goldoni's amusing *I rusteghi*. Moratín, unlike his predecessor Garcia de la Huerta, was a great admirer of Molière, of whose *École des maris* and *Médecin malgré lui* he made spirited translations. He also translated *Hamlet* into Spanish. Moratín edited the texts of many early Spanish plays and was the author of a critical study of the theatre, *Los orígenes del teatro español* (1830), which, though sharing the prejudices of the age to some extent, threw much light on the period before Lope de Vega.

MORATORIA, OROSMÁN (1859–98), see SOUTH AMERICA, 1.

MOREAU LE JEUNE (1741–1814), see COSTUME, 7.

MOREHOUSE, WARD (1898–), American dramatic critic, born in Savannah, Georgia. While a student at North Georgia College he joined a professional Shakespeare reader on a southern tour. Afterwards he served as a reporter on *The Atlanta Journal*, and in 1919 went to New York. Morehouse could be recommended for his sheer readability, but that would be an injustice to his many other talents. He is an expert theatrical journalist and historian and the green-room interviewer *par excellence*. His love of the theatre and his interpretation of that love are in everything he writes about it. Long before he was appointed dramatic critic of *The New York Sun*, his column for that paper, 'Broadway After Dark', and his lively book of memoirs concerning the American theatre of the nineteen-twenties and thirties, *Forty-Five Minutes After Eight*, revealed him as a delightful raconteur who caught with admirable cunning the tempo and rhythm of the Great White Way. Like most critics he has on occasion succumbed to the wiles of the theatre and turned dramatist, and like most of them with indifferent results. That generous understanding of actors and actresses, of directors and producers, and even of press-agents, which one finds in his reporting, never blinds him when he takes up the critical pen, but if talent flashes for a moment in some small 'bit' role he will see it and welcome it with encouraging praise. Among his plays are *Gentlemen of the Press* and *Miss Quis*. He has also written the biography of George M. Cohan.   T. Q. C.

MORETO Y CABAÑA, AGUSTÍN (1618–69), Spanish dramatist, author of a number of plays, many of which are lost. He had not the force of his predecessors, Lope de Vega and Calderón, nor even of his contemporary Rojas, but his poetry is delicate and his wit elegant and subtle. He excelled in stagecraft, especially in the setting of plots with relevant contemporary details. His best plays are *El Lindo Don Diego* and *El desdén con el desdén* (adapted by Molière in *La Princesse d'Élide*), which some critics consider to be the most representative comedy of Old Spain. In this charming piece the Countess Diana treats all her suitors with coldness, but piqued by the apparent indifference of the Count of Urgel, falls in love with him and finally marries him. A number of Moreto's plays were really rewritings of older themes from Lope, Tirso, and others, to suit the taste of the time, but they are none the less excellent, and in most cases exceed their originals in dramatic force and clarity. He excelled in the *comedia de figurón*, in which the chief character is a caricature of a particular trait in human nature rather than a portrait.

MORGAN, CHARLES LANGBRIDGE (1894–   ), English novelist and essayist, who succeeded A. B. Walkley as dramatic critic of *The Times* in 1926, a position which he held until 1939, invariably writing with discernment and distinction of literary style. His play, *The Flashing Stream*, was produced in 1938 at the Lyric Theatre, where it ran for six months. It has for its theme mental absolutism—'the power to assimilate and have repose in an idea, as one of the conditions precedent to singleness of mind'. The writing is marked by the same fastidious care that distinguishes all this author's work, the characters are drawn with nervous vitality, and in the theatre the piece displayed a striking command of stage technique.   T. C. K.

MORICZ, ZSIGMOND (1879–1942), Hungarian dramatist, author of a number of problem plays in which the Hungarian peasants are no longer idealized, as in Szigligeti's comedies, but sharply and realistically drawn.

MORLEY, HENRY (1822–94), Professor of Literature at University College, London, whose varied work included a number of dramatic criticisms published in 1891 as *The Journal of a London Playgoer, from 1851 to 1866*. Morley was also a member of the committee of a School of Dramatic Art opened with a view to raising the standard of acting and drama. He was much concerned with the relations between literature and the stage. The vogue for plays lifted entire from the French caused him much concern, and he pointed out the greater advantage of the English dramatists borrowing the Frenchmen's tools and using them to make their own plays.   T. C. K.

MOROSCO THEATRE, NEW YORK, on 45th Street west of Broadway. It was built by the Shubert brothers, and named in honour of Oliver Morosco, a well-known West Coast producer, who was responsible for the initial attraction, *Canary Cottage*, which opened on 5 Feb. 1917. Important productions at this theatre were O'Neill's *Beyond the Horizon* and Bennett's *Sacred and Profane Love*, while in 1920 *The Bat* had a record run with 867 performances and set the fashion for mystery thrillers. A long series of negligible plays was followed by *The Firebrand*, a Renaissance romance in which Joseph Schildkraut scored a personal triumph. The Pulitzer Prize-winner, *Craig's Wife*, was seen here with Chrystal Herne and Josephine Hull, and had 289 performances, and Katharine Cornell was success-

ful with *The Letter*. The Theatre Guild production of *Call It a Day* ran for six months, and an interesting experiment was Wilder's revision of *A Doll's House*, with Ruth Gordon and Paul Lukas. Two English plays which found favour were *Bachelor Born* (done in London as *Housemaster*) and *Spring Meeting*, in which Jean Cadell returned to Broadway with Gladys Cooper and A. E. Matthews. Later successes at this theatre have been *Skylark, Old Acquaintance, Blithe Spirit*, and *The Voice of the Turtle*.   G. F.

MORRIS [MORRISON], CLARA (1848–1925), American actress, who was on the stage as a child, and after touring the provinces appeared at Daly's first Fifth Avenue Theatre, making an immense impression as Cora the Creole in his *Article 47*. She was seen in a large range of parts, and in spite of a strong accent and an extravagant, unrestrained manner was popular both in New York and on tour. Though not a good actress, she had an extraordinary power of moving an audience, and could always be relied on to fill the theatre whenever she appeared. Her emotional sweep and range was best seen in such parts as Camille, but she also essayed Lady Macbeth, Julia in *The Hunchback*, and a number of modern heroines. She appeared for some years under the management of Palmer, but in 1885 was compelled by ill health to retire from the stage, spending her time in the writing of short stories and novels. In 1904 she appeared once more in the theatre, playing in an all-star revival of *The Two Orphans*, and subsequently went into vaudeville.

MORRIS. (1) OWEN (*fl.* late 18th cent.), actor who was with the American Company from 1759 to 1790. He was apparently a good low comedian, at his best in the portrayal of humorous old men. Among his parts were Sir Oliver Surface, Dogberry, and Polonius, all of which he played for the first time in New York. His first wife, also an actress, who played Ophelia in the first New York production of *Hamlet*, was drowned in a ferry accident in New York in 1767. Morris had married again by 1773, and his new wife who is only known as (2) MRS. OWEN MORRIS (1753–1826) figures in the playbills with him, becoming one of the outstanding actresses of the American Company. She played Charlotte in *The Contrast*, the first American comedy, and was also seen as Lady Teazle, Ophelia, and Beatrice. For some years she was the toast of New York, which she left after the season of 1789, with her husband, to join Wignell's new company at the Chestnut Street Theatre, Philadelphia. Here she was soon eclipsed by the lovely Mrs. Merry (see BRUNTON, 2), and on returning to New York with the company for a season in 1797 she was thought little of. She probably continued to act too long, and had in her heyday relied too much on her fine appearance and high spirits. She remained in Philadelphia until 1810, during which time her husband is believed to have died, and Odell (*Annals of the New York*

Stage) thinks she may have been the Mrs. Morris who appeared at the Commonwealth Theatre in New York as late as 1815.

MORRIS (MORRICE) DANCE, an English dance popular at all village festivals. Different authorities derive it either from the Germanic sword-dance, or from the Morisco, or Moorish dance, the latter on account of the blackened faces of the dancers or their companions. Chambers, however, sees in this custom a relic of the old pagan rite of smearing the face with ash from the sacrificial fire. In the same way the fool who accompanies the dancers, with his bladder and cow's tail, would be a survival of the primitive worshipper in sacrificial costume. The dancers, usually six in number, wear bells on their legs, and carry handkerchiefs or short staves in their hands. The music is traditionally supplied by a pipe and tabor, or by bagpipes, though in recent times a fiddler has been used. With the dancers went the fool, the hobby-horse, and, at Maytime, a Jack-in-the-Green; sometimes a dragon and a Maid Marian. From its popularity at Maytime the Morris came to be associated with Robin Hood and his Merry Men. It was also an essential part of the mumming play. It can be traced all over England and Scotland, and reached the height of its popularity under Henry VIII, when it appeared at Court. Among the people, it still survives, notably at Bampton in Oxfordshire, and in the early twentieth century it had a fostered revival under the auspices of the English Folk Dance Society. The Morris dance can be either stationary or processional, and both forms can be seen in the streets of Oxford on May morning.

MORTON, CHARLES (1819–1904), known as 'the father of the halls', opened the Canterbury, the first organized music-hall, in 1849, and the Oxford in 1861, and was called in at various times to retrieve the failing fortunes of the Tivoli, the Pavilion, and other halls, which he did most successfully. He had a wonderful flair for picking his performers, and hardly ever had a failure. Although he was the favourite target of the puritan element at that time, Chevalier calls him, in his *Before I Forget*, 'a gentleman of experience and refinement', and says that under him the Pavilion came nearer the ideal variety theatre than any other in London. Although Morton appreciated and employed purveyors of hearty vulgarity, he was opposed to innuendo and salacity, and demanded a high standard of all his entertainers.

MORTON. (1) THOMAS (c. 1764–1838), English dramatist, famous for having created the character of Mrs. Grundy, who does not appear, but is frequently referred to, in his *Speed the Plough* (1800), as the embodiment of British respectability. The play is otherwise unimportant, being a sentimental comedy of a type popular at the time. Morton wrote several others in the same vein—*The Way to Get Married* (1796), *A Cure for the Heart-Ache* (1797), and *Secrets Worth Knowing* (1800).

He was also the author of two spectacular melodramas, of an amusing comedy, *The School of Reform* (1805), frequently revived, notably by Irving, and of an historical play with music in which Macready played the hero, Henri IV. His *Children in the Wood* (1793) passed into the repertory of the Juvenile Drama. His son (2) JOHN MADDISON (1811–91) was a prolific writer of farces, mainly taken from the French, which helped to build up the reputation of such comedians as Buckstone, Wright, Harley, the Keeleys, and others. One of the most popular was *Lend Me Five Shillings* (1846), while he wrote, first as *The Double-Bedded Room* and then as *Box and Cox* (1847), the farce on which Burnand and Sullivan based their musical farce, *Cox and Box* (1867).

MOSCOW ART THEATRE. This famous theatre, now dedicated to Maxim Gorky, is the best known of all Russian theatrical organizations outside Russia. It was founded in 1898 by Stanislavsky and Nemirovich-Danchenko, and its name is indissolubly linked with that of Chekhov, whose plays were first given there with success. Its original company was drawn partly from the amateur actors of the Society for Art and Literature, and partly from the graduates of the dramatic class of the Philharmonic Society, and it was a co-operative venture, issuing shares to its members. It was also supported financially by rich patrons of the bourgeois intelligentsia, among whom the most active was Savva Morozov.

The theatre opened with *Tsar Feodor Ivanovich* before an audience which was almost equally hostile and appreciative, and much intrigued by the new 'naturalistic' style of acting. The seal was set on the success of the new enterprise when it gave, as its fifth production, Chekhov's *The Seagull*, which had previously been given without success at the Alexandrinsky Theatre. This was followed by *Uncle Vanya*, *Three Sisters*, and *The Cherry Orchard*. Stanislavsky's system of dramatic training, which is fully set forth in his books, and has achieved world-wide fame, scored a signal triumph, and the Moscow Art Theatre, which in longevity ranks next to the Moscow Maly, soon had an unassailable reputation. It has indeed been a mirror of the times, and the ferment of society that led to the abortive Revolution of 1905 was reflected in its production of Gorky's great play of the underworld, *The Lower Depths*. His *Children of the Sun* was in the bill at the Moscow Art Theatre when the Revolution actually took place. The repertory in pre-Revolutionary days included also a number of European classics, but the only Shakespearian play to be produced at this time was *Julius Caesar*.

The failure of the 1905 rising produced a period of uncertainty and unrest, which was reflected by the Moscow Art Theatre's productions of mystic, pacifist, or merely superficial plays. The October Revolution caught the directors unaware, as Stanislavsky himself admitted, and had it not been for the tolerance

and foresight of Lunacharsky, this great institution might have been swept away, a loss not
only to the Soviet theatre, but to those of
Europe and America. Given time to find its
feet in the new world, with which it was fundamentally in sympathy, though as yet a little dis-
orientated, the Moscow Art Theatre company
left Russia for a long tour of Europe and
America, fêted and applauded wherever it
went. Back in Moscow it tentatively tried out
a Soviet play, *Pugachov* (1925), but with little
success; *The Last of the Turbins*, which followed in 1926, was a step in the right direction,
and the theatre finally resumed its leadership
of the Russian stage with a fine production of
Armoured Train 14-69. Gorky's last play,
Yegor Bulichev, followed in 1934. Since then
the Moscow Art Theatre has staged a number
of interesting new plays, including *Platon
Krechet* (1937), *Kremlin Chimes* (1942), *The
Russian People*, and *Depth Prospecting* (both
1943). It has also continued its work on the
classics, approaching and interpreting them in
the spirit of realism combined with the most
brilliant theatrical art. Some of the actors who
appeared in the first productions—notably
Ivan Moskvin, Vasili Kachalov, and Olga
Knipper-Chekhova (the widow of Chekhov and
a brilliant interpreter of his plays)—passed the
rest of their careers with the company, while a
gifted younger generation shows every promise
of carrying on the traditions of the theatre.

From the studios established for training
and experiment by the Moscow Art Theatre a
number of important individual groups have
developed (see REALISTIC and VAKHTANGOV
THEATRES). The First Studio was started in
1913 under the leadership of L. A. Sulerzhitsky
(1872-1916), who worked on Stanislavsky's
methods. His most successful production was
an adaptation of *The Cricket on the Hearth*. In
1924 the First Studio was reconstituted as the
Moscow Art Theatre II, under the direction of
Michael Chekhov, who opened with a production of *Hamlet* in which he himself played the
title-role. For some years after the Revolution
this theatre held aloof from Soviet Realism.
Its productions, brilliant in form, masterly in
technique, still remained foreign to the new
life. The position improved after the departure of Michael Chekhov, who emigrated in
1927, and a number of classic and modern
plays were produced with a high degree of
realism and artistic excellence.

MOSCOW STATE JEWISH THEATRE,
known in Yiddish as Melucha and in Russian
as Goset. This was founded as the Jewish
Theatre Studio in Leningrad in 1919 by Alexander Granovsky, for the production of plays
in Yiddish. After a visit to Vitebsk, it went to
Moscow, where it was first known as the
Jewish Chamber Theatre, later receiving its
present name. Its first performance in Moscow
in 1921 was given in the Chagall Hall seating
90 people and was devoted to short comedy
sketches by Sholom Aleichem. The company
became so popular that in 1922 it was able to

move to the Romanov Hall, which seats 500.
The present theatre seats 766. In 1928 the
company undertook a European tour, during
which Granovsky resigned his directorship and
was succeeded by his assistant and chief actor,
Mikhoels, who had been one of the original
members. In 1941 the company was evacuated
to Tashkent, returning to Moscow in 1943.
One of its finest productions was *King Lear* in
1935, directed by Radlov, with scenery by
Tishler, in which Mikhoels was outstanding
in the name-part.   E. H.

MOSES, MONTROSE JONAS (1878-1934), an
American dramatic critic and editor of a number of anthologies of drama, both American
and European. His works reflect the wideness
of his interests and his scholarly knowledge
of the history of the stage. They include a
survey of famous actor families in America,
published in 1906, a study of Ibsen, a life of
the actor Edwin Forrest, and *The American
Dramatist* (3rd ed., 1925), the last an interesting contribution to the history of the theatre
in the United States. Moses also contributed
a number of articles on the theatre to periodicals
and encyclopaedias. In 1911 he married the
daughter of the American dramatist, James A.
Herne. She died in 1921 after the birth of a son.

MOSKVIN, IVAN MIKHAILOVICH (1874-   ),
outstanding Russian actor, who, after the
deaths of Stanislavsky and Nemirovich-
Danchenko, became director of the Moscow
Art Theatre. He studied for the stage under
Nemirovich-Danchenko in the Moscow Philharmonic Society, which he joined in 1893, and
then worked for two years in provincial theatres.
He was a member of the Moscow Art Theatre
from its foundation, and came immediately to
the fore, playing the lead in its first production.
Among his later roles were Luka in *The Lower
Depths*, Nozdrev in *Dead Souls*, and Epihodov
in *The Cherry Orchard*. He again appeared in
this last play in the 1938 revival, together with
others of the original cast, and had one of the
leading roles in the play about Lenin, *Kremlin
Chimes* (1942).

M.O.S.P.S. THEATRE, MOSCOW, see MOS-
SOVIET THEATRE.

MOSS, SIR EDWARD (1852-1912), an English
showman who began life among booths and
circuses, built an 'Empire' in Edinburgh and
elsewhere, and went to London in 1900, having
joined forces with Stoll in Moss Empires Ltd.
He built the Hippodrome and, having dissolved
his partnership with Stoll, ran his own circuit.
He was knighted for his services to the entertainment industry.

MOSSOP, HENRY (1729-74), Irish actor,
who, despite much ability and good sense, so
wrecked his life by his jealousy of Garrick that
he finally died in poverty in a Chelsea garret,
and was only saved from a pauper's funeral
by the intervention of a condescending uncle.
Mossop went to Drury Lane from Ireland, and
proved himself good in tragedy, being at first

an excellent ally to Garrick in his rivalry with Barry. He took over the parts of Quin, and was seen as Richard III, Zanga, Horatio to Garrick's Lotario, and Theseus to Mrs. Pritchard's Phaedra. He was also good as Macbeth, Othello, Wolsey, and Orestes. A foolish insistence on playing young lover parts, to which he was quite unsuited, led to some failure and ridicule, and the hot-tempered actor visited his resentment on Garrick. He then left London and went back to Ireland, opening the Smock Alley Theatre in Dublin in 1761 in opposition to Barry and Woodward at the Crow Street Theatre. He was soon plunged into financial difficulties, which he aggravated by gambling and general dissipation, and at last, ruined in pocket and health, he crept back to London. Too proud to appeal to Garrick, and impatient of advice or correction, he was gradually deserted by all his friends and died of starvation.

MOSSOVIET THEATRE, Moscow. This theatre, now under the direction of Zavadsky, was founded in 1923 as the Moscow Trades Unions Theatre (M.O.S.P.S.), with the object of encouraging young playwrights to tackle Soviet and political themes. It specialized in producing topical plays to celebrate Soviet or other revolutionary anniversaries, and its earliest and best dramatist was Bill-Belotserkovsky, whose *Hurricane* was produced there in 1926. It lapsed somewhat from its high standards in later years, dabbling in formalism and realism, but after it had been reconstructed as the Theatre of the Moscow Soviet (or Council), it seemed to mature and become more theatrical in the best sense, and less a living newspaper. During the Second World War the theatre was evacuated. It returned to Moscow with a number of interesting productions to its credit, and a company strengthened by the inclusion of some experienced actors from elsewhere and some promising youngsters. In the same year a Mossoviet studio under Zavadsky was opened for the training of young pupils, the course to last three years.

MOTION, a name given in the sixteenth and seventeenth centuries to the puppet-plays of the itinerant showmen. The earliest dealt with biblical subjects, and Shakespeare refers in *The Winter's Tale* to 'a motion of the Prodigal Son'. Later the range of subjects was extended, and episodes were used from medieval romance, mythology, and contemporary history.

MOULIN-ROUGE, Paris, a well-known dance-hall which opened on 5 Oct. 1889, including in its boundary a large garden used for dancing and entertainment in the summer. A feature of the Moulin-Rouge has always been its cabaret show, and it was there that the can-can made its first appearance, the dancers in 1893 being Grille d'Égout, la Goulue, la Môme Fromage, and Nini-patte-en-l'air. Mistinguett was for some years part-proprietor of the Moulin-Rouge and frequently appeared there, as did most of the stars of variety and music-hall.

For the Moulin Rouge, New York, see NEW YORK THEATRE (2).

MOUNET. (1) JEAN SULLY (1841–1916), known as Mounet-Sully, a famous French actor who, after studying under Bressant at the Conservatoire, made his début at the Comédie-Française in 1872 as Oreste in *Andromaque*. His fine physique, beautifully modulated voice, and sombre, penetrating gaze, added to fiery, impetuous acting and great originality, soon brought him into prominence. His career was one of unclouded success, and he appeared in all the great tragic roles of the French classical repertory. He was also outstanding in the plays of Victor Hugo when they were finally given at the Comédie-Française. His younger brother (2) PAUL (1847–1922) was trained as a doctor, but deserted his profession for the stage. He appeared at the Odéon, mainly in tragic roles, and went to the Comédie-Française in 1889, where, though not as great an actor as his brother, he was an important member of the company.

MOUNTFORT. (1) WILLIAM (1664–92), English actor and author of several comedies, including a harlequinade in the Italian manner, *The Life and Death of Dr. Faustus*. He specialized in 'fine gentleman' parts, where the dramatist's witty lines seemed to come spontaneously from his lips. He was an excellent Sparkish in *The Country Wife* and created the part of Sir Courtly Nice in Crowne's play of that name. He was brutally murdered at the instigation of a certain Captain Hill, who had been annoying Mrs. Bracegirdle and suspected Mountfort of being a successful rival in her affections. His early death was a great loss to the stage. Six years previously he had married a young actress, (2) SUSANNA PERCIVAL (1667–1703). Herself the daughter of an actor, she had been on the stage since she was a child. She was equally good in broad comedy or subtle satire, and her playing of Melantha, in Dryden's *Marriage à la Mode*, as described by Colley Cibber, must have been superb. She was a natural mimic, and in spite of her beauty was sufficiently free from vanity to don grotesque clothes or make-up when the part called for it. In her younger days she was much admired in male attire, and was persuaded to play Bayes in Buckingham's *The Rehearsal*, which she did 'with true coxcombly spirit!' Her second husband was the actor Verbruggen.

MOUNT VERNON GARDEN THEATRE, NEW YORK, a playhouse in a summer resort opened in 1800 by one Corre. At first it gave open-air performances three times a week, with actors from the winter stock companies, mainly of light comedy, interspersed with concerts, fireworks, al fresco entertainments, and the Placides in a tight-rope-walking exhibition. By 1802 it had reached the stage of giving good five-act comedies with practically the whole of the Park Theatre company, but this ambitious achievement led to its downfall, as the following summer the actors went to Albany, and the Mount Vernon Garden Theatre was closed.

MOWATT, Anna Cora (née Ogden) (1819–70), American author and actress, mainly remembered for her social comedy, *Fashion* (1845), which usually ranks as the best, if not the first, of the early satiric treatments of American life. It was first produced at the Park Theatre, under Simpson, and was successfully revived in 1924. Mrs. Mowatt, who had already been giving Readings, was encouraged by its reception to become an actress, which she did very successfully, making her début as Pauline in *The Lady of Lyons* in 1845. She had a season at Niblo's, and then formed her own company, with E. L. Davenport as her leading man, being seen with him in London in 1848–50. She made her last appearance at Niblo's in 1854, shortly after the appearance of her *Autobiography*, and lived in retirement with her second husband, a Mr. Ritchie, dying in London. She wrote other plays, as well as novels, short stories, and magazine articles, but *Fashion* is the only one that has survived in more than name. Quinn, in his *History of the American Drama*, says of her:

Real as her contribution to our drama was, her influence upon our theatre was probably even greater. . . . She proved triumphantly that an American gentlewoman could succeed in it without the alteration of her own standard of life. She took into the profession her high heart, her utter refinement, her keen sense of social values, and her infinite capacity for effort, and her effect was a real and great one.

MULTIPLE SETTING, a term applied to the stage décor of the medieval play (known in France as *décor simultané* and in Germany as *Standort-* or *Simultanbühne*). This was an inheritance from the liturgical drama, with its numerous 'mansions' or 'houses' disposed about the church, thus enabling the actors to pass from one place to another without any break in the action, the spectators agreeing to ignore the 'houses' not in use. When the medieval play first moved from the church, the 'mansions' were disposed on three sides of an unlocalized 'platea' or acting space, but by the sixteenth century, at any rate in France, they are found in a straight line, or on a very slight curve. In England the different scenes of a Mystery cycle were on perambulating pageants, and the multiple setting was not needed. It continued in France, and possibly in Germany, for a long time, and was still in use at the Hôtel de Bourgogne in Paris in the early seventeenth century. It is even possible that Corneille's early plays, done at the Marais, were staged in a multiple setting, which was finally routed by the development of the 'machine' play. The set scenes of the Renaissance stage in Italy were single composite backgrounds, and not multiple settings in the original sense, though the unlocalized acting space in front of the tragic or comic houses corresponds to the medieval 'platea'. The Elizabethan public stage, such as the Globe, did not employ the multiple

setting, though something of the kind may have been used in the early days of the private, roofed, playhouse, and was certainly a feature of the elaborate Court masque up to the beginning of the seventeenth century.

MUMMING BIRDS, see Karno, Fred.

MUMMING PLAY. The nature of any primitive folk drama in the British Isles is rather a subject for speculation than for detailed analysis, but there almost certainly existed, from primitive times, semi-dramatic funeral rites and certain ceremonies marking the different periods of the agricultural year. It seems possible that the old English mumming play has preserved traces of some such early spring festival.

The mumming play is still performed in a handful of English villages, usually at Christmas time. Up to the middle of the nineteenth century it was performed all over the country by rustic amateurs; although there were numerous local variants, and the text had in some places degenerated into jingling nonsense, there is a surprising uniformity in the plot and even in the wording of the text of the many versions that have been recovered from widely separated districts.

The main features of the plot are as follows: St. George introduces himself as a gallant Christian Knight and is challenged by the Turkish Knight. A terrific combat ensues, in which one of them is slain. A Doctor is then introduced, who recites a litany of the diseases he can cure, and eventually restores the stricken warrior to life. The performance concludes with a collection. Upon this framework were always superimposed a number of subsidiary stock characters, varying with the district—a Fool in cap and bells, Beelzebub, Father Christmas, and Jack Finney (or Johnny Jack) the Sweeper. The play is spoken throughout in rhyming couplets of which the following are a fair sample, both in their vigour and in a certain almost surrealist obscurity into which the original text has often slipped:

I am King George, this noble Knight
Came from foreign lands to fight
To fight that fiery dragon who is so bold
And cut him down with his blood cold.

Father Christmas has his own distinctive lines, which recur usually in some such form as this:

In come I, old Father Christmas,
Welcome or welcome not,
I hope old Father Christmas
Will never be forgot.

It will be seen that the central feature of the drama is the death and resurrection of one of the protagonists. By analogy with similar ceremonies throughout the world it is not entirely fanciful to see in this episode a relic of a spring festival in which the reawakening of the earth from the death of winter is enacted with human characters. Beyond this legitimate supposition it is not possible to go; there are no records of the enacting of any such ceremonies in England at any time, nor are there any indications of the performance of such a play during the Middle Ages. It is not until the close of the eighteenth century that contemporary references to the mumming play are to be found.

The general plot of the play as it has been preserved for us can hardly be earlier than the beginning of the seventeenth century. The legend of St. George and the Seven Champions of Christendom, upon which the play is apparently founded, was not popularized in England until the end of the sixteenth century; Richard Johnson's *Famous History of the Seaven Champions of Christendom* was first printed in 1596. During the succeeding centuries it took a prominent position in native folk-literature, and was the subject of numerous ballads, chap-books, drolls, and puppet-plays. This legend elaborates the Dragon story endlessly and introduces various single combats with heathen Champions. But there is no suggestion of any resurrection of a defeated warrior.

During the eighteenth century, for the first time, travelling troupes of barnstormers and portable fairground theatrical booths began to penetrate to the most remote country villages; and it is not unlikely that the village folk borrowed the most popular subject-matter and characters from the drolls and puppet-plays that they saw, and tried to emulate them for their own amusement and profit. The most likely theory of the origin of the mumming play is that the distorted version of the legend of St. George was grafted upon some ancient and otherwise unknown traditional game involving the death and restoration to life of a human character.

This theory does not entirely explain the fact that performances so extremely similar grew up in such widely separated counties of England and Scotland. If there was a common original it must have enjoyed an exceptional and widespread popularity; but the existence of it cannot be proved—it has entirely disappeared from human records. Yet the only alternative to the existence of a common origin is the acceptance of the mumming play as a remarkable product of mass telepathy.

Once established in its main outlines, the mumming play preserved its traditional form without fearing to shed old characters or take on new ones. St. George soon became King George, and the Napoleonic Wars, and even the European War of 1914, left their mark. The texts were invariably handed down by word of mouth, growing more and more corrupt in the process; every Christmas time a group of mummers would go from house to house—much like carol-singers—giving their performance and taking their collection wherever they were welcomed. With the steady urbanization of the country-side the old custom, like many others, has nearly disappeared. Yet, quite apart from its historical interest, the mumming play possesses a rough dramatic vigour which is well worth preserving for its own sake.

The scanty information regarding the mummers' play which it has been possible to collect has been collated and commented on exhaustively by Sir E. K. Chambers in *The English Folk-Play* (1933), which also contains a 'normalized' text, to use the editor's own expression. This gives a fair idea of the general run of the play and the order of the incidents.   G. S.

MUNCH, ANDREAS (1811–84), Norwegian dramatist (see SCANDINAVIA, 2).

MUNDAY, ANTHONY (*c.* 1553–1633), English actor and dramatist. He may have acted with the company of the Earl of Oxford, but was later active as a pamphleteer, ballad-maker, translator, and general literary hack. He wrote a good deal for Henslowe, mainly in collaboration, and much of his work is lost. With Chettle he was responsible for two plays on Robin Hood, and with several others for the lost plays on Sir John Oldcastle. He also had some part in *Sir Thomas More*, as the manuscript is in his handwriting. Some of his *John a Kent and John a Cumber* (1594), done by the Admiral's Men, may have suggested to Shakespeare the comic scenes of Bottom and his companions in *A Midsummer Night's Dream*, which was probably acted by the rival company a year later.

MUNDEN, JOSEPH SHEPHERD (1758–1832), English comedian, who after a hard apprenticeship in the provinces was seen at Covent Garden in 1790, taking over the parts of John Edwin, who had just died. His first great original part was Old Dornton in *The Road to Ruin*, which raised him to the front rank. Liston and Quick thought him the finest living actor, and he was particularly good in drunken scenes, seeming to find some fresh 'business' every night. In repose he had a sedate look, but could make his features assume fantastic forms, and Lamb, who had an unbounded admiration for him, wrote of his face: 'Munden has none that you can properly pin down and call *his*. . . . If his name could be multiplied like his countenance, it might fill a play-bill. He, and he alone, literally *makes faces*. . . . Out of some invisible wardrobe he dips for faces. . . . In the grand grotesque of farce, Munden stands out as single and unaccompanied as Hogarth.' The breadth of his acting would scarcely be conceivable nowadays, and even in his own time he was censured for caricature. But his acting made the fortune of many a poor play, transforming its shadows into living realities. He remained at Covent Garden for over twenty years, and then went to Drury Lane, retiring in 1824, when, though he had amassed a good fortune, he lived sparingly, thus lending colour to former accusations of meanness.

MUNK, KAJ (1898–1944), Danish priest and playwright, whose name sprang into prominence when he became a victim of Nazi aggression during the 1939–45 war. From 1924 until his death—he was shot by the Nazis on 4 Jan. 1944—he was parish priest at Vedersø, and during the occupation, which he resisted unceasingly, published his banned sermons and his last and best-known play, *Niels Ebbesen* (1943), a stirring patriotic drama. He had previously been well known in Denmark for a number of historical and contemporary plays, of which the first, dealing with Herod, appeared in 1929. One of his earliest successes was *Cant* (1934), on Henry VIII and Anne Boleyn, but *Ordet* (1932), on a contemporary religious theme, is considered by some critics to be his best work. A play on the life of the Danish philosopher Georg Brandes had some success, while Munk had already shown his opposition to the Axis by *Sejren* (1936), dealing with Italian aggression in Abyssinia, and *Han Sidder ved Smeltediglen* (1938), dealing with Nazi anti-Semitism.

MURDOCH. (1) JAMES EDWARD (1811–93), an American actor, considered by many of his contemporaries the finest light comedian of his day. He was especially noted for his excellent elocution. He began his career at the Chestnut Street Theatre in Philadelphia, his birthplace, and played there with Fanny Kemble in 1833. He remained on the stage until 1858, appearing in England in 1856 in several of his best-known parts, in which he was well received. Jefferson, who played Moses to his Charles Surface in 1853, admired his acting immensely. In his *Autobiography* he says:

[Murdoch] stood alone, and I do not remember any actor who excelled him in those parts that he seemed to make his own. . . . There was a manliness about his light comedy that gave it more dignity than the flippant style in which it was usually played. . . . It was the finish and picturesque style of Murdoch's acting that agreeably surprised the audience of the Haymarket Theater when he played there. . . . The public was unprepared to see comely old English manners so conspicuous in an American actor, and he gained its sympathy at once.

Among his other parts were Benedick, Orlando, Mercutio, Mirabel, and The Rover. On the outbreak of the Civil War in 1861, in which his only son was killed, Murdoch came out of his retirement to give readings and lectures to, and on behalf of, the wounded, the last being at the dramatic festival in Cincinnati in 1883, in which town he died. His nephew (2) FRANK HITCHCOCK (? –1872), also an actor, was the author of an excellent frontier play, *Davy Crockett*, produced only a few weeks before his death. Frank Mayo made a success in the name-part, after a cool initial reception, and it was later played by his son Edwin.

MURPHY, ARTHUR (1727–1805), English actor and dramatist, who was encouraged by Samuel Foote to go on the stage, but was not a particularly good actor. He retired in 1756 and devoted all his energies to play-writing, beginning with four farces and continuing with an adaptation of one of Voltaire's plays as *The Orphan of China* (1759). Among his later tragedies the best were *The Grecian Daughter* (1772) and *Alzuma* (1773), while of his comedies, several of which were based on Molière and other French writers, the outstanding ones were *The Way to Keep Him* (1760), *All in The Wrong* (1761), *The School for Guardians* (1767), and *Know Your Own Mind* (1777). Murphy had little originality, but was an adept at choosing and combining the best elements of the work of others, and had his

place in the revival of the comedy of manners which led up to *The School for Scandal*.

MURRAY, THOMAS CORNELIUS (1873–   ), modern Irish dramatist. His subjects are drawn from the peasant and farming life of his native county of Cork and are distinguished, even among Irish dramatic works for sympathetic perception of the deeply religious and sometimes actually mystical quality in the minds of those peasants. Tragedy, or potential tragedy, is most natural to him; the strict realism of situation, the penetration into the minds of his characters, and the excellence of his dialogue—which seem to bring the actual speech of his people upon the stage—combine to give his work at its finest a quality which distinguishes it clearly from any other of the present day. Despite success in America and England, it would seem that Murray's work should be estimated yet more highly than it at present is.

He made his name in *Birthright*, produced at the Abbey in 1910. This is a play of rivalry and family jealousy in which passion and concentration produce genuine tragedy. *Maurice Harte* (1912) is a remarkable play, not only for its theme, the conflict between spiritual honesty and family affection in the mind of a young peasant, but for the imaginative sympathy with which the characters are portrayed, the directness of the dialogue, the concentration and economy of material in its two acts, and the fineness of the resultant tragic balance. *The Briery Gap* (published in 1917 but not produced) is an exquisite brief tragedy; *Spring* (1918) is a one-act study of poverty and the greed engendered by it; *Aftermath* (1922) is a full-length tragedy on the theme of the arranged marriage; and *Autumn Fire* (1924), another tragedy of mis-mating, is probably the author's best work in the three-act form. *The Pipe in the Fields* (1927) is a fine, brief study of the sudden flowering of the mind of an artist. *The Blind Wolf* (1928), the first of Murray's plays which is not set in Ireland, is again a peasant tragedy. His later plays include *A Flutter of Wings* (1929), *Michaelmas Eve* (1932), *A Stag at Bay* (1934), *A Spot in the Sun* (1938), *Illumination* (1939).   U. E.-F.

MURRAY, WALTER, see KEAN, THOMAS.

MUSE, of Comedy, Thalia; of Dancing, Terpsichore; of Tragedy, Melpomene.

MUSICAL COMEDY, a popular type of light entertainment, which derives from a fusion of burlesque and light opera, taking from the latter the tradition of a sketchy plot, songs arising from it, and concerted finales for each act. Burlesque provided topicality and an intermission of speciality sketches. The first English show to approximate to a musical comedy was *In Town* (1892), which George Edwardes transferred from the Prince of Wales's to his own Gaiety, following it with *The Shop Girl* (1894) and thus inaugurating the series of musical comedies connected with his name. From America, where the foundations of musical comedy had been laid by Tony Pastor, and by the great names of vaudeville, came the swift-moving and tuneful *Belle of New York* (1898), while England sent back to America such things as *Floradora* (1899) and the English versions of *The Merry Widow* (1907) and *The Chocolate Soldier* (1910). In both countries the talent of composers, librettists, comedians, and beautiful chorus-girls was poured out on a host of light-hearted frolics whose tunes are still sung.

The war of 1914–18 brought about many changes, but the essentials of musical comedy remained. The chief differences lay in the importation of large spectacular effects and the increased efficiency of the chorus, which led to the accent being on dancing rather than singing. Among the highlights of this period were *Rose-Marie* and *No, No, Nanette* (both 1925), *The Desert Song* (1927), and the outstanding *Showboat* (1928), based on the novel by Edna Ferber.

In England musical comedy then suffered something of a setback, attention being concentrated on spectacular or intimate revue, or on the big musical plays of Ivor Novello and Noel Coward. In America, however, the genre flourished, first with such song-and-dance satires as *Of Thee I Sing* (1932), *Let 'Em Eat Cake* (1933), and *I'd Rather Be Right* (1937), and later with the musical metamorphosis of such plays as *Green Grow the Lilacs* and *Liliom* into *Oklahoma!* (1943), and *Carousel* (1945), which mingled good music, a strong plot, and professional ballet dancing in a way which marked a great advance on the earlier somewhat haphazard concoction of the typical musical comedy in its less palmy days. America has marked this advance by dropping the 'comedy' connotation of the term, and ticketing its productions merely 'musicals'.

MUSIC BOX, NEW YORK, between Broadway and Eighth Avenue, one of the most popular theatres in New York, which has had surprisingly few failures. A spacious and comfortable house, seating 1,000, it opened on 22 Sept. 1921 with a revue by Irving Berlin, which ran into several editions. Several other revues followed, as did *Once in a Lifetime*, one of the best farces yet written about Hollywood, and *Of Thee I Sing* (1932), the first musical show to win the Pulitzer Prize. Later successes have been *Dinner at Eight*, with Constance Collier as, recognizably, the late Maxine Elliott, *Of Mice and Men* (1937), winner of the Critics' Prize, the hilarious *Man Who Came to Dinner* (1939), based on the antics of the late Alexander Woollcott, and the charming *I Remember Mama* (1944).   G. F.

MUSIC-HALL. I. HISTORY. When Victorian publicans shouted, 'This way, gents, to the music-hall', they meant the one on their own premises—tavern annexes which had developed into gilt-and-plush 'palaces' devoted to comic songs, varied with acrobatics, conjuring, juggling, and dancing. These temples or theatres of variety were always known as music-halls to the British people, and also to the French, though to the American such entertainments were first 'variety' then 'vaudeville' then 'vodeville' (see VAUDEVILLE, 2).

Music-halls of this type began at small taverns in the early eighteenth century. These begat musick-houses, such as Sadler's Wells, to whose programmes of song, dance, and acrobatics were added pageant and pantomime until they outshone the Theatres Royal, in defiance of the law to protect the stage monopoly. These law-breakers were law-makers; attempts to suppress them changed them into minor theatres. Meanwhile the old demand for wine-and-song was supplied by music clubs, which flourished everywhere in the time of the four Georges. All, whatever trade, class, or district they catered for, fostered the comic song. Their history is influenced by street-lighting, for while the age-long black-out still persisted men liked to find entertainment at the next street-corner. As gas-lighting spread they flocked to more glamorous haunts. Evans's Song-and-Supper Rooms at the King Street corner of Covent Garden were celebrated for midnight concerts in the eighteen-forties, under 'Paddy' Green, an Adelphi actor (for later history, see PLAYERS' THEATRE). There was a choir with an academic repertory of part-songs relieved by the long-winded burlesque ballads of Sam Cowell, now remembered more for 'Villikins and his Dinah' and 'The Rat-catcher's Daughter'.

Every tavern had its music-room. In laughter-loving Lambeth the Canterbury Arms was so thronged that Charles Morton, the publican, opened a special building with a stage as well as a space for tables and chairs, and so became 'the father of the halls'. Throughout the eighteen-fifties many a publican bought the house, school, or chapel next door and transformed it into 'the music-hall'. The process changed the volunteer entertainers of the tavern 'free-and-easy' into red-nosed comics and buffo vocalists. Urgent calls for 'turns' from all quarters—street-lighting had now improved—sent up earnings. In fashionable clothes the 'comic' blossomed into the 'lion comique', notably in the person of George Leybourne, the singer of 'Champagne Charlie'. Women performers had promptly decided that the halls were a suitable place for the display of their talents, and Charles Morton responded by engaging sopranos of note. When his taste reverted from the operatic to the domestic, the female 'serio-comic' appeared in the fleshings and spangles of burlesque to sing of menaced virtue one minute and washing-day the next. Sudden success set a feverish pace that killed. Few stars of those early days lived to be fifty years old. One generation of them vanished with Sam Cowell, who died in 1864, and another with George Leybourne twenty years later. Jenny Hill, 'the Vital Spark', whose brave spirit shone in all her studies of pathetic little cockneys, was consistently praised as the brightest star of all. She retired broken in health a few years before she died in 1896.

The halls themselves changed with the changing stars. The tavern annexe survived until its licence to serve alcohol was taken away. All links with the bar-parlour were broken, even in those halls which still had the parent 'pub' firmly embedded in the oft-enlarged façade. In the provinces 'Empires' were being run with twice-nightly programmes by two managers who joined forces to capture London and then split, Moss installing his headquarters at the Hippodrome and Stoll his at the Coliseum. 'Variety' now meant variety. Despite a protest from the theatres, recalling that which was made against the musick-houses over a century earlier, drama (legally confined to performances occupying not more than thirty minutes) was included in the bill when Sir Herbert Tree, Sir George Alexander, and Sarah Bernhardt consented to appear on the music-hall stage. To meet the competition of talking-films, novelties of many kinds, from a Wild West Rodeo to symphony orchestras and bouts of professional tennis or pugilism, were tried at the Coliseum. Still the menace of the 'talkies' was felt until George Black, a manager from the north, caught the taste of the music-hall public. He banded the best knockabout comedians together in a 'Crazy Gang' which acted in the foyer and auditorium as well as on the stage, and interrupted other acts as well as performing their own. They made the Palladium more popular than it had ever been before; but this was an isolated example. Where there had been many hundreds of music-halls in Great Britain, there were now only survivors here and there. Most of the others were cinemas; those that were still variety theatres went in mainly for revue. 'Non-stop' variety was tried at the Windmill, near Piccadilly Circus, where it continued despite the Second World War; and the music-hall comedian comes annually into his own in that typically British institution, the Christmas pantomime.　　　　　　　　　M. W. D.

II. DEVELOPMENT. Unlike the actor of the legitimate stage, the music-hall artist—or performer, as he called and still calls himself—was never blinded by the glamour of the West End. To him London was a 'date', just the same as Manchester, Liverpool, Leicester, or elsewhere, a place in which he would 'work' (not 'play', as an actor would say), and where he would give the same act in the same way, apart from any local 'gag' he might interpolate. This difference between 'work' and 'play' is one of the great distinctions between the music-hall and the theatre. It stands for much, and it marks the individualism which distinguishes the music-hall. However eminent actors or actresses may be, they are still cogs in a play. The music-hall performer is identical with his act. Not for him the carefully prepared 'entrance' contrived by every artifice of a practised dramatist.

The music-hall artist had so many minutes allotted for his turn, and had to make good in that time. The 'stars' (with whom the word originated before it was annexed by the cinema) sang songs written to suit their own style. They had their individual make-up, which was their trade-mark—Robey his eyebrows, Harry Tate his moustache, Mark Sheridan his frock coat and bell-bottomed trousers tied round the knee, Eugene Stratton his black face, George Lashwood his faultless tailoring and air of Beau Brummel; Gus Elen, Alec Hurley, and Albert Chevalier shared the 'coster' role, though Chevalier was the 'pearliest' of the Pearly Kings; George Formby, the plaintive dare-devil and would-be royster, who wasn't going home 'till a quarter past nine', exploited the Lancashire accent; R. G. Knowles never appeared without his opera hat, frock coat, and white duck trousers; Wilkie Bard had his high forehead and deliberate air; Kate Carney her 'Arriet's feathers; Grock his fiddle; Harry Lauder his kilts and curly stick; Happy Fanny Fields her Dutch costume; and T. E. Dunville his tight-fitting black suit. Some, on the other hand, varied their attire. Dan Leno, in whatever guise he appeared, was always Dan Leno, while his pantomime partner, Herbert Campbell, was beloved for his bulky figure. Marie Lloyd was always Marie Lloyd, the epitome of Cockney London, and although Little Tich might represent a variety of characters from a jockey to a fireman, still his diminutive size was his greatest asset, and he seldom failed to complete his act without using his elongated boots for his famous dance. Chirgwin was the unalterable 'white-ey'd Kaffir', and relied almost wholly upon two songs, 'My Fiddle is My Sweetheart' and 'The Blind Boy', asking the audience in his queer falsetto voice: 'Which will you have, ladies and gempmuns, The Fiddler or the Blind 'Un?' They always wanted both. Harry Champion specialized in songs about food—'Boiled Beef and Carrots'—delivered at terrific speed, and ending with a 'breakdown' which was his own particular property. They even had their own posters, which were as individual as themselves, and T. E. Dunville would advise the patrons of, say, the Hackney Empire that 'I'm Sticking Here for a Week'. To their public they were old friends, and that public never wanted them to change.

The tremendous efficiency of it all proved that these people were specialists at their jobs. To watch Cinquevalli juggling was to see perfection in that particular art. There was the neatness of dapper Vesta Tilley, the supreme clowning of Grock, the perfect understanding and timing of Clarice Mayne and 'That' (Jas. W. Tate), the dainty appeal and daring of Ella Retford, the humour of Vesta Victoria. The same applied to the trapezists, the acrobats, the Risley Acts, the trampolinists and the dancers who went to make up a music-hall 'bill'. They worked hard, often playing at three or four widely-separated halls a night, even in the days before motor transport, and keeping to a strict time-table. At halls like the Tivoli, the Oxford, the London Pavilion, could habitually be seen a programme of some twenty 'star turns'. Much the same was true of the Holborn Empire, which kept the banner of variety flying up to the end, until it was practically destroyed by enemy action in 1941.

At the Empire and the Alhambra in Leicester Square things were rather different. For years these two halls were the home of ballet, and each had its famous promenade. The Empire was always the finer of the two, and was known as 'the Cosmopolitan Club of the World'. An exile returning to London from foreign parts, and going straight there, could be sure of meeting an old friend. There was an air of almost regal splendour there—marble, gilt, thick rich carpets, its promenade as much a feature as its stage—there is nothing like it to-day. Champagne flowed, people chattered and laughed, gazing down at the ballet through an atmosphere of blue smoke from innumerable good cigars which tinged the golden glow of the lighting. These two halls were peculiar to London, as was the Palace at Cambridge Circus, which having begun as a Grand Opera House became one of the smartest Theatres of Varieties ever seen, replete with evening dress and titles in the audience, and 'stars' and novelties on the stage. It was at the Palace that music-hall received its accolade, when King George V commanded a performance there in 1912. Although a Royal Performance attended by the Sovereign became an annual event, that was the only real 'Command' performance. Later, the London Coliseum struck an individual note as a refined and respectable music-hall to which one could safely take children. But by then the whole of music-hall was growing anaemic, and was already losing grip upon that full-bodied vulgar humour which has been part of the British national 'make-up' since the days of Chaucer through those of Shakespeare and Dickens.

In its heyday the music-hall represented the type of entertainment most loved by the masses. It was gay, raffish, carefree. Its themes were fully understood and appreciated by the multitude, for they dealt with their own emotions, their own troubles, their own perplexities, their own meat and drink, and their own raw humour. The lodger, the mother-in-law, the brokers, the overdue rent, the kipper and bloater, the annual seaside holiday, beer, the state of being stony broke; and by way of contrast, mother love, true hearts that beat as one, the old home with its apple-trees, its ivy-clad walls and its village bells—these were the music-hall's great stand-bys. It embraced, too, husbands both errant and hen-pecked—wives, both domineering and downtrodden—unfaithful swains and lasses, Gay Paree and midnight revelry. And it was very sound on the subject of patriotism: it told the British people that they were the salt of the earth and could never be beaten, and it glorified the Red, White, and Blue. It gave the people songs they could join in singing, songs they could whistle and remember. And they remember them still. It may be said to have supplied this country with the folk-songs of an era. You went to a music-hall to have a good time, and you had it. You found yourself surrounded by people in the same frame of mind, laughing, joking, smoking, having their drinks freely either at the bar inside the auditorium, or—in the earlier days—served to them in their seats. You soon surrendered to their virile, boisterous mood, joining in the choruses and the shouting, the whistling and the acclamation, which made up 'the spirit of the halls'. Nothing was restrained, nothing was sophisticated: it was all high spirits, and every day was a Bank Holiday. That was what the halls were like, the Oxford, the London Pavilion, the Middlesex, the Holborn Empire, the South London, the Canterbury in its varying phases, the Metropolitan; and, to much the same degree, Collins's and the hundreds of outlying halls like the Bedford, the Granville (Walham Green), the Star (Bermondsey), the Queen's (Poplar), the Paragon, and the countless Empires and Hippodromes of the suburbs and provinces.

III. SOME NOTABLE HALLS (for their histories as theatres, see under their own names).

1. *The Alhambra.* This was first opened as a music-hall by E. T. Smith, the showman, who failed. After an interlude as a circus, it became a music-hall again under William Wilde of Norwich. During his tenancy the great Leotard, trapeze artist and wire-walker, drew crowds. He returned again in 1866, when Hollingshead, founder of the Gaiety Theatre, was in charge, and was paid as much as £180 a week. He never had an accident, and died in his bed of consumption at the age of 30. Other stars of this period were the Two Farinis, the Kiralfys, the Foucarts, and the Georgia Magnet. At one time in the Alhambra's career, when things were very shaky, Charles Morton, the 'father of the halls', was called in. He not only stemmed the tide of failure, but made the theatre a very profitable proposition. Its greatest period as a music-hall was from 1890 to 1910.

2. *The Canterbury.* This was the original music-hall. The Canterbury Arms, which gave it birth, occupied the site of an old tavern, which had stood for centuries in the Westminster Bridge Road. In 1848 it was taken over by Charles Morton and his brother-in-law, Frederick Stanley. They ran concerts on Saturday evenings, which soon became very popular. No charge was made for admission—they made their profit on the drinks sold. Later a Thursday concert was added, and within a year they had built a hall on the site of their old skittle-alley adjoining, which held 700 people. Morton had enlivened his concerts by engaging professionals. In the new hall he went yet further and charged for admission. There was no stage, only a platform at the end of the room. John Caulfield was Chairman and Jonghmann was musical director. Charles Morton spared no expense to make the venture successful, paying his artists as much as £30 a week. Augustus Braham, son of the great tenor, sang there, as did Miss Turpin (Mrs. Henry Wallack) and Miss Russell, the latter as Marguerite in selections from Gounod's 'Faust' given at the Canterbury before the first full performance at His Majesty's on 11 June 1863.

No less a person than Mlle Tietjens was in the audience on that occasion. Sam Cowell, E. W. Mackney, and a host of other 'comics' appeared at the Canterbury, and the place was packed nightly. Later a new hall was constructed round the old one, and on a Saturday night the old one was finally demolished, the new one opening on the following Monday. It had a picture gallery, which *Punch* called 'The Royal Academy over the Water'. The entrance fee was 6*d.* downstairs and 9*d.* in the Circle. The audience sat at small tables, and had their food or drinks brought to them there.

In 1863 Stanley retired and Morton remained in sole charge until Boxing Night 1867, when William Holland took over. He had the hall redecorated regardless of cost, and when he was told that his 1,000 guinea carpet might make some of his humbler patrons feel awkward, he put out posters inviting them to come and spit on it.

Classical music vanished from the bill, and comedy predominated. George Leybourne, just coming into prominence, was engaged at £20 a week, which was soon increased, billed as the 'lion comique', and given a carriage and four to drive about in. He always drank champagne, as befitted the singer of 'Champagne Charlie'. In 1876 the house passed to Villiers, and was enlarged at a cost of £40,000. The bills at this time included those friendly rivals, Leybourne and The Great Vance, Fred Coyne, Arthur Roberts, and numerous others, while Phyllis Broughton and Florence Powell were the chief dancers in the ballet which now became a popular feature. One of the most successful was a spectacular and topical ballet called 'Plevna', followed by an equally successful 'Trafalgar'. The Canterbury was at that time the only hall where good ballet could be seen, and the public flocked to it. Edward VII (as Prince of Wales), the Duke of Cambridge, and the Duke and Duchess of Teck were among the royal visitors. Prices soared, but when the attendances began to slacken a drastic lowering of them brought success back again. For many years the Canterbury bar was a favourite place of call for the entire music-hall profession, as was only fitting in the hall that saw the birth of variety. It was later taken over by a limited company.

3. *The City Music-Hall.* This was originally the Dr. Johnson public-house and supper-room, a most popular place of entertainment in Bolt Court, Fleet Street. It was noted for the excellence of its brown beer, chops, kidneys, and oysters, and for the high standard of the entertainment offered to its patrons while they ate and drank. It closed in 1863.

4. *The Coliseum.* This famous house opened as a variety theatre on 24 Dec. 1904. It gave four performances daily and staged vast shows, including a reproduction of the Derby with real racehorses and jockeys. Later it became a regular music-hall, featuring ballet, musical acts, and even Sir Henry Wood, while stars of the legitimate stage appeared there in short sketches. After being used as a

theatre for some time it went back to variety for a short period just before the Second World War. When it was first opened it had a miniature railway intended to convey royal visitors from the Royal Entrance to the Royal Box. This broke down the first time it was used, with King Edward VII on board, and was never used again.

5. *Collins's.* This was originally the Lansdowne Arms. It was taken over by Sam Collins, the popular Irish vocalist, and opened by him, after a brush with the licensing authorities, on 4 Nov. 1863. Collins, whose real name was Sam Vagg, and who had been a chimney-sweep, ran it successfully until his death in 1865, when his widow took over. It stands in Upper Street, Islington, and is still open.

6. *Deacon's.* This hall was opened on 14 Dec. 1861 (the day the Prince Consort died) by J. Deacon. It stood in Islington near Sadler's Wells Theatre, and Arthur Roberts made his début there, as did Fred Williams, a clever comedian and sketch-writer who became its Chairman. Harry Randall also appeared there. The hall vanished in the 1890s during street improvements.

7. *The Eagle.* This tavern, in the Mile End Road, was originally owned by A. Ward. W. Lusby took it from him and, erecting a platform in the grounds, opened it as Lusby's Summer and Winter Garden. Later he built a hall on the site, which he sold to Crowder and Payne in 1878. This was burnt down and rebuilt as the Paragon, a very successful music-hall for many years.

8. *The Empire Theatre of Varieties.* This famous hall stood in Leicester Square on the site of Savile House, which had been a royal residence, an exhibition gallery and a café-chantant, and had been destroyed by fire in 1865. The site lay vacant until Nicols, proprietor of the Café Royal, built a theatre there and opened it on 17 Apr. 1884. After failing as a theatre it became a music-hall and was a great success. The promenade, which was one of its chief features, was attacked as a haunt of vice by Mrs. Ormiston Chant in her Purity Campaign in 1894. She only succeeded in publicizing it further, and making herself the most popular 'guy' of that year. The Empire ballets were another of its great features. Katti Lanner was ballet-mistress, many of the ballets were created by Wilhelm, while Zanfretta, Adeline Genée, Lydia Kyasht, and Phyllis Bedells were its ballerinas. A famous male dancer who appeared there was Fred Farren, a master of mime and a wonderful actor. His sensational apache dance thrilled London. The Empire is now a cinema.

9. *Gatti's.* There were two Gattis, one in Villiers Street, Charing Cross, where Sloman, the famous improvisator, made his last appearance. It was known also as Gatti's-under-the-Arches (it stood below Charing Cross Station) and later became a restaurant. Gatti's-in-the-Road (Westminster Bridge Road) was opened by Carlo Gatti, a caterer, in 1865. It flourished for many years, and saw Harry Lauder's first London appearance. It is now a cinema.

10. *The Hippodrome.* This was opened by Moss Empires on 15 Jan. 1900 to house circus and variety. It staged many famous 'turns' and big spectacular shows, in which Marceline the Clown was a great attraction. Later it became purely a Theatre of Varieties, then a home of revue, and finally a theatre, as it is to-day. It stands in Cranbourn Street, Leicester Square.

11. *The London Pavilion.* This was opened by Loibl and Sonnenhammer as a café-chantant. It was originally a stable-yard roofed in, and had in its time housed waxworks and Napoleon's coach. It was continually enlarged and altered, becoming more prosperous each time, and took its final shape in 1885, when its bill included all the great names of the music-hall. Jenny Hill, billed as The Vital Spark, made her sensational début there; The Great Macdermott sang 'We don't want to fight, but by Jingo, if we do, We've got the ships, we've got the men, and got the money too!' (words and music by G. H. Hunt); it was the spiritual home of Dan Leno, and its bills were magnificent, with twenty 'stars' at a time. Under the management of C. B. Cochran it housed several spectacular revues, but reverted to non-stop variety under John Southern in the 1930s. It is now a cinema.

12. *The Marylebone.* This was originally the Rose of Normandy tavern (still standing) which had been the centre of a vanished pleasure-garden resort known as Marylebone Gardens. Sam Collins converted it into a music-hall, but it was not a success, and he gave it up in 1861. His successor, W. Botting, ran it as a music-hall into the 1890s.

13. *The Metropolitan.* This was originally the White Lion in the Edgware Road, one of the old concert-rooms. As the Turnhams, named from its proprietor, it opened as a music-hall on 6 Dec. 1862 and held 4,000 people. It was later taken over by one of the limited companies which under the Act of 1862 were springing up everywhere, and opened as the Metropolitan on Easter Monday 1864. It passed through many hands before success came, and is still a prosperous music-hall, practically the last which retains the genuine old-time music-hall atmosphere. It was one of the first London halls at which The Great Vance appeared, with his Cockney songs like 'The Chickaleery Cove'.

14. *The Middlesex.* This famous house in Drury Lane, affectionately known as the Old Mo, started as the Great Mogul, and was little more than a public-house singing-room. It was transformed into the Middlesex Music-Hall by W. Winder, who left it to convert the White Lion into the Metropolitan. It was rebuilt in 1872, with further alterations three years later. In 1878 J. L. Graydon made the hall so popular that he had to enlarge it. Many music-hall stars made their début at the Old Mo, including Sam Collins, singing 'Paddy's Wedding', and it claimed to be the first London hall at which Dan Leno appeared. It was also connected with the early days of Marie Lloyd. Just before the war of 1914–18, at a time when revue was paramount, it made a sensation by staging a series of French revues, the Ba-ta-ta-Clan, featuring 'the Girl with the Muff'—who appeared to be otherwise unclothed. It was one of the last halls to have a Chairman. Taken over by Sir Oswald Stoll, rebuilt and renamed the Winter Garden Theatre, it had no further music-hall history.

15. *The Oxford.* Morton, who had had a big success with the Canterbury, and had noticed that Weston was being successful with a hall in Holborn, decided to invade the West End. He took over the Boar and Castle Inn, at the corner of Oxford Street and Tottenham Court Road, an old coaching house dating back to at least Jacobean times, and probably further, built a music-hall on the site, and opened it as the Oxford on 26 Mar. 1861. The first bill included Madame Parepa (Mme Carl Rosa) and Santley, as well as a host of other singers, which showed that Morton was pursuing the plan adopted at the Canterbury of offering his patrons good music. Sims Reeves was offered his own terms to sing at the opening, but declined. When first built the Oxford was the finest music-hall in London. It was 94 ft. long and 41 ft. high, lighted by 28 crystal stars, which were later superseded by four chandeliers suspended from the roof with smaller ones in the galleries. An immense mirror fixed at the back of the stage reflected the whole hall, in which food and drink were served at that time, while the 'turns' were performed on a platform stage. It was burned down on 11 Feb. 1868, but was rebuilt and reopened on 9 Aug. 1869 under the control of Syers and Taylor. It was burnt down again on 1 Nov. 1872 and reopened on 17 March of the following year, much enlarged. In 1891 it passed under the control of a company which ran the Tivoli and the London Pavilion, and so became one of those which were known as the Syndicate Halls. It was rebuilt and modernized, the new foundation stone being laid by Charles Morton on 15 Aug. 1892, the opening taking place on the following 31 Jan. It was a most successful hall, at which all the great stars appeared. On its act drop was a painting of Magdalen College Tower, which was also emblazoned on its programmes. It ran Saturday matinées, at which, for 6*d.*, all the old stars could be seen and sometimes a new one spotted, for George Robey and Harry Tate both made their débuts at one. It was a typical music-hall, where men could stand at the bar, order a drink, and watch the show. It finally became a theatre.

16. *The Palace.* When this had failed as opera house and theatre, though run by Sir Augustus Harris, the company which owned it called in Charles Morton, then an old man, to see what he could do with it. He made it the smartest Theatre of Varieties in London, and died there in harness, to be succeeded by Alfred Butt, who had joined with Morton to reorganize the financial side. Under him its prestige increased. Pavlova introduced real Russian ballet to London there, Maud Allan made a sensation with her bare-legged dancing

and her *Vision of Salome*. Datas the memory-man appeared there, and the first Royal Command music-hall performance, ordered by George V in 1912, took place at the Palace. Just before 1914 the house switched over to revue, and only went back to variety once more, for a short season in 1921, when Harry Lauder occupied the entire second half of the programme, and packed the theatre. In its palmy days Herman Finck was its conductor, and while there composed his well-known waltz *In the Shadows*, to which the justly celebrated Palace Girls performed a skipping-rope dance. Marie Lloyd nearly failed there, for once in her life, but when she introduced, to the tune of the then popular *Narcissus*, a song which began 'There they are, the two of them on their own', the audience could no longer resist her, and she triumphed once again.

17. *The Palladium*. This very successful music-hall, built on the site of Hengler's Circus in Argyll Street, Oxford Circus, was opened in 1910. During its career it has also housed revue and been a theatre. It reverted to variety under George Black, and was the home of his 'Crazy Gang' before they went to the Victoria Palace.

18. *The Rotunda*. Variety performances were given in this hall in Blackfriars Road as early as 1829, when Sloman, the improviser of topical rhymes, played there. It may be considered the original home of organized variety, but not of the music-hall, a distinction which the Canterbury yields to none. Dan Leno's parents appeared at the Rotunda as duettists and dancers. It was closed because a cockfight was given within its walls. Later it became the Ring, the home of boxing and pugilism for many years, and the scene of some Shakespearian performances, notably of *Henry V*, under Robert Atkins in 1936.

19. *The Royal Holborn*. This was the first music-hall to challenge the supremacy of the Canterbury. Some time in the early 1850s the Holborn National Schools were transformed into a music-hall by Edward Weston, and proved most successful. This encouraged Morton to build the Oxford, a short distance away, though not without opposition from Weston, who tried unsuccessfully to obtain an injunction. Its name was later changed from Weston's to the Royal Holborn, and it continued on its successful career, with many stars making early appearances there. It was the home of J. H. Stead, 'The Perfect Cure', and Bessie Bellwood, the most exuberant 'serio' of the halls, made a very early appearance there, being told she was too quiet. It had a consistently high standard, and one of its Chairmen, for many years, was W. B. Fair, famous as the singer of 'Tommy, Make Room for Your Uncle'. Bad times came upon it at the beginning of the twentieth century, but it was rescued by George Gray, who staged sketches there, such as *The Fighting Parson*, and others. It then became the Holborn Empire, and except for special theatrical matinées, remained a music-hall throughout its career, being the last surviving hall playing variety in

the West End when it was destroyed during the blitz in 1941. The site is now for sale.

20. *The Stoll*. Originally the London Opera House, opened unsuccessfully by Oscar Hammerstein on 13 Nov. 1911, this building stands on the site of the old Vere Street Theatre (Gibbon's Tennis-court). It was acquired by Sir Oswald Stoll, who gave it his name, and ran it as a music-hall. For many years it was a cinema, but has reverted to a policy of alternate musical productions and variety.

21. *The South London*. This was the third music-hall to succeed in London, following the Canterbury and Weston's (Holborn Empire). It was a handsome hall, built and decorated like a Roman villa, standing on the site of a Roman Catholic Chapel, and it opened on 30 Dec. 1860, with E. W. Mackney, the original black-faced comedian, in the bill. It was burnt down in 1869, but speedily rebuilt. In 1874 it was taken over by J. J. Poole, a most enterprising man, who produced excellent spectacles and ballets there. Among his discoveries were Barrington Foote, Connie Gilchrist, and J. J. Dallas. It was Poole who gave Leybourne his nickname of the 'lion comique'. The Great MacDermott appeared there, singing his 'Scamp' song, and Fred Coyne made his last appearance at the South London, which later saw the début of Florrie Forde. One of its Chairmen was 'Baron' Courtney. It was badly damaged by enemy action during the Second World War.

22. *The Strand*. This hall stood on the site of the old Exeter 'Change in the Strand. It opened in 1871, and called itself the Strand Musick-Hall to emphasize its superiority over the less refined music-halls. It was charmingly decorated and upholstered, but proved a little too refined for the public, and had to alter its policy. Jolly Johnnie Nash was made Chairman, the 'comics' were called in, including The Great Vance and Leybourne, but all to no purpose. In its place arose the old Gaiety Theatre, a position now marked by the island site at the end of Aldwych and Wellington Street.

23. *The Surrey*. This hall, originally The Grapes in Southwark Bridge Road, became the Surrey Music-Hall in the 1840s. The Vokes family appeared there at the then enormous salary of £20 a week. Other early stars were Louie Sherrington, Willie and Emma Ward of 'The Gingham Umbrella' fame, Pat P. Fannin, a famous dancer, and Mr. and Mrs. Jack Carroll, negro banjoists and dancers. When the Surrey Gardens were opened it changed its name to the Winchester, which title it retained until its demolition in 1878. At one time it was owned by W. B. Fair.

24. *The Sutton Arms*. A hall in Little Sutton Street, Clerkenwell, also known as the Goldsmith's Arms, which was open on Mondays, Fridays, and Saturdays. Fred Albert was one of its great attractions. The late Henry Sampson, founder of the Sunday newspaper, *The Referee*, used to give exhibitions of sparring in this hall. Its owner, George Clark, backed Sampson in his running matches.

25. *The Tivoli*. This was one of London's most famous halls. It stood in the Strand when that thoroughfare was a great centre of amusement and night-life, and was erected in 1890 on the site of a beer-hall of the same name. At first it was unlucky, but when Charles Morton was called in it soon picked up, and the Tivoli, or the 'Tiv', as it was affectionately called, became a favourite resort. It gave excellent programmes, often with twenty stars at a time, including Lottie Collins singing 'Ta-Ra-Ra-Boom-de-Ay'. One of the earliest revues was staged at the Tivoli, which later became a cinema.

26. *The Trocadero*. This was a handsome hall put up on the site of the old Argyll Rooms in Windmill Street, Piccadilly. It had many ups and downs. In 1893 it was put up for auction, but the reserve price of £10,000 was not reached, and it was finally acquired by Hugh J. Didcott, the music-hall agent, who had as sleeping partner in his venture the Coster comedian Albert Chevalier. It did not succeed, and eventually became a restaurant. It was at one time run by Sam Adams, a famous music-hall figure.

27. *The Victoria Palace*. This opened in 1863 as the Royal Standard Music-Hall, Pimlico. It was a successful house, though its early history was uneventful. All the 'stars' of the day played there, and a unique feature of the building was the inscription 'Artistes' Entrance' over the stage door. It was rebuilt and modernized in 1911, and after the First World War was used as a theatre (see VICTORIA PALACE).

28. *The Washington*. This music-hall in Battersea supplanted a previous one called the Magpie. It was run by 'Pony' Moore, of the Moore and Burgess Minstrels, and had quite a good career. It has now vanished.

29. *The William IV*. This was one of the very early halls—practically a supper-room. Sam Cowell once dodged an engagement here to attend the audition at the Canterbury which made him a great 'star'.

30. *The Windmill*. This opened as a theatre in 1931, and became a music-hall playing a formula of its own, known as 'Revudeville', most successfully. Situated in Great Windmill Street, Piccadilly, it was the only London place of entertainment to remain open all through the Second World War, even at the height of the blitz, an achievement which has been made the subject of an American film.

MUSIC IN THE THEATRE, see INCIDENTAL MUSIC.

MUSICOS, see CAFÉ-CONCERT.

MUSSATO, ALBERTINO (1261–1329), the first Italian dramatist to write a tragedy, *Eccerinus*, dealing with a recent event of Italian history. Written in Latin in about 1315, it was probably never acted, but is important as showing the influence on the old religious drama of the classic form, particularly of Seneca (see ITALY, 1 b i).

MUSSET, LOUIS CHARLES ALFRED DE (1810–57), French poet and novelist of the Romantic school, and the one man who might have fused the new drama with the classical tradition of the French theatre. But the failure of his first play, *La Nuit vénitienne* (1830), due partly to an unfortunate accident, partly to organized opposition, turned him from the stage, and he wrote his later plays to be read. Consequently he had no influence on the stage in his own day, and it was not until 1847 that *Un Caprice* was put on at the Comédie-Française. It was immediately successful, and was followed by *Il faut qu'une porte soit ouverte ou fermée* and *Il ne faut jurer de rien*. To a theatre under the dual influence of Scribe and Balzac, de Musset brought back the poetry and fantasy which it was in danger of losing. Excellent examples of de Musset's method, which he himself explained as a fusion of the romantic and classical traditions, are *Les Caprices de Marianne*, first given in 1851, and *On ne badine pas avec l'amour*, which was seen ten years later. His best work is undoubtedly to be found, however, in *Fantasio*, given in 1866, and *Lorenzaccio*, written in Venice in 1834, after his tragic liaison with George Sand. De Musset's plays, which show a mingling of eighteenth-century France, Italian Renaissance, Shakespeare, and Marivaux, may also be considered a source of Symbolism. They have atmosphere, but an unlocalized action, for which scenery is unnecessary. Being liberated, by the conditions of their composition, from the conventions of theatrical presentation, they represent a world in which anything can and does happen. De Musset was a wonderful painter of women, and more than any other writer of his time recognized the tragedy of unrequited love.

MYNNISCUS, a Greek tragic actor who played for Aeschylus.

MYSTERY PLAY, a medieval religious entertainment, so called because it was produced by the Guilds as part of their 'mysteries'. These plays are found all over Europe and the term is synonymous with the earlier Miracle play. Based on the Bible, from the Creation to the Second Coming, and on the lives of the saints, they were mostly given at Whitsuntide or on the Feast of Corpus Christi. Each was really a cycle of plays, a different guild being responsible for the performance of each episode. The few surviving English Mystery plays are known by the names of the towns where they are believed to have been performed—the Chester, probably written by Ralph Higden on Latin and French sources, the Coventry, which contains the fine carol 'Lullay thou littel tiny child', the Towneley (or Wakefield), rougher in humour and containing the farcical 'Second Shepherd's Play' with Mak the sheep-stealer, and finally the York, the longest extant, with forty-eight plays and one fragment, of which the manuscript is in the British Museum (see also AUTO; ENGLAND, 1; FRANCE, 1; ITALY, 1; SACRA RAPPRESENTAZIONE and SPAIN, 1).

N

NADIR, MOSES (1885–1943), writer of Yiddish plays produced in New York by Maurice Schwartz (see JEWISH DRAMA, 6).

NAEVIUS, GNAEUS (c. 270–c. 199 B.C.), one of the most original of Latin writers, was the first successor of Andronicus in drama. In 235 B.C. he produced a play at the Ludi Romani, and he continued to bring out a series of translations from Greek tragedy and comedy, as well as two original plays on Roman historical subjects, until the end of the war with Hannibal. The surviving fragments show that in style he altogether surpassed his predecessor; we see in him a man of daring and energy, one who loved liberty and had a gift for social and political satire which was to cost him dear. Into his translations he infused a strong Roman element; it is not surprising that his chief dramatic work was in comedy. A celebrated piece of characterization is his description of a flirt in *The Girl from Tarentum*. The Roman historical play (see FABULA, 4. *Praetexta*) was his creation; the surviving fragments scarcely enable us to say more than that one of his two *praetextae* dealt with Romulus, the other with the victory won at Clastidium by Naevius's great contemporary, M. Claudius Marcellus, in 222 B.C. Naevius's turn for satire brought him into collision with the powerful family of the Metelli, and after undergoing a period of imprisonment he is said to have died an exile in Africa, about the end of the century.

W. B.

NAHARRO, BARTOLOMÉ DE TORRES (c. 1480–c. 1530), was, with Encina and Vicente, one of the earliest of Spanish dramatists. Like Encina also, he spent much time in Italy and enjoyed the favour of Leo X. He published his plays, which had all been first performed in Italy, in 1517 with other works under the general title of *Propalladia*. They are witty, sometimes at the expense of religion, written in fluent verse with some regard for the principles of dramatic unity, and contain occasional excellent dramatic effects. The sallies against the clergy caused them to be banned in Spain for some time. *La Himenea*, a *comedia a fantasia*, is a foreshadowing of the cloak-and-sword plays later to be so important and popular a feature of the Spanish theatre, while the distinction in the preface to his works between realistic and romantic comedy may rank as the first attempt at dramatic criticism in Spain. Naharro also carried further the characterization and unity of plot already apparent in Encina.

NAOGEORG, see KIRCHMAYER, THOMAS.

NARES, OWEN (1888–1943), English actor, and for many years one of the most popular matinée idols of London. He had great personal beauty, which at times obscured his very real gifts as an actor. On his mother's side he was the grandson of the famous scene-painter Beverley, some of whose talent he inherited and appeared to have passed on to his son, who unhappily predeceased him, being killed in 1942 at the age of 25. The father made his first appearance in 1908, after studying with Rosina Filippi, and was at the St. James's in 1910, where he appeared in *Old Heidelberg*. Among his later successes were Lord Monkhurst in *Milestones*, and Julian Beauclerc in *Diplomacy*, Peter Ibbetson, and the dual role of the Bishop and Thomas Armstrong in *Romance*. In 1923 he took over the management of the St. James's, where he appeared as Mark Sabre in a dramatization of *If Winter Comes*, in which he had previously been seen on tour, and in 1925 went to South Africa with a repertory which included *Romance* and *Diplomacy*. Of his later parts the most successful were Roger Hilton in *Call it a Day*, Robert Carson in *Robert's Wife*, in which he played opposite Edith Evans, and Max de Winter in *Rebecca*. His sudden death at the early age of 55 was a great loss to the English stage, since the excellence of his later work had given indications of much depth and maturity, and he seemed about to draw on greater reserves of strength and authority than he had previously been credited with.

NARR, the Fool of the German Carnival play (see GERMANY, 1).

NASH, JOHN (1828–1901), a comedian who was a well-known star of the music-halls in their early period. Known as Jolly, or Jolly John, Nash, he had a singing contest in 1864 with another performer called Taylor for a hundred pounds a side at Weston's (afterwards the Holborn Empire). Both sang six songs, and Taylor won by a small margin. But Nash went on to become a great star, one of his most famous songs being 'Rackety Jack', which he once sang before Edward VII, who joined in the chorus. Nash became Chairman of the Strand Musick-Hall which, in its endeavours to become refined, failed to amuse, and was replaced by the Gaiety Theatre. W. M. P.

NASHE, THOMAS (1567–1601), English pamphleteer, noted for his part in the Martin Marprelate controversy and for his attacks on Gabriel Harvey, which arose from his friendship with Lyly. He was also a friend and collaborator of Greene, and with Christopher Marlowe wrote *Dido, Queen of Carthage*, his earliest extant essay in dramatic form. In 1597 he was concerned with Jonson in the ill-fated *Isle of Dogs*, played at the Swan on Bankside, which sent the actors and Jonson, and possibly Nashe also, to prison on account of its supposedly seditious nature. This play is lost, and the only extant dramatic work of Nashe's is *Summer's Last Will and Testament* (1592–3), a mixture of comedy and masque designed for performance in the house of a nobleman, probably Archbishop Whitgift at Croydon. It was used as the basis of Constant Lambert's masque for orchestra, chorus, and baritone solo, first given in 1936.

NASSAU STREET THEATRE, or, more properly, the Theatre in Nassau Street, was probably the first place used for professional stage plays in New York. It consisted of a large room in a house on Nassau Street where in 1750 Walter Murray and Thomas Kean brought their company from Philadelphia to play *Richard III* as rewritten by Colley Cibber, together with a repertory of tragedies and farces. In 1751 Robert Upton, probably an actor sent over from London by Lewis Hallam, gave a short and unsuccessful season, which included *Othello*, and in 1753 the elder Hallam, arriving from his tour of the southern cities, caused the old theatre to be dismantled and a new one, known as the New Theatre, or Hallam's in Nassau Street, to be built. Here he and his famous company stayed for a long season, opening in the autumn with *The Conscious Lovers*, and ending in March of the following year with *The Gamester*. After Hallam's departure the theatre was devoted to more mundane uses, and disappears from theatre history.

NATANSON, JACQUES (1901–   ), French dramatist, whose plays were produced at the Théâtre de l'Œuvre in the years following the First World War. He was an ironic and unsentimental portrayer of the contemporary scene in the 1920s, and two of his plays, *Le Greluchon délicat* (1925) and *Je t'attendrais* (1928) were given in translation in New York. A more serious and subtle play was *L'Été* (1934), the story of lost happiness between two wars.

NATHAN, GEORGE JEAN (1882–   ), American dramatic critic, who needs no introduction to anyone even remotely acquainted with the American theatre or the American scene; he has been a leading figure of both for many years. He was born in Fort Wayne, Indiana, and educated at Cornell and the University of Bologna in Italy. In 1905 he joined the staff of *The New York Herald* and began his career as a dramatic critic. It is doubtful whether any other individual exercised a more important influence in the transformation of the native stage. When Nathan first went to work the American theatre was an intellectual wilderness. The works of Augustus Thomas and David Belasco cluttered the playhouses to the exclusion of almost everything else. Nathan fought for the drama of ideas and in those days it was a fight against great odds. He introduced the modern plays of Europe—Ibsen, Shaw, Hauptmann, and Strindberg—and derided the contemporary American producers and playwrights. His most important discovery in the U.S.A. was Eugene O'Neill, whose early work he published in *The Smart Set*, a magazine he edited with H. L. Mencken. There, too, appeared James Joyce, Brieux, Wedekind,

Molnar, Melchior Lengyel, Lord Dunsany, Harold Brighouse and a host of others, all hitherto unknown to the general public. Thus the American audience as well as the American theatre slowly came to change its outlook, and by the end of the First World War the stage was cleared for the modern drama, foreign and domestic.

In more recent years Nathan has championed Sean O'Casey—he was largely responsible for the New York production of *Within the Gates* —and William Saroyan, whose first theatre effort, *My Heart's in the Highlands,* he praised enthusiastically when there was still much doubt as to its worth.

He has written over thirty books on the theatre and now does an annual volume on each New York season. Among his best-known works are *The Critic and the Drama, Mr. George Jean Nathan Presents, The World in False Face, The Autobiography of an Attitude, The House of Satan, Art of the Night, The Intimate Notebooks of George Jean Nathan* (especially interesting for its portraits of O'Neill, Dreiser, Sinclair Lewis and others), *Testament of a Critic* and *Encyclopaedia of the Theatre.*   T. Q. C.

NATION, THÉÂTRE DE LA, see COMÉDIE-FRANÇAISE.

NATIONAL OPERATIC AND DRAMATIC ASSOCIATION (N.O.D.A.), see AMATEUR THEATRE IN GREAT BRITAIN, 2.

NATIONAL THEATRE, LONDON. The lack of an exemplary theatre in the capital of the Empire, endowed by the State, or by private generosity, and so preserved from the changes and chances of profit and loss, has been, from the time of David Garrick, a cause of sorrow and complaint on the part of almost every lover of the drama. In other European countries endowed theatres are the rule rather than the exception (e.g. Comédie-Française), but for us the Puritan Revolution shattered the old relationship between the Stage and the Court, and at the Restoration the two 'Patent Theatres', and the Lord Chamberlain's subsidiary office as censor of plays, were the only relics that remained of State patronage. Bulwer Lytton, early in the nineteenth century, and later on Sir Henry Irving, were both fervent supporters of the National Theatre idea; but it was left to a younger group of professional actor-managers, dramatists, and critics to take positive action for the preparation of a practical scheme. This group included such men as Sir Herbert Tree, Arthur Bourchier, George Bernard Shaw, William Archer, and Harley Granville-Barker. In 1910 the two last collaborated in a volume entitled *The National Theatre: A Scheme and Estimates,* which immediately became the recognized handbook of the movement. For a complete exposition of the theory and practice of National Theatre work, readers are referred to this book, and to its sequel, rewritten and brought up to date by Granville-Barker alone, and published in 1930.

At the time the National Theatre group was establishing itself, a separate movement was on foot to celebrate the coming tercentenary of the death of William Shakespeare, in 1916, by the erection of a monument to his memory in some central position in London. Articles in the *Daily News* and *Daily Chronicle* urged that the only appropriate monument to Shakespeare would be a National Theatre. A fusion of the two schemes was effected, and a single joint Committee was set up with the avowed object of founding a National Theatre which should include a statue of Shakespeare as a prominent feature of its architecture. Sir Israel Gollancz became the Secretary of this 'Shakespeare Memorial National Theatre Committee', and the project was launched under the highest auspices in the social, literary, and theatre worlds at a Public Meeting at the Theatre Royal, Drury Lane, in the summer of 1908. The appeal for funds was headed by a donation of £70,000 from Sir Carl Meyer; propaganda on a national scale was started; and it seemed quite likely that the necessary funds would be collected in time to lay the foundation stone of the theatre in 1916 according to plan. The outbreak of the war, however, involved the total suspension of the appeal; but in 1919 the Committee started again with the prospect that the then ascendant Labour Party might agree to government support for an enterprise which seemed so consonant with their avowed programme of post-war social and cultural reform. But attention was soon deflected to more urgent problems, and it was not till 1930 that a direct approach was made to the Cabinet, in reply to which it was stated that no help from that quarter could be looked for until evidence was forthcoming of a demand for a National Theatre by the people as a whole. However immediately discouraging, this reply at least made it clear that the principle of State aid was accepted, and the Committee was encouraged to undertake a further propaganda effort. For the success of this they largely relied on the new interest in good theatre which had been conspicuous throughout the country since the end of the First World War. The Earl of Lytton was now Chairman of the Committee, and Mr. Geoffrey Whitworth had been appointed Hon. Secretary in succession to Sir Israel Gollancz.

Meanwhile, the sum subscribed up to 1914 had increased by compound interest and capital appreciation to a total of £150,000. In 1938 a site for the theatre facing the Victoria and Albert Museum in South Kensington was purchased; architectural designs for the theatre by Sir Edwin Lutyens and Mr. Cecil Masey were completed, and a new and nation-wide appeal for funds was launched. By the summer of 1939 it appeared that the National Theatre was once again in process of realization. That a new war, more terrible even than the last, brought an end to these hopes for a second time was disheartening. But the faith of the Committee did not weaken. Dame Edith Lyttelton, who from the first had been one of its most active members, was appointed Acting-Chairman of the Committee, and the war period was utilized in the preparation of plans for the ultimate completion of the scheme. The coming of peace enabled the committee to consider an even more ambitious scheme. By arrangement with the London County Council the site at South Kensington is to be exchanged for a larger one in a central position on the south bank of the Thames, and an amalgamation is in prospect with the Old Vic, who will provide the theatre with a Company of the highest artistic merit as soon as it is built.

There can, indeed, be little doubt that if a National Theatre was desirable in the past, it is now a necessity. Private enterprise can never achieve the results which may be expected to follow the building and adequate endowment of a permanent home for the revival of British drama. The case for this assertion could be argued at length. Here it can best be illustrated by the following statement of 'aims and methods' which, since its inception, has formed the official programme of the National Theatre Movement.

1. To provide in the capital of the Empire a theatre where the people may have continual opportunities of seeing the best drama, past and present, produced with the utmost distinction and played by a permanent company of the highest merit.

2. To maintain the efficiency and dignity of the art of acting by providing opportunities for its exercise in its highest classical departments.

3. To keep the plays of Shakespeare in its repertory.

4. To revive whatever is vital in British drama.

5. To prevent recent plays of merit from falling into oblivion.

6. To produce new plays and to further the development of modern drama.

7. To produce translations of representative works of foreign drama, ancient and modern.

8. To organize National Theatre tours throughout the country, and overseas.

9. To stimulate the art of the theatre through every possible and suitable means.

In conclusion, it is important to realize that 'national' in this connexion does not mean 'nationalized'; nor has it any political connotations whatsoever. This theatre will have precisely the same relation to authority as all other theatres. Like them, and no less than them, it will be subject to the jurisdiction of the Lord Chamberlain. Within that limit, the National Theatre will be experimental as well as, in the best sense, the school of a great tradition. It is called National because, when it is built, equipped, and endowed, the theatre will be presented to the nation, and will be administered by a body of public trustees, with a Director who will have full control of the artistic side of the management.   G. W.

For a theatre in London called the National, see QUEEN'S THEATRE (2).

For the People's National Theatre, see PRICE, NANCY.

NATIONAL THEATRE, NEW YORK. (1)
Originally the Italian Opera House, this opened
as a theatre in 1836 under Tom Flynn and
H. E. Willard. It had a good season from 1837
to 1838, when it was under the management of
J. W. Wallack. Its fine company, perfect stage
management, and Wallack's eye for detail made
it a serious rival to the Park, and in opposition
to the latter's nickname of 'Old Drury' it was
often referred to as 'Covent Garden'. John
Vandenhoff was seen at the National under
Wallack, and was the first great English actor
who did *not* appear at the Park. In the same
year W. E. Burton came from Philadelphia
to make his first appearance in New York,
being engaged for a further season in Feb.
1839. After Wallack's withdrawal, Hackett
was seen in a season of his own plays, and
Charlotte Cushman came as Lady Macbeth
and a female Romeo. Apart from straight plays
the theatre housed a number of operas and
ballets, and some negro minstrelsy. It was
burnt down on 23 Sept. 1839. Rebuilt, it was
again destroyed on 29 May 1841, after a somewhat uneventful period, in which the Vanden-
hoffs made their last appearance in New York.
The theatre had not been a financial success,
except under Wallack, and as the neighbourhood was unsalubrious, it was never rebuilt.

(2) On 41st Street between Seventh and
Eighth Avenues. This opened on 1 Sept. 1921
with Sidney Howard's first play, *Swords*, which
had only a short run. The first success of the
new theatre, after an unsuccessful revival of
Trilby, was *The Cat and the Canary*, a thriller
which ran for nearly a year. Early in 1923 came
Will Shakespeare, in a production by Winthrop
Ames, with Katharine Cornell, Cornelia Otis
Skinner, Otto Kruger, and Haidée Wright,
while the end of the same year saw Walter
Hampden in his popular revival of *Cyrano de
Bergerac*. The next success was *The Trial of
Mary Dugan* (1927) with 437 performances,
while a record for the house was set up by
Grand Hotel (1930) with 459 performances.
This last play was produced by Herman
Shumlin with décor by Aline Bernstein and a
superb cast. The next play of any distinction
was *Within the Gates* (1934), while two years
later came a successful dramatization of *Ethan
Frome*, with a cast which included Pauline
Lord, Ruth Gordon, and Raymond Massey.
The end of 1936 saw the success of Noel
Coward's *To-night at 8.30*, with the author and
Gertrude Lawrence. It was withdrawn at the
height of its success because of Coward's
other commitments. Later successes at this
theatre were *The Little Foxes* (1939), with
Tallulah Bankhead, and *The Corn is Green*
(1940), in which Ethel Barrymore gave a fine
performance as the elderly school-teacher.
After structural alterations the theatre reopened on 11 Nov. 1941 with Maurice Evans
in *Macbeth*, and in 1946 *Call Me Mister* began
its long run.   G. F.

For the New National Theatre, New York,
see CHATHAM THEATRE (2).

NATIONWIDE THEATRE, U.S.A. Any
consideration of the non-commercial theatre in
the United States must perforce group together
its two main divisions, the community and the
university theatres. They have had similar
backgrounds; they have been committed to
like objectives; and, following World War II,
they have moved together towards what it is
fitting to call a Nationwide Theatre.

This Nationwide Theatre grew from the
Tributary Theatre (1925–40) which, in turn,
resulted from a metamorphosis of the Little
Theatre which preceded it (1910–25). So,
properly to understand the present impulses
towards a full national theatre, it is necessary
to go back to the Little Theatre Movement
from which the non-commercial theatres, in
town and on campus, sprang.

In such a discussion it would be best to trace
first the rise and development of the community
theatre to its present state; and then to examine
the parallel growth of the university theatre.

1. COMMUNITY THEATRE. Around 1910
amateur theatres were established in many
communities. Some were in the large cities—
Boston, Chicago, Detroit; others in smaller
places like Ypsilanti, Michigan, and Galesburg,
Illinois. But wherever located, they all derived
their impetus, their idealism, and the bulk of
their repertory from the Free Theatres of
Europe.

Like their models they were revolt theatres.
They protested against the American professional stage as then exhibited on Broadway,
in road shows, and in the scores of country-
wide stock companies. Most of these they
adjudged to be meretricious, inartistic, and
without significance. In their place the
pioneering amateurs proposed to set up art
theatres devoted to experiment. To their
audiences they would introduce the theories
and methods of Craig, Stanislavsky, and Reinhardt, displayed in dramas of worth from the
British Isles, from the continent, and even,
too, from the new-burgeoning branch of
American playwriting.

In essence, then, this was the 'Little Theatre
Movement'. Among its leaders in the com-
munity theatres were men and women of dis-
crimination, courage, and creative ability—
Gilmor Brown, Frederic McConnell, Oliver
Hinsdell, Irving Pichel, Sam Hume, Maurice
Brown, Ellen Van Volkenburg, Mr. and Mrs.
Burton James, Maurice Gneisen, Thomas
Wood Stevens, and Jaspar Deeter—to name a
few.

The credo of the groups which they led was:
'Create your own theatre with the talent at
hand.' Of necessity this had to be the rallying-
cry, for most of these units operated in small
playhouses whose limited capacity (like the 91
seats in Maurice Brown's Chicago theatre, or
the 60 at Ypsilanti, Michigan) did not make for
a large box-office return. Moreover, it was
considered a point of pride with these groups
(since it reflected the nature of the movement)
to have a cross-section of the local citizenry
listed on their play-bills as members of the cast

or of the several business and production staffs.

Fundamentally, then, the Little Theatre was a 'theatre for participation' rather than a 'theatre for audiences'. This does not mean that it neglected its audience; but it did stress, unduly at times, the opportunities afforded its members for self-expression. Such an attitude, in fact, was passed on to succeeding generations of community theatres and, in many cases, is part of their operating policy even to-day.

At this point it should be noted that the major changes in the course of the development of the non-commercial theatre have been occasioned by a shift in emphasis from 'the theatre for participation' towards the 'theatre for audiences'. As the weight inclined in that direction the Little Theatre gave way to the Tributary Theatre; as it inclined still more the Nationwide Theatre emerged.

The first of these shifts became evident in the 1920s. Directors began to feel the need for more satisfactory playhouses to replace the inadequate and frequently makeshift plants in which their limited means had forced them to work. This meant money; which, in turn, implied a larger public attendance at the plays. No longer would coterie audiences, and the dilettantism that they encouraged in many cases, serve the day.

Besides, the commercial theatre outside New York City was falling into a sorry decline. This was caused partly by the flank attacks that the non-commercial theatre had made upon it, partly by its own low standards of production, and partly by the greater accessibility and the consequent popularity of the motion picture. As a result, the community theatre became in most sections of the country the only available place for the presentation of living drama. The potential audience for the Little Theatre had increased; and its directors were quick to realize this fact.

This larger audience proved more exacting in its demands. It agreed to amateurism in principle; but it asked for professional competence in the productions. Scenery and costumes had to be better; acting on a higher level; directing equal to the best in New York.

These insistences pushed organizations which were otherwise amateur towards a modified professionalism. At the very inception of the Little Theatre Movement it had been recognized that if a theatre was to make progress it must have a salaried director. So the better units paid their director a yearly wage. And by 1925 all theatres of consequence had professional directors. By this time, too, there were paid designer-technicians and paid business managers. Some, like the Cleveland Playhouse, even went so far as to employ professional actors as the core of a permanent company.

Coupled with this desire to improve the quality of productions was a deep-seated idealism. The pioneers who had founded Little Theatres were not blatant showmen but artists with vision and social concern. And so were the second generation of leaders that followed them. They all realized that their theatres should be manifestations of the community which supported them. They went further than that: they saw that their theatres were under obligation to the sum-total—the American theatre as an institution. In addition, they suddenly recognized that their organizations, along with those dedicated to similar purpose in the universities, had become the very seed-bed of any American theatre of the future.

Awareness of these responsibilities, imperceptibly but surely, changed the Little Theatre into the Tributary Theatre. This designation was excogitated by Edith J. R. Isaacs, who explained it in this way:

The center of America's professional theatre life will probably always be New York. The center, yes, but not the source. The Tributaries must feed the main stream; the states must feed New York. As long as New York feeds the states the American Theatre will remain only a backwash for the waters that run by the market place. And don't think for a moment that it is Maine, Wyoming, and Wisconsin that suffer most from this. The theatre in New York is the greatest sufferer.[1]

This label was distasteful in so far as it connoted an inferior or an ancillary position. It was satisfactory only in so far as it stressed the regional and the national aspects of the implied relationship. Far better was it, however, than the somewhat apologetic epithet 'little' which in most local instances had been discarded in favour of 'civic' or 'community'.

But whatever the appellations of the individual units, the Tributary Theatre did become more community-conscious, more civic-conscious. Such feeling was intensified by the progressive artistic impoverishment of the professional theatre. By 1940 even the Broadway stage was losing some ground, in competition with the radio and the talkies. The theatre, as far as the United States as a whole, was concerned, was, artistically, geographically, and numerically, in the non-profit-making playhouses.

Once again the community theatres, in conjunction with their university counterparts, reached out for larger audiences. The shift was still farther away from the 'theatre for participation'.

In consequence, after World War II a marked inclination towards further professionalization of the non-profit-making theatre (especially of its acting companies) was evident. Employment for actors in places other than on Broadway fitted in handily with the theories for 'decentralizing' the American theatre which had been rampant since 1925.

In a number of instances, then, the paid actor has been making his way into the community theatre. On the other hand, there are still many governing boards that are reluctant to have the amateur actor dispossessed. The 'theatre for participation' is by no means dead; it flourishes in many places.

[1] *Theatre Arts Monthly*, Sept. 1928, vol. xii, No. 9, page 620.

Hence, there are to-day three distinct types of non-commercial theatres in the United States. First, there are the theatres which are wholly professionalized, like the Dallas Theatre. Second, there are the ones which are professionalized in part, like the Pasadena (Cal.) Playhouse. And third, there are the theatres which are entirely dependent on the amateur actor, such as the Harrisburg Community Theatre.

Though they may use a various nomenclature, and though they may differ on the question of thorough and complete professionalization,[1] these theatres and many others like them are agreed on one thing: they are no longer lesser streams to a main stream; they are the main stream itself.

Believing this, with their sister theatres in the universities they wish to be regarded, collectively, as the new Nationwide Theatre.

2. UNIVERSITY THEATRE. The universities and colleges were affected by the Little Theatre Movement at about the same time that the community theatres were. At Harvard University in 1912 Professor George Pierce Baker inaugurated what was to become the famous '47 Workshop'. Here plays written in his English 47 class were given a careful and rehearsed performance. This was a complete innovation, for never before had an attempt been made to correlate academic instruction with practical theatre. The experiment was posited on the belief that viable drama could better be studied under the conditions of a staged performance than, as was the usual practice, in the confines of a class-room. Not only playwriting but all the other arts and crafts of the theatre were thus encouraged.

At the Carnegie Institute of Technology in 1914 Thomas Wood Stevens (who had come there from the Wisconsin Players, a group founded in 1911 by Thomas H. Dickenson and Zona Gale, and unofficially identified with the state university) went even further. He established, for the first time in any American institution of learning, a four-year course in theatre arts leading to an academic degree. Shortly thereafter Alexander Drummond introduced similar subject-matter into the curriculum of Cornell University.

It will be observed that these projects were taking place in the eastern universities. However, the educational institutions of the broad prairies and rich farm-lands of the deep Midwest were active with experiment, too. Their efforts inclined towards folk-drama—plays about a particular region, its people, and its lore. Pioneers in this work were Alfred Koch (who was later to transfer his work in this field to the University of North Carolina) at the University of North Dakota. Somewhat later Edward C. Mabie encouraged folk-playwriting at the University of Iowa.

From beginnings of this sort the drama, as an academic subject and as a practised art, made its way into the curricula of colleges and universities the country over. As an adjunct to such study Little Theatres, resembling in all details the community Little Theatres, were set up in auditoriums, assembly halls, class-rooms, or in buildings especially adapted for the purpose.

However, these gains were not in all cases achieved without opposition from the academic authorities. Even Baker at Harvard had to conduct his work more or less as an extra-curricular activity; and officially he was teaching rhetoric and public speaking and not theatre at all. In many cases these new subjects were accepted only as incidental courses to either the Speech or the English Departments. It took all of fifteen years—a span corresponding in the community theatre to the Little Theatre period—for the preceptor-regisseur (for the university theatre director had to be, and still is, an administrator and a teacher as well as a theatre artist) to assert and establish himself and his work.

But by 1925, and increasingly thereafter, Drama Departments, Theatre Arts Departments, Schools of the Theatre, Divisions of Drama, began to appear in their own rights. They offered a corpus of material on both the undergraduate and graduate levels that led not only to the bachelor's but to the master's and doctor's degrees as well.

Moreover, both state universities and privately endowed ones in the 1920s and 1930s began to build theatres for their drama departments which were a far cry from the 'laboratory theatres', 'workshops', and other makeshift arrangements that had been used. Some of these buildings were million-dollar structures like the ones at the University of Wisconsin, Yale University, the University of Iowa, and Indiana University, and far surpassed the Broadway commercial theatres in size and equipment. Even the more modest playhouses that were built had facilities sufficient for first-rate performances.

Likewise at this time scene designers, costume designers, and stage technicians of considerable competence were added to the faculties. Part of their time they spent in the class-room, the rest in the rehearsal hall and shop. And the university theatres profited in much the same way by such professionalization of their staffs as did the community theatres at a corresponding point in their development.

It should be noted, too, that universities were inclining to some degree away from a 'theatre for participation', just as were the community theatres of the period. Of course, in an educational institution a theatre has to attend to the training of its students. But the realization dawned that this training might rightly include the students in the audience as well as the students on the stage and backstage. Less stress was put on avocational theatre; more on 'theatre for audiences'—audiences made up of both students and townsfolk alike.

Like community and civic theatres, college and university theatres began to see that they could not be cloistered and apart; that they had

[1] See 'A Young Man's War', by Sawyer Falk, *Theatre Arts Monthly*, July 1946, vol. xxx, No. 7.

obligations to the communities in which they functioned; that they must project their activities and their influence beyond the strict boundaries of their campuses; and that in many instances they must assume the full custodianship of the drama not only for their towns or cities but for the neighbouring country-side and even for their entire state or region. They, too, were a part of the Tributary Theatre which was transforming itself, by its assumption of larger obligations, into the Nationwide Theatre of to-morrow.

The energy directed to this purpose expressed itself in various forms from university to university, depending upon the local situation and the predilection of the particular director. A list of some of the directors and their special achievements will show both the protean nature of the university theatre and the immense potential strength it can bring to bear in the building of a people's theatre.

Included on this list would be: Glenn Hughes of the University of Washington for reintroducing and popularizing the arena technique of production, and for maintaining a year-around schedule of plays for the entire community; Hallie Flanagan Davis at Smith College for experimenting with new types of production and playwriting, especially those that give opportunity for social comment; Marian Stebbins of Mills College for performances annually of the Greek classics out of doors; Walter Kerr at Catholic University for the presentation of many original scripts, some of which have found their way to the professional stage; Barclay Leatham of Western Reserve University for effecting a collaboration between the activities of his drama department and the productions of the Cleveland Playhouse; Alexander Drummond at Cornell University for his encouragement of the writing and production of rural drama in New York State; Albert McCleery at Fordham University for conducting a successful theatre within the very orbit of the Broadway stage itself; Sawyer Falk of Syracuse University for the 'Civic-University Idea' which allows for the inclusion of community theatre within the framework of a university drama department, and for his experiments in fusing the screen with the stage; C. Lowell Lees of the University of Utah for envisioning a State Theatre which would have its genesis at the university; Paul Baker at Baylor University for innovations in theatre construction and for setting up a university company which tours the wide South-west; Samuel Seldon of the University of North Carolina for carrying on the folk-play tradition of Frederick Koch, and for directing for a decade Paul Green's pageant-play *The Lost Colony* at Roanoke Island; Boyd Smith at Yale University for carrying on the traditions and practices that George Pierce Baker had brought there from his '47 Workshop'; Lee Norvelle of Indiana University for his interest in state-wide play festivals, and for his touring company project which will use professional actors; C. R. Kase of the University of Dela-

ware for fostering dramatic activity throughout the state by the formation of The Delaware Dramatic Association; Henry Boettcher of the Carnegie Institute of Technology for successfully maintaining the department established by Thomas Wood Stevens; Randolph Somerville of New York University for the Shakespearian repertory he has built up, and for using, before all others, professional actors as the core of a university company; E. C. Mabie of the University of Iowa for making his theatre the focal centre of a region-wide culture; Hubert Heffner of Stanford University for bringing together students and professionals in the work of the department, and especially for the 'artists-in-residence' plan whereby young professional theatre artists find employment on a university campus; and Arthur Cloethingh of Pennsylvania State College for setting up an extension service which helps units in and out of the state with the mounting and directing of plays.

Work of equal importance and influence has been done by Warner Bentley at Dartmouth College, Herschel Bricker at the University of Maine, Rupel Jones at the University of Oklahoma, Valentine Windt at the University of Michigan, David Itkin of DePaul University, Theodore Fuchs at Northwestern University, Frank Fowler at the University of Kentucky, Albert Johnson at Cornell (Iowa) College, John Dolman at Swarthmore College, Homer Abeggler at Miami University, Frank Whiting at the University of Minnesota, Mary Virginia Heinlein at Vassar College, and Robert Masters at Indiana State Teachers College. Many others could be added.

It appears at the present time (1949) that the university and community theatres are moving irresistibly in the same general direction. So identical have their interests always been that some fifteen years ago many of them banded into a single organization—the National Theatre Conference. The declared purpose of this organization is collectively to serve the non-commercial theatre and to assure its stability and permanence. It shares the belief of its individual units that what was once called the Little Theatre, and later on the Tributary Theatre, will to-morrow be a national theatre composed of such community and university theatres (both within and without its fold) as are capable of serving their own regions while being, at the same time, national enough in character to effect a plausible concatenation with their fellows.   S. F.

NATURALISM, a movement in the theatre of the late nineteenth century which arose in revolt against the artificial theatricality of contemporary forms of playwriting and acting. The citadel had already been breached by the realism of Ibsen and his followers, but it was a selective realism. Naturalism discarded all compromise and came out strongly on the side of stark reality. The forerunner of the movement was probably Strindberg, with *Miss Julie*, and Zola raised it to the importance of a literary creed, with his demand for a 'slice of life'. His dramatization of his own novel *Thérèse Raquin* (1873) was the first consciously conceived naturalistic drama; but it was Becque, as author, and Antoine, as producer, who established naturalism in the theatre. The Théâtre Libre, as Antoine's new venture was called, had much influence in Europe. It led to the formation of Brahm's Freie Bühne in Germany, where naturalism found its most triumphant expression with such plays as *Die Familie Selicke* and the realistic dramas of Hauptmann and Schönherr, and to Grein's Independent Theatre in England, where Shaw was the apostle of the new movement, which, however, languished in uncongenial soil. In Russia, on the other hand, it flourished, and attained world recognition in the work of Stanislavsky and the Moscow Art Theatre, particularly with their production of Gorky's *The Lower Depths*. In Spain naturalism is represented by *La Malquerida*, and in America by the early works of O'Neill, by some facets of Maxwell Anderson's works, and by the dramatized novels of Steinbeck.

NAUMACHIA, at Rome, a mimic sea-fight of great splendour, staged in an arena flooded for the purpose—also the name given to an amphitheatre specially built for this purpose by Augustus on the right bank of the Tiber. Naumachiae, or water-pageants, were given in Italy at the time of the Renaissance (see MACHINERY). For English nineteenth-century aquatic spectacles see CIRCUS.

NAVARRO, PEDRO (*fl.* sixteenth century), a Spanish actor-manager, mentioned by Cervantes, who says that he succeeded Lope de Rueda, and was famous in the part of the cowardly ruffian. He discarded the clothes-sack of former travelling companies, substituting boxes and trunks. He also, according to the same authority, brought the singers from behind the curtain into the full view of the audience, and abolished the universal false beard, retaining it only for old men and disguises. He is credited with the invention, or perfecting, of stage effects of thunder, lightning, clouds, battles, and so on, although in this, says Cervantes, 'he did not reach the present sublime heights'.

NAZIMOVA, ALLA (1879–1945), Russian actress, who received her training in Moscow, and in 1904 was leading lady of a St. Petersburg theatre. She toured Europe and America with a Russian company, and in 1906, having learnt English in less than six months, made her first appearance in an English-speaking part —Hedda Tesman—at the Princess's Theatre, New York, under the management of the Shuberts. She remained in America, where she was considered an outstanding exponent of Ibsen's heroines, and in 1910 took possession of the Thirty-Ninth Street Theatre, rechristened the Nazimova, with *Little Eyolf*. After some years in films, she returned to the stage, playing with the Civic Repertory Theatre and the

Theatre Guild in Ibsen, Chekhov, Turgeniev, and O'Neill. She was a superb actress, vibrant and passionate, and vividly sensitive to every subtlety of her many great roles.

NEGRO IN THE AMERICAN THEATRE. On the early American colonial stage Negro characters were rare, since the repertory came from England. The outstanding exceptions, Shakespeare's *Othello* and the African Prince in Thomas Southerne's *Oroonoko*, had little appeal for audiences of slave-holders. In 1799 the latter play was enlivened and made more congenial by a song 'The Gay Negro Boy' sung in black-face to banjo strumming. A popular comedy, *The Padlock* (1769), had a West Indian slave, Mungo, who was a singing, bibulous, profane clown of little authenticity. Played by Lewis Hallam, who supposedly sought realism, Mungo fathered a long line of comic Negroes in American drama. In *Robinson Crusoe and Harlequin Friday* (1786) and *The Buccaneers; or, the Discovery of Robinson Crusoe* (1817) the dialect imitated Defoe's pidgin-English instead of actual Negro speech.

Minor Negro characters appeared in *The Candidates* (written probably before the Revolutionary War), in *The Fall of British Tyranny* (1776), where slaves, released by the British, promise to kill their masters, and in *The Yorker's Stratagem* (1792), which shows a New Yorker marrying a West Indian mulatto. The Negro servant, serving chiefly for comic relief, appears first in *Triumphs of Love* (1795) and *The Politicians* (1797). This comic stereotype, which roughly resembles the stage Irishman in buffoonery, far-fetched dialect, and singing, ranges from William Dunlap's *A Trip to Niagara* (1830) to Anna Cora Mowatt's *Fashion* (1845).

Meanwhile another tradition was hardening. Songs in alleged Negro dialect were interspersed in *A New Way To Win Hearts* (1802), *The Battle of Lake Champlain* (1815), and *Tom and Jerry* (1820–1), which found a spot for gay singing and dancing even in a Charleston slave-market. In 1823 Edwin Forrest's black-faced acting in *The Tailor in Distress* was praised as the first realistic representation of the plantation Negro. Finding no white actress willing to blacken her face to play opposite him, Forrest had to hire an old Negro washerwoman, but this squeamishness of white actresses did not last very long. In the 1820s George Nichols popularized 'Zip Coon' and other songs and dances learned from Negroes in the Mississippi Delta, and George Washington Dixon impersonated Negroes in songs like 'Coal Black Rose', 'Long Tailed Blue', and in Negro burlettas. It became a rule to interpolate Negro songs in theatre programmes, whether farce or tragedy; they were sung by circus clowns, sometimes from the backs of cantering horses.

In 1828 along the Ohio River (whether in Louisville, Cincinnati, or Pittsburgh is not clear) Thomas 'Daddy' Rice imitated the singing and shuffling of a Negro hostler. The skit was enthusiastically received. In 1833, as a new fillip to the act, 'Daddy' Rice dumped a four-year-old burnt-corked urchin from a bag on to the stage; this was Joseph Jefferson the third, who perfectly mimicked Rice's ungainly dancing. Rice was not content with single songs but wove them together; his organized *Bone Squash* is probably the first 'Ethiopian Opera'. Rice's phenomenal popularity called for imitation in the thirties; P. T. Barnum featured Ethiopian breakdowns; the American Museum exhibited the Ethiopian Comic Statues; and a popular circus act was 'Jim Crow, Esquire, on Horseback'. In 1843 the first regular minstrel troupe, a quartette including Daniel Emmett, the composer of 'Dixie', appeared on the stage in gala costume, performing on the fiddle, banjo, bones, and tambourine, telling jokes, and ending with a grand breakdown. Ethiopian minstrelsy was born.

Contemporary rivals, the Kentucky Minstrels, the Congo Melodists, and the Original Christy Minstrels, along with many others, swept the nation. It was for the Christys, who retired wealthy, that Stephen Foster wrote his best-known songs. The minstrel craze saw its heyday in the decades from 1850 to 1870. Among the numerous companies that sprang up after the Civil War, McIntyre and Heath, the Al G. Fields Minstrels, Haverly's Mastodons, and Dan Bryant's Minstrels were among the best-known. At the end of the seventies, companies attempted to whip up a waning demand by quantity of performers and extravaganza. From spontaneity the minstrel show descended into ritualized conventionality. The end of this peculiar American phenomenon (which was extremely popular in England also) came during the second decade of the twentieth century. Amateur companies, however, still perform minstrelsy, and its influence remains in vaudeville, in the moving pictures, and on the radio.

The minstrel show consisted of three parts. At the rise of the curtain the black-faced company with a lone white-faced middleman stood in a semicircle. Then the middleman, 'Mister Interlocutor', ordered 'Gentlemen, be seated'. The interlocutor, painfully correct, 'father of all the foils in vaudeville', engaged in badinage with Mr. Bones and Mr. Tambo, the two endmen, who were the chief punsters and wisecrackers. Quips and conundrums, interpolated comic and sentimental songs, with a gay song by full chorus and a grand walk-around, filled out the first part. The second part was the 'olio', a variety bill of dances, vocal and instrumental music, and stump speeches, ending with a 'hoe-down dance' accompanied by singing and hand-clapping. The third part consisted of after-pieces—farces, comic opera, or burlesque —at first supposed to be based on Negro life; but later any short play was used (even *Box and Cox*).

Though black-face minstrelsy started out with rudimentary realism, it soon degenerated into fantastic artificiality. It must be remem-

bered that Ethiopian minstrelsy was white masquerade; Negro performers were not allowed to appear in it until after the Civil War; it was composed by whites, acted and sung by whites in burnt cork, for white audiences. It succeeded in fixing one stereotype deeply in the American consciousness: the shiftless, lazy, improvident, loud-mouthed, flashily-dressed Negro, with kinky hair and large lips, over-addicted to the eating of watermelon and chicken (almost always purloined), the drinking of gin, the shooting of dice, and the twisting of language into ludicrous malformations. Life was a perennial joke or 'breakdown'. Black-face minstrelsy underestimated and misrepresented the American Negro in much the same way that the English drama treated the stage Irishman.

Though minstrelsy generally showed an easy-going, amusing way of life, occasionally a few sentimental plaints about the woes of slavery—e.g.'Darling Nelly Gray' (1856)—were ventured in the North. The first anti-slavery protest entered legitimate drama with *The Gladiator* (1831). Though this play dealt with the uprising of slaves in ancient Rome, the author feared that if produced in a slave state he and the actors would be 'rewarded with the penitentiary'. Two little-known abolitionist melodramas, *The Captured Slave* and *The Branded Hand*, appeared in 1845, but are not known to have been acted.

For full use of anti-slavery protest the American stage, like American fiction, had to wait for the appearance of *Uncle Tom's Cabin* in 1852. Within six months of the enormous success of Mrs. Stowe's novel, two adaptations were produced in New York. Opposed to the theatre on religious grounds and unprotected by copyright, Mrs. Stowe received no share of the large profits made from dramatizations of her book. She did, however, attend incognito a performance of the play in the fifth year of its amazing run. There were many adaptations; two versions appeared in Paris; in 1878 five London theatres presented the play concurrently. *Uncle Tom's Cabin* has been America's most popular play by far; from 1852 to 1931 it never left the American boards, and since then it has been revived, notably in George Abbott's very free *Sweet River* (1936).

The best-known version of *Uncle Tom's Cabin* was by George L. Aiken, who heightened the sentimentality and melodrama. His treatment of Topsy lacked Mrs. Stowe's understanding and was close to black-face minstrelsy; Eliza's crossing the ice was theatrical sensationalism. Over the years the abolitionist edge of the material was dulled, and the treatment veered toward melodrama and farce. Harriet Beecher Stowe's second anti-slavery novel *Dred* was thrice dramatized in 1856, by C. W. Taylor, John Brougham, and H. J. Conway. Though *Dred* had many good points as a novel, none of the dramatizations succeeded. For all of their great anti-slavery service *Uncle Tom's Cabin* and, to a lesser degree, *Dred* have helped in the stereotyping of Negroes on the American stage.

More than the novel, the widely popular *Uncle Tom* plays have been too persuasive in supporting the generalizations that impish, light-fingered Topsy, and the ideally forgiving and submissive Uncle Tom, are 'typical Negroes', and that it is only the mixed-blood Negroes who are, as a result of their biological inheritance, aggressive, intelligent, and willing to fight for freedom.

The same sort of 'tragic mulatto stereotype' is constant in other abolitionist dramas. In 1857 J. T. Trowbridge dramatized his novel *Neighbor Jackwood*, which dealt with a beautiful octoroon who escapes from Louisiana to Vermont and there marries her Yankee benefactor. The revelation of Northern dislike for the Fugitive Slave Law gives the play more reality than the idealized characterization. William Wells Brown, the Negro author and anti-slavery agent, wrote *Escape; or, a Leap For Freedom* (1858), the first play by an American Negro. It is not known to have been produced, but Brown gave readings of it to great applause. As a play it is inept and imitative; even the comic scenes are closer to blackface minstrelsy than Brown's own experiences of slavery should have allowed. The heroine is the octoroon beauty, by this time becoming a stage familiar. Dion Boucicault's *The Octoroon* (1859) is the most theatrical in the gallery of doomed mixed-blood heroines. Canny artificer that he was, Boucicault wrote a play calculated to give offence to neither North nor South in those critical years. Slavery is shown as kindly; the slaves are happy-go-lucky sleepy-heads; only Zoe, the octoroon, is tragic because she cannot marry the white man she loves. Zoe is a strange mixture of abjectness, of pride in her white blood, of forgiveness equal to Uncle Tom's, and of devotion to her dead white father who had failed to guarantee her freedom. Boucicault provided two separate endings so the audience could take their choice, and the play reaped great financial returns.

Ossawatomie Brown (1859), the first dramatization of the Harper's Ferry Raid, significantly portrayed John Brown's Negro comrades. But in the numerous plays of the Old South and the Civil War, Negro characters were generally inconsequential and almost interchangeable. *The Guerrillas* (1863) showed the faithful slave indignantly refusing freedom, revealing to the Richmond audience its wish rather than the pressing actuality. On the other hand, *For A Brother's Life* (1885) portrayed Negro refugees to the Union camps. Augustus Thomas's version of *Colonel Carter of Cartersville* (1892) conventionally stressed the mutual affection between master and slave, but unconventionally had a real Negro in the role of the faithful servant. The favourite tragic octoroon appeared in *The White Slave* (1882), which rivalled in popularity *The Octoroon*, and in *Captain Herne, U.S.A.* (1895). A much more convincing octoroon appeared the same year in Frank Mayo's dramatization of Mark Twain's *Pudd'nhead Wilson*, a mordant exposé of slavery. Winston Churchill's dramatization

of *The Crisis* (1902) contained a vivid slave auction. *The New South* (1893) by J. R. Grismer and Clay Greene showed something of the uneasy side of slave life. In this play James A. Herne played the part of a Negro murderer named Sampson. In *The Reverend Griffith Davenport* (1899), Herne's own play about slavery and the Civil War, Sampson is the name of a runaway Negro who takes his own life. Herne's view of the cruelties of slavery is soberly realistic. So is Steele Mackaye's dramatization (1881) of Albion Tourgee's *A Fool's Errand*, a sympathetic treatment of the problems of the newly freed in a hostile South. In Thomas Dixon's *The Clansman* (1906), however, the Ku Klux Klan is glorified and Negroes are characterized as brutes whose emancipation was a grievous mistake.

As an answer to this kind of propaganda a Negro, Joseph S. Cotter, Sr., wrote *Caleb, The Degenerate* (1906), more of a tract than a play. In 1909 William Vaughn Moody portrayed in *The Faith Healer* something of the superstition, religious fervour, and eloquence of Negro folk-life. The height of the problem play of the period was *The Nigger* (1910). Using a popular framework Sheldon shows a politically ambitious hero suddenly discovering that he has Negro blood. After advancing to the governorship and finding himself unable to help Negroes, he confesses his race and pledges himself to its service. As a writer of advanced ideas, Sheldon said bolder things about lynching and miscegenation than had been heard on the American stage before him. *Pride of Race* (1916) by Michael Landman also dealt with miscegenation, but less convincingly.

The comic Negro was continued in the 1880s and 1890s in Edward Harrigan's *Mulligan* cycle of vaudeville sketches about Negro life, dealing with dialect-speaking Irishmen, Germans, and Negroes. Harrigan's *The Doyle Brothers* (1874) and *Pete* (1887) glorify the faithful old Negro servant, but his metropolitan characters have a rough realism. Negro entertainers now began to appear in black-face minstrelsy, using not only the same make-up as the whites but the same artificial pattern. Early companies were Lew Johnson's Plantation Company, the Georgia Minstrels, later Callender's Original Georgia Minstrels, and the Colored Hamtown Singers. Famous Negro Minstrels were Billy Kersands ('King Rastus'), Sam Lucas, and James Bland, the composer of 'Carry Me Back to Ol' Virginny', and 'In the Evening by the Moonlight'. The minstrel show gave apprenticeship to song-and-dance comedians who were later to make their names on Broadway.

In 1890 *The Creole Burlesquers* emerged from the minstrel pattern; John W. Isham's *The Octoroons* (1895) and *Oriental America* (1896) followed. Where the minstrel shows had been all-male, these shows glorified the Negro girl both in the chorus and as principals. *Black Patti's Troubadours* (1896) kept the minstrel form until the finale in which the splendid-voiced Black Patti sang operatic selections. In

1898, with Bob Cole's *A Trip To Coontown*, the first show to be produced and managed by Negroes, the Negro show arrived. Within a decade Negro shows such as *Clorindy, The Origin of the Cakewalk, Jes' Lak White Folks, The Policy Players, The Sons of Ham, In Dahomey, Bandana Land, The Red Moon*, and *The Darktown Follies* had been produced and were definitely part of America's theatrical scene.

For about a decade Negro shows lost favour because of repetitiousness. In 1921 *Shuffle Along*, produced by Miller and Lyles, a really new black-face team, and Noble Sissle and Eubie Blake, masters of the jazz music that was taking New York by storm, started a long series of successes. Their high-spirited gaiety in dancing, jazzed-up music, fresher comedy, lavish costumes and sets, put a definite stamp on American entertainment. Some of the hits were *Liza* and *Running Wild* (both 1923), *From Dixie to Broadway* and *Chocolate Dandies* (both 1924), *Plantation Revue* (1925), Lew Leslie's annual *Blackbirds* (1927–30) and his *Brown Buddies* (1930) and *Rhapsody in Black* (1931). Florence Mills, Josephine Baker, Adelaide Hall, Ada Ward, Ethel Waters, Bill Robinson, and Johnny Hudgins were a few of the headliners.

The Negro musical show was part of America's discovery of Harlem, and that, of course, only on its gay and colourful side. Realistic drama of Negro folk-life, with Negroes as major characters, came first to Broadway with Ridgely Torrence's *Three Plays for a Negro Theatre* (1917). Influenced by The Abbey Theatre's folk plays of the Irish, Torrence recognized the dignity in the lives of his characters. *The Rider of Dreams* is a gentle portrait of a music-loving wastrel and his severely tried, hard-working wife; *Granny Maumee* is a harsh portrait of an old woman who bitterly remembers that a mob burned her son. *Simon the Cyrenian* told of the black Simon who bore Christ's cross for him to Calvary. The presentation of these plays was significant in American theatre history.

Similarly historic was *The Emperor Jones* (1920), produced by the Provincetown Players. O'Neill had already shown interest in Negroes in *The Moon of the Caribees* (1918) and in *The Dreamy Kid* (1919), a one-act tragedy of a young Negro gangster in Harlem. *The Emperor Jones* was something new on the American stage; Brutus Jones, crafty, bold, arrogant, and truculent, is far from the comic servant or naïve folk type. Though social protest is absent, certain pressures upon Negro life (slavery, the chain-gang) are clearly portrayed. The atavism is debatable if Brutus Jones is intended to symbolize *the* Negro; but it is possible that Brutus is another instance of O'Neill's study of man, not of a particular race. The new tech niques, the use of the throbbing tom-tom, the exotic setting, the monologues delivered so powerfully by Charles Gilpin and later Paul Robeson made theatre history. The *Emperor Jones* is remote from Negro experience in America. *All God's Chillun Got Wings* (1923) is a closer approach to the problem play. In this study of intermarriage and the tragic effects of race prejudice, O'Neill has selected an extreme case, with the Negro too selfless and inept, and the white girl too weak and stupid, for credence. Even so the play was threatened with riots.

In 1923 the Ethiopian Art Players, organized by Raymond O'Neil and Mrs. Sherwood Anderson, indicated lines that Negro performances were to take, producing a jazzed-up *Comedy of Errors*, a revival of *Salome*, and a folk-play, *The Chip Woman's Fortune*, by a Negro playwright, Willis Richardson. The one-act *Rackey* (1919) and *Goat Alley* (1922) presented something of the drab misery of Negro slums. There is more colour and music and knowledge of folk-life in *Roseanne* (1923), a sympathetic study of southern church life. *Black Boy* (1926) chronicled the rise and fall of a Negro pugilist, but the presence of the newly discovered Paul Robeson in the lead could not save it. Another play dealing with the meaner aspects of life is *Lulu Belle* (1926), the melodrama of a Harlem harlot's progress, with Lenore Ulric in the title-role. David Belasco's realistic sets of Harlem were notable. In 1929 the Negro novelist, Wallace Thurman, collaborated with William Rapp on *Harlem*, a swiftly paced melodrama of the seamier aspects of life, seen from the inside. Its racketeers, gamblers, loose women, its murder and rent party could have been matched in life. *Singing the Blues* (1931), by John McGowan, continued the exploitation of the gaudier Harlem.

Greater respect for his material was shown by Em Jo Basshe in his *Earth* (1927), a lyrical drama of a conflict in the deep South between Christianity and voodooism, featured by weird music composed by Hall Johnson. This was a production of the New Playwrights Theatre. Another of their productions was *Hoboken Blues* (1927), an expressionistic play combining realism and fantasy, vaudeville and tragedy. Subtitled *The Black Rip Van Winkle*, contrasting Harlem at the turn of the century and in the gaudy boom twenty-five years later, the play contained much sharp protest at the economic plight of the Negro. A 'native opera' was attempted in *Deep River* (1926), another short-lived experiment. More in the older tradition was *Showboat* (1927), one of America's most popular, most revived musicals. One of the high spots of this colourful melodrama of river life has always been the singing of 'Old Man River', first by Jules Bledsoe, then by Paul Robeson, and more recently by Kenneth Spencer.

Of all American playwrights, Paul Green has made most thorough use of Negro folk-life in drama. His one-act plays, better known to the Tributary than to the Broadway theatres, range from *The No 'Count Boy* (1924), depicting a musical vagabond reminiscent of Synge's Playboy, to stark snapshots of life among Negro farmhands such as *The Hot Iron* (1926),

White Dresses (1926), and *The End of the Row* (1926). Folk superstitions are dealt with amusingly in *The Man Who Died At Twelve O'Clock* (1925) and gruesomely in *Aunt Mahaly's Cabin* (1925). Green's honesty in dealing with subjects generally taboo in the South and his recognition of the harshness of Negro life are apparent in *In Abraham's Bosom* (1926), a play about the last century. Abraham McCranie, the Negro son of a slave-owner, dreams and labours to bring education to his needy people, but meets with distrust and dislike from other Negroes, even his own family, and with hostility from the whites. When a white mob breaks up a meeting that he has called he is tormented beyond endurance and kills his white half-brother after a bitter quarrel. The mob, already formed, comes to his house and shoots him down. *In Abraham's Bosom* was awarded the Pulitzer Prize for its imagination, sympathy, and power. In *The House of Connelly* (1931) the Negro characters are minor but well characterized. *Roll, Sweet Chariot* (1935), an acting version of *Potter's Field* (1931), is experimental, with speech, chant, and song alternating. It gives a fluent cross-section of the loose morality and violence of a southern shanty-town. Green does not make this material something picturesque; his chain-gang scene is brutal and true; the general tone is depressing. There is more social protest in *Hymn to the Rising Sun* (1936), an ironic, forceful drama of the horror of southern convict camps; both Negro and white convicts are victims of their sadism. Paul Green has stated that his plays are not meant to be 'generally representative of the Negro race', that he has been chiefly concerned with 'the more tragic and uneasy side of Negro life'. This he has conveyed with authentic knowledge and imaginative insight.

Rather than the tragic and uneasy phases, the exotic attracted Du Bose Heyward and Dorothy Heyward in *Porgy* (1927), dramatized from the former's novel. Cleon Throckmorton's elaborate sets of Catfish Row, a waterside slum of Charleston, were background for an appealing story of primitive passion, hatred, murder, humour, superstition, faith, and sorrow. The crippled beggar Porgy and his doomed girl Bess were characterized with great sympathy. Rouben Mamoulian directed the production with a flair for the picturesque, especially in the wake and storm scenes. The same authors' *Mamba's Daughters* (1939), also adapted from a novel by Du Bose Heyward, is a more conventional tale of fierce devotion on the part of Mamba, a cunning grandmother, and Hagar, a slow-witted Amazon mother, both of them single-tracked in their determination to make something of Hagar's daughter. *Mamba's Daughters* was Ethel Waters's first appearance on the legitimate stage, and she was highly praised for the power and dignity with which she played Hagar. Du Bose Heyward's *Brass Ankle* (1931), the tragedy of a woman of Negro-Indian-white stock who bears a son who is a 'throw-back' to some unknown Negro

ancestor, is unconvincing. In 1935 George Gershwin selected *Porgy* as the basis of the 'first American folk-opera', for which Ira Gershwin wrote many lyrics. Presented by the Theatre Guild in 1935 and revived in 1942, directed by Mamoulian, and introducing Todd Duncan and Anne Brown to the American stage, *Porgy and Bess* has become one of America's best-loved and most influential entertainments.

One result of *Porgy's* success was the dramatization (1930) of the best-selling novel, *Scarlet Sister Mary*. Ethel Barrymore in black-face played the scarlet sister of the Negro plantation, but the play was a failure. Another skilful and informed writer about South Carolina Negroes, E. C. L. Adama, failed in *Potee's Gal* (1929), a play about the primitive life in the Congaree swamps. Marc Connelly, a comparative outsider, succeeded where these comparative insiders failed. *The Green Pastures* (1930) is derived from Roark Bradford's *Ol' Man Adam an' His Chillun*, a book of burlesques purporting to be a Negro preacher's version of the Bible. Connelly retained some of the burlesque such as a God in frock-coat and fedora, smoking a ten-cent cigar, and walking the earth like 'a natural man'. But Connelly infused much tenderness and reverence into Bradford's farces, aided by Richard Harrison as 'de Lawd', by a cast that performed with simplicity and dignity, and by the well-placed spirituals beautifully sung by Hall Johnson's Choir. Inexactly termed 'an attempt to present certain aspects of a living religion in the terms of its believers', *The Green Pastures* would probably shock the Negro folk as sacrilegious, and is really Marc Connelly's version of what Roark Bradford said was a Negro preacher's version of religion. Still, the kindly perplexed father of his people is like the God of the spirituals. There are some charming vignettes of Negro folk-life on its less uneasy side, and the majestic scene of the exodus to the Promised Land, with the ragged crowds of the heavy-laden, their faces lighted with hope and faith, marching to the swelling choruses of 'I'm Noways Weary', touches upon profound reality.

In 1933 a Negro playwright's version of folk religion appeared in *Run, Little Chillun*, the first successful play of Negro authorship on Broadway. Based, as was Basshe's *Earth*, on a conflict between Christianity and a pagan cult, *Run, Little Chillun* made full use of spectacle, the dance, and music. It inclined to the exotic and melodramatic, but unquestionably had the authenticity of the inside view. The church scenes especially were distinguished by moving realism, with superb musical effects. Kenneth Burke pointed out that *The Green Pastures* was 'essentially a white man's play . . . exploiting the old conception of the Negro (naïve, good-natured, easily put upon)', whereas *Run, Little Chillun* emphasizes 'an aspect of the Negro symbol with which our theatre-going public is not theatrically at home: the power side of the Negro'. Lacking the stagecraft of

The Green Pastures, its best scenes had greater verisimilitude.

Black Souls (1932) was a well-intentioned play, using educated Negroes for propaganda purposes, but it lacked the force of reality. One of the strongest anti-lynching plays was *Never No More* (1932), written after the author, an ex-cotton-planter, had accidently witnessed a Negro's being burned at the stake. There is more than horror in the play; sympathetic understanding marks the portrait of the Negro tenant family ruled over by the mother (admirably played by Rose McLendon). The burning of the scapegoat son while the family is barricaded in their cabin was a scene of almost intolerable tension. Another powerful social indictment of the same year was *Bloodstream*, which showed the brutality of Negro and white convict labour in the mines. In 1934 John Wexley dramatized the notorious Scottsboro case in *They Shall Not Die*, throwing light on the travesty of justice, the violence of the police system and the mobs, and the poverty and ignorance of both Negroes and whites. *Mulatto*, in the same year, is a mordant sensational account of an illicit relationship in the South, showing the hatred of a mulatto son for his white father. *White Man* (1936) was an unconvincing tragedy of the near-white.

The most successful play of radical protest was *Stevedore* (1934). The frame-up of a Negro organizer, who is accused of rape in order to check his militancy, is prevented when the concerted action of white and black dockhands turn back a mob. Lonnie Thompson, who is class- rather than race-conscious, the spunky Binnie, keeper of a lunch-room, and Blacksnake, a man full of fight, are new Negroes on the American stage. In 1937 *Marching Song* also presented Negro life and characters in terms of social analysis and protest. A large number of left-wing plays followed *Stevedore* in urging that Negroes must organize and fight for their rights and that white and Negro labour must unite their forces. One of the best of these, *A Mighty Wind A-Blowin'* (1936), urged the union of white and Negro sharecroppers. Of the New Theatre League's 'agit-prop' plays, one Negro hero was Angelo Herndon, who was jailed for leading a march of the unemployed in Atlanta. Another hero was John Henry, the champion steel-driver, whom both Herbert Kline, editor of *New Theatre*, and Frank Wells stressed as a working-class hero. In 1939 the commercial theatre presented Roark Bradford's *John Henry*, but even with Paul Robeson and Josh White in the cast the play failed. Bradford revealed little sympathy with the essential dignity of John Henry.

Wells's *John Henry* had to wait for the Federal Theatre to produce it. The Federal Theatre Project was fortunate in having as its director Hallie Flanagan, who wanted a theatre that would fearlessly present problems touching American life; she was also greatly interested in a Negro theatre. Federal Theatre did more for Negroes than give employment to the many unemployed Negro actors; it

served as a needed apprenticeship in acting, playwriting, producing, and designing; and it brought the people into the theatre.

The plays produced in Harlem and in such cities as Boston, Hartford, Philadelphia, Newark, Chicago, Seattle, San Francisco, Los Angeles, and Birmingham, were of many sorts. The most popular was *The Haitian Macbeth* (1936), which with Jack Carter, Edna Thomas, and Canada Lee in the leading roles, directed by Orson Welles and John Houseman, and with tropical settings by Nat Karson, made theatre history. The witchcraft scenes in a Haitian jungle, the weird dances performed to frenzied drumming, set a type of adaptation of the classics that has prevailed. Somewhat in the same vein was *Haiti* (1938), a melodrama of the revolt of Toussaint L'Ouverture and Christophe against the French. *The Swing Mikado* by the Theatre Project of Chicago was the hit of 1939; the free swinging of Gilbert and Sullivan, the exotic stage settings, and the enthusiastic abandon of actors, singers, and dancers swept away even confirmed Savoyards. Other adaptations, of *Lysistrata*, *The Taming of the Shrew*, *Androcles and the Lion*, and *Noah*, met with less success. *The Emperor Jones*, *In Abraham's Bosom*, *Run, Little Chillun*, and *Stevedore* were revived by project units.

Of great importance were the plays of Negro authorship which but for the Federal Theatre Project might never have received a professional hearing. Noteworthy among these are Frank Wilson's two treatments of folk life, *Brother Mose* (which appeared briefly on Broadway in 1929) and *Walk Together, Chillun* (1936); also a dramatization of a detective novel of Harlem, *The Conjure Man Dies* (1936), and *The Trial of Dr. Beck*, *The Case of Philip Lawrence*, and *The Natural Man* (all 1937), another treatment of the John Henry myth. Especially marked by social realism were *Turpentine* (1936), which dealt with the hardships of labour in Florida swamps, and *Big White Fog* (1938), a play about the depression. *Battle Hymn* (1936) dramatized John Brown's historic thrust for freedom; *Sweet Land* (1937) showed the Negro's continuing struggle. In *How Long Brethren?* (1937) Tamiris and her group danced to Lawrence Gellert's 'Negro Songs of Protest' sung by a Negro chorus. In 1939, with a text by Carlton Moss, *Prelude to Swing*, a dramatic history of the development of Negro music, was presented by a dance unit, a choral group, and a swing orchestra. *Bassa Moona* (1936) brought the real African jungle dance-drama to Broadway.

The success of the Federal Theatre's *Swing Mikado* stimulated private producers to stage the *Hot Mikado* (1939) which was less primitive but smarter, and, with Bill Robinson stopping the show, more commercially successful. Riding the crest, *Swingin' The Dream* (1939) jazzed up *A Midsummer Night's Dream* with the swing artists Louis Armstrong and Maxine Sullivan in key roles, but the result was more of a stunt than a play. *Cabin in The Sky* (1940) capitalized somewhat on *The Green Pastures*.

[570]

The acting of Ethel Waters, Rex Ingram, Dooley Wilson, Todd Duncan, and Katherine Dunham made for a long run, but the play was sentimental, amusing fantasy, not drama of Negro life. The all-Negro musical show continued in *Jump For Joy* (1940), *Harlem Cavalcade* (1942), *Blue Holiday*, and *Memphis Bound* (both 1945). The last two, though studded with famous stars, had only short runs. With a good story around which to build the singing and dancing, the all-Negro *Carmen Jones* (1943) was an immense success. This spectacle was adapted by Oscar Hammerstein from Bizet's 'Carmen' and gorgeously produced by Billy Rose. In contrast, the curiosity value of *Lysistrata* as played by a Negro cast in Gilbert Seldes's adaptation did not succeed. A later all-Negro success was *St. Louis Woman* (1946). The story of the love-life of a flashy jockey at the turn of the century, this was a gay, loud extravaganza with gorgeous costumes and striking sets. Katherine Dunham and her troupe have been popular in their performances of exotic, chiefly Caribbean, dancing in *Tropical Revue* (1944), *Carib Song* (1945), and *Bal Nègre* (1946). Haitian dancing by Josephine Premice, and African and American Negro dancing by Pearl Primus, have also been popular. From *Kykunkor* (1934) to *A Tale of Old Africa* (1946) Asadata Dafora has presented occasional African dance-dramas in New York, with full knowledge of and respect for his native traditions.

No earlier play explored Negro life with such tragic intensity as *Native Son* (1941). Staged and directed for maximum excitement, more melodramatic and less clarified than Richard Wright's novel, the drama was highly successful in its portrait of Bigger Thomas, trapped like a rat in his Chicago slum home, warped into a killer. Canada Lee's understanding creation of the role of Bigger had much to do with the play's gripping power. Candour and insight marked the dramatization of *Strange Fruit* (1945). Losing some of the novel's depth, the adaptation conveyed movingly the tragedy of a love affair between a young white Southerner and a Negro girl, as well as a most convincing cross-section of a Southern town. Critics were more pleased by *Deep Are The Roots* (1945), which skilfully handled timely problems. A Negro lieutenant, decorated in war, returns to his native South to devote himself to educating his people. The play displays frankly the forces opposed to Negro development in the South, the problem of intermarriage (discussed more openly than ever before), Southern liberalism, and the intelligent Negro's determination to achieve full citizenship. *Jeb* (1946) posed another problem of the veteran, that of unemployment. It was sincere and sympathetic, but lacked the excitement of *Deep Are The Roots*. On *Whitman Avenue* (1946) dramatized the problem of restricted housing in Northern cities. A Negro family's living in a white neighbourhood causes ugly violence. The play hits hard on a significant theme, and the self-respecting average middle-class Negro family was new on the American stage.

A recent trend of integration is observable on Broadway, particularly in musical comedy. More and more Negro performers have been 'folded into' supporting casts, rather than made to stand out as something particular, like Bert Williams in the *Ziegfeld Follies* and Ethel Waters in *As Thousands Cheer*. From the Federal Theatre *Sing For Your Supper* (1939) through *This Is The Army* (1942), *On The Town* (1944), and *Sing Out, Sweet Land* (1944) ('A salute to American Folk and Popular Music'), Negroes have been part and parcel of the shows. The height of this integration is seen in *Call Me Mister* (1946), a musical of the returning veteran, in *Bloomer Girl* (1944), and especially in *Finian's Rainbow* (1947), a sharp, original satire of racism with Negroes sharing in major and minor roles. In 1943 the late Thomas 'Fats' Waller and George Marion, a Negro and white team, produced successfully *Early to Bed*, but in 1946 the even more significant *Beggar's Holiday*, based on Gay's *Beggar's Opera*, resulted from uniting the talents of two Negroes: the composer Duke Ellington and the designer and co-producer Perry Watkins, with those of two whites: co-producer John R. Sheppard and lyric-writer John La Touche; the play was cast without regard to colour; the male lead was white, the female was Negro; the rest of the cast interracial. Broadway took kindly to the innovation. A few Negro actors, notably Canada Lee as Caliban in Margaret Webster's production of *The Tempest* (1945) and as Bosola in the revival of *The Duchess of Malfi* (1946), have been assigned roles hitherto closed to Negroes. In 1946 the Equity-Library Theatre presented a mixed cast in *Outward Bound*. A further instance of integration was the choice of Langston Hughes to do the lyrics to Kurt Weill's score for the musical production of Elmer Rice's *Street Scene* (1947).

In the early 1940s over one hundred plays on Broadway included Negro actors in roles numbering nearly a thousand. But serious drama of Negro life was rare, and the Negro playwright noticeably absent. Even the few plays that dealt realistically with Negro life were most often by white authors. Except for the short-lived Federal Theatre Project, the Negro playwright has been without experience in the professional theatre. He has turned to the tributary theatre—community, college, and semi-professional groups—to learn and practise his craft. American Negroes by and large see little of the theatre; below the Mason-Dixon line they are not allowed in the legitimate theatres, except infrequently in segregated sections. Negro stock companies played at the Pekin Theatre in Chicago and the Lincoln and the Lafayette Theatres in New York. These theatres, especially the Lafayette, introduced many outstanding performers to the legitimate stage, but their repertory consisted of the melodramatic standbys of Broadway. Early amateur groups in

Washington, D.C., presented *Star of Ethiopia* (1913), a pageant of race progress, and *Rachel* (1920), a play denouncing race prejudice. The Negro Little Theatre movement, however, generally followed the lead of Alain Locke and Montgomery Gregory, founders of the Howard University Players, in exploring the drama of Negro folk-life, though some Negro amateur groups refuse to do plays of Negro life.

The most productive playwright for the thriving college theatres has been Randolph Edmonds, whose *Six Plays for a Negro Theatre* about historic Negroes or the folk take well with college audiences. His *In the Land of Cotton* (1942), showing the harshness of sharecropping life, was performed by the People's Community Theatre of New Orleans, directed by Thomas Richardson, who has organized several working-class theatres.

A product of collegiate drama, Abram Hill was a moving force in the establishment of the American Negro Theatre, the most firmly established semi-professional group. Hill's *On Striver's Row* (1942), produced at the 135th Street Library Theatre, has taken well with the Harlem that is gaily satirized; Hill's dramatization of Len Zinberg's *Walk Hard, Talk Loud* (1944), a novel of the prize-fighting world, did not take so well. The American Negro Theatre's most signal success was its production of *Anna Lucasta* (1944). This play by Philip Yordan about a Polish family was adapted to Negro life and first presented in Harlem. The skill of the production warranted its removal down town, where it had a phenomenal run, introducing such stars as Hilda Simms and Frederick O'Neal. It also had a long run in London. The American Negro Theatre has also produced Owen Dodson's *The Garden of Time*, a retelling of the Medea story. Dodson is the author of other poetic plays, *The Divine Comedy*, a play suggested by Father Divine's movement (produced at the Yale University Theatre, 1938), and *The Amistad*, a play on the historic mutiny. He has been influential in college drama and is a member of the Negro Playwrights Company. Another member of the company is Theodore Ward, whose *Big White Fog* was one of the strongest of the Federal Theatre Project's plays, and whose *Our Lan'*, a play of social realism, tried out in the spring of 1947, received Theatre Guild encouragement for a more thorough-going production in the fall.

In 1821, while white actors were smearing their faces with burnt cork to mimic Negroes, a Negro group, the African Company, led by James Hewlett, was performing Shakespeare in New York City. Shortly thereafter, Ira Aldridge, finding no opportunities for his acting abilities in America, went to Europe, where he became famous, particularly as Othello to Charles Kean's Iago. Negroes have since played Shakespeare, notably Edward Sterling Wright in *Othello* at the Lafayette Theatre in 1915, but generally in a Negro theatre before a Negro audience. About a century after Aldridge, Paul Robeson matched his triumph in a London performance of *Othello*, with Maurice Browne as Iago; and in 1943 Margaret Webster's magnificent production of *Othello*, with José Ferrer's Iago and Uta Hagen's Desdemona supporting Robeson's Othello, achieved the longest recorded run of consecutive performance of any Shakespearian play. S. A. B.

NEIGHBORHOOD PLAYHOUSE, NEW YORK, at 466 Grand Street. This theatre, which for the first five years of its life was occupied by amateurs, was built and endowed in 1915 by Alice and Irene Lewisohn. It later housed a professional company which performed the plays of Shaw, O'Neill, and others, and did a certain amount of experimental work in music and drama. It closed in 1927, but the organization became a corporation sponsoring occasional productions of interest, and in 1935, to mark its 20th anniversary, it presented at the Lyceum Theatre a Spanish play entitled *Bitter Oleander*.

NEILSON, ADELAIDE (1846–80), English actress, child of a strolling player, whose real name was Elizabeth Ann Brown. Born at Leeds, she had an unhappy childhood, and in 1865 made her first appearance on the stage as Julia in *The Hunchback*, always one of her best and favourite parts. After several years in London and the provinces, where she was much admired in Shakespeare and other productions, including a number of dramatizations of Scott, she made her first visit to the United States in 1872, touring the country with a fine repertory. She became exceedingly popular, and had just returned from a second extended tour of that country when she died. Beloved and admired by the public and by members of her own profession, her early death was a great loss to the stage. A beautiful woman, with dark eyes and a most expressive countenance, she was considered to be at her best in the part of Juliet, though she was also much admired as Viola. She made an unhappy marriage, and divorced her husband in 1877.

NEILSON, JULIA, see TERRY (9).

NEMIROVICH-DANCHENKO, VLADIMIR IVANOVICH (1859–1943), co-founder and director of the famous Moscow Art Theatre, and one of the outstanding personalities of the Russian stage, both Imperial and Soviet. He studied at Moscow University, and during his student days was already writing dramatic criticism. He later wrote a number of novels and eleven plays, mostly conventional and successful comedies which were done at the Maly Theatre. In 1891 he was in charge of the Drama Course of the Moscow Philharmonic Society, and among his pupils were Moskvin, Olga Knipper, and Meyerhold. It was at this time that he first began to realize that all was not well with the Russian stage, and took advantage of his opportunities at the Maly to introduce reforms there, including more rehearsals and a less rigid style of acting.

In 1897 took place his meeting and discussion

with Stanislavsky which resulted in the founding of the Moscow Art Theatre, to which he brought a number of his pupils. He was responsible for the literary quality of the theatre's repertory, as Stanislavsky was for the high standard of its acting, and it was he who persuaded Chekhov to allow a second production of *The Seagull* after its failure at the Alexandrinsky. He was personally responsible for a number of the theatre's most widely admired productions both classic and modern, and shortly before his death received a Stalin award for his work on the new play about Lenin, *Kremlin Chimes* (1942).

While the Moscow Art Theatre was touring abroad under Stanislavsky in the difficult days after the October Revolution, Nemirovich-Danchenko remained in the U.S.S.R. and founded a Musical Studio, now called after him, where he developed a new style and standard of production for opera and operetta, in which he proved that the methods of the Moscow Art Theatre could be applied with as much success to the operatic as to the dramatic stage. Nemirovich-Danchenko has written an account of the founding of the Moscow Art Theatre, and expounded his own philosophy of the drama, in his *My Life in the Russian Theatre* (1937). A second volume of memoirs, written just before his death, is also to appear.

NERO, Emperor of Rome from A.D. 54 to 68, was a devotee of the theatre, and himself appeared frequently on the stage. Not only did he perform as a dancer in pantomime—thus we are told that he wished to 'dance' the role of Virgil's Turnus, and that he was moved by jealousy to put the pantomimus Paris to death —but his pride in his 'divine voice' led him to appear as a tragic actor in such parts as the Mad Hercules, the Blind Oedipus, the Matricide Orestes, even Canace in Travail. These were evidently scenes taken from tragedy or modelled on tragedy, and intended to be 'sung' by a single performer. On such occasions the emperor, like other actors, wore a mask to indicate his role; but the features of the mask were modelled on his own, or on those of his mistress for the time being. From his famous theatrical tour of Greece (A.D. 66–7) he returned with 1,808 triumphal crowns. Even his worst crimes do not seem to have shocked conservative opinion in Rome so much as these antics—a fact which illustrates the low status of professional entertainers, at any rate under the Empire.   w. b.

NERONI, Bartolomeo (*c.* 1500–71/3), builder of the Siena Theatre (see MACHINERY and SCENERY, 2).

NESTROY, Johann Nepomuk (1801–62), Austrian actor and dramatist, who was in his youth a singer at the Viennese Opera House. He soon deserted opera for the drama, and proved himself a fine comedian. From 1854 to 1861 he directed the Karl-Theater. His plays, which are closely bound up with the evolution

of the Viennese fairy-tale play, are witty and cynical, and were long popular in Austria and Germany, though little known outside. A collected edition in twelve volumes was published in 1890.

NEUBER, Frederika Carolina (née Weissenborn) (1697–1760), one of the earliest and best-known of German actress-managers. After a childhood made unhappy by a tyrannical father she eloped at the age of nineteen with a young clerk, Johann Neuber(1697–1759), whom she afterwards married, and with him joined the theatrical company of Spiegelberg, then acting in Weissenfels. Here, and with another company run by Haak, they remained for ten years, and at the end of that time formed a company of their own, with a patent which enabled them to play at the Leipzig fairs. 'Die Neuberin', as she was called, was at this time a fine actress, at the height of her powers. She was much admired in breeches parts, and had already attracted the notice of Gottsched, who planned to make use of her art in the reforming of the German theatre. She was quite willing to carry out his ideas, as she had herself formed the project of raising and purifying the standard of both acting and repertory, and in 1727 she started on the production of French classic tragedies and comedies adapted by Gottsched and his adherents. Ideally the old improvised comedy and the popular farces and harlequinades should have been entirely abolished, but this was not immediately possible, and proved a bone of contention between actors, reformers, and the public which finally wrecked the whole enterprise. Caroline Neuber was a high-spirited woman, intolerant of restraint and criticism, and she was bound sooner or later to come into conflict with the rigid principles of Gottsched. The first break came when the company, in 1739, having learnt one translation of *Alzire*, refused to replace it with a new translation by Gottsched's wife, and even the famous enactment of Harlequin's banishment from the stage, though ostensibly a gesture in Gottsched's favour, was aimed more at the Neubers' rival, the old harlequin-player Müller, at that moment delighting Leipzig audiences, who found the regular plays of the new drama rather dull. Once she had broken with Gottsched, Caroline Neuber's star waned, and her fortunes rapidly declined. Some disastrous appearances at Hamburg, where she offended her audience by outspoken criticisms of their taste, were followed in 1740 by an unfortunate visit to Russia, curtailed by the death of the Empress. The company, however, and particularly the acting of its leading lady, had been favourably noticed, and left their imprint on the Russian theatre, then struggling into being. Returning to Leipzig, the Neubers found themselves ousted by a former associate, Schönemann, and further offended Gottsched by ridiculing his *Der sterbende Cato*. He had insisted on Roman dress for this, a sensible innovation but one too far in advance of his time, and Caroline Neuber retorted by dressing the actors in flesh-pink leggings. She also satirized her former patron in a curtain-raiser written by herself, now lost, in which he was depicted as a bat-winged censor. These sallies, however, and the comforting admiration of the young Lessing, could not retrieve her lost fortunes. The company broke up, but the Neubers struggled along until the outbreak of the Seven Years War, which reduced them to complete poverty, and they died within a year of each other.

Caroline Neuber's association with Gottsched, in spite of its unfortunate conclusion, is generally regarded as the turning-point in German theatre history, and the starting-point of modern German acting. She certainly did a great deal for her profession, training her actors and actresses well, ruling them with a firm hand, and insisting on regularity and order. She produced the plays Gottsched provided for her not for financial gain, since the old popular comedy would probably have been more profitable, but because she realized that the theatre had fallen on evil times artistically and believed in the superior qualities of the well-written, regular French classic play. Though her style of acting, which was pompous in tragedy and affected in comedy, later went out of fashion, it was in its day a vast improvement on the old clowning and farcical horse-play, and prepared the way for the subtle, natural style of Ekhof and Schröder. Her husband, of whom little is known, was evidently no actor, but he appears to have been a sensible man of business, quiet and modest, entirely devoted to his wife and an unfailing support through good times and bad. Both domestically and in their work they offered an example worthy of emulation to their colleagues, and were the first to bring about a relationship between the stage and men of letters which had hitherto seemed impossible.

NEUE FREIE VOLKSBÜHNE, BERLIN, see FREIE BÜHNE.

NEVILLE, (THOMAS) HENRY (GARTSIDE) (1837–1910), English actor, son of a theatre manager, and the twentieth child of a twentieth child (both by second marriages). He was on the stage as a boy, and as an adult made his début in the provinces in 1857. He was first seen in London at the Lyceum on 8 Oct. 1860, and was for many years connected with the Olympic, where on 2 May 1863 he played Bob Brierley in *The Ticket-of-Leave Man*, always his finest part. A flamboyant and romantic actor, he was at his best in strong characters, and played in Drury Lane melodramas for fourteen years, making his last appearance in April 1910, shortly before his death.

NEW AMSTERDAM THEATRE, NEW YORK, on West 42nd Street, renowned as the home of the famed Ziegfeld Follies. It opened on 26 Oct. 1903 with Nat Goodwin in the Klaw and Erlanger production of *A Midsummer Night's Dream*, while later in the same year

came the Drury Lane pantomime *Mother Goose*, which ran for three months. Among visiting stars who appeared at this theatre in its early years were Mrs. Pat Campbell in Sardou's *The Sorceress*, H. B. Irving and Dorothea Baird in *Paolo and Francesca*, and the Forbes-Robertsons in *Caesar and Cleopatra*. *Brewster's Millions* and *The Merry Widow* were both successful productions here, while the first of the Ziegfeld shows was seen in 1914. Two years later Tree came in *Henry VIII*, but the theatre was mainly occupied by musical comedy and revue until, in 1933, Eva Le Gallienne brought *Alice in Wonderland* and *The Cherry Orchard* from the Civic Repertory for a successful run. The last production at this theatre, which is now a cinema, was Walter Huston in *Othello* (1937) produced by Robert Edmond Jones.   G. F.

NEW BOWERY THEATRE, NEW YORK, see BOWERY THEATRE (2).

NEW BROADWAY THEATRE, NEW YORK, see DALY'S THEATRE (1).

NEW CHATHAM THEATRE, NEW YORK, see CHATHAM THEATRE (2).

NEW CHELSEA THEATRE, LONDON, see COURT THEATRE.

NEW COMEDY, see GREECE.

NEW ENGLISH OPERA HOUSE, LONDON, see ROYALTY THEATRE (2).

NEW LYCEUM THEATRE, LONDON, see PANHARMONIUM.

NEW NATIONAL THEATRE, NEW YORK, see CHATHAM THEATRE (2).

NEW ORLEANS, see PIONEER THEATRE IN THE U.S.A.

NEW OXFORD THEATRE, LONDON, see OXFORD MUSIC-HALL.

NEW PARK THEATRE, NEW YORK, on the site of the old Aquarium, opened 15 Oct. 1883. It was furnished with a good deal of material bought when Booth's Theatre was demolished, and began with a series of musical plays. It was then occupied for a short time by Belasco, and by the company from the Windsor Theatre (destroyed by fire), who imported mainly melodrama. On 11 Aug. 1884 little Minnie Maddern, later Mrs. Fiske, was seen in *Caprice*, and the theatre then became a museum, occasionally housing itinerant companies and light opera.

See also PARK THEATRE (2).

NEW QUEEN'S THEATRE, LONDON, see ALBION THEATRE.

NEW ROYALTY THEATRE, LONDON, see ROYALTY THEATRE (2).

NEW STRAND THEATRE, London, see STRAND THEATRE (1).

NEW THEATRE, London, in St. Martin's Lane, built in 1903 by Sir Charles Wyndham, who opened it with a revival of *Rosemary*. Forbes-Robertson transferred *The Light that Failed* there from the Lyric; Mrs. Patrick Campbell produced Sudermann's *The Joy of Living*, which belied its title and failed, giving way to a revival of *The Second Mrs. Tanqueray*. *Mrs. Gorringe's Necklace*, transferred from Wyndham's, finished its long run at the New, which has been a consistently successful theatre. Among its many successes must be counted *The Scarlet Pimpernel* with Fred Terry and Julia Neilson; *Grumpy* with Cyril Maude; seasons by Matheson Lang with *The Wandering Jew* and other plays; Shaw's *St. Joan* with Sybil Thorndike; *The Constant Nymph* with Edna Best and Noel Coward; and John Gielgud's productions of *Richard of Bordeaux*, *Hamlet*, and *Romeo and Juliet*. After the bombing of the Old Vic and Sadler's Wells Theatres the companies were housed at the New in alternate seasons of ballet and repertory until in 1945 the ballet went to Covent Garden, leaving the Old Vic in sole possession.   W. M. P.

For the New Theatre, New York, see CENTURY THEATRE and PARK THEATRE (1).

NEW YORK, see BROADWAY.

NEW YORK THEATRE, New York. (1) Originally the Church of the Messiah, at 728 Broadway, this had been used for concerts and lectures before, on 23 Dec. 1865, Lucy Rushton, an actress of little ability but great personal charm, opened it as her own theatre, appearing with the veteran Charles Walcot in *The School for Scandal*, *The Lady of Lyons*, and *As You Like It*. On 3 Sept. 1866, re-christened the New York, it opened under Mark Smith and Lewis Baker. It was here that Daly took his company after the destruction by fire of his first Fifth Avenue Theatre, remaining there the whole of 1873. After his departure the theatre was known as Fox's Broadway, and eventually became a home of variety as the Globe.

(2) On Broadway between 44th and 45th Streets. Originally the Olympia Music-Hall, this was opened by Hammerstein on 25 Nov. 1895. Vaudeville of a superior kind flourished with such stars as Yvette Guilbert and diverse attractions which included midgets, aerial ballet, acrobats, and a Bal Champêtre in the roof-garden. On 24 Apr. 1899 the theatre was renamed the New York, and among the many successes staged there were a dramatization of *Mrs. Wiggs of the Cabbage Patch* (1906), several of George M. Cohan's plays, and the musical comedy *Naughty Marietta*. In 1912 the theatre was known as the Moulin Rouge. It returned to vaudeville, films being added in 1915, and was finally pulled down in 1935.
G. F.

For the New York Theatre, Bowery, see BOWERY THEATRE (1).

NEW YORKER THEATRE, New York. This opened as the Gallo in 1927, with Margaret Anglin in *Electra*, followed by the Abbey Players in *Juno and the Paycock*. On 12 May 1930, the theatre opened under its present name with a handsome production of Ibsen's rarely-seen *The Vikings*, for which Thomas Wilfred created backgrounds of colour and light in moving patterns in the place of realistic scenery. These, however, proved somewhat distracting in performance, and tended to take attention off the actors. In 1932 a fine Spanish company under Fernando Diaz de Mendoza and Maria Guerrero occupied the theatre for five weeks in an impressive repertory which ranged from Lope de Vega to the Quintero Brothers. It was later devoted to music-hall and musical comedy, under various managements, including that of the Federal Music Project in 1937, but in 1939 it reverted to its present name.   G. F.

NEWINGTON BUTTS, London. It is not known whether a theatre was built at Newington, or whether plays were merely given in an inn-yard there, or in an enclosure in the open air; but there can be no doubt that it was a theatrical centre of some importance. This is proved by many references to it, and by an entry in Henslowe's *Diary*, which states: 'in the name of God, Amen, beginning at Newington, my Lord Admiralle and my Lord Chamberlain's men, as followeth, 1594. . . .' Then follows an entry of receipts from various plays performed there by these companies, and of expenses incurred. Newington was an excellent place for a theatre, inasmuch as it was the equivalent on the south side of Finsbury Field on the north, where the first theatres arose (see THEATRE and CURTAIN), and was a place of public resort for archery and general recreation. In 1586 the Privy Council desired that the Lord Mayor of London should restrain and prohibit plays at the Theatre and other places about Newington, out of his charge. Howes, in his *Continuation to Stow's Annals* in 1631, gives a list of London's theatres 'besides one in former times at Newington Butts'. But there is no record or description of such a theatre, only clear evidence of plays being given there. The accepted site is now known as the Elephant and Castle.

NEWTON, JOHN (?–1625), English actor, who was with Prince Charles's Men. It is thought that he played the lean clown to Rowley's fat clown, since he is several times referred to as gaunt and 'spiny', and is noted as having played 'A Fasting-Day' in *The Inner Temple Masque* in 1619. He was evidently an important person in the company, representing, again with Rowley, Prince Charles's Men before the Privy Council when Heminge and Burbage represented the King's Men.

NIBLO'S GARDEN, New York, originally a summer resort opened by William Niblo at the corner of Broadway and Prince Street on the site of the Columbia Garden. Here, in 1828, he built a small Sans Souci Theatre, which was used in the summer for concerts and varied entertainments. The greatest attraction was the amazing performance of the Ravel troupe, a family of tight-rope acrobats and pantomimists who entertained New York for some thirty summers. The theatre was also used for plays, notably after the burning of the first Bowery and Wallack's National Theatres, and for the visits of such stars as Jefferson, Burton, Mrs. John Drew, and Mrs. Mowatt. On 18 Sept. 1846 the theatre was itself burnt down, and not rebuilt until 1849, when, on 30 July, a new theatre destined to be used the whole year round made a good start. It was improved and enlarged in 1853, and saw the last appearance in New York of Rachel two years later. Niblo finally retired in 1861, and under the management of Wheatley was produced *The Black Crook*, with which the name of Niblo's is indissolubly linked. This was a fantastic mixture of drama and spectacle, with wonderful scenery and transformations, for which the entire stage was remodelled, and with an amazing ballet of scantily clad dancers —it has been called New York's first 'leg-show'. Opening on 12 Sept. 1866, it ran for 475 performances, and was three times revived. It was followed by a similar melodrama-spectacle, *The White Fawn*, which was less successful. On 16 Nov. 1868 came Bouci-cault's elaborate mechanistic melodrama, as given at the Adelphi, London, *After Dark; or, London by Night*, followed by Lydia Thompson and her blondes, then at the height of their popularity in burlesque. The theatre which had housed so many fine plays and players was now given over to melodrama and spectacle, and to such popular performances as Lotta in *Heartsease* and Chanfrau in *Kit, the Arkansas Traveller*, until on 6 May 1872 it was again burnt down. Rebuilt, it opened on 30 Nov. with a ballet-extravaganza which ran for six months, and then housed another panto-mime family, the Vokes. But its great days were nearly over, and it was now finding itself too far down-town for a front-rank theatre. After remaining closed for nearly a year, it reopened in 1876 as a combination house for the accommodation of visiting stars with their own companies, but it continued its tradition of scenic splendour, particularly in ballet and opera, until 1895, when it was demolished.

NICOLET, JEAN BAPTISTE (*c.* 1728–96), French acrobat and entertainer, son of a puppet-master, who played at the fairs of St. Germain and St. Laurent. In 1760 he had a booth on the Boulevard du Temple, which he soon transformed into a small permanent theatre, with a good troupe of acrobats and animal turns. His monkey, Turco, was well known as a clever performer on the tight-rope, and died of eating too many sugared almonds given him by female admirers. Nicolet himself played young lovers and harlequins when he replaced his puppets by living actors, and his

theatre flourished in spite of the opposition of the Comédie-Française. In 1772 he was summoned to Court by Louis XV, who allowed him to call his theatre the Spectacle des Grands Danseurs du Roi, a title which it retained until 1792, when it became the Théâtre de la Gaîté. The freedom of the theatres under the Revolution allowed Nicolet to play the repertory of the Comédie-Française, which he did, choosing for preference the lighter pieces, until in 1795 he retired and his associate Ribié took over. Nicolet may be said to have started the Boulevard du Temple on its glorious career as the central point of Paris's minor theatres, many of which attained notoriety, particularly in melodrama, before Haussmann's rebuilding scheme swept them away in 1862.

NICOLL, ALLARDYCE (1894–   ), English theatre historian, successively Professor of English Language and Literature in London and Birmingham Universities, and at one time head of the Department of Drama in Yale University, where he began a vast and comprehensive file of photographs of theatrical material from all over Europe which is constantly being enriched, and forms a precious deposit of valuable material for the theatre research worker. Nicoll is the author of a number of useful and well-illustrated books on specialized aspects of the theatre, including *Masks, Mimes, and Miracles*, and *Stuart Masques and the Renaissance Stage*, and of more popular works, such as *British Drama*, *The English Theatre*, and *Readings in British Drama*, intended for the use of young students and non-specialists. In 1946 he brought to a close, with the publication of his two-volume *Nineteenth Century Drama, 1850–1900*, a series of eight volumes, begun in 1923, covering the history of the English theatre from the Restoration, each period having an invaluable hand-list of plays arranged under dramatists. He is a lecturer and writer on Shakespeare, and annually convenes a meeting of Shakespearian experts at Stratford-on-Avon during the Festival season.

NICOSTRATOS, a Greek tragic actor, famous for his skill in delivering messenger-speeches.

NIGGER MINSTRELS, a form of entertainment which originated from the negro patter songs of Jim Crow [T. D. Rice] and from his burlesques of Shakespeare and opera, to which negro songs were added. From 1840 to 1880 the Minstrel Show was the most popular form of entertainment in the United States (see NEGRO IN THE AMERICAN THEATRE). It came to England in the eighteen-forties and was essentially a family entertainment—as distinct from the music-hall, which was for adults only—and took place usually in a hall, notably in St. James's Hall, Piccadilly, and not in a theatre. The performers, originally, as in the United States, white men with blacked faces (whence the term Burnt-cork Minstrels), but later true negroes, sat in a semicircle with their instruments, banjos, tambourines, one-stringed fiddles, bones, &c., singing their haunting, plaintive coon songs and sentimental ballads, varied by soft-shoe dances and outbursts of back-chat between the interlocutor and Bones—the latter a permanent feature, and the butt of the party. The jokes were very elementary and relied for much of their humour on repetition, and after a great vogue the Nigger Minstrels gradually disappeared. Some of the performers migrated to the music-hall stage (see CHIRGWIN and STRATTON), while the last remnants of the fashion lingered on at the seaside, where two or three strollers in traditional nigger-minstrel costume—tight striped trousers and waistcoat and tall white hat, or straw boater—would wander along the sands with a banjo. Among the most famous minstrel troupes were the Christy Minstrels, the Burgess and Moore, and the Mohawks. A revival of the Minstrel Show, as the Kentucky Minstrels, formed a popular B.B.C. programme in the 1940s.

NIJINSKY, VASLAV (1890–1950), a famous male dancer, who first appeared in Western Europe with Diaghilev's Ballets Russes. His name has become almost legendary, and the details of his career, which terminated tragically with a complete mental breakdown, must be looked for in his wife's biography and in the ballet memoirs of the period. He was technically a superb dancer, with an amazing power of elevation which made him seem almost to hover in the air. He was also a choreographer, but the only one of his ballets to survive is 'L'Après-midi d'un Faune', which caused a scandalized outcry on its first production in 1912, as did 'Le Sacre du Printemps' in the following year (see also BALLET, 8). Nijinsky's sister, Bronislava, is a choreographer who has worked for Diaghilev, for Ida Rubenstein, for whom some of her best work was done, and for her own company. She has had an immense influence on ballet through her pupils, among them Lifar, Dolin, and Ashton.

NOAH, MORDECAI MANUEL (1785–1851), early American playwright, author of several plays on national historical themes. His first effort, however, produced in Charleston in 1812 was a translation of Pixérécourt's most popular melodrama, *Le Pélerin blanc* (1801). It was later given at Covent Garden, with alterations by John Kerr, and in its new form returned to New York, where it remained popular for many years. Noah's later plays were produced at the Park Theatre, and it was after the third night of *The Siege of Tripoli* (1820), now lost, that the theatre was destroyed by fire. In a later play, *The Grecian Captive* (1822), the hero and heroine made their entrances on an elephant and a camel respectively, a spectacular device due, no doubt, to the fertile brain of the manager, Stephen Price, who later imported real tigers into Drury Lane. Noah's plays are simply written, with a good deal of action and sustained interest, and with the aid of lavish

scenery, transparencies, and illuminations they held the stage for many years. He had an active life in politics and journalism, and in the prefaces to his printed plays gives an amusing account of his experiences in the theatre, and of the difficulties of the native American playwright in competition with the established English drama. He was, however, a great admirer of the English theatre, and in 1820 proposed the health of Edmund Kean at a banquet given in New York in the latter's honour. There is an account of him in Dunlap's *History of the American Stage.*

NOBILI, LAUDIVIO DE' (*fl.* fifteenth century), early Italian dramatist, whose *De Captivitate ducis Jacobi* (1464), written in Latin, and probably never performed, shows an interesting mingling of Senecan tragedy and the *sacre rappresentazioni* (see ITALY, 1 *b* i).

NOISES OFF, a term embracing such effects as Rain, Wind, Thunder, Galloping Hooves, &c. (see MACHINERY and TRICKWORK ON THE ENGLISH STAGE).

NOKES, JAMES (?–1696), English actor, and a member of Davenant's company at the Duke's House. He was a fine comedian, of whom Colley Cibber has left a masterly pen-portrait, and usually played foolish old husbands, and clumsy fops, as well as a few ridiculous old-lady parts. He could set audiences laughing by his mere looks, and indulged in such expressive dumb-show that, to quote Cibber, 'his silent perplexity (which would sometimes hold him several minutes) gave your imagination as full content as the most absurd thing he could say'. He and Anthony Leigh played much together and were excellent foils for each other. Nokes's best part, among many that he created in Restoration drama, seems to have been Sir Martin Mar-all in Dryden's comedy of that name, produced at Lincoln's Inn Fields in 1667. He amassed a considerable fortune and retired from the stage some years before his death. He is believed to have kept a toy-shop. His elder brother Robert, of whom little is known, was also in Davenant's company.

NŌ PLAY, see JAPAN.

NORA BAYES THEATRE, NEW YORK, see FORTY-FOURTH STREET THEATRE.

NORTON, THOMAS (1532–84), a member of the Inner Temple who, with Thomas Sackville, wrote *Gorboduc, or Ferrex and Porrex*, the first surviving example of regular Senecan tragedy in English dramatic literature. It was given on New Year's Day 1561–2 at an entertainment before Queen Elizabeth in Inner Temple Hall. Written in blank verse throughout, it is divided into five acts, of which Norton apparently wrote the first three and Sackville the last two. In theme it resembles *King Lear*, with Gorboduc, king of Britain, dividing his kingdom between his two sons, who quarrel and are both killed.

[577]

NORWAY, see SCANDINAVIA, 2.

NORWICH PLAYERS, see MONCK, NUGENT.

NORWORTH THEATRE, NEW YORK, see BELMONT THEATRE.

NOVELLI, ERMETE (1851–1919), Italian actor, son of the prompter to a travelling company, who was connected with the stage from early infancy. He made his first appearance, however, at the age of 18, and was not at first successful; but perseverance, joined to his natural genius, soon made him the outstanding actor of the Italian stage in his day. A large man, weighing some eighteen stone, he was nevertheless light on his feet and quick in action, with a fine, expressive head and mobile features. He was excellent in comedy, which he at first played exclusively, but it was in tragedy that he made his reputation. He toured extensively, and after appearing in several European countries visited the United States, South America, and Egypt. His greatest roles were Othello, Lear, Shylock, Macbeth, and Hamlet; in the last he played the death-scene with brutal realism—indeed, from contemporary accounts his acting appears to have been exceedingly forceful and melodramatic—and it was said that in the scene with the ghost he seemed to impart to the audience the certainty of a visitation from another world, merely by the concentration of his whole attention upon the inexplicable phenomenon. Another part in which he excelled was the title-role in a translation of Aicard's *Le Père Lebonnard*, a play originally given at Antoine's Théâtre Libre, in which Novelli was acclaimed by the author and the French critics for the excellence of his acting. In 1900 he attempted to found a permanent theatre in Rome, as La Casa di Goldoni, but the enterprise failed through lack of public support and had to be abandoned.

NOVELLO, IVOR (1893–1951), English actor-manager, dramatist, and composer, and one of the most consistently successful men of the London theatre. Born in Cardiff, the son of musical parents—his mother Clara Novello was a well-known choral conductor—he showed from his earliest days ability and ease in the composition of light music. During the First World War he was responsible for part of the score of several successful musical comedies,

and also wrote 'Keep the Home Fires Burning', a popular song of the time, which was first sung at a National Sunday League Concert at the old Alhambra. His parents were for some time averse to his taking up the stage as a career, but in 1921 he made his first appearance at the Ambassadors' Theatre, as Armand Duval in *Deburau*. Three years later he wrote his first play, *The Rat*, in collaboration with Constance Collier, and appeared in it himself. Since then he has written more than twenty plays, both comedies and musical comedies, playing in most of them himself, and, for the latter, composing also the musical score. Among his straight plays are *Symphony in Two Flats* (1929), *I Lived With You* (1932), and *We Proudly Present* (1947). He set up a record by being the author, composer, and leading man of four successive musical plays at Drury Lane from 1935 to 1945, where he also played *Henry V* in a spectacular revival in 1938. His work is distinguished by his complete understanding of the theatre, and of the needs of the entertainment world.   W. M. P.

NOVELTY THEATRE, LONDON, see KINGSWAY THEATRE.

NOVERRE, JEAN GEORGES (1727–1810), one of the great figures in the early history of ballet-dancing. He led a somewhat roving existence, being for some time ballet-master at Stuttgart, and succeeded the great Vestris at the Paris Opéra, where he had an opportunity to put into practice the theories enunciated in his *Lettres sur la danse* (1760). Garrick, for whom Noverre worked at Drury Lane, called him 'the Shakespeare of the dance', and he was much esteemed by Voltaire.

NOVIUS, see FABULA (1) *Atellana*.

NURSERY, THE, a training school for young actors during the Restoration period. There may for a short time have been two Nurseries—the point is obscure—but the name generally refers to that set up by Killigrew in Hatton Garden, which some time in 1668 moved to the old theatre in Gibbon's Tennis-Court (see VERE STREET THEATRE). This disappeared in 1671, when Lady Davenant built a new Nursery in the Barbican. This flourished until at least 1682, when it is referred to in Dryden's *MacFlecknoe*.

O

OBERAMMERGAU, see PASSION PLAY.

OBEY, ANDRÉ (1892–   ), French dramatist, whose early plays were written for the Compagnie des Quinze (see COPEAU and SAINT-DENIS). He had already collaborated in one play when he joined them in 1929, and remained their titular dramatist for three years. During that time he wrote *Noé*—given in an English translation in 1935 at the New Theatre, with John Gielgud as Noah—*Le Viol de Lucrèce*, which was later used as the basis of an opera by Benjamin Britten, and *La Bataille de la Marne* (all 1931). All three plays were written and presented according to the ideas of Copeau, and the fine performances which the Compagnie des Quinze gave of them went far to prove the excellence of his method, even though he was no longer in control. *Noé* was remarkable for the liveliness of its beasts, while *Le Viol de Lucrèce* and *La Bataille de la Marne* made fine use of a modified Greek chorus.

O'CASEY, SEAN (1884–   ), is known primarily as the dramatist of the Dublin slums, for, though others had used this setting, his popularity was far greater, both in Ireland and England. He knew intimately the people of whom he wrote and the events of the years from 1915 to 1922 which formed the material of the three plays by which his name was made. His treatment is closely related to that of the Irish realists before him; grim, clear-cut, and satiric, his reading of life is yet at bottom that of a poet. He belongs to a class of writers rare in all literature and very rare in drama, the tragic satirists, in whom the comedy of satire points directly to tragic implications. In two plays he approaches greatness, in *Juno and the Paycock*, whose universality and balance have tragic quality, and in *The Plough and the Stars*, where the satiric use of antithesis gives form to the play and, as a result, carries it beyond photography of life into interpretation.

The first of O'Casey's plays to be produced was *The Shadow of a Gunman* (1923), a melodramatic story of the war in 1920 and its effects on the lives of a group of people in a Dublin tenement house. This anticipates, in its subject, setting, and some of its implicit commentary, the finer plays that followed; the men who talk, live, and die for ideas are contrasted with women who live and die for actualities. Already the method of revelation by antithesis that gives force to his later work is beginning to be seen. *Juno and the Paycock* (1924), a moving, realistic tragedy, set in 1922, with similar materials and some of the same antitheses, impressed both English and Irish audiences (though differently) and had, like its successor, great popularity in both countries. *The Plough and the Stars*, a play of the Easter Rising of 1916, which caused a riot in Dublin

when it appeared in 1926, has been highly esteemed since in both countries, the two audiences differing somewhat in the nature of their misinterpretation. In *The Silver Tassie* (1928) he began to change his style and to abandon in part his setting; in the war scenes in France (Act II) satiric reaction is crossed by stylization and sometimes by what is virtually symbolism. *Within the Gates* (1933) is set in London and, remarkable though the play is in certain ways, it is doubtful whether the extension of stylization and symbolism has helped O'Casey to master his material or his thought. Moreover, he is no more successful in portraying the processes of the Cockney mind than an English dramatist would expect to be in tackling O'Casey's own Dubliners. Certain other plays have been written since; *The End of the Beginning* and *A Pound on Demand* (both one-act), *The Star Turns Red* and *Purple Dust* (both 1940 and in three acts), *Oak Leaves and Lavender* (1946), *Red Roses for Me* (1947). A contribution to dramatic criticism, *Essays in the Theatre*, appeared in 1937, and has since been followed by other critical and autobiographical works: *I Knock at the Door, Pictures in the Hallway, Drums under the Window*, and *Inishfallen, Fare Thee Well* (1939 to 1948).

OCTAVIA. The manuscripts of Seneca's plays include a drama of this name, dealing with the misfortunes of Nero's wife. Among the characters are Nero himself and Seneca. A prophecy describing in circumstantial language the death of Nero is strong evidence that the play was written after that event, and cannot therefore be the work of Seneca. As our only example of the *praetexta* (see FABULA, 4) the play has some interest, but in style and content it displays the faults of Seneca's own plays without his brilliance.   W. B.

ODEON, THÉÂTRE ROYAL DE L', the second theatre of Paris, which ranks next to the Comédie-Française. It was opened in 1816 by Picard, and two years later destroyed by fire. Rebuilt, it was again managed by Picard until his retirement in 1821. Its repertory, of which Picard himself wrote the greater part, helped by such authors as Andrieux, consisted mainly of light opera, or comedies with music. It was not until Harel took over its management in 1829 that music was left to the Opéra and the Opéra-Comique, and the Odéon built up a classical and contemporary repertory which gave it the position it holds to-day.

ODETS, CLIFFORD (1906–   ), American dramatist, and the most gifted of the American playwrights who developed a theatre of social protest during the 1930s. Born in Philadelphia, but growing up in New York, he tried his hand at writing and became an actor after graduation from high school. After joining the Group Theatre in 1931, he participated in that organization's effort to create a theatre devoted to social realities and ensemble acting along the lines laid down by Stanislavsky and the Moscow Art Theatre. When the tensions of the depression period drove the Group and Odets far to the political left, he aroused world-wide attention with a long one-act taxicab-strike play, *Waiting for Lefty* (1935), consisting of union-meeting scenes and vignettes descriptive of personal conversions to radicalism. For the Broadway production, the author added another multi-scened one-acter, *Till the Day I Die* (1935), a drama of the anti-Nazi underground in Germany. Encouraged by his success, Odets refurbished an earlier written full-length drama, *Awake and Sing* (1935), about a financially-embarrassed Jewish family's frustration and revolt. Notable for its realism, contrapuntal technique, and mingling of humour with explosive passion, the play brought Odets recognition as the most promising new American playwright. Although his next work, *Paradise Lost* (1935), dealing with the bankruptcy of a middle-class family, met with a tepid reception, he retrieved his reputation with *Golden Boy* (1937), the story of a sensitive Italian youth's deterioration after economic pressures turn him from music to professional prize-fighting. The author's star declined, however, after 1937. *Rocket to the Moon* (1938) failed as a social parable in spite of excellent characterization and considerable pathos. In *Night Music* (1940), an extravaganza expressing the struggles of disoriented youth, Odets dissipated his fire in too many directions. In *Clash by Night* (1941) he attempted to create political allegory out of the personal humiliations of an unemployed labourer, but the play emerged as a laboured domestic triangle. Each of these plays displayed a turbulent talent that had become turbid.

J. G.

OEHLENSCHLAEGER, ADAM GOTTLOB (1779–1850), Danish poet and dramatist, was born at Vesterbro in Denmark and as a young man came in contact with the theatre in Copenhagen, first (and temporarily) as an actor and then as a playwright. Poetry was his natural medium and he began early to write. His first attachments were to the *bürgerliche Trauerspiel* of Kotzebue and his German contemporaries, to Shakespeare, and to the Danish poet Johannes Ewald to whom he was in some ways a successor. As his genius defined itself he became more deeply attached to the myths and history of Scandinavia, and in his hands the saga-play reaches a power which makes him the greatest influence in Danish drama except Holberg. At a comparatively early stage his art was influenced by the work of Schiller and by the study of Greek drama, but some of the finest of his plays fall at the beginning of his career—*Sanct Hans Aften-Spil* (*Saint John's Night*) in 1802, *Aladdin* in 1804–5, and *Hakon Jarl* in 1805—though the steady development of thought and of the reading of character

gives dramatic depth to his later plays that these have not. Of the plays of his maturity perhaps the most famous are *Hagbarth og Signe* (1815) and *Væringerne i Miklagård* (1827), both tragedies. Oehlenschlaeger's output in plays alone is very great, without reference to his lyric and narrative poetry. Between 1802 and 1845 he wrote some thirty-odd, which ranged from tragedy (most numerous) through lyric drama and dramatic idyll to comedy.   U. E.-F.

OENSLAGER, DONALD (1902–   ), American scenic designer. A graduate of Harvard, where he was a member of Baker's famous '47 Workshop', and later teacher of scenic design there; he has been responsible for the décor of many important Broadway productions (see U.S.A., II).

ŒUVRE, THÉÂTRE DE L', see LUGNÉ-POË.

OFF STAGE (towards, or beyond, the sides of the acting area), see STAGE DIRECTIONS.

OHEL, the theatrical company of the Palestine Jewish Labour Federation, with its headquarters in Tel Aviv. It was founded on 21 April 1925 by Moses Halevy (1895–   ) and is supported by the various institutions of the Labour Federation. It has a portable stage for touring the agricultural settlements, taking its name from the Jewish word for tent. Halevy, who was one of the original members of Habima, and a pupil of Stanislavsky, organized a year's intensive training for the thirty students who first presented themselves, and on 24 May 1926 gave his first public performance in Tel Aviv with dramatizations of stories by Isaac Leib Peretz dealing with life in the Hassidic villages. The style of presentation was fresh and humorous, with scenery modelled on the designs of the Russian-Jewish artist Chagall. Ohel, which went on a European tour in 1934, has specialized in comedy, and has produced a number of plays, some by non-Jewish authors.   E. H.

OHIO ROSCIUS, see ALDRICH, LOUIS.

OHNET, GEORGES (1848–1918), French novelist and dramatist, some of whose plays were taken from his own books, notably the best-known, *Le Maître de forges*. This was given at the Gymnase in 1883 and ran for a year. It had been published the previous year as a novel, and in both forms was a success. Ohnet had a big popular following, but his work aroused a good deal of controversy and he was mercilessly treated by the critics, particularly Jules Lemaître, who condemned his false idealism and sentiment, and the banality of his style, attributes which no doubt contributed to his enormous though short-lived success. The opinion of the critics finally prevailed, and the tide of fortune turned against Ohnet; nothing of his is now known except the play mentioned above, which as *The Iron-master*, in an adaptation by Pinero, was given in London in 1884.

O'KEEFFE, JOHN (1747–1833), Irish dramatist, who wrote his first play at the age of 15, and was for twelve years a member of Mossop's stock company in Dublin. At 23 his eyesight began to fail and he eventually went blind. This kept him from the stage, but did not prevent his writing a number of plays, mainly farces and light operas, the latter containing many well-known songs. The most popular of these was *The Poor Soldier* (1783), which had a great vogue in America also, as did the comedy *Wild Oats* (1791), first seen at Covent Garden. Hazlitt called O'Keeffe 'the English Molière', but in view of the total disappearance of all his work from the stage, this comparison can hardly be justified. In 1826 he published *Recollections of the Life of John O'Keeffe written by Himself.*

OKHLOPKOV, NIKOLAI PAVLOVICH (1900–), Soviet actor and producer, a Siberian who first worked as a carpenter in his local theatre, studied the 'cello, and painted. In 1924 he put on his first production, May-Day spectacle in the central square of his birth-place, Irkutsk, of which he was dramatist, producer, and chief actor. His stage was a central platform, and his audience formed part of his cast. Here can be found the root of that original style which he later developed more fully at the Realistic Theatre in Moscow. He was also influenced by the Mongol-Chinese conventions, the Japanese *kabuki*, and the highly stylized presentations of the Yakut theatre. During the early days of the October Revolution Okhlopkov was a follower of the theories of Mayakovsky. In 1925 he went to Moscow, and studied under Meyerhold, and in 1932 became artistic director of the Realistic Theatre (formerly a Moscow Art Theatre Studio). Here he produced a number of plays—*Mother, The Iron Flood, Aristocrats*—setting up a different stage, or set of stages, for each, and drawing the spectators into the whirlpool of action. In all his productions, which aroused much interest and controversy, he developed in the theatre Eisenstein's theory of *montage*, the uninterrupted flow of action, as in Shakespeare and the Greek dramatists. His work was necessarily experimental, and had a somewhat limited appeal. As a result the Realistic Theatre was closed in 1938, and Okhlopkov went to the Vakhtangov Theatre, where his production of *Cyrano de Bergerac* was notable for the originality of its setting and interpretation. In 1943 he became director of the Theatre of the Revolution, and bids fair to develop the promise of his early days. For a detailed description of Okhlopkov's work at the Realistic Theatre see André van Gyseghem's *Theatre in Soviet Russia* (1943).

OLD BOWERY THEATRE, NEW YORK, see BOWERY THEATRE (1).

OLD COMEDY, see GREECE. The term was used in the nineteenth century, particularly in America, to denote English comedy from Shakespeare to Sheridan.

OLDFIELD, ANNE [NANCE] (1683–1730), one of the most famous of English actresses, successor to Mrs. Bracegirdle. She was first induced to go on the stage by Farquhar, who heard her reading aloud and recommended her to Christopher Rich; but it was not until Cibber, struck by her playing of Leonora in *Sir Courtly Nice*, produced her as Lady Betty Modish in his own *Careless Husband* (1703) that she made much stir. From then onwards her career was one of unbroken triumph. She was particularly good as Sylvia in *The Recruiting Officer* (1706) and as Mrs. Sullen in *The Beaux' Stratagem* (1707), and was the first Jane Shore. This, and Calista in *The Fair Penitent*, were her best parts in tragedy. She played with much majesty and power, particularly in *Cato* (1713) and as Andromache in *The Distressed Mother* (1712), whose first night was nearly wrecked by the partisans of Mrs. Rogers, Oldfield's rival. She was, however, always reluctant to undertake tragedy, and preferred comedy, in which she excelled. Her Lady Townley in *The Provoked Husband* (1727), which was her last new part in comedy, was particularly admired. She was buried in Westminster Abbey, near Congreve, and Savage, whom she had rescued from destitution, wrote her epitaph. Beautiful in face and figure, she had a most distinctive speaking voice, and was the only English actress Voltaire could follow without effort.

OLD MAN—WOMAN, see STOCK COMPANY.

OLDMIXON, MRS. [née Georgina Sidus] (?–1835/6), an English singer who, as Miss George, was a favourite at the Haymarket and Covent Garden, London, before she became a member of Wignell's company at the Chestnut Street Theatre, Philadelphia, in May 1793. There she took the lead in light opera, and also appeared in straight plays. She gave a concert in New York in 1797 and in the following year became a member of Dunlap's company at the newly built Park Theatre, playing Mrs. Candour in *The School for Scandal*. She also played Ophelia, and appeared in *Inkle and Yarico*, in which she had been seen at the Haymarket in 1787. For some years she was away from the stage, during which time no doubt her seven children were born, but in 1806 she reappeared under Cooper, playing the Nurse in *Romeo and Juliet*, and other elderly parts, though her singing was as good as ever. She retired some time before 1813, and in later years appeared only on the concert platform. She was the daughter of an Oxford clergyman, and married a grandson of the John Oldmixon mentioned in *The Dunciad*. After leaving the stage she kept a seminary for young ladies.

OLD MO, THE, see MUSIC-HALL III. 14.

OLD VIC THEATRE, LONDON, in the Waterloo Road, world-famous for its productions of Shakespeare. It was originally the Coburg Theatre, whose foundation-stone came from the old Savoy Palace. It was built by subscription, Princess Charlotte and Prince Leopold heading the list, and was named in their honour. In spite of royal patronage it was in danger of remaining unfinished, until a tallow-chandler named Glossop, who loved the drama, advanced a considerable sum and the theatre was completed at a cost of £12,000. It opened on 11 May 1818 with *Trial by Battle; or, Heaven Defend the Right*, a play based on a much-talked-of murder trial which had taken place a few weeks before. In addition there was a Grand Asiatic Ballet and a harlequinade. Although the proprietors promised protection, the roads were still too unsafe for the rank and fashion of town to risk the journey across the river, so the Coburg became a local house for melodrama of the most sensational kind. It was a handsome theatre, its great feature being the act-drop installed in 1822, a huge mirror reflecting the whole auditorium. Its weight put such a strain upon the roof that it had to be done away with. Plays appear to have been well staged at the Coburg, and many actors enshrined in the 'penny plain, twopence coloured' toy-theatre sheets appeared there. Occasionally a star came from the West End. Edmund Kean made five appearances there in June–July 1831, at £50 a night. But the Coburg patrons preferred their own star, Tom Cobham, to Kean, and for years the theatre remained a very local house. In 1833 it was renamed the Victoria, from the fact that Princess (later Queen) Victoria visited it once. It soon became affectionately known as the Old Vic, and made itself a niche in theatreland as a house of most extravagant melodrama. Its audience was even rougher than its shows, and there were frequent accidents, in one of the worst of which, in 1858, sixteen people lost their lives in a false alarm of fire. In 1871, under the management of J. A. Cave, it became a music-hall, and on 9 Sept. of that year, to celebrate its expected end, the play with which it had opened was revived. Then Emma Cons, first woman member of the L.C.C., bought the freehold, and reopened the theatre on Boxing Day 1880 as a temperance music-hall, naming it the Royal Victoria Hall and Coffee Tavern. It became a favourite family resort, with music and orchestral selections, and lectures given there laid the foundations of Morley College. Later, under the management of Lilian Baylis, niece of Emma Cons, films were introduced and then opera, for which a dramatic licence was obtained. In 1914 the Old Vic gave its first Shakespeare seasons and in 1923 celebrated the Tercentary of the publication of the First Folio by a performance of *Troilus and Cressida*, thus completing the production of all Shakespeare's plays at this theatre under Miss Baylis's management. Continuous seasons of Shakespeare, with occasional other revivals, were given, often with fine actors, until in 1940–1 the theatre suffered badly from enemy action and was closed. Its work continued, however, and the Old Vic company, whether

on tour or in a temporary West End home, upheld the honourable traditions of pre-war days. The damaged building was used as a centre for the training of actors, under Michel Saint-Denis, until repairs were effected, and on 14 Nov. 1950 the Old Vic reopened with *Twelfth Night*, produced by Hugh Hunt. (See also BAYLIS, LILIAN.)

OLIMPICO THEATRE, VICENZA, see SPECTACLE THEATRES.

OLIVIER, SIR LAURENCE (1907–), English actor and producer, knighted in 1947 for his services to the theatre. He studied for the stage under Elsie Fogerty, and made his first appearance at Stratford in 1922, as Katharina in an all-male production of *The Taming of the Shrew*. From 1926 to 1928 he was with the Birmingham Repertory company, and in 1937, after a somewhat varied career, which ranged from many modern parts to an alternation of Romeo and Mercutio with John Gielgud at the New Theatre in 1935, he joined the Old Vic Theatre company, with which his reputation was chiefly made. A fine, virile actor and athlete, a good fencer and a somewhat robust elocutionist, he is at his best in strong romantic costume parts, to which his dark good looks give an added attraction. His Hamlet, which he played in its entirety at the Old Vic in 1937 and later at Elsinore, is a fine, vigorous piece of work in which, however, some of the subtler shades evaporate. His versatility may be judged by his playing on one evening Hotspur and Justice Shallow, on another Oedipus and Mr. Puff. He has been responsible for the production of several plays, and has appeared in a number of films, of which the finest were his own productions of *Henry V* and *Hamlet*. During part of the 1939–45 war he served in the Fleet Air Arm.

OLUFSEN, OTTO CARL (1764–1827), Danish dramatist of the early nineteenth century (see SCANDINAVIA, 1).

OLYMPIA MUSIC-HALL, NEW YORK, see NEW YORK THEATRE (2).

OLYMPIC PAVILION, LONDON, see OLYMPIC THEATRE (1).

OLYMPIC THEATRE. (1) LONDON, built in 1805 on the site of a public house, the Queen of Bohemia, by Philip Astley, mostly of timber from the old French warship *Ville de Paris*, the deck being used for the stage. There was very little brickwork, and the roof was of tin. No trace of the theatre now remains, the Aldwych rebuilding having swept away all the streets thereabout.

The original cost of the Olympic was £800. It was built in the shape of a tent and was known as Astley's Middlesex Amphitheatre. Astley obtained a licence through the influence of Queen Charlotte and opened in 1806. The venture proved a complete failure, and not even pugilism could fill the theatre. Having lost £10,000 Astley tried to let, and in April 1813 Elliston took over, giving Astley £2,800 for the building and an annuity of £20 a year for life. Astley died the following year.

The theatre was then known as the Olympic Pavilion. Elliston changed the name to Little Drury Lane and opened on 19 Apr. 1813. The Patent Theatres caused him to close, but in Dec. he managed to get a licence and reopened, going back to the old name. This theatre was nearly the scene of Edmund Kean's début, for Elliston had a claim upon him which he ceded to Drury Lane for a small sum. In 1818 Elliston rebuilt the theatre at a cost of £2,500 and engaged a fine company, for which Planché wrote. A year later Elliston became lessee of Drury Lane, and many people lost fortunes by trying their luck at the Olympic. In 1824, having ruined himself at Drury Lane, Elliston sold the Olympic and all its contents for £4,860 to John Scott, builder of the Sans Souci and Adelphi, who ran melodrama there. At the end of 1830 Mme Vestris became Scott's tenant and opened on 3 Jan. 1831 with a drama about Mary Queen of Scots, with Miss Foote as the Queen, and an extravaganza by Planché, called *Olympic Revels*. Her policy of low prices, and light entertainment beautifully staged and played, brought success and made the Olympic a front-rank theatre with a hall-mark of its own. In 1835 Charles J. Mathews first appeared there, and three years later he and Mme Vestris were married. They visited America, and in their absence things went badly at the Olympic, which they left in 1839 to go to Covent Garden. During the next ten years the theatre led a precarious existence. In 1848 Walter Watts, a clerk in the Globe Insurance Company, took it and ran it on the firm's money, introducing Gustavus Brooke to London. On 29 Mar. 1849 it was burned down, and there was a strong suspicion of incendiarism. Watts rebuilt it and opened it again the following year, but it was closed down when he was arrested for enormous defalcations and forgery. George Bolton, who had previously ventured there, tried again and failed, and then Farren, now an old man, moved in with a splendid company which included Mrs. Stirling. He had no success, though during his tenancy Frederick Robson made his first appearance, in 1853, in which year Alfred Wigan became manager. Besides Robson, the great attraction, he engaged Mrs. Stirling and Emery. Wigan retired in 1857 and Robson took over; but his powers failed him, he lost his health, and died in 1864. It was during this period that *The Ticket-of-Leave Man* drew crowded houses.

Horace Wigan then leased the theatre and ran romantic plays, making a small 'Olympic drama' tradition, with himself, Henry Neville, and Kate Terry as the stars. After four years of this Webster succeeded him and produced *The Woman in White*. In 1871 Ada Cavendish became manageress. A large sum was spent on improvements, but the venture was not a success and, though Neville and many others tried their luck, in 1890 the theatre closed. Entirely rebuilt, enlarged, and redecorated, it was opened by Wilson Barrett in Dec. 1890, but he was unfortunate, and in the following year Lago tried opera with a production of 'Eugene Onegin'. This also failed. In 1895 an Anglo-American syndicate produced a version of *The Pilgrim's Progress*, with a ballet and a woman playing the part of Christian on the lines of a Principal Boy. The Olympic finally closed in 1899.　　　　　　　　　w. m. p.

(2) NEW YORK, a handsome theatre at 444 Broadway, on the site of the old Broadway Circus. This was built for H. E. Willard and W. R. Blake and opened on 13 Sept. 1837 with a mixed bill. It was not a success, and it passed through many hands before on 9 Dec. 1839 Mitchell started it on its glorious career as a house for light entertainment—burletta, burlesque, and extravaganza. As Mitchell's Olympic it flourished for over ten years, guying the productions at the big New York playhouses in a constant succession of light-hearted frolics. It even weathered the depression of 1842–3 which proved fatal to many other enterprises, and was the first theatre in New York to play a weekly matinée. Among its outstanding successes were *Hamlet Travestie*, a dramatization of part of *Nicholas Nickleby* with Mitchell as Vincent Crummles and La Petite Céleste as The Infant Phenomenon, burlesques of Fanny Elssler, of *Richard III* with Mitchell as Richard, cad, and later driver, to Omnibus No. 3, of *London Assurance*, and of *The Bohemian Girl* as *The Bohea-Man's Girl*. The season of 1847–8 saw Planché's *The Pride of the Market*, and Chanfrau in *A Glance at New York in 1848*, in which he played Mose, his famous fireman character. In 1849 the theatre was redecorated, but Mitchell was failing in health and took to importing stars. This policy was disastrous, and on 9 Mar. 1850 the Olympic closed abruptly, much to the distress of those who had for so long enjoyed the gaiety and beauty of its productions. After a short spell under Burton the theatre became a home of German drama and finally closed on 25 June 1851. A shop was later built on the site.

(3) On 8 Oct. 1863 Laura Keene's Theatre (see KEENE, LAURA) opened as the Olympic under Mrs. John Wood. Among the plays produced in her first season was Daly's second effort, adapted from Sardou's *Le Papillon*. This management also sponsored the first appearance in New York of Mrs. G. H. Gilbert, later a much-loved star and player of aristocratic dowagers under Daly. She played Sairey Gamp, hitherto considered a man's part. Mrs. Wood's last season was memorable for the début of G. F. Rowe, who appeared as Micawber and Silas Wegg in his own adaptations of Dickens. She had had no settled policy, however, and in 1866 was replaced by Leonard Grover, who presented Joseph Jefferson in Boucicault's version of *Rip Van Winkle*, which had already had some success in London. Later productions at this theatre, which was for some time used for opera, were

A Midsummer Night's Dream with a panorama by Telbin of London, in which Cornelia Jefferson played Titania, Clara Fisher Peasblossom, and G. L. Fox Bottom, and Fox's famous pantomime of *Humpty-Dumpty* with himself as Clown and Emily Rigl as Columbine. This opened on 10 Mar. 1868 and ran for a year. It was followed by another pantomime, by Daly's *Horizon*, with Agnes Ethel, and in 1872 the theatre became a home of variety. It finally closed on 17 Apr. 1880, and was demolished, shops being built on the site.

(4) The New Olympic, New York, a hall built in 1856 on Broadway to house Buckley's Serenaders, was taken over in the following year by Chanfrau, who intended to revive the mixed bills of Mitchell's Olympic. He was unsuccessful, and after a few weeks the theatre became a music-hall, as Buckley's Olympic.

The Anthony Street Theatre was opened in 1812 as the Olympic for one year. There was a circus known as the Olympic Arena in 1858, a short-lived Olympic on Eighth Avenue in 1860, and an Olympic Music-Hall at 600 Broadway on the site of the old Alhambra, which functioned from 1860 to 1861. Wallack's old theatre was renamed the Olympic in 1862 under Fox (see BROADWAY THEATRE).

OMBRES CHINOISES, see SHADOW SHOW.

OMNIBUS BOX, see AUDITORIUM, 3 and BOX.

ONE-ACT PLAY, see AMATEUR THEATRE IN GREAT BRITAIN, CURTAIN-RAISER, and NATION-WIDE THEATRE.

O'NEILL, ELIZA (1791–1827), English actress, who made her first appearance on the stage in her birthplace, Drogheda, where her father was actor-manager of the local theatre. Going to Belfast and Dublin, she soon made a name for herself and in 1814 was engaged on Mathews's recommendation for Covent Garden. Her first appearance as Juliet was overwhelmingly successful and for five years she had a career of unbroken triumph, being particularly admired in comedy—her Lady Teazle was excellent—but appearing also in tragedy. Her reputation stood high, and her worst enemies could accuse her of nothing more than some meanness over money matters. On 13 July 1819 she made her last appearance on the stage as Mrs. Haller in *The Stranger*, and retired to marry Mr. (later Sir William) Becher. On her début she was looked on as the worthy successor of Mrs. Siddons, with less nobility perhaps, but greater sweetness and charm. A classical beauty, with a deep, clear voice, she was much admired by Hazlitt, and her early retirement was a great loss to the stage.

O'NEILL, EUGENE GLADSTONE (1888–   ), American playwright, born in New York City, son of the well-known romantic actor James O'Neill (1847–1920). His early education, which was of a fragmentary nature, was received at various private schools. He attended Princeton University for one year only, took various temporary business jobs, signed as seaman on several voyages to South America, South Africa, and elsewhere, and worked as a reporter on a newspaper in New London, Conn. After a few months' apprentice work there, his health broke down,

my lungs [as he wrote in 1919] being affected, and I spent six months in a sanatorium thinking it over. It was in this enforced period of reflection that the urge to write first came to me. The next fall ... I began my first play—*The Web*. In 1914–15 I was a student in Professor Baker's English 47 at Harvard. The summer of 1916 I spent at Provincetown. It was during that summer the Provincetown Players, who have made the original productions of nearly all my short plays in New York, were first organized.

Although O'Neill had written several one-act plays and a few long ones before 1920, it was not until that year that his first full-length play was professionally produced. This was *Beyond the Horizon*, a starkly effective study in character, laid in rural New England. It was clear, both to the public and to the critics, that the young author was not only a man who was deeply concerned with the more tragic aspects of life, but that he was a playwright of genuine talent and considerable skill. In spite of ill-health, which has continued almost without interruption to the present time, he has been able to devote a large part of his energies and thought to playwriting. By temperament a man who prefers privacy to public life, he has apparently allowed nothing in the external world to interrupt his writing. *Beyond the Horizon* was followed almost immediately by productions of four other plays—a one-act *Exorcism*; *Diff'rent*, a grim bit of dramatic irony in two acts; *The Emperor Jones*, one of his best-known and most popular plays; and an early version of what was to become *Anna Christie*. The last-named (1921) tells the story of a young woman who is, presumably, 'purified' by the love of a man; its popularity was based largely on the romantic and external theatrical qualities of the acting and production. In quick succession other O'Neill plays were brought to the stage—*Gold*, *The Straw*, and *The First Man*—each of them 'failures' with the playgoing public, yet each revealing new aspects of their author's persistent attempts to show life and character honestly and effectively. In 1922 came *The Hairy Ape*, a rather experimental symbolic work which stemmed, according to the author, from *The Emperor Jones* rather than from the work of the European Expressionists, which it in many ways resembles. In 1924 three new plays were produced—*Welded*, *All God's Chillun Got Wings*, and *Desire Under the Elms*. The first, a compact and rather bloodless study in marriage, was a quick failure; the second a moving character study about a Negro and his white wife; and the last the most mature work he had yet written. *Desire Under the Elms*, the scene of which is laid on a New England farm in the 1850s, again shows the dramatist's deep concern with the tortured soul of man under the stress of extreme passion. *The Great God Brown* (1926) was preceded by a romantic, pseudo-historical play about Ponce de Leon and his quest for the Fountain of Youth. This was *The Fountain* (1925), a play that had only a short run. *The Great God Brown* remains to this day one of the most tortuous and complicated of the O'Neill plays. It is a study of the multifarious inter-relationships that exist between a man and his family on the one hand, and a man and his soul (to put it simply) on the other. In the author's own somewhat long explanation of his play, in which he made extensive use of elaborate masks, he says that his 'background pattern of conflicting tides in the soul of Man' should always be 'mystically within and behind them, giving them a significance beyond themselves'. *The Great God Brown*, though it had some success as a stage piece in the theatre, is more interesting and significant as showing the direction of the author's thinking and his dissatisfaction with surface realism as a means of revealing character. *Marco Millions* (1928) is a far more serene work than anything O'Neill had done so far. It is pleasantly ironic and full of comedy and romantic colour, even though it is also a bitter satire on the aggressive business man who has lost touch with beauty and the eternal verities. *Strange Interlude* (1928), a play in nine acts, almost twice the length of an ordinary stage piece, is a work of extraordinary power, and another of the O'Neill plays which, aided somewhat and somewhat confused by the copious use of asides and soliloquies, seeks to probe deep into the usually hidden motives of human character. It is a far cry from the earlier plays, and it shows, for all its digressions, an ever-increasing tendency on the author's part to explain the thoughts and emotional reactions of the characters. In this play and in certain others that followed it, O'Neill seems to have endeavoured to clarify his ideas on the soul of man and the destiny of the human race to the detriment of his art as a playwright. A consideration of his later work, however, will show that he has never wholly neglected the maxim about the proper study of mankind, nor has he ever allowed himself to stray too far away from the fundamental ends of drama as a spectacle of human life. *Lazarus Laughed* (1928) is the author's most pronounced philosophical affirmation of his belief in humanity, a munificent spectacle, its scene laid in ancient Rome. It tells the story of the resurrection of Lazarus and his ultimate triumph over death. 'Fear is no more!', runs the refrain, 'Death is dead!' The play has never been professionally produced in the United States. In 1929 came *Dynamo*, an unsuccessful piece, originally planned as the first part of a trilogy on man's efforts to find a lasting faith. After its production O'Neill decided not to continue with the other two plays. Meantime he had been labouring at another trilogy, *Mourning Becomes Electra*. In many respects his most successful work, it was first seen in 1931. In this impressive tragic work we have a 'retelling of the tragic

tale of Agamemnon and Clytemnestra, Orestes and Electra ... O'Neill has reconceived the old doctrine of Nemesis in terms of the more or less biological and psychological doctrine of cause and effect ... A Puritan has transgressed the moral code of his time and people ... and the son of his victim turns upon the living representatives of his family in order to have revenge.' A nostalgic comedy, *Ah, Wilderness!* (1933), and a somewhat barren and over-intellectualized play about faith, *Days Without End* (1934), followed *Mourning Becomes Electra*; then for twelve years O'Neill retired from the theatre, refusing to allow any of his new work to be staged. But from 1934 until 1946 he did an enormous amount of writing, which included several plays that are parts of a series of nine interrelated plays, and three or four that do not belong to the 'cycle'. In late 1946 *The Iceman Cometh* was seen in New York, where it enjoyed a long run and aroused a vast amount of critical comment. Like its later companion piece, *A Moon for the Misbegotten* (1947), it is partly expository drama and partly a philosophical disquisition on faith. Both plays are technically in the best O'Neill manner, and neither one in any way indicates a diminution of the playwright's grasp of the essentials of his art. They are both clearly the work of a man who from the very first determined, by the help of his extraordinary talent as a craftsman, to illuminate so far as possible the soul of modern man at odds both with his fellowmen and with a world which has fallen far short of the dramatist's conception of what it should be.   B. H. C.

O'NEILL, MAIRE, see ALLGOOD (2).

ON STAGE (in view of the audience, also toward the centre line), see STAGE DIRECTIONS.

O.P. (Opposite Prompt), see STAGE DIRECTIONS.

OPEN AIR THEATRE, LONDON, founded by Sydney Carroll in 1933, is an enclosure in Regent's Park, suitable for the presentation of pastoral plays, by Shakespeare and others. In bad weather plays are given under cover. It is open during the summer months, and has given some excellent productions with well-known actors.

OPERA. A dramatic composition, intended to be represented on the stage, in which vocal and instrumental music plays an essential part. In a stricter sense, opera has been defined as a drama of which every word is sung. This definition, however, would exclude all operas with spoken dialogue, and it is therefore more convenient to make two divisions: operas in which the lyrical parts (airs, duets, &c.) are connected, and the action carried on, by 'recitative', i.e. musical declamation midway between speech and song; and operas in which ordinary spoken dialogue, whether in prose or verse, is used for the connecting passages.

There were operatic elements in many stage

productions long before opera proper came into being, for instance in the Italian pastorals of the Renaissance period, in the English Court masque or in the French *ballet-mascarade* (see BALLET DE COUR, MASQUE, and PASTORAL). Yet, as the American music critic O. G. T. Sonneck has said, 'no historical subtleties will ever succeed in proving that opera really existed before the Florentine Camerata stumbled on it. All the undercurrents of their time might have been converging towards opera, yet of themselves they would not have led to opera without the new element of dramatic musical speech.'

1. ORIGINS. The Camerata was a group of Florentine noblemen, poets, and musicians. One of the objects of their gatherings was the revival, or imitation, of ancient Greek tragedy, which in their opinion had originally been for the greater part recited to music. It was from these literary experiments that accidentally, as it were, the first opera resulted, a short play on the subject of Daphne, the nymph who was loved by Apollo and turned into a laurel. It was written by Ottavio Rinuccini (1562–1621), set to music by Jacopo Peri (1561–1633), and produced at a Florentine palace during the Carnival of 1597–8. A second opera by the same authors followed in 1600, treating for the first time the myth of Orpheus and Eurydice which has remained a favourite operatic subject throughout the centuries. Peri's 'Euridice' music has been preserved, and so has a rival setting by Giulio Caccini (c. 1545–1618). Judging from these early scores, it can be said that the music was definitely subordinate to the words (or libretto), and was intended to heighten and intensify the poetry rather than to achieve an importance of its own. Luckily for the future development of opera, the next composer to try his hand at the new genre was a musician of genius, Claudio Monteverdi (1567–1643), who realized its immense possibilities and in his 'Orfeo' (1607) produced a masterpiece which in the course of the centuries has lost nothing of its dramatic power and beauty.

In the first forty years of operatic history operas were written and produced, not with any regularity, but for special occasions only. The form developed on a broader and more popular basis from 1637, when the first opera-house was opened to the general public in Venice. This was followed by a dozen others in the course of the seventeenth century. There were regular opera seasons, and schools of composers, librettists, stage-painters, and singers came into being. Venetian operas were exported to other towns where in turn local theatres were built and local schools originated. Within a few decades opera was safely and permanently established all over Italy, having reached Naples in 1651 and Palermo in 1658.

Between 1637 and the close of the century 360 operas by 66 composers were produced at Venice alone. Their names are of merely antiquarian interest to-day, as are the names of the early librettists, adroit craftsmen who knew exactly what the public wanted—ingenious

plots with a vivid historical background, the more complicated the better, with an invariably happy ending, generally achieved by a *deus ex machinâ*. Above all, these libretti were full of opportunities for the painter and the engineer to work their miracles. The seventeenth century was the great age of scenic art and stage machinery, and the richest effects and most startling inventions were reserved for opera. The brothers Parigi represent the first generation of artists who worked for opera. The comparative simplicity of their designs corresponds to the classical attitude of the early Florentine scores. Among the Venetians Giacomo Torelli (1608–78), called by his contemporaries 'il gran stregone'—the great wizard —held first place.

The subjects of the earliest operas were myths and legends drawn from Homer, Virgil, and Ovid. The epic poems of Tasso and Ariosto were other sources of inspiration. Monteverdi's 'Incoronazione di Poppea' (1642) was the first opera founded on history, and from that time onwards history and romance yielded an inexhaustible supply of Greek and Roman, Oriental and Nordic, kings, queens, and generals and their followers, enemies, and slaves. The plots grew more complicated from year to year; in 1662 an opera on the subject of Hercules had 33 singing characters, and in 1671 one on Darius had 15 changes of scenery, all compressed into the customary three acts.

Towards the end of the seventeenth century the influence of the great French dramatists, Corneille and Racine, makes itself felt, particularly in the libretti of the first literary reformer of the operatic stage, Apostolo Zeno (1668–1750). He tried to bring some order into the confusion of the degenerate libretti of the period, by observing to a certain extent the (French) Aristotelian unities of time, place, and action, by restricting the number of characters, and by suppressing the scenic extravagances. Zeno's reform became convention in the hands of his famous successor, Pietro Metastasio (1698–1782). No words of any man were ever set to music as often as his. He wrote only about thirty different libretti, but there were more than a thousand settings of them between 1724 and 1840. Practically every operatic composer of the eighteenth century used one or more of his libretti. His lyrics are of great poetic beauty, and attracted musicians like Handel, Gluck, and Mozart.

2. DEVELOPMENT. Italian opera first crossed the Alps as early as 1618. The first stopping-place was Vienna, which, under the Emperor Leopold I, became, next to Venice, the most important operatic centre of the seventeenth century. It was here that Lodovico Burnacini (1636–1707) worked, the greatest representative of stage baroque at its richest and most typical. From Vienna Italian opera spread to Munich, Dresden, and Hanover, and by 1750 there was no German Court without its Italian company, complete with composer, poet, painter, and singers. Nor was the foreign influence limited to Austria and Germany.

Brussels, Amsterdam, and Warsaw had Italian opera before 1700; London and Madrid, Stockholm and Lisbon, Copenhagen and St. Petersburg followed in the eighteenth century. On the artistic side, the members of the Galli-Bibiena family must be mentioned here. One of them worked at almost every European Court at some time or other. To Ferdinando Galli-Bibiena (1657–1743) belong the innovations in diagonal perspective (see SCENERY) which took the place of the central perspective as used in the seventeenth century, and opened up undreamed-of possibilities for stage effects of all kinds. Ferdinando's son Giuseppe (1696–1757) was the first to use, in 1723, transparent scenery lighted from behind (see BIBIENA).

3. FRANCE. A notable exception to this Italian cult was France, where in 1671 the *Académie Royale des Opéras* was inaugurated. Its first great composer and absolute musical ruler, Jean-Baptiste Lully (1632–87), though a native of Florence, never set any but French words to music, and his literary collaborator, Philippe Quinault (1635–88), holds a place of honour in French drama. Together they established a tradition which lasted for well over a hundred years. Under Lully's successors, particularly Jean-Philippe Rameau (1683–1764), French opera developed independently of Italian influence. Features of the *tragédie-lyrique* of this time are its frequent choruses and elaborate dances. A typical French product which came into vogue about 1700 was the *opéra-ballet*, divided into scenes, or 'entrées', with alternate singing and dancing, the whole loosely held together by a unifying theme (see MOLIÈRE).

4. ITALY. In Italy meanwhile the centre of operatic activity had passed from Venice to Naples. Under the leadership of the great Alessandro Scarlatti (1660–1725) the southern capital had become the source which supplied the whole of Europe with an unending stream of gifted musicians, composers, instrumentalists, and, above all, singers. While Venetian opera at its worst had been a mere pretext for the antics of the scenic designer, Neapolitan opera tended more and more to be dominated completely by the voice. The 'spectacle for the eye' turned into a 'concert in costume'. The positive achievements of the school of Naples (including the rise of comic opera) should not be underrated; but the final results of its influence upon serious opera proved disastrous.

Famous prima donnas and even more celebrated castrato singers (like Senesino and Farinelli) aroused a general adoration which, particularly in the case of the castrati, it is difficult to understand to-day. In time, the superficial cult of the voice began to overshadow all other considerations. Composers were expected to provide constant opportunities for the star singers to show off their trills and graces. The librettist mattered least of all—if indeed there was one, for the greater part of Italian operas produced between 1720 and 1760 consisted of settings of existing dramas by Zeno, Metastasio, and a few others. Audiences

paid scarcely any attention to the action, chatted through the recitatives, and waited for the arias, which they knew by heart. A new type of opera developed, called *pasticcio*—a pie—made up of favourite airs strung together on a thin thread of recitative by some local hack composer.

It was against these abuses that the reforms of Christoph Willibald Gluck (1714–87) were directed. His experiences as a travelling conductor must have shown him how far the opera of his time had deviated from the ideals once set forth by the Florentines and by Monteverdi. In the poet Raniero da Calzabigi (1714–95) he found a congenial librettist, and 'Orfeo' (1762) was the first-fruit of their collaboration. The preface to the score of 'Alceste' (1767) embodies the principles of Gluck's musical-dramatic creed, the return to a pure and noble representation of character and sentiment, regardless of sensual gratification, preferring, as it were, 'the Muses to the Sirens'. In 1774 Gluck went to Paris, where since the death of Rameau the *Académie* was without a musical leader, and his later works, especially 'Iphigénie en Tauride' (1779), gave a new impulse to French opera. Gluck's personal style could not easily be imitated, and there were no immediate repercussions; but slowly his ideas gained ground, and his influence is clearly discernible in the general high standard of opera in Paris, Vienna, and some Italian towns at the time of his death.

5. COMIC OPERA. After some isolated early instances, a steady development of comic opera is first observed in Naples at the beginning of the eighteenth century. For some time Neapolitan composers and playwrights had specialized in adapting Venetian opera to local taste by adding comic scenes which were placed at the ends of the acts. Though at first they were connected with the main plot, the tendency was to make them more and more independent, until at last they became little operas in themselves, called *intermezzi*, performed between the acts of the serious opera. More often than not they formed the most popular part of the evening's entertainment and were gradually introduced into other operas, or detached altogether. The most famous example is 'La Serva Padrona' (1733), with music by Giovanni Battista Pergolesi (1710–36), which soon became a stock piece for travelling companies.

The visit of a comic opera or opera buffa company to Paris in 1752 gave a decisive start to French *opéra-comique*, which had itself developed from the *pièces en vaudevilles* (the equivalent of the English ballad opera, with spoken dialogue). Jean-Jacques Rousseau (1712–78) wrote his *intermède* 'Le Devin du village' (1752) in direct imitation of Italian intermezzi, and the success achieved by this little piece gave rise to a whole school of similar ones, written by such excellent dramatists as Favart, Anseaume, and Sedaine, and set to music by composers like François André Philidor (1726–95) and André Grétry (1742–1813). In Italy, meanwhile, the intermezzi had grown into three-act comic operas, the popularity of which increased from year to year. The Venetian playwright Carlo

Goldoni (1707–93) lifted the somewhat primitive Neapolitan types to a higher literary level, and his character-comedies attracted the best contemporary musicians. Giovanni Paisiello (1740–1816), who wrote on the Barber of Seville thirty years before Rossini, and Domenico Cimarosa (1749–1801), whose 'Matrimonio segreto' (1792) still holds the stage, were the most brilliant representatives of Italian opera buffa at the end of the eighteenth century.

6. ENGLAND. The general attitude of England towards opera is commented on in *The Gentleman's Journal* for 1693: 'Operas abroad are plays where every word is sung; this is not rellished in England.' But before this time there had been some very original English solutions of the operatic problem. Davenant's *The Siege of Rhodes* (1656, music by Locke and others) is regarded by some authorities as the first English opera, and was called a 'representation by the art of prospective in scenes and the story sung in recitative musick'. Two little chamber operas, the 'Venus and Adonis' (c. 1684) of John Blow (1649–1708) and Purcell's 'Dido and Aeneas' (c. 1689), show a perfection of style completely untouched by the influence of foreign models. Henry Purcell (1659–95) might have become the Lully of his country but for his untimely death, as is shown by the excellence of his other two important stage works, 'King Arthur' (1691) and 'The Fairy Queen' (1692).

The further history of English opera is a series of scattered attempts rather than a steady progression. This is partly due to the fact that in 1705 Italian opera was established in London, and that the overpowering personality of George Frederick Handel (1685–1759) and the bulk of his thirty-five Italian operas stood in the way of a parallel development of opera in English. An occasional success like the 'Artaxerxes' (1762) of Thomas Arne (1710–78) (on his own translation of Metastasio's libretto 'Artaserse') merely serves to emphasize the fact that England had no serious opera fit to compare with that of Italy and France.

7. BALLAD OPERA. An entirely novel contribution to the musical stage was Gay's *Beggar's Opera* (1728), a play with music arranged by John Christopher Pepusch (1667–1752). This was the first and best example of the ballad opera, a play of popular and often topical character with spoken dialogue and a large number of songs fitted to existing tunes. After a few years of unbroken success the new genre disappeared as suddenly as it had sprung up; but traces of it remained in the English theatre, in plays which contained a good deal of compiled music, as, for example, Sheridan's *The Duenna* (1775). Among the dramatists who took an active interest in the progress of English opera were many illustrious writers, from Dryden and Addison to Fielding, Garrick, and Sheridan. The most famous English scene-painter of operatic scenery was a pupil of Inigo Jones, John Webb (1611–72), who painted the scenery for *The Siege of Rhodes*. The designs for it still exist. James Thornhill (1675–1734), father-in-

law of Hogarth, painted the scenery for one of the earliest operas in the Italian style produced in London, 'Arsinoe' (1705), arranged by Thomas Clayton (c. 1670–c. 1730).

8. GERMANY. Disregarding some isolated earlier attempts, German opera began in 1678, when the first regular opera-house in Hamburg opened its doors. It was here that young Handel started on his operatic career. The prolific Reinhard Keiser (1674–1739) was the chief composer. After 1700 Italian airs began to creep into German opera, and from that time onwards there was a steady decline towards the *pasticcio* until in 1738 German opera was abandoned altogether and an Italian company took over. About 1750 the German *Singspiel* originated as a popular reaction against the absolute reign of the Italians; at the beginning it was little more than a play with incidental songs, in imitation of the English ballad opera and the French *opéra-comique*. With Mozart's 'Die Entführung aus dem Serail' (1782) the genre reached its artistic peak; in a more elaborate form it was carried on well into the nineteenth century. Among the German dramatists interested in the *Singspiel* must be mentioned Goethe, who provided a few libretti for it.

9. MOZART. The various styles and tendencies of eighteenth-century opera came to a head in the work of Wolfgang Amadeus Mozart (1756–91). Mozart was not a revolutionary innovator. He did not break with tradition, he rather used what was good in it as a foundation upon which to build. His first opera on a large scale, 'Idomeneo' (1781), seems to fulfil Gluck's ideal in a new and youthful spirit, while 'La Clemenza di Tito' (1791) (libretto by Metastasio) brings the old-type Italian serious opera to a dignified conclusion. The somewhat feeble genre of the German *Singspiel* culminates in 'Die Entführung aus dem Serail' (1782), while the progress of Italian comic opera is crowned by the masterpieces of 'Le Nozze di Figaro' (1786) and 'Così fan tutte' (1790). 'Don Giovanni' (1787) stands by itself, a tragi-comedy which has no parallel in musical drama, and 'Die Zauberflöte' (1791), though rooted in age-old traditions of the Viennese fair and puppet-shows, prophetically heralds the romantic opera of the future. The scope and variety of Mozart's work has never been surpassed, not even by Gluck, Wagner, or Verdi, who all reached twice Mozart's age, for like Purcell and Pergolesi, Mozart, 'beloved of the gods', died young.

10. ROMANTIC OPERA. The fifty years between the death of Mozart and the rise of Wagner may conveniently be labelled the age of romantic opera, although the main stream is not always clearly visible among a number of tributary currents. Operatic fashions were now dictated from Paris. The French Revolution had given a startling impulse to opera, as to the theatre in general. There was no great master in Paris worthy to be called the successor of Gluck; but there were many talented composers and dramatists, men full of ideas and

imagination who grasped the demands of the new era, Frenchmen as well as emigrated Italians like Luigi Cherubini (1760–1842), attracted by the vigorous musical life of the capital of the new republic. Dozens of new theatres were opened in Paris between 1791 and 1805, many of them devoted to opera in some form, and to them flocked a new public to whom the gods of mythology and the shepherds of Arcady meant nothing. They wanted to see full-blooded heroes, villains, and lovers, melodramatic stories and effects, exciting rescues from tyranny, noble bandit chiefs, haunted castles, and subterranean dungeons. The English 'Gothic' novels of Ann Radcliffe and 'Monk' Lewis exercised a strong influence on French revolutionary opera.

Napoleon severely restricted the number of theatres; the opera of his Empire is marked by a short revival of classicism, and by imperialistic works on a grandiose scale such as the 'Fernand Cortez' (1809) of Gasparo Spontini (1774–1851). This was the forerunner of what is now generally called French grand opera, by which is meant the lavish and spectacular operas of Auber (1782–1871) ('La Muette de Portici', 1828), Halévy (1799–1862) ('La Juive', 1835), and, most typical, Meyerbeer (1791–1864) ('Les Huguenots', 1836). The romantic movement was carried on at the Opéra-Comique by a number of highly successful operas with spoken dialogue, of which Boïeldieu's (1775–1834) 'La Dame blanche', Auber's 'Fra Diavolo', and Hérold's (1791–1833) 'Zampa' are the best examples. On the literary side mention must be made of Eugène Scribe (1791–1861), a prolific and proficient dramatist. His libretti were coveted and set to music by the greatest composers of his time, and he helped to make French opera a model of theatrical effectiveness and accomplishment.

The different types of French opera were duly taken up and imitated in Germany and, to a lesser degree, in Italy and other countries. Ludwig van Beethoven's (1770–1827) solitary contribution to the lyric stage, 'Fidelio' (1805), is, as far as the literary material is concerned, directly derived from a French source, a typical rescue-story set in an operatic Spain of an indefinite period, but filled with very real characters of the composer's own time, and expressing his personal feelings and ideals. For the first time in its history German opera gained general recognition with 'Der Freischütz' of Carl Maria von Weber (1786–1826). On its appearance in 1821 the work was hailed as the fulfilment of the old German desire for a national opera, and it has remained a favourite of the people ever since, with the strong popular appeal of its rural setting against a folk-lore background, its melodious freshness, and the highly dramatic scene in the Wolf's Glen. A more sombre, supernatural element is predominant in the operas of Heinrich Marschner (1795–1861) ('Der Vampyr', 1828, and 'Hans Heiling', 1833), which form the perfect historical link between Weber and the early Wagner. Italian opera of this period is represented by

the works of Gioacchino Rossini (1792–1868), Vincenzo Bellini (1801–1835), and Gaetano Donizetti (1797–1848), but it is only in a limited sense that the term 'romantic' can be applied to some of them, although the novels of Walter Scott were largely exploited by Italian librettists, as they were also in France and Germany. Then, as always, Italian opera was foremost a singers' opera, and opportunities for vocal display were more important than dramatic subtleties. Most of Rossini's florid and brilliant operas which took the world by storm are now forgotten outside Italy; but his 'Barbiere di Siviglia' (1816) will live on as the last masterly manifestation of the true eighteenth-century buffo spirit of which there is no more than a pale reflection in Donizetti's 'Elisir d'Amore' (1832) and 'Don Pasquale' (1843). Of serious works of this time, Bellini's 'La Sonnambula' and 'Norma' (both 1831) and Donizetti's 'Lucia di Lammermoor' (1835) are still in the Italian repertory. The chief librettist of this period was Felice Romani (1788–1865), who undoubtedly had a flair for well-woven plots and effective situations.

The most important English romantic opera was the work of a foreigner, Weber's 'Oberon', produced at Covent Garden in 1826. An English school may be dated from John Barnett's (1802–90) 'Mountain Sylph' (1834) and is best represented by Michael William Balfe's (1808–70) 'Bohemian Girl' (1843) and William Vincent Wallace's (1812–65) 'Maritana' (1845), unpretentious works of popular appeal which were also successful on the continent. Musically they speak the universal European language of their time, the Donizetti-Auber idiom. As in Germany, development was seriously hampered by the lack of good libretti, and the effusions of Edward Fitzball (1792–1873) and Alfred Bunn (1798–1860) helped largely to discredit English opera at home and abroad.

11. WAGNER. The second half of the nineteenth century is dominated by the powerful personality of Richard Wagner (1813–83), and by his peculiar creation, the music-drama. There never was—and probably never will be —another opera composer whose work stood for fifty years and more in the centre of heated controversy everywhere, and who divided the whole musical world into two camps, ardent adherents and bitter enemies. As a result of his unceasing struggles, opera was at last taken seriously, not only by a small circle but by the general public, as seriously as Handel's 'Messiah' or Beethoven's Ninth Symphony. Wagner never had to rely upon the whims of a literary collaborator; from the beginning he wrote the words as well as the scores of his music-dramas, a fact which may partly account for the perfect unity of thought and expression found in the best of them. His 'Rienzi' (1842) is an historical grand opera in the florid style of Meyerbeer, and the three operas that followed, 'Der fliegende Holländer' (1843), 'Tannhäuser' (1845), and 'Lohengrin' (1850), to-day appear as the natural outcome of the German romantic movement. With 'Tristan und Isolde'

(1865), still the most revolutionary work in the whole history of opera, Wagner completely breaks away from operatic traditions and conventions, to return to them again, at least in part, in 'Die Meistersinger' (1868). The tetralogy of 'Der Ring des Nibelungen' ('Das Rheingold', 'Die Walküre', 'Siegfried', and 'Götterdämmerung', 1869–76) and the 'sacred festival play' of 'Parsifal' (1882) complete the list of his works.

The purely musical features of Wagner's reform (and there are many, including the famous *leitmotif*) do not here concern us. On the dramatic side may be mentioned the abandoning of the chorus (completely achieved only in parts of 'Der Ring des Nibelungen') and the abolishing of 'set numbers' by substituting a continuous flow of melody for the old alternation of recitative and air. Wagner dreamed of a *Gesamtkunstwerk*—a unity of all arts in the service of music-drama—and never have an artist's dreams come truer than his. In 1876 he built the Festspielhaus at Bayreuth, an opera-house devoted exclusively to his own works, where he controlled singers, conductors, instrumentalists, and scenic artists, chosen by himself and performing before an enthusiastic and faithful audience. He was his own composer, librettist, and producer, and the complicated machinery called for in many of his operas was contrived and executed according to his own plans. So was the scenery, but as this was unfortunately one of the worst periods in the history of German fine arts, the reproductions of the original settings appear to-day repulsive in their Teutonic realism. Professor Dent in 1940 drew attention once again to the theories and designs of the Swiss artist Adolphe Appia, made about 1896, as a solution of the difficult problems confronting the modern producer of 'Der Ring des Nibelungen'.

The number of Wagner's imitators in Germany and elsewhere is legion. Hundreds of pompous and ambitious music-dramas, complete with heavy orchestration and elaborate leitmotifs, bear testimony to his overwhelming influence. They were soon forgotten, and of all the many German operas written in the shadow of the master, there are perhaps only two which still live, the 'Barbier von Bagdad' (1858) by Peter Cornelius (1824–74), and 'Hänsel und Gretel' (1893) by Engelbert Humperdinck (1854–1921). What survives of European opera composed between 1850 and 1900 are those works which were hardly influenced by Wagnerism or were written in conscious or unconscious revolt against it. There is certainly nothing of Wagner in the most successful French opera of the period, the 'Carmen' (1875) of Georges Bizet (1838–75), a colourful and passionate drama of love and jealousy which became the starting-point for the Italian school of 'Verismo', best known through Pietro Mascagni's (1863–1945) 'Cavalleria Rusticana' (1890) and Ruggiero Leoncavallo's (1858–1919) 'Pagliacci' (1892). A typical French product of the nineteenth century is the *drame-lyrique*, represented by such works as Ambroise Tho-

mas's (1811–96) 'Mignon' (1866) and Charles Gounod's (1818–93) 'Faust' (1859), culminating in the sentimental charm of Jules Massenet's (1842–1912) 'Manon' (1884). Mention should be made too of Hector Berlioz (1803–69), whose chief operatic work, 'Les Troyens' (1863), stands by itself, indebted, if to anyone, to the great Gluck.

12. VERDI. The most important contemporary of Wagner was the Italian Giuseppe Verdi (1813–1901), who succeeded in erecting, under the eyes of his German rival, an operatic kingdom of his own, not perhaps of the same unity and consistency, but no less impressive in its proportions and infinite variety. Verdi started his career about 1840 as a rival of Donizetti, Saverio Mercadante (1795–1870), and Giovanni Pacini (1796–1867), but he was soon recognized as the greatest Italian master of the century. Nearly all his libretti were taken from literary works of a high standard—from Shakespeare, Schiller, Byron, Hugo—and the composer's letters show his keen interest and active co-operation in their shaping, down to the smallest detail. 'Macbeth' (1847), 'Rigoletto' (1851), and 'La Traviata' (1853) are perhaps the most significant works of Verdi's middle period. In 'Don Carlos' (1867) he paid tribute to France, while 'Aida' (1871) is a magnificent example of Italian grand opera, the splendour of which has never been surpassed. In his last operas, 'Othello' (1887) and 'Falstaff' (1893), Verdi reached truly Shakespearian depths of passion and heights of humour; in the dramatist Arrigo Boito (1842–1918), himself an opera composer of some importance ('Mefistofele' 1868), Verdi found the perfect literary collaborator.

13. SLAVONIC OPERA. It is at this period that east European opera comes to the fore for the first time. About the middle of the nineteenth century national schools of opera had sprung up in many countries, inspired by native poetry, folk-lore, and folk-music. While the Hungarian operas of Ferenc Erkel (1810–93) and the Polish operas of Stanislaw Moniuszko (1819–72) are little known outside their own countries, Czechoslovakia scored an international success with 'The Bartered Bride' (1866) by Bedřich Smetana (1824–84), a simple tale of Bohemian peasant life produced a year later than Wagner's 'Tristan und Isolde', and as un-Tristanlike as possible. Smetana wrote many other successful operas, as did his younger contemporary, Antonín Dvořák (1841–1904). (For a further note on Czech opera see CZECHOSLOVAKIA, 2.) In Russia, after feeble attempts in the eighteenth century which came to nothing, a national school of opera started with Michael Glinka's (1804–57) 'A Life for the Czar' (1836) (known also as 'Ivan Susanin'), and among the greatest achievements of Russian opera are Modest Mussorgsky's (1839–81) 'Boris Godunov' (1874), a stirring musical drama taken from Russian history, Peter Tchaikovsky's (1840–93) 'Eugene Onegin' (1879), and the scores of Nicholas Rimsky-Korsakov (1844–1908) and Alexander Borodin (1833–87),

full of vivid oriental colouring. The chief sources of inspiration for many of these operas were the poems and plays of the great Russian poet, Alexander Pushkin (1799–1837).

14. LIGHT OPERA. Another form of anti-Wagnerian reaction was the rise of light opera which began in Paris, where the *opéra-bouffe* of Jacques Offenbach (1819–80) and his successors ousted *opéra-comique* of the old style. Parallel movements in other countries caused the rise of the Spanish *zarzuela*, the Viennese waltz operetta of Johann Strauss (1825–99), and the Savoy operas of Sir William Schwenck Gilbert (1836–1911) and Sir Arthur Sullivan (1842–1900), a model of collaboration between librettist and composer. After 1900 there came a general decline of all the lighter genres towards musical comedy and revue.

15. MODERN OPERA. Wagner, and Verdi in his last works, had shown the importance of the literary side of opera, which should be something more than a mere libretto. As few musicians were able to equal Wagner in this respect, or to find a second Boito, composers of the early twentieth century took to using existing dramas of high literary quality, as they stood, a method which seems to have been first employed by the Russian composer Alexander Dargomizhsky (1813–69) in 1868, with 'The Stone Guest', based on Pushkin's play of that name. This was produced after the composer's death, in 1872. Richard Strauss (1864–1949), the outstanding German opera composer after Wagner, set Oscar Wilde's (1856–1900) *Salome* in a German translation (1905), and four years later *Elektra* by Hugo von Hofmannsthal (1874–1929), thus inaugurating a collaboration which continued with 'Der Rosenkavalier' (1911), 'Ariadne auf Naxos' (1912), and other works. Claude Debussy (1862–1918) was attracted by the mystic symbolism of Maurice Maeterlinck (1862–1949) and in 'Pelléas et Mélisande' (1902) created the masterpiece of modern impressionistic French music; the same poet's *Ariane et Barbe-Bleue* was set by Paul Dukas (1865–1935) in 1907. In Italy, Gabriele d'Annunzio's (1863–1938) plays were used by Ildebrando Pizzetti (1880–   ) and others, while one of the most-discussed operas of modern times, Alban Berg's (1885–1935) 'Wozzeck' (1925), is a setting of a play by Georg Büchner (1813–37) written in 1836. The modern opera composer with the greatest popular appeal, Giacomo Puccini (1858–1924), proceeded in the old manner, and had libretti written to order. The world success of 'La Bohème' (1896), 'La Tosca' (1900), and 'Madame Butterfly' (1904) is partly due to the skill of his literary collaborators, Giuseppe Giacosa (1847–1906) and Luigi Illica (1857–1919).

After the First World War of 1914–18 there was a great revival of interest in opera, and conditions were very favourable for young and progressive composers and for experiments of all kinds. National opera-houses were opened in all the new states of Europe from the Baltic to the Balkans, and international festivals at Salzburg, Baden-Baden, Florence, Glyndebourne, and elsewhere fostered the cause of opera. Strauss and Debussy had shown that there were unthought-of possibilities of creating something new and successful even after Wagner and Verdi, and about 1920 opera composers started a hectic search for ways that would lead beyond Strauss and Debussy to an opera of the future. Strauss himself, in 'Ariadne' (1912) and 'Intermezzo' (1924), hinted at possible directions, away from romantic subjects, back to the eighteenth century or forward to the realism of the machine age.

New slogans and battle-cries followed one another in quick succession. New forms of opera, or forms similar to opera, were tried out by the Russian Igor Stravinsky (1882–   ), the Austrian Arnold Schönberg (1874–1951), the German Paul Hindemith (1895–   ), the Frenchman Darius Milhaud (1892–   ), the Italian Francesco Malipiero (1882–   ), the Spaniard Manuel de Falla (1876–1946), the Czech Ernst Křenek (1900–   ), the Hungarian Bela Bartók (1881–1945), the Swiss Arthur Honegger (1892–   ), the Englishman Ralph Vaughan Williams (1872–   ), the American Virgil Thomson (1896–   ), to mention but one composer of each country. Old forms, long discarded, opera-oratorio, opera-ballet, monodrama, ballad opera, were revived and adapted to the new spirit, and the customary forms were carried on by composers who chose as their starting-point either Wagner, as did Franz Schreker (1878–1934) and Rutland Boughton (1878–   ), Strauss, as did Ottorino Respighi (1879–1936), Debussy, as did Maurice Ravel (1875–1937), or who took traditional elements from their own countries' musical past, as did Ermanno Wolf-Ferrari (1876–1948) in Italy, Benjamin Britten (1913–   ) in England, Zóltan Kodály (1882–   ) in Hungary, Leoš Janáček (1854–1928) and Jaromir Weinberger (1896–   ) in Czechoslovakia, Dmitri Shostakovich (1906–   ) and Ivan Dzerjinsky (1909–   ) in Russia.

These different manifestations of energy had not yet been directed into distinct channels when the Second World War broke out in 1939. There was not time between the two conflicts for a new main style to take shape, and no one can venture to form an opinion of twentieth-century opera, nor foretell what direction it will take.   A. L.

OPERA COMIQUE, LONDON. This theatre stood in the East Strand, near the old Globe (see GLOBE THEATRE, 2). The two playhouses were back to back, and were known as the Rickety Twins. It was badly built and was probably erected in the hope of compensation when the expected improvements led to the replanning and rebuilding of the district around. It had as entrance long narrow tunnels from three thoroughfares, and was frequently referred to as Theatre Royal, Tunnels. It was so draughty that the audience could not sit in comfort, and many of them caught cold. In case of fire its stairs would have occasioned much loss of life, but, like its companion the Globe, it was never burned down, for which playgoers of the time had much reason to be grateful. Its very name was a mistake, for the public did not take to a foreign title. It opened in 1871 with a musical play, based on Molière and called by the clumsy title of *The Doctor in Spite of Himself*, with music by D'Oyly Carte, which was a failure. Then the company of the Comédie-Française, driven from Paris by the Franco-Prussian war, played there, their first appearance outside France in the whole of their history. In 1873 Ristori appeared there, and then followed the famous Gilbert and Sullivan partnership, which had started at the Royalty with *Trial by Jury*. In Nov. 1877 appeared *The Sorcerer*, followed by *H.M.S. Pinafore*, *The Pirates of Penzance*, and *Patience*, which was later transferred to D'Oyly Carte's new theatre, the Savoy. With this the short heyday of the theatre closed, and the last production was seen there in 1899.   w. m. p.

OPERA HOUSE, New York, see GRAND OPERA HOUSE and NATIONAL THEATRE (1).

OPITZ, MARTIN (1597–1639), German author of a short handbook of poetics which turned the attention of his contemporaries to the classics, France, and Italy, and so brought about a break with the native theatre tradition, replacing it with a somewhat lifeless academic literature. He himself translated a number of Seneca's plays, and some Italian plays, into stately but monotonous alexandrines.

O.P. RIOTS, see COVENT GARDEN.

ORANGE MOLL, see MEGGS.

ORANGE STREET THEATRE, London, in Chelsea, a private theatre, used by amateurs about 1831.

ORATOR, the name given in the early French theatre to the actor—usually the most distinguished member of the company—who drew up the playbill, and at the end of each performance addressed the audience, telling them what play would be given next, offering a graceful compliment to any royal or eminent visitor, and giving out any notices of general theatrical interest. He was often called on to quell riots, or silence interrupters, and the position called for wit, courage, and good-humour as well as authority and prestige. Among the early actors who filled the position were Montdory, Floridor, Laroque, Molière, and his successor La Grange.

ORCHESTRA. In the Elizabethan theatre the musicians sat aloft in a small gallery in the tiring-house and above the inner stage. In the Restoration theatre, though Killigrew tried unsuccessfully to bring them to the ground, they were housed in a box over the proscenium opening. In Georgian times the orchestra finally achieved the pit, or well, in front of and somewhat below the stage, which they now occupy, unless ousted by mechanical music (see also INCIDENTAL MUSIC).

ORCHESTRA STALLS, see AUDITORIUM, 3 and STALLS.

ORCHESTRA, THEATRE, see INCIDENTAL MUSIC.

ORIENTAL THEATRE, LONDON, a music-hall in Poplar which became a theatre in 1867. It was later called the Albion, and was used for melodrama for some time. It then reverted again to a music-hall as the Queen's Palace of Varieties.

ORRERY, LORD (Roger Boyle, first Earl of Orrery) (1621–79), a Restoration nobleman and man of letters, to whom Dryden generously, though not perhaps accurately, gave the credit for first writing rhymed heroic drama. He started his career as a dramatist by writing some forgotten comedies, but adopted the heroic theme of 'love and honour' in his later and more successful plays, notably *Mustapha* (1665) and *The Black Prince* (1667). These, and one or two other plays by him, are useful in their printed versions on account of their detailed stage directions.

OSTLER, WILLIAM (?–1614), a boy-actor with the Children of the Chapel Royal, who appeared in *The Poetaster* in 1601. As an adult he was taken on by the King's Men, with whom he appeared in *The Alchemist* and was the original Antonio in *The Duchess of Malfi*. His excellent reputation is attested by a contemporary epigram which calls him 'sole King of Actors'. He married the daughter of Heminge, joint-editor of Shakespeare's plays, in 1611, and had shares in both the Globe and Blackfriars, which Heminge tried to acquire from his widow.

OSTROVSKY, ALEXANDER NIKOLAIVICH (1823–86), Russian dramatist, who was born in Moscow and studied law at the University. He left before qualifying, and spent the next five years as a clerk in the Moscow Juvenile and Commercial Courts. Both there, and at home —his father was a lawyer with many clients among business men—he was able to study the merchant class, and so gathered the material for his plays, realistic studies of corruption and sharp practice, which have earned him the title of 'the Balzac of the Muscovite merchant'. He first came into prominence in 1848, as the author of *The Bankrupt* (later renamed *It's All in the Family*), an outspoken commentary on the faked bankruptcy of certain commercial magnates which lost him his job. It was banned for thirteen years, but circulated in manuscript and through private readings. After this Ostrovsky wrote a number of historical plays, a fairy-play which served as the basis for the libretto of Rimsky-Korsakov's opera 'Snow-Maiden', and finally the series of realistic contemporary satires by which he is best known.

Some of these have been translated into English, a difficult task owing to the richness and local colouring of Ostrovsky's style. They include *Even a Wise Man Stumbles* (also known as *Enough Stupidity in Every Wise Man*), *Easy Money*, and *Wolves and Sheep*, published in 1944 in a translation by David Magarshack; the second of these is based on *The Taming of the Shrew*. But the best-known of Ostrovsky's plays outside his own country is *The Storm*, a study in religious intolerance.

Most of Ostrovsky's plays were produced at the Maly Theatre in Moscow, where he found a champion and ideal interpreter in the actor Prov Sadovsky. In return he championed the stage, and in 1882 wrote a memorandum on the People's Theatres, urging the establishment of a National Theatre. He also founded the Society of Russian Playwrights, and in 1885 was appointed manager of the Moscow Imperial Theatres.

The statue of Ostrovsky is at the entrance to the Maly—as is the bust of Molière in the entrance to the Comédie-Française—each man commemorated by the theatre he had made so peculiarly his own.

OTWAY, THOMAS (1652–85), English dramatist, who was educated at Winchester and Oxford, and in 1670 made his first and last appearance on the stage in Aphra Behn's *The Forced Marriage*. Disappointed in his ambition to be an actor, he turned to playwriting, and in 1675 produced *Alcibiades*, a tragedy which provided Mrs. Barry with her first great part. Otway was madly in love with her, though she gave him no encouragement, and in 1678, after the production of *Don Carlos*, a tragedy in rhymed verse, and a comedy entitled *Friendship in Fashion*, he enlisted in the army and went to Holland. Back in London, he returned to playwriting, and produced his two finest tragedies, *The Orphan; or, The Unhappy Marriage* (1680), and *Venice Preserved; or, a Plot Discovered* (1681), in both of which Betterton and Mrs. Barry appeared. They have been often revived, and contain some of the finest poetry of the day. Otway has been called 'an Elizabethan born out of his time', and his best work certainly shows a greater depth and sincerity, coupled with fine writing, than any other writing of the period. He was highly esteemed by his contemporaries. One of his most successful plays was his translation of *Les Fourberies de Scapin*. This was given at Dorset Garden as an after-piece to his *Titus and Berenice* (1676) (based on Racine), which remained on the London stage until 1812, and was played even later at the minor theatres and in the provinces.

O.U.D.S., see OXFORD.

OUVILLE, ANTOINE LE METEL D' (*c.* 1590–1656/77), French dramatist, elder brother of the abbé-dramatist Boisrobert. He lived for some time in Spain, and was the first to introduce Calderón to France. He led a profligate and irregular life, which is reflected in the subject-matter of his comedies. The most successful of these was *L'Esprit folet* (1638–9), an adaptation of Calderón's *Dama duende*. Molière may have drawn on d'Ouville's *Trahisons d'Arbiran* (1638) for some of *Tartuffe*.

OVERSKOU, THOMAS (1798–1873), Danish dramatic critic and historian, also the author of a number of plays, of which the best-known is *Pak* (1845).

OWENS, JOHN EDMOND (1823–86), American actor, born in London, but taken to the United States at the age of 5. He went on the stage at 17, and had a slow start; but after some initial success, he became known as an eccentric comedian and as an outstanding interpreter of 'Yankee' characters. His most famous part was that of Solon Shingle in *The People's Lawyer*, in which Dickens saw him in London in 1865. He was also good as Toodles, Dr. Pangloss, Caleb Plummer, Paul Pry, and Aminadab Sleek. In 1876 he played Perkyn Middlewick in *Our Boys*, and some years later joined the Madison Square stock company, where he played with Annie Russell. He retired in 1885. Owens is described by Joseph Jefferson in his *Autobiography* as 'the handsomest low comedian I had ever seen. He had a neat, dapper little figure, and a face full of lively expression. His audience was with him from first to last, his effective style and great flow of animal spirits capturing them.' He relied for his effects on his comic personality, and was somewhat extravagant in his acting, his Yankees being stage-folk rather than portraits from life. He was, however, popular and amusing, and made many successful tours throughout the United States.

OXBERRY. (1) WILLIAM (1784–1824), English actor, editor, and publisher, the son of an auctioneer. He was apprenticed in youth to a printer enamoured of acting. With him and his friends Oxberry acted *Douglas*, and other plays, in a converted stable. Emboldened by this experience, he broke his indentures at 18, and took to the professional stage, appearing at Watford as Antonio in *The Merchant of Venice*. After a round of the provinces he married, came to London, and appeared unsuccessfully at Covent Garden under Kemble. His performance was harshly criticized in *The Monthly Mirror*, a paper which, by an ironic twist of fate, he later edited. Discouraged, Oxberry set off for Scotland, where he appeared mostly in tragedy. On his return to London he made spasmodic appearances in small parts at the Lyceum and Drury Lane, and starred in minor suburban theatres. He was for a short time (1821) manager of the Olympic, but without much success. Shortly before his death he took over the Craven's Head Chophouse near Drury Lane, where his powers of mimicry and his readiness to drink made him a popular host and a boon companion. In addition to his histrionic activities, he was also a publisher and printer, and was responsible for a number of volumes of theatrical interest. He gave his name to *Oxberry's Dramatic Biography*, published posthumously by his widow, probably with the assistance of her second husband, Leman Rede. He was the author of a little farce, *The Actress of All Work* (1819), which was probably inspired by Colman's *Actor of All Work*, written for Mathews in 1817. This play, which has been wrongly attributed to Oxberry's son, a lad of 11 at the date of its composition, shows one actress in six different roles, and was a favourite with little Clara Fisher, the child prodigy. Oxberry was a tall man, fat in his later years, dark in complexion, with a small and piercing eye. Passionate and of a difficult temper, he was yet considered a good friend, though a mediocre actor. His portrait hangs in the Garrick Club. His son (2) WILLIAM HENRY (1808–52) was also an actor, and was one of the company who went with Miss Smithson to Paris in 1833. He succeeded the Keeleys in the management of Covent Garden, after managing the Lyceum without success, and was later with Mme Vestris. He was also for a time manager of the Windsor theatre. A contemporary said of him: 'There were few theatres at which he was not seen.' In contrast to his father he was a very little man, a lively actor and dancer in burlesque with a quaint manner; he is said never to have known his part on first nights. He wrote a number of plays, mostly adapted from the French, of which *Matteo Falcone* (1836) was the most successful.

OXFORD. In common with other centres, Oxford probably had its performances of medieval religious plays, and the constant association of play-acting with education practised in the song- and other schools may have led to undergraduate performances of which no trace remains. The earliest record is of a liturgical play at Magdalen towards the close of the fifteenth century, while in the following century several colleges put on Latin plays written by Nicholas Grimald. In 1566 Elizabeth visited Oxford and was entertained by two plays in Christ Church Hall, thus setting a fashion which was followed by other famous visitors, notably Charles I in 1636. These, however, were all in the nature of academic exercises, and incursions of professional companies seem to have been discouraged, as in later years, though Strange's Men were seen in an inn-yard in 1590–1, the King's Men in a tennis-court in 1680, and Betterton's company in 1703. The eighteenth century was unfavourable to the development of dramatic talent, though there were occasional private theatricals and some quasi-official performances at Commemoration. It was not until the middle of the nineteenth century that colleges began to form their own dramatic societies, Brasenose being first in the field. These have now become a regular feature of undergraduate life, but officially the theatre has as yet no place in the university nor in its curriculum, though a movement is on foot to found a Drama Department with its own experimental theatre. The town has the New Theatre, for touring companies, and a repertory company which, under J. B. Fagan from 1923 to 1925, made a mark in theatre annals. Playing in a converted Big-Game Museum, the company, which at various times included Tyrone Guthrie, Raymond Massey, Flora Robson, Glen Byam Shaw, Robert Morley, and John Gielgud, put on a fine programme of English and continental plays. The venture was, however, ill supported, and after two seasons, during which the theatre was closed in the summer vacation, Fagan gave up the struggle. The Playhouse continues to function, but has deserted its old quarters for a new intimate building in Beaumont Street, provided by Eric Dance, which opened in 1938.

Another manifestation of theatrical activity in Oxford is that provided by the University Dramatic Society, commonly known as O.U.D.S. This was founded in 1885, mainly through the exertions of Arthur Bourchier, then an undergraduate at Christ Church, and his friends, among them W. L. Courtney and Cosmo Gordon Lang, future Archbishop of Canterbury and cousin of Matheson Lang. The first production, given in the Town Hall, was *Henry IV, Part I*, in which Bourchier played Hotspur, and Lang spoke the prologue. From then until the outbreak of war in 1914 thirty-two productions were given, mainly of Shakespearian comedies, in the former New Theatre. During the war the society was disbanded, but started again in 1919, helped by the generous co-operation of the professional theatre, many of whose stars were past members of O.U.D.S. The first production of the new series was Hardy's *Dynasts*, which the author himself went to see. This was followed by a varied assortment of comedies and tragedies, and to the indoor winter show was added an annual open-air performance in different college gardens which became a feature of the summer term. At all these performances the women's parts—female members of the university being debarred from participation—were played by professional actresses of the front rank, and a number of professional producers were also employed as an alternative to undergraduates. On the outbreak of war in 1939 the society was again suspended, but a new society, known as the Friends of the O.U.D.S., was formed under the auspices of senior members, and was successful during the war years not only in maintaining the high level of previous productions, but in paying off outstanding bills and laying aside funds for the future. O.U.D.S. was re-formed in 1949.

Mention should also be made of the Greek plays given in Oxford, the first, in 1880, being the *Agamemnon* of Aeschylus, under the patronage of Dr. Jowett, then Master of Balliol. It was given in the new hall at Balliol, before a scene designed by Burne-Jones. Among the actors were Frank Benson and W. L. Courtney, later prominent in O.U.D.S. Later productions were the *Alcestis* in 1887, the *Frogs* in 1892, and the *Knights* in 1897.

OXFORD MUSIC-HALL, London, built in Oxford Street and opened by Charles Morton in 1861. This became a very prosperous Theatre of Varieties. It was taken over by C. B. Cochran and made into a theatre in 1917, in which year he produced *The Better 'Ole*, a musical play by Bruce Bairnsfather, the famous war cartoonist, which ran for 811 performances. In 1921 the theatre was rebuilt and modernized. It opened with a revue, *The League of Notions*, followed by *Mayfair and Montmartre*. In 1926 the site and building were sold, and the theatre demolished to make way for a restaurant. (See also under MUSIC-HALL.) W. M. P.

OXFORD'S MEN. The first mention of a company of players under this name occurs as early as 1492, and in 1547 the players of the 16th Earl of Oxford caused a scandal by playing in Southwark while a dirge was being sung for Henry VIII at St. Saviour's. This company may have been disbanded in 1562, but later the 17th Earl, himself a playwright, became patron of the Earl of Warwick's Men, who in 1580 appeared under Oxford's name in Burbage's Theatre during the absence on tour of its usual players. They got into trouble for brawling, and were banished to the provinces, not appearing at Court until 1584, when John Lyly was with them. The company included a number of boys, who, with some of the Children of the Chapel and of Paul's, played at Blackfriars. It was eventually (1602) merged in that of Worcester.

OZEROV, Vladislav Alexandrovich (1770–1816), Russian dramatist, who was educated at the Cadet College for the sons of the nobility, where he became interested in the theatre and in languages, particularly French. He held many military posts, and worked in the Forestry Department. In 1808 he retired without a pension, and spent the last years of his life in poverty in a village. His first play, written in 1798, was a failure, but some of his later ones, though written in a frigid classical style much influenced by the neo-classicism of France, achieved a certain popularity. He took his heroes from widely different ages and countries—Oedipus, Ossian, Dmitry—but subjected them all to the same treatment, and their foreign origin was manifest in the ease with which they were translated into German and French. Ozerov is almost forgotten now, but one of his patriotic plays, dealing with the fourteenth-century leader of the Russians against the Tartars, Dmitry of the Don, was revived in 1943 by the Kamerny Theatre.

P

PACUVIUS, MARCUS (220–130 B.C.), one of the leading dramatists of Rome, and the first to specialize in tragedy. We possess the titles of twelve tragedies and one *praetexta*; the fragments amount to about 400 lines. Pacuvius seems to have liked pathetic scenes, philosophical discussions, and complicated plots— ancient critics ranked him first in point of learning, Accius first in force—while his language, though sometimes awkward and obscure, shows pictorial power (he was a painter as well as a writer) and careful attention to sound-effects. Many of his plays enjoyed great popularity down to the end of the Republic. A canticum from his *Armorum Iudicium* was sung at the funeral of Julius Caesar; one of its lines was very apposite: 'To think that I saved the men who were to murder me!' Perhaps the most famous scene in Roman tragedy was the opening of Pacuvius's *Iliona*. The play dealt with Polydorus, youngest son of Priam, who was entrusted to the care of his sister Iliona, wife of Polymestor, King of Thrace. Iliona brought up Polydorus as her son, pretending to Polymestor that their child was Polydorus. On the fall of Troy Polymestor murdered the supposed Polydorus—really his own son. The play opened with the ghost of the murdered boy rising to implore his sleeping mother for burial. In the half-light of early morning the sleeping form of Iliona was discovered on the stage; presently the ghost made its appearance from a recess in the stage-floor. Unfortunately, on one occasion in the first century, Fufius, the actor playing the part of Iliona, had got drunk and really fallen asleep, thus failing to hear the ghost's appeal until the whole theatre took up the words: 'Mother, I cry to thee.' Another favourite scene, in the *Chryses*, showed Orestes and Pylades brought captive before Thoas; he wished to punish Orestes alone, and there was a generous rivalry between the two friends, each claiming to be Orestes—a passage which, as Cicero tells us, brought the spectators to their feet in applause. Cicero claims that in the final scene of the *Niptra* Pacuvius has improved on Sophocles; whereas Sophocles allowed the mortally wounded hero to express all his agony, Pacuvius makes him die with a Stoic self-control.

W. B.

PAGEANT. In medieval times the word referred to the movable stage on which a scene of the processional religious play was performed. This stage on wheels consisted usually of two rooms, the lower one curtained off as a dressing-room, though it could on occasion be used to represent Hell. Later the name was transferred to the ambulating entertainments, not entirely religious, of which we retain a survival in the Lord Mayor's Show, and, when the dramatic part of the proceedings had lapsed, to the dumb-show tableaux, sometimes accompanied by explanatory verse. From this meaning of the word comes its modern connotation of 'a spectacular procession', as applied to the elaborate civic pageants so fashionable in England in the early nineteen hundreds. The first was that produced by Louis N. Parker at Sherborne in 1905, and it was followed by others at Warwick, Dover, York, Oxford, and many other places. These mingled short dramatic sketches with displays of dancing, songs, and processions to music, the whole having some bearing on the history of the locality. During the 1914–18 war several patriotic pageants were produced at London theatres, while Drury Lane celebrated its own history in *The Pageant of Drury Lane* (1918), again with Louis Parker as pageant-master.

A further extension of the medieval meaning is found in the pageants, or stationary stages, set up out- or in-doors, to welcome royal or distinguished visitors, or to celebrate a marriage or an embassy. These were popular in Tudor and Elizabethan times, and consisted of songs and speeches, with a dramatic entertainment, usually allegorical, specially written for the occasion.

The word pageant was also applied to the elaborate structures of wood and painted canvas which were used in the Tudor masques. These were often ingenious machines, fixed or movable, designed and built at considerable expense for the purposes of a single night's entertainment (SEE MASQUE).

PAGEANT LANTERN, see LIGHTING, 2 *g.*

PAILLERON, ÉDOUARD (1834–99), French dramatist, author of a number of light comedies which show a penetrating analysis of contemporary society, and an equal disregard of the problems of social conduct so popular on the stage at that time. Pailleron may be said to provide the light-hearted pendant to the later work of the younger Dumas and of Henri Becque. His plays are comedies of character, but they do not belong to any school, and have little affinity with the earlier comedy to which this label is given. His first plays were performed under the Second Empire, but his best, of which *Le Monde où l'on s'ennuie* (1881) and *La Souris* (1887) were the most successful, belong to the Third Republic. The former, a satire on pedantry and intellectual preciosity, was extremely successful, and has been several times revived. Unfortunately Pailleron's work dates, and the excellence of the dialogue does little to compensate for the loss of interest inevitable with the passage of time. His last plays, which included *Cabotins* (1894), a study in false pretences, were less successful, and soon forgotten.

PAINT FRAME, a device suspended at the

back of the stage to carry the canvas while the scene-painter is at work on it (see STAGE, 5).

PAIR OF FLATS, see FLAT.

PALACE THEATRE, LONDON, opened by D'Oyly Carte on 31 Jan. 1891 as the English Opera House. It proved as unsuccessful as others of the same name. Sullivan's grand opera, 'Ivanhoe', was the first production, but neither it nor its successor attracted the public. Sarah Bernhardt appeared there in 1892 and Harris tried to run a mixture of music and melodrama, but failed. Then, under Charles Morton, it became a Theatre of Varieties and had a long and successful career. Morton was succeeded by Alfred Butt, with variety and from 1914 with revue, of which the first, *The Passing Show*, introduced Elsie Janis to England. Since then, except for a short season in 1921, the theatre has never reverted to variety, but under successive managements has staged all types of shows, and has sometimes been used for special film productions. For some years Jack Hulbert and Cecily Courtneidge were its resident stars. It is now controlled by Tom Arnold.   W. M. P.

PALAIS-ROYAL, THÉÂTRE DU. The first theatre of this name in Paris was a small private playhouse in the home of Cardinal Richelieu, which he rebuilt at great expense in the last years of his life, importing all the newest stage machinery, with superb interior decoration. It was long and narrow, the floor rising in a series of shallow steps, with two balconies on each side, and held about 600 people. It was formally inaugurated on 14 Jan. 1641, with a spectacular performance of *Mirame*, in whose composition Richelieu is believed to have had a hand, though it was attributed to Desmarets. The splendid audience was headed by the King and Queen, and admittance was restricted to the great nobles of the Court and their immediate families. After Richelieu's death in the following year the theatre, with all his other possessions, became the property of the King and was used intermittently for Court entertainments until 1660, when it was given to Molière in the place of the demolished Petit-Bourbon. After some hasty repairs and redecoration it remained in use until 1670, when it was rebuilt and enlarged and once more equipped with new machinery necessary for spectacular productions of opera. It opened with *Psyché*, and Molière played there until the night of his death, 17 Feb. 1673, after a performance of *Le Malade imaginaire*. Lully, who held a monopoly of music in France, immediately claimed the Palais-Royal for his new Academy of Music, and it was so called until it was burnt down in 1763. Rebuilt, it was again destroyed by fire in 1781.

The whole area occupied by the Palais-Royal then underwent reconstruction by its owner, the Duc de Chartres, as a vast pleasure-garden, and several theatres were built there, most of which at some time called themselves Palais-Royal. One of them housed Talma and his companions during the Revolution, and after the reconstruction of the company by Napoleon in 1803 became the present Comédie-Française. The second Palais-Royal of any importance opened under Dormeuil in 1831 and saw, among other things, the first night of Labiche's famous comedy, *Le Chapeau de paille d'Italie*.

PALAPRAT, JEAN DE BIGOT (1650–1721), French dramatist, of good family. He went to Paris in 1671 and became friendly with Molière and Dominique. He also made the acquaintance of Brueys, with whom he later collaborated in several plays for the Comédie-Française, in which the actor J. B. Raisin, a friend of both authors, played leading parts. They were successful at the time, but soon forgotten, as were the plays which Palaprat wrote on his own, or with Dominique, for the Italian actors. Palaprat was a witty and amusing companion, a true Gascon, and Étienne later wrote a play dealing with his friendship and collaboration with Brueys.

PALESTINE, see JEWISH DRAMA, 7.

PALLADIO, ANDREA (1518–80), Italian architect, whose surname was bestowed on him by his benefactor J. G. Trissino (from Pallas) and has in turn given its name to the Palladian style of architecture, based on the principles of antiquity as Palladio interpreted them in his work, and in his *Quattro libri dell' Architettura*, published in Venice in 1570. This was translated into English with notes by Inigo Jones, who was a pupil and admirer of Palladio, and imported his ideas into England, influencing both the theatre and public architecture. Palladio built, among other things, the Teatro Olimpico, Vicenza, the most important theatre of the Italian Renaissance, which was finished by his pupil Scamozzi.

PALLENBERG, MAX (1877–1934), German actor, who worked for some time with Reinhardt, and proved himself a versatile and subtle comedian. He made his first appearance on the stage in 1895, and was later in Vienna and in Berlin, where in 1914 he was an outstanding member of the Deutsches Theater. He was excellent at improvisation and in broad comedy, but could also play more serious parts, as was proved by his performance of the barker in *Liliom*. He was the husband of the eminent Viennese comedienne, Fritzi Massary.

PALLIATA, see FABULA (3).

PALMER, ALBERT MARSHMAN (1838–1905), American theatre manager, who controlled successively the Union Square Theatre, the Madison Square Theatre, and Wallack's old theatre, to which he gave his own name. He retired in 1896, and became manager for Richard Mansfield, who had made his first appearance under Palmer at Union Square

Theatre. Palmer, who was well educated and a man of much taste, sought to rival Daly and Wallack, and built up in each of his theatres a good, well-disciplined company. He did not, like Daly, create stars, but chose his actors wisely and set many on the road to fame. In his early years he followed Wallack's lead in producing imported plays, but later turned to new American works, producing *Hazel Kirke*, *Beau Brummel*, *Alabama*, and other native dramas, and encouraging such American playwrights as Augustus Thomas, Clyde Fitch, Bronson Howard, and William Gillette. In 1882 he was instrumental in founding the Actors' Fund. Palmer did a great deal for the American theatre, and his influence on staging, back-stage conditions, and the fostering of native talent was extremely beneficial.

PALMER. (1) JOHN (1728–68), known as 'Gentleman' Palmer, an English actor who died young after making a good reputation in small comic parts, like that of Brush in *The Clandestine Marriage*. He married the daughter of Mrs. Pritchard, who proved an indifferent actress. He was an extremely vain young man, and would no doubt have hated to be confused, as he often is, with (2) JOHN (1742–98), apparently no relation, who made his first appearance at the Haymarket under Foote, and in 1766 was taken on by Garrick for Drury Lane. He succeeded to many of the parts of Robert Palmer, a worthy actor mentioned in *The Rosciad*, and not, as far as is known, related to either of the Johns. The younger John was the first Joseph Surface, and Lamb, who has left a description of him in the part, said that when he appeared he was the hero of the play, a feat achieved in our own day by John Gielgud. He was also good as Falstaff and as Sir Toby Belch, and in such impudent parts as Captain Absolute, Young Wilding, and Dick Amlet. Tragedy was beyond him, and he rarely attempted it. Sheridan nicknamed him 'Plausible Jack', and he was as famous for his mendacity as for his acting. He built the Royalty Theatre in Wellclose Square, opening in 1787 with a fine company, Braham, aged 14, singing between the acts of the play. Palmer, who had no licence, was summonsed by the Patentees, but wriggled his way out of any unpleasantness and rejoined the Drury Lane company. He died on the stage, while acting in *The Stranger* at Liverpool.

PALMO'S OPERA HOUSE, NEW YORK, see BURTON, W. E.

PALSGRAVE'S MEN, see ADMIRAL'S MEN.

PANHARMONIUM, LONDON. This stood in New-road, King's Cross. It was a curious-looking building with a small portico, built originally by Lanza, a teacher of singing, for musical entertainments and displays by his pupils. In 1832 Mrs. Fitzwilliam and Buckstone opened it as the Clarence Theatre with the interior decorated to represent a Chinese pavilion. They soon left, and in 1838 it was known as the New Lyceum. Many obscure managers ran it, but it sank so low that box tickets to admit four were sold for threepence. So disreputable did it become that it was closed by order of the magistrates. In 1870 an attempt to reopen it ended in failure, and it was heard of no more.   W. M. P.

PANOPTICON, LONDON, see ALHAMBRA.

PANTALOON, the old man—later Columbine's father, guardian, or husband—in the harlequinade, where he is the butt of Clown's practical jokes. He comes from Pantalone, who, in the *commedia dell'arte*, was an elderly Venetian, a caricature of the city merchant, by turns avaricious, suspicious, amorous, and gullible (see ITALY, 2). In Elizabethan England the term was applicable to any old man—as witness Shakespeare's reference to 'the lean and slipper'd pantaloon, with spectacles on nose and pouch on side'.

PANTHEON, LONDON, in Oxford Street, built by James Wyatt. This opened on 28 Apr. 1772, and was designed as an indoor Ranelagh or Vauxhall. It was a popular place for balls, routs, and, above all, masquerades. When the Opera House in the Haymarket was burned down in 1789 the Pantheon was used in its stead, and Wyatt reconstructed it for the purpose. It was itself burned down in 1792, only the façade, so long a London landmark, remaining. Wyatt rebuilt it again, but its day had passed. Various attractions were tried, and in 1812 a Colonel Greville, who ran an entertainment in the Argyll Rooms called 'The Pic Nic', opened it as the Pantheon Theatre in partnership with a wine merchant called Cundy. They relied on opera, and lost £50,000 in just over a month. Greville retired, but Cundy tried to carry on with opera, unsuccessfully. At Christmas 1813 he staged pantomime and ballet, with boxes at 5s., pit at 3s., and gallery at 2s., but he could not compete with Drury Lane, Covent Garden, and Sadler's Wells, and in 1814 the building, with the rent in arrears, was put up for sale. The creditors sold everything, even stripping the paper from the walls. Clear of debt Cundy tried again, and the Duke of Norfolk sought unsuccessfully to get him a licence. Elliston, too, negotiated for the Pantheon, but nothing came of it. The theatre remained closed for many years, reopened as a bazaar, and was then used for over seventy years as the offices of Gilbeys, the wine merchants. It was pulled down in 1937.   W. M. P.

PANTOMIME has seven distinct meanings, confused by persistent efforts to read into the word *pantomimus* the associated idea of performance wholly in dumbshow. Until this error takes root early in the eighteenth century, pantomime in English literature means 'player of every part'. The various meanings can be classified as follows:

(1) The Greek label for a type of actor peculiar to Imperial Rome. By means of a mask with three compartments each carved to represent the face of a different person—Mars, Venus, and Vulcan, for example—he suggested by gesture alone all the characters in a fable, as well as birds or beasts, tempest, fire, or flood, to illustrate a narrative sung by the chorus. (For further details see MIME, 2 and PANTOMIMUS.)

(2) Eighteenth-century ballets with subjects taken from classical mythology. Inspired by a knowledge of *pantomimus* derived from Lucian's *Dialogues* without reference to other sources, the Duchesse du Maine staged *ballets-pantomimes* at Sceaux in the belief that she was reviving an ancient art. 'The Loves of Mars and Venus' at Drury Lane in March 1717 was billed as a 'New dramatic entertainment after the manner of the ancient pantomimes'.

(3) Traditional Christmas entertainments of the British Empire, originating in the comic dances of Arlequins from the Paris fairs (see COMMEDIA DELL'ARTE and HARLEQUINADE). By 1715 rivalry in such entertainments between London's leading theatres had become keen. At Lincoln's Inn Fields John Rich, the manager, appeared under his stage name of Lun as Harlequin. Drury Lane devised more and more elaborate harlequinades, then tried 'The Loves of Mars and Venus', and a month later showed Harlequin as Perseus with Columbine as Andromeda in a ballet called 'The Shipwreck'. This confused the public who (despite a managerial protest that harlequinades were 'not in the least designed for an imitation of the ancient pantomimes, Harlequin, Scaramouche, Punch, and Pierrot being of the present Italian theatre') made 'pantomime' the label for their favourite after-piece. None can be acclaimed as the first of a species whose peculiarity is that it has been shaped less by authors than by audiences. Public approval caused the harlequinades to lengthen until their style had to be varied to provide rest for the dancers. In *Tom Jones* Fielding describes how harlequinade and classic fable alternated incongruously, but this was one device among many. The story of Dr. Faustus was thus Italianized so that trick-scenery could be employed, and Jack Sheppard so that Harlequin could demonstrate that criminal's prison-breaking exploits. Usually Harlequin was a comic character until he was romanticized as the lover of Columbine. Their elopement, with Pantaloon, as her father, in pursuit through scenes that reflected the tastes and topics of the day, became a steadfast pattern. But the opening scenes, where some immortal bestowed the magic wand upon Harlequin, had to be novel. Classic mythology went out of fashion at the turn of the eighteenth century, and tales from chapbooks gradually took its place. In the nineteenth century the opening was elaborated in cast and scenery until it took the form of the fashionable burlesques or extravaganzas—not in dumbshow—with actresses in the heroes'

parts. Victorian pantomimes gradually softened the burlesque, especially when pantomime troupes of dancers, notably the Vokeses at Drury Lane, acted fairy-tales dramatized at such length that the pantomime ceased to be an 'after-piece', though preceded for some years by a one-act comedy. When Augustus Harris became manager of Drury Lane he prompted a music-hall invasion throughout the country, which replaced theatrical companies in pantomimes by casts of variety artists. This brought comic relief uppermost, but the glamour was ensured by restricting the choice of subject mainly to tales that had the seal of nursery approval upon them. These tales, after contact with a century of Christmas audiences, have been artfully adapted to the stage. *Cinderella* uses another of Perrault's stories (*Les Fées*) as a kind of prologue, and absorbs part of the plot of Rossini's unfairylike opera, 'La Cenerentola', with its character of Dandini for second boy. *The Babes in the Wood* has Robin Hood and his Merry Men to make happy the ending. *Red Riding Hood* for over a hundred years has had a demon wolf on two legs from a Paris opera instead of the ordinary wolf of Perrault's story. *Aladdin* is based on a burlesque by H. J. Byron in the eighteen-sixties which bestowed on the hero's mother the name of Widow Twankey at a time when tea-clippers raced home from the East with cargoes of twankay. *Robinson Crusoe* has a survivor in its villain, Will Atkins, of Pixerécourt's *mélodrame* about Crusoe's densely-populated isle. *Mother Goose*, merely a name on Perrault's title-page and little more than a figure in the piece with this title in which Grimaldi played, is a modern pantomime written by J. Hickory Wood for Dan Leno at Drury Lane. *Blue Beard* persistently disguises itself as the 1002nd Arabian Nights' Entertainment, for though Perrault knew it to be a legend of France, the Christmas pantomime decided otherwise. Oliver Goldsmith's *Goody Two-Shoes* includes in its pantomime form Bo-Peep, Tommy Tucker, Little Boy Blue, and other nursery-rhyme children. Thus pantomime has added another chapter to folk-lore, although the incongruity of such plots as the background for acrobatics, topical songs, and patriotic tableaux is such that the word 'pantomime' (or more particularly the words 'a proper pantomime') signifies in colloquial English 'a state of confusion'.

(4) Wordless Pierrot plays, first inspired by the performance of English pantomimes in Paris. Comparing Grimaldi's *Mother Goose* with the French version played at the Funambules by Deburau shows how such very dissimilar entertainments were once related. The Gallic mentality, trying to rationalize the monstrous hotch-potch of the visitors, had first to get rid of Clown. All these tricks and transformations were a nightmare to be seen not through the eyes of the very spirit of them but in the mind of one who suffers them. For this Deburau invented a new Pierrot, not the

clumsy half-wit of the Italians, but a wistful mourner in the light of the moon. 'Le Napoléon de la Pantomime' Banville called him when to devise a pantomime for the Funambules was the ambition of every Paris romantic. Through Deburau's son the line of French Pierrots continued until Severin died in 1930. They rarely made so much stir abroad as when *L'Enfant prodigue*, with a girl to play Pierrot, was acted in all parts of the world during the eighteen-nineties.

(5) Melodrama in dumbshow. In the eighteenth century stage monopolies both in England and France forbade dialogue except at Theatres Royal. Unlicensed theatres presented wordless spectacles, displays of pageantry which developed into tales of adventure with songs, recitatives, and notice-boards or scrolls to explain the plot in between battles or single combats. In London the popularity of such shows at Sadler's Wells and the Royal Circus caused Drury Lane and Covent Garden to engage special pantomime companies to act after-pieces in imitation of their humble rivals. The label was either *ballet d'action* or 'serious pantomime' (see MELODRAMA). These terms continued during the following period (early nineteenth century) when similar pieces had some scenes in dialogue and some 'in pantomime'. Brief wordless versions of famous melodramas were played by the troupe of Paul Martinetti (1851–1924) in the variety theatres of several countries. His pantomimes included *The Duel in the Snow* (from *The Corsican Brothers*) and *Robert Macaire*. These were highly popular on the halls in England at a time when the dramatic sketch with dialogue was still forbidden—last relic of the stage monopoly.

(6) Acrobatic-cum-scenic spectacles. Circus troupes, bent on exhibiting their talents in world-wide theatrical tours under their own management, borrowed ideas from both the Grimaldi and the Deburau traditions while devising pantomimes of a type that became peculiarly their own. From the eighteen-sixties to the eighteen-nineties the Ravels and the Hanlon-Lees excited astonishment with their nightmare spectacles, and in Paris the theatrical species called *la féerie*, notably *Les Pilules du Diable* at the Châtelet, adapted such antics for Christmas festivities. The American pantomime of *Humpty-Dumpty*, in which Fox, the most celebrated of American clowns, toured throughout the United States, may perhaps be included in this category, although it was of an earlier date, and in its style unique.

(7) A term variously employed to describe what is seen in acting or dancing. It is applied to passages in plays when ideas are silently conveyed; to expressive movements made by actors with arms, legs, or face when not speaking; to passages in ballet which cannot strictly be described as dancing; to expressive movements made by a ballet dancer's arms, face, or anatomical parts other than legs. The technique thus baldly stated is an important

characteristic of modern acting and modern ballet.

In order to dissociate themselves from popular entertainments, modern exponents of dumbshow describe their art as 'mime' (see MIME, 3), although it has nothing in common with the mimicry, or the performances based on that idea, of Ancient Rome.   M. W. D.

PANTOMIMUS, THE, was a performer whose art consisted in representation by means of rhythmical gesture alone. This form of entertainment, popular in Magna Graecia (it was called the 'Italian dance'), was brought into fashion at Rome during the reign of Augustus by Pylades of Cilicia and Bathyllus of Alexandria. As a form of art it took itself seriously; though passionate and often demoralizing, it was not coarse or farcical like the mime, its chief competitor for the favour of the theatre-going public throughout the period of the Roman Empire (see MIME, 2). The central figure was the masked dancer, usually a solo performer, who with steps, postures, and gestures of every kind represented in turn each of the characters of the story; thus if the theme was the love of Mars and Venus, he would show first the Sun bringing the bad news to Venus's husband Vulcan, then Vulcan setting the net to entrap the guilty pair, then the other gods coming, one by one, to survey the confusion of the lovers, then the embarrassed Venus and the alarmed Mars. Lucian assures us that a performer of Nero's time was able when put on his mettle to represent all this by gesture alone, without the aid of chorus or musical accompaniment, to the satisfaction of his critic. The dancer might on occasion have an assistant; thus we hear of a pantomimus who so overacted the part of the mad Ajax that not only did he tear the costume of one of the *scabillarii* and seize the flute of one of the musicians, but he dealt with it so violent a blow to Odysseus, who was standing beside him in a triumphant attitude, that only his head-dress saved him from fatal injury; finally Ajax descended from the stage and took his seat between two alarmed spectators, while the crowd applauded what they considered a supreme display of acting. The better performers were more restrained; thus when his pupil, Hylas, could think of no better way of representing 'great Agamemnon' than by standing on his toes, Pylades showed him a subtler method by merely assuming an air of reflection. Language and facial expression were alike denied to the actor by his mask with its closed mouthpiece; his most important instrument was his 'speaking hands'. The art of gesture was carried to heights beyond our comprehension; Lucian tells us of a visitor to Rome from the Pontus who, though he knew no Greek and was thus unable to follow the words of the chorus, found the gestures of the pantomimus so lucid that he wanted to take him home as an interpreter. It is clear, however, that many of the gestures employed were conventionalized; thus there were certain steps prescribed by tradition for

Thyestes when in the act of eating his children.

The performance usually took place in the theatre; the pantomimus wore the costume of a tragic actor, a cloak and a silken tunic reaching to the feet. A graceful, supple figure was essential. The mask was dignified in expression; in contrast with the mask of tragedy, the mouth was closed. The performer might wear a different mask for each role; thus we hear of five masks being used for one pantomime. The musical instruments employed by the orchestra included flutes, pipes, cymbals, and trumpets. During the performance the chorus sang the libretto, usually in Greek. The time was given by the *scabillarii*, who wore under their sandals the *scabillum*, a box of wood or metal capable of emitting a clear note under pressure.

The subjects of the pantomime, according to Lucian, might include anything from Chaos to Cleopatra, i.e. any theme taken from mythology or past history. Anything, it would seem, could be set to music and adapted for dancing; Nero wished to 'dance' the Turnus of Virgil, and we hear of poems and even speeches being so treated; in general, however, the pantomime took its themes from tragedy. The favourite subject was love. The songs of the chorus, like the accompanying music, were usually of but small artistic merit, though well-known poets sometimes enriched themselves by writing libretti for pantomimes. Everything turned on the skill of the dancer. A single unrhythmical movement on his part would ruin the performance. His beauty and skill, his intoxicating gestures and the seductive nature of the theme, were calculated to have a potent, indeed a disastrous, effect, especially on female spectators. St. Augustine regarded the pantomime as more dangerous to morals than the circus, and Zosimus, writing in the fifth century, traces the moral decline of the Roman Empire to the introduction of the pantomime. So great was its popularity that fights between the supporters of rival pantomimi became a menace to the public peace. The performers found their way into private houses; Ummidia Quadratilla owned a troupe of them, whose performances were shunned by her puritanical grandson. Seneca speaks of privately-owned and pampered female performers. Pantomimi were legally *infames*, members of a dishonourable profession; sometimes their performances were banned by the government, and any immoral behaviour on their part might be visited with the severest punishment. Still they continued to flourish, particularly under such emperors as Nero, themselves interested in the theatre. Nero's favourite pantomimus was Paris, who was eventually put to death owing to the emperor's professional jealousy. Large fortunes were made by successful pantomimi, and the Emperor Marcus Aurelius had to fix a maximum fee for their performances. So great was the place which the pantomime occupied on the stage of Imperial times that the old word for actor, *histrio*, came to have the meaning of 'performer of pantomime'.   W. B.

PARADE, see BOBÈCHE and FAIRS.

PARAGUAY, see SOUTH AMERICA, 1.

PARALLEL, the American equivalent of the English rostrum, or stage platform.

PARFAICT, two brothers, (1) FRANÇOIS (1698–1753) and (2) CLAUDE (1701–77), who collaborated in a number of works on French theatre history. Their chief publications were an *Histoire générale du théâtre français depuis son origine* (1745–9), in 15 volumes; *Mémoires pour servir à l'histoire des spectacles de la foire* (1743), in 2 volumes; *Histoire de l'ancien théâtre italien depuis son origine jusqu'à sa suppression en 1697* (1753); and *Dictionnaire des théâtres de Paris* (1756–67), in 7 volumes. Although painstaking, they were not always accurate and their judgement was sometimes at fault, but their work is valuable and full of information which cannot be found elsewhere. François was also something of a dramatist, but nothing of his dramatic work has survived.

PARIGI. (1) GIULIO (?–1635) and (2) ALFONSO (?–1656), two brothers, and the first generation of scenic designers to work for opera. Their designs were comparatively simple, compared with later developments, and correspond to the classical simplicity of the early Florentine scores. Giulio, who appears to be the elder of the two, was a pupil of Buontalenti (see also OPERA, 1 and SCENERY, 2).

PARIS. There were two popular Roman actors (pantomime dancers) of this name, of whom one was executed under Nero (A.D. 67), owing, it is said, to Nero's jealousy of his art, the other under Domitian (A.D. 83). For the second Paris the Roman poet Statius wrote the libretto of a pantomime, *Agave*, now lost.

(For the theatres of Paris, see under their own names and FRANCE.)

PARKER, HENRY TAYLOR (1867–1934), an American critic of music and the drama, first on the New York *Globe*, and later, for thirty years, on the Boston *Transcript*, where his articles on both branches of art were remarkable for their integrity and scholarship. His energy and enthusiasm were alike admirable, and he had the gift of conveying to his reader a vivid picture of what he had himself seen or heard. His assessment of acting was based on a wide knowledge of the history and traditions of the American stage, and of the careers of individual actors. He published only one volume of his collected articles, which, as a fellow critic said, 'forms one of the finest chapters in newspaper drama criticism in America'. An individualist among the critics of his day, he was respected by theatre people and the general public alike.

PARKER, JOHN (1875–   ), English dramatic critic and theatrical journalist who has put all writers on the contemporary English theatre in his debt by editing *Who's Who in the Theatre*. This valuable publication appeared first in 1912, in succession to the editor's previous *Green Room Book*, and has since run through numerous editions, each of which has been carefully revised and brought up to date. It now contains more than 3,000 biographical entries, much useful information on performances of notable plays, and genealogical tables of famous theatrical families prepared by the late Dr. J. E. M. Bulloch. John Parker is also honorary secretary of the Critics' Circle.

T. C. K.

PARKER, LOUIS NAPOLEON (1852–1944), English dramatist, author of over 100 plays and adaptations. He was for some time a music-master at Sherborne. The success of his early plays enabled him to resign in 1892, and he went to London to devote the rest of his long life to the theatre. Among his plays, the most successful were *Rosemary* (1896), *Pomander Walk* (1910), and *Disraeli* (1911), the latter having a long run in America. Parker was in great demand for the civic pageants so much in vogue in Edwardian England, and produced among others the pageants at Sherborne (1905), Warwick (1906), Dover (1908), and York (1909). During the 1914–18 war he produced several patriotic pageants in London, and was the author of *The Pageant of Drury Lane* (1918). His work is uneven and diffuse, at its best admirable, at its worst hack-work. The partitioning of his undoubted talents among varied interests was amusingly underlined by the title of his reminiscences, *Several of My Lives* (1928).

PARKER, P.C., see AUSTIN, CHARLES.

PARK LANE THEATRE, NEW YORK, see DALY'S THEATRE (3).

PARK THEATRE. (1) NEW YORK, the first outstanding theatre of the United States, known as the ' Old Drury ' of America. Built by Hallam and Hodgkinson, it was originally called the New Theatre, and was opened on 29 Jan. 1798 with *As You Like It*. Hodgkinson played Jaques and Hallam Touchstone, while the cast contained many of the members of the former John Street Theatre company. The second production, on 31 Jan., was *The School for Scandal* with the Hallams as Sir Peter and Lady Teazle, and Jefferson in his later famous part of Moses. Prosperity first came to the theatre with the engagement of Thomas Abthorpe Cooper, then only 21, and on the threshold of a brilliant career. He made his first appearance on 28 Feb. as Hamlet, and was soon accounted one of the finest actors yet seen in New York. In spite of a good company, however, and of the popularity of plays by Kotzebue, and by Dunlap, one of the managers of the theatre, the fortunes of the venture were constantly jeopardized by quarrels between the managers, until finally Dunlap took over entirely, engaging his former associates as salaried

actors. His repertory was mainly modern, consisting of contemporary successes from London, translations from the continent, and his own plays, though a few classics were given, including *Twelfth Night*, first seen in New York on 11 June 1804.

In spite of enthusiasm and hard work, Dunlap went bankrupt in 1805, and a year later the theatre was bought by Beekman and Astor, who installed Cooper as sole manager, with Dunlap as his salaried assistant. Still the theatre did not prosper; Cooper was not a good business man, and a new era was inaugurated in the autumn of 1808, when Stephen Price bought a controlling interest in the management. Neither an actor, like Cooper, nor a dramatist, like Dunlap, he was able to devote himself to management. Under him the first indigenous American drama, *The Indian Princess; or, La Belle Sauvage*, was given on 14 June 1809, with a success which was later repeated at Drury Lane. Price also engaged the young American actor, John Howard Payne, whose first play was performed at the Park when he was 14, and added the parents of Edgar Allan Poe to his stock company.

It was Price who inaugurated the policy of importing foreign stars, a policy directly responsible for the decline of the old stock company. The first great English actor to appear at the Park was George Frederick Cooke, who, in Nov. 1810, began an engagement which lasted for two seasons. He was successful at first, but his popularity declined as his habitual vice of drunkenness overcame him, and as the stock company was still good, stars were not really necessary; nor was it possible to import them during the war with England, from 1812 to 1815. It was not until 1818 that the stock system was abandoned, and the company were retained purely to support visiting stars. One of the greatest of these was Kean, who was booked to appear at the Park when, on 24 May 1820, it was totally destroyed by fire. The company moved to the old Anthony Street Theatre, and there Kean made his first appearance in New York. The Park was rebuilt, and opened on 1 Sept. 1821 for the era of its greatest prosperity and importance. Practically every actor of importance at the time, whether English, American, or continental, appeared at the Park—the Keans, the Mathews, Charles and Fanny Kemble, the Wallacks, Hackett, the Keeleys, Buckstone, Forrest, Vandenhoff, and Cushman, to name only a few. This period saw also the emergence of the American playwright, and the theatre was no longer dependent on importations. In 1824 the success of the newly opened Chatham Theatre led to the introduction of vast spectacular shows like *The Cataract of the Ganges*, but the constant succession of guest artists helped the retention of Shakespearian and other classic plays in the repertory. In the autumn of 1827 the Park was first lit by gas, and two years later, during a bad financial panic, it was closed for a time, and given over to masquerades and lectures. It was redecorated in 1834, and again in 1837, when it was forced to contend with the rivalry of Wallack's National Theatre. This year saw the appearance of Jean Davenport, aged 11, believed to be the original of Dickens's Ninetta Crummles, in a range of parts which included Sir Peter Teazle, Young Norval, Richard III, Shylock, and Little Pickle. The theatre was now losing its monopoly of New York acting, and was becoming out of date, clinging to the old system of frequent changes of bill, with all its attendant evils of under-rehearsal and over-fatigue. On 20 Jan. 1840 Stephen Price, who had managed it for over 30 years, with the assistance of Simpson, died suddenly, and the Park entered on a bad period. In June 1841 everything was put up for sale to pay the rent. The theatre was intermittently used as a circus and, in spite of a few flickers of its former brilliance, such as the three-weeks run of Boucicault's first play, *London Assurance*, in Oct. 1841, and another visit by Macready in 1843, it became more and more of a liability. After the death of Simpson in 1848 the theatre was taken over by Hamblin, who ran it in conjunction with his own theatre, the Bowery; but, in spite of extensive rebuilding, he could not restore its lost glory, and on 16 Dec.' 1848 it was burnt down, thus breaking the last link with the Hallams and the John Street Theatre, and the coming of professional drama to the New World.

(2) A second Park Theatre, on Broadway and 22nd Street, opened on 13 Apr. 1874, with Fechter in the last new part he was to create, in his own adaptation of a French play. This theatre had been intended for Boucicault, but after continuous litigation its real history began on 16 Sept. 1874, when John T. Raymond appeared there in his famous part of Colonel Sellars. Later successes were *The Mighty Dollar* with the Florences in 1875, and G. F. Rowe in his own play, *Brass*, in 1876. Henry E. Abbey, later manager of the Metropolitan Opera House, took over the new Park late in 1876, and started it on a prosperous career which lasted until, on 30 Oct. 1882, the day on which Lily Langtry was to have made her New York début there, the theatre was totally destroyed by fire and never rebuilt.

(3) The first professional theatre established in Brooklyn, after nearly forty years of unsuccessful tentatives, was the Park, which opened on 14 Sept. 1863, and soon passed into the hands of Mrs. Conway. She remained there until 1871, and established the theatre firmly in the affections of its audience, playing herself with a good company, and frequently importing stars for short seasons. After her departure it languished for a while, but housed the Florences, Minnie Maddern in *Oliver Twist*, and, in the season of 1873–4, an amazing array of stars—Lester Wallack, Adelaide Neilson, Chanfrau, Owens, Sothern, and others. The theatre tended more and more to be merely a halting-place for travelling companies. In 1876 it fell a victim to the craze for variety and burlesque, but after the burning of the Brooklyn Theatre it regained its monopoly of acting

and turned again to legitimate drama. It was the last theatre in New York to have a stock company supporting visiting stars (for a later Park Theatre in New York, see MAJESTIC THEATRE).

(4) Scotland's first Little Theatre, founded in Glasgow in 1941 by John Stewart, and conducted on club lines, was named the Park. One production is given each month, and the usual run is for a fortnight.

(5) For the Park Theatre, Camden Town, London, see ALEXANDRA THEATRE (2).

PASO, the name given in the seventeenth-century Spanish theatre to a one-act comic scene. As exploited by Lope de Rueda it became synonymous with *entremés*. With the addition of dancing and singing it later developed into the *sainete*, a genre popularized by Ramón de la Cruz.

PASQUINO, one of the minor *zanni* or servant roles of the *commedia dell' arte*. The name is said to have originated in Rome at the end of the fifteenth century. It was taken up by the *commedia dell'arte*, and passed into French comedy, possibly by the intermediary of the actor Baron, being found as the name of the valet in the plays of Destouches. In the French seventeenth-century theatre the expression 'the Pasquin of the company' became general, and designated the actor charged with the satiric roles found in Regnard and Dufresny.

PASS DOOR, a fireproof door placed in an inconspicuous part of the proscenium wall, leading from the auditorium to the side of the stage and so backstage. It is usually used only by those connected with the theatre, ordinary members of the audience penetrating behind the scenes by means of the Stage Door which opens on to the street.

PASSION PLAY. The secular development of the Passion Play was widespread throughout western Europe, and led to a tradition of open-air pageant productions of the Good Friday story in many small towns and villages. Most of them died out during the fifteenth century, but helped by the Catholic counter-reformation in the following century a few were revived in Switzerland, Austria, and Germany. They continue spasmodically in a few remote villages in Germany, but the only one to become famous is that given decennially (from 1633) at Oberammergau, in Bavaria. A fusion of two Augsburg cycles, this was first performed during a visitation of plague, and remains entirely amateur, the villagers dividing the parts among themselves, and being responsible also for the production and scenery.

PASTICCIO (PASTICHE), see OPERA, 4.

PASTORAL, a dramatic form which evolved in Italy from pastoral poetry, by way of the dramatic eclogue or rustic (shepherd) play.

There had previously been some pastoral elements in drama, notably in Agostino Beccari's *Sacrificio* (1554), which was labelled a *favola pastorale*, but the first outstanding pastoral play was Tasso's *Aminta* (1573), a tale of rustic love written in fine poetry with superb choruses. It was followed by Guarini's *Il Pastor Fido*, published about 1590, but probably not performed before 1596. Both were translated and performed in France and England, and had a widespread influence, *Il Pastor Fido* being given several times after the Restoration, once in a version by Settle, and continuing to be revived up to 1809. The latest of many versions of *Aminta* was that prepared by Leigh Hunt in 1820.

These two plays mark the highest achievements of the genre, but the pastoral continued in favour in Italy for some time (see ITALY, 2). The first English play to be called a pastoral was Peele's *Arraignment of Paris* (1581), but it does not appear to have been influenced by either of the above as were, later, Lyly and Samuel Daniel, while in 1608–9 Fletcher tried to give the English stage a native pastoral with *The Faithful Shepherdess*. It was a failure at first, but proved a success in revival, being full of poetry and invention. Pepys saw it in 1663, and called it 'a most simple thing, and yet much thronged after and often shown, but it is only for the scenes' sake, which is very fine indeed and worth seeing'. Jonson's *Sad Shepherd* was never finished, and it cannot be said that the pastoral ever became acclimatized in England, though it had some influence on the masque and so on Shakespeare. Dr. Greg, in *Pastoral Poetry and Pastoral Drama* (1906), claims that *Comus*, though called a masque, is essentially a pastoral, directly dependent upon previous pastoral works.

The pastoral bears no relation to real rustic life; it is entirely artificial, and must be judged accordingly. It cannot flourish at the same time as romantic drama, which may account for its slight success in England. It was more at home in France, where it inspired a number of authors, notably Hardy, who wrote one pastoral; Racan, whose *Bergeries* (1623), though placed in France, shows definite traces of Italian influence; and Théophile de Viau, whose *Pyrame* (1621) was publicly burnt, but for its author's faults, not its own. The pastoral disappeared from French dramatic literature in the mid-1630s, but not before it had served as a vehicle for the introduction of the Unities in Mairet's *Sylvanire* (1630).

PATENT THEATRES, LONDON, see COVENT GARDEN and DRURY LANE.

PAVILION, LONDON, in Whitechapel. This was opened by Wyatt and Farrell in 1829. Fanny Clifton (Mrs. Stirling) went there from the City Theatre and made her first success. The theatre was burned down in 1856 and rebuilt. Under the management of Morris Abrahams it was a very efficient house, catering largely for the big Jewish population of the neighbourhood. Isaac Cohen also gave good plays and pantomimes there, and many famous Jewish actors appeared at it. It was for a time a cinema, and then returned to Jewish drama. It has not been used for some time.

W. M. P.

PAVILION THEATRE, LONDON, see WEST LONDON THEATRE; NEW YORK, see ANTHONY STREET THEATRE and CHATHAM THEATRE (1).

PAVLOVA, ANNA (1882–1931), a famous and much-loved ballerina, who for many years toured the world with her own company, a revelation and an inspiration to all who saw her. Trained in the strict tradition of the Russian Imperial School, she was with Diaghilev's Ballets Russes when they first went to Western Europe in 1909 and 1910; she broke away to form her own company, in which she had a number of English dancers, an unusual occurrence at that time, and one for which the English ballet has had reason to be grateful. Pavlova was a dancer of great versatility, but will probably be best remembered for her 'Dying Swan' (1905), a solo dance by Fokine.

PAVY, SALATHIEL (or SALMON) (1590–1603), a child-actor in the Boy Company at the Blackfriars, who is best remembered by Ben Jonson's epitaph on his early death at the age of 13. He was apparently noted for his excellence in playing the parts of elderly men.

PAY BOX, see AUDITORIUM, 2 and BOX.

PAYNE, JOHN HOWARD (1791–1852), an American actor and dramatist, best known as the author of 'Home, Sweet Home'. This, with music by Henry Bishop based on a Sicilian air, was first sung by Miss Marie Tree in 1821. Payne was a precocious boy, whose first play was produced in New York when he was only 14. Three years later, in spite of parental opposition, he went on the stage, and made a great reputation in such parts as Young Norval, Romeo, Tancred, and Hamlet. After a successful début in New York, he toured the larger American cities, and in 1811 appeared at the Chestnut Street Theatre, Philadelphia, as Frederick in his own version of Kotzebue's *Das Kind der Liebe*. As *Lovers' Vows*, this had already been translated by Mrs. Inchbald, Benjamin Thompson, Anne Plumptre, and William Dunlap. Payne's version, based on the first two of these, is interesting, in the opinion of A. H. Quinn, as 'showing his methods of work, and also his sense of the theatrically effective'. Frederick always remained one of his favourite parts, in which he was much admired.

In spite of his early successes, or perhaps because of them, Payne later found it difficult to establish himself in New York, and his efforts were further frustrated by the jealousy of George Frederick Cooke. So in 1813 he sailed for England, and appeared at Drury Lane, and in the provinces, with great success. A visit to Paris brought him the friendship of

Talma and the freedom of the Comédie-Française, and for many years Payne was engaged in the translation and adaptation of current French successes for the English stage. These were also performed in the United States, but in spite of continued success in both countries Payne received very little money for his work.

Among his many plays—he has been credited with some fifty or sixty—the best were probably *Brutus; or, the Fall of Tarquin*, a tragedy played by Charles Kean in London in 1818 and in Paris in 1827, and *Charles II; or, the Merry Monarch* (1824), based on a play by Alexandre Duval and written in collaboration with Washington Irving, a lifelong friend. Payne was also responsible for *Therese; or, the Orphan of Geneva* (1821), for one of the many versions of *The Maid and the Magpie* (1815), and for translations of several of Pixerécourt's melodramas. He had little originality, but a good sense of the theatre and a deft touch in handling his material. His work undoubtedly had some influence on the course of American drama, in spite of his continued residence abroad. At one time he tried, unsuccessfully, to manage Sadler's Wells Theatre, but only landed himself in prison for debt, and he was for a couple of years editor of a theatrical paper, *The Opera-Glass*. In 1842 he was appointed American Consul at Tunis, where he remained until his death.

PECKHAM. There was a theatre in Peckham High Street, and a local legend held that Nell Gwynn played there, though no proof can be adduced. The theatre was occasionally used for dramatic purposes up to 1822, the last time by Penley, a Drury Lane actor. It was finally converted into a school.

PEDROLINO, see PIERROT.

PEELE, GEORGE (*c.* 1558–*c.* 1597), English dramatist, of good family and well educated, but a shiftless, dissolute fellow, companion of Greene, Nashe, and Marlowe, who lived by his wits and by such small sums as he could earn at play-writing and play-acting. He wrote a good deal of miscellaneous verse, some pageants, and a number of plays, of which the best are *The Arraignment of Paris*, given at Court, probably in 1581, *David and Bethsabe* (*c.* 1587), *Edward I* (1591), which survives only in a mutilated form, and his best-known and most popular work, *The Old Wives' Tale*, written probably in 1590. This 'pleasant conceited comedie', as it is called on the title-page of the first edition (1595), is a mixture of high romance and English folk-tale, which was long dismissed by critics as negligible and pretentious nonsense. Bullen was the first to appreciate its qualities, in his edition of 1888, and it is now considered something of a landmark in the development of English comedy, bringing a new and more subtle strain of humour into the farce of earlier days. Peele had a fine command of language and was the author of some charming lyrics.

PEEP-SHOW. The art of theatrical production leaves no legacy to the future, and it is often extremely difficult for us to reconstruct the physical appearance of the stage of even the last few centuries. The actual stage scenery has almost always been destroyed, and ordinary pictorial views and designs tend to give a hopelessly romanticized impression of the intended effect. But, when the ordinary channels of information are unsatisfactory, it is sometimes found that surprisingly accurate representations of stage effects have been preserved in such unconsidered trifles as children's toys and rich men's playthings. Such was the nineteenth-century English Toy Theatre, and such was the Peep-show.

The essence of a peep-show is that it is a device in which one can view a perspective; it usually takes the form of a box, with a small eyepiece, inside which are arranged the receding elements of a perspective view; the scenes were sometimes painted on glass and illuminated from behind, in the manner of transparencies, but more usually consisted of a number of cut-out sheets of wood or cardboard. Some such device is said to have been constructed by Leon Battista Alberti in 1437; in the sixteenth and early seventeenth centuries we find some highly elaborate moving scenes incorporated in the horological automata of the period; these appear to be closely based on the pageants of the Renaissance stage, representing the stately processions of gods and goddesses in classical and mythological settings. Some examples of these stage models have been preserved in the Kunsthistorisches Museum at Vienna, and they provide an interesting record of the Court entertainments of the Renaissance period.

In the latter part of the seventeenth century dramatic spectacle was confined more and more behind the stage proscenium, and the peep-shows reflect this tendency by concentrating upon producing an effect of vast distances within the narrow framework of their wooden box; at the same time what had originated as a scientific toy for the educated rich became popularized as a public entertainment, a fairground side-show, and a children's plaything. While the eighteenth-century peep-shows throw a valuable light on the state of perspective scene-painting, their subjects tend to diverge from the theatrical tradition and to be concerned rather with the representation of famous views and historical events. An important innovation was the placing of a lens in the eyepiece. Throughout the eighteenth century a large variety of stage models, moving pictures, musical clocks, and other types of scenic automata—many of them constructed in Germany and Holland—were exhibited throughout England by Penkethman and other lesser showmen; unfortunately, none of these seems to have been preserved. Within living memory small peep-shows were still being exhibited in the streets; these usually consisted of a number of single pictures, depicting legendary or contemporary sensational events, that were lowered, one after the other, before the view of the spectator, while the showman kept up a running commentary upon them.

Although the public peep-shows have vanished, some of the children's peep-shows have been preserved; the most exquisite of these were those made at Augsburg by the brothers Engelbrecht at the beginning of the eighteenth century; they provide some charming examples of the contemporary art of perspective-drawing in the representation of baroque halls, formal gardens, and the country scene.

The juvenile peep-show is dealt with in Grober's *Children's Toys in Bygone Days*, and there is a detailed description of the Renaissance models by Dr. Wolfgang Born in *The Connoisseur* for February and April 1941.

G. S.

PÉLISSIER, HARRY GABRIEL (1874–1913), English composer and entertainer, of French origin, and the first husband of Fay Compton. He was the originator of the famous Pélissier Follies, who earned their spurs on the sands and promenades and even al fresco at Earl's Court, and then appeared at the Apollo Theatre, London, where they delighted packed audiences for many seasons. They wore ordinary pierrot costume, alternately black with white pompons and white with black pompons, against a drape of black and white curtains, and were compèred by Pélissier, who wrote a good deal of their material himself. Their show was one of the best things of its kind, with good music, topicality, wit, and observation, and it has never been equalled, in spite of several efforts to revive it by employing the same formula.

W. M. P.

PELLESINI. (1) GIOVANNI (c. 1526–1612), an actor of the *commedia dell'arte*. By 1576 he evidently had a company of his own, but shortly afterwards he joined the Confidenti, and became their director, and the husband of their star actress, (2) VITTORIA PIISSIMI (*fl.* 1575–94), whom he may have married about 1582. He played as Pedrolino, a *zanni* role which is considered to be the origin of Pierrot.

PEMBERTON, THOMAS EDGAR (1849–1905), English dramatist and stage historian, most of whose work was done in connexion with the theatre in Birmingham, where he was head of an old-established firm of brass-founders. From 1882 to 1900 he was dramatic critic of the *Birmingham Daily Post*, and was on intimate terms with many of the leading actors of the day. His memoirs of Sothern, the Kendals, Robertson, Hare, Ellen Terry, and Wyndham were written from personal knowledge, and are therefore interesting, but have no literary distinction. Pemberton lectured frequently on the theatre, and was a governor of the Memorial Theatre, Stratford-on-Avon. His plays, none of which has survived on the stage, were done mainly in the provinces. He was also the author of a book on Dickens and the stage, and of a history of the Birmingham theatres.

PEMBROKE'S MEN, an Elizabethan theatrical company with which Shakespeare is assumed to have been connected in about 1592–3. It was under the patronage of the Earl of Pembroke, and was first mentioned in late 1592. Among the play-books which its actors parted with to the booksellers a year later were Marlowe's *Edward II*, *The Taming of a Shrew*, and *The True Tragedy of Richard Duke of York*. Shakespeare's *Taming of the Shrew* and *Richard III* may have been revisions for Pembroke's Men of the two last titles. The company's name is also on the title-page of *Titus Andronicus*, which Shakespeare had refashioned from *Titus and Vespasian* for Sussex's Men. The revised draft of parts 2 and 3 of *Henry VI* was also in their repertory, the first part (a rewriting of *The Contention of York and Lancaster*) belonging still to Strange's Men. Chambers thinks it possible that Shakespeare also wrote at this time, and for this company, a first draft of *Henry VIII*, now lost; but his connexion with the company ceased in 1594, when he joined the newly formed Chamberlain's Men. The company itself underwent an eclipse until 1597, when a group of players, calling themselves Pembroke's Men, but seemingly made up of Admiral's and Chamberlain's Men, leased the Swan from Langley. Here they got into trouble with the authorities for their production of Nashe's and Jonson's *Isle of Dogs*. The theatre was closed, and some of the actors, including Jonson, were put in prison. This disaster broke up the group, and most of its members returned to play with the Admiral's Men under Henslowe at the Rose. A few remained faithful to the Swan, and formed the nucleus of a new company of Pembroke's Men which appeared in provincial records under that name during the next few years, and at the Rose for a day or so in 1600. Their visit was apparently unsuccessful, and no further record of them is found. It is surmised that they joined Worcester's Men, a company formed shortly afterwards.

PENÇO DE LA VEGA, JOSEPH (1650–1703), author of the first printed Hebrew drama (see JEWISH DRAMA, 3).

PENKETHMAN, WILLIAM (?–1725), English comedian, whose name is also spelt Pinkethman. He had a booth at Bartholomew and other Fairs, where he was very popular, being nicknamed Pinkey, or, more disdainfully, the 'Idol of the Rabble'. He also managed a theatre at Richmond and at one time travelled the country with peep-shows and scenic automata introduced from the continent. His early years are obscure, but he is believed to have played small comic parts with the United Company as early as 1682. Montague Summers, however, thinks that his first part was Stitchum, a tailor, in *The Volunteers*, in 1692. He was a member of the Drury Lane company under Cibber, who wrote for him Don Lewis, in *Love Makes a Man*, and Trappanti in *She Would and She Would Not*. Doran says he was remarkable as a speaking Harlequin in such plays as *The*

Emperor of the Moon, playing in a mask, and losing all his wit and piquancy when he discarded it. He took unpardonable liberties with author and audience, gagging and fooling with his part until even his admirers complained. He continued to act until a year before his death.

PENLEY, WILLIAM SYDNEY (1852–1912), English actor-manager who came of a theatrical family, and as a child was at the Chapel Royal and a chorister at Westminster Abbey. He made his first appearance on the stage at the old Court Theatre under Marie Litton on 26 Dec. 1871, in farce, and then toured in light and comic opera. He was for some years at the Strand, playing burlesque under Mrs. Swanborough; he appeared in Gilbert and Sullivan, and was with the Hanlon-Lees, going with them to America. The first outstanding success of his career came when he succeeded Tree in the title-role of *The Private Secretary* (1884), with which he has become so identified that he is often believed to have been the first to play the part. He appeared in it for two years, and in frequent revivals. He is also closely identified with the farce *Charley's Aunt* (1892), in which he played Lord Fancourt Babberley during its run of 1,466 performances, a record for its time. In 1900 he opened the Novelty Theatre as the Great Queen Street Theatre, appeared in revivals of his most successful parts, and retired in 1901. Much of his success as a comedian lay in his dry humour, his serious, rather pathetic, face, and the solemnity of his voice and manner contrasting with the farcical lines of his part.

PENN, WILLIAM (*c.* 1592–?), a boy-actor in 1609, when he appeared in *Epicoene*, and from 1616 to 1625 an adult member of the Prince's Men, whom he left to join the King's Men. He seems to have played small parts, usually of heavy fathers or dignified old men, and by 1629 he was a shareholder in the company. He was still with them in 1636, after which there is no further trace of him.

PENNA, LUÍZ CARLOS MARTINS (1815–48), see SOUTH AMERICA, 2.

PENNYCUICKE, ANDREW (1620–?), who published several plays when the theatres were shut under Cromwell, claiming to have been an actor and to have played in them himself. Though there is no evidence of this beyond his bare word, it is probable that he was one of Beeston's Boys at the Cockpit, and he may have been one of the actors who were found playing surreptitiously there and in the Red Bull.

PENNY GAFF, see GAFF.

PENNY PLAIN, TWOPENCE COLOURED. For the origin of this phrase, see TOY THEATRE.

PEOPLE'S NATIONAL THEATRE, see PRICE, NANCY.

PEOPLE'S THEATRE, NEWCASTLE, see AMATEUR THEATRE IN GREAT BRITAIN, 1 *d*.

PEPYS, SAMUEL (1633–1703), English diarist, and Secretary of the Navy Office, deserves mention here for the information given in his diary on the world of the theatre during the early years of the Restoration. Pepys, whose passion for the theatre was nearly as great as his love for music, kept a note of the plays he saw, recorded his impression of their actors, and related many stray items of backstage gossip imparted to him by one or other of his theatrical friends. To him we owe many illuminating glimpses of the green room, of the theatre under reconstruction, and of the rowdy talkative audiences of his day.

PERETZ, ISAAC LEIB (1852–1915), Jewish writer and lawyer. Born in Poland, he became secretary to the Warsaw Jewish community, and in 1876 published his first work, a volume of poems in Hebrew. Later, however, he turned to Yiddish as his medium. Similarly, in his philosophy—there is a definite struggle of ideas in Peretz—he changed from the rationalism of the Haskala (or Enlightenment) Movement to the symbolism and mysticism of Hassidism, which henceforth permeated his whole outlook. Some of his short stories dealing with life in Hassidic villages were dramatized and produced by Ohel on its first public appearance in Tel Aviv in 1926. His dramatic poem, *Night in the Old Market*, was dramatized by Granovsky and produced in 1925 at the Moscow State Jewish Theatre.   E. H.

PÉREZ GALDÓS, BENITO, see GALDÓS.

PERFECT CURE, THE, see STEAD, J. H.

PERIAKTOI, see ACOUSTICS, 3, GREECE, 1 *b*, and MACHINERY.

PERKINS, RICHARD (?1585–1650), English actor, one of the Queen's Men, and probably the best known and most experienced of them. He is first heard of in 1602, when he appeared as one of Worcester's Men in a play by Heywood, with whom he remained friendly for many years. Heywood and Webster both praised his acting, and he seems to have had a large range of parts.

PERTH REPERTORY THEATRE, see SCOTLAND.

PERU, see SOUTH AMERICA, 1.

PERUZZI, BALDASSARE (1481–1537), Italian scenic designer, and the first to apply the science of perspective to theatrical scenery. His flat work was as convincing as built pieces. He was responsible for the scenery of Bibbiena's *Calandria* when it was given at Rome in 1514, the year after its first production (see SCENERY, 1).

PETIPA, MARIUS (1822–1910), a French ballet-master, who was engaged at the Russian Imperial Ballet School in 1847, and became ballet-master there in 1862. He had an immense influence on the history and development of the Russian ballet, training many of its

most prominent dancers, and being responsible for the choreography of 'Swan Lake' and
'The Sleeping Beauty' to Tchaikovsky's music.

PETIT-BOURBON, SALLE DU, the first
Court theatre of France, in the long gallery of
the palace of the Dukes of Bourbon. This had
been falling into disrepair since the treachery
of the Constable (who went over to the
Spaniards in 1527) but was finally rescued and
used for Court balls and other entertainments.
It was a long, finely proportioned room, with
a stage at one end, and the first recorded
professional company to play on it was the
commedia dell'arte troupe, the Gelosi, in May
1577, though they may have appeared there on
an earlier visit. The stage was frequently used
by visiting Italian companies after this, and in
1604 the famous Isabella Andreini played
there for the last time, dying on the return
journey to Italy. In 1645 Mazarin invited the
great Italian scene-painter and machinist
Torelli to supervise the production of the
opera 'Orpheus and Euridice', given at the
Petit-Bourbon two years later, and in 1658,
when the theatre was again in the possession
of a *commedia dell'arte* troupe under Tiberio
Fiorillo, the famous Scaramouche, Molière's
company, fresh from the provinces, was allowed
to share it. For this privilege Molière paid a
heavy rent, and was given the less profitable
days for his appearances—Mondays, Wednesdays, Thursdays, and Saturdays—the Italians
keeping the more lucrative Tuesdays and
Sundays.

Molière opened on 2 November 1658 with
five plays of Corneille in succession, and not
until the end of the month did he put on one
of his own farces, *L'Étourdi*, followed by *Le
Dépit amoureux*. The Petit-Bourbon saw also
the first night of *Les Précieuses ridicules* and
Sganarelle, ou le cocu imaginaire before it was
suddenly scheduled for demolition by the
Superintendent of the Royal Buildings in
October 1660. Work was begun without
reference to Molière—the Italians had departed
before this—on some flimsy pretext, probably
at the instigation of Molière's rivals and
detractors, and the company, in full tide of
success, found itself homeless. However,
Louis XIV gave them Richelieu's disused
theatre in the Palais-Royal, and the Petit-
Bourbon disappeared. Molière took the boxes
and fittings with him, but Vigarani, at that
time Court architect and scene-painter,
claimed Torelli's scenery and machinery for
the Salle des Machines which he was building
for the king in the Tuileries. When they had
been handed over, he burnt them, hoping no
doubt to destroy all traces of his admired predecessor, of whom he was extremely jealous.

PETRI, OLAVUS (1493–1552), Swedish humanist, usually credited with the authorship of the
first Swedish play in the vernacular, *Tobiae
Comedia*, published in 1550.

PHELPS, SAMUEL (1804–78), English actor

and manager, and the first to run Sadler's
Wells Theatre as the home of Shakespeare. He
was originally a journalist, but after appearing
with success in some amateur theatricals
decided to make the stage his career. He
toured the provinces for several years,
particularly the northern cities on the York
circuit, and made a great reputation as a tragedian, being engaged by Macready for Covent
Garden. He first appeared in London, however, at the Haymarket under Webster, playing Shylock, Hamlet, Othello, and Richard III,
repeating his Othello to Macready's Iago
at Covent Garden. After the abolition of
the Patent monopoly in 1843 he took over
Sadler's Wells Theatre, and did much to
redeem the English stage from the triviality
into which it had fallen, particularly in respect
of poetic drama, by his fine and imaginative
productions of Shakespeare. Among them the
most important were *Macbeth* in 1847 and
Antony and Cleopatra in 1849, the first revival
for a hundred years. His *Pericles* was the first
performance of the play since Restoration
times. By the time he retired in 1862 he had
produced all Shakespeare's plays with the
exception of *Henry VI*, *Titus Andronicus*,
Troilus and Cressida, and *Richard II*, appearing
in most of them himself. Though primarily a
tragedian, he gave an excellent performance
as Bottom, and was also much admired as
Sir Pertinax McSycophant, giving a highly
coloured but forcible rendering of the part.
Lear and Othello were considered his best
parts. His lovers were cold, and his delivery
in love scenes tended to be harsh, though he
revelled in the pathetic. After leaving Sadler's
Wells he appeared in London and the provinces in Shakespeare and dramatizations of
Sir Walter Scott's novels, in which he was
much admired. He remained on the stage
until almost the end of his life, his last appearance being as Cardinal Wolsey on 31 Mar.
1878 at the Aquarium Theatre under Miss
Litton, at which time he was already in poor
health. Phelps was a hard-working, conscientious actor, who made the theatre his life,
and during his long period at Sadler's Wells
needed all his fortitude and obstinacy to
enable him to maintain a consistently high
standard, often in the face of much opposition.
His productions were remarkable for their
scenic beauty, though he never succumbed to
the prevailing desire for mere exhibition and
pageantry. His work was continued by a
number of young actors whom he had trained,
and whose boast it later was that they had
played Shakespeare at Sadler's Wells under
Phelps.

PHERECRATES, an Athenian comic poet,
slightly earlier than Aristophanes. He probably won his first victory in 437 B.C. In one
of his plays, *The Savage*, referred to by Plato
in the *Protagoras*, he poked fun at the idea of
the Noble Savage, and suggested that even
certain contemporary Athenians were preferable to him.

PHILADELPHIA, a town which from the beginning of American history has been closely connected with theatrical enterprise. A company under Kean and Murray acted *Cato* there in 1749, and it was the third town to be visited by the elder Hallam, in 1754. Douglass brought the American Company there in 1759, and built the first permanent theatre building in the United States (see SOUTHWARK THEATRE). This saw the production in 1766 of the first American play. Later theatres were the Chestnut Street and the Walnut Street, opened in 1794 and 1811 respectively, and the Arch Street, which, although it suffered severely, as did the other two theatres, from the theatre slump in 1829, had a brilliant season in 1831–2, mainly through the efforts of Edwin Forrest, whose brother was one of the managers. In contrast to its rivals it gave the preference to American actors in American plays, instead of relying on imported stars in their own repertory. The Arch Street Theatre became famous again under the management of Mrs. John Drew. It was not until the 1830s that Philadelphia lost its foremost position in the theatrical world, the lead passing to New York. This was mainly due to the intense rivalry between the theatres in the town, and the vicious system of importing foreign stars, which ruined all the managements. From then on Philadelphia supported stock companies, or visiting touring companies, and continued to enjoy good plays, but without regaining its former supremacy.

PHILEMON (*c.* 361–263 B.C.), an Athenian poet of the New Comedy, who was considered almost the equal of Menander. He was freely imitated by Roman comic poets. Plautus's *Mercator, Trinummus,* and *Mostellaria* are perhaps adaptations from Philemon.

PHILHARMONIC, LONDON, see GRAND THEATRE.

PHILIPPIN, see VILLIERS (1).

PHILLIPS, AUGUSTINE (?–1605), one of the actors in Shakespeare's plays, who after playing with Strange's and the Admiral's Men, joined the Chamberlain's Men on its formation in 1594. In his will he left 30s. to Shakespeare, Condell, and Christopher Beeston respectively. He was one of the original shareholders in the Globe.

PHILLIPS, STEPHEN (1864–1915), English poet and dramatist, whose poetic drama *Paolo and Francesca,* when produced by Sir George Alexander in 1902 with the young Henry Ainley as Paolo, was believed to have inaugurated a new era of poetry in the English theatre. Phillips, who had been for a short time an actor in the company of his cousin, Frank Benson, had already achieved some success with *Herod* (1901), produced by Tree, but his later works failed to reach a like standard, and his early promise was not fulfilled.

PHILLPOTTS, EDEN (1862–   ), English dramatist and novelist, author of a number of light comedies of English rural life, of which the most successful was *The Farmer's Wife.* First seen at the Birmingham Repertory Theatre in 1916, it was revived in 1924 with Cedric Hardwicke as Churdles Ash. Transferred to the Court Theatre, London, it ran for over 1,300 performances and has several times been revived with success. Also produced at the Birmingham Repertory Theatre were *Devonshire Cream* (1924), *Jane's Legacy* (1925), and *Yellow Sands* (1926), in the last of which Phillpotts had the collaboration of his daughter Adelaide, also a novelist and dramatist in her own right. Kemp, in *The Birmingham Repertory Theatre,* contends that *Yellow Sands,* which was transferred to the Haymarket, London, successfully, is a better play than *The Farmer's Wife.* 'The plot is trim, tidy and probable; the characters are wholesome, and the wit springs easily from the situation.' He also adds: 'There has been no one quite so adept at staging a party as Phillpotts. Thirza Tapper's teaparty in *The Farmer's Wife* is, of course, the classic example of fun among the tea-cups; but *Jane's Legacy* has its own bright bout of celebration', while there is another grand 'do' in *Yellow Sands,* in which Jennifer Varwell assesses her relatives when the wine is in.

PHILOCLES. The writer of the Argument to the *Oedipus Tyrannus* of Sophocles says that the trilogy of which it formed part was placed second to a trilogy by Philocles 'whoever he was'. He was in fact a nephew of Aeschylus.

PHOENIX SOCIETY, THE, was founded in 1919 under the auspices of the Stage Society for the adequate presentation of the plays of the older English dramatists. Little work of this kind had been seen in London since the productions of Philip Carr's Mermaid Theatre early in the twentieth century, and, Shakespeare alone excepted, the plays of the Elizabethan, Jacobean, and Restoration dramatists appeared to have fallen completely out of the theatrical repertory. The Stage Society began the work of revival in 1915, and continued annually to produce one Restoration comedy by Farquhar, Congreve, or Vanbrugh until 1919. The Phoenix was then constituted, and a committee of four appointed, to continue the work on a wider scale. In the six years of its existence, up to 1925, twenty-six plays were produced; the authors included Marlowe, Ben Jonson, Beaumont and Fletcher, Heywood and Ford, Dryden, Otway, Wycherley, and Congreve. From the beginning enthusiastic support was given by actors and actresses, many of them already of well-established reputation; two permanent adaptable sets were designed by the late Norman Wilkinson; and the productions were directed by Edith Craig (2) and Allan Wade (24). In 1923 a brilliant performance of Fletcher's *Faithful Shepherdess,* with special and elaborate scenes and dresses, was given in conjunction with Sir Thomas

Beecham, who arranged and conducted the musical accompaniment.

There can be little doubt that the influence of these performances helped considerably to combat the indifference—in some cases the hostility—shown to early English drama; several of the plays revived by the Phoenix have since been frequently and successfully acted on the public stage; and a large section of English drama, once neglected, has been enabled to prove in the theatre its continuing vitality.

PHOENIX THEATRE, LONDON, in the Charing Cross Road, built by Sidney Bernstein, with décor by Komisarjevsky. Its first production was *Private Lives* by Noel Coward, who appeared in his own play with Gertrude Lawrence under the management of C. B. Cochran on 24 Sept. 1930. It later passed into the hands of Victor Luxembourg, and was then run by a syndicate. Tom Arnold produced several successful musical plays there during his term of management, including Ivor Novello's *Arc de Triomphe* and an ambitious version of Tolstoy's *War and Peace. To-night at 8.30* was seen there in 1936, and a revival of *Love for Love* in 1943 with John Gielgud and an all-star cast. Later outstanding successes were *Under the Counter* and a revival, with Cyril Ritchard and Madge Elliott, of *The Relapse, or Virtue in Danger.* The Phoenix is named after an old theatre which stood in Drury Lane (see COCKPIT). W. M. P.

PHRYNICHUS. (1) A Greek tragic poet, slightly earlier than Aeschylus, who won victories in 512 and 476 B.C. He was fined for his *Capture of Miletus* (see GREECE, 4. Censorship), and wrote also another historical play, *Phoenician Women*, on the defeat of Xerxes. In his drama the chorus was more prominent and the actor less so than in Aeschylus. Aristophanes, more than half a century later, refers to Phrynichus's 'sweet lyrics' as being still very popular.

(2) An Athenian comic poet, contemporary with Aristophanes. He gained several victories, but little is known of his work. H. D. F. K.

PICARD, LOUIS BAPTISTE (1769–1828), one of the few successful dramatists of France under Napoleon, a period singularly barren in good literature. Intended for the law, he was irresistibly drawn to the theatre, and became, like Molière, actor, author, and manager. He was always cheerful, and rode the storms of the Revolution, the Empire, and the Restoration with an unquenchable gaiety, flourishing under all of them. Napoleon found in him his ideal comic author, ready to amuse the public without touching on thorny questions of the day. Yet he had a caustic humour, which under more auspicious circumstances might have flowered into satire, and did not spare the newly rich and newly risen. He excelled in depicting bourgeois or provincial interiors, and was the originator of a mingling of light satiric prose comedy with music which proved immensely popular in its day. Indeed, one of his plays, *La Petite ville* (1801), went to Germany as *Die lustige Witwe* and so to England as *The Merry Widow.* He may be regarded as a transitional author, since his comedies bear out Beaumarchais's prophecy of a continued corruption of society, and yet are often moral and full of a naïve belief in the future. His published texts give careful directions for settings and costume, in which he aimed above all at pictorial effect, and he can be credited with the creation of one new character, the valet Deschamps. But most of his plays are forgotten, since he lacked a touch of genius to kindle his undoubted talents. He was the founder and for many years the manager of the Odéon, which ranks second in importance only to the Comédie-Française. He gave up acting in 1807 in order to qualify for admission to the French Academy and for the award of the Légion d'Honneur, which Napoleon himself did not dare give to an actor, not even to Talma. Among his plays *Médiocre et rampant* (1797), whose title comes from a speech by Figaro, is perhaps the best in its picture of contemporary society, while *Le Passé, le présent et l'avenir* (1791) pays tribute to the new ideas of his time. Far more amusing, however, is the lighthearted *Le Collatéral, ou la Diligence à Joigny* (1799) which with *La Vieille tante* (1811) and *Les Deux Philibert* (1816) ranks among the best of Picard's work.

PICCADILLY THEATRE, LONDON, in Denman Street. It opened under Edward Laurillard on 7 Apr. 1928 with a musical comedy, *Blue Eyes*, which was followed by several notable productions. Shortly before the outbreak of war in 1939 the theatre was taken over by H. M. Tennent, Ltd., who transferred there at popular prices their long-running successes from other theatres. After 1939 Robert Donat starred there in a successful revival of *The Devil's Disciple*, John Gielgud was seen in *Macbeth*, and Noel Coward's record-breaking *Blithe Spirit* began its run there, transferring later to the Duchess. In 1943 *Panama Hattie* started a successful run, interrupted by enemy action in 1944, when the theatre suffered slight damage. *Jacobowsky and the Colonel* was produced there in 1945, while Ian Hay's naval comedy *Off the Record* later had a long run. W. M. P.

PICCOLOMINI, ENEA SILVIO (1405–64), early Italian dramatist, author of a comedy, *Chrysis* (1444), written in Latin verse in imitation of Terence and Plautus. Unlike other comedies of the time, most of which were based on Italian student life and follies, and owed little to classical models, *Chrysis* contains a number of characters who are recognizably Roman, and derive from the *Asinaria* and the *Curculio* (see ITALY, 1 b iii).

PICKARD, HELENA, see HARDWICKE, SIR CEDRIC.

PICKELHERRING, see REYNOLDS, ROBERT.

PIECE. This term originally covered any element of a scene, apart from the Drop and the Flat, including such things as Ground Rows and Set Pieces, and adjuncts like Cottage Pieces, Foot Pieces, and Set Waters.

PIERROT. The original of this famous character must be looked for in the *commedia dell'arte*, where he started life as Pedrolino, a *zanni* or servant role, of which Giovanni Pellesini was the earliest and best-known exponent. The character had in it something of Pulcinella (Punch), and one of its offshoots is the clown, hero of Leoncavallo's 'Pagliacci'. Although only one among many *zanni*, Pedrolino seems to have ranked high, judging by the place he occupies in the *scenarii* of Flaminio Scala, published in 1611. The credit of bringing this role into France, and transforming it into the earliest version of the French Pierrot, is usually given to an Italian actor named Giuseppe Giaratone, or Giratoni, who joined the Italian company in Paris about 1665. He accentuated Pierrot's simplicity and awkwardness, so important a feature of his later manifestations, and dressed him in the familiar costume, loose white garments with long sleeves, ruff, and large hat whose soft brim flapped round his whitened face. This, with some slight alterations, has remained his distinguishing garb ever since, but his character has been strangely altered. He soon made a place for himself in the affections of the French audience at the fairs, where, in company with other characters from the *commedia dell'arte*, he was played by some excellent actors. He might have remained but one good thing among many had it not been for the genius of Deburau, who made the character his own, and for twenty years, at the Funambules, acted nothing else. Without speaking a word, he mimed the naïveté, the clumsiness, the childish joys and sudden despairs of this comic yet often pathetic figure, which became almost legendary. Deburau, who drew the whole of Paris to his little theatre, and was praised by critics and fellow-actors alike, created, from the scattered offshoots of the *commedia dell'arte* Pedrolino, a character which lived in its own right, a French, indeed a Parisian, figure which retained little of its Italian origin beyond white clothes and its incurable, yet somehow appealing, stupidity. He was followed in the part by his son, and later by Paul Legrand at the Folies-Dramatiques (later Théâtre Déjazet), but Legrand made Pierrot less amusing and more sentimental, a trait which was later developed by a host of imitators until the robust country lad of early days had become a lackadaisical, lovesick youth pining away from unrequited love, and much addicted to singing mournful ballads under a full moon.

Meanwhile the Pierrot of Deburau had been given a new lease of life as the hero of the wordless play, *L'Enfant prodigue*, which was produced at the Cercle Funambulesque in 1890. Although Pierrot had come to England with pantomime, it was *L'Enfant prodigue* which established him in London, excellently mimed as it was at the Prince of Wales's Theatre in 1891 by Jane May, Zanfretta, Courtis, and others. The popularity of Pierrot brought the first English pierrot-troupe to Henley Regatta, under the genial management of Clifford Essex, and soon they had spread all over England, ousting the black-faced Minstrels from the beaches and pier-pavilions of English seaside towns. Formed into 'concert parties', they toured the country, the girls in short frilly white frocks, the men in loose black or white suits, all enlivened by coloured buttons, ruffs, and ruffles. The men, following Deburau in this, covered Giratoni's bald head by a tightly stretched black handkerchief, knotted behind, and the floppy hat of Pedrolino was replaced by a dunce's cap, also ornamented with coloured buttons. In this costume, augmented on occasion by 'token' accessories, the various members of the company—singers, dancers, conjurors, comedians—went through their acts, and, ignoring the solitariness of their prototype, formed a gregarious 'Pierrot troupe'. The apotheosis of this form of entertainment, which has largely been replaced by the more sophisticated and individual agglomeration of turns known as revue, was reached by Pélissier's Follies, who, having conquered the provinces, came to London in the early 1900s and became a permanent feature of theatrical life there until their final break-up. A successful revival of the old Pierrot show, staged by the Co-Optimists under Davy Burnaby, enlivened London for several seasons in the 1920s. Present-day concert parties, which, despite competition from the cinema and radio, still figure among the attractions of the seaside in summer, have mostly discarded the Pierrot costume, though some smaller groups retain it, last vestige of a long tradition.

PIGEON-HOLES, a term applied to a box in a theatre auditorium framed by a small arched opening (see AUDITORIUM, 3).

PIKE'S GRAND OPERA HOUSE, NEW YORK, see GRAND OPERA HOUSE.

PILGRIM PLAYERS. (1) see BIRMINGHAM REPERTORY THEATRE and JACKSON, SIR BARRY; (2) see BROWNE, E. MARTIN.

PINERO, SIR ARTHUR WING (1855–1934), English dramatist, was born in Islington. After leaving school at the age of 10 he was apprenticed to the law. The study of it he relieved with much amateur acting, and from it he presently escaped and obtained employment as an actor in the Edinburgh stock company, making his first appearance at the Theatre Royal, Edinburgh, on 22 June 1874. He was an actor for ten years, but only as a means to achieve his real purpose. On 6 Oct. 1877 he had his first play, *Two Hundred A Year,* produced at the Globe. Many minor pieces followed. With *The Money Spinner* in 1881 Pinero arrived at the St. James's. Popularity came with *The Magistrate* (1885), the first of the Court Theatre farces which became all the rage. It is often maintained still that in *The Magistrate*, *The Schoolmistress* (1886), *Dandy Dick* (1887), *The Cabinet Minister* (1890), and (in its rather more romantic way) *The Amazons* (1893), not only Pinero but also farce were at their best. *Sweet Lavender* (1888), a frank appeal to sentimentality, confirmed its author in prosperity.

With *The Profligate* (1889) Pinero made his first memorable venture into what was then considered the 'unpleasant' in drama. Not very important in itself, this piece at least hinted at possibilities in the author's development which were to be made clear when, at the end of May 1893, *The Second Mrs. Tanqueray* appeared at the St. James's and, with the assistance of Mrs. Patrick Campbell, startled the town. On the thought of the world at large it can have had no direct influence at all; but in a theatrical world so much and so long given over to farce, burlesque, and melodrama, Pinero's play was revolutionary. It was a serious English play with an idea—and it made money. *The Second Mrs. Tanqueray* had the effect of breaking down a host of fearful prejudices and clearing the intellectual air. During the next thirty years Pinero was regularly productive. *The Notorious Mrs. Ebbsmith* (1895) was Paula Tanqueray's successor. *Trelawny of the 'Wells'* enjoyed 135 performances from Jan. 1898. *The Gay Lord Quex* (1899), a brilliant piece of theatricalism, contained a third act which is perhaps the author's masterpiece of contrivance. With the turn of the century began a long succession of serious plays from *Iris* (1901) and *Letty* (1903) to *His House in Order* (1906) and *Mid-Channel* (1909). Of these *Iris* may be reasonably considered as Pinero's best study of a woman. In 1909, the year of the production of *Mid-Channel*, Pinero was knighted. His reputation was at its zenith. Thereafter his hold on the public slipped, and an attempt to renew it in *A Cold June* (1932), two years before his death, was a pathetic failure.

Pinero's thought moved easily in response to the currents of fashionable interest. He preached only to discover that London was already half-way to elegant conversion. He had a remarkable gift for setting a spark to polite controversy, but where he shocked his countrymen he shocked them within the range of their pleasure. Success was a necessary consequence, and when the fashion in which he had risen disappeared, a part of his reputation went with it. Though hailed as a disciple of Ibsen he was, on the contrary, a successor to Scribe and Sardou, and the hope that later generations will re-discover his serious plays must rest on his magnificent powers of telling a story for the stage. Not even his tendency to stilted language in naturalistic scenes can spoil the eagerness of his audiences to know what is going to happen next.   A. V. C.

PIN-RAIL, another name for the Fly-rail to which the lines are made fast (see ENGLISH PLAYHOUSE, 2 *a*).

PIONEER THEATRE IN THE UNITED STATES.

Perhaps nowhere in the history of the theatre has man's instinctive craving for drama, whether as an outlet for self-expression or as a form of diversion, been more strikingly demonstrated than in the United States of the first half of the nineteenth century. Nowhere else is its vitality more significantly underlined. As far back as 1698, Spanish soldiers had staged plays in the territory now embraced in the states of Texas and New Mexico, but from these regions the drama had disappeared with the Spaniards. The eighteenth century had witnessed its rebirth on the continent, and seen it, gradually winning over tremendous odds, achieve an accepted place on the Eastern seaboard. Then, after 1800, national expansion over the Alleghenies and down into the valley of the Mississippi gained in impetus and volume as a young people pushed with determination into the wilderness. The hardships and dangers they encountered have been recounted many times, but they were not great enough to extinguish the inborn passion for acting and the stage.

First came the military, who were giving plays at Fort Pitt, the Pittsburgh of to-day, as early as 1790, and on the site of present-day Detroit eight years later. Then, as the civilians moved in, there sprang up in one crude frontier settlement after another equally crude Roscian and Thespian societies, almost invariably wholly male in composition. The ebullient Kentuckians did not wait for the new century, but began their histrionic experiments in Lexington in 1799. By 1801 tyros were busy in Cincinnati, presenting O'Keeffe's *The Poor Soldier* 'between a ragged roof and sorry floor', as the dedicatory poem states. Pittsburgh was only two years behind with its civilian enthusiasts. In whatever the town, the amateurs held forth in any sort of room or hall they could press into service, and both acting and staging were of the roughest type. For the most part, the pieces offered were trivial in quality, but occasionally, being ambitious, the would-be tragedians tried their hands at Shakespeare.

Close upon the heels of the amateurs came the professionals, sometimes, in ability and experience, scarcely distinguishable from their predecessors. In 1806 they invaded Pittsburgh. In 1812 came the Turners, William, his wife, and their offspring. Sophia had played Montreal, and had even trod the boards of the famous Park Theatre in New York. Moreover, in their journeys they had picked up assorted satellites, including such veterans as Mrs. Giles Barrett and Thomas Caulfield, and also various novices who preferred the stage to less glamorous vocations. This little corps remained in Pittsburgh three years, and then turned their faces westward, spending two months in Cincinnati. It had been Turner's plan to cross the Ohio into Kentucky, where he had leased quarters in Frankfort, Lexington, and Louisville, but he had found himself dispossessed even before arriving on the scene.

In this same year, 1815, 'Old Sam' Drake (1772–1847), surrounded by his family and a few attendant outsiders, including Noah Miller Ludlow (1795–1886) and Frances Ann Denny (1798–1875) (later, as Mrs. Alex Drake, the tragedy queen of the West), accomplished a hazardous journey from Albany to Pittsburgh, and thence into Kentucky, where he occupied the buildings for which Turner had contracted, and put the drama on a permanent footing in the Blue Grass State. He did not, however, limit his activities to any restricted region, but travelled about from place to place, including Cincinnati, where in about 1826 his son and daughter-in-law, Mr. and Mrs. Alex Drake, assumed direction and delighted even so severe a critic as Mrs. Trollope. After Alex's death in 1830, his widow withdrew, leaving the field to James H. Caldwell (1793–1863), who set about raising the standards of audience behaviour. Such a reform was badly needed. If even in the 'Old Country' decorum had not yet wholly possessed the play-going public, little could be expected of these uncouth spectators on the mid-Western frontier. Like their Elizabethan forebears, they crunched nutshells; they also chewed tobacco and spat—not always accurately. Men wore their hats, and there was much obstreperous by-play with the helpless actors. There was also the never-absent threat of a fight. Until these conditions were corrected, ladies were prone to stay away from the theatre unless their potential escorts were satisfied that they would not be disturbed.

Far to the south in New Orleans the drama had first asserted itself in 1791, when some French comedians had fled thither from a Negro revolt on the island of Santo Domingo. The English theatre was first introduced in 1806, in a tavern, but the roots did not grow deep, and, despite sporadic performances, it did not flourish before 1818, when Ludlow, then himself a mere beginner, brought his modest forces to the St. Philippe Street Theatre. In 1821 the lordly Caldwell assumed dominion, and made the Louisiana metropolis his kingdom. He opened the American Theatre in Camp Street, and later, in 1835, his great St. Charles, which gave the drama its first really worthy home in the south. But by this time the frontier was a long way from New Orleans, and its later fortunes do not come within the scope of this article.

While these events were taking place, itinerant companies were trying their luck in various communities in the south-eastern states, and on the banks of the Mississippi, notably at Natchez, Vicksburg, and St. Louis. The most important, theatrically, of the river towns was unquestionably St. Louis, twenty miles below the mouth of the Missouri. Here amateurs, as usual, blazed the trail when in 1815 they gave two plays in an abandoned log blacksmith shop which served also as a courthouse, ballroom, and church. Thither headed Turner after dis-

appointments farther east, but he did not arrive until January 1818. After about six months he again moved on, abandoning the town to the amateurs until 1820, when Ludlow, with the Drakes hard upon his heels, landed on the water front. St. Louis not proving large enough to support two companies at once, the rivals merged their forces, but even so, times being bad, business was unprofitable, and they departed. The same misfortune attended the Collins and Jones troupe in the fall. These companies used the Thespian Theatre, a frame structure erected by the amateurs, and this in turn gave way in 1826 to the notorious Salt House, a ventilation-proof hot-box fashioned from an abandoned warehouse, which held its own until 1837, when it went up in flames. On 3 July of that year Ludlow, together with his new partner, the celebrated comedian Sol Smith (1801–69), dedicated the New St. Louis Theatre, the handsomest 'Temple of the Muses' yet built west of the Mississippi. (It actually had individual seats in the parquet.) St. Louis now took its place as the theatrical capital of the West, a position it maintained until it was dethroned by Chicago after the Civil War.

Chicago had been late in falling into line. In fact, until 1830 or thereabouts, there had been no Chicago. Farther to the north-west in Feb. 1834, officers at Fort Crawford, now Prairie-du-Chien, Wisconsin, staged *Who Wants a Guinea?* Ten days later a company composed of four adults and a child essayed *The Woodman's Hut* in an unfinished house with horses stabled beneath the floor in Galena, Illinois. In 1837 Chicago had its first taste when two young actors, Isherwood and McKenzie, began giving plays in the dining-room of the Sauganash Hotel, in front of which quail still wandered. The following year McKenzie was joined by his brother-in-law, Joseph Jefferson II (1804–42), and a considerable segment of the family circle, including two young boys who were in time to attain wide fame as Rip Van Winkle; these were his stepson, Charles Burke (1822–54), and his celebrated son Joseph III (1829–1905). Failing to find the pot of gold at the foot of the rainbow in Chicago, the little group cheerfully set out for points south, and spent the next few years barnstorming in the hinterlands of the Mississippi and Missouri Rivers, and so on down to Mobile on the Gulf, where Joseph II succumbed to yellow fever.

In 1847 John B. Rice (1809–74) raised the curtain of a new frame theatre in Chicago and welcomed an array of celebrities, but the frontier had by now moved away. Meanwhile, in Nauvoo, thirty miles to the south, the Mormons were diligently cultivating the tragic and the comic muses, the great Brigham Young himself playing a priest in *Pizarro*. But it was not, apparently, until 1851 that the future metropolis of St. Paul enjoyed its first taste of the drama, when George Holland (1791–1870) presented his company in a converted hall. A frame store served as the first playhouse in

Omaha in 1857. Three years later the lovely Julia Dean (1830–68) (grand-daughter of 'Old Sam' Drake) took her bow in the dining-room of the Herndon House. Omaha prospered theatrically because it was on a direct route from East to West.

By Western standards it was not far from there to Denver, and there in 1859 a room in Apollo Hall saw Charles R. Thorne (1814–93) and his sons, also the later favourite Mike Dougherty (?–1865). Very shortly the Thornes went their ways, but the local forces were greatly strengthened by the arrival of John S. Langrishe (1829–95), who, soon joining with his fellow Hibernian, the irresistible Mike, was taking the drama up into the mining gulches and the rowdy mountain hamlets, where human life was cheap and entertainment dear.

Though farther removed from the centres of civilization, Salt Lake City actually anticipated the Colorado communities. The Mormons had always relished play-acting, and soon after settling down in their distant Eden, they turned to their favourite amusement, putting on productions, first, in 1850, in a small building called 'the Bowery' and subsequently in the Social Hall, both men and women participating enthusiastically. Federal troops sent to keep an eye on them set up a canvas theatre at Camp Floyd on the shores of the great lake. Lacking the conventional materials for constructing scenery, the soldiers fell back on chalk and mustard for colouring materials. These makeshifts sufficed, but a carelessness in the matter of rehearsal almost proved the undoing of the military Thespians. Common love of the drama actually seems to have served to bind the watching army and the watched Mormons together, and ladies from Salt Lake sometimes acted at the camp. In 1860 Brigham Young, remembering the pleasure he had derived from his participation in *Pizarro* back in the Nauvoo days, ordered the construction of an imposing theatre, which was finally dedicated with solemn religious services in 1862.

Just as the Mormons welcomed all forms of dramatic entertainment, so the early settlers of the future great state of Texas opened their arms, and in the late 1830s both Houston and Matagordo had theatres before they had churches. Even during the turbulent days of the republic stars from the East made their way to the Texas towns.

Far to the west on the Pacific coast, as in the Colorado Rockies, the gold-seekers demanded their plays—and got them. The first California performances are thought to have been staged in a rough one-story building in Monterey shortly before 1850, about the same time that soldiers were demonstrating their histrionic mettle in Los Angeles, almost on the site of present-day Hollywood. By 1849 Sacramento had its Eagle Theatre, a flimsy structure of canvas and wood which is reputed to have cost the almost incredible sum of $75,000 and more. As in Colorado, admission was paid in gold dust, and when there was high water the spectators clambered up on the benches to keep

their extremities dry. The year 1850 witnessed the opening of the first theatre in San Francisco, over a saloon. Soon thereafter building after building was put up and almost as speedily burned down. Yet the proprietors never admitted defeat, and to California flocked the great and the near-great of the theatrical world, some of them to write their names large in the flamboyant history of the state. Outshining all others in brightness was that of the appealing child-actress Lotta Crabtree (1847–1924), whose mother took her from mining-camp to mining-camp, risking her limbs but guarding her morals. In a sense a child-actress Lotta always remained, and to this day her memory is cherished by the Golden Gate.

After the Civil War, the railroad united the East and the West, and, although for years the desperate Indians remained in places a deadly menace, the frontier soon disappeared. The recent wilderness was dotted with towns and villages, the inhabitants of which, like their pioneering forebears, demanded plays and players. Dion Boucicault (1822–90) fathered 'the Road', and the theatre had come to stay— until the movies rudely and crudely thrust it aside. Yet even to-day it is far from dead. The vitality which survived heat, cold, fire and flood, impromptu stages, and often unspeakable acting, has not succumbed before the advances of cinema and radio. It has changed, adapted itself to new conditions, but died it has not. (See also UNITED STATES.)

W. G. B. C.

PIRANDELLO, LUIGI (1867–1936), one of the most important and widely known of modern Italian dramatists. He began his literary career by writing poems, novels, and short stories which already foreshadowed the philosophy most strongly expressed in his plays—the illusion of life, and the hopelessness of man's attempt to create a reality for himself and for others—a bitter and destructive creed which the unhappy circumstances of Pirandello's private life did nothing to ameliorate. His characters are mainly nameless, in humble circumstances, but from the drama of their lives he draws conclusions vast and far-reaching in their implications, indicative of deep personal anguish and a destructive force of unbelief. There can be no truth, since truth varies with different individuals, and with each individual in different circumstances; there can be no communication with others, since words interpret what seems to be, and not what is; and in the last resort there can be no sanity, since sanity demands a stable foundation, and for Pirandello there is nothing but flux and uncertainty. The influence of his works on a disillusioned post-war generation was profound, and it spread rapidly, through the productions at his own theatre in Rome, founded in 1925, and through the tours of America and Europe which he undertook with his company. The best-known of his plays, in translation, are probably *Sei personaggi in cerca d'autore* (1921), which roused great interest when done in Paris in 1923 by Pitoëff, and as *Six Characters in Search of an Author* was equally successful in England and the U.S.A.; *Così è, se vi pare* (1918) (*Right you are, if you think you are*); *Come tu mi vuoi* (1930) (*As You Desire Me*); and what is probably his finest work, *Enrico IV* (1922) (*Henry IV*).

PIRON, ALEXIS (1689–1773), French dramatist. He was educated for the law, but the bankruptcy of his father sent him to seek his fortune in Paris. There he wrote farces for Francisque's Théâtre de la Foire, and overcame the difficulty of not employing more than one speaking actor, as enacted by the law of 1718, by a series of monologues, of which the first was *Arlequin Deucalion* (1722). Encouraged by his success, he sent a comedy, *L'École des pères*, to the Comédie-Française, where it was produced in 1728. It is an interesting mingling of the old and new theatre, for it stands on the threshold of the *comédie larmoyante*, though its author still holds to the theory that comedy should seek to amuse first, and only incidentally instruct. Piron's best work, and one of the outstanding comedies of the eighteenth century, was *La Métromanie* (1738), while of his tragedies *Gustave Wasa* (1734) remained in the repertory for some time. Piron was a gay and witty companion, who frequented the salon of Mme de Tencin, and was a friend of Rousseau. He suffered all his life from some scurrilous verses which he wrote in his youth; they turned up at the most inopportune moments, and finally lost him his seat in the French Academy.

PISCATOR, ERWIN (1893–   ), German producer, and a disciple of Max Reinhardt. He worked in Berlin from 1919 to 1930, and then went to the United States, where he became director of the Dramatic Workshop of the New School for Social Research. His outstanding production was probably his adaptation of a Czech novel as *Die Abenteuer des braven Soldaten Schweik* (1927). His settings are stylized, and he makes use of films in his productions to enlarge their horizons and speed up the action. He attempts, as it were, to replace both naturalism and expressionism by an intellectual clarity which is not without its own emotion, and makes use of all possible mechanical devices which can drive home the argument of the play. He has had a big influence on the trends of modern European and American play-production.

PISISTRATUS, tyrant of Athens, on and off, from 560 B.C. to his death in 528 B.C. He did much for the economic and cultural development of Athens. In particular he reorganized on a grand scale the festivals of Dionysus, instituting contests in dithyramb and in tragedy, this being the first official recognition of tragedy (see GREECE).

PISTOIA, IL, see CAMINELLI, ANTONIO, and ITALY, 1 *b* i.

PIT, the name given to the ground floor of the theatre auditorium, generally excavated below ground level. In the early playhouses the stage and lower boxes were approximately at ground level, and the whole space sunk between these was called the pit, from the Elizabethan cockpit, used for cock-fighting. In the early nineteenth century the lower boxes were replaced by a raised circle, with the pit extending underneath; shortly after, the old rows of pit seats near the orchestra were replaced by the higher-priced Stalls, and the name 'pit' was applied only to the more distant rows (see also AUDITORIUM).

PITOËFF. (1) GEORGES (1887–1939), Russian actor who settled in Paris after the 1914–18 War and, with his wife (2) LUDMILLA (1896–1951), exerted a great influence on the French theatre up to the time of his death. Like Copeau, he believed that the French theatre, and indeed the theatre everywhere, was suffering from bankruptcy, both of ideas and of imagination. Pitoëff's attempt to remedy this state of affairs consisted in the presentation of the best work of foreign dramatists, as well as the plays of such innovators in the French theatre as Claudel, Cocteau, and Anouilh. The value of his work lay not only in the plays he presented, but in the subtle and entirely personal interpretation which he gave them. He had already had some experience of the theatre before he came to Paris, having for two years directed his own amateur company in St. Petersburg. After appearing in various theatres of Paris, including that of Copeau, he took his company to the Théâtre des Arts in 1924, and from there to the Mathurins. Much of his best work was done in these two theatres, particularly after 1934 when he finally settled at the Mathurins. There he proved himself a fine actor and a complete man of the theatre, adapting, translating, producing, and acting at one and the same time. Among the dramatists whom he introduced to Paris three particularly stand out—Shaw, Shakespeare, and Pirandello—and it was perhaps in Shakespeare that his genius found its fullest scope. He was nobly assisted in his task, which brought him much hard work and little money, by his wife, an excellent actress, who after her husband's death continued to direct the company, taking it on an extended tour of America and Canada. Among the many parts which she played to perfection were Nora in *A Doll's House*, Marthe in Claudel's *L'Échange*, and the hostess in Goldoni's *La Locandiera*. She was also extraordinarily moving as Joan of Arc.

PITT, see DIBDIN.

PITTSBURG, see PIONEER THEATRE IN THE U.S.A.

PIXERÉCOURT, RENÉ CHARLES GUILBERT DE (1773–1844), French dramatist, called by his contemporaries 'the Corneille of Melodrama', of which he wrote more than fifty, ranging from fairy-tale plots to dramas of contemporary life in realistic settings. His early life, which no doubt influenced his writing, was as tormented and extravagant as that of any of his heroes. Seventeen when the Revolution broke out, he escaped to Coblenz, came back to serve in the Revolutionary army, was saved from the wrath of Robespierre by Carnot, and penniless, with a wife and child to support, he painted fans for a living for eighteen long months. He had already written sixteen plays, some of which had been accepted by various theatres but not yet produced, when in 1797 the Ambigu-Comique put on *Les Petits Auvergnats*. It was successful enough to warrant his abandoning the fans for ever, and the rest of his life was devoted to the theatre. Alone or in collaboration he wrote nearly 100 plays, and for thirty years provided the staple fare of the secondary theatres. The first of the long series of melodramas by which he is mainly remembered was *Victor, ou l'enfant de la forêt* (1798), and the most successful *Coelina, ou l'enfant de mystère* (1800), which was soon translated into German, English, and Dutch. Many of his later plays suffered from too much collaboration, but they made money, most of which he lost when the Théâtre de la Gaîté, of which he was a director, and where his best plays were given, was burnt down in 1835. This disaster, joined to the effects of a serious illness, ended his career, and he retired to Nancy to die a lingering death. He was an odd, tormented creature, who in his extraordinary plays seems to typify the Revolution, that mixture of ferocity and idealism, when blood and tears were shed with equal facility. Yet he had an appreciation of good literature, formed a fine library which he wept to see dispersed, and took his work very seriously, setting forth his credo in *Le Mélodrame* and *Dernières réflexions sur le mélodrame*, being the first writer to use the word in its present sense (see MELODRAMA). He wrote quickly, but spent a long time over the production and scenery of his plays, for which he often invented new machinery and provided spectacular effects. He said himself: 'I write for those who cannot read', a large, enthusiastic, but unlettered public, whom he never failed, and whose counterpart to-day is catered for mainly by the films. Pixérécourt, who was the undisputed king of the lesser theatres, marked the extent of German influence in the early nineteenth-century theatre, and in his turn influenced the Romantic dramatists. Hugo and Dumas, among others, saw and enjoyed the melodramas of Pixérécourt, and their own plays are often only melodrama raised to a literary status by the beauties of style and lyric poetry. He also had a great influence in England, where the main characteristics of his theatre are preserved in the drawings of the Penny Plain, Tuppence Coloured Toy Theatre.

PLABILISCHIKOV, PETER ALEXEIVICH (1760–1812), Russian actor and dramatist, educated at Moscow University, where he first became interested in the theatre. On leaving the university he went to St. Petersburg and appeared in revivals of Sumarokov's plays. In 1779 he joined the Court theatre company, playing the roles of heroes and lovers to which his handsome appearance made him eminently suitable. He later became Inspector of Russian Theatres, and in 1793 returned to Moscow, where he was much admired. He wrote a number of plays, of which the historical tragedies are negligible; but those dealing with the everyday life of merchants and peasants are of greater interest, and may be considered the forerunners of social realistic comedy in Russia. A year before his death he was elected a member of the Society of Russian Writers at Moscow University.

PLACIDE, a family of actors, of whom the first (1) ALEXANDRE (? –1812) was rope dancer to the King of France. He left the continent on the outbreak of the Revolution, was seen in Dublin, Bath, Bristol, and Norwich, and in 1791 landed at Charleston, U.S.A., where he gave a display of 'agility and pantomime' which he repeated in New York. He also danced in a ballet, danced a hornpipe, played a fiddle while on the tight-rope, and was seen to 'somerset backward and forward, over a table and chair'. At some point he married an actress, daughter of Mrs. Pownall and of James Wrighten, prompter at Drury Lane, who from 1793 to 1795 was a good leading actress and singer at the John Street Theatre, New York. They had a large family, of whom the eldest girl married William Rufus Blake, and with her two sisters was on the stage. Of the boys the younger became a popular comedian, while the other (2) HENRY (1799–1870) was the best-known of the family. As a child he appeared at the Anthony Street Theatre, New York, and in 1823 made his adult début at the Park in *The Heir-at-Law*. He remained there for many years, except for short tours to other American towns, and one somewhat unsuccessful appearance in London in 1841, and was later at Burton's. Like John Gilbert, he represented the best traditions of polished acting in old comedy, and was excellent in the role of the high-bred English gentleman, Sir Peter Teazle being one of his best parts. He was also good in eccentric humour, particularly in broken-English parts and in dialect, and in his youth was a good singer and farce-player.

PLANCHÉ, (JEAN-BAPTISTE) GUSTAVE (1808–57), French dramatic critic, mainly remembered for his attacks on the Romantics, by which he aroused the enmity of Victor Hugo. A clever man, but much embittered by early poverty, he became critic of the *Revue des Deux Mondes* in 1831, and his somewhat morose and sarcastic temperament was naturally antipathetic to the excesses of the young writers of the time. Later he became the friend of Alfred de Vigny, George Sand, and Balzac, who recognized the sincerity of his work and the justification, according to his own lights, of his strictures on their fellow writers.

PLANCHÉ, JAMES ROBINSON (1796–1880), English dramatist, of Huguenot descent, who was interested in the theatre from an early age, and appeared with some success in amateur theatricals. He was a most prolific writer, mainly of burlesques, extravaganzas, and pantomimes, though he also wrote a few melodramas and comedies. His first play, a burlesque, was given at Drury Lane in 1818, and for the next few years he produced several plays a year, many of them being given at the Adelphi. He was associated with the Vestris–Mathews management at the Lyceum, and wrote for it what many considered his best work, *The Island of Jewels* (1849), for which the scene-painter Beverley produced some remarkable effects. Planché's adaptation of a French melodrama as *The Vampyre; or, the Bride of the Isles* (1820) first introduced to the English stage the so-called 'vampire' trap. Planché was a serious student of art, and designed and supervised the costumes for Charles Kemble's production of *King John* in 1824, the first to approximate to historical accuracy. He was also a good musician, and from 1826 to 1827 was musical director of Vauxhall Gardens. He wrote a quantity of libretti for opera, including Weber's 'Oberon', and English versions of 'William Tell' and 'The Magic Flute'. An unauthorized production of one of his plays led him to press for reform in the laws governing theatrical copyright, and it was mainly his efforts that led to the passing of the Act 3 William IV, c. 15 giving protection to dramatic authors. He published in 1834 a *History of British Costume* which long remained a standard work. Among his many interests he included the study of heraldry, and in his capacity as Rouge Croix Pursuivant of Arms at the Heralds' College he several times went abroad to confer the Order of the Garter on foreign royalties. His work for the theatre seems strangely at variance with his more scholarly activities, but it was enormously successful. It appears to have no literary merit whatever, and divorced from its music and spectacular effects is quite unreadable. It depended largely on its staging and topicality, and taken as a whole provides an excellent picture of the English stage during sixty years.

PLATO. (1) An Athenian comic poet, contemporary with Aristophanes. He gained several victories, but only a few fragments of his work survive. He is often referred to as Plato Comicus, to distinguish him from the philosopher.

(2) The philosopher (427–348 B.C.), of Athens, of highly aristocratic family. In his youth he composed tragedies and other forms of poetry, but on coming under the influence of Socrates and his rigorous intellectualism, he burnt his plays and devoted his life to philosophy and mathematics. However, a few of his epigrams survive, and are among the best in the Greek language.

The philosophical work that he published was put into a dialogue form which was a development of the mime (see MIME, 1 *b*). In the more abstruse works, and in most of the *Republic*, the dialogue is only nominal; elsewhere it is consistently dramatic, with occasional passages of astonishing vividness and power. The character-sketches of Euthyphro or Ion, or the opening scenes of the *Protagoras*, are good examples of Plato's dramatic skill; his mastery of ironic comedy is shown by his picture of the sophists in the *Euthydemus*; of tragedy by the scene of Socrates' death in the *Phaedo*.

Plato's theories of literature and drama have had immense influence. His 'inspirational' theory of poetry is the direct source of the idea of the *furor poeticus*—'the poet's eye in a fine frenzy rolling', through a sixteenth-century translation of Plato's *Ion*, which greatly influenced the French Pléiade. In other dialogues Plato is much less sympathetic to literature; his idea that a conception of 'the Good' can be reached only through the intellectual process of dialectic led him, apparently, to mistrust 'inspiration'; and in the *Republic*, and elsewhere, Plato would admit poetry into his ideal society only under a paralysing censorship. He objects in particular to drama because it appeals especially to the ignorant, seeks what is agreeable rather than what is good, and debilitates the community by appealing to emotions, not to reason, by representing characters as being overcome by their emotions, and by propagating blasphemous and impossible ideas about the deity (e.g. by repeating stories of strife between gods). There was also the more metaphysical objection, against art in general, that since it makes only a copy of sensible objects, themselves only a copy of 'reality', it is further from the truth even than the imperfect world of sense. These criticisms were important chiefly for the reply which they drew from Aristotle.   H. D. F. K.

PLATT, the Elizabethan theatrical term for 'plot', which consisted of a prompter's outline of the action of a play, with division into acts, actors' entrances and exits, and other notes, drawn up and posted somewhere behind the scenes for the help and convenience of organizing calls and properties. It should not be confused with an author's synopsis, nor with the *scenarii* of the *commedia dell'arte*, which were used as the groundwork for improvisation. The 'platt' was a purely utilitarian device, of which a few stray specimens have been preserved among Henslowe's papers.

PLAUTUS, Roman playwright. The twenty-one plays (one of them a mere fragment) contained in his extant manuscripts must be the twenty-one selected by Varro as universally admitted to be authentic out of the 130 which had come by his time (first century B.C.) to be attributed to Plautus. The authenticity of the *Mercator* and the *Asinaria* may be questioned; but in general the plays which have come down to us possess a unity of style and display the qualities which Roman writers attribute to Plautus—command of language and metre, wit, high spirits, and indifference to form.

Neither Plautus's full name, nor the dates of his birth and death, nor any details concerning his life, can be regarded as established. The prologues to his plays, our earliest documents, refer to him as 'Plautus'; whether the 'Maccus' who wrote the *Asinaria* and the 'Maccus (or Maccius) Titus' who wrote the *Mercator* are to be identified with each other and with him is difficult to say. A passage in the *Cistellaria* (*ll.* 197–202) speaks of the Hannibalic War as drawing to a close; and according to notes in the oldest extant manuscript the *Stichus* was produced in 200 and the *Pseudolus* in 191 B.C. The traditional account is scarcely wrong in saying that Plautus knew poverty and hardship, that he acquired a practical knowledge of the theatre at an early age, and that he depended for his livelihood on the success of his plays. These plays, the earliest complete works of Latin literature which we possess, are all free translations from Greek New Comedy. There is no evidence that Plautus deliberately re-modelled the plots or characters given him by his Greek originals; what he did was to choose which plays he would like to translate and to infuse his translations with his own personality. He seems to have liked complicated plot, strongly marked characters, and scenes of love-making, revelry, trickery, and debauchery; he was himself able to supply song, repartee, jests, puns, and topical allusions, often with small regard for what was dramatically appropriate. The fate of Naevius was a warning to all dramatists to abstain from political and personal satire, but there seems to have been no absolute ban on indecency; several of Plautus's plays, such as the *Bacchides*, the *Pseudolus*, and the *Truculentus*, portray the life of the brothel; and the concluding scenes of the *Casina* (a favourite play with the public, to judge by its prologue, which was written for a revival performance) carry farce to outrageous lengths, while suggesting by their lack of form that they are largely the independent work of Plautus himself. There appears indeed to have been some reaction on the part of the public against the prevailing licence of comedy, for the prologue and epilogue to the *Captivi* boast of the high moral tone of that particular play. We note, too, that nowhere does Plautus venture to jest where the honour of a respectable woman is concerned.

Among the better-known plays the *Menaechmi* (source of Shakespeare's *Comedy of Errors*) and the *Amphitruo* deal with the complications caused by mistaken identity; the *Aulularia* shows us a poor old man, Euclio, not free from some traits of miserliness, who has been half-crazed by the discovery of a buried treasure; the *Mostellaria* or 'Ghost Story' displays the endless fertility of invention whereby amid growing difficulties the slave Tranio contrives to baffle his young master's father, unexpectedly returned from abroad; the *Rudens* tells of storm and shipwreck on the lonely shore of Libya; a treasure recovered from the sea, and a long-lost daughter restored to her parents; in the *Captivi* the noble courage and devotion of a slave enable his master to escape from captivity, while he himself eventually finds that his captor is his own father. Considering the limits imposed by New Comedy, the variety of plot in Plautus's plays is considerable; and, if we miss in him the subtle effects of Menander and Terence, we have instead a flow of wit and a vigour of language which explain his supreme popularity on the Roman stage. Within a few years of his death Plautus had become a classic; and even when his plays were ceasing or had long ceased to be acted they provided a source of merriment for generations of readers, from Cicero to St. Jerome.   W. B.

PLAY, a generic term applied to any work written to be acted, and covering such more limiting terms as tragedy, comedy, farce, drama, &c. It may range from a spirited exchange of backchat between two mountebanks in the market-place to a full-length work given in a special building—a theatre—with a cast of highly trained professional actors aided by all the appurtenances of lighting, costuming, and production. The one essential requisite is that it should be entirely or mainly spoken; if given without dialogue it ranks as mime or ballet, if all the dialogue is sung, as opera. Hybrid forms give rise to Ballad Opera, Burletta, and Musical Comedy (for the use of music as an adjunct to a play, see INCIDENTAL MUSIC).

A play can be read, either alone or in company, but only fulfils its original intention when it is acted. The text may therefore be regarded as a skeleton, a dead thing to which the producer, actor, and audience must contribute before it can be brought to life. Although the fundamental principles of drama remain constant—action, conflict, unity of purpose, resolution—the form of a play may conform to certain conventions—five-act, three-act, unity of time and place, separation (or alternatively fusion) of tragedy and comedy—which vary from age to age, and even from country to country. The form, however, comes first, the rules afterwards, even with Aristotle. In the same way, although the art of acting is to some extent dependent on the type of play in favour at the moment, it has an independent life of its own, and at certain points in the history of the theatre there may be conflict between the text and its interpreters. Just as a bad play may succeed temporarily because of some topical allusion or contemporary fashion or because of superlative acting, so a good play may be temporarily eclipsed in its own day, and only appreciated in revival. Generally speaking, plays written to be read—Closet drama—remain outside the main stream of the theatre, though this theory is refuted by the success of Alfred de Musset's *Comédies et Proverbes* on the stage many years after they were written, and by the enormous influence on European drama of the tragedies of Seneca, which were probably not acted, but read aloud.

The poetic drama of the nineteenth century, which from a purely literary point of view contains many fine things, has not yet proved successful in action. A change in theatrical fashion may bring it into prominence, but it seems likely that an inherent lack of dramatic impulse allied to too great a weight of pure poetry may always hinder its immediate effect on an audience (see POETICAL DRAMA). The author alone cannot produce a play in the full sense of the word, and his work demands the co-operation of many other people, among whom he is merely the furnisher of the text. This aspect is lost sight of in our modern use of the word dramatist, but the earlier playwright, in its affinity with such words as wheelwright, reveals it clearly, and makes the author a fellow worker in the theatre with actor, producer, designer, stage-carpenter, and so on. Some of the finest of our plays have been written by men labouring under all the advantages and disadvantages of actual daily participation in the work of the theatre.

PLAYBILL, PROGRAMME (ENGLISH). The playbill, which is the earliest form of the theatrical programme as we know it, occurs comparatively late in the history of dramatic art. What means of publicity were adopted by the Elizabethan players on Bankside are unknown, but it may be assumed that the managers relied upon word of mouth and the services of what in the modern circus is called a 'barker'. Small 'bills' or tickets, giving only the name of the play and the theatre, were apparently scattered in the gentry's coaches, or delivered at their houses by hand, and the earliest known of these (1692) is reprinted by W. J. Lawrence in his *Elizabethan Play-House* (2nd series). But if anything more elaborate from this period ever existed, it is lost, and it is not until about the middle of the eighteenth century that we find examples of anything that might properly be called a playbill.

About this period it became the custom to print an announcement of the play on a small quarto sheet, which was then stuck up on the wall outside the theatre and distributed to the coffee-houses. The earliest specimens in the Gabrielle Enthoven Collection at the Victoria and Albert Museum (the largest collection of London playbills and programmes in the world) were issued by the managements of Covent Garden and Drury Lane and are dated 1737. They are well printed on roughish paper with the Royal Arms at the top and 'Vivat Rex' at the bottom, and are dated each day. At first very few details are given, but the following night's performance is also advertised by means of a note at the foot. As the text grows the Royal Arms disappear, but the legend 'His (or Their) Majesty's Servants present . . .' goes on for some time, and this applies to Lincoln's Inn Fields, Goodman's Fields, and the Haymarket Theatre as well as to the two patent houses.

Gradually more and more details are given, with full list of cast and even, towards the end

of the eighteenth century, mention of the stage decorator (e.g. de Loutherbourg, who worked for Garrick). The playbill was therefore the equivalent of a modern programme, but it also served the purpose of a theatre poster. It was issued daily and dated, a practice which continued until about 1860, when weekly or half-weekly changes occurred. Towards 1810 it grows larger, about foolscap size, and shortly afterwards it becomes a double sheet, in order to accommodate the elaborate descriptions of scenery and painters' names which the new triumphs of the landscape school (Telbin, Clarkson Stanfield, &c.) had made fashionable. The size of the playbill was soon about 19½ inches square folded in the middle. By 1850 it had grown to 26 by 17 inches, and in 1856, during Charles Kean's management of the Princess's Theatre, to 20 by 30 inches folded in three, one column being devoted to lengthy dissertations on his Shakespearian productions. Pantomime characters of this period were also provided with descriptions of a humorous nature, consisting almost entirely of puns in the taste of the time.

The effect of these developments was to make the playbill extremely unwieldy for use as a theatre programme, and about 1850 the Olympic Theatre, London, began to issue small playbills on a quarto sheet about 12 by 9 inches as well as the larger bills. These smaller bills were printed on one side and folded in the middle, and were probably supplied to occupants of the more expensive seats without charge. Drury Lane soon followed, and the other theatres came slowly into line.

No use had yet been made of the theatre programme as a medium of advertisement, but in the eighteen-sixties the firm of Eugene Rimmel, 'Perfumers of London and Paris', began printing, by arrangement with the theatres, notepaper-size programmes with stamped paper-lace borders, some very elaborate. The fourth page of the programme was devoted to Rimmel's advertisement and the whole was perfumed. This practice continued until the eighteen-eighties, and the changes in the details of the advertisements often make it possible to date otherwise undated programmes.

In 1869 the St. James's Theatre, London, began to issue a kind of magazine programme called *Bill of the Play*. The second and third pages were filled with literary matter—notes on the theatre, the current production, &c.—while the fourth page provides a list of omnibus routes, cab fares from different parts of London, and Spiers and Pond's Refreshment Department charges. Similar details of transport facilities appeared on a few other theatre programmes in the eighteen-seventies, but the only other 'magazine' programme of the period was that issued by the Criterion Theatre under the title of *The Firefly*.

The same theatre, in the later eighteen-seventies, began to adorn its programmes with sketches of scenes from the play and actors in character. These appeared on the front and on the borders of the middle pages. All details of the play itself were now confined to the latter. The Haymarket Theatre followed a similar practice, but most other programmes were still very simple, consisting of a single sheet of notepaper with no advertisements. They were issued free, while the legend 'No fees or gratuities of any kind' gives a hint of a controversy which still agitates the theatre from time to time. At the Gaiety Theatre John Hollingshead was a no-fee enthusiast. He issued a four-sheet programme (9½ by 19 inches), which grew to eight sheets in the later eighteen-seventies, with pages 2, 3, 6, 7, and 8 devoted to advertisements. The fanciful design on the cover varied from year to year.

About 1880 thin cardboard programmes came into use, often printed in colour. The Savoy, which opened in 1881 and was the first theatre to be lighted solely by electricity, issued some very elaborate cardboard programmes, printed at first by Marcus Ward & Co., with complicated borders on gold, featuring electric bulbs as decorative motifs. Subsequently Savoy programmes showed coloured sketches of the characters in various Gilbert and Sullivan operettas. Some of these are admirable examples of colour printing and must have been quite costly to produce. The Haymarket Theatre in the period 1886–96 provided cardboard programmes for stalls and dress-circle, paper ones for pit and gallery. These were adorned with a view of the façade of the theatre and a group from *The School for Scandal* as depicted on the drop-curtain.

In the eighteen-eighties appeared for the first time a type of programme which still lingers in provincial music-halls. This was the threefold card, each panel measuring about 8 by 3 inches. These were originally printed by the Edwardes Menu Co. and had small advertisements on either side of the programme-matter and all over the two backs. These programmes, which cost 6d., were used at nearly all the 'fee' theatres and continued in decreasing numbers until well into the twentieth century.

Irving at the Lyceum revived the practice of issuing a programme freshly dated for each performance. This began in the autumn of 1880 and continued for the greater part of his management. Augustin Daly followed the same practice at the various theatres in which his company appeared. After the uniformity of earlier programmes, those of the eighteen-eighties show astonishing variety. Sizes varied enormously, and almost every theatre had its own cover-design. The St. James's Theatre under Alexander used a Beefeater as a kind of symbolic mark. Tree at His Majesty's reproduced many of Charles Buchel's posters of himself. Some theatres showed views of the interior and exterior on the front cover. Aubrey Beardsley's poster design for the season at the Avenue Theatre in 1894 was reproduced in monochrome on the programme. At the Savoy

in 1912 Granville-Barker made a similar use of Albert Rutherston's costume-designs for *The Winter's Tale* and of William Nicholson's for *Twelfth Night*.

After 1910 the 6 by 9 inches type of programme became common. Programmes were now usually issued by the refreshment contractors and this made for greater uniformity. After the war of 1914–18 'magazine' programmes on American lines were used by many theatres. These cost 6d. and contained a certain amount of light reading-matter or theatrical gossip. Other theatres issued a programme of as much as twenty pages with photographs of the performers, scenes from the play, and a very large number of advertisements, the actual programme-matter being confined to the middle sheet. The increasing commercialization of the theatre affected even the actual programme-matter. Whereas formerly only theatrical purveyors had been mentioned, credit was now given to dressmakers, milliners, and the suppliers of shoes, stockings, furniture, typewriters, cigarettes, and properties of all kinds. Programmes were then sold in all theatres at prices varying from 3d. to 6d. (Old Vic, 2d.) except on first nights when they were usually presented free of charge. When paper restrictions came into force during the 1939–45 war programmes were reduced to a single folded sheet, or were cut to a size of about 3 by 5½ inches.

'Gala' programmes form a class by themselves. In the early nineteenth century we find them printed on fringed silk or satin, a practice which continued into the twentieth century. In the late nineteenth century the programmes of the St. James's Theatre were printed in gold on cardboard for first nights, and for similar occasions. Irving had his printed on imitation vellum. Some of the programmes issued for performances of the Russian Ballet were artistic productions of a high order. These Gala programmes were often very expensive (5s.). Attempts to introduce a transparent programme which could be read when held up to the light were not very successful, for such a programme is necessarily confined to a single sheet (see also POSTERS, THEATRICAL).

G. E.

PLAYERS' CLUB. (1) NEW YORK. This was founded in 1888 on the lines of the Garrick Club in London, on the initiative of Lawrence Barrett, Augustin Daly, Albert M. Palmer, and Edwin Booth, the last-named donating and endowing his house at 16 Gramercy Park for the purpose. He continued to occupy a suite of rooms in it, and died there in 1893. The Players', which admits ladies only to a ceremonial dinner held on the Sunday nearest to Shakespeare's birthday, has a large collection of theatrical relics, including jewellery and weapons owned by famous actors, paintings of American and foreign actors, death-masks, and a fine library, which is continually being added to. Edwin Booth's rooms are still as he left them, though other parts of the house have been altered to provide accommodation for members. One of the features of the Players' is an open-air courtyard at the back of the house, with a veranda round, where members may dine in summer. John Drew was for many years president of the Players', and in 1947 the library and theatre collection were catalogued and arranged by May Davenport Seymour and Elizabeth P. Barrett, of the New York Public Library Theatre Department.

(2) TORONTO. This was founded in 1913 as a university dramatic society. It gave its first performance in the hall of Victoria College, its repertory consisting mainly of established one-act plays, though occasional new Canadian short plays were given. Its first producer was the American-trained actor and director, Roy Mitchell, who in 1919 took the company to the newly opened Hart House Theatre, where they gave an interesting season of classical plays, accompanied by a programme of lectures and musical matinées. The organization of what was virtually an undergraduate society, however, was not adapted to the management of a permanent theatre with technical and financial problems, and on the emergence of the Board of Syndics, with nine members under the Chairmanship of Vincent Massey, the Players' Club withdrew and re-formed as a separate body. Among its later productions was an outstanding *Way of the World*. Sir Ernest Macmillan was for some years Director of Music for the Club (see also CANADA and HART HOUSE THEATRE).

PLAYERS' THEATRE, a small private theatre in Villiers Street (formerly in Evans's Song-and-Supper Rooms, King Street, Covent Garden, and in Albemarle Street), started by Peter Ridgeway and Leonard Sachs in 1936. Plays were sometimes given, but the main feature was *Late Joys*, a song-and-supper cabaret of Victorian burlesques, dances, and turns, introduced in true music-hall style by a Chairman.

PLAYFAIR, SIR NIGEL (1874–1934), English actor, producer, and manager, who gained his early experience with the O.U.D.S. and other amateur societies. He was intended for the law, but in 1902 made his first appearance on the stage, and later toured with Benson, and was in Shaw's plays at the Court Theatre. He also appeared in a number of Shakespearian parts at His Majesty's under Tree, and played Bottom in Granville-Barker's production of *A Midsummer Night's Dream* at the Savoy in 1912. In 1918 he took over the Lyric Theatre, Hammersmith, and remained there until 1932, making it one of the most popular and stimulating centres of theatrical activity. He produced there *Abraham Lincoln*, a revival of *The Beggar's Opera* with settings by Claude Lovat Fraser which ran for nearly 1,500 performances, *Lionel and Clarissa*, *Riverside Nights*, an intimate revue by A. P. Herbert and others, *The Way of the World* and *The Beaux' Stratagem*, both with Edith Evans, a stylized black-and-white revival of *The Importance of* *Being Earnest*, with John Gielgud as Worthing, *When Crummles Played*, a burlesque of *The London Merchant* set in the theatrical background of *Nicholas Nickleby*, and numerous other plays old and new, in many of which he himself appeared. He was also responsible for the production of *The Insect Play*, given at the Regent in 1923, being part-author of the translation. He wrote an account of his Hammersmith management in *The Story of the Lyric Theatre, Hammersmith* (1925) and *Hammersmith Hoy* (1930). In 1928 he was knighted for his magnificent services to the English theatre, on which he had a profound and lasting influence.

PLAYHOUSE. (1) LONDON, at the Embankment end of Northumberland Avenue. This theatre was built by Sefton Parry as a speculation. It was for a time thought that the South Eastern Railway Co. would require the site for the extension of Charing Cross station, but they did without it, and the theatre, then known as the Avenue, opened on 11 Mar. 1882, with 'Madame Favart', the cast including Florence St. John, Fred Leslie, and Marius. After a series of light operas the Avenue had its first big success with Arthur Roberts in such plays as *The Old Guard*, while in 1890 George Alexander started his career as actor-manager in *Dr. Bill*. A year later *The Crusaders* was a success, as was a revival of *Judah*. Mr. and Mrs. Kendal appeared in 1893 in *A White Lie* and *The Silver Shell*, while 1894 saw the first production of *Arms and the Man*.

Mrs. Patrick Campbell and Forbes-Robertson were at the Avenue in 1899, and in the same year Charles Hawtrey staged one of the theatre's greatest successes, *A Message from Mars*, which opened on 22 Nov. and ran for 544 performances. In 1905 Cyril Maude, who had severed his partnership with Harrison at the Haymarket, took the Avenue, demolished and rebuilt it. On the night of 5 Dec. the roof of Charing Cross Station collapsed and wrecked the new building. It was again rebuilt, and opened as the Playhouse on 28 Jan. 1907, with Cyril Maude in *Toddles*. He remained there until Sept. 1915, producing and playing in many successful plays, both new and revivals, together with his wife, Winifred Emery. He was succeeded, in 1917, by Gladys Cooper, who, with Frank Curzon until 1928, and later by herself, staged and appeared in many plays, including a distinguished revival of *The Second Mrs. Tanqueray*. She left in 1933, and since then the theatre has had no settled policy.

W. M. P.

(2) NEW YORK, on 48th Street, between Broadway and Fifth Avenue. This was built by William A. Brady, and opened on 15 Apr. 1911. It had its first success with *Bought and Paid For*, which ran up 431 performances, and in 1915–16 Grace George, wife of Brady, appeared there in a repertory which included *The Liars*, the first American performance of *Major Barbara*, and a revival of *Captain Brassbound's Conversion*. Later successful new plays

were *For the Defence* (1919) and *The Wonderful Thing* (1920) with Jeanne Eagels, and in 1924 came *The Show-Off*, with a fine performance by Louis Jean Bartels, which ran for 571 performances. The next important production was *The Road to Rome* (1927), followed by *Street Scene* (1929) in its original form. This gained the Pulitzer Prize, and is considered by many to be Elmer Rice's finest play to date. After a somewhat blank period the theatre had a further success with *Three Men on a Horse* (1935). *Yes, My Darling Daughter* (1937) had 405 performances, and was followed by several successful revivals, including *The Circle*, *Outward Bound*, and *Kind Lady*. In 1945 *The Glass Menagerie*, in which Laurette Taylor made her last appearance as The Mother, began a long run at this theatre.   G. F.

PLOUGH (or PLOW) MONDAY, in English folk festivals the Monday after Twelfth Night. Fragmentary texts of a Plough Monday play have been recovered from the East Midlands, similar in character to the Christmas Mumming Play, with which it was probably assimilated. The main differences between the two are that the characters of the Plough Monday play are farm-hands and their like, not heroes, as in the Mumming Play, and the central incident, the death of one of the characters, is due to an accident and not to a fight. Both plays are probably survivals, later influenced by literary trends, of a primitive folk festival of Winter and Spring (see MUMMING PLAY).

PLYMOUTH THEATRE, NEW YORK, on West 45th Street, opened on 10 Oct. 1917. This theatre has a commodious stage, and is the official home of Arthur Hopkins, who has presented many of his most successful ventures there. Among the more interesting of the early productions was *The Wild Duck* (1918), this being the first time the play had been given in New York in English. Nazimova starred in it, and also appeared in *Hedda Gabler* and *A Doll's House*. Later in the year John Barrymore appeared in a dramatization of Tolstoy's *Redemption*, entitled *The Living Corpse*, and, in 1919, in *The Jest*, with his brother Lionel. Among later successes the most memorable was *What Price Glory?* (1924), a realistic portrayal of war which, with a fine cast, ran for 433 performances. In 1925 came Winthrop Ames's delightful revivals of Gilbert and Sullivan, while later successes at this theatre include *Burlesque* (1927), which established Barbara Stanwyck as a star, *Counsellor-at-Law* (1931) with Paul Muni, *Tovarich* (1936), the Pulitzer Prize-winner *Abe Lincoln in Illinois* (1938), the anti-Nazi melodrama *Margin for Error* (1939), and the charming *Lute Song* (1946), an adaptation by Sidney Howard of a Chinese play, in which Mary Martin gave a fine performance.   G. F.

POCKETS (the American name for Dips), see LIGHTING, 2 *f*.

POCOCK, ISAAC (1782–1835), English painter and dramatist, mainly remembered to-day for his melodrama, *The Miller and his Men* (1813), which, with its romantic scenery, strong situations, and incendiary denouement, has proved the most popular play of the nineteenth-century Juvenile Drama, and is still occasionally revived in cardboard. Pocock was the author of several other popular melodramas—including one of the many versions of the thieving magpie story as *The Magpie, or the Maid?* (1815), another Toy Theatre favourite—of a number of farces, written mainly at the beginning of his career, and of innumerable adaptations of Scott's novels. He had little originality, and is merely one of the many writers of the period whose work in a more literary age would have been relegated to the minor theatres. However, in the general poverty of play-writing at the time, he was usually accorded production at Covent Garden and Drury Lane, or at the very least at the Haymarket. It was Pocock's *Rob Roy Macgregor* (1818) that first brought Macready into prominence, while his farce, *Hit or Miss* (1810), gave Mathews a good part as Dick Cypher. Pocock was a pupil of Romney and a good artist, exhibiting several times at the Royal Academy.

PODESTA, JOSÉ J., see SOUTH AMERICA, 1.

POEL, WILLIAM (1852–1934), English actor and producer, son of William Pole. He changed his name in deference to his father's dislike of his chosen profession, and made his first appearance on the stage in 1876. His first production was an episode from *Don Quixote*, given at the King's Cross Theatre in 1880. For two years Poel was manager of the Old Vic, then a music-hall, and many of his early productions were adaptations made by himself from novels and stories. He was for many years general instructor to the Shakespeare Reading Society, for which he produced a number of plays, and it was with a donation from them, and one from Mr. Arthur Dillon, that in 1894 he founded the Elizabethan Stage Society, whose work had such an enormous influence on the staging and production of Shakespeare in the following century. The Society appeared in various halls and courtyards, and, on a stage modelled in accordance with Poel's idea of an Elizabethan stage, produced Shakespeare (beginning with *Twelfth Night* in 1895), Marlowe, Beaumont and Fletcher, Jonson, Middleton, Rowley and Ford, and a translation of *Everyman*, its first performance for 400 years. Much of the incidental music was written and played by Arnold Dolmetsch and his family, and the plays were given with the minimum of scenery and the maximum of poetic effect. Shaw, reviewing Poel's work, said:

The more I see of these performances by the Elizabethan Stage Society, the more I am convinced that their method of presenting an Elizabethan play is not only the right method for that particular sort of play, but that any play performed on a platform amidst the audience gets closer home to its hearers than when it is presented as a picture framed by a proscenium.

The last production of the Elizabethan Stage Society was *Romeo and Juliet* in 1905. Financially the venture had not been a success but artistically it vindicated Poel's theories, and stimulated others to experiment with simple settings and so free Shakespeare from the cumbersome trappings of the late 19th century. Poel continued to work in the theatre until his death, and was responsible for the revivals, under various auspices, of the old improvised *Hamlet* play of the English Comedians, *Fratricide Punished*, given for the first time in England at the Oxford Playhouse in 1924; of *Arden of Feversham* in 1925; and of *David and Bethsabe* in 1932, for the first time since 1599. He was President of the London Shakespeare League, and author of several plays and books on the theatre.

POETIC DRAMA. The use of poetry for plays was constant in early times all over Europe, and continued for tragedy long after comedy had suffered the incursion of prose. From the prose comic scenes of Shakespeare, interpolated among some of his sublimest poetry, it was an easy step to the complete prose comedies of, for example, Dryden, who continued to use poetry for tragedy. But even the latter usage waned, and it finally became the fashion for all plays intended for the stage to be written throughout in prose, a fashion that was intensified in the late nineteenth and early twentieth centuries by the growing commercialism of the theatre, which effectively ousted the poet from the stage. In return many poets conceived their dramatic works as pure poetry, often not intended for production. But some, uneasily aware of the unhappy gulf between what had originally been the component parts of a good play, tried to effect a reconciliation. The term 'poetic drama', which would at one time have been unnecessary, was then adopted to signalize their attempts to bring poetry back to the theatre as a living organism and is applied also to plays written in a deliberately 'poetic' manner, even if not in verse-form. ED.

The rebirth of the theatre in the age of Goethe and Schiller and the still-rising tide of romanticism in literature stimulated the growth of poetic drama (poetic plays written to be acted) in Europe.

In nineteenth-century England most of the leading poets, who usually lacked skill in playwriting, joined with star performers such as Kean, Macready, and Irving in presenting poetic drama of varying literary and dramatic merits. Byron's *Werner* (1830), Browning's *A Blot in the 'Scutcheon* (1843), Shelley's *The Cenci* (1886), and Tennyson's *Becket* (1893) were outstanding, but the rhetorical dramas of James Sheridan Knowles and Sir Edward Bulwer-Lytton's *The Lady of Lyons* (1838) and *Richelieu* (1839) were more popular and more frequently performed. The plays of John Davidson, which contain much excellent poetry, have gone unproduced, and it has been possible to perform only portions of Thomas Hardy's magnificent epic drama, *The Dynasts* (pub. 1904–8). Stephen Phillips, probably the most successful combination of poet and dramatist of his time, brought blank verse back into the commercial theatre of London for a brief period with his plays *Herod* (1900), *Ulysses*, and *Paolo and Francesca* (both 1902). But he was also the last of the poetic dramatists in the tradition of the nineteenth century, a century which had seen a gradual estrangement of poetic drama from the main body of plays written for the theatre.

About the turn of the century, poetic drama, under such diverse influences as the Nō drama of Japan, Ibsen, and the advance of realism, and the writings of the French symbolist poets, began to take on a more experimental tone, and poetic dramatists began to think in terms of a theatre of their own. The leaders of the Irish literary revival, William Butler Yeats, John Millington Synge, and Lady Gregory, produced many plays of great poetic beauty and sound dramatic structure. Yeats, with his short verse-plays such as *The Land of Heart's Desire* (1894), *Cathleen Ni Houlihan* (1902), *The King's Threshold* (1903), and *Deirdre* (1906), was never able to establish a poetic theatre as he wished, but his integrity as a poet and dramatist raised the standards of poetic drama and deeply influenced his Irish and English contemporaries. Synge's plays, though written in prose, are the work of a true poet, as are those of O'Casey.

Among the English poetic dramas of the early twentieth century, John Masefield's *The Tragedy of Nan* (1908) (in poetic prose), John Drinkwater's *Rebellion* (1914), James Elroy Flecker's *Hassan* (1923), Gordon Bottomley's *King Lear's Wife* (1915) and *Gruach* (1923), were the most important. In the 1930s a number of poets, including T. S. Eliot, Stephen Spender, W. H. Auden, and Christopher Isherwood, broke away from the traditional verse play and laid new foundations for poetic drama with free verse, modern symbolism, satire, and social consciousness. Eliot's plays, *Murder in the Cathedral* (1935) and *The Family Reunion* (1939), are notable for their fine poetry; *The Dog Beneath the Skin* (1936) and *The Ascent of F.6* (1937) by Auden and Isherwood, for their intellectual wit, penetrating satire, and social criticism.

The first important American poetic dramatist, William Vaughn Moody, won his principal success with a prose play, *The Great Divide* (1906), but his work and teachings have influenced many others, such as Josephine Preston Peabody and Percy MacKaye. Maxwell Anderson has carried on a long and valiant fight to establish poetic drama in the American theatre. *Mary of Scotland* (1933) and *Winterset* (1935) are his best works so far, but in these, as in his other plays, the poetry is definitely not of the first rank and his dramatic construction frequently leaves something to be desired.

Among contemporary American poets, E. E. Cummings, Edna St. Vincent Millay, Robinson Jeffers, Wallace Stevens, Alfred Kreymborg, and Archibald MacLeish have all written distinguished poetic dramas, only a few of which have been widely produced. Their work is, for the most part, characterized by great freedom and individuality and considerable experiment.

As the cleavage between the poetic theatre and the commercial theatre has become more acute in the twentieth century, the production of poetic drama has had to depend mainly on university theatres, dramatic schools, and groups which have been formed specifically for that purpose. In England, the Mercury Theatre, which began in London in the 1930s, is exclusively devoted to the production of poetic drama, and its successful presentation in 1945 of Ronald Duncan's *This Way to the Tomb*, and Anne Ridler's *The Shadow Factory*, indicates that there is still an audience for poetic drama. Plays in verse, including *The Zeal of Thy House*, by Dorothy Sayers, and *Christ's Comet*, by Christopher Hassall, have been written for production in the Chapter House of Canterbury Cathedral, as part of a revival of religious drama in England. Poetic plays by Christopher Fry, including *A Phoenix Too Frequent* and *The Lady's Not For Burning*, have been successfully produced in London. Since the death of the Federal Theatre Project in the United States in 1939 there has been very little production of poetic drama in America. Radio broadcasting, particularly in England, has given thousands an opportunity to hear new poetic drama written especially for radio by such poets as Louis MacNeice, Archibald MacLeish, and Norman Corwin.

The history of poetic drama on the continent of Europe in the nineteenth and twentieth centuries is frequently a history of poets who wrote their dramas in prose, a development common in nineteenth-century Europe but not strongly felt in England and Ireland until the 1890s. In France, such verse-dramas as Hugo's *Hernani* (1830) and *Ruy Blas* (1838), Coppée's *Pour la Couronne* (1895), and Rostand's *Cyrano de Bergerac* (1897) must be considered with the prose plays of Musset, Vigny, Claudel, Vildrac, Cocteau, and the Belgian symbolist, Maurice Maeterlinck, for a comprehensive picture of poetry on the stage. In Germany, Hebbel's *Judith* (1840) and *Maria Magdalena* (1846), the plays of Hauptmann, particularly *Die versunkene Glocke* (1896), the short verse plays and libretti of Hofmannsthal, and the plays of Berthold Brecht are significant contributions to poetic drama. In their own countries Chekhov, Ibsen, Strindberg, Grillparzer, D'Annunzio, Valle-Inclán, Martínez Sierra, and Garcia Lorca, writing in poetry or prose, sometimes in both, have made eminent contributions to the development of their national dramas and to the growth of the modern poetic theatre.

In the last century and a half poetic drama has developed from the traditional blank-verse pattern to the most experimental forms of poetry and prose. It has been at the heart of many important literary movements, notably French symbolism and the Irish literary renaissance, and never far from the frontiers of modern literature. The competition of the commercial theatre has been severe and the position of poetic drama in the modern theatre is not so assured as it deserves to be, but poetic dramatists still have faith in the theatre as a medium of expression and the future lies in the development of their art.   H. C.

POGODIN, NIKOLAI FEDOROVICH (1900–   ), Soviet dramatist, who has steadily consolidated his reputation, and is now one of the outstanding figures of the Soviet stage. By profession a journalist, he entered the theatre in 1929, with a play which was rehearsed by the Moscow Art Theatre, but for some reason not performed. This was followed by *Tempo*, which shows a group of Soviet workers, helped by an American engineer, constructing a building in record time. This play, which is based on fact, and is hardly more than a 'documentary', was produced in 1930 at the Vakhtangov Theatre, and was translated into English by Irving Talmadge in *Six Soviet Plays* (1934). *Poem About an Axe*, which deals with the trials of a blacksmith who finds a new process for the manufacture of steel and then forgets how he did it, was produced by Popov at the Theatre of the Revolution in 1931, as was *My Friend* in the following year. This, a more human and profound piece of work, paved the way for Pogodin's most famous play, *Aristocrats*, an extraordinary piece of stagecraft as well as an intensely moving human document. It deals with the regeneration of a gang of criminals engaged on the digging of a canal from the Baltic to the White Sea and also appeared in *Six Soviet Plays*, in a translation by Anthony Wixley. It was first produced at the Vakhtangov Theatre in 1934, and by Okhlopkov in the same year at the Realistic Theatre, while in 1938 it was seen at the Unity Theatre in London. But even in this play Pogodin had not yet succeeded in making his characters individuals rather than types, nor in evolving action credibly from within rather than imposing it from without. In these and other respects his next play, *The Man with the Gun*, a play about Lenin produced at the Vakhtangov Theatre in 1937, showed a great advance, which appears to have been maintained in his later plays, such as *Kremlin Chimes* (1942), a sequel to the above, and in his war plays, *The Ferryboat Girl*, which deals with the defence of Stalingrad, and *Moscow Nights*. With so much excellent work behind him at a comparatively early age, Pogodin is one of the contemporary Soviet authors of whom much may be expected.

POISSON, a family of actors who served the French stage during three generations. The first, (1) RAYMOND (*c*. 1630–90), known as Belleroche, was intended for the medical profession, but joined a provincial company in about 1650, and a few years later was at the Hôtel de Bourgogne, where his wife played the parts given up by Mlle Bellerose, wife of the famous tragedian. A big man, with an expressive face and a large mouth, Poisson was an excellent comic actor, in spite of a slight stutter, and was a favourite of Louis XIV, who liked both his acting and his companionship, and of Colbert, who stood godfather to one of his children. He took from Scarron's *Écolier de Salamanque* (1654) the character of the valet Crispin, and made it peculiarly his own, introducing it into several of his plays and playing the part himself. His many light comedies have been forgotten, since they had none of the gaiety of his acting. One, however, is interesting—*Le Baron de la Crasse* (1663)—since it shows a strolling company performing before some local gentry, and its leader may be intended as a satirical portrait of Molière. Two of Poisson's daughters were on the stage and married actors (see DAUVILLIERS and LA TUILLERIE), while his second son, with an actress wife, was a member of a company maintained by the King of Poland. Of all his children, however, it was (2) PAUL (1658–1735) who best carried on the family tradition. He joined the Comédie-Française in 1688, playing his father's old parts, including Crispin, with the same stutter, and remained with the company until 1724, except for a short retirement between 1711 and 1715. He married (3) ANGÉLIQUE (1657–1756), actress daughter of Du Croisy, who was on the stage at 13, and a member of the Comédie-Française from its foundation until she retired in 1694. Her sons (4) PHILIPPE (1682–1743) and (5) FRANÇOIS ARNOULD (1696–1753) were both actors, though the elder disliked the life and retired in 1722. He was, like his grandfather, a dramatist, and wrote a number of comedies, of which the best was *L'Impromptu de campagne* (1733). François Arnould, on the contrary, ran away from the army to join a company of strolling players, and was admitted to the Comédie-Française against his father's wish. He was excellent in valets and heavy humorous characters, and he too inherited Raymond's stutter. His most admired role was Lafleur in *Le Glorieux*. His sister (6) MADELEINE-ANGÉLIQUE (1684–1770) married a Spaniard named Le Gomez, and was the author of four tragedies, of which one, *Habis*, given at the Comédie-Française in 1714 and frequently revived, was the most successful.

POLIZIANO [ANGELO AMBROZINI] (1454–91), early Italian dramatist, friend and protégé of Lorenzo de' Medici (the Magnificent). His *La Favola di Orfeo* was one of the first plays by an Italian to be written in the vernacular, and to make use of a classical-mythological, instead of a biblical, subject. Written in 1472 at the request of the Cardinal of Mantua, it may have been given in that year, and in any case was probably performed before 1483, when the Cardinal died. In form the *Orfeo* resembles a *sacra rappresentazione*, but its content points

forward to the imminent development of the secular forms of Renaissance drama, especially of the pastoral (see ITALY, 1).

POLLARD, THOMAS (*fl.* first half of seventeenth century), English actor, a comedian with the King's Men. He probably began his acting career as Shank's apprentice in the Palsgrave's Company in about 1610. By 1623, when he was already a member, though not a shareholder, in the King's Company, he had achieved some eminence as a player of comic roles, and he added considerably to his reputation in later years. With the actor Bowyer he was accused of having embezzled the wardrobe and effects of the company on the closing of the theatres in 1642, but there may be an element of exaggeration in this, since Pollard was still *persona grata* with his old companions after this date, and with them signed the dedication of the Beaumont and Fletcher folio of 1647.

POLUS, the most famous Greek tragic actor of the fourth century B.C. (see GREECE, 3 *d*).

POMPONIUS, see FABULA (1) *Atellana*.

PONSARD, FRANÇOIS (1814–67), French dramatist, whose somewhat frigid neo-classical plays came as a relief to a public wearied by the excesses of Romanticism. Ponsard, who was a lawyer by profession, was first attracted to the theatre by seeing the great actress, Mlle Rachel, at Lyons, where she appeared in a number of plays by Racine and Corneille, and his first play, *Lucrèce*, based directly on Livy and Corneille, ignored entirely the poetry and passion of the Romantic school. Given in 1843, the year which saw the failure of Hugo's *Les Burgraves*, it was an instantaneous success. Some of the credit for this must go to its actors, headed by Bocage and Mlle Dorval, some to the reactions of an audience who found in its sobriety, says a contemporary critic, some dignity, some reticence, and much common sense, above all a subject and a style which they could understand and appreciate. Ponsard, who followed up this play with several other tragedies, thus found himself the champion of order and seemliness, in opposition to the licence of Romanticism, and the founder of what was known as *le théâtre du bon sens*. His most successful play, based on a contemporary theme, was *L'Honneur et l'argent* (1853), which opened to him the doors of the French Academy in 1855. He did not, however, enjoy writing these moralizing bourgeois plays, which were coming into fashion with Augier and the younger Dumas, and returned to his earlier methods in *Le Lion amoureux* (1866) and *Galilée* (1867). The first was successful, but the second aroused the opposition of the clerical party. It had not been intended for production, and the slowness of the action was not compensated for by the beauty of the verse. Ponsard, whose works are now completely forgotten, kept up a steady level of talented mediocrity, and his initial success was due more to the reaction against the Romantics than to his intrinsic merits. He wrote a charming idyll, *Horace et Lydie* (1850), for Mlle Rachel, who had refused to play the heroine in his *Charlotte Corday* earlier in the year, a part interpreted with much success by Mlle Judith.

PONTI, DIANA DA (*fl.* 1582–1605), an actress of the *commedia dell'arte*, known as Lavinia, who, after appearing with the Confidenti and possibly Gelosi troupes, had a company of her own, which may have been the Desiosi. She appeared in Lyons in 1601, and is last heard of at the head of a company under the patronage of the Duke of Mirandola in 1605. She played young lover parts.

POPE, JANE (1742–1818), English actress, who played as a child with Garrick, and made her first appearance as an adult on 27 Sept. 1759, as Corinna in *The Confederacy*. She was immediately successful, and soon succeeded Kitty Clive, playing hoydens, chambermaids, and pert ladies, with a brilliance that made Churchill in 1761 call her 'lively Pope'. She was the original Mrs. Candour in *The School for Scandal* and Tilburina in *The Critic*, and played Portia to Macklin's Shylock on his last appearance in 1789. She only relinquished young characters when age and obesity forced her to, and then proved herself equally good in elderly duenna parts, and in such parts as Mrs. Heidelberg. She retired in May 1808.

POPE, THOMAS (?–1604), one of the actors in Shakespeare's plays, and an original shareholder in the Globe and the Curtain. In 1586–7 he went with Kempe and other actors to Denmark and Germany, and joined the Chamberlain's Men on their formation in 1594. He is referred to as 'a clown' and may have played some of the parts of Kempe.

POPOV, ALEXEI DMITREVICH (1892–   ), outstanding Soviet producer, who joined the Moscow Art Theatre in 1912 and worked there for six years. He then went to Kostroma to become director of a drama studio organized by local students, and under him the theatre achieved professional status. While there he produced plays, such as *The Cricket on the Hearth* and *The Devil's Disciple*, on which he had previously worked either in Moscow or independently. From 1923 to 1930 he worked at the Vakhtangov Theatre, where his six main productions played an important part in the development of the company. In 1931 he was invited to become artistic director of the Theatre of the Revolution, where his outstanding productions were *Poem About an Axe*, *My Friend*, and *Romeo and Juliet*: In 1936 he went to the Central Theatre of the Red Army in Moscow, where his production of *The Taming of the Shrew* in 1937 made theatre history.[1] He also did there *Field-Marshal Suvorov* (1939),

[1] For a detailed account of this see Joseph Macleod's *New Soviet Theatre* (1943).

and a lavishly spectacular *Midsummer Night's Dream* (1940). During the Second World War he went with his theatre into evacuation, producing a number of plays, among them *Long, Long Ago* (1942) and the brilliant and topical *Stalingrad* (1944). Popov, the keynote of whose work is humanity, has always been kind to young writers, and was the first to encourage Pogodin by producing his early plays at the Theatre of the Revolution. He is probably the most important figure of the Soviet theatre at the present time.

PORTA, GIAMBATTISTA DELLA, see DELLA PORTA.

PORTABLE THEATRES, see ENGLISH FAIRGROUND AND PORTABLE THEATRES.

PORTER, HENRY (*fl.* 1596–9), English dramatist, mentioned by a contemporary as one of 'the best for comedy amongst us'; he worked for Henslowe, but of the several plays recorded in Henslowe's Diary only one survives. This is *The Two Angry Women of Abingdon* (*c.* 1598), a comedy of English rural life which, says Lamb, is 'full of business, humour and merry malice'. Nothing is known of Porter's life, though he appears to have been at Oxford, and he can be identified equally well with any of the numerous Henry Porters listed there towards the end of the sixteenth century.

PORTER, MARY ANN (?–1765), English actress, who understudied Mrs. Barry, and later succeeded her in tragic parts. She had been on the stage as a child, and was a pupil of Betterton. In later life she was an ideal tragedy queen, tall, well-formed, with a deep, modulated voice which rendered her unsuitable for comedy. Barton Booth, who did not admire Anne Oldfield in tragedy, was in raptures over Mrs. Porter's Belvidera. In parts where passion predominated she seemed to be inspired with an enthusiastic ardour capable of raising the coldest spectator to animation. Yet, when grief and tenderness were called for, she was capable of the most affecting softness. Among her original parts were Hermione in *The Distressed Mother* and Alicia in *Jane Shore*. She made her first appearance at Lincoln's Inn Fields in 1699, and her last at Covent Garden in 1742. In private life she was a quiet, respectable person, and enjoyed a long retirement in the society of her friends.

PORTER'S HALL, LONDON (or Rosseter's Blackfriars) a playhouse in the precincts of Blackfriars, erected by Philip Rosseter in 1615. It was never finished, as the authorities intervened, but plays seem to have been given there by the Lady Elizabeth's and the Prince's Men.

PORTE-SAINT-MARTIN, THÉÂTRE DE LA, PARIS. This theatre was built on its present site in 1781 after the burning of the Opéra, and housed the company of the latter until 1794. It was then used for various purposes and did not open again as a theatre until

1810, after which it was used exclusively for strong drama and spectacular works. In 1822 a company of English actors tried unsuccessfully to give *Othello* there. Later the plays of Delavigne and Hugo were given, as were the big fairy-tale shows, *La Biche au bois* and *Pied de mouton*. It was at this theatre, under the management of Harel, that Frédérick-Lemaître made his first triumphant appearances with Mme Dorval. The building was destroyed by fire in 1871, but was rebuilt on the same site from the original plans, and continued its successful career.

PORTMAN THEATRE, London, see WEST LONDON THEATRE.

PORTUGUESE-AMERICAN THEATRE, see SOUTH AMERICA, 2.

POSSART, Ernst von (1841–1921), German actor and theatre manager, who made his first appearance on the stage at Breslau in 1860, where he played Iago. This began his apprenticeship to tragedy, of which he was a distinguished exponent in later years, some of his finest parts being Shylock, Franz Moor, Mephistopheles, Carlos in *Clavigo*, and Nathan the Wise in Lessing's play of that name. In 1864 von Possart was in Munich, where he became manager of the theatre in 1875, and Intendant General of the Royal Theatres in 1893. He was the founder of the Prinz Regent Theater, and of festivals in commemoration of Wagner and Mozart, held between 1893 and 1905. In 1910 he appeared in New York in a repertory of distinguished plays, with much success. A fine-looking man, with an alert, intelligent face and flashing eyes, he was noted for the beauty of his voice and the dignity and ease of his movements. He adapted a number of plays for the German stage, including some of Shakespeare's, and was given an honorary doctorate by the University of Munich.

POSTERS, THEATRICAL. If the poster may be defined as a temporary public announcement by means of letters or pictures, or both, it is at least as old as the Egypt of Ptolemy, for there is in existence a papyrus of about 150 B.C. giving details of two slaves escaped from the neighbourhood of Alexandria. The Greeks were in the habit of inscribing notices on white-washed walls or on wooden boards. They used in addition a kind of rotating square column on the four faces of which inscriptions were either painted or engraved. It is probable that some of these inscriptions referred to theatrical performances. Theatrical publicity was certainly known to the Romans, for considerable evidence has survived of the way in which the problem was handled in such a representative town as Pompeii. A so-called 'album' was discovered in the ruins in the early years of the nineteenth century. It consisted of a wall divided by pilasters with panels, and on these it was the custom to announce in red and black paint the details of gladiatorial shows and other attractions. It is believed not only that these advertisements had the names of the principal actors in large letters, in the modern manner, but that it was at least sometimes the custom to add a pictorial representation of one of the scenes of the play. At all events Pliny mentions a certain Calludes as excelling in this kind of painting.

There follows a long gap in the history of the poster. In the Dark Ages the times were too disturbed, and most people, even among the upper classes, illiterate. The Middle Ages made use not of posters but of heraldry and criers. It was not until the end of the fifteenth century that posters, used for political purposes, once more appeared. With the rise of the printing press their usage became of such importance that governments were forced to take notice of it, and to make stringent laws for its regulation. Official posters (e.g. royal proclamations) were among the first to have any pictorial content, usually merely the Royal Arms.

About the middle of the seventeenth century, in France, both the actors and the religious confraternities began to make use of posters. In England, according to Brewer's *Dictionary of Phrase and Fable*, before the Fire of London (1666) the posts which protected pedestrians in the street were used for affixing theatrical and other announcements, whence the name of 'posters'. But no specimen seems to have survived. The earliest English play-bill in the Gabrielle Enthoven Collection in the Victoria and Albert Museum is of the year 1737, and it is not pictorial (see also PLAY-BILL).

However, before this pictorial posters had been used, at least in France, for recruiting purposes. The illustrations were in woodcut, and were sometimes coloured by hand in a similar manner to the broadsheets of the period. The *Cabinet des Estampes* in Paris has also pictorial posters issued by troupes of acrobats in the early years of the eighteenth century. Woodcut continued to be the approved method of embellishing posters until the rise of commercial lithography in the first half of the nineteenth century.

In this development France took the lead, and some of the finest artists of the Romantic period produced posters, generally advertising books or periodicals, and for the most part in one tint only. Various attempts were made to add the colour which was felt to be necessary. Roucher tried to introduce the methods which had proved successful in the production of wallpapers, others reverted to the more primitive practice of stencilling. The honour of bringing the true colour-poster to perfection belongs to Jules Chéret.

Jules Chéret was born in 1836 in Paris, but he served his apprenticeship as a lithographer in England. In 1866, profiting by the introduction of machines making use of large lithographic stones, he launched out on his career as probably the most prolific poster-artist of all time. He produced nearly a thousand posters, all of them good and some of them masterpieces. Working for the most part directly on the stone, he was able, with the limited number of colours at his disposal, to produce the most diverse effects. He was an excellent draughtsman with a pronounced individual style, and the very narrowness of his range was an advantage in his work for the theatres, music-halls, and 'dancings' of Paris. From 1867, when he announced the appearance of Sarah Bernhardt in *La Biche au Bois*, to the end of the century, his gay and dancing figures called the passers-by to a perpetual carousal at the Folies-Bergère, at the Alcazar d'Hiver, at the Cirque Fernando, or the Moulin Rouge.

His example inspired a host of others, some of whom, like the brothers Choubrac, followed his manner closely, while others, like Eugène Grasset and Ibels, struck out a line of their own. But the artist who took up the manner of Chéret and transformed it most completely was Toulouse-Lautrec. Other well-known French artists have designed posters—Forain, Willette, Valloton, Métivel, Anquetin, Bonnavel, Guillaume, and Steinlen—but, with the possible exception of the last, none has so completely fused his own personality with the theatrical poster as the artist who gave the world such masterpieces as 'Aristide Bruant dans son cabaret', 'Jane Avril', and 'La Goulue—Moulin Rouge'. Among the finest *affiches* of Steinlen may be mentioned his 'Yvette Guilbert' and his 'Mothu et Doria—Scènes Impressionnistes'. Posters—theatrical posters in particular—have never reached a higher standard than that attained on the Paris hoardings in the eighteen-nineties.

The first English theatrical poster of any note was designed by Fred Walker to advertise a dramatized version of *The Woman in White*, produced in 1871. This, however, was not a lithograph but a wood-engraving. The Beggarstaff brothers (William Nicholson and James Pryde) were among the first pioneers of the poster in England, and most of their work was done for the theatre. Their method was the highly original one of building up the design in cut-out layers of different shades of brown paper. Their work was commissioned by Irving for *Hamlet* and *Don Quixote*, and the original cut-out designs for these have been preserved.

English artists in general took longer to assimilate the lessons of Impressionism than their French colleagues, so that while the Frenchmen were already thinking in terms of flat colour and the balance of masses, the English had not yet shaken themselves free from the trammels of academic realism. So we find advertisers buying pictures (the classic example is Millais's 'Bubbles') and transforming them into advertisements by the simple process of adding a caption. However, in the mid eighteen-nineties posters by Aubrey Beardsley for the Avenue Theatre began to appear, and the admirable poster artist Dudley Hardy produced simple and effective designs for a number of plays.

In any purely aesthetic evaluation the melodrama poster is usually left out of account, but it must be admitted that it loomed much larger on the hoardings of the last twenty-five years of the nineteenth century and the first decade of the twentieth than any other kind of theatrical advertisement. Its method was one of blatant realism turned to the service of situations highly coloured in both senses of the word. The lurid incident, the pathetic situation, the improving sentiment—these were the stock-in-trade of the designer, who was more concerned to move the emotions than to produce a work of art. For such plays as *It's Never Too Late To Mend, The Lights of London, The Silver King, Uncle Tom's Cabin* (with its almost unbroken run of eighty years), *East Lynne, The Streets of London*, and the Irish dramas of Dion Boucicault, immense numbers of posters were produced, for the most part designed by men whose names have faded into obscurity. This kind of poster is now no longer used to advertise plays, but the same style still lingers in cinema advertisements, and presumably appeals to the same public as that of the old melodrama.

The traditions of the artistic poster were carried on in the early years of the twentieth century by Frank Brangwyn, Cecil Aldin, Phil May, John Hassall, Maurice Greiffenhagen, Will Owen, and others. In more recent years some excellent theatrical posters have been produced by Lovat Fraser (notably for *The Beggar's Opera*), Aubrey Hammond, Doris and Anna Zinkeisen, Guy Kortright, Bert Thomas, Norman Wilkinson of Four Oaks, Thomas Derrick, M. H. Lawrence, Charles A. Buchel, and John Garside.

The poster all over the continent of Europe was much influenced by the French school of designers. In Germany artists of the calibre of Max Klinger and Franz Stück did not disdain to design for the hoardings, but for a whole generation advertising art in central Europe was dominated by the figure of Ludwig Hohlwein. The stimulus given to the German theatre by the work of Reinhardt was manifest also in the sphere of theatrical publicity. In Austria Emil Orlik produced some excellent posters. In Belgium the work of Meunier, V. Mignot, H. Cassiers, and Toussaint did much to improve prevailing standards. The Russian theatre had few poster-designers of note, but the Diaghilev Ballet employed first-rate artists not only for its costumes and décor, but for its public announcements. Some of the costume designs of Léon Bakst made excellent posters with hardly any change. The best Spanish posters are those advertising bull-fights. They are generally bold in conception and striking in colour, but their designers are, for the most part, anonymous.

Before 1900 American posters, with the exception of some designs by Matt Morgan, were of the kind described above as advertising English melodrama. With the eighteen-nineties a new era began, Louis J. Mead and W. H. Bradley leading, for the most part with small decorative placards. Then such well-known artists as Maxfield Parrish, James Montgomery Flagg, Will Denslow, and Charles Dana Gibson took up the work, to be followed by Harrison Fisher, Norman Rockwell, Karl Johnson, McClelland Barclay, and others. Not all of these, however, worked exclusively or even chiefly for the theatre. Indeed, of recent years theatrical advertising has found it difficult to compete with the ampler funds of the vendors of other products. On a Paris hoarding of the eighteen-nineties most of the posters displayed were advertisements of theatres, music-halls, or some other kind of entertainment. To-day most posters seem to advertise alcoholic beverages. Theatre managers are now compelled to content themselves with more modest displays, and there has therefore been a revival of something like the old playbill: a small announcement giving the name of the theatre and play, the principal actors, &c., adorned sometimes, but by no means always, by an appropriate design. This seems to be true of most countries, and so it may be said that the theatrical advertisement in poster form has come full circle and ended where it began, as a simple announcement affixed to a wall or post or column. With the advance of other methods of publicity (the name of the principal actors 'in lights', &c.) it seems unlikely that the ambitious theatrical poster will ever be revived in any quantity. As for quality, that can hardly surpass the standard reached in Paris in 1895.

J. L.

POTIER DES CAILLETIÈRES, CHARLES-GABRIEL (1774–1838), French actor, considered by Talma the greatest comedian of his day. Of good family, he was in the army during the Revolution, but in 1796 went to Paris and decided to adopt the stage as a profession. He was for some years in the provinces, and in May 1809 made his début at the Théâtre des Variétés. He was slow in making his way into popular favour, but once established he never lost his hold on the affection of the public. His last years were spent at the Palais-Royal, where he first appeared in 1831. His one fault was a weak voice, but this was offset by the subtlety and vivacity of his acting, which conveyed his meaning without words. He had two sons, of whom one was a good actor, though overshadowed by the memory of his father, and author of a number of vaudevilles.

POTTER, MRS. JAMES BROWN- [*née* CORA URQUHART] (1859–1936), one of the first American society women to go on the stage. She was trained by David Belasco, though she never appeared under his management, being first seen as a professional, after innumerable amateur performances for charity, in London in 1886. With Kyrle Bellew as her leading man

she toured Australia and the Far East, preceded by immense publicity, and returned to London in 1892. During the Boer War she raised large sums of money for war charities by her recitation of such poems as 'The Absent-Minded Beggar', and in 1904 became manager of the Savoy. Her venture was unsuccessful, and ended in bankruptcy, after which she went on tour, retiring from the stage in 1912.

POWELL, GEORGE (1668–1714), English actor, who between 1687 and the year of his premature death created many gallant and tragic roles. He was Bellamour in *The Old Bachelor* (1693), and the first to play Lothario in *The Fair Penitent* (1703), and, says Barton Baker, 'he wanted only sobriety and industry to have risen to be one of the finest actors of his time'. As it was, drink and brawling kept him back, and he was soon outdistanced by Wilks. He caused many disturbances in the theatre, was usually imperfect in his part and drunk on the stage, where, it is said, he made such violent love that Vanbrugh grew nervous for the actress. In spite of his debaucheries Christopher Rich tolerated him because, in his capacity as director of rehearsals, he kept the actors content on low salaries. He was the author of two tragedies given at Drury Lane, and of several comedies.

POWELL, WILLIAM (1735–69), English actor, a pupil and protégé of David Garrick at Drury Lane, where he was the first to play Lovewell in *The Clandestine Marriage* (1766). During Garrick's absence abroad in 1763–4 Powell played his parts, with great success, and later, tiring of a subordinate position, joined Colman and Harris as part-patentee of Covent Garden, where he played Honeywell in the first production of *The Good-Natured Man* (1768). He died suddenly, at the height of his success, 'having every perfection but experience', while in Bristol, where he was managing a theatre.

POWELL (POWEL). There appear to have been two puppet showmen of this name, who flourished in about 1710–15. They may, of course, have been the same. Martin, a crippled dwarf, had his puppet theatre under the Piazza in Covent Garden, while Robert is referred to in Disher's *Clowns and Pantomimes* as 'a showman popular in France, Germany, and Spain as well as England'. This 'Shakespeare of the minor stage' composed several of his own plays, mostly on popular tales and ballads or on biblical subjects.

POWER. (1) TYRONE (1795–1841), Irish actor, son of a strolling player, who essayed both the army and the navy before he finally took to acting in 1815. For some years he played light comedy in the provinces and minor theatres of London, but made little mark in the theatrical world until in 1826 he was unexpectedly called upon to play a comic Irish role. This he did with such success that he succeeded to the stage Irishmen left vacant by the death of Charles Connor, and appeared at both the Patent Theatres and the Haymarket in such parts as Murtoch Delany, Dennis Brulgruddery, Lucius O'Trigger, Major O'Flaherty, and Dr. O'Toole. A handsome, high-spirited man with thick curling hair, a rich brogue, and a fine singing voice, he quickly became a favourite with the public. He also turned to authorship and produced a number of light comedies and farces—*St. Patrick's Eve* (1832), *Paddy Cary, the Boy of Clogheen* (1833), *O'Flannigan and the Fairies* (1836)—in which he appeared himself. His last appearance in London was made in 1840. He then left for America, where he had already made two visits and was much admired, and on the return journey was drowned in the sinking of S.S. *President*. His death was a great loss, both financially and artistically, to the English and Irish theatres, where he was always sure of packed houses. It was a sad coincidence that his friend and fellow actor, E. W. Elton, was also drowned two years later, in the wreck of the *Pegasus*. Power left a wife and eight children, none of whom went on the stage, though one, Harold, was the father of (2) TYRONE (1869–1931), whose stage career was mainly in America, where he was leading man for such actresses as Mrs. Fiske, Julia Marlowe, Mrs. Leslie Carter, and Henrietta Crosman. He was also a prominent member of Augustin Daly's company from 1890 to 1898, appearing with it in London, his birth-place, where he played also with Tree and Irving. In his later years he appeared mainly in Shakespearian parts. His son (3) TYRONE (1913–) was playing with Katharine Cornell in *Saint Joan* in 1936 when he was offered a contract with Twentieth-Century Fox. He has since had a distinguished career in films.

PRADON, JACQUES (1632–98), a French dramatist remembered only for his rivalry with Racine. Little is known of his early years, but he had some facility in verse-writing, and Racine's detractors, looking round for a figure-head, found in him just what they wanted. His *Phèdre* (1677) was applauded at the expense of Racine's, a verdict which has been reversed by posterity. Pradon's first play was *Pirame et Thisbé* (1674), done at the Hôtel de Bourgogne with some success, due again to the cabal against Racine. Pradon owes whatever posthumous fame he has achieved to the greatness of the enemies he roused against him, including the redoubtable Boileau, and so the names, at least, of his plays are remembered, though they are seldom read or acted.

PRAETEXTA, see FABULA (4).

PRATINAS (*fl.* 496 B.C.) of Phlius, an important figure in pre-Aeschylean drama (see SATYR-DRAMA).

PRESTON, THOMAS (*fl.* 1570), the unknown author of a popular early English tragi-comedy, *Cambyses King of Persia*, written with bombastic eloquence, thus giving rise to Falstaff's remark that he must speak in passion, and would do it in 'King Cambyses' vein'. The play helps to mark the transition from the medieval Morality play to the Elizabethan historical drama. Its author, who may also have written the heroical romance, *Sir Clyomon and Sir Clamydes*, given at about the same time, and some broadside ballads, should not, according to Chambers, be confused with the academic Thomas Preston (*fl.* 1569–89) who was a Fellow of King's, Cambridge, and later Vice-Chancellor. In 1592 the latter, as Master of Trinity Hall, was one of a number of petitioners who asked for the banning of plays in Cambridge.

PRÉVILLE [PIERRE LOUIS DUBUS] (1721–99), French actor, who was perhaps, after J. B. Raisin, the greatest comedian the Comédie-Française had yet known. He had an unhappy childhood, and was befriended by a wealthy man who put him into a lawyer's office and forbade him to go to the Comédie-Française, hoping thus to put an end to his hankerings after an actor's life. On the death of his benefactor, Dubus, as he then was, considered himself released from his promise, and went to see *Le Légataire universel*, with F. A. Poisson as Crispin. He afterwards gave so masterly an imitation of Poisson that his employer allowed him to join a company of provincial actors. He went to the Comédie-Française in 1753, replacing Poisson in comic roles. He was also excellent in Marivaux's plays, partnered by Mlle Dangeville. Of less than medium height, he had sharp features and expressive eyes. His only faults, in the eyes of his companions, were his hasty temper and his excessive devotion to the pleasures of the table. He made a great personal success as the six characters in one in a revival of Boursault's *Mercure galant*. He retired in 1786, and with his wife, also an actress at the Comédie-Française, went to live at Senlis, returning to the theatre for a short time in 1791.

PRICE, NANCY (1880–), English actress and theatre manager, who first appeared on the stage with Benson's company, and in 1902 made a success as Calypso in *Ulysses*. Among her later parts were Olivia in *Twelfth Night*, Rosa Dartle in *Em'ly*, a dramatization of *David Copperfield*, and Hilda Gunning in *Letty*. She continued to enhance her reputation in a wide variety of parts, but it is as the founder and guiding spirit of the People's National Theatre that she is best remembered. This venture began in 1930 with a revival at the Fortune Theatre of *The Man from Blankley's*, and during the next few years Nancy Price was responsible for the production of over fifty plays, ranging from Euripides to Pirandello, and including *Alison's House, Lady Precious Stream*, and *Whiteoaks*, in which she played for two years the part of old Adeline Whiteoaks. These were all produced at the Little Theatre (since destroyed by enemy action), which was for some years the headquarters of the People's National Theatre. Nancy Price has also written a number of books on various open-air subjects, and a volume of reminiscences, *Shadows on the Hill*, published in 1935. She became a C.B.E. in 1950.

PRICE, STEPHEN (1783–1840), the first outstanding American theatre manager who was neither an actor, like Hallam and Douglass, nor a playwright, like Dunlap. In 1808 he bought a share in the management of the Park Theatre, New York, and gradually assumed complete control. Odell, in his *Annals of the New York Stage*, calls him 'a theatrical speculator', since to him was due the constant importation of famous European actors, beginning with G. F. Cooke in 1810–11, which by 1830 had wrecked the old resident companies of the larger American towns. He also likens him to Barnum in his love of spectacular and freakish effects—real horses and tigers on the stage, for example. It was this trait which caused many people to disapprove of his tenancy of London's Drury Lane in 1826. Price, whose whole theatrical career was closely bound up with that of the Park Theatre, died opportunely just as its fortunes were beginning to decline.

PRIESTLEY, JOHN BOYNTON (1894–   ), English dramatist, novelist, and critic. He was born at Bradford and educated there and at Trinity Hall, Cambridge. He served during the war of 1914–18 with the Duke of Wellington's and the Devon Regiments. His writing career, beginning in 1918 with a volume of verse, *The Chapman of Rhymes*, brought him in 1931 to *The Good Companions*, a vastly successful novel which the author in collaboration with Edward Knoblock successfully dramatized. Any doubts of Mr. Priestley's innate theatrical capacity were soon set at rest. *The Roundabout* was quickly followed by *Dangerous Corner* (both 1931), perhaps the most ingenious play ever put together, and *Laburnum Grove* (1933) confirmed him as a successful dramatist. *Eden End* (1934) mingled gentle melancholy and rich humour in a rounded beauty which he has not since matched. Out of modern conceptions of time he succeeded in making two excellent plays, *Time and the Conways* and *I Have Been Here Before*, both written in 1937. A brief period of experimental work followed. In *Music At Night* (1938) and *Johnson Over Jordan* (1939) he sought with courage, skill and sincerity to give modern drama a new depth, but the technical means he employed were not to the taste of the public, and he turned during the war to less ambitious comedies. It is possible that in his strenuous endeavour to entertain a public much in need of amusement he wrote too quickly, for he also did much miscellaneous writing and a famous series of broadcasts; nor did he forget that he was a novelist and an essayist. *They Came To A City* (1943) may be excepted from this generalization; it was an earnest political tract which the public absorbed with every sign of enjoyment.

Priestley has some affinities with H. G. Wells. So long as he is satisfied to draw from human character, especially Yorkshire character, its simple fun and pathos, his judgement of what the public wants is pretty nearly infallible. *When We Are Married* (1938), for instance, was a gorgeous farce with its roots firm in Yorkshire nature. He can enrich a good story with touches of shrewd, humorous, and sentimental observation. But there is a pertinacious reformer at work in his composition. He would be a politician and a dramatic innovator. As a political thinker he tends to over-simplify problems, and as a serious dramatist in search of new forms he would seem to prefer fresh combinations of dubious stage devices to some heightened form of speech through which his ambitions might be realized. Fortunately, there is no need at present to attempt a final estimate of a dramatist whose work is still capable of development in many different directions.

A. V. C.

PRIME MINISTER OF MIRTH, see ROBEY, GEORGE.

PRINCE CHARLES'S MEN, usually known as the Prince's Men, a theatrical company formed in 1616 on the death of Henslowe by his son-in-law Alleyn from an amalgamation of the Lady Elizabeth's Men and the Duke of York's Men. Their first settled home was the Phoenix, where Beeston installed them after he had ousted the remnants of the Queen's Men, and here they enjoyed some measure of prosperity. In 1622 they were themselves ousted by the new Lady Elizabeth's Company, and went to the Curtain. The company broke up when Charles succeeded to the throne, and many of its important players transferred to the King's Men. In 1631 a new company was formed under the patronage of the young Prince Charles, and appeared at Salisbury Court. Just before the closing of the theatres the Prince's Men were connected with the Fortune, where one of their chief actors was Fowler, a player of 'conquering parts'.

PRINCE EDWARD, LONDON, a large theatre in Old Compton Street, Soho. It opened in 1930 with *Rio Rita* under the management of Lee Ephraim. It did not prove a very successful theatre, and its principal productions were musical comedies and revues, of which *Nippy* in 1930 was outstanding, and a play based on the adventures of Sexton Blake. The theatre then became a restaurant-cabaret, as the London Casino, where one dined or supped and watched a spectacular stage show. After the outbreak of war in 1939 it became the Queensberry All-Services Club, but subsequently resumed operations as a theatre, with variety shows, spectacle, and pantomime. W. M. P.

PRINCE HENRY'S MEN, see ADMIRAL'S MEN.

PRINCE OF WALES'S THEATRE, LONDON, in Coventry Street. This opened as the

Prince's Theatre on 18 Jan. 1884 under Edgar Bruce, with a revival of *The Palace of Truth*. Kyrle Bellew, Tree, Miss Lingard, and Sophie Eyre were in the cast. In March of the same year a free adaptation of *A Doll's House*, called *Breaking a Butterfly*, was produced there. Miss Lingard, totally miscast, played the lead and adverse criticism led to the play's being withdrawn in less than a month. *The Private Secretary*, with Tree as the Rev. Robert Spalding, was produced there on 29 Mar. 1884, afterwards going to the old Globe. Tree also made a success in *Called Back*. In 1885–6 Mrs. Langtry ran a season at the Prince's, and in 1891 *L'Enfant prodigue*, superbly mimed by Jane May, Zanfretta, and others, was a great success. The theatre now became the Prince of Wales's, and Arthur Roberts played there in burlesques, and in *In Town*, the first modern musical comedy, which was later transferred to the Gaiety. Roberts also made a great hit in *Gentleman Joe*. In 1899 Forbes-Robertson and Mrs. Patrick Campbell appeared at this theatre in *The Moonlight Blossom*, and in 1900 Marie Tempest, forsaking musical comedy, produced, in association with Frank Curzon, *English Nell*, *Peg Woffington*, and *Becky Sharp*, playing the name-parts herself. In 1901 Hawtrey produced *The Man from Blankley's*, and later George Edwardes produced many musical comedies at this theatre, including *The School Girl*, with Edna May, Marie Studholme, G. P. Huntley, George Graves, and James Blakeley, Billie Burke in a small part, and Pauline Chase (later a famous Peter Pan) in the chorus. Frank Curzon controlled the theatre for many years, presenting both musical and straight plays, the most memorable of the former being, perhaps, *Miss Hook of Holland*. From 1914 to 1918 Charlot ran revue, and in 1923 the Co-Optimists had a season at the theatre. *Alibi* and *By Candle Light*, in the same year, were both successful. The theatre was reconstructed and for a time staged non-stop revue and variety. It then passed under the control of George Black, who presented plays and musical shows, in one of which, *Strike a New Note*, the comedian Sid Field scored an outstanding success.　　　　　　　　　　　　　W. M. P.

The Scala, under the management of the Bancrofts, was also known as the Prince of Wales's Theatre.

PRINCE'S THEATRE, LONDON, in Shaftesbury Avenue, was built by Walter and Frederick Melville, who controlled the Lyceum for so many years. It opened on 26 Dec. 1911 with a revival of *The Three Musketeers*. Sarah Bernhardt played a season there, as did Sacha Guitry and Yvonne Printemps, and for some years there was an annual Gilbert and Sullivan season. The theatre has never had a settled policy, but has ranged from drama to pantomime, and its successes include *Monsieur Beaucaire*, *Alf's Button*, and *Funny Face*; during the run of this last, production and theatre alike were imperilled by a burst gas-main. Seymour Hicks produced plays at the Prince's

and Charles Macdona ran revivals including *Diplomacy*, *The Wandering Jew*, and *Sweet Nell of Old Drury*, with all-star casts and seats at half-price. Firth Shephard also produced successful shows there. The theatre was badly blasted in 1940 and twice in 1941, but was able to stay open.　　　　　　　　　　　　　W. M. P.

The Prince of Wales's Theatre in Coventry Street, London, was first named the Prince's, as was the St. James's for a short while.

PRINCESS THEATRE, NEW YORK, at 104 West 49th Street, one of the city's smallest and most perfect playhouses. Holding 299 people, it was built by F. Ray Comstock on the site of an old livery stable, and named for his old second-floor theatre on 29th Street. It opened on 14 Mar. 1913 with the Princess Players in one-act plays. The first outstanding production was a translation of Brieux's *Maternité* in 1915, while, after a series of musical comedies and intimate revues, the Princess saw in 1920–1 the Provincetown Players in several of their productions, including *The Emperor Jones*. In the same year Brock Pemberton produced *Six Characters in Search of an Author*, which ran for 17 weeks, while in 1922 came Maxwell Anderson's first New York production with *White Desert*, which speedily failed. In 1928 the theatre was renamed the Lucille La Verne, but after two productions reverted to its original name, only to change it for the Assembly in 1929. It then became a cinema, except for a short interval in 1937, when as the Labour Stage—after it had become the recreation centre of the International Ladies Garment Workers Union—it staged a topical revue, *Pins and Needles*, which caught the fancy of the town and ran into three editions with 1,108 performances.　　　　　　　G. F.

PRINCESS'S THEATRE, LONDON. This was built by a silversmith named Hamlet, on the site of a building called the Queen's Bazaar, on the north side of Oxford Street, near the Circus. This was used for the sale of fancy and miscellaneous goods. It was destroyed by fire in 1829 and rebuilt to house exhibitions. Hamlet transformed it into a theatre and opened it on 5 Oct. 1840. Its reconstruction evidently took some time, since it had been named by permission after Queen Victoria before her accession. It was advertised as being 'fitted up in a style and splendour never before equalled in this country', and the first attractions were promenade concerts, for which the prices were 1s. and 2s. These were not very successful, and after further alteration the theatre reopened on 26 Dec. 1842 with Bellini's 'La Sonnambula' and other operas and light dramatic pieces. In 1843 Hamlet went bankrupt and Maddox took over. He staged several of Balfe's operas, and General Tom Thumb, the circus midget, also appeared. In 1845 Charlotte Cushman and Edwin Forrest made their London début there in a tragedy called *Fazio*. In 1850 Maddox gave up the theatre, which was taken over by Charles Kean, with Keeley as his partner for the first year. Kean's management was memorable, both for his productions of Shakespeare and for his success in transforming French drama into entertainment palatable to English popular taste. Queen Victoria was so thrilled by *Pauline* that she clutched the curtain of her box in a convulsive grasp until the tense situation was over. *The Corsican Brothers* was a great personal success for Kean, as was *Louis XI*. In his *Henry VIII* limelight was used for the first time, and the burning of the palace in *Sardanapalus* was a great piece of realism. Here Ellen Terry, as a child, had her first engagement under Kean, who gave up the Princess's on 29 Aug. 1859, when he appeared as Wolsey. In the following September Augustus Harris, father of the future manager of Drury Lane, took over, and engaged Henry Irving, then a stock actor at the Theatre Royal, Edinburgh. He failed, and returned to the provinces. In 1860 Harris brought Fechter to the Princess's, where his portrayal of Hamlet in what was then a novel fashion caused a sensation. In Oct. 1862 Harris retired and a Mr. Lindus took the theatre to please his wife, sustaining a heavy loss. George Vining was the next tenant, and he inaugurated the epoch of melodrama, for which the theatre became famous, with *The Huguenot Captain* (starring Adelaide Neilson), *The Streets of London*, including the thrilling fire scene, and *Arrah-Na-Pogue*. In Oct. 1865 *It's Never Too Late To Mend* began with a riotous first night, when the audience objected to the savagery of one of the scenes, showing a boy in prison being flogged. The critics railed against it, but the play ran for 148 nights and made a profit of £8,000. In the same year Kean gave a farewell season, dying three years later. Benjamin Webster succeeded Vining as manager in 1869, Chatterton joining him the following year and becoming sole manager in 1872. Chatterton ran seasons of Shakespeare, alternating Phelps with Creswick in an attempt to revive the glories of Kean's management, but he had to go back to melodrama, including *Lost in London* and *The Lancashire Lass*. In 1875 Joseph Jefferson revived *Rip Van Winkle* with great success, and in 1879 Charles Warner startled theatre-goers with his amazing performance as Coupeau in *Drink*. After a short and unsuccessful venture by Booth, Wilson Barrett, with Modjeska, took the theatre. His first success was *The Lights of London*, and on 16 Nov. 1882 came *The Silver King*, which ran a year and became, perhaps, the classic example of melodrama. In 1886 Barrett left, and the importance of the theatre waned. The last successful play staged there was *The Fatal Wedding* in 1902. Shortly afterwards it was taken over by an American syndicate, but owing to difficulties with the lease, and considerable requirements in the way of alterations, it was never reopened and became a warehouse.

W. M. P.

PRINCIPAL BOY, the chief character in the modern pantomime—Aladdin, Idle Jack, Prince Charming, Robinson Crusoe—traditionally played by a woman. This custom appears to have originated partly in the playing of young boys' parts in opera by women singers (as for example Cherubin in Mozart's 'Nozze di Figaro'), and partly in the extravaganzas and burlesques of the nineteenth century, which popularized the blond wig, short tunics, fleshings, and high heels of the typical hero. Some authorities, however, derive the custom from the fact that the pantomime may be looked on as a survival of the Roman Feast of Saturnalia, which took place approximately at what is now our Christmas season. One of the features of the Saturnalia was the exchange of costume between the sexes, an example of topsy-turvydom which is well in the spirit of the pantomime and intensified there by the fact that the 'dame' is usually played by a man. The Principal Boy was not firmly established until the 1880s, and it was Augustus Harris, at Drury Lane, who insisted on opulent curves, as with Harriet Vernon, a 'magnificent creature of ample figure'. Others were Nellie Stewart and Queenie Leighton. In our own day the tradition, with less emphasis on curves, has been carried on by such Principal Boys as Phyllis Neilson-Terry and Madge Elliot as Prince Charming, Marie Burke as Jack and Prince Charming, Fay Compton as Robin Hood (*The Babes in the Wood*), and Anne Ziegler as Prince Silverthistle (*The Sleeping Beauty*); while at the Coliseum in 1937 Jill Esmond appeared in *Beauty and the Beast* as a slim and lovely Prince Hal, ungallantly disguised for most of the evening under a shaggy bearskin.

PRINTEMPS, YVONNE (1895–   ), see GUITRY (3).

PRITCHARD, HANNAH (1711–68), English actress, who as Miss Vaughan made some reputation at the fairgrounds and around London. She married a poor actor, and as Mrs. Pritchard had a short engagement at the Haymarket, going on to Drury Lane, where she was established some ten years before Garrick appeared. At first she played only in comedy, but in later years she turned to tragedy, and was a fine Lady Macbeth. She was also the first and only interpreter of Dr. Johnson's *Irene*. Her acting was somewhat mannered and old-fashioned, as she had been formed in the school of Quin, and she was not seen to advantage in artificial comedy. In later life, as Churchill does not fail to point out in *The Rosciad*, she became somewhat stout, but could still play young heroines with charm. She remained with Garrick until her retirement a few months before her death, appearing for the last time as Lady Macbeth on 24 April 1768, after which Garrick never played Macbeth again. Doran said of her: 'Her distinguishing qualities were natural expression, unembarrassed deportment, propriety of action, and an appropriateness of delivery which was the despair of all her contemporaries, for she took care of her consonants, and was so exact in her articulations, that, however voluble her enunciation, the audience never lost a syllable of it.' She was considered to have given more prominence than is usual to the part of Gertrude in *Hamlet*, and her Queen Katharine in *Henry VIII* was equally fine. She had a brother on the stage, and her daughter, who married the first John Palmer, was also an actress for a short time, retiring on her mother's death.

PRIVATE BOX, see AUDITORIUM, 2 and BOX.

PROCTOR, FREDERICK FRANCIS (1851–1929), American manager, who made a good deal of money in vaudeville and built a number of theatres in New York, the first being the Twenty-Third Street Theatre, which opened on 5 May 1890 with *Shenandoah*, transferred from the Star Theatre. Later productions at this theatre were *All the Comforts of Home* and *Men and Women*. Procter was first the rival and then the partner of that other vaudeville pioneer, B. F. Keith, and was known as the 'dean of vaudeville', being owner of a chain of music-halls.

PRODUCER. (1) In America, the man responsible for the financial side of play-production, for the buying of the play, the renting of the theatre, the engagement of actors and staff, and the handling of receipts. In England the American producer is known as the manager.

(2) In England the man responsible for the general interpretation of the play, and for the conduct of rehearsals, during which he guides and advises the actors, welding them into a corporate body. He has no responsibility for the financial or business side of the production, but only for its artistic and dramatic integration. In America the English producer is known as the director, on the continent as the *régisseur*. It is only since the beginning of the twentieth century that play-production has become a separate profession, distinct from that of actor or author, and that the producer has achieved a paramount position in the theatre. In early days a play was directed by its author, who might also, as with Molière, be the chief actor; the eighteenth-century 'star' produced his own play, as did the nineteenth-century actor-manager; often only new plays were rehearsed, merely to perfect lines and cues, and settle entrances and exits. A newcomer in an old play was left to learn his way about by trial and error, while a visiting star might walk through his lines with the principals of the stock company, and leave the lesser people to accommodate themselves to his acting during the actual performance. From a perusal of memoirs and letters, it seems as if many actors were engaged merely on recommendation or recitation—as Mrs. Jordan was by Tate Wilkinson at Leeds—and appeared on the stage with no previous rehearsal, trusting to the older members to carry them along until they found their feet. Study of one's lines was a personal matter, and in

tragedy particularly—the chief preoccupation of the great actors of the past—each production was regarded as a series of bravura performances, with the star scoring 'points'. Comedy was approached somewhat differently, but even there co-ordination of the different actors was left to the stage-manager, usually also the prompter, from whose humble functions the modern omnipotence of the producer takes its origin. Belasco, one of the first American producers, was in his early days stage-manager and prompter in San Francisco. Possibly the first producer (or director) in its modern sense was George, Duke of Saxe-Meiningen. Stanislavsky, the first great Russian producer, appeared in the plays he directed, which most modern producers do not. Among those producers who have achieved international fame are Max Reinhardt, Granville-Barker, Gordon Craig—more in theory than in practice—Jacques Copeau, Meyerhold, Taïrov, and Komisarjevsky. England and America can each boast of a number of competent men whose fame has not, however, spread much beyond their own countries, and who are in many cases still young enough in 1949 for their best work to lie before them. The requirements of modern producers may be summed up in the words of Ivor Brown in *Parties of the Play*:

> They must know acting from within, and be perfectly acquainted with its technical difficulties and with the use of stage mechanism. . . . Their chief task is to take a detached view of the point which the author seeks to establish. . . . They must relate the word to the appearance, the idea to the atmosphere, the movement to the scene. They are working, accordingly, in terms of mind and of matter in order to fuse them in the service of the whole artistic conception. . . . Their implements are their own sensibility, the plasticity of others, and the mechanical equipment of the playhouse from its footlights to its 'floats'.

It has also been said that the ideal producer must be an actor, an artist, an architect, an electrician, an expert in geography, history, costume, accessories, and scenery, and have a thorough understanding of human nature—the last trait being the most essential.

PROFILING, an edging of $\frac{1}{4}$ in. board added to the straight edge of a flat, and cut to a required shape (see FLAT).

PROGRAMME, see PLAYBILL.

PROJECTED SCENERY, see LIGHTING, 1 and 2 *i*.

PROJECTOR LAMP, see LIGHTING, 2.

PROLETCULT THEATRE, MOSCOW, see TRADES UNIONS THEATRE.

PROLOGUE, an introductory poem or speech, which originally explained or commented on the action of the play which it preceded. It was first used by Euripides (see

GREECE, 1 c), and later by the Elizabethans, who applied to it the name Chorus. Together with the Epilogue, which closed the action, the Prologue was extensively used during the Restoration period, and survived well into the eighteenth century. It disappeared with the crowded bills of the nineteenth century, and is now used only on special occasions. At their best the Prologue and Epilogue were witty and sometimes scurrilous commentaries on the politics and social conditions of the day, written by outstanding men of the theatre, of whom Dryden and Garrick were the greatest, and spoken by the finest actors of the day.

PROMPT BOOK — BOX — CORNER — SIDE, see STAGE DIRECTIONS.

PROPERTY ROOM, a storage space behind the stage where everything used in the presentation of plays, not connected with the wardrobe, the lighting, or the scenery, is stored. These are known shortly as Props, and may range from stuffed animals to trinket boxes. Hand-props are those which an actor handles—as for example a document, or a candlestick. All are under the control of a Property man, whose function it is to prevent the unauthorized removal by the company of oddments from the store, and to produce from it anything that may be required at a moment's notice.

PROPS, the usual term for Stage Properties. It includes everything essential to the action of the play which does not come under the heading of costume, scenery, or furniture. Hand-props are letters, photographs, revolvers, glasses, newspapers, knitting. Others are dinner-plates, inkpots, food in general, telephones, &c. They are in the charge of a Property man, working under the direction of the stage-manager, and are kept in a special props cupboard or room, not by the actors who use them. The latter are usually given their hand-props before the entry when they need them, and relieved of them as they come off the stage.

PROSCENIUM. The proscenium with its opening—the portal of the stage—is the frame which the auditorium affords for the stage picture. The meaning of the word has changed with time, since it originally meant that which was before the 'scene' or actors' tiring-room, and so the stage itself. It was then used more specifically for what is now called the 'fore-stage' or 'apron', that is, the part of the stage in front of the curtain, and later became applied to the surroundings of the forestage, probably by extension of its meaning in such compounds as 'proscenium door' and 'proscenium balcony', which originally signified a door leading on to the forestage or a balcony overlooking it. Hence the word proscenium came to mean the wall itself in which the door and balcony were situated, and so the whole surround of the stage opening.

The forestage in the seventeenth century was the principal acting area. The stage itself was a scenic area behind, used only in certain scenes. Thus the proscenium of the Restoration theatre, flanking the forestage, had a very important function, since it had to supply the acting accessories which, in the Elizabethan theatre, had become essential to the players—entrances to the stage and the means of inter-playing on different levels. It was even called upon, in Wren's Dorset Garden Theatre, to supply an equivalent to the Elizabethan central musicians' gallery, over the stage opening—before the musicians found their present home in a well at the foot of the stage.

The Proscenium Doors or Doors of Entrance in the Restoration theatre might number as many as six, three in a row on either side of the deep forestage, continuing the façade of the lower box tier. There is evidence of six doors in the stage directions of plays acted at the Theatre Royal, Bridges Street, and at Rich's Little Theatre, Lincoln's Inn Fields. There is similar evidence, but now only of four doors, at Duke's Theatre, Lincoln's Inn Fields, at Duke's Theatre, Dorset Garden, at Wren's Drury Lane, at the Opera House in 1707, and at the Little Theatre, Haymarket, as late as 1737. Highly interesting conventions attended the use of these doors in early times; they were the usual means of entrance for an actor to the stage—if he were to enter 'in the scene' it was a singular enough occasion to be specifically marked in the stage directions. The doors had knockers and bells, and could be locked at need. They could also be used to represent what in effect amounted to a change of scene, as in *The Adventures of Five Hours,* produced at the Duke's Theatre, Lincoln's Inn Fields, in 1663. Here two adjacent proscenium doors were employed to represent, the first, one side of a given door, the second, the other side of the same door. Thus it was possible for a character to leave the stage (and the room it stood for) by one proscenium door and immediately re-enter by the neighbouring door on to the same stage now representing a different room. It is probable that a generalized stock back-scene remained unchanged for the two rooms. Full play was made of this cinema technique in sword chases and in cut-and-thrust adventure dramas.

This raises a point important for the proper understanding of the early function of stage scenery in England. It was intended to present an accompaniment, or decoration, to the play, but never to transform the stage to a naturalistic similitude of the place where the scene was supposed to occur. Early English scenery may have been, on occasion, closely relevant; it was not, generally, directly illustrative. It was the proscenium, and its doors and balconies, which were the real and concrete adjuncts of dramatic action.

The number of doors may have been a variable quantity, not only in different theatres, but in the same theatre at different periods. Further, it is not impossible that in some late Restoration theatres the door was not in the architecture of the proscenium, but in a specially built piece inside it, constructed maybe on the lines of those Special Frontispieces (or inner prosceniums) which were 'joyn'd to the Great Pilasters' of the proscenium proper to frame the scenery (as in the masque tradition) on those occasions when an opera was produced. Just as, in the presentation of a play in an opera-house, the essential doors would have to be added in some such way as suggested above, so, in the presentation of an opera at a playhouse, the different conventions of opera would render the proscenium doors unnecessary. They might even be objectionable, since they smacked of another technique. There are indications that on such occasions the permanent doors were hidden by specially constructed frontispieces or proscenium wings, which would probably be in front of the curtain.

At some time in stage history, probably in the early eighteenth century, the proscenium doors were reduced to one on each side. Many examples of their use by Restoration playwrights, and of the conventions attaching to them, are to be found in Montague Summers's *The Restoration Theatre* (1934).

During the eighteenth century, with the turn towards naturalism, the custom of entering 'within the scene' grew, and the doors were used less and less until at the beginning of the nineteenth century they tended to be reserved for one occasion only, namely the entry of each actor, after the show, to 'take his bow'. He came on at one side, crossed the stage amid applause or hisses, and made his exit by the other door. They were then named Call Doors.

With the decay in the function of the doors, the balcony above, once so necessary to the performance of Restoration scenes, became obsolescent, and by the nineteenth century it was often no more than a blind niche. It had been, however, highly enough developed in the late eighteenth century to achieve its own sash windows, in accordance with the convention of using it in house-exterior scenes. Even in Victorian times, there are notes of surviving proscenium windows bearing gay boxes of red geraniums.

The presence of this solid architectural feature, the proscenium side—this fixed backbone of practicalities in the frame of the scenic picture—must have exercised a great influence on the form of late seventeenth- and early eighteenth-century drama. Every actor had to 'make an entrance'. There must have been a whole-heartedness bestowed upon the action, and a welcome touch of formalized fascination in the peeping of a character over a balcony so near in architectural unity to that in which one sat oneself.

A further department of the proscenium, linking it with the scenery, is sometimes found in the form of a sort of inner arch of a more temporary nature, situated just inside the curtain. Such a 'beading' between frame and picture (to speak figuratively) is as old as the playhouse. On the Restoration stage a Special Frontispiece was, on occasion, set up, joined to the real proscenium, to provide a decorative frame, like the frontispiece of a Court masque, for the performance of operas. It was the need for such a linking feature that gave rise to the Proscenium Wings and Border. It is not generally realized that the fitting of a scene to a given stage is often a matter for much compromise and even adaptation. Especially when the scene has to tour a number of theatres of various sizes, and with very different proscenium openings, is some means required to vary in effect the size of the opening, and fit it to the scene, without too much alteration of the scene itself. Thus we find, in all periods of the English playhouse, a tendency to push the scenery proper somewhat upstage, and to insert between it and the actual proscenium a non-scenic mount. This had to be decorative and theatrical in effect, yet of a design that would render it suitable to whatever scene was behind it. The traditional subject adopted to satisfy these requirements was a composition of hanging drapery; the folds, swags, fringes, cords, and tassels offered wide possibilities to a scene-painter, and yet, of its nature, a curtain could easily suffer considerable alteration of position, and be arranged to provide a smaller or a wider opening.

An interesting variation of subject appears to have obtained at Rich's new Lincoln's Inn Fields Theatre, in the early eighteenth century, and at his subsequent Covent Garden; the idea may also have been used in other theatres. The proscenium wings were not treated purely as folds of curtain but had certain architectural features added. Of these the most characteristic and notable was a pair of striking, life-sized Proscenium Statues cut out in profile, and situated one at the foot of either wing, projecting from them on to the stage. The statues were probably changeable, for draped female figures and crouching fawns are to be seen, among others, in pictures of the time.

It is because of the existence of this variable frame in the theatre that such an unexpectedly wide interval appears on most early stage plans between the first grooves and the proscenium sides—an interval so wide as to leave a gap in the picture were nothing provided to fill it. Yet, possibly because this 'filling' was variable in position, it is rarely marked on plans, and thus its existence is often overlooked.

Generally speaking the 'filling' appears to have taken the form of a pair of booked wings, opened to a right angle or more, and set on either side of the stage. The on-stage edge of each is profiled and cut to the shape of a draped curtain, and connecting the two opposite sides across the top of the scene is a deep border, its edge similarly cut to the shape of a festooned curtain or a decorative pelmet. The whole is elaborately painted. Thus we have an inner proscenium of painted drapery behind the actual architectural proscenium of the theatre itself. Something of this arrangement is unescapable in any theatre. In France the curtain frame stood, as indeed it might be said to do in England, as a symbol of the theatre almost as widely accepted as the conventional masks of tragedy and comedy, and the French have the colourful name for it of *Manteau d'Arlequin*.

Because of their construction, these proscenium wings could, in England, be easily pulled off to give a wide opening, or pushed on till their angle opened out almost flat, so reducing the opening. Similarly the border above might be raised or lowered to suit the set. Sometimes the off-stage half of each pair of wings had a door cut in it, irrespective of the drapery pattern—so that players might enter on the narrow space of stage between, even when a front cloth was lowered immediately behind the proscenium wings. This arrangement may still be seen in some music-halls.

Another means of varying the width of the opening was to have the two pieces of each proscenium wing separate, but arranged to slide one behind the other in a sort of 'fork' projecting down from the fly-floor above. The name for such a sliding extension of the proscenium wing appears to have been Tormentor, and the word is still applied in the theatre to-day to the development mentioned in the next paragraph. A name of a similar sort is used for the proscenium border in America—it is there called the Teaser, but the word is not commonly found in English stage parlance.

In the modern theatre, the proscenium wings are often replaced by a fixed pair of narrow flats covered with black velvet, which supply the same insulating link between scenery and proscenium. These may carry peep-holes for the stage manager or prompter to view the stage. The names of Inner Proscenium or False Pros. (the word is scarcely ever spoken in full on the stage) are used for such developments of the proscenium wings.

The term False Proscenium is, moreover, also employed to cover a further variation of the inner frame idea. Here there is an additional motive—the saving of scenery. A pair of wide flats, generally containing a door, are stood one either side the stage facing each other. A third special flat, or ceiling piece, is suspended face-down between their tops. Thus a sort of tunnel or bridge is formed, and the scenery is set beyond, with a consequent saving of all the more forward, or down-stage, pieces. Considerable additions may be made to such a system until the result bears the appearance of an elaborately modelled piece of built architecture, or the false proscenium is treated in bare simplicity and associated with a cyclorama behind in such a way that a complete stage-setting is provided, and the scenery reduced to a single small set piece, on the system of 'detail setting'.

Thus the proscenium, though to-day thought of as little more than an opening, within which hangs the curtain in all its variations (see CURTAIN), has certain elements associated with it which speak of a long tradition. It once stood as a feature of considerable architectural complexity, forming an essential link between the auditorium and the scene.   R. S.

PROTAGONIST. The Greek tragic poet was restricted to three actors (apparently; the point is disputed). These came to be known as Protagonist, Deuteragonist, Tritagonist: first, second, and third actor (from *agôn*, contest). When contests between actors were instituted (see GREECE, 3 *a*) only the protagonists came into question. In the early Aeschylean drama there was one preponderant part for the protagonist; later, this was not necessarily true. In Sophocles he must often have taken several roles, and the distinction between him and the deuteragonist was of little dramatic significance.   H. D. F. K.

PROVINCETOWN PLAYERS, an experimental group of American actors and playwrights which in 1916 staged the first of O'Neill's plays to be produced, *Bound East for Cardiff*. This was given at the Wharf Theatre, Provincetown, but the group later moved to New York, where they continued to produce the plays of O'Neill, who was for a time one of their directors, and of other American playwrights. For some years they operated in conjunction with the Greenwich Village Theatre under O'Neill, Robert Edmond Jones, and Kenneth Macgowan, and had successfully fulfilled their avowed purpose of giving 'American playwrights a chance to work out their ideas in freedom' when in 1929, after an unsuccessful move to the Garrick Theatre, they disbanded. At the same time the Greenwich Village Theatre, which had seen the first production of *Desire Under the Elms*, as well as of many foreign contemporary plays and some classical revivals such as *Love for Love*, closed and reopened for a year as the Irish Theatre, being demolished in 1930. Both these organizations were intimately connected with the work of O'Neill, probably America's greatest playwright, their ardent experimentalism giving him the opportunities he needed for freedom of expression and an unhampered development.

PROVINCIAL THEATRES IN GREAT BRITAIN. 1. GENERAL SURVEY. (*a*) *Strolling Players up to 1700*. In medieval times the larger towns outside London had their own performances of plays based on the Bible (see ECCLESIASTICAL DRAMA, ENGLAND, 1, MYSTERY PLAY, and PAGEANT). These were the monopoly of the town guilds and were acted by local amateurs, both lay and clerical. For ephemeral amusement the people depended on wandering minstrels, tumblers, acrobats, and their own May-day games and Harvest revels. Elizabethan England had a fairly large body of strolling players, of whom little is known. London companies, under licence and permission from their patron, toured the country in the summer, or when plague drove the Court from town, and there may have been a number of unlicensed companies, living largely on their wits and liable at any time to be hauled up before the magistrates as rogues and vagabonds. The universities (see OXFORD and

CAMBRIDGE) had their own academic exercises, which were not intended for the townspeople. There were at this time no theatre buildings outside London, and any touring company, however important, had to put up with an inn-yard or a makeshift arrangement in a barn, or at the best in a hall. Civil war no doubt laid as heavy a hand on provincial drama as on that of London, but immediately after the Restoration strolling companies began to operate once more in the provinces. It is impossible to estimate how many of them there were, or to what extent they covered the country. Records at Norwich reveal the existence of several companies, and elsewhere parish registers have entries relating to them. They travelled with Letters Patent from the King or licences from the Master of the Revels or the Lord Chamberlain, which they presented to the Mayor's Court in order to obtain leave to play. It was difficult for the Mayor to refuse a licence, though at Norwich he got permission to curtail the stay of the players, and he frequently made it a condition that a benefit should be given for the poor, a custom that persisted in later years when an annual benefit for charity was usually given. Some companies—the Duke of Monmouth's, the Duke of Grafton's, and Lord Strange's— were still under the protection of noblemen, as they had been in Elizabethan times, and performances took place in inns, barns, and booths temporarily adapted or specially set up for the purpose.

(b) *The Circuit System and the First Theatres.* As more companies came into the field at the beginning of the eighteenth century they gradually adopted a number of towns in their district which they visited regularly. These formed what was known as their 'circuit'. This was not accomplished, however, without disputes between rival companies. The Duke of Norfolk's and the Duke of Grafton's Servants clashed at Norwich, and in Newcastle Herbert's and Keregan's companies produced rival performances of *The Beggar's Opera* on the same night. One town in the circuit naturally became the headquarters of the troupe, and between 1720–30 companies began to be known by the name of their chief town instead of by that of their manager or patron. The circuit was arranged so that the larger towns could be visited during Race or Assize weeks when they were full of people, while lesser towns and villages were visited biennially or occasionally. Towns were sometimes changed from one circuit to another; Beverley for instance changed hands three or four times.

The establishment of regular circuits naturally led to the building of the first provincial playhouses, since a company that was sure of acting once or twice a year in a town found that it was better to have its own specially erected building rather than to depend on inns, Town Halls, and other makeshifts. Among the earliest playhouses built in the provinces were those of Bath (1705), Jacob's Wells, Bristol (1729), York (1734), and Ipswich (1736).

(c) *Licensing Act, 1737.* The increased activities of the players met with a great deal of Puritan opposition. Power's company was twice chased away from Bristol, but fulminations against the players, issued from press and pulpit until well into the nineteenth century, resulted often in nothing but bigger audiences. The usual indictments were of the immorality of the plays, and of their ill effects on the workers who wasted time and money attending them. This opposition culminated in the passing of the Licensing Act of 1737 which at one blow abolished the right of all provincial companies to act for hire, gain, or reward, branded the players once again as rogues and vagabonds, and put them at the mercy of informers. The Bath and York theatres were closed down, though acting continued elsewhere in both towns; but in practice the Act made singularly little difference, though informers did sometimes cause the suspension of performances and the imprisonment of players. Justices still granted licences to play and performances continued unless information was lodged against the players. Several companies evaded the law by charging for entry to a concert and giving a play free in the interval; but many did not even trouble to do this, and simply took the risk of fine and imprisonment.

(d) *Sharing System.* All the companies in the first half of the eighteenth century worked on shares. After the expenses of the night had been paid, the profits, even down to the remains of the candles, were shared among all members of the company equally, except that the manager took four extra shares, known as dead shares, for his expenses in connexion with the scenery, the wardrobe, and so on. Every night an account was made up and the money paid out, the youngest and least experienced member of the company receiving the same as the leading actors. This commonwealth system, though good in many ways, was open to abuse by unscrupulous managers, for the accumulation of important bills which the management owed, known as the stock debt, sometimes figured among the expenses though it had long since been paid off. Such abuses led to the system falling out of favour in the mid-century and being replaced by the payment of salaries. The actors, however, depended more on their benefits, of which they had one or more during the year, either single or shared, according to their importance, than on either their shares or their salaries. In the larger companies in the latter part of the century a benefit night for a popular favourite might bring in as much as £200–£300.

(e) *Strolling Companies.* Throughout the eighteenth and the beginning of the nineteenth centuries the established circuit companies were supplemented by many lesser troupes who played in haylofts, stables, and booths in the small towns and villages, and even sometimes intruded on the circuit towns. These troupes were generally very poor; they frequently fled from a town by night leaving their debts behind and were as frequently left stranded by rascally managers who escaped with what cash there was. Such companies were continually changing personnel and were recruited from London pot-houses or from each other. They travelled on foot, sometimes with their scenery and properties on their backs, though the better of them had wagons. They sent ahead a player or two to take the town, i.e. to obtain a licence from the local justice, and on arrival the drum was beaten and play-bills distributed. Their resources in scenery, properties, and wardrobe were often pitiful and their paucity of numbers necessitated doubling and trebling of parts. They also continued to work on the sharing system long after the circuit companies had abandoned it. But they did bring drama, however inadequately, to many places which otherwise would have been without it. A good idea of their life may be obtained from the autobiography of Mrs. Charlotte Charke, daughter of Colley Cibber, and the volumes of Ryley's *The Itinerant*.

(*f*) *Companies from London.* Some provincial towns depended wholly or largely for their entertainment on the visits of London actors during the long vacation. Troupes of minor players from both patent houses and minor theatres paid annual visits to Bristol, Canterbury, Liverpool, Birmingham, and other towns. With one such company in Ipswich Garrick made his first appearance on the stage.

(*g*) *The Provinces as Training Centres.* By the middle of the eighteenth century Bath, Norwich, and York had become the important centres in the provinces, and engagements there were eagerly sought after, as they were looked upon as stepping-stones to the London boards. Before the days of dramatic schools experience in the provinces was almost the only way in which an actor could learn his job; and the wide variety of plays and audiences that the circuit companies offered proved invaluable to him. A large proportion of the great actors and actresses of the latter half of the eighteenth and the early nineteenth centuries received their first chance on the stage and years of training in provincial companies. To give only a few examples: J. P. Kemble trained in Wolverhampton and York, Mrs. Siddons and Macready at Bath, Elizabeth Farren at Liverpool, G. F. Cooke at Manchester, Chester, and Newcastle, Mrs. Jordan and Samuel Phelps at York, Elliston at Bath and York, Edmund Kean at Exeter, E. A. Sothern at Birmingham. Much of the credit for the fact that the eighteenth century was a period of great acting must go to the provincial theatres.

(*h*) *The Heyday of Provincial Theatres, 1750–1810.* The latter half of the eighteenth century saw many theatres arise all over England. The circuit companies flourished and commanded, first as learners and then as stars, most of the theatrical talent of the time. Seasons in the principal towns lasted two to four months, performances being given three or four times a week. Sometimes there was a second shorter season. Royal patents were granted to Bath and Norwich in 1768, York and Hull 1769, Liverpool 1771, Manchester 1775, Bristol 1778, and Newcastle 1788, thus legalizing the position of these theatres. Brighton, Windsor, and Richmond, Surrey, being places of royal residence, operated under licences from the Lord Chamberlain. In 1788 an Act was passed legalizing acting in the provinces by giving justices powers to license players for sixty days at one time. This gave a further stimulus to theatre-building: thus Samuel Butler opened six theatres in his Yorkshire circuit between 1788 and 1805, and Fisher eleven in his East Anglian one between 1809 and 1828. The chief circuit companies now concentrated on the larger centres and left the smaller towns and villages to lesser circuits, many of which were formed in this half-century. A list in *The Authentic Memoirs of the Green Room* (*c.* 1815) gives 25 main circuits in England and 3 in Wales; a fuller list of principal provincial managements in England and Wales in L. T. Rede's *Road to the Stage* (1827) gives a total of 41, a few of which were independent of circuits; and in addition 8 sharing companies are mentioned which mostly visited towns where the theatres had long been closed; these do not include companies which merely acted at fairs. Managers such as Tate Wilkinson of York, Watson of Cheltenham, Mrs. Baker of Canterbury, and James Augustus Whitley of Chester became famous figures in the theatrical world of their period.

(*i*) *Theatres.* There were several ways in which money was raised to erect theatres, but usually it was done by subscription, the subscribers then being the proprietors of the theatre. Subscribers took shares of a certain sum on which they generally received interest as well as silver tickets admitting them to all performances. In other cases, viz. Ipswich, speculators built the theatre in return for a concession such as receipts from the gallery. Frequently, as at Doncaster and York, the theatre was built on ground leased from the corporation. The circuit manager then became lessee of the theatre for a term of years. The theatres were of widely differing size and cost: Liverpool cost £6,000, Huddersfield £2,400, Winchester only £1,000. The larger theatres such as Liverpool and Beaufort Street, Bath, held £300, the smaller ones anything from £40–£80. Sometimes the theatre was built after a London model, sometimes on an original plan. Bristol Theatre Royal claims to be the first semicircular auditorium, and subsequently other provincial playhouses were converted from square to horseshoe shape: Brighton in 1796, Liverpool in 1803, and York in 1822. Only two Georgian theatres still survive for their original purpose: that at Bristol, built in 1766, is an example of a larger theatre of the time and retains some early machinery, and that at Richmond, Yorks., dating from 1788, is small, rectangular in shape, and retains its proscenium. Both are of great interest and value to the theatre historian.

Other shells survive but have been adapted as warehouses, chapels, auction-rooms, and the like.

(*j*) *Charges*. Prices of seats varied from 2*s*. to 3*s*. for boxes, later rising to 4*s*. and 5*s*.; pit 2*s*. or 2*s*. 6*d*.; upper boxes 1*s*. 6*d*. or 2*s*.; gallery 1*s*. or 1*s*. 6*d*.; upper gallery 6*d*. Seats on the stage were abolished as the century progressed, and stage boxes took their place. Half-price was usual except on first nights, on the visits of stars, and when expensive pantomimes were given. Manchester did not allow half-price. Many theatres also offered a subscription season for a certain number of nights, this being followed by a series of benefits.

(*k*) *Scenery*. The best companies had good resources. The initial layout on scenery for the Newcastle Theatre Royal in 1788 was £800, and Tate Wilkinson spent £500 on scenery at York in one season, 50 guineas on one scene. Wilkinson tells us that though he had treble the scenery of any other provincial theatre, his stage was too confined for many sliding scenes, and the drop scenes from fixtures could not be added to unless the work of the play were to be hindered. Thus pieces and pantomimes with a long scene-plot could not be properly staged, and an apartment often did duty for a farm-house, and prisons and chambers appeared with palace wings. The question of how the smaller theatres managed needs investigation. Most companies of importance had their own scene-painters, who were sometimes also responsible for house decorations. In the Norwich circuit the scene-painter was more highly paid than the actors. He prepared scenery for the whole tour at Norwich, but certain stock scenes were kept at each circuit theatre. London scene-painters were also employed, for instance Greenwood and Carver at Brighton, and Grieve and Capon at Bath. In smaller companies the scene-painter was also an actor. Local views were often introduced into drop scenes and act drops.

(*l*) *Lighting and Heating*. Tallow candles and oil-lamps were the means of illumination on the stage and in the auditorium until they were replaced by wax candles (Salisbury in 1777, Ipswich in 1787, Birmingham in 1795, Liverpool in 1800). Gas was used at Exeter in the same year that it was introduced into the London theatres (1817), but owing to explosions a reversion to candles took place shortly after. Other theatres which early adopted gas lighting were Brighton and Liverpool in 1818, Cheltenham in 1819, and York in 1822. Theatres were warmed by braziers or stoves, but there were many complaints of damp in winter and lack of ventilation in summer. Theatres frequently suffered destruction by fire: Birmingham and Manchester twice and Exeter three times.

(*m*) *Plays*. As in London, the main play was followed by an afterpiece, sometimes by two or even occasionally three. In addition, with one or two exceptions such as Liverpool, there were interludes of singing, dancing, and recitation, so that performances lasted five hours or more. London successes appeared on the provincial stage a few weeks after their metropolitan presentation. Provincial managers did not wait for plays to be printed, but obtained copies by various direct or devious means. Sometimes the London manager was induced to lend the manuscript, sometimes agents were instructed to take copies at the play, or prompters were bribed to supply them. Garbled versions were often presented. Authors were paid no fees in the provinces until after the Act of 1842 (see COPYRIGHT). A few plays by local dramatists appeared at Manchester, Liverpool, York, Whitby, Worcester, and elsewhere; licences to act them were sometimes, but by no means always, obtained, as by law they had to be, from the Lord Chamberlain. Plays were rarely given more than two or three times during the season, but each new production was repeated at every town in the circuit. The companies had large repertories; Butler's company, for example, performed 100 plays and afterpieces during their year's travels. Taste in general followed London, though Wilkinson records that some successes from the capital failed in York and some London failures succeeded there.

(*n*) *Players*. The advantage to the actor of the circuit system was that he could reckon on employment all the year round, as the chief companies generally articled players for a term of months or years. Many of the strolling and some of the circuit companies were very much family affairs. Actors' children started to appear on the stage at the ages of three and four, and Dickens's picture of the Crummles family in *Nicholas Nickleby* is hardly exaggerated. Typical weekly salaries at different periods are: York, 1736, 12*s*., 1785, £2; Richmond, Yorks., 1780, 15*s*.; Norwich 35*s*. to 2 guineas. At Exeter Kean received 2 guineas in 1811, and in 1821 the highest salary paid at Liverpool was £2. 10*s*. L. T. Rede (*op. cit.*) gives the average salaries of all the circuits, the lowest being 15*s*., the highest £5, and the majority varying from one guinea to £1. 10*s*. An actor in Bath or York could realize £400–£500 a year. The tragedian commanded the best salary and was considered the leading actor in the company. Actors were expected to supply a good part of their wardrobe, and actresses all of it. The starring system, whereby special actors and actresses were brought from London to play for a few nights or weeks, started in the 1790s. One or two theatres, as at York and Portsmouth, realized the danger to their stock players and at first refused to engage visitors. But the demand for stars grew rapidly and their prices rose accordingly. Thus Cooke was paid £20 a night in Bath in 1805. Soon the stars refused a salary and demanded half profits or even whole receipts. Kemble refused 30 guineas at York and by taking a share instead made £150. Even the lesser companies were compelled to engage stars for one or two nights, and the principal actors and actresses often returned as stars to play with the companies in which they had trained.

(*o*) *The Audience.* The audience, itself often noisy and ill behaved, demanded humility and acquiescence from the players. The manager had to give thanks on leave-taking and frequently to appear on the stage to apologize for various real or supposed shortcomings or misdemeanours. Riots were often the result of raised prices or other proceedings objectionable to the audience. Requests not to go behind the scenes were couched in begging terms. Bespeaks were granted by the gentry, military, freemasons, schools, race stewards, &c. Keen playgoers often undertook hazardous coach journeys in winter to see the play, and playbills used to advertise moonlight nights for their encouragement.

(*p*) *The Decline in the Nineteenth Century.* In the second and third decades of the nineteenth century the provincial theatres, like the London ones, showed a rapid decline. Audiences dwindled, managers went bankrupt, and theatres changed lessees with bewildering frequency. Many theatres ceased to function or stood empty for seasons at a time. Lesser circuits began to break up, Butler's of Richmond, Yorks., for instance, in 1822, Fisher's of Norfolk and Suffolk in 1844. Stock companies confined themselves to fewer theatres, and the lesser towns had either no drama at all or had to rely on occasional visits from scratch companies. Many reasons are adduced for the general decline: the rise of Methodist opposition, the unrest and uncertainty caused by the industrial revolution, the poverty of the drama and consequent craze for melodrama with expensive effects, the coming in of later dining hours. To these, as far as the provinces are concerned, may be added the bad effects of the starring system. The more stars, or 'auxiliaries' as they were called, that were brought at exorbitant fees from London the more the audiences demanded. They ceased to be satisfied with the efforts of the stock company, and the stock companies in turn declined in talent because of the poor rewards the provincial theatres now afforded. Once the principal theatres engaged stars of note to play leads they ceased to become the great schools of acting that they had been in the preceding century.

In 1843 an Act for Regulating the Theatres (see DRAMATIC CENSORSHIP) attempted to stimulate dramatic activity. The monopoly of the patent houses was finally ended; freedom was granted to all theatres to present legitimate drama, and all had a right to be licensed by the justices. Restrictions with regard to length of seasons were abolished, so that a stock company could stay in one theatre all the year round. This was a death-blow to many circuits, since the minor theatres, which had been functioning in most big towns as circuses, amphitheatres, music-halls, and the like, presenting only pantomimes and burlettas, could now obtain licences as regular theatres. As they were usually large buildings, holding 2,000–3,000 spectators, their competition proved a serious embarrassment to the old-established theatres.

(*q*) *Touring Companies.* Another factor hastened the end of the system of stock companies with or without circuits: this was the rise of the touring company. Already in the late 1820s the rage for foreign operas, which could not be satisfied by the stock companies, had led to the formation of opera companies which toured the country, performing for a week or two at each theatre. These were followed by English light opera companies playing either one opera or a series of operas. Some London theatre companies started to send their productions on tour, though often they relied on the local stock companies to fill the minor roles. Indeed from 1850 to 1880 the two systems existed side by side, the stock companies being used to reinforce the travelling companies, as well as to give some performances on their own account, especially the Christmas pantomime which had become an annual custom at most theatres by mid-century. The enormously increased facilities for travel afforded by the development of the railways, however, ensured the final triumph of the touring over the stock system. The circuits were finally broken up, and lessees were able to run theatres at different ends of the country. It was a bad day for the provincial stage when this happened, because all local and regional interests were lost, whilst touring companies provided no variety of experience for the actor. The provincial theatres ceased to be independent centres of theatrical life and by the 1880s relied almost entirely on the visits of weekly touring companies bringing their versions of the latest London successes. The few remaining stock companies ceased at about the same time.

(*r*) *The Twentieth Century. Cinema and Repertory.* Thus when the cinema entered into the provincial field about 1910 the theatres rapidly succumbed. Many were converted to cinema-houses, with the result that large towns, often with long theatrical histories, ceased to have any theatre at all, until the repertory movement started to supply the deficiency (see REPERTORY), returning to the principle of a local stock company though not to that of a nightly change of play. Many towns now have flourishing repertory theatres, notably Bristol, Liverpool, and Birmingham.

In 1943 theatre history was made by the reopening of the old Bristol Theatre Royal with the help of C.E.M.A., this being the first theatre in England to be state-aided. A movement is on foot to establish a system of civic theatres partly supported by municipal authorities with opportunity of interchange of companies. Undoubtedly a revival of theatrical life in the provinces has set in.

2. INDIVIDUAL TOWNS. The following brief summaries give the theatrical history of some typical towns.

(*a*) *Bath.* The first theatre was built in 1705 by subscription at a cost of £1,300 for John Power. On the passing of the Licensing Act in 1737 this theatre was demolished, and the players adapted a room under Lady Hawley's Assembly Rooms, which in 1745 came under the management of Simpson. In 1750 a new theatre was erected in Orchard Street, the shell of which still exists. The two continued in rivalry until 1756 when John Palmer, manager of Orchard Street, bought out Simpson's. The Orchard Street Theatre was reconstructed by Arthur in 1767 and again in 1774–5, a royal patent being obtained in 1768. The Palmers, father and son, were succeeded in management by Keasberry and Dimond. Mrs. Siddons was a member of the stock company from 1778 to 1782 at a salary of £3 a week. In 1805 a new theatre in Beaufort Square was erected on a tontine scheme by Palmer, the city architect, in conjunction with George Dance. In 1817 a long connexion with the Bristol Theatre was broken and from 1822 a decline set in. A succession of short-lived lessees included Mrs. Macready and J. H. Chute, who partially revived the theatre's fortunes. In 1862 it was destroyed by fire and a new theatre opened on the same site, designed by C. J. Phipps and financed by a limited liability company. Since 1884 the theatre has been used by touring companies.

(b) *Birmingham.* Two theatrical booths existed before 1730 but the first theatre was built in Moor Street about 1740. Richard Yates brought a company from London every season. A theatre in King Street opened in 1751, and another in New Street in 1774. This last was twice rebuilt after fires in 1792 and 1820. The elder Macready succeeded Yates as lessee in 1795 and was granted a royal patent in 1807. R. W. Elliston and Alfred Bunn were followed by a quick-changing succession of managers, the most important of whom was Mercer Simpson in 1840. His son introduced touring companies in 1849, but the stock company lingered on, frequently acting in Shakespeare revivals, until 1878. The theatre was closed in 1901 and rebuilt in 1904. In addition to the Theatre Royal and the Alexandra, Birmingham possesses a famous Repertory Theatre. Another theatre, the Prince of Wales's, was destroyed by enemy action in the Second World War.

(c) *Brighton.* The first permanent theatre was built in North Street in 1774 by Samuel Paine, a bricklayer. Roger Johnstone, the first lessee, was succeeded by Fox, who erected a new theatre in Duke Street in 1790 at a cost of £500. Fox died in 1792 and a succession of lessees followed. The theatre was remodelled in horseshoe form in 1796, and a royal box was fitted. The house closed in 1806, and a theatre in New Road was built by Hewitt Cobb in 1807, the lessee being John Brunton. In spite of royal patronage this theatre ruined a number of managers. It was temporarily closed and the properties sold by auction in 1820. The first Christmas pantomime was presented in 1823. In 1854 Nye Chart became lessee and in 1866 he purchased the theatre, demolished it, and commissioned C. J. Phipps to build another on the same site. His management lasted until his death in 1876, when he was succeeded by his widow. It was while playing at this theatre in October

1891 that Julia Neilson and Fred Terry were married. Touring companies started in 1868, but the stock company existed up to 1873.

(d) *Bristol.* Puritan opposition to the theatre was strong in Bristol, but the Bath players succeeded none the less in establishing themselves there, and in 1729 John Hippisley built the first regular theatre at Jacob's Wells. This was visited annually by a mixed company from the London theatres, whilst the Bath company continued to provide a spring season. In 1766 a new theatre in King Street was erected by subscription at a cost of £5,000. The architect was John Paty, the decorations by Michael Edkins. Paty had plans from Saunders, a Drury Lane carpenter, and many features echo that building. The royal patent was granted in 1778. John Palmer jun., of the Bath Theatre, was lessee in 1779 and made extensive alterations both that year and in 1800, when he added a new gallery. The connexion with Bath, broken in 1817, was renewed by the younger Macready in 1837. The stock company came to an end in 1878. The Theatre Royal became the home of variety and pantomime until it was reopened in 1943 under the auspices of the Arts Council (then known as C.E.M.A.). It, and Richmond (see below), are the most historic existing playhouses in England, and the only survivals from the eighteenth century.

(e) *Liverpool.* In the early part of the eighteenth century cockpits were used for dramatic performances. The Old Ropery Theatre, c. 1740, was a converted room and was visited by Irish companies. In 1749 or 1750 a theatre without boxes was built in Drury Lane, which comedians from the London theatres visited in the summer. Boxes were added in 1759 and green- and dressing-rooms provided in 1767. Letters patent were granted in 1771 and a new theatre erected in 1772 at a cost of £6,000, Sir William Chambers being the architect. The engagement of a provincial company in 1778 caused a riot. Among lessees were Joseph Younger and George Mattocks, the latter of whom was ruined in 1786. In 1789 Francis Aickin and J. P. Kemble were lessees. Under W. T. Lewis and Thomas Knight the theatre was rebuilt in 1803 in horseshoe shape. The Liverpool season ran nearly all the year round and was independent of a circuit. In 1884 the theatre was adapted as a circus and later was purchased by the corporation for a cold storage company. Liverpool has now four theatres and a repertory company.

(f) *Norwich.* A series of taverns, including the White Swan, served as theatres until 1758, when Thomas Ivory built the first permanent theatre on Theatre (then Assembly) Plain. The Norwich company's circuit included Ipswich, Bury, Colchester, Yarmouth, and many lesser Norfolk towns. Ivory obtained a royal patent in 1768 and was succeeded by William Wilkins, who appointed a series of managers, including Brunton, to run the circuit. A new Theatre Royal was built in 1826 at the cost of £6,000 on a site adjoining the old one. Its most notable manager was William Sidney, 1854–85. The

Norwich circuit broke up about 1852, and the latter part of Sidney's régime marked the change-over from stock to touring companies. This theatre, enlarged in 1913, was burnt down in 1934 and reopened in 1936. Nugent Monck's Maddermarket company was started in 1910, and since 1921 has acted in a theatre constructed on Elizabethan lines. The company is an amateur one and has performed all Shakespeare as well as many other classes.

(g) *Richmond, Yorkshire.* The theatre here is one of the two surviving eighteenth-century English playhouses. Smaller than Bristol, the Richmond playhouse also differs in having a rectangular auditorium, and is unique in preserving the original proscenium. It was opened in 1788 by Samuel Butler the elder on Corporation ground. His circuit included Harrogate, Beverley, Northallerton, Whitby, Kendal, and Ulverston. After Butler's death in 1812 his widow, who was a member of the Jefferson family, ran the circuit until her son Samuel Butler was old enough to take it over in 1821. Soon after the circuit started to break up, and Butler's connexion with the Richmond Theatre ended in 1830. For a few years it was rented for short seasons to various managers, and in 1848 it was converted into a wine cellar and auction room, the sunk pit being boarded over. In 1943 it was restored to use as a theatre in commemoration of the 850th year of the enfranchisement of the borough.

(h) *York.* The first theatre in York was adapted from a tennis-court for Keregan's company in 1734. Previously his and other companies had acted at the Merchant Taylors' Hall, Banks's Cockpit, and elsewhere. From 1732 the season was on a subscription basis, and the company was one of the first to be a salaried instead of a sharing one. The second theatre was built by Joseph Baker, adjoining the site of the present Theatre Royal. Baker erected another and larger theatre in 1765. In the same year Tate Wilkinson, most famous of provincial managers, succeeded him, and under his régime many actors and actresses were trained. Hull, Leeds, Doncaster, Wakefield, Pontefract, and other towns were in the York circuit. Wilkinson died in 1803 and was succeeded by his son John Wilkinson, who later sub-let to a succession of lessees. The theatre was remodelled in 1822, the cost being defrayed by subscription. Further improvements were made in 1835. J. L. Pritchard, Henry Beverley, W. S. Thorne, and John Coleman were the lessees from 1848 to 1878. Coleman employed famous authors to write plays and pantomimes for his circuit, but eventually went bankrupt. The theatre was reconstructed in 1875 and 1880 and rebuilt in 1901. Waddington's stock company was given up about 1880 in favour of touring companies. The Theatre Royal is now used by a repertory company.   S. R.

PUBLILIUS SYRUS, see MIME, 2 *b*.

PUDDLE WHARF THEATRE, see PORTER'S HALL and ROSSETER, PHILIP.

PULCINELLA, one of the comic servants of the *commedia dell'arte* who may have originated with the actor 'Ciuccio' (Andrea Calcese). A hump-backed, doltish fellow, Pulcinella is regarded, by those who look for the origin of the Italian improvised comedy in the Atellan farces, as identical with the Maccus, or stupid servant, of Latin popular comedy. In his original Italian form he is regarded as typical of the Neapolitan district; as Polichinelle he stands to some for the quick wit of France; while as Punch (and Punchinello) he epitomizes English humour. His name first appears in the early seventeenth century, and the character, wherever it originated, was probably firmly established by Silvio Fiorillo, otherwise famous as Capitano Mattamoros. Pulcinella has no part in the English harlequinade, unless we consider that some of his characteristics may have passed to Clown, but, still in his Italian clothes, and with his humped back and hooked nose, he is the chief figure in the ubiquitous travelling puppet-booth (see PUNCH AND JUDY). In the opinion of competent critics, the popularity of Pulcinella, and the disproportionate attention paid to his buffoonery, was one of the main causes of the decline of the *commedia dell' arte* (see ITALY, 2).

PULITZER PRIZE for drama, one of several literary awards established under the will of Joseph Pulitzer (1847–1911), given annually for the best 'original American play performed in New York'. It was first awarded in 1918, and Eugene O'Neill and Robert Sherwood had each won it three times by the year 1949.

PUNCH AND JUDY. This old puppet-show, sometimes still to be seen in the streets and at the seaside, dates in its present form from about 1800. The familiar story is briefly as follows: Punch, a grotesque hunchback with hooked nose and chin and usually a protruding belly, is left to mind the baby while Judy, his wife, goes shopping. The baby begins to cry, ignores Punch's attempts to soothe it, and only screams louder when he chastises it; at last in anger and desperation Punch throws it out of the window. Judy returns, is furious with Punch, and belabours him with a stick; whereupon Punch seizes the stick, beats Judy senseless, and kills her. There then follow a number of encounters between Punch and various characters, most of whom he beats and kills—these usually include a Doctor, a Negro, and a Beadle. Eventually, however, Punch is captured and taken off to be hanged. At the last moment he tricks Jack Ketch, the hangman, persuading him to put his head into the noose, and then quickly pulling the rope. After his triumph over all human adversaries he is sometimes, however, frightened by the ghost of Judy, and then by the Devil, who arrives to carry him off; after a tremendous fight Punch usually emerges the victor, and hoists the lifeless body of the Devil upon his triumphant stick. Punch has a friendly companion in Joey, the Clown, and a scene is often introduced with a real live dog—Toby. Not the least remarkable aspect of this 'horrific' drama is that it invariably moves an audience to roars of laughter.

The origin of Punch is an obscure subject, about which it is tempting to romanticize; it is nevertheless not entirely fanciful to see his early prototype in the masked mimes of the popular Greek and Roman theatre; here we find grotesque figures, masked sometimes with hooked noses, and padded absurdly or obscenely about their bodies; their drama dealt with popular mythological stories and was enlivened with slap-stick and buffoonery. Puppet-shows were popular at that period, and almost certainly reproduced the traditions of the mime. Throughout the obscurity of the Dark and Middle Ages it appears that this tradition, though suppressed by the Church, never entirely disappeared, and in the sixteenth century we find an essentially popular drama growing up in Italy, a drama of stock characters, improvised by masked figures, some of them grotesquely padded—the *commedia dell' arte* (see ITALY, 2). It is not impossible that this tradition was largely preserved through a thousand years in the puppet-shows.

Among the characters of the Italian comedy was one Pulcinella—a sly comic servant, always getting into scrapes and cleverly escaping punishment; he invariably had a hooked nose, and a hump-back, and was a great favourite in the district of Naples; but it was as a puppet that he gained his greatest success, for as a puppet his physical disfigurements could be comically exaggerated in a manner impossible to a living actor.

The Italian comedy spread all over Europe, and was firmly established in Paris; with it went the Italian puppet theatres, and in France Pulcinella became Polichinelle—a witty Gallic character destined to preside over the French puppet stage for 150 years. When, in 1660, the English Court returned to England, and King Charles II once again threw the theatres open to every kind of entertainment, the Italian puppets were not slow to take advantage of the fields that had been so fruitful earlier in the century; in 1662 Samuel Pepys, passing through Covent Garden, notes 'the Italian puppet-play, which is very pretty, the best that ever I saw, and great resort of gallants', and in 1666 at Moorfields he saw 'Polichinello, which pleases me mightily, . . . and I like the more I see it'.

England took 'Polichinello' to her heart, and soon anglicized him from 'Punchinello' to plain Punch. But it was not only in name that he was translated; he retained all his physical grotesqueries, but was adopted as a ubiquitous English buffoon in every puppet-play of the period. At this time the old biblical stories that had been banished from the living theatre were still the staple fare on the puppet stage, and Punch was introduced as a vulgar 'farceur' into the Garden of Eden, Noah's Ark, or the Court of Solomon; he turned up unexpectedly in the story of Dick Whittington or of Doctor Faustus. This apparent incongruity was in effect no more than the traditional stage 'business' of the English clown; with the decline of the Morality plays, towards the end of the sixteenth century, the character of the Vice, who was accustomed to run through every play as a perpetual trouble-maker among the more virtuous characters, declined into a mere buffoon or clown, but continued to crop up as light relief throughout the whole body of Elizabethan drama; his distracting antics were gradually banished from the stage, but he found a home in the character of Punch upon the puppet stage—always a sure preserver of popular dramatic tradition.

Thus it will be seen that the character of Punch is derived partly from the early Mediterranean mimes through the Italian comedy, and partly from the tradition of the English medieval fool through the dramatic types of the Vice and the Clown; he has evolved into a character quite different from both Pulcinella and Polichinelle. Throughout the eighteenth century Punch continued as the chief and presiding character on the puppet stage; there was no such thing as a Punch play, but merely hundreds of biblical, legendary, and sometimes literary stories, in all of which Punch appeared; for a few years (1710–14) Punch's theatre in Covent Garden was the rage of the town, but long after the fashion had died away puppet-plays were still popular at fairs and country wakes among the ordinary common people. It was during these years that Punch's character was formed: he was a quarrelsome nuisance to the rest of the actors, he had a wife called Joan, who nagged him, and whom he beat, the Devil usually appeared at the end to take him away—and sometimes succeeded—and he spoke in a high squeak, formed by inserting a 'swazzle' or squeaker into the mouth of the speaker. He was the beloved favourite of the people.

Gradually, however, the popularity of an essentially Elizabethan stage technique began to fade, even on the puppet stage; Punch and Joan were often banished to a comic afterpiece, or entirely ousted by the new craze for Fantoccini, or Trick Figures, and the old fairground puppet plays degenerated into a mere jumble of nonsensical and indecent absurdities. It was at this point, at the end of the eighteenth century, that Punch must have seemed on the verge of extinction.

To understand what happened now it is important to appreciate the distinction between the various types of puppet-show (see MARIONETTE and PUPPET). The early English puppet-shows were probably presented by hand- or glove-puppets; the puppet-play in Ben Jonson's *Bartholomew Fair* (1614) appears to be designed for this type of puppet. The Italian puppets brought over after the Restoration were probably marionettes, and it was undoubtedly as a marionette that Punch developed in England. English puppet-shows of the eighteenth century were almost invariably presented by marionettes. A marionette theatre, however, is difficult to transport—it requires at least a cart—and by the end of the eighteenth century Punch had declined so much in favour that it was no longer economically worth while to transport all the apparatus of a marionette theatre presenting Punch plays from one village or fair to another. Punch nearly died—but instead he became a hand-puppet. The old tradition had never been entirely lost, and hand-puppet booths, presenting short knock-about turns between Punch and Joan, or Punch and the Devil, had been set up outside fairground puppet theatres as a sort of 'trailer' for the full-length puppet-plays inside. Now Punch was relegated solely to the open-air hand-puppet booth; it was easily portable, for one man could carry it on his back, and present an entire show single-handed, with the indispensable aid of a mate to 'bottle' or collect the pennies from the audience. In this transformation Punch found a new lease of life.

It is important to realize that the form taken by the Punch and Judy show has been dictated far more by these practical and economic considerations than by any literary or symbolical fantasies of later commentators. The essential features of every hand-puppet show are that only two characters can appear at a time (unless there is more than one manipulator), that there is very little opportunity for elaborate staging effects, and that the gestures of the figures are extremely limited; it is, therefore, almost essential for a hand-puppet show to concentrate on fast, witty dialogue, or on broad and vulgar effects, with plenty of slapstick and fighting, which hand-puppets can do to perfection. That is precisely what the Punch and Judy show provides. Punch is on the stage the whole time, occupying the manipulator's right hand; on the left hand are introduced one after another a whole procession of lively characters, each to do battle and fall before Punch's furious assaults. The scheme of the play can be seen as a not unnatural development from the earlier Punch dramas, but the dialogue has been cut to the bone to suit the new medium, and there appears indeed little rhyme or reason in Punch's pugnacity; Judy—probably a corruption from the familiar 'Joaney'—hardly has time to show herself a shrew before she is slaughtered; the Doctor comes from the commedia dell'arte; Joey was introduced early in the nineteenth century in honour of Grimaldi the famous clown; the trick of hanging the hangman is found in the Italian comedy; the Beadle, now usually a Policeman, is an obvious native growth; the combat with the Devil was a feature of the late Morality plays.

Throughout the nineteenth century Punch and Judy prospered, and Punch's squeak was familiar in the streets of London and throughout the country-side. From time to time new characters were added or old ones were transformed—'Shallaballah', an obscure Oriental, became Jim Crow the Negro minstrel; Mr. Jones, a respectable tradesman, appeared as the owner of Toby; a boxing match was introduced; but the main outlines of the story have remained exactly the same. To-day Punch

and Judy is not often seen in the streets, but it is not defunct; a survey carried out by *The World's Fair* showed that in the summer of 1938 there were resident Punch and Judy shows at over forty English and Welsh seaside towns; at the larger of these the showmen have to pay a rent for the right to perform, and rely on collecting throughout the season not only enough to cover that, but enough to keep themselves during the winter until Christmas time, when there are plenty of parties to be attended. There are probably about a hundred men in this country able to perform Punch and Judy; many of them belong to families who have been doing it for generations, but there have also recently been new-comers from the music-halls, and amateurs who have turned a hobby into a part-time source of income. Some of the work of these new-comers is excellent: Punch and Judy demands a strong and extremely adaptable voice, an ability to gag in the true *commedia dell'arte* tradition, perfect timing of minute finger-movements, and considerable physical toughness—the strain of holding one's arms above one's head for half an hour and of throwing one's body about during the fights is most exhausting.

Punch's continued existence in modern England is something of a miracle, but he is still popular, and is still genuinely funny, and there seems no reason why he should disappear now; the details of his drama may change in the future as they have done in the past, but the type seems to be immortal and the tradition is too strong to die.

The text of Punch and Judy was first taken down in 1827 by J. Payne Collier and published with illustrations by George Cruikshank. This text is not free from suspicion, and has probably been edited and 'improved' with literary emendations, but it has remained in print to this day. The early editions contained a 'History of Punch and Puppets' by Payne Collier that was certainly very good for its period, but can now be shown to contain some inaccuracies and inventions. There is a chapter on Punch, including the Payne Collier text, in *Popular Entertainments through the Ages* by Samuel McKechnie; Mayhew's *London Labour and the London Poor* (1851) contains a verbatim transcription of an actual mid-Victorian street performance, while a modern version of the story, played in Scotland by a travelling company, is given in George Baker's *Playing with Punch* (1944).   G. S.

PUNCH AND JUDY THEATRE, NEW YORK, a delightful playhouse, holding only 300 people, situated on the north side of 49th Street. It opened on 10 Nov. 1914 with *The Marriage of Columbine*, and one of its first successes was a dramatization of *Treasure Island*. Charles Hopkins and his wife had been identified with this theatre from its opening, and in 1926 it was renamed the Charles Hopkins and opened with *The Makropoulos Secret*. A record for the house of 321 performances was set up by *Mrs. Moonlight*, while in 1928 a translation of Reynal's *Le Tombeau sous l' Arc de Triomphe* ran for a week. In 1932 the theatre became a cinema for the showing of special films.   G. F.

PUNCH'S PLAYHOUSE, LONDON, see STRAND THEATRE (1).

PUPPET. A puppet, strictly speaking, is any inanimate figure controlled by human agency. There are many different types of puppets, and in their long history they have been put to many different uses.

Probably their earliest appearance was in connexion with religious ceremonies or as a medium for popularizing religious legends; for the temples of Egypt and Greece statues were constructed that could incline their heads and make other movements under the direction of concealed controls; similar figures were known in the churches of medieval Europe; and among African tribes, idols have been found that could be secretly operated in the same manner. The dividing line between charlatanry and religious drama was, perhaps, sometimes finely drawn. To this day, in the Far East—China, Burma, the islands of Java and Bali—the traditional epics of Buddhist mythology are still performed by puppets, and the puppet-showman is venerated as a great popular educator. In Europe, in the Middle Ages, religious dramas performed by puppets developed from the Christmas crib plays and, especially in Italy, came to have an important part in the instruction and entertainment of the people.

With the disappearance of the living religious drama in Europe the puppet-shows still continued to present biblical stories, since they were the popular traditional stories of the common people. Even in England, plays like *The Creation of the World* or *The Court of Solomon* were performed by itinerant puppet-shows almost to the beginning of the nineteenth century—250 years after they had been banished from the stage. The puppet-show is essentially the drama of the people and has preserved, often for centuries, age-old dramatic types and popular legends; puppet-showmen are usually simple and unlearned men who earn a modest livelihood by enacting what their fathers have taught them.

Throughout western Europe, up to the end of the nineteenth century, the travelling puppet theatres were regular visitors to country fairs and remote villages; their performances were usually crude and sometimes vulgar, but they carried the drama where even the strolling players never ventured. It was not only dramatic and literary traditions that were preserved by puppets—when Bohemia lay under Austrian domination the puppet-showmen played a great part in fortifying the national culture of the people as they travelled from village to village performing native Czech plays in their own language. To-day the cinema has, unfortunately, driven most of the travelling puppet theatres off the roads.

Perhaps not far removed from the religious puppet-show is the puppet designed to arouse wonder; at certain periods of its history the puppet has been admired for its mechanistic rather than its dramatic qualities; its movements have been regarded as a sort of conjuring trick, the secret of its construction jealously guarded, and great ingenuity has been displayed in devising clever and intricate effects. This aspect of puppetry was probably first highly developed in the Fantoccini of the late eighteenth century by those masters of puppetry, the Italians, and was soon absorbed into the English and other native traditions; in the nineteenth century this development was still further advanced by the clever English marionette showman, Thomas Holden, and in the twentieth century the brilliant Podrecca's Piccoli represented further advances in intricate articulation. There are a few companies still to be seen on the English music-halls, notably Delvaine's, that keep alive this particular branch of the puppet tradition: among the favourite tricks are the 'Dissecting Skeleton' whose bones gradually float apart and dance separately in the four corners of the stage and then reunite, and the 'Grand Turk' whose arms, legs, head, and finally trunk fly apart, each turning into a separate small figure.

Puppets have always been popular among the common people, but in their time they have also provided fashionable entertainment for high society. The Italian puppets that went to London soon after the Restoration were summoned to several command performances by Charles II; the famous Puppet Theatre under the Piazza in Covent Garden, under the direction of a brilliant dwarf, Martin Powell, was one of the most fashionable and successful entertainments of its day (1710–14); later in the same century the Italian puppets, presenting opera and Fantoccini, again took London by storm; the Prince of Wales himself was a subscriber at Lord Barrymore's select Puppet Theatre in Savile Row in 1790. In sixteenth-century Italy there were many princes who patronized puppets in their private theatres—Lorenzo de' Medici, Cosimo I and Francesco I among them. In Germany in the 1770s there was an elaborate private Puppet Theatre belonging to Prince Esterházy, for which Haydn was commissioned to write several operettas.

The fashionable puppet-show, as might be expected, emancipated itself from the traditional legacies of the folk-puppet theatre, and developed in their place a sophisticated charm and a keen sense of satire. The puppet is indeed particularly well suited for mimicry and satire and has often been employed for that purpose. That twisted genius, Samuel Foote, used to introduce an act with puppets into his entertainments with the object of impersonating and mimicking popular actors of the period, and in 1773 produced an entire puppet-play at his theatre in the Haymarket as a satire on the popular taste in sentimental comedy. Charles Dibdin, another gifted eccentric of the English stage, erected his own Puppet Theatre at Exeter 'Change in 1775, and mocked at his contemporaries on its boards. Satire has flourished even more happily across the Channel than in England—so much so that the Roman puppet theatres were closed down in about 1850 by the state authorities owing to their thinly disguised political references. In France, in the 1860s, a clever journalist, Lemercier de Neuville, developed a puppet-show whose political and literary allusions made it in great demand in the *salons*; in the same period Maurice Sand, at Nohant, diverted himself and his sister with a puppet theatre which, with its witty contemporary allusions, was designed to appeal essentially to their own literary circle.

The fortunes of the puppet-show waxed and waned through many centuries without anyone, at least in Europe, regarding it very seriously, or thinking of it as anything other than a crude entertainment or, at most, an amusing diversion. However, the closing years of the nineteenth and the early years of the twentieth centuries saw a marked revival, in which puppets were 'discovered' by the artists, and accorded a serious respect that they had never enjoyed before. In 1862 the 'Theatron Erotikon' in Paris was the scene of a series of puppet performances devised by a group of young artists who permitted a certain sophisticated impropriety to enliven their productions; the puppet-show has continued to exercise a great attraction upon many French writers and artists ever since. In England, Gordon Craig, with his emphasis on the actor's role as an 'uebermarionette', campaigned with enthusiasm for the puppet as a worthwhile artistic and dramatic medium. From these early efforts the present puppet revival has sprung; to-day the self-consciously 'artistic' puppet-show still remains largely an affair of the studio, but it has its limited circle of devotees, and it seems possible that its influence on the specifically 'entertainment' puppet may lead to a rejuvenation of the old art. Among contemporaries who have devoted themselves, with promising results, to the art of the puppet one might mention Walter Simmonds for a delightful one-man show, Olive Blackham, who has founded the Roel Puppet Theatre, Margaret Hoyland for her expressive paper figures, and Jan Bussell for a technique of puppet ballet. In France Marcel Temporal, Jacques Chesnais, and the Arc-en-ciel Theatre group, work with intelligence and wit, usually with hand-puppets. In Germany Paul Brann, who founded the Munich Art-Puppet Theatre in the great tradition of south German woodcarving, and Harro Siegel, with his more delicate productions of opera, also deserve mention.

The most recent development of puppetry has been its widespread adoption by schools in Germany, Czechoslovakia, England, and America as a handicraft subject. Educationalists welcome the puppet-show as a means of self-expression and as a happy vehicle for instruction; it seems likely that the practice of school puppetry will be even more widely extended in the future. The old school of traditional puppet-showmen sometimes tend to look askance at this 'interference from amateurs';

but it seems probable that—quite apart from its educational value—school puppetry will breed a new appreciation of the puppet-show in the coming generation and encourage a considerable revival in its public presentation.

To-day, in England and America, the puppet is being talked and written about as never before; there are societies—the British Puppet Guild and the Puppeteers of America—devoted to encouraging the art; there are a host of simple technical handbooks; there are summer schools, and conferences, and exhibitions. Most of this activity is the work of amateurs; the puppet is welcomed as a fascinating hobby —the interest usually lies in the making rather than in the performing; the results often lack dramatic or artistic value, but it is perhaps a mistake to expect a high standard at this stage of the revival. A few of the more enterprising puppeteers have launched professional shows of their own; they have all had to face a hard struggle to earn a living, but in America there are now several well-established puppet troupes, and in England a few companies have weathered their difficulties to find growing appreciation. The puppet revival is only gradually breaking upon the general public, and there is an unfortunate prejudice that a puppet-show is essentially a children's entertainment; children do make an ideal audience for puppets, as they accept their incongruities as perfectly natural, but the scope of the puppet is very wide and it is a pity to limit it entirely to juvenile entertainment. New fields in which puppets have appeared with success are as advertising shows and in television, for which they have proved extremely suitable. The dramatic and entertainment values of our puppet-shows often leave room for considerable improvement, but the seeds of a revival have been sown, and there is no lack of enthusiasm to carry it forward to a successful conclusion in which the puppet will be reinstated as a widely accepted popular entertainment.

More or less permanent puppet theatres are to be found, but only by diligent search, throughout Europe. Sometimes they cater exclusively for the local working-class or peasant population, and are situated in obscure side streets and down cellars; here the traditions of the folk-puppet plays are preserved intact. Sometimes the productions have been brought technically up to date, and theatres have been specially built for them in the public parks. The following list, compiled in 1939, takes no account of many small and semi-private puppet theatres, but includes only the best-known public theatres, at which more or less regular repertory performances are presented throughout the year; they are, however, usually closed during the summer months. It is impossible to tell how many of these theatres have survived, but puppets have weathered a good many wars in their history, and it is hoped that these details will have a more than historical interest and prove of some practical value to European travellers.

Puppet Theatres in Europe [1939]

AUSTRIA
Salzburg: Aicher's Marionette Theatre. Delicate production, with a feeling for the eighteenth-century 'Mozartian' atmosphere, has made this a fashionable and famous entertainment.

BELGIUM
Antwerp, Brussels: Traditional style.
Liége: Traditional Tchantchès drama.

CZECHOSLOVAKIA
Pilsen: Marionette Theatre of Prof. Skupa.
Prague: 'The Realm of Puppets' at the Central Library. 'The Theatre of Artistic Education' at the Club of Technical and Art Students.
Semi-private puppet theatres attached to schools, colleges, sokols, &c., are to be found in almost every town in Czechoslovakia.

ENGLAND
Fleetwood: Bilton's Marionettes. A summer season of children's pantomimes in an open-air theatre at the Marine Gardens.
Malvern: The Lanchester Marionette Theatre. Seasons of variety, short plays, &c., at frequent intervals throughout the year.
Manchester: Belle Vue Park. Daily performances of Punch and Judy during the summer, presented by Professor Le Fay in an indoor theatre.
Morecambe: D'Albert's Marionettes on an open-air stage.
Punch and Judy outdoor shows are to be seen on the beach at almost every seaside resort during the summer season.

FRANCE
Amiens: Traditional 'Lafleur' drama.
The Pajot-Walton Marionettes are to be found touring the country with music-hall turns and traditional puppet repertoire.
Lyons: The original Guignol Theatre, conducted by Pierre Nichthauser.
Paris: Luxembourg Gardens. Hand-Puppets (Guignol) and Marionettes; a charming theatre, run, mainly for children, by Robert Deshartis.
Numerous open-air Guignol booths in the parks, Champs-Élysées, &c.

GERMANY
Aachen: Schaengehent (Rod-Puppet) Theatre. Traditional Rhineland drama.
Max Radestock Hand-Puppet Theatre.
Baden-Baden: Puhonny Marionette Theatre. A particularly artistic expression of the German tradition.
The Schichtl and Iwowski Puppet Theatres conduct tours through the country with repertoires of Marionettes, Hand-Puppets, and Shadow Shows.
Cologne: Hänneschen (Rod-Puppet) Theatre. Traditional Rhineland drama.
Zangerle Marionette Theatre. The Rhineland dramas in a modern technique.
Dortmund: Kastner Marionette Theatre.
Elberfeld-Wuppertal: Fritz Gerhard's Marionette Theatre. The official centre of State Puppetry.
Hohnstein: Hand-Puppet Theatre of Max Jacob. A brilliant example of this medium.
Leipzig: Kuenstlerhaus Hand-Puppet Theatre.
Munich: Binter's Marionette Theatre, historic and long established.
Radebeul: Carl Schröder Hand-Puppet Theatre.
Stuttgart: Deininger's Marionette Theatre.
Würzburg: Bendel and Flach Marionette Theatre.
This is far from exhausting the list of German puppet theatres; in no other country has the tradition been preserved so healthily. Often the puppet theatres are subsidized by the municipalities.

GREECE
Athens: Karagöz Shadow Theatre at the Café Molos.

ITALY
Milan: Teatro Gerolamo. These theatres have retained in their comedies and operas some of the *commedia dell'arte* characters.
Palermo: Traditional Sicilian drama.
Rome: The famous Teatro dei Piccoli of Vittorio Podrecca, with its brilliant Fantoccini and potted opera.
Turin: Teatro Gianduja.

JAPAN
Osaka: Traditional Japanese drama with unique life-size puppets, manipulated in full view of the audience.
Tokyo: Asakusa Park.

SPAIN
Travelling shows are occasionally found on temporary pitches. Faydella, a very old-established company from Barcelona, was showing in Majorca in 1940.

SWITZERLAND
Geneva: Les Petits Tréteaux, with an imaginative repertory directed by Marcelle Moynier.
St. Gallen: Children's Marionette Theatre, with traditional repertory.
Zürich: Marionette Theatre of Alfred Altherr, attached to the School of Art.

U.S.A.
Apart from certain small puppet theatres preserving the folk drama of the national minorities, permanent public puppet theatres have not yet been established in the U.S.A. There are, however, a number of touring companies which have brought a technical skill and freshness of outlook to their art with most encouraging results—Tony Sarg, Rufus Rose, Remo Bufano, and the Tattermann Marionettes are among a host of enthusiastic innovators. In recent years there seems to have been a reaction in favour of the simplified cabaret puppet-show; among several exponents Bob Bromley, who performs with one figure at a time, in a plain 'spot', and without any stage or scenery, has achieved particular success.

U.S.S.R.
Moscow: The Central Puppet Theatre, directed by Obratzov, whose theatre acts as a training centre for puppeteers throughout the Union. Each constituent republic of the U.S.S.R. has its own national puppet theatre, sending out touring shows of educational value. The greater part of Russian puppetry is with Hand-Puppets.

The history of puppets was written by Charles Magnin in 1852 (*Histoire des marionnettes en Europe*); later histories—in French by Ernest Maindron, in Italian by 'Yorrick', in German by Max von Boehn, and in English by Helen Joseph—have embroidered the subject further. For later developments, Cyril Beaumont's *Puppets and the Puppet Stage* (1938) is an excellent pictorial survey; the annual *Puppetry*, published in the U.S.A. since 1930, is an invaluable record; and reference should also be made to the weekly 'Puppet Column', in the English showman's journal, *The World's Fair*.

There are many different types of puppets, including (*a*) the HAND- (or GLOVE-) PUPPET, which is the simplest form of rounded puppet. It is constructed with a firm head and hands, upon a loose open costume; the performer inserts his hand into the costume, with his first finger placed in the head and the second finger and thumb each in a hand; he stands behind a screen and holds the puppets above it. The head and hands of a hand-puppet are usually made of wood, but this has the disadvantage of being heavy, and they are sometimes now made of papier mâché, which is very light and strong. The disadvantages of the hand-puppets are that the gestures of the figures are limited to the twitching of a man's fingers, and that one performer cannot introduce more than two characters at a time; the great advantages of hand-puppets are that they are quickly and simply made and very light and easy to carry about. The successful hand-puppet play concentrates on broad simple effects, witty dialogue, or knock-about comedy. Many of the popular national puppet characters are hand-puppets, carried in this form across Europe by wandering showmen. Such are Punch and Judy in England; in France, Guignol, the type of the Lyonnais silk-weaver, generous, bibulous, and witty; in Germany, Kasperl, a sly clever peasant type; in Russia, Petrouchka, from the same stock at Punch; and in Italy, Pulcinella, the father of them all; even in China there is a family of hand-puppets not very dissimilar from the European breed. All these folk-puppet shows make a great point of beatings, terrific fights, and broad low comedy.

The satiric and literary puppet-shows that sprang up in France towards the end of the nineteenth century, the puppets of Edmond Duranty, Lemercier de Neuville, and Maurice Sand, were all hand-puppet shows. Among modern exponents of the hand-puppet who have developed their shows on their own individualistic lines one might mention Walter Wilkinson in England, the author of several books describing his life as a travelling showman, and Nina Efimova in the U.S.S.R., who has contributed a charming account of her work in *Adventures of a Russian Puppet Theatre.* The continental-style theatre, allowing several manipulators to work together, permits considerably more ambitious productions than the one-man booth used for Punch and Judy.

(*b*) The ROD-PUPPET is an extension of the hand-puppet; it is a full-length rounded figure, supported and manipulated by rods from below. Its movements are necessarily slow and very limited, but the control is absolute, and broad gestures of rare beauty with the arms can be obtained. The most famous and beautiful rod-puppets are found in the island of Java; in Europe the only native tradition is in the Rhineland. In Paris, in the 1880s, Henri Signoret opened a puppet theatre with the intention of reviving the great plays of classical antiquity; the medium he adopted was figures controlled from below the stage by strings passing through their bodies and operated from a sort of keyboard. To-day Gera Blattner in Paris is experimenting along the same lines. The most striking recent work with rod-puppets has been achieved by Richard Teschner in Vienna; his stage is seen through a great golden framed convex lens, thus enlarging the figures and lending an air of mystery and enchantment to a highly polished

performance. In America Majorie Batcheldor is experimenting with rod-puppets with great success

Other important different types of puppets are described under the following headings:

MARIONETTES: Rounded figures controlled by wires or strings from above the stage.

PUNCH AND JUDY: Rounded figures fitting upon the performer's hands and held over a screen above his head.

SHADOW SHOW: The shadows of flat figures cast upon a translucent screen.

TOY THEATRE: Flat figures cut from cardboard.

There are several other less well known types, notably the intricate and almost life-size Japanese puppets, held in full view of the audience by sometimes as many as three manipulators, and operated by small wires and levers concealed in their backs. Some of the finest Japanese dramatists of the eighteenth century composed plays for the puppet stage, which was closely linked with the popular *Kabuki* drama and recognized as an integral form of theatrical art (see JAPAN). The 'Cheeky Boys' and other dummies used by ventriloquists represent humbler examples of the same type of puppet.

Then there are 'Jigging Puppets' or 'Marionnettes à la planchette', consisting of one or two figures with a string passing horizontally through their breasts from an upright post to the performer's knee, and made to jig or dance about to the bagpipes or similar instrument. These were for many centuries a popular street entertainment.

One cannot do more than mention the Giant Figures carried in street processions, or the many different types of mechanical automata—the peep-show, the water theatres, the moving pictures, and so on. These may all be included in the sphere of puppetry, but, interesting and charming though they may often be, they belong rather to the non-dramatic aspect of the subject and lie outside the scope of the present volume.   G. S.

PURDY'S NATIONAL THEATRE, NEW YORK, see CHATHAM THEATRE (2).

PURIM PLAYS.
The Jewish Festival of Purim on the 14th Adar (roughly early March), commemorating the events described in the Book of Esther, is a semi-religious holiday which acquired particular importance during the Jewish persecutions of the Middle Ages. Its secular character is attributed by some authorities to a Babylonian or Persian influence, and amusements of all kinds have always been associated with it. Purim Plays appear to have been extemporized in France and Germany as early as the fourteenth century, but they take their origin mainly from the improvised songs and masquerades in which the mummers impersonated the characters of the Book of Esther under the influence of the Italian carnival. These masquerades were at first opposed by the spiritual authorities, but later tolerated as

long as they did not overstep the bounds of decency.

The plays were mostly in one act. Costumes and style were fixed by tradition. Prose and verse were intermingled. All had songs, amusing interludes featuring comic rabbis, apothecaries, midwives, and devils, panto-mimic dances, and a final chorus foretelling Israel's salvation. The dialogue was largely improvised, and based on such subjects as the story of Esther and Haman, the sale of Joseph by his brethren, the story of David and Goliath, and sometimes the life of Moses. These plots, which show one man fighting with God's help against overwhelming odds, could be adapted to local conditions within the traditional frame-work. Until recently they were still given in Eastern Europe in barns, stables, workshops, and in the house of the rich man of the village. Some idea of the dramatic possibilities of these primitive plays may be gathered from the account of one given as late as the end of the nineteenth century in Jerusalem, where life was still unaffected by the Jewish renaissance. The subject was the sale of Joseph. The scene was laid in front of the tomb of his mother Rachel—a well-known landmark in Jerusalem —represented by two chairs covered by a white cloth. Joseph, being led away into captivity, broke away from the slave-dealers and clung weeping to the tomb, from which his mother's voice was heard issuing, bidding him not to fear, for one day he would be a king in Egypt.

The Purim Plays, which have had a con-siderable influence on the development of Jewish drama, took on a literary form in the early seventeenth century. Their technique was borrowed from the *commedia dell'arte*, the Capitano becoming Goliath or Haman, Panta-lone Abraham or Jacob, Arlecchino Satan. Certain non-Jewish plays also had an influence on them; for English readers the most interest-ing are those done in Germany by the English Comedians, which included a version of *Esther and Haman* printed in the 1640 collection of their repertory. There was probably an Eng-lish original of this, but if so it is lost. The popularity of the German version helped to raise the standard of Purim Plays by making them studies in ambition. With the Hebrew revival in Holland and Italy comes a dramatiza-tion of the Book of Esther by Usque and de Graziano, which was produced at Ferrara in 1619, while at the end of the century Enriquez wrote a *Comedia famosa de Aman y Mordechai* (1699), also intended for general representation.

The first-known Purim Play in Germany was a very poor *Ahasuerus* given at Frankfurt-am-Main in 1708. In the same city in 1712 Beer-man von Limburg's play on the sale of Joseph proved so popular that it was printed, and produced as late as 1858 at Minsk. It appears to have been very spectacular in production, with fire, thunder, and other wonders. A point of interest is the appearance in it of the Pickel-herring of the English Comedians, who hence-forth becomes the traditional Purim clown. Another Purim Play by Beerman dealt with David and Goliath, and, like the earlier one, proved so popular that Christians were for-bidden by the authorities to attend it.

Purim Plays became increasingly vulgar as time went on, and in 1720 the reaction set in with the production in Prague of a new play on Esther, shorn of much extraneous matter. This proved popular, and was reprinted for the third time at Amsterdam in 1774. The fight against vulgarity was continued energeti-cally by the Haskala groups, which improved the Purim Plays by relegating the comic figures to the background, and introducing a serious educational element. By the early nineteenth century the Purim Plays were covering the whole range of drama, and with the founding by Goldfaden of a permanent Yiddish theatre which embodied in its productions much of the spirit and method of the Purim Plays, their days were numbered.   E. H.

PURITAN INTERREGNUM. The Puritan opposition to the theatre, which had been growing steadily since the beginning of the seventeenth century, culminated in the closing of the theatres in 1642 by a Parliamentary Ordinance which stated that 'whereas public sports do not well agree with private calamities, nor public stage-plays with the seasons of humiliation . . . while these . . . do continue public stage-plays shall cease and be forborne'. It will be seen that public plays only were forbidden. There is no direct evidence that the Puritans as a whole were hostile to drama. Their objections to the public theatres were partly social, partly political, and only in ex-treme cases religious. Under the early Stuarts the London theatre, its plays, and its drama-tists had become increasingly attached to the Royalist cause, and the assembling of an audience at the playhouse provided excellent opportunities for subversive activities. Plays continued to be acted under the Common-wealth in schools—with the approbation of Cromwell himself—and possibly in private houses, and in 1656 Davenant was allowed to produce publicly his 'entertainment with music'—*The Siege of Rhodes*—now regarded as the first English opera. But for 18 years the professional actors were deprived of their means of livelihood, and their theatres stood derelict, many of them never to be used again. Some actors joined the army, some drifted into the provinces, some, like Andrew Cane, re-turned to earlier, half-forgotten trades. Only the boldest, or most desperate, tried to evade the ban. Evidence of surreptitious perform-ances is given by records of the fining or im-prisoning of the actors concerned. Among them were Richard Baxter, William Beeston, and Robert Cox, who took refuge in the For-tune, and in the smaller theatres, such as the Cockpit, Gibbon's Tennis-Court, and the Red Bull.

PUSHKIN, ALEXANDER SERGEIVICH (1799–1837), Russia's first and greatest national poet, born in Moscow. His father was a civil servant and his mother was descended from Peter the

Great's famous Moor Hannibal. Pushkin, whose uncle Vasily was a well-known poet, was educated privately, and at the age of eight, according to his brother, wrote little plays in French, which he acted with his sister. At 15 he included among his favourite writers the French dramatists, Molière, Racine, and Voltaire—and the Russians Ozerov and Fonvizin. But two of the greatest influences on him were Byron and Shakespeare. He valued the former for his progressive romanticism and his poetry of the rebel-hero, the latter for his superb characterization and the profundity of his philosophy. He once compared Shakespeare and Molière thus:

Characters created by Shakespeare are not types of such and such a passion, or such and such a vice, as with Molière, but living beings, filled with many passions, many vices . . . Molière's miser is miserly and no more; Shakespeare's miser is miserly, keen-witted, vengeful, ambitious, sagacious.

It was under the influence of Shakespeare that Pushkin started work on his great drama *Boris Godunov*. He had already realized that Russia had no truly national drama, only an imitation of the neo-classic French school, and that it could only be created by returning to Russian themes and Russian folk-lore, and by making the Russian language a literary instrument fit to rank with the French and German languages for which it had been so often discarded in its own country. His association with the Decembrist Revolutionaries shows that he realized also the social implications of his literary search for the soul of Russia.

It is evident from his letters and from fragments of unpublished works that Pushkin contemplated a series of dramatic works of which *Boris Godunov* alone was completed. It is notable in being the first Russian tragedy on a political theme—the relationship between a tyrant and his people—which though set back in time was actually a burning contemporary problem; and it does not rely on a love-intrigue. In other respects, too, it was revolutionary: it was broken up into scenes and episodes, it mingled poetry with prose, and made use of colloquial Russian speech. It was not published until six years after its completion in 1825, owing to trouble with the censorship, and was not seen on the stage for nearly fifty years, being given its first production in 1870. It became the basis of an opera by Moussorgsky, in which form it is usually seen nowadays.

Just before his death in a duel, Pushkin completed a series of one-act tragedies, little psychological portraits presented with great subtlety. One deals with Don Juan, one with the rivalry of Mozart and Salieri, and shows the latter, envious of Mozart's genius, poisoning him, while a third, depicting the character of a miser, owes something to Harpagon, but more to Shylock. With some unfinished scenes from Russian folk-lore and from the age of feudalism, this makes up the tale of Pushkin's work for the theatre. Though he is not primarily remembered as a dramatist—for his fine poems must take pride of place—and had little direct contact with the stage, the Russian theatre owes him a great debt, since it was he who first made Russian a literary language and so ushered in the work of the late nineteenth and twentieth centuries. It is of interest that his name, and even long quotations from his verses, are still on the lips of modern Russians.

PYLADES, a Roman pantomime actor (see PANTOMIMUS).

Q

'Q' THEATRE, Kew Bridge, see SUBURBAN THEATRES.

QUAGLIO, a family of artists, extending over several generations, many of whom worked for the theatre. They were of Italian origin, but late in the seventeenth century moved from Lake Como to Munich, where at least three generations were connected with the Court theatre, while a descendant was working at the Berlin Court theatre as late as 1891 (see SCENERY, 4).

QUARTERMAINE. (1) LEON (1876–), English actor, who made his first appearance on the stage at Sheffield in 1894. He was first seen in London in 1901, with Forbes-Robertson, and was a member of Granville-Barker's company at the St. James's in 1913, where he played in Shaw, Galsworthy, and Ibsen. He is a fine Shakespearian actor, and in later years his Banquo, John of Gaunt, and Cymbeline were memorable. He also gave a fine performance as the Nobleman's Man in *The Man with a Load of Mischief* (1925). He has appeared many times in America with great success. His brother (2) CHARLES (1877–) is also an actor, whose later career has been mainly in films. He was first seen in London in 1900, with Benson's company, and was for some years with Tree at His Majesty's.

QUAYLE, ANTHONY (1913–), English actor and producer, who made his first appearance on the stage in 1931, after training at the R.A.D.A. He was seen in a variety of parts, and in 1937 went with the Old Vic company to Elsinore, playing Laertes, and subsequently toured the continent and Egypt with them. He had already given proof of solid qualities, notably as Essex in *Elizabeth la Femme sans Homme*, when the Second World War interrupted his career. From 1939 to 1945 he served with the Royal Artillery, and from his experiences of guerrilla warfare in Albania came his first novel, *Eight Hours from England*, followed by *On Such a Night*. Meanwhile he had returned to the stage, where his acting revealed a maturity and breadth which proved that his war-service had in no way hindered, but rather had furthered, his artistic development. This was abundantly proved by his production in 1946 of *Crime and Punishment*, and by his work as actor and producer at the Stratford Memorial Theatre, of which he became director in 1948, in succession to Sir Barry Jackson.

QUEEN ANNE'S MEN, a company—usually known as the Queen's Men—formed on the accession of James I, from the combination of Worcester's and Oxford's Men which had previously been at the Hope. They played at the Curtain, and among them in the beginning were Christopher Beeston, Richard Perkins, and Thomas Heywood. By 1609 they were playing also at the Red Bull, and seem to have had a successful career, both in London and in the provinces; but in 1616 internal dissension and the pressure of outward circumstances had combined to trouble them, and Beeston, who was their manager, moved them to his new playhouse, the Cockpit, or Phoenix. Their tenancy started off with a Shrove Tuesday riot of the London apprentices. This was a bad omen and they never prospered, it being left to the Prince's Men under Taylor to make a success of the new theatre. The Queen's Men broke up on the death of their patron, the best of them remaining at the Red Bull, the rest going into the provinces, while Beeston joined the Prince's Men, now his tenants at the Cockpit.

QUEEN ELIZABETH'S MEN, the most famous of London's theatrical companies in the 1580s–90s, was formed in 1583 by Tilney, acting under orders from Walsingham. Originally twelve in number, its members were appointed Grooms of the Chamber. Among them was the famous jester, Tarleton, favourite of Queen Elizabeth until he offended her with jokes against Raleigh and Leicester. The company made its first appearance at Court in December and in the following March, and then went on tour, returning to play, among other things, Tarleton's *Five Plays in One*, later revived as *The Seven Deadly Sins, Part 1*. The death of Tarleton in 1588 was a great blow. The company was superseded by the Admiral's Men, to whom the dramatist Greene in 1591 sold *Orlando Furioso* after having previously sold it to the Queen's. He probably took advantage of the fact that the latter company was touring the provinces, and not in great favour in London. The last performance of the Queen's Men at Court was given in 1594, though they appeared at one of Henslowe's theatres later in the year, and from then onwards they dwindled away in the provinces, having sold their playbooks to Henslowe.

QUEEN HENRIETTA'S MEN, usually known as the Queen's Men, a theatrical company whose early origins are obscure. It was formed under Beeston some time in 1625, probably after the plague of that year had shut the theatres and disrupted the existing companies. The chief actors seem to have come from the late Queen Anne's Men and from the Lady Elizabeth's Men, among them Perkins, Bowyer, Turner, and Timothy Reade. They appear to have flourished, and among their successful plays were those which their official dramatist, James Shirley, wrote for them, some twenty, alone or in collaboration, from 1625–37. They also appeared with great success before the Court in Heywood's masque, *Love's Mistress*, for which Inigo Jones designed some admirable scenery. They might have continued to flourish, but for the plague of 1636 which closed the theatres. This gave Beeston the excuse to disband the company and form another, Beeston's Boys, which took over the Cockpit, while the Queen's Men were absorbed into other companies. Later a new Queen's company was formed, and played at Salisbury Court, its official dramatist being Richard Brome. Little more is known of its existence, which must have been somewhat precarious, and it disappeared at the final closing of the theatres in 1642.

QUEEN OF BOHEMIA'S MEN, see LADY ELIZABETH'S MEN.

QUEEN STREET THEATRE, LONDON, see KINGSWAY THEATRE.

QUEEN'S THEATRE, LONDON. (1) In the Haymarket. This theatre owed its inception to the mismanagement of Christopher Rich at Drury Lane, troubles there inspiring Sir John Vanbrugh to build a new theatre, for which he raised £3,000 in £100 shares, the thirty subscribers having the right to free admission for life. Colley Cibber saw the foundation-stone laid, and in 1705 the theatre was ready. Betterton and his company left Lincoln's Inn Fields Theatre and went there under the direction of Congreve and Vanbrugh. But although the building was ornate, it lay off the beaten track, and the acoustics were disastrously ineffective. Opera proved a complete failure, and Vanbrugh's comedy, *The Confederacy*, fared no better. Vanbrugh then let the theatre to Owen Swiney, who did a little better, but when the actors were commanded back to their allegiance at Drury Lane, the house was entirely given over to opera. It passed through many phases, being known as the King's and the Royal Italian Opera House. It was finally destroyed by fire in 1876, and the Carlton Hotel and Her (later His) Majesty's Theatre arose on the site.

(2) In Long Acre, originally St. Martin's Hall, which was reconstructed as a theatre and opened on 24 Oct. 1867. Alfred Wigan was in charge, but the real manager was Henry Labouchère. The theatre had a short but lively existence. The first production was an adaptation of Charles Reade's novel, *White Lies*. Liston, afterwards of the Olympic, followed Wigan and then came Ernest Clifton, who brought success. Mrs. Rousby made her London début there in 1869 in *The Fool's Revenge*, and helped by Tom Taylor made a success.

There was always an excellent company at the Queen's, which for a time included Toole and Lionel Brough. Henry Irving played there, as did Charles Wyndham and Phelps, Ellen Terry, and Salvini, the last, in 1875, giving a fine performance as Othello. The theatre was well appointed with an excellently equipped stage, and in size it ranked next to Drury Lane. In 1878 it ceased to be a theatre, and was occupied by the Clerical Co-operative Stores. It now forms part of Odhams Press, and its outer walls still stand, while up to a short time ago the old direction signs were still to be seen inside the building. At one time it was known as the National Theatre.

(3) In Shaftesbury Avenue, sister theatre to the Globe, which it adjoins. This was opened on 8 Oct. 1907 by J. E. Vedrenne with *The Sugar Bowl*. In 1908 a musical play, *The Belle of Brittany*, ran for 147 performances, and a year later H. B. Irving gave a season of revivals which included *The Bells* and *Robert Macaire*. In 1912 the theatre housed the fashionable tango teas, and in 1916 it had its first big success with *Potash and Perlmutter*, which ran for 665 performances. In 1919 Owen Nares, in association with Alfred Butt, became actor-manager of the Queen's and later appeared there in a revival of *The Little Minister*. Among the fine productions at this theatre were *And So To Bed*, *The Apple Cart*, *The Barretts of Wimpole Street*, which ran for 529 performances, *Evensong*, and *Jane Eyre*. From 1937 to 1938 a distinguished company under John Gielgud appeared in Shakespeare, Sheridan, and Chekhov. The last play produced at the theatre was *Rebecca*, during whose run, on the night of 24 Sept. 1940, the building was badly damaged by enemy action—the first London theatre to become a war casualty. It has been closed since.   W. M. P.

QUEUE. In London the formation of a queue outside the entrances to the theatre, whether to book seats in advance or to pay on entering, is a recent phenomenon in the theatre world, dating only from the early 1900s. Before that an unruly mob would assemble before the theatre and rush the doors as soon as they were opened, women and elderly persons being ruthlessly thrown aside. It is possible now, for seats which cannot be booked in advance, to hire a small folding stool, to which is attached a label bearing the hirer's name, and this stands deputy until half-an-hour or so before the opening of the doors. These can only be obtained from the attendant in charge on the day of the performance, beginning at some fixed time, which obviates the queueing-up overnight which was a feature of some important first-nights in the 1920s, though it is still occasionally indulged in.

QUICK-CHANGE ROOM, a small, closed recess opening off the stage, used by actors for changing their clothes when the time of their absence from the stage does not allow of a return to their dressing-rooms.

QUICK, JOHN (1748–1831), English actor, who as a boy of 14 joined a provincial company, and in 1767 was engaged for the Haymarket summer season by Foote. Here his good work caused him to be taken on at Covent Garden, where he was Postboy in *The Oxonian in Town* and in *The Good-Natured Man*. He remained at Covent Garden for the rest of his career, except for occasional visits to the provinces, and a brief managership of the King Street Theatre, Bristol. He had a vast repertory of comic parts, which ranged from Shallow and Polonius to the Clown in pantomime, through numerous rustics and comic servants. He inherited the roles of Ned Shuter and of Woodward, and was the original Tony Lumpkin and Bob Acres. He hankered after tragedy, and for his benefit in 1790 chose to appear as Richard III, only to be laughed off the stage. After that he remained faithful to comedy until his retirement in 1798, from which he occasionally emerged, being seen at the Lyceum in 1800. His last appearance was at the Haymarket as Don Felix in *The Wonder*, at a benefit for Mrs. Mattocks. A small, impetuous man, Quick was the favourite actor of George III, and his pleasant and somewhat chubby face was painted by Zoffany and others, in portraits which now hang in the Garrick Club, London.

QUIN, JAMES (1693–1766), English actor, who made his first appearance at the Smock Alley Theatre in Dublin in 1712. Two years later he was playing small parts at Drury Lane, where he made a sudden success in the part of Bajazet in *Tamerlane* when the actor billed to play it was taken ill. In 1718 he went to Lincoln's Inn Fields Theatre, where he remained for fourteen years, appearing first as Hotspur, and then in a range of parts which included Othello, Lear, Falstaff, the Ghost in *Hamlet*, and Buckingham in *Richard III*. In 1732 he went to Covent Garden, and from there returned to Drury Lane, where he remained for several years, playing leading roles in tragedy. He was a declaimer rather than an actor, and almost the last representative of the school of Betterton, whose manner he may have caught from Booth. He was also a stickler for the old traditional costumes, and would not alter one detail. A portrait of him as Coriolanus, in Thomson's play (1748), shows him equipped with plumes, peruke, full spreading short skirt, and truncheon. Pope refers to 'Quin's high plume', as does Addison in *The Spectator*. But Quin's supremacy was soon to be challenged by the rising star of Garrick, of whom he said, 'if the young fellow is right, I and the rest of the players have been all wrong.' In 1751 he retired to Bath, having spent the last years of his career in constant rivalry with Garrick. A man of great gifts, he had had little formal education, and despised book-learning. Vain, obstinate, and quarrelsome, he was yet generous and warm-hearted, and was esteemed by some, notably Walpole, above Garrick. He was immortalized by Smollett in *Humphry Clinker*. His epitaph was written by Garrick, with whom he was reconciled in his last years.

QUINAULT, a family of French actors, of whom the father and five children were all members of the Comédie-Française. The most famous was the second son (for whom see DUFRESNE), while of the three daughters the eldest, known as Mlle de Nesle, died young, and the youngest, known as Quinault la Cadette, shared soubrette roles with Mlle Dangeville.

QUINAULT, PHILIPPE (1635–88), French dramatist and librettist. The son of a baker, he became valet to Tristan L'Hermite, through whose influence his first play, *Les Rivales* (1653), was put into rehearsal at the Hôtel de Bourgogne as being by Tristan. When the actors discovered the truth, they wanted to halve the money that they were paying for the play, and the result of the negotiations was that the author was given a stipulated share in the receipts of each performance, and not, as hitherto, in those of the first few nights only. This has been cited by Fabien, Pill, and others as the origin of the royalty system, but the point is disputable. By 1666 Quinault had written sixteen plays, of which *La Mère coquette* (1665) was much praised by La Harpe. He was, however, maligned by Boileau, who found him insipid and sentimental, and much disliked by Racine. The last of his plays to profit from the advice of Tristan was *La Comédie sans comédie* (1655), which was a great success. Several of the characters in it bore the names of the actors playing the parts. Quinault later married a wealthy young widow, whom he had loved before her first marriage. She persuaded him to give up writing for the stage, which she considered a low pastime, but having been elected to the French Academy in 1670, he felt he ought to return to literature, so collaborated with Molière in the lyrics for *Psyché* (1671). He then contributed to 'Les Fêtes de l'Amour et de Bacchus', other parts of which were written by Molière and Benserade. This led to a meeting with Lully, composer of the music, and to a fruitful collaboration between the two. Quinault wrote a libretto for Lully every year, and his work was much admired by Louis XIV, who often, with royal condescension, suggested subjects for his pen. Such is the purifying power of music that his wife did not object to his engaging in such tasks. Quinault appeared to be at the height of his powers when he wrote what proved to be his last libretto, that for 'Armide'. The death of Lully and the influence of the religious ideas of the time then turned him finally against the stage. In the opinion of a contemporary critic, his verses were already music before Lully set them, in which respect he approached Racine, though with nothing of the latter's strength and passion.

QUINTERO, THE BROTHERS. (1) SERAFÍN ÁLVAREZ (1871–1938) and (2) JOAQUÍN ÁLVAREZ (1873–1944), joint authors of about 150 modern Spanish plays, of which the best known are *Los Galeotes* and *El Patio* (both 1900), *Abanicos y panderetas* (1902), *Mañana de Sol* (1905), *Las de Cain* (1908), and *Doña Clarines* (1909). Many of the brothers' early plays were *sainetes* or short farces, based on the manners and customs of the Andalusian folk. In general, their work is amusing, conventionally sentimental, and suffused with kindliness and good-humoured tolerance. Many of their plays have been translated and successfully performed abroad, in England in the translations of Helen and Harley Granville-Barker—*Fortunato*, *The Lady from Alfaqueque*, *A Hundred Years Old*, and *Don Abel writes a Tragedy*.

R

RACAN, MARQUIS DE (1589–1670), French dramatist who, with Théophile de Viau, marks the entry into French dramatic literature of the poet and courtier. He was a page at Court, and as a boy frequented the theatre, where he much enjoyed the plays of Hardy. But his own play, a pastoral entitled *Les Bergeries*, given in 1620, is more influenced by the *Aminta* of Tasso and Guarini's *Pastor Fido* than by the ranting tragi-comedies of Hardy. It was written in accordance with the Unities and helped to popularize their vogue. It is weak in construction, but, under the influence of Malherbe, who was then working hard to purify and ennoble the French language, the author paid great attention to style, and the play contains some good lyric passages. Racan, who preferred the pleasures of the country to the pains of Court life, had an uneventful history, and died peacefully at an advanced age.

RACHEL [ELISA FÉLIX] (1820–58), child of a poor Jewish family, and one of the greatest actresses France, or perhaps the world, has ever known. She had an unhappy childhood, but was given some instruction in verse-speaking by her father, in which her cousin Julie Bernat, later the actress Mlle Judith, also shared. After singing in the streets, she was befriended by Choron, who passed her on to Saint-Aulaire. She studied at the latter's dramatic school in the old Théâtre Molière, played an astonishing number of parts between the ages of 13 and 16, and made a reputation for herself as a most promising young actress. A short course at the Conservatoire was cut short by her father, who was anxious to make money out of her undoubted gifts, and she was engaged by Poisson, manager of the Gymnase-Théâtre, where she appeared in the early part of 1837 in *La Vendéenne* by Dupont, based on a scene from Scott, an ephemeral play which would be forgotten but for Rachel's connexion with it. She was lucky enough to win the favourable opinion of Jules Janin, the powerful critic of the *Journal des Débats*. But she still had a lot to learn and Samson, himself a pupil of Talma, was willing to teach her. Coached by him, she entered the Comédie-Française in 1838, appearing as Camille in *Horace*. This and later parts brought her some success, but the public did not become fully aware of her until Janin had more than once eulogized her in the *Journal des Débats*. His enthusiasm for his 'discovery' was laughed at, but he was listened to, and encouraged by him Rachel revived the glories of French tragedy, which had been almost entirely neglected since the death of Talma. Phèdre was destined to be her greatest part, but she was excellent in all the great plays of Corneille and Racine, as well as in a number of modern plays, including a revival of *Marie Stuart* by Lebrun and the first production of *Adrienne Lecouvreur* (1849) by Scribe and Legouvé. But it was in classical roles that she excelled—Hermione, Roxane, Camille—and it was mainly in these that she appeared on tour, either in the French provinces, in Europe, going as far as Russia, in London, where she first appeared in 1841 with outstanding success, or in America, where, on her one visit in 1855, she finally aggravated her tubercular condition, the result of early hardships and later overwork, combined with a feverish succession of amorous intrigues. She died at the age of 38, leaving a great memory, and a tradition of tragic acting which has never been surpassed. Two of her sisters were also on the stage; the elder played mainly at the Odéon, but the younger, who died at 25, shortly before Rachel's death, was at the Comédie-Française, where she delighted Victor Hugo by her acting in a revival of his *Angelo* in which Rachel also appeared.

RACINE, JEAN (1639–99), French playwright and poet, with Corneille the greatest dramatist of the seventeenth century. Orphaned at the age of 4, he was brought up by his grandparents and his aunt Agnès, later Abbess of Port-Royal, where Racine was educated after a few years at the Collège de Beauvais. He was an excellent scholar, though somewhat undisciplined, an enthusiastic admirer of the Greek dramatists, and at 19 already a good poet. He soon escaped from the restraining influence of Port-Royal and the Jansenists, and led a free, though not particularly dissipated, life. His close friends at this time were La Fontaine, Boileau, and Molière, and it was the last who was instrumental in putting Racine's early work before the public, when in 1664 he produced *La Thébaïde, ou les frères ennemis*, at the Palais-Royal. It was moderately successful, and Molière was emboldened to accept another play by the same author.

Racine had already shown that he had little gratitude for those who helped him, and this was abundantly proved when he let the Hôtel de Bourgogne produce his second play, *Alexandre et Porus* (1665), a fortnight after Molière, thus causing the receipts at the Palais-Royal to drop perceptibly. The only excuse for this conduct was that the Hôtel de Bourgogne had a greater reputation in tragedy than Molière's company, and Racine did indeed say that he was not satisfied with the Palais-Royal production. It is, however, believed that feminine intrigue was at the bottom of the affair, particularly as Mlle Du Parc, a fine tragic actress, and Racine's mistress, left Molière to play the lead in *Andromaque*, produced at the Hôtel de Bourgogne in 1667, with Montfleury, Floridor, and Mlle Desœillets. After this double betrayal Molière never spoke to Racine again. The latter did not long enjoy his triumph, however, since Mlle Du

Parc died suddenly the following year. Many years later the infamous Catherine Voisin accused Racine of having poisoned her to make room for Mlle Champmeslé, who came from the Marais to play the part of Hermione during the illness of Mlle Desœillets. She certainly became Racine's mistress, and is particularly associated with his later work, creating, among other parts, his Phèdre and Bérénice.

It was with the production of *Andromaque* that Racine achieved recognition as a great dramatist, rival of the ageing Corneille, and in some ways superior to him. He assisted in the production of his plays, and got many of his best stage-effects by declaiming his verses aloud as he wrote, and by studying the parts closely with the actors.

Andromaque, which was translated into English as *The Distressed Mother* by Ambrose Philips in 1712, when Anne Oldfield played the leading part, was followed by Racine's one comedy, *Les Plaideurs* (1668). It was originally intended for the Italian troupe, and was based to some extent on Aristophanes' *Wasps*, but on the departure of Scaramouche from Paris it was given at the Hôtel de Bourgogne. It was not successful at first, but after it had been applauded at Court its popularity was assured, and frequent revivals have intensified the regret that Racine did not again venture to compose a comedy. His next tragedy, *Britannicus* (1669), was not very successful, though it was much admired for its exquisite poetry, and the example of Nero is said by Boileau to have deterred Louis XIV from featuring himself any more in Court ballets and entertainments. With his next play Racine once again found himself at odds with Corneille, for either by coincidence or design they were both working on the same subject, and the production of Racine's *Bérénice* (1670) took place a week before that of Corneille's *Tite et Bérénice* at Molière's theatre. Racine's was more generally applauded, and was followed by *Bajazet* (1672) and *Mithridate* (1673), oriental subjects treated in a completely French and contemporary style, a reproach often levelled at Racine. They enhanced his reputation, however, and assured his position as the leading tragic dramatist of his day.

For his next play he returned to Greek tragedy, a field which was at that time being exploited by two of his rivals, Thomas Corneille and Quinault. His *Iphigénie* (1674) was a brilliant success and it seemed likely that it would be followed by a succession of equally fine plays. But with his next composition Racine's career as a dramatist came to an abrupt end. He had made many enemies, and they, looking about for someone to set against him, since he seemed to have vanquished Corneille, hit on Pradon, a pleasant, mediocre, and sugary writer, who adapted his subjects to the sentiments of the time. When they discovered that Racine was writing *Phèdre*, they persuaded Pradon to compose a tragedy on the same theme. This he did, and to Racine's chagrin Pradon's play was slightly more successful than his when both were produced at the rival theatres in 1677.

This, and perhaps even more Racine's appointment by Louis XIV as historiographer-royal, caused him to give up the theatre. He married, had seven children, made his peace with Port-Royal, and turned his gifts to the studying and recording of contemporary French history. He retained his interest in the theatre, however, and at the request of Mme de Maintenon—who, it should be remembered, was once the wife of the dramatist Scarron—produced, for her school of young ladies at St. Cyr, the tender and poetic play, *Esther* (1689). It was given at the school with great success, but by Racine's express desire was not performed in public, and it had to wait until 1721, when Baron, Duclos, Legrand, Dufresne, and Adrienne Lecouvreur appeared in it at the Comédie-Française. By then the vogue for biblical subjects was over, and the play failed. The beauty of the poetry did not compensate for the lack of action.

Esther was followed by an even finer play for the same purpose, *Athalie* (1691), which was given in a much simpler form than *Esther*, with no costumes and far less pomp. Perhaps some of the youthful actresses had had their heads turned by their previous success. It was given at the Comédie-Française in 1716, and has since proved to be one of Racine's most admired works.

Racine was not a particularly estimable character. He had a bitter wit, was ungrateful, cold-hearted, and bad-tempered; but as a dramatist, within the strictly defined limits of French classical tragedy, he was a master spirit. He was restricted by the conventions of his time, which forbade excess in any form, but the abounding vitality and passion of his characters, particularly of his women, seems all the greater for the limitations imposed on them. It may be said that the rules he chose to observe served only to enhance his genius, while his great poetic gifts saved his plays from monotony or rigidity. In his own field he has never been surpassed.

R.A.D.A., London, see BARNES, SIR KENNETH.

RADIO CITY MUSIC HALL, New York, the largest theatre in the world. Situated in the Rockefeller Centre, it opened with a galaxy of talent and a staff made up of well-known theatre personalities, including Robert Edmond Jones and Martha Graham. It closed almost immediately, to open again with a combined cinema and stage show which has proved extremely popular. New full-length films alternate with a programme of music-hall turns which for speed and precision would be hard to beat. Owing to its enormous size and superb equipment the theatre is eminently suitable for spectacular effects, to which the well-drilled chorus, known as the Rockettes, contributes in no small degree. G. F.

RADIO DRAMA IN GREAT BRITAIN. In the earliest days of broadcasting there was, of course, no such thing as a broadcast play in the strict sense of the term. The first example of radio drama ever broadcast in England was the Tent Scene from *Julius Caesar*, and the technique of such broadcasting was limited to placing the microphone conveniently adjacent to stage actors and hoping for the best; that the best was not achieved is not altogether surprising. It was not long, however, before it became abundantly realized that the use of material originally composed to satisfy the demands both of eye and ear was unlikely to prove adequate to supply a medium which could satisfy the ear only. Accordingly, although the difficulties for the most part continued to be surmounted by various forms of adaptation of stage material, enthusiasts for radio drama looked more and more anxiously towards something in the nature of a breakaway from the stage play. This finally took place in two forms. In 1927 Cecil Day Lewis's adaptation of Conrad's novel *Lord Jim* pointed the way to a completely new field of adaptable material unhampered by the conventions of the stage. At about the same time Richard Hughes, in his original radio play, *Danger*, whose setting was the bowels of a coal-mine, demonstrated how drama, in the best sense of the word, existed which could be conveyed to the audience by the microphone and could not possibly be conveyed to the audience by the stage. From this point, radio drama ceased to be purely an experiment, and became something of a phenomenon.

The invention of the dramatic control panel, which enabled several studios to be used simultaneously for a single production, and made it possible for the producer to balance the relative output of those studios against each other, and to fade the output of one studio into that of another, was the next milestone along the road. It is true that this multiple-studio technique had to be almost entirely abandoned, from 1939–41, but although circumstances for a time forced radio drama back within the confines of single-studio technique, that technique was no longer what it was before the control panel was invented. The experience achieved by the use of the panel was brought to bear on the gear then at the disposal of radio producers, and there was little concrete loss. The only severe casualty, admittedly a very severe one, inflicted on radio drama by the Second World War was the enforced loss of the experimental radio play, which proved impracticable without the devices of the dramatic control panel.

Since 1930 the radio play has continued to develop along three main lines. There is first the studio production of classical works, both British and foreign. A series of Shakespearian plays is broadcast regularly every year, and such authors as Chekhov, Ibsen, Shaw, Wilde, Strindberg, and the great Greek dramatists have found on the air a survival likely to be denied them under the harsh conditions of commercial management in the normal theatre. Secondly, there is a steady output of adapted novels and short stories, particularly of the latter. Both the short story of atmosphere such as Walter de la Mare's, and the short story of strong characterization and plot, like the *Ashenden* tales of Somerset Maugham, have proved themselves in their several ways to be ideal microphone material. The advantage of the short story over the novel for adaptation lies partly in the fact that the former has, as a rule, comparatively few characters, a most important consideration in dealing with all radio drama, and partly in the increasing tendency to shorten all broadcast programmes. One of the most successful adaptations of a novel in the early days was probably that made of Compton Mackenzie's *Carnival* by Holt Marvell (Eric Maschwitz). It ran for two hours and a quarter, and in the period at his disposal the adapter managed not only to cover space and time but to build up living characters. Time-periods of this length are now, however, few and far between, if not actually non-existent. It is doubtful whether, under present conditions of broadcasting, the novel can be adapted except in serial form. In her handling of *David Copperfield* Audrey Lucas proved how successful this method can be. Thirdly, there is the radio play proper. On this front progress has not been as fast, nor gone as far, as might reasonably have been expected. Authors of standing have shown considerable reluctance to try their hand at the new medium, probably owing to a comprehensible unwillingness to sacrifice their ideas in a market comparatively unremunerative if considered in relation to the hypothetical rewards of stage and screen work. Yet even the younger authors, without the excuse of such sacrifice, have been curiously unwilling to try their 'prentice hands at the radio play. Here the reason may have been a singular atmosphere of mumbo-jumbo perhaps inseparable from any medium closely connected with machinery, which has made the writer believe that it is impossible to work for the radio without an exhaustive knowledge of studios, microphones, and thermionic valves. There have, however, been notable exceptions. Tyrone Guthrie wrote two admirable plays for broadcasting, and then somewhat unaccountably abandoned the field. Patrick Hamilton, in *Money with Menaces* and *To the Public Danger*, both pointed a moral and adorned a tale. L. du Garde Peach in *The Path to Glory* wrote one of the most brilliant of existing radio plays. And a study of the files of the *Radio Times* during past years reveals a perhaps unexpected amount, in both quality and quantity, of original radio dramatic output. The war gave the radio play a new lease of life. In 1938 the spotlight was beginning inevitably to shift towards the television play; two-dimensional material was coming back into its own. The temporary halt to the progress of television contributed considerably towards postponing the death of the ordinary radio play.

Indeed, to some extent the war proved, in this particular instance, some sort of blessing, however considerably disguised. The blackout, difficulties of transport, and sheer physical inability on the part of many people to visit the theatre, all combined to increase the number of listeners to plays broadcast and encouraged them to give such plays the concentrated attention which they require for success. For the first time, during the war years, the broadcast play ceased from being a programme item of minority appeal and, as far as its more popular examples were concerned, came to compete on equal terms with even such established favourites as 'Music-Hall'. The Saturday Night Theatre series achieved listening figures which would have been considered out of the question before 1939. This was an encouraging fact which augured well for the prospects of the later and even more important series 'World Theatre', now firmly established.

It may be worth while to add to this note a brief sketch of acting for the microphone. It is desirable to destroy the illusion that what is needed is less an actor than a trained elocutionist. The latter, with his acute self-consciousness and elaborately false inflexions, makes the worst of broadcast actors. The quality essential above all others for work before the microphone is sincerity. Radio acting calls for that quality in actors which has so often been sicklied over by the conventions of 'ham' Shakespearian training, or the brittle cocktail and cup-and-saucer technique of the modern comedy. The actor at the microphone *must make believe*; he must, in short, not only act, but be. It is, perhaps, superfluous to add that while personality will certainly carry across the microphone, personal beauty, even when referred to by other characters, can hardly hope to do so.   V. G.

RADLOV, SERGEI, Soviet actor, dramatist, and producer, who, after a varied career during which he wrote and produced his own plays in Leningrad, and was responsible for operatic as well as dramatic performances, opened his own studio-theatre in 1932 (again in Leningrad). There he staged *Ghosts*, *Romeo and Juliet*, and an excellent *Othello* (1935), a production which he repeated for the Moscow Maly Theatre. His outstanding achievement to date, however, has been his production of *King Lear* for the Moscow Jewish Theatre, with Mikhoels in the title-role. In spite of some good productions of contemporary plays, it seems as if he is at his best in Shakespeare, whom he has studied deeply, written about, and pondered on. In this he is helped by his wife, who is his translator.

RAHERE (*d.* 1144), a jester attached to the service of Henry I, as a permanent member of the Royal Household. He amassed a large fortune by his wit, and used it to found the priory of St. Bartholomew at Smithfield, later the famous hospital. He entered the Church and became prebendary of St. Paul's in 1111 (see MINSTRELS and BARTHOLOMEW FAIR).

RAIL, the piece of timber forming the top or bottom of a flat.

RAIMUND, FERDINAND (1790–1836), Austrian playwright and actor, akin to Molière by

the deep-seated melancholy beneath his wit. He first won popularity by his acting in farce, but despite the success of his folk-comedies at the Leopoldstädter Theater in Vienna, of which he became manager, he was more interested in tragedy, and had already shown signs of mental disturbance when he committed suicide in 1836. Among his best plays were *Das Mädchen aus der Feenwelt, oder der Bauer als Millionär* (1826), which preaches with the help of magical forces and a host of allegorical personages the doctrine of contentment on small means, and *Der Alpenkönig und der Menschenfeind* (1828), in which a kindly mountain spirit cures a misanthropist by assuming his shape and character, while the misanthropist, disguised as his own brother-in-law, has to watch the havoc caused by his suspicions and ill will. Needless to say all ends happily.   W. E. D.

RAISIN, a family of French actors, consisting of (1) CATHERINE (1650–1701), (2) JACQUES (1653–1702), and (3) JEAN-BAPTISTE (1655–93). As children they were brought to the Foire Saint-Germain in 1662 by their father, an organist of Troyes, who mystified the crowd, and later the Court, with a mechanical spinet which proved on investigation to have Jean-Baptiste, aged 7, inside it. Louis XIV was so amused by the elder Raisin's ingenuity that he allowed him to form a company of child-actors under the patronage of the Dauphin. Among its members were Jean de Villiers, destined to be the husband of Catherine, whom she married in 1679, and Baron, who was later taken by Molière into his own company. After the death of the elder Raisin his widow took the children into the provinces. Jean-Baptiste came back to the Hôtel de Bourgogne in 1679, with his wife (4) FRANÇOISE PITEL DE LONGCHAMP (1661–1721), known as Fanchon, who was related to the famous actress Mlle Beauval. They were both members of the original troupe of the Comédie-Française, and after her husband's death Fanchon became the mistress of the Dauphin, by whom she had two daughters. Jean-Baptiste was an excellent comedian, known as 'little Molière', but it was not until after the death of Rosimond in 1686 that he was given leading parts to play. His early death was much regretted. His elder brother joined the Comédie-Française four years after its foundation. He appeared mostly in tragedy, and was a tall, thin, solemn, reserved man, very different from Jean-Baptiste. He wrote some successful comedies, and also composed music for the theatre.

RAKE, the slope of the stage floor upward from the audience. It is not now universal, but originally aided the illusion of scenes painted in perspective (see STAGE).

RAKING PIECE, a canvas-covered wooden frame with a sloping top edge, used as a small groundrow or to conceal a ramp on the stage.

RÁKOSI, JENÖ (1842–1928), Hungarian dramatist, and with Dóczy the leader of the neo-romantic drama of the late nineteenth century in Hungary, which forsook the popular realistic and social problems of the day for legend and fantasy.

RAMBERT, Marie [Mrs. Ashley Dukes], Russian dancer, founder of the Ballet Club and the Marie Rambert Ballet, which have played an important part in the development of English ballet. During the years between the death of Diaghilev, with whose Ballets Russes she had danced, and the arrival of Colonel de Basil's company, she got together a group of young English dancers, who for the first time did not find it necessary to adopt foreign names, as Ninette de Valois and Alicia Markova had had to do. Together with the Camargo Society, which she helped to found, she fostered the growing interest in and practice of ballet-dancing until the foundation of the Vic-Wells Ballet, which took many of her best dancers. She has also had a share in the development of English choreography and design, and has proved herself an inspired teacher, and above all an enthusiastic fosterer of talent in her young pupils, many of whom have left her to become world-famous elsewhere. The performances which she has sponsored at the little Mercury Theatre, though on a necessarily small scale, have always been marked by originality and technical excellence, and from the beginning have been taken seriously by those who have the future of English ballet at heart.

RAMP, an inclined approach to a rostrum.

RANCH, Hieronymus Justesen (1539–1607), early Danish dramatist (see SCANDINAVIA, 1).

RANDALL, Harry (1860–1932), a music-hall performer who as a child played minor parts in pantomime, but left the stage and went into business. A few amateur appearances at Saturday night shows brought him offers from the halls which he finally accepted, and he became one of the great names of music-hall and pantomime. He was a pillar of the famous pantomimes at the Grand, Islington, in which he appeared continuously, with only one break, from 1891 to 1901, playing both male and 'dame' parts. He appeared in Dan Leno's last Drury Lane pantomime, *Humpty-Dumpty*, and was a worthy successor of that great comedian, whose intimate friend he was.

RANKIN. (1) Arthur McKee (1842–1914), American actor, who had already had some experience as an amateur before in 1865 he made his first appearance on the professional stage at the Arch Street Theatre, Philadelphia, under Mrs. John Drew. Four years later he married (2) Kitty Blanchard (1847–1911), with whom he starred at the Union Square Theatre, and later in a series of long tours, mainly in somewhat crude melodrama. The most famous play in his repertory was *The Danites*, first given in 1877, and in London in 1880. He was for some time manager of the Third Avenue Theatre, New York. He later separated from his wife, and with Nance O'Neil as his leading lady toured all over the world, visiting London again in 1902. Of his three daughters, Phyllis became Mrs. Harry Davenport, Doris Mrs. Lionel Barrymore, and Gladys Mrs. Sidney Drew.

RASTELL, John (?–1536), brother-in-law of Sir Thomas More, and father-in-law, through the marriage of his daughter Elizabeth, of John Heywood, author of early English interludes, some of which were printed by John and his son William Rastell. John Rastell is believed to have been the author of *Calisto and Meliboea*, an adaptation of part of de Rojas's *Celestina*, and of *The Dialogue of Gentleness and Nobility*, both of which were acted in his own garden at Finsbury in about 1527, and printed by him in the same year. He may also have been the author of an earlier interlude entitled *The Play of the Four Elements* (c. 1517).

RAUCOURT [Françoise Marie Antoinette Josèphe Saucerotte] (1756–1815), a somewhat turbulent French actress, daughter of a provincial actor who had tried without success to join the Comédie-Française. Having profited by the lessons of Mlle Clairon, and gained experience in the provinces and abroad, she appeared at the Comédie-Française in 1771 with great success. She was excellent in stern, tragic parts, for which her queenly figure and deep voice were eminently suitable. Unfortunately she led a wild life, got into debt, lost the affection of the audience, and fled from Paris in 1776. Recalled by Marie Antoinette, she returned and was with some difficulty reinstated at the theatre, where she immediately came into conflict with the all-powerful Mme Vestris. She also took a leading part in the troubles of the revolutionary period, when she opposed Talma's secession from the company, and was herself imprisoned with a number of her comrades.

RAVENSCROFT, Edward (*fl.* 1671–97), English dramatist, of whose life little is known. His career as a playwright was a long one, extending from *Mamamouchi; or, the Citizen turned Gentleman*—based on *Le Bourgeois gentilhomme*—in 1671 to *The Italian Husband* in 1698. His best work was done in farce, and his outrageous *The London Cuckolds* (1681) came to be traditionally given at both Patent Theatres on Lord Mayor's Day until Garrick stopped it at Drury Lane in 1751 and Covent Garden dropped it three years later. It was revived in 1782 for the benefit night of Quick, and then disappeared for ever. Among Ravenscroft's other plays, which he took from many sources, were the comedies of *The Careless Lovers* (1673) and *The Wrangling Lovers* (1676), *Dame Dobson* (1683), and *The Anatomist; or, the Sham Doctor* (1696). He also wrote a Harlequin play, based on *Les Fourberies de Scapin*, which was forestalled by Otway's version, an English adaptation of the Latin play *Ignoramus*, and an 'improved' version of *Titus Andronicus*. Ravenscroft has achieved some notoriety on account of his quarrel with Dryden, but none of his plays survives on the stage.

RAYMOND, John T. [really John O'Brien] (1836–87), American actor, famous for his playing of Colonel Mulberry Sellers in a dramatization of Mark Twain's *The Gilded Age* (1874). He made his first appearance in 1853, and was immediately hailed as a fine comedian. He toured and worked in stock companies for some years, and in 1861 joined Laura Keene in New York, taking over the part of Asa Trenchard in *Our American Cousin* from Jefferson. He was also seen as Tony Lumpkin and Crabtree, with great success. In 1867 he went with Sothern to England, where his Asa Trenchard was well received; but his Colonel Sellars, which he did there in 1880, seven years after its first production, was a disappointment. Jefferson, who knew him well, preferred him in the part of Ichabod Crane (in a dramatization of Washington Irving's *Wolfert's Roost*), and said of his performance, 'It was quaint and strong; his love scene with Katrina was acted in the best spirit of comedy; the serio-comic expression that he threw into this woe-begone, love-sick swain was irresistibly droll.' Raymond, who was an able and energetic man and remained on the stage until his death, had a long imperturbable face, and a slow seriousness which made his comedy even more appealing. He was popular with the public and with his fellow actors, and once he was established as a star appeared mainly in plays by and about Americans, except for *The Magistrate*, in which he was excellent as Posket. His second wife was the daughter of the actress Rose Eytinge.

RAYNER'S NEW SUBSCRIPTION THEATRE IN THE STRAND, London, see STRAND THEATRE (1).

READE, Charles (1814–84), English novelist, who was also the author of a number of plays. Of these the best-known are *Masks and Faces* (1852), dealing with Garrick and Peg Woffington, which he wrote in collaboration with Tom Taylor, *The Courier of Lyons* (1854), which became famous as *The Lyons Mail*, and was revived by Irving and Sir John Martin-Harvey, and *It's Never Too Late To Mend* (also 1854). Among Reade's later plays the most outstanding was a version of Zola's *L'Assommoir* as *Drink* (1879), written in collaboration with Charles Warner. He also dramatized Tennyson's *Dora* in 1867. Reade was essentially a novelist, and his best work for the stage was done in collaboration with more theatrically-minded men, or based on existing foreign plays. He also dramatized some of his own novels.

READE, Timothy (*fl.* first half of seventeenth century), a comedian popular in London prior to the closing of the theatres in 1642. He probably began his career as a boy-actor in 1626, and later was at Salisbury Court with the King's Revels, rejoining the Queen's Men at a later date. From contemporary allusions it is evident that he was renowned as a dancer, and in 1641 *The Stage-Players' Complaint* was issued with the sub-title *In a Pleasant Dialogue between Cane of the Fortune and Reed of the Friers*, with a woodcut of two dancers, one of which was probably intended for Reade. The prologue to *The Careless Shepherdess* (1656) refers also to his fame as a comedian in the lines 'I never saw Rheade peeping through the Curtain, But ravishing joy enter'd into my heart'. Reade—'Tim Reade the Fool'—was one of the actors who tried to break the law by acting in 1647, but was stopped and apprehended, and Gayton later referred to him as 'the most incomparable mimicke upon the face of the Earth'.

REALISM, which may be accounted a modified form of naturalism, sought, at the end of the nineteenth century, to substitute for the well-made play and the traditional declamatory acting of the period, dramas which should approximate in speech and situation to the social and domestic problems of every day, played by actors who rejected all artifice and spoke and moved naturally, against scenery which reproduced with fidelity the usual surroundings of the people they represented. The movement began with Ibsen, and spread rapidly across Europe, upsetting the established theatre, and demanding the evolution of a new type of actor to interpret the new playwrights. Realism, with some extension to its grosser offshoot, Naturalism, and some reaction as in Symbolism and Impressionism, has dominated the serious stage of Europe and America in some form or another since the 1880s, with modifications of time and circumstance, but always recognizably 'real'.

REALISTIC THEATRE, Moscow. This small theatre, also known as the Krasnya Presnya Theatre from the district in which it is situated, had its origin in a group of actors from the Moscow Art Theatre who in 1918 became a mobile unit touring local Working Clubs. In 1921 it was reorganized as the Fourth Studio of the Moscow Art Theatre, when its first production was *The Promised Land* by Somerset Maugham. This, and *The Brave Soldier Schweik*, were the only good productions of this early period, followed by *Cement*, the theatre's first Soviet play, in 1927. From the beginning of its activities the theatre was based on the methods of the Moscow Art Theatre, but the decisive change in its history came with the appointment in 1932 of Nikolai Okhlopkov as its artistic director. All his productions, which include *Razbeg, Mother, The Iron Flood*, and *Aristocrats*—the last being the one which made him virtually world-famous—called for an entire reconstruction of the playing space in the theatre, and the use of a cinema technique, with several stages in various parts of the auditorium, used simultaneously or in quick succession, while actors and audience mingled freely, the latter sometimes being called on to take part in the action of the play.

This experimental technique, while interesting and valuable, had necessarily a limited appeal and in 1938 the theatre was closed (see also OKHLOPKOV).

REBHUN, PAUL (*c.* 1500–46), a German Protestant playwright, whose *Susanna* (1535), written under direct encouragement from Luther, shows in its multiple setting and division into five acts an interesting mingling of medievalism and humanism (see GERMANY, 2).

RECITAL THEATRE, NEW YORK, see DALY'S THEATRE (3).

RED ARMY THEATRE, MOSCOW. This theatre was founded in 1919, in a building holding about 900 spectators, as a permanent centre for the production of plays about the Red Army which might interest the public, and also for plays of any description which might be supposed to interest the Red soldiers. In 1940 it moved into a vast new building with the exterior shape of a five-pointed star, containing a theatre and stage equipped with all the most modern devices obtainable and with a seating capacity of 2,000. The original staff was drawn from the small groups of amateur soldier-actors who had been catering for the amusement of their fellows since 1917. The first director was Yuri Zavadsky, followed by Alexei Popov, who rapidly became one of the outstanding producers of the U.S.S.R. A list of plays staged at this theatre would show a wide range, from Shakespeare to Pogodin, from the Napoleonic days of *Suvorov* (1939) to the actuality of *People of Stalingrad* (1944). During the Second World War the theatre was evacuated, but returned with an imposing list of productions in hand (see also POPOV).

RED BULL THEATRE, LONDON. There is a reference to the fact that part of the Red Bull fell down during the performance of a puppet-play in 1599; but it may then have been an inn, one of whose galleries collapsed under the strain of a large audience. The Red Bull playhouse was built about 1605 by Aaron Holland in Upper Street, St. John Street, Clerkenwell. It was occupied by the Queen's Men until 1617, and then by other companies. It was renovated and partly rebuilt in 1625, and may have been roofed in, either then or later; opinions are divided, Hotson claiming that it was always an open-air theatre, while W. J. Lawrence inclines to the view that it was roofed, anyhow by the Restoration period. Contemporary dramatists frequently sneered at it, and it appears to have been what is usually known in theatrical circles as a 'blood tub'. But it served to start on his theatrical career no less a person than Thomas Killigrew, for Pepys reports of him: 'He would go to the Red Bull and when the man cried to the boys "Who will go and be a devil and he shall see the play for nothing?" then he would go in and be a devil upon the stage and so get to see the plays.' This gives an insight into the type of play performed there —hot and strong dramas, with plenty of devils and red fire, very popular with the people of the neighbourhood. When the theatres were closed under the Commonwealth, surreptitious shows and puppet-plays were sometimes given at the Red Bull, and at the Restoration Killi-

grew's company played there before going to Vere Street. Pepys went there on 23 Mar. 1661:

Out to the Red Bull ... up to the tireing-room, where strange the confusion and disorder that there is among them in fitting themselves, especially here, where the clothes are very poor, and the actors but common fellows. At last into the pitt, where I think there was not above ten more than myself, and not one hundred in the whole house. And the play, which is called *All's Lost by Lust*, poorly done; and with so much disorder, among others, that in the musique-room the boy that was to sing a song not singing it right, his master fell about his ears and beat him so that it put the whole house in an uprore.

The theatre fell into disuse soon afterwards, but was still standing in 1663.   W. M. P.

REDE. (1) LEMAN THOMAS TERTIUS (1799–1832), English actor, who in 1824 married the widow of Oxberry and was responsible for many publications under the latter's name, particularly the posthumous *Oxberry's Dramatic Biography*. Rede was also the author of *The Road to the Stage* (1827), a useful manual of acting, interesting for a study of the contemporary theatre (see MAKE-UP). He continued to act after his marriage and was seen at Sadler's Wells a fortnight before his death. His younger brother (2) WILLIAM LEMAN (1802–47) was a prolific playwright, who began his career in 1823 with a version of *Sixteen String Jack* given at the Coburg Theatre. Among his many farces the best-known was *The Old and Young Stager* (1835), written for the début of the younger Mathews, in which he appeared at the Olympic with Liston as the Old Stager. Rede also wrote *The Peregrinations of Pickwick*, based on Dickens, and a burlesque of *Douglas* (both 1837), and was responsible for a number of dramas played at the minor theatres in London.

RED LION INN, see INNS USED AS THEATRES.

REFLECTORS, see LIGHTING, 2 *c*.

REGENCY THEATRE OF VARIETIES, LONDON, see SCALA THEATRE.

REGENT THEATRE, LONDON. This began as the Euston Music-Hall, and became a playhouse in 1922. Among its most interesting productions were *The Insect Play* in 1923, and the successful play with music, *The Immortal Hour*, in 1931. It later became a cinema.

RÉGISSEUR, see PRODUCER.

REGNARD, JEAN-FRANÇOIS (1655–1709), French dramatist. He had an adventurous early life, for while on a journey he was captured by Algerian pirates and spent two years as a slave in Constantinople. Being ransomed, he travelled all over Europe, but at last settled in Paris, and put his undoubted talent for versification at the service of the Comédie-Italienne from 1688 to 1696, often in collaboration with Dufresny. From 1694 to 1708 he wrote also for the Comédie-Française. He ranks immediately after Molière as a writer of comedies. His first successful production at the Comédie-Française, where he made good use of the experience he had attained elsewhere, was *Attendez-moi sous l'orme* (1694). He followed it up with several other comedies, the best being *Le Joueur* (1696) and *Le Légataire universel* (1708); the latter remained in the repertory of the Comédie-Française until the early twentieth century. Though Regnard had a great gift for devising comic situations, and wrote witty dialogue, he inevitably suffers by comparison with his illustrious predecessor, and his comedies have been labelled 'Molière caricatured' or 'Molière with all that makes him immortal omitted'. But it is interesting to note, in Regnard's plays, the gradual emergence of the valet as the central figure, forerunner of Figaro. Regnard's greatest fault is a weakness in character development, due to the introduction of circumstantial evidence in no way essential to the present traffic of the stage, a vice which got steadily worse during the eighteenth century, particularly in the moral *drame* of the period, and was still prevalent in the nineteenth century.

RÉGNIER [FRANÇOIS JOSEPH PIERRE TOUSEZ] (1807–85), French actor, who studied painting and architecture and then went on the stage under his mother's maiden name. In 1831 he went to the Comédie-Française, and made a great success in a revival of *Le Mariage de Figaro*. He was soon in possession of all the leading classical comic parts, and was good in modern plays also, particularly *Gabrielle*, *L'Aventurière*, *La Joie fait peur*, and *Supplice d'une femme*. He retired in 1872, and was for some years a professor at the Conservatoire, where he trained a number of outstanding actors. He published a volume of memoirs and essays on the theatre and collaborated in two plays.

REHAN [CREHAN], ADA (1860–1916), American actress, and for many years the leading lady of Augustin Daly's company. Born in Ireland, she went to the United States at the age of 5. Her elder sisters were on the stage, and she herself first played at the age of 13, with her brother-in-law, who was instrumental in getting her into Mrs. John Drew's company at the Arch Street Theatre, Philadelphia. It was there that, by a printer's error, she was first billed by the name she afterwards retained and made famous. She was with several stock companies, playing opposite famous stars of the day, and in 1879 was engaged by Daly for New York. Her first part on Broadway was in Daly's version of *L'Assommoir*, and when Daly first opened his own theatre she played Nelly Beers in *Love's Young Dream*. She became one of the best-loved actresses in New York and in London, where she made her first appearance in 1884 at Toole's. She was later seen at Daly's own theatre in London, of which she laid the corner-stone in 1891. Her most famous part, in a repertory which covered Shakespearian and classic comedies as well as

adaptations of foreign farces, was probably Katharina in *The Taming of the Shrew*. She first played this in New York in 1887, when the Induction to the play was also given there for the first time. Other parts in which she was much admired were Lady Teazle and Rosalind. She was essentially a comedienne, at her best in parts of arch and somewhat artificial comedy, and that side of her art was developed by Daly to the exclusion of all others. This was unfortunate in that the turn of the century saw a new style of play which demanded a new style of acting, and made her, while still young, seem outmoded. The precision and sparkling technique of old comedy could not be adapted to the new drama. After Daly's death she continued to present plays of his former repertory, but with dwindling success, in spite of her attractive personality, and she made her last public appearance in May 1905. Her life had been entirely devoted to the theatre, and she never married.

REHEARSAL, see PRODUCER.

REINHARDT, MAX [really GOLDMANN] (1873–1943), Austrian actor, manager, and outstanding producer of plays. He first appeared on the stage in Salzburg in 1893, and in the following year went to the Deutsches Theater in Berlin, where under the tuition of Otto Brahm he became noted as a masterly portrayer of old men. In 1903 he ceased to act, and devoted all his time to production. A new era in theatrical presentation was at hand, helped on by the work of such men as Taïrov and Craig. It was to involve the use of new mechanical devices, of new methods of lighting, of well-schooled crowd work as opposed to the star-actor system of the past. Reinhardt gathered together these multiple activities of the theatre, ably supported by keen young actors trained in his methods, and by equally zealous scenic, musical, and choreographic experts. It was his avowed intention to free the theatre from the shackles of literature, to set it on its own feet. Creative vision of a high order, infectious enthusiasm, and a gift for attracting devoted collaboration enabled him to brush obstacles on one side. In order to create intimacy of contact between actors and audience, such as had existed in the days of ancient Greece, he projected the stage into the arena, into the midst of the spectators. Scenery he replaced by highly stylized architecture, using vertical lines where the actor required to be dwarfed, horizontal where his stature was to be magnified. By the use of rhythmic mass movement—and very few producers have equalled Reinhardt in the management of crowds—he sought to sweep the spectators into the very heart of the play. No place was too vast for him. He produced the *Oedipus Rex* in the Zirkus Schumann in Vienna in 1910, and in 1911 was brought to London by C. B. Cochran to produce *The Miracle* at Olympia. The following year saw his production of *Oedipus Rex* with Martin-Harvey at Covent Garden, and among other outstanding productions must be reckoned his *Midsummer Night's Dream*—which he produced again for O.U.D.S. at Oxford in 1933, and in Hollywood in 1934—*Macbeth, Julius Caesar, Agamemnon*, his season of plays in New York in 1927–8, his *Helen* in London in 1932, again under C. B. Cochran's management, and his numerous productions of light and comic opera. In 1920 Reinhardt founded the Salzburg Festival, where every year he staged in front of the Cathedral a lavish and exciting production of the old Morality play, *Jedermann*, adapted by von Hofmannsthal, and in the theatre a number of plays which included Goethe's *Faust*. He also ran the first school for the training of producers. It was inevitable that Reinhardt should be accused of vulgarizing the theatre, but it must not be forgotten that in addition to his vast spectacular shows in which he appealed to the multitude, in his smaller theatres, such as the Kammerspiele and the Kleines Theater, he staged intimate productions intended to appeal to the connoisseur, and gave to many masterpieces a subtly individualized atmosphere characterized by simple line and subdued lighting. When Hitler came into power in 1933 Reinhardt left Germany, and spent the rest of his life in America, where he continued to work until his death (see also SCENERY, 6).

RÉJANE [GABRIELLE CHARLOTTE RÉJU] (1857–1920), famous French actress, who made her first appearance in 1875, at the Vaudeville, whose manager she afterwards married and divorced. She was soon recognized as a leading player of comedy and appeared at many Parisian theatres. She was frequently seen in London, making her first appearance there in 1894, and Shaw, in *Our Theatres in the Nineties*, while despising her choice of play, says of her acting 'it has the quick sensibility which is the really moving quality in fine comic acting, and it is perfectly honest and self-respecting in its impudence'. Few of her parts were memorable, with the exception of Madame Sans-Gêne, in which she was seen in New York in 1895, and she never ventured to approach the classics. But in her own line of light comedy she was unapproachable. In 1906 she opened her own theatre in Paris, and also took over the Royalty in London, intending to run it as a French repertory theatre. In 1909 she toured South Africa, and retired in 1915.

RELIEVE, see MASQUE and FLAT.

REMOTE CONTROL, see LIGHTING, 2 *k*.

RENAISSANCE, THÉÂTRE DE LA, PARIS. (1) The first theatre of this name was built by Aténor Joly, and opened on 8 Nov. 1838 with a licence for plays both with and without music. This aroused the jealousy of the Comédie-Française and the Opéra, who finally caused it to close in 1841, but not before it had done some good work. The actors were headed by Frédérick-Lemaître and Mme Dorval, and the first play given there was *Ruy Blas*. Among

later productions was a ballet in which Carlotta Grisi made her first appearance in Paris.

(2) The second Renaissance opened in 1873, on the site cleared by the burning of the Théâtre de la Porte Saint-Martin in 1871. It was a small theatre, and unwisely endeavoured to play strong drama. This soon gave way to light operas, the most successful being those by Lecocq. Between 1884 and 1892 the theatre was in a bad way, passing through many hands, and finally it closed. Sarah Bernhardt, returning from a long tour abroad, took it over and made it successful, appearing there with the elder Guitry, de Max, and sometimes Coquelin. Among her successful productions there were *La Princesse lointaine, Magda*, and a revival of *Phèdre*. The theatre was also leased to the companies of Duse and Novelli, and to the Spanish actress Maria Guerrero. Sarah Bernhardt later went to the Châtelet and the Renaissance became the Théâtre-Lyrique, playing musical shows only.

REPERTORY THEATRE MOVEMENT. It is impossible to name any one person as the sponsor of the Repertory Movement in England, but no one can deny that it owes much to the vision and courage of J. T. Grein, who in 1891 launched his Independent Theatre, where the plays of Ibsen and Shaw were first presented to London audiences. Up till then it may be said that the British theatre in the nineteenth century had contented itself chiefly with unrealities—plays which failed to reflect life truthfully. Grein's venture was something of an upheaval, and the year 1891 proved to be a significant date in the history of British drama.

The Stage Society carried on Grein's work nobly, but not until the memorable Vedrenne–Barker season at the Court Theatre, London, from 1904 to 1907 did the word 'Repertory' become widely popularized. Eleven of Shaw's plays were produced there, five of them for the first time, as well as the works of Euripides, Ibsen, Hauptmann, Yeats, *The Voysey Inheritance* by Barker, and *The Silver Box* by a new dramatist named John Galsworthy. The aim of the management was 'truth as opposed to effect', and they believed that the play was more important than the actor. Yet the acting and teamwork of the company was a revelation, even the smallest part being played to perfection.

Other London Repertory seasons which aroused interest were those run by Lena Ashwell at the Kingsway in 1907 and Gertrude Kingston at the Little in 1910. But although all these experiments were of inestimable value to the movement in general, the real impetus had been given by the activities of Miss A. E. F. Horniman, affectionately known as 'Queen Horniman', who started Repertory Theatres in Dublin and Manchester. She acquired the lease of the Abbey Theatre, Dublin, rebuilt it, and in 1903 opened it as the Repertory Theatre of Ireland, having given it free for six years to the Irish Players. According to W. B. Yeats it was 'the only theatre in any English-speaking country that is free for a certain number of years to play what it thinks worth playing and to whistle at the timid'. The Abbey created a school of acting which became famous, and an equally famous school of dramatists. This unique little theatre, which has survived riots, curfews, rebellions, and civil war, is still one of the most remarkable and successful Repertory Theatres in the world, and Irish play-goers owe much to the Englishwoman who founded it. (See also IRELAND.)

Having established the Abbey, Miss Horniman then purchased the Gaiety Theatre, Manchester, and in 1908 established there the first Repertory Theatre in Great Britain. She collected round her a fine group of actors and dramatists, and produced many important British and continental plays. 'Local' dramas were also staged, and it is probable that the Gaiety audiences wearied of Lancashire in-teriors, which, they said, reminded them too much of home. Whatever the reason, public apathy forced the theatre to close in 1921, and the most distinguished Repertory Theatre in this country became a cinema. But it had been a magnificent adventure; it had discovered great players and playwrights, and all existing Repertory Theatres, as well as the British theatre in general, owe a great debt of grati-tude to Miss Horniman.

Mention should be made here of a spectacu-lar Repertory season which Charles Frohman, the American impresario, ran at the Duke of York's Theatre, London, in 1910. In spite of a galaxy of stars and plays of distinction the season proved unsuccessful, possibly because, in spite of the Vedrenne–Barker season at the Court, London audiences were still unwilling to accept frequent changes of bill.

In 1909 the Glasgow Repertory Theatre opened under the skilful direction of Alfred Wareing, who was eager to make the city 'independent of the touring drama London might please to send it'. The company included many well-known players, and Glasgow audiences became acquainted with Repertory acting and production of a high standard. The outbreak of war in 1914 closed the theatre just as it was beginning to get its head above water financially (see GLAS-GOW and SCOTLAND).

While the Manchester and Glasgow Reper-tory Theatres were still running, another Repertory Theatre began its career. This was the Liverpool Repertory, which opened in 1911 and has remained open continuously ever since, being the longest-lived Repertory Theatre in Great Britain. It can justifiably claim to be a 'citizens' theatre', for instead of being the property of one or two persons, it is owned by a great number of small shareholders, and was the first English Repertory Theatre to be founded by this means (see LIVERPOOL REPERTORY THEATRE).

In 1913 the Birmingham Repertory Theatre was opened, and under its patron and founder, Sir Barry Jackson, this attractive little play-house attained an international reputation. It would be difficult to find any theatre whose programme of plays could rival that of Birmingham. It trained many young players, several of whom became famous; it gave many a dramatist his first audience, and it was here that John Drinkwater's chronicle and other plays had their first production. Also it was owing to Sir Barry Jackson's initiative that the successful Malvern Festivals were orga-nized, where 'Repertory' was presented in the true sense of the word with constant changes of bill (see BIRMINGHAM REPERTORY THEATRE).

The pioneer work of all these theatres stimulated an ever-growing interest in Reper-tory, and one of the most phenomenal aspects of British drama has been the remarkable growth and success of the Repertory Theatre Movement, resulting in the establishment of over 100 Repertory Theatres in Great Britain. In addition to these, which have their own resident companies, one must not ignore what is being done by the many small touring Repertory companies.

No article on Repertory would be complete without at least a passing reference to the great achievements of the Old Vic Theatre in London and the provinces, and of the Shake-speare Memorial Theatre at Stratford-on-Avon. At the Maddermarket Theatre, Norwich, many distinguished plays have been performed on its Elizabethan stage under the scholarly direction of Nugent Monck. Then there was J. B. Fagan and his gallant enterprise at the Playhouse, Oxford, and Terence Gray, whose seasons at the Festival Theatre, Cam-bridge, excited great interest, chiefly owing to his experimental and imaginative settings. Organizations like the Masque Theatre, and Jevan Brandon-Thomas's and Wilson Barrett's companies in Scotland, also brought prestige to the Repertory Movement. London saw the successful repertory season of John Gielgud at the Haymarket and of the Old Vic Company at the New.

With Repertory Theatres now firmly esta-blished all over the country it is interesting to remember that in the early days of the movement the word 'Repertory' was consi-dered synonymous with failure. There was then a certain significance in that much-quoted story about Beerbohm Tree, who, on being asked 'When is a Repertory Theatre not a Repertory Theatre?' replied cynically, 'When it is a success.' Repertory then meant to most people a theatrical venture constantly facing disaster, or a group of well-meaning amateurs appearing in some dreary lecture-hall in the provinces. It did not occur to them that these Repertory Theatres were then fostering the talents of many actors and drama-tists who were later to become famous. Even now many citizens of towns which possess a Repertory Theatre regard it as an educational institute, and imagine every play produced there to be shrouded in Russian gloom or Lancashire fog. But now that Repertory has come into its own the word is no longer used solely in derision or pity, and Repertory has brought the living theatre within the reach of thousands who otherwise were wholly dependent on the cinema for entertainment.

Critics often complain that Repertory Theatres have no right to such a title, and the charge is justified. Ivor Brown once said that 'Repertory is a silly name—both dull and inaccurate'. Frank Vernon tells how Miss Horniman hated the word, and never used it. The true Repertory Theatre is one in which a number of plays are always ready for production, so that as many as five or six can be performed weekly, with new ones in preparation. Such a scheme, ideal though it may be, bristles with difficulties, chiefly economic, and is rarely attempted. Most present-day Repertories produce one play at a time, giving it a run of from one to three weeks, sometimes longer. Some perform twice nightly, with a different play every week. Undoubtedly the original aim of Manchester, Liverpool, and Birmingham was true repertory, on the lines of the Comédie-Française, but, says Sir Barry Jackson, 'two things mitigated against the fulfilment of this ideal; entirely inadequate theatres to cope with the frequent change of bill, and the conservatism of English audiences ... both of these will have to be overcome sooner or later. A real Repertory Theatre should be able to retain its successes several nights a week and experiment on the others. This is the one and only solution which will have the desired effect of not overworking the actors, and making the public's mind more alert as to what is going on. Short runs are no good to anyone.'

The use of the word Repertory may be unwarranted, but some such title is necessary to distinguish such a theatre, with its own resident company engaged for a season, from the ordinary provincial theatres which house a touring company playing one play only for a week, and the London theatres where one play may run six months or a year.

Repertory theatres have become great training schools for the ambitious young actor or actress eager to learn the intricate art of acting, and the experience gained on a Repertory stage is invaluable. The list of famous actors in London, New York, and Hollywood who have graduated from Repertory is a long one, and it is rare to open the programme of a West End theatre without finding in the cast the names of three or four actors who owe everything to their Repertory training. A long London run or provincial tour may mean financial security, and in such a tragically overcrowded profession as that of the theatre this cannot be ignored. But long runs have a depressing effect on an actor's work, while the frequent changes of part inherent in Repertory work have a stimulating effect. True, much of the work is performed under exhausting conditions; a new play every week or two, endless rehearsals, constant learning of new parts, frequent first nights—all these demand much mental and physical endurance.

But the advantages outweigh the difficulties. Acting in Repertory makes for resourcefulness and versatility, is excellent for training the memory, and will give a nervous actor confidence. Also Repertory audiences are quite different from those of the ordinary theatre. There is an unusual bond of interest and even of affection between Repertory playgoers and their players. The latter become part of the social and artistic life of the city, and it is rare to meet a famous player who has had Repertory experience, and does not admit, in all sincerity, that those exciting and adventurous years were the happiest of his life.

Repertory audiences are invariably critical and able to discriminate between a good play and a poor one. They are no longer satisfied with that local and even parochial drama which was so popular in the early days of the movement. They now demand from their Repertory Theatres what might be termed 'the universal mind'. They enjoy colour, romance, beauty, poetry, Shakespeare, and tragedy if it is not depressing and drab. The 'cocktail school' of drama, with its amusing but worthless characters, has a limited appeal for audiences who, outside the theatre, are too often faced with the stern realities of life. The dialect play, too, has lost much of its former appeal, possibly because those true-to-life back parlours, with incandescent gas-mantles, plush tablecloths, and decaying aspidistras, afforded the minimum of escape. It is often interesting to see plays which have conspicuously failed in London prove successful in Repertory theatres, and London successes, in like manner, fail provincially.

To sum up, the Repertory Theatre Movement has played an all-important part in the world of British drama, and many people, known and unknown, have contributed to its present-day success. It would be difficult to find more fitting words with which to conclude this survey than those spoken many years ago by John Drinkwater, a Repertory actor and dramatist, when he said 'the future of English drama depends on the standing of the provincial Repertory Theatres as much as on any form of theatre now open'.   W. A.

REPUBLIC THEATRE, New York, on 42nd Street west of Times Square. This was built by Oscar Hammerstein and opened on 27 Sept. 1900 with a play by James A. Herne, in which he appeared himself, with his two daughters, Mrs. Sol Smith, and the young Lionel Barrymore. Two years later the theatre was leased to David Belasco, given his name, and used for a number of his outstanding productions, including *The Darling of the Gods*, *Sweet Kitty Bellairs*, *The Music Master*, *Adrea*, *The Girl of the Golden West*, and *The Rose of the Rancho*. When Belasco's second theatre, the Stuyvesant, was renamed the Belasco, the Republic reverted to its original name. Among the distinguished actors who subsequently appeared there were Jane Cowl and Lou Tellegen, while successful plays included *Abie's Irish*

Y

Rose, transferred from the Fulton. The last play seen at the Republic, before it became a burlesque house and then a cinema named the Victory, was *Frankie and Johnny*, which opened on 25 Sept. 1930 and closed after 61 performances.   G. F.

RÉPUBLIQUE, THÉÂTRE DE LA, see COMÉDIE-FRANÇAISE.

RETURN, a narrow flat set back in the walls of a Box Set to produce a break.

REVEAL, a false thickness-piece used in a Box Set to give solidity to the openings.

REVELS OFFICE, see MASTER OF THE REVELS.

REVERE, GIUSEPPE (1812–89), Italian poet and patriot, whose historical drama, *Lorenzino de' Medici*, had some success when produced in 1839. It was followed by a number of others, published in 1860. Though of interest from a literary and historic point of view, Revere's plays are not particularly well adapted for the stage.

REVOLVES, see STAGE, 5.

REVOLVING STAGE, see ARCHITECTURE, MACHINERY, and SCENERY.

REVUE, a term of French origin, used to describe a survey, mainly satiric, of contemporary events, with songs, sketches, burlesques, monologues, and so on. No satisfactory English term has ever been found for this mixture, and the French continues in use. It is first found in Planché's *Recollections* (1872), where he says he was responsible for the first Revue on the English stage with his *Success; or, a Hit if you Like It*, produced at the Adelphi in 1825. This was however a 'Review' of the dramatic productions of the past season. The first real revue seen in England was *Under the Clock*, produced at the Court Theatre in 1893, and written by Seymour Hicks and Charles Brookfield.

A few years before the war of 1914–18 what is now known as revue became very popular, but it was still revue in its British form, and had little to do with the continental variety. Revues were produced at the Empire, the Alhambra, and the London Hippodrome. They were spectacular, with a smattering of topicality, but that, and the wit, was subdued by excessive spectacle, and they became parades of singing, dancing, and costume-display, with a few sketches thrown in. The names most closely associated with these productions were those of Albert de Courville at the London Hippodrome and of André Charlot at the Alhambra. Austen Hurgon took revue to the provinces through the music-halls, where it soon began to crowd out variety entertainment.

In 1914 Alfred Butt started a series of revues of great beauty and good taste at the Palace Theatre, beginning with *The Passing Show*, which introduced Elsie Janis to England. Much of the revue music, and many of its artists, came from America, for at this period Ragtime was sweeping the world, and *Hullo Ragtime* (1912), produced by de Courville and starring Ethel Levey, was a typical example.

In America revue was inaugurated in 1907 by Florenz Ziegfeld, with his Ziegfeld Follies, which ran through twenty-four editions. A later producer of American revue was George White, whose Scandals, inaugurated in 1919, became a regular annual feature of the New York stage.

The greatest exponent of revue in England was Sir Charles Cochran. At the Ambassadors' Theatre in 1914 his *Odds and Ends* was a serious attempt at an intimate revue, which relied on cleverness and wit more than on dress and dancing. He followed it up with other shows at the Oxford, and then at the London Pavilion. Taste, good music, wit, and beauty abounded. Meanwhile all over the country entertainments of a formless nature were being performed under the general title of revue, though they bore little resemblance to it. Even the Theatre Royal, Drury Lane, staged one.

So popular did revue become in the West End of London that certain managements presented it continuously from 2 p.m. till midnight. One theatre, the Windmill, made a special feature of this, and remained open right through the London Blitz of 1940–2, with a form of entertainment known as Revuedeville, and also as 'non-stop variety' (see MUSIC-HALL, III. 30).

English revue reached a high standard at the private Gate Theatre and was just beginning to emerge from there when the war started in 1939. At the Ambassadors', where Cochran had launched his Intimate Revue, it again found a home. *Sweet and Low*, staged there in 1943, ran for over 1,000 performances, and remained, in its various editions, the nearest thing to true revue to be seen in London. Noel Coward did some excellent revues for Sir Charles Cochran, in which music and wit were set above mere scenic splendour. One of the best librettists of revue in England was undoubtedly the late Herbert Farjeon, whose Little Revues were a feature of London's theatrical life in the years immediately preceding the Second World War.   W. M. P.

REYNOLDS, FREDERICK (1764–1841), English dramatist, author of over 200 plays of which the most notorious was *The Caravan; or, the Driver and his Dog*. This netted him £350, a good sum for those days, and saved Drury Lane from disaster when it was first produced in 1803, mainly because of the appearance on the stage of a real dog, Carlos, who dived into a tank of water to save a child from drowning. Reynolds's first play was a translation of *Werther*, produced at Bath in 1785, but in the main his plays were either light comedies, like *How to Grow Rich* (1793), melodramas, or adaptations of Shakespeare for light opera. In 1827 he published an interesting volume of reminiscences, containing many side-lights on the contemporary stage, entitled *The Life and Times of Frederick Reynolds, Written by Himself*.

REYNOLDS, ROBERT (*fl.* 1610–40), English actor who was a Queen's Man but by 1616 had gone to Germany, where he was one of the popular English Comedians under Robert Browne and John Green, succeeding the latter as leader of the company. As a clown, Pickelherring, he made an enviable reputation on the continent, where he is recorded up to 1640.

RHINTHONICA, see FABULA (5).

RHODES, JOHN (*c.* 1606–?), a London bookseller, said by Downes in *Roscius Anglicanus* to have been connected before the Commonwealth with Blackfriars Theatre, probably as wardrobe-keeper or prompter. At the Restoration he obtained a licence to reopen the Cockpit—of which he had become Keeper in 1644—with a small company of players, among whom were his young apprentices Thomas Betterton and Edward Kynaston. His licence was rendered null by the patent granted to Killigrew and Davenant, and his actors were taken over by them, Betterton becoming leading man in Davenant's company, and later the leading actor of his day. There was also a John Rhodes, presumably a different man, who was part-owner of the Fortune Playhouse in 1637.

RICCOBONI. (1) ANTONIO (*fl.* 1675–95), an actor of the *commedia dell'arte*, who played Pantalone, and was seen in this part in London when the Italian actors paid a visit there in 1679. His son (2) LUIGI (*c.* 1675–1753), known as Lelio, was a fine actor, and was entrusted with the task of selecting and directing the Italian company which returned to Paris in 1716. With him were his wife and brother-in-law, who played the young lovers, Silvia, later the interpreter of Marivaux's heroines, and the famous Harlequin Thomassin. It was under Riccoboni that the Italian company first played in French. He was also the author of several books on the theatre in French and Italian, of which one was published in an English translation in 1741. They form one of the main sources of our knowledge of the *commedia dell'arte*.

RICE [REIZENSTEIN], ELMER (1892–   ), American dramatist, born in New York. He studied and practised law, and became a successful writer with his first effort, the melodrama *On Trial* (1914), the first American play to employ the flashback technique of the screen. It was followed by two unsuccessful anti-militaristic dramas during World War I, another trial melodrama, *For the Defense* (1919), a collaboration with Hatcher Hughes, *Wake Up Jonathan* (1921), and *It Is the Law* (1922). Rice's other collaborations, of no particular merit, were *Close Harmony* (1924) and *Black Sheep* (1932). His first major contribution was the expressionistic fantasy *The Adding Machine* (1923), which satirized the growing regimentation of man in the machine-age through the life and death of the arid book-keeper 'Mr. Zero'. *Street Scene* (1929) won the Pulitzer Prize for its realistic chronicle of life in the slums. *The Left Bank* (1931) described

expatriation from America as an ineffectual escape from materialism, and *Counsellor-at-Law* (1931) drew a realistic picture of the legal profession.

The depression of the 1930s inspired the polemical *We, the People* (1933), the Reichstag Trial was paralleled in *Judgement Day* (1934), and conflicting American and Soviet ideologies formed the subject of the conversation-piece *Between Two Worlds* (1934). When these plays failed on Broadway their author retired from the theatre after venting his wrath on dramatic critics and composing a satire on the stage, *Not for Children*, published in 1935. Rice returned to Broadway in 1937 to write and direct for the Playwrights' Producing Company which he helped to establish. He employed fantasy and recapitulated history in *American Landscape* (1938) to press a plea for racial tolerance and peace between capital and labour. He dispensed with preachment in the romantic *Two on an Island* (1940), but returned to the political scene with *Flight to the West* (also 1940), a fervent denunciation of the 'rational madness' of Nazism, punctuated with melodrama when a refugee tries to assassinate a German diplomat on a transatlantic clipper. *A New Life* (1942) presented a mild conflict between youthful idealism and social snobbery. Rice recaptured the success of his early plays with the fantasy *Dream Girl* (1945), in which a too imaginative girl encounters unexpected romance in reality, and there was much distinction in his operatic version of *Street Scene* (1947), to which Kurt Weill supplied the music.   J. G.

RICE, JOHN (*c.* 1596–?), an Elizabethan boy-actor apprenticed to Heminge, who lent him to the Merchant Taylors' Company to deliver a speech before King James in 1607. In 1610 he appeared with Burbage in a water-pageant, as Corinea, a nymph. He joined the King's Men, probably in succession to Nathan Field, in 1619, and remained with them some years. He is presumed to have taken Holy Orders, since Heminge in his will of 1630 leaves 20s. to 'John Rice, clerk, of St. Saviour's in Southwark'. Rice appears in the actor-list of Shakespeare's plays, and was in the original production of *The Duchess of Malfi*, playing the part of the Marquis of Pescara.

RICE, THOMAS DARTMOUTH (1806–60), an American vaudeville performer and negro impersonator, known as Jim Crow, from the refrain of his most famous song. This, according to one account, was based on a song and shuffling dance done by an old negro while grooming a horse, and Rice, having arranged it to his satisfaction, first gave it in 1828, while playing in Ludlow and Smith's Southern Theatre in Louisville, Kentucky, as an intermission between the acts of a play. It caught the public fancy, was published in several editions and performed all over the United States. In 1833 Rice visited Washington, and there had as partner in his turn the four-year-old Joseph Jefferson (1829–1905), later one of America's most famous actors. Dressed as a miniature Jim Crow—a ragged nondescript costume and a white hat, his face blacked with burnt cork—he was tumbled out of a sack at the conclusion of Rice's song, and performed the song and dance himself. In 1836 Rice appeared at the Surrey Theatre, London, and started the enormous vogue of Nigger Minstrels in England. In spite of this, and of his burlesques into which he introduced old negro songs, and which formed the basis of the later Ethiopian Operas, he never himself became part of a troupe, preferring to work alone. Rice was an eccentric man, and died in poverty. In 1837 he married an Englishwoman, but she and their children predeceased him.

RICH. (1) CHRISTOPHER (?–1714), a lawyer who in 1689 bought Alexander Davenant's share of the Theatre Royal Patent, and by 1693 had got complete control of the theatre. He soon became known as a tyrant, a twister, and a mean man, and under his management the company went from bad to worse. Salaries were cut, expenses pared to the minimum, and Rich was constantly involved in lawsuits. In the end Betterton, with most of the better actors, broke away and formed his own company, leaving Rich to carry on with a mediocre group of players. He was finally forced out of management, and took over the deserted theatre in Lincoln's Inn Fields. He died before it was ready, but his son (2) JOHN (c. 1682–1761) managed it, and was responsible for the production there of *The Beggar's Opera* in 1728. John Rich was the first to make pantomime popular in England, and, as Lun, played Harlequin himself with great success (see COVENT GARDEN, DRURY LANE, LINCOLN'S INN FIELDS THEATRE, and PANTOMIME).

RICHARDSON, SIR RALPH (1902–   ), English actor who was knighted in 1946 for his services to the English theatre, which he has served well and unobtrusively since his first appearance on the stage in 1921, at the Little Theatre, Brighton, as Lorenzo in *The Merchant of Venice*. He was with the Birmingham Repertory Company in 1926, and later appeared in London in several plays by Priestley, giving an exceptionally fine performance in *Johnson over Jordan* (1939). He first played with the Old Vic Company, with whom his reputation was chiefly made, in the season of 1930, and on the opening of Sadler's Wells Theatre in the following year he played Sir Toby Belch in the initial production of *Twelfth Night*. He also appeared several times at the Malvern Festival. After some years in the Fleet Air Arm during the 1939–45 war, he returned to the Old Vic, being much admired as Peer Gynt and Sir John Falstaff. In 1949, after leaving the Old Vic, he gave a fine performance as the father in *The Heiress* at the Haymarket. An unspectacular and unselfish actor, his range of parts is wide, and to each he brings the same integrity of purpose and subtle interpretation. With a few exceptions he is not at his best in romantic costume parts, but excels in the delineation of baffled humanity, with all its suppressed poetry, humorous resignation, and deep springs of pity and humility, at odds with a complex and contradictory society.

RICHELIEU, ARMAND JEAN DU PLESSIS DE, CARDINAL (1585–1642), famous statesman, and for many years virtual ruler of France. He did a great deal for the theatre, and by his patronage of the actor Montdory, whom he often summoned to play before him, helped to establish a permanent professional theatre in Paris, and to raise the status of the actor. He had strong leanings towards dramatic authorship, and wrote a number of plays in collaboration with a committee of five—Corneille, Rotrou, Boisrobert, Colletet, and Claude de L'Étoile. They were not very successful, and Corneille resigned after helping with two, having incurred the Cardinal's wrath by making a trifling alteration to his part of the plot. Richelieu built a very well-equipped theatre in his palace, which later, as the Palais-Royal, became famous under Molière. It was opened on 14 January 1641, in the presence of the king and queen and a brilliant audience, with a production of *Mirame*, attributed to Desmarets, but partly the work of Richelieu himself. The new machinery and splendid settings, which heralded the later vogue for such accessories in opera, were received with admiration and applause, but the play had nothing like the ovation given to Corneille and others in the less splendidly equipped public theatres, and is now forgotten. Richelieu is mainly remembered in theatrical history for his association with Corneille, whom he alternately befriended and rebuked, as in the famous quarrel over *Le Cid*.

RICHEPIN, JEAN (1849–1926), French poet and dramatist, a brilliant but undisciplined man, who was for a short time an actor. He is perhaps best known for his novels and poetry, and like them his plays, of which the first was *L'Étoile* (1873), are somewhat marred by an insistent morbidity. They represent, nevertheless, an important part of his work, and include *Nana Sahib* (1883), *Monsieur Scapin* (1886), *Le Filibustier* (1888), *Par la glaive* (1892), *Le Chien de garde* (1898), and *Don Quichotte* (1905). They were mostly given at the Comédie-Française, though *Le Chemineau* (1897), having been accepted there subject to correction, was taken by the author to the Odéon, and had an immense success. Richepin also wrote words for music by Massenet and Georges.

RICHMOND HILL THEATRE, NEW YORK. This opened on 14 Nov. 1831, in the converted house of Aaron Burr, with *The Road to Ruin*. It had a good company under able management, and was probably intended to give scope to the talents of Mrs. Duff, who played there for two seasons, mainly in revivals. The theatre had the temerity to stage *The Hunchback* on the same night as the Park Theatre, 18 June 1832, and was prospering when it was closed on account of plague, which claimed one of its best actors, Woodhull. It then housed Italian opera, sponsored by Lorenzo da Ponte (1749–1838), Mozart's librettist and Professor of Italian at Columbia University. In 1836 Mrs. Hamblin opened it for a couple of seasons, and the famous comedian James E. Murdoch made there his first appearance in New York, while later Miss Nelson took it over and made a hit in *The Mountain Sylph*. For a few seasons it opened as the Tivoli Gardens, and from 1845 to 1848 was again advertised as the Richmond Theatre, but mainly housed circus and variety. It then disappears from theatrical records.

RICHMOND THEATRE, LONDON, first built about 1765 and pulled down in 1884. It was quite an important playhouse, and many great actors appeared there. The elder Mathews, as a stage-struck youth, paid 7½ guineas to be allowed to play Richard III. Dibdin appeared there, and so did Edmund Kean, who died in the house next door. Helen Faucit made her début there in 1833. The present theatre was built in 1899, and has had an interesting, though not spectacular, history, being used mainly for revivals, and try-outs of new plays, many of which have subsequently found their way to the West End.   w. m. p.

For the Richmond Theatre, Yorkshire, see PROVINCIAL THEATRES.

RICINIATA, see FABULA (6) and MIME (2).

RICKETTS, CHARLES (1866–1931), see COSTUME, 10 c.

RISE AND SINK, a method of effecting a Transformation Scene (see TRICKWORK ON THE ENGLISH STAGE).

RISTORI, ADELAIDE (1822–1906), Italian actress, celebrated far beyond the confines of her native country, particularly as a player of tragic parts. The daughter of actors, she was on the stage as a child, and at 14 gave a successful interpretation of the part of Francesca da Rimini in Silvio Pellico's version of the play. At 18 she played for the first time a part which she made peculiarly her own—Maria Stuart in Schiller's tragedy. She retired from the stage for a short time on marriage, but returned and in 1855 went to Paris, where, after a somewhat quiet début, she soon became an outstanding figure and a serious rival to Rachel. From Paris she went to England, Spain, and the United States, where she first appeared in 1866, and then toured the country with great success. In 1882 she was seen in London as Lady Macbeth and was much praised by the critics. Mrs. Kendal, in a characteristic remark, said of her that she was a greater actress than Sarah Bernhardt because she had no sex-appeal. She retired in 1885, and three years later published her memoirs, which provide an interesting account of her life, and a penetrating study of her approach to her art.

RITTERDRAMA, an offshoot of the *Sturm und Drang* drama, which followed on Goethe's *Götz von Berlichingen* (1773) and Klinger's *Otto* (1774). It might perhaps be translated as 'feudal' drama. In it the valour and doughty independence of the medieval knights was shown amidst battle scenes, jousting, and pageantry, often with a marked vein of Bavarian local patriotism. Among the authors of such plays were Josef August von Törring (1753–1826), Bavarian Minister of State, with *Kasper der Thorringer* (publ. 1785) and *Agnes Bernauerin* (1780), and Joseph Marius Babo (1756–1822), for some time Director of the Court theatre in Munich, with *Otto von Wittelsbach* (1782). Like the *Sturm und Drang* drama, the *Ritterdrama* is written in prose, is irregular in form, and has as its theme strong passions and a contempt for conventions. These plays did much to foster the taste for romantic and medieval settings kindled by *Götz von Berlichingen*, and it is significant that Schiller's *Die Räuber* was given in sixteenth-century costume. Reactionary influences caused the *Ritterdrama* to be banned from the Munich stage, but its vogue continued elsewhere, notably in Austria, where Karl Friedrich Hensler (1761–1825) fused this type of drama with the native operatic fairy-tale in *Das Donauweibchen* (1797).

RITZ THEATRE, NEW YORK, on 48th Street west of Broadway. This opened on 21 Mar. 1921 with Clara Eames in Drinkwater's *Mary Stuart*. It was a failure, as was his *Robert E. Lee*. In 1922 came *It Is the Law*, and in 1924 a successful production of *Outward Bound*. A year later Winthrop Ames produced *Old English* with George Arliss, which ran for 183 performances, while later in the same year *The Man with a Load of Mischief*, with Ruth Chatterton and Robert Loraine, had a short run. A series of failures was broken in 1927 by the 27-weeks' run of *Excess Baggage*, a comedy on the heartbreaks of vaudeville, while in the autumn of 1932 Ruth Draper gave a three-weeks' season of monologues. In 1937 the theatre was taken over by the Federal Theatre Project, which presented there Arthur Arent's living newspaper *Power* for 118 performances. A year later *Murder in the Cathedral* was given 21 performances and, after a Federal Theatre production of *Pinocchio*, the theatre became a cinema.   G. F.

R.K.O. CENTRE, and **R.K.O. ROXY,** NEW YORK, see CENTRE THEATRE.

ROBERTS, ARTHUR (1852–1933), one of the earliest of music-hall comedians and, unlike many others, neither red-nosed nor shabby. At 19 he sang in tavern entertainments, and all through the 1870s he appeared on the halls, where his first successful song was 'If I Was Only Long Enough, a Soldier I Would Be'. In 1881 he first appeared in pantomime, under Harris at Drury Lane, and later appeared as immaculate guardsmen and men-about-town in burlesques and musical comedies. In the first of these, *In Town*, as Captain Coddington, he set a fashion in male headgear. He celebrated his jubilee in 1925, and later appeared in one of Cochran's revues at the London Pavilion. He was a great 'gagster'. It was not necessary to write him a part; he did that for himself, and altered it every night.

W. M. P.

ROBERTSON, THOMAS WILLIAM (1829–71), English dramatist, eldest of the twenty-two children of an actor. Several of his brothers and sisters were on the stage, the most famous being the youngest girl, Madge (see KENDAL). Robertson himself acted as a child, and after some years' schooling went as an adult actor to Lincoln, where he made himself generally useful, painting scenery, writing songs and plays, and acting small parts. He was in fact trained in the old school which he was later to destroy, a process which can be studied, with reservations, in Pinero's *Trelawny of the 'Wells'* (1898). Yet his earliest plays were in no way remarkable. He wrote them quickly and sold them cheaply to Lacy, the theatrical publisher, and his first success was achieved with *David Garrick* (1864), based on a French play and written for Sothern. Though built up very largely on the old formulae and abounding in 'type' characters, the printed copy of this play, with its elaborate directions for realistic scenery and costume, and its wealth of stage directions, is a definite pointer in the direction which Robertson was to take almost immediately with such plays as *Society* (1865), *Ours* (1866), *Caste* (1867), *Play* (1868), and *School* (1869). Their monosyllabic titles alone come as a refreshing change after the flowery nomenclature of earlier and even contemporary plays. They were all given at the Prince of Wales's Theatre, where the success of *Society* established the reputation not only of the author but of the newly formed Bancroft management. With these plays Robertson founded what has been called 'the cup-and-saucer drama'—that is, the drama of the realistic, contemporary, domestic interior. His rooms were recognizable, his dialogue credible, his plots, though they now seem somewhat artificial, were true to his time, and an immense advance on anything that had gone before. *Caste* in particular still holds the stage, and some of the others would revive well.

Robertson, who was a robust and convivial creature, with red hair and beard and a brilliant flow of conversation, directed his own plays, and has sometimes been accounted the first of the modern producers. Years of hard work and continual rebuffs embittered him, but with the coming of success his naturally sweet temper reasserted itself, and he was able to enjoy a few years of fame before his tragically early death at the height of his career. He had, however, left a permanent mark on the theatre of his time, and the work of many modern dramatists is adumbrated in his early efforts at realism.

ROBESON, PAUL (1898–   ), American negro actor and singer, who abandoned a legal career for the stage, where he first appeared in 1921. A year later he was seen in England, playing opposite Mrs. Patrick Campbell in *The Voodoo*, and on his return to New York created a great sensation by his performances with the Provincetown Players in O'Neill's plays, particularly *The Emperor Jones*. It was his singing of 'Ole Man River' in *Showboat* that first revealed the haunting quality of his superb bass voice, and for many years afterwards he toured Europe and America with a programme of negro spirituals. He returned to the stage in 1930, when he was seen in London in *Othello*, which in 1943 in New York achieved the longest recorded run of any Shakespearian play. Robeson has also appeared in a number of films, and is the subject of a biography, written by his wife and published in 1930.

ROBEY, GEORGE (1869–   ), one of the most successful and popular comedians of the English music-halls, where he has been given the nickname of 'the Prime Minister of Mirth'. He made his first appearance at the Aquarium in 1891, and after a trial at the Oxford in the same year was engaged for most of the leading music-halls of London and the provinces. He has also played in a number of pantomimes. Apart from popular songs, he has been very successful in a series of humorous caricatures and sketches, and in 1916 he appeared for the first time in revue as Lucius Bing in *The Bing Boys are Here*, followed by *The Bing Boys on Broadway*. Other ventures have been an interesting Falstaff in *Henry IV, Part I*, Menelaus in *Helen*, stage appearances in farces, and tours in England and elsewhere with his own revue company, which he later put on in London in *Bits and Pieces*. Robey's humour is robust, and he appears to consist largely of a bowler hat and two enormous black eyebrows. He is a painter, having exhibited both at the Academy and at the Royal Institute of Painters in Water Colours, a writer—his first book was published in 1908—a violin-maker, a good cricketer, and a student of Egyptology. In 1919 he was created a C.B.E. for services during the war.

ROBIN HOOD, an English legendary hero, whose name first appears in *Piers Plowman* (1377). He typifies the chivalrous outlaw from oppression, champion of the poor against the tyranny of the rich. Though his story may have some basis in fact, it is impossible to identify him with any historical personage, though an Elizabethan playwright, Anthony Munday, made him the exiled Earl of Huntingdon. Since he is always dressed in green, he may be a survival of the Wood-man, or Jack-in-the-Green, of the early pagan spring festivities, or he may have been imported by minstrels from France (see ADAM DE LA HALLE, *Le Jeu de Robin et Marion*). By the end of the fifteenth century he and his familiar retinue of Maid Marian, Little John, Friar Tuck, and the Merry Men, with their accompanying Morris Dance, were inseparable from the May-Day revels, and the protagonists of many a rustic drama. These, however, cannot be considered folk plays, as were the Mumming and

Plough Monday Plays, since they were written by minstrels. The May-Day festivities found their way to Court, where they became mixed up with allegory and pseudo-classicism. Henry VIII, in particular, enjoyed many splendid Mayings, including one in which he was entertained by Robin Hood to venison in a bower. After that their popularity waned, and they were finally suppressed by the Puritans. The story of Robin Hood and his Merry Men has been a favourite subject for nineteenth- and twentieth-century pantomime.

ROBINS, ELIZABETH (1865–   ), American actress, who passed the greater part of her professional life in England, and was prominently identified with the introduction of Ibsen to the London stage. She made her first appearance, however, with the Boston Museum stock company in 1885, and remained with them for some years, afterwards touring with Booth and Barrett. She was first seen in London in 1889, and in June of that year appeared as Martha Bernick in *The Pillars of Society*. A visit to Norway had awakened her interest in Ibsen, and in 1891 she played Mrs. Linden in *A Doll's House* and the title-role in *Hedda Gabler*, in which she gave a remarkable performance. Two years later she played Hilda in *The Master Builder*, Rebecca West in *Rosmersholm*, and Agnes in *Brand*. *Little Eyolf* followed in 1896 and *John Gabriel Borkman* in 1897. She held the stage rights of most of these plays, and was responsible, sometimes in conjunction with such advanced groups as the Independent Theatre, for their initial productions. She was seen also in a wide variety of other parts, notably as Mariana in Echegaray's play of that name. She then retired, apart from a brief return to the stage as Lucrezia in *Paolo and Francesca* (1902), and devoted herself to literature, publishing a number of novels and two volumes of theatrical reminiscences.

ROBINSON, (ESMÉ STUART) LENNOX (1886–   ), whether as actor, playwright, producer, manager, director, or dramatic critic, has been connected with the main stream of Irish drama since his first play appeared at the Abbey in 1908 and he himself became producer there in 1910 (see IRELAND, 1). His long association has meant continuity, the importance of which, in a movement of such recent foundation, is very considerable. His close connexion began immediately after the death of Synge in the days when Yeats and Lady Gregory were still the dominant forces in the theatre and immediately before the expansion of its international reputation with the first American tour in 1911. His plays have continued to appear steadily, and with very few intervals, from that day to this, and neither in theme nor in technique has he ever shown signs of stagnation. It is hard to say whether his continuous prominence as an Abbey playwright owes more to his technical skill (he is one of the finest craftsmen in Irish or English drama) or to the liveness of his sympathy and imagination, which have kept him abreast of

each new phase of Irish drama and frequently its leader. His work began with *The Clancy Name* (1908), which marked him at once as a clear-sighted realist, independent in choice of material and already possessed of a firm sense of form. In this play and its immediate successors, such as *Harvest* (1910), he and a group of young realistic playwrights presented by degrees a series of fresh aspects of the life of Ireland, opening up areas not touched by Yeats, Lady Gregory, and Synge. The comedy *The White-Headed Boy* (1916) was immediately appreciated also in England and America and has remained popular in all three countries. In the earlier *Patriots* (1912), *The Dreamers* (1913), and in *The Lost Leader* (1918) he treated political and patriotic themes as matter of tragedy, with no danger of weakening into sentimentalism. Already in these plays—and especially in *The White-Headed Boy* and *Crabbed Youth and Age* (1922)—Robinson's skill, not only as a structural craftsman but as a creator of character in the direction of comedy of manners, was becoming clear. That capacity has never faltered in its development.

In *The Big House* (1926) Robinson was still abreast of the times and its problems and was the first man in Ireland to write a play on the changing order of its civilization—a theme touched also by Yeats, notably in his last play, *Purgatory*. In *The Far-Off Hills* (1928) and in *Church Street* (1934) he returned to that comedy in which his most precise work had been done, achieving in *Church Street* not only a fine and skilful piece of dramatic structure, but a tragi-comedy or 'mingled drama' whose satire was genial and whose mingled ironies were tragic. His later works include *Give a Dog* (1928), *Ever the Twain* (1929), *All's Over, Then?* (1932), *Is Life Worth Living?* (also known as *Drama at Inish*) (1933), *When Lovely Woman* (1936), and *Killycreggs in Twilight* (1937). His contribution to dramatic history and criticism includes *The Irish Theatre* (1939), a collection of lectures given by him and other leaders of this theatre in 1938, and *Curtain Up* (1941).   U. E.-F.

ROBINSON, MARY (*née* DARBY) (1758–1800), English actress who, after a short career on the stage, left it to become the mistress of the Prince Regent, making her last appearance as Perdita, by which name she is best known. She was the spoiled child of a spendthrift, and at 16 made an unhappy marriage with a dissolute young man, with whom she shortly afterwards went to prison for debt. She was coached for her first appearance, as Juliet, by Garrick, and appeared at Drury Lane in 1776, her success being already assured by her reputation for beauty and profligacy. Yet some critics saw in her the makings of a fine actress, better suited to heavy tragedy than to the light, girlish parts she usually played. After her short-lived affair with the Regent, for which she was much pitied and considered the less blamable of the two, she would probably have returned to the theatre; but she was strongly advised not to, and a severe attack of rheumatic fever left her, at 24, too helpless to do so. She spent the rest of her life wandering from one spa to another, seeking relief, and supporting herself by writing poems and novels, now forgotten.

ROBINSON, RICHARD (? –1648), English actor, who appears in the actor-list of Shakespeare's plays. He was probably a boy-actor at the Blackfriars, and was certainly one of the King's Men from 1611 onwards. As a young lad he played women's parts, and was much praised by Ben Jonson. Later he witnessed Burbage's will and possibly married his widow, which has inclined some to think that he may have been apprenticed to Burbage. He signed the dedication of the Beaumont and Fletcher folio in 1647.

ROBSON, FLORA (1902–   ), English actress, trained at the R.A.D.A., who first appeared at the Shaftesbury Theatre, London, 1921, in Clemence Dane's *Will Shakespeare*. Her chief successes have been in parts demanding controlled nervous tension (e.g. Mrs. Christie in *Black Chiffon*, 1949). She was also memorable as Mary Paterson (1931) in Bridie's *The Anatomist*, and (1948) showed a latent ability for comedy in *Captain Brassbound's Conversion*. Her performances in films are of a correspondingly high standard.

ROBSON, FREDERICK (1821–64), English actor, whose real name was Thomas Robson Brownbill, was apprenticed to an engraver, but made a number of appearances in amateur companies before deserting his trade for the stage. After several engagements in the provinces he appeared at the Grecian in 1844, and became famous as the singer of 'Villikins and his Dinah' and 'The Country Fair'. In 1850 he went to Dublin but returned to become one of the mainstays of burlesque at the Olympic, of which he later became joint manager with Emden. He was very short and ugly, but an actor of great power, and was affectionately known as 'the great little Robson'. Among his most popular parts were Jim Baggs in *The Wandering Minstrel*—in which he continued to sing 'Villikins and his Dinah' with as much success as at the Grecian—Jacob Earwig in *Boots at the Swan*, Daddy Hardacre in the sketch of that name, and Sampson Burr in *The Porter's Knot*. Robson died at the early age of 43, a victim to intemperance.

ROBSON, STUART [HENRY ROBSON STUART] (1836–1903), American comedian, whose odd voice and quaint personality provided his stock-in-trade for over fifty years of acting. He began as a boy of 16, and after ten years with leading stock companies went to Laura Keene's Theatre in New York as principal comedian. He also spent some years with Mrs. John Drew at the Arch Street Theatre in Philadelphia and with Warren in Boston. In 1873 he was seen in London, and shortly afterwards he began a long association with Crane, playing with him in light farce, in *The Hen-*

rietta, which was specially written for them, and as one of the two Dromios in *The Comedy of Errors*; he was also Falstaff to Crane's Slender. In 1889 the two parted amicably, and Robson produced several new plays, dying suddenly while on tour shortly after celebrating his stage jubilee.

RODE, HELGE (1870–1937), Danish dramatist (see SCANDINAVIA, 1).

ROD-PUPPET, see PUPPET.

ROGERS, WILLIAM PENN ADAIR (1879–1935), American comedian, better known as Will Rogers. He had Red Indian blood in him and spent his youth on the range, later, after a good though erratic education, becoming a cowboy. In 1902 he joined a Wild West circus in the Argentine, being billed as the Cherokee Kid. After a tour in Australia he returned to the States to appear at the St. Louis exhibition. In 1905 he made his first appearance in New York, where he soon became very popular, joking informally with his audience. He appeared in musical comedy for the first time in 1912, and rapidly became a star on Broadway, reaching the height of success in a series of Ziegfeld Follies shows. His personality was more important than his material, and his wisecracks were quoted everywhere. In the 1920s the stage lost him to Hollywood, and he also became a newspaper correspondent, a lecturer, and a radio commentator. An enthusiast about flying, he was killed on a flight with the aviator Wiley Post. In contrast to the exotic background of his Broadway shows and the publicity accorded to his every movement, his domestic life, with a devoted wife and three children, was quiet and happy.

ROJAS, FERNANDO DE (?–*c.* 1541), Spanish author of a dramatic dialogue in twenty-one acts, the *Tragicomedia de Calisto y Melibea*, usually known as *La Celestina*. The earliest known edition is 1499, though it may have been published, and was certainly written, earlier. There is no evidence of its having been acted—and indeed its length and structure would probably have made this impossible—but it is essentially dramatic in form, and deals with the conflict between good and evil, between Celestina, the personification of the Seven Deadly Sins, and Calisto, the incarnation of the Renaissance idea of Platonic love. It shows a curious mingling of medieval and Renaissance elements, and was not without a profound influence on the course of the drama. A later dramatist, Joaquín Romero de Cepeda, wrote a *Comedia Salvaje*, based on part of *La Celestina*, while an English interlude, *Calisto and Melibea*, of unknown authorship, published by John Rastell about 1530, is drawn from the first part of the book, and is considered one of the first English dramatic works to approach true comedy. A complete translation of *La Celestina* was made by James Mabbe (1631).

ROJAS ZORRILLA, FRANCISCO DE (1607–48), a Spanish dramatist of great dramatic skill, whose tragedy, *El Rey abajo ninguno* (also known as *El labrador mas honrado, García del Castañar*), ranks with the best work of the Spanish theatre. It is still acceptable to the public, and many of its chivalrous and resounding lines are known by heart. His comedies, in which the *gracioso*, or clown, is often the chief personage, are distinguished by wit and neatness of versification. The best known is *Entre bobos anda el juego*. Modern critics have admired in Rojas his independence of contemporary theatrical convention, which gives his work a personal flavour sometimes missing in those who were overwhelmed by the preponderance of Lope de Vega and Calderón. He was forgotten after his death, and rediscovered by Solís. He owes much of his posthumous fame to the genius of the actor Isidore Maíquez. Rojas also wrote a number of *autos*. He was in his day much admired and pillaged by the French, notably by Scarron, Thomas Corneille, Le Sage, and many others.

ROLL-OUT, a loose flap of canvas at the bottom of a piece of scenery, which enables an actor to appear suddenly on the stage by rolling through it and springing quickly to his feet.

ROMAGNESI, a family of actors belonging to the *commedia dell'arte*. Little is known of the father, (1) NICCOLO (?–1660), beyond his stage name, Orazio, and the fact that he married (2) BRIGIDA BIANCHI (1613–*c.* 1703), the daughter of a player, and herself a good actress, known as Aurelia. Her son (3) MARC' ANTONIO (*c.* 1633–1706) first appeared in young lover parts, and later as the Pedant-Doctor. He must at some time have appeared in London, since his wife died there in 1675. Two of his sons were actors, one, (4) Carlo VIRGILIO (1670–1708), known as Leandro, making his début at the Théâtre-Italien in Paris in 1694, and remaining there until the theatre was closed. He was accounted a fine player of young lovers.

ROMANELLI OF MANTUA, SAMUEL (1757–1814), writer of plays in Hebrew, into which language he translated Metastasio and other Italian authors (see JEWISH DRAMA, 3).

ROMANI, FELICE (1788–1865), Italian poet, a writer of great charm and distinction, who wrote some excellent libretti for Italian operas. Two of these are from Shakespeare, whom he probably knew only through the French adaptations of Ducis—*Hamlet* for Mercadante (1822), and *Romeo and Juliet*, which was set by Vaccai in 1827 and by Bellini in 1833. Perhaps his best, and certainly his best-known, work was done for Bellini's 'La Sonnambula' (1831).

ROMANTIC COMEDY, see COMEDY.

ROMASHOV, BORIS SERGEIVICH (1895–), Soviet dramatist, whose first play, *Meringue Pie*, a satire on the pretensions of bourgeois elements in Soviet society, was produced as early as 1924. Among his later plays, which

were mainly melodramatic dramatizations of episodes in the Civil War, the most important was *Fighters* (1934), which dealt with the Red Army in peacetime, and the clash between private and public interests among the officers. In 1942 a play dealing with the defence of Moscow, *The Stars Cannot Fade*, was put on at the Sverdlovsk theatre, less than a year after the events it deals with took place. This play, whose theme is the courage of a young student, galvanized by war into a man of action, proved very popular.

ROME. 1. FROM THE ORIGINS TO THE END OF THE REPUBLICAN PERIOD. Roman drama was produced by a succession of writers who strove to adapt Greek originals to the native taste for rhetoric, spectacle, and sensationalism and also for buffoonery, homely wit, and biting repartee. Livy tells us that out of a blend of the primitive 'Fescennine Verses', or interchanges of jest by clowns at harvest and other festivals, with music and dance imported from Etruria, there grew a 'medley' (*satura*) which we may perhaps liken to the music-hall entertainment of Edwardian days. The advance to true drama was made by Livius Andronicus, who in 240 B.C. produced at the public games a Greek play in translation. From then till the end of the Republic, Greek tragedies and comedies in translation continued to be produced in Rome. Attempts at original composition consisted of a very few plays on Roman historical themes (see FABULA, 4), and a considerable number of comedies on middle-class or humble life in Italy (see FABULA, 9), but such pieces were probably slight. We have no reason for attributing to any Latin writer the invention of plot or character on a grand scale. The Roman crowd, who were also the electorate, wanted entertainment. The State and the magistrates were anxious to satisfy them and to pay those who could supply the entertainment; the easy and obvious method of translating Greek plays for public performance provided a livelihood for Latin writers in days when there was as yet no reading public in Rome. In general the method adopted was to select a Greek play hitherto untranslated, and to render it freely into Latin, introducing modifications in detail which aimed at pleasing the audience, such as the expression of Roman sentiments in Roman rhetorical style or the addition, in comedy, of jests and topical allusions, however incongruous with their context. Only in the case of Terence can we discern a conscious artistic impulse to improve on the Greek model; in general we may say that the creation of plot and character was neither aimed at by the Roman dramatists nor expected of them by their audience. They were neither men of independent means nor (usually, at any rate) slaves, but hard-working folk, dependent for a livelihood on their pens, and organized, along with the scribes, into a trade guild, the *collegium poetarum*.

Dramatic performances formed part of the entertainment provided free to the public at the games. The actors had to compete with rival attractions such as boxing or rope-dancing; even after the play had begun, a rumour that better fare was to be found elsewhere might cause the spectators to desert in a body. The authorities, however anxious to please the public, were alive to the danger of allowing so large a body of people to hear any utterance on the stage which might reflect on the government or on members of the governing classes; political and personal allusions were therefore in general banned, though it would have been difficult to prevent the actors and the audience from occasionally finding a topical reference in the words of an old play (thus a line in honour of 'Tullius', i.e. Servius Tullius the king, was on one occasion taken by the audience as referring to their own contemporary, M. Tullius Cicero). With moral and religious matters the censorship was less concerned; the *Amphitruo* of Plautus shows the gods Jupiter and Mercury as heartless deceivers, and it is precisely those plays of Plautus and Terence which we know to have been particularly popular (the *Casina* and the *Eunuchus*) which strike us as being the most improper works of their authors. But Plautus's boast in the prologue and epilogue to the *Captivi* that this play is of a higher moral tone than most Greek comedies suggests that Roman public taste itself might impose limits on the dramatist's freedom; in general our extant Latin comedies are fairly free from indecency.

To judge from the prologues, admission to the games was open to all—citizens and slaves, matrons and courtesans, even nurses and their squalling charges. Performances began in the morning; a play could be got through by lunch time. All performances were in the open air. At first there was no permanent theatre; the simple buildings required—the stage and behind it the scene-building—could be put up where required. We have several references in the prologues and plays to a seated audience; no doubt tiers of wooden scaffolding could be erected for a performance and taken down afterwards. What the spectators saw was an open stage with behind it a building, the front wall of which was pierced by three doors. The stage itself represented the open street running from the centre of the town to the harbour or country, or the space in front of a palace, a cottage, or other building. Our modern stage convention allows us to see what is happening inside a house; the spectators of a Roman comedy were in the position of people standing in the public street and observing what was taking place in front of two or three houses which fronted on that street. Interior scenes and changes of setting within the course of a play were unknown. The absence of a front curtain during the period when our extant comedies were written made it necessary to begin and end each play with an empty stage. Act-division, interludes, and intervals were unknown; on one occasion only do we hear of a solo by the flute-players to cover the momentary absence of the chief actor.

Every care was taken that the audience should follow the plot and realize the significance of each means of entrance and the identity of each character. The characters in comedy were types rather than individuals—old gentlemen, usually rather close-fisted, young gentlemen, usually extravagant and spineless, intriguing slaves, jealous wives, boastful captains, treacherous pimps—and custom prescribed the appropriate costume, wig, and mask for each of these types. Unmarried women of the respectable classes were excluded by Greek convention from appearing in public, except at religious or other festivals; consequently the unmarried heroines of Greek New Comedy and its Latin derivatives are something below respectability —courtesans or maidens who have by some misfortune been separated from their parents and brought up in humble circumstances. A common form of plot shows a young gentleman in love with a slave-girl and anxious to raise the money for her purchase; if marriage is to be the outcome, it must be shown in the course of the play that the girl is not only chaste but the long-lost child of respectable parents. In general the plots of comedy turn on intrigues, attempts to raise money, and swindling and deception of many kinds.

The use of costumes and masks (Terence uses *persona*, mask, in the sense of 'character') enabled small companies of five or six actors to perform almost any play by doubling of parts. The leading actor might himself be the producer. Such leading actors might rise to fame and fortune; the careers of Ambivius Turpio, in the second century B.C., and of Cicero's contemporaries, Aesopus and Roscius, seem to prove that the theatrical profession was not yet regarded as in itself degrading. We hear nothing of slaves appearing on the stage until Cicero's day, when Roscius trained a slave named Panurgus for the stage.

Much of what in the Greek originals had been spoken was in the Latin adaptations sung or chanted by the actors to a musical accompaniment supplied by a flute-player. On the other hand, the chorus of fifth-century Greek tragedies was in the Latin adaptations probably represented by a single speaker, attended perhaps by mutes, who appeared on the stage with the other actors. Actors complain of the strain on their voices; indeed, when we consider that they were performing in the open air before large audiences and amid considerable noise, we see that strength of voice must have been one of an actor's chief qualifications.

As for the production of plays, it seems that the authorities responsible for the public games would commission a producer to procure a good play and arrange for its performance. Although revivals of old and successful plays were not unknown, the attraction of novelty would naturally suggest, at least during the productive period of Latin drama, the purchase of a newly written work from its author. The author probably sold his manuscript outright to the producer, who also paid the company, hired the costumes from the *choregus*, and in general took all business details on his shoulders, hoping to reap a profit from the sum handed him by the magistrates or other persons responsible for the giving of the games. Somehow the manuscripts of plays managed to survive to later generations, sometimes with modifications, such as the addition of an alternative final scene, which indicate the hand of a later producer; but even the archaic plays of Livius Andronicus, which can hardly have enjoyed much popularity on the stage, survived, perhaps as school texts, to the time of Cicero, who read them and pronounced them not worth a second reading. Such a manuscript would naturally include the prologue if there was one —or prologues, if the play had been given a revival performance; the author's name would appear on the title-page, and notes of opening or later performances might also be included. From such information scholars of a later generation seem to have derived their accounts of theatrical activities and their biographical information with regard to the early dramatists. It is only too clear that the records were soon confused; there was much dispute as to which were the genuine plays of Plautus, and no means of settling such a controversy, while the tendency to fill in biographical details from inference and even imagination is indicated by the discrepancies in the 'Life' of Terence. The only safe basis for the study of Latin drama is the text of the plays and prologues.

Though tragedy seems to have attracted fewer writers than comedy, the popularity and influence of the leading tragic writers appears to have been great. In general they seem to have selected as models the more melodramatic of the Greek originals. Exciting plots, flamboyant characters, gruesome scenes, violent rhetoric were more attractive to the Roman crowd than the qualities for which we chiefly prize our extant Greek tragedies. By comparing the fragments we can see how Roman translators modified their originals to suit national taste. In substance there was probably little alteration; the changes were in matters of style and detail, the chief feature being the development of rhetoric at the expense of truth and naturalness. In comedy the free-and-easy methods of the early writers appear to have been succeeded by greater fidelity to the Greek originals; but that something was felt to be lost thereby is suggested by the contemporary development of the comedy of Italian manners (see FABULA, 9). By the end of the second century B.C. Turpilius, the last writer of comedy for the stage, was dead, while Accius, the last writer of tragedy, died some fifteen or twenty years later.

From about the time of Sulla we notice new developments. While old plays are still produced (actors such as Aesopus in tragedy and Roscius in comedy made large fortunes), we gather on the whole that new plays were not being written for the stage. The writing of tragedy and comedy appears now to be regarded as a purely literary affair and is practised by persons of the governing class, e.g. Julius Caesar Strabo and Quintus Cicero; such writers seem to have composed original plays, not translations. While the theatres become more splendid, the standard of theatrical entertainment seems to sink; rustic farce (see FABULA, 1) and mime enjoy increasing popularity, and even the revivals of old plays are marred by tasteless extravagance of production. The introduction of the drop-curtain makes possible elaborate scenic effects and quick changes of setting. A divorce sets in between drama and the stage; Cicero seems to think of drama as something to be read, while theatrical performances are for him little more than a vulgar form of popular entertainment.

2. THE EMPIRE. Many plays were written during the Empire, and theatres arose in Europe, Asia, and Africa; but these plays and these theatres had little or nothing to do with each other. As public taste had been found to prefer mime and pantomime (see MIME, 2, and PANTOMIMUS), the stage was almost monopolized by these light performances, though we have a few references to the revival of old plays. The tragedies and comedies now written are independent compositions intended to be read aloud among friends. The tragedies ascribed to Seneca, including the *praetexta*, *Octavia*, are examples of this Closet drama; though full of clever rhetoric, they are clearly not designed for the stage, and were probably never performed. As the only examples of Latin tragedy to reach the modern world, they were destined nevertheless to exercise great influence on the drama of the Renaissance.

3. THE ROMAN THEATRE AND STAGE. Unlike the Greek theatre, the central feature of the Roman theatre was from the first not the orchestra but the raised stage, on which all the performers appeared. As every seat had to command a view of the stage, the *cavea*, or portion occupied by the seating, could not exceed semicircular form. The orchestra, immediately in front of the stage, was unused except to accommodate distinguished spectators. As in the Greek theatre, the 'scene-building' behind the stage must from early times have been used both as the back-scene and as the actors' dressing-room. The spectators sat on tiers of wooden benches (*spectacula*) supported by scaffolding, or on the ground below; we see a similar arrangement in an Etruscan tomb-painting. The whole structure was a temporary affair during the productive period of Latin drama. There was no curtain; the back-scene, with its regulation three doors, was open to view throughout the play. Characters could enter from any one of the house-doors, each of which might represent a different house in the play, or from the side-entrances in the wings; the side-entrance to the spectators' right denoted the near distance, that to their left the farther distance. Thus, if the scene was laid in a town, a character going off to the spectators' right was supposed to be going to the forum; if he went off to their left he might, according to circumstances, be supposed to be on his way to the country or the harbour. Near

the side-entrances, and illustrating their significance at the moment, stood the *periaktoi*, revolving stands indicating the scenery in the neighbourhood. If for some reason it was necessary to move a character from one house to another, or to the forum or harbour, without bringing him on the stage, which represented the street, he was supposed to use the back door and the *angiportum*, an imaginary street running behind the houses. Of scenery, other than the front wall of the scene-building and the *periaktoi*, there was little or none; interior scenes could not be represented; all action had necessarily to take place in front of the houses shown in the background. If a banquet was to be shown, the tables and couches had to be brought on the stage for the purpose and taken indoors again at the end of the scene. The rocks of the *Rudens* (*l.* 206) were probably left to the imagination. The stage-building had a practicable roof.

In the first century B.C. theatres and scenery grew more elaborate; finally, in 55 B.C. Pompey built the first stone theatre in the Campus Martius. In 13 B.C. Cornelius Balbus built another theatre, while the theatre of Marcellus, also erected in the reign of Augustus, is still in existence. In fulfilment of the Roman policy of keeping the crowd entertained, theatres were erected all over the Empire; splendid examples are still to be seen at Orange, in the south of France, at Aspendus, in Asia Minor, and at Sabratha, in Africa. The only theatre so far excavated in Britain, that at Verulamium (St. Albans), is of the 'cock-pit' type designed for gladiatorial and animal combats as well as for stage-shows. As many of these theatres were erected on sites where there was no natural slope to carry the tiers of seats, these were supported by masonry, through which passages led from outside to the orchestra or to a corridor at the top of the auditorium; thence, by means of flights of steps, each spectator could find his way to his place, assisted, perhaps, by the picture, name, and number on his ticket, of which numerous examples are extant. Meanwhile the *aulaeum* or drop-curtain, first mentioned by Cicero, had come into use. It was lowered at the beginning of the performance into a recess under the stage and raised at the end to conceal the stage from view. It seems that it was not until the second century A.D. that the curtain came to be operated in the modern manner, being raised to reveal and lowered to conceal the stage. We see in Apuleius, *Metamorphoses*, x. 29–34, how behind the curtain an elaborate scene could be built up on the stage. Over it was a wooden roof, protecting actors and scenery from the weather. The vast auditorium was also protected by means of coloured linen awnings attached to masts fixed in the enclosing wall. For the further comfort of spectators cooling artificial showers were sometimes provided, as we see in a public notice in Pompeii, which shows, incidentally, that the Romans knew the uses of the theatrical poster. In these vast, splendid, and luxurious theatres were staged the trivial shows of Imperial Rome, which, however magnificent, catered, it must be confessed, for a debased public taste (see also ACOUSTICS, 3).   W. B.

4. DECADENCE AND DESTRUCTION. To the other disintegrating factors working against the serious theatre in Imperial Rome was added the constant hostility of the Christian Church. No Christian could be an actor, under pain of excommunication, and all priests and devout persons refrained from attendance at theatrical performances of any kind. Tertullian in *De Spectaculis* urged the Christian to look for spectacle to the services of the Church, not perhaps foreseeing that he would later be taken literally. As far back as the Code of Theodosius, A.D. 435, public performances were forbidden on Sundays, a prohibition which still holds good in England, and in the sixth century the theatres in Europe were finally closed, the much-harassed actors being forced to rely on private hospitality, or take to the road. In Constantinople the rules were relaxed, possibly at the instance of the Empress Theodora, herself, according to contemporary gossip, an actress, and the government still considered the provision of actors and public performances as being among its duties. The theatre in the East perished in the Saracen invasions of the seventh and eighth centuries. In the West, in spite of a continued interest in drama as literature, an interest which St. Augustine in *Civitate Dei* upholds as a means of education, the theatre as organized entertainment vanished under the onslaught of the barbarians, who despised it. The last reference to it is in A.D. 533.

From then until the tenth century there was nothing but an undercurrent of itinerant mimes and acrobats (see MIME, 2 and MINSTREL), while the Church quietly absorbed pagan rites (see FOLK PLAY and MUMMING PLAY) into its own ritual, and unconsciously prepared the way for a revival of the theatre it had tried to suppress (see ECCLESIASTICAL DRAMA, and the separate countries of Europe).

ROPE HOUSE, the name given to a theatre which follows the traditional practice of working the scenery by lines from a fly-floor—also known as a Hand-worked House—as against the modern counterweight system (see ENGLISH PLAYHOUSE, 2 *a* and STAGE).

RORKE, KATE (1866–1945), English actress, a member of an old theatrical family. She made her first appearance at the Court Theatre under the management of Sir John Hare in 1878 as one of the school-children in *Olivia*, and in 1880 was engaged by Wyndham for the Criterion, where she remained for a considerable time, playing in a great variety of parts and growing in experience and popularity. In 1885 she made a great success as Lucy Preston in *The Silver Shield*. In 1889 she returned to Hare as his leading lady, and during her six years with him gave some fine performances, including Mrs. Goldfinch in *A Pair of Spectacles* (1890). A handsome and imposing woman, she was leading lady for many of the outstanding actor-managers of the day, including Tree, with whom she went to America, Alexander, Waller, and others. In 1906 she was appointed Professor of Dramatic Art at the Guildhall School of Music, and there trained a number of young players who afterwards became famous. As time went on she made fewer appearances on the professional stage, although she occasionally took part in gala performances. In 1917 she appeared in her old part when *A Pair of Spectacles* was revived at the New Theatre and Wyndham's. For many years she had her own school of acting, and was accounted one of the best instructors in dramatic art of her day.   w. m. p.

ROSCIUS, QUINTUS (?–62 B.C.), Roman comic actor, and the most famous of his day, liked and admired by Cicero, who delivered on his behalf the speech *Pro Roscio Comoedo*. Roscius's success was the result of careful study; he thought out and practised every gesture before employing it on the stage. He was awarded a gold ring, the symbol of equestrian rank, by the dictator Sulla. Pliny tells us that his yearly takings amounted to fifty million sesterces (half a million pounds in our money).   w. b.

For the American Roscius, see ALDRIDGE, IRA; for the Dublin, or Hibernian, Roscius, see BROOKE, G. V.; for the Ohio Roscius, see ALDRICH, LOUIS; for the Scottish Roscius, see JOHNSTON, H. E.; for the Young American Roscius, see COWELL (2); for the Young Roscius, see BETTY, WILLIAM.

ROSE TAVERN, see WILL'S COFFEE HOUSE.

ROSE THEATRE, LONDON. This owed its name to the fact that it stood in what had been a rose garden. It was built by one James Grigges, carpenter, for Henslowe and his partner, John Cholmley, citizen and grocer of London, and was probably opened at Michaelmas 1587. It is not known what company first played there, but five years later, after extensive repairs and alterations, Lord Strange's Men were there, followed by other companies until in 1594 the Admiral's Men settled there and stayed till their transfer in 1600 to the Fortune. It was at this theatre that Alleyn made his great reputation, and it is probable that the First Part of Shakespeare's *Henry VI* was given there. From Henslowe's accounts it can be inferred that the theatre was of wood and plaster on a brick foundation, partly thatched, and octagonal in shape. After 1600 various companies occupied the theatre until in 1605 Henslowe's lease ran out, and the building was deserted. It was pulled down some time before 1606.

ROSENBLÜT, HANS (*fl.* fifteenth century), a writer of German popular farces, who lived in Nuremberg and was probably a Mastersinger, like his contemporary Hans Folz (see GERMANY, 1).

ROSIMOND [CLAUDE LA ROZE] (*c.* 1640–86), a French actor who, after playing in the provinces and joining the Théâtre du Marais in 1668, was invited by the remnants of Molière's company to join them after the latter's death. This he did, playing as his first part Molière's role in *Le Malade imaginaire*. He was already known as a dramatist, and it may have been his double reputation that induced La Grange and his companions to look to him for a successor to Molière. If so, he proved a disappointment, as he produced only one more play, and that not a very successful one. He was an educated man, something of a scholar, and he had one of the finest libraries of plays in Paris. He was said to have been very intemperate and to have died of drink, but this was denied by Mlle Desmares, who had acted with him. His comedies were often revived during his lifetime, but are now forgotten. His play about Don Juan was the source of Shadwell's *The Libertine* (1675).

ROSSETER, PHILIP (*c.* 1575–1623), English musician, friend of Campion, who left him all his property, with the wish that it had been more. Rosseter became involved in theatrical affairs when he obtained a patent, with other musicians, to train the Children of the Revels. He was later associated in management with Henslowe, and was a lessee of Whitefriars. In 1615 he built a new playhouse in Blackfriars, known as Porter's Hall or Puddle Wharf Theatre, but it was never finished, for the civic authorities succeeded in having its licence taken away. After this Rosseter retired from the theatre, but continued as royal lutanist until his death.

ROSSI, ERNESTO FORTUNATO GIOVANNI MARIA (1827–96), Italian actor, at his best in tragedy. He was early enamoured of the stage, and at the age of 10 formed a company of children which played with some success in private houses. At 18 he made his début on the professional stage of Leghorn, his birthplace, in the troupe of Calloud. He later joined the company of Gustave Modena, and in 1852 was acting with the great Italian actress, Adelaide Ristori, with whom he went to Paris in 1855. He quickly proved himself a fine interpreter of the Italian classic tragedies, and of Shakespeare, being the first Italian actor to play *Othello* (in 1856), in the blank-verse translation by Carcano, following it with *Hamlet* in an early version by Rosconia. He was also good as Lear. He travelled widely, being much admired in Paris and Germany, and died while returning from a successful season in St. Petersburg. His method of interpreting Shakespeare was not, however, acceptable in England or America. In 1886 and 1888 he published two volumes of theatrical memoirs, and also translated *Julius Caesar* into Italian.

ROSTAND, EDMOND (1868–1918), French romantic dramatist, whose colourful poetic plays came as a relief after the drab realities of the naturalistic school. Born in Marseilles, he was a true son of the south, and his plays are full of colour and movement, with a saving grace of humour which usually redeems their sentimentality. His first play was a delicious satire on the aspirations of young lovers, *Les Romanesques* (1894), which was followed by the more serious but infinitely tender and lyrical *Princesse lointaine* (1895). A biblical play, *La Samaritaine* (1897), was less successful, but in *Cyrano de Bergerac* (1898), written for the elder Coquelin, Rostand achieved a wonderful fusion of romantic *bravura*, lyric love, and theatrical craftsmanship which has made his play a perennial favourite, both in France and in America and England, where something of its quality survives even a pedestrian translation. A later play, *L'Aiglon* (1900), in which Sarah Bernhardt played the ill-fated son of Napoleon, had less vigour, but appealed by its pathetic evocation of fallen grandeur, and the frank sentimentality of its theme. Rostand's last complete play—he died at 49 after years of ill health—was *Chantecler* (1910), which, though not as popular as his earlier works, is by some critics accounted his best, as it is certainly his most profound. The verse is masterly, and the allegory unfolds effortlessly on two planes of consciousness, the beast's and man's. A further play, *La Dernière Nuit de Don Juan*, was left unfinished, but indicates how much Rostand's undoubted talent might have matured had he been given longer in which to perfect it. The two plays by which he is best known are obviously youthful works, frankly romantic and sentimental, but they appealed to a public wearied by naturalism and somewhat disconcerted by symbolism. Their influence has not been obvious, nor has Rostand had many followers, but he made a valiant attempt to break through the meshes of the 'useful' and 'realistic' theatre and recapture the glamour and poetry of an earlier age.

ROSTRUM, any platform, from a small dais for a throne to a vast battlement, placed on the stage. It is usually made with a removable top and hinged sides, to fold flat for packing. It is reached by steps or a ramp, and quitted offstage by 'lead-off' steps. A rostrum-front is a canvas-covered flat placed to conceal the front of the platform.

ROSWITHA, see HROSWITHA.

ROTROU, JEAN (1609–50), French dramatist, and next to Corneille the best and most important of his day. He was only 19 when he had two plays produced at the Hôtel de Bourgogne, where he may have succeeded Hardy as official dramatist to the troupe. His work shows some originality and a true feeling for the theatre, and his popularity may be gauged from the fact that he had four plays given in Paris in 1636, the year of Corneille's *Le Cid*. More than thirty of his works survive, some of them the best examples extant of the popular tragi-comedy of the time. Rotrou was much interested in Spanish literature, and translated one of Lope de Vega's plays as *La Bague de l'oubli* (1629), important as being the first extant French play to be based on one from Spain. It was also the first French comedy, as

distinct from farce. Rotrou was the author of one of the numerous versions of the story of Amphitryon, which, as *Les Sosies*, is considered his best play. His *Venceslas* (1647), a tragedy based on a play by Francisco de Rojas, was sold to pay a gambling debt, and long remained in the repertory of the French theatre, providing an excellent part in Ladislas for such actors as Baron, Lekain, and Talma. Its first interpreter was probably Montfleury. Rotrou was a man of great charm and nobility of character, which endeared him even to his rivals. He loved Paris, but remained faithful to his native town of Dreux, where he held important municipal offices. He died during a plague in the city, having refused to relinquish his post and seek safety elsewhere.

ROTUNDA, LONDON, in Blackfriars Road. This was a museum and a concert hall, and in 1833 it was opened as a theatre—the Globe. It had an undistinguished career for about five years. At one time it was a music-hall, then a storehouse, and a centre for boxing. It was at length scheduled for demolition, reverting meanwhile to use as a warehouse.

ROUSSEAU, JEAN-BAPTISTE (1671–1741), French man of letters who wrote some comedies before being banished from France for the publishing of libellous verse. They were given at the Comédie-Française with some success. He also translated Machiavelli's *Mandragola*, and based a play on Ben Jonson's *Epicoene*. These two plays were apparently never acted. Rousseau was also responsible for the libretti of two operas.

ROUSSEAU, JEAN-JACQUES (1712–78), French philosopher and man of letters. He was the author of two light operas, of which 'Le Devin du village', containing many simple and charming songs, was a great success. Paradoxically—though perhaps it may be accounted for by his quarrel with Diderot—Rousseau in his *Lettre à d'Alembert contre les spectacles* (1758) opposed the favourite eighteenth-century view that the stage can be used for political and moral teaching, and declared that, being only intended for amusement, it is harmful and useless and should be suppressed. Incidentally, this may also be meant as an attack on Voltaire, whose passion for the theatre was well known. Yet, though no dramatist himself, Rousseau is important through the influence of his ideas on the drama, as well as on French and European literature in general.

ROWE, GEORGE FAWCETT (1834–89), American actor, who made his first appearance in New York, at the Olympic, in 1866, billed as 'from the London and Australian theatres'. Little is known of his early years, but he became popular in America, and for some time played young lovers, to which his fair, handsome, boyish face and elegant figure were eminently suited. In 1872 he made a great success as Digby Grant—Irving's part—in Albery's *Two Roses*, and later toured extensively in character parts. Among his best performances were Micawber in *Little Em'ly*, Waifton Stray in *Brass*, and Hawkeye in *Leatherstocking*, Rowe's own adaptation of *The Last of the Mohicans*. He was also responsible for the adaptation of Feuillet's *Sphinx* (1875), in which Clara Morris gave a powerful and horrifying performance.

ROWE, Nicholas (1674–1718), English dramatist of the Augustan age, and one of the few to display any real dramatic power. Of his seven tragedies, the early ones were written in a somewhat frigid neo-classic style, but his masterpieces, *The Fair Penitent* (1703) (based on Massinger's *The Fatal Dowry*) and *The Tragedy of Jane Shore* (1714), have genuinely moving and poetic passages, and both were frequently revived, Mrs. Siddons being particularly good in the parts first played by Mrs. Barry and Anne Oldfield respectively. Rowe, who was in love with the unresponsive Mrs. Bracegirdle, was also the author of *Tamerlane* (1701), in which Betterton was outstanding in the name-part, of *The Tragedy of Lady Jane Grey* (1715), and of one unsuccessful comedy. He was made Poet Laureate in 1715, published a translation of Lucan which was much admired by Dr. Johnson, and edited Shakespeare's plays in 1709, adding stage directions, act- and scene-divisions, and working to make the text less corrupt. He was not a great dramatist; he had many talents and a feeling for the theatre, but, either through his own weakness or because of the general decline of tragedy at the time, he failed to infuse his work with any vitality. The only one of his plays which has been revived in recent times is *Jane Shore*.

ROWLEY, Samuel (? –1624), English actor and dramatist, who is credited with having had a hand in a number of plays which preceded, and possibly provided material for, some of Shakespeare's, including *The Taming of a Shrew*. His only extant play is a chronicle drama on the life of Henry VIII, acted in 1603 by the Admiral's Men, *When You See Me, You Know Me*. He is believed to have revised Marlowe's *Dr. Faustus* for Henslowe in 1602, mainly by adding some comic passages. A number of lost plays were given by Palsgrave's Men in 1623–4, of whom Rowley, an actor of some repute, was a member, having joined the company in 1597 when it was known as the Admiral's, and remained with it under successive changes of patron.

ROWLEY, William (c. 1585–c. 1637), English actor and dramatist, whose best work was done in collaboration with Middleton, notably in *The Changeling* (1622). Of his own plays the most important is *All's Lost by Lust* (1622), in which he himself played the clown. He had previously played the fat clown, Plumporridge, in *The Inner Temple Masque* in 1619, as a foil to John Newton's thin clown, and was the fat bishop in Middleton's *A Game at Chess* (1624). Otherwise little is known of him, though he was at one time credited with colla-

boration with no less a person than Shakespeare in *The Birth of Merlin*. This, however, is now discredited, and Dekker, Middleton, Beaumont, and Fletcher have been suggested in the place of Shakespeare.

ROYAL ACADEMY OF DRAMATIC ART, London, see BARNES, SIR KENNETH.

ROYAL ALFRED THEATRE, London, see WEST LONDON THEATRE.

ROYAL BOROUGH THEATRE, London, in Tooley Street. This was used between 1834–6, and then pulled down, as the land on which it stood was required by a railway company.

ROYAL BOX, see AUDITORIUM and BOX.

ROYAL CIRCUS, London, see SURREY THEATRE.

ROYAL COURT THEATRE, London, see COURT THEATRE.

ROYAL ENGLISH OPERA HOUSE, London, see PALACE THEATRE.

ROYAL GROVE, London, see ASTLEY'S AMPHITHEATRE.

ROYAL ITALIAN OPERA HOUSE, London, see QUEEN'S THEATRE (1).

ROYAL KENT THEATRE, London. This stood in High Street, South Kensington, between 1834 and 1840. It held only about 250 people, but had a Royal Entrance down a back court, though there is no evidence that it was ever used. Brown, a well-known comedian of the time, played there, as did Wyatt, brother of G. A. Sala. It was at the Royal Kent that Bunn saw Denvil and engaged him to play Manfred at Drury Lane. The theatre took its name from the Duke of Kent, who gave it his patronage.

            W. M. P.

ROYAL MANOR HOUSE THEATRE, London, stood in the King's Road, Chelsea, from 1838 to about 1841. It was for a time under the management of E. L. Blanchard, but otherwise little is known about it.

ROYAL PANTHEON THEATRE, London. This was a small nineteenth-century playhouse in Catherine Street, Strand, known also as Jessop's Hall, and the Little Catherine Street Theatre. It was used chiefly by amateurs, many of whom afterwards became professionals. It was possible here, as at other minor theatres, such as the King's Cross, to purchase the privilege of playing principal parts. Henry Neville is said to have appeared at this theatre in his early days, and Mrs. Sumbel Wells, a well-known actress, gave imitations of Mrs. Siddons there. The site of the theatre was incorporated in the Aldwych rebuilding scheme. Its exact location is uncertain, but it stood somewhere near the second Gaiety Theatre. W. M. P.

ROYAL STANDARD THEATRE, LON-
DON, see STANDARD THEATRE (1).

ROYAL SUSSEX THEATRE, LONDON,
see WEST LONDON THEATRE.

ROYAL VICTORIA HALL, LONDON, see
OLD VIC.

ROYALE THEATRE, NEW YORK. Built by
the Chanins on West 45th Street, this opened
on 11 Jan. 1927 with a musical comedy,
followed by further musical shows, and by
Winthrop Ames's productions of Gilbert and
Sullivan. In 1928 came Mae West in *Diamond
Lil*, which ran for nearly a year, and in 1933
Both Your Houses, a Pulitzer Prize-winner
sponsored by the Theatre Guild. The controversial *They Shall Not Die*, based on the
Scottsboro case, with a distinguished cast and
settings by Lee Simonson, was seen at this
theatre in 1934, while in the autumn of the
same year the theatre was renamed the Golden,
and presented a series of moderately successful
comedies. From 1936 to 1940 it was used for
broadcasting, but then returned to drama
under its old name.   G. F.

ROYALTY. The custom of paying a dramatist a royalty, or small percentage of the receipts, for every night his play is performed is
of comparatively recent origin. In Elizabethan
times plays were either bought outright, as can
be seen from Henslowe's accounts, or formed,
as with Shakespeare, part of the stock-in-trade
of the co-operative society of which the author
was a member, and from which he drew moneys
under various headings. For the printing of
plays the publisher sometimes, though not
always, paid a small sum down, but the practice of printing the text of plays was not encouraged, as they could then be played freely by
companies other than that to which the manuscript belonged. Conditions under the Restoration were much the same, in that the
dramatist received very little for his work, and
that only at the whim of the management.
The system of patronage was universal, and a
needy author—it should be remembered that
many Restoration dramatists were men of substance or had other, less chancy, sources of
income—might be given the entire profits of a
benefit night; but it was not until the second
half of the eighteenth century that a playwright
could expect to live on the proceeds of his
works. Thus, for instance, Dr. Johnson and
Oliver Goldsmith were given the proceeds of
the third, sixth, and ninth nights of *Irene*
(1748) and *The Good-Natured Man* (1768)
respectively. From scattered references in the
period it seems that the third night was traditionally the author's night. With only two or
three playhouses, a small audience, and consequently a continual change of bill, many plays
failed to achieve even three nights. Towards
the end of the eighteenth century—by which
time Beaumarchais had established the royalty
system in France—a return was made to the

custom of buying plays outright, Morton
receiving a thousand pounds for one of his
comedies, and Mrs. Inchbald eight hundred
for *Wives as they Were, and Maids as they Are*
(1797). By this time reputable publishers were
also willing to pay several hundred pounds for
the right to publish a play, a custom by this
time almost universal, and this, in spite of
piracies, added considerably to a dramatist's
income.

With the nineteenth century the prestige,
and consequently the money-value, of the
dramatist declined sharply. The lightest farces
and musical pieces earned the most money,
and even that was very little when mounting
costs and the expense of the star system involved managers in heavier outlays. This led
to an enormous amount of hack-work at pitiable
prices, and may help to explain the constant
stream of thefts, plagiarisms, and adaptations
from French and German sources which
flooded the English stage at its worst period.

The first movement to secure proper recognition of authorship was made by Planché, and
it was mainly due to his efforts that the Copyright Bill of 1832 was passed, and the Dramatic
Authors' Society formed. This, however, only
gave protection to plays written after 1833, and
the copyright of plays printed before that date
remained the property of the publisher and not
the author. It was also extremely difficult to
collect acting fees from provincial managements, and from America, and cases are on
record of actors attending a theatre, memorizing
a play, and reproducing it without payment
(see FLORENCE and HOLCROFT).

Apparently the first English dramatist to
receive a royalty, or at any rate a definite share
in the profits irrespective of what they might
be, was Boucicault, who had for some years
been receiving roughly £100 down for each
new play, and in 1860 suggested to Webster
that for his next play, in which he and his wife
were as usual appearing in the leading parts,
he should, as author, be given a fixed percentage of the takings. The play in question being
either *The Colleen Bawn* or *The Octoroon*—
accounts vary; but the new method netted
Boucicault some £10,000, and the more astute
of his fellow authors were quick to follow his
example. The American critic, William Winter, says that the first play in America to be
paid for on this system was Belasco's *Valerie*
(1886), written for Lester Wallack, but as the
author received a flat rate of 250 dollars a week,
that was not a royalty in the generally accepted
sense—though a great advance on the £2 or
£3 a night that some authors in England were
still accepting at this time. By degrees the
standard rate of royalty became 5 to 10 per
cent., rising perhaps to 20 per cent. in the case
of established dramatists, while piracy was
finally checked by the International Copyright
Agreement of 1887 and the American Copyright Bill of 1891. These made it possible for
the author to enjoy the additional income
derived from publication without at the same
time losing his acting fees.

ROYALTY THEATRE, LONDON. (1) In 1787 John Palmer, of Drury Lane Theatre, with another actor named Lee Lewes, erected a theatre in Wells Street, Wellclose Square in East London, and engaged Quick, Ryder, Bannister, Mrs. Johnson, and Mrs. Gibbs for it. They appeared to be under the impression that the Lieutenant of the Tower of London and the magistrates of Tower Hamlets had the power to grant them a licence, and had announced the opening before they discovered their mistake. Drury Lane and Covent Garden threatened them with penalties, but on 20 June 1787 the Royalty, as the theatre was named, gave *As You Like It*, though with a much weaker company than had originally been intended. There was a minor riot, probably inspired by the Patent Theatres, and the theatre closed until 3 July. Palmer was summoned before the local magistrates to produce his licence, and could not do so, although he tried every subterfuge. He was arrested but released on bail, and subsequently rejoined the Drury Lane company. In 1788 Macready, father of the great tragedian, got permission from the Lord Chamberlain to do burlettas and pantomimes at the Royalty, but with little success. The theatre led a precarious existence for a long time. In 1810 it was known as the East London, and in 1826 was burned down, but rebuilt and reopened in 1828 as the Brunswick. So badly was it constructed that on 28 Feb., three days after the opening, it collapsed while the company was rehearsing *Guy Mannering*, killing fifteen people and injuring twenty.

(2) The New Royalty, originally Miss Kelly's Theatre, was an offshoot of her school of acting in Dean Street, Soho. An engineer named Stevenson had interested her in an invention of his whereby stage and scenery could be worked by machinery. By a series of wheels and cogs, scenes were to be altered, and even the stage raised and lowered. A complete revolution of stage technique was expected. The new playhouse opened on 25 Mar. 1840, with a drama called *Summer and Winter*; but the machinery proved a failure. The hopeful engineer had said that it could be worked by one man, but a test proved that a horse was necessary. The theatre was so small that the tramping of the horse and the roar of the machinery not only drowned the voices of the actors but made the building vibrate so that everything in it, including the audience, shook like a jelly. The result was that the theatre had to be closed after five nights, and the building almost pulled down before the machinery could be removed. Miss Kelly endeavoured to reopen, but without success, and she retired for good. In 1850 a new management opened the theatre as the New English Opera House, perhaps the most ominous title which can be given to an English theatre, and the whole scheme failed. As the New Royalty, the theatre opened again in 1861, under the direction of Mrs. Selby, who, like Miss Kelly, ran a school of acting. The theatre was mainly used for performances by her pupils, one of whom, Ada Cavendish,

became famous. In 1862 Charles Wyndham made his London début at this theatre, as did Adelaide Neilson in 1865, playing Juliet with immediate success. *Trial by Jury* was staged in 1875, and *Crutch and Toothpick* was a success in 1881. In 1883 Kate Stanley took over the theatre, reconstructed it, and ran comic opera. For some years there was an annual season of French plays. An important event in 1891 was the first performance in English of Ibsen's *Ghosts*, while in the following year *Charley's Aunt* began its non-stop run at the Royalty, and *Widowers' Houses* was produced there by the Independent Theatre. In 1900 Mrs. Patrick Campbell redecorated the theatre, and with herself as actress-manageress staged a number of plays, including *Magda*, *The Fantasticks*, *Pelleas and Melisande*, and Bjørnson's *Beyond Human Power*. The management which brought most repute to the theatre was that of J. E. Vedrenne and Dennis Eadie. The former had already done splendid work at the Court with Granville-Barker, and, with Eadie, a fine actor, produced such plays as *Milestones* and *The Man who Stayed at Home*. Among the younger players encouraged by this management may be mentioned Owen Nares and Gladys Cooper. After this, the Royalty had no settled policy. *The Co-Optimists*, under Archie de Bear, began its career there in 1921. The theatre still stands.   W. M. P.

RUCELLAI, GIOVANNI (1475–1525), Italian dramatist of the Renaissance, whose *Oreste* (c. 1514) and *Rosmunda* (1516) are tragedies constructed on the Greek model, as laid down by Trissino. The second is taken from Gothic history, while the first, on a classical theme, seems to owe something to the *Iphigenia in Tauris* of Euripides.

RUEDA, LOPE DE (1510–65), Spain's first actor-manager and popular dramatist. A goldsmith by trade, he forsook his workshop for the theatre. He gathered together a company which he led himself, and wrote mainly for them and for the popular audiences before which they appeared in the big towns of Spain. In contrast to the more sophisticated playwrights of Court and college, he wrote in prose, and was more influenced by the Italian *commedia dell'arte* than by his contemporaries. His dialogue is natural, easy, and idiomatic, with a strong sense of the ridiculous and a happy satirizing of the manners of his day. His main purpose was to amuse, and in this he seems to have succeeded admirably. Cervantes speaks of him as 'a brilliant actor and a man of sound sense'. He was the originator of the *paso*, or one-act prose incident (such as *Las Aceitunas*, the best one-act play written in Spain in the sixteenth century), which was later introduced into longer plays, though extraneous in subject. One of his plays, *Eufemia*, turns on the 'point of honour' later so important in the Spanish theatre. Rueda's four vigorous comedies anticipate Lope de Vega. One of them, *Los engañados*, is drawn from the same Italian source as

Shakespeare's *Twelfth Night*. Witty and entertaining, Rueda had a great influence on the Spanish theatre, which was considered by Cervantes and Lope de Vega to have truly begun with him.

RUGGLE, GEORGE (1575–1622), a scholar of Cambridge who in 1615 wrote a satire on the lawyers, *Ignoramus,* partly in English and partly in Latin. This was seen by James I on a visit to the town, and so pleased him that he made another visit to see it again a week later. The play is based to a great extent on the *Trappolaria* (1596) of Della Porta, but the chief part is a satire of the then Cambridge recorder, Francis Brackyn. Ruggle is believed to have written two other comedies played at the University.

RUNDHORIZONT, see LIGHTING, 1 *d.*

RUSHTON, LUCY, see NEW YORK THEATRE (1).

RUSSELL, ANNIE (1864–1936), American actress, who was on the stage as a child and after touring South America and the West Indies in a juvenile opera company, returned to New York to make a big success in the name-part of *Esmeralda* (1881). At the height of her subsequent popularity she was forced to retire from the stage through illness, but in 1894 she returned, playing in a number of new plays, among them *Sue,* in which she was also seen in London for the first time in 1898. On a subsequent visit in 1905 she appeared at the Court Theatre under the Barker–Vedrenne management as the heroine of *Major Barbara*. She had essayed several Shakespearian parts before in 1912 she organized an Old English Comedy Company, for which she played Kate Hardcastle, Beatrice, and Lydia Languish, later appearing as Lady Teazle in a revival of *The School for Scandal*. She retired in 1918.

RUSSELL, LILLIAN (1861–1922), American actress and singer, whose real name was Helen Louise Leonard. A beautiful woman, both in face and figure, with a vivid and flamboyant personality, she made her first appearance at Tony Pastor's Theatre in 1881, soon made a name for herself in burlesque and light opera, and was nicknamed 'The American Beauty'. She was four times married.

RUSSELL, SOL SMITH (1848–1902), American actor, who was on the stage at the age of 12. He was for a time in Daly's company, and also toured America with a company of his own, one of his most successful productions being *A Poor Relation* (1888). He was also good in *A Bachelor's Romance,* by Martha Morton.

RUSSIA. 1. PRE-SOVIET. (*a*) *Up to the Seventeenth Century*. Compared with the rest of Europe the Russian theatre had a late start, and its early history is mainly that of a struggle for the establishment of a national art in the face of competition from imported and experienced foreign companies, usually German or French. These companies, few of which

remained for any length of time, were supported by the authorities, who considered, no doubt correctly, that a stable national theatre would prove too great a threat to their security.

The causes for the late development of the Russian, as opposed to the European, theatre were many and various, and included in early times the hostility of the Church, later the iron hand of absolutism, the almost complete illiteracy of the bulk of the population, and the neglect of the Russian language among the nobility. Yet there must have been in Russia, as elsewhere, from the very earliest times, nomadic entertainers, jesters, clowns, buffoons, and puppet-masters, who played musical instruments, and sang or recited ancient historical ballads and tales. They were a necessary part of every holiday gathering, especially at such religious festivals as Christmas and Easter, at carnivals and at weddings. The varied nature of such of their performances as have been recorded shows not only the primitiveness of their art, but also the way in which they adapted it to suit their audiences. Jesters belonging to the feudal nobility praised the deeds of their patron and his ancestors; those attached to religious bodies served in the ritual and ceremonies of the Church; while the wandering entertainers of the country fairs were often accompanied by performing animals, particularly bears, and indulged in little but rough farce and horseplay, or gave their crude puppet-shows in hastily erected booths.

But these sporadic amusements cannot be said to constitute a theatre. That might have come, as it did elsewhere, through the Church. Ecclesiastical drama certainly made its way into Russia from Byzantium, and later, in the sixteenth and seventeenth centuries, was a powerful weapon in the struggle against Roman Catholicism; but it never became so widespread or so highly developed as in western Europe, nor did it prove, as there, the forerunner of a national drama. It constituted a transitional episode in the history of Russian civilization, and passed without leaving a trace. The origin of the Russian theatre must be looked for elsewhere.

The nomadic entertainers, who had been, in the eleventh century, if not encouraged at least countenanced by the Church, were, from the fourteenth century onwards, severely treated and forced to go underground. They formed themselves into bands and wandered from village to village, from fair to fair, earning a living when they could by their art, and when they could not, by thieving. Deprived of the protection of Church and nobility, they were driven out of Muscovy—the then very limited area actually ruled by the Moscow Dukes—and eventually settled in the North, where whole villages of these strolling players were to be found. They were, however, made use of by the Moscow Tsars in their struggle with the Church, and Ivan the Terrible had the Archbishop led through the streets dressed as a clown. He also employed professional entertainers at royal weddings, and at carnival time, when, it is said, he himself danced in a masquerade, 'along with the clowns'; but whether these were real clowns, or merely a means of insulting his enemies by comparing them with clowns, is not known.

(b) *Seventeenth Century*. There is no information available regarding Tsarist amusements in later times, but it seems most likely that during the period of reaction under Boris there were none, while the so-called 'Time of the Troubles' left little leisure for play-acting. As soon as the country had recovered, however, and the first Romanov became Tsar in 1613, a 'house of amusement' was built by royal command. Since 'amusement' in the seventeenth century was synonymous with 'theatre', and since the Russian strolling entertainers are known to have played only a very secondary role, the chief actors at this first Russian theatre were experienced foreigners, most probably Germans. It is, however, significant that at the wedding celebrations of the Tsar in 1626 the traditional church choir was replaced by a company of Russian nomadic entertainers, and this example was followed by the leading nobles of the Court. Thus, by an ironic twist of fortune, the jesters, who in the sixteenth century had been forced into the remote country-side, in the first half of the seventeenth century found themselves installed in the palaces of the Tsar and his courtiers. Their triumph, however, was short-lived, for in 1648 a decree of the Tsar Alexis, then in a reactionary mood, forbade all types of worldly amusement, ordered all musical instruments and other theatrical properties to be broken and burnt, and anyone found making use of them to be severely punished. Jesters once more disappeared from Court, and at Alexis's wedding the traditional church choir again replaced secular music and play-acting.

Meanwhile, away from the Court, School Drama, as in Europe, was coming into being. The events of the 'Time of the Troubles' had brought Russia into conflict with the West, particularly with the Jesuits who sought to convert the Russians to Roman Catholicism. It was necessary for the Russian Church to defend itself and its dogmas, and, for this, education and training in theology were essential. In the early part of the seventeenth century Russian theological schools were founded on the lines of existing Jesuit schools in Europe, while the first Latin academy on the western pattern was established in 1632.

The Jesuits had long used the theatre as a means of instruction and propaganda (see JESUIT DRAMA) and Russian churchmen realized that they must do the same. The plays they gave appear to have been entirely medieval in character, and the subjects were taken either from the Bible or from Jesuit plays, translated and adapted into Russian from Polish. Later, as the students inevitably took control of the acting, local farcical elements crept in, and new plays by Russian authors made their appearance. One of the earliest-known writers of Russian School Drama was Simon Polotsky (1629–80), who in 1664 became tutor to the

Tsar's sons, and produced two plays, of which one, based on the story of the prodigal son, shows a great advance in characterization and dramatic action on the purely scholastic exercises that had preceded it.

It was at about this time that the secular theatre again reared its head in the Russian Court. The Tsar, reversing his former attitude towards the theatre under the influence of his journeys in Poland and his Anglophile second wife, sought to bring his Court in line with the brilliance of western European Courts, and realized that for this a flourishing Court theatre was necessary. A play was planned as part of the celebrations for the birth of a royal infant (later Peter the Great) in 1672, and an envoy was sent abroad to recruit actors. He was unsuccessful. Russia was a distant and almost unknown country, and few actors were willing to risk the journey. In this quandary Court officials looked to the 'free' German quarter of Moscow, where plays had not been banned, and where, as early as 1664, the English Ambassador of Charles II was present at a comedy, unfortunately not specified. It would be interesting to know what was in the German repertory at this time; possibly the plays imported into Germany by the English Comedians, for when a young German priest, Johann Gottfried Gregory, was given a group of untrained children and told to produce a play at short notice, he and his assistant Rinhuber cast their minds back to the plays which had been in vogue when they left Germany, and wrote a tragi-comedy of Ahasuerus and Esther based on the play included in the 1620 repertory of the English Comedians (see ENGLISH COMEDIANS, GERMANY, and PURIM PLAYS). This, at least, is surmised by B. Malnick (see Slavonic Year-Book, Vol. XIX: *The Origin and Early History of the Theatre in Russia*), who points out that later plays given under Gregory's tuition included one on Judith, from the same source, and one on Tamberlaine, distantly related to Marlowe's, written by Georg Huebner, Gregory's assistant.

Gregory's first actors were probably German children, who played in Russian and German in a hastily constructed wooden theatre lit by candles. A central seat was provided for the Tsar, while the rest of the audience sat on wooden benches. Incidental music was provided, also scenery—perspectives by the Dutch painter Engles—and elaborate costumes. The first performance was a success, in spite of the young actors' difficulties with the Russian language, which was later avoided by handing over Russian children to be trained by Gregory. They too were a success, and both theatre and theatrical school were in a flourishing condition when in Feb. 1675 Gregory died. His place was taken by Huebner, who tended to sharpen the secular development of the Court play, away from the biblical subjects which had lent themselves so admirably to Imperialist propaganda. For example, the story of Esther had been represented as the struggle of the absolute monarch to retain his autocracy, and that of

Judith had been preceded by a prologue emphasizing the autocratic dominion of the Tsar over the whole of Russia. Huebner therefore proved unacceptable to the reactionary party, and was dismissed in Dec. 1675, being replaced by Stepan Chizinsky, a former teacher of Latin in a Russian theological college, and author of two plays, one biblical, on the story of David and Goliath, one a secular trifle from Greek mythology, both of which are lost.

With the death of Alexis in 1676 the theatre was closed, the building which had housed it was cleared and all its appurtenances thrown out; and the century which had seen a tentative beginning of a Court, though not a national, theatre in Russia ended in the complete disintegration of all that had been accomplished.

(c) *Eighteenth Century*. When, under Peter the Great, a return was made to more liberal ideas, the work of Gregory and his assistants had all to be done again. A Hungarian puppet-master, Ivan Splavsky, was sent from Moscow to Danzig to hire a troupe of actors, one of the requirements being that they should speak Russian. However, the company that eventually came, led by Johann Kunst, described as 'an eminent master of theatrical science', could play only in German, so Kunst, like Gregory before him, was given a group of Russian youths to instruct. Peter the Great, who intended to use his new theatre more for political propaganda than for amusement, immediately instructed Kunst to write a play dealing with one of his recent victories, and built the first public theatre in Russia—in the Red Square—for it to be performed in. Kunst was quite willing to obey instructions, but for some reason the play was never written, and a year later he died. One of his company, Bendler, carried on his work, and was later replaced by Otto First, but neither of them was successful with the Russian students, and the theatre, which had been a continual expense, was disbanded in 1707. Peter had intended to make it a public institution, and for this purpose had issued a special decree encouraging people, especially foreigners, to attend. On days of performance, for instance, certain gates of the city were kept open till 9 o'clock, and no toll was levied. The price of admission to the theatre was the equivalent of a few pence, and according to contemporary figures, the average attendance was 124, though during the summer festivals it rose to as much as 400.

Peter the Great's attempts to establish a popular theatre for his own purposes having been thus frustrated, drama, particularly the spectacular ballet and opera, became once more the prerogative of Court circles. The Tsar's sister had her own private theatre, and wrote a number of plays herself, some based on old Russian legends. These filtered down to the people eventually through the bands of wandering students and apprentices who intermittently gave shows in improvised barn-theatres and public places.

Meanwhile the School Drama flourished quietly, and in 1702 the Moscow Religious Academy produced a panegyric play on the Second Coming, an allegory which eulogized Peter the Great in his struggle against Sweden, and was mainly directed against the Poles for their refusal to aid Russia. A further play of the same kind was projected for the Tsar's birthday, but had to be postponed because he was at the front. It was produced, however, with suitable alterations, when he returned victorious, and was followed in the course of the next few years by similar plays dealing allegorically with contemporary political events.

An attempt was made at this time, by Feofan Prokopovich (1681–1736), an ardent adherent of the reforms of Peter the Great, to found a secular, as distinct from an ecclesiastical, School Drama, similar to that which had flourished in many great scholastic establishments of the West. He produced a tragicomedy, played in 1705 in the theatre in the Red Square, which was based on a Russian historical theme. This shows a prince of Kiev who completely changes the life of his people by his acceptance of Christianity. The three heathen priests who oppose his reforms are thinly veiled caricatures of the worst type of contemporary Russian clergy, who opposed the reforms of Peter the Great, typified by the hero, Vladimir. This play, which is quite unlike anything which had preceded it, shows some psychological insight and is written in a style which is, for its period, brilliantly realistic. Prokopovich's experiment was, however, destined to fail, and after a period of further subjugation, Russian School Drama manifested a new spirit when it began to introduce a larger comic and peasant element into the interludes. This at times overshadowed the more orthodox main theme, and a national peasant drama might have evolved had conditions been more favourable. But the dead weight of authority, and the popularity of foreign actors, added to the rigid moral and educational purpose of the School Drama, alien to the spirit of an age and Court which sought only amusement, combined to stifle it; and after a last splendid effort at panegyric plays for the coronation of the Empress Elizaveta Petrovna in 1742, the Russian School Drama disappeared. It had served a useful purpose. It had given its exponents experience in the writing and producing of plays, and in the mechanics of stagecraft and acting, and something of its tradition lingered on into the next century, particularly among students and enthusiasts in remote places. In this way it brought its small contribution to the main stream of Russian culture which was to produce so sudden and glorious a theatrical flowering. Some of the comic interludes of the School Drama remained in the repertory of the puppet theatres when its more serious themes had been forgotten.

With the death of Peter the Great in 1725 the official Court theatre languished, to revive on the accession of Anna in 1730. First came several visiting Italian *commedia dell'arte* companies, who gave elaborate pantomimic performances with a lavish use of machinery and incidental music. There were still no Russian actors, however, though this period saw the establishment of the Imperial School of Ballet, and the development of a school of Russian singers in the Italian style. In 1740 the Italian actors were replaced by a German company under Caroline Neuber, and for the first time the Russian Court made the acquaintance of the neo-classical acting and plays of western Europe. This polished literary drama might have found favour, but the death of Anna in 1741 caused the dismissal of the company. It was replaced two years later by a French company with a repertory of comedies by Molière, Regnard, Destouches, and La Chaussée, varied by the tragedies of Voltaire. This company remained in Russia for fifteen years, and had a great influence. French became the fashionable language of the Court, completely ousting German, and when eventually Russia produced some professional actors they owed a great deal to the French tradition.

For the time was coming when the Russian theatre as a social force, and not as a mere adjunct of Church or State, could no longer be suppressed. It arose in connexion with the formation of a Court intelligentsia, and the increasing power of the bourgeoisie. In 1732 a Cadet College had been founded for the education of the sons of the nobility. It aimed primarily at a military training, but the curriculum embraced also theology and poetics, self-defence and deportment, riding, fencing, and dancing, music, recitation, sculpture, and miniature-painting. The foundation of this institute may be regarded as the starting-point of Russian national drama. The cadets, who had already been employed in Court festivities, and had given the necessary impetus to the founding of the Imperial School of Ballet, now founded a Society of Lovers of Russian Literature. One of its members was Alexei Petrovich Sumarokov (1718–77), the first great Russian dramatist, whose tragedy *Khorev* was performed by the cadets in 1749. Three other plays followed, and soon the cadets were summoned to Court to play before the Empress Elizabeth.

Sumarokov, whose plays were the first outstanding dramatic contribution to Russian literature, wrote in the neo-classical style imported from Europe, particularly from France. His works are distinguished by their economy of expression; he used few characters, and the epic speeches of his heroes have great dramatic quality. He fought hard to establish a truly national theatre, and to purge the Russian literary language of gallicisms. Seven of his nine tragedies deal with Russian history, mainly in the period which saw the establishment of Russian feudalism.

Sumarokov's plays, however, would have been of little use without actors to interpret them, and it was here that the long tradition of the School Drama came in useful. The cadets who had first performed in *Khorev* were, and remained, amateurs; the Court singers whom

Elizabeth sent to the college to be trained as actors were not strong enough in numbers or talent to found a theatre; but in the provincial town of Yaroslavl, from about 1750 onwards, a good company of amateurs, headed by two brothers named Volkov, had given performances, probably of adapted School Dramas, whose excellence was brought to the notice of the Empress. She summoned them to Court, where they gave a Morality play, repeating it for the general public in the theatre which had been used by Caroline Neuber. Feodor Volkov (1729–63), and another member of the company, Ivan Dmitrevsky (1734–1821), were chosen to go to the Cadet College, and later appeared in a performance at Court of Sumarokov's *Sinav and Truvor* (1755). Other students, including women, joined the company, and by 1757 they had been given a Court subsidy—negligible compared with that of the French and Italian companies, but at least a sign of official recognition—and permission to perform once a week in the Opera House. The cadets then ceased to appear on the stage, and the first Russian professional theatrical company came into being. It was State-subsidized and State-controlled, and was destined to remain for a long time a tool in the hands of authority. Its repertory, which as time went on included some Russian plays, was nevertheless composed entirely of pieces acceptable to the existing régime, and the few liberal ideas of the eighteenth century which found their way into the theatre were severely dealt with. The main influences were those of the French *comédie larmoyante* and the German realistic bourgeois tragedy. Comedies and light operas, many of them based on scenes of village life, were numerous, but none of them are worth more than a mention. Superficial, charming, and tuneful, they served to pass the time, as did the plays of the Empress Catherine herself —comedies based on Russian folk-lore and fairy tales, or historical scenes in the style of Shakespeare which show a break with the neo-classic tradition. Almost the only dramatist of any importance in this period was Denis Ivanovich Fonvizin (1744–92), whose play *The Minor*, first produced in 1782, and considered by Gorky to be his best, still remains popular in present-day repertories.

(d) *Nineteenth Century.* Before the end of the nineteenth century Russia was destined to produce a body of dramatic literature second to none in Europe, and actors whose traditions were to be an inspiration to their successors. But little of this was apparent in the early years. The first plays seen then were translations of Racine and Corneille, or native imitations of French tragedies. The only writer of any importance was Vladislav Alexandrovich Ozerov (1770–1816), whose heroes, ranging from Oedipus to Ossian, were all cast in the sublime mould, while his study of a Russian hero, Dmitry Donskoy, was intended not as a truthful picture of the past, but as a panegyric of his own autocratic monarch. Modern problems and contemporary life had as yet no place on the Imperial stage, which the Tsar Nicholas I had recently brought into line with other official organizations by arrogating to himself, as head of the Third Department (the Secret Police), the supervision of the repertory, and the distribution of roles among the actors. There were at this time two theatres in St. Petersburg, both Imperial—the Bolshoy (or Great), built in the seventeenth century, and the Maly (or Little), formerly a private theatre. These should not be confused with the theatres of the same names in present-day Moscow, nor should the name Bolshoy be linked with Bolshevik. There were theatres of that name long before the present régime was established in Russia.

The St. Petersburg Bolshoy Theatre was used mainly for ballet and opera, the Maly for drama. To them was added a third, the Youth Theatre, built by the dramatist-prince, Alexander Alexandrovich Shakhovsky (1777–1846), where light comedy was played, mainly by graduates of the Government Theatrical School. This latter establishment had been founded with the idea of educating the children of officials and the bourgeoisie, and of using the theatre as a direct means of political propaganda. There was also in St. Petersburg at this time a circus in which dramatic performances were sometimes given. In Moscow the theatres were crowded into various buildings, since the Bolshoy there had been burnt down in 1805, at the time of the Napoleonic invasion. It was later rebuilt, and in 1824 the Moscow Maly was re-housed in a converted private house.

Two popular but otherwise unimportant dramatists who emerged under the supervision of the Tsar were Kukolnik and Polevoy. The former began his career in 1833 with a play on the life of Tasso, an unsuccessful attempt to establish in Russia the new romanticism which was sweeping over Europe. A year later, probably after some pressure had been applied by the Secret Police, he concocted a patriotic drama dealing with the saving of Moscow by Minin and Pozharsky, and the election of a Romanov to the throne. This play made Kukolnik famous, and he continued to write in the same strain, adapting foreign plays, or writing to order topical dramas which gave all the characters a chance to assert their loyalty to the Tsar.

Polevoy, another opportunist, became a dramatist late in life. He was a merchant of Siberia who turned literary critic, and in his journal dared to criticize the plays of Kukolnik. As a result the paper was suppressed, and Polevoy was advised to employ his talents elsewhere. He turned to the theatre, and in 1837 produced a romantic drama, following it with a series of patriotic plays which earned the approbation of the Tsar and the Third Department.

Apart from patriotic plays, which many considered the invention of Nicholas I himself, melodrama, both imported and home-made, was flourishing. Critics denounced it as lacking in any aesthetic value, and harmful in its moral influence; but the Tsar encouraged it, as offering 'an emotional lightning-conductor which grounded the energy of social protest'. All that was necessary, in the case of imported melodrama, was to make it 'safe'. How this was done is shown by the handling of a dramatized version of *Notre-Dame de Paris*. Instead of Notre-Dame, the décor showed the Antwerp Town Hall. The clerical characters became laymen, and the dissolute young rake was transformed into a moral and platonic lover.

Meanwhile Nicholas I safeguarded himself against criticism by issuing decrees which laid down minute instructions for the guidance of dramatic critics. They must be 'moderate and well-intentioned, restrained in criticizing artists, remembering that they are in the royal service'. In spite of this, such men as the redoubtable Belinsky savagely criticized the plays, the authors, and the actors. The Tsar, tired of trying to muzzle him, at last ordered his arrest and exile, but Belinsky cheated him at the last moment by dying before the police came for him.

The tradition of Russian acting, begun by Volkov and his associates, was upheld at this time by two very different men—Vasily Andreyevich Karatygin (1802–53) and Pavel Stepanovich Mochalov (1800–48). The former represented the official romanticism of the Court bureaucratic circles, while the latter portrayed the rebellious romanticism of the bourgeoisie. Karatygin, who had an expressive face and a fine voice and figure, was eminently suited to tragic parts. His acting was worked out to the last detail, and Shchepkin, an eminent contemporary critic, said of him that he 'appeared in uniform, buttoned up to the last button, acting on the stage as if on parade'. He was a master of stage effects, his make-up, costume, and movements were carefully studied, and Belinsky said, 'When I saw him act my whole being was shaken.' Mochalov, on the other hand, was an emotional, romantic actor, who began his career in sentimental drama. One of his best roles in his early days was that of Meinau in *Menschenhass und Reue*, and by the force of his acting he raised melodrama to the heights. According to Belinsky again, his best part was that of Hamlet, to whom he imparted less melancholy and gloom than was then usual, replacing them by strength and energy.

The political role which the theatre was called on to play under the Tsar Nicholas I demanded suitable premises. The former Maly Theatre of St. Petersburg could no longer accommodate its audience, so the larger and more imposing Alexandrinsky Theatre was built in 1832. This was the home of drama, intended for the delight and education of the bourgeoisie. From its stage came the resonant voice of Karatygin in the patriotic monologues of Kukolnik and Polevoy, while the Bolshoy Theatre continued to put on ballet and opera, mainly for Court circles. In Moscow, the Maly Theatre, famous as the home of dramatic spectacles, resounded to the emotional tirades of Mochalov. But the theatre was no longer confined to the two capitals. This period of Russian theatrical history is characterized by a great increase in the number of playhouses in the provinces. Formerly they had been part of the feudal or landed estates, and had belonged —both building and actors—to the prince or noble of the region; now some of them were being taken over and run commercially by serf-owners or landlords, to make money. From private they had become public theatres. By the middle of the nineteenth century there had also been a great increase in the number of theatres owned by merchants. All these theatres came under the jurisdiction of the Secret Police, and could produce only plays allowed by the authorities. A play might be permitted in one town and forbidden in an-other, depending on the social composition of the audience. It is not surprising that the artistic level of these provincial theatres was very low, while the conditions under which the actors lived, particularly in the travelling com-panies, were sordid in the extreme. Good local actors were drawn away to Moscow or St. Petersburg. Even there standards of produc-tion and acting were not high. Scenery was crude and apt to collapse, costumes bedraggled and often unsuitable, while, apart from a few stars, the actors were poorly paid and under-rehearsed. There was no producer, and the work of the stage-manager was confined to getting the actors on and off the stage at the right moment. Even in the theatrical schools no time was given to teaching people to act, only to sing, or dance, or fence. They were supposed to act by instinct, and so arose, as elsewhere, a style of acting which relied on stage-tricks, on hard-won experience of what gesture or tone of voice would bring applause or laughter, a stereotyped pattern which suited the fustian for which it was designed, but which was death to any realism of character or situa-tion.

Alongside this unreal theatre there was the growing popularity of vaudeville, imported from France. It consisted of one-act comedies in couplets (*chastushki*) with a sharp, satirical content, in which the petty town bourgeois laughs at the troubles of the government and the habits of the ruling classes. It was tolerated by the authorities because it encouraged in its audience a light-hearted attitude to reality. Its gossipy intrigues transformed life into a naïve, cheerful joke, an atmosphere in which reforms would have little chance to flourish. Starting at Court, vaudeville quickly became plebeian, and adapted itself to its new milieu. Costume, décor, and acting became more realistic, more intimate. The new authors of vaudeville were not drawn from the aristocracy, but from people closely associated with the theatre, who knew their actors and what they were capable of. Chief among them were Koni, editor of a theatrical journal, and the actors Peter Kara-tygin and Peter Grigoreyev, who had been a strolling player and later an unsuccessful writer of patriotic plays.

It would seem impossible for a free national drama to flourish in such an atmosphere. Yet, in spite of all difficulties, in spite of the dead hand of authority, the paucity of good acting and good theatres, the inertia of the audiences, and the danger of independent thought, the nineteenth century, from the defeat of Napoleon in 1812 onwards, saw the emergence of the great dramatists of Imperial Russia—Pushkin, Tolstoy, Gogol, Turgeniev, Chekhov, and Gorky.

The reasons for this are not far to seek. Up to the beginning of the nineteenth century, as we have seen, Russia was in a state of lethargy. The absolute rule of the aristocracy led to sterility in art. The theatres of the two capital cities were controlled by the police, and as late as 1882 it was still forbidden to open any new ones. Court life existed wholly on imported European ideas, and all persons of culture spoke French or German. Russian was for the rabble. Even those writers who used their native tongue produced only slavish imitations of European models. Then came the Napoleonic invasion, which raised the people to heights of patriotism undreamed of previously, and did more than anything to pave the way for the growth of a truly national drama. This war of freedom against foreign dictatorship proved an inspiration to many writers, and since litera-ture had become of importance to the State, it obviously had to be written in the mother tongue. Even the nobility woke up to the emergence of a national consciousness, and the first great writer to use Russian as a lite-rary medium—Alexander Sergeivich Pushkin (1799–1837)—was universally acclaimed. It is impossible to exaggerate his influence on Russian literature as a whole, and on the theatre in particular. His works, important in them-selves, proved also a storehouse of plots on which his contemporaries and successors drew for the themes of their operas and dramas. Both he and Mikhail Yurevich Lermontov (1814–41), author of *Masquerade* (written 1835; prod. 1852 in a cut version, 1864 in full), represented the lesser nobility who had suffered under the oppression of the Court and the higher bureaucratic circles, and were more closely in sympathy with the people. Their plays—tragedies in verse—were implicit criti-cisms of the life of the aristocracy, while their contemporary Alexander Sergeivich Griboye-dov (1795–1829) chose comedy for his scathing criticisms of authority. *Woe from Wit* (pub. 1833) is his most famous play. It is also known as *Wit Works Woe* and by some half-dozen other titles, though the Russian title *Gore ot Ooma* is perhaps best translated as *The Dis-advantages of Being Clever*. It depicts the moral corruption of the ruling class and the stupidity of the politician, and is the first social play in Russian drama, organically linked up with the literature of the Decembrist revolt in 1825.

For the first time Russian dramatists were writing about living people, and were concerned to write the truth about the existing order. Had these authors lived longer and reached maturity, they might have changed the course of Russian drama considerably. As it was, they all died young; but they had prepared the ground, and it was left to the dramatist Nikolai Vasileivich Gogol (1809–52) and the actor Mikhail Semenovich Shchepkin (1788–1863) to effect the necessary reform of the Russian stage.

Although Gogol was only in his early forties when he died, he had written two long plays and a number of short ones, which, in their pointed criticism and their truthful delineation of a corrupt and wastrel society, opened the way for later dramatists. His *Inspector-General* (also known as *The Government Inspector* and *Revizor*) (1836) was produced, surprisingly enough, at the Court theatre in the presence of the Tsar, with Shchepkin as the Mayor, but it was so bitterly attacked that Gogol left Russia, under-estimating the breach he had made in the walls of absolutism, and the number of people who were going forward with him.

The period of reaction which followed the revolt of 1825 was ended by the accession of Alexander II, on the whole the most liberal of the Tsars, under whom the nobility tended to become more and more mere figure-heads, while the emerging bourgeoisie split into two groups, the intelligentsia on the one hand, the industrial and mercantile capitalists on the other. The intelligentsia got material support from the wealthy burghers, who were themselves of humble origin for the most part, and felt themselves despised by the aristocrats. Consequently they were in sympathy with the poorer classes in their fight against privilege and absolutism.

The change-over from feudalism to capitalism was expressed in the theatre in the works of Alexander Nikolaevich Ostrovsky (1823–86), prolific author of a number of realistic middle-class comedies, whose themes embraced practically the whole of contemporary Russian life and society. Like Balzac, his whole life was devoted to the writing of one great dramatic work in many chapters, which might equally well be summed up under the title of the Human Comedy. During more than forty years of dramatic activity he had over fifty plays produced on the Russian stage, of which some half-dozen have been translated into English.

Parallel with this new realistic drama came a reorientation of the material side of the theatre—settings, design, and style of acting. Ostrovsky's first play, produced in 1853, startled the audience by its simple and photographically exact presentation. For the first time a heroine appeared in a cotton frock, with naturally smooth hair. Before this, silk and French hairdressing were obligatory. These innovations naturally affected all aspects of stage technique. The older actors had to adapt themselves to the new demands, or give way to younger men. Shchepkin was the leader of the new theatre, though others, notably Alexander Martynov (1816–60) and Prov Sadovsky (1818–72), ably assisted his reforms. Stage setting also underwent a change. The previous system

of hanging drapes gave way to the box set, and a room depicted on the stage had walls, doors, and windows, while articles of everyday use which entered into the action of the play were really placed on the stage for the actors to handle. Real furniture, instead of painted canvas, was used for the first time. Ostrovsky took a practical interest in the work of the theatre, and participated in the running of the Moscow Maly Theatre, which is now known as the House of Ostrovsky. Writing to him, the famous Russian author Goncharov said: 'You have erected a building whose foundation-stones were laid by Fonvizin, Griboyedov, Gogol. Only after you can we Russians say with pride, Now we have our own Russian National Theatre.'

Meanwhile, in western Europe, naturalism, first brilliantly manifested in Zola's works, began to invade the theatre, and found expression in the Meiningen system, so called from the theatre company under Chronegk attached to the Court of Duke George II of Saxe-Meiningen. It created a sensation by the historical accuracy of its productions, and the artistic harmony of its ensemble. The company paid two visits to Russia in the 1880s, and had a great influence on the private theatres which had sprung up with the removal of the ban in 1882. Created and maintained by the newly emerging bourgeoisie, these theatres, though still under police censorship, had greater freedom than the Court theatre to experiment with new styles, and put on new plays. The most important of them was that run by an entrepreneur named Korsh, where the early plays of Anton Pavlovich Chekhov (1861–1904) were produced. Another was run by one Lentovsky, who first used electric light, and among other innovations actually 'produced' his plays, instead of allowing the actors to do as they thought best.

The acting of the Meiningen company, the influence of Ibsen and Hauptmann, and the breakdown of the Imperial Theatre when it tried to stage Chekhov's full-length plays, fully revealed the inadequacy of contemporary acting. Something new and vital in the theatre was needed to match the new drama. The time brought forth the men, and in 1898 Vladimir Ivanovich Nemirovich-Danchenko (1859–1943), a successful playwright, and Konstantin Sergeivich Alexeyev (1865–1938), an amateur actor and producer whose stage name was Stanislavsky, founded the Moscow Art Theatre, where the great writers of the new naturalistic movement—Ibsen, Hauptmann, and not least Chekhov—found their ideal interpreters.

Only one more outstanding dramatist was to appear in Russia before the Revolution of 1917 changed the face of the Russian theatre almost beyond recognition. This was Alexei Maximovich Pyeshkov (1868–1936), better known as Maxim Gorky—the Stormy Petrel of the Revolution, and the bridge between old and new, for he was the only dramatist whose plays were first produced both in Imperial and in

Soviet Russia. Prophet of the Revolution and one of its builders, he represents the new power entering the Russian theatre—the proletariat. Unlike Chekhov, he is little known outside Russia, and although the progressive Moscow Art Theatre produced his first two plays, *The Philistine* and *The Lower Depths*, in 1902, the ones written after the 1905 Revolution were not produced at all. Only after the Revolution of 1917 did Gorky come into his own, his last, and one of his best, plays, *Yegor Bulichev*, being produced in 1934 by the Moscow Art Theatre which, like the dramatist, had survived the stress and storm of a period which had swept much of the old Imperial theatre into oblivion.

2. SOVIET THEATRE. (*a*) *General*. The nineteenth century and earliest years of the twentieth saw the emergence and establishment of a national Russian theatre. It had produced the great names listed above, one of which at least, Chekhov's, has since transcended all frontiers. It may be said that in the last years of the old régime the theatre (at its best in the Moscow Art Theatre), the Imperial opera, and the Imperial ballet were among the few purely efficient and beautiful things that Tsardom either encouraged by patronage or allowed to develop without too much interference.

It is one of the glories of the succeeding Soviet régime that it had the intelligence to take over the best of what it inherited, and immensely to foster its extension. The mere physical development of the stage under Soviet rule is enormous. Before the outbreak of the Second World War there were nearly a thousand professional theatres in the Soviet Union, of which 410 staged plays in non-Russian languages. The present Georgian Republic, for example, which in 1913 had three theatres, in 1938 had 39. And the same rapid expansion is to be found in all the provinces, apart from the big increase in the number of theatres in the capital cities. To these must be added the children's theatres, a factor of great importance in the training of the younger generation. The first of these, which in 1939 numbered about 200, many of them puppet theatres, was opened in Moscow on 7 Nov. 1918, on the first anniversary of the Revolution. They are essentially theatres for, not by, children. The actors and staff are adults, young certainly, but specially trained for their work, and chosen from the best material available, while the repertory is selected to appeal to the children of the age-group for which the particular theatre caters. Outside the vast professional theatre there are again innumerable amateur groups, tens of thousands of them, mostly attached to farms, factories, and other institutions. They are equipped with stages, and receive invaluable help and encouragement from the professional actors and producers. Each amateur group is usually affiliated to a professional theatre, in Moscow or elsewhere, and special facilities are given for the training of promising youngsters, who often graduate from these amateur groups to the professional stage.

This vast expansion and diffusion of the theatre, reaching into regions where no stage play had probably ever penetrated before, could not have been achieved without sympathetic encouragement, and above all practical assistance, from the new government. Indeed, the Bolshevik treatment of the theatre is probably one of the brightest spots in its history, and those who, in the first flush of victory, would have swept away the Moscow Art Theatre with other pre-Soviet organizations were properly rebuked when Lunacharsky, first Commissar for Education, gave it generous support. He made it financially independent, and allowed it time to readjust itself to the new régime—a forbearance which has been amply repaid by the fine work it has done since it regained its balance in about 1924-7. Among other theatres inherited and absorbed by Soviet Russia mention must be made of the Alexandrinsky and the Theatres for the People in Petrograd (Leningrad), and of the Maly, the Kamerny, and the various offshoots of the Moscow Art Theatre in Moscow. The history of these is given under their separate headings.

To the inherited theatres, which in spite of trained actors and a seasoned repertory started anew with the handicap of being out of touch with the new audiences, were now added the innumerable theatres founded and directly organized by the cultural department of the People's Commissar of Finance, in fulfilment of the promise made by the Eighth Congress of the Bolshevik Party: 'To open and make accessible to the working masses the treasures of classic art.' These, though in sympathy with their audiences, and intended partly as instruments of education in the new social order, were on their side handicapped by the lack of highly trained theatre men, and by a dearth of plays suitable for their purpose, a dearth which developments in Soviet dramatic art before 1939 were going some way to remedy. The first steps were necessarily tentative and experimental, and a beginning was made by assisting the various groups of the bourgeois artistic intelligentsia, some of which had already attempted a minor reorganization, as in the short-lived Theatre of Artistic Drama and Theatre of Tragedy.

It would be impossible to enumerate all the theatres which have sprung into being as a result of the rapid uprising, under active government encouragement, of the Russian love of and aptitude for the drama. Mention must, however, be made of the Lenkom, the Lensoviet (T.R.A.M.), the Meyerhold, the Mossoviet (M.O.S.P.S.), the Realistic, the Red Army, the Theatre of the Revolution, the Trades Unions Theatre (V.Ts.P.S.), the Vakhtangov and the Yermolova, all in Moscow; and in Leningrad of the Theatre of Comedy (see AKIMOV), the Grand Gorky, the Radlov, and the Theatre of the Baltic Sailors. All these are dealt with under their own names. There are also in Moscow and elsewhere theatres of the national minorities, such as the State Jewish Theatre (see JEWISH DRAMA, 6), and the

Gipsy Theatre, founded in 1931 as a small travelling show of simple turns. This latter has now reached the stage where it is able to handle efficiently full-length plays on gipsy themes.

Theatres which produce only ballet and opera, such as the Bolshoy in Moscow and the Kirov (formerly the Marinsky) in Leningrad, are outside the scope of this book. It has also been necessary to omit a number of small studio theatres which nevertheless do good work, and the whole gamut of light, ephemeral entertainments, music-hall, musical comedy, circus, &c., which flourish all over the U.S.S.R., but in which information is not easily obtainable in translation.

(b) *Theatres of the People in Petrograd.* Among the theatres of pre-Revolutionary Russia inherited by the Soviets, a special place is occupied by the so-called 'Theatres of the People'. They began on the eve of 1900, at a time when the shadow of coming events caused various sections of Tsarist society to take more interest than before in the influence which could be wielded by the theatre on the democratic petty bourgeois and working-class public.

i. The first was due to the influence of the ruling class exercised through theatres under the control of the Tsarist Ministry of Finance. The chief theatre of this type was the 'People's House dedicated to Nicholas II'. Its barrack-like architecture, asphalt floor, and spiked iron railings were in striking contrast to the gold and plush of the Imperial theatres. Its director was a Major-General Cherepanov, and its chief productions were patriotic plays written to order. These theatres were not of sufficient importance to justify their being nursed through the stormy years, and once the police and the military directors had been removed, there remained little more than an acting and technical staff of about the level of a provincial company, more easily assimilated by the new régime than the complex and sensitive organism of such bodies as the Moscow Art Theatre, for instance. Lunacharsky himself began the alterations even before the October Revolution, and tried to soften the barrack-like atmosphere by carpets over the asphalt and tapestries on the walls. It was not so easy to change the acting, however, though the repertory was completely overhauled, and five plays by Gorky and one each by Galsworthy and Tolstoy were produced under the direction of N. N. Arbatov, a former member of the People's Theatre. In 1920 plays by Molière, Lope de Vega, and Lunacharsky himself were introduced, produced by I. M. Lapitsky, with settings by B. A. Almadingen. But they were no more successful than the previous offerings had been, and a third change took place, with the production under A. R. Kugel of chronicle plays dealing with the reigns of Alexander I, Nicholas II, and so on. This led eventually to artistic bankruptcy, and shortly afterwards the theatre closed. The experiment had proved that a genuine Soviet theatre could not evolve from a so-called 'People's Theatre' of mediocre quality and limited outlook; and Lenin and the

other Bolshevik leaders were shown to be correct in their contention that genuine 'socialist' art must come from the assimilation of the fine cultural heritage of the past, and that only the best, in actors and plays, was good enough for the theatre of the people. The old theatres must be encouraged to take their place in the new society, and at the same time they must influence and stimulate the growth of the new theatres, particularly those organized for specific tasks, such as the theatre for young workers (see LENKOM THEATRE), for the Red Army, and for the children.

ii. A second type of pre-Revolutionary People's Theatre was that favoured by the advanced units of the industrial bourgeoisie, who counted the theatre among the various means which they employed to extend their hold over the workers. The theoreticians of this movement included even Ostrovsky, who in 1882 submitted to the Emperor Alexander III a memorandum on the construction in Moscow of a Russian People's Theatre, which, he said, was needed for the merchants: 'They will build it, they will run it, and they know what they want. . . . This theatre will be a genuine consolation for the simple, fresh Russian public.' Towards the end of the 1890s Petrograd industrialists realized Ostrovsky's ideal by founding the Vasili-Ostrovsky Theatre for the Workers, and in the years previous to 1914 similar theatres were opened in some Petrograd factories, including the famous Thornton Textile Works, where Lenin first began his political work.

iii. The third type of 'People's Theatre' was that of the cultural sections of the Co-operative Societies, the Society for People's Universities, and the Factory Mutual Aid Societies. These dramatic groups produced both old and modern plays, particularly those dealing with social problems which were rejected by the commercial and Imperial theatres. They included plays by Gorky and Tolstoy, plays on local working-class problems, and finally plays of the western European social drama by Hauptmann and others. The theatres were hampered by the operation of the Tsarist censorship, but in spite of that they played an important and progressive part in the days before the final struggle.

These three types had no strict lines of demarcation, and tended at various times to overlap, but they had in common a swift expansion after the 1905 Revolution, and a number of internal crises of various kinds before they were swept up into the October Revolution.

(c) *Organization of the Soviet Theatre.* It is significant that the Soviet theatre, even in the capital cities, can best be studied under the headings of the separate theatres. The reason for this lies in the organization, peculiar to itself, which the U.S.S.R. has set up for the supply of personnel, both actors and staff, to the numerous theatres under its charge. These call for a continual intake of actors, producers, technicians, and workers in all branches of theatrical art, who are supplied by the State

Technical Schools of Drama, of which the chief is the State Institute of Theatrical Art (GITIS) in Moscow. Before 1917 there were only three theatrical schools in Russia, at which the total attendance was less than 100 persons, while the total number of actors was under 8,000. By 1939 the number of students at the 46 theatrical institutes of the U.S.S.R. amounted to 4,000.

The organization of the Soviet theatre, which is a State concern run on State money and supported by State authority, has a parallel in the Comédie-Française, the Paris Opéra, and various other 'leading' theatres in most civilized countries (except England) that are run on a system of State (or Municipal) endowments, a permanent company, and a changing repertory. The difference in the Soviet approach is that this system applies without exception to every full-time professional theatre up and down the Union. Elsewhere in Europe the life of the actor, outside State and Municipal theatres, is at best a chancy affair, devitalized and rendered more precarious by the commercial necessity for long runs. In the U.S.S.R. the keynote of theatrical life is security and permanence. The students receive their training free, and may in addition be granted free living accommodation and a monetary grant. On finishing their training they join a company, which is a permanent body attached to a particular theatre building, where they may perhaps remain for the rest of their lives. There is no question of engaging actors who may happen to be free in order to present a certain play, nor of disbanding the company at the end of the run; indeed, there are no 'runs', since each theatre has a true repertory, and gives a number of different plays each season, varying the programme nightly, as is done in London by the Old Vic company, and at the Memorial Theatre, Stratford-on-Avon. This close association of actor and theatre makes for excellent team-work, the building up of a 'house' tradition, and a smooth running of every detail obtainable only by constant working together of actor, producer, and theatre staff. At the same time it tends to stress the differences between the various theatre-groups, and to exalt the producer above the dramatist, a situation which may undergo alteration when the new Soviet dramatists grow in strength and authority.

Until recent years the dearth of contemporary dramatists was the one weak spot in the Soviet theatre, and may account for the number of revivals of Russian and European classics. These tended at one time to bulk too large in the repertory, but they will no doubt fall into the background as the body of Soviet plays grows larger. The lack of good dramatists is understandable. Soviet actors, producers, and technicians, who are admittedly among the best in the world, could be, and were, found among the men of the Revolution. Some had been in but not of the old régime, and after a quick adjustment were able to lead and train younger men. They were essentially men of action. For the writer, the thinker, the break was more complete. Gorky was the only dramatist to ride out the storm he had helped to raise. The early years of the new régime were too troubled, too close, for dramatization, and such plays as were written were crudely melodramatic, instruments of propaganda rather than works of art. Then came the epoch of 'socialist realism'—a phrase difficult to explain, but meaning roughly that all plays, old and new, had to be interpreted in the light of the new society in which they were being presented. In other words, the balance had to be kept between excessive naturalism on the one hand, and formalism on the other. The play and its production must reflect not only the outlook of its original period but also that of the later changed circumstances. It must be interpreted yet not falsified. This led to some interesting, if mistaken, reorientations of classical works, and to a marked falling-off of purely propaganda plays, since the dramatist was no longer concerned to teach but to interpret. It was necessary for Soviet dramatists to grow up with the régime, for it to be part of themselves and not imposed from outside, before they could synthesize it, and evolve from its many aspects a picture that would be true spiritually as well as factually. Given the necessary artistic freedom, Soviet dramatists will find their material becoming easier to handle, their technique more sure, and their characterization more vivid, until their plays take their rightful place among the other glories of a great theatrical epoch. But it is as yet too early to attempt any evaluation of individuals. Among the many dramatists whose work it is not possible yet rightly to assess, a few stand out, either by reason of their success in their own country, or because their work has been made known to the English-speaking world in translation. Among the former may be ranked Trenev, Pogodin, and Korneichuk; among the latter Ivanov, whose *Armoured Train 14–69* (1927) was the first outstanding Soviet play; Afinogenov, author of *Fear* (1931) and *Distant Point* (1934); Bulgakov, whose *Days of the Turbins* (1926) was seen in London as *The White Guard* (1938); and Simonov, author of *The Russians* (1943). The plays of the war years, when mass evacuations of theatres took place, and when travelling companies played to the fighting forces right up to the front line, are not as yet known; but a cursory glance seems to show that they are not lacking in quantity, and, it is to be hoped, in quality.

(d) *Soviet Stage Design.* From its earliest days the Soviet theatre has been remarkable for the vitality and variety of its scenic design, which deserves a place to itself in this survey. In the theatres of Moscow, Leningrad, Kharkov, Tiflis, and other centres, all styles of stage-setting, from conventional operatic decoration to naturalistic representation, from modernized baroque to abstract constructivism and scenic architecture, have been seen, each in turn dominating the stage.

Before the Revolution stage design fell into two categories—the naturalism of the legitimate drama, and the impressionistic and symbolic settings of opera, ballet, and the experimental theatres. Naturalism in Russia found its finest expression in the early Moscow Art Theatre productions, when Stanislavsky was striving for a complete illusion of reality. His chief designer was V. A. Simov (1858–1935), leader of the naturalistic school, who prepared the settings for such outstanding productions as *Brand*, *Julius Caesar*, and *The Seagull*. The other extreme is seen in the work of Mstislav Dobujinsky (1875–   ) and Alexander Niko-laievich Benois (1870–   ). The former was responsible for the décor of *Woe from Wit* and *A Month in the Country*, among other plays; while the latter designed the settings for productions of *La Locandiera* and *Le Malade imaginaire*. Both these artists are outstanding in their use of colour, the sweep of their composition, and their symbolism. Dobujinsky's setting for the opera 'Queen of Spades' was a genuine Dance of Death, with its macabre columns and arches. It was a pity that both these artists emigrated, as they were among the greatest designers of their generation; but Benois continued to do good work elsewhere in Europe (see BALLET), and it is interesting to note in passing that at one time he worked in the Moscow Art Theatre. His employment there is proof of the catholicity of Stanislavsky, and the falsity of labelling him merely 'naturalistic'.

In the period immediately following the Revolution the obvious tendency was a reaction from the naturalistic school on the one hand and the aesthetic on the other, which produced a technique known as Constructivism. The pioneer of this method was Meyerhold, whose pre-Soviet productions in St. Petersburg had owed much to his designer, Alexander Golovin (1863–1930). Golovin's settings, particularly for *Masquerade* at the Alexandrinsky, were outstanding examples of colourist-impressionist work in the theatre.

Meyerhold, in an access of enthusiasm, worked with Shestakov, Popova, Shlepanov, and Rodchenko to clear away the 'old rubbish' that cluttered the stage. Away went wings, painted drops, borders, and all the rest of the old-fashioned paraphernalia. The theatre became a factory, with actors as the workers, and the performance as a process of production. Movable platforms, revolving wheels, ladders, lifts, stairs, and stands emphasized the dynamic nature of the new theatre. This was an excellent symbolic gesture—the stage stripped to the bare essentials for the resurgence of the theatre —but it went too far, and as a permanent feature proved monotonous in form and colour. The new, alive, untutored audiences crowding into the theatres for the first time wanted something more colourful and evocative; they wanted the setting to express the substance of the play, and its epoch. So Constructivism went; but it had served its purpose, and some traces of it still remained—in the productions

of Okhlopkov at the Realistic Theatre, for instance, and in the three-dimensional use of the stage which is so widespread in the Soviet Union. It is interesting to note that most constructivist artists became either architects or industrial designers. They were least concerned with the stage picture, and most with the dynamics of action. Their décor made no attempt to give the audience the impression of a factory or a house, but reflected the inherent dynamics of the events taking place on the stage. From them the designers of to-day have learnt to consider the sociological angle of the play, an essential part of Soviet production and design, while retaining from the pre-Revolutionary theatre, with its stylized presentation of a given epoch, the richness of colour and line.

The designers' quest for the architectural image has led to such different manifestations as the stylized architectural settings of Rabinovich and V. Beyer, the architectural constructivism of some of Rindin's settings, the rich romantic architecture of Tishler, and the satirical romanticism of Nikolai Akimov, and of Levin. The conflict between Akimov's romantic and sceptical tendencies was most noticeable in his production of *Hamlet* at the Vakhtangov Theatre in 1932. Levin has many fine designs to his credit, particularly in opera, but he is so many-sided that it would be difficult to assign him to any particular school. His work is to be found everywhere, from Grand Opera to Music-Hall, and some of his designs, particularly those for the Maly Theatre production of Gorky's *Enemies* in 1933, were strongly naturalistic. This influence is also paramount in the work of Dmitriev, who was responsible for the décor of Gorky's last plays when they were done at the Vakhtangov Theatre.

Architectural theatre design was carried to its apotheosis in the work of Y. Schtoffer (1906–   ) for Okhlopkov at the Realistic Theatre, where the whole auditorium was taken as the stage space in which the scene is set, each production involving a totally different arrangement of seating and view-points for the audience. This method was brilliantly successful in the productions of *Mother*, *The Iron Flood*, and *Razbeg*. Another outstanding scenic designer is N. A. Schrifin, one of whose fine settings for Popov's production of *The Taming of the Shrew* in 1937 was reproduced at the Soviet Theatre Exhibition in London in 1946. Throughout the play the use of tapestries combined with solid furniture gave a vivid and evocative picture of a mingled Elizabethan and Italian Renaissance scene. Schrifin designed equally lovely settings for Popov's production of *A Midsummer Night's Dream* in 1940, and later some realistic décor, from sketches made on the spot, for a play by a Red Army soldier on the siege of Stalingrad.

In the last few years four outstanding artists have made their name in the theatre—Tishler, referred to above; Peter Vladimirovich Williams (1902–48), who created some most original settings for *The Pickwick Club*, done at the Moscow Art Theatre in 1934, with full use of backcloths (this play was a wonderfully alive stage-transcript of the novel, satisfying even to an English idolater of Dickens); V. Bassov (1901–   ), whose settings for such productions as *Romeo and Juliet* and *Othello*, the latter at the Maly, show him to be an artist on a monumental scale; and lastly V. Favorsky (1886–   ), who enchanted his audiences with his first stage designs, for *Twelfth Night*, which made use of an architectural synthesis of the Renaissance with a painted backcloth panorama.

It is impossible, in the space available here, to deal with the numerous artists and designers of the National Republics of the Union, whose theatres are dealt with below. Their work, in general, shows an equal variety of styles, to which is added the richness of their national traditions. The Ukrainian theatre, for example, has two great scenic artists in Valim Meller and Anatole Petritsky. The former works chiefly in the Berezil theatre, most of its designs being by himself or his pupils. At first a Constructivist, Meller in his later work has achieved a synthesis of architecture, painting, and sculpture, with striking results. Petritsky, an artist of temperamental brilliance, sonorous colouring, and entrancing fancy, has specialized in design for opera. He has also worked in Moscow, where he did some dynamic settings for Dikie at the V.Ts.P.S.

In Georgia the Rustavelli State Theatre in Tiflis, to mention only one other, has given fine productions of plays on national themes which owe much to the settings of Heracles Gamrekel. Other important Georgian artists are Otakelli, M. Arutchyan, and Arurnav.

(e) The National theatres. Mention of the Ukrainian and Georgian theatres introduces the question of the theatrical life of the people in the States affiliated to Soviet Russia. From the fact that the national theatre of Azerbaijan celebrated its 60th anniversary in 1933, that of the Tartars its 30th in 1934, and that of the Jews its 30th in 1935, it might be assumed that all these theatres had developed unchecked under Tsarist rule. But this illusion is quickly dispelled if one considers their history a little more closely. The theatres, even of those peoples who had possessed an ancient and rich culture, knew no normal, organic development. The Georgian theatre began in the latter half of the eighteenth century, but after the conquest of the country in 1801 its existence was suspended until 1861. The Jewish theatre founded by Abraham Goldfaden in 1876 lasted only seven years. During the reign of Alexander III performances in Yiddish were forbidden, and such as were given were labelled 'German'. Equally in White Russia the theatre founded in 1851 by Dunin-Martsinkevich lasted only for 12 years, and, like the printing of books in the White Russian language, was banned after the Polish insurrection of 1863. Occasional performances were disguised as 'Ukrainian'.

Almost the only people to found and hold on to a national theatre before 1917 were the Ukrainians. It had a brilliant galaxy of actors and playwrights, and in modern times has produced the fine dramatist Korneichuk; but even in the Ukraine the theatre did not enjoy full freedom, and for a long time Ukrainian plays were only allowed if accompanied by Russian vaudeville numbers.

In Western Ukraine (Little Poland) a theatre of a sort had been in existence since 1864, but its resources were meagre, its actors persecuted and ill paid, and its repertory negligible. It held a jubilee performance, practically its last, just before the outbreak of war in 1914. With no permanent theatre, the company constantly touring and always short of funds, this group had no chance of developing, though at times it numbered among its members some excellent actors. M. L. Kropivnitsky, the founder of the Ukrainian Theatre in Russia, played with the company in 1875, and was horrified by its wretchedness and poverty. In his reminiscences he wrote:

The dresses are sorry, the scenery poor. The orchestra consists of six musicians, the chorus of four girls and five boys. ... In Tarnopol and Czernowitz we at least had decent theatres, but in Kizman, Borogobuzh, Salishchiki, Snyatyn and some other towns the performances were given in stables. These were divided in two, the scenery set up and the floor strewn with sand. The actors had to sing in one half, while the horses were neighing in the other. The repertory was very dull, and I had nothing to do.

The years passed, but brought no change in the position of the theatre. In 1904 M. Sadovsky was invited to come from the Ukraine to be producer and manager, and a well-known actress, Sankovetskaya, joined the company. It was hoped that these importations would help to overcome the difficulties in which the theatre found itself, but little improvement was possible, and the guest-artists soon left. 'I met the troupe in Chertkov,' Sadovsky related subsequently, 'where they had pitched a tent, just as the Punch and Judy shows do at our fairs.' After thirty years the company was still giving its performances in premises that 'resembled either a stable or a shippen'.

In 1919 a new theatre group started in Lvov, full of hope, but was quickly suppressed, not to re-appear until 1939. Since its affiliation with Soviet Russia the Western Ukraine has seen the opening of theatres playing in Polish, Russian, Yiddish, and Ukrainian. The last has found its task the easiest, because of the existence of a strong Ukrainian national theatre in that part of the country which came under Soviet rule in 1917.

Azerbaijan, which had already possessed a fine playwright in the nineteenth century in Ilya Elvin Akhundov, now has a vigorous theatrical life. Plays are given by different groups in Armenian, Russian, and Turkish, and in 1938 the State Dramatic Theatre produced *Macbeth*. The country has also its contemporary playwrights. The same is true of Armenia, which under the Tsarist government had no theatre at all, in spite of its long cultural history. It now has 24, which, in addition to

the works of such Armenian playwrights as
Deremik Demirchyan, gives the plays of
Russian and European writers—*Othello, Masquerade, Kabale und Liebe*. In 1939 the Armenian Theatre was invited to perform in
Moscow.

One of the outstanding national theatres of
the U.S.S.R. is undoubtedly that of Georgia.
Here the culture of the Georgians had been
intensely russianized, but the first Georgian
theatre was founded about 1870, and a little
later a travelling company started to tour the
country under the management of Shalva
Dadiani, who also wrote the plays which they
performed. His work, and his theatre, survived
the October Revolution, and in 1930 one of his
plays was produced in Moscow, where Dadiani
himself worked for a time before returning to
Georgia. The chief of the 48 theatres of
Georgia is the Rustavelli State Theatre in
Tiflis, directed by Sandro Akhmeteli. Another
outstanding theatre is that of K. A. Marjanishveli, also in Tiflis, which in 1938 gave a fine
performance of *Othello*.

Of the 150 nationalities that inhabited the
former Russian Empire, the majority had no
national theatre at all. Their dramatic activities
were limited to games, to musical and sporting
contests, to religious and family ceremonies,
and to the narrations of story-tellers. In some
countries, such as Uzbekistan, there was a
widespread development of the puppet theatre
and the shadow show. But there was no 'stage'
in the European sense of the word.

These regions have now created—and been
encouraged from Moscow to create—their own
theatres. The five republics of the old Tsarist
province of Turkestan have fine theatre buildings, with a repertory which includes national,
Russian, and European plays. Audiences in
the Arctic Circle were first introduced to the
theatre by travelling companies. The Travelling Arctic Theatre set out in 1935 to bring plays
to the backward communities, and was followed by a company from the Maly Theatre of
Moscow in 1936, with the result that the
Eskimos and kindred peoples are now writing
and producing plays in their own languages.

On the whole, according to data which are
still incomplete, more than one-half of the
people in the U.S.S.R. are actively engaged in
building up their own theatrical culture. The
predominant tendency is naturally realism, but
romanticism is creeping in, particularly in the
older centres, Georgia, Ukraine, and White
Russia. The greatest achievements to date, as
in Moscow and Leningrad, lie more in the
domain of play-producing than play-writing,
but one will probably follow the other in due
course. Each region has utilized the material
to hand—the puppets, the shadow shows, the
wandering circus-folk and minstrels of such
districts as Uzbekistan, the folk-song and folk-dance, and primitive instruments of the nomadic
tribes; while the influence of China is shown,
in those theatres that border her, by the use of
masks and the stylization of external portrayal
of character. To these native elements has

been added the rich heritage of the Western
theatre, which has not, however, succeeded in
swamping the national characteristics. Those
who have seen productions in Latvia, Armenia,
Kirghizia, in the Gipsy or the Jewish theatres,
can testify to the variation in the manner of the
actors, each bringing from his national heritage
some new note, facial expression, richness of
gesture, and so on. An equally wide difference
can be seen in the décor, which takes colour
from its surroundings, as when the State
Theatre at Baku produced *Macbeth* with
costumes 'from some barbarous feudal age of
the East'.

In conclusion, it is worth noting the tremendous role played by the central Russian
theatre in the building up of all these national
theatres throughout the Union. Thus the early
Uzbek actors were trained by the pupils of
Vakhtangov; the Latvian theatrical organization is under the direction of an actor from the
Vakhtangov Theatre, to which the producer of
the Armenian Theatre, Simonov, also belongs.
This, with the constant arrival in Moscow and
Leningrad of promising pupils from distant
provinces, who take back the newest methods
to help them in dealing with local problems,
contributes enormously to the rapid growth
and improvement, both technically and
artistically, of the new theatres; and this, in its
turn, cannot but react favourably upon the
native playwrights, of whom we may expect to
see an ever-increasing number in years to come.

The same close co-operation is found among
the directors of the various national theatres.
Goldblatt, for example, an actor in the State
Jewish Theatre in Moscow, is also art director
of the Gipsy Theatre, while Litvinov, the
director of the White-Russian Theatre, came
from the State Jewish Theatre of that province.
Equally important, though not as yet so
apparent, is the influence of such men as
Akhmeteli of Georgia, and Alexander Granovsky of the State Jewish Theatre of Moscow,
upon a considerable number of Soviet productions. The national theatres, in spite of their
comparative youth, can be said to have made
already a considerable contribution to the
general history of the Soviet theatre, and have
to a certain extent influenced its style. From
them comes the element of Revolutionary
romanticism which is so characteristic of young
communities conscious of their destiny. While
the Georgians excel in the presentation of
Revolutionary romanticism in the form of
dramatic tragedy, the Jewish actors have given
no less brilliant presentations of the same spirit
in comedy and satire. It must suffice here to
mention the names of Tamara Petroziantz and
Kari Yakubov of Uzbekistan, of Horava,
Vasadre, and Zulukidze of Georgia, of Vladimirsky and Krylovich of White Russia, of that
most eminent Armenian tragedian, Papazyan,
of the great Jewish actors Mikhoels and Zuskin.
By the united efforts of all the nationalities of
the U.S.S.R. a Soviet theatre is being built up
which, differing as to its outward form and
language according to the region which it

serves, is national in form and socialist in content. In exact contradistinction to the policy of Imperial Russia, which was avowedly to 'russify' its dependencies from Finland to the Chinese border, and even as far as was possible to outlaw the native languages and cultures, one of the most brilliant experiments of the Soviet Government has been, from its very beginnings, deliberately to develop local languages and encourage local cultures by all and every means in its power. The best companies of the outlying nationalities are officially invited to Moscow to give performances in their own languages and in accordance with their own traditions, while members of the Central Government, including Stalin himself, attend the performances.

RUTEBEUF (*c.* 1230–*c.* 1285), a medieval minstrel who, with Adam de la Halle and Jean Bodel, stands at the beginning of French secular drama. Very little is known of his life; he was always poor and never very successful, though he ranked slightly above some of the humbler brethren in the hierarchy of minstrels, since at one time he possessed a horse. He married a plain, elderly wife, and though uneducated and of humble birth, his skill as a rhymer and singer made him a welcome guest in the halls of the feudal barons. His most important play was *Le Miracle de Théophile*, which in the 1930s was revived by Gustave Cohen's students at the Sorbonne, who took from it their name of 'Les Théophiliens'.

RUZZANTE, see BEOLCO and ITALY, 2.

RYAN, LACY (1694–1760), an English actor, of great talent, almost amounting to genius, who lacked physical advantages and the help of careful training. He first appeared as Seyton to Betterton's Macbeth, in a full-bottomed wig, and was Marcus in the original production of *Cato* (1713). He had a steady, uneventful career, mostly at Covent Garden, where he played big Shakespearian roles in opposition to Garrick at Drury Lane, with little success. It is said that Garrick went to see his Richard III, intending to scoff, but was astonished and moved by the genius and power which he saw striving to make itself felt through the burden of bad training, uncouth gestures, and slovenly figure. Ryan continued to play youthful lovers and heroes until his death, and was all his life a friend of the actor Quin, whom he had befriended in early days.

RYER, PIERRE DU (*c.* 1600–58), French dramatist, who though well educated and the holder of several important positions, was always handicapped by poverty, and relied for his living on hackwork translations of Greek and Latin authors. He wrote a number of plays, of which the earliest were tragicomedies in the style of Hardy, three being given in the year 1628–9. They were spectacular, calling for elaborate staging in the old-fashioned simultaneous style, and ignored the Unities of time and place. Several comedies followed, containing good parts for the comedian Gros-Guillaume, of which the best was *Les Vendanges de Suresne* (1633), and then, under the influence of Mairet's *Sophonisbé* (1634), du Ryer turned his attention to tragedy. The most successful of several tragedies, which included some on biblical subjects, was *Scévole* (1644). This remained in the repertory of the Comédie-Française for over 100 years, and was one of the plays given by Molière's short-lived Illustre-Théâtre. In the opinion of competent critics, du Ryer did more than anyone, except Mairet and Corneille, to establish French classical tragedy, though his range was wide, and included also pastorals like *Clitophan et Leucippe* (1629), which survives only in manuscript. Most of du Ryer's plays were given by the company at the Hôtel de Bourgogne.

S

SAAVEDRA, Ángel, EL DUQUE DE RIVAS (1791–1865), important in the history of the Spanish theatre as having written one of the first successful Romantic dramas of the nineteenth century, in revolt against the neo-classic poverty of the contemporary Spanish stage, for which he had previously written several classic and somewhat frigid plays. This was *Don Álvaro, o la fuerza del sino*, a Romantic verse-drama given in 1835. Rivas, who was in Paris in 1830, was much influenced by Victor Hugo, and on his return to Spain was acclaimed as a leader in the movement which was to sweep the youth of the country back to a just estimate of their national drama. His attention to detail and to stage setting was something new in the Spanish theatre, as was his handling of the crowd as an articulate entity.

SABBATTINI, Nicola (c. 1574–1654), Italian architect, designer of the Teatro del Sole in Pesaro, and author of a treatise on stage designing, *Pratica di fabricar scene e machine ne' teatri* (1638) (see LIGHTING, 1 a and MACHINERY).

SABBIONETTA THEATRE, see SCENERY, 2 and SPECTACLE THEATRES.

SACHS, Hans (1494–1576), German dramatist and Mastersinger, a cobbler by profession, whose main dramatic activity began about 1518. Immensely proud of his facility, he turned out long tragedies and comedies, and short brisk Carnival plays. His range is enormous: the Bible, legend, history, the classics, and the vast store of popular anecdote furnished him with material. His subjects are treated without the faintest historical perspective, sense of poetry, or tragic depth, and were merely used to serve his purpose of moral betterment. Most of the tragedies, such as *Die mörderisch Königin Clytemnestra* or *Der Hörnen Sewfriedt*, strike the modern reader as travesties, but the comedies— that is, plays with a happy ending, though not necessarily humorous—are more successful. In *Die ungleichen Kinder Eve* the Lord pays a friendly visit to the cottage of Adam and Eve, and examines their progeny—six good and six bad—in the Lutheran Catechism (Sachs was one of the first poets of his day to support Luther), dealing out appropriate rewards and punishments.

Sachs's fame rests chiefly on his Carnival plays, of which he wrote about 200, notable for their vivid folk-pictures and homespun humour. He may be said to have turned the horseplay of Shrovetide into a folk-play in simple form. Comparison with his sources shows that he did not aim at originality, but deft omissions and additions, and many telling touches, reveal his power of characterization and a sense of dramatic economy. The dialogue is often very natural and the rough and ready verse is not unpleasing.

Sachs, who is the hero of Wagner's opera 'Die Meistersinger', united in himself the healthiest tendencies of past and present, combining naïveté with shrewdness, humanity, and a glorious gift of laughter.   W. E. D.

SACKVILLE, Thomas, first Earl of Dorset (1536–1608), English lawyer and politician, Lord Treasurer under Elizabeth and James I. In 1561 he collaborated with his fellow student Thomas Norton in the writing of the first regular Senecan English tragedy in blank verse, *Gorboduc, or Ferrex and Porrex*. This was given before Queen Elizabeth on New Year's Day in the hall of the Inner Temple. He also contributed, to the second edition of *A Mirror for Magistrates* (1563), the *Induction* and *The Complaint of Buckingham*, the only contributions having any literary merit. (For the actor Sackville, see ENGLISH COMEDIANS.)

SACRA RAPPRESENTAZIONE, the fifteenth-century religious play of Italy, comparable in many respects with the *auto* of Spain and the Mystery play of France and England, for which modern criticism has now coined the generic name of 'Bible-histories'. As elsewhere, the Italian religious drama began in the church, but migrated to the market-place, where the original solemnity of the Bible story was gradually enlivened by humorous and contemporary elements, and by material imported from the lives of the saints (see ITALY, 1 a ii).

SADLER'S WELLS THEATRE, London. The discovery of a medicinal spring in the grounds of a Mr. Sadler in the year 1683–4 led to the establishment of a popular pleasure-garden there, which became known as Sadler's Wells. Entertainments of a varied nature were given, and Sadler, in partnership with a dancing-master named Forcer, erected a wooden 'Musick House' with a platform to serve as a stage. Sadler's Wells then stood in open country, and though it seems to have been a well-conducted place as a rule, a murder was committed there in 1712, when a naval lieutenant was killed by a lawyer 'near the organ loft'.

Sadler apparently retired in 1699 in favour of one Miles, who with Forcer ran the place as Miles' Musick House. He died in 1724 and Forcer in 1730. The son of the latter, a barrister, carried on the place, again called Sadler's Wells, and added musical interludes, the first stage performances on record there. The Princesses Amelia and Caroline visited it in 1735. In 1746 Rosoman, a local builder (after whom a nearby street is now named), took over the Wells, which had rather lost its reputation, and restored its good name. In 1765 he pulled down the old Musick House, and raised a stone theatre at the cost of £4,225, the whole thing being done in seven weeks. He had evidently engaged a company before this date, however, for in 1755 the Rural Calendar says 'this theatre —for such it is—is now so well regulated, under the present manager, that a better company is not anywhere to be met with'. *The Tempest* —possibly in Dryden's version—was performed there in 1764.

Rosoman retired in 1772, with a fortune of £40,000, and Tom King, a Drury Lane actor and the original Sir Peter Teazle, was manager from 1772 to 1782. He ran the place well, and for some time employed Charles Dibdin. In 1781 a child of just over two years old danced at Sadler's Wells. His name was Joseph Grimaldi, and he played a 'sprite'. After King, the managers were Arnold, Wroughton, and Siddons, husband of the great tragedienne. Under the last-named, a small boy named Carey recited at Sadler's Wells. He was to become known as Edmund Kean.

In 1783 a troupe of performing dogs caused a sensation. In 1786 Miss Romanzini, better known as Mrs. Bland, sang, and in 1788 a success was made by Master Abrahams—who later shed the first and last letters of his name, and became the famous Braham. In 1804 Sadler's Wells became the home of Aquatic Drama, mostly the work of the younger Dibdin. A large tank filled from the New River was installed, in which boats floated, naval battles took place, heroines were rescued by heroes, and children by Newfoundland dogs. *The Siege of Gibraltar*, complete with naval bombardment, was the first of these spectacles, and their vogue continued for some years.

In 1807 a false alarm of fire caused a panic in the theatre; twenty-three people were killed and many injured. In 1818 Grimaldi took over and sustained a heavy loss. He made his farewell appearance at Sadler's Wells on 17 Mar. 1828, broken in health and fortune. Tom Mathews succeeded him as clown.

For the next fifteen years there was nothing much of interest at the Wells, until in 1844 it was let to Samuel Phelps and Mrs. Warner. They opened with *Macbeth* on 27 May 1844. Mrs. Warner retired the following year, but Phelps, with Greenwood, made theatre history with his productions of Shakespeare and classical plays. Artistically the Wells was probably the foremost London theatre of its time. Phelps, a magnificent actor, held sway there, covering the theatre and himself with glory, until 1863. After that its fame faded. Morton Price and Miss Lucette gave light entertainments there, Robert Edgar ran it for six years with his wife, Miss Marriott, a noted female Hamlet, as its leading lady; but it soon became a skating-rink and a venue for prize-fights, and in 1878 it was closed as a dangerous structure.

In 1879 Mrs. Bateman, on leaving the Lyceum, reconstructed the interior, and tried to revive the glories of the past. After her, her daughter Isabel carried on for a while. But the theatre never attained the heights reached under Phelps, and sank to be a house of indifferent twice-nightly shows. For a long time it was derelict. In 1921 Ernest Rolls planned to make it into a music-hall, but nothing came of it.

Then Lilian Baylis conceived the idea of making it a North London pendant to the Old Vic in South London, and a new theatre arose on the site of the old one, opening on 6 Jan. 1931 with *Twelfth Night*. Since 1934 Sadler's Wells has had its own companies, distinct from those of the Old Vic, and has become a permanent home of opera and ballet. The theatre suffered superficial damage by bombing in 1940–1, and was temporarily closed, reopening in 1945.   W. M. P.

SADOVSKY [really Ermilov], Prov Michailovich (1818–72), one of the best of early Russian actors. He was born in Moscow, and educated for the stage by a well-known provincial actor, Sadovsky, a relative on his mother's side, from whom the young Ermilov took his professional name. He appeared on the provincial stage, in Tula, at the age of 14, and in 1839 went to Moscow and joined the company of the Imperial Maly Theatre. He occupied a modest place at first, but came to the fore in Ostrovsky's plays, of whose comic roles he proved to be the ideal interpreter, as Shchepkin was of Gogol's. With Sadovsky it may be said that the internal psychological development of the character was at one with the external, life-like presentation. It was largely due to Sadovsky's championship that Ostrovsky's plays were first done and then kept in the repertory until they received due recognition from the public. Unlike the earlier actors, Kachalov and Mochalov, Sadovsky followed Shchepkin in a realistic approach to his art.

Sadovsky's son and daughter-in-law were also members of the Maly company, and his grandson, also named Prov, is still with the theatre, thus maintaining a family connexion which dates back over a century.

SAFETY CURTAIN, an iron or fireproof sheet which falls in front of the ordinary curtain of a theatre, and is designed to separate the stage and auditorium in the event of fire. By law it must be lowered once at every performance and this is generally done during an interval. The earliest reference to this device, which is sometimes nicknamed 'the Iron', occurs at Drury Lane in 1794.

SAINETE, in early Spanish drama a short, comic, rough-and-tumble farce synonymous with the *entremés*, which was inserted between the acts of a longer play, or followed it as an extra turn. It developed from the *paso* of Lope de Rueda, and the best examples were written by Ramón de la Cruz, who, during a period of inertia and general apathy under the neoclassic régime, kept alive the comic spirit of Old Spain. *Sainetes* on Andalusian folkthemes have been written in modern times by the Quintero brothers.

SAINT-DENIS, Michel (1897–   ), French actor and producer, founder of the

Compagnie des Quinze and head of the Old Vic Theatre Centre. He began his career with his uncle Jacques Copeau at the Vieux-Colombier, where he was stage-manager and assistant producer, and went with him to Burgundy when he founded his theatre school there. He then went with the company on tour throughout the continent and to England, and in 1930 took over the direction of the Compagnie des Quinze, for whom he produced *Noé*, *Le Viol de Lucrèce*, and *Bataille de la Marne*, all by Obey, as well as other plays, appearing in all of them himself. The company achieved a great reputation, but was finally disbanded and in 1936 Saint-Denis, who had already produced *Noah* (in English) and *The Witch of Edmonton* in London, founded the London Theatre Studio for the training of young actors. Several public performances were later given, and the work of the school had already made an interesting contribution to the English theatre, when the outbreak of war in 1939 caused it to close down. Meanwhile Saint-Denis had done several more productions, including *Macbeth*, *Three Sisters*, *The White Guard*, and *The Marriage of Blood*, to all of which he brought the same fastidious intellect, clarity of vision, and refusal to be bound by tradition which had marked the productions of the Compagnie des Quinze. It is unfortunate that his work as producer and as director of the Old Vic Theatre Centre has withdrawn him from acting, since he is a subtle exponent of the finest shades of French classical comedy.

SAINTE - BEUVE, CHARLES AUGUSTIN (1804–69), one of the greatest of French critics, who from 1848, after a short excursion into politics, settled down peaceably to write an essay every Monday for one of several journals. These were later collected and published in a series of volumes—*Causeries du lundi, Nouveaux lundis, Premiers lundis*—which provide a panorama of the French theatre during his lifetime. As a young man he wrote his first article on Victor Hugo, who became his friend and initiated him into the delights of Romanticism, which he first encouraged but later criticized with much acrimony. He also wrote plays and novels, but finally gave up creative work and became, as he said himself, 'merely a spectator, an analyst'. He was a friend of the actor Molé, and little that went on in the theatre escaped him. He wrote well and fluently, though rather too much, and besides his Monday articles was responsible for many books of theatrical and literary criticism.

ST. JAMES THEATRE, NEW YORK, on 44th Street and Eighth Avenue. This opened as Erlanger's on 26 Sept. 1927. It was intended as a house for musical and spectacular shows, and received its present name in 1932. Among its early productions was an all-star revival of *She Stoops to Conquer* with Mrs. Leslie Carter as Mrs. Hardcastle, followed after two weeks by a revival of *Diplomacy*. In 1929 Mrs. Fiske

made one of her last stage appearances in the highly amusing *Ladies of the Jury*, while a year later came *Jew Süss*, followed by light opera until 1932. A return to straight drama was made with *Lost Horizon* (1934), but the house reverted to musical shows, with some success, until in 1937 critics and public alike acclaimed Margaret Webster's production of *Richard II*, with Maurice Evans in the namepart. The same combination was responsible for *Hamlet* in 1938 and for *Henry IV, Part I*, with Evans as Falstaff, in 1939. The following year saw Helen Hayes and Maurice Evans in *Twelfth Night*, produced under the auspices of the Theatre Guild, and the poignant *Native Son*, in which Canada Lee gave a fine performance. The theatre was for a long time occupied by the Theatre Guild's production of *Oklahoma!*, a musical play based on *Green Grow the Lilacs*, which opened in 1943.   G. F.

ST. JAMES'S THEATRE, LONDON, built by John Braham in 1835, on a site occupied by an old hostelry dating back to Charles II. He was then 58, and invested in it his life savings of £26,000. He opened on 14 Dec. with *Agnes Sorel*, styled a burletta to evade the ban on plays, singing the tenor role himself. With him were Streeton, Priscilla Horton, afterwards Mrs. German Reed, and Miss Glossop—her first appearance. Boxes were 5*s.*, pit 3*s.*, and gallery 2*s.*, with half-price to all parts. But nothing succeeded, neither Braham's own productions nor the importations of a French company. In 1836 came a series of comic plays and operettas by Dickens, none of which succeeded. Braham hung on until 1838, but by then he was penniless, and had to start all over again. The theatre continued to be unsuccessful. Bunn staged opera there to empty benches. The only things that drew money were a wild beast show, and a German company, which profited by the fashion for all things German due to the influence of the Prince Consort, in whose honour the theatre was renamed the Prince's. When Bunn went bankrupt at Drury Lane the theatre closed, to be reopened in 1842 under its old name by Mitchell. He ran it for twelve years, almost entirely with French companies, Rachel appearing there in 1846 and, for the last time in England, in 1853. Three years later Mitchell gave up his tenancy, having lost much money by it.

The theatre then went through a period of short and not very successful managements. Toole had his first regular engagement in London there, Braham's son essayed his fortune with an opera which ran for five nights, Miss Herbert, under the management of Frank Matthews, thrilled the town in *Lady Audley's Secret*, Irving made his second London appearance as Doricourt in *The Belle's Stratagem*, and in 1879 Hare and the Kendals assumed joint management, which lasted successfully until 1888, breaking the spell of bad luck which had for so long dogged the theatre. After a further short period of failure the theatre was opened on 31 Jan. 1891 by George Alexander, whose long tenancy as actor-manager was the most brilliant the theatre had ever known. In May 1893 there was a sensation when Mrs. Patrick Campbell appeared as Paula in *The Second Mrs. Tanqueray*, and among Alexander's other successes were *The Importance of Being Earnest*, *The Prisoner of Zenda*, *Paolo and Francesca*, which brought Henry Ainley to London, *Old Heidelberg*, and *His House in Order*. In 1900 the auditorium of the theatre was entirely reconstructed. In 1911 Alexander was knighted. The last play in which he appeared at the St. James's was *The Aristocrat*, in Jan. 1917. He died the following year, at the age of 59, and after him managements came and went, one of the most successful being Gilbert Miller's, partnered, for a short time, by Henry Ainley. Gerald du Maurier produced, among other plays, *The Last of Mrs. Cheyney* with Gladys Cooper, and later successes were *The Green Goddess* with George Arliss, an adaptation of *Pride and Prejudice*, and a fine revival of *A Month in the Country*. The theatre suffered some damage by enemy action during both world wars, but is still in use.

W. M. P.

ST. LOUIS, see PIONEER THEATRE IN THE U.S.A.

ST. MARTIN'S THEATRE, LONDON, in West Street, St. Martin's Lane, a small intimate theatre, built by Bertie A. Meyer, who was its first lessee. It opened on 23 Nov. 1916 with C. B. Cochran's production of *Hoop-La*, followed by Brieux's *Damaged Goods*, which created a sensation. Seymour Hicks appeared in *Sleeping Partners* in 1917, and in 1920 Alec L. Rea took over the theatre, and the Reandean and Reandco managements, of which he was chairman, produced a number of plays, many of them by new authors. They included *The Skin Game*, *A Bill of Divorcement*, *Loyalties*, *Berkeley Square*, *Strange Orchestra*, and *The Wind and the Rain*, which ran for 1,001 performances. In 1937-8 Basil Dean, who had been the producer for Reandean, had a season with J. B. Priestley, whose Yorkshire comedy, *When we are Married*, had its first London performance there.

In the foyer of the theatre is a plaque in memory of Meggie Albanesi, the young actress whose early death was a great loss to the stage, and who made her earliest successes at the St. Martin's Theatre.   W. M. P.

ŚAKUNTALĀ, see INDIA.

SALISBURY COURT, LONDON, the last theatre built in London before the Civil War. It was erected in 1629 by Richard Gunnell and William Blagrove at a cost of one thousand pounds. It stood on part of the site of Dorset House, where Salisbury Square, Fleet Street, now stands. It was a 'private' theatre, with a roof; built of brick, it occupied a piece of ground 140×40 ft. It was in the possession

of the King's Revels from 1629 to 1631, of Prince Charles's Men, 1631-5, of the Queen's Men, 1637-42. During the Commonwealth surreptitious performances were given there, but the interior fittings were destroyed by soldiers in Mar. 1649. William Beeston restored it in 1660, and Rhodes's company played there, as did Davenant's before he built his own theatre near by. In 1661 George Jolly was there, and Beeston himself had a company there from 1663 to 1664. It was burned down in the Great Fire of London, 1666.

W. M. P.

SALLE DES MACHINES, a small but well-equipped theatre, built by Vigarani in 1660 to house the spectacular shows in honour of the marriage of Louis XIV. It continued in use for many years for Court entertainment, and was later under the control of the artist and scenic designer Jean Bérain. It was, however, under Servandony that it reached the height of its splendour, many magnificent spectacles being given there with his designs and machinery.

SALLÉ, MARIE (1710-56), a famous ballerina, contemporary with Camargo, and one of the first to attempt some reform in the dress of the dancer. Camargo had already shortened her full skirts, but Sallé discarded them altogether, replacing the cumbersome paniers and elaborate head-dresses of the day by flowing draperies and loose hair. Thus attired, she appeared at Covent Garden in 1734 in a ballet entitled 'Pygmalion', but her efforts were unavailing, and it was left to Isadora Duncan, nearly two hundred years later, to popularize the classical Greek chiton.

SALTICA, see FABULA (7).

SALTIKOV-SHCHEDRIN, MIKHAIL EVGRAFOVICH (1826-89), one of the most brilliant satirists in Russian literature, and the author of one outstanding play, *The Death of Pazukhin*, published during his lifetime, but not performed until 1901. It was revived by the Moscow Art Theatre in 1914, and done by them in New York in 1924. Another, *Shadows*, was found among his papers and first produced in 1914. Both plays reveal the rottenness and corruption of the Tsarist society of the time, a theme to which Saltikov-Shchedrin returned again and again in his other writings. Many of these were subsequently dramatized, though they, and his so-called 'Dramatic Essays', written in dialogue form, were not intended for the stage.

SALT LAKE CITY, see PIONEER THEATRE IN THE U.S.A.

SALVIATI, FRANCESCO (1510-63), see MACHINERY.

SALVINI, TOMMASO (1829-1916), Italian actor, child of actors, who was on the stage at

[699]

14, appearing with much success in the comedies of Goldoni. In 1847 he joined the company of Adelaide Ristori, then just beginning her successful career, and with her made his first success in tragedy. His life was a succession of triumphs, and he was known all over Europe and America, visiting England frequently, and the U.S.A. five times between 1873 and 1889. On one visit he played Othello to the Iago of Edwin Booth. Othello was always his finest part, and he sensibly refused to play it more than four times a week. He was also good as Macbeth and as King Lear, and in the plays of Alfieri. Among modern parts his best was Conrad in Giacometti's *La Morte Civile* (1861). He retired in 1890, but in 1902 returned to the stage to take part in the celebrations in Rome in honour of Adelaide Ristori's 80th birthday. He published a volume of memoirs, part of which appeared in English as *Leaves from the Autobiography of Tommaso Salvini* (1893). His son Alessandro (1861–96) was also an actor, and had some success in the United States.

SAM H. HARRIS THEATRE, NEW YORK, on the south side of 42nd Street between Broadway and Eighth Avenue. This opened on 7 May 1914 and was originally a cinema, as it is to-day. In between it saw the production of several successful plays, including *On Trial*, *Justice*, and *The Greeks Had a Word For It*, while in 1922 John Barrymore, under the direction of Arthur Hopkins, played Hamlet 101 times, thus breaking by one performance Booth's former record for the part. The theatre reverted to films on 18 Mar. 1933.   G. F.

SAMSON, JOSEPH ISIDORE (1793–1871), French actor, who entered the Conservatoire at 16, and subsequently spent several years in the provinces. In 1819 he appeared in Paris at the opening of the new Odéon theatre, and made such a good impression that the manager, Picard, retained him as leading man until 1826, when the Comédie-Française claimed his services. There he found himself overshadowed by several older actors, and resigned in order to go to the Palais-Royal. After a few years he returned to the Comédie-Française, where he remained for the rest of his career, making his first success as Bertrand de Rantzau in 1833. In 1843 he became Doyen of the company, and retired in 1863. A handsome man, with a fine profile and a mass of curly hair, he was accounted a good actor, but it is as the teacher of Rachel that he is chiefly remembered. In was his influence that enabled her, at 15, to enter the Conservatoire, and though her father soon took her away in order that she might earn money by acting, she returned to Samson for private lessons. By instructing her in the classical tradition, which he had himself received from Talma, Samson contributed not a little to the revival of French tragedy with which Rachel is associated. He is said to have been one of the finest teachers of acting ever known at the Conservatoire, where he remained on the staff until his death, and many of his pupils became famous. He was also the author of a number of comedies.

SAM S. SHUBERT THEATRE, NEW YORK, see SHUBERT.

SÁNCHEZ, FLORENCIO (1875–1910), see SOUTH AMERICA, 1.

SANDERSON, MARY (?–1712), see BETTERTON (2).

SANDFORD, SAMUEL (*fl.* 1660–99), Restoration actor, a member of Davenant's company at Dorset Garden, and a master of facial expression. He specialized in somewhat wicked characters, and Charles II called him 'the best Villain in the world'.

SAN FRANCISCO, see PIONEER THEATRE IN THE U.S.A.

SAN GALLO, BASTIANO DA (1481–1551), see MACHINERY.

SANGER'S AMPHITHEATRE, LONDON, see ASTLEY'S.

SANQUIRICO, ALESSANDRO (1780–1849), see BALLET, 4 and SCENERY, 4.

SANSKRIT DRAMA, see INDIA.

SANS PAREIL, LONDON, see ADELPHI THEATRE (1).

SANS SOUCI, LONDON, a small theatre built by Charles Dibdin at the corner of Leicester Place, Leicester Square, in 1796. Here he appeared in his one-man 'Table Entertainments', of which he was author, composer, narrator, singer, and accompanist, until 1805, when he sold it. Edmund Kean, as a boy, gave acrobatic performances there. Although described as 'an elegant little theatre', it was too small for any save special shows, and became a place for amateur entertainments and benefits. In 1832 it was given over to vaudeville, and in 1834 a French company occupied it. After that it was disused and was eventually pulled down.   W. M. P.

For the Sans Souci, New York, see NIBLO'S GARDEN.

SANTURINI, FRANCESCO (1627–82), see SCENERY, 3.

SARAT, AGNAN (?–1613), French provincial actor, who in 1578 took a company to Paris and leased the theatre of the Hôtel de Bourgogne from the Confraternity of the Passion. After a short stay he disappeared again into the provinces, and in 1600 returned to Paris as chief comedian in the company of Valleran-Lecomte, with whom he remained until his death.

SARCEY, FRANCISQUE (1827–99), French dramatic critic, who had an immense following, and by his numerous writings and lecture-tours could make or unmake a dramatist. Himself convinced of the rightness of his opinion, he could convince his audience, and knew how to gain their confidence from the beginning. He personified for the polyglot audiences that flocked to hear him all over Europe the fat, jolly, gesticulating Frenchman whose common sense one could trust. Many of his dramatic judgements—which were not always correct, since he distrusted originality in any form— were reprinted in his books, notably *Comédiens et comédiennes* (1878) and *Quarante ans de Théâtre* (1900).

SARDOU, VICTORIEN (1831–1908), French dramatist, and one of the most uniformly successful of his day. Like Scribe, whose successor he was, Sardou wrote copiously on a number of subjects, with expert craftsmanship and superficial brilliance. His first successful play was a comedy, *Les Pattes de mouche* (1860), done in London as *A Scrap of Paper*, but he was equally at home in historical drama, of which the best known is probably *Madame Sans-Gêne* (1893), in melodrama— *Fédora* (1882) and *La Tosca* (1887), later used by Puccini for his opera—and in social drama. Of the last, his *Dora* (1877) and *Divorçons* (1880) are typical. The former, as *Diplomacy*, in a translation by Clement Scott, was for a long time popular with London audiences. Many of Sardou's plays were written for Sarah Bernhardt, to whom they owed much of their success. Sardou, who brought everything to a commonplace level, and judged a play solely as a vehicle for a popular success, has been the cockshy of many critics. Shaw, who disliked everything he stood for, coined the word Sardoodledom to epitomize his 'well-made' play, while Henry James called him 'that supremely clever contriver'. Yet he had great gifts theatrically, and his characters lack only life—but it is a fatal lack.

SAROYAN, WILLIAM (1908–   ), American writer whose plays are marked by improvisatory exuberance and rhapsodic celebration of the common man. He was born of Armenian parents in Fresno, California. After a little schooling, he sold newspapers, carried telegrams, worked in a vineyard, and started writing short stories, first attracting attention with *The Daring Young Man on the Flying Trapeze* (1934). His first-produced long one-acter, *My Heart's in the Highlands* (1939), was a tender treatment of a poet's struggle to maintain his integrity in a materialistic world. The carefree spirit of the play affirmed its author's faith in man's ability to triumph over bleak reality. Saroyan's next rhapsody, the Pulitzer Prize and Drama Critics' Award play, *The Time of Your Life* (1939), assembled a motley group of characters whose hungers were counterpointed by a sense of comradeship and assertions of their individuality. Hovering over them was a disenchanted man who dispensed encouragement and money to them on the principle that 'in the time of your life, live—so that in that good time there shall be no ugliness or death for

yourself or for any life your life touches'. Less successful but also suffused with sympathy for delicate and frustrated souls was *Love's Old Sweet Song* (1940), which treated the awakening of a genteel spinster by a salesman of bottled panaceas, and *The Beautiful People* (1941), which celebrated the spiritual beauty of a sensitive girl and her shiftless father. The lynching of an innocent tramp was the theme of a distinguished one-act play *Hello Out There* (1942), and an irrepressible young writer's conflict with a ruthless Hollywood mogul was the subject of *Get Away, Old Man* (1943). Saroyan wrote a number of other elusive professionally-unproduced plays, which suffered from chaotic dramaturgy and failed to win support.   J. G.

SATYR-DRAMA. The Greek tragic poet had to present four plays at one performance— three tragedies (whether a connected 'trilogy' or not) and a satyr-play. This was a burlesque, in which a hero of myth, often a hero from the trilogy, was introduced in some ludicrous situation, and always in association with a chorus of satyrs. Satyrs, or Sileni, were conceived as creatures of the wild, half-human, half-animal; their stage-costume was indecent, and gave them the ears and tail of a horse.

The origin of this surprising association of tragedy and the satyr-drama is not clear. Aristotle speaks of tragedy 'developing out of the satyric, with its short plots and ludicrous diction'; some modern scholars, naturally, find this difficult to believe. Certainly the dramatic form of the satyr-drama resembled that of tragedy—definite episodes were separated, or linked, by choral odes; and the metre was the metre of tragedy, not of comedy—but this may be due to imitation. The characteristics of the satyr-drama were rude action, vigorous dancing, boisterous fun, and indecency in speech and gesture.

Arion is said to have been the first to make the satyr-revel metrical in form; elsewhere Pratinas, a century later, is said to have been the 'first to write satyr-plays'. It seems that the satyr-play must have formed part of the tragic contest when that was instituted by Pisistratus at the festival of Dionysus; though the connexion between satyrs and Dionysus is not clear either. Pratinas and Aeschylus are regarded as the great masters of the satyr-drama. One satyr-play survives entire, the *Cyclops* of Euripides; another in part, the *Ichneutae* (Trackers) of Sophocles. During the fifth century there was at least a partial modification of the tradition, inasmuch as Euripides' *Alcestis*, a tragi-comedy, was presented in lieu of a satyr-play.

There is no connexion whatever between satyric drama and satire, or between it and any form of Greek comedy.   H. D. F. K.

SAURIN, BERNARD JOSEPH (1706–81), French dramatist, originally a lawyer. A pension from a wealthy friend enabled him at 40 to retire and devote himself entirely to literature, for which he had great aptitudes. He was the author of a successful tragedy, *Spartacus* (1760), of a comedy, *Les Mœurs du temps* (1759) and of a *drame bourgeois*, *Béverlei* (1768), based on Moore's *The Gamester*. It was probably taken from Diderot's translation of the latter, for there is no evidence that Saurin knew English, and represents the most serious of several attempts to introduce contemporary English drama to France. But Saurin omits much of the melodrama, and concentrates on the pathetic situation of Béverlei's family, including Tomi, his infant son. Of all Saurin's plays it is the most interesting to read nowadays. Of the rest, the actors, says Clairon, who played in it, had great hopes of *Blanche et Guiscard* (1763), but it was disappointingly received. This too is based on an English play, Thomson's *Tancred and Sigismunda*, given at Drury Lane in 1745.

SAVILLE THEATRE, LONDON, in Shaftesbury Avenue. This opened on 8 Oct. 1931, under the management of Jack Waller, with *For the Love of Mike*, a musical play which proved successful. It was followed by other equally successful musical and straight productions. The theatre was badly damaged by enemy action in 1940–1, but reopened and carried on. Firth Shephard produced successful revues there, and later straight plays.

W. M. P.

SAVOY THEATRE. (1) LONDON, built and opened by D'Oyly Carte in Oct. 1881 with *Patience*, transferred from the Opera Comique. With its delicate colouring, quilted silk curtain, and electric lighting, it struck a new note in theatres. Here were staged the Gilbert and Sullivan light operas, and all, including those which first appeared at the Royalty or the Opera Comique, are now labelled with the name of the Savoy. Later works with Sullivan's music, but libretti by other hands, also produced at the Savoy, had not the same success, nor was Gilbert successful with other composers.

Apart from the Savoy operas, the theatre had a success in *Merrie England*. It then had a run of bad luck and was closed for a time, but the Vedrenne–Barker partnership was successful there in 1907 with revivals of Shaw, while in 1912–14 Barker produced there *The Winter's Tale*, *Twelfth Night*, and *A Midsummer Night's Dream*. Other notable plays staged there have been *Paddy the Next Best Thing*, *Young Woodley*, *Journey's End*, and *The Man Who Came To Dinner*. The theatre was reconstructed and redecorated in 1929. Its main entrance is in the forecourt of the Savoy Hotel, Strand, and the theatre is built partly underground.

W. M. P.

(2) NEW YORK. This theatre opened as Schley's Music-Hall in Feb. 1900, playing only vaudeville, and in October of the same year changed its name and policy. It housed a number of musical shows, and transfers of successful plays from other theatres, but had a somewhat uneventful history and finally became a cinema.

G. F.

SAXE-MEININGEN, see MEININGEN PLAYERS.

SCALA, FLAMINIO (*fl.* 1600–21), an important figure of the *commedia dell'arte*, known as Flavio. He was concerned with the second group of Confidenti, and more occupied with their business management, of which his letters reveal many interesting details, than with acting. He was the author of a collection of *scenarii* printed in 1611.

SCALA THEATRE, LONDON. In the late eighteenth century Signor Paschali built a concert room in Tottenham Street, Tottenham Court Road, which was purchased and enlarged by the committee for the Concerts of Antient Music, whose performances were patronized by Royalty. In 1802 the building was taken over by an amateur society called the Pic Nics, whose success earned them the hostility of the Patent Theatres. In 1808 they were replaced by a circus, which was not successful. The hall was closed for a time and reopened by Mr. Paul, a gunsmith in the Strand, to gratify his wife's theatrical ambitions. These brought him to the Bankruptcy Court. In Dec. 1814 the building was sold to Harry Beverley for £315, the purchaser taking over the scenery, wardrobe, &c., for another £300. Rent was £177 a year, and taxes £35. Considerably altered, it opened in 1815 as the Regency Theatre of Varieties. The stage was 21 ft. wide and 36 ft. deep, and prices ranged from 1s. to 4s., with a capacity of about £130. After a six years' struggle it was taken over by Brunton, who called it the West London Theatre and starred his daughter Elizabeth, afterwards Mrs. Yates of the Adelphi.

In 1826 French companies visiting London played there, but without success. During 1829 Tom Dibdin, Watkins Burroughs, and Mrs. Waylett all ventured, but to no avail. In Jan. 1831, after being known as the Tottenham Street Theatre, it was rechristened the Queen's, and, altered and redecorated, was opened by Mrs. Nisbett with Mrs. Glover, Mrs. Humby, and a good company. In spite of this, and of the fact that Mme Céleste made her first London appearance here, the new management had little but misfortune, and left during 1837–8, having been financed by Ephraim Bond, a money-lender and gaming-house proprietor. After Mrs. Nisbett, Madame Vestris and Charles Mathews took the theatre, calling it the Fitzroy, as it had been for a short time in 1833. In Oct. 1839 it became the Queen's again, and under the management of C. J. James, a scenic artist, it was known as the Dust Hole. Prices went as low as a shilling, eightpence, sixpence, and fourpence, with half-price for boxes and pit, and lurid melodrama was the attraction. The theatre shared with the Bower Saloon the doubtful reputation of being the lowest-grade playhouse in London, and the neighbourhood matched it. At this point

Marie Wilton and Squire Bancroft took the theatre on a borrowed capital of £1,000 (of which only £150 remained when the curtain went up on the opening night in 1865), renamed it the Prince of Wales's, by permission of the heir to the throne, and, starting with burlesque, proceeded to revolutionize British stage comedy with the works of T. W. Robertson, whose most famous plays they produced and played in. An outstanding feature of their management was the introduction of 'practicable' stage settings. When they left the Prince of Wales's to go to the Haymarket in 1879 they had made the despised Dust Hole into a famous and fashionable theatre. On 21 Feb. 1880 Geneviève Ward appeared there in a revival of *Forget-Me-Not*, playing Stéphanie de Mohrivart to the Prince Maleotti of the young Beerbohm Tree. In 1882 the theatre was closed owing to a dispute and the necessity of structural alterations. It was rebuilt and improved by Dr. Distin Maddick, who opened it in 1905 as the Scala with Forbes-Robertson in *The Conqueror*. It has had a somewhat chequered career since, but is still in use, though slightly damaged by enemy action in 1940–1. The old main entrance is retained as its stage door.

W. M. P.

SCAMMACCA, ORTENSIO (1562–1648), an Italian Jesuit, author of nearly fifty plays on sacred or moral themes, intended ostensibly for the edification of the faithful, but containing a good deal of sensational matter, eked out with love intrigues, and interlarded with piety. The religious element is, however, preponderant, and even in plays drawn from classical sources angels and devils make their appearance, while women, contrary to the usual practice of Jesuit drama, are given important parts.

SCAMOZZI, VINCENZO (1552–1616), Italian architect, pupil of the great Palladio, whose Teatro Olimpico at Vicenza he finished after his master's death. He was also responsible for the building of the Sabbionetta theatre (see ARCHITECTURE and SCENERY, 2).

SCANDINAVIA. Of the four Scandinavian countries, each of which has produced a remarkable literature, only Denmark has what might be termed a typical European dramatic history, beginning, like England, France, Germany, and Italy, with medieval religious drama and the later School Drama, or its equivalent, and thereafter producing plays, now predominantly native, now influenced in varying degrees by the great movements of general European literary history: seventeenth-century classicism, the Romantic period, and so forth. Like the other European literatures, it has had periods predominantly dramatic or marked by the emergence of great dramatists, alternating with others relatively unproductive in this field, but has never for long since the seventeenth century been entirely sterile. In this way, it may be said to correspond with the broad pattern of European drama, possessing, like other literatures, though not necessarily in the same order as any other, its systole and diastole.

But the dramatic history of each of the others is, in one way or another, peculiar to itself. Iceland, even in the great saga period (approximately thirteenth century), produced no drama, though often showing a strong underlying dramatic instinct; not until the late nineteenth and early twentieth centuries did a drama begin to grow up under the stimulus of the rest of Scandinavia, Europe, and America. Norway, whose literary history in every branch is affected by the union with Denmark in the late fourteenth century and the gradual substitution of the Danish for the native language, produced indeed, in the eighteenth and early nineteenth centuries, dramatists whose spirit, and sometimes subject-matter, was essentially Norwegian, but who wrote in Danish and were partially assimilated into Danish literature. Its great native contributions to drama did not come until the second half of the nineteenth century with Bjørnson and Ibsen. Then, at one stroke, by the work of Ibsen, it produced the most potent influence in European drama for what is now nearly a century. A glance over Norwegian literature, however, makes it clear that the genius of the nation has always been, potentially if not actually, dramatic and that the leading place it has taken in European drama since the rise of Ibsen has not been accidental. The history of Swedish drama has been completely different again from the other three. Here, on the contrary, it would seem that the genius of the race was not essentially dramatic. All the facilities for drama have been there, as they were in Denmark and the rest of Europe, from the sixteenth century, and there has in fact been a continuous stream of dramatists adequate to maintain the supply. But most of them were either imitators of the Danish, German, French, or English, or poets who, engaging more happily in some other form of literary expression, found there their distinction and international reputation. Not until the coming of Strindberg at the end of the nineteenth century did Sweden, in spite of its advantages, produce a dramatist who, *as a* dramatist, had even a limited reputation outside Scandinavia.

1. DENMARK. The history of Danish drama begins in the sixteenth century, where the presence of relatively late medieval forms suggests that there had been, to some extent, an earlier drama also. No records remain to indicate a body of Danish drama comparable with that of England, France, and Holland in the thirteenth, fourteenth, and fifteenth centuries, and only the School Drama of Christiern Hansen (?–post 1545) (*Den Utro Hustru* (*The Unfaithful Wife*) and *Dorothiae Komedie*), and of Hieronymus Justesen Ranch (1539–1607), and the anonymous *Ludus de Sancto Kanuto Duce* (1530), survive to indicate varying degrees of independence in the use of native sources. Most important of these are

perhaps Ranch's *Salomon's Hylding (Homage to Solomon)* (1584), *Kerrig Niding* (1598), and *Samson's Fængsel (The Captivity of Samson)* (1599). The absence of vernacular plays throughout the seventeenth century (a fact remarked upon by Holberg himself), coupled with the tradition of producing French and German plays in the Copenhagen theatre in the early eighteenth century, suggests that, with the disappearance of the ecclesiastical and scholastic Latin or vernacular School Drama, dramatic writing ceased for a time in Denmark. It was re-created at one stroke by Holberg.

Ludvig Holberg (1684–1754), though a Norwegian by birth, worked in Copenhagen and was the first dramatist to use the Danish language. He had a strong influence upon Danish drama, setting an example of realistic comedy combining the technique of the classics and of Molière, that was the more important in that Danish literature was soon afterwards exposed to strong German influences. Without the steadying effects of Holberg's authority in native comedy, Danish poets and dramatists, who assimilated the influence of Klopstock and the 'bardic' German poetry that the Norwegians resisted, might have postponed the development of a native Danish drama.

Johannes Ewald (1743–81) was the first to experience this sympathy with contemporary German inspiration and to carry it over into drama. He followed Holberg in so far as he wrote in Danish, but in little else. One of Denmark's great lyric poets, he wrote its first tragedies, beginning with the dramatic poem, *Adam og Eva* (pub. 1769), and passing on to drama proper with *Rolf Krage* (1770) and *Balder's Død (The Death of Balder)* (1774). His genius gradually freed itself from the German influence and in *Fiskerne (The Fishers)* in 1778 his power as a dramatic poet and native dramatist produced the finest of his works. This and two fragments that his early death left unfinished show tendencies and potentialities so far unknown in Europe.

At the death of Ewald, Denmark was on the verge of the *Guldalderen* (the Golden Age) in which her poets were from time to time dramatists and her dramatists poets. Ole Samsøe with the *Dyveke* (1796) marks the end of the eighteenth century, and the nineteenth opens with the names of Otto Carl Olufsen (1764–1827), whose *Gulddaasen (The Golden Box)* (1793) was probably the best comedy since Holberg, and with the work of Peter Andreas Heiberg (1758–1841), leading on to the astonishing succession of Oehlenschlaeger, J. L. Heiberg, Hertz, and Hauch.

Adam Oehlenschlaeger (1779–1850) is generally considered to have had a greater influence upon Danish drama than any other writer except Holberg, and it was an influence that balanced Holberg's. He was a writer of tragedies upon native themes, some of them historical or legendary, but essentially northern, a romantic whose romanticism led on from the later work of Ewald, converting rather than counteracting the German influences of the eighteenth century. At a period when the energies of Norwegians were necessarily preoccupied with establishing their constitution and their nationality, Danish nationalism was rich in imaginative, poetic, and dramatic expression. Oehlenschlaeger's most characteristic plays are *St. Hans Aften-Spil (Saint John's Night)* (1802), *Aladdin* (1804), *Hakon Jarl* (1805), *Palnatoke* (1808), *Stærkodder* (1812), *Hagbarth og Signe* (1815), and *Væringerne i Miklagård (The Varangians at Miklagård)* (1827).

Johan Ludwig Heiberg (1791–1860) was a writer of a wholly different kind, whose popular romantic dramas gradually took precedence over the tragedy of Oehlenschlaeger. His gifts were varied, extending to realistic comedy on one side and strongly influential literary criticism upon the other. His familiarity with Paris and Parisian culture was of no little value at this period of Denmark's dramatic history. Between 1847 and 1854 his directorship of the National Theatre gave him yet another sphere of influence. Characteristic of his romantic plays are *Elverhøj (The Elf-Hill)* (1828) and *Fata Morgana* (1838), and of his comedies and satires *En Sæjl efter Døden (A Soul after Death)* (1841) and *Nøddeknækkerne (The Nutcrackers)* (1845). At the other extreme are his vaudevilles, realistic comedies with songs on topical Danish themes though on French models.

The sentimental drama of Bernhard Severin Ingemann (1789–1862) had great popularity and he sometimes threw the work of Oehlenschlaeger into the shade in the affections of the Danish public by his national, historical novels. He was a prolific writer, perhaps best remembered as a dramatist by his *Sulamith og Salomon* (1839).

Henrik Hertz (1797–1870), who was of Jewish parentage, wrote chiefly comedies, realistic or romantic, but he is remembered also for at least one romantic national drama and two tragedies. He also made a notable excursion into criticism in sympathy with J. L. Heiberg. His most characteristic comedies are, perhaps, *Herr Burchardt og hans Familie (Mr. Burchardt and his Family)*, and *Flyttedager (Quarter-days)* (both 1827). These were followed by other comedies until 1836, and in 1837 by *Svend Dyrings Hus (The House of Svend Dyring)*, a national drama drawn from folk-tales, and the famous *Kong René's Datter (King René's Daughter)*, which was widely translated. The tragedy *Ninon* (1848) and the romantic comedy *Tonietta* (1849) represent the work of his middle years. From the later plays may be mentioned *Et Offer (A Sacrifice)* (1854), *En Kurmethode (The Cure)* (1861), and *Tre Dage i Padua (Three Days in Padua)* (1869), his last play.

Thomas Overskou (1798–1873), the dramatic critic and historian, also left a number of plays, of which *Pak* (1845) is probably the best known.

From the middle of the century onwards come the tragedies and historical dramas of

Johannes Carsten Hauch (1790–1872), of which the best known is probably *Marsk Stig* (*Marshal Stig*) (1850). He, with Jens Christian Hostrup (1818–92), bridges the gulf between the dramatists of the Golden Age and the group in the later nineteenth century forming part of the movement that originated with Georg Brandes (1842–1927). This eminent critic swayed literary opinion in Denmark and far beyond, and was one of the first, as he is still the best, of the supporters of Ibsen.

Earliest of this circle to leave a considerable mark was Holger Drachmann (1846–1908), poet and lyric dramatist, who was at the end of the century the most popular playwright of Denmark. Best known of his plays are, perhaps, *Der var en Gang* (*Once upon a time*) (1885), *Vølund Smed* (1894), *Brav Karl* (1898) in which he made his name, *Gurre* (1899), *Halfred Vandraadeskjald* (1900), and *Det Grönne Haab* (*The Evergreen Hope*). His strength was in the poetic and lyrical quality of his dramas rather than in their structure and form.

With Edvard Brandes (1847–1931) and Otto Benzon (1856–1927) the characteristic modern drama sets in, analytical and critical of contemporary society as that of Norway, France, and England also became, as soon as the influence of Bjørnson and Ibsen was felt. Edvard Brandes' *Et Besøg* (*A Visit*) (1882) and Benzon's *En Skandale* (*A Scandal*) (1884) show the tendency clearly. From the late nineteenth century to the present day the Danish drama may be roughly divided into two phases, that of the period before the nineteen-thirties and that of the thirties onwards.

The early twentieth century was a period of fertility; there were few major dramatists but a number of plays of some distinction. The most familiar names are those of Einar Christiansen, Sven Lange, Henri Nathansen (the dramatist of Jewish problems), Olaf Hansen, and, outstanding among their contemporaries, Hjalmar Bergström, Gustav Wied, and Helge Rode.

Helge Rode (1870–1937) is a poetic dramatist of religious and national problems, whose plays are less well known outside Scandinavia than those of Bergström and Wied. Hjalmar Bergström (1868–1914) is a dramatist of social problems closely related to Ibsen's tradition, whose best-known plays are, perhaps, *Lynggaard & Co.* (1905), *Karen Bornemann* (1907), and *Dame-Te* (1910). Gustav Wied (1858–1914) is a highly original novelist and dramatist with close affiliations, this time to Strindberg. He began his dramatic career with a series of small satirical plays distinguished by their wit and the quality of their dialogue. His best-known play is probably *Ranke Viljer* (1906), translated into English as *2 × 2 = 5*.

The two outstanding dramatists of recent years are Kaj Munk and Kjeld Abell.

Kaj Munk (1898–1944) represents a drama unlike that of his immediate forerunners, a theatre of action and not of psychological dissection. Many of his plays are historical, *En Idealist* (1928), *Cant* (1934), *De Udvalgte* (*The Elect*) (1933), *Sejren* (*The Victory*) (1936),

Pilatus (1937), and finally *Niels Ebbesen* (1943), the play by which his name is best known, by reason of the associations which surround it. Notable among his non-historical plays are *I Brændingen* (*In the Breakers*) (1929), *Ordet* (*The Word*) (1932), which will probably prove to be his greatest play, and *Han Sidder ved Smeltediglen* (*He Sits by the Melting-Pot*) (1938).

Kjeld Abell (1902–) is a brilliant man of the theatre who has written some extremely interesting plays. Best known, perhaps, in Denmark and elsewhere, are *Melodien, der blev væk* (1935), a lyrical play done in England as *The Melody that got Lost*, and the more serious *Anna Sophie Hedvig* (1939), a play whose ideological implications link with the work of Kaj Munk and Nordahl Grieg (see NORWAY).

2. NORWAY. As has been said above, the drama of Norway is bound up with that of Denmark—in fact until the separation of 1814, and in effect for some years longer. There is some evidence that Norway had a share in the School Drama of the late sixteenth century, probably in the form of plays in Norse and Latin mixed; there would appear to have been no other regular theatrical activity apart from that afforded by Denmark. A fresh development is indicated by the opening of the theatre in Christiania in 1837 (its predecessor having been burnt in 1835), but its personnel remained Danish for some years. The first national theatre (Den nationale scene) was created at Bergen by the initiative of Ole Borneman Bull (1810–80), the musician, and opened only in 1850. The early years of Norwegian dramatic history are thus somewhat confused, as it is difficult to say to what extent the three earliest dramatists, Holberg, Brun, and Wessel, can be regarded as Norwegian, seeing that they owed to Copenhagen their theatrical education, the production of their plays, and their audiences. A measure of acclimatization is inevitable, since the nature of an audience and the traditions of a theatre have a powerful shaping influence upon the work of a dramatist. It has, however, seemed best to regard them here as Norwegian, and the significant history of that drama may therefore be said to begin in 1721.

In that year Ludvig Holberg became director of the Danish theatre in Copenhagen (doubling the post with that of Professor of Metaphysics in the University), and began to write plays in Danish, or Dano-Norwegian, the language of the educated classes throughout the *Tvillingrikene* (the 'twin-kingdoms'). Hitherto the Danish Theatre had produced only plays in French or German, but for the next six years Holberg poured out comedies written not only in the native language but about native types, Danish or Norwegian or both. He was a scholar who knew his Aristophanes, his Plautus, his Terence, but above all his Molière and his *commedia dell'arte*. But he was primarily a comic genius who, while using the technique and forms of the great comedy-writers of the past, drew his material from what lay at hand. The Danish people saw for the first time their customs, habits, and civilization presented in the mirror of comedy, the Danish and Norwegian literatures (as yet unseparated) were founded, the native language acclimatized, if only temporarily, upon the stage, and for this, as much as for his activities as a historian and a philosopher, the early eighteenth century in Denmark and Norway is known as 'The Age of Holberg'. His first play, *Den politiske Kandestøber (The Political Tinker)* (1722), and the later *Erasmus Montanus* (1723) are among the best-known.

After Holberg the output flags. The lead in drama passes from Norway to Denmark with the work of Ewald, but among the Norwegian writers resident in Copenhagen and forming Det Norske Selskab (The Norwegian Club) some were dramatists, if only to the extent of one remarkable play. Nordahl Brun (1745–1816) produced in 1772 a tragedy, *Zarine*, in the fashionable French tradition, and a little later *Einer Tambeskielver*, an early example of the patriotic saga-dramas popular for the next hundred years. *Zarine* was one of those plays which call for parody, and it got it. A parody by Johan Wessel (1742–85), *Kjærlighed uden Strømper (Love Without Stockings)*, a brilliant mock-tragedy, destroyed not only *Zarine*, but the outworn tradition it represented. Wessel was a comedy-writer of Holberg's own kind, but he wrote very little more: *Lykken bedre end Forstanden (More Lucky than Wise)* (1776) is perhaps the best-known.

Nor did the period that followed present any activity comparable with Holberg's. During the next half century some of Norway's most distinguished poets from time to time wrote plays and, more fortunate than their contemporaries in England, had their plays produced. But, coinciding with the Golden Age in Denmark, it is a barren period. The energies of the nation appear to have been absorbed in the political efforts leading up to and following the creation of the Constitution and the separation from Denmark in 1814.

Henrik Bjerregaard (1792–1842) produced a musical play, *Fjeldeventyret (The Adventure on the Mountain)* (1824), which was native in material and setting, and Henrik Arnold Wergeland (1808–45), though it was not his medium, wrote several plays. Of these, the first was *Irreparabile Tempus* (1828) and the finest *Venetianerne (The Venetians)* (1841); he wrote also some plays, such as *The Campbells* (1837), on English subjects. Andreas Munch (1811–84), son of Johan Storm Munch, again turned sometimes from verse to playwriting, contributing *Kong Sverres Ungdom (King Sverre's Youth)*, the prize-winning play of 1838, an English-history play, *Lord William Russell* (1857), which was the subject of much discussion, and the unfortunate *Hertug Skule* which, appearing in 1864, was immediately eclipsed by Ibsen's *Kongsemnerne (The Pretenders)*. Finally, the great linguist and philologist Ivar Aasen (1813–96) produced *Ervingen (The Heir)*, a popular musical play, in

1855 (one of its songs, 'Millom bakkar og berg', being the most popular national song even to-day).

But in that year Henrik Johan Ibsen (1826–1906) had already written his earliest plays and Bjørnstjerne Bjørnson (1832–1910) was just beginning. Between them these two dramatists revolutionized Norwegian thought, literature, and language, and carried the dramatic reputation of the country ahead of that of any other in Europe. Bjørnson's work in drama was less than Ibsen's both in quantity and in power, but he carried great weight in his own day because of his further reputation as a novelist and songwriter and his immense popularity as a political leader. Ibsen's influence upon Norwegian civilization is occasionally lost sight of only because the world has been primarily concerned with estimating his influence upon the world's. Bjørnson's early historical plays and Ibsen's great poetic dramas, *Brand* (1865) and *Peer Gynt* (1867), stirred the national imagination, and Ibsen's astounded Europe. Bjørnson's realistic and contemporary analyses and condemnation of the errors of society, culminating in *En Handske (A Gauntlet)* in 1883, in part preceded Ibsen's similar but graver and more profound studies of social evils. Both brought some salutary shocks and disturbance to the complacency of the society they condemned and, at least in Ibsen's case, to many similar societies outside Norway. When Ibsen died in 1906 Scandinavian drama was established among the great dramatic literatures of history.

The modern period has produced until recently no outstanding figures except Heiberg and Kinck, though again, men of great reputation as novelists or poets have from time to time written plays. Jonas Lie is known for *Lystige Koner (Merry Wives)* (1894), a social comedy, and *Lindelin* (1897); Alexander Kielland for *Paa Hjemveien (Homewards)* (1878), a comedy on business morality, *Hans Majestats Foged (His Majesty's Sheriff)*, and *Det Hele er Ingenting (It Is All Nothing)* (both 1880), *Betty's Formynder (Betty's Guardian)* (1887), a study of modern women, and *Professoren (The Professor)* (1888), on the conflict between the old and the new worlds in University life; Arne Garborg for *Uforsonlige (The Irreconcilables)* (1888) and *Læraren (The Teacher)* (1896); Knut Hamsun for a number of plays, some of them comparable with his novels, of which the best-known are, perhaps, the trilogy *Ved Rikets Port (At the Gate of the Kingdom)* (1895), *Livets Spil (The Play of Life)* (1896), and *Aftenrode (Afterglow)* (1898). To these may be added *Livet Ivold (In the Grip of Life)* and the eight-act dramatic poem *Munken Vendt* (1903).

Gunnar Heiberg (1857–1929) is, however, essentially a dramatist, a writer of great skill and originality, often satiric and often showing some affinity with Ibsen's latest phase. His *Tante Ulrikke (Aunt Ulrikke)* appeared in 1884, *Kong Midas (King Midas)* in 1890, and the two plays by which he is best known, *Balkonen (The Balcony)* and *Kjærlighedens*

Tragedie (*The Tragedy of Love*), in 1894 and 1904. To these may be added *Det Store Lod* (*The Grand Prize*) (1895), *Folkeraadet* (*The People's Council*) (1897), *Harald Svan's Mor* (*Harald Svan's Mother*) (1899), *Kjærlighed til Næsten* (*Charity Begins at Home*) (1902), *Jeg vil verge mit Land* (*I Will Defend My Country*), and *Paradesengen* (*The Lying-in-State*).

Another fine dramatic artist is Hans Kinck (1865–1926), whose *Drifte karen* (*The Drover*), a play on the theme of the erratic emergence of genius, with its sequel *Paa Rindalslægret* (*At Rindal Camp*) (1925), is sometimes compared with *Peer Gynt*. His plays on Italian themes are, in addition, works of learning: *Agilulf den Vise* (*Agilulf the Wise*) (1906), *Den Sidste Gjest* (*The Last Guest*) (1910), *Mot Karneval* (*Towards the Carnival*), *and Paa Ekrenes Gaard* (*On the Ekre Estate*) (both 1913). To the early years of this century belong also the works of Peter Egge; Hans Aanrud—*Storken* (1895), *Höit til hest* (*On the High Horse*) (1901), *Hanen* (*The Cock*) (1906); Gabriel Scott—*Himmeluret* (*The Clock of Heaven*) (1905), and *Babelstaarn* (1910); Hans Wiers-Jenssen—*Anne Pedersdotter* (1908); Gabriel Finne; Sigurd Ibsen; Anders Stiloff; Nils Collett Vogt; Johan Bojer; Vilhelm Krag—*Baldevins Bryllup* (*Baldevin's Wedding*) (1900). Outstanding slightly later is Nils Kjær (1870–1924), with satirical comedy and the drama of contemporary political and religious problems: *Regnskabets dag* (*The Day of Reckoning*) (1902), *Mimosa's Hjemkomst* (*Mimosa's Homecoming*) (1907), *Det lykkelige Valg* (*The Happy Election*) (1913), and *For Træet er det Haab* (*There is Hope for the Tree*) (1917). Here too should be mentioned the Landsmaal writers, Vetlie Vislie and Olaf Hoprekstad and Sigurd Christiansen.

The most notable names in Norwegian drama of the immediate past and present are Helge Krog (1889–) and Nordahl Grieg (1902–43); the difference between them is considerable and obvious. Krog is an acute and subtle psychologist whose perception of the undertones of human relations remains his chief characteristic whatever material he uses and whatever the mood of his play. His dialogue has the skill and fineness of finish associated with certain schools of modern French dramatists. Some of his most remarkable plays are *Det store Vi* (*The Great We*) (1919), *Jarlshus* (*The House of Jarl*) (1913), *På Solsiden* (*On the Sunny Side*) (1927), *Blåpapiret* (*The Copy*) (1928), *Konkylien* (*The Sounding Shell*) (1929), *Underveis* (*On the Way*) (1931), *Treklang* (*Triad*) (1933), and, perhaps the most notable of all, *Opbrud* (*Break-up*) (1936).

Nordahl Grieg, whose death in action in 1943 robbed Norway and Europe of one of their most promising younger dramatists, was a writer of power and of passionate thought, an experimenter in material and technique whose final form had hardly declared itself. His two most notable plays made a strong impression both in Scandinavia and abroad; the first, *Vår Aere og Vår Makt* (*Our Honour and Our Power*) (1935), was an anti-war play of overwhelming force and originality, and the second, *Nederlaget* (*The Defeat*) (1936), was a tragedy of the Paris Commune which has become famous far beyond Scandinavia. His earlier plays were *En Ung Mands Kjærlighet* (*A Young Man's Love*) (1927), *Barabbas* (1927), and *Atlanterhavet* (*The Atlantic*) (1932), to which should be added *Men imorgen* (*But To-morrow*) (1936).

3. SWEDEN. Although Swedish drama has a history of nearly equal length with Dano-Norwegian, there is a marked contrast in the significance of its contribution; until the work of Strindberg appeared no Swedish dramatist had reached European fame and exerted an influence upon European drama. The history of Swedish drama is, then, on the one hand, a succession of reflections of the prevailing tendencies in European drama—Italian, French, Dutch, English, German, Danish, and Norwegian—mirrored in the work of writers who were often skilled dramatists but of no great original genius and, on the other hand, a record of single, often remarkable, plays written by poets whose chief claim to fame rests upon their work in other forms. It would then, until the coming of Strindberg, appear to be the history of a race distinguished in other branches of literature but lacking any powerful dramatic tendency. Nor can this be entirely explained away by the presence of easily accessible drama in the neighbouring countries, for the history of Danish drama shows, in the early nineteenth century, the victory of a powerful native instinct over a vogue for translation and adaptation. The submission to such vogues which governed, for example, the English theatre from the middle of the eighteenth century until nearly the close of the nineteenth seems, in the case of Sweden, to have had a duration of nearly three hundred years.

The presence of the early School Drama, or Reformation Bible-play, suggests that Sweden had already some dramatic tradition in the mid-sixteenth century and had made some contribution to the medieval drama proper in which many literatures of Europe shared. But, as in the case of Denmark, there appears to be no record of those earlier phases which played a considerable, if not impressive, part in the history of English and of French drama. As it is, the history of Swedish drama begins with the vernacular *Tobiae Comedia* (pub. 1550), generally attributed to the humanist Olavus Petri (1493–1552). Unlike Denmark, Sweden has an almost continuous, if not particularly distinguished, series of vernacular plays from that point onwards, though when the School Drama dies down in the early seventeenth century, there is little to record until we find the work of the first foreign imitators in the middle of that century.

To the early School Drama proper belong such plays as *Josephi Historia* (pub. 1601) and *Dawidhs Historia* (pub. 1604), but modifications soon begin to set in. As in England and France at an earlier date, native comedy begins to mingle with the religious material and to fuse with the imitations of classical drama which soon appear. Johannes Messenius (1579–1636) and his followers begin to draw their material from Swedish saga and history, using dialogue as the vehicle for secular instead of sacred history. Messenius intended to cover Swedish history in 50 plays, but six only are extant, of which *Disa* (1611) is the first. In similar tradition are Nikolaus Holgeri Catonius with *Troijenborg* (*Troy Town*) (1632), sometimes reckoned the best play of the period, and Andreas Johannis Prytz with *Olof Skottkonung* (1620) and other chronicle plays, all with a religious trend. In *Judas Redivivus* (1614), Jacobus Rondeletius produced a 'Christian tragi-comedy' with more dramatic power, especially in its comic parts. All this, though imitative and perhaps on the whole more notable for quantity than quality, seems about to lead on to a healthy, native drama. Yet when the work of this group ceases nothing rises to take its place, and the coming of foreign influences in the middle of the century found no native stock strong enough to resist them. Except for Urban Hiärne (1641–1724), who belatedly carries the School Drama to its climax in the famous and popular *Rosimunda* (1665), the native drama is left to the University circles, while the Court patronizes the new French masque and the imitations of it in Swedish by Georg Stiernhielm (1598–1672): *Then fångne Cupido* (1649) and *Parnassus Triumphans* (1651).

By the beginning of the last decade Swedish actors were established in Stockholm (though the Royal Swedish Theatre itself did not open until 1737), but this in no way loosened the hold of the classical French drama, which carried over into the eighteenth century the traditions of seventeenth-century France and led to heavy Voltairean tragedies, and comedies (with rather more vitality) after Molière.

Olof Dalin (1708–63) is the most eminent writer of the mid-eighteenth century in Sweden, a man of genius who now and again also wrote plays, showing the influence of French tragedy, of Molière and Holberg in comedy, and of his English contemporaries, Addison, Pope, and Swift in general. His *Brynhilda* (1738) was the first Swedish tragedy of pure French classical derivation, and his comedy, *Den afundsjuke* (*The Jealous Man*), of the same year, points to Molière and Holberg. Genuine comedy, sometimes nearer to Holberg than to the English or French tradition, was contributed by Carl Gyllenborg (1679–1746), whose *Den Svenska sprätthöken* (*The Swedish Fop*) opened the Royal Swedish Theatre in 1737, and by R. G. Modée (1698–1752), who presented bourgeois comedy material in classical form. Erik Wrangel (1686–1765) produced between 1739 and 1748 two tragedies and one comedy; and translations—among other dramatists, of Holberg—played some part.

The influence of King Gustav III (1746–92) upon the drama of the latter part of the

eighteenth century was very strong. He encouraged dramatists, supported the National Theatre at Stockholm (opened in 1773), and himself wrote or collaborated in plays for Court performances. He gathered about him a group of playwrights: Carl Israel Hallman (1732–1800); Johan Henrik Kellgren (1751–95), who between 1780 and 1788 had some share in a number of historical plays; Carl Gustaf Leopold (1756–1829), with his Scandinavian legendary themes; Gudmund Jöran Adlerbeth (1751–1818), with his imitations of Racine and Voltaire at the turn of the century; Olof Kexél (1748–96), with his comedies of French and English derivation; and Carl Envallsson (1756–1806), who parodied the classical form with his *Iphigenie den andra* in 1800. In all this abundance there was little independence. In content, theme, or form (or in all of them) the French influence still held.

But even in the Romantic period that follows there is little emancipation in the drama and there are fewer dramatists. In Sweden, as in England, there is little drama worthy of note in the early nineteenth century except that written by poets who were primarily concerned with other kinds of literature. The Swedish poets, however, unlike their English contemporaries, had every encouragement to write drama, and the work of Atterbom and Stagnelius thus reached the stage.

Per Daniel Amadeus Atterbom (1790–1835) produced in the dramatic form what is often considered his masterpiece, *Lycksalighetens Ö* (*The Isle of Bliss*) (1824), but wrote no other plays. The highly original plays of Erik Johann Stagnelius (1793–1823) are, similarly, the work of a poet who was not primarily a dramatist: *Martyrerna* (*The Martyrs*) (1821); *Bacchanterna* (*The Bacchantes*) (1822); and *Thorsten Fiskare* (*Thorsten the Fisher*) and *Sigurd Ring* (posthumous). To the next period belong the historical dramas and the criticism of Bernhard von Beskow (1796–1868), beginning to show the influence of Schiller, and the dramatic work of Carl Jonas Love Almqvist (1793–1866).

Between this period and the coming of Strindberg in the late nineteenth century stand the names of Blanche, Börjessen, Dahlgren, and Jolin. August Theodore Blanche (1811–68) acclimatized in his comedies the art of J. L. Heiberg and Scribe; of some 36 plays may be mentioned *Positivhataren* (*The Man Who Hated the Barrel-Organ*) (1843); *Magister Bläckstadius* (1844); *Rika Morbror* (*The Rich Uncle*) (1845); *Hittebarnet* (*The Foundling*) (1847); *En Tragedi i Vimmerby* (1848). Johan Börjessen (1790–1866) wrote romantic drama influenced by his interpretation of Shakespeare, recently made accessible in K. A. Hagberg's translation. Fredrik August Dahlgren (1816–95), who also shows the influence of Shakespeare (as well as of Calderón), produced at least one popular play, his peasant play *Vermländingarne* (*The Vermlanders*) (1846).

By the late nineteenth century the influence

of Ibsen and Bjørnson was growing strong and was soon modified and then reinforced in Sweden by the work of Strindberg in the 1880s. To this period of Swedish drama belong the names of Agrell, Leffler, Ahlgren, and Hedberg, though the later work of Hedberg continues into the twentieth century. Alfhild Agrell (1849–1923) is remembered chiefly by the impression made by her *Räddad (Saved)* in 1882. Closer still to the influence of Ibsen is perhaps the work of Anne Charlotte Leffler (1849–92). In her *Sanna kvinnor (True Women)* (1883) we find the best of the 'indignationslitteratur'. It was followed by *Hur man gör godt (How to do Good)* (1885), and in 1891 by three more comedies. Ernst Ahlgren (Victoria Benedictsson) (1849–88) among her other writings is known by one play, *Final* (1885). The early work of Tor Hedberg (1862–1931) follows immediately upon these and much of it has close association with Ibsen: *En Tvekamp (Single Combat)* (1892); *Nattrocken (The Dressing-Gown)* (1893); *Judas* (1895); *Gerhard Grim* (1897); *Guld och gröna skogar (Gold and Green Forests)* (1903). His later work belongs to the twentieth century, but a few plays may be mentioned here: *Johan Ulfstjerna* (1907); his most notable play, *Karlavagnen (Charles's Wain)* (1910); and *Perseus och vidundret (Perseus and the Monster)* (1917).

August Strindberg (1849–1912) brought vitality into Swedish drama, though his themes sometimes provoked hostility as great as that raised by Ibsen's in Norway. In him Swedish drama ceased to be imitative and offered instead an art whose originality, in both matter and form, has inspired a succession of imitators, acknowledged and unacknowledged. Strindberg's name is remembered abroad for the realistic plays of the first half of his career and for the sometimes mystical impressionist drama of the second half. To these, for Sweden, must be added the fifteen major dramas on Swedish history, the popularity of which recalls the fact that the story of Swedish secular drama begins with a group of native history plays.

Since Strindberg's day he has been regarded as a classic in Sweden (and abroad). His work as a dramatist and man of the theatre may be said to have led first to the raising of the famous Swedish theatres to the position they still hold among the connoisseurs of theatrical art in Europe, and then to a tendency to imitation among the Swedish dramatists of the early twentieth century. This in turn gave place to a drama of some originality which holds considerable promise for the future.

From the beginning of this century to the outbreak of the First World War, Swedish drama is best represented by the later plays of Strindberg, the earlier plays of Per Hallström (1866–   ), the later work of Tor Hedberg, and such plays as *Elna Hall* (1917), by Ernst Didring (1868–1931), which had international success. Per Hallström is remembered chiefly as a poet and story-writer; his plays, beginning with *Grefven af Antwerpen*

(The Count of Antwerp) (1899), are dramas and tragedies on classical or Swedish history.

In the period between the wars a group of dramatists came to the fore, the most notable of whom were Hjalmar Bergman (1883–1931) and Pär Lagerkvist (1891–   ). Bergman, who is also famous as a novelist, is closely linked with Strindberg both by theme and mood and by his constant and often fruitful experimentation in dramatic form and technique. His earlier work (until about 1925) generally took the form of subtle, psychological tragedy; his later, no less experimental, was almost entirely high comedy. Pär Lagerkvist represents the group of still more recent Swedish playwrights who are concerned with the problems of modern life, political, economic, and psychological. Even more than Bergman, he derives from Strindberg in mood, theme, and technique, but his work is far from being merely derivative and it is chiefly with Strindberg's last phase that he is associated. The most representative of his early plays is *Himlens hemlighet (The Secret of Heaven)* (1919), which shows a powerful imagination at work upon an interpretation of life whose despair is almost unalleviated. His later work, though still essentially tragic, admits a certain resolution of the tragic elements, or at least an indication of a balancing, redemptive element. This remarkable dramatist is also distinguished by the elliptical, suggestive form of his dialogue which appears at times to have some relation to the corresponding technique in the French dramatist, J.-J. Bernard.

Mention should also be made of a number of recent Swedish dramatists, most of whom can only be represented by one or two plays: Runar Schildt by *Galgamannen (The Gallows-Man)* (1922); Vilhelm Moberg by *Hustrun (The Wife)* (1929) and *Våld (Violence)* (1932); Ragnar Josephson by *Kanske en diktare (Perhaps a Poet)* (1932); Rudolf Värnlund by *Den heliga familjen (The Holy Family)* and *Vägen till Kanaan (The Road to Canaan)* (both 1932), and *Modern och stjärnan (The Mother and the Star)* (1940); Sigfrid Siwertz by *En hederlig man (An Honourable Man)* and *Skönhet (Beauty)* (both 1933); Herbert Grevenius by *Första maj (The First of May)* and *Som folk är mest (As People Mostly Are)* (both 1935); Karl Ragnar Gierow by *Varulven (The Were-Wolf)* (1941) and *Av hjärtans lust (With All One's Heart)*.

To these should be added the names of Lars-Levi Laestadius, Rüne Lindström, Sven Stolpe, and Marika Stjernstedt.   U. E.-F.

SCAPINO, one of the *zanni* or servant roles of the *commedia dell' arte*. Like Brighella, he is crafty and unprincipled, but in moments of danger he does not belie his name, which means 'to run off' or 'to escape'. The first actor to play him was Francesco Gabrielli, a prominent member of the Confidenti, and one of a company which went with the younger Andreini to Paris in 1624. He made the part an important one, but it dwindled later, until with Molière Scapino passed into French comedy as a quick-witted and unscrupulous valet, as in *Les Fourberies de Scapin*.

SCARAMUCCIA, a character of the *commedia dell' arte* which is usually classed with the *zanni* or servant roles, but considered by some to have approximated more to the blustering braggart soldier. The actor most closely associated with the part, though he may not actually have created it, was Tiberio Fiorillo, a magnificent actor who won fame all over Italy before proceeding to Paris, where at one time his company shared the Petit-Bourbon with Molière. He returned to Italy intermittently, but from 1661 the greater part of his time was spent in Paris. He went several times to England. The life of Scaramouche was written, rather inaccurately, by his companion Mezzetin (Angelo Costantini), and he was one of the *commedia dell' arte* actors who had the greatest influence on Molière and so on the development of the French theatre.

SCARRON, PAUL (1610–60), French playwright and novelist. He had an unhappy childhood, and after a visit to Rome began to study for the Church. He was quite unsuited to it, and soon began to lead a riotous life. A foolish adventure led to his being crippled by rheumatism at the age of 30. Unable to move, he was forced to rely on his pen for a livelihood. He turned his attention to the theatre, and wrote a number of witty though slightly scabrous farces, of which the first two, *Jodelet, ou le maître-valet* (1643) and *Jodelet souffleté* (1645), were acted by the comedian of that name at the Théâtre du Marais. They were followed by others, all equally successful, some of them based on Spanish plays to which Scarron added a good deal of his own, modernizing the originals. Meanwhile Scarron's house had become the rendezvous of the literary figures—including Corneille—whom he amused with his wit, mocking at the world as he mocked at his own infirmities. In 1652 Scarron married the beautiful but penniless orphan, Françoise d'Aubigné, who as Mme de Maintenon was destined to be the second wife of Louis XIV and the virtual ruler of France. Meanwhile Scarron continued to write for the theatre. His *Don Japhet d'Arménie* (1647) had been extremely successful, and was later to be frequently revived by Molière. *L'Écolier de Salamanque* (1654) was barefacedly plagiarized by Boisrobert; but Scarron was revenged, for Boisrobert's version is forgotten, while that of Scarron is remembered, particularly on account of the valet Crispin, played for so long by the actor-family Poisson. Scarron, whose interest in Spanish literature has already been noted, may have taken from *La Viaje Entretenido* of de Rojas the idea of his great novel, *Le Roman comique* (1651), which depicts the adventures and miseries of a band of strolling players, for whose leader, Leandro, the provincial actor-manager Filandre is believed to have served as a model.

SCENARIO. This word, which is now used mainly for the script of a motion picture, or for a synopsis of the action of a musical play, was originally applied to the skeleton plots of the *commedia dell'arte*, replacing some time in the early eighteenth century the older word *soggetto*. These are not such synopses as might be drawn up by an author for his written drama, nor should they be confused with the Elizabethan 'platts', chiefly charts of entrances and exits and properties drawn up for the convenience of the prompter. They are theatrical documents, prepared for the use of the professional companies either by their leader or most gifted member, or by enthusiastic amateur admirers of the *commedia dell'arte* style. They consist of a scene-by-scene résumé of the action, together with some note of locality and special effects. Their informal elasticity allowed the insertion of extraneous 'business' according to the discretion or ability of the company or player presenting them (see ITALY, 2).

SCENE BAY, or Dock, rooms opening off the stage proper, and used for the storing of scenery.

SCENE-PAINTING, see MACHINERY and SCENERY.

SCENERY, THEATRICAL. 1. ORIGINS. Scenery is a comparatively recent invention in the history of the theatre. The drama of ancient Greece was played before a background of ever-increasing elaboration, which background in Roman times had become a grandiose architectural façade. But, if we except the mysterious *periaktoi* (which are supposed to have been revolving prisms painted with different scenes and fitting, it is hard to see how, into the permanent setting of the classical stage), the ancient world knew nothing of what we should call stage-scenery (but see also ACOUSTICS, ARCHITECTURE, GREECE, MACHINERY, and ROME).

The same is true of the medieval period. Sacred drama had begun to be played inside the churches by the tenth century. Soon it moved outside, and the west front of a cathedral provided a 'permanent setting' more splendid than anything even the Romans had imagined. Then, as drama grew steadily more profane, performances were given in town squares and market-places, and special structures had to be built to represent the various scenes. But these 'houses', as they were called, were more in the nature of 'properties' than of scenery. Even when there was an effort, towards the end of the medieval period, to group the 'houses' on one raised platform or stage, no attempt was made to present a coherent or unified stage picture. The 'simultaneous setting' had Heaven in one corner, Hellmouth in the other, and, in between, Pilate's House, or Golgotha.

2. RENAISSANCE. The unification of the stage picture was the work of the princely Courts of the Renaissance, and it is no accident that stage scenery and the new Absolutism arose at the same time. In Italy, throughout the fifteenth

century, the New Learning had resulted in a growing interest in the classical drama. Plautus was revived by the Roman Academy towards the end of the century, and in 1486 by Ercole d'Este at Ferrara. Humanists and Princes combined to see that plays should be as 'classical' as learning could make them and that they should form part of Court festivities. Many such festivities took place in the open air, but there was what might be called a natural tendency to move indoors, and in 1491, also at Ferrara, a play was performed in a closed room. In these circumstances there was no room for the old methods, the stage-picture was unified perforce and an attempt was made to make the space available seem larger by the use of perspective painting. This perspective painting, rendered possible by the researches of artists and scholars during the second half of the fifteenth century, was perhaps originally intended merely to enlarge the apparent size of the room. The greatest artists of the period, Leonardo da Vinci, Raphael, Bramante, were employed in the decoration of princely fêtes. Of these the last-named might almost be called a specialist in using perspective for this purpose; he had done so with great effect as early as 1480, in the sacristy of San Satiro in Milan and in the church itself. It was probably under his influence that Baldassare Peruzzi (1481–1531) applied the newly perfected science to the deliberate construction of theatrical decoration.

In this project he was helped by the spread of the influence of the architectural writings of Vitruvius (c. 70–15 B.C.). This precious legacy from the ancient world had been discovered in manuscript at St. Gall in 1414, but it was not until 1511 that the first printed, illustrated edition appeared, and not until 1521 that the work was first translated into Italian. Some of the scenery which Peruzzi designed for Pope Leo X and Pope Clement VII is described by Vasari, who also records that 'he began a book on the antiquities of Rome, with a commentary on Vitruvius'. His notes and drawings were utilized by his pupil Sebastiano Serlio (1475–1554) in the preparation of his great work *Architettura*, the part of which dealing with perspective appeared in 1545. Serlio wrote with the banqueting-hall of a prince in mind, and he described three kinds of stage sets for different dramatic genres. The 'houses' of his sets were arranged on both sides of a street receding at right angles from the front of the stage, and were two-sided and carefully foreshortened.

In 1560 Bartolomeo Neroni (c. 1500–71/3) built a theatre in Siena in a great hall behind the Palace of the Senate (that is, he erected a proscenium in a building already existing) and he provided it with scenery on the Serlio model. An engraving of this has fortunately been preserved.

Other influences, however, were at work, and there were those who strove for theatres more completely faithful to the Roman model,

that is, consisting of a semicircle of ascending seats and, at the back of the stage, an elaborate, permanent architectural façade. The Teatro Olimpico at Vicenza was begun, it is said, by the great Andrea Palladio (1518–80) in 1580, but as he died in the same year the work was entrusted to Vincenzo Scamozzi (1552–1616), who completed it in 1584. It is probable that the three arches in the architectural façade were originally closed either by doors or by painted cloths, but Scamozzi had the brilliant idea of building behind each arch a street of houses diminishing in perspective. Five scenic runways (one for each of the archways and one for each of the side doors) were added by him on the occasion of the visit of the Empress Maria of Austria in 1585.

Scamozzi was also responsible for the erection in 1588 of a *teatro all' antica* in the little town of Sabbionetta. This theatre, although much smaller than either the Teatro Olimpico or the Teatro Farnese (erected at Parma in 1618) is a vital link between the two, but is perhaps of more importance in the history of theatrical architecture than of stage scenery.

The passion for plays in the second half of the sixteenth century could not be confined to those who were able or willing to have special theatres erected. Performances continued to be given in the halls of palaces, converted for the purpose, and among the most important of these were the Florentine *Intermezzi* of 1589.

These were of such importance in theatrical history that they are worth considering in some detail. The festivals in honour of the marriage of the Grand Duke Ferdinand I of Tuscany lasted throughout May 1589, and included masquerades, animal-hunts, a Naumachia, or water-pageant, on the Arno, and three comedies. These comedies were enlivened by *intermezzi* or interludes, a series of spectacular pantomimes *sul gusto antico* interspersed with madrigals, the seed from which the whole of opera took its origin. We are not concerned, however, with their importance in the history of music (for which see OPERA) but only with the manner of their presentation. The machinist and designer was Bernardo Buontalenti (1536–1608), called delle Girandole, i.e. of the Fireworks. He entered the service of the Medici family in 1547 and for nearly sixty years was laying out palaces, villas, fortresses, and gardens, as well as presiding over all Grand Ducal festivities, constructing theatrical machinery, arranging firework displays, and ordering funeral ceremonies. He was in fact a typical 'architect' of the period, including in his scope everything from stage costume to military engineering. Both drawings and engravings of his work for the *Intermezzi* of 1589 have been preserved and are among the most important early documents of scenic history.

There is some dispute as to whether the side-pieces shown in his sets are true theatrical 'wings', i.e. whether they were flat pieces of painted canvas stretched on wooden frames and able to slide in and out when it was desired to change the scene. Buontalenti is usually considered to have worked with *telari*, that is, three-sided prisms constructed in supposed imitation of the classical *periaktoi*, but whether this be so or not the scenery he devised created immense interest, as can be seen from the number of contemporary accounts, and became the ancestor of a long progeny.

His pupils were Giulio Parigi (?–1635) and Agostino Migliori (*fl.* 1610). The former was in charge of the Florentine festivities of 1606, 1608, and 1615, and we are fortunate in having representations of these in the engravings of Canta-Gallina, Stefano della Bella, and Callot. Jacques Callot (1592–1635) was himself a designer at the Court of Tuscany until 1622, and when he went to Nancy he carried the seed with him and devised *entrées* in the Florentine manner. Another foreign pupil was Josef Furtenbach (1591–1667). He was unable to put his knowledge into practice in Germany owing to the Thirty Years War, but he produced a work on architecture which included some valuable engravings of stage settings. But from our point of view the most interesting disciple of Parigo was Inigo Jones (1573–1652). He was not formally a pupil, but he paid several visits to Italy in the early years of the seventeenth century, and the influence of the Italian designers on his work is beyond question.

He was fortunate in that James I shared the passion of contemporary princes for courtly festivities, especially for the masque, which gave Jones his opportunity. As elsewhere, stage scenery in England was confined to the Court. The public theatres still used the bare apron stage derived from the medieval tradition, and the most prodigious dramatic achievement of all time was just drawing to its close unaided by any scenic illusion whatever. At the most Shakespeare had only the curtained alcove at the back of the stage which might by any stretch of imagination rank as 'scenery'. He was compelled to put the scenery into the language of the play, and the world is the richer for it. Yet it is tempting to speculate what use he might have made of the new art of theatrical decoration if it had become known in England twenty years or so earlier.

A large number of drawings by Inigo Jones for the scenery and costume of Court masques has fortunately been preserved at Chatsworth, and these, together with the texts by Ben Jonson and others, provide a complete enough picture of performances at Whitehall under James I and Charles I. What we find is a simplified version of the Italian system, Jones never using more than four wings on each side. It is probable that his influence would have spread to the public theatres, but the outbreak of the Civil War put an end to developments and it is not until after the Restoration that the story can be resumed.

3. SEVENTEENTH CENTURY. Meanwhile the new art of opera, with its inevitable elaboration of scenery, was spreading from Florence all over Italy. Magnificent musical plays were

mounted at Milan and at Viterbo. In Parma the Teatro Farnese already mentioned was inaugurated towards the end of 1618 and provided with a complete system of 'wings'. Perhaps these were invented by Giambattista Aleotti (1546–1636), the architect of the theatre, perhaps by his pupil Giacomo Torelli (1608–78), but whoever devised them, they were to have an enormous influence on the development of the theatre, and to last, unmodified in their essential principles, until the end of the nineteenth century.

In Rome the fury for opera knew no bounds, a future Pope writing some of the libretti. The powerful Barbarini family built an immense theatre capable of holding 3,000 spectators, furnished it with complicated machinery, and employed artists like Giovanni Lorenzo Bernini (1598–1680) to design the décor. The opera of 'Sant' Alessio' was performed there in 1634 in the presence of Alexander Charles of Poland and afterwards published with engravings showing the principal scenes. Such illustrated commemorative volumes became increasingly frequent as the century progressed, and are the source from which much of the history of the *settecento* theatre has been compiled.

Torelli was one of the first, if not the first, of the professional scene-painters who were nothing else. He was called 'il gran stregone', the great wizard, of the theatre, and he spread the system which he had learned at Parma through the princely houses of Italy, all of whom wished to be in the fashion and have a theatre of their own. It was at Venice, however, that his influence was felt with most far-reaching effect, for it was there that commercial opera with spectators paying for their seats took its rise. The first public performance of opera took place at Venice in the San Cassiano Theatre in 1637. In general the commercial theatre offered a simplified version of the new stage-craft, a mere perspective of columns or pilasters with a changing background. An exception was the Teatro Novissimo, and Torelli acted as decorator there from 1641 until 1645. A large number of commemorative volumes which have come down to us make it easy to form an estimate of his style and methods.

In 1645 Cardinal Mazarin invited Torelli to Paris, and an engraving by Stefano della Bella shows the scene which he devised for an opera produced at the Petit-Bourbon in 1647. Although some of the Paris theatres, such as the theatre in the Hôtel de Bourgogne, clung to a kind of permanent setting with doors in an architectural façade, the Italian system made rapid headway, and when Torelli returned to Italy in 1662 his work was carried on in France by his followers and pupils, the architect Amanadini (*fl.* 1660) and the machine-master Gaspare Vigarani (1586–1663). It was the latter who constructed the Salle des Machines in the Tuileries, which was to reach the height of its fame in the next century under the celebrated Servandony (see below).

In England, as we have noted, there was a gap in theatrical development during the Puritan domination, but even before Cromwell's death tentative efforts were made to revive the drama, played this time not on the old, bare Elizabethan stage, but with all the elaboration of the new technique. The influence of the Shakespearian theatre persisted in the survival of the apron stage, with the proscenium arch placed behind it. Professor Allardyce Nicoll has acutely suggested that 'just as in Italy the scene space developed out of the *periaktoi*, set within the archways, so in England the scenic part of the stage developed from that room in which Shakespeare had shown Ferdinand and Miranda playing their amorous game of chess'. But the development was arrested, as it were, halfway, and until well on into the eighteenth century much of the action still took place on the projecting apron.

English audiences had their first taste of opera when Davenant in May 1656 produced *The Siege of Rhodes*, a play with music by Locke (considered to be the first English opera). It was first given privately at Rutland House in Aldersgate and later at the Cockpit or Phoenix. He entrusted the décor to John Webb (1611–72), the kinsman and pupil of Inigo Jones, and, as might be expected, his designs show a direct descent from the scenery of the Jacobean and Caroline masques, modified to some extent by the new wave of Italian influence. After the Restoration the new London theatres adopted the Italian system, Dorset Garden leading the way with operas by Dryden, Shadwell, and D'Urfey. The scenery painted for these filtered down to the ordinary theatrical performances, but it was long before England had anything to rival the work of the great continental designers. There are, however, in the Victoria and Albert Museum, some very interesting designs by Sir James Thornhill (1675–1734) for operatic performances in the early years of the eighteenth century.

The influence of the Italians was not only maintained by foreign artists who studied their work, but by the actual migration of the Italian scenic painters themselves. In the second half of the seventeenth century the rage for Italian opera spread all over Europe, and every prince and princeling wanted to make it a part of his Court festivities. Reference has already been made to developments in France. In Germany, the end of the Thirty Years War was followed by a period of recovery. In 1652 a theatre was built in Vienna by Giovanni Burnacini (?–1655), who designed the scenery also. When he died he was succeeded by his son Lodovico Ottavio Burnacini (1636–1707), who became a great favourite of the Emperor Leopold I. Munich saw its first opera in 1654, 'La Ninfa ritrosa', with decorations by Francesco Santurini (1627–82). He was succeeded by Domenico (*fl.* 1685–93) and Gasparo (*fl.* 1662–86), sons of Francesco Mauro. The Mauri later migrated to Dresden. They were among the first of the great Italian

families of scenic artists. There were five brothers, of whom three were decorators and two machinists, and they made their enormous reputation first in Venice. They passed to Piacenza, to Parma, and thence to wider fields beyond the Alps; and it was while they were at Parma that they were assisted by a young beginner who was to be the founder of a still more famous dynasty of decorators.

Ferdinando Galli da Bibiena (1657–1743) was left an orphan at the age of eight. He showed a talent for theatrical design from his earliest years, and at 28 we find him installed at Parma as 'primario pittore ed architetto'. After devising many princely fêtes there he was called to Barcelona for the wedding of Charles and Elizabeth, afterwards Emperor and Empress. They invited him to Vienna, where he remained for the greater part of his life. Many of his original drawings have been preserved, and he is credited with a revolution in the art of theatrical design by his discovery of the diagonal perspective setting.

His brother Francesco (1659–1739) worked at Rome, Mantua, Genoa, and Naples. He built a theatre in Vienna, and, but for an engagement at Nancy, might have gone to London. He built theatres at Verona and Rome and, like his brother, ended his career as a teacher of the art of scene-painting at Bologna. Ferdinando had four sons of whom two, Giuseppe (1696–1757) and Antonio (1700–74), followed their father's and uncle's profession. Giuseppe was the more important and prolific of the two. He assisted his father in Barcelona and Vienna, decorated his first opera in 1716, worked at Prague, Dresden, Munich, Breslau, and Graz, and was responsible, with his son Carlo (1728–1787), for the decoration of the Opera House at Bayreuth. Carlo, while still a youth, entered the service of the Margrave of Bayreuth, and later worked in Italy, France, Holland, Flanders, England (about 1763), and perhaps in Russia. In three generations the Galli da Bibiena family had spread the principles and practice of baroque theatre décor over the whole continent.

An almost parallel career was followed by the Galliari, a Piedmontese artist family. Like the Galli, two of a family of brothers left orphans at an early age set up as scene-painters and became the originators of the school of theatrical decoration which had its centre at Turin and Milan. Bernardino Galliari (1707–94) worked at both places, before being summoned to Innsbruck, where, with his brother Fabrizio (1709–90), he was entrusted with the decorations for royal festivals. It would be tedious to enumerate all the places where he worked; but in 1772 he was summoned to Berlin by Frederick the Great, and there, with the aid of his nephew Giovanni (1746–1818), he designed six scenes and a curtain for the Royal Opera House. Another nephew, Gasparo (1760–1818), was also a scenic artist.

4. EIGHTEENTH CENTURY. By this time the

whole character of theatrical decoration had changed. The elaborate architectural backgrounds of the baroque had yielded on the one hand to a more classical style and on the other to the growing interest in landscape. Fabrizio Galliari himself, although he had specialized in the diagonal perspective invented by Ferdinando Galli and carried to its ultimate extreme by Giuseppe Galli, was one of the first to introduce romantic naturalistic landscape into the architectural stage picture.

Neo-classicism had long been evident in real architecture; indeed, there is a sense in which the whole movement inaugurated by Ferdinando Galli was a deliberate turning away from the formal tendencies of Palladian classicism and symmetry. The influence of the ultra-baroque persisted longer in the theatre than elsewhere, but towards the middle of the eighteenth century the fight was joined again. The reaction against the baroque style in the theatre began in Paris, and even Germany, which had hitherto been completely under Italian masters, now began to yield to the influence of the French. One of the most influential of these was Jean Nicolas Servandony (1695-1766), who in the early part of his career as a scenic artist called himself Servandoni, and made out that he was a Florentine. He was actually born at Lyons, but had studied in Italy. After much decorative work in Portugal and France, he assumed control of the Salle des Machines at the Tuileries and mounted a whole series of magnificent spectacles. Later he worked at Dresden, Vienna, and other cities in central Europe. He even went to London. He represented the neo-classical impulse which was soon to be supreme, and after the death of the last Galli da Bibiena to be plainly manifested in the work of such later Italian artists at foreign Courts as the Quaglio brothers, Lorenzo (1730-1804) and Giuseppe (1747-1828), Paolo Landriani (1770-1838), and Alessandro Sanquirico (1780-1849).

England, which had escaped by its isolation both the splendours and the excesses of the baroque theatre, was not much influenced by neo-classicism in stage decoration. But the new enthusiasm for romantic landscape, and the abandonment of the idea, which had lasted from the middle of the sixteenth century, that a stage setting was almost inevitably architectural, gained rapid ground. One of its first exponents was the Strasbourg artist Philippe Jacques de Loutherbourg (1735-1810), who came to England in 1771 and was soon afterwards employed to design the scenery for Drury Lane. Even if some of his *maquettes* had not been preserved, his well-known paintings would give a sufficient idea of his romantic tendencies. Most of his work was done for the pantomimes and 'Entertainments' which under Garrick's management varied the theatrical fare provided for the audiences of Drury Lane; and by his invention of transparent scenery—moonshine, fire, volcanoes—and by 'cut-out' scenery he did much to increase the attractiveness of the stage picture.

The neo-Gothic enthusiasm entered the English theatre some twenty years later with the romantic architectural settings of William Capon (1757-1827). For J. P. Kemble's revivals of Shakespeare he devised a number of flats and backcloths based upon authentic documents, and so began the progress towards antiquarian 'correctness'. Not only Shakespeare but the new school of historical drama represented by such a play as George Colman's *The Iron Chest* offered scope for his talents, and his work and that of de Loutherbourg provided the basis for the development of English scenic design during the first half of the nineteenth century.

5. NINETEENTH CENTURY. Spectacular equestrian shows were very popular in the early eighteen-hundreds, and Astley's playhouse gave an opportunity for the talents of John Henderson Grieve (1770-1845) and other members of his family. Indeed it may be said that the Grieve family, like the Galli da Bibiena family of a century before, dominated scene-painting for nearly a hundred years. Thomas Grieve (1799-1882) and William Grieve (1800-44) carried the family tradition through a second generation, and Thomas's son through a third. Another great name in scene-painting was that of Clarkson Stanfield (1793-1867), whose somewhat histrionic talent was less at home in his innumerable landscape-paintings than on the stage of a theatre. So popular did his work become that the playbills of the period display his name in larger type than the name of the principal actor.

The antiquarian tendency inaugurated by Capon was carried still further in the Kemble productions of the eighteen-twenties, and to its logical or illogical conclusion in the series of Shakespeare revivals put on by Charles Kean at the Princess's Theatre in the fifties. The principal artists employed were T. Grieve, F. Lloyds, H. Cuthbert, J. Day, and William Telbin (1813-73). The last named was the founder of a scene-painting family which persisted into the twentieth century. The second half of the century showed little change in the methods of presentation, and under Irving at the Lyceum we find that Hawes Craven (1837-1910) employed the same transparencies, cut-out scenes, &c. which de Loutherbourg had used a hundred years before.

But by the time the nineteenth century had reached the final quarter the theatrical traditions inherited from the baroque and romantic periods were in full decay. For spectacular pieces—pantomimes and the like—the cut-cloth, or series of cut-cloths, had been developed to such excess that the stage-picture resembled lace-work, or a cut-paper valentine. In serious plays audiences were growing dissatisfied with the artificial conventions of walls of rooms which were no walls, but a row of flats, of doors, windows, and even furniture painted on stretched canvas. There was a cry for realism, in tune with the contemporary realism of painting and literature, and realism was in its turn the first essential of reform. Interiors were in future to be represented by the Box Set with three solid walls and a ceiling; furniture and accessories, sometimes even food, were to be real.

6. THE MODERN PERIOD. It was in 1887 that Antoine founded the Théâtre Libre in Paris in order, as he and his supporters firmly believed, to apply the principles of stage naturalism in all their completeness. As he was a producer of genius he actually did much more than this, for he used the scenery and stage properties to reinforce the mood of a play in a way which had never been attempted before. Perhaps Antoine himself, with his passion for real meat, real fountains, and the like, never realized the force of some of his *mises-en-scène*, and as his repertoire was wilfully limited to the works of the new naturalistic school of drama he was deprived of plays which might have lent themselves to any great novelty of staging.

The reaction against realism came from the group of young writers and artists known as the *Symbolistes*, who, led by Paul Fort, attacked the Théâtre Libre for its search for the exact and for giving no help to authors of fantasy and imagination. Fort founded the Théâtre Mixte which, after two performances, became the Théâtre d'Art, and in his manifesto enunciated many of the principles which were later to become the commonplaces of the modernist school. Scenery was to be simplified, evocative rather than descriptive; there was to be frank stylization, complete harmony between scenery and costume, and the absolute abandonment of the perspective backcloth. Among the painters who joined in the battle against naturalism and painted decorations for the Théâtre d'Art were Vuillard, Bonnard, Maurice Denis, Odilon Redon, and K. X. Roussel.

The works of some new dramatists, especially Maeterlinck, were sufficiently imaginative to give scope to the new method, and in 1892, when the Théâtre d'Art had become the Théâtre de l'Œuvre, Lugné-Poë, collaborating with Camille Mauclair and Édouard Vuillard, presented *Pelléas et Mélisande* at the Bouffes-Parisiens. The great Konstantin Stanislavsky (1863–1938) was present at this performance, and afterwards admitted how much he owed to the decorations by Vogler, and to all the experimental work which was being carried out in Paris towards the end of the last century.

Shortly afterwards Stanislavsky returned to Russia, and in 1897 founded the Art Theatre of Moscow. His object was the reform of the Russian stage, but he began by proclaiming the gospel of naturalism according to Antoine, and by striving to emulate the realistic effects of the Meiningen company which, under Chronegk, had visited Moscow only a few years before. In fact, naturalism was pushed to an extreme, an attempt being made to reproduce actual conditions of life, with all its accumulated detail, and in particular its merging of the principal characters of a drama in the mass of the participants. The abolition of the 'star' system, and the rehearsing of crowds to a point never before attempted, was perhaps Stanislavsky's greatest individual contribution to the new movement. By the very perfection of their technique the actors in his theatre transcended realism and evolved a kind of symbolic rhythm which was to prove a perfect instrument for the presentation of the plays of Chekhov.

Meanwhile, a German-speaking Swiss, Adolphe Appia (1862–1928), had, in 1899, published his epoch-making work on the reform of staging, *Die Musik und die Inscenierung*. Some years before he had issued a smaller work dealing with Wagner's operas, moved thereto by the unsatisfactory nature of the scenery at Bayreuth. His aesthetic sense was offended in particular by the glaring contrast between the flatness of the scenery and the inevitable three dimensions of the actor. Appia declared that the essentials of good stage-presentation were, first, a plastic scene which would give the actors' attitudes and movements all their value, and, second, lighting which would emphasize instead of destroying the solidity of the human form. His suggested designs for Wagner, Shakespeare, &c., which were marked by an extreme simplicity and by the use of dramatic lighting, had an immense influence on the future of stage décor.

It was, of course, the invention of electric lighting and its adaptation to stage purposes which made Appia's ideas practicable. Gas had made it possible to use light not only for illumination but for effect, but electricity opened up a much wider range of possibilities. By the Fortuny system which was worked out in Germany at the beginning of the twentieth century it became possible to obtain a uniform illumination approximating to real daylight. The essence of the system was the reflection of light from bands of coloured silk and its diffusion thence on to a sky-dome or cyclorama occupying the back of the stage. The original Fortuny system of illumination has been largely abandoned, but the sky-dome has remained as one of the most potent devices for attaining complete scenic illusion. Fortuny's sky-dome of silk which could be shut up like a carriage-hood and transported from one theatre to another has been replaced in many theatres, chiefly in Germany and America, by the sky-dome of plaster which, no longer semicircular (for that blocked the side entrances to the stage), takes the form of a flattened shell, bending inwards sharply at the top and at the sides. Whitewashed plaster makes an admirable surface for light to play upon, and the effect seen from the front of the stage is of infinite distance, open sky. Its more realistic possibilities have been worked out in the Swedish Ars system which permits photographs of real clouds to be projected upon the artificial sky. But it is also capable of more imaginative use. (See also LIGHTING, 1 *d*.)

Simultaneously with improvements in lighting came other mechanical contrivances, which placed new power in the hands of the producers, for good or ill. Chief among these was the revolving stage, installed in 1896 by Lautenschläger at Munich. This enabled three or even more settings to exist at the same time on the revolve and to be moved into view of the audience in turn. The scenery itself could be of the most solid type, although of course considerable ingenuity was needed to fit the various scenes into segments of the circle. This raised so many difficulties in practice that an attempt was made to avoid them by the invention of sliding stages, rising and falling stages, and the like. One of the most elaborate was installed in the Théâtre Pigalle in Paris in the late twenties. But the living actor should beware of too much machinery. It is merely the end of a logical process that the Théâtre Pigalle is now a cinema.

Such developments were the very opposite of those envisaged by a prophet like Appia, and there were others who sought the salvation of stagecraft not in an ever-increasing elaboration but in a drastic simplicity. A leading place among these was taken by Edward Gordon Craig (1872–   ), whose influence has been out of all proportion to the number of his actual productions. His writings are a permanent inspiration to all workers in the theatre, but his actual system resolved itself into a series of large screens with a limited number of movable features such as flights of steps, and with these he endeavoured to build up an imaginative stage picture with no concessions to realism at all. His production of *Hamlet* at the Moscow Art Theatre in 1912 is still capable of arousing controversy, but his ideas have undoubtedly had a large progeny. But before dealing with these and with other attempts to escape from the tyranny of the picture-stage it is necessary to say something of one of the most extraordinary outbursts of creative activity that the modern theatre has known.

While all these tendencies had been taking shape, scene-painting had not entirely vanished even from progressive stages; indeed it had reached a new and wonderful flowering in the Russian Ballet, or, as it should be called to distinguish it from the traditional ballet which remained in Russia, the Diaghilev Ballet. It sprang from a painters' movement, a group of young St. Petersburg painters inspired by Wronbel to attempt the complete transformation of the art of scenic design. Serge Diaghilev (1872–1929), with his gift for organization, collected them under the banner of his review, *Mir Iskousstva*, or *The World of Art*. The members of this group, of which the most famous were Léon Bakst (1866–1924) and Alexandre Benois (1870–   ), practised a kind of mannered archaism which proved particularly suited to the decoration of ballet. In opposition to them was a Moscow group, more in touch with such Parisian movements as Cubism, and these artists also were enlisted in Diaghilev's service. The most famous names

were Larionov, Gontcharova, and Barthe, and it was in succession to their work that it seemed natural and logical to Diaghilev to call in the services of French painters like Picasso and Derain.

These developments, however, were still in the future when the Diaghilev Ballet burst like a bombshell upon the Paris of 1909. Its triumph in France and in England are matters of history (see BALLET, 7), but its influence on stage design was perhaps less than on the arts in general. From the point of view of stage décor, indeed, Bakst and Benois were not the beginning of anything; they were the flowering of an age-long process. The Russian Ballet was the gorgeous sunset of scene-painting. In its glorious career it reflected every changing phase of painting, but (except for late attempts by Diaghilev to make use of some of the developments of the post-Revolutionary Russian theatre) it did not reflect the history of the contemporary theatre in its effort to break away from the old traditions of presentation.

Craig, in his desire for artistic unity in presentation, had dreamed of a theatre entirely controlled by one man; a super-man at once author, producer, decorator, and costumier. For the actor himself he preferred to substitute the 'über-marionnette'. Extreme as this notion was, it was in tune with the rise of the producer during the first decade of the twentieth century to a commanding and almost dictatorial position in the theatre. Such a producer, or *régisseur*, animating the whole enterprise, had Diaghilev been. An even more typical figure was Max Reinhardt (1873–1943)—more typical and more important for our purpose, because he summed up in his career nearly all the developments of the contemporary theatre, and his extensive travels made his influence world-wide.

He was the complete eclectic, changing his manner completely in accordance with the mood of the play. His choice of play ranged from the most realistic to the most imaginative, and his presentations varied no less. He used the revolving stage, the semi-permanent setting, simultaneous settings, runways, flights of steps. Refusing to be confined within the framework of the proscenium arch, his productions spilled over into the orchestra and then out of the theatre altogether, into the circus, the public hall, the street, and finally back into the church from which the modern European theatre had emerged. In 1910 he produced *Oedipus Rex* in the Zirkus Schumann in Vienna. His most famous production, *The Miracle*, was staged at Olympia in London in 1911. After the First World War he found even wider opportunities, and at Salzburg turned, as it were, the whole city into a stage, setting *Jedermann* in front of the façade of the cathedral. In Vienna the authorities turned over to him the old ballroom in the Hofburg where he erected a formalized permanent setting, harmonizing with the character of the room, and staged upon it plays by Goethe, Calderón, and Beaumarchais. There for a quarter of a century he dominated the stage of Central Europe and summed up every vital impulse of the theatre, with the exception of some of the Parisian developments of the early nineteen-twenties. His activity continued until the advent of the Nazi régime when he went to America, where he died.

In the years immediately following the First World War the dominant aesthetic movement in Germany was known as Expressionism. So far as scenic design was concerned this reduced itself to an attempt to 'make the décor act'. This meant on the one hand a drastic simplification of scenery—playing *Richard III*, for example, on a single flight of blood-red steps—and on the other the twisting of the shapes of inanimate objects to emphasize the mood of a play. Curiously enough, the most complete example of this was not in a play, but in a film, the famous *Cabinet of Dr. Caligari*. In Russia Evreinov's theory of 'monodrama' took up the same theme, and the Dutch director Herman Rosse experimented in the theatre with animated backgrounds, some of them projected by a cinematograph machine. The designs of the American designer Robert Edmond Jones (1887–   ) for *Macbeth* in 1921 show lopsided cardboard archways as crazily insecure as the fortunes of the hero whose mind they reflected and emphasized. In the same year another American designer, Norman-Bel Geddes (1893–   ), schemed to build in Madison Square Gardens a gigantic theatre specially for the production of Dante's *Divine Comedy*, with a kind of permanent setting for Heaven, Hell, and Purgatory; but this ambitious project was never realized.

In England the theatre remained for the most part indifferent to continental and American developments. The designs of artists like Charles Ricketts (1866–1931) broke no new ground, magnificent as some of them were, but Lovat Fraser (1890–1921), had he lived, might have inaugurated a movement of far-reaching significance. His famous designs for *The Beggar's Opera* made use of a very simple semi-permanent setting which could be either indoors or out by the expedient of changing two small painted panels. It should not be forgotten, however, that one of Reinhardt's most revolutionary productions was ordered for, and produced in, London by Charles B. Cochran—*The Miracle* at Olympia. In general the English theatre has remained faithful to realism and the Box Set, and the large number of good stage-designers who exist find little scope for their talents.

France produced no stage director with the sweep and variety of Reinhardt, but important developments took place in the French theatre in the years immediately before and immediately after the First World War. The scenic traditions of the Russian Ballet were carried on by the Ballets Suédois, by Comte Étienne de Beaumont's Soirées de Paris, and to a lesser extent by Jacques Rouché, who took

over the direction of the Théâtre d'Art in 1910 and employed such artists as Dethomas Drésa and Dunoyer de Segonzac. But the most interesting of the *régisseurs* were those who strove to get away from the whole tradition of the painted scene. The greatest of these was Jacques Copeau (1878–1949), who at the Vieux-Colombier arranged, in very small space, a permanent setting in which the classics could be played in a new (or a very old) way. Later Copeau went round the country with a troupe of actors who played, in barns and market-places, pieces written by themselves or improvised on the spot (see COMPAGNIE DES QUINZE). We are back in the world of the medieval theatre and the *commedia dell' arte*, and have parted company with the whole question of scenic design.

Charles Dullin (1885–1949) founded the Théâtre de l'Atelier in 1921 and two years later began production in a regular theatre in Montmartre. His décors were extremely simple, formed for the most part of easily movable screens. The special flavour of a scene was less a matter of scenic design than of costume and manner of playing, but Dullin sought also by a modified Constructivism to allow the action three dimensions to move in instead of only two. The actual painted décor was reduced to a system of movable panels.

Louis Jouvet (1887–1951), a great actor as well as producer, learned much from Copeau, but struck out on his own original lines. He believed that there could be no rebirth of the theatre without rebuilding it from the beginning. In his actual productions at the Comédie des Champs-Élysées he strove for an extreme simplicity, a scene in which the décors were merely indicated without any attempt at illusion. A later worker at the same theatre was Gaston Baty (1885–   ). He asked of his actors a minimum of gesture and emphasis. His décors also were simple, but he strove to make each detail significant and bearing a part in the action. At the Théâtre des Arts, and particularly at the Mathurins, Georges Pitoëff (1896–1939), a Russian actor who settled in Paris, had many successes, of which the most notable was Shaw's *Saint Joan*, but his characteristic style was seen most clearly in a play like *Les Ratés*, with its division of the scene into a series of compartments, like the 'houses' of the medieval stage.

In Russia itself the Revolution left Stanislavsky in charge of the Art Theatre of Moscow, but there were some who had studied under him who were dissatisfied with the methods of Realism. Chief among these was Vsevolod Meyerhold (1873–   ). He wished to restore the primacy of the actor, and at the same time to abolish the 'mystic gulf' which had for so long separated the actor from his audience. Hence a frank theatricality, with the action spilling over among the spectators and drawing them into the communion of the represented drama. In revolt against any kind of realism he thrust the scene-painter out of the theatre and reduced scenery to a few scaffoldings on a bare stage. An even more drastic exponent of Constructivism was Alexander Taïrov (1885–   ) of the Moscow Kamerny Theatre. After the Revolution, academic art was swept away and artists of the advanced school found scope for their talents not only in the actual theatre but in organizing popular manifestations, military reviews, and open-air fêtes. The destruction and disorder everywhere apparent gave birth to Constructivism, which was partly the result of a natural desire to stabilize life, and partly an echo of the theories of the Futurists with all their admiration for the bare lines of the machine. Constructivism for Taïrov developed into a system of stage scaffolding with the various actions of the play taking place at different levels, up flights of wooden steps, across ladders, or on little jutting platforms far above the stage. Decoration was reduced to the frankly symbolic, to an almost mathematical abstraction. For certain modern plays, especially those which are assumed to take place in a workshop or factory, Constructivism was very effective, but it was hardly a universal formula and was soon abandoned by its chief exponents. In Rabinovitch's sets for the Moscow Art Theatre production of the *Lysistrata* of Aristophanes the scenery was simplified almost to the point of abstraction, but did suggest Greek architecture in a non-naturalistic way. Within recent years the Russian theatre would appear to have swung back to a kind of stylized realism and even to a certain romanticizing tendency when dealing with plays of the past. Certainly the almost fanatical extravagances of the early years of Soviet rule have been abandoned, but it is too early to say what direction Russian stage-design will ultimately take.

Throughout Europe the period of fundamental innovation ended with the nineteen-twenties. The thirties were, almost from the first, overshadowed by the threat of coming war, and no new and vital experiments seem to have been made. Now that the Second World War has come to an end, it may again be followed by a long period of aesthetic (as of other) confusion and some years will undoubtedly elapse before the dominant style of the new epoch becomes apparent. At least it can be said that the stage designer and stage director of the future will not be confined within any single manner of presentation. He will be able to choose the frank rhetoric of the platform stage, the revived traditions of the baroque set-piece, the built-up Box Set of Realism, or any degree of abstraction and stylization. The art of scenic design has, as it were, come full circle; all styles are possible, and the only question the artist has to ask himself is which of these is most in harmony with the mood and message of the play.   J. L.

SCHILLER, JOHANN CHRISTOPH FRIEDRICH VON (1759–1805), German dramatist and poet, who ranks as one of the chief playwrights of Germany. He was the son of an army surgeon, and after receiving a good education at the school founded by the Duke of Württemberg for the sons of his officers, he was himself destined for the medical profession. Literature, however, was his passion, and he was only 22 when his first play, *Die Räuber*, was accepted by Dalberg for production, after the action had been relegated to the safe distance of the sixteenth century. The play, which deals with the hostility of two brothers, was an outburst of pent-up resentment, and thrilled the younger generation. Schiller, who was now an army doctor, twice attended performances without leave of absence. A severe reprimand and a fortnight's imprisonment left him smarting and resentful, and in 1782 he took refuge in Mannheim. He was not unkindly received, though his uncouth manners were at variance with his new surroundings, and his relationship with Dalberg, who appointed him author and stage-manager to the Mannheim Theatre, was cordial. In spite of this, and of the success of *Kabale und Liebe* in 1784, Schiller, who was living in Mannheim under an assumed name, found life difficult. He was heavily in debt, and might have starved had not a kindly friend, Frau von Wolzogen, offered him her country cottage as a refuge. He was also befriended by Charlotte von Kalb, one of the many cultured women of the period who sought in literary patronage compensation for a marriage of convenience. Her influence may be traced in *Don Carlos* (1787), Schiller's first attempt at historical tragedy in the grand style. While he was engaged on it he went to Leipzig, where he first met Gottfried Körner, one of his admirers, who became a lifelong friend. Under Körner's influence Schiller made Posa, the friend who lays down his life in a vain effort to save Don Carlos, the champion of religious tolerance, prepared to carry his ideals into the presence of Philip II himself.

This play, which was produced in 1787, marks the transition to Schiller's later style, though twelve years were to elapse before another play came from his pen. Meanwhile he married and was appointed unsalaried professor of history at Jena, eking out his meagre income from students' fees by historical essays and the editorship of *Thalia*, in which he and Körner published the results of their aesthetic discussions. The two main works of this period were historical, *Die Geschichte des Abfalls der vereinigten Niederlande*, written before he went to Jena, and *Die Geschichte des dreissigjährigen Kriegs*.

The intensive study necessary for this latter work provided him with the material for his great trilogy of *Wallenstein*, which was finally completed in 1799, and translated into English by Coleridge in the following year. He was by this time, after a period of rest and recuperation from illness, which he spent mainly in an intensive study of Kant, settled in Weimar, where he enjoyed the friendship and collaboration of Goethe in pursuit of their common goal—an ordered, self-disciplined, and seemly society—and in the denunciation of mediocrity and low aims. Nothing now remained but the delimitation in *Naive und sentimentalische Dichtung* of his own reflective poetic temperament from Goethe's spontaneous genius before he strode forward from achievement to achievement until his regrettably early death from tuberculosis in 1805.

These last few years saw the appearance of *Maria Stuart* in 1800, of *Die Jungfrau von Orleans* in 1801, of *Die Braut von Messina* in 1803, and of Schiller's last play, *Wilhelm Tell*, in 1804 (for a detailed discussion of these, see GERMANY, 4). W. E. D.

SCHIMMEL, HENDRIK JAN (1823–1906), see HOLLAND.

SCHLEGEL. (1) JOHANN ELIAS VON (1719–49), German dramatist, author of some good comedies, and of tragedies, some of which are historical. He received his literary training from Gottsched in Leipzig, but though his own plays are conservative in style, and he employs the alexandrine line in tragedy, he soon emancipated himself from Gottsched's yoke in thought and in aesthetic judgement, a process which was helped by his appointment to Copenhagen, where a more liberal atmosphere prevailed. His objective valuation of the drama of different nations, and his views on the relation of art and nature are well in advance of his time. He was, however, destined to be eclipsed by Lessing's more trenchant mind and greater forcefulness of expression. His nephew, (2) AUGUST WILHELM (1767–1845), is remembered more as a sensitive and discerning critic of enormous range, and a highly talented translator of Shakespeare, Dante, Cervantes, and Calderón, than as a creative artist, though he wrote some sixteen plays. He had little originality, but avoided the extravagances of his fellow Romantics. In his famous lectures given at Vienna, *Über dramatische Kunst und Literatur,* published from 1809 to 1811, he was the first to trace the development of drama in all nations. W. E. D.

SCHLEY'S MUSIC-HALL, NEW YORK, see SAVOY THEATRE (2).

SCHNITZLER, ARTHUR (1862–1931), Austrian dramatist, a doctor by profession, who brought to his plays something of the dispassionate attitude of the consulting-room. His first work for the theatre, and the one which is usually associated with his name, was *Anatol,* a series of sketches of an irresponsible gallant. This was written in 1893, and was followed two years later by the darker side of the picture in *Liebelei,* where the working-class girl kills herself on learning of the death of the young aristocrat who had been merely trifling with her. Although in this play, and in many others, notably *Reigen*(1902), *Der Ruf des Lebens*(1905), and *Der einsame Weg*(1904), a sensitive play of delicate half-lights, Schnitzler handles the entanglements of sex with a sure touch, he pursues also the swiftness of change from irresponsible make-believe to grim reality in *Der grüne*

Kakadu (1899), and in *Dr. Bernhardi* (1912), his one contribution to the problem play, views from all angles the repercussions of an anti-Semitic incident in a Viennese hospital. Schnitzler may be taken as typical of the light-hearted cynicism of Vienna before 1914. It has been said of him: 'He remains an exquisite artist who transferred the objectivity of the naturalist method to the romantic field.'

SCHOOL DRAMA, a term applied to the academic, educational type of play which developed under the influence of the humanists, and is found in the early dramatic literature of all European countries. Written by scholars for performance by schoolboys, as part of their educational curriculum, they were originally all in Latin, a tradition which persisted longest in the Jesuit colleges (see JESUIT DRAMA). Elsewhere they tended quickly to slip into the vernacular, and had some influence on the development of the non-academic, popular and later professional drama. There was a great deal of dramatic activity in English schools and colleges in the first half of the sixteenth century, and the first two 'regular English comedies'—*Ralph Roister Doister* and *Gammer Gurton's Needle*—were given at Eton (or Westminster), and at Christ's College, Cambridge, respectively. (For further information on School Drama, see the separate countries of Europe.)

SCHÖNEMANN, JOHANN FRIEDRICH (1704–82), German actor, originally a harlequin in a travelling troupe. He later joined the company of Caroline Neuber, where he acted a variety of parts, and was particularly admired in the valets of French comedy. He married an actress, Anna Rachel Weigler, and after the Neubers' break with Gottsched and their departure for Russia Schönemann formed his own company and took Caroline Neuber's place in Leipzig. Into this new company he took Sophie Schröder, Ekhof, and Ackermann, all destined to play so large a part in the theatrical development of Germany. Schönemann, who was 36 when he formed his company, was at first an able and astute leader, though he lacked the idealism which had inspired the young Caroline Neuber. He continued to act well in comedy, but was less successful in tragedy, retaining to the end the stiff and pompous declamatory style evolved by Gottsched and Caroline Neuber. Later he became completely immersed in his hobby of horse-dealing and left the company to Ekhof, and, when financial ruin could no longer be avoided, he abandoned his profession entirely and retired into private life.

SCHREYVOGEL, JOSEF (1768–1832), manager of the Vienna Hofburgtheater during its most successful period. He first became involved in theatrical matters in 1802, and by 1814 was in charge of the choice, casting, and production of plays at the Hofburgtheater. He continued in this position, in spite of financial and other difficulties, introducing many excellent and much-needed reforms, until he was finally dismissed in 1832 for outspokenness unpalatable to his employers. Among the authors he encouraged and produced, often in the face of opposition from the censor, was Grillparzer, while he was instrumental in bringing to the Hofburgtheater Heinrich Anschutz, who became one of the leading actors of Vienna. Schreyvogel's own plays are now forgotten.

SCHRÖDER, FRIEDRICH LUDWIG (1744–1816), the greatest name in German theatrical annals, a fine actor and the first to introduce Shakespeare to Germany. He was the son of Sophie Schröder (see ACKERMANN, 2) by her first marriage, and grew up in the theatrical company of her second husband, Konrad Ackermann. He was acting at three years old, and had a hard, unhappy childhood, which is described in his biography by his friend F. L. W. Meyer. On the outbreak of war in 1756 the Ackermann company left Königsberg, where Schröder was then at school, and he was unaccountably left behind. He lived in the deserted theatre, which he occasionally was able to let to wandering companies, and earned his living somehow. From his tenants he learnt acrobatics and dancing, and at 13 was befriended by an English rope-dancer and acrobat, Michael Stuart, and his charming Danish wife. A year or two later, after a hazardous journey on foot, he succeeded in rejoining the Ackermanns in Switzerland. He worked with the company, but was contemptuous of acting, which he thought a puerile occupation compared to the rigours of tumbling.

The turning-point of his career came when Ekhof, then at the height of his powers, joined the company. Schröder, though outwardly as contemptuous and ill-mannered as usual, saw at last what acting could be, and for the five years that Ekhof remained with them he studied him closely, deepening and purifying his own art in the process. Conscious of his growing mastery, he manœuvred Ekhof into such a difficult position that the older man retreated, leaving his young rival—he was then about 25—a clear field. During the Ackermanns' occupation of the new National Theatre at Hamburg Schröder was much admired, particularly in the parts of the quick-witted, light-heeled valets of French comedy, but when a new management was installed he declined to remain under it, and joined a popular but somewhat inferior travelling company run by Joseph von Kurz, which continued to give the old improvised comedy. Here he remained for a year, with little profit to himself, and then returned to Hamburg, where, the successive managements having failed, and Ackermann being now too old and indolent to take over, the young Schröder grasped the reins of management with a firm hand. He married in 1773 a young actress named Christine Hart (? –1829), who made him an excellent wife, and though the financial side of the company was still under the control of his mother, now a widow, he took complete responsibility for the artistic side. He seemed to grow up overnight, and to his excellent

qualities as a brilliant actor he added those of astute manager and inspiring producer. At the head of a brilliant company, which included his two half-sisters, Dorothea and Charlotte Ackermann, he was in the forefront of the new movement in Germany. His first independent production was *Emilia Galotti*; he encouraged the *Sturm und Drang* writers, and was the first to play the name-part in *Götz von Berlichingen*, in which he abolished the last remnants of French costume—powdered wigs and lace ruffles—not only reforming the costumes and scenery, but directing the new approach to acting necessitated by the new type of play.

The chief enterprise with which Schröder's name is imperishably linked, however, is the introduction of Shakespeare to the German stage. He was known on the printed page to all the ardent youngsters of the new generation, but they had not had an opportunity of seeing him acted. Even now, they saw him only in the adapted versions made by Schröder himself, where Hamlet survived, as did Cordelia, but even so each production was a revelation, and probably as much as audiences could have stomached at the time. The series started in 1776 with *Hamlet*, in which Brockmann played the name-part and Schröder the Ghost (he later played Laertes, the Grave-digger, and Hamlet), and by 1780 eleven plays had been given, of which *Othello* was a failure and *King Lear* an outstanding success.

With this pioneer work Schröder also combined the production of a more conservative repertory, including the once popular but now forgotten plays and monodramas of Brandes, ballets, and even light musical pieces. He continued to dance himself till 1778, the year in which he did Lear, and made the rest of the company do the same. He worked his actors hard—indeed, he was considered to have caused the death by overwork and worry of his gifted half-sister Charlotte—but he taught them the value of application, of steady consistent progress, and of team-work. This first phase of Schröder's Hamburg management, which brought him in nothing financially, since his mother kept the profits and gave him a beggarly salary, was perhaps the most glorious of his career. It ended when friction between himself and the company caused him to go with his wife to Vienna, where he remained for four years as an honoured guest-artist of the Burgtheater. This period contributed little to his own development, but he left a mark on the Viennese stage. Under his influence it quietened down considerably and lost much of its pompous ranting in tragedy and its old-fashioned foolery in comedy. Indeed, Schröder may be said to have laid the foundations of the subtle and refined ensemble playing of the Vienna Burgtheater company which was later to become their distinguishing mark.

Back in Hamburg in 1786 Schröder took over the theatre again, and raised it from the slough of despond into which a series of incompetent managements had plunged it. For twelve years he kept it orderly and prosperous, and at the head of the theatrical world in Germany. It was a less glorious period than his previous one. His ideals had flagged a little, and the stage that should have seen the triumphs of the mature Goethe and Schiller was given over to the trivialities of Kotzebue and Iffland. But it was a prosperous time, and at 54, having achieved financial independence, Schröder gave up the stage entirely, buying a country estate in Holstein where he spent the rest of his life in intellectual activity and honourable retirement. It is interesting to note, in passing, that Schröder and his sister figure in Goethe's *Wilhelm Meister* as Serlo and Aurelie.

SCHUCH, FRANZ (*c.* 1716–64), German harlequin-player, leader of a company of travelling actors to which the great actor Ekhof belonged for a short time after he left Schönemann. Brandes, a poor actor and a prolific dramatist, who afterwards obtained some success, had his first stable engagement with Schuch, and describes him in his memoirs as a fine comedian and improviser, homely without descending to triviality, humorous without vulgarity. He was a shrewd business man, and much esteemed by his company and by the audiences of the towns where he played. Lessing thought highly of him, and attended his performances whenever possible. After his death his three sons, who had inherited some of his talents but not the probity of his character, undertook the management of the troupe, which they soon reduced to bankruptcy. It was then taken over by Döbbelin, who had previously been a member of the company, and established by him in Berlin, where it prospered.

SCHWARTZ, MAURICE (1888–   ), Jewish actor and producer. Born in the Ukraine, he was to have gone to America with his family in 1899, but owing to some misunderstanding over the steamship passages he was left behind in England. There he lived by his wits, working in a rag factory, doing odd jobs in the Yiddish theatre in London, and singing in a synagogue choir. Two years later his family traced him and took him to New York. In 1905 he joined the Delancey Street Dramatic Club, where his first appearance earned him a job in a Baltimore theatre. After several years in Yiddish theatres there and in Cincinnati, Chicago, and Philadelphia, he joined David Kessler's company in New York. In 1912 he produced his first play, a translation from the English, following it a year later with an original play. In 1918 he became a partner in the Irving Place Theatre, where, after a short period of management on his own elsewhere, he opened his Jewish Art Theatre. This was successful, and in 1924 he embarked on a tour of Europe. On his return to New York Schwartz moved his theatre to Broadway, hoping to attract assimilated Jewry. The result was disappointing, and he returned to Second Avenue, traditional New York home of the Yiddish theatre. Since then he has toured the Argentine, visited Palestine, where

he worked with Ohel, and appeared in films. His repertory is extensive, including both Jewish and other classics, and he has encouraged the development of many Yiddish playwrights by his careful productions of their early plays.   E. H.

SCISSOR CROSS, see STAGE DIRECTIONS.

SCISSOR STAGE, see STAGE, 5.

SCOTLAND. The position of Scotland as regards the theatre is on a parallel with her geographical position in relation to Europe. Both lie on the outposts. Drama did not begin to flourish in her cities until the nineteenth century, and it was not until the 1920s that her native authors concerned themselves at all seriously with the writing of plays in the vernacular, or in English on Scottish themes for production on a Scottish stage. But the seemingly belated appearance of a Scottish drama was really a revival after early arrested growth, for in the fifteenth and sixteenth centuries moralities and festival pageants flourished in Scotland as elsewhere, and in Sir David Lyndsay's *Ane Pleasant Satyre of the Thrie Estaitis* (produced at Cupar in 1540 and revived during the Edinburgh Festival of 1948) there are traces of a beginning of indigenous drama. Indeed, the Scottish Renaissance seemed at one time to be tending towards the theatre. The country's turbulent history, in which the clash of individuals had free play, and the natural humour of the people, offered a fitting soil for it, while dramatic imagination shone richly in the great ballads. But a Scots parallel to the Elizabethan stage did not develop, the green shoots being blighted by the civil and religious strife that blanketed the country during the seventeenth century. Satire, fantasy, humour, and a taste for the macabre—these elements in Lyndsay's Morality and in the non-dramatic writings of the Makars have found free expression in the plays of a modern Scottish dramatist like Bridie, thus suggesting that the roots of the modern Scottish dramatic movement are embedded deeply in the past.

From the close of the sixteenth until the opening of the twentieth century the most prominent of the very few manifestations of indigenous drama in Scotland was the tragedy *Douglas* by John Home. This laborious work was produced in 1756 in a theatre in the Canongate, Edinburgh, where an ill-paid company of English actors led an underworld existence. A few years previously, in 1736, the poet Allan Ramsay had ventured to build a theatre in one of the closes of the Scottish capital, but it was immediately closed under the licensing laws. Towards the end of the eighteenth century the theatre fared a little better, existing more or less regularly in both Edinburgh and Glasgow, and throughout the nineteenth century it flourished. Day bills issued between 1815 and 1817 by the Theatre Royal, Edinburgh, and the Theatre Royal, Glasgow, reveal the existence of a stirring theatrical life. Stock companies played Shakespeare and the eighteenth-century classics regularly, and introduced new comedies and farces every week. Itinerant stars from the London stage—Kean, the Kembles, and others—paid regular visits. Dramatic versions of Sir Walter Scott's novels were popular. *Guy Mannering* (published in 1815) appeared on the stage in Glasgow and Edinburgh in 1817. Many of the melodramas and romances produced had a Scottish flavour, and a popular 'grand Scottish National Pantomime', entitled *Oscar and Malvina*, drew inspiration from Macpherson's *Ossian*. Among other pantomimes were *Sawney Bean's Cave* and *The Falls of Clyde*. *Deacon Brodie* (1880), by R. L. Stevenson and W. E. Henley, and the early plays of Barrie, were heralds of the distinctly Scottish drama that was to arise in the twentieth century (see also EDINBURGH and GLASGOW).

Scotland's first real contribution to the theatre was made in the five years 1909–14, when the repertory movement that followed the impact of Ibsen made its way north of the Border, inspiring the Glasgow Repertory Theatre; this did excellent work and during its five seasons produced plays by prominent English and continental dramatists, as well as a few Scottish plays, the most notable being John Ferguson's *Campbell of Kilmohr*, a one-act tragedy of exceptional merit. But the theatre never envisaged forming a Scottish company of actors, relying on a professional stock company, many of whose members later went to London.

The outbreak of war in 1914 forced the Glasgow Repertory Theatre to close down. Its work in fostering Scots drama was not forgotten, however, and what remained of its funds (about £400) was transferred to the St. Andrew's Society, which used the money to launch the movement that produced the Scottish National Players. This body of active and talented actors, mainly amateur, formed between 1921 and 1936 the chief focal point of native Scots drama. It soon ceased to be part of the St. Andrew's Society and functioned independently. In January 1922 the Scottish National Theatre Society was formed to support it. Its aims were to develop Scottish drama, to found a Scottish National Theatre, and to encourage the taste of the public for good drama of any type. These aims were only partially fulfilled. The society never acquired a theatre building of its own, and the development of a school of Scottish dramatists proceeded very slowly. The movement unfortunately failed to establish in Glasgow a Scottish counterpart of the Abbey Theatre in Dublin, mainly owing to the absence of financial backing, the prevalence of economic depression, the industrialization of the modern Lowland Scot, and the magnetic force of the London stage, which drew away producers and players, and was the Mecca of the best dramatists. Nevertheless the Scottish National Players shaped a number of excellent actors and produced the works of over thirty Scottish

dramatists, in addition to many plays by Shakespeare, Shaw, Chekhov, Sierra, and others.

When the energies of the Scottish National Players flagged towards the 1930s a new company of Glasgow amateurs, the Curtain Theatre, became the pioneering vehicle for the production of new plays in the vernacular. In the meantime various theatrical ventures of a repertory nature appeared and disappeared on the Scottish scene. The Masque Theatre, the Brandon-Thomas Players, and the Howard and Wyndham Players conducted seasons of varying length with a fair amount of success in Glasgow and Edinburgh. From 1936 onwards a Repertory Theatre in Perth, directed by David Steuart and Marjorie Dence, ploughed a gallant furrow, producing plays by authors old and new, and in the summer of 1939 the first Scottish Theatre Festival was successfully launched there, at which the plays presented were Chekhov's *Three Sisters*, Bridie's *The Golden Legend of Shults* (a first performance), Shaw's *Caesar and Cleopatra*, and Shakespeare's *Romeo and Juliet*.

The Community Drama movement has flourished successfully in Scotland, and the annual Festivals organized by the Scottish Community Drama Association have two achievements to their credit—the raising of amateur standards of acting and production, and the creation of a fairly large body of one-act plays in the vernacular, among which Joe Corrie's may be given pride of place. They have also popularized the drama in rural and urban Scotland, and helped to keep the theatre alive in a period dominated by the cinema. But this amateur movement has on the whole dissipated effort, preventing, by proliferation and individualism, the concentration of talent in the service of either Scottish drama or Little Theatre ideals.   W. J.

SCOTT, CLEMENT WILLIAM (1841–1904), English dramatic critic, on the *Daily Telegraph* from 1872 until within a few years of his death. He wrote several plays under the pseudonyms 'John Doe' and 'Saville Rowe' and often in collaboration with B. C. Stephenson. Some of these were translations from Sardou, of which *Diplomacy* (1878), from *Dora*, was the most notable. He was the editor of *The Theatre*, a monthly magazine devoted to the drama, which ran from 1877 to 1897.

As a dramatic critic Scott was in the forefront of the Old Guard that put up a determined resistance to the new drama. He was at the opposite pole of contemporary criticism from William Archer, whose translations of Ibsen's plays caused such distress to Scott when they were performed in London. Scott's well-known attack on *Ghosts* was marked by that obstinate refusal to look at anything outside conventional morality which tinged his whole outlook on the theatre.

When Scott published *From 'The Bells' to 'King Arthur'*, a critical record of first-night productions at the Lyceum Theatre from 1871 to 1895, Bernard Shaw reviewed the book and wrote of the author:

Mr. Clement Scott is not the first of our great dramatic critics but he is the first of the great dramatic reporters . . . the main secret of his popularity is that he is, above all, a sympathetic critic . . . an average young university graduate would hang himself sooner than wear his heart on his sleeve before the world as Mr. Scott does, and that is just why the average young university graduate never interests anyone in his critical remarks. . . . Mr. Scott is not a thinker: whatever question you raise with him you must raise as a question of conduct, which is a matter of feeling, and not of creed, which is a matter of intellectual order . . . the drama which asserts and argues will never be tolerated by him . . .

This was borne out by Scott's assessment of Ibsen's *Ghosts* as 'a wretched, deplorable, loathsome history, as all must admit. It might have been a tragedy had it been handled by a man of genius. Handled by an egotist and a bungler, it is only a deplorably dull play.'

T. C. K.

SCOTTISH COMEDIANS. These form a distinctive school. They flourish in variety and in pantomime in Scotland, and the greatest of them, such as Sir Harry Lauder and Will Fyffe, have gone forth from their native heath to entertain the Empire. They are modern minstrels and raconteurs, providing an outlet for the wild spirit, cousin of the Highland reel, and the pawky and sentimental humours that seethe beneath the stolid Scots exterior. They specialize in a conventional pastoralism. The foremost of the indigenous Glasgow comedians was Tommy Lorne (born Hugh Corcoran in a slum), who for a decade or two reigned in the Princess's and Theatre Royal pantomimes. He was highly skilled in impersonations, and his Dame, based on the personality of the working-class woman who finds the world menacing and incomprehensible, was an individual creation. Lorne's successor at the annual Princess's pantomime, George West, followed the Grimaldi tradition in make-up and in a flair for fantastic costume. He is a fertile humorist. Comedians of a less supple nature are Dave Willis and Tommy Morgan.

W. J.

SCOTTISH COMMUNITY DRAMA ASSOCIATION (S.C.D.A.), see AMATEUR THEATRE IN GREAT BRITAIN, 2.

SCOTTISH NATIONAL PLAYERS, THE, made their first appearance under the auspices of the St. Andrew's Society in a hall in Glasgow, presenting three one-act plays. Three months later, in April 1921, they produced three new plays in the Athenaeum Theatre, and soon ceased to be part of the St. Andrew's Society, having an independent life of their own. They aimed at producing plays in the vernacular by Scottish authors, and in fact were the first to produce the works of over thirty Scottish dramatists, including James Bridie, John Brandane, Joe Corrie, John Ferguson, Neil Gunn, Robins Millar, and others.

A body of plays was thus written for the Players that reflected Scottish life from every angle. Many excellent actors, some of whom later found their way to London and New York, were trained by the Players. When the company's energies flagged in the early 1930s their work for indigenous Scottish drama was taken over by the Curtain Theatre, Glasgow.

W. J.

SCOTTISH ROSCIUS, see JOHNSTON, H. E.

SCRIBE, (AUGUSTIN) EUGÈNE (1791–1861), French dramatist, the originator and exponent of the 'well-made play'. A prolific writer, he was responsible, alone or in collaboration, for more than 400 plays, comprising tragedies, comedies, vaudevilles, and libretti for light opera. His collaborators, of whom Legouvé, Dupin, Delavigne, Mélèsville, and Saintine are the best known, all brought much to the common stock, but the stagecraft was Scribe's. Yet his early plays, which began in 1810 with a protest against Romanticism, were failures, and it was not until 1815 that he achieved fame with *Une Nuit de la Garde Nationale.* Some years later the first night of *Un Verre d'eau* (1820) occasioned a stormy scene at the Comédie-Française, as it saw the first appearance of a young actress whose success was unpalatable to Mlle Mars. The most successful of Scribe's plays, and the one best remembered, was *Adrienne Lecouvreur* (1849), written in collaboration with Legouvé, who in 1874 wrote Scribe's biography. The play, though incorrect historically, provided a fine part for Rachel, and later for Sarah Bernhardt. In translation it was played by Mme Ristori, Mme Modjeska, Helen Faucit, and many others.

Scribe's popularity has not guaranteed him against almost complete oblivion. His plays, which in their banality and pettiness reflect very faithfully the bourgeois epoch of the Restoration and the Monarchy of July, are constructed with the utmost neatness and economy, a relief to his middle-class audiences after the incoherence of the Revolution and the excesses of the Romantics. They are still interesting as examples of dramatic construction, though seldom revived nowadays. He had no depth, no delicacy of perception. But though he was not a literary figure, though his language was poor, and although he has not created a single figure, with the possible exception of Adrienne Lecouvreur, who has remained in theatrical memory, he was an excellent craftsman. He had an uncanny flair for theatrical effect, and was unrivalled in judging what would appeal to an audience at any given moment. He wrote successfully for a number of theatres for more than thirty years, and his example weighed heavily on the European theatre for long after his death. Indeed, he was blamed for all the shortcomings of the dramatists who succeeded him, and in France his influence was strong on Labiche and Sardou. His much-sought-after libretti helped to make French romantic opera a model of theatrical effectiveness.

SCRUTO, a device used in effecting a Transformation Scene (see TRICKWORK ON THE ENGLISH STAGE).

SCUDÉRY, GEORGES DE (1601–67), French author, brother of the famous Madeleine de Scudéry, *précieuse* and novelist, with whom he collaborated in the well-known romantic novel, *L'Astrée*. Georges was in the French Guards in his youth, and always retained a soldierly bearing, and a touch of the gentleman-adventurer. His first play was produced in 1630, and during the next thirteen years he wrote some sixteen more, mostly tragicomedies. He played a leading part in the attack on *Le Cid*, probably in order to conciliate his patron Richelieu, who at one time, by way of indirect reproach to Corneille, made much of him. He was annoyed at not being one of the five dramatists chosen to write Richelieu's plays, but consoled by his election as a foundation member of the French Academy, an honour which he had done little to deserve. His plays are now forgotten. One of them, *Le Trompeur puni* (1631), was done at the Cockpit in London by Floridor's company in 1635.

SÉDAINE, MICHEL JEAN (1719–97), French dramatist, who, owing to the early death of his father, was forced to leave school and work as a stone-cutter. He was befriended by the painter David and by the architect Buron (whose kindness he was later to repay by adopting Buron's grandson) and rapidly made good the deficiencies in his education. Finding himself endowed with a facility for writing amusing lyric verse, he turned out a number of excellent libretti for light operas, with music by Grétry, Philidor, Monsigny, and others. His 'On ne s'avise jamais de tout' (1761) was the last light opera given at the Théâtre de la Foire Saint-Laurent before it was closed at the request of the Comédie-Italienne, who then amalgamated with it to form the Opéra-Comique. One of Sedaine's most successful libretti was 'Le Roi et le Fermier', based, probably by way of Collé's *La Partie de chasse d'Henri IV*, on Dodsley's *King and the Miller*. Sedaine's most important work, however, and the one by which he is best remembered, is *Le Philosophe sans le savoir* (1765), a *drame bourgeois* written under the influence of Diderot, and interpreting his dramatic theories better than their originator could do in his own plays. It shows little imagination, but has a lively wit, and delicately drawn characters, and is the only play of its type to have remained in the repertory. Sedaine became a member of the French Academy in 1789.

SEDLEY, SIR CHARLES (c. 1639–1701), Restoration dramatist, wit, and man of letters, friend of Rochester and Etherege. He wrote several plays, of which the best are *The Mul-*

berry-Garden (1668), a comedy of contemporary manners which owes something to Molière's *École des Maris* and something to Etherege's *Comical Revenge* (1664), and the lively but licentious *Bellamira, or the Mistress* (1687), based on the *Eunuchus* of Terence. Sedley was also the author of a dull tragedy on the subject of Antony and Cleopatra, written in imitation of Dryden's heroic drama.

SEDLEY-SMITH, WILLIAM HENRY (1806–72), an American actor, of good English parentage, who at 14 ran away from home to escape the unkindness of his step-father, and joined a company of strolling players, adding Smith to his real name of Sedley. He toured the English provinces for some years, and in 1827 went to America, making his first appearance at the Walnut Street Theatre, Philadelphia, as Jeremy Diddler in *Raising the Wind*. A year later he was seen in Boston, where he became extremely popular. He managed the Boston Museum from 1836 to 1860, during which time he also appeared in New York, being first seen there in a number of Shakespeare plays in 1840. He made his last appearance there in 1865 and then went to San Francisco, where he became manager of the California Theatre until his death, and was able to be of service to the young David Belasco. Winter, in his life of the latter, says of Sedley-Smith: 'Robust, rosy, stately, with a rich, ringing voice, a merry laugh, and a free and noble courtesy of demeanour . . . he played all parts well, and in some he was superlatively excellent.' Among the latter Winter mentions Sir Oliver Surface, Old Dornton, and the Stranger. Sedley-Smith married a charming actress, by whom he had one daughter, Mary, later the wife of Sol Smith.

SELWYN THEATRE, NEW YORK, on the north side of 42nd Street. This theatre opened on 2 Oct. 1918 and one of the most successful plays staged there was *The Royal Family* (1927), a saga of the Drew and Barrymore families, seen in England as *Theatre Royal*. *Battling Butler*, with Charles Ruggles, was seen here, as was *The Constant Nymph*, while *Wake Up and Dream* introduced Jessie Matthews to the New York stage, in company with Tilly Losch and Jack Buchanan. The last outstanding event in the theatre's history was a series of six matinées of *Electra* with Blanche Yurka and Mrs. Pat Campbell, after which it became a cinema.							G. F.

SEMENOVA, EKATERINA SEMENOVNA (1786–1849), famous Russian actress. The daughter of a serf and of a teacher in the St. Petersburg Cadet Corps, she was attached to the theatre school in St. Petersburg at the age of ten, and studied under Dmitrevsky. She made her first appearance in 1803, and came to the fore in the tragedies of Ozerov. Later she played the heroines of Racine, Shakespeare, and Schiller. Having had little education she could not work out her roles unaided, and was coached first by Prince Shakovsky, the dramatist, and Head of the Repertory of the Alexandrinsky Theatre, and then by Gnedich, the famous poet and translator of the *Iliad*. She made a great impression on her contemporaries by her beauty and her lovely contralto voice. Pushkin dedicated some of his poems to her, and wrote of her with ecstasy in his essay on the Russian theatre. According to him she had no peer on the Russian stage, though her acting lacked continuity, and was marred by gusts of emotion. Her rivalry with another actress caused her to leave the stage for a time. She returned after two years, and in 1823 appeared successfully in *Phèdre*. Two years later she married a Senator Prince, and played only in the private theatres of Moscow and St. Petersburg. She has been called the Russian Mrs. Siddons.

SEMPER, GOTTFRIED (1803–79), German theatre architect, designer of the Dresden Opera House. He was connected with Wagner in the planning of a Festival Theatre for Munich, which was never built, but of which many features were incorporated later into the Festspielhaus at Bayreuth. The story of his relations with Wagner and Bayreuth has been told by his son, who was also an architect (see also Ernest Newman's *Life of Wagner*, Vol. iii, Ch. 17). (See ACOUSTICS and ARCHITECTURE.)

SENECA, LUCIUS ANNAEUS (*c.* 4 B.C.–A.D. 65), Roman dramatist, philosopher, satirist, statesman, the tutor and later the victim of Nero. Under his name we have nine Latin tragedies: *Hercules (Furens)*, *Phoenissae* (or *Thebais*), *Troades*, *Medea*, *Phaedra* (or *Hippolytus*), *Oedipus*, *Agamemnon,Thyestes,Hercules (Oetaeus)*. Some manuscripts add the *Octavia*, a Roman historical play dealing with the unfortunate wife of Nero. Of these plays the *Octavia* at any rate can hardly be the work of Seneca: it brings Seneca on the stage as a character, it refers to Nero in terms which would never have been permitted during the emperor's lifetime, and it contains a prophetic passage describing his death too circumstantial to have been written by one who died three years before him. The authenticity of the other nine plays is generally accepted by modern scholars; their style, their Stoic outlook, and their occasional touches of humane sentiment and moral elevation are paralleled in Seneca's other writings, and Quintilian quotes part of a line from the *Medea* as Seneca's. As our only extant Latin tragedies, and the only dramas of any kind which have come down to us from the Roman Empire, these plays have great historical importance, and their influence on the development of drama in modern times has been profound.

As a dramatist Seneca seems to owe little to the old dramatists of the Republic, whose style he would probably have despised. His plays are not translations from the Greek but independent works, though based on Greek models. His metres are strictly quantitative, unlike the half-accentual metres of the Republican dramatists, yet at the same time quite unlike the metres of Greek drama. Seneca's plays differ

from anything bequeathed to us by the stage of earlier times, whether Greek or Roman; and one reason for the difference is that his plays were designed not for the stage but for reading, especially dramatic reading to a select audience —the so-called *recitatio*. There are scenes in Seneca which could not be staged: Hercules shoots down his wife and children, the dismembered body of Hippolytus is pieced together by his sorrowing father, Medea kills her son and flings his body down to his father from the palace roof. We do not see the actors coming and going as in a real play: characters speak, then relapse into silence, and we cannot always be sure whether a character not actually speaking is conceived of as present or absent. Objects which in a real play would be visible to all are strangely ignored: thus though Phaedra kills herself under her husband's eyes, he makes no reference to her action, and does not deign to notice her corpse until the very end of the play. The pervading atmosphere is not that of a stage-play, in which the dramatist must visualize every scene and every movement, but that of a *recitatio*, where the speaker takes now one part, now another, and where he can ignore everything but the idea or emotion which the author desires to have expressed at the moment. Character-drawing is too crude to be convincing: Hercules will of course utter heroic sentiments, Ulysses will be crafty, and so on; but all the characters speak with the overstrained voice of the reciter. It is the nature of the *recitatio* to aim at immediate, often merely verbal, effects; plot and character tend to be subordinated to the constant search for smart and surprising turns of speech, for hyperbole and epigram. The grand object seems to be to startle the audience into applause by novel excesses in emotion or expression. The pleasure we as readers may derive from even the best passages is qualified by our apprehension of suddenly meeting with some absurd conceit or some wearisome display of learning.

It is evident that Seneca departed widely from his Greek models, and that his alterations were usually for the worse: compare, for example, his *Oedipus* with the *Oedipus Tyrannus* of Sophocles, or his *Phaedra* with the *Hippolytus* of Euripides. Nevertheless it would be unfair to deny the dramatic power of many scenes in such plays as the *Medea* and the *Troades*, or the beauty of many choral passages. There is perhaps some dramatic quality even in the atmosphere of gloom and horror, of treachery, brutality, and witchcraft, which pervades these plays, and which is itself to some extent a reflection of the times in which Seneca lived. After all, when Seneca writes of the fears and suspicions of Court life, the instability of power, the anxieties of princes and the crimes to which tyranny can lead, or the courage and inward peace which can sustain a man in direst peril and in the pangs of death, that is something more than mere literary reminiscence and commonplace.

For the Renaissance Seneca was the model writer of tragedy. He wrote in Latin, and his language could be understood; his plays were regularly constructed in five acts, according to the Horatian precept; they dealt with emotions and catastrophes which, if they seem to us overdrawn, were universally intelligible; even his rant and rhetoric appealed to the prevailing taste. His rattling line-by-line interchange of dialogue, his chorus, his tyrants, ghosts, and witches, his corpse-strewn stage, all reappear in Elizabethan drama. In 1551–2 his *Troades* was performed at Trinity College, Cambridge. Shakespeare's *Titus Andronicus* is a gruesome example of Senecan influence, while in his *Richard III* we see the splendid effects which Senecan material can be made to yield when employed by dramatic genius.   W. B.

SENTIMENTAL COMEDY, see COMEDY.

SERLIO, SEBASTIANO (1475–1554), Italian painter and architect, who after working for many years on theatrical problems produced a treatise on Architecture, of which the part dealing with perspective in the theatre appeared in 1545. It was immediately translated into French, and had an important influence on the development of scenic design. An English edition, *The Second Book of Architecture*, was published in 1611 (see LIGHTING, 1 *a* and SCENERY, 2).

SERVANDONY, JEAN NICOLAS (1695–1766), a French scenic artist, born in Lyons, who was one of the first to react against the baroque style. After working in various parts of Europe, and particularly in Italy he settled in Paris and took over the control of the Salle des Machines in the Tuileries. There he produced some interesting work, which influenced the stage designing of Italy and Germany. He was in London in 1749, and married there (see also COSTUME, 7 and SCENERY, 4).

SET. This word has developed far from its original meaning, and has now become a noun covering any 'set' of pieces arranged to make a stage scene. Originally the word was used only in 'set scene'—that is, a scene set up in concealment because of the complication of its parts and revealed as a discovery at the opening of a front scene, as against the flat scene whose two simple parts slide on or off the stage in view of the audience (see FLAT). This was the customary procedure in the English theatre up to the time of Irving, and it is not too much to say that a nice mixture of flat scene and set scene was one of the most important formative elements in English drama. It allowed the speedy transition from scene to scene so essential to a drama based on the unique Elizabethan tradition, and at the same time allowed of peak moments of grandiose scenic depth, and multiplane elaboration, that permitted the fantasy of the theatre to have full play. With time the elaboration of the set scene grew, and by early Victorian times it was a serious matter, involving much built stuff as well as painted. A specially contrived short front scene, known as the Carpenter's Scene and devised by the play-

wright to permit the building of an elaborate set behind, was developed as a makeshift device, but soon proved inadequate, and, with Irving, visible scene-change finally died, a curtain being dropped to conceal the scene-shifting during an interval. The flat scene was no longer used, and the set scene became general, till now all scenes may be labelled 'sets', while the term 'setting' has become the general name for the whole theatrical art of designing and staging the scenery of a play
                                                           R. S.

SET PIECE. (1) Scenery of canvas stretched on a wooden frame cut to the silhouette of, for example, a house or a fountain (see FLAT).
(2) The solid three-dimensional elements of full scenery (see BUILT PIECES).

SET SCENE, see FLAT and SET.

SETTLE, ELKANAH (1648–1724), a Restoration dramatist now chiefly remembered for his quarrel with Dryden, who considered his popularity at Court endangered by the success of his rival's bombastic dramas. Settle figures as Doeg in *Absalom and Achitophel*. He began his career by staging drolls at the Fairs, but fired by the favourable reception given to Dryden's *Conquest of Granada*, he put on, with the help of Rochester, Dryden's bitter enemy, an equally elaborate and heroic *Empress of Morocco* (1671). This, with Betterton in the cast, was well enough received to warrant the publication of the text embellished with most valuable scenic illustrations—perhaps the first play to be so published. It was also parodied in a farce by Doggett. Settle wrote a number of other plays, but never again achieved such a success, and in the last years of his life he returned to Bartholomew Fair, playing a dragon in green leather in Mrs. Myn's booth in one of his own productions. The Elkanah Settle Collection of seventeenth-century illustrations is in the Library of the Guildhall, London.

SET WATERS, a series of groundrows set one behind the other to represent a lake, river, or sea, and by their arrangement capable of permitting the passage of a stage boat between them.

SEYLER, ABEL (1730–1801), a merchant of Hamburg, who fell in love with the actress Sophie Hensel, took her part in her quarrels with Ackermann, and eventually became manager of the Hamburg theatre. He might have proved successful but for the intrigues and hot temper of Sophie Hensel, whom he married and took on tour in her own company. Ekhof was with them for a time, and took over the management of the company when it was faced with financial ruin, which caused Sophie to retire in high dudgeon to Vienna. She soon returned, however, and she and Seyler started a new company with varying success. In 1779 Seyler was invited by Dalberg to take over the management of the new Mannheim theatre, but there again his wife's ungovernable temper and jealous disposition caused their dismissal, and forced them to resume their travels. He remained faithful to her in spite of her faults, which must have caused him much suffering, and on her death found a little peace in the hospitable house of Schröder at Holstein.

SEYMOUR [really CUNNINGHAM]. (1) JAMES (1823–64), a comedian, born in Belfast, who began his stage career in Ireland as a boy. From 1840 to 1864 he was well known in the United States as an interpreter of stage Irishmen. He married an American actress, Lydia Eliza Griffith (1832–97). Their only son, (2) WILLIAM GORMAN (1855–1933), made his first appearance on the stage at the age of 2, and at 7 played the Duke of York to Lawrence Barrett's Richard III. He continued to play children's parts with most of the stars of the day, and in 1869, while call-boy at Booth's Theatre, played François to Edwin Booth's Richelieu and the Player Queen to his Hamlet. He was Henrick in the run of 149 consecutive performances of *Rip Van Winkle* with Jefferson, and in 1871 he joined the stock company at the Globe Theatre, Boston, appearing with Edwin Forrest at his final performance. From 1875 until his retirement in 1927 he continued to act, and was also manager of a number of theatres, being general stage director for Charles Frohman and the Empire Theatre, New York, from 1901 to 1919. He married May Davenport, daughter of E. L. Davenport and sister of Fanny (see DAVENPORT, 4), and of their five children three went on the stage. After his death his library was presented to Princeton University to form the nucleus of a William Seymour Theatre Collection.

SHADOW SHOW. The shadow theatre is a puppet-show in which flat figures are passed between a strong light and a translucent screen; the audience, on the other side of the screen, sees their shadows passing across it. Limited of necessity to a highly stylized convention, the shadow show has proved itself an artistic medium of rare and delicate charm.

The oldest form of shadow theatre is found in the Far East—particularly in China and the islands of Java and Bali, where there are still potent shadow-show traditions in which ancestor-worship and magic play their part. The grotesque Javanese figures are particularly striking and well known. Gradually the shadow show seems to have spread westwards in a cruder and more decadent form; there are traces of it in Arabia, along the north coast of Africa, and in Turkey. From Turkey the shadow theatre was taken to Greece, where it took root and evolved into a native popular entertainment; in the Greek shadow show a witty, vulgar, Greek type, 'Karagöz', appears in every play, invariably getting the better of unpopular characters—Turks, tax-collectors, and—perhaps—Italians.

Shadow shows of some kind must have existed in western Europe from very early times—there is a complete shadow-show performance indicated in Ben Jonson's *Tale of a Tub* (1640)—but it was not till the second half of the eighteenth century that travellers returning from the East brought the Eastern shadow show with them and the 'Ombres Chinoises' sprang into popularity. In 1774 Dominique Séraphin established a Shadow Theatre at Versailles, which was extensively patronized by the Court, and in the next year Ambroise introduced this entertainment to England; the craze for 'Ombres Chinoises' did not last for very long, but in its time it was a constant attraction and must have been a pretty and clever entertainment; the plays seem to have consisted of amusing episodes rather than dramatic pieces—the great classic was *The Broken Bridge*, in which a traveller indulges in a pantomime argument with a workman on the other side of a river. This was first given by Séraphin after he moved to the Palais-Royal in 1784. His theatre there continued under his nephew (who succeeded him in 1799) until 1859, and was the delight of successive generations of Parisian children.

The 'Ombres Chinoises' were preserved in the English Galanty Show, which was often given in a Punch and Judy booth with a sheet stretched across the opening and lit by candles from inside. The old favourite of *The Broken Bridge* was still performed in the London streets up to the end of the nineteenth century, but the Galanty Show seems to have disappeared completely now.

Towards the end of the nineteenth century there was something of a revival of the shadow show in France; a group of artists and writers who gathered at the Chat Noir café in Montmartre, led by Henri Rivière and Caran d'Ache, combined during the 1880s and 1890s in presenting a series of shadow-show performances that became famous for their wit and artistry.

In our own day the art of the shadow theatre has seen a most welcome revival in the shadow films of Lotte Reiniger; their method of production varies slightly from the ordinary shadow technique: the figures, cut from tin and fully jointed, are laid upon a translucent 'table', brightly illuminated from below, and moved gradually while a 'stop camera' above records each position.

Shadow figures can be made of cardboard, but are much better constructed of tin (as in the Chat Noir and Galanty Show), of leather (as in Java and Bali), or of some coloured transparent material (as in China and Greece). There are several methods of manipulation:

1. By thin bamboo rods, held by the operator from *below* the screen (as in the Far East).
2. By rods held at *right angles* to the screen (as in Greece).
3. By concealed strings or wires passing down behind the figures and operated from *below* (as in the Chat Noir and Galanty Shows).
4. Figures that do not possess any actions of their own can be drawn across the screen from the *sides*.

The history of the shadow theatre has been written by George Jacob in *Geschichte des Schattentheaters* (1907). (See also MALAY and PUPPET.)   G. S.

SHADWELL, THOMAS (*c.* 1642–92), Restoration dramatist, whose best comedies, *Epsom Wells* (1672), *The Squire of Alsatia* (1688), and *Bury Fair* (1689), give interesting though somewhat scurrilous pictures of contemporary manners. His first play, *The Sullen Lovers; or, the Impertinents* (1668), was based on Molière's *Les Fâcheux*, but on the whole Shadwell was more indebted to Jonson, whose disciple he claimed to be. Indeed, it was his devotion to Jonson that led to his quarrel with Dryden, whom he succeeded as Poet Laureate. Shadwell has been much criticized for his adaptations from Shakespeare, particularly for his version of *The Tempest* as 'The Enchanted Island' (1674) in operatic form, following the example of Davenant and Dryden. Here everything was subordinated to the machinery and scenery, as in his own opera 'Psyche', which cost Dorset Garden £800 in scenery alone. Shadwell, who disliked and satirized the heroic tragedy of Dryden as well as the early Restoration comedies, was a competent dramatist whose plays were most successful in his own day, though they no longer bear revival, mainly owing to their coarse and topical humour. Nicoll says of him: 'Many might laugh at his idiosyncrasies, his love of beer and his habit of declaring that his plays were written in unconscionably brief spaces of time, but for all that he remains one of the chief of the comic dramatists outside of the school of manners.' He married an actress, Anne Gibbs, who was in Davenant's first company. She outlived him, and published posthumously his last comedy, which was given in 1692, and was rated below some of his earlier work.

SHAFTESBURY THEATRE, LONDON, the first playhouse to be built in Shaftesbury Avenue. It opened in 1888 under the direction of Miss Wallis, who had played leading parts at many London theatres. The first production was *As You Like It*, followed by *The Lady of Lyons*. The season was a failure, but in the following year E. S. Willard had more success with *The Middleman* and *Judah*. There was a season of Italian Opera in 1891, when Lago introduced 'Cavalleria Rusticana' to London. Miss Wallis reappeared, without success, and later Letty Lind, a beautiful dancer, drew the town. In 1896 £15,000 was lost over comic opera. In the following year a dramatized version of Marie Corelli's *The Sorrows of Satan* was produced with Lewis Waller in the lead, but it was not until 1898 that the Shaftesbury had its first real success, when *The Belle of New York*, produced there on 12 Apr., ran for 697 performances. It revolutionized musical comedy as then known, and introduced Edna May to London. Later Fred Terry and Julia Neilson had one of their few failures at the Shaftesbury, with a play called *For Sword or*

Song. In 1903 a musical play, *In Dahomey*, with a complete negro cast, was a success. The theatre, after many vicissitudes, had another success in *The Arcadians* (1909), under the direction of Robert Courtneidge. This was a delightful musical comedy which had a record run for this theatre, 809 performances. In 1933 Werner Krauss, an eminent German actor, appeared at the Shaftesbury at a time when political feeling ran high, and there was a disturbance in the theatre on the first night. On 17 Apr. 1941 the building was completely demolished by enemy action.   W. M. P.

SHAKESPEARE. 1. LIFE AND WORKS. William Shakespeare (1564–1616), first son and third child of John Shakespeare, a glover yeoman of Stratford-on-Avon, and his wife, Mary Arden, a minor heiress of Wilmcote, was christened on 26 Apr. 1564; tradition asserts that his birthday was 23 Apr., St. George's Day. Presumably the boy attended the grammar school of his native town, but the first record of his activities is that of his marriage, evidently a hasty one, to a lady whom extant documents almost certainly (but not positively) identify as Anne Hathaway of Shottery. The wedding took place about the end of Nov. 1582; a daughter, Susanna, was born in May 1583, and twins followed in 1585. Another gap in our knowledge extends from this time until 1592, when a pamphlet written by the dying Robert Greene shows Shakespeare evidently well established in London as actor and dramatist. There is a story that he left Stratford because of a deer-stealing escapade at Charlecote; another tale asserts that he served as a schoolmaster in the country; it is possible that he was the William Shakeshafte (a variant of 'Shakespeare' used by the poet's grandfather) who has been recorded as a private player in the service of a Lancashire gentleman, Alexander Lea. Whatever his activities, during those years he must have added to his education and gained experience of life in circles higher than his own domestic surroundings. From this time contemporary documents yield us more information. In 1593 and 1594 he dedicated his poems *Venus and Adonis* and *The Rape of Lucrece* to the Earl of Southampton, in terms that suggest familiarity, and by the beginning of 1595 he had evidently become a 'sharer' in the Lord Chamberlain's company. Evidence of his rise in the world appears in his father's successful application (1596) to the herald's office for a coat of arms, and by the poet's purchase in 1597 of the large house known as New Place, in Stratford. Other documents show him, in 1596, associated with Francis Langley, builder of the Swan Theatre, in a complicated quarrel involving William Gardiner, a Justice of the Peace in London, and at the same time concerned with Stratford interests (the only extant letter addressed to him was from his fellow townsman Richard Quiney, in 1598). About that time he was resident at St. Helens, Bishopsgate, but by 1599 he had moved to the Liberty of the Clink, and in 1604 was a lodger in the house of Christopher Mountjoy in Cripplegate. In 1610 he seems to have taken up residence at New Place, although his presence in London during the summer of 1612, the spring of 1613, and the winter of 1614, together with his purchase of some Blackfriars property in 1613, demonstrates his continued association with the metropolis. His will, signed on 25 Mar. 1616, preceded his death (23 Apr.) by about a month; tradition says he died after a too convivial evening with Drayton and Jonson. He was buried in the chancel of Stratford church.

There are other documents, but these mainly concern business transactions at Stratford, and do not add much to our knowledge of the man. The record of his life can, however, be expanded both by relating his literary work to those meagre facts, and by cautiously making use of traditional material. The prefatory matter to the First Folio shows how highly he was esteemed by his fellow actors and by his great contemporary, Ben Jonson: tradition speaks, with probable truth, of royal esteem as well. There must be a personal story behind the sonnets, and with that story the puzzling narrative of *Willobie his Avisa* (1594) is likely to be connected. It has been recorded that he 'died a Papist', and this suggestion is not without some vague corroborative evidence.

Bare factual information, however, and legends regarding his adventures fade into insignificance when we confront the extraordinary range of his poetic achievement. He came just at the right moment to make full and fresh use of the teeming drama of his time, finding a novel and flexible stage apt for his purposes, and an eager audience representative of all classes in the community to encourage and inspire. The man and the time were in harmonious conjunction. Starting to write probably about 1590, he contributed at least thirty-six plays to the theatre. Of these, sixteen were printed in quarto during his lifetime, but, apart from the fact that some are obviously bad texts, surreptitiously obtained, the publishing conditions of the age make it probable that he himself did not read the proofs. In 1623 Heminge and Condell of the King's Men, the company to which he had belonged, issued the entire body of his dramatic work in folio form; this volume presents the only texts of another twenty plays, and is probably the most important single volume in the entire history of literature. Arranging the contents under the headings of Comedies, Histories, and Tragedies, the editors of the Folio give no indication of the dates of composition of the separate items, but from a careful scrutiny of such external evidence as exists, and from 'internal' tests (the quality of the blank verse, use of prose and rhyme, &c.), most scholars are agreed, at least in general terms, concerning their chronology—although the problem is complicated by the fact that some editors find evidence of different layers of textual strata in individual plays: thus, for example, Professor J. Dover Wilson believes

that *A Midsummer Night's Dream* was originally written in 1592, revised in 1594, and again revised four years later. Any attempt to date the dramas exactly must, therefore, be hazardous and uncertain.

One thing seems certain, that Shakespeare started his career by penning, unaided or in collaboration, an historical tetralogy consisting of the three parts of *Henry VI* and *Richard III*. In all probability Parts II and III of *Henry VI* came first in 1591, followed by Part I in 1592 and by *Richard III* in 1593. The great Elizabethan actor Burbage won fame in the role of Richard, and *Richard III* was still being performed in 1633, as a record of a Court performance shows. The success of these plays no doubt urged Shakespeare to write his *King John*, probably based on an older two-part dramatization of that monarch's reign. This tragedy stands alone, but shortly afterwards, about 1595, another historical tetralogy was started with *Richard II*, which, during the Essex conspiracy in 1601, won notoriety because of its abdication scene; it was still in the Globe repertory in 1631, and from the year 1607 comes an interesting record of its popularity, when it was produced on the high seas by sailors in the fleet of William Keeling. The two parts of *Henry IV* (probably about 1597 or 1598) carry on the story of Henry Bolingbroke and introduce a richly contrasting comic element with the character of Falstaff (originally named Oldcastle), while the general theme is rounded off with *Henry V* (probably 1598). With this play Shakespeare closed his career as a writer of histories, save for the late *Henry VIII*, produced in the summer of 1613, in which he certainly collaborated with another playwright, whom many believe to have been Fletcher.

Very early in his career he started to try his hand at comedy, experimenting during the early 1590s in gay satire (*Love's Labour's Lost*), in the style of Plautus (*Comedy of Errors*), and in that of Ariosto (*The Taming of the Shrew*). One has the impression here of a young dramatist unsure of his orientation, yet all these plays are skilful and succeeded in holding the stage. The first was revived in 1605 and was still being played in 1631; the second, which is known to have been acted at Gray's Inn in 1594, was revived in 1604; a quarto of the third, issued in 1631, indicates that it was still in the playhouse repertory, and a Court performance is recorded in 1633. In *The Two Gentlemen of Verona* the lack of assurance persists, although here a definite approach is made towards the comedy of humour, and immediately afterwards, probably between 1595 and 1599, this kind of comic drama finds rich and lyrical expression in *A Midsummer Night's Dream, Much Ado About Nothing, As You Like It*, and *Twelfth Night*. Little is known concerning the stage-history of these plays. *A Midsummer Night's Dream* was given a Court performance in 1604; *Twelfth Night* was acted at the Middle Temple in 1602, was given at Court in 1618 and 1623, and was still popular in 1640. Some time following the production of *Henry IV* comes *The Merry Wives of Windsor*, an aberration in this series; probably tradition is right in saying it was written at the command of Queen Elizabeth, who wanted to see Falstaff in love. It was revived at Court in 1604 and 1638. In *The Merchant of Venice* a break in the almost perfect balance observable in the other comedies is patent, and this leads to a couple of so-called 'dark comedies'—*All's Well that Ends Well* and *Measure for Measure* (given at Court in 1604), in which the romantic material is strained almost to breaking. With these may be associated the cynically bitter *Troilus and Cressida*, which possibly was acted not on the public stage but privately.

These were composed at the same time as Shakespeare was reaching towards deepest expression of tragic concepts. Already at the very beginning of his career he must have had some part (but how great is questionable) in *Titus Andronicus*, a play which, despite or because of its bloodiness, seems to have remained popular with less critical audiences. Again, in the midst of his lyrical comedies, the dramatist made a second, but a false, attempt at creating the tragic spirit—*Romeo and Juliet* (about 1595), evidently a popular play although there are no definite records of early performances. Then came the great series of tragedies and Roman plays. *Julius Caesar*, which was seen by a visitor to London in 1599, was probably the first, but the final *Hamlet* must have come very soon after. *Othello* may have been new when it was presented at Court in 1604; it was evidently very popular. Performances are recorded in 1610, 1629, 1635, and there were Court productions in 1612 and 1636. Burbage acted Othello and Taylor Iago. *King Lear* must have followed not many months later; it appeared at Court in 1606, and about the same time came *Macbeth*, which, tied in theme with *Julius Caesar*, clearly addresses itself to a Jacobean Court. The classical subject-matter of *Julius Caesar* is paralleled in *Antony and Cleopatra*, in *Coriolanus*, and in the almost hysterical *Timon of Athens* (all probably about 1607 or 1608).

In *King Lear* Shakespeare had turned to ancient British history, and the atmosphere of this play is reproduced, albeit with a changed tone, in *Cymbeline*. Seen by Forman in 1611, it was written probably about 1610; there was a revival at Court in 1634. Another play seen in 1611 by Forman, *The Winter's Tale*, is similar in spirit, darker than the early comedies of humour and including incidents reminiscent of the tragedies, yet ending with solemn happiness. Evidently popular, it had Court productions in 1611, 1613, 1618, 1619, 1624, and 1634. *The Tempest*, gravest and serenest of all the dramas, was presented at Court in 1611 and in the following year.

To Shakespeare have been attributed, in whole or in part, several other dramas. His hand in *Pericles*, which had been printed as his in 1609, and which was added to the Third Folio of 1664, has generally been accepted, and recent scholarship suggests that we may actually have some pages of his own writing in the manuscript of *Sir Thomas More*. Less likely, although still possible, is his participation in *Edward III* (printed in 1596), and in *The Two Noble Kinsmen*, which was printed in 1634 as by him and Fletcher.

Of his non-dramatic work, *Venus and Adonis* was (carefully) printed in 1593, and *The Rape of Lucrece* in 1594; the *Sonnets* were first printed in 1609, with a dedication to 'Mr. W. H.' over which a lively, acrimonious, but inconclusive controversy has raged for many years. Some of his work appeared in *The Passionate Pilgrim* (1599) and in *Love's Martyr* (1601).

Although there is some reason for believing that a few of Shakespeare's plays were originally written for private or for Court performance, his strength rests in the fact that he was essentially a 'public' dramatist, addressing himself to the demands of a widely representative audience, eager to listen to rich poetic utterance, keenly interested in human character, and apt to welcome both the delicacy of the romantic comedy and the rigours of tragedy. There is little known concerning the contemporary production of his dramas, but sufficient information concerning the Elizabethan stage is extant to give us a general impression of the methods used in their presentation. The absence of scenery helps to explain the strong emphasis on poetic utterance; for the Elizabethans the visual appeal lay in the rich costumes worn by the actors, which threw stress on the persons speaking rather than on dumb, inanimate properties. Here was an opportunity for the dramatist to reveal essential reality that has kept his plays vivid over three centuries. Again and again commentators have spoken of Shakespeare as a 'child of nature', or as one who vied with nature in his creative power, and possibly there is no other author who so harmoniously and with such ease reveals the basic power of the great playwright—the power at once to create the characters of his imagination and to enter into them. Transcendence and immanence are the two bases of his genius, and it is the presence of these qualities that explains the prime paradox—that Shakespeare himself belongs in a sphere beyond our grasp even while we have the impression of knowing him intimately; it likewise explains that peculiar irony which is the characteristic feature both of his comedy and his tragedy. This quality is, of course, dependent upon the nature of his own literary genius, yet one cannot too firmly assert that for its expression in these plays the Elizabethan theatre and the contemporary audience were definitely responsible.   A. N.

2. PRODUCTION IN ENGLISH. Although some of Shakespeare's plays remained continuously in the repertory of the English theatre, from the Restoration until the end of the nineteenth century few people had an opportunity of seeing them in their original form. For this the change in theatre building and theatrical

technique was partly responsible, but the main onus lay on those who, while professing their admiration for Shakespeare, deliberately altered his texts to make them conform to the requirements of a new age. During the Commonwealth his comedies were pillaged to provide short entertainments or drolls, like that of 'Bottom the Weaver', taken from *A Midsummer Night's Dream*. There was every excuse for this, in the precarious state of the theatre at that time, since a full-length production would have had little chance of survival. But there was no excuse for later remodellings except that, to a small sophisticated audience much under the influence of French classical tragedy, Shakespeare was a barbarian, whose occasional poetic beauties entitled him to some consideration, but whose work stood in need of purification and revision.

It was in this spirit that the Restoration and early eighteenth-century theatre approached Shakespeare. Davenant embellished *Macbeth* with singing and dancing; *Romeo and Juliet* was given a happy ending. Neither play was revived in its proper form until 1744. *The Tempest* formed the basis of an opera by Shadwell, *A Midsummer Night's Dream* provided a libretto for Purcell, and Lacy the actor made a new version of *The Taming of the Shrew*.

If Davenant was the first of Shakespeare's adapters, Nahum Tate was undoubtedly the worst. In 1681 he rewrote *King Lear*, omitting the Fool, who was not seen again until 1838, and keeping Cordelia alive in order that she might marry her lover Edgar. He also tackled *Richard II* and *Coriolanus*, but with less success. An adaptation which survived even longer than Tate's *Lear* was the *Richard III* of Colley Cibber. First given in 1700, it proved immensely popular, and provided an excellent part for a tragic actor, containing as it did passages from *Henry IV*, *Henry V*, *Henry VI*, and *Richard II*, as well as a good deal of Cibber's own invention. This hybrid thing was probably the first so-called Shakespearian play to be given in America, since Kean and Murray produced it at their Nassau Street Theatre in New York in 1751. As was only natural, the plays popular in England in the first half of the eighteenth century were those most frequently given in the New World, with the same cuts or emendations. But early actors there were forced to an amusing subterfuge in some of the more puritanical towns like Boston, where *Othello*, for example, was given as 'a Moral Dialogue against the Sin of Jealousy'. Otherwise they used the well-tried versions of Tate, Cibber, Shadwell, and later Garrick. For this great actor, though in some ways he tried to prune back the excrescences of the Restoration texts, and produced *Antony and Cleopatra* for the first time since 1660, retained Cibber's *Richard III*, allowed Macbeth to die on the stage, and Juliet to awake before the death of Romeo. He even made short versions of four of the comedies, and his *Catharine and Petruchio* (1756) held the stage until Ben Webster revived *The Taming of the*

Shrew at the Haymarket in 1844. It is, however, Garrick's tampering with *Hamlet*, and his omission of the Grave-diggers, that marks the end of this phase in Shakespearian production. The tide had already begun to turn slowly in favour of the original texts, and in 1741 Macklin had rescued Shylock, in the so-called *Jew of Venice*, from the hands of the low comedian, and by his interpretation of the part caused Pope to exclaim: 'This is the Jew, That Shakespeare drew.' It was a long time before actors and producers scrupulously respected the text, and Kemble still thought it necessary to cut, combine, and edit each play before producing it. He did, however, try to follow the lead, again given by Macklin, who in 1773 had dressed Macbeth in Highland costume, in reforming the costuming of Shakespeare's plays. His Othello was still a scarlet-coated general, his Richard III wore silk knee-breeches and Lear defied the storm in a flowered dressing-gown. But, helped by his sister Sarah Siddons, who was the first to discard the hoops, flounces, and enormous headgear of tragic heroines, he made an effort to combine picturesqueness with accuracy, and his Coriolanus wore what in contemporary thought approximated to a Roman costume. The *Examiner* scoffed at his innovations, but they bore fruit in Charles Kemble's *King John*, staged in Jan. 1824 with historically accurate costumes designed by Planché.

The battle for a fairly accurate text was almost won by this time, and Kean had taken a step in the right direction in the same year when he restored the original ending to *King Lear*. Helped by the patience and research of scholars, and by the criticisms of such men as Coleridge and Hazlitt, the original plays were gradually emerging from the accretions of more than a century's rewriting. Madame Vestris and the younger Mathews revived *Love's Labour's Lost* and *A Midsummer Night's Dream* in 1839–40 with the original text, and the freedom of the theatres in 1843 enabled Phelps to embark on his fine series of productions at Sadler's Wells, while Charles Kean staged his equally remarkable Shakespeare seasons at the Princess's.

Shakespeare was now presented in a reasonably correct form, but he suffered a new distortion at the hands of his admirers by their emphasis on detail, scenery, and pageantry. The archaeological correctness—which apparently led also to dullness—of Charles Kemble heralded the magnificent spectacles of Macready at Covent Garden from 1837 to 1843. He should be credited with having restored the Fool to Lear, though played by a woman, and with having revived *The Tempest* without Dryden's interpolations, which included a male counterpart of Miranda. But he helped forward the smothering process, which continued at the Princess's, and reached its height at the Haymarket and His Majesty's under Tree, and at the Lyceum under Irving. Phelps, who in 1845 restored a male Fool, and in 1847 put on *Macbeth* without Locke's singing witches, as well

as reviving *The Winter's Tale*, was more concerned with the text than with the scenery,
which was pleasantly sober and unobtrusive.
But elsewhere the newly restored text was in
danger of disappearing under the elaboration
of detail, while the action of the play, designed
for an untrammelled stage, was constantly
held up by the necessity for elaborate scene-
changes.

It was the publication in 1888 of de Witt's
drawing of the Swan Theatre which first turned
men's minds to the possibility of reproducing
not only the text of Shakespeare's plays but
also the physical conditions in which they were
first seen. The main interest had already
switched from the problem of the text to the
problem of interpretation, a problem which
became ever more important as the producer
gained the upper hand in the theatre. To this
was added the problem of a suitable building,
or failing that an approximation of the Elizabethan stage. The latter was tackled by William
Poel with the founding of the Elizabethan
Stage Society, and later by Nugent Monck in
the Maddermarket at Norwich, the former by
Sir Frank Benson when he reduced scenery to
a minimum and insisted on clear, controlled
speaking of Shakespeare's poetry.

One of the landmarks in the history of Shakespearian production was Granville-Barker's
season at the Savoy in 1912; another was the
founding of the Old Vic, whose swiftness and
simplicity brought Shakespeare back to the
English theatre in an intimate and personal
way. Many experiments have been tried, from
Sir Barry Jackson's modern-dress *Hamlet* in
1925 to the fantastications of Komisarjevsky
and the elaborations of Reinhardt. But, with
all its divergencies, the main trend from 1900
onwards has been the simplification of the
background, either by a permanent set, a bare
stage, or symbolic settings, and a consequent
insistence on the importance of the text, the
free flow of the verse, and the unhampered
action of the plot. A happy combination of
scholarly research and theatrical experience
seems the best method of dealing with the many
problems that inevitably arise in producing
plays written in haste, printed without the
author's supervision, and designed for a
vanished playhouse—plays, moreover, which
have suffered from the over-zealous attentions
of erudite editors on the one hand and the
mutilations of hack-writers or 'star' actors on
the other.

In America, where, as in England, the nineteenth century saw first intense preoccupation
with the leading role and the personality of the
actor, and later the accumulation of scenery
and detail, the twentieth century saw also the
new scholarly approach to the text, and the
invasion of the commercial theatre by the universities—a phenomenon more marked in the
United States than in England (see NATION-
WIDE THEATRE). The widespread use of an
experimental theatre as part of a university
course has led to some interesting experiments,
and efforts have been made to disentangle

Shakespeare from tradition, erudition, and
decoration, and to get at the heart of the matter.
The influence of the new approach to Shakespeare has been manifest in such productions
as those of Margaret Webster, and the modern-
dress *Julius Caesar* of Orson Welles.

3. PRODUCTION IN TRANSLATION. Shakespeare remained almost entirely unknown outside England until well into the eighteenth
century, when Voltaire first drew attention to
him in the *Lettres philosophiques* (1734), and for
a long time the prevalent opinion on his plays
was that of the contemporary English theatre—
that he was an undisciplined genius whose faults
might be forgiven, but whose influence on
young dramatists was to be deplored. Even his
first admirer in Germany, Herder, had no wish
to see him on the stage. Nor were the early
translations such as to alter the general outlook.
A frigid version of *Julius Caesar* in 1741, by
C. W. von Borck, written in alexandrines, a
prose summary of a number of his plays in
French by Laplace, with dull verse renderings
of some of the more important poetic scenes, a
bowdlerized version in German prose by Wie-
land—none of these had any success. The first
translation to be widely read was that in fairly
faithful prose by Le Tourneur, published in
1776–82. This was the only one known to
Italy, where it was warmly defended by Dr.
Johnson's friend Baretti, until Leoni's Italian
versions in 1819–22; it was read by Manzoni,
the first Italian to be profoundly influenced by
Shakespeare, and it provided Ducis, who knew
no English, with the basis of the first French
stage versions used by Molé at the Comédie-
Française between 1769 and 1792. These were
tailored to fit the Unities, so that Desdemona,
for instance, was wooed, wedded, and murdered in the space of a day, while *Hamlet*,
Romeo and Juliet, and *King Lear* were provided
with happy endings on the lines of the English
adaptations mentioned above.

In Germany Lessing's *Hamburgische Dramaturgie* (1767–9) first drew the general attention
to Shakespeare, but it was the great actor
Schröder who put him on the stage. The
success of *Götz von Berlichingen* in 1773 had
breached the fortress of classicism, and in 1776
—the year of Le Tourneur's first French
translations—Schröder ventured to produce
Hamlet in Hamburg. It was an adapted *Hamlet*, but even so it proved something of a
shock to his audience, though when they had
recovered from the Ghost they broke into
applause. Thus encouraged, Schröder put on
Othello, which was a failure, *The Merchant of
Venice*, and *Measure for Measure*, which had
a cool reception, and finally, in 1778, *King
Lear*, which was an unqualified success. This
encouraged other German towns to take the
plunge, particularly after Schröder had taken
his productions to Berlin, Mannheim, and elsewhere, and new translations were provided by
J. J. Eschenburg in his Mannheim Shakespeare
(1775–8) and by A. W. Schlegel, whose seventeen plays were somewhat closer to the original, though still bowdlerized. Schlegel was

completed later by Tieck and others, and republished with revisions and additions by F. Gundolf in 1908. In passing it may be noted that good acting versions of the main plays were provided between 1869 and 1871 by Emil Devrient.

The struggle to acclimatize Shakespeare in Germany is pictured in the first part of Goethe's novel *Wilhelm Meisters Lehrjahre*. The incomplete early version points to a climax in which *Hamlet* in its entirety was to have been performed on a regenerated German stage, the hero by this time having come to stand for the young idealist of Goethe's generation. In a discussion with Serlo, who represents Schröder, and his companions, Wilhelm gives the first consistent reading of Hamlet's character—'a costly vessel in which an oak-tree has been planted'. Even in the later version, where Wilhelm yields to Serlo's demand for a compromise, the adapting is mild compared with what the play suffered at Schröder's hands. But, like Ducis, he knew how much his audience could stand, and was careful to give them no more. That was reserved for a more enlightened future, which would, however, have had no chance if Schröder had not blazed a trail. Once introduced into Germany Shakespeare prospered, until he was finally claimed as 'unser' Shakespeare. His genius was thought akin to that of the Teutons. In the Romance countries he fared somewhat otherwise. In France the rising tide of Romanticism swept him into favour, and the visit of Macready and Miss Smithson to Paris in 1828 set the seal on his reputation. In 1839 came a new translation by Laroche with an introduction by Dumas *père*, and from 1856 to 1867 a translation of the complete works by Victor Hugo. As knowledge of Shakespeare spread and his influence was more profoundly felt, earlier translations were found to be inadequate. In Italy he established himself more slowly. Rusconi's *Hamlet* did not appear until 1839 and Carcano's standard translation was not begun until 1843. This, in blank verse, was finally completed in 1882. The great actor Gustavo Modena could not reconcile his audience to *Othello* in 1843, and the first Italian to succeed in the role was his pupil Ernesto Rossi, in 1856. He was also good as Hamlet, Macbeth, Lear, Coriolanus, Shylock, and Romeo, while Salvini triumphed as Othello and Adelaide Ristori as Lady Macbeth. These were all tragic roles, and although Zacconi and Ermete Novelli made a success of Petruchio, and a fine production of *A Midsummer Night's Dream* with Mendelssohn's music was given in Rome in 1910, it still seems as if the tragic aspect of Shakespeare's genius appeals more to the Latin races than his comic spirit—witness the success of the 1947 version of *Hamlet* in French, by André Gide, interpreted by Jean-Louis Barrault.

In Spain, where the exuberance of the Golden Age, and its proximity in time to Elizabethan drama, might have led one to expect some interest in Shakespeare, little was heard of him until the late nineteenth century,

while adequate translations were not forthcoming until the twentieth, nor have the outstanding actors, as in Italy, done anything to popularize him on the stage.

Interest in Shakespeare was not, however, confined to the above countries. The first Swedish translation was made in 1847–51 by Carl August Hagberg, a Danish actor. Peter Folsom published, before he died in 1817, four volumes of translations, beginning with *Hamlet*, which were later added to by others. Per Hallström's magnificent translations, upon which he worked for ten years, were published in the 1920s and 1930s. In 1911–13 came a Polish translation done by the outstanding Polish poets in collaboration. Hungary, where Shakespeare productions are frequent and well attended, saw its first *Hamlet* in 1794—a translation of Schröder's version—and in 1864 a complete translation by the foremost poets and writers was published under the auspices of the Kisfaludy Society. These versions are invariably used on the Hungarian stage, and are performed more frequently than those of any other European dramatist. In Soviet Russia eighteen of Shakespeare's plays are in the permanent repertory of the main theatres, the most popular being *Hamlet, Othello, King Lear*—a fine performance of the last was given in the State Jewish Theatre with Mikhoels in the name-part—*Romeo and Juliet, Twelfth Night, Much Ado About Nothing*, and *The Taming of the Shrew*. It will be seen that three of the comedies are included in this list, which suggests that England and Soviet Russia may eventually meet on the common ground of humour. The plays have been translated into seventeen of the languages of the U.S.S.R., while an annual Shakespeare Conference is held at which scholars, producers, actors, and critics meet to discuss and plan productions of the plays. Shakespeare has also appeared in the Jewish languages, in Hebrew as early as 1874 (*Othello*), in Yiddish—in Goldfaden's *Two Kune Lemels*, a version of *Romeo and Juliet*—in 1880. Since then the Habima, Ohel, and Haifa Players have produced several of his plays in Hebrew, including *Hamlet, King Lear, Twelfth Night, The Merchant of Venice*, and *The Merry Wives of Windsor*, while *The Merchant of Venice, Othello*, and particularly *King Lear* have been popular in Yiddish. None of the plays have been performed in Ladino, but two, *The Comedy of Errors* and *Romeo and Juliet*, have formed the basis of novels in that language.

From the nineteenth century onwards Shakespeare has proved popular in Japan, where his plays have been given in translations by Tsubouchi, while Tokyo possessed a fine Shakespeare Museum.

SHAKESPEARE THEATRE, LONDON, in Curtain Road. There exist scarcely any records of this early-nineteenth-century theatre, which seems at one time to have been given over to feats of horsemanship. Grimaldi played there once. Later it became a house for legitimate drama. It may have stood on the site of the Standard Theatre.

SHAKHOVSKY, ALEXANDER ALEXANDROVICH (1777–1846), Russian dramatist, author of many plays, mainly comedies, though he also wrote a few tragedies. He is regarded as the founder of the Court vaudeville. Born near Smolensk, he was privately educated, and joined the army, retiring with the rank of staff-captain. In 1795 his first comedy was given at the Hermitage Theatre, of which he later became a director. His work there was interrupted by the Napoleonic invasion, during which time he led a troop of civilian volunteers against the French, but was resumed in 1819. A quarrel with the director, Prince Tyuafyakin, led to his dismissal, but in 1824 he was back once more, taking part in production and administration. In 1808 he founded and edited a theatrical journal, and built the third theatre in St. Petersburg, the Youth Theatre, for light comedy, played mainly by graduates of the Government Theatrical School.

SHANK, JOHN (?–1636), English actor, who appears in the actor-list of Shakespeare's plays, and whose name is found in many different spellings. He apparently began his career with the Queen's Men, but no record of this beyond his own asseveration has been found. He was, however, a member of the King's Men, joining them either shortly before, or at the time of, the death in 1615 of Armin, whose position as chief clown he inherited. He was a comedian, well thought of as a singer and dancer of jigs, and appears to have been very popular with his audience, and though the written lines of his roles are often few, it seems that he was allowed considerable licence in gagging. From the number of boy-apprentices with whom his name is connected, and from the fact that so many people were buried from his house in Cripplegate, it has been inferred that one of his functions in the company was the training of apprentices, who lodged with him. He had a son John, also an actor, who played at the Fortune. He led a dissolute life, and was court-martialled in 1642 for cowardice while fighting on the Parliamentary side in the Civil War.

SHARER, the name given to a member of an Elizabethan theatrical company who owned a share in the wardrobe and playbooks, as distinct from the apprentice or hired man. If he had also a share in the actual playhouse building, he was known as a 'housekeeper' as well.

SHARING SYSTEM, see PROVINCIAL THEATRES, 1 d.

SHARPE, RICHARD (c. 1602–32), an excellent actor with the King's Men, who from 1625 until his early death played the parts of romantic young heroes. Since he is known to have played the name-part in *The Duchess of Malfi* and to have been acting several years previous

to that, it is evident that he started his career as a young boy and quickly gave proof of much ability. His other women-roles are not known, but he is conjectured to have played queens and haughty young women. It was probably Sharpe who ran up a bill with young Condell for 41s. 10d. for stockings.

SHATTERELL. There were two actors of this name, Edward and Robert, who may have been father and son, but more likely brothers. Edward was evidently the elder, since he is found among the actors on the continent after the closing of the theatres, and must therefore have had some experience of acting before 1642. He was also one of those who contrived to put on surreptitious plays at the Red Bull as early as 1654, where he is found again in Mohun's company immediately on the Restoration. Robert was one of Beeston's Boys at the Cockpit, may have served in the army during the Civil War, and with Edward joined Killigrew's first company. Edward disappears from the records soon after this, but Robert flourished, and was evidently a man of substance, since he was one of those who could afford to build themselves houses near the new Drury Lane in 1663. He remained with Killigrew until his death, which took place some time shortly before 1684.

SHAW, GEORGE BERNARD (1856–1950), dramatist, critic, and writer on public affairs, born in Dublin, son of George Carr Shaw (a pensioned sinecure-office-holder of the Four Courts) and Lucinda Elizabeth (Gurly) Shaw. The impecunious ways of her husband led Mrs. Shaw to adopt a career as vocalist and teacher of singing, and it was from this circumstance that G.B.S. obtained the early knowledge and love of classical music which qualified him later to become a music critic in London. Following a sketchy formal education which began at the Wesleyan Connexional School in Dublin, he started work in his early teens as a land-agent's office-boy at 18s. a month and became cashier when 16. In the spring of 1876, having risen to a salary of £84 a year, he migrated to London, where he worked for a few months with the Edison Telephone Company. During the next nine years he earned a total of £6 (for an article, a patent-medicine advertisement, and a set of verses), his keep being provided by his mother. Between 1879 and 1883 he wrote five unsuccessful novels (all of which have since been included with his collected works) and made himself an effective speaker on political and other subjects, joining the Fabian Society in 1884.

Through William Archer, Shaw became a book-reviewer for the *Pall Mall Gazette* and art critic on *The World* (he had qualified for this by haunting the Dublin National Gallery in boyhood), and gradually extended his journalistic connexions. From 1888 to 1890 he wrote music criticism for the *Star* (using the pseudonym Corno di Bassetto), and then until 1894 for *The World*. Admirable though

his music articles were, their quality was surpassed by that of the dramatic criticism he contributed to the *Saturday Review* between Jan.
1895 and May 1898. These essays on plays
and players (later reissued as *Our Theatres in
the Nineties*), as fresh and invigorating fifty
years afterwards as at the time they were
written, set a new standard in English theatre
criticism.

   Though Shaw professed no love of the stage,
he quickly recognized its value as a platform
for the transmission of ideas of social and
political reform to which he had dedicated
himself. He also became an ardent disciple of
Ibsen, whose works in translation were at that
time bringing a stimulating breath of reality
into the stale atmosphere of a drama which
had been for many generations remote from life
outside the theatre. Bernard Shaw therefore
turned to the writing of plays, and *Widowers'
Houses* (begun in 1885) opened in 1892 his long
career as the most notable dramatist of his
time. This first play was produced on 9 Dec.
at the Royalty Theatre by J. T. Grein as part
of his Independent Theatre venture. *Arms and
the Man* was played at the Avenue Theatre on
21 Apr. 1894, but *The Philanderer* and *Mrs.
Warren's Profession* had been written in the
previous year. The last-named play did not
reach the stage before 1902, when it was produced privately by the Stage Society, the
Censor's ban on public performances being
maintained until the 1920s. These early
dramatic works caused Shaw to be regarded
in many quarters as subversive, since he was
attacking vested interests and bringing into
the light social evils considered unfit for open
discussion. He had embarked upon a crusade
designed to introduce to the stage subjects—
such as slum landlordism, prostitution, war,
religion, family disturbances, health, economics
—previously confined to political meetings,
the courts, or the pulpit. Deliberately turning
his back upon the variations and vagaries of
sex attraction, the stock material of a vast
majority of plays, Shaw aimed at the minds of
playgoers instead of at their emotions and
physical sensations. He wanted 'a pit of philosophers', not merely a theatre full of folk
seeking meretricious titillating entertainment.
Thought, not action, was therefore the staple
of the Shavian theatre; but, as several generations of playgoers came to learn and to acknowledge with gratitude and enthusiasm, thought
salted with humour and talk enlivened with
wit and eloquence provide a more rewarding
type of entertainment than any that the modern
stage had previously offered.

   When the early antagonism to Shaw died
down and cooler judgement displaced it, the
two main charges laid against him were that
he had no sense of human character and could
create nothing but mouthpieces for the utterance of his own views, and that he was nothing
but a destructive critic. Time has already
answered the first of those charges, for plays
do not live in full vigour for half a century and
more on 'views' alone. The second charge

could only be sustained if audiences and
readers were held to be under no obligation to
draw plain and, indeed, inescapable inferences
from the material before them.

   The popularity of Shaw's work dates from
the Court Theatre repertory season under the
management of H. Granville-Barker and J. E.
Vedrenne, 1904–7, during which 701 performances were given of 11 of his plays. His
since-familiar leading idea of the Life Force
as the governing factor in human affairs was
first embodied in dramatic form in *Man and
Superman* (1903). In the author's opinion the
masterpiece among his nearly fifty plays is
Back to Methuselah (1921), though this opinion
is not widely shared. In film versions, based
upon faithful transcriptions of the original text,
Pygmalion, *Major Barbara*, and *Caesar and
Cleopatra* have reached millions who do not
frequent the theatre. It is difficult to assess
the relative popularity of the other plays, most
of which have been performed throughout the
world in many languages. In England *Saint
Joan* probably outstrips the rest in general
favour, with *Candida*, *Arms and the Man*, *The
Doctor's Dilemma*, and *You Never Can Tell*
following. *Heartbreak House* stands in high
esteem with critical judges.

   Since *Plays: Pleasant and Unpleasant* first
appeared in two volumes in 1898 Shaw has
consistently given careful attention to the
presentation of his plays in print. In typo-
graphical layout he set a revolutionary high
standard which others have followed, and his
detailed stage-directions amount to a commentary which greatly assists the reader to
visualize the author's intentions for the actors.
As a producer at rehearsals Shaw earned unanimous praise and respect in the theatre.

   The famous Prefaces to the plays form an
independent branch of the author's writings
and are largely responsible for his reputation
as one of the great masters of English prose. A
book demanding special mention here is *Ellen
Terry and Bernard Shaw: A Correspondence*
(1931), which on both sides is rich in graces
and virtues impossible to characterize in
measured terms. Shaw's major critical writings include *The Quintessence of Ibsenism* (1891;
revised 1913) and *The Complete Wagnerite*
(1898).

SHAW, ROBERT GOULD, see HARVARD.

SHCHEPKIN, MIKHAIL SEMENOVICH (1788–
1863), one of the greatest of Russian actors,
born in Kursk Province, the son of a serf.
He had his first reading lessons from a baker's
wife and a priest, and then entered the county
school. His interest in the theatre was aroused
when he accidentally witnessed a play in a
nobleman's private theatre, and at school he
played in one of Sumarokov's comedies. In
1802 he was sent back to Kursk to attend the
Provincial Public School. He was an excellent
scholar and a great reader. Through a school-
friend he became acquainted with Bafsov,
owner of the Kursk theatre, where he was
admitted to prompt and copy music. He also

appeared in private theatricals with some success. At fifteen he finished school, and being a serf could go no further. During the next year or two he appeared in public performances during the summer, and in private shows in Kursk during the winter. In Nov. 1805 a benefit performance for the actress Lykova was given. The leading actor got drunk and could not appear, and Shchepkin offered his services. He gave a brilliant performance, and was rewarded with some good roles, though until 1808 he worked mainly as an understudy. In that year he joined the troupe to play ·comic roles, and remained until the company was dissolved in 1816. He was then invited to join the Stein and Kalinovsky troupe in Kharkov, and went with them at the invitation of Prince Repin to play in Poltava, where he met the actor Uragov. In 1818 a movement, inaugurated by Prince Repin, was set on foot to purchase Shchepkin's freedom from his owner Volkenstein; and shortly after his liberation the manager of the Moscow Maly Theatre invited him to join the Imperial company. He made his début in Nov. 1822 in Zagoskin's *Gospodin Bogatonov; or, a Provincial in the Capital*. He was already an accomplished actor, but Moscow offered him great opportunities which he was not slow to take advantage of. From 1825 to 1828 he played in St. Petersburg. Griboyedov's *Woe from Wit* and Gogol's *Inspector-General* provided him with some fine roles, and he was at his best during the 1840s. After that he declined and his acting lost its grip, though that does not detract from his great influence on the Russian theatre. He was a convinced and militant realistic actor, and the Russian critic Belinsky saw in his work a synthesis of Mochalov's passion and Karatygin's technical perfection, which demanded of its exponent a perpetual observation of life and its truthful presentation on the stage. Shchepkin's greatest roles were in the comic characters of Shakespeare, Schiller, and Gogol. He created from the varied tendencies of his time a school of acting which realized itself in the plays of Ostrovsky, Chekhov, and Gorky. Encouraged by Pushkin, Shchepkin wrote his autobiographical notebooks, which are of great artistic and historic theatrical interest.

SHCHUKIN, BORIS VASILIEVICH (1894–1939), Soviet actor whose early death robbed the Russian stage of one of its outstanding figures. He was for twenty years at the Vakhtangov Theatre, where he played leading roles. In his last years he gave some exceptionally fine performances, notably in the title-role of *Yegor Bulichev*, in Afinogenov's *Distant Point*, and as Lenin, whom he was the first actor to impersonate. Joseph Macleod, in *The New Soviet Theatre*, wrote of him that, as befitted a man so essentially of the theatre, 'if he did not die in harness, he very nearly did—in bed, reading Diderot's *Paradoxe sur le Comédien*'. After his death the street in which he lived was renamed in his honour.

SHELDON, EDWARD BREWSTER (1886–1946), American dramatist, and one of the first to graduate from Baker's '47 Workshop'. His first play, *Salvation Nell* (1908), was produced when he was only 22, and, with Mrs. Fiske as the heroine and her husband as director, proved a great success. Sheldon was immediately hailed as the rising hope of the American theatre, and as the leader of the new school of realistic writers. His next play, *The Nigger* (1909), was a theatrical but courageous handling of the negro problem, while *The Boss* (1911) was a study of modern industrial conditions. But all Sheldon's serious work was overshadowed by the success of his popular romantic play, *Romance* (1913), which, with Doris Keane as the Italian opera singer who attracts the young idealistic clergyman, had a long run both in New York and London. It made an immense emotional appeal to audiences all over the world, and was translated into French and other languages. Handicapped by serious illness, Sheldon did most of his later work in collaboration, and also translated and adapted anonymously a number of popular successes. Summing up his work, Quinn in his *History of American Drama* says of him:

He is the celebrator of the aspiration of those who strive to lift themselves out of circumstances or a mode of life to something higher and his sympathy is always with them, even if they are doomed to disappointment from the beginning.... In this general attitude of sympathy with the aspiring soul, Sheldon points forward to Eugene O'Neill. But as in O'Neill the poet dominates the dramatist, so in Sheldon the playwright limits or at least defines the poet's power.

SHELLEY, PERCY BYSSHE (1792–1822), famous English romantic poet, and author of several plays in poetry, of which the best known is *The Cenci*. Published in 1819, this was first acted by the Shelley Society in 1886, and has been several times revived and broadcast; it is, however, pure poetry but poor drama, being confused in action and somewhat too dependent upon Shakespeare, and it is unlikely to find a permanent place even in the repertory of poetic drama on the stage.

SHEPHERD, EDWARD (c. 1670–1747), English architect, designer of Shepherd's Market, Mayfair, and of the first theatre built in Covent Garden in 1732 (see ARCHITECTURE and COVENT GARDEN).

SHERIDAN, MARK (? –1917), a musichall comedian, whose specialty was Cockney songs with rousing choruses, often descriptive of seaside delights. One which is still sung was 'I do like to be beside the seaside'. He was at his best in the 1890s, but during the 1914–18 war—whose soldiers marched to his rousing 'Here we are again'—he was beset by melancholy and, feeling that his powers were failing, he committed suicide in a Glasgow park while appearing in pantomime. He always wore a top hat, a frock coat, bell-bottomed trousers, fastened round the knee with a strap in imitation of the old-time navvies, big boots, and carried a cane.   W. M. P.

SHERIDAN, RICHARD BRINSLEY (1751–1816), English dramatist, theatre manager, and politician, whose best play, *The School for Scandal*, stands as the masterpiece of English comedy of manners, with all the wit, but none of the licentiousness, of the Restoration comedy from which it derives. Sheridan, who was the son of an actor and of an authoress—his mother, Mrs. Frances Sheridan (1724–66), wrote both plays and novels—was born in Dublin, educated at Harrow, and intended for the law. But at 21 he made a romantic marriage with the daughter of the singer and composer Linley, and two years later his first play, *The Rivals*, was produced at Covent Garden, followed by a farce, *St. Patrick's Day; or, the Scheming Lieutenant*, and a comic opera, 'The Duenna', all given in 1775. In 1776 Sheridan bought Garrick's share in Drury Lane and rebuilt the theatre in 1794. He remained there until its destruction by fire in 1809, always in financial difficulties. His later plays, all produced at Drury Lane, included *A Trip to Scarborough*, altered from Vanbrugh's *The Relapse*, and the famous *School for Scandal* (both 1777), with Mrs. Abington as the first Lady Teazle; *The Critic; or, a Tragedy Rehearsed* (1779), the best of the many burlesques stemming from Buckingham's *The Rehearsal*, and the only one to have been constantly revived; and, many years later, when Sheridan had practically deserted the theatre for politics, *Pizarro* (1799), an adaptation of a popular drama by Kotzebue. He was also part author of several entertainments, and wrote the pantomime of *Robinson Crusoe* for Drury Lane in Jan. 1781, as an after-piece to *The Winter's Tale*, as well as three new spectacular scenes for a revival of *Harlequin Fortunatus* in 1780. Sheridan is said by Oulton to have appeared as Harlequin for one night, but there is no proof of this. He certainly exploited to the full the popular taste for spectacle and pantomime, helped by Noverre and de Loutherbourg, and *The Critic*, for example, was produced with remarkable scenic effects and lavish costumes. His management of Drury Lane was marked by a succession of quarrels with the managers of the smaller theatres—Astley's, Sadler's Wells, the new Royalty—whose success alarmed him, and with his co-partners, Linley and Ford, he was several times successful in embroiling his rivals with the authorities, though he failed to retain the monopoly he was striving for. The pressure of the unlicensed theatres was too great. Sheridan became a Member of Parliament in 1780, rose rapidly in his new profession, and made some remarkable speeches at the trial of Warren Hastings. But his last years were unhappy, and he never recovered from the destruction of Drury Lane, though he endeavoured to bear the blow with equanimity. He died in 1816 and was buried in Westminster Abbey.

SHERIDAN, WILLIAM EDWARD (1840–87),

American actor, with a virile and forceful personality and a fine resonant voice. He made his first successes in Philadelphia, and in the last years of his brief career was extremely popular in San Francisco, where he first appeared in 1880. Among his best parts were Louis XI, Othello, and Shylock, and he was also good in *A New Way to Pay Old Debts* and *The Lyons Mail*. During the Civil War he was a captain in the Union Army, returning to the stage afterwards, when he appeared at Niblo's Garden as the first American Beamish McCoul in *Arrah-na-Pogue*. His first wife dying in 1872, he married Louise Davenport, and with her embarked on a long tour of Australia, where he died.

SHERLOCK, WILLIAM (*fl.* first half of seventeenth century), English actor, probably the keeper of Beeston's Cockpit from its opening in 1616 until he was succeeded by John Rhodes some time between 1637 and 1644. He was a Queen's Man from 1625 until the closing of the theatres in 1642, and was transferred with them in 1637 to Salisbury Court. From his extant list of parts it is obvious that he played both comic and villainous parts, though he was stronger as a comedian.

SHERRIFF, ROBERT CEDRIC (1896–   ), English dramatist and novelist, who became widely known with his war-play, *Journey's End* (1928), which gives a realistic and yet emotionally moving picture of the reactions of a small group of men in a dug-out just before an attack. It was the first play dealing with the 1914–18 war to achieve success, and its phenomenal popularity came as a surprise even to those who had ventured to back their faith in it. First produced on a Sunday night by the Stage Society, it was brought to the commercial theatre by Maurice Browne, whom it established as a manager and producer, and ran for two years, the small cast of men only including such actors as Colin Clive, Maurice Evans, and Robert Speaight. Translated and played all over the world, and frequently revived by amateur societies, it remains one of the few plays dealing with modern warfare to be both artistically and theatrically acceptable. Sherriff also wrote a comedy on village cricket, *Badger's Green* (1930); a play on Napoleon's last years, *St. Helena* (1935); *Miss Mabel* (1948), *Home at Seven* (1950), in which Sir Ralph Richardson gave an impressive study of amnesia.

SHERWOOD, ROBERT EMMET (1896–   ), American dramatist, who distinguished himself as a writer of both comedy and plays of social and political content. He was born in New Rochelle, near New York, and was graduated from Harvard University in 1918. After seeing service in the First World War and writing for periodicals, Sherwood scored a success with his first play, *The Road to Rome* (1927), a satirical treatment of Hannibal's march which deflated military glory. *The Love Nest* (also 1927) was a trivial dramatization of a Ring Lardner short story, and *The Queen's Husband* (1928) drew a moderately amusing portrait of a henpecked king. The melodrama *Waterloo Bridge* (1930) was more successful in London than in New York, and *This is New York* (also 1930), a melodrama of blackmail and scandal, was a total failure. Sherwood's next effort, however, was the brilliant high comedy *Reunion in Vienna* (1931), which revived the embers of a pre-war romance between a dashing Hapsburg archduke and the wife of a psycho-analyst who is hoist with his own petard of intellectual complacency.

With *The Petrified Forest* (1935) and the almost simultaneously written *Acropolis* (a well-regarded failure in London, never professionally produced in America) Sherwood addressed himself to the deteriorating world situation. He drew a parallel between the decline of Periclean civilization and the rising tide of Fascism in *Acropolis*, and composed an allegory on intellectual bankruptcy in the melodrama *The Petrified Forest*, which recounted the disintegration and virtual suicide of a young writer. Sherwood's pessimism grew darker in the ironic Pulitzer Prize-winner *Idiot's Delight* (1936), in which he foretold a second World War and postulated further bankruptcy for Western civilization. *Tovarich* (also 1936), from the French of Jacques Deval, was only a pleasant detour for Sherwood, who next wrote the stirring democratic affirmation *Abe Lincoln in Illinois* (1938). This chronicle paralleled contemporary political struggles with those of the past and characterized Abraham Lincoln as a man of peace who entered the political arena reluctantly. *There Shall Be No Night* (1941), written in response to the invasion of Finland, showed a pacifistic scientist choosing war as a preferable alternative to slavery. At about this time Sherwood himself entered upon a life of action as a friend of Franklin D. Roosevelt and as a leading interventionist prior to Pearl Harbour, writing no new plays until *The Rugged Path* (1945), a rather disjointed account of an idealistic journalist's conflict with his isolationist family and his death on a Pacific Island.   J. G.

SHIELS, GEORGE (1886–1949), one of the most popular and versatile playwrights in Ireland, esteemed alike in the North and in the South for his serious as for his humorous work. He had a range of experience that was somewhat uncommon and he drew upon a wide knowledge of character and social relations in both parts of Ireland and in America. His treatment of this material is realistic without bitterness or harshness, humorous or fanciful without becoming farcical, and sympathetic without forfeiting that humour or the satire into which it merges.

He was first known by his comedies, humorous and satirical pictures of contemporary life, one of which, *Bedmates* (1921), made his name. Among the most popular of them were *Paul Twyning* (1922), *Professor Tim* (1925), and *The New Gossoon* (1930).

But his serious plays, such as *The Passing Day* (1936) and *The Rugged Path* (1940), show clearly that he was not limited to comedy; the second of these had an unprecedented run at the Abbey Theatre.

Other plays by George Shiels are *Away from the Moss, The Tame Drudge, Old Bob, Insurance Money, First Aid, The Retrievers, Cartney and Kevney, Neal Maquade, The Summit, The Jailbird*, and *The Fort Field*.   U. E.-F.

SHIRLEY, JAMES (1596–1666), the leading dramatist of London when the Puritans shut the playhouses in 1642. He survived the Commonwealth, only to die of exposure during the Great Fire of London. A university man, he took orders in the Church of England, but became a Roman Catholic and a schoolmaster, and wrote some forty plays, most of which have survived in print, though not on the stage. These include tragedies like *The Maid's Revenge* (1626); *The Traitor* (1631), Shirley's most powerful play, a horror-and-revenge tragedy into which has been imported a masque of the Lusts and Furies; *Love's Cruelty* (1631); and *The Cardinal* (1641), of which Wilson in Vol. VI of the *Cambridge History of English Literature* says, '[It] brings to a fitting close the tremendous file of English tragedy.' Shirley's best work, however, was done in comedy, in which he provides a link between Jonson and the Restoration. This is particularly true of *The Lady of Pleasure* (1635), in which, it has been said, 'the cool and calculated intrigue of Aretina is thoroughly typical of the degradation of love in the seventeenth-century comedy of manners'. Other comedies by Shirley are *The Witty Fair One* (1628), *Hyde Park* (1632), *The Gamester* (1633), which was later adapted by Garrick, and *The Sisters* (1642). A prompt-book of this last, dating from the early years of the Restoration, supplies some interesting stage-directions, and is now in the library of Sion College. Shirley was popular in the early days of the Restoration, no less than eight of his plays being revived, including *The Cardinal*, which Pepys saw in 1667.

SHOLOM ALEICHEM, see ALEICHEM.

SHOP, theatrical slang for engagement. To be out of a shop, or 'resting', means to be unemployed.

SHOWBOAT, the name given to the floating theatres of the great North American rivers of the West, particularly the Mississippi and the Ohio, which represent an early and most successful attempt to bring drama to the pioneer settlements. It is not known who first built a showboat, or at what date. In fact, the entire history of the floating theatre, being mainly preserved by oral tradition, is confused and obscure, and has gathered about itself such an accretion of legend that it is difficult to disentangle the facts. But from the earliest pioneering days boats were thick on the rivers, for trade, for freight, and for less legitimate purposes, such as gambling and drinking, and it would require little ingenuity to transform a keel-boat or a raft into a passable show-place. Doubtless many of the early itinerant companies of the West moored their boats to the bank and built on deck a rough cabin to shelter and enclose the players. The first recorded instance of this, however, dates from 1817, when that intrepid pioneer player, Noah Miller Ludlow (1795–1866), took his company along the Cumberland river to the Mississippi in a flat-boat with a shelter at one end. In general, however, Ludlow played on land, even if he moved by water, and it is William Chapman (1764–1839), formerly an actor in London and New York, who has the honour of heading the list of showboat managers. Ludlow, in his memoirs, has left a description of Chapman's showboat, as he saw it in about 1831. He describes the structure as being 'a large flat-boat with a rude kind of house built upon it, having a ridge-roof, above which projected a staff with a flag attached, upon which was plainly visible the word Theatre'. The interior was apparently long and narrow, with a shallow stage at one end and benches in front across the width of the boat, the whole lighted by guttering candles. Here the Chapman family, consisting of husband and wife and five children, large enough to dispense with much outside help, played one-night stands along the rivers wherever a sizeable settlement made it feasible. The average entrance fee was about 50 cents, and the staple fare strong melodrama or fairy-tale plays, ranging from *The Stranger* to *Cinderella*. There are some interesting references to the Chapmans in the memoirs of Tyrone Power (1798–1841), one of which deserves to be quoted: 'Chapman's practice is to have a building suitable to his views erected upon a raft at some point high up the Mississippi, or one of its tributaries, whence he takes his departure early in the fall, with scenery, dresses, and decorations, all prepared for representation. At each village or large plantation he hoists banner and blows trumpet and few who love a play suffer his ark to pass the door, since they know it is to return no more until the next year; for, however easy may prove the downward course of the drama's temple, to retrograde, upwards, is quite beyond its power. . . . When the Mississippi theatre reaches New Orleans, it is abandoned and sold for firewood; the manager and troop returning in a steamer to build a new one.' The use of trumpet and flag suggests an interesting parallel with the practice of the early English theatres (see ELIZABETHAN PLAYHOUSE). Later, showboats made use of steam-tugs for the journey up river, coming in time to own their own steamships as an integral part of the outfit.

After Chapman's death his widow sold the showboat to that other pioneer player, Sol Smith (1801–69), who lost it in the following year in a collision. It is not known what happened to Chapman's children, though they probably remained on the stage, and one of his sons may have been the Henry Chapman (1822–65), well known as an actor, whose two daughters, Blanche and Ella, both handsome and proficient actresses, appeared in burlesque for many years on tour. Ella also visited England, making her début there in 1876 and later appearing in pantomime at the Grand, Islington, and Her Majesty's Theatre.

Another showboat captain of the early days was Henry Butler (dates unknown), an old theatre manager who took a combined museum and playhouse up and down the Erie Canal from about 1836 until his death, showing stuffed animals and waxworks by day, and at night, since he had a good sailor-actor in Jack Turner, playing such nautical dramas as *Black-Eyed Susan*.

A showboat about which a certain amount of information is available is the Floating Circus Palace of Spaulding and Rodgers. Built in Cincinnati in 1851, it was shorter and wider than the river steamboats of the time, and was intended for elaborate, usually equestrian, shows. It had a central arena with several tiers of benches, capable of accommodating a large audience, kitchens, dressing-rooms, stables, and living-quarters. In addition to circus, vaudeville, and minstrel acts, concerts, and a museum, the Floating Circus Palace also gave dramatic performances. Its history coincides with the heyday of the showboats, which increased in numbers and popularity until the outbreak of war in 1861 drove them off the river, never again to return in such numbers.

The spirit of showmanship survived, however, and in 1878 a Captain A. B. French (? –1902) took his *New Sensation* along the Mississippi. He had to live down a good deal of prejudice, but the high moral tone of his productions, and the good behaviour of his small company, soon won favour, and the showboat was again considered respectable. Captain French's wife was the first woman to hold a pilot's licence in those waters, and the only one to hold both that and master's papers. At one time she and her husband ran two showboats, piloting one each.

A formidable rival to French was Captain E. A. Price (dates unknown), owner of the *Water Queen*, built in 1885. This had a stage nineteen feet across, lit by oil, a good stock of scenery, a company of some fifty persons, and that indispensable adjunct to all showboats, a steam calliope. After a long and honourable career as a showboat it became a floating dance-hall in Tennessee, and in 1935 was used in the filming of Edna Ferber's *Showboat*. This excellent, though fictionized, account of life on a floating theatre was the first to bring the Mississippi showboat prominently before the general public, and had a well-deserved success as novel, play, and film.

Incidentally, another river boat which figured in a film was the sidewheeler *Kate Adams*, built in 1898, the third of her line, which in 1926 appeared as *La Belle Revere* in

Uncle Tom's Cabin. She was later burnt to the waterline.

Among the many other showboat managers of the time was Captain E. E. Eisenbarth (dates unknown), owner of the first boat to bear the name *Cotton Blossom.* This was capable of seating a large audience, and on a stage twenty feet by eleven feet presented a three-hour entertainment of straight solid drama, usually popular melodrama, though in 1904 Eisenbarth made showboat history by producing *Faust.* The *Cotton Blossom* was one of the first showboats to be lit by electricity. The name persisted, and a later *Cotton Blossom* was owned by Captain Otto Hitner, who produced adaptations of such novels as *The Little Shepherd of Kingdom Come* made by his wife.

It was in 1907 that a famous showboat personality, Captain Billy Bryant, author of the fascinating *Children of Ol' Man River* (1936), first entered the profession, when his father launched *The Princess* with a programme featuring himself and his family. Among the early productions of the Bryant family were a somewhat unusual version of *Hamlet* and such popular melodramas as *East Lynne.* By 1918 the Bryants were able to build their own boats, on which they gave successful revivals of many good old melodramas—*Jesse James, From Rags to Riches, Bertha the Sewing Machine Girl, The Bird in the Gilded Cage,* and, most popular of all, *Ten Nights in a Bar Room.* Vaudeville, interspersed with songs and magic-lantern shows, filled up the intervals, while Captain Billy's own speeches before and after the show became famous. A typical one was printed in *The New York Times* for 12 Oct. 1930.

Another well-known showboat family is the Menkes, four brothers who in 1917 bought French's *New Sensation* from Price, who had purchased it from French's widow in 1902. They kept the old name, though the boat has been several times replaced, and in 1922–3, under Captain J. W. Menke, it made a trip lasting a year and covering 5,000 miles. Other boats owned by the Menkes were *Golden Rod* and *Hollywood* (which, with their headquarters at St. Louis, are still operating), *Wonderland, Sunny South,* and *Floating Hippodrome.* Their repertory was again melodrama, including such favourites as *The Trail of the Lonesome Pine,* though in the late 1920s they made an innovation by presenting a musical comedy.

In the years before the slump of 1929 a number of new managements made their appearance on the water—the *Majestic* under Nico and Reynolds, the *America,* the *River Maid,* another *Princess,* a new *Water Queen* under Captain Roy Hyatt—mostly offering melodrama and variety; but they were hard hit by the economic depression, and for some time Menke's *Golden Rod* and Bryant's *Showboat* were the only ones still functioning. Things picked up again later, however, and in 1938 Ben Lucien Burman, in his book on the Mississippi, *Big River to Cross,* was able to mention five by name as still working, as well as many other smaller and less well-known ones on distant waters. That the structure of the showboat has altered little with the years can be seen by his description of it as

resembling an old-time packet whose owner, in a fit of anger, has knocked off both the smokestacks and the pilot house; moored behind is a small steamboat, to move it on its journeyings . . . At one end (of the vessel) is the stage, its wings piled high with scenes of ruined castles or a dusty, lamp-lit street corner of Old Chicago; the curtain depicts a bridge over some precipitous valley high in the Alps, or a horde of white-robed men and women fleeing terror-struck from the flames of Vesuvius. . . . At the side of the curtain is a hole, through which the proprietor can peep unobserved and count the audience in the seats before him; when he has mentally translated the spectators into money that seems sufficient for the evening, he smiles with content and gives the orchestra the signal to begin. . . . The plays on the larger boats are either melodrama or musical spectacles, the melodramas being acted in burlesque fashion when the boat is anchored at the wharf of a metropolis, but losing all such artificial quality the moment the vessel points its prow toward the wilderness. Always their programs are broken with vaudeville: a Swiss bell ringer: a musician who can play Dixie on the flute as he swings from a horizontal bar: an artist who can draw a picture of the President in red, white, and blue chalk upside down, and balance a huge American flag on his right shoe during the entire creation of the masterpiece.

These talented vaudevillians are performers in the main drama as well. For an actor on a showboat is nothing if not versatile. He must play the cornet in the orchestra . . . when the drama begins he must portray the bearded father. . . . He must sell popcorn and ice cream cones during the first intermission, and stop to play an accordion solo; when the play begins again, he must enact the hind-end of a horse. . . . He must do a tap dance; play the piano strings with a nail as though it were a harp; ride roller skates on a barrel; and one minute before the final curtain be thrown to his death to the Indians waiting in triumph at the foot of Grand Canyon.

The actors on the showboats are of infinite variety. Some are carnival troupers, dancers and acrobats, come from the tents of the sideshows; some are country boys and girls, lured by the glamor of the theater from the cornfields . . . some are professional actors, like those in the old stock companies, weary of trouping in one night stands and the vagaries of the metropolis. The smaller boats are family affairs, a man and his wife, with any roving performer they may chance upon in their travels.

The life of the showboat player is hard and hazardous, but it has the charm of individualism and the unexpected and will not be corralled into the classification of the modern theatre. Found nowhere but in the United States, it represents, in all its aspects, a survival of the old and colourful pioneering days in the Golden West.

SHUBERT. (1) LEE (1875–   ), (2) SAM S. (1876–1905), and (3) J. J. (1880–   ), American theatre managers and producers. After varied experience in theatre business they formed the Shubert Theatre Corporation, which controls the major part of the theatres in New York and other principal cities. They have their offices on the upper floors of the Sam S. Shubert Theatre on 44th Street, which opened on 29 Sept. 1913 with the Forbes-Robertsons in *Hamlet* and other plays. The first American play seen there was *A Thousand Years Ago* (1914). The theatre has housed mainly musical comedy, but among its straight successes have been *Copperhead* (1918) with Lionel Barrymore, *And So To Bed* (1927) with Yvonne Arnaud, and *Dodsworth* (1934). Elisabeth Bergner made her Broadway début at this theatre in *Escape Me Never*, under the auspices of the Theatre Guild, who were also responsible for the appearance of the Lunts in *Idiot's Delight* and *Amphitryon 38*. It was at this theatre that *Bloomer Girl* opened on 5 Oct. 1944, running until 27 Apr. 1946.   G. F.

SHUTER, EDWARD (NED) (1728–76), English actor, of whom Doran said:

> There are few comic actors who have had such command over the muscles of the face as Shuter. He could do what he liked with them, and vary the laughter as he worked the muscles. Not that he depended on grimace; that was only the ally of his humour, and both were impulsive—as the man was, by nature; he often stirred the house with mirth, by saying something better than the author had put down for him.

Shuter, whose portrait was painted by Zoffany, made his first appearance on the stage at Richmond in 1744, and his last as Falstaff at Covent Garden in the year of his death. In June 1746 he played Osric and the Third Witch to Garrick's Hamlet and Macbeth, and during his long and arduous professional life he created a number of parts, among them Justice Woodcock, Druggett, Old Hardcastle, and Sir Anthony Absolute.

SIDDONS, SARAH (1755–1831), the greatest tragic actress of the English stage. She was the eldest of the twelve children of Roger Kemble, a midland actor-manager, and spent her childhood travelling in his company. At 18 she married William Siddons, also a member of the company, and together they appeared in the provinces, Sarah first showing her mettle at Cheltenham. A tentative appearance at Drury Lane under Garrick in 1775 was a failure, and she returned to the provinces, playing at York under Tate Wilkinson and at Bath under John Palmer. A second attempt in London in 1782 was more successful, and Mrs. Siddons was instantly acclaimed a tragic actress without equal, a position she maintained until the end of her career. She began, however, at the zenith of her powers and unlike her great brother, John Philip Kemble, did not improve with age. Among her early parts were Isabella in *The Fatal Marriage*, Belvidera in *Venice Preserved*, and Jane Shore, while she was later outstanding as Constance in *King John*, Zara in *The Mourning Bride*, and above all as Lady Macbeth, the part in which she made her farewell appearance on 29 June 1812. She returned to the stage on 9 June 1819 as Lady Randolph in *Douglas* for the benefit of her younger brother Charles and his wife, but she was only

a shadow of her former self. Macready called it 'the last flicker of a dying flame'. But at her best there was no one to touch her, and contemporary critics were unanimous in their praise of her beauty, tenderness, and nobility. Hazlitt said of her: 'Power was seated on her brow; passion emanated from her breast as from a shrine. She was tragedy personified. . . . To have seen Mrs. Siddons was an event in everyone's life'; and after her retirement he wrote: 'Who shall make tragedy stand once more with its feet upon the earth, and its head above the stars, weeping tears and blood?' A superbly built and extremely dignified woman, with a rich resonant voice and great amplitude of gesture, Mrs. Siddons wisely left comedy alone, and appeared almost exclusively in tragic and heroic parts. She was not much liked behind the scenes, being unapproachable and avaricious, and she had a great dislike of publicity which led her to be somewhat uncivil to her admirers. Yet her intelligence and her good judgement made her the friend of such men as Dr. Johnson and Horace Walpole, while Reynolds, Lawrence, and Gainsborough delighted in painting her, the first immortalizing her beauty as the Tragic Muse. Towards the end of her career she became somewhat stout, and her acting was considered monotonous and outmoded. She was also extremely prudish, even in her youth, and jibbed at the breeches in Rosalind, appearing in a costume which was that neither of a man nor of a woman, and extremely unbecoming. In any case she was poor in the part, and seldom played it. Yet her brother once referred to her as 'one of the best comic singers of the day', though as no record exists of her having appeared before the public in that role, one can only surmise that she unbent in private. She was the mother of two girls, who died young, and of a son, Henry (1775–1815), who was for a long time connected with the Edinburgh theatre, but was accounted a poor actor (see also KEMBLE).

SIDE BOX, see AUDITORIUM and BOX.

SIERRA, GREGORIO MARTÍNEZ, see MARTÍNEZ SIERRA.

SILL IRONS, flat strips of metal used as strengthening pieces across the bottom of openings in flats.

SILVA, ANTÓNIO JOSÉ DA (1705–39), see SOUTH AMERICA, 2.

SIMON [SIMEON], JOSEPH (1594–1671), see JESUIT DRAMA.

SIMONOV, KONSTANTIN MIKHAILOVICH (1915–   ), Soviet dramatist, whose first play, *The Russian People*, dealing with the impact of war on a group of civilians and soldiers near the front line, was produced in 1942 and frequently revived. It was given in London in 1943 as *The Russians* by the Old Vic Theatre company. His next play, *A Fellow from Our Town* (1942), was awarded a Stalin prize, while a third, *Wait for Me* (1943) (the title is taken from one of Simonov's own poems), has been played all over the U.S.S.R., and has set a definite seal of approval on the reputation of this young dramatist. It is perhaps too soon to assess his quality as yet, but such early and competent work augurs hopefully for the future.

SIMONOV, REUBEN NIKOLAIVICH (1899–   ), Soviet actor and producer, who has made a name for himself as a serious and original worker in the theatre. He began his career during the First World War at the Chaliapin Studio, which was much influenced by the Moscow Art Theatre, and in 1920 joined that theatre's Fourth Studio, later to become the Vakhtangov Theatre. His first production was *Intervention* (1933), with settings by Rabino-vich. He was also one of the producers of the first play given by the Uzbek National Theatre, and in 1931 he organized a group of students, trained by himself in the methods of Stanis-lavsky and Vakhtangov, which later became a State theatre. Among its notable productions was a dramatization of Sholokov's novel, *Virgin Soil Upturned*. For a description of Simonov at work, see Norris Houghton's *Moscow Rehearsals*, published in 1936.

SIMONSON, LEE (1888–   ), American theatrical designer, author of *The Stage is Set* (1932) and of a volume of memoirs, *Part of a Lifetime* (1943). His first work for the theatre was done in connexion with the Washington Square Players, and he later became one of the founders and directors of the Theatre Guild, for whose productions much of his finest work has been done. He was Director of the Inter-national Exhibition of Theatre Art held in New York in 1934, and is a director of the National Theatre and Academy and of the Museum of Costume Art in New York (see also UNITED STATES, 2).

SIMPSON, EDMUND SHAW (1784–1848), American actor and manager, who made his first appearances in 1806 in the English pro-vinces, and was playing in Dublin when Cooper and Price engaged him for the Park Theatre, New York. He made his first appearance there in Oct. 1809, and remained for thirty-eight years, being possibly the most important man to come into the American theatre since Cooper. He played Richmond to the Richard III of Kean, Cooke, and the elder Booth, and remained a prime favourite with the audience until 1833, when he retired from the stage because of lameness caused by an accident. He had been appointed acting manager of the theatre in 1812, and Price's partner in 1815, and had kept the theatre running well, in spite of the disastrous fire of 1820, mainly by im-porting English stars and encouraging the fashion for Italian opera. He continued in management after his retirement from acting, and in 1837, by which time the prestige of the Park was on the wane, he became sole lessee.

He struggled to maintain his former position in the theatrical world, but his theatre was in a bad state of repair and his methods out of date. In 1848 he surrendered it to Hamblin, manager of the Bowery, against an annuity, and died almost immediately. He was held in high esteem by his public, both for his long and devoted service to the theatre, and for his brave struggle against adversity in his declining years.

SINCLAIR, ARTHUR (1883–   ), Irish actor, husband of Maire O'Neill, who made his first appearance on the stage as Daire in *On Baile's Strand* (1904) with the Irish National Theatre Society, and was with the Abbey Theatre, Dublin, until 1916, playing in all the notable productions of that time. He then formed his own company and toured Ireland and England, subsequently appearing in variety theatres in Irish sketches. He built up a great reputation as an Irish comedian, some of his finest parts being Flaherty in *The Playboy of the Western World*, John Duffy in *The White-Headed Boy*, in which he toured America and Australia, Boyle in *Juno and the Paycock*, Fluther Good in *The Plough and the Stars*, Shields in *The Shadow of a Gunman*, and James in *Spring Meeting*. Most of these he has revived several times. He has also been seen as Christopher Sly in *The Taming of the Shrew* and as Smee in *Peter Pan*.

SINGSPIEL, see OPERA, 8.

SKELTON, JOHN (*c.* 1460–1529), see ENG-LAND, 2.

SKINNER. (1) OTIS (1858–1942), American actor, best remembered for his performance as Hajj in the oriental fantasy *Kismet* (1911), in which he appeared for two years and fre-quently revived on tour. He had, however, had a long and distinguished career before this, making his first appearance on the stage in Philadelphia in 1877, and in New York at Niblo's Garden in 1879. After some years with Booth and Lawrence Barrett, he joined Augustin Daly and with him made his first appearance in London, where he was again seen in 1890 as Romeo. For two years he toured with Modjeska, playing such parts as Orlando, Benedick, and Major Schubert in *Magda*, and with Joseph Jefferson played Young Absolute in *The Rivals*. Among his later successes were *His Grace de Grammont* (1894), in which his wife, Maud Durbin, played opposite him as Mistress Hamilton, *The Honour of the Family* (1907), *Your Humble Servant* (1909), and *Mr. Antonio* (1916), the last two written for him by Booth Tarkington. In 1926 he appeared as Falstaff in *Henry IV, Part I* and two years later as the same character in *The Merry Wives of Windsor*. Among his last appearances were Shylock, with Maude Adams, and Thersites in *Troilus and Cressida*. He wrote several volumes of reminiscences, including *Footlights and Spotlights* (1924) and

The Last Tragedian (1939). His daughter (2) CORNELIA OTIS (1902–   ) is celebrated as a diseuse, and has toured extensively in solo performances all over the United States and in London. She was trained for the stage by Jacques Copeau, and made her first appearance in her father's company in 1921. She is the author of a number of entertaining books, including a volume of reminiscences of continental travel, *Our Hearts Were Young and Gay*.

SKY BORDER, see BORDER, SCENERY, and STAGE, 3.

SKY-DOME, see LIGHTING, 1 *d* and SCENERY, 6.

SLIP BOX (another name for Green Box), see AUDITORIUM, 3 and BOX.

SLIPS, a name used in the late eighteenth and early nineteenth centuries to designate the ends or near-stage extremities of the upper tiers of seats in the theatre (see AUDITORIUM, 3).

SLOAT (or SLOTE), a term used in Victorian stage-management for a device which conveyed (*a*) scenery and (*b*) persons.

(*a*) The Sloat below the stage enabled flat scenes, groundrows, or footpieces to be raised through a cut in the stage. A Sloat Box contained a rolled and painted cloth which could be raised during, for example, a Transformation Scene (see ENGLISH PLAYHOUSE, 2 *c* and STAGE, 1).   R. S.

(*b*) Elaborate stage-directions in *The Orange Girl* (Surrey, 1864) show that the Slote carried the heroine from a height downwards to a trap. In a letter to the *Era Almanack* of 1887 Irving says 'the slote in *Faust* struck me on the head, instead of carrying me up into the flies above'; in mentioning this accident Brereton's *Life of Irving* uses the word 'slide'. The contrivance is described by Herman Merivale, in *Bar, Stage and Platform*, as having been invented by Charles Kean so that the angels in *Faust* and *Henry VIII* should be without wires. The ghost in *The Corsican Brothers*, as staged under the management of Charles Kean and of Irving, entered on a 'sliding-trap', a similar apparatus between mezzanine and stage level. A detailed account of the 'Corsican trap' is given by Sir John Martin-Harvey in his autobiography.   M. W. D.

SLOMAN, CHARLES (1808–70), a performer in the early music-halls, and the original of Young Nadab in Thackeray's *The Newcomes*. He is best remembered for his doggerel verses improvised on subjects given him by members of the audience, or on the appearance and dress of those in front of him, but he was also a writer of songs, both comic and serious, for himself and for other music-hall performers, including Sam Cowell and Ross. He was at the height of his fame in the 1840s but fell on hard times. One of his last engagements was as Chairman of the Middlesex Music-Hall in

Drury Lane, and he died soon after, a pauper, in the Strand Workhouse.

SLOTE, see ENGLISH PLAYHOUSE, 2 *c*, SLOAT and STAGE, 1.

SLOVAK THEATRE, see CZECHOSLOVAKIA, 1 *b*.

SLY, WILLIAM (?–1608), English actor, who appears in the actor-list of Shakespeare's plays. He was connected with the theatre from about 1590, when his name appears in the cast of *Seven Deadly Sins* (part 2), and he joined the Chamberlain's Men on its formation in 1594. He was not one of the original shareholders of the Globe, but became one at some time, since he mentions it in his will, and he also had a seventh share in the Blackfriars, later taken over by Richard Burbage.

SMITH, ALBERT (1816–60), an interesting but somewhat forgotten figure of literary and theatrical London in the mid-nineteenth century, whose novels are very like those of Dickens. He dramatized several of the latter's works for the stage, and also produced some original but forgotten plays of his own. His main claim to fame lay in his one-man entertainments, of which the first was *The Overland Mail*, given in 1850. This was an amusing and no doubt exaggerated account of a recent trip to India, interspersed with topical songs and stories, and illustrated by scenery specially painted for the occasion by the famous scene-painter, William Beverley. It proved such a success that Smith followed it up with *The Ascent of Mont Blanc*, given at the Egyptian Hall, Piccadilly, again with scenery by Beverley, who had accompanied Smith to Switzerland to gather material for the display, and by a similar 'lecture' on China. During the run of the last he married Mary, actress daughter of the Keeleys, leaving her a widow in less than a year. His death was caused by his insistence on giving his lecture in spite of a sharp attack of bronchitis, which turned to pneumonia. For the last ten years of his life he had enjoyed enormous popularity. His simple entertainment, whose charm lay as much in its spontaneity and wit as in the actual material, was reckoned among the things to be visited in London, and was frequently patronized by Queen Victoria and the royal children. Smith was also a prolific journalist and a contributor to *Punch* for many years.

SMITH, EDWARD TYRRELL (1804–77), English theatre manager, was the son of an admiral. He became a policeman, an auctioneer, and finally the most reckless theatrical speculator of his day. In 1850 he took over the Marylebone Music-Hall, and later rented Drury Lane, then in very low water, for £3,000, and opened it in 1852 with *Uncle Tom's Cabin* and one of Blanchard's pantomimes. He also bought the Panopticon in Leicester Square, renamed it the Alhambra, and reopened it in 1858 as a circus, after having disposed of all the scientific para- phernalia with which it was filled, and sold the famous organ to St. Paul's Cathedral. He exhibited Sayers and Heenan there, and then ran it as a music-hall. Smith was an amazing man, to whom nothing came amiss. At Drury Lane he had Gustavus Brooke, the younger Mathews, and operatic singers. He mixed opera with drama and with Shakespeare, he intro- duced Chinese conjurors and a 'Human Fly' who crawled about the ceiling. He presented Rachel, the tragedienne, and followed her with a circus. He was lessee of Her Majesty's for Italian opera, of the Lyceum, of Astley's, and of the Surrey. He was the proprietor of High- bury Barn, and of the Regent Music-Hall, West- minster; he was also landlord of the Radnor Tavern, in Chancery Lane, a wine merchant, a picture dealer, a land agent, a bill discounter, and a newspaper proprietor. In the multitude of activities there was no wisdom and he eventually ruined himself. In his day he was a noted character, and in spite of his many follies he made friends everywhere and kept them. He was also the first to inaugurate the morning performance, which under Hollings- head became the modern afternoon matinée.

W. M. P.

SMITH, RICHARD PENN (1799–1854), Ameri- can dramatist, one of the leading members of the Philadelphia group, and a lawyer by pro- fession. He was the author of some twenty plays, of which fifteen were acted. They are of all types, ranging from farce to romantic tragedy, and represent the transition in the American theatre from the play imported or inspired by Europe and the true native produc- tion of later years. Most of his comedies were adaptations from the French, while his roman- tic plays were mainly based on incidents of American history. What is believed to be his finest piece of work, a tragedy entitled *Caius Marius*, has not survived. It was produced by Edwin Forrest in 1831, with himself in the title-role, and proved extremely successful. It was possibly Forrest's aversion to the printing of plays in which he appeared that caused it to be lost. Another interesting play, also lost, was *The Actress of Padua* (1836), which was based on Hugo's *Angelo*, one of the first echoes of French romanticism in American theatrical history. It was revived by Charlotte Cushman in the early 1850s, and was seen in New York as late as 1873, probably with some alterations by John Brougham, to whom the play has been attributed.

SMITH. (1) SOLOMON FRANKLIN (1801–69), a pioneer of the American theatre on the fron- tier, usually known as Sol Smith. He had a hard childhood, and at 16 ran away from his brother's shop, where he was employed, in the hope of becoming an actor. He was forced to return for a while, but eventually achieved his ambition, travelling with the Drakes and other itinerant companies, and eking out a livelihood by spasmodic journalism. By 1823 he had got together a company of his own, but marriage and financial difficulties caused him to look about for a more stable position, and in 1827 he and his wife, a singer, joined the company of J. H. Caldwell, with whom they visited St. Louis and other Mississippi towns. Smith eventually went into partnership with Noah Ludlow. The combination prospered and dominated the St. Louis stage until 1851, building there the first permanent theatre west of the Mississippi. Smith, who appeared as a star at the Park Theatre, New York, under Simpson, and in Philadelphia under the management of Wemyss, was at his best in low comedy, particularly in such parts as Mawworm in *The Hypocrite*. He was a man of upright character, popular, and much re- spected, and published three books on the theatre, the last, *Theatrical Management in the West and South* (1868), being a combination of the two earlier ones. In 1853 he dissolved his partnership with Ludlow and became a lawyer. Two of his sons were on the stage, (2) MARCUS (1829–74), better known as Mark, making his first appearance as a child in his father's theatre, and then going to New York, where he was a member of Burton's until it closed. He excelled in the portrayal of the English gentle- man of old comedy, and was with Wallack's from 1862 to 1863. In London, under Mrs. John Wood, he made a good impression, and returned to New York to play his last part at Union Square Theatre in *One Hundred Years Old*, in which he made a great hit. His daughter became an opera singer.

SMITH, WILLIAM (? –1696), English actor, friend of Betterton, a tall, handsome man who was the original player of Pierre and Chamont in Otway's famous tragedies, and also of Sir Fopling Flutter and Scandal. He became em- broiled behind the scenes with a nobleman, who struck him and was severely reprimanded by the king for doing so; upon which a party of gentlemen combined to drive Smith from the stage by their hisses and cat-calls. Being a wealthy man, he retired and lived quietly, but later returned to the theatre, and died while playing in *Cyrus the Great*.

SMITH, WILLIAM (1730–1819), English actor, known as 'Gentleman Smith', on account of his elegant figure, fine manners, and handsome face. Sent down from Cambridge, he took to the stage, and after being coached by Spranger Barry he made his first appearance at Covent Garden on 1 Jan. 1753. He remained there until 1774, and then went to Drury Lane, where he was the first to play Charles Surface. He was also Mrs. Siddons's first Macbeth, and alternated Hamlet and Richard III with Gar- rick, whom he greatly admired, though his own style was more that of Quin. He was in possession of most of the big tragic parts when John Philip Kemble came to Drury Lane in 1783, and kept them until his retirement in 1788. He then went to Bury St. Edmunds and spent his time hunting and attending race- meetings, though he reappeared once more in his famous part of Charles Surface in 1798, for the benefit of his friend King, the original Sir Peter Teazle. In an age which expected its actors to turn their hands to anything, from tragedy to pantomime—Garrick himself is said to have played Harlequin—Smith's proudest boast was that he had never blackened his face, never played in a farce, and never ascended through a trap-door. He would also never consent to appear at the theatre on a Monday during the hunting season, as he was a zealous rider to hounds.

SMITHSON, HARRIET CONSTANCE (1800–54), an English actress who made her first appearance in London in 1818 as Letitia Hardy in *The Belle's Stratagem* at Drury Lane. She then played Lady Anne and Desdemona to the Richard III and Othello of Edmund Kean, and was seen also at Covent Garden and the Haymarket, returning to Drury Lane in 1822 as Countess Wilhelm in *Adeline*. Little is known of her early days, but she seems to have been a promising but not particularly well-known actress when in 1828 she went with Macready to Paris, and was received with acclamation. Her Desdemona and Ophelia excited enormous enthusiasm, and the young romantics of the day covered her with adulation, even Janin declaring that she had revealed Shakespeare to France, and had made his tragedies the prerogative of the actress, thus forestalling Rachel, who called her many years later 'a poor woman to whom I am much indebted'. Her fame was short-lived, as she soon afterwards made an ill-judged and unhappy marriage with Berlioz, the French composer, and retired from the stage.

SMOCK ALLEY THEATRE, see DUBLIN.

SOCIALIST REALISM, the name given to the theatrical method and approach expounded in Soviet Russia by Lunacharsky, on the lines laid down by Lenin, and carried out, often with excellent and unexpected results, by the producers of the U.S.S.R. Apparently the term was first used in 1932, as a protest against the dry, formalist productions of such men as Meyerhold and Taïrov. It reasserted the importance of the individual and summed up the work of the theatre as 'a representation which must not be untrue, either to present-day facts or to the facts of the past; but it must express that truth in such terms that the worker-audience of to-day gets a perspective of either the Socialism it is helping to build, or of the factors of the past out of which that Socialism has come'. This naturally affects the producer's attitude to the classics, as can be seen by the accounts of recent Shakespearian and other revivals which have conformed to the method. It also influences the playwright, as the personal problems of his characters are increasingly bound up with their general surroundings, and with the forces which led to, or arise from, the upheaval of 1917.

SOCIÉTÉ JOYEUSE, see FRANCE, 1.

SOCK, from the Latin *soccus*, referring to the light, soft shoe worn by the comic actor, in contrast to the heavy boot of the tragedian (see COTHURNUS and BUSKIN). By extension, the word is used to denote comedy. Milton uses it in this sense in *L'Allegro*: 'Then to the well-trod stage anon, If Jonson's learned sock be on.'

SOGGETTO, the earlier name for the *scenario* of the *commedia dell' arte*, which was also known as *commedia a soggetto* (see ITALY, 2).

SOLDENE, EMILY (1840–1912), a music-hall performer who first appeared as Miss Fitzhenry at the Canterbury, where she sang in the excerpts from opera which Morton made such a feature of his programmes there. When he opened the Oxford she appeared there also, and became the leading lady of the Light Opera and Opera Bouffe company at the old Philharmonic (later the Grand) Theatre, Islington. She scored many successes there, and the Prince of Wales (afterwards Edward VII) went frequently to see her, as did many West End playgoers. She accompanied Morton to America when he took his light opera company there, but retired on marriage and went to live in Australia. She published in 1897 a volume of reminiscences giving much interesting information on the stage and music-hall of her time.   W. M. P.

SOMI, LEONE DE (1527–92), see JEWISH DRAMA, 3 and LIGHTING, 1 a.

SOPHOCLES (496–406 B.C.), Greek dramatist, son of Sophillus, was born of good family at Colonus, near Athens. As a boy he was celebrated for the beauty of his voice and figure, and took part in a boys' dance which celebrated the victory of Salamis (480 B.C.). (Aeschylus fought in the battle, and a neat but inaccurate tradition caused Euripides to be born on the day of the battle—four years too late.) Sophocles is said to have written over a hundred plays; seven are extant, as well as substantial parts of a not very amusing satyr-play, the *Ichneutae* (Trackers), and many fragments. He won eighteen victories, the first—over Aeschylus—in 468. He is said to have won the second prize very often, and never to have been third. The extant plays are: *Ajax* (c. 450 B.C.), *Antigone* (c. 442), *Trachiniae*, *Oedipus Rex* (? c. 425), *Electra*, *Philoctetes* (409), and *Oedipus Coloneus* (posthumous).

Aeschylus represents the heroic period of Athenian democracy, Sophocles its triumphant maturity. The first part of his active life coincided with the Periclean Age, in which Sophocles was a distinguished and congenial figure. In 440 he was elected (for the year) to the high military and administrative post of *Stratêgos* (General), and apparently on at least one other occasion held public office. He lived through the greater part of the long struggle with Sparta, dying, in his native Colonus, a few months after Euripides, and just before the final defeat of Athens in the Peloponnesian

War. Cicero is the earliest authority for the story that, towards the end of his long life, Sophocles was brought into court by his sons on the charge of being incapacitated by old age from managing his affairs; and that, having read to the jury an ode from the play which he was composing, the *Oedipus Coloneus*, he was triumphantly acquitted. The truth of the story is doubted, but it does seem that Sophocles did at least complete this remarkable play at the age of 90 or thereabouts. All the ancient references to him agree in giving a picture of a serene, distinguished, and greatly loved figure.

This serenity pervades his drama; but it is a serenity that comes from the triumph over suffering, not from its avoidance. Few things in drama are more poignant than Sophocles' tragic climaxes. Sophocles approached drama in a very different spirit from Aeschylus, and therefore modified the form considerably (see GREECE, 1 *b*). In addition to this, he developed a poetic style which, while always beautiful and dignified, was amazingly supple, reflecting character and emotion with a subtlety approached, in Greek, only by Plato; outside Greek, by nobody. These new complexities and delicacies were used by Sophocles with a logic and an economy which make him as powerful a dramatist as any.

Aristotle's analysis of tragedy is based, in the main, on the Sophoclean drama, since he regarded this as the mature form of tragedy, and therefore neglected others (e.g. the Aeschylean).   H. D. F. K.

SOPHRON of Syracuse, a writer of mimes (see MIME, 1 *b*).

SORGE, REINHARD JOHANNES (1892–1916), German poet, who began as a disciple of Nietzsche, and fell, a devout Catholic, in the 1914–18 war. His most important play, *Der Bettler* (written in 1912, but not performed until 1917), was a drama of social protest written in an expressionist style. It foreshadows the revolt of the young generation against the old, and the striving for a higher spiritual orientation, two of the most insistent themes of the expressionist movement. His later plays are expressions of religious ecstasy.

SORMA [ZAREMBA], AGNES (1865–1927), German actress, who was on the stage as a child, and in 1883 was engaged for the newly founded Deutsches Theater, where she soon became popular in young girls' parts. As her powers developed, however, she began to be recognized as an outstanding actress, some of her first successes being scored in revivals of Grillparzer's works, particularly *Weh dem, der lügt!* in which she played opposite Joseph Kainz. She was also seen as Juliet, Ophelia, and Desdemona, and later as Nora, a part which she continued to play for many years, notably on a visit to Paris, and on an extended tour of Europe. She also made her first appearance in New York in that part, appearing at the Irving Place Theatre in Apr. 1897 with a German company. She was a distinguished interpreter of the heroines of Sudermann and Hauptmann, and, in lighter vein, was successful as the Hostess in *La Locandiera*. A beautiful woman, with dark hair and eyes, and a charming smile, she was for many years the best-known actress of Germany, and from 1904 to 1908 worked under Max Reinhardt in Berlin.

SOTHERN. (1) EDWARD ASKEW (1826–81), English actor who made his name in New York, as Lord Dundreary in *Our American Cousin* (1858), a part which he practically created, and with which he is always associated. He first appeared on the stage in the English provinces, and later, as Douglas Stuart, went to Boston, where he was not at first very successful, being considered by a contemporary critic 'undertaught and over-praised'. After some years on tour he joined Wallack's in New York, and reverted to his original name of Sothern. Jefferson, who played in the original production of *Our American Cousin*, says in his *Autobiography* that Sothern had at first little opinion of the small part he had been offered by Laura Keene, 'and as the dismal lines of Dundreary were read, he glanced over at me with a forlorn expression, as much as to say "I am cast for that dreadful part", little dreaming that the character of the imbecile lord would turn out to be the stepping-stone of his fortune'. Jefferson then goes on to describe how, during the first weeks of the run, Sothern began to introduce 'extravagant business' into his part. This went down well, and by the end of a month he was the equal of any other character; at the end of the run he was the whole play. He was equally successful in London, where long side-whiskers as he wore them became known as 'dundrearies'. The play became almost a series of monologues, and several other sketches were written round Sothern's creation. Another of Sothern's great parts was *Brother Sam*, which Jefferson, and also Clement Scott, thought even better than his Dundreary. Sothern had ambitions towards the playing of romantic drama, but though parts of his *David Garrick* (1864) were excellent, Scott says 'his love scene that ends the play acted as a soporific on many of us'. *A Crushed Tragedian* (1874), in which he played the part of an old actor, was also a failure in London, though well received in New York. Sothern was essentially an eccentric comedian, and it was in that line that he did his best and most memorable work. He had three sons on the stage, some of whom (2) EDWARD HUGH (1859–1933) inherited the major share of his father's talent and charm. Educated in England, he intended to take up painting, but heredity led him to the stage. He started slowly, toured with McCullough in the United States, and in 1884 became leading man of Frohman's Lyceum company, where he remained until 1898. A light comedian and a charming romantic hero in cloak-and-sword plays like *The Prisoner of Zenda*, he was immensely popular, both in New York and on tour. He was seen as Hamlet in 1900, and later opened the new Lyceum in New York with *If I Were King*. For some years he headed a Shakespearian repertory company with Julia Marlowe, who became his second wife in 1911. After her retirement in 1916 he continued to appear intermittently, being last seen in 1927. He devoted much of his later years to public readings and lectures and wrote his autobiography as *The Melancholy Tale of 'Me'* (1916). A small but dignified man, with a handsome, sensitive face, he was the ideal romantic hero of the late nineteenth century, and although by hard work he achieved some success in tragedy, his real talent lay in light comedy and romance. He was good as Malvolio, and several times revived his father's old part of Lord Dundreary.

SOTIE, the topical and satirical play of medieval France, whose best-known author is Pierre Gringore, the *mère-sotte* or chief fool of the Parisian *enfants sans souci*. The *sotie* was not a farce, though they had elements in common, and was often inspired by political or religious intrigue. It was intended for amusement only, and is not to be compared with the Mystery or Morality play, to which it often served as a curtain-raiser. The actors, or *sots* (fools), wore the traditional fool's costume, dunce's cap, short jacket, tights, and bells on their legs. Modern research inclines to the idea that the *soties* were acted not only by such amateur associations as the *enfants sans souci* and the *clercs de la basoche*, but by semi-professional and more or less permanent companies, somewhat in the tradition of the *commedia dell'arte*, each with its own repertory. The point is, however, still obscure, and needs further elucidation. There are a number of extant texts, of which the Recueil Trepperel is the most representative.

SOUND EFFECTS, see MACHINERY and TRICKWORK ON THE ENGLISH STAGE.

SOUTH AMERICA. For the purposes of this article the term South America is stretched to cover all territory south of the Rio Grande River, which is to say that it includes Central America and Mexico. Strictly speaking, that takes in the theatres of twenty nations, speaking four European languages and many native dialects, but in reality only a few of these have a native theatre of any real importance.

Those characteristics of the theatre in South America which distinguish it from that in other nations of European extraction can be understood only in the light of the continent's history and of the Spanish and Portuguese who, invading at the start of the sixteenth century, brought with them not only new languages and a new religion, but also what was then the most brilliant theatre tradition in Europe. They found among Indian tribes native to the new land a dramatic tradition expressed in terms of religious ceremonial. This skill and this custom were utilized by the priests who came with the soldiers; they changed the content of dramatic recital to that prescribed in Catholic pastorals and Miracle plays. Hardly was the conquest completed when the plays of Lope de Vega, Juan de Encina, Gil Vicente, which had been popular at home, were imported to the new land.

These two double roots of the South American theatre, the native and the European, the lay and the religious, have continued to flourish through four centuries and a half, sometimes blooming separately and sometimes intertwined. To them should be added, particularly in the case of Brazil and Cuba, a racial heritage out of Africa which is only now being studied. Their influence extends throughout the continent, and sometimes shows itself in strange ways. When Mozart's 'Magic Flute' was presented in Mexico City not long ago the arias and choruses were sung in German, but the recitative was in Mexican Spanish; the scene in the temple was set and costumed as in an Aztec temple. The Mexican audience found nothing peculiar in the mixture. In the same spirit, Indians in various villages enliven holiday festivals with pageants presenting the fifteenth-century Spanish struggle between the Moors and the Christians—a struggle still fresh to their conquerors when they reached America, and impressed on the primitive Indian mind with such force that though it took place in an alien land it has become a Mexican folk-theme.

A third root of continuing importance is the colonial attitude of dependence and uncertainty imposed by four centuries of European rule exercised by viceroys governing on the order of distant kings. At times this still shows itself in an immaturity of workmanship and a lack of confidence which hamper dramatic development of the first order.

1. SPANISH AMERICA. The theatre in those parts of South America conquered by the Spaniards developed earlier and with more abundance than in Portuguese-settled Brazil. The Spaniards took Mexico in 1521, and in 1538 put on their first recorded performance in the European manner. They had a 'House of Comedies' in Mexico City by 1597—only twenty years after the first permanent theatre was established in Madrid itself. In Peru, the earliest touring company arrived in 1599. In Chile, thirty-four years later, on 11 Sept. 1633, 'comedies were presented by captains, sergeants major, scribes and nobles' on a stage a span and a half high.

Meanwhile the priests, using Miracle plays as vehicles for teaching Indian converts in monastery schools the content as well as the speech and the ways of the conquering religion, trained them to present *pasos, entremeses*, and *entradas a Jerusalén*. The natural result, among a natively dramatic people, was the emergence of Indian versions of the *nacimiento* and the *pastorela*, which in some instances became native village festivals with the chief roles handed down by inheritance.

Not much from the sixteenth and seventeenth centuries has survived intact excepting plays which had been imported from Europe. Three plays by Lope de Vega are said to have been translated into Quechua (a native dialect), but there are few records of a Quechuan play surviving in Spanish other than the famous historical fake *Ollantay*, thought for years to be a vestige from pre-Spanish days. It was written in the eighteenth century and performed in 1780 before Tupac Amaru, the last great Inca rebel against Spanish rule. It was shortly afterward banned by the ruling Spanish Viceroy, and therefore a few copies were carefully guarded. It has been translated into many tongues.

Three early playwrights represent the best of that first period. Juan Ruiz de Alarcón (1581–1639) was born in Mexico and is eagerly claimed there, but he went to Madrid at an early age, and there made his reputation as one of Lope de Vega's competitors. Fernán González de Eslava (*fl.* last third of the sixteenth century) was a Spaniard who made a dramatic career in Mexico; he is seldom read by others than scholars, to whom he is important because he preserved in his plays the popular speech of the time. A more famous playwright and one authentically Mexican is the poetess Sor Juana Inés de la Cruz, born Juana Inés de Asbaje y Ramírez de Cantillana (1651–95). Known to her admiring compatriots as 'the tenth Muse', she was rich, learned, determined, and beautiful; she seems to have been a distracting influence in high circles, and no convent could silence her pen. Her fame as poet and playwright survives.

Of eighteenth-century plays two are occasionally revived, the pretended Inca romance *Ollantay*, and *Siripo*, written in 1789 by Manuel J. Labardén of Argentina. The first concerns the love of a minor chieftain for the daughter of an Inca chief and, while written in Quechua, is Spanish in form and situation. The second is the melodramatic story of Lucía Miranda, a heroine of the colonizing period. In both instances the subject-matter is South American, but the manner of writing and of development is European. That balance continues.

The nineteenth century brought independence from Spain, and a breaking apart of the old vice-royalties into smaller units, self-governing within and competitive without. The cultural influences that had centred in vice-regal capitals persisted, but with independence came an effort on the part of the small proportion of the cultured to create national literatures which should be expressive of national ideals and free from the repressive effect of royal edicts issued at long distance. During the nineteenth century they sought to escape from the hampering influence of Spain; during the twentieth they are trying to escape from the crippling effect of the colonial mentality.

Of the score of South American countries which owe their heritage to Spain, there is hardly one which fails to honour a favourite playwright. For foreign students, however, those whose fame extends beyond the borders of their own countries hold most interest. The modern theatre in South America (meaning by that the theatre which shows the influence of the Ibsen revolution) has flourished with most promise in Argentina, Chile, and Mexico. In Argentina it began in 1884, when José J. Podestá, a circus clown turned impresario, took one of the famous gaucho legends and acted it out for a country audience. The gauchos were the cowboys of the great South American plains, and dear to all Argentinians. The South American theatre had found its first native source, and one that continues to be active to this day. *Juan Moreiro* (1884) was the name of that first gaucho play, and it was full of blood, thunder, and galloping hooves down the centre aisle. *Calandria* (written in 1896), by Martíniano Leguizamón (1858–1935), a dramatist with literary pretensions, was the next step, but still rough. *Juan Soldao*, by Orosmán Moratoria (1859–98), had its gallopings better timed and placed, and now ranks as the most famous of the gaucho plays.

Late in the nineteenth century echoes of Ibsen, come by way of Echegaray out of Spain, began appearing in Buenos Aires. The gauchos grew older, acquired sons and problems—and playwrights to deal with them in the new manner. *M'Hijo el Dotor* (1903), written by Florencio Sánchez (1875–1910), Montevideo newspaper man and the most famous playwright of the region, deals with the gaucho's son who took to city ways, and his old gaucho father who understood neither the son's ambitions nor his weaknesses. Sánchez was followed by Ernesto Herrera (1887–1917), whose biographer considers him the equal as well as the disciple of the older man. He explored further into social problems which had no gaucho heritage, and his plays picture early twentieth-century society there, especially in the lower strata.

The Argentine theatre is thought by many to be the most hospitable and most fruitful in South America. It plays French and Italian drama in those tongues for big immigrant populations, and it has the reputation of translating and adapting anything that comes to hand. Touring companies bring plays, ballets, opera from Europe and North America, and are warmly welcomed by avid audiences. Buenos Aires is the only South American city to boast a regular opera season, though Rio de Janeiro makes attempts.

Thanks to a law passed in 1910 which gives playwrights a larger share of royalties than is customary, author-managers flourish in Argentina. Leonidas Barletta, creator and manager of the Teatro del Pueblo, which offers good plays to workers at a low price, is the best known of these, though he and his theatre became less prominent after President Perón came into power. The star system prevails here, as in the rest of South America, and Lola Membrives is its leading luminary. She has her own company, and plays are tailored or arranged for her by the best native or visiting dramatists.

The most famous Argentine playwright to-day is Samuel Eichelbaum (1894–   ), who is also a dramatic critic. He too lost favour when social protest became suspect. His best-known plays are *Un Hogar*, *Un Tal Servando Gómez*, and *Un Guapo del 900*. He follows in the tradition of Florencio Sánchez and Ernesto Herrera, with more attention to psychological complications than those earlier playwrights attempted. Two famous teams write popular comedies with style and finish—Camilo Darthés and Carlos Damel, whose most applauded play is *Los Hijos Crecen* (1937), and Pedro E. Pico and Rodolfo González Pacheco, famous for *Que La Agarre Quien Quiera*. In addition there are playwrights who work for the library rather than the stage.

Mexico's theatre is also hospitable, also fruitful, but it has developed few playwrights of dramatic importance and few plays of lasting value. In compensation, it has certain spontaneous and popular qualities which make its activities important to the participants and to the audience. On the literary plane, it enlists poets and writers of high quality—Xavier Villaurrutia and Rodolfo Usigli, Celestino Gorostiza, who was in 1938 named director of Mexico's Department of Fine Arts, the famous poet and diplomat Alfonso Reyes, the novelist Mauricio Magdaleno. These men write for experimental groups, or for famous actresses, rather than for the general stage. Their plays —e.g. *La Hiedra* of Villaurrutia, or *Noche de Estío* of Usigli—are written in the tradition made famous by Europe's *avant-garde*.

Professional companies in Mexico devote themselves mostly to revivals of popular Spanish plays or to adaptations of plays which have proved their drawing power in Europe or the United States. Between them and the literary playwrights flourishes a mutual scorn. They must please an audience hungry for novelty, and this means a repertory schedule calling for a new play every week. The company meets on Monday to plan the next week's programme. They may have a new play, adapt an old one, or find a new way of presenting an individual speciality of an individual actor. In such circumstances an absent playwright gets short shrift. Performances are put together with more haste than finish, and they have no time or money for fine décor or brilliant costumes.

Mexico's important contributions to the theatre are the popular 'carpa' in cities, and the Indian pageant in towns. The 'carpa' is a tent in which players working along *commedia dell' arte* lines put on two 'tandas' or revues for a small entrance fee. Their material is topical, their plots are sketched, their lines improvised according to the mood and the news of the day. Out of the 'carpas' has come a procession of clowns, led by the famous Cantinflas, who, on stage and screen, have made America laugh.

The Indian ceremonial pageants are the fruit of four and a half centuries of Indian persis-tence under Spanish rule and influence. The dances of the 'concheros' at San Miguel de Allende, for example, celebrate Christ's conquest of the savage Otomites. Some villages tell the story of Cortés and the Indian girl Malinche, others send troupes to the Shrine of the Virgin of Guadalupe to put on feast-day pageants in her honour.

Outside of Argentina and Mexico the theatre is not so well organized. In Chile, Antonio Acevedo y Hernández and Armando Moock have won fame that echoes through the continent. The latter is acclaimed by many as South America's leading dramatist. Chile's theatre is profiting from the residence there of Margarita Xirgu, Spain's most famous actress of modern times, who, having left Spain when General Franco seized power, founded and directs the Academia Dramática in Santiago. Chile has honoured her work by making her academy an integral part of the Teatro Nacional.

Colombia has a trio of dramatists famous in this century—Antonio Alvarez Lleras, Alejandro Mesa Nicholls, Luís Enrique Osorio— whose plays show colour and originality in a land too prone to imitate Spanish models. Bolivia has a famous playwright, Mario Flores, whose reputation was won in Argentina. Paraguay's most celebrated playwriting is unexportable, being written not in Spanish but in a native Indian dialect called Guaraní which is widely spoken among the lower classes. Julio Correa, playwright, actor, and director, organized the Elenco Teatral Guaraní in Asunción, and makes it the headquarters for his highly original and locally popular drama. Peru likes plays that celebrate its pre-Spanish Inca culture, and in 1946 a spectacle called *Inca Taky*, which included war and religious dances, native songs and recitations, went on tour. Famous for the escapades of the eighteenth-century actress La Perricholi, Peru still keeps certain Indian ceremonials intact.

Of Latin-American stars, Fernando Soler, Virginia Fábregas, María Teresa Montoya, and the clown Cantinflas make their home in Mexico, and their fame throughout the continent. Argentina boasts Lola Membrives and the comedian Luís Sandrini, also of continental fame. In many of these countries there lingers an almost Elizabethan tradition of the theatrical way of life, in which participants can turn their hands to any tasks. In Mexico, Luís G. Basurto is playwright, impresario, director. In Argentina, Pepita Serrador is leading lady and director. Luís Sandrini and José Cibrián are actors as well as directors.

Theatre buildings throughout the continent tell of a people's pride in supplanting kings and emperors who were patrons of the stage and counted a magnificent opera house as a ruler's proper jewel. The cities are proud of their theatres. Rio de Janeiro, Santiago de Chile, Lima in Peru, have municipal theatres, elaborately baroque, where prize performances are given under municipal patronage. The Municipal Theatre in Rio, and the famous

Teatro Colón which is the official theatre in Buenos Aires, are primarily opera houses, and both cities have in addition several big commercial theatres. The official theatre in Mexico City is the Palacio de Bellas Artes, begun in 1904 by the Dictator Porfirio Díaz; built of marble, it was opened in 1934. It has elaborate stage machinery but its resources are seldom put to full use. In summary, it might be said that the great days of the South American theatre are still to come.

2. BRAZIL. The Brazilian theatre stems directly from the Portuguese. In addition to the difficulties suffered by the theatre in Spanish-American countries, it struggles under the load of a frail heritage, except for the brilliant work of Gil Vicente (c. 1465–c. 1539) and Francisco Sá de Miranda (1485–1558), and of the repressive influence exercised by monarchs even more fond than were the Spaniards of banning theatre enterprises for long periods. Moreover, it lacked the favourable competition of a chain of colonial capitals to which the stage was a source of pride. Only Rio de Janeiro had, until modern times, claims to being both a cultural and a governmental centre. Other South American countries emerged from European rule without benefit of monarch, but Brazil, freed from Portugal in 1821 by the royal rebel Prince Pedro, was by him proclaimed an empire, and continued under the rule of the Bragança family until 1889. Thus it came late to popular sovereignty, and the consequent extension of the colonial mentality into modern times added a further bar to the development of drama of the highest quality.

Brazil's first theatre genius was António José da Silva (1705–39), known as Judeu (the Jew). He was born in Rio, but taken to Lisbon at the age of eight. His extraordinary dramatic talent was developed during a short and stormy life in the Portuguese capital; though he was spectacularly murdered by the Inquisition, both colony and mother country claim him as their greatest playwright. Witty and malicious, he satirized that false and precious period of the early eighteenth century to the delight of audiences and the annoyance of officials. A century later his life and tragic fate formed the theme of Brazil's first national play, *António José* (1838), written by the romantic poet Domingo José Gonçalves de Magalhães (1811–82).

Brazil's first playhouse, the baroque Royal Theatre of St. John, was the gift of King João VI of Portugal, who fled to the colony with his nobles in 1807 when Napoleon invaded the Iberian peninsula. For eleven years it welcomed drama imported from Europe and the Argentine; then it burned down, and was replaced by the Royal Theatre of St. Peter.

The first major dramatist to write on Brazilian themes was Luíz Carlos Martins Penna (1815–48). His work consists of nineteen comedies, of which *O Juiz de Paz na Roça* (1838) is considered Brazil's first national comedy, seven dramas, and one tragi-farce. *O Noviço* is one of the most famous of his plays, but all of them picture the life of the period with wit and grace.

His dramas constitute almost the only solid body of theatre writing of any value (not excluding a volume by the famous novelist Machado de Assis (1839–1908) called *Theatre*), for Brazil's plays are mostly fugitive productions by men who earn their living in other fields.

With Martins Penna stands the novelist José Mariniano de Alencar (1829–77), who wrote eight plays of a moralizing nature as well as the famous novel *O Guarani*, which has been made into a play. His *O Demonio Familiar* (1864) is still acted and was re-adapted for the modern stage by Procópio Ferreira in Rio de Janeiro in 1941. There is also Joaquim José da França Junior (1838–90), who wrote gay comedies, of which the most successful are *Tres Candidatos* and the satire *As Doutoras*. Among moderns may be mentioned Mello Nobrega, J. Barroso, Gutta Pinho, Lirival Coutinho, and Amara Gurgel, who wrote *O Pão Duro* (1941).

To-day's theatre in Brazil has one famous actor-producer, Procópio Ferreira, who revives native classics, imports European drama, and plays local modern comedy. Brazilian audiences are hospitable and fun-loving, native farces are plentiful and popular, student groups in São Paulo as well as Rio are reverent in revivals, but serious writing is mostly lacking. President Vargas made an effort, during his régime, to stimulate it with an ambitious plan (approved in 1943 and furnished with the equivalent of seven and a half million American dollars) for the 'cultural uplift of our national theatre'. This was to include the establishing of a Comedia Brasileira along the lines of the Comédie-Française, a School of the Theatre, an experimental theatre, a theatre magazine, an Opera Brasileira, a Children's Theatre, and a scheme for enlisting audience support. The promoter and director was a man of wide theatrical experience, Alexandre Abbadie Faria Rosa.

The Brazilian masses, with their admixture of African heritage, have more than their share of dramatic impulse and tend toward folk pageantry, but these show themselves in the famous carnivals rather than on the stage. So far, the mixture of black and white which is so important a factor in modern Brazil has not been exploited as a source of dramatic inspiration. Brazil's theatre is still described by critics as in a state of amused decadence, with farce its most popular and characteristic product. M. A.

SOUTHERNE, THOMAS (1660–1746), English dramatist, friend of Dryden (for whose plays he wrote a number of prologues and epilogues) and of Mrs. Aphra Behn, two of his plays, *The Fatal Marriage; or, the Innocent Adultery* (1694) and *Oroonoko* (1695), being based on her novels. These are both tragedies, as was his first play, *The Loyal Brother; or, the Persian Prince* (1682). These show a mingling of heroic and sentimental drama which was not without influence on the development of eighteenth-century tragedy as typified in Rowe.

Southerne was also the author of three comedies of manners which enjoyed much success when they were first produced. They contain some witty scenes, but are weak in construction and overloaded with unnecessary detail. It was on Southerne's advice that Colley Cibber's first play was produced at Drury Lane in 1696.

SOUTH STREET THEATRE, see SOUTH-WARK THEATRE.

SOUTHWARK THEATRE, PHILADELPHIA, the first permanent theatre in America. Built in 1766 by Douglass, manager of the American Company, it was a rough brick and wood structure, painted red, its stage lit by oil. From its position it was sometimes called the South Street Theatre. During its first season, which opened on 12 Nov. with *The Provoked Husband* and *Thomas and Sally*, it saw the production of *The Prince of Parthia*, the first American play to be produced professionally in America. During the War of Independence the theatre was closed, but after the departure of the British was reopened for a short time in the autumn of 1778. In 1784 the younger Hallam and John Henry, who had assumed the management of the American Company, returned to the Southwark before proceeding to New York, and the building continued to be used for theatrical purposes until in 1821 it was partly destroyed by fire. Rebuilt and used as a distillery, it was not finally demolished until 1912.

SOVIET THEATRE, see RUSSIA, 2.

SPAIN. 1. ORIGINS. The fall of Rome meant the end in Europe of a sustained dramatic tradition of any literary value, and in Spain, as in all European countries, the modern secular drama grew out of the services of the Church (see ECCLESIASTICAL DRAMA). The medieval Church had many dramatic moments—symbolic rites like the burial of the Crucifix on Good Friday and its restoration on Easter Sunday—the Byzantine liturgy, introduced into Spain in the fourth century, with its dialogued sequences and alternating choirs—the living narrative style of the Evangelists and, above all, the cycle of Church festivals, especially of Christmas and Easter. A regular part of festival celebrations was the presentation of familiar scenes from the New Testament, such as the Christmas story, the Passion and Resurrection, the raising of Lazarus, and the conversion of Paul, scenes designed to bring home to an illiterate people simple religious truths. The Roman mime and pantomime, and love of spectacle, which had prevailed in the last epoch of Roman supremacy, cannot have been altogether extinguished; and perhaps its influence may be seen in the definitely mimetic nature of early liturgical drama; as in the gestures of the 'juglar' reciting epic verse or ballads; as in the dances of the people, and in their pageants and processions on feast-days. So the pre-formal

dramatic traditions in Spain were essentially spectacular and popular. The first liturgical plays were acted entirely within the church, and only as they became more elaborate and more independent of the sacred offices did they move outside to the market-square or inn-yard.

The earliest extant play in the vernacular is a fragment of an Epiphany performance known as the *Auto* (or *Misterio*) *de los Reyes Magos.* It is a dramatic account of the visit of the Three Kings to the child Jesus, including the appearance of the star, together with Herod's anxiety, and his consultation with his wise men and rabbis. The text is interrupted, for it is only a fragment of 147 lines; but it is the earliest example of independent dramatic composition in Spanish, and is attributed to the middle of the twelfth century, although the manuscript may belong to a later date. In the three hundred years that follow this piece, evidence of dramatic activity is only indirectly obtained, but from various archives and edicts it is clear that the festivals continued to be an occasion for dramatic display, frequently accompanied by processions of great pomp. A secular tradition of crude burlesque, 'juegos de escarnio', must have existed concurrently. An important document in this respect is the *Siete Partidas* of Alfonso X promulgated in 1263:

... The clergy must not take part in 'juegos de escarnio' and if other men do, the clergy must not attend them. ... Nor ought these things to be done within the churches. ... But there are subjects which the clergy may represent such as the birth of Our Lord, and how the angel came to the shepherds and told them Christ was born ... but this should be done decently and with great devotion ... and not in small villages or unsuitable places, nor to make money thereby. ...

In 1264 the festival of Corpus Christi (on the Thursday after Trinity Sunday) was established in honour of the Holy Sacrament, and it was soon adopted as an important day in the Church's year. There was nothing in this festival to limit the thoughts of Christians to single scenes or passages of the Scriptures, and as a result Corpus Christi plays, later known as *autos sacramentales*, might deal allegorically with any subject from the Creation to the Day of Judgement. Their nature did not demand chronological so much as doctrinal exactitude, and the prevailing tone was devotional rather than historical. Corpus Christi became increasingly a municipal festival—deputies appointed by the city would take charge, and the city arms would be fixed over chosen sites. Meanwhile the Holy Sacrament was placed in the middle of the principal chapel of the Cathedral, and there the *auto* was first performed in the presence of the town council and the Cathedral Chapter. The performance was followed by divine service, mass, and a sermon, and then dancing in the place where the *auto* had been presented, until evening, when all emerged from the Cathedral and formed a procession, moving from street to street and performing the *auto* at the appointed sites. Performances varied considerably in the use of scenery and costume. Archives yield interesting details. In the early fifteenth century there is mention of an elaborate allegory, where the platform held a castle with four towers, and a centre tower with a wheel of allegorical figures. Other details are more primitive. God the Father was distinguished by his gilded face; and expenses include:

Keys for St. Peter which cost 2 reales and 18 little gilded lamps and 230 roses gilded and plated with leaves of tin to adorn the sky in which is God the Father; the gilding at 2 maravedís and for the plating, 1 maravedí.

2. RENAISSANCE. The next development in Spanish dramatic art is the work of individual poets, for with the Renaissance the age of anonymity is over. The stress is now on the literary form of drama, and on the lyrical quality of the verse. While Church festivals continued to offer popular entertainment, craftsmanship and learning were demanded by the more refined audiences of Court and cloister. To the middle of the fifteenth century belong the courtly masquerades and Nativity plays of Gómez Manrique (1412–90), and although these pieces are hardly dramatic, their elegance and polish indicate the effects of secular patronage. There were still plays wholly religious in subject and in tone, but the late fifteenth and early sixteenth centuries saw a definite move toward secularization. The profane comic element of the 'juegos de escarnio' acquired a more intellectual form in the satire and criticism of Renaissance comedy. Medieval traditions were not discarded, but while the primitive dramatists of Spain aimed at converting literary material into popular theatre, the Renaissance poets strove to give the popular theatre a literary form.

The first dramatist of this period was Juan del Encina (1468–*c.* 1537). Encina, musician, actor, and playwright in the household of the Duke of Alba, emancipated the Spanish dramatic tradition from its medieval limitations, and gave it the more general and secular orientation of the Renaissance. In his early productions, the religious outline is still insistent and sometimes exclusive, but occasionally the shepherd scenes are drawn energetically and with true, if primitive, comic spirit. In these early devotional pieces Encina reflects the trends of the Middle Ages without adding much originality except in the lyrical charm of their execution. However, a further development is soon noticeable in the *Églogas Representadas en Recüesta de Amores* (1494, 1495) or in the *Representación del Amor* (1497), where the shepherds have been promoted to the chief place, and the tone and incidents are wholly secular. A repeated theme is the transforming power of love, even on a crude and ignorant shepherd. But Encina's analysis of the symptoms of love-sickness comes nearer to the great medieval idealization of love than to the spirit of the Renaissance, which must be looked for in his later plays, written after

years in Rome, where he absorbed the Italian fashions. Then the term 'Égloga' has a greater significance, and the *Égloga de Tres Pastores*, the *Égloga de Cristino y Febea*, or the *Égloga de Plácida y Victoriano*, are good examples of a completely new and pagan treatment of the shepherd theme. Thus, within the work of Encina alone there is clearly marked the rapid advance of dramatic form, from the simple shepherd incidents of Nativity and other festival plays to a completely secular outlook, which is, in its turn, transformed by the spirit of the Italian Renaissance.

A significant product of this period is the *Tragicomedia de Calisto y Melibea*, published in 1499, and attributed to Fernando de Rojas. It is really a novel in dramatic form and can never have been staged; but it is the first work in which truly life-size characters are portrayed. One of them, the evil old woman go-between, La Celestina, has achieved general acknowledgement as a character of independent life, becoming a traditional type, not merely in literary conventions, but in popular speech.

The development initiated by Encina was consolidated by the work of his later contemporaries, Lucas Fernández, Torres Naharro, and Gil Vicente.

Lucas Fernández (*c.* 1474–1542) was not so fully imbued with the Renaissance spirit as Encina, and his greatest work is a religious Easter play, the *Auto de la Pasión*, which was performed on Good Friday by the clergy in Salamanca Cathedral. It is an ambitious play, combining Old and New Testament figures for symbolic value. The scene of Christ's suffering is deliberately evoked by description and narrative rather than by direct representation, and the general effect is one of powerful rhetoric and almost cruel intensity. The graphic narration of suffering is interrupted by exclamations of grief and, with a keen and skilful artistic sense, the poet obtains all the emotional effect possible out of the situation. At the culminating point the stage directions require an *Eccehomo* to appear on high, 'to provoke the people to devotion'. The expression of grief then reaches its height, and when words can go no further, the play resumes with the organ and a well-known devotional hymn: 'O crux, ave, spes unica.'

Bartolomé de Torres Naharro (*c.* 1480–*c.* 1530) was the first dramatic critic in Spain. Little is known of his life; but most of his dramatic compositions were produced in Rome, and show Italian influence. He distinguishes between two types of comedy: comedy of manners and romantic comedy, and in his volume of plays, the *Propalladia*, he gives examples of both types. They are full length, with a fairly complex plot. His comedies of manners portray a great variety of stock characters, and are often full of satire and cynical criticism of social conditions. On the other hand, his romantic comedies are based on the conflict of love and honour, and so anticipate the *comedias* of Lope de Vega. His *gracioso* shows an interesting development of the Spanish theatre at this time, corresponding to the fool on the Elizabethan stage. His humble rank exempts him from the cult of chivalrous honour, and his remarks, apart from giving comic relief, are frequently a commentary on the play, sometimes in the form of burlesque, sometimes as a reminder of practical wisdom. If Torres Naharro is, as claimed, the originator of the *gracioso*, it is only because he gave artistic and dramatic justification to an already popular figure. The stage technique of Naharro's plays is comparatively primitive, as is evident from the devices he is obliged to use to convey the narrative clearly. For example, most of his sketches are preceded by an *introito*, or prologue, which concludes in every case with a fairly detailed summary of the plot. Lope de Vega would have considered this most undramatic, destroying dramatic suspense, but in Naharro it is essential because dramatic art had not advanced far enough to present a series of scenes that would be intelligible to an audience without explanation. Some of his plays require a street scene (for example *La Himenea*) and it is quite probable that they were staged in the Italian setting of converging streets, making use of the balcony and street doors of the foremost houses.

Gil Vicente (*c.* 1465–*c.* 1539) is perhaps the most prominent of these early dramatists. He was Portuguese by birth and wrote chiefly for the Portuguese Court, but several of his plays are in Spanish. They show an increasing maturity in dramatic composition. Their scope is considerably widened, and includes comic scenes from everyday life, as well as national, chivalresque, pastoral, or allegorical themes. One of his most famous works is the *Trilogís de las Barcas*, a series of three allegorical plays, only one of which is in Spanish. The allegorical element lies in the outline, the three vessels of Death, destined to carry passengers to Hell, to Purgatory, and to Glory. The selection of the passengers offers Vicente an opportunity for humanist satire, and the potentialities of the theme are obvious. Vicente handles a chivalresque subject with equal interest, as for example in his dramatized version of *Amadís de Gaula*. Like Encina, the texture of his work is essentially lyrical and his *autos* contain many fine songs and lullabies. Vicente's art is deliberate and courtly, but he incorporates into his verse the rhythms and refrains of popular poetry.

The best drama of the early sixteenth century was produced mainly for private entertainment, and so its chief contribution to the public stage was to shape literary convention. Encina gave to popular drama the independent status of art, and by experiment in material and form his immediate successors consolidated his lead. Already many features distinguished the Spanish style. The custom of presenting more than one play in a single performance made less natural the strict division of tragedy and comedy and encouraged the short topical sketch, the *entremés*, which generally accompanied a full-length play. The scenes of comic relief in Encina's plays are developed into

independent *pasos*, or comic interludes, and later are isolated into a separate genre, the *sainete*. From the earliest days drama was closely associated with music. Incidental songs and occasionally whole plays had musical settings. Some of Encina's scores are still on record, and the custom persisted in the seventeenth-century *zarzuela*.

A significant trait is the absence of so-called realism as an ultimate criterion. The audience is not always needing to be convinced of actuality; but convention plays a large part in this theatre. The dramatist is expected to give a stylized version of nature. Observation accommodates itself to artistic imagination. In the same way, events do not speak for themselves, but are given full artistic expression, a relief for the author and for the audience, and no doubt one way of ensuring the right response. This tendency affects even the style of acting, and from the beginning Spanish drama required a rhetorical rather than 'psychological' manner.

The early part of the sixteenth century had been a time of general dramatic activity. The religious drama still flourished and a number of anonymous *autos* of this period survive, together with those of known writers, amongst them the *Cain y Abel* of Jaime Ferrúz, and *La Vida de Santa Orocia* by Bartolomé Paláu, which dramatizes the legendary fate of Don Rodrigo, the last of the Gothic kings in Spain; then there is the Old Testament story of Joseph, *La Tragedia Josefina*, of Micael de Carvajal; parallel with these original compositions runs a spate of translations, free versions, and imitations of Greek and Latin masterpieces, made by the scholars and humanists of the day, which had very little influence on the development of popular drama. Hernán Pérez de la Oliva (1492–1531), Rector of the University of Salamanca, made free translations of Sophocles, Euripides, and Plautus. Pedro Simón Abril (1530–90) translated Terence. Among the many imitations were the three verse tragedies of the lyric poet Lupercio Leonardo de Argensola (1562–1613), *Isabela*, *Filis*, and *Alejandra*. Efforts were also made to adapt the classic formula to national subjects. The most important of these tentatives was that of a Portuguese poet, Antonio de Ferreira (1528–69), whose *Doña Inés de Castro* was translated into Spanish and adapted as two plays by Fray Jerónimo Bermudez (*c.* 1530–99).

*3. THE ESTABLISHMENT OF THE PROFESSIONAL THEATRE. During this period, however, there were no permanent public theatres. Lope de Rueda (1510–65) was Spain's first professional actor-manager, and he travelled with his company from one town to another, performing his own plays by daylight in the market-place or inn-yard. Naturally his stage equipment and technique were of the simplest, and in his plays he developed most successfully the realistic comic vein of Torres Naharro and popular tradition. Cervantes as a young man was present at one of his performances given in the square before the cathedral of Segovia, and always retained a vivid impression of it. In the Prologue to his own plays he has left a description of a travelling company of his youth:

Their whole baggage would go into a single sack and consisted of four white sheepskins ornamented with gilt leather, four beards and wigs, and four crooks. . . . The stage was formed of four benches set square with four or six planks on them, the whole rising two feet above the ground. . . . An old blanket moving two ways on cords was the adornment of the theatre . . . and behind it unaccompanied musicians sang some old ballad. . . .

Rueda's greatest strength lies in his use of popular speech and incident, and his most important contribution to dramatic tradition is the prose *paso*, or short comic sketch, rather than the Italianate *comedia* with its elaborate intrigue and character study. Some of his *pasos* have become proverbial; for instance *Las Aceitunas*, where a man and his wife quarrel over the price they will ask for olives that are not yet planted. These scenes have a simple dramatic point, and a definite popular appeal. Addressed to the public, they are conditioned by their audience and in this way show a movement towards a national drama.

By far the best description of the life of a travelling company in the early days of the Spanish theatre was written by one of Rueda's actors, Agustín de Rojas, in his *El Viaje Entretenido* (1630). He describes the various companies which pass through the villages, from the *bululú*, or single player on foot, who recites various pieces in a narrative rather than dramatic manner, to the *cambaleo*, or company of five men and one woman, 'with luggage that could be carried by a spider'; or better still, the *bojiganga*, which comprised six or seven men, two women, and a boy, and—highest point of all—the *compañía* of thirty players, a carriage, and a large wardrobe. Evidently the extent of the repertory was in relation to the size of the company.

By the end of the sixteenth century there were permanent theatres established in Seville, Valencia, and Madrid. The development in Madrid may perhaps be taken as representative. In 1560 Madrid had become the official capital of Spain, and with the growth of the city it was necessary to find some fixed place for the players to perform. Appointment and control of such places were granted to certain charitable institutions, or '*cofradías*', in order that they might absorb the profit. There were at first some five *corrales* of the primitive type, really nothing more than the yards of houses, open to the air. The stage was at the rear, and the general audience would stand in the yard or *patio*. More distinguished spectators looked on from the windows and balconies of the surrounding houses. There was originally no roof to stage or *patio* and performances were quite likely to be interrupted by rain. In 1574 an Italian company visiting the *Corral de la Pacheca* and unwilling to suffer loss through rainy weather built a roof over the stage and part of the yard, leaving an awning for the rest. Later, in 1582, a building arose on the site of the old *corral*, renamed the *Corral del Príncipe*. It was modelled on another theatre of Madrid, the *Corral de la Cruz*, which had been built in 1579, retaining the traditional features of the open-air theatre. The balconies became boxes, or *palcos*. The groundlings still stood, but some rising seats, or *gradas*, for men only were placed behind them, and behind that again a special gallery for women, called the *cazuela*. The stage was a platform stage jutting out into the audience. Behind the backcloth or *manta* was the green room, the *vestuario*. The building was probably roofed, and when a proscenium arch was later introduced a drop curtain was added, and painted scenery, long confined to the Court theatre, made its appearance. By 1587 the *Corral del Príncipe* and the *Corral de la Cruz* had ousted all the other public theatres in Madrid.

In the early days performances had been limited to Sundays and feast-days; with the growing demand for popular entertainment two representations were authorized during the week, generally on Tuesdays and Thursdays. The afternoon was the regular time for performances. An interesting document of this time, compiled to assess the rent, shows the annual number of performances to be only 198, allowance made for

46 days of Lent, 77 days of summer, 34 Saturdays and 10 days for the making of scenery, St. James's and St. Sebastian's days, and because of the small number of spectators and the rain.

The programme was not limited to a single play, but included short comic pieces, musical interludes, ballads, and dances of a popular nature. This variety is in line with tradition, for a precedent may be found for it in the early festival celebrations.

Music was always an important feature and the public theatres replaced the national *vihuela* with a small orchestra of five violins, which later increased under the influence of opera. Scenic effects and properties were very simple. When a change of scene was required by the plot, it was either implied in the text and left to the imagination of the audience, or else sketchily indicated by drawing the curtain from the recess at the back of the stage, where the clues to the new scene would be displayed. A favourite device was the miraculous appearance of an angel, let down by a *tramoya*, or of a devil shooting up through a trap door, or *escotillón*. On the whole, however, the use of scenery and effects at this stage depended not on art, but on circumstances, or on the producer's resources. The use of costume is interesting, since stage directions show that nationality, rank, or profession were indicated by it, and in Lope de Vega's plays costume supplements scenery to some extent. However, a visitor to Madrid complained that Greeks and Romans on the Spanish stage wore Spanish costume. This is comparable perhaps to modern performances of *Hamlet* or *Macbeth* where conventional Elizabethan styles are used regardless of the historical setting. The Spanish costume was in fact a conventional style of the theatre, and not the contemporary fashion of Spain.

The establishment of public theatres assisted the movement towards a national drama. In Seville, the most important transitional dramatist was Juan de la Cueva (1550–1610). With other heroic subjects, Cueva introduced on to the stage familiar episodes of national history and legend. Tales of the Cid, of the seven princes of Lara, of the defence of Spain against Charlemagne, familiar to the people in epic or ballad form, were dramatized and given new circulation. In this particular respect Cueva prepared the way for Lope de Vega; but his dramatic technique is still clumsy. He does not handle his material dramatically, but action filters through narrative. In his versification also he experiments, combining traditional and Italian elements. Other important figures were Juan de Timoneda, bookseller, publisher, and author, whose long life stretched across the entire sixteenth century, and his younger contemporaries, Andrés Rey de Artieda (1549–1613), author of Los Amantes de Teruel, (a play based on a popular Spanish legend and later treated by Tirso de Molina, Pérez de Montalván, and Eugenio Hartzenbusch); and Cristobal de Virués (1550–1609), author of five tragedies on classic lines, of which Elisa Dido is the best.

Barely confined within this period is Miguel de Cervantes (1547–1616), author of Don Quixote, who also contributed considerably to the theatre. He drew on his own experiences for some of his plays, notably El Trato de Argel, reminiscent of his captivity in Algiers, and his work includes comedies, interludes, and one tragedy, El Cerco de Numancia, which was revived in 1937. His dialogue was easy and natural, and he was as far removed from the pedantry of the pseudo-classicists as from the licence and buffoonery of more popular entertainers. His interludes contain some of his best dramatic work. He was not, however, altogether successful in his approach to the theatre, and no one, not even Cervantes, could stand up against the overwhelming success of Lope de Vega, who for more than fifty years filled the Spanish theatres to overflowing.

4. THE GOLDEN AGE. Lope Félix de Vega Carpio (1562–1635) was the acknowledged prince and potentate of the Spanish theatre in the Golden Age. He found the theatre in its infancy, and by the imprint of his personality imposed on it a direction and a form which are essentially characteristic. He left a massive accumulation of plays, but although he wrote more than any of his contemporaries or successors, he also repeated himself less. Invention was clearly his supreme gift. He drew his subjects from the Bible, from mythology, hagiography, history, chronicle, medieval romance, from ballads, legends, and song, and interspersed his rapid fluent verse with music and dancing. The whole world was his province and he pillaged it with both hands. His work is so varied, and his style so enigmatic, that it is impossible to select any plays by him

as typical, and they all evade classification. It is significant that later dramatists always found in Lope material which repaid further development. They might do much with him, developing an idea or a scene, but the development itself is not in Lope, and is foreign to his nature, for he proceeds by experiment. His work is a series of discoveries, each of which he rapidly tires of, and he does not probe into questions he would rather avoid. Action is stimulating, and replaces argument and abstraction. Lope's plays are scraps of dramatic excitement. They have no consistent orientation, no continuity. In this way, his Arte nuevo de hacer comedias is disappointing, for he was neither a partisan nor the leader of a school. He discovered that action could be successfully portrayed on the stage, and with this formula ready to hand, and an accurate knowledge of popular taste, his production was almost mechanical. It may even be said that the public helped to write Lope's plays.

Many other dramatists continued on the lines suggested by Lope. Among the Valencian group was Guillén de Castro y Bellvís (1569–1631), who is remembered particularly for his Las mocedades del Cid, two plays on the life and exploits of Rodrigo Díaz, the traditional Spanish hero. Castro includes almost every episode of the great Cid legend, so that occasionally passages are merely ballad-sequences; but on the whole his dramatic productions have a certain vigour and originality and, like Lope, he provided later writers with material for major dramatic triumphs: for example Corneille's Le Cid and Moreto's El Lindo Don Diego.

The most outstanding Andalusians of this period were Antonio Mira de Amescua (1574–1644), whose best play, El Esclavo del Demonio, was later freely drawn on by Calderón, and Luis Vélez de Guevara (1579–1644), author of the picaresque novel, El Diablo Cojuelo, on which Le Sage based his Le Diable Boiteux, as well as of a fine play on Inés de Castro, Reinar después de morir, a subject he treated with lyric and dramatic power. Lope's admirer and biographer, Juan Pérez de Montalván, also wrote a number of plays, historical and religious, and some of romantic intrigue. A younger man, whose best work was done before the death of Lope, was Luis Quiñones de Benevente (? –1652). He was a writer of entremeses, witty and vivid sketches of contemporary life and manners, and diverted every sort of audience by his adroit handling of the smaller types of farce, such as the loa and the sainete. Benevente was the heir of Rueda and Cervantes, and the real ancestor of Ramón de la Cruz and the Quintero brothers.

Among all the dramatists of this time, two alone are generally conceded worthy to rank with Lope—Tirso de Molina and Alarcón. Tirso (or Fray Gabriel Téllez, 1584–1648) was an enthusiastic follower of Lope. He shares his inventiveness and erratic powers of execution, and his great plays are effective pieces of impressionistic composition. Contrasting scenes are held together by a powerful idea or dramatic climax rather than by a formal co-ordination. His penetration into motive and emotion gives his characters individuality and life, and his version of the Don Juan type in *El Burlador de Sevilla* has not been surpassed.

On the other hand the work of Juan Ruíz de Alarcón y Mendoza (*c.* 1581–1639) indicates a movement away from this free and imaginative style of composition. In his early plays he puts most emphasis on the intrigue in its mechanical aspects, and even in his later and more mature work, where he handles a social or ethical theme, there is a characteristic organization and economy. In Alarcón the use of comedy is deliberate, and manipulated to enforce a very personal point of view.

With regard to the actual staging of these plays, the school of Lope de Vega relied very little on stage machinery or effects. The scene shifts constantly, and every play is full of movement, but the audience responds imaginatively to the text, and does not demand visual assistance. In the same way, what is required of an actor is eloquence and animation, and the popularity of the *dama* and the *galán* tended to develop somewhat stereotyped leading roles at the expense of the rest of the company. In May 1598 Philip II had shut the theatres for two years, but they opened again under Philip III. During the lifetime of Lope de Vega Madrid had, besides its two main public theatres and the Court theatres of El Buen Retiro and Aranjuez, several smaller ones, and a multitude of actors. The most famous actor of this time was Rios y Pinedo, while Damien Arias de Penafiel first acted many of the chief roles in the plays of the Golden Age. Jerónimo Velásquez, though probably not an actor himself, was manager of the company which gave Lope de Vega's first plays, and father of Elena, who, though already married to an actor, deserted him to become the mistress of Lope, and the Filís of his lyrics.

Among the famous actresses of the seventeenth century were María Calderón, who had a son by Philip IV (the second Don John of Austria); Antonia Granados, known as the divine Antandra, who married a nobleman, Don Pedro de Castro, and founded a family of actors; Mariana Vaca, wife and mother of actors; Micaela Fernández, who in defiance of regulations appeared on the stage in man's clothes, a popular feature of many plays throughout Spanish drama; Francisca Bezona, who appeared before Philip IV of Spain, Louis XIV of France, and Charles II ot England; and finally Manuela Escamilla, singer, dancer, and actress, who was on the stage at the age of seven. Of the men the chief were Alonso de Olmedo, a man of good family who became an actor because he fell in love with an actress, and toured Spain with his own company; Fernán López, who died on the stage; and Ortiz, Avendano, Roque de Figueroa, Jacinto de Barrios, and Heredia, who are all noted as having acted in the plays of Tirso de Molina.

The next development in the history of Spanish drama is to be found in the work of Pedro Calderón de la Barca (1600–81). He was sufficiently distant from Lope de Vega to recast his formula, and exploit the resources of the stage in his own way. Superficially there are many similarities between Lope and Calderón, the movement and excitement of the plot, the lyrical eloquence, the exacting *pundonor*, or 'point of honour'; but instead of Lope's careless prodigality and conventional treatment, Calderón's approach is essentially artistic, and shows a marked affinity to the baroque style prevalent at the time in the plastic arts and architecture. The baroque is perhaps the final expression of the Spanish Golden Age. It includes the great cathedrals, Seville, Santiago de Compostela, together with the baroque painters (El Greco, for example), and gongorism in poetry. In Calderón this baroque style is expressed in the energy and abruptness of the transitions of the plot. Just as in architecture smooth contours, arches, straight lines, were interrupted to intensify the feeling of movement, so in Calderón's plays the plot is disrupted in order to preserve the effect of force and energy. There is an extreme superficial excitement although the basic idea is sober enough, and simple. For Calderón's drama is an artistic exposition of Catholic dogma, and in several plays it is possible to conceive of the action as demonstrating a syllogism. The language is highly rhetorical, figures ascend and descend, a dark, wild, and uncultivated scene fades into a brilliant palace interior, a typical chiaroscuro effect. Certain characters are given more attention than others. This law of subordination to the main theme is essentially baroque, indicating an attention to design and perspective exemplified more concretely in the peculiar type of scenic effect in which Calderón indulged—tiers of scenery arranged symmetrically with especial emphasis on perspective. In *La vida es sueño*, for example, the foremost wings of scenery draw aside to reveal the setting of the next scene. Stagecraft and music had advanced very quickly in Calderón's time, and he was prompt to make use of every new device, in association with Cosmo Lotti, the famous stage engineer. His comedy *Casa con dos puertas mala es de guardar* turns on a mechanical feature—the two entries to the stage by which the characters appear and disappear to their mutual embarrassment. An interesting development in Calderón's stagecraft is found in his *comedias palaciegas*, comedies given in the palace gardens, with a combination of real and artificial scenery. Among Calderón's finest productions are his *autos sacramentales*. They continued a long tradition of religious drama, becoming almost the last word on the subject. The genre was peculiarly suited to Calderón's powers, to his synthetic, intellectual, and dogmatic view of life, and its symbolic character was most easily expressed by his stage technique.

Francisco de Rojas Zorrilla (1607–48) was a dramatist of great powers whose work was influenced by Calderón. Both in comic and in tragic themes he reveals energy and understanding of character, and his solution to familiar situations is by no means conventional. Like Calderón he pays careful attention to the staging, and by the use of circumstantial detail gains a powerful comic effect. In this respect he resembles Agustín Moreto y Cabaña (1618–69). With delicate wit and a fine sense of caricature, Moreto lays the comic stress on contemporary manners and customs, on the social contacts and relations of men and women, a stress more in sympathy with the neo-classicism of France than with the traditions of Spain.

Around Calderón, Rojas, and Moreto are grouped a vast number of minor playwrights, all contributing to the general traffic of the stage at that time. One or two plays are worthy of mention: *El Pastelero de Madrigal* by Jerónimo de Cuellar (? –*c.* 1666), a play on the pastry-cook who tried to supplant the King of Portugal; *El Conde de Essex* or *Dar vida por su dama* by Antonio Cuello y Ochoa (1611–82), a theme taken from English history; and *La piedra filosofal* by Francis Antonio de Bances Candamo (1662–1704), which follows the philosophic-mythological style of Calderón, being a successful imitation of *La vida es sueño*. Juan Bautista Diamante (1625–87) is an interesting study in reciprocal influence, for he is indebted to Corneille's *Le Cid*, itself based on Guillén de Castro's play, for his *Honrador de su padre*, one of the first plays in which can be traced the French influence in Spain, soon to become so preponderant.

5. EIGHTEENTH CENTURY. It was during the next century, with the accession of a Bourbon to the Spanish throne, that the French influence was really insistent, imposing upon native genius the formulated rules and rigidity of a foreign tradition. The great Spanish dramatists were tried in the balance of the neo-classicists, and found wanting. Their plays were forgotten or derided, while feeble imitations of French masterpieces occupied the stage. One of the first Court festivities, after the accession of Philip V, grandson of Louis XIV, was a Spanish translation of a play by Corneille. In 1713 a Spanish Academy was founded on the lines of the French Academy. Contemporary critics explained the advantages of the French approach, and Lope de Vega stood self-condemned by his boast that he 'shut the Unities under lock and key, before he began to write'; Luzán's *Poética*, published in 1737, was the manifesto of the new régime. In it he attempts to bring Spanish art under the control of 'those precepts which are observed among polished nations'. He was obsessed by the idea that the Spanish genius needed restraint. This age of arbitrary theorizing was, however, remarkably unproductive. Two inferior authors alone are worth recording in the first part of the century, Antonio de Zamora (1664–1728) and José de Canizares (1676–1750). Zamora, whose work includes a version of the Don Juan legend,

No hay plazo que no se cumpla y Convidado de piedra, had a certain realistic vigour, but Canizares was far inferior, tending to clumsy burlesque. One result of this unproductivity was the increasing vogue for opera. The Court, bored with frigid copies of French classics forced on them by the assiduity of the Conde de Aranda and his circle, turned more and more to Italian opera, brought into Spain by Isabel Farnese, the second wife of Philip V. The traditional theatre architecture of Spain, based on the *corral*, had already been abandoned as far back as 1708, when the director of an Italian company had built a new theatre, the *Caños del Peral*, on French and Italian lines. Now the old *Corrales* of *la Cruz* and *el Príncipe* were also rebuilt, and the Court theatre of *El Buen Retiro*, which had so often seen the triumphs of Calderón, was decorated with all the luxury and contrivances of the new 'machine-theatre' by Farinelli, summoned to Spain by Fernando VI. In 1765 the *autos*, last relics of the old Spanish drama, were finally forbidden. María Ladvenant (1741–67), an actress of the time, played the part of the Madonna in the last production of an *auto*. The way was clear for the neo-classicists. Yet, strangely enough, translations of French plays and imitations of them by such writers as Nicolás Fernández de Moratín (the elder) (1737–80), José Cadalso (1741–82), and Tomás de Iriarte (1750–91), though favoured by the purveyors of Court amusement and supported by the critics, achieved no success. One play alone, *La Raquel* (1778), by Vicente García de la Huerta (1734–87), deserves mention. While conforming to the Unities it took its subject from an old play by Amescua, and is the one successful result of a blending of such diverse elements.

In the general poverty of the time, one native talent alone stands out—that of Ramón de la Cruz (1731–94). His short farces, none lasting longer than a quarter of an hour, depicted the daily life of the Madrid populace, and had an immediate and well-merited success; their humour, observation, and lively dialogue recall the *pasos* of Lope de Rueda. Ramón de la Cruz was also author of some amusing parodies on the prevailing taste for tragedy.

For a long time the only form in which the public knew and could assess their national drama was in the *refundiciones*, or remodelled versions, by writers like Candido María Trigueros and Dionisio Solís. For contemporary amusement they turned to the worthless comedies of Luciano Francisco Comella (1751–1812), which so aroused the scorn of Leandro Fernández de Moratín the younger (1760–1828) that he satirized them mercilessly in his *El Café* or *La Comedia Nueva* (1792). Moratín observes the Unities; he keeps to a strict economy of form and his admiration for Molière is quite evident; but his plays have a certain sincerity of emotion and observation that lends them independent value. He gives to the neo-classic formula a characteristic development, by combining native and imported elements in just proportions. *El Sí de las Niñas* (1806) is the best example of his style. His *El Barón* (1803) was the occasion of a riotous evening in the theatre. Antonio Pinto, actor and friend of Moratín, together with Ponce, Querol, and María Ribera, was acting in Moratín's play when it was howled down. He insisted on performing it again the next day, and it was an immediate success. Two other actresses of this period were Rosalia Fernández (?-1803), more popularly known as La Tirana, an actress of great tragic power, and her rival Maria Antonia Vallejo, or La Caramba.

An interesting feature of Moratín's work is that in spite of his neo-classical form his interpretation of comedy is somewhat romantic. In his hands comedy no longer implies the vigilance of an objective criterion, the classical norm of behaviour, or social propriety. Most of his plays illustrate a moral, but the moral is perhaps determined more by sentiment than by satire.

6. NINETEENTH CENTURY. The nineteenth century saw the development of the Romantic Revival. As a literary movement it was not destined to have a long life, but it was important dramatically, as it re-established the prestige of the dramatists of the Golden Age, and restored continuity to Spanish dramatic tradition. The first signs of Romanticism may be seen in the work of Francisco Martínez de la Rosa (1787-1862). His early work is in the neo-classic style, and the sentimental, moral tone of his comedies is taken directly from Moratín, but his *Conjuración de Venecia* (1834) has all the features of Romanticism. It was followed a few months later by the romantic tragedy, *Macías*, by Mariano José de Larra (1809-37), and in 1835 by the *Don Alvaro, o la fuerza del sino* of Ángel Saavedra, el Duque de Rivas (1791-1865). Other works appeared in the same vein: *Los Amantes de Teruel*, an energetic version of an old theme by Juan Eugenio Hartzenbusch (1806-80), and the plays of Antonio García Gutiérrez (1812-84) and of Gil y Zárate (1796-1861); but *Don Álvaro* is considered to be the most complete example in Spanish dramatic literature of the Romantic mood, a mood to which the general character of the Spanish style is unsympathetic. It is the more lyrical, antiquarian, picturesque side of Romanticism that was most thoroughly adopted in Spain, as in the plays of José Zorrilla y Moral (1817-93). Zorrilla turns to the early ballads and legends for his material, as for example in his *El Zapatero y el Rey* and *El puñal del godo*, or in his rehandling of the Don Juan story in *Don Juan Tenorio*, his major success. The end of the Romantic movement is perhaps best indicated in the work of Manuel Bretón de los Herreros (1796-1873), in whose plays the sentimental tradition of Moratín is replaced by satire and realism. *Marcela, o ¿cual de los tres?* (1831) is a simple comedy with a variety of types and picturesque detail. Among his contemporaries were Ventura de la Vega (1807-65) and Rodríguez Rubí (1817-90).

The increased popularity of the *zarzuela*, which seemed at times to overshadow the whole theatre, together with the vogue of the *teatro por horas* (see GÉNERO CHICO), led to a narrowing of interests in the serious theatre, and the Romantic drama was followed by a transitional period which inclined towards a non-lyrical treatment of contemporary subjects. The main dramatists of this period were Manuel Tamayo y Baus (1829-98), Luis de Eguilaz (1830-74), and Adelardo López de Ayala (1828-79). Tamayo y Baus came from a family of actors, and his plays show some skill in handling the resources of the stage. In character they generally follow the lines of Moratín, and frequently illustrate a moral or sentiment, as in *Lo Positivo* (1862). His most ambitious play is perhaps *Un drama nuevo* (1837), built around the character of Shakespeare's Yorick, and requiring dramatic staging of a play within a play. Eguilaz, who was more prolific but less profound than Tamayo, wrote historical dramas on literary themes, and comedies of contemporary manners; while Ayala's successful drama shares many of the characteristics of Tamayo's. His most important plays are *El tanto por ciento* (1861) and *Consuelo* (1878).

From the theatrical point of view, however, the most important dramatist of this period was undoubtedly José Echegaray (1832-1916), who was awarded the Nobel Prize for Literature in 1904. He was an engineer by profession, and made use of every theatrical device for dramatic effect; for example, of dimly lit scenes to create an atmosphere of sinister and emotional power. For his plot he chooses the moment of climax in a difficult situation, and does not unfold character through the emotional reactions of dialogue, but forces a solution, or a choice of alternatives. His language and elaborate staging are highly artificial, so that the character of his work approaches that of melodrama. His best plays were composed with a definite actor or actress in mind; *O locura o santidad* (1877), *El gran Galeoto* (1881), and many others were written for Antonio Vico, Rafael and Ricardo Calvo, Elisa Boldun, or Elisa Mendoza Tenorio, all outstanding players of the time.

Among the immediate disciples of Echegaray may be mentioned Eugenio Sellés (1844-1926), author of the triangle drama, *El nudo gordiano* (1878), and Leopoldo Cano (1844-1934). The work of Benito Pérez Galdós (1843-1920) is important not so much for its dramatic quality as for its gradual unfolding of character, and its insistent realism. Enrico Gaspar (1842-1902) wrote a number of realistic thesis-plays which proved successful, and the working-class tragedy, *Juan José*, by Joaquín Dicenta (1863-1917), belongs to this school. Ángel Guimerá (1847-1924), author of *Terra baixa* (1897), and Feliú y Codina (1847-97), author of *La Dolores* (1892), also deserve mention.

7. THE MODERN PERIOD. The greatest name in the contemporary Spanish theatre is undoubtedly Jacinto Benavente (1866-   ). He brought to his playwriting a vast knowledge of

contemporary European drama, and his remarkable versatility, his observation and philosophical overtones, created a many-sided drama, mingling realism and romanticism, cynicism and kindliness. In his successors, Gregorio Martínez Sierra (1881–1947) and the Quintero brothers, the kindliness predominates. The religious note in Martínez Sierra's plays is a reminder of the long history of religious drama in Spain, while the gentle humour of the Quintero brothers has been much appreciated in England and America. The sterner thesis-plays of Manuel Linares Rivas (1867–) have proved popular in Spain; while experiments in poetic drama, sometimes epic or historical in theme, have found an able exponent in Eduardo Marquina (1879–). The contemporary Spanish theatre has also been deeply influenced by the philosophy of Miguel de Unamuno (1864–1937), and by the 'generation of '98', including the literary plays of Ramón María de Valle-Inclán (1869–). A tendency of this 'generation', inspired by the final loss to the *patria* of her colonies, is to turn to the history and character of Spain, and seek to interpret *lo español*. This is perhaps the explanation of the *modernismo* of twentieth-century Spanish drama, with its folk-lore motifs given intellectual significance, as for example in the lyrical drama of Federico García Lorca (1898–1936) or of Rafael Alberti (1903–).

So ends for the moment this summary of a rich and varied theatre. In the Golden Age it found its most original and independent expression, assuming then a national individuality, and now, after years of submission to various foreign influences and ideals, it seems to be moving once more towards its native orientation.

SPANISH-AMERICAN THEATRE, see SOUTH AMERICA, I.

SPECTACLE THEATRES, the name given to the lavish theatres and opera houses of early Italy. The first was built in about 1486 at Ferrara by the d'Este family, but the three most famous examples are the Teatro Olimpico of Vicenza, the Court theatre at Sabbionetta, and the Teatro Farnese at Parma. The first was begun by Palladio in 1579, and was modelled strictly on Vitruvius. It was finished by his pupil Scamozzi, who also built the theatre at Sabbionetta, which was intended for intimate drama and held only 250 people. The Teatro Farnese, built by Aleotti, was a superb edifice, holding 3,500 people. All these theatres were sumptuously decorated inside, and had finely equipped stages which could deal with the most elaborate settings and machinery (see also ACOUSTICS, ARCHITECTURE, LIGHTING, MACHINERY, and SCENERY).

SPECTATORY, see AUDITORIUM.

SPEECH. The appeal of drama is both visual and auditive. Its sound-element, like that of poetry, consists of significant words, both logical and emotional in their appeal. Speech may be considered the most vital element in drama, and the actor's speech is the chief factor in expressing the dramatist's conception of character, particularly in the absence of stage directions, an innovation not generally employed until the first half of the nineteenth century. The dramatist's lines must reach our ear with the exact shade of intonation, of emphasis, and of phrasing required by him. His dialogue and spoken descriptions must convey all we need to know of the two elements of dramatic conflict, character, and circumstance.

Speech times the action of a play, and must be timed to suit that action. It is the principal factor in establishing the illusion of time. The author writes the play, but is dependent on those who are trained as actors, and who are the living medium of its representation, for its presentation to the public. The dramatist may, like Shakespeare, have left no stage directions but those implicit in the text, or, like Shaw, he may have left a continuous commentary in the form of directions which make his plays as readable as a novel. In either case the actor must mould his speech to the action, and time his action to the speech, as a dancer moulds himself to the rhythm of his dance music.

The history of dramatic representation makes this clear. Greek drama originated in a ritual-dance, set to choric words. Its earliest form was a narrative commentary on the dance action. The first great progressive step was the introduction of dialogue, probably antiphonal in character, between the chorus and an actor. In comedy this took a more impromptu and jesting form. The distinction between choric and dramatic delivery may not at first have been clearly marked. Choral lyrics were in the nature of chanted odes illustrated by vivid ritual and mimetic action. There were a number of lyric forms, each with their prescribed ritual character, the very perfection of their traditional form giving significant variety to the scheme of choric action in each different play. The need to blend, and also to contrast, with this ritual measure necessitated a contrasting uniformity in the dramatic passages. This was at first marked by long soliloquy or narrative passages. But with the advent, under Aeschylus, of the second actor, dialogue proper begins, and contrasted character plays its part. Though the outward curve of the forehead in the actor's mask may have helped audibility, yet the huge theatres of Athens or of Epidaurus imposed a measured delivery, orchestral and lyric in character.

It is interesting to note that the site chosen and the construction of the Greek theatre gave almost perfect acoustics. The seats rose from the orchestra tier after tier to a huge wall of rock; the actor, standing below, at the central point of the orchestra, or dancing-floor, or against the sounding-board of the wall that hid the *skênê* or dressing pavilion, can, even in the ruined theatres left us to-day, make every word audible while his speech maintains its rhythmic character. We know that the Greek audiences were most critical of rhythm and stress, as in the French theatre of 1900.

As we pass from *Prometheus* to the *Oresteia* and on to the Tauric Iphigenia of Euripides, we see clearly the steady growth in characterization as the actors gained in power of execution, and as the audience demanded a greater reality in the acting. The action develops through the dialogue, and the contrasting character of speech in each person is shown by choice of words, and by the vivid cut-and-thrust of the dialogue. All that was at one time implied by the term 'classic' is foreign to the wild incoherent cries of the Furies, though they never lose their rhythmic pattern, or to the poignant suspense and change of mood in the recognition of Orestes, and the flight of the brother and sister from Thoas' vengeance. Every tradition and comment which has come down to us points to a high, even unique, standard of speech in the Greek theatre. Action, in our sense of the word, was very limited for the tragic actor; the chorus was the orchestration of the play. Without programmes or books of the words, audibility and intelligibility must have demanded unending study. This is stressed by the comparative rarity of the dramatic festivals, and the high estimation in which great interpreters of drama were held.

All this goes to prove that the two great arts of speech and of plastic rhythm in movement must have transcended any modern achievement. It implies a harmony of author and executant, and demands the technical skill of perfect verse-writing and of diction which is as definite and finished as a musical performance. (See also ACOUSTICS and GREECE.)

To come to modern times, Italian drama was essentially a 'mime' drama, that is, a drama of gesture and action in which only stock characters were employed. The Latin tradition of the Renaissance produced certain splendid plots, but character, and therefore speech, had no free play. Poetry took over the task, and the glorious enrichment of our mother tongue, which culminated in the Authorized Version of the Bible (1611), prepared the way for the miracle of speech which we call Elizabethan drama. The discovery by Marlowe of the perfect vehicle for dramatic speech—blank verse —was the result of many earlier lyric experiments, and of the revival of classical learning. In blank verse we have a line where every verse stress is a sense stress. The stresses must recur at regular intervals of time, but they may be divided by a varying number of unstressed syllables, and the number of the stresses themselves may vary from line to line. The manner of writing, and speaking, this great metric unit varies with every shade of character. Compare Rosalind's 'measure' with that of Beatrice, Hamlet's with Prospero's, Henry V's with Antony's. Then again, it is adjusted to suit the individual actor. Hamlet's 'rant' was made to fit Burbage like a glove; the acquisition of a singing clown gave rise to the lyrics of *Twelfth Night*. Young men trained as women impersonators, with voices which had been carefully safeguarded from too harsh a break, played the Queen in *Hamlet*, Lady Macbeth, Cleopatra. In one magnificent scene the whole technical theory of acting and speech in the theatre is tabulated for us, by a dramatist who is himself an actor (see *Hamlet*, Act III, Scene ii). Shakespeare was no university dramatist unable to endure vigour and breadth of delivery. His impeccable ear carries him on from prose to blank verse, from blank verse to couplet, from couplet to lyric. His young lover can speak a sonnet almost unperceived, his clown can jingle his mockery. Lady Macbeth can find a music so incredible in its significance that she can stand motionless almost throughout her part and chain us to her words. Shakespeare's greatest music coincides with his greatest freedom of metric form. Yet he can give Caliban blank verse and Ariel a form of lyric music unique in all our literature. Here again in the Elizabethan theatre we have an hour of perfect achievement; master dramatists, a public all lovers of their language and its triumphs, and a theatrical tradition still fresh and vigorous, which one supreme genius rules for over twenty years. This music reaches us only at second hand, and our theatrical tradition was sacrificed to Puritan intransigeance. When the theatre revived in 1660 it followed a magnificent, but alien, tradition, that of French diction, as created by Molière, together with the formal music of Corneille and Racine. A Court where manners ruled gave us the supreme comedy of manners. The stuff itself was not so great, but the technique of its utterance achieved perfection, and the country it served had the intelligence to see in perfectly spoken drama the one supreme school of a nation's speech. Hence the foundation of the Comédie-Française (1680), and for lack of any such living school of speech in this country we still bear the reproach of speaking our own language worse than any nation.

Simplicity is Molière's ideal. His comedy is full of sharply-defined contrasted character-drawing. His people spoke to their audience in the language of their own day. Like Shakespeare he mocks the pedant, the *précieux*, with fanciful vocabulary and stilted diction; like him he derides heroic rant, and even more than Shakespeare he demands contrasted team-work in people who are almost all of one social standing and period. Next to the scene in *Hamlet* referred to above, Molière's *Impromptu de Versailles* is the finest lesson to actors ever written, finer than *The Critic* because the end to be achieved is perfection, not the parodying of theatrical faults.

Something of Molière's quality of speech is translated into our own Restoration comedy, particularly in the case of Mirabel and Millamant (*The Way of the World*). Sheridan and his lovely Linley have behind them the great school of song, in which she excelled. The dialogue of *The Rivals* and *The School for Scandal*, and also of *She Stoops to Conquer*, demands diction, not to be confused with the monstrous horror of 'elocution' which was to descend on the untrained, uneducated players of the early nineteenth century, with their perpetual swinging between exaggerated melodrama and stereotyped comedy. The cause of this plague is not far to seek; there were no new plays of contemporary value. Opera had absorbed the interest of the fashionable world, and the evangelical dislike of the theatre closed the door to many lines of dramatic activity. The star actor counted his eccentricities of speech as an asset, and up to the 1860s there was no real sense of style in dialogue. Even then a trifling realism disfigured the real value of the 'cup-and-saucer' comedy. Scenery, production, lighting, crowd effects, costume—these were the standbys of great nineteenth-century revivals. Realism was a matter of *mise en scène* and construction rather than of dialogue. The greatest tragedian of the time maintained, until almost the end of his career, an artificial eccentricity of speech which was the delight of the caricaturist. The women did better, but worked on the principle of imitation only. Stage delivery was not human delivery. The reaction to realism suffered from the low standard of everyday speaking, and only with the close of the nineteenth century did saner and more rhythmic standards of utterance return. The Vedrenne–Barker management, with Shaw as its teacher, showed the final swing of the pendulum. Modern players, particularly the women, are fine interpreters of verse, and as good comedians, probably, as England has ever known. Modern speech is, however, threatened by the distortion of the microphone, and by the gradual extinction of the art of singing, and no effort should be spared in keeping up the present high standard.

What makes up the equipment of the good speaker? Not an artificial and imitative production, but a diction which physiologically, phonologically, and aesthetically represents the most perfect functional action of which he is individually capable. The true stage voice is a voice physiologically faultless, allied to a mind which can take in accurately, before attempting to give out.

The question of speech training for the stage is a big one, but a brief analysis of the elements needed for success may be helpful. Speech includes vocabulary, pronunciation, articulation, utterance, and significant phrasing by stress, pause, and pitch.

Vocabulary may be defined as a knowledge of words and the custom of using them with the most perfect sense of their accepted significance. It is the actor's lifelong study, since he must possess an historical as well as a contemporary knowledge of his own language, and a quick capacity for the acquisition of certain foreign words and idioms.

Pronunciation is based on phonetic standard and customary use. It includes the quick recognition of vowel quality and of syllabic stress. The noun 're'cord' and the verb 'recor'd', for instance, are distinguished by a change of stress, and a modification of the quality of the first vowel sound. Historically, Hamlet should substitute the verbal for the substantive pronunciation in the phrase 'I'll wipe away all trivial fond recor'd'.

Articulation is the muscular action of jaw, lips, and tongue in framing the rhythm of speech. Its characteristics are lightness, precision, and unconscious control. A speaker may select the correct combination for the word 'thermometer', and stress the word correctly. Defective dentition may confer the knighthood of 'Sir Nometer' on the word, or a bad cold in the head reduce it to 'Der-bo-be-tah'. Good articulation is a matter of physical training.

Utterance implies the addition of vocal tone to the perfect articulatory action. It calls for the co-ordination of breath, phonation, resonation, and pitch variety, with the previous qualities of speech listed above. Above all, it aims at a perfect co-ordination of sound and significance which in the actor must become altogether automatic. Its standard is not a matter of opinion but of physiological correctness and aesthetic perfection.

Phrasing links all preceding qualities into the significant expression of a complete thought: a sentence, affirmative or interrogative; a command, or a plea; a parenthesis or a contradiction. Every line of the actor's part requires this knowledge and the power of instantly imitating a given reading from the producer, or in response to a comrade's line. It is the basis of all team-work in speech. The unending study of rhythmic speech in great prose or verse is the basis of the whole achievement. The aim is unconscious automatic perfection.

The success of the performer depends on his capacity first for receiving sound-impressions and translating them into sense, secondly for giving out such impressions with original significance even though the words themselves are none of his choosing and convey a meaning foreign to his character and mood. The French stage is our master in all that concerns this great art, which is called the Art of Diction. Behind the actor's success lies always the combination of imagination and technique. The question of emotional self-transformation or technical skill at the time of performance is a purely personal one. It may vary during the repetitions of a long run, or according to the mental philosophy of a Coquelin or a Kean, but one thing is certain: speech is fundamentally a technical matter, a question of perfect motor action placed at the service of the mind. Passion will no more render a hideous phonation endurable than extra acceleration will improve the running of a motor-car with a flat tyre.

The following suggestions may be helpful to the beginner who aspires to speak well. Study your great language unceasingly, unrelentingly. Learn its fundamental rhythm in force, time, and space. Practise its greatest patterns, its sharpest significant contrasts. Submit yourself to the strictest training as a vocal instrument. Learn your vocal and articulatory resources as you would learn to play the violin; as a matter of exact training, of physical mastery over a perfect instrument, an instrument, remember, which developed primarily to help you to eat soup safely, rather than to vocalize in perfection, so that it tends to work in reverse, swallowing instead of sounding when you most feel things. Remember also that you will not sing more in tune because you 'feel' the words of a song, nor will you speak better because you like the words you have to say. Your business is not to enjoy speaking, but to make your audience enjoy listening. Personal eccentricities interfere with the writer's intention and the audience's enjoyment. They condemn an actor to the vicissitudes of typecasting, the more inevitably as he who indulges in them becomes over-individualized, and so narrows the range of his own personality. Cut out everything from your daily life and practice which will hurt your speech. Never coddle or doctor your instrument, but respect it as if it were a violin worth five thousand pounds. It is a wind instrument; see that your breathing apparatus is faultlessly clean. It has an exquisitely adjusted resonator; see that it is clean and unclogged. It has an ivory keyboard; keep it clean and faultlessly alined. It has a touch infinitely more delicate and soft than a violin or a flute. Master its movements and keep them flexible.

What is it then to speak badly? It is to use an impoverished vocabulary eked out with slang and an utterance depending on custom and on phonetic standard, not on phonological principles and the practice of great poets. The nature of good speech is like that of all good art. It is not a mimicry of any artificial standard. It is a perfect fitting of our physiological instrument for significant and emotional and aesthetic uses. It is not an artificial constancy of pronunciation. It is no great matter whether you say I-there or EE-ther; what excoriates the listener's ear is the yapping nasal whine of something for which our alphabet has no symbol, a tight-shut nasal 'Oife'.

Our national art is the drama. Our national inheritance is the greatest and most widespread language man has ever spoken. Every Englishman should know, and practise his knowledge of, these facts.   E. F.

SPENCER, GABRIEL (?–1598), an Elizabethan actor often described by his first name only. He was a member of the Admiral's Company at the time of his death, and was killed by Ben Jonson during a duel in Hoxton Fields on 22 Sept., having himself two years previously killed his opponent in a duel.

SPENCER, JOHN (?), one of the best known of the English Comedians on the continent, where he first appears in 1605. He continued to tour the Netherlands and Germany until 1623, and was known evidently as a clown, taking for his pseudonym the name Hans Stockfisch, analogous to the Pickelherring of Robert Reynolds.

SPERONI, SPERONE(1500–88), Italian dramatist, whose *Canace* (1543) is considered the most horrible of the many bloodthirsty tragedies of this period. Dealing with incestuous love, and ending with a pile of corpses, it caused fierce controversy when it was first performed at Padua (see ITALY, 1 *b* i).

SPIEGELBERG, CHRISTIAN (? –1732), a German actor-manager, who first acted under Velten, and later assumed the leadership of a young company which toured extensively, from Scandinavia, across Europe, to Russia. It was with this company that the famous German actress, Caroline Neuber, made her first appearance.

SPOTBLOCK, a pulley block set in the grid for a special purpose, such as the suspension of a chandelier.

SPOTLIGHT, see LIGHTING, 2.

STAGE. Behind the proscenium of the modern theatre lies that technical province of which the stage proper and its adjacent offices form the major part. A stage floor alone is inadequate for the presentation of a play. Of almost equal importance is the Grid, an open floor above the stage, whence all suspended scenery hangs. In addition to this, there is often a smaller space—the Fly-floor—at the side of the stage, or suspended gallery-wise over its side, where the lines controlling the scenes and effects are worked. And finally there is the dim and mysterious forest of timbers and platforms below the stage where, at least in the older theatres, the secrets of many spectacular marvels lie hidden. There are therefore at least four storeys to be considered—the cellar, the stage, the fly galleries, and the grid.

1. THE STAGE FLOOR. In the modern theatre this is often no more than an unbroken rectangle of level boarding, but in the past the stage was neither a simple rectangle, nor was it level, nor was it an unbroken surface. To-day, though the stage floor is, in England at least, reduced to one of the simplest and least enterprising phases of its history, there are still theatres, some traditional and some advanced, which possess highly developed technicalities of 'revolves', 'bridges', and 'scissors'. Simplicity of stage floor was not a feature of the late Georgian and the early Victorian playhouses. These—even small theatres in the provinces—had a rich collection of fascinating technicalities, and owned a long tradition in their arrangement.

To begin with, the whole floor possessed a Stage Rake, or slope, down from the back to the footlights in front. This tradition of a raked stage is long and conservative, but it brought more than one serious complication. To-day the highest authorities point out that stage rake is not of the slightest value in the presentation of a modern show, and is highly undesirable. The belief that it enables the actors to be seen better, or that it gives a dancer a slightly better basis for a leap, have both been proved fallacies. No rake is of the slightest help in displaying the actors at the back of a stage above those in front unless it is so steep as to become impractical. Even extreme stage rake is limited in practice to a slope of 4 per cent., and is often as small as $1\frac{1}{2}$ per cent. The only proper solution for the display of up-stage groups is to raise them on rostrums at the very least a foot above the group in front.

Moreover, a sloping stage brings serious disadvantages in the setting of scenery—any pieces set diagonally cannot join neatly to squarely vertical neighbours; the side flats of a box-set need Fox Wedges under the base of each to compensate for the slope, or they have to be built out of true with sloping bottom rails, when, of course, they cease to be inter-changeable and can never be of use save on the one side of the stage. Moreover, any setting of pieces upon a boat truck (see below, 5. OTHER ELEMENTS) becomes dangerous, since the truck may make away on its own down the incline.

Thus stage rake is now discountenanced. It once had, however, a very definite purpose, in that it aided the illusion of scenes painted in perspective. With the passing of perspective scene-painting it ceases to have any justification at all.

The floor of the traditional stage consists of boards running up- and down-stage, laid on a specially arranged system of joists running across the stage. Because of the business of stage working, no considerable timber below the floor boards could run in any direction but across-stage; consequently the floor joists could not be supported on cross bearers, but each had to be upheld separately by its own system of vertical posts from the floor of the cellar. Thus the structure below a stage floor resembled a series of independent frameworks, all parallel to the audience. Owing to the rake of the early stage, a certain stress was exerted in long use, which tended to make the stage slide in the direction of the slope, and no permanent agent was allowable in the structure below to brace against, or counteract, this thrust—any cross-braces would have hindered the movement of bridges. Consequently, beneath old stages there is seen a system of metal strap-hooks, linking one row of uprights with the next behind, and so knitting the whole together. These tie-bars could be unhooked at need to allow the passage of a machine or piece of scenery.

Above the floor joists are the Boards (so positive and intimate a part of the actor's craft as to have become a second name for it—as in the phrase 'on the boards', which signifies 'in the profession'). The boards were arranged in such a fashion that it was practically possible to open the stage over the whole extent of the acting area, leaving only the floor in the wing spaces at the sides untouched. The joists of the floor were then revealed, and between them worked a variety of contrivances which gave a reason and plan for the whole scheme.

The first aperture, with its accompanying contrivance, was at the very forefront of the stage before the curtain. This was the Foot-lights Trap, a long rectangular aperture with a post below at either end. Between the posts a framework slid up and down, and upon this the lamps of the footlights were arranged. They were lowered (according to an account of 1810) not only to enable a stage hand in the cellar to trim them, but so that the stage might, upon occasion, be darkened. For this purpose a pair of lines was taken up from the ends of the framework over pulleys at the heads of the posts and down again to the drum of a central shaft in the cellar. A line led from this same drum in the opposite direction to a counter-weight, designed to balance the framework, and from the shaft an endless line was brought by pulleys to a point at the side under the stage floor, where it ascended to a winch in the prompter's corner, so that the whole operation of dimming the footlights could be conducted from the stage without going into the cellar (see also LIGHTING).

The next aperture—found in many stages to-day—is the Carpet Cut. This is a long, narrow cut, stretching nearly the width of the proscenium opening, and just behind the curtain. Its aperture is closed by one or more flaps, hinged on the down-stage side. When these are lifted, the edge of any carpet or stage-cloth that may be needed in the scene is dropped through for an inch or two, and the flap closed to trap it. This is neatly and instantaneously fixed, and so cannot trip up the player.

The next apertures are of a different nature. In the traditional stage they are two or more square openings, placed symmetrically, and about two feet across. For these the joists are cut, and a special framing, with trap doors, constructed. They are termed the Corner Traps, and they are accompanied by a com-plicated mechanism below, whose purpose is to raise a standing figure from the cellar to make a spectacular appearance on the stage. The trap door of this opening may be con-structed in various ways. Sometimes it is a mere square of boards, battened out. Some-times it is an arrangement of thin strips, hinged together or mounted on a flexible back-ing, and capable of sliding like a roll-top desk. Sometimes the door is taken away altogether and replaced for the occasion by a closure of a special type, to allow of a sudden appearance as if by magic. Of such, the most famous is the Star Trap, which is a circular opening filled by a series of triangle-like segments of wood, fitted radially, and hinged to the circum-ference of the opening with leather; as the figure shoots through, the flaps open like a crown, and immediately fall again as the player passes. In other examples, a diaphragm of rubber is used with a slit across it; and in others again, when it is desired to allow no opening at all save that exactly needed by the player's body as it ascends, a Bristle Trap is inserted, in which bristles are attached radiating inwards from the edge of the circular opening to be pressed aside as the player ascends, returning at once to their original position.

The commonest method of getting rid of a trap door is, however, by means of the Slider system. In this the door section itself is supported at one edge on a fillet in the joist below, and at the opposite edge by a lever, which, when vertical, takes the weight of the door and holds it in position. When the lever is pulled, the edge of the door drops a couple of inches, and its sides come to rest in a pair of sloping grooves cut in the face of the side frames of the opening. These sloping ways are continued under the stage floor so that the whole trap door can be slid along them till it is completely concealed under the stage, leaving the opening free. The trap platform is then raised with the figure upon it, and itself becomes the filling to the aperture, till the trap is again lowered, and the original door slid back, and, by its lever, lifted to a flush position.

Beyond the corner traps comes a similar, but larger, single trap, centrally placed. This is the Grave Trap. It may be 6 ft. long and 3 ft. wide. It has a platform below, which can be raised or lowered, and its traditional use is in the grave scene in *Hamlet* (whence its name), though it was pressed into service on many other occasions. Again, many varieties of ingenious development are to be found for the mechanism of the trap. Sometimes it opens by the dropping of a pair of longitudinal flaps, counterweighted by levers to close again at need, and it may have a cushioned trough below to break a player's leap-down. Sometimes the door is so arranged that by the dropping of a pair of bars the sections of the floor descend severally on to a sloping timber cut like the stringer of a stair, thus forming a flight of steps. Most frequently, the mechanism is in the form of a counterweighted platform, like a larger edition of the footlight trap.

A similar, but square, trap is more rarely found, also central, and farther up-stage, called the Cauldron Trap. This owed its name to the cauldron scene in *Macbeth*. (See also ENGLISH PLAYHOUSE, 2.)

There now follows a complicated system of apertures of a different nature. From this point to the back of the acting-area the stage was divided into a series of successive sections, about three to five in number, each repeating the same arrangement. Each section was between 4 and 5 ft. deep, and stretched from side to side of the acting-area. Detailed arrangement of all these apertures varied in various stages, but a typical scheme for each section was as follows: the first three joists in each case remained intact. Between the first and second, and between the second and third, the floor-boards were divided centrally, and the two half-sections arranged to drop as sliders and run apart, drawn by ropes, to lie concealed under either side of the stage. The long, narrow opening so revealed was a Cut. Below it were Sloats (sometimes spelt Slote), by means of which flat scenes, and groundrows or footpieces, could be raised to the stage-level.

On occasion a cloth might be attached to the base of a groundrow and be drawn up from its rolled position in a Sloat Box below the cut, by lines from the grid, as the groundrow rose in the air during a transformation scene. With two sloat sets in each of three sections, one was able to raise elements of six separate scenes from below the stage (see ENGLISH PLAYHOUSE, 2 *c*).

Directly behind these cuts a wider opening occupied the remainder of each section. For this the joists were cut and the aperture framed. The opening was effected similarly by sliders, but the mechanism below was different; here a great platform, framed and tied, rose in corner-grooves with the aid of counterweights and a winch, to lift complete groups of posed figures to the stage—as, for instance, a tableau of fairies. These machines were called Bridges, and great variety is found in their design, until to-day the electrically controlled bridges of a large theatre may reach a high degree of engineering complexity.

The narrow strips of stage floor remaining over the tops of the joists, and separating the openings, were called Fillets.

This arrangement of sloat-cut, sloat-cut, and bridge-cut was repeated in the next section, and so on until the end of the acting-area was reached.

At the back of the stage was frequently a recess, or Inner Stage, a legacy of the inner stage of the Elizabethans and of the 'relieve' space of the masques. Here was often found the last opening—a large lift for the occasional raising of pieces from the cellar or carpenter's shop below to the stage-level. Its purpose was generally limited, and it was rarely used for stage effects.

2. THE CELLAR. In considering the Cellar below the stage, where so much of this machinery is worked, another characteristic in which the English stage differs from the continental is at once apparent. The English cellar was, in general, far shallower. This was because the English stage possessed a system of grooves, which allowed any tall framed pieces to be slid to the sides of the stage in a change. In the continental theatre the wings alone, in general, slid sideways; any framed backgrounds (as opposed to hanging drops) had to be lowered beneath the stage. This, in a theatre or opera house, already greater in average dimensions than the more intimate, dramatic, English playhouse, entailed a greater depth, so that the continental cellar, or *dessous*, often descended for four or five storeys.

The English cellar usually consisted of a Mezzanine Floor below the stage floor, where most of the machines were worked, and beneath this a Well in the central part of the area, into which the base of the traps and the bridges descended, and at the bottom of which were the drums and shafts which worked them. The Band-Room, a retiring-room for the members of the orchestra, is frequently found under the stage.

3. THE FLY-FLOOR. This variation in size and complexity marked the working floors above

the English stage as well as those below. In the continental theatre there might be as many as three stages of Fly-floors or Fly-galleries, before the Grid was reached. In the English stage there is rarely more than one on either side.

The Fly-floor is a gallery running along the sides of the stage above the wing space. Its purpose to-day is to supply a working floor for the Fly-men working the lines of the grid, and to keep the huge complexity of ropes and their ends, which these men have to handle, from cumbering the working space of the stage below. The gallery itself is protected by a heavily built railing, carrying two rows of cleats, an upper and a lower. The lines are made off to the cleats on the lower rail when a cloth or border is trimmed, or 'deaded', that is, hung squarely at its correct height. When the cloth is 'flown', the lines are not taken off the lower cleats, but pulled in from above until the scenery is at a sufficient height, when they are made off, in a bight, upon the upper rail. Thus, when the cloth has to be lowered into position, the lines have only to be detached from the upper rail and lowered out, and their attachment to the lower rail will ensure the cloth being roughly in its correct position (roughly, because variations in temperature and humidity noticeably affect the length of the ropes).

There may be a fly-floor on either side of a stage, though generally one side (the prompt side) is chiefly used for tying-off. Between these floors there were formerly Catwalks, or narrow communicating bridges, slung on iron stirrups from the grid, so that the fly-men might get out to any point over the stage to see to the proper working of scenery. Generally there was one catwalk above each set of grooves.

Often the borders in an eighteenth-century and early nineteenth-century theatre were a simple stock of three types—arch borders, sky borders, and tree borders. These could, of course, be supplemented upon occasion, but the stock borders were so commonly used that in Foulston's Theatre Royal, Plymouth, in 1811, the borders of each set were all connected with their own shafts, and these three shafts, together with a fourth from which the groove-arms worked, were situated over the stage-left fly-floor, and worked by hanging endless lines, round drums at the extremities of the shafts.

4. THE GRID. Above the fly-floors comes the Grid, an open floor of metal or timber bearers, covering the whole of the stage area and bearing the regular pulley blocks and the Spotblocks (that is, blocks put in temporarily for a special use, such as the suspension of a chandelier in the scene).

Above the grid again may be a crowning area where certain drums and shafts are disposed whose purpose was formerly to serve the working of cloud machines and such celestial appearances. These are now very rarely seen.

On the traditional English stage, ground-rows and traps were, generally speaking, worked from the cellar—wings and flats from the stage, by means of grooves—borders, occasional cloths, and the hinged groove-arms, from the grid and fly-floor—and aerial ascents and descents from the shafts over the grid.

Stages to-day are divided into two classes according to the method of working the fly-lines. The older traditional theatres, where the system described above is used, are known as Rope, or Handworked, Houses, the others, which employ a more modern system of counterweights and endless lines, as Counterweight Houses; since here no great lengths of spare rope need to be accommodated when scenery is flown, these commonly have no fly-floors, and the flying system is worked from the stage-level.

5. OTHER ELEMENTS. The rectangle of the traditional English stage often has a small recess, a Backstage, or Inner Stage, opening out of the back-wall, which was used for the setting of the final pieces of deep, spectacular scenes of great vistas. Upon normal occasions it serves as a subsidiary scene dock. The strips at either side of the main area which come directly behind the proscenium sides are termed the Wing Spaces, or the Wings, from the scenery which separated them from the acting-area. Opening from the stage proper are the Scene Docks, or Bays, where scenery is stored; the Quick-change Room, where hurried changes of costume are made; the Property Room (where are stored all the special adjuncts of a presentation which do not come under the heads of wardrobe, scenery, or lighting; these may vary from carpets to nosegays, from weapons to meals, from snuff-boxes to coffins, from apples to animals, and from thunder-sheets to glass-crashes). There may also be the Furniture Store, and possibly the Green Room, that sitting-room of the waiting players, whose name is, so far, a mystery of which little is known with certainty, save that the room was formerly also known as the Scene Room, which term was only applied to the scene store at a later time. In the early theatres more than one green room sometimes existed, and they were strictly graded in use according to the salary of the player, who was fined for presuming to use a green room above his rank.

At the back of some of the older stages is the Paint Frame, a huge frame suspended from the grid, and designed to carry the stretched canvas that the scene-painter turns into cloths. Sometimes the painter works on the level of the fly-floor, and drops the frame by means of a winch to any required level for his work; sometimes the frame is fixed and he works at it on a moving bridge raised and lowered by a winch.

Between the stage and the auditorium is generally a fireproof Pass-door, situated in an inconspicuous part of the proscenium wall.

Though the average stage floor to-day in England is a simple surface, many developments of hydraulic and electrical devices have been made on the continent and in the larger theatres at home. The Asphaleian System is one of the earliest of the modern elaborate mechanical systems; in it the whole stage area is divided into individual platforms, upon hydraulic pistons, each of which may be separately raised, lowered, or tipped. Revolves, in many varieties, have been experimented with, and the elaboration of electric Bridges may be considerable. Valuable use is often made of Boat Trucks, or large, low platforms, only a few inches high, and running on castors; upon them whole scenes, or sections of scenes, can be moved. The idea may be extended in various ways, as when two trucks are used in successive scenes, and pivoted each at the down-stage and off-stage corner, so as to swing in over the acting-area, or out of sight in the wing-space at need. Sometimes such a system is known as a Scissor Stage. Or the trucks may reach a high degree of elaboration and run on a system of rails and lifts, until as many as five separate Waggon Stages are to be found in one theatre, all capable of moving aside from the acting position, or of rising and sinking in the cellar, each bearing a full set of scenery.

Detailed accounts of such developments upon the continent can be found in Kranich's *Bühnentechnik der Gegenwart* (2 vols., 1933), and a scissor stage is illustrated in Doris Zinkeisen's *Designing for the Stage* (1938).

R. S.

STAGE BOX, see AUDITORIUM and BOX.

STAGE BRACE, an extensible rod which supports a flat, or piece, being hooked to the back of the flat at one end and attached to the floor by a stage screw, or weighted by a braceweight, at the other end. A variant, composed of a right-angled triangle of wood hinged to the flat, opened out and weighted, is known as a French Brace.

STAGE-CLOTH, see CLOTH.

STAGE DIRECTIONS, or notes added to the script of a play to convey information about its performance not already explicit in the dialogue itself. Generally speaking, they are concerned with (*a*) the actor's movements, (*b*) the scenery or stage effects.

Stage directions concerning the actor's movement are, in the English theatre, based on two important peculiarities: they are all relative to the position of an actor facing the audience—right and left are therefore reversed from the spectator's point of view—and they are derivative from the period when the stage was raked, or sloped upwards, towards the back. Thus, any advancing movement towards the audience is said to proceed Down-stage, and any retiring movement is termed a movement Up-stage. (A derivative use of the latter word arises in stage slang when any haughty behaviour is said to be 'up-stage'.)

The simplest examples of stage directions relating to the actor's movements are such single words as 'enters', 'sits', 'stands', 'turns'. To these may be added two traditional instructions whose grammar is hallowed by tradition, and in the latter of which a very interesting convention is recalled—they are *Exit* and *Manet*. *Exit* ('he goes out', originally *Exeat*, 'let him go out') has to-day become an English word in its own right, inflected by theatrical people as a normal verb; hence, 'you exit here', 'he exits', 'they exit', and so forth are now common usage, while *Exeunt* has become pedantic save in the conventional phrase *Exeunt omnes*, and *Exeant* is almost unknown. The antithesis, *Manet* ('he remains'), is far less commonly seen, but it was used as far back at least as 1698 to indicate the remaining of a character on the stage while the others went off—especially at the end of a scene, when it implied that the player remained through the visible change of scenery and proceeded with the action directly the following scene was in place, thus carrying on the flow of the play without a break.

Directions may also indicate change of position on the stage, such, for instance, as the word 'Crosses', which is an instruction to the player to go across the stage, either for practical reasons, so as to reach a given object, or for technical reasons, so as to provide a break in a passage otherwise without action. A 'Scissor Cross' is the crossing of two characters from opposite directions simultaneously and (unless arranged as an intentional effect) is regarded as an ugly move significant of clumsy technique.

It is when actual direction of movement is indicated that the two conventional peculiarities of English usage become apparent. The acting area of the stage is supposed to be divided approximately into nine main zones, three situated Down-stage (that is, in front), three Up-stage (that is, at the back), and three across the centre between the other two. The zones are called (front) Down Left, Down Centre, and Down Right; (back) Up Left, Up Centre, and Up Right; (middle) Left, Centre, and Right. Further subdivisions are indicated around the centre zone by Up Left Centre, Down Left Centre, and similarly for the right side. Three further terms relating to the back-wall of the scene are Centre Back, Left and Right Centre Back. All these terms are usually abbreviated to initials when writing. Lateral movements to or from the centre line of the stage are described as movements On or Off respectively, the extent of the movement being generally qualified by an adverb; thus, while 'to go off' is equivalent to *exit*, 'to go off a little' is limited to partial withdrawal to the side.

Movement around an object is, according to the conventional usage, expressed in terms of height, alluding to the old sloping stage. Thus an actor is not told to go 'behind' or 'in front of' a table, but 'above' it or 'below' it. Such an apparently odd form of direction becomes justified in considering a movement round, say, a sofa, when it will be seen that 'Go in front of the sofa' is an equivocal instruction if the sofa has its back to the audience.

A further variety of stage directions is found in melodrama and earlier plays, where such terms as R.U.E. and L.2.E. are found. These relate to the times when all side-walls of scenes were composed of separate wings, and the Entrance was the passage between one wing and its neighbour. Thus R.U.E. signifies Right Upper Entrance, and L.2.E. Left Second Entrance—the first entrance being that between the proscenium wing and the first wing of the scene proper. A further, and earlier, variant of this method of terminology (found as far back as 1748) was to indicate an entrance, or the position of a piece of scenery, as 'in the second [&c.] grooves'; this signified that the piece of scenery slid in, and was supported by, those particular grooves, or that the entrance took place immediately behind them. In 1887, moreover, it was possible to say that a backcloth hung 'in the 3rd grooves', though that backcloth had nothing to do with the grooves, save that, in this particular case, it hung in the space between the third and fourth sets.

Any note on stage directions must include mention of the two curious and apparently redundant terms Prompt Side and Opposite Prompt. Rarely in actual stage conversation is the former term ever alluded to by initials, while its opposite is as rarely alluded to in full. But in writing, P.S. and O.P. are generally used. This applies only to the English-speaking theatre, where the Prompt Side is usually accepted as the stage left, and O.P. as the stage right (though in some theatres the prompter's corner is found on the right). The Prompt Corner, in the British theatre, is a desk against the inner side of the proscenium wall where the prompter installs his Prompt Book (a copy of the play, generally interleaved, and carrying the full directions and warnings necessary to the management of the production), and where a board of switches for signals, communicating to various parts of the theatre, is generally situated. Among the signals is the Bar Bell to warn patrons in the bars and foyers of the approaching end of an interval. On the continent the Prompter's Box is usually sunk beneath a coved hood in the centre of the footlights. Hence in English theatres presenting opera the central prompter's box is sometimes seen.

Stage directions covering scenery are, to-day, generally self-explanatory descriptions of the layout and appearance of the stage for the scene in question, and offer little for special comment beyond the conventions for describing positions explained above. The history of stage directions does, however, contain some special expressions. In Elizabethan and Restoration plays the location of the scene is often not specified, and was, in fact, frequently not held as of great importance; in the earlier period the location of a scene was the stage, and there was little serious attempt to make the stage look like, or mean, some other place.

This attitude remained to some extent after the introduction of scenery, but, though actual location was still sometimes not specified (or limited to, say, 'Don Diego's House', without indication of any particular room, or even whether exterior or interior), a new direction was now needed indicating what happened at the scene-change, though how the scene appeared might be left to the presenter. Thus we read 'The scene draws' or 'draws off', indicating that the two flats of the back-scene were opened to disclose the next scene. Or we have 'The scene draws over' or 'closes in' (the latter term used in a poetic sense even as late as 1892 when all reference to its original significance had passed). Further, we have what is so frequently misunderstood, the simple 'The scene closes' and 'The scene opens'; such directions referred to the actual movement of the scenery.

Many technical directions have crept unintended into published plays based on original prompter's scripts. These are often of high interest to students, as when in Shirley's *The Sisters* ('prepared for performance between 1668 and 1671', see Montague Summers, *The Restoration Theatre*, p. 142), the initials U.D.P.S., M.D.O.P., and L.D.P.S. (indicating Upper, Middle, or Lower Doors on Prompt or Opposite Prompt Sides) show the use of six proscenium doors in the Restoration playhouse.

A further development in the form of stage directions, but one chiefly intended to facilitate the wider reading of plays by the general public, came about the end of the nineteenth century. Ibsen's descriptions of the appearance of the details of his scenes and his characters were full and careful. Bernard Shaw went even further in this direction in his printed plays, and Granville-Barker, Barrie, and others all tended to change the stage direction from a technical thing to a readable thing, designed to refer less and less to the means of the stage itself, but to define more and more the effects those means must achieve.   R. S.

STAGE DIRECTOR, see PRODUCER, 2.

STAGE DOOR. This, situated at the back or side of the theatre, provides the link between the street and the stage. Through it pass the actors and stage hands, and authorized visitors, to gain the dressing-rooms, rehearsal-rooms, and various offices. Access to these, and to the business offices, can also be obtained via the front entrance of the theatre. Immediately inside the stage door is the cubicle, usually with a glass front, of the stage-door keeper (more properly designated the hall keeper), a permanent and important member of the theatre staff. It is his business to check the arrival and departure of all who frequent the theatre, to prevent unauthorized persons from entering, to receive and transmit telephone and other messages. He keeps a jealously guarded list of the home addresses and telephone numbers of actors in the current show, not to be divulged except under extreme pressure, receives their letters and parcels, and occasionally executes commissions for them. A good stage-door keeper is a valuable adjunct to any theatre, and often the staunch friend and ally of the actor, particularly of the leading players, protecting them from the curiosity of 'fans', who gather outside the stage door after the performance to see the actors leave, and to obtain autographs. Just inside the stage door is the Call Board or Notice Board on which calls for rehearsal and all important information for the company is posted, including the dreaded 'Notice' informing them of the end of the play's run. In Elizabethan times the Stage door—or Tiring House door—was the only entrance to the theatre except for the main front entrance, and was used by those members of the audience who had seats on the stage.

STAGE EFFECTS, see MACHINERY and TRICKWORK ON THE ENGLISH STAGE.

STAGE-KEEPER, a functionary of the Elizabethan theatre who was responsible for the sweeping and clearing of the acting space, and probably for other odd jobs.

STAGE LIGHTING, see LIGHTING.

STAGE PROPERTIES, see STAGE, 5 and PROPS.

STAGE SETTING, a term sometimes used to define the arrangement of a stage (with curtains, &c.) in such a way as to provide a general background suitable for any play, as distinct from scenery, which is suitable for one play or part of a play only (see ENGLISH PLAYHOUSE, 3 and SET).

STAGE SOCIETY, THE INCORPORATED, LONDON. This was founded in 1899 for the production of plays of artistic merit which stood very little chance of performance in a commercial theatre. These were to be given with a West End cast at a West End theatre for one, or at most two, performances. One consequence of this policy has been that productions were, of necessity, given on Sunday nights, since only then were West End theatres available. This led to a police raid on the Royalty Theatre on 26 Nov. 1899, when the Society's first production took place there. This was Shaw's *You Never Can Tell*, incidentally the first performance of this play.

The original group of sponsors, which included Frederick Whelen, William Sharp (Fiona Macleod), W. Lee Mathews, Sydney Olivier (afterwards Lord Olivier), Hector Thomson, and H. A. Hertz, were enthusiasts for the theatre and dissatisfied with its condition at that time, but they had little professional connexion with it, and it may be that much of their success was attributable to that fact. They were 'amateurs' in the best sense. How firmly they adhered to their original admirable intentions may be seen by the list

of the Society's productions, which number more than 200. It includes the first production in England of a number of Shaw's plays, as well as of plays by such foreign dramatists as Hauptmann, Gorky, Gogol, Wedekind, Kaiser, Pirandello, J. J. Bernard, Afinogenov, Cocteau, and Odets.

In 1930 the then Council of the Stage Society considered that its work was done, owing to the emergence of such groups as the Gate Theatre, and suggested that it should be wound up. The proposal was defeated by an overwhelming majority, and a leading article in *The Times* for 2 Dec. 1930 said: 'The Stage Society has by its own excellence created for itself a trust which cannot lightly be abandoned.' With the outbreak of war in 1939 the work of the Society fell into abeyance, but it was hoped that later on—when the Ibsen and Shaw and Chekhov of a new age made their unheralded and unwelcomed appearance—the Society might resume its fruitful work, much of which was done under the aegis of W. S. Kennedy, who was elected to the Council in 1907 and served it in various capacities until 1938. It is interesting to note that the Stage Society was the first body to sponsor plays on Sunday since the days of Charles I, and that the Vedrenne–Barker management at the Court Theatre may be said to have arisen out of its activities. The Stage Society was at one time associated with the Three Hundred Club, also a Sunday play-producing society, founded by Phyllis Bell, wife of Geoffrey Whitworth, which in the years after 1918 produced some interesting plays, including *Young Woodley, Don Juan* (by Flecker), and Lawrence's *David*.

STAGE SWITCHBOARD, see LIGHTING, 2 *j*.

STAGG, CHARLES and his wife MARY (*fl.* early eighteenth century), actors and teachers of dancing, who in 1716 were in possession of a theatre built by a merchant in Williamsburg. Nothing is known of their activities, but after the death of Charles in 1735 his widow was in charge of dancing assemblies in the same town. There is a possibility that the Staggs may have prepared and produced a play given in 1718 before the Governor of Virginia. Their names figure in the earliest records of professional entertainment in the New World.

STAGNELIUS, ERIK JOHANN (1793–1823), Swedish poet, author of a number of poetic plays staged in Stockholm (see SCANDINAVIA, 3).

STAIRCASE-SIDE, see FLAT.

STALL, the name given in the modern theatre to the individual seats between the stage front and the pit, those nearest the stage being known as Orchestra Stalls. They first appeared in the 1830s to 1840s, after the raising of the first circle had allowed the pit to extend farther back, and are considered by most people to be the best seats in the house, an honour claimed by some, however, for the central seats of the front row of the Dress Circle. The Stalls are, with the exception of Boxes, the most expensive seats in the theatre. They were at one time called by their French name of *fauteuils*, which was then taken by extension to mean the whole area of stalls, including the Orchestra Stalls. In some theatres the term Balcony Stalls was applied to the front rows of the Dress Circle.

R. S.

STANDARD THEATRE. (1) LONDON, in Shoreditch. This theatre opened in 1835 as the Royal Standard and in 1837, when its records begin, was under the management of Johnson and Lee. They remodelled it in 1845 and called it the New Standard. It was up for sale in 1849, and was taken over by John Douglass, who, like Nelson Lee, had been a showman. After his death it was run by his sons. It was burned down in 1866 and rebuilt on a larger scale, reopening in 1868 as the Standard. It had a good stock company, and was the first of the north-east suburban theatres to attract visiting stars from the West End. This gave it a position of some importance and drew good audiences. It was one of the largest theatres in London, and while Richard Douglass was in charge its pantomimes rivalled those of Drury Lane and the neighbouring Hoxton Britannia. The Melville family, afterwards connected for so long with the Lyceum, ran it successfully for a considerable period, a feature of their management being the annual visit of the J. W. Turner Opera Company. The growth of other suburban theatres eventually robbed the Standard of its audiences and, like so many others of its kind, it became a cinema. It was destroyed by enemy action in 1940–1. W. M. P.

For the Standard Theatre, Pimlico, London, see VICTORIA PALACE.

(2) NEW YORK. This opened as the Eagle on 18 Oct. 1875, and had a prosperous career as a home of variety and light entertainment. Re-christened the Standard, it saw on 15 Jan. 1879 the first production in New York of *H.M.S. Pinafore*, which had a sensational success. It ran for 175 nights, and was soon being played everywhere. An unsuccessful season in 1880 had for its only success Annie Pixley as M'liss in Bret Harte's play, and shortly afterwards the theatre changed hands at a very low price. *Patience*, beginning on 22 Sept. 1881, ran for a whole season, as did *Iolanthe* in the following year. On 14 Dec. 1883 the theatre was destroyed by fire, but it was rebuilt and reopened on 23 Dec. 1884, again as a home of light opera. In 1897, renamed the Manhattan, it opened again as a playhouse with *What Happened to Jones*.

STANFIELD, CLARKSON (1793–1867), English scenic artist, son of an actor and author. He was for some years in the Merchant Navy, and first painted scenery for the Royalty Theatre in Wellclose Square. In 1831 he

worked in the Theatre Royal, Edinburgh, and returned to London to become scenic director at the Coburg and eventually at Drury Lane. By 1834 he had exhibited with such success at the Royal Academy that he gave up scene-painting as a profession, though he did some work for Macready's pantomime in 1837 and again in 1842. He was also a friend of Charles Dickens, for whose private production of *The Frozen Deep* at Tavistock House he painted the backcloth. His last theatrical work was a drop-scene for the New Adelphi which he painted for his friend Ben Webster in 1858.

STANISLAVSKY, KONSTANTIN SERGEIVICH (1865–1938), Russian actor, producer, and teacher, whose real name was Alexeyev. He began by acting in amateur productions at his own home and elsewhere. With a growing interest in the professional theatre he observed and analysed the great actors of the time— Salvini, Rossi, Yermolova, Sadovsky, Lensky— attended a theatrical school, and finally began a more systematic course of study under F. P. Komisarjevsky, father of Vera and Theodore, himself a dramatist and producer. He played in vaudeville, operetta, drama, and comedy, and was at one time prepared to embark on an operatic career. In all these ways he revealed his passion for work, his profound self-criticism, and his rare quality for systematizing and generalizing his experience. In 1888, together with the elder Komisarjevsky and Fedotov (son of a well-known actor), he founded the Society of Literature and Art, whose aim was to bring together workers from all spheres of art for the systematic presentation of good plays. At first Stanislavsky was an actor in the amateur group of the society, later he became its producer. In 1891 he produced for the first time on the Russian stage Tolstoy's *The Fruits of Enlightenment*, and a dramatization of Dostoievsky's *Sela Stepanchikov*. These brought him to the notice of the public; his further productions brought him fame.

At this period Stanislavsky was working mainly under the influence of the Meiningen Company, famed for its historically exact décor and costumes and for the elaborately-worked-out detail of its productions, especially in the crowd scenes. From it he took the striving for historical truth, the superb method of producing crowd scenes, and the smooth running of the whole. He rejected its somewhat declamatory style of acting, seeking rather simplicity and truth. In 1898 he and Nemirovich-Danchenko jointly founded the Moscow Art Theatre, with which their names are indissolubly linked. This created a new epoch in the development of Russian, and indeed of world, theatre art. In its first productions (Tolstoy's *Tsar Feodor Ivanovich*, 1898; Ostrovsky's *Snow Maiden*, 1900; Tolstoy's *Power of Darkness*, 1902; Shakespeare's *Julius Caesar*, 1903) Stanislavsky continued and developed the ideals he had expounded for the Society of Literature and Art. Away with all theatricality, all pompous, stereotyped mannerisms; the stage and the actor must give the complete illusion of reality. Thus the Moscow Theatre became the home of theatrical naturalism.

Among Stanislavsky's greatest achievements were the productions of Chekhov's plays, *The Seagull* in 1898, *Uncle Vanya* in 1899, *Three Sisters* in 1901, and *The Cherry Orchard* in 1904. These mark a further stage in the development of Stanislavsky's style, the accent being transferred from the external to the internal, from the truth of history, manners, and customs to the truth of feelings, moods, and expressions. He produced the plays as lyric dramas, underlining the emotional elements with music, and showing how Chekhov's apparently passive dialogue demands great subtlety, and a psychological internal development of the role with great simplicity of external expression.

During the years of upheaval leading to the uprising of 1905 Stanislavsky produced the plays of that 'stormy petrel of the Revolution', Maxim Gorky, including *The Lower Depths*. In the years of reaction (1905–16) he turned to the Symbolists—Maeterlinck and Andreyev —and aestheticized, stylized productions. Under the Soviet régime, after an initial period of adjustment, he continued his work as a fine producer of both old and new plays (see MOSCOW ART THEATRE). He was himself a superb character actor, and through long and persistent practice he raised his technique to a high pitch of perfection. His temperament was deep, powerful, but controlled. Among his best roles were Astrov in *Uncle Vanya*, Vershinin in *Three Sisters*, Gayev in *The Cherry Orchard*, Dr. Stockman in *An Enemy of the People*, and Rakitin in *A Month in the Country*. In later years, owing to ill health, he gave up acting, but continued to work as a producer and teacher. He left a record of his ideas and methods in his books, *My Life in Art* (1924) and *An Actor Prepares* (1926), and in two works published posthumously, *Stanislavsky Rehearses Othello* (1948) and *Building a Character* (1950).

STARKE, JOHANNE CHRISTIANE (1731–1809), a fine tragic and emotional German actress, who became the leading lady of Koch's company at Leipzig. Her only rival in her own line was Sophie Hensel, but the latter's evil temper and intriguing nature often lost her the sympathy of the audience, whereas Johanna Starke retained her friends, on stage and off. She was excellent as Miss Sara Sampson in Lessing's play of that name, and later played older, maternal and lachrymose roles to perfection. When her tragic style became somewhat outmoded she turned to comedy, and was a great success as comic elderly women. She played for a time under Ekhof at Gotha, and went with the company to Mannheim after his death.

STAR THEATRE, NEW YORK. This was Lester Wallack's second theatre, and when he left it became the home of plays in German until 23 Mar. 1882, when it opened as the Star, taking the place of Booth's. It was at this theatre on 29 Oct. 1883 that Irving made his first appearance in New York, appearing with Ellen Terry and his Lyceum company under the management of Henry E. Abbey. He confined himself to modern plays, not wishing to challenge Booth in Shakespeare, and his staging, lighting, and acting proved a revelation to New York audiences. Later visitors to the Star were Booth himself, Modjeska in Barrymore's *Nadjezda*, John McCullough on his farewell visit to New York, Mary Anderson, returning after two years in London, Bernhardt in her most popular parts, and Wilson Barrett.

STEAD, JAMES HENRY (?–1886), a music-hall performer who achieved fame with one song from which he took his nickname 'The Perfect Cure'. It was written by a song-writer named Tom Perry, and Stead first sang it at Weston's Music-Hall (afterwards the Holborn Empire). All through the 1870s it created a furore, not so much on account of the song, perhaps, as of the curious dance which accompanied it. Dressed in a suit with very broad stripes running down it, his pale face painted with red cheeks like a Dutch doll and adorned with a small moustache and imperial, the whole surmounted by a clown's hat, Stead bounded up and down all the time he was singing, with his hands held tightly by his side. He is said to have made as many as sixteen hundred leaps at each performance. He never found another song to equal 'The Perfect Cure', and when its vogue waned he fell on bad times, and died in poverty in an attic in Seven Dials.   W. M. P.

STEELE, SIR RICHARD (1672–1729), English soldier, politician, essayist, pamphleteer, and incidentally dramatist, in which capacity he was one of the first to temper the licentiousness of the Restoration drama with sentimental moralizing. His work for the theatre falls into two periods, the first covering his three early comedies, *The Funeral* (1701), a satire on the fashionable parade of grief, *The Lying Lover* (1703), an amusing trifle spoiled by a priggish last act, and *The Tender Husband* (1705), which, like its predecessors, had only a short run and a moderate success. Steele then turned his energies to *The Tatler* and *The Spectator*, though remaining in close touch with the theatrical world, particularly Drury Lane, and it was not until 1722 that he produced his last, and most important, play, *The Conscious Lovers*, a sentimentalized adaptation of Terence's *Andria*, marked throughout by a high moral tone and given under Colley Cibber's supervision with an excellent cast which included Booth, Wilkes, and Mrs. Oldfield. It was a great success, and was immediately translated into German and French, exercising an immense influence on the current European drift towards *la comédie larmoyante*. Steele was the founder and editor of the first English theatrical paper, *The Theatre*, which appeared twice a week from 1719 to 1720.

STEINBECK, JOHN (1902–   ), American writer, best known as a novelist, who qualified as a playwright with dramatizations of his short published novels *Of Mice and Men* and *The Moon Is Down*, which were already actually dramatic in structure and dialogue. Born in Salinas, California, of German and Irish descent, Steinbeck worked as an itinerant farm-hand in his youth, and later as foreman on a ranch and as a chemist in a sugar refinery. After some desultory education at Leland Stanford University he worked as a manual labourer and as a reporter in New York. Returning to California, he began to write the novels that won him a reputation without assuring him a livelihood until he published *Of Mice and Men*. The play, taken from that novel, was produced in 1937 and won the Drama Critics' Prize in 1938 for its realistic picture of itinerant labour and the tragic story of a feeble-minded farm-hand. Steinbeck's second play, *The Moon Is Down* (1942), which was more favourably received in Europe than in New York, dramatized the occupation of a peaceful town by the Germans, and the resistance movement.   J. G.

STERNHEIM, KARL (1878–1943), German dramatist, whose bitter anti-bourgeois satires have caused him to be likened to Molière and Wycherley. The son of a banker, he took delight in flaying the snobbery and petty-mindedness of his immediate circle. His plays deal with social climbers, newly-enriched millionaires, weak-kneed would-be gallants, and financial jugglers. His biting humour, enhanced by his telegraphic style, reminiscent of the expressionists, struck a new note in the German theatre at this time, and he ranked as one of the few modern German dramatists to succeed in comedy. Among his plays the most successful were *Bürger Schippel* (1913), *Tabula Rasa* (1916), *Libussa* (1922), and *Der Nebbich* (1922). One of his later plays dealt with the subject of Oscar Wilde.

STEVENSON, WILLIAM (?–1575), a Fellow of Christ's College, Cambridge, who is believed to have been the author of *Gammer Gurton's Needle*, a play which, with Udall's *Ralph Roister Doister*, stands at the beginning of English comedy. No definite date can be assigned for its performance, but it was probably given at Cambridge between 1552 and 1563. It was printed in 1575, the year of Stevenson's death, and may be identical with a play referred to as *Diccon the Bedlam*, the name of the chief character in *Gammer Gurton's Needle*. This play has also been attributed, with little likelihood, to Dr. John Still, Bishop of Bath and Wells in 1593, and to Dr. John Bridges, who is mentioned as its author in the *Martin Marprelate* tracts. It is possible that Bridges may have assisted Stevenson in the composition of the play, since he is known to have been a prolific writer of verse and a noted wit; or he may have revised it for a later performance. Although structurally the play conforms to the classic type, its material is native English, and one of its characters, Hodge, has

given his name to the conventional English farm labourer.

STICHOMYTHIA, a type of dialogue employed occasionally in Greek classical drama, in which two characters speak single lines of verse alternately during passages of emotional tension or forceful disputation. The device has been likened to 'alternate strokes of hammers on the anvil'. It has been used in English drama, notably in Shakespeare's *Richard III* (e.g. Act I, Scene ii, lines 193–203), and the clipped prose dialogue in some of the plays of the 1920s (Noel Coward's among them) may be thought to derive, however remotely and indirectly, from the Greek practice. It is, however, essentially a poetic device, and its effectiveness even in verse drama depends upon a carefully limited employment. It is sometimes referred to as 'cut-and-parry' or 'cut-and-thrust' dialogue.

STIERNHIELM, GEORG (1598–1672), Swedish dramatist, author of a number of imitations of contemporary French masques, much patronized by the Court.

STILE, the vertical side-piece of a flat.

STILL, JOHN, see STEVENSON, WILLIAM.

STIRLING. (1) FANNY (really MARY ANNE KEHL) (1815–95), English actress, who made her first appearance at the Coburg in 1832 under the name of Fanny Clifton. Here she met and married an actor (2) EDWARD STIRLING (really LAMBERT) (1809–94), who had made his first appearance on the stage in 1828. He wrote some 200 plays, many of them based on the novels of Dickens, and produced either at the Lyceum or at the Adelphi, of which he was stage-manager with Frederick Yates. He was also the author of a volume of reminiscences published in 1881. His wife appeared under his management at the Adelphi, and had a successful career in soubrette and comedy roles, though she was not good in Shakespeare or in tragedy. In later years her acting was thought somewhat extravagant, but she was one of the last exponents of the grand style in comedy. Peg Woffington in *Masks and Faces* supplied her with one of her best parts, while in her later years she had no equal as Mrs. Malaprop, Mrs. Candour, and Juliet's Nurse. In 1870 she retired from the stage, but gave recitals and taught elocution. On her husband's death she married again, becoming Lady Gregory, but died a year later.

STOCK COMPANY, a theatrical troupe which was regularly attached to a particular theatre or group of theatres, operating on a true repertory basis with a nightly change of bill. The term seems to have come into use about the mid-nineteenth century, probably in order to distinguish a regular, resident company from a touring one. The system was, however, in existence long before that, and the name would have been applicable to the companies attached to the Patent Theatres in London from the Restoration onwards, and to the eighteenth-century circuit companies in the provinces. The early nineteenth-century theatres in New York, Boston, Philadelphia, and other centres in the United States, were also occupied by stock companies, which, as in England, found themselves threatened by the establishment of the long run, and, in the provinces, by the competition of the touring companies. By 1880 the touring company, assisted by cheap and easy railway transport, had triumphed, and the stock companies had practically ceased to exist. They had been excellent training grounds for young actors, giving them variety of acting experience, together with some permanence and security. Something of the same function is now performed by the repertory companies, but their weekly change of bill gives a less wide range of parts, with practically no repetition, while such companies as the Old Vic present only four or five plays in a season. The State-subsidized theatres of the continent, such as the Comédie-Française, and the theatres of Soviet Russia, approximate to the old stock company, but the enormous increase in the size of the potential audience has made the constant change of bill unnecessary and uneconomic, added to which the modern audience has come to rely on a continuous run and tends to be bewildered by the true repertory system. An attempt to establish something of the kind in New York has not yet proved successful.

The old stock company was formed of a group of actors each of whom undertook some special line of business. The Tragedian, who was also the leading man, took such parts as Hamlet and Macbeth—though he also appeared in comedy. The Old Man played Sir Anthony Absolute and Sir Peter Teazle, and was a person of consequence. The Old Woman took Juliet's Nurse. The Heavy Father or Heavy Lead was a term which came into use about 1830 to describe tyrants and villains in tragedy and melodrama; while the Heavy Woman played the more mature parts in tragedy, such as Lady Macbeth, or Emilia in *Othello*. The Juvenile Lead was the young lover and hero, and the Juvenile Tragedian took on Macduff or Laertes, often combining such parts with light comedy roles. The Low Comedian played leading comic parts of a broad, farcical, or clownish type, and was usually apportioned minor roles in tragedy, while the Walking Lady or Gentleman played secondary parts in comedy, such as Careless in *The School for Scandal*. These roles were usually given to beginners and the salary was low. General Utility played minor roles in any and every type of play—'to have the most to do'—the least notice of doing it—and receive the lowest salary' was how Leman Rede described it in *The Road to the Stage* (1827). A Super, or Supernumerary, was an actor or actress who was engaged merely to walk on in a particular play in addition to the regular company, and

had nothing to say. Such persons were often not paid at all. Among other members of a stock company were such specialists as the Leading or First Singer, or Vocalist, the Principal Dancer, and so on (see also PROVINCIAL THEATRES). S. R.

STOCKFISCH, see SPENCER, JOHN.

STOLL, SIR OSWALD (1866–1942), English theatre manager, an Australian of Irish parentage, whose real name was Gray. He took his stepfather's name, however, and gained his first theatrical experience at the Parthenon in Liverpool under his mother's management. He then joined forces with Moss and built Empires all over the provinces; but when they came to London the original Empire in Leicester Square was not for sale, so Moss built the Hippodrome and Stoll the Coliseum. When first opened the latter gave four shows a day, which did much to change the old-style music-hall show into the present Variety. Stoll was one of the quietest showmen that ever lived. He spoke very softly, and was always inaudible. He made the Coliseum a most respectable place, with more music than comedy, and cleaned up Variety, refusing to allow any comedian to use an expletive, however mild. He controlled the Stoll Circuit and gave his name to the Stoll Theatre, formerly the London Opera House. In 1919 Stoll was knighted, not only for his services to the stage, but for his benevolent works and his War Seals Foundation during the 1914–18 war. He sometimes wrote songs, among them one for Vesta Tilley which was a great success. W. M. P.

STOLL THEATRE, LONDON. This was opened in 1911 by Oscar Hammerstein the first, as the London Opera House, with *Quo Vadis?*; but this palatial playhouse had only a short operatic career, and was soon staging revue and pantomime, with long intervals of closure. Soon after war broke out in 1914 a strange entertainment, half dramatic, half musical, was seen there under the title of *England Expects*. The building was eventually acquired by Sir Oswald Stoll who gave it his name and ran it as a cinema for a long time. During the Second World War it became a music-hall and, under Prince Littler, a home of musical plays. It stands in Kingsway, near the junction with Aldwych, and part of its site was once Gibbon's tennis-court (see VERE STREET THEATRE). The head of Hammerstein, carved on the façade, was obliterated when the theatre passed into other hands. W. M. P.

STONE, JOHN AUGUSTUS (1801–34), American dramatist, author of *Metamora*, one of the first plays to be based on American history. This was awarded a prize by Forrest for 'the best tragedy, in five acts, of which the hero, or principal character, shall be an original of this country'. It was given in New York in 1829, and was a great success, being revived as late as 1887. After playing in it for some years Forrest commissioned Bird to rewrite it, but as no complete manuscripts of either version exist, it is not possible to say how much Bird altered it. Stone, who was a mediocre actor, wrote also a number of romantic historical plays which have not survived. Disappointed as actor and author, he committed suicide, according to Wood, by throwing himself into the river at Philadelphia.

STORER, see HENRY, JOHN.

STORM AND STRESS, see STURM UND DRANG.

STRAND LIGHT CONSOLE, see LIGHT-ING, 2 k.

STRAND THEATRE, LONDON. (1) In 1831 Benjamin Lionel Rayner, a celebrated Yorkshire comedian, acquired a building which from 1820 to 1828 had housed panoramas. In seven weeks he transformed it into a theatre and opened it on 25 Jan. 1832, as Rayner's New Subscription Theatre in the Strand. It was decorated in white, gold, and silver, and, as it had no licence, tickets were sold off the premises at 4s., 3s., and 2s. There was no gallery. At this time the last battles between the unlicensed houses and the Patent Theatres were being waged, and the opening attraction at the new theatre was a skit on the situation, called *Professionals Puzzled; or, Struggles at Starting*. There was also a special little play for Mrs. Waylett, the star actress, and Rayner appeared in one of his former successes, *The Miller's Maid*. A few weeks after the opening Mrs. Waylett took sole charge, and in Nov. 1832 the theatre closed down. It reopened in February of the following year, when Fanny Kelly gave a monologue entertainment, and in October Wrench and Russell tried drama there. But the Patent Theatres caused it to be closed. In 1834 Mrs. Waylett tried again, resorting to every expedient to evade the Patent Laws, such as free admission on the purchase of an ounce of lozenges for 4s. A real Red Indian chief and his squaw appeared, as did Mrs. Nisbett, while the greatest success was Gilbert à Becket's burlesque of *Manfred*. But in 1835 the theatre was again closed at the behest of the Patent Houses. At last, in 1836, it was put on the same footing as the Olympic and the Adelphi, and on 1 May Douglas Jerrold and James Hammond reopened it. The partnership did not last long, but Hammond remained until 1839. A gallery had been added to the theatre, holding 800 people at 1s. 6d. each. Dickens's novels in dramatic form were played there, notably *Pickwick Papers* under the title of *Sam Weller*, and *Nicholas Nickleby*; but the dramatic fare was always reinforced by extravaganza.

In 1841 a conjuror named Jacobs took the theatre. The Keeleys starred there, and Mrs. Stirling appeared in *Aline*. Fox Cooper took over in 1847, followed by Oxberry and Edward Hooper in rapid succession. From 1848 to 1850 William Farren took command. Under him Mrs. Stirling appeared in *Adrienne Lecouvreur* and as Olivia in *The Vicar of Wakefield*—Farren playing Dr. Primrose and Mrs. Glover making her last stage appearance as Mrs. Primrose. William Copeland of Liverpool was the next tenant. He renamed the theatre Punch's Playhouse, but though he engaged good actors he lasted only two seasons. After a varied career, during which the theatre sank very low, W. H. Swanborough, in Feb. 1858, started a scheme which seemed certain to fail. He starred his daughter in H. J. Byron's burlesques, and success came their way. *Fra Diavolo, The Miller and His Men, The Lady of Lyons*, were all popular and the public flocked to see the Swanborough shows, with a cast that also included James Thorne, Edward Terry, Miss Raynham, Mrs. Raymond, and Marie Wilton (afterwards Lady Bancroft). The last of the Swanborough burlesques was given in 1872. In 1882 the theatre was condemned, rebuilt, and reopened. A period of failure followed, with *Vice Versa* as the only bright spot. Swanborough died, and J. S. Clarke became lessee, with a notable season of old English comedies. In the early nineties Willie Edouin took the theatre, and with *Our Flat* scored a run of 600 nights. Later *Niobe*, with Beatrice Lamb and Harry Paulton in the leading roles, ran for several hundred performances, and it became the fashion for wedding-parties to visit this play—why, no one ever knew! A period of farce followed, and then came the record-breaking musical comedy, *The Chinese Honeymoon*, which ran for 1,075 performances. The theatre was demolished in 1905, and its site is now covered by the Aldwych Underground station.

(2) The present Strand Theatre opened on 22 May 1905 as the Waldorf, Aldwych, under the direction of the Shubert Brothers, of New York, with Italian Opera. Duse then played a season there, and Tree transferred *Oliver Twist* from His Majesty's when the proscenium arch of the latter developed a crack. An American, F. C. Whitney, then took the theatre and gave it his name. Some musical plays of little importance were produced, and in 1910 the theatre took its present name. Successful productions there were Matheson Lang's *Mr. Wu* in 1913, and a revival of *The Scarlet Pimpernel*, with Fred Terry and Julia Neilson, in 1915. During their tenancy the theatre was damaged by a bomb dropped from a Zeppelin. In 1917 a dramatization of Elinor Glyn's *Three Weeks* was produced, and later Arthur Bourchier took over the theatre and ran it successfully for many years, producing, among other plays, *Treasure Island* and *Stop Flirting*, the latter with Adele and Fred Astaire. After Bourchier's death his second wife, Kyrle Bellew, took command, and in association with Firth Shephard and Leslie Henson produced several successful farces, notably *It's a Boy* in 1930. In 1940, during the air bombardment of London, Donald Wolfit played Shakespeare at the Strand during the lunch hour, and on 8 Oct. 1940 the theatre was badly blasted. Although all the

dressing-rooms were damaged, and costumes had to be dug out, while actors had to scramble over debris to reach the stage, the show went on. The theatre was later repaired and is still in use.   W. M. P.

STRANGE'S MEN, an Elizabethan theatre company, presumed to be the first by which Shakespeare was employed, either as actor and playwright, or as playwright only, in 1592. The company had been in existence before this, playing mainly in the provinces. At the same time a company called the Earl of Derby's Men, under the patronage of Lord Strange's father, was also in existence, a duplication which has caused some confusion. Both companies were at Court in 1582, Strange's Men being referred to as 'tumblers'. Their chief actor was a John Symons, who joined the Queen's Men in 1588, while the rest of Strange's Men amalgamated with the Admiral's Men at the Theatre under James Burbage, with Edward Alleyn as their chief actor. After quarrelling with Burbage, they left the Theatre and went together to the Rose, Henslowe's new playhouse, where the joint company played sometimes under one name, sometimes under the other, though Alleyn always kept his personal status as an Admiral's Man. In Court records the company is invariably referred to as Strange's, as it is also in Henslowe's diary during their six weeks' season in 1592. It is at this time that Shakespeare probably wrote for them, or perhaps rewrote from an older play, the first part of his *Henry VI*, and he may, in the following year, have written for them *The Comedy of Errors*, under the title of *The Jealous Comedy*. Among their other plays were *Titus and Vespasian*, which later became *Titus Andronicus* for Sussex's Men, and *A Knack to know a Knave*, while the older plays in their repertory included *The Jew of Malta*, *Orlando Furioso*, and *Friar Bacon and Friar Bungay*, as well as a number of plays now lost. The company, which separated itself from the Admiral's in 1594, included Kempe, Heminge (later the friend and editor of Shakespeare), Pope, and Phillips. On the death of their patron in 1594 (he had succeeded his father as Earl of Derby only six months before) and on the general reshuffling of the companies which took place with the formation of the Chamberlain's Men in that year, the company vanished into the provinces, to reappear at Court in 1599–1600. The last mention of them is at Islington in 1618.

STRANITZKY, JOSEPH ANTON (1676–1726), an Austrian actor, originally a medical student. He was at one time a member of Velten's company, and in 1699 and 1702 emerges as a puppet-master. A few years later he settled in Vienna and founded the popular stage there, adopting for his clowning the dress and dialect of a Salzburg peasant. He has himself in his writings described the stage appearance of the clown Hanswurst, as he became known, probably from his sausage-shaped satchel—green-peaked hat, hair tied up in a tuft on the top of his head, huge black eyebrows and beard, a thick neck, a large collar, green-edged braces with an immense heart in front, inscribed H.W., wide yellow trousers, and buttons as big as a fist. Lady Mary Wortley Montagu gives an amusing account in her letters of her visit to one of Hanswurst's performances in 1716. Stranitzky prospered and grew rich, and was able to acquire his own theatre in Vienna.

                                                W. E. D.

STRATFORD-ON-AVON, the birth-place of Shakespeare and scene of a yearly festival devoted to his works, given at the Shakespeare Memorial Theatre. This festival, now firmly established and running every year from April till October with a repertory of six to eight plays, has been growing since the 1860s, slowly, persistently, and always impredictably. In 1947 it was once more at a critical stage. A period of rising profits and falling standards of acting ended in 1946, and the direction of the Memorial Theatre was taken over by Sir Barry Jackson. He was commissioned by the Governors to re-establish a Stratford tradition of fine theatrical art and, incidentally, to create a permanent company which great cities at home and abroad would receive with delight. Sir Barry Jackson's directorship ended in 1948, and the outcome of his policy is matter for future historians. It is still imperilled by the remoteness of Stratford from film studios and the unwillingness of eminent Shakespearian actors to absent themselves from London for the best part of a year. Yet the history of the festival encourages the hope that this, together with other formidable difficulties, will be overcome. It is a history which would never have been possible without a great deal of that generosity of spirit which Shakespeare's name is able to evoke not only in men of the theatre but in the theatre's patrons; and the patrons of Stratford have belonged to many different races.

The famous Jubilee of 1769 turned the town into a stage—for Garrick; and its feasting and fireworks, its commemorative odes and masquerades, were perhaps the beginning of Stratford as a centre of Bardolatry. The origins of the festival come much later. The notion of celebrating the Tercentenary with the performance of a play on the birthday emanated from Stratford in 1861, and, despite lack of enthusiasm and some discouraging opposition from London, was carried into effect three years later. Its moving spirit was E. F. Flower; and it was his son, Charles Edward Flower, who first conceived the idea of a permanent memorial theatre. A committee was formed, but the first result of its activities was a renewal of London's hostility to Stratford's claim to have a special interest in its son. C. E. Flower, ignoring metropolitan gibes, issued a national appeal for £20,000. The response was generally poor, and the greater part of the money came from his own purse. He also presented the Governors of the theatre with the riverside site. So that it was in 1879 that the festival as we know it to-day began. *Much Ado About Nothing* was the first play to be performed. Barry Sullivan was Benedick, and Helen Faucit came out of her retirement to play Beatrice. So delighted was Sullivan by the triumph of his first festival that he returned the following year. It was through the influence of Sullivan that Edward Compton took over the festival plays for 1881, and he also returned the following year. The festival tradition had been established. Young Frank Benson came in 1886, and remained in control of the spring and summer festivals for the next thirty years. He produced every play in the folio except *Titus Andronicus* and *Troilus and Cressida*. He made theatre history by giving festival audiences an uncut version of *Hamlet*. His local popularity was so great that the whole town turned out to welcome him at the station, and he was drawn in a horseless carriage to his hotel. The Bensonians created an atmosphere of athleticism and conviviality which still lingers about the festival.

The year 1925 had a character of its own. A Royal Charter was granted to the Memorial Theatre, and the festival made a profit for the first time in its forty-six years of life. On Saturday, 6 Mar. 1926, the theatre—something of a Victorian monstrosity—was destroyed by fire. The festival was due to open in six weeks' time. A local fund of £1,600 was raised almost overnight, a cinema was converted into a theatre, and for the next six seasons W. Bridges-Adams, who had succeeded Sir Frank Benson in 1919, contrived in spite of all difficulties to please visitors with swift and well-balanced productions. More than half of the large sum required to build a new theatre was raised in America, and both there and in this country it was again a Flower—this time Sir Archibald Flower—who was the moving spirit of the appeal. The new theatre, designed by Elizabeth Scott, was opened by the Prince of Wales on 23 Apr. (Shakespeare's birthday) 1932, with *King Henry IV, Parts I and II*. Some interesting productions have been seen there, notably Komisarjevsky's *King Lear* and *Macbeth*. Under the directorship of Ben Iden Payne, who succeeded W. Bridges-Adams in 1934, there was a marked improvement in the speaking of verse, while Robert Atkins carried out, during a brief directorship, a number of useful reforms. On Sir Barry Jackson's retirement in 1949 his place was taken by Anthony Quayle, who had played with the company during the previous season.   A. V. C.

STRATTON, EUGENE (1861–1918), an American negro impersonator who, like Chirgwin, became a well-known music-hall star. He was born in Buffalo, U.S.A., his real name being Eugene Augustus Ruhlmann. At the age of 17, after some experience as a solo turn, he joined the Haverly Minstrels, with whom he went to London in 1880. He was for many years with the Moore and Burgess Minstrels. When their popularity began to wane he took to the music-hall stage, making his first appearance at the Royal Holborn in 1892. As a white-faced performer he was not successful, but on resuming his negro make-up he made an instant appeal, and became the outstanding black-face performer of the halls, particularly when he sang 'Lily of Laguna' and other coon songs by Leslie Stuart—wistful ballads to which he whistled a refrain while dancing on a darkened, spotlighted stage in soft shoes, a noiseless, moving shadow. He retired in 1914, making his last appearance at the Queen's, Poplar.

STREATER [STREETER], ROBERT (1624–80), English painter, who was responsible for the decorations of the Sheldonian Theatre, Oxford. He was said to excel in architectural and decorative paintings on a large scale, especially those in which perspective and a knowledge of foreshortening were required. Evelyn, in his diary for 9 Feb. 1671, says he saw 'at White-hall Theater' 'the famous play call'd *The Siege of Granada* two days acted successively; there were indeed very glorious scenes and perspectives, the worke of Mr. Streater, who well understands it'.

STRINDBERG, AUGUST (1849–1912), Swedish dramatist, was born in Stockholm in 1849. He was the author of some fifty-odd plays (as well as poems, novels, stories, and autobiographical works) besides being a proficient scholar in several unrelated branches of knowledge. His genius was of that passionate and sensitive kind which is driven to, though not satisfied by, never-resting mental activity and exploration. His life, and the consequent matter of his plays, was divided by the crisis thus brought on in his middle years (about 1895–1897). His earlier plays, after the experimental stage usual to young dramatists, are first historical and then realistic. These latter offer a reading of life whose implications denounce, not so much the accidental corruption of society already analysed by his Norwegian predecessors, Bjørnson and Ibsen, as certain of the basic tendencies of human nature. The later plays, from 1898 onwards, are either, again, historical (histories now of some power and originality) or attempts to reveal, in expressionist forms of which he was often the first master, the unexplored areas, the inarticulate impulses and processes, of the human mind. In many of these it would seem that a genuine mystical experience lies behind the implications of the play and that a resolution of the earlier problems has been found. On the strictly technical side his genius is no less fertile than it is in the discovery of subject and theme. The variety and abundance of his technical invention and theatrical devices is astounding. Much of the structural virtuosity which has until lately been fashionable in Europe and America has, in fact, either been anticipated by Strindberg or actually derived from him (consciously or unconsciously) by playwrights who have merely dotted his 'i's' and crossed his 't's'. He is one of the most difficult of modern dramatists to measure, for the raw force and copiousness of his genius still dazzles the judgement. He has been both over- and under-estimated, now being regarded as the equal of Ibsen (which, for lack if only of artistic wholeness, he could not be) and now merely as a brilliant theatre-man, remarkable only for novelty of theme and form.

His principal plays may be grouped roughly in the following way. The early plays, including the first group of histories, fall between 1870 and 1882: *Fritänkaren (The Free-Thinker)* (1870); *Den Fredlöse (The Outlaw)* (1871); *Gillets Hemlighet (The Secret of the Guild)* (1880); *Anno Fyrtiåotta (In the Year Forty-eight)* (1881); *Herr Bengt's Hustru (Sir Bengt's Wife)* and *Lycko-Pers Resa (The Wanderings of Lucky Per)* (both 1882). A sharp change, already anticipated in his fiction, enters his dramatic work with *Fadren (The Father)* (1887); this, together with *Fröken Julie (Miss Julie)* (1888) and its famous preface, contains the clear revelation of Strindberg's growing preoccupation with sin, crime, and abnormality and his reading of human nature in terms of these. The dramatic technique of these plays and the corresponding comments in the preface also mark an advance in power and definition. Other plays of this second phase, some of which have been widely produced, show also some interesting experiments in length, ranging from the full play to brief studies such as *Den Starkare (The Stronger)* (1890), with only one speaking part. This period includes *Kamraterna (Comrades)*, (1886–7); *Fordringsägare (Creditors)* (1888); *Paria* and *Samum* (both 1890); *Himmelrickets Nycklar (The Keys to the Kingdom of Heaven)* (1892); *Inför Döden (Facing Death)*, *Första Varningen (The First Warning)*, *Debet och Kredit*, *Moderskärlek (Mother-love)*, *Das Band*, and *Das Spiel mit dem Feuer* (all 1892–3) (both these last were translated into Swedish in 1897 as *Bandet* and *Leka med Elden*).

The main division in Strindberg's work, in thought and technique, may perhaps best be made at this point. For the plays that follow in 1899, such as *Advent* on the one hand and *Brott och Brott (Crimes and Crimes)* on the other, reveal, in their widely different styles, the presence of those governing conceptions of spiritual reality which are apparent during the remaining ten years of Strindberg's work. The other plays of this last period are *Till Damaskus I* and *II (To Damascus)* (1898); *Folkungasagan (The Folkungs' Saga)*, *Gustaf Vasa*, the first of his fifteen major historical dramas, and *Erik XIV* (all 1899); *Gustaf Adolf* (1900); *Påsk (Easter)*, *Midsommar*, *Dödsdansen I* and *II (The Dance of Death)*, and *Carl XII* (all 1901); *Kronbruden (The Bride with the Crown)*, *Svanehvit (Swanwhite)*, and *Ett Drömspel (A Dream Play)* (all 1902); *Engelbrekt* (1901); *Kristina*, *Gustaf III*, and *Näktergalen i Wittenberg (The Nightingale of Wittenberg)* (all 1903); *Till Damaskus III* (1904); *Oväder (The*

Thunderstorm), *Brända Tomten (The Site of the Burnt House)*, *Spöksonaten (The Spook Sonata)*, and *Pelikanen* (all 1907); *Sista Riddaren (The Last Knight)* and *Abu Casems Tofflor (The Slippers of Abu Casem)* (both 1908); *Riksföreståndaren (The Regent)*, *Bjälbojarlen (The Earl of Bjälbo)*, *Svarta Handsken (The Black Glove)*, and *Stora Landsvägen (The Great Highway)* (all 1909). In 1907 Strindberg, together with August Falck, founded the famous Intima Teatern in Stockholm.   U. E.-F.

STURM UND DRANG, the name given to a phase of eighteenth-century German literature and drama which carried to its farthest consequences the doctrine of the rights of the individual as preached by the protagonists of enlightenment. The writers of this movement espoused Rousseau's doctrine of a return to nature, but they meant by that something far more elemental than Rousseau had intended. In drama Shakespeare was their idol. Characteristic themes reappear again and again in their work, among them the Faust legend, treated by Goethe and Klinger, and the tragedy of the unmarried mother executed for the murder of her child while her seducer goes free. This latter was an injustice which weighed heavily on the conscience of these young writers, and it was treated by H. L. Wagner in *Die Kindesmörderin* and by Lenz in *Die Soldaten* (both 1776), as well as by Goethe in his *Faust*. Other subjects were the hostile brothers, incompatible natures fettered by malignant fate in a close relationship, and in love with the same woman—Klinger's *Die Zwillinge* (1776) and Schiller's *Die Räuber* (1781)—and the over-mastering power of love, hurling even honourable natures into crime—Müller's *Genoveva* and again Goethe's *Faust*. The movement had repercussions all over Europe, and its influence can be clearly seen in the late eighteenth- and early nineteenth-century melodrama of England. Of its progenitors Goethe and Schiller went on to greater things; Klinger, from one of whose plays the movement took its name, lapsed into mediocrity; Lenz wrote no more.   W. E. D.

STUYVESANT THEATRE, NEW YORK, see BELASCO.

SUBURBAN THEATRES, LONDON. All through the 1890s and the early 1900s there was a great deal of theatrical activity in the London suburbs, and many theatres were built. The best known, with their dates of opening, are:

Balham, The Duchess, 1899; The Brixton (destroyed by enemy action, 1940), 1896; Camberwell, The Metropole, 1894; The Camden, in Camden Town, 1900; Clapham, The Shakespeare, 1896; Crouch End Opera House, 1897; The Dalston, 1898; Deptford, The Broadway, 1897; Fulham, The Grand, 1897; Hammersmith, The Kings (still used as a theatre), 1902; Holloway, The Marlborough, 1903; The Kennington, 1898; The Kilburn, 1895; Notting Hill Gate, The Coronet, 1898;

Peckham, The Crown, 1898; Poplar, The Prince's, 1905; Rotherhithe, The Terriss, 1899; Stoke Newington, The Alexandra (still a theatre), 1897; Stratford, The Borough, 1896, The Theatre Royal (still a theatre), 1884; Woolwich, The Grand, 1900.

These theatres were used solely for the visits of touring companies and for an annual pantomime. Some later became repertory theatres, some music-halls, but the majority are now cinemas. There was a small theatre called the Parkhurst at the junction of Holloway Road and Camden Road, which has now vanished. There was a large theatre inside the Crystal Palace, and there is also one inside the Alexandra Palace, which was rebuilt in 1922, but it remained in use for a short time only. It is now used by the B.B.C. in connexion with television.

More recent suburban theatres are those at Wimbledon, opened in 1910, at Lewisham (The Hippodrome), opened in 1912, at Golders Green (The Hippodrome), opened in 1913 as a music-hall, and as a theatre in 1923, and at Streatham (Streatham Hill), opened in 1929. These last have been very successful with touring companies and shows before and immediately after London production, and with annual pantomimes. The Intimate Theatre, Palmers Green, opened by John Clements in 1935, has done excellent work as a repertory theatre whose new plays have sometimes been transferred to the West End. The 'Q' Theatre at Kew Bridge, opened on 26 Dec. 1924 by J. and D. De Leon, is also used for try-outs and revivals. (See also ARTILLERY, EMBASSY, EVERYMAN, LYRIC (2), MERCURY, and RICHMOND THEATRES.)   W. M. P.

SUDAKOV, ILYA YAKOVLEIVICH (1890–   ), Soviet actor and producer, who received his training at the Moscow Art Theatre, and was one of the founders of the Second Studio, where he first tackled production. When the studio was merged with the Moscow Art Theatre he continued to direct, first under Stanislavsky and Nemirovich-Danchenko, and then independently, without however ceasing to act. He taught in a number of Theatre Schools, and in 1933 was invited to become director of the Moscow Theatre of the Leninist Komsomol (see LENKOM), which he reorganized and revitalized on the lines of the Moscow Art Theatre. He then became artistic director of the Maly Theatre, where one of his best productions was Uriel Acosta in 1940, with sets by Rabinovich.

SUDERMANN, HERMANN (1857–1928), German dramatist, a writer of the realistic era whose first play, Die Ehre, was given at the Lessing theatre (founded by Oskar Blumenthal in 1888) in 1889, the same year as Hauptmann's Vor Sonnenaufgang at the Freie Bühne. Sudermann became the oustanding exponent of German middle-class drama, and helped to make a facile form of naturalism acceptable to the general public. He was much influenced by Ibsen, as may be seen by his Das Glück im Winkel (1895) and Johannisfeuer (1900); and even his histori-

cal plays, Johannes (1898) and Die drei Reiherfedern (1898), have an obstinately modern and naturalistic atmosphere. The play by which he is best remembered, however, is Die Heimat (1893), known to England and America as Magda, which combines the theatrical effectiveness of the 'well-made' play with the social significance of Magda, the 'new woman'.

SŪDRAKA, see INDIA.

SUE, EUGÈNE (1804–57), French dramatist, who trained as a naval surgeon and was present at the battle of Navarino in 1827. After running through a fortune and getting involved in several scandals, he wrote a series of novels which had a great and unexpected success and were immediately adapted for the stage. They had little literary quality, but all the ingredients for popularity, being full of bloodshed, horrors, and melodramatic events. Among them were Les Mystères de Paris, which was translated into English and had a great influence, and Le Juif errant, a version of the Wandering Jew legend which gained wide popularity.

SUETT, RICHARD (1755–1805), English comedian, commonly known as Dicky Suett. As a boy he sang in the choir at St. Paul's, and made his first appearance at Drury Lane in 1780, when he was considered extremely comical, though with a little too much gag and grimace. He was at his best in the fools of Shakespeare, which seemed to have been specially written for him. Lamb, who called him the Robin Goodfellow of the stage, said: 'They have all the true Suett stamp, a loose and shambling gait and a slippery tongue.' Off the stage he was somewhat melancholic, a tall, thin, ungainly man much given to solemn practical jokes and outrageous puns. He was a heavy drinker, which doubtless hastened his death.

SUKHOVO-KOBYLIN, ALEXANDER VASILEIVICH (1817–1903), Russian dramatist, whose whole life was overshadowed by the death of his mistress, whom he was suspected of having murdered. He had already started to write a play, Krechinsky's Wedding, before this tragic event, and during the time he spent in jail—the case dragged on for many years—he finished it, averring that many of the best scenes had been written in prison. It was finally staged at the Moscow Maly Theatre in 1855. Its subject, like that of his two other plays—one written in 1862 and performed at the Alexandrinsky twenty years later, and the other written in 1868 and staged in 1900 in the Theatre of the Literary Society—was the decay of the patriarchial life of old Russia, the breaking-up of the great country estates, the decadence of the nobility, and the growing power of a corrupt bureaucracy. Although Sukhovo-Kobylin truly asserted that he was not a revolutionary, he was regarded as a dangerous man and his plays were banned by the censor. He was a great friend and admirer of Gogol, whose influence is seen in the character of Krechinsky. Sukhovo-Kobylin was also much influenced by that other great satirist of the time, Saltikov-Schedrin. Worn out by his struggles with the censorship, Sukhovo-Kobylin gave up the theatre for philosophy, and retired to France, where he died.

SULLIVAN, (Thomas) Barry (1821–91), Irish actor, who joined a touring company after seeing Macready act, and played for some years in Ireland, mainly in Cork. From 1841 to 1852 he was seen in the English provinces and in Scotland, where he managed a theatre in Aberdeen for three years. He then made his first appearance in London as Hamlet under Buckstone at the Haymarket, and achieved sufficient recognition to warrant a season at Sadler's Wells with Phelps. In the autumn of 1858 he went to New York and at the Broadway Theatre was seen in a wide range of leading parts. He also toured extensively, being exceedingly well received in San Francisco. He made a long visit to Australia, and returned to England to play Benedick to Helen Faucit's Beatrice for the inaugural performance of the Shakespeare Memorial Theatre in 1879. After this he was seldom seen in London, but continued to be popular in the provinces and Ireland. He made his last appearance on the stage in 1887 as Richard III in Liverpool. He was never a really first-class actor, but his vigorous action and forcible delivery made him a success in tragedy with less sophisticated audiences, for whom he kept alive the good old traditions of Shakespearian acting. His sturdy build and face much pitted with small-pox, as well as his natural roughness, rendered him unsuited to comic or romantic parts, which he wisely did not attempt.

SUMAROKOV, Alexei Petrovich (1718–77), the first Russian dramatist. He was born in Finland, of an old and noble family, and at 14 entered the newly founded Cadet College for the education of the sons of the nobility. Here his natural talent for elocution and his love of literature led him to join the Society of Lovers of Russian Literature, of which he was one of the first members. On leaving the college he worked in various government departments, but continued his literary avocations, and in 1749 his first play, a tragedy, *Khorev*, was acted by the cadets, as were the plays which followed. He wrote in the neo-classical style which had been imported into Russia from France, but took his subjects from Russian history, and endeavoured to refine and purify the Russian literary language. He took an active part in the organization of the Cadet College amateur dramatic performances, and when the Yaroslavl actors arrived in St. Petersburg it was largely owing to his efforts that the leading actors were admitted to the College for training, and afterwards allowed to organize the first professional Russian company. In 1756 Sumarokov was appointed head of the Russian (as distinct from the Italian and French) Theatre in St. Petersburg, and three years later he founded a journal in which to air his literary and dramatic

opinions, and wage war against his numerous detractors. In 1761 his liberal outspokenness caused him to be dismissed from office, and thereafter he confined himself to literature. He moved in theatrical circles in Moscow, but the Court banned his plays, which may nevertheless be regarded as the starting-point of a native Russian drama.

SUMMERS, the Rev. (Alphonsus Joseph-Mary Augustus) Montague (1880–1946), English critic and theatre historian. He wrote widely upon Restoration drama and in 1919 founded the Phoenix, a society for the production of old plays. He also edited the plays of Congreve, Wycherley, Otway, Shadwell, and Dryden. His *Bibliography of Restoration Drama* is a valuable compilation, covering a period on which he was one of the foremost authorities. At the time of his death he was working on nineteenth-century melodrama, and had just completed the writing of his autobiography.
T. C. K.

SUPER, SUPERNUMERARY, see STOCK COMPANY. The term is still in use for soldiers, crowds, servants, who are essential to a play but have no lines to speak.

SURREY THEATRE, London. In 1771 an equestrian performer named Charles Hughes opened a riding-school and exhibition in opposition to Philip Astley. Some years later he and Charles Dibdin built, at the cost of £15,000, an amphitheatre near the Obelisk in Blackfriars Road, and opened it in 1782 as the Royal Circus. It was here that the equestrian drama, made famous by Astley, really started. The Royal Circus had a very troubled existence and was burned down in 1803. Rebuilt in 1804, it continued its previous course, until in 1809 Elliston, the Great Lessee, converted it into a theatre. To evade the Patent Act, he put a ballet into all the plays, which included *Macbeth, Hamlet*, and *The Beaux' Stratagem*. In 1814 he gave up, and the building became a circus again until in 1816 Thomas Dibdin reopened it and named it the Surrey. He failed in 1823 and the theatre sank very low. Elliston took it over again in 1827, when he left Drury Lane. Douglas Jerrold, then a struggling young playwright, brought him *Black-Eyed Susan*, which he accepted at once. T. P. Cooke was engaged for it at £60 a week and a 'half clear' benefit every sixth week, and it was produced on 8 June 1829. It drew all London, and on the 300th night the theatre was illuminated. The author, who wrote many more plays for the Surrey, received no more than £70 as remuneration for a successful run of 400 nights.

Elliston made his last appearance at the theatre on 24 June 1831, and died a fortnight later. Osbaldiston then took over, and among other things produced *Jonathan Bradford; or, the Murder at the Roadside Inn*, a poor play which ran successfully for 260 nights. It had a novel stage-set divided into four, with four actions going on simultaneously.

Osbaldiston was succeeded by Davidge, a miserly man, and then by Bunn, from Drury Lane, who essayed opera. In 1848 'Dick' Shepherd, the originator of the rough-and-tumble melodrama now associated with the Surrey, took over, with Osbaldiston back as his partner. This soon ended, however, and Creswick, a fine legitimate actor, joined Shepherd, who was broad and vulgar. Yet their association was successful and lasted, with a short break, from 1848 to 1869. During this time the theatre was burned down and rebuilt. Nothing of importance then took place until 1880, when George Conquest, actor, playwright, and pantomimist, took over. He ran sensational dramas, many of them written by himself, which proved very much to the taste of his patrons, and every Christmas he put on a fine pantomime. The house flourished until his death in 1901. It declined after this and became a cinema from 1920 to 1924, with a brief season of opera. Several attempts were made to reopen it, but there were too many restrictions in the lease and it became derelict. Eventually the land was purchased by the Royal Ophthalmic Hospital, and the building was pulled down in 1934.   W. M. P.

SUSARION, of Megara, is said to have 'invented the comic chorus' (i.e. made it other than a simple improvisation) in Icaria, Attica, between 580 and 560 B.C.

SUSSEX'S MEN, a company of players with whom Shakespeare may have been connected for a short time. They were attached to the service of three Earls of Sussex in succession, from 1569 to about 1618. They first appeared at Court in 1572, when their patron became Chamberlain, and for a time were referred to as the Chamberlain's Men, not to be confused with the later brilliant company of the Chamberlain's Men which emerges in 1594. They appeared in many provincial towns, and made periodic visits to London. On one of these, in 1594, they played for six weeks under Henslowe at the Rose, and their one new play was *Titus Andronicus*, revised for them from an earlier play, which had belonged to Pembroke's Men, by the hand of Shakespeare. They may have had in their repertory at this time other plays by Shakespeare, and they also appeared in *The Jew of Malta*, the property of Henslowe, in *Speed the Plough*, and in *Friar Bacon and Friar Bungay*.

SWANSTON, ELIARD or HILLIARD [he himself spells it Eyllaerdt] (?-1651), a prominent actor with the King's Men from 1624 to the closing of the theatres in 1642. He had been an actor at least two years previously to 1624, and took a prominent part, not only in the acting, but in the management of the company, being associated with Lowin and Taylor in business affairs. He played a variety of roles—Othello, Bussy d'Ambois, and various villains, including Richard III. During the Civil War he turned Parliamentarian, in contrast to most of the other actors, who remained staunchly Royalist, and became a jeweller. Shadwell refers to his reputation in *The Virtuoso* when Snarl says: 'I ... have seen ... Swanstead: Oh a brave roaring Fellow! Would make the house shake again.'

SWAN THEATRE, LONDON. The actual date of the building and opening of the Swan is uncertain, but it was probably about 1596. It was a Bankside Theatre standing in Paris (or Parish) Garden, near the Bear Gardens, a popular place of resort. It was consequently well situated for its purpose, and had the advantage of being near several landing-stairs for boats bringing visitors from the north bank of the Thames. It was built by Francis Langley, a substantial and respectable citizen of London. He was in favour at Court, but this did not prevent his having trouble over his projected theatre; in 1594 the Lord Mayor addressed a complaint to the Lord Treasurer, begging that the building of this playhouse might be stopped, on account of the evils arising therefrom. This may have delayed Langley, but did not prevent him from carrying out his design. The theatre arose, and probably took its name from the great number of swans which then frequented the river and its banks near by.

Although the Swan had by no means a glorious career, a good deal is known about it. It served Henslowe as a model for the Hope Theatre, and is frequently mentioned in his *Diary*. John de Witt, of Utrecht, when in England, not only visited the Swan, but wrote a description and made a sketch of it.

Of all the theatres, however, the largest and most distinguished is that whereof the sign is a Swan ... since it contains three thousand persons, and is built of a concrete of flint stones (which greatly abound in Britain) and supported by wooden columns painted in such exact imitation of marble that it might deceive even the most cunning. Since its form seems to approach that of a Roman structure, I have depicted it above.

We have only a copy of De Witt's drawing, which shows three galleries, the stage with a play in progress on the apron (but not the 'heavens' above the stage, i.e. the canopy over the players), the flag flying, and a man blowing a trumpet. The flint-and-mortar-work probably filled up the spaces between the wooden pillars, for the theatre was essentially a wooden building on a brick foundation. De Witt has been criticized for his estimate of 3,000 spectators, which has been regarded as a slip of the pen for 300. H. B. Wheatley, however, estimated the capacity of the galleries at 2,000, while the contemporary theatre, the Fortune, is thought to have held well over that number.

The Swan does not seem to have housed a permanent company, and was as much in request for sports, fencing and so on, as for plays. There was trouble in 1597 over the production of *The Isle of Dogs*, a seditious comedy by Nashe and Jonson, which led to a temporary closing of all theatres, and imprisonment for the actors and Jonson (Nashe managed to escape). In 1598 Robert Wilson challenged all comers to a contest of wit and extempore versification, a popular form of entertainment at that time, and defeated them all. In 1600 Peter Bromville, an expert fencer, exhibited his skill, while two years later, during a bout of fencing, a man called Dun was thrust in the eye and killed. In the same year Richard Vennar announced a spectacular show called *England's Joy*, to be played at the Swan by gifted amateurs, but after taking the money at the door he decamped, while the infuriated audience wreaked vengeance on the theatre. Vennar was caught and punished. *A Chaste Maid of Cheapside* (1611) was produced at the Swan, but after that few plays seem to have been given there. The last mention of the theatre is found in a pamphlet issued in 1632 (*Holland's Leaguer*), which, after referring to the Globe and the Hope, says 'the last . . . was now fallen to decay, and like a dying Swanne, hanging downe her head, seemed to sing her owne dierge'.   W. M. P.

SWEDEN, see SCANDINAVIA, 3.

SWINEY, OWEN (*c.* 1675–1754), Irish actor and manager, who in his youth may have been in the army. In about 1700 he was at Drury Lane, where for a time he acted as right-hand man to Christopher Rich. In 1705 he joined with Cibber and others in an attempt to break Rich's stranglehold over his actors by leasing Vanbrugh's old theatre in the Haymarket, where he produced *The Beaux' Stratagem* with Anne Oldfield as Mrs. Sullen. This brought him into conflict with the licensing laws, and he was forbidden to do plays. He was for a time able to stave off ruin by pandering to the popular taste for opera, but after an unsuccessful attempt to run Drury Lane in partnership with Wilks, Doggett, and Cibber, from which he was ousted by William Collier, he was forced to leave England to escape his creditors. He went to Venice, and remained in exile from 1710 to 1730. On his return he called himself MacSwiney, by which name he is sometimes known. He became the friend and patron of Peg Woffington, to whom he imparted the traditions of Anne Oldfield, and on his death he left her all his property.

SYMBOLISM IN THE THEATRE. Symbols have been used on the stage since the earliest times. Much of Elizabethan 'stage furniture' was symbolic, as a throne for a Court, a tent for a battlefield, a tree for a forest. Symbolic elements are found in Chekhov, and in the later plays of Ibsen and Strindberg. But Symbolism as a conscious art-form, conceived as a reaction against realism, came into the theatre with Maeterlinck, writing under the influence of Mallarmé and Verlaine. His characters have no personality of their own, but are symbols of the poet's inner life. This aspect was intensified in Yeats's early plays in verse. Other dramatists to come under the influence of Symbolism include Andreyev and Evreinov in

Russia, Hugo von Hofmannsthal and the later Hauptmann (with *Die versunkene Glocke*) in Germany, Synge (*The Well of the Saints*) and O'Casey (*Within the Gates*) in Ireland, and O'Neill in the United States.

SYNDICATE, see THEATRICAL SYNDICATE.

SYNGE, JOHN MILLINGTON (1871–1909), Irish dramatist and with Yeats one of the leading figures in the Irish Dramatic Movement (see IRELAND). Unlike Yeats, whose reputation rests equally upon his poetry, his drama, and his imaginative prose, Synge is remembered primarily as a dramatist. In him the expression of poetic imagination took an inevitable dramatic form. Although he died prematurely, while his art was still developing rapidly and continuously, he left enough in his six plays not only to show the unmistakable quality of his poetic and dramatic power, but to establish himself as the greatest of modern Irish dramatists, one who claims consideration beside the finest achievements of the twentieth century. His control of dramatic structure—whether in comedy or tragedy—is firm and powerful; his revelation of the characters and processes of mind of a subtle and imaginative peasantry is sure and penetrating; his language, and especially his imagery, is rich, live, and essentially poetic. The two prose works, *The Aran Islands* and *In Wicklow and West Kerry*, form a background to the plays and reflect, like them, an intent preoccupation with nature and with the minds and lives of Irish peasants in close and living contact with nature.

Yeats, meeting Synge in Paris, and divining the nature of his genius before he himself had done so, induced him to go back to Ireland and settle in the far west, among those peasants whose ways of life and speech gave him the material of most of his plays. His first, *In the Shadow of the Glen* (1903), begins the series of grave, original studies of Irish character and thought which from time to time drew upon Synge the hostility of his audiences, but are now appreciated wherever Irish drama is played. *Riders to the Sea* followed in 1904, a one-act tragedy whose brevity and economy of form and intensity and simplicity of passion make it one of the finest, if not the finest, of all modern short plays. *The Well of the Saints* (1905) is a comedy in which poetic beauty is mingled with underlying irony that is potentially tragic. *The Tinker's Wedding*, which may have been written earlier than these, was not produced; the theme would have made it unsuitable, but its comedy, drawn from the life of the roads, is richer and more jovial than any other that Synge wrote. The climax of his achievement in the comedy of bitter, ironic yet imaginative realism comes with *The Playboy of the Western World*. The keen and unsparing (though sympathetic) portraiture in this play raised riots in the Abbey in 1907, and again among certain Irish patriots in America in 1911. But it has long been accepted as his finest work; his power is here seen at its full capacity, as it could not be in the later but unfinished

Deirdre. This last play, which turns back to the ancient legends of Ireland for its subject, while still characteristic of Synge in its language and imagery, is nobly planned and all but greatly carried out.   U. E.-F.

SZERDAHELYI, Kálmán (1829–72), Hungarian actor, and leading man, with Egressy, of the company which played at the first Hungarian National Theatre opened in Budapest in 1837.

SZIGLIGETI, Ede (1814–78), Hungarian dramatist, author of a number of plays with music which portray in light comedy a series of idealized peasant types from the Hungarian countryside.

SZÖMÖRY, Dezső (1869–1945), Hungarian dramatist, best known for his dramas on subjects drawn from Hungarian history. He also wrote plays on contemporary social problems.

T

TABARIN [Antoine Girard] (? –1626), a popular figure in the streets of Paris for many years. Nothing is known of his birth or early years, but in about 1618 he set up a booth on the Pont-Neuf with his brother Philippe, better known as the quack-doctor, Mondor. Here, and in the Place Dauphine, Tabarin and a few companions, among whom was his wife Francisquine, would mount their trestle-platform and put the holiday crowd into a good humour before Mondor began the serious business of the day, selling his nostrums and boluses. Most of his material Tabarin wrote himself, or rather sketched out in the style of the *commedia dell'arte* scenarii, and from 1622 to 1632 a number of small volumes, entitled *Les Subtilités tabariniques*, were published, containing his farces, puns, jokes, and monologues. There is reason to believe that he was much influenced by the Italian actors who so often played in Paris, and from them he took the 'sack-beating' joke which Molière later borrowed for *Les Fourberies de Scapin* (1671). Tabarin himself never trod the boards of the legitimate theatre, but his fame long outlasted him, both La Fontaine and Boileau mentioning him years after his death, while his name passed into everyday speech (*faire le tabarin* = play the fool). It survives to-day in the name of a dance-hall in Montmartre.

TABERNARIA, see FABULA (8) and (9).

TABS (short for Tableau Curtain), used originally of an act-drop which parted and rose sideways towards the outer top corners, and by extension to any front curtain, or, mistakenly, to curtain settings on the stage.

TADEMA, Sir Lawrence Alma- (1836–1912), English artist, of Dutch origin, who worked for Irving and Tree, designing for the first the costumes and scenery of *Cymbeline* (1896) and *Coriolanus* (1901), and for the second *Hypatia* (1893) and *Julius Caesar* (1898).

TAGLIONI. (1) Filippo (1777–1871), an Italian ballet-master, and the father of (2) Marie (1804–84), the most celebrated ballerina of her day. It was for her that her father composed the great romantic ballet 'La Sylphide' (1832). Neither this nor any other of his ballets have survived in the repertory, though there is an evocation of its name in Fokine's 'Les Sylphides' (1908), where the dancers are dressed in the costume of Taglioni's day.

TAILS, see BORDER.

TAÏROV, Alexander Yakovlevich (1885–   ), Soviet producer, who in 1914 founded the Kamerny Theatre with which he has since been associated. Starting with experimental productions, he evolved a system which negatived humanity and the naturalism then in vogue with the Moscow Art Theatre, and reduced his actors to the status of puppets, a part only of what he envisaged as 'synthetic theatre', that is, a fusion of all theatrical arts under the sole control of the producer. This served to carry him through the stormy aftermath of the October Revolution, but proved inadequate when confronted with the demands of a new audience, ignorant but avid of warmth and colour, unused to theatrical convention and closely in touch with reality. In spite of his production of the contemporary play, *An Optimistic Tragedy*, in 1934 it was felt that he was out of touch with his audience, and the Kamerny Theatre was taken over by a committee. Taïrov continued to work under supervision, acclimatizing himself to the principles of Socialist Realism, and gradually evolving a new philosophy which has become apparent in some of his later productions. These aroused favourable comment, notably *Madame Bovary* in 1939. Under Taïrov the Kamerny has always been a channel for modern Western drama as well as classical; Shaw, O'Neill, and many others have been staged there. Taïrov's wife, Alice Koonen, is the leading lady of the Kamerny, and one of the outstanding actresses of the U.S.S.R.

TALFOURD, Sir Thomas Noon (1795–1854), English lawyer and man of letters, best known in the theatre for his tragedies, *Ion* (1836), *The Athenian Captive* (1838), and *Glencoe* (1840). The first, finely acted by Macready, was a success on its production at Covent Garden, and belongs to the small group of poetic plays with which the more literary-minded authors of the day sought to re-establish poetry on the stage. A classic and somewhat frigid production, it is modelled on the lines of French tragedy, with careful observance of the Unities and a somewhat uninspired flow of blank verse. The two later plays were also written for Macready, but were eventually produced at the Haymarket, with less success than *Ion*, which was several times revived up to 1850. Talfourd wrote a good deal of dramatic criticism, and was the literary executor of Lamb, whose works he edited after the latter's death, as he did the posthumous publications of Hazlitt. He supported the rights of authorship in the agitation over the Copyright Bill, and was an intimate friend of Dickens and Bulwer-Lytton, the first dedicating to him *The Pickwick Papers* and the second *The Lady of Lyons*.

TALMA, François Joseph (1763–1826), French actor, educated in England. The son of a dentist, he followed his father's profession for a time, but abandoned it in favour of the theatre. In 1787, with the help of the actor Molé, he made his début at the Comédie-Française, and soon attracted attention by his talent, as well as by his costume, since he was the first to play Roman parts in a toga instead of in modern dress. He also made many reforms in theatrical speech, suppressing the exaggerations of the tragic declamatory style, and allowing the sense rather than the metre to determine the pauses. He supported the Revolution, and in 1789 declaimed with much fervour the inflammatory speeches in *Charles IX* predicting the fall of the Bastille. This led to friction with some of the older members of the company, and he left them. Under the patronage of Danton and Desmoulins he opened the Théâtre de la République, on the site of the present Comédie-Française, and played there with some of the bolder spirits who had accompanied him, until the National Theatre was again reconstituted under Napoleon, who had a great admiration for Talma. In 1808 he took him to Erfurt and made him play *La Mort de César* before an audience which included five crowned heads. He also took him on a ceremonial visit to Dresden. Talma, who was a fine actor and exercised a salutary influence on the French theatre, remained on the stage until his death with no failing of power. His last part was in Delaville's *Charles VI* (1826), which, like many another poor play, he raised to success by the excellence of his acting. He occasionally played comedy, but preferred tragedy, particularly in its more sombre and pathetic aspects. He has left some interesting reflections on theatrical art and acting, which were published as a preface to the memoirs of Lekain, whom Talma much admired. His second wife, Charlotte Vanhove (1771–1860), also wrote a book on acting. She was the daughter of an actor at the Comédie-Française and was herself a member of the company from 1785 to 1811.

TAMAYO Y BAUS, Manuel (1829–98), Spanish dramatist, with Ayala the chief representative of the transition period from romanticism to realism. Under his own name, and also as Joaquín Estébañez, he wrote a number of plays, some historical, as *La locura de amor* (1855), which shows the queen Doña Juana driven mad by jealousy of her husband, others dealing with modern domestic and social problems, as *Lo Positivo* (1862), which deals with the conflict between sentiment and interest. One of Tamayo's most interesting plays is *Un drama nuevo* (1837), written in simple, powerful prose, in which Shakespeare appears, and in which Yorick, the central figure, kills on the stage, during a mock fight, his supposed rival in love.

TARKINGTON, (Newton) Booth (1869–1946), American novelist, and author of a number of plays, of which the best-known is the romantic costume drama, *Monsieur Beaucaire* (1901). This was based in collaboration on his own novel, but was spoilt artistically by the substitution of a conventionally happy ending for the ironic ending implicit in the novel. It was nevertheless very successful in

America, with Richard Mansfield in the name-part, and also in London, where it later provided the material for a musical play with a score by Messager. Among Tarkington's other plays were two for Otis Skinner, *Your Humble Servant* (1909) and *Mr. Antonio* (1916), a charming comedy of youth entitled *Clarence* (1919), and a social drama on the theme of snobbery, *Tweedles* (1923), which failed in production. Tarkington appears to have taken his plays far less seriously than his novels, and produced little of permanent value for the stage.

TARLETON, Richard (? –1588), the most famous of Elizabethan clowns, probably the original of Yorick 'the king's jester', as described by Hamlet, and the 'pleasant Willy' of Spenser's *The Tears of the Muses*, 'with whom all joy and jolly merriment Is also deaded'. A drawing of him preserved in a manuscript of the British Museum and reproduced in *Tarleton's Jests* (a posthumous work) shows that he was short and broad, with a large, flat face, curly hair, a wavy moustache, and a small starveling beard. Tarleton himself tells us that he had a flat nose and a squint, a peculiarity well brought out in a second portrait of him discovered by W. J. Lawrence in 1920. His usual clown's dress was a russet suit and buttoned cap, with short boots strapped at the ankle, as commonly worn by rustics at this time. A leather money-bag hung on a belt at his waist, and he is depicted playing on a tabor and pipe. He was one of the Queen's Men, and though few of his original parts are definitely known, he is believed to have been the Mouse of *Mucedorus*, possibly Bullethrumble in *Selimus*, and conjecturally Pedringano in *The Spanish Tragedy*. A great deal of his clowning was probably extempore, and Shakespeare may have had him in mind when he said 'Let those set down for them', and Marlowe, when he railed at 'clownage' in the Prologue to *Tamburlaine*. W. J. Lawrence, in a penetrating study *On the underrated genius of Dick Tarleton*, ascribes to Shakespeare's desire to organize the gagging Clown such richly comic parts as Launce, Speed, Bottom, and Dogberry, and the Grave-digger in *Hamlet*. There can be no doubt that the genius of Tarleton led to a persistent mingling of tragedy and farce in early Elizabethan plays; but his great *tour de force* was the Jig—'dear delight of the Elizabethan multitude'—a farce in rhyme, sung and danced to a series of popular tunes. The music for some of Tarleton's jigs has been preserved, but the only libretto, *Tarltons Jigge of a horse loade of Fooles* (c. 1579), is considered by Chambers and others to be one of Collier's forgeries. Tarleton is, however, known to have written for the Queen's Men a composite play, now lost, entitled *The Seven Deadly Sins*, in two parts, the first containing five short plays, the second three. The plot, or outline, of the second part has been preserved in manuscript, and was for some time thought to be a scenario for an improvised play after the manner of the

Italian *commedia dell'arte*. It seems now to be accepted, however, that this plot (or 'platt', as it is sometimes called) was merely a helpful indication of the sequence of events for the use of the actors and prompter. A number of books published under Tarleton's name after his death are probably spurious, the authors having annexed his name to ensure their sales. His popularity may be judged from the number of taverns named after him, of which one, *The Tabour and Pipe Man*, with a sign-board taken from *Tarleton's Jests*, still stood in the Borough two hundred years after his death, while the action of *Cuck-queans and Cuckolds Errant* (1601) takes place in the Tarlton Inn, Colchester. Tarleton himself at some time had an eating-house in Paternoster Row.

TASSO, TORQUATO (1544–95), famous Italian poet, whose play *Torrismondo* (pub. 1587) is a mingling of tragedy and romance. Though classic in form, it deals in romantic fashion with the love of Torrismondo for Rosmonda, who turns out to be his sister, and whom he has married on behalf of a friend. Thus proved traitor and incestuous, Torrismondo dies, fulfilling the prophecy that his sister would cause his death. Tasso was also the author of a pastoral, *L'Aminta* (1573), which, with Guarini's *Pastor Fido* (1598), stands at the head of a long line of similar plays, their influence spreading all over Europe (see ITALY, 1 *b* and PASTORAL).

TATE, HARRY (1872–1940), a comedian of the music-halls, best remembered for his series of sketches on Golfing, Motoring, Fishing, and so on. He made his first appearance at the Oxford in 1895, though he had previously done a good deal of work as an entertainer at concerts. He took his stage name from the firm of Henry Tate & Sons, Sugar Refiners, by whom he was at one time employed, his real name being Ronald Macdonald Hutchison. He appeared in the earliest revues at the London Hippodrome, but returned to the music-halls, and in 1935 played the King in *The Sleeping Beauty* pantomime, in which Nellie Wallace appeared as the Witch.

TATE, NAHUM (1652–1715), a poor poet and worse playwright, who collaborated with Dryden in the second part of *Absalom and Achitophel* and with Nicholas Brady in a metrical version of the Psalms. His plays were mainly adaptations, and he is chiefly remembered for his tamperings with Shakespeare—in *King Lear* he makes Cordelia survive to marry Edgar—and for his trouncing by Pope in *The Dunciad*.

TAVISTOCK HOUSE THEATRE, a perfectly-fitted and well-appointed private theatre in the London residence of Charles Dickens, where amateur performances were frequently given (see DICKENS).

TAYLOR, JOSEPH (*c.* 1585–1652), English actor, with Lowin the chief business manager

of the King's Men after the death of Condell and Heminge. He joined the company in 1619, at which date he was already a well-known actor, and took over many of Burbage's parts. He also appeared as the handsome young lovers, or the handsome dashing villains, in the plays of Beaumont and Fletcher. The third edition of *The Faithful Shepherdess*, which was acted at Court on Twelfth Night, contains a eulogy of Taylor, presumably for his acting in, and his production of, the play. Some of the costumes used were given to Taylor by the Queen 'the year before of her owne pastorall'. Taylor was one of the actors caught playing in the Cockpit when it was raided by Commonwealth soldiers, and Downes, writing during the Restoration, says that Davenant had seen Taylor act Hamlet, in which he had been coached by Shakespeare. This is unlikely, since Shakespeare was dead before Taylor joined the King's Men, but he may well have seen Burbage, the original player of the part, and modelled his performance on that. He is certainly said to have played it 'incomparably well', and also to have been good as Ferdinand in *The Duchess of Malfi*, another of Burbage's parts, as Iago, as Truewit in *Epicoene*, and as Face in *The Alchemist*. His name long remained synonymous with good acting.

TAYLOR, LAURETTE (1884–1946), see MANNERS (2).

TAYLOR, TOM (1817–80), English dramatist and editor of *Punch*. He was for some years Professor of English in London University, but from 1850 to 1871 was a civil servant in the Health Department. From his youth he was attracted to the theatre, and in 1844, his first year in London, had a play produced by the Keeleys at the Lyceum. He continued to write copiously until two years before his death, and was one of the most popular dramatists of his day. His chief successes were scored in domestic drama, though he also attempted plays on historical themes. He had little dramatic genius, and borrowed his material freely from various sources; but his excellent stagecraft and his skilful handling of contemporary themes makes him always interesting, and in some respects a forerunner of the reforms of Robertson. Among his plays, which number over seventy, the best-known are *To Parents and Guardians* (1846); *Masks and Faces* (1852), a comedy on the life of Peg Woffington written in collaboration with Charles Reade and frequently revived; *Still Waters Run Deep* (1855), a play based on a French novel and remarkable in its time for its frank discussion of sex; *Our American Cousin* (1858), first done in New York and noteworthy because of the appearance in it of Sothern as Lord Dundreary, a part which he enlarged until it practically swamped the play; *The Overland Route* (1860); *The Ticket-of-Leave Man* (1863), a melodrama on a contemporary theme of low life which had much influence on such later works as *The Silver King*; and finally two plays written in collaboration, *New Men and Old Acres* (1869) and *Arkwright's Wife* (1873). Taylor was himself an enthusiastic amateur actor, playing at Tavistock House in Dickens's private theatre and being one of the leading members of the Canterbury Old Stagers. A genial, though sometimes irascible, man, he was extremely popular in London literary society, and an excellent journalist. There are some interesting glimpses of him in Ellen Terry's *Story of My Life*.

TCHEHOV, TCHEKHOV, see CHEKHOV.

TEARLE. (1)(GEORGE) OSMOND (1852–1901), English actor, who made his début at Liverpool on 26 Mar. 1869 and two years later appeared at Warrington as Hamlet, a part he subsequently played many times. After six years in the provinces he appeared in London and soon formed his own company, with which he toured. On 30 Sept. 1880 he joined the stock company at Wallack's, New York, making his first appearance there as Jaques, and later alternated between London and New York. In 1888 he organized a Shakespearian company which appeared with much success at Stratford-on-Avon, and proved an invaluable training-ground for young actors. He was himself a fine Shakespearian actor, combining excellent elocution with a natural elegance and dignity. He had a high reputation in the provinces, and made his last appearance on the stage at Carlisle in 1901, dying a week later. His second wife (2) MARIANNE LEVY (*née* Conway) (1854–96) was the granddaughter of the English actor William August Conway, whose son married an American actress, later manageress of the Brooklyn Theatre, where Minnie, as she was known, made her first appearances. Her sons were both on the stage, (3) GODFREY (1884–   ) making his first appearance in his father's company, and remaining with him until his death. He has had a long and illustrious career on the London stage, and in films, one of his outstanding parts being Commander Edward Ferrers in *The Flashing Stream*. He was also good as Othello, as Hamlet, and as Antony.

TEASER (a term used in America for the proscenium border), see PROSCENIUM.

TEATRO ESPAÑOL and **TEATRO REAL,** see MADRID THEATRES, 1 and 2.

TEATRO FARNESE, TEATRO OLIMPICO, see SPECTACLE THEATRES.

TEATRO POR HORAS, see GÉNERO CHICO.

TELARI, see SCENERY, 2.

TELBIN, a family of English scene-painters, of whom (1) WILLIAM (1813–73) worked at Drury Lane under Macready in 1840. He had previously been connected with several provincial theatres, and was later at Covent Garden and at the Lyceum. His son (2) WILLIAM LEWIS (1846–1931) was at Manchester Theatre Royal for many years, and later in London, where in 1902, after a visit to Italy, he designed the settings and costumes for Alexander's production of *Paolo and Francesca* at the St. James's Theatre. Two sisters of the elder Telbin were on the stage in New York.

TEMPEST, MARIE [MARY SUSAN ETHERINGTON] (1864–1942), English actress, who in 1937 was created D.B.E. in recognition of her services to the stage. She was trained as a singer, and her first appearances were made in light opera and musical comedy. It was not until 1899 that she forsook music for straight acting, subsequently appearing only in comedy. Her first successes were made as Nell Gwynn, Peg Woffington, and Becky Sharp, and as Kitty in *The Marriage of Kitty*, in which she appeared during her engagement at the Duke of York's under Frohman. She subsequently revived this several times, in London and New York, and also on an extensive tour which took her all over the world. On her return she continued to appear in modern comedy, and soon became noted for her playing of charming and elegant middle-aged women—Judith Bliss in *Hay Fever*, Olivia in *Mr. Pim Passes By*, the title-role in *The First Mrs. Fraser*, and Fanny Cavendish in *Theatre Royal*. In 1935 she celebrated her stage jubilee with a matinée at Drury Lane in the presence of King George V and Queen Mary, the proceeds going to endow a ward for the theatrical profession in St. George's Hospital. She continued to act until her death, and retained to the end her elegant appearance, enhanced by an excellent taste in dress, and the subtlety and sureness of her superb technique.

TENNIS-COURT. Many early theatres in France and in Restoration England were housed in converted tennis-courts (see ARCHITECTURE, ENGLISH PLAYHOUSE, 1, ILLUSTRE-THÉÂTRE, LINCOLN'S INN FIELDS THEATRE and VERE STREET THEATRE).

TENNYSON, ALFRED, LORD (1809–92), Poet Laureate after the death of Wordsworth. Though not gifted dramatically nor very much in touch with the contemporary stage, he nevertheless contributed to the poetic drama of his day. His first play, *Queen Mary* (1876), a somewhat frigid tragedy in blank verse on Elizabethan lines, was adapted and produced by Irving, as were *The Cup* (1881), with Ellen Terry as Camma, and *Becket* (1893), the last being considered by many the finest achievement of Irving's career. Of Tennyson's other plays in verse *The Falcon*, based on an episode in the Decameron, was given at the St. James's by the Kendals in 1879, *The Promise of May* (1882), a drama of modern village life, was unsuccessful at the Globe, and *The Foresters* (1892), with music by Sullivan, was seen at the Lyceum. A play on Harold was printed, but not performed until 1928. Like many other poets of his day, Tennyson failed to amalgamate fine poetry and good theatre, and the success of *Becket* was mainly due to the beauty and compelling power of Irving's interpretation. It has not been revived since his death.

TERENCE (*c.* 190–159 B.C.), Roman dramatist. We possess six plays by Publius Terentius Afer, produced between the years 166 and 160 B.C. From the prologues prefixed to these plays scholars of later ages attempted to reconstruct the life of the author, but their results were conflicting and should be treated with reserve. All Terence's prologues were written to meet the criticisms of his enemies. They said that he accepted literary help from his noble friends, that his plays were not accurate versions of his originals, and that he sometimes introduced scenes or characters from plays which had already been translated by other Roman dramatists. Terence's replies are evasive, but we can see that he endeavoured to improve on his Greek originals, thereby displaying an originality which we find in no other Roman writer of tragedy or comedy. Evidently he had his own artistic standards. He held that a play should explain itself, and ought not to require an explanatory prologue; on more than one occasion he altered monologue into dialogue to secure a more dramatic effect; he added to Menander's *Eunuchus* a swaggering captain and his attendant parasite in order to make the play more amusing; in the *Andria* he added a second lover who wishes to marry the girl destined by the parents as the bride of Pamphilus, who is himself in love with a girl of humble family. Everywhere in Terence we find contrasts of character; thus, for example, in the *Adelphi*, between Demea, the strict father, and his genial bachelor brother Micio; again there is a contrast between Demea's two sons, the headstrong if generous Aeschinus and the timid Ctesipho. Throughout his plays we find an atmosphere of culture and refinement, not unnatural in the works of a writer who had some contact with the aristocracy. The contrast with Plautus is complete; there are few jokes and no buffoonery or topical allusions or irrelevancy; we find ourselves in a world which is not strikingly Greek or Roman, but independent of place and time. When Terence added Charinus to the *Andria* he introduced a situation not to be paralleled in Greek comedy—a young gentleman in love with a young lady of his own station. The oriental seclusion of young ladies in Athens, as reflected in comedy, made it practically impossible for a young man to meet any young woman of his own class. The greater freedom of women in Rome made it possible to develop the love-interest in literature on almost modern lines.

That Terence had his difficulties with the public as well as with his critics is shown by the two failures of the *Hecyra*. The turbulent Roman audience was only too ready to leave the theatre if bored, and seek the entertainment presented by rope-dancers and gladiators. We can well understand Julius Caesar's criticism that Terence lacked *vis comica*. Nevertheless he achieved success, even during his short career as a dramatist; and after his death the polish of his style made him one of the favourite Roman authors. Terence's interest was above all things in humanity at large; the fine and

famous remark of one of his characters, 'I am a human being and think all human affairs my concern', is true of Terence himself, and gives his work an abiding charm. In the schools of the Middle Ages the plays of Terence were read and acted. In the tenth century the nun Hroswitha wrote the well-known plays in which she tried to imitate Terence's style while improving on his morality. At the Renaissance his works were translated into several languages, and his influence was particularly marked in France.   W. B.

TERPSICHORE, the Muse of Dancing.

TERRISS. (1) WILLIAM [really WILLIAM CHARLES JAMES LEWIN] (1847–97), English actor, known affectionately by the British public as 'Breezy Bill' and 'No. 1, Adelphi Terriss', since his best work was done at the Adelphi Theatre. In his early days he was a sailor, but, irked by the monotony, he left; nor did medicine and engineering, both suggested careers, attract him. He looked for excitement, action, and rapid movement, and found them on the stage. His first professional appearance—he had been an enthusiastic amateur—was made in Birmingham in 1867, and was by no means successful. Nothing daunted, he applied to Bancroft and was engaged. Still he made no mark, and with his wife, Amy Fellowes, also an actress, he emigrated to the Falkland Islands, where he bred sheep and broke-in wild horses. Eventually he returned to England, tried the stage again—as Doricourt in *The Belle's Stratagem*—and this time was successful. One of his first big successes was as Nicholas Nickleby at the Adelphi, but he made his name as Squire Thornhill in *Olivia* at the Court Theatre in 1878, playing opposite Ellen Terry. Later he played Romeo to Adelaide Neilson's Juliet, and in 1880 he joined Irving at the Lyceum, where he remained for some time. He was one of the few actors who were not afraid to stand up to the great actor-manager. But he is best remembered as the hero of a famous series of melodramas at the Adelphi. His charm and gusto delighted the audience, and the success of such plays as *Harbour Lights*, *The Girl I Left Behind Me*, and *One of the Best* (which Bernard Shaw reviewed under the heading of 'One of the Worst') owed much to his handsome, debonair presence and vigorous acting. He was one of the most popular actors of his time, as he was also one of the kindest and most generous of men, and his untimely assassination by a madman in 1897 outside the Adelphi Theatre was a great grief to his numerous admirers, and a loss to the English stage. His daughter (2) ELLALINE (1871–   ), who was born during her parents' stay in the Falkland Islands, married Seymour Hicks, a partnership which proved ideal both on and off stage. She made her first appearance under Tree at the Haymarket in 1888, and has had a long and varied career, appearing with her husband in many of his own plays, including *Bluebell in Fairyland*, first produced in 1901 and many times revived. One of her outstanding appearances was as Phoebe Throssel in *Quality Street*. She accompanied her husband on tour, both in straight plays and on the music-halls, and went with him to France in 1914. She has published her reminiscences (1928) (see also HICKS, SEYMOUR).

TERRY, a family of English actors which has given many illustrious players to the stage. The first was (1) BENJAMIN (1818–96), son of an innkeeper at Portsmouth, a handsome man with a beautiful speaking voice and fine elocution, gifts which he has transmitted to his descendants through several generations. Some of their good looks may also have come from his wife (2) SARAH BALLARD (1819–1892), the daughter of a Scottish minister, who adopted her husband's profession and as Miss Yerrit proved herself a good actress. Of her eleven children two died in infancy, the rest were connected with the stage, three sons in business or managerial capacities. Her eldest daughter (3) KATE (1844–1924) was on the stage as a child, and at eight years of age went to London to play Prince Arthur in Charles Kean's production of *King John* at the Princess's. She remained there until the Keans left that theatre, playing also Cordelia. She then went to the Bristol stock company, returned to London to play Ophelia to Fechter's Hamlet, appeared in several of Tom Taylor's plays, and seemed to be heading for a brilliant career when in 1867 she left the stage on her marriage to Arthur Lewis. Of her two daughters, one, also Kate, became the mother of Val and John Gielgud, while the other, (4) MABEL TERRY-LEWIS (1872–   ), went on the stage, making her first appearance on 17 Jan. 1895 with John Hare in *A Pair of Spectacles*. She retired on her marriage in 1905, but lost her husband during the 1914–18 war, and returned to the theatre in 1920, playing in *The Grain of Mustard Seed* at the Ambassadors'. Her retirement had in no way impaired her excellence, and she immediately embarked on a long and successful career.

The most distinguished member of the Terry family was Benjamin's second daughter, (5) ELLEN ALICE (1847–1928), who made her first appearance on the stage at the Princess's Theatre as Mamillius in *The Winter's Tale* at the age of 9. She too remained with the Keans until their retirement in 1859, and in the summer of that and succeeding years toured with her sister Kate in *A Drawing-Room Entertainment*, in which they each played several parts in some small sketches. Ellen then joined the Bristol stock company and returned to London to appear at the Haymarket. It was while acting there that she left the stage to marry the painter G. F. Watts, an ill-judged union which soon came to an end. Returning to the theatre for a short while, she again left it, this time for six years, during which time her two children were born (see CRAIG, EDITH and EDWARD GORDON, and GODWIN, E. W.). When she reappeared as Philippa in *The Wandering Heir*, at the insistence of the author, Charles Reade, to replace Mrs. John Wood, she was as brilliant as ever, and the long rest seemed only to have increased the excellence of her acting. This was particularly noticeable in Portia, which she played at the Prince of Wales's under the management of the Bancrofts. She remained with them for a year, and then went to the Court Theatre under Hare, playing one of her few 'original' parts—Olivia in an adaptation of *The Vicar of Wakefield*. It was during the run of this play that Ellen Terry married her second husband, Charles Kelly, who died in 1885.

In 1878 Irving, who had recently begun his tenancy of the Lyceum, engaged Ellen Terry as his leading lady, thus inaugurating a partnership which became one of the glories of the English stage. It lasted until 1902, and ranged over a wide field, including a good deal of Shakespeare, revivals of modern plays like *The Lady of Lyons* and *Robert Macaire*, and plays specially written for Irving, *Charles I*, *Becket*, and *The Bells*. Ellen Terry accompanied Irving on his American tours, and subsequently toured there under the management of Charles Frohman. After leaving the Lyceum she became manager of the Imperial Theatre, where she produced *The Vikings* and *Much Ado About Nothing*, with sets designed by her son Gordon Craig, and then appeared in two new plays, *The Good Hope*, by Heijermans, and Barrie's *Alice-Sit-By-The-Fire*. In 1906 she celebrated her stage jubilee with a mammoth matinée at Drury Lane at which all the stage personalities of the day assisted, as well as 24 members of her own family. She was at this time appearing at the Court Theatre in *Captain Brassbound's Conversion*. In 1907 she married as her third husband James Carew, and after that appeared rarely on the stage. Instead she toured America and Australia, giving lectures on Shakespeare, four of which were published in 1931, proving once again how excellent was her critical faculty and how masterly her handling of the written word. These qualities had already appeared in her autobiography, published in 1908 (republished with notes and an additional section by Christopher St. John in 1933), and can be seen in her correspondence with Bernard Shaw, published in 1931. Throughout her career she was an inspiration to those who played with her, and Matheson Lang, who once played Benedick to her Beatrice—which many considered her finest part—said that he learnt more of the real art of acting from that experience than from all the work of the seven years before. It is difficult to convey any impression of her luminosity and joyousness. She was not at her best in tragedy, though some critics thought her Lady Macbeth very fine, and she never played Rosalind, which seemed above all other parts to have been written for her. But as Beatrice, as Olivia, as Portia, as Lilian in *New Men and Old Acres*, as Lady Teazle, as Desdemona, as Viola, as Cordelia, and in a hundred other parts, she played with a freshness and vitality which gave life to the dullest moment. She was created D.B.E. in 1925.

Two more Terry sisters were on the stage, (6) MARION (1852–1930), who made her first appearance as Ophelia in Tom Taylor's version of *Hamlet*, and (7) FLORENCE (FLOSS) (1854–96), who also made her first appearance as a child in one of Tom Taylor's plays. She played Nerissa to Ellen's Portia, and was much admired in her elder sister's part of Olivia, which she played on tour. She was apparently a young actress of great promise, but left the stage on her marriage in 1882. Her daughter and granddaughter followed the family tradition. Marion continued her career as an able and attractive actress, playing, among many other parts, Dorothy in *Dan'l Druce, Blacksmith* (1876), and the young ladies of T. W. Robertson's comedies. She went with the Bancrofts to the Haymarket and later, with Alexander at the St. James's, was the first Mrs. Erlynne in *Lady Windermere's Fan*. She also played in some of H. A. Jones's plays, and was the original Susan Throssel of *Quality Street*. She was not often seen in Shakespeare, though on occasion she deputized for her sister Ellen, and was at her best in light comedy. Her last appearance on the stage was as the Princess in *Our Betters* in 1923, after which she retired on account of ill health. It was said of her by a critic in her young days that she represented the type of woman whom all good Englishmen love.

The youngest child of Benjamin and Sarah was (8) FRED (1863–1933), a handsome romantic actor, who made his first appearance on the stage at the Haymarket under the Bancrofts in 1880. In 1884 he played Sebastian to his sister Ellen's Viola at the Lyceum, and was an immediate success. He is mainly remembered for his performance of Sir Percy Blakeney in *The Scarlet Pimpernel*, which he frequently revived, but he was also much admired in *Sweet Nell of Old Drury, Dorothy o' the Hall, Matt o' Merrymount*, and *Henry of Navarre*. In these and many other productions he played with his wife (9) JULIA NEILSON (1868–   ), who was a student at the Royal Academy of Music and went on the stage on the advice of Gilbert, playing Cynisca to Mary Anderson's Galatea at the Lyceum, 21 Mar. 1888. She later appeared as Galatea, and was in *Broken Hearts* and *The Wicked World* at the Savoy. After touring with Tree she returned with him to the Haymarket, where she remained for five years, making an outstanding success as Drusilla Ives in *The Dancing Girl* and as Hester Worsley in *A Woman of No Importance*. It was here that she first met her future husband, whom she describes in her memoirs as 'tall, taller than I; handsome as a picture; ardent about the theatre. He had all the gay charm of his already famous family, beautifully courteous manners and a passion for hard work.' She appeared for a short time under other managements, notably as Princess Flavia in *The Prisoner of Zenda*, but from 1900 to 1930 she and her husband toured or played in London with their own company. They were ideally suited, and though some may have thought her a finer player than her husband it was truly said in his obituary notice that 'the public which only remembers him as the actor-manager ... playing a strictly limited type of role, have really no conception of what a sound all-round actor Fred Terry really was'. Both his children were on the stage, his son (10) DENNIS (1895–1932) dying suddenly while on tour in South Africa before he had had time to develop the promise of his youth. He has, however, left a daughter by his actress-wife, Mary Glynne, whose career promises well. His sister (11) PHYLLIS (1892–   ) made her first appearance in *Henry of Navarre* under her father's management, and later was much admired as Viola. She has appeared in a number of Shakespeare productions, toured in vaudeville, and played Principal Boy in pantomime. It was under her management that her cousin, John Gielgud, made his first professional appearance.

Two nieces of Ellen Terry, Minnie and Beatrice, daughters of her brother Charles, were also on the stage.

TERRY, DANIEL (1789–1829), English actor, friend of Sir Walter Scott, several of whose novels he dramatized for Covent Garden, where they were given with elaborate scenery, and music by Bishop. Terry, who was no relation to the above family as far as is known, was trained as an architect, and later applied his knowledge to the designing of Abbotsford, but in 1803 he joined a company in Sheffield under the father of Macready. Two years later he was with Stephen Kemble, and then went to Edinburgh with Henry Siddons. A good-looking man, with a fine voice and a sensitive, alert face, he made his first appearance in London at the Haymarket, playing the fop, Lord Ogleby, in *The Clandestine Marriage*. From 1813 to 1822 he was a member of the Covent Garden company, and went to Edinburgh in 1815 to support Mrs. Siddons in her farewell engagement there. He was also seen at Drury Lane. In 1825, in partnership with Frederick Yates, he took over the Adelphi, but the venture was not a financial success, and Terry soon retired. He was at his best in character parts, particularly those of old men, or in strong emotional drama, but he had little tenderness or subtlety, and seldom attempted young lovers or the serious gentlemen of old comedy.

TERRY, EDWARD O'CONNOR (1844–1912), English actor and manager, not connected with any of the actors listed above. He made his first appearances in amateur theatricals and in 1863 appeared in several provincial towns with a touring company, notably in the Isle of Man with Irving, then young and unknown, and in Belfast, where he supported a number of visiting stars. He was first remarked for his playing of such Shakespearian parts as Touchstone and Dogberry at Manchester under Calvert, and was seen in London at the Surrey in 1867. A year later he played the First Grave-digger at the Lyceum, and then spent several years with Mrs. Swanborough at the Strand, playing in burlesque and light comedy. This led to his engagement by Hollingshead for the Gaiety, where from 1876 he was a member of the famous 'Gaiety Quartette' with Nellie Farren, Kate Vaughan, and Edward Royce. In 1887 he opened his own theatre (see below), where his first success was *Sweet Lavender*. Later productions were *The Times*, a revival of *The Magistrate*, and *Love in Idleness*, of which he was part-author. He toured extensively in Australia, South Africa, and America, and in 1904 married as his second wife the widow of Sir Augustus Harris. He was active in theatrical affairs, and associated with many stage charities. Though not an outstanding actor, he was a good eccentric comedian, and a careful and conscientious manager.

TERRY'S THEATRE, LONDON, in the Strand, was built on the site of a famous supper-room and music-hall called the Coal Hole. It took its name from the actor, Edward Terry, who opened it in 1887 with *The Churchwarden* and *The Woman Hater*. His first success at this short-lived theatre was *Sweet Lavender*, produced there on 21 Mar. 1888, with Terry as Dick Phenyl—his best part. It ran for 684 performances, and its author, Pinero, had two other plays produced at Terry's, *The Times* (1891) and a revival of *In Chancery*. Terry's later became a cinema, and was pulled down during improvements in the Strand in 1923.
W. M. P.

THALIA, the Muse of Comedy.

THALIA, NEW YORK, see BOWERY THEATRE (1).

THEATRE, THE, the first—and most appropriately named—playhouse to be erected in London, was built by James Burbage, who on 13 Apr. 1576 obtained a twenty-one years' lease of houses and land situated between Finsbury Fields and the public road from Bishopsgate to Shoreditch Church. The site became Holywell Lane, Shoreditch, at the south-west corner of the Fields. It was a definite article of the lease that a playhouse should be erected on the land. Burbage took his father-in-law, John Braynes, into partnership, and they built a circular wooden building, without a roof, for theatrical and other entertainments. It cost between £600 and £700; the actual sum advanced by Braynes was one thousand marks, roughly about £660. Burbage was his own architect and builder. The actual dimensions are not known, but the building was apparently commodious, with scaffolding for galleries and what would now be described as boxes. It opened in the autumn of 1576. Admission was one penny for standing room on the ground, and a second penny for admission to the galleries; for a further penny one could obtain a stool, or what was described as 'a quiet standing' out of the crowd on the floor into the less crowded galleries.

The history of the Theatre is stormy. The Corporation of the City of London strongly disapproved of plays and players, and consequently of this innovation of playhouses, and kept up a continual persecution. But the public evidently flocked there, for the authorities and the preachers of the day complained constantly of the crowds which resorted to the playhouse. Burbage was made to pay an extra £10 in rent 'in respect of the great profit and commoditie which he had made and in time to come was further likely to make out of the Theatre'. That profit, however, seems problematical.

The Theatre did not have a very distinguished dramatic career. Its chief use for a while, and at intervals throughout its existence, was for exhibitions and competitions of sword-play, fencing, quarterstaff, and athletic exercises. But naturally Burbage used it for the company with which he was connected, the Earl of Leicester's Men: Warwick's Men played there too. The Queen's Men and other players were there in 1583–91. Strange's and the Admiral's Men played there in 1590–1, and then the Chamberlain's Men, the most distinguished company of the time, which Burbage and the best of Leicester's Men had joined. Plays performed there include the lost and anonymous *Blacksmith's Daughter* and *The History of Caesar and Pompey, Cataline's Conspiracies*, probably the original *Hamlet* on which Shakespeare based his play, and *Dr. Faustus*, during a performance of which the theatre cracked, to the alarm of the audience. Tarleton and Kempe also performed 'jigges and drolls' there.

In spite of the claim that he was doing good business, Burbage found it hard to pay the higher rent for which he was always being pressed, and also the interest on the original loan. The City Corporation, too, made things difficult for him, and when in 1597 Giles Allen, the ground landlord, declared that he intended to end the lease, Burbage's sons, Richard and Cuthbert, who had succeeded their father, now dead, took advantage of a clause which enabled them to remove from the site 'all such buildings and other things as should be builded'. They pulled down the Theatre, transported the timber and material across the river to Bankside, and used them to build the famous Globe.
W. M. P.

THEATRE ACOUSTICS, see ACOUSTICS.

THEATRE ARCHITECTURE, see ARCHITECTURE.

THEATRE ARTS, an American magazine of international interest, which monthly surveyed the theatre all over the world in essays, reviews, and photographs. Founded in Detroit in 1916, as a quarterly under the name of *Theatre Arts Magazine*, its first editor was Sheldon Cheney. From the beginning the magazine set itself a high standard, which was consistently maintained under the subsequent editorships of Edith J. R. Isaacs and Rosamond Gilder. It was also responsible for the publication of a number of important theatrical books, and of portfolios of stage designs (see also ISAACS, EDITH J. R.). In Feb. 1948 it changed hands, and was renamed *New Theatre Arts*.

THEATRE COLLECTIONS, see COLLECTIONS.

THÉÂTRE D'ART, PARIS, see LUGNÉ-POË.

THÉÂTRE DE L'ATELIER, PARIS, see DULLIN.

THÉÂTRE DE L'ŒUVRE, PARIS, see LUGNÉ-POË.

THÉÂTRE DE MADAME, PARIS, see GYMNASE-DRAMATIQUE.

THÉÂTRE-FRANÇAIS, PARIS, see COMÉDIE-FRANÇAISE.

THEATRE GUILD, NEW YORK, a membership society for the presentation of distinguished and uncommercial American and foreign plays, which made its first public appearance in 1919 with *The Bonds of Interest*. Its second production, which scored an unexpected success, was *John Ferguson*, since when the Theatre Guild has been the means of introducing many notable plays and players to America. Its influence, in its early years particularly, was very great, and although success later modified its original programme somewhat, it maintains its high standard and its preference for what is new and unusual in the world's theatre. The precursor of the Theatre Guild was the group known as the Washington Square Players, which was formed in 1914, under Edward Goodman, and for the next three years presented intermittently at the Bandbox Theatre a programme of non-commercial plays with some success. Katharine Cornell made one of her earliest appearances with this group. The first productions of the Theatre Guild were given at the Garrick, and in 1925 the society built its own playhouse (see GUILD THEATRE).

THÉÂTRE-ITALIEN, PARIS, see COMÉDIE-ITALIENNE.

THEATRE LIBRARY ASSOCIATION, an organization founded in 1937 by H. M. Lydenberg, then head of the New York Public Library, at the suggestion of George Feedley, with the intention of fostering the preservation of theatrical books, pamphlets, playbills, programmes, relics, and ephemera, by the exchange of material and ideas between private and public collectors all over the world. The Association publishes a *Broadside* three times a year on theatre work, research in progress, and the location of theatrical material, and since 1942 a *Theatre Annual*.

THÉÂTRE LIBRE, PARIS, see ANTOINE.

THEATRE MACHINERY, see MACHINERY and TRICKWORK ON THE ENGLISH STAGE.

THÉÂTRE MIXTE, PARIS, see THÉÂTRE DE L'ŒUVRE.

THEATRE MUSIC, see INCIDENTAL MUSIC.

THEATRE OF COMEDY, LENINGRAD, see AKIMOV.

THEATRE OF DRAMA, MOSCOW, see THEATRE OF THE REVOLUTION.

THEATRE OF THE BALTIC FLEET. This was first formed in 1930 by an amateur group of sailors in the Baltic Fleet which was based on Leningrad. It began with concerts on board and in Baltic ports. By degrees its members achieved professional status, and it was reinforced by professional actors conscripted into the Navy. In 1934 A. V. Pergament, a Leningrad producer, became its director, and its repertory ranged from Russian classics to plays specially written for it, mainly about the sea. It continued to perform during the Second World War, suffering many casualties, and was in Leningrad during the siege, when a new topical play, *To Meet the Squadron*, was performed (1942). It also continued to give concerts and revues. In 1943 Vishnevsky wrote for it *At the Walls of Leningrad* and, in collaboration with Kron and Azarov, a musical play, with excellent crowd scenes, dealing with the siege of Leningrad.

THEATRE OF THE REVOLUTION, Moscow. This theatre, which is now merged with the Moscow Theatre of Drama, and has a seating capacity of 1,320, is directed by Okhlopkov. It was founded in 1922 as an organ of propaganda, and under Meyerhold produced a series of new plays, mostly dealing with problems of the day. It was perhaps too early for such dramatization of events, and when in 1924 Meyerhold left to direct his own theatre, the Theatre of the Revolution became, in the words of one critic, 'a sort of large-scale News Theatre'. Popov, later to rank so high in the history of the Soviet theatre, became its director in 1930, and an immediate deepening of serious purpose was apparent. An earlier manifestation of this had been apparent in *The Man with the Portfolio* (1928), produced by Dikie, but it was strengthened by such productions as *Poem About an Axe*, *My Friend*, and *Joy Street*. Under Popov the theatre also tackled *Romeo and Juliet* with such success that it has remained in the repertory ever since. During the Second World War the theatre was evacuated, but returned under Okhlopkov with a programme of new and interesting plays.

THEATRE ORCHESTRA, see INCIDENTAL MUSIC.

THEATRE ROYAL, BRIDGES STREET, see DRURY LANE.

THEATRE ROYAL, HOLBORN, see CONNAUGHT THEATRE.

THEATRE ROYAL, MARYLEBONE, see WEST
LONDON THEATRE.

THEATRE ROYAL, STRAND, see STRAND
THEATRE (1).

THEATRE ROYAL, WESTMINSTER, see
ASTLEY'S AMPHITHEATRE.

THEATRE SCENERY, see SCENERY.

THEATRICAL COMMONWEALTH. (1)
The name taken by a group of disgruntled
actors in Philadelphia in 1812, who tried unsuccessfully to start a profit-sharing company
of their own, in opposition to the established
theatres.

(2) A group of actors who seceded from the
Park Theatre, New York, in the autumn of
1813, and set up for themselves in a converted
circus on Broadway. The company included
Holman and his daughter, Gilfert, later Holman's son-in-law, Leigh, Wareing, Mrs.
Twaits, and Mrs. Goldson. Twaits was the
manager, and the company gave some good
plays—an excellent *School for Scandal*, and
good productions of *The Rivals* and *As You
Like It*. Emboldened by their popularity, the
rebels had the temerity to put on *The Virgin of
the Sun* on the same night as the Park, with
some success. The theatre closed in Dec. 1813
on the death of Mrs. Twaits, and the company
finally disbanded in Jan. 1814, several of the
actors returning to the Park.

THEATRICAL SYNDICATE, an association of American business men in the theatre,
formed in 1896, which included the firm of
Klaw and Erlanger, Charles Frohman, Al Hayman, Sam Nixon (Samuel F. Nirdlinger), and
J. Fred Zimmerman. For about 16 years they
controlled most of the theatres of New York
and many of those in other big towns, and
gradually exerted a stranglehold over the entertainment life of the country. They were powerful enough to harm those who opposed their
monopoly, forcing Mrs. Fiske to play in
second-rate theatres on tour, and Sarah Bernhardt to appear in a tent. Both these actresses,
however, with the assistance of Daly and
Belasco, helped in the end to break the syndicate, whose original good intentions of organizing the theatre and preventing exploitation
and wastage had been overlaid by a desire to
make money without reference to aesthetic
values, and a determined elimination of healthy
competition.

THEODORUS, a Greek tragic actor of the
fourth century B.C.

THEOGNIS, a Greek tragic poet who, according to Aristophanes, was so frigid that
when his play was produced in Athens the
rivers froze in Thrace.

THÉOPHILE DE VIAU (1590–1626), French
dramatist, author of *Pirame et Thisbé*, a

pastoral given in 1621. It was most successful,
and helped to establish the vogue of the
Unities. It was revived at Court in 1627 with
Mlle de Rambouillet as Pyramus. With his
contemporary the Marquis de Racan, Théophile marks the entry into French drama of the
poet and courtier, but unlike his companion he
had a stormy life. He was suspected of being
—as a Huguenot and a *libertin*—part-author of
Le Parnasse satirique, and therefore exiled.
Though he later returned to France and became a Catholic, he was again accused of
atheism and immorality, and condemned to be
burnt at the stake. Escaping this fate, he was
banished, and died shortly afterwards at the
home of his friend and benefactor Montmorency.

THEORIC FUND, a grant of two obols distributed to the poorer citizens of Athens to
enable them to pay for admission to the theatre
at the Dionysiac festivals. It was introduced
in the time of Pericles, suppressed during the
Peloponnesian War, and revived by the demagogue Agyrrhius in 394 B.C., when it was raised
to one drachma a head. It was finally abolished
by the intervention of Demosthenes after
Chaeronea.

THESPIS, of Icaria, in Attica, a Greek poet
who has good claims to be considered the
founder of drama, since he was the first to use
an actor in his plays, in addition to the chorus
and its leader. He won the prize at the first
tragic contest in Athens, *c.* 534 B.C. Titles only
of his plays are preserved, and even these may
not be genuine.   H. D. F. K.

'Tradition has it that Thespis took his actors
round in a cart, which formed their stage (cf.
Horace, *Ars Poetica*, and Dryden's prologue
to Lee's *Sophonisba*). The adjective Thespian
has come to be used of actors and acting in
general, and often figures in the names of
amateur companies, while 'the Thespian art' is
journalese for the art of acting.

THIRTY-NINTH STREET THEATRE,
NEW YORK. This had a short but brilliant
career as a playhouse. It was opened by the
Shuberts on 18 Apr. 1910 as the Nazimova,
with that actress in the first New York production of *Little Eyolf*, which ran for six weeks. A
year later, re-christened, it opened again with
Green Stockings, and later saw Charles Quartermaine and Madge Titheradge in *A Butterfly on
the Wheel*. Towards the end of 1912 Annie
Russell conducted a repertory season of English
classics at this theatre, and a year later John
Barrymore appeared there in the Harvard Prize
Play, *Believe Me, Xantippe*. In 1919 Walter
Hampden appeared as Hamlet, and the theatre
continued to flourish until 1925, when it was
pulled down. An office building now stands
on the site.   G. F.

THOMAS, AUGUSTUS (1857–1934), American
dramatist, whose numerous plays are mainly
based on themes of American life and thought.

He was associated as a young man with an amateur dramatic club in St. Louis, his birthplace, both as actor and author, and a sketch, *Editha's Burglar*, written for production by the club, was later rewritten as a full-length play and produced in 1889 with Maurice Barrymore in the role of the burglar. Thomas succeeded Boucicault as adapter of foreign plays at the Madison Square Theatre under Palmer, but his first popular success, an original drama entitled *Alabama* (1891), enabled him to resign and devote his time to his own work. Among his later plays were several others based on a definite locality—*In Mizzoura* (1893), *Arizona* (1899), *Colorado* (1901), and *Rio Grande* (1916). His best play was *The Copperhead* (1918), in which Lionel Barrymore made a hit as Milt Shanks. An interest in hypnotism and faith-healing was shown in *The Witching Hour* (1907), *Harvest Moon* (1909), and *As A Man Thinks* (1911), but on the whole Thomas's plays are not profound, and provided entertainment of a kind acceptable to his audience. He probably wrote too much and too unevenly, but he is of significance in the development of the modern American play by his consistent use of native material. In 1922 he published his autobiography under the title of *The Print of My Remembrance*.

THOMPSON, JOHN (?–1634), English actor, who was with the King's Men for some years as their leading boy-player. In about 1621 he played the Cardinal's Mistress in *The Duchess of Malfi*, and for the next ten years continued to appear as a woman, mostly in queenly or haughty parts, sometimes as a regal villainess. Since several of his roles comprised songs, it is reasonable to suppose that he was something of a singer. He does not appear to have fulfilled as an adult player the promise of his youth, but since he only lived for a short time after attaining male roles, it is probable that he lacked time and opportunity to show what he could do. He was closely associated with the actor Shank, and may have been apprenticed to him.

THOMPSON, LYDIA (1836–1908), English actress, who was first a dancer, appearing at His Majesty's in 1852, and then went into burlesque, with which her name is chiefly connected. She became well known in the provinces, and in 1868 took a troupe of golden-haired English beauties to the United States, where she remained six years, joining forces with Willie Edouin and introducing burlesque to America. She also went to Australia and India, and on returning to England in 1874 alternated between there and New York until her death. From 1886 to 1888 she was manageress of the Strand Theatre, London, and made her last appearance at the Imperial in 1904.

THOMSON, JAMES (1700–48), English poet, author of the long poem *The Seasons*, and possibly of 'Rule Britannia', which first ap-

peared in his masque of *Alfred* (1740). He was celebrated in his own day for some forgotten tragedies on classical lines: *Sophonisba* (1730); *Agamemnon* (1738), in which the Cibbers and Quin appeared, though with little success; *Tancred and Sigismunda* (1744), possibly his best work, in which, says Allardyce Nicoll in *Eighteenth Century Drama*, 'while the treatment is classical to a degree, the theme shows clearly Thomson's move from the duller realms of pseudo-classicism to the spacier realms of romantic enthusiasm'; and *Coriolanus* (1749), given posthumously, again with Quin, and a failure. Thomson's only other play, *Edward and Eleonora*, which deals classically with the romantic theme later treated by Scott in *The Talisman*, was banned by the censor and not produced. Thomson was one of the best dramatists of his day, in the opinion of Pope and others, but the permanent eclipse of his theatrical work shows to what a low ebb the English theatre had fallen at this time in its endeavours to ape the stately measures of French classical tragedy.

THORNDIKE. (1) SYBIL (1882–   ), distinguished English actress, wife of Sir Lewis Casson, three of whose children are also on the stage. In 1931 she was created D.B.E. for her services to the English theatre. She began her career under Ben Greet, touring with him in England and the United States, and was leading lady for several seasons at Miss Horniman's Repertory Theatre in Manchester, where she laid the foundations of her later career, Shaw calling her even then his ideal Candida. From 1914 to 1918 she was at the Old Vic, where she played not only a long series of Shakespearian and other heroines, but also such parts as Prince Hal, Puck, Launcelot Gobbo, the Fool in *King Lear*, and Ferdinand in *The Tempest*. She returned to the Vic many times, and during the 1939–45 war toured mining towns and villages with an Old Vic company as Lady Macbeth, Candida, and Medea. Among the outstanding performances of her long and distinguished career have been Hecuba in *The Trojan Women*, Saint Joan in Shaw's play of that name, and the elderly schoolmistress in *The Corn is Green*. Her versatility has been shown by her appearances in Grand Guignol, in modern comedy, in Greek tragedy, in poetic drama, and in English and foreign classics. Her biography was written in 1929 by her brother (2) (ARTHUR) RUSSELL (1885–   ), with whom she collaborated in a life of Lilian Baylis. Like his sister, Russell Thorndike, actor, dramatist, and novelist, has been associated with Ben Greet and the Old Vic, where he was leading man for several seasons. One of his finest performances was given in the title-role of his own play, *Dr. Syn* (1925). His younger sister (3) EILEEN (1891–   ) was also an actress, making her first appearance at the Court Theatre in 1909, after studying at the R.A.D.A. From 1912 to 1917 she was at the Liverpool Repertory Theatre, but retired from the stage on her marriage, and did not act again until 1930. From 1933 to 1939 she was principal of the Embassy School of Acting, and was also connected with the Central School of Speech Training.

THORNE. (1) CHARLES ROBERT, senior (c. 1814–93), American actor, son of a New York merchant, who made his first appearance on the stage at the Park Theatre in 1829. A year later he starred at the Bowery, where he met and married (2) ANN MARIA MESTAYER (? –1881), member of a famous circus family. He appeared with her at many theatres and was for some time manager of the Chatham, but though his work was good he had no settled policy, and contributed little to the development of the American stage. He toured extensively, and managed theatres in several large towns, notably San Francisco. Of his five children the best-known was (3) CHARLES ROBERT, junior (1840–83), who as a child toured with his parents, and in 1860 was with Jefferson in New York, where he played in the latter's revival of *Our American Cousin* at Laura Keene's Theatre. He was later in Boston, but his career really began when in 1871 he joined the Union Square Theatre under Palmer, where he was for many years immensely popular as the dashing young heroes of melodrama. A good-looking, athletic, and attractive person, not over-intelligent, he represented the ideal romantic hero of the time. In 1874 he was seen in London with some success. He made his last appearance in 1883 in *The Corsican Brothers*, but was forced to retire from the cast owing to illness, and died soon afterwards.

THORNE, SARAH (1837–99), English actress and theatre manager, who for many years ran the stock company at the Theatre Royal, Margate, where she trained a number of young players, including Louis Calvert, Granville-Barker, and Violet and Irene Vanbrugh. She came of good theatrical stock, her father being Richard Samuel Thorne, a provincial actor-manager. Of her seven brothers and sisters, who all went on the stage, the best-known is (2) THOMAS (1841–1918), for many years actor-manager at the Vaudeville, where with David James he presented and played in *Our Boys.* This ran for many years and made fortunes for its author, H. J. Byron, and the two partners. Sarah's son (3) GEORGE (1856–1922) was also an actor, and made his first appearance at his mother's theatre at the age of two. He toured India, and played Grossmith's parts in D'Oyly Carte's principal touring company. In addition he wrote a number of burlesques and pantomimes and adapted several of Dickens's novels for the stage.   W. M. P.

THREE HUNDRED CLUB, LONDON, see STAGE SOCIETY.

THROWLINE, a cord used to join the flats forming a wall, as in a Box Set (see FLAT).

THUNDER. The noise of thunder is usually produced off-stage by the shaking of a suspended iron sheet known as the Thunder Sheet. An earlier, Georgian device was the Thunder Run, consisting of two long, inclined wooden troughs down which iron balls were rolled past releasing-doors, to produce an effect whose sound not only came from overhead but whose reverberations shook the building with a trembling as awful as the true peals of Jove himself. For an account of the existing Thunder Run at the Theatre Royal, Bristol, see an illustrated article by Richard Southern in *The Architectural Review* for May 1944.

TICH, LITTLE, see LITTLE TICH.

TIE-BARS, metal strap-hooks, linking the upright posts under a raked stage (see STAGE, 1).

TIECK, LUDWIG (1773–1853), German romantic poet and playwright, whose early plays were fairy-tales treated in a vein of Aristophanic satire. Among these were *Der gestiefelte Kater* (1797), *Ritter Blaubart* (1797), and *Die verkehrte Welt* (1798). His wit and his mental acrobatics are often engaging, but they tend to pall as the absence of any positive standard becomes apparent. He followed his short plays in prose with long, often very long, very long, dramas such as the *Leben und Tod der heiligen Genoveva* (1799) and *Kaiser Oktavianus* (1804). In 1824 Tieck was appointed director of the Dresden Court theatre, where he insisted on clear diction and simplified staging. He became an influential critic, and his writings on the theatre, afterwards collected as *Dramaturgische Blätter* (1826), reveal him as a man of insight and taste, but without the moral force of a great reformer. His interest in the Elizabethan age is reflected in his novels, *Dichterleben* (1826) and, with echoes of *Wilhelm Meister*, in *Der junge Tischlermeister* (1836), in his translations of Ben Jonson, and in his completion of Schlegel's translations of Shakespeare, whose cult he furthered in Germany.

TILLEY, VESTA (1864–   ), a famous music-hall performer, at her best in male impersonations. She was on the stage at the age of 3½, and made her first appearance in male attire at 5. Before she went to London in 1878 she was well known in the provinces as the Great Little Tilley, her real name being Matilda Ball (or Bowles). Her success in London was equally great, and for many years she was known as the London Idol. She married Colonel Sir Walter de Frece, and in 1920 retired from the stage after a final appearance before an enthusiastic audience at the Coliseum. Among the songs she made famous were 'Burlington Bertie', 'Jolly Good Luck to the Girl Who Loves a Soldier', 'The Army of To-day's All Right', 'Following in Father's Footsteps', and 'The Piccadilly Johnny With the Little Glass Eye'.

TILNEY, SIR EDMUND, see MASTER OF THE REVELS.

TIMES SQUARE THEATRE, NEW YORK,

on the north side of West 42nd Street. This was opened by the Selwyns on 30 Sept. 1920 with *The Mirage*, which ran for 192 performances. Several musical plays were followed by *The Fool*, and by a short-lived version of *Pelleas and Melisande*, with Jane Cowl. Two later successes were André Charlot's Revue, with a large cast of London favourites, and *Gentlemen Prefer Blondes*, while *Front Page* occupied the season of 1928–9 with 199 performances. In Jan. 1931 came Coward's *Private Lives*, with the author, Gertrude Lawrence, Jill Esmond, and Laurence Olivier; in spite of changes in the cast, it ran for 256 performances. The last play at this theatre, which then became a cinema, was *Forsaking All Others*, which introduced Tallulah Bankhead to Broadway.   G. F.

TIREMAN, the Elizabethan equivalent of the modern Wardrobe Master (or Mistress). Chambers sums up his duties as follows: He 'fitted the dresses and the beards, furnished stools, and in the private theatres took charge of the lights'.

TIRSO DE MOLINA, see MOLINA.

TITINIUS, see FABULA (9) *Togata.*

TIVOLI GARDENS, NEW YORK, see RICHMOND HILL THEATRE.

TOBY, the dog of the Punch and Judy show. He joined Punch after the latter had become established in England, and has no connexion with the *commedia dell'arte*; nor does he figure in the harlequinade, though Clown is sometimes accompanied by a mongrel puppy. In early Punch and Judy shows there was sometimes a puppet-dog, but there is no evidence that he was called Toby. The name seems to have come into use with the introduction of a live dog, somewhere between 1820 and 1850, possibly because the first dog to be employed was already so called. It has also been suggested that the name has some connexion with Tobit or Tobias, a favourite subject for a seventeenth-century puppet-show, where Tobias and the angel are accompanied by a dog. Toby is usually a small, quick-witted, mongrel terrier. Wearing a ruff round his neck, he sits on the sill of the puppet-booth window, taking little part in the action, though he may be fondled by Punch in a moment of lachrymose sentimentality, or incited to bite the heads off some of Punch's enemies, not excepting the baby. In the end he usually seizes Punch by the nose, and is killed. After the show he goes round among the audience, with whom he is a firm favourite, collecting pennies in a little bag which he holds in his mouth.

TOGATA, see FABULA (9).

TOGGLE RAIL, a wooden bar across the back of a canvas flat, used to strengthen it and

to counteract the drawing power of size paint as it dries (see FLAT).

TOLLER, ERNST (1893–1939), German dramatist, and one of the best and most mature writers of the expressionist school. His first play, *Wandlung* (1918), written during his imprisonment as a pacifist, is a plea for tolerance and the abolition of war. Three years later came his best-known work, *Masse-Mensch*(1921), followed by *Die Maschinenstürmer* (1922), which deals with the Luddite riots of 1815 in England, and was done in London by the Stage Society as *The Machine Wreckers*. It is less expressionist in technique than *Masse-Mensch*, and less pessimistic, since Toller, in the person of his hero, Jim Cobbett, foreshadows the day when the rebellious workers will be an organized and stable body of intelligent men. But Toller's later plays, which failed to reach the heights of his earlier work, were progressively less hopeful in tone as he watched the domestic tragedy of Germany unfold itself, and the man who had been imprisoned for his part in the communist rising of 1919 left Germany in 1933 to become a British subject. He went to America, lecturing and advising on drama, and committed suicide in the summer of 1939.

TOLSTOY, ALEXEI KONSTANTINOVICH(1817–75), Russian diplomat, friend of Alexander II, who was born in St. Petersburg, of a noble family, and held many important posts. He was the author of a number of poems, and of a fine historical trilogy, containing excellent crowd scenes and written with much semi-oriental imagery, in which he idealized old feudal Russia. They are *The Death of Ivan the Terrible*, *Tsar Feodor Ivanovich*, and *Tsar Boris*. Written between 1866 and 1870, they were banned by the censor, who finally allowed the second to be put on as the opening production of the Moscow Art Theatre in 1898. Later the complete trilogy was given.

TOLSTOY, ALEXEI NIKOLAEVICH (1882–1945), one of the outstanding writers of early Soviet Russia, whose first work was published under the Imperial régime, in 1908. Member of an aristocratic family, he received a good education, and devoted himself to literature. His first play was written after the October Revolution, and showed the influence of it reaching even to Mars. Later works included a trilogy on Peter I, based on his own novel, and another historical trilogy on Ivan the Terrible, of which the first part, dealing with Ivan's youth and marriage, was produced by the Maly in 1943, and the second part, dealing with Ivan's struggles to unite Russia, by the Moscow Art Theatre later in the same year. Among plays on a modern theme an outstanding one was *The Road to Victory* (1939), dealing with an episode of the Revolution, in which both Stalin and Lenin appear.

TOLSTOY, LEO NIKOLAEVICH (1828–1910), one of the great names in Russian literature and social history, the bulk of whose work lies outside the theatre. He was first encouraged to try his hand at playwriting in the 1850s, under the influence of Turgeniev and Ostrovsky, and started some comedies which, however, remained unfinished. It was not until 1886 that he once more turned to the theatre, and by then his whole philosophy of life had undergone a change. Under the influence of M. V. Lentovsky, director of one of the Moscow People's Theatres, who was looking for plays dealing with the life of the people—a subject few fashionable authors cared to touch at that time —Tolstoy wrote *The Power of Darkness*, possibly the most forceful peasant play ever written. The material for it came from real life, since the main outline was taken from a criminal case heard at Tula. In the hands of such an artist as Tolstoy the sordid tale of crime became a stark naturalistic document, comparable with Hauptmann's *Vor Sonnenaufgang*, and as such for many years banned by the censor. It was first acted abroad, in Paris, and then in Berlin. In it Tolstoy revealed to what depths of degradation the 'idiocy of village life' could reduce human beings, until their most ordinary instincts were perverted and grew unnatural.

His second play, *The Fruits of Enlightenment*, which was also begun in 1886, arose out of a visit to a spiritualist séance. Published in 1891 and produced at the Moscow Maly Theatre in the following year, this satirizes the parasitic life of the country gentry, their preoccupation with trifles, their exploitation of the poverty-stricken peasants, and the latter's growing resentment. It is one of the world's classics, and rings as true to-day as when it was written. In presentation it is probably possible to give it greater truth to-day than at its first production, since the Imperial Theatres were ill equipped to enact the peasant characters, which even the Moscow Art Theatre could not at first fully develop.

Tolstoy's last plays were both unfinished, and bring into the theatre the theory of 'passive resistance' which he was developing in his other work at the time. *Redemption* (or *The Living Corpse*, as it is sometimes called) is a problem play centring upon the conflict between the Christian doctrine of self-sacrifice and the marriage laws of the State. It made a great impression when it was first seen in Europe, and Lenin, in his analysis of Tolstoy's work, said 'it is a wonderfully powerful, direct and truthful protest against social lies and hypocrisy'. It was produced by the Moscow Art Theatre in 1911.

The Light that Shines in Darkness was Tolstoy's last work for the theatre, and its final act exists only in outline. In it he tried to sum up all his hopes, experiences, and opinions on life. Here again he uses the method of parallel conflict, in which the useless life of the wealthy Sarintsev family alternates with that of the poverty-stricken, overworked, and helpless peasants.

Two of Tolstoy's novels, *Resurrection* and *Anna Karenina*, were also dramatized and produced with great success at the Moscow Art Theatre and elsewhere.

TOOLE, JOHN LAURENCE (1830–1906), English actor and theatre manager. Born in London, where his father was Toastmaster to the East India Company, he was for a short time, like Garrick, clerk to a wine-merchant, but success in amateur theatricals, notably as Jacob Earwig in *Boots at the Swan*, turned his thoughts to the stage. Encouraged by Dickens, he joined Dillon's company in Dublin in 1852 as a low comedian, and two years later made a fleeting appearance in London, returning to establish himself, after further experience in the provinces, in 1856. He was seen at the Lyceum as Fanfaronade in *Belphegor*, in which Marie Wilton, later Lady Bancroft, also made her first appearance in London. On the recommendation of Dickens, Toole was engaged by Ben Webster for the New Adelphi in 1858, and remained there nine years. Among his successful parts were Bob Cratchit in *A Christmas Carol* (1859) and Caleb Plummer in *Dot* (1862), Boucicault's dramatization of *The Cricket on the Hearth*. In this he combined humour with a pathos which showed how well he might have played serious character parts; but the public preferred him in farce. He was for many years a close friend of Irving, with whom he first played at the Queen's, Long Acre, in 1857, and subsequently on tour. In 1869 he began a long association with Hollingshead at the Gaiety, being excellent in burlesque and opéra bouffe, and in 1879 he went into management at the Charing Cross Theatre, with a good resident stock company, giving it his own name in 1882. The most important production of his last years was Barrie's first play, a farce entitled *Walker, London* (1892). He habitually toured the provinces in summer, with a good company, gaining thereby much profit and reputation. Crippled by gout, he left the stage in 1895, when his theatre was pulled down, and retired to Brighton, where he died. He made one appearance in New York, in 1874, at Wallack's, but was not very successful, his humour being too cockneyfied for the Americans. Clement Scott called him 'one of the kindest and most genial men who ever drew breath. . . . No one acted with more spirit or enjoyed so thoroughly the mere pleasure of acting.' He was much respected in his profession, and always on good terms with his audience, being particularly good at end-of-performance speeches.

TOOLE'S THEATRE, LONDON, in King William Street, Charing Cross. This was originally the Polygraphic Hall, where Woodin gave monologue entertainments. In 1869 it became a small theatre, known as the Charing Cross, but nothing of any importance happened there until J. S. Clarke revived *The Rivals* in 1872, himself playing Bob Acres with Mrs. Stirling as Mrs. Malaprop, her first appearance in this, her best, part. Alexander Henderson became manager in 1876, and renamed the theatre the Folly. His wife, Lydia Thompson, starred under him in burlesque. In 1878 the theatre had a tremendous success with Violet Cameron and Shiel Barry in Planquette's *Les Cloches de Corneville*.

In 1879 Toole took over, and three years later gave the theatre his own name. Pinero's early comedy, *Imprudence*, was produced there in 1881, followed by *Boys and Girls*. Both failed, but burlesques by H. J. Byron were successful. Daly's company made their first London appearance at Toole's in 1884, and in 1892 Barrie's first play, *Walker, London*, began a successful run. Toole had enlarged and improved the theatre, but it never held more than 900 people. His last production there was *Thoroughbred*, in Feb. 1895. It closed in the same year, the land having been acquired for an extension of the Charing Cross Hospital.

W. M. P.

TOOLEY, NICHOLAS (*c.* 1575–1623), English actor whose real name was Wilkinson. He was with the King's Men from about 1605 to his death and was an intimate friend of the Burbage family. He may indeed have been apprenticed to Richard, whose will he witnessed, and he was lodging in Cuthbert Burbage's house at the time of his death. It is not known with any certainty what roles he played, except for that of Forobosco in *The Duchess of Malfi*. His name appears in the actor-list of Shakespeare's plays.

TOP DROP, another name for Border.

TORELLI, GIACOMO (1608–78), the first professional scene-painter who was not primarily an artist. He was working at the Teatro Novissimo in Venice in 1641–3, where, it is said, the magical effects of his stage mechanisms gave rise to a suspicion that he was in league with the devil. He thereupon went to Paris, remaining there from 1645 until 1662. In 1650 he devised some fine scenic effects for Corneille's spectacle-play *Andromède*, given at Molière's first theatre, the Petit-Bourbon, which Torelli had refurbished backstage. He was above all a practical man of the theatre, and made many important innovations in the setting and designing of scenery, being the first inventor of a device for moving several sets of wings on to the stage simultaneously. His achievements earned him the nickname of 'il gran stregone' (the great wizard or magician), but much of the work he did in Paris was destroyed by his rival Vigarani (see also ARCHITECTURE, COSTUME, MACHINERY, OPERA, and SCENERY).

TORMENTOR, a term originally applied to a sliding extension of the proscenium wing, now to the fixed narrow flat, covered in black velvet, which has replaced it.

TORRES NAHARRO, BARTOLOMÉ DE, see NAHARRO.

TOTTENHAM STREET THEATRE, LONDON, see SCALA THEATRE.

TOURING COMPANY, see PROVINCIAL THEATRES, 1 *q*.

TOURNEUR, CYRIL (1575–1626), English dramatist, of whose life very little is known, though he was connected with the Cecils and may have been used by them on secret missions abroad. In the year before his death he was secretary to the council of war at Cadiz under Sir Edward Cecil. Two extant plays are doubtfully assigned to him, *The Revenger's Tragedy*, published in 1607 and probably played a year or two previously, and *The Atheist's Tragedy*, published in 1611 and probably written in 1606, since echoes of *King Lear* have been noted in it. The manuscript of a further play, *The Nobleman*, was destroyed by Warburton's cook.

TOWERS, SAMUEL, see AGGAS, ROBERT.

TOWNELEY CYCLE, see ENGLAND, 1 and MYSTERY PLAY.

TOWSE, JOHN RANKIN (1845–1927), American dramatic critic, who was born at Streatham, Surrey, England, and studied at Cambridge. In 1869 he went to the United States and found work as a reporter on *The New York Post*. His early journalistic career was an eventful one. His stories of conditions on Blackwell's Island aroused the anger of Tammany Hall, and won the young Englishman an immediate reputation. Later he covered the Tweed ring exposures trial, the 'criminal charges' trial of Henry Ward Beecher, and the Westbrook ferryboat disaster. In 1874 he became dramatic critic of *The New York Post*, an assignment he held for fifty years, until his retirement in 1927. Imbued with the traditions of Drury Lane, the Haymarket, and Sadler's Wells, he remained ever faithful to the theatre of his youth. Ibsen and Shaw he held in slight esteem and on many matters he saw eye to eye with William Winter. But Towse had a more judicial temper and never descended to abuse. On his retirement, however, he denounced the modern theatre as destitute of morality. Apart from his newspaper work he has left a volume of theatrical memoirs, *Sixty Years of the Theatre*, in which he recalls the golden age of Augustin Daly, Salvini, Samuel Phelps, Modjeska, Adelaide Neilson, and Edwin Booth.

T. Q. C.

TOY THEATRE. One of the most delightful of the many charming ephemeral publications of the nineteenth century was the 'Juvenile Drama'—a sort of miniature edition of the contemporary theatre. In the year 1811 a Mr. William West, who kept a small stationer's shop in Exeter Street, off the Strand, was publishing sheets of theatrical characters copied from the latest productions at Covent Garden, Drury Lane, and the minor theatres; each plate of figures contained about eight small drawings depicting the various characters in their most dramatic moments. Soon scenery, consisting of back drops and side wings, was also included. Considerable care was apparently taken to make an accurate copy of the details of costume and scenery, and even the faces of the actors were sometimes faithfully reproduced. Each play consisted of some ten or twenty sheets, usually sold at a 'penny plain, or twopence coloured'. The colouring was done by hand in bold, vivid hues that are as fresh to-day as when they were first applied.

These toy-theatre plays were probably first intended as some form of theatrical souvenir, but the idea proved immensely popular and was very soon adapted as a children's plaything; between the years 1815 and 1835 the Juvenile Drama seems to have been quite a thriving industry, with some fifty different publishers engaged in it; as soon as a new production at any of the theatres showed signs of popularity it was quickly issued in a toy-theatre version; the sheets would be stuck on cardboard and carefully cut out, and eventually the drama would be re-enacted in countless nurseries and drawing-rooms. As the trade came to cater more and more for children the fine quality of the early engraving and colouring began to fall off, but several publishers continued to produce new plays in the original style until the 1850s and even later.

In the second half of the nineteenth century toy-theatre plays were sometimes given away with boys' magazines, or cheaply printed on a single sheet and sold for a penny; but the genuine Juvenile Drama never quite disappeared, and is still obtainable to-day. As late as 1932 there were two shops in the Hoxton district of London, kept by Mr. Webb and Mr. Pollock, where these old plays were still printed and sold; both these gentlemen are now dead, but Pollock's shop has been transferred to Bloomsbury under new management, and toy-theatre material is still available there.

The Juvenile Drama is of unique interest, as it has preserved with astonishing fidelity the appearance of the early nineteenth-century theatre and even the gestures and mannerisms of its actors; here is recorded the theatre of J. P. Kemble, Edmund Kean, Madame Vestris, Liston, and Grimaldi; the productions, not only of the Patent Theatres, but of the Surrey, the Olympic, Astley's Amphitheatre, and other minor theatres; plays like *The Miller and his Men*, *George Barnwell*, *The Corsican Brothers*, with a total repertory of some three hundred melodramas and pantomimes in all the bright colours and heroic gestures of their first performance.

Among the best publishers of toy-theatre plays were West, Jameson, Hodgson, Skelt, Green, Park, and Webb. There are good collections in the Print Room of the British Museum and at the London Museum; the history of the subject is recorded in *Juvenile Drama*, by George Speaight (1947), and in *Penny Plain, Twopence Coloured*, by A. E. Wilson (1932); while in an essay under the same title (1884) Robert Louis Stevenson paid a graceful tribute to the charm of the Juvenile Drama.

Other countries have their own toy theatres —notably Germany, Denmark, and Spain— but they have usually grown up rather later than that of England and are printed by colour lithography; their plays are directly prepared for children and are not adapted from the living theatre. Efforts to revive the toy theatre in England in a modern form have been made by the British Puppet and Model Theatre Guild.   G. S.

TRABEATA, see FABULA (9) and (10).

TRADES UNIONS THEATRE, Moscow. This theatre, which is affiliated to the Central Council of the Trades Unions of the U.S.S.R. and is known as the V.Ts.P.S., was created in 1932 from the Proletcult Theatre, started immediately after the October Revolution by Sergei Eisenstein. A pupil of Meyerhold, Eisenstein (who later belonged entirely to the cinema) turned his stage into a circus ring and staged shows of which no trace remains except in the heightened apprehension of the audiences which came freshly to them. After Eisenstein left, the Proletcult Theatre passed through many vicissitudes until it received its new name at the same time as a new director, Alexei Dikie. His first production, *Sailors of Cattaro*, showed that he had combined with his Moscow Art Theatre training a modicum of the Proletcult Theatre's formalism, an amalgam which determined the future line of the theatre's development. Another interesting production at this theatre was *Nonsense*, of which André van Gyseghem gives a detailed description in his *Theatre in Soviet Russia*. Later productions were less successful, and in 1936 the theatre was closed (see also DIKIE).

TRAFALGAR SQUARE THEATRE, LONDON, see DUKE OF YORK'S THEATRE.

TRAGÉDIE-LYRIQUE, see OPERA, 3.

TRAGEDY, a term applied to plays dealing in an elevated, poetic style with the grandeur and misery of man in his loftier aspects, as the plaything of fate and yet superior to it. The word is of Greek origin, and Greek tragedy, as written by Aeschylus, Euripides, and Sophocles, set a standard for world drama that has never yet been surpassed (see GREECE, 1). Rome knew only the tragedies of Seneca, written to be read and not acted, which had nevertheless a remarkable influence on European tragedy, through the translations of the humanists. On the continent Italian tragedy, derived directly from the Greek, developed early, but had to wait for its finest expression in the plays of Alfieri in the eighteenth century. Both France and England took to tragedy by way of Seneca, but the latter mingled with it less learning and more romance. Marlowe and Shakespeare in England and Calderón in Spain remained impervious to the French classical tragedy, which reigned supreme elsewhere until the Romantic Revival. Its greatest exponents were Corneille and Racine, who constructed their plays according to the French interpretation of Aristotle's *Poetics*, but with a touch of genius denied to their successors. It was the letter and not the spirit of French tragedy that was imported into England after the Restoration, and resulted in such plays as Addison's *Cato*, while in Germany Gottsched, aided by the actress Caroline Neuber, endeavoured to impose it on the somewhat chaotic German theatre. In neither country did it become acclimatized, nor was Luzán more successful in Spain. Germany had to wait for Schiller and Goethe before she could claim to have produced any great playwrights, while the English and Spanish genius had already shown its true bent with the plays of Lope de Vega and Shakespeare. The influence of the latter spread over Europe in the last years of the eighteenth century, and so helped to produce the highly-coloured tragedies of the Romantic Revival.

An effort to apply the formula of classical tragedy to the misfortunes of the domestic interior was made in the eighteenth century, resulting in such plays as those of Lillo in England, Lessing in Germany, and Mercier in France. These, however, cannot be classified as true tragedy, and are known as *tragédie bourgeoise* or domestic tragedy. Nor can the realistic dramas of Ibsen and his disciples rank as tragedy, though their implications are often tragic enough. In the narrow theatrical sense of the word, tragedy demands a cast of princes and demi-gods, an unfamiliar background—exotic, romantic, or imaginary—and a sense of detachment whose effect is heightened by the use of verse or rhetorical prose. The modern revival of the poetic drama is closely allied with a renewal of interest in the tragic aspects of life. Efforts are again being made to tame tragedy and bring it within the family circle, and it seems as if the use of admittedly poetic language will always help the expression of a strong personal feeling which demands a universal response, and is characteristic of a tragic situation. It is interesting that T. S. Eliot's *Murder in the Cathedral*, dealing with politics in high places, has been the most successful of the new poetic plays, while the same author's *Family Reunion*, containing some equally fine poetry, failed.

An offshoot of pure tragedy is the tragi-comedy, a play dealing with a story inherently tragic, and having an unhappy end, which yet contains certain elements of comedy. Under such a definition some critics have classified *Hamlet* as a tragi-comedy, but the perfect example of the type is *Le Cid*, while the most prolific writer of tragi-comedies was undoubtedly Corneille's predecessor, Alexandre Hardy.

The Tragedy of Revenge was the name given to those Elizabethan plays of which Kyd's *Spanish Tragedy* (1592) was the first. Dealing with bloody deeds which demand retribution, their motto was 'an eye for an eye and a tooth for a tooth', and their sublimity could easily turn to melodrama; and indeed in a cruder

form the revenge motif underlay many of the melodramas of the nineteenth century. In the range of Shakespeare's plays *Titus Andronicus* may be considered the lowest form of the Revenge Tragedy, *Hamlet* its perfect flowering. Under the same heading come the great tragedies of Webster, those of Tourneur, and such plays as *Bussy d'Ambois* and *The Changeling*.

The playing of tragedy makes great demands on the actor, who must have a stately presence —Garrick notwithstanding—fine features, and a resonant and perfectly controlled voice. The stately alexandrine of French tragedy developed a somewhat static style of acting, with slow impressive gestures, which was carried into England after the Restoration and was exemplified by Quin.

TRAGIC CARPET, a green baize stage cloth, spread before the performance of a tragedy to prevent the corpses from soiling their clothes on the dusty boards. It may originally have been a permanent covering, though early references to green cloth coverings seem to refer to the benches in the auditorium rather than to the stage itself. By the end of the seventeenth century its appearance was invariably restricted to and heralded the performance of tragedy. It continued in use into the nineteenth century, and is frequently referred to in theatrical letters and memoirs.

T.R.A.M. THEATRE, Moscow, see LEN-KOM THEATRE.

TRAMPOLINE has so far not been recognized as part of the English language, though it has often appeared on music-hall programmes. It is the apparatus resembling a spring mattress upon which acrobats bounce, and usually has a gymnast's horizontal bar at either end. The word comes from *tremplin*, the wedge-shaped springboard used by acrobats of many generations. In the announcements of Philip Astley, father of the circus, it was anglicized as tramplin and then trampline.   M. W. D.

TRANSFORMATION SCENE, TRANSPARENCY, see TRICK-WORK ON THE ENGLISH STAGE.

TRANSPONTINE MELODRAMA, a term applied, usually in genial derision, to a type of crude and extravagantly sensational play staged in the mid-nineteenth century in London theatres 'across the bridges' (i.e. on the south side of the Thames) such as the Surrey Theatre and the Old Vic. By extension the term was later attached to such plays wherever performed.

TRAP, a device by which scenery or actors can be projected on to the stage from below. It is mainly used in pantomime, in transformation scenes, and for ghostly apparitions. The best known is the Star Trap, which projects an actor on to the stage at great speed (or its variant, the Bristle Trap, which just allows the passage of a body), and is used for the arrival of the Demon King. The Cauldron Trap, a larger square trap not found very frequently, takes its name from a scene in *Macbeth*, while the Grave Trap, a useful oblong trap in the centre of the stage, is named from the scene of the burial of Ophelia in *Hamlet*. Corner Traps are small square ones on each side of the stage behind the curtain, used to raise a standing figure. The Corsican Trap, or Ghost Glide, by which a rising figure appears to drift across the stage, was first used in *The Corsican Brothers*, and the Vamp Trap, by which an actor appears to pass through solid scenery, in the melodrama *The Vampire*.

An exception to the above is the Footlights Trap, in front of the curtain in early theatres, which enabled the lamps to be sunk for trimming or to darken the stage (see ENGLISH PLAYHOUSE, 2 c, LIGHTING, and STAGE).   R. S.

TRAVERSE CURTAIN, see ENGLISH PLAYHOUSE, 3.

TREE BORDER, see BORDER, SCENERY, and STAGE, 3.

TREE, ELLEN (1806–80), see KEAN (3).

TREE. (1) SIR HERBERT DRAPER BEERBOHM (1853–1917), English actor-manager, the second son of Julius Ewald Beerbohm and Constance Draper, and the half-brother of Max Beerbohm. His father, a naturalized British subject, was of German, Dutch, and Lithuanian extraction. Herbert was educated first at a school at Frant, in Kent, and afterwards at Schnepfenthal College, Thuringia. He became at the age of 17 a clerk in the city office of his father, who was a grain merchant. Soon afterwards he began to be known as an amateur actor, and in 1878 he went on the stage professionally. His chief successes in the early eighties were his impersonations of the Rev. Robert Spalding in *The Private Secretary*, and of Macari in *Called Back*. In Apr. 1887 he became manager of the Comedy Theatre, where he produced *The Red Lamp*. Later in that year he took over the management of the Haymarket Theatre. Among his productions were *Captain Swift* (1888), *The Merry Wives of Windsor* (1888), *The Dancing Girl* (1891), *Hamlet* (1892), *A Woman of No Importance* (1893), and *Trilby* (1895), the most echoing of his successes. He built Her (later His) Majesty's Theatre, which was completed early in 1897, opening with a production of *The Seats of the Mighty*.

In this theatre Tree carried on the sumptuously illustrative Lyceum tradition of Shakespearian production, lavishing upon largely visual interpretation all the resources of a generously imaginative romantic mind and achieving effects of magnificence much to the taste of the day. 'It was the whole tradition that was wrong,' declared a contemporary critic, 'not the way he carried it out.' Between 1888 and 1914 Tree produced eighteen of Shakespeare's plays, and once at least, in

Richard II, he succeeded in reinforcing and exhibiting, not merely supplementing by ingenious 'business', his author's imagination. Interspersed with these were such pieces as *Herod* (1900), *The Last of the Dandies* (1901), *Ulysses* (1902), *The Darling of the Gods* (1903), *Colonel Newcome* (1906), *Faust* (1908), *Drake* (1912), *Pygmalion* and *David Copperfield* (both 1914). Tree was knighted in 1909. His versatility found outlet in lecturing and in authorship. He wrote three books: *An Essay on the Imaginative Faculty* (1893), *Thoughts and Afterthoughts* (1913), and *Nothing Matters* (1917).

Tree was a romantic actor, delighting naturally in grandiose effects and in the representation of fantastic, eccentric, bizarre characters. It was in such characters that his own imagination had freest play. When his imagination happened not to be interested in some aspect of a play he had the amateur's fault of 'walking through' the supposedly dull passage. He often chose parts outside his temperamental and physical range. His tragic acting lacked fundamental force. Yet when all his limitations and waywardness are taken into account he must still be reckoned a romantic actor of erratic brilliance and a fine character actor. Connoisseurs would discover even in his extravagances redeemingly delicate strokes of characterization, thrown off as by a sudden impulse.

In 1883 Tree married (2) HELEN MAUD HOLT (1863–1937), an actress of remarkable versatility who excelled in high comedy. Born in London and educated at Queen's College, where she took honours in classics, she married at the age of twenty. Her marriage proved the starting-point of a distinguished stage career, and for the next half a century she was seen in a great variety of parts. She excelled in comedy, playing in Shakespeare, Sheridan, Shaw, and Barrie among other authors. Lady Tree's earliest hit was at the Court Theatre in 1883, as Hester Gould in *The Millionaire*. She appeared in the following year as heroine of her husband's one-act play, *Six and Eightpence*. In 1887 she joined him at the Haymarket and acted with him in *The Red Lamp*. Other parts followed, and in 1897 she was Madame de Cournal in *The Seats of the Mighty* at the opening of Her Majesty's Theatre. As hostess and as leading lady, she shared Herbert Tree's reign, and played in most of the lavish productions which gave His Majesty's its special place in the theatrical history of the time. When the South African war broke out Lady Tree was instrumental in handing over to the War Fund £1,700 in three weeks, her salary for reciting Kipling's 'Absent-Minded Beggar'. In 1902 she assumed for a while the direction of Wyndham's Theatre. After Tree's death she continued to be a familiar figure on the London stage. At the age of 70 she played Mistress Quickly at His Majesty's. Her last part was the Duchess of Stroud in *Our Own Lives* at the Ambassadors' in 1935.

Of the three daughters of Sir Herbert and

Lady Tree, the eldest, (3) VIOLA (1884–1938), followed in the family tradition and in 1904 made her first appearance at the Theatre Royal, Edinburgh, playing Viola in her father's production of *Twelfth Night*. During the next four years she was frequently seen in Shakespeare at His Majesty's, and in 1906 appeared in *The Winter's Tale* as Perdita to the Hermione of Ellen Terry. It was in 1908 that she began seriously to study singing, and in 1910 she sang Eurydice to the Orpheus of Marie Brema in Gluck's opera with some success. The stage, however, regained her interest, and she appeared in a variety of parts till shortly before her death. She was a woman whose gifts far exceeded her ambitions. She wrote with ease and vivacity and published several books. In 1912 she married the dramatic critic Alan Parsons. Her son David also became an actor.   A. V. C.

TREMONT THEATRE, see BOSTON.

TRENEV, KONSTANTIN ANDREIVICH (1884–), Soviet dramatist, son of a peasant, who by great efforts, after a poverty-stricken childhood, became a school-teacher and editor of a Ukrainian newspaper. He soon began to write, and his first volume of short stories was published in 1914. After the Revolution he turned to the theatre, and his first play, dealing with an eighteenth-century peasant insurrection, was staged by the Moscow Art Theatre in 1925. This was the theatre's first attempt at a Soviet play, and was not particularly successful, but it served to establish Trenev as a playwright, a position which he strengthened in the following year when the Maly Theatre produced the first version of his *Lyubov Yarovaya*. This, in a second, much-altered form, with five acts instead of four, was one of the outstanding productions of the Moscow Art Theatre in 1937, and was awarded a Stalin Prize in 1940. It tells the story of an intelligent and progressive school-teacher, who is an active Revolutionary, but whose husband has joined the White Russians. Finally she is forced to choose between love and loyalty, and betrays her husband. This play, which abounds in excellent characterizations, with the sailor Shvandya and the peasant-soldier Pikalov typifying old and new Russia, has proved popular all over the U.S.S.R., and is so far the most important work to come from Trenev. He has, however, kept up a steady output, and may yet do better.

TRETYAKOV, SERGEI MIKHAILOVICH (1892–), one of the earliest Soviet dramatists, whose best-known play, *Roar China*, was produced by Meyerhold in 1926. Though somewhat elementary and melodramatic, and written for propaganda purposes, it is a vivid historical document, presenting with intense conviction the conflict between Chinese coolies and foreign imperialists.

TRIBUTARY THEATRE, U.S.A., see NATIONWIDE THEATRE.

TRICKWORK ON THE ENGLISH STAGE. It was in their tricks, with the high skill they demanded from the carpenter and the acrobatic actor, that the English actors were, in the nineteenth century, acknowledged leaders of the world. Perhaps less attention than it deserves has in the past been paid at home to the startling brilliance achieved by English trickwork, though several admiring and almost envious references were made to it on the continent.

Tricks may involve scenery, or supply an accompanying 'effect' to a scene, or may involve the person of the player himself, and depend not on their working alone but on the skill and brilliant timing of the man or woman who takes part in them.

Tricks with scenery generally involve some change in its appearance, either wholly or in part. Methods for effecting such changes were many, but possibly the most widely used was that of Falling Flaps. An account of 1803 mentions 'those double flat scenes, which are also used to produce instantaneous changes. The whole scene being covered with pieces of canvas, framed and moving upon hinges, one side [of each of these hinged flaps] is painted to represent a certain scene, and the other to represent one totally different.' Before the working of the trick, these flaps are all 'elevated above the joints', that is to say each flap is raised and presents its obverse face to the audience, making, with its fellows, a complete picture. 'The contrivances for moving them are very various. In general, however, they are kept in the elevated situation by catches, which being suddenly relieved, they fall by their own weight', presenting the reverse face to the audience, and displaying thus the painting of a completely different subject.

An interesting example of such a system of flaps is to be found in the Victorian toy-theatre sheets. Here the sheets for certain back scenes bear the legend 'Trick Scene', and close inspection will show that across part of the design are one or more rows of dotted lines. On a separate sheet of 'Tricks' one or more smaller pieces correspond with the scene and fit in the area marked by the dotted lines. The piece, or pieces, are to be cut out, hinged in position on the back-scene sheet, and worked to effect the trick change in exactly the same way as the framed canvas flaps mentioned above.

Such a system is generally applied only to part of a scene, as for instance to one shop front out of a row of shops in a street scene. For the magic transformation of the whole scene other methods are available, and the skilled development of these led to the great erstwhile feature of every pantomime, the Transformation Scene. In later years much of the transformation has been effected by gauze cloths, and by straightforward flying of cloths, but the Rise and Sink was once an effective variant, in which the upper part of the scene detached itself from the lower and ascended to the low grid (which was formerly not high enough to allow the flying of more than half a back scene at most), while the lower part, framed out and possibly with a profiled upper edge, descended into the cellar upon sloats. The Fan Effect was also sometimes employed, where sectors of the back scene, pivoted centrally at the foot of the scene, sank sideways upon each other like a pair of collapsing fans.

Again, a quick transition of scene might be achieved by dividing the back scene into a series of vertical strips, each of which was wound on its own vertical roller. The set of rollers is stationed across the stage like a row of columns, with another scene visible behind as a backcloth. Upon the change, lines from the top and bottom of each roller are pulled sideways, and the new scene is drawn out from the 'columns' to fill the intercolumnar spaces, hiding the view behind, and presenting, in a flash, a new scene.

Scruto may also be employed. Scruto is the name given to a surface made by attaching a number of narrow strips of thin wood side by side on a canvas backing, so as to form a continuous flexible sheet, like the cover of a roll-top desk. Upon the scruto a subject may be painted and the whole attached to a scene so as to roll down or up, at cue, and replace the old painting with a new.

The intricacies of inventiveness by which these methods may be applied and developed are amazing. One extension of the Falling Flap method, for instance, was used to transform a set piece instantaneously before the eyes of the audience, at a touch, maybe, of Harlequin's baton. In its simplest form, the set piece—a small one, let us say, representing a square bale labelled 'Shag Tobacco'—possesses half its subject painted on the normal surface, but the other half is on one face of a hinged flap, turning, in this case, vertically. On the action of a simple trick-line, this flap is swung over, like the page of a book, to lie over the first portion of the piece, so discovering the remaining portion and the reverse face of the hinged flap. Hereon is painted perhaps a large cabbage with a watering-can beside it—the quality of the tobacco is revealed in its source!

But this is not all. When one withdraws a letter from an envelope, it may be a small sheet folded once; the act of opening the letter is then the simple pivoting of a 'flap'. But the letter may be larger, and folded not once, but again. Now, upon pulling it open, it exhibits in effect not only a turning flap, but also a couple of rising flaps within, which must spring up before the whole sheet is revealed. So in trick set pieces a series of separate flaps may all be spring-hinged together to lie compactly flat when folded, but upon release all fly out to present not only a totally different painted subject but one which considerably exceeds the original piece in size, so augmenting the wonder of the trick. The complication of a large *châssis à développement*, as the French so well call this type of set piece, is illustrated in a cut in Moynet's *L'Envers du Théâtre* (1873).

Possibly an early reference to such a trick-piece in England lies in an item to be found in the Covent Garden Inventory of 1743 (now in the British Museum), where, under the head *Painted Pieces in Great Room*, is listed a 'front of garden that changes to house'; or again in the inventory of scenery at the Crow Street Theatre, Dublin, 1776, where we find a 'Changeable flat in Mercury Harlequin'.

Associated with such tricks are the 'effects' of sounds—that of a body falling into water after a leap behind a sea row (accompanied maybe with the 'splash' of a flung-up shower of rice); that of the Glass Crash, where a quantity of broken glass and china is flung from one bucket into another; that of the Thunder Sheet, where a suspended iron sheet is vigorously shaken to produce the sound of the rolling of a storm; that of the Wind Machine, where a ribbed drum is revolved against a sheet of silk, or other material, producing a variable singing note admirably suggestive of howling wind; and there are many others, some detailed in A. Rose's *Stage Effects*, in A. E. Peterson's articles on 'Stage Effects and Noises Off' included in *Theatre and Stage* (1934), or Frank Napier's *Noises Off* (1936). Georgian thunder was, however, frequently produced by the far better method of a Thunder Run—two long inclined wooden troughs, down which iron balls were rolled.

Possibly one of the most effective visual tricks is the Transparency. Here part or all of the back-scene is painted, not upon canvas, but upon linen or calico, and executed, not in opaque size-paint, but in transparent dye. The appearance of the painting is normal when lit from the front, but as lights are brought up behind, the subject fades or becomes supplemented by further painting on the back of the linen, until the whole effect is changed, and a normal building, for instance, appears given over to the ravages of fire, or a quiet country landscape blossoms into the glow of a lurid sunset. Any features of the former scene required to remain in dark silhouette after the change are, of course, executed in opaque paint.

From these beginnings the resources of tricks develop to the most advanced and closely guarded secrets of first-class conjuring, passing on the way such fascinating phantoms as Pepper's Ghost, or those of Young and Poole—perfectly transparent actors, capable of moving to any part of the stage, and of being stabbed or walked-through with impunity. Such an effect is based on the principle of reflection, the image of an actor walking in the orchestra-well appearing upon a sheet of glass suspended at a critical angle in, or near, the proscenium opening, together with a judicious balancing of lights. Many applications of tricks to the theatre are to be found in two French books, wherein much English procedure is described, namely Georges Moynet's *Trucs et Décors* (1893), and A. de Vaulabelle and Ch. Hémardinquer's *La Science au Théâtre*. It is perhaps significant of the wide influence of English trick-work that one of the most frequently mentioned traps in these two books is the *trappe anglaise.*

But the final apotheosis of the trick, where the highest art of the theatre in this direction is reached, comes with the union of actor and effect—where the trick is the combination of brilliant timing and acrobatic skill in the player with the sureness and ingenuity of the experienced stage-carpenter.

The humblest example of this union, in bare simplicity, is the Roll-out, a mere flap of loose canvas left at the bottom of a piece of scenery, through which a player can suddenly roll from behind, and leap to his feet on the scene. After this comes the famous Vamp Trap, consisting of two spring-leaves, either in the stage or in the scenery, through which the body of an actor can pass like a spirit through a solid. The name is stated by J. R. Planché to be derived from the title of his melodrama *The Vampire; or, the Bride of the Isles,* produced at the Lyceum (then called the English Opera House) in 1820.

The Leap is the supreme test of the trick player. In essence, it is no more than an acrobat's jumping through a trap in the scenery; but by the skilful interplaying of a group of highly trained players, and the clever multiplication and placing of types of traps, it can produce a notable piece of theatre, and one able to occupy on its own merits a place in a programme. Such was the Dumb Ballet, of which acts like *Fun in a Bakehouse,* or *Ki Ko Kookeeree,* are examples. A diagrammatic plot of the latter remains, in the form of a coloured sketch of the scene, with hinged flaps, made to be forwarded each week to the stage manager of the next house to inform him of the practicalities of the show. In the sketch are seen at least eight varieties of trap, all to be used in dazzling succession as the flashing troupe went through their evolutions in the Victorian back-yard they took as their setting. Mr. A. E. Peterson, present owner of this drawing, states that the act visited, among other places, the Adelphi Theatre, Liverpool, about 1871.

Many names in English stage history are associated with such trickwork, from 'Don Jumpedo', who jumped 'down his own throat', through the immortal Grimaldi, and along the line of the Lupinos and that of the Conquests, till international and almost royal eminence was achieved by the staggering 'entortillationists', exhibiting 'zampillerostation' and countless other acts, who were known as the Hanlon-Lees.

These men brought trickwork, leaps, and tumbling to the height of an art, and to an eminence recognized throughout the world as peculiarly English. R. S.

TRIGG, WILLIAM (*fl.* first half of seventeenth century), a boy-actor in the King's Company, who played women's parts from about 1626 to 1632. He was probably one of Shank's apprentices, and by 1636 he had graduated to adult parts, and was a hired man. He may have joined Beeston's Boys at about this time, and is still found with them in 1639. There is a possibility that during the Civil War he started as a royalist but turned parliamentarian; this, however, is not certain. The date of his death is unknown, but he was still alive in 1652. He does not appear to have returned to his old profession after the Restoration.

TRISSINO, GIAN GIORGIO (1478–1550), Italian dramatist whose *Sofonisba* shows the first direct contact with Greek drama during the Renaissance. This tragedy, whose material is taken from Livy and remodelled on the familiar lines of Greek tragedy, was published in 1515 and many times reprinted before its first production at Vicenza in 1524. Somewhat lifeless and uninteresting in itself, it is important in its implications, since it marked out the way of rigid adherence to Greek models for future writers of Italian tragedy.

TRISTAN L'HERMITE, FRANÇOIS (1601–55), French dramatist, considered by his contemporaries a formidable rival to Corneille. He had a stormy youth, as having killed a man in a duel he was forced to fly to England. He then started out for Spain, but in passing through Poitiers he met and was befriended by Scévole de Sainte-Marthe, generous and learned patron of literature, who found him work and secured the king's pardon for him. Tristan was thus enabled to return to Paris, and in 1636 his first play, *Mariamne,* was given at the Théâtre du Marais with almost unprecedented success, largely due to the acting of Montdory as Herod, with Mlle de Villiers as his leading lady. The play, taken from various sources, including one by Hardy, held the boards for nearly 100 years. Corneille is said to have praised its last act. Encouraged by this initial success, Tristan continued to write plays, but none of them equalled his first, and all are forgotten. Two were in the repertory of Molière's short-lived Illustre-Théâtre. Tristan was a great gambler and often in debt, but he was generous and kind-hearted, and a good friend. The dramatist Quinault was in his youth befriended by Tristan, who left him a large sum of money in his will.

TRITAGONIST, see PROTAGONIST.

TRUCKS, low platforms on castors, to take previously-arranged scenery on and off the stage. Also called Boat Trucks (see STAGE, 5).

TUCCIO, STEFANO (1540–97), see JESUIT DRAMA.

TUKE, SIR SAMUEL (?–1674), a gentleman at the Court of Charles II, who, on the suggestion of the king, wrote *The Adventures of Five Hours,* a tragi-comedy adapted from Calderón, which was given at Lincoln's Inn Fields on 8 Jan. 1663. It was seen by Pepys, who praised it rather extravagantly, and also spoke of his liking for the author, in spite of his evident conceit. This was Tuke's only venture into playwriting, the rest of his time being spent in attendance on, and secret missions for, Charles II, who held him in high favour because of his support of the royalist party during the Civil War, when he fought at Marston Moor, and in Paris during the Commonwealth.

TUMBLER (a loose roller inside a rolled-up cloth), see DROP.

TURGENIEV, IVAN SERGEIVICH (1818–83), Russian novelist and dramatist, whose best-known play is *A Month in the Country*. He belonged to a wealthy landowning family, but had an unhappy childhood. After private lessons from French and German tutors he entered Moscow University, where he soon turned to literature, translating Shakespeare, and writing poems and articles. He was sent to Berlin University to finish his education, and in 1843 published his first play, a romantic swashbuckling drama set in Spain. In the same year he met Belinsky, the great Russian critic, who had an important influence on his development. His second play, a satirical comedy in the style of Gogol's *Inspector-General*, was published in 1846. Entitled *Penniless; or, Scenes from the Life of a Young Nobleman*, its leading character is a gentleman adventurer who sums up the theme of the play in its last words: 'You have passed, golden times, you have gone, noble breed.' Two years later he wrote a one-act comedy in the style of Alfred de Musset's *Comédies et Proverbes, Where It's Thin, It Breaks*, and in 1847 a play intended for the benefit night of the actor Shchepkin. This, however, was banned by the censor, and did not appear in print until 1857. It finally reached the stage in 1861. Meanwhile Turgeniev had written another play for Shchepkin, a delicate and touching comedy entitled *The Bachelor*. Written with one eye on the censor, this inoffensive trifle shows an elderly man and his young ward deceived and disappointed by the girl's fiancé, the bachelor's protégé, who turns out to be a hypocrite and a coward. The role of the old man gave Shchepkin, and later Martynov and Karatygin, an excellent opportunity to show their talents. It was produced and published in 1849, and was followed by *The Boarder*, a further study of unhappy old age, and by a lively comedy dealing with a partition of land between brother and sister (according to the old Russian custom) and the quarrels that ensue.

In 1850 Turgeniev wrote his masterpiece for the theatre, *A Month in the Country*, originally entitled *The Student*. It was prematurely announced for publication, but the censors held it up for five years, and it was not staged until 1872. It is important as the first psychological drama in the Russian theatre. It did not fit into the acknowledged genres of 'comedy of manners' or 'comedy of characters', and was considered, even by its author, a 'novel in dramatic form'. In it Turgeniev proves himself to be the forerunner of Chekhov, in that he shifted the dramatic action from external to internal conflict. A similar shifting of interest was taking place in all European literature, and Turgeniev might have pursued the matter even farther had not his battles with the censorship, and his subsequent imprisonment and exile, caused him to give up writing plays and to concentrate on short stories. His last play was a light comedy of no great significance. He certainly had no opinion of himself as a dramatist, and intended his plays mainly for reading. But his insight and inner realism could not fail to make them effective in performance when they were staged and interpreted as they should be—a feat which has only become possible in recent years. *A Month in the Country* has become popular in the repertory of the European theatre, particularly in Great Britain.

TURLUPIN [HENRI LEGRAND] (c. 1587–1637), a player of farcical comedy at the Hôtel de Bourgogne, where he was partnered by Gaultier-Garguille and Gros-Guillaume. Tradition has it that they were all three originally bakers, and evolved their comic turns when throwing flour at each other. They probably all three played at the Paris fairs before joining a professional company, which Turlupin did after his companions, in 1615. He excelled in broad comedy, playing roguish valets, and with the rest of the company figures as himself in *La Comédie des comédiens* (1633), by Gougenot. As Belleville he also played serious parts, but it is as a farce-player that he is best remembered. His wife, Marie Durand, was anxious to go on the stage. This he would not permit, but after his death, being left with five small children, she married another actor, d'Orgemont, who succeeded Montdory at the Théâtre du Marais.

TURNER, ANTHONY (?), English actor, who is first found at the Cockpit in 1622. He remained there with the Queen's Men for the next fifteen years, but was evidently not one of the leading men. The parts in which he is known to have appeared include that of an old man. In 1637 he was one of those who remained in Beeston's new company at the Cockpit, and he seems then to have become slightly more important. He was arrested in 1659 for playing illegally at the Red Bull, and was evidently one of the more active theatrical law-breakers under the Commonwealth, in company with Edward Shatterell.

TURPILIUS, see ROME and FABULA (3) *Palliata*.

TURPIO, AMBIVIUS, a Roman actor-producer of the second century B.C. (see ROME, 1 and CAECILIUS STATIUS).

TWAITS, WILLIAM (?–1814), a low comedian who was appearing with some success under the elder Macready in Birmingham and Sheffield when Wood engaged him for the Philadelphia theatre. He played there opposite Jefferson, and in 1805 made his first appearance in New York at a benefit night for Dunlap, who describes him as short, with stiff carroty hair, a mobile and expressive face, and a powerful asthmatic voice which he used with great comic effect. He was at his best in farce and broad comedy, and in accordance with the tradition of the day he appeared as Polonius. He was also seen as Richard III, and, somewhat incongruously, as Mercutio. More suited to his peculiar talents were the parts of the First Grave-digger, Dogberry, Launcelot Gobbo, and Goldfinch in *The Road to Ruin*, all of which he played under Cooper's management at the Park Theatre, New York. In 1813 Twaits was one of the recalcitrant players who formed the Theatrical Commonwealth, which played in the old circus on Broadway. He withdrew on the death at the end of the year of Mrs. Twaits, one of the lovely Westray sisters, previously known on the stage as Mrs. Villiers, and shortly before his own death appeared at the newly opened Anthony Street Theatre.

TWELVEPENNY PLACES, see AUDITORIUM, 1 c.

TWOPENNY GAFF, see GAFF.

TYLER, ROYALL (1757–1826), author of the first American comedy, *The Contrast*. Born in Boston, he graduated from Harvard, served in the army, and was then admitted to the Bar. While in New York he made the acquaintance of Thomas Wignell, at that time the leading comedian of the American Company, and it was probably due to his interest and influence that *The Contrast* was produced at the John Street Theatre on 16 Apr. 1787. In return for his help Tyler gave Wignell the copyright of the play, which was published in 1790 with George Washington heading the list of subscribers. The play, which is a light comedy in the style of *The School for Scandal*, was a success and was several times revived, though when given in Tyler's birthplace it had, like *Othello*, to be disguised as a Moral Lecture in Five Parts.[1] Tyler wrote several other plays, some of which are lost, but never again achieved the excellence of his first.

[1] In 1917 it was given at Philadelphia under the supervision of Otis Skinner.

U

UDALL, NICHOLAS (1505–56), English scholar, headmaster in turn of Eton and Westminster, and the author of *Ralph Roister Doister*, the earliest-known English comedy. Written while he was at Eton for performance by the boys in place of the usual Latin comedy, it was probably performed there between 1534 and 1541, though efforts have been made to connect it with Udall's headmastership at Westminster and date it 1552. In any case, it was not printed until about 1566–7. This comedy, the first play in English to deserve that name, is much influenced by Terence and Plautus, and turns on the efforts of a vainglorious fool to win the heart and hand of a wealthy London widow, egged on by the parasite Merygreeke, and finally thwarted by Gawin Goodluck, the lucky suitor. Although Udall is known to have written several other plays, as well as Dialogues and Pageants for Court festivities, where he was connected with the Revels Office under Mary, they are now lost, or survive only in fragmentary form. Udall is sometimes credited with the authorship of *Thersites*, an interlude acted at Court in 1537 which A. W. Pollard considers to be the work of John Heywood.

UKRAINE, see RUSSIA, 2 e.

ULSTER GROUP THEATRE, see IRELAND, 3.

UNAMUNO, MIGUEL DE (1864–1937), a Spanish philosopher, and author of a number of literary and poetic plays in which the characters are essentially static entities. These have never been acted, and were not intended for the stage; Unamuno has nevertheless had an important influence on Spanish drama, mainly through his philosophical writings, particularly *Del sentimiento trágico de la vida en los hombres y en los pueblos* (1913), published in English in 1921 as *The Tragic Sense of Life*.

UNDERHILL, CAVE (*c.* 1634–*c.* 1710), an actor of the Restoration period well equipped by nature for the playing of boobies and lumpish louts, such as Clodpate in *Epsom Wells*, Lolpoop in *The Squire of Alsatia*, Drydrubb in *The Maid's Last Prayer*, and Sir Sampson in *Love for Love*. He was also much admired as the Grave-digger in *Hamlet*, and it was in this part that he made his last appearance shortly before he died, at a benefit performance given at the instigation of *The Tatler*. Colley Cibber, in his *Apology*, has left an excellent portrait of Underhill, who was esteemed one of the best actors of his day.

UNDERWOOD, JOHN (*c.* 1590–1624), a boy-actor at the Blackfriars, where he appeared in *Cynthia's Revels* and *The Poetaster*. As an adult actor he joined the King's Men, and from 1608 to his death played with them regularly, though his only known role is that of Delio in *The Duchess of Malfi*. It has been conjectured that he played juvenile leads, princes, gallants, and libertines. He owned shares in the Blackfriars, Globe, and Curtain Theatres.

UNION SQUARE THEATRE, NEW YORK, on the south side of Union Square. This opened as a variety hall on 11 Sept. 1871. Among the initial attractions were the Vokes family—Jessie, Victoria, Rosina, Fred, and Fawdon—in their pantomime-spectacle *The Belles of the Kitchen*. On 1 June 1872 A. M. Palmer took over, and for ten years made the theatre one of the finest in New York. Many of the best actors in the United States appeared there, and its stock company was remarkable. Among its outstanding productions were *Agnes*, which ran for 100 nights, Mark Smith in *One Hundred Years Old*, Charlotte Thompson in *Jane Eyre*, and Clara Morris in *Camille*. *The Two Orphans*, produced in Dec. 1874, made a fortune for Palmer and a star of Kate Claxton. Maude Granger and W. H. Gillette both made their first appearances in New York under Palmer, while Stoddart, who played at the Union Square Theatre in 1875–6, remained with the stock company until it was disbanded in 1885, and then went to Madison Square with Palmer. The last play done under Palmer's management was *A Parisian Romance* (1883), which saw the début of Richard Mansfield in a small part that made him famous overnight. The theatre then opened under new management, but the stock company, though somewhat depleted by death and withdrawals, continued to function, being almost the last to resist the combination houses. After it was disbanded the theatre was used by travelling stars until in Feb. 1888 it was burnt down. It was rebuilt but never regained its former brilliance, and was mostly devoted to continuous vaudeville under various names. It later became a burlesque house and then a cinema, and in 1936 it was demolished.

UNION THEATRE, NEW YORK, see CHATHAM THEATRE (2).

UNITED STATES OF AMERICA. I. GENERAL SURVEY. The history of the theatre in the United States of America is complex—complex because of the vast geographical extent of the country and because of its gradual settlement and growth during the eighteenth and nineteenth centuries. To appreciate the way in which the stage has developed there it is best to think of it as divided into a number of clearly marked, yet interrelated, sections. First comes the colonial period, ending about the year 1775; from the establishment of the new nation on to about 1820 is a period when theatre-lovers, proud of their independence, endeavour to set up a national playhouse; rapid progress is evident in the period 1820–70, and still more during the thirty years (1870–1900) to the close of the century, when the American stage draws well abreast of the European in technical skill, if not in dramatic artistry; thereafter comes an age of interesting experiment (1900–30), with the modern years seeing the fruits of many earlier efforts.

1. THE COLONIAL THEATRE: FROM THE BEGINNINGS TO 1776. Long before any English plays were presented in the New World, what is now Latin America and the west coast of the United States had witnessed performances, directly or indirectly sponsored by the Catholic Church, which carried back in spirit to medieval times. From the year 1538, for example, comes a record of the production in Mexico, on the traditional Corpus Christi Day (the Thursday after Trinity Sunday), of a series of religious plays—*La Anunciación de la Natividad de San Juan Bautista hecha a su padre Zacarias, La Anunciación de Nuestra Señora, La Visitación de Nuestra Señora a Santa Isabel*, and *La Natividad de San Juan*. The following year yields a *Conquista de Rodas*, succeeded by a *Conquista de Jerusalén*. As early as 1598 there was a performance in New Mexico of 'an original play on a subject connected with the conquest of New Mexico', while professional Spanish actors were presenting dramas in the New World colonies by the beginning of the seventeenth century. From far off to the northward, too, comes a record of early dramatic activity: in 1606 a masque in French was performed, in honour of the Sieur de Poutrincourt, at Port Royal in Acadia.

While the ancient religious plays were still to be found in the eighteen-thirties and while the early productions (whether religious or secular) unquestionably succeeded in leaving some sporadic traces behind them, it is not from this source that the theatre known as 'American' fundamentally springs. From England, not Spain or France—from Shakespeare, not from Lope de Vega—stems the American playhouse.

This American playhouse, however, starts late. The initial attempts to establish an English-speaking community in the New World were made in the first decade of the seventeenth century—just in time to find an imaginative echo in Shakespeare's *Tempest*: but it was long before the uneasy conditions of life in the struggling colonies permitted of such luxuries as attendance at plays. A few sparse records from this century hint that the drama was not entirely unknown and that, in the more leisured and latitudinarian South at least, men were dreaming of reproducing in their new homes the theatrical delights they had left behind them in London: even in the very home of austere Puritanism, Increase Mather had, to his vivid alarm, heard in 1687 'much discourse of beginning Stage-Plays in New England'. At the same time, although it is certain that some men were thinking of these things, it is equally certain that, whatever occasional and surreptitious endeavours may have been made in this

way, nothing was attempted beyond one or two amateur—and no doubt woefully crude—productions.

The distinction of being the first professional actor to exhibit his talents to the colonists must, it seems, go to the eccentric and not over-respectable Tony Aston (*fl.* first half of eighteenth century), who apparently found his way in 1703 to 'Charles-Town', South Carolina, and, a few months later, to New York. Since he had no company with him, we are bound to assume that any performances he gave were in the nature of monologues and readings only. He was, however, the swallow heralding a coming summer, and it is significant that between 1699 and 1702 a certain Richard Hunter, otherwise unknown, asked for a licence to act plays in New York (which then had a populaton of scarcely 4,000). Another decade had barely passed when Williamsburg, Virginia, had a playhouse built in its midst; here a certain Charles Stagg, with his wife Mary, presented a few dramas. Thereafter accounts of stage performances begin to come from many localities. In the thirties Charleston, South Carolina, had its Dock Street Theatre, and audiences there were able, from time to time, to see such Restoration tragedies as *The Orphan* and such almost contemporary comedies as *The Recruiting Officer*—although, without a doubt, in the most primitive of surroundings. If we may judge of these early playhouses by their successors on the frontier, they consisted simply of a plain wooden hut, with a platform at one end concealed by a frayed front curtain; scenery was nothing more than some paper wings, while dingy illumination came from a meagre array of smoking candles.

By the middle of the century, circumstances of life along the eastern coast had become such as to warrant the appearance of professional companies more stable, and presumably much more competent, than those which tentatively preceded them. In 1750 what had been but villages were becoming towns; road travel was less hazardous; the industry of the original settlers had produced a small but active leisured society. The time was ripe for the formal introduction of the theatre to America.

All through the period immediately following this date we hear of increasing dramatic effort, associated rather with Philadelphia and the South than with New York. It was in Philadelphia that a company led by Thomas Kean and Walter Murray constructed a playhouse in 1749 out of a warehouse; after presenting an interesting repertory (including *Richard III*) they formed the 'Virginia Company of Comedians', playing at Williamsburg, Annapolis, and elsewhere in that vicinity. A few years later, in 1752, Williamsburg welcomed another company, newly arrived from England, headed by the elder Lewis Hallam (1714–56) and consisting of twelve persons in all—the first theatrical group especially dispatched from London to America and now recognized as responsible for establishing the professional theatre, in a form not too far removed from contemporary English standards, in the colonies. During the fifties, this company, later headed by David Douglass (? –1786), contributed much to the youthful American theatre. They introduced many hitherto unrepresented plays (*King Lear*, for example, *Romeo and Juliet*, *Hamlet*, and *The Merchant of Venice*); they were active, too, in the building of new theatres, among which were the Southwark, or South Street, in Philadelphia (1766) and the John Street in New York (1767). The latter, a wooden house, had two rows of boxes, a pit, and a gallery; proscenium doors with boxes above them flanked the stage. In 1785 this theatre was repainted 'at a vast expense, beautified and illuminated in a style to vie with European splendour'. (Preceding this house were New York's first Nassau Street Theatre (1750), Hallam's Nassau Street Theatre (1753), Cruger's Wharf Theatre (1758), and the Chapel (or Beekman) Street Theatre (1761)—all short-lived and of minor importance.)

By the time when the years of the Revolutionary War drew men's thoughts to things other than the theatre the playhouse had established a hold, as yet perhaps infirm but nevertheless tenacious, on the imagination of the States. Nothing can demonstrate this better than the facts that in 1777 the John Street Theatre, renamed the Theatre Royal, was used by British soldiers anxious to display their acting talents and that the following year (1778) Addison's *Cato* was performed, in the other camp, at Valley Forge before a 'splendid audience' which included George Washington himself.

2. THE BEGINNINGS OF THE AMERICAN THEATRE: 1776–1820. Just at first, after winning success in the war, some of the infant States tried to prohibit the playhouse, but soon professional acting was proceeding on a still more extended scale. Lewis Hallam junior (1740–1808) returned from Jamaica (whither he had gone during the disturbances) in 1784, and the following year, by entering into partnership with John Henry (1738–94), broadened the scope of what was already known as the American Company. This group, with the comedian Thomas Wignell (1753–1802) and the second Mrs. Owen Morris (1753–1826), won considerable fame, was honoured by Washington, and maintained for several years a virtual monopoly over New York, Philadelphia, Baltimore, and Annapolis. It had the distinction of producing in 1787 Royall Tyler's *The Contrast*, the first native comedy written for professionals, and of attracting some English actors (of minor eminence at least) to American shores.

By the close of the century rivals began to appear, for the rapidly growing cities were now such as could provide audiences for more than one histrionic troupe. Under the inspiration of Wignell, who had seceded from the American Company in 1791, a new body of actors, which included Mrs. Oldmixon (?–1835/6), Thomas Jefferson (1732–1807), James Fennell (1766–

1816), Mrs. Merry (1769–1808), and later young Thomas Cooper (1776–1849), started performances in 1794 in Philadelphia, at a new house, the Chestnut Street Theatre. Built on the model of the Theatre Royal at Bath, this playhouse, capable of seating 2,000 persons, with its Corinthian columns outside and with its well-equipped stage, marked a definite milestone in the progress of the American theatre. We are now in the transition period between two ages. More attention is being paid to scenic effects and the standard of acting is rising; comfort is creeping in for the audience, and the better-class patrons can enjoy reserved seats in the boxes: yet manners remain rough, notices respectfully requesting the spectators 'not to spit in the stove', managers finding it difficult to prevent those in the gallery from throwing 'apples, nuts, bottles, and glasses on the stage and into the orchestra'. On the one hand we hear of the engagement of competent scene-painters; on the other, of 'dirty pieces of canvas' serving to represent a landscape, and of backcloths showing a street 'while the side-scenes represent a wood'. Success attended the Wignell company: soon it spread its activities southward beyond Philadelphia and was responsible for the erection of other theatres at Baltimore (1794) and Washington (1800).

Meanwhile, signs were evident that rising New York was about to challenge the supremacy of Philadelphia. Four years after the opening of the Chestnut Street Theatre, the Park Theatre in New York was opened (1798), and this was immediately hailed as marking another distinct advance in theatre architecture. A stone building, it had three tiers of boxes, a gallery and a pit; the seating capacity was about 2,000. Here William Dunlap (1766–1839), whose first drama, *The Father; or, American Shandyism*, had been produced at the John Street Theatre in 1789 and who, in 1796, became associated with the American Company, pursued a chequered career until 1805, distraught by quarrels and jealousies among his actors but winning fame by his own plays and some success by his exploitation of the mediocre, but then highly esteemed, dramatic talents of the German playwright Kotzebue.

In 1805 Dunlap's efforts to keep the Park Theatre going ended in failure: the house was sold to John Jacob Astor and John K. Beekman, who put in charge of it the well-established actor Thomas Cooper. A sum of $15,000 was laid out in the embellishment of the interior; new actors were engaged, notably the eccentric comedian William Twaits (? –1814); 'stars' were called in for short seasons (thus denting, if not shattering, the structure of the old stock companies); and once more a landmark in theatre history was reached when John Howard Payne (1791–1852), who had appeared at the Park as Young Norval in 1809, reversed the theatrical flow by travelling to England (1813) and acting at Drury Lane. The American theatre was truly beginning to come of age.

If Payne went to England (and there later

thrilled all good sentimental hearts by his composition of 'Home, Sweet Home'), excited American audiences hailed the arrival of George Frederick Cooke (1756–1812), the most brilliant tragedian that the States had so far seen, but one whom intemperance rendered hopelessly unreliable. In 1810 he played at the Park and thereafter, until his death two years later, toured to various cities, leaving behind him many memories of his Richard III and other roles. Not long after (1820) appeared the equally brilliant and equally unreliable Edmund Kean (1787–1833).

The old Park Theatre was burned to the ground in 1820, and a new Park, with improved lighting facilities and other advances on its predecessor, opened the following season. Already this house had set New York as the leader of the American cities in dramatic affairs. The fact that in 1809 it was taken over by the first theatre 'manager', Stephen Price (1783–1840), indicates the position it had gained. Commercially active, this Price, according to the English manager Alfred Bunn, 'lured away to the shores of America every performer of any distinction (and what is of equal importance—utility) whom gold could tempt, or speculation seduce'. The new Park seated 2,500 persons, and boasted of 'patent' oil lamps hung in three chandeliers each containing thirty-five lights—a wonder to the age. For long, Philadelphia struggled to maintain its rivalry, but the traditions of 'Broadway'—if not as yet on Broadway itself—were surely being formed.

At the same time, as we leave this period of growth and concentration of power, it is important to note that, while the influence of the South began to decline, the force of events was carrying the stage into the Puritanic North. There, at the first, plays had to be disguised as 'moral lectures' and theatres as 'exhibition rooms', but a spade is still a spade by whatever name it may be called, and Boston's 'New Exhibition Room' (1792) was nothing but a playhouse. Under the irrepressible enthusiasm of Joseph Harper the society of Boston, Providence, and Newport were initiated into the pleasant mysteries of the stage. How rapidly circumstances were changing is shown by the erection, despite the still strong Puritan bias, of the Federal Street Theatre in Boston (1794), followed two years later by the Haymarket. The former was constructed of brick, with a stage opening of 31 feet; some improvements were introduced in 1798 when it had to be rebuilt after a disastrous fire. Elsewhere, to the West, Albany, which had welcomed a visit by Hallam's company in 1769, got its first permanent theatre—the brick-built, 'neat and commodious' Green Street Theatre—in 1812.

3. THE STARS OF NEW YORK: 1820–70. For a short time the new Park Theatre of New York dominated theatrical life in America. Here Junius Brutus Booth (1796–1852), Kean's rival, made his new York début in 1821, after a few initial performances at Richmond, Virginia; here in 1822 appeared the elder Mathews

(1776–1835), whose particular style in comedy was so highly acclaimed on both sides of the Atlantic.

Soon, however, conditions altered. New York had crushed the rivalry of Philadelphia, but the city had grown sufficiently large to produce rivalry within its own boundaries. In 1824 the Chatham Garden Theatre was opened with a distinguished company that included Joseph Jefferson (1774–1832), as well as the founder of a great theatrical dynasty, Henry Wallack (1790–1870). Graciously planned, it retained the useful old forestage which was so rapidly disappearing in England, together with the proscenium doors (also vanishing relics of the past) set in a framework that is almost reminiscent of the Elizabethan stage. Two years later the Lafayette Theatre was introduced to the public: recognized as one of 'the most splendid theatres in the Union', it was particularly well equipped for those equestrian and aquatic shows which made such an appeal to contemporaries. Although it vanished in a fire a few years later, already in 1826 still another playhouse, the Bowery, had appeared on the scene. This theatre, with a name destined to evoke many fond memories, was a classic structure holding nearly 3,500 persons, with a huge stage lit by the new medium of gas. (Gas lighting had been introduced at the Chestnut Street Theatre in Philadelphia ten years before, and at the Camp Street Theatre in New Orleans two years before, its use for theatrical purposes in New York.) Fire took its toll of this house also (1828), but ninety days after its destruction a new Bowery, with a stage 84 feet deep and considerable improvements in the auditorium, took its place. When this likewise was destroyed in a conflagration in 1836, a third Bowery appeared (1837). This lasted for only a year (fire, again) and a fourth Bowery was built in 1839. In 1845, after still another fire, a fifth Bowery was opened; this pursued a fairly successful, but chequered, career into the present century.

From the thirties onward theatrical development was swift. In 1835 came the Franklin Theatre, a small house holding only six hundred spectators. Two years previously New York acquired its first Italian Opera House. (Another, Palmo's, was opened in 1844, and a third, the Astor Place Opera House, in 1847; the theatre of the Academy of Music, with an audience capacity of 4,600, was constructed in 1854, enduring till the Metropolitan appeared in 1883. It was pulled down in 1926.) In 1836 the Opera House ceased to fulfil its original purpose and the following year came under the management of James William Wallack (1791–1864) as the National Theatre: here a formidable company, including many distinguished players, won considerable fame until its destruction by fire three years later. Although this house thus suffered from the prevailing menace, its place was taken by the New Chatham Theatre (otherwise called the New National). At the same time appeared the

Olympic Theatre, where, between 1839 and 1850, the comedian William Mitchell (1798–1856) entertained audiences with burlesques, farces, and adaptations of Dickens's novels. In 1850 John Brougham (1810–80), already well known on the English stage, built the Lyceum on Broadway. A few years before this, Palmo's Opera House was transformed into Burton's Theatre (1848): here, and in other houses with which he was associated, William Evans Burton (1804–60) presented productions more ambitious than any so far seen in America. Brougham's Lyceum became, in 1852, Wallack's Lyceum, and what Burton had achieved found a fitting rival. The company assembled here was probably more brilliant than any in the past and it established a tradition which was carried on to a New Lyceum (1861) and which endured until 1882 under the famous actor Lester Wallack (1820–88). It was with this theatre that Dion Boucicault (1822–90), a stormy petrel in theatres on both sides of the Atlantic, was closely associated. Still another highly popular playhouse was that of Laura Keene (1826–73), opened in 1856, also situated on Broadway—a theatre distinguished by many triumphs, not least of which was the production of *Our American Cousin*, with Edward Askew Sothern (1826–1881) and Joseph Jefferson III (1829–1905) (best remembered for his Rip Van Winkle of 1859) in the cast. Just at the end of the period came Booth's Theatre on Sixth Avenue (1869). Erected at a great cost, with a capacity of 1,800, this house possessed special facilities for scenic effects; the wide stage could be made to sink and hydraulic rams were introduced for the handling of the sets. It was the home of Edwin Booth (1833–93), an outstanding actor, son of Junius Brutus Booth (1796–1852), and brother of that John Wilkes Booth (1839–65) who assassinated Abraham Lincoln in 1865 during a performance of *Our American Cousin* at Ford's Theatre in Washington. The same year that Booth's was opened, a new era was being ushered in by the opening of the Fifth Avenue Theatre (originally built in 1867), soon to be under the management of Augustin Daly (1838–99): in this playhouse standards of production were set which surpassed even the notable and worthy efforts of its predecessors.

As the very names given to the theatres indicate, these fifty years from 1820 to 1870 were a period of star actors and managers. They formed a period, too, when the stages of the United States and of England, despite many attempts to establish a native American tradition, became as one. In early years it had been mainly the minor London players who hazarded the long and then exhausting journey across the Atlantic, but now, following the visits of Cooke and Kean, almost all the actors prominent on London's boards arranged American tours. W. C. Macready (1793–1873) arrived in 1826, Charles Kean (1811–68) in 1830, Charles Kemble (1775–1854) in 1832.

While this is true, there is evident another paradoxical truth. The New York stage during this time was not simply an echo of London's: in tragedy and in comedy alike an individual style was being born among American players. James Henry Hackett (1800–71) was the perfect Yankee. Edwin Forrest (1806–72) rose slowly to become the most representative American actor of his age, one who introduced a peculiar style of his own and who was instrumental in encouraging much native dramatic talent. In 1835 the great Charlotte Cushman (1816–76) came before the public, while Mrs. John Drew (Louisa Lane) (1820–97), whose long stage career extended from her appearance as a crying baby at twelve months old on to the very last years of the nineteenth century, provided in herself almost a history of the American playhouse.

4. THE OPENING OF THE FRONTIER: 1820–70. While New York, notwithstanding its close association with London, was thus beginning to strike an individual note, other parts of the United States, from proud and genteel Boston to the farthest of rough frontiers, was awakening theatrically. The famous 'Boston Museum' was opened in 1843 and was destined to prove of some considerable significance in the future; in 1854 a new Federal Street Theatre, with an auditorium seating 3,000 persons and with an excellent stage, showed that the capital of Massachusetts was in process of forgetting the austerity of the Pilgrim Fathers.

Meanwhile, a great stirring was to be felt everywhere in the South and West of the Alleghenies. Already in 1791 a group of French actors had appeared in New Orleans and soon the city boasted a St. Pierre Theatre (1807), a St. Philippe (1808), and an Orleans (1809). A few years later, in 1817–18, Noah Miller Ludlow (1795–1886), later to win much repute in the circuits, brought his American Theatrical Commonwealth Company to this largely French-speaking town, and his initial success there led to the building of the American Theatre by James H. Caldwell (1793–1863) in 1822. This man, Caldwell, rapidly assumed almost complete power in the district. Anxious to introduce the latest improvements to his southern audiences, he was one of the first in America to install gas lighting in a theatre, while in the St. Charles Theatre (1835), erected at a cost of $350,000, he gave New Orleans what was then the most magnificent playhouse in the States.

During these years his predecessor, Ludlow, had been active elsewhere. To St. Louis he carried a company in 1820; four years later he constructed a small brick theatre at Mobile. For some time he was associated with Joshua Collins and William Jones (who built (1820) an important Columbia Street Theatre at Cincinnati), but later joined his fortunes with the picturesque Sol Smith (1801–69), a stage-struck farmer's son who, with many vicissitudes, played a significant part in opening up the theatre of the West. Their united efforts were responsible for the erection (1837) of a new theatre in St. Louis, a large three-tiered building with a capacity of 1,500. Here they maintained a local monopoly until in 1851 John Bates opened another theatre, which in turn was followed by the Varieties (1852), the People's (1852), and the Olympic (1866).

All over the speedily growing States the record was similar. A theatre had been established at Washington already in 1800 but this must have been but a humble affair. By 1835 the 'Nation's Capital' possessed, in the National Theatre, an adequate playhouse, with a stage 68 feet by 71; in 1862 this was followed by Ford's, where Lincoln met his end. The first performances at Indianapolis, in the West, were given in 1823; thirty years later, in 1858, that city had, in the Metropolitan, a theatre seating 1,500 persons, while a couple of decades after that date it claimed that its Opera House (1875) was 'the best arranged theatre in the United States'. During the early years of the century Chicago was nothing but a village; even towards the end of the thirties it had no stage save an improvised affair set up in an hotel dining-room. By 1847, however, the time had arrived for the construction of a permanent theatre, and from then on progress was rapid. A fine playhouse was built in the rising city in 1857 (McVicker's Theatre), and others followed both before and after the disastrous fire of 1871. Crosby's Opera House (1865) cost $600,000, and in 1889 the Auditorium was reputed to be the largest theatrical building in America.

In the Far West, San Francisco experienced similar theatrical development during the fifties: the Mormon State of Utah rejoiced, by 1862, in the possession of its handsome Salt Lake Theatre; while up and down the wide Mississippi the showboats—calliopes screaming, bands blaring, flags flying—splashed their colourful way. It has been calculated that, whereas in 1800 there were no more than 150 professional actors in the United States performing in a bare handful of theatres, by 1885 over 3,500 towns, with a total of more than 5,000 theatres, were witnessing dramatic productions, and much of this growth took place during the period (1820–70) in question.

5. THE BEGINNINGS OF THE AMERICAN DRAMA: 1820–70. During all this time English plays, classic and contemporary, formed the main bill of fare, both in New York's star theatres and in the rude theatres of the frontier. Signs, however, were not lacking, both in New York and in the newly explored theatrical territory, that a native drama was in the making. Far back in 1767 Thomas Godfrey's (1736–63) *Prince of Parthia* had started the ball rolling, while *The Contrast* of Royall Tyler (1757–1826) in 1787 had made comic use of local types. Slightly later came the plays of William Dunlap, the first American professional dramatist. In 1808 the Chestnut Street Theatre in Philadelphia saw the first acted drama by an American author on an Indian theme—*The Indian Princess*, by James Nelson Barker (1784–1858); this play, presented in 1820 at Drury Lane as *Pocahontas; or, the Indian Princess*,

appears also to have been the first American dramatic work produced, after performance in the New World, on a London stage. John Howard Payne carried native playwriting a stage farther, as did Robert Montgomery Bird (1806–54), and George Henry Boker (1823–90), whose *Francesca da Rimini* (1855), still remembered, is one of the best poetic plays written in English during the course of the century.

Nearly all of these, however, despite the utilization in many of American scenes and characters, were dominated by English models, and although some are worthy of note little was provided in them of an individual spirit. In less literary realms, on the other hand, new possibilities were being discovered. When T. D. Rice (1808–1860) in 1828 listened to an old Negro outside the theatre at Louisville, persuaded him to repeat the song he was singing, and later, in blackface, reproduced the song—'Jump Jim Crow'—in a native play, he was responsible for starting the vogue of the Minstrel Show. Within a little more than a decade (1842) the famous Christy Minstrels had been formed as a company and something entirely fresh had been given to the stage. The minstrel shows may have been a travesty of the Negro song and dance from which ultimately they took their being, but alongside of them others were beginning to forget the classic, romantic, melodramatic, sentimental, and diverse dramatic traditions and, forgetting, were listening to the actual forms of speech used by persons around them. In the earliest plays introducing Indian characters, the feathered braves communicated their noble thoughts in bombastic classic or romantic style: when Boucicault introduced into *The Octoroon* (1859) an Indian who merely grunted he carried contemporaries truly from an old world into a new.

6. THE TRIUMPH OF REALISM: 1870–1900. In 1869 the opening of Daly's Theatre was a landmark greater even than any in the past. Augustin Daly was a theatrical genius, a man who had at once the ability to engage the best talent of his time and the personality to exert a very definite influence upon those, no matter how talented, with whom he worked. Under his direction appeared a company of brilliant players, and, when one considers that to their contributions were added the results of his own meticulous and sensitive direction, it is not surprising to find that he moved on from success to success, opening a second Daly's Theatre in 1879, taking his actors to London in 1884, and completing the eastward trend by setting up a Daly's Theatre there in 1893. The care he took with his rehearsals is now proverbial: almost legendary are the stars of his cast—John Drew, Jr. (1853–1927), Adelaide Neilson (1848–80), Maurice Barrymore (1847–1905), and others. Nor was his inspiration confined entirely to the practical work of the stage: it was Daly who introduced to New York audiences *Saratoga* (1870), by Bronson Howard (1842–1908), a play which firmly placed this

forerunner of the modern American dramatists in the theatrical firmament.

Despite the excellence of his directorship, sharp rivalry was given to Daly's, between 1872 and 1883, by the Union Square Theatre under the management of Albert Marshman Palmer (*c.* 1840–1905), a man of vastly different calibre but one who had the skill (some said, the luck) to make use of the services of others more gifted than himself.

Theatre after theatre sprang up during this time. The 14th Street Theatre (which had been opened originally in 1866 as the Théâtre Français) appeared in 1870, came under the management of Laura Keene in 1871, and two years later, after extensive alterations, became the Lyceum, under Fechter. Increasing sums of money were put into these buildings. The Park of 1874 cost $100,000, Wallack's in 1882 cost $250,000, and so on to Oscar Hammerstein's Manhattan Theatre (1892), the foyer of which was said to be equalled only by the great opera-houses of Paris and Vienna. The New Park (1883), the Bijou Opera House (1880, renamed the Bijou Theatre in 1883), the Lyceum (1885), the Broadway (1888), the Garrick (1890), the Empire (1893), the American (1893), Hammerstein's Olympia (rechristened the Lyric, 1895)—these and others gave to New York a theatrical world fit to be compared with that of any other metropolis.

In some respects New York went beyond the other capitals, for among her new theatres was one, the Madison Square Theatre (1879), which was the marvel of its time, introducing stage equipment of the kind which later brought fame to the theatres of Germany. With justification a newspaper of the time declared that 'anyone in doubt that New York is rapidly becoming the theatre centre of the world must have been convinced of it at the opening of the new Madison Square Theatre'. The seats were more commodiously arranged than in any other house; air-conditioning provided freshness to the auditorium; the balconies, no longer in the old horseshoe form, were 'broken into three flowing bays, like Moorish archways laid horizontally', with lower boxes 'like moresque pavilions—octagonal in form, guarded by lattices of carved wood, embossed with old ivory and gold'. Revolutionary as was the auditorium, however, it was the stage that caused greatest wonder. The orchestra was set, not below the stage but above the proscenium arch, in a recess which could be concealed by curtains, while beyond the arch there was a 'double elevator stage' by means of which sets could be prepared above or below that which was being shown to the audience and raised or lowered, when necessary, into position. The inventor of all these wonders was Steele MacKaye (1842–94), dramatist, visionary, actor, and manager. From his fertile brain flowed idea after idea for the improvement of theatres. The double stage was one, but from him came also such devices, simple and grandiose, as the folding theatre chair, the 'curtain of light' to take the place of the ordinary drop-curtain, the cloud-machine,

the sliding stage, and the proscenium adjuster (altering the size of the stage opening). For the Lyceum (1885) he introduced electric light and gave to the auditorium a delicacy of form and colouring well in accord with the latest views of the aesthetes, while in the Spectatorium, designed for the Chicago World Fair of 1893, he planned a house for spectacles far beyond the dreams of any contemporary.

This was a time of great actors, American and other. Robert Mantell (1854–1928), William Gillette (1855–1937), Richard Mansfield (1857–1907), Mrs. Fiske (1865–1932), Julia Marlowe (1866–1950), Maude Adams (1872–), Ethel Barrymore (1879–) played during these years on the same stages as saw Henry Irving (1838–1905), Benoît Coquelin (1841–1909), Sarah Bernhardt (1845–1923), Ellen Terry (1847–1928), and Mrs. Patrick Campbell (1865–1940). It was a time, too, when new methods of directing came to supersede the old. Daly had set up fresh standards and the age found its most characteristic producer in the realist David Belasco (1859–1931). Those in charge of the theatre had become tired of the artificialities of the past and their dreams were set on achieving ever more and more of an approximation to the actual: the qualities essential to the cinema were being exploited in those years when the cinema had not as yet been born. For the achievement of this realism Steele MacKaye invented new devices; for it Belasco trained his actors; for it the new playwrights penned their dramas. As yet the American drama did not acknowledge the hard austerity of an Ibsen, but even though the plays of the time seem now to be unduly sentimental, and reminiscent of the melodramatic form against which they reacted, it is possible to see how the path was being made smooth for the future. Augustus Thomas (1859–1934), whose first great success was *Alabama* (1891)—a study of North and South after the Civil War—and who contributed many later dramas to the stage, introduced New York audiences to the 'play of ideas'. American history and contemporary social life were exploited in the interesting works of Clyde Fitch (1865–1909). Realistic observation of native types gives distinction to the writings of James A. Herne (1839–1901), whose *Margaret Fleming* (1890) is still remembered. Perhaps these men did not accomplish much, but, poor as most of their plays now seem to us, it is clearly evident that collectively they were evolving a style characteristically American.

To a large extent the promise of this age was vitiated at the very close of the century by the arising of a new force in the theatre—the theatrical trust. The stars and the acting managers had, it is true, dealt a serious blow to the old stock-company tradition, but the fact that these men were creatively concerned with practising the art of the stage gave their work a liveliness and vigour which cannot come from a playhouse dominated by commercial interests. The first Theatrical Syndicate, under Sam Nixon, Fred Zimmerman, Al Hayman, Charles Frohman, Marc Klaw, and Abraham

Erlanger, was formed in 1896, and gradually extended its control not only over New York but over the entire country. Belasco and others fought bitterly to preserve their independence, but it was obvious that the concentration of power in the hands of business men was destined to triumph. The days of the actor-manager, like the days of the stock company, were over.

7. THE GROWTH OF A NEW THEATRE: 1900–30. In 1900 there were no less than forty-three theatres in New York, and still the building of playhouses continued apace. Abbey's Theatre, which was opened by Henry Irving and Ellen Terry in 1893, became, after alterations, the Knickerbocker in 1896. Oscar Hammerstein (1847–1919) constructed the Republic in 1900: this became the Belasco two years later. The Savoy appeared as Schley's Music-Hall in 1900, while another variety house, the Gotham, came into being in 1901. The year following saw the erection of the handsome Majestic; Daniel Frohman's Lyceum was opened in 1903, and Hammerstein's gorgeous Manhattan Opera House, constructed at a cost of $2,000,000, in 1906. One after another they came—the Gaiety and the Stuyvesant (the present Belasco) (1907), the Maxine Elliott (1908), the New (1909), the Globe (1910), the Winter Garden (1912), the Cort (1912), the Booth (1913), the Longacre (1913), the Henry Miller (1918), the Music Box (1921), the Earl Carroll (1922), the Imperial (1923), the Guild (1924). And these are the names of only a few among the important buildings constructed during the first quarter of the century. By 1926 New York had sixty-eight playhouses in active use; two years later there were eighty.

Significant things were happening during these decades. The commercialism which had taken such a hold of the stage in the last years of the nineteenth century and the first years of the present century was now being fought with other weapons than Belasco had used. In New York the attempt of Winthrop Ames (1871–1937) to re-establish repertory at the New Theatre in 1909 failed, but other efforts in that direction were to prove more fortunate. In 1915 and 1916 two groups were formed, destined to wield considerable influence on the playwrights of the age: one of these was the Washington Square Players who, after preliminary performances at the Bandbox, moved to the Garrick and transformed themselves into the Theatre Guild; the second was the Provincetown Players, so closely identified with the introduction to the American public of the early plays of O'Neill—indeed, when this body was reconstituted in 1924, that dramatist shared with Robert Edmond Jones (1887–) and Kenneth Macgowan (1888–) the task of directing it. Less concerned with producing the work of living American authors but nevertheless of considerable importance in bringing the new drama to the attention of playgoers was another venture of 1915—the Neighborhood Playhouse, sponsored by Alice and Irene Lewisohn, while in

1926, came Eva Le Gallienne's (1899–) experiments at the Civic Repertory.

A new generation of actors was arising, a new generation of producers and scene-designers. Above all, there was arising a new generation of playwrights. The century opens with the work of a number of authors, among whom were William Vaughn Moody (1869–1910) (whose *The Great Divide* appeared in 1906) and Edward Sheldon (1886–1946) (creator of *Romance*, 1913), able craftsmen, inheritors of the late nineteenth-century tradition, adding to that tradition something characteristic of their own but in no wise striking out fresh dramatic paths. By the middle of the second decade the Provincetown Players were presenting some one-act plays by a young writer, Eugene O'Neill (1888–), whose entire approach to the theatre was revolutionary. Hailed at first only by a small group of enthusiasts, O'Neill startled large numbers of his contemporaries in the twenties by his daring in *Beyond the Horizon* and *The Emperor Jones* (both 1920), *The Hairy Ape* (1922), *All God's Chillun Got Wings* and *Desire Under the Elms* (both 1924), *The Great God Brown* (1926), *Marco Millions* and *Lazarus Laughed* (both 1927). His *Strange Interlude*, with its deliberate use of the 'aside' expanded into fundamental dialogue, came in 1928; the thirties saw the tense *Mourning Becomes Electra* (1931) and the nostalgic *Ah, Wilderness!* (1933); the forties *The Iceman Cometh* (1946) and *A Moon for the Misbegotten* (1947). In O'Neill the American theatre recognized a master, and he did more than any of his predecessors to bring the world to realization of the existence in the New World of a self-conscious independent stage. It is possible that now, looking back on his works in the perspective of time, we are forced to acknowledge that they do not possess to the fullest degree those excellences which once we thought were there. All too clearly we see now that O'Neill has missed the heights of genius by his lack of that infinite capacity for taking pains which is the hall-mark of the supreme artist; as clearly do we see that, during the period of his stormy apprenticeship, he did not train himself sufficiently as a master of words—so that in most of his plays scenes of crisis and emotional intensity cry out for a peerless expression which he is incapable of producing. Yet the fact remains that in O'Neill the American theatre came to own one of the world's most dominating dramatic figures, a man who, potentially if not in actual realization, may stand on the same exalted level as the most distinguished masters of past eras.

And with O'Neill arrived a whole school of other writers who, in contradistinction to the dramatist-craftsmen of preceding years, aimed at high artistry in their works. Sidney Howard (1891–1939) enlarged the scope of the realistic play in *They Knew What They Wanted* (1924), *The Silver Cord* (1926), and *Yellow Jack* (1934). In the last of these, indeed, he showed that his talent was capable of embracing much more than domestic issues, and of utilizing dramatic conventions beyond those of the naturalistic stage. In Robert Emmett Sherwood (1896–) the theatre welcomed an author of rich qualities who passed from the gently sceptical and ironic comic effects of *The Road to Rome* (1927) and *Reunion in Vienna* (1931) to serious reflection on the very fundamentals of our modern civilization (*The Petrified Forest*, 1934; *Idiot's Delight*, 1936). To Broadway, Elmer Rice (1892–) brought an inventive mind and a vigorous willingness to experiment; his expressionistic *Adding Machine* appeared in 1923, his ultra-naturalistic *Street Scene* in 1929. Maxwell Anderson's (1888–) first play, *White Desert*, came in 1923, to be followed by the vastly successful *What Price Glory?* (1925), written in collaboration with Laurence Stallings (1894–), which, although it did not by any means indicate what this author was later to do in the field of poetic drama, at once revealed the presence of a young playwright of worth. In these years, too, were presented Hatcher Hughes's (1883–1945) vigorous *Hell Bent for Heaven* (1924) and John Howard Lawson's (1895–) experimental *Processional* (1925). Without a doubt the twenties proved that the American drama had achieved its majority.

Not less active were the scene-designers. Norman-Bel Geddes (1893–) and Robert Edmond Jones (1887–), although both practical men, had visions of visual grandeur for the theatre which carried it far from the ideals of Belasco. For long identified with the Theatre Guild, Lee Simonson (1888–), without aiming at the majesty of conception which inspired Geddes and Jones, has contributed to the New York stage a long series of fresh and imaginative settings, all characteristic yet widely varied in their technique. In the work of these men the theatre was displaying its willingness to harmonize with the achievements of the new playwrights.

8. THE MODERN AMERICAN THEATRE. During the nineteen-thirties the theatre in the United States seemed to be progressing yet farther, to be moving towards realization of things as yet but dimly dreamed. There was an electric tension on Broadway and beyond. The Federal Theatre Project appeared to many to have within it the makings of a national dramatic movement; theatres of the Left, such as the Theatre Union and the Group Theatre, brought new vigour to the stage; in the ordinary commercial playhouses audiences were being amused or moved by a series of dramas which, excellent in themselves, were thought by many to betoken still greater things in the future.

These were the days when Maxwell Anderson seemed about to usher in a great era of poetic drama—*Winterset*(1935) following *Mary of Scotland* (1933), *High Tor* (1937) following *Winterset*. Archibald MacLeish (1892–) was hailed by those who saw in this poetic drama the hope of succeeding years for turning, in *Panic* (1935), from lyrical poetry to the theatre. At the same time Sam Behrman's (1893–) skilful and mellowed comedies,

Biography (1932) and *End of Summer* (1936), evoked a gracious spirit, lost for a moment in *No Time for Comedy* (1939) and recaptured in *Jakobowsky and the Colonel*(1943). Philip Barry (1896–1949), less skilful and more inclined towards sentiment yet gifted with a fine ear for word values, presented then his *Hotel Universe* (1930), *The Animal Kingdom* (1932), and *Philadelphia Story*(1939). The atmosphere of Gilbert and Sullivan, made modern and mordant, seemed to be reborn in *Of Thee I Sing* (1931), in which George Kaufman (1889–) collaborated with Morrie Ryskind (1895–). Collaborating later with Moss Hart (1904–), Kaufman might have been thought to have been establishing, in *You Can't Take It With You* (1936), a fresh kind of American comedy-farce, a form which was also enriched by George Abbott's(1887–) fantastic *Three Men on a Horse* (1935). Marc Connelly (1891–) came forward with his sensitive dramatic treatment of Negro religion, *Green Pastures* (1930); Paul Green (1894–) with his imaginative *House of Connelly* (1931); Clare Boothe (1903–) with her viciously (and perhaps superficially) witty *The Women* (1936); Lillian Hellman(1904–) with her incisive *Children's Hour* (1934) and *Little Foxes* (1938); John Steinbeck (1901–) with his psychopathic study *Of Mice and Men* (1937). From the Leftist theatre issued John Wexley's(1902–) angry *They Shall Not Die*(1934) and the melodramatic *Stevedore*(1934) of Paul Peters(1908–) and George Sklar—above all, the *Waiting for Lefty* (1935) of Clifford Odets (1906–), to be followed by his *Awake and Sing* (1935), *Golden Boy* (1937), and *Rocket to the Moon* (1938).

It was a glorious decade, yet, in retrospect, it must be confessed, regretfully, that its glory now seems a trifle tarnished. Even by the end of these ten years the hopes for the future were by no means so roseate as they had been at its start. In particular, it could be observed that, with the exception of Clifford Odets (who soon deserted Broadway for Hollywood), no young playwright of any real outstanding potentialities had risen to carry on the torch from the men of the older generation—O'Neill, Anderson, Rice, Behrman, Sherwood. It was as though, instead of keeping forces in reserve, the American theatre had, within this brief space of time, expended all its strength. The Federal Theatre Project came, bringing with it such memorable productions as that of the Negro *Macbeth*, and went—condemned by its unfortunate foundation as a relief measure—to leave behind it but few permanent relics. The theatres of the Left faded away. True, the last years of the decade were clouded with the darkness preceding the storm, while in the midst of the war itself one could not expect to see much in the way of powerful writing for the stage. Yet the rapid ease with which the New York theatre slipped at that time into the presentation of musical comedy and farce might well be taken to indicate either that the earlier force was spent or that the American stage had not gained genuine and enduring strength. *Oklahoma!* and *Bloomer Girl* are no doubt splendid things of their kind, but their kind is not that on which a richer drama can be based.

There seems to be real justification for the judicial summing-up made in 1939 by a distinguished American critic, Joseph Wood Krutch, of the century's achievements in drama:

The fact remains that no playwright who has emerged since 1918, not even O'Neill, has produced an impact even remotely comparable to that produced by Ibsen or Shaw. Nor does the surviving corpus of dramatic writing seem to justify entirely the sense which one has had from year to year that excellent plays were being produced in considerable number. Too many of these plays seem to have fulfilled their function of keeping alive a vital and interesting theatre without actually achieving any permanent place in dramatic literature. The 'best play of the year' has very often owed its popularity to some novelty of theme or dramatic method which seemed exceptionally interesting at the moment but which failed to remain so for very long, and some of these 'best plays' have already been almost completely forgotten.

9. THE THEATRE OUTSIDE NEW YORK. One development of major import, however, is to be chronicled in the history of the modern American theatre. In New York few new play-houses were built between 1930 and 1946 (although among them was the immense RKO or Centre Theatre (1932) in Rockefeller Centre): but, outside New York, inspired by the enthusiasm of what has come to be known as 'The Tributary (or Nationwide) Theatre', dozens of new houses have appeared in every part of the United States. Whatever the final estimate of their importance, they represent a new element in the theatrical world.

The first Little Theatre in America was constructed in 1900 for the Hull House Players of Chicago; the first introduction of drama into the academic world was G. P. Baker's (1866–1935) '47 Workshop' at Harvard University in 1912. Now the number of Little Theatres is legion; college drama departments are to be reckoned by the score. Although the Department of Dramatic Arts at Pittsburg's Carnegie Institute of Technology was founded in 1914, and in 1918 came Frederick Koch's (1877–1944) Carolina Playmakers at the University of North Carolina, the Yale Theatre of 1926 was the first of the large university playhouses, while it was during the thirties and early forties that most of the other important academic houses were opened—at the University of Iowa in 1934, at Stanford University in 1937, at Amherst College in 1938, at the University of Indiana in 1940, and at Williams College in 1941. Maybe the most interesting among all of these is the Penthouse Theatre (1940) at the University of Washington—designed specifically for 'arena' productions.

A similar story is to be told of the civic theatres. Here too development has been rapid. In 1919 the Théâtre du Vieux Carré in New Orleans was constructed, followed by the Pasadena Playhouse in 1925, the Goodman

Theatre in Chicago (1925), the Little Theatres of Dallas, Texas, Omaha, Nebraska (both 1928), and San Antonio, Texas (1929)—the last-named entirely owned and controlled by the city. The idea of a 'civic centre', with a theatre in its midst, was now more than a vision, finding realization at Kalamazoo (1931) and Colorado Springs (1936). Most of these theatres are strictly amateur (although the majority engage professional producers); among the exceptions is the successful and rightly esteemed Cleveland Playhouse, which, under the skilful direction of Frederick McConnell, produces fourteen plays each season with a company some of whom are amateur, some professional.

Without question the achievements of these university and civic ventures have been note-worthy, and those concerned with them have now become conscious of their mission—partly through the unflagging enthusiasm of Mrs. Edith J. Isaacs (1878–   ), editor till 1945 of *Theatre Arts*, partly through the organization known as the National Theatre Conference. *Theatre Arts*, till its demise in 1948, constantly championed the cause of the 'Tributary Theatre', while the Conference, with the financial help of the Rockefeller Foundation, has endeavoured to secure common action in the larger and more important non-commercial playhouses in the various States. These play-houses have brought opportunities for seeing dramas before hundreds of communities; they provide socially useful avocational activities for over a million people; they have contributed to the professional stage not a few actors and technicians.

Without minimizing in the least their positive accomplishment, it may, however, be suggested that as yet the impact of the Little Theatres on the New York stage has not been as great as might have been expected. The reason perhaps is threefold. First of all, in many of these centres eyes are directed towards distant Broadway, and anxious thought is given, not to vital experimentation, but to securing, at the earliest possible release date, the latest popular New York hit. Such playhouses, while no doubt serving a useful purpose in bringing the new plays to the attention of audiences which otherwise might see no plays at all, are thus simply reproducing in amateur terms the offerings of the professional stage and therefore cannot expect to have any wider influence. Secondly, in those non-commercial playhouses (and they are many) that possess well-equipped stages, since it is relatively easier to emulate the professional in material settings and costumes than in subtler forms of theatrical expression, much stress has been laid on the visual appeal of the productions, and this in turn has had a regrettable influence on young apprentice dramatists even in those areas where a serious effort is made to encourage local writing talent. Thirdly, in those quarters in which an attempt is made to do other than simply reproduce the professional, there commonly exists an attitude towards Broadway either antagonistic or paradoxically bivalent. On the one hand, some directors express open contempt for the professional and claim that the future should be devoted to the cultivation of regional drama on Little Theatre lines; on the other, there are directors who, while professing to despise, confuse the issue by seizing avidly on what Broadway offers even while at the same time they seek to promote the regional.

The progressive decline from the high hopes of earlier years has nowhere been more trenchantly expressed than in the writings of the scene-designer Robert Edmond Jones, who, surveying the entire field in 1941, decided that the well-equipped stages with their effective sets were in reality killing the rich promise of the American drama. If only, he declared, we could go back to a bare stage for a time, training producers and actors and dramatists to do without the scenic accessories, a vital theatre might come to take the place of that which so graced the earlier years of the century. Without a doubt, if the time for rejuvenation comes, the United States possesses in the Nationwide Theatre a potential force for the invigoration of the stage. What the future will yield is unsure, but if that force is wielded effectively in the direction of experimentation designed to aid the professional theatre, the years to come may well bring the playhouse that was born barely two hundred years ago—and yet is the inheritor of all the traditions that created Shakespeare—truly before the world as inspirer and leader. At the moment the sense of direction has not been found: the accomplishments of the future, It would seem, must depend entirely on the particular orientation to be adopted in the years immediately ahead. Technically, the American theatre—amateur and professional alike—is well abreast, and in many respects is well ahead, of stages in other lands; what is still uncertain, despite its truly great achievements, is what it wishes to do spiritually with its technical skill.

A. N.

(See also BROADWAY, NATIONWIDE THEATRE, NEGRO IN THE AMERICAN THEATRE, PIONEER THEATRE, and American actors, dramatists, and theatres under their own names.)

II. SCENIC DESIGN. Scenic design in the United States, originally known as 'the new stagecraft', has become a recognized, artistic profession and an integral part of theatrical production. A designer's name appears on every programme directly under that of the play's director, in recognition of the fact that the designer is considered an essential collaborator in interpreting a script. As such, he (or she) is expected to provide not only a background that is pictorially effective, but one that can, by its arrangement of playing areas and the emphasis of its lighting, sustain dramatic action, reflect the mood, and heighten the emotional values of a performance. Very few settings seen in the course of a theatrical season fail to do so. American designers as a group display great versatility, maintain a high level of taste, technical skill in both plan and execution, and, as frequently as playwrights provide the opportunity, fantasy and imagination.

The development of scenic design in the American theatre began shortly before the First World War and was directly influenced and inspired by its previous development in Europe: the doctrines and designs of Gordon Craig, Adolphe Appia's theory of stage lighting and the drawings with which he illustrated it, the work of Emil Orlik and Ernst Stern for Max Reinhardt's first repertory seasons in Berlin, Linnebach's at Dresden, the productions of the Moscow Art Theatre, and those of other continental stages. A pioneer volume by an American critic, H. K. Motherwell, *The Theatre of To-day* (1914), illustrated and analysed the successive innovations in style and technique of European productions. The *Theatre Arts* magazine, founded in 1917 by Sheldon Cheney, continued to provide a valuable focus for critical discussion of stage design and direction both in America and abroad. The first experiments in the simplification and stylization of stage settings as well as atmospheric lighting were in part a revolt against traditional scene-painting, but also part of an insurgent movement in the American theatre directed against stereotyped methods of acting, stage direction, and conventional subject-matter. The new stagecraft appeared, within the course of a few years, in Little, semi-amateur, or experimental theatres which were recruiting new audiences for modern playwrights, such as the Washington Square Players, the Neighborhood Playhouse, and the Provincetown Players, who staged the early plays of Eugene O'Neill; on the operatic stage, in musical revues and ballets, as well as on the professional stage, centred in New York City and known as 'Broadway'.

Among the first stylized settings were those of Sam Hume (1913) at the Arts and Crafts Theatre in Detroit, based on rearrangements of simplified architectural units. Robert Edmond Jones was the first designer to make a successful professional début with his setting and costumes for *The Man Who Married a Dumb Wife*, as part of Granville-Barker's repertory season (1915), when New York audiences also saw Norman Wilkinson's festooned forest for *A Midsummer Night's Dream*, and its gilded fairies. Jones's setting was almost poster-like in its decorative simplification, the silver grey of a house front, the black accent of its door and window, without any suggestion of medieval ornament or architectural detail, and the brilliant contrast of the women's costumes of clear yellow and orange with their towering hennins and exaggerated trains; it was accepted as a manifesto of 'the new movement'. But Jones presently achieved a more subtle, dramatic, and romantic chiaroscuro both in stage lighting and three-dimensional composition (after designing a ballet for Nijinsky, 'Till Eulenspiegel') in a series of notable productions directed by Arthur Hopkins that included *Redemption*, *The Jest* (*La Cena delle Beffe*), *Richard III*, and *Hamlet* with John Barrymore. These productions had the dignity and simplicity, almost austerity, of composition, the balance of large masses and simplified architectural form which remained characteristic of all of Jones's subsequent work.

Lee Simonson, who had served his apprenticeship with the Washington Square Players, established his reputation at the Theatre Guild —founded in 1919—with *The Faithful, Power of Darkness, Liliom, Heartbreak House, Back to Methuselah, Peer Gynt,* and *Marco Millions.* Joseph Urban, Viennese architect and decorator, who had demonstrated the values of continental stagecraft in a series of operatic settings for the Boston Opera Company in 1913, achieved nation-wide popularity with his investiture of the *Ziegfeld Follies,* a lavish annual revue 'glorifying the American Girl'. Among Norman-Bel Geddes's first designs were those for the operas 'Shanweis' and 'La Nave', a musical comedy, and a revue. His most spectacular production was *The Miracle,* when he replaced a conventional gilded proscenium with the soaring, full-scale apse of a cathedral for Max Reinhardt's presentation of that medieval pageant. His most typical work, besides his projects for *King Lear* and *The Divine Comedy,* were his settings for *Lazarus Laughed, Hamlet,* and *Lysistrata,* architectonic units of plinths, ramps, and terraced levels, so-called 'abstract settings', the plastic forms used being an integral part of the total patterns of movement of the actors and the variations in emphasis of the stage lighting.

This first group of designers was speedily followed by another, most of whose members are still active in the theatre to-day. These, with some of their more important productions, are: Cleon Throckmorton (*The Hairy Ape, The Emperor Jones, All God's Chillun Got Wings*); Aline Bernstein (*The Little Clay Cart, The Dybbuk, Romeo and Juliet, Grand Hotel*); Raymond Sovey (*St. Joan, Wings over Europe*); Woodman Thompson (*What Price Glory?, Beggar on Horseback, Iolanthe*); James Reynolds and Albert Johnson, in the field of musical revues; Mordecai Gorelik (*Processional* and the Group Theatre's repertory); Jo Mielziner (*The Guardsman, Street Scene, Romeo and Juliet, Hamlet* (for John Gielgud), *Saint Joan, The Barretts of Wimpole Street, Glass Menagerie,* the ballet 'Pillar of Fire', and numerous musical comedies); Donald Oenslager (*The Doctor's Dilemma, Pygmalion,* and the operas 'Tristan and Isolde', 'Salomé', and 'Abduction from the Seraglio'); Stewart Chaney (*Life with Father, Voice of the Turtle, Hamlet* (for Leslie Howard), *Winter's Tale, Merry Wives of Windsor*); and later Howard Bay (*One-Third of a Nation, Carmen Jones*); Cecil Smith, ballets and musical comedies; and Lemuel Ayres (*Oklahoma!*).

The above list can serve only as an indication of the work of American scenic artists, many of whom have designed from fifty to a hundred productions or more, the most successful from ten to twenty or more productions a season. Their designs have been widely reproduced, including excellent photographs of many settings as lighted in performance. A verbal description being inadequate, the interested

reader is referred to the illustrations in such volumes as *Settings and Costumes of the Modern Stage* (the London Studio Year Book for 1933); *Stage Decoration,* by Sheldon Cheney (1928); *20th Century Stage Decoration,* by S. J. Hume and W. R. Fuerst, vol. ii (1929); *Tendances nouvelles du théâtre,* by L. Moussinac (1931); *Das amerikanische Theater,* by Gregor Fülöp-Miller (1931); the files of *Theatre Arts,* as well as the books written by American scenic designers themselves analysing the artistic problems and possibilities of their craft: R. E. Jones, *Drawings for the Theatre* (1925); Mordecai Gorelik, *New Theatres for Old* (1940); Donald Oenslager, *Scenery Then and Now* (1936); Lee Simonson, *The Stage is Set* (1932) and *Part of a Lifetime* (Drawings and Designs 1919-40); and Norman-Bel Geddes, *Horizons; A Project for a Theatrical Presentation of the Divine Comedy* (1924).

In general, the work of American designers displays a great variety of method and style, ranging from realism to decorative simplification and formalization. This is in part the consequence of the conditions under which the American theatre operates. There are virtually no permanent companies or endowed playhouses as in Europe; every production is financed as a separate enterprise, the director as well as the cast recruited for each play. Designers in America rarely have the opportunity of working consecutively with a director, such as Copeau, Meyerhold, or Taïrov, who has developed a single method of production. Realism remains as vital and predominant a form of expression for American playwrights as for the American novelists; contemporary poets have not developed an effective dramatic form; revivals of classic or poetic drama are still infrequent. Nevertheless Jones, in his barroom for O'Neill's *The Iceman Cometh,* displays, in naturalistic terms, subtlety and artistry in conveying an atmosphere of forlorn despair; *Liliom* and *Winterset* were imbued with poetic intensity and a certain degree of tragic grandeur. And many period settings underline the satiric interest of a script or, as lighted, dramatize its emotional force.

The importance attached to lighting a stage-setting, and the careful supervision of every detail involved in its execution, are also characteristic of American designing. Architectural blue-prints to a half-inch scale are supplied for the constructing carpenter. The colour sketch is frequently no more than a record of the artist's intention. The technical problem of preserving its quality in enlarging it to theatrical dimensions is a matter of active collaboration between the designer and the painters of various scenic studios. Flat uniformity of pigment is avoided; some method of breaking even a solid tone of a wall is employed, whether by spattering, stippling, or puddling to secure contrasts of colour of approximately the same value which will vibrate under stage light. Responsibility for the successful execution of his ideas is considered an essential part of the designer's job.

The setting itself is conceived as a surface to receive light—as Appia first contended; and lighting rehearsals often occupy a total of eighteen hours or more.

The apparatus used consists predominantly of both sharp and soft focus spotlights of from 500 to 1,000 W. These are usually placed in groups of eight or ten on stanchions at either side of the stage, often mounted on a small truck, masked by a wing with a flexible fifteen-inch flipper, and are known as light tormentors. Overhead spotlights, from twenty-five to fifty or more, are hung from pipes between the light tormentors. Three-circuit colour borders are, as a rule, used sparingly for general atmospheric tone or colour, except where a sky-drop or cyclorama is an important part of the setting. Footlights are either used to a very low intensity, or are frequently dispensed with, being replaced by groups of eighteen to twenty-four spotlights hung from the front of the first balcony and angled to catch actors as they near the setting line, beyond the area of overhead and side spotlighting. The spotlights are dimmer-controlled, the colour, angle, and intensity of each set being directed to establish the relative values of the scenic background and the playing areas, within a range that will evoke the mood of an act or a scene. Apart from cues required by the script as to time of day, changes from day to dusk or night, &c., this requires subtle and shifting change of emphasis, each lamp or group of lamps being set to a 'mark', on a range of dimmer points marked from zero to 100, and then changing to another set of marks, for another interrelated balance of groups of lights, each change being accomplished slowly enough so that the mechanics of the shift are imperceptible to an audience. The motivation of such a light-plot depends on the artistic sensibility of the designer as well as the director; the pictorial and theatrical values of a stage setting are inseparable from its lighting. The consensus of opinion among American designers is that no setting is designed until it is successfully lighted.

The professional theatre, being an itinerant one, is limited to portable switchboards and somewhat antiquated resistance dimmers, which are cumbersome to interlock and master mechanically, and require an excessive amount of labour and rehearsal time to ensure accurate timing for complicated light-cues. Several types of remote dimming control have been developed recently; in these the control panel is a pilot board, on which one to ten light-cues can be pre-set and electrically interlocked. Controls for as many as fifty to sixty circuits, each with a variable capacity of 5 to 5,000 W. each, can be assembled in a space of approximately 3 by 4 feet, and proportional dimming of the most elaborate lighting changes handled by a single operator from a single master control, the reactor units being placed below stage. Being permanent installations these have been used principally outside New York City (see also LIGHTING, 3).

No theatre has been built in New York for a generation. In 1928 there were 80 'legitimate' theatres (i.e. those not used for motion pictures); by 1945 the number had declined to 36, in 1947 to 32. Despite the boom of war-time prosperity, theatre owners found it more profitable to convert their property or lease it to motion-picture companies. The mounting costs of production, which have doubled within the last five years, tend to limit the number of experimental productions and also the development of new playwrights.

The only playhouses that are modern, both technically and architecturally, are those erected, or now being planned, for university theatres, and other which are to serve as War Memorials as part of civic centres. The development of scenic design in the United States, as part of another era of technical and artistic experiment in play-production, may depend on the number of permanent professional companies which may be established in the near future at such theatres (see above, I. 9).

L. S.

UNITI, The, a *commedia dell'arte* company which has caused much discussion, since it is possible that the word refers not to a distinct company, as did the words Gelosi and Confidenti, for example, but means a combined troupe of actors from different companies formed for a special occasion. Because of this some critics consider the Uniti to be part of the history of the Gelosi, some of the Confidenti. Whatever the facts, it remains certain that a company under that name was directed by Drusiano Martinelli and his wife Angelica in 1584, and for some years afterwards. A company calling itself the Uniti is noted in 1614, but this may have been a temporary amalgamation. Among its members were Silvio Fiorillo and his son.

UNITIES, The Three, of Time, Place, and Action, see ARISTOTLE, DRAMATIC CRITICISM, and FRANCE.

UNITY THEATRE, GLASGOW. This theatre was formed in 1941 by the amalgamation of four amateur companies, the Transport, the Clarion, the Jewish Institute, and the Workers' Theatre, and has achieved more than local fame for able productions and catholic choice of play. In the summer of 1945 the company were the guests of the London Unity Theatre (see AMATEUR THEATRE IN GREAT BRITAIN) and received high commendation. They aspire to form a professional company and to establish a school of acting. Their first production was *Major Operation*, by the Glasgow dramatist, James Barke, and their repertory has included *Distant Point*, *Juno and the Paycock*, *Golden Boy*, and *The Lower Depths*.   W. J.

UNIVERSITY THEATRE, U.S.A., see NATIONWIDE THEATRE, 2 and UNITED STATES OF AMERICA, I. 9.

UPPER GALLERY, see AUDITORIUM, I *c*.

UPSTAGE (the acting area farthest from the audience), see STAGE DIRECTIONS.

URBAN, JOSEPH (1872–1933), architect and stage designer, born in Vienna, where he worked for many years before going to Boston in 1911–12 to design sets for the opera there. He was also in New York, where he designed settings for the Ziegfeld Follies, the Metropolitan, and James K. Hackett's Shakespearian productions. He built the Ziegfeld Theatre in New York, with its egg-shaped interior, and introduced much of the new continental stage-craft to American theatre-audiences, making use of broad masses of colour and novel lighting effects on costume and scenery.

USIGLI, RODOLFO, see SOUTH AMERICA, 1.

U.S.S.R., see RUSSIA.

UTILITY, see STOCK COMPANY.

UZBEKISTAN, see RUSSIA, 2 *e*.

V

VADSTENA, a small town in Sweden which has, in the middle of a row of early nineteenth-century houses, a small private theatre. This was built in 1826, and the last professional production was given there in 1878. Its origin, architect, and original owner are unknown. The theatre is still in working order, and is occasionally used for amateur performances.

VAKHTANGOV, EUGENE V. (1883–1922), Soviet Russian actor and producer, and founder of the theatre in Moscow which now bears his name. As a young man he joined the Moscow Art Theatre, and became the devoted pupil and friend of Stanislavsky. In 1914 he was put in charge of a studio attached to the theatre, which made a great success with a production of *Macbeth*, with Vakhtangov, a fine, sensitive actor, in the title-role. In 1920 the company was reorganized as the Third Studio, and under its young, dynamic leader began to break away from the parent theatre, which at that time was rather uncertain. While the latter still limited itself to naturalism, and to a striving towards the complete illusion of reality, Vakhtangov made the widest possible use of theatre-forms, though he never allowed form, as such, to overpower the production as a whole, and always sought for an ensemble which would correspond to the basic idea of the play under consideration. It was in his constant striving for truth that he developed that unsurpassed use of the grotesque which is so typical of his work. The culminating point of his career was his production of *Turandot*, which he did not live to see. It has remained in the repertory of the theatre ever since, exactly as he conceived it. In the same year (1922) his brilliant production of *The Dybbuk* was given at the Habima Theatre (see JEWISH DRAMA), another offshoot of the Moscow Art Theatre, founded by Vakhtangov.

Since his death the Vakhtangov Theatre, under the management of his widow, has continued to do good and stimulating work, still under the inspiration of his short but glorious leadership. The first Soviet play was given in 1924, and was followed by such contemporary works as *Yegor Bulichev* and *Aristocrats*. In 1932 Akimov's production of an unorthodox *Hamlet* aroused a storm of protest, and was withdrawn, but not before it had focused the attention of the theatrical world on this vital young theatre, which has had in its company men of the calibre of Okhlopkov, and the late Boris Shchukin, who made a great impression as Bulichev, and as Lenin in *The Man with the Gun*.

During the early part of the Second World War the Vakhtangov Theatre was evacuated to Omsk, and returned to find its premises damaged by bombing. Repairs were put in hand, and it is hoped that the theatre suffered no permanent damage.

VALERIO, see BENDINELLI.

VALLERAN-LECOMTE (*fl.* 1590–*c.* 1613), early French actor-manager, who is first heard of at Bordeaux in 1592. Shortly afterwards he had his own company, with Marie Venier, wife and daughter of actors and the first French actress to be known by name, as his leading lady. As author for his company he engaged the prolific Alexandre Hardy, often considered the first professional dramatist of France, and by the early years of the seventeenth century was established intermittently at the Hôtel de Bourgogne as the tenant of the Confraternity of the Passion. The old actor, Agnan Sarat, who more than twenty years before had brought his own company to Paris, was Valleran-Lecomte's chief comedian, and remained with him until his death in 1613, Valleran-Lecomte himself dying or retiring shortly afterwards. Little is known of Valleran-Lecomte's acting, though he appears to have been good in farcical parts as well as in serious plays, and it is interesting to note that when the company first came to Paris he took the entrance-money at the door himself—or so says Tallemant des Réaux in his *Historiettes*.

VALOIS, NINETTE DE [really EDRIS STANNUS] (1898–), the first great name in English ballet, and the person who has, more than any other, been responsible for its development as a serious art in its own right, and no longer a tolerable imitation of the Russian ballet. An Irishwoman, trained by Diaghilev, her romantic pseudonym is a relic of the days when no English dancer could hope to succeed without a foreign name, a custom which Ninette de Valois, though forced to observe it herself, has happily rendered obsolete by her foundation of an English school of ballet. After leaving Diaghilev she founded her own ballet school, and was also responsible for the production of ballets at Dublin, Cambridge, and elsewhere. The founding of the Camargo Society in 1930 gave her her first big chance, which she took with 'Job', a fine ballet which remains in the repertory. She was then engaged by Lilian Baylis to train the *corps de ballet* for the Old Vic opera, and her work there led to the foundation of a separate ballet company. This eventually took possession of Sadler's Wells, and later of Covent Garden, and was able to rely on English dancers and choreographers trained in its own school, as well as on the further fine productions of Ninette de Valois, which include such outstanding ballets as 'Checkmate' and 'The Rake's Progress' (see also BALLET, 8).

VAMP TRAP, a device to enable the body of an actor to pass through a solid piece of scenery. It takes its name from Planché's melodrama *The Vampire* (1820), where it was first, or most

[819]

extensively, used (see TRICKWORK ON THE ENGLISH STAGE).

VANBRUGH, SIR JOHN (1664–1726), English dramatist and architect, in which latter capacity he was responsible for Blenheim Palace, Castle Howard, the Clarendon Building, Oxford (with Hawksmoor), and the Queen's Theatre in the Haymarket (not to be confused with the present Haymarket), which was also known as the King's, and the Opera House. It was built to house Betterton's company, and three of Vanbrugh's own plays were given there, including *The Confederacy* (1705), a comedy based on Dancourt's *Les Bourgeoises à la mode*. He was responsible for several other translations, of Dancourt, Boursault, Molière, and a Spanish play, but his best work undoubtedly went into *The Relapse; or, Virtue in Danger* (1696), a sequel to and parody of Cibber's *Love's Last Shift*, produced the previous year, and *The Provoked Wife* (1697), written, according to tradition, while Vanbrugh was imprisoned in Paris for some unspecified offence, the two countries being then at war. The unequal quality of Vanbrugh's work, and the comparative smallness of his output, are due to the fact that the theatre was to him merely a spare-time amusement, though he often proves himself a master dramatist. His last two plays were much castigated by Jeremy Collier in his diatribe against the stage, and Vanbrugh was moved to reply to his accusations. But as his fame as an architect grew he left the theatre, and his last play, originally called *A Journey to London*, was left unfinished at his death. It was completed and produced by Colley Cibber in 1728 as *The Provoked Husband*. Vanbrugh, who had the Restoration traits of coarseness, pungent wit, and cynicism, has perhaps been underrated as a dramatist, and holds an important place in the evolution of English comedy. 'He helped', says Professor Thaler, 'to extend the range of the comedy of manners . . . and he packs into his best plays much solid food for thoughtful laughter.' It should be noted that *The Relapse* was later adapted for a more prudish stage by Sheridan as *A Trip to Scarborough* (1777), but in its original form had a long run at the Phoenix Theatre, London, in 1947–8.

VANBRUGH. (1) VIOLET AUGUSTA MARY (1867–1942), a distinguished English actress, daughter of the Rev. Prebendary Reginald Barnes of Exeter. She made her first appearance at Toole's Theatre, London (now destroyed), in burlesque, in 1886, and in 1888 joined the stock company at Margate, where she first appeared as Ophelia. Under the capable management of Sarah Thorne she perfected herself in her chosen profession, and later joined the Kendals, accompanying them to America. On her return she was engaged by Irving, making her appearance as Anne Boleyn in *Henry VIII* with great success, and understudying Ellen Terry. In 1894 she married the actor-manager Arthur Bourchier, and appeared

at the Royalty as his leading lady, playing a great number of parts, always with distinction, polish, and versatility. Indeed, much of the success of her husband's ventures then and later at the Garrick and on tour may be said to have been due to her talent and popularity. With Tree at His Majesty's she was a fine Queen Katharine (*Henry VIII*) and Lady Macbeth, and her later appearances included an outstanding performance in *Thunder in the Air* at the Duke of York's in 1928. She celebrated her golden jubilee in 1937 shortly after appearing as Mistress Ford in *The Merry Wives of Windsor* at the Ring, Blackfriars, and in the Open Air Theatre, Regent's Park. Tall and distinguished-looking, she was a fine actress, much loved and respected in her profession. Her sister (2) IRENE (1872–1949), who married the younger Dion Boucicault, was also trained by Sarah Thorne, and made her first appearance at the Theatre Royal, Margate, as Phoebe in *As You Like It* in 1888. The same year saw her début at the old Globe in London, where she played the White Queen in *Alice in Wonderland*. She then gained experience under various managements, with Tree at the Haymarket, with Alexander at the St. James's, where she played Ellean in *The Second Mrs. Tanqueray* and Gwendolen Fairfax in *The Importance of Being Earnest*, and with Hare at the old Globe. It was there that she scored her first great success, as Sophie Fullgarney in *The Gay Lord Quex*. She became the outstanding interpreter of Pinero's heroines, and her Nina Jesson in *His House in Order* and her Letty in the play of that name were memorable performances. At the Duke of York's under Charles Frohman she appeared in *The Admirable Crichton*, and then and later proved herself a perfect player of Barrie parts. Among the portraits with which she enriched the English stage her Rose Trelawny and Norah Marsh (in *The Land of Promise*) should not be forgotten. She celebrated her golden jubilee in 1938 by a matinée at His Majesty's, and in 1941 was created D.B.E. Dark, with wonderfully expressive eyes, she was an actress of great charm, and represented all that was best in the acting of her generation (see also BARNES, SIR KENNETH). W. M. P.

VAN CAMPEN, JACOB (*c.* 1590–1657), Dutch architect, builder of the first theatre in Amsterdam in 1637, on the lines of Palladio's Teatro Olimpico in Vicenza (see ARCHITECTURE).

VANCE, THE GREAT (1839–88), a music-hall 'lion comique', friend and rival of Leybourne. He was employed in a solicitor's office in Lincoln's Inn, but forsook it for the halls, and became best known for his comic cockney songs in the style of Sam Cowell, such as 'The Chickaleery Bloke'. Inspired by the success of Leybourne's 'Champagne Charlie' he countered with the praises of Cliquot, and between them they went through the whole wine-list. Vance, whose real name was Alfred Peck

Stevens, was also a fine singer of moral 'motto' songs, such as 'Act on the Square, Boys'. He died during an appearance at the Sun, Knightsbridge, on Boxing Day 1888.

VANDENHOFF. (1) JOHN (1790–1861), English actor, who made his first appearance on the stage in 1808, and spent many years in the provinces. He was for some time in Bath, and from 1815 to 1820 was a favourite with audiences in Liverpool, Manchester, and other big towns. He was also much liked in Edinburgh, particularly as Coriolanus. In 1820 he was seen at Covent Garden as Lear, following it with other leading parts, being much admired as Iago. He remained in London about eighteen years, and in 1834 played Hamlet at the Haymarket, going to Drury Lane in 1838. In spite of a good voice and features and a certain manly dignity, he failed to reach a commanding position, being somewhat deficient in pathos and passion, and from 1839 onwards was mainly seen in the provinces. His son (2) GEORGE (1813–85) made his first appearance in 1839 at Covent Garden, where among other parts he played Mercutio in Mme Vestris's production of *Romeo and Juliet*. In 1842 he went to New York and made his début at the Park as Hamlet. A tour which followed brought him friends and financial success, and he decided to remain in the United States. From 1843 to 1853 he taught elocution and gave poetry readings, and appeared on the stage in New York and elsewhere, being at one time leading man at the Chestnut Street Theatre, Philadelphia, and at Palmo's Opera House. In 1845 he staged an English translation of Sophocles' *Antigone*, with music by Mendelssohn, and a stage approximating to the contemporary idea of a Greek theatre. He returned to London in 1853 and was seen as Hamlet, but he had little liking for his profession and retired in 1856. He was then called to the bar, but continued to give poetry readings, and in 1860 published his reminiscences as *Leaves from an Actor's Notebook*. A tall, scholarly man of good sense and good breeding, but somewhat aloof, he made a final appearance on the stage with Geneviève Ward in 1878, playing Wolsey, and Gloster in *Jane Shore*. His sister (3) CHARLOTTE ELIZABETH (1818–60), a small, fair, gentle woman, was an excellent actress in parts requiring delicacy and pathos. She made her first appearance in 1836 as Juliet, and among her later parts were Cordelia, Julia, and Pauline. She was the first to play Parthenia in *Ingomar* and Lydia in *The Love Chase*, and was much admired as Antigone and Alcestis in translations from the Greek.

VANDERBILT THEATRE, NEW YORK, a modest but handsome playhouse on the south side of 48th Street, east of Broadway. It opened on 2 Nov. 1921 with Pauline Lord and a fine cast in *Anna Christie*, which was a success with critics and public alike. Later productions were less successful, though *Lazybones*, with George Abbott, ran for ten weeks in 1924, and

Mulatto (1935) had 373 performances. But *See Naples and Die, Days to Come,* and a revival of *London Assurance,* proved unacceptable to the public. The last play of any importance at this theatre, which in 1939 was taken over for broadcasting, was an all-star revival of *The Importance of Being Earnest.*   G. F.

VAN DRUTEN, JOHN (1901–   ), dramatist, of Dutch extraction, born in London, where his first plays were produced, but later an American citizen. He first came into prominence with *Young Woodley* (1928), a slight but charming study of adolescence which was unaccountably banned by the censor, and produced by the Stage Society as a protest. When the ban was removed, it was seen in London and had a long run. It was also successful in New York. Van Druten's later plays, which are mainly light comedies, include *After All* (1929), a study of family relationships, *London Wall,* a comedy of office life, and *There's Always Juliet* (both 1931), which contains one of the few successful efforts by an Englishman to portray an American girl. His gift for the delineation of women was further shown in *The Distaff Side* (1933), in which Sybil Thorndike gave a moving performance as the mother, and *Old Acquaintance* (1940), a study of two disparate women writers which was successful on both sides of the Atlantic. *The Voice of the Turtle* (1943), a war-time comedy which had an extremely long run in New York, was coldly received in London, where the philanderings of its three characters seemed trivial and pointless. Van Druten has also been responsible for several dramatizations and translations, sometimes in collaboration, and in 1938 published a volume of reminiscences as *The Way to the Present.*

VAN VONDEL, JOOST (1587–1679), see HOLLAND and JEWISH DRAMA, 3.

VARIETY. When the music-halls were rebuilt, in their era of prosperity, so as to exclude the individual supper-tables, the resulting entertainment lost much of the free-and-easy sparkle of the old days, and a good deal of the boisterous element, both on the stage and among the audience, and was more properly known as 'variety', while the buildings themselves were called Theatres of Varieties. For the old evening-long series of single turns was substituted the twice-nightly programme, first instituted by Maurice de Frece at the Alhambra, Liverpool; ballets and spectacular shows were imported, and the whole elaborate set-up was far removed from the old 'music-hall'. The old name clung, however, side by side with the new, and the history of this form of entertainment must be looked for under MUSIC-HALL, and, for America, under VAUDEVILLE.

VARIETY THEATRE, Hoxton, a music-hall near the Britannia. It was used for plays during 1871, but only produced a programme of farce blended with variety. It has no history as a playhouse.

VARIUS RUFUS, Lucius (*c.* 74–14 B.C.), the friend of Virgil and Horace, and author of a lost tragedy *Thyestes*, which was given in 29 B.C. at the games in celebration of the victory of Actium. The author is said to have received the equivalent of £8,000 for it from Augustus, and Quintilian said that in his opinion it was as good as any Greek tragedy.

VAUDEVILLE, a name of French origin, applied to plays of a light or satiric nature, interspersed with songs; later a form of light or comic opera. In the United States the term has become synonymous with the English 'music-hall', and is now often used in England with that sense.

1. Vaudeville, which has undergone several changes of form and meaning, may have originated in the fifteenth century, when a workman in Normandy, named Olivier Basselin, composed satiric couplets on popular airs, directed against the English invaders. These became popular throughout the region where he lived and took their name from it—chansons du Vau (or Val) de Vire—songs of the valley of Vire. Another writer of these early couplets was Jean le Houx. Or the word may derive from 'voix de villes'—song of the city streets. By 1674 it had already received its present form, and Boileau in his *Art Poétique* published in that year describes it as a satiric and often political ballad. It passed into theatrical parlance by way of the little theatres of the Paris fairs, where, owing to the monopoly of the Comédie-Française, plays could only be given in dumb-show, with interpolated choruses on well-known tunes, often parodying the productions of the legitimate theatre. These *pièces en vaudevilles*, as they were called, were the staple fare of the Opéra-Comique, and were written by such men as Piron, Collé, Le Sage, Fuzelier, Favart, Autreau—to name only the best-known—and corresponded roughly to the English ballad opera. Their popularity paved the way for the immense vogue of light opera in the Paris of the mid-nineteenth century, catered for by the prolific Scribe and his many collaborators and rivals—Mélèsville, Désaugiers, Ancelot, Mazères, Dumersan, Theaulon, the Cogniard brothers, and many more. When these vaudevilles lost their popularity the use of the word was restricted to the variety stage, whence its present meaning in America.   ED.

2. VAUDEVILLE IN AMERICA (for England see MUSIC-HALL). On the night of 24 Oct. 1881 Tony (Antonio) Pastor (1837–1908) staged a novel entertainment in his new Fourteenth Street theatre. It proved to be an innovation—a straight, clean, variety show—the inaugural of what America came to know as vaudeville. Pastor had been a singer in the 'dumps' and 'slabs', as the earlier variety performers called the miserable settings in which they played. An operator of beerhalls, he had booked variety acts of the 1870s. These were coarse, vulgar, often obscene, their patrons masculine, save for the prostitutes who solicited the tipplers.

Pastor was an astute showman. He reasoned, wisely, that if he cleaned up his bills he could double his audience by attracting respectable women patrons and their escorts. For his opening he presented eight contrasting acts—comedy, acrobatic, song, and dance—headed by Ella Wesner, a male impersonator of the dandies of the day, who varied her presentation with English music-hall songs. To Pastor's delight a mixed audience of good douce people attended, and the box-office revenue was gratifying. But he never realized that his eventful October entertainment had sealed the type of vaudeville that was to enrich his successors. Exploiting his showmanship, they made a bonanza of a theatrical expression vital in its social as well as artistic aspects, for vaudeville's *jeux d'esprit* were largely topical fun. That Benjamin Franklin Keith (1846–1914) and his subsequent partners, Edward Franklin Albee (1857–1930) and Frederick Francis Proctor (1851–1929), were the first to take vaudeville out of the beerhalls is not wholly borne out by the facts. Pastor's clean vaudeville was offered two years before Keith entered this branch of theatrical business.

The transition from the lustier variety acts of dungboot days to the 'refined' vaudeville of the 1890s and 1900s was welcomed by seasoned performers, who enjoyed working in the spacious theatres built by the new managers. They relished their comfortable dressing-rooms, the new scenery, good furniture, and props. Best of all, the more responsive audiences attracted by this burnished type of vaudeville spurred their efforts to entertain, and a new theatrical presentation, of impact, subtlety, neatness, and realism, was developed.

New sketches, written to a specific 'punch' formula (all acts were limited to twenty minutes or less), replaced the blowzy afterpieces of the 1870s, and they looked fine in the bright settings provided. Realistic mountings intensified dramatic portrayals, and animal acts improved one hundred per cent. in fresh landscapes of light wood with cut borders. Trainers shed their undertakerish Prince Alberts for hunting or riding costume, and put snappy uniforms on their assistants. Mechanical betterments fell like a benison on sight acts, magic, musical, and spectacular numbers. And there was more employment, for the managers increased their bills to ten, twelve, sometimes fifteen acts. A new technique in comedy, drama, and novelty acts came out of all this. Elaborate gestures, distorted facial expressions, the unlovely prattfall, were curbed—noticeable improvements over the excessive slapstick methods of comics in pre-Pastor times. An example of the new technique was the act of James J. Morton (1862–1933) and Maude Ravel. This was one of the funniest acts of the mid-1890s, and the team played the circuits for years. Morton's smooth delivery, the economy of his art, was astonishing. The audiences of the 1870s, accustomed to bladder clouts and stuffed clubs, would have looked askance at Morton's cadaverous, expressionless countenance as he presented his material. He would make heart-scalding attempts to help Maude with her songs—earnest, futile efforts that never accomplished anything—except to throw his audience into unbuttoned laughter.

Another development was the headline system. The more intelligent audiences of later vaudeville began to rate their favourites, and the managers responded with top billing and increased salaries for performers with such box-office appeal. This led to the abuse of 'name' billing. A 'name' act was just that. What other appeal in vaudeville had Sarah Bernhardt, Emma Calvé, Lily Langtry, or Mrs. Patrick Campbell? But to the true vaudeville artist soaring salaries gave incentive to create new styles either of thrust, persuasion, or zany routines. The latter acts, which were burlesque or 'nut' acts—Collins and Hart, or Duffy and Sweeney, are incomparable examples —were popular. For vaudeville was America in motley, the national relaxation. It was a dig in the nation's ribs, its brassy assurance but a mask for an emotional simplicity, a beguiling sincerity, that was often as naïve as a circus.

Here one recalls some of the great names that graced vaudeville in its halcyon days— roughly a thirty-year span from the mid-1890s to 1925, when the inroads of motion pictures, especially the talkies, which followed in 1927, hastened its decline. Among them were Charlie Case (1858–1916), Joe Jackson (?– 1942), Joe Cook (1890–   ), Ed Wynn (1886–), Bert Williams (1873–1922), W. C. Fields (1879–1946), Frank Tinney (1878–1940), Bill Robinson (1878–   ), the Howards, Eugene (1880–   ) and Willie (1883–1949), Eddie Cantor (1893–   ), Lou Holtz (1898–   ), and Jimmy Durante (1893–   ). Their feminine foils in acclaim were Nora Bayes (1880–1928), Eva Tanguay (1878–1947), Elsie Janis (1889–   ), Irene Franklin (1876–1941), Cissie Loftus (1876–1943), Marie Cahill (1874– 1933), Fay Templeton (1865–1939)—the snows, alas, of yesteryear. There were outstanding teams, too, three acts and four acts. But the single artist predominated as the headliner. There is not space to discuss the merits of each of these performers whom we salute for their effortless pleasantries—indeed, much of their art was ineffable. But two selected at random—a monologist and a silent act—will admirably illustrate the flourishing art of the vaudeville before it withered and died of no home. The first is Charlie Case, whose quiet monologue was one of the most entrancing acts in the vaudeville of the 1900s. His unassuming presentation, the while he twiddled the piece of string that was his only prop, and without which he could not go on, shrunk him to a parity with the little man in his audience. In a land of racial conflict no one remembered he was a negro. He was your true comic, likeably sad; winning, never bargaining for,

favour. For pathos is akin to comedy, and sympathy a spur to tearful laughter. All this was part of Case's art. A part too of Joe Jackson's. His bicycling tramp was the acme of pantomime. In fright wig and red nose he accomplished by eye-work, by his slightest, sometimes feigned, gesture, by his furrowed, quizzical brow, by an awkwardness born of grace, the poignancy that Case conveyed in words—a magnificent intimate act was this of Jackson's.

No doubt the insistence of the managers on clean acts provoked a delicacy and restraint that made for subtlety and the vigour of hint. The force of restriction is a powerful challenge. Yet all the performers mentioned, especially the women, owed a debt to the English and French artists of the halls. Their invasion of the American vaudeville theatres was an incalculable influence. These splendid performers —Sir Harry Lauder (1870–1950), Albert Chevalier (1861–1923), Marie Lloyd (1870– 1922), Yvette Guilbert (1866–1944), Vesta Victoria (1873–1951), Vesta Tilley (1864–   ), Wilkie Bard (1874–1944), accented sophistication, satire, characterization. They employed the *mot*, were alive to their pitch of acceptance, and played up, not down, to American audiences; a superb illustration of the universal quality of art.

The life of American vaudeville was incredibly brief—but fifty-odd years from Pastor's experiment to the closing in 1932 of Broadway's Palace Theatre as a two-a-day. The precise reasons for its demise are critical and touching. Motion pictures and radio dealt it a death wound. But an indifferent public had also learned to amuse itself with sports, automobiles, and cocktail parties, and now finds its intimate entertainment in night-clubs.

D. G.

VAUDEVILLE THEATRE, LONDON, in the Strand, was built in 1870 for three of the most popular actors of the day, H. J. Montague, David James, and Thomas Thorne. It opened on 16 Apr. with *Love and Money* and a burlesque, which attracted little attention; but the production of Albery's *Two Roses* later in the same year brought success, and served to introduce Irving to the notice of the public in the character of Digby Grant. The play ran for a long time. At its conclusion Montague left the management, but the next success, Byron's *Our Boys*, had both David James and Thorne in the cast. It ran from 16 Jan. 1875 to 18 Apr. 1879, and had many revivals later. After a period of success with straight plays the theatre was devoted to farce, one of which, *Confusion*, ran for a year. A less successful period followed, but in 1891 Ibsen's *Hedda Gabler* and *Rosmersholm* were given for the first time in England, at matinées. In the same year the theatre's somewhat self-effacing exterior was extended, and it was entirely redecorated and much improved. In 1893 the Gattis, who still own it, bought it and revived *Our Boys*. Later Seymour Hicks and his wife had a successful run there with straight plays, and with a succession of musical comedies which proved most popular. In 1926 the theatre was rebuilt and reconstructed, and is still in use.   W. M. P.

VAUDEVILLE, THÉÂTRE DU, Paris. This was opened on 2 Jan. 1792 by the actors who were forced to leave the Comédie-Italienne when its licence was renewed for musical plays only. The company was headed by Rozières, and was frequently in trouble for the topical and political allusions found in its productions by the vigilance of the censor. It eventually fell back on the safety of semi-historical pieces, based on anecdotes of heroic figures, and in 1838 was burnt down. The company moved to the Théâtre des Nouveautés, where plays by Dumas *fils* and others were given with some success, but the theatre fell on bad times and was frequently closed. In 1868 the present building was opened, under the old name, and has since had a steady, though somewhat uneventful, career.

VAUDEVILLES, PIÈCES EN, see OPERA, 5.

VAUGHAN, KATE [CATHERINE CANDELON] (*c.* 1852–1903), English comedy actress, child of a theatre musician. She was trained as a dancer by Mrs. Conquest and with a sister made her début in the music-halls in 1870. For some years she continued her career as a dancer, inaugurating a new school of skirt dancing, and also played in burlesque; from 1876 to 1883 she was a member of the famous Gaiety quartet, with Nellie Farren, Edward Terry, and Royce. She then abandoned dancing, and was seen only in standard comedy, playing Lydia Languish, Miss Hardcastle, Peg Woffington, and Lady Teazle during her tenancy of the Opéra Comique in 1887. With H. B. Conway she organized a company to tour the provinces in these and similar parts, and scored a great hit as Peggy in *The Country Girl*.

VAUXHALL, a place of entertainment in London, originally known as Spring Gardens, Foxhall, which opened in 1660, and was frequented by Pepys. Writing of it in 1700 Tom Brown said: 'In the close walks the most experienced mothers have often lost themselves in looking for their daughters.' During the eighteenth century it was used extensively for concerts, glee-singing, fireworks, and occasional spectacular dramatic shows. It figures in many memoirs of the period, and in Fanny Burney's *Evelina* (1779). In the early nineteenth century it was known as the Royal Gardens, Vauxhall, and a mimic battle of Waterloo was staged there, as were some of Bishop's operettas. It first opened during the day in 1836, and was lit by gas-lamps in 1849. It was described by Dickens, and was often in trouble owing to rioting and disorders, which finally led to its closing in 1859, the site being built over, though the name persists.

There was a Vauxhall in New York in the

early part of the nineteenth century, which had a small open-air theatre for summer shows. This was burnt down in 1808, but the gardens long remained a favourite resort, and several seasons of plays were given there in the 1840s.

VEDRENNE, JOHN E. (1867–1930), English theatre manager, best remembered for his association with Granville-Barker at the Court Theatre from 1904 to 1907, and at the Savoy in 1907, during which time they presented a number of outstanding plays, including some of Shaw's for the first time. Vedrenne, who was originally in commerce, became a concert agent and business-manager for several theatres, and was associated with such stars as Benson, Forbes-Robertson, Lewis Waller, and Dennis Eadie.

VEGA, VENTURA DE LA (1807–65), Spanish dramatist, pupil of Alberto Lista, and author of *El hombre del mundo* (1845), which continued the tradition of Moratín, in opposition to the extravagances of the Romantic Revival. It was extremely successful, and was included by Carlos de Ochoa in his volume of seven contemporary *chefs-d'œuvre*. Vega, who was at one time director of the Teatro Español, was also the author of a number of comedies (see also BRETÓN DE LOS HERREROS).

VEGA CARPIO, LOPE FÉLIX DE (1562–1635), famous Spanish playwright and the most prolific dramatist of all time, credited with over 2,000 plays, though the actual number of known titles is 725, and the existing texts about 470. This 'monster of nature'—or 'phoenix of genius', to give him another of his titles—has suffered from the quantity of his works. Several dozen authors could have become famous, dividing his output among them.

His own life-story reads like a melodrama. He was the child of humble parents, a precocious scholar, a soldier at fifteen, a member of the ill-fated Armada expedition, from which he returned safely, a clerk in minor orders, twice married, hero of many intrigues, a devoted father, a wit, a novelist, a poet, and a dramatist. There is hardly any subject on which he did not write a play, from the lives of the saints to the flimsiest of farces. He found the Spanish theatre still in its infancy, but awake to the possibilities of a new era—a true Renaissance theatre, ready to embrace all subjects within its ever-expanding boundaries. Lope ruled it as supreme master for more than fifty years. In his *Arte nuevo de hacer comedias* he fixed the form of the classic Spanish play for at least two centuries—three acts of verse dialogue in varying metres, far removed from the five acts of steady alexandrines as in the French theatre, or from the formless mingling of verse and prose as in Shakespeare. His best plays show a skilful mingling of comic and heroic elements, and hold the balance equally between the popular and the learned, a characteristic also of the earlier Spanish dramatists of Valencia and Seville. His fine, free-flowing verse, complexity of intrigue, and keen sense of the theatrically effective can still hold the stage, as was shown by a successful revival of *La dama boba* in Buenos Aires in the 1930s. A similar success might await the revival of other works much applauded in their day—*El acero de Madrid, Amar sin saber a quien, Los melindres de Belisa, Juana,* and *La moza de cántaro*. Lope de Vega excelled in the traditional Spanish cloak-and-sword plays, with their mingling of gallantry and intrigue, jealousy and devotion, the action often turning on the *pundonor*, or 'point of honour' so dear to the Spanish soul. But from a modern standpoint his greatest plays are perhaps those which dramatize the struggles of the Spanish peasantry against injustice—*El mejor alcalde el Rey, Peribáñez y el Comendador de Ocaña,* and *Fuenteovejuna,* the last hailed in Russia as the first proletarian play, and equally acclaimed, on other grounds, in London. The influence of this many-sided genius was felt not only in his own country, but all over Europe. Lord Holland (whose account of the life and writings of Lope de Vega was published in 1806) said that he never began to read a play by Lope without having to continue feverishly to the end, and was of the opinion that, without the inspiration and example of Lope de Vega, Corneille and Molière would not have written their masterpieces.

VELTEN, JOHANNES (1640–95), German actor, a man of culture who studied at the universities of Wittenberg and Leipzig, but deserted science for the stage. There is a theatrical tradition that he was attracted to acting by taking part in an undergraduate production of Corneille's *Polyeucte,* but Mantzius points out that this is presumed to have taken place in 1669, when Velten was long past the age of an undergraduate and indeed had probably been a member of Carl Andreas Paulsen's troupe for some years. Here he remained, touring in the usual heterogenous repertory of the time, to which he added translations of some of Molière's plays, and, in 1686, a version of *Hamlet* as *Der bestrafte Brüdermord*. In 1678, having married the daughter of an actor, he took over the company himself and managed it until his death, when it was carried on by his wife Catharina Elizabeth Velten. Under different names, and with many fluctuations of fortune, this company held together until in 1771, after passing through the hands of Caroline Neuber, Schönemann, Koch, and Ackermann, it came under the leadership of Schröder.

VENICE THEATRE, NEW YORK, see CENTURY THEATRE (2).

VENIER [VERNIER], MARIE (*fl.* 1590–1619), the first French actress to be known by name. She was the daughter of Pierre Venier, a provincial actor-manager who established himself at the Foire St. Germain in 1600, and later played at the Hôtel d'Argent on payment of a daily levy to the Confraternity of the

Passion, holders of the monopoly of acting in Paris. At that time Marie Venier, with her husband Laporte, also an actor, was at the Hôtel de Bourgogne with Valleran-Lecomte, with whom she had probably already appeared in the provinces. According to contemporary accounts Marie Venier was a beautiful and accomplished actress, at her best as tragedy queens.

VENNE, LOTTIE (1852–1928), English actress, best known for her work in burlesque under Ada Swanborough at the Strand Theatre, where she played from 1873 to 1877. She then turned to straight comedy, and was seen in *The Young Mrs. Winthrop, The Magistrate,* and other plays, though she continued intermittently to appear in musical comedy and farce. She was an excellent mimic, and her imitations of Marion Terry in *Lady Windermere's Fan* and of Lady Tree in *Hamlet* made the fortune of Brookfield's travesty, *The Poet and the Puppets*. A fine-looking woman, high-spirited and good-humoured, she had the good sense to take over in later years the parts of saucy matrons in the place of her earlier soubrette roles, and thus retained the affection of her public and the respect of the critics. Her son and daughter were both on the stage, the latter being the wife of the actor James Welch.

VERBRUGGEN, MRS., see MOUNTFORT (2).

VERE STREET THEATRE, LONDON, originally a tennis-court built in 1634, and belonging to, or named after, a man called Gibbon, stood in Clare Market. The out-of-work actors tried to play there after the closing of the theatres, but were betrayed by one of the company, whom a contemporary calls 'an ill Beest . . . causing the poor actors to be routed by the soldiery'. In 1656 Davenant gave one of his entertainments with music and dancing there. In 1660 Killigrew converted it into a theatre, opening with *Henry IV, Part I,* on 8 Nov., and used it while he got ready to build Drury Lane. As he had a Royal Charter and his company was the King's, Vere Street has been regarded by some as the first Theatre Royal; but that title properly belongs to Drury Lane, to which Killigrew moved in 1663. Vere Street under George Jolly was then used as a Nursery, or training-school for young actors, by both Killigrew and Davenant (who later had his own) until 1671. From 1675 to 1682 it was a Nonconformist meeting-house. It later became a carpenter's shop and a slaughterhouse, and was finally destroyed by fire in 1809. On its site another playhouse stands to-day—the Stoll Theatre (London Opera House).

w. m. p.

VERGERIO, PIER PAOLO (1370–1444), an early Italian dramatist, author of *Paulus,* the first extant Italian comedy (since one believed to have been written earlier by Petrarch is lost). Written in Latin, probably at Bologna in 1389, where Vergerio was a student, it is a study of contemporary university life, a satiric, licentious comedy which owes little to the classics, though it has some superficial resemblance to the comedies of Terence (see ITALY, 1 *b*).

VERNEUIL, see LA GRANGE (3).

VESTRIS [VESTRI]. An Italian family of dancers and actors which has ramifications in France and England. The first to come into prominence was (1) GAETAN APOLLINE BALTHASAR (1728–1808), who went to Paris in 1747 with his parents and numerous brothers and sisters, all but one of whom were dancers and actresses. Two years later he appeared at the Paris Opéra, and was immediately successful. He joined the regular ballet company there, and remained with it until his retirement. Fulsomely called 'le dieu de la danse' by one of his brothers, the nickname stuck, not without some gentle irony in its application, since he was as vain as he was talented. He was a difficult, quarrelsome man, often in trouble with the authorities and the audience, but all his faults were forgiven him because of the excellence of his dancing. He was twice married, the second time in his old age to the dancer Anne Heinel (1752–1808), who had been one of his bitterest opponents in her early days at the Paris Opéra. His son by another dancer, Marie Allard (1742–1802), (2) MARIE JEAN AUGUSTIN, known as Auguste (1760–1842), was trained by his parents, and at the age of twelve made his début at the Opéra with his father. He joined the company in 1775, and went with his father to London in 1781, when they were pelted with orange-peel because the price of the seats had been raised, and later applauded to the echo for the beauty of their performance. After the Revolution he went again to London, and was ballet-master at the King's Theatre in 1791 when Haydn's compositions were given there. Later he returned to Paris, and taught. Taglioni was one of his pupils. His son (3) (AUGUSTE) ARMAND (1788–1825) made his début at the Opéra in 1800, dancing with his father and grandfather. He later went to London, where he married Lucia Elizabeth Bartolozzi, whom he left in 1820. Eighteen years later she married the younger Mathews (see MATHEWS, 3). The brother of Gaetan, (4) ANGELO MARIE GASPARD (1730–1809), was a mediocre dancer, who was tolerated at the Opéra and later at the Comédie-Italienne on account of his name. In 1766, while at Stuttgart in the troupe of the Duke of Württemburg, he married (5) FRANÇOISE GOURGAUD (1743–1804). She was the daughter of a provincial actor, her brother and sister being members of the Comédie-Française (see DUGAZON). She herself made her début there in 1768, and though not an outstanding actress, she had some success. She engaged in constant quarrels with her rival, Marie Blanche Sainval, whose début at the Comédie-Française she managed by her intrigues to get retarded for

several years. An indiscretion on the part of Sainval later caused her to be exiled, and Mme Vestris was blamed. It took her some time to regain the favour of the public. On the outbreak of the Revolution she left the stage, but returned and continued to act until just before her death. She created a number of tragic heroines, and was much admired by Voltaire in his *Irène* (1778). She was also good as Catherine de' Medici in *Charles IX* (1789), and in the death scene of *Gabrielle de Vergi* (1772). She was not tall, but was very dignified, and owed much to the teaching of Lekain. In later years the passionate temper of her acting became much modified, and Janin said of her, 'Toute froide et toute blanche, cette femme avait du feu dans les yeux et pas de sang dans ses veines.' She was a great admirer of the work of André Chénier, and managed to secrete a copy of his *Timoléon* when he had been ordered to destroy it.

VEZIN. (1) HERMANN (1829–1910), English actor, born in the U.S.A., who came to England in 1850 and made his first appearance on the stage at York. After further experience in the provinces and two years in America, he took the Surrey Theatre, London, and appeared there in a fine series of classic parts. Phelps then engaged him for Sadler's Wells, and by 1861 he was recognized as an outstanding actor in both comedy and tragedy, being excellent as Macbeth, Othello, Jaques, Sir Peter Teazle, and Dr. Primrose, which he was the first to play. He also appeared as Iago to the Othello of John McCullough, and was with Irving at the Lyceum, making his last appearance under Tree on 7 Apr. 1909. A scholarly, intellectual man, of small stature, with clear-cut features, a dignified bearing, and a very lovely voice, he lacked only warmth and personal magnetism. In 1863 he married an Australian actress (2) JANE ELIZABETH THOMSON (1827–1902), formerly the wife of the American actor, Charles Young. She was on the stage as a child, and was an admirable actress, with much romantic fervour and a sweet voice. She made her first appearance in England in 1857, at Sadler's Wells, and from 1858 to 1875 she had few rivals as an exponent of Shakespearian and poetic drama.

VICE, see FOOL.

VICENTE, GIL (*c.* 1465–*c.* 1539), by trade a goldsmith, maker of the famous monstrance in the church at Belén and one of the founders of modern Spanish drama. He wrote a number of plays in Portuguese (his native language), some in Spanish, and some in a mixture of the two. His first play was given in 1502 before the Portuguese king, Manuel el Grande. He became the sole purveyor of drama to the Court and soon became famous. Erasmus is said to have learnt Portuguese solely in order to read him in the original. His poetry is fresh and spirited, with a strong Renaissance feeling for the beauties of nature. The themes of his longer plays are courtly, while his shorter farces are full of colour and gaiety, and are perfect examples of their kind. He was helped in their composition and representation by his daughter, Paula, a good actress much esteemed in Lisbon.

VICTORIA PALACE, LONDON, opposite Victoria Station. This was for many years a popular music-hall, having formerly been the Standard, Pimlico. In 1930 Archie de Bear produced a successful revue there, called *Chelsea Follies*. In 1934 a most curious production took place there, Reynolds's *Young England*, which, although meant to be a serious patriotic play, was treated with ridicule, and drew vast crowds who came to laugh, jeer, and interrupt the performance. It went to various other theatres, including Daly's, where a riot occurred which endangered the licence of the theatre. In 1935 Seymour Hicks turned the Victoria Palace into a proper theatre, and produced *The Miracle Man*, following it with revivals. Lupino Lane succeeded him, and on 16 Dec. 1937 presented a musical play called *Me and My Girl*, which ran for 1,065 performances up to the temporary war-time closing of the theatres in Sept. 1939. The play was afterwards revived, and Lupino Lane did other productions there, as did Jack Hylton. (See also MUSIC-HALL.)   W. M. P.

VICTORIA THEATRE, LONDON, see OLD VIC.

VIENNA. Austria, whose dramatists are dealt with under Germany and their own names (see also HUNGARY, and, for Bohemia, CZECHOSLOVAKIA), had, in spite of the use of the German language, a distinct theatrical tradition of her own, centring upon Vienna. The first theatre building there was the Kärntnerthor, followed in 1741 by the famous Burgtheater, first known as the Theater an der Burg, later as the Hofburgtheater. In 1776 it was reorganized by the Emperor Joseph II, who made it a National Theatre on the lines of the Comédie-Française, which it has remained ever since. It had a long succession of distinguished directors, of whom the best was Heinrich Laube (1806–84). Under him the company, which included such actors as Sonnenthal, later a director, Lewinsky, Bauermeister, and Charlotte Wolter, gave some fine performances, particularly of Shakespeare. In later years the Burgtheater, which was partially destroyed by bombing in the 1939–45 war, became somewhat out of date, and tended to adhere strictly to a classical repertory and a safe and somewhat uninspired policy in acting and direction. Among other theatres in Vienna are the Opera, also destroyed by bombing, the Theater an der Wien, home of light opera, the Redoutensaal, used for intimate classical and modern drama, and Max Reinhardt's old Theater in der Josephstadt.

VIEUX-COLOMBIER, THÉÂTRE DU, PARIS, see COPEAU.

VIGANÒ, SALVATORE (1769–1821), a pupil of Noverre, and ballet-master at La Scala, Milan,

where he produced vast spectacular ballets, assisted by the splendid designs prepared for him by Sanquirico. He was the first to make the *corps de ballet* a group of individuals rather than a perfectly regimented but lifeless whole. His wife, Maria Medina, an excellent dancer, caused a sensation in 1793 when she appeared at Vienna in a simple clinging muslin dress, with her hair hanging loose, a reform attempted unsuccessfully by Marie Sallé in 1734, and finally established by Isadora Duncan in the 1920s.

VIGARANI. (1) GASPARE (1586–1663), Italian stage-designer and machinist, inventor of many new stage tricks and superb effects. He was working in Modena when in 1659 he was called to Paris by Mazarin to supervise the entertainments to be given in honour of Louis XIV's approaching marriage. For these he built the Salle des Machines in the Tuileries, and designed its stage machinery. As Molière's first theatre, in the Petit-Bourbon, was then being demolished, Vigarani claimed the scenery and machinery for use in his new theatre, and burnt it all, probably in the hope of destroying the work of his rival Torelli. After his death his son (2) CARLO, who had been working with him, was responsible for the mechanics of *Les Plaisirs de l'île enchantée*, an entertainment given at Versailles with the collaboration of Molière and Lully. He became a naturalized Frenchman, lived in an apartment in the Louvre, and was frequently employed by Lully for operatic spectacles. His dates are uncertain; he was still alive in 1693 and his widow, a Frenchwoman, in 1716.

VIGSZINHÁZ THEATRE, see HUNGARY.

VILLAURRUTIA, XAVIER, see SOUTH AMERICA, I.

VILLIERS. (1) CLAUDE DESCHAMPS DE (1600–81), French actor and author of several plays, including farces and a version of Don Juan which may have had some influence on Molière. He played in farce himself as Philippin, his name being often given to the character he was to portray. He was a member of a company formed in 1624 which included Lenoir and Montdory, and with his second wife (2) MARGUERITE BÉGUET (?–1670) was with them again when they came to Paris in 1630. Husband and wife remained at the Théâtre du Marais until the retirement of Montdory, when they went to the Hôtel de Bourgogne. Both were excellent actors, and the wife is best remembered for having been the first to play the part of Chimène in *Le Cid* (1636). De Villiers is caricatured in Molière's *Impromptu de Versailles* (1664) together with the rest of the company of the Hôtel de Bourgogne. He retired from the stage on the death of his wife, who had not acted since about 1664. (3) JEAN DE VILLIERS (1648–1701), who as a child appeared with the Raisin children in the Troupe du Dauphin, and was a member of the

Comédie-Française from 1679 to 1680, was possibly related to the above. He was better in comedy than in tragedy, and was much admired in the part of a ridiculous marquis. He married Catherine Raisin, who gave up the stage on her marriage in 1679. Their son and daughter were both actors.

VILLIERS, GEORGE, Duke of Buckingham, see BUCKINGHAM.

VILNA TROUPE. This company was founded at Vilna in 1916 by David Hermann (1876–1930) as the Union of Yiddish Dramatic Artists (called Fado, from the initials of the original name), with the intention of continuing Peretz Hirschbein's reform of the Yiddish stage. The first production was Sholom Asch's *Landsleute*, which was immediately successful. The company attracted the attention of Jewish intellectuals in the German Army of Occupation, and in 1917, partly on their advice, moved to Warsaw, where Hermann scored an immense success with his production, a month after the author's death, of Ansky's *The Dybbuk*, in Yiddish. This was taken on tour to Berlin, London, and New York. Returning to Warsaw in 1924 the company found that they had lost their theatre, and at the end of the year they moved to Vienna. There they split up, one section going to America, where it joined forces with Maurice Schwartz, the other, led by Hermann, going to Rumania. This latter group returned to Warsaw in 1927 and remained there until Hermann's death. The repertory of the Vilna Troupe was at first fairly extensive, and included a number of Yiddish classics, but later it became associated with and entirely dependent on a single play, *The Dybbuk*, a limitation which probably accounts for its decline.   E. H.

VINCENT, MARY ANN (née FARLOW) (1818–87), American actress, born in England, where she joined a provincial company and married an actor named Vincent. She went with her husband in 1846 to act at the National Theatre, Boston, where he died shortly afterwards. She continued to act as Mrs. J. R. Vincent, and in 1852 joined the stock company at the Boston Museum, staying there thirty-five years, first as its leading comedienne and later in duenna and old-lady parts. She was exceedingly popular, and a great personality, being described as a 'jolly, chubby little figure, with a pleasant voice, kindhearted, fond of animals and children'. At her jubilee in 1885 she appeared in two of her finest roles, Mrs. Hardcastle and Mrs. Malaprop. The Vincent Memorial Hospital in Boston was founded in her memory.

VIRGINIA COMPANY OF COMEDIANS, the name given by Walter Murray and Thomas Kean to the troupe with which they toured the southern cities of America in 1753, in opposition to that of the elder Hallam.

VISĀKHADATTA, see INDIA.

VISHNEVSKY, VSEVOLOD VITALEVICH (1900–), Soviet dramatist, of whom it has been said, that 'the fanaticism of the revolution sings through his plays'. After three plays dealing with the Civil War, he wrote *The Optimistic Tragedy*, which was produced with great success by Taïrov at the Kamerny Theatre in 1934. It dealt with the work and final death in battle of a woman commissar with the Red Fleet during the early days of the Soviet régime. The part of the heroine was played by Taïrov's wife, Alice Koonen. The play was published in *Four Soviet Plays* (1937) in a translation by H. G. Scott and Robert S. Carr. Since then Vishnevsky has had several plays produced, but nothing equal to *The Optimistic Tragedy*. In 1943, however, he collaborated with Alexander Kron, author of *Depth Prospecting*, and Alexander Azarov, in a musical play, *Wide Spreads the Sea*, and also wrote *At the Walls of Leningrad*. Both these plays were produced at the Baltic Fleet Theatre, and seem to have been well received.

VITAL SPARK, THE, see HILL, JENNY.

VITRUVIUS POLLIO, MARCUS (*fl.* 70–15 B.C.), the Roman author of a treatise in ten books, *De Architectura*, which deals among other things with theatre construction, illustrated by diagrams. Discovered in manuscript at St. Gall in 1414, it was printed in 1511 and translated into Italian in 1521. It had a great influence on the building of Renaissance theatres (see also ACOUSTICS, ARCHITECTURE, MACHINERY, and SCENERY).

VOKES, a family of English pantomimists, popular in England and America, consisting of (1) FREDERICK MORTIMER (1846–88), (2) JESSIE CATHERINE BIDDULPH (1851–84), (3) VICTORIA (1853–94), and (4) ROSINA (1854–94). Children of a theatrical costumier in business at 19 Henrietta Street, London, they played child parts on the legitimate stage, and first appeared as a family group at Edinburgh in 1861, their numbers augmented by (5) WALTER FAWDON (?–1904), who also took the name of Vokes. They toured for some years, and in 1865 appeared at the Lyceum in *Humpty-Dumpty*. From 1869 to 1879 they were the mainstay of the Drury Lane pantomime, where, says Disher in *Clowns and Pantomimes*, '[the Vokes] set the claims of the fairy-tale high and made an attempt to keep the humour within its limits'. They were also seen at the Adelphi and elsewhere in two amusing burlesque and pantomimic sketches, *The Belles of the Kitchen* and *A Bunch of Berries*, and made their first appearance in America in the latter in 1871. The first member of the family to break away was Rosina, 'the pick of the bunch' according to a contemporary critic. Her place was taken by Fred's wife, Bella, daughter of 'Pony' Moore of Minstrelsy fame, while Rosina married the composer Cecil Clay, and after some years in retirement went back to the stage. In 1885 she took a light comedy and burlesque company to the United States and Canada, and became a great favourite there. The family group broke up finally on the death of Jessie.

VOLKOV, FEDOR GREGORYEVICH (1729–63), a Russian actor of great talent, and one of the founders of the Russian national theatre. He was the son of a merchant, and was born in Kostroma. He organized an amateur theatre in Yaroslavl which gave performances in the houses of the merchants, and in Jan. 1752 was summoned with his troupe to St. Petersburg, where he gave a private performance before the Court. In 1754 Volkov, with Dmitrevsky, a member of his company, was sent to the Cadet College for the sons of the nobility, where he was trained as an actor for the Court theatre, and received in addition a good general education. He appeared at Court again in 1755, and in August of the following year joined what may be regarded as the first professional Russian theatrical company, organized by the dramatist Sumarokov. Volkov became its leading actor and Sumarokov's chief assistant. At first the company was hampered by lack of money, but its production soon attracted the attention of those Court circles later responsible for the overthrow of Peter III and the accession of Catherine the Great. Volkov and his brother, who was also an actor, took part in the revolt, and were rewarded with Court offices. Fedor Volkov also organized the celebrations in honour of Catherine's coronation in Moscow, and it was there, while directing a street masquerade entitled *The Triumph of Minerva*, that he caught cold and died.

VOLTAIRE [FRANÇOIS MARIE AROUET] (1694–1778), has an important place in the history of the theatre, the only aspect of his many-sided activity which need concern us here. Before his visit to England in 1726, a turning-point in his life, he had written one good tragedy, *Œdipe* (1718), which was successful enough to be parodied by Dominique at the Théâtre-Italien, and two mediocre ones, *Artémire* (1720) and *Mariamne* (1724). The latter promised well, but failed when a joke from the pit as Adrienne Lecouvreur drank poison set the audience laughing. A few months later Voltaire, who had by this time adopted the name by which he is known, an anagram of Arouet l(e) i(eune), rewrote it, and it was then successful. The firstfruits of his visit to England, during which he discovered Shakespeare, and appreciated him as far as was possible for a Frenchman raised in an entirely different tradition, were *Brutus* (1730), inspired by *Julius Caesar*, and *Zaïre* (1732), which owes something to *Othello*. The latter was extremely successful and ranks with the later *Mérope* as Voltaire's best play. In the same year as his famous *Lettres philosophiques* appeared *Adélaïde du Guesclin* (1734), which failed after two performances. It also was rewritten and given eighteen years later as *Amélie, ou le Duc de Foix* with some success, while in yet another thirteen years, under its

original title, and in its original form, it was extremely successful, a reversal of fortune which afforded Voltaire much amusement. This constant remodelling of old plays, of which *Mariamne* and *Mérope* are further examples, shows Voltaire's continual preoccupation with the theatre, a passion which remained with him all his life, and to which he owed many of his happiest hours. He was an indefatigable promoter of theatrical performances, himself no mean actor, and he built several private theatres, having the means to indulge so expensive a taste. The best of these was at Ferney, his last home. Meanwhile *Mérope* (1743), written for Mlle Dumesnil, and the first French play at which the audience called for the author, had been preceded by *La Mort de César* (1735), *Alzire* and *L'Enfant prodigue* (both 1736)—the last pure eighteenth-century *drame*, with comedy and tragedy mingling, a practice Voltaire later condemned—and *Mahomet, ou le fanatisme* (1741), first given at Lille by La Noue, who successfully played the name-part in Paris. By this time Voltaire's enemies had opposed to him as France's greatest dramatist the aged writer of tragedies, Crébillon. Voltaire's reply to that was to take the subjects of six of Crébillon's plays—though not his best—and write on them himself. The first, *Sémiramis*, was given in 1748, and Voltaire himself later admitted that it contributed to the continued decline of French classical tragedy by its lavish use of spectacular effects. But it had one important consequence, since its crowd scenes and spectacular effects led the author to insist on the removal of the audience from the stage, a reform long overdue which finally took place in 1759.

Voltaire's next play, *Nanine* (1749), based on Richardson's *Pamela*, is again a *drame*, and well illustrates the dangers of an excess of sensibility. From this period dates Voltaire's friendship with the great actor Lekain, who made his début in *Rome sauvée* (1754), another rival to Crébillon, as was *Oreste* (1749). Voltaire had by this time left France for the Court of Frederick the Great, and several years elapsed before his next play was seen in Paris. This was *L'Orphelin de la Chine* (1755), followed by *Tancrède* (1760), Voltaire's last good play, for six further tragedies are negligible, though one, *Irène* (1778), deserves a passing mention, since it was to see it that Voltaire made his last journey to Paris, dying there in a moment of triumph, for the audience applauded the author, if not the play. Of four comedies written in this last period one, *L'Écossaise* (1760), owed its success to its satire, while *Le Droit du seigneur* (1762) failed completely. The others were only given on the less exacting stage of Ferney.

Voltaire was not a great dramatist, nor a great poet, but his plays show a breadth of treatment and force of description hardly surpassed in his own day. He had the gift of attracting and interesting his audience, and if his works are now never revived, the fault lies in his facility, which led him to write too carelessly and too much, and in the fact that he lived in an age of transition, reflecting its momentary preoccupations. He considered himself a traditionalist, yet contributed not a little to the decay of French tragedy. The form of his best plays is seventeenth century, the contents eighteenth. Many of his later works were marred by the introduction of philosophical propaganda, as in *Les Guèbres*, which was never acted. He inaugurated the romantic melodrama that was to flourish in the early nine-teenth century, and to him, rather than to the Romantics, goes the honour of having first introduced local colour into the theatre. By slackening the rigid form of tragedy to something more acceptable to the larger but less educated audience for which he was writing he drove tragedy a step farther on the road which led to melodrama, *drame bourgeois*, and *opéra-comique*.

V.Ts.P.S., Moscow, see TRADES UNIONS THEATRE.

W

WADE, ALLAN (1881–   ), English actor, manager, and producer. He was one of the four original founders of the Phoenix Society and responsible for the productions of nearly all the plays staged by it. He made his first appearance on the stage in 1904, and shortly afterwards was with Frank Benson, leaving him in 1906 to become assistant to Granville-Barker at the Court Theatre, where he was instrumental in arranging the first visit of the Irish Players in 1909. Most of his work has been done as play-reader and producer for various managements, but he has appeared in a number of plays both in London and New York, and in 1935 he was appointed adjudicator in the Canadian Dominion Drama Festival. Author of a *Bibliography of W. B. Yeats* (1908), he was also responsible for the translations, done by the Stage Society, of *Intermezzo* (1934) and *The Infernal Machine* (1935).

WAGGON STAGE, see STAGE, 5.

WAGNER, RICHARD (1813–83), see GERMANY, 5 and OPERA, 11.

WAITS, a lesser order of minstrels attached to the service of a noble household, or to the municipal corporations. The name survives in the term applied to the modern itinerant, though usually local, carol-singers of Christmas.

WAKEFIELD CYCLE, see ENGLAND, 1 and MYSTERY PLAY.

WALCOT. (1) CHARLES MELTON (1816–68), American actor, born in London, where he trained as an architect, going in 1837 to the United States. His handsome person and fine voice turned his thoughts to the stage, as did his marriage to an actress in New York. He made his first appearance in 1842, and was for many years connected with Mitchell's famous Olympic, both as an eccentric comedian and as a dramatist, writing a number of topical burlesques which have not survived, but which were popular in their day. From 1852 to 1859 he was one of the leading members of Wallack's company, where he played such parts as Charles Surface and Bob Acres. He had an alert, intelligent face with a high domed forehead, which was inherited by his son (2) CHARLES MELCOT (1840–1921); but whereas the father had side-whiskers and in his later years looked like a venerable clergyman, the son wore a moustache and the jovial expression of a genial British squire. The latter first went on the stage as Brown, but later resumed his own name, and in 1863 married (3) ISABELLA NICKINSON (1847–1906), an accomplished actress who has for many years with him at the Walnut Street Theatre, Philadelphia. They then joined Daniel Frohman's stock company at the Lyceum, where from 1887 onwards they appeared in comic or dignified elderly parts in most of the Lyceum successes. Walcot, who like his wife was beloved by the public and his fellow actors alike, bridged the gap between the old romantic actors and the newer realism, and brought to the modern Lyceum plays an intelligent interest combined with the authority of the old school of comedy.

WALDIS, BURKHART (*fl.* sixteenth century), at one time a monk, later author of a virulent anti-Catholic play in support of the Reformation given at Riga (see GERMANY, 2).

WALDORF THEATRE, NEW YORK, on the south side of 50th Street, between Sixth and Seventh Avenues. This opened on 20 Oct. 1926 and had its first hit with a musical comedy in the following year, while in 1929 and 1930 it was used for the Little Theatre Tournament. In 1930 also came Leo Bulgakov's production of *The Lower Depths* as *At the Bottom*, which had 72 performances, and was followed by five performances of *The Seagull*. A revival of *An American Tragedy* in 1931 ran for 17 weeks, and *Dangerous Corner* in 1933 was the last production at this theatre, which became a cinema, and was later demolished.   G. F.

For the Waldorf Theatre, London, see STRAND THEATRE (2).

WALKING GENTLEMAN—LADY, see STOCK COMPANY.

WALKLEY, ALFRED BINGHAM (1855–1926), English dramatic critic, on *The Times* from 1900 to 1926. Previously he had written criticisms for the *Speaker*, the *National Observer*, and the *Star*. He republished a volume of his earlier criticisms as *Playhouse Impressions* (1892); and selections from his *The Times* criticisms as *Drama and Life* (1907), *Pastiche and Prejudice* (1921), *More Prejudice* (1923), and *Still More Prejudice* (1925).

Walkley in an essay on criticism wrote: 'Your critic is a sedentary person with a literary bias. His instinct is to bring to the play the calm lotos-eating mind with which he day-dreams over a book in his library. To this frame of mind the boisterous flesh-and-blood element of the actor comes as a rude distraction.' No working theatre critic could live up to the letter of this declaration, yet it gives some indication of Walkley's critical quality. His criticisms were more literary than theatrical. He devoted more of his space to the play than to the players: although he was always critical of what he called 'coterie criticism'.

Walkley was a cultured and conscientious writer who took himself and his duties seriously. He wrote as well as the theatre of his time demanded; and this, in view of the productive period in which he worked, is high praise. In 1903 he delivered three lectures on dramatic criticism at the Royal Institution. These were published in the same year, and they sum up Walkley's outlook on the profession to which he brought an urbane distinction.   T. C. K.

WALLACE, EDGAR (1875–1932), English journalist, novelist, and playwright, the first to make a speciality of detective drama. Many of his plays were based on his own books, the twentieth-century equivalent of Mrs. Radcliffe's 'horror' novels. Among the most successful were *The Ringer* (1926), *The Terror* (1927), *The Squeaker* (1928), *The Flying Squad* (1929), *On the Spot* and *Smoky Cell* (both 1930), and *The Case of the Frightened Lady* (1931). Wallace showed extraordinary perfection of detail, narrative skill, and inside knowledge of police methods and criminal psychology, the fruit of his apprenticeship as a crime reporter.

WALLACE, NELLIE (1870–1948), one of the greatest women comedians of the English music-halls. She first appeared at Birmingham in 1888 as a clog-dancer, and later toured as one of the three Sisters Wallace. Then followed a long apprenticeship of touring in various plays before she returned to the halls as a single turn. She also appeared in revue, and in pantomime, notably as the Wicked Witch Carabosse in *The Sleeping Beauty* at the Vaudeville in 1935. One of her most famous songs was 'I Lost Georgie in Trafalgar Square'. Nellie Wallace was a mistress of the grotesque, and one of the few successful women Dames in pantomime. In private life she was Mrs. Eleanor Jane Liddy. Her husband and her only child, a daughter, predeceased her.

WALLACK, a family of actors, of English origin, important in connexion with the development of the theatre in New York. The first, (1) HENRY JOHN (1790–1870), was born in London, where his parents were leading players at Astley's Amphitheatre, and later at the Surrey. There young Wallack, with his brother and sisters, made his first appearance at an early age. In 1819 he was engaged to go to the United States, making his début at Baltimore, and first playing in New York at the Anthony Street Theatre, where he was seen in tragedy and heroic drama. In 1824 he was leading man of the Chatham Garden Theatre, but he later returned to London, and was for some years at Covent Garden, returning to New York in 1837 to manage the first Wallack Theatre, and in 1847 playing Sir Peter Teazle at the Broadway. He was later manager of the Theatre Royal, Manchester, and he made his last appearance on the stage as Falstaff in 1858. One of his sisters was popular at the Coburg Theatre, London, as Mrs. Stanley, the other married an actor named Pincott, and was the mother of Leonora, later Mrs. Alfred Wigan. His brother (2) JAMES WILLIAM (1791–1864) also made his early appearances in London, and was for several years at Drury Lane, playing such parts as Laertes, Young Absolute, Joseph Surface, Richmond, Faulconbridge, and Iago. In 1818 he made his first appearance in New York, and proved himself an actor of the school of Kemble. He was extremely handsome, with a distinguished bearing, dark hair and eyes, fine features, a rich, sonorous voice, and great vitality. He divided his time between England and the United States, and was said to have crossed the Atlantic thirty-five times. In 1837 he took over the management of the National Theatre, New York, with his elder brother as stage-manager, and when two years later it burnt down he went first to Niblo's Garden, and then on tour. He made his last appearance in London in 1851, and in the following year opened Brougham's old Lyceum, New York, as Wallack's. Elegantly redecorated, well equipped, and furnished with a good stock company in a repertory of Shakespeare and standard comedies, with some modern plays, it flourished for ten years. Wallack himself made his last stage appearance there in 1859, but continued in management, opening a new theatre on Broadway and 13th Street in 1861. His inaugural speech marked his last public appearance, and three years later he died, leaving the traditions he had established to be carried on by his nephew (3) JAMES WILLIAM (1818–73) and two nieces, Fanny and Julia, and by his son (4) JOHN JOHNSTONE (1820–88), known as Lester. James served his apprenticeship under his father and uncle, being at Covent Garden with the former, and in 1837 joined the latter's company at the National, where he rose from walking gentleman to leading juvenile. A man of rugged physique, with a deep powerful voice, he was at his best in tragedy and strong sombre drama—Macbeth, Othello, Iago, Richard III. Fagin, in a dramatization of *Oliver Twist* (1867), was one of his finest parts, and at Booth's in 1872–3 he played Mathias in *The Bells* most terrifyingly. He was not at home in comedy, except for Jaques and Mercutio. In 1865 he was a member of Wallack's stock company under his cousin, who had made his first appearances on the stage in the English provinces, first as Allan Field, later as John Lester, retaining the Lester when he eventually resumed the surname of Wallack. He was for some time in Dublin, and in 1845 played at Manchester with Helen Faucit and Charlotte Cushman. He then made his first appearance in New York at the Broadway, presented himself and his cousin in his own adaptation of *The Three Musketeers*, and in 1850 was with Burton at the Chambers Street Theatre, where he proved excellent as Aguecheek and Charles Surface. He was stage-manager for his father when the latter took over Brougham's Lyceum, and played a wide range of parts, comic and romantic. He was the real manager of the new Wallack's even before his father's death. Under him the theatre flourished until 1882, but kept to its former policy of staging mainly English plays, becoming as much identified in New York with Robertson's comedies as the Bancrofts were in London. Shakespeare, however, lapsed somewhat, Lester appearing as Benedick in 1867–8, and doing nothing further until *As You Like It* in 1880. Among the new plays produced there was Lester's own dramatization of a novel, *Rosedale* (1863), in which he gave a fine performance for many years as the hero, Elliot Grey. From about 1870 Wallack's began to feel the competition of Booth's and Daly's Theatres, but it continued on its well-bred and somewhat old-fashioned way, and was still capable of attracting such players as young H. L. Montague and Rose Coghlan, and of being redecorated in 1880 in red and gold. A year later it closed (for its later history see STAR THEATRE), and on 4 Jan. 1882 a new Wallack's opened on Broadway and Thirtieth Street with yet another revival of *The School for Scandal*. Mrs. Langtry, who was to have made her New York début at the Park on the day it was burnt down, went to Wallack's instead, and a year later melodrama, in the person of *The Silver King*, made its appearance at the home of old comedy, which was sinking fast. In 1887 Lester transferred the lease to other hands, allowing them to retain the old name, and the last stock season was given under Abbey in 1888, in which year Lester died. His memoirs were published a year later. The theatre was then leased by Palmer, but reverted to its original name in 1896 and finally closed in 1915 in a last blaze of glory with Granville-Barker's productions there of *A Midsummer Night's Dream*, *Androcles and the Lion*, and other plays. It was then demolished.

A Wallack Theatre, which flourished from 1924 until it became a cinema in 1931, was originally opened as the Lew Fields in 1904, and renamed the Hackett in 1906, James K. Hackett appearing there in 1908 in a revival of *The Prisoner of Zenda*. The same year saw the production of *Salvation Nell*, with Mrs. Fiske, and in 1911 the theatre again changed its name, this time to Harris. One of its most successful productions was *Dulcy* (1921), with Lynn Fontanne, while a year later the Theatre Guild gave twenty-four performances of *From Morn to Midnight* there.

WALLER, EMMA (1820–99), American actress, who with her husband went to New York from London, and there became one of the leading players of the day. She made her first appearance at the Walnut Street Theatre as Ophelia to her husband's Hamlet in Oct. 1857, was seen in New York the following year, and from then until her retirement in 1878 played leading roles all over the United States. A tall, stately woman, with an interesting and expressive face, she was good as Lady Macbeth, as Queen Margaret in Cibber's version of *Richard III*, which she played with Edwin Booth, as Meg Merrilies, and as Julia in *The Hunchback*. She also, in the fashion of the time, played Hamlet and Iago. After her retirement she continued to give readings in public, and was also a teacher of elocution.

WALLER. (1) LEWIS [really WILLIAM WALLER LEWIS] (1860–1915), English actor-manager, and one of the outstanding romantic actors of his day. Born in Spain, of English parents, he was an enthusiastic amateur before he went on the professional stage, making his first appearance at Toole's Theatre in 1883. During a long and varied career he appeared in a number of famous romantic parts, including Monsieur Beaucaire—perhaps the supreme example of his talent—Brigadier Gerard, and D'Artagnan. A robust and dynamic actor, with a magnificent voice, he was at his best in costume parts, and particularly in Shakespeare. His Brutus, his Faulconbridge, and particularly his Henry V, were memorable. He was one of the first so-called matinée idols, but entirely without conceit, and the hysteria of his more fervid supporters was a cause of much embarrassment to him. In modern-dress comedy he did not appear to such advantage, and *An Ideal Husband*, with which he first went into management at the Haymarket, was not a suitable medium for his particular gifts. He has, somewhat unkindly, been called 'the high-priest of dignified tushery', a two-edged tribute which has at least the merit of conceding something more than flamboyance and spectacle to his romantic productions. He married an actress, (2) FLORENCE WEST (1862–1913), sister-in-law of the dramatic critic Clement Scott, who appeared with her husband in many of his outstanding successes, notably as Miladi in *The Three Musketeers*.

W. M. P.

WALNUT STREET THEATRE, PHILADELPHIA. Built as a circus in 1809, this was first used as a playhouse in 1811, when it entered into competition with the successful and well-established Chestnut Street Theatre. It is still in use, and is the oldest playhouse in the United States. It flourished until 1829, when intense rivalry between the various managements in the city brought about the bankruptcy of them all. From then onwards it had a good stock company, which supported visiting stars, but contributed little to the development of American theatrical life, whose centre moved to New York.

WALTER, EUGENE (1874–1941), American dramatist, whose early plays, though somewhat melodramatic, seemed to point the way towards a more realistic and sober approach to social problems. The best of them were *Paid in Full* (1908) and *The Easiest Way* (1909). A later play, *Fine Feathers* (1913), was good also, but less successful. Unfortunately Walter failed to live up to his early promise, and his last plays are negligible. Among them were dramatizations of two popular novels by John Fox, Jr., *The Trail of the Lonesome Pine* (1912) and *The Little Shepherd of Kingdom Come* (1916). He was also the author of a handbook on dramatic technique, entitled *How to Write a Play* (1925).

WARD, (LUCY) GENEVIÈVE TERESA (1838–1922), an American actress equally well known in England, and, in her earlier career, as an opera singer under the name of Mme Guerrabella. While on tour in Cuba she lost her singing voice, as a result of diphtheria and overwork, and became an actress, making her début as Lady Macbeth in Manchester in 1873. The following year she appeared in London, where she achieved success in a wide variety of roles, which included Antigone, Mrs. Haller, Belvidera, Portia, and Emilia in *Othello*. A fine linguist, she played Lady Macbeth in French at the Porte-Saint-Martin in Paris, and after further appearances in London was first seen as an actress in New York in 1878. A year later she produced under her own management in London the famous *Forget-Me-Not*, which proved such a success that she played it all over the world. Playing opposite her in the original production was the young Johnston Forbes-Robertson as Sir Horace Welby. After her last visit to the United States in 1891 she joined Irving at the Lyceum, playing Queen Eleanor in *Becket*, Queen Katharine in *Henry VIII*, and Queen Margaret in *Richard III*. From 1900 onwards she played more rarely, but was seen several times with Benson's company, and shortly before her death played Queen Margaret at the Old Vic. A tall, commanding woman, with aquiline features, she bore some resemblance in her youth to Adelaide Ristori, with whom she was often compared. She was created D.B.E. in 1921.

WARDE, FREDERICK BARKHAM (1851–1935), an American actor and lecturer on Shakespeare and the drama. He was intended for the law, but in 1867 joined a small touring company, and after several years in stock companies, where he played with such stars as Irving and Adelaide Neilson, he went to Booth's Theatre, New York, making an immediate success. He remained there for three years, playing in Shakespeare with McCullough, Booth, and Charlotte Cushman, and then toured with Janauschek and the Lingards. In 1881 he began a long career of starring in his own company, mainly in Shakespeare and such old favourites as *Virginius*, *The Gladiator*, and *The Lady of Lyons*, since he was unable to find any modern plays to his taste. He did not appear on the stage after 1919, though he made several films of Shakespeare and classical novels. In 1907 he began lecturing, and in 1913 published *The Fools of Shakespeare*. He was also the author of a charming book of reminiscences, *Fifty Years of Make-Believe* (1920). He was a scholarly man, and received an Hon. D.Litt. from the University of S. California for his services to literature.

WARFIELD, DAVID (1866–1951), American actor, associated at the height of his fame with David Belasco. Warfield had been a programme-seller and later an usher at the San Francisco theatre—where Belasco incidentally spent many of his early years—and in 1888 joined a travelling company, playing Melter Moss in *The Ticket-of-Leave Man*. This failed after a week, and he went into variety, appearing in New York in 1890 in vaudeville and musical comedy. He was Karl in the original production of *The Belle of New York*, and later spent three years in a burlesque company. He was adept

at presenting the New York East Side Jew of his day, and had already given proof of fine qualities in his acting when in 1901 Belasco starred him in *The Auctioneer*. This was an instantaneous success and had a long run, but it was as the gentle, pathetic, self-sacrificing Anton von Barwig in *The Music Master* (1904) that Warfield set the seal on his growing reputation. He played nothing else, in New York and on tour, for three years. Among his later successes were Wes Bigelow in *A Grand Army Man* (1907), and the title-roles in *The Return of Peter Grimm* (1911) and *Vanderdecken* (1915). He was also seen as Shylock in Belasco's 1922 production of *The Merchant of Venice*.

WARNER, CHARLES (1846–1909), English actor, son of an actor named James Lickfold who was in Phelps's company at Sadler's Wells. Here the son made his first appearance at the age of 15, but was then put to study with an architect. The theatre soon drew him back, and he left home to play in the provinces under the name of Warner, which he later retained. He was first seen in London in 1864 as Paris in *Romeo and Juliet*, and in 1869 played Steerforth in *Little Em'ly*. Two years later he succeeded Irving as Jingle, and then toured with Adelaide Neilson. He was the first Charles Middlewick in *Our Boys* (1875), but he was at his best in melodrama, playing at the Adelphi for many years. His finest part was Coupeau in *Drink* (1879). He made his last appearance under Tree, playing Leontes to the Hermione of Ellen Terry in *The Winter's Tale* in 1906. He then went to America, where he committed suicide. Two of his children were on the stage.

WARREN. (1) WILLIAM (1767–1832), American actor, of English birth, who made his early appearances in the English provinces, where he was at one time in the same company as Thomas Jefferson. In 1788 Warren was with Tate Wilkinson, and played in support of Sarah Siddons. His real career began, however, when in 1796 he was invited by Wignell to join his Philadelphia company, and there, except for a number of short visits to New York, the rest of his life was passed. He succeeded Wignell as manager of the Chestnut Street Theatre, in partnership with William Wood, and it was under them that the great American actor Edwin Forrest made his first appearance, as Young Norval. Warren was a fine actor of old men, Sir Anthony Absolute, Old Dornton, Sir Toby Belch, Falstaff, and Sir Peter Teazle being accounted his best parts. He had a long and successful career, somewhat saddened towards the end by financial reverses and domestic sorrows, and retired in 1829, making a final farewell appearance the year before his death. He was three times married, his second wife being the famous actress Mrs. Merry, and his third the sister-in-law of the first Joseph Jefferson. His six children were all connected with the theatre, his four daughters marrying actors or managers, and one son being himself a manager and the father-in-law of the third Joseph Jefferson. The best known was (2) WILLIAM (1812–88), who spent most of his professional life at the Boston Museum. He made his first appearance at the Arch Street Theatre, Philadelphia, shortly after his father's death, as Young Norval. He then toured for some years, and was a member of several good stock companies. He was seldom seen in New York, and only once in England, in 1845. He began his long association with the Boston Museum in 1847, and remained there over forty years, becoming one of the leading citizens of the town. In his early days he acted a wide variety of parts, but later specialized in comedy, being particularly admired as Touchstone, Polonius, Bob Acres, and Sir Peter Teazle. He appeared also in a number of new plays, which his excellent acting often redeemed from mediocrity. In 1882 he celebrated his jubilee, playing Dr. Pangloss and Sir Peter Teazle, and in 1883 retired after playing Old Eccles in *Caste*, to spend the rest of his life pleasantly and happily in the company of his many friends. He was never married. It was said of him that 'his acting seems the fine flower of careful culture, as well as the free outcome of a large intelligence and native genius'.

WASHINGTON SQUARE PLAYERS, NEW YORK, see THEATRE GUILD.

WATER RATS, THE GRAND ORDER OF, a British association of members of the music-hall profession which originated in 1889 from an up-river (Thames) party to celebrate the successes of the Water Rat, a racing pony. Joe Elvin was a prime mover in the formation of the Society. Its present name was adopted in 1890, the objects being Philanthropy, Conviviality, and Social Intercourse. It has raised large sums for needy artistes and for public charities.

WATTS, Jr., RICHARD (1898–   ), American dramatic critic, who was born in Parkersburg, West Virginia, and attended Columbia University. He was a reporter on *The Brooklyn Eagle* in 1922 and in 1924 joined *The Herald-Tribune* as film critic. He was one of the first Americans to write seriously of the films, and his work in that field has historic as well as critical value. In 1936 he became *The Herald-Tribune* dramatic critic, though prior to that he had acted as assistant dramatic critic to the late Percy Hammond in addition to writing on the cinema. During the Second World War he served in the OWI in China and in Ireland and is now dramatic critic of *The New York Post.*   T. Q. C.

WEBB, JOHN (1611–72), English artist. He was a pupil of Inigo Jones, and was employed by Davenant to design and paint scenery for his productions, beginning with *The Siege of Rhodes.* For this Webb prepared landscapes showing the general layout of the town and harbour, based probably on actual engravings of the scene. In the Epilogue to *The World in the Moon* Settle emphasizes the native origin

of his elaborate scenery, in contrast to the French fashion of the time, with his play on the scene-painter's name, ''Tis all home-spun Cloth; All from an English Web'.

WEBER AND FIELDS' NEW MUSIC-HALL, NEW YORK, see FORTY-FOURTH STREET THEATRE.

WEBSTER. (1) BENJAMIN NOTTINGHAM (1797–1882), English actor, manager, and dramatist, descended from a long line of theatrical and musical people. He had numerous brothers and half-brothers, all of whom were connected with the stage, one of them, Frederick (1802–78), being stage-manager at the Haymarket for many years. Frederick's grandchild, Florence Ann (1860–99), who was an actress and dancer, married George Lupino. Ben himself was first a dancer, playing Harlequin and Pantaloon in the provinces and at Drury Lane. He then took to broad comedy, proving himself a useful actor, and was with Mme Vestris at the Olympic. In 1837 he became lessee of the Haymarket, which he managed for sixteen years, engaging all the best actors of the day and putting on many notable plays, in which he himself frequently appeared. In 1844 he took over the Adelphi as well, and was associated with Mme Celeste, and with Dion Boucicault, collaborating with the latter in two plays. He made an adaptation of *The Cricket on the Hearth*, in which he appeared with great success as John Peerybingle, but his finest part was Triplet in *Masks and Faces*, which he produced at both the Haymarket and the Adelphi in 1852. He opened the New Adelphi in 1859, and continued in management until his retirement in 1874. He retained his faculties to the end, and some of his latest parts were outstanding. In his own line as a character actor he was unsurpassed in his own day, but he had little liking for farce, in spite of having written a number of successful ones, and tempered his comedy with a somewhat grim humour. Two of his children were on the stage, and his namesake, by profession a barrister, wrote a number of plays, mainly melodramatic, none of which has survived. The first Ben's grandson (2) BENJAMIN (1864–1947), who had three sisters on the stage, was intended for his father's profession, the law, but deserted it for the theatre. He made his first appearances with Hare and Kendal, and was subsequently with Irving at the Lyceum and on tour in the United States. He was also in the companies of Alexander, Ellen Terry, and Boucicault, and appeared in the plays of Shaw, Shakespeare, Pinero, Barrie, and others, including *Richard of Bordeaux* and *Mr. Pim Passes By.* On the outbreak of war in 1939 he went to America, where his reputation stood as high as in England, and remained there till his death, making his last appearance on Broadway as Montague in *Romeo and Juliet* with Laurence Olivier and Vivien Leigh. In 1892 he married (3) MAY WHITTY (1865–1948), who made her first appearance at the Court Theatre, London, in 1881. Under her maiden name she was for many years an outstanding figure of the English and American stages, and she and her husband both had distinguished careers in films also. In 1918 she was made Dame Commander of the British Empire for work in connexion with the war. Her daughter (4) MARGARET (1905–) was on the stage for some years, making her first appearance in 1917, and her adult début in 1924 with Sybil Thorndike in *The Trojan Women*. She was a member of Fagan's Oxford Repertory Company, toured with Ben Greet, and was with the Old Vic 1929–30. In 1936 she went to New York and, while continuing to act, has made an outstanding reputation as a producer, particularly of Shakespeare, on which subject she has written a book arising out of her experiences, *Shakespeare without Tears*. She has made numerous lecture tours in the United States and supervised the Shakespearian productions at the New York World's Fair in 1939.

WEBSTER, JOHN (?–1634), English dramatist, whose fame rests almost entirely on two plays, *The White Devil* (1612) and *The Duchess of Malfi* (1614). Both are founded on Italian *novelle* and are passionate dramas of love and political intrigue in Renaissance Italy, compound of crude horror and sublime poetry. Indeed, in the latter respect Webster approached Shakespeare more nearly than any of his contemporaries, and both these plays have held the stage down to the present day. They provide scope for great acting and fine settings, and in the category of poetic drama remained unsurpassed by any later work, except that of Otway, until a new conception of tragedy was imported into European literature by Ibsen. Webster's other work is of little importance. Apart from *Appius and Virginia* (c. 1608) and *The Devil's Law Case* (1623), his other plays, including some now lost, were written in collaboration, chiefly with Dekker. It has been suggested that Webster had a hand in Tourneur's *Revenger's Tragedy*, but there is no proof of this. Practically nothing is known of his life, and Chambers has surmised that he may have come late to play-writing and previously have been an actor, possibly the John Webster who appears among the English Comedians in Germany under Browne in 1596.

WEDEKIND, FRANK (1864–1918), German dramatist and actor, who, after working as a journalist, and secretary to a circus, appeared in cabaret in songs which he had written and composed. He then formed a theatrical company, with himself and Gertrud Eysoldt as chief actors, and toured in a repertory of his own plays. These, which show the influence of Hauptmann and the new realistic school of drama, nevertheless in their fantasy and symbolism point the way towards expressionism. In fierce revolt against the secrecy imposed on adolescents in sex matters he wrote *Die junge Welt* (1890) and *Frühlings Erwachen* (1891), both dealing with the problems of youth, while in *Der Erdgeist* (1895) and its sequel *Die Büchse*

der Pandora (1903) he portrays sex in its most raw and lustful aspects. Here, and in later plays, his sex-ridden males and females, his gentlemen crooks, as in *Der Marquis von Keith* (1900), and his grotesque yet vital cranks, in *Hidalla* (1904), are typical of that feverish, violent, almost demoniac spirit which preluded the catastrophe of 1914.

WEIMAR, a German town important in theatre history because of its association with Goethe. He first went there in 1775 as a young man, and was closely connected with the amateur theatricals at Court, producing some fine out-door pageants and plays, and being himself a good actor in comedy, though somewhat wooden and unyielding in tragedy. He then busied himself with other matters until in 1790, finding that the new Court theatre built ten years previously was not doing very well, he took over its management, and for twenty-six years maintained a steady flow of productions, hampered always by poor equipment, lack of money, and a company which, though eager and interested, contained no outstanding stars. Iffland visited Weimar during 1796 and played some fourteen parts of his wide repertory, but the greatest glory of the theatre was its productions of the plays of Schiller, who settled in Weimar in 1800. His influence on German and indeed European drama was immense, but in Weimar his direction, though it resulted in improved settings and ensemble playing, tended to make the actors even more stilted in their declamation and wooden in their gestures. After Schiller's death in 1805 Goethe reduced the company to a set of well-trained but lifeless marionettes, whose acting was in no way comparable to that of Schroeder's company at Hamburg. He was by this time fond of the theatre which had caused him so much work and worry, but was finally forced by the machinations of a temperamental opera singer to retire, the last straw being the importation of a performing poodle in a melodrama, *The Forest of Bondy*.

WEISE. (1) CHRISTIAN (1642–1708), German dramatist, headmaster of a school at Zittau, where he wrote and produced a number of long plays, on subjects taken from many and varied sources. He made good use of the Narr, or fool, to point the moral, and in contrast to the exuberant, ranting verse of Lohenstein and his imitators used a plain, dry, prose style which he coached his boys to speak clearly and simply. He should not be confused with (2) CHRISTIAN FELIX WEISSE (1726–1804), friend and contemporary of the young Lessing, with whom Weisse collaborated in translating a number of French and English plays for Caroline Neuber's company.

WEITER, AISIG (1878–1919), Russian-Jewish writer of plays on contemporary themes, produced at the Moscow State Jewish Theatre.

WELL, the lower part of the cellar beneath the stage (see STAGE, 1). The Orchestra Well for the accommodation of the theatre musicians is in front of and below the stage itself.

WEMYSS, FRANCIS COURTNEY (1797–1859), English actor and manager, who spent most of his professional life in the United States. He made his first appearances in the English provinces, and in 1821 was seen in London, where he was engaged for the Chestnut Street Theatre company. He made his début there the following year with such fine actors as Warren, Wood, Henry Wallack, and the elder Jefferson, and in 1824 made his first appearance in New York. He was a good actor, but not of the first rank, playing mainly small parts in revivals. He was Duncan to Macready's Macbeth on the occasion of the Astor Place Opera House riot. Nor was he more successful as a manager, though he was at various times in charge of the Chestnut Street Theatre, Barnum's American Museum, and theatres in many big American cities. In spite of his shortcomings, he has a high place in the history of the American theatre, which he served devotedly till the end of his life with impeccable taste and integrity. He was the author of a most entertaining autobiography, *Twenty-Six Years of the Life of an Actor and Manager* (1847), and also edited the Philadelphia series of standard plays, published as *The Acting American Theatre*, with fine frontispieces of American actors by Neagle. A pleasant, cultured, and courtly man, he was extremely popular in America, but never ceased to be regarded as an Englishman. He helped to found and administer the Theatrical Fund.

WERFEL, FRANZ (1890–1945), Austrian novelist and dramatist, whose trilogy, *Der Spiegelmensch* (1921), is an interesting resumption of the Faust-Mephistopheles theme. This symbolic drama was followed by two historical plays, which had some success, *Juarez und Maximilian* (1924) and *Paulus unter den Juden* (1926). A chronicle-play dealing with the history of Jewry, *The Eternal Road* (1936), though elaborately staged and produced by Max Reinhardt in New York, was little more than a pageant. Werfel's most original contribution to the theatre, however, was his adaptation of his novel, *Bocksgesang* (1921) (known in English as *The Goat Song*), in which the crazy brutality of man in rebellion is symbolized by the monster, half-goat, half-man, who leads a peasants' revolt in the eighteenth century. He is eventually killed, but not before he has passed on his heritage of cruelty and bestiality to his child by a young nobleman's wife.

WERGELAND, HENRIK ARNOLD (1808–45), Norwegian poet and dramatist, famous in the first place for his epic, *Skabelsen, Mennesket og Messias* (*Creation, Man, and the Messiah*), wrote, besides his other poetry, a number of plays. The earlier of these were farces (written under a pen-name) and were later followed by plays written under the influence of Shakespeare: *Sinclars Død* (*The Death of Sinclair*) (1828); a comedy, *Opium* (1831); and to some extent also *Irreparabile Tempus* (1828). In his later plays there is less of this influence and more of Wergeland's fertile, fantastic, and sometimes apocalyptic imagination. *Den indiske Cholera* (*The Indian Cholera*), *Barnemordersken* (*Infanticide*), and *De sidste Kloge* (*The Last Wise Men*), ranging from tragedy to farce, all belong to 1834; two more political farces follow in 1837, and then the drama *Campbellerne* (*The Campbells*), the cause of a controversy better known than the play. To the last group, written after 1839, belong more political farces, the drama *Venetianerne* (*The Venetians*) in 1841, and the posthumous *Søkadetterne iland* (*Midshipmen Ashore*).   U. E.-F.

WERNER, FRIEDRICH LUDWIG ZACHARIAS (1768–1823), author of the one-act tragedy, *Die vierundzwanzigste Februar* (1810), which established the so-called Fate Drama in Germany. He was a poet and mystic who became a Roman Catholic priest in Vienna, where he was renowned for his preaching. His plays, which include *Das Kreuz an der Ostsee* (1806), *Martin Luther* (1807), and *Kunigunde, die Heilige* (1815), bear a strong religious imprint, and mingle scenes of telling realism with weird fantasies. They were among the few German romantic verse-dramas to obtain success on the stage.

WESSEL, JOHAN (1742–85), Norwegian dramatist (see SCANDINAVIA, 2).

WEST, FLORENCE (1862–1913), see WALLER(2).

WEST LONDON THEATRE. In 1831 a theatre was opened in Church Street, Marylebone, called the Royal Sussex. A year later it was renamed the Pavilion, and was an unlicensed theatre for crude melodrama and comic songs. In 1835 it was renamed the Portman Theatre, and two years later was pulled down and rebuilt. The new theatre, known as the Marylebone, opened on 13 Nov. 1837. It continued to offer the same fare as before, and was closed several times. In 1842 it was again largely rebuilt and given the name of the Theatre Royal, Marylebone. Under the direction of John Douglass it knew a period of prosperity, playing popular melodrama and pantomime. Douglass retired in 1847, and the theatre was taken over by Mrs. Warner, the Drury Lane actress who had recently been with Phelps at Sadler's Wells. She failed, as also did E. T. Smith and J. W. Wallack, her successors. In 1858 it was taken over by Joseph Cave, who had appeared there as a boy. He remained for some years, and in 1864 the old house was rebuilt and enlarged, being renamed the Royal Alfred in 1866, when it made an effort to provide better entertainment. Charles Harcourt brought Henrietta Hodson and the company from the Queen's Theatre, Long Acre, there, but in 1870 it reverted to its old name of the Marylebone, and to melodrama. Towards the end of the nineteenth century it was again rebuilt and renamed the West London, still remaining faithful to melodrama. It became a cinema in 1932 and was damaged by enemy action in 1941, since when it has been used as a storehouse.   W. M. P.

The Scala was at one time (1820) known as the West London.

WESTERN. (1) (PAULINE) LUCILLE (1843–77), and (2) HELEN (1844–68), American actresses, daughters of a comedian and of his actress-wife, who by a second marriage after his death became Mrs. Jane English, the name by which she is usually known. The children toured with their mother and step-father in a mixed entertainment which gave plenty of scope for their precocious talents in acting and dancing. Helen died before she could become well known as an adult actress, but Lucille was noted for her playing of strong emotional parts in such plays as *East Lynne, Camille, Masks and Faces,* and *The Stranger.* One of her finest performances was given as Nancy in a dramatization of *Oliver Twist,* with E. L. Davenport as Bill Sikes and the younger J. W. Wallack as Fagin. She died at the height of her career.

WESTMINSTER PLAY, LONDON. It is now generally recognized that the contribution made to the early history of the English stage by the older schools and universities, and by the companies of Boy Players, was a considerable one. For a time, and mainly owing to the patronage of Queen Elizabeth and King James I, the acting of plays both in English and Latin by the 'little eyases', as Hamlet called them, had a considerable vogue, and their popularity was such that they were viewed with dislike by the recognized adult companies. Apart from the plays produced by the Children of the Chapel Royal and by the Children of Paul's, there are records of theatrical performances during the sixteenth century by the boys of Eton, Winchester, Westminster, Shrewsbury, St. Paul's, and other schools, and by the undergraduates of Oxford and Cambridge. In the first years of the seventeenth century their popularity began to wane, and in the twentieth century the annual Latin Play at Westminster School alone survived, and preserved a more or less unbroken tradition from the sixteenth century.

Some confusion has, however, resulted from the fact that those who have written on the early history of the Westminster Play have failed to realize that there were three distinct 'sets' of boys at Westminster who presented plays. First the Queen's or King's Scholars, who are invariably referred to in the records as 'the Children of the grammar school'. They acted an annual play, usually at Christmas, and always in Latin, and this is the ancestor of the modern Westminster Play. It has always been acted by the boys who are in 'College'. Secondly, there were the Town Boys or Oppidans, as distinct from the Scholars, who from time to time acted a play in English. This was known as the Town Boys' Play and was probably always an unofficial production. Lastly, there were the Choir Boys of Westminster, who were a separate school with their own

schoolmaster. They are always referred to in sixteenth-century records as 'the Children of Westminster' and their plays were invariably in English and suitable to their education and upbringing.

The origin of the Westminster Play is probably to be found in the Christmas ceremonies connected with the election of the Boy Bishop in medieval times, but there is definite evidence to show that the acting of plays by Terence and Seneca was introduced at Westminster during the headmastership of Dr. Alexander Nowell (1543–55), who has a further claim to fame both as the writer of the Shorter Catechism and as the inventor of bottled beer. When the school was re-founded by Queen Elizabeth in 1560 a clause was inserted in the Statutes enjoining the annual presentation of a Latin play by the Scholars on the grounds of the advantages to be derived by them from a habit of correct action and pronunciation. The Latin Play thereby became an annual event. Several of the bills of expenses for these plays have been preserved among the muniments of Westminster Abbey (see L. E. Tanner, *Westminster School,* pp. 123–6, and Motter, pp. 272–4, where they are printed). It was perhaps natural that Terence and Plautus should hold the stage, but occasionally performances were given of plays by other authors. The most interesting of these was, probably, the performance of the *Sapientia Salomonis* given in the College Hall in January 1566 in the presence of Queen Elizabeth and the Princess Cecilia of Sweden. The Queen had also been present two years before at the performance of the *Miles Gloriosus* when the exertions of the youthful actors were such that xijd. had to be expended 'for buttered beere for ye children being horse'. All these performances took place in the ancient and still existing College Hall, formerly the Abbot's Dining Hall. The Play was given every Christmastide until the outbreak of the Civil War in 1642.

It is a curious fact that there is no further record of the Play until sixty years later, when it reappears in 1704 apparently as a well-established annual event. The missing period covers most of the long headmastership (1638–95) of the famous Dr. Richard Busby (1605–95). He was himself, however, no enemy to acting, for as an undergraduate he had acted in *The Royal Slave* (1636) before the King and Queen at Christ Church, Oxford, with such success that he had contemplated taking up the stage as a profession. It is probable that the Play was in fact revived at the Restoration, for James Russell, writing as a Westminster boy (c. 1660–6), states that the boys 'are to act a play very shortly', and it is recorded that Barton Booth, who was at the School from 1689 to 1698, received his 'first encouragement in acting from his Master . . . Dr. Busby at the rehearsals of a Latin play acted at that school'. At any rate in 1704 the *Amphitruo* was acted complete with Prologue and Epilogue, and in this form and from that date the records are continuous. 'At first the Epilogue was a monologue; in due course it became a dialogue, and it has finally developed into a witty and scholarly satire in Latin on contemporary events, in which all the characters [in the Play] play a part and appear in modern dress. The Prologue, on the other hand, has tended more and more to become a serious review of the events of the past school year. To the student of the last centuries the Prologues and Epilogues of the Westminster Play are an invaluable storehouse of allusions, and not infrequently preserve the memory of events or words of topical interest which would otherwise have passed into oblivion.' (L. E. Tanner, *Westminster School*, p. 61.)

The cycle of plays has always included the *Adelphi*, *Andria*, and *Phormio*, but the fourth play has varied. The *Eunuchus* was acted until 1860, when the *Trinummus* of Plautus took its place. In 1907 the *Eunuchus* was revived as the *Famulus*, but in 1926 it gave place to a revival of the *Rudens*, which now appears to have established itself in the cycle.

The Play was originally acted in the College Hall. After the Restoration it was transferred to the Old Dormitory of the King's Scholars in Dean's Yard. In 1730 it was again transferred to the New Dormitory in Little Dean's Yard and continued to be acted there until 1938. In May 1941 the Dormitory was gutted by an incendiary bomb.

Apart from the usual 'properties' there is evidence that in the sixteenth century there was some attempt at providing scenery. In 1565, for instance, a painter was paid for 'drawing the cytee and temple of Jerusalem and for paynting towres' for the *Sapientia Salomonis*. This may, perhaps, have been exceptional, and in general no doubt the Hall with its 'screens' and musicians' gallery provided a simple and adequate setting. In the eighteenth century a back-scene representing Covent Garden was considered sufficient, but in 1758 'Athenian' Stuart devised a more suitable classical background. This 'impossible mountain with a temple perched on the top of it', lit by a chandelier which 'with glittering improbability' hung from the skies in the middle of the stage, remained until 1858, when Professor C. R. Cockerell, R.A., an Old Westminster, designed a drop-scene representing the Bay of Salamis and a back-scene of Athens and the Acropolis. These exceedingly beautiful scenes, painted by Fenton, Phelps's scene-painter, remain in use, though a special back-scene was designed for the revival of the *Rudens*.

In early days the dresses of the actors were hired from the Office of the Revels and thousands of pins seem to have been required to make them fit the children. No doubt they were glad to take what they could get without much regard to suitability. Those playing unusual parts, such as the Furies in the *Mostellaria*, had special clothes made for them. In the eighteenth century, following the convention of the time, the actors appeared more or less in the ordinary dress of the period, and it was not felt to be incongruous if Choerea appeared in the full uniform of the Guards, or Davus in the livery of an eighteenth-century footman. It was not until 1839 that classical costumes were introduced; but the older convention survives in the Epilogue, where the actors wear the modern dress appropriate to their parts. The Prologue is always spoken in front of the curtain by the Captain in knee-breeches, buckled shoes, evening dress, gown, and bands.

Other stage traditions may also be noticed—some of which alone survive on the Westminster stage. The auditorium is still divided into separate 'pits'—Seniors, Masters, Ladies, &c. The Dean presides on the second night, and the senior or most distinguished Old Westminster present on the third and last night. At the conclusion of the Epilogue they call for the 'Cap'—an ancient custom suggestive of the hunting-field rather than the theatre. The audience pass through the King's and other 'Bars' (i.e. Toll Bars) to their seats. The boys are seated in the 'Gods' under the control of two 'Gods' Monitors' who, by waving their tanning-canes at traditional places in the text, ensure that applause is not withheld.

Not the least important part of the Play is the audience, which in distinction finds no parallel elsewhere, and, oddly enough, the traditional custom of wearing medals and decorations is still observed. Not only has the Play been the annual meeting-place for Westminsters of all generations, but ambassadors, statesmen, judges, and bishops are usually numbered in the audience, and indeed there are but few who have held high place in Church or State during the last two hundred and fifty years who have not at some time been present. We have noted the visits of Queen Elizabeth. In 1800 the Prince Regent was present, and in 1834 King William IV attended a performance of the *Eunuchus*. The Prince Consort came more than once and brought the young Prince of Wales. In 1937, King George VI and Queen Elizabeth attended a performance of the *Adelphi*, and, in accordance with ancient custom when members of the Royal Family are present, were escorted by King's Scholars bearing torches as they crossed the Yard to the Dormitory (see also ACOUSTICS, 5).   L. E. T.

WESTMINSTER THEATRE, LONDON. (1) This was built by an undertaker named Gale in 1832 on the site now covered by the Wesleyan Central Hall. T. D. Davenport, reputed to have been the original of Dickens's Vincent Crummles, was its first manager. Dibdin Pitt and John Douglass followed. The theatre never obtained a licence in the four years of its existence, but William Davidge, Joseph Raynor, and Munyard, all of whom eventually achieved fame, appeared there.

(2) The present Westminster Theatre in Palace Street, near Victoria Station, was opened

on 7 Oct. 1931, under the direction of Anmer Hall (A. B. Horne), with *The Anatomist*. Numerous interesting plays have been produced there, including *The Lake*, *The Zeal of Thy House*, a revival of *The Doctor's Dilemma*, and *Troilus and Cressida* in modern dress. In 1944 it staged a distinguished revival of *An Ideal Husband*, and produced Bridie's *It Depends What You Mean*. The Westminster was the first London theatre to reopen after the compulsory war-time closing in Sept. 1939.

W. M. P.

WESTON, THOMAS (1737–76), an English actor, whose father was head cook to George II. He joined a strolling company, and thinking himself a tragedian, played Richard III abominably. He found his true vocation in comedy, and after playing in Shuter's and Yates's booths at Bartholomew Fair, he was engaged for small parts at the Haymarket. Foote thought highly of his comic talents, and wrote for him the part of Jerry Sneak in *The Mayor of Garret* (1763). He went also to Drury Lane, alternating seasons at both theatres, being considered second to none in comedy, and surpassing even Garrick in the part of Abel Drugger. The German critic Lichtenberg has left a fine description of his playing of Scrub in *The Beaux' Stratagem*, and of his acting in general. He was somewhat dissipated, constantly in debt, and finally died of drink.

WESTRAY, a family of actresses, consisting of a mother and three beautiful daughters, who were all at the Park Theatre, New York, where the mother married as her second husband an actor in the company named Simpson. Of the three girls, Ellen became Mrs. John Darley, and after twenty years in New York joined her sister Juliana, wife of W. B. Wood, in Philadelphia, where she was extremely successful. The third sister, Elizabeth, married the comedian Twaits.

WHARF THEATRE, NEW YORK, see CRUGER'S WHARF THEATRE.

WHEATLEY. (1) FREDERICK (? –1836), an Irish entertainer who in 1803 appeared with much success at the Park Theatre, New York, and spent the rest of his life on the American stage. He married (2) SARAH ROSS (1790–1872), who made her début at the Park in 1805 and was for many years an outstanding actress of comic elderly women, including Mrs. Malaprop and Juliet's Nurse. Her son (3) WILLIAM (1816–76) made his début at the Park at the age of ten, playing a juvenile role with Macready, whom he then accompanied on tour. He was for several years the chief player of children's parts at the Park, and after careful schooling made his adult début there in 1834. A hard worker, an excellent actor, and a good manager, he was at Niblo's Garden from 1862–8, where his greatest achievement was the production of the spectacular ballet-extravaganza, *The Black Crook* (1866). Its success netted him a fortune, on which he retired. His sister Julia was a singer, but (4) EMMA (1822–54) was a highly

accomplished and popular actress. Frederick had also a brother Samuel on the stage, whose wife, a Mrs. Williams from London, was at the Park at the same time as Sarah and later went to Boston.

WHELAN, ALBERT (1875–　), a music-hall comedian, who was the first to use a signature tune ('Lustige Brüder'). He was born in Melbourne, and first appeared as a red-nosed comedian in a mining camp. Back in Melbourne he joined the company of *The Belle of New York*, in which he subsequently played in England. In 1901 he appeared at the Empire, Leicester Square, and all other principal halls. A clever performer, he never altered his style. His whistled entrance tune, his immaculate evening dress, his tall hat, his stick, his white gloves, and his wrist-watch were unchanged. But his songs were always new and entertaining.

WHITE-EYED KAFFIR, THE, see CHIRGWIN, G. H.

WHITEFRIARS THEATRE, LONDON. This seems to have been the refectory hall of the Whitefriars monastery, situated on ground in and around where Bouverie Street and adjoining thoroughfares stand to-day. Some stones of the old monastery can still be seen incorporated in the offices of the *News of the World*. The hall was adapted for use as a 'private' theatre, on the lines of the first Blackfriars Theatre, by Thomas Woodford and Michael Drayton in 1606, though it may have been used earlier. Its dimensions were about 35×85 ft. It was used by the Children of the King's Revels from 1608 to 1609; by the Queen's Revels, 1609–13; by the Lady Elizabeth's Men, 1613–14; and possibly by the Prince's Men thereafter. It was still in use in 1621, but its later history is obscure. Pepys, in his diary for 1660, records a visit there to see Massinger's *The Bondman*, one of his favourite plays, but he may have meant Salisbury Court, which replaced it in 1629, and with which it is sometimes confused. W. M. P.

WHITEHALL THEATRE, LONDON, built on the site of the historic Old Ship Tavern, is a small, intimate, modern playhouse. It was opened on 29 Sept. 1930 by Walter Hackett with his own play, *The Way to Treat a Woman*, transferred from the Duke of York's. He and his wife, Marion Lorne, controlled the theatre until 1933, he writing the plays and she appearing in them. For a time the theatre housed revue. W. M. P.

WHITNEY THEATRE, LONDON, see STRAND THEATRE (2).

WHITTLE, CHARLES R. (?–1947), a music-hall performer from the North, singer of a dozen songs with the word 'girl' in the title, of which the best was 'The Girl in the Clogs and Shawl'. The most popular of his songs, however, was 'Let's All Go Down the Strand'.

WHITTY, DAME MAY (1865–1948), see WEBSTER (3).

WHITWORTH, GEOFFREY (1883–1951), founder of the British Drama League (see AMATEUR THEATRE IN GREAT BRITAIN, 2), which he directed from its inception in 1919 until 1948, when he retired and was succeeded by E. Martin Browne. He was also active in the cause of the National Theatre, which formed the subject of two of his books—*The Theatre of My Heart* (1930) and *The Making of a National Theatre* (1951). On 13 July 1951, two months before his death, he saw his work begin to bear fruit when Her Majesty Queen Elizabeth laid the Foundation-stone of a National Theatre on the South Bank of the Thames. Whitworth was for many years on the Executive Committee of Governors of the Shakespeare Memorial Theatre, Stratford-upon-Avon, and a member of the Critics' Circle. Although his work lay mainly with amateurs, it was of considerable benefit to the English theatre as a whole.

WIED, GUSTAV (1858–1914), Danish dramatist, best known outside his own country by his satiric comedy *Ranke Viljer* (1906), which, as $2 \times 2 = 5$, had a great success in Germany in 1908, and later in New York, where it was given in 1928 at the Civic Repertory Theatre.

WIGNELL, THOMAS (1753–1802), American actor, of English extraction. He was a cousin of the younger Hallam, by whom he was induced in 1774 to join the American Company, in which he quickly became leading man. He was instrumental in getting the first American comedy, Tyler's *The Contrast*, put on in New York in 1787, and in 1789 he spoke the prologue to, and played the comic doctor in, Dunlap's first play, *The Father; or, American Shandyism*. He was much admired by Washington, who attended his benefit night at the John Street Theatre in Nov. 1789. Shortly afterwards Wignell left New York and went to England, where he recruited a company to play at the new Chestnut Street Theatre in Philadelphia. Among its members were James Fennell, Mrs. Merry, Mrs. Oldmixon, and the Morrises, whom Wignell had brought with him from New York. The theatre was designed on the lines of the Theatre Royal, Bath, and saw a number of distinguished performances under Wignell and his successors in management, Warren and Wood. In 1797 Wignell took his company to New York for a season, playing in Ricketts's Circus. They were considered superior to the American Company, but Wignell took them back to Philadelphia, and never again essayed New York, remaining at the Chestnut Street Theatre till his death. Seven weeks before he died he married his leading lady, Mrs. Merry, who later became the wife of William Warren.

WILDE, OSCAR FINGAL O'FLAHERTIE WILLS (1856–1900), Irish wit and dramatist. Educated in Dublin, he then went to Oxford, where he won the Newdigate Prize for English Verse, and, in spite of a reputation for idleness, took a First Class degree in Classics. He was the leader of a new aesthetic cult, satirized in *Patience*, where he figures as Bunthorne. In 1882 he went on a lecture tour in the United States, and had a play, *Vera*, produced in New York. It was not a success, and for some years he confined himself to the writing of novels, poems, and short tales, though a blank-verse tragedy, *The Duchess of Padua*, was also seen in New York in 1891. It was, however, with his light comedies that Wilde ultimately achieved fame on the stage—*Lady Windermere's Fan* (1892), *A Woman of No Importance* (1893), *An Ideal Husband* (1895), and finally, his most characteristic play, *The Importance of Being Earnest* (1895). In this he discarded his former vein of sentiment, which he knew to be false and a concession to the times, and returned to the pure formula of Congreve. Though all his plays have been revived, *The Importance of Being Earnest* wears best and has proved the most successful. Few comedies of the English stage have as much wit, elegance, and theatrical dexterity. His poetic play, *Salomé*, was banned in England, but produced in Paris by Sarah Bernhardt in 1894, and later set to music by Richard Strauss, since when it has occasionally been revived in England. In 1895 Wilde was sentenced to two years' imprisonment with hard labour on conviction for a moral offence, and afterwards went to Paris, where, broken in health and fortune, he soon died. His life was made the subject of a play by Leslie and Sewell Stokes, given in London in 1936. He was married, and had two sons.

WILDENBRUCH, ERNST VON (1845–1909), German dramatist, who paid tribute to the new unity of Germany under the Hohenzollerns in his historical dramas, *Die Karolinger* (1882), *Die Quitzows* (1888), *Heinrich und Heinrichs Geschlecht* (1896), which earned him the approbation of Kaiser Wilhelm II. His one realistic play, *Die Haubenlerche* (1890), was written under the influence of the new spirit of naturalism. He also wrote a play on Christopher Marlowe. His style is lively but platitudinous, with frequent repetitions of important statements, and his characters are without psychological depth. He has been termed a 'belated romanticist', and was a capable rather than an inspired playwright.

WILDER, THORNTON NIVEN (1897–   ), American novelist and dramatist, whose most important work for the theatre has been done in his two stimulating and provocative plays, *Our Town* (1938), a picture of a small American community, and *The Skin of Our Teeth* (1942), a survey of man's hairbreadth escape from disaster through the ages, both of which have been awarded the annual Pulitzer Prize. The latter provided an excellent part in Sabina for Tallulah Bankhead in New York and Vivien Leigh in London, where Sir Laurence Olivier was responsible for its production. Among Wilder's earlier works for the theatre were *The Trumpet Shall Sound*, a play about the American Civil War done by students of the American Laboratory Theatre in 1927, a translation of Obey's

Lucrèce for Katharine Cornell in 1932, a new
version of *A Doll's House* for Ruth Gordon in
1937, and an adaptation of one of Nestroy's
farces as *The Merchant of Yonkers* (1938).
Wilder is an original and unconventional
dramatist, who arouses fierce controversy, but
whose work forms a permanent contribution
to the American scene.

WILKINSON, NORMAN (1882–1934), English artist, designer of some of the most beautiful settings and costumes seen in the English theatre, particularly in the years immediately before the war of 1914–18. His first work was done for Charles Frohman at the Duke of York's in 1910, but he sprang into prominence with his costumes and scenery for Granville-Barker's Shakespeare season at the Savoy, (1912–14), *A Midsummer Night's Dream* being particularly memorable, with its gilded fairies and 'magical and iridescent forest'. He also designed the costumes and settings for a production of Euripides' *Iphigenia in Tauris*, given in London in 1912. He was with Playfair at the Lyric, Hammersmith, worked for C. B. Cochran and for the Phoenix and Stage Societies, and in 1932 designed *A Midsummer Night's Dream* for the Memorial Theatre at Stratford-on-Avon, of which he was a Governor. To distinguish him from a marine artist of the same name he was usually referred to as Norman Wilkinson of Four Oaks.

WILKINSON, TATE (1739–1803), English actor and provincial theatre manager whose passion for the theatre led him, though of good family, to adopt the stage as a profession. He was given a small part by Shuter and then recommended to Garrick, who engaged him for Drury Lane. He became well known for his imitations of living actors, and Peg Woffington, offended by his mimicry of her, tried to keep him out of the theatre. They later became friends, however, and it was on his arm that she left the stage after her last appearance in 1757. Wilkinson played only minor parts until Foote, liking his imitations, took him to Dublin, where he was most successful. He failed, however, to rouse much enthusiasm in a London audience, and eventually took himself off to the provinces. After some restless years he took over the York circuit, which included also Hull and Leeds, and conducted it for some 30 years with conspicuous success. Many well-known actors, among them Mrs. Jordan, Kemble, Fawcett, Suett, Emery, and the elder Mathews 'owed their first advancement to his discrimination'. As he grew older he became very eccentric, and the elder Mathews used to do a charming monologue in imitation of him. Foote, after a violent but short-lived quarrel, satirized him as Shift in *The Minor* (1760). In spite of his many foibles he was much loved and respected, and his death was greatly regretted. He has left an interesting account of his life in his *Memoirs* (1790) and *Wandering Patentee* (1795).

WILKS, ROBERT (1665–1732), a gifted English actor, good in tragedy but better in comedy, who to the end of his life could play young men. He was first engaged by Christopher Rich for Drury Lane, on the recommendation of Betterton, and after a season in Ireland returned to play the parts of Mountfort, who had just been assassinated. He became very popular with the public and with his fellow actors, but on being appointed joint manager of Drury Lane he found himself constantly at odds with the parsimonious Doggett, who eventually retired in favour of Booth. Wilks was the first to play the fine gentlemen of Cibber's plays and the heroes of Farquhar, his most famous part being Sir Harry Wildair. In tragedy he was at his best in the portrayal of manly sorrow, as in Macduff, when he always drew tears from his audience. He was also good as Hamlet. He was a conscientious, hard-working actor, but his fiery temper often led him into trouble, and caused several of the company to migrate to Lincoln's Inn Fields Theatre.

WILLARD, EDWARD SMITH (1853–1915), English actor, chiefly remembered for his villains in contemporary melodrama. He made his first appearance on the stage at Weymouth in 1869, and remained in the provinces, except for a short engagement at Covent Garden in 1875, until 1881, in which year he first came prominently before the public as Clifford Armytage in *The Lights o' London*. His reputation was enhanced by his Captain Skinner in *The Silver King* (1882), and he remained with Wilson Barrett until 1886, playing in all the latter's subsequent productions. Among Willard's later successes were *Jim the Penman* (1886) at the Haymarket, and Jem Dalton in a revival of *The Ticket-of-Leave Man* at the Olympic in 1888. In the following year he went into management at the Shaftesbury, where he produced among other things *The Middleman* (1889), himself playing Cyrus Blenkarn. He then went to America with such success that he returned there annually for some years, touring the United States and Canada with a repertory of successful plays. Among them was *The Professor's Love Story* (1894) in which he made a great hit, thus proving, what his earlier performances in *Arkwright's Wife* and as Tom Pinch had made apparent, that he could handle tenderness and emotion with the same skill as villainy. He retired from the stage in 1906.

WILLIAM STREET THEATRE, NEW YORK, used, probably by amateurs, in 1790 for entertainments and comedies. Among the plays produced there were *The Miller of Mansfield* and *George Barnwell*, and Dunlap's farce, *The Soldier's Return*. There was also a pantomime of Robinson Crusoe with a display of transparencies and Italian Shades, or shadow show.

WILLIAMS, BARNEY (1823–76), American actor, who with his wife, the sister of Mrs. W. J. Florence, toured extensively in the United States, mainly in Irish comedies. They were both seen in London in 1855 in *Rory O'More*, and remained for four years, returning to New York to continue their Irish impersonations, which became a tradition in the theatre. Williams was for two years manager of Wallack's old theatre, which he rechristened the Broadway, but soon found that touring was both pleasanter and more profitable, and once more took to the road. He made his first appearance in 1836 and his last in 1875, and to the end remained not so much an actor as an entertainer, a much-loved, jovial, rollicking, drinking, stage Irishman on the boards and off.

WILLIAMS, BRANSBY (1870–   ), a top-line music-hall performer who for many years specialized in the presentation of characters from Dickens and Shakespeare, musical monologues, and imitations of famous actors. He had made many appearances as an enthusiastic amateur, in the intervals of tea-tasting in Mincing Lane, before, encouraged by William Terriss, he joined a provincial stock company, playing a variety of parts which laid the foundation of his excellent technique. He deserted the theatre for the music-hall in 1896, making his first appearance as an impersonator at the London, Shoreditch. Shortly afterwards he deputized at short notice for Dan Leno at the Tivoli with such success that he was immediately engaged on his own account, and he soon became one of the most popular entertainers of his day, both in England and America. In 1904 he was commanded to Sandringham to play before King Edward VII. He was a fine low comedian in pantomime, and in his later years a star of radio.

WILLIAMS, EGBERT AUSTIN (c. 1876–1922), negro comedian, usually known as Bert Williams, who came from the Bahamas as a child and later joined a minstrel troupe. In 1895 he teamed up with George Walker, also a negro comedian, and their vaudeville act was successfully produced at Koster and Bial's, New York, in the following year, after some time spent on tour in perfecting it. By 1903 Williams was in a position to produce an all-negro musical comedy, *In Dahomey*, which was given with much success in New York and London. It was followed by several others, but after the death of his partner in 1909 Williams gave up management and went as leading comedian to the Ziegfeld Follies, writing his own material. Off-stage he was a tall, serious, and scholarly man, light in colour, but for his performances he blacked himself and portrayed the shuffling, shiftless nigger of tradition. He had great gifts, and might, had circumstances permitted, have become a great actor. In his chosen line he did excellent work, and was a pioneer for his race in the American theatre.

WILLIAMS, EMLYN (1905–   ), Welsh actor, dramatist, and producer. He was a member of the O.U.D.S. while at Oxford, and in 1927 made his first appearance on the professional stage in *And So to Bed*. Among his early plays was an adaptation of *Prenez garde à la*

peinture as *The Late Christopher Bean*, which ran for over a year with Edith Evans as Gwenny; but his first outstanding success, both as actor and author, was scored with *Night Must Fall*, in which he played Danny. It was a success both in London and New York. Among other excellent performances were those of Angelo in *Measure for Measure* at the Old Vic in 1937, and Sir Robert Morton in *The Winslow Boy* in 1946. But Williams has mainly confined his acting to his own plays, which he also produces. Among them are *The Corn is Green* (1938), *The Light of Heart* (1940), *The Wind of Heaven* (1945), and *Trespass* (1947).

WILLIAMS. (1) (ERNEST GEORGE) HARCOURT (1880–   ), English actor and producer, who at the end of 1947 celebrated his stage jubilee while appearing as William the Waiter in a revival of *You Never Can Tell*. He made his first appearance in Belfast with Benson, after studying for the stage under Kate Bateman (Mrs. Crowe), and with the same company first appeared in London in 1900. He was associated with a number of leading actors, including Kate Rorke, Ellen Terry, H. B. Irving, whom he accompanied to America, and George Alexander, and was seen in many interesting new plays, including those of Ibsen, Shaw, and Granville-Barker. His career was interrupted by war service, but in 1919 he was seen in *Abraham Lincoln*, and later appeared as the Player King in John Barrymore's *Hamlet*. From 1929 to 1934 he was producer at the Old Vic, where his innovations in Shakespearian production were first criticized and later hailed as epoch-making, based as they were upon Granville-Barker's Prefaces, and Williams's own love of and feeling for the swiftness and splendour of Elizabethan verse. In 1937 he gave a fine performance as William of Sens in *The Zeal of Thy House*, which he also produced, and some years later returned to the Old Vic company, with whom he visited New York in 1946. In 1935 he published a volume of reminiscences, *Four Years at the Old Vic*. In 1908 he married the distinguished actress (2) JEAN STERLING MACKINLAY (1882–   ), who studied for the stage with Dame Geneviève Ward, made her first appearance in 1901 with Benson, and was later with both Hare and Alexander. She has been prominently associated with the movement for a Children's Theatre in England, and for many years staged a unique series of children's matinées at Christmas-time.

WILLIAMS, TENNESSEE [THOMAS LANIER] (1914–   ), American playwright, who in 1939 was awarded a Theatre Guild prize for four one-act plays entitled *American Blues*. He first came into prominence with the production of *The Glass Menagerie* (1945), in which Laurette Taylor made her last appearance, as the Mother. This play, which was awarded the New York Drama Critics' Circle Award, was later seen in London, as was Williams's next play, *A Streetcar named Desire* (1947).

WILLIAMSBURG, Virginia, U.S.A., one of the first towns in the New World to witness theatrical performances. In 1736 *Cato* was given there, probably by a group of amateurs, also *The Busybody* and, at a slightly later date, *The Drummer; or, the Haunted House.* It was at Williamsburg that Hallam's (professional) company first played on their arrival from England, opening on 15 Sept. 1752 with *The Merchant of Venice* and *The Alchemist.*

WILL'S COFFEE HOUSE, also known as the Rose Tavern, was situated at No. 1, Bow Street, Covent Garden, on the west side, at the corner of Russell Street. It was kept by one Will Unwin, and here the Restoration wits resorted after the play, to praise or damn it. They mainly congregated in a room on the first floor. There are many references in contemporary literature to this famous tavern.

WILSON, Francis (1854–1935), an American actor, who at 14 appeared in a black-face song-and-dance act which toured successfully for many years. He then worked on the staff of the Chestnut Street Theatre, Philadelphia, and subsequently appeared in a number of plays, mainly musical. It was not, however, until his appearance as Cadeaux in *Erminie* (based on *Robert Macaire*) at the Casino, 10 May 1886, that he made money and reputation. From then until 1904 he appeared in a succession of musical comedies, finally turning to straight comedy with a play by Clyde Fitch. In 1907 he appeared in *When Knights were Bold,* following it with his own play, *The Bachelor's Baby,* which ran for three years and earned him a fortune. In 1913 Wilson was elected President of the newly formed Actors' Equity Association, resigning in 1921, when he also left the stage, except for a few sporadic appearances on special occasions. An ardent book-collector, particularly of Boothiana, he wrote several volumes of reminiscences, and books on J. W. Booth and on his friends Eugene Field and Joseph Jefferson.

WILSON, John (1585–? 1641), a member of Shakespeare's company who has been confused with the eminent lutanist and Oxford Professor of Music of the same name. He was evidently a musician, since a stage direction of *Much Ado about Nothing* puts 'Jacke Wilson' for Balthasar. He must therefore have been the original singer of 'Sigh no more, Ladies'. He may have been concerned in a performance of *A Midsummer Night's Dream,* played in 1631 on a Sunday, which gave much offence to the Puritans; but this may have been the other John Wilson, or even another actor and lute-player, Henry Wilson.

WILSON, Robert (?–*c.* 1600), an Elizabethan actor and playwright, who was very well thought of in his own day and referred to as a rare man 'for a quicke, delicate, refined, extemporall witt'. He was originally one of Leicester's Men, and joined the Queen's Men in about 1583. On the breaking-up of this

company during the plague of 1592–3 Wilson probably gave up acting and devoted himself to playwriting, mainly for Henslowe's Admiral's Men, and to extemporizing, a favourite Elizabethan pastime in which he is noted as having indulged at the Swan on Bankside.

WILTON, Marie (1839–1921), see BANCROFT.

WIND MACHINE, a device used off-stage to reproduce the stormy howling of wind (see TRICKWORK ON THE ENGLISH STAGE).

WINDMILL THEATRE, London, in Great Windmill Street, Shaftesbury Avenue. This is a small intimate playhouse which was opened in 1931 by J. E. Watts-Phillips with a play called *Inquest.* It had previously been a cinema. It did not succeed as a theatre, and passed into the hands of Mrs. Laura Henderson, who, with her manager Vivian Van Damm, ran continuous variety and revue, which still occupy it. It was the only West End theatre to remain open continuously during the air bombardment of London in 1940–1, and adopted the slogan 'We never closed'.   W. M. P.

WINDSOR THEATRE, New York, see FORTY-EIGHTH STREET THEATRE.

WING, a canvas-covered flat placed at the side of the stage, either facing or obliquely towards the audience, used in conjunction with a backcloth to mask-in the side of the set. There may be anything from one to eight wings on each side of the stage. Their use has been largely superseded by the closed-in Box Set, except in pantomime and spectacular musical shows and in exteriors. To be 'in the wings' means to be standing in the space behind the wings, out of sight of the audience; here actors normally await their cues.

WINTER GARDEN THEATRE. (1) London, in Drury Lane, on the site of the Middlesex Music-Hall. It was opened on 20 May 1919 by Grossmith and Laurillard with Leslie Henson in *Kissing Time,* transferred from the Gaiety. This ran for 430 performances. *The Cabaret Girl* had a successful run at this theatre in 1922, and in 1927 *The Vagabond King* had 480 performances. The fortunes of the theatre then underwent a change, and it was closed for long periods. In 1933 Charles Macdona produced *On the Rocks* at popular prices. *Walk this Way* was also a success. The theatre was slightly damaged by blast in 1944, but Tom Arnold was able to produce a successful pantomime there the following Christmas and in 1946 *No Room at the Inn* had a long and successful run.   W. M. P.

(2) New York, originally the Metropolitan. This theatre was managed by Burton in his last years. After some vicissitudes it opened as the Winter Garden on 14 Sept. 1859 with a good company under Dion Boucicault. The first production was *Dot,* Boucicault's dramatization of *The Cricket on the Hearth,* with Joseph Jefferson as Caleb Plummer and Agnes Robertson as Dot. They later played Newman Noggs

and Smike in *Nicholas Nickleby*, but Boucicault's own plays occupied most of the first season. An interesting production at this theatre was that of Joseph Jefferson's early version of *Rip Van Winkle*, while the appearance in quick succession of John Sleeper Clarke, Charlotte Cushman, Edwin Booth, Sothern, and the Florences proved how completely the United States could depend on her own great actors, and no longer needed to import them from Europe. It was at the Winter Garden that the three Booths appeared on 25 Nov. 1864 in *Julius Caesar*, a performance given to raise money for the Shakespeare statue in Central Park. Edwin played Brutus, Junius Brutus played Cassius, and John Wilkes played Antony. This was the second and final appearance in New York of Lincoln's assassin. *Julius Caesar* was followed by Edwin Booth's run of *Hamlet* for 100 performances, a record not broken until John Barrymore and John Gielgud both surpassed it; and it was at this theatre that Edwin Booth appeared in public for the first time after Lincoln's murder, to be greeted by an enthusiastic audience. They were again assembling to see Booth as Romeo when, on 23 Mar. 1867, this historic old theatre was burnt down. It was not rebuilt.

(3) NEW YORK, on the site of the American Horse Exchange, 50th Street. This theatre was opened by the Shuberts on 20 Mar. 1911 with a musical show, since when it has had a glamorous and eventful life. It has been mainly given over to musical comedies and revues, including that in which Gaby Deslys made her first appearance in New York in 1911, and to the various editions of *The Passing Show*. Most of the outstanding personalities of the vaudeville stage have appeared at the Winter Garden, including Mistinguett, Al Jolson, Ed Wynn, Eddy Cantor, Bert Lahr, and many others. For some years it was a cinema but returned to live drama in 1933.

WINTER, WILLIAM (1836–1917), American dramatic critic whose conservative attitude towards innovators and new tendencies in the theatre made him the transatlantic counterpart of the London critic Clement Scott. They adopted a closely similar attitude to the stage and their tastes and preferences in relation to acting—especially Shakespearian acting—were almost identical. Both indulged in sentimental eulogy of popular players of their time; both consistently upheld the view that conventional morality must take precedence in any conflict with aesthetic principle; and both struggled stubbornly but in vain against the insurgence of realism in modern drama. In retrospect, however, Scott can be seen to have had merits not possessed by Winter, who is unlikely—despite his contemporary prominence and repute—to be remembered in the history of criticism except, possibly, as the last champion of provincial puritanism in the theatre.

Born in Gloucester, Massachusetts, and schooled at Harvard, he descended upon New York in 1859 as literary editor of *The Saturday Press*. Two years later he became dramatic critic of *The Albion* and in 1865 went to work for *The New York Tribune*, where he served as dramatic critic until 1909. His reign was a long and severe one, and his enormous success —he was the most conspicuous figure in American dramatic criticism of the period— rested solely on the mentality of his readers. During his long career he rarely committed himself to an opinion at variance with that of the great majority of his readers, who were not concerned with the fundamental tenets of sound criticism. He was undisguisedly antagonistic to foreign visiting performers—the English excepted—and his notices of Eleonora Duse, Sarah Bernhardt, and Réjane were disfigured by violent irrelevancies concerning their private lives. He denounced both Ibsen and Shaw. 'The slimy mush of Ibsen', he wrote, 'and the lunacy of Maeterlinck are made to trickle into the public mind and turn the public stomach.' And again: 'There is more true drama in Wills's *Olivia*, Young's *Jim the Penman*, Thomas's *Witching Hour*, and McLellan's *Leah Kleschna* than there is in a round dozen of the works of Ibsen.'

After his retirement from *The Tribune*, he continued to write, contributing to *Harper's Weekly* and other periodicals. He also wrote biographies of Henry Irving, Joseph Jefferson, Edwin Booth, Ada Rehan, Tyrone Power, Sr., Richard Mansfield, and David Belasco. There is much valuable information in these books but, unfortunately, they are composed in such a pompous style that they make almost intolerable reading. Another book, *Other Days*, is a backward glance at the actors of an earlier generation.   T. Q. C.

WOFFINGTON, PEG [MARGARET] (*c.* 1714–60), celebrated English actress. Born in Dublin, the daughter of a bricklayer who died when she was very young, she was befriended and educated by the famous rope-dancer Madame Violante, and at 10 was playing Polly and other parts in a children's company. She was then engaged at the Smock Alley Theatre, Dublin, where she appeared in a wide range of parts, including old ladies, Ophelia, and her later famous breeches part, Sir Harry Wildair, in which she was first seen in Apr. 1740. She was immediately engaged by Rich for Covent Garden, and as Sir Harry became the toast of the town. She was the only one who could act the part with the spirit and elegance of the original, Wilks, and for a long while no male actor dared attempt to rival her. She had a fine figure, vivacious features, and flashing dark eyes, and her one defect was her harsh voice, which, though she managed to subdue it, rendered her unfit for tragedy. But her high-born ladies—Millamant, Lady Townly, Lady Betty Modish—her women of spirit and elegance, her homely humorous females, were all excellent. Her company was sought as much by men of sense as by the fops, for she had a good wit and charmed them by her conversation. She was known as the most beautiful and least vain woman of her day, but her good nature did not extend to her fellow actresses, and she was constantly at odds with Kitty Clive, Mrs. Cibber, and George Ann Bellamy, whom she is said to have driven from the stage and wounded with a dagger in a fit of rage. She was for some years the mistress of Garrick, who wrote for her the charming song 'My Lovely Peggy', and played opposite him both in London and Dublin before going to Covent Garden. The last male part she created was Lothario, and the last original part Lady Randolph in *Douglas*, playing opposite Barry as Young Norval. She made her last appearance on the stage as Rosalind in *As You Like It* on 3 May 1757, being taken ill at the beginning of the epilogue. She lingered on for three years, and gave herself to good works and repentance for her former life, endowing almshouses at Teddington in expiation of the past. She is the subject of the play *Masks and Faces* (1852), written by Charles Reade and Tom Taylor, on which Reade later based his novel, *Peg Woffington*. Peg's younger sister Mary was also on the stage for a short time, but left it to make a brilliant marriage with Robert, second son of the Earl of Cholmondeley.

WOLHEIM, LOUIS ROBERT (1881–1931), American stage and screen actor, who had been a teacher of mathematics and a mining engineer before, in 1922, he appeared with the Provincetown Players in *The Hairy Ape* as a very realistic and brawny stoker. He then appeared at the Plymouth Theatre, New York, as the brutally aggressive Flagg in *What Price Glory?*, and from then onwards his career was entirely in the films. A tall, heavily built man, he had been a fine athlete in his youth, and had a broken nose which gave him the truly tough appearance necessary for his parts, though in private life he was gentle and scholarly.

WONDERLAND, LONDON, see EFFINGHAM SALOON.

WOOD, MRS. JOHN (née MATILDA CHARLOTTE VINING) (1831–1915), actress and manageress well known in England and the United States. Member of a big theatrical family, she was first cousin to Mrs. E. L. Davenport. Born in Liverpool, she made her first appearance at Brighton as a child, and had already built up a good reputation in the English provinces when in 1854 she went to America. Widowed in 1863, she took over the Olympic, New York, later to be made famous by Mitchell, and ran it successfully for three years, leaving to make her first appearance on the London stage in 1866 as Miss Miggs in *Barnaby Rudge*. She appeared frequently in London and New York, and was for nearly ten years manageress of the Court Theatre, London, where she was highly respected by her company and popular with the public. A woman of liberal views, she spared no expense in the conduct of her affairs, and ruled her actors firmly but kindly. Clement

Scott, who had a great admiration for her, said of her in 1899:

In a certain line of character she stood alone . . . I have seldom seen an actress so brimming over with fun, with such a keen sense of a ludicrous situation, or one who has that remarkable gift of being able to get her nature and individuality over the footlights. . . . She brings to her work . . . training and experience; she possesses all the glow and style of the old school, with the polish, nature, and finesse of the new.

WOOD, WILLIAM BURKE (1779–1861), the first American-born actor to hold a high place in the American theatre. With Warren he was for many years manager of the Chestnut Street Theatre, Philadelphia, and his diary, which he kept in detail from 1810 to 1833, contains much of interest in the history of the early American theatre. The list of plays given each season shows a marked preponderance of Shakespeare, and of plays imported from England, but in later years more native offerings crept in. Wood's predilection for the English classics may have been due to his own admirable playing of polished comedy, but he was also good in the lighter parts of tragedy. He married Juliana Westray, who with her two sisters had been at the Park Theatre, New York. She appeared for many years under her husband's management, and was extremely popular and a good actress.

WOOD'S BROADWAY THEATRE, NEW YORK, see BIJOU THEATRE (3).

WOOD'S MUSEUM, NEW YORK, see DALY'S THEATRE (1).

WOODWARD, HARRY (1717–77), an English comedian, who was with Garrick at Drury Lane, and wrote a number of pantomimes for him, basing them on the fairy-tales which later became so popular for this purpose. He played Harlequin himself, and was accounted a fine performer, being a nimble dancer and a master of expressive gestures. Educated at the Merchant Taylors' School, Woodward made his first appearance on the stage in 1730, playing under Rich at Covent Garden, where he was known as Lun Junior. He went to Drury Lane in 1738 and remained there for twenty years. Apart from his Harlequin, he was also considered excellent in such parts as Mercutio, Bobadil, Touchstone, Marplot, Captain Absolute (which he was the first to play), and Petruchio, with Kitty Clive as Katharina. In 1758 he went to Dublin and engaged with Macklin (who soon withdrew) and Barry in the management of the Crow Street Theatre, in which they ruined themselves and Mossop, their rival at Smock Alley. Returning to London in 1763, Woodward went back to Covent Garden, but the vogue for harlequinades was passing, and he turned his talents to burlesque and topical skits. He remained on the stage until his death, and was perhaps the last of the great Harlequins, since in the early nineteenth century Grimaldi made Clown the central figure of the pantomime.

WOODWORTH, SAMUEL (1785–1842), early American dramatist, whose best play is *The Widow's Son* (1825), based on an actual incident in the War of Independence, and first given at the Park Theatre in New York. Woodworth, who was also a journalist, and collaborated with another American dramatist, John Howard Payne, in the editing of a Boston newspaper, wrote two domestic dramas in the European tradition, *The Deed of Gift* (1822) and *The Forest Rose* (1825). The latter, which had a musical accompaniment, contains the popular Yankee character Jonathan Ploughboy, which provided Henry Placide and Dan Marble with fine opportunities in comedy. The play was also given successfully in London. Woodworth's other plays are of less importance, but one of them, based on an incident in the life of Lafayette, was played before the latter on his visit to New York in 1824.

WOOLGAR, SARAH JANE (BELLA), see MELLON, MRS. ALFRED.

WOOLLCOTT, ALEXANDER (1887–1943), American dramatic critic, who will probably be better remembered as the prototype of Sheridan Whiteside in the Kaufman–Hart farce, *The Man Who Came to Dinner*. He was born in Phalanx, New Jersey, and attended Hamilton College. Some years before the First World War he went to New York and worked as a police reporter on *The New York Times*. Later he graduated to the drama department and in 1914—when only twenty-seven—he was made dramatic critic. During the war he served as an enlisted man in the A.E.F. for two years, including one on the editorial council of the service paper, *Stars and Stripes*. In 1919 he returned as dramatic critic for *The New York Times*. In 1922 he went to *The New York Herald* and the following year was transferred to *The Sun*. From 1925 to 1928 he was dramatic critic for *The New York World* but after 1928 he retired from active newspaper reviewing and devoted himself to radio broadcasting, lecture tours, and magazine articles.

Woollcott's judgements were capricious in the extreme. It has been said that he had every aptitude for literature except a taste for the first-rate. His critical opinions were certainly extravagant. Unqualifiedly he nominated Charlie Chaplin as 'the greatest living actor' and *The Skin of Our Teeth* as 'head and shoulders above anything else ever written for our stage'. On the other hand, he found some of Eugene O'Neill's work (*Strange Interlude* and *Mourning Becomes Electra*) completely worthless and seems to have missed much of importance that came before him during his reviewing years. Actually he was more interested in players than in plays. He wrote the lives of Mrs. Fiske, Irving Berlin, Charlie Chaplin, and the Marx Brothers, and discoursed—in print and over the radio—on Maude Adams, Helen Hayes, Maxine Elliott, Ruth Gordon, and Katharine Cornell.

A fat, owlish man, both sharp-tongued and sentimental, he cut a colourful figure on the Broadway of his period. His idiosyncrasies, foibles, and *bons mots* have been recorded by many of his contemporaries, and Samuel Hopkins Adams has written an informative and full-length biography. Woollcott's criticism was of the ephemeral variety, but he wrote in a bright manner and with a shrewd understanding of the popular taste. He turned playwright on two occasions, collaborating with George Kaufman on *The Channel Road* (1929) and *The Dark Tower* (1923), and actor on three—*Brief Moment, Wine of Choice*, and in the road company of *The Man Who Came to Dinner*.

His books include *The Command Is Forward, Mr. Dickens Goes to the Play, Enchanted Aisles, Going to Pieces, While Rome Burns, Long, Long Ago*, and *As You Were*.   T. Q. C.

WORMS, GUSTAVE HIPPOLYTE (1836–1910), French actor, who studied under Beauvallet and in 1858 made his début at the Comédie-Française, playing young lovers in comedy and tragedy. He soon proved himself a good actor but, tired of the internal politics which hindered his reception as a member of the company, he left it to go to Russia, where he spent several successful and profitable years. Back in Paris in 1877, he was to have gone to the Gymnase, but the Comédie-Française, recognizing their mistake in letting him go, asked him to return. This he did, making a great success as Don Carlos, with Mounet-Sully as Hernani, and Sarah Bernhardt as Doña Sol. Zola, who admired his intelligence and his artistic integrity, said that he gave the monologue in his part so well, and so calmly, that all the applause was for him, and 'the realist beat the romantic on his own ground'. Dumas *fils*, in several of whose plays Worms appeared, said his voice 'was the voice of honour itself', and he was at his best in heroic parts or in the gentlemanly heroes of old comedy. For many years he was a professor at the Conservatoire.

WREN, SIR CHRISTOPHER (1631–1723), English architect, designer of St. Paul's Cathedral and the Sheldonian Theatre, Oxford, and of the 1674 Drury Lane Theatre (see ARCHITECTURE, DRURY LANE, and ENGLISH PLAYHOUSE).

WYCHERLEY, WILLIAM (1640–1716), Restoration dramatist, whose comedies, though coarse and often frankly indecent, show so much strength and savagery in attacking the vices of the day that their author has been labelled 'a moralist at heart'. Educated in France and at Oxford, Wycherley was to some extent influenced by Molière, but he transmuted his borrowings by his own particular genius, and his style has an individuality seldom found in other writers of the time. His first play, which brought him the patronage of the Duchess of Cleveland, was *Love in a Wood; or, St. James's Park* (1671), followed by *The Gentleman Dancing Master* (1672), based on Calderón and the least characteristic of Wycherley's plays. His best-known work is

The Country Wife (1674–5), in which the comedy hinges upon the efforts of a jealous husband to keep his young but naturally wanton country wife from the temptations of London life, which she takes to only too easily. It was revived several times and in 1766 was adapted by Garrick as *The Country Girl* and produced at Drury Lane. The part of the heroine was a favourite with Mrs. Jordan, who played it inimitably, though she might have shone even more in the original version. This was not seen in London again until revived in 1924 by the Phoenix Society, with a fine cast. The play was later seen at the Old Vic. Wycherley's last play, considered by many critics to be his finest work, was *The Plain Dealer* (1676), which Dryden called 'one of the best, most general and most useful satires that has ever been presented on the English Theatre'. This view has been often disputed, and Wycherley's morality called in question, but the play was certainly successful in its own day, and its author was dubbed 'Manly' Wycherley from the name of its hero, with whose outspoken and misanthropic bent he doubtless had much sympathy. It was frequently revived up to the turn of the century, and in 1925 was given in London by the Renaissance Society. Wycherley, who contracted a secret marriage with the widowed Countess of Drogheda, which brought him into disfavour with Charles II and later landed him in prison for debt, was somewhat unhappy in his later years, but was cheered by the friendship of the young Alexander Pope, who revised many of his poems.

WYLIE, JULIAN (1878–1934), English theatre manager, whose real name was Samuelson. He was born in Southport and proud of being a Lancastrian. He showed a leaning towards the theatre and showmanship from his earliest youth, and Barnum himself was anxious to adopt him. Having built up a big connexion in Manchester as an agent, he went to London, married, and started out to conquer the metropolis with a pound, lent him by his wife, to whom he was all his life devoted and she to him. His business grew, and he added to it an 'ideas department', advising the artistes whom he represented how best to use their talents and build up their acts. He was himself a very accomplished illusionist and invented a 'talking head', which, without any body attached, answered questions put to it by the audience. In addition to his mastery of stage magic he was well versed in theatre mechanics, and was probably one of the best technical producers of his day. When pantomime was at a low ebb, he rescued it, producing some magnificent specimens in the true old tradition. He became the unchallenged Pantomime King of his time, and one of his proudest moments was when he produced *The Sleeping Beauty* at Drury Lane in Dec. 1929, when the traditional home of pantomime had been without one for ten years. Although pantomime was his chief concern, he will be remembered also for his production of *Mr. Cinders* and *The Good Companions*. Under a brusque exterior which covered his shyness, he had a kind and gentle nature, and he adored children. This was probably the reason for his success with pantomime, for he never really grew up. His love and enthusiasm for the theatre, and his capacity for work in its service, were boundless. He died suddenly while producing his second Drury Lane pantomime.   W. M. P.

WYNDHAM. (1) SIR CHARLES (1837–1919), son of a surgeon named Culverwell, was one of the finest of English actor-managers, whose long and brilliant career covers the story of an epoch. He trained as a doctor in Dublin, but was an enthusiastic amateur actor, and finally appeared on the professional stage at the Royalty Theatre, London, in 1862. Some months later he went to the United States, and joined the Confederate Army as a surgeon, being present at most of the big engagements of the war. He returned to the stage in New York in the following year, but without much success, and two years later was back in England, where he appeared at Manchester in a farce written by himself. Returning to the Royalty, he started on a series of performances of Shakespearian and other parts. This gave him a varied experience that proved useful later on. Venturing into management without much success, he returned to America (in 1869) and remained there for two years, becoming known as an excellent light comedian. He was also one of the first actors to take his own company on tour in the United States. His first big success after his return to England in 1871 was *Brighton* (1874), which he subsequently took to the Criterion, thus inaugurating an association with that theatre which was to last the rest of his life. He made it one of the foremost playhouses of London, and also built and managed the New Theatre and Wyndham's, making them equally successful. A tall, handsome man, with a mobile expressive face and a distinguished presence, he had a voice which, though at times a little husky, had great charm. A fine light comedian, he could play serious roles also, and in dramatic scenes, such as his deadly cross-examination of Felicia Hindmarsh in *Mrs. Dane's Defence*, he had few equals. His judgement and his productions were alike impeccable. He delighted in roles where, in the last act, he had a long speech which put everything and everyone to rights, and in the delivery of it he was superb. Among his roles the greatest was perhaps that of David Garrick in Tom Robertson's play, which he made peculiarly his own. He was also outstanding in *Rosemary*, *The Liars*, *The Case of Rebellious Susan*, and *The Mollusc*, to name but a few. He was knighted in 1902, and few actors have better deserved the honour, for he did much for the stage. He married as his second wife (2) MARY MOORE (1862–1931), widow of the playwright James Albery. A fine actress, she remained under Wyndham's management, playing leading roles with him, until his death, when she continued in the management of his theatres. She made her first appearance on the stage at the Gaiety, under John Hollingshead, but gave up acting on her first marriage, not returning to the theatre until 1881, when she first appeared (as Miss M. Mortimer) under Wyndham. She too was outstanding in *David Garrick*, in which she played Ida Ingot, and in that and other roles had few equals. Her performance in *The Mollusc*, which contained only four characters, and in which she, as leading lady, scarcely stirred from a settee, was a *tour de force*. A woman of great beauty and charm, she retained her energy, her business acumen, and her quick intelligence to the end. After her death her son (see ALBERY, 2) and Sir Charles's by his first wife, (3) HOWARD (1865–1947), who had long been associated with his father's theatres, took joint control of them, and produced a number of successful new plays and revivals.

WYNDHAM'S THEATRE, LONDON, in Charing Cross Road, was built by Charles Wyndham. It opened on 16 Nov. 1899, with a revival of *David Garrick*, in which Wyndham had already appeared with great success. A number of plays followed, among them *Mrs. Dane's Defence*, in which Wyndham and Lena Ashwell gave remarkable performances, and *Glittering Gloria*, with James Welch and a bull-dog in the leading parts. Another early success was *When Knights were Bold*, which ran for 579 performances. In 1909 a play by Guy du Maurier dealing with the invasion of England, called *An Englishman's Home*, caused a sensation and materially increased the recruiting for the newly established Territorial Army. A year later Gerald du Maurier and Frank Curzon took over Wyndham's and remained there with success for many years. Among their productions were *A Kiss for Cinderella*, *Dear Brutus*, and *The Ringer*, by Edgar Wallace, who was for a time manager of the theatre. Among its later successes were *George and Margaret*, *Quiet Wedding*, its long-running sequel, *Quiet Week-End*, and *No Medals*. W. M. P.

Y

YAKOVLEV, ALEXEI SEMENOVICH (1773–1817), Russian actor, a member of the St. Petersburg Imperial Theatre company. He was a member of a merchant family and had practically no education. His parents died when he was young, and all schooling ended when at 13 he was set to work in a wine-merchant's shop. In 1793, under the influence of the playwright Perepechin, he wrote his first play, and was persuaded by the actor Dmitrevsky to go on the stage, where he made his first appearance in 1794 as Oskold in *Semir*. Helped by his excellent presence and powerful voice, and by the counsels of Dmitrevsky, he was soon playing leading roles. His acting was mainly intuitive, and his temperament rebelled against craftsmanship and technical detail. His performances were therefore very unequal, but he had some perceptions of greatness, and tried to initiate reforms which were later carried out by Shchepkin. He was a heavy drinker, and at one time tried to commit suicide, subsequently leaving the stage for a while. On his return the public welcomed him back warmly, but his talent was declining. In Oct. 1817 he played Othello, and was carried from the stage in a state of collapse, dying shortly afterwards.

YALE. This American university had theatrical performances in its very early days, since in 1771 an annual series of plays was inaugurated to which the students invited their friends. The performance, held in the early summer and accompanied by a garden party, was usually given at a large house in the town. Among the plays performed were *The Conscious Lovers, The Beaux' Stratagem*, and in 1785 an original play, *The Mercenary Match*, written by one Bidwell, an undergraduate in his senior year. There has been for many years an amateur dramatic society for the students, and in 1925 the official Drama Department was inaugurated, with an excellent little experimental theatre built and endowed by Edward Harkness, of which Professor George Baker, fresh from the triumphs of his playwriting course and '47 Workshop' at Harvard, was the first Director. The curriculum comprises an elaborate post-graduate course, and gives instruction in design, lighting, costuming, and production, as well as the opportunity of writing plays for subsequent production. There is also in the University Library a Theatre Collection which houses among other things a vast dossier of photographs of theatrical material collected from all over Europe. This was begun under the supervision of Professor Allardyce Nicoll during his term of office as head of the Drama Department, and is constantly being added to.

YATES. (1) FREDERICK HENRY (1795–1842), English actor, friend of the elder Mathews, with whom—Yates being then in the army—

he played to the troops of the Duke of Wellington near Cambrai. Mathews persuaded him to go on the stage, and he was first seen in Edinburgh, where it is said 'precocity and consummate self-confidence enabled him to play leading parts in Shakespeare with distinction'. In 1818 he went to London, where he was Iago to the Othello of Charles Mayne Young, and in the following year Falstaff to Macready's Hotspur. Having no pretensions to be anything but a useful actor, he played everything that was offered to him, and always well, but he eventually deserted tragedy for comedy, where his real talent lay. In 1825, with Daniel Terry, he took over the Adelphi and gave a series of melodramas, farces, and burlesques, being joined on Terry's death in 1829 by his old friend Mathews. Some of the best authors of the day wrote for him, and he himself was excellent in such parts as Fagin, Mantalini, and Miss Miggs. In his company, besides T. P. Cooke, Rice, and the low comedian Wright, was his wife, Elizabeth Brunton, sister of the famous Mrs. Merry. She was an excellent actress, and mother of (2) EDMUND (1832–94), a well-known journalist, friend of Albert Smith and Clement Scott, and the author of a number of light ephemeral plays. It was in a dramatization of one of his novels as *A Millionaire* (1883) that Lady Tree made her first big success.

YATES. (1) RICHARD (1706–96), English comedian, accounted in his day almost as good a speaking Harlequin as the famous Woodward. He was with Giffard's company when Garrick made his first appearance there, and was the first to play Sir Oliver Surface. His style in comedy was modelled on that of Doggett, and he was a careful and conscientious actor, seldom resorting to trickery. He was excellent in all Shakespeare's fools, and was considered the only actor of the time to have a just notion of how to play them. In all characters of low humour he was unsurpassed, but fine gentlemen and serious comedy lay outside his range. His second wife, (2) MARY ANN GRAHAM (1728–87), was a fine tragic actress. Coached by her husband, Garrick, and Murphy, she made her first appearance at Drury Lane in 1754, and was at first unnoticed, owing to the ascendancy of Mrs. Cibber. On the latter's death, however, she was considered the first exponent of classical heroines in eighteenth-century tragedy, to which her dignified presence and powerful, though monotonous, voice were eminently suitable. She was somewhat frigid in her deportment, and of little use in the portrayal of tenderness, pathos, or comedy. She made her last appearance on the stage in 1785, at a benefit for George Ann Bellamy.

YEATS, WILLIAM BUTLER (1865–1939), Irish poet and dramatist, and a founder of the Irish

Dramatic Movement at the end of the nineteenth century (see IRELAND). It was to his determination and foresight that it owed its beginning, and it was his courage, his eloquence, and his acute business intelligence that combined with Lady Gregory's work to keep it alive through the first precarious years. It was his criticism that defined and guided it; it was his name that gave it distinction when little else was known of it. But these things might have been done by another man; what Yeats alone could contribute was poetic drama, which he brought back to life in the English-speaking countries, beginning with Ireland. Before he began his work, poetry was virtually unknown in the contemporary theatre; nineteenth-century poets had either avoided drama or written plays primarily for reading. Yeats lived to see poetic drama acclimatized in Ireland, England, and America almost as it had been in Elizabethan England. This was the more remarkable in that Yeats's genius does not appear to have been primarily dramatic. But, like Ben Jonson before him, he was determined to become a dramatist, and he mastered the details of technique. His belief in the theatre, and in an Irish theatre in particular, was enough; the plays of his maturity are essentially dramatic.

The early plays, *Land of Heart's Desire* (1894), *The Countess Cathleen* (1899), and *Shadowy Waters* (1897–1906), are poetic plays which appeal to the innate imagination of their audiences; their themes are remote; the experience they present, though universal, is not revealed in terms of actual, contemporary life. They thus separate clearly from the contemporary European tradition in serious drama, which was based on that of Ibsen's middle plays. The next three, *The Hour Glass* (1903, 1912), *The King's Threshold* (1903), and *The Unicorn from the Stars* (1907), are, dramatically and poetically, an advance. The thought and the poetry are deepened and clarified, but the plays are also more dramatic. The first is virtually a modern morality, the third a bold piece of speculative thinking, and both are based on a similar mystical experience; in *The King's Threshold* the function of poetry and of the poet is the major theme. During, or just after, this period come the two brief peasant plays, *Cathleen ni Houlihan* and *The Pot of Broth* (1902), and those based on the heroic legends of Ireland, *On Baile's Strand* (1904), *Deirdre* (1906 seq.), and *The Green Helmet* (1908). The 'Four Plays for Dancers' follow in 1916 and 1917: *At The Hawk's Well*, *The Only Jealousy of Emer* (1916), *The Dreaming of the Bones*, and *Calvary* (1917). In these, extreme simplicity of design and setting is matched by brevity of expression and severity of thought. In the latest plays of all, this plainness and severity, characteristic also of his poetry after 1916, reaches fulfilment, and the underlying thought makes stricter demands than ever upon the intelligence and imagination of the audience. Perhaps most characteristic of these are the last two, *The Words*

upon the Window Pane (1934) and *Purgatory* (1938).

His work, whether in prose or verse, was essential poetry; and he was unexcelled in his own time by any other poetic dramatist writing in English.   U. E.-F.

YERMOLOVA, MARIA NIKOLAIEVNA (1853–1928), tragic actress of pre- and post-Revolutionary Russia, whom Stanislavsky considered the greatest actress he had ever known, not excepting Duse. She was the daughter of the prompter at the Maly Theatre, and, after attending a theatre school, made her début there as Emilia Galotti in 1870. She approached this, and her other leading roles, in a new way, making her heroines active, independent members of society in contrast to the passive, unreal presentations of the past. She was outstanding in such plays as *Maria Stuart*, *Die Jungfrau von Orleans*, *Phèdre*, *La Estrella de Sevilla*, and *Macbeth*. On the occasion of her benefit in 1876 she chose to appear in Lope de Vega's *Fuenteovejuna*, in which she scored such a success with the more liberal-minded among her audience that it was promptly banned. Yermolova was in no whit disconcerted by the October Revolution, which her large humanity and progressive liberalism rather welcomed, and her fifty years on the stage were celebrated in 1920 with full honours and the title of People's Artist of the Republic, which may be compared with the English D.B.E. In 1930 the students of the Maly Theatre named a studio in her honour, which later became the Yermolova Theatre. After its break with the parent body it adopted the methods of the Moscow Art Theatre, and adapted them to the problems of adolescent youth in the modern world. During the Second World War it was evacuated, but returned with an impressive programme. From its early days the company has grown until it numbers about sixty members, while its small permanent home, of which it took possession in 1933, seats nearly 400.

YEVREINOV, NIKOLAI, see EVREINOV.

YIDDISH ART THEATRE, NEW YORK, see JEWISH DRAMA (6).

YIDDISH DRAMA, see JEWISH DRAMA.

YORK CYCLE, see ENGLAND, 1 and MYSTERY PLAY.

YOUNG, CHARLES (?–1874), American actor, about whom very little information is available. He was for a time in Australia, and managed a theatre in Hobart. He appears to have been eccentric and undisciplined, though erratically good in tragedy. He was for a short time the husband of Mrs. Duff, though the marriage was never consummated, and he was also the first husband of Jane Elizabeth Thomson, later well known on the London stage as Mrs. Hermann Vezin.

YOUNG, Charles Mayne (1777–1856), celebrated English actor, and one of the finest disciples of the Kemble school of acting. The son of a doctor, he was well educated, but owing to financial and other difficulties had to support his mother at an early age. He became a clerk, but amateur theatricals gave him a taste for the stage, and in 1798, as Mr. Green, he made his début at Liverpool. From there he went to Manchester and Edinburgh, and became an intimate friend of Sir Walter Scott. Two years later he married a young actress who had recently appeared at the Haymarket as Juliet with much success. She died in childbirth the following year, her son becoming a clergyman and author of a life of his father, who never married again. It was through the good offices of the elder Mathews, always his close friend, that Young was first seen in London, playing Hamlet at the Haymarket with much success, Mathews appearing with him as Polonius. Both actors appeared in the same parts when Young took his farewell of the stage in May 1832, with Macready as the Ghost. During his years in the London theatre he proved himself a sterling actor and an ornament to his profession. He played with John Philip Kemble, Mrs. Siddons, Macready, and Miss O'Neill, and in 1822 was with Kean at Drury Lane. The only new part of any importance which he created was Rienzi, but he was good both in tragedy and comedy, as Falstaff, Macheath, McSycophant, Falkland, Cassius, Iago, the Stranger, Hamlet, and Macbeth. Equable in temper, with a steady confidence in and knowledge of his own powers, he was welcomed everywhere, and in private life was a delightful companion, enjoying his long retirement to the full.

YOUNG, Stark (1881–), American dramatic critic, who was born in Como, Mississippi, and attended the universities of Mississippi and Columbia. Afterwards he was an instructor in English at the University of Texas and at Amherst College. In 1921 he joined the editorial staff of *The New Republic* and has been that magazine's dramatic critic ever since. During the season of 1924–5 he was also dramatic critic of *The New York Times*. Stark Young is without question the finest critic of acting at work in America to-day and has written brilliantly of the many foreign artists who have come before him: of the Moscow Art Company, of Mei Lan-fang, of Duse, and of Bernhardt. He has written several plays, and has directed productions of Lenormand's *Failures* and O'Neill's *Welded*. An expert linguist, he has translated Chekhov's *The Seagull* and plays from Spanish and Italian. His novel, *So Red the Rose*, a nostalgic picture of the ante-bellum South, achieved great success some years ago and was subsequently made into a film.   T. Q. C.

YOUNG ROSCIUS, see BETTY.

Z

ZACCONI, ERMETE (1867–1948), Italian actor, child of strolling players, who made his first appearance on the stage at the age of 7. After many years on tour, during which he perfected his art without attracting undue attention, he became, in 1884, leading man in a company run by Giovanni Emanuel. He was soon recognized as one of the outstanding actors of the Italian stage, equalled only by Novelli, and was able to found and direct his own company. He was the first Italian actor to put on *Ghosts*, playing Oswald Alving himself, and with Duse was instrumental in reconciling the Italian public to Ibsen's plays. He produced translations of plays by Tolstoy, Hauptmann, and Strindberg, and also appeared in a number of Italian plays and in the great roles of Shakespeare. In 1899 he played with Duse in *La Gioconda* and Dumas's *Le Demi-monde*, but with small success, and they separated to tour each with their own company. He penetrated as far as Russia, being well received, and was also seen in Austria and Germany. He was accounted a most versatile actor, equally at home in old and modern plays, and in tragic and comic parts, being particularly good as Hamlet, and as the name-part in Testoni's *Il Cardinale Lambertini* (1905), a comedy of intrigue based on a seventeenth-century cardinal of Bologna.

ZAKHAVA, BORIS EVGENEVICH (1896–   ), Soviet actor and producer, who in 1913 entered the students' dramatic studio which became, under Vakhtangov, the Third Moscow Art Studio, and then the Vakhtangov Theatre. He was one of the most active members of the studio, and a close friend and collaborator of Vakhtangov, participating with him in his productions, notably the famous *Turandot*, in which he played Timur. After the death of Vakhtangov, Zakhava produced independently many plays by Ostrovsky, Leonov, Schiller, Gorky, and others, of which the most important was *Yegor Bulichev* in 1935. He continued to act, and worked for two years in Meyerhold's theatre in order to study his methods. He is the author of several books in which he expounds and develops the methods of Stanislavsky and Vakhtangov.

ZANGWILL, ISRAEL (1864–1926), Jewish author and philanthropist, who established his literary reputation with a fine novel, *The Children of the Ghetto* (1892). He also wrote some plays, of which *The Melting Pot*, a study of Jewish immigrant life in the United States, was the most important. First produced in New York in 1908, it was a great success, and was several times revived, being first seen in London in 1914.

ZANY, the anglicized form of the Italian *zanni*, a term which covers all the male servant masks of the *commedia dell'arte*. Among them were the prototypes of the English Harlequin (Arlecchino) and Punch (Pulcinella), who have changed greatly in appearance and function; and Scapin, Scaramouche, and Pasquin, who are perhaps more famous in their French form than in their Italian—Scapino, Scaramuccia, and Pasquino. The lovesick French Pierrot and the English Pierrot of concert-parties are also distantly derived from a zany, Pedrolino. In Elizabethan usage the word, which is now rarely used, always carried the idea of a 'clumsy imitator'.

ZARZUELA, a Spanish musical play, which took its name from the royal shooting-lodge near Madrid, where such diversions were the favourite amusement of Philip IV. From the earliest times Spanish plays were accompanied by music, and often designed to be sung, and among the writers of *zarzuelas* were Lope de Vega and Calderón. They were, however, more frequently handled by the *entremesistas*, of whom Quiñones de Benevente was the chief. A *Teatro de la Zarzuela*, devoted entirely to this type of entertainment, was opened in Madrid on 10 Oct. 1856. The rise of the *género chico*, however, challenged the vogue of the sentimental nineteenth-century *zarzuela*, and the name is now chiefly applied to a light entertainment, in one act, lasting about an hour. Several of these may be given in an evening. They may be comic, satiric, melodramatic, but seldom if ever tragic.

ZAVADSKY, YURI ALEXEIVICH (1894–   ), Soviet actor and producer, who began his career at the Moscow Art Theatre. He then went with Vakhtangov to the Third Studio, and was in the latter's production of *Turandot*, but left shortly afterwards. In 1927 he opened his own studio with a group of students. As a producer he works on the system of Stanislavsky, as modified by Vakhtangov, but insists less on depth than on lightness of touch and a free-flowing line. His first production was *On ne badine pas avec l'amour*, and he later made a success with *The Devil's Disciple*. In 1940 he was appointed director of the Mossoviet Theatre, and on returning from evacuation during the Second World War he prepared to stage a series of plays in groups—a group of Ostrovsky, for example, and a group of Goldoni. He had previously supervised the production of Afinogenov's last play, *Mashenka*. Zavadsky ranks among the outstanding producers of the U.S.S.R.

ZENO, APOSTOLO (1668–1750), for many years Court poet at Vienna, the predecessor there of Metastasio, and like him a writer of libretti for plays where words and music have equal weight. These have since been used by numerous composers as operatic libretti. He had his first resounding success in 1695, when *Gl'Inganni felici*, with music by Carlo Francesco Pollardo (1653–1722), was first performed at the Teatro Sant'Angelo in Venice. A later *Lucio Vero* (1700), with music by the same composer, was also successful, and has been set by about twenty composers since. Zeno produced a drama every year for the Court at Vienna, some of them in collaboration with Pariati. Most of his subjects were taken from classical history and mythology.

ZIEGFELD, FLORENZ (1867–1932), American theatre manager, son of the President of the Chicago Musical College. He originated and perfected the American theatrical revue in a series of productions called the Ziegfeld Follies, which began in 1907 and ran for twenty-four consecutive editions under the caption 'An American Institution'. He borrowed his pattern largely from the Folies-Bergère, Paris, basing the emphasis on beautiful girls, scenic invention, comic sketches, and noteworthy vaudeville specialities. His name connotated prodigality in both his theatrical and his personal life. He spent thousands on production numbers which he discarded after a first night. He outbid other managers for stars whose services he wanted, and when he travelled it was in luxurious style with a retinue of attendants—chauffeurs, secretaries, and a valet. His slogan, 'Glorifying the American Girl', resulted in making the Ziegfeld girl symbolize perfect American beauty for more than three decades. His standard of female perfection was adopted largely by the early motion pictures, many of whose first stars were Ziegfeld girls, including Olive Thomas, Mae Murray, Marion Davies, Irene Dunne, Martha Mansfield, and Paulette Goddard.

Engagement in a Ziegfeld production was counted a primary theatrical honour because of the producer's superb taste and critical selectivity. He was a star-maker and a discoverer of talent, chiefly responsible for bringing into prominence such famous stars of the stage, screen, and radio as Fannie Brice, W. C. Fields, Eddie Cantor, and Bert Williams. Among the artists, national and international, who played under his aegis were Anna Held, Maurice Chevalier, Fred and Adele Astaire, Lupino Lane, Billie Burke, Nora Bayes, Marilyn Miller, Sophie Tucker, and Evelyn Laye. Among those associated with him in his productions were Joseph Urban, scenic artist; Victor Herbert, Irving Berlin, Sigmund Romberg, George Gershwin, and Richard Rodgers, composers; J. P. McEvoy, Irving Caesar, Ring Lardner, William Anthony McGuire, and Oscar Hammerstein II, librettists and lyricists. His productions included, in addition to the Follies, *The Red Feather, The Comic Supplement, Kid Boots, Sally, Showboat*—one of the finest musical comedies in the history of the American stage—and numerous straight plays. Ziegfeld's second wife (the first was Anna Held) was Billie Burke (1885–   ),

who made her stage début in London and went to America to be John Drew's leading lady. She became one of the most popular comediennes of the American stage, and later appeared extensively in films and on the radio. The life of Ziegfeld was the subject of a film by M.G.M. B. S.

ZIEGFELD THEATRE, NEW YORK. This opened on 2 Feb. 1927, and was one of the handsomest playhouses in the city, superbly designed by Joseph Urban to provide more than adequate backstage space, a handsome auditorium, and a fine, stark exterior. Its life was a short one, for the great American showman for whom it was built and named was nearly at the end of his career, but he saw several successes there before he died in 1932. Among them were *Rio Rita*, the opening attraction, *Showboat, Bitter Sweet*, and the Ziegfeld Follies of 1931. In 1932 the theatre became a cinema, but on 7 Dec. 1944 it was reopened as a theatre by Billy Rose, with Beatrice Lillie in *Seven Lively Arts*. G. F.

ZIEGLER, CLARA (1844–1909), German actress, who from 1867 to 1868 was in Leipzig, and later went to Munich for some years as guest artist. A beautiful woman with a particularly lovely voice, she was at her best in such parts as Joan of Arc, Penthesilea, and Medea; she also, in the tradition of her day, played Romeo. She was the author of several plays, and on her death left her house and library to the city of Munich, as a theatre museum, together with money for its maintenance as a theatre collection. The idea of such a museum first came to her in 1892, when visiting the International Music and Theatre Exhibition in Vienna, and it was formally opened in 1910. Its curator for many years was the famous German theatre historian, Franz Rapp. Several other collections have been added to it, and in 1932 extra space for display was acquired elsewhere, the house being used for the books and catalogues, and such special treasures as the first film made by UFA and unique records of broadcast plays.

ZILAHY, LAJOS (1891–   ), Hungarian dramatist, author of a number of plays dealing realistically with the social problems of the post-1914 period.

ZOFFANY, JOHN (1733/5–1810), a painter, of Bohemian extraction, who in 1758 settled in London and remained there until his death. Among his works were many theatrical portraits, particularly of David Garrick—as Abel Drugger, as Jaffier (with Mrs. Cibber), as Macbeth (with Mrs. Pritchard), as Sir John Brute and so on. He also painted Samuel Foote, Shuter, King, and other actors, either singly or in groups from a particular play, as for example King and Mrs. Baddeley in *The Clandestine Marriage*, and a scene from *Love in a Village*. Many of his paintings are in the possession of the Garrick Club.

ZOLA, Émile (1840–1902), French novelist and dramatist, leader of the naturalistic school. He much disliked the facile, optimistic plays of Scribe and his followers, and thought that a play should be a 'slice of life', thrown on the stage without embellishment or artifice. His own plays, particularly *Thérèse Raquin* (1873), which he dramatized from his novel of that name, carry out this theory, which he developed at greater length in his critical articles, later republished in two volumes as *Le Naturalisme au théâtre* and *Nos auteurs dramatiques*. The second volume castigates the major dramatists of the time, of whom Zola had a very poor opinion, and is less interesting than the first, in which he deals mainly with his own ideas of reform. It is as a novelist that Zola is chiefly remembered, but he had an important influence on the development of the French, and through that of the European, theatre of his day and afterwards.

ZORRILLA, Francisco de Rojas, see rojas zorrilla.

ZORRILLA Y MORAL, José (1817–93), the outstanding poetic dramatist of the Romantic movement in Spain. His most famous play is the extraordinarily popular *Don Juan Tenorio* (1844), which added yet another version to the numerous interpretations of the Don Juan legend. For many years it was given annually on All Saints' Day in all the theatres of Spain. Among Zorrilla's other plays mention should be made of *El puñal del godo* (1842), *El Zapatero y el Rey*, a historical play in two parts (1840 and 1841), and *Traidor; inconfeso y mártir* (1849), based on the supposed life of Dom Sebastian of Portugal, a legendary figure whose existence is doubtful. Zorrilla is also the author of some cloak-and-sword comedies, and of a book of memoirs, interesting for the history of the theatre.

ZUCKMAYER, Carl (1896–   ), German dramatist, whose folk-comedy, *Der fröhliche Weinberg* (1925), was typical of the new realism. He made his name with *Der Hauptmann von Köpenick*, based on an actual incident to which he gave a satiric twist, since the local shoemaker who, disguised as a captain, causes all the trouble, only achieves his end because of the Prussian obedience to a uniform. This play has been successfully translated into English, and has also been filmed. Zuckmayer's other plays, also based on popular tales, as in *Der Schelm von Bergen*, are less satiric.

BIBLIOGRAPHY

THIS list covers more than 1,000 books on the history of the theatre, its drama, its dramatists, and its actors, classified under several heads. In order to avoid duplication of titles, books are entered once only, and cross-references have been made where necessary from one section to another, except to the General and Technical sections, which readers are advised to consult on all occasions. Where a number of different countries, regions, or buildings have been grouped together (as Far Eastern Theatres; London Theatres; Regional Theatres, U.S.A.) cross-references are given for each item. The only person to have a separate bibliography is Shakespeare. All other persons should be looked for under their country of origin.

In order to facilitate reference, the longer bibliographies have been divided into several main chronological groups, with the general books on each section listed alphabetically by authors or editors, followed by memoirs and biographies listed alphabetically by the name of the subject. Thus, the main section on English Restoration and Eighteenth-Century Drama is followed by books on Congreve, Farquhar, Sheridan, and Wycherley, and then by entries ranging from Colman to Macklin. Students of the English and American theatres should consult all the bibliographies, as most of them will be seen to contain books touching on those two theatres.

With a few exceptions, plays and collections of plays have been omitted, as have the collected criticisms of modern dramatic critics.

Abbreviations: B. = Bibliography
Ed. = edition, editor
Ill. = Illustrations
N.Y. = New York
n.d. = no date
rev. = revised
tr. = translated, translation

The Bibliography on *Jesuit Drama* was compiled by Dr. Edna Purdie, and that on *South America* by Miss Mildred Adams. The others have been compiled by the Editor, with assistance from Miss Ena Sheen in London and Mrs. Elizabeth Barrett in New York.

GENERAL BOOKS

1. Reference Books

W. DAVENPORT ADAMS: *A Dictionary of the Drama*. A Guide to the Plays, Playwrights, Players, and Playhouses of the United Kingdom and America, from the Earliest Times to the Present, Vol. I: A–G (no other pub.), London and Philadelphia, 1904.

BLANCH M. BAKER: *Dramatic Bibliography*. An annotated list of books on the History and Criticism of the Drama and Stage and on the allied arts of the Theatre. Introduction by Milton Smith. N.Y., 1933.

ROSAMOND GILDER: *A Theatre Library, a Bibliography of 100 Books relating to the Theatre*, N.Y., 1932.

—— and GEORGE FREEDLEY: *Theatre Collections in Libraries and Museums; an International Handbook*, N.Y., 1936.

LILLIAN ARVILLA HALL: *Catalogue of Dramatic Portraits in the Theatre Collection of the Harvard College Library*, 4 vols., Harvard U.P., 1930–4.

BAMPTON HUNT (Ed.): *Green Room Book, or Who's Who on the Stage*. An Annual Biographical Record of the Dramatic, Musical, and Variety World, Ill., London, 1906.

PAUL LACROIX: *Catalogue of the Soleinne Library*, Paris, 1843.

ROBERT W. LOWE: *A Bibliographical Account of English Theatrical Literature from the Earliest Times to the Present Day*, London, 1888.

PAUL ALFRED MERBACH: *Bibliographie für Theatergeschichte, 1905–10*, Berlin, 1913.

JOHN PARKER (Ed.): *Green Room Book, or Who's Who on the Stage*, Ill., London, annually, 1907–11.

—— *Who's Who in the Theatre, A Bibliographical Record of the Contemporary Stage*, London, 1912; tenth ed., 1947.

ARTHUR POUGIN: *Dictionnaire historique et pittoresque du Théâtre, et des Arts qui s'y rattachent*, Ill., Paris, 1885.

AUGUSTE RONDEL: *Catalogue analytique sommaire de la Collection théâtrale Rondel*, suivi d'un Guide pratique à travers la Bibliographie théâtrale et d'une Chronologie des Ouvrages d'information et de critique théâtrales, Paris, 1932, B.

BERNARD SOBEL (Ed.): *The Theatre Handbook and Digest of Plays*, N.Y., 1940, B.

ROY STALLINGS and PAUL MYERS: *A Guide to Theatre Reading*, [prepared] under the editorial supervision of George Freedley. Foreword by Rosamond Gilder, N.Y., 1949.

2. Drama and General History

ROBERT HAMILTON BALL: *The Amazing Career of Sir Giles Overreach*, Ill., Princeton and London, 1939, B.

ALFRED BATES (Ed.): *The Drama*, 22 vols., London, 1913.

GEORGE BRANDES: *Main Currents in 19th Century Literature*, tr. from the Danish, 6 vols., Ill., London and N.Y., 1906.

SHELDON WARREN CHENEY: *The Theatre. Three Thousand Years of Drama, Acting and Stagecraft*, Ill., London and N.Y., 1929, B.

WILLIAM CREIZENACH: *Geschichte des neueren Dramas*, 5 vols., Halle, 1893–1916. (*See* ENGLAND for a tr. of Vol. 4.)

LUCIEN DUBECH, JACQUES DE MONTBRIAL, MADELEINE HORN-MONVAL: *Histoire générale illustrée du théâtre*, 5 vols., Ill., Paris, 1931–4.

ASHLEY DUKES: *Drama*, London, 1926; rev. ed., 1936 (Home University Library), B.

GEORGE FREEDLEY and JOHN A. REEVES: *A History of the Theatre*, Ill., N.Y., 1941, B.

JOHN GASSNER: *Masters of the Drama*, N.Y., 1940, B.

ROSAMOND GILDER: *Enter the Actress. The First Women in the Theatre*, Ill., London and Boston, 1931.

HARLEY GRANVILLE-BARKER: *The Use of the Drama*, London, 1946.

GLENN HUGHES: *The Story of the Theatre, a Short History of Theatrical Art from the Beginning to the Present Day*, Ill., London and N.Y., 1928, B.

KARL MANTZIUS: *A History of Theatrical Art in Ancient and Modern Times*, authorized tr. from the Danish by Louise von Cossel (vols. 1–5) and C. Archer (vol. 6), 6 vols., Ill., London, 1903–21.

BRANDER MATTHEWS: *The Development of the Drama*, N.Y., 1903.

—— and LAURENCE HUTTON (Eds.): *Actors and Actresses of Great Britain and the United States from the Days of David Garrick to the Present Time*, 5 vols., N.Y., 1886.

MALCOLM MORLEY: *The Theatre*. Foreword by George Arliss. London, 1935.

ALLARDYCE NICOLL: *The Development of the Theatre. A Study of Theatrical Art from the Beginnings to the Present Day*, Ill., London, 1927; new and rev. ed., 1948, B.

—— *Masks, Mimes and Miracles, Studies in the Popular Theatre*, Ill., London and N.Y., 1931.

HELEN ORMSBEE: *Backstage with Actors, from the time of Shakespeare to the Present Day*, Ill., N.Y., 1938.

LUIGI RICCOBONI: *An Historical and Critical Account of the Theatres in Europe*, London, 1741.

THOMAS WOOD STEVENS: *The Theatre from Athens to Broadway*, Ill., N.Y., 1932.

DONALD CLIVE STUART: *The Development of Dramatic Art*, N.Y., 1928, B.

ENID WELSFORD: *The Fool, his Social and Literary History*, Ill., London, 1935, B.

N. SCARLYN WILSON: *European Drama*, London, 1937, B.

3. Modern Drama

JOHN ANDREWS and OSSIA TRILLING (Eds.): *International Theatre*, London, 1949.

JOHN MASON BROWN: *The Modern Theatre in Revolt*, N.Y., 1929, B.

HUNTLY CARTER: *The New Spirit in the European Theatre, 1914–1924*. A comparative study of the changes effected by the war and revolutions, Ill., London and N.Y., 1925.

FRANK W. CHANDLER: *Modern Continental Playwrights*, N.Y., 1931, B.

BARRETT H. CLARK: *A Study of the Modern Drama*; a Handbook for the Study and Appreciation of Typical plays, European, English, and American, of the last three-quarters of a century, N.Y., 1934; rev. ed., 1938, B.

—— and GEORGE FREEDLEY (Eds.): *A History of Modern Drama*, N.Y., 1947, B.

THOMAS H. DICKINSON: *An Outline of Contemporary Drama*, Boston, 1927, B.

—— (Ed.): *The Theatre in a Changing Europe*, Ill., London and N.Y., 1937.

HALLIE FLANAGAN: *Shifting Scenes of the Modern European Theatre*, Ill., N.Y., 1928.

ISAAC GOLDBERG: *The Drama of Transition*, Cincinnati, 1922.

MORDECAI GORELIK: *New Theatres for Old*, Ill., N.Y., 1940, London, 1947, B.

ARCHIBALD HENDERSON: *European Dramatists*, Ill., N.Y., 1913; rev. ed., 1926.

THEODORE KOMISARJEVSKY: *Myself and the Theatre*, Ill., London, 1929.

KENNETH MACGOWAN: *The Theatre of Tomorrow*, Ill., N.Y., 1922, B.

ANNA IRENE MILLER: *The Independent Theatre in Europe, 1887 to the Present*, N.Y., 1931, B.

HIRAM KELLY MODERWELL: *The Theatre of Today*, Ill., London and N.Y., 1915; new ed. with Introduction by John Mason Brown, 1927.

WILLIAM LYON PHELPS: *The Twentieth Century Theatre, Observations on the Contemporary English and American Stage*, N.Y., 1918.

GUIDO RUBERTI: *Il teatro contemporaneo in Europa*, Bologna, 1921.

(Consult also the files of *The Mask*, ed. Gordon Craig, Ill., Florence, 1908–29; and *Theatre Arts*, various editors, Ill., N.Y., 1916–48.)

TECHNICAL BOOKS

1. General Stagecraft, including Scenery

VICTOR ED. D'AMICO: *Theater Art*, Ill., Peoria, Illinois, 1931, B.

DENYS AMIEL et HENRI FESCOURT (Eds.): *Les Spectacles à travers les Âges*, 3 vols., Ill., Paris, 1931–2.

ADOLPHE APPIA: *La mise en scène du drame wagnérien*, Paris, 1895.

—— *Die Musik und die Inscenierung*, Ill., Munich, 1899.

GERMAIN BAPST: *Essai sur l'histoire du théâtre. La mise en scène, le décor, le costume, l'architecture, l'éclairage, l'hygiène*, Ill., Paris, 1893.

PHILIP W. BARBER: *The Scene Technician's Handbook*, Ill., New Haven, 1928.

PETER BAX: *Stage Management*. Introduction by William Armstrong. Ill., London, 1936, B.

HAROLD BURRIS-MEYER and EDWARD C. COLE: *Scenery for the Theatre*. The organization, processes, materials, and techniques used to set the stage. Introduction by Arthur Hopkins. London and Boston, 1939, B.

LUDOVIC CELLER: *Les décors, les costumes et la mise en scène au XVIIe siècle, 1615–80*, Paris, 1869.

SHELDON WARREN CHENEY: *Stage Decoration*, Ill., London and N.Y., 1928.

RAYMOND COGNIAT: *Décors de Théâtre*, Ill., Paris, 1930.

EDWARD GORDON CRAIG: *On the Art of the Theatre*, Ill., London, 1911, N.Y., 1925; *Scene*, Ill., London and N.Y., 1923.

LOUISE DAMERON: *Bibliography of Stage Settings*, Baltimore, 1936.

W. G. FAY: *A Short Glossary of Theatrical Terms*, London, 1930.

GIULIO FERRARI: *La Scenografia*, Ill., Milan, 1902, B.

OSKAR FISCHEL: *Das Moderne Bühnenbild*, Ill., Berlin, 1923.

DARIEL FITZKEE: *Professional Scenery Construction*, Ill., San Francisco, 1930.

WALTER RENÉ FUERST and SAMUEL J. HUME: *Twentieth Century Stage Decoration*. Introduction by Adolphe Appia. 2 vols., Ill., London, 1928, B.

WILLIAM BURT GAMBLE: *The Development of Scenic Art and Stage Machinery* (a Bibliography), N.Y., 1920; rev. ed., 1928.

JOSEPH GREGOR: *Wiener szenische Kunst.* 1: Die Theaterdekoration. 2: Das Bühnenkostüm, 2 vols., Ill., Vienna, 1924–5.

—— *Monumenta Scenica. Denkmäler des Theaters*, 12 portfolios, Vienna, 1925–30.

—— *Weltgeschichte des Theaters*, Ill., Zürich, 1933, B.

HAROLD HELVENSTON: *Scenery, a Manual of Scene Design*. Foreword by Kenneth Macgowan. Ill., Stanford U.P., 1931.

LESLIE ALLEN JONES: *Scenic Design and Model Building*, Ill., Boston, 1939.

ROBERT EDMOND JONES: *Drawings for the Theatre*. Introduction by Arthur Hopkins. Ill., N.Y., 1925.

GEORGE R. KERNODLE: *From Art to Theatre. Form and Convention in the Renaissance*, Ill., Chicago, 1943, B.

THEODORE KOMISARJEVSKY and LEE SIMONSON: *Settings and Costumes of the Modern Stage*, Ill., London and N.Y., 1933.

FRIEDRICH KRANICH: *Bühnentechnik der Gegenwart*, 2 vols., Ill., Berlin, 1929, 1933, B.

KENNETH MACGOWAN and ROBERT EDMOND JONES: *Continental Stagecraft*, Ill., N.Y., 1922.

VALERIO MARIANI: *Storia della Scenografia Italiana*, Ill., Florence, 1930, B.

A. HYATT MAYOR: *The Bibiena Family*, Ill., N.Y., 1945.

LÉON MOUSSINAC: *The New Movement in the Theatre, a Survey of Recent Developments in Europe and America*, tr. from the French. Introduction by R. H. Packman, Foreword by Gordon Craig. Ill., London, 1931, B.

CARL NIESSEN: *Das Bühnenbild, ein kulturgeschichtlicher Atlas*, Bonn, 1924–7.

DONALD OENSLAGER: *Scenery Then and Now*, Ill., N.Y., 1936.

CAMILLE POUPEYE: *La mise en scène théâtrale d'aujourd'hui*, Ill., Brussels, 1927, B.

CORRADO RICCI: *La Scenografia italiana*, Ill., Milan, 1930, B.

SAMUEL SELDEN and HUNT D. SELLMAN: *Stage Scenery and Lighting*, Ill., N.Y., 1930.

GEORGE SHERINGHAM and JAMES LAVER (Eds.): *Design in the Theatre* (Studio Special Number), Ill., London, 1927, B.

LEE SIMONSON: *The Stage is Set*, Ill., N.Y., 1932, B.

PIERRE SONREL: *A Study of Scene Design*, tr. from the French by Richard Southern, Ill., London, 1950, B.

RICHARD SOUTHERN: *Stage-Setting for Amateurs and Professionals*, Ill., London, 1937, B.

GEOFFREY WHITWORTH: *Theatre in Action*, Ill., London and N.Y., n.d.

DORIS ZINKEISEN: *Designing for the Stage*, Ill., London, 1938.

PAUL ZUCKER: *Die Theaterdekoration des Barock*, Ill., Berlin, 1925, B.

—— *Die Theaterdekoration des Klassizismus*, Ill., Berlin, 1927, B.

(*See also* AMATEUR THEATRE.)

2. Architecture and Acoustics

STANLEY BELL, NORMAN MARSHALL, and RICHARD SOUTHERN: *Essentials of Stage Planning*. Foreword by Geoffrey Whitworth, Ill., London, 1949, B.

MARTIN HAMMITZSCH: *Der moderne Theaterbau. Der höfische Theaterbau, der Anfang der modernen Theaterbaukunst, ihre Entwicklung und Betätigung zur Zeit der Renaissance, des Barock und des Rokoko*, Ill., Berlin, 1906, B.

EDITH J. R. ISAACS (Ed.): *Architecture for the New Theatre*, Ill., N.Y., 1935.

EDWARD BERNARD KINSILA: *Modern Theatre Construction*, Ill., N.Y., 1917.

ARTHUR S. MELOY: *Theatres and Motion Picture Houses*; a Practical Treatise on the proper planning and construction of such buildings, containing useful suggestions, rules, and data for the benefit of architects, prospective owners, &c., Ill., N.Y., 1916.

FREDERIC PAWLEY: *Theatre Architecture, a Brief Bibliography*, N.Y., 1932.

IRVING PICHEL: *Modern Theatres*, Ill., N.Y., 1925, B.

PAUL E. SABINE: *Acoustics and Architecture*, Ill., London and N.Y., 1932, B.

EDWIN O. SACHS and ERNEST A. E. WOODROW: *Modern Opera Houses and Theatres*. Examples selected from playhouses recently erected in Europe. With descriptive text, a treatise on theatre planning and construction, and supplements on stage machinery, theatre fires, and protective legislation, 3 vols., Ill., London, 1896–8.

MANFRED SEMPER: *Handbuch der Architektur*, Vol. IV: Theater, Ill., Stuttgart, 1904, B.

R. W. SEXTON and B. F. BETTS: *American Theatres of Today*, 2 vols., Ill., N.Y., 1927–30.

P. MORTON SHAND: *Modern Theatres and Cinemas*, Ill., London, 1930.

RICHARD SOUTHERN: *The Georgian Playhouse*, Ill., London, 1948.

JOSEPH URBAN: *Theatres*, Ill., N.Y., 1930.

PAUL ZUCKER: *Theater- und Lichtspielhäuser*, Ill., Berlin, 1926.

3. Costume

LUCY BARTON: *Historic Costume for the Stage*. Foreword by B. Iden Payne. Ill., London and Boston, 1935, B.

MAX VON BOEHN: *Das Bühnenkostüm in Altertum, Mittelalter und Neuzeit*, Ill., Berlin, 1921, B.

ADOLPHE JULLIEN: *Histoire du costume au théâtre depuis les origines du théâtre en France jusqu'à nos jours*, Ill., Paris, 1880.

CARL KÖHLER: *A History of Costume*, ed. and augmented by Emma von Sichart, tr. from the German by Alexander K. Dallas, Ill., London, 1928, B.

THEODORE KOMISARJEVSKY: *The Costume of the Theatre*, Ill., London, 1931.

M. CHANNING LINTHICUM: *Costume in the Drama of Shakespeare and his Contemporaries*, Ill., Oxford and N.Y., 1936, B.

ISABEL MONRO and DOROTHY COOK (Eds.): *Costume Index*, N.Y., 1937.

GEORGE SHERINGHAM and R. BOYD MORRISON (Eds.): *Robes of Thespis*. Costume Designs by Modern Artists. Preface by Rupert Mason. Ill., London, 1928.

NEVIL TRUMAN: *Historic Costuming*. Foreword by C. B. Cochran. Ill., London, 1936.

AGNES BROOKS YOUNG: *Stage Costuming*, Ill., N.Y., 1927, B.

(*See also* BALLET, *and* OPERA.)

4. Lighting

ALFRED VON ENGEL: *Bühnenbeleuchtung*; Entwicklung und neuester Stand der lichttechnischen Einrichtungen an Theaterbühnen, Ill., Leipzig, 1926, B.

THEODORE FUCHS: *Stage Lighting*, Ill., London and Boston, 1929, B.

LOUIS HARTMANN: *Theatre Lighting. A Manual of the Stage Switchboard*. Foreword by David Belasco. Ill., London and N.Y., 1930, B.

W. J. LAWRENCE: 'Early English Stage- and Theatre-Lighting, 1580–1800' (in *Stage Year Book*), Ill., London, 1927.

MATTHEW LUCKIESH: *Lighting Art; Its Practice and Possibilities*, Ill., N.Y., 1917.

STANLEY R. McCANDLESS: *A Method of Lighting the Stage*, Ill., N.Y., 1932; 3rd ed., 1947.

—— *A Syllabus of Stage Lighting*, New Haven, 1931.

—— *Glossary of Stage Lighting*, New Haven, 1926; 5th ed., 1941.

W. PERREN MAYCOCK: *Electric Wiring, Fittings, Switches, and Lamps*, London, 1899; 6th ed. rev. by Philip Kemp, 1928.

ALVIN LESLIE POWELL: *Lighting of Theatres and Auditoriums*, Ill., N.Y., 1923.

—— and A. RODGERS: *Lighting for the Non-Professional Stage Production*, Ill., N.Y., 1931.

C. HAROLD RIDGE: *Stage Lighting*. Preface by Norman Marshall. Ill., Cambridge, 1928, B.

—— and F. S. ALDRED: *Stage Lighting; Principles and Practice*. Introduction by Herbert M. Prentice. Ill., London, 1935, N.

R. GILLESPIE WILLIAMS: *The Technique of Stage Lighting*, Ill., London, 1947.

(*See also* AMATEUR THEATRE.)

5. Machinery

DIDEROT et D'ALEMBERT: *L'Encyclopédie* (*Machines de Théâtre*), Paris, 1772.

GEORGES MOYNET: *La Machinerie Théâtrale; Trucs et Décors.* Explication raisonnée de tous les moyens employés pour produire les illusions théâtrales, Ill., Paris, 1895.

M. J. MOYNET: *L'Envers du théâtre; Machines et Décorations,* Ill., Paris, 1874; 3rd ed., 1888.

FRANK NAPIER: *Noises Off; a Handbook of Sound Effects.* Foreword by Tyrone Guthrie. Ill., London, 1936.

ARTHUR ROSE: *Stage Effects. How to make and work them,* Ill., London and N.Y., 1928.

ACOUSTICS, *see* TECHNICAL BOOKS, 2.

ALBANY, *see* REGIONAL AND PIONEER THEATRE.

ALFRED DE VAULABELLE et CH. HÉMARDINQUER: *La Science au Théâtre,* Ill., Paris, 1908.

6. Scene-painting

LESLIE ALLEN JONES: *Painting Scenery,* Ill., Boston, 1935.

F. LLOYDS: *Practical Guide to Scene-Painting and Painting in Distemper,* Ill., London, 1875.

VLADIMIR POLUNIN: *The Continental Method of Scene-Painting,* ed. by Cyril W. Beaumont, Ill., London, 1927.

ARTHUR ROSE: *Scenes for Scene-Painters, a Practical Handbook,* Ill., London, 1925.

AMATEUR THEATRE

JEVAN BRANDON-THOMAS: *Practical Stagecraft for Amateurs,* ed. by David C. Keir. Preface by Marie Tempest. Ill., London, 1936.

WAYNE CAMPBELL: *Amateur Acting and Play Production,* Ill., N.Y., 1931.

LESLIE CRUMP: *Directing for the Amateur Stage,* Ill., N.Y., 1935.

HAROLD DOWNES (Ed.): *Theatre and Stage.* A Modern Guide to the Performance of all Classes of Amateur Dramatic, Operatic, and Theatrical Work, 2 vols., Ill., London, 1934.

W. G. ELLIOTT (Ed.): *Amateur Clubs and Actors,* Ill., London, 1898.

WILLIAM PERDUE HALSTEAD: *Stage Management for the Amateur Theatre,* with an Index

to the Standard Works on Stagecraft and Stage Lighting, Ill., London and N.Y., 1938, B.

FRANCES MACKENZIE: *The Amateur Actor,* London, 1935, 2nd ed. enlarged and rev., 1936, B.

ALAN MACKINNON: *The Oxford Amateurs; a Short History of Theatricals at the University,* Ill., London, 1910.

CHARLES S. PARSONS: *Amateur Stage-Management and Production.* Foreword by Leslie Henson, Ill., London, 1931.

EMANUEL D. SCHONBERGER: *Play Production for Amateurs,* Ill., N.Y., 1938.

(*See also* NATIONWIDE THEATRE, U.S.A., *and* PROVINCIAL AND REPERTORY THEATRES.)

AMERICA, *see* SOUTH AMERICA, *and* U.S.A.

ARCHITECTURE, *see* TECHNICAL BOOKS, 2.

ARGENTINE, *see* SOUTH AMERICA, 2.

ART OF ACTING

SARAH BERNHARDT: *The Art of the Theatre,* tr. from the French by H. J. Stenning. Preface by James Agate. London, 1924.

RICHARD BOLESLAVSKY: *Acting; the First Six Lessons.* Introduction by Edith J. R. Isaacs. N.Y., 1933; London, 1950.

HALLAM BOSWORTH: *Technique in Dramatic Art.* Foreword by Oliver Hinsdell. Ill., N.Y., 1926; rev. ed., 1934.

LOUIS CALVERT: *Problems of the Actor.* Introduction by Clayton Hamilton. London and N.Y., 1918.

TOBY COLE and HELEN KRICH CHINOY (Eds.): *Actors on Acting,* an anthology with introduction and biographical notes, N.Y., 1950, B.

CONSTANT BENOÎT COQUELIN: *The Art of the Actor,* tr. from the French. London, 1932.

LANE CRAUFORD: *Acting; Its Theory and Practice,* with illustrative examples of Players

past and present. Foreword by H. Chance Newton. London, 1930.

DENIS DIDEROT: *The Paradox of Acting,* tr. from the French ed. of 1864 with annotations by Walter Herries Pollock. Preface by Henry Irving. London, 1883.

GUSTAVE GARCIA: *The Actor's Art, a Practical Treatise on Stage Declamation, Public Speaking and Deportment,* for the use of Artists, Students, and Amateurs, including a Sketch on the History of the Theatre, Ill., London, 1882; 2nd ed., 1888.

GEORGE HENRY LEWES: *On Actors and the Art of Acting,* London, 1875.

SAMUEL SELDON: *A Player's Handbook; the Theory and Practice of Acting,* Ill., N.Y., 1934, B.

ROBERT SPEAIGHT: *Acting, its Idea and Tradition,* London, 1939, B.

BIBLIOGRAPHY

KONSTANTIN STANISLAVSKY: *An Actor Prepares*, tr. from the Russian by Elizabeth Reynolds Hapgood, London and N.Y., 1936.

—— *Building a Character*, tr. from the Russian, Ill., London and N.Y., 1950.

FRANÇOIS JOSEPH TALMA: *On the Actor's Art*, tr. from the French. Preface by Henry Irving. London, 1883.

(*See also* DRAMATIC CRITICISM, *and* MAKE-UP.)

AUSTRIA, *see* GERMANY.

AUTOS SACRAMENTALES, *see* ECCLESIASTICAL DRAMA, *and* SPAIN.

BALLET

CYRIL W. BEAUMONT: *Complete Book of Ballets, a Guide to the Principal Ballets of the 19th and 20th centuries*, Ill., London, 1937.

—— *Supplement to the Complete Book of Ballets*, Ill., London, 1942.

—— *Five Centuries of Ballet Design*, Ill., London and N.Y., 1939.

—— *The Diaghilev Ballet in London, a Personal Record*, London, 1940; Ill. ed., 1945.

ALEXANDRE BENOIS: *Reminiscences of the Russian Ballet*, tr. by Mary Britnieva, Ill., London, 1941.

CARYL BRAHMS (Ed.): *Footnotes to the Ballet*, Ill., London, 1936.

ARNOLD HASKELL: *Ballet* (Penguin Books), Ill., London, 1938, B.

JANET LEEPER: *English Ballet* (King Penguin series), Ill., London, 1944.

PRINCE PETER LIEVEN: *The Birth of Ballets-Russes*, tr. by L. Zarine, Ill., London, 1936.

JOHN MARTIN: *The Dance, the Story of the Dance in Pictures and Text*, Ill., N.Y., 1946.

WALTER ARCHIBALD PROPERT: *The Russian Ballet in Western Europe, 1909–1920, with a Chapter on the Music by Eugene Goossens*, Ill., London, 1921.

—— *The Russian Ballet, 1921–29*, Ill., London, 1931.

ADRIAN STOKES: *To-Night the Ballet*, Ill., London, 1934.

W. J. TURNER: *English Ballet* (Britain in Pictures series), Ill., London, 1944.

NINETTE DE VALOIS: *Invitation to the Ballet*, Ill., London, 1937, B.

BATH, *see* PROVINCIAL AND REPERTORY THEATRES.

BELGIUM

JETHRO BITHELL: *Contemporary Belgian Literature*, London and N.Y., 1915, B.

A. DUPONT: *Répertoire dramatique belge*, 2 vols., Liége, 1884.

GEORGES DOUTREPONT: *Histoire illustrée de la littérature française en Belgique*, Ill., Brussels, 1939, B.

F. FABER: *Histoire du théâtre français en Belgique depuis son origine jusqu'à nos jours d'après*

des documents inédits, Brussels and Paris, 1878–80.

MAURICE GAUCHEZ: *Histoire des lettres françaises de Belgique des origines à nos jours*, Brussels, 1922, B.

JETHRO BITHELL: *Life and Writings of Maurice Maeterlinck*, London and N.Y., 1913, B.

UNA TAYLOR: *Maurice Maeterlinck*, a Critical Study, London, 1914.

BIBLE-HISTORIES, *see* ECCLESIASTICAL DRAMA, ENGLAND, *and* FRANCE.

BIRMINGHAM, *see* PROVINCIAL AND REPERTORY THEATRES.

BOLIVIA, *see* SOUTH AMERICA, 3.

BOSTON, *see* REGIONAL AND PIONEER THEATRE.

BRAZIL, *see* SOUTH AMERICA, 4.

BRIGHTON, BRISTOL, *see* PROVINCIAL AND REPERTORY THEATRES.

BURLESQUE, *see* POPULAR ENTERTAINMENT, 1 and 2.

BURMA, *see* FAR EASTERN THEATRES, 1.

CALIFORNIA, CHARLESTON, *see* REGIONAL AND PIONEER THEATRE.

CHILE, *see* SOUTH AMERICA, 5.

CHINA, *see* FAR EASTERN THEATRES, 2.

CIRCUS

BERTHA BENNET BURLEIGH: *Circus*, Ill., London, 1937.

JOHN S. CLARKE: *Circus Parade, A Pictorial Review of the Circus*, Ill., London, 1936.

MAURICE WILLSON DISHER: *Greatest Show on Earth*. Introduction by D. L. Murray. Ill., London, 1937.

—— *Fairs, Circuses and Music Halls* (Britain in Pictures series), Ill., London, 1942.

THOMAS FROST: *Circus Life and Circus Celebrities*, London, 1875.

CHARLIE KEITH: *Circus and Amusement (Equestrian, Dramatic and Musical) in all Nations*, Derby, 1879.

A. H. KOBER: *Circus Nights and Circus Days, Extracts from the Diary of a Circus Man*, tr. from the German by Claude W. Sykes, Ill., London, 1928.

LADY ELEANOR SMITH: *British Circus Life*, ed. by W. R. Turner, Ill., London, 1948.

SIR GARRARD TYRWHITT-DRAKE: *The English Circus and Fair Ground*, Ill., London, 1946.

M. R. WERNER: *Barnum*, Ill., N.Y., 1923, B.

COLOMBIA, *see* SOUTH AMERICA, 6.

COMÉDIE-FRANÇAISE, *see* FRANCE.

COMEDY, *see* TRAGEDY, 2.

COMMEDIA DELL' ARTE

M. APOLLONIO: *Storia della commedia dell' arte*, Milan, 1930, B.

ARMAND BASCHET: *Les comédiens italiens à la cour de France sous Charles IX, Henri III, Henri IV et Louis XIII*, Paris, 1882.

CYRIL W. BEAUMONT: *The History of Harlequin*. Preface by Sacheverell Sitwell. Ill., London, 1926, B.

ÉMILE CAMPARDON: *Les Comédiens du Roi de la Troupe Italienne pendant les deux derniers siècles*, 2 vols., Paris, 1880.

PIERRE LOUIS DUCHARTRE: *The Italian Comedy, the Improvisation, Scenarios, Lives, Attributes, Portraits and Masks of the Illustrious Characters of the Commedia dell' arte*, tr. from the French by Randolph T. Weaver, Ill., London and N.Y., 1929, B.

K. M. LEA: *Italian Popular Comedy, a Study in the Commedia dell' arte, 1560–1620*, 2 vols., Ill., Oxford, 1934, B.

C. MIC: *La Commedia dell' arte, ou, le théâtre des comédiens italiens des XVIe, XVIIe, et XVIIIe siècles*, Ill., Paris, 1927, B.

LOUIS MOLAND: *Molière et la comédie italienne*, Ill., Paris, 1867.

LES FRÈRES PARFAICT: *Histoire de l'ancien théâtre italien depuis son origine en France jusqu'à sa suppression en l'année 1697*, Paris, 1753.

E. PETRACCONE: *La commedia dell' arte, Storia, Tecnica, Scenari*, Naples, 1927.

LUIGI RICCOBONI: *Nuovo Teatro Italiano, che contiene le comedie stampate e recitate dal S. L. Riccoboni, detto Lelio*, 3 vols., Paris, 1733.

MAURICE SAND: *Masques et Buffons — Comédie Italienne*, 2 vols., Ill., Paris, 1860. In an English Translation as *The History of the Harlequinade*, 2 vols., Ill., London, 1915.

WINIFRED SMITH: *The Commedia dell' arte, a Study in Italian Popular Comedy*, Ill., N.Y., 1912, B.

—— *Italian Actors of the Renaissance*, Ill., N.Y., 1930.

(*See also* FRANCE, *and* ITALY.)

COMMUNITY THEATRE, *see* AMATEUR THEATRE, NATIONWIDE THEATRE, PROVINCIAL AND REPERTORY THEATRES, *and* REGIONAL AND PIONEER THEATRE.

COSTUME, *see* TECHNICAL BOOKS, 1 and 3.

COURT THEATRE, COVENT GARDEN THEATRE, CRITERION THEATRE, *see* LONDON THEATRES.

DENMARK, *see* SCANDINAVIA, 2.

DRAMATIC CRITICISM

JAMES AGATE (Ed.): *The English Dramatic Critics, 1660–1932*, an Anthology, London, 1932.

—— *These Were Actors, Extracts from a Newspaper Cuttings Book, 1811–33*, Ill., London, 1943.

—— *Those Were the Nights, an Anthology of Criticism, 1880–1906*, Ill., London, 1946.

ANNE BRADBY (Ed.): *Shakespeare Criticism, 1919–1935*, London, 1936 (The World's Classics series).

H. J. CHAYTOR: *Dramatic Theory in Spain. Extracts from Literature before and during the Golden Age*, Cambridge, 1925.

BARRETT H. CLARK: *European Theories of the Drama, with a Supplement on the American Drama; an Anthology of Dramatic Theory and Criticism from Aristotle to the Present Day, in a series of selected texts, with Commentaries, Biographies and Bibliographies*, N.Y., 1947, B.

CHARLES HAROLD GRAY: *Theatrical Criticism in London to 1795*, N.Y., 1931, B.

CLAYTON HAMILTON: *The Theory of the Theatre, and other Principles of Dramatic Criticism*, London and N.Y., 1910; rev. ed. with Foreword by Burns Mantle, N.Y., 1939.

ELEANOR JOURDAIN: *Dramatic Theory and Practice in France, 1690–1808*, London, 1921.

—— *The Drama in Europe in Theory and Practice*, London, 1924, B.

SAM R. LITTLEWOOD: *Dramatic Criticism.* Foreword by Sir Barry Jackson. London, 1939, B.

MONTROSE J. MOSES and JOHN MASON BROWN (Eds.): *The American Theatre as seen by its Critics, 1752–1934*, N.Y., 1934.

J. G. ROBERTSON: *Lessing's Dramatic Theory, being an Introduction to, and a Commentary on, his Hamburgische Dramaturgie*, Cambridge, 1939, B.

GEORGE SAINTSBURY: *A History of Criticism and Literary Taste in Europe from the Earliest Texts to the Present Day*, 3 vols., London, 1900–4.

DAVID NICHOL SMITH (Ed.): *Shakespeare Criticism; A Selection*, London, 1916, new ed., 1946 (The World's Classics series).

FELIX SPER: *The Periodical Press of London: Theatrical and Literary (excluding the daily Newspaper), 1800–30.* With a Foreword by Allardyce Nicoll. Boston and London, 1937.

A. C. WARD (Ed.): *Specimens of English Dramatic Criticism, XVII–XX Centuries*, London, 1945 (The World's Classics series).

DRURY LANE THEATRE, *see* LONDON THEATRES.

DUBLIN, *see* ENGLAND, *and* IRELAND.

EAST ANGLIA, *see* PROVINCIAL AND REPERTORY THEATRES.

ECCLESIASTICAL DRAMA

ALLESSANDRO D'ANCONA: *Origini del teatro in Italia, Studi sulle sacre rappresentazioni*, 2 vols., Florence, 1877.

KATHARINE LEE BATES: *The English Religious Drama*, London and N.Y., 1893, B.

E. K. CHAMBERS: *The Mediaeval Stage*, 2 vols., Oxford and N.Y., 1903, B.

STANLEY W. CLARKE: *The Miracle Play in England, an Account of the Early Religious Drama*, Ill., London, 1897, B.

GUSTAVE COHEN: *Histoire de la mise en scène dans le théâtre religieux français du moyen âge*, Paris, 1906; new ed., 1926, B.

—— *Le Livre de conduite du régisseur et le compte des dépenses pour le Mystère de la Passion joué à Mons en 1501*, Paris, 1925.

—— *Le Théâtre en France au moyen âge*, I: *Le Théâtre Religieux*, Ill., Paris, 1928, B.

VICTOR MICHELS: *Studien über die ältesten deutschen Fastnachtspiele*, Strassburg, 1896.

ALEXANDER A. PARKER: *The Allegorical Drama of Calderón, an Introduction to the autos sacramentales*, Oxford, 1943.

LOUIS PETIT DE JULLEVILLE: *Histoire du Théâtre en France — Les Mystères*, 2 vols., Paris, 1880.

ALFRED W. POLLARD: *English Miracle Plays, Moralities, and Interludes*, Ill., Oxford, 1927.

M. J. RUDWIN: *Historical and Bibliographical Survey of the German Religious Drama*, Pittsburgh, 1924.

KARL YOUNG: *The Drama of the Mediaeval Church*, 2 vols., Ill., Oxford, 1933, B.

(*See also* the general histories of ENGLAND, FRANCE, GERMANY, ITALY, *and* SPAIN.)

EDINBURGH, *see* PROVINCIAL AND REPERTORY THEATRES.

ELIZABETHAN PLAYHOUSE, *see* ENGLAND, *and* SHAKESPEARE.

ENGLAND

JOHN ANDREWS and OSSIA TRILLING (Eds.): *Dobson's Theatre Year Book 1948*, London, 1949.

DAVID ERSKINE BAKER: *The Companion to the Playhouse*; or, an Historical Account of all the Dramatic Writers of Great Britain and Ireland from the commencement of our theatrical exhibitions down to 1764, 2 vols., London, 1764; new ed., as *Biographia Dramatica; or, a Companion to the Playhouse*, enlarged and continued from 1764 to 1782 by Isaac Reed, 2 vols., 1782; continued to 1811 by Stephen Jones, 3 vols., 1812.

REGINALD CLARENCE (Ed.): *The Stage Cyclopaedia, a Bibliography of plays*, London, 1909.

T. and J. EGERTON: *The Theatrical Remembrancer*, containing a Complete List of all the dramatic performances in the English language, London, 1788.

MALCOLM ELWIN: *The Playgoer's Handbook to Restoration Drama*, London, 1928, B.

HORACE FOOTE: *A Companion to the Theatres; and Manual of the British Drama*, Ill., London, 1829.

WALTER WILSON GREG: *A List of English Plays written before 1643 and printed before 1700*, London, 1900.

ALFRED HARBAGE: *Annals of English Drama, 975–1700*, London and Philadelphia, 1940.

GERARD LANGBAINE: *An Account of the English Dramatick Poets*, Oxford, 1691.

AGNES MURE MACKENZIE: *The Playgoer's Handbook to the English Renaissance Drama*, London, 1927, B.

PETER NOBLE: *British Theatre Yearbook*, Ill., London, 1946.

EDWIN NUNGEZER: *A Dictionary of Actors and of Other Persons associated with the Public Representation of Plays in England before 1642*, Yale and Oxford, 1929, B.

MONTAGUE SUMMERS: *A Bibliography of the Restoration Drama*, London, n.d.

HENRY BARTON BAKER: *Our Old Actors*, 2 vols., London, 1878; rev. ed. in 1 vol., 1881.

—— *The London Stage; Its History and Traditions from 1576 to 1888*, 2 vols., London, 1889.

—— *History of the London Stage and its Famous Players, 1576–1903*, London, 1904.

BENJAMIN BRAWLEY: *A Short History of the English Drama*, London, 1921, B.

W. BRIDGES-ADAMS: *The British Theatre* (British Life and Thought series), Ill., London, 1944.

DONALD BROOK: *The Romance of the English Theatre*, Ill., London, 1945.

W. R. CHETWOOD: *A General History of the Stage*, from its Origin in Greece down to the present Time, with the Memoirs of most of the principal Performers that have appeared on the English and Irish stage for the last Fifty years, London, 1749.

DUTTON COOK: *Hours with the Players*, London, 1883.

W. A. DARLINGTON: *The Actor and His Audience* (Studies of Burbage, Betterton, Garrick, Siddons, Kean, Irving), Ill., London, 1949.

DR. JOHN DORAN: *Their Majesties' Servants; or, Annals of the English Stage from Betterton to Kean*, 2 vols., Ill., London, 1864; rev. and ed. by Robert W. Lowe as *Annals of the English Stage from Thomas Betterton to Edmund Kean*, 3 vols., Ill., London, 1888.

JOHN DOWNES: *Roscius Anglicanus, or a Historical Survey of the Stage*, London, 1708; Facsimile reprint with historical preface by Joseph Knight, 1886; Reprint of the original edition with notes by Montague Summers, 1930.

B. IFOR EVANS: *A Short History of English Drama* (Penguin Books), London, 1948.

JOHN GALT: *The Lives of the Players*, Ill., 2 vols., London, 1831.

THOMAS GILLILAND: *The Dramatic Mirror*, containing the History of the Stage from the Earliest Period to the Present time; including a Biographical and Critical Account of all the Dramatic Writers from 1660; and also of the most distinguished Performers from the Days of Shakespeare to 1807; and a History of the Country Theatres in England, Ireland, and Scotland, Ill., 2 vols., London, 1808.

GRAHAM GREENE: *British Dramatists* (Britain in Pictures series), Ill., London, 1942.

WILLIAM HAZLITT: *A View of the English Stage; or, a Series of Dramatic Criticisms*, London, 1818 (and many later editions).

—— *Lectures on the English Comic Writers*, London, 1818; ed. by Brimley Johnson (The World's Classics series), 1907.

EDMOND MALONE: *An Historical Account of the Rise and Progress of the English Stage*, and of the Economy and Usage of our Ancient Theatres and of the Original Actors in Shakespeare's Plays (Vol. 2 of Malone's edition of Shakespeare, 10 vols.), London, 1790 (and later editions).

BERNARD MILES: *The British Theatre* (Britain in Pictures series), Ill., London, 1948.

ALLARDYCE NICOLL: *British Drama. An Historical Survey from the Beginning to the Present Time*, Ill., London and N.Y., 1925; new ed. 1932, B.

—— *The English Theatre, a Short History*, Ill., London, 1936, B.

FELIX E. SCHELLING: *English Drama*, London and N.Y., 1914.

R. FARQUHARSON SHARP: *A Short History of the English Stage from its Beginnings to the Summer of the Year 1908*, London and N.Y., 1909.

ERNEST SHORT: *Theatrical Cavalcade*, Ill., London, 1942.

ALWIN THALER: *Shakspere to Sheridan, a Book about the Theatre of Yesterday and To-Day*, Ill., Harvard U.P. and Oxford, 1922.

ASHLEY H. THORNDIKE: *English Comedy*, N.Y., 1929, B.

A. W. WARD: *A History of English Dramatic Literature to the Death of Queen Anne*, 3 vols., London, 1875; rev. ed., 1899.

—— and A. R. WOLTER (Eds.): *The Cambridge History of English Literature*, 15 vols., Cambridge and N.Y., 1907–16, B.

E. K. CHAMBERS: *The English Folk-Play*, Oxford, 1933.

R. J. E. TIDDY: *The Mummers' Play, with a Memoir*, Oxford, 1923.

T. H. VAIL-MOTTER: *The School Drama in England*, Ill., London, 1929.

(*See also* ECCLESIASTICAL DRAMA.)

F. S. BOAS: *An Introduction to Tudor Drama*, Ill., Oxford, 1933.

A. W. REED: *Early Tudor Drama—Medwall, the Rastells, Heywood and the More Circle*, Ill., London, 1926.

JOHN BAKELESS: *Christopher Marlowe; The Man in his Time*, London and N.Y., 1938.

F. S. BOAS: *Marlowe and his Circle. A Biographical Survey*, Ill., London, 1929.

—— *Christopher Marlowe; a Biographical and Critical Study*, Ill., Oxford, 1940.

MARK ECCLES: *Christopher Marlowe in London.* Introduction by Leslie Hotson. Harvard U.P., 1934.

UNA ELLIS-FERMOR: *Christopher Marlowe*, London, 1927.

PHILIP HENDERSON: *And Morning in his Eyes, a Book about Christopher Marlowe*, Ill., London, 1937, B.

LESLIE HOTSON: *The Death of Christopher Marlowe*, Ill., Harvard U.P. and London, 1925.

JOHN H. INGRAM: *Christopher Marlowe and his Associates*, Ill., London, 1904, B.

J. QUINCY ADAMS: *Shakespearean Playhouses, a History of English Theatres from the Beginning to the Restoration*, Ill., Boston, 1917.

F. S. BOAS: *Shakespeare and his Predecessors*, London, 1896.

M. C. BRADBROOK: *Themes and Conventions of Elizabethan Tragedy*, London and N.Y., 1935, B.

C. F. TUCKER BROOKE: *The Tudor Drama, a History of English National Drama to the Retirement of Shakespeare*, Ill., London and Boston, 1912.

E. K. CHAMBERS: *The Elizabethan Stage*, 4 vols., 1923, B.

WILLIAM CREIZENACH: *The English Drama in the Age of Shakespeare* (Vol. 4 of *Geschichte des neueren Dramas*), tr. from the German by Cécile Hugon, London, 1916, B.

FREDERICK G. FLEAY: *A Biographical Chronicle of the English Drama, 1559–1642*, 2 vols., London, 1891.

WALTER WILSON GREG: *Pastoral Poetry and Pastoral Drama, a literary inquiry, with special reference to the pre-Restoration stage in England*, London, 1906, B.

—— *Dramatic Documents from the Elizabethan Playhouses, Stage Plots, Actors' Parts, Prompt Books, Commentary*, Ill., Oxford, 1931.

G. B. HARRISON: *The Story of Elizabethan Drama*, Ill., Cambridge and N.Y., 1924, B.

W. J. LAWRENCE: *The Elizabethan Playhouse and Other Studies*, Ill., Stratford-on-Avon and N.Y., 1912. Second Series, 1913, B.

—— *Pre-Restoration Stage Studies*, Ill., Harvard U.P., 1927.

—— *The Physical Conditions of the Elizabethan Public Playhouse*, Ill., Harvard U.P., 1927.

—— *Old Theatre Days and Ways*, Ill., London, 1935.

—— *Those Nut-Cracking Elizabethans, Studies of the Early Theatre and Drama*, Ill., London, 1935.

—— *Speeding Up Shakespeare, Studies of the Bygone Theatre and Drama*, Ill., London, 1937.

GEORGE SAINTSBURY: *A History of Elizabethan Literature*, London, 1887.

FELIX E. SCHELLING: *Elizabethan Drama 1558–1642.* A History of the Drama from the Accession of Queen Elizabeth to the Closing of the Theaters, to which is prefixed a Résumé of the Earlier Drama from its Beginnings, 2 vols., London and N.Y., 1908, B.

—— *Elizabethan Playwrights.* A Short History of the English Drama from Mediaeval Times to the Closing of the Theaters in 1642, N.Y., 1925, B.

JOHN ADDINGTON SYMONDS: *Shakspere's Predecessors in the English Drama*, London, 1884; 2nd ed., 1900.

ARTHUR SYMONS: *Studies in the Elizabethan Drama*, London and N.Y., 1920.

CHARLES WILLIAM WALLACE: *The Evolution of the English Drama up to Shakespeare*, with a History of the first Blackfriars Theatre, a Survey based upon original records now for the first time collected and published, Berlin, 1912.

HENRY WILLIS WELLS: *Elizabethan and Jacobean Playwrights*, N.Y., 1939.

L. C. KNIGHTS: *Drama and Society in the age of Jonson*, London, 1937, B.

JOHN PALMER: *Ben Jonson*, Ill., London and N.Y., 1934.

G. E. BENTLEY: *The Jacobean and Caroline Stage; Dramatic Companies and Players*, 2 vols., Oxford, 1941, B.

F. S. BOAS: *An Introduction to Stuart Drama*, Oxford, 1946.

UNA ELLIS-FERMOR: *The Jacobean Drama, an Interpretation*, London, 1936, B.

(*See also* GREECE AND ROME, 6, MASQUE, *and* SHAKESPEARE.)

F. W. BATESON: *English Comic Drama, 1700–1750*, Oxford, 1929, B.

ELEANORE BOSWELL: *The Restoration Court Stage, 1660–1702*, with a particular account of the production of *Calisto*, Ill., Harvard U.P., 1932, B.

BONAMY DOBRÉE: *Restoration Comedy, 1660–1720*, Oxford, 1924, B.

—— *Restoration Tragedy, 1660–1720*, Oxford, 1929, B.

PERCY FITZGERALD: *A New History of the English Stage from the Restoration to the Liberty of the Theatres in connection with the Patent Houses*, 2 vols., London, 1882.

JOHN GENEST: *Some Account of the English Stage. From the Restoration in 1660 to 1830*, 10 vols., Bath, 1832.

LESLIE HOTSON: *The Commonwealth and Restoration Stage*, Ill., Cambridge, Mass., and Oxford, 1928.

GEORGE HENRY NETTLETON: *English Drama of the Restoration and Eighteenth Century, 1642–1780*, N.Y., 1914, B.

ALLARDYCE NICOLL: *A History of Restoration Drama, 1660–1700*, Cambridge, 1923; 3rd rev. ed., 1940.

—— *A History of Early Eighteenth Century Drama, 1700–1750*, Cambridge, 1925; 2nd ed., 1929.

—— *A History of Late Eighteenth Century Drama, 1750–1800*, Cambridge, 1927.

ARTHUR COLBY SPRAGUE: *Beaumont and Fletcher on the Restoration Stage*, Ill., Harvard U.P. and Oxford, 1926, B.

MONTAGUE SUMMERS: *The Restoration Theatre*, an account of the Staging of Plays in the Restoration Theatre, Ill., London and N.Y., 1934.

—— *The Playhouse of Pepys. A Description of the Drama produced in the Years 1660–82*, Ill., London, 1935.

AUTREY NELL WILEY: *Rare Prologues and Epilogues, 1642–1700*, Ill., London, 1939.

RICHARD HINDRY BAKER: *Mr. Cibber of Drury Lane*, N.Y., 1939, B.

COLLEY CIBBER: *An Apology for the Life of Colley Cibber, with an Historical View of the Stage during his own time*, London, 1740; new ed. with notes and supplement by Robert W. Lowe, 2 vols., Ill., London, 1889; in Everyman's Library, 1914.

JOHN C. HODGES: *William Congreve, the Man. A Biography from New Sources*, Ill., N.Y., 1944, B.

D. CRANE TAYLOR: *William Congreve*, Oxford, 1931.

WILLARD CONNELY: *Young George Farquhar*, Ill., London and N.Y., 1949.

E. M. BUTLER: *Sheridan; a Ghost Story*, London, 1931.

WILLIAM C. DARLINGTON: *Sheridan*, London, 1933.

KENELM FOSS: *Here Lies Richard Brinsley Sheridan*, N.Y., 1940.

LEWIS GIBBS: *Sheridan*, London, 1947.

WALTER SYDNEY SICHEL: *Sheridan*, 2 vols., Ill., Boston, 1909, B.

WILLARD CONNELY: *Brawny Wycherley*, London and N.Y., 1930.

EUGENE R. PAGE: *George Colman the Elder, Essayist, Dramatist and Theatrical Manager, 1732–94*, N.Y., 1935, B.

WILLIAM DUNLAP: *Memoirs of George Frederick Cooke, late of the Theatre Royal, Covent Garden*, 2 vols., London, 1813.

WILLIAM COOKE: *Memoirs of Samuel Foote*, with a collection of his genuine bon-mots, anecdotes, opinions, etc., mostly original, and three of his dramatic pieces not published in his works, 3 vols., London, 1805.

RYLLIS CLAIR ALEXANDER (Ed.): *The Diary of David Garrick*, being a record of his memorable trip to Paris in 1751, Ill., London and N.Y., 1928.

MARGARET BARTON: *Garrick*, Ill., London, 1948, B.

THOMAS DAVIES: *Memoirs of the Life of David Garrick*, interspersed with characters and anecdotes of his theatrical contemporaries, the whole forming a history of the stage which includes a period of 36 years, 2 vols., London, 1780.

PERCY FITZGERALD: *Life of David Garrick*, from original family papers and numerous published and unpublished sources, 2 vols., London, 1868; new and rev. ed., 1899.

FRANK A. HEDGCOCK: *A Cosmopolitan Actor. David Garrick and his French Friends*, Ill., London, 1912, B.

JOSEPH KNIGHT: *Garrick*, London, 1894.

ARTHUR MURPHY: *Life of David Garrick*, 2 vols., London, 1801.

MRS. CLEMENT PARSONS: *Garrick and his Circle*, Ill., London, 1906, B.

ELIZABETH P. STEIN: *David Garrick, Dramatist*, Ill., N.Y., 1938, B.

WILLIAM COOKE: *Memoirs of Charles Macklin, Comedian*, with the Dramatic Characters, Manners, Anecdotes, etc. of the age in which he lived, and a chronological list of all the parts played by him; forming an History of the Stage during almost the whole of the last century, London, 1804.

JAMES THOMAS KIRKMAN: *Memoirs of the Life of Charles Macklin, Esq.*, 2 vols., London, 1799.

EDWARD ABBOTT PARRY: *Charles Macklin*, London, 1891.

C. F. ARMSTRONG: *A Century of Great Actors, 1750–1850*, London, 1912.

ALFRED BUNN: *The Stage*, both before and behind the Curtain, from observations taken on the spot, 3 vols., London, 1840.

EDWARD FITZBALL: *Thirty-Five Years of a Dramatic Author's Life*, 2 vols., London, 1859.

THOMAS HOLCROFT: *Memoirs*, written by himself, and continued to the time of his death from his Diary, Notes, and other Papers by William Hazlitt, 3 vols., London, 1816.

CHARLES MATHEWS: *Memoirs*, ed. by Mrs. Mathews, 4 vols., Ill., London, 1838–9.

ALLARDYCE NICOLL: *A History of Early Nineteenth Century Drama, 1800–1850*, 2 vols., Cambridge, 1930.

H. SIMPSON and C. BROWN: *A Century of Famous Actresses, 1750–1850*, London, 1913.

ERNEST BRADLEE WATSON: *Sheridan to Robertson, a study of the Nineteenth-Century London Stage.* Foreword by George Pierce Baker. Ill., Harvard U.P., 1926, B.

F. W. HAWKINS: *The Life of Edmund Kean*, from published and original sources, 2 vols., London, 1869.

H. M. HILLIBRAND: *Edmund Kean*, N.Y., 1933.

J. FITZGERALD MOLLOY: *The Life and Adventures of Edmund Kean, Tragedian, 1787–1833*, 2 vols., London, 1888.

GILES PLAYFAIR: *Kean*, Ill., London, 1939.

J. W. COLE: *The Life and Theatrical Times of Charles Kean*, 2 vols., London, 1859.

HERSCHEL BAKER: *John Philip Kemble: The Actor in his Theatre*, Harvard U.P. and London, 1942, B.

JAMES BOADEN: *Memoirs of the Life of John Philip Kemble*, including a history of the stage from the time of Garrick to the present day, 2 vols., London, 1825.

PERCY FITZGERALD: *The Kembles*, 2 vols., London, 1871.

(*For* FANNY KEMBLE *see* U.S.A.)

WILLIAM ARCHER: *W. C. Macready*, London, 1890.

WILLIAM CHARLES MACREADY: *Reminiscences and selections from his diaries and letters*, ed. by Sir Frederick Pollock, 2 vols., London, 1875.

LADY POLLOCK: *Macready as I knew Him*, London, 1885.

JOHN COLEMAN: *Memoirs of Samuel Phelps*, London, 1886.

W. MAY PHELPS and JOHN FORBES-ROBERTSON: *The Life and Life-Work of Samuel Phelps*, Ill., London, 1886.

JAMES BOADEN: *Memoirs of Mrs. Siddons*, interspersed with anecdotes of authors and actors, 2 vols., London, 1827.

THOMAS CAMPBELL: *Life of Mrs. Siddons*, 2 vols., London, 1834.

YVONNE FFRENCH: *Mrs. Siddons; Tragic Actress*, Ill., London, 1936, B.

MRS. CLEMENT PARSONS: *The Incomparable Siddons*, Ill., London, 1909, B.

WILLIAM ARCHER: *English Dramatists of Today*, London, 1882.

J. W. CUNLIFFE: *Modern English Playwrights, a Short History of the English Drama from 1825*, London and N.Y., 1927, B.

F. J. HARVEY DARTON: *Vincent Crummles, his Theatre and his Times*, with an Historical Introductory Note and Appendixes, Ill., London, 1926.

SHAW DESMOND: *London Nights of Long Ago*, Ill., London, 1927.

CHARLES DICKENS (Ed.): *The Life of Charles J. Mathews*, 2 vols., Ill., London, 1879.

MAURICE WILLSON DISHER: *Blood and Thunder*, Ill., London, 1949.

AUGUSTIN FILON: *The English Stage, being an account of the Victorian drama*, tr. from the French by Frederic Whyte. Introduction by Henry Arthur Jones. London, 1897.

H. CHANCE NEWTON: *Crime and the Drama, or Dark Deeds Dramatized.* Introduction by Sir John Martin-Harvey. Ill., London, 1927.

ALLARDYCE NICOLL: *A History of Late 19th Century Drama, 1850–1900*, 2 vols., Cambridge, 1946.

ERNEST REYNOLDS: *Early Victorian Drama, 1830–70*, Cambridge, 1936, B.

CLEMENT SCOTT: *The Drama of Yesterday and Today*, 2 vols., Ill., London, 1899.

SIR SQUIRE and LADY BANCROFT: *Mr. and Mrs. Bancroft on and off the Stage*, written by themselves, 2 vols., London, 1888.

(*For* DION BOUCICAULT *see* U.S.A.)

AUSTIN BRERETON: *The Life of Henry Irving*, 2 vols., Ill., London, 1905.

EDWARD GORDON CRAIG: *Henry Irving*, Ill., London, 1930.

CHARLES HIATT: *Henry Irving, a Record and Review*, Ill., London, 1899.

H. A. SAINTSBURY and CECIL PALMER (Eds.): *We Saw Him Act; a Symposium on the Art of Sir Henry Irving*, Ill., London, 1939.

CLEMENT SCOTT: *From 'The Bells' to 'King Arthur'; a critical record of the first-night productions at the Lyceum Theatre from 1871 to 1895*, Ill., London, 1897.

BRAM STOKER: *Personal Reminiscences of Henry Irving*, 2 vols., Ill., London, 1906.

RICHARD A. CORDELL: *Henry Arthur Jones and the Modern Drama*. Prefatory Note by William Lyon Phelps. N.Y., 1932.

DORIS ARTHUR JONES: *The Life and Letters of Henry Arthur Jones*, Ill., London, 1930; in an American edition as *Taking the Curtain Call*, N.Y., 1930.

T. EDGAR PEMBERTON: *The Kendals*, Ill., London, 1900.

HAMILTON FYFE: *Sir Arthur Pinero's Plays and Players*, Ill., London, 1930.

T. EDGAR PEMBERTON: *The Life and Writings of T. W. Robertson*, Ill., London, 1893.

ELIZABETH ROBINS: *Theatre and Friendship* (Correspondence with Henry James), Ill., London and N.Y., 1932.

MAURICE COLBOURNE: *The Real Bernard Shaw*, Ill., London, 1949.

ARCHIBALD HENDERSON: *George Bernard Shaw, His Life and Works:* a Critical Biography, Ill., N.Y., 1932.

HESKETH PEARSON: *Bernard Shaw: His Life and Personality*, Ill., London, 1942; in an American ed. as *G.B.S.; a Full-Length Portrait*, N.Y., 1942, B.

G. B. SHAW: *Dramatic Opinions and Essays, 1894–98*, ed. by James Huneker, 2 vols., N.Y., 1907.

—— *Our Theatres in the Nineties; criticisms contributed week by week to the* Saturday Review *from Jan. 1895 to May 1898*, 3 vols., London, 1931.

CHRISTOPHER ST. JOHN (Ed.): *Ellen Terry and Bernard Shaw: A Correspondence*, London, 1931; new ed. with Ill., London, 1949.

EDWARD GORDON CRAIG: *Ellen Terry and her Secret Self*, Ill., London, n.d.

CHARLES HIATT: *Ellen Terry and her Impersonations*, Ill., London, 1898.

T. EDGAR PEMBERTON: *Ellen Terry and her Sisters*, Ill., London, 1902.

CHRISTOPHER ST. JOHN: *Ellen Terry*, Ill., London, 1907.

ELLEN TERRY: *The Story of My Life*, Ill., London, 1908; reprinted as *Memoirs*, with Preface, Notes, and Biographical Chapters by Edith Craig and Christopher St. John, London, 1933.

MAX BEERBOHM (Ed.): *Herbert Beerbohm Tree; some Memories of him and his Art*, Ill., London, 1920.

ANDRÉ GIDE: *Oscar Wilde, a Study*, London, 1905.

HESKETH PEARSON: *The Life of Oscar Wilde*, Ill., London, 1946; in an American edition as *Oscar Wilde; his Life and Wit*, N.Y., 1946, B.

ARTHUR RANSOME: *Oscar Wilde*, London, 1912.

JAMES AGATE: *A Short View of the English Stage, 1900–26*, London, 1926.

WILLIAM ARCHER: *The Old Drama and the New*, London and Boston, 1923.

SIR GEORGE ARTHUR: *From Phelps to Gielgud, Reminiscences of the Stage through Sixty-five Years*. Ill., London, 1936.

MAX BEERBOHM: *Around Theatres, 1898–1910*, 2 vols., London and N.Y., 1930.

MARIO BORSA: *The English Stage of Today*, tr. from the Italian and ed. by Selwyn Brinton, London and N.Y., 1908.

THOMAS H. DICKINSON: *The Contemporary Drama of England*, Boston and London, 1920; rev. ed., 1931, B.

PHILIP GODFREY: *Backstage, a Survey of the Contemporary English Theatre from Behind the Scenes*, Ill., London, 1933.

J. T. GREIN: *The New World of the Theatre, 1923–4*. Preface by G. K. Chesterton. London, 1924.

NORMAN MARSHALL: *The Other Theatre*, Ill., London, 1947.

CAMILLO PELLIZZI: *English Drama; the Last Great Phase*, tr. from the Italian by Rowan Williams. Foreword by Orlo Williams. London, 1935.

ERNEST REYNOLDS: *Modern English Drama*, Ill., London, 1949.

ROBERT SPEAIGHT: *Drama since 1939* (The Arts in Britain series), Ill., London, 1947.

(*For* SIR GEORGE ALEXANDER *and* LILIAN BAYLIS *see* LONDON THEATRES.)

W. A. DARLINGTON: *J. M. Barrie*, London, 1938.

JAMES A. ROY: *James Matthew Barrie*, N.Y., 1938.

EDWARD GORDON CRAIG: *On the Art of the Theatre*, Ill., London, 1911.
JANET LEEPER: *Edward Gordon Craig; Designs for the Theatre* (King Penguin series), Ill., London, 1948.
ENID ROSE: *Gordon Craig and the Theatre, a Record and an Interpretation*, Ill., London and N.Y., 1931, B.

CHRISTOPHER HASSALL: *Notes on the Verse Drama* (The Masque, No. 6), Ill., London, 1948.
RONALD PEACOCK: *The Poet in the Theatre*, London and N.Y., 1946.
PRISCILLA THOULESS: *Modern Poetic Drama*, Oxford, 1934, B.
(Consult also the files of *The Era*, 1881–1939, and *Era Almanacks*; *Play Pictorial*, 1902–40, and *Theatre World*, 1925– ; and *The Theatre*, ed. Clement Scott, 1877–97.)

ENGLISH COMEDIANS, *see* ENGLAND, GERMANY, *and* SHAKESPEARE.

ENGLISH PLAYHOUSE, *see* TECHNICAL BOOKS, I and 2, ENGLAND, LONDON THEATRES, *and* PROVINCIAL AND REPERTORY THEATRES.

EXETER, *see* PROVINCIAL AND REPERTORY THEATRES.

FAIRS AND FAIRGROUNDS, *see* CIRCUS, *and* POPULAR ENTERTAINMENT, I.

FAR EASTERN THEATRES

1. *Burma*

MAUNG HTIN AUNG: *Burmese Drama, a study, with Translations of Burmese Plays*, London, 1937.

2. *China*

L. C. ARLINGTON: *The Chinese Drama from the Earliest Times until To-Day. A Panoramic Study of the Art in China, tracing its Origin and describing its Actors (in both Male and Female Rôles); their Costumes and Make-Up, Superstitions and Stage Slang; the accompanying Music and Musical Instruments; concluding with Synopses of Thirty Chinese Plays*. With a *Pien* by Mei Lan-fang; Foreword by H. A. Giles. Ill., Shanghai, 1930, B.
KATE BUSS: *Studies in the Chinese Drama*, Ill., Boston, 1922; rev. ed., N.Y., 1930.
JACK CHEN: *The Chinese Theatre*, Ill., London, 1949.
HERBERT ALLEN GILES: *A History of Chinese Literature*, London and N.Y., 1901; rev. ed. 1931, B.
REGINALD FLEMING JOHNSTON: *The Chinese Drama*, Ill., Shanghai, 1921.
A. E. ZUCKER: *The Chinese Theater*, Ill., Boston and London, 1925, B.
CECILIA S. L. ZUNG: *Secrets of the Chinese Drama, a complete explanatory guide to actions and symbols as seen in the performance of Chinese dramas*, Ill., London and Shanghai, 1937.

3. *India*

HERBERT H. GOWEN: *A History of Indian Literature from Vedic Times to the Present Day*, London and N.Y., 1931, B.

P. GUHA-THAKURTA: *The Bengali Drama, its Origin and Development*, London, 1930, B.
GEORG JACOB, HANS JENSEN, HANS LOSCH (Eds.): *Das indische Schattentheater*, Ill., Stuttgart, 1931.
A. BERRIEDALE KEITH: *The Sanskrit Drama in its Origin, Development, Theory and Practice*, Oxford and N.Y., 1924.
STEN KONOW: *Das indische Drama*, Berlin, 1920.
ARTHUR A. MACDONELL: *A History of Sanskrit Literature*, London, 1913, B.
MONTGOMERY SCHUYLER, Jr.: *A Bibliography of the Sanskrit Drama, with an Introductory Sketch of the Dramatic Literature of India*, Columbia U.P., N.Y., 1906.
R. K. YAJNIK: *The Indian Theatre. Its Origins and its Later Developments under European Influence, with special reference to Western India*, London and N.Y., 1934.

4. *Japan*

W. G. ASTON: *A History of Japanese Literature*, London, 1899, B.
ANDRÉ BEAUJARD: *Le théâtre comique des Japonais, Introduction à l'étude des Kyôghén*, Paris, 1937, B.
A. BÉNAZET: *Le théâtre au Japon, ses rapports avec les cultes locaux*, Ill., Paris, 1901, B.
OSMAN EDWARDS: *Japanese Plays and Playfellows*, Ill., London, 1901.
ZOE KINCAID: *Kabuki, the Popular Stage of Japan*, Ill., N.Y., 1925.

FRANK ALANSON LOMBARD: *An Outline History of the Japanese Drama*. Introduction by George Pierce Baker. Ill., London and N.Y., 1929, B.

ALBERT MAYBON: *Le théâtre japonais*, Ill., Paris, 1926.

MARIE C. STOPES and PROFESSOR JOJI SAKURAI:

Plays of Old Japan: The 'Nō': Together with translations of the dramas. Preface by His Excellency Baron Kato, the Japanese Ambassador. Ill., London, 1913, B.

ARTHUR WALEY: *The Nō Plays of Japan*. With letters by Oswald Sickert. Ill., London and N.Y., 1922, B.

FASTNACHTSSPIEL, *see* ECCLESIASTICAL DRAMA, *and* GERMANY.

FEDERAL THEATRE, *see* U.S.A.

FRANCE

SAMUEL CHAPPUZEAU: *Le Théâtre françois divisé en trois livres où il est traité*: (1) *De l'Usage de la Comédie*. (2) *Des Autheurs qui soutiennent le Théâtre*. (3) *De la conduite des Comédiens*. 3 vols., Paris, 1674.

JULES JANIN: *Histoire de la littérature dramatique*, 6 vols., Ill., Paris, 1853–8.

GUSTAVE LANSON: *Manuel bibliographique de la Littérature française moderne, 1500–1900*, 4 vols., Paris, 1909–12.

EUGÈNE LINTILHAC: *Histoire générale du théâtre en France*, 5 vols., Paris, 1904–10, B.

HENRY LYONNET: *Dictionnaire des comédiens français*, 2 vols., Geneva, 1911–12.

GEORGES MONVAL: *Liste des Sociétaires de la Comédie-Française, 1658–1900*, Paris, 1900.

LES FRÈRES PARFAICT (Claude et François): *Histoire du Théâtre françois depuis son origine jusqu'à présent*, 15 vols., Amsterdam and Paris, 1735–49.

—— *Mémoires pour servir à l'histoire des spectacles de la foire*, 2 vols. in 1, Paris, 1743.

LOUIS PETIT DE JULLEVILLE: *Le théâtre en France, Histoire de la Littérature dramatique depuis ses origines jusqu'à nos jours*, Paris, 1889; rev. ed., 1921.

ARTHUR POUGIN: *Acteurs et actrices d'autrefois. Histoire anecdotique des théâtres à Paris depuis 300 ans*, Ill., Paris, 1896.

GEORGE SAINTSBURY: *A Short History of French Literature*, Oxford, 1882.

JEAN VALMY-BAYSSE: *Naissance et vie de la Comédie-Française*, Ill., Paris, 1945, B.

GUSTAVE COHEN: *Le théâtre en France au moyen âge*, 2 vols., Ill., Paris, 1931, B.

LOUIS PETIT DE JULLEVILLE: *La Comédie et les Mœurs en France au moyen âge*, Paris, 1885.

—— *Les Comédiens en France au moyen âge*, Paris, 1885.

VICTOR FOURNEL: *Le théâtre au XVIIe siècle — La Comédie*, Paris, 1892.

ELEANOR F. JOURDAIN: *An Introduction to the French Classical Drama*, London, 1912.

HENRY CARRINGTON LANCASTER (Ed.): *Le Mémoire de Mahelot, Laurent et d'autres décorateurs de l'Hôtel de Bourgogne et de la Comédie-Française au XVIIe siècle*, Ill., Paris, 1920.

—— *A History of French Dramatic Literature, 1610–1700*, 9 vols., Baltimore and Paris, 1929–42, B.

—— *Sunset: A History of Parisian Drama in the Last Years of Louis XIV, 1701–15*, Baltimore and Paris, 1945.

GUSTAVE LANSON: *Esquisse d'une histoire de la tragédie française*, Paris, 1927.

JULES MARSAN: *La Pastorale dramatique en France à la fin du XVIe et au commencement du XVIIe siècles*, Ill., Paris, 1905, B.

PIERRE MÉLÈSE: *Le théâtre et le public à Paris sous Louis XIV, 1659–1715*, Ill., Paris, 1934, B.

M. GUIZOT: *Corneille and His Times*, tr. from the rev. French ed., N.Y., 1852.

GUSTAVE LANSON: *Corneille*, Paris, n.d. (Les Grands Écrivains Français), B.

H. ASHTON: *Molière*, London, 1930, B.

H. C. CHATFIELD-TAYLOR: *Molière, a biography*. Introduction by T. F. Crane. Ill., London and N.Y., 1906, B.

BRANDER MATTHEWS: *Molière, his Life and his Works*, Ill., N.Y., 1910.

LOUIS MOLAND: *Molière, sa vie et ses œuvres, avec une notice sur le théâtre et la troupe de Molière*, Ill., Paris, 1887.

W. G. MOORE: *Molière, a new criticism*, Oxford, 1949.

JOHN PALMER: *Molière, His Life and Works*, Ill., London and N.Y., 1930, B.

ARTHUR TILLEY: *Molière*, Cambridge and N.Y., 1921.

A. F. B. CLARKE: *Jean Racine*, Harvard U.P., 1937, B.

MARY DUCLAUX: *The Life of Racine*, London and N.Y., 1925, B.

DANIEL MORNET: *Jean Racine*, Paris, 1943.

DENIS DIDEROT: *Entretiens avec Dorval*, Paris, 1875 (*see also* ART OF ACTING).

F. GAIFFE: *Le drame en France au XVIIIe siècle*, Ill., Paris, 1910, B.

GUSTAVE LANSON: *Nivelle de la Chaussée et la comédie larmoyante*, Paris, 1887; 2nd ed., 1903 (Les origines du drame contemporain).

JULES LEMAÎTRE: *La Comédie après Molière et le théâtre de Dancourt*, 1882; 2nd ed., 1903.

L. S. MERCIER: *Du Théâtre*, Amsterdam, 1773.

D. MORNET: *Le Romantisme au XVIIIe siècle*, Paris, 1912.

PAUL FRISCHAUER: *Beaumarchais; Adventurer in a Century of Women*, N.Y., 1935.

ANDRÉ HALLAYS: *Beaumarchais*, Paris, n.d. (Les Grands Écrivains Français), B.

MLLE CLAIRON: *Mémoires et Réflexions sur l'art dramatique*, Paris, 1799 (An VII).

E. DE GONCOURT: *Mlle Clairon*, Ill., Paris, 1890.

HENRI LOUIS LEKAIN: *Mémoires*, suivis d'une correspondance inédite, Paris, 1801 (An IX).

GASTON DESCHAMPS: *Marivaux*, Paris, n.d. (Les Grands Écrivains Français), B.

RICHARD ALDINGTON: *Voltaire* (Republic of Letters series), London, 1925, B.

GUSTAVE LANSON: *Voltaire*, Paris, n.d. (Les Grands Écrivains Français), B.

JEAN-JACQUES OLIVIER: *Voltaire et les comédiens interprètes de son théâtre*, Paris, 1899.

F. W. M. DRAPER: *The Rise and Fall of the French Romantic Drama, with special reference to the influence of Shakespeare, Scott and Byron*, London, 1923, B.

D. O. EVANS: *Le Théâtre pendant la période romantique (1827–50)*, Paris, 1925.

PIERRE NEBOUT: *Le drame romantique*, Paris, 1895.

CHARLES-MARC DES GRANGES: *La Comédie et les mœurs sous la Restauration et la Monarchie de Juillet (1815–48)*. Préface de Jules Lemaître. Paris, 1904.

JULES LEMAÎTRE: *Theatrical Impressions*, tr. from the French by Frederic Whyte, London, 1924.

CHARLES LENIENT: *La Comédie en France au XIXe siècle*, 2 vols., Paris, 1898.

BRANDER MATTHEWS: *French Dramatists of the 19th century*, London and N.Y., 1882; rev. ed. 1905.

—— *The Theatres of Paris*, Ill., London and N.Y., 1880.

JULES JANIN: *Deburau: histoire du Théâtre à quatre sous*. Préface par Arsène Houssaye. Paris, 1881.

L. HENRY LECOMTE: *Un comédien au XIXe siècle, Frédérick-Lemaître*. Étude biographique et critique d'après les documents inédits, 2 vols., Paris, 1888.

A. BARBOU: *Victor Hugo et son siècle*, Paris, 1889.

JAMES D. BRUNER: *Studies in Victor Hugo's Dramatic Characters*, London and Boston, 1908.

F. FLUTRE: *Victor Hugo*, Ill., Paris, 1927.

R. DE BEAUVOIR: *Mémoires de Mlle Mars*, 2 vols., Paris, 1849.

W. G. HARTOG: *G. de Pixerécourt*, Paris, 1913.

JAMES AGATE: *Rachel*, London, 1928, B.

LOUIS BARTHOU: *Rachel*, Ill., Paris, 1926.

JULES JANIN: *Rachel et la Tragédie*, Ill., Paris, 1859.

NEIL COLE ARVIN: *Eugène Scribe and the French Theatre, 1815–60*, Harvard U.P., 1924, B.

A. DUMAS: *Mémoires de Talma*, 4 vols., Paris, 1852–4.

(*See also* ART OF ACTING.)

FRANK WADLEIGH CHANDLER: *The Contemporary Drama of France*, Boston, 1920, B.

BARRETT H. CLARK: *Contemporary French Dramatists*, Cincinnati, 1915, B.

AUGUSTIN FILON: *The Modern French Drama, Seven Essays*, tr. from the French by Janet E. Hogarth. Introduction by W. L. Courtney. London, 1898.

S. A. RHODES: *The Contemporary French Theatre*, N.Y., 1942, B.

HUGH ALLISON SMITH: *Main Currents of Modern French Drama*, Ill., N.Y., 1925.

SAMUEL MONTEFIORE WAXMAN: *Antoine and the Théâtre Libre*, Cambridge, Mass., 1926, B.

MAY AGATE: *Madame Sarah*, London, 1945.

SIR GEORGE ARTHUR: *Sarah Bernhardt*, London, 1923.

MAURICE BARING: *Sarah Bernhardt*, London, 1933.

G. G. GELLER: *Sarah Bernhardt*, tr. from the French by E. S. G. Potter, Ill., London, 1933.

REYNALDO HAHN: *Sarah Bernhardt: Impressions*, tr. from the French. Introduction by Ethel Thompson. Ill., London, 1932.

JULES HURET: *Sarah Bernhardt*, tr. from the French by G. A. Raper. Introduction by Edmond Rostand. Ill., Paris, 1899.

ANTHONY CURTIS: *New Developments in the*

French Theatre, a Critical Introduction to the Plays of Jean-Paul Sartre, Simone de Beauvoir, Albert Camus, and Jean Anouilh (The Masque, No. 8), Ill., London, 1948.

(*See also* ART OF ACTING, ECCLESIASTICAL DRAMA, COMMEDIA DELL' ARTE, DRAMATIC CRITICISM, OPERA, *and* SHAKESPEARE.)

GAIETY THEATRE, *see* LONDON THEATRES.

GERMANY AND AUSTRIA

JULIUS BAB: *Die Chronik des deutschen Dramas*, 5vols., Berlin, 1922 ff.

—— *Deutsche Schauspieler*, Berlin, 1908.

EDUARD DEVRIENT: *Geschichte der deutschen Schauspielkunst*, 5 vols., Leipzig, 1848–74; new ed. rev. by W. Stuhlfeld, Berlin, 1929.

KUNO FRANCKE: *A History of German Literature as determined by Social Forces*, N.Y., 1901.

MAX LITTMAN: *Die königlichen Hoftheater in Stuttgart*, Ill., Darmstadt, 1912.

BAYARD QUINCY MORGAN: *A Critical Bibliography of German Literature in English Translation, 1481–1927; Supplement, 1928–35*, Stanford U.P., 1939.

J. W. NAGL und J. ZEIDLER: *Deutsche-Oesterreichische Literaturgeschichte*, ed. by Eduard Castle, 4 vols., Vienna, 1899 ff.

W. SPEMANN: *Goldenes Buch des Theaters*, Ill., Berlin, 1902.

CALVIN THOMAS: *A History of German Literature*, N.Y., 1928.

M. J. RUDWIN: *The Origin of the German Carnival Comedy*, N.Y., 1920, B.

B. AIKIN-SNEATH: *Comedy in Germany in the First Half of the 18th Century*, Ill., Oxford, 1936, B.

JOHANN CHRISTIAN BRANDES: *Meine Lebensgeschichte*, ed. P. A. Merbach, Ill., Berlin, 1924. In a French translation as *Mémoires de Brandes, auteur et comédien allemand*, 2 vols., Paris, 1823.

JOSEPH ANTON CHRIST: *Schauspielerleben im 18. Jahrhundert*, ed. by Rudolf Schirmer, Ill., Leipzig, 1912.

BERTHOLD LITZMANN: *Der grosse Schröder* Ill., Berlin, 1904.

CAMILLO VON KLENZE: *From Goethe to Hauptmann, Studies in a Changing Culture*, N.Y., 1926, B.

GEORG WITKOWSKI: *German Drama of the 19th Century*, tr. from the German by L. E. Horning, N.Y., 1900.

GEORG BRANDES: *Wolfgang Goethe*, authorized translation from the Danish by Allen W. Porterfield, 2 vols., N.Y., 1925.

G. H. LEWES: *The Life and Works of Goethe, with sketches of his age and contemporaries, from published and unpublished sources*, 2 vols., 1855 (also in Everyman's Library, with a Preface by Havelock Ellis, 1908).

EMIL LUDWIG: *Goethe, the History of a Man*, tr. from the German by Ethel Colburn Mayne, 2 vols., Ill., London and N.Y., 1928.

JOHN G. ROBERTSON: *Goethe*, London, 1927. (The Republic of Letters series), B.

GUSTAV POLLAK: *Franz Grillparzer and the Austrian Drama*, Ill., N.Y., 1907.

PAUL SCHLENTHER: *Gerhard Hauptmann: Leben und Werke*, rev. ed. by A. Eloesser, Berlin, 1922.

KARL J. NAEF: *Hugo von Hofmannsthals Wesen und Werk*, Zürich, 1938.

MAX GRUBE: *Geschichte der Meininger*, Ill., Berlin, 1926.

THOMAS CARLYLE: *The Life of Schiller*, London, 1825.

HENRY W. NEVINSON: *Life of Schiller*, N.Y., 1899.

SOLOMON LIPTZIN: *Arthur Schnitzler*, N.Y., 1932.

ROBERT F. ARNOLD (Ed.): *Das deutsche Drama*, Munich, 1925, B.

JULIUS BAB: *Das Theater der Gegenwart: Geschichte der dramatischen Bühne seit 1870*, Ill., Leipzig, 1928, B.

FÉLIX BERTAUX: *Panorama of German Literature from 1871 to 1931*, tr. by J. J. Troustine, N.Y., 1935, B.

JETHRO BITHELL: *Modern German Literature, 1880–1938*, Ill., London, 1939, B.

ARTHUR ELOESSER: *Modern German Literature*, tr. from the German by Catherine A. Phillips. Introduction by Ludwig Lewisohn. London and N.Y., 1933.

ERNST FEISE: *Fifty Years of German Drama*, a Bibliography of Modern German Drama, 1880–1930, based on the Loewenberg Collection in the Johns Hopkins University Library, Baltimore, 1941.

WILHELM KNEVELS: *Das moderne Drama, Gesicht unserer Zeit. Darstellung, Deutung, Wertung*, Brunswick, 1930.

BERTHOLD LITZMANN: *Das deutsche Drama in den litterarischen Bewegungen der Gegenwart*, Hamburg, 1894.

HUNTLY CARTER: *The Theatre of Max Reinhardt*, Ill., London, 1914.

FRANZ HORCH: *Die Spielpläne Max Reinhardts, 1905–30*, Munich, 1930.

SIEGFRIED JACOBSOHN: *Max Reinhardt*, Ill., Berlin, 1910.

HANS ROTHE: *Max Reinhardt, 25 Jahres Deutsches Theater*, Ill., Munich, 1930.

OLIVER M. SAYLER (Ed.): *Max Reinhardt and His Theatre*, Ill., N.Y., 1924.

ERNST STERN und HEINZ HERALD (Eds.): *Reinhardt und seine Bühne, Bilder von der Arbeit des Deutschen Theaters*, Ill., Berlin, 1918.

(*See also* ECCLESIASTICAL DRAMA, DRAMATIC CRITICISM, *and* SHAKESPEARE.)

GLASGOW, *see* PROVINCIAL AND REPERTORY THEATRES.

GREECE AND ROME

1. General

JAMES TURNEY ALLEN: *Stage Antiquities of the Greeks and Romans and their Influence*, Ill., London and N.Y., 1927, B.

MARGARETE BIEBER: *The History of the Greek and Roman Theatre*, Ill., Princeton U.P., 1939, B.

EDWARD CAPPS: *Vitruvius and the Greek Stage*, Chicago, 1893.

VITRUVIUS: *The Ten Books on Architecture*, tr. from the Latin by Morris Hicky Morgan, Ill., Cambridge, Mass., 1914.

2. Greece—General

ROY C. FLICKINGER: *The Greek Theater and its Drama*, Ill., Chicago and Cambridge, 1918; 4th ed., 1936, B.

ARTHUR ELAM HAIGH: *The Attic Theatre: a Description of the Stage and Theatre of the Athenians, and of the Dramatic Performances at Athens*, Ill., Oxford, 1889; 3rd ed. rev. and ed. by A. W. Pickard-Cambridge, 1907.

A. W. PICKARD-CAMBRIDGE: *The Theatre of Dionysus in Athens*, Ill., Oxford, 1946, B.

—— *Dithyramb, Tragedy and Comedy*, Ill., Oxford, 1927.

JOHN ADDINGTON SYMONDS: *Studies of the Greek Poets*, 2 vols., London, 1893; new ed., 1920.

3. Aristotle

ARISTOTLE: *On the Art of Poetry*, a revised text with Critical Introduction, Translation, and Commentary by Ingram Bywater, Oxford, 1909. An Analytical Commentary and Notes on the Preceding, by A. S. Owen, Oxford, 1931.

S. H. BUTCHER: *Aristotle's Theory of Poetry and Fine Art*, with a critical text and translation of the *Poetics*, London, 1895; 4th ed., 1911.

LANE COOPER: *Aristotle on the Art of Poetry*, an amplified version with supplementary illustrations for students of English, N.Y., 1913.

4. Comedy—Aristophanes and Menander

FRANCIS MACDONALD CORNFORD: *The Origin of Attic Comedy*, London, 1914.

PHILIPPE E. LEGRAND: *New Greek Comedy*, tr. from the French by James Loeb, N.Y., 1917.

GILBERT NORWOOD: *Greek Comedy*, N.Y. and London, 1931.

LOUIS E. LORD: *Aristophanes: His Plays and His Influence*, Boston, 1925, B.

GILBERT MURRAY: *Aristophanes, a Study*, Oxford, 1933.

5. Tragedy—Aeschylus, Euripides, and Sophocles

ARTHUR ELAM HAIGH: *The Tragic Drama of the Greeks*, Ill., Oxford, 1896.

H. D. F. KITTO: *Greek Tragedy, a Literary Study*, London, 1939.

AUGUST C. MAHR: *The Origin of the Greek Tragic Form, a Study in the Early Theatre in Attica*, Ill., N.Y., 1938, B.

GILBERT NORWOOD: *Greek Tragedy*, London and N.Y., 1920.

J. T. SHEPPARD: *Greek Tragedy*, Ill., Cambridge, 1920.

—— *Aeschylus and Sophocles: their Work and Influence*, Ill., London and N.Y., 1927, B.

GILBERT MURRAY: *Aeschylus, the Creator of Tragedy*, Oxford, 1940.

HERBERT WEIR SMYTH: *Aeschylean Tragedy*, Berkeley, Cal. and Cambridge, 1924.

PAUL DECHARME: *Euripides and the Spirit of his Dramas*, tr. from the French by James Loeb, N.Y., 1906.

G. M. A. Grube: *The Drama of Euripides,* London, 1941, B.

F. L. Lucas: *Euripides and his Influence,* London, 1928, B.

Gilbert Murray: *Euripides and his Age,* London and N.Y., 1913; 2nd ed. 1946 (Home University Library).

C. M. Bowra: *Sophoclean Tragedy,* Oxford, 1944.

T. B. L. Webster: *An Introduction to Sophocles,* Oxford, 1936.

6. *Rome—Plautus, Terence, and Seneca*

William Beare: *The Roman Stage,* Ill., London, 1950, B.

Harold N. Fowler: *A History of Roman Literature,* Oxford and N.Y., 1932.

W. W. Fowler: *The Roman Festivals of the Period of the Republic,* London, 1899.

Plautus: *Three Plays,* tr. with an introduction by F. A. Wright and H. Lionel Rogers, N.Y., 1925.

John W. Cunliffe: *The Influence of Seneca on Elizabethan Tragedy,* London and N.Y., 1893.

Léon Herrman: *Le théâtre de Sénèque,* Paris, 1924, B.

F. L. Lucas: *Seneca and Elizabethan Tragedy,* Cambridge and N.Y., 1922.

Clarence W. Mendell: *Our Seneca* (on the connexion between English and Greek drama via Seneca), London and N.Y., 1941.

Gilbert Norwood: *The Art of Terence,* Oxford, 1923.

GROUP THEATRE, *see* U.S.A.

HAYMARKET THEATRE, *see* LONDON THEATRES.

HEBREW DRAMA, *see* JEWISH DRAMA.

HULL, *see* PROVINCIAL AND REPERTORY THEATRES.

INDIA, *see* FAR EASTERN THEATRES, 3.

IRELAND

Stephen Gwynn: *Irish Literature and Drama in the English Language, a Short History,* London, 1936.

Robert Hitchcock: *Historical View of the Irish Stage,* 2 vols., Dublin, 1788–94.

Peter Kavanagh: *The Irish Theatre, being a History of the Drama in Ireland from the Earliest Period up to the Present Day,* Ill., Tralee, 1946, B.

R. M. Levey and J. O'Rorke: *Annals of the Theatre Royal, Dublin, from its opening in 1821 to its destruction by fire, Feb. 1880, with occasional notes and observations,* Dublin, 1880.

J. Fitzgerald Molloy: *The Romance of the Irish Stage, with Pictures of the Irish Capital in the 18th Century,* 2 vols., Dublin, 1897.

La Tourette Stockwell: *Dublin Theatres and Theatre Customs, 1637–1820,* Ill., Kingport, Tenn., 1938, B.

Ernest Boyd: *Ireland's Literary Renaissance,* N.Y., 1916; new ed., London and N.Y., 1923, B.

—— *The Contemporary Drama of Ireland,* Dublin and N.Y., 1918, B.

Dawson Byrne: *The Story of Ireland's National Theatre, The Abbey Theatre, Dublin,* Ill., Dublin, 1929.

Una Ellis-Fermor: *The Irish Dramatic Movement,* London, 1939, B.

W. G. Fay and Catherine Carswell: *The Fays of the Abbey Theatre, an Autobiographical Record.* Foreword by James Bridie. Ill., London and N.Y., 1935.

Augusta, Lady Gregory: *Our Irish Theatre,* London and N.Y., 1913.

—— *Journals 1916–1930.* Edited by Lennox Robinson, London, 1946.

Micheal MacLiammoir: *All for Hecuba, an Irish Theatrical Autobiography,* Ill., London, 1946.

Andrew E. Malone: *The Irish Drama, 1896–1928,* London and N.Y., 1929.

Lennox Robinson (Ed.): *The Irish Theatre. Lectures delivered during the Abbey Theatre Festival held in Dublin in August 1938,* London, 1939, B.

Cornelius Weygandt: *Irish Plays and Playwrights,* Ill., London and Boston, 1913.

Francis Bickley: *J. M. Synge and the Irish Dramatic Movement,* London and N.Y., 1912, B.

Maurice Bourgeois: *John Millington Synge and the Irish Theatre,* Ill., London, 1913, B.

Daniel Corkery: *Synge and Anglo-Irish Literature, a Study,* Dublin and London, 1931, B.

P. P. Howe: *J. M. Synge, a Critical Study,* London, 1912, B.

Horatio Sheafe Krans: *W. B. Yeats and the Irish Literary Revival,* N.Y., 1904, B.

William Butler Yeats: *Autobiography,* London and N.Y., 1938.

(*See also* ENGLAND.)

ITALY

G. Antonini: *Il teatro contemporaneo in Italia*, Milan, 1927.

M. Apollonio: *Storia del teatro italiano*, Florence, 1940.

Antonio Belloni: *Il Seicento, Cap. 5: Il teatro*, Milan, 1905; 3rd ed., 1929 (Storia letteraria d'Italia), B.

Emilio Bertana: *La Tragedia*, Milan, 1910; 3rd ed., 1929 (Storia dei Generi Letterari Italiani), B.

Giuseppe Costetti: *Il teatro italiano nel 1800*, Turin, 1901.

Benedetto Croce: *La letteratura della nuova Italia*, 6 vols., Bari, 1921–40, B.

Joseph Spencer Kennard: *The Italian Theatre*, Vol. I: *From the Beginning to the Close of the Seventeenth Century*, Vol. II: *From the Close of the Seventeenth Century*, 2 vols., Ill., N.Y., 1932, B.

Lander MacClintock: *The Contemporary Drama of Italy*, Boston, 1920, B.

Addison McLeod: *Plays and Players in Modern Italy*, Ill., London, 1912.

Luigi Rasi: *I Comici Italiani, Biografia, Bibliografia, Iconografia*, 2 vols., Florence, 1897, 1905.

Luigi Riccoboni: *Histoire du théâtre italien depuis la décadence de la comédie latine, avec un catalogue des tragédies et comédies italiennes imprimées depuis l'an 1500 jusqu'à l'an 1660 et une dissertation sur la tragédie moderne*, 2 vols., Paris, 1728; enlarged ed., 1730.

Giovanni e Carlo Salvioli: *Bibliografia universale del teatro drammatico italiano*, Venice, 1894–1903.

Ireneo Sanesi: *La Commedia*, 2 vols., Milan, 1911, 1935 (Storia dei Generi Letterari Italiani), B.

Adriano Tilgher: *Studi sul teatro contemporaneo*, Rome, 1923, 3rd ed., 1928.

—— *La scena e la vita, nuovi studi sul teatro contemporaneo*, Rome, 1925.

Luigi Tonelli: *L'Evoluzione del teatro contemporaneo in Italia*, Palermo, 1913.

—— *Il teatro italiano dalle origini ai giorni nostri*, Milan, 1924.

Joseph Cooper Walker: *Historical Memoir on Italian Tragedy*, Ill., London, 1799.

Édouard Schneider: *Eleonora Duse: Souvenirs, Notes et Documents*, Paris, 1925, B.

Arthur Symons: *Eleonora Duse*, London, 1926.

Carlo Goldoni: *Memoirs*, tr. from the French by John Black, 2 vols., London, 1828.

H. C. Chatfield-Taylor: *Goldoni, a Biography*, Ill., London and N.Y., 1914, B.

Carlo Gozzi: *Memoirs*, tr. from the Italian by J. Addington Symonds, 2 vols., Ill., London, 1890, B.

Walter Starkie: *Luigi Pirandello, 1867–1936*, London, 1926; rev. ed., London and N.Y., 1937.

Domenico Vittorini: *The Drama of Luigi Pirandello*, Philadelphia, 1935, B.

Tommaso Salvini: *Leaves from the Autobiography of Tommaso Salvini*, London and N.Y., 1893.

(*See also* COMMEDIA DELL' ARTE, OPERA, *and* SHAKESPEARE.)

JAPAN, see FAR EASTERN THEATRES, 4.

JESUIT DRAMA

A. and A. Backer et C. Sommervogel: *Bibliothèque de la Compagnie de Jésus: Bibliographie*, Brussels and Paris, 1890 ff.

P. Bahlmann: *Jesuiten-Dramen der niederrheinischen Ordensprovinz*, Leipzig, 1896.

E. Boysse: *Le Théâtre des Jésuites*, Paris, 1880.

F. Colagrosso: *Saverio Bettinelli e il teatro gesuitico*, 2nd ed., Florence, 1901.

B. Duhr, S.J.: *Geschichte der Jesuiten in den Ländern deutscher Zunge*, Freiburg i/Brg., 1907.

A. P. Farrell: *The Jesuit Code of Liberal Education. Development and Scope of the Ratio Studiorum*, Ill., Milwaukee, 1938, B.

L. Ferrari: 'Appunti sul teatro tragico dei Gesuiti in Italia' (in *Rassegna Bibliografica della Letteratura Italiana VII*, 1899).

W. Flemming: *Geschichte des Jesuitentheaters in den Länder deutscher Zunge (Schriften der Gesellschaft für Theatergeschichte 32)*, Berlin, 1923.

L. V. Gofflot: *Le Théâtre au Collège du moyen âge à nos jours*, Ill., Paris, 1907, B.

J. Jouvancy, S.J.: *Magistris Scholarum inferiorum Soc. Jesu de ratione discendi et docendi*, Florence, 1703.

F. Lang, S.J.: *Dissertatio de actione scenica, cum Figuris eandem explicantibus, et Observationibus quibusdam de Arte comica*, Ill., Munich, 1727.

W. H. McCabe: *An Introduction to the Early Jesuit Theatre*, Cambridge, 1929.

C. F. Menestrier, S.J.: *Des ballets anciens et modernes*, Paris, 1682.

J. Müller, S.J.: *Das Jesuitendrama in den Ländern deutscher Zunge vom Anfang (1555) bis zum Hochbarock (1665)*, 2 vols., Augsburg, 1930.

G. M. Pachtler, S.J. (Ed.): *Ratio Studiorum et Institutiones Scholasticae Societatis Jesu (Monumenta Germaniæ Pædagogica*, ed. Kehrbach, Vols. II and V), 2 vols., Berlin, 1887.

C. Rahlenbeck: 'Le théâtre des Jésuites en Belgique (1540–1640)' (in *Revue de Belgique* LX), Brussels, 1888.

W. Richter: 'Paderborner Jesuitendramen von 1592–1770' (in *Mitteilungen der Gesellschaft für deutsche Erziehungs- und Schulgeschichte* IV), Berlin, 1894.

B. Soldati: *Il Collegio Mamertino e le origini del teatro gesuitico*, Turin, 1906. (Contains the text of S. Tuccio's *Juditha*, 1564.)

J. Gar ca Soriano: 'El Teatro de Colegio en España' (in *Boletín de la Real Academia Española* XIV, 1927, XV, 1928, and XVI, 1929.)

J. Zeidler: *Studien und Beiträge zur Geschichte der Jesuitenkomödie und des Klosterdramas* (Theatergeschichtliche Forschungen 4), Hamburg and Leipzig, 1891.

JEWISH DRAMA

Edward Davison Coleman: *Plays of Jewish Interest on the American Stage, 1752–1821*, Baltimore, 1934.

—— *Habimah, Hebrew Theatre of Palestine*, Ill., Tel Aviv, 1937. (This is available also in French, German, Hebrew, and Yiddish.)

Jewish Encyclopaedia, a descriptive record of the History, Religion, Literature, and Customs of the Jewish People from the Earliest Times to the Present Day, 12 vols., Ill., London and N.Y., 1901.

A. A. Roback: *The Story of Yiddish Literature*, Ill., N.Y., 1940, B.

Meyer Waxman: *A History of Jewish Literature*, Ill., N.Y., 1941, B.

JUVENILE DRAMA, *see* POPULAR ENTERTAINMENT, 5.

KABUKI, KYOGEN, *see* FAR EASTERN THEATRES, 4.

LIGHTING, *see* TECHNICAL BOOKS, 1 and 4.

LITTLE THEATRE, *see* AMATEUR THEATRE, NATIONWIDE THEATRE, PROVINCIAL AND REPERTORY THEATRES, *and* REGIONAL AND PIONEER THEATRE.

LITURGICAL DRAMA, *see* ECCLESIASTICAL DRAMA.

LIVERPOOL, *see* PROVINCIAL AND REPERTORY THEATRES.

LONDON THEATRES

T. Fairman Ordish: *Early London Theatres (In the Fields)*, Ill., London, 1894.

Erroll Sherson: *London's Lost Theatres of the 19th Century, with Notes on Plays and Players seen there*. Foreword by Dame Madge Kendal. Ill., London, 1925.

Desmond MacCarthy: *The Court Theatre, 1904–7, a Commentary and Criticism*, London, 1907.

Henry Saxe-Wyndham: *The Annals of Covent Garden, from 1732–1897*, 2 vols., Ill., London, 1906.

Desmond Shawe-Taylor: *Covent Garden*, Ill., London, 1948.

T. Edgar Pemberton: *The Criterion Theatre, 1875–1903*, Ill., London, 1903.

D. Forbes-Winslow: *Daly's; the Biography of a Theatre*, Ill., London, 1944.

Dougald MacMillan (Ed.): *Drury Lane Calendar, 1747–76*, compiled from the Playbills, Oxford, 1938.

W. Macqueen-Pope: *Theatre Royal Drury Lane*, Ill., London, 1945.

Edward Stirling: *Old Drury Lane; Fifty Years' Recollections of Author, Actor, and Manager*, 2 vols., London, 1881.

John Hollingshead: *Gaiety Chronicles*, Ill., London, 1898.

—— '*Good Old Gaiety*': *an Historiette and Remembrance*, Ill., London, 1903.

W. Macqueen-Pope: *Gaiety, Theatre of Enchantment*, Ill., London, 1949.

W. Macqueen-Pope: *Haymarket, Theatre of Perfection*, Ill., London, 1948.

Cyril Maude: *The Haymarket Theatre, some Records and Reminiscences*, Ill., London, 1903.

NIGEL PLAYFAIR: *The Story of the Lyric Theatre, Hammersmith.* Introduction by Arnold Bennett; Epilogue by A. A. Milne. Ill., London, 1925.

JOHN BOOTH: *A Century of Theatre History, 1816–1916: The Old Vic.*, Ill., London, 1917.

EDWARD J. DENT: *A Theatre for Everybody; The Story of the Old Vic and Sadler's Wells,* Ill., London, 1945, B.

CICELY HAMILTON and LILIAN BAYLIS: *The Old Vic,* Ill., London, 1926.

HARCOURT WILLIAMS: *Four Years at the Old Vic, 1929–33,* Ill., London, 1935.

—— *Vic-Wells, the Work of Lilian Baylis,* Ill., London, 1938.

AUDREY WILLIAMSON: *Old Vic Drama, a Twelve Years' Study of Plays and Players.* Foreword by Dame Sybil Thorndike. Ill., London, 1948.

A. E. W. MASON: *Sir George Alexander and the St. James's Theatre,* Ill., London, 1935. (*See also* ENGLAND.)

LYRIC THEATRE, HAMMERSMITH, *see* LONDON THEATRES.

MACHINERY, *see* TECHNICAL BOOKS, 1 and 5.

MADDERMARKET THEATRE, NORWICH, *see* PROVINCIAL AND REPERTORY THEATRES.

MAKE-UP

JOHN F. BAIRD: *Make-Up, a Manual for the use of Actors, Amateur and Professional,* Ill., London and N.Y., 1930.

T. W. BAMFORD: *Practical Make-Up for the Stage.* Foreword by Ernest Thesiger. Ill., London, 1940.

AD. BRACHART: *L'art de se maquiller et de se grimer,* Ill., Paris, 1912.

RUDOLPH G. LISZT: *The Last Word in Make-Up* (Make-Up Encyclopedia), Ill., London and N.Y., 1939.

CAVENDISH MORTON: *The Art of Theatrical Make-Up,* Ill., London, 1909.

CHARLES S. PARSONS: *A Guide to Theatrical Make-Up.* Foreword by Cedric Hardwicke. Ill., London, 1932.

SERGE STRENKOVSKY: *The Art of Make-Up,* ed. by Elizabeth S. Taber, Ill., N.Y., 1937, B.

ERIC WARD: *A Book of Make-Up,* Ill., London, 1930.

N. E. B. WOLTERS: *Modern Make-Up for Stage and Screen.* Introduction by Matheson Lang. Ill., London, 1935.

(*See also* ART OF ACTING.)

MANCHESTER, *see* PROVINCIAL AND REPERTORY THEATRES.

MARIONETTES, *see* POPULAR ENTERTAINMENT, 5.

MASQUE

LILY B. CAMPBELL: *Scenes and Machines on the English Stage during the Renaissance, a Classical Revival,* Ill., N.Y. and Cambridge, 1923.

J. ALFRED GOTCH: *Inigo Jones,* Ill., London, 1928.

W. W. GREG: *A List of Masques, Pageants, etc.,* Supplementary to a List of English Plays (*see* ENGLAND), London, 1901.

INIGO JONES: *Designs for Masques and Plays at Court,* a descriptive catalogue of Drawings for Scenery and Costumes. Introduction and Notes by Percy Simpson and E. F. Bell. Oxford, 1924. (Publications of the Walpole Society, Vol. XII.)

ALLARDYCE NICOLL: *Stuart Masques and the Renaissance Stage,* Ill., London, 1937.

PAUL REYHER: *Les masques anglais,* Paris, 1909.

MARY SUSAN STEELE: *Plays and Masques at Court during the Reigns of Elizabeth, James, and Charles,* New Haven, 1926, B.

MARY SULLIVAN: *The Court Masques of James I,* Ill., N.Y., 1913.

ENID WELSFORD: *The Court Masque, a Study in the Relationship between Poetry and the Revels,* Ill., Cambridge and N.Y., 1928.

(*See also* ENGLAND.)

MEININGEN PLAYERS, *see* GERMANY.

MEXICO, *see* SOUTH AMERICA, 7.

MINSTRELSY, *see* ENGLAND, NEGRO IN THE THEATRE, POPULAR ENTERTAINMENT, 3, *and* U.S.A.

MIRACLE PLAY, *see* ECCLESIASTICAL DRAMA, ENGLAND, *and* FRANCE.

MUSIC-HALL, *see* POPULAR ENTERTAINMENT, 2.

MYSTERY PLAY, *see* ECCLESIASTICAL DRAMA, ENGLAND, *and* FRANCE.

NATIONWIDE THEATRE, U.S.A.

ALFRED G. ARVOLD: *The Little Country Theatre*, Ill., N.Y., 1922, B.

LOUISE BURLEIGH: *The Community Theatre, in Theory and Practice*, Ill., Boston, 1917, B.

ALEXANDER DEAN: *Little Theatre Organization and Management for Community, University, and School, including a History of the Amateur in Drama.* Preface by Walter Prichard Eaton, London and N.Y., 1926.

THOMAS HERBERT DICKINSON: *The Insurgent Theatre; Organisation and Management of the Non-commercial Theatre*, N.Y., 1917.

CLARENCE J. DE GOVEIA: *Community Playhouse*, Ill., N.Y., 1923, B.

NORRIS HOUGHTON: *Advance from Broadway*, N.Y., 1941.

ALBERT McCLEERY and CARL GLICK: *Curtains Going Up*, Ill., N.Y., 1939, B.

KENNETH MACGOWAN: *Footlights across America; Towards a National Theater*, Ill., N.Y., 1929, B.

CLARENCE ARTHUR PERRY: *The Work of the Little Theatres*, N.Y., 1933, B.

(*See also* REGIONAL AND PIONEER THEATRE, *and* U.S.A.)

NEGRO IN THE THEATRE

FREDERICK W. BOND: *The Negro and the Drama*, Washington, 1940, B.

STERLING A. BROWN: *Negro Poetry and Drama*, Washington, 1937, B.

FRANCIS P. GAINES: *The Southern Plantation*, N.Y., 1925, B.

EDITH J. R. ISAACS: *The Negro in the American Theatre*, Ill., N.Y., 1947.

JAMES WELDON JOHNSON: *Black Manhattan*, Ill., N.Y., 1930.

HILDA LAWSON: *The Negro in American Drama* (Bibliography of Contemporary Negro Drama), Ill., Urbana, 1939.

(*See also* POPULAR ENTERTAINMENT, 3, *and* U.S.A.)

NEWCASTLE-UPON-TYNE, *see* PROVINCIAL AND REPERTORY THEATRES.

NIGGER MINSTRELS, *see* NEGRO IN THE THEATRE, *and* POPULAR ENTERTAINMENT, 3.

NŌ PLAYS, *see* FAR EASTERN THEATRES, 4.

NORTH SHIELDS, NORTHAMPTON, *see* PROVINCIAL AND REPERTORY THEATRES.

NORWAY, *see* SCANDINAVIA, 3.

NORWICH, *see* PROVINCIAL AND REPERTORY THEATRES.

OLD VIC, *see* LONDON THEATRES.

OPERA

WALLACE BROCKWAY and HUBERT WEINSTOCK: *The Opera; a History of its Creation and Performance, 1600–1941*, Ill., London and N.Y., 1941.

RICHARD CAPELL: *Opera, its Nature and History*, London, 1930.

E. J. DENT: *Foundations of English Opera, a Study of Musical Drama in England during the Seventeenth Century*, Cambridge, 1928.

—— *Opera* (Pelican Books), London, 1940.

OLIN DOWNES: *The Home Book of the Opera*, N.Y., 1937.

ARTHUR ELSON: *A History of Opera*, Boston, 1926.

CARLOS FISCHER: *Les Costumes de l' Opéra*, Ill., Paris, 1931, B.

DYNELEY HUSSEY: *Eurydice, or the Nature of Opera*, London, 1929.

GUSTAV KOBBÉ: *The Complete Opera Book; the Stories of the Operas, together with 410 of the leading Airs and Motives in Musical Notation*, London and N.Y., 1922; rev. ed., 1924.

HENRY E. KREHBIEL: *A Book of Operas; their Histories, Plots, and Music*, 2 vols. in 1, N.Y., 1919.

DR. ALFRED LOEWENBERG: *Annals of Opera, 1597–1940, compiled from original sources*, Cambridge, 1943.

LEO MELITZ: *The Opera Goer's Complete Guide*, London and N.Y., 1924.

PERCY A. SCHOLES: *A Miniature History of Opera for the General Reader and the Student*, Oxford, 1931.

O. G. SONNECK: *Early Opera in America*, N.Y., 1915.

R. A. STREATFEILD: *The Opera, a Sketch of its Development, with full Descriptions of all Works in the Modern Repertory*, 5th ed. rev. and enlarged by E. J. Dent, London and N.Y., 1925.

PANTOMIME, see COMMEDIA DELL' ARTE, *and* POPULAR ENTERTAINMENT, 4.

PHILADELPHIA, see REGIONAL AND PIONEER THEATRE.

PIONEER THEATRE, U.S.A., see REGIONAL AND PIONEER THEATRE.

POETIC DRAMA, see ENGLAND.

POPULAR ENTERTAINMENT

1. General

VICTOR FOURNEL: *Les Spectacles populaires et les artistes des rues*, Paris, 1863.

THOMAS FROST: *The Old Showmen, and the Old London Fairs*, London, 1874.

SAMUEL McKECHNIE: *Popular Entertainments through the Ages*, Ill., London, 1931.

GEORGE JEAN NATHAN: *The Popular Theatre*, N.Y., 1918.

2. Burlesque, Music-Hall, Variety, Vaudeville

W. H. ('BILLY') BOARDMAN: *Vaudeville Days*, ed. by David Whitelaw. Foreword by Andrew Soutar. Ill., London, 1935.

DION CLAYTON CALTHROP: *Music-Hall Nights*, Ill., London, 1925.

MAURICE WILLSON DISHER: *Winkles and Champagne, Comedies and Tragedies of the Music-Hall*, Ill., London, 1938.

S. THEODORE FELSTEAD: *Stars who made the Halls, a Hundred Years of English Humour, Harmony, and Hilarity*, Ill., London, 1946.

PERCY FITZGERALD: *Music-Hall Land*, Ill., London, 1891.

DOUGLAS GILBERT: *American Vaudeville, its Life and Times*, Ill., N.Y., 1940.

—— *Lost Chords, a Social History of American Popular Songs*, N.Y., 1942.

ARCHIBALD HADDON: *The Story of the Music-Hall*, Ill., London, 1935.

W. H. MORTON and H. CHANCE NEWTON (Eds.): *Sixty Years' Stage Service; being a Record of the Life of Charles Morton, 'The Father of the Halls'*, Ill., London, 1905.

H. CHANCE NEWTON: *Idols of the 'Halls', being my Music-Hall Memories*. Foreword by Sir Oswald Stoll. Ill., London, 1928.

EDWARD RENTON: *The Vaudeville Theatre. Building, Operation, Management*, N.Y., 1918.

HAROLD SCOTT: *The Early Doors, Origins of the Music-Hall*, Ill., London, 1948, B.

ERNEST SHORT: *Fifty Years of Vaudeville, 1894–1945*, Ill., London, 1946.

BERNARD SOBEL: *Burleycue*, Ill., N.Y., 1931.

CHARLES DOUGLAS STUART and A. J. PARK: *The Variety Stage; a History of the Music-Halls from the Earliest Period to the Present Time*, London, 1895.

3. Minstrels

LAURENCE HUTTON: *Curiosities of the American Stage*, Ill., N.Y., 1891.

DAILEY PASKMAN and SIGMUND SPAETH: *'Gentlemen, be seated!' A parade of the old-time minstrels, profusely illustrated from old prints and photographs and with complete music for voice and piano*. Foreword by Daniel Frohman. Garden City, N.Y., 1928.

HARRY REYNOLDS: *Minstrel Memories: the Story of Burnt Cork Minstrelsy in Great Britain from 1836 to 1927*, Ill., London, 1928.

EDWARD LeRoy RICE: *Monarchs of Minstrelsy, from 'Daddy' Rice to date*, Ill., N.Y., 1911.

CARL WITTKE: *Tambo and Bones, a History of the American Minstrel Stage*, Durham, N.C., 1930, B.

4. Pantomime

R. J. BROADBENT: *A History of Pantomime*, London, 1901.

CHARLES DICKENS (Ed.): *Memoirs of Joseph Grimaldi*, Ill., London, 1838.

MAURICE WILLSON DISHER: *Clowns and Pantomimes*, Ill., London, 1925.

LEOPOLD WAGNER: *The Pantomimes and all about them*, London, c. 1881.

A. E. WILSON: *Christmas Pantomime, the Story of an English Institution*, Ill., London, 1934, B.; as *King Panto*, N.Y., 1935.

—— *Pantomime Pageant, a Procession of Harlequins, Clowns, Comedians, Principal Boys, &c.*, Ill., London and N.Y., 1946.

5. Puppets, Marionettes, Punch and Judy, Toy Theatre

MARJORIE BATCHELDER: *The Puppet Theatre Handbook*. Introduction by George Speaight. Ill., London, 1948, B.

MAX VON BOEHN: *Dolls and Puppets*, tr. from the German by Josephine Nicoll, Ill., London, 1932, B.

J. PAYNE COLLIER: *Punch and Judy*, Ill., London, 1870.

NINA EFIMOVA: *Adventures of a Russian Puppet Theatre*, tr. from the Russian by Elena Mitcoff, Ill., Birmingham, Mich., 1935.

HELEN HAIMAN JOSEPH: *A Book of Marionettes*, Ill., N.Y., 1920.

GEORGE SPEAIGHT: *Juvenile Drama, The History of the English Toy Theatre*, Ill., London, 1946.

A. E. WILSON: *Penny Plain, Twopence Coloured, a History of the Juvenile Drama*. Foreword by Charles B. Cochran. Ill., London and N.Y., 1932.

(*See also* CIRCUS, COMMEDIA DELL' ARTE, FRANCE, NEGRO IN THE THEATRE, *and* SPAIN.)

PORTUGAL, *see* SPAIN, 2.

PROVIDENCE, R.I., *see* REGIONAL AND PIONEER THEATRE.

PROVINCIAL AND REPERTORY THEATRES
(INCLUDING SCOTLAND AND WALES)

CECIL CHISHOLM: *Repertory, an Outline of the Modern Theatre Movement, Production, Plays, Management*, Ill., London, 1934, B.

BASIL DEAN: *The Repertory Theatre*, Liverpool, 1911.

DR. ALFRED LOEWENBERG (Ed.): *A Bibliography of the Theatres of the British Isles (excluding London)*, London, 1950.

SYBIL ROSENFELD: *Strolling Players and Drama in the Provinces, 1660–1765*, Ill., Cambridge, 1939.

SAMUEL WILLIAM RYLEY: *The Itinerant, or Memoirs of an Actor*, 6 vols., London, 1808.

TATE WILKINSON: *Memoirs of His Own Life*, 4 vols., York, 1790.

BELVILLE S. PENLEY: *The Bath Stage, a History of Dramatic Representations in Bath*, Ill., London and Bath, 1892.

M. F. K. FRASER: *Alexandra Theatre, the Story of a Popular Playhouse*, Ill., Birmingham, 1948.

T. C. KEMP: *The Birmingham Repertory Theatre. The Playhouse and the Man*. Foreword by Sir Barry Jackson. Ill., Birmingham, 1943; rev. ed., 1948.

BACHE MATTHEWS: *A History of the Birmingham Repertory Theatre*. Introduction by Barry V. Jackson. Ill., London, 1924.

PHYLLIS PHILIP RODWAY and LOIS RODWAY SLINGSBY: *Philip Rodway and a Tale of Two Theatres*, Ill., Birmingham, 1934.

M. E. BOARD: *The Story of the Bristol Stage, 1490–1925*, London, 1926.

MARY THERESA ODELL: *Mr. Trotter of Worthing and the Brighton Theatre, 1814–19*, Ill., Worthing, 1944.

WILLIAM COTTON: *The Story of the Drama in Exeter during its best period, 1787–1823, with Reminiscences of Edmund Kean*, Ill., London and Exeter, 1887.

THOMAS SHEPPARD: *Evolution of the Drama in Hull and District*, Ill., Hull, 1927.

R. J. BROADBENT: *Annals of the Liverpool Stage from the Earliest Period to the Present Time, Together with Some Account of the Theatres and Music-Halls in Bootle and Birkenhead*, Ill., Liverpool, 1908.

GRACE WYNDHAM GOLDIE: *The Liverpool Repertory Theatre, 1911–34*, Ill., Liverpool, 1935.

HAROLD OSWALD: *The Theatres Royal in Newcastle-upon-Tyne. Desultory papers relating to the Drama and its homes in that place*, Ill., Newcastle, 1936.

ROBERT KING: *North Shields Theatres, a history of the theatres at North Shields and the adjoining village of Tynemouth, from 1765, including an account of the travelling booths*, Ill., Gateshead, 1948, B.

AUBREY DYAS: *Adventure in Repertory (Northampton Repertory Theatre, 1927–48)*. Foreword by J. B. Priestley. Ill., Northampton, 1948.

T. L. G. BURLEY: *Playhouses and Players of East Anglia*, Ill., Norwich, 1928.

R. H. MOTTRAM: *The Maddermarket Theatre*, Norwich, 1929.

—— *The Norwich Players*. Introduction by Nugent Monck; Epilogue by J. Sprott. Ill., Norwich, 1936.

M. C. DAY and J. C. TREWIN: *The Shakespeare Memorial Theatre*. Forewords by Sir Frank Benson and W. Bridges-Adams. Ill., London, 1932.

RUTH ELLIS: *The Shakespeare Memorial Theatre*, Ill., London, 1948, B.

WILLIAM SENIOR: *The Old Wakefield Theatre*, Wakefield, 1894.

MARY THERESA ODELL: *The Old Theatre, Worthing, 1807–55*, Ill., Worthing, 1938.

TATE WILKINSON: *The Wandering Patentee, or a History of the Yorkshire Theatre from 1770 to the Present Day*, 4 vols., York, 1795.

JAMES C. DIBDEN: *The Annals of the Edinburgh Stage, with an Account of the Rise and Progress of Dramatic Writing in Scotland*, Ill., Edinburgh, 1888.

JOHN JACKSON: *The History of the Scottish Stage, the whole interspersed with Memoirs of his own life*, Edinburgh, 1793.

SAMUEL WILLIAM RYLEY: *The Itinerant in Scotland*, 3 vols., London, 1827.

CECIL PRICE: *The English Theatre in Wales in the 18th and early 19th Centuries*, Ill., Cardiff, 1948, B.

PUNCH AND JUDY, PUPPETS, *see* POPULAR ENTERTAINMENT, 5.

REGIONAL AND PIONEER THEATRE, U.S.A.

HENRY PITT PHELPS: *Players of a Century; a Record of the Albany Stage*, Albany, 1880; rev. ed., 1890.

CLAIR EUGENE WILLSON: *Mimes and Mines: a Historical Study of the Theatre in Tombstone*, Tucson, Arizona, 1935.

WILLIAM WARLAND CLAPP, jr.: *A Record of the Boston Stage*, Boston, 1853.

CLAIRE McGLINCHEE: *The First Decade of the Boston Museum*, Ill., Boston, 1940, B.

KATE RYAN: *Old Boston Museum Days*, Ill., Boston, 1915.

EUGENE TOMPKINS and QUINCY KELBY: *The History of the Boston Theatre, 1854–1901*, Ill., Boston, 1908.

GEORGE R. MacMINN: *The Theater of the Golden Era in California*, Ill., Caldwell, Idaho, 1941, B.

CONSTANCE ROURKE: *Troupers of the Gold Coast, or the Rise of Lotta Crabtree*, Ill., N.Y., 1928.

WILLIAM STANLEY HOOLE: *The Ante-bellum Charleston Theatre*, Ill., University of Alabama, 1946, B.

EOLA WILLIS: *The Charleston Stage in the 18th Century*, Ill., Columbia, S.C., 1924, B.

MELVIN SCHOBERLIN: *From Candles to Footlights; a Biography of the Pike's Peak Theatre, 1859 to 1876.* Preface by Barrett H. Clark. Ill., Denver, 1941, B.

JOSEPH S. SCHICK: *The Early Theatre in Eastern Iowa: Cultural Beginnings and the Rise of the Theatre in Davenport and Eastern Iowa, 1836–1863*, Ill., Chicago, 1939, B.

REECE DAVIS JAMES: *Old Drury of Philadelphia; a History of the Philadelphia Stage, 1800–1835*, Ill., Philadelphia, 1932.

THOMAS CLARK POLLOCK: *The Philadelphia Theatre in the 18th Century.* Foreword by Arthur Hobson Quinn. Philadelphia, 1933, B.

ARTHUR HERMAN WILSON: *A History of the Philadelphia Theatre, 1835–1855.* Foreword by Arthur Hobson Quinn. Philadelphia, 1935, B.

WILLIAM B. WOOD: *Personal Recollections of the Stage, embracing notices of actors, authors and auditors during a period of forty years*, Philadelphia, 1855.

CHARLES BLAKE: *An Historical Account of the Providence Stage*, Ill., Providence, R.I., 1868.

GEORGE O. WILLARD: *History of the Providence Stage, 1762–1891*, Providence, R.I., 1891.

WILLIAM G. B. CARSON: *The Theatre on the Frontier. The Early Years of the St. Louis Stage*, Ill., Chicago, 1932, B.

NOAH M. LUDLOW: *Dramatic Life as I Found It*, St. Louis, 1880.

SOL SMITH: *Theatrical Management in the West and South for Thirty Years*, Ill., N.Y., 1868.

MYRTLE E. HENDERSON: *History of the Theatre in Salt Lake City*, Ill., Evanston, Illinois, 1934, B.

ALEXANDER HUNTER and J. H. POLKINHORN: *The New National Theater, Washington, D.C. A Record of 50 Years*, Ill., Washington, 1885.

(*See also* NATIONWIDE THEATRE, *and* U.S.A.)

REPERTORY THEATRES, *see* PROVINCIAL AND REPERTORY THEATRES.

ROME, *see* GREECE AND ROME, 1 and 6.

RUSSIA

ALEXANDER BAKSHY: *The Path of the Modern Russian Stage, and other Essays*, Ill., London, 1916.

HUNTLY CARTER: *The New Theatre and Cinema of Soviet Russia, being an analysis and synthesis of the unified theatre produced in Russia by the 1917 Revolution, and an account of its growth and development from 1917 to the Present Day*, Ill., London and N.Y., 1924.

—— *The New Spirit in the Russian Theatre, 1917–28*, Ill., London and N.Y., 1929.

ARTHUR P. COLEMAN: *Humour in the Russian Comedy from Catherine to Gogol*, N.Y., 1925, B.

HENRY WADSWORTH LONGFELLOW DANA: *Handbook on Soviet Drama*, N.Y., 1938, B.

—— *Drama in Wartime Russia*, Ill., 1943.

RENÉ FÜLÖP-MILLER and JOSEPH GREGOR: *The Russian Theatre; Its Character and History, with especial reference to the Revolutionary Period*, tr. from the German by Paul England, Ill., London and Philadelphia, 1930.

WILLIAM GERHARDI: *Anton Chekhov, a Critical Study*, London, 1923.

ANDRE VAN GYSEGHEM: *Theatre in Soviet Russia*, Ill., London, 1943.

NORRIS HOUGHTON: *Moscow Rehearsals*, Ill., N.Y., 1936.

JANKO LAVRIN: *Gogol*, London, 1925, B.

JOSEPH MACLEOD: *The New Soviet Theatre*, Ill., London, 1943.

JOSEPH MACLEOD: *Actors Cross the Volga*, Ill., London, 1946.

P. A. MARKOV: *The Soviet Theatre*, Ill., London, 1934.

PRINCE D. S. MIRSKY: *Modern Russian Literature*, Ill., Oxford, 1925, B.

—— *Contemporary Russian Literature, 1881–1925*, London and N.Y., 1926, B.

VLADIMIR NEMIROVICH-DANCHENKO: *My Life in the Russian Theatre*, tr. from the Russian by John Cournos, Ill., London and Boston, 1936.

GEORGE RAPALL NOYES (Ed.): *Masterpieces of the Russian Drama*, selected and edited with Introductions, N.Y., 1933, B.

OLIVER M. SAYLER: *Inside the Moscow Art Theatre*, Ill., N.Y., 1925.

—— *The Russian Theatre*, Ill., N.Y., 1922; rev. and enlarged ed., 1923.

KONSTANTIN STANISLAVSKY: *My Life in Art*, tr. from the Russian by J. J. Robbins, Ill., N.Y. and London, 1924.

—— *Stanislavsky Produces Othello*, tr. from the Russian, Ill., London and N.Y., 1948.

—— *Stanislavsky on the Art of the Stage*, tr. from the Russian by David Magarshack, Ill., London, 1950.
(*See also* ART OF ACTING.)

LEO WIENER: *The Contemporary Drama of Russia*, Boston, 1924, B.

(*See also* BALLET, POPULAR ENTERTAINMENT, 4, *and* SHAKESPEARE.)

SACRE RAPPRESENTAZIONI, *see* ECCLESIASTICAL DRAMA, *and* ITALY.

SADLER'S WELLS THEATRE, *see* LONDON THEATRES.

SCANDINAVIA

1. *General*

FREDERIKA BLANKNER (Ed.): *The History of the Scandinavian Literatures*, N.Y., 1938, B.

EDMUND GOSSE: *Northern Studies*, London, 1890.

H. G. TOPSÖE-JENSEN: *Scandinavian Literature from Brandes to Our Day*, translated from the Danish by Isaac Anderson, Ill., N.Y., 1939, B.

2. *Denmark*

P. HANSEN: *Illustreret dansk Litteraturhistorie*, 3 vols., Ill., Copenhagen, 1902.

THOMAS OVERSKOU: *Den danske Skueplads*, 4 vols., Copenhagen, 1854–62.

CARL S. PETERSEN og VILHELM ANDERSEN: *Illustreret dansk Litteraturhistorie*, Vol. 4, Ill., Copenhagen, 1925, B.

3. *Norway and Ibsen*

FRANCIS BULL: *Fra Holberg til Nordahl Brun, studier til Norskaandshistorie*, Kristiania, 1916.

FRANCIS BULL, FREDERIK PAASCHE, og A. H. WINSNES: *Norsk Litteraturhistorie*, Vol. 4, 1–2, Ill., Kristiania, 1937, B.

ILLIT GRØNDAHL and OLA RAKNES: *Chapters in Norwegian Literature*, London, 1923.

THEODORE JORGENSON: *History of Norwegian Literature*, N.Y., 1933.

A. H. WINSNES: *Det norske Selskab, 1772–1812*, Kristiania, 1924, B.

IDA TEN EYCK FIRKINS: *Henrik Ibsen: a Bibliography of Criticism and Biography*, N.Y., 1921.

EDMUND GOSSE: *Henrik Ibsen*, Ill., London, 1908, N.Y., 1911.

OTTO HELLER: *Henrik Ibsen: Plays and Problems*, Boston, 1912.

HENRIK JAEGER: *Henrik Ibsen: a Critical Biography*, tr. from the Norwegian by W. M. Payne, Ill., Chicago, 1901.

HALVDAN KOHT: *The Life of Ibsen*, tr. from the Norwegian by Ruth Linna McMahon and Hanna Astrup Larsen, 2 vols., Ill., London and N.Y., 1931 (The standard Life).

JANKO LAVRIN: *Ibsen and his Creation, a Psycho-critical Study*, London, 1921.

MONTROSE J. MOSES: *Henrik Ibsen, the Man and his Plays*, N.Y., 1908; new ed., 1920, B.

G. B. SHAW: *The Quintessence of Ibsenism*, London, 1891; new ed., London and N.Y., 1913.

H. J. WEIGAND: *The Modern Ibsen: a Reconsideration*, N.Y., 1925.

A. E. ZUCKER: *Ibsen the Master Builder*, Ill., N.Y., 1929, B.

4. Sweden and Strindberg

G. E. KLEMMING: *Sveriges dramatiska litteratur till och med 1875*, Stockholm, 1863–79.

O. SYLWAN: *Svenska Litteraturens Historia*, 3 vols., Ill., Stockholm, 1919–21, B.

JOAN BULMAN: *Strindberg and Shakespeare: Shakespeare's Influence on Strindberg's Historical Drama*, London, 1933, B.

ERIK HEDÉN: *Strindberg: en ledtråd vid studiet av hans verk*, Stockholm, 1921; rev. ed., 1926. In a German tr. by Julia Koppel as *Strindberg: Leben und Dichtung*, Munich, 1921.

MARTIN LAMM: *Strindbergs dramer*, 2 vols., Stockholm, 1924–6.

—— *August Strindberg*, 2 vols., Stockholm, 1940–2.

V. T. McGILL: *August Strindberg, the Bedeviled Viking*, Ill., N.Y., 1930, B.

ELIZABETH SPRIGGE: *The Strange Life of August Strindberg*, London, 1949, B.

VANCE THOMPSON: *Strindberg and his Plays*, N.Y., 1921.

SCENERY, SCENE-PAINTING, see TECHNICAL BOOKS, 1 and 6.

SCOTLAND, see PROVINCIAL AND REPERTORY THEATRES.

SHADOW SHOW, see FAR EASTERN THEATRES, 3.

SHAKESPEARE, WILLIAM (1564–1616)

WALTER EBISCH and LEVIN L. SCHÜCKING: *A Shakespeare Bibliography*, Oxford, 1931. Supplement (1930–5), 1937.

HARLEY GRANVILLE-BARKER and G. B. HARRISON (Eds.): *A Companion to Shakespeare Studies*, Cambridge, 1934, B.

JOSEPH QUINCY ADAMS: *A Life of William Shakespeare*, Ill., London and N.Y., 1923.

GEORGE BRANDES: *William Shakespeare, a Critical Study*, tr. from the Danish, 2 vols., London, 1898.

IVOR BROWN: *Shakespeare*, London, 1949.

E. K. CHAMBERS: *William Shakespeare, a Study of Facts and Problems*, 2 vols., Ill., Oxford, 1930, B. In an abridgment by Charles Williams as *A Short Life of Shakespeare*, Ill., Oxford, 1933, B.

A. E. G. LAMBORN and G. B. HARRISON: *Shakespeare, the Man and his Stage*, Ill., London, 1923 (The World's Manuals series).

SIR SIDNEY LEE: *A Life of William Shakespeare*, Ill., London and N.Y., 1898; new ed. rewritten and enlarged, 1915.

HESKETH PEARSON: *A Life of Shakespeare* (Penguin Books), London, 1942.

GEORGE PIERCE BAKER: *The Development of Shakespeare as a Dramatist*, Ill., N.Y., 1907.

A. C. BRADLEY: *Shakespearean Tragedy*. Lectures on Hamlet, Othello, King Lear, and Macbeth, London, 1904.

H. B. CHARLTON: *Shakespearian Comedy*, London and N.Y., 1938.

SAMUEL TAYLOR COLERIDGE: *Essays and Lectures on Shakespeare*, London, 1849 (also Everyman's Library, 1907).

—— *Shakespearian Criticism*, ed. by T. M. RAYSOR, 2 vols., London, 1930.

HELENA FAUCIT: *Some of Shakespeare's Female Characters*, London, 1893.

GEORGE GORDON: *Shakespearian Comedy*, and other Studies, London and N.Y., 1944.

HARLEY GRANVILLE-BARKER: *Prefaces to Shakespeare*, 5 vols., London. (1) *Love's Labour's Lost, Julius Caesar, King Lear*, 1927; rev. ed., 1933. (2) *Romeo and Juliet, The Merchant of Venice, Antony and Cleopatra, Cymbeline*, 1930; rev. ed. 1935. (3) *Hamlet*, 1937. (4) *Othello*, 1945. (5) *Coriolanus*, 1947.

F. E. HALLIDAY: *Shakespeare and his Critics*, Ill., London, 1949, B.

WILLIAM HAZLITT: *Characters of Shakespear's Plays*, London, 1817 (Everyman's Library, 1906; World's Classics, 1916).

GEORGE C. D. ODELL: *Shakespeare from Betterton to Irving*, 2 vols., Ill., London and N.Y., 1921.

BIBLIOGRAPHY

JOHN PALMER: *Political Characters of Shake-speare*, London, 1945.

—— *Comic Characters of Shakespeare*, London, 1946.

ELLEN TERRY: *Four Lectures on Shakespeare.* Ed. with an Introduction by Christopher St. John. London, 1932.

CHARLES EDGAR LEWIS WINGATE: *Shakespeare's Heroines on the Stage*, Ill., N.Y., 1895.

—— *Shakespeare's Heroes on the Stage*, Ill., N.Y., 1896.

THOMAS BALDWIN: *The Organization and Personnel of the Shakespearean Company*, Princeton U.P., 1927.

ALFRED HARBAGE: *Shakespeare's Audience*, Columbia U.P., 1941, B.

A. C. SPRAGUE: *Shakespeare and the Audience, a Study in Exposition*, Harvard U.P., 1935.

—— *Shakespeare and the Actors, the Stage Business in his Plays, 1660–1905*, Ill., Harvard U.P., 1944, B.

ASHLEY H. THORNDIKE: *Shakespeare's Theater*, Ill., N.Y., 1916, B.

ESTHER CLOUDMAN DUNN: *Shakespeare in America*, N.Y., 1939.

C. M. HAINES: *Shakespeare in France*, London, 1925.

JEAN JULES JUSSERAND: *Shakespeare in France under the Ancien Régime*, tr. from the French, Ill., London, 1899.

ALBERT COHN: *Shakespeare in Germany in the 16th and 17th Centuries; an Account of English Actors in Germany and the Netherlands and of Plays performed by them during the same Period*, London, 1865.

LACY COLLISON-MORLEY: *Shakespeare in Italy*, Ill., Stratford-on-Avon, 1916, B.

J. CALINA: *Shakespeare in Poland*, London, 1923.

MIKHAIL M. MOROZOV: *Shakespeare on the Soviet Stage*, tr. from the Russian by David Magarshack. Introduction by J. Dover Wilson. Ill., London, 1947.

V. POPOVIC: *Shakespeare in Serbia*, London, 1928.

(*See also* ENGLAND, DRAMATIC CRITICISM, PROVINCIAL AND REPERTORY THEATRES, and SCANDINAVIA, 4.)

SOUTH AMERICA

1. *General*

ARTHUR COESTER: *The Literary History of Spanish America*, N.Y., 1916; new ed., 1938, B.

WILLIS KNAPP JONES: 'Latin-American Drama, a Reading List' (in *Books Abroad*, Vol. XVII, No. 1), 1943, B.

LUÍS ALBERTO SÁNCHEZ: *Historia de la literatura americana*, Santiago de Chile, 1937, B.

PEDRO HENRÍQUEZ UREÑA: *Literary Currents in Hispanic America*, Harvard U.P. and London, 1945, B.

2. *Argentine*

RUTH RICHARDSON: *Florencio Sánchez and the Argentine Theatre*, N.Y., 1933, B.

EDWARD HALE BIERSTADT: *Three Plays of the Argentine*, N.Y., 1920.

3. *Bolivia*

ENRIQUE FINOT: *Historia de la literatura boliviana*, Ill., Mexico City, 1943.

4. *Brazil*

RONALD DE CARVALHO: *Pequena história da literatura brasileira*, Ill., Rio de Janeiro, 1919; 6th ed., 1937, B.

ISAAC GOLDBERG: *Brazilian Literature*, N.Y., 1922, B.

ARTHUR MOTTA: *História da literatura brasileira*, São Paulo, 1930.

MUCIO DA PAIXÃO: *O teatro no Brasil*, Rio de Janeiro, 1936.

ERICO VERISSIMO: *Brazilian Literature—an Outline*, N.Y., 1945, B.

5. *Chile*

ARMANDO DE MARÍA Y CAMPOS: *Breve historia del teatro en Chile y su vida taurómaca*, Mexico City, 1940.

DOMINGO AMUNÁTEGUI Y SOLAR: *Las letras chilenas*, Santiago de Chile, 1925; new ed., 1934.

6. *Colombia*

GUSTAVO OTERO MUÑOZ: *Resumen de historia de la literatura colombiana*, Ill., Bogotá, 1937; 3rd ed., 1940.

7. *Mexico*

ARMANDO MARÍA Y CAMPOS: *Memoria de teatro — Crónicas (1943–1945)*, Mexico City, 1946, B.

—— *Archivo de teatro — Crónicas de enero a diciembre de 1946*, Mexico City, 1947, B.

BIBLIOGRAPHY

ANTONIO MAGAÑA ESQUÍVEL: *Imagen del teatro*, Ill., Mexico City, 1940, B.

RODOLFO USIGLI: *Méjico en el teatro*, Mexico City, 1932, B.

8. *Uruguay*

ALBERTO ZUM FELDE: *Proceso intelectual de* *Uruguay y crítica de su literatura*, Montevideo, 1941.

9. *Venezuela*

JUAN JOSÉ CHURIÓN: *El teatro en Caracas*, Caracas, 1924.

SOVIET THEATRE, see RUSSIA.

SPAIN AND PORTUGAL

1. *Spain*

AUBREY F. G. BELL: *Contemporary Spanish Literature*, N.Y., 1925.

J. P. W. CRAWFORD: *The Spanish Pastoral Drama*, Philadelphia, 1915.

—— *Spanish Drama before Lope de Vega*, London and Philadelphia, 1922; rev. ed., 1937, B.

JAMES FITZMAURICE-KELLY: *Lope de Vega and the Spanish Drama*, London, 1902.

—— *Spanish Bibliography*, Oxford and N.Y., 1925.

—— *A New History of Spanish Literature*, Oxford and N.Y., 1926, B.

HALFDAN GREGERSEN: *Ibsen and Spain, a Study in Comparative Drama*, Harvard U.P., 1936, B.

HENRY RICHARD, LORD HOLLAND: *Some Account of the Life and Writings of Lope Felix de Vega Carpio*, London, 1806.

GEORGE HENRY LEWES: *The Spanish Drama, Lope de Vega and Calderón*, London, 1846.

HENRI LYONNET: *Le théâtre en Espagne*, Ill., Paris, 1897.

ERNEST MÉRIMÉE: *A History of Spanish Literature*, tr., rev. and enlarged by S. Griswold Morley, Ill., London and N.Y., 1931, B.

ALFRED MOREL-FATIO: *La comedia espagnole au XVIIe siècle*, Paris, 1885; 2nd ed., 1923.

GEORGE TYLER NORTHUP: *An Introduction to Spanish Literature*, Chicago, 1925, B.

E. ALLISON PEERS: *A History of the Romantic Movement in Spain*, 2 vols., London, 1940, B.

HUGO ALBERT RENNERT: *The Life of Lope de Vega*, Philadelphia, 1904.

—— *The Spanish Stage in the time of Lope de Vega, with an Alphabetical List of Spanish Actors and Actresses, 1560–1680*, N.Y., 1909.

WILLIAM HUTCHINSON SHOEMAKER: *The Multiple Stage in Spain during the 15th and 16th Centuries*, Princeton U.P., 1935, B.

WALTER STARKIE: *Jacinto Benavente*, London, 1924, B.

ÁNGEL VALBUENA: *Literatura dramatica española*, Ill., Barcelona, 1930, B.

RONALD BOAL WILLIAMS: *The Staging of Plays in the Spanish Peninsula Prior to 1555* (University of Iowa Studies, Spanish, No. 5), 1934, B.

MARCIANO ZURITA: *Historia del Género Chico*, Madrid, 1920.

2. *Portugal*

AUBREY F. G. BELL: *Portuguese Bibliography*, N.Y. and Oxford, 1922 (Hispanic Society Monographs).

—— *Portuguese Literature*, Oxford, 1922.

(*See also* ECCLESIASTICAL DRAMA, *and* DRAMATIC CRITICISM.)

STAGECRAFT, see TECHNICAL BOOKS, *and* AMATEUR THEATRE.

STRATFORD-ON-AVON, see PROVINCIAL AND REPERTORY THEATRES, *and* SHAKESPEARE.

SWEDEN, see SCANDINAVIA, 4.

THEATRE GUILD, see U.S.A.

TOY THEATRE, see POPULAR ENTERTAINMENT, 5.

TRAGEDY AND COMEDY

1. Tragedy

WILLIAM MACNEILE DIXON: *Tragedy*, London, 1924; 3rd ed., 1929.

F. L. LUCAS: *Tragedy in Relation to Aristotle's Poetics*, London, 1927.

C. E. VAUGHAN: *Types of Tragic Drama*, London, 1908.

(*See also* ENGLAND, FRANCE, GREECE, ROME, ITALY, *and* SHAKESPEARE.)

2. Comedy

JOHN PALMER: *The Comedy of Manners*, Ill., London, 1913, B.

JOHN PALMER: *Comedy*, London, 1914.

HENRY TEN EYCK PERRY: *Masters of Dramatic Comedy and their Social Themes*, Harvard U.P., 1939, B.

ATHENE SEYLER and STEPHEN HAGGARD: *The Craft of Comedy, a Correspondence*, London, 1943.

WILLARD SMITH: *The Nature of Comedy*, Boston, 1930, B.

(*See also* ENGLAND, FRANCE, GREECE AND ROME, ITALY, RUSSIA, SHAKESPEARE, *and* SPAIN.)

TRIBUTARY THEATRE, U.S.A., *see* NATIONWIDE THEATRE.

URUGUAY, *see* SOUTH AMERICA, 8.

U.S.A.

JOHN ANDERSON: *The American Theatre*, Ill., N.Y., 1938, B.

BEN BLAKE: *The Awakening of the American Theatre*, Ill., N.Y., 1935.

T. ALLSTON BROWN: *History of the American Stage*, Ill., N.Y., 1870.

—— *A History of the New York Stage from the First Performance in 1732 to 1901*, 3 vols., N.Y., 1903.

ORAL SUMNER COAD and EDWIN MIMS, jr.: *The American Stage* (Vol. 14 of *The Pageant of America*), New Haven, Ill., 1929.

WILLIAM DUNLAP: *History of the American Theatre*, 2 vols., London, 1833.

JOSEPH GREGOR und RENÉ FÜLÖP-MILLER: *Das amerikanische Theater und Kino*, Ill., Zürich, 1931.

DANIEL CARL HASKELL: *List of American Dramas in the New York Public Library*, N.Y., 1916.

FRANK P. HILL: *American Plays printed 1714–1830, a Bibliographical Record*, Palo Alto, Cal., 1934.

ARTHUR HORNBLOW: *A History of the Theatre in America from its Beginnings to the Present Time*, 2 vols., Ill., Philadelphia, 1919.

MARGARET G. MAYORGA: *A Short History of the American Drama; Commentaries on Plays prior to 1920*, Ill., N.Y., 1932, B.

MONTROSE J. MOSES: *The American Dramatist*, Ill., Boston, 1911; rev. ed., 1925, B.

—— *Famous Actor Families in America*, Ill., N.Y., 1906, B.

GEORGE C. D. ODELL: *Annals of the New York Stage*, 15 vols., Ill., N.Y., 1927–49.

ARTHUR HOBSON QUINN: *A History of the American Drama*, N.Y. and London. Vol. I: *From the Beginnings to the Civil War*, 1923; new ed., 1943. Vol. II: *From the Civil War to the Present Day*, 1937.

LEWIS CLINTON STRANG: *Players and Plays of the Last Quarter Century*, 2 vols., Boston, 1903.

OSCAR WEGELIN: *Early American Plays, 1714–1830*, N.Y., 1900; rev. ed., 1905.

WILLIAM WINTER: *The Wallet of Time; containing personal, biographical, and critical reminiscences of the American theatre*, 2 vols., Ill., N.Y., 1913.

WILLIAM WINTER: *The Life of David Belasco*, 2 vols., Ill., N.Y., 1920.

CLEMENT FOUST: *Life and Dramatic Works of Robert Montgomery Bird*, Philadelphia, 1919.

E. S. BRADLEY: *George Henry Boker, Poet and Patriot*, Philadelphia, 1927, B.

ASIA BOOTH CLARKE: *The Elder and the Younger Booth*, Ill., London and Cambridge, Mass., 1882.

LAURENCE HUTTON: *Edwin Booth*, Ill., N.Y., 1893.

STANLEY KIMMEL: *The Mad Booths of Maryland*, Ill., N.Y., 1940, B.

WILLIAM WINTER: *Life and Art of Edwin Booth*, Ill., London and N.Y., 1893.

TOWNSEND WALSH: *The Career of Dion Boucicault*, N.Y., 1915.

BIBLIOGRAPHY

JOE COWELL: *Thirty Years Passed Among the Players in England and America*, N.Y., 1844.

MAURICE WILLSON DISHER (Ed.): *The Cowells in America, being the Diary of Mrs. Sam Cowell, 1860–61*, Ill., London, 1934.

(*For* LOTTA CRABTREE, *see* REGIONAL AND PIONEER THEATRE.)

E. A. DITHMAR: *The Life of Augustin Daly*, N.Y., 1917. (*See also* ENGLAND, *and* LONDON THEATRES.)

ORAL SUMNER COAD: *William Dunlap, a Study of his Life and Works, and of his Place in Contemporary Culture*, Ill., N.Y., 1917, B.

OSCAR WEGELIN: *A Bibliographical Checklist of the Plays and Miscellaneous Writings of William Dunlap, 1766–1839*, N.Y., 1916.

ARCHIE BELL: *The Clyde Fitch I Knew*, N.Y., 1909.

MONTROSE J. MOSES and VIRGINIA GERSON: *Clyde Fitch and His Letters*, Boston, 1924.

WILLIAM R. ALGER: *The Life of Edwin Forrest*, 2 vols., Ill., Philadelphia, 1877.

LAWRENCE BARRETT: *Edwin Forrest*, Ill., London and Cambridge, Mass., 1882.

GABRIEL HARRISON: *Edwin Forrest, the Actor and the Man*, Ill., Brooklyn, 1889, B.

JAMES REES: *The Life of Edwin Forrest*, Philadelphia, 1874.

DANIEL FROHMAN: *Memories of a Manager, Reminiscences of the Old Lyceum and of some Players of the Last Quarter Century*, Ill., London, 1911.

—— *Daniel Frohman Presents*, N.Y., 1935.

JOSEPH JEFFERSON: *Autobiography*, Ill., London and N.Y., 1890; new ed., 1950.

WILLIAM WINTER: *The Jeffersons*, Ill., London and Cambridge, Mass., 1881.

—— *The Life and Art of Joseph Jefferson*, Ill., N.Y., 1894.

MARGARET ARMSTRONG: *Fanny Kemble, a Passionate Victorian*, Ill., London and N.Y., 1938.

DOROTHY DE BEAR BOBBÉ: *Fanny Kemble*, Ill., London and N.Y., 1932, B.

LEOTA S. DRIVER: *Fanny Kemble*, Ill., Chapel Hill, N.C., 1933, B.

FANNY KEMBLE (Mrs. Frances Anne Butler): *Journals*, 2 vols., London and Philadelphia, 1835.

MICHAEL BENNETT LEAVITT: *Fifty Years in Theatrical Management*, Ill., N.Y., 1912.

(*For* NOAH LUDLOW, *see* REGIONAL AND PIONEER THEATRE.)

PERCY MACKAYE: *Epoch. The Life of Steele MacKaye*, 2 vols., Ill., N.Y., 1927, B.

PAUL WILSTACH: *Richard Mansfield, the Man and the Actor*, Ill., London and N.Y., 1908, B.

WILLIAM WINTER: *Life and Art of Richard Mansfield*, 2 vols., N.Y., 1910.

DAVID D. HENRY: *William Vaughn Moody, a Study*, Boston, 1934.

MRS. ANNA CORA MOWATT: *Autobiography of an Actress, or Eight Years on the Stage*, Boston, 1854.

ROSA P. CHILES: *John Howard Payne*, N.Y., 1930.

GABRIEL HARRISON: *John Howard Payne, Dramatist, Poet, Actor, and Author of 'Home, Sweet Home'*, Albany, N.Y., 1875; rev. ed. as *The Life and Writings of John Howard Payne*, Philadelphia, 1885.

JOHN HOWARD PAYNE: *Memoirs*, London, 1815.

(*For* SOL SMITH, *see* REGIONAL AND PIONEER THEATRE.)

AUGUSTUS THOMAS: *The Print of My Remembrance*, N.Y., 1922.

LESTER WALLACK: *Memories of Fifty Years*. Introduction by Laurence Hutton. Ill., N.Y., 1889.

FRANCIS COURTNEY WEMYSS: *Twenty-Six Years of the Life of an Actor and Manager*, Glasgow, 1848.

DANIEL BLUM (Ed.): *Theatre World* (A pictorial and statistical record of the American Theatre), Ill., N.Y., annually since 1944–5.

JOHN MASON BROWN: *The American Theatre as it is To-day*, N.Y., 1930.

RICHARD BURTON: *The New American Drama*, N.Y., 1913.

THOMAS H. DICKINSON: *Playwrights of the New American Theater*, N.Y., 1924.

WALTER PRICHARD EATON: *Plays and Players: Leaves from a Critic's Scrapbook*. Preface by Barrett H. Clark. Ill., Cincinnati, 1916.

ELEANOR FLEXNER: *American Playwrights, 1918–38; the Theatre Retreats from Reality*. Preface by John Gassner. N.Y., 1938.

NORMAN HAPGOOD: *The Stage in America, 1897–1900*, N.Y., 1901.

JOSEPH WOOD KRUTCH: *The American Drama since 1918*, N.Y., 1939.

BURNS MANTLE: *American Playwrights of To-day*, N.Y., 1926.

BOYD MARTIN: *Modern American Drama and Stage*, Ill., London, 1943.

BIBLIOGRAPHY

JOSEPH VERNER REED: *The Curtain Falls*, N.Y., 1935.

OLIVER M. SAYLER: *Our American Theatre, Important Productions on the American Stage, 1908–23*, Ill., N.Y., 1923.

BARRETT H. CLARK: *Maxwell Anderson, the Man and his Work*, N.Y., 1933, B.

JOHN BARRYMORE: *Confessions of an Actor*, Indianapolis, 1926.
GENE FOWLER: *Goodnight, Sweet Prince* (*The Life and Times of John Barrymore*), Ill., N.Y., 1944; London, 1949.

HALLIE FLANAGAN: *Arena* (The Federal Theatre), Ill., N.Y., 1940, B.
WILLSON WHITMAN: *Bread and Circuses, a Study of Federal Theatre*, London and N.Y., 1937, B.

HAROLD CLURMAN: *The Fervent Years, the Story of the Group Theatre and the Thirties*, N.Y., 1945; London, 1949.

BARRETT H. CLARK: *Eugene O'Neill, the Man and his Plays*, Ill., London and N.Y., 1926; rev. ed. 1933; new and rev. ed., 1947, B.
—— *A Bibliography of the Works of Eugene O'Neill*, N.Y., 1931.
HELEN DEUTSCH and STELLA HANAU: *The Provincetown, a Story of the Theatre*. Introduction by Kenneth Macgowan. Ill., N.Y., 1931.
RICHARD DANA SKINNER: *Eugene O'Neill, a Poet's Quest*, N.Y., 1935.
SOPHUS KEITH WINTHER: *Eugene O'Neill, a Critical Study*, N.Y., 1934.

WALTER PRICHARD EATON: *The Theatre Guild; The First Ten Years*, with articles by the Directors, Ill., N.Y., 1929.

(*See also* CIRCUS, DRAMATIC CRITICISM, ENGLAND, NATIONWIDE THEATRE, NEGRO IN THE THEATRE, OPERA, POPULAR ENTERTAINMENT, REGIONAL AND PIONEER THEATRE.)

VARIETY, VAUDEVILLE, *see* POPULAR ENTERTAINMENT, 2.

VENEZUELA, *see* SOUTH AMERICA, 9.

WAKEFIELD, WALES, WORTHING, *see* PROVINCIAL AND REPERTORY THEATRES.

YIDDISH DRAMA, *see* JEWISH DRAMA.

YORKSHIRE, *see* PROVINCIAL AND REPERTORY THEATRES.

PRINTED IN GREAT BRITAIN
AT THE UNIVERSITY PRESS, OXFORD
BY CHARLES BATEY, PRINTER TO THE UNIVERSITY

SUPPLEMENT

(Page references are to the Main volume unless otherwise stated)

AMATEUR THEATRE IN GREAT BRITAIN (p. 22). The Questors Theatre was founded in 1929, and after some success in British Drama League Festivals, embarked on a policy of producing only plays of unusual interest and literary merit. Seven productions are given annually, each for about ten performances. These are mainly revivals—Shaw, Ibsen, Pirandello, and others—with an occasional Shakespeare production and a sprinkling of new plays. Rodney Ackland's *The Dark River* (1943) and *The Diary of a Scoundrel* (1946), based on a play by Ostrovsky, had their first performances at The Questors, as did the English translation of Marcel Aymé's *Clérambard* (1953). The Director of the theatre is Alfred Emmet, who has been connected with The Questors since its inception. In order to save the high cost of renting halls, the company decided to acquire its own theatre, and from 1933 to 1938 shared premises in Mattock Lane, Ealing, with the Boy Scouts' Association. In 1938 it took over the whole building, reseating and redecorating the auditorium, and in 1952 purchased the freehold of the site. A theatre is being built there—one of the few new theatre buildings in England since 1939—to hold about 350, with an adaptable stage which can be used for proscenium, forestage, open stage, arena, and 'space stage' productions, with a separate block of rehearsal and administrative rooms. A good deal of the work is being done by the members, and the first block, consisting of a foyer, servery, and cloakrooms, is now (1957) nearly completed.

The Tavistock Repertory Theatre, formerly at the Mary Ward Settlement, was re-formed after the war and took possession in Sept. 1952 of Canonbury Tower, Islington, formerly the home of, among others, Francis Bacon and Goldsmith. In the adjoining hall the members built a stage and proscenium, put in lighting and seating, and, after redecoration, opened it on 15 Feb. 1953 as the Tower Theatre. The first production was a translation of Obey's play on Don Juan as *Man into Ashes*. Extensive work was also carried out in the Tower itself to equip it as a club with living accommodation for a warden. Most of the money needed for these purposes was raised by the members, with the help of a grant from the Pilgrim Trust. The theatre is licensed by the Lord Chamberlain, and therefore open to the public, and Sunday performances are given for members only. Fourteen productions are given each year, with a minimum of six performances of each play.

Unity Theatre came into being on 5 Jan. 1936 and opened on 19 Feb. in a converted church hall in Britannia Street, Kings Cross. The first important production, in April, was Odets's *Waiting for Lefty*, with which the pre-sent premises in Goldington Street opened in Oct. 1937. Other productions at Britannia Street were Irwin Shaw's *Bury the Dead* and Ben Bengal's *Plant in the Sun*, which, produced by Herbert Marshall with Paul Robeson in the lead, ran for six weeks. It was in Jan. 1938 that Unity introduced from America the Living Newspaper technique with a play on a London bus-strike, *Busmen*, produced by John Allen. Other Living Newspaper productions were given in 1938 (*Crisis*), in 1952 (*Barrier across Europe*), and in 1956 (*World on Edge*). Interesting productions have been Pogodin's *Aristocrats* (1937), Afinogenov's *Distant Point*, and O'Casey's *The Star Turns Red* (both 1940), and the first production in English of Lope de Vega's *Fuente Ovejuna* (1943). Simonov's *Russian Question* and *The Whole World Over* were given in 1948 and 1949, both produced by Bill Rowbotham, who was responsible for the dramatization of Robert Tressall's *Ragged-Trousered Philanthropists* in the latter year. In 1956 Sartre showed his appreciation of the work done by Unity by permitting the theatre to give the first English production of his *Nekrassov* on 6 Jan. Unity was professional from Jan. 1946 to March 1947. It is now amateur. Other Unity Theatres still extant are in Chingford, Manchester, on Merseyside, Thamesside, and in New Zealand.

(p. 23) Scotland. The Scottish Community Drama Association has since 1945 paid increasing attention to the production of full-length plays; the production of one-act plays by clubs and for festivals has now become the exception rather than the rule.

ASHCROFT, PEGGY (1907–), English actress, who was trained at the Central School, and made her first appearance at the Birmingham Rep. as Margaret in *Dear Brutus* (1926). In the following year she was seen briefly in London at Playroom Six, but her first impact on the public was made as Naemi in *Jew Süss* (1929), a part in which she showed that simplicity and sense of poetic tragedy which have made so many of her later performances memorable. During the next few years she was seen in a variety of parts, among them Desdemona to Paul Robeson's Othello, Pervaneh in *Hassan* and Juliet in *Romeo and Juliet* (for O.U.D.S.), and spent a year at the Old Vic. But it was with her Juliet in Gielgud's production at the New Theatre in 1935 that her growing reputation was finally consolidated. With a youthful gaiety and innocence she combined a strict integrity and a deepening maturity of purpose which again served to make her Nina in *The Seagull* the following year an outstanding experience. That she was also an excellent player of comedy was shown in her Lady Teazle, Cecily Cardew, Beatrice, and Mistress Page, while her aptitude for modern drama showed itself in *Edward My Son*, in *The Heiress*, and in Rattigan's *The Deep Blue Sea*. In 1956 she appeared in Enid Bagnold's *The Chalk Garden*, and at the Court Theatre in an amazing dual role, as the prostitute and the prostitute's male cousin, in Brecht's *The Good Woman of Setzuan*. One of her finest performances was undoubtedly Hedda Gabler (1954), which she played in London and on tour in Norway. For this performance she was awarded the King's Medal by the King of Norway. She was created C.B.E. in 1951 and D.B.E. in 1956 for her services to the theatre, honours richly deserved and worthily borne.

BAKER, SARAH (1736/7–1812), English theatre proprietor and manageress, whose activities in Kent over a period of more than fifty years have been summarized by Mrs. Norma Hodgson in an article in *Studies in English Theatre History* (1952) from which the following details are taken. She was the daughter of an acrobatic dancer (Ann Wakelin, who toured with her own company) and in about 1761 married a member of her mother's company. Left a widow some time in 1769, with three small children, she made her first ventures into management, probably with a puppet-theatre; but from 1772 to 1777 she took over the management of her mother's old company. Mrs. Wakelin then retired, and Mrs. Baker formed a new company, with an ambitious repertory which included Shakespeare and Sheridan. With this she established herself as a regular visitor to Canterbury, Rochester, Faversham, Maidstone, and Tunbridge Wells, with occasional visits to Folkestone, Deal, Sandwich, Lewes, and Sittingbourne. At first she used a portable theatre, later she played in any suitable building, but from about 1789 onwards she built her own theatres—some ten in all. Among the actors who appeared early in their careers under Mrs. Baker were Edmund Kean, Thomas Dibdin, and Fawcett. Her daughter Sally married William Dowton (see p. 193), who, with his son William, tried unsuccessfully to run the theatres after Mrs. Baker's death.

BETTI, UGO (1892–1953), Italian dramatist, by profession a lawyer and a High Court judge, whose plays, much influenced by Pirandello, dramatize the precarious situation in the modern world of the innocent individual who cannot prove his innocence before a hostile society. His first play, which won first prize in a competition organized by a theatrical review, was *La Padrona*. It was done in Rome in 1927 by Odescalchi with some success. Among his later plays the most important are *Frana allo scalo Nord* (1933), *Il Paese delle vacanze* (1942) (see illus. No. 122), and *Corruzione al Palazzo di giustizia* (1949), which was broadcast by the B.B.C. in 1954 as *The Sacred Scales*. *Il Giocatore* (1951) was seen in translation in New York in 1952; *La Regina e gli insorti* (1951) and *L'Aiuola bruciata* (posthumously produced in 1953) were done in London in 1955–6 as *The Queen and the Rebels* and *The Burnt Flower-*

Bed respectively. *Investigations* was given an amateur performance in 1956 by the University of Bristol Dramatic Society.

BOUCICAULT (p. 89). (4) NINA (1867–1950), daughter of the elder Boucicault, was born in London, but made her first appearance on the stage in her father's company in America, playing Eily O'Connor in a revival of his *Colleen Bawn*. She first appeared in London as Flossie Trivett in *The New Wing* in 1892. In 1903 she gave excellent performances as Bessie Broke in *The Light that Failed*, and as Mona Loiney in *Little Mary*, but she is chiefly remembered for her Peter in Barrie's *Peter Pan*, which she played on its first production in Dec. 1904. She continued to appear on the London stage until 1927, and in 1935 returned for a few months as Lady Bernice Jeune in *Frolic Wind*. Her last appearance was as the Countess Mortimer in *Waste* (1936).

BRECHT, BERTOLT (p. 94). Brecht died suddenly in 1956 just as his company, the Berliner Ensemble, which he founded in 1949, was about to give its first season in London at the Palace Theatre, with a repertory which included *Mutter Courage und ihre Kinder*, *Pauken und Trompeten* (based on Farquhar's *The Recruiting Officer*), and *Der kaukasische Kreidekreis*. This gave Londoners an opportunity of seeing for themselves Brecht's much-discussed Epic Theatre, and his 'method of alienation' (*Verfremdungseffekt*), which has given rise to much controversy. It is as yet too soon to judge of Brecht's influence on the contemporary English theatre, but there are signs that it will be effective and far-reaching. Brecht, whose reputation had been steadily increasing since the war, is now regarded as one of the major dramatists and poets of his generation, and has even been hailed as the greatest dramatist Germany has ever produced (see Sebastian Haffner's article in the *Observer*, 19 Aug. 1956). Several of his plays have been seen in England in translation. In 1938 *Señora Carrar's Rifles* was produced by John Fernald at Unity Theatre. Theatre Workshop did *Mother Courage* at the Taw and Torridge Festival in 1955, with Joan Littlewood in the title-role, while in 1956 *The Good Woman of Setzuan* was seen at the Court Theatre with Peggy Ashcroft, *The Rule and the Exception* at Unity, and *Galileo* at Birmingham University. In New York *Galileo* was done by ANTA in 1947 and by the Berliner Ensemble at the Paris Festival in 1957.

BRISTOL UNIVERSITY DEPARTMENT OF DRAMA. One of the most striking developments of the last few years has been the gradual acceptance of the theatre (apart from dramatic literature) as a subject suitable for academic study. This has resulted in the foundation at Bristol University of a Department of Drama (the only one in Great Britain at the moment), on the lines of those found in American universities, but unique in being closely linked with a professional company and training school, housed in an historic theatre (the Bristol Old Vic).

The Bristol Department of Drama was established within the Faculty of Arts of Bristol University in the 1946-7 session. The syllabus covers the history of drama from classical to modern times, and the three-year course, combined with other subjects, leads eventually to the degree of Bachelor of Arts. Instruction is also given on the practical side of the theatre, for which purpose a drama studio, designed by Richard Southern, was opened in Feb. 1951. Built in a disused squash-racket court, the studio provides a lecture-room which can be transformed into a picture-frame theatre, an open-stage theatre, or an arena theatre. It was financed by part of a grant from the Rockefeller Foundation, which has also helped to equip the library, and provides each year a visiting lecturer, usually a person of eminence in the theatre, such as Michael Redgrave (1952) or Hugh Hunt (1953). The Department provides facilities for postgraduate study, and for research work leading to the degrees of M.A. and Ph.D.

BROADWAY (p. 97). I am indebted to Mr. Robert Downing of The Players' Club, New York, for the following information on Broadway's theatres. Those which have been pulled down since 1951 include the Belmont (p. 72), the Centre (p. 118), the Empire (p. 221), the Forty-Eighth and Forty-Fourth Street (with the Nora Bayes) (p. 273), the Klaw (p. 441), the Majestic (p. 498), now the site of the New York Coliseum, the Savoy (p. 702), and the Vanderbilt (p. 821). No new theatres have been built.

Other theatres which appear to be permanently lost to stage attractions and are now used only for radio and television broadcasts include the Adelphi (p. 12), the Biltmore (p. 80), the Century (p. 119), the Concert (p. 145), the Hudson (p. 374), the Manhattan (p. 512), the Mansfield (p. 512), the New Yorker (p. 575), and the Ritz (p. 669).

The Central Theatre (p. 118), which in 1928 became a cinema, has now reverted to legitimate theatre under a new name, as the Holiday. Daly's (p. 178) was demolished in 1957. The Fulton (p. 294) has been renamed the Helen Hayes. The Gaiety (p. 297) is now used for films only, and has changed its name to the Victoria. The Guild (p. 346) now houses the stage productions of ANTA (see American National Theatre and Academy, p. 24). The Hollywood (p. 370) has been renamed the Mark Hellinger.

BROOK, PETER STEPHEN PAUL (1925–), English producer, whose early work aroused much controversy, but produced interesting results. He was in his late teens when he produced *Dr. Faustus* and *The Infernal Machine* on the minute stages of the Torch and Chanticleer theatres. At twenty he was with Sir Barry Jackson at the Birmingham Rep., where his production of *King John*, with Scofield as the Bastard, attracted much attention. In 1946

he followed Sir Barry to Stratford-upon-Avon, and there did an enchanting *Love's Labour's Lost*, costumed *à la Watteau*. In the same year he produced, in London, *The Brothers Karamazov* and Sartre's *Vicious Circle*, both with Alec Guinness. Returning to Stratford in 1947, he was responsible for a *Romeo and Juliet* which unleashed the fury of the critics, mainly on account of the clumsy cutting and handling of the verse. In the same year he continued his association with Sartre's plays by producing *Men Without Shadows* and *The Respectable Prostitute*, both at the Lyric, Hammersmith, and was appointed Director of Productions at Covent Garden Opera House. Here his 'Salome', with designs by Salvador Dali, again started a stimulating argument over the value and purpose of his work. He vindicated himself triumphantly with *Ring Round the Moon* (1950) in London, and with *Measure for Measure* (Stratford, 1950) and *The Winter's Tale* (1951), both with Gielgud. These were followed by a revival of *Venice Preserv'd* at the Lyric, Hammersmith (1953) which did honour to all concerned. Brook's later productions include Fry's *The Dark is Light Enough* (1954), Anouilh's *The Lark*, and *Titus Andronicus* (both 1955). Also in 1955 he produced *Hamlet*, with Scofield, not altogether successfully. After a short tour, and a season in London, this company went to Moscow—the first English company to appear there since 1917.

CANADA (p. 113). A professional theatre has now come into being in Canada, with the opening in 1952 of the Shakespeare Playhouse at Stratford, Ontario (see Shakespeare Festivals, S., p. 15). From it a touring company, The Canadian Players, has been sent out with a repertory which includes Shakespeare, Shaw, and Ibsen. In Toronto there are now three professional theatre groups: The Crest, run on a two-weekly repertory basis, the Avenue, and the Circle. The Théâtre du Nouveau Monde, from Montreal, played at the Paris Festival in 1955, and was also seen at Edinburgh in 1956, together with the famous comedian Fridolin (Gratien Gelinas).

CENTRES DRAMATIQUES, LES. The French dramatic centres, five in number, were founded between 1947 and 1952 with the object of fostering drama in the provinces, which had for too long been starved of live entertainment by the centralization of all theatrical activities in Paris. The idea of such a theatre in the provinces was first mooted by Gémier in 1912, with his Théâtre Ambulant, and later developed by Copeau, whose Copiaus lived and worked in Burgundy from 1924 to 1929.

The centres, supported by the State and by the municipality, are based on university towns, from which a permanent professional company, with portable sets, lighting, and costumes, goes out on tour. In large towns it may play for two or three nights, elsewhere for one night only. Where there is no theatre the performance is given in a cinema or hall. The repertory consists mainly of French classics—comedy in preference to tragedy—good new plays, and translations of foreign classic and modern plays. New French plays are scarce, since most authors look to Paris for their first production, but the centres hope eventually to encourage and establish good regional playwrights.

The first centre to be founded was that in the east, covering Colmar, Haguenau, Metz, Mulhouse, and Strasbourg. It gave its first performance in Jan. 1947. It was then based on Colmar, but later moved to Strasbourg, where it runs a Drama School also. Here, in a building specially designed by Pierre Sonrel, students are given a three-year training. The school opened in 1954, and is run by Michel Saint-Denis, who in 1952 took over the direction of the centre from André Clavé.

The centre at St. Étienne, which serves the Lyonnaise, the Valley of the Rhône, Burgundy, and the Alps, is directed by Jean Dasté, who was a pupil of Copeau and a member of Les Copiaus and of the Compagnie des Quinze. In 1942 he founded an amateur company named Les Comédiens de Grenoble, which was absorbed by the centre on its establishment in Sept. 1947.

In 1945 Maurice Sarrazin founded an amateur company called Le Grenier de Toulouse, which in 1946 won first prize in a competition held in Paris. In Jan. 1949 this became the basic company of a centre covering the area from the Atlantic at Bordeaux to the banks of the Rhône. It is still directed by Sarrazin, and is proving extremely popular. One of its most successful performances, which was seen in Paris, was a translation of *The Taming of the Shrew* as *La Mégère apprivoisée*.

The western centre, under Hubert Gignoux, was also based on a good amateur company. It opened in Nov. 1949 and covers Brittany, Normandy, and the Valley of the Loire, with its centre in Rennes. In 1951 it gave a number of open-air performances of *Cymbeline*.

A Provençal centre was founded by Baty in 1952, just before his death, and is now run by Douking. It serves the eastern Midi, and the coast from Perpignan to Nice.

CHILDREN'S THEATRES. The twentieth century has seen a remarkable development all over the world in the direction of the establishment of theatres specifically for children. Previously, as in the Elizabethan era with its boy companies, or as in the nineteenth century, with its children's companies in such productions as the juvenile *H.M.S. Pinafore*, children played for adult audiences. Now the tendency is to appeal directly to the child audience; the actors may be adults, children, or even puppets, but in all cases the material will be plays, sketches, or a mixed programme written or adapted for children. Some of the earliest tentatives towards a children's theatre were made by Jean Sterling Mackinlay, with her Children's Matinées, held annually for about six weeks in the winter from 1914 to

1939. In France a similar venture was Chancerel's Théâtre de l'Oncle Sébastien, founded in 1935. After the Second World War a more ambitious project in England was The Young Vic, founded and directed by George Devine, which, though artistically a great success, particularly on its continental tours, was defeated by financial problems, the cause of most problems encountered by pioneers in this field. There are, however, a number of groups still working, mainly in connexion with educational or social bodies, such as Toynbee Hall.

The whole question of children's theatres, even when conducted by professional actors, is inextricably bound up with the problems of education, and cannot be entirely divorced from the use of drama in schools. For example, the Mobile Theatre of Caryl Jenner (founded in 1948) gives 70 per cent. of its productions actually in school buildings, and so helps to reinforce the work of the teacher of English who includes improvisation, mime, playwriting, and acting in the curriculum. This work should not be confused with the annual school production of a classic (usually Shakespeare or Sheridan) which has become a recognized activity of many schools (notably of Harrow, Bryanston, the Sloane School, and many others), and continues the tradition of medieval and Renaissance school and university performances. Nor has it anything in common with school matinées at the Old Vic and Stratford-upon-Avon.

On the Continent the problems of children's theatre are continually under review, and many companies exist, too many to list here. In Russia alone there are more than fifty permanent children's theatres, some catering for the juniors, up to about 11 or 12 years of age, others for older children. The movement was started soon after the Revolution by Natalie Satz, who opened the first children's theatre in Moscow. In America, where, unlike Russia and the satellite countries, children's theatres are not subsidized, they are mainly run by independent groups, and are much helped by the fact that one publishing firm, the Children's Theatre Press (founded 1935), devotes its resources exclusively to the publication of plays suitable for performance to children. The Press was the moving spirit behind the Children's Theatre Conference held by the American Educational Theatre Association (AETA) recently. The question has also been taken up by the International Theatre Institute (a branch of U.N.E.S.C.O.) and was the subject of a special issue of *World Theatre*, vol. ii, No. 3, entitled *Youth and the Theatre*, from which some of the above details were taken.

CONQUEST (p. 147). I am indebted to Miss Frances Fleetwood, author of a book on the Conquest family (see S. Bibl., p. 24), for the following note, which clears up some confusions and errors in the original article.

(1) BENJAMIN OLIVER (1804–72) was lessee of the Garrick Theatre in Leman Street from its opening in 1830, with brief intervals, until its destruction by fire in 1846. In 1851 he acquired

[4]

the Grecian Theatre, which he managed until his death. He married a dancer and ballet-mistress, Clarissa Ann Bennett, by whom he had three daughters and a son, who were all on the stage. His step-daughter Clara (1825–88) married the tragedian Charles Dillon. His only son (2) GEORGE AUGUSTUS (1837–1901) (who established his father's stage-name of Conquest as the family surname by deed poll in 1883) acted as a child at the Garrick Theatre. He was then educated in France, where the famous French actor Coquelin was his fellow-pupil. Originally intended for the musical profession, George preferred to be an acrobat and pantomimist. In collaboration with Henry Spry he wrote and produced nearly fifty pantomimes, celebrated for their brilliant acrobatic effects (on one occasion no less than thirty traps were used). In these pantomimes the flying ballet was brought to perfection. George also wrote, alone or in collaboration (often with Paul Meritt or Henry Pettitt), over one hundred melodramas, for production at the Grecian, and later at the Surrey. Many of these were translations or adaptations from the French. He was also a competent artist, designing and painting stage scenery, properties, and masks. He was a powerful character actor and an excellent animal impersonator. Off-stage he stammered badly, but this defect was not apparent in his acting. When his father died he succeeded to the management of the Grecian, which he sold in 1879 to T. G. Clark. He then visited America, intending to make a lengthy tour, but a serious accident at the outset obliged him to abandon the project and return to England. In August 1881 he took the Surrey Theatre (see illustr. No. 68), which he made famous for its melodramas and pantomimes. His eldest son (3) GEORGE (1858–1926) was known as a good comedian and a pantomime Dame. In 1904 he sold the Surrey Theatre, but in 1910 for a short time managed the Britannia, Hoxton. His younger brothers (4) FRED (1871–1941) and (5) ARTHUR (1875–1945) were competent actors and notable animal impersonators, the former being especially remarkable for his pantomime Goose, and the latter (who played for nearly twenty years in pantomime at Covent Garden and Drury Lane) for his music-hall act 'Daphne, the Chimpanzee'. Another distinguished member of this family was the grand-nephew of the elder George, Francis Lister (1899–1951), for thirty years a leading man in the West End and on Broadway.

CORNISH ROUNDS. There are in Cornwall, particularly in the west, remains of circular earthworks which are believed to have been open-air theatres used for annual performances of Mystery plays. These could accommodate, on banks (usually seven) cut in the rising ground, and sometimes faced with granite, a large number of spectators grouped round a central area or 'playing-place' (*plen an gwary*). Some of them were still in use in the seventeenth century. The surviving plans for a trilogy consisting of a play on the Creation,

one on the Passion, and one on the Resurrection, and for a two-day play on the life of St. Meryasek, show that Heaven was at the eastern end, with Hell on the north. This is probably a survival from the days of Church performances. There must also, from the stage directions, have been rostrums or stages of varying levels on the central area.

One feature of the Cornish playing-place which has given rise to some controversy is the 'conveyour', which Chambers took to be a person, i.e. a stage-manager, charged with the duty of shepherding or 'conveying' a character to his appointed place. R. Morton Nance, however (see *Journal of the Royal Institution of Cornwall*, vol. xxiv, pp. 190–211), thinks that by 'conveyour' is meant a central covered pit with a tunnel running to it from the side of the 'playing-place', by which characters could 'appear' unexpectedly, as from a nineteenth-century trap, and he equates it with the so-called Devil's Spoon at Perran Round, a long shallow trench running from a depression in the first bank of seats to a central pit.

DEVINE, GEORGE ALEXANDER CASSADY (1910–   ), English actor and producer, who in the early part of his career was closely associated with John Gielgud and Michel Saint-Denis. As President of O.U.D.S. in 1932 he was instrumental in inviting Gielgud to Oxford to produce *Romeo and Juliet*, a memorable production in which Peggy Ashcroft and Edith Evans played Juliet and the Nurse, Christopher Hassall Romeo, and Devine himself Mercutio. Making his professional début later the same year, in *The Merchant of Venice* at the St. James's, he spent a season at the Old Vic, and was then again associated with Gielgud, being with him in *Hamlet* (1934), *Romeo and Juliet*, and *Noah* (1935) (the latter produced by Saint-Denis), *The Seagull* (1936) (produced by Komisarjevsky), and in his season at the Queen's (1937–8) he was in Saint-Denis's productions of *The White Guard* and *Twelfth Night* (both 1938), and from 1936 to 1939 was with him at the London Theatre Studio as teacher and producer. From 1932 to 1935 he was associated with the firm of Motley, scenic designers, and married Sophia Harris, one of the partners in the firm, in 1940. After six years in the army, he returned to the theatre, and was again with Saint-Denis at the Old Vic School, being also director of the Young Vic, two enterprises whose early deaths were both a reproach and a loss to the English theatre. Among the parts played by Devine since the war mention must be made of his outstanding Tesman in Peggy Ashcroft's *Hedda Gabler* in 1954, in which year he also produced William Walton's opera, *Troilus and Cressida*, at Covent Garden. In 1956 he was appointed Artistic Director of the newly-founded English Stage Company at the Royal Court, which has already done interesting work, notably with its discovery of the young playwright, John Osborne. In addition to producing some of the plays in the repertory, Devine has given some fine performances, particularly as Mr. Shu Fu in *The Good Woman of Setzuan*, and Mr. Pinchwife in *The Country Wife*.

EDINBURGH. The Edinburgh International Festival of Music and Drama, which lasts for three weeks from, roughly, the middle of Aug. to early Sept., started in 1947. Drama has always been the weakest side of the programme, but some interesting events have taken place. The practice of inviting foreign companies to appear at the Royal Lyceum Theatre was begun in the Festival's first year, when Jouvet's company from the Athénée was seen in *L'École des femmes* and Giraudoux's *Ondine*. In 1948 Barrault appeared in Gide's translation of *Hamlet* and in Marivaux's *Les Fausses Confidences*. Since then companies from Düsseldorf, from the Atelier, from the Comédie-Française, from the Théâtre National Populaire, and the mime-artist Marcel Marceau, have been seen in Edinburgh. In 1955 Edwige Feuillère appeared in *La Dame aux camélias*. New plays which have had their first productions during the Festival include T. S. Eliot's *The Cocktail Party* and *The Confidential Clerk* (both commissioned by the Festival Society), Charles Morgan's *The River Line*, Thornton Wilder's *The Matchmaker* (a new version of *The Merchant of Yonkers*, based on a play by Nestroy), and his *A Life in the Sun*. This was produced on a specially-constructed stage in the Assembly Hall, where Tyrone Guthrie had previously been responsible for Edinburgh's first production in the round, an adaptation by Robert Kemp of Sir Davyde Lyndesay's *Ane Satyre of the Thrie Estaites*, last performed nearly three hundred years before. Other performances at the Assembly Hall have included the Old Vic in *Bartholomew Fair*, and Hugh Hunt's production of *Romeo and Juliet*. In 1950 the Glasgow Citizens' Theatre presented three plays by Scottish writers (including Bridie's *The Queen's Comedy*) at the Lyceum. In the same year there was a revival there of the famous *Douglas* by John Home, with Sybil Thorndike and Lewis Casson. (From information supplied by Iain Crawford, Glasgow.)

ENGLISH STAGE COMPANY, an organization formed in 1956 to present modern plays, both English and foreign, and to encourage young dramatists. After an unsuccessful attempt to reopen the bomb-damaged Kingsway Theatre, the company, under the artistic direction of George Devine, with Tony Richardson as assistant director, opened at the Royal Court Theatre in Sloane Square on 2 April 1956 with Angus Wilson's *The Mulberry Bush*, previously produced at the Bristol Old Vic. The most successful play of this first season, which included Arthur Miller's *The Crucible*, Ronald Duncan's *Don Juan* and *The Death of Satan*, and Nigel Dennis's *Cards of Identity*, was *Look Back in Anger*, the first play of the 26-year-old John Osborne. Originally included in the repertory, this was given a separate run of some two months, and was followed on 31 Oct. by the first production in English of Brecht's *The Good Woman of Setzuan*, with Peggy Ashcroft as guest artist, and by a revival on 12 Dec. of *The Country Wife*. The first English production of *The Member of the Wedding* by Carson McCullers followed on 5 Feb. 1957, and on 10 Apr. John Osborne's second play, *The Entertainer*, was warmly received with Laurence Olivier giving a splendid performance as Archie Rice.

ETHIOPIA. In Ethiopia, as in Europe, drama grew out of the rites of religious festivals. The Hamites, the original inhabitants of the country, worshipped the sun and stars, trees, and the spirits of earth and water. Their earliest dramas were probably mimes, acted in the open under trees, beside rivers, or on mountain tops. Later these were transferred to temples. The remains of such a temple, with inscriptions that reveal the worship of south-Arabian deities, has been found in Aksum, an ancient city in the north of the country.

These early rites appear to have died out when the Semitic tribes, and particularly the Amhara, penetrated into Ethiopia, and took over its political and cultural affairs. Ancient Ethiopian traditions say that their Queen Mekeda (the Biblical Queen of Sheba) visited Jerusalem and had a son by Solomon. This son, Menelik I, returned to Ethiopia in 1000 B.C. to found the first Amharic-Ethiopic dynasty. With him went the first-born sons of the high priests and nobles of Israel, bearing with them the sacred Ark of the Covenant. On arriving at Aksum they built a temple to house the Ark, and in the courtyard the priests performed Semitic dances which they had learnt at King Solomon's court. From these developed a form of Dance-Drama, to the accompaniment of drums, staves, and percussion instruments, whose influence is still apparent today. Later, rudimentary forms of drama began to develop, with choral speaking accompanied by the beating of a gong, drum, or other instrument. Each ceremony had its own mime—the Burnt Offering, the Meal Offering, the Peace Offering, the Guilt Offering, the Sin Offering—while three times a year the male members of the community performed open-air religious dramas in which women had no part. One of these commemorated, in a procession of brightly clad priests, the bringing to Ethiopia of the Ark of the Covenant.

Early in the fourth century missionaries from Egypt and Syria brought Christianity to Ethiopia, and in A.D. 334 it became the State religion of the Empire. New ceremonies were introduced in an endeavour to combine Christian dogma with Jewish and pagan rites. Among these was the annual three-day dance-drama of Timket, which took place in the third week of January. This retained the ceremony of the Ark, but added to it the Baptism of Christ.

Another drama of this time was *Kadam Souarir* (The Forsaken Saturday) which celebrated the giving-up of the Jewish Sabbath for the Christian Sunday. *Maskal*, which took place in Sept. at the end of the rainy season, also shows a blending of pagan, Jewish, and Christian elements. It began with the actors collecting the bright yellow flower called Maskal which grows in profusion at this time of the year, and presenting it to the audience as a reminder of the beginning of spring. This was probably a survival of early nature-worship. It was followed by a Jewish episode based on the belief that the smoke of sacrifice ascends to heaven and returns to bless the earth. The actors collected dry branches and tied them together in bundles. Then, with songs and dances accompanied by musical instruments, they cast the bundles into a fire kindled round a tall pole stuck in the ground. The Christian interpretation of this episode is based on an old legend which says that an Ethiopian queen named Helena went with other Christians to search for the cross on which Christ was crucified. When the search proved successful, the queen commanded that a long pole should be set up and set fire to, so that the Christians in Constantinople could see it and learn the good news. These early church dramas were acted in Ge'ez, which belongs to one of the southern groups of Semitic languages, but as time went on, and secular drama developed, this was replaced by Amharic, the language of the ruling tribe.

Secular drama first developed when people gathered together to act plays, improvising their dialogue and action on a given plot, usually an episode from their own tribal history. Scenery was rarely used, except for leaves and branches to denote out-door scenes. Most of the plays began at sunset and lasted for two to four hours.

Through the centuries music, dance, and drama played an ever-increasing part in the social life of the Ethiopians, but it was not until the reign of the present Emperor Haile Selassie I that an organized movement, sponsored by the Government, came into being. A National Theatre was opened in Addis Ababa, in which only Ethiopian artists are employed, to preserve and stimulate the folk-art of the country. No make-up is worn, except by clowns and comic characters. The programme, made up of variety turns, lasts about three hours, during which time the audience can enter and leave freely, and refreshments can be obtained. National songs and dances are performed, and sometimes comic dramatic sketches on current events. In these the actors improvise round a given plot, and the actor usually plays the same character in a number of different sketches— the young heroine, her lover, the rogue, the comedian, and the clown. The clown always wears a white wig, eyebrows, moustache and beard, and a long black cloak, which he wraps round himself when making his entrances and exits. He is often a skilled acrobat and contortionist.

In 1956, to commemorate the Silver Jubilee of the Emperor Haile Selassie I, a magnificent theatre of contemporary design, seating about 2,000 people, was opened in Addis Ababa.

Since its inception artists of international fame from many countries have performed in it, and at other times it is used for the production of modern Ethiopian plays in Amharic. These are not, as at the National Theatre, improvised on a set plot, but written out in full, and carefully rehearsed and produced, with full use of the elaborate stage lighting, and of costume, scenery, and make-up. A regular State Company of sixty actors is attached to the theatre. Among the many new playwrights of Ethiopia is Berhanu Denqé, author of a verse-play on the Queen of Sheba's visit to Solomon entitled *Negest Azeb* (1951). The Prime Minister of Ethiopia has also written several historical plays. The prose-tragedy *Ya-dam dins* (1948) —The Voice of Blood—tells the story of the Ethiopian patriot-bishop Abuna Petros, who was killed by the Italians. *Asab-enne-sau* (1951) —Man and His Thought—deals with an episode at the court of King David, while *Salsawit Dawit* (also 1951)—David III—tells the story of an Ethiopian emperor of the eighteenth century. Kabbada Mika'el, the present (1956) Minister of Education, has written some plays in verse, of which *Ya-tinbit qutaro* (1946) has been translated and published in English as *Fulfilment of Prophecy*; he has also made a translation and adaptation of *Romeo and Juliet* (1953). Another playwright, Germanchau Takla-Hawaryat, is the author of a verse-drama *Tewodros* (1950), which tells the story of the nineteenth-century Ethiopian Emperor Theodore, who fought against the English and later committed suicide. Among the women playwrights Senedu Gabru has written two verse-dramas, published in her book *Yalibbe Mashaf* (1949)—The Book of My Heart; and Romana-Warq Kasahun has written, among other works, *Mahtota Tebab* (1951)—The Lamp of Science—on the subject of Princess Tsahai, the daughter of the present emperor, who was trained as a nurse and died in the service of her profession.

Through the advance of education, and with the help and encouragement given to writers and actors by the Imperial family and the Government, a new era for the theatre is beginning in this ancient land. (Information supplied by Miss Olivia Hasler, of Addis Ababa.)

FERNALD, JOHN BAILEY (1905–), English producer, who in 1955 was appointed Principal of the Royal Academy of Dramatic Art in succession to Sir Kenneth Barnes. Educated at Marlborough and Oxford, he was President of O.U.D.S. in 1927, and in 1929, after some experience with amateur productions, did his first professional production at the Arts Theatre. He has since had a long and successful career as a producer, broken only by war service at sea 1940–5, after which he went to the Liverpool Playhouse for three years, 1946–9. During this time he was Shute Lecturer on the Art of the Theatre at Liverpool University (1948). In 1949 he was associated with Roy Rich in the direction of the Arts Theatre, London. He continues to produce, both at R.A.D.A. and in the professional West End Theatre, and is the author of *The Play Produced: An Introduction to the Technique of Producing Plays* (1933), and, with his second wife, the actress Jenny Laird, of a play, *And No Birds Sing* (1955). He produced at Unity, in its early amateur days, the first translation of a play by Brecht to be done in England, *Señora Carrar's Rifles*.

FINLAND. The first attempt to introduce the theatre into Finland seems to have been made at the Academy of Abo/Turku in 1640, when a student company acted translations of Renaissance dramas, moralities, and Latin comedies on a raised stage with classical columns and tapestry hangings. With the prevalence of war and plague, however, this had little effect, and during the eighteenth century Finland depended mainly on Swedish travelling actors, or French companies from Sweden, for dramatic entertainment. In the early nineteenth century, after the annexation of Finland by Russia, German influence was particularly strong, and it was not until after the First World War that Finland was free to develop her own theatre.

As in many countries today, Belgium and South Africa for instance, the theatre in Finland is bilingual, and the two halves, the Finnish-speaking and the Swedish-speaking, develop independently, with occasional shifts of actors and technicians from one to the other. There are also two National Theatres. The Finnish-speaking one was founded in 1872, the Swedish-speaking in 1916, though the theatre and company on which this latter is based was founded as early at 1866. The moving spirit in the foundation of the Finnish-speaking National Theatre was Kaarlo Juhan Bergbom (1843–1906), who gathered round him a company which included the great actress Ida Aalberg (1857–1915). Bergbom was a great lover of Ibsen, and the first performance of *John Gabriel Borkman* was given at his theatre in 1897. The acquisition of Adolf Lindfors (1857–1929), an excellent actor in Molière, who had previously been with the Swedish-speaking company, established the tradition of Molière-acting which eventually led to the appearance of the Finnish National Theatre in a translation of *L'Avare* at the Paris International Theatre Festival in May 1955. The history of the Finnish-speaking theatre, from its inception to 1902 (the date of the company's installation in its present theatre) has been written by Eliel Aspelin-Haapkylä (in 4 vols.). A further volume, by Rafael Koskimies, brings the story down to 1917. The father of Finnish drama was Kivi (Aleksis Stenvall, 1834–72), whose statue, outside the Finnish National Theatre, was unveiled on 10 Oct. 1939. The production of his *Lea* in Helsinki/Helsingfors on 10 May 1869 marks the inauguration of a Finnish dramatic literature. He wrote also a play on Kullervo (a character in the great Finnish epic *Kalevala*), but his most important plays are undoubtedly his comedies of village life, of which *Nummisuutarit* (*The Village*

Shoemakers, 1864) is still in the repertory. Other important Finnish dramatists are Minna Canth (1844–97), whose realistic plays deal with contemporary problems, and particularly those of the emancipation of women, and two poetic dramatists, Juhana Henrik Erkko (1849–1906) and Eino Leino (1878–1926). The former drew on the *Kalevala* for his two most important plays, the latter on Finnish history. Later dramatists include Maria Jotuni (1880–1943), author of satirical comedies of rural life; Erkki Kivijärvi (1882–1942); Yrjö Soini (1896–), commonly known as Agapetus, writer of farces; Hella Vuolijoki (1888–1954), much influenced by Russian dramatists, whom she translated into Finnish (she was director of the Finnish Radio from 1945 to 1949); and Lauri Haarla (1890–1944).

The Swedish-speaking stage in Finland owes much to the Swedish actor Carl Gottfried Seuerling (1727–95), who, with his wife, brought to Finland his own translations of Shakespeare (beginning with *Romeo and Juliet* in 1780), as well as translations of Racine, Molière, Voltaire, Calderón, and Holberg. One of the outstanding actresses of the Swedish National Theatre in Finland was Marie Elisabeth Silfvan (1801–65), whose life was written by Yrjö Hirn. The leader of the company today is Erik Lindström (1906–), who played Hamlet at Elsinore in July 1947 and was seen in 1950 in Stockholm in a production of *The Taming of the Shrew* directed by Tyrone Guthrie, which had opened previously in Helsinki. In a playwriting competition held in 1955, for which scripts were received from Denmark, Sweden, Norway, Iceland, and Finland, the first prize was won by a Swedish-language author, Walentin Chorell, with his *Systrarna* (The Sisters).

There are in Finland (with a population of 4 million inhabitants, of which one-tenth is Swedish-speaking) 30 professional Finnish theatres (8 in Helsinki) and 5 Swedish (2 in Helsinki, 1 at Abo, 1 at Vasa, and a travelling company which tours the provinces). There are also at least 7,000 amateur groups. (Information from the Finnish Embassy in London, Dr. von Frenckell and J. B. Olli.)

FREEDLEY, GEORGE (1904–), American theatre historian, founder and director of the Theatre Department of the New York Public Library, which in 1956 celebrated its 25th anniversary. On this occasion Freedley was awarded the Kelcey Allen Award for distinguished services to the American theatre. A graduate of the Baker Workshop at Yale, he became an actor for a short time, and was then associated with the Theatre Guild. In 1931 he joined the staff of the New York Public Library. In addition to the Theatre Department there, he founded the Theatre Library Association, the Equity Library Theatre, is a director of ANTA, and secretary of the New York Drama Critics' Circle. He lectures and writes extensively on the theatre, and was at one time dramatic critic of the New York *Morning Telegraph*, for which he is now drama feature writer and book editor. He is part-author of *A History of the Theatre* (with John Reeves), of *A History of Modern Drama* (with Barrett H. Clark), and of *Theatre Collections in Libraries and Museums* (with Rosamond Gilder).

GATE THEATRE (p. 301). A certain amount of confusion over this theatre needs clearing up. The first Gate Theatre was a club theatre with premises on the top floor of a warehouse in Floral Street, off the Strand. It opened on 30 Oct. 1925, under the management of Peter Godfrey, with Susan Glaspell's *Bernice*, and had its first success with Toller's *From Morn till Midnight*, which was favourably reviewed by James Agate. In 1927 the theatre moved to Villiers Street, Strand, and opened on 22 Nov. with Gantillon's *Maya*. From then until 1931 Charles Spencer was joint manager with Godfrey. Among the plays seen there were a number of translations or adaptations, some of them by Godfrey, who also produced most of them. Margaret Rawlings and Flora Robson were among the actresses who appeared there. In 1934 Norman Marshall took over the Gate, and reopened it with Toller's *Miracle in America*. He continued to run it as a successful non-commercial venture until the outbreak of war. It was badly damaged in 1941, and has not been reopened.

GÉMIER, FIRMIN (1865–1933), French actor and producer, pupil of Antoine, whom he succeeded as director of the Odéon in 1906. After walking-on in one of Antoine's productions in 1887, he spent four years in the suburban theatres of Paris, and then joined Antoine at the Théâtre-Libre, where he proved himself an excellent actor, both in classic and modern roles. He was also a good producer, but it was as a teacher that his influence made itself felt in the modern French theatre, since he was the first to emphasize the importance of improvisation and systematic exercises in the training of young actors, in the style of Stanislavsky, whose contemporary and disciple he was. One of his most famous pupils was Charles Dullin, who, after developing his methods still further, passed them on to those outstanding figures in the Parisian theatre today, Barrault, Vilar, and Valde. The germ of the present Centres Dramatiques and the Théâtre National Populaire (see S., pp. 3, 16) was implicit in Gémier's early tentatives, both before and after the First World War, to found such a theatre, with his Théâtre National Ambulant (1911–12) and his Théâtre National Populaire (1920). An excellent life of Gémier, by Paul Blanchart, was published in 1954.

GUINNESS, ALEC (1914–   ), English actor, who, after training at the Fay Compton Studio of Dramatic Art, where he won First Prize at the annual Public Show, made his first appearance as Osric in Gielgud's *Hamlet* in 1934, a part which he played again at the Old Vic (1936–7). It was during this season that he first attracted notice by his Sir Andrew Aguecheek. He then joined Gielgud's company at the Queen's, playing Aumerle in *Richard II* with great simplicity and pathos, Snake in *The School for Scandal*, Fedotik in *Three Sisters*, and Lorenzo in *The Merchant of Venice*, the last with a magically poetic quality which seemed to foreshadow a career in romantic parts. Much of the same quality was apparent in his modern-dress Hamlet (produced by Tyrone Guthrie in 1938), a remarkably sincere, straightforward performance which had in it some unforgettable moments. It contrasted admirably with his Arthur Gower (in *Trelawny of the 'Wells'*) and his extremely amusing Bob Acres in the same season. Among his later parts have been Herbert Pocket and Mitya in his own adaptations of *Great Expectations* and *The Brothers Karamazov*, Garcin in Sartre's *Vicious Circle (Huis-Clos)*, and, with the Old Vic, an outstanding Fool in *King Lear*, and two excellent performances as Abel Drugger in *The Alchemist* and Hlestakov in *The Government Inspector*; he also appeared at Edinburgh as Harcourt Reilly in *The Cocktail Party*. In 1951 he appeared in his own production of *Hamlet*, an effort to break with tradition and present Hamlet in Shakespeare's own image which failed, but even in its failure left some of the audience more stirred and interested than by other less unorthodox Hamlets. In 1953 he played in the opening season of the Shakespeare Theatre at Stratford, Ontario, and in the following year was seen again in London in the title-role of Bridget Boland's *The Prisoner*. His success in films, which cannot be dealt with here, has been as great as on the stage. He is an unpredictable and protean creature, who constantly delights his audience with his wit and mimicry, or chills them with his revelations of the abysses in the mind of man. No one can say what he will do next. But whatever he does it will be worth watching.

INTERNATIONAL FEDERATION FOR THEATRE RESEARCH. A meeting of delegates from over twenty countries, held in London in July 1955 at the invitation of the Society for Theatre Research, resulted in the formation of an international body devoted to the collection, preservation, and dissemination of theatrical material throughout the world. A further meeting in Paris in 1956, presided over by the Chairman of the English parent body, Mr. Ifan Kyrle Fletcher, resulted in the drafting of a constitution and the founding of an international magazine, *Theatre Research/Recherches Théâtrales*. It is hoped that at a meeting to be held in Venice in July 1957 the draft constitution will be accepted and the Federation established on a firm basis. At present (Apr., 1957) the committee consists of delegates representing seventeen countries, and has its headquarters in Rome.

INTERNATIONAL THEATRE INSTITUTE (I.T.I.). This body, which exists to promote international co-operation and exchange of ideas among all workers in the theatre, was founded as a branch of U.N.E.S.C.O. in July 1947, at a meeting in Paris presided over by J. B. Priestley. It works through national centres, with headquarters in Paris, and publishes a monthly bulletin of *World Premières*, as well as a quarterly illustrated review, *World Theatre*. It has also been responsible for the holding of a yearly (latterly two-yearly) conference, usually in one of the capital cities of Europe, and for specialist conferences at the Paris headquarters on such subjects as 'Theatre and Youth'. The British Centre, one of the first to be founded (April 1948), was particularly active in this field, and was asked to collect and report on information from all member countries as to the work that was being done by and for young people in the theatre of today. It hopes in due course to be able to bring foreign theatrical companies to London. At the moment it has to content itself with receiving, entertaining, and advising those, whether students or young theatre workers, who come to study the English theatre and helping those who go abroad to study the foreign theatre. It also endeavours to bring together members of the teaching and theatrical professions, between whom, in England, there is a great gulf fixed. Above all, it serves as an information bureau about the theatre at home and abroad. In this it is assisted by its department of Theatre Architecture and Planning, under the direction of Dr. Richard Southern, whose Theatre Collection is housed at the Centre. The British Centre has also founded, as an adjunct to its work, an International Theatre Association, which enables its members to meet and discuss theatrical problems with foreign theatre workers visiting London.

The American Centre works through ANTA (The American National Theatre and Academy, see p. 24), and covers much the same ground as that outlined above.

JONES, MARGO (1913–55), American director and producer, founder of an experimental theatre in Dallas. After an academic education from which she emerged with a degree in psychology, she turned to the theatre which she had loved since childhood, and after studying at the Southwestern School of the Theatre in Dallas, she worked with the Ojai Community Players, and at the Pasadena Playhouse in California. In 1939 she was associated with community and university drama in Houston, Texas, and in 1943 she staged an early play of Tennessee Williams, *You Touched Me*, at the Cleveland Playhouse. Two years later she established the theatre which will always be associated with her name in Dallas. Here she encouraged the work of new playwrights, and gave experimental productions of older plays, which she has described in her book, *Theatre-in-the-Round*, published in 1951. Her work was first seen on Broadway in 1945, when she directed, with Eddie Dowling, Tennessee Williams's *The Glass Menagerie*. Later productions included *Summer and Smoke*, *Joan of Lorraine*, and *Southern Exposure*. She died at the height of her powers, and her early death was a great loss to the American theatre, which

she had sought to revitalize, on and off Broadway, both by her own abounding energy and by a new approach to the problems of staging plays.

LAMBS, The, a London supper club founded in the 1860s by a group which included the actors John Hare, Harry Montague, Henry Irving, and Squire Bancroft. It consisted of twenty-four members, under a Chairman called The Shepherd, who wore a badge with the motto Floreant Agni, and carried a crook surmounted by a silver bell. The club had no regular premises, but met for many years at the Gaiety Restaurant and subsequently at the Albemarle Hotel. It survived until the 1890s. Meanwhile, Montague, who had returned to America, founded a similar club in New York in 1875, with himself as the first Shepherd. At first the club had no regular premises, but in 1880 a clubhouse was acquired at 34 West 26th Street. The first Gambol took place in the same year, with Edmund S. Holland, one of the original five members, as the Collie. The present constitution was adopted in 1893, a new club-house taken in 1897, and on the dissolution of the London Lambs the Shepherd's crook, bell, and badge were presented to the American Shepherd. The surviving London members were elected honorary members of the New York club, and Hare was designated Shepherd Emeritus. In 1904 the club moved to its present (1957) premises at 128 West 144th Street, which have been several times enlarged to accommodate a growing membership which now stands at over a thousand. The first Ladies' Day was held on Sunday, 6 Jan. 1952. The Lambs in its present form is roughly the equivalent of the London Savage Club, as the Players is of the Garrick.

LEIGH, VIVIEN [Vivian Mary Hartley] (1913–   ), English actress, wife of Sir Laurence Olivier. After a short period of study in Paris and at the R.A.D.A., a few appearances in films and one small part at the 'Q' Theatre in 1935, she made a sensational success in May of the same year as Henriette in *The Mask of Virtue*. In 1936 she played Jenny Mere in *The Happy Hypocrite*, and in 1937 went with the Old Vic to Elsinore, playing Ophelia to the Hamlet of Olivier. After appearing as Titania at the Old Vic and Serena Blandish at the Gate, she went to America, and was seen as Juliet. Later successes included Jennifer Dubedat in *The Doctor's Dilemma*, Sabina in *The Skin of our Teeth*, and a number of parts with the Old Vic on tour. It was, however, with her Blanche du Bois in *A Streetcar Named Desire* (1949) that she gave proof of greater powers as an actress than she had hitherto shown (her work in films, which cannot be considered here, was already outstanding), and she became one of London's leading actresses. During the Festival of Britain she appeared with her husband in Shaw's *Caesar and Cleopatra* and Shakespeare's *Antony and Cleopatra*, both in London and New York, the general consensus of opinion being that she was more successful as Shaw's Cleopatra than as Shakespeare's. In 1953 she appeared, again with her husband, in Rattigan's *The Sleeping Prince*.

LIGHTING, STAGE. 2. MODERN (*k*) Remote Control (p. 475). Of the two types of remote control previously outlined, the multi-pre-set tends to be found in theatres devoted mainly to legitimate drama—the Old Vic, the Saville, and the New Theatre in London, the Shakespeare Memorial Theatre at Stratford-upon-Avon—the Light Console in the theatres which stage ballet, musicals, and large spectacular shows—Drury Lane, the Coliseum, the Adelphi, Her Majesty's, and the Royal Festival Hall. Since 1951 a further division has arisen. Previously the multi-pre-set board used either direct electronic dimmers or electronically-controlled saturable reactors, whereas the Light Console employed electro-mechanically-operated dimmer banks. The latter could not accurately pre-set intermediate dimmer positions. However fast its operation, the positioning of the dimmers was rather rough and ready, and dependent on the dexterity of the operator. However, the advantage of the mechanical system is that once dimmers are brought to their levels they do not require to be energized from the control panel. Thus, the controls can be freed to be set for the next change of lighting. On all other systems of dimming a set of levers is needed to hold the lighting while the next change is pre-set on another set. Practical application of these systems has led to the inclusion of a large number of pre-sets in the shape of repeat dimmer levers to each dimmer circuit. In America ten, or even twenty, pre-sets or sets of repeat levers are not unknown. The difficulty is that even when the levers are very small they take up a lot of room, and it is also confusing to have a control for say 200 dimmers which may need 4,000 dimmer levers. In England Frederick Bentham, the inventor of the Light Console, has replaced the electronic dimmer system by a mechanically-driven dimmer bank which now gives two complete dimmer pre-sets from the desk which previously gave only one. This was first installed at the New Theatre, London. He followed it by his Strand System CD, which combines the light console with the multiplicity of levers. This has been installed at the Palace and Sadler's Wells. The principle involved is known as 'Lit Move', and exploits the static nature of the electro-mechanical dimmer bank. Dimmer levers are used to pre-set only those circuits required to move, and then only if an intermediate position is needed.

In lighting equipment the main development has been the use of 'tungsten' spotlights, both in England and in America, to replace arc lamps for following. In New York following technique is used even for straight plays, for example, in *Cat on a Hot Tin Roof*. The operator, using a beam which hardly registers, discreetly follows actors into stage areas which

it would be difficult to light. In London in a similar situation all possible areas would be covered by a large number of baby mirror spots under dimmer control. (Article by L. G. Applebee. See illustrs. Nos. 61–62.)

MERMAID THEATRE, a structure originally designed by Michael Stringer and C. Walter Hodges for Bernard Miles, which reproduces, in general terms, the main features of the Elizabethan stage. Erected first in a hall in Acacia Road, St. John's Wood, it opened on 9 Sept. 1951 with a performance of 'Dido and Aeneas' in which Kirsten Flagstad sang Dido. This was followed a week later by *The Tempest*. In 1952 Middleton's *A Trick to Catch the Old One* was performed. In Coronation Year (1953) The Mermaid was erected in the quadrangle of the Royal Exchange in the City of London, and performances were given of 'Dido', *As You Like It*, *Macbeth*, and *Eastward Ho!* On 17 Oct. 1956 the foundations were laid of a new Mermaid Theatre at Puddle Dock in Upper Thames Street, near Blackfriars Station, a site previously chosen for a theatre in 1616, but unused owing to the opposition of the City Fathers. It is hoped that the new theatre will open early in 1958. It is to be a portable building, framed in steel arches, to seat 650 persons. Prices will be low, and there will be a restaurant on the premises. Modern plays as well as plays by Shakespeare and other Elizabethan dramatists will be done. According to *The Times* correspondent, who attended the inaugural ceremony, the theatre when finished will resemble 'something between a modern church and Mr. Peggotty's house made from an upturned boat'. It was designed by Mr. Elidir Davies, F.R.I.B.A.

MILLER, ARTHUR (1915–), American dramatist, who while a student at Michigan University won three drama prizes, one of which, the Theatre Guild National Award of 1937, he shared with Tennessee Williams. On leaving the University he joined the Federal Theatre Project. His first play, *The Man Who Had All the Luck* (1944), ran for only five performances on Broadway, but in 1947 *All My Sons* had a long run and was given the Drama Critics' Award. It was produced in London (in 1948), as was *Death of a Salesman*, which on its production in New York in 1949 again gained the Critics' Award, and the Pulitzer Prize. Two further plays, *The Crucible* (1952) and *A View from the Bridge* (1955), consolidated Miller's position in the theatre as a first-rate craftsman, and a writer who is not afraid to tackle contemporary problems. His aim, in his own words, has been to present 'man as the creature of society, and at the same time as its creator'. *The Crucible* was done in London by the English Stage Company at the Court in 1956, and *A View from the Bridge* by the Watergate Theatre Club at the Comedy in the same year, during Miller's visit to England after his marriage to the film-star Marilyn Monroe.

PLAYERS' THEATRE (p. 621). Some confusion having arisen in this article, the following note has kindly been supplied by Raymond Mander and Joe Mitchenson.

A small studio theatre on the first floor at 6 New Compton Street opened in Jan. 1927 as Playroom Six. It was here that Peggy Ashcroft made her first London appearance, as Bessie in *One Day More* (May 1927). In Nov. 1929, on its removal to ground-floor premises, with John Fernald as producer, the club changed its name to The Players' Theatre. It moved again in Apr. 1934 to premises in 43 King Street, Covent Garden—the building which in Victorian times had housed Evans' (late Joy's) Song and Supper Rooms. It soon closed, but in Dec. 1936 it was reopened by Peter Ridgeway as The New Players' Theatre. It was here, in Dec. 1937, that Harold Scott produced the first Victorian cabaret, so inaugurating the entertainment that later became famous in London as Ridgeway's Late Joys. After Ridgeway's death in 1938, a mixture of plays and Victorian music-hall items continued to fill the bill until 1940, when, because of the blitz, the Club, now directed by Leonard Sachs, and known simply as the Players' Theatre, moved to 13 Albemarle Street. In 1945 it acquired the premises under the arches of Charing Cross station which had originally been the Hungerford Music Hall, and later been known as Gatti's-Under-the-Arches to distinguish them from Gatti's-Over-the-Water (in Westminster Bridge Road). Here, under the direction of Don Gemmell, Reginald Woolley and Gervase Farjeon, the theatre continues to run an old-time Victorian music-hall, with other entertainments which include an annual Victorian pantomime.

PLINGE, WALTER, a name used on English playbills to conceal a doubling of parts, particularly in a Shakespeare play (for the American equivalent, see SPELVIN, S., p. 16). Sir St. Vincent Troubridge has kindly supplied the following note on his career. 'There are two versions of the origin of Walter Plinge, and though they differ somewhat, both connect him with drinking in the early and great days of the Benson Company. The more frequent version, which I have read in the memoirs of old Bensonians and heard from them in the 1920s, claims him as the landlord of a pub opposite or near the stage door of the Lyceum when Benson played his first season there in 1900. His geniality, good beer, and easy credit endeared him to the company, who thought he should be immortalized in print, and started using his name in the programme for their second and third appearances covered with crêpe hair. Matheson Lang, in *Mr. Wu Looks Back* (pp. 207-8) gives the other version. "Walter Plinge is a mystery. He has appeared not only in several of my plays, but also at the same time in casts of other productions in other London theatres. . . . The dreadful truth is simply this. During Benson's first London season there was, close to the stage-door of the theatre, a pleasant and cheery little bar to

which members of the company would sometimes 'step aside'. When an interval during rehearsals gave rise to such an opportunity, H. O. Nicholson invented a kind of code-word for this delectable stepping. As thus: 'If you have time, Mr. Plinge is waiting to see you outside the stage-door.' In other words that meant: 'Have we time for a quick one?'." It can readily be understood from this that Mr. Plinge became a very important and a very popular personage in the Benson Company. Where he got the name Walter I don't really know, but someone—I've got an idea it was Oscar Asche—had a brain-wave one day and used the name for a double on a programme. Thus Plinge grew into quite a popular actor of small parts.' The name was never, as in America, used for doll or animal actors, but still makes occasional appearances on London and provincial playbills.

POLAND. The origins of the theatre in Poland, as in all European countries, must be looked for in the liturgy of the Church (see ECCLESIASTICAL DRAMA, p. 213). It was Jan Kochanowski (1530–84), the foremost Polish poet of the Renaissance, who gave Poland its first secular play of any importance (*The Dismissal of the Grecian Envoys*, 1578), but moralities and popular farces continued to flourish until well into the seventeenth century. A typical example of the latter was P. Baryka's *A Peasant Made King* (1637).

The agricultural nature of the country, and the comparatively small size of the towns, favoured the activities of strolling companies rather than of permanent theatres (John Green's English Comedians visited Poland as early as 1616), but a theatre was erected in the Royal Castle in Warsaw in 1637, which for a time housed a resident Italian opera company. French and Italian plays were given, as well as elaborate masks and an increasing number of Polish plays. School drama flourished under the Jesuits and the Piarists.

The first public theatre, the Teatr Narodowy, opened in Warsaw in 1765. In 1783 Wojciech Boguslawski (1757-1829), who had joined the company five years earlier, became its director, and in the next thirty years he laid the foundations of theatrical life throughout the country, financing, building, and directing theatres in a number of towns. He encouraged new playwrights, and he himself wrote and translated some sixty plays, of which *The Miracle* (1794) was the most popular. Other important dramatists of this period were Franciszek Zablocki (1754-1812), and J. U. Niemcewicz (1758-1841).

In the nineteenth century the theatre became, for a country under foreign domination, both an instrument of national aspiration, and a means of escape. The former was expressed by the Romantic poets—Adam Mickiewicz (1798–1855), Juliusz Slowacki (1809-49), Zygmunt Krasinski (1812-59)—followed by the writers of the Young Poland movement, of whom the Cracow poet Stanislaw Wyspianski (1867-1907) was the most important, while comedy flourished with such writers as Aleksander Fredro (1793–1876), Michal Balucki (1837–1901), Jozef Blizinski (1827–93) and others. Later, drama became more concerned with social realities, and among the writers of this period were Aleksander Swietochowski (1849–1938), Gabriela Zapolska (1860–1921), Stanislaw Przybyszewski (1868–1927), Tadeusz Rittner (1873–1921), J. A. Kisielewski (1876–1918), K. H. Rostworowski (1877–1938), and Wlodzimierz Perzynski (1878–1930).

The efficiency of the theatres in the nineteenth century depended partly on the degree of freedom allowed to them. In Warsaw the theatres were nationalized after the 1830 Rising, and Russian police officials were nominally in charge. The Teatr Narodowy, the Teatr Rozmaitosci (1829), and the Teatr Wielki (1833), maintained a high standard during the second half of the century with such outstanding actors as Modjeska (see p. 536), Boleslaw Leszczynski (1840–1916), Wincenty Rapacki (1841–1924), and Mieczyslaw Frenkiel (1859–1934). In Vilna, where Boguslawski had appeared in 1785, and established a theatre, performances in Polish were forbidden from 1864 to 1906. In Poznan, the main theatre centre of the Prussian part of Poland, a permanent theatre was not established until 1870. Conditions were more favourable in the Austrian part. Boguslawski appeared in Lwow in 1790, and six years later he settled there for a time and built a permanent theatre. He was succeeded by J. N. Kaminski (1777–1855), who opened a new theatre in 1817, and remained in management for twenty years. Two other theatres were built, one in 1842 and one in 1900. The latter reached a high standard under Tadeusz Pawlikowski, manager until 1906, and L. Heller, who succeeded him until 1918.

Cracow had its first permanent theatre in 1799, and a second—the Stary—opened in 1842. In 1893, when the new Juliusz Slowacki Theatre opened, Cracow became for a time the chief theatre centre of Poland.

After the First World War the theatre in Poland was able to develop freely. One of its finest theatres was the Polski in Warsaw, which opened in 1912 under Arnold Szyfman (1882–), who still directs it. *The Apple-Cart*, by Shaw, had its world première in this theatre, and two other Shaw plays their European premières. Also important was the Reduta Theatre, founded in Warsaw in 1919 by the eminent actor-producer, Juliusz Osterwa (1885–1947). It later transferred to Vilna, and split into two sections, one playing in the city, the other touring the small towns of Eastern Poland. Also deserving of mention are the *avant-garde* theatre Ateneum, which was directed by the distinguished actor Stefan Jaracz (1883–1945), and the Boguslawski Theatre in Warsaw, founded by Leon Schiller (1887–1954), one of the finest Polish producers of this century. Among the great actors of this period was Ludwik Solski (1855–1954), for many years the doyen of the Polish stage. He retained his full powers until the end of his long life, and was at his best in comedy, where his wit, dexterity, and perfect timing had full play.

The Second World War brought total destruction to the Polish theatre. All theatre buildings, archives, and libraries in Warsaw, as well as in many other cities, were destroyed or deprived of all their equipment, and many eminent theatre men were killed or driven out of the country. But as soon as the war ended, companies sprang up again, and theatres were rebuilt with official financial help. In 1949 all theatres were subjected to a central authority, which controlled their organization and repertory, but this was abolished in 1956, and replaced by decentralization which gives each theatre a large measure of freedom in choice of repertory and manner of presentation. There are many new theatres, such as the People's Theatre in the new town of Nowa Huta, directed by Krystyna Skuszanka, and the Teatr Nowy in Lodz, directed by Kazimierz Dejmek. Nor is there any lack of talented young producers and designers, while, in addition to older writers, well known before the war—Jerzy Szaniawski, L. H. Morstin, Jaroslaw Iwaszkiewicz, and Leon Kruczkowski—there are younger men, like Jerzy Zawieyski and Roman Brandstaetter, whose success belongs to the post-war years. (Article by Boleslaw Taborski.) (For the influence of the Polish theatre in Russia,[1] see p. 683; for the Yiddish theatre in Poland, see pp. 425–7 and 828.)

RATTIGAN, TERENCE (1911–), English dramatist, whose first play, written in collaboration with Philip Heimann, was *First Episode* (1933). This was followed in 1936 by an immensely successful light comedy, *French Without Tears*, and in 1939 by *After the Dance*. Two plays in collaboration in 1940, *Follow My Leader* (with Anthony Maurice) and *Grey Farm* (with Hector Bolitho), were followed by *Flare Path* (1942), *While the Sun Shines* (1943), and *Love In Idleness* (1944). The last provided an excellent vehicle for the Lunts, who played in it in London, and also in America under the title of *O Mistress Mine*. Rattigan, who had hitherto been considered an astute purveyor of light entertainment, now began to show signs of a more serious purpose in *The Winslow Boy* (1946), the story of a father's fight to clear his young son of a charge of petty theft. This won for its author the Ellen Terry Award for the best play of the year, and in 1947 the New York Critics' Award for the best foreign play. *Playbill*, consisting of two plays, *Harlequinade* and *The Browning Version*, followed in 1948, and also received the Ellen Terry Award. *Adventure Story* (1949), with Paul Scofield as Alexander the Great, was an interesting failure, and with *Who is Sylvia?* (1950) Rattigan appeared ready to return to his former vein of comedy. In 1952, however, he produced *The Deep Blue Sea*, an 'emotional drama' in which a charming middle-aged woman (played successively by Peggy Ashcroft, Celia Johnson, and Googie Withers) falls in love with a feckless, drunken, ex-R.A.F. fighter-pilot, and twice attempts suicide. The play, though well written and theatrically exciting, failed to come to grips with the central problem. An excursion into Ruritanian romance, *The Sleeping Prince*, in which Laurence Olivier and Vivien Leigh appeared, followed in 1953, and in 1955 Margaret Leighton and Eric Portman gave excellent performances in the two plays which made up *Separate Tables*.

Rattigan's *Collected Plays* were published in 1953 in 2 vols., each with a long introduction by the author.

REDGRAVE, MICHAEL SCUDAMORE (1908–), English actor, son of the well-known players Margaret Scudamore and Roy Redgrave. Educated at Clifton and Cambridge, he first became a schoolmaster, but had made a number of amateur, and some professional, appearances—notably with the A.D.C. and in his own productions at Cranleigh School—before he joined the Liverpool Rep. in 1934. He remained there for two years, playing a wide variety of parts, and married a fellow member of the company, Rachel Kempson, who has since appeared with him in many plays. They were together at the Old Vic in 1936, where, among other parts, Redgrave played Mr. Horner in a revival of *The Country Wife*. Although some critics found him miscast, he gave an excellent performance which long remained in the memory of those who saw it. In this, and in his Aguecheek in 1938, he displayed a gift for comedy which he has too rarely exploited. In 1937 he was with Gielgud's company at the Queen's, and in 1940 played Macheath in Gielgud's production of *The Beggar's Opera*. At his best in nervous, intellectual parts which carry overtones of internal conflict, he was good as Lord Monchensey in *The Family Reunion* in 1939. In the same year he first appeared in films, and has since—except for war service in the Royal Navy—divided his time between stage and screen. He returned to the stage after the war with a fine performance in the short-lived *Duke in Darkness*, and has since been seen in a number of Shakespearian parts, for which he is well equipped by a fine presence and a beautiful speaking voice. These include Hamlet at the Old Vic and at Elsinore, Macbeth, in which he made his first appearance in New York, Richard II, Prospero, Shylock, Antony, and Lear, all at Stratford-upon-Avon. He has also been seen in modern plays, some of which he produced himself—*Thunder Rock*, *Uncle Harry*, *Jacobowsky and the Colonel*. His last and so far (1957) finest performance was a superb delineation of Hector in Giraudoux's *La Guerre de Troie n'aura pas lieu* (done in London as *Tiger at the Gates*), which he subsequently repeated in New York. Although at the start of his career his acting may have suffered from the inhibitions induced by an academic background, the effort of overcoming these has meant that in his later years he has become a finer actor than many who were more precociously successful. He is the author of two plays, produced in Liverpool, and of *The Actor's Ways and Means*, based on a series of lectures given at Bristol University in 1952. An account of his life and work, by Richard Findlater, was published in 1956.

SALACROU, ARMAND (1899–), French dramatist, whose finest, but perhaps least characteristic, play is *Les Nuits de la colère*, which deals with the German occupation of France during the Second World War. Superbly acted by Barrault and his company, this was first seen at the Marigny in 1947, and in London during the visit of Barrault in 1951. It was broadcast by the B.B.C. as *Men of Wrath*, but has not yet been seen on the stage in English. Unlike Anouilh and Sartre, Salacrou has not yet made contact with the English public, though performances have been given, mainly by student groups, of *L'Archipel Lenoir*, *L'Inconnue d'Arras*, and *Une Femme libre*. The Arts Theatre produced a translation of *Histoire de Rire* as *No Laughing Matter* (by Lucienne Hill) in Jan. 1957. Salacrou's other plays include *Un Homme comme les autres*, *La Terre est ronde*, *Les Fiancés du Havre*. During the season of 1946–7 three of Salacrou's plays were running simultaneously in Paris. Several of them have been translated into Italian. Detailed studies of his work were written in 1947 by José van den Esch, and in 1951 by Serge Radine.

SARTRE, JEAN-PAUL (1905–), one of the most controversial of modern French playwrights, and the one who, with Anouilh, has become best known abroad. His philosophy of existentialism, which he has propagated not only in his plays but in novels and essays, became extremely popular with young people everywhere after the war. His first play, *Les Mouches*, dealt with the legend of Orestes, and was translated into English as *The Flies*; it was followed by *Huis-Clos* (known in English as *Vicious Circle* or *No Exit*), *Morts sans sépulture* (*Men Without Shadows*), *La Putain respectueuse* (*The Respectable Prostitute*), *Les Mains sales* (known in English as *Crime Passionnel* or *Red Gloves*), and *Le Diable et le Bon Dieu*, which has not yet (1957) been seen in England. Sartre's plays pose the problem of liberty, with the conclusion that each person must find his or her own solution. In 1956 Unity Theatre gave the first English production of *Nekrassov*.

SCOFIELD, PAUL (1922–), English actor who, after appearing in a variety of parts in a students' repertory company, and on tour for C.E.M.A. during the war, joined the Birmingham Rep. in 1945. Here he scored a great success as the Bastard in *King John*, and in the following year moved to Stratford-upon-Avon with Sir Barry Jackson, who had been appointed Director of the Memorial Theatre. There he remained until 1948, as a fantastical Don Armado in Peter Brook's production of *Love's Labour's Lost*, an endearing Clown in

The Winter's Tale, a suavely ironic Lucio in *Measure for Measure*, a fiery Mercutio, a wistful Aguecheek, and a Hamlet whose excellences had to struggle against unbecoming Victorian trappings. This part he played again, in more favourable circumstances, in 1955, first in London and then at the Moscow Art Theatre, in the first English company to appear in Russia since the Revolution. For this, and for his services to the stage, he was appointed C.B.E. in the New Year Honours of 1956. In the intervening years he had been seen in a wide variety of parts, to each of which he brought some new facet of his many-sided personality. He was Tegeus-Chromis in *A Phoenix Too Frequent* at the Arts Theatre (1946), Alexander in Rattigan's ill-fated historical pageant, *Adventure Story* (1949), and made a great impression as the twin brothers Hugo and Frederic in *Ring Round the Moon* (1950), which ran for two years. One of his few modern parts was Sturgess in *The River Line* (1952), and he also played the drunken priest in *The Power and the Glory* (1956). One of his finest performances was as Pierre in *Venice Preserv'd* in 1953 at the Lyric, Hammersmith, where he had previously been seen as the foppish Witwoud in *The Way of the World*. With his strongly-moulded face, his curious voice, sometimes harsh, sometimes bell-like, but always arresting, and his astonishing versatility, Scofield is an actor who escapes classification, but has already proved himself one of the finest of our younger players.

SHAKESPEARE FESTIVALS. Two festivals devoted to summer seasons of Shakespeare have been inaugurated recently. The first was at Stratford, Ontario, Canada, where a temporary tent-theatre, in a modified Elizabethan style, opened in 1953 with *All's Well That Ends Well* and *Richard III*, both produced by Tyrone Guthrie. A new permanent building, incorporating many of the tent features, is now being built, and will be ready for the 1957 Festival.

The second Shakespeare Festival is held at Stratford, Connecticut, U.S.A., and owes its inception to the initiative and energy of Lawrence Langner. The building, designed by Edwin Howard, stands on the banks of the Housatonic, and opened on 12 July 1955 with *Julius Caesar*, followed by *The Tempest*. Attached to the theatre is an Academy, under the direction of Helen Menken, where students are trained in Shakespearian acting. Both these enterprises are wholly professional.

The Oregon Shakespeare Festival, at Ashland, is mainly amateur. It is a much older venture than the above, having been founded in 1935. Plays were first given by college students in a frame structure with no roof, a former domed Chautauqua building. This was damaged by fire in 1940 and the festival was suspended until 1947, when a new stage was built, and professional actors were engaged for the first time. Five or six plays are given during the festival, which is held during the summer vacation. Attached to the theatre is an Insti-tute of Renaissance Studies under Professor Margaret Bailey of Stanford University.

SOCIETY FOR THEATRE RESEARCH, The, was founded in 1948, after a meeting held at the Old Vic Theatre Centre on 15 June, which brought together all those interested in the problems of theatre history and the preservation of ephemeral and other material relating to the theatre. The Society holds monthly meetings during the winter, with an occasional summer meeting, at which lectures, with discussion, are given on specific points of theatrical history (including ballet and opera). Members receive an illustrated quarterly, *Theatre Notebook*, and an annual publication, as well as occasional pamphlets, and are entitled to use the library which the Society is gradually building up by gift and purchase. The preservation of source material on the theatre, and of photographic records, is encouraged, and the Society aims at establishing local groups in the large provincial towns, most successful so far being that in Manchester. In the summer of 1955 the Society held in London the first international conference on theatre history, attended by representatives of twenty-two countries, which resulted in the formation of the International Federation for Theatre Research (see S., p. 9). The first President of the Society was Mrs. Gabrielle Enthoven, who was succeeded on her death in 1950 by Professor Edward J. Dent.

SOUTH AFRICA. The theatre in South Africa is beset by problems similar to those found in the other Dominions, particularly Canada, and indeed in most countries that do not have the metropolitan pivot of their language within their own frontiers. When Captain Cook visited the Cape of Good Hope in 1771 he remarked: 'There are no public entertainments.' However, towards the end of the century this deficiency was made good, first by French troops stationed in Cape Town and, after 1795, by the British occupying garrison. The African Theatre, in Hottentot Square, was opened in 1800 or 1801, and until, in 1839, it was closed by a wave of puritanism, it saw much amateur performance in English, Dutch, French, German, and even occasional appearances by voyaging professionals from England. By 1843 puritanism had subsided sufficiently to permit the conversion of two wine stores into little theatres, and when Sefton Parry, the English theatrical manager, opened the Drawing-Room Theatre on 13 July 1855, he inaugurated a system—a professional management with a semi-professional company—which is still found in South Africa today (1957).

The Diamond Rush of the 1860s brought with it a number of theatrical adventurers, notably Captain Disney Roebuck (c. 1821–85), who from 1873 provided Cape Town with regular entertainment; with the Gold Rush of the 1880s came real prosperity, a much inflated population, and an endless variety of theatrical activity. Excellent theatres were built in Cape Town (the Opera House, 1893,

[15]

the Tivoli, 1903), Johannesburg (the Standard, 1891, the Globe (later the Empire), 1892, the Gaiety, 1893, His Majesty's, 1903), Pretoria, Durban, Port Elizabeth, Bloemfontein, Kimberley, Grahamstown, and other smaller towns; almost every great name of the time came out and played in them. The central figure during this period was Leonard Rayne, (1869–1925), lessee of many of the theatres, who, besides importing overseas artists, had his own company and, with his wife, Freda Godfrey, played leading roles. After his death the South African theatre suffered the decline then common to all theatres. Many of the old buildings were converted into cinemas, others were torn down. However, this decline was accompanied by the rise of the Amateur Theatre movement, and by the emergence of the Afrikaans professional theatre. A Hollander, Paul de Groot (1882–1942), led the first company to tour in this language in 1926. He was followed by many others, including André Huguenet, the Hanekoms, Wena Naude, Pikkie Uys, and Anton Ackermann. During the 1930s and 1940s they toured continuously throughout the country, giving European plays in translation, and simple, somewhat melodramatic and sentimental works by the many folk-dramatists who arose to satisfy their needs. The emergence of an Afrikaans literature was not paralleled by that of an English; the amateur companies perform West End and Broadway popular fare, with considerable personal success, and the two leading groups, the Cape Town Repertory Theatre Society, founded in 1921, and the Johannesburg Rep., founded in 1927, have built their own theatres. In Cape Town the Drama Department of the University has presented in its Little Theatre (founded in 1931) an international repertory of the classics.

The war years, 1939–45, saw a brilliant renaissance of the English-speaking professional theatre, opera, and ballet. The company formed by Gwen Ffrangcon-Davies and Marda Vanne gave, from 1941 to 1946, in association with African Consolidated Theatres (the monopoly group now owning almost all the theatres and cinemas), seasons of distinction in the larger towns. Since the war their standard has been maintained by other companies, notably by Brian Brooke, who has established theatres in Cape Town (1946–56) and Johannesburg (1955), and presents continuous seasons of repertory. His wife, Petrina Fry, is recognized as the country's leading actress.

To correlate South Africa's diverse theatrical activities, and to improve the standard of the touring companies, the Government was approached to subsidize a parent group, and in 1947 the National Theatre Organization was instituted. With headquarters in Pretoria, under the direction of P. P. Breytenbach, this body has gone from strength to strength. Numerous companies, playing in both official languages, tour all the large and most of the small towns, and on occasion South-West Africa and Rhodesia, successfully presenting work of quality where often none was known before. Local writing, particularly by Afrikaans dramatists, has been encouraged, and played before an audience constantly more enthusiastic and more discerning. (Article by Victor Glasstone, Cape Town.)

SPELVIN, GEORGE, a fictitious stage name used in the cast lists of American theatrical productions. It is first found in New York in 1886, in Charles A. Gardiner's play, *Karl the Peddler*. Spelvin's usefulness as a playbill identity to cover doubling persisted through the managements of George C. Tyler and William Collier, Sr. The latter, with his partner, Charles Reed, even gave him credit for gags used in a comedy, *Hoss and Hoss* (1895). He appeared in almost all the plays of Winchell Smith, and the late John Golden carried the tradition into the contemporary theatre. It is estimated that George Spelvin or his relatives (for several variations of the Christian name have been used) have figured in more than 10,000 Broadway performances since George's début. The name has also been applied, theatrically, to dead bodies, dolls substituting for babes in arms, and animal actors. *Theatre Arts* magazine has sporadically featured a critic of the critics who masquerades under Spelvin's name. (Information supplied by Mr. Robert Downing, The Players', N.Y. For the English counterpart of Spelvin, see PLINGE, S., p. 12.)

THÉÂTRE NATIONAL POPULAIRE. In 1920 Firmin Gémier sought to establish in France a popular theatre which should appeal to, and be supported by, the masses. After a chequered career, this enterprise found itself in 1937 in the Palais de Chaillot, with a newly-built theatre seating 2,700 spectators, a stage 70 feet deep and a proscenium opening 80 feet wide. It languished from lack of funds and audiences, until in 1951 Jean Vilar became its Director. He removed the footlights and batten lights from the theatre, and extended the forestage into the audience, thus providing a flexible stage for experimental productions. He inaugurated in Nov. 1951, with the 'Weekend de Suresnes', a series of suburban performances in large halls, where, for a small inclusive fee, the public was offered two plays, a lecture or discussion with the actors, a concert, two meals, and a dance. As well as these and other activities in Paris, the T.N.P., as it is usually called, plays at the Avignon Festival (founded by Vilar) and tours France and other countries. It was seen at Edinburgh in 1953 and in London in April 1956. Subsidized by the State, it is bound to give at least 150 performances in and around Paris every year, and must keep its prices low. Otherwise the Director is free to choose his plays and his company, which consists of some eighteen to twenty-five actors, on a yearly contract. Under Vilar's able direction, the T.N.P. has flourished, and is now one of the most important theatrical enterprises in France.

THEATRE WORKSHOP, a company founded in Kendal in the spring of 1946 by a group of actors, some of whom, according to their manifesto, were 'dissatisfied with the commercial theatre on artistic grounds . . . others . . . on social and political grounds'. Some of the original members had worked together in the north of England before 1939, and among them was Joan Littlewood, now producer and director of Theatre Workshop. For seven years the company toured Great Britain and Europe, seldom remaining more than a few weeks in the same place. It had no financial backing or official support, and all income was shared equally among the members. In 1953 they took over the derelict Theatre Royal at Stratford, London, E. 15, and after repairing and redecorating the interior they opened in February with a production of *Twelfth Night*. They were invited by the French organizers to represent Great Britain at the Paris International Theatre Festivals in 1955 and 1956, playing *Arden of Feversham* and *Volpone* on the first occasion, and *The Good Soldier Schweik* (adapted by Ewan McColl) on the second. On both occasions they were highly praised. One of their most interesting and controversial productions has been *Richard II*. On 24 May 1956 they produced a new Irish play on prison life, *The Quare Fellow*, which was later transferred to the Comedy Theatre. Their list of productions covers a wide range, and they have given first performances of a number of new plays and adaptations from English and foreign novels. In 1955 they gave the first performance in England of Brecht's *Mother Courage* at the Taw and Torridge Festival.

TOBY, a stock character in the folk theatre of the United States, a bucolic comedy juvenile leading man in provincial repertory companies of the Mississippi Valley and the Great Southwest. Most travelling dramatic tent shows, playing one-week stands in rural communities, feature a Toby-comedian, and he is also popular aboard the remaining show boats on inland American waters. Deriving from the *commedia dell'arte*, the Shakespeare clown, the conventional stage 'silly boy', and the Yankee comedian, Toby is the only standard character in the American theatre who is permitted to improvise within the framework of his background. He represents the country bumpkin triumphant over evil (usually personified as 'city slickers'). With a freckled face and a blacked-out front tooth, he wears a rumpled red wig, battered hat, calico shirt, baggy jeans, and large, ill-fitting boots or shoes. He first emerges in the 1900s, and Frederick R. Wilson, member of a touring tent show company known as Horace Murphy's Comedians, was the first of a long line of actors to specialize in Toby roles; plays have been specially written for him, and Broadway successes have been plagiarized with titles and plots altered to include Toby as the chief character. Toby-comedy includes generous use of the topical 'ad-lib', and expert use of such theatrical gymnastics as the pratt-fall, glides, splits, and rubber-legs. Toby sometimes leaves the stage during the play, and conducts his fooling in the audience. It is traditional in revivals of *Uncle Tom's Cabin* for the Toby-comedian of the troupe to don black-face and a gunnysack costume to impersonate Topsy. Toby frequently has a feminine counterpart in the company, the grand-daughter of the old-time 'rough soubrette', by the name of Susie. (Information supplied by Mr. Robert Downing, of The Players', New York.)

USTINOV, PETER ALEXANDER (1921–), English actor, dramatist, and producer, who through his mother Nadia is the grand-nephew of Alexandre Benois (see p. 74). His best work has a fantastic fairy-tale quality which nevertheless contains a hard core of commonsense and a shrewd perception of the problems of life today, in their international rather than their insular aspect. He combines these same qualities in his acting, joined to a great gift of mimicry. Trained under Saint-Denis at the London Theatre Studio, he made his first appearance in London in Aug. 1939, at the Players' Late Joys, in his own sketches, and was memorable as the aging opera-singer, Madame Liselotte Beethoven-Finck. After some miscellaneous experiences in repertory, revue, and straight plays in and around London, during which time his first play, a translation of Sarment's *Le Pêcheur d'ombres* as *Fishing for Shadows* (1940), was done at the Threshold Theatre, he joined the army. He returned to the stage in June 1946, playing Petrovitch in Rodney Ackland's adaptation of *Crime and Punishment*. In 1948 he appeared in his own adaptation of Ingmar Bergman's *Hets* (*Frenzy*), and in the following year produced and acted in Linklater's *Love in Albania*. Since then he has appeared mainly in his own plays, which include *House of Regrets* (1942), *Blow Your Own Trumpet* (1943), *The Banbury Nose* (1944), *The Tragedy of Good Intentions* (1945), *The Indifferent Shepherd* (1948), *The Moment of Truth* (1951), and *No Sign of the Dove* (1953). His first popular success in London was *The Love of Four Colonels* (1951), followed by the equally successful *Romanoff and Juliet* (1956), in both of which he gave excellent performances.

VILAR, JEAN (1912–), French actor and producer, who in 1951 was appointed head of the Théâtre National Populaire (T.N.P.). As a boy he showed great musical talent, but while studying in Paris in 1932 he attended a rehearsal of Dullin's production of *Richard III* at the Atelier, and decided to make the stage his career. He worked as Dullin's stage-manager for some years, playing also small parts, and after war service joined a company of young actors who toured the provinces. In 1943 he was seen in Paris in Synge's *The Well of the Saints*, and then took over the Théâtre de Poche, which seats only a hundred people. In 1945 he produced, first at the Vieux-Colombier and later in front of the Abbey of Bec-Hellouin, T. S. Eliot's *Murder in the*

Cathedral, with himself as Becket. This aroused general interest, and in 1947 Vilar was asked to organize a dramatic open-air summer festival at Avignon. This opened with the first production in France of *Richard II* and has since become an annual event. Plays by Shakespeare, Molière, Brecht, Kleist, as well as new plays by such authors as Claudel, Supervielle, and Montherlant, are given on an open stage in the Cour d'Honneur in the Palace of the Popes before an audience of some 2,700 people. Vilar, who is an excellent actor as well as a masterly and inspiring producer, has appeared in many of his own productions, notably as Macbeth, Don Juan, Ruy Blas, and Richard II. He was also seen in 1951 as Heinrich in Sartre's *Le Diable et le Bon Dieu*, and played Œdipe with the company of Jean-Louis Barrault and Madeleine Renaud.

WOLFIT [WOOLFITT], DONALD (1902–), English actor-manager, whose career has been spent mainly in the service of Shakespeare. He made his first appearance on the stage in York, walking on in *The Merchant of Venice* in Sept. 1920. After touring with Fred Terry, he appeared in London in Nov. 1924 as Phirous in *The Wandering Jew*. He was at the Old Vic from 1929 to 1930, toured Canada as Robert Browning in *The Barretts of Wimpole Street* during 1931–2, and in 1933 was Thomas Mowbray in *Richard of Bordeaux*. He was at Stratford-upon-Avon in 1936, and in the following year formed his own company, touring extensively in a Shakespearian repertory, with which he also appeared for a season at the Kingsway in 1940. During the Battle of Britain he gave over a hundred lunch-time performances of scenes from Shakespeare, which were much appreciated by those whom war and black-out would otherwise have debarred from the theatre. He continued to tour in Shakespeare and other classics, two of his best performances being as Volpone and Sir Giles Overreach (in *A New Way to Pay Old Debts*). He was excellent at the Old Vic in 1951 as Tamburlaine, and as Lord Ogleby in *The Clandestine Marriage*. In 1957 he appeared at the Lyric, Hammersmith, in two plays by Montherlant, *The Master of Santiago* and *Malatesta*. He is the author of an autobiography, *First Interval*, and in 1950 was created C.B.E. for his services to the English stage, and to Shakespeare in particular.

YUGOSLAVIA. The early history of the theatre in Yugoslavia is similar to that of other European countries. Greek and Roman spectacle-theatres (the ruins of which still exist and are sometimes used for performances) gave way to folk-drama of the indigenous peoples, and to mystery plays in the vernacular. The Jesuit school drama flourished, as elsewhere, and there were numerous visits from French and German companies. Yugoslavia has a dual-language theatre. The first performance in the Slovene language was given in 1789, but the aftermath of the Napoleonic wars prevented further developments. The first performance in the Croat language was given in 1840 in Zagreb, in a theatre built in 1834. The actors were the Novi Sad, Yugoslavia's first professional company, based on an amateur company founded by 'the father of the Serbian theatre', Joakim Vujic, in 1838. He also organized a Court theatre for the ruling prince, Milos, at Kragujevac. The Novi Sad was in Belgrade in 1842, but in the absence of a theatre building had to act in converted halls. The first workers' theatre was opened in Idrija in 1850, where plays in Slovene were given for the mining community there.

The theatre in Zagreb became a national institution with a State subsidy in 1861, and Croatian drama developed rapidly under D. Demetar and J. Frajdenrajh. In 1869 the present theatre in Belgrade was built (it has been rebuilt and modernized after damage during both world wars), and it was there that a permanent theatre, established in 1870, began its work. Meanwhile a Slovene theatre had been established in Ljubljana, where by 1867 no less than thirty-six plays in the Slovene language had been performed. Here, and in Belgrade and Zagreb, drama and opera flourished, though often under difficulties. The years between the two world wars were equally difficult, but new playwrights made their appearance until in 1941 all theatrical life came to a standstill with the German invasion. After the liberation companies of young actors were quickly formed, and played before soldier audiences and in the liberated towns. As in many other countries, there was a sudden expansion in theatrical activities, and Yugoslavia, which in 1939 had had twelve professional theatres, in 1949 had sixty-six. Many of these were in industrial towns and in remote places which had hitherto had no drama. In Macedonia, for instance, there are six theatres giving plays in Macedonian. Nor are the other minorities neglected. A Hungarian theatre was founded in Subotica in 1945. There is another at Backa Topola, a Shiptar theatre at Pristina, an Italian one at Rijeka, a Rumanian one at Vrsac, and a Turkish one at Skoplje. In 1948 a Yugoslav Dramatic Theatre was founded in Belgrade, with a company drawn from all parts of the country. This achieved great success at the International Dramatic Festival in Paris in July 1954 with a performance of Marin Drzic's *Dundo Maroje*. The repertory of the Yugoslav theatre now includes plays by such writers as the Serbian nineteenth-century author, Popović, the Slovene Ivan Cankar, and the contemporary playwright Miroslav Krleza, as well as plays by Shakespeare, Shaw, Gogol, Molière, Lope de Vega, and other classics, and modern English and American dramas.

ADDENDA AND CORRIGENDA

THIS list contains dates of death not given in the main volume, emendations of detail based on recent research, corrections of misprints, and a few brief additional notes.

p. 11. **ADAMS**, MAUDE, d. 1953.

p. 18. **ALEXANDRA THEATRE** (2), in Park Street, Camden Town. Opened 31 May 1873 (not 1874). *Friendship* was by Robert Reece.

p. 19. **ALFIERI**, l. 4. He was born in Asti (not Turin).

p. 20. **ALLGOOD** (2) MAIRE O'NEILL, b. 1887; d. 1952.

p. 28. **ANZENGRUBER**, LUDWIG, l. 6, *for* 1867 *read* 1870.

p. 33. **ARCHITECTURE, THEATRE**, 1st column, l. 15 from bottom, Max Littmann (not Littman) d. 1931.

p. 35. **ARMSTRONG**, WILLIAM, d. 1952. C.B.E. 1951.

p. 37. **ASCHE** (2) LILY BRAYTON, d. 1953.

—— **ASHWELL**, LENA, d. 1957.

p. 47. **BALIEFF**, NIKITA. A. E. Wilson points out that he was not 'a monkey-faced little man', but 'a big, burly man with a vast moon-face, who must have weighed at least 16 stone'.

p. 51. **BALLET**, 2nd column, l. 40, *for* Rubenstein *read* Rubinstein.

p. 58. **BARON** (4) ETIENNE, d. 1711 (not 1911).

pp. 61–62. **BARRYMORE** (3) LIONEL, d. 1954. In 1951 he published an autobiography, *We Barrymores, as told to Cameron Shipp*.

(6) The London WILLIAM BARRYMORE (1758–1830) opened the Old Vic, as the Royal Coburg (see illustr. No. 47), in 1818, with *Trial by Battle; or, Heaven Defend the Right*.

p. 62. **BASSERMANN** (2) ALBERT, d. 1952. He returned to Europe in 1945 and died at Zurich.

p. 63. **BATY**, GASTON, d. 1952.

p. 66. **BECK**, HEINRICH, l. 11, *for* Siegler *read* Ziegler.

—— **BECQUE**, *for* HENRI *read* HENRY.

p. 67. **BEERBOHM**, MAX, d. 1955.

p. 71. **BELL**, JOHN JOY, d. 1934 (not 1938).

p. 73. **BENAVENTE**, JACINTO, d. 1954.

p. 76. **BERNSTEIN**, ALINE, d. 1955.

p. 94. **BRAYTON**, LILY, d. 1953.

p. 100. **BROCHET**, HENRI, d. 1952.

p. 104. **BULGAKOV**, M. A., d. 1940.

p. 107. **BYRON**, LORD, l. 9, *for* Charles Kean *read* Macready; l. 11, *for* 1837 *read* 1838; l. 13, *for* 1814 *read* 1815. Macready first played *Werner* in 1830, Phelps revived it at Sadler's Wells in 1844, Irving at the Lyceum in 1887.

p. 113. **CANADA**, 2nd column, l. 33, *for* mitigated *read* militated.

p. 124. **CHEKHOV** (3) M. A., d. 1955.

p. 132. **CLAUDEL**, PAUL, d. 1955.

p. 138. **COLLIER**, CONSTANCE, d. 1955.

p. 144. **COMEDY THEATRE** (1) LONDON. Now the home of the New Watergate Theatre Club, which opened on 11 Oct. 1956 with Arthur Miller's *A View from the Bridge*.

(2) NEW YORK. The Washington Square Players were at this theatre from 1916 to 1918.

p. 157. **COSTANTINI**, l. 11, *for* soubriquet, *read* sobriquet.

p. 162. **COSTUME**, 10 (*a*), l. 13, *for* Ernst, *read* Ernest; l. 31, *for* 'Turan', dot *read* 'Turandot'.

p. 163. —— 10 (*c*), 2nd column, l. 22, *for* Parkes *read* Parks (b. 1905; d. 1955).

p. 164. **COURT THEATRE**, see ENGLISH STAGE COMPANY (S., p. 6).

p. 182. **DAVIS**, OWEN, d. 1956.

p. 186. **DEVRIENT** (8) HANS, d. 1927.

p. 190. **DODD**, LEE, l. 10, *for* 1920 *read* 1929.

p. 193. **DOWTON**, WILLIAM, l. 6, *for* 1795 *read* 1796.

p. 205. **DRURY LANE**, 1st column, l. 5 from bottom, *for* 1869 *read* 1889.

p. 208. **DUFRESNE**, l. 4, *for* d'Éperon *read* d'Épernon.

p. 221. **EMBASSY THEATRE**, closed 1955; taken over by the Central School, 1957.

p. 247. **ESMOND**, l. 3 from bottom, Eva Moore, d. 1955.

p. 250. **EVREINOV**, NIKOLAI, d. 1953.

—— **EYSOLDT**, GERTRUD, d. 1955.

p. 261. **FIELDING**, HENRY, l. 6, *for* 1736 *read* 1730.

p. 266. **FLECKER**, JAMES ELROY. Both *Don Juan* and *Hassan* have been revived, the former as an unofficial venture at the Gateway Theatre, Edinburgh, during the 1950 Festival, the latter by Basil Dean, with much splendour but little success, at the Cambridge Theatre, London, during the Festival of Britain (6 May 1951).

p. 268. **FOLIES-MARIGNY**. A circular building for a panorama was erected on the site of this theatre and is still standing. It became a music-hall in 1896, Marigny-Théâtre in 1901, Comédie-Marigny in 1913. In 1925 it was bought by Léon Volterra, whose widow still owns it. From 1946 to 1956 it housed the Barrault-Renaud company in a distinguished repertory of plays.

p. 273. **FORTUNY**, MARIANO, d. 1949.

p. 287. **FRANCE**, 2nd column, l. 34, *for* mitigated *read* militated.

p. 291. —— 1st column, l. 8, *for* tragedienne

read comedienne; 2nd column, l. 10 from bottom Henry (not Henri) Bernstein, d. 1953; l. 16 from bottom, *for* Porte-Riche *read* Porto-Riche; l. 24 from bottom, Paul Claudel, d. 1955.

p. 292. —— 1st column, l. 44. Henri René Lenormand, d. 1951 (not 1938); l. 45, Jean-Jacques Bernard, d. 1951; l. 55, Gaston Baty, d. 1952; 2nd column, l. 20, Mistinguett, d. 1956.

p. 296. **GAIETY THEATRE** (1) LONDON, 2nd column, l. 4, *for* Charles *read* Alfred; l. 3 from bottom, *The Toreador* was 1901.

p. 301. **GARRICK THEATRE** (1). Its first managers were Freer, Wyman, and the elder Conquest. It was burnt down in 1846 (not 1845). After Howe's bankruptcy in 1875 it remained empty for some time, but in 1879 Tree appeared there, under the management of Miss May Bulmer, and made a great success as Bonneteau in *A Cruise to China*. Shortly afterwards the building was demolished and a police station erected on the site.

p. 311. **GERMANY**, 1st column, l. 16, *for* 1710 *read* 1712.

p. 316. —— 2nd column, l. 5, Albert Bassermann, d. 1952.

p. 317. —— 1st column, l. 4 from bottom, Gertrud Eysoldt, d. 1955; 2nd column, l. 1, *for* Karl *read* Carl.

p. 318. —— 1st column, l. 20, Herbert Eulenberg, d. 1949; l. 20 from bottom, Leopold Jessner, d. 1945; 2nd column, l. 3, Bertolt Brecht, d. 1956 (see S., p. 2).

p. 319. **GHÉON**, HENRI, l. 18, Henri Brochet, d. 1952.

p. 321. **GILBERT**, SIR WILLIAM SCHWENCK. His first collaboration with Sullivan was not *Trial by Jury* but an operatic extravaganza *Thespis; or, The Gods Grown Old*, given at the Gaiety on 26 Dec. 1871.

p. 331. **GRAND THEATRE**, Islington, 2nd column, l. 10. Burnt down in Dec. 1887, this theatre was rebuilt and reopened in Aug. 1888.

p. 332. **GRECIAN THEATRE.** This opened in 1832 as a Concert Hall. The theatre licence was not issued until Benjamin Conquest took over in 1851.

p. 339. **GREENE**, ROBERT, 2nd column, l. 7. The 'malicious remark' was: 'An upstart crow beautified with our feathers, and in his opinion the only Shake-scene in the country.' l. 19. The 'romantic drama influenced by Marlowe' was *Alphonsus King of Aragon*, probably acted in 1587 (the year of *Tamburlaine*) or 1588, and now lost.

p. 342. **GRIFFITH**, HUBERT, d. 1953.

—— **GRILLPARZER**, FRANZ, 2nd column, last lines. *Libussa* was produced at the Burgtheater in Vienna two years after his death, with Charlotte Wolter in the title-role.

p. 345. **GUARINI**, *for* BATTISTA *read* GIOVANNI BATTISTA.

p. 351. **HAMPDEN**, WALTER, d. 1956.

p. 357. **HAYES**, HELEN. In 1956 the Fulton Theatre in New York was renamed the Helen Hayes in celebration of this actress's fifty years' services to the American stage.

p. 363. **HERCZEG**, FERENC, d. 1954.

p. 368. **HOLBORN THEATRE**, l. 10, *for* Herman *read* Hermann.

p. 369. **HOLLAND**, 1st column, l. 17 from bottom, *for* Pel *read* Pels; l. 26 from bottom, *for* Joost van Vondel *read* Joost van den Vondel.

p. 375. **HUNEKER**, JAMES, 2nd column, l. 18, comma after *Ivory*.

p. 376. **HUNGARY**, 2nd column, l. 21, Ferenč Molnar, d. 1952; l. 6 from bottom, Ferenč Herczeg, d. 1954.

p. 387. **INSET.** Sir St. Vincent Troubridge adds to this note: 'An inset is also a small set, such as a triangular room or attic, lowered from the flies, or set inside (i.e. in front of) a full set that does not have to be struck.'

p. 392. **ISAACS**, EDITH J., d. 1956.

p. 396. **ITALY**, 1st column, l. 18, *for* 1471 *read* 1472.

p. 407. ——, 1st column, l. 6 from bottom, Luigi Chiarelli, d. 1947; 2nd column, l. 18, Luigi Antonelli, d. 1942; l. 19, Enrico Cavacchioli, d. 1954; l. 45, Pier Maria Rosso di San Secondo, d. 1956.

p. 425. **JEWISH DRAMA.** 2nd column, l. 6, Leo Kobrin, d. 1946; l. 8, Solomon Libin is dead; date not known. 6. THE ART THEATRE PERIOD, l. 37, *for* Schwartz (1888–) *read* Schwartz (1889–).

p. 426. —— 1st column, l. 47. Peretz Markish, d. 1952; 2nd column, l. 8, Menahem Gnessin, d. 1953; l. 11, Isaac Daniel, d. 1935.

p. 430. **JONES**, ROBERT EDMOND, d. 1954.

p. 431. **JONSON**, BEN, 1st column, ll. 32–33, for *Cataline* read *Catilina*, for *Batholomew Fair* read *Bartholomew Fair*.

p. 436. **KEENE**, LAURA, 2nd column, l. 5 from end, *for* 15 Apr. *read* 14 Apr.

p. 437. **KEMBLE** (1) ROGER. His wife died on 24 Apr. 1807.

(2) JOHN PHILIP. His wife's first husband was William Brereton (1751–87). Her parents, Elizabeth and William Hopkins, were both on the stage. William acted in Edinburgh and in the provinces before coming to Drury Lane in 1761. He remained there as prompter until his death in 1780. Elizabeth died in 1801.

p. 440. **KINGSLEY**, SIDNEY, l. 1, *for* 1906 *read* 1907.

p. 441. **KINGSWAY THEATRE**, last line. This theatre is not in a fit state to be used.

p. 442. **KNICKERBOCKER THEATRE.** The last production was Philip Dunning's *Sweet Land of Liberty*, which opened on 23 Sept. and ran for eight performances.

p. 444. **KOMISARJEVSKY**, THEODORE, d. 1954.

p. 460. **LEWIS**, WILLIAM, l. 3, *for* soubriquet *read* sobriquet.

p. 470. **LIGHTING**, 2nd column, l. 33, Mariano Fortuny, d. 1949.

p. 478. **LINDSAY**, HOWARD, l. 3, *for* Russell *read* Russel.

p. 482. **LONSDALE**, FREDERICK, d. 1954.

p. 489. **MACCARTHY**, DESMOND, d. 1952. He was knighted in 1951 for services to the drama and to literature.

p. 494. **MACKAYE** (2) PERCY, d. 1956.

p. 512. **MALY THEATRE**, 1st column, l. 4, Alexander Ostuzhev, d. 1953.

p. 521. **MATHEWS** (3) LUCIA, l. 4, *for* Daughter *read* Grand-daughter.

p. 523. **MAYNE**, RUTHERFORD, l. 23, for *The Goneril* read *The Gomeril*.

p. 530. **MEYERHOLD**, V. E., d. 1943.

p. 535. **MISTINGUETT**, d. 1956.

p. 536. **MODJESKA**, HELENA, l. 1, *for* 1844 *read* 1840.

p. 537. **MOLIÈRE**, 2nd column, l. 22 from bottom, *for* Éperon *read* Épernon.

p. 539. **MOLNÁR**, FERENČ, d. 1952.

p. 546. **MOSKVIN**, I. M., d. 1946.

p. 550. **MURRAY**, T. C., l. 4, *delete comma after* distinguished.

p. 551. **MUSICAL COMEDY**, 1st column, l. 6, for *Floradora* read *Florodora*.

p. 552. **MUSIC-HALL**, 2nd column, l. 8, *for* Brummel *read* Brummell.

p. 555. ——— III. 11. *The London Pavilion*, l. 14, *for* G. H. Hunt *read* G. W. Hunt.

p. 556. ——— 1st column, l. 12, *In the Shadows* is not a waltz, but a dance written in 4/4.

p. 557. ——— 25. *The Tivoli*. This was closed in 1956, its contents sold by auction and the building demolished to make way for a block of offices.

p. 563. **NATIONWIDE THEATRE**, 1st column, l. 9 from bottom, *for* Alfred Koch *read* Frederick Koch.

p. 570. **NEGRO IN THE AMERICAN THEATRE**, 1st column, l. 8, *for* accidently *read* accidentally; l. 13, *for* McLendon *read* McClendon.

p. 581. **OKHLOPKOV**, N. P., l. 5, *insert* a *before* May-Day.

p. 584. **O'NEILL**, EUGENE, d. 1953. He was awarded the Nobel Prize for Literature in 1936. His posthumous play *A Long Day's Journey into Night* (written in 1941, publ. 1956) was first performed in Sweden in 1955, in Germany early in 1956, in New York later in the same year.

p. 586. **OPERA**, 2nd column, l. 10, the Parigi were not brothers but father and son.

p. 591. **OPERA COMIQUE**. This theatre opened 29 Oct. 1870 (not 1871) with a French company headed by Mlle Déjazet. The company of the Comédie-Française which came in 1871 was headed by Gôt. The theatre was reconstructed in 1885. The Gilbert and Sullivan collaboration did not start with *Trial*

by Jury at the Royalty, but with *Thespis; or, The Gods Grown Old* at the Gaiety in 1871.

p. 597. **PALACE THEATRE**. Sullivan's 'Ivanhoe' had 160 performances. Its successor was Messager's 'La Basoche', which failed. In recent years the Palace has been used for companies of foreign actors and dancers (T.N.P., Barrault, Berliner Ensemble, Antonio, &c.) brought to London by the initiative of Peter Daubeny.

p. 598. **PALMER**, ALBERT, 1st column, l. 10, *for* Brummel *read* Brummell.

p. 601. **PARIGI**, l. 2, they were not brothers but father and son. Giulio b. 1590, d. 1636 (not 1635).

——— **PARKER**, JOHN, d. 1952.

p. 603. **PARK THEATRE** (2), l. 9, *for* Sellars *read* Sellers.

——— **PASSION PLAY**. The first performance at Oberammergau was 1634 (not 1633).

p. 625. **POLIZIANO** (sometimes spelt, particularly in American books, Politian), l. 1, *for* Ambrozini *read* Ambrogini.

p. 653. **QUEUE**, l. 12, *for* name *read* number.

p. 660. **RAYMOND**, JOHN T., l. 15, *for* Sellars *read* Sellers.

p. 666. **REVOLVING STAGE**, delete ARCHITECTURE and MACHINERY.

p. 668. **RICH** (2) JOHN. Paul Sawyer, in *Theatre Notebook*, vol. viii, No. 2, p. 48, points out that John Rich must have been born c. 1692, not c. 1682. He cites as evidence Rich's tombstone and several contemporary estimates of his age as 69–70 when he died in 1761.

p. 670. **ROBEY**, GEORGE, d. 1954. Knighted for services to the stage 1954.

p. 671. **ROBINS**, ELIZABETH, b. 1862 (not 1865), d. 1952.

p. 715. **SCENERY, THEATRICAL**, 6. THE MODERN PERIOD, 2nd column, l. 11, *for* German-speaking *read* French-speaking.

p. 717. ——— 1st column, l. 29, Robert Edmond Jones, d. 1954; 2nd column, l. 10 from bottom, Vsevolod Meyerhold, d. 1943; l. 28 from bottom, Gaston Baty, d. 1952.

p. 718. ——— 1st column, l. 2, Alexander Taïrov, d. 1950.

p. 721. **SCHWARTZ**, MAURICE, l. 1, *for* 1888 *read* 1889.

p. 733. **SHAKESPEARE**, 2nd column. The first paragraph should read: The first Swedish translations were made in 1847–51 by Carl August Hagberg. Per Hallström's magnificent translations into Swedish, on which he worked for ten years, were published in the 1920s and 1930s. A Danish actor, Peter Foersom (not Folsom), published, before he died in 1817, four volumes of translations. . . . There are also modern Norwegian translations of outstanding value.

p. 737. **SHERWOOD**, ROBERT, d. 1955.

p. 740. **SHUBERT** (1) LEE, d. 1953.

p. 742. **SINCLAIR**, Arthur, d. 1951.

p. 758. **SPAIN**, 6. Nineteenth Century, l. 18, for *del sino* read *de sino*; 2nd column, l. 2 from bottom, Jacinto Benavente, d. 1954.

p. 759. —— 1st column, l. 14, Manuel Linares Rivas, b. 1878 (not 1867), d. 1938; l. 17, Eduardo Marquina, d. 1946; l. 22, Ramón María de Valle-Inclán, d. 1936; l. 32, Rafael Alberti, who now lives in South America, was born in 1902 (not 1903).

p. 762. **SPEECH**, l. 9 from end, *for* I-there *read* I-ther.

p. 767. **STAGE DIRECTIONS**. Edward A. Langhans points out (*The Theatre Annual*, 1956, p. 51) that the references given at the end of this article are not from *The Sisters*, but from Theobald's *The Perfidious Brother*, published in 1715 and produced at Lincoln's Inn Fields a year later.

p. 772. **STOLL**, Sir Oswald. His first experience was gained at the Star Music Hall, Cardiff, under his mother's management, before he went to Liverpool. l. 16 *for* always *read* almost.

p. 776. **SUBURBAN THEATRES**. The Fulham Grand and the Stoke Newington Alexandra have been closed, The Kings, Hammersmith, is a B.B.C. studio and the Kilburn is a cinema. Some fifteen other surburban theatres have also been closed or adapted for other uses.

p. 778. **SURREY THEATRE**. Elliston (not Thomas Dibdin) named it the Surrey in 1809. The name was used permanently from 1819 onwards. George Conquest took over in 1881 (not 1880).

p. 782. **TAÏROV**, A. Y., d. 1950.

p. 785. **TEARLE** (3) Godfrey, d. 1953. Knighted for services to the stage in the Birthday Honours of 1951.

—— **TENNYSON**, l. 19. *Harold* was given by the Birmingham Repertory Company at the Court Theatre, London, in Apr. 1928, with Laurence Olivier as Harold. Robert Speaight, Ralph Richardson, and Gwen Ffrangcon-Davies were also in the cast.

p. 787. **TERRY** (3) Kate, l. 12, *for* two daughters *read* four daughters.

p. 789. **THEATRE ARTS**. This magazine was amalgamated with *Stage* in 1948, and under its original name (not *New Theatre Arts*) and the editorship of John D. MacArthur continues to appear monthly.

p. 790. **THEATRE GUILD**. Kenneth Macgowan writes: 'The Washington Square Players were founded in 1914, began productions in 1915, and moved from the Bandbox to the Comedy in 1916.'

—— **THEATRE LIBRARY ASSOCIATION**, l. 4, *for* Feedley *read* Freedley. The first number of *Broadside* was published in May 1940.

p. 792. **THORNDIKE** (3) Eileen, d. 1953.

p. 793. **TIECK**, Ludwig. It was not Tieck who completed Schlegel's translations of Shakespeare, but his daughter Dorothea Tieck.

—— **TILLEY**, Vesta, d. 1952.

p. 800. **TRENEV**, K. A., d. 1945.

p. 811. **UNITED STATES OF AMERICA**, 2nd column, l. 14, Maude Adams, d. 1953.

p. 812. —— 1st column, l. 8 from bottom, Robert Edmond Jones, d. 1954; 2nd column, l. 18, Eugene O'Neill, d. 1953.

p. 813. —— 1st column, l. 2, Robert Sherwood, d. 1955; l. 30, Robert Edmond Jones, d. 1954; 2nd column, l. 27, *for* 1904 *read* 1905.

p. 814. —— 2nd column, l. 21, Mrs. Edith J. Isaacs, d. 1956.

p. 815. —— 2nd column, l. 17, *for* 1917 *read* 1916.

p. 816. —— 1st column, l. 18, *for* 'Shanweis' *read* 'Shanewis'.

p. 823. **VAUDEVILLE**, 1st column, l. 23 from bottom, Elsie Janis, d. 1956; 2nd column, l. 24, Vesta Tilley, d. 1952.

p. 825. **VELTEN**, Johannes, d. 1692 (not 1695).

p. 828. **VISHNEVSKY**, V. V., d. 1951.

p. 831. **WADE**, Allan, d. 1954.

p. 846. **WOODWARD**, Harry. He made his first appearance, not in 1730, but on 2 Jan. 1729 in a performance of *The Beggar's Opera* given by a children's company known as the Lilliputians. He played three small parts.

p. 851. **YOUNG**, Charles, l. 3. He was born in Australia.

p. 853. **ZACCONI**, Ermete, b. 1856 (not 1867); d. 1948.

p. 855. **ZUCKMAYER**, Carl. *Der Teufels General* was done in London, as *The Devil's General*, in Sept. 1953 at the Savoy Theatre.

p. 860. **AMATEUR THEATRE**, 4th item, *for* Downes *read* Downs.

p. 861. **BALLET**, W. J. Turner, for *English Ballet* read *The English Ballet*.

p. 880. 1st column, 2nd item, *for* 1870 *read* 1828.

p. 881, 1st column, 3rd item, *for* Dibden *read* Dibdin.

SUPPLEMENTARY BIBLIOGRAPHY

THIS short-title list contains a selection of books on the theatre (not including Ballet and Opera) published in England and America between 1949 and 1956. A few earlier works, and some foreign books, have been included. Except in the General and Technical sections, books are arranged alphabetically by authors. The same abbreviations have been used as in the Main Bibliography.

Attention is drawn to the lavishly-illustrated *Enciclopedia dello Spettacolo* (text in Italian), which is in course of publication. This covers the history of all forms of theatrical entertainment throughout the world. It will be complete in eight volumes, of which three have so far (1957) appeared.

GENERAL BOOKS

1. Reference Books

The Player's Library: The Catalogue of the Library of the British Drama League, London, 1950; First Supplement, 1951; Second Supplement, 1954; Third Supplement (with a catalogue of Plays in French), 1956.

The Theatre of the British Isles, excluding London, a Bibliography compiled by ALFRED LOEWENBERG, London, 1950.

2. Drama and General History

GEORGE ALTMAN, RALPH FREUD, KENNETH MACGOWAN, WILLIAM MELNITZ: *Theater Pictorial*, Ill., California U.P., 1953.

DANIEL C. BOUGHNER: *The Braggart in Renaissance Comedy*, Minnesota U.P. and London, 1954, B.

KENNETH MACGOWAN and WILLIAM MELNITZ: *The Living Stage. A History of World Theater*, Ill., N.Y., 1955, B.

A. M. NAGLER: *Sources of Theatrical History*, Ill., N.Y., 1952, B.

ALLARDYCE NICOLL: *World Drama from Aeschylus to Anouilh*, Ill., London, 1949.

3. Modern Drama

ERIC BENTLEY: *In Search of Theater*, Ill., N.Y., 1953, London, 1955.

JOHN GASSNER: *The Theatre in our Times*, N.Y., 1954.

MARTIN LAMM: *Modern Drama*, tr. from the Swedish, Oxford, 1952.

RAYMOND WILLIAMS: *Drama from Ibsen to Eliot*, London, 1952.

TECHNICAL BOOKS

1. General Stagecraft, including Scenery

The English translation of Sonrel's book has not yet appeared. Readers are referred to the original volume, *Traité de scénographie*, Ill., Paris, 1943, B.

W. P. BOYLE: *Central and Flexible Staging*, Ill., California U.P. and London, 1956.

TOBY COLE and HELEN KRICH CHINOY (Eds.): *Directing the Play. A Sourcebook of Stagecraft*, Ill., N.Y. and London, 1953, B.

E. CROFT-MURRAY: *John Devoto, a Baroque Scene Painter*, Ill., London, 1953.

J. E. DIETRICH: *Play Direction*, Ill., N.Y., 1953, London, 1955.

NICOLE DECUGIS et SUZANNE REYMOND: *Le Décor de Théâtre en France du Moyen-Âge à 1925*, Ill., Paris, 1953, B.

GUIDO FRETTE: *Stage Design, 1909–54*, Ill., London, 1956.

PETER GOFFIN: *The Art and Science of Stage Management*, London, 1953.

WILFRID A. GRANVILLE: *A Dictionary of Theatrical Terms*, London, 1952.

HUGH HUNT: *The Director in the Theatre*, London, 1954.

STEPHEN JOSEPH: *Theatre-in-the-Round*, Ill., London, 1955.

JANOS SCHOLZ (Ed.): *Baroque and Romantic Stage Design*, Ill., N.Y., 1955, B.

LEE SIMONSON: *The Art of Scenic Design*, Ill., N.Y. and London, 1950.

RICHARD SOUTHERN: *The Open Stage*, Ill., London, 1953.

—— *Changeable Scenery: Its origin and development in the British Theatre*, Ill., London, 1951.

ERNEST STERN: *My Life, My Stage*, Ill., London, 1951.

A. NICHOLAS VARDAC: *Stage to Screen. Theatrical Method from Garrick to Griffith*, Ill., Harvard U.P. and London, 1949.

2. Architecture and Acoustics

C. WALTER HODGES: *The Globe Restored*, Ill., London, 1953.

RICHARD LEACROFT: *Civic Theatre Design*, Ill., London, 1949.

HÉLÈNE LECLERC: *Les Origines italiennes de l'architecture théâtrale moderne*, Ill., Paris, 1946, B.

Manual of Safety Requirements in Theatres and other places of public entertainment (H.M. Stationery Office), London, latest ed., 1949.

H. BURRIS MEYER and E. C. COLE: *Theatres and Auditoriums*, Ill., N.Y., 1949.

A. CARRI RAMELLI: *Edifici per gli Spettacoli*, Ill., Milan, 1945.

[23]

3. Costume

WOLFGANG BRUHN and MAX TILKE: *A Pictorial History of Costume*, tr. from the German, Ill., London, 1955.

MILLIA DAVENPORT: *The Book of Costume*, 2 vols., Ill., N.Y., 1948, London, 1954.

HENNY HARALD HENSEN: *Costume Cavalcade*, tr. from the Danish, Ill., London, 1956, B.

JAMES LAVER: *Drama; its costume and décor*, Ill., London, 1951, B.
—— (Ed.): *Costume of the Western World*, Vol. 3 (in six parts); *The Tudors to Louis XIII*, Ill., London, 1951.

MARGOT LISTER: *Stage Costume*, Ill., London, 1954.

4. Lighting

FREDERICK BENTHAM: *Stage Lighting*, Ill., London, 1950.

P. CORRY: *Lighting the Stage*, Ill., London, 1954, B.

5. Scene-painting

ROBERT FORMAN: *Scene Painting*, Ill., London, 1950.

AMATEUR THEATRE

P. CORRY: *Stage Planning and Equipment for Multi-Purpose Halls*, Ill., London, 1949.

WILLARD J. FRIEDERICH and JOHN H. FRAZER: *Scenery Design for the Amateur Stage*, Ill., N.Y. and London, 1951.

NORAH LAMBOURNE: *Dressing the Play*, Ill., London, 1953, B.
—— *Staging the Play*, Ill., London, 1956, B.

CALLUM MILL: *Make-Up for the Amateurs*, Ill., London, 1955, B.

ALAN NELSON-SMITH: *The Business Side of the Amateur Theatre*, London, 1953.

NOVA PILBEAM: *Acting on the Amateur Stage*, Ill., London, 1953.

ART OF ACTING

S. D. BALUKHATY (Ed.): *'The Seagull' produced by Stanislavsky*, tr. from the Russian, Ill., London, 1952.

JEAN-LOUIS BARRAULT: *Reflections on the Theatre*, tr. from the French, Ill., London, 1951.

TOBY COLE (Ed.): *Acting and the Stanislavski Method*, Ill., N.Y. and London, 1947.

NIKOLAI M. GORCHAKOV: *Stanislavsky Directs*, tr. from the Russian, N.Y. and London, 1955.

B. L. JOSEPH: *Elizabethan Acting*, London, 1951.

MICHAEL REDGRAVE: *The Actor's Ways and Means*, Ill., London, 1953.

COMMEDIA DELL'ARTE

G. ATTINGER: *L'Esprit de la commedia dell'arte dans le théâtre français*, Paris, 1950.

THELMA NIKLAUS: *Harlequin Phoenix, or the Rise and Fall of a Bergamask Rogue*, Ill., London, 1956, B.

DRAMATIC CRITICISM

HAROLD DOWNS: *The Critic in the Theatre*, London, 1953.

HAROLD HOBSON: *Verdict at Midnight. Sixty Years of Dramatic Criticism*, London, 1952.

LEIGH HUNT: *Dramatic Criticism, 1808–1831*, N.Y., 1949, London, 1950.

HENRY JAMES: *The Scenic Art. Notes on acting and the drama, 1872–1901*, London, 1949.

CHARLES RICE: *The London Theatre in the Eighteen-Thirties*, London, 1950.

KENNETH TYNAN: *He That Plays the King. A View of the Theatre*, London, 1950.

ECCLESIASTICAL DRAMA

HARDIN CRAIG: *English Religious Drama of the Middle Ages*, Oxford, 1955, B.

GRACE FRANK: *The Medieval French Drama*, Oxford, 1954, B.

CARL J. STRATMAN (Ed.): *Bibliography of Medieval Drama*, California U.P. and London, 1955.

P. R. VINCENT: *The 'Jeu de Saint Nicholas' of Jean Bodel of Arras: a literary analysis*, Oxford, 1955.

ENGLAND

Attention is drawn to the importance of Henslowe's *Diary* (2 vols., 1904–8) and *The Henslowe Papers* (1907), both edited by Walter Greg, as essential documents for the Elizabethan theatre.

WINIFRED BANNISTER: *James Bridie and his theatre*, London, 1955.

G. E. BENTLEY: *Jacobean and Caroline Stage*, Vols. 3–5, Oxford, 1956.

FREDERICK BOAS: *An Introduction to 18th-Century Drama, 1700–80*, Oxford, 1953.

J. W. BOWYER: *The celebrated Mrs. Centlivre*, Ill., London, 1953, B.

M. C. BRADBROOK: *Growth and Structure of Elizabethan Comedy*, London, 1955.

CHARLES DIBDIN (the younger): *Memoirs*, ed. by G. Speaight, London, 1956.

MAURICE WILLSON DISHER: *Melodrama. Plots that Thrilled*, Ill., London, 1955.

RICHARD FINDLATER: *The Unholy Trade*, London, 1952, B.

FRANCES FLEETWOOD: *Conquest. The Story of a Theatre Family*, Ill., London, 1953, B.

THOMAS H. FUJIMURA: *The Restoration Comedy of Wit*, Princeton and London, 1952, B.

G. L. HOSKING: *The Life and Times of Edward Alleyn*, Ill., London, 1951.

LEE HUGHES: *A Century of English Farce (Restoration to Mid-18th Century)*, Princeton and London, 1956, B.

SUPPLEMENTARY BIBLIOGRAPHY

LAURENCE IRVING: *Henry Irving. The Actor and his World*, Ill., London, 1951, B.

JAMES J. LYNCH: *Box, Pit and Gallery. Stage and Society in Johnson's London*, Ill., Cambridge, 1953.

RAYMOND MANDER and JOE MITCHENSON: *Theatrical Companion to the Plays of Shaw*, Ill., London, 1955.

—— *Theatrical Companion to Maugham*, Ill., London, 1955.

HESKETH PEARSON: *The Last Actor-Managers*, Ill., London, 1956.

—— *Beerbohm Tree. His Life and Laughter*, Ill., London, 1956.

HARRY WILLIAM PEDICORD: *The Theatrical Public in the time of Garrick*, N.Y., 1954, B.

REX POGSON: *Miss Horniman and the Gaiety Theatre, Manchester*, Ill., London, 1952.

ROBERT RENTOUL REED: *Bedlam on the Jacobean Stage*, Harvard and London, 1952, B.

SYBIL ROSENFELD: *Foreign Theatrical Companies in Great Britain in the 17th and 18th Centuries*, London, 1955.

A. P. ROSSITER: *English Drama from Early Times to the Elizabethans*, London, 1950.

GEORGE ROWELL: *The Victorian Theatre, a survey*, Ill., London, 1956, B.

PERCY SIMPSON: *Studies in Elizabethan Drama*, Oxford, 1955.

JOHN HARRINGTON SMITH: *The Gay Couple in Restoration Comedy*, Harvard and London, 1948.

ROBERT SPEAIGHT: *William Poel and the Elizabethan Revival*, Ill., London, 1954.

Studies in English Theatre History, in memory of Gabrielle Enthoven, London, 1952.

ALINE MACKENZIE TAYLOR: *Next to Shakespeare. Otway . . . on the London Stage*, Ill., Duke U.P., 1950, B.

J. C. TREWIN: *Mr. Macready, a 19th-Century Tragedian and his Theatre*, Ill., London, 1955, B.

EUGENE M. WAITH: *The Pattern of Tragicomedy in Beaumont and Fletcher*, Yale and London, 1952.

A. C. WARD: *Bernard Shaw*, Ill., London, 1951, B.

AUDREY WILLIAMSON: *Theatre of Two Decades*, Ill., London, 1951.

A. E. WILSON: *Edwardian Theatre*, Ill., London, 1951.

W. J. WIMSATT (Ed.): *English Stage Comedy*, N.Y. and London, 1955.

FAR EASTERN THEATRES

MULK RAJ ANAND: *The Indian Theatre*, Ill., London, 1950.

FAUBION BOWERS: *Japanese Theatre*, Ill., N.Y. and London, 1954.

—— *Theatre in the East*, Ill., N.Y. and London, 1956, B.

EARLE ERNST: *The Kabuki Theatre*, Ill., London, 1956.

U. P. NI: *Konmara Pya Zat. An Example of Popular Burmese Drama in the 19th-Century*, tr. from the Burmese by H. Pe, London, 1952.

E. R. SARATHCHANDRA: *The Sinhalese Folk Play and the Modern Stage*, Ill., Colombo, 1953.

A. C. SCOTT: *The Kabuki Theatre of Japan*, Ill., London, 1955, B.

—— *The Classical Theatre of China*, Ill., London, 1956, B.

FRANCE

GEOFFREY BRERETON: *Jean Racine, a critical biography*, Ill., London, 1951, B.

J. CHIARI: *The Poetic Drama of Paul Claudel*, N.Y. and London, 1954.

MARGARET CROSLAND: *Jean Cocteau*, Ill., London, 1955, B.

MAY DANIELS: *The French Drama of the Unspoken*, Edinburgh, 1953, B.

HAROLD HOBSON: *The French Theatre of Today, an English View*, London, 1953.

GRACE PAULINE IHRIG: *Heroines in French Drama of the Romantic Period, 1829–48*, N.Y., 1950, B.

HENRY CARRINGTON LANCASTER: *French Tragedy in the Time of Louis XV and Voltaire, 1715–44*, 2 vols., Baltimore and London, 1950, B.

—— *French Tragedy in the Reign of Louis XVI and the Early Years of the French Revolution, 1774–92*, Baltimore and London, 1953, B.

T. E. LAWRENSON: *The French Stage in the 17th Century*, Ill., London, 1956.

JAMES C. MCLAREN: *The Theatre of André Gide*, Oxford, 1953, B.

EDWARD OWEN MARSH: *Jean Anouilh, poet of Pierrot and Pantaloon*, Ill., London, 1953.

JOANNA RICHARDSON: *Rachel*, Ill., London, 1956, B.

E. VINAVER: *Racine and Poetic Tragedy*, tr. from the French, Manchester, 1955.

GERMANY AND AUSTRIA

W. H. BRUFORD: *Theatre, Drama and Audience in Goethe's Germany*, London, 1950, B.

H. B. GARLAND: *Schiller*, N.Y., 1950.

HUGH F. GARTEN: *Hauptmann*, London, 1954, B.

RICHARD MARCH: *Heinrich von Kleist*, London, 1954, B.

E. L. STAHL: *Friedrich Schiller's Drama. Theory and Practice*, Oxford, 1954, B.

GREECE AND ROME

GEORGE E. DUCKWORTH: *The Nature of Roman Comedy*, Ill., Princeton and London, 1952, B.

[25]

L. H. G. Greenwood: *Aspects of Euripidean Tragedy*, London, 1953.

H. D. F. Kitto: *Form and Meaning in Drama. A Study of Six Greek Plays and Hamlet*, London, 1956.

F. J. H. Letters: *Life and Work of Sophocles*, London, 1953.

Katherine Lever: *The Art of Greek Comedy*, London, 1956.

F. L. Lucas: *Greek Drama for Everyman*, London, 1954.

Gilbert Norwood: *Essays in Euripidean Drama*, London, 1954.

A. W. Pickard-Cambridge: *The Dramatic Festivals of Athens*, Ill., Oxford, 1953, B.

A. J. M. Waldock: *Sophocles the Dramatist*, Cambridge, 1951, B.

T. B. L. Webster: *Studies in Later Greek Comedy*, Ill., Manchester, 1953.

—— *Greek Theatre Production*, Ill., London, 1956.

POPULAR ENTERTAINMENT

V. C. Clinton-Baddeley: *The Burlesque Tradition in the English Theatre after 1660*, Ill., London, 1952, B.

—— *All Right on the Night*, Ill., London, 1954.

Marjorie Batchelder: *Rod Puppets and the Human Theatre*, Ill., N.Y., 1947, B.

Jacques-Charles: *Cent ans de Music-Hall*, Ill., Paris, 1956.

Jacques Chesnais: *Histoire générale des marionnettes*, Ill., Paris, 1947, B.

Richard Findlater: *Grimaldi, King of Clowns*, Ill., London, 1955, B.

André-Charles Gervais: *Marionnettes et marionnettistes de France*, Ill., Paris, 1947, B.

James Grant: *Penny Theatres* (from *Sketches in London, 1838*), Ill., London, 1952.

Karagöz: son histoire, ses personnages, son esprit mystique et satirique, Ill., Istanbul, 1951.

Paul McPharlin: *The Puppet Theatre in America*, Ill., N.Y., 1949.

Tristan Rémy: *Jean-Gaspard Deburau*, Ill., Paris, 1954.

G. Le Roy: *Music-Hall Stars of the Nineties*, Ill., London, 1952.

Bernard Sobel: *A Pictorial History of Burlesque*, Ill., N.Y., 1956.

George Speaight: *A History of the English Puppet Theatre*, Ill., London, 1955, B.

RUSSIA

Ronald Hingley: *Chekhov*, Ill., London, 1950, B.

J. Lavrin: *Nikolai Gogol*, London, 1952.

David Margarshack: *Chekhov*, Ill., London, 1952, B.

David Margarshack: *Stanislavsky*, Ill., London, 1953.

—— *Turgenev*, Ill., London, 1954, B.

B. V. Vareke: *A History of the Russian Theatre*, N.Y., 1951.

(See also Art of Acting.)

WILLIAM SHAKESPEARE
1564–1616

Cécile de Banke: *Shakespearean Stage Production, then and now*, Ill., N.Y. and London, 1954, B.

Marchette Chute: *Shakespeare of London*, N.Y. and London, 1951, B.

F. E. Halliday: *A Shakespeare Companion, 1550–1950*, Ill., London, 1952, B.

Alfred Harbage: *A Theatre for Shakespeare*, Toronto and London, 1955.

Charles Beecher Hogan: *Shakespeare in the Theatre, a Record of Performances in London, 1701–50*, N.Y. and Oxford, 1952.

Leslie Hotson: *The First Night of 'Twelfth Night'*, N.Y. and London, 1954.

T. C. Kemp and J. C. Trewin: *The Stratford Festival*, Ill., Birmingham, 1953.

Allardyce Nicoll (Ed.): *Shakespeare Survey*, Ill., London, annually since 1948, B.

Jaroslav Pokorny: *Shakespeare in Czechoslovakia*, Ill., Prague, 1955.

Arthur Colby Sprague: *Shakespearian Players and Performances*, Ill., Harvard and London, 1953.

—— *The Stage Business in Shakespeare's Plays: A Postscript*, London, 1954.

Margaret Webster: *Shakespeare Today*, London, 1957.

U.S.A.

Daniel Blum: *A Pictorial History of the American Theatre, 1900–50*, Ill., N.Y., 1950.

Alan S. Downer: *Fifty Years of American Drama, 1900–50*, Chicago, 1951.

Edwin A. Engel: *The Haunted Heroes of Eugene O'Neill*, Harvard and London, 1953.

Edmond N. Gagey: *Annals of the San Francisco Stage*, Ill., N.Y. and London, 1950, B.

Philip Graham: *Showboats. The History of an American Institution*, Ill., Austin, Texas, 1951, B.

Margo Jones: *Theatre-in-the-Round*, Ill., N.Y., 1951, B.

Wisner Payne Kinne: *George Pierce Baker and the American Theatre*, Ill., N.Y., 1954, B.

Felix Sper: *From Native Roots. A Study of American Folk Drama*, Ill., Idaho, 1948.

LIST OF ILLUSTRATIONS

LIST OF ILLUSTRATIONS

LIST OF ILLUSTRATIONS

1. Theatre at Epidaurus

2. Theatre at Priene

3. Marble mask (male)

4. Marble mask (female)

5. Actor (terracotta)

6. Actor (ivory)

7. Iphigenia in Tauris

8. The Revenge of Medea

9. Theatre at Verulamium (St. Albans)

10. Menander with masks

11. A tragic scene

12. A comic scene

13. Actor with mask

14. A performance in Pekin

15. The Monkey God   16. Mei-Lan-Fang

17. A Kabuki stage

18. A Nō stage

19. Javanese rod-puppets

20. Javanese shadow-figures

21. A shadow-play

22. Javanese shadow-figures

23. A religious drama

24. Hell-mouth

25. A secular comedy

26. La Ballerina

27. Coviello

28. Pantalone

29. Harlequino

30. Pagliaccio

31. Scaramuccia

32. Il Capitano Spezzafer

33. Colombine

34. A Harlequinade at Covent Garden, *c.* 1770

35. Punch and Judy, 1888

36. *Dick Whittington and his Cat*, 1852

37. *Puss in Boots*, 1887

38. Teatro Olimpico, Vicenza

39. Theatre at Sabbioneta

40. The Swan Theatre, London

41. A Commonwealth stage, London

42. Dorset Garden, London

43. Bristol Theatre Royal

44. Chestnut Street Theatre, Philadelphia

45. Drury Lane, London

46. Covent Garden, London

47. The Royal Coburg, London

48. Theatre at Eastbourne

49. The Old Vic, London

50. Penthouse Theatre, U.S.A.

51. The Old Burgtheater, Vienna

52. The New Burgtheater, Vienna

53. The Comédie-Française, Paris

54. The Athénée Saint-Germain, Paris

55. The Bolshoi, Moscow

56. The Grosses Schauspielhaus, Berlin

57. The first Schouwburg, Amsterdam

58. The rebuilt Schouwburg, Amsterdam

59. Drottningholm, Sweden

60. The City Theatre, Malmö, Sweden

61. The San Carlos, Lisbon

62. Drury Lane, London

63. The Bolshoi, Moscow

64. The Bolshoi, Minsk

65. The Bowery Theatre, New York

66. The Cleveland Playhouse, Ohio, U.S.A.

67. The Globe Playhouse, London

68. The Surrey Theatre, London

69. The old theatre at Stratford-upon-Avon

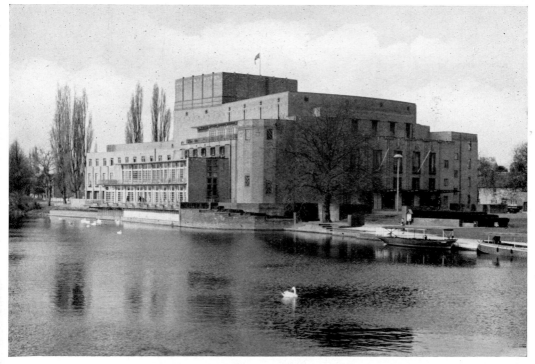

70. The new theatre at Stratford-upon-Avon

71. Rustic Scene

72. Comic Scene

73. Tragic Scene

Serlio, 1545

74. Buontalenti

75. Parigi

76. Torelli

77. Galli-Bibbiena family

78. Schinkel, *Die Jungfrau von Orleans*

79. Saxe-Meiningen, *Miss Sara Sampson*

80. Inigo Jones

81. Eighteenth century

82. Early nineteenth century

83. Late nineteenth century

84. *Othello, 1837*

85. *Macbeth, 1853*

86. *Romeo and Juliet*, 1882

87. *Hamlet*, 1900

88. *Henry VIII*, 1910

89. *Twelfth Night*, 1912

90. *Hamlet* 1913

91. *Macbeth,* 1928

92. *The Taming of the Shrew*, 1937

93. *Henry VIII*, 1949

94. *King Lear*, 1955

95. *The Merry Wives of Windsor,* 1955

96. *Twelfth Night*, 1914

97. *Romeo and Juliet*, 1930

98. Othello, 1937

99. Antony and Cleopatra, 1947

100. *Henry IV, Part I,* in Germany, 1912

101. *The Merchant of Venice* in Czechoslovakia, 1931

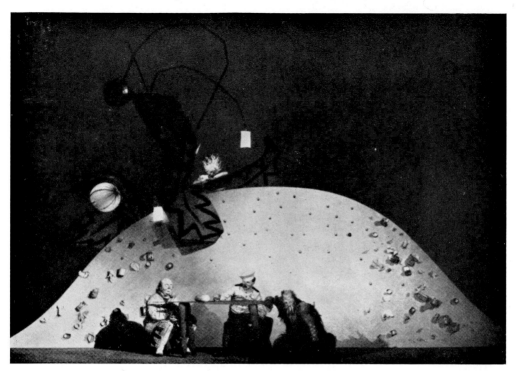

102. *The Tempest* in Sweden, 1934

103. *Hamlet* in Russia, 1954

104. *Rosmersholm*, Oslo, 1906

105. *Peer Gynt*, London, 1944

106. *The Three Sisters*, 1901

107. *Marriage*, 1950

108. *Le malade imaginaire*, 1674

109. *Le bourgeois gentilhomme*, 1952

110. *La Folle de Chaillot*, 1945

111. *L'Annonce faite à Marie*, 1955

112. *St. Joan*, 1924

113. *Gammer Gurton's Needle*, 1933

114. *Love for Love*, 1943

115. *The Lady's Not for Burning*, 1949

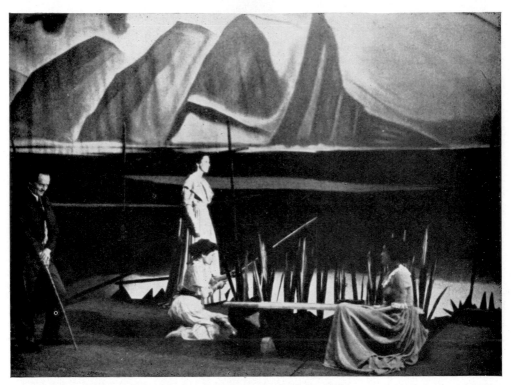

116. *The Lady from the Sea*, 1934

117. *Amphitryon 38*, 1937

118. *All My Sons*, 1947

119. *Death of a Salesman*, 1948

120. *The Armoured Train*, Russia, 1927

121. *The Travels of Benjamin III*, Israel, 1942

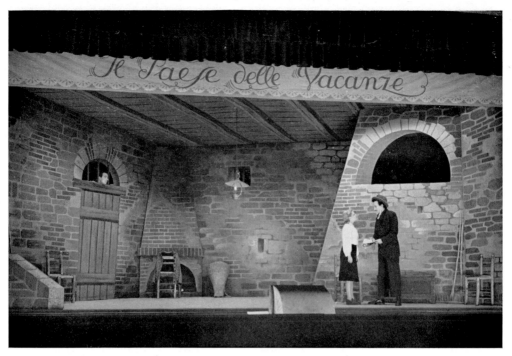

122. *Il Paese delle Vacanze*, Milan, 1942

123. *Mother Courage and her children*, Berlin, 1949

124. *Romeo and Juliet*

125. *The School for Scandal*

126. *Henry VIII*

127. *A New Way to Pay Old Debts*

128. Inigo Jones   129. Della Bella   130. Gissey

131. Bérain   132. Burnacini   133. Gillot

134. Planché   135. Meininger   136. Wilhelm

COSTUME DESIGNS

137. Albert Rutherston

138. Ernest Stern

139. Alexander Golovin

140. Lovat Fraser

141. Michael Weight

142. Titina Rota

143. Stewart Chaney

144. Mariano Andreu

145. Roger Furse

146. 1777

147. 1856

148. 1859

149. 1864

150.   1899

151.   1893

152.   1895

153.   1920

154.   1948